Current Law

STATUTES

1996

VOLUME ONE

AUSTRALIA
The Law Book Company
Brisbane • Sydney • Melbourne • Perth

CANADA
Carswell
Ottawa • Toronto • Calgary • Montreal • Vancouver

Agents:
Steimatzky's Agency Ltd., Tel Aviv;
N. M. Tripathi (Private) Ltd., Bombay;
Eastern Law House (Private) Ltd., Calcutta;
M.P.P. House, Bangalore;
Universal Book Traders, Delhi;
Aditya Books, Delhi;
MacMillan Shuppan KK, Tokyo;
Pakistan Law House, Karachi

Current Law

STATUTES

1996

VOLUME ONE

SWEET & MAXWELL EDITORIAL TEAM

SARAH ANDREWS   CAROL LOCKE
SHIRLEY ARCHER   CERI PICKERING
RACHAEL ARMITAGE   JANICE SAYER
MELANIE BHAGAT   MELISSA TEMPLE
HANNAH CASEY   SUZANNE WARREN

W. GREEN EDITORIAL TEAM

STEPHEN HARVEY   PETER NICHOLSON
JANIE BRASH

LONDON

SWEET & MAXWELL

EDINBURGH

W. GREEN

1997

Published by
SWEET & MAXWELL LIMITED
of 100 Avenue Road, London,
and W. GREEN LIMITED
of Alva Street, Edinburgh,
Typeset by MFK Information Services Limited, Hitchin, Herts.
and printed in Great Britain
by The Bath Press,
Bath.

ISBN This Volume only : 0 421 56570 5
As a set : 0 421 56610 8

CONTENTS

CHRONOLOGICAL TABLE

VOLUME ONE

Annotators' names are in italic

VOLUME ONE

*c.*1. Humber Bridge (Debts) Act 1996
   2. Hong Kong (Overseas Public Servants) Act 1996
      Professor Paul Jackson, University of Reading
   3. Wild Mammals (Protection) Act 1996
      Mike Radford, Lecturer in Law, University of East Anglia
   4. Consolidated Fund Act 1996
   5. Health Service Commissioners (Amendment) Act 1996
      Jonathan Montgomery, B.A., LL.M., Senior Lecturer in Law, University of Southampton and Non-Executive Director of Southampton Community Health Services NHS Trust
   6. Chemical Weapons Act 1996
      Amanda Perry, Lecturer in Law, Centre for Legal Studies, University of Sussex
   7. Prevention of Terrorism (Additional Powers) Act 1996
      Sandeep Savla, Sarah Phillimore and Gary Scanlan of City University
   8. Finance Act 1996
      Ian Ferrier, Barrister, 8 Gray's Inn Square
   9. Education (Student Loans) Act 1996
      William Hinds, Lecturer in Law, University of Leeds
  10. Audit (Miscellaneous Provisions) Act 1996
  11. Northern Ireland (Entry to Negotiations, etc.) Act 1996
  12. Ratings (Caravans and Boats) Act 1996
  13. Non-Domestic Rating (Information) Act 1996
  14. Reserve Forces Act 1996
      G. R. Rubin, Professor of Law, University of Kent in Canterbury

ALPHABETICAL INDEX OF SHORT TITLES

STATUTES 1996

(References are to chapter numbers of 1996)

HUMBER BRIDGE (DEBTS) ACT 1996

(1996 c.1)

An Act to confer power on the Secretary of State to provide that sums payable to him by the Humber Bridge Board shall not be so payable.

[29th February 1996]

PARLIAMENTARY DEBATES
  Hansard, H.C. Vol. 268, col. 1551. H.L. Vol. 568, cols. 12, 1610; Vol. 569, cols. 723, 1144.

INTRODUCTION
  This Act allows the Secretary of State, with the consent of the Treasury, to make an order providing that any sums payable in accordance with an agreement under s.5(3) of the Humber Bridge Act 1971, shall not be so payable.

Power of Secretary of State

1.—(1) The Secretary of State may by order provide that any sum (including interest) which would otherwise be payable to the Secretary of State by the Humber Bridge Board in accordance with an agreement under section 5(3) of the Humber Bridge Act 1971, and which is specified in the order, shall not be so payable.

(2) No order shall be made under subsection (1) without the consent of the Treasury.

(3) The power to make an order under subsection (1) shall be exercisable by statutory instrument which shall be subject to annulment in pursuance of a resolution of the House of Commons.

Short title

2. This Act may be cited as the Humber Bridge (Debts) Act 1996.

INDEX

References are to sections

HONG KONG (OVERSEAS PUBLIC SERVANTS) ACT 1996*

(1996 c. 2)

An Act to confer power to make provision for the making of payments to, and to permit early retirement by, certain Hong Kong overseas public servants; to authorise the provision of resettlement services to certain Hong Kong overseas public servants who retire early; and to confer power to make provision for the making in certain circumstances of payments to supplement pensions and gratuities paid to or in respect of retired overseas public servants in respect of service in Hong Kong.

[29th February 1996]

PARLIAMENTARY DEBATES
Hansard, H.C. Vol. 267, col. 849; Vol. 268, col. 1248. H.L. Vol. 568, col. 1268; Vol. 569, cols. 471, 1203.

INTRODUCTION AND GENERAL NOTE
This Act is an enabling measure which confers powers on Her Majesty by Orders in Council to make provision for overseas public servants in Hong Kong. Section 3 allows for early retirement during a period running from July 1, 1996 to June 30, 1997. Section 4 allows for the supplementation of pensions and gratuities.

The colonial service was renamed Her Majesty's Overseas Civil Service in 1954, following the publication of a White Paper which dealt with the consequences of decolonisation on the Service. A further White Paper in 1960 dealt with financial assistance to former colonies to enable them to keep the services of expatriate officers. Since then, 42 British dependent territories have become independent. This Act, in the words of the Minister of State, Foreign and Commonwealth Office, recognises the Government's responsibilities to the last serving members of the Overseas Civil Service (*Hansard,* H.C. Vol. 267, col. 862).

The principle of the legislation was accepted on all sides in both Houses. The main, indeed only, bone of contention was the extent of protection to be given to civil servants falling within the terms of the Act which turned entirely on the provisions of Orders in Council to be made under the Act.

COMMENCEMENT
The Act comes into effect on the date of the Royal Assent, February 29, 1996.

Hong Kong overseas public servants

1. For the purposes of this Act a person is a Hong Kong overseas public servant at any time if at that time—

(a) he is, or is treated by the Secretary of State as being, a member of Her Majesty's Overseas Civil Services or Her Majesty's Overseas Judiciary, and

(b) he is on the pensionable establishment of the government of the colony of Hong Kong.

DEFINITIONS
"Hong Kong overseas public servant": subss. (a), (b).

GENERAL NOTE
The section defines the persons falling within the scope of the Act by reference to membership of Her Majesty's Overseas Civil Service or Her Majesty's Overseas Judiciary. Her Majesty's Overseas Civil Service was constituted by the Secretary of State for the Colonies in 1954 (Colonial Office Paper O.C.S.1. HMSO (1955)). For the purposes of the Act there is no need to distinguish Her Majesty's Overseas Judiciary from the Overseas Civil Service.

A person may fall within the terms of the Act if he *is* a member of the Overseas Civil Service or Judiciary or *is treated* by the Secretary of State as being such a member. In the former case, a refusal by the Secretary of State to accept that an applicant is within the class will be subject to

---

* Annotations by Professor Paul Jackson, University of Reading.

judicial review. Membership of the class is a "precedent fact" which is to be determined as a matter of law, not according to the belief of the minister: see *R. v. Secretary of State for the Home Department, ex p. Khawaja* [1984] A.C. 74. Where, however, an applicant seeks to be *treated* as a member of the service, judicial review in the case of an adverse decision by the minister must be confined to a challenge on the grounds of unfairness or irrationality. "Treated" is clearly appropriate to confer a subjective discretion on the Secretary of State.

Payments on entering service of Hong Kong SAR

2. Her Majesty may by Order in Council make provision for the making by the Secretary of State of payments to persons who—
   (a) are Hong Kong overseas public servants throughout the period begining with 1st May 1993 and ending with 30th June 1997, and
   (b) enter the service of the government of the Hong Kong Special Administrative Region on the ending of Her Majesty's sovereignty and jurisdiction over Hong Kong on 1st July 1997.

DEFINITIONS
   "Hong Kong overseas public servants": s.1.

GENERAL NOTE
   The cessation of British rule over Hong Kong and the establishment of the Hong Kong Special Administrative Region with effect from July 1, 1997 were agreed between the Government of the U.K. and the People's Republic of China following negotiations which resulted in the Joint Declaration which was ratified by both Governments on May 27, 1985. The necessary legislative authority for giving legal effect to the Joint Declaration was provided in the Hong Kong Act 1985 (c. 15).

Early retirement before 1st July 1997

3.—(1) Her Majesty may by Order in Council make provision—
   (a) permitting early retirement during the relevant period by persons who are Hong Kong overseas public servants throughout the period beginning with 1st May 1993 and ending with their retirement, and
   (b) for the making by the Secretary of State of payments to persons who retire in accordance with the Order in Council.
   (2) The Secretary of State may provide—
   (a) advice about suitable alternative employment, and
   (b) other resettlement services,
to persons who, having been Hong Kong overseas public servants throughout the period beginning with 1st May 1993 and ending with their retirement, retire early during the relevant period (whether or not in accordance with an Order in Council under subsection (1)).
   (3) In this section "the relevant period" means the period beginning with 1st July 1996 and ending with 30th June 1997.

DEFINITIONS
   "Hong Kong overseas public servants": s.1.
   "relevant period": subs. (3).

Pension supplements

4.—(1) Her Majesty may by Order in Council make provision for the making by the Secretary of State, in specified circumstances, of payments to supplement pensions and gratuities paid under any specified provision of the law of Hong Kong to or in respect of persons who—
   (a) have at any time been Hong Kong overseas public servants, or
   (b) have been on the pensionable establishment of the government of the colony of Hong Kong either as members of any of the relevant colonial Services or in specified circumstances.
   (2) In subsection (1)(b) "the relevant colonial Services" means the Services listed in the Schedule to the Special Regulations constituting Her

Majesty's Overseas Civil Service which were appended to Colonial No. 306 (1954).

DEFINITIONS
"Hong Kong overseas public servants": s.1.
"relevant colonial services": subs. (2).

Payments under Orders in Council

5.—(1) An Order in Council under this Act may make provision for the amount of payments under the Order in Council to be determined in any specified manner.

(2) The manner of determining the amount of payments under such an Order in Council need not be similar to the manner of determining the amount of other overseas public service payments.

(3) The circumstances specified in an Order in Council under section 4 for the making of payments need not be similar to those for the making of other overseas public services payments.

(4) The references in subsections (2) and (3) to other overseas public service payments are to payments to public servants in connection with the ending of Her Majesty's sovereignty or jurisdiction over any colony or other territory apart from Hong Kong.

(5) An Order in Council under section 2 or 3 may include provision authorising the Secretary of State to satisfy any liability to United Kingdom tax incurred by any person in respect of the making to him of a payment under the Order in Council.

DEFINITIONS
"other overseas public service payments": subs. (4).

GENERAL NOTE
This section provides the authority for determining the amounts to be paid under the Act and in particular, provides that payments to Hong Kong overseas public servants may be at different rates from those applicable to other overseas public servants. This provision ensures that account can be taken in calculating payments of such factors as the variation in exchange rates of currencies as against the pound sterling, differences in the various territories concerned in calculating pensions and difficulties in comparing grades of public servants in different jurisdictions.

Supplementary

6.—(1) An Order in Council under this Act—
(a) may make different provision in relation to different cases,
(b) may except specified cases from any of its provisions, and
(c) may contain provisions which are incidental or supplementary.

(2) An Order in Council under section 3 may provide that any specified provision of the Order in Council shall form part of the law of the colony of Hong Kong.

(3) In this Act "specified", in relation to an Order in Council, means specified in the Order in Council.

(4) A statutory instrument containing an Order in Council under this Act shall be subject to annulment in pursuance of a resolution of either House of Parliament.

DEFINITIONS
"specified": subs. (3).

GENERAL NOTE
The application to Hong Kong as part of Hong Kong law, of Orders in Council made under s.3 of the Act (as provided in subs. (2)) is in addition to the Crown's continued right to legislate for Hong Kong by prerogative. The application of English law in Hong Kong is currently governed by the Application of English Law Ordinance 1971.

Financial provision

7. Any expenditure incurred by the Secretary of State under or by virtue of this Act shall be met out of money provided by Parliament.

Short title

8. This Act may be cited as the Hong Kong (Overseas Public Servants) Act 1996.

INDEX

References are to sections

WILD MAMMALS (PROTECTION) ACT 1996*

(1996 c.3)

An Act to make provision for the protection of wild mammals from certain cruel acts; and for connected purposes.   [29th February 1996]

PARLIAMENTARY DEBATES
Hansard, H.C. Vol. 270, col. 553; H.L. Vol. 569, col. 700.

INTRODUCTION AND GENERAL NOTE

This Act extends, for the first time, to the generality of wild mammals in Great Britain statutory protection against specified acts of cruelty. Domestic and captive animals are already protected by the terms of the Protection of Animals Act 1911 (c.27) and the Protection of Animals (Scotland) Act 1912 (c.14); birds, reptiles and fish living wild remain unprotected from acts of cruelty except so far as other legislation, most notably Pt. I of the Wildlife and Countryside Act 1981 (c.69), imposes restrictions on the way in which certain species may be treated.

Private Members' Bills were introduced into the House of Commons in the 1991–92 and 1994–95 sessions of Parliament with the intention of providing protection for wild mammals, including a clause which would have made it an offence to carry out hunting with dogs. Both Bills foundered as a result of this provision. In an attempt to speed its progress through Parliament, the clause which would have effectively prohibited hunting was eventually dropped from the second Bill and a consensus reached between pro- and anti-hunting members of both Houses and interested organisations including the British Field Sports Society, the National Farmers' Union, the Royal Society for the Prevention of Cruelty to Animals and the League Against Cruel Sports, on a form of words which would offer some protection against cruelty to wild mammals without adversely affecting field sports. That Bill was ultimately unsuccessful due to lack of parliamentary time, but was re-introduced in its revised form by a Private Member in the 1995–96 session. On the basis of the agreement as to its terms which had been reached previously, the Bill attracted widespread support and no serious opposition during its passage through both Houses of Parliament. The extent of the agreement is evidenced by the fact that no amendments were tabled and the total time spent debating its provisions throughout the entire legislative process was less than two-and-a-half-hours.

Section 1 makes it an offence to subject a wild mammal to any one of a catalogue of specific acts with intent to inflict unnecessary suffering; to do so accidentally or unintentionally does not amount to an offence. If the intent is present, there is no requirement to show that unnecessary suffering has actually been caused.

Section 2 specifies five important exceptions, the circumstances in which no offence is committed. These include consequences arising from the pursuit of field sports. Hunting, shooting and coursing are not, therefore, affected by the provisions of the Act. To remove any doubt on this point, the Bill's supporters, with reference to the House of Lords' decision in *Pepper v. Hart* [1993] A.C. 593, specifically confirmed as much during the Second Reading in the House of Commons.

Section 5 provides that a person guilty of an offence under the Act is liable to a fine not exceeding level 5 on the standard scale, or up to six months' imprisonment, or both. Where more than one wild mammal is involved and a fine is imposed, the maximum amount is to be determined as if the person had been convicted of a separate offence in respect of each animal. In addition, s.6(1) empowers courts in England and Wales to order confiscation of any vehicle or equipment which was used in the commission of the offence.

The Act does not affect the statutory protection which is extended to specific species of mammal such as deer (the Deer Act 1991 (c.54)), badgers (Protection of Badgers Act 1992 (c.51)), or those included in Scheds. 5, 6 and 9 of the Wildlife and Countryside Act 1981.

The Act comes into force on April 29, 1996 by virtue of s.7(2).

The Act does not apply to Northern Ireland, where more extensive provisions to protect wildlife from cruelty than are contained in this Act are already in force. Under the Welfare of Animals Act (Northern Ireland) 1972 it is an offence, *inter alia*, to cruelly beat, kick, ill-treat, torture, infuriate or terrify any animal, including birds, fish and reptiles, regardless of whether they are domestic, captive or wild (ss.13 and 29). However, there are similar exclusions relating to acts done in the pursuit of hunting and coursing (s.15(c)(d)).

Offences

1. If, save as permitted by this Act, any person mutilates, kicks, beats, nails or otherwise impales, stabs, burns, stones, crushes, drowns, drags or asphyxiates any wild mammal with intent to inflict unnecessary suffering he shall be guilty of an offence.

---

*Annotations by Mike Radford, Lecturer in law, University of East Anglia.

Exceptions from offence under the Act

2. A person shall not be guilty of an offence under this Act by reason of—

(a) the attempted killing of any such wild mammal as an act of mercy if he shows that the mammal had been so seriously disabled otherwise than by his unlawful act that there was no reasonable chance of its recovering;

(b) the killing in a reasonably swift and humane manner of any such wild mammal if he shows that the wild mammal had been injured or taken in the course of either lawful shooting, hunting, coursing or pest control activity;

(c) doing anything which is authorised by or under any enactment;

(d) any act made unlawful by section 1 if the act was done by means of any snare, trap, dog, or bird lawfully used for the purpose of killing or taking any wild mammal; or

(e) the lawful use of any poisonous or noxious substance on any wild mammal.

Interpretation

3. In this Act "wild mammal" means any mammal which is not a domestic or captive animal within the meaning of the Protection of Animals Act 1911 or the Protection of Animals (Scotland) Act 1912.

Powers of constable

4. Where a constable has reasonable grounds for suspecting that a person has committed an offence under the provisions of this Act and that evidence of the commission of the offence may be found on that person or in or on any vehicle he may have with him, the constable may—

(a) without warrant, stop and search that person and any vehicle or article he may have with him; and

(b) seize and detain for the purposes of proceedings under any of those provisions anything which may be evidence of the commission of the offence or may be liable to be confiscated under section 6 of this Act.

Penalties

5.—(1) A person guilty of an offence under this Act shall be liable on summary conviction to a fine not exceeding level 5 on the standard scale, or a term of imprisonment not exceeding six months, or both.

(2) Provided that where the offence was committed in respect of more than one wild mammal, the maximum fine which may be imposed shall be determined as if the person had been convicted of a seperate offence in respect of each such wild mammal.

Court powers of confiscation &c.

6.—(1) The court before whom any person is convicted under this Act may, in addition to any other punishment, order the confiscation of any vehicle or equipment used in the commission of the offence.

(2) The Secretary of State may, by regulations made by statutory instrument and subject to annulment in pursuance of a resolution of either House of Parliament, make provision for the disposal or destruction in prescribed circumstances of any vehicle or equipment confiscated under this section.

Citation, commencement and extent

7.—(1) This Act may be cited as the Wild Mammals (Protection) Act 1996.

(2) This Act shall come into force with the expiration of the period of two months beginning with its passing.

(3) This Act shall not apply to Northern Ireland.

(4) Section 6 of this Act shall not apply to Scotland, and so much of section 4 as refers to that section shall also not apply there.

INDEX

References are to sections

CONSOLIDATED FUND ACT 1996

(1996 c. 4)

An Act to apply certain sums out of the Consolidated Fund to the service of the years ending on 31st March 1995 and 1996.   [21st March 1996]

PARLIAMENTARY DEBATES
Hansard, H.C. Vol. 273, 807; H.L. Vol. 570, cols. 851, 1155.

INTRODUCTION
This Act makes provision for the application of £148,670,792.82 from the Consolidated Fund for the service of the year ended March 31, 1995 and for the application of £3,446,089,000 for the service of the year ending on March 31, 1996.

Most Gracious Sovereign,

We, Your Majesty's most dutiful and loyal subjects, the Commons of the United Kingdom in Parliament assembled, towards making good the supply which we have cheerfully granted to Your Majesty in this Session of Parliament, have resolved to grant unto Your Majesty the sums hereinafter mentioned; and do therefore most humbly beseech Your Majesty that it may be enacted, and be it enacted by the Queen's most Excellent Majesty, by and with the advice and consent of the Lords Spiritual and Temporal, and Commons, in this present Parliament assembled, and by the authority of the same, as follows:—

Issue out of the Consolidated Fund for the year ended 31st March 1995

1. The Treasury may issue out of the Consolidated Fund of the United Kingdom and apply towards making good the supply granted to Her Majesty for the service of the year ended on 31st March 1995 the sum of £148,670,792.82.

Issue out of the Consolidated Fund for the year ending 31st March 1996

2. The Treasury may issue out of the Consolidated Fund of the United Kingdom and apply towards making good the supply granted to Her Majesty for the service of the year ending on 31st March 1996 the sum of £3,446,089.00.

Short title

3. This Act may be cited as the Consolidated Fund Act 1996.

INDEX

References are to section number

HEALTH SERVICE COMMISSIONERS (AMENDMENT) ACT 1996*

(1996 c. 5)

ARRANGEMENT OF SECTIONS

An Act to make provision about the Health Service Commissioners.

[21st March 1996]

PARLIAMENTARY DEBATES
   Hansard, H.C. Vol. 268, col. 266; Vol. 269, col. 411; Vol. 270, cols. 148, 490. H.L. Vol. 568, col. 1267; Vol. 569, cols. 479, 1670; Vol. 570, col. 1125.

INTRODUCTION AND GENERAL NOTE

The Health Service Commissioners Act 1996 amends the Health Service Commissioners Act 1993 (c. 46). It extends the scope of the Commissioners' jurisdiction in order to ensure that all aspects of NHS services are covered. Previously the Commissioners were prohibited from examining matters of clinical judgment, but s.6 of the 1996 Act removes that prohibition. In addition the exclusion in the 1993 Act of matters relating to family health services is removed by ss.1–3 of the 1996 Act.

The jurisdiction of the Commissioners has also been extended in response to developments in the NHS market. NHS patients are now sometimes treated by independent providers who are under contract to the NHS to provide services. The Commissioner can now investigate the actions of such providers when NHS patients are concerned (see ss.1–3 of the 1996 Act). The purchasing functions of GP Fund-holders are specifically brought within the Commissioners' remit (see the new s.3(1B) of the 1993 Act, as inserted by s.2 of this Act).

The Health Service Commissioners now provide the final tier of a complex but uniform NHS complaints procedure that was implemented on April 1, 1996. Under those procedures most complaints should be speedily resolved internally by the bodies complained against. If such local resolution cannot be achieved, there is provision for a semi-independent panel to review that complaint. As a final, and wholly independent process, complainants who remain unsatisfied can seek an investigation by the Health Service Commissioner. The Commissioner will not usually investigate until the first two levels of the NHS procedure have been completed (*see* s.5 of the 1996 Act).

---

* Annotations by Jonathan Montgomery, B.A. LL.M. Senior Lecturer in Law, University of Southampton and Non-Executive Director of Southampton Community Health Services NHS Trust.

The internal NHS complaints procedures are governed by Directions and Guidance issued to NHS bodies. There are three relevant documents; 'Directions to NHS trusts, health authorities and special health authorities for special hospitals on hospital complaints procedures' made on March 7, 1996 and issued with EL(96)19, 'Miscellaneous directions to health authorities for dealing with complaints' made on March 15, 1996, and NHS Executive, *Complaints: Listening ... Acting ... Improving. Guidance on the implementation of the NHS Complaints Procedure* (NHSE 1996). These complaints procedures are described in J. Montgomery, *Health Care Law* (Oxford University Press, 1996) Chap. 5.

Complaints procedures in the NHS are conceived as entirely separate from disciplinary matters. The 1996 Act does not remove the proscription of the Health Service Commissioners investigating complaints about personnel matters. Although complaints arising from family health services can now be entertained, the system of complaints in that sector was amended in April 1996 so as to separate disciplinary matters from the handling of complaints by patients (the two were previously dealt with by a single procedure).

COMMENCEMENT

The Act was brought into force on April 1, 1996, by the Health Service Commissioners (Amendment) Act 1996 (Commencement) Order 1996 (S.I. 1996 No. 970). Sections 2(2), 4(2) and 6(1) of the Act apply in relation to actions beginning on or after April 1, 1996, and actions beginning before that date where it can reasonably be said that part of the same action occurs on or after that date.

ABBREVIATIONS

HSC Act 1993 : Health Service Commissioners Act 1993 (c. 46).

NHS Act 1977 : National Health Service Act 1977 (c. 49).

Providers of services

Providers to be subject to investigation

1. In the Health Service Commissioners Act 1993 (the 1993 Act) after section 2 there shall be inserted—

"Persons subject to investigation

Health service providers subject to investigation

2A.—(1) Persons are subject to investigation by the Health Service Commissioner for England if they are persons (whether individuals or bodies) undertaking to provide in England general medical services, general dental services, general ophthalmic services or pharmaceutical services under the National Health Service Act 1977.

(2) Persons are subject to investigation by the Health Service Commissioner for Wales if they are persons (whether individuals or bodies) undertaking to provide in Wales general medical services, general dental services, general ophthalmic services or pharmaceutical services under the National Health Service Act 1977.

(3) Persons are subject to investigation by the Health Service Commissioner for Scotland if they are persons (whether individuals or bodies) undertaking to provide in Scotland general medical services, general dental services, general ophthalmic services or pharmaceutical services under the National Health Service (Scotland) Act 1978.

(4) In this Act—

(a) references to a family health service provider are to any person mentioned in subsection (1), (2) or (3);

(b) references to family health services are to any of the services so mentioned.

Independent providers subject to investigation

2B.—(1) Persons are subject to investigation by the Health Service Commissioner for England if—

(a) they are persons (whether individuals or bodies) providing services in England under arrangements with health service bodies or family health service providers, and

(b) they are not themselves health service bodies or family health service providers.

(2) Persons are subject to investigation by the Health Service Commissioner for Wales if—

(a) they are persons (whether individuals or bodies providing services in Wales under arrangements with health service bodies or family health service providers, and

(b) they are not themselves health service bodies or family health service providers.

(3) Persons are subject to investigation by the Health Service Commissioner for Scotland if—

(a) they are persons (whether individuals or bodies) providing services in Scotland under arrangements with health service bodies or family health service providers, and

(b) they are not themselves health service bodies or family health service providers.

(4) The services provided under arrangements mentioned in subsection (1)(a), (2)(a) or (3)(a) may be services of any kind.

(5) In this Act references to an independent provider are to any person providing services as mentioned in subsection (1), (2) or (3)."

DEFINITIONS

"Commissioner": HSC Act 1993, s.1.

"family health services": HSC Act 1993, s.2A(4), as inserted by this section.

"general dental services": NHS Act 1977, s.35, NHS (General Dental Services) Regulations 1992 (S.I. 1992 No. 661) (England and Wales); NHS (Scotland) Act 1978, s.25, NHS (General Dental Services) (Scotland) Regulations 1996 (S.I. 1996 No. 177).

"general medical services": NHS Act 1977, s.29, NHS (General Medical Services) Regulations 1992 (S.I. 1992 No. 635) (England and Wales); NHS (Scotland) Act 1978, s.19, NHS (General Medical Services) (Scotland) Regulations 1995 (S.I. 1995 No. 416).

"general ophthalmic services": NHS Act 1977, s.38, NHS (General Ophthalmic Services) Regulations 1986 (S.I. 1986 No. 975) (England and Wales); NHS (Scotland) Act 1978, s.26, NHS (General Ophthalmic Services) (Scotland) Regulations 1986 (S.I. 1986 No. 965).

"health service body": HSC Act 1993, s.2(4).

"pharmaceutical services": NHS Act 1977, s.41, NHS (Pharmaceutical Services) Regulations 1992 (S.I. 1992 No. 662) (England and Wales); NHS (Scotland) Act 1978, s.27, NHS (Pharmaceutical Services) (Scotland) Regulations 1995 (S.I. 1995 No. 414).

GENERAL NOTE

The new s.2A extends the jurisdiction of the Health Services Commissioner to cover family health services; delivered by general medical practitioners, community dentists, opticians and pharmacists. These persons were previously excluded from the Commissioner's remit and came within the jurisdiction of the NHS Service Tribunals. Those tribunals have now been abolished. Their disciplinary jurisdiction has been transferred to new "Disciplinary Committees" and the complaints functions are dealt with by the NHS complaints procedures and the Health Service Commissioner.

The new s.2B extends the jurisdiction of the Health Service Commissioner to cover the actions of non health service bodies who are contracted to provide services for the NHS. The Commissioner can only investigate complaints about services provided for the NHS, not private services (see the new s.3(1C), as inserted by s.2 of this Act).

Commissioners' general remit as to providers

2.—(1) Section 3 of the 1993 Act (general remit of Commissioners) shall be amended as follows.

(2) After subsection (1) there shall be inserted—

"(1A) Where a family health service provider has undertaken to provide any family health services and a complaint is duly made to a Commissioner by or on behalf of a person that he has sustained injustice or hardship in consequence of—

(a) action taken by the family health service provider in connection with the services,

(b) action taken in connection with the services by a person employed by the family health service provider in respect of the services,

(c) action taken in connection with the services by a person acting on behalf of the family health service provider in respect of the services, or

(d) action taken in connection with the services by a person to whom the family health service provider has delegated any functions in respect of the services,

the Commissioner may, subject to the provisions of this Act, investigate the alleged action.

(1B) Where the family health service provider mentioned in subsection (1A) is a member of a recognised fund-holding practice, references there to action taken by any person in connection with family health services include references to action taken by the person concerned in connection with any allotted sum paid to the members of the practice.

(1C) Where an independent provider has made an arrangement with a health service body or a family health service provider to provide a service (of whatever kind) and a complaint is duly made to a Commissioner by or on behalf of a person that he has sustained injustice or hardship in consequence of—

(a) a failure in the service provided by the independent provider,

(b) a failure of the independent provider to provide the service, or

(c) maladministration connected with any other action taken in relation to the service,

the Commissioner may, subject to the provisions of this Act, investigate the alleged failure or other action.

(1D) Any failure or maladministration mentioned in subsection (1C) may arise from action of—

(a) the independent provider,

(b) a person employed by the provider,

(c) a person acting on behalf of the provider, or

(d) a person to whom the provider has delegated any functions."

(3) After subsection (4) there shall be inserted—

"(5) Nothing in this Act authorises or requires a Commissioner to question the merits of a decision taken without maladministration by—

(a) a family health service provider,

(b) a person employed by a family health service provider,

(c) a person acting on behalf of a family health service provider, or

(d) a person to whom a family health service provider has delegated any functions.

(6) Nothing in this Act authorises a Commissioner to question the merits of a decision taken without maladministration by—

(a) an independent provider,

(b) a person employed by an independent provider,

(c) a person acting on behalf of an independent provider, or

(d) a person to whom an independent provider has delegated any functions."

DEFINITIONS

"action": HSC Act 1993, s.19.

"allotted sum": HSC Act 1993, s.19 (as amended by Sched. 1 para. 6(2) of this Act).

"Commissioner": HSC Act 1993, s.1.

"complaint duly made": HSC Act 1993, ss.8–10.

"family health services": HSC Act 1993, s.2A(4), as inserted by s.1 of this Act.
"family health service provider": HSC Act 1993, s.2A(4), as inserted by s.1 of this Act.
"functions": HSC Act 1993, s.19.
"independent provider": HSC Act 1993, s.2B(5), as inserted by s.1 of this Act.

GENERAL NOTE
The new subsections inserted by this section make amendments to s.3 of the HSC Act 1993 consequential upon the extension of the Commissioners' remit by the new ss.2A and 2B. The Commissioners' powers will be essentially the same in respect of the new jurisdiction as in relation to those areas already overseen.

New subs. 3(1B) of the 1993 Act. Fund-holding practices exercise purchasing powers for a limited range of clinical services using a budget devolved to them and known as the "allotted sum". General medical practitioners in fund-holding practices have a dual role, as providers of family health services and as purchasers of other care. Both of these functions are now within the remit of the Health Service Commissioners. The "provider" function falls within the new subs. 3(1A), and the "purchaser" function comes under the new subs. 3(1B).

New subs. 3(5) of the 1993 Act. The drafting of this subsection is slightly different from that of the existing subs. (4) which makes equivalent provisions for those matters already within the remit of the Commissioners before the 1996 Act. Subsection (4) excludes decisions taken without maladministration in the exercise of a discretion. Subsection (5) prevents the Commissioners' investigation decisions being taken without maladministration, whether or not a discretion is involved.

New subs. 3(6) of the 1993 Act. See the note on the new subs. 3(5).

Providers: other provisions

3. Schedule 1 (which contains other provisions relating to family health service providers and independent providers, including provisions consequential on sections 1 and 2) shall have effect.

DEFINITIONS
"Commissioner": HSC Act 1993, s.1.
"Mental Welfare Commissioner for Scotland": Mental Health (Scotland) Act 1984, s.2.

GENERAL NOTE
This section introduces Sched. 1, which makes consequential amendments to the 1993 Act. Only one of which requires annotation here.

New s.7(3A) of the 1993 Act, inserted by para. 2(5). This subsection prevents the parties to an arrangement by which family health services are provided using the Commissioners to investigate that arrangement or its implementation.

Other matters

Mental Welfare Commission for Scotland

4.—(1) In section 2(3) of the 1993 Act (bodies subject to investigation by Health Service Commissioner for Scotland) the word "and" at the end of paragraph (c) shall be omitted and after paragraph (d) there shall be inserted "and

(e) the Mental Welfare Commission for Scotland".

(2) In section 4(3) of the 1993 Act (no investigation where protective functions of Mental Welfare Commission for Scotland applicable) after "action" there shall be inserted "by a health service body other than the Mental Welfare Commission for Scotland if it is action".

(3) After section 7 of the 1993 Act there shall be inserted—

"Certain functions of Mental Welfare Commission for Scotland

7A. A Commissioner shall not conduct an investigation in respect of action taken by the Mental Welfare Commission for Scotland under section 33 (orders for discharge of hospital patients), 35I (revocation of community care orders) or 50 (orders discharging patients from guardianship) of the Mental Health (Scotland) Act 1984."

GENERAL NOTE
  The effect of the amendments made by this section is to align the position in Scotland with that in England and Wales. The Mental Health Act Commission (which deals with England and Wales) is already subject to the Commissioner's jurisdiction. The functions of the Mental Welfare Commission for Scotland include some which in England and Wales are carried out by Mental Health Review Tribunals (which are not subject to investigation by the Health Service Commissioner). The new s.7A excludes from the Commissioner's remit the equivalent functions of the Scots Commission.

Availability of other remedy

  5. In section 4 of the 1993 Act (availability of other remedy) after subsection (3) there shall be inserted—
    "(4) Subsection (5) applies where—
      (a) action by reference to which a complaint is made under section 3(1), (1A) or (1C) is action by reference to which a complaint can be made under a procedure operated by a health service body, a family health service provider or an independent provider, and
      (b) subsection (1), (2) or (3) does not apply as regards the action.
      (5) In such a case a Commissioner shall not conduct an investigation in respect of the action unless he is satisfied that—
      (a) the other procedure has been invoked and exhausted, or
      (b) in the particular circumstances it is not reasonable to expect that procedure to be invoked or (as the case may be) exhausted.
      (6) Section 1(2) of the Hospital Complaints Procedure Act 1985 (which provides that no right of appeal etc. conferred under section 1 of that Act is to preclude an investigation under this Act) shall have effect subject to subsection (5) above."

DEFINITIONS
  "Commissioner": HSC Act 1993, s.1.
  "family health service provider": HSC Act 1993, s.2A(4), as inserted by s.1 of this Act.
  "health service body": HSC Act 1993, s.2(4).
  "independent provider": HSC Act 1993, s.2B(5), as inserted by s.1 of this Act.

GENERAL NOTE
  The amendments effected by this section ensure that where complaints are made to the Health Service Commissioners they should not be investigated unless the NHS complaints procedures have been used, and exhausted, or it would not be reasonable to expect the complainant to use, or continue to use, them. The intention is that most grievances will be resolved within the revised NHS procedures introduced from April 1, 1996, which already provide the opportunity for independent review (see the Introduction and General Note, above). The Commissioners will provide a final review of the handling of grievances within those procedures.
  There are no criteria laid down in the Act to determine when it would be unreasonable to expect the complainant to use or continue to use the local NHS procedures (so that the Commissioner might investigate before they have been completed). In the House of Lords, the Health Minister, Baroness Cumberlege, adopted the present Commissioner's suggestion that two examples might be where there had been excessive delay in dealing with the complaint, and where the complainant had lost all confidence in the local complaints arrangements (*Hansard*, H.L. Vol. 569, col. 1677).

Exercise of clinical judgment

  6.—(1) Section 5 of the 1993 Act (no investigation to be conducted of action taken in consequence of exercise of clinical judgment) shall be omitted.
    (2) In section 3 of the 1993 Act (general remit of Commissioners) after subsection (6) (inserted by section 2 above) there shall be inserted—

"(7) Subsections (4) to (6) do not apply to the merits of a decision to the extent that it was taken in consequence of the exercise of clinical judgment."

GENERAL NOTE
The amendments made by this section extend the remit of the Health Service Commissioners to clinical judgment. The Commissioners now have jurisdiction to examine clinical decisions, and this examination can include consideration of the merits of such decisions because subss. 3(4)–(6) of the 1993 Act are disapplied by the new subs. 3(7) (inserted by subs. (2) of this section). Thus while previously clinical judgment could not be examined by the Commissioners at all, now it can be scrutinised more closely than administrative decisions.

No definition of "clinical judgment" is given in the Act. The Under-Secretary of State for Health, Mr John Horam, offered the following tentative explanation: "The essence of the concept is that clinical judgment is that which a health professional makes by virtue of his or her particular skills, expertise and training, and that which a lay person could not make." (*Hansard*, H.C. Vol. 268, col. 898). In Standing Committee E he also accepted that it included diagnosis of an illness and the care and treatment of patients (January 9, 1996, *per* col. 45).

The Commissioner will usually seek advice from experts from the appropriate profession on the merits of clinical judgment, under the powers provided by Sched. 1, para. 13 to the 1993 Act.

General health services

7.—(1) Section 6 of the 1993 Act (general health services etc.) shall be amended as follows.

(2) The following provisions shall be omitted—

(a) subsection (1) (no investigation to be conducted of action taken by person providing general medical services etc. under National Health Service Act 1977);

(b) subsection (2) (no investigation to be conducted of action taken by medical practitioners etc. in pursuance of contracts under Part II of National Health Service (Scotland) Act 1978).

(3) After subsection (4) there shall be inserted—

"(5) A Commissioner shall not conduct an investigation in respect of action taken by a Health Authority in the exercise of its functions under regulations made under section 29, 36, 39 or 42 of the National Health Service Act 1977 by virtue of section 17 of the Health and Medicines Act 1988 (investigations of matters relating to services).

(6) A Commissioner shall not conduct an investigation in respect of action taken by a Health Board in the exercise of its functions under regulations made under section 19, 25(2), 26(2) or 27(2) of the National Health Service (Scotland) Act 1978 by virtue of section 17 of the Health and Medicines Act 1988."

DEFINITION
"Commissioner": HSC Act 1993, s.1.

GENERAL NOTE
The two subsections omitted by subs. (2) are no longer appropriate because of the extension of the jurisdiction of the Commissioners to the actions of those providing family health services. However, that extension applies to the supervision of complaints by patients, not to the investigation of disciplinary matters by health authorities. Together with the existing subss. 6(3) and 6(4) of the 1993 Act, the new subss. 6(5) and 6(6) exclude such disciplinary investigations from the remit of the Commissioners.

Personnel matters

8.—(1) Section 7 of the 1993 Act (personnel, contracts etc.) shall be amended as follows.

(2) In subsection (1) (Commissioner not to investigate personnel matters) after "1978" there shall be inserted "or the National Health Service and Community Care Act 1990".

(3) After subsection (3A) (inserted by Schedule 1 to this Act) there shall be inserted—

"(3B) Nothing in the preceding provisions of this section prevents a Commissioner conducting an investigation in respect of action taken by a health service body in operating a procedure established to examine complaints."

DEFINITIONS
"Commissioner": HSC Act 1993, s.1.
"health service body": HSC Act 1993, s.2(4).

GENERAL NOTE
This section introduces two amendments that clarify and tidy up the law. The main effect of subs. (2) is to amend the 1993 Act to ensure that personnel matters concerning the staff of NHS trusts (which were established under the 1990 Act not the earlier legislation) are excluded from the jurisdiction of the Commissioners. This regularises the position of those employees with that of other NHS staff. Subsection (3) ensures that staff may invoke the Commissioner's jurisdiction where they feel that they have suffered injustice due to the maladministration of their employer's complaints procedure. This clarification follows from the fact that complaints procedures are to be understood as being quite separate from disciplinary procedures.

Complaints: requirements to be met

9. In section 9 of the 1993 Act (requirements to be complied with as regards complaints) the following subsections shall be omitted—
  (a) subsection (5) (Commissioner must be satisfied that health service body has been afforded reasonable opportunity to investigate complaint);
  (b) subsection (6) (subsection (5) to be disregarded in certain circumstances).

GENERAL NOTE
The two subsections removed by this section are no longer necessary because they would duplicate the provisions of the new s.4(4)–(6) of the 1993 Act, as inserted by s.5 of this Act.

Reports

10.—(1) Section 14 of the 1993 Act (reports by Commissioners) shall be amended as follows.
  (2) In subsection (1) for paragraph (c) there shall be substituted—
      "(c) to the health service body who at the time the report is made provides the service, or has the function, in relation to which the complaint was made,".
  (3) In subsection (2)—
  (a) the word "and" shall be inserted at the end of paragraph (a);
  (b) paragraph (c) and the word "and" at the end of paragraph (b) shall be omitted.
  (4) In subsection (3) for the words from "make a special report" to the end of the subsection there shall be substituted "lay before each House of Parliament a special report on the case."
  (5) for subsection (4) there shall be substituted—
      "(4) Each of the Commissioners—
      (a) shall annually lay before each House of Parliament a general report on the performance of his functions under this Act, and
      (b) may from time to time lay before each House of Parliament such other reports with respect to those functions as he thinks fit."

DEFINITIONS
"Commissioner": HSC Act 1993, s.1.
"functions": HSC Act 1993, s.19.
"health service body": HSC Act 1993, s.2(4).

GENERAL NOTE
The main effect of the amendments made by this section is to ensure that the Health Service Commissioners report directly to Parliament, rather than through the Secretary of State for Health as previously. The new s.14(1)(c) also ensures that health service bodies who have arranged for their functions to be performed by other providers will receive a copy of the Commissioner's report. It also ensures that where the functions of the NHS body against who the complaint was made have been transferred to another body (such as where a NHS trust is dissolved and its functions transferred to another), the body carrying out those functions at the time the report is made will receive a copy.

Information

11.—(1) Section 15 of the 1993 Act (information) shall be amended as follows.

(2) In subsection (1) (information not to be disclosed except for certain purposes) the word "or" at the end of paragraph (c) shall be omitted and after paragraph (d) there shall be inserted "or

(e) as permitted by subsection (1B)."

(3) After subsection (1) there shall be inserted—

"(1A) Subsection (1B) applies where, in the course of an investigation, a Commissioner or any of his officers obtains information which—

(a) does not fall to be disclosed for the purposes of the investigation or any report to be made in respect of it, and

(b) is to the effect that a person is likely to constitute a threat to the health or safety of patients.

(1B) In such a case the Commissioner may disclose the information to any persons to whom he thinks it should be disclosed in the interests of the health and safety of patients; and a person to whom disclosure may be made may, for instance, be a body which regulates the profession to which the person mentioned in subsection (1A)(b) belongs or his employer or any person with whom he has made arrangements to provide services.

(1C) If a Commissioner discloses information as permitted by subsection (1B) he shall—

(a) inform the person mentioned in subsection (1A)(b) that he has disclosed it, and

(b) inform him of the identity of any person to whom he has disclosed it."

(4) In subsection (2) (neither a Commissioner nor his officers to be called on to give evidence) after "nor his officers" there shall be inserted "nor his advisers".

(5) After subsection (2) there shall be inserted—

"(3) The reference in subsection (2) to a Commissioner's advisers is a reference to persons from whom the Commissioner obtains advice under paragraph 13 of Schedule 1."

DEFINITION
"Commissioner": HSC Act 1993, s.1.

GENERAL NOTE
The new s.15(1A), (1B) of the 1993 Act provides the Commissioner, and his officers, with the power to disclose otherwise confidential information if they think that it is necessary to do so to protect patients.

The amendment to s.15(2) ensures that those who advise the Commissioner during the course of investigation cannot be required to give evidence on the information they obtain. This will prevent them being forced to disclose their advice in malpractice litigation. The officers of the Commissioner were already exempt from giving such evidence.

General

Finance

12. There shall be paid out of money provided by Parliament any increase attributable to this Act in the sums payable out of money so provided under any other Act.

Repeals

13. The enactments set out in Schedule 2 are repealed to the extent there specified.

Commencement

14.—(1) This Act shall come into force in accordance with provision made by the Secretary of State by order made by statutory instrument.

(2) An order (or different orders) may make different provision—

(a) for different provisions of this Act;

(b) for different purposes, whether framed by reference to different parts of the United Kingdom or otherwise.

(3) An order may provide that a prescribed provision of this Act shall apply in relation to—

(a) action beginning on or after a prescribed date;

(b) action beginning before that date if it can reasonably be said that part of the same action occurs on or after that date.

(4) In subsection (3)—

(a) "action" includes failure to act;

(b) "prescribed" means prescribed by the order.

GENERAL NOTE

The Act was brought into force on April 1, 1996, by the Health Service Commissioners (Amendment) Act 1996 (Commencement) Order 1996 (S.I. 1996, No. 970). Sections 2(2), 4(2) and 6(1) of the Act apply in relation to actions beginning on or after April 1, 1996, and actions beginning before that date where it can reasonably be said that part of the same action occurs on or after that date.

Northern Ireland

15. The following provisions of this Act extend to Northern Ireland—

(a) sections 3, 11, 13, 14 and this section,

(b) Schedule 1 so far as it amends any enactment which extends to Northern Ireland, and

(c) Schedule 2 so far as it repeals any enactment which extends to Northern Ireland.

Citation

16. This Act may be cited as the Health Service Commissioners (Amendment) Act 1996.

SCHEDULES

Section 3   SCHEDULE 1

PROVIDERS OF SERVICES

Introduction

1. The 1993 Act shall be amended as mentioned in the following provisions of this Schedule.

Matters excluded from investigation

2.—(1) Section 7 (Commissioner not to investigate certain matters) shall be amended as follows.

(2) In subsection (2) the word "and" at the end of paragraph (a) shall be omitted.

(3) In subsection (2), in paragraph (b) (exception for arrangements between bodies) for the words from "a body which" to the end of the paragraph there shall be substituted "an independent provider for the provision of services by the provider".

(4) In subsection (2), after paragraph (b) there shall be inserted "and

(c) matters arising from arrangements between a family health service provider and an independent provider for the provision of services by the independent provider."

(5) After subsection (3) there shall be inserted—

"(3A) A Commissioner shall not conduct an investigation in pursuance of a complaint if—

(a) the complaint is in respect of action taken in any matter relating to arrangements made by a health service body and a family health service provider for the provision of family health services,

(b) the action is taken by or on behalf of the body or by the provider, and

(c) the complaint is made by the provider or the body."

Investigations

3.—(1) Section 11 (procedure in respect of investigations) shall be amended as follows.

(2) In subsection (1) for "this Act" there shall be substituted "section 3(1)".

(3) After subsection (1) there shall be inserted—

"(1A) Where a Commissioner proposes to conduct an investigation pursuant to a complaint under section 3(1A), he shall afford—

(a) to the family health service provider, and

(b) to any person by reference to whose action the complaint is made (if different from the family health service provider),

an opportunity to comment on any allegations contained in the complaint.

(1B) Where a Commissioner proposes to conduct an investigation pursuant to a complaint under section 3(1C), he shall afford—

(a) to the independent provider concerned, and

(b) to any other person who is alleged in the complaint to have taken or authorised the action complained of,

an opportunity to comment on any allegations contained in the complaint."

(4) In subsection (5) after the word "investigation" (where it first appears) there shall be inserted "pursuant to a complaint under section 3(1)".

(5) After subsection (5) there shall be inserted—

"(5A) The conduct of an investigation pursuant to a complaint under section 3(1A) or (1C) shall not affect any action taken by the family health service provider or independent provider concerned, or any power or duty of that provider to take further action with respect to any matters subject to the investigation."

4.—(1) Section 12 (evidence) shall be amended as follows.

(2) In subsection (1) after the word "investigation" (where it first appears) there shall be inserted "pursuant to a complaint under section 3(1)".

(3) After subsection (1) there shall be inserted—

"(1A) For the purposes of an investigation pursuant to a complaint under section 3(1A) or (1C) a Commissioner may require any person who in his opinion is able to supply information or produce documents relevant to the investigation to supply any such information or produce any such document."

Reports

5.—(1) Section 14 (reports by Commissioners) shall be amended as follows.

(2) In subsection (1) for the words from "A Commissioner" to "by him" there shall be substituted "In any case where a Commissioner conducts an investigation pursuant to a complaint under section 3(1) he shall send a report of the results of the investigation".

(3) In subsection (2) after "investigation" there shall be inserted "pursuant to a complaint under section 3(1)".

(4) After subsection (2) there shall be inserted—

"(2A) In any case where a Commissioner conducts an investigation pursuant to a complaint under section 3(1A) he shall send a report of the results of the investigation—

(a) to the person who made the complaint,

(b) to any member of the House of Commons who to the Commissioner's knowledge assisted in the making of the complaint (or if he is no longer a member to such other member as the Commissioner thinks appropriate),

(c) to any person by reference to whose action the complaint is made,

(d) to the family health service provider (if he does not fall within paragraph (c)),

(e) to any health service body with whom the family health service provider is subject to an undertaking to provide family health services, and

(f) to the Secretary of State.

(2B) In any case where a Commissioner decides not to conduct an investigation pursuant to a complaint under section 3(1A) he shall send a statement of his reasons—

(a) to the person who made the complaint, and

(b) to any such member of the House of Commons as is mentioned in subsection (2A)(b).

(2C) In any case where a Commissioner conducts an investigation pursuant to a complaint under section 3(1C) he shall send a report of the results of the investigation—

(a) to the person who made the complaint,

(b) to any member of the House of Commons who to the Commissioner's knowledge assisted in the making of the complaint (or if he is no longer a member to such other member as the Commissioner thinks appropriate),

(c) to any person who is alleged in the complaint to have taken or authorised the action complained of,

(d) to the independent provider,

(e) to the health service body or family health service provider with whom the independent provider made the arrangement to provide the service concerned, and

(f) to the Secretary of State.

(2D) In any case where a Commissioner decides not to conduct an investigation pursuant to a complaint under section 3(1C) he shall send a statement of his reasons—

(a) to the person who made the complaint, and

(b) to any such member of the House of Commons as is mentioned in subsection (2C)(b)."

(5) In subsection (3)(a) after "3(1)" there shall be inserted ", (1A) or (1C)".

Interpretation

6.—(1) Section 19 (interpretation) shall be amended as follows.

(2) After the definition of "action" there shall be inserted—

" "allotted sum" shall be construed in accordance with section 15 of the National Health Service and Community Care Act 1990 or, in Scotland, section 87B of the National Health Service (Scotland) Act 1978;".

(3) After the definition of "Court" there shall be inserted—

" "family health services" has the meaning given by section 2A;

"family health service provider" has the meaning given by section 2A;".

(4) After the definition of "health service body" there shall be inserted—

" "independent provider" has the meaning given by section 2B;".

(5) At the end of the definition of "patient" the word "and" shall be omitted.

(6) In the definition of "person aggrieved" after "3(1)" there shall be inserted ", (1A) or (1C)".

(7) After the definition of "person aggrieved" there shall be inserted—

" "recognised fund-holding practice" shall be construed in accordance with section 14 of the National Health Service and Community Care Act 1990 or, in Scotland, section 87A of the National Health Service (Scotland) Act 1978."

The Commissioners

7. In Schedule 1 (the Commissioners) the following paragraph shall be inserted after paragraph 3—

"3A.—(1) A person who is a relevant family health service provider shall not be appointed a Commissioner or acting Commissioner; and a person so appointed shall not, during his appointment, become a relevant family health service provider.

(2) For this purpose a "relevant family health service provider" means—

(a) in relation to the Health Service Commissioner for England or for Wales or a person appointed to act as such, a person mentioned in section 2A(1) or (2), and

(b) in relation to the Health Service Commissioner for Scotland or a person appointed to act as such, a person mentioned in section 2A(3)."

SCHEDULE 2

REPEALS

Chapter	Short title	Extent of repeal
1993 c. 46.	The Health Service Commissioners Act 1993.	In section 2(3) the word "and" at the end of paragraph (c). Section 5. Section 6(1) and (2). In section 7(2) the word "and" at the end of paragraph (a). Section 9(5) and (6). In section 14(2), paragraph (c) and the word "and" at the end of paragraph (b). In section 15(1) the word "or" at the end of paragraph (c). In section 19 the word "and" at the end of the definition of "patient".

INDEX

References are to sections and Schedules

CHEMICAL WEAPONS ACT 1996*

(1996 c. 6)

---

*Annotations by Amanda Perry, Lecturer in Law, Centre for Legal Studies, University of Sussex.

An Act to promote the control of chemical weapons and of certain toxic chemicals and precursors; and for connected purposes.   [3rd April 1996]

PARLIAMENTARY DEBATES

Hansard, H.C. Vol. 267, col. 810; Vol. 268, col. 413. H.L. Vol. 567, col. 1049; Vol. 568, col. 1364; Vol. 569, col. 1428; Vol. 570, col. 1071; Vol. 571, col. 148.

INTRODUCTION AND GENERAL NOTE

The Convention on the Prohibition of the Development, Production, Stockpiling and Use of Chemical Weapons and on their Destruction, 1993
(see generally Perry Robinson 1, and the *CWC Bulletin*)

The Chemical Weapons Act 1996 (c. 6) is designed to implement the U.K.'s obligations arising under the *Convention on the Prohibition of the Development, Production, Stockpiling and Use of Chemical Weapons and on their Destruction, 1993* ('CWC' or 'the Convention'). It is only through passing implementing legislation that the U.K. is able to ratify an international convention.

At the time this Act was given Royal Assent, the CWC had 160 signatures, but only 49 instruments of ratification deposited with the UN Secretary General. It needs 65 ratifications in order to come into force. Having placed itself in a position to be among the first 65 States Parties to ratify the Convention, the U.K. is now able to offer its nationals for administrative and inspectorate positions in the international Organisation for the Prohibition of Chemical Weapons ('OPCW') to be set up in The Hague to govern the implementation of the CWC. It should be noted that the Chemical Weapons Act does not mirror the provisions of the CWC exactly, as it is envisaged that some parts of the Convention will be implemented using prerogative powers (Watson: 1995, 24).

The CWC is 'the first treaty to provide for a verifiable world-wide ban on an entire class of weapons of mass destruction' (*Hansard*, H.C. Vol. 267, col. 810). While, for example, the Biological Weapons Convention, (implemented by the Biological Weapons Act 1974 (c. 6) outlawed the use of biological materials as weapons, it did not provide for a verification regime. The CWC bans the use, production, *etc.*, of chemical weapons, and demands the destruction of existing chemical weapons. It backs up these demands with an intrusive verification regime. Existing stocks of chemical weapons and chemical weapons production facilities must be declared to an international body (the OPCW). The stipulated nature of such declarations varies according to the class of danger presented by the chemical. Chemicals which are listed in the first of the three schedules to the annex Convention are subject to a quantitative limit on production and stockpiling. Other chemicals, known as 'discrete organic chemicals', must be declared if they are produced in amounts above a certain limit (*Hansard*, H.L. Vol. 568, col. 1365). States Parties declarations and general compliance levels can be verified through site inspections by OPCW officials. Trading in chemicals related to chemical weapons with states not party to the Convention is also controlled under the Convention.

The CWC, and therefore the Act, place heavy administrative burdens upon the DTI and upon persons and companies dealing with certain chemicals and buildings, whether they be researchers, industries, defence or otherwise. Compliance costs to industry alone are expected to be up to £8 million (*Hansard*, H.C. Vol. 267, col. 812). The Act will affect not only those involved in military-related research or industry, but also any academic and commercial enterprises which handle chemicals. This will include chemicals which have a 'dual function', allowing them to be used either for chemical weapons or for the production of completely benign products.

Under Art. VII CWC:
1. Each State Party shall, in accordance with its constitutional process, adopt the necessary measures to implement its obligations under this Convention ...
4. In order to fulfil its obligations under this Convention, each State Party shall designate or establish a National Authority to serve as the national focal point for effective liaison with the [OPCW] and other States Parties.
The DTI is the U.K.'s National Authority for the purposes of the Convention.

The Role of the DTI

The DTI volunteered to be the National Authority for the purposes of the CWC, and therefore the body responsible for the implementation of the Act. It felt itself to be the most appropriate conduit for CWC matters, on the grounds that the U.K. chemical weapons industry was a civil rather than a military affair, and that therefore much of the impact of the Act would be on the conduct of industry (Perry Robinson 2: 1996, 5–6). The DTI announced that, 'In the U.K. we intend that the National Authority should be established within the DTI and will not be a separate body of agency. Its functions will therefore be vested in the Secretary of State' (Watson: 1995, 31). The DTI will be responsible for 'collecting information from industry and others affected by the convention, processing it and presenting it to the OPCW. It will help inspected sites to deal with the inspection process and will monitor compliance with the convention' (*Hansard*, H.C. Vol. 267, col. 812).

The suitability of the DTI for the task of National Authority under the Convention was discussed in the House of Commons. Particular concerns were raised in regard to the need for accountability and transparency in the fulfilment of the obligations arising under the CWC (*Hansard*, H.C. Vol. 267, col. 818), and the availability of expertise in the DTI to cope with the rigours of the Act and Convention (*Hansard*, H.C. Vol. 267, col. 841). During its passage through Parliament, it was suggested in both Houses that the Bill should be amended to provide for the compulsory creation of a National Advisory Committee, charged with the duty of advising the Secretary of State on the CWC and the Act (*Hansard*, H.C. Vol. 268, col. 433; H.L. Vol. 569, col. 1428). However, the Government announced in the House of Lords that 'it was indeed the intention of the Secretary of State to establish an advisory committee, albeit not on a statutory basis' (*Hansard*, H.L. Vol. 569, col. 1434). The Government also announced that the views of the advisory committee would be sought on a draft of each annual report to Parliament on the operation of the Act, and that the committee would be able to draw any concerns 'to the attention of the Secretary of State directly' (*Hansard*, H.L. Vol. 570, col. 1074).

Outline of Act

The Act is divided into nine parts. The first part, the central section, is concerned with defining chemical weapons. The second and third parts create offences in relation to the use, *etc.*, of chemical weapons and the construction, *etc.*, of chemical weapons production facilities, and provide the Secretary of State with the powers necessary to detect and put an end to the commission of such crimes. The fourth part of the Act deals with the limited occasions on which chemicals, which might otherwise be considered to be chemical weapons, are permitted to be used under a licensing system. The fifth part of the Act creates a wide ranging power on behalf of the Secretary of State to demand that information be provided by members of the public in connection with the Act. The sixth part of the Act deals with the inspections which will be made on U.K. territory in pursuance of the CWC. The final parts of the Act lay down miscellaneous provisions, including various powers of search and arrest to be exercised by persons authorised by the Secretary of State.

Offences and Delegated Legislation

This Act allows for delegated legislation to be introduced by the Secretary of State under ss.20, 23 and 36.

New offences created under the Act are of three types. The most serious offences of use, *etc.*, of chemical weapons, and creating, *etc.*, chemical weapons production facilities under ss.2 and 11 are punishable by life imprisonment. The middle range offences of providing false or misleading information under ss.9, 17, 20, 21, 22 and 23, disclosure of confidential information under s.32, and use of Schedule 1 chemicals under s.19 are each punishable by a fine, imprisonment, or both. The lesser offences of failure to provide information under s.9, failure to comply with a notice under s.22, failure to comply with a regulation under s.23, offences connected with inspections under s.26, and destruction of objects, *etc.*, under s.17 attract fines alone.

COMMENCEMENT

The Act received Royal Assent on April 3, 1996. Under s.39(1), the Secretary of State has the power to determine by statutory instrument the date on which the Act will come into force.

ABBREVIATIONS

CWC	:	*Convention on the Prohibition of the Development, Production, Stockpiling and Use of Chemical Weapons and on their Destruction 1993.*
CWC Bulletin	:	*Chemical Weapons Convention Bulletin*, Quarterly Journal of the Harvard Sussex Programme on CBW Armament and Arms Limitation.
DTI Notes on Clauses	:	*House of Lords Chemical Weapons Bill: Notes on Clauses*, December 1995, DTI.
OPCW	:	Organisation for the Prohibition of Chemical Weapons, established under Art. VIII CWC.
Perry Robinson 1	:	Perry Robinson, J.P. "*Implementing the Chemical Weapons Convention*" *International Affairs* (1996), Vol. 72, pp. 73–89.

Perry Robinson 2   : Perry Robinson, J.P. *"Aspects of the Chemical Weapons Bill now before the Lords"*, January 23, 1996, a paper prepared for, and distributed by, the Royal Society of Chemistry as its Background Brief for the 2nd Reading of the Bill by the House of Lords.

Perry Robinson 3   : Perry Robinson, J.P. *"The Verification System for the Chemical Weapons Convention" The Convention on the Prohibition and Elimination of Chemical Weapons: A Breakthrough in Disarmament* (1994), Hague Academy of International Law Workshop, Martinus Nijhoff Publishers: London, pp. 489–508.

Watson   : Watson, Fiona M. *The Chemical Weapons Bill*, House of Commons Library Research Paper 95/116: 1995, November 21, 1995.

Introduction

General interpretation

1.—(1) Chemical weapons are—

(a) toxic chemicals and their precursors;

(b) munitions and other devices designed to cause death or harm through the toxic properties of toxic chemicals released by them;

(c) equipment designed for use in connection with munitions and devices falling within paragraph (b).

(2) Subsection (1) is subject to sections 2(2) and (3), 10(1) and 11(2) (by virtue of which an object is not a chemical weapon if the use or intended use is only for permitted purposes).

(3) Permitted purposes are—

(a) peaceful purposes;

(b) purposes related to protection against toxic chemicals;

(c) legitimate military purposes;

(d) purposes of enforcing the law.

(4) Legitimate military purposes are all military purposes except those which depend on the use of the toxic properties of chemicals as a method of warfare in circumstances where the main object is to cause death, permanent harm or temporary incapacity to humans or animals.

(5) A toxic chemical is a chemical which through its chemical action on life processes can cause death, permanent harm or temporary incapacity to humans or animals; and the origin, method of production and place of production are immaterial.

(6) A precursor is a chemical reactant which takes part at any stage in the production (by whatever method) of a toxic chemical.

(7) References to an object include references to a substance.

(8) The Convention is the Convention on the Prohibition of the Development, Production, Stockpiling and Use of Chemical Weapons and on their Destruction, signed at Paris on 13 January 1993.

(9) This section applies for the purposes of this Act.

DEFINITIONS

"chemical weapons": subss. (1), (2) and (3), and ss.10(1) and 11(2).

"Convention, the": subs. (8).

"legitimate military purposes": subs. (4).

"object": subs. (7).

"permitted purpose": subs. (3).

"precursor": subs. (6).

"toxic chemical": subs. (5).

GENERAL NOTE

This section highlights the Act's role as the domestic legislation implementing the CWC, and outlines what will constitute a chemical weapon for the purpose of the Act. The Act employs definitions which are derived from Art. II of the CWC but are not always verbatim. The CWC defines chemical weapons in Art. II as follows:

'1. "Chemical Weapons" means the following, together or separately:

(a) Toxic chemicals and their precursors, except where intended for purposes not prohibited under this Convention, as long as the types and quantities are consistent with such purposes;

(b) Munitions and devices, specifically designed to cause death or other harm through the toxic properties of those chemicals specified in subparagraph (a), which would be released as a result of the employment of such munitions and devices;

(c) any equipment specifically designed for use directly in connection with the employment of munitions and devices specified in subparagraph one. . . .'

In contrast, the Act first gives a broad definition of what constitutes a chemical weapon, and then excludes those things which are used or intended to be used for permitted purposes. The effect of the CWC and Act approached is substantially the same, and both aim to capture all chemical weapons, including those which technology has yet to create, within the scope of the legislation (DTI Notes on Clauses: 1).

Subss. (1), (5) and (6)

Chemical weapons include toxic chemicals and their precursors (chemical reactants involved in the production of toxic chemicals), and munitions and other devices and equipment which are designed to use chemicals in order to cause death or harm. An example of equipment designed for use with munitions which use chemical weapons is a container designed to be used for the storage of chemical weapons (DTI Notes on Clauses: 3). Equipment originally designed for a purpose other than for use with chemical weapons, and which is later used in connection with chemical weapons is not covered by this section.

Toxic chemicals are further defined as chemicals which can cause death, permanent harm or temporary incapacity to humans or animals, regardless of the purposes for or methods by which they were created. Chemicals which attack vegetation are not included in the definition of toxic chemicals, but their use is restricted by the Convention on the Prohibition of Military and Any Other Hostile Uses of Environmental Modification Techniques which prevents any attempts to attack vegetation as a method of warfare. The U.K. is a signatory to that Convention (DTI Notes on Clauses: 5).

Subss. (2) and (3)

The subs. (1) definition of a chemical weapon must be read subject to ss.2(2) and (3), 10(1) and 11(2). These sections explain that where the intention of a person is to use an object which could otherwise be a chemical weapon for a permitted purpose, then it will not be a chemical weapon. In those cases, the use (s.2) or possession (s.10) of such an object, or the creation or improvement of facilities for the production of such an object (s.11) will not be contrary to the Act.

Subsections (2) and (3) echo Art. II, para. 9 of the CWC, which states:

9. "Purposes Not Prohibited Under this Convention" means:

(a) Industrial, agricultural, research, medical, pharmaceutical or other peaceful purposes;

(b) Protective purposes, namely those purposes directly related to protection against toxic chemicals and protection against chemical weapons;

(c) Military purposes not connected with the use of chemical weapons and not dependent on the use of the toxic properties of chemicals as a method of warfare;

(d) Law enforcement including domestic riot control purposes.

The U.K. Act does not follow the exact wording of the CWC because the DTI felt that the CWC definition contained 'an element of circularity.' Article II, para. 9 CWC, which forms part of the definition of chemical weapons, twice uses the phrase 'chemical weapons.' Subsections (2) and (3) are intended to avoid this type of self referential definition (DTI Notes on Clauses: 3).

The term "peaceful purposes" includes the industrial, agricultural, research, medical and pharmaceutical purposes spelt out in Art. II, para. 9 CWC (DTI Notes on Clauses: 4).

It should be noted that s.19 of the Act states that it is an offence to use, produce or possess any of the serious toxic chemicals or precursors set out in the Schedule to the Act for permitted purposes. See notes to s.19 for further details of its effect.

Subs. (4)

Subsection 4 defines the permitted purpose of 'legitimate military purposes'. Essentially it allows the use by the military of objects which might otherwise be chemical weapons, as long as they are not used in a way which defeats a major purpose of the Act—namely to eradicate the use of chemical warfare.

As noted above, Art. II, para. 9(c) CWC contains a circular definition of chemical weapons. In order to avoid this problem, the Act refers to military purposes other than those which use the toxic properties of chemicals as a method of warfare, rather than referring directly to 'chemical weapons'. Whilst being unwieldy and complicated, it would seem that the Act successfully manages to avoid the theoretical circularity of the CWC on this point. Although disparity between the Act and the CWC is unlikely to cause serious difficulties in interpretation, it is doubtless safer to use the exact wording of an international agreement when implementing it. The 'circular' elements of the CWC were not unclear in their purpose, and it may be that the choice to veer away from the original Convention text will cause some interpretational complexities in the future. It is precisely because of the overt nature of the intentions behind the CWC provisions in question that there is little serious risk of conflicting interpretations.

Subs. (7)

Subsection 7 provides that the term shall include substances, and therefore chemicals. This improves the drafting of ss.2–10 by removing the need for repetition.

Chemical weapons

Use etc. of chemical weapons

2.—(1) No person shall—
(a) use a chemical weapon;
(b) develop or produce a chemical weapon;
(c) have a chemical weapon in his possession;
(d) participate in the transfer of a chemical weapon;
(e) engage in military preparations, or in preparations of a military nature, intending to use a chemical weapon.

(2) For the purposes of subsection (1)(a) an object is not a chemical weapon if the person uses the object only for permitted purposes; and in deciding whether permitted purposes are intended the types and quantities of objects shall be taken into account.

(3) For the purposes of subsection (1)(b), (c), (d) or (e) an object is not a chemical weapon if the person does the act there mentioned with the intention that the object will be used only for permitted purposes; and in deciding whether permitted purposes are intended the types and quantities of objects shall be taken into account.

(4) For the purposes of subsection (1)(d) a person participates in the transfer of an object if—
(a) he acquires or disposes of the object or enters into a contract to acquire or dispose of it, or
(b) he makes arrangements under which another person acquires or disposes of the object or another person enters into a contract to acquire or dispose of it.

(5) For the purposes of subsection (4)—
(a) to acquire an object is to buy it, hire it, borrow it or accept it as a gift;
(b) to dispose of an object is to sell it, let it on hire, lend it or give it.

(6) In proceedings for an offence under subsection (1)(a), (c) or (d) relating to an object it is a defence for the accused to prove—
(a) that he neither knew nor suspected nor had reason to suspect that the object was a chemical weapon, or
(b) that he knew or suspected it to be a chemical weapon and as soon as reasonably practicable after he first so knew or suspected he took all reasonable steps to inform the Secretary of State or a constable of his knowledge or suspicion.

(7) Nothing in subsection (6) prejudices any defence which it is open to a person charged with an offence under this section to raise apart from that subsection.

(8) A person contravening this section is guilty of an offence and liable on conviction on indictment to imprisonment for life.

DEFINITIONS
"chemical weapons": ss.1(1)–1(3), 10(1) and 11(2).
"object": s.1(7).
"permitted purpose": s.1(3).
"to acquire": subs. (5)(a).
"to dispose": subs. (5)(b).

GENERAL NOTE

Section 2 implements the obligations of the U.K. under Arts. I and VII of the CWC by prohibiting the use, development, production and possession of chemical weapons, as well as participation in their transfer and their use or intention to use them in a military operation. Offences
under this section carry a maximum penalty of life imprisonment. Specific defences of lack of
knowledge or suspicion and reporting to the appropriate authorities are provided for.

Subs. (1)

The wording of the subsection is similar to that used in Art. I, para. 1 CWC. However, it was
felt unnecessary to include in the Act the offences of assisting, encouraging and inducing
another to act in a way contrary to the Convention which are outlined in Art. I, para. 1(d) CWC.
These offences are provided for under s.8 of the Accessories and Abettors Act 1861 (c. 94),
which makes it possible to prosecute as a principal, any person who aids, abets, counsels or
procures the commission of an indictable offence (DTI Notes on Clauses: 8).

The Act also fails to make mention either in this section or in others, of riot control agents.
Under Art. I, para. 5 CWC, each party 'undertakes not to use riot control agents as a method of
warfare' (Watson: 1995, 34).

Furthermore, no provision has been made for the destruction of chemical weapons which the
U.K. has abandoned on the territory of another since January 1, 1925, as stipulated in Arts. I,
para. 3, and II, para. 6 of the CWC. It is entirely unclear how the Government will fulfil its
obligations to clear up such chemical weapons in the absence of legislative provisions on the
matter.

No mention is made in the Act of exporting and importing chemical weapons. The Government announced in the House of Commons that it was not necessary to ban the import or export
of chemical weapons because a DTI license must be obtained in order to import or export from
the U.K., to trade in chemical weapons is banned under the CWC, and therefore the DTI would
never issue a license for the import or export of chemical weapons. In any case, the Government
pointed out, to possess a chemical weapon is an offence, and chemical weapons are unlikely to be
the subject of licence applications (*Hansard*, H.C. Vol. 267, col. 845). It is, however, likely that
applications will be made for the import and export of chemicals and objects which have a dual
use—that is, which both fall within the wide definition of chemical weapons given in s.1 of the
Act, and which can be used for entirely innocent purposes. It is therefore a significant feature of
the Act that it fails to comment upon the legality or otherwise of importing and exporting chemical weapons, or upon the obligations of the DTI in relation to the issuing of import and export
licences.

Subss. (2) and (3)

In subs. (2), the 'permitted purpose' exception referred to in s.1(2) is explained in relation to
the use of chemical weapons. Under subs. (2) where an object is *actually used*, within the meaning of subs. (1)(a), for a permitted purpose within s.1(3), it is not a chemical weapon under the
Act.

In parallel with subs. (2), subs. (3) provides that where a person develops, produces or possesses an object, or is involved in its transfer or use or intended use in military preparations, and
the person does that act with the *intention* that the object will be used for a permitted purpose
within s.1(3), it is not a chemical weapon for the purpose of the Act.

Under subss. (2) and (3), when determining whether an object is used, *etc.*, within subs. (1) for
a permitted purpose, the amount and type of the object in question should be considered. This
requirement implements Art. II, para. 1(a) CWC, which states that toxic chemicals and precursors intended for purposes which are not prohibited under the Convention are not chemical
weapons if the types and quantities in which these substances are held are consistent with purposes not prohibited (DTI Notes on Clause: 10).

It should be noted that s.19 of the Act states that it is an offence to use, produce or possess any
of the serious toxic chemicals or precursors set out in the Schedule to the Act for permitted
purposes. See notes of s.19 for further details of its effect.

Subss. (6) and (7)

In subs. (6), two defences are outlined to the offences of using and possessing a chemical
weapon, and participating in the transfer of a chemical weapon under subs. (1)(a)(c) and (d).
Firstly, it is a defence to those offences if the defendant can prove that he or she, did not know,
did not suspect, and did not have reason to suspect the object in question to be a chemical
weapon. In its notes to the House of Lords, the DTI suggested that a lorry driver who was found
to have transported a chemical weapon could have a defence if he or she did not *know* that the
object was a chemical weapon (DTI Notes on Clauses: 11). This is not strictly true, as the driver
would also have to show that he or she had no reason to *suspect* that the object was a chemical
weapon. The defence involves a degree of objectivity, and is therefore likely to be narrow. The
exact width of the defence will be determined by the interpretation given to the phrase 'nor had

reason to suspect'. The second defence is available to the defendant who did know or have reason to suspect that the object in question was a chemical weapon, but who took all reasonable steps to inform the Secretary of State or a constable of such knowledge or suspicion, as soon as it was reasonably practicable to do so.

No specific defence is given to the offences of developing and producing a chemical weapon or engaging in military preparations intending to use a chemical weapon. This is presumably because it is virtually impossible to lack knowledge or suspicion of the nature of the object in those circumstances.

Subsection 7 ensures that any defences normally available to a defendant will not be excluded by the inclusion of specific defences in subs. (6).

Subs. (8)

The maximum penalty for the commission of an offence under subs. (1) is life imprisonment. Similar offences under the Biological Weapons Act 1974 also attract a maximum penalty of life (DTI Notes on Clauses: 12).

Application of section 2

3.—(1) Section 2 applies to acts done in the United Kingdom or elsewhere.

(2) So far as it applies to acts done outside the United Kingdom, section 2 applies to United Kingdom nationals, Scottish partnerships, and bodies incorporated under the law of any part of the United Kingdom.

(3) Her Majesty may by Order in Council extend the application of section 2, so far as it applies to acts done outside the United Kingdom, to bodies incorporated under the law of any of the Channel Islands, the Isle of Man or any colony.

(4) For the purposes of this section a United Kingdom national is an individual who is—

(a) a British citizen, a British Dependent Territories citizen, a British National (Overseas) or a British Overseas citizen,

(b) a person who under the British Nationality Act 1981 is a British subject, or

(c) a British protected person within the meaning of that Act.

(5) Proceedings for an offence committed under section 2 outside the United Kingdom may be taken, and the offence may for incidental purposes be treated as having been committed, in any place in the United Kingdom.

DEFINITIONS

"United Kingdom national": subs. 3(4).

GENERAL NOTE

See generally Harvard Draft Research Proposal on Jurisdiction with Respect to Crime [1935] 29 AJIL Supp. 443, and Warbrick, 'Criminal Jurisdiction' (1994) 43 ICLQ 460–464.

Section 3 implements the jurisdiction requirements of Art. VII, para. 1 CWC. The section determines the acts to which s.2 will apply. The scope of the section is widely defined to give the U.K. jurisdiction over crimes on the basis of the nationality of the offender as well as on territorial grounds. This ground for jurisdiction (known as the 'active personality principle'), is found in other conventions which create international crimes, such as the International Convention Against the Taking of Hostages 1979, the Tokyo Convention on Offences and Certain other Acts Committed on Board Aircraft 1963. In providing for active personality jurisdiction, the CWC and the Act have ensured that the impact of the legislation is able to spread beyond the borders of the States Parties.

Subss. (1) and (2)

Subsection (1) lays down the principle that s.2 can apply to acts both inside and outside of U.K. territorial boundaries. Acts within s.2 which are committed inside the U.K., by U.K. or other nationals, whether individuals or companies, will be offences under the Act. Where acts within s.2 are committed outside of the U.K., the U.K. courts will have jurisdiction to deal with resulting prosecutions, where the facts fall within subs. (2).

Subsection (2) limits the extra territorial impact of s.2 to the actions abroad of U.K. nationals, Scottish partnerships, and bodies incorporated under the law of any part of the U.K. The extension of jurisdiction to the crimes of U.K. companies abroad goes beyond the requirements of Art. VII, para. 1 CWC. Subsection (3) provides that s.2 may later be extended by Order in Council to apply to acts done abroad by companies incorporated in the Channel Islands, Isle of Man, or a colony.

Subs. (5)
This subsection simplifies prosecutions of acts abroad falling under s.2, by stating that they can be conducted as if the offence were committed in the U.K.

Suspicious objects

4.—(1) If—

(a) the Secretary of State has grounds to suspect that an object is a chemical weapon, and

(b) at least one person falls within subsection (2),

the Secretary of State may serve on any person falling within that subsection a copy of a notice falling within subsection (3).

(2) The persons falling within this subsection are—

(a) any person who appears to the Secretary of State to have the object in his possession, and

(b) any person not falling within paragraph (a) and who appears to the Secretary of State to have an interest which the Secretary of State believes is materially affected by the notice.

(3) A notice falling within this subsection is a notice which—

(a) describes the object and states its location;

(b) states that the Secretary of State suspects that the object is a chemical weapon and gives the reasons for his suspicion;

(c) states that he is considering whether to secure its destruction under sections 5 to 7;

(d) states that any person may make representations that the object is not a chemical weapon;

(e) states that a person on whom the notice is served and who has the object in his possession must not relinquish possession before a date specified in the notice.

DEFINITIONS
"chemical weapons": ss.1(1)–1(3), 10(1) and 11(2).
"destroyed": s.10(2).
"notice falling within": subs. (3).
"object": s.1(7).
"persons falling within": subs. (1).

GENERAL NOTE
The purpose of s.4 is to provide the Secretary of State with powers to investigate the possibility that an object may be a chemical weapon, and to prevent such an object from being disposed of before proper action can be taken in relation to it.

Subss. (1) and (2)
Where the Secretary of State has grounds to suspect that an object is a chemical weapon, then he may serve persons appearing to be in possession of the object in question, or persons appearing to be materially affected by a notice, with a copy of a notice. The arrangement for serving notice or a copy of a notice under the Act is outlined in s.34. There are no restrictions on the source of information which may lead the Secretary of State to form such a suspicion.

Subs. (3)
A notice should contain a description of the object and where it is located. It should also inform the recipient that the Secretary of State suspects the object to be a chemical weapon and on what grounds, and that the Secretary of State is considering whether to destroy the object under ss.5–7. Article 1, para. 2 of the CWC provides that all chemical weapons in States Parties must be destroyed.

The notice must specify that anyone wishing to do so can make representations denying that the object is a chemical weapon, on the grounds that it is intended for a permitted purpose under s.10(1), or contains no toxic chemicals or precursors within s.1. The purpose of s.4 was described by the DTI to allow the Secretary of State to obtain the information necessary in order to determine whether an object is a chemical weapon (DTI Notes on Clauses: 17). However, s.4(3)(d) merely provides that persons notified should be told that they may defend the object if they wish—there is no requirement to provide information. What information is given may lead to the institution of searches under s.5.

The notice must explain that the possessor of the object must maintain possession of that object until the date stated in the notice. Failure to maintain possession until the date specified in the notice is an offence under s.9(1).

Power to remove or immobilise objects

5.—(1) If the Secretary of State has reasonable cause to believe that—

(a) an object is on premises to which the public has access or which are occupied by a person who consents to action being taken under this subsection, and

(b) the object is a chemical weapon,

the Secretary of State may authorise a person to enter the premises and to search them.

(2) If—

(a) a justice of the peace is satisfied on information on oath that there is reasonable cause to believe that an object is on premises (of whatever nature) and that it is a chemical weapon, or

(b) in Scotland a justice, within the meaning of section 307 of the Criminal Procedure (Scotland) Act 1995, is satisfied by evidence on oath as mentioned in paragraph (a),

he may issue a warrant in writing authorising a person acting under the authority of the Secretary of State to enter the premises, if necessary by force, at any time within one month from the time of the issue of the warrant and to search them.

(3) A person who acts under an authorisation given under subsection (1) or (2) may take with him such other persons and such equipment as appear to him to be necessary.

(4) If a person enters premises under an authorisation given under subsection (1) or (2) and the object is found there he may make the object safe and—

(a) he may seize and remove it if it is reasonably practicable to do so, or

(b) he may in any other case affix a warning to the object or to something in a conspicuous position near the object, stating that the object is not to be moved or interfered with before a date specified in the warning.

(5) For the purposes of subsection (4) an object is made safe if, without being destroyed, it is prevented from being an immediate danger (as where a fuse is neutralised or the object is smothered in foam).

(6) The powers conferred on an authorised person under this section shall only be exercisable, if the authorisation under subsection (1) or the warrant so provides, in the presence of a constable.

(7) This section applies whether or not any copy of a notice has been served under section 4.

DEFINITIONS

"chemical weapons": ss.1(1)–1(3), 10(1) and 11(2).

"destroyed": s.10(2).

"object": s.1(7).

"object made safe": subs. (5).

"premises": s.10(3).

GENERAL NOTE

Section 5 provides the Secretary of State with the power to authorise searches of premises and there to make safe, seize, or remove objects or to affix warnings. Searches are divided into two types. Searches of premises to which the public has access, or whose owner consents can be conducted by persons authorised by the Secretary of State. Searches by force with one month's notice can be made with a warrant. 'Premises' is defined in s.10(2), and includes vehicles, vessels, aircraft and hover craft. There is no right to make objections to searches under s.5, and attempts to obstruct them constitute an offence under s.9(2). Rights to be heard do arise in relation to the destruction of objects under ss.6 and 7.

Subss. (1) and (3)

Where the Secretary of State has reasonable cause to believe that an object is a chemical weapon and is in premises either to which the public have access, or to a search of which the occupier consents, then the Secretary of State may authorise a person to enter and search those premises. The powers of an authorised person during such a search are outlined in subss. (3) to (6). Subsection (3) allows an authorised person to take with them whatever equipment and persons they deem necessary.

While s.4(1) requires that a Secretary of State have *a suspicion* that an object is a chemical weapon, before a s.4(3) notice can be served, subs. (1) requires the Secretary of State to have *reasonable cause to believe* that an object is a chemical weapon before the powers to remove, immobilise and destroy under ss.5 and 6 are activated. The reasonableness of a belief in these circumstances will be governed by the standards of administrative law.

It should further be noted that in order to authorise the performance of a search without a warrant, a Secretary of State need only have (apart from the reasonable belief that there is a chemical weapon on the premises) a reasonable *belief* that a premises is either open to the public or occupied by a person who would consent to a search. In particular, knowledge by the Secretary of State of consent by the occupier is not required.

Subss. (4) and (5)

If an object is found during a search by authority under subs. (1) or by warrant under subs. (2), it can be made safe. To make an object safe is, according to subs. (5), to prevent it from being an immediate danger without destroying it. If it is reasonably practicable to do so, the object may be seized and removed. Where it is not possible to remove an object, for example because it is a toxic chemical in a dangerous state, then the authorised person may place a warning on or near the object stating that the object must be left untouched for a specified period.

Subs. (7)

The search, warning and seizure procedures outlined in this section are available even without the issue of a notice of suspicion under s.4. This provision may ensure that s.5 actions can be taken with an element of surprise. Search of private property can be made without consent under subs. (2) at any time during the month for which the warrant is valid.

Power to destroy removed objects

6.—(1) This section applies if an object is removed from premises under section 5, and for the purposes of this section—

    (a) the first six-month period is the period of six months beginning with the day after the removal;

    (b) the second six-month period is the period of six months beginning with the day after the first six-month period ends.

(2) If at any time in the second six-month period the Secretary of State decides that the object should be destroyed he may authorise a person to destroy it; but this is subject to subsections (3) to (5).

(3) If at any time in the first six-month period—

    (a) any person appears to the Secretary of State to have had the object in his possession immediately before its removal, or

    (b) any person not falling within paragraph (a) appears to the Secretary of State to have an interest which the Secretary of State believes would be materially affected by the object's destruction,

the Secretary of State must serve on such a person a copy of a notice falling within subsection (4).

(4) A notice falling within this subsection is a notice which—

    (a) describes the object and states its location;

    (b) states that the Secretary of State proposes to secure its destruction and gives the reasons for his proposal;

    (c) states that the person on whom the copy of the notice is served may object to the Secretary of State's proposal;

    (d) states that an objection (if made) must be made in writing to the Secretary of State before such date as is specified in the notice and must state why the object should not be destroyed.

(5) Before he reaches a decision under subsection (2) the Secretary of State must—

(a) allow any person on whom a copy of a notice has been served under subsection (3) time to respond, and

(b) take into account any objections to the object's proposed destruction (whether made in response to a notice or otherwise).

(6) If an object is removed from premises under section 5 and destroyed under this section the Secretary of State may recover from a responsible person any costs reasonably incurred by the Secretary of State in connection with the removal and destruction; and a responsible person is any person who had possession of the object immediately before its removal.

(7) If—

(a) an object is removed from premises under section 5,

(b) at the end of the second six-month period the Secretary of State has not authorised the destruction of the object, and

(c) a person had possession of the object immediately before its removal, the Secretary of State must return the object to the person mentioned in paragraph (c) or, if there is more than one, to such of them as the Secretary of State thinks appropriate.

DEFINITIONS
"destroyed": s.10(2).
"first six-month period": subs. (1)(a).
"notice falling within": subs. (4).
"object": s.1(7).
"premises": s.10(3).
"responsible person": subs. (6).
"second six-month period": subs. (1)(b).

GENERAL NOTE
This section governs the powers of the Secretary of State and authorised persons to destroy objects which have been removed from premises during a s.5 search. It is at this stage that those persons who have an interest in an object are first allowed to make representations to try to persuade the Secretary of State not to destroy the object. However, attempts to prevent a person authorised under subs. (2) from destroying an object constitute an offence under s.9(2)(c).

Powers are divided into those which arise in the first six-month period (six months from the day after the removal of the object) and those which arise in the second six-month period (six months from the day after the first six-month period ends). During the first six-month period, notices must be given of the imminent destruction of an object to interested parties, and the Secretary of State must take account of any objections raised in response. During the second six-month period, the object may be destroyed.

Subs. (5)
Decisions to destroy an object under subs. (2) must not be taken before persons served with copies of the subs. (3) notice have had time to respond, and any objections which they or others may have made, have been taken into account. Knowingly making false or misleading statements in a representation is an offence under s.9(5).

The time to be allowed for such objections will be guided by the requirements of reasonableness, and the need for the Secretary of State to make a decision before the expiry of the second six-month period if destruction is to be ordered. Obviously, no objection made to the destruction of an object will be heeded unless it contains a convincing assertion that the object is not a chemical weapon (DTI Notes on Clauses: 27).

Power to enter premises and destroy objects

7.—(1) This section applies if a warning has been affixed under section 5, and for the purposes of this section—

(a) the first six-month period is the period of six months beginning with the day after the warning was affixed;

(b) the second six-month period is the period of six months beginning with the day after the first six-month period ends.

(2) If at any time in the second six-month period the Secretary of State decides that the object should be destroyed it may be destroyed as provided by subsections (6) to (9); but this is subject to subsections (3) to (5).

(3) If at any time in the first six-month period—

(a) any person appears to the Secretary of State to have had the object in his possession immediately before the warning was affixed, or

(b) any person not falling within paragraph (a) appears to the Secretary of State to have an interest which the Secretary of State believes would be materially affected by the object's destruction,

the Secretary of State must serve on such a person a copy of a notice falling within subsection (4).

(4) A notice falling within this subsection is a notice which—

(a) describes the object and states its location;

(b) states that the Secretary of State proposes to secure its destruction and gives the reasons for his proposal;

(c) states that the person on whom the copy of the notice is served may object to the Secretary of State's proposal;

(d) states that an objection (if made) must be made in writing to the Secretary of State before such date as is specified in the notice and must state why the object should not be destroyed.

(5) Before he reaches a decision under subsection (2) the Secretary of State must—

(a) allow any person on whom a copy of a notice has been served under subsection (3) time to respond, and

(b) take into account any objections to the object's proposed destruction (whether made in response to a notice or otherwise).

(6) If—

(a) at any time in the second six-month period the Secretary of State decides that the object should be destroyed, and

(b) the object is on premises to which the public has access or which are occupied by a person who consents to action being taken under this subsection,

the Secretary of State may authorise a person to enter the premises and to destroy the object if it is found there.

(7) If (whatever the nature of the premises concerned)—

(a) a justice of the peace is satisfied on information on oath that a warning has been affixed under section 5, and that the Secretary of State has decided at any time in the second six-month period that the object should be destroyed, or

(b) in Scotland a justice, within the meaning of section 307 of the Criminal Procedure (Scotland) Act 1995, is satisfied by evidence on oath as mentioned in paragraph (a),

he may issue a warrant in writing authorising a person acting under the authority of the Secretary of State to enter the premises, if necessary by force, at any time within one month from the time of the issue of the warrant and to destroy the object if it is found there.

(8) A person who acts under an authorisation given under subsection (6) or (7) may take with him such other persons and such equipment as appear to him to be necessary.

(9) The powers conferred on an authorised person under this section shall only be exercisable, if the authorisation under subsection (6) or the warrant so provides, in the presence of a constable.

(10) Where an object is destroyed under this section the Secretary of State may recover from a responsible person any costs reasonably incurred by the Secretary of State in connection with the destruction; and a responsible person is any person who had possession of the object immediately before the warning was affixed under section 5.

DEFINITIONS

"destroyed": s.10(2).

"first six-month period": subs. (1)(a).

"notice falling within": subs. (4).
"premises": s.10(3).
"responsible person": subs. (10).
"second six-month period": subs. (1)(b).

GENERAL NOTE

This section deals with the powers of the Secretary of State to arrange for the *in situ* destruction of an object which was found during a s.5 search, and which could not be removed from the site. In such situations a s.5(4) warning will have been affixed on or near the suspicious object, ordering that it must not be interfered with. The section is similar to s.6, but incorporates added considerations relating to entry to and destruction of the premises.

Powers are divided into those which arise in the first six-month period (six months from the day after the placing of a warning on or near the object) and those which arise in the second six-month period (six months from the day after the first six-month period ends). During the first six-month period, the Secretary of State must serve notices on relevant persons, informing them of the object's imminent destruction and inviting their comments. As under s.6, the Secretary of State can destroy an object during the second six-month period, but only if requirements relating to notification and the hearing of objections have been fulfilled.

Decisions to destroy an object under subs. (2) must not be taken before persons served with copies of the subs. (3) notice have had time to respond, and any objections which they or others may have made, have been taken into account. The time to be allowed for such objections will be guided by the requirements of reasonableness, and the need for the Secretary of State to make a decision before the expiry of the second six-month period if destruction is to be ordered. No objection made to the destruction of an object will be heeded unless it contains a convincing assertion that the object is not a chemical weapon (DTI Notes on Clauses: 27). Knowingly making false or misleading statements in a representation is an offence under s.9(5).

The decision of the Secretary of State to destroy an object is not subject to appeal, although judicial review can be sought. If an object is wrongly destroyed, then compensation might be available under s.8, but only where no notice was given of the intention to destroy the object. Attempts to prevent an authorised person from destroying an object constitute an offence under s.9(2)(c).

Subss. (6) and (7)

There are two methods by which entry into a premises and the destruction of an object found there can be sanctioned. Under subs. (6), the Secretary of State is empowered during the second six-month period to authorise the destruction of an object which is located on property either which is open to the public, or whose owner consents to entry and destruction. Subsections (6) and (7) have similarities to ss.5(1) and (2). However, the problems relating to the words "reasonable cause to believe" in s.5(1) are not repeated in subs. (6).

Under subs. (7), a justice of the peace or a justice (in Scotland) can provide a warrant to enter a premises and destroy an object, by force if necessary, within a month. The justice of the peace need only be satisfied that a s.5 warning has been made, and the Secretary of State has decided to destroy the object.

Compensation for destruction

8.—(1) This section applies if a person claims that—
(a) an object has been destroyed under section 6 or 7,
(b) he had an interest which was materially affected by the destruction and he sustained loss as a result, and
(c) no copy of a notice was served on him under the section concerned (whether or not one was served on any other person).

(2) If the person concerned makes an application under this section to the High Court or in Scotland the Court of Session, and the Court finds that his claim is justified, the Court may order the Secretary of State to pay to the applicant such amount (if any) by way of compensation as the Court considers just.

(3) If the Court believes that the object would have been destroyed even if a copy of a notice had been served on the applicant under the section concerned the Court must not order compensation to be paid under this section.

DEFINITIONS

"destroyed": s.10(2).
"object": s.1(7).
"premises": s.10(3).

Section 8 concerns the provision of compensation to those persons who had an interest in an object, which was materially affected when the object was destroyed under ss.6 or 7, causing a loss, and where no copy of a notice was served on that person. If notice has been sent to the claimant then it will have been possible to make representations under s.6(4) and (5) or s.7(4) and (5), and the Secretary of State might, if convinced that the object was not a chemical weapon, have desisted from destroying the object. Therefore, where notice has been served and the object has been destroyed, then the claimant has been given due opportunity to make representations, has failed to make convincing arguments in defence of the object, and will not be compensated.

The claimant must make an application to the High Court or the Court of Session in Scotland which, if satisfied that the claim is justified, will order the Secretary of State to pay to the claimant such compensation as the court sees fit. There are no limits on the amount of compensation which the court can award, but nor is there any obligation on the courts to award compensation at all. The court shall not order compensation for the claimant if it believes that even if the notice had been duly served, the object would have been destroyed. For example, if the courts finds that the object would have been destroyed as a chemical weapon, then the claimant would undoubtedly have been guilty of the offence under s.2, and could not rightly receive compensation.

Offences relating to destruction etc.

9.—(1) If—
- (a) a copy of a notice is served on a person under section 4,
- (b) the notice relates to an object in his possession at the time the copy is served,
- (c) he relinquishes possession before the date specified under section 4(3)(e), and
- (d) he has no reasonable excuse for so relinquishing possession,

he is guilty of an offence.

(2) If a person wilfully obstructs a person in—
- (a) entering or searching premises under an authorisation given under section 5(1) or (2) or 7(6) or (7),
- (b) making an object safe, seizing or removing an object, or affixing a warning, under section 5(4),
- (c) destroying an object under an authorisation given under section 6(2) or 7(6) or (7), or
- (d) attempting to do anything mentioned in paragraphs (a) to (c),

the person so obstructing is guilty of an offence.

(3) If—
- (a) a warning is affixed under section 5(4),
- (b) a person interferes with the warning, or moves or interferes with the object before the date specified in the warning, and
- (c) he has no reasonable excuse for doing so,

he is guilty of an offence.

(4) A person guilty of an offence under any of the preceding provisions of this section is liable—
- (a) on summary conviction, to a fine of an amount not exceeding the statutory maximum;
- (b) on conviction on indictment, to a fine.

(5) A person who knowingly makes a false or misleading statement in response to a copy of a notice served under section 4, 6 or 7 is guilty of an offence and liable—
- (a) on summary conviction, to a fine of an amount not exceeding the statutory maximum;
- (b) on conviction on indictment, to imprisonment for a term not exceeding two years or to a fine or to both.

DEFINITIONS
"destroyed": s.10(2).
"making an object safe": s.5(5).
"object": s.1(7).
"premises": s.10(3).

This section creates a series of offences relating to interference with the exercise of powers by the Secretary of State and authorised persons under ss.4–7. The object of this section is to ensure that ss.4–7 procedures run smoothly.

Subss. (1) to (4)
It is an offence to give up possession of an object which has been the subject of a notice under s.4, where there is no reasonable excuse for doing so. Such notices are a means by which the Secretary of State can discover information about a particular object, and they are required to specify that the possessor of the object in question may not give up its possession for a stated period. It is also an offence to wilfully obstruct searches, seizure, removals, destructions and the making safe of objects which have been authorised under ss.5–7. It is also an offence to interfere without reasonable excuse with a warning posted under s.5(4), or with an object which is the subject of such a warning before the date specified in the warning. These offences are punishable by a fine.

Subs. (5)
It is an offence knowingly to make false or misleading statements in response to notices served under ss.4, 6 or 7. Such offences are punishable by more severe penalties than the offences under subss. (1) to (3), in recognition of the fact that providing false information may completely conceal the existence of a chemical weapon, rather than merely delaying the discovery of the chemical weapon. On summary conviction the punishment for providing false information is a fine. On conviction on indictment, the punishment is imprisonment up to 2 years, or a fine, or both.

Destruction etc: supplementary

10.—(1) If an object is in the possession of a person who intends that it will be used only for permitted purposes, it is not a chemical weapon for the purposes of sections 4(1) and (3) and 5(1) and (2); and in deciding whether permitted purposes are intended the types and quantities of objects shall be taken into account.

(2) For the purposes of sections 4 to 9—

(a) to the extent that an object consists of a toxic chemical or precursor, it is destroyed if it is permanently prevented from being used other than for permitted purposes;

(b) to the extent that an object consists of a munition or other device designed to cause death or harm through toxic chemicals released by it, it is destroyed if it is permanently prevented from doing so;

(c) to the extent that an object consists of equipment designed for use in connection with a munition or other device, it is destroyed if it is permanently prevented from being so used.

(3) In sections 5 to 9 "premises" includes land (including buildings), moveable structures, vehicles, vessels, aircraft and hovercraft.

(4) Nothing in sections 4 to 7 affects any power arising otherwise than by virtue of those sections (such as a power to dispose of property in police possession in connection with the investigation of a suspected offence).

DEFINITIONS
"chemical weapons": ss.1(1)–1(3), 10(1) and 11(2).
"object": s.1(7).
"permitted purpose": s.1(3).
"precursor": s.1(6).
"toxic chemical": s.1(5).

GENERAL NOTE
This section provides definitions and rules for application to ss.4–9.

Subs. (1)
Subsection (1), in conjunction with ss.1(2), 2(2) and 11(2), forms a framework to protect from the powers of the Act dealings with objects which would otherwise be considered to be chemical weapons, where such dealings constitute, or are intended to constitute, a permitted purpose within s.1(3). Here, as in each of the relevant sections, it is specified that in determining whether

a permitted purpose was intended in a particular case, reference shall be made to the types and quantities of the objects in question. This requirement implements Art. II, para. 1(a) CWC, which states that toxic chemicals and precursors intended for purposes which are not prohibited under the Convention are not chemical weapons if the types and quantities in which those substances are held are consistent with purposes not prohibited (DTI Notes on Clauses: 10).

Subs. (2)

Subsection (2) defines a separate meaning for the word "destroyed" for toxic chemicals and precursors, munitions and other devices, and equipment for the purposes of ss.4–9. This subsection implements Pt. IV(A) of the Verification Annex to the CWC. There, destruction is defined as any "process by which chemicals are converted in an essentially irreversible way to a form unsuitable for production of chemical weapon and which in an irreversible manner renders munitions and other devices unusable as such." This definition is purposely loose, in order to allow for States Parties to choose the method of destruction individually suited to them (DTI Notes on Clauses: 40).

Subs. (3)

Subsection (3) provides a broad definition of what constitutes 'premises' for the purposes of the sections of the Act relating to identification, search, seizure, removal and destruction, *i.e.* ss.4–9. For those sections, land, buildings, movable structures, vehicles, vessels, aircraft and hover craft all constitute premises in which chemical weapons might be found. The word takes on a normal restricted meaning for the purpose of later sections relating to the production of chemical weapons. Presumably it is anticipated that vehicles, vessels, aircraft and hover craft make unlikely sites or chemical weapons production facilities.

Subs. (4)

The powers held by the police under other legislation, such as the Police and Criminal Evidence Act 1984 (c. 60) and the Police (Property) Act 1897 (c. 30), are not affected by the provisions of ss.4–7. Police will continue to be able to search premises and dispose of objects under those Acts (DTI Notes on Clauses: 41).

Premises for producing chemical weapons etc.

Premises or equipment for producing chemical weapons

11.—(1) No person shall—

(a) construct premises he intends to be used to produce chemical weapons;

(b) alter premises in circumstances where he intends that they will be used to produce chemical weapons;

(c) install or construct equipment he intends to be used to produce chemical weapons;

(d) alter equipment in circumstances where he intends that it will be used to produce chemical weapons;

(e) permit the construction on land he occupies of premises he intends to be used to produce chemical weapons;

(f) permit premises on land he occupies to be altered in circumstances where he intends that they will be used to produce chemical weapons;

(g) permit the installation or construction on land he occupies of equipment he intends to be used to produce chemical weapons;

(h) permit equipment on land he occupies to be altered in circumstances where he intends that it will be used to produce chemical weapons.

(2) For the purposes of subsection (1) an object is not a chemical weapon if the person intends that the object will be used only for permitted purposes; and in deciding whether permitted purposes are intended the types and quantities of objects shall be taken into account.

(3) A person contravening this section is guilty of an offence and liable on conviction on indictment to imprisonment for life.

DEFINITIONS

"chemical weapons": ss.1(1)–1(3), 10(1) and 11(2).

"object": s.1(7).

"permitted purpose": s.1(3).

GENERAL NOTE

Subss. (1) and (3)

Subsection (1) states that the construction or alteration of premises and the construction, alteration, or installation of equipment where the intention is that such things be used to produce chemical weapons is an offence. It is also an offence for the occupier of land to allow such activities to occur on it with the intention that such activities leads to the production of chemical weapons. This addition is intended to catch those who are responsible for the construction, *etc.*, of the facility, as well as those who actually construct it. It is therefore the intention of the occupier of the land that is relevant to the offence (DTI Notes on Clauses: 42).

According to s.10(2), the definition of premises used for ss.5–9 does not apply to s.11(1). This means that 'premises' for the purpose of s.11(1) will bear a more limited meaning than that listed in s.10(2), and will not be taken to include such thing as hover craft, aircraft, vessels, *etc.*

These offences are punishable by imprisonment for life. Section 31(1), (3), (4) and (5) applies to these offences.

Subs. (2)

Subsection (2), in conjunction with ss.1(2), 2(2) and 10(1), forms a framework to protect from the powers of the Act dealings with objects which would otherwise be considered to be chemical weapons, where such dealings constitute, or are intended to constitute, a permitted purpose within s.1(3). Here, as in each of the relevant sections, it is specified that in determining whether a permitted purpose was intended in a particular case, reference shall be made to the types and quantities of the objects in question. This requirement implements Art. II, para. 1(a) CWC, which states that toxic chemicals and precursors intended for purposes which are not prohibited under the Convention are not chemical weapons if the types and quantities in which those substances are held are consistent with a purposes not prohibited (DTI Notes on Clauses: 10).

Suspicious equipment or buildings

12.—(1) If—

  (a) the Secretary of State has grounds to suspect that any equipment or building is a chemical weapons production facility, and

  (b) at least one person falls within subsection (2),

the Secretary of State may serve on any person falling within that subsection a copy of a notice falling within subsection (3).

(2) The persons falling within this subsection are—

  (a) any person who appears to the Secretary of State to occupy the land on which the equipment or building is situated,

  (b) if the Secretary of State's suspicion relates to equipment, any person not falling within paragraph (a) and who appears to the Secretary of State to have the equipment in his possession, and

  (c) any person not falling within paragraph (a) or (b) and who appears to the Secretary of State to have an interest which the Secretary of State believes is materially affected by the notice.

(3) A notice falling within this subsection is a notice which—

  (a) describes the equipment or building and states its location;

  (b) states that the Secretary of State suspects that the equipment or building is a chemical weapons production facility and gives the reasons for his suspicion;

  (c) states that he is considering whether to require the equipment or building to be destroyed or altered;

  (d) states that any person may make representations that the equipment or building is not a chemical weapons production facility.

(4) If the notice relates to equipment it must state that a person on whom the notice is served and who has the equipment in his possession must not relinquish possession of, or alter or use, the equipment before a date specified in the notice.

DEFINITIONS

  "chemical weapons production facility": s.18(1).

  "destroyed": s.18(2).

  "notice falling within": subs. (3).

  "persons falling within": subs. (2).

GENERAL NOTE
This section provide the Secretary of State with an opportunity to acquire information about any equipment or building suspected of being a chemical weapons facility. Equipment and buildings involved in the production of chemical weapons can be destroyed or altered under ss.13–15. This fulfils the U.K.'s obligation under Art. I, para. 4 CWC to "destroy chemical weapons production facilities it owns or possesses or that are located in any place under its jurisdiction or control, in accordance with the provisions of this Convention." Sections 12–15 provide for a procedure similar to the ss.4–9 procedure relating to suspicious objects. However, there is no need for provisions relating to destruction *in situ* as under s.7.

There is no obligation on persons served with notice to make representations with regard to the nature of the building or equipment in question. However, knowingly to make false or misleading statements is an offence under s.17(5).

It should be noted that where the Secretary of State has reasonable cause to believe that buildings or equipment are a chemical weapons facility, and does not require any further information, ss.13–15 can be used without a s.12 notice having been given (DTI Notes on Clauses: 49).

An important limitation to these powers is that under s.18(1), 'chemical weapons production facility' has the meaning given to it by the Convention. This means that ss.12–15 powers can only be used in relation to the production of Sched. 1 and other highly dangerous chemicals, and not to lesser chemicals that might constitute chemical weapons for the purpose of s.1. This is entirely in conformity with the provisions of the CWC. However, it is still an offence to construct, *etc.*, premises or equipment for producing all s.1 chemical weapons under s.11. Furthermore, to use, *etc.*, chemical weapons is an offence under s.2, and where a chemical weapons production facility is suspected, the Secretary of State would probably find grounds for exercising powers under ss.4–7 to assess and control the situation. Finally, if a defendant were convicted of altering, *etc.*, premises with the intention of using them for the purpose of producing lesser chemical weapons (*i.e.* less dangerous that Sched. 1 chemicals), then s.30 might allow for the confiscation and destruction of the premises and equipment (DTI Notes on Clauses: 50–51).

Notice requiring destruction or alteration

13.—(1) If—

(a) the Secretary of State has reasonable cause to believe that any equipment or building is a chemical weapons production facility, and

(b) at least one person falls within subsection (2),

the Secretary of State may serve on each person falling within that subsection a copy of a notice falling within subsection (3).

(2) The persons falling within this subsection are—

(a) any person who appears to the Secretary of State to occupy the land on which the equipment or building is situated,

(b) if the Secretary of State's belief relates to equipment, any person not falling within paragraph (a) and who appears to the Secretary of State to have the equipment in his possession, and

(c) any person not falling within paragraph (a) or (b) and who appears to the Secretary of State to have an interest which the Secretary of State believes would be materially affected by the destruction or alteration of the equipment or building.

(3) A notice falling within this subsection is a notice which—

(a) describes the equipment or building and states its location;

(b) states that the Secretary of State believes the equipment or building is a chemical weapons production facility;

(c) requires the equipment or building to be destroyed or altered (as the case may be) in a manner, and before a date, specified in the notice.

(4) If a notice under this section requires any equipment or building to be altered, a further notice under this section may—

(a) revoke the first notice, and

(b) require the equipment or building to be destroyed;

and the preceding provisions of this section shall apply to the further notice accordingly.

(5) This section applies whether or not any copy of a notice has been served under section 12.

DEFINITIONS
"chemical weapons production facility": s.18(1).
"destroyed": s.18(2).
"notice falling within": subs. (3).
"persons falling within": subs. (2).

GENERAL NOTE
Section 13 provides procedures for the destruction of suspected chemical weapons production facilities, in fulfilment of Art. I, para. 4 CWC. The Secretary of State is empowered under this section to require recipients of a copy of a notice to destroy or alter a suspected chemical weapons production facility. It is considered that the destruction of a chemical weapons production facility can be left up to the recipients of a notice, whereas the destruction of a chemical weapon is dangerous and must be done by a specialist (DTI Notes on Clauses: 72). The method by which chemical weapons facilities shall be destroyed is outlined in the verification annex to the CWC. Destruction of a building is defined in s.18(2) as 'complete demolition'. Section 13 runs in parallel with ss.5–7, which relate to identifying and destroying chemical weapons themselves. Section 18(3) ensures that these and other provisions do not affect existing powers of authorities to deal with suspicious objects.

There is no opportunity for the recipients of notices to make representations as to the legality of the building or equipment concerned. This is because the definition of chemical weapons production facilities is so detailed and objective that it is not necessary to inquire into the intentions behind the construction of the facility (DTI Notes on Clauses: 55). However, the usual administrative law procedures of judicial review remain open to them. It is an offence under s.17(2) to fail to fulfil the requirements of a notice without reasonable cause.

Subs. (4)
Special provision is made in subs. (4) for those circumstances in which a plant already modified under s.13 needs to be further altered, again using s.13, in order to bring it out of the category of chemical weapons production facility. This subsection fulfils obligations taken on under the Convention. The general rule under Art. V of the CWC is that chemical weapons production facilities should normally be destroyed outright. However, under Art. V, para. 13, "in cases of exceptional and compelling need," the OPCW can give permission to States Parties to modify chemical weapons production facilities to be used for the first six years of the Convention's operation for permitted purposes, as long as it was used for such purposes before the Convention came into operation (DTI Notes on Clauses: 55). Under Art. V, para. 12 CWC, a chemical weapons production facility 'may be temporarily converted for destruction of chemical weapons. ... Such a converted facility must be destroyed as soon as it is no longer in use for the destruction of chemical weapons but, in any case, not later than 10 years after entry into force of this Convention.' This subsection will allow for a temporary chemical weapons destruction facility to be altered or destroyed in accordance with the Convention.

Powers derived from ss.12–15 can only be used in relation to the production of Sched. 1 and other highly dangerous chemicals, and not to lesser chemicals that might constitute chemical weapons for the purpose of s.1. See notes to s.12 for further details.

Power where notice not complied with

14.—(1) For the purposes of this section the qualifying condition is that—
(a) a notice has been prepared under section 13,
(b) the provisions of section 13(1) to (3) have been complied with in relation to the notice,
(c) the notice has not been revoked, and
(d) any requirement set out in the notice has not been complied with.
(2) If—
(a) a justice of the peace is satisfied on information on oath that the qualifying condition is fulfilled, or
(b) in Scotland a justice, within the meaning of section 307 of the Criminal Procedure (Scotland) Act 1995, is satisfied by evidence on oath that the qualifying condition is fulfilled,
he may issue a warrant in writing authorising a person acting under the authority of the Secretary of State to take remedial action under this section.
(3) If a person is authorised by a warrant to take remedial action under this section he may—

   (a) enter the land on which the equipment or building is situated, if necessary by force;

   (b) do whatever is required to secure that the equipment or building is destroyed or altered in a manner specified in the notice;

   (c) take with him such other persons and such equipment as appear to him to be necessary to help him to exercise the powers mentioned in paragraphs (a) and (b).

   (4) The powers conferred on an authorised person under this section shall only be exercisable, if the warrant so provides, in the presence of a constable.

   (5) If anything is done in exercise of the powers mentioned in this section, the Secretary of State may recover from a responsible person any costs reasonably incurred by the Secretary of State in connection with the exercise of those powers; and a responsible person is—

   (a) in the case of equipment, any person in possession of the equipment at the time the land is entered;

   (b) in the case of a building, any person occupying the land at the time it is entered.

DEFINITIONS
   "destroyed": s.18(2).
   "qualifying condition": subs. (1).
   "responsible person": subs. (5).

GENERAL NOTE
   Where a notice has been properly served under s.13 demanding that a building be destroyed or altered, and that notice has not been fully complied with, then s.14 provides that a person authorised by the Secretary of State can apply to a Magistrate or Justice (in Scotland) for a warrant to enter, search, and destroy or alter the building or equipment concerned. Reasonable costs incurred during action taken under the warrant can be reclaimed by the Secretary of State from occupiers of land or possessors of equipment which are the subject of the warrant. This is in acknowledgement of the fact that these are 'the persons most likely to be directly responsible for the failure to implement a notice' (DTI Notes on clauses: 60).

   The DTI itself has described the powers under this section as 'drastic,' but justified, on the grounds of public safety and the need to fulfil the obligations of the U.K. under the CWC (DTI Notes on Clauses: 60).

   Under s.18(3), the existing powers of authorities to deal with suspicious objects are not affected by ss.12–14.

   It should be noted that powers given under ss.12–15 powers can only be used in relation to the production of Sched. 1 and other highly dangerous chemicals, and not to lesser chemicals that might constitute chemical weapons for the purpose of s.1. See notes on s.12 for further details.

Subs. (4)
   As with other warrants available under the Act (see for example, s.15(5)), the warrant may provide that actions taken under it be in the presence of a constable. These provisions are made where it is anticipated that a breach of the peace may result from the action taken under the warrant (DTI Notes on Clauses: 60).

Position where no notice can be served

   15.—(1) For the purposes of this section the qualifying condition is that—

   (a) the Secretary of State has reasonable cause to believe that any equipment or building is a chemical weapons production facility,

   (b) in the period of six months beginning with the day after he formed his belief it has not been possible to serve a copy of a notice under section 13 because of the circumstances mentioned in subsection (2), and

   (c) the Secretary of State has drawn up proposals for the destruction or alteration of the equipment or building in a manner specified in the proposals.

   (2) The circumstances are that—

   (a) no person appeared to the Secretary of State to occupy the land on which the equipment or building is situated,

   (b) if the Secretary of State's belief relates to equipment, no person appeared to the Secretary of State to have the equipment in his possession, and

   (c) no person appeared to the Secretary of State to have an interest which the Secretary of State believed would be materially affected by the destruction or alteration of the equipment or building.

(3) If—

   (a) a justice of the peace is satisfied on information on oath that the qualifying condition is fulfilled, or

   (b) in Scotland a justice, within the meaning of section 307 of the Criminal Procedure (Scotland) Act 1995, is satisfied by evidence on oath that the qualifying condition is fulfilled,

he may issue a warrant in writing authorising a person acting under the authority of the Secretary of State to take remedial action under this section.

(4) If a person is authorised by a warrant to take remedial action under this section he may—

   (a) enter the land on which the equipment or building is situated, if necessary by force;

   (b) do whatever is required to secure that the equipment or building is destroyed or altered in a manner specified in the proposals drawn up by the Secretary of State;

   (c) take with him such other persons and such equipment as appear to him to be necessary to help him to exercise the powers mentioned in paragraphs (a) and (b).

(5) The powers conferred on an authorised person under this section shall only be exercisable, if the warrant so provides, in the presence of a constable.

(6) If anything is done in exercise of the powers mentioned in this section, the Secretary of State may recover from a responsible person any costs reasonably incurred by the Secretary of State in connection with the exercise of those powers; and a responsible person is—

   (a) in the case of equipment, any person in possession of the equipment at the time the land is entered;

   (b) in the case of a building, any person occupying the land at the time it is entered.

DEFINITIONS

"circumstances": subs. (2).
"chemical weapons production facility": s.18(1).
"destroyed": s.18(2).
"qualifying condition": subs. (1).

GENERAL NOTE

This section concerns those cases in which it has not been possible to issue a notice to destroy or alter a suspected chemical weapons production facility under s.13, because a suitable recipient could not be identified by the Secretary of State within six months of forming a suspicion regarding the building or equipment. Because no notice has been issued, such cases fall outside the limits of ss.13 and 14.

The section provides that a person authorised by the Secretary of State can apply to a Magistrate or Justice (in Scotland) for a warrant to enter, search, and destroy or alter the building or equipment concerned. Reasonable costs incurred during action taken under the warrant can be reclaimed by the Secretary of State from occupiers of land or possessors of equipment which are the subject of the warrant. This is to cover the instance where a responsible person appears after the six-month waiting period and a decision has been taken by the Secretary of State to act under s.15 (DTI Notes on Clauses: 65).

The DTI itself has described the powers under this section as 'drastic,' but justified, on the grounds of public safety and the need to fulfil the obligations of the U.K. under the CWC (DTI Notes on Clauses: 66).

Powers provided for under ss.12–15 can only be used in relation to the production of Sched. 1 and other highly dangerous chemicals, and not to lesser chemicals that might constitute chemical weapons for the purpose of s.1 . See notes to s.12 for further details.

Under s.18(3), the existing powers of authorities to deal with suspicious objects are not affected by ss.12–14.

Subs. (4)

As with other warrants available under the Act (see for example, s.14(5)), the warrant may provide that actions taken under it be in the presence of a constable. These provisions are made where it is anticipated that a breach of the peace may result from the action taken under the warrant (DTI Notes on Clauses: 60).

Compensation for destruction or alteration

16.—(1) This section applies if a person claims that—

  (a) any equipment or building has been destroyed or altered in compliance with a notice falling within section 13(3) or has been destroyed or altered under section 14,

  (b) he had an interest which was materially affected by the destruction or alteration and he sustained loss as a result, and

  (c) no copy of a notice was served on him under section 13.

(2) This section also applies if a person claims that—

  (a) any equipment or building has been destroyed or altered under section 15, and

  (b) he had an interest which was materially affected by the destruction or alteration and he sustained loss as a result.

(3) If the person concerned makes an application under this section to the High Court or in Scotland the Court of Session, and the Court finds that his claim is justified, the Court may order the Secretary of State to pay to the applicant such amount (if any) by way of compensation as the Court considers just.

(4) If the Court believes that the equipment or building would have been destroyed or altered even if a copy of a notice had been served on the applicant under section 13 the Court must not order compensation to be paid under this section.

DEFINITIONS

"destroyed": s.8(2).

GENERAL NOTE

This section concerns the provision of compensation to those persons whose interest in any equipment or building was materially affected by the destruction or alteration of that equipment or building pursuant to s.13(3) or s.14, without notice to the claimant.

Subs. (3)

The claimant must make an application to the High Court or the Court of Session in Scotland which, if satisfied that the claim is justified, will order the Secretary of State to pay to the claimant such compensation as the court sees fit. There are no limits on the amount of compensation which the court can award, but nor is there any obligation on the courts to award compensation at all.

Subs. (4)

The court shall not order compensation for the claimant if it believes that even if the notice had been duly served, the building or equipment would have been destroyed. For example, if the courts finds that the building or equipment would have been destroyed because it was a chemical weapon production facility within s.18(1), then the claimant would undoubtedly have been guilty of an offence under s.2, and could not rightly receive compensation.

There is no formal procedure for the making of representations to the Secretary of State as to whether a building or piece of equipment which is the subject of a s.13 notice is a chemical weapons production facility. This is because it is felt that the definition of a chemical weapons production facility in s.18(1) is detailed enough that extensive representations are unlikely to be necessary. However, compensation is given to those who are not notified, in recognition of the fact that such persons will not even be able to challenge the Secretary of State's intentions to destroy equipment or buildings in advance by letter or judicial review, because they will not be aware of such intentions. It appears from the DTI notes on the Act that s.13 notices are expected to be on occasion, a serious security risk, and that in those cases where it is too dangerous to publish a description of a suspected chemical weapons production facility, compensation is intended to be a "long-stop" (DTI Notes on Clauses: 69). This may cause trouble, given that the destruction or alteration of buildings or equipment under ss.14 or 15 can only be legally allowed where a notice has actually been issued or was impossible to issue.

Offences relating to destruction etc.

17.—(1) If—
(a) a copy of a notice is served on a person under section 12,
(b) the notice relates to equipment in his possession at the time the copy is served,
(c) he relinquishes possession of, or alters or uses, the equipment before the date specified under section 12(4), and
(d) he has no reasonable excuse for doing so,
he is guilty of an offence.
(2) If—
(a) a copy of a notice is served on a person under section 13,
(b) the notice relates to equipment in his possession at the time the copy is served or to a building situated on land he occupies at that time,
(c) any requirement set out in the notice is not fulfilled, and
(d) he has no reasonable excuse for the requirement not being fulfilled,
he is guilty of an offence.
(3) If a person wilfully obstructs—
(a) a person exercising, or attempting to exercise, the powers mentioned in section 14(3)(a) or (b) or 15(4)(a) or (b), or
(b) any other person taken with him as mentioned in section 14(3)(c) or 15(4)(c) and helping him, or attempting to help him, to exercise those powers,
the person so obstructing is guilty of an offence.
(4) A person guilty of an offence under any of the preceding provisions of this section is liable—
(a) on summary conviction, to a fine of an amount not exceeding the statutory maximum;
(b) on conviction on indictment, to a fine.
(5) A person who knowingly makes a false or misleading statement in response to a notice served under section 12 is guilty of an offence and liable—
(a) on summary conviction, to a fine of an amount not exceeding the statutory maximum;
(b) on conviction on indictment, to imprisonment for a term not exceeding two years or to a fine or to both.

General Note
   This section runs in parallel with s.9 by creating offences in order to prevent any unauthorised attempts to impede the destruction or alteration of a chemical weapons production facility by the Secretary of State.
   Failure to comply with a notice either by dealing with buildings or equipment in a way contrary to the notice, or by failing to comply with a requirement in a notice, is an offence punishable by fine. It is also an offence to supply false or misleading information in a representation, punishable by fine or imprisonment. The provision of false information carries a higher penalty than the obstruction of the exercise of powers because while obstruction may delay proceedings, false information may 'frustrate the whole process and prevent the Secretary of State from dealing with a potentially dangerous chemical weapons production facility' (DTI Notes in Clauses: 74).
   Section 31(2)–(5) applies these offences.

Destruction etc: supplementary

18.—(1) In sections 12 to 15 "chemical weapons production facility" has the meaning given by the definition of that expression in the Convention, and for this purpose—

(a) expressions used in the definition in the Convention shall be construed in accordance with the Convention, and

(b) section 1 shall be ignored.

(2) For the purposes of sections 12 to 16 "destroyed" and "destruction", in relation to a building, mean demolished and demolition.

(3) Nothing in sections 12 to 15 affects any power arising otherwise than by virtue of those sections (such as a power to dispose of property in police possession in connection with the investigation of a suspected offence).

DEFINITIONS

"Convention, the": s.1(8).

GENERAL NOTE

Section 18 provides definitions of "chemical weapons production facility," "destroyed" and "destruction" for the purposes of ss.12–15.

Subs. (1)

"Chemical weapons production facility" is defined for the purpose of ss.12–15 according to the CWC and *not* according to s.1 of the Act. Article II, para. 8 of the CWC defines chemical weapons production facilities as follows:

'8. "Chemical Weapons Production Facility":

(a) Means any equipment, as well as any building housing such equipment, that was designed, constructed or used at any time since 1 January 1946:

(i) As part of a stage in the production of chemicals ("final technological stage") where the material flows would contain, when equipment is in operation:

(1) Any chemical listed in Schedule 1 in the Annex on Chemicals; or

(2) Any other chemical that has no use, above 1 tonne per year on the territory of a State Party or in any other place under the jurisdiction or control of a state Party, for purposes not prohibited under this Convention but can be used for chemical weapons purposes;

or

(ii) For filling chemical weapons, including, *inter alia*, the filling of chemicals listed in Schedule 1 into munitions, devices or bulk storage containers; the filling of chemicals into containers that form a part of assembled binary munitions and devices or into chemical sub munitions that form part of assembled unitary munitions and devices, and the loading of the containers and chemical sub munitions into the respective munitions and devices;

(b) Does not mean :

(i) Any facility having a production capacity for synthesis of chemicals specified in subparagraph (a)(i) that is less than 1 tonne;

(ii) Any facility in which a chemical specified in subparagraph (a)(i) is or was produced as an unavoidable by-product of activities for purposes not prohibited by the Convention, provided that the chemical does not exceed 3 percent of the total product and that the facility is subject to declaration and inspection under the Annex on Implementation and Verification (hereinafter referred to as the Verification Annex);

(iii) The single small-scale facility for production of chemicals listed in Schedule 1 for purposes not prohibited under this Convention as referred to in Part VI of the Verification Annex.'

In brief, for the purposes of ss.12–15, a chemical production facility is buildings and or equipment which are (a) designed to produce chemicals listed in the Schedule to the Act (and Sched. 1 of the Convention) or (b) designed to produce other chemicals which have no permitted use, can be used for chemical weapons purposes, and are present in large amounts or (c) used in filling or loading munitions with either of those categories of chemical. The CWC definition focuses on the most dangerous of chemicals, and is narrower than the definition of a chemical weapon under s.1 of the Act.

It should be noted that as far as the offence of producing a chemical weapon under s.11 is concerned, the wider definition of s.1 of the Act is to be used.

Subs. (3)

Subsection (3) ensures that common law and statutory powers such as those of a police officer when investigating a suspected offence are not affected by ss.12–15. This may be of particular importance where police officers accompany authorised searchers under ss.14 or 15 (DTI Notes on Clauses: 77).

Chemicals for permitted purposes

Restriction on use etc.

19.—(1) Subject to section 20 (which relates to licences) no person shall—

(a) use a Schedule 1 toxic chemical or precursor for a permitted purpose, or

(b) produce or have in his possession a Schedule 1 toxic chemical or precursor with the intention that it will be used for a permitted purpose.

(2) A Schedule 1 toxic chemical or precursor is a toxic chemical or precursor listed in Schedule 1 to the annex on chemicals to the Convention; and for ease of reference that Schedule is set out in the Schedule to this Act.

(3) A person contravening this section is guilty of an offence and liable—

(a) on summary conviction, to a fine of an amount not exceeding the statutory maximum;

(b) on conviction on indictment, to a fine.

DEFINITIONS

"Convention, the": s.1(8).
"permitted purpose": s.1(3).
"precursor": s.1(6).
"Schedule 1 toxic chemical or precursor": subs. (2).
"toxic chemical": s.1(5).

GENERAL NOTE

It is an offence to use, produce, or have in one's possession, for a permitted purpose, a chemical listed in Sched. 1. The punishment for such an offence is a fine. To use, produce, or have in one's possession a chemical listed in Sched. 1 where such actions are *not* intended to be for a permitted purpose is already made an offence under s.2(1). The ss.2(1) and 19 ban on the use of Sched. 1 chemicals is broken only in favour of those producers who obtain a s.20 licence. The impact of these sections is to control the production of the particularly dangerous Sched. 1 chemicals to a selected and clearly identifiable group.

Sections 19 and 20 together implement the obligations of the U.K. under Pt. VI of the Verification Annex to the CWC, which provides that the production of Sched. 1 facilities can be licensed by States Parties. Pt. VI states that:

'2. A State Party shall not produce, acquire, retain, transfer or use Schedule 1 chemicals unless:

(a) The chemicals are applied to research, medical, pharmaceutical or protective purposes; and

(b) The types and quantities of chemicals are strictly limited to those which can be justified for such purposes; and

(c) The aggregate amount of such chemicals at any given time for such purposes is equal to or less than 1 tonne; and

(d) The aggregate amount for such purposes acquired by a State Party in any year through production, withdrawal from chemical stocks and transfer is equal to or less than 1 tonne.

...

8. Each State Party that produces Schedule 1 chemical, for research, medical, pharmaceutical or protective purposes shall carry out the production at a single small-scale facility approved by the State Party, except as set forth in paragraphs 10, 11 and 12.

...

10. Production of Schedule 1 chemicals in aggregate quantities not exceeding 10 KG over a year may be carried out for protective purposes at one facility outside a single small-scale facility. This facility shall be approved by the State Party.

11. Production of Schedule 1 chemicals in quantities of more than 100 g per year may be carried out for research medical or pharmaceutical purposes outside a single small-scale facility in aggregate quantities not exceeding 10 kg per year per facility. These facilities shall be approved by the State Party.

12. Synthesis of Schedule 1 chemicals for research, medical or pharmaceutical purposes, but not for protective purposes, may be carried out in aggregate quantities of less than 100 g per year per facility. These facilities shall not be subject to any obligation relating to declaration and verification as specified in D and E.'

Licences

20.—(1) Section 19 does not apply to anything done in accordance with the terms of a licence granted by the Secretary of State and having effect at the time it is done.

(2) The Secretary of State may—

(a) grant a licence in such circumstances and on such terms as he thinks fit;

(b) vary or revoke a licence by serving a notice to that effect on the person to whom the licence was granted.

(3) A variation or revocation shall take effect at such reasonable time as is specified in the notice served under subsection (2)(b).

(4) The Secretary of State may by order make provision with respect to appealing against a refusal to grant, renew or vary a licence or against a variation or revocation of a licence.

(5) An order under subsection (4) shall be made by statutory instrument subject to annulment in pursuance of a resolution of either House of Parliament.

(6) A person who knowingly makes a false or misleading statement for the purpose of obtaining a licence or a renewal or variation of a licence, or of opposing a variation or revocation of a licence, is guilty of an offence and liable—

(a) on summary conviction, to a fine of an amount not exceeding the statutory maximum;

(b) on conviction on indictment, to imprisonment for a term not exceeding two years or to a fine or to both.

GENERAL NOTE

Section 20 ensures that the s.19 ban on the use, production or possession of Sched. 1 chemicals will not apply to acts done under licence. It lays down the powers of the Secretary of State to grant, vary, revoke and renew such licences as well as the method by which appeals can be made against such decisions. It is an offence to make false or misleading statements in the course of seeking a decision in relation to a licence.

Sections 19 and 20 together implement the obligations of the U.K. under Pt. VI of the Verification Annex to the CWC, which provides that the production of Sched. 1 facilities can be licensed by States Parties. See the notes to s.19 for the relevant text of the CWC.

Subss. (1), (2) and (3)

The s.19 ban on using Sched. 1 chemicals, even for a permitted purpose does not apply to acts done under a licence granted by the Secretary of State. There are no guidelines laid down regarding what types of applications should be accepted or rejected. In particular, it was pointed out in the House of Commons that it is not clear 'who will decide what is or is not acceptable research' and therefore whether academics will be granted licences to use chemicals on application (*Hansard*, H.C. Vol. 267, col. 832).

According to the DTI, it is intended that licences granted by the Secretary of State will include conditions which will ensure that production of Sched. 1 chemicals in the U.K. will conform to the rules laid down in paras. 2, 8, 10, 11 and 12 of Pt. VI of the Verification Annex (DTI Notes on Clauses: 83). Licences may be varied or revoked by notice. During debates in the Committee stage in the House of Commons, the Government indicated that it expected to reduce the administrative burden falling on the DTI by issuing an open licence to possess, *etc.*, chemicals listed in Sched. 1 up to about 5 g. 'It would be difficult to issue open licences for larger levels such as 100 g because that would take us outside the convention's requirements to limit schedule 1 chemicals to 1 tonne.' The Government expressed particular interest in the issuing of open licences for research purposes (*Hansard*, H.C. Vol. 268, col. 441. H.L. Vol. 568, col. 1381).

Subss. (4) and (5)

The Secretary of State is empowered to create procedures for appeal against decisions made in relation to licences. Such provisions will be established in statutory instruments to be passed through Parliament by negative resolution procedure. Attempts made during the Committee Stage in the House of Commons to require statutory instruments passed under this section and s.23 to be positively approved (by affirmative procedure) by Parliament were resisted by the Government (*Hansard*, H.C. Vol. 268, col. 413).

The structure for appeals is left entirely at the discretion of the Secretary of State. During the Committee stages in both Houses, the Government stated its intention to use the model appeal procedures soon to be proscribed by order under the Deregulation and Contracting Out Act 1994 (c. 40). Any appeals committee for these purposes would include members of a variety of backgrounds, including research, academic and medical (*Hansard*, H.L. Vol. 569, col. 1438. H.C. Vol. 268, col. 416).

No provision is made for appeals against the granting of a licence.

Information and records

Information for purposes of Act

21.—(1) If the Secretary of State has grounds to suspect that a person is committing or has committed an offence under this Act the Secretary of State may by notice served on the person require him to give in such form as is specified in the notice, and within such reasonable period as is so specified, such information as—

(a) the Secretary of State has reasonable cause to believe will help to establish whether the person is committing or has committed such an offence, and

(b) is specified in the notice.

(2) A person who without reasonable excuse fails to comply with a notice served on him under subsection (1) is guilty of an offence and liable—

(a) on summary conviction, to a fine of an amount not exceeding the statutory maximum;

(b) on conviction on indictment, to a fine.

(3) A person on whom a notice is served under subsection (1) and who knowingly makes a false or misleading statement in response to it is guilty of an offence and liable—

(a) on summary conviction, to a fine of an amount not exceeding the statutory maximum;

(b) on conviction on indictment, to imprisonment for a term not exceeding two years or to a fine or to both.

GENERAL NOTE

The Secretary of State is empowered to demand information from a person where there are grounds to suspect that they have committed or are committing an offence under the Act. It is an offence to fail to provide information, or knowingly to provide false or misleading information in response to a notice issued under subs. (1). Punishment for the former is a fine, and for the latter a fine and or imprisonment for up to two years. Presumably a more severe punishment is given for fraudulent or misleading statements because these are considered to be more dangerous than failure to disclose information at all.

Sections 30 and 31(2)–(5) apply to offences under this provision.

Information and records for purposes of Convention

22.—(1) The Secretary of State may by notice served on any person require him to give in such form as is specified in the notice, and within such reasonable period as is so specified, such information as—

(a) the Secretary of State has reasonable cause to believe is or will be needed in connection with anything to be done for the purposes of the Convention, and

(b) is specified in the notice;

and the information required by a notice may relate to a state of affairs subsisting before the coming into force of this Act or of the Convention.

(2) The Secretary of State may by notice served on any person require him to keep such records as—

(a) the Secretary of State has reasonable cause to believe will facilitate the giving of information the person may at any time be required to give under subsection (1), and

(b) are specified in the notice.

(3) A person who without reasonable excuse fails to comply with a notice served on him under subsection (1) or (2) is guilty of an offence and liable—

(a) on summary conviction, to a fine of an amount not exceeding the statutory maximum;

(b) on conviction on indictment, to a fine.

(4) A person on whom a notice is served under subsection (1) and who knowingly makes a false or misleading statement in response to it is guilty of an offence and liable—

(a) on summary conviction, to a fine of an amount not exceeding the statutory maximum;

(b) on conviction on indictment, to imprisonment for a term not exceeding two years or to a fine or to both.

DEFINITIONS
"Convention, the": s.1(8).

GENERAL NOTE
In contrast to s.21, here the Secretary of State is empowered to demand the supply of information and the keeping of records where there is reasonable cause to believe this is needed in connection with the CWC.

The need for the far reaching powers in ss.22 and 23 to be vested in the Secretary of State is clear. The CWC has wide ranging requirements for the supply of information. For example, under Art. III, para. 1, "each State Party shall submit to the Organisation, not later than 30 days after this Convention enters into force for it, the following declarations, in which it shall" disclose, *inter alia*, the amount and location of any chemical weapons and chemical weapons production facilities which it owns, and or which are found within its jurisdiction. Riot control agents must also be declared under Art. III, para. 1(e). In addition, there is a wide range of information which falls outside these specific declarations which the DTI will require in order to fulfil its obligation under Art. VII CWC to "adopt the necessary measures to implement its obligations under this Convention." More specifically, Art. VI, para. 2 CWC states that "each State Party shall adopt the necessary measures to ensure that toxic chemicals and their precursors are only developed, produced, otherwise acquired, retained, transferred or used within its territory or in any other place under its jurisdiction or control for purposes not prohibited under this Convention."

Section 22 gives the Secretary of State the power to obtain the information needed to fulfil these obligations. It is an offence to fail to provide information, or knowingly to provide false or misleading information in response to a notice issued under subs. (1). Punishment for the former is a fine, and for the latter a fine and or imprisonment for up to two years. The provision of false or misleading information in response to a notice may lead to submission of a false declaration to the OPCW under Art. III of the Convention, and therefore attracts a more severe penalty than total failure to disclose information (DTI Notes on Clauses: 90).

Identifying persons who have information

23.—(1) The Secretary of State may make regulations requiring persons of any description specified in the regulations to inform him that they are of such a description.

(2) Any such description must be so framed that persons within it are persons on whom the Secretary of State is likely to want to serve a notice under section 22.

(3) If regulations are made under this section the Secretary of State shall arrange for a statement of the fact that they have been made to be published in such manner as is likely to bring them to the attention of persons affected by them.

(4) A person who without reasonable excuse fails to comply with a requirement imposed by the regulations is guilty of an offence and liable—

(a) on summary conviction, to a fine of an amount not exceeding the statutory maximum;

(b) on conviction on indictment, to a fine.

(5) A person who knowingly makes a false or misleading statement in response to a requirement imposed by the regulations is guilty of an offence and liable—

    (a) on summary conviction, to a fine of an amount not exceeding the statutory maximum;

    (b) on conviction on indictment, to imprisonment for a term not exceeding two years or to a fine or to both.

(6) The regulations shall be made by statutory instrument subject to annulment in pursuance of a resolution of either House of Parliament.

GENERAL NOTE

Section 23 empowers the Secretary of State to place a degree of responsibility for the volunteering of information for the purposes of s.22 (*i.e.* the vast amounts of information required by the Secretary of State for the purposes of declarations and general monitoring under the CWC) upon individuals and companies in the U.K., by requiring certain categories of individual and companies to identify themselves as likely to be of interest to the Secretary of State under s.22. According to the DTI, it was not possible to define within the Act itself, which persons will be required to make themselves known to the Secretary of State, as the State Parties to the CWC have yet to agree on the extent of the information which States Parties will need to provide in declarations under the Convention. This was a primary reason for leaving the determination of this matter to the Secretary of State (DTI Notes on Clauses: 92, *Hansard*, H.C. Vol. 268, col. 417). The section provides the Secretary of State with the power to define the categories of person affected by regulation to be passed through the Houses of Parliament by negative resolution procedure.

The fact that such a regulation has been passed must be made known to the people who may be affected by it. Failure to comply with regulations is an offence punishable by a fine, and the conscious making of false or misleading statements is an offence punishable by fine and or imprisonment. Sections 30 and 31(2) apply to these offences.

The fact that this section provides for the passing of delegated legislation by negative procedure, as well as a similar provision in s.20, was debated at length in the House of Commons (*Hansard*, Vol. 268, col. 414).

Inspections under Convention

Inspections: interpretation

24. For the purposes of sections 25 to 28—

    (a) the verification annex is the annex on implementation and verification to the Convention;

    (b) a routine inspection is an inspection conducted pursuant to Parts II to IX of that annex;

    (c) a challenge inspection is an inspection conducted pursuant to Parts II and X of that annex;

    (d) an assistance inspection is an inspection conducted pursuant to Parts II and XI of that annex;

    (e) "in-country escort", "inspector", "inspection team" and "observer" have the meanings given by Part I of that annex.

DEFINITIONS

"verification annex": subs. (a).

GENERAL NOTE

See generally Perry Robinson 3.

The definitions used in relation to inspections in the Act are tied firmly to those in the Convention. In the CWC, a routine inspection is a regular inspection of countries' relevant sites to ensure that declarations made by States Parties to the OPCW are accurate. They are governed by Pts. IV–IX of the Verification Annex to the CWC. A 'Challenge inspection' is an inspection of a country's relevant sites, whether declared or not, conducted in response to a request by another State Party. These are governed by Pts. II and X of the Verification Annex. An assistance inspection is initiated by the OPCW, in response to fears of another State Party that it is or is likely to be under threat from acts conducted by another state, which are prohibited by the Convention, such as attacks by chemical weapons or riot control agents. These are governed by Pts. II and XI of the Verification Annex.

Inspections have been described as one of a series of 'devices for generating confidence that benefits promised by the treaty would actually materialise, if not fully then at least to a cost-compensating extent ... Thus conceived, the function of verification is not to ascertain that States Parties are complying with their obligations. That would anyway be impossible, for many of the obligations are negative ones ... Rather, the function of verification is to build sufficient confidence in the elimination of chemical weapons for States Parties to continue accepting the burdens and restrictions of the regime' (Perry Robinson 3 1994: p.489).

Other pieces of legislation dealing with international inspectors include the Nuclear Safeguards and Electricity (Finance) Act 1978 (c. 25) (involving inspections by the International Atomic Energy Agency) and the Arms Control and Disarmament (Inspections) Act 1991 (c. 41) (involving inspections under the Conventional Forces in Europe Treaty).

Rights of entry etc. for purposes of inspections

25.—(1) If it is proposed to conduct a routine inspection, a challenge inspection or an assistance inspection in the United Kingdom, the Secretary of State may issue an authorisation under this section in respect of that inspection.

(2) An authorisation under this section shall—

(a) contain a description of the area (the specified area) in which the inspection is to be conducted,

(b) specify the type of inspection concerned,

(c) state the names of the members of the inspection team by whom the inspection is to be carried out, and

(d) in the case of a challenge inspection, state the name of any observer who may accompany the team.

(3) Such an authorisation shall have the effect of authorising the inspection team—

(a) to exercise within the specified area such rights of access, entry and unobstructed inspection as are conferred on them by the verification annex, and

(b) to do such other things within that area in connection with the inspection as they are entitled to do by virtue of the verification annex (including things concerning the maintenance, replacement or adjustment of any instrument or other object).

(4) Such an authorisation shall in addition have the effect of—

(a) authorising an in-country escort to accompany the inspection team in accordance with the provisions of the verification annex, and

(b) authorising any constable to give such assistance as the in-country escort may request for the purpose of facilitating the conduct of the inspection in accordance with the verification annex;

and the name of the person in charge of the in-country escort shall be stated in the authorisation.

(5) An authorisation under this section in the case of a challenge inspection shall in addition have the effect of authorising the observer to exercise within the specified area such rights of access and entry as are conferred on him by the verification annex.

(6) Any constable giving assistance in accordance with subsection (4)(b) may use such reasonable force as he considers necessary for the purpose mentioned in that provision.

(7) The occupier of any premises—

(a) in relation to which it is proposed to exercise a right of entry in reliance on an authorisation under this section, or

(b) on which an inspection is being carried out in reliance on such an authorisation,

or a person acting on behalf of the occupier of any such premises, shall be entitled to require a copy of the authorisation to be shown to him by a member of the in-country escort.

(8) The validity of any authorisation purporting to be issued under this section in respect of any inspection shall not be called in question in any court of law at any time before the conclusion of that inspection.

(9) Accordingly, where an authorisation purports to be issued under this section in respect of any inspection, no proceedings (of whatever nature) shall be brought at any time before the conclusion of the inspection if they would, if successful, have the effect of preventing, delaying or otherwise affecting the carrying out of the inspection.

(10) If in any proceedings any question arises whether a person at any time was or was not, in relation to any routine, challenge or assistance inspection, a member of the inspection team or a member of the in-country escort or the observer, a certificate issued by or under the authority of the Secretary of State stating any fact relating to that question shall be conclusive evidence of that fact.

(11) If an authorisation is issued under this section the Secretary of State may issue an amendment varying the specified area, and—

(a) from the time when the amendment is expressed to take effect this section shall apply as if the specified area were the area as varied;

(b) subsection (8) shall apply to the amendment as it applies to the authorisation;

(c) the Secretary of State may issue further amendments varying the specified area and in such a case paragraphs (a) and (b) shall apply.

DEFINITIONS

"assistance inspection": s.24(d).
"challenge inspection": s.24(c).
"in country escort": s.24(e).
"inspection team": s.24(e).
"inspector": s.24(e).
"observer": s.24(e).
"routine inspection": s.24(b).
"verification annex": s.24(a).

GENERAL NOTE

This section concerns empowering the Secretary of State to facilitate inspections by OPCW officials, as required under the CWC.

Subss. (8) and (9)

In order to ensure that inspections are not delayed, in contravention of the CWC, the Act provides that no legal action can be brought in relation to an inspection where to do so would interfere with its timely completion. In particular, no authorisation can be challenged prior to completion of the inspection.

Offences in connection with inspections

26.—(1) If an authorisation has been issued under section 25 in respect of any inspection, a person is guilty of an offence if he—

(a) refuses without reasonable excuse to comply with any request made by any constable or a member of the in-country escort for the purpose of facilitating the conduct of that inspection in accordance with the verification annex,

(b) interferes without reasonable excuse with any container, instrument or other object installed in the course of that inspection in accordance with the verification annex, or

(c) wilfully obstructs any member of the inspection team or of the in-country escort, or the observer, in the conduct of that inspection in accordance with the verification annex.

(2) Subsection (1)(b) applies to interference which occurs at any time while the container, instrument or other object is retained in accordance with the verification annex.

(3) A person guilty of an offence under this section is liable—

(a) on summary conviction, to a fine of an amount not exceeding the statutory maximum;

(b) on conviction on indictment, to a fine.

"in country escort": s.24(e).
"inspection team": s.24(e).
"object": s.1(7).
"observer": s.24(e).
"verification annex": s.24(a).

GENERAL NOTE

This section ensures the smooth running of inspections made under the CWC, by providing that various methods of impeding an inspection are offences punishable by fine. For example, paras. 9 and 10 of the verification annex allow inspection teams to leave such things as monitoring devices and information collection containers to store collected information on premises for the purpose of future monitoring (DTI Notes on Clauses: 104). Special provision is made in this section of the Act to protect such objects during and after the inspection.

It is not an offence knowingly to give false or misleading information to an inspection team. This matter was debated in the House of Commons Committee stage (*Hansard*, H.C. Vol. 268, col. 421). The Parliamentary Under Secretary of State for Trade and Industry stated that it was not advisable to create such an offence because,

"it would be extreme to penalise a person who might just be a plant worker who knows little about the chemical weapons convention, and who may not have been warned formally not to make a misleading or false statement, especially bearing in mind that the inspectors may well be international and not U.K. citizens, which might lead to some confusion. Also, given that the chemical industry competes internationally, plant workers might be keen not to breach commercial confidentiality, which is understandable" (*Hansard*, H.C. Vol. 268, col. 421). Sections 30 and 31(2)–(5) apply to offences under this section.

Privileges and immunities in connection with inspections

27.—(1) Members of inspection teams and observers shall enjoy the same privileges and immunities as are enjoyed by diplomatic agents in accordance with the following provisions of the 1961 Articles, namely—

(a) Article 29,

(b) paragraphs 1 and 2 of Article 30,

(c) paragraphs 1, 2 and 3 of Article 31, and

(d) Article 34.

(2) Such persons shall, in addition, enjoy the same privileges as are enjoyed by diplomatic agents in accordance with paragraph 1(b) of Article 36 of the 1961 Articles, except in relation to articles the importing or exporting of which is prohibited by law or controlled by the enactments relating to quarantine.

(3) Samples and approved equipment carried by members of an inspection team shall be inviolable and exempt from customs duties.

(4) The privileges and immunities accorded to members of inspection teams and observers by virtue of this section shall be enjoyed by them at any time when they are in the United Kingdom—

(a) in connection with the carrying out there of a routine inspection, a challenge inspection or an assistance inspection, or

(b) while in transit to or from the territory of another party to the Convention in connection with the carrying out of such an inspection there.

(5) If—

(a) immunity from jurisdiction of a member of an inspection team is waived in accordance with the verification annex, and

(b) a notice made by the Secretary of State and informing the member of the waiver is delivered to him in person,

then, from the time the notice is so delivered, this section shall not have effect to confer that immunity on the member.

(6) If in any proceedings any question arises whether a person is or is not entitled to any privilege or immunity by virtue of this section, a certificate issued by or under the authority of the Secretary of State stating any fact relating to that question shall be conclusive evidence of that fact.

(7) In this section—

"the 1961 Articles" means the Articles which are set out in Schedule 1 to the Diplomatic Privileges Act 1964 (Articles of Vienna Convention on Diplomatic Relations of 1961 having force of law in United Kingdom);

"approved equipment" and "samples" shall be construed in accordance with the verification annex;

"enactment" includes an enactment comprised in subordinate legislation (within the meaning of the Interpretation Act 1978).

DEFINITIONS
"approved equipment": subs. (7).
"assistance inspection": s.24(d).
"challenge inspection": s.24(c).
"Convention, the": s.1(8).
"enactment": subs. (7).
"in country escort": s.24(e).
"inspection team": s.24(e).
"observer": s.24(e).
"routine inspection": s.24(b).
"samples": subs. (7).
"verification annex": s.24(a).
"1961 Articles": subs. (7).

GENERAL NOTE
The purpose of this section is to ensure that inspectors and observers are given the privileges and immunities necessary for the efficient and objective exercise of their duties. Part II, para. 11 of the verification annex to the CWC requires that such privileges and immunities are to be granted to inspectors for the sake of this Convention and not for the personal benefit of the individuals themselves.

Subss. (1) , (2) and (7)
The privileges and immunities set out in the CWC are itemised in the Act by reference to their original sources in other international conventions. In particular, inspectors are guaranteed rights to inviolability of person, living quarters, offices, papers, correspondence, samples, equipment, and exemption from taxes and customs duties. No mention is made in the Act of the Pt. II, para. 11(h) verification annex statement that 'the members of the inspection team shall be accorded the same currency and exchange facilities as are accorded to representatives of foreign Governments on temporary official missions.'

The U.K. has bound itself, in accordance with the CWC to give such privileges and immunities to inspectors where they are either operating in the U.K., or are passing through the U.K. en route to performing an inspection in another state.

Subs. (5)
Under Pt. II, para. 11 of the verification annex to the CWC, the immunity of an inspector from the jurisdiction of a State Party can be waived by the Director General of the OPCW where "that immunity would impede the course of justice." Subsection (5) provides that such a waiver is to have effect from the time that notice of the waiver is delivered.

Under Pt. II, para. 11(i) and 13 of the verification annex, inspection team members are obliged to respect the laws of States Parties and are obliged not to undertake paid employment. Furthermore, State Parties are empowered to discuss alleged abuses of privileges and immunities with the Director General of the OPCW.

Reimbursement of expenditure

28. The Secretary of State may reimburse any person in respect of expenditure incurred in connection with a routine inspection, a challenge inspection or an assistance inspection.

DEFINITIONS
"assistance inspection": s.24(d).
"challenge inspection": s.24(c).
"routine inspection": s.24(b).

This section authorises the Secretary of State to reimburse expenses incurred by any person in relation to CWC inspections. The Pt. II, para. 26 of the Verification Annex to the CWC states that the State Party being inspected by an inspection team must make available to the team the necessary amenities. Expenditure of this kind is to be reimbursed under the Annex to the Secretary of State by the OPCW. Section 28 allows the Secretary of State to use those funds to reimburse private bodies who have provided such amenities to the teams (DTI Notes on Clauses: 109).

Offences: miscellaneous

Power to search and obtain evidence

29.—(1) If—

(a) a justice of the peace is satisfied on information on oath that there is reasonable ground for suspecting that an offence under this Act is being, has been or is about to be committed on any premises or that evidence of the commission of such an offence is to be found there, or

(b) in Scotland a justice, within the meaning of section 307 of the Criminal Procedure (Scotland) Act 1995, is satisfied by evidence on oath as mentioned in paragraph (a) above,

he may issue a warrant in writing authorising a person acting under the authority of the Secretary of State to enter the premises, if necessary by force, at any time within one month from the time of the issue of the warrant and to search them.

(2) A person who enters the premises under the authority of the warrant may—

(a) take with him such other persons and such equipment as appear to him to be necessary;

(b) inspect any document found on the premises which he has reasonable cause to believe may be required as evidence for the purposes of proceedings in respect of an offence under this Act;

(c) take copies of, or seize and remove, any such document;

(d) inspect, seize and remove any device or equipment found on the premises which he has reasonable cause to believe may be required as such evidence;

(e) inspect, sample, seize and remove any substance found on the premises which he has reasonable cause to believe may be required as such evidence;

(f) search or cause to be searched any person found on the premises whom he has reasonable cause to believe to be in possession of any document, device, equipment or substance;

but no woman or girl shall be searched except by a woman.

(3) The powers conferred by a warrant under this section shall only be exercisable, if the warrant so provides, in the presence of a constable.

Justices of the peace and justices in Scotland are empowered to issue warrants for entry into and searching of premises if they are satisfied that there are reasonable grounds for suspecting that it is or will be the scene of an offence, or that it houses evidence relating to an offence under the Act. The Secretary of State will then have a month during which to authorise persons to investigate the possibility of an offence. Persons authorised for such a search of premises can, *inter alia*, inspect, copy, seize and remove documents and substances, and search people found on the premises. However such activities can only be conducted where there is a reasonable cause to believe that the document, substance or person is connected to the suspected offence in a way specified in the subsection.

As under s.5, warrants issued under s.29 may provide that the search may only be carried out in the presence of a constable.

Forfeiture in case of conviction

30.—(1) The court by or before which a person is convicted of an offence under this Act may order that anything shown to the court's satisfaction to relate to the offence shall be forfeited, and either destroyed or otherwise dealt with in such manner as the court may order.

(2) In particular, the court may order the thing to be dealt with as the Secretary of State may see fit; and in such a case the Secretary of State may direct that it be destroyed or otherwise dealt with.

(3) Where—

(a) the court proposes to order anything to be forfeited under this section, and

(b) a person claiming to have an interest in it applies to be heard by the court,

the court must not order it to be forfeited unless he has been given an opportunity to show cause why the order should not be made.

GENERAL NOTE

Goods involved in offences under the Act may be forfeited or dealt with by the Secretary of State. Provision is made for persons with an interest in the thing to make representations as to why it should not be forfeited.

Offences: other provisions

31.—(1) Proceedings for an offence under section 2 or 11 shall not be instituted—

(a) in England and Wales, except by or with the consent of the Attorney General;

(b) in Northern Ireland, except by or with the consent of the Attorney General for Northern Ireland.

(2) Proceedings for an offence under any provision of this Act other than section 2 or 11 shall not be instituted except by or with the consent of the Secretary of State; but the preceding provisions of this subsection do not apply to Scotland.

(3) Where an offence under this Act is committed by a body corporate and is proved to have been committed with the consent or connivance of, or to be attributable to any neglect on the part of—

(a) a director, manager, secretary or other similar officer of the body corporate, or

(b) any person who was purporting to act in any such capacity,

he as well as the body corporate shall be guilty of that offence and shall be liable to be proceeded against and punished accordingly.

(4) In subsection (3) "director", in relation to a body corporate whose affairs are managed by its members, means a member of the body corporate.

(5) Where an offence under this Act is committed by a Scottish partnership and is proved to have been committed with the consent or connivance of a partner, he as well as the partnership shall be guilty of that offence and shall be liable to be proceeded against and punished accordingly.

DEFINITIONS

"director": subs. (4).

GENERAL NOTE

Subss. (1) and (2)

The most serious offences which are listed in ss.2 and 11 of the Act, and include the possession, manufacture, use and transfer of chemical weapons and the creation of a chemical weapons production facility, may only be prosecuted at the instigation of the Irish or English Attorney General. Prosecutions for lesser offences under the Act can only be brought by the Secretary of State, except in Scotland. The result is a division of responsibility for the bringing of prosecutions under the Act. In the case of less serious offences, the Secretary of State will be both 'the regulating authority and the prosecuting authority' (*Hansard*, H.C. Vol. 268, col. 425). This matter was debated at length in the House of Commons (*Hansard*, H.C. Vol. 268, col. 424). According to the DTI, the subsections are intended to ensure consistency and integrity in prosecutions by preventing private actions (DTI Notes on Clauses: 115).

Subsection (1) does not need to deal with the Lord Advocate of Scotland, who in any case is generally the only competent instigator of criminal prosecutions in Scotland (DTI Notes on Clauses: 115).

Subss. (3), (4) and (5)

These subsections ensure that members of companies shall be liable for offences committed by their company if the member added, by connivance, consent or neglect, to the commission of the offence. Partners in Scottish partnerships are only liable to be prosecuted if they exhibited consent or connivance in the offence. Neglect by a Scottish partner is apparently not enough to incur liability.

Other miscellaneous provisions

Disclosure of information

32.—(1) This section applies to information if—

   (a) it was obtained under, or in connection with anything done under, this Act or the Convention, and

   (b) it relates to a particular business or other activity carried on by any person.

(2) So long as the business or activity continues to be carried on the information shall not be disclosed except—

   (a) with the consent of the person for the time being carrying on the business or activity,

   (b) in connection with anything done for the purposes of the Convention,

   (c) in connection with anything done for the purposes of this Act,

   (d) in connection with the investigation of any criminal offence or for the purposes of any criminal proceedings,

   (e) in connection with the enforcement of any restriction on imports or exports,

   (f) in dealing with an emergency involving danger to the public,

   (g) with a view to ensuring the security of the United Kingdom, or

   (h) to the International Court of Justice for the purpose of enabling that Court to deal with any dispute referred to it under the Convention.

(3) The reference to this Act in subsection (2)(c) does not include a reference to section 33.

(4) A person who discloses information in contravention of this section is guilty of an offence and liable—

   (a) on summary conviction, to a fine of an amount not exceeding the statutory maximum;

   (b) on conviction on indictment, to imprisonment for a term not exceeding two years or to a fine or to both.

(5) Where a person proposes to disclose information to which this section applies in circumstances where the disclosure would by virtue of paragraphs (b) to (h) of subsection (2) not contravene this section, he may disclose the information notwithstanding any obligation not to disclose it that would otherwise apply.

DEFINITIONS

"Convention, the": s.1(8).

GENERAL NOTE

The information which will be collected by various authorities under the Act and internationally under the CWC will be of a highly delicate nature. Information concerning types and amounts of chemically related materials, equipment and substances will be considered to be sensitive by both governments, in relation to national security, and industry in relation to the threat of industrial espionage.

Under Art. VII, para. 6 CWC;

'Each State Party shall treat as confidential and afford special handling to information and data that it receives in confidence from the Organisation in connection with the implementation of this Convention. It shall treat such information and data exclusively in connection with its rights and obligations under this Convention and in accordance with the provisions set forth in the Confidentiality Annex.'

The U.K. is perhaps less concerned than others about the question of national security, having stopped using chemical weapons in the 1950's (Watson: 1995, p.33). However, the government did express concern as to the possibility that information published might provide members of the public with a 'how to' guide to making chemical weapons (*Hansard*, H.L. Vol. 570, col. 1072). During the passage of the Bill through Parliament, the Chemical Industries Association and the Royal Society of Chemistry expressed concerns that the release of statistics concerning amounts and types of chemicals held by various private bodies might result in inadvertent publication of trade secrets. Academic institutions will also be concerned that confidential data relating to their research may be divined from collected information (*Hansard*, H.C. Vol. 268, col. 437. H.L. Vol. 570, col. 1072).

It is for these reasons that the Act provides that information which relates to business or other activities and is collected in connection with the Act, shall not be disclosed except where there is consent, or in connection with the implementation of the Act or the CWC, or where there is one of four public interest type reasons listed in subs. (2)(d)–(g) for doing so. To contravene this section is an offence punishable by fine or imprisonment.

Whoever discloses information in circumstances falling within the exceptional circumstances allowed in subs. (2) shall not be liable for the breach of any other rules preventing the release of the information. So for example, an action for breach of confidentiality could not be brought in contract against such a person. However, this exemption from liability does not apply to information released with the consent of the person carrying out the business or other activity concerned under subs. (2)(a). Of course if the disclosure has been made with consent under subs. (2)(a), then an action for breach of confidence could not be brought in any case. The more important result of this subsection is that where a person discloses information with consent, they may still be liable under the Official Secrets Act 1989 (c. 6) (DTI Notes on Clauses: 119).

Annual reports by Secretary of State

33. The Secretary of State shall in each calendar year—
(a) prepare a report on the operation of this Act, and
(b) lay a copy of the report before each House of Parliament.

GENERAL NOTE

The Secretary of State's annual report on the operation of the Act is to be submitted to the Houses of Parliament. The section makes no stipulation as to what type of information should be included in the report. Attempts made in the House of Commons Committee stage to amend the Act so as to require the report to contain certain information, failed on the grounds that the information required would threaten the needs of industry and researchers to maintain confidentiality (*Hansard*, Vol. 268, col. 427). In deciding what information to release in such a report, the Secretary of State will not be bound by the confidentiality rule in s.32. However, the concerns expressed in relation to s.32 will be important in that decision. A balance will have to be struck between the desire to maintain transparency in the monitoring of chemical weapons, and the need to protect confidential industrial, military and academic information.

During its passage through the Houses of Parliament, attempts were made to amend the Bill so as to ensure that the Secretary of State would be bound to make arrangements for an annual seminar which would provide an opportunity for a two way exchange of information concerning the operation of the Act between the government and academics and industrial representatives. This suggestion was rejected by the Government (*Hansard*, Vol. 569, col. 1442).

Service of notices

34. A notice under any provision of this Act, or a copy of a notice under any such provision, may be served on a person—
(a) by delivering it to him in person,
(b) by sending it by post to him at his usual or last-known residence or place of business in the United Kingdom, or
(c) in the case of a body corporate, by delivering it to the secretary or clerk of the body corporate at its registered or principal office or sending it by post to the secretary or clerk of that body corporate at that office.

GENERAL NOTE
    Notices can be served by the Secretary of State under ss.4, 6, 7, 12, 13, 21 and 22 of the Act.

Amendment of Army, Air Force and Naval Discipline Acts

35. In each of the following provisions, namely—
(a) section 70(4) of the Army Act 1955 (civil offences),
(b) section 70(4) of the Air Force Act 1955 (civil offences), and
(c) section 48(2) of the Naval Discipline Act 1957 (exclusion of jurisdiction of courts-martial),
after the words "Biological Weapons Act 1974" there shall be inserted "or an offence under section 2 or 11 of the Chemical Weapons Act 1996".

GENERAL NOTE
    Section 35 provides for the amendment of the Army Act 1955 (c. 18), Air Force Act 1955 (c. 19), and Naval Discipline Act 1957 (c. 53) in order that when service personnel commit the most serious offences of the Act, under s.2 (making, possessing, using, *etc.*, a chemical weapon) and s.11 (creation of a chemical weapons production facility), they shall be tried not in court martial, but in civil law, by a judge and a jury. This provision has already been made with regard to offences under the Biological Weapons Act 1974 committed by service personnel (DTI Notes on Clauses: p.123).

Power to amend this Act

36.—(1) The Secretary of State may by order make such additions to, omissions from or other modifications to this Act as he considers necessary or desirable to give effect to any amendment of the Convention made in pursuance of its provisions.
    (2) The power to make an order under this section shall, if the order solely modifies the Schedule to this Act, be exercisable by statutory instrument subject to annulment in pursuance of a resolution of either House of Parliament.
    (3) The power to make any other order under this section shall be exercisable by statutory instrument, and no such order shall be made unless a draft of it has been laid before and approved by resolution of each House of Parliament.

DEFINITIONS
    "Convention, the": s.1(8).

GENERAL NOTE
    Section 36 provides for the amendment of the Act by three methods, by order, by statutory instrument subject to negative resolution, and by statutory instrument subject to positive resolution.

Subs. (1)
    The CWC can be amended under the procedures outlined in Art. XV of the CWC. The Secretary of State is empowered under subs. (1) to amend the Act in order to keep up with changes to the CWC. This section is not meant for any other purpose than to provide for amendments in keeping with the alteration of the CWC.

Subss. (2) and (3)
    Where the Secretary of State simply wishes to modify the Schedule to the Act containing a list of Scheduled Toxic Chemicals and Precursors, subs. 2(2) provides that a statutory instrument subject to annulment by either House of Parliament will suffice. When the adequacy of the so called 'negative resolution procedure' as a control of delegated legislation on this subject was doubted in the House of Lords, the Government stressed that the speed with which amendments to the CWC must be mirrored in domestic legislation did not allow for anything more time consuming than the 'negative resolution procedure' (*Hansard*, H.L. Vol. 569, col. 1444). The addition of the word 'solely' was the result of an Opposition amendment. This is the second time in 25 years that 'an unamended Opposition amendment has been accepted' (*Hansard*, H.C. Vol. 268, col. 432).
    Under subs. (3), where the Secretary of State wishes to amend by order through statutory instrument anything other than the Schedule to the Act, the statutory instrument concerned must be positively approved by a resolution in each House of Parliament.

The Crown

37.—(1) Subject to the following provisions of this section, this Act binds the Crown.

(2) No contravention by the Crown of a provision made by or under this Act shall make the Crown criminally liable; but the High Court or in Scotland the Court of Session may, on the application of a person appearing to the Court to have an interest, declare unlawful any act or omission of the Crown which constitutes such a contravention.

(3) Notwithstanding subsection (2), the provisions made by or under this Act apply to persons in the public service of the Crown as they apply to other persons.

(4) Nothing in this section affects Her Majesty in her private capacity; and this subsection shall be construed as if section 38(3) of the Crown Proceedings Act 1947 (meaning of Her Majesty in her private capacity) were contained in this Act.

GENERAL NOTE

While the Crown and its servants will not be criminally liable for any contravention of the Act, an interested party can apply to a High Court or Court of Session in Scotland to have such an act or omission declared unlawful. Furthermore, according to subs. (4), the Act will not bind the Queen in her personal capacity. However, under subs. (3), a Crown servant can be held liable for contraventions of the Act where made in their personal capacity, because the Act applies to crown servants as it applies to other people.

General

Finance

38.—(1) Any expenses of the Secretary of State incurred in consequence of this Act shall be paid out of money provided by Parliament.

(2) Any sums received by the Secretary of State in consequence of this Act shall be paid into the Consolidated Fund.

GENERAL NOTE

Expenditure incurred by the Secretary of State in implementing the Act is to be paid for by Parliament. Activities such as information gathering, destroying of objects and the reimbursement under s.28 of expenses incurred during Convention inspections will result in costs to the Secretary of State. Sums received by the Secretary of State in implementing the Act are to be paid to the Consolidated Fund. The Secretary of State will receive funds when the costs of destruction are repaid under ss.6(6), 7(10) and 15(6) (DTI Notes on Clauses: 128).

Commencement, extent and citation

39.—(1) This Act (except this section) shall come into force on such day as the Secretary of State may appoint by order made by statutory instrument.

(2) It is hereby declared that this Act extends to Northern Ireland.

(3) Her Majesty may by Order in Council make provision for extending any of the provisions of this Act, with such exceptions, adaptations or modifications as may be specified in the Order, to any of the Channel Islands, the Isle of Man or any colony.

(4) This Act may be cited as the Chemical Weapons Act 1996.

GENERAL NOTE

The Act, apart from s.39, will come into force on the day appointed by order of the Secretary of State under statutory instrument, and will apply to Northern Ireland.

Subs. (3)

Subsection (3) provides for the extension in future, of the whole of the Act by Order in Council to the Channel Islands, the Isle of Man and any colony. The CWC cannot be fully complied with unless the Act is extended to cover all territories under U.K. sovereignty (DTI Notes on Clauses: 129). This section is to be contrasted with s.3(2) which merely allows an Order in Council to extend the jurisdiction of the U.K. to cover offences under s.2 committed outside the U.K. by companies or nationals of Channel Islands, the Isle of Man and any colony.

SCHEDULE

SCHEDULED TOXIC CHEMICALS AND PRECURSORS

(CAS registry
number)

A.   TOXIC CHEMICALS:

(1)   O-Alkyl ($\leq C_{10}$, incl. cycloalkyl) alkyl
       (Me, Et, n-Pr or i-Pr)-phosphonofluoridates
       e.g. Sarin: O-Isopropyl methylphosphonofluoridate   (107-44-8)
             Soman: O-Pinacolyl methylphosphonofluoridate   (96-64-0)
(2)   O-Alkyl ($\leq C_{10}$, incl. cycloalkyl) N,N-dialkyl
       (Me, Et, n-Pr or i-Pr) phosphoramidocyanidates
       e.g. Tabun: O-Ethyl N,N-dimethyl
                          phosphoramidocyanidate   (77-81-6)
(3)   O-Alkyl (H or $\leq C_{10}$, incl. cycloalkyl) S-2-dailkyl
       (Me, Et, n-Pr or i-Pr)-aminoethyl alkyl
       (Me, Et, n-Pr or i-Pr) phosphonothiolates and
       corresponding alkylated or protonated salts
       e.g. VX: O-Ethyl S-2-diisopropylaminoethyl
                        methyl phosphonothiolate   (50782-69-9)
(4)   Sulfur mustards:
       2-Chloroethylchloromethylsufide   (2625-76-5)
       Mustard gas: Bis (2-chloroethyl) sulfide   (505-60-2)
       Bis (2-chloroethylthio) methane   (63869-13-6)
       Sesquimustard: 1,2-Bis (2-chloroethylthio) ethane   (3563-36-8)
       1,3-Bis (2-chloroethylthio)-n-propane   (63905-10-2)
       1,4-Bis (2-chloroethylthio)-n-butane   (142868-93-7)
       1,5-Bis (2-chloroethylthio)-n-pentane   (142868-94-8)
       Bis (2-chloroethylthiomethyl) ether   (63918-90-1)
       O-Mustard: Bis (2-chloroethylthioethyl) ether   (63918-89-8)
(5)   Lewisites:
       Lewisite 1:   2-Chlorovinyldichloroarsine   (541-25-3)
       Lewisite 2:   Bis (2-chlorovinyl) chloroarsine   (40334-69-8)
       Lewisite 3:   Tris (2-chlorovinyl) arsine   (40334-70-1)
(6)   Nitrogen mustards:
       HN1:   Bis (2-chloroethyl) ethylamine   (538-07-8)
       HN2:   Bis (2-chloroethyl) methylamine   (51-75-2)
       HN3:   Tris (2-chloroethyl) amine   (555-77-1)
(7)   Saxitoxin   (35523-89-8)
(8)   Ricin   (9009-86-3)

B.   PRECURSORS:

(9)   Alkyl (Me, Et, n-Pr or i-Pr) phosphonyldifluorides
       e.g. DF: Methylphosphonyldifluoride   (676-99-3)
(10) O-Alkyl (H or $\leq C_{10}$, incl. cycloalkyl) O-2-dialkyl
       (Me, Et, n-Pr or i-Pr)-aminoethyl alkyl
       (Me, Et, n-Pr or i-Pr) phosphonites
       and corresponding alkylated or protonated salts
       e.g. QL: O-Ethyl O-2 diisopropylaminoethyl
       methylphosphonite   (57856-11-8)
(11) Chlorosarin: O-Isopropyl
                            methylphosphonochloridate   (1445-76-7)
(12) Chlorosoman: O-Pinacolyl
                            methylphosphonochloridate   (7040-57-5)

Notes:

1. This Schedule sets out Schedule 1 to the annex on chemicals to the Convention as corrected.
2. In this Schedule the reference to the CAS registry is to the chemical abstract service registry.

3. This Schedule must be read subject to the following proposition, which is based on a note in the Convention: where reference is made to groups of dialkylated chemicals, followed by a list of alkyl groups in parentheses, all chemicals possible by all possible combinations of alkyl groups listed in the parentheses must be taken to be listed in the Schedule.

GENERAL NOTE

The Schedule is a replica of Sched. 1 to the annex on chemicals to the CWC.

INDEX

References are to sections and the Schedule

PREVENTION OF TERRORISM (ADDITIONAL POWERS) ACT 1996*

(1996 c. 7)

An Act to extend powers of search in connection with acts of terrorism and terrorist investigations; confer powers on constables in relation to areas on which police cordons are imposed in connection with terrorist investigations; and confer powers in connection with the prevention of acts of terrorism to impose prohibitions and restrictions in relation to vehicles on roads.   [3rd April 1996]

PARLIAMENTARY DEBATES
Hansard, H.C. Vol. 275, col. 152. H.L. Vol. 571, cols. 276, 290.

INTRODUCTION AND GENERAL NOTE

This Act amends the Prevention of Terrorism Act 1989 ("1989 Act") in order to give the police and in some circumstances other examining officers additional statutory powers which it is intended will help either to prevent, or to aid in the investigation of, acts of terrorism.

The enactment of this legislation must be seen in the context of the event which followed the resumption of violence by the IRA on February 9, 1996 when a bomb at South Quay in London killed two and brought the cease-fire effectively to an end.

A number of concerns were expressed as the Bill passed through the House of Lords, at the speed at which the legislation had been prepared, but there was a general recognition that the circumstances were extreme and demanded extreme measures; Mr Jack Straw, the Shadow Home Secretary agreed with the general provisions of the new Bill and the new investigative and other powers prescribed therein.

The Act creates five specific new powers for the police, building on the existing framework of anti-terrorist legislation and on the common law powers already exercised. The Act also makes a number of amendments to the 1989 Act with the objective being to clarify and strengthen police powers—the common law powers in existence were felt to be obscure and in need of such statutory underpinning.

It was intended for the Act to be clear and practical while being subject to equally clear and sensible safeguards; thus maintaining the balance between the fight against terrorism and recognising the importance of preserving the civil rights of individuals. In addition, the Government has given assurances that the operation of the powers will be scrutinised annually by an independent reviewer.

The provisions of the Act are summarised below:

Section 1: Enables the police to stop and search pedestrians for articles which can be used in the commission, preparation or instigation of terrorist offences.

Section 2: Enables the police to search non-residential premises for evidence which will be of value to police investigations concerned with terrorism.

Section 3: Enables an examining officer to search unaccompanied freight in ports.

Section 4: Enables the police to cordon off areas to search for explosive devices or to collect forensic evidence following an explosion.

Section 5: Enables the police to impose temporary parking restrictions in response to a general threat to vulnerable sites.

---

* Annotations by Sandeep Savla, Sarah Phillimore and Gary Scanlan of City University.

Section 6: Makes consequential amendments to s.19(1) of the 1989 Act which concerns the prosecution of offences requiring the consent of the D.P.P.

COMMENCEMENT
   This Act was enacted on April 3, 1996 and inserted new provisions into the Prevention of Terrorism (Temporary Provisions) Act 1989 (c. 4).

ABBREVIATIONS
   "PACE"   : Police and Criminal Evidence Act 1984 (c. 60).
   "1989 Act" : Prevention of Terrorism (Temporary Provisions) Act 1989 (c. 4).

Power to stop and search pedestrians

   1.—(1) In the 1989 Act insert, after section 13A—

   "Power to stop and search pedestrians
   13B.—(1) Where it appears to a police officer of the rank mentioned in subsection (1)(a), (b) or (as the case may be) (c) of section 13A above that it is expedient to do so in order to prevent acts of terrorism to which that section applies, he may give an authorisation that the powers to stop and search persons conferred by this section shall be exercisable at any place within his area or a locality in his area which is specified in the authorisation.
   (2) This section confers on any constable in uniform power to stop any pedestrian and search him, or anything carried by him, for articles of a kind which could be used for a purpose connected with the commission, preparation or instigation of such acts of terrorism.
   (3) A constable may exercise his powers under this section whether or not he has any grounds for suspecting the presence of articles of that kind.
   (4) Nothing in this section authorises a constable to require a person to remove any of his clothing in public other than any headgear, foot-wear, outer coat, jacket or gloves.
   (5) A person is guilty of an offence if he—
   (a) fails to stop when required to do so by a constable in the exercise of his powers under this section; or
   (b) wilfully obstructs a constable in the exercise of those powers.
   (6) A person guilty of an offence under subsection (5) above shall be liable on summary conviction to imprisonment for a term not exceeding six months or a fine not exceeding level 5 on the standard scale or both.
   (7) An authorisation under this section may be given in writing or orally but if given orally must be confirmed in writing by the person giving it as soon as is reasonably practicable.
   (8) A person giving an authorisation under this section must cause the Secretary of State to be informed, as soon as is reasonably practicable, that it was given.
   (9) An authorisation under this section—
   (a) may be cancelled by the Secretary of State with effect from such time as he may direct;
   (b) ceases to have effect if it is not confirmed by the Secretary of State before the end of the period of 48 hours beginning with the time when it was given; but

(c) if confirmed, continues in force—

(i) for such period, not exceeding 28 days beginning with the day on which it was given, as may be specified in the authorisation; or

(ii) for such shorter period as the Secretary of State may direct.

(10) If a person is stopped by a constable under this section, he shall be entitled to obtain a written statement that he was stopped under the powers conferred by this section if he applies for such a statement not later than the end of the period of twelve months from the day on which he was stopped.".

(2) Section 13A of the 1989 Act (powers to stop and search vehicles etc. and person carrying things) is amended as follows.

(3) Subsection (3)(c) (power to stop and search pedestrians) is repealed and, in consequence, the following words are also repealed—

(a) in subsection (6)(a), "or (as the case may be) to stop"; and

(b) in subsection (9), "and similarly as respects a pedestrian who is stopped under this section for a search of anything carried by him".

(4) For subsection (4) substitute—

"(4) A constable may exercise his powers under this section whether or not he has any grounds for suspecting the presence of articles of that kind.

(4A) Nothing in this section authorises a constable to require a person to remove any of his clothing in public other than any headgear, footwear, outer coat, jacket or gloves."

(5) In subsection (8) for "specified" substitute "mentioned".

(6) For subsection (10) substitute—

"(10) An authorisation under this section may be given in writing or orally but if given orally must be confirmed in writing by the person giving it as soon as is reasonably practicable.

(10A) In this section "specified" means specified in an authorisation under this section."

(7) In subsection (1)(a) for "area" substitute "district".

GENERAL NOTE

This section was subjected to the most severe criticism as the Bill was debated in the House of Lords; it was recognised as the most important clause with regard to the creation of powers of stop and search. It was regarded as inevitable that legislation such as this, produced at short notice and as an immediate response to recent events, would give rise to confusion in the exercise of the new powers and therefore the wording and ambit of the provisions of the Act should be subject to some form of consultation procedure. Various amendments were suggested, for example that subs. (1) should explicitly require the police to act reasonably in the exercise of these new powers. Concerns were expressed as to the extent to which these powers were to be exercised solely on the authorisation of and by the police themselves.

However, following assurances from the Government, such amendments were withdrawn. The Government gave assurances that the police were well aware that the new powers would need to be exercised with sensitivity and care. Immediate guidance on the provisions was to be issued and for the short term the police have undertaken to apply the relevant PACE Code voluntarily, namely Code A. In due course the PACE Code will be formally amended to govern the exercise of the new stop and search powers created by the Act. Assurances were also given that Parliament would receive regular reports from law enforcement agencies on the operation of the new powers (*Hansard*, H.L. Vol. 571, col. 292).

Subs. (2)

Section 13A of the 1989 Act which was inserted by the Criminal Justice and Public Order Act 1994 (c. 33), allows a constable to stop and search any vehicle, its driver and passengers; to stop any pedestrian and search anything he is carrying for articles which could be used in preparing, committing or instigating an act of terrorism. But s.13A did not permit a constable to search the pedestrian himself for anything he may have concealed, for example, in his pockets. Section 13B is intended to correct this omission in the current powers of stop and search and is deemed necessary because incendiary devices may easily be of a size that may be concealed about the person.

Subs. (4)

Concerns were expressed about the precise nature of such "rub-down" searches and in particular the difficulties that might arise if juveniles were searched or women searched by a male officer. However it seems clear that such concerns were misplaced—the "rub-down" search is clearly not as intrusive as a strip-search and does not permit the taking of intimate or non-intimate samples. If the need is felt to carry out a more intrusive body search it would require an arrest of the individual concerned. During the passage of the Bill, the Government offered assurances that the police in exercising these extensive new powers of stop and search would act in accordance with guidelines already adopted in respect of the exercise of other police powers of stop and search.

Subs. (6)

The stop and search powers in this section are seen as being in need of enforcement. Prosecution for either offence will proceed only by or with the agreement of the D.P.P.—see s.6 below and accompanying notes.

Searches of non-residential premises

2.—(1) Schedule 7 to the 1989 Act (terrorist investigations) is amended as follows.

(2) After paragraph 2 insert—

"*Search of non-residential premises*

2A.—(1) A justice of the peace may, on an application made by a police officer of at least the rank of superintendent, issue a warrant under this paragraph if satisfied that a terrorist investigation is being carried out and that there are reasonable grounds for believing—

    (a) that there is material which is likely to be of substantial value (whether by itself or together with other material) to the investigation to be found on one or more of the premises specified in the application; and

    (b) that the material does not consist of or include items subject to legal privilege, excluded material or special procedure material.

(2) The officer making an application under this paragraph may not include in the premises specified in the application any which he has reasonable cause to believe are used wholly or mainly as a dwelling.

(3) A warrant under this paragraph shall authorise a constable to enter any of the premises specified in the warrant and to search the premises and any person found there and to seize and retain anything found there or on any such person, other than an item subject to legal privilege, if he has reasonable grounds for believing—

    (a) that it is likely to be of substantial value (whether by itself or together with other material) to the investigation; and

    (b) that it is necessary to seize it in order to prevent it from being concealed, lost, damaged, altered or destroyed.

(4) Entry and search under a warrant issued under this paragraph must be within 24 hours from the time when the warrant is issued."

(3) In paragraph 6(1) (power of Circuit judge to order person to provide an explanation of material seized in pursuance of a warrant under paragraph 2 or 5), after "2" insert ", 2A".

(4) In paragraph 7(1), (power of police officer of at least the rank of superintendent, in cases of great urgency, to give constable the authority given by a search warrant under paragraph 2 or 5), after "2" insert ", 2A".

(5) After paragraph 11 insert—

"*Search of non-residential premises*

11A.—(1) A procurator fiscal may, for the purposes of a terrorist investigation, apply to a sheriff for a warrant under this paragraph in relation to two or more premises specified in the application.

(2) A procurator fiscal making an application under this paragraph may not include in the premises so specified any which he has reasonable cause to believe are used wholly or mainly as a dwelling.

(3) On such an application a sheriff may issue a warrant authorising a constable to enter and search the premises specified in the application if the sheriff is satisfied that—

    (a) a terrorist investigation is being carried out; and

    (b) there are reasonable grounds for believing that there is material which is likely to be of substantial value (whether by itself or together with other material) to the investigation to be found on one or more of those premises.

(4) A warrant under this paragraph shall authorise a constable to enter any of the premises specified in the warrant and to search those premises and any person found there and to seize and retain any material found there or on any such person, if he has reasonable grounds for believing that—

    (a) it is likely to be of substantial value (whether by itself or together with any other material) to the investigation; and

    (b) it is necessary to seize it in order to prevent it being concealed, lost, damaged, altered or destroyed.

(5) Entry and search under a warrant issued under this paragraph must be within 24 hours from the time when the warrant is issued.

(6) A warrant issued under this paragraph may authorise persons named in the warrant to accompany a constable who is executing it.".

(6) In paragraph 15(1) (power of sheriff to order explanation of material produced to or seized by a constable) after second "paragraph" insert "11A or".

(7) In paragraph 16(1) (power of police officer of at least the rank of superintendent, in cases of great urgency, to give constable authority given by search warrant under paragraph 14) after "paragraph" insert "11A or".

(8) In paragraph 17(2) (power of constable acting under this Schedule to open lockfast places) after second "paragraph" insert "11A or".

DEFINITIONS
"excluded material": Sched. 7, para. 1 to the 1989 Act.
"items subject to legal privilege": Sched. 7, para. 1 to the 1989 Act.
"premises": s.20(1) of the 1989 Act.
"special procedure material": Sched. 7, para. 1 to the 1989 Act.
"terrorist investigation": s.17(1) of, and Sched. 7, para. 1 to the 1989 Act.

GENERAL NOTE
The search powers available under Sched. 7, paras. 2 and 14 to the 1989 Act are extended by this section. It is no longer required that the material which is likely to be of substantial value to the investigation is on premises specified in the application, and there is no need to satisfy the conditions in Sched. 7, para. 2(2) or Sched. 7, para. 14(3).

Subss. (2) and (5)
A justice of the peace, or a sheriff in Scotland, may issue a warrant for the police to search if there are reasonable grounds for believing that the material is to be found on one or more of the premises specified in the application. The application must be made by a police officer of at least the rank of superintendent, or the procurator fiscal in Scotland, and may not include premises which he has reasonable cause to believe are used wholly or mainly as a dwelling. Entry and search must be within 24 hours of the issue of the warrant.

Searches of unaccompanied goods

3.—(1) In Schedule 5 to the 1989 Act (port and border controls) insert, after paragraph 4—

"Powers to search goods

4A.—(1) For the purpose of determining whether they are or have been involved in the commission, preparation or instigation of acts of terrorism to which paragraph 2 above applies, an examining officer may search any goods which have arrived in or are about to leave Great Britain or Northern Ireland on any ship, aircraft or vehicle.

(2) An examining officer may board any ship or aircraft or enter any vehicle for the purpose of determining whether there are goods on the ship, aircraft or vehicle in respect of which he may wish to exercise his power of search.

(3) Where an examining officer has power to search under this paragraph, he may, instead, authorise a search to be carried out on his behalf by a person who is not an examining officer.

(4) Where a person who is not an examining officer is authorised to carry out a search in accordance with sub-paragraph (3) above he may—

   (a) board any ship or aircraft or enter any vehicle for the purpose of determining whether there are goods on the ship, aircraft or vehicle in respect of which he may wish to exercise his power of search; and

   (b) if necessary, use reasonable force for the purpose of carrying out his functions under this paragraph.

(5) In Scotland any person employed by a police authority for the assistance of constables under section 9 of the Police (Scotland) Act 1967 may perform any functions conferred on examining officers by this paragraph, and may, if necessary, use reasonable force for the purpose of performing those functions.

(6) Any person carrying out a search under this paragraph may, for the purpose of examining it, detain for a period not exceeding seven days anything found on the search.

(7) If, on examining anything so found, the person examining it is of the opinion that it may be needed for use as evidence in criminal proceedings he may detain it until he is satisfied that it will not be so needed.

(8) In this paragraph "goods" includes—

   (a) stores,

   (b) baggage,

   (c) substances, whether natural or manufactured, and whether or not incorporated in or mixed with other goods, and

   (d) in relation to Scotland, also all corporeal moveables,

and any transport container or other container in which goods may be placed."

(2) In paragraph 11 of Schedule 5 to the 1989 Act (offences), after "this Schedule" insert ", or otherwise wilfully obstructs, or seeks to frustrate the object of, a search under this Schedule,".

(3) In section 16(1) of that Act (scope of Schedule 5), after "persons" insert "or goods".

DEFINITIONS

"aircraft": s.20(1) of the 1989 Act.
"examining officer": Sched. 5, para. 1 to the 1989 Act.
"goods": s.4A(8) of the 1989 Act, as inserted by s.3.
"ship": s.20(1) of the 1989 Act.
"vehicle": s.20(1) of the 1989 Act.

GENERAL NOTE

This section extends the search powers available under Sched. 5, para. 4 to the 1989 Act, which were previously restricted to the search of a person or his baggage, or any ship or aircraft and anything on board it, or anything taken off or about to be taken aboard a ship or aircraft, for the purpose of determining whether the person is or has been concerned with the commission, preparation or instigation of acts of terrorism within Sched. 5, para. 2.

    Section 3, which inserts a new s.4A into the 1989 Act, means that for the purpose of determining whether a person has been involved in the commission, preparation or instigation of acts of terrorism within Sched. 5, para. 2, an examining officer may search unaccompanied goods which have arrived in or are about to leave Great Britain or Northern Ireland on any ship, aircraft or vehicle. Section 4A(7) provides that if anything is found on a search, and if the person examining it is of the opinion that an item may be needed for use as evidence in criminal proceedings, then he may detain it until he is satisfied that it will not be so needed.

Subs. (2)
    Schedule 5, para. 11 is amended so that it is an offence wilfully to obstruct, or seek to frustrate the object of a search under the Schedule.

Police cordons

    4.—(1) In the 1989 Act insert, after section 16B—

"PART IVB

CORDONS AND PROTECTIVE POWERS

Power to impose a police cordon
    16C.—(1) If it appears to a police officer of at least the rank of superintendent that it is expedient to do so in connection with an investigation into the commission, preparation or instigation of an act of terrorism to which this section applies, he may authorise a cordon to be imposed on an area specified by him in the authorisation.
    (2) If it appears to a constable below the rank of superintendent that it is necessary for him to do so as a matter of great urgency, he may exercise the power given to a superintendent by subsection (1) above.
    (3) The acts of terrorism to which this section applies are—
    (a) acts of terrorism connected with the affairs of Northern Ireland; and
    (b) acts of terrorism of any other description except acts connected solely with the affairs of the United Kingdom or any part of the United Kingdom other than Northern Ireland.
    (4) The powers that may be exercised within an area on which a cordon has been imposed under this section are set out in Schedule 6A to this Act.
    (5) Schedule 6A also makes further provision with respect to cordoned areas."
    (2) The new Schedule 6A to the 1989 Act is inserted by the Schedule to this Act.

DEFINITIONS
    "authorisation": Sched. 6A to the 1989 Act.
    "cordoned area": Sched. 6A to the 1989 Act.
    "police tape": Sched. 6A to the 1989 Act.
    "terrorist investigation": s.17(1) of, and Sched. 6A to the 1989 Act.

GENERAL NOTE
    This inserts a new s.16C into the 1989 Act, and places the limited and uncertain common law powers that were available to the police to impose cordons on a new statutory basis.

Subs. (1)
    Section 16C(1) provides that a police officer of at least the rank of superintendent may authorise a cordon to be imposed on an area specified by him, if it appears to him that it is *expedient* to do so in connection with an investigation into the commission, preparation or instigation of an act of terrorism as defined in s.16C(3). By s.16C(2) a constable below the rank of superintendent may exercise this power if it is necessary for him to do so as a matter of great urgency.
    In the House of Lords, Lord McIntosh of Haringey moved an amendment which was subsequently withdrawn, that the clause read, "Where it appears reasonable to a police officer of the

rank … that it is expedient to do so" (*Hansard*, H.L. Vol. 571, col. 321). Baroness Blatch, on behalf of the Government, pointed out that any unreasonable exercise of the powers could be challenged by way of judicial review (*Hansard*, H.L. Vol. 571, col. 325).

The powers that may be exercised within an area on which a cordon has been imposed are set out in a new Sched. 6A to the 1989 Act (inserted by section 4(2) of this Act). By Sched. 6A, para. 4, the initial period of the authorisation must not exceed 14 days, although the period may be extended by a written variation of a police officer of at least the rank of superintendent. The overall period for which an authorisation is in force must not exceed 28 days. Schedule 6A, para. 9 creates criminal offences in relation to the powers in cordoned areas. Although this section places the common law powers of the police on a statutory basis, Sched. 6A, para. 10 provides that this does not derogate from other powers available to a constable at common law or under any other enactment.

Parking prohibitions and restrictions and the removal of vehicles

5. In Part IVB of the 1989 Act insert, after section 16C—

"Parking prohibitions and restrictions and the removal of vehicles

16D.—(1) If it appears to an appropriate officer that it is expedient to do so in order to prevent acts of terrorism to which section 16C above applies he may give an authorisation for the purposes of this section.

(2) An authorisation—

(a) may be given in writing or orally but if given orally must be confirmed in writing by the person giving it as soon as is reasonably practicable; and

(b) has effect—

(i) in relation to such roads, or parts of roads, as may be specified; and

(ii) for such period, not exceeding 28 days, as may be specified.

(3) Only roads, or parts of roads, which are within the police area of the officer giving the authorisation may be specified.

(4) An authorisation gives any constable power to prohibit or restrict the leaving of vehicles, or their remaining at rest, on any specified road, or part of a road.

(5) The power conferred by subsection (4) above is to be exercised by placing the appropriate traffic sign on, or on any structure which is on, the road or part of the road concerned.

(6) If the driver or other person in charge of a vehicle which has been permitted to remain at rest in contravention of any prohibition or restriction imposed under subsection (4) above fails to move the vehicle when ordered to do so by a constable in uniform, he is guilty of an offence.

(7) A person is guilty of an offence if he leaves a vehicle, or permits a vehicle to remain at rest, on a road in contravention of a prohibition or restriction imposed under this section.

(8) It is a defence for any person charged with an offence under this section to prove that he had lawful authority or some other reasonable excuse for the act or omission in question.

(9) A person guilty of an offence under subsection (6) above is liable on summary conviction to imprisonment for a term not exceeding three months or a fine not exceeding level 4 on the standard scale or both.

(10) A person guilty of an offence under subsection (7) above is liable on summary conviction to a fine not exceeding level 4 on the standard scale.

(11) If it appears to an appropriate officer that the exercise of the powers conferred by this section ought to continue beyond the period

for which their exercise has been authorised under this section he may, from time to time, authorise the exercise of those powers for a further period, not exceeding 28 days.

(12) The fact that a person has a current disabled person's badge does not—

(a) exempt him from any prohibition or restriction imposed under this section; or

(b) constitute lawful authority, or a reasonable excuse, for failing to comply with any order given under this section.

(13) In this section—

"appropriate officer" means—

(a) any police officer of or above the rank of commander of the metropolitan police, as respects the metropolitan police district;

(b) any police officer of or above the rank of commander of the City of London police, as respects the City of London; or

(c) any police officer of or above the rank of assistant chief constable of a force maintained for any other police area;

"authorisation" means an authorisation given under this section;

"disabled person's badge" has the same meaning as in section 142 of the Road Traffic Regulation Act 1984;

"driver" means, in relation to a vehicle which has been left on any road, the person who was driving it when it was left there;

"road" has the same meaning as in the Road Traffic Act 1988;

"specified" means specified in an authorisation;

"traffic sign" has the meaning given in section 142(1) of the Road Traffic Regulation Act 1984; and

"vehicle" has the same meaning as in section 99(5) of the Act of 1984.

(14) A constable exercising powers under this section may suspend a parking place; and any such suspension is to be treated for the purposes of section 99 of the Act of 1984 (removal of vehicles illegally parked etc.), and any regulations in force under that section, as a restriction imposed under this section.

(15) The powers conferred by this section are additional to any other powers which a constable has either at common law or under or by virtue of any other enactment and are not to be taken to affect any of those other powers."

DEFINITIONS

"appropriate officer": s.16D(13) of the 1989 Act, as inserted by s.5.

"authorisation": s.16D(13) of the 1989 Act, as inserted by s.5.

"disabled person's badge": s.16D(13) of the 1989 Act, as inserted by s.5.

"driver": s.16D(13) of the 1989 Act, as inserted by s.5.

"road": s.16D(13) of the 1989 Act, as inserted by s.5.

"specified": s.16D(13) of the 1989 Act, as inserted by s.5.

"traffic sign": s.16D(13) of the 1989 Act, as inserted by s.5.

"vehicle": s.16D(13) of the 1989 Act, as inserted by s.5.

GENERAL NOTE

By this section, a new s.16D is inserted into the 1989 Act, which provides statutory powers to the police to impose parking prohibitions and restrictions upon vehicles and to facilitate the removal of vehicles. The section therefore provides statutory underpinning to the uncertain common law powers, although by s.16D(15) the powers conferred by this section are in addition to any other powers which a constable has, either at common law or under any other enactment. If it appears to a police officer of or above the rank of commander (in respect of the metropolitan police district and the City of London) or assistant chief constable that it is expedient to do so in order to prevent acts of terrorism to which s.16C applies, he may give an authorisation. By s.16D(4) such an authorisation gives any constable the power to prohibit or restrict the leaving of vehicles or their remaining at rest on any specified road, or part of a road.

Section 16D(7) creates a criminal offence if a person leaves a vehicle, or permits a vehicle to remain at rest on a road in contravention of a prohibition or restriction, but by s.16D(8) it is a defence to prove that he had lawful authority or some other reasonable excuse for the act or omission. The consent of the Director of Public Prosecutions is required before a prosecution may be brought (see s.6 below). This section does not state what constitutes lawful authority or some other reasonable excuse, except that it does state by s.16D(12)(b) that a current disabled person's badge does not constitute lawful authority or a reasonable excuse for failing to comply with the order given under this section.

Consent to prosecutions

6. In section 19(1) of the 1989 Act (proceedings to be instituted in England and Wales only with consent), in paragraph (aa) (consent of Director of Public Prosecutions required in England and Wales)—
  (a) after "13A", insert "13B"; and
  (b) for "or 16B" substitute "16B or 16D or under Schedule 6A".

GENERAL NOTE
  The consent of the Director of Public Prosecutions is required in relation to prosecutions under the new ss.13B, 16D and Sched. 6A of the 1989 Act.

Short title, interpretation and extent etc.

7.—(1) This Act may be cited as the Prevention of Terrorism (Additional Powers) Act 1996.
  (2) In this Act "the 1989 Act" means the Prevention of Terrorism (Temporary Provisions) Act 1989.
  (3) Section 3 and this section extend to the United Kingdom.
  (4) Paragraph 7 of the Schedule inserted in the 1989 Act by the Schedule to this Act extends only to England and Wales.
  (5) Paragraph 8 of the Schedule so inserted extends only to Scotland.
  (6) Otherwise, the provisions of this Act extend only to Great Britain.
  (7) In section 28(2) of the 1989 Act (extent of Act)—
  (a) in paragraph (a) (provisions not extending to Northern Ireland)—
          (i) after "13A", insert "13B"; and
          (ii) for "Part IVA" substitute "Parts IVA and IVB";
  (b) in paragraph (b) (provisions extending only to England and Wales), the first "and" is repealed and after "Schedule 5" insert ", paragraph 7 of Schedule 6A and paragraph 2A of Schedule 7";
  (c) in paragraph (c) (provisions extending only to Scotland), after "Schedule 4" insert ", paragraph 8 of Schedule 6A"; and
  (d) in paragraph (d) (provisions extending only to England and Wales and Northern Ireland) after "Schedule 7" insert "except paragraph 2A".
  (8) For the purposes of section 27 of the 1989 Act, any amendments made in that Act by a provision of this Act shall be treated as having been continued in force by the order under subsection (6) of that section which has effect at the time when this Act is passed.

GENERAL NOTE

Subs. (8)
  Section 27(6)(b) of the 1989 Act states that the Secretary of State may, by order made by statutory instrument, provide that all or any of the provisions under the 1989 Act which are for the time being in force, shall cease to be in force. This would apply also to the new amendments to that Act which are inserted by subs. (8) of this Act.

SCHEDULE

NEW SCHEDULE 6A TO THE 1989 ACT

In the 1989 Act insert, after Schedule 6—

"SCHEDULE 6A

POLICE CORDONS

1. In this Schedule—
"authorisation" means an authorisation given under section 16C of this Act;
"cordoned area" means an area on which a cordon has been imposed by an authorisation which remains in force;
"police tape" means any plastic or other tape which is generally used by the police force concerned to indicate an area to which members of the public should not attempt to gain access;
"terrorist investigation" means any investigation to which section 17(1) of this Act applies.

Authorisation

2.—(1) Authorisation may be given in writing or orally but if given orally must be confirmed in writing by the person giving it as soon as is reasonably practicable.
(2) A constable who gives an authorisation by virtue of section 16C(2) above must, as soon as is reasonably practicable—
(a) make a written record of the time at which he gave it; and
(b) cause a police officer of at least the rank of superintendent to be informed that it was given.
(3) An officer to whom such a report is made may give a direction in writing—
(a) confirming the authorisation; or
(b) if he considers that it should not be confirmed, cancelling it.
(4) If a direction is given under sub-paragraph (3)(b), the officer giving it must record in writing—
(a) the fact that the authorisation was given; and
(b) the reason for giving it.

Area on which cordon is imposed

3.—(1) An authorisation must specify the area on which the cordon is being imposed.
(2) That area must be within the police area of the person giving the authorisation.

Period for which cordon is imposed

4.—(1) An authorisation must specify the period for which it will be in force.
(2) The period initially specified must not exceed 14 days.
(3) The specified period may be extended by one or more written variations made by an officer of at least the rank of superintendent.
(4) The overall period for which an authorisation is in force must not exceed 28 days.

Marking the area

5. The area on which a cordon is imposed must, so far as is reasonably practicable, be indicated by means of police tape or in such other manner as appears to the police officer responsible for carrying out the arrangements for applying the cordon to be appropriate.

Police powers in cordoned area

6.—(1) A person who is in a cordoned area must immediately leave the area if ordered to do so by a constable in uniform.
(2) A person who is on any premises which abut or are wholly or partly within a cordoned area must immediately leave the premises if ordered to do so by a constable in uniform.

(3) The driver or other person in charge of a vehicle which is in a cordoned area must immediately move the vehicle from the area if ordered to do so by a constable in uniform.

(4) A constable may—
- (a) remove from a cordoned area any vehicle which is in that area; or
- (b) move any such vehicle to another place within that area.

(5) A constable in uniform may prohibit or restrict any vehicular or pedestrian access to a cordoned area.

Powers of search in cordoned area: England and Wales

7.—(1) If a police officer of at least the rank of superintendent has reasonable grounds for believing—
- (a) that there is material which is likely to be of substantial value (whether by itself or together with other material) to a terrorist investigation to be found on premises which are wholly or partly within a cordoned area, and
- (b) that the material does not consist of or include items subject to legal privilege, excluded material or special procedure material,

he may give written authority for a search of the premises.

(2) If written authority is given under this paragraph, a constable may enter the premises specified in the authority, search the premises and any person found there and seize and retain anything found there or on any such person, other than items subject to legal privilege, if he has reasonable grounds for believing—
- (a) that it is likely to be of substantial value (whether by itself or together with other material) to the investigation; and
- (b) that it is necessary to seize it in order to prevent it being concealed, lost, damaged, altered or destroyed.

(3) Entry and search under an authority given under this paragraph may be at any time (and on more than one occasion) while the area concerned is a cordoned area.

(4) Nothing in this paragraph authorises a constable to require a person to remove any of his clothing in public other than any headgear, footwear, outer coat, jacket or gloves.

(5) Any power of seizure conferred by this Schedule is without prejudice to the powers conferred by section 19 of the Police and Criminal Evidence Act 1984 and for the purposes of sections 21 and 22 of that Act (access to, and copying and retention of, seized material), a terrorist investigation is to be treated as an investigation of or in connection with an offence.

(6) In this paragraph "items subject to legal privilege", "excluded material" and "special procedure material" have the meaning given in sections 10 to 14 of the Police and Criminal Evidence Act 1984.

Powers of search in cordoned areas: Scotland

8.—(1) If a police officer of at least the rank of superintendent has reasonable grounds for believing that there is material which is likely to be of substantial value (whether by itself or together with other material) to a terrorist investigation to be found on premises which are wholly or partly within a cordoned area, he may give written authority for a search of the premises.

(2) If written authority is given under this paragraph, a constable may enter the premises specified in the authority, search the premises and any person found there and seize and retain anything found there or on any such person if he has reasonable grounds for believing that it is such material as is mentioned in sub-paragraph (1) above and that it is necessary to seize it in order to prevent it being concealed, lost, damaged, altered or destroyed.

(3) Under an authority given under this paragraph a constable may—
- (a) enter and search the premises specified in the authority at any time (and on more than one occasion) while the area concerned is a cordoned area; and
- (b) if necessary, for the purpose of the exercise of his powers under sub-paragraph (2) above, open lockfast places on such premises.

(4) Nothing in this paragraph authorises a constable to require a person to remove any of his clothing in public other than any headgear, footwear, outer coat, jacket or gloves.

(5) Nothing in this paragraph shall prejudice any rule of law whereby—
- (a) communications between a professional legal adviser and his client, or
- (b) communications made in connection with or in contemplation of legal proceedings and for the purpose of those proceedings,

are in legal proceedings protected from disclosure on grounds of confidentiality.

Offences

9.—(1) A person who—

(a) fails to comply with an order given under paragraph 6(1), (2) or (3) above,

(b) contravenes a prohibition or restriction imposed under paragraph 6(5) above, or

(c) wilfully obstructs a constable in the execution of his duty under paragraph 6 above,

is guilty of an offence.

(2) A person who wilfully obstructs, or seeks to frustrate the object of, a search under paragraph 7 or 8 above, is guilty of an offence.

(3) It is a defence for a person charged with an offence under sub-paragraph (1)(a) or (b) above to prove that he had lawful authority or some other reasonable excuse for the failure or contravention.

(4) A person who is guilty of an offence under this paragraph is liable on summary conviction to imprisonment for a term not exceeding three months or to a fine not exceeding level 4 on the standard scale or both.

Powers to be in addition to other powers

10. The powers conferred by this Schedule are additional to any other powers which a constable has either at common law or under or by virtue of any other enactment and are not to be taken to affect any of those other powers."

INDEX

References are to sections and the Schedule

FINANCE ACT 1996*

(1996 c. 8)

---

* Annotations by Ian Ferrier, Barrister.

Chapter VI

Miscellaneous provisions

Reliefs

An Act to grant certain duties, to alter other duties, and to amend the law relating to the National Debt and the Public Revenue, and to make further provision in connection with Finance.   [29th April 1996]

PARLIAMENTARY DEBATES
Hansard, H.C. Vol. 268, col. 266; Vol. 269, col. 411; Vol. 270, cols. 148, 490; Vol. 274, cols. 1045, 1179. H.L. Vol. 571, cols. 148, 1357.

INTRODUCTION AND GENERAL NOTE

This Act continued the trend towards ever lengthier fiscal legislation. It is virtually the same length as the Finance Act 1993 (c. 34), itself the longest on record. The last four Finance Acts have added more than 1,600 pages to the statute book. This is not the result of innovative departures in the tax law but rather of ever increasing complexity and a tendency to spell out in detail matters which were previously left to practice and judicial interpretation.

Three groups of measures primarily contributed to the length of the Act, accounting for nearly half its content:

(1) the introduction of landfill tax, levied on the disposal of material as waste at a landfill site (ss.39–71 and Sched. 5);

(2) a new system for the taxation of debt held by companies (ss.80–105 and Scheds. 8–15);

(3) a further instalment of provisions relating to the introduction of self-assessment and the abolition of the preceding year basis of assessment under Sched. D (ss.121–142 and Scheds. 19–25).

Although economic recovery continued, it was not as buoyant as the government expected, and a public sector borrowing requirement (PSBR) of nearly £30 billion left little scope for tax cuts. However, the basic rate of income tax was reduced from 25 per cent to 24 per cent, and the charge on bank and building society interest was reduced from the basic rate to the lower rate (20 per cent). There was a substantial increase in the inheritance tax threshold from £154,000 to £200,000.

ABBREVIATIONS

"ACT"	:	advance corporation tax.
"ADP"	:	acceptable distribution policy.
"BLAGAB"	:	basic life assurance and general annuity business.
"CFC"	:	controlled foreign companies.
"EEA"	:	European Economic Area.
"ESC"	:	extra-statutory concession.
"ESOT"	:	employee share ownership trust.
"FID"	:	foreign income dividend.
"FOTRA"	:	free of tax to residents abroad.
"IHC"	:	international headquarters companies.
"LIFO"	:	"last in, first out".
"MEA"	:	Mineral Extraction Allowances.
"QCB"	:	qualifying corporate bonds.
"repos"	:	sales and repurchase agreements.
"SDRT"	:	stamp duty reserve tax.
"SORP"	:	Statement of Recommended Practice.
"SRA"	:	Scientific Research Allowances.
"UKCS"	:	U.K. continental shelf.
"VCT"	:	venture capital trust.
"VTR"	:	vocational training relief.
"CAA"	:	Capital Allowances Act 1990.
"FA"	:	Finance Act.
"ICTA"	:	Income and Corporation Taxes Act 1988.
"IHTA"	:	Inheritance Tax Act 1984.
"SDMA"	:	Stamp Duties Management Act 1891.
"TCGA"	:	Taxation of Chargeable Gains Act 1992.
"TMA"	:	Taxes Management Act 1970.
"VATA"	:	Value Added Tax Act 1994.

PART I

EXCISE DUTIES

Alcoholic liquor duties

Spirits: rate of duty

1.—(1) In section 5 of the Alcoholic Liquor Duties Act 1979 (spirits), for "£20.60" there shall be substituted "£19.78".

(2) This section shall be deemed to have come into force at 6 o'clock in the evening of 28th November 1995.

GENERAL NOTE

A reduction of four per cent is applied to the duty on spirits.

Wine and made-wine: rates

2.—(1) In the Table of rates of duty in Schedule 1 to the Alcoholic Liquor Duties Act 1979 (wine and made-wine)—

(a) in Part I of the Table for "200.64", where it appears as the rate for wine or made-wine of a strength exceeding 15 per cent. but not exceeding 22 per cent., there shall be substituted "187.24"; and

(b) in Part II of that Table (wine or made-wine of a strength exceeding 22 per cent.), for "20.60" there shall be substituted "19.78".

(2) Paragraph (a) of subsection (1) above shall be deemed to have come into force on 1st January 1996 and paragraph (b) shall be deemed to have come into force at 6 o'clock in the evening of 28th November 1995.

GENERAL NOTE
The rate of duty on wine (or made-wine) of a strength exceeding 15 per cent but not exceeding 22 per cent is reduced by 6.7 per cent and on such wine exceeding 22 per cent by four per cent.

Cider: rate of duty

3.—(1) In subsection (1) of section 62 of the Alcoholic Liquor Duties Act 1979 (cider), for "rate of £23.78 per hectolitre" there shall be substituted "rates shown in subsection (1A) below."

(2) After that subsection there shall be inserted the following subsection—
"(1A) The rates at which the duty shall be charged are—
(a) £35.67 per hectolitre in the case of cider of a strength exceeding 7.5 per cent.; and
(b) £23.78 per hectolitre in any other case."

(3) This section shall come into force on 1st October 1996.

GENERAL NOTE
The single rate of excise duty on cider (including perry) is replaced by two rates, depending on the strength of the cider. The existing rate will continue to apply to cider of a strength under 7.5 per cent but the rate on higher strength cider is increased by 50 per cent.

Hydrocarbon oil duties

Rates of duty and rebate

4.—(1) In section 6(1) of the Hydrocarbon Oil Duties Act 1979, for "£0.3614" (duty on light oil) and "£0.3132" (duty on heavy oil) there shall be substituted "£0.3912" and "£0.3430", respectively.

(2) In section 8(3) of that Act (duty on road fuel gas), for "£0.3314" there shall be substituted "£0.2817".

(3) In section 11(1) of that Act (rebate on heavy oil), for "£0.0166" (fuel oil) and "£0.0214" (gas oil) there shall be substituted "£0.0181" and "£0.0233", respectively.

(4) In subsection (1) of section 13A of that Act (rebate on unleaded petrol), for "the rate of £0.0482 a litre" there shall be substituted "the rate specified in subsection (1A) below"; and after that subsection there shall be inserted the following subsections—
"(1A) The rate of rebate shall be—
(a) £0.0150 a litre in the case of higher octane unleaded petrol; and
(b) £0.0482 a litre in any other case.
(1B) For the purposes of this section unleaded petrol is 'higher octane' if—
(a) its research octane number is not less than 96 and its motor octane number is not less than 86;
(b) it is delivered for home use as petrol which satisfies the condition set out in paragraph (a) above;
(c) it is delivered for home use as petrol which is suitable to be used as fuel for engines for which leaded petrol is suitable by virtue of being leaded; or
(d) it is delivered for home use under such a description, or in such a manner, as tends, in the circumstances, to suggest that it is—
(i) petrol satisfying the condition set out in paragraph (a) above; or
(ii) petrol suitable to be used as fuel for engines for which leaded petrol is suitable by virtue of being leaded.

(1C) The method of testing unleaded petrol for ascertaining, for the purposes of this section, its research octane number or motor octane number shall be such as the Commissioners may direct."

(5) In subsection (2) of that section (meaning of "unleaded"), for the words from "or, if" onwards there shall be substituted "; and petrol is 'leaded' for the purposes of this section if it is not unleaded."

(6) In section 14(1) of that Act (rebate on light oil for use as furnace fuel), for "£0.0166" there shall be substituted "£0.0181".

(7) Subsections (1) to (3) and (6) above shall be deemed to have come into force at 6 o'clock in the evening of 28th November 1995; and subsection (4) above shall come into force on 15th May 1996.

GENERAL NOTE

This section increases the rates of excise duties on most chargeable fuels and reduces the rate of duty on gas used as road fuel. It also provides for a further duty increase on higher octane unleaded fuel. In response to trade concerns, the definition of higher octane petrol was amended in committee to add to the products so comprised. The purpose of this measure was to protect the revenue from an increased use of super unleaded petrol, which could be blended with other additives to make it usable in cars that require leaded petrol [Standing Committee E, January 30, 1996, col. 29].

Subs. (1)
The rates of excise duty on light and heavy oils are increased by about 3p per litre.

Subs. (2)
The duty on road fuel gas is reduced by about 5p per kilogram.

Subs. (3)
The alteration in the rebates on heavy oil results in an increase of duty of about 0.15p per litre on fuel oil and 2p per litre on gas oil.

Subs. (4)
This creates a new rate of rebate applicable to higher octane unleaded petrol, resulting in an additional duty liability of 3.5p per litre on such petrol delivered for home use.

Subs. (6)
The duty rebate on light oil used as furnace fuel is altered, producing an effective increase in duty of 0.15p per litre.

Misuse of rebated kerosene

5.—(1) The Hydrocarbon Oil Duties Act 1979 shall be amended as mentioned in subsections (2) to (5) below.

(2) In section 11(1) (rebate on heavy oil), for "and 13" there shall be substituted "13, 13AA and 13AB".

(3) In section 12(2) (restriction on use of rebated heavy oil for road vehicles), after "allowed" there shall be inserted "(whether under section 11(1) above or 13AA(1) below)".

(4) After section 13 there shall be inserted the following sections—

"Restrictions on use of rebated kerosene
13AA.—(1) If, on the delivery of kerosene for home use, it is intended to use the kerosene as fuel for—
    (a) an engine provided for propelling an excepted vehicle, or
    (b) an engine which is used neither for propelling a vehicle nor for heating,
a declaration shall be made to that effect and thereupon rebate shall be allowed at the rate for rebated gas oil which is then in force, instead of at the rate then in force under section 11(1)(c) above.

(2) Subject to subsection (3) below, no kerosene on whose delivery for home use a rebate at the rate given by section 11(1)(c) above has been allowed shall—

(a) be used as fuel for an engine provided for propelling an excepted vehicle;

(b) be used as fuel for an engine which is used neither for propelling a vehicle nor for heating; or

(c) be taken into the fuel supply of an engine falling within paragraph (a) or (b) above.

(3) Subsection (2) above does not apply to any quantity of kerosene in respect of which there has been paid to the Commissioners an amount equal to duty on the same quantity of gas oil at the rate for rebated gas oil which is in force at the time of the payment.

(4) A payment under subsection (3) above shall be made in accordance with regulations made under section 24(1) below for the purposes of this section.

(5) For the purposes of this section and section 13AB below—

'excepted vehicle' means a vehicle which is an excepted vehicle under any provision of Schedule 1 to this Act; and

'kerosene' means heavy oil of which more than 50 per cent. by volume distils at a temperature of 240°C or less.

(6) For the purposes of this section and section 13AB below the rate for rebated gas oil which is in force at any time is the rate of duty which at that time is in force under section 6(1) above in the case of heavy oil as reduced by the rate of rebate allowable at that time under section 11(1)(b) above.

Penalties for misuse of kerosene

13AB.—(1) If a person uses kerosene in contravention of section 13AA(2) above—

(a) the Commissioners may recover from him, in respect of the quantity of kerosene used, an amount equal to duty on the same quantity of gas oil at the rate for rebated gas oil which is in force at the time of the contravention;

(b) his use of the kerosene shall attract a penalty under section 9 of the Finance Act 1994 (civil penalties); and

(c) if he uses the kerosene with the relevant intent, he shall be guilty of an offence.

(2) If a person is liable for kerosene being taken into a fuel supply of an engine in contravention of section 13AA(2) above—

(a) the Commissioners may recover from him, in respect of the quantity of kerosene taken into the fuel supply, an amount equal to duty on the same quantity of gas oil at the rate for rebated gas oil which is in force at the time of the contravention;

(b) his becoming so liable shall attract a penalty under section 9 of the Finance Act 1994 (civil penalties); and

(c) if he has the relevant intent in relation to the kerosene being taken into the fuel supply, he shall be guilty of an offence.

(3) For the purposes of subsection (2) above, a person is liable for kerosene being taken into a fuel supply of an engine if at the time—

(a) he has the charge of the engine; or

(b) subject to subsection (4) below, he is the owner of the engine.

(4) If a person other than the owner is for the time being entitled to possession of the engine, that other person and not the owner is liable.

(5) If—

(a) a person supplies kerosene having reason to believe that it will be put to a particular use, and

(b) that use is one which, if a payment is not made under subsection (3) of section 13AA above, will contravene subsection (2) of that section,

his supplying the kerosene shall attract a penalty under section 9 of the Finance Act 1994 (civil penalties) and, if he makes the supply with the relevant intent, he shall be guilty of an offence.

(6) In this section 'the relevant intent' means the intent that the restrictions imposed by section 13AA(2) above shall be contravened.

(7) A person guilty of an offence under this section shall be liable—

(a) on summary conviction, to a penalty of the statutory maximum, or to imprisonment for a term not exceeding 6 months, or to both;

(b) on conviction on indictment, to a penalty of any amount, or to a term of imprisonment not exceeding 7 years, or to both.

(8) Any kerosene falling within subsection (9) or (10) below is liable to forfeiture.

(9) Kerosene falls within this subsection if it is taken into a fuel supply in contravention of section 13AA(2) above.

(10) Kerosene falls within this subsection if—

(a) it has been supplied in circumstances in which there is reason to believe that it will be put to a particular use; and

(b) that use is one which, if payment is not made under subsection (3) of section 13AA above, will contravene subsection (2) of that section."

(5) In section 24 (control of use of duty-free and rebated oil)—

(a) in subsection (1), after "section 13A" there shall be inserted "section 13AA"; and

(b) in subsection (2), after "section 12" there shall be inserted "or section 13AA".

(6) This section shall have effect in relation to cases where kerosene is—

(a) used as fuel, or

(b) taken into a fuel supply,

on or after such day as the Commissioners of Customs and Excise may by order made by statutory instrument appoint.

GENERAL NOTE

This section was added at report stage. It imposes a positive rate of duty on kerosene when it is used not as heating oil, but as motor fuel in off-road vehicles or in certain other excepted vehicles, such as those used for road construction.

Penalties are provided for failure to declare the use and pay the duty [*Hansard*, H.C. Vol. 274, col. 1048].

Mixing of rebated oil

6.—(1) The Hydrocarbon Oil Duties Act 1979 shall be amended as mentioned in subsections (2) to (4) below.

(2) In section 20 (contaminated or accidentally mixed oil), after subsection (3) there shall be inserted the following subsection—

"(4) The power to make a payment to a person under subsection (2) above in relation to oils that have become accidentally mixed does not apply in relation to a mixture in respect of which he is liable to pay duty under section 20AAA below."

(3) After section 20A there shall be inserted the following sections—

"**Mixing of rebated oil**

20AAA.—(1) Where—

(a) a mixture which is leaded or unleaded petrol is produced in contravention of Part I of Schedule 2A to this Act, and

(b) the mixture is not produced as a result of approved mixing,

a duty of excise shall be charged on the mixture.

(2) Where—

(a) a mixture of heavy oils is produced in contravention of Part II of Schedule 2A to this Act,

(b) the mixture is not produced as a result of approved mixing, and

(c) the mixture is supplied for use as fuel for a road vehicle or an excepted vehicle, a duty of excise shall be charged on the mixture.

(3) The person liable to pay the duty charged under subsection (1) above is the person producing the mixture.

(4) The person liable to pay the duty charged under subsection (2) above is the person supplying the mixture.

(5) The Commissioners may exempt a person from liability to pay duty charged under this section in respect of the production or supply of a mixture if they are satisfied—

(a) that the mixture has been produced or (as the case may be) supplied accidentally; and

(b) that, having regard to all the circumstances, the person should be exempted from liability to pay the duty.

(6) Part III of Schedule 2A to this Act makes provision with respect to rates and amounts of duty charged under this section.

(7) In this section—

'approved mixing' has the meaning given by section 20A(5) above; and

'excepted vehicle' means a vehicle which is an excepted vehicle under any provision of Schedule 1 to this Act.

Mixing of rebated oil: supplementary

20AAB.—(1) A person who—

(a) produces a mixture on which duty is charged under section 20AAA(1) above, or

(b) supplies a mixture on which duty is charged under section 20AAA(2) above,

must notify the Commissioners that he has done so within the period of seven days beginning with the date on which he produced or (as the case may be) supplied the mixture.

(2) A person is not required to give a notification under subsection (1) above if, before he produced or (as the case may be) supplied the mixture, he notified the Commissioners that he proposed to do so.

(3) Notification under subsection (1) or (2) above must be given in such form and in such manner, and must contain such particulars, as the Commissioners may direct.

(4) Subject to subsection (7) below, where it appears to the Commissioners—

(a) that a person has produced or supplied a mixture on which duty is charged under section 20AAA above, and

(b) that he is the person liable to pay the duty,

they may assess the amount of duty due from him to the best of their judgement and notify that amount to him or his representative.

(5) An assessment under subsection (4) above shall be treated as if it were an assessment under section 12(1) of the Finance Act 1994.

(6) The Commissioners may give a direction that a person who is, or expects to be, liable to pay duty charged under section 20AAA above—

(a) shall account for duty charged under that section by reference to such periods ('accounting periods') as may be determined by or under the direction;

(b) shall make, in relation to accounting periods, returns in such form and at such times and containing such particulars as may be so determined;

(c) shall pay duty charged under that section at such times and in such manner as may be so determined.

(7) The power to make an assessment under subsection (4) above does not apply in relation to a person who is for the time being subject to a direction under subsection (6) above.

(8) Where any person—

(a) fails to give a notification which he is required to give under subsection (1) above, or

(b) fails to comply with a direction under subsection (6) above,

his failure shall attract a penalty under section 9 of the Finance Act 1994 (civil penalties)."

(4) After Schedule 2 there shall be inserted the Schedule set out in Schedule 1 to this Act.

(5) This section and Schedule 1 to this Act shall have effect in relation to—

(a) the production on or after the appointed day of a mixture which is leaded or unleaded petrol; and

(b) the supply on or after the appointed day of a mixture of heavy oils;

and "the appointed day" here means such day as the Commissioners of Customs and Excise may by order made by statutory instrument appoint.

GENERAL NOTE

This section, similar in intent to s.5 above, was also added at report stage. It allows Customs and Excise to charge duty when oils of different descriptions are mixed after the normal duty point and the duty liability of the resultant mixture exceeds that originally paid. This provision has been made necessary by an increase in both deliberate and accidental mixing of a variety of fuels, especially kerosene with diesel road fuel and kerosene with rebated gas oil, sometimes called red diesel. There was no current provision, except in limited circumstances to recover duty if mixing took place after the normal duty point.

The section imposes a duty on such mixed fuels, requires the producer or supplier to notify the Customs and Excise, and provides penalties for failure to do so.

See further the General Note to Sched. 1 [*Hansard*, H.C. Vol. 274, col. 1048].

Marked oil used as fuel for road vehicles

7.—(1) After section 24 of the Hydrocarbon Oil Duties Act 1979 (control of use of duty free and rebated oil) there shall be inserted the following section—

"Penalties for misuse of marked oil

24A.—(1) Marked oil shall not be used as fuel for a road vehicle.

(2) For the purposes of this section marked oil is any hydrocarbon oil in which a marker is present which is for the time being designated by regulations made by the Commissioners under subsection (3) below.

(3) The Commissioners may for the purposes of this section designate any marker which appears to them to be used for the purposes of the law of any place (whether within or outside the United Kingdom) for identifying hydrocarbon oil that is not to be used as fuel for road vehicles, or for road vehicles of a particular description.

(4) For the purposes of this section marked oil shall be taken to be used as fuel for a road vehicle if, but only if, it is used as fuel for the engine provided for propelling the vehicle or for an engine which draws its fuel from the same supply as that engine.

(5) Where a person uses any hydrocarbon oil in contravention of subsection (1) above, his use of the oil shall attract a penalty under section 9 of the Finance Act 1994 (civil penalties).

(6) If a person who uses any marked oil in contravention of subsection (1) above does so in the knowledge that the oil he is using is marked oil, he shall be guilty of an offence and liable—

(a) on summary conviction, to a penalty of the statutory maximum, or to imprisonment for a term not exceeding 6 months, or to both;

(b) on conviction on indictment, to a penalty of any amount, or to a term of imprisonment not exceeding 7 years, or to both.

(7) Any marked oil which is in a road vehicle as part of the fuel supply for the engine which propels the vehicle shall be liable to forfeiture.

(8) Where in any proceedings relating to this section a question arises as to the nature of any substance present at any time in any hydrocarbon oil—

(a) a certificate of the Commissioners to the effect that that substance is or was a marker designated for the purposes of this section shall be sufficient, unless the contrary is shown, for establishing that fact; and

(b) any document purporting to be such a certificate shall be taken to be one unless it is shown not to be."

(2) In section 24(1) of that Act (purposes for which regulations may be made), for "or section 19A above" there shall be inserted ", section 19A or section 24A of this Act".

GENERAL NOTE
This section provides powers to penalise the use of oils as road fuel where they are released within or outside the U.K. for use other than as road fuel. Penalties are introduced to cover the use of marked fuel in both private and commercial vehicles.
Use of the fuel attracts a civil penalty (a criminal penalty in the case of deliberate use) and liability to forfeiture of the vehicle.
Marked oil is to be defined by regulation.

Relief for marine voyages

8.—(1) The following provisions of the Hydrocarbon Oil Duties Act 1979 are hereby repealed—

(a) section 18 (fuel for ships in home waters), and

(b) in subsection (1) of section 19 (fuel used in fishing boats, etc.), paragraph (a) and the words from "by the owner" to "be".

(2) This section shall come into force on such day as the Commissioners of Customs and Excise may by order made by statutory instrument appoint.

GENERAL NOTE
The section enacts an existing concessionary relief for commercial operators of small petrol driven vessels (other than fishing boats, which already enjoyed relief). This includes vessels involved in commercial transport, diving support, marine surveying, inshore rescue and safety work, and fish farming at sea [Standing Committee E, February 1, 1996, col. 49].

Tobacco products duty

Rates of duty

9.—(1) For the Table of rates of duty in Schedule 1 to the Tobacco Products Duty Act 1979 there shall be substituted—

"TABLE

1.	Cigarettes	An amount equal to 20 per cent. of the retail price plus £62.52 per thousand cigarettes.
2.	Cigars	£91.52 per kilogram.
3.	Hand-rolling tobacco ...	£85.94 per kilogram.
4.	Other smoking tobacco and chewing tobacco	£40.24 per kilogram."

(2) This section shall be deemed to have come into force at 6 o'clock in the evening of 28th November 1995.

GENERAL NOTE
The rates of duty, except for hand-rolling tobacco, are increased. The increase is 8.5 per cent for cigarettes, 6.9 per cent for cigars and 6.9 per cent for pipe and chewing tobacco.

Betting duties: rates

General betting duty

10.—(1) In section 1(2) of the Betting and Gaming Duties Act 1981 (rate of general betting duty), for "7.75 per cent." there shall be substituted "6.75 per cent.".

(2) This section shall apply in relation to bets made on or after 1st March 1996.

The rate of general betting duty is reduced from 7.75 per cent to 6.75 per cent. This is done to help the betting and horse and greyhound racing industries, which have suffered due to a reduction in betting as a result of the introduction of the National Lottery.

Pool betting duty

11. In section 7(1) of the Betting and Gaming Duties Act 1981 (rate of pool betting duty), for "32.50 per cent" there shall be substituted—
   (a) in relation to bets the stake money on which has been or is paid on or after 3rd December 1995 and before the first Sunday to follow the day on which this Act is passed, "27.50 per cent."; and
   (b) in relation to bets the stake money on which is paid on or after that first Sunday, "26.50 per cent.".

The rate of pool betting duty is reduced from 32.5 per cent to 27.5 per cent from December 3, 1995 to May 4, 1996 and to 26.5 per cent from May 5, 1996 (the first Sunday after the day on which the Finance Act was passed). The reduction is to mitigate the effects on the pool betting industry of the National Lottery. The second reduction of one per cent is to be passed on to the Football Trust and the Foundation for Sport and the Arts.

Amusement machine licence duty

Licences for machines as well as premises

12.—(1) In subsection (1) of section 21 of the Betting and Gaming Duties Act 1981 (requirement for amusement machine licence with respect to premises), at the end there shall be inserted "or the machine".

(2) In subsection (2) of that section (licences to be known as amusement machine licences), at the end there shall be inserted "and, if it is granted with respect to a machine, rather than with respect to premises, as a special amusement machine licence.".

(3) After subsection (3) of that section there shall be inserted the following subsections—

"(3AA) A special amusement machine licence shall not be granted except where—
   (a) the machine with respect to which it is granted is of a description of machine for which special amusement machine licences are available;
   (b) such conditions as may be prescribed by regulations made by the Commissioners are satisfied in relation to the application for the licence, the machine and the person by whom the application is made; and
   (c) the licence is for twelve months.

(3AB) Special amusement machine licences shall be available for amusement machines of each of the following descriptions—
   (a) machines that are not gaming machines; and
   (b) small prize machines."

(4) In section 24(4) of that Act (provision of unlicensed machines), at the end there shall be inserted "or the machines".

(5) In paragraph 4 of Schedule 4 to that Act (seasonal licences), after sub-paragraph (7) there shall be inserted the following sub-paragraph—

"(7AA) Sub-paragraphs (4) and (5) above shall have effect where—
   (a) an amusement machine is provided on any premises at any time in a winter period, and
   (b) the provision of that machine on those premises at that time is authorised by a special amusement machine licence,
as if an amusement machine licence had been granted in respect of those premises for that winter period."

(6) Paragraph 5 of that Schedule shall become sub-paragraph (1) of that paragraph, and after that sub-paragraph there shall be inserted the following sub-paragraphs—

"(2) Regulations may provide for this Schedule to have effect in relation to special amusement machine licences with such exceptions, adaptations and modifications as may be prescribed.

(3) Without prejudice to the generality of sub-paragraphs (1) and (2) above, regulations may include provision requiring—

(a) a special amusement machine licence to be displayed on such premises and in such manner, and

(b) the machine to which such a licence relates to bear such labels and marks,

as may be determined by directions given, in accordance with the regulations, by the Commissioners."

GENERAL NOTE

The section amends the Betting and Gaming Duties Act 1981 (c. 63) to allow for the issue of special licences for amusement machines. A special licence applies to a machine rather than to the premises where it is situated. Licences last for 12 months and apply to all licensable amusement machines. To prevent abuse, machines subject to special licences cannot be used between November and February on premises which are subject to seasonal licences the other eight months of the year.

Air passenger duty

Pleasure flights

13.—(1) In section 31 of the Finance Act 1994 (air passenger duty: exceptions for certain passengers) after subsection (4) there shall be inserted—

"(4A) A passenger is not a chargeable passenger in relation to a flight if under his agreement for carriage (whether or not it is evidenced by a ticket)—

(a) the flight is to depart from and return to the same airport, and

(b) the duration of the flight (excluding any period during which the aircraft's doors are open for boarding or disembarkation) is not to exceed 60 minutes."

(2) In section 32 of that Act (change of circumstances after ticket issued etc.)—

(a) in subsection (1) (which provides that that section applies where a person's agreement for carriage is evidenced by a ticket) for the words "This section applies" there shall be substituted the words "Subsections (2) and (3) below apply";

(b) after subsection (3) there shall be added—

"(4) Where—

(a) at the time a passenger's flight begins, by virtue of section 31(4A) above he would not (assuming there is no change of circumstances) be a chargeable passenger in relation to the flight, and

(b) by reason only of a change of circumstances not attributable to any act or default of his, the flight does not return to the airport from which it departed or exceeds 60 minutes in duration (excluding any period during which the aircraft's doors are open for boarding or disembarkation),

he shall not by reason of the change of circumstances be treated as a chargeable passenger in relation to that flight."

GENERAL NOTE

Certain short pleasure flights are exempted from air passenger duty. These are flights of not more than 60 minutes' duration departing from and returning to the same airport. An unforeseen extension or diversion of a flight will not make the passenger chargeable.

Vehicle excise duty

Increase in general rate

14.—(1) In Schedule 1 to the Vehicle Excise and Registration Act 1994 (annual rates of duty), in paragraph 1(2) (the general rate), for "£135" there shall be substituted "£140".

(2) Subsection (1) above applies in relation to licences taken out after 28th November 1995.

GENERAL NOTE
    The rate of vehicle excise duty for cars, taxis, vans, etc., is increased from £135 to £140.

Electrically propelled vehicles

15.—(1) In Schedule 1 to the Vehicle Excise and Registration Act 1994 (annual rates of duty), in paragraph 2(1)(a) (rate for motorcycles with low cylinder capacity), after "150 cubic centimetres" there shall be inserted "or the motorcycle is an electrically propelled vehicle".

(2) In paragraph 4F of that Schedule (electrically propelled vehicles are special concessionary vehicles)—

    (a) in sub-paragraph (1), after "electrically propelled vehicle" there shall be inserted "other than a motorcycle (within the meaning of Part II of this Schedule)"; and

    (b) sub-paragraph (2) shall be omitted.

(3) In section 62 of that Act (definitions), after subsection (1) there shall be inserted the following subsection—

    "(1A) For the purposes of this Act, a vehicle is not an electrically propelled vehicle unless the electrical motive power is derived from—

        (a) a source external to the vehicle, or

        (b) an electrical storage battery which is not connected to any source of power when the vehicle is in motion."

(4) Subsections (1) to (3) above apply in relation to licences taken out after 28th November 1995.

(5) In Schedule 2 to that Act (exemptions), after paragraph 2 there shall be inserted the following paragraph—

"Electrically assisted pedal cycles

2A.—(1) An electrically assisted pedal cycle is an exempt vehicle.

(2) For the purposes of sub-paragraph (1) an electrically assisted pedal cycle is a vehicle of a class complying with such requirements as may be prescribed by regulations made by the Secretary of State for the purposes of this paragraph."

GENERAL NOTE
    The vehicle excise duty for electrically propelled motorcycles is reduced to the rate equivalent to the lowest cylinder capacity for petrol vehicles (*i.e.* £15). Electrically assisted pedal cycles, to be defined by secondary legislation, are exempted from duty.

Steam powered vehicles etc.

16.—(1) In Schedule 1 to the Vehicle Excise and Registration Act 1994 (annual rates of duty), after paragraph 4E there shall be inserted the following paragraph—

    "4EE. A steam powered vehicle is a special concessionary vehicle."

(2) In paragraph 3 of that Schedule (buses), in sub-paragraph (2)(b) (vehicles which are not buses), after "excepted vehicle" there shall be inserted "or a special concessionary vehicle".

(3) In paragraph 4(2) of that Schedule (meaning of "special vehicle"), for "and is" there shall be substituted "which is not a special concessionary vehicle and which is".

(4) In paragraph 5 of that Schedule (recovery vehicles), after sub-paragraph (5) there shall be inserted the following sub-paragraph—

"(5A) A vehicle is not a recovery vehicle if it is a special concessionary vehicle."

(5) In paragraph 6(1) of that Schedule (vehicles used for exceptional loads), after paragraph (b) there shall be inserted—

"and which is not a special concessionary vehicle."

(6) In paragraph 7(2) of that Schedule (meaning of "haulage vehicle"), after "Part IV," there shall be inserted "IVA,".

(7) In paragraph 16 of that Schedule (application of Part VIII of the Schedule), in sub-paragraph (1)(a), after "Part II, IV," there shall be inserted "IVA,".

(8) This section applies in relation to licences taken out after 28th November 1995.

GENERAL NOTE

Steam powered vehicles are accorded the status of special concessionary vehicles, the annual duty for which is £35.

Consequential amendments are made to exclude certain classes of vehicles from the special concessionary vehicle group.

Vehicles capable of conveying loads

17.—(1) Schedule 1 to the Vehicle Excise and Registration Act 1994 (annual rates of duty) shall be amended in accordance with subsections (2) to (8) below.

(2) In paragraph 4(2) (meaning of "special vehicle"), immediately before paragraph (c) there shall be inserted the following paragraph—

"(bb) a vehicle falling within sub-paragraph (2A) or (2B),".

(3) After sub-paragraph (2) of paragraph 4 there shall be inserted the following sub-paragraphs—

"(2A) A vehicle falls within this sub-paragraph if—
   (a) it is designed or adapted for use for the conveyance of goods or burden of any description; but
   (b) it is not so used or is not so used for hire or reward or for or in connection with a trade or business.

(2B) A vehicle falls within this sub-paragraph if—
   (a) it is designed or adapted for use with a semi-trailer attached; but
   (b) it is not so used or, if it is so used, the semi-trailer is not used for the conveyance of goods or burden of any description."

(4) In paragraph 9(2) (rigid goods vehicles which are subject to basic goods vehicle rate), after paragraph (b) there shall be inserted "and
   (c) to any rigid goods vehicle which is used loaded only in connection with a person learning to drive the vehicle or taking a driving test,".

(5) In paragraph 10(1) (trailer supplement), after "exceeding 12,000 kilograms" there shall be inserted ", which does not fall within paragraph 9(2)(b) or (c)".

(6) In paragraph 11(2) (tractive units which are subject to basic goods vehicle rate), after paragraph (b) there shall be inserted "and
   (c) to any tractive unit to which a semi-trailer is attached which is used loaded only in connection with a person learning to drive the tractive unit or taking a driving test,".

(7) In paragraph 16(1) (cases where Part VIII of Schedule 1 does not apply), paragraph (b), and the word "or" immediately preceding it, shall be omitted.

(8) After paragraph 18 there shall be inserted the following paragraph—

"Other expressions

19.—(1) In this Part 'driving test' means any test of competence to drive mentioned in section 89(1) of the Road Traffic Act 1988.

(2) For the purposes of this Part a vehicle or a semi-trailer is used loaded if the vehicle or, as the case may be, the semi-trailer is used for the conveyance of goods or burden of any description."

(9) In section 7 of the Vehicle Excise and Registration Act 1994 (issue of licences), in subsection (2) (declarations and particulars in relation to goods vehicles)—

(a) after "goods vehicle" there shall be inserted "or a special vehicle"; and

(b) after "goods vehicles" there shall be inserted "or, as the case may be, special vehicles".

(10) After subsection (7) of that section there shall be inserted the following subsection—

"(8) In this section 'special vehicle' has the same meaning as in paragraph 4 of Schedule 1."

(11) Subject to subsection (13) below, subsections (1) to (8) above apply in relation to licences taken out after 28th November 1995.

(12) Subsection (13) below applies where a vehicle licence is taken out—

(a) on or before 28th November 1995, and

(b) at the rate applicable (at the time it is taken out) under Schedule 1 to the Vehicle Excise and Registration Act 1994.

(13) While the licence is in force duty shall not, by virtue of this section, become chargeable under section 15 of that Act (vehicle used in manner attracting higher rate).

(14) Subsections (9) and (10) above apply in relation to applications made after 28th November 1995.

(15) Paragraph 15 of Schedule 1 to that Act (which is unnecessary) shall be omitted.

General Note

Vehicles over 3.5 tonnes which are constructed or adapted to carry goods or burden but are used unladen privately are included in the "special vehicle" class, or if used laden for driver training or testing purposes, are included in the heavy goods vehicle class. In either case the annual rate is £150.

Subs. (5)

Island goods vehicles and goods vehicles used for driver training or testing purposes are excluded from the trailer supplement.

Subs. (6)

The basic rate is also applied to laden articulated vehicles used for driver training or testing.

Old vehicles

18.—(1) In Schedule 2 to the Vehicle Excise and Registration Act 1994 (exempt vehicles), immediately before paragraph 2 there shall be inserted the following paragraph—

"Old vehicles

1A.—(1) A vehicle of a description mentioned in sub-paragraph (2) is an exempt vehicle at any time if it was constructed more than 25 years before the beginning of the year in which that time falls.

(2) The descriptions of vehicles are—

(a) a vehicle in respect of which no annual rate is specified by any provision of Parts II to VIII of Schedule 1;

(b) a motorcycle which does not exceed 450 kilograms in weight unladen.

(3) In sub-paragraph (2)(b) 'motorcycle' has the same meaning as in Part II of Schedule 1."

(2) In Schedule 1 to that Act (annual rates of duty), in paragraph 1 (rate for vehicle for which no other rate is specified)—

(a) for paragraphs (a) and (b) of sub-paragraph (1) there shall be substituted "the general rate"; and

(b) sub-paragraphs (3) to (5) shall be omitted;
and, in paragraph 2 (motorcycles), sub-paragraph (2) shall be omitted.
(3) In section 2(4) of that Act (rate of duty for vehicle not currently in use and for which no previous licence issued), for the words from "whichever" to the end there shall be substituted "the general rate currently specified in paragraph 1(2) of Schedule 1".
(4) In that Act—
(a) in section 13 (trade licences), in subsection (3)(b),
(b) in section 13 as substituted under paragraph 8 of Schedule 4, in subsection (4)(b), and
(c) in section 36(3)(b) (additional liability where cheque dishonoured), for "1(1)(a)" there shall be substituted "1".
(5) This section has effect in relation to times after 28th November 1995.

GENERAL NOTE
A new exempt class is introduced for general rate vehicles (private/light goods), motor bicycles and motor tricycles more than 25 years old [Standing Committee E, February 2, 1996, col. 77].

Old vehicles: further provisions

19.—(1) In Schedule 2 to the Vehicle Excise and Registration Act 1994 (exempt vehicles), for paragraph 1A (inserted by section 18 above) there shall be substituted the following paragraph—

"Old vehicles

1A.—(1) Subject to sub-paragraph (2), a vehicle is an exempt vehicle at any time if it was constructed more than 25 years before the beginning of the year in which that time falls.
(2) A vehicle is not an exempt vehicle by virtue of sub-paragraph (1) if—
(a) an annual rate is specified in respect of it by any provision of Part III, V, VI, VII or VIII of Schedule 1; or
(b) it is a special vehicle, within the meaning of Part IV of Schedule 1, which—
(i) falls within sub-paragraph (3) or (4); and
(ii) is not a digging machine, mobile crane, works truck or road roller.
(3) A vehicle falls within this sub-paragraph if—
(a) it is designed or adapted for use for the conveyance of goods or burden of any description;
(b) it is put to a commercial use on a public road; and
(c) that use is not a use for the conveyance of goods or burden of any description.
(4) A vehicle falls within this sub-paragraph if—
(a) it is designed or adapted for use with a semi-trailer attached;
(b) it is put to a commercial use on a public road; and
(c) in a case where that use is a use with a semi-trailer attached, the semi-trailer is not used for the conveyance of goods or burden of any description.
(5) In sub-paragraph (2) 'digging machine', 'mobile crane' and 'works truck' have the same meanings as in paragraph 4 of Schedule 1.
(6) In sub-paragraphs (3) and (4) 'commercial use' means use for hire or reward or for or in connection with a trade or business."
(2) This section has effect in relation to times on or after 1st June 1996.

GENERAL NOTE
This section, inserted at committee stage, extends the exemption for vehicles more than 25 years old, to preserved vehicles such as fire engines, road rollers, steam traction engines, agricultural, ex-military and ex-commercial vehicles. It does not apply to commercially operated buses, coaches, heavy goods vehicles or recovery vehicles [Standing Committee E, March 7, 1996, col. 719].

Exemptions for vehicle testing: general

20.—(1) Paragraph 22 of Schedule 2 to the Vehicle Excise and Registration Act 1994 (exemption for vehicle testing) shall be amended as follows.

(2) In sub-paragraph (1) (use for the purposes of submitting a vehicle to, or bringing it away from, a compulsory test), after the words "compulsory test", in each place where they occur, there shall be inserted "or a vehicle weight test".

(3) After sub-paragraph (1) there shall be inserted the following sub-paragraph—

"(1A) A vehicle is an exempt vehicle when it is being used solely for the purpose of—

(a) taking it (by previous arrangement for a specified time on a specified date) for a relevant re-examination, or

(b) bringing it away from such a re-examination."

(4) In sub-paragraph (2) (use by an authorised person in the course of compulsory test)—

(a) after "compulsory test" there shall be inserted ", a vehicle weight test or a relevant re-examination and is being so used"; and

(b) in paragraphs (a) and (b), after the words "the test", in each place where they occur, there shall be inserted "or re-examination".

(5) After sub-paragraph (2) there shall be inserted the following sub-paragraph—

"(2A) A vehicle is an exempt vehicle when it is being used by an authorised person solely for the purpose of warming up its engine in preparation for the carrying out of—

(a) a compulsory test, or

(b) a relevant re-examination that is to be carried out for the purposes of an appeal relating to a determination made on a compulsory test."

(6) In sub-paragraph (3) (exemption applying where the relevant certificate is refused), after "a vehicle" there shall be inserted "or as a result of a relevant re-examination,".

(7) In sub-paragraph (5) (relevant examinations)—

(a) for paragraph (a), there shall be substituted the following paragraph—

"(a) an examination under regulations under section 49(1)(b) or (c) of the Road Traffic Act 1988 (examination as to compliance with construction and use or safety requirements)";

(b) the word "and" shall be inserted at the end of paragraph (b); and

(c) paragraph (c) (examinations for the purpose of an appeal under section 60 of the Road Traffic Act 1988) shall be omitted.

(8) After sub-paragraph (6) there shall be inserted the following sub-paragraphs—

"(6A) In this paragraph 'a vehicle weight test' means any examination of a vehicle for which provision is made by regulations under—

(a) section 61A of this Act,

(b) section 49(1)(a) of the Road Traffic Act 1988 (tests for selecting plated weights and other plated particulars), or

(c) Article 65(1)(a) of the Road Traffic (Northern Ireland) Order 1995.

(6B) In this paragraph 'a relevant re-examination' means any examination or re-examination which is carried out in accordance with any provision or requirement made or imposed for the purposes of an appeal relating to a determination made on a compulsory test or vehicle weight test."

(9) Subject to section 21(3) below, in sub-paragraph (7) (meaning of "authorised person")—

(a) the word "and" at the end of paragraph (b) shall be omitted;

(b) at the end of paragraph (c) there shall be inserted the word "and"; and
(c) after that paragraph there shall be inserted the following paragraph—
    "(d) in the case of a relevant re-examination—
            (i) the person to whom the appeal in question is made, or
            (ii) any person who, by virtue of an appointment made by
        that person, is authorised by or under any enactment to carry
        out that re-examination."
    (10) This section shall be deemed to have come into force on 28th November 1995.

GENERAL NOTE
    Vehicles are exempted from duty when used on public roads for certain purposes connected
with a compulsory test. This section extends the exemption to the use of a vehicle by an authorised person to warm up its engine before a compulsory test and to taking a vehicle to or from a
pre-arranged examination for the issue of a design weight certificate. It also makes provision
regarding the taking of a vehicle to or from a pre-arranged goods vehicle plating examination
and its use in connection with an appeal following such a test or examination.

Exemptions for vehicle testing in Northern Ireland

    21.—(1) Paragraph 22 of Schedule 2 to the Vehicle Excise and Regis-
tration Act 1994 (exemption for vehicle testing) shall be further amended as
follows.
    (2) For sub-paragraph (6) (meaning of "compulsory test" in Northern Ire-
land) there shall be substituted the following sub-paragraph—
        "(6) In this paragraph 'compulsory test' means, as respects Northern
    Ireland—
        (a) an examination to obtain a test certificate under Article 61 of the
            Road Traffic (Northern Ireland) Order 1995 without which a
            vehicle licence cannot be obtained for the vehicle,
        (b) an examination to obtain a goods vehicle test certificate under
            Article 65 of that Order, or
        (c) an examination to obtain a public service vehicle licence under
            Article 60(1) of the Road Traffic (Northern Ireland) Order
            1981."
    (3) For paragraph (c) of sub-paragraph (7) (as amended by section 20(9)
above) there shall be substituted the following paragraph—
        "(c) in the case of an examination within sub-paragraph (6), an
            authorised examiner within the meaning of Article 61(3)(a)
            of the Road Traffic (Northern Ireland) Order 1995 or a
            vehicle examiner within the meaning of Part III of that
            Order; and".
    (4) In sub-paragraph (9) (meaning of "relevant certificate" in Northern
Ireland), for paragraphs (a) and (b) there shall be substituted the following
paragraphs—
        "(a) a test certificate (within the meaning of Article 61(2) of the
            Road Traffic (Northern Ireland) Order 1995),
        (b) a goods vehicle test certificate (within the meaning of Article
            65(2) of that Order), or".
    (5) In sub-paragraph (10)(a) (meaning of "relevant work"), the words
"(or, in Northern Ireland, a vehicle test certificate)" shall be omitted.
    (6) This section shall be deemed to have come into force on the date of the
coming into operation of Articles 61 and 65 of the Road Traffic (Northern
Ireland) Order 1995 ("the operational date").
    (7) Subsections (2), (4) and (5) above do not have effect in relation to a
compulsory test carried out in Northern Ireland before the operational date
except for the purpose of construing, in relation to such a test, the reference
to a further compulsory test in paragraph 22(10)(a) of Schedule 2 to the
Vehicle Excise and Registration Act 1994.

GENERAL NOTE
The section provides further necessary amendments to apply s.20 to Northern Ireland.

Other provisions relating to Northern Ireland

22.—(1) In section 42 of the Vehicle Excise and Registration Act 1994 (not fixing registration mark), in subsection (5)(b), for "Article 34 of the Road Traffic (Northern Ireland) Order 1981" there shall be substituted "Article 63 of the Road Traffic (Northern Ireland) Order 1995".

(2) In subsection (6) of that section, for paragraph (b) there shall be substituted—

> "(b) it is being driven for the purposes of, or in connection with, its examination under Article 61 of the Road Traffic (Northern Ireland) Order 1995 in circumstances in which its use is exempted from paragraph (1) of Article 63 of that Order by regulations under paragraph (6) of that Article."

(3) In section 60A(11) of that Act (special maximum weight in Northern Ireland), for "Article 29(3) of the Road Traffic (Northern Ireland) Order 1981" there shall be substituted "Article 60(1) of the Road Traffic (Northern Ireland) Order 1995".

(4) In section 61(6) of that Act (meaning of "weight unladen"), for paragraph (b) there shall be substituted—

> "(b) in Northern Ireland, has the same meaning as it has for the purposes of the Road Traffic (Northern Ireland) Order 1995 by virtue of Article 7 of that Order."

(5) In paragraph 6 of Schedule 1 to that Act (vehicles used for exceptional loads), in sub-paragraph (2) for paragraph (b) there shall be substituted—

> "(b) Article 60 of the Road Traffic (Northern Ireland) Order 1995,".

(6) In that paragraph—

(a) in sub-paragraph (3)(a), for "Article 28 of the Road Traffic (Northern Ireland) Order 1981" there shall be substituted "Article 55 of the Road Traffic (Northern Ireland) Order 1995"; and

(b) in sub-paragraph (4), for "the Road Traffic (Northern Ireland) Order 1981" there shall be substituted "the Road Traffic (Northern Ireland) Order 1995".

(7) In paragraph 17 of Schedule 3 to that Act (amendments of the Road Traffic (Northern Ireland) Order 1981)—

(a) in sub-paragraph (1), "29(2)," and "34(6)," shall be omitted, and

(b) sub-paragraph (2) shall be omitted.

GENERAL NOTE
The amendments made by this section update the statute to take account of the Road Traffic (Northern Ireland) Order 1995.

Licensing and registration

23. Schedule 2 to this Act (which makes provision in connection with powers conferred on the Secretary of State by the Vehicle Excise and Registration Act 1994) shall have effect.

GENERAL NOTE
The section introduces Sched. 2, which brings in a number of changes to the procedure for the licensing and registration of vehicles. The purpose of the changes is to reduce evasion of vehicle excise duty and to enforce the requirement governing registration and transfer more effectively.
See further the General Note to Sched. 2 [Standing Committee E, February 1, 1996, col. 85].

Repeal of certain drawbacks and allowances

Repeal of certain drawbacks and allowances

24. The following provisions (which provide for repayments, drawbacks or allowances in the case of certain excise duties) shall cease to have effect, that is to say—

(a) section 3 of the Finance Act 1977 (repayment in respect of tobacco used in the manufacture of a tobacco product after having borne duty under section 4 of the Finance Act 1964);
(b) section 22(6) of the Alcoholic Liquor Duties Act 1979 (additions in respect of waste which are deemed to be made to tinctures exported or shipped as stores);
(c) section 23 of that Act of 1979 (allowances in respect of British compounded spirits);
(d) section 92(6) of that Act of 1979 (transitional right to drawback); and
(e) section 9(2) and (3) of the Isle of Man Act 1979 (removal to the Isle of Man treated as export for the purposes of drawback).

GENERAL NOTE
The repayment provisions specified are repealed. They had become redundant because of changes to the law permitting duty to be suspended rather than having to be paid and then reclaimed from Customs.

PART II

VALUE ADDED TAX

EC Second VAT Simplification Directive

EC Second VAT Simplification Directive

25. Sections 26 to 29 of and Schedule 3 to this Act are for the purpose of giving effect to requirements of the directive of the Council of the European Communities dated 17th May 1977 No. 77/388/EEC and the amendments of that directive by the directive of that Council dated 10th April 1995 No. 95/7/EC (amendments with a view to introducing new simplification measures with regard to value added tax).

GENERAL NOTE
The section introduces ss.26–29 and Sched. 3, which implement the second VAT simplification directive of the European Community. Among the changes made to the system are the introduction of fiscal warehousing arrangements, standardisation of the rules for calculating VAT due on imports, and simplification of the rules regarding process work carried out on goods.

Fiscal and other warehousing

26.—(1) The provisions of Schedule 3 to this Act shall have effect.
(2) Subject to subsection (3) below, this section and Schedule 3 to this Act shall come into force on such day as the Commissioners of Customs and Excise may by order made by statutory instrument appoint, and shall apply to any acquisition of goods from another member State and any supply taking place on or after that day.
(3) In so far as the provisions inserted by Schedule 3 to this Act confer power to make regulations they shall come into force on the day this Act is passed.

GENERAL NOTE
This section provides that Sched. 3, which implements the new system for fiscal warehousing, will come into effect on a day to be appointed by the Customs and Excise, except for the power to make regulations, which comes into effect on the passage of the Act. The Appointed Day for these purposes was June 1, 1996 by virtue of S.I. 1996 No. 1249 (c. 21).
See further the General Note to Sched. 3.

Value of imported goods

27.—(1) Section 21 of the Value Added Tax Act 1994 (value of imported goods) shall be amended as follows.
(2) In subsection (2) of that section at the end of paragraph (a) the word "and" shall be omitted.
(3) For paragraph (b) of that subsection there shall be substituted—

"(b) all incidental expenses, such as commission, packing, transport and insurance costs, up to the goods' first destination in the United Kingdom; and

(c) if at the time of the importation of the goods from a place outside the member States a further destination for the goods is known, and that destination is within the United Kingdom or another member State, all such incidental expenses in so far as they result from the transport of the goods to that other destination;

and in this subsection "the goods' first destination" means the place mentioned on the consignment note or any other document by means of which the goods are imported into the United Kingdom, or in the absence of such documentation it means the place of the first transfer of cargo in the United Kingdom."

(4) This section shall have effect in relation to goods imported on or after 1st January 1996.

GENERAL NOTE

The value of imported goods for VAT will be taken to include incidental expenses up to their first destination in the U.K. and to their further destination if that is known at the time of importation.

Adaptation of aircraft and hovercraft

28.—(1) Section 22 of the Value Added Tax Act 1994 shall be omitted.

(2) This section shall apply to supplies made on or after 1st January 1996.

GENERAL NOTE

The repeal of the Value Added Tax Act 1994 (c. 23), s.22, which contained special valuation provisions applying to the adaptation of aircraft and hovercraft, follows from the enactment of s.29 below, which deals with this in a wider context.

Work on materials

29.—(1) The Value Added Tax Act 1994 shall be amended as follows.

(2) After subsection (2) of section 30 there shall be inserted the following subsection—

"(2A) A supply by a person of services which consist of applying a treatment or process to another person's goods is zero-rated by virtue of this subsection if by doing so he produces goods, and either—

(a) those goods are of a description for the time being specified in Schedule 8; or

(b) a supply by him of those goods to the person to whom he supplies the services would be of a description so specified."

(3) In subsection (5) of section 55 (supplies of gold), after paragraph (b) there shall be inserted the following—

"; or

(c) any supply of services consisting in the application to another person's goods of a treatment or process which produces goods a supply of which would fall within paragraph (a) above.";

and the word "or" at the end of paragraph (a) shall be omitted.

(4) Paragraph 2 of Schedule 4 (which provides that the treatment or processing of another person's goods shall in certain circumstances be a supply of goods) shall be omitted.

(5) This section shall apply to supplies made on or after 1st January 1996.

GENERAL NOTE

This section introduces amendments changing the VAT treatment of process or repair work carried out on a customer's materials.

Subs. (2)
Process work carried out on a customer's materials is zero-rated where that work results in the production of goods which are themselves zero-rated (*e.g.* food, children's clothes, books and newspapers).

Subs. (3)
The special VAT accounting scheme for gold continues to cover supplies of treatment or processing work where the goods produced are fine gold, gold grain or gold coins of any purity.

Subs. (4)
Process work on a customer's materials will be treated as a supply of services rather than a supply of goods [Standing Committee E, February 6, 1996, col. 99].

Other provisions relating to charges to VAT

Refunds in connection with construction and conversion

30.—(1) For subsection (1) of section 35 of the Value Added Tax Act 1994 (refund of VAT to persons constructing certain buildings) there shall be substituted the following subsections—
   "(1) Where—
      (a) a person carries out works to which this section applies,
      (b) his carrying out of the works is lawful and otherwise than in the course or furtherance of any business, and
      (c) VAT is chargeable on the supply, acquisition or importation of any goods used by him for the purposes of the works,
   the Commissioners shall, on a claim made in that behalf, refund to that person the amount of VAT so chargeable.
   (1A) The works to which this section applies are—
      (a) the construction of a building designed as a dwelling or number of dwellings;
      (b) the construction of a building for use solely for a relevant residential purpose or relevant charitable purpose; and
      (c) a residential conversion.
   (1B) For the purposes of this section goods shall be treated as used for the purposes of works to which this section applies by the person carrying out the works in so far only as they are building materials which, in the course of the works, are incorporated in the building in question or its site.
   (1C) Where—
      (a) a person ('the relevant person') carries out a residential conversion by arranging for any of the work of the conversion to be done by another ('a contractor'),
      (b) the relevant person's carrying out of the conversion is lawful and otherwise than in the course or furtherance of any business,
      (c) the contractor is not acting as an architect, surveyor or consultant or in a supervisory capacity, and
      (d) VAT is chargeable on services consisting in the work done by the contractor,
   the Commissioners shall, on a claim made in that behalf, refund to the relevant person the amount of VAT so chargeable.
   (1D) For the purposes of this section works constitute a residential conversion to the extent that they consist in the conversion of a non-residential building, or a non-residential part of a building, into—
      (a) a building designed as a dwelling or a number of dwellings;
      (b) a building intended for use solely for a relevant residential purpose; or

(c) anything which would fall within paragraph (a) or (b) above if different parts of a building were treated as separate buildings."

(2) In subsection (2) of that section (method of making claim), after "may by regulations prescribe" there shall be inserted "or, in the case of documents, as the Commissioners may determine in accordance with the regulations".

(3) After subsection (3) of that section there shall be inserted the following subsections—

"(4) The notes to Group 5 of Schedule 8 shall apply for construing this section as they apply for construing that Group.

(5) The power of the Treasury by order under section 30 to vary Schedule 8 shall include—

(a) power to apply any variation made by the order for the purposes of this section; and

(b) power to make such consequential modifications of this section as they may think fit."

(4) This section applies in relation to any case in which a claim for repayment under section 35 of the Value Added Tax Act 1994 is made at any time on or after the day on which this Act is passed.

GENERAL NOTE

The section introduces amendments to VATA 1994, s.35, to provide that a non-business builder who creates a dwelling for the first time by the conversion of an existing building, *e.g.* a barn, can reclaim most of the VAT on goods and services paid out in the course of that conversion.

The subsections have been extensively revised to take account of the differing elements of the DIY (do-it-yourself) builders and DIY converters' relief. The existing DIY builder's scheme provides for refunds of VAT on goods purchased by the DIY builder. Services supplied together with goods by tradesmen are already zero-rated. Work to existing buildings is always standard rated, but the amended scheme now allows this VAT to be reclaimed by DIY converters [Standing Committee E, February 6, 1996, col. 102].

Groups: anti-avoidance

31.—(1) In section 43 of the Value Added Tax Act 1994 (groups of companies), after subsection (8) there shall be inserted the following subsection—

"(9) Schedule 9A (which makes provision for ensuring that this section is not used for tax avoidance) shall have effect."

(2) After Schedule 9 to that Act there shall be inserted the Schedule set out in Schedule 4 to this Act.

(3) In section 83 of that Act (appeals), after paragraph (w) there shall be inserted the following paragraph—

"(wa) any direction or assessment under Schedule 9A;".

(4) In section 84 of that Act (further provisions relating to appeals), after subsection (7) there shall be inserted the following subsection—

"(7A) Where there is an appeal against a decision to make such a direction as is mentioned in section 83(wa), the cases in which the tribunal shall allow the appeal shall include (in addition to the case where the conditions for the making of the direction were not fulfilled) the case where the tribunal are satisfied, in relation to the relevant event by reference to which the direction was given, that—

(a) the change in the treatment of the body corporate, or

(b) the transaction in question,

had as its main purpose or, as the case may be, as each of its main purposes a genuine commercial purpose unconnected with the fulfilment of the condition specified in paragraph 1(3) of Schedule 9A."

(5) Subsection (1A) of section 43 of that Act shall not have effect in relation to supplies on or after the day on which this Act is passed.

GENERAL NOTE
This section, and Sched. 3, which were considerably amended in committee and at the report stage, are designed to combat an increasing use of groups of companies in the avoidance of VAT. It follows on an earlier provision in the Finance Act 1995 (c. 4), s.25.

Subs. (4)
On appeals to a tribunal against a direction given under Sched. 4, a general commercial purpose defence applies, as well as invalidity of the direction.
See further the General Note to Sched. 4 [Standing Committee E, February 6, 1996, col. 108].

Supplies of gold etc.

32.—(1) In section 55 of the Value Added Tax Act 1994 (supplies of gold), for paragraph (a) of subsection (5) there shall be substituted the following paragraph—
> "(a) any supply of goods consisting in fine gold, in gold grain of any purity or in gold coins of any purity; or".

(2) This section applies in relation to any supply after 28th November 1995.

GENERAL NOTE
The special VAT accounting scheme for gold is extended to cover gold grain of any purity. This is a measure intended to combat fraud.

Small gifts

33.—(1) In Schedule 4 to the Value Added Tax Act 1994 (matters to be treated as supply of goods or services), in paragraph 5(2)(a) (gift of goods in the course or furtherance of a business not a supply if cost to donor is not more than £10), for "£10" there shall be substituted "£15".

(2) At the end of paragraph 5 of Schedule 4 to that Act there shall be inserted the following sub-paragraph—
> "(7) The Treasury may by order substitute for the sum for the time being specified in sub-paragraph (2)(a) above such sum, not being less than £10, as they think fit."

(3) In section 97(4) of that Act (orders which are subject to affirmative procedure), after paragraph (a) there shall be inserted the following paragraph—
> "(ab) an order under paragraph 5(7) of Schedule 4 substituting a lesser sum for the sum for the time being specified in paragraph 5(2)(a) of that Schedule;".

(4) Subsection (1) above shall apply where a gift is made after 28th November 1995.

GENERAL NOTE
The exemption limit for business gifts, £10 since the introduction of VAT in 1973, is raised to £15. Future changes are to be made by Treasury order, subject to the affirmative resolution procedure in the case of a reduction.

Payment and enforcement

Method of making payments on account

34. In section 28 of the Value Added Tax Act 1994 (payments on account of VAT), after subsection (2) there shall be inserted the following subsection—
> "(2A) The Commissioners may give directions, to persons who are or may become liable by virtue of any order under this section to make payments on account of VAT, about the manner in which they are to make such payments; and where such a direction has been given to any person and has not subsequently been withdrawn, any duty of that person by virtue of such an order to make such a payment shall have effect

as if it included a requirement for the payment to be made in the manner directed."

GENERAL NOTE

The power given by this section will be used to require traders using the payment on account scheme to pay by electronic means [Standing Committee E, February 6, 1996, col. 145].

Default surcharges

35.—(1) The Value Added Tax Act 1994 shall be amended as follows.

(2) After section 59 (default surcharge) there shall be inserted the following section—

"Default surcharge: payments on account

59A.—(1) For the purposes of this section a taxable person shall be regarded as in default in respect of any prescribed accounting period if the period is one in respect of which he is required, by virtue of an order under section 28, to make any payment on account of VAT and either—

  (a) a payment which he is so required to make in respect of that period has not been received in full by the Commissioners by the day on which it became due; or

  (b) he would, but for section 59(1A), be in default in respect of that period for the purposes of section 59.

(2) Subject to subsections (10) and (11) below, subsection (4) below applies in any case where—

  (a) a taxable person is in default in respect of a prescribed accounting period; and

  (b) the Commissioners serve notice on the taxable person (a 'surcharge liability notice') specifying as a surcharge period for the purposes of this section a period which—

      (i) begins, subject to subsection (3) below, on the date of the notice; and

      (ii) ends on the first anniversary of the last day of the period referred to in paragraph (a) above.

(3) If—

  (a) a surcharge liability notice is served by reason of a default in respect of a prescribed accounting period, and

  (b) that period ends at or before the expiry of an existing surcharge period already notified to the taxable person concerned,

the surcharge period specified in that notice shall be expressed as a continuation of the existing surcharge period; and, accordingly, the existing period and its extension shall be regarded as a single surcharge period.

(4) Subject to subsections (7) to (11) below, if—

  (a) a taxable person on whom a surcharge liability notice has been served is in default in respect of a prescribed accounting period,

  (b) that prescribed accounting period is one ending within the surcharge period specified in (or extended by) that notice, and

  (c) the aggregate value of his defaults in respect of that prescribed accounting period is more than nil,

that person shall be liable to a surcharge equal to whichever is the greater of £30 and the specified percentage of the aggregate value of his defaults in respect of that prescribed accounting period.

(5) Subject to subsections (7) to (11) below, the specified percentage referred to in subsection (4) above shall be determined in relation to a prescribed accounting period by reference to the number of such periods during the surcharge period which are periods in respect of which the taxable person is in default and in respect of which the value of his defaults is more than nil, so that—

(a) in relation to the first such prescribed accounting period, the specified percentage is 2 per cent.;

(b) in relation to the second such period, the specified percentage is 5 per cent.;

(c) in relation to the third such period, the specified percentage is 10 per cent.; and

(d) in relation to each such period after the third, the specified percentage is 15 per cent.

(6) For the purposes of this section the aggregate value of a person's defaults in respect of a prescribed accounting period shall be calculated as follows—

(a) where the whole or any part of a payment in respect of that period on account of VAT was not received by the Commissioners by the day on which it became due, an amount equal to that payment or, as the case may be, to that part of it shall be taken to be the value of the default relating to that payment;

(b) if there is more than one default with a value given by paragraph (a) above, those values shall be aggregated;

(c) the total given by paragraph (b) above, or (where there is only one default) the value of the default under paragraph (a) above, shall be taken to be the value for that period of that person's defaults on payments on account;

(d) the value of any default by that person which is a default falling within subsection (1)(b) above shall be taken to be equal to the amount of any outstanding VAT less the amount of unpaid payments on account; and

(e) the aggregate value of a person's defaults in respect of that period shall be taken to be the aggregate of—

(i) the value for that period of that person's defaults (if any) on payments on account; and

(ii) the value of any default of his in respect of that period that falls within subsection (1)(b) above.

(7) In the application of subsection (6) above for the calculation of the aggregate value of a person's defaults in respect of a prescribed accounting period—

(a) the amount of outstanding VAT referred to in paragraph (d) of that subsection is the amount (if any) which would be the amount of that person's outstanding VAT for that period for the purposes of section 59(4); and

(b) the amount of unpaid payments on account referred to in that paragraph is the amount (if any) equal to so much of any payments on account of VAT (being payments in respect of that period) as has not been received by the Commissioners by the last day on which that person is required (as mentioned in section 59(1)) to make a return for that period.

(8) If a person who, apart from this subsection, would be liable to a surcharge under subsection (4) above satisfies the Commissioners or, on appeal, a tribunal—

(a) in the case of a default that is material for the purposes of the surcharge and falls within subsection (1)(a) above—

(i) that the payment on account of VAT was despatched at such a time and in such a manner that it was reasonable to expect that it would be received by the Commissioners by the day on which it became due, or

(ii) that there is a reasonable excuse for the payment not having been so despatched,

or

 (b) in the case of a default that is material for the purposes of the surcharge and falls within subsection (1)(b) above, that the condition specified in section 59(7)(a) or (b) is satisfied as respects the default,

he shall not be liable to the surcharge and for the purposes of the preceding provisions of this section he shall be treated as not having been in default in respect of the prescribed accounting period in question (and, accordingly, any surcharge liability notice the service of which depended upon that default shall be deemed not to have been served).

 (9) For the purposes of subsection (8) above, a default is material to a surcharge if—

 (a) it is the default which, by virtue of subsection (4) above, gives rise to the surcharge; or

 (b) it is a default which was taken into account in the service of the surcharge liability notice upon which the surcharge depends and the person concerned has not previously been liable to a surcharge in respect of a prescribed accounting period ending within the surcharge period specified in or extended by that notice.

 (10) In any case where—

 (a) the conduct by virtue of which a person is in default in respect of a prescribed accounting period is also conduct falling within section 69(1), and

 (b) by reason of that conduct, the person concerned is assessed to a penalty under section 69,

the default shall be left out of account for the purposes of subsections (2) to (5) above.

 (11) If the Commissioners, after consultation with the Treasury, so direct, a default in respect of a prescribed accounting period specified in the direction shall be left out of account for the purposes of subsections (2) to (5) above.

 (12) For the purposes of this section the Commissioners shall be taken not to receive a payment by the day on which it becomes due unless it is made in such a manner as secures (in a case where the payment is made otherwise than in cash) that, by the last day for the payment of that amount, all the transactions can be completed that need to be completed before the whole amount of the payment becomes available to the Commissioners.

 (13) In determining for the purposes of this section whether any person would, but for section 59(1A), be in default in respect of any period for the purposes of section 59, subsection (12) above shall be deemed to apply for the purposes of section 59 as it applies for the purposes of this section.

 (14) For the purposes of this section references to a thing's being done by any day include references to its being done on that day."

 (3) In section 59, at the beginning of subsection (1) (circumstances amounting to a default in respect of any prescribed accounting period), there shall be inserted "Subject to subsection (1A) below"; and after that subsection there shall be inserted the following subsection—

 "(1A) A person shall not be regarded for the purposes of this section as being in default in respect of any prescribed accounting period if that period is one in respect of which he is required by virtue of any order under section 28 to make any payment on account of VAT."

 (4) After subsection (10) of that section there shall be inserted the following subsection—

 "(11) For the purposes of this section references to a thing's being done by any day include references to its being done on that day."

 (5) After the section 59A inserted by subsection (2) above there shall be inserted the following section—

"**Relationship between sections 59 and 59A**

59B.—(1) This section applies in each of the following cases, namely—

    (a) where a section 28 accounting period ends within a surcharge period begun or extended by the service on a taxable person (whether before or after the coming into force of section 59A) of a surcharge liability notice under section 59; and

    (b) where a prescribed accounting period which is not a section 28 accounting period ends within a surcharge period begun or extended by the service on a taxable person of a surcharge liability notice under section 59A.

(2) In a case falling within subsection (1)(a) above section 59A shall have effect as if—

    (a) subject to paragraph (b) below, the section 28 accounting period were deemed to be a period ending within a surcharge period begun or, as the case may be, extended by a notice served under section 59A; but

    (b) any question—

        (i) whether a surcharge period was begun or extended by the notice, or

        (ii) whether the taxable person was in default in respect of any prescribed accounting period which was not a section 28 accounting period but ended within the surcharge period begun or extended by that notice,

were to be determined as it would be determined for the purposes of section 59.

(3) In a case falling within subsection (1)(b) above section 59 shall have effect as if—

    (a) subject to paragraph (b) below, the prescribed accounting period that is not a section 28 accounting period were deemed to be a period ending within a surcharge period begun or, as the case may be, extended by a notice served under section 59;

    (b) any question—

        (i) whether a surcharge period was begun or extended by the notice, or

        (ii) whether the taxable person was in default in respect of any prescribed accounting period which was a section 28 accounting period but ended within the surcharge period begun or extended by that notice,

were to be determined as it would be determined for the purposes of section 59A; and

    (c) that person were to be treated as having had outstanding VAT for a section 28 accounting period in any case where the aggregate value of his defaults in respect of that period was, for the purposes of section 59A, more than nil.

(4) In this section 'a section 28 accounting period', in relation to a taxable person, means any prescribed accounting period ending on or after the day on which the Finance Act 1996 was passed in respect of which that person is liable by virtue of an order under section 28 to make any payment on account of VAT."

(6) In section 69(4)(a) and (9)(b) (disregard in connection with penalties for breach of regulations of conduct giving rise to a surcharge), after the words "section 59", in each case, there shall be inserted "or 59A".

(7) In section 76(1) and (3)(a) (assessments for surcharges), after the words "section 59", in each case, there shall be inserted "or 59A".

(8) This section applies in relation to any prescribed accounting period ending on or after 1st June 1996, but a liability to make a payment on account

of VAT shall be disregarded for the purposes of the amendments made by this section if the payment is one becoming due before that date.

This section introduces new ss.59A and 59B and modifies the existing s.59 of the Value Added Tax Act 1994. They provide for default surcharge to be applied as a sanction when traders under the payment on account scheme (those paying more than £2 million VAT per annum) fail to make required payments on account, or fail to pay the balance payment due with the VAT return, on time.

Subs. (2)
This introduces new s.59A of VATA 1994, which provides for a default surcharge where payment on account traders are late in making payments of VAT. The surcharge applies to traders who have been in default during the previous 12 months and have received a surcharge liability notice from Customs and Excise. Liability to surcharge extends for 12 months from the first default. A trader will remain liable to surcharge until he has been free from default for 12 months. Liability to surcharge will not arise unless a payment is due and a minimum of £30 applies. A scale of surcharge from two per cent to five, 10 and 15 per cent applies, depending on the number of periods for which the trader has been in default.

The value of defaults and of outstanding VAT is the aggregate of payments on account and payments due with the return.

A defence of due diligence and reasonable excuse applies, both to a surcharge and to a surcharge liability notice. A surcharge under s.59A and a penalty under s.69 cannot both be imposed in relation to the same conduct.

The Customs and Excise may direct, after consultation with the Treasury, that a specific period should be left out of the surcharge reckoning.

Payment must be made so that the money becomes available to Customs and Excise by the due date (this also applies to payments due with the VAT return by payment on account traders under s.59).

Subs. (3)
A payment on account trader cannot be liable to surcharge under both s.59 and s.59A.

Subs. (5)
This introduces new s.59B of VATA 1994 which provides for co-ordination between s.59 and s.59A so that a trader joining or leaving the payment on account scheme will carry any surcharge liability with him.

Repeated misdeclaration penalty

36.—(1) In section 64 of the Value Added Tax Act 1994 (repeated misdeclaration penalty), the following subsections shall be substituted for subsections (6) and (7) (inaccuracies treated as not material)—

"(6) Subject to subsection (6A) below, where by reason of conduct falling within subsection (1) above—

    (a) a person is convicted of an offence (whether under this Act or otherwise), or

    (b) a person is assessed to a penalty under section 60 or 63,

the inaccuracy concerned shall not be regarded as material for the purposes of this section.

    (6A) Subsection (6) above shall not prevent an inaccuracy by reason of which a person has been assessed to a penalty under section 63—

    (a) from being regarded as a material inaccuracy in respect of which the Commissioners may serve a penalty liability notice under subsection (2) above; or

    (b) from being regarded for the purposes of subsection (3) above as a material inaccuracy by reference to which any prescribed accounting period falling within the penalty period is to be treated as the first prescribed accounting period so falling in respect of which there is a material inaccuracy.

    (7) Where subsection (5) or (6) above requires any inaccuracy to be regarded as not material for the purposes of the serving of a penalty liability notice, any such notice served in respect of that inaccuracy shall be deemed not to have been served."

(2) This section has effect in relation to inaccuracies contained in returns made on or after the day on which this Act is passed.

GENERAL NOTE
The amendments to s.64 of VATA 1994 made by this section ensure that an error which triggers the misdeclaration penalty for single large underdeclarations in s.63 also counts in the reckoning towards the misdeclaration penalty for repeated errors in s.64.

Penalties for failure to notify

37.—(1) In section 67 of the Value Added Tax Act 1994 (penalty for failure to notify liability to be registered under Schedule 1, etc.)—
    (a) in subsection (1)(a), after "6" there shall be inserted ", 7"; and
    (b) in subsection (3)(a), for "or 6" there shall be substituted ", 6 or 7".
(2) Subject to subsection (3) below, subsection (1) above shall apply in relation to—
    (a) any person becoming liable to be registered by virtue of sub-paragraph (2) of paragraph 1 of Schedule 1 to the Value Added Tax Act 1994 on or after 1st January 1996; and
    (b) any person who became liable to be registered by virtue of that sub-paragraph before that date but who had not notified the Commissioners of the liability before that date.
(3) In relation to a person falling within subsection (2)(b) above, section 67 of the Value Added Tax Act 1994 shall have effect as if in subsection (3)(a) for the words "the date with effect from which he is, in accordance with that paragraph, required to be registered" there were substituted "1st January 1996".

GENERAL NOTE
The amendments to s.67 of VATA 1994 made by this section reinstate the penalty provision, inadvertently removed by the Finance Act 1990 (c. 29), s.10, when a trader who acquires a business as a going concern fails to notify a liability to be registered.

VAT invoices and accounting

38.—(1) Paragraph 2 of Schedule 11 to the Value Added Tax Act 1994 (regulations about accounting for VAT, VAT invoices etc.) shall be amended as follows.
(2) After sub-paragraph (2) there shall be inserted the following sub-paragraph—
    "(2A) Regulations under this paragraph may confer power on the Commissioners to allow the requirements of any regulations as to the statements and other matters to be contained in a VAT invoice to be relaxed or dispensed with."
(3) In sub-paragraph (10) (adjustments of VAT accounts), at the end of paragraph (c) there shall be inserted "and
    (d) for a person, for purposes connected with the making of any such entry or financial adjustment, to be required to provide to any prescribed person, or to retain, a document in the prescribed form containing prescribed particulars of the matters to which the entry or adjustment relates; and
    (e) for enabling the Commissioners, in such cases as they may think fit, to dispense with or relax a requirement imposed by regulations made by virtue of paragraph (d) above."

GENERAL NOTE
Customs and Excise are given power to allow businesses to omit information from their invoices which would otherwise be mandatory. Regulations may also be made requiring businesses to issue a document containing prescribed information to adjust VAT on an invoice when a change in price of goods or services alters the amount of VAT to be charged after the invoice has been issued.

PART III

LANDFILL TAX

The basic provisions

Landfill tax

39.—(1) A tax, to be known as landfill tax, shall be charged in accordance with this Part.

(2) The tax shall be under the care and management of the Commissioners of Customs and Excise.

GENERAL NOTE
This section introduces the landfill tax, announced originally in the 1994 Budget. The proceeds, estimated at £450 million per annum, will be used to fund a reduction of 0.2 per cent in employers' national insurance contributions. It will be administered by the Customs and Excise.

Charge to tax

40.—(1) Tax shall be charged on a taxable disposal.

(2) A disposal is a taxable disposal if—
(a) it is a disposal of material as waste,
(b) it is made by way of landfill,
(c) it is made at a landfill site, and
(d) it is made on or after 1st October 1996.

(3) For this purpose a disposal is made at a landfill site if the land on or under which it is made constitutes or falls within land which is a landfill site at the time of the disposal.

GENERAL NOTE
The tax is imposed on a disposal of material as waste by way of landfill at a landfill site (see further ss.64–66) [*Hansard*, H.C. Vol. 270, col. 148].

Liability to pay tax

41.—(1) The person liable to pay tax charged on a taxable disposal is the landfill site operator.

(2) The reference here to the landfill site operator is to the person who is at the time of the disposal the operator of the landfill site which constitutes or contains the land on or under which the disposal is made.

GENERAL NOTE
The landfill site operator is made liable to pay the tax [Standing Committee E, February 6, 1996, col. 148].

Amount of tax

42.—(1) The amount of tax charged on a taxable disposal shall be found by taking—
(a) £7 for each whole tonne disposed of and a proportionately reduced sum for any additional part of a tonne, or
(b) a proportionately reduced sum if less than a tonne is disposed of.

(2) Where the material disposed of consists entirely of qualifying material this section applies as if the reference to £7 were to £2.

(3) Qualifying material is material for the time being listed for the purposes of this section in an order.

(4) The Treasury must have regard to the object of securing that material is listed if it is of a kind commonly described as inactive or inert.

GENERAL NOTE
    The rate of tax is £7 per tonne, but qualifying material, to be listed in a Treasury order, attracts
the lower rate of £2 per tonne. The intention is that inactive or inert material should enjoy the
lower rate [Standing Committee E, February 8, 1996, col. 155].

Exemptions

Material removed from water

43.—(1) A disposal is not a taxable disposal for the purposes of this Part if
it is shown to the satisfaction of the Commissioners that the disposal is of
material all of which—
  (a) has been removed (by dredging or otherwise) from water falling
      within subsection (2) below, and
  (b) formed part of or projected from the bed of the water concerned
      before its removal.
  (2) Water falls within this subsection if it is—
  (a) a river, canal or watercourse (whether natural or artificial), or
  (b) a dock or harbour (whether natural or artificial).
  (3) A disposal is not a taxable disposal for the purposes of this Part if it is
shown to the satisfaction of the Commissioners that the disposal is of
material all of which—
  (a) has been removed (by dredging or otherwise) from water falling
      within the approaches to a harbour (whether natural or artificial),
  (b) has been removed in the interests of navigation, and
  (c) formed part of or projected from the bed of the water concerned
      before its removal.
  (4) A disposal is not a taxable disposal for the purposes of this Part if it is
shown to the satisfaction of the Commissioners that the disposal is of
material all of which—
  (a) consists of naturally occurring mineral material, and
  (b) has been removed (by dredging or otherwise) from the sea in the
      course of commercial operations carried out to obtain substances such
      as sand or gravel from the seabed.

GENERAL NOTE
    This section, together with the following three, was introduced at report stage, to reflect vari-
ous concerns which had been expressed inside and outside the House of Commons. It exempts
from landfill tax material produced by dredging or similar activities in fresh or sea water [*Hansard*, H.C. Vol. 274, col. 1052].

Mining and quarrying

44.—(1) A disposal is not a taxable disposal for the purposes of this Part if
it is shown to the satisfaction of the Commissioners that the disposal is of
material all of which fulfils each of the conditions set out in subsections (2) to
(4) below.
  (2) The material must result from commercial mining operations (whether
the mining is deep or open-cast) or from commercial quarrying operations.
  (3) The material must be naturally occurring material extracted from the
earth in the course of the operations.
  (4) The material must not have been subjected to, or result from, a non-
qualifying process carried out at any stage between the extraction and the
disposal.
  (5) A non-qualifying process is—
  (a) a process separate from the mining or quarrying operations, or
  (b) a process forming part of those operations and permanently altering
      the material's chemical composition.

GENERAL NOTE
Material produced as a by-product from mining and quarrying is exempt from landfill tax.

Pet cemeteries

45.—(1) A disposal is not a taxable disposal for the purposes of this Part if—

    (a) the disposal is of material consisting entirely of the remains of dead domestic pets, and

    (b) the landfill site at which the disposal is made fulfils the test set out in subsection (2) below.

(2) The test is that during the relevant period—

    (a) no landfill disposal was made at the site, or

    (b) the only landfill disposals made at the site were of material consisting entirely of the remains of dead domestic pets.

(3) For the purposes of subsection (2) above the relevant period—

    (a) begins with 1st October 1996 or (if later) with the coming into force in relation to the site of the licence or resolution mentioned in section 66 below, and

    (b) ends immediately before the disposal mentioned in subsection (1) above.

GENERAL NOTE
Pet cemeteries are exempted from landfill tax.

Power to vary

46.—(1) Provision may be made by order to produce the result that—

    (a) a disposal which would otherwise be a taxable disposal (by virtue of this Part as it applies for the time being) is not a taxable disposal;

    (b) a disposal which would otherwise not be a taxable disposal (by virtue of this Part as it applies for the time being) is a taxable disposal.

(2) Without prejudice to the generality of subsection (1) above, an order under this section may—

    (a) confer exemption by reference to certificates issued by the Commissioners and to conditions set out in certificates;

    (b) allow the Commissioners to direct requirements to be met before certificates can be issued;

    (c) provide for the review of decisions about certificates and for appeals relating to decisions on review.

(3) Provision may be made under this section in such way as the Treasury think fit (whether by amending this Part or otherwise).

GENERAL NOTE
The Treasury is given power to extend or reduce exemptions by statutory order. It is intended to use the power, *inter alia*, to exempt historically contaminated land from the tax [*Hansard*, H.C. Vol. 274, col. 1052].

Administration

Registration

47.—(1) The register kept under this section may contain such information as the Commissioners think is required for the purposes of the care and management of the tax.

(2) A person who—

    (a) carries out taxable activities, and

    (b) is not registered,

is liable to be registered.

(3) Where—

    (a) a person at any time forms the intention of carrying out taxable activities, and

(b) he is not registered,
he shall notify the Commissioners of his intention.

(4) A person who at any time ceases to have the intention of carrying out taxable activities shall notify the Commissioners of that fact.

(5) Where a person is liable to be registered by virtue of subsection (2) above the Commissioners shall register him with effect from the time when he begins to carry out taxable activities; and this subsection applies whether or not he notifies the Commissioners under subsection (3) above.

(6) Where the Commissioners are satisfied that a person has ceased to carry out taxable activities they may cancel his registration with effect from the earliest practicable time after he so ceased; and this subsection applies whether or not he notifies the Commissioners under subsection (4) above.

(7) Where—
(a) a person notifies the Commissioners under subsection (4) above,
(b) they are satisfied that he will not carry out taxable activities,
(c) they are satisfied that no tax which he is liable to pay is unpaid,
(d) they are satisfied that no credit to which he is entitled under regulations made under section 51 below is outstanding, and
(e) subsection (8) below does not apply,
the Commissioners shall cancel his registration with effect from the earliest practicable time after he ceases to carry out taxable activities.

(8) Where—
(a) a person notifies the Commissioners under subsection (4) above, and
(b) they are satisfied that he has not carried out, and will not carry out, taxable activities,
the Commissioners shall cancel his registration with effect from the time when he ceased to have the intention to carry out taxable activities.

(9) For the purposes of this section regulations may make provision—
(a) as to the time within which a notification is to be made;
(b) as to the form and manner in which any notification is to be made and as to the information to be contained in or provided with it;
(c) requiring a person who has made a notification to notify the Commissioners if any information contained in or provided in connection with it is or becomes inaccurate;
(d) as to the correction of entries in the register.

(10) References in this Part to a registrable person are to a person who—
(a) is registered under this section, or
(b) is liable to be registered under this section.

GENERAL NOTE

This contains the basic administrative structure for landfill tax. Customs and Excise will keep a register of persons carrying out taxable activities, as defined in s.69. Provision is made for removing persons from the register in appropriate circumstances. The section will be supplemented by regulations.

It is anticipated that about 1,400 landfill site operators will be liable to register.

Information required to keep register up to date

48.—(1) Regulations may make provision requiring a registrable person to notify the Commissioners of particulars which—
(a) are of changes in circumstances relating to the registrable person or any business carried on by him,
(b) appear to the Commissioners to be required for the purpose of keeping the register kept under section 47 above up to date, and
(c) are of a prescribed description.

(2) Regulations may make provision—
(a) as to the time within which a notification is to be made;
(b) as to the form and manner in which a notification is to be made;

(c) requiring a person who has made a notification to notify the Commissioners if any information contained in it is inaccurate.

GENERAL NOTE

Customs and Excise are empowered to make regulations concerning information required to keep the landfill tax register up to date.

Accounting for tax and time for payment

49. Regulations may provide that a registrable person shall—
(a) account for tax by reference to such periods (accounting periods) as may be determined by or under the regulations;
(b) make, in relation to accounting periods, returns in such form as may be prescribed and at such times as may be so determined;
(c) pay tax at such times and in such manner as may be so determined.

GENERAL NOTE

The provisions regarding accounting for tax and dates for payment are to be made by regulation.

Power to assess

50.—(1) Where—
(a) a person has failed to make any returns required to be made under this Part,
(b) a person has failed to keep any documents necessary to verify returns required to be made under this Part,
(c) a person has failed to afford the facilities necessary to verify returns required to be made under this Part, or
(d) it appears to the Commissioners that returns required to be made by a person under this Part are incomplete or incorrect,
the Commissioners may assess the amount of tax due from the person concerned to the best of their judgment and notify it to him.

(2) Where a person has for an accounting period been paid an amount to which he purports to be entitled under regulations made under section 51 below, then, to the extent that the amount ought not to have been paid or would not have been paid had the facts been known or been as they later turn out to be, the Commissioners may assess the amount as being tax due from him for that period and notify it to him accordingly.

(3) Where a person is assessed under subsections (1) and (2) above in respect of the same accounting period the assessments may be combined and notified to him as one assessment.

(4) Where the person failing to make a return, or making a return which appears to the Commissioners to be incomplete or incorrect, was required to make the return as a personal representative, trustee in bankruptcy, receiver, liquidator or person otherwise acting in a representative capacity in relation to another person, subsection (1) above shall apply as if the reference to tax due from him included a reference to tax due from that other person.

(5) An assessment under subsection (1) or (2) above of an amount of tax due for an accounting period shall not be made after the later of the following—
(a) two years after the end of the accounting period;
(b) one year after evidence of facts, sufficient in the Commissioners' opinion to justify the making of the assessment, comes to their knowledge;
but where further such evidence comes to their knowledge after the making of an assessment under subsection (1) or (2) above another assessment may be made under the subsection concerned in addition to any earlier assessment.

(6) Where—

(a) as a result of a person's failure to make a return in relation to an accounting period the Commissioners have made an assessment under subsection (1) above for that period,

(b) the tax assessed has been paid but no proper return has been made in relation to the period to which the assessment related, and

(c) as a result of a failure to make a return in relation to a later accounting period, being a failure by the person referred to in paragraph (a) above or a person acting in a representative capacity in relation to him, as mentioned in subsection (4) above, the Commissioners find it necessary to make another assessment under subsection (1) above,

then, if the Commissioners think fit, having regard to the failure referred to in paragraph (a) above, they may specify in the assessment referred to in paragraph (c) above an amount of tax greater than that which they would otherwise have considered to be appropriate.

(7) Where an amount has been assessed and notified to any person under subsection (1) or (2) above it shall be deemed to be an amount of tax due from him and may be recovered accordingly unless, or except to the extent that, the assessment has subsequently been withdrawn or reduced.

(8) For the purposes of this section notification to—

(a) a personal representative, trustee in bankruptcy, receiver or liquidator, or

(b) a person otherwise acting in a representative capacity in relation to another person,

shall be treated as notification to the person in relation to whom the person mentioned in paragraph (a) above, or the first person mentioned in paragraph (b) above, acts.

(9) Subsection (5) above has effect subject to paragraph 33 of Schedule 5 to this Act.

(10) In this section "trustee in bankruptcy" means, as respects Scotland, an interim or permanent trustee (within the meaning of the Bankruptcy (Scotland) Act 1985) or a trustee acting under a trust deed (within the meaning of that Act).

GENERAL NOTE

Where the taxpayer has failed to meet his obligations, the Customs and Excise can raise an assessment to the best of their judgment. There is a general time limit of two years after the end of the relevant accounting period or one year after the Customs and Excise have become aware of evidence justifying an assessment. This does not preclude a later assessment if further evidence comes to light. Where another assessment becomes necessary for a later period, the Customs and Excise may assess an amount greater than would otherwise have been considered appropriate.

The time limits in this section are extended by virtue of Sched. 5, para. 33. See further the General Note to that Schedule.

Credit

Credit: general

51.—(1) Regulations may provide that where—

(a) a person has paid or is liable to pay tax, and

(b) prescribed conditions are fulfilled,

the person shall be entitled to credit of such an amount as is found in accordance with prescribed rules.

(2) Regulations may make provision as to the manner in which a person is to benefit from credit, and in particular may make provision—

(a) that a person shall be entitled to credit by reference to accounting periods;

(b) that a person shall be entitled to deduct an amount equal to his total credit for an accounting period from the total amount of tax due from him for the period;

(c) that if no tax is due from a person for an accounting period but he is entitled to credit for the period, the amount of the credit shall be paid to him by the Commissioners;

(d) that if the amount of credit to which a person is entitled for an accounting period exceeds the amount of tax due from him for the period, an amount equal to the excess shall be paid to him by the Commissioners;

(e) for the whole or part of any credit to be held over to be credited for a subsequent accounting period;

(f) as to the manner in which a person who has ceased to be registrable is to benefit from credit.

(3) Regulations under subsection (2)(c) or (d) above may provide that where at the end of an accounting period an amount is due to a person who has failed to submit returns for an earlier period as required by this Part, the Commissioners may withhold payment of the amount until he has complied with that requirement.

(4) Regulations under subsection (2)(e) above may provide for credit to be held over either on the person's application or in accordance with directions given by the Commissioners from time to time; and the regulations may allow directions to be given generally or with regard to particular cases.

(5) Regulations may provide that—

(a) no benefit shall be conferred in respect of credit except on a claim made in such manner and at such time as may be determined by or under regulations;

(b) payment in respect of credit shall be made subject to such conditions (if any) as the Commissioners think fit to impose, including conditions as to repayment in specified circumstances;

(c) deduction in respect of credit shall be made subject to such conditions (if any) as the Commissioners think fit to impose, including conditions as to the payment to the Commissioners, in specified circumstances, of an amount representing the whole or part of the amount deducted.

(6) Regulations may require a claim by a person to be made in a return required by provision made under section 49 above.

(7) Nothing in section 52 or 53 below shall be taken to derogate from the power to make regulations under this section (whether with regard to bad debts, the environment or any other matter).

GENERAL NOTE

Customs and Excise are given power to make regulations permitting credit to be given to taxpayers. For similar provisions relating to insurance premium tax and the relevant regulations, see FA 1994, s.55 and S.I. 1994 No. 1774, regs. 17–19.

Bad debts

52.—(1) Regulations may be made under section 51 above with a view to securing that a person is entitled to credit if—

(a) he carries out a taxable activity as a result of which he becomes entitled to a debt which turns out to be bad (in whole or in part), and

(b) such other conditions as may be prescribed are fulfilled.

(2) The regulations may include provision under section 51(5)(b) or (c) above requiring repayment or payment if it turns out that it was not justified to regard a debt as bad (or to regard it as bad to the extent that it was so regarded).

(3) The regulations may include provision for determining whether, and to what extent, a debt is to be taken to be bad.

  Regulations under s.51 may allow credit for bad debts incurred by landfill site operators.

Bodies concerned with the environment

53.—(1) Regulations may be made under section 51 above with a view to securing that a person is entitled to credit if—
  (a) he pays a sum to a body whose objects are or include the protection of the environment, and
  (b) such other conditions as may be prescribed are fulfilled.
  (2) The regulations may in particular prescribe conditions—
  (a) requiring bodies to which sums are paid (environmental bodies) to be approved by another body (the regulatory body);
  (b) requiring the regulatory body to be approved by the Commissioners;
  (c) requiring sums to be paid with the intention that they be expended on such matters connected with the protection of the environment as may be prescribed.
  (3) The regulations may include provision under section 51(5)(b) or (c) above requiring repayment or payment if—
  (a) a sum is not in fact expended on matters prescribed under subsection (2)(c) above, or
  (b) a prescribed condition turns out not to have been fulfilled.
  (4) The regulations may include—
  (a) provision for determining the amount of credit (including provision for limiting it);
  (b) provision that matters connected with the protection of the environment include such matters as overheads (including administration) of environmental bodies and the regulatory body;
  (c) provision as to the matters by reference to which an environmental body or the regulatory body can be, and remain, approved (including matters relating to the functions and activities of any such body);
  (d) provision allowing approval of an environmental body or the regulatory body to be withdrawn (whether prospectively or retrospectively);
  (e) provision that, if approval of the regulatory body is withdrawn, another body may be approved in its place or its functions may be performed by the Commissioners;
  (f) provision allowing the Commissioners to disclose to the regulatory body information which relates to the tax affairs of persons carrying out taxable activities and which is relevant to the credit scheme established by the regulations.

  Regulations under s.51 may also allow credit for contributions to approved bodies whose purpose is, or includes the protection of the environment.
  It is intended to use this power to encourage the setting up of environmental trusts for approved environmental purposes. Site operators making payments to these trusts will be able to claim a rebate of 90 per cent of their contribution, up to a maximum of 20 per cent of their landfill tax bill [Standing Committee E, February 8, 1996, col. 175].

Review and appeal

Review of Commissioners' decisions

54.—(1) This section applies to the following decisions of the Commissioners—
  (a) a decision as to the registration or cancellation of registration of any person under this Part;
  (b) a decision as to whether tax is chargeable in respect of a disposal or as to how much tax is chargeable;

   (c) a decision as to whether a person is entitled to credit by virtue of regulations under section 51 above or as to how much credit a person is entitled to or as to the manner in which he is to benefit from credit;

   (d) a decision as to an assessment falling within subsection (2) below or as to the amount of such an assessment;

   (e) a decision to refuse a request under section 58(3) below;

   (f) a decision to refuse an application under section 59 below;

   (g) a decision as to whether conditions set out in a specification under the authority of provision made under section 68(4)(b) below are met in relation to a disposal;

   (h) a decision to give a direction under any provision contained in regulations by virtue of section 68(5) below;

   (i) a decision as to a claim for the repayment of an amount under paragraph 14 of Schedule 5 to this Act;

   (j) a decision as to liability to a penalty under Part V of that Schedule or as to the amount of such a penalty;

   (k) a decision under paragraph 19 of that Schedule (as mentioned in paragraph 19(5));

   (l) a decision as to any liability to pay interest under paragraph 26 or 27 of that Schedule or as to the amount of the interest payable;

   (m) a decision as to any liability to pay interest under paragraph 29 of that Schedule or as to the amount of the interest payable;

   (n) a decision to require any security under paragraph 31 of that Schedule or as to its amount;

   (o) a decision as to the amount of any penalty or interest specified in an assessment under paragraph 32 of that Schedule.

(2) An assessment falls within this subsection if it is an assessment under section 50 above in respect of an accounting period in relation to which a return required to be made by virtue of regulations under section 49 above has been made.

(3) Any person who is or will be affected by any decision to which this section applies may by notice in writing to the Commissioners require them to review the decision.

(4) The Commissioners shall not be required under this section to review any decision unless the notice requiring the review is given before the end of the period of 45 days beginning with the day on which written notification of the decision, or of the assessment containing the decision, was first given to the person requiring the review.

(5) For the purposes of subsection (4) above it shall be the duty of the Commissioners to give written notification of any decision to which this section applies to any person who—

   (a) requests such a notification,

   (b) has not previously been given written notification of that decision, and

   (c) if given such a notification, will be entitled to require a review of the decision under this section.

(6) A person shall be entitled to give a notice under this section requiring a decision to be reviewed for a second or subsequent time only if—

   (a) the grounds on which he requires the further review are that the Commissioners did not, on any previous review, have the opportunity to consider certain facts or other matters, and

   (b) he does not, on the further review, require the Commissioners to consider any facts or matters which were considered on a previous review except in so far as they are relevant to any issue not previously considered.

(7) Where the Commissioners are required in accordance with this section to review any decision it shall be their duty to do so; and on the review they may withdraw, vary or confirm the decision.

(8) Where—

(a) it is the duty under this section of the Commissioners to review any decision, and

(b) they do not, within the period of 45 days beginning with the day on which the review was required, give notice to the person requiring it of their determination on the review,

they shall be deemed for the purposes of this Part to have confirmed the decision.

GENERAL NOTE

Taxpayers are given a right to require the Customs and Excise to review their decisions on the matters listed. The right must be exercised within 45 days of the decision. If the Customs and Excise have not responded within a further 45 days, they will be deemed to have confirmed the decision.

The section follows the precedent set in relation to decisions regarding customs and excise duties and insurance premium tax (see FA 1994, ss.14–15 and 48).

Appeals: general

55.—(1) Subject to the following provisions of this section, an appeal shall lie to an appeal tribunal with respect to any of the following decisions—

(a) any decision by the Commissioners on a review under section 54 above (including a deemed confirmation under subsection (8) of that section);

(b) any decision by the Commissioners on such review of a decision referred to in section 54(1) above as the Commissioners have agreed to undertake in consequence of a request made after the end of the period mentioned in section 54(4) above.

(2) Where an appeal is made under this section by a person who is required to make returns by virtue of regulations under section 49 above, the appeal shall not be entertained unless the appellant—

(a) has made all the returns which he is required to make by virtue of those regulations, and

(b) has paid the amounts shown in those returns as payable by him.

(3) Where an appeal is made under this section with respect to a decision falling within section 54(1)(b) or (d) above the appeal shall not be entertained unless—

(a) the amount which the Commissioners have determined to be payable as tax has been paid or deposited with them, or

(b) on being satisfied that the appellant would otherwise suffer hardship the Commissioners agree or the tribunal decides that it should be entertained notwithstanding that that amount has not been so paid or deposited.

(4) On an appeal under this section against an assessment to a penalty under paragraph 18 of Schedule 5 to this Act, the burden of proof as to the matters specified in paragraphs (a) and (b) of sub-paragraph (1) of paragraph 18 shall lie upon the Commissioners.

GENERAL NOTE

Where a taxpayer is dissatisfied with the outcome of a review, he can appeal to the VAT and duties tribunal (see s.70). Any tax must be paid before the appeal, except in cases of hardship. Where dishonesty is alleged in relation to a civil penalty for tax evasion under Sched. 5, para. 18, the burden of proof lies on the Customs and Excise.

Appeals: other provisions

56.—(1) Subsection (2) below applies where the Commissioners make a decision falling within section 54(1)(d) above and on a review of it there is a further decision with respect to which an appeal is made under section 55 above; and the reference here to a further decision includes a reference to a deemed confirmation under section 54(8) above.

(2) Where on the appeal—

(a) it is found that the amount specified in the assessment is less than it ought to have been, and

(b) the tribunal gives a direction specifying the correct amount,

the assessment shall have effect as an assessment of the amount specified in the direction and that amount shall be deemed to have been notified to the appellant.

(3) Where on an appeal under section 55 above it is found that the whole or part of any amount paid or deposited in pursuance of section 55(3) above is not due, so much of that amount as is found not to be due shall be repaid with interest at such rate as the tribunal may determine.

(4) Where on an appeal under section 55 above it is found that the whole or part of any amount due to the appellant by virtue of regulations under section 51(2)(c) or (d) or (f) above has not been paid, so much of that amount as is found not to have been paid shall be paid with interest at such rate as the tribunal may determine.

(5) Where an appeal under section 55 above has been entertained notwithstanding that an amount determined by the Commissioners to be payable as tax has not been paid or deposited and it is found on the appeal that that amount is due the tribunal may, if it thinks fit, direct that that amount shall be paid with interest at such rate as may be specified in the direction.

(6) Without prejudice to paragraph 25 of Schedule 5 to this Act, nothing in section 55 above shall be taken to confer on a tribunal any power to vary an amount assessed by way of penalty except in so far as it is necessary to reduce it to the amount which is appropriate under paragraphs 18 to 24 of that Schedule.

(7) Without prejudice to paragraph 28 of Schedule 5 to this Act, nothing in section 55 above shall be taken to confer on a tribunal any power to vary an amount assessed by way of interest except in so far as it is necessary to reduce it to the amount which is appropriate under paragraph 26 or 27 of that Schedule.

(8) Sections 85 and 87 of the Value Added Tax Act 1994 (settling of appeals by agreement and enforcement of certain decisions of tribunal) shall have effect as if—

(a) the references to section 83 of that Act included references to section 55 above, and

(b) the references to value added tax included references to landfill tax.

GENERAL NOTE

On appeal, the tribunal can increase an assessment, or order the repayment of tax or the payment of a credit with interest. The payment of interest may also be ordered where the taxpayer loses an appeal, heard without payment of tax. The tribunal has no power to vary an amount assessed as penalty or interest under Sched. 5, paras. 18–24 and paras. 26–27, except in pursuance of paras. 25 and 28. This allows the tribunal to mitigate the penalty or interest, or increase it to its original level, if it has already been mitigated by the Customs and Excise.

The provisions in ss.85 and 87 of VATA 1994, regarding the settling of appeals by agreement and the enforcement of tribunal decisions applies for landfill tax.

Review and appeal: commencement

57. Sections 54 to 56 above shall come into force on—

(a) 1st October 1996, or

(b) such earlier day as may be appointed by order.

GENERAL NOTE

The right to require a review and the powers of the tribunal are activated on October 1, 1996, when the tax commences to be charged (see s.40), or earlier if the Customs and Excise so order (see s.71(1)).

Miscellaneous

Partnership, bankruptcy, transfer of business, etc.

58.—(1) As regards any case where a business is carried on in partnership or by another unincorporated body, regulations may make provision for determining by what persons anything required by this Part to be done by a person is to be done.

(2) The registration under this Part of an unincorporated body other than a partnership may be in the name of the body concerned; and in determining whether taxable activities are carried out by such a body no account shall be taken of any change in its members.

(3) The registration under this Part of a body corporate carrying on a business in several divisions may, if the body corporate so requests and the Commissioners see fit, be in the names of those divisions.

(4) As regards any case where a person carries on a business of a person who has died or become bankrupt or incapacitated or whose estate has been sequestrated, or of a person which is in liquidation or receivership or in relation to which an administration order is in force, regulations may—

(a) require the first-mentioned person to inform the Commissioners of the fact that he is carrying on the business and of the event that has led to his carrying it on;

(b) make provision allowing the person to be treated for a limited time as if he were the other person;

(c) make provision for securing continuity in the application of this Part where a person is so treated.

(5) Regulations may make provision for securing continuity in the application of this Part in cases where a business carried on by a person is transferred to another person as a going concern.

(6) Regulations under subsection (5) above may in particular—

(a) require the transferor to inform the Commissioners of the transfer;

(b) provide for liabilities and duties under this Part of the transferor to become, to such extent as may be provided by the regulations, liabilities and duties of the transferee;

(c) provide for any right of either of them to repayment or credit in respect of tax to be satisfied by making a repayment or allowing a credit to the other;

but the regulations may provide that no such provision as is mentioned in paragraph (b) or (c) of this subsection shall have effect in relation to any transferor and transferee unless an application in that behalf has been made by them under the regulations.

GENERAL NOTE

The section deals with various special situations by empowering the Customs and Excise to make regulations covering them. Those included are partnerships (subss. (1) and (2)), companies carrying on business in divisions (subs. (3)), bankruptcy (subs. (4)), and the transfer of a business as a going concern (subss. (5) and (6)).

Groups of companies

59.—(1) Where under the following provisions of this section any bodies corporate are treated as members of a group, for the purposes of this Part—

(a) any liability of a member of the group to pay tax shall be taken to be a liability of the representative member;

(b) the representative member shall be taken to carry out any taxable activities which a member of the group would carry out (apart from this section) by virtue of section 69 below;

(c) all members of the group shall be jointly and severally liable for any tax due from the representative member.

(2) Two or more bodies corporate are eligible to be treated as members of a group if the condition mentioned in subsection (3) below is fulfilled and—

(a) one of them controls each of the others,

(b) one person (whether a body corporate or an individual) controls all of them, or

(c) two or more individuals carrying on a business in partnership control all of them.

(3) The condition is that the prospective representative member has an established place of business in the United Kingdom.

(4) Where an application to that effect is made to the Commissioners with respect to two or more bodies corporate eligible to be treated as members of a group, then—

(a) from the beginning of an accounting period they shall be so treated, and

(b) one of them shall be the representative member,

unless the Commissioners refuse the application; and the Commissioners shall not refuse the application unless it appears to them necessary to do so for the protection of the revenue.

(5) Where any bodies corporate are treated as members of a group and an application to that effect is made to the Commissioners, then, from the beginning of an accounting period—

(a) a further body eligible to be so treated shall be included among the bodies so treated,

(b) a body corporate shall be excluded from the bodies so treated,

(c) another member of the group shall be substituted as the representative member, or

(d) the bodies corporate shall no longer be treated as members of a group,

unless the application is to the effect mentioned in paragraph (a) or (c) above and the Commissioners refuse the application.

(6) The Commissioners may refuse an application under subsection (5)(a) or (c) above only if it appears to them necessary to do so for the protection of the revenue.

(7) Where a body corporate is treated as a member of a group as being controlled by any person and it appears to the Commissioners that it has ceased to be so controlled, they shall, by notice given to that person, terminate that treatment from such date as may be specified in the notice.

(8) An application under this section with respect to any bodies corporate must be made by one of those bodies or by the person controlling them and must be made not less than 90 days before the date from which it is to take effect, or at such later time as the Commissioners may allow.

(9) For the purposes of this section a body corporate shall be taken to control another body corporate if it is empowered by statute to control that body's activities or if it is that body's holding company within the meaning of section 736 of the Companies Act 1985; and an individual or individuals shall be taken to control a body corporate if he or they, were he or they a company, would be that body's holding company within the meaning of that section.

GENERAL NOTE

This section allows two or more companies to be treated as a group for the purposes of landfill tax. In such a situation the tax is the liability of the representative member, subject to an overriding joint and several liability (subs. (1)). The normal rules for defining a group apply (subs. (2) and (9)). The representative member must have a place of business in the U.K. (subs. (3)). Members may be added to or excluded from the group, or the representative member may be changed, or the group itself dissolved (subs. (5)). Applications for treatment as a group or for additions to the group or change of representative member can be refused by the Customs and

Excise only for the protection of the revenue (subss. (4) and (6)). The Customs and Excise may terminate a group registration with regard to a company where it appears that the necessary control no longer exists (subs. (7)).

Applications for group treatment must be made not less than 90 days before the effective date, or such later time as the Customs and Excise may allow (subs. (8)).

Information, powers, penalties, etc.

60. Schedule 5 to this Act (which contains provisions relating to information, powers, penalties and other matters) shall have effect.

GENERAL NOTE

This section introduces Sched. 5, which sets out the provisions relating to information, sundry powers, recovery of tax, criminal and civil penalties, interest and other matters in relation to landfill tax.

See further the General Note to Sched. 5.

Taxable disposals: special provisions

61.—(1) Where—

(a) a taxable disposal is in fact made on a particular day,

(b) within the period of 14 days beginning with that day the person liable to pay tax in respect of the disposal issues a landfill invoice in respect of the disposal, and

(c) he has not notified the Commissioners in writing that he elects not to avail himself of this subsection,

for the purposes of this Part the disposal shall be treated as made at the time the invoice is issued.

(2) The reference in subsection (1) above to a landfill invoice is to a document containing such particulars as regulations may prescribe for the purposes of that subsection.

(3) The Commissioners may at the request of a person direct that subsection (1) above shall apply—

(a) in relation to disposals in respect of which he is liable to pay tax, or

(b) in relation to such of them as may be specified in the direction,

as if for the period of 14 days there were substituted such longer period as may be specified in the direction.

GENERAL NOTE

A disposal may be treated as being made on the date of an invoice within 14 days, or later if the operator so requests.

Taxable disposals: regulations

62.—(1) For the purposes of this Part, regulations may make provision under this section in relation to a disposal which is a taxable disposal (or would be apart from the regulations).

(2) The regulations may provide that if particular conditions are fulfilled—

(a) the disposal shall be treated as not being a taxable disposal, or

(b) the disposal shall, to the extent found in accordance with prescribed rules, be treated as not being a taxable disposal.

(3) The regulations may provide that if particular conditions are fulfilled—

(a) the disposal shall be treated as made at a time which is found in accordance with prescribed rules and which falls after the time when it would be regarded as made apart from the regulations, or

(b) the disposal shall, to the extent found in accordance with prescribed rules, be treated as made at a time which is found in accordance with prescribed rules and which falls after the time when it would be regarded as made apart from the regulations.

(4) In finding the time when the disposal would be regarded as made apart from the regulations, section 61(1) above and any direction under section 61(3) above shall be taken into account.

(5) The regulations may be framed by reference to—
(a) conditions specified in the regulations or by the Commissioners or by an authorised person, or
(b) any combination of such conditions;
and the regulations may specify conditions, or allow conditions to be specified, generally or with regard to particular cases.

(6) The regulations may make provision under subsections (2)(b) and (3)(b) above in relation to the same disposal.

(7) The regulations may only provide that a disposal is to be treated as not being a taxable disposal if or to the extent that—
(a) the disposal is a temporary one pending the incineration or recycling of the material concerned, or pending the removal of the material for use elsewhere, or pending the sorting of the material with a view to its removal elsewhere or its eventual disposal, and
(b) the temporary disposal is made in an area designated for the purpose by an authorised person.

GENERAL NOTE
The Customs and Excise may make regulations providing for taxable disposals to be treated as non-taxable or as occurring at a later time and prescribing rules and conditions applicable to such treatment. Temporary storage pending incineration, recycling, etc., is the specific situation envisaged [Standing Committee E, February 8, 1996, col. 210].

Qualifying material: special provisions

63.—(1) This section applies for the purposes of section 42 above.

(2) The Commissioners may direct that where material is disposed of it must be treated as qualifying material if it would in fact be such material but for a small quantity of non-qualifying material; and whether a quantity of non-qualifying material is small must be determined in accordance with the terms of the direction.

(3) The Commissioners may at the request of a person direct that where there is a disposal in respect of which he is liable to pay tax the material disposed of must be treated as qualifying material if it would in fact be such material but for a small quantity of non-qualifying material, and—
(a) a direction may apply to all disposals in respect of which a person is liable to pay tax or to such of them as are identified in the direction;
(b) whether a quantity of non-qualifying material is small must be determined in accordance with the terms of the direction.

(4) If a direction under subsection (3) above applies to a disposal any direction under subsection (2) above shall not apply to it.

(5) An order may provide that material must not be treated as qualifying material unless prescribed conditions are met.

(6) A condition may relate to any matter the Treasury think fit (such as the production of a document which includes a statement of the nature of the material).

GENERAL NOTE
The Customs and Excise may direct, subject to Treasury order, that material may be taxed at the lower rather than the higher rate if there is only a small quantity of non-qualifying material in it (see s.42).

Interpretation

Disposal of material as waste

64.—(1) A disposal of material is a disposal of it as waste if the person making the disposal does so with the intention of discarding the material.

(2) The fact that the person making the disposal or any other person could benefit from or make use of the material is irrelevant.

(3) Where a person makes a disposal on behalf of another person, for the purposes of subsections (1) and (2) above the person on whose behalf the disposal is made shall be treated as making the disposal.

(4) The reference in subsection (3) above to a disposal on behalf of another person includes references to a disposal—

(a) at the request of another person;

(b) in pursuance of a contract with another person.

GENERAL NOTE

A disposal of material as waste occurs when a person making the disposal intends to discard the material.

Disposal by way of landfill

65.—(1) There is a disposal of material by way of landfill if—

(a) it is deposited on the surface of land or on a structure set into the surface, or

(b) it is deposited under the surface of land.

(2) Subsection (1) above applies whether or not the material is placed in a container before it is deposited.

(3) Subsection (1)(b) above applies whether the material—

(a) is covered with earth after it is deposited, or

(b) is deposited in a cavity (such as a cavern or mine).

(4) If material is deposited on the surface of land (or on a structure set into the surface) with a view to it being covered with earth the disposal must be treated as made when the material is deposited and not when it is covered.

(5) An order may provide that the meaning of the disposal of material by way of landfill (as it applies for the time being) shall be varied.

(6) An order under subsection (5) above may make provision in such way as the Treasury think fit, whether by amending any of subsections (1) to (4) above or otherwise.

(7) In this section "land" includes land covered by water where the land is above the low water mark of ordinary spring tides.

(8) In this section "earth" includes similar matter (such as sand or rocks).

GENERAL NOTE

A disposal of material as landfill occurs when it is deposited on or under the land. This definition may be changed by Treasury order.

Landfill sites

66. Land is a landfill site at a given time if at that time—

(a) a licence which is a site licence for the purposes of Part II of the Environmental Protection Act 1990 (waste on land) is in force in relation to the land and authorises disposals in or on the land,

(b) a resolution under section 54 of that Act (land occupied by waste disposal authorities in Scotland) is in force in relation to the land and authorises deposits or disposals in or on the land,

(c) a disposal licence issued under Part II of the Pollution Control and Local Government (Northern Ireland) Order 1978 (waste on land) is in force in relation to the land and authorises deposits on the land,

(d) a resolution passed under Article 13 of that Order (land occupied by district councils in Northern Ireland) is in force in relation to the land and relates to deposits on the land, or

(e) a licence under any provision for the time being having effect in Northern Ireland and corresponding to section 35 of the Environmental Protection Act 1990 (waste management licences) is in force in relation to the land and authorises disposals in or on the land.

GENERAL NOTE
A landfill site is land which is authorised for the purpose by the appropriate authority.

Operators of landfill sites

67. The operator of a landfill site at a given time is—

(a) the person who is at the time concerned the holder of the licence, where section 66(a) above applies;

(b) the waste disposal authority which at the time concerned occupies the landfill site, where section 66(b) above applies;

(c) the person who is at the time concerned the holder of the licence, where section 66(c) above applies;

(d) the district council which passed the resolution, where section 66(d) above applies;

(e) the person who is at the time concerned the holder of the licence, where section 66(e) above applies.

GENERAL NOTE
The operator of a landfill site is either the licensee or the authority occupying the site.

Weight of material disposed of

68.—(1) The weight of the material disposed of on a taxable disposal shall be determined in accordance with regulations.

(2) The regulations may—

(a) prescribe rules for determining the weight;

(b) authorise rules for determining the weight to be specified by the Commissioners in a prescribed manner;

(c) authorise rules for determining the weight to be agreed by the person liable to pay the tax and an authorised person.

(3) The regulations may in particular prescribe, or authorise the specification or agreement of, rules about—

(a) the method by which the weight is to be determined;

(b) the time by reference to which the weight is to be determined;

(c) the discounting of constituents (such as water).

(4) The regulations may include provision that a specification authorised under subsection (2)(b) above may provide—

(a) that it is to have effect only in relation to disposals of such descriptions as may be set out in the specification;

(b) that it is not to have effect in relation to particular disposals unless the Commissioners are satisfied that such conditions as may be set out in the specification are met in relation to the disposals;

and the conditions may be framed by reference to such factors as the Commissioners think fit (such as the consent of an authorised person to the specification having effect in relation to disposals).

(5) The regulations may include provision that—

(a) where rules are agreed as mentioned in subsection (2)(c) above, and

(b) the Commissioners believe that they should no longer be applied because they do not give an accurate indication of the weight or they are not being fully observed or for some other reason,

the Commissioners may direct that the agreed rules shall no longer have effect.

(6) The regulations shall be so framed that where in relation to a given disposal—

(a) no specification of the Commissioners has effect, and

(b) no agreed rules have effect,

the weight shall be determined in accordance with rules prescribed in the regulations.

GENERAL NOTE

The weight of materials disposed of will be determined by regulations made by the Customs and Excise.

Taxable activities

69.—(1) A person carries out a taxable activity if—

(a) he makes a taxable disposal in respect of which he is liable to pay tax, or

(b) he permits another person to make a taxable disposal in respect of which he (the first-mentioned person) is liable to pay tax.

(2) Where—

(a) a taxable disposal is made, and

(b) it is made without the knowledge of the person who is liable to pay tax in respect of it,

that person shall for the purposes of this section be taken to permit the disposal.

GENERAL NOTE

The section defines the ambit of taxable activities (see s.47). A person will be liable even where disposals are made without his knowledge.

Interpretation: other provisions

70.—(1) Unless the context otherwise requires—

"accounting period" shall be construed in accordance with section 49 above;

"appeal tribunal" means a VAT and duties tribunal;

"authorised person" means any person acting under the authority of the Commissioners;

"the Commissioners" means the Commissioners of Customs and Excise;

"conduct" includes any act, omission or statement;

"material" means material of all kinds, including objects, substances and products of all kinds;

"prescribed" means prescribed by an order or regulations under this Part;

"registrable person" has the meaning given by section 47(10) above;

"tax" means landfill tax;

"taxable disposal" has the meaning given by section 40 above.

(2) A landfill disposal is a disposal—

(a) of material as waste, and

(b) made by way of landfill.

(3) A reference to this Part includes a reference to any order or regulations made under it and a reference to a provision of this Part includes a reference to any order or regulations made under the provision, unless otherwise required by the context or any order or regulations.

(4) This section and sections 64 to 69 above apply for the purposes of this Part.

GENERAL NOTE

This section contains further definitions.

Supplementary

Orders and regulations

71.—(1) The power to make an order under section 57 above shall be exercisable by the Commissioners, and the power to make an order under any other provision of this Part shall be exercisable by the Treasury.

(2) Any power to make regulations under this Part shall be exercisable by the Commissioners.

(3) Any power to make an order or regulations under this Part shall be exercisable by statutory instrument.

(4) An order to which this subsection applies shall be laid before the House of Commons; and unless it is approved by that House before the expiration of a period of 28 days beginning with the date on which it was made it shall cease to have effect on the expiration of that period, but without prejudice to anything previously done under the order or to the making of a new order.

(5) In reckoning any such period as is mentioned in subsection (4) above no account shall be taken of any time during which Parliament is dissolved or prorogued or during which the House of Commons is adjourned for more than four days.

(6) A statutory instrument containing an order or regulations under this Part (other than an order under section 57 above or an order to which subsection (4) above applies) shall be subject to annulment in pursuance of a resolution of the House of Commons.

(7) Subsection (4) above applies to—

(a) an order under section 42(3) above providing for material which would otherwise be qualifying material not to be qualifying material;

(b) an order under section 46 above which produces the result that a disposal which would otherwise not be a taxable disposal is a taxable disposal;

(c) an order under section 63(5) above other than one which provides only that an earlier order under section 63(5) is not to apply to material;

(d) an order under section 65(5) above providing for anything which would otherwise not be a disposal of material by way of landfill to be such a disposal.

(8) Any power to make an order or regulations under this Part—

(a) may be exercised as regards prescribed cases or descriptions of case;

(b) may be exercised differently in relation to different cases or descriptions of case.

(9) An order or regulations under this Part may include such supplementary, incidental, consequential or transitional provisions as appear to the Treasury or the Commissioners (as the case may be) to be necessary or expedient.

(10) No specific provision of this Part about an order or regulations shall prejudice the generality of subsections (8) and (9) above.

GENERAL NOTE

Regulations (and an order under s.57) may be made by the Customs and Excise. Orders may be made by the Treasury. Both are to be by statutory instrument. The affirmative resolution procedure applies to orders under ss.42(3), 46, 63(5) and 65(5), which would alter the incidence of the tax. In the case of other orders and of regulations the negative procedure applies.

PART IV

INCOME TAX, CORPORATION TAX AND CAPITAL GAINS TAX

CHAPTER I

PRINCIPAL PROVISIONS

Income tax charge, rates and reliefs

Charge and rates of income tax for 1996–97

72.—(1) Income tax shall be charged for the year 1996–97, and for that year—

(a) the lower rate shall be 20 per cent.;

(b) the basic rate shall be 24 per cent.; and
(c) the higher rate shall be 40 per cent.
(2) For the year 1996–97 section 1(2) of the Taxes Act 1988 shall apply—
(a) as if the amount specified in paragraph (aa) (the lower rate limit) were £3,900; and
(b) as if the amount specified in paragraph (b) (the basic rate limit) were £25,500;
and, accordingly, section 1(4) of that Act (indexation) shall not apply for the year 1996–97.
(3) Section 559(4) of the Taxes Act 1988 (deductions from payments to sub-contractors in the construction industry) shall have effect—
(a) in relation to payments made on or after 1st July 1996 and before the appointed day (within the meaning of section 139 of the Finance Act 1995), with "24 per cent." substituted for "25 per cent."; and
(b) in relation to payments made on or after that appointed day, as if the substitution for which section 139(1) of the Finance Act 1995 provided were a substitution of "the relevant percentage" for "24 per cent."

GENERAL NOTE
The basic rate of income tax is reduced from 25 to 24 per cent. The lower and higher rates remain at 20 and 40 per cent respectively.
The lower rate threshold is increased from £3,200 to £3,900 and the higher rate threshold from £24,300 to £25,500.
In line with the reduction in the basic rate, the deduction rate for payments to sub-contractors in the construction industry is reduced to 24 per cent.

Application of lower rate to income from savings

73.—(1) After section 1 of the Taxes Act 1988 there shall be inserted the following section—

> "**Application of lower rate to income from savings and distributions**
> 1A.—(1) Subject to sections 469(2) and 686, so much of any person's total income for any year of assessment as—
> (a) comprises income to which this section applies, and
> (b) in the case of an individual, is not income falling within section 1(2)(b),
> shall, by virtue of this section, be charged for that year at the lower rate, instead of at the rate otherwise applicable to it in accordance with section 1(2)(aa) and (a).
> (2) Subject to subsection (4) below, this section applies to the following income—
> (a) any income chargeable under Case III of Schedule D other than—
> (i) relevant annuities and other annual payments that are not interest; and
> (ii) amounts so chargeable by virtue of section 119 or 120;
> (b) any income chargeable under Schedule F; and
> (c) subject to subsection (4) below, any equivalent foreign income.
> (3) The income which is equivalent foreign income for the purposes of this section is any income chargeable under Case IV or V of Schedule D which—
> (a) is equivalent to a description of income falling within subsection (2)(a) above but arises from securities or other possessions out of the United Kingdom; or
> (b) consists in any such dividend or other distribution of a company not resident in the United Kingdom as would be chargeable under Schedule F if the company were resident in the United Kingdom.
> (4) This section does not apply to—

(a) any income chargeable to tax under Case IV or V of Schedule D which is such that section 65(5)(a) or (b) provides for the tax to be computed on the full amount of sums received in the United Kingdom; or

(b) any amounts deemed by virtue of section 695(4)(b) or 696(6) to be income chargeable under Case IV of Schedule D.

(5) So much of any person's income as comprises income to which this section applies shall be treated for the purposes of subsection (1)(b) above and any other provisions of the Income Tax Acts as the highest part of his income.

(6) Subsection (5) above shall have effect subject to section 833(3) but shall otherwise have effect notwithstanding any provision requiring income of any description to be treated for the purposes of the Income Tax Acts (other than section 550) as the highest part of a person's income.

(7) In this section 'relevant annuity' means any annuity other than a purchased life annuity to which section 656 applies or to which that section would apply but for section 657(2)(a)."

(2) In section 4 of that Act (construction of references to deduction of tax), after subsection (1) there shall be inserted the following subsection—

"(1A) As respects deductions from, and tax treated as paid on, any such amounts as constitute or (but for the person whose income they are) would constitute income to which section 1A applies, subsection (1) above shall have effect with a reference to the lower rate in force for the relevant year of assessment substituted for the reference to the basic rate in force for that year."

(3) Subsection (1) above has effect in relation to the year 1996–97 and subsequent years of assessment and subsection (2) above has effect in relation to payments on or after 6th April 1996.

(4) Schedule 6 to this Act (which makes further amendments in connection with the charge at the lower rate on income from savings etc.) shall have effect.

(5) Where any subordinate legislation (within the meaning of the Interpretation Act 1978) falls to be construed in accordance with section 4 of the Taxes Act 1988, that legislation (whenever it was made) shall be construed, in relation to payments on or after 6th April 1996, subject to subsection (1A) of that section.

General Note

This section, together with Sched. 6, implements a new system for the taxation of income from savings. The tax charge on income such as bank and building society interest is reduced from the basic rate to the lower rate of 20 per cent. The rate at which tax is deducted at source from payments of savings income is similarly reduced to 20 per cent. Existing provisions which already charge dividends at the lower rate, are subsumed into the new s.1A of the Income and Corporation Taxes Act 1988 (c. 1) ICTA 1988.

Subs. (1)

For an individual, the higher rate applies to any savings income falling above the basic rate limit. The scheme does not apply to unauthorised unit trusts and discretionary trusts.

Subs. (2)

The scheme applies to virtually all income chargeable under Case III of Sched. D, any income chargeable under Sched. F, and any equivalent foreign income.

Subs. (3)

Equivalent foreign income is defined as Case IV or Case V income which would be charged under Case III if it arose in the U.K., and dividends from non-resident companies which would be similarly chargeable under Sched. F.

Subs. (4)
　Income charged on the remittance basis (because the recipient is not domiciled in the U.K.) and payments from foreign estates of deceased persons are excluded from the scheme.

Subss. (5) and (6)
　Savings income is treated as the highest part of a person's income after employment termination payments and gains on life insurance policies treated as income of the policyholder.

Subs. (7)
　Life annuities, other than those covered by s.656 of the ICTA 1988, are excluded from the scheme.
　Further amendments to existing legislation are made by Sched. 6.

Personal allowances for 1996–97

　74.—(1) For the year 1996–97 the amounts specified in the provisions mentioned in subsection (2) below shall be taken to be as set out in that subsection; and, accordingly, section 257C(1) of the Taxes Act 1988 (indexation), so far as it relates to the amounts so specified, shall not apply for the year 1996–97.
　(2) In section 257 of that Act (personal allowance)—
　(a)　the amount in subsection (1) (basic allowance) shall be £3,765;
　(b)　the amount in subsection (2) (allowance for persons aged 65 or more but not aged 75 or more) shall be £4,910; and
　(c)　the amount in subsection (3) (allowance for persons aged 75 or more) shall be £5,090.

GENERAL NOTE
　The personal allowance for 1996–97 is set at £3,765 for those under 65, at £4,910 for those aged 65 to 74, and at £5,090 for those aged 75 or over, an increase of £240, £280 and £290 respectively.

Blind person's allowance

　75.—(1) In section 265(1) of the Taxes Act 1988 (blind person's allowance), for "£1,200" there shall be substituted "£1,250".
　(2) This section shall apply for the year 1996–97 and subsequent years of assessment.

GENERAL NOTE
　The blind persons' allowance is increased from £1,200 to £1,250 [Standing Committee E, February 13, 1996, col. 290].

Limit on relief for interest

　76. For the year 1996–97 the qualifying maximum defined in section 367(5) of the Taxes Act 1988 (limit on relief for interest on certain loans) shall be £30,000.

GENERAL NOTE
　The limit on loans qualifying for mortgage interest relief remains at £30,000.

Corporation tax charge and rate

Charge and rate of corporation tax for 1996

　77. Corporation tax shall be charged for the financial year 1996 at the rate of 33 per cent.

GENERAL NOTE
　The rate of Corporation tax remains at 33 per cent.

Small companies

　78. For the financial year 1996—
　(a)　the small companies' rate shall be 24 per cent.; and

(b) the fraction mentioned in section 13(2) of the Taxes Act 1988 (marginal relief for small companies) shall be nine four-hundredths.

GENERAL NOTE

The small companies' rate of corporation tax is reduced from 25 to 24 per cent in line with the basic rate of income tax. The fraction providing marginal relief for profits between £300,000 and £1.5 million is increased from one-fiftieth to nine four-hundredths, giving a marginal rate of 35.25 per cent [Standing Committee E, February 15, 1996, col. 298].

Abolition of Schedule C charge etc.

Abolition of Schedule C charge etc.

79.—(1) The charge to tax under Schedule C is abolished—
(a) for the purposes of income tax, for the year 1996–97 and subsequent years of assessment;
(b) for the purposes of corporation tax, for accounting periods ending after 31st March 1996.

(2) Schedule 7 to this Act (which, together with Chapter II of this Part of this Act, makes provision for imposing a charge under Schedule D on descriptions of income previously charged under Schedule C, and makes connected amendments) shall have effect.

GENERAL NOTE

The charge to tax under Sched. C, which covers interest on U.K. and foreign government debt, is abolished. Such interest will in future be covered by a new charge under Sched. D, Cases III, IV or V, as appropriate.

Schedule 7 makes consequential amendments.

CHAPTER II

LOAN RELATIONSHIPS

Introductory provisions

GENERAL NOTE

This Part of the Act provides for the repeal of a variety of complex rules for different types of bond and their replacement with a single set of rules covering all debt. The new rules in general apply to companies only. The proposals originated in consultative documents issued by the Treasury and the Bank of England on May 25, 1995 dealing respectively with the taxation of gilts and bonds, and possible developments in the gilts market, in particular the introduction of an official gilt strips market (see ss.95 and 202). Formal intention to proceed was given in a written answer from the Chancellor [*Hansard*, H.C. Vol. 263, Pt. 2, col. 377].

The new rules make it possible to repeal the accrued income scheme, so far as applies to companies, and the provisions dealing with deep discount, deep gain, qualifying indexed securities and qualifying convertible securities.

Taxation of loan relationships

80.—(1) For the purposes of corporation tax all profits and gains arising to a company from its loan relationships shall be chargeable to tax as income in accordance with this Chapter.

(2) To the extent that a company is a party to a loan relationship for the purposes of a trade carried on by the company, profits and gains arising from the relationship shall be brought into account in computing the profits and gains of the trade.

(3) Profits and gains arising from a loan relationship of a company that are not brought into account under subsection (2) above shall be brought into account as profits and gains chargeable to tax under Case III of Schedule D.

(4) This Chapter shall also have effect for the purposes of corporation tax for determining how any deficit on a company's loan relationships is to be brought into account in any case, including a case where none of the compa-

ny's loan relationships falls by virtue of this Chapter to be regarded as a source of income.

(5) Subject to any express provision to the contrary, the amounts which in the case of any company are brought into account in accordance with this Chapter as respects any matter shall be the only amounts brought into account for the purposes of corporation tax as respects that matter.

GENERAL NOTE

This section introduces the new system. It provides that for the purposes of corporation tax, "loan relationships" should be dealt with in accordance with Chap. II. Profits from trading loan relationships are taken into trading profits and profits from other loan relationships are taxable under Case III. In either case, relief is to be given on a "deficit" arising from a loan relationship.

Meaning of "loan relationship" etc.

81.—(1) Subject to the following provisions of this section, a company has a loan relationship for the purposes of the Corporation Tax Acts wherever—
  (a) the company stands (whether by reference to a security or otherwise) in the position of a creditor or debtor as respects any money debt; and
  (b) that debt is one arising from a transaction for the lending of money; and references to a loan relationship and to a company's being a party to a loan relationship shall be construed accordingly.

(2) For the purposes of this Chapter a money debt is a debt which falls to be settled—
  (a) by the payment of money; or
  (b) by the transfer of a right to settlement under a debt which is itself a money debt.

(3) Subject to subsection (4) below, where an instrument is issued by any person for the purpose of representing security for, or the rights of a creditor in respect of, any money debt, then (whatever the circumstances of the issue of the instrument) that debt shall be taken for the purposes of this Chapter to be a debt arising from a transaction for the lending of money.

(4) For the purposes of this Chapter a debt shall not be taken to arise from a transaction for the lending of money to the extent that it is a debt arising from rights conferred by shares in a company.

(5) For the purposes of this Chapter—
  (a) references to payments or interest under a loan relationship are references to payments or interest made or payable in pursuance of any of the rights or liabilities under that relationship; and
  (b) references to rights or liabilities under a loan relationship are references to any of the rights or liabilities under the agreement or arrangements by virtue of which that relationship subsists; and those rights or liabilities shall be taken to include the rights or liabilities attached to any security which, being a security issued in relation to the money debt in question, is a security representing that relationship.

(6) In this Chapter "money" includes money expressed in a currency other than sterling.

GENERAL NOTE

This sets out the basic scope of a "loan relationship". Companies are party to a "loan relationship" when they stand either as debtor or creditor for a money debt, and that debt arises from a loan of money, whether expressed in sterling or any other currency [Standing Committee E, February 29, 1996, col. 613].

Taxation of profits and gains and relief for deficits

Method of bringing amounts into account

82.—(1) For the purposes of corporation tax—
  (a) the profits and gains arising from the loan relationships of a company, and

(b) any deficit on a company's loan relationships,
shall be computed in accordance with this section using the credits and debits given for the accounting period in question by the following provisions of this Chapter.

(2) To the extent that, in any accounting period, a loan relationship of a company is one to which it is a party for the purposes of a trade carried on by it, the credits and debits given in respect of that relationship for that period shall be treated (according to whether they are credits or debits) either—

(a) as receipts of that trade falling to be brought into account in comput-ing the profits and gains of that trade for that period; or

(b) as expenses of that trade which are deductible in computing those profits and gains.

(3) Where for any accounting period there are, in respect of the loan relationships of a company, both—

(a) credits that are not brought into account under subsection (2) above ("non-trading credits"), and

(b) debits that are not so brought into account ("non-trading debits"),
the aggregate of the non-trading debits shall be subtracted from the aggre-gate of the non-trading credits to give the amount to be brought into account under subsection (4) below.

(4) That amount is the amount which for any accounting period is to be taken (according to whether the aggregate of the non-trading credits or the aggregate of the non-trading debits is the greater) to be either—

(a) the amount of the company's profits and gains for that period that are chargeable under Case III of Schedule D as profits and gains arising from the company's loan relationships; or

(b) the amount of the company's non-trading deficit for that period on its loan relationships.

(5) Where for any accounting period a company has non-trading credits but no non-trading debits in respect of its loan relationships, the aggregate amount of the credits shall be the amount of the company's profits and gains for that period that are chargeable under Case III of Schedule D as profits and gains arising from those relationships.

(6) Where for any accounting period a company has non-trading debits but no non-trading credits in respect of its loan relationships, that company shall have a non-trading deficit on its loan relationships for that period equal to the aggregate of the debits.

(7) Subsection (2) above, so far as it provides for any amount to be deduct-ible as mentioned in paragraph (b) of that subsection, shall have effect not-withstanding anything in section 74 of the Taxes Act 1988 (allowable deductions).

Non-trading deficit on loan relationships

83.—(1) This section applies for the purposes of corporation tax where for any accounting period ("the deficit period") there is a non-trading deficit on a company's loan relationships.

(2) The company may make a claim for the whole or any part of the deficit to be treated in any of the following ways, that is to say—

(a) to be set off against any profits of the company (of whatever descrip-tion) for the deficit period;

(b) to be treated as eligible for group relief;

    (c) to be carried back to be set off against profits for earlier accounting periods; or

    (d) to be carried forward and set against non-trading profits for the next accounting period.

(3) So much of the deficit for the deficit period as is not the subject of a claim under subsection (2) above shall be carried forward so as to be brought into account for the purposes of this Chapter as a non-trading debit ("a carried-forward debit") for the accounting period immediately following the deficit period.

(4) No claim shall be made under subsection (2)(a) to (c) above in respect of so much (if any) of the non-trading deficit of a company for any accounting period as is equal to the amount by which that deficit is greater than it would have been if any carried-forward debit for that period had been disregarded.

(5) No part of any non-trading deficit of a company established for charitable purposes only shall be set off against the profits of that or any other company in pursuance of a claim under subsection (2) above.

(6) A claim under subsection (2) above must be made within the period of two years immediately following the end of the relevant period, or within such further period as the Board may allow.

(7) In subsection (6) above "the relevant period"—

    (a) in relation to a claim under subsection (2)(a), (b) or (c) above, means the deficit period; and

    (b) in relation to a claim under subsection (2)(d) above, means the accounting period immediately following the deficit period.

(8) Different claims may be made under subsection (2) above as respects different parts of a non-trading deficit for any period, but no claim may be made as respects any part of a deficit to which another claim made under that subsection relates.

(9) Schedule 8 to this Act (which makes provision about what happens where a claim is made under subsection (2) above) shall have effect.

GENERAL NOTE

    Where a non-trading deficit arises, this may be set against any other profits of the company for that period, or treated as eligible for group relief or carried back to be set against earlier profits from loan relationships, or carried forward to be set against non-trading profits for the next period. This treatment is dependent on a claim within two years or such longer period as the Revenue may allow.

    In the absence of a claim, the deficit is carried forward as a non-trading debit, but any amount carried forward is not then available for other forms of relief.

    A charity cannot obtain relief under this section.

    Claims may split a deficit between the various reliefs, provided that double relief is unavailable.

    Schedule 8 provides further detail on the effect of claims [Standing Committee E, February 29, 1996, col. 617].

Computational provisions etc.

Debits and credits brought into account

84.—(1) The credits and debits to be brought into account in the case of any company in respect of its loan relationships shall be the sums which, in accordance with an authorised accounting method and when taken together, fairly represent, for the accounting period in question—

    (a) all profits, gains and losses of the company, including those of a capital nature, which (disregarding interest and any charges or expenses) arise to the company from its loan relationships and related transactions; and

    (b) all interest under the company's loan relationship and all charges and expenses incurred by the company under or for the purposes of its loan relationships and related transactions.

(2) The reference in subsection (1) above to the profits, gains and losses arising to a company—

(a) does not include a reference to any amounts required to be transferred to the company's share premium account; but

(b) does include a reference to any profits, gains or losses which, in accordance with normal accountancy practice, are carried to or sustained by any other reserve maintained by the company.

(3) The reference in subsection (1)(b) above to charges and expenses incurred for the purposes of a company's loan relationships and related transactions does not include a reference to any charges or expenses other than those incurred directly—

(a) in bringing any of those relationships into existence;

(b) in entering into or giving effect to any of those transactions;

(c) in making payments under any of those relationships or in pursuance of any of those transactions; or

(d) in taking steps for ensuring the receipt of payments under any of those relationships or in accordance with any of those transactions.

(4) Where—

(a) any charges or expenses are incurred by a company for purposes connected—

(i) with entering into a loan relationship or related transaction, or

(ii) with giving effect to any obligation that might arise under a loan relationship or related transaction,

(b) at the time when the charges or expenses are incurred, the relationship or transaction is one into which the company may enter but has not entered, and

(c) if that relationship or transaction had been entered into by that company, the charges or expenses would be charges or expenses incurred as mentioned in subsection (3) above,

those charges or expenses shall be treated for the purposes of this Chapter as charges or expenses in relation to which debits may be brought into account in accordance with subsection (1)(b) above to the same extent as if the relationship or transaction had been entered into.

(5) In this section "related transaction", in relation to a loan relationship, means any disposal or acquisition (in whole or in part) of rights or liabilities under that relationship.

(6) The cases where there shall be taken for the purposes of this section to be a disposal and acquisition of rights or liabilities under a loan relationship shall include those where such rights or liabilities are transferred or extinguished by any sale, gift, exchange, surrender, redemption or release.

(7) This section has effect subject to Schedule 9 to this Act (which contains provision disallowing certain debits and credits for the purposes of this Chapter and making assumptions about how an authorised accounting method is to be applied in certain cases).

GENERAL NOTE

This section, which was heavily amended in committee, provides for debits and credits from loan relationships to reflect all profits and losses, interest and allowable expenses arising from the relationship or the acquisition or disposal of it. These must be calculated in accordance with an authorised accounting method (see s.85). Amounts carried to share premium account are not included, but amounts carried to other reserves are.

Schedule 9 provides further computational rules for a variety of special situations. See further the General Note to that Schedule [Standing Committee E, February 29, 1996, col. 618].

Authorised accounting methods

85.—(1) Subject to the following provisions of this Chapter, the alternative accounting methods that are authorised for the purposes of this Chapter are—

(a) an accruals basis of accounting; and

(b) a mark to market basis of accounting under which any loan relationship to which that basis is applied is brought into account in each accounting period at a fair value.

(2) An accounting method applied in any case shall be treated as authorised for the purposes of this Chapter only if—

(a) it conforms (subject to paragraphs (b) and (c) below) to normal accountancy practice, as followed in cases where such practice allows the use of that method;

(b) it contains proper provision for allocating payments under a loan relationship to accounting periods; and

(c) where it is an accruals basis of accounting, it does not contain any provision (other than provision comprised in authorised arrangements for bad debt) that gives debits by reference to the valuation at different times of any asset representing a loan relationship.

(3) In the case of an accruals basis of accounting, proper provision for allocating payments under a loan relationship to accounting periods is provision which—

(a) allocates payments to the period to which they relate, without regard to the periods in which they are made or received or in which they become due and payable;

(b) includes provision which, where payments relate to two or more periods, apportions them on a just and reasonable basis between the different periods;

(c) assumes, subject to authorised arrangements for bad debt, that, so far as any company in the position of a creditor is concerned, every amount payable under the relationship will be paid in full as it becomes due;

(d) secures the making of the adjustments required in the case of the relationship by authorised arrangements for bad debt; and

(e) provides, subject to authorised arrangements for bad debt and for writing off government investments, that, where there is a release of any liability under the relationship, the appropriate amount in respect of the release is credited to the debtor in the accounting period in which the release takes place.

(4) In the case of a mark to market basis of accounting, proper provision for allocating payments under a loan relationship to accounting periods is provision which allocates payments to the accounting period in which they become due and payable.

(5) In this section—

(a) the references to authorised arrangements for bad debt are references to accounting arrangements under which debits and credits are brought into account in conformity with the provisions of paragraph 5 of Schedule 9 to this Act; and

(b) the reference to authorised arrangements for writing off government investments is a reference to accounting arrangements that give effect to paragraph 7 of that Schedule.

(6) In this section "fair value", in relation to any loan relationship of a company, means the amount which, at the time as at which the value falls to be determined, is the amount that the company would obtain from or, as the case may be, would have to pay to an independent person for—

(a) the transfer of all the company's rights under the relationship in respect of amounts which at that time are not yet due and payable; and

(b) the release of all the company's liabilities under the relationship in respect of amounts which at that time are not yet due and payable.

GENERAL NOTE
    This section authorises two types of accounting method to be used for tax purposes, the "accruals" basis and the "mark to market" basis, and sets out the criteria which each basis has to fulfil in order to qualify [Standing Committee E, March 5, 1996, col. 637].

Application of accounting methods

86.—(1) This section has effect, subject to the following provisions of this Chapter, for the determination of which of the alternative authorised accounting methods that are available by virtue of section 85 above is to be used as respects the loan relationships of a company.

(2) Different methods may be used as respects different relationships or, as respects the same relationship, for different accounting periods or for different parts of the same accounting period.

(3) If a basis of accounting which is or equates with an authorised accounting method is used as respects any loan relationship of a company in a company's statutory accounts, then the method which is to be used for the purposes of this Chapter as respects that relationship for the accounting period, or part of a period, for which that basis is used in those accounts shall be—

(a) where the basis used in those accounts is an authorised accounting method, that method; and

(b) where it is not, the authorised accounting method with which it equates.

(4) For any period or part of a period for which the authorised accounting method to be used as respects a loan relationship of a company is not determined under subsection (3) above, an authorised accruals basis of accounting shall be used for the purposes of this Chapter as respects that loan relationship.

(5) For the purposes of this section (but subject to subsection (6) below)—

(a) a basis of accounting equates with an authorised accruals basis of accounting if it purports to allocate payments under a loan relationship to accounting periods according to when they are taken to accrue; and

(b) a basis of accounting equates with an authorised mark to market basis of accounting if (without equating with an authorised accruals basis of accounting) it purports in respect of a loan relationship—

(i) to produce credits or debits computed by reference to the determination, as at different times in an accounting period, of a fair value; and

(ii) to produce credits or debits relating to payments under that relationship according to when they become due and payable.

(6) An accounting method which purports to make any such allocation of payments under a loan relationship as is mentioned in subsection (5)(a) above shall be taken for the purposes of this section to equate with an authorised mark to market basis of accounting (rather than with an authorised accruals basis of accounting) if—

(a) it purports to bring that relationship into account in each accounting period at a value which would be a fair value if the valuation were made on the basis that interest under the relationship were to be disregarded to the extent that it has already accrued; and

(b) the credits and debits produced in the case of that relationship by that method (when it is properly applied) correspond, for all practical purposes, to the credits and debits produced in the case of that relationship, and for the same accounting period, by an authorised mark to market basis of accounting.

(7) In this section "fair value" has the same meaning as in section 85 above.

(8) In this section "statutory accounts", in relation to a company, means—

(a) any accounts relating to that company that are drawn up in accordance with any requirements of the Companies Act 1985 or the Companies (Northern Ireland) Order 1986 that apply in relation to that company;

(b) any accounts relating to that company that are drawn up in accordance with any requirements of regulations under section 70 of the Friendly Societies Act 1992 that apply in relation to that company;

(c) any accounts relating to that company which are accounts to which Part I of Schedule 21C to the Companies Act 1985 or Part I of Schedule 21D to that Act (companies with UK branches) applies;

(d) in the case of a company which—

    (i) is not subject to any such requirements as are mentioned in paragraphs (a) or (b) above, and

    (ii) is a company in whose case there are no accounts for the period in question that fall within paragraph (c) above,

any accounts relating to the company drawn up in accordance with requirements imposed in relation to that company under the law of its home State; and

(e) in the case of a company which—

    (i) is not subject to any such requirements as are mentioned in paragraphs (a), (b) or (d) above, and

    (ii) is a company in whose case there are no accounts for the period in question that fall within paragraph (c) above,

the accounts relating to the company that most closely correspond to the accounts which, in the case of a company formed and registered under the Companies Act 1985, are required under that Act.

(9) For the purposes of subsection (8) above the home State of a company is the country or territory under whose law the company is incorporated.

GENERAL NOTE

This section determines whether a company is to use an authorised accruals or an authorised mark to market basis. A company will account for a loan relationship for tax purposes on an authorised mark to market basis if this is used in its statutory accounts. Otherwise it must use an authorised accruals basis. These criteria apply irrespective of whether a company is a party to a loan relationship as a creditor or as a debtor [Standing Committee E, March 5, 1996, col. 650].

Accounting method where parties have a connection

87.—(1) This section applies in the case of a loan relationship of a company where for any accounting period there is a connection between the company and—

(a) in the case of a debtor relationship of the company, a person standing in the position of a creditor as respects the debt in question; or

(b) in the case of a creditor relationship of the company, a person standing in the position of a debtor as respects that debt.

(2) The only accounting method authorised for the purposes of this Chapter for use by the company as respects the loan relationship shall be an authorised accruals basis of accounting.

(3) For the purposes of this section there is a connection between a company and another person for an accounting period if (subject to subsection (4) and section 88 below)—

(a) the other person is a company and there is a time in that period, or in the two years before the beginning of that period, when one of the companies has had control of the other;

(b) the other person is a company and there is a time in that period, or in those two years, when both the companies have been under the control of the same person; or

(c) there is a time in that accounting period, or in those two years, when the company was a close company and the other person was a participator in that company or the associate of a person who was such a participator at that time.

(4) Two companies which have at any time been under the control of the same person shall not, by virtue of that fact, be taken for the purposes of this section to be companies between whom there is a connection if the person was the Crown, a Minister of the Crown, a government department, a Northern Ireland department, a foreign sovereign power or an international organisation.

(5) The references in subsection (1) above to a person who stands in the position of a creditor or debtor as respects a loan relationship include references to a person who indirectly stands in that position by reference to a series of loan relationships.

(6) Subsections (2) to (6) of section 416 of the Taxes Act 1988 (meaning of "control") shall apply for the purposes of this section as they apply for the purposes of Part XI of that Act.

(7) Subject to subsection (8) below, in this section "participator" and "associate" have the meanings given for the purposes of Part XI of the Taxes Act 1988 by section 417 of that Act.

(8) A person shall not for the purposes of this section be regarded as a participator in relation to a company by reason only that he is a loan creditor of the company.

GENERAL NOTE

This section provides that where the parties to a loan relationship are connected, then the only accounting method which can be used for tax purposes is an authorised accruals method. Connection is defined in terms of control during a two year period. Close companies are also connected with participators and their associates. There is an exemption for state companies and international organisations [Standing Committee E, March 5, 1996, col. 653].

Exemption from section 87 in certain cases

88.—(1) Subject to subsection (5) below, where a creditor relationship of a company is one to which that company is a party in any accounting period in exempt circumstances, any connection for that accounting period between the company and a person who stands in the position of a debtor as respects the debt shall be disregarded for the purposes of section 87 above.

(2) A company having a creditor relationship in any accounting period shall, for that period, be taken for the purposes of this section to be a party to that relationship in exempt circumstances if—

(a) the company, in the course of carrying on any activities forming an integral part of a trade carried on by that company in that period, disposes of or acquires assets representing creditor relationships;

(b) that period is one for which the company uses an authorised mark to market basis of accounting as respects all the creditor relationships represented by assets acquired in the course of those activities;

(c) the asset representing the creditor relationship in question was acquired in the course of those activities;

(d) that asset is either—
   (i) listed on a recognised stock exchange at the end of that period; or
   (ii) a security the redemption of which must occur within twelve months of its issue;

(e) there is a time in that period when assets of the same kind as the asset representing the loan relationship in question are in the beneficial ownership of persons other than the company; and

(f) there is not more than three months, in aggregate, in that accounting period during which the equivalent of 30 per cent. or more of the assets of that kind is in the beneficial ownership of connected persons.

(3) An insurance company carrying on basic life assurance and general annuity business and having a creditor relationship in any accounting period shall, for that period, be taken for the purposes of this section to be a party to that relationship in exempt circumstances if—

(a) assets of the company representing any of its creditor relationships are linked for that period to its basic life assurance and general annuity business;

(b) that period is one for which the company uses an authorised mark to market basis of accounting as respects all the creditor relationships of the company represented by assets that are so linked;

(c) the asset representing the creditor relationship in question is so linked;

(d) that asset is either—

(i) listed on a recognised stock exchange at the end of that period; or

(ii) a security the redemption of which must occur within twelve months of its issue;

(e) there is a time in that period when assets of the same kind as the asset representing the creditor relationship in question are in the beneficial ownership of persons other than the company; and

(f) there is not more than three months, in aggregate, in that accounting period during which the equivalent of 30 per cent. or more of the assets of that kind is in the beneficial ownership of connected persons.

(4) For the purposes of subsections (2) and (3) above—

(a) assets shall be taken to be of the same kind where they are treated as being of the same kind by the practice of any recognised stock exchange, or would be so treated if dealt with on such a stock exchange; and

(b) a connected person has the beneficial ownership of an asset wherever there is, or (apart from this section) would be, a connection (within the meaning of section 87 above) between—

(i) the person who has the beneficial ownership of the asset, and

(ii) a person who stands in the position of a debtor as respects the money debt by reference to which any loan relationship represented by that asset subsists.

(5) Where for any accounting period—

(a) subsection (1) above has effect in the case of a creditor relationship of a company, and

(b) the person who stands in the position of a debtor as respects the debt in question is also a company,

that subsection shall not apply for determining, for the purposes of so much of section 87 above as relates to the corresponding debtor relationship, whether there is a connection between the two companies.

(6) Subsection (5) of section 87 above shall apply for the purposes of this section as it applies for the purposes of that section.

(7) In this section "basic life assurance and general annuity business" and "insurance company" have the same meanings as in Chapter I of Part XII of the Taxes Act 1988, and section 432ZA of that Act (linked assets) shall apply for the purposes of this section as it applies for the purposes of that Chapter.

GENERAL NOTE

This section, added at the committee stage, provides further exemptions from the operation of s.87. These relate to companies carrying on a trade which involves the acquisition and disposal of securities and to insurance companies holding securities linked to their "BLAGAB" business. The securities must be either quoted or redeemable within 12 months, there must be other holders and not more than 30 per cent can be held by connected persons over a period of more than three months.

Inconsistent application of accounting methods

89.—(1) Where there is any inconsistency or other material difference between the way in which any authorised accounting method is applied as respects the same loan relationship in successive accounting periods, a balancing credit or balancing debit shall be brought into account in the second of those periods ("the second period").

(2) The amount of the balancing credit or debit shall be computed as respects the relationship in question by—

(a) taking the amount given by subsection (3) below and the amount given by subsection (4) below; and

(b) then aggregating those amounts (treating any debit as a negative amount) to produce a net credit or net debit.

(3) The amount given by this subsection is whichever of the following is applicable—

(a) a debit equal to the amount (if any) by which the first of the following amounts exceeds the second, that is to say—

(i) the aggregate of the credits actually brought into account for all previous periods in which the accounting method was used; and

(ii) the aggregate of the credits that would have been brought into account if that method had been applied in those periods in the same way as it was applied in the second period;

(b) a credit equal to the amount (if any) by which the second aggregate mentioned in paragraph (a) above exceeds the first; or

(c) if both those aggregates are the same, nil.

(4) The amount given by this subsection is whichever of the following is applicable—

(a) a credit equal to the amount (if any) by which the first of the following amounts exceeds the second, that is to say—

(i) the aggregate of the debits actually brought into account for all previous periods in which the accounting method was used; and

(ii) the aggregate of the debits that would have been brought into account if that method had been applied in those periods in the same way as it was applied in the second period;

(b) a debit equal to the amount (if any) by which the second aggregate mentioned in paragraph (a) above exceeds the first; or

(c) if both those aggregates are the same, nil.

(5) In this section "previous period" means any accounting period before the second period.

GENERAL NOTE

Where a company alters the way in which it applies an authorised basis of accounting to a loan relationship, any difference in the debits or credits arising from the change is brought into charge or relieved as appropriate.

Changes of accounting method

90.—(1) This section applies where different authorised accounting methods are used for the purposes of this Chapter as respects the same loan relationship for different parts of the same accounting period or for successive accounting periods.

(2) Where, in the case of any loan relationship, the use of any authorised accounting method is superseded in the course of any accounting period by the use of another—

(a) the assumptions specified in subsection (4) below shall be made;

(b) each method shall be applied on those assumptions as respects the part of the period for which it is uscd; and

(c) the credits and debits given by the application of those methods on those assumptions shall be brought into account in the accounting period in which the change of method takes effect.

(3) Where, in the case of any loan relationship, the use of any authorised accounting method is superseded as from the beginning of an accounting period by the use of another—

(a) a net credit or debit shall be computed (treating any debit used in the computation as a negative amount) by—

(i) aggregating the credits and debits which, on the assumptions specified in subsection (4) below, would have been given in respect of that relationship for the successive accounting periods by the use for each period of the accounting method actually used for that period;

(ii) aggregating the credits and debits so given without the making of those assumptions; and

(iii) subtracting the second aggregate from the first; and

(b) the net credit or debit shall be brought into account for the purposes of this Chapter in the accounting period as from the beginning of which the change of method takes effect.

(4) The assumptions mentioned in subsections (2) and (3) above are—

(a) that the company ceased to be a party to the relationship immediately before the end of the period, or part of a period, for which the superseded method is used;

(b) that the company again became a party to that relationship as from the beginning of the period or, as the case may be, part of a period for which the other authorised accounting method is used;

(c) that the relationship to which the company is deemed to have become a party is separate and distinct from the one to which it is deemed to have ceased to be a party;

(d) that the amount payable under the transaction comprised in each of the assumptions specified in paragraphs (a) and (b) above was equal to the fair value of the relationship; and

(e) so far as relevant, that that amount became due at the time when the company is deemed to have ceased to be a party to the relationship or, as the case may be, to have again become a party to it.

(5) Where—

(a) a mark to market basis of accounting is superseded by an accruals basis of accounting in the case of any loan relationship, and

(b) the amount which would have accrued in respect of that relationship in the period or part of a period for which the accruals basis of accounting is used falls to be determined for the purposes of this section in accordance with the assumptions mentioned in subsection (4) above,

that amount shall be taken for those purposes to be equal to the amount resulting from the subtraction of the amount given by subsection (6)(a) below from the amount given by subsection (6)(b) below.

(6) Those amounts are—

(a) the amount which by virtue of the assumptions mentioned in subsection (4) above is given as an opening value for the period or part of a period; and

(b) the amount equal to whatever, in the computation in accordance with an authorised accruals basis of accounting of the amount accruing in that period or part of a period, would have been taken to be the closing value applicable as at the end of that period or part of a period if such a basis of accounting had always been used as respects the relationship.

(7) In this section "fair value" has the same meaning as in section 85 above.

GENERAL NOTE

Where a company changes the authorised accounting method which it uses for a loan relationship from an accruals basis to a mark to market basis, or vice versa, debits and credits are computed for each accounting method by reference to the fair value (see s.85(6)) of the loan as the closing value under the former accounting method and the opening value for the new method.

Payments subject to deduction of tax

91.—(1) This section applies where—

(a) any company receives a payment of interest on which it bears income tax by deduction; and

(b) in the case of that company, a credit relating to that interest has been brought into account for the purposes of this Chapter for an accounting period ending more than two years before the receipt of the payment.

(2) On a claim made by the company to an officer of the Board, section 7(2) or, as the case may be, 11(3) of the Taxes Act 1988 (deducted income tax to be set against liability to corporation tax) shall have effect in relation to the income tax on the payment as if the interest had fallen to be taken into account for the purposes of corporation tax in the accounting period in which the payment of that interest is received.

(3) In determining for the purposes of this section which accounting period is the accounting period for which a credit relating to interest paid subsequently was brought into account, every payment of interest to a company under a loan relationship of that company shall be assumed to be a payment in discharge of the earliest outstanding liability to that company in respect of interest payable under the relationship.

(4) For the purposes of this section, the earliest outstanding liability to interest payable under a loan relationship of a company shall be identified, in relation to any payment of such interest, according to the authorised accounting method most recently used as respects that relationship, so that—

(a) if that method is an authorised accruals basis of accounting, it shall be determined by reference to the time when the interest accrued; and

(b) if that method is an authorised mark to market basis of accounting, it shall be determined by reference to the time when the interest became due and payable.

(5) In subsection (4) above the reference, in relation to a payment of interest made to a company in any accounting period, to the authorised accounting method most recently used as respects that relationship is a reference to the authorised accounting method which, in the case of that company, has been used as respects that relationship for the accounting period which, when the payment is made, is the most recent for which amounts in respect of that relationship have been brought into account for the purposes of this Chapter.

(6) A claim under this section shall not be made in respect of any payment of interest at any time after the later of the following, that is to say—

(a) the time two years after the end of the accounting period in which the payment is received; and

(b) the time six years after the end of the accounting period for which the credit in respect of the interest was brought into account for the purposes of this Chapter.

(7) Where—

(a) there is a payment of interest to a company under a loan relationship of that company, and

(b) the company is prevented by virtue of subsection (6) above from making any claim under this section in respect of that payment,

the company shall not be entitled to make any claim under paragraph 5 of Schedule 16 to the Taxes Act 1988 (set off of income tax borne against income tax payable) in respect of that payment.

GENERAL NOTE

This section deals with the treatment of income tax where companies receive payments net of tax more than two years after they are taken into account for corporation tax. In such a case the income tax will be available for set-off against the corporation tax for the accounting period in which the payment is received. No matter how long payment is delayed a company has a minimum of two years within which to make a claim.

Special cases

Convertible securities etc.

92.—(1) This section applies to an asset if—

(a) the asset represents a creditor relationship of a company;

(b) the rights attached to the asset include provision by virtue of which the company is or may become entitled to acquire (whether by conversion or exchange or otherwise) any shares in a company;

(c) the extent to which shares may be acquired under that provision is not determined using a cash value which is specified in that provision or which is or will be ascertainable by reference to the terms of that provision;

(d) the asset is not a relevant discounted security within the meaning of Schedule 13 to this Act;

(e) at the time when the asset came into existence there was a more than negligible likelihood that the right to acquire shares in a company would in due course be exercised to a significant extent; and

(f) the asset is not one the disposal of which by the company would fall to be treated as a disposal in the course of activities forming an integral part of a trade carried on by the company.

(2) The amounts falling for any accounting period to be brought into account for the purposes of this Chapter in respect of a creditor relationship represented by an asset to which this section applies shall be confined to amounts relating to interest.

(3) Only an authorised accruals basis of accounting shall be used for ascertaining those amounts.

(4) Amounts shall be brought into account in computing the profits of the company for the purposes of corporation tax as if the Taxation of Chargeable Gains Act 1992 had effect in relation to any asset to which this section applies as it has effect in relation to an asset that does not represent a loan relationship.

(5) For the purposes of that Act the amount or value of the consideration for any disposal or acquisition of the asset shall be treated as adjusted so as to exclude so much of it as, on a just and reasonable apportionment, relates to any interest which—

(a) falls to be brought into account under subsections (2) and (3) above as accruing to any company at any time; and

(b) in consequence of, or of the terms of, the disposal or acquisition, is not paid or payable to the company to which it is treated for the purposes of this Chapter as accruing.

(6) In subsection (5) above the references to a disposal, in relation to an asset, are references to anything which—

(a) is a disposal of that asset (within the meaning of the Taxation of Chargeable Gains Act 1992); or

(b) would be such a disposal but for section 127 or 116(10) of that Act (reorganisations etc.);

and the references to the acquisition of an asset shall be construed accordingly.

GENERAL NOTE

This section sets out how convertible debt securities are to be treated when held otherwise than for trading purposes. They will escape the full scope of the charge normally imposed by this Chapter if, broadly, the conversion option was a genuine one judged at the time of issue, and the convertible cannot be redeemed in the event of non-conversion for more than the issue price. In such cases, only the interest on the convertible will be charged as income, on an accruals basis.

Any gain or loss on disposal will be dealt with under the rules for tax on chargeable gains. Any other convertibles will be subject to the same rules as other loan relationships [Standing Committee E, March 5, 1996, col. 665].

Relationships linked to the value of chargeable assets

93.—(1) This section applies in the case of any loan relationship of a company that is linked to the value of chargeable assets unless it is one the disposal of which by the company would fall to be treated as a disposal in the course of activities forming an integral part of a trade carried on by the company.

(2) The amounts falling for any accounting period to be brought into account for the purposes of this Chapter in respect of the relationship shall be confined to amounts relating to interest.

(3) Only an authorised accruals basis of accounting shall be used for ascertaining those amounts.

(4) Amounts shall be brought into account in computing the profits of the company for the purposes of corporation tax as if the Taxation of Chargeable Gains Act 1992 had effect in relation to the asset representing the relationship as it has effect in relation to an asset that does not represent a loan relationship.

(5) For the purposes of that Act the amount or value of the consideration for any disposal or acquisition of the asset shall be treated as adjusted so as to exclude so much of it as, on a just and reasonable apportionment, relates to any interest which—

(a) falls to be brought into account under subsections (2) and (3) above as accruing to any company at any time; and

(b) in consequence of, or of the terms of, the disposal or acquisition, is not paid or payable to the company to which it is treated for the purposes of this Chapter as accruing.

(6) For the purposes of this section a loan relationship is linked to the value of chargeable assets if, in pursuance of any provision having effect for the purposes of that relationship, the amount that must be paid to discharge the money debt (whether on redemption of a security issued in relation to that debt or otherwise) is equal to the amount determined by applying a relevant percentage change in the value of chargeable assets to the amount falling for the purposes of this Chapter to be regarded as the amount of the original loan from which the money debt arises.

(7) In subsection (6) above the reference to a relevant percentage change in the value of chargeable assets is a reference to the amount of the percentage change (if any) over the relevant period in the value of chargeable assets of any particular description or in any index of the value of any such assets.

(8) In subsection (7) above "the relevant period" means—

(a) the period between the time of the original loan and the discharge of the money debt; or

(b) any other period in which almost all of that period is comprised and which differs from that period exclusively for purposes connected with giving effect to a valuation in relation to rights or liabilities under the loan relationship.

(9) If—

(a) there is a provision which, in the case of any loan relationship, falls within subsection (6) above,

(b) that provision is made subject to any other provision applying to the determination of the amount payable to discharge the money debt,

(c) that other provision is to the effect only that the amount so payable must not be less than a specified percentage of the amount falling for the purposes of this Chapter to be regarded as the amount of the original loan, and

(d) the specified percentage is not more than 10 per cent., that other provision shall be disregarded in determining for the purposes of this section whether the relationship is linked to the value of chargeable assets.

(10) For the purposes of this section an asset is a chargeable asset, in relation to a loan relationship of a company, if any gain accruing on the disposal of the asset by the company on or after 1st April 1996 would, on the assumptions specified in subsection (11) below, be a chargeable gain for the purposes of the Taxation of Chargeable Gains Act 1992.

(11) Those assumptions are—

   (a) where it is not otherwise the case, that the asset is an asset of the company;

   (b) that the asset is not one the disposal of which by the company would fall to be treated for the purposes of corporation tax as a disposal in the course of a trade carried on by the company; and

   (c) that chargeable gains that might accrue under section 116(10) of that Act (postponed charges) are to be disregarded.

(12) In subsection (5) above references to a disposal, in relation to an asset, are references to anything which—

   (a) is a disposal of that asset (within the meaning of the Taxation of Chargeable Gains Act 1992); or

   (b) would be such a disposal but for section 127 or 116(10) of that Act (reorganisations etc.);

and the references to the acquisition of an asset shall be construed accordingly.

(13) For the purposes of this section neither—

   (a) the retail prices index, nor

   (b) any similar general index of prices published by the government of any territory or by the agent of any such government,

shall be taken to be an index of the value of chargeable assets.

GENERAL NOTE

   This section ensures that treatment under the Taxation of Chargeable Gains Act 1992 (c. 12) will continue to apply to loan relationships linked to the value of chargeable assets, for example, via a share index. This does not apply where the company is trading in such securities. A *de minimis* limit of 10 per cent in enhancement of value applies. The retail prices index and similar indices are not relevant for the section.

Indexed gilt-edged securities

94.—(1) In the case of any loan relationship represented by an index-linked gilt-edged security, the adjustment for which this section provides shall be made in computing the credits and debits which fall, for any accounting period, to be brought into account for the purposes of this Chapter in respect of that relationship as non-trading credits or non-trading debits.

(2) The adjustment shall be made wherever—

   (a) the authorised accounting method applied as respects the index-linked gilt-edged security gives credits or debits by reference to the value of the security at two different times, and

   (b) there is any change in the retail prices index between those times.

(3) Subject to subsection (4) below, the adjustment is such an adjustment of the amount which would otherwise be taken for the purposes of that accounting method to be the value of the security at the earlier time ("the opening value") as results in the amount in fact so taken being equal to the opening value increased or, as the case may be, reduced by the same percentage as the percentage increase or reduction in the retail prices index between the earlier and the later time.

(4) The Treasury may, in relation to any description of index-linked gilt-edged securities, by order provide that—

(a) there are to be no adjustments under this section; or

(b) that an adjustment specified in the order (instead of the adjustment specified in subsection (3) above) is to be the adjustment for which this section provides.

(5) An order under subsection (4) above—

(a) shall not have effect in relation to any gilt-edged security issued before the making of the order; but

(b) may make different provision for different descriptions of securities.

(6) For the purposes of this section the percentage increase or reduction in the retail prices index between any two times shall be determined by reference to the difference between—

(a) that index for the month in which the earlier time falls; and

(b) that index for the month in which the later time falls.

(7) In this section "index-linked gilt-edged securities" means any gilt-edged securities the amounts of the payments under which are determined wholly or partly by reference to the retail prices index.

GENERAL NOTE

This section provides a measure of relief where companies hold indexed gilts other than for the purposes of a trade. The profits or losses otherwise to be brought into account for an accounting period are to be adjusted by the value of the indexed gilts at the start of the period, multiplied by the movement in the retail price index over the period.

The Treasury is given power to modify the section by order to cater for possible future types of index-linked gilts [Standing Committee E, March 5, 1996, col. 670].

Gilt strips

95.—(1) This section has effect for the purposes of the application of an authorised accruals basis of accounting as respects a loan relationship represented by a gilt-edged security or a strip of a gilt-edged security.

(2) Where a gilt-edged security is exchanged by any person for strips of that security—

(a) the security shall be deemed to have been redeemed at the time of the exchange by the payment to that person of its market value; and

(b) that person shall be deemed to have acquired each strip for the amount which bears the same proportion to that market value as is borne by the market value of the strip to the aggregate of the market values of all the strips received in exchange for the security.

(3) Where strips of a gilt-edged security are consolidated into a single gilt-edged security by being exchanged by any person for that security—

(a) each of the strips shall be deemed to have been redeemed at the time of the exchange by the payment to that person of the amount equal to its market value; and

(b) that person shall be deemed to have acquired the security received in the exchange for the amount equal to the aggregate of the market values of the strips given in exchange for the security.

(4) References in this section to the market value of a security given or received in exchange for another are references to its market value at the time of the exchange.

(5) Without prejudice to the generality of any power conferred by section 202 below, the Treasury may by regulations make provision for the purposes of this section as to the manner of determining the market value at any time of any gilt-edged security (including any strip).

(6) Regulations under subsection (5) above may—

(a) make different provision for different cases; and

(b) contain such incidental, supplemental, consequential and transitional provision as the Treasury may think fit.

(7) In this section "strip" means anything which, within the meaning of section 47 of the Finance Act 1942, is a strip of a gilt-edged security.

GENERAL NOTE
The section provides specific rules for the treatment of the stripping or reconstitution of gilts if an authorised accruals method of accounting is to be used. Specific rules are not needed if a mark-to-market basis is used.
For further provisions regarding gilt strips see s.202 [Standing Committee E, March 5, 1996, col. 671].

Special rules for certain other gilts

96.—(1) This section applies as respects any loan relationship of a company if—
   (a) it is represented by a security of any of the following descriptions—
       (i) 3½% Funding Stock 1999–2004; or
       (ii) 5½% Treasury Stock 2008–2012;
   and
   (b) it is one to which the company is a party otherwise than in the course of activities that form an integral part of a trade carried on by the company.
(2) The amounts falling for any accounting period to be brought into account for the purposes of this Chapter in respect of a loan relationship to which this section applies shall be confined to amounts relating to interest.
(3) Only an authorised accruals basis of accounting shall be used for ascertaining those amounts.

GENERAL NOTE
In the case of the two specific low-coupon gilts listed, only amounts relating to interest are brought into charge, where they are held by a company for non-trading purposes.

Manufactured interest

97.—(1) This section applies where—
   (a) any amount ("manufactured interest") is payable by or on behalf of, or to, any company under any contract or arrangements relating to the transfer of an asset representing a loan relationship; and
   (b) that amount is, or (when paid) will fall to be treated as, representative of interest under that relationship ("the real interest").
(2) In relation to that company the manufactured interest shall be treated for the purposes of this Chapter—
   (a) as if it were interest under a loan relationship to which the company is a party; and
   (b) where that company is the company to which the manufactured interest is payable, as if that relationship were the one under which the real interest is payable.
(3) Any question whether debits or credits falling to be brought into account in the case of any company by virtue of this section—
   (a) are to be brought into account under section 82(2) above, or
   (b) are to be treated as non-trading debits or non-trading credits,
shall be determined according to the extent (if any) to which the manufactured interest is paid for the purposes of a trade carried on by the company or is received in the course of activities forming an integral part of such a trade.
(4) Where section 737A(5) of the Taxes Act 1988 (deemed manufactured payments) has effect in relation to a transaction relating to an asset representing a loan relationship so as, for the purposes of section 737 of, or Schedule 23A to, that Act, to deem there to have been a payment representative of interest under that relationship, this section shall apply as it would have applied if such a representative payment had in fact been made.
(5) This section does not apply where the manufactured interest is treated by virtue of paragraph 5(2)(c) or (4)(c) of Schedule 23A to the Taxes Act 1988 (manufactured interest passing through the market) as not being income of the person who receives it.

GENERAL NOTE
Amounts paid in place of real interest (manufactured interest) are treated as equivalent to real interest on loan relationships.

Collective investment schemes

98. The provisions of this Chapter have effect subject to the provisions of Schedule 10 to this Act (which makes special provision in relation to certain collective investment schemes).

GENERAL NOTE
This section introduces Sched. 10, which modifies the rules in this Chapter so far as they relate to certain collective investment schemes (see Financial Services Act 1986 (c. 60), s.75).
See further the General Note to Sched. 10.

Insurance companies

99. The preceding provisions of this Chapter have effect subject to Schedule 11 to this Act (which makes special provision in relation to certain insurance companies and in relation to corporate members of Lloyd's).

GENERAL NOTE
This section introduces Sched. 11, which adapts the loan relationship provisions for insurance companies, in particular those carrying on life assurance business.
See further the General Note to Sched. 11.

Miscellaneous other provisions

Interest on judgments, imputed interest, etc.

100.—(1) This Chapter shall have effect in accordance with subsection (2) below where—
 (a) interest on a money debt is payable to or by any company;
 (b) that debt is one as respects which it stands, or has stood, in the position of a creditor or debtor; and
 (c) that debt did not arise from a loan relationship.
(2) It shall be assumed for the purposes of this Chapter—
 (a) that the interest is interest payable under a loan relationship to which the company is a party; but
 (b) that the only credits or debits to be brought into account for those purposes in respect of that relationship are those relating to the interest.
(3) References in this section to interest payable on a money debt include references to any amount which, in pursuance of sections 770 to 772 of the Taxes Act 1988 (transactions at an undervalue or overvalue), as those sections have effect by virtue of section 773(4) of that Act, falls to be treated in pursuance of those sections as—
 (a) interest on a money debt; or
 (b) interest on an amount which is treated as a money debt.
(4) Any question whether debits or credits falling to be brought into account in accordance with this section in relation to any company—
 (a) are to be brought into account under section 82(2) above, or
 (b) are to be treated as non-trading debits or non-trading credits,
shall be determined according to the extent (if any) to which the interest in question is paid for the purposes of a trade carried on by the company or is received in the course of activities forming an integral part of such a trade, or (in the case of deemed interest) would be deemed to be so paid or received.

(5) This section has effect subject to the provisions of Schedules 9 and 11 to this Act.

GENERAL NOTE
Amounts previously taxed as interest continue to be so taxed even though they do not arise from an existing loan relationship. These include notional interest on deemed loan relationships with connected persons and interest on awards of compensation [Standing Committee E, March 5, 1996, col. 682].

Financial instruments

101.—(1) Chapter II of Part IV of the Finance Act 1994 (provisions relating to certain financial instruments) shall not apply to any profit or loss which, in accordance with that Chapter, accrues to a company for any accounting period on a qualifying contract by virtue of which the company is a party to any loan relationship if—
  (a) an amount representing that profit or loss, or
  (b) an amount representing the profit or loss accruing to that company on that contract,
is brought into account for that period for the purposes of this Chapter.
  (2) After section 147 of that Act (qualifying contracts) there shall be inserted the following section—

"Debt contracts and options to be qualifying contracts
  147A.—(1) For the purposes of this Chapter a debt contract or option is a qualifying contract as regards a qualifying company if the company becomes entitled to rights, or subject to duties, under the contract or option at any time on or after 1st April 1996.
  (2) For the purposes of this Chapter a qualifying company which is entitled to rights, or subject to duties, under a debt contract or option both immediately before and on 1st April 1996 shall be deemed to have become entitled or subject to those rights or duties on that date.
  (3) This section has effect subject to paragraph 25 of Schedule 15 to the Finance Act 1996 (transitional provisions)."
  (3) After section 150 of that Act (qualifying contracts) there shall be inserted the section set out in Schedule 12 to this Act (which defines debt contracts and options by reference to contracts and options conferring rights and duties to participate in loan relationships).
  (4) In section 151 of that Act (provisions that may be included in contracts and options), for the words "or a currency contract or option,", in each place where they occur, there shall be substituted "a currency contract or option or a debt contract or option".
  (5) In section 152(1) of that Act (disregard of provisions for relatively small payments in contracts and options), after "150" there shall be inserted "or 150A".
  (6) In section 153(1) of that Act (qualifying payments), for the word "and" at the end of paragraph (c) there shall be substituted—
    "(ca) in relation to a qualifying contract which is a debt contract, a payment falling within section 150A(5) or (6) above; and".

GENERAL NOTE
This section, together with Sched. 12, extends the rules in the FA 1994, ss.147–177 and Sched. 18 relating to the taxation of financial instruments used by companies for managing interest rate and currency risks.
  The new FA 1994, s.147A, ensures that debt contracts and options are treated as qualifying contracts for the FA 1994 provisions. It also provides transitional rules through Sched. 15, para. 25.
  For the definition of debt contracts and options, see Sched. 12 [Standing Committee E, March 5, 1996, col. 683].

Discounted securities: income tax provisions

102. Schedule 13 to this Act (which, in connection with the provisions of this Chapter relating to corporation tax, makes provision for income tax purposes about discounted securities) shall have effect.

<small>GENERAL NOTE</small>
This section introduces Sched. 13, which provides new rules for the taxation of profits and losses made by individuals on the transfer or redemption of securities which were issued at a discount.
See further the General Note to Sched. 13.

Supplemental

Interpretation of Chapter

103.—(1) In this Chapter—
"authorised accounting method", "authorised accruals basis of accounting" and "authorised mark to market basis of accounting" shall be construed in accordance with section 85 above;
"creditor relationship", in relation to a company, means any loan relationship of that company in the case of which it stands in the position of a creditor as respects the debt in question;
"debt" includes a debt the amount of which falls to be ascertained by reference to matters which vary from time to time;
"debtor relationship", in relation to a company, means any loan relationship of that company in the case of which it stands in the position of a debtor as respects the debt in question;
"gilt-edged securities" means any securities which—
　　(a) are gilt-edged securities for the purposes of the Taxation of Chargeable Gains Act 1992; or
　　(b) will be such securities on the making of any order under paragraph 1 of Schedule 9 to that Act the making of which is anticipated in the prospectus under which they are issued;
"an independent person" means a knowledgeable and willing party dealing at arm's length;
"international organisation" means an organisation of which two or more sovereign powers, or the governments of two or more sovereign powers, are members;
"loan" includes any advance of money, and cognate expressions shall be construed accordingly;
"money" shall be construed in accordance with section 81(6) above and subsection (5) below;
"money debt" shall be construed in accordance with section 81(2) above;
"non-trading credit" and "non-trading debit" shall be construed in accordance with section 82(3) above;
"retail prices index" has the same meaning as it has, by virtue of section 833(2) of the Taxes Act 1988, in the Income Tax Acts;
"share", in relation to a company, means any share in the company under which an entitlement to receive distributions may arise.
(2) For the purposes of this Chapter a company shall be taken to be a party to a creditor relationship for the purposes of a trade carried on by that company only if it is a party to that relationship in the course of activities forming an integral part of that trade.
(3) For the purposes of this Chapter, and of so much of any other enactment as contains provision by reference to which amounts fall to be brought into account for the purposes of this Chapter, activities carried on by a company in the course of—
　　(a) any mutual trading, or

(b) any mutual insurance or other mutual business which is not life assurance business (within the meaning of Chapter I of Part XII of the Taxes Act 1988),

shall be deemed not to constitute the whole or any part of a trade.

(4) If, in any proceedings, any question arises whether a person is an international organisation for the purposes of any provision of this Chapter, a certificate issued by or under the authority of the Secretary of State stating any fact relevant to that question shall be conclusive evidence of that fact.

(5) For the purposes of this Chapter the European currency unit (as for the time being defined in Council Regulation No. 3180/78/EEC or in any Community instrument replacing it) shall be taken to be a currency other than sterling.

GENERAL NOTE
    This section provides definitions for, and other aids to interpretation of, the loan relationships legislation.

Subs. (2)
    Companies are to be regarded as party to a creditor relationship for the purposes of their trade only in the course of activities forming an integral part of it.

Subs. (3)
    Mutual trading and mutual insurance are not to be treated as trading for this purpose.

Minor and consequential amendments

104. Schedule 14 to this Act (which, for the purposes of both corporation tax and income tax, makes certain minor and consequential amendments in connection with the provisions of this Chapter) shall have effect.

GENERAL NOTE
    The section introduces Sched. 14, which makes minor and consequential amendments to other legislation.
    See further the General Note to Sched. 14.

Commencement and transitional provisions

105.—(1) Subject to Schedule 15 to this Act, this Chapter has effect—
    (a) for the purposes of corporation tax, in relation to accounting periods ending after 31st March 1996; and
    (b) so far as it makes provision for the purposes of income tax, in relation to the year 1996–97 and subsequent years of assessment.

(2) Schedule 15 to this Act (which contains transitional provisions and savings in connection with the coming into force of this Chapter) shall have effect.

GENERAL NOTE
    The loan relationship provisions have effect for corporation tax for accounting periods ending after March 31, 1996 and for income tax from 1996–97 onwards.
    Transitional provisions are contained in Sched. 15. See further the General Note to that Schedule.

CHAPTER III

PROVISIONS RELATING TO THE SCHEDULE E CHARGE

Living accommodation provided for employees

106.—(1) In subsection (1) of section 145 of the Taxes Act 1988 (living accommodation provided for employees), the words "and is not otherwise made the subject of any charge to him by way of income tax" shall be omitted.

(2) After section 146 of that Act there shall be inserted the following section—

"Priority of rules applying to living accommodation

146A.—(1) This section applies where, within the meaning of section 145, living accommodation is provided in any period for any person by reason of his employment.

(2) The question whether the employee is to be treated under section 145 or 146 as in receipt of emoluments in respect of the provision of the accommodation shall be determined before any other question whether there is an amount falling to be treated in respect of the provision of that accommodation as emoluments.

(3) Tax under Schedule E in respect of the provision of the accommodation shall be chargeable on the employee otherwise than in pursuance of sections 145 and 146 to the extent only that the amount on which it is chargeable by virtue of those sections is exceeded by the amount on which it would be chargeable apart from those sections."

(3) This section applies for the year 1996–97 and subsequent years of assessment.

General Note

This section is introduced to counter a scheme known as a reverse *Heaton v. Bell* ((1969) 46 T.C. 211), under which an employee forgoes a certain amount of salary in return for accommodation, which is less than the value of the accommodation for tax purposes. The lesser amount may be chargeable under s.19 rather than the greater amount under ss.145 and 146.

The new s.146A provides that ss.145 and 146 take priority with respect to charges on living accommodation [Standing Committee E, February 15, 1996, col. 307].

Beneficial loans

107.—(1) For section 160(1B) of the Taxes Act 1988 (aggregation of loans) there shall be substituted the following subsections—

"(1B) Where, in relation to any year—
  (a) there are loans between the same lender and borrower which are aggregable with each other,
  (b) the lender elects, by notice given to the inspector, for aggregation to apply in the case of that borrower, and
  (c) that notice is given before the end of the period of 92 days after the end of that year,
all the loans between that lender and that borrower which are aggregable with each other shall be treated for the purposes of subsections (1) and (1A) above and Part II of Schedule 7 as a single loan.

(1BA) For the purposes of subsection (1B) above loans are aggregable with each other for any year where—
  (a) in the case of each of the loans, there is a time in that year, while the loan is outstanding as to any amount, when the lender is a close company and the borrower a director of that company;
  (b) the benefit of each of the loans is obtained by reason of the borrower's employment;
  (c) in the case of each of the loans, there is no time in that year when a rate of interest is applied to the loan which is equal to or more than whatever is the official rate at that time;
  (d) the loans are loans made in the same currency; and
  (e) none of the loans is a qualifying loan."

(2) In paragraph 5 of Schedule 7 to that Act (alternative method of calculation)—
  (a) in sub-paragraph (1)(a), for the words from "for the purpose" to "appeal)" there shall be substituted "at a time allowed by sub-paragraph (2) below"; and
  (b) in sub-paragraph (1)(b), for "within the time allowed by sub-paragraph (2) below" there shall be substituted "at such a time".

(3) For sub-paragraph (2) of that paragraph there shall be substituted the following sub-paragraph—

"(2) A notice containing a requirement or election for the purposes of sub-paragraph (1) above is allowed to be given at any time before the end of the period of 12 months beginning with the 31st January next following the relevant year."

(4) This section has effect for the year 1996–97 and subsequent years of assessment and applies to loans whenever made.

GENERAL NOTE
This section eases the rules governing the calculation of the value of the benefit from cheap or interest-free loans to employees. The requirement for aggregation of relevant loans is ended, so that there will now be separate reporting of individual loans. Special rules, allowing aggregated reporting to continue, apply with respect to directors of close companies. The rules on the time limit for election for the daily method of calculation are changed to fit with the general self-assessment time limits [Standing Committee E, February 15, 1996, col. 309].

Incidental benefits for holders of certain offices etc.

108.—(1) After section 200 of the Taxes Act 1988 (expenses of Members of Parliament) there shall be inserted the following section—

"Incidental benefits for holders of certain offices etc.

200AA.—(1) A person holding any of the offices mentioned in sub-section (2) below shall not be charged to tax under Schedule E in respect of—

(a) any transport or subsistence provided or made available by or on behalf of the Crown to the office-holder or any member of his family or household; or

(b) the payment or reimbursement by or on behalf of the Crown of any expenses incurred in connection with the provision of transport or subsistence to the office-holder or any member of his family or household.

(2) Those offices are—

(a) any office in Her Majesty's Government in the United Kingdom, and

(b) any other office which is one of the offices and positions in respect of which salaries are payable under section 1 of the Ministerial and other Salaries Act 1975 (whether or not the person holding it is a person to whom a salary is paid or payable under the Act).

(3) Nothing in this section shall prevent a person from being chargeable to tax under Schedule E in respect of the benefit of a mobile telephone (within the meaning of section 159A).

(4) References in this section to a member of the family or household of an office-holder shall be construed in accordance with section 168(4).

(5) References in this section to the provision of transport to any person include references to the following—

(a) the provision or making available to that person of any car (whether with or without a driver);

(b) the provision of any fuel for a car provided or made available to that person;

(c) the provision of any other benefit in connection with a car provided or made available to that person.

(6) In this section—

'car' means any mechanically propelled road vehicle; and

'subsistence' includes food and drink and temporary living accommodation."

(2) This section has effect for the year 1996–97 and subsequent years of assessment.

GENERAL NOTE
This section, introduced at report stage, ensures that ministers and their families are protected from a tax charge on the use of their official cars and incidental living expenses. The Inland Revenue had been advised that the existing legislation did not cover this [*Hansard*, H.C. Vol. 274, col. 1067].

Charitable donations: payroll deduction schemes

109.—(1) In section 202(7) of the Taxes Act 1988 (which limits to £900 the deductions attracting relief), for "£900" there shall be substituted "£1,200".

(2) This section has effect for the year 1996–97 and subsequent years of assessment.

GENERAL NOTE
The annual limit on donations to charity qualifying for relief under the payroll giving scheme is increased from £900 to £1,200 [Standing Committee E, February 15, 1996, col. 311].

PAYE settlement agreements

110. After section 206 of the Taxes Act 1988 there shall be inserted the following section—

"PAYE settlement agreements

206A.—(1) PAYE regulations may make provision falling within subsection (2) below about the sums which, as sums in respect of income tax under Schedule E on emoluments of a person's employees, are to be the sums for which the employer is to be accountable to the Board from time to time.

(2) That provision is provision under which the accountability of the employer, and the sums for which he is to be accountable, are to be determined, to such extent as may be prescribed, in accordance with an agreement between the Board and the employer ('a PAYE settlement agreement'), instead of under PAYE regulations made otherwise than by virtue of this section.

(3) PAYE regulations may provide for a PAYE settlement agreement to allow sums for which an employer is to be accountable to the Board in accordance with the agreement—

(a) to be computed, in cases where there are two or more persons holding employments to which the agreement relates, by reference to a number of those persons all taken together;

(b) to include sums representing income tax on an estimated amount taken, in accordance with the agreement, to be the aggregate of the cash equivalents and other amounts chargeable to tax in respect of—

(i) taxable benefits provided or made available by reason of the employments to which the agreement relates; and

(ii) expenses paid to the persons holding those employments;

and

(c) to be computed in a manner under which the sums for which the employer is accountable do not necessarily represent an amount of income tax payable in respect of income which (apart from the regulations) is assessable under Schedule E on persons holding employments to which the agreement relates.

(4) PAYE regulations may provide—

(a) for an employer who is accountable to the Board under a PAYE settlement agreement for any sum to be so accountable without that sum, or any other sum, being treated for any prescribed purpose as tax deducted from emoluments;

(b) for an employee to have no right to be treated as having paid tax in respect of sums for which his employer is accountable under such an agreement;

(c) for an employee to be treated, except—

(i) for the purposes of the obligations imposed on his employer by such an agreement, and

(ii) to such further extent as may be prescribed,

as relieved from any prescribed obligations of his under the Income Tax Acts in respect of emoluments from an employment to which the agreement relates; and

(d) for such emoluments to be treated as excluded from the employee's income for such further purposes of the Income Tax Acts, and to such extent, as may be prescribed.

(5) For the purposes of any PAYE regulations made by virtue of this section it shall be immaterial that any agreement to which they relate was entered into before the coming into force of the regulations.

(6) PAYE regulations made by virtue of this section may—

(a) make different provision for different cases; and

(b) contain such incidental, supplemental, consequential and transitional provision as the Board may think fit.

(7) Without prejudice to the generality of subsection (6) above, the transitional provision that may be made by virtue of that subsection includes transitional provision for any year of assessment which—

(a) for the purposes of the regulations, treats sums accounted for in that year before the coming into force of the regulations as accounted for in accordance with an agreement as respects which the regulations have effect after they come into force; and

(b) provides, by reference to any provision made by virtue of paragraph (a) above, for income arising in that year before the coming into force of the regulations to be treated as income in relation to which modifications of the Income Tax Acts contained in the regulations apply.

(8) Without prejudice to the generality of subsection (6) above, any power of the Board to make PAYE regulations with respect to sums falling to be accounted for under such regulations shall include power to make the corresponding provision with respect to sums falling, by virtue of this section, to be accounted for in accordance with a PAYE settlement agreement.

(9) In this section—

'employment' means any office or employment the emoluments from which are (or, apart from any regulations made by virtue of this section, would be) assessable to tax under Schedule E, and cognate expressions shall be construed accordingly;

'PAYE regulations' means regulations under section 203;

'prescribed' means prescribed by PAYE regulations;

'taxable benefit', in relation to an employee, means any benefit provided or made available, otherwise than in the form of a payment of money, to the employee or to a person who is, for the purposes of Chapter II of this Part, a member of his family or household;

and references in this section to a time before the coming into force of any regulations include references to a time before the commencement of section 110 of the Finance Act 1996 (by virtue of which this section was inserted in this Act)."

GENERAL NOTE

This section provides the authority for the introduction of regulations covering PAYE settlement agreements. The intention is to provide a statutory framework for arrangements—currently known as "annual voluntary settlements"—under which employers may meet their employees' tax liabilities on a range of minor benefits in kind or expenses payments, *e.g.* staff functions, relocation costs exceeding the £8,000 limit and reimbursement of telephone expenses.

The new s.206A sets out the main characteristics of a PAYE settlement agreement and provides for regulations to ensure that the tax liability on any item included in such an agreement will be the employer's and not the employee's [Standing Committee E, February 15, 1996, col. 316].

CHAPTER IV

SHARE OPTIONS, PROFIT SHARING AND EMPLOYEE SHARE OWNERSHIP

Share options

Amount or value of consideration for option

111.—(1) Section 149A of the Taxation of Chargeable Gains Act 1992 (consideration for grant of option under approved share option schemes not to be deemed to be equal to market value of option) shall be amended as follows.

(2) In subsection (1)(b) (restriction to approved share option schemes) for "as mentioned in section 185(1) of the Taxes Act (approved share option schemes)" there shall be substituted "by an individual by reason of his office or employment as a director or employee of that or any other body corporate".

(3) In subsection (2) (grantor to be treated as if the amount or value of the consideration was its actual amount or value) for "The grantor of the option" there shall be substituted "Both the grantor of the option and the person to whom the option is granted".

(4) Subsection (4) (section not to affect treatment under that Act of person to whom option granted) shall cease to have effect.

(5) For the side-note to that section there shall be substituted "Share option schemes."

(6) This section has effect in relation to any right to acquire shares in a body corporate obtained on or after 28th November 1995 by an individual by reason of his office or employment as a director or employee of a body corporate.

GENERAL NOTE

The purpose of this section is to align the treatment of unapproved share options with that of approved share options as regards their treatment for capital gains tax purposes on their grant. For unapproved as well as approved schemes the TCGA 1992, s.149A, will treat the consideration for the option as the amount actually paid rather than the market value [Standing Committee E, February 15, 1996, col. 321].

Release and replacement

112.—(1) After section 237 of the Taxation of Chargeable Gains Act 1992 there shall be inserted—

"Share option schemes: release and replacement of options

237A.—(1) This section applies in any case where a right to acquire shares in a body corporate ("the old right") which was obtained by an individual by reason of his office or employment as a director or employee of that or any other body corporate is released in whole or in part for a consideration which consists of or includes the grant to that individual of another right ("the new right") to acquire shares in that or any other body corporate.

(2) As respects the person to whom the new right is granted—
  (a) without prejudice to subsection (1) above, the new right shall not be regarded for the purposes of capital gains tax as consideration for the release of the old right;

(b) the amount or value of the consideration given by him or on his behalf for the acquisition of the new right shall be taken for the purposes of section 38(1) to be the amount or value of the consideration given by him or on his behalf for the old right; and

(c) any consideration paid for the acquisition of the new right shall be taken to be expenditure falling within section 38(1)(b).

(3) As respects the grantor of the new right, in determining for the purposes of this Act the amount or value of the consideration received for the new right, the release of the old right shall be disregarded."

(2) Section 238(4) of that Act (which provides that the release of an option under an approved share option scheme in exchange for another option, in connection with a company take-over, is not to involve a disposal, and which is superseded by subsection (1) above) shall cease to have effect.

(3) This section has effect in relation to transactions effected on or after 28th November 1995.

GENERAL NOTE

The new TCGA s.237A provides that where an employee gives up an option in exchange for a replacement option there is no charge to capital gains tax. Any gain (or loss) will be brought into account when the new option is disposed of, or when shares obtained by exercising the option are sold [Standing Committee E, February 15, 1996, col. 331].

Savings-related share option schemes

Exercise of rights by employees of non-participating companies

113.—(1) In paragraph 21 of Schedule 9 to the Taxes Act 1988 (provisions which an approved savings-related share option scheme may make with respect to the exercise of rights under the scheme) in sub-paragraph (1), the word "and" immediately preceding paragraph (e) shall be omitted and after that paragraph there shall be inserted "and

(f) if, at the bonus date, a person who has obtained rights under the scheme holds an office or employment in a company which is not a participating company but which is—

(i) an associated company of the grantor, or

(ii) a company of which the grantor has control,

those rights may be exercised within six months of that date."

(2) After sub-paragraph (3) of that paragraph there shall be inserted—

"(4) Where a scheme approved before the date of the passing of the Finance Act 1996 is altered before 5th May 1998 so as to include such a provision as is specified in sub-paragraph (1)(f) above, the scheme may apply the provision to rights obtained under the scheme before the alteration takes effect, whether the bonus date in relation to the rights occurred before or after the passing of that Act; and where the provision is applied to such rights by virtue of this sub-paragraph, its application to such rights shall not itself be regarded as the acquisition of a right for the purposes of this Schedule.

This sub-paragraph has effect subject to paragraph 4 above."

(3) In paragraph 26(3) of that Schedule (only directors or employees of grantor or participating company to be eligible to participate, except as provided by paragraph 19 or pursuant to such a provision as is referred to in paragraph 21(1)(e)) after "21(1)(e)" there shall be inserted "or (f)".

GENERAL NOTE

This section enables employees participating in Save-As-You-Earn share option schemes to exercise their options, notwithstanding that at that time they are working for a company which is not participating in the scheme, provided the company is associated with or controlled by the company which set up the scheme [Standing Committee E, February 15, 1996, col. 332].

Other share option schemes

Requirements to be satisfied by approved schemes

114.—(1) Part IV of Schedule 9 to the Taxes Act 1988 (requirements applicable to approved share option schemes which are not savings-related) shall be amended in accordance with subsections (2) and (3) below.

(2) In paragraph 28 (scheme must impose limit on aggregate market value of shares which may be acquired in pursuance of rights obtained under the scheme or certain related schemes)—

    (a) in sub-paragraph (1) (aggregate market value of shares not to exceed the appropriate limit) for "the appropriate limit" there shall be substituted "£30,000"; and

    (b) sub-paragraphs (2) and (4) (meaning of the appropriate limit and, for the purposes of that definition, the relevant emoluments) shall cease to have effect.

(3) In paragraph 29 (price at which shares may be acquired to be stated and to be not manifestly less than the market value, or, in certain circumstances, 85 per cent. of the market value, of shares of the same class) for sub-paragraphs (1) to (6) there shall be substituted—

    "(1) The price at which scheme shares may be acquired by the exercise of a right obtained under the scheme—

    (a) must be stated at the time the right is obtained, and

    (b) must not be manifestly less than the market value of shares of the same class at that time or, if the Board and the grantor agree in writing, at such earlier time or times as may be provided in the agreement."

(4) Section 185 of the Taxes Act 1988 (approved share option schemes) shall be amended in accordance with subsections (5) to (7) below.

(5) In subsection (2), for "Subject to subsections (6) to (6B) below" there shall be substituted "Subject to subsection (6) below".

(6) For subsections (6) to (6B) there shall be substituted—

    "(6) Where, in the case of a right obtained by a person under a scheme which is not a savings-related share option scheme, the aggregate of—

    (a) the amount or value of any consideration given by him for obtaining the right, and

    (b) the price at which he may acquire the shares by exercising the right,

is less than the market value, at the time he obtains the right, of the same quantity of issued shares of the same class, he shall be chargeable to tax under Schedule E for the year of assessment in which he obtains the right on the amount of the difference; and the amount so chargeable shall be treated as earned income, whether or not it would otherwise fall to be so treated."

(7) In subsections (7) and (8) for "(6A)" there shall be substituted "(6)".

(8) In section 120 of the Taxation of Chargeable Gains Act 1992 (increase in expenditure by reference to tax charged in relation to shares etc) in subsection (6) (which defines the applicable provision) for paragraph (b) (which refers to subsection (6A) of section 185 of the Taxes Act 1988) there shall be substituted—

    "(b) subsection (6A) of that section (as that subsection has effect in relation to rights obtained before the day on which the Finance Act 1996 was passed), or

    (c) subsection (6) of that section (as that subsection has effect in relation to rights obtained on or after that day)."

(9) Schedule 16 to this Act, which makes provision with respect to share option schemes approved before the day on which this Act is passed, shall have effect.

(10) Subsections (3) to (7) above have effect in relation to rights obtained on or after the day on which this Act is passed.

GENERAL NOTE
This section, together with Sched. 16 and s.115, provides for the replacement of the executive share option scheme with a new relief for company share option plans. The main changes are a limit of £30,000 on the value of shares under option which may be held by an employee at any one time, measured by their value at the time the option was granted, and a condition that the options must not be granted at a discount.

The section was introduced as the result of public indignation with generous options granted to directors of recently privatised utilities [*Hansard*, H.C. Vol. 270, col. 191].

Transitional provisions

115.—(1) If, during the period—
(a) beginning with 17th July 1995, and
(b) ending with the day preceding the passing of this Act,
any rights have been obtained by a person under an approved share option scheme in circumstances falling within subsection (2) below, the rights shall be treated for the purposes of sections 185 to 187 of, and Schedule 9 to, the Taxes Act 1988 as being rights obtained otherwise than in accordance with the provisions of an approved share option scheme.

(2) The circumstances mentioned in subsection (1) above are circumstances such that, on the assumptions in subsection (3) below, there would, by virtue of paragraph 28 or 29 of Schedule 9 to the Taxes Act 1988 (limit on what may be obtained and requirements with respect to price), have been, with respect to the operation of the scheme, a contravention of any of the relevant requirements or of the scheme itself.

(3) The assumptions mentioned in subsection (2) above are—
(a) that the amendments made by subsection (2) of section 114 above had effect at all times on and after 17th July 1995;
(b) that the amendments made by subsections (3) to (7) of that section had effect in relation to rights obtained at any time on or after that date; and
(c) that the provisions of paragraphs 1(1) and 2 to 5 of Schedule 16 to this Act had effect at all times on and after 17th July 1995, but with the substitution for references to the day on which this Act is passed of references to that date.

(4) For the purposes of this section, rights obtained by a person on or after 17th July 1995 shall be treated as having been obtained by him before that date if—
(a) the scheme in question is one approved before that date;
(b) an offer of the rights or an invitation to apply for them was made in writing to that person before that date; and
(c) he obtained the rights within the period of thirty days beginning with the day on which the offer or invitation was made.

(5) In this section—
"approved share option scheme" means an approved share option scheme, within the meaning of section 185 of the Taxes Act 1988, other than a savings-related share option scheme;
"relevant requirements" has the meaning given in paragraph 1(1) of Schedule 9 to the Taxes Act 1988;
"savings-related share option scheme" has the meaning given by Schedule 9 to the Taxes Act 1988.

GENERAL NOTE
The previous relief, for executive share options will apply to those granted before July 17, 1995, when the proposed change in the law was announced. Options granted between that date and Royal Assent will qualify under the new scheme, provided they do not breach £30,000 and were not granted at a discount [Standing Committee E, February 15, 1996, col. 346].

Profit sharing schemes

The release date

116.—(1) In section 187(2) of the Taxes Act 1988 (interpretation of sections 185 and 186 of, and Schedules 9 and 10 to, that Act) in the definition of "release date" (the fifth anniversary of the date on which shares were appropriated to a participant in a profit sharing scheme) for "fifth" there shall be substituted "third".

(2) The amendment made by subsection (1) above shall have effect in relation to shares of a participant in a profit sharing scheme if the third anniversary of the appropriation of the shares to the participant occurs on or after the day on which this Act is passed.

(3) If the third anniversary of the appropriation of any shares to a participant in a profit sharing scheme has occurred, but the fifth anniversary of their appropriation to him has not occurred, before the passing of this Act, then, in the application of sections 186 and 187 of, and Schedules 9 and 10 to, the Taxes Act 1988 in relation to those shares, the release date shall be the day on which this Act is passed.

GENERAL NOTE

Together with the next two sections, this reduces from five to three years the period during which shares in an approved profit-sharing scheme must be held in trust if an employee is to receive them tax free. This section amends the definition of "release date" [Standing Committee E, February 15, 1996, col. 347].

The appropriate percentage

117.—(1) In Schedule 10 to the Taxes Act 1988 (further provisions relating to profit sharing schemes) for paragraph 3 (the appropriate percentage) there shall be substituted—

"3.—(1) For the purposes of any of the relevant provisions charging an individual to income tax under Schedule E by reason of the occurrence of an event relating to any of his shares, the "appropriate percentage" in relation to those shares is 100 per cent., unless sub-paragraph (2) below applies.

(2) Where the individual—

(a) ceases to be a director or employee of the grantor or, in the case of a group scheme, a participating company as mentioned in paragraph 2(a) above, or

(b) reaches the relevant age,

before the event occurs, the "appropriate percentage" is 50 per cent., unless paragraph 6(4) below applies."

(2) In section 187(8) of that Act (determination of certain values and percentages where shares are appropriated to a participant at different times) paragraph (b) (which relates to the appropriate percentage), and the word "and" immediately preceding it, shall cease to have effect.

(3) Subsections (1) and (2) above have effect in relation to the occurrence, on or after the day on which this Act is passed, of events by reason of whose occurrence any provision of section 186 or 187 of, or Schedule 9 or 10 to, the Taxes Act 1988 charges an individual to income tax under Schedule E.

GENERAL NOTE

The provisions relating to the "appropriate percentage" of charge to income tax where shares are withdrawn prematurely from a profit-sharing trust are amended. In future the appropriate percentage will be either 100 per cent, or 50 per cent in certain special circumstances.

The appropriate allowance

118.—(1) In section 186(12) of the Taxes Act 1988 (determination of the appropriate allowance for the purposes of the charge to tax on capital receipts by a participant in an approved profit sharing scheme)—

(a) for "£100" there shall be substituted "£60"; and
(b) for "five years" there shall be substituted "three years".
(2) Subsection (1) above has effect for the year 1997–98 and subsequent years of assessment.

GENERAL NOTE
　The "appropriate allowance" available to set against the tax charge under s.117 is reduced from £100 to £60.

Employee share ownership trusts

Removal of requirement for at least one year's service

119.—(1) In Schedule 5 to the Finance Act 1989 (employee share ownership trusts) in paragraph 4(5)(a) (for a trust to be a qualifying ESOT, its beneficiaries must have been employees or directors of the company for at least one year) the words "not less than one year and" shall cease to have effect.
　(2) This section applies to trusts established on or after the day on which this Act is passed.

GENERAL NOTE
　The requirement of at least one year's service before an employee can join an ESOT (employee share ownership trust) is removed [Standing Committee E, February 15, 1996, col. 353].

Grant and exercise of share options

120.—(1) In Schedule 5 to the Finance Act 1989 (employee share ownership trusts), in paragraph 4 (the trust deed must contain provision as to the beneficiaries) after sub-paragraph (2) there shall be inserted—
　　"(2A) The trust deed may provide that a person is a beneficiary at a given time if at that time he is eligible to participate in a savings-related share option scheme within the meaning of Schedule 9 to the Taxes Act 1988—
　　　(a) which was established by a company within the founding company's group, and
　　　(b) which is approved under that Schedule.
　　(2B) Where a trust deed contains a rule conforming with sub-paragraph (2A) above it must provide that the only powers and duties which the trustees may exercise in relation to persons who are beneficiaries by virtue only of that rule are those which may be exercised in accordance with the provisions of a scheme such as is mentioned in that sub-paragraph."
　(2) In consequence of the amendment made by subsection (1) above, section 69 of, and Schedule 5 to, the Finance Act 1989 (which respectively make provision about chargeable events in relation to the trustees of qualifying employee share ownership trusts and the requirements to be satisfied by such trusts) shall be amended in accordance with the following provisions of this section.
　(3) In subsection (4) of that section (meaning of "qualifying terms" for the purposes of the provision that the transfer of securities to beneficiaries is a chargeable event if it is not on qualifying terms)—
　　(a) in paragraph (a) (securities which are transferred at the same time must be transferred on similar terms) after "time" there shall be inserted "other than those transferred on a transfer such as is mentioned in subsection (4ZA) below";

(b) in paragraph (b) (securities must have been offered to all the persons who are beneficiaries), after "trust deed" there shall be inserted "by virtue of a rule which conforms with paragraph 4(2), (3) or (4) of Schedule 5 to this Act"; and

(c) in paragraph (c) (securities must be transferred to all such beneficiaries who have accepted the offer) for "beneficiaries" there shall be substituted "persons".

(4) After subsection (4) of that section there shall be inserted—

"(4ZA) For the purposes of subsection (1)(b) above a transfer of securities is also made on qualifying terms if—

(a) it is made to a person exercising a right to acquire shares, and

(b) that right was obtained in accordance with the provisions of a savings-related share option scheme within the meaning of Schedule 9 to the Taxes Act 1988—

(i) which was established by, or by a company controlled by, the company which established the trust, and

(ii) which is approved under that Schedule, and

(c) that right is being exercised in accordance with the provisions of that scheme, and

(d) the consideration for the transfer is payable to the trustees."

(5) In sub-paragraph (4) of paragraph 4 of that Schedule (trust deed may provide for charity to be beneficiary if there are no beneficiaries falling within a rule conforming with sub-paragraph (2) or (3)) after "sub-paragraph (2)" there shall be inserted ", (2A)".

(6) In sub-paragraph (7) of that paragraph (trust deed must not provide for a person to be a beneficiary unless he falls within a rule conforming with sub-paragraph (2), (3) or (4)) after "sub-paragraph (2)" there shall be inserted ", (2A)".

(7) In sub-paragraph (8) of that paragraph (trust deed must provide that person with material interest in founding company cannot be a beneficiary) after "at a particular time (the relevant time)" there shall be inserted "by virtue of a rule which conforms with sub-paragraph (2), (3) or (4) above".

(8) In paragraph 5(2) of that Schedule (trust deed must be so expressed that it is apparent that the general functions of the trustees are as mentioned in paragraphs (a) to (e)) after paragraph (c) there shall be inserted—

"(cc) to grant rights to acquire shares to persons who are beneficiaries under the terms of the trust deed;".

(9) In paragraph 9 of that Schedule (trust deed must provide that transfers of securities to beneficiaries must be on qualifying terms and within the qualifying period) in sub-paragraph (2) (meaning of qualifying terms)—

(a) in paragraph (a) (securities which are transferred at the same time must be transferred on similar terms) after "time" there shall be inserted "other than those transferred on a transfer such as is mentioned in sub-paragraph (2ZA) below";

(b) in paragraph (b) (securities must have been offered to all the persons who are beneficiaries) after "trust deed" there shall be inserted "by virtue of a rule which conforms with paragraph 4(2), (3) or (4) above"; and

(c) in paragraph (c) (securities must be transferred to all such beneficiaries who have accepted the offer) for "beneficiaries" there shall be substituted "persons".

(10) After sub-paragraph (2) of that paragraph there shall be inserted—

"(2ZA) For the purposes of sub-paragraph (1) above a transfer of securities is also made on qualifying terms if—

(a) it is made to a person exercising a right to acquire shares, and

(b) that right was obtained in accordance with the provisions of a savings-related share option scheme within the meaning of Schedule 9 to the Taxes Act 1988—

(i) which was established by, or by a company controlled by, the founding company, and

(ii) which is approved under that Schedule, and

(c) that right is being exercised in accordance with the provisions of that scheme, and

(d) the consideration for the transfer is payable to the trustees."

(11) In paragraph 10 of that Schedule (trust deed must not contain features not essential or reasonably incidental to purposes mentioned in that paragraph)—

(a) after "acquiring sums and securities," there shall be inserted "granting rights to acquire shares to persons who are eligible to participate in savings-related share option schemes approved under Schedule 9 to the Taxes Act 1988, transferring shares to such persons,"; and

(b) for "Schedule 9 to the Taxes Act 1988" there shall be substituted "that Schedule".

(12) This section has effect in relation to trusts established on or after the day on which this Act is passed.

GENERAL NOTE

The purpose of this section is to make it possible for an ESOT to operate in conjunction with a savings-related share option scheme. Existing legislation enables an ESOT to be used in conjunction with an approved profit-sharing scheme. The amendments to the FA 1989 make the following principal changes:

(i) they allow persons who are eligible to participate in a savings-related share option scheme to be beneficiaries of an ESOT;

(ii) they enable the trustees of an ESOT to grant options under savings-related share option schemes, and to transfer shares to option holders when options are exercised;

(iii) they ensure that there will be no tax charge when the trustees of an ESOT transfer shares to option holders when the options are exercised.

Provision is also made to cover the situation where some employees who are eligible to participate in the option scheme may not also be beneficiaries of the ESOT. There will be, in effect, two potentially overlapping classes of ESOT beneficiary: participants in the option scheme and beneficiaries of the ESOT itself. The participants in the option scheme would be entitled to receive shares only in terms of the scheme. The beneficiaries of the ESOT would be entitled to receive any shares (or cash) acquired and held by the ESOT trustees.

CHAPTER V

SELF ASSESSMENT, GENERAL MANAGEMENT ETC.

General

Returns and self assessment

121.—(1) In subsection (1) of section 8 of the Taxes Management Act 1970 (personal return), and in subsection (1) of section 8A of that Act (trustee's return), after the words "year of assessment," there shall be inserted the words "and the amount payable by him by way of income tax for that year,".

(2) In subsection (1A) of each of those sections, the words from "and the amounts referred to" to the end shall cease to have effect.

(3) After that subsection of each of those sections there shall be inserted the following subsection—

"(1AA) For the purposes of subsection (1) above—

(a) the amounts in which a person is chargeable to income tax and capital gains tax are net amounts, that is to say, amounts which take into account any relief or allowance a claim for which is included in the return; and

(b) the amount payable by a person by way of income tax is the difference between the amount in which he is chargeable to income tax and the aggregate amount of any income tax deducted at source and any tax credits to which section 231 of the principal Act applies."

(4) For subsection (1) of section 9 of that Act (returns to include self-assessment) there shall be substituted the following subsection—

"(1) Subject to subsection (2) below, every return under section 8 or 8A of this Act shall include a self-assessment, that is to say—

(a) an assessment of the amounts in which, on the basis of the information contained in the return and taking into account any relief or allowance a claim for which is included in the return, the person making the return is chargeable to income tax and capital gains tax for the year of assessment; and

(b) an assessment of the amount payable by him by way of income tax, that is to say, the difference between the amount in which he is assessed to income tax under paragraph (a) above and the aggregate amount of any income tax deducted at source and any tax credits to which section 231 of the principal Act applies."

(5) In subsection (1)(b) of section 11AA of that Act (return of profits to include self-assessment), for the words ", allowance or repayment of tax" there shall be substituted the words "or allowance".

(6) In subsection (1)(a) of section 12AA of that Act (partnership return), after the words "so chargeable" there shall be inserted the words "and the amount payable by way of income tax by each such partner".

(7) For subsection (1A) of that section there shall be substituted the following subsection—

"(1A) For the purposes of subsection (1) above—

(a) the amount in which a partner is chargeable to income tax or corporation tax is a net amount, that is to say, an amount which takes into account any relief or allowance for which a claim is made; and

(b) the amount payable by a partner by way of income tax is the difference between the amount in which he is chargeable to income tax and the aggregate amount of any income tax deducted at source and any tax credits to which section 231 of the principal Act applies."

(8) This section and sections 122, 123, 125 to 127 and 141 below—

(a) so far as they relate to income tax and capital gains tax, have effect as respects the year 1996–97 and subsequent years of assessment, and

(b) so far as they relate to corporation tax, have effect as respects accounting periods ending on or after the appointed day for the purposes of Chapter III of Part IV of the Finance Act 1994.

GENERAL NOTE

This section makes changes to the provisions relating to returns, self-assessments and partnership statements to define what constitutes the self-assessment return and the components of the self-assessment and partnership statement [*Hansard*, H.C. Vol. 270, col. 506].

Notional tax deductions and payments

122.—(1) At the end of subsection (1) of section 9 of the Taxes Management Act 1970 (as substituted by section 121(4) above) there shall be inserted the words "but nothing in this subsection shall enable a self-assessment to show as repayable any income tax treated as deducted or paid by virtue of section 233(1), 246D(1), 249(4), 421(1), 547(5) or 599A(5) of the principal Act."

(2) At the end of subsection (1) of section 59B of that Act (payment of income tax and capital gains tax) there shall be inserted the words "but nothing in this subsection shall require the repayment of any income tax treated as

deducted or paid by virtue of section 233(1), 246D(1), 249(4), 421(1), 547(5) or 599A(5) of the principal Act."

(3) In subsection (1) of section 233 of the Taxes Act 1988 (taxation of certain recipients of distributions), for paragraphs (a) and (b) there shall be substituted the following paragraphs—

"(a) that person shall be treated as having paid income tax at the lower rate on the amount or value of the distribution;

(b) no repayment shall be made of any income tax treated by virtue of paragraph (a) above as having been paid;".

(4) In paragraph (a) of subsection (1A) of that section—

(a) for sub-paragraph (i) there shall be substituted the following sub-paragraph—

"(i) income on which that person falls to be treated as having paid income tax at the lower rate by virtue of paragraph (a) of subsection (1) above, or"; and

(b) for the words "that assessment" there shall be substituted the words "that subsection".

(5) In the following enactments, namely—

(a) subsection (2)(a) of section 246D of that Act (individuals etc.); and

(b) subsection (4)(a) of section 249 of that Act (stock dividends treated as income),

for the words from "no assessment" to "on it" there shall be substituted the words "the individual shall be treated as having paid income tax at the lower rate on that income".

(6) In subsection (1)(b) of section 421 of that Act (taxation of borrower when loan released), for the words "no assessment shall be made on him in respect of" there shall be substituted the words "he shall not be liable to pay".

(7) The following shall cease to have effect, namely—

(a) in subsection (5)(a) of section 547 of that Act (method of charging to tax), the words from "no assessment" to "but";

(b) in subsection (6) of section 599A of that Act (charge to tax: payments out of surplus funds), the words from "subject" to "and"; and

(c) subsection (7) of that section.

GENERAL NOTE
The changes made by this section allow for the inclusion in the self-assessment return of items of income which are treated for tax purposes as having been received after deduction of tax. Such tax, being "notional", is not repayable.

Liability of partners

123.—(1) In subsection (2) of section 12AA of the Taxes Management Act 1970 (partnership return) after the words "with the notice" there shall be inserted the words "or a successor of his".

(2) In subsection (3) of that section after the words "the partner" there shall be inserted the words "or a successor of his".

(3) In subsection (7)(a) of that section, the words "any part of" shall cease to have effect.

(4) At the end of that section there shall be inserted the following subsections—

"(11) In this Act 'successor', in relation to a person who is required to make and deliver, or has made and delivered, a return in pursuance of a notice under subsection (2) or (3) above, but is no longer available, means—

(a) where a partner is for the time being nominated for the purposes of this subsection by a majority of the relevant partners, that partner; and

(b) where no partner is for the time being so nominated, such partner as—

(i) in the case of a notice under subsection (2) above is identified in accordance with rules given with that notice; or

(ii) in the case of a notice under subsection (3) above, is nominated for the purposes of this subsection by an officer of the Board;

and 'predecessor' and 'successor', in relation to a person so nominated or identified, shall be construed accordingly.

(12) For the purposes of subsection (11) above a nomination under paragraph (a) of that subsection, and a revocation of such a nomination, shall not have effect in relation to any time before notice of the nomination or revocation is given to an officer of the Board.

(13) In this section 'relevant partner' means a person who was a partner at any time during the period for which the return was made or is required, or the personal representatives of such a person."

(5) In subsection (1) of section 12AB of that Act (partnership return to include partnership statement)—

(a) in paragraph (a), for the words "each period of account ending within the period in respect of which the return is made" there shall be substituted the words "the period in respect of which the return is made and each period of account ending within that period";

(b) in sub-paragraph (i) of that paragraph, for the words "that period" there shall be substituted the words "the period in question";

(c) after that sub-paragraph there shall be inserted the following sub-paragraph—

"(ia) the amount of the consideration which, on that basis, has accrued to the partnership in respect of each disposal of partnership property during that period,";

and

(d) in paragraph (b), after the words "such period" there shall be inserted the words "as is mentioned in paragraph (a) above" and after the word "loss," there shall be inserted the word "consideration,".

(6) In subsection (2) of that section—

(a) in paragraph (a) after the words "to that person" there shall be inserted the words "or a successor"; and

(b) in paragraph (b) for the words from "partnership statement" to "he" there shall be substituted the words "or a predecessor's partnership statement as to give effect to any amendments to the return in which it is included which he or a predecessor".

(7) In section 12AC of that Act (power to enquire into partnership return)—

(a) in subsection (1)(b), after the word "person" there shall be inserted the words "or a successor of that person"; and

(b) subsection (6) (which is superseded by subsection (4) above) shall cease to have effect.

(8) In subsection (1)(b) of section 93A of that Act (failure to make partnership return), after the word "he" there shall be inserted the words "or a successor of his".

(9) In subsections (3) and (4) of that section, after the words "the representative partner" there shall be inserted the words "or a successor of his".

(10) In subsection (6) of that section—

(a) after the words "the representative partner" there shall be inserted the words "or a successor of his"; and

(b) after the words "that partner", in both places where they occur, there shall be inserted the words "or successor".

(11) In subsection (7) of that section, for the words "the representative partner had a reasonable excuse for not delivering the return" there shall be substituted the words "the person for the time being required to deliver the

return (whether the representative partner or a successor of his) had a reasonable excuse for not delivering it".

(12) In subsection (1)(a)(ii) of section 95A of that Act (incorrect partnership return or accounts), for the words "such a return" there shall be substituted the words "a return of such a kind".

(13) In subsection (3) of that section—

(a) after the words "the representative partner" there shall be inserted the words "or a successor of his"; and

(b) after the words "that partner", in both places where they occur, there shall be inserted the words "or successor".

(14) In subsection (1) of section 118 of that Act (interpretation), for the definition of "successor" there shall be substituted the following definition—

" 'successor', in relation to a person who is required to make and deliver, or has made and delivered, a return under section 12AA of this Act, and 'predecessor' and 'successor', in relation to the successor of such a person, shall be construed in accordance with section 12AA(11) of this Act;".

GENERAL NOTE
The section makes minor changes to the rules relating to partnership returns under self-assessment. Principally, it provides that where the partner responsible for dealing with any matters relating to the return ceases to be available to do so, the remaining partners may nominate a replacement as "successor" [Standing Committee E, February 15, 1996, col. 358].

Retention of original records

124.—(1) The Taxes Management Act 1970, as it has effect—

(a) for the purposes of income tax and capital gains tax, as respects the year 1996–97 and subsequent years of assessment, and

(b) for the purposes of corporation tax, as respects accounting periods ending on or after the day appointed under section 199 of the Finance Act 1994 for the purposes of Chapter III of Part IV of that Act (self-assessment management provisions),

shall be amended in accordance with the following provisions of this section.

(2) In section 12B (records to be kept for purposes of returns) in subsection (4) (which permits the duty to preserve records to be discharged by the preservation of the information contained in them, and provides for the admissibility in evidence of copy documents) at the beginning there shall be inserted the words "Except in the case of records falling within subsection (4A) below,".

(3) After that subsection there shall be inserted—

"(4A) The records which fall within this subsection are—

(a) any statement in writing such as is mentioned in—

(i) subsection (1) of section 234 of the principal Act (amount of qualifying distribution and tax credit), or

(ii) subsection (1) of section 352 of that Act (gross amount, tax deducted, and actual amount paid, in certain cases where payments are made under deduction of tax),

which is furnished by the company or person there mentioned, whether after the making of a request or otherwise;

(b) any certificate or other record (however described) which is required by regulations under section 566(1) of the principal Act to be given to a sub-contractor (within the meaning of Chapter IV of Part XIII of that Act) on the making of a payment to which section 559 of that Act (deductions on account of tax) applies;

(c) any such record as may be requisite for making a correct and complete claim in respect of, or otherwise requisite for making a correct and complete return so far as relating to, an amount of tax—

(i) which has been paid under the laws of a territory outside the United Kingdom, or

(ii) which would have been payable under the law of such a territory but for a relief to which section 788(5) of the principal Act (relief for promoting development and relief contemplated by double taxation arrangements) applies."

(4) In subsection (5) of that section (penalty for failure to comply with section 12B(1) or (2A)) for "Subject to subsection (5A)" there shall be substituted "Subject to subsections (5A) and (5B)".

(5) After subsection (5A) of that section there shall be inserted—

"(5B) Subsection (5) above also does not apply where—

(a) the records which the person fails to keep or preserve are records falling within paragraph (a) of subsection (4A) above; and

(b) an officer of the Board is satisfied that any facts which he reasonably requires to be proved, and which would have been proved by the records, are proved by other documentary evidence furnished to him."

(6) In Schedule 1A (claims etc not included in returns) in paragraph 2A (keeping and preserving of records) in sub-paragraph (3) (which makes corresponding provision to section 12B(4)) at the beginning there shall be inserted "Except in the case of records falling within section 12B(4A) of this Act,".

(7) In sub-paragraph (4) of that paragraph (penalty for failure to comply with paragraph 2A(1)) at the beginning there shall be inserted "Subject to sub-paragraph (5) below,".

(8) After that sub-paragraph there shall be inserted—

"(5) Sub-paragraph (4) above does not apply where—

(a) the records which the person fails to keep or preserve are records falling within paragraph (a) of section 12B(4A) of this Act; and

(b) an officer of the Board is satisfied that any facts which he reasonably requires to be proved, and which would have been proved by the records, are proved by other documentary evidence furnished to him."

(9) The amendments made by this section shall not have effect in relation to—

(a) any time before this Act is passed, or

(b) any records which a person fails to preserve before this Act is passed.

GENERAL NOTE

The section extends the rules for keeping records to enable returns to be completed, and claims to be made, under self-assessment. The obligation to keep records can normally be satisfied by taking copies of the information or by recording it in the books of a business. However, vouchers, or other documentary evidence, showing that domestic or foreign tax has been suffered must be kept in their original form. Examples of these are dividend or interest certificates and vouchers issued under the subcontractor's scheme [Standing Committee E, February 20, 1996, col. 366].

Determination of tax where no return delivered

125.—(1) For subsection (1) of section 28C of the Taxes Management Act 1970 (determination of tax where no return delivered) there shall be substituted the following subsections—

"(1) This section applies where—

(a) a notice has been given to any person under section 8 or 8A of this Act (the relevant section), and

(b) the required return is not delivered on or before the filing date.

(1A) An officer of the Board may make a determination of the following amounts, to the best of his information and belief, namely—

(a) the amounts in which the person who should have made the return is chargeable to income tax and capital gains tax for the year of assessment; and

(b) the amount which is payable by him by way of income tax for that year;

and subsection (1AA) of section 8 or, as the case may be, section 8A of this Act applies for the purposes of this subsection as it applies for the purposes of subsection (1) of that section."

(2) In subsection (3) of that section the words "or 11AA" shall cease to have effect.

(3) In subsection (6) of that section for the words ", section 8A(1A) or, as the case may be, section 11(4)" there shall be substituted the words "or, as the case may be, section 8A(1A)".

(4) After subsection (5) of section 59B of that Act (payment of income tax and capital gains tax) there shall be inserted the following subsection—

"(5A) Where a determination under section 28C of this Act which has effect as a person's self-assessment is superseded by his self-assessment under section 9 of this Act, any amount of tax which is payable or repayable by virtue of the supersession shall be payable or (as the case may be) repayable on or before the day given by subsection (3) or (4) above."

GENERAL NOTE

Changes are made to the provisions relating to determination of tax when a return has not been filed by the appropriate time to maintain consistency with the Taxes Management Act 1970 (c. 9), ss.8 and 9.

Companies are excluded, since tax determinations for them are dealt with under s.137.

PAYE regulations

126.—(1) After subsection (9) of section 59A of the Taxes Management Act 1970 (payments on account of income tax) there shall be inserted the following subsection—

"(10) Regulations under section 203 of the principal Act (PAYE) may provide that, for the purpose of determining the amount of any such excess as is mentioned in subsection (1) above, any necessary adjustments in respect of matters prescribed by the regulations shall be made to the amount of tax deducted at source under that section."

(2) After subsection (7) of section 59B of that Act (payment of income tax and capital gains tax) there shall be inserted the following subsection—

"(8) Regulations under section 203 of the principal Act (PAYE) may provide that, for the purpose of determining the amount of the difference mentioned in subsection (1) above, any necessary adjustments in respect of matters prescribed by the regulations shall be made to the amount of tax deducted at source under that section."

GENERAL NOTE

Provision is made for PAYE regulations to ensure that adjustments can be made in arriving at the amount of tax deducted at source which falls to be taken into account for the purposes of the TMA 1970, ss.59A and 59B.

Repayment postponed pending completion of enquiries

127. After subsection (4) of section 59B of the Taxes Management Act 1970 (payment of income tax and capital gains tax) there shall be inserted the following subsection—

"(4A) Where in the case of a repayment the return on the basis of which the person's self-assessment was made under section 9 of this Act is enquired into by an officer of the Board—

(a) nothing in subsection (3) or (4) above shall require the repayment to be made before the day on which, by virtue of section 28A(5) of this Act, the officer's enquiries are treated as completed; but

(b) the officer may at any time before that day make the repayment, on a provisional basis, to such extent as he thinks fit."

GENERAL NOTE

A repayment reflected in a return under self-assessment need not be made immediately where the Revenue have commenced an enquiry into the return [Standing Committee E, February 20, 1996, col. 409].

Claims for reliefs involving two or more years

128.—(1) In section 42 of the Taxes Management Act 1970 (procedure for making claims etc.)—

(a) subsections (3A) and (3B) (which are superseded by subsection (2) below) shall cease to have effect;

(b) in subsection (7)(a), the words "534, 535, 537A, 538" shall cease to have effect; and

(c) after subsection (11) there shall be inserted the following subsection—

"(11A) Schedule 1B to this Act shall have effect as respects certain claims for relief involving two or more years of assessment."

(2) After Schedule 1A to that Act there shall be inserted, as Schedule 1B, the provisions set out in Schedule 17 to this Act (claims for reliefs involving two or more years).

(3) For subsection (9) of section 96 of the Taxes Act 1988 (relief for fluctuating profits of farming etc.) there shall be substituted the following subsection—

"(9) Where a person makes a claim under this section, any claim by him for relief under any other provision of the Income Tax Acts for either of the two years of assessment—

(a) shall not be out of time if made before the end of the period during which the claim under this section is capable of being revoked; and

(b) if already made, may be amended or revoked before the end of that period;

and, in relation to a claim made by being included in a return, any reference in this subsection to amending or revoking the claim is a reference to amending the return by amending or, as the case may be, omitting the claim."

(4) In section 108 of that Act (election for carry-back)—

(a) for the words "the inspector within two years after" there shall be substituted the words "an officer of the Board within one year from the 31st January next following"; and

(b) the words from "and, in any such case" to the end shall cease to have effect.

(5) For subsection (5) of section 534 of that Act (relief for copyright payments) there shall be substituted the following subsections—

"(5) A claim under this section with respect to any payment to which it applies by virtue only of subsection (4)(b) above—

(a) shall have effect as a claim with respect to all qualifying payments, that is to say, all such payments in respect of the copyright in the same work which are receivable by the claimant, whether before or after the claim; and

(b) where qualifying payments are so receivable in two or more years of assessment, shall be treated for the purposes of the Management Act as if it were two or more separate claims, each in respect of the qualifying payments receivable in one of those years.

(5A) A claim under this section may be made at any time within one year from the 31st January next following—

(a) in the case of such a claim as is mentioned in subsection (5) above, the latest year of assessment in which a qualifying payment is receivable; and

(b) in the case of any other claim, the year of assessment in which the payment in question is receivable.

(5B) For the purposes of subsections (5) and (5A) above, a payment shall be regarded as receivable in the year of assessment in computing the amount of the profits or gains of which it would, but for this section, be included."

(6) After subsection (6) of that section there shall be inserted the following subsection—

"(6A) In the case of persons carrying on a trade, profession or business in partnership, no claim may be made under any of the following provisions, namely—

(a) this section and section 535;

(b) section 537 as it has effect in relation to this section and section 535; and

(c) section 537A and section 538,

in respect of any payment or sum receivable on or after 6th April 1996; and nothing in any of those provisions shall be construed as applying to profits chargeable to corporation tax."

(7) In section 535 of that Act (relief where copyright sold after ten years or more), the following shall cease to have effect, namely—

(a) in subsection (4), the words "Subject to subsection (5) below";

(b) subsections (5) and (7); and

(c) in subsection (6), the words from "unless the author" to the end.

(8) After subsection (8) of that section there shall be inserted the following subsection—

"(8A) No claim for relief made under subsection (1) above shall be allowed unless it is made within one year from the 31st January next following the year of assessment in which the payment is receivable; and for the purposes of this subsection a payment shall be regarded as receivable in the year of assessment in computing the amount of the profits or gains of which it would, but for this section, be included."

(9) For subsection (5) of section 537A of that Act (relief for payments in respect of designs) there shall be substituted the following subsections—

"(5) A claim under this section with respect to any payment to which it applies by virtue only of subsection (4)(b) above—

(a) shall have effect as a claim with respect to all qualifying payments, that is to say, all such payments in respect of rights in the design in question which are receivable by the claimant, whether before or after the claim; and

(b) where qualifying payments are so receivable in two or more years of assessment, shall be treated for the purposes of the Management Act as if it were two or more separate claims, each in respect of the qualifying payments receivable in one of those years.

(5A) A claim under this section may be made at any time within one year from the 31st January next following—

(a) in the case of such a claim as is mentioned in subsection (5) above, the latest year of assessment in which a qualifying payment is receivable; and

(b) in the case of any other claim, the year of assessment in which the payment in question is receivable.

(5B) For the purposes of subsections (5) and (5A) above, a payment shall be regarded as receivable in the year of assessment in computing the amount of the profits or gains of which it would, but for this section, be included."

(10) After subsection (3) of section 538 of that Act (relief for painters, sculptors and other artists) there shall be inserted the following subsection—

"(4) No claim for relief made under subsection (1) above shall be allowed unless it is made within one year from the 31st January next following the year of assessment in which the payment is receivable; and for the purposes of this subsection a payment shall be regarded as receivable in the year of assessment in computing the amount of the profits or gains of which it would, but for this section, be included."

(11) This section (except subsections (1)(b) and (6) above) and Schedule 17 to this Act have effect as respects claims made (or deemed to be made) in relation to the year 1996–97 or later years of assessment.

(12) Subsection (1)(b) above has effect as respects claims made in relation to the year 1997–98 or later years of assessment.

GENERAL NOTE

This section, together with Sched. 17, makes a number of changes designed to make claims affecting more than one year's tax work better under self-assessment.

Subss. (1) and (2)

These abolish the existing provisions cited for claims for loss relief and pave the way for the new TMA 1970, Sched. 1B, inserted by Sched. 17 below. See further the General Note to that Schedule.

Subs. (3)

Claims for averaging farming profits, coupled with claims or revocation of claims for other reliefs, may continue up to the finality date for the tax return for the year in question or, if later, the finality date for the averaging claim.

Subs. (4)

The time limit for carry-back of post-cessation receipts is amended from two years after the year of assessment in which the sum was received to one year after the January 31 next following the year of assessment in which the sum is received.

Subs. (5)

The new ICTA 1988, ss.534(5), (5A) and (5B) modifies the provisions regarding backward spreading of copyright payments. The time limit for making claims is reduced to 22 months.

Subs. (6)

Partnerships and companies are excluded from the backward spreading provisions.

Subs. (7)

The power to elect for forward spreading on death or cessation is withdrawn.

Subs. (8)

The time limit for forward spreading claims is reduced to January 31 following one year after the end of the year of assessment following the relevant year.

Subs. (9)

Claims in respect of designs are placed on the same basis as those in respect of copyright (see subs. (5)) above.

Subs. (10)

A similar time limit applies for backward spreading for painters, sculptors and other artists. See further the General Note to Sched. 17 [Standing Committee E, February 20, 1996, col. 413].

Claims for medical insurance and vocational training relief

129.—(1) Nothing in section 42 of the Taxes Management Act 1970 (procedure for making claims etc.), or Schedule 1A to that Act (claims etc. not included in returns), shall apply in relation to—

(a) any claim under subsection (6)(b) of section 54 (medical insurance relief) of the Finance Act 1989 ("the 1989 Act"); or

(b) any claim under subsection (5)(b) of section 32 (vocational training relief) of the Finance Act 1991 ("the 1991 Act").

(2) In section 54(6)(b) of the 1989 Act and section 32(5)(b) of the 1991 Act, after the words "on making a claim" there shall be inserted the words "in accordance with regulations".

(3) In section 57(1) of the 1989 Act (medical insurance relief: supplementary), after paragraph (a) there shall be inserted the following paragraph—

"(aa) make provision for and with respect to appeals against a decision of an officer of the Board or the Board with respect to a claim under section 54(6)(b) above;".

(4) In section 33(1) of the 1991 Act (vocational training relief: supplementary), after paragraph (a) there shall be inserted the following paragraph—

"(aa) make provision for and with respect to appeals against a decision of an officer of the Board or the Board with respect to a claim under section 32(5)(b) above;".

(5) Subsection (1)(a) above shall not apply in relation to claims made before the coming into force of regulations made by virtue of section 57(1)(aa) of the 1989 Act.

(6) Subsection (1)(b) above shall not apply in relation to claims made before the coming into force of regulations made by virtue of section 33(1)(aa) of the 1991 Act.

GENERAL NOTE

Regulations will be made to cover claims made by insurers and educational institutions to recover tax deducted at source from payments made to them under the tax relief schemes for private medical insurance and vocational training.

Procedure for giving notices

130.—(1) Section 42 of, and Schedule 1A to, the Taxes Management Act 1970, as they have effect—

(a) for the purposes of income tax and capital gains tax, as respects the year 1996–97 and subsequent years of assessment, and

(b) for the purposes of corporation tax, as respects accounting periods ending on or after the day appointed under section 199 of the Finance Act 1994 for the purposes of Chapter III of Part IV of that Act (self-assessment management provisions),

shall be amended in accordance with the following provisions of this section.

(2) In subsection (7) of section 42 (which contains a list of provisions, claims under which must be made in accordance with subsection (6)) the following words shall cease to have effect, that is to say—

(a) in paragraph (a), "62A," and "401,"; and

(b) in paragraph (c), "30,", "33,", "48, 49," and "124A,".

(3) In subsection (10) of that section (section 42 to apply in relation to elections and notices as it applies in relation to claims) the words "and notices" shall cease to have effect.

(4) In subsection (11) of that section (Schedule 1A to apply as respects any claim, election or notice made otherwise than in a return under section 8 etc.) for the words ", election or notice" there shall be substituted "or election".

(5) In paragraph 1 of Schedule 1A (claims etc. not included in returns), in the definition of "claim", for the words "means a claim, election or notice" there shall be substituted "means a claim or election".

GENERAL NOTE

The current position for giving notices, under which there is no formal procedure, is maintained for self-assessment [Standing Committee E, February 20, 1996, col. 419].

Interest on overdue tax

131.—(1) Section 110 of the Finance Act 1995 (interest on overdue tax) shall be deemed to have been enacted with the insertion after subsection (3) of the following subsection—

"(4) So far as it relates to partnerships whose trades, professions or businesses were set up and commenced before 6th April 1994, subsection (1) above has effect as respects the year 1997–98 and subsequent years of assessment."

(2) In subsection (3) of section 86 of the Taxes Management Act 1970 (which was substituted by the said section 110), for the words "section 93" there shall be substituted the words "section 92".

(3) In Schedule 19 to the Finance Act 1994, paragraph 23 (which is superseded by the said section 110) shall cease to have effect.

GENERAL NOTE

The section corrects a minor defect in the FA 1995, s.110, dealing with interest on overdue tax. It charges interest on tax paid late by partnerships in respect of 1996–97 on the established basis as originally intended, rather than on the new basis that will apply under self-assessment [Standing Committee E, February 20, 1996, col. 421].

Overdue tax and excessive payments by the Board

132. Schedule 18 to this Act (which amends enactments relating to overdue tax or excessive payments by the Board) shall have effect.

GENERAL NOTE

The section introduces Sched. 18, which clarifies the interest position where certain tax is paid late and enables excessive payments made by the Revenue to be recovered by assessment after the introduction of self-assessment.

See further the General Note to Sched. 18.

Claims and enquiries

133. Schedule 19 to this Act (which, for purposes connected with self-assessment, further amends provisions relating to claims and enquiries) shall have effect.

GENERAL NOTE

The section introduces Sched. 19, which provides for the Revenue to be able to enquire into claims that are not reflected in a self-assessment in the same way as other claims and to make enquiries where there are alternative bases of taxation and an option for the Revenue to choose between them.

See further the General Note to Sched. 19.

Discretions exercisable by the Board etc.

134.—(1) Schedule 20 to this Act (which in connection with self-assessment modifies enactments by virtue of which a decision or other action affecting an assessment may be or is required to be taken by the Board, or one of their officers, before the making of the assessment) shall have effect.

(2) Subject to subsection (3) below, the amendments made by that Schedule shall have effect—

(a) for the purposes of income tax and capital gains tax, as respects the year 1996–97 and subsequent years of assessment; and

(b) for the purposes of corporation tax, as respects accounting periods ending on or after the day appointed under section 199 of the Finance Act 1994 for the purposes of Chapter III of Part IV of that Act (self-assessment management provisions).

(3) Paragraphs 22 and 23 of that Schedule shall have effect in relation to shares issued on or after 6th April 1996.

GENERAL NOTE
This section introduces Sched. 20 which makes further amendments reflecting the change to self-assessment. The current system requires the Revenue to be satisfied with a return before it makes the tax assessment on the figures contained in the return. Many claims for relief also require the Revenue to be satisfied as to the validity of the claim, or for the taxpayer to show or prove entitlement or for the Revenue to exercise its judgment before effect can be given to the claim. Under self-assessment the taxpayer is required to include a self-assessment as part of the return, and where possible also to make claims as part of the return. The provisions which require a decision or other action to be taken by the Revenue before the making of an assessment are therefore no longer appropriate, and Sched. 20 makes the necessary changes to remove those requirements from the Taxes Acts.
See further the General Note to Sched. 20.

Time limits for claims etc.

135.—(1) Schedule 21 to this Act (which in connection with self-assessment modifies enactments which impose time limits on the making of claims, elections, adjustments and assessments and the giving of notices, and enactments which provide for the giving of notice to the inspector) shall have effect.

(2) Subject to subsections (3) to (5) below, the amendments made by that Schedule shall have effect—
  (a) for the purposes of income tax and capital gains tax, as respects the year 1996–97 and subsequent years of assessment; and
  (b) for the purposes of corporation tax, as respects accounting periods ending on or after the day appointed under section 199 of the Finance Act 1994 for the purposes of Chapter III of Part IV of that Act (self-assessment management provisions).

(3) The amendments made to the Capital Allowances Act 1990 and the Finance Act 1994 by that Schedule, in their application to trades, professions or vocations set up and commenced before 6th April 1994, shall (so far as relating to income tax) have effect as respects the year 1997–98 and subsequent years of assessment.

(4) The Capital Allowances Act 1990, as it has effect for the year 1996–97 in relation to trades, professions or vocations set up and commenced before 6th April 1994, shall (so far as relating to income tax) have effect as respects that year with the following modifications, that is to say, as if—
  (a) in sections 25(3)(c), 30(1), 31(3) and 33(1) and (4), for "two years after the end of" there were substituted "the first anniversary of the 31st January next following";
  (b) in section 37(2)(c), for "more than two years after the end of the chargeable period or its basis period" there were substituted "later than the first anniversary of the 31st January next following the year of assessment in which ends the basis period";
  (c) in section 53(2), for "before the expiry of the period of two years beginning at the end of" there were substituted "on or before the first anniversary of the 31st January next following";
  (d) in section 68(5), for "two years after the end of that period" there were substituted "the first anniversary of the 31st January next following the year of assessment in which the relevant period ends";
  (e) in section 68(9A)(b), for "two years after the end of" there were substituted "the first anniversary of the 31st January next following the year of assessment in which ends";
  (f) in section 129(2), for "not more than two years after the end of" there were substituted "on or before the first anniversary of the 31st January next following";

(g) in section 141(3), for "the inspector not later than two years after the end of" there were substituted "an officer of the Board on or before the first anniversary of the 31st January next following".

(5) Section 118 of the Finance Act 1994, as it has effect for the year 1996–97 in relation to trades, professions or vocations set up and commenced before 6th April 1994, shall (so far as relating to income tax) have effect as respects that year as if, in subsection (3), for "two years after the end of" there were substituted "the first anniversary of the 31st January next following".

GENERAL NOTE

This section, together with Sched. 21, amends sections of the Taxes Acts which impose time limits for making claims and elections, adjustments to assessments and the giving of notices, so as to align them with the time limits within which a taxpayer has to file a return or can amend a self-assessment, or with the ordinary time limit within which an assessment can be made.

Subss. (3)–(5)

These deal with the situation where, for 1996–97 only, the new definition of "chargeable period" in the Capital Allowances Act 1990 (c. 1), s.161 (introduced by the FA 1994, s.212(2)) does not apply for certain taxpayers. For income tax, various references to two years are amended so as to align with the normal time limit for taxpayer amendment to a self-assessment.

See further the General Note to Sched. 21.

Appeals

136. Schedule 22 to this Act (which makes provision, in connection with self-assessment, about appeals) shall have effect.

GENERAL NOTE

This section introduces Sched. 22, which makes a number of changes to the rules for assigning appeals and other proceedings under self-assessment to the appropriate body of commissioners and, in the case of the General Commissioners, establishing which body has jurisdiction.

See further the General Note to Sched. 22.

Companies

Schedules 13 and 16 to the Taxes Act 1988

137.—(1) Schedule 23 to this Act shall have effect.

(2) The amendments made by that Schedule shall have effect as respects return periods ending on or after the appointed day for the purposes of Chapter III of Part IV of the Finance Act 1994.

(3) In subsection (2) above "return period" means—

(a) so far as relating to Schedule 13 to the Taxes Act 1988, a period for which a return is required to be made under paragraph 1 of that Schedule; and

(b) so far as relating to Schedule 16 to that Act, a period for which a return is required to be made under paragraph 2 of that Schedule.

GENERAL NOTE

The section introduces Sched. 23, which amends the rules in the ICTA 1988, Scheds. 13 and 16, when self-assessment is introduced for companies. Schedule 13 deals with advance corporation tax (ACT) and Sched. 16 with returns of income tax deducted from payments made by the company. The changes will come into force when self-assessment is introduced for companies, for accounting periods ending on or after a day to be appointed by the Treasury.

See further the General Note to Sched. 23.

Accounting periods

138. Schedule 24 to this Act (which makes provision, in connection with self-assessment, in relation to accounting periods) shall have effect.

GENERAL NOTE

The section introduces Sched. 24, which provides rules for the case where there is any uncertainty about, or dispute over the proper accounting period of a company making a return under self-assessment, and relaxes the rules for companies in liquidation which make such returns. It also ensures that the rules under the self-assessment system for determinations of tax where no return is made will operate properly for companies.

See further the General Note to Sched. 24.

Surrenders of advance corporation tax

139. Schedule 25 to this Act (which makes provision, in connection with self-assessment, about surrenders of advance corporation tax) shall have effect.

GENERAL NOTE

This section introduces Sched. 25, which provides for amendments to be made to the way in which companies will make surrenders of advance corporation tax to their subsidiaries when self-assessment is introduced.

See further the General Note to Sched. 25.

Chargeable gains

Transfer of company's assets to investment trust

140.—(1) In section 101 of the Taxation of Chargeable Gains Act 1992 (transfer of company's assets to investment trust) after subsection (1) there shall be inserted—

"(1A) Any chargeable gain or allowable loss which, apart from this subsection, would accrue to the company on the sale referred to in subsection (1) above shall be treated as accruing to the company immediately before the end of the last accounting period to end before the beginning of the accounting period mentioned in that subsection."

(2) This section shall have effect as respects accounting periods ending on or after the day appointed under section 199 of the Finance Act 1994 for the purposes of Chapter III of Part IV of that Act (self-assessment management provisions).

GENERAL NOTE

The amendment to the TCGA 1992, s.101, provides that where a charge arises on a company becoming an investment trust following a no gain/no loss transfer under s.139, the charge will accrue in the accounting period immediately before the one in which the transferee company becomes an investment trust, rather than the one in which the transfer took place. This will fit better with self-assessment.

Roll-over relief

141.—(1) In subsection (4) of section 152 of the Taxation of Chargeable Gains Act 1992 (roll-over relief)—

(a) after the word "making" there shall be inserted the words "or amending"; and

(b) after the word "assessments", in the second place where it occurs, there shall be inserted the words "or amendments".

(2) After section 153 of that Act there shall be inserted the following section—

"Provisional application of sections 152 and 153

153A.—(1) This section applies where a person carrying on a trade who for a consideration disposes of, or of his interest in, any assets ('the old assets') declares, in his return for the chargeable period in which the disposal takes place—

(a) that the whole or any specified part of the consideration will be applied in the acquisition of, or of an interest in, other assets ('the new assets') which on the acquisition will be taken into use, and used only, for the purposes of the trade;

(b) that the acquisition will take place as mentioned in subsection (3) of section 152; and

(c) that the new assets will be within the classes listed in section 155.

(2) Until the declaration ceases to have effect, section 152 or, as the case may be, section 153 shall apply as if the acquisition had taken place and the person had made a claim under that section.

(3) The declaration shall cease to have effect as follows—

(a) if and to the extent that it is withdrawn before the relevant day, or is superseded before that day by a valid claim made under section 152 or 153, on the day on which it is so withdrawn or superseded; and

(b) if and to the extent that it is not so withdrawn or superseded, on the relevant day.

(4) On the declaration ceasing to have effect in whole or in part, all necessary adjustments—

(a) shall be made by making or amending assessments or by repayment or discharge of tax; and

(b) shall be so made notwithstanding any limitation on the time within which assessments or amendments may be made.

(5) In this section 'the relevant day' means—

(a) in relation to capital gains tax, the third anniversary of the 31st January next following the year of assessment in which the disposal of, or of the interest in, the old assets took place;

(b) in relation to corporation tax, the fourth anniversary of the last day of the accounting period in which that disposal took place.

(6) Subsections (6), (8), (10) and (11) of section 152 shall apply for the purposes of this section as they apply for the purposes of that section."

(3) In section 175 of that Act (replacement of business assets by members of a group)—

(a) in subsections (2A) and (2B), after the words "Section 152" there shall be inserted the words "or 153"; and

(b) in subsection (2C), for the words "Section 152 shall not" there shall be substituted the words "Neither section 152 nor section 153 shall".

(4) In section 246 of that Act (time of disposal or acquisition), the words from "or, if earlier" to the end shall cease to have effect.

(5) In subsection (5)(b) of section 247 of that Act (roll-over relief on compulsory acquisition), for the words "subsection (3)" there shall be substituted the words "subsections (3) and (4)".

(6) After that section there shall be inserted the following section—

"Provisional application of section 247

247A.—(1) This section applies where a person who disposes of land ('the old land') to an authority exercising or having compulsory powers declares, in his return for the chargeable period in which the disposal takes place—

(a) that the whole or any specified part of the consideration for the disposal will be applied in the acquisition of other land ('the new land');

(b) that the acquisition will take place as mentioned in subsection (3) of section 152; and

(c) that the new land will not be land excluded from section 247(1)(c) by section 248.

(2) Until the declaration ceases to have effect, section 247 shall apply as if the acquisition had taken place and the person had made a claim under that section.

(3) For the purposes of this section, subsections (3) to (5) of section 153A shall apply as if the reference to section 152 or 153 were a refer-

ence to section 247 and the reference to the old assets were a reference to the old land.

(4) In this section 'land' and 'authority exercising or having compulsory powers' have the same meaning as in section 247."

GENERAL NOTE

This section provides that roll-over relief for the replacement of business assets and on the acquisition of land may be allowed in a self-assessment on a provisional basis. This relief will be withdrawn if a valid claim has not been made by the normal due date of the return for the period in which the third anniversary of the disposal falls, or earlier if the taxpayer indicates that the declaration of an intention to reinvest no longer holds good.

Subs. (2)
The new TCGA 1992, s.153A, implements the provisional roll-over relief.

Subs. (3)
This amendment ensures that the new provisional relief works satisfactorily in the context of members of a group of companies.

Subs. (4)
The time of disposal and acquisition of land acquired by an authority under compulsory purchase will always be the time the compensation is agreed and not, if earlier, the time the authority enters the land. This ensures that provisional roll-over relief will not be withdrawn before actual roll-over relief is available.

Subs. (6)
The new TCGA 1992, s.247A, enacts provisional roll-over relief on compulsory acquisition to be given on the same basis as under new s.153A for replacement of business assets.

Premiums for leases

142.—(1) Paragraph 3 of Schedule 8 to the Taxation of Chargeable Gains Act 1992 (premiums for leases) shall be amended as follows.

(2) In sub-paragraph (2), for the words "for the period" to the end there shall be substituted the words ", being a premium which—
  (a) is due when the sum is payable by the tenant; and
  (b) where the sum is payable in lieu of rent, is in respect of the period in relation to which the sum is payable."

(3) In sub-paragraph (3), for the words "for the period" to the end there shall be substituted the words ", being a premium which—
  (a) is due when the sum is payable by the tenant; and
  (b) is in respect of the period from the time when the variation or waiver takes effect to the time when it ceases to have effect."

(4) For sub-paragraphs (4) to (6) there shall be substituted the following sub-paragraphs—

"(4) Where under sub-paragraph (2) or (3) above a premium is deemed to have been received by the landlord, that shall not be the occasion of any recomputation of the gain accruing on the receipt of any other premium, and the premium shall be regarded—
  (a) in the case of a premium deemed to have been received for the surrender of a lease, as consideration for a separate transaction which is effected when the premium is deemed to be due and consists of the disposal by the landlord of his interest in the lease; and
  (b) in any other case, as consideration for a separate transaction which is effected when the premium is deemed to be due and consists of a further part disposal of the freehold or other asset out of which the lease is granted.

(5) If under sub-paragraph (2) or (3) above a premium is deemed to have been received by the landlord, otherwise than as consideration for the surrender of the lease, and the landlord is a tenant under a lease the duration of which does not exceed 50 years,this Schedule shall apply—

(a) as if an amount equal to the amount of that premium deemed to have been received had been given by way of consideration for the grant of the part of the sublease covered by the period in respect of which the premium is deemed to have been paid; and

(b) as if that consideration were expenditure incurred by the sub-lessee and attributable to that part of the sublease under section 38(1)(b)."

(5) This section has effect as respects sums payable on or after 6th April 1996.

GENERAL NOTE

This section amends the treatment for capital gains tax purposes of capital sums paid by a tenant and received by a landlord in respect of the variation, waiver or surrender of a lease, or commutation of the rent due under a lease. From April 6, 1996 such sums are to be taken into account in the year in which they are payable rather than the year in which the lease was first granted. This will avoid the need for adjustments to the assessment for the earlier year [Standing Committee E, February 20, 1996, col. 436].

CHAPTER VI

MISCELLANEOUS PROVISIONS

Reliefs

Annual payments under certain insurance policies

143.—(1) After section 580 of the Taxes Act 1988 there shall be inserted the following sections—

"Relief from tax on annual payments under certain insurance policies

580A.—(1) This section applies (subject to subsection (7)(b) below) in the case of any such annual payment under an insurance policy as—

(a) apart from this section, would be brought into charge under Case III of Schedule D; or

(b) is equivalent to a description of payment brought into charge under Case III of that Schedule but (apart from this section) would be brought into charge under Case V of that Schedule.

(2) Subject to the following provisions of this section, the annual payment shall be exempt from income tax if—

(a) it constitutes a benefit provided under so much of an insurance policy as provides insurance against a qualifying risk;

(b) the provisions of the policy by which insurance is provided against that risk are self-contained (within the meaning of section 580B);

(c) the only annual payments relating to that risk for which provision is made by that policy are payments in respect of a period throughout which the relevant conditions of payment are satisfied; and

(d) at all times while the policy has contained provisions relating to that risk, those provisions have been of a qualifying type.

(3) For the purposes of this section and section 580B a qualifying risk is any risk falling within either of the following descriptions, that is to say—

(a) a risk that the insured will (or will in any specified way) become subject to, or to any deterioration in a condition resulting from, any physical or mental illness, disability, infirmity or defect;

(b) a risk that circumstances will arise as a result of which the insured will cease to be employed or will cease to carry on any trade, profession or vocation carried on by him.

(4) For the purposes of this section the relevant conditions of payment are satisfied in relation to payments under an insurance policy for so long as any of the following continues, that is to say—

(a) an illness, disability, infirmity or defect which is insured against by the relevant part of the policy, and any related period of convalescence or rehabilitation;

(b) any period during which the insured is, in circumstances insured against by the relevant part of the policy, either unemployed or not carrying on a trade, profession or vocation;

(c) any period during which the income of the insured (apart from any benefits under the policy) is less, in circumstances so insured against, than it would have been if those circumstances had not arisen; or

(d) any period immediately following the end, as a result of the death of the insured, of any period falling within any of paragraphs (a) to (c) above;

and in this subsection 'the relevant part of the policy' means so much of it as relates to insurance against one or more risks mentioned in subsection (3) above.

(5) For the purposes of subsection (2)(d) above provisions relating to a qualifying risk are of a qualifying type if they are of such a description that their inclusion in any policy of insurance containing provisions relating only to a comparable risk would (apart from any reinsurance) involve the possibility for the insurer that a significant loss might be sustained on the amounts payable by way of premiums in respect of the risk, taken together with any return on the investment of those amounts.

(6) An annual payment shall not be exempt from income tax under this section if it is paid in accordance with a contract the whole or any part of any premiums under which have qualified for relief for the purposes of income tax by being deductible either—

(a) in the computation of the insured's income from any source; or

(b) from the insured's income.

(7) Where a person takes out any insurance policy wholly or partly for the benefit of another and that other person pays or contributes to the payment of the premiums under that policy, then to the extent only that the benefits under the policy are attributable, on a just and reasonable apportionment, to the payments or contributions made by that other person—

(a) that other person shall be treated for the purposes of this section and section 580B as the insured in relation to that policy;

(b) this section shall have effect in relation to those benefits, so far as comprised in payments to that other person or his spouse, as if the reference in subsection (1)(a) above to Case III of Schedule D included a reference to Schedule E; and

(c) subsection (6) above shall have effect as if the references to the premiums under the policy were references only to the payments or contributions made by that other person in respect of the premiums.

(8) Where—

(a) payments are made to or in respect of any person ('the beneficiary') under any insurance policy ('the individual policy'),

(b) the rights under the individual policy in accordance with which the payments are made superseded, with effect from the time when another policy ('the employer's policy') ceased to apply to that person, any rights conferred under that other policy,

(c) the employer's policy is or was a policy entered into wholly or partly for the benefit of persons holding office or employment under any person ('the employer') against risks falling within subsection (3)(a) above,

(d) the individual policy is one entered into in pursuance of, or in accordance with, any provisions contained in the employer's policy, and

(e) the beneficiary has ceased to hold office or employment under the employer as a consequence of the occurrence of anything insured against by so much of the employer's policy as related to risks falling within subsection (3)(a) above,

this section shall have effect as if the employer's policy and the individual policy were one policy.

(9) In the preceding provisions of this section references to the insured, in relation to any insurance policy, include references to—

(a) the insured's spouse; and

(b) in the case of a policy entered into wholly or partly for purposes connected with the meeting of liabilities arising from an actual or proposed transaction identified in the policy, any person on whom any of those liabilities will fall jointly with the insured or his spouse.

(10) References in this section and section 580B to insurance against a risk include references to any insurance for the provision (otherwise than by way of indemnity) of any benefits against that risk, and references to what is insured against by a policy shall be construed accordingly.

Meaning of 'self-contained' for the purposes of s.580A

580B.—(1) For the purposes of section 580A the provisions of an insurance policy by which insurance is provided against a qualifying risk are self-contained unless subsection (2) or (3) below applies to the provisions of that policy so far as they relate to that risk; but, in determining whether either of those subsections so applies, regard shall be had to all the persons for whose benefit insurance is provided by that policy against that risk.

(2) This subsection applies to the provisions of an insurance policy so far as they relate to a qualifying risk—

(a) that insurance policy contains provision for the payment of benefits other than those relating to that risk;

(b) the terms of the policy so far as they relate to that risk, or the manner in which effect is given to those terms, would have been significantly different if the only benefits under the policy had been those relating to that risk; and

(c) that difference is not one relating exclusively to the fact that the amount of benefits receivable by or in respect of any person under the policy is applied for reducing the amount of other benefits payable to or in respect of that person under the policy.

(3) This subsection applies to the provisions of an insurance policy ('the relevant policy') so far as they relate to a qualifying risk if—

(a) the insured under that policy is, or has been, the insured under one or more other policies;

(b) that other policy, or each of those other policies, is in force or has been in force at a time when the relevant policy was in force or at the time immediately before the relevant policy was entered into;

(c) the terms of the relevant policy so far as relating to that risk, or the manner in which effect is given to those terms, would have been significantly different if the other policy or policies had not been entered into; and

(d) that difference is not one relating exclusively to the fact that the amount of benefits receivable by or in respect of any person under the other policy, or any of the other policies, is applied for reducing the amount of benefits payable to or in respect of that person under the relevant policy.

(4) In subsections (2)(b) and (3)(c) above the references to the terms of a policy so far as they relate to a risk include references to the terms fixing any amount payable by way of premium or otherwise in respect of insurance against that risk."

(2) This section has effect for the year 1996–97 and subsequent years of assessment in relation to—

(a) any payment which under the policy in question falls to be paid at any time on or after 6th April 1996; and

(b) any payment not falling within paragraph (a) above in relation to which the conditions mentioned in subsection (3)(a) and (b) below are satisfied.

(3) This section shall also be deemed to have had effect for earlier years of assessment in relation to any payment in relation to which the following conditions are satisfied, that is to say—

(a) the payment was made under a policy in relation to which the requirements of subsection (4) below were fulfilled; and

(b) the policy in question provided for the right to annual payments under the policy to cease when all the liabilities in question were discharged.

(4) The requirements of this subsection are fulfilled in relation to any policy if—

(a) the only or main purpose of the insurance under the policy was to secure that the insured would be able to meet (in whole or in part) liabilities that would or might arise from any transaction;

(b) the policy expressly identified the transaction or, as the case may be, all the transactions (whether actual or proposed) by reference to which the insurance was taken out; and

(c) none of the transactions which would or might give rise to the liabilities mentioned in paragraph (a) above could be one entered into after any of the circumstances insured against arose.

(5) In subsection (4) above "transaction" includes any arrangements for the provision of credit or for the supply of services to residential premises.

GENERAL NOTE

The section introduces the new ICTA 1988, ss.580A and 580B, which provide exemption from tax, subject to certain conditions, for benefits paid under insurance policies to those who make arrangements to protect themselves financially in the event of accident, sickness, disability, infirmity or unemployment. The benefits covered will include those paid under some kinds of long-term care insurance. Benefits received under group policies taken out by employers to meet the cost of sick pay and passed on to the employee are also exempt if and to the extent that he has contributed to the premiums.

Benefits are not exempt when they fall to be taken into account in computing the insured's trading or similar profits, or where the insured was entitled to deduct the premiums in computing his income tax liability. In general the section takes effect on April 6, 1996, but if the insurance policy provides benefits that are linked to mortgage repayments or other specified commitments, the exemption has retrospective effect.

The section originated from public concern over the tax position of payments under a mortgage protection policy and this resulted in a comprehensive examination of a range of other types of insurance.

The new s.580A lays down the basic scope of and conditions for the exemption. The four basic conditions are:

(i) the benefit is paid under a policy which covers a "qualifying risk" (see subs. (3));

(ii) the provisions of the policy under which the benefits are paid are "self-contained" (see s.580B);

(iii) the policy provides for payment only while all the necessary conditions for payment are satisfied;

(iv) the provisions of the policy are of a kind on which the insurer runs the risk of making a loss. The new s.580B provides that a policy is "self-contained" unless:

(i) where it provides different benefits, the terms of the policy in relation to a qualifying risk are significantly different from what they would have been had it provided benefits only in relation to that risk (unless the only difference is a reduction in the amount of the benefits receivable);

(ii) where there are other policies, the terms of the policy covering the qualifying risk would have been significantly different had the other policies not existed (unless the only difference is a reduction in the amount of the benefits receivable under the relevant policy) [Standing Committee E, February 22, 1996, col. 439].

Vocational training

144.—1 Section 32 of the Finance Act 1991 (vocational training relief) shall be amended in accordance with the following provisions of this section.

(2) In subsection (1) (application of section) for paragraph (ca) (individual has attained school leaving age etc. at time of paying for the course) there shall be substituted—

"(ca) at the time the payment is made, the individual—

(i) in a case where the qualifying course of vocational training is such a course by virtue only of paragraph (b) of subsection (10) below, has attained the age of thirty, or

(ii) in any other case, has attained school-leaving age and, if under the age of nineteen, is not a person who is being provided with full-time education at a school,".

(3) For subsection (10) (meaning of "qualifying course of vocational training") there shall be substituted—

"(10) In this section "qualifying course of vocational training" means—

(a) any programme of activity capable of counting towards a qualification—

(i) accredited as a National Vocational Qualification by the National Council for Vocational Qualifications; or

(ii) accredited as a Scottish Vocational Qualification by the Scottish Vocational Education Council; or

(b) any course of training which—

(i) satisfies the conditions set out in the paragraphs of section 589(1) of the Taxes Act 1988 (qualifying courses of training etc.),

(ii) requires participation on a full-time or substantially full-time basis, and

(iii) extends for a period which consists of or includes four consecutive weeks,

but treating any time devoted to study in connection with the course as time devoted to the practical application of skills or knowledge."

(4) This section applies to payments made on or after 6th May 1996.

GENERAL NOTE

Under the FA 1991, s.32, individuals funding their own training may obtain vocational training relief (VTR) if their course is capable of leading to a National or Scottish Vocational Qualification. This section widens the scope of the relief. Individuals over the age of 30 will be able to get VTR for fees they pay for full time vocational courses lasting between four weeks and a year, whether or not the course leads to a Vocational Qualification. The course must, however, satisfy the test in the ICTA 1988, s.589(1). *i.e.* it must be designed to give skills or knowledge relevant to, and intended to be used in, gainful employment or self-employment [Standing Committee E, February 22, 1996, col. 454].

Personal reliefs for non-resident EEA nationals

145.—(1) In section 278(2)(a) of the Taxes Act 1988 (exclusion of non-residents from entitlement to personal reliefs not to apply to Commonwealth citizens or citizens of the Republic of Ireland), for "a citizen of the Republic of Ireland" there shall be substituted "an EEA national".

(2) After subsection (8) of that section (claims to be made to the Board) there shall be added the following subsection—

"(9) In this section 'EEA national' means a national of any State, other than the United Kingdom, which is a Contracting Party to the Agreement on the European Economic Area signed at Oporto on 2nd May 1992, as adjusted by the Protocol signed at Brussels on 17th March 1993."

(3) This section has effect for the year 1996–97 and subsequent years of assessment.

GENERAL NOTE

This section extends the entitlement to U.K. personal reliefs to all nationals of States within the European Economic Area (EEA), even when they are not resident in the U.K. Currently this entitlement only applies to citizens of the Commonwealth and the Republic of Ireland. The change will also mean that EEA nationals will be entitled to tax credits in respect of dividends paid by a U.K. company.

The EEA comprises the states of the European Union plus Norway, Iceland and Liechtenstein [Standing Committee E, February 22, 1996, col. 463].

Exemptions for charities

146.—(1) Section 505(1) of the Taxes Act 1988 (exemptions for charities) shall be amended as follows.

(2) For paragraph (a) (rents etc.) there shall be substituted the following paragraph—

"(a) exemption from tax under Schedules A and D in respect of any profits or gains arising in respect of rents or other receipts from an estate, interest or right in or over any land (whether situated in the United Kingdom or elsewhere) to the extent that the profits or gains—

(i) arise in respect of rents or receipts from an estate, interest or right vested in any person for charitable purposes; and

(ii) are applied to charitable purposes only;".

(3) For sub-paragraph (ii) of paragraph (c) (yearly interest and annual payments) there shall be substituted the following sub-paragraphs—

"(ii) from tax under Case III of Schedule D,

(iia) from tax under Case IV or V of Schedule D in respect of income equivalent to income chargeable under Case III of that Schedule but arising from securities or other possessions outside the United Kingdom,

(iib) from tax under Case V of Schedule D in respect of income consisting in any such dividend or other distribution of a company not resident in the United Kingdom as would be chargeable to tax under Schedule F if the company were so resident, and".

(4) In paragraph (e) (trading profits), after "by a charity" there shall be inserted "(whether in the United Kingdom or elsewhere)".

(5) This section has effect—

(a) for the purposes of income tax, for the year 1996–97 and subsequent years of assessment; and

(b) for the purposes of corporation tax, in relation to accounting periods ending after 31st March 1996.

GENERAL NOTE
This section enacts an existing extra-statutory concession (B9) which exempts from tax certain investment income, such as bank interest, accruing to charities. The concession also applied to overseas rents and dividends [Standing Committee E, February 22, 1996, col. 472].

Withdrawal of relief for Class 4 contributions

147.—(1) In section 617 of the Taxes Act 1988 (social security benefits and contributions), subsection (5) (relief for Class 4 contributions) shall cease to have effect.

(2) In consequence of the provision made by subsection (1) above, in paragraph 3(2) of Schedule 2 to—

(a) the Social Security Contributions and Benefits Act 1992, and

(b) the Social Security Contributions and Benefits (Northern Ireland) Act 1992,

the words "(e) section 617(5) (relief for Class 4 contributions);" shall be omitted.

(3) This section shall have effect in relation to the year 1996–97 and subsequent years of assessment.

GENERAL NOTE
Self-employed individuals are currently allowed to deduct one half of their Class 4 National Insurance contributions from their taxable trading profits. To make the operation of self-assessment easier, this relief is being withdrawn. As a compensatory measure, the rate at which Class 4 contributions are computed is being reduced from 7.3 per cent to six per cent.

Mis-sold personal pensions etc.

148.—(1) Income tax shall not be chargeable on any payment falling within subsection (3) or (5) below.

(2) Receipt of a payment falling within subsection (3) below shall not be regarded for the purposes of capital gains tax as the disposal of an asset.

(3) A payment falls within this subsection if it is a capital sum by way of compensation for loss suffered, or reasonably likely to be suffered, by a person in a case where that person, or some other person, acting in reliance on bad investment advice at least some of which was given during the period beginning with 29th April 1988 and ending with 30th June 1994,—

(a) has, while eligible, or reasonably likely to become eligible, to be a member of an occupational pension scheme, instead become a member of a personal pension scheme or entered into a retirement annuity contract;

(b) has ceased to be a member of, or to pay contributions to, an occupational pension scheme and has instead become a member of a personal pension scheme or entered into a retirement annuity contract;

(c) has transferred to a personal pension scheme accrued rights of his under an occupational pension scheme; or

(d) has ceased to be a member of an occupational pension scheme and has instead (by virtue of such a provision as is mentioned in section 591(2)(g) of the Taxes Act 1988) entered into arrangements for securing relevant benefits by means of an annuity contract.

(4) A payment chargeable to income tax apart from subsection (1) above may nevertheless be regarded as a capital sum for the purpose of determining whether it falls within subsection (3) above.

(5) A payment falls within this subsection if and to the extent that it is a payment of interest, on the whole or any part of a capital sum such as is mentioned in subsection (3) above, for a period ending on or before the earliest date on which a determination (whether or not subsequently varied on an appeal or in any other proceedings) of the amount of the particular capital sum in question is made, whether by agreement or by a decision of—

(a) a court, tribunal or commissioner,

(b) an arbitrator or (in Scotland) arbiter, or

(c) any other person appointed for the purpose.

(6) In this section—

"bad investment advice" means investment advice in respect of which an action against the person who gave it has been, or may be, brought—

    (a) in or for negligence;

    (b) for breach of contract;

    (c) by reason of a breach of a fiduciary obligation; or

    (d) by reason of a contravention which is actionable under section 62 of the Financial Services Act 1986;

"investment advice" means advice such as is mentioned in paragraph 15 of Schedule 1 to the Financial Services Act 1986;

"occupational pension scheme" means—

    (a) a scheme approved, or being considered for approval, under Chapter I of Part XIV of the Taxes Act 1988 (retirement benefit schemes);

    (b) a relevant statutory scheme, as defined in section 611A(1) of that Act; or

    (c) a fund to which section 608 of that Act applies (superannuation funds approved before 6th April 1980 etc.);

"personal pension scheme" has the meaning given by section 630(1) of the Taxes Act 1988;

"relevant benefits" has the meaning given by section 612(1) of the Taxes Act 1988;

"retirement annuity contract" means a contract made before 1st July 1988 and approved by the Board under or by virtue of any provision of Chapter III of Part XIV of the Taxes Act 1988.

(7) This section shall have effect, and be taken always to have had effect, in relation to any payment falling within subsection (3) or (5) above, whether made before or after the passing of this Act.

GENERAL NOTE

Following the introduction of personal pension schemes in 1988, many individuals, such as postal workers, nurses and miners, were wrongly advised to leave their occupational pension schemes and take out a personal pension scheme. About 400,000 cases are thought to be involved. The institutions involved in the mis-selling of the pensions are to compensate the individuals concerned. This section exempts from income tax and capital gains tax amounts received in respect of such compensation. The exemption applies where between April 29, 1988 (when the Financial Services Act was introduced) and June 30, 1994 (when the problem had been fully identified) an individual was wrongly advised to transfer from, opt out of or not to join an occupational pension and instead to take out a personal pension scheme, buy-out contract or retirement annuity contract [*Hansard*, H.C. Vol. 270, col. 490].

Annual payments in residuary cases

149.—(1) Section 347A of the Taxes Act 1988 (annual payments not a charge on the income of a payer) shall apply to any payment made on or after 6th April 1996—

(a) in pursuance of any obligation which falls within section 36(4)(a) of the Finance Act 1988 (existing obligations under certain court orders), and

(b) for the benefit, maintenance or education of a person (whether or not the person to whom the payment is made) who attained the age of 21 before 6th April 1994,

as if that obligation were not an existing obligation within the definition contained in section 36(4) of the Finance Act 1988.

(2) Subsection (1) above does not apply to any payment to which section 38 of the Finance Act 1988 (treatment of certain maintenance payments under existing obligations) applies.

Certain annual payments, made under court orders dating from 1988 or earlier (and unchanged since 1988) will no longer be treated as a charge on the income of the payer, nor as taxable income of the recipient. The change affects payments made on or after April 6, 1996 to or for the benefit of a person (normally an adult son or daughter of the payer) who reached the age of 21 before April 6, 1994.

The change does not affect maintenance paid under court orders which qualifies for relief under transitional provisions in the FA 1988, s.38. This covers payments to a former husband or wife for their own benefit, or that of a child under 21, under court orders and written agreements dating from 1988 or earlier, including orders which have subsequently been amended [Standing Committee E, February 22, 1996, col. 480].

Income tax exemption for periodical payments of damages and compensation for personal injury

150.—(1) The sections set out in Schedule 26 to this Act shall be inserted after section 329 of the Taxes Act 1988.

(2) The first of those sections supersedes sections 329A and 329B inserted by the Finance Act 1995 and applies to payments received after the passing of this Act irrespective of when the agreement or order referred to in that section was made or took effect.

(3) Subsections (1) and (2) of the second of those sections supersede section 329C inserted by the Criminal Injuries Compensation Act 1995 and apply to payments received after the passing of that Act.

(4) The repeal of sections 329A and 329B does not affect the operation of those sections in relation to payments received before the passing of this Act.

GENERAL NOTE
The FA 1995, s.142, inserted the new ICTA 1988, ss.329A, 329B and 329C which exempted from tax annuities payable under structured settlements for damages for personal injury.

This section introduces Sched. 26, which replaces the previous provisions with the new ICTA 1988, ss.329AA and 329AB.

The new provisions widen the previous relief in the following ways:
(i) payments made under court order are covered, as well as those made by agreement;
(ii) annuities purchased by a third party, *e.g.* the Motor Insurers' Bureau, are covered;
(iii) payments made to trustees are covered;
(iv) structured settlements payable by the Criminal Injuries Compensation Board are covered. This had already been enacted by the Criminal Injuries Compensation Act 1995 (c. 53), s.8, which inserted the new ICTA 1988, s.329C [Standing Committee E, March 7, 1996, col. 736].

Taxation of benefits

Benefits under pilot schemes

151.—(1) The Treasury may by order make provision for the Income Tax Acts to have effect in relation to any amount of benefit payable by virtue of a Government pilot scheme as if it was, as they think fit, either—
  (a) wholly or partly exempt from income tax and, accordingly, to be disregarded in computing the amount of any receipts brought into account for income tax purposes; or
  (b) to the extent specified in the order, to be brought into account for the purposes of income tax as income of a description so specified or as a receipt of a description so specified.

(2) The Treasury may by order provide for any amount of benefit payable by virtue of a Government pilot scheme to be left out of account, to the extent specified in the order, in the determination for the purposes of section 153 of the Capital Allowances Act 1990 (subsidies etc.) of how far any expenditure has been or is to be met directly or indirectly by the Crown or by an authority or person other than the person actually incurring it.

(3) In this section "Government pilot scheme" means any arrangements (whether or not contained in a scheme) which—

(a) are made, under any enactment or otherwise, by the Secretary of State or any Northern Ireland department;

(b) make provision for or about the payment of amounts of benefit either—

(i) for purposes that are similar to those for which any social security or comparable benefit is payable; or

(ii) for purposes connected with the carrying out of any functions of the Secretary of State or any such department in relation to employment or training for employment;

(c) are arrangements relating to a temporary experimental period; and

(d) are made wholly or partly for the purpose of facilitating a decision as to whether, or to what extent, it is desirable for provision to be made on a permanent basis for or in relation to any benefit.

(4) In subsection (3)(b) above the reference to making provision for or about the payment of amounts of benefit for purposes that are similar to those for which any social security or comparable benefit is payable shall include a reference to making provision by virtue of which there is a modification of the conditions of entitlement to, or the conditions for the payment of, an existing social security or comparable benefit.

(5) An order under this section may—

(a) make different provision for different cases, and

(b) contain such incidental, supplemental, consequential and transitional provision (including provision modifying provision made by or under the Income Tax Acts) as the Treasury may think fit.

(6) In this section "benefit" includes any allowance, grant or other amount the whole or any part of which is payable directly or indirectly out of public funds.

(7) The power to make an order under this section—

(a) shall be exercisable for the year 1996–97 and subsequent years of assessment; and

(b) so far as exercisable for the year 1996–97, shall be exercisable in relation to benefits, allowances and other amounts paid at times on or after 6th April 1996 but before the making of the order.

(8) The Treasury shall not make an order under this section containing any such provision as is mentioned in subsection (1)(b) above unless a draft of the order has been laid before, and approved by a resolution of, the House of Commons.

GENERAL NOTE

This section provides the authority to introduce Treasury Orders governing the tax treatment of payments made under Government pilot schemes. A pilot scheme is a new work incentive scheme or social security benefit which may be "piloted" on a trial basis and the results evaluated before a decision on full implementation is taken. A new social security benefit, Earnings Top-Up will be piloted next year. The method of setting tax treatment by Treasury Order will create a flexible and responsive way of dealing with this which suits the temporary nature of pilot schemes.

Subs. (2)

Assets purchased with grants under pilot schemes may be eligible for capital allowances.

Subs. (8)

Orders imposing a charge to tax are subject to the affirmative resolution procedure.

Jobfinder's grant

152.—(1) The Income Tax Acts shall have effect, and be deemed always to have had effect, as if jobfinder's grant were exempt from income tax and, accordingly, were to be disregarded in computing the amount of any receipts brought into account for income tax purposes.

(2) In this section "jobfinder's grant" means grant paid under that name by virtue of arrangements made in pursuance of section 2 of the Employment and Training Act 1973 or section 1 of the Employment and Training Act (Northern Ireland) 1950 (arrangements for assisting persons to select, train for, obtain or retain employment).

GENERAL NOTE

Jobfinder's Grant is made exempt from tax since its inception in April 1995. It is a grant made to individuals who have been unemployed for two years or more to enable them to meet the costs of starting work, for example, paying for tools or work clothing. It is payable after a claimant has taken up employment of 30 or more hours per week which pays less than £150 per week [Standing Committee E, February 22, 1996, col. 480].

Investments

Foreign income dividends

153. Schedule 27 to this Act (which makes provision relating to foreign income dividends) shall have effect.

GENERAL NOTE

This section introduces Sched. 27, which amends the foreign income dividend (FID) scheme. This came into force on July 1, 1994. The main amendments include changes both in the calculation of distributable foreign profits and notional foreign source ACT to allow more relief for foreign tax in certain cases; a relaxation of the qualifying rules for international headquarters companies (IHCs) owned by foreign quoted companies through intermediate holding companies; and changes clarifying how the FID scheme operates.

See further the General Note to Sched. 27.

FOTRA securities

154.—(1) The modifications which, under section 60 of the Finance Act 1940, may be made for the purposes of any issue of securities to the conditions about tax exemption specified in section 22 of the Finance (No. 2) Act 1931 shall include a modification by virtue of which the tax exemption contained in any condition of the issue applies, as respects capital, irrespective of where the person with the beneficial ownership of the securities is domiciled.

(2) Subject to subsections (3) to (5) below, nothing in the Tax Acts shall impose any charge to tax on any person in respect of so much of any profits or gains arising from a FOTRA security, or from any loan relationship represented by a FOTRA security, as is expressed to be exempt from tax in the tax exemption condition applying to that security.

(3) Exemption from tax shall not be conferred by virtue of subsection (2) above in relation to any security unless the requirements imposed as respects that exemption by the conditions with which the security is issued (including any requirement as to the making of a claim) are complied with.

(4) The tax exemption condition of a FOTRA security shall not be taken to confer any exemption from any charge to tax imposed by virtue of the provisions of Chapter IA of Part XV or Chapter III of Part XVII of the Taxes Act 1988 (anti-avoidance provisions for residents etc.)

(5) Nothing in this section shall entitle any person to any repayment of tax which he has not claimed within the time limit which would be applicable under the Tax Acts (apart from this section) to a claim for the repayment of that tax.

(6) A person with the beneficial ownership of a FOTRA security who would, by virtue of this section, be exempt from tax in respect of some or all of the profits and gains arising from that security, or from any loan relationship represented by it, shall not be entitled for the purposes of income tax or corporation tax to bring into account any amount—

(a) in respect of changes in the value of that security;
(b) as expenses or disbursements incurred in, or in connection with, the holding of the security or any transaction relating to the security; or
(c) as a debit given, in respect of any loan relationship represented by that security, by any provision of Chapter II of this Part of this Act in respect of such a relationship.

(7) Schedule 28 to this Act (which contains amendments consequential on the provisions of this section) shall have effect.

(8) References in this section to a FOTRA security are references to—
(a) any security issued with such a condition about exemption from taxation as is authorised in relation to its issue by virtue of section 22 of the Finance (No. 2) Act 1931; or
(b) any 3½% War Loan 1952 Or After which was issued with a condition authorised by virtue of section 47 of the Finance (No. 2) Act 1915;
and references, in relation to such a security, to the tax exemption condition shall be construed accordingly.

(9) This section and Schedule 28 to this Act shall have effect—
(a) for the purposes of income tax, for the year 1996–97 and subsequent years of assessment; and
(b) for the purposes of corporation tax, for accounting periods, ending after 31st March 1996.

GENERAL NOTE

The section, together with Sched. 28, modifies the Treasury's powers to issue securities on FOTRA (free of tax to residents abroad) terms. These securities, sometimes also known as "exempt gilts", are exempt from income tax for persons normally resident abroad, and from capital taxes for persons normally resident and domiciled abroad. To facilitate the introduction of a gilt strips market (see s.202), the requirement of overseas domicile for exemption from capital taxes is removed. Otherwise a non-resident would be liable for capital gains on gilt strips, which have the character of capital.

See further the General Note to Sched. 28 [Standing Committee E, March 7, 1996, col. 715].

Directions for payment without deduction of tax

155. After section 51 of the Taxes Act 1988 there shall be inserted the following section—

"Commencement of direction under section 50 or 51

51AA. A direction under section 50 or 51 that any security shall be deemed to have been issued subject to the condition that the interest thereon shall be paid without deduction of tax may provide that the direction is to have effect in relation only to payments of interest made on or after such date as may be specified in the direction."

GENERAL NOTE

The new ICTA 1988, s.51AA, provides that a direction by the Treasury under ss.50 or 51 that interest on certain securities be paid gross of tax may specify the date from which the direction is to apply.

Paying and collecting agents etc.

156. Schedule 29 to this Act (which amends the rules relating to paying and collecting agents) shall have effect.

GENERAL NOTE

This section introduces Sched. 27, which sets out the framework for the new arrangements under which U.K. paying and collecting agents—mainly banks and stockbrokers—will have to deduct tax from certain foreign dividends and interest. These arrangements also apply to interest on U.K. Government stock.

The Revenue has power to make regulations to provide the detailed rules for the new arrangements.

See further the General Note to Sched. 27.

Stock lending fees

157.—(1) After section 129A of the Taxes Act 1988 (interest on cash collateral paid in connection with stock lending arrangements) there shall be inserted the following section—

> **"Stock lending fees**
> 129B.—(1) The income which, as income deriving from investments of a description specified in any of the relevant provisions, is eligible for relief from tax by virtue of that provision shall be taken to include any relevant stock lending fee.
> (2) For the purposes of this section the relevant provisions are sections 592(2), 608(2)(a), 613(4), 614(3) 620(6) and 643(2).
> (3) In this section 'relevant stock lending fee', in relation to investments of any description, means any amount, in the nature of a fee, which is payable in connection with an approved stock lending arrangement relating to investments which, but for any transfer under the arrangement, would be investments of that description.
> (4) In this section 'approved stock lending arrangement' has the same meaning as in Schedule 5A."

(2) This section has effect in relation to any arrangements entered into on or after 2nd January 1996.

GENERAL NOTE

The new ICTA 1988, s.129B, removes the existing tax charge on fees received by pension funds in relation to approved stock lending arrangements [Standing Committee E, February 22, 1996, col. 486].

Transfers on death under the accrued income scheme

158.—(1) In section 710(5) of the Taxes Act 1988 (meaning of "transfer" in sections 711 to 728), after "or otherwise" there shall be inserted ", but—
> (a) does not include the vesting of securities in a person's personal representatives on his death; and".

(2) Subsection (1) of section 721 of that Act (transfer of securities on death) shall cease to have effect.

(3) For subsection (2) of that section (transfers by personal representatives to legatees) there shall be substituted—
> "(2) Where—
> (a) an individual who is entitled to securities dies, and
> (b) in the interest period in which the individual died, the securities are transferred by his personal representatives to a legatee,
> section 713 shall not apply to the transfer."

(4) Subsection (4) of that section (interest period treated as ending with death) shall cease to have effect.

(5) This section has effect as respects deaths on or after 6th April 1996.

GENERAL NOTE

The accrued income scheme (see the ICTA 1988, ss.710–738) will no longer apply to the transfer of securities on an individual's death to his personal representatives. Where the securities are transferred to a legatee within an interest period the transfer from the personal representatives to the legatee is also disregarded [Standing Committee E, March 5, 1996, col. 707].

Manufactured payments, repos, etc.

159.—(1) Sections 729, 737A(2)(b) and 786(4) of the Taxes Act 1988 (provisions applying to sale and repurchase agreements) shall cease to have effect except in relation to cases where the initial agreement to sell or transfer the securities or other property was made before the appointed day.

(2) In section 737 of that Act—

(a) in subsection (5) (manufactured dividends paid to UK residents by non-residents), for the words from "a person resident in the United Kingdom" to "the United Kingdom recipient shall" there shall be substituted "a United Kingdom recipient, that recipient shall"; and

(b) after that subsection there shall be inserted the following subsection—

"(5AAA) For the purposes of subsection (5) above a person who receives a manufactured dividend is a United Kingdom recipient if—

(a) he is resident in the United Kingdom; or

(b) he is not so resident but receives that dividend for the purposes of a trade carried on through a branch or agency in the United Kingdom."

(3) In section 737C of that Act (deemed manufactured payments), the following subsection shall be inserted after subsection (11A) in relation to cases where the initial agreement to sell the securities is made on or after the appointed day, that is to say—

"(11B) The preceding provisions of this section shall have effect in cases where paragraph 2, 3 or 4 of Schedule 23A would apply by virtue of section 737A(5) but for paragraph 5 of that Schedule as they have effect in a case where the paragraph in question is not disapplied by paragraph 5; and where—

(a) the gross amount of the deemed manufactured interest, or

(b) the gross amount of the deemed manufactured overseas dividend,

falls to be calculated in such a case under subsection (8) or (11) above, it shall be so calculated by reference to the provisions of paragraph 3 or 4 of Schedule 23A that would have applied but for paragraph 5 of that Schedule."

(4) In sub-paragraph (3) of paragraph 4 of Schedule 23A to that Act (manufactured overseas dividends paid to UK residents by non-residents), for the words from "a person resident in the United Kingdom" to "the United Kingdom recipient shall" there shall be substituted "a United Kingdom recipient, that recipient shall".

(5) After that sub-paragraph there shall be inserted the following sub-paragraphs—

"(3A) For the purposes of sub-paragraph (3) above a person who receives a manufactured overseas dividend is a United Kingdom recipient if—

(a) he is resident in the United Kingdom; or

(b) he is not so resident but receives that dividend for the purposes of a trade carried on through a branch or agency in the United Kingdom.

(3B) Dividend manufacturing regulations may make provision, in relation to cases falling within sub-paragraph (3) above, for the amount of tax required under that sub-paragraph to be taken to be reduced, to such extent and for such purposes as may be determined under the regulations, by reference to amounts of overseas tax charged on, or in respect of—

(a) the making of the manufactured overseas dividend; or

(b) the overseas dividend of which the manufactured overseas dividend is representative."

(6) In sub-paragraph (7) of paragraph 4 of that Schedule (regulations for off-setting), for the words from "against" to "and account" in the words after paragraph (b) there shall be substituted "in accordance with the regulations and to the prescribed extent, amounts falling within paragraph (a) of sub-paragraph (7AA) below against the sums falling within paragraph (b) of that sub-paragraph, and to account"; and after that sub-paragraph there shall be inserted the following sub-paragraph—

"(7AA) Those amounts and sums are—
(a) amounts of overseas tax in respect of overseas dividends received by him in that chargeable period, amounts of overseas tax charged on, or in respect of, the making of manufactured overseas dividends so received by him and amounts deducted under sub-paragraph (2) above from any such manufactured overseas dividends; and
(b) the sums due from him on account of the amounts deducted by him under sub-paragraph (2) above from the manufactured overseas dividends paid by him in that chargeable period."

(7) In sub-paragraph (1) of paragraph 8 of that Schedule (power to modify provisions of Schedule)—
(a) before the "or" at the end of paragraph (a) there shall be inserted—
"(aa) such persons who receive, or become entitled to receive, manufactured dividends, manufactured interest or manufactured overseas dividends as may be prescribed,"
and
(b) in the words after paragraph (b), for "paragraph 2, 3 or 4 above" there shall be substituted "paragraphs 2 to 5 above".

(8) After sub-paragraph (1) of paragraph 8 of that Schedule there shall be inserted the following sub-paragraph—
"(1A) Dividend manufacturing regulations may provide, in relation to prescribed cases where a person makes or receives the payment of any amount representative of an overseas dividend, or is treated for any purposes of this Schedule or such regulations as a person making or receiving such a payment—
(a) for any entitlement of that person to claim relief under Part XVIII to be extinguished or reduced to such extent as may be found under the regulations; and
(b) for the adjustment, by reference to any provision having effect under the law of a territory outside the United Kingdom, of any amount falling to be taken, for any prescribed purposes of the Tax Acts or the 1992 Act, to be the amount paid or payable by or to any person in respect of any sale, repurchase or other transfer of the overseas securities to which the payment relates."

(9) Subsections (2), (4) and (5) above have effect—
(a) for the purposes of corporation tax, in relation to accounting periods ending after 31st March 1996; and
(b) for the purposes of income tax, in relation to the year 1996–97 and subsequent years of assessment.

(10) In this section "the appointed day" means such day as the Treasury may by order appoint, and different days may be appointed under this subsection for different purposes.

GENERAL NOTE
This section makes a number of provisions about the tax treatment of manufactured overseas dividends and related matters. In particular, it will enable a simpler alternative to the existing rules for deducting tax from manufactured overseas dividends to be introduced by regulations. This will enable the related revenue protection measure in the ICTA 1988, s.737A, to be brought into effect in relation to overseas securities. The section also corrects anomalies and repeals redundant legislation.

Subs. (1)
This repeals some existing provisions relating to repos (sale and repurchase agreements) with effect from an appointed day. The provisions will become redundant only once a day is appointed under s.737B(9) to bring s.737A into effect for overseas securities. Accordingly, the same day will be appointed for both measures.

Subs. (2)
This inserts new s.737(5AAA) and repeals some redundant wording in s.737(5). The new subsection removes an anomaly by extending the operation of the section from persons resident in the U.K. to persons not so resident but who trade in the U.K. through a branch or agency.

Subs. (3)
The new s.737C(11B) corrects a drafting error.

Subs. (4)
Together with the new Sched. 23A, para. 4(3A), inserted by subs. (5), this makes changes to Sched. 23A, para. 4, mirroring those made to s.737 by subs. (2) above.

Subs. (5)
This also inserts a new Sched. 23A, para. 4(3B), which together with subss. (6)–(8) below amends the regulation making powers in Sched. 23A so that regulations will be able to:
(i) take account of tax suffered on manufactured overseas dividends in the same way that account is presently taken of foreign tax suffered on "real" overseas dividends;
(ii) provide for the alternative treatment of manufactured overseas dividends;
(iii) resolve conflicts between the tax treatment of such transactions in other countries and the tax treatment under domestic law.

Investments in housing

160. Schedule 30 to this Act (which makes provision conferring relief from corporation tax on companies that invest in housing) shall have effect.

GENERAL NOTE
This section introduces Sched. 30, which amends the rules for approved investment trusts to enable them to invest in residential properties as well as shares or securities. The purpose of the change is to attract more capital into the rented housing market. See further the General Note to Sched. 30 [Standing Committee E, February 22, 1996, col. 486].

Venture capital trusts: control of companies etc.

161.—(1) Schedule 28B to the Taxes Act 1988 (venture capital trusts: meaning of qualifying holdings) shall have effect, and be deemed always to have had effect, subject to the amendments in subsections (2) and (3) below.

(2) In paragraph 9 (requirements as to subsidiaries etc. of the relevant company), the following shall be omitted—
(a) in sub-paragraph (1), the words "subject to sub-paragraph (2) below"; and
(b) sub-paragraph (2).

(3) In paragraph 13 (interpretation), for sub-paragraphs (2) and (3) ("connected" and "control" to be construed in accordance with sections 839 and 416(2) to (6)) there shall be substituted the following sub-paragraphs—
"(2) For the purposes of paragraphs 5(2) and 9 above, the question whether a person controls a company shall be determined in accordance with subsections (2) to (6) of section 416 with the modification given by sub-paragraph (3) below.
(3) The modification is that, in determining whether a person controls a company, there shall be disregarded—
(a) his or any other person's possession of, or entitlement to acquire, relevant fixed-rate preference shares of the company; and
(b) his or any other person's possession of, or entitlement to acquire, rights as a loan creditor of the company.
(4) Section 839 shall apply for the purposes of this Schedule, but as if the reference in subsection (8) to section 416 were a reference to subsections (2) to (6) of section 416 with the modification given by sub-paragraph (3) above.
(5) For the purposes of sub-paragraph (3) above—
(a) relevant fixed-rate preference shares are fixed-rate preference shares that do not for the time being carry voting rights; and

(b) 'fixed-rate preference shares' has the same meaning as in section
95.' '

GENERAL NOTE
This section, introduced at committee stage, implements a concession announced by the
Government in September 1995 (see [1995] STI 1391). The original legislation governing venture capital trusts (VCTs) in the FA 1995 debarred a VCT from controlling any company in
which it invested. Control was to be construed in accordance with the ICTA 1988, s.416. This was
considered to be too restrictive. The amendments to the ICTA 1988, Sched. 28B, permit control
to be construed without regard to non-voting, fixed-rate preference shares and loans [Standing
Committee E, March 7, 1996, col. 738].

Insurance policies

Qualifying life insurance policies: certification

162.—(1) Section 55 of the Finance Act 1995 (removal of certification
requirements for qualifying policies with respect to any time on or after 5th
May 1996 etc) shall have effect—
  (a) with the substitution for "5th May 1996", wherever occurring, of "the
      appointed date"; and
  (b) with the addition of the following subsection after subsection (8)—
      "(9) In this section "the appointed date" means such date as may be
      specified for the purpose in an order made by the Board."
  (2) In Schedule 15 to the Taxes Act 1988 (qualifying policies) paragraphs
24(2A) and 25(2) shall have effect with the substitution for "5th May 1996" of
"the appointed date for the purposes of section 55 of the Finance Act 1995
(removal of certification requirements)".

GENERAL NOTE
The certification by the Revenue of qualifying policies of life assurance, due to end from May
5, 1996, has been extended to an appointed date to be fixed by the Revenue by statutory order.
This is to allow more time for the Revenue to consult with the insurance industry regarding new
rules governing qualifying policies.

Insurance companies

Life assurance business losses

163. Schedule 31 to this Act, which makes provision about losses arising to
insurance companies in the carrying on of life assurance business, shall have
effect.

GENERAL NOTE
This section, tabled at report stage following a discussion in committee (see Standing Committee E, March 12, 1996, col. 869) introduces Sched. 31, which modifies the measures introduced in the FA 1995 regarding losses incurred by life assurance companies. The changes
prevent an anti-avoidance rule from operating in a way which might inhibit new companies from
starting up life assurance operations, but will strengthen it in the situations where it is intended
to operate.
See further the General Note to Sched. 31.

Limits on relief for expenses

164.—(1) For subsections (2) to (5) of section 76 of the Taxes Act 1988
there shall be substituted the following subsections—
      "(2) Where, in the case of any such company, the amount mentioned
      in paragraph (a) of subsection (2A) below exceeds for any accounting
      period the amount mentioned in paragraph (b) of that subsection, the
      amount which by virtue of this section is to be deductible by way of man-
      agement expenses for that period shall be equal to the basic deduction
      for that period reduced by the amount of the excess.

(2A) Those amounts are—

(a) the amount which would be the profits of the company's life assurance business for that period if computed in accordance with the provisions applicable to Case I of Schedule D and adjusted in respect of losses; and

(b) the amount (including any negative amount) produced by deducting the following aggregate amount from the company's relevant income for that period from its life assurance business, that is to say, the aggregate of—

    (i) the basic deduction,

    (ii) any non-trading deficit on the company's loan relationships which is produced for that period in relation to that business by a separate computation under paragraph 2 of Schedule 11 to the Finance Act 1996,

    (iii) any amount which in pursuance of a claim under paragraph 4(3) of that Schedule is carried back to that period and (in accordance with paragraph 4(5) of that Schedule) applied in reducing profits of the company for that period, and

    (iv) any charges on income for that period so far as they consist in annuities or other annual payments that are referable to the company's life assurance business and, if they are not annuities, are payable by the company wholly or partly in satisfaction of claims under insurance policies.

(2B) For the purposes of subsection (2A) above a company's relevant income for any accounting period from its life assurance business is the sum of the following—

(a) the income and gains of the company's life assurance business for that accounting period; and

(b) the relevant franked investment income of the company for that period so far as it arises from assets held for the purposes of that business and is not included in the income and gains mentioned in paragraph (a) above.

(2C) The adjustment in respect of losses that is to be made for any accounting period under paragraph (a) of subsection (2A) above is a deduction of the amount equal to the unused part of the sum which—

(a) by reference to computations made in respect of the company's life assurance business in accordance with the provisions applicable to Case I of Schedule D, and

(b) disregarding section 434A(2),

would fall, in the case of the company, to be set off under section 393 against the company's income for that period.

(2D) For the purposes of subsection (2C) above, an amount is unused to the extent that it has not been taken into account for any previous accounting period in determining the amount by reference to which the following question was answered, namely, the question whether, and by how much, the amount deductible by virtue of this section by way of management expenses was less than the basic deduction.

(5) Subject to paragraph 4(11) to (13) of Schedule 11 to the Finance Act 1996, where the basic deduction for any period exceeds the amount which for that period is to be deductible by virtue of this section by way of management expenses, the amount to be carried forward by virtue of section 75(3) (including the amount to be so carried forward for the purpose of computing the amount of the basic deduction for any period) shall be increased by the amount of the excess."

(2) In subsection (8) of that section—

(a) after the definition of "authorised person" there shall be inserted the following definition

" 'basic deduction', in relation to an accounting period of an insurance company, means the amount which, by virtue of this section, would be deductible by way of management expenses for that period but for subsection (2) above;"
and

(b) after the definition of "recognised self-regulating organisation" there shall be inserted the following definition—

" 'relevant franked investment income', in relation to any insurance company, means any franked investment income of the company in so far as it is not income the tax credits comprised in which may be claimed by the company under section 438(4) or 441A(7);".

(3) In paragraph 5 of Schedule 19AC to the Taxes Act 1988 (modification of section 76)—

(a) in sub-paragraph (1), in the subsection (6B) treated as inserted in section 76, for "their" there shall be substituted "its" and the words "and subsections (2) and (3)(b) above" shall be omitted; and

(b) after that sub-paragraph there shall be inserted the following sub-paragraph—

"(1A) In section 76 references to franked investment income shall be treated as being references to UK distribution income within the meaning of paragraph 5B of this Schedule."

(4) In section 56(4) of the Taxes Act 1988 (which contains a reference to the computation required by section 76(2) of that Act), for "by" there shall be substituted "for the purposes of".

(5) Subject to subsection (6) below, this section has effect in relation to accounting periods beginning on or after 1st January 1996.

(6) Notwithstanding anything in the previous provisions of this section, section 76 of the Taxes Act 1988 has effect in relation to accounting periods beginning on or after 1st January 1996—

(a) as if the reference in subsection (2D) of that section to a previous accounting period included a reference to an accounting period beginning before that date, and

(b) in relation to such a previous accounting period, as if the references—

(i) to the amount deductible by virtue of this section, and
(ii) to the basic deduction,

were to be construed by reference to whatever provisions had effect in relation to that previous period for purposes corresponding to those of that section as amended by this section.

GENERAL NOTE
This section changes and simplifies the rules that govern the limit on the relief that can be given in any one accounting period to a life insurance company in respect of the expenses of managing its life assurance business.

Subs. (1)
This amends the existing rules in the ICTA 1988, s.76, by replacing the current subs. (2)–(5).

The new subs. (2), (2A) and (2B) provide the basic rule for the calculation that must be made in order to determine whether or not the management expenses being claimed by an insurance company will need to be restricted. A comparison is made between the profits of the life assurance business calculated on Sched. D Case I principles and on the "I minus E" basis. If the first figure is greater than the second the expenses to be allowed are correspondingly reduced.

The new subs. (2C) and (2D) explain what losses may be set against the Case I profit of the year when making the comparison. These are losses in previous periods which have neither been used in the comparison in those periods nor used in other ways, *e.g.* surrender or set-off. The losses are, however, calculated without regard to a rule that restricts the amount of a loss that can actually be set-off or surrendered.

The new subs. (5) ensures that any management expenses that cannot be taken into account as a result of the restriction in new subs. (2A) can be carried forward.

Subss. (2)–(6)

These contain further consequential amendments and commencement and transitional provisions [Standing Committee E, February 22, 1996, col. 504].

Annual payments under insurance policies: deductions

165.—(1) In section 337 of the Taxes Act 1988 (deductions in computing income), the following subsections shall be inserted after subsection (2)—

"(2A) In computing any profits or losses of a company in accordance with the provisions of this Act applicable to Case I of Schedule D, subsection (2)(b) above shall not prevent the deduction of any annuity or other annual payment which is payable by a company wholly or partly in satisfaction of any claim under an insurance policy in relation to which the company is the insurer.

(2B) The reference in subsection (2A) above to an annuity payable wholly or partly in satisfaction of a claim under an insurance policy shall be taken, in relation to an insurance company (within the meaning of Chapter I of Part XII), to include a reference to every annuity payable by that company; and the references in sections 338(2) and 434B(2) to an annuity paid wholly or partly as mentioned in subsection (2A) above shall be construed accordingly."

(2) In section 338(2) of that Act, in the words after paragraph (b) (payments which are not charges on income), after "corporation tax" there shall be inserted "nor any annuity or other annual payment which (without being so deductible) is paid wholly or partly as mentioned in section 337(2A)".

(3) In section 434B of that Act (treatment of interest and annuities in the case of insurance companies), subsection (1) shall cease to have effect; and in subsection (2), for the words from the beginning to "mentioned in subsection (1) above" there shall be substituted—

"(2) Nothing in section 337(2A) or 338(2) shall be construed as preventing any annuity or other annual payment which is paid wholly or partly as mentioned in section 337(2A)".

(4) Subject to subsection (5) below, this section has effect in relation to accounting periods beginning on or after 1st January 1996.

(5) In relation to any accounting period beginning on or after 1st January 1996 but ending before 1st April 1996, this section shall have effect as if any reference in provisions inserted by this section to an annuity payable or paid by an insurance company included a reference to any such interest as was mentioned in section 434B(1) of the Taxes Act 1988 before its repeal by virtue of this section.

GENERAL NOTE

This section clarifies the way in which insurance companies get relief in their tax computations for annuities they pay and for some other claims under insurance policies. Those currently treated as charges on income will in future be allowed as an expense of the trade.

Subs. (1)

This inserts the new ICTA 1988, s.337(2A) and (2B), which allow any annuity and annual payment in satisfaction of a claim to be deducted as a trading expense. These include some payments under mortgage payment protection and other creditor insurances, and income withdrawals from personal pension schemes.

Subs. (2)

This makes a consequential amendment to prevent annuities and annual payments that are the subject of this section from being treated as charges on income.

Subs. (3)

This repeals the ICTA 1988, s.434B(1), which is no longer necessary and makes changes to s.434B(2) to preserve the existing relief for annuities and annual payments relating to BLAGAB business when a life insurer is taxed on the "I minus E" basis rather than on its trading profits.

Subss. (4) and (5)
These subsections contain commencement and transitional provisions.

Equalisation reserves

166. Schedule 32 to this Act (which makes provision about the tax treatment of equalisation reserves maintained by insurance companies) shall have effect.

GENERAL NOTE
This section introduces Sched. 32, which provides for a new scheme of tax relief on equalisation reserves maintained in respect of certain lines of general insurance. Under a new DTI regulatory framework, insurance companies will be required to set aside each year a proportion of premiums from specified types of business into a reserve to be drawn upon when claims experience is exceptionally poor. Transfers into such reserves will be allowed as a deduction from profits and transfers out will be taxed.
See further the General Note to Sched. 32.

Industrial assurance business

167.—(1) In section 432 of the Taxes Act 1988, subsection (2) (industrial assurance business treated as separate business for the purposes of Chapter I of Part XII) shall cease to have effect.

(2) In section 432A(2) of the Taxes Act 1988, for paragraphs (d) and (e) (different categories of basic life assurance and general annuity business, including and not including industrial assurance business), there shall be substituted the following paragraph—

"(d) basic life assurance and general annuity business; and".

(3) In section 86 of the Finance Act 1989 (spreading of relief for acquisition expenses)—

(a) in subsection (1)(a), for "in respect of industrial life assurance business carried on by the company" there shall be substituted "for persons who collect premiums from house to house"; and

(b) in subsection (2), for "in respect of industrial life assurance business" there shall be substituted "for persons who collect premiums from house to house".

(4) In section 832 of the Taxes Act 1988 (interpretation), in the definition of "industrial assurance business" for "has" there shall be substituted "means any such business carried on before the day appointed for the coming into force of section 167(4) of the Finance Act 1996 as was industrial assurance business within".

(5) In Schedule 14 to the Taxes Act 1988 (ancillary provisions about relief in respect of life assurance premiums), in paragraph 8, at the beginning of sub-paragraph (4) (policy which is varied so as to increase benefits, etc. to be treated as issued after 13th March 1984) there shall be inserted "Subject to sub-paragraph (8) below,".

(6) After sub-paragraph (7) of that paragraph there shall be inserted the following sub-paragraph—

"(8) Sub-paragraph (4) above does not apply in the case of a variation so as to increase the benefits secured, if the variation is made—

(a) on or after such day as the Board may by order appoint, and

(b) in consideration of a change in the method of payment of premiums from collection by a person collecting premiums from house to house to payment by a different method."

(7) In Schedule 15 to the Taxes Act 1988 (qualifying policies)—

(a) in paragraph 1(6) (calculation of amount included in premiums of whole life and term insurances in respect of their payment otherwise than annually), for "and if the policy is issued in the course of an industrial assurance business," there shall be substituted "and if the policy provides for payment otherwise than annually without providing for the amount of the premiums if they are paid annually,"; and

(b) in paragraph 2(2) (the equivalent calculation for endowment assurances), for "issued in the course of an industrial assurance business" there shall be substituted "that provides for the payment of premiums otherwise than annually without providing for the amount of the premiums if they are paid annually,".

(8) After paragraph 8 of that Schedule there shall be inserted the following paragraph—

"8A.—(1) Paragraphs 7 and 8 above shall have effect in relation to any policy issued on or after the appointed day as if the references to the issue of a policy in the course of an industrial assurance business were references to the issue of a policy by any company in a case in which—

(a) the company, before that day and in the course of such a business, issued any policy which was a qualifying policy by virtue of either of those paragraphs; and

(b) the policies which on 28th November 1995 were being offered by the company as available to be issued included policies of the same description as the policy issued on or after the appointed day.

(2) In this paragraph 'the appointed day' means such day as the Board may by order appoint."

(9) In paragraph 18(3) of that Schedule (certain variations of a policy not to affect whether policy is a qualifying policy), after paragraph (b) there shall be inserted "or

(c) any variation so as to increase the benefits secured or reduce the premiums payable which is effected—

(i) on or after such day as the Board may by order appoint, and

(ii) in consideration of a change in the method of payment of premiums from collection by a person collecting premiums from house to house to payment by a different method."

(10) Subsections (1) to (3) above have effect in relation to accounting periods beginning on or after 1st January 1996.

(11) Subsection (4) above shall come into force on such day as the Board may by order appoint.

(12) Subsection (7) above shall have effect in relation to policies issued on or after such day as the Board may by order appoint.

GENERAL NOTE

This section removes the distinction between "industrial" and "ordinary" life assurance business for tax purposes. Industrial business involves collecting premiums in cash from policy holders' homes, often at weekly intervals. The Treasury are now proposing to repeal the Industrial Assurance Acts 1923 to 1968 as a deregulatory measure and the distinction between industrial and ordinary business has become less important for tax purposes as industrial business has declined. Accordingly, the distinction between the classes of business will be removed for accounting periods ending on or after January 1, 1996.

The section also includes measures to ensure that the tax treatment of existing policy holders will not suffer as a result of the disappearance of industrial assurance business as a distinct category. These measures will come into force on a day to be appointed by the Revenue, which will coincide with the proposed repeal of the Industrial Assurance Acts.

Capital redemption business

168.—(1) For subsection (3) of section 458 of the Taxes Act 1988 (meaning of capital redemption business) there shall be substituted the following subsection—

"(3) In this section 'capital redemption business' means any business in so far as it—

(a) is insurance business for the purposes of the Insurance Companies Act 1982, but not life assurance business; and

(b) consists in effecting on the basis of actuarial calculations, and carrying out, contracts under which, in return for one or more fixed payments, a sum or series of sums of a specified amount become payable at a future time or over a period."

(2) Schedule 33 to this Act (which makes provision for the application of the I minus E basis of charging tax to companies carrying on capital redemption business) shall have effect.

(3) In Chapter I of Part XII of the Taxes Act 1988, after section 458 (capital redemption business) there shall be inserted the following section—

"Capital redemption business: power to apply life assurance provisions
458A.—(1) The Treasury may by regulations provide for the life assurance provisions of the Corporation Tax Acts to have effect in relation to companies carrying on capital redemption business as if capital redemption business were, or were a category of, life assurance business.

(2) Regulations under this section may provide that the provisions applied by the regulations are to have effect as respects capital redemption business with such modifications and exceptions as may be provided for in the regulations.

(3) Regulations under this section may—
(a) make different provision for different cases;
(b) include such incidental, supplemental, consequential and transitional provision (including provision modifying provisions of the Corporation Tax Acts other than the life assurance provisions) as the Treasury consider appropriate; and
(c) include retrospective provision.

(4) In this section references to the life assurance provisions of the Corporation Tax Acts are references to the following—
(a) the provisions of this Chapter so far as they relate to life assurance business or companies carrying on such business; and
(b) any other provisions of the Corporation Tax Acts making separate provision by reference to whether or not the business of a company is or includes life assurance business or any category of insurance business that includes life assurance business.

(5) In this section 'capital redemption business' has the same meaning as in section 458."

(4) In section 539(3) of that Act, in the definition of "capital redemption policy" for "insurance" there shall be substituted for "contract".

(5) In section 553(10) of that Act, in paragraph (a) of the definition of "new offshore capital redemption policy", for "an insurance" there shall be substituted "a contract".

(6) Subsection (1) above shall have effect as respects accounting periods ending on or after the day appointed under section 199 of the Finance Act 1994 for the purposes of Chapter III of Part IV of that Act (self-assessment management provisions), and subsections (4) and (5) above shall have effect as respects contracts effected on or after that day.

GENERAL NOTE

This section makes a number of changes to the taxation of capital redemption business, which is a form of investment business carried on by a few insurance companies and which does not involve any contingency dependent on human life. Changes are necessary with the introduction of self-assessment because the way the business is taxed at present, and in particular the way expenses are relieved, relies on concessions and practices. It is desirable that these should be spelt out in legislation if the company is to be able to assess itself correctly.

See further the General Note to Sched. 33.

Subs. (1)
This changes the definition of capital redemption business and brings it into line with the wording of the E.C. Life Insurance Directives.

Subs. (3)
The new ICTA 1988, s.458A, confers a power on the Treasury to make regulations adapting the existing rules applying to life assurance business, and specifically BLAGAB business, to capital redemption business.

Subss. (4)–(6)
These provide consequential amendments and commencement provisions. The legislation will apply from the general commencement day for corporation tax self-assessment.

Provisional repayments in connection with pension business

169.—(1) Schedule 19AB to the Taxes Act 1988 (pension business: payments on account of tax credits and deducted tax) shall be amended in accordance with the provisions of Part I of Schedule 34 to this Act.

(2) Schedule 19AC to the Taxes Act 1988 (modification of that Act in relation to overseas life insurance companies) shall be amended in accordance with the provisions of Part II of Schedule 34 to this Act.

(3) The amendments made by Schedule 34 to this Act shall have effect in relation to provisional repayment periods, within the meaning of Schedule 19AB to the Taxes Act 1988, falling in accounting periods ending on or after the day appointed under section 199 of the Finance Act 1994 for the purposes of Chapter III of Part IV of that Act (self-assessment management provisions).

GENERAL NOTE
The section introduces Sched. 34, which makes a number of amendments to the ICTA 1988, Sched. 19AB. This sets out the rules under which an insurance company carrying on pension business can make provisional repayment claims during a year for repayments of income tax deducted at source, and payments of tax credits on distributions it receives which relate to its pension business. The changes are needed to ensure that the Schedule works appropriately for self-assessment.
See further the General Note to Sched. 34.

Time for amending and enquiring into returns

170.—(1) After section 11AB of the Taxes Management Act 1970 there shall be inserted the following sections—

"Modifications of sections 11AA and 11AB in relation to non-annual accounting of general insurance business

11AC.—(1) This section applies in any case where a company carrying on insurance business in any period delivers a return for that period under section 11 of this Act which is based wholly or partly on accounts which the company is required or permitted to draw up using the method described in paragraph 52 of Schedule 9A to the Companies Act 1985 (accounting for general insurance business on a non-annual basis).

(2) Where this section applies, section 11AA(2) of this Act shall have effect as if after paragraph (b) there were added "and
> (c1) where a company has delivered a return which is based wholly or partly on accounts drawn up as mentioned in section 11AC(1) of this Act, then, at any time before the end of the period of twelve months beginning with the date on which any particular technical provision constituted in the case of those accounts as described in paragraph 52 of Schedule 9A to the Companies Act 1985 is replaced as described in sub-paragraph (4) of that paragraph, the company may by notice to an officer of the Board so amend its self-assessment as to give effect to any amendments to the return—

    (i) which arise from the replacement of that technical provision, and

    (ii) which the company has notified to such an officer."

(3) Where this section applies, section 11AB of this Act shall have effect—

  (a) as if in subsection (1)(b) after "subsection (2)(b)" there were inserted "or (c1)"; and

  (b) as if in subsection (2) for the words from "is" to the end of paragraph (b) there were substituted—

    "(a1) in the case of a return (whenever delivered) which is based wholly or partly on accounts drawn up as mentioned in section 11AC(1) of this Act, is whichever of the following periods ends the later, that is to say—

      (i) the period of two years beginning with the date (or, if there is more than one such date, the latest date) on which any technical provision constituted in the case of those accounts as described in paragraph 52 of Schedule 9A to the Companies Act 1985 is replaced as mentioned in sub-paragraph (4) of that paragraph; or

      (ii) the period ending with the quarter day next following the first anniversary of the day on which the return was delivered; and

    (b1) in the case of an amendment of such a return—

      (i) if the amendment is made on or before the filing date, is the period of twelve months beginning with that date; or

      (ii) if the amendment is made after that date, is the period ending with the quarter day next following the first anniversary of the day on which the amendment was made;".

Modifications of sections 11AA and 11AB for insurance companies with non-annual actuarial investigations

11AD.—(1) This section applies in any case where a return under section 11 of this Act is delivered by an insurance company which is permitted by an order under section 68 of the Insurance Companies Act 1982 to cause investigations to be made into its financial condition less frequently than is required by section 18 of that Act.

(2) Where this section applies, section 11AA(2) of this Act shall have effect as if, after paragraph (b), there were added "and

    (c2) where a company falling within section 11AD(1) of this Act has delivered a return for any period, then, at any time before the end of the period of twelve months beginning with the date as at which the relevant investigation is carried out, that is to say—

      (i) if the return is for a period as at the end of which there is carried out an investigation under section 18 of the Insurance Companies Act 1982 into the financial condition of the company, that investigation, or

      (ii) if the return is not for such a period, the first such investigation to be made into the financial condition of the company as at the end of a subsequent period,

    the company may by notice to an officer of the Board so amend its self-assessment as to give effect to any amendments to its return which arise from that investigation and which the company has notified to such an officer."

(3) Where this section applies, section 11AB of this Act shall have effect—

  (a) as if in subsection (1)(b) after "subsection (2)(b)" there were inserted "or (c2)"; and

(b) as if in subsection (2) for the words from "is" to the end of paragraph (b) there were substituted—

"(a2) in the case of a return delivered at any time by a company falling within section 11AD(1) of this Act, is the period of two years beginning with the date as at which the relevant investigation, as defined in section 11AA(2)(c2) of this Act, is carried out; and

(b2) in the case of an amendment of such a return—

  (i) if the amendment is made on or before the filing date, is the period of twelve months beginning with that date; or

  (ii) if the amendment is made after that date, is the period ending with the quarter day next following the first anniversary of the day on which the amendment was made;".

Modifications of sections 11AA and 11AB for friendly societies with non-annual actuarial investigations

11AE.—(1) This section applies in any case where a return under section 11 of this Act is delivered by a friendly society which is required by section 47 of the Friendly Societies Act 1992 to cause an investigation to be made into its financial condition at least once in every period of three years.

(2) Where this section applies, section 11AA(2) of this Act shall have effect as if, after paragraph (b), there were added "and

(c3) where a friendly society falling within section 11AE(1) of this Act has delivered a return for any period, then, at any time before the end of the period of fifteen months beginning with the date as at which the relevant investigation is carried out, that is to say—

  (i) if the return is for a period as at the end of which there is carried out an investigation under section 47 of the Friendly Societies Act 1992 into the financial condition of the society, that investigation, or

  (ii) if the return is not for such a period, the first such investigation to be made into the financial condition of the society as at the end of a subsequent period,

the society may by notice to an officer of the Board so amend its self-assessment as to give effect to any amendments to its return which arise from that investigation and which the society has notified to such an officer."

(3) Where this section applies, section 11AB of this Act shall have effect—

(a) as if in subsection (1)(b) after "subsection (2)(b)" there were inserted "or (c3)"; and

(b) as if in subsection (2) for the words from "is" to the end of paragraph (b) there were substituted—

"(a3) in the case of a return delivered at any time by a friendly society falling within section 11AE(1) of this Act, is the period of twenty seven months beginning with the date as at which the relevant investigation, as defined in section 11AA (2)(c3) of this Act, is carried out; and

(b3) in the case of an amendment of such a return—

  (i) if the amendment is made on or before the filing date, is the period of twelve months beginning with that date; or

  (ii) if the amendment is made after that date, is the period ending with the quarter day next following the first anniversary of the day on which the amendment was made;"."

(2) The amendment made by subsection (1) above shall have effect as respects accounting periods ending on or after the day appointed under section 199 of the Finance Act 1994 for the purposes of Chapter III of Part IV of that Act (self-assessment management provisions).

GENERAL NOTE

This section provides for the extension of time limits for both amending and enquiring into a corporation tax self-assessment return in the case of certain insurers. It will apply to general insurance companies which base their returns on recognised forms of non-annual accounting and to life insurance companies and friendly societies which are permitted to have actuarial valuations less frequently than annually. For these insurers, the normal time limits for amending corporation tax self-assessments will not be long enough to allow them to submit revised figures when their accounts are finalised. The Revenue's power of enquiry into these returns is similarly extended.

The new TMA 1970, s.11AC, extends the time limit for amending a corporation tax self-assessment for general insurance companies which base their returns on recognised forms of non-annual accounting. An amendment may be made up to 12 months after the accounts are finalised. The inspector is allowed two years after the accounts are finalised to raise enquiries.

The new TMA 1970, ss.11AD and 11AE, make similar changes for life insurance companies and friendly societies which are permitted to have actuarial valuations less frequently than annually for supervisory purposes. In the case of friendly societies the limits are extended to 15 months and 27 months respectively.

Friendly societies

Life or endowment business

171.—(1) In section 466 of the Taxes Act 1988 (interpretation of Chapter II of Part XII) for subsection (1) (meaning of "life or endowment business") there shall be substituted—

"(1) In this Chapter "life or endowment business" means, subject to subsections (1A) and (1B) below,—

(a) any business within Class I, II or III of Head A of Schedule 2 to the Friendly Societies Act 1992;

(b) pension business;

(c) any other life assurance business;

(d) any business within Class IV of Head A of that Schedule, if—

(i) the contract is one made before 1st September 1996; or

(ii) the contract is one made on or after 1st September 1996 and the effecting and carrying out of the contract also constitutes business within Class I, II or III of Head A of that Schedule.

(1A) Life or endowment business does not include the issue, in respect of a contract made before 1st September 1996, of a policy affording provision for sickness or other infirmity (whether bodily or mental), unless—

(a) the policy also affords assurance for a gross sum independent of sickness or other infirmity;

(b) not less than 60 per cent. of the amount of the premiums is attributable to the provision afforded during sickness or other infirmity; and

(c) there is no bonus or addition which may be declared or accrue upon the assurance of the gross sum.

(1B) Life or endowment business does not include the assurance of any annuity the consideration for which consists of sums obtainable on the maturity, or on the surrender, of any other policy of assurance issued by the friendly society, being a policy of assurance forming part of the tax exempt life or endowment business of the friendly society."

(2) In subsection (2) of that section (other definitions) there shall be inserted at the appropriate places—

(a) " "insurance company" shall be construed in accordance with section 431;"; and

(b) " "long term business" shall be construed in accordance with section 431;".

(3) In section 266 of that Act (life assurance premium relief) in subsection (6) (deduction from total income where relief given for part of certain payments to friendly societies) after paragraph (b) there shall be inserted "and

(c) the insurance or contract is not excluded by subsection (6A) below,".

(4) After that subsection there shall be inserted—

"(6A) For the purposes of subsection (6)(c) above, an insurance or contract is excluded by this subsection if it is made on or after 1st September 1996 and affords provision for sickness or other infirmity (whether bodily or mental), unless—

(a) it also affords assurance for a gross sum independent of sickness or other infirmity;

(b) not less than 60 per cent. of the amount of the premiums is attributable to the provision afforded during sickness or other infirmity; and

(c) there is no bonus or addition which may be declared or accrue upon the assurance of the gross sum."

(5) In section 463(1) of that Act (Corporation Tax Acts to apply to friendly societies' life or endowment business as they apply to insurance companies' mutual life assurance business) after "mutual life assurance business" there shall be inserted "(or other long term business)".

(6) The amendment made by subsection (5) above shall have effect in relation to accounting periods ending on or after 1st September 1996.

GENERAL NOTE

This section, introduced as a backbench amendment at committee stage, assists Friendly Societies created after June 1, 1973 to carry out non-life and non-endowment business such as critical illness benefit. Such societies are subject to a tax regime under the ICTA 1988, s.461, which prevents the development of products with modern features such as provision for the payment of benefit upon the occurrence of a serious illness.

Subs. (1)

This inserts a new definition of life or endowment business in the ICTA 1988, s.466(1). Apart from re-enacting existing rules, it provides that when a contract is made on or after September 1, 1996, it is included in life or endowment business if it constitutes in part the carrying out of life assurance business of the types within Friendly Societies Act 1992 (c. 40), Sched. 2, Head A, Class I, II or III, or sickness business under Class IV.

The new ss.461(1A) and (1B) reproduce the existing restrictive rule.

Subs. (2)

This inserts a definition of "insurance company" which had been lacking before, and of "long-term business", which is needed for the purposes of subs. (5).

Subss. (3) and (4)

These amend the ICTA 1988, s.266, which deals with life assurance premium relief. The existing vestigial relief is preserved, but the widening of life or endowment business made by subs. (1) does not provide an opportunity for more extensive relief.

Subs. (5)

This extends the scope of the ICTA 1988, s.463(1), to cover sickness business which is not life assurance business.

Subs. (6)

The new provisions are effective for accounting periods ending on or after September 1, 1996. Since Friendly Societies have accounting periods coinciding with the calendar year this means that they will apply from 1997 onwards [Standing Committee E, March 12, 1996, col. 858].

Personal pension schemes

Return of contributions on or after death of member

172.—(1) In section 633(1) of the Taxes Act 1988 (Board not to approve a personal pension scheme which makes provision for any benefit other than those specified in paragraphs (a) to (e)) in paragraph (e) (payment on or after the death of a member of a lump sum satisfying the conditions in section 637A) for the words following "a lump sum" there shall be substituted "with respect to which the conditions in section 637A (return of contributions) are satisfied".

(2) For section 637A of that Act (return of contributions on or after death of member) there shall be substituted—

"Return of contributions on or after death of member

637A.—(1) The lump sum payable under the arrangements in question (or, where two or more lump sums are so payable, those lump sums taken together) must represent no more than the return of contributions together with reasonable interest on contributions or bonuses out of profits, after allowing for—

(a) any income withdrawals, and

(b) any purchases of annuities such as are mentioned in section 636.

To the extent that contributions are invested in units under a unit trust scheme, the lump sum (or lump sums) may represent the sale or redemption price of the units.

(2) A lump sum must be payable only if, in the case of the arrangements in question,—

(a) no such annuity as is mentioned in section 634 has been purchased by the member;

(b) no such annuity as is mentioned in section 636 has been purchased in respect of the relevant interest; and

(c) no election in accordance with subsection (5)(a) of section 636 has been made in respect of the relevant interest.

(3) Where the member's death occurs after the date which is his pension date in relation to the arrangements in question, a lump sum must not be payable more than two years after the death unless, in the case of that lump sum, the person entitled to such an annuity as is mentioned in section 636 in respect of the relevant interest—

(a) has elected in accordance with section 636A to defer the purchase of an annuity; and

(b) has died during the period of deferral.

(4) In this section "the relevant interest" means the interest, under the arrangements in question, of the person to whom or at whose direction the payment in question is made, except where there are two or more such interests, in which case it means that one of them in respect of which the payment is made.

(5) Where, under the arrangements in question, there is a succession of interests, any reference in subsection (2) or (3) above to the relevant interest includes a reference to any interest (other than that of the member) in relation to which the relevant interest is a successive interest."

(3) This section—

(a) has effect in relation to approvals, of schemes or amendments, given under Chapter IV of Part XIV of the Taxes Act 1988 (personal pension schemes) after the passing of this Act; and

(b) does not affect any approval previously given.

GENERAL NOTE

This section was introduced as a government amendment at report stage.

The new ICTA 1988, s.637A, provides that where a member of a personal pension scheme dies without purchasing an annuity and the survivor, *i.e.* the spouse or dependent, also dies before purchasing an annuity, the fund may pass to the survivor's heir, however long a time has elapsed since the original member's death. Previously this was possible within two years of the member's death [*Hansard*, H.C. Vol. 274, col. 1082].

Participators in close companies

Loans to participators etc.

173.—(1) Section 419 of the Taxes Act 1988 (loans to participators etc.) shall be amended in accordance with subsections (2) to (4) below.

(2) For subsection (3) (time when tax becomes due) there shall be substituted the following subsection—

"(3) Tax due by virtue of this section in relation to any loan or advance shall be due and payable on the day following the expiry of nine months from the end of the accounting period in which the loan or advance was made."

(3) After subsection (4) (relief in respect of repayment) there shall be inserted the following subsection—

"(4A) Where the repayment of the whole or any part of a loan or advance occurs on or after the day on which tax by virtue of this section becomes due in relation to that loan or advance, relief in respect of the repayment shall not be given under subsection (4) above at any time before the expiry of nine months from the end of the accounting period in which the repayment occurred."

(4) In subsection (6) (application to loans and advances to certain companies who are participators etc.), the words "and to a company not resident in the United Kingdom" shall be omitted.

(5) In section 826(4) of that Act (interest on repayment of tax by virtue of section 419), for paragraph (a) there shall be substituted the following paragraph—

"(a) the date when the entitlement to relief in respect of the repayment accrued, that is to say—

(i) where the repayment of the loan or advance (or part thereof) occurred on or after the day mentioned in section 419 (4A), the date nine months after the end of that accounting period; and

(ii) in any other case, the date nine months after the end of the accounting period in which the loan or advance was made; or".

(6) This section has effect in relation to any loan or advance made in an accounting period ending on or after 31st March 1996.

GENERAL NOTE

The section amends the rules which charge tax when a close company makes a loan to a participator. The main changes are to the dates on which the tax charge and any relief in respect of a repayment fall due. For any loan repaid within nine months after the end of the accounting period in which it was made, relief can be claimed as soon as the tax is payable.

Subs. (2)

This provides for the tax to become payable nine months after the end of the company's accounting period in which the loan is made, rather than 14 days after the end of that period as at present.

Subs. (3)

Where a loan is repaid more than nine months after the end of the accounting period in which it is made, relief is due nine months after the end of the accounting period in which it is repaid. Where it is repaid within nine months of the end of the accounting period in which it was made, the existing rules apply and relief can take effect as soon as the tax falls due.

Subs. (4)
The rules no longer apply to loans made to non-resident companies.

Subs. (5)
Interest under the ICTA 1988, s.826(4), payable by the Revenue when a loan has been repaid will be calculated from the date which is the later of the date the relief is due, the date the tax falls due and the date the tax is paid [Standing Committee E, February 27, 1996, col. 513].

Attribution of gains to participators in non-resident companies

174.—(1) Section 13 of the Taxation of Chargeable Gains Act 1992 (attribution of gains to members of non-resident companies) shall be amended in accordance with subsections (2) to (9) below.

(2) In subsection (2) (persons subject to charge on gain to company), for "holds shares" there shall be substituted "is a participator".

(3) For subsections (3) and (4) (part of gain attributed to person subject to charge) there shall be substituted the following subsections—

"(3) That part shall be equal to the proportion of the gain that corresponds to the extent of the participator's interest as a participator in the company.

(4) Subsection (2) above shall not apply in the case of any participator in the company to which the gain accrues where the aggregate amount falling under that subsection to be apportioned to him and to persons connected with him does not exceed one twentieth of the gain."

(4) In subsection (5), paragraph (a) (section not to apply where gain distributed within two years) shall be omitted; and after that subsection there shall be inserted the following subsection—

"(5A) Where—

(a) any amount of capital gains tax is paid by a person in pursuance of subsection (2) above, and

(b) an amount in respect of the chargeable gain is distributed (either by way of dividend or distribution of capital or on the dissolution of the company) within 2 years from the time when the chargeable gain accrued to the company,

that amount of tax (so far as neither reimbursed by the company nor applied as a deduction under subsection (7) below) shall be applied for reducing or extinguishing any liability of that person to income tax in respect of the distribution or (in the case of a distribution falling to be treated as a disposal on which a chargeable gain accrues to that person) to any capital gains tax in respect of the distribution."

(5) In subsection (7) (deduction of tax paid in computing gain on shares in the company)—

(a) for "not reimbursed by the company)" there shall be inserted "neither reimbursed by the company nor applied under subsection (5A) above for reducing any liability to tax)"; and

(b) for "the shares by reference to which the tax was paid" there shall be substituted "any asset representing his interest as a participator in the company."

(6) After subsection (7) there shall be inserted the following subsection—

"(7A) In ascertaining for the purposes of subsection (5A) or (7) above the amount of capital gains tax or income tax chargeable on any person for any year on or in respect of any chargeable gain or distribution—

(a) any such distribution as is mentioned in subsection (5A)(b) above and falls to be treated as income of that person for that year shall be regarded as forming the highest part of the income on which he is chargeable to tax for the year;

(b) any gain accruing in that year on the disposal by that person of any asset representing his interest as a participator in the company shall be regarded as forming the highest part of the gains on which he is chargeable to tax for that year;

(c) where any such distribution as is mentioned in subsection (5A) (b) above falls to be treated as a disposal on which a gain accrues on which that person is so chargeable, that gain shall be regarded as forming the next highest part of the gains on which he is so chargeable, after any gains falling within paragraph (b) above; and

(d) any gain treated as accruing to that person in that year by virtue of subsection (2) above shall be regarded as the next highest part of the gains on which he is so chargeable, after any gains falling within paragraph (c) above."

(7) In subsection (9) (cases where person charged is a company)—

(a) for "the person owning any of the shares in the company" there shall be substituted "a person who is a participator in the company"; and

(b) for the words from "to the shares" onwards there shall be substituted "to the participating company's interest as a participator in the company to which the gain accrues shall be further apportioned among the participators in the participating company according to the extent of their respective interests as participators, and subsection (2) above shall apply to them accordingly in relation to the amounts further apportioned, and so on through any number of companies."

(8) In subsection (10) (application to trustees), for "owning shares in the company" there shall be substituted "who are participators in the company, or in any company amongst the participators in which the gain is apportioned under subsection (9) above,".

(9) After subsection (11) there shall be inserted the following subsections—

"(12) In this section 'participator', in relation to a company, has the meaning given by section 417(1) of the Taxes Act for the purposes of Part XI of that Act (close companies).

(13) In this section—

(a) references to a person's interest as a participator in a company are references to the interest in the company which is represented by all the factors by reference to which he falls to be treated as such a participator; and

(b) references to the extent of such an interest are references to the proportion of the interests as participators of all the participators in the company (including any who are not resident or ordinarily resident in the United Kingdom) which on a just and reasonable apportionment is represented by that interest.

(14) For the purposes of this section, where—

(a) the interest of any person in a company is wholly or partly represented by an interest which he has under any settlement ('his beneficial interest'), and

(b) his beneficial interest is the factor, or one of the factors, by reference to which that person would be treated (apart from this subsection) as having an interest as a participator in that company, the interest as a participator in that company which would be that person's shall be deemed, to the extent that it is represented by his beneficial interest, to be an interest of the trustees of the settlement (and not of that person), and references in this section, in relation to a company, to a participator shall be construed accordingly.

(15) Any appeal under section 31 of the Management Act involving any question as to the extent for the purposes of this section of a person's interest as a participator in a company shall be to the Special Commissioners."

(10) In paragraph 1(3) of Schedule 5 to the Taxation of Chargeable Gains Act 1992 (application of section 86 to section 13 gains)—

    (a) in paragraph (a), for "hold shares in a company which originate" there shall be substituted "are participators in a company in respect of property which originates";

    (b) in paragraph (b), for "the shares" there shall be substituted "so much of their interest as participators as arises from that property"; and

    (c) at the end there shall be added—

    "Subsections (12) and (13) of section 13 shall apply for the purposes of this sub-paragraph as they apply for the purposes of that section."

(11) This section applies to gains accruing on or after 28th November 1995.

GENERAL NOTE

This section amends the TCGA 1992, s.13. This applies to chargeable gains accruing to a company which is not resident in the U.K. and which would be a close company if it were so resident. Such gains were apportioned to U.K. residents and domiciliaries in proportion to the assets of the company to which the shareholder would be entitled on a liquidation. This made s.13 easy to avoid by minimising the share of assets to which the taxpayer would be entitled on a winding-up. The amendments tackle this by making the apportionment depend on the extent of the shareholder's participation in the non-resident company.

Subs. (3)

This substitutes new subss. (3) and (4) which provide for gains to be apportioned among participators, subject to a *de minimis* limit of one twentieth.

Subs. (4)

These amendments provide that where tax has been paid under s.13 and then a dividend or capital distribution is received in respect of that gain, tax paid on the gain can be used to reduce or eliminate liability to income tax or capital gains tax on the dividend or capital distribution.

Subs. (5)

This makes changes consequential to subs. (4).

Subs. (6)

New subs. (7A) provides rules for charging capital gains tax and income tax on amounts received as a dividend or capital distribution in respect of the gain.

Subs. (7)

This amends the existing s.13(9) to apply the new subs. (3) to apportion gains to non-resident companies which are themselves participators in the non-resident company in which the gain arises.

Subs. (8)

This amends s.13(10) to provide for apportionment where trustees are participators.

Subs. (9)

This inserts new subss. (12)–(15). Subsection (12) imports the definition of "participator" from the ICTA 1988, s.417. Subsection (13) clarifies the scope of references to participators and provides for apportionment to be on a just and reasonable basis. Subsection (14) provides that where a person's interest in a company is through a settlement, the trustees shall be deemed to be the participators. Subsection (15) provides for appeals to the Special Commissioners.

Subss. (10) and (11)

These contain consequential and commencement provisions [Standing Committee E, February 27, 1996, col. 518].

Cancellation of tax advantages

Transactions in certain securities

175.—(1) In section 704 of the Taxes Act 1988 (which relates to the cancellation of tax advantages and specifies the circumstances mentioned in section

703(1)) in paragraph D(2)(b) (companies which do not satisfy the conditions there specified with respect to their shares or stocks) for "are authorised to be dealt in on the Stock Exchange, and are so dealt in (regularly or from time to time)" there shall be substituted "are listed in the Official List of the Stock Exchange, and are dealt in on the Stock Exchange regularly or from time to time".

(2) The reference in paragraph D(2)(b) of section 704 of the Taxes Act 1988 to being listed in the Official List of the Stock Exchange and being dealt in on the Stock Exchange regularly or from time to time shall be taken to include a reference to being dealt in on the Unlisted Securities Market regularly or from time to time, but this subsection is subject to subsection (3) below.

(3) Subsection (2) above—

(a) so far as relating to sub-paragraph (2) of paragraph D of section 704 of the Taxes Act 1988 as it applies for the purposes of sub-paragraph (1) of that paragraph or paragraph E of that section, shall not have effect where the relevant transaction takes place after the date on which the Unlisted Securities Market closes;

(b) so far as relating to paragraph D of that section as it applies for the purposes of section 210(3) or 211(2) of that Act (which relate to bonus issues following, and other matters to be treated or not treated as, repayment of share capital) shall not have effect—

(i) in the case of section 210(3), in relation to share capital issued after that date; or

(ii) in the case of section 211(2), in relation to distributions made after that date.

(4) Except as provided by subsection (3) above, this section—

(a) so far as relating to sub-paragraph (2) of paragraph D of section 704 of the Taxes Act 1988 as it applies for the purposes of sub-paragraph (1) of that paragraph or paragraph E of that section, shall have effect where the relevant transaction takes place after the passing of this Act; and

(b) so far as relating to paragraph D of that section as it applies for the purposes of section 210(3) or 211(2) of that Act, shall have effect—

(i) in the case of section 210(3), in relation to share capital issued after the passing of this Act; or

(ii) in the case of section 211(2), in relation to distributions made after the passing of this Act.

(5) In this section "the relevant transaction" means—

(a) the transaction in securities mentioned in paragraph (b) of section 703(1) of the Taxes Act 1988, or

(b) the first of the two or more such transactions mentioned in that paragraph,

as the case may be.

General Note

This section amends the definition of securities caught by the anti-avoidance provisions of the ICTA 1988, ss.703–709. It takes account of recent developments on the Stock Exchange by providing that only those companies under the control of more than five persons and whose securities are listed on the Official List of the Stock Exchange or, until it is closed, are traded on the Unlisted Securities Market, will retain exemption from the provisions [Standing Committee E, February 27, 1996, col. 525].

Chargeable gains: reliefs

Retirement relief: age limits

176.—(1) In each of sections 163 and 164 of, and paragraph 5 of Schedule 6 to, the Taxation of Chargeable Gains Act 1992 (retirement relief), for "the age of 55", wherever occurring, there shall be substituted "the age of 50".

(2) The amendments made by this section shall apply in relation to disposals on or after 28th November 1995.

GENERAL NOTE
The minimum qualifying age for capital gains tax retirement relief is reduced from 55 to 50.

Reinvestment relief on disposal of qualifying corporate bond

177. Section 164A of the Taxation of Chargeable Gains Act 1992 (reinvestment relief) shall have effect, and be deemed always to have had effect, as if the following subsections were inserted after subsection (2)—

"(2A) Where the chargeable gain referred to in subsection (1)(a) above is one which (apart from this section) would be deemed to accrue by virtue of section 116(10)(b)—

(a) any reduction falling to be made by virtue of subsection (2)(a) above shall be treated as one made in the consideration mentioned in section 116(10)(a), instead of in the consideration for the disposal of the asset disposed of; but

(b) if the disposal on which that gain is deemed to accrue is a disposal of only part of the new asset, it shall be assumed, for the purpose only of making a reduction affecting the amount of that gain—

(i) that the disposal is a disposal of the whole of a new asset,

(ii) that the gain accruing on that disposal relates to an old asset consisting in the corresponding part of what was in fact the old asset, and

(iii) that the corresponding part of the consideration deemed to be given for what was in fact the old asset is taken to be the consideration by reference to which the amount of that gain is computed;

and in this subsection 'new asset' and 'old asset' have the same meanings as in section 116.

(2B) Where a chargeable gain accrues in accordance with subsection (12) of section 116, this Chapter shall have effect—

(a) as if that gain were a gain accruing on the disposal of an asset; and

(b) in relation to that deemed disposal, as if references in this Chapter to the consideration for the disposal were references to the sum of money falling, apart from this Chapter, to be used in computing the gain accruing under that subsection."

GENERAL NOTE
This section ensures that where a gain arises on the disposal of Qualifying Corporate Bonds (QCBs) which have been exchanged for shares, that gain is eligible for capital gains tax reinvestment relief. Presently, shares may be exchanged for QCBs without giving rise to an immediate charge to tax. Instead, any gain on the shares is brought into charge when the QCBs themselves are disposed of. Due to an anomaly in the rules for reinvestment relief the gain which comes back into charge on disposal of the QCBs is not eligible for relief. The section corrects this anomaly by inserting a new TCGA 1992, s.164A(2A)(a). The new s.164A(2A)(b) deals with the position where there is a disposal of only some of the QCBs. The new s.164A(2B) deals with cases where shares are exchanged partly for cash and partly for QCBs and makes the cash element eligible for reinvestment relief.

Special cases

Sub-contractors in the construction industry

178.—(1) In section 566 of the Taxes Act 1988 (powers to make regulations in connection with the provisions relating to sub-contractors in the construction industry), after subsection (2) there shall be inserted the following subsection—

"(2A) The Board may by regulations make provision—

(a) for the issue of documents (to be known as 'registration cards') to persons who are parties, as sub-contractors, to any contract relating to construction operations or who are likely to become such parties;

(b) for a registration card to contain all such information about the person to whom it is issued as may be required, for the purposes of any regulations under this section, by a person making payments under any such contract;

(c) for a registration card to take such form and to be valid for such period as may be prescribed by the regulations;

(d) for the renewal, replacement or cancellation of a registration card;

(e) for requiring the surrender of a registration card in such circumstances as may be specified in the regulations;

(f) for requiring the production of a registration card to such persons and in such circumstances as may be so specified;

(g) for requiring any person who—
  (i) makes or is proposing to make payments to which section 559 applies, and
  (ii) is a person to whom a registration card has to be produced under the regulations,
to take steps that ensure that it is produced to him and that he has an opportunity of inspecting it for the purpose of checking that it is a valid registration card issued to the person required to produce it.

(2B) A person who fails to comply with an obligation imposed on him by virtue of subsection (2A)(g) above shall be liable to a penalty not exceeding £3,000.

(2C) Subject to subsection (2D) below, where—

(a) a person who is a party to a contract relating to any construction operations ('the contractor') makes or is proposing to make payments to which section 559 applies,

(b) the contractor is required by regulations under this section to make statements about another party to the contract ('the sub-contractor') in any return, certificate or other document,

(c) a registration card containing the information to be stated should have been produced, in accordance with any such regulations, to the contractor, and

(d) the statements made in the return, certificate or other document, so far as relating to matters the information about which should have been obtainable from the card, are inaccurate or incomplete in any material respect,
the contractor shall be liable to a penalty not exceeding £3,000.

(2D) A person shall not be liable to a penalty under subsection (2C) above if—

(a) a valid registration card issued to the sub-contractor, or a document which the contractor had reasonable grounds for believing to be such a card, was produced to the contractor and inspected by him before the statements in question were made; and

(b) the contractor took all such steps as were reasonable, in addition to the inspection of that card, for ensuring that the statements were accurate and complete.

(2E) A person liable to a penalty under subsection (2C) above shall not, by reason only of the matters in respect of which he is liable to a penalty under that subsection, be liable to any further penalty under section 98 of the Management Act.

(2F) Regulations under this section may make different provision for different cases."

(2) In the second column of the Table in section 98 of the Taxes Management Act 1970 (penalties in respect of certain information provisions), for the entry relating to regulations under section 566(1) and (2) of the Taxes Act 1988 there shall be substituted the following entry—

"regulations under section 566(1), (2) or (2A);".

GENERAL NOTE

This section provides for the introduction of mandatory registration cards for those subcontractors in the construction industry who are unable to qualify for Form 714 exception certificates under the revised conditions introduced by the FA 1995, Sched. 27, para. 4. The Revenue are empowered to make regulations under which subcontractors will have to present a registration card to contractors. The contractors will have to inspect and record details from the cards of subcontractors they engage, on pain of a penalty of up to £3,000. The penalties under the TMA 1970, s.98 also apply, but not cumulatively. The penalty for failing to record details accurately does not apply where a valid card, or one which could be reasonably taken to be such, was inspected by the contractor and he took all reasonable steps to ensure that the statement was accurate and complete.

Roll-over relief in respect of ships

179. Schedule 35 to this Act (which amends sections 33A to 33F of the Capital Allowances Act 1990) shall have effect.

GENERAL NOTE

This section, brought in by the Government at report stage following a discussion in committee, introduces Sched. 35, which extends rollover relief for balancing charges arising on ships so that it will apply across groups of companies.

See further the General Note to Sched. 35 [Standing Committee E, March 12, 1996, col. 835].

Scientific research expenditure: oil licences

180.—(1) The Capital Allowances Act 1990 shall have effect, and be deemed always to have had effect, with the following sections inserted after section 138 (assets ceasing to belong to traders)—

"Disposal of oil licences etc.

138A.—(1) For the purposes of section 138 where—

(a) a person ('the transferor') disposes of any interest in an oil licence to another ('the transferee'), and

(b) part of the value of that interest is attributable to any allowable exploration expenditure incurred by the transferor,

that disposal shall be deemed (subject to section 138B) to be a disposal by which an asset representing the allowable exploration expenditure to which that part of the value is attributable ceases to belong to the transferor.

(2) Section 138 shall have effect in relation to the disposal of an interest in an oil licence, to the extent that the disposal is treated by virtue of subsection (1) above as a disposal of an asset representing allowable exploration expenditure, as if the disposal value of the asset were an amount equal to such part of the transferee's expenditure on acquiring the interest as it is just and reasonable to attribute to the part of the value of that interest that is attributable to the allowable exploration expenditure.

(3) In this section and section 138B references to allowable exploration expenditure are references to any allowable scientific research expenditure of a capital nature incurred on mineral exploration and access.

(4) In this section and section 138B—

'foreign oil concession' means any right to search for or win overseas petroleum, being a right conferred or exercisable (whether or not by virtue of a licence) in relation to a particular area;

'interest' in relation to an oil licence, includes, where there is an agreement which—

    (a) relates to oil from the whole or any part of the area to which the licence applies, and

    (b) was made before the extraction of the oil to which it relates,

any entitlement under that agreement to, or to a share of, either that oil or the proceeds of its sale;

'mineral exploration and access' has the same meaning as in Part IV;

'oil'—

    (a) except in relation to a UK licence, means any petroleum; and

    (b) in relation to such a licence, has the same meaning as in Part I of the Oil Taxation Act 1975;

'oil licence' means any UK licence or foreign oil concession;

'overseas petroleum' means any petroleum that exists in its natural condition at a place to which neither the Petroleum (Production) Act 1934 nor the Petroleum (Production) Act (Northern Ireland) 1964 applies;

'petroleum' has the same meaning as in the Petroleum (Production) Act 1934; and

'UK licence' means a licence within the meaning of Part I of the Oil Taxation Act 1975.

Disposal of oil licences: election for alternative tax treatment

138B.—(1) Subsections (2) and (3) below apply where—

    (a) a person ('the transferor') disposes of any interest in an oil licence to another ('the transferee') during the transitional period;

    (b) part of the value of the interest is attributable to allowable exploration expenditure incurred by the transferor; and

    (c) an election is made in accordance with this section specifying an amount as the amount to be treated as so attributable.

(2) Section 138 shall have effect in relation to the disposal as if—

    (a) the disposal were a disposal by which an asset representing the allowable exploration expenditure ceases to belong to the transferor; and

    (b) the disposal value of that asset were an amount equal to the amount specified in the election.

(3) For the purposes of Part IV, the amount of any expenditure incurred—

    (a) by the transferee in acquiring the interest from the transferor, or

    (b) by any person subsequently acquiring the interest (or an interest deriving from the interest),

which is taken to be attributable to expenditure incurred, before the disposal to the transferee, on mineral exploration and access shall be the lesser of the amount specified in the election and the amount which, apart from this subsection, would be taken to be so attributable.

(4) An election—

    (a) shall be made by notice to the Board given by the transferor; and

    (b) subject to subsection (5) below, shall not have effect unless a copy of it is served on the transferee and the transferee consents to it.

(5) If the Special Commissioners are satisfied—

    (a) that the disposal was made under or in pursuance of an agreement entered into by the transferor and the transferee on the mutual understanding that a quantified (or quantifiable) part of the value of the interest disposed of was attributable to allowable exploration expenditure, and

(b) that the part quantified in accordance with that understanding and the amount specified in the election are the same,

they may dispense with the need for the transferee to consent to the election.

(6) Any question falling to be determined by the Special Commissioners under subsection (5) above shall be determined by them in like manner as if it were an appeal; but both the transferor and the transferee shall be entitled to appear and be heard by those Commissioners or to make representations to them in writing.

(7) Subject to subsection (8) below, an election may specify any amount, including a nil amount, as the amount to be treated as mentioned in subsection (1)(c) above.

(8) Where—

(a) a return has been made for a chargeable period of the transferor, and

(b) the return includes, at the time when it is made, an amount which, disregarding the provisions of this section, would be treated under section 138 as a trading receipt accruing in that period,

the election must not specify an amount less than the amount included in the return unless the Board agrees the lesser amount in question.

(9) An election made in accordance with this section—

(a) is irrevocable; and

(b) shall not be varied after it is made.

(10) For the purposes of this section a disposal is a disposal made during the transitional period if it is one made—

(a) before 13th September 1995; or

(b) on or after that date in pursuance of any obligation to make the disposal which, immediately before that date, was an unconditional obligation.

(11) For the purposes of subsection (10) above, the fact that a third party who is not connected with the transferor or the transferee may, by exercising any right or withholding any permission, prevent the fulfilment of an obligation does not prevent the obligation from being treated as unconditional.

(12) In subsection (11) above the reference to a third party is a reference to any person, body, government or public authority, whether within or outside the United Kingdom; and section 839 of the principal Act (connected persons) applies for the purposes of that subsection.

(13) All such assessments and adjustments of assessments shall be made as may be necessary to give effect to this section."

(2) Section 151(1) of the Capital Allowances Act 1990 (procedure on apportionments under Parts I, III to VI and Part VIII) shall have effect, and be deemed always to have had effect, as if for "VI" there were substituted "VII".

(3) In section 118 of the Capital Allowances Act 1990 (mineral extraction licences in the case of assets formerly owned by non-traders), the existing provisions shall become subsection (1) of that section and the following subsection shall be inserted after that subsection—

"(2) Section 138A shall have effect for the purposes of subsection (1) above in relation to expenditure on mineral exploration and access as it has effect for the purposes of section 138 in relation to allowable scientific research expenditure of a capital nature."

(4) Subsection (3) above applies in relation to any sale taking place on or after 13th September 1995.

(5) In any case to which enactments re-enacted in the Capital Allowances Act 1990 apply instead of that Act, this section shall have effect as if it

required amendments equivalent to those made by subsections (1) and (2) above to have effect, and be deemed always to have had effect, in relation to those enactments.

GENERAL NOTE
The purpose of this section is to prevent capital allowances being given twice on the same oil exploration expenditure. An oil company can generally claim Scientific Research Allowances (SRA) on expenditure which it incurs on exploration and appraisal. When an asset representing expenditure on which SRA has been given is sold, some or all of the SRA is clawed back as a trading receipt under the Capital Allowances Act 1990 (c. 1), s.138.

For the oil industry this provision had been interpreted on the basis that an interest in an oil licence represented exploration and appraisal expenditure in the licensed area on which SRA had been given. Thus, SRA previously given to the seller could be clawed back on the disposal of the oil licence. The buyer could then claim Mineral Extraction Allowances (MEA) limited to the seller's exploration expenditure. However, legal advice did not support this interpretation for SRA clawback in cases where the contract for sale did not provide that the licence sold represented scientific research expenditure, although the ability of the buyer to claim MEA was not affected. The section ensures that the SRA clawback can be made in appropriate cases to avoid double capital allowances being claimed. It applies to past as well as future disposals, but there are transitional provisions for disposals prior to September 13, 1995, when the prospective change in the law was announced, which will allow companies to ensure that their tax liabilities on these past disposals match their expectations at the time of the disposal.

Overseas petroleum

181.—(1) In subsection (1) of section 196 of the Taxation of Chargeable Gains Act 1992 (interpretation of sections 194 and 195), for "licence" there shall be substituted "UK licence".

(2) After subsection (1) of section 196 of that Act there shall be inserted the following subsection—

"(1A) For the purposes of section 194 a licence other than a UK licence relates to an undeveloped area at any time if, at that time—

(a) no development has actually taken place in any part of the licensed area; and

(b) no condition for the carrying out of development anywhere in that area has been satisfied—

(i) by the grant of any consent by the authorities of a country or territory exercising jurisdiction in relation to the area; or

(ii) by the approval or service on the licensee, by any such authorities, of any programme of development.";

and in subsection (2) of that section for "subsection (1) above" there shall be substituted "subsections (1) and (1A) above".

(3) For subsection (5) of section 196 of that Act there shall be substituted the following subsections—

"(5) In sections 194 and 195 and this section—

'foreign oil concession' means any right to search for or win overseas petroleum, being a right conferred or exercisable (whether or not by virtue of a licence) in relation to a particular area;

'interest' in relation to a licence, includes, where there is an agreement which—

(a) relates to oil from the whole or any part of the licensed area, and

(b) was made before the extraction of the oil to which it relates,

any entitlement under that agreement to, or to a share of, either that oil or the proceeds of its sale;

'licence' means any UK licence or foreign oil concession;

'licensed area' (subject to subsection (4) above)—

(a) in relation to a UK licence, has the same meaning as in Part I of the Oil Taxation Act 1975; and

(b) in relation to a foreign oil concession, means the area to which the concession applies;

'licensee'—

(a) in relation to a UK licence, has the same meaning as in Part I of the Oil Taxation Act 1975; and

(b) in relation to a foreign oil concession, means the person with the concession or any person having an interest in it;

'oil'—

(a) except in relation to a UK licence, means any petroleum (within the meaning of the Petroleum (Production) Act 1934); and

(b) in relation to such a licence, has the same meaning as in Part I of the Oil Taxation Act 1975;

'overseas petroleum' means any oil that exists in its natural condition at a place to which neither the Petroleum (Production) Act 1934 nor the Petroleum (Production) Act (Northern Ireland) 1964 applies; and

'UK licence' means a licence within the meaning of Part I of the Oil Taxation Act 1975.

(5A) References in sections 194 and 195 to a part disposal of a licence shall include references to the disposal of any interest in a licence."

(4) Subsections (1) to (3) above shall have effect in relation to any disposal on or after 13th September 1995 and subsection (3) shall also have effect, and be deemed always to have had effect, for the construction of section 195 of the Taxation of Chargeable Gains Act 1992 in its application to disposals before that date.

(5) Where enactments re-enacted in the Taxation of Chargeable Gains Act 1992 apply, instead of that Act, in the case of any disposal before 13th September 1995, this section shall have effect as if it required amendments equivalent to those made by subsection (3) above to have effect, and be deemed always to have had effect, for the construction of any enactment corresponding to section 195 of that Act.

GENERAL NOTE

This section extends a relief for chargeable gains and capital allowances purposes. At present when a company sells an interest in an oil licence covering an undeveloped area in the U.K. or on the U.K. Continental Shelf (UKCS) and the consideration for the disposal is a licence for another undeveloped area or an agreement to undertake exploration work in the licensed area, the consideration is treated as being nil. As a result, no chargeable gain arises to the company and there is no SRA clawback or MEA balancing charge. If the consideration consists of another licence interest then the acquisition cost of that second licence is deemed to be nil for chargeable gains purposes and the buyer cannot claim MEA on the seller's exploration expenditure. The section extends this treatment to oil licences and equivalent agreements overseas. The purpose is primarily deregulatory in that it will avoid the need to value non-cash considerations for disposals in many circumstances.

The section also makes it clear that where there is an SRA clawback on the disposal of any overseas oil licence, the expenditure on which there is an SRA clawback will be treated as allowable expenditure when computing any chargeable gain or allowable loss on the disposal of the licence. This provision is retrospective.

The existing reliefs for disposals of an oil licence for an undeveloped area in the U.K. or UKCS are in the Taxation of Chargeable Gains Act 1992 (c. 12), ss.194 and 196 and the Capital Allowances Act 1990 (c. 1), s.118A. Where the qualifying conditions are met, the TCGA 1994, s.194, treats the consideration as nil for chargeable gains purposes and the CAA 1990, s.118A, treats the consideration as nil for capital allowance purposes. The definitions of a licence are derived from the TCGA 1996, s.196, to which the main changes made by this section apply.

Controlled foreign companies

182. Schedule 36 to this Act (which contains amendments of Chapter IV of Part XVII of the Taxes Act 1988) shall have effect in relation to accounting periods of a controlled foreign company, within the meaning of that Chapter, beginning on or after 28th November 1995.

GENERAL NOTE

This section introduces Sched. 36, which makes changes to the controlled foreign companies (CFC) legislation. No charge arises under that legislation if a CFC makes an acceptable distribution back to the U.K. Hitherto, trading CFCs have had to distribute 50 per cent of their available profits, broadly the profits shown by their accounts. In future, they will have to distribute 90 per cent of their profits calculated as if they were chargeable to tax in the U.K., as is the case for non-trading companies.

The purpose of the charge is to prevent abuse of the previous provisions using captive insurance companies and other devices. The yield to the revenue is expected to be £100m.

See further the General Note to Sched. 36 [Standing Committee E, February 27, 1996, col. 526].

PART V

INHERITANCE TAX

Rate bands

183.—(1) For the Table in Schedule 1 to the Inheritance Tax Act 1984 shall be substituted—

TABLE OF RATES OF TAX

Portion of value		Rate of tax
Lower limit £	Upper limit £	Per cent.
0	200,000	Nil
200,000	—	40

(2) Subsection (1) above shall apply to any chargeable transfer made on or after 6th April 1996; and section 8 of that Act (indexation of rate bands) shall not have effect as respects any difference between the retail prices index for the month of September 1994 and that for the month of September 1995.

GENERAL NOTE

The threshold for inheritance tax is increased from £154,000 to £200,000 and the single rate of 40 per cent is maintained [Standing Committee E, February 27, 1996, col. 534].

Business property relief

184.—(1) The Inheritance Tax Act 1984 shall be amended as follows.

(2) In section 105(1) (relevant business property for the purposes of business property relief)—

    (a) in paragraph (b) (unquoted shares and securities attracting 100 per cent. relief where they gave the transferor control of a company)—
        (i) the words "shares in or" shall be omitted; and
        (ii) for the words "shares or securities owned by the transferor" there shall be substituted "securities owned by the transferor and any unquoted shares so owned";
    (b) for paragraph (bb) (unquoted shares attracting 100 per cent. relief in other cases) there shall be substituted the following paragraph—

"(bb) any unquoted shares in a company;"
and

(c) paragraph (c) (unquoted shares attracting 50 per cent. relief) shall be omitted.

(3) In section 107(4) (replacement of property with unquoted shares), for the words from the beginning to "such shares" there shall be substituted—

"(4) Without prejudice to subsection (1) above, where any shares falling within section 105(1)(bb) above which are".

(4) In section, 113A(3A)(b) (which contains a reference to shares and securities falling within paragraph (b) of section 105(1)), after "(b)" there shall be inserted "or (bb)".

(5) For the removal of any doubt, the following subsection shall be inserted in section 113A (provisions applying to business property relief where there is a transfer within seven years of death) after subsection (7)—

"(7A) The provisions of this Chapter for the reduction of value transferred shall be disregarded in any determination for the purposes of this section of whether there is a potentially exempt or chargeable transfer in any case."

(6) This section—

(a) so far as it inserts a new subsection (7A) in section 113A, has effect in relation to any transfer of value on or after 28th November 1995; and

(b) so far as it makes any other provision, has effect—

(i) in relation to any transfer of value on or after 6th April 1996, and

(ii) for the purposes of any charge to tax by reason of an event occurring on or after 6th April 1996, in relation to transfers of value before that date.

GENERAL NOTE

The existing 100 per cent business property relief for holdings of more than 25 per cent of unquoted shares in qualifying companies is extended to all holdings of such shares, with effect from April 6, 1996.

Subs. (5)

This adds a new subs. (7A) to the Inheritance Tax Act 1984 (c. 51), s.113A, which contains rules for granting business property relief where tax, or extra tax, is chargeable on a transfer made within seven years of death. It provides, for the avoidance of doubt, that the availability of business property relief is to be disregarded in deciding whether a transfer falls within those rules [*Hansard*, H.C. Vol. 274, col. 1196].

Agricultural property relief

185.—(1) Chapter II of Part V of the Inheritance Tax Act 1984 (agricultural property) shall be amended as follows.

(2) In section 116 (relief for transfers of agricultural property) after subsection (5) there shall be inserted—

"(5A) Where, in consequence of the death on or after 1st September 1995 of the tenant or, as the case may be, the last surviving tenant of any property, the tenancy—

(a) becomes vested in a person, as a result of his being a person beneficially entitled under the deceased tenant's will or other testamentary writing or on his intestacy, and

(b) is or becomes binding on the landlord and that person as landlord and tenant respectively,

subsection (2)(c) above shall have effect as if the tenancy so vested had been a tenancy beginning on the date of the death.

(5B) Where in consequence of the death on or after 1st September 1995 of the tenant or, as the case may be, the last surviving tenant of any property, a tenancy of the property or of any property comprising the whole or part of it—

    (a) is obtained by a person under or by virtue of an enactment, or

    (b) is granted to a person in circumstances such that he is already entitled under or by virtue of an enactment to obtain such a tenancy, but one which takes effect on a later date, or

    (c) is granted to a person who is or has become the only or only remaining applicant, or the only or only remaining person eligible to apply, under a particular enactment for such a tenancy in the particular case,

subsection (2)(c) above shall have effect as if the tenancy so obtained or granted had been a tenancy beginning on the date of the death.

    (5C) Subsection (5B) above does not apply in relation to property situate in Scotland.

    (5D) If, in a case where the transferor dies on or after 1st September 1995,—

    (a) the tenant of any property has, before the death, given notice of intention to retire in favour of a new tenant, and

    (b) the tenant's retirement in favour of the new tenant takes place after the death but not more than thirty months after the giving of the notice,

subsection (2)(c) above shall have effect as if the tenancy granted or assigned to the new tenant had been a tenancy beginning immediately before the transfer of value which the transferor is treated by section 4(1) above as making immediately before his death.

    (5E) In subsection (5D) above and this subsection—

    "the new tenant" means—

        (a) the person or persons identified in a notice of intention to retire in favour of a new tenant as the person or persons who it is desired should become the tenant of the property to which that notice relates; or

        (b) the survivor or survivors of the persons so identified, whether alone or with any other person or persons;

    "notice of intention to retire in favour of a new tenant" means, in the case of any property, a notice or other written intimation given to the landlord by the tenant, or (in the case of a joint tenancy or tenancy in common) all of the tenants, of the property indicating, in whatever terms, his or their wish that one or more persons identified in the notice or intimation should become the tenant of the property;

    "the retiring tenant's tenancy" means the tenancy of the person or persons giving the notice of intention to retire in favour of a new tenant;

    "the tenant's retirement in favour of the new tenant" means—

        (a) the assignment, or (in Scotland) assignation, of the retiring tenant's tenancy to the new tenant in circumstances such that the tenancy is or becomes binding on the landlord and the new tenant as landlord and tenant respectively; or

        (b) the grant of a tenancy of the property which is the subject of the retiring tenant's tenancy, or of any property comprising the whole or part of that property, to the new tenant and the acceptance of that tenancy by him;

    and, except in Scotland, "grant" and "acceptance" in paragraph (b) above respectively include the deemed grant, and the deemed acceptance, of a tenancy under or by virtue of any enactment."

    (3) In consequence of subsection (2) above, subsection (2A) of that section (which made, in relation to Scotland, provision which is superseded by the subsection (5A) inserted by subsection (2) above) shall cease to have effect.

(4) For the removal of any doubt, the following subsection shall be inserted in section 124A (provisions applying to agricultural property relief where there is a transfer within seven years of death) after subsection (7)—

"(7A) The provisions of this Chapter for the reduction of value transferred shall be disregarded in any determination for the purposes of this section of whether there is a potentially exempt or chargeable transfer in any case."

(5) Subsection (2) above—

(a) so far as relating to subsections (5A) to (5C) of section 116 of the Inheritance Tax Act 1984, has effect in any case where the death of the tenant or, as the case may be, the sole surviving tenant, occurs on or after 1st September 1995; and

(b) so far as relating to subsections (5D) and (5E) of that section, has effect in any case where the death of the transferor occurs on or after 1st September 1995.

(6) Subsection (3) above has effect in any case where the death of the tenant or, as the case may be, the sole surviving tenant, occurs on or after 1st September 1995.

(7) Subsection (4) above has effect in relation to any transfer of value on or after 28th November 1995.

GENERAL NOTE

This section amends the provisions on 100 per cent agricultural property relief to include let farmland involving succession to an agricultural tenancy due to the tenant's retirement or death. The new provisions apply from September 1, 1995.

Subs. (2)

This inserts five new subsections into the IHTA 1984, s.116.

The new subs. (5A), which deals with succession to tenancies in Scotland, treats a tenancy acquired by succession following the previous tenant's death as a tenancy starting from the date of that death for the purposes of determining the rate of agricultural property relief under s.116(2)(c).

The new subs. (5B) makes parallel provision for succession to tenancies other than in Scotland.

The new subs. (5C) disapplies (5B) in the case of Scotland.

The new subs. (5D) deals with the situation where the landowner dies before succession to a tenancy has taken effect following a notice of retirement given before the death. For the purposes of determining the rate of relief, it treats the tenancy granted to the new tenant as a tenancy starting just before the death. The grant must be within 30 months after the notice is given.

The new subs. (5E) contains various definitions.

Subs. (4)

This is a parallel provision to s.184(5) above.

PART VI

STAMP DUTY AND STAMP DUTY RESERVE TAX

Stamp duty

Transfers of securities to members of electronic transfer systems etc.

186.—(1) Stamp duty shall not be chargeable on an instrument effecting a transfer of securities if the transferee is a member of an electronic transfer system and the instrument is in a form which will, in accordance with the rules of the system, ensure that the securities are changed from being held in certificated form to being held in uncertificated form so that title to them may become transferable by means of the system.

(2) In this section—

"certificated form" has the same meaning as in the relevant regulations;

"electronic transfer system" means a system and procedures which, in accordance with the relevant regulations, enable title to securities to be evidenced and transferred without a written instrument;

"member", in relation to an electronic transfer system, means a person who is permitted by the operator of the system to transfer by means of the system title to securities held by him in uncertificated form;

"operator" means a person approved by the Treasury under the relevant regulations as operator of an electronic transfer system;

"the relevant regulations" means regulations under section 207 of the Companies Act 1989 (transfer without written instrument);

"securities" means stock or marketable securities;

"uncertificated form" has the same meaning as it has in the relevant regulations.

(3) This section applies in relation to instruments executed on or after 1st July 1996.

(4) This section shall be construed as one with the Stamp Act 1891.

GENERAL NOTE

This section provides for transfers of shares into electronic transfer systems to be exempted from stamp duty. It was introduced in anticipation of the inception on the Stock Exchange of the CREST system of paperless share transfers expected in July 1996. The fixed 50p stamp duty charge that would otherwise have arisen will not apply. However, such transfers could be liable to stamp duty reserve tax (SDRT), usually at 0.5 per cent (see s.189) [Standing Committee E, February 27, 1996, col. 556].

Stamp duty reserve tax

Territorial scope of the tax

187.—(1) In section 86 of the Finance Act 1986 (introduction) after subsection (3) there shall be added—

"(4) Stamp duty reserve tax shall be chargeable in accordance with the provisions of this Part of this Act—

(a) whether the agreement, transfer, issue or appropriation in question is made or effected in the United Kingdom or elsewhere, and

(b) whether or not any party is resident or situate in any part of the United Kingdom."

(2) The amendment made by subsection (1) above shall have effect—

(a) in relation to an agreement, if—

(i) the agreement is conditional and the condition is satisfied on or after 1st July 1996; or

(ii) the agreement is not conditional and is made on or after that date; and

(b) in relation to a transfer, issue or appropriation made or effected on or after that date.

GENERAL NOTE

This section makes it clear that the charge to SDRT on agreements to transfer securities applies whether or not the transaction is effected in the U.K., and whether or not any of the parties to it are resident or situated in the U.K.

Removal of the two month period

188.—(1) In section 87 of the Finance Act 1986 (the principal charge) in subsection (2) (tax charged on the expiry of the period of two months beginning with the relevant day unless the first and second conditions are fulfilled before that period expires) the following shall be omitted—

(a) the words "the expiry of the period of two months beginning with", and

(b) the words from "unless" to the end.

(2) In section 88 of that Act (special cases) in subsection (1) (which provides for instruments on which stamp duty is not chargeable by virtue of certain enactments to be disregarded for the purposes of section 87(4) and (5)) before paragraph (a) there shall be inserted—

"(aa) section 65(1) of the Finance Act 1963 (renounceable letters of allotment etc),

(ab) section 14(1) of the Finance Act (Northern Ireland) 1963 (renounceable letters of allotment etc.),".

(3) Subsections (2) and (3) of that section (which are superseded by subsection (2) above) shall cease to have effect.

(4) In section 92(1) of that Act (repayment or cancellation of tax where the conditions in section 87(4) and (5) are shown to have been fulfilled after the expiry of the period of two months beginning with the relevant day but before the expiry of six years so beginning)—

(a) for "after the expiry of the period of two months (beginning with the relevant day, as defined in section 87(3))" there shall be substituted "on or after the relevant day (as defined in section 87(3))"; and

(b) for "(so beginning)" there shall be substituted "(beginning with that day)".

(5) The amendments made by this section shall have effect in relation to an agreement to transfer securities if—

(a) the agreement is conditional and the condition is satisfied on or after 1st July 1996; or

(b) the agreement is not conditional and is made on or after that date.

GENERAL NOTE

The existing two-month delay before an SDRT charge arises on an agreement to transfer shares is removed. At present an agreement will usually be followed by a transfer document chargeable to stamp duty, but this will not apply in the case of transfers of shares within electronic transfer systems. Accordingly the delay is no longer appropriate. The delay in repayment or cancellation of SDRT where an instrument is executed and, if chargeable to stamp duty, duly stamped, is also removed.

Transfers to members of electronic transfer systems etc.

189.—(1) In section 88 of the Finance Act 1986 (special cases) after subsection (1) there shall be inserted—

"(1A) An instrument on which stamp duty is not chargeable by virtue of section 186 of the Finance Act 1996 (transfers of securities to members of electronic transfer systems etc) shall be disregarded in construing section 87(4) and (5) above unless—

(a) the transfer is made by a stock exchange nominee; and

(b) the maximum stamp duty chargeable on the instrument, apart from section 186 of the Finance Act 1996, would be 50p;

and in this subsection "stock exchange nominee" means a person designated for the purposes of section 127 of the Finance Act 1976 as a nominee of The Stock Exchange by an order made by the Secretary of State under subsection (5) of that section."

(2) This section has effect in relation to an agreement to transfer securities if an instrument is executed on or after 1st July 1996 in pursuance of the agreement.

GENERAL NOTE

This section provides that the stamp duty exemption given by s.186 does not prevent a charge to SDRT if such a transfer is for consideration in money or money's worth. As CREST takes over settlement of share transactions, shares held by the Stock Exchange nominee SEPON on behalf of Exchange members will be transferred into CREST accounts. Technically, these transfers would be liable to SDRT although the shares were being credited to the same member's account within CREST. The section exempts them from SDRT unless they involve a sale.

Transfers between associated bodies

190.—(1) In section 88 of the Finance Act 1986 (special cases) after subsection (1A) there shall be inserted—

"(1B) An instrument on which stamp duty is not chargeable by virtue of section 42 of the Finance Act 1930 or section 11 of the Finance Act (Northern Ireland) 1954 (transfer between associated bodies corporate) shall be disregarded in construing section 87(4) and (5) above in any case where—

> (a) the property mentioned in section 42(2)(a) of the Finance Act 1930 or, as the case may be, section 11(2)(a) of the Finance Act (Northern Ireland) 1954 consists of chargeable securities of any particular kind acquired in the period of two years ending with the day on which the instrument was executed; and
>
> (b) the body corporate from which the conveyance or transfer there mentioned is effected acquired the chargeable securities—
>
>> (i) in a transaction which was given effect by an instrument of transfer on which stamp duty was not chargeable by virtue of section 81 above;
>>
>> (ii) in pursuance of an agreement to transfer securities as regards which section 87 above did not apply by virtue of section 89 below; or
>>
>> (iii) in circumstances with regard to which the charge to stamp duty or stamp duty reserve tax was treated as not arising by virtue of regulations under section 116 or 117 of the Finance Act 1991."

(2) At the end of that section there shall be added—

"(4) For the purposes of subsection (1B) above, if the securities mentioned in paragraph (a) of that subsection cannot (apart from this subsection) be identified, securities shall be taken as follows, that is to say, securities of the same kind acquired later in the period of two years there mentioned (and not taken under this subsection for the purposes of any earlier instrument) shall be taken before securities acquired earlier in that period.

(5) If, in a case where subsection (4) above applies, some, but not all, of the securities taken in accordance with that subsection were acquired as mentioned in paragraph (b) of subsection (1B) above by the body corporate mentioned in that paragraph, the stamp duty reserve tax chargeable under section 87 above by virtue of subsection (1B) above shall not exceed the tax that would have been so chargeable had the agreement to transfer the securities related only to such of the securities so taken as were so acquired.

(6) Where a person enters into an agreement for securities to be transferred to him or his nominee, the securities shall be treated for the purposes of subsections (1B)(a) and (4) above as acquired by that person at the time when he enters into the agreement, unless the agreement is conditional, in which case they shall be taken to be acquired by him when the condition is satisfied."

(3) This section has effect where the instrument on which stamp duty is not chargeable by virtue of section 42 of the Finance Act 1930 or section 11 of the Finance Act (Northern Ireland) 1954 is executed on or after 4th January 1996 in pursuance of an agreement to transfer securities made on or after that date.

GENERAL NOTE

This section prevents a company from obtaining shares free of stamp duty or SDRT through a combination of the stamp duty group relief and one of the special reliefs for market makers, brokers and dealers. If the latter acquired the shares by a transfer which was exempted from stamp duty or SDRT, an SDRT charge is to be imposed on a subsequent intra-group transfer to the company within two years by the market maker. If the particular securities being transferred by a market maker cannot be identified with an earlier acquisition, a "last in, first out" (LIFO) rule operates. Where some, but not all, of the securities were acquired by the market maker free of stamp duty or SDRT, the charge will be limited to such of the securities as were acquired free of duty. Under an agreement of transfer, securities are treated as acquired at the time of the agreement, unless the agreement is conditional, in which case the date of acquisition is the date on which the condition is satisfied.

The section operates from January 4, 1996.

Stock lending and collateral security arrangements

191.—(1) After section 89A of the Finance Act 1986 (exceptions from section 87 for public issues) there shall be inserted—

"Section 87: exceptions for stock lending and collateral security arrangements

89B.—(1) Where a person (P) has contracted to sell chargeable securities of a particular kind in the ordinary course of his business as a market maker in chargeable securities of that kind and, to enable him to fulfil the arrangements contract, he enters into an arrangement under which—

(a) another person (Q) is to transfer chargeable securities to P or his nominee, and

(b) in return, chargeable securities of the same kind and amount are to be transferred (whether or not by P or his nominee) to Q or his nominee,

section 87 above shall not apply as regards an agreement to transfer chargeable securities which is made for the purpose of performing the obligation to transfer chargeable securities described in paragraph (a) or (b) above.

(2) Where the arrangement mentioned in subsection (1) above is also one under which—

(a) an amount of chargeable securities of some other kind is to be transferred by P or his nominee to Q or his nominee by way of security for the performance of the obligation described in paragraph (b) of that subsection, and

(b) on performance of that obligation, the securities mentioned in paragraph (a) above, or chargeable securities of the same kind and amount as those securities, are to be transferred to P or his nominee,

section 87 above shall also not apply as regards an agreement to transfer chargeable securities which is made for the purpose of performing the obligation to transfer chargeable securities described in paragraph (a) or (b) above.

(3) Where, to enable Q to make the transfer to P or his nominee which is mentioned in paragraph (a) of subsection (1) above, Q enters into an arrangement under which—

(a) another person (R) is to transfer chargeable securities to Q or his nominee, and

(b) in return, chargeable securities of the same kind and amount are to be transferred (whether or not by Q or his nominee) to R or his nominee,

section 87 above shall not apply as regards an agreement to transfer chargeable securities which is made for the purpose of performing the obligation to transfer chargeable securities described in paragraph (a) or (b) above.

(4) Where the arrangement mentioned in subsection (3) above is also one under which—

    (a) an amount of chargeable securities of some other kind is to be transferred by Q or his nominee to R or his nominee by way of security for the performance of the obligation described in paragraph (b) of that subsection, and

    (b) on performance of that obligation, the securities mentioned in paragraph (a) above, or chargeable securities of the same kind and amount as those securities, are to be transferred to Q or his nominee,

section 87 above shall also not apply as regards an agreement to transfer chargeable securities which is made for the purpose of performing the obligation to transfer chargeable securities described in paragraph (a) or (b) above.

(5) For the purposes of this section a person is a market maker in chargeable securities of a particular kind if he—

    (a) holds himself out at all normal times in compliance with the rules of The Stock Exchange as willing to buy and sell chargeable securities of that kind at a price specified by him, and

    (b) is recognised as doing so by The Stock Exchange.

(6) The Treasury may by regulations provide that for subsection (5) above (as it has effect for the time being) there shall be substituted a subsection containing a different definition of a market maker for the purposes of this section.

(7) Regulations under subsection (6) above shall apply in relation to any agreement to transfer chargeable securities in pursuance of an arrangement entered into on or after such day after 1st July 1996 as is specified in the regulations.

(8) The power to make regulations under subsection (6) above shall be exercisable by statutory instrument subject to annulment in pursuance of a resolution of the House of Commons."

(2) This section applies in relation to agreements to transfer chargeable securities in pursuance of an arrangement entered into on or after 1st July 1996.

GENERAL NOTE

    This section provides for the treatment for SDRT of stock lending arrangements made by Stock Exchange market makers. Both the return of stock to the lender, and the transfer of collateral to the lender, will be exempted from SDRT. Transfers involving an intermediary, as middleman between borrower and lender, are eligible for the broker-dealer relief provided by current legislation. There are already stamp duty rules for stock lending transactions in paper form. The new rules provide for dematerialised stock lending and replace extra-statutory concessions, which will continue until the section comes into operation on July 1, 1996 [Standing Committee E, February 27, 1996, col. 562].

Repayment or cancellation of tax

    192.—(1) In consequence of section 188(1) above, subsections (4), (5) and (8) of section 87 of the Finance Act 1986 (exemption from stamp duty reserve tax where an instrument is executed etc) shall cease to have effect.

    (2) In section 88 of that Act (which provides for instruments on which stamp duty is not chargeable by virtue of certain enactments to be disregarded for the purposes of section 87(4) and (5)) in subsections (1), (1A) and (1B) for "section 87(4) and (5) above" there shall be substituted "section 92(1A) and (1B) below".

    (3) In section 92 of that Act (repayment or cancellation of tax) in subsection (1) (which refers to the conditions in section 87(4) and (5))—

(a) for "section 87(4) and (5)" there shall be substituted "subsections (1A) and (1B) below"; and

(b) for "the following provisions of this section shall apply" there shall be substituted "subsections (2) to (4A) of this section shall apply".

(4) After that subsection, there shall be inserted—

"(1A) The first condition is that an instrument is (or instruments are) executed in pursuance of the agreement and the instrument transfers (or the instruments between them transfer) to B or, as the case may be, to his nominee all the chargeable securities to which the agreement relates.

(1B) The second condition is that the instrument (or each instrument) transferring the chargeable securities to which the agreement relates is duly stamped in accordance with the enactments relating to stamp duty if it is an instrument which, under those enactments, is chargeable with stamp duty or otherwise required to be stamped."

(5) At the end of that section there shall be added—

"(6) In this section "the enactments relating to stamp duty" means the Stamp Act 1891 and any enactment which amends or is required to be construed together with that Act."

(6) The amendments made by this section shall have effect in relation to an agreement to transfer securities if—

(a) the agreement is conditional and the condition is satisfied on or after 1st July 1996; or

(b) the agreement is not conditional and is made on or after that date.

GENERAL NOTE

This section reorganises existing legislation as a consequence of the removal of the two-month period before a charge to SDRT arises on an agreement to transfer securities. The removal of the two-month period by s.188 means that an SDRT charge will arise in all cases, but will be cancelled or repaid where the necessary conditions are met. The conditions for cancellation or repayment, presently in the FA 1986, s.87, are transferred to s.92, where they more naturally belong under the new system.

Depositary receipts

193.—(1) Section 93 of the Finance Act 1986 (depositary receipts) shall be amended in accordance with the following provisions of this section.

(2) In subsection (1) (charge to stamp duty reserve tax where certain things are done in pursuance of an arrangement) in paragraph (b) (transfer or issue to, or appropriation by, a person falling within subsection (3))—

(a) after "transferred or issued to" there shall be inserted "the person mentioned in paragraph (a) above or"; and

(b) for "such a person" there shall be substituted "the person mentioned in paragraph (a) above or a person falling within subsection (3) below".

(3) In subsection (6) (payment by instalments) in paragraph (d) (instrument received by person falling within subsection (3)) for "subsection (3)" there shall be substituted "subsection (2) or (3)".

(4) This section has effect—

(a) so far as relating to the charge to tax under section 93(1) of the Finance Act 1986, where securities are transferred, issued or appropriated on or after 1st July 1996 (whenever the arrangement was made);

(b) so far as relating to the charge to tax under section 93(10) of that Act, in relation to instalments payable on or after 1st July 1996.

GENERAL NOTE

This section amends the law to provide that the higher rate charge of 1.5 per cent to SDRT applies where the shares underlying the depositary receipts are to be held by the issuer. Currently the SDRT charge applies only to the normal arrangements where the shares are to be held by a nominee or agent for the issuer, but a transfer to the issuer may be liable to stamp duty.

Rates of charge expressed as percentages

194.—(1) In section 87 of the Finance Act 1986, in subsection (6) (which specifies the rate at which stamp duty reserve tax under that section is charged) for "50p for every £100 or part of £100" there shall be substituted "0.5 per cent."

(2) In section 93 of that Act (depositary receipts)—

    (a) in subsection (4) (rate of charge) for "£1.50 for every £100 or part of £100" there shall be substituted "1.5 per cent.";

    (b) in subsection (5) (which applies subsection (4) with modifications in certain cases where the securities are transferred by a chargeable instrument) for the words from "as if "£1.50" read" onwards there shall be substituted "as if "1.5 per cent." read "1 per cent.""; and

    (c) in subsection (10) (payment in instalments etc) in paragraph (b), for "£1.50 for every £100 or part of £100" there shall be substituted "1.5 per cent. of the amount".

(3) Section 94(8) of that Act (which defines "the day of The Stock Exchange reforms" for the purposes of section 93(5) and which becomes unnecessary in consequence of the amendment made by subsection (2)(b) above) shall be omitted.

(4) In section 96 of that Act (clearance services)—

    (a) in subsection (2) (rate of charge) for "£1.50 for every £100 or part of £100" there shall be substituted "1.5 per cent.";

    (b) in subsection (3) (which applies subsection (2) with modifications in certain cases where the securities are transferred by a chargeable instrument) for the words from "as if "£1.50" read" onwards there shall be substituted "as if "1.5 per cent." read "1 per cent.""; and

    (c) in subsection (8) (payment in instalments etc) in paragraph (b), for "£1.50 for every £100 or part of £100" there shall be substituted "1.5 per cent. of the amount".

(5) Section 96(12) of that Act (which defines "the day of The Stock Exchange reforms" for the purposes of subsection (3) and which becomes unnecessary in consequence of the amendment made by subsection (4)(b) above) shall be omitted.

(6) In section 99 of that Act (interpretation) after subsection (12) there shall be added—

    "(13) Where the calculation of any tax in accordance with the provisions of this Part results in an amount which is not a multiple of one penny, the amount so calculated shall be rounded to the nearest penny, taking any ½p as nearest to the next whole penny above."

(7) Subsections (1) to (5) above have effect in accordance with the following provisions of this subsection, that is to say—

    (a) in relation to the charge to tax under section 87 of the Finance Act 1986, subsection (1) above applies where—

        (i) the agreement to transfer is conditional and the condition is satisfied on or after 1st July 1996; or

        (ii) the agreement is not conditional and is made on or after 1st July 1996;

    (b) in relation to the charge to tax under section 93(1) of that Act, paragraphs (a) and (b) of subsection (2) above apply where securities are transferred, issued or appropriated on or after 1st July 1996 (whenever the arrangement was made) and subsection (3) above has effect accordingly;

    (c) in relation to the charge to tax under section 93(10) of that Act, paragraph (c) of subsection (2) above applies in relation to instalments payable on or after 1st July 1996;

    (d) in relation to the charge to tax under section 96(1) of that Act, paragraphs (a) and (b) of subsection (4) above apply where securities are

transferred or issued on or after 1st July 1996 (whenever the arrangement was made) and subsection (5) above has effect accordingly;

(e) in relation to the charge to tax under section 96(8) of that Act, paragraph (c) of subsection (4) above applies in relation to instalments
payable on or after 1st July 1996.

GENERAL NOTE
This section amends the FA 1986 in order to convert the existing rates of SDRT from 50p per
£100 or part of £100 (£1.50 per £100 or part of £100 in the case of the higher rate charge) to flat
percentages. This will facilitate calculation of the tax, particularly for transfers into or within
electronic transfer systems such as CREST, and result in small reductions in the amounts of tax
payable.

Regulations concerning administration: sub-delegation to the Board

195. In section 98 of the Finance Act 1986 (Treasury regulations with
respect to administration etc) after subsection (1) there shall be inserted—
"(1A) The power conferred on the Treasury by subsection (1) above
includes power to make provision conferring or imposing on the Board
functions which involve the exercise of a discretion."

GENERAL NOTE
The Treasury's regulation-making power under the FA 1986, s.98, is extended to include
power to confer or impose discretionary functions on the Revenue. Regulations made under
s.98 deal with the administration, assessment, collection and recovery of SDRT.

Clearance services

Election by operator for alternative system of charge

196.—(1) In section 70 of the Finance Act 1986 (clearance services) in subsection (1) (which, subject to subsection (9), makes provision with respect to
stamp duty on transfers into clearance services) after "Subject to subsection
(9)" there shall be inserted "and section 97A".

(2) In section 96 of that Act (clearance services) in subsection (1) (which,
subject to subsection (5) and section 97, provides for stamp duty reserve tax
to be chargeable on transfers into clearance services) for "section 97" there
shall be substituted "sections 97 and 97A".

(3) After section 97 of that Act (exceptions) there shall be inserted—

"Clearance services: election for alternative system of charge

97A.—(1) A person whose business is or includes the provision of
clearance services for the purchase and sale, of chargeable securities or
relevant securities (an "operator") may, with the approval of the Board,
elect that stamp duty and stamp duty reserve tax shall be chargeable in
accordance with this section in connection with those clearance services.

(2) An election under subsection (1) above—
(a) shall come into force on such date as may be notified to the operator by the Board in giving their approval; and
(b) shall continue in force unless and until it is terminated in accordance with the following provisions of this section.

(3) If and so long as an election under subsection (1) above is in force,
stamp duty or stamp duty reserve tax (as the case may require) shall, in
connection with the clearance services to which the election relates, be
chargeable in relation to—
(a) a transfer or issue falling within section 70(1) or 96(1) above,
(b) an agreement falling within section 90(4) above by virtue of section 96(1) above, or
(c) an agreement falling within section 90(5) above,
as it would be chargeable apart from sections 70, 90(4) and (5) and 96
above.

(4) Where stamp duty or stamp duty reserve tax is chargeable by virtue of subsection (3) above in relation to a transfer, issue or agreement, sections 70, 90(4) and (5) and 96 above shall not have effect in relation to that transfer, issue or agreement.

(5) Nothing in subsection (3) or (4) above affects the application of section 70 or 96 above in relation to a transfer falling within section 70(1) or 96(1) above by the operator or his nominee to, or to a nominee of, another operator in relation to whom no election under subsection (1) above is for the time being in force.

(6) The Board may require the operator, as a condition of the approval of his election under subsection (1) above, to make and maintain such arrangements as they may consider satisfactory—

    (a) for the collection of stamp duty reserve tax chargeable in accordance with this section, and

    (b) for complying, or securing compliance, with the provisions of this Part and of regulations under section 98 below, so far as relating to such tax.

(7) Where the operator is not resident in the United Kingdom and has no branch or agency in the United Kingdom, the Board may require him, as a condition of the approval of his election under subsection (1) above, to appoint and, so long as the election remains in force, maintain a tax representative.

(8) A person shall not be an operator's tax representative under this section unless that person—

    (a) has a business establishment in the United Kingdom, and

    (b) is approved by the Board.

(9) A person who is at any time an operator's tax representative under this section—

    (a) shall be entitled to act on the operator's behalf for the purposes of stamp duty and stamp duty reserve tax in connection with the clearance services to which the operator's election under subsection (1) above relates,

    (b) shall secure (where appropriate by acting on the operator's behalf) the operator's compliance with and discharge of the obligations and liabilities to which the operator is subject, in connection with the clearance services to which the operator's election under subsection (1) above relates, by virtue of legislation relating to stamp duty or stamp duty reserve tax (including obligations and liabilities arising before he became the operator's tax representative), and

    (c) shall be personally liable in respect of any failure to secure the operator's compliance with or discharge of any such obligation or liability, and in respect of anything done for purposes connected with acting on the operator's behalf,

as if the obligations and liabilities imposed on the operator were imposed jointly and severally on the tax representative and the operator.

(10) An election under subsection (1) above may be terminated—

    (a) by not less than thirty days' notice given by the operator to the Board or by the Board to the operator; or

    (b) if there is or has been a breach of a condition of the approval of the election imposed by virtue of subsection (6) or (7) above, by a notice

        (i) given by the Board to the operator,

        (ii) taking effect on the giving of the notice or at such later time as may be specified in the notice, and

        (iii) stating that it is given by reason of the breach of condition.

(11) Where an election under subsection (1) above is terminated, section 96 above shall have effect as if chargeable securities of the same amounts and kinds as are, immediately before the termination, held by the operator or his nominee in connection with the provision of the clearance services, had, immediately after the termination, been transferred to the operator or, as the case may be, to the nominee by a transfer falling within subsection (1) of that section.

(12) In this section "relevant securities" has the same meaning as in section 70 above."

(4) Section 97(2) of that Act (no charge to tax under section 96 on transfers to a stock exchange nominee or to, or to a nominee of, a recognised investment exchange or recognised clearing house) shall not have effect in relation to any transfer effected on or after 1st July 1996.

(5) In section 99(10) of that Act (interpretation of "chargeable securities" in sections 93, 94 and 96) for "and 96" there shall be substituted ", 96 and 97A".

(6) Subsections (1), (2), (3) and (5) above shall come into force on 1st July 1996.

GENERAL NOTE

This section provides an option for an alternative charging regime for clearance services, instead of the 1.5 per cent higher rate charge to stamp duty or SDRT that is now mandatory on transfers of securities into clearance services. Subject to conditions, the section enables clearance services to elect for SDRT at the appropriate rate to apply to transactions within the service, instead of the initial 1.5 per cent charge.

Subs. (3)

This inserts a new FA 1986, s.97A, which implements the election for the alternative system of charge.

The new s.97A(6) empowers the Revenue to require a clearance service operator, as a condition of approval of his election, to make suitable arrangements for collecting SDRT and for compliance with the relevant provisions relating to such tax.

The new s.97A(7) enables the Revenue to require a clearance service operator, as a condition for approval of his election, to appoint and maintain a tax representative if the operator is not resident in the U.K. and has no branch or agency in the U.K.

The new s.97A(8) provides that a person may not be a tax representative unless he has a business establishment in the U.K. and is approved by the Revenue.

The new s.97A(9) provides that a tax representative is entitled to act on the operator's behalf, shall secure the operator's compliance with relevant obligations and liabilities, if necessary by acting on his behalf, and is personally liable for failure so to secure the operator's compliance.

The new s.97A(10) provides for termination of an election by 30 days' notice from the operator or by the Revenue on a breach of the conditions, with immediate effect unless otherwise specified.

The new s.97A(11) provides that on termination of an election, the higher rate 1.5 per cent charge to SDRT shall apply to the shares then held by the operator in connection with the clearance service.

Subs. (4)

This subsection repeals the exemption from the higher rate charge for transfers to a Stock Exchange nominee and certain other bodies and nominees. The exemption is superseded by the option for the alternative charging system.

PART VII

MISCELLANEOUS AND SUPPLEMENTAL

Miscellaneous: indirect taxation

Setting of rates of interest

197.—(1) The rate of interest applicable for the purposes enactment to which this section applies shall be the rate which for the purposes of that enactment is provided for by regulations made by the Treasury under this section.

(2) This section applies to—

(a) paragraphs 7 and 9 of Schedule 6 to the Finance Act 1994 (interest payable to or by the Commissioners of Customs and Excise in connection with air passenger duty);

(b) paragraphs 21 and 22 of Schedule 7 to that Act (interest on amounts of insurance premium tax and on amounts payable by the Commissioners in respect of that tax);

(c) sections 74 and 78 of the Value Added Tax Act 1994 (interest on VAT recovered or recoverable by assessment and interest payable in cases of official error); and

(d) paragraphs 26 and 29 of Schedule 5 to this Act (interest payable to or by the Commissioners in connection with landfill tax).

(3) Regulations under this section may—

(a) make different provision for different enactments or for different purposes of the same enactment,

(b) either themselves specify a rate of interest for the purposes of an enactment or make provision for any such rate to be determined, and to change from time to time, by reference to such rate or the average of such rates as may be referred to in the regulations,

(c) provide for rates to be reduced below, or increased above, what they otherwise would be by specified amounts or by reference to specified formulae,

(d) provide for rates arrived at by reference to averages or formulae to be rounded up or down,

(e) provide for circumstances in which changes of rates of interest are or are not to take place, and

(f) provide that changes of rates are to have effect for periods beginning on or after a day determined in accordance with the regulations in relation to interest running from before that day, as well as in relation to interest running from, or from after, that day.

(4) The power to make regulations under this section shall be exercisable by statutory instrument subject to annulment in pursuance of a resolution of the House of Commons.

(5) Where—

(a) regulations under this section provide, without specifying the rate determined in accordance with the regulations, for a new method of determining the rate applicable for the purposes of any enactment, or

(b) the rate which, in accordance with regulations under this section, is the rate applicable for the purposes of any enactment changes otherwise than by virtue of the making of regulations specifying a new rate,

the Commissioners of Customs and Excise shall make an order specifying the new rate and the day from which, in accordance with the regulations, it has effect.

(6) The words "the rate applicable under section 197 of the Finance Act 1996" shall be substituted—

(a) for the words "the specified rate" in each of paragraphs 7(1) and (3) and 9(1) of Schedule 6 to the Finance Act 1994 (air passenger duty);

(b) for the words "the prescribed rate" in each of sub-paragraphs (1) and (3) of paragraph 21 of Schedule 7 to that Act (insurance premium tax);

(c) for the words from "such rate" onwards in sub-paragraph (2) of paragraph 22 of that Schedule; and

(d) in the Value Added Tax Act 1994—

(i) for the words "the prescribed rate" in each of subsections (1), (2) and (4) of section 74, and

(ii) for the words from "such rates" onwards in subsection (3) of section 78.

(7) Subsections (1) and (6) above shall have effect for periods beginning on or after such day as the Treasury may by order made by statutory instrument appoint and shall have effect in relation to interest running from before that day, as well as in relation to interest running from, or from after, that day; and different days may be appointed under this subsection for different purposes.

GENERAL NOTE

This section introduces a more streamlined procedure for setting Customs and Excise interest rates in relation to late payments and repayments for air passenger duty, insurance premium tax, value added tax and landfill tax. At present charges are made by Treasury order, which is a slow and cumbersome procedure. The section enables Treasury regulations to be made permitting interest rates to be set without the need for a statutory instrument each time one of the rates changes. The rates could be set by reference to market rates, for instance by reference to the average of the base rates used by the clearing banks, as is already done for Inland Revenue interest by Treasury regulations under the FA 1989, s.178 (see S.I. 1989 No. 1297). Changes in the interest rates will be announced by way of an order made by the Customs and Excise.

Miscellaneous: direct taxation

Banks

198. Schedule 37 to this Act (which re-defines "bank" for certain purposes, and makes related amendments) shall have effect.

GENERAL NOTE

This section introduces Sched. 37, which provides a definition of "bank" to be used in a number of tax provisions. The main purpose of the schedule is to ensure that where interest payments are made on loans that have been transferred from a bank to a non-resident bank or other party that is not liable for corporation tax, such as an individual, the party that pays interest must do so under deduction of tax.

See further the General Note to Sched. 37.

Quotation or listing of securities

199. Schedule 38 to this Act (which contains amendments of enactments referring to the quotation or listing of securities) shall have effect.

GENERAL NOTE

This section introduces Sched. 38, which ensures that various provisions with reference to the Stock Exchange treatment of shares and securities, retain their intended meaning in the light of forthcoming changes. Price quotes for some shares and securities will no longer be included in the Stock Exchange Official List from April 1, 1996. Schedule 38 ensures that the tax treatment of such shares and securities remains unchanged.

See further the General Note to Sched. 38.

Domicile for tax purposes of overseas electors

200.—(1) In determining—
(a) for the purposes of inheritance tax, income tax or capital gains tax where a person is domiciled at any time on or after 6th April 1996, or
(b) for the purposes of section 267(1)(a) of the Inheritance Tax Act 1984 (deemed UK domicile for three years after ceasing to be so domiciled) where a person was domiciled at any time on or after 6th April 1993,
there shall be disregarded any relevant action taken by that person (whether before, on or after that date) in connection with electoral rights.

(2) Relevant action is taken by a person in connection with electoral rights where—
(a) he does anything with a view to, or in connection with, being registered as an overseas elector; or
(b) when registered as an overseas elector, he votes in any election at which he is entitled to vote by virtue of being so registered.

(3) For the purposes of this section, a person is registered as an overseas elector if he is—

(a) registered in any register mentioned in section 12(1) of the Representation of the People Act 1983 (right to be registered of persons entitled
to vote at parliamentary elections) on account of any entitlement to
vote conferred on him by section 1 of the Representation of the People
Act 1985 (extension of parliamentary franchise to certain non-resident British citizens); or
(b) registered under section 3 of that Act of 1985 (certain non-resident
peers entitled to vote at European Parliamentary elections).

(4) Nothing in subsection (1) above prevents regard being had, in determining the domicile of a person at any time, to any relevant action taken by
him in connection with electoral rights if—
(a) his domicile at that time falls to be determined for the purpose of
ascertaining his or any other person's liability to any of the taxes mentioned in subsection (1)(a) above; and
(b) the person whose liability is being ascertained wishes regard to be had
to that action;
and a person's domicile determined in accordance with any such wishes shall
be taken to have been so determined for the purpose only of ascertaining the
liability in question.

GENERAL NOTE
This section, introduced on backbench initiative at report stage, removes an anxiety felt by
expatriates in relation to domicile. It provides that in determining a person's domicile for tax
purposes no regard shall be had to any action taken by him to register as an overseas elector or to
vote in an election. There is a proviso that the action can be taken into account for determining
any person's liability to tax if that person so wishes. The domicile so ascertained applies only for
that purpose [*Hansard*, H.C. Vol. 274, col. 1106].

Enactment of Inland Revenue concessions

201. Schedule 39 to this Act has effect for the purpose of enacting certain
extra-statutory concessions relating to income tax, corporation tax, capital
gains tax, and stamp duty.

GENERAL NOTE
This section introduces Sched. 39, which enacts 11 Inland Revenue extra-statutory
concessions.
See further the General Note to Sched. 39.

Miscellaneous: other matters

Gilt stripping

202.—(1) In section 47 of the Finance Act 1942 (Treasury regulations with
respect to the transfer and registration of Government stock), after paragraph (bb) of subsection (1) there shall be inserted the following
paragraphs—
"(bc) for the exchange of any such stock and bonds (whenever
issued) for strips thereof;
(bd) for exchanges by which such strips (whether deriving from the
same security or from different securities) are consolidated
into a single security of a description so specified;".

(2) After subsection (1A) of that section (transfer of deceased persons'
stocks and bonds) there shall be inserted the following subsections—
"(1B) In this section 'strip', in relation to any stock or bond, means a
security issued under the National Loans Act 1968 which—
(a) is issued for the purpose of representing the right to, or of
securing—

          (i) a payment corresponding to a payment of interest or principal remaining to be made under the stock or bond, or

          (ii) two or more payments each corresponding to a different payment remaining to be so made;

  (b) is issued in conjunction with the issue of one or more other securities which, together with that security, represent the right to, or secure, payments corresponding to every payment remaining to be made under the stock or bond; and

  (c) is not itself a security that represents the right to, or secures, payments corresponding to a part of every payment so remaining.

(1C) For the purposes of subsection (1B) of this section, where the balance has been struck for a dividend on any stock or bond, any payment to be made in respect of that dividend shall, at times falling after that balance has been struck, be treated as not being a payment remaining to be made under the stock or bond.

(1D) Without prejudice to the generality of the powers conferred by the preceding provisions of this section (but subject to subsection (1E) of this section), regulations made by virtue of paragraph (bc) or (bd) of subsection (1) of this section may—

  (a) provide, for the purpose of authorising the making of exchanges, for any stock or bonds to be treated as issued on such terms as may be specified in the regulations;

  (b) contain such provision as the Treasury think fit about the circumstances in which and the conditions subject to which exchanges may be effected; and

  (c) contain any such provision as could be contained in rules made under section 14(3) of the National Loans Act 1968 (Treasury rules as to exchange of securities).

(1E) Regulations made by virtue of subsection (1)(bc) or (bd) of this section shall not make provision for the exchange of any stock or bonds, or of any strips, in any cases other than those where the exchange is at the request of the holder or in accordance with an order made by a court.

(1F) Regulations under this section may make different provision for different cases and contain such exceptions and exclusions as the Treasury think fit; and the powers of the Treasury to make regulations under this section are without prejudice to any of their powers under the National Loans Act 1968.”

(3) After section 2 of the National Debt (Stockholders Relief) Act 1892 (date for striking balance for a dividend on stock) there shall be inserted the following section—

“Payment of dividend on stock stripped after balance struck

    2A.—(1) Where—

  (a) any stock is exchanged for strips of that stock, and

  (b) that exchange takes place after the balance has been struck for a dividend on that stock but before the day on which that dividend is payable,

any person who would have been entitled to that dividend but for the exchange shall remain entitled to that dividend notwithstanding the exchange.

(2) The Treasury may by order made by statutory instrument provide that for the purposes of this section and section 47(1C) of the Finance Act 1942, the balance for any dividend on any stock is to be deemed to be struck at a time which, by such a period as is specified in the order, precedes the time when the balance is actually struck.

(3) A period specified in an order under subsection (2) above shall not exceed 7 days; and an order made under that subsection may make different provision for different cases.

(4) In this section 'strip', in relation to any stock, has the meaning given by section 47 of the Finance Act 1942."

(4) In section 16 of the National Loans Act 1968 (supplemental provisions as to national debt), after subsection (4) there shall be inserted the following subsection—

"(4A) In subsections (3) and (4) above the references to stock or registered bonds issued under this Act include references to a strip (within the meaning of section 47 of the Finance Act 1942) of any stock or bond (whether the stock or bond is issued under this Act or otherwise)."

(5) The Treasury may by regulations make provision for securing that enactments and subordinate legislation which—

(a) apply in relation to government securities or to any description of such securities, or

(b) for any other purpose refer (in whatever terms) to such securities or to any description of them,

have effect with such modifications as the Treasury may think appropriate in consequence of the making of any provision or arrangements for, or in connection with, the issue or transfer of strips of government securities or the consolidation of such strips into other securities.

(6) Regulations under subsection (5) above may—

(a) impose a charge to income tax, corporation tax, capital gains tax, inheritance tax, stamp duty or stamp duty reserve tax;

(b) include provision applying generally to, or to any description of, enactments or subordinate legislation;

(c) make different provision for different cases; and

(d) contain such incidental, supplemental, consequential and transitional provision as the Treasury think appropriate.

(7) The power to make regulations under subsection (5) above shall be exercisable by statutory instrument subject to annulment in pursuance of a resolution of the House of Commons.

(8) Schedule 40 to this Act (which makes provision in relation to strips for taxation purposes) shall have effect.

(9) The enactments that may be modified by regulations under this section shall include section 95 above and the enactments contained in Schedule 40 to this Act.

(10) In this section—

"government securities" means any securities included in Part I of Schedule 11 to the Finance Act 1942;

"modifications" includes amendments, additions and omissions; and

"subordinate legislation" has the same meaning as in the Interpretation Act 1978;

and expressions used in this section and in section 47 of the Finance Act 1942 have the same meanings in this section as in that section.

GENERAL NOTE

This section, together with Sched. 40, makes provisions to facilitate a market in strips of gilt-edged securities. Stripping is the process of exchanging a gilt for a number of quite separate securities, each one taking the place of the right to one or more of the payments which would have been received by the holder of an unstripped gilt. The section defines strips and enables regulations to be made to set out the terms on which gilts can be exchanged for strips.

Subs. (1)

The new FA 1942, s.47(1)(bc) and (bd) enables the Treasury to make regulations covering the transfer and registration of strips.

Subs. (2)

The new FA 1942, s.47(1B)–(1F), defines a strip and enables regulations to make provision about the exchange of stocks for their constituent strips, in particular making it clear that no holder of stock will be obliged to strip it.

Subs. (3)
The new National Debt (Stockbrokers Relief) Act 1892, s.2A, provides for a dividend on a security stripped during ex-dividend periods to remain payable to the previous holder.

Subs. (4)
The new National Loans Act 1968 (c. 13), s.16(4A), is a consequential amendment.

Subss. (5)–(10)
These subsections provide further regulation-making powers, provide definitions and introduce Sched. 40. The power to impose tax by regulation is unusual.
See further the General Note to Sched. 40 [Standing Committee E, March 5, 1996, col. 710].

Modification of the Agriculture Act 1993

203.—(1) Part I of Schedule 2 to the Agriculture Act 1993 (taxation provisions applying to the reorganisation of the milk marketing boards) shall have effect, and be deemed always to have had effect, in accordance with subsections (2) to (4) below where—
  (a) any approved scheme has made provision as to the functions of a milk marketing board in the period after the transfers taking effect on the vesting day under section 11 of that Act;
  (b) regulations have been made by virtue of section 14(2) of that Act (provision following re-organisation) for giving effect to that provision; and
  (c) a transaction is or has been entered into by that board in pursuance of any obligation under those regulations to carry out those functions so far as they relate to a subsidiary of the board.
  (2) For the purposes of that Part of that Schedule—
  (a) anything done by way of entering into the transaction, or for the purpose of carrying it out, shall be deemed to have been done under and in accordance with the scheme; and
  (b) the terms and other provisions having effect in relation to that transaction by virtue of anything contained in, or anything done in exercise of powers conferred by, any regulations under section 14(2) of the Agriculture Act 1993 shall be deemed to be terms for which the scheme provided or, as the case may be, to be provisions of the scheme.
  (3) Sub-paragraph (1) of paragraph 16 of Schedule 2 to the Agriculture Act 1993 (distributions) shall have effect, and be deemed always to have had effect, in a case where the terms and provisions mentioned in subsection (2)(b) above involved or involve—
  (a) the issue or transfer of any shares in, or securities of, any body,
  (b) the conferring of any right to a distribution out of the assets of any body,
  (c) the conferring of any right to, or to acquire, shares in any body, or
  (d) the transfer to any person of any property or rights of a milk marketing board, or of the subsidiary of such a board,
as if the references to the vesting day in paragraphs (a), (c), (d) and (e) of that sub-paragraph were references to the day on which the winding up of the board is completed.
  (4) Sub-paragraph (4) of paragraph 31 of Schedule 2 to the Agriculture Act 1993 (condition to be satisfied if body to be qualifying body by virtue of sub-paragraph (1)(c)) shall have effect, and be deemed always to have had effect, as if—
  (a) the reference, in relation to a company, to 90 per cent. of its ordinary share capital were a reference to 70 per cent. of its ordinary share capital; and
  (b) the references to shares having been issued to any person included references to their having been allotted to that person.

(5) Paragraph 1 of Schedule 2 to the Agriculture Act 1993 (tax continuity with successor bodies) shall have effect, and be deemed to have had effect, in relation to any relevant transfer after 31st December 1995 to a society registered under the Industrial and Provident Societies Act 1965 of—

(a) a trade, or part of a trade, of a milk marketing board, or

(b) any property, rights or liabilities of such a board,

as it has effect in relation to any transfer under section 11 of that Act to a qualifying body.

(6) Paragraphs 16, 20, 25, 26, 28 and 29 of Schedule 2 to the Agriculture Act 1993 shall have effect, and be deemed to have had effect, in relation to any relevant transfer after 31st December 1995 of assets of a milk marketing board to a society registered under the Industrial and Provident Societies Act 1965 as if—

(a) the terms and other provisions of the transaction for effecting the transfer were contained in an approved scheme;

(b) the society were a relevant successor of that board; and

(c) references in those paragraphs to the vesting day were references to the day on which the winding up of the board is completed.

(7) For the purposes of subsections (5) and (6) above, a transfer of anything to a society registered under the Industrial and Provident Societies Act 1965 is a relevant transfer if—

(a) it is a transfer in pursuance of regulations made by virtue of section 14(2) of the Agriculture Act 1993;

(b) it is not a transfer of shares in a subsidiary of a milk marketing board; and

(c) the condition mentioned in sub-paragraph (5) of paragraph 31 of Schedule 2 to that Act would have been met in relation to that society if the provision made as to the persons to whom the membership of the society is open were contained in an approved scheme providing for the transfer.

(8) Paragraph 20 of Schedule 2 to the Agriculture Act 1993 (treatment of acquisition of certain shares and securities) shall not apply, and shall be deemed never to have applied, in relation to the acquisition of any security after 31st December 1995 if the indebtedness acknowledged by that security does not fall, for the purposes of the Taxation of Chargeable Gains Act 1992, to be treated as a debt on a security (as defined in section 132 of that Act of 1992).

(9) For the purposes of Chapter II of Part IV of this Act, so far as it has effect for any accounting period ending after 31st March 1996 in relation to any creditor relationship represented by a debenture issued on or after 31st December 1995, paragraph 25 of Schedule 2 to the Agriculture Act 1993 shall have effect as if sub-paragraph (2)(a) of that paragraph (deemed consideration for issue of debenture issued under approved scheme) were omitted.

(10) For the purposes of the Taxation of Chargeable Gains Act 1992, where any debenture to which paragraph 25 of Schedule 2 to the Agriculture Act 1993 applies has been or is issued at any time after 31st December 1995, the indebtedness acknowledged by that debenture shall be deemed (where that would not otherwise be the case) to be, and always to have been, a debt on a security (as defined in section 132 of that Act of 1992).

(11) Expressions used in this section and in Part I of the Agriculture Act 1993 have the same meanings in this section as in that Part.

GENERAL NOTE

The Agriculture Act 1993 (c. 37) provided for the winding up of the Milk Marketing Boards and their replacement by successor bodies. The Act contained provisions to prevent a tax charge arising on the Boards, their successors or the dairy producers when the Boards were reorganised if the reorganisations were carried out on or before vesting day. The section extends this relief to disposals after vesting day and caters for various options for the flotation of Dairy Crest [Standing Committee E, February 29, 1996, col. 577].

Supplemental

Interpretation

204. In this Act "the Taxes Act 1988" means the Income and Corporation Taxes Act 1988.

Repeals

205.—(1) The enactments mentioned in Schedule 41 to this Act (which include spent provisions) are hereby repealed to the extent specified in the third column of that Schedule.

(2) The repeals specified in that Schedule have effect subject to the commencement provisions and savings contained in, or referred to, in the notes set out in that Schedule.

Short title

206. This Act may be cited as the Finance Act 1996.

SCHEDULES

Section 6   SCHEDULE 1

MIXING OF REBATED OIL

The following is the Schedule which shall be inserted after Schedule 2 to the Hydrocarbon Oil Duties Act 1979—

"SCHEDULE 2A

MIXING OF REBATED OIL

PART I

LIGHT OIL

Converting unleaded petrol into leaded petrol

1.—(1) A mixture which is leaded petrol is produced in contravention of this paragraph if such a mixture is produced by—
  (a) adding lead to unleaded petrol in respect of which a rebate has been allowed under subsection (1) of section 13A of this Act at the rate given by subsection (1A)(a) of that section;
  (b) adding lead to unleaded petrol in respect of which a rebate has been allowed under subsection (1) of that section at the rate given by subsection (1A)(b) of that section; or
  (c) adding lead to a mixture of unleaded petrol of a description mentioned in paragraph (a) above and unleaded petrol of a description mentioned in paragraph (b) above.

(2) In sub-paragraph (1) above the reference to adding lead to unleaded petrol includes a reference to adding leaded petrol to unleaded petrol.

(3) This paragraph is subject to any direction given under paragraph 3 below.

Adding octane enhancers to low octane unleaded petrol

2.—(1) A mixture which is super-unleaded petrol is produced in contravention of this paragraph if such a mixture is produced by adding an octane enhancer to unleaded petrol in respect of which a rebate has been allowed under subsection (1) of section 13A of this Act at the rate given by subsection (1A)(b) of that section.

(2) For the purposes of sub-paragraph (1) above 'super-unleaded petrol' means unleaded petrol—

(a) whose research octane number is not less than 96; and

(b) whose motor octane number is not less than 86.

(3) Subsection (1C) of section 13A applies for the purposes of this paragraph as it applies for the purposes of that section.

(4) This paragraph is subject to any direction given under paragraph 3 below.

Power to create exceptions

3. The Commissioners may give a direction that, in such description of circumstances as may be specified in the direction, a mixture is not produced in contravention of paragraph 1 above or (as the case may be) paragraph 2 above.

PART II

HEAVY OIL

Mixing partially rebated heavy oil with unrebated heavy oil

4. A mixture of heavy oils is produced in contravention of this paragraph if such a mixture is produced by mixing—

(a) gas oil in respect of which a rebate has been allowed under section 11(1)(b) of this Act; and

(b) heavy oil in respect of which, on its delivery for home use, a declaration was made that it was intended for use as fuel for a road vehicle.

Mixing fully rebated heavy oil with unrebated heavy oil

5. A mixture of heavy oils is produced in contravention of this paragraph if such a mixture is produced by mixing—

(a) heavy oil which is neither fuel oil nor gas oil and in respect of which a rebate has been allowed under section 11(1)(c) of this Act; and

(b) heavy oil in respect of which, on its delivery for home use, a declaration was made that it was intended for use as fuel for a road vehicle.

Mixing fully rebated heavy oil with partially rebated heavy oil

6. A mixture of heavy oils is produced in contravention of this paragraph if such a mixture is produced by mixing—

(a) heavy oil which is neither fuel oil nor gas oil and in respect of which a rebate has been allowed under section 11(1)(c) of this Act; and

(b) gas oil in respect of which a rebate has been allowed under section 11(1)(b) of this Act.

Complex mixtures of heavy oils

7. A mixture of heavy oils is produced in contravention of this paragraph if such a mixture is produced in contravention of more than one paragraph of paragraphs 4 to 6 above.

PART III

RATES OF DUTY, ETC.

Rate for mixtures of light oil

8.—(1) Subject to paragraph 10 below, duty under section 20AAA(1) of this Act shall be charged at the following rates.

(2) In the case of a mixture produced in contravention of paragraph 1 above, the rate is the rate for light oil in force at the time that the mixture is produced.

(3) In the case of a mixture produced in contravention of paragraph 2 above, the rate is the rate produced by deducting from the rate for light oil in force at the time the mixture is produced the rate of rebate which at that time is in force under section 13A(1A)(a) of this Act.

(4) In this paragraph 'the rate for light oil' means the rate given in the case of light oil by section 6(1) of this Act.

Rate for mixtures of heavy oil

9.—(1) Subject to paragraph 10 below, duty charged under subsection (2) of section 20AAA of this Act shall be charged at the rate for heavy oil in force at the time when the mixture is supplied as mentioned in that subsection.

(2) In this paragraph 'the rate for heavy oil' means the rate given in the case of heavy oil by section 6(1) of this Act.

Credit for duty paid on ingredients of mixture

10. Where duty is charged under section 20AAA of this Act in respect of any mixture, the amount of duty produced by applying paragraph 8 or 9 above shall be reduced by the amount of any duty under section 6 of this Act which the Commissioners are satisfied has been paid in respect of any ingredient of the mixture.

Interpretation

11. In this Schedule—
'fuel oil' and 'gas oil' have the same meanings as in section 11 of this Act;
'leaded petrol' and 'unleaded petrol' shall be construed in accordance with section 13A of this Act."

GENERAL NOTE
The Schedule is supplemental to s.6, which imposes a duty on fuels which are mixed after the normal duty point. It defines the types of mixture caught by s.6 and specifies the duty applicable.

Section 23   SCHEDULE 2

VEHICLE LICENSING AND REGISTRATION

1. In this Schedule "the 1994 Act" means the Vehicle Excise and Registration Act 1994.

Vehicle licences

2.—(1) Section 7 of the 1994 Act (issue of vehicle licences) shall be amended in accordance with this paragraph.
(2) After subsection (3) there shall be inserted the following subsections—
"(3A) A person applying for a licence shall not be required to make a declaration specified for the purposes of subsection (1)(a) if he agrees to comply with such conditions as may be specified in relation to him by the Secretary of State.
(3B) The conditions which may be specified under subsection (3A) include a condition that particulars for the time being specified for the purposes of subsection (1)(b) are furnished by being transmitted to the Secretary of State by such electronic means as he may specify."
(3) Sub-paragraph (2) above applies to applications made on or after the day on which this Act is passed.
(4) In subsection (6)—
(a) after "may provide for—" there shall be inserted the following paragraph—
"(aa) the return of any vehicle licence which is damaged or contains any particulars which have become illegible or inaccurate,";
(b) in paragraph (a), after "or damaged", there shall be inserted "or which contains any particulars which have become illegible or inaccurate"; and
(c) at the end of paragraph (b) there shall be inserted "in any of those circumstances".

Trade licences

3. In section 11 of the 1994 Act (trade licences), after subsection (1) there shall be inserted the following subsection—
"(1A) The power to prescribe conditions under subsection (1) includes, in particular, the power to prescribe conditions which are to be complied with after the licence is issued."

Registration regulations

4.—(1) Subsection (1) of section 22 of the 1994 Act (registration regulations) shall be amended in accordance with this paragraph.
(2) In paragraph (d), after "a person by", there shall be inserted ", through".
(3) In paragraph (dd), after "a person by", there shall be inserted "or through".
(4) At the end of paragraph (h) there shall be inserted "or which contain any particulars which have become illegible or inaccurate".
(5) After paragraph (h) there shall be inserted the following paragraph—
"(i) provide for a fee of such amount as appears to the Secretary of State to be reasonable to be paid on the issue of new registration documents in any of the circumstances mentioned in paragraph (h)."

5. In subsection (1B)(a) of section 22 of the 1994 Act, for "the other person there mentioned or to the Secretary of State or to both;" there shall be substituted "another person there mentioned or to the Secretary of State or to another such person and to the Secretary of State;".

6. After subsection (1B) of section 22 of the 1994 Act there shall be inserted the following subsection—

"(1C) Regulations under subsection (1)(e) may, in particular, provide that registration documents need not be issued in respect of the registration of a vehicle until the vehicle has been inspected by a person specified by the Secretary of State."

7. After subsection (1C) of section 22 of the 1994 Act there shall be inserted the following subsections—

"(1D) The Secretary of State may by regulations require a person—

(a) who surrenders a vehicle licence under section 10(2),

(b) who does not renew a vehicle licence for a vehicle kept by him, or

(c) who keeps an unlicensed vehicle at any place in the United Kingdom,

to furnish such particulars and make such declarations as may be prescribed by the regulations, and to do so at such times and in such manner as may be so prescribed.

(1E) For the purposes of subsection (1D)(b) a person shall be regarded as not renewing a vehicle licence for a vehicle kept by him if—

(a) he keeps a vehicle for which a vehicle licence is in force, and

(b) he does not, at such time as may be prescribed by the regulations or within such period as may be so prescribed, take out a vehicle licence to have effect from the expiry of the vehicle licence mentioned in paragraph (a).

(1F) For the purposes of subsection (1D)(c) a vehicle is unlicensed if no vehicle licence is in force for the vehicle.

(1G) Regulations under subsection (1D) may make such transitional provision as appears to the Secretary of State to be appropriate."

Surrender of licences: repayments

8. In section 19 of the 1994 Act (surrender of licences), after subsection (2), there shall be inserted the following subsection—

"(3) Subsection (1) does not apply if the holder of the licence does not comply with regulations made by virtue of section 22(1D)(a)."

Offences

9.—(1) In section 29 of the 1994 Act (penalty for using or keeping unlicensed vehicle), at the beginning of subsection (3) there shall be inserted "Subject to subsection (3A)", and after subsection (3) there shall be inserted the following subsection—

"(3A) In the case of a person who—

(a) has provided the Secretary of State with a declaration or statement (in pursuance of regulations under section 22) that the vehicle will not during a period specified in the declaration or statement be used or kept on a public road, and

(b) commits an offence under subsection (1) within a period prescribed by regulations,

subsection (3) applies as if the reference in paragraph (a) to level 3 were a reference to level 4."

(2) This paragraph applies in relation to offences committed on or after the day on which this Act is passed.

10. In section 33 of the 1994 Act (not exhibiting licence), after subsection (3) there shall be inserted the following subsection—

"(4) The Secretary of State may make regulations prohibiting a person from exhibiting on a vehicle in respect of which excise duty is chargeable anything—

(a) which is intended to be, or

(b) which could reasonably be,

mistaken for a licence which is for, or in respect of, the vehicle and which is for the time being in force."

11.—(1) Section 45 of the 1994 Act (false or misleading declarations and information) shall be amended in accordance with this paragraph.

(2) After subsection (2) there shall be inserted the following subsection—

"(2A) A person who makes a declaration or statement which—

(a) is required to be made in respect of a vehicle by regulations under section 22, and

(b) to his knowledge is either false or in any material respect misleading,

is guilty of an offence."

(3) In subsection (3) (offence of furnishing false or misleading particulars), in paragraph (a), after "required by" there shall be inserted "virtue of".

Offences: information and admissions

12. After section 46 of the 1994 Act there shall be inserted the following—

"Duty to give information: offences under regulations
    46A.—(1) Subsection (2) applies where it appears to the Secretary of State—
    (a) that a person is a person by, through or to whom a vehicle has been sold or disposed of
        and that he has failed to comply with regulations made by virtue of section 22(1)(d)
        requiring him to furnish particulars prescribed by the regulations;
    (b) that a person is a person by or through whom a vehicle has been sold or disposed of
        and that he has failed to comply with regulations made by virtue of section 22(1)(dd)
        requiring him to furnish a document prescribed by the regulations; or
    (c) that a person is a person who is surrendering a vehicle licence, or who is not renewing
        a vehicle licence for a vehicle kept by him or who is keeping an unlicensed vehicle and
        that he has failed to comply with regulations made by virtue of section 22(1D) requir-
        ing him to furnish particulars or make a declaration prescribed by the regulations.
    (2) The Secretary of State may serve a notice on the person in question requiring him to
give the Secretary of State such information as it in his power to give—
    (a) as to the identity of any person who is keeping a specified vehicle or who has kept it at
        a specified time or during a specified period;
    (b) as to the identity of any person by, through or to whom a specified vehicle has been
        sold or disposed of at a specified time or during a specified period; or
    (c) which may lead to the identification of a person falling within paragraph (a) or (b).
    (3) A person who fails to comply with a notice under subsection (2) is guilty of an offence.
    (4) A person guilty of an offence under subsection (3) is liable on summary conviction to
a fine not exceeding level 3 on the standard scale.
    (5) In this section 'specified' means specified in a notice under subsection (2)."
13. After section 51 of the 1994 Act there shall be inserted the following section—

"Admissions: offences under regulations
    51A.—(1) Subsection (2) applies in relation to any proceedings in England, Wales or
Northern Ireland against a person for an offence on the grounds that—
    (a) a vehicle has been sold or disposed of by, through or to him and he has failed to
        furnish particulars prescribed by regulations made by virtue of section 22(1)(d);
    (b) a vehicle has been sold or disposed of by or through him and he has failed to furnish a
        document prescribed by regulations made by virtue of section 22(1)(dd); or
    (c) he has surrendered, or not renewed, a vehicle licence, or is keeping an unlicensed
        vehicle, and has failed to furnish any particulars or make a declaration prescribed by
        regulations made by virtue of section 22(1D).
    (2) If—
    (a) it is appropriately proved that there has been served on the accused by post a require-
        ment under section 46A to give information as to the identity of the person keeping
        the vehicle at a particular time, and
    (b) a statement in writing is produced to the court purporting to be signed by the accused
        that he was keeping the vehicle at that time,
the court may accept the statement as evidence that the accused was keeping the vehicle at
that time.
    (3) In subsection (2) 'appropriately proved' has the same meaning as in section 51."

Proceedings in respect of offences

14.—(1) In—
    (a) section 47(1) and (2) of the 1994 Act (institution and conduct of proceedings in England
        and Wales or Northern Ireland), and
    (b) section 48(3) of the 1994 Act (proceedings in Scotland),
after "section 29, 34" there shall in each case be inserted ", 35A".
    (2) In section 55(1) of the 1994 Act (guilty plea by absent accused), for paragraphs (a) and (b)
there shall be substituted "an offence under section 29 or 35A".
    (3) This paragraph applies in relation to proceedings commenced on or after the day on which
this Act is passed.

Compounding of offences

15. In section 59 of the 1994 Act (regulations: offences), after subsection (5), there shall be
inserted the following subsection—

"(6) The Secretary of State may, if he sees fit, compound any proceedings for an offence—
(a) under subsection (1), or
(b) under regulations under section 24 or 28."

Regulations

16. In section 57(1) of the 1994 Act (regulations generally), the words "(other than sections 7(2) and (3), 8, 26, 27, 52 and 54)" shall be omitted.

GENERAL NOTE
The Schedule makes changes to the licensing and registration system in order to reduce evasion.

Para. 7
This provides for regulations requiring a declaration, known as an "off-road declaration" to be made when a licence is surrendered for a refund and when a licence is not being renewed and the vehicle is to be kept off the road. The practice aimed at is "month skipping", where a licence is not renewed until some time after the due date.

Para. 9
The penalty for "month skipping" is level 4 on the standard scale (£2,000).

Paras. 10–16
These provide for the creation of further offences in connection with the registration and transfer of vehicles and for proceedings with regard to them.

Section 26   SCHEDULE 3

VALUE ADDED TAX: FISCAL AND OTHER WAREHOUSING

1. In subsection (1) of section 6 of the Value Added Tax Act 1994, for the words "section 18" there shall be substituted the words "sections 18, 18B and 18C".
2. In subsection (1) of section 7 of the Value Added Tax Act 1994, for the words "sections 14 and 18" there shall be substituted the words "sections 14, 18 and 18B".
3. In subsection (1) of section 12 of the Value Added Tax Act 1994, for the words "section 18" there shall be substituted "sections 18 and 18B".
4. In subsection (1) of section 13 of the Value Added Tax Act 1994, for the words "section 18" there shall be substituted "sections 18 and 18B".
5. The following sections shall be inserted in the Value Added Tax Act 1994 after section 18.

"Fiscal warehousing
18A.—(1) The Commissioners may, if it appears to them proper, upon application approve any registered person as a fiscal warehousekeeper; and such approval shall be subject to such conditions as they shall impose.
(2) Subject to those conditions and to regulations made under section 18F such a person shall be entitled to keep a fiscal warehouse.
(3) "Fiscal warehouse" means such place in the United Kingdom in the occupation or under the control of the fiscal warehousekeeper, not being retail premises, as he shall notify to the Commissioners in writing; and such a place shall become a fiscal warehouse on receipt by the Commissioners of that notification or on the date stated in it as the date from which it is to have effect, whichever is the later, and, subject to subsection (6) below, shall remain a fiscal warehouse so long as it is in the occupation or under the control of the fiscal warehousekeeper or until he shall notify the Commissioners in writing that it is to cease to be a fiscal warehouse.
(4) The Commissioners may in considering an application by a person to be a fiscal warehousekeeper take into account any matter which they consider relevant, and may without prejudice to the generality of that provision take into account all or any one or more of the following—
(a) his record of compliance and ability to comply with the requirements of this Act and regulations made hereunder;
(b) his record of compliance and ability to comply with the requirements of the customs and excise Acts (as defined in the Management Act) and regulations made thereunder;
(c) his record of compliance and ability to comply with Community customs provisions;

(d) his record of compliance and ability to comply with the requirements of other member States relating to VAT and duties equivalent to duties of excise;

(e) if the applicant is a company the records of compliance and ability to comply with the matters set out at (a) to (d) above of its directors, persons connected with its directors, its managing officers, any shadow directors or any of those persons, and, if it is a close company, the records of compliance and ability to comply with the matters set out at (a) to (d) above of the beneficial owners of the shares of the company or any of them; and

(f) if the applicant is an individual the records of compliance and ability to comply with the matters set out at (a) to (d) above of any company of which he is or has been a director, managing officer or shadow director or, in the case of a close company, a shareholder or the beneficial owner of shares,

and for the purposes of paragraphs (e) and (f) "connected" shall have the meaning given by section 24(7), "managing officer" the meaning given by section 61(6), "shadow director" the meaning given by section 741(2) of the Companies Act 1985 and "close company" the meaning given by the Taxes Act.

(5) Subject to subsection (6) below, a person approved under subsection (1) shall remain a fiscal warehousekeeper until he ceases to be a registered person or until he shall notify the Commissioners in writing that he is to cease to be a fiscal warehousekeeper.

(6) The Commissioners may if they consider it appropriate from time to time—

(a) impose conditions on a fiscal warehousekeeper in addition to those conditions, if any, which they imposed under subsection (1), and vary or revoke any conditions previously imposed;

(b) withdraw approval of any person as a fiscal warehousekeeper, and

(c) withdraw fiscal warehouse status from any premises.

(7) Any application by or on behalf of a person to be a fiscal warehousekeeper shall be in writing in such form as the Commissioners may direct and shall be accompanied by such information as they shall require.

(8) Any approval by the Commissioners under subsection (1) above, and any withdrawal of approval or other act by them under subsection (6) above, shall be notified by them to the fiscal warehousekeeper in writing and shall take effect on such notification being made or on any later date specified for the purpose in the notification.

(9) Without prejudice to the provisions of section 43 concerning liability for VAT, in subsections (1) and (2) above "registered person" includes any body corporate which under that section is for the time being treated as a member of a group.

Fiscally warehoused goods: relief

18B.—(1) Subsections (3) and (4) below apply where—

(a) there is an acquisition of goods from another member State;

(b) those goods are eligible goods;

(c) either—

    (i) the acquisition takes place while the goods are subject to a fiscal warehousing regime; or

    (ii) after the acquisition but before the supply, if any, of those goods which next occurs, the acquirer causes the goods to be placed in a fiscal warehousing regime; and

(d) the acquirer, not later than the time of the acquisition, prepares and keeps a certificate that the goods are subject to a fiscal warehousing regime, or (as the case may be) that he will cause paragraph (c)(ii) above to be satisfied, and the certificate shall be in such form and be kept for such period as the Commissioners may by regulations specify.

(2) Subsections (3) and (4) below also apply where—

(a) there is a supply of goods;

(b) those goods are eligible goods;

(c) either—

    (i) that supply takes place while the goods are subject to a fiscal warehousing regime; or

    (ii) after that supply but before the supply, if any, of those goods which next occurs, the person to whom the former supply is made causes the goods to be placed in a fiscal warehousing regime;

(d) in a case falling within paragraph (c)(ii) above, the person to whom the supply is made gives the supplier, not later than the time of the supply, a certificate in such form as the Commissioners may by regulations specify that he will cause paragraph (c)(ii) to be satisfied; and

(e) the supply is not a retail transaction.

(3) The acquisition or supply in question shall be treated for the purposes of this Act as taking place outside the United Kingdom if any subsequent supply of those goods is while they are subject to the fiscal warehousing regime.

(4) Where subsection (3) does not apply and the acquisition or supply in question falls, for the purposes of this Act, to be treated as taking place in the United Kingdom, that acquisition or supply shall be treated for the purposes of this Act as taking place when the goods are removed from the fiscal warehousing regime.

(5) Where—

(a) subsection (4) above applies to an acquisition or a supply,

(b) the acquisition or supply is taxable and not zero-rated, and

(c) the acquirer or supplier is not a taxable person but would be were it not for paragraph 1(9) of Schedule 1, paragraph 1(7) of Schedule 2 and paragraph 1(6) of Schedule 3, or any of those provisions,

VAT shall be chargeable on that acquisition or supply notwithstanding that the acquirer or the supplier is not a taxable person.

(6) In this section "eligible goods" means goods—

(a) of a description falling within Schedule 5A;

(b) upon which any import duties, as defined in article 4(10) of the Community Customs Code of 12th October 1992 (Council Regulation (EEC) No.2913/92), either have been paid or have been deferred under article 224 of that Code or regulations made under section 45 of the Management Act;

(c) (in the case of goods imported from a place outside the member States) upon which any VAT chargeable under section 1(1)(c) has been either paid or deferred in accordance with Community customs provisions, and

(d) (in the case of goods subject to a duty of excise) upon which that duty has been either paid or deferred under section 127A of the Management Act.

(7) For the purposes of this section, apart from subsection (4), an acquisition or supply shall be treated as taking place at the material time for the acquisition or supply.

(8) The Treasury may by order vary Schedule 5A by adding to or deleting from it any goods or varying any description of any goods.

Warehouses and fiscal warehouses: services

18C.—(1) Where—

(a) a taxable person makes a supply of specified services;

(b) those services are wholly performed on or in relation to goods while those goods are subject to a warehousing or fiscal warehousing regime;

(c) (except where the services are the supply by an occupier of a warehouse or a fiscal warehousekeeper of warehousing or fiscally warehousing the goods) the person to whom the supply is made gives the supplier a certificate, in such a form as the Commissioners may by regulations specify, that the services are so performed;

(d) the supply of services would (apart from this section) be taxable and not zero-rated; and

(e) the supplier issues to the person to whom the supply is made an invoice of such a description as the Commissioners may by regulations prescribe,

his supply shall be zero-rated.

(2) If a supply of services is zero-rated under subsection (1) above ("the zero-rated supply of services") then, unless there is a supply of the goods in question the material time for which is—

(a) while the goods are subject to a warehousing or fiscal warehousing regime, and

(b) after the material time for the zero-rated supply of services,

subsection (3) below shall apply.

(3) Where this subsection applies—

(a) a supply of services identical to the zero-rated supply of services shall be treated for the purposes of this Act as being, at the time the goods are removed from the warehousing or fiscal warehousing regime or (if earlier) at the duty point, both made (for the purposes of his business) to the person to whom the zero-rated supply of services was actually made and made by him in the course or furtherance of his business,

(b) that supply shall have the same value as the zero-rated supply of services,

(c) that supply shall be a taxable (and not a zero-rated) supply, and

(d) VAT shall be charged on that supply even if the person treated as making it is not a taxable person.

(4) In this section "specified services" means—

(a) services of an occupier of a warehouse or a fiscal warehousekeeper of keeping the goods in question in a warehousing or fiscal warehousing regime;

(b) in relation to goods subject to a warehousing regime, services of carrying out on the goods operations which are permitted to be carried out under Community customs provisions or warehousing regulations as the case may be; and

(c) in relation to goods subject to a fiscal warehousing regime, services of carrying out on the goods any physical operations (other than any prohibited by regulations made under section 18F), for example, and without prejudice to the generality of the foregoing words, preservation and repacking operations.

Removal from warehousing: accountability

18D.—(1) This section applies to any supply to which section 18B(4) or section 18C(3) applies (supply treated as taking place on removal or duty point) and any acquisition to which section 18B(5) applies (acquisition treated as taking place on removal where acquirer not a taxable person).

(2) Any VAT payable on the supply or acquisition shall (subject to any regulations under subsection (3) below) be paid—

(a) at the time when the supply or acquisition is treated as taking place under the section in question; and

(b) by the person by whom the goods are removed or, as the case may be, together with the excise duty, by the person who is required to pay that duty.

(3) The Commissioners may by regulations make provision for enabling a taxable person to pay the VAT he is required to pay by virtue of subsection (2) above at a time later than that provided by that subsection; and they may make different provisions for different descriptions of taxable persons and for different descriptions of goods and services.

Deficiency in fiscally warehoused goods

18E.—(1) This section applies where goods have been subject to a fiscal warehousing regime and, before being lawfully removed from the fiscal warehouse, they are found to be missing or deficient.

(2) In any case where this section applies, unless it is shown to the satisfaction of the Commissioners that the absence of or deficiency in the goods can be accounted for by natural waste or other legitimate cause, the Commissioners may require the fiscal warehousekeeper to pay immediately in respect of the missing goods or of the whole or any part of the deficiency, as they see fit, the VAT that would have been chargeable.

(3) In subsection (2) "VAT that would have been chargeable" means VAT that would have been chargeable on a supply of the missing goods, or the amount of goods by which the goods are deficient, taking place at the time immediately before the absence arose or the deficiency occurred, if the value of that supply were the open market value, but where that time cannot be ascertained to the Commissioners' satisfaction, that VAT shall be the greater of the amounts of VAT which would have been chargeable on a supply of those goods—

(a) if the value of that supply were the highest open market value during the period (the relevant period) commencing when the goods were placed in the fiscal warehousing regime and ending when the absence or deficiency came to the notice of the Commissioners, or

(b) if the rate of VAT chargeable on that supply were the highest rate chargeable on a supply of such goods during the relevant period and the value of that supply were the highest open market value while that rate prevailed.

(4) This section has effect without prejudice to any penalty incurred under any other provision of this Act or regulations made under it.

Sections 18A to 18E: supplementary

18F.—(1) In sections 18A to 18E and this section—

"duty point" has the meaning given by section 18(6);

"eligible goods" has the meaning given by section 18B(6);

"fiscal warehouse" means a place notified to the Commissioners under section 18A(3) and from which such status has not been withdrawn;

"fiscal warehousekeeper" means a person approved under section 18A(1);

"material time"—

(a) in relation to any acquisition or supply the time of which is determined in accordance with regulations under section 6(14) or 12(3), means such time as may be prescribed for the purpose of this section by those regulations;

(b) in relation to any other acquisition, means the time when the goods reach the destination to which they are despatched from the member State in question;

(c) in relation to any other supply of goods, means the time when the supply would be treated as taking place in accordance with subsection (2) of section 6 if paragraph (c) of that subsection were omitted; and

(d) in relation to any other supply of services, means the time when the services are performed;

"warehouse", except in the expression "fiscal warehouse", has the meaning given by section 18(6);

"warehousing regulations" has the same meaning as in the Management Act.

(2) Any reference in sections 18A to 18E or this section to goods being subject to a fiscal warehousing regime is, subject to any regulations made under subsection (8)(e) below, a reference to eligible goods being kept in a fiscal warehouse or being transferred between fiscal warehouses in accordance with such regulations; and any reference to the removal of goods from a fiscal warehousing regime shall be construed accordingly.

(3) Subject to subsection (2) above, any reference in sections 18C and 18D to goods being subject to a warehousing regime or to the removal of goods from a warehousing regime shall have the same meaning as in section 18(7).

(4) Where as a result of an operation on eligible goods subject to a fiscal warehousing regime they change their nature but the resulting goods are also eligible goods, the provisions of sections 18B to 18E and this section shall apply as if the resulting goods were the original goods.

(5) Where as a result of an operation on eligible goods subject to a fiscal warehousing regime they cease to be eligible goods, on their ceasing to be so sections 18B to 18E shall apply as if they had at that time been removed from the fiscal warehousing regime; and for that purpose the proprietor of the goods shall be treated as if he were the person removing them.

(6) Where—

(a) any person ceases to be a fiscal warehousekeeper; or

(b) any premises cease to have fiscal warehouse status,

sections 18B to 18E and this section shall apply as if the goods of which he is the fiscal warehousekeeper, or the goods in the fiscal warehouse, as the case may be, had at that time been removed from the fiscal warehousing regime; and for that purpose the proprietor of the goods shall be treated as if he were the person removing them.

(7) The Commissioners may make regulations governing the deposit, keeping, securing and treatment of goods in a fiscal warehouse, and the removal of goods from a fiscal warehouse.

(8) Regulations may, without prejudice to the generality of subsection (7) above, include provisions—

(a) in relation to—

(i) goods which are, have been or are to be subject to a fiscal warehousing regime,

(ii) other goods which are, have been or are to be kept in fiscal warehouses,

(iii) fiscal warehouse premises, and

(iv) fiscal warehousekeepers and their businesses,

as to the keeping, preservation and production of records and the furnishing of returns and information by fiscal warehousekeepers and any other persons;

(b) requiring goods deposited in a fiscal warehouse to be produced to or made available for inspection by an authorised person on request by him;

(c) prohibiting the carrying out on fiscally warehoused goods of such operations as they may prescribe;

(d) regulating the transfer of goods from one fiscal warehouse to another;

(e) concerning goods which, though kept in a fiscal warehouse, are not eligible goods or are not intended by a relevant person to be goods in respect of which reliefs are to be enjoyed under sections 18A to 18E and this section;

(f) prohibiting the fiscal warehousekeeper from allowing goods to be removed from the fiscal warehousing regime without payment of any VAT payable under section 18D on or by reference to that removal and, if in breach of that prohibition he allows goods to be so removed, making him liable for the VAT jointly and severally with the remover,

and may contain such incidental or supplementary provisions as the Commissioners think necessary or expedient.

(9) Regulations may make different provision for different cases, including different provision for different fiscal warehousekeepers or descriptions of fiscal warehousekeeper, for fiscal warehouses of different descriptions or for goods of different classes or descriptions or of the same class or description in different circumstances."

6. In subsection (1) of section 20 of the Value Added Tax Act 1994, there shall be inserted at the beginning the words "Subject to section 18C,".

7. In section 30 of the Value Added Tax Act 1994 the following subsection shall be added after subsection (8)—

"(8A) Regulations may provide for the zero-rating of supplies of goods, or of such goods as may be specified in regulations, in cases where—

(a) the Commissioners are satisfied that the supply in question involves both—

(i) the removal of the goods from a fiscal warehousing regime within the meaning of section 18F(2); and

(ii) their being placed in a warehousing regime in another member State, or in such member State or States as may be prescribed, where that regime is established by provisions of the law of that member State corresponding, in relation to that member State, to the provisions of sections 18A and 18B; and

(b) such other conditions, if any, as may be specified in the regulations or the Commissioners may impose are fulfilled.",

and in subsection (10) for the words "subsection (8) or (9)" there shall be substituted the words "subsection (8), (8A) or (9)" and for the words "subsection (6), (8) or (9)", there shall be substituted the words "subsection (6), (8), (8A) or (9)"

8.—(1) Section 62 of the Value Added Tax Act 1994 shall be amended as follows.

(2) In paragraph (a) of subsection (1), after the words "a person" there shall be inserted the words "by whom one or more acquisitions or", the words "or" at the end of sub-paragraph (i) and "and" at the end of sub-paragraph (ii) shall be omitted and the following additional sub-paragraphs shall be inserted—

"(iii) prepares a certificate in accordance with section 18B(1)(d) or gives a supplier a certificate in accordance with section 18B(2)(d); or

(iv) gives the supplier a certificate in accordance with section 18C(1)(c); and".

(3) In the passage following paragraph (b) of subsection (1) and in subsections (3) and (4), after the word "giving" wherever it appears there shall be inserted the words "or preparing".

(4) In subsection (3) after the words "gave" and "given" there shall be inserted in each case the words "or prepared".

9. In subsection (1) of section 69 of the Value Added Tax Act 1994 after paragraph (f) the following shall be added—

"; or

(g) section 18A in the form of a condition imposed by the Commissioners under subsection (1) or (6) of that section,".

10. In section 73 of the Value Added Tax Act 1994 the following subsections shall be added after subsection (7)—

"(7A) Where a fiscal warehousekeeper has failed to pay VAT required by the Commissioners under section 18E(2), the Commissioners may assess to the best of their judgment the amount of that VAT due from him and notify it to him.

(7B) Where it appears to the Commissioners that goods have been removed from a warehouse or fiscal warehouse without payment of the VAT payable under section 18(4) or section 18D on that removal, they may assess to the best of their judgment the amount of VAT due from the person removing the goods or other person liable and notify it to him."

11. In sections 73(9) and 76(5) of the Value Added Tax Act 1994 for the words "or (7)" there shall be substituted ", (7), (7A) or (7B)".

12. In section 83 of the Value Added Tax Act 1994 the following paragraph shall be added after paragraph (d)—

"(da) a decision of the Commissioners under section 18A—

(i) as to whether or not a person is to be approved as a fiscal warehousekeeper or the conditions from time to time subject to which he is so approved;

(ii) for the withdrawal of any such approval; or

(iii) for the withdrawal of fiscal warehouse status from any premises;",

and in paragraph (p)(ii) for "subsection (7)" there shall be substituted "subsections (7), (7A) or (7B)".

13. In paragraph 1 of Schedule 1 to the Value Added Tax Act 1994, the following sub-paragraph shall be added after sub-paragraph (8)—

"(9) In determining the value of a person's supplies for the purposes of sub-paragraph (1) or (2) above, supplies to which section 18B(4) (last acquisition or supply of goods before removal from fiscal warehousing) applies and supplies treated as made by him under section 18C(3) (self-supply of services on removal of goods from warehousing) shall be disregarded.".

14. In paragraph 1 of Schedule 2 to the Value Added Tax Act 1994, the following sub-paragraph shall be added after sub-paragraph (6)—

"(7) For the purposes of sub-paragraphs (1) and (2) above supplies to which section 18B(4) (last acquisition or supply of goods before removal from fiscal warehousing) applies shall be disregarded.".

15. In paragraph 1 of Schedule 3 to the Value Added Tax Act 1994, the following sub-paragraph shall be added after sub-paragraph (5)—

"(6) In determining the value of a person's acquisitions for the purposes of sub-paragraph (1) or (2) above, acquisitions to which section 18(B)(4) (last acquisition or supply of goods before removal from fiscal warehousing) applies shall be disregarded.".

16. In paragraph 8(1) of Schedule 11 to the Value Added Tax Act 1994 after the words "another member State" there shall be inserted the words ", or in the possession of a fiscal warehousekeeper,".

17. In paragraph 10(2) of Schedule 11 to the Value Added Tax Act 1994, after the words "on those premises" there shall be inserted the words ", or that any premises are used as a fiscal warehouse,".

18. The following Schedule shall be added to the Value Added Tax Act 1994.

"SCHEDULE 5A

GOODS ELIGIBLE TO BE FISCALLY WAREHOUSED

Description of goods	*Combined nomenclature code of the European Communities*
Tin	8001
Copper	7402
	7403
	7405
	7408
Zinc	7901
Nickel	7502
Aluminium	7601
Lead	7801
Indium	ex 811291
	ex 811299
Cereals	1001 to 1005
	1006: unprocessed rice only
	1007 to 1008
Oil seeds and oleaginous fruit	1201 to 1207
Coconuts, Brazil nuts and cashew nuts	0801
Other nuts	0502
Olives	071120
Grains and seeds (including soya beans)	1201 to 1207
Coffee, not roasted	0901 11 00
	0901 12 00
Tea	0902
Cocoa beans, whole or broken, raw or roasted	1801
Raw sugar	1701 11
	1701 12
Rubber, in primary forms or in plates, sheets or strip	4001
	4002
Wool	5101
Chemicals in bulk	Chapters 28 and 29
Mineral oils (including propane and butane; also including crude petroleum oils)	2709
	2710
	2711 12
	2711 13
Silver	7106

Description of goods	Combined nomenclature code of the European Communities
Platinum (palladium, rhodium)	7110 11 00
	7110 21 00
	7110 31 00
Potatoes	0701
Vegetable oils and fats and their fractions, whether or not refined, but not chemically modified	1507 to 1515"

GENERAL NOTE

The Schedule implements the new system for fiscal warehousing. It also applies to existing Customs and Excise warehouses.

Paras. 1–4

These make consequential amendments to other sections of the VATA 1994.

Para. 5

This introduces new ss.18A–F.

Section 18A empowers the Customs and Excise to approve registered persons as fiscal warehousekeepers, subject to conditions and regulations.

Section 18B grants relief from VAT for goods entering a fiscal warehouse, so long as they remain there. The goods which are eligible are listed in new Sched. 5A (see para. 18 below).

Section 18C. Certain services in connection with goods which are under a warehousing regime are zero-rated for VAT. These are restricted to warehousekeeping services, the carrying out of approved operations on the goods under the existing warehouse system, and (for fiscal warehousing) such physical operations on the goods as preservation and repacking.

Section 18D provides for the payment of VAT which becomes due on the removal of goods from warehouses. Detailed rules are to be provided by regulation.

Section 18E makes the fiscal warehousekeeper responsible for the payment of VAT on goods which go missing. Tax will be charged on the highest open market value and the highest VAT rate applicable, where the precise time of disappearance cannot be ascertained.

Section 18F contains various definitions and supplementary provisions. It also defines the scope of the regulations which may be made by the Customs and Excise.

Para. 7

This allows the Customs and Excise to make regulations zero-rating supplies of goods from a U.K. fiscal warehouse to one in another member state.

Paras. 8–17

These introduce amendments to the existing provisions regarding penalties, assessments, recovery of tax, rights of appeal, registration, power to take samples and powers of entry and search to accommodate the fiscal warehousing regime.

Para. 18

This lists and specifies the goods that will be eligible for fiscal warehousing.

Section 31   SCHEDULE 4

VALUE ADDED TAX: ANTI-AVOIDANCE PROVISIONS

The following is the Schedule which shall be inserted after Schedule 9 to the Value Added Tax Act 1994—

"SCHEDULE 9A

ANTI-AVOIDANCE PROVISIONS: GROUPS

Power to give directions

1.—(1) Subject to paragraph 2 below, the Commissioners may give a direction under this Schedule if, in any case—

    (a) a relevant event has occurred;

    (b) the condition specified in sub-paragraph (3) below is fulfilled;

    (c) that condition would not be fulfilled apart from the occurrence of that event; and

    (d) in the case of an event falling within sub-paragraph (2)(b) below, the transaction in question is not a supply which is the only supply by reference to which the case falls within paragraphs (a) to (c) above.

(2) For the purposes of this Schedule, a relevant event occurs when a body corporate—

(a) begins to be, or ceases to be, treated as a member of a group; or

(b) enters into any transaction.

(3) The condition mentioned in sub-paragraph (1) above is that—

(a) there has been, or will or may be, a taxable supply on which VAT has been, or will or may be, charged otherwise than by reference to the supply's full value;

(b) there is at least a part of the supply which is not or, as the case may be, would not be zero-rated; and

(c) the charging of VAT on the supply otherwise than by reference to its full value gives rise or, as the case may be, would give rise to a tax advantage.

(4) For the purposes of this paragraph the charging of VAT on a supply ('the under-charged supply') otherwise than by reference to its full value shall be taken to give rise to a tax advantage if; and only if, a person has become entitled—

(a) to credit for input tax allowable as attributable to that supply or any part of it, or

(b) in accordance with regulations under section 39, to any repayment in respect of that supply or any part of it.

(5) The cases where a person shall be taken for the purposes of sub-paragraph (4) above to have become entitled to a credit for input tax allowable as attributable to the under-charged supply, or to a part of it, shall include any case where—

(a) a person has become entitled to a credit for any input tax on the supply to him, or the acquisition or importation by him, of any goods or services; and

(b) whatever the supplies to which the credit was treated as attributable when the entitle-ment to it arose, those goods or services are used by him in making the undercharged supply, or a part of it.

(6) For the purposes of sub-paragraphs (4) and (5) above where—

(a) there is a supply of any of the assets of a business of a person ('the transferor') to a person to whom the whole or any part of that business is transferred as a going con-cern ('the transferee'), and

(b) that supply is treated, in accordance with an order under section 5(3), as being nei-ther a supply of goods nor a supply of services,

the question, so far as it falls to be determined by reference to those assets, whether a credit for input tax to which any person has become entitled is one allowable as attributable to the whole or any part of a supply shall be determined as if the transferor and the transferee were the same person.

(7) Where, in a case to which sub-paragraph (6) above applies, the transferor himself acquired any of the assets in question by way of a supply falling within paragraphs (a) and (b) of that sub-paragraph, that sub-paragraph shall have the effect, as respects the assets so acquired, of requiring the person from whom those assets were acquired to be treated for the purposes of sub-paragraphs (4) and (5) above as the same person as the transferor and the transferee, and so on in the case of any number of successive supplies falling within those paragraphs.

(8) For the purposes of this paragraph any question—

(a) whether any credit for input tax to which a person has become entitled was, or is to be taken to have been, a credit allowable as attributable to the whole or any part of a supply, or

(b) whether any repayment is a repayment in respect of the whole or any part of a supply,

shall be determined, in relation to a supply of a right to goods or services or to a supply of goods or services by virtue of such a right, as if the supply of the right and supplies made by virtue of the right were a single supply of which the supply of the right and each of those supplies constituted different parts.

(9) References in this paragraph to the full value of a supply are references to the amount which (having regard to any direction under paragraph 1 of Schedule 6) would be the full value of that supply for the purposes of the charge to VAT if that supply were not a supply falling to be disregarded, to any extent, in pursuance of section 43(1)(a).

(10) References in this paragraph to the supply of a right to goods or services include references to the supply of any right, option or priority with respect to the supply of goods or services, and to the supply of an interest deriving from any right to goods or services.

Restrictions on giving directions

2. The Commissioners shall not give a direction under this Schedule by reference to a relevant event if they are satisfied that—

(a) the change in the treatment of the body corporate, or

(b) the transaction in question,

had as its main purpose or, as the case may be, as each of its main purposes a genuine commercial purpose unconnected with the fulfilment of the condition specified in paragraph 1(3) above.

Form of directions under Schedule

3.—(1) The directions that may be given by the Commissioners under this Schedule are either—

  (a) a direction relating to any supply of goods or services that has been made, in whole or in part, by one body corporate to another; or

  (b) a direction relating to a particular body corporate.

(2) A direction under this Schedule relating to a supply shall require it to be assumed (where it would not otherwise be the case) that, to the extent described in the direction, the supply was not a supply falling to be disregarded in pursuance of section 43(1)(a).

(3) A direction under this Schedule relating to a body corporate shall require it to be assumed (where it would not otherwise be the case) that, for such period (comprising times before the giving of the direction or times afterwards or both) as may be described in the direction, the body corporate—

  (a) did not fall to be treated, or is not to be treated, as a member of a group, or of a particular group so described; or

  (b) fell to be treated, or is to be treated, as a member of any group so described of which, for that period, it was or is eligible to be a member.

(4) Where a direction under this Schedule requires any assumptions to be made, then—

  (a) so far as the assumptions relate to times on or after the day on which the direction is given, this Act shall have effect in relation to such times in accordance with those assumptions; and

  (b) paragraph 6 below shall apply for giving effect to those assumptions in so far as they relate to earlier times.

(5) A direction falling within sub-paragraph (3)(b) above may identify in relation to any times or period the body corporate which is to be assumed to have been, or to be, the representative member of the group at those times or for that period.

(6) A direction under this Schedule may vary the effect of a previous direction under this Schedule.

(7) The Commissioners may at any time, by notice in writing to the person to whom it was given, withdraw a direction under this Schedule.

(8) The refusal or non-refusal by the Commissioners of an application under section 43 shall not prejudice the power of the Commissioners to give a direction under this Schedule requiring any case to be assumed to be what it would have been had the application not been refused or, as the case may be, had it been refused.

Time limit on directions

4.—(1) A direction under this Schedule shall not be given more than six years after whichever is the later of—

  (a) the occurrence of the relevant event by reference to which it is given; and

  (b) the time when the relevant entitlement arose.

(2) A direction under this Schedule shall not be given by reference to a relevant event occurring on or before 28th November 1995.

(3) Subject to sub-paragraphs (1) and (2) above, a direction under this Schedule—

  (a) may be given by reference to a relevant event occurring before the coming into force of this Schedule; and

  (b) may require assumptions to be made in relation to times (including times before 29th November 1995) falling before the occurrence of the relevant event by reference to which the direction is given, or before the relevant entitlement arose.

(4) For the purposes of this paragraph the reference, in relation to the giving of a direction, to the relevant entitlement is a reference to the entitlement by reference to which the requirements of paragraph 1(4) above are taken to be satisfied for the purposes of that direction.

Manner of giving directions

5.—(1) A direction under this Schedule relating to a supply may be given to—

  (a) the person who made the supply to which the direction relates, or

  (b) any body corporate which, at the time when the direction is given, is the representative member of a group of which that person was treated as being a member at the time of the supply.

(2) A direction under this Schedule relating to a body corporate ('the relevant body') may be given to that body or to any body corporate which at the time when the direction is given is, or in pursuance of the direction is to be treated as, the representative member of a group of which the relevant body—

(a) is treated as being a member;

(b) was treated as being a member at a time to which the direction relates; or

(c) is to be treated as being, or having been, a member at any such time.

(3) A direction given to any person under this Schedule shall be given to him by notice in writing.

(4) A direction under this Schedule must specify the relevant event by reference to which it is given.

Assessment in consequence of a direction

6.—(1) Subject to sub-paragraph (3) below, where—

(a) a direction is given under this Schedule, and

(b) there is an amount of VAT ('the unpaid tax') for which a relevant person would have been liable before the giving of the direction if the facts had accorded with the assumptions specified in the direction,

the Commissioners may, to the best of their judgement, assess the amount of unpaid tax as tax due from the person to whom the direction was given or another relevant person and notify their assessment to that person.

(2) In sub-paragraph (1) above the reference to an amount of VAT for which a person would, on particular assumptions, have been liable before the giving of a direction under this Schedule is a reference to the aggregate of the following—

(a) any amount of output tax which, on those assumptions but not otherwise, would have been due from a relevant person at the end of a prescribed accounting period ending before the giving of the direction;

(b) the amount of any credit for input tax to which a relevant person is treated as having been entitled at the end of such an accounting period but to which he would not have been entitled on those assumptions; and

(c) the amount of any repayment of tax made to a relevant person in accordance with regulations under section 39 but to which he would not have been entitled on those assumptions.

(3) Where any assessment falls to be made under this paragraph in a case in which the Commissioners are satisfied that the actual revenue loss is less than the unpaid tax, the total amount to be assessed under this paragraph shall not exceed what appears to them, to the best of their judgement, to be the amount of that loss.

(4) For the purposes of the making of an assessment under this paragraph in relation to any direction, the actual revenue loss shall be taken to be equal to the amount of the unpaid tax less the amount given by aggregating the amounts of every entitlement—

(a) to credit for input tax, or

(b) to a repayment in accordance with regulations under section 39,

which (whether as an entitlement of the person in relation to whom the assessment is made or as an entitlement of any other person) would have arisen on the assumptions contained in the direction, but not otherwise.

(5) An assessment under this paragraph relating to a direction may be notified to the person to whom that direction is given by being incorporated in the same notice as that direction.

(6) An assessment under this paragraph shall not be made—

(a) more than one year after the day on which the direction to which it relates was given, or

(b) in the case of any direction that has been withdrawn.

(7) Where an amount has been assessed on any person under this paragraph and notified to him—

(a) that amount shall be deemed (subject to the provisions of this Act as to appeals) to be an amount of VAT due from him;

(b) that amount may be recovered accordingly, either from that person or, in the case of a body corporate that is for the time being treated as a member of a group, from the representative member of that group; and

(c) to the extent that more than one person is liable by virtue of any assessment under this paragraph in respect of the same amount of unpaid tax, those persons shall be treated as jointly and severally liable for that amount.

(8) Sub-paragraph (7) above does not have effect if or to the extent that the assessment in question has been withdrawn or reduced.

(9) Sections 74 and 77(6) apply in relation to assessments under this paragraph as they apply in relation to assessments under section 73 but as if the reference in subsection (1) of section 74 to the reckonable date were a reference to the date on which the assessment is notified.

(10) Where by virtue of sub-paragraph (9) above any person is liable to interest under section 74—

(a) section 76 shall have effect in relation to that liability with the omission of subsections (2) to (6); and

(b) section 77, except subsection (6), shall not apply to an assessment of the amount due by way of interest;

and (without prejudice to the power to make assessments for interest for later periods) the interest to which any assessment made under section 76 by virtue of paragraph (a) above may relate shall be confined to interest for a period of no more than two years ending with the time when the assessment to interest is made.

(11) In this paragraph 'a relevant person', in relation to a direction, means—

(a) the person to whom the direction is given;

(b) the body corporate which was the representative member of any group of which that person was treated as being, or in pursuance of the direction is to be treated as having been, a member at a time to which the assumption specified in the direction relates; or

(c) any body corporate which, in pursuance of the direction, is to be treated as having been the representative member of such a group.

Interpretation of Schedule etc.

7.—(1) References in this Schedule to being treated as a member of a group and to being eligible to be treated as a member of a group shall be construed in accordance with section 43.

(2) For the purposes of this Schedule the giving of any notice or notification to any receiver, liquidator or person otherwise acting in a representative capacity in relation to another shall be treated as the giving of a notice or, as the case may be, notification to the person in relation to whom he so acts."

GENERAL NOTE

Para. 1
This confers powers on the Customs and Excise to give directions if certain conditions appear to them to be satisfied. The power becomes applicable when a company enters or leaves a VAT group or enters into any transaction. The condition is that there is or may be a supply on which VAT is not charged on its full value, through being supplied within a group. The power also applies where transfers of assets of a business as a going concern form part of the chain of transactions.

Para. 2
The power may not be exercised where there is a genuine commercial purpose in the transaction.

Para. 3
This specifies the form of directions under the Schedule. The direction must include assumptions regarding the status of supplies and the entering and leaving of groups.

Para. 4
A six-year time limit applies for directions.

Para. 5
Directions may be issued to the person making the supply in question or to the representative member of the group. Directions relating to a particular company may be given to the company or to past, present or future representative members.

Para. 6
Assessments may be raised in pursuance of a direction, but must not exceed the actual loss of tax. The assessment may be incorporated in a direction and must follow within one year of the direction. Normal recovery procedures apply. The assessment may be served on the person to whom the direction is given or to the representative member of an actual or assumed group.

SCHEDULE 5

LANDFILL TAX

PART I

INFORMATION

General

1.—(1) Every person who is concerned (in whatever capacity) with any landfill disposal shall furnish to the Commissioners such information relating to the disposal as the Commissioners may reasonably require.

(2) The information mentioned in sub-paragraph (1) above shall be furnished within such time and in such form as the Commissioners may reasonably require.

Records

2.—(1) Regulations may require registrable persons to make records.

(2) Regulations under sub-paragraph (1) above may be framed by reference to such records as may be stipulated in any notice published by the Commissioners in pursuance of the regulations and not withdrawn by a further notice.

(3) Regulations may—

(a) require registrable persons to preserve records of a prescribed description (whether or not the records are required to be made in pursuance of regulations) for such period not exceeding six years as may be specified in the regulations;

(b) authorise the Commissioners to direct that any such records need only be preserved for a shorter period than that specified in the regulations;

(c) authorise a direction to be made so as to apply generally or in such cases as the Commissioners may stipulate.

(4) Any duty under regulations to preserve records may be discharged by the preservation of the information contained in them by such means as the Commissioners may approve; and where that information is so preserved a copy of any document forming part of the records shall (subject to the following provisions of this paragraph) be admissible in evidence in any proceedings whether civil or criminal, to the same extent as the records themselves.

(5) The Commissioners may, as a condition of approving under sub-paragraph (4) above any means of preserving information contained in any records, impose such reasonable requirements as appear to them necessary for securing that the information will be as readily available to them as if the records themselves had been preserved.

(6) A statement contained in a document produced by a computer shall not by virtue of sub-paragraph (4) above be admissible in evidence—

(a) in criminal proceedings in England and Wales, except in accordance with sections 69 and 70 of the Police and Criminal Evidence Act 1984 and Part II of the Criminal Justice Act 1988;

(b) in civil proceedings in Scotland, except in accordance with sections 5 and 6 of the Civil Evidence (Scotland) Act 1988;

(c) in criminal proceedings in Scotland, except in accordance with Schedule 8 to the Criminal Procedure (Scotland) Act 1995;

(d) in civil proceedings in Northern Ireland, except in accordance with sections 2 and 3 of the Civil Evidence Act (Northern Ireland) 1971;

(e) in criminal proceedings in Northern Ireland, except in accordance with Article 68 of the Police and Criminal Evidence (Northern Ireland) Order 1989 and Part II of the Criminal Justice (Evidence, Etc.) (Northern Ireland) Order 1988.

(7) In the case of civil proceedings in England and Wales to which sections 5 and 6 of the Civil Evidence Act 1968 apply, a statement contained in a document produced by a computer shall not be admissible in evidence by virtue of sub-paragraph (4) above except in accordance with those sections.

Documents

3.—(1) Every person who is concerned (in whatever capacity) with any landfill disposal shall upon demand made by an authorised person produce or cause to be produced for inspection by that person any documents relating to the disposal.

(2) Where, by virtue of sub-paragraph (1) above, an authorised person has power to require the production of any documents from any person, he shall have the like power to require pro-

duction of the documents concerned from any other person who appears to the authorised person to be in possession of them; but where any such other person claims a lien on any document produced by him the production shall be without prejudice to the lien.

(3) The documents mentioned in sub-paragraphs (1) and (2) above shall be produced—

(a) at such place as the authorised person may reasonably require, and

(b) at such time as the authorised person may reasonably require.

(4) An authorised person may take copies of, or make extracts from, any document produced under sub-paragraph (1) or (2) above.

(5) If it appears to him to be necessary to do so, an authorised person may, at a reasonable time and for a reasonable period, remove any document produced under sub-paragraph (1) or (2) above and shall, on request, provide a receipt for any document so removed; and where a lien is claimed on a document produced under sub-paragraph (2) above the removal of the document under this sub-paragraph shall not be regarded as breaking the lien.

(6) Where a document removed by an authorised person under sub-paragraph (5) above is reasonably required for any purpose he shall, as soon as practicable, provide a copy of the document, free of charge, to the person by whom it was produced or caused to be produced.

(7) Where any documents removed under the powers conferred by this paragraph are lost or damaged the Commissioners shall be liable to compensate their owner for any expenses reasonably incurred by him in replacing or repairing the documents.

PART II

POWERS

Entry and inspection

4. For the purpose of exercising any powers under this Part of this Act an authorised person may at any reasonable time enter and inspect premises used in connection with the carrying on of a business.

Entry and search

5.—(1) Where—

(a) a justice of the peace is satisfied on information on oath that there is reasonable ground for suspecting that a fraud offence which appears to be of a serious nature is being, has been or is about to be committed on any premises or that evidence of the commission of such an offence is to be found there, or

(b) in Scotland a justice, within the meaning of section 307 of the Criminal Procedure (Scotland) Act 1995, is satisfied by evidence on oath as mentioned in paragraph (a) above,

he may issue a warrant in writing authorising any authorised person to enter those premises, if necessary by force, at any time within one month from the time of the issue of the warrant and search them.

(2) A person who enters the premises under the authority of the warrant may—

(a) take with him such other persons as appear to him to be necessary;

(b) seize and remove any documents or other things whatsoever found on the premises which he has reasonable cause to believe may be required as evidence for the purposes of proceedings in respect of a fraud offence which appears to him to be of a serious nature;

(c) search or cause to be searched any person found on the premises whom he has reasonable cause to believe to be in possession of any such documents or other things;

but no woman or girl shall be searched except by a woman.

(3) The powers conferred by a warrant under this paragraph shall not be exercisable—

(a) by more than such number of authorised persons as may be specified in the warrant,

(b) outside such times of day as may be so specified, or

(c) if the warrant so provides, otherwise than in the presence of a constable in uniform.

(4) An authorised person seeking to exercise the powers conferred by a warrant under this paragraph or, if there is more than one such authorised person, that one of them who is in charge of the search shall provide a copy of the warrant endorsed with his name as follows—

(a) if the occupier of the premises concerned is present at the time the search is to begin, the copy shall be supplied to the occupier;

(b) if at that time the occupier is not present but a person who appears to the authorised person to be in charge of the premises is present, the copy shall be supplied to that person;

(c) if neither paragraph (a) nor paragraph (b) above applies, the copy shall be left in a prominent place on the premises.

(5) In this paragraph "a fraud offence" means an offence under any provision of paragraph 15(1) to (5) below.

Arrest

6.—(1) Where an authorised person has reasonable grounds for suspecting that a fraud offence has been committed he may arrest anyone whom he has reasonable grounds for suspecting to be guilty of the offence.

(2) In this paragraph "a fraud offence" means an offence under any provision of paragraph 15(1) to (5) below.

Order for access to recorded information etc.

7.—(1) Where, on an application by an authorised person, a justice of the peace or, in Scotland, a justice (within the meaning of section 307 of the Criminal Procedure (Scotland) Act 1995) is satisfied that there are reasonable grounds for believing—
  (a) that an offence in connection with tax is being, has been or is about to be committed, and
  (b) that any recorded information (including any document of any nature whatsoever) which may be required as evidence for the purpose of any proceedings in respect of such an offence is in the possession of any person,
he may make an order under this paragraph.

(2) An order under this paragraph is an order that the person who appears to the justice to be in possession of the recorded information to which the application relates shall—
  (a) give an authorised person access to it, and
  (b) permit an authorised person to remove and take away any of it which he reasonably considers necessary,
not later than the end of the period of 7 days beginning with the date of the order or the end of such longer period as the order may specify.

(3) The reference in sub-paragraph (2)(a) above to giving an authorised person access to the recorded information to which the application relates includes a reference to permitting the authorised person to take copies of it or to make extracts from it.

(4) Where the recorded information consists of information contained in a computer, an order under this paragraph shall have effect as an order to produce the information in a form in which it is visible and legible and, if the authorised person wishes to remove it, in a form in which it can be removed.

(5) This paragraph is without prejudice to paragraphs 3 to 5 above.

Removal of documents etc.

8.—(1) An authorised person who removes anything in the exercise of a power conferred by or under paragraph 5 or 7 above shall, if so requested by a person showing himself—
  (a) to be the occupier of premises from which it was removed, or
  (b) to have had custody or control of it immediately before the removal,
provide that person with a record of what he removed.

(2) The authorised person shall provide the record within a reasonable time from the making of the request for it.

(3) Subject to sub-paragraph (7) below, if a request for permission to be allowed access to anything which—
  (a) has been removed by an authorised person, and
  (b) is retained by the Commissioners for the purposes of investigating an offence,
is made to the officer in overall charge of the investigation by a person who had custody or control of the thing immediately before it was so removed or by someone acting on behalf of such a person, the officer shall allow the person who made the request access to it under the supervision of an authorised person.

(4) Subject to sub-paragraph (7) below, if a request for a photograph or copy of any such thing is made to the officer in overall charge of the investigation by a person who had custody or control of the thing immediately before it was so removed, or by someone acting on behalf of such a person, the officer shall—
  (a) allow the person who made the request access to it under the supervision of an authorised person for the purpose of photographing it or copying it, or
  (b) photograph or copy it, or cause it to be photographed or copied.

(5) Subject to sub-paragraph (7) below, where anything is photographed or copied under sub-paragraph (4)(b) above the officer shall supply the photograph or copy, or cause it to be supplied, to the person who made the request.

(6) The photograph or copy shall be supplied within a reasonable time from the making of the request.

(7) There is no duty under this paragraph to allow access to, or to supply a photograph or copy of, anything if the officer in overall charge of the investigation for the purposes of which it was removed has reasonable grounds for believing that to do so would prejudice—

(a) that investigation,

(b) the investigation of an offence other than the offence for the purposes of the investigation of which the thing was removed, or

(c) any criminal proceedings which may be brought as a result of the investigation of which he is in charge or any such investigation as is mentioned in paragraph (b) above.

(8) Any reference in this paragraph to the officer in overall charge of the investigation is a reference to the person whose name and address are endorsed on the warrant concerned as being the officer so in charge.

9.—(1) Where, on an application made as mentioned in sub-paragraph (2) below, the appropriate judicial authority is satisfied that a person has failed to comply with a requirement imposed by paragraph 8 above, the authority may order that person to comply with the requirement within such time and in such manner as may be specified in the order.

(2) An application under sub-paragraph (1) above shall be made—

(a) in the case of a failure to comply with any of the requirements imposed by sub-paragraphs (1) and (2) of paragraph 8 above, by the occupier of the premises from which the thing in question was removed or by the person who had custody or control of it immediately before it was so removed, and

(b) in any other case, by the person who had such custody or control.

(3) In this paragraph "the appropriate judicial authority" means—

(a) in England and Wales, a magistrates' court;

(b) in Scotland, the sheriff;

(c) in Northern Ireland, a court of summary jurisdiction, as defined in Article 2(2)(a) of the Magistrates' Court (Northern Ireland) Order 1981.

(4) In England and Wales and Northern Ireland, an application for an order under this paragraph shall be made by way of complaint, and sections 21 and 42(2) of the Interpretation Act (Northern Ireland) 1954 shall apply as if any reference in those provisions to any enactment included a reference to this paragraph.

Power to take samples

10.—(1) An authorised person, if it appears to him necessary for the protection of the revenue against mistake or fraud, may at any time take, from material which he has reasonable cause to believe is intended to be, is being, or has been disposed of as waste by way of landfill, such samples as he may require with a view to determining how the material ought to be or to have been treated for the purposes of tax.

(2) Any sample taken under this paragraph shall be disposed of in such manner as the Commissioners may direct.

PART III

RECOVERY

General

11. Tax due from any person shall be recoverable as a debt due to the Crown.

Preferential and preferred debts

12.—(1) In the Insolvency Act 1986, in section 386(1) (preferential debts) the words "landfill tax," shall be inserted after "insurance premium tax," and in Schedule 6 (categories of preferential debts) the following paragraph shall be inserted after paragraph 3A—

"3B. Any landfill tax which is referable to the period of 6 months next before the relevant date (which period is referred to below as "the 6-month period").

For the purposes of this paragraph—

(a) where the whole of the accounting period to which any landfill tax is attributable falls within the 6-month period, the whole amount of that tax is referable to that period; and

(b) in any other case the amount of any landfill tax which is referable to the 6-month period is the proportion of the tax which is equal to such proportion (if any) of the accounting period in question as falls within the 6-month period;

and references here to accounting periods shall be construed in accordance with Part III of the Finance Act 1996."

(2) In the Bankruptcy (Scotland) Act 1985, Schedule 3 (preferred debts) shall be amended as mentioned in sub-paragraphs (3) and (4) below.

(3) In paragraph 2 the following sub-paragraph shall be inserted after sub-paragraph (1A)—

"(1B) Any landfill tax which is referable to the period of six months next before the relevant date."

(4) The following shall be inserted after paragraph 8A—

"Periods to which landfill tax referable

8B.—(1) For the purpose of paragraph 2(1B) of Part I of this Schedule—

(a) where the whole of the accounting period to which any landfill tax is attributable falls within the period of six months next before the relevant date ("the relevant period"), the whole amount of that tax shall be referable to the relevant period; and

(b) in any other case the amount of any landfill tax which shall be referable to the relevant period shall be the proportion of the tax which is equal to such proportion (if any) of the accounting period in question as falls within the relevant period.

(2) In sub-paragraph (1) above "accounting period" shall be construed in accordance with Part III of the Finance Act 1996."

(5) In the Insolvency (Northern Ireland) Order 1989, in Article 346(1) (preferential debts) the words "landfill tax" shall be inserted after "insurance premium tax" and in Schedule 4 (categories of preferential debts) the following paragraph shall be inserted after paragraph 3A—

"3B. Any landfill tax which is referable to the period of 6 months next before the relevant date (which period is referred to below as "the 6-month period").

For the purposes of this paragraph—

(a) where the whole of the accounting period to which any landfill tax is attributable falls within the 6-month period, the whole amount of that tax is referable to that period; and

(b) in any other case the amount of any landfill tax which is referable to the 6-month period is the proportion of the tax which is equal to such proportion (if any) of the accounting period in question as falls within the 6-month period;

and references here to accounting periods shall be construed in accordance with Part III of the Finance Act 1996."

Distress and diligence

13.—(1) Regulations may make provision in respect of England and Wales and Northern Ireland—

(a) for authorising distress to be levied on the goods and chattels of any person refusing or neglecting to pay any tax due from him or any amount recoverable as if it were tax due from him;

(b) for the disposal of any goods or chattels on which distress is levied in pursuance of the regulations;

(c) for the imposition and recovery of costs, charges, expenses and fees in connection with anything done under the regulations.

(2) In respect of Scotland, where any tax or any amount recoverable as if it were tax is due and has not been paid, the sheriff, on an application by the Commissioners accompanied by a certificate by the Commissioners—

(a) stating that none of the persons specified in the application has paid the tax or other sum due from him,

(b) stating that payment of the amount due from each such person has been demanded from him, and

(c) specifying the amount due from and unpaid by each such person,

shall grant a summary warrant in a form prescribed by act of sederunt authorising the recovery, by any of the diligences mentioned in sub-paragraph (3) below, of the amount remaining due and unpaid.

(3) The diligences referred to in sub-paragraph (2) above are—

(a) a poinding and sale in accordance with Schedule 5 to the Debtors (Scotland) Act 1987;

(b) an earnings arrestment;

(c) an arrestment and action of forthcoming or sale.

(4) Subject to sub-paragraph (5) below and without prejudice to paragraphs 25 to 34 of Schedule 5 to the Debtors (Scotland) Act 1987 (expenses of poinding and sale) the sheriff officer's fees, together with the outlays necessarily incurred by him, in connection with the execution of a summary warrant shall be chargeable against the debtor.

(5) No fee shall be chargeable by the sheriff officer against the debtor for collecting, and accounting to the Commissioners for, sums paid to him by the debtor in respect of the amount owing.

(6) Regulations may make provision for anything which the Commissioners may do under sub-paragraphs (2) to (5) above to be done by an officer of the Commissioners holding such rank as the regulations may specify.

Recovery of overpaid tax

14.—(1) Where a person has paid an amount to the Commissioners by way of tax which was not tax due to them, they shall be liable to repay the amount to him.

(2) The Commissioners shall only be liable to repay an amount under this paragraph on a claim being made for the purpose.

(3) It shall be a defence, in relation to a claim under this paragraph, that repayment of an amount would unjustly enrich the claimant.

(4) No amount may be claimed under this paragraph after the expiry of six years from the date on which it was paid.

(5) A claim under this paragraph shall be made in such form and manner and shall be supported by such documentary evidence as may be prescribed by regulations.

(6) Except as provided by this paragraph, the Commissioners shall not be liable to repay an amount paid to them by way of tax by virtue of the fact that it was not tax due to them.

PART IV

CRIMINAL PENALTIES

Criminal offences

15.—(1) A person is guilty of an offence if—
 (a) being a registrable person, he is knowingly concerned in, or in the taking of steps with a view to, the fraudulent evasion of tax by him or another registrable person, or
 (b) not being a registrable person, he is knowingly concerned in, or in the taking of steps with a view to, the fraudulent evasion of tax by a registrable person.

(2) Any reference in sub-paragraph (1) above to the evasion of tax includes a reference to the obtaining of a payment under regulations under section 51(2)(c) or (d) or (f) of this Act.

(3) A person is guilty of an offence if with the requisite intent—
 (a) he produces, furnishes or sends, or causes to be produced, furnished or sent, for the purposes of this Part of this Act any document which is false in a material particular, or
 (b) he otherwise makes use for those purposes of such a document;
and the requisite intent is intent to deceive or to secure that a machine will respond to the document as if it were a true document.

(4) A person is guilty of an offence if in furnishing any information for the purposes of this Part of this Act he makes a statement which he knows to be false in a material particular or recklessly makes a statement which is false in a material particular.

(5) A person is guilty of an offence by virtue of this sub-paragraph if his conduct during any specified period must have involved the commission by him of one or more offences under the preceding provisions of this paragraph; and the preceding provisions of this sub-paragraph apply whether or not the particulars of that offence or those offences are known.

(6) A person is guilty of an offence if—
 (a) he enters into a taxable landfill contract, or
 (b) he makes arrangements for other persons to enter into such a contract,
with reason to believe that tax in respect of the disposal concerned will be evaded.

(7) A person is guilty of an offence if he carries out taxable activities without giving security (or further security) he has been required to give under paragraph 31 below.

(8) For the purposes of this paragraph a taxable landfill contract is a contract under which there is to be a taxable disposal.

Criminal penalties

16.—(1) A person guilty of an offence under paragraph 15(1) above is liable—
 (a) on summary conviction, to a penalty of the statutory maximum or of three times the amount of the tax, whichever is the greater, or to imprisonment for a term not exceeding six months or to both;
 (b) on conviction on indictment, to a penalty of any amount or to imprisonment for a term not exceeding seven years or to both.

(2) The reference in sub-paragraph (1) above to the amount of the tax shall be construed, in relation to tax itself or a payment falling within paragraph 15(2) above, as a reference to the aggregate of—
 (a) the amount (if any) falsely claimed by way of credit, and
 (b) the amount (if any) by which the gross amount of tax was falsely understated.

(3) A person guilty of an offence under paragraph 15(3) or (4) above is liable—

(a) on summary conviction, to a penalty of the statutory maximum (or, where sub-paragraph (4) below applies, to the alternative penalty there specified if it is greater) or to imprisonment for a term not exceeding six months or to both;

(b) on conviction on indictment, to a penalty of any amount or to imprisonment for a term not exceeding seven years or to both.

(4) Where—

(a) the document referred to in paragraph 15(3) above is a return required under this Part of this Act, or

(b) the information referred to in paragraph 15(4) above is contained in or otherwise relevant to such a return,

the alternative penalty is a penalty equal to three times the aggregate of the amount (if any) falsely claimed by way of credit and the amount (if any) by which the gross amount of tax was understated.

(5) A person guilty of an offence under paragraph 15(5) above is liable—

(a) on summary conviction, to a penalty of the statutory maximum (or, if greater, three times the amount of any tax that was or was intended to be evaded by his conduct) or to imprisonment for a term not exceeding six months or to both;

(b) on conviction on indictment, to a penalty of any amount or to imprisonment for a term not exceeding seven years or to both;

and paragraph 15(2) and sub-paragraph (2) above shall apply for the purposes of this sub-paragraph as they apply respectively for the purposes of paragraph 15(1) and sub-paragraph (1) above.

(6) A person guilty of an offence under paragraph 15(6) above is liable on summary conviction to a penalty of level 5 on the standard scale or three times the amount of the tax, whichever is the greater.

(7) A person guilty of an offence under paragraph 15(7) above is liable on summary conviction to a penalty of level 5 on the standard scale.

(8) In this paragraph—

(a) "credit" means credit for which provision is made by regulations under section 51 of this Act;

(b) "the gross amount of tax" means the total amount of tax due before taking into account any deduction for which provision is made by regulations under section 51(2) of this Act.

Criminal proceedings etc.

17. Sections 145 to 155 of the Customs and Excise Management Act 1979 (proceedings for offences, mitigation of penalties and certain other matters) shall apply in relation to offences under paragraph 15 above and penalties imposed under paragraph 16 above as they apply in relation to offences and penalties under the customs and excise Acts as defined in that Act.

PART V

CIVIL PENALTIES

Evasion

18.—(1) Where—

(a) for the purpose of evading tax, a registrable person does any act or omits to take any action, and

(b) his conduct involves dishonesty (whether or not it is such as to give rise to criminal liability),

he is liable to a penalty equal to the amount of tax evaded, or (as the case may be) sought to be evaded, by his conduct; but this is subject to sub-paragraph (7) below.

(2) The reference in sub-paragraph (1)(a) above to evading tax includes a reference to obtaining a payment under regulations under section 51(2)(c) or (d) or (f) of this Act in circumstances where the person concerned is not entitled to the sum.

(3) The reference in sub-paragraph (1) above to the amount of tax evaded or sought to be evaded is a reference to the aggregate of—

(a) the amount (if any) falsely claimed by way of credit, and

(b) the amount (if any) by which the gross amount of tax was falsely understated.

(4) In this paragraph—

(a) "credit" means credit for which provision is made by regulations under section 51 of this Act;

(b) "the gross amount of tax" means the total amount of tax due before taking into account any deduction for which provision is made by regulations under section 51(2) of this Act.

(5) Statements made or documents produced by or on behalf of a person shall not be inadmissible in any such proceedings as are mentioned in sub-paragraph (6) below by reason only that it has been drawn to his attention—

(a) that, in relation to tax, the Commissioners may assess an amount due by way of a civil penalty instead of instituting criminal proceedings and, though no undertaking can be given as to whether the Commissioners will make such an assessment in the case of any person, it is their practice to be influenced by the fact that a person has made a full confession of any dishonest conduct to which he has been a party and has given full facilities for investigation, and

(b) that the Commissioners or, on appeal, an appeal tribunal have power under paragraph 25 below to reduce a penalty under this paragraph,

and that he was or may have been induced thereby to make the statements or produce the documents.

(6) The proceedings referred to in sub-paragraph (5) above are—

(a) any criminal proceedings against the person concerned in respect of any offence in connection with or in relation to tax, and

(b) any proceedings against him for the recovery of any sum due from him in connection with or in relation to tax.

(7) Where, by reason of conduct falling within sub-paragraph (1) above, a person is convicted of an offence (whether under this Part of this Act or otherwise) that conduct shall not also give rise to liability to a penalty under this paragraph.

19.—(1) Where it appears to the Commissioners—

(a) that a body corporate is liable to a penalty under paragraph 18 above, and

(b) that the conduct giving rise to that penalty is, in whole or in part, attributable to the dishonesty of a person who is, or at the material time was, a director or managing officer of the body corporate (a named officer),

the Commissioners may serve a notice under this paragraph on the body corporate and on the named officer.

(2) A notice under this paragraph shall state—

(a) the amount of the penalty referred to in sub-paragraph (1)(a) above (the basic penalty), and

(b) that the Commissioners propose, in accordance with this paragraph, to recover from the named officer such portion (which may be the whole) of the basic penalty as is specified in the notice.

(3) Where a notice is served under this paragraph, the portion of the basic penalty specified in the notice shall be recoverable from the named officer as if he were personally liable under paragraph 18 above to a penalty which corresponds to that portion; and the amount of that penalty may be assessed and notified to him accordingly under paragraph 32 below.

(4) Where a notice is served under this paragraph—

(a) the amount which, under paragraph 32 below, may be assessed as the amount due by way of penalty from the body corporate shall be only so much (if any) of the basic penalty as is not assessed on and notified to a named officer by virtue of sub-paragraph (3) above, and

(b) the body corporate shall be treated as discharged from liability for so much of the basic penalty as is so assessed and notified.

(5) No appeal shall lie against a notice under this paragraph as such but—

(a) where a body corporate is assessed as mentioned in sub-paragraph (4)(a) above, the body corporate may require a review of the Commissioners' decision as to its liability to a penalty and as to the amount of the basic penalty as if it were specified in the assessment;

(b) where an assessment is made on a named officer by virtue of sub-paragraph (3) above, the named officer may require a review of the Commissioners' decision that the conduct of the body corporate referred to in sub-paragraph (1)(b) above is, in whole or in part, attributable to his dishonesty and of their decision as to the portion of the penalty which the Commissioners propose to recover from him;

(c) sections 55 and 56 of this Act shall apply accordingly.

(6) In this paragraph a "managing officer", in relation to a body corporate, means any manager, secretary or other similar officer of the body corporate or any person purporting to act in any such capacity or as a director; and where the affairs of a body corporate are managed by its members, this paragraph shall apply in relation to the conduct of a member in connection with his functions of management as if he were a director of the body corporate.

Misdeclaration or neglect

20.—(1) Where, for an accounting period—

(a) a return is made which understates a person's liability to tax or overstates his entitlement to credit, or

(b) an assessment is made which understates a person's liability to tax and, at the end of the period of 30 days beginning on the date of the assessment, he has not taken all such steps as are reasonable to draw the understatement to the attention of the Commissioners,

the person concerned is liable, subject to sub-paragraphs (3) and (4) below, to a penalty equal to 5 per cent. of the amount of the understatement of liability or (as the case may be) overstatement of entitlement.

(2) Where—

(a) a return for an accounting period overstates or understates to any extent a person's liability to tax or his entitlement to credit, and

(b) that return is corrected, in such circumstances and in accordance with such conditions as may be prescribed by regulations, by a return for a later accounting period which understates or overstates, to the corresponding extent, that liability or entitlement,

it shall be assumed for the purposes of this paragraph that the statement made by each such return is a correct statement for the accounting period to which the return relates.

(3) Conduct falling within sub-paragraph (1) above shall not give rise to liability to a penalty under this paragraph if the person concerned furnishes full information with respect to the inaccuracy concerned to the Commissioners—

(a) at a time when he has no reason to believe that enquiries are being made by the Commissioners into his affairs, so far as they relate to tax, and

(b) in such form and manner as may be prescribed by regulations or specified by the Commissioners in accordance with provision made by regulations.

(4) Where, by reason of conduct falling within sub-paragraph (1) above—

(a) a person is convicted of an offence (whether under this Part of this Act or otherwise), or

(b) a person is assessed to a penalty under paragraph 18 above,

that conduct shall not also give rise to liability to a penalty under this paragraph.

(5) In this paragraph "credit" means credit for which provision is made by regulations under section 51 of this Act.

Registration

21.—(1) A person who fails to comply with section 47(3) of this Act is liable to a penalty equal to 5 per cent. of the relevant tax or, if it is greater or the circumstances are such that there is no relevant tax, to a penalty of £250; but this is subject to sub-paragraph (4) below.

(2) In sub-paragraph (1) above "relevant tax" means the tax (if any) for which the person concerned is liable for the period which—

(a) begins on the date with effect from which he is, in accordance with section 47 of this Act, required to be registered, and

(b) ends on the date on which the Commissioners received notification of, or otherwise became aware of, his liability to be registered.

(3) A person who fails to comply with section 47(4) of this Act is liable to a penalty of £250.

(4) Where, by reason of conduct falling within sub-paragraph (1) above—

(a) a person is convicted of an offence (whether under this Part of this Act or otherwise), or

(b) a person is assessed to a penalty under paragraph 18 above,

that conduct shall not also give rise to liability to a penalty under this paragraph.

Information

22.—(1) If a person—

(a) fails to comply with any provision of paragraph 1 or 3 above, or

(b) fails to make records as required by any provision of regulations made under paragraph 2 above,

he is liable to a penalty of £250; but this is subject to sub-paragraph (4) below.

(2) Where—

(a) a penalty (an initial penalty) is imposed on a person under sub-paragraph (1) above, and

(b) the failure which led to the initial penalty continues after its imposition,

he is (subject to sub-paragraph (4) below) liable to a further penalty of £20 for each day during which (or any part of which) the failure continues after the day on which the initial penalty was imposed.

(3) A person who fails to preserve records in compliance with any provision of regulations made under paragraph 2 above (read with that paragraph and any direction given under the regulations) is liable to a penalty of £250; but this is subject to sub-paragraph (4) below.

(4) Where by reason of a failure falling within sub-paragraph (1) or (3) above—

(a) a person is convicted of an offence (whether under this Part of this Act or otherwise), or

(b) a person is assessed to a penalty under paragraph 18 above,

that failure shall not also give rise to liability to a penalty under this paragraph.

Breach of regulations

23.—(1) Where regulations made under this Part of this Act impose a requirement on any person, they may provide that if the person fails to comply with the requirement he shall be liable to a penalty of £250; but this is subject to sub-paragraphs (2) and (3) below.

(2) Where by reason of any conduct—

(a) a person is convicted of an offence (whether under this Part of this Act or otherwise), or

(b) a person is assessed to a penalty under paragraph 18 above,

that conduct shall not also give rise to liability to a penalty under the regulations.

(3) Sub-paragraph (1) above does not apply to any failure mentioned in paragraph 22 above.

Walking possession agreements

24.—(1) This paragraph applies where—

(a) in accordance with regulations under paragraph 13(1) above a distress is authorised to be levied on the goods and chattels of a person (a person in default) who has refused or neglected to pay any tax due from him or any amount recoverable as if it were tax due from him, and

(b) the person levying the distress and the person in default have entered into a walking possession agreement.

(2) For the purposes of this paragraph a walking possession agreement is an agreement under which, in consideration of the property distrained upon being allowed to remain in the custody of the person in default and of the delaying of its sale, the person in default—

(a) acknowledges that the property specified in the agreement is under distraint and held in walking possession, and

(b) undertakes that, except with the consent of the Commissioners and subject to such conditions as they may impose, he will not remove or allow the removal of any of the specified property from the premises named in the agreement.

(3) If the person in default is in breach of the undertaking contained in a walking possession agreement, he is liable to a penalty equal to half of the tax or other amount referred to in sub-paragraph (1)(a) above.

(4) This paragraph does not extend to Scotland.

Mitigation of penalties

25.—(1) Where a person is liable to a penalty under this Part of this Schedule the Commissioners or, on appeal, an appeal tribunal may reduce the penalty to such amount (including nil) as they think proper.

(2) Where the person concerned satisfies the Commissioners or, on appeal, an appeal tribunal that there is a reasonable excuse for any breach, failure or other conduct, that is a factor which (among other things) may be taken into account under sub-paragraph (1) above.

(3) In the case of a penalty reduced by the Commissioners under sub-paragraph (1) above an appeal tribunal, on an appeal relating to the penalty, may cancel the whole or any part of the reduction made by the Commissioners.

PART VI

INTEREST

Interest on under-declared tax

26.—(1) Sub-paragraph (2) below applies where—

(a) under section 50(1) of this Act the Commissioners assess an amount of tax due from a registrable person for an accounting period and notify it to him, and

(b) the assessment is made on the basis that the amount (the additional amount) is due from him in addition to any amount shown in a return made in relation to the accounting period.

(2) The additional amount shall carry interest for the period which—

(a) begins with the day after that on which the person is required by provision made under section 49 of this Act to pay tax due from him for the accounting period, and

(b) ends with the day before the relevant day.

(3) For the purposes of sub-paragraph (2) above the relevant day is the earlier of—

(a) the day on which the assessment is notified to the person;

(b) the day on which the additional amount is paid.

(4) Sub-paragraph (5) below applies where under section 50(2) of this Act the Commissioners assess an amount as being tax due from a registrable person for an accounting period and notify it to him.

(5) The amount shall carry interest for the period which—

(a) begins with the day after that on which the person is required by provision made under section 49 of this Act to pay tax due from him for the accounting period, and

(b) ends with the day before the relevant day.

(6) For the purposes of sub-paragraph (5) above the relevant day is the earlier of—

(a) the day on which the assessment is notified to the person;

(b) the day on which the amount is paid.

(7) Interest under this paragraph shall be payable at the rate applicable under section 197 of this Act.

(8) Interest under this paragraph shall be paid without any deduction of income tax.

(9) Sub-paragraph (10) below applies where—

(a) an amount carries interest under this paragraph (or would do so apart from that sub-paragraph), and

(b) all or part of the amount turns out not to be due.

(10) In such a case—

(a) the amount or part (as the case may be) shall not carry interest under this paragraph and shall be treated as never having done so, and

(b) all such adjustments as are reasonable shall be made, including adjustments by way of repayment by the Commissioners where appropriate.

Interest on unpaid tax etc.

27.—(1) Sub-paragraph (2) below applies where—

(a) a registrable person makes a return under provision made under section 49 of this Act (whether or not he makes it at the time required by such provision), and

(b) the return shows that an amount of tax is due from him for the accounting period in relation to which the return is made.

(2) The amount shall carry interest for the period which—

(a) begins with the day after that on which the person is required by provision made under section 49 of this Act to pay tax due from him for the accounting period, and

(b) ends with the day before that on which the amount is paid.

(3) Sub-paragraph (4) below applies where—

(a) under section 50(1) of this Act the Commissioners assess an amount of tax due from a registrable person for an accounting period and notify it to him, and

(b) the assessment is made on the basis that no return required by provision made under section 49 of this Act has been made by the person in relation to the accounting period.

(4) The amount shall carry interest for the period which—

(a) begins with the day after that on which the person is required by provision made under section 49 of this Act to pay tax due from him for the accounting period, and

(b) ends with the day before that on which the amount is paid.

(5) Sub-paragraph (6) below applies where—

(a) under section 50(1) of this Act the Commissioners assess an amount of tax due from a registrable person for an accounting period and notify it to him, and

(b) the assessment (the supplementary assessment) is made on the basis that the amount (the additional amount) is due from him in addition to any amount shown in a return, or in any previous assessment, made in relation to the accounting period.

(6) The additional amount shall carry interest for the period which—

(a) begins with the day on which the supplementary assessment is notified to the person, and

(b) ends with the day before that on which the additional amount is paid.

(7) Sub-paragraph (8) below applies where under section 50(2) of this Act the Commissioners assess an amount as being tax due from a registrable person for an accounting period and notify it to him.

(8) The amount shall carry interest for the period which—

(a) begins with the day on which the assessment is notified to the person, and

(b) ends with the day before that on which the amount is paid.

(9) Sub-paragraph (10) below applies where under paragraph 32 below the Commissioners—

(a) assess an amount due from a person by way of penalty under Part V of this Schedule and notify it to him, or

(b) assess an amount due from a person by way of interest under paragraph 26 above and notify it to him.

(10) The amount shall carry interest for the period which—

(a) begins with the day on which the assessment is notified to the person, and

(b) ends with the day before that on which the amount is paid.

(11) Interest under this paragraph shall be compound interest calculated—

(a) at the penalty rate, and

(b) with monthly rests;

and the penalty rate is the rate found by taking the rate at which interest is payable under paragraph 26 above and adding 10 percentage points to that rate.

(12) Interest under this paragraph shall be paid without any deduction of income tax.

(13) Where—

(a) the Commissioners assess and notify an amount as mentioned in sub-paragraph (5)(a) or (7) or (9)(a) or (b) above,

(b) they also specify a date for the purposes of this sub-paragraph, and

(c) the amount concerned is paid on or before that date,

the amount shall not carry interest by virtue of sub-paragraph (6) or (8) or (10) above (as the case may be).

(14) Sub-paragraph (15) below applies where—

(a) an amount carries interest under this paragraph (or would do so apart from that sub-paragraph), and

(b) all or part of the amount turns out not to be due.

(15) In such a case—

(a) the amount or part (as the case may be) shall not carry interest under this paragraph and shall be treated as never having done so, and

(b) all such adjustments as are reasonable shall be made, including adjustments by way of repayment by the Commissioners where appropriate.

28.—(1) Where a person is liable to pay interest under paragraph 27 above the Commissioners or, on appeal, an appeal tribunal may reduce the amount payable to such amount (including nil) as they think proper.

(2) Where the person concerned satisfies the Commissioners or, on appeal, an appeal tribunal that there is a reasonable excuse for the conduct giving rise to the liability to pay interest, that is a factor which (among other things) may be taken into account under sub-paragraph (1) above.

(3) In the case of interest reduced by the Commissioners under sub-paragraph (1) above an appeal tribunal, on an appeal relating to the interest, may cancel the whole or any part of the reduction made by the Commissioners.

Interest payable by Commissioners

29.—(1) Where, due to an error on the part of the Commissioners, a person—

(a) has paid to them by way of tax an amount which was not tax due and which they are in consequence liable to repay to him,

(b) has failed to claim payment of an amount to the payment of which he was entitled in pursuance of provision made under section 51(2)(c) or (d) or (f) of this Act, or

(c) has suffered delay in receiving payment of an amount due to him from them in connection with tax,

then, if and to the extent that they would not be liable to do so apart from this paragraph, they shall (subject to the following provisions of this paragraph) pay interest to him on that amount for the applicable period.

(2) The applicable period, in a case falling within sub-paragraph (1)(a) above, is the period—

(a) beginning with the date on which the payment is received by the Commissioners, and

(b) ending with the date on which they authorise payment of the amount on which the interest is payable.

(3) The applicable period, in a case falling within sub-paragraph (1)(b) or (c) above, is the period—

(a) beginning with the date on which, apart from the error, the Commissioners might reasonably have been expected to authorise payment of the amount on which the interest is payable, and

(b) ending with the date on which they in fact authorise payment of that amount.

(4) In determining the applicable period for the purposes of this paragraph, there shall be left out of account any period referable to the raising and answering of any reasonable enquiry relating to any matter giving rise to, or otherwise connected with, the person's entitlement to interest under this paragraph.

(5) In determining for the purposes of sub-paragraph (4) above whether any period is referable to the raising and answering of such an enquiry as is there mentioned, there shall be taken to be so referable any period which begins with the date on which the Commissioners first consider it necessary to make such an enquiry and ends with the date on which the Commissioners—

(a) satisfy themselves that they have received a complete answer to the enquiry, or

(b) determine not to make the enquiry or (if they have made it) not to pursue it further;

but excluding so much of that period as may be prescribed by regulations.

(6) For the purposes of sub-paragraph (5) above it is immaterial—

(a) whether any enquiry is in fact made;

(b) whether any enquiry is or might have been made of the person referred to in sub-paragraph (1) above or of an authorised person or of some other person.

(7) The Commissioners shall only be liable to pay interest under this paragraph on a claim made in writing for that purpose.

(8) No claim shall be made under this paragraph after the expiry of six years from the date on which the claimant discovered the error or could with reasonable diligence have discovered it.

(9) Any reference in this paragraph to receiving a payment from the Commissioners includes a reference to the discharge, by way of set-off, of their liability to make it.

(10) Interest under this paragraph shall be payable at the rate applicable under section 197 of this Act.

30.—(1) Where—

(a) any interest is payable by the Commissioners to a person on a sum due to him under this Part of this Act, and

(b) he is a person to whom regulations under section 51 of this Act apply,

the interest shall be treated as an amount to which he is entitled by way of credit in pursuance of the regulations.

(2) Sub-paragraph (1) above shall be disregarded for the purpose of determining a person's entitlement to interest or the amount of interest to which he is entitled.

PART VII

MISCELLANEOUS

Security for tax

31. Where it appears to the Commissioners requisite to do so for the protection of the revenue they may require a registrable person, as a condition of his carrying out taxable activities, to give security (or further security) of such amount and in such manner as they may determine for the payment of any tax which is or may become due from him.

Assessments to penalties etc.

32.—(1) Where a person is liable—

(a) to a penalty under Part V of this Schedule, or

(b) for interest under paragraph 26 or 27 above,

the Commissioners may, subject to sub-paragraph (2) below, assess the amount due by way of penalty or interest (as the case may be) and notify it to him accordingly; and the fact that any conduct giving rise to a penalty under Part V of this Schedule may have ceased before an assessment is made under this paragraph shall not affect the power of the Commissioners to make such an assessment.

(2) In the case of the penalties and interest referred to in the following paragraphs of this sub-paragraph, the assessment under this paragraph shall be of an amount due in respect of the accounting period which in the paragraph concerned is referred to as the relevant period—

(a) in the case of a penalty under paragraph 18 above relating to the evasion of tax, and in the case of interest under paragraph 27 above on an amount due by way of such a penalty, the relevant period is the accounting period for which the tax evaded was due;

(b) in the case of a penalty under paragraph 18 above relating to the obtaining of a payment under regulations under section 51(2)(c) or (d) or (f) of this Act, and in the case of interest under paragraph 27 above on an amount due by way of such a penalty, the relevant period is the accounting period in respect of which the payment was obtained;

(c) in the case of interest under paragraph 26 above, and in the case of interest under paragraph 27 above on an amount due by way of interest under paragraph 26 above, the relevant period is the accounting period in respect of which the tax was due;

(d) in the case of interest under paragraph 27 above on an amount of tax, the relevant period is the accounting period in respect of which the tax was due.

(3) In a case where the amount of any penalty or interest falls to be calculated by reference to tax which was not paid at the time it should have been and that tax cannot be readily attributed to any one or more accounting periods, it shall be treated for the purposes of this Part of this Act as tax due for such period or periods as the Commissioners may determine to the best of their judgment and notify to the person liable for the tax and penalty or interest.

(4) Where a person is assessed under this paragraph to an amount due by way of any penalty or interest falling within sub-paragraph (2) above and is also assessed under subsection (1) or (2) of section 50 of this Act for the accounting period which is the relevant period under sub-paragraph (2) above, the assessments may be combined and notified to him as one assessment, but the amount of the penalty or interest shall be separately identified in the notice.

(5) Sub-paragraph (6) below applies in the case of an amount due by way of interest under paragraph 27 above.

(6) Where this sub-paragraph applies in the case of an amount—

(a) a notice of assessment under this paragraph shall specify a date, being not later than the date of the notice, to which the amount of interest which is assessed is calculated, and

(b) if the interest continues to accrue after that date, a further assessment or further assessments may be made under this paragraph in respect of amounts which so accrue.

(7) If, within such period as may be notified by the Commissioners to the person liable for the interest under paragraph 27 above, the amount referred to in paragraph 27(2), (4), (6), (8) or (10) above (as the case may be) is paid, it shall be treated for the purposes of paragraph 27 above as paid on the date specified as mentioned in sub-paragraph (6)(a) above.

(8) Where an amount has been assessed and notified to any person under this paragraph it shall be recoverable as if it were tax due from him unless, or except to the extent that, the assessment has subsequently been withdrawn or reduced.

(9) Subsection (8) of section 50 of this Act shall apply for the purposes of this paragraph as it applies for the purposes of that section.

Assessments: time limits

33.—(1) Subject to the following provisions of this paragraph, an assessment under—

(a) any provision of section 50 of this Act, or

(b) paragraph 32 above,

shall not be made more than six years after the end of the accounting period concerned or, in the case of an assessment under paragraph 32 above of an amount due by way of a penalty which is not a penalty referred to in sub-paragraph (2) of that paragraph, six years after the event giving rise to the penalty.

(2) Subject to sub-paragraph (5) below, an assessment under paragraph 32 above of—

(a) an amount due by way of any penalty referred to in sub-paragraph (2) of that paragraph, or

(b) an amount due by way of interest,

may be made at any time before the expiry of the period of two years beginning with the time when the amount of tax due for the accounting period concerned has been finally determined.

(3) In relation to an assessment under paragraph 32 above, any reference in sub-paragraph (1) or (2) above to the accounting period concerned is a reference to that period which, in the case of the penalty or interest concerned, is the relevant period referred to in sub-paragraph (2) of that paragraph.

(4) Subject to sub-paragraph (5) below, if tax has been lost—

(a) as a result of conduct falling within paragraph 18(1) above or for which a person has been convicted of fraud, or

(b) in circumstances giving rise to liability to a penalty under paragraph 21 above,

an assessment may be made as if, in sub-paragraph (1) above, each reference to six years were a reference to twenty years.

(5) Where after a person's death the Commissioners propose to assess an amount as due by reason of some conduct of the deceased—

(a) the assessment shall not be made more than three years after the death, and

(b) if the circumstances are as set out in sub-paragraph (4) above, the modification of sub-paragraph (1) above contained in that sub-paragraph shall not apply but any assessment which (from the point of view of time limits) could have been made immediately after the death may be made at any time within three years after it.

Supplementary assessments

34. If, otherwise than in circumstances falling within subsection (5)(b) of section 50 of this Act, it appears to the Commissioners that the amount which ought to have been assessed in an assessment under any provision of that section or under paragraph 32 above exceeds the amount which was so assessed, then—

(a) under the like provision as that assessment was made, and

(b) on or before the last day on which that assessment could have been made,

the Commissioners may make a supplementary assessment of the amount of the excess and shall notify the person concerned accordingly.

Disclosure of information

35.—(1) Notwithstanding any obligation not to disclose information that would otherwise apply, the Commissioners may disclose information to—

(a) the Secretary of State,
(b) the Environment Agency,
(c) the Scottish Environment Protection Agency,
(d) the Department of the Environment for Northern Ireland,
(e) a district council in Northern Ireland, or
(f) an authorised officer of any person (a principal) mentioned in paragraphs (a) to (e) above,

for the purpose of assisting the principal concerned in the performance of the principal's duties.

(2) Notwithstanding any such obligation as is mentioned in sub-paragraph (1) above, any person mentioned in sub-paragraph (1)(a) to (f) above may disclose information to the Commissioners or to an authorised officer of the Commissioners for the purpose of assisting the Commissioners in the performance of duties in relation to tax.

(3) Information that has been disclosed to a person by virtue of this paragraph shall not be disclosed by him except—

(a) to another person to whom (instead of him) disclosure could by virtue of this paragraph have been made, or
(b) for the purpose of any proceedings connected with the operation of any provision of, or made under, any enactment in relation to the environment or to tax.

(4) References in the preceding provisions of this paragraph to an authorised officer of any person (the principal) are to any person who has been designated by the principal as a person to and by whom information may be disclosed by virtue of this paragraph.

(5) The Secretary of State shall notify the Commissioners in writing of the name of any person designated by the Secretary of State under sub-paragraph (4) above.

(6) No charge may be made for a disclosure made by virtue of this paragraph.

The register: publication

36.—(1) The Commissioners may publish, by such means as they think fit, information which—

(a) is derived from the register kept under section 47 of this Act, and
(b) falls within any of the descriptions set out below.

(2) The descriptions are—

(a) the names of registered persons;
(b) the addresses of any sites or other premises at which they carry on business;
(c) the registration numbers assigned to them in the register;
(d) the fact (where it is the case) that the registered person is a body corporate which under section 59 of this Act is treated as a member of a group;
(e) the names of the other bodies corporate treated under that section as members of the group;
(f) the addresses of any sites or other premises at which those other bodies carry on business.

(3) Information may be published in accordance with this paragraph notwithstanding any obligation not to disclose the information that would otherwise apply.

Evidence by certificate etc.

37.—(1) A certificate of the Commissioners—

(a) that a person was or was not at any time registered under section 47 of this Act,
(b) that any return required by regulations made under section 49 of this Act has not been made or had not been made at any time, or
(c) that any tax shown as due in a return made in pursuance of regulations made under section 49 of this Act, or in an assessment made under section 50 of this Act, has not been paid,

shall be sufficient evidence of that fact until the contrary is proved.

(2) A photograph of any document furnished to the Commissioners for the purposes of this Part of this Act and certified by them to be such a photograph shall be admissible in any proceedings, whether civil or criminal, to the same extent as the document itself.

(3) Any document purporting to be a certificate under sub-paragraph (1) or (2) above shall be taken to be such a certificate until the contrary is proved.

Service of notices etc.

38. Any notice, notification or requirement to be served on, given to or made of any person for the purposes of this Part of this Act may be served, given or made by sending it by post in a letter addressed to that person at his last or usual residence or place of business.

39.—(1) This paragraph applies to directions, specifications and conditions which the Commissioners or an authorised person may give or impose under any provision of this Part.

(2) A direction, specification or condition given or imposed by the Commissioners may be withdrawn or varied by them.

(3) A direction, specification or condition given or imposed by an authorised person may be withdrawn or varied by him or by another authorised person.

(4) No direction, specification or condition shall have effect as regards any person it is intended to affect unless—

(a) a notice containing it is served on him, or

(b) other reasonable steps are taken with a view to bringing it to his attention.

(5) No withdrawal or variation of a direction, specification or condition shall have effect as regards any person the withdrawal or variation is intended to affect unless—

(a) a notice containing the withdrawal or variation is served on him, or

(b) other reasonable steps are taken with a view to bringing the withdrawal or variation to his attention.

No deduction of penalties or interest

40. In section 827 of the Taxes Act 1988 (no deduction for penalties etc.) the following subsection shall be inserted after subsection (1B)—

"(1C) Where a person is liable to make a payment by way of—

(a) penalty under Part V of Schedule 5 to the Finance Act 1996 (landfill tax), or

(b) interest under paragraph 26 or 27 of that Schedule,

the payment shall not be allowed as a deduction in computing any income, profits or losses for any tax purposes."

Destination of receipts

41. All money and securities for money collected or received for or on account of the tax shall—

(a) if collected or received in Great Britain, be placed to the general account of the Commissioners kept at the Bank of England under section 17 of the Customs and Excise Management Act 1979;

(b) if collected or received in Northern Ireland, be paid into the Consolidated Fund of the United Kingdom in such manner as the Treasury may direct.

Set-off of amounts

42.—(1) Regulations may make provision in relation to any case where—

(a) a person is under a duty to pay to the Commissioners at any time an amount or amounts in respect of landfill tax, and

(b) the Commissioners are under a duty to pay to that person at the same time an amount or amounts in respect of any tax (or taxes) under their care and management.

(2) The regulations may provide that if the total of the amount or amounts mentioned in sub-paragraph (1)(a) above exceeds the total of the amount or amounts mentioned in sub-paragraph (1)(b) above, the latter shall be set off against the former.

(3) The regulations may provide that if the total of the amount or amounts mentioned in sub-paragraph (1)(b) above exceeds the total of the amount or amounts mentioned in sub-paragraph (1)(a) above, the Commissioners may set off the latter in paying the former.

(4) The regulations may provide that if the total of the amount or amounts mentioned in sub-paragraph (1)(a) above is the same as the total of the amount or amounts mentioned in sub-paragraph (1)(b) above no payment need be made in respect of the former or the latter.

(5) The regulations may include provision treating any duty to pay mentioned in sub-paragraph (1) above as discharged accordingly.

(6) References in sub-paragraph (1) above to an amount in respect of a particular tax include references not only to an amount of tax itself but also to other amounts such as interest and penalty.

(7) In this paragraph "tax" includes "duty".

43.—(1) Regulations may make provision in relation to any case where—

(a) a person is under a duty to pay to the Commissioners at any time an amount or amounts in respect of any tax (or taxes) under their care and management, and

(b) the Commissioners are under a duty to pay to that person at the same time an amount or amounts in respect of landfill tax.

(2) The regulations may provide that if the total of the amount or amounts mentioned in sub-paragraph (1)(a) above exceeds the total of the amount or amounts mentioned in sub-paragraph (1)(b) above, the latter shall be set off against the former.

(3) The regulations may provide that if the total of the amount or amounts mentioned in sub-paragraph (1)(b) above exceeds the total of the amount or amounts mentioned in sub-paragraph (1)(a) above, the Commissioners may set off the latter in paying the former.

(4) The regulations may provide that if the total of the amount or amounts mentioned in sub-paragraph (1)(a) above is the same as the total of the amount or amounts mentioned in sub-paragraph (1)(b) above no payment need be made in respect of the former or the latter.

(5) The regulations may include provision treating any duty to pay mentioned in sub-paragraph (1) above as discharged accordingly.

(6) References in sub-paragraph (1) above to an amount in respect of a particular tax include references not only to an amount of tax itself but also to other amounts such as interest and penalty.

(7) In this paragraph "tax" includes "duty".

Amounts shown as tax on invoices

44.—(1) Where—
(a) a registrable person issues an invoice showing an amount as tax chargeable on an event, and
(b) no tax is in fact chargeable on the event,
an amount equal to the amount shown as tax shall be recoverable from the person as a debt due to the Crown.

(2) Where—
(a) a registrable person issues an invoice showing an amount as tax chargeable on a taxable disposal, and
(b) the amount shown as tax exceeds the amount of tax in fact chargeable on the disposal,
an amount equal to the excess shall be recoverable from the person as a debt due to the Crown.

(3) References in this paragraph to an invoice are to any invoice, whether or not it is a landfill invoice within the meaning of section 61 of this Act.

Adjustment of contracts

45.—(1) This paragraph applies where—
(a) material undergoes a landfill disposal,
(b) a payment falls to be made under a disposal contract relating to the material, and
(c) after the making of the contract there is a change in the tax chargeable on the landfill disposal.

(2) In such a case the amount of any payment mentioned in sub-paragraph (1)(b) above shall be adjusted, unless the disposal contract otherwise provides so as to reflect the tax chargeable on the landfill disposal.

(3) For the purposes of this paragraph a disposal contract relating to material is a contract providing for the disposal of the material, and it is immaterial—
(a) when the contract was made;
(b) whether the contract also provides for other matters;
(c) whether the contract provides for a method of disposal and (if it does) what method it provides for.

(4) The reference in sub-paragraph (1) above to a change in the tax chargeable is a reference to a change—
(a) to or from no tax being chargeable, or
(b) in the amount of tax chargeable.

46.—(1) This paragraph applies where—
(a) work is carried out under a construction contract,
(b) as a result of the work, material undergoes a landfill disposal,
(c) the contract makes no provision as to the disposal of such material, and
(d) the contract was made on or before 29th November 1994 (when the proposal to create tax was announced).

(2) In such a case the amount of any payment which falls to be made—
(a) under the construction contract, and
(b) in respect of the work,
shall be adjusted, unless the contract otherwise provides, so as to reflect the tax (if any) chargeable on the disposal.

(3) For the purposes of this paragraph a construction contract is a contract under which all or any of the following work is to be carried out—
(a) the preparation of a site;
(b) demolition;

(c) building;
(d) civil engineering.

Adjustment of rent etc.

47.—(1) This paragraph applies where—
(a) an agreement with regard to any sum payable in respect of the use of land (whether the sum is called rent or royalty or otherwise) provides that the amount of the sum is to be calculated by reference to the turnover of a business,
(b) the agreement was made on or before 29th November 1994 (when the proposal to create tax was announced), and
(c) the circumstances are such that (had the agreement been made after that date) it can reasonably be expected that it would have provided that tax be ignored in calculating the turnover.

(2) In such a case the agreement shall be taken to provide that tax be ignored in calculating the turnover.

GENERAL NOTE
This Schedule contains the usual panoply of powers and penalties considered necessary for enforcing landfill tax. Much of it covers well-travelled ground (see, for example, the FA 1994, Sched. 7, in relation to insurance premium tax).

Para. 1
The Customs and Excise are given a general power to require information.

Para. 2
The records which must be kept will be prescribed by regulation. Restrictions are placed on the use of computer-generated documents in court proceedings.

Para. 3
This establishes the conditions under which the Customs and Excise may require documents to be produced to them.

Para. 4
The Customs and Excise are empowered to enter premises.

Para. 5
They may also, with a warrant from a J.P. in cases of suspected fraud, enter premises forcibly and search the premises and any individuals therein.

Para. 6
They are also given a power of arrest.

Para. 7
A J.P. may also issue an order, in cases of a suspected tax offence, requiring access for the Customs and Excise to recorded information.

Para. 8
Where documents are removed by the Customs and Excise under paras. 5 or 7, the owner retains a right to access and to obtain copies unless it would prejudice the investigation.

Para. 9
If the Customs and Excise fail to comply with para. 8, the aggrieved person can get an order from the magistrates (or, in Scotland, the sheriff) to enforce compliance.

Para. 10
Samples of landfill waste may be taken.

Para. 11
Landfill tax is recoverable as a debt due to the Crown. A proposal to make company directors jointly and severally liable was removed in committee [Standing Committee E, February 8, 1996, col. 188].

Para. 12
Landfill tax due from any person is a preferential debt in insolvency.

Para. 13
The Customs and Excise are empowered to make regulations covering distraint against the assets of non-payers. In Scotland, diligence may be invoked.

Para. 14
Overpaid tax is recoverable, subject to a six-year time limit [*Hansard*, H.C. Vol. 274, col. 1181].

Para. 15
Various criminal offences are created in relation to landfill tax.

Para. 16
The penalties range up to unlimited fines and seven years' imprisonment.

Para. 17
The provisions of the Customs and Excise Management Act 1979 (c. 2), ss.145–155, apply for the purposes of landfill tax.

Para. 18
As with other excise taxes such as VAT, a system of civil penalties is also provided for landfill tax. This paragraph applies to fraudulent evasion and provides for a penalty equal to the amount of tax evaded. It does not debar criminal proceedings.

Para. 19
Penalties under para. 18 may be levied on individual officers of companies where it appears to the Customs and Excise that their conduct was wholly or partly responsible for the default.

Para. 20
Misdeclaration or neglect also attracts a civil penalty. The penalty is five per cent of the tax misdeclared.

Para. 21
Failure to register attracts a penalty of £250 or, if greater, five per cent of the relevant tax.

Para. 22
Failure to provide information and/or documents or to keep records under paras. 1–3 attracts a penalty of £250 plus £20 per day for continuing default.

Para. 23
Breach of any regulations regarding landfill tax attracts a £250 penalty.

Para. 24
Breach of a walking possession agreement made by regulations under para. 13(1) attracts a penalty of half the tax due.

Para. 25
The Customs and Excise or the tribunal may mitigate any penalty under paras. 18–24.

Para. 26
Interest is charged on under-declared tax at the rate applicable under s.197.

Para. 27
Interest at a penalty rate is charged on unpaid tax, interest and penalties. The rate is compound interest with monthly rests at 10 per cent over the para. 26 rate.

Para. 28
Interest under para. 27 may be mitigated by Customs and Excise or the tribunal.

Para. 29
Interest at the rate applicable under s.197 is payable by the Customs and Excise on refunds of tax delayed by official error. The interest must be claimed in writing.

Para. 30
Interest payable by the Customs and Excise is treated as a credit under s.51.

Para. 31
The Customs and Excise may require security for the payment of landfill tax.

Para. 32
Assessments for penalties or interest under paras. 18–27 may be made and recovered as if they were assessments to tax.

Para. 33
A general time limit of six years is provided for assessments under s.50 or para. 32. For penalties or interest under para. 32 a two-year time limit applies. In cases of fraud, a 20-year time limit applies. A three-year limit applies in the case of deceased individuals [Standing Committee E, February 8, 1996, col. 193].

Para. 34
Supplementary assessments, other than under s.50(5)(b), may be raised by the Customs and Excise within the time limits of the original assessment.

Para. 35
The Customs and Excise can disclose information to environmental agencies about landfill site operators and *vice versa.*

Para. 36
The Customs and Excise are permitted to publish the register compiled under s.47. This information is already in the public domain [Standing Committee E, February 8, 1996, col. 194].

Para. 37
The Customs and Excise may provide evidence of certain facts by certificate.

Para. 38
Notices may be served on a person by posting it to his residence or place of business.

Para. 39
The Customs and Excise may withdraw or vary any directions, specifications and conditions imposed by them.

Para. 40
Landfill tax interest and penalties cannot be offset against any direct tax liabilities.

Para. 41
Landfill tax is paid into the Customs and Excise account at the Bank of England (or the Consolidated Fund in the case of Northern Ireland).

Para. 42
Provision is made for regulations to set off moneys owed by a person in respect of landfill tax against moneys owed to him in respect of other Customs and Excise taxes [Standing Committee E, February 8, 1996, col. 195].

Para. 43
Similarly, regulations may provide for the set-off of moneys due by a person in respect of other Customs and Excise taxes against moneys due to him in respect of landfill tax.

Para. 44
Amounts shown on invoices as landfill tax are recoverable as a debt due to the Crown, whether or not it is in fact due.

Para. 45
A contract for the disposal of landfill material will be adjusted to reflect landfill tax unless the contract otherwise provides [*Hansard*, H.C. Vol. 274, col. 1181].

Para. 46
A construction contract which involves landfill disposal made on or before November 29, 1994 will also be adjusted to reflect tax, unless it provides otherwise.

Para. 47

Rents or royalties in respect of the use of land, where the agreement was made on or before November 29, 1994, will be calculated on the basis of ignoring landfill tax in turnover, if this appears a reasonable assumption.

Section 73   SCHEDULE 6

TAXATION OF SAVINGS AT THE LOWER RATE

The Taxes Management Act 1970 (c. 9)

1. In section 86 of the Taxes Management Act 1970 (interest on tax assessed in addition to deducted tax etc.), so far as it has effect without the substitutions made by paragraph 23 of Schedule 19 to the Finance Act 1994 and section 110 of the Finance Act 1995, in subsection (2)(b) after "the basic rate" there shall be inserted "or the lower rate".

The Taxes Act 1988

2. In section 4(2) of the Taxes Act 1988 (meaning of "relevant year of assessment" for the purposes of deductions etc.), for "subsection (1) above" there shall be substituted "this section".

3. In section 5(4) of that Act (time when tax in addition to deducted tax etc. becomes due), after "basic rate" there shall be inserted "or the lower rate".

4.—(1) Subject to sub-paragraph (2) below, in subsection (1)(b) of section 51B of that Act (periodic returns of tax on gilts), for "basic rate" there shall be substituted "lower rate".

(2) Sub-paragraph (1) above has effect for the purposes only of the exercise on or after the day on which this Act is passed of the Treasury's power to make regulations under that section; but that power may be exercised on or after that day for the purpose of making provision, with retrospective effect, on the basis that the assumption to be applied in relation to all payments made on or after 6th April 1996 was an assumption that such payments bear tax at the lower rate.

5. In paragraph (c) of section 246D(2) of that Act (application of section 207A to certain foreign income dividends), for the words from "as income" to the end of the paragraph there shall be substituted "(without prejudice to paragraph (a) above) as if it were income to which section 1A applies;".

6. In section 249(4)(c) of that Act (application of section 207A), for the words from "as income" to "but" there shall be substituted "(without prejudice to paragraph (a) above) as if it were income to which section 1A applies, but".

7.—(1) In subsection (2)(b)(ii) of section 326B of that Act (loss of exemption for TESSAs), for the words from "basic rate on" to the end of the sub-paragraph there shall be substituted "applicable rate on any interest or bonus paid on the account before that time;".

(2) After subsection (2) of that section there shall be inserted the following subsection—

"(2A) In subsection (2)(b)(ii) above 'the applicable rate' means—

(a) in the case of interest or bonus paid before 6th April 1996, the basic rate for the year of assessment in which the payment was made; and

(b) in any other case, the lower rate for the year of assessment in which it was made."

(3) This paragraph has effect as respects withdrawals on or after 6th April 1996.

8. In section 350 of that Act (charge to tax where payments made subject to deduction), in subsection (1) for "basic rate" there shall be substituted "applicable rate"; and after that subsection there shall be inserted the following subsection—

"(1A) In subsection (1) above 'the applicable rate' means the rate which is applicable to the payment under section 4."

9. In section 421(1)(c) of that Act (application of section 207A), for the words from "as income" to "but" there shall be substituted "(without prejudice to paragraph (b) above) as if it were income to which section 1A applies, but".

10.—(1) In section 468 of that Act (authorised unit trusts to be subject to corporation tax), the following subsection shall be inserted after subsection (1)—

"(1A) In relation to any authorised unit trust the rate of corporation tax for the financial year 1996 and subsequent financial years shall be deemed to be the rate at which income tax at the lower rate is charged for the year of assessment which begins on 6th April in the financial year concerned."

(2) Sub-paragraph (1) above has effect in relation to any accounting period ending after 31st March 1996.

(3) Sections 468E and 468EE of that Act (rate of corporation tax on authorised unit trusts) shall not apply in relation to any accounting period ending after 31st March 1996 except so far as those sections relate to the financial year 1995.

11.—(1) In section 468L of that Act (interest distributions), after subsection (1) there shall be inserted the following subsection—

"(1A) For the purposes of this Chapter no amount shall be shown as so available unless the authorised unit trust in question satisfies the qualifying investments test throughout the distribution period."

(2) After subsection (7) of that section there shall be inserted the following subsections—

"(8) For the purposes of this section an authorised unit trust satisfies the qualifying investments test throughout a distribution period ('the relevant period') if at all times in that period, the market value of the qualifying investments exceeds 60 per cent. of the market value of all the investments of that trust.

(9) Subject to subsection (13) below, in this section 'qualifying investments', in relation to an authorised unit trust, means the investments of that trust which are of any of the following descriptions—

    (a) money placed at interest;

    (b) securities;

    (c) shares in a building society;

    (d) qualifying entitlements to a share in the investments of another authorised unit trust.

(10) For the purposes of subsection (9) above an entitlement to a share in the investments of another authorised unit trust is a qualifying entitlement at any time in the relevant period if, and only if, the other authorised unit trust would itself (on the relevant assumption) satisfy the qualifying investments test throughout that period.

(11) For the purposes of subsection (10) above the relevant assumption is that the only investments of the other authorised unit trust which are to be regarded as qualifying investments are those falling within paragraphs (a) to (c) of subsection (9) above.

(12) In this section 'security' does not include shares in a company; and references in this section to investments of an authorised unit trust are references to investments subject to the trusts of that authorised unit trust but do not include references to cash awaiting investment.

(13) The Treasury may by order amend subsection (9) above so as to extend or restrict the descriptions of investments of an authorised unit trust that are qualifying investments.

(14) An order made by the Treasury under subsection (13) above may—

    (a) make different provision for different cases; and

    (b) contain such incidental, supplemental, consequential and transitional provision as the Treasury may think fit;

and, without prejudice to the generality of paragraph (b) above, such an order may make such incidental modifications of subsection (11) above as the Treasury may think fit."

(3) This paragraph has effect in relation to distribution periods ending on or after 1st April 1996.

12. In section 469(2) of that Act (taxation of income of unauthorised unit trusts), after the words "unit holders)", in the first place where they occur, there shall be inserted "and, in the case of income to which section 1A applies, chargeable to income tax at the basic rate, instead of at the lower rate".

13. In sections 549(2), 686(1), 699(2) and 819(2) of that Act (which refer to income tax being chargeable at the lower rate in accordance with section 207A), for "section 207A" there shall be substituted "section 1A".

14.—(1) In paragraph (a)(i) of subsection (2) of section 582 of that Act (funding bonds), for "basic" there shall be substituted "applicable".

(2) After that subsection there shall be inserted the following subsection—

"(2A) In subsection (2) above 'the applicable rate', in relation to a year of assessment, means whichever of the basic rate and the lower rate for that year is the rate at which the person by or through whom the bonds are issued would have had to deduct income tax from the amount of interest in question if that amount had been actually paid by or through him."

15. In section 686 of that Act (liability to additional rate in the case of trustees of discretionary trusts), after subsection (2A) there shall be inserted the following subsection—

"(2B) For the purposes of subsection (2A) above where the income tax borne by any income arising to trustees is limited in accordance with section 128 of the Finance Act 1995 (limit on income chargeable on non-residents), the income arising to the trustees which shall be taken not to bear tax by reason wholly or partly of their not having been resident in the United Kingdom shall include so much of any income arising to them as—

    (a) is excluded income within the meaning of that section; and

(b) is not income which is treated for the purposes of subsection (1)(b) of that section as income the tax on which is deducted at source."

16. In Part XV of that Act (settlements), at the end of Chapter IC there shall be inserted the following Chapter—

"CHAPTER ID

TRUST MANAGEMENT EXPENSES

Disregard of expenses where beneficiary non-resident
689A.—(1) This section applies where—
(a) there is income ('the distributed income') arising to trustees in any year of assessment which (before being distributed) is income of a person ('the beneficiary') other than the trustees;
(b) the trustees have any expenses in that year ('the management expenses') which are properly chargeable to that income or would be so chargeable but for any express provisions of the trust; and
(c) the beneficiary is not liable to income tax on an amount of the distributed income ('the untaxed income') by reason wholly or partly of—
(i) his not having been resident in the United Kingdom, or
(ii) his being deemed under any arrangements under section 788, or any arrangements having effect by virtue of that section, to have been resident in a territory outside the United Kingdom.
(2) Where this section applies, there shall be disregarded in computing the income of the beneficiary for the purposes of the Income Tax Acts such part of the management expenses as bears the same proportion to all those expenses as the untaxed income bears to the distributed income.
(3) For the purpose of computing the proportion mentioned in subsection (2) above, the amounts of the distributed income and of the untaxed income shall not, in either case, include so much (if any) of the income as is equal to the amount of income tax, or of any foreign tax, chargeable on the trustees (by way of deduction or otherwise) in respect of that income.
(4) In subsection (3) above, 'foreign tax' means any tax which is—
(a) of a similar character to income tax; and
(b) imposed by the laws of a territory outside the United Kingdom.
(5) For the purposes of this section, where the income tax chargeable on any person is limited in accordance with section 128 of the Finance Act 1995 (limit on income chargeable on non-residents), the income of that person on which he is not liable to tax by reason of not having been resident in the United Kingdom shall be taken to include so much of any income of his as—
(a) is excluded income within the meaning of that section; and
(b) is not income which is treated for the purposes of subsection (1)(b) of that section as income the tax on which is deducted at source.

Order in which expenses to be set against income
689B.—(1) The expenses of any trustees in any year of assessment, so far as they are properly chargeable to income (or would be so chargeable but for any express provisions of the trust), shall be treated—
(a) as set against so much (if any) of any income as is income falling within subsection (2) or (3) below before being set against other income; and
(b) as set against so much (if any) of any income as is income falling within subsection (2) below before being set against income falling within subsection (3) below.
(2) Income falls within this subsection if it is—
(a) so much of the income of the trustees as is income the amount or value of which is determined in accordance with section 233(1A);
(b) income which is treated as having arisen to the trustees by virtue of section 246D(4) or 249(6); or
(c) income which is treated as received by the trustees by virtue of section 421(1)(a).
(3) Income falls within this subsection if it is income to which section 1A applies but which does not fall within subsection (2) above.
(4) This section has effect—
(a) subject to sections 686(2A) and 689A, but
(b) notwithstanding anything in section 1A(5) and (6)."

17. In section 698A of that Act (taxation at the lower rate of the income of beneficiaries)—

(a) in subsection (1), for the words from "section 207A" to the end there shall be substituted "section 1A shall have effect as if that income were income to which that section applies."; and

(b) in subsection (2), for the words from "section 207A" to the end there shall be substituted "section 1A shall have effect as if the payment made to the trustee were income of the trustee to which that section applies."

18.—(1) In subsection (1) of section 737 of that Act (deductions from manufactured payments), after "shall apply" there shall be inserted "(subject to subsection (1A) below)", and for subsection (1A) of that section there shall be substituted the following subsection—

"(1A) The deduction of tax which is deemed to have been made under subsection (1) above shall be taken to have been made at the lower rate as if the deemed annual payment were income to which section 1A applied; and—

(a) the reference to the applicable rate in subsection (1) of section 350, so far as it has effect by virtue of subsection (1) above, and

(b) Schedule 16, so far as it so has effect,

shall be construed accordingly."

(2) This paragraph has effect in relation to payments on or after 6th April 1996.

19. In section 737C(6) of that Act (computation of amount of deemed manufactured interest), for "basic" there shall be substituted "lower".

20. In section 743(1) of that Act (supplemental provisions relating to transfers of assets abroad)—

(a) after the words "the basic rate", in the first place where they occur, there shall be inserted "or the lower rate"; and

(b) for "income that has borne tax at the basic rate", there shall be substituted "any income to the extent that it has borne tax at that rate".

21. In section 789(2) of that Act (old double taxation relief agreements), for "to bear income tax at the basic rate and" there shall be substituted "—

(a) to bear income tax at the basic rate or, where that income is income to which section 1A applies, at the lower rate; and

(b) ".

22. In paragraph (a) of section 821(1) of that Act (under-deductions from payments made before passing of annual Act to be charged under Case VI of Schedule D), for the words from "under Schedule D in respect" to the end of the paragraph there shall be substituted "under Case III of Schedule D in respect of those payments; and".

23. In section 822(1) of that Act (over-deductions from interest on loan capital etc. made before the passing of annual Act where basic rate for the year is lower than in the previous year), for "basic rate lower" there shall be substituted "lower rate less".

24. In section 835(6)(a) of that Act (estimating total income), after "basic rate" there shall be inserted "or the lower rate".

25.—(1) In Schedule 3 to that Act (public revenue dividends etc.—

(a) in paragraph 1(c), for "basic" there shall be substituted "lower";

(b) in paragraph 6A—

(i) in sub-paragraph (1), for "applicable" there shall be substituted "lower"; and

(ii) sub-paragraph (4) shall cease to have effect.

(2) This paragraph has effect in relation to payments made on or after 6th April 1996 and before the day on which this Act is passed.

The Finance Act 1989 (c. 26)

26.—(1) In section 88(1) of the Finance Act 1989 (rate of corporation tax on policy holders' fraction of profits to be equal to the basic rate), after "subsection (2)" there shall be inserted "and section 88A".

(2) After section 88 of that Act there shall be inserted the following section—

"Lower corporation tax rate on certain insurance company profits

88A.—(1) Subject to subsection (2) below, in the case of a company carrying on basic life assurance and general annuity business, the rate of corporation tax chargeable for any financial year on so much of the company's BLAGAB profits for any accounting period as represents the company's lower rate income for the period shall be deemed to be the rate at which income tax at the lower rate is charged for the year of assessment which begins on 6th April in the financial year concerned.

(2) Subsection (1) above does not apply in relation to profits charged under Case I of Schedule D.

(3) In this section, references to a company's lower rate income for any accounting period are references to so much of the income and gains of its basic life assurance and general annuity business for the period as consists in income of any of the following descriptions—

   (a) income falling within paragraph (a) of Case III of Schedule D, as that Case applies for the purposes of corporation tax;

   (b) purchased life annuities to which section 656 of the Taxes Act 1988 applies or to which that section would apply but for section 657(2)(a) of that Act;

   (c) any such dividends or other distributions of a company not resident in the United Kingdom as would be chargeable under Schedule F if the company were resident in the United Kingdom;

   (d) so much of—

        (i) any dividend distribution (within the meaning of section 468J of the Taxes Act 1988), or

        (ii) any foreign income distribution (within the meaning of section 468K of that Act),

   as is deemed by subsection (2) of section 468Q of that Act (or by that subsection as applied by section 468R(2) of that Act) to be an annual payment.

(4) Where for any period—

   (a) an insurance company's basic life assurance and general annuity business is mutual business,

   (b) the policy holders' share of the company's relevant profits is equal to all those profits, or

   (c) the policy holders' share of the company's relevant profits is more than the company's BLAGAB profits,

the amount to be taken for the purposes of this section as the amount of the company's BLAGAB profits for that period representing its lower rate income for that period shall be the amount equal to the applicable proportion of its BLAGAB profits.

(5) Where subsection (4) above does not apply in the case of an insurance company for any period, the amount to be taken for the purposes of this section as the amount of the company's BLAGAB profits for the period representing its lower rate income for that period shall be the amount produced by multiplying the following, that is to say—

   (a) the applicable proportion of those profits; and

   (b) the fraction given by dividing the policy holders' share of the relevant profits of the company for the period by its BLAGAB profits for that period.

(6) For the purposes of this section the applicable proportion of a company's BLAGAB profits for any period is the amount which bears the same proportion to those profits as the aggregate amount of the company's lower rate income for that period bears to the total income and gains for that period of the company's basic life assurance and general annuity business.

(7) For the purposes of this section, the BLAGAB profits of a company for an accounting period are the income and gains of the company's basic life assurance and general annuity business reduced by the aggregate amount of—

   (a) any non-trading deficit on the company's loan relationships,

   (b) expenses of management falling to be deducted under section 76 of the Taxes Act 1988, and

   (c) charges on income,

so far as referable to the company's basic life assurance and general annuity business.

(8) Section 88(3) above applies for the purposes of this section as it applies for the purposes of section 88(1) above."

(3) In section 89 of that Act (meaning of "policy holders' share" of profits), in subsection (1)—

(a) for "section 88" there shall be substituted "sections 88 and 88A";

(b) after "life assurance business" there shall be inserted "or, as the case may be, basic life assurance and general annuity business"; and

(c) for "the business" there shall be substituted "its life assurance business";

and in subsection (2), in each of paragraphs (b) and (c), for "the business" there shall be substituted "the company's life assurance business".

(4) This paragraph shall have effect for the financial year 1996 and subsequent financial years.

The Taxation of Chargeable Gains Act 1992 (c. 12)

27. In section 4(3A) of the Taxation of Chargeable Gains Act 1992 (disregard of income chargeable at lower rate in accordance with section 207A of the Taxes Act 1988), for "section 207A" there shall be substituted "section 1A".

Commencement of Schedule

28. Subject to any express provisions as to commencement that are contained in the preceding provisions of this Schedule, this Schedule has effect for the year 1996–97 and subsequent years of assessment.

GENERAL NOTE

The Schedule makes consequential amendments to existing legislation in relation to the application of lower rate tax to income from savings.

Para. 10

The corporation tax rate for all authorised unit trusts is reduced to 20 per cent. Previously this only applied if a claim was made and the test set out in para. 11 was satisfied.

Para. 11

An authorised unit trust may make a distribution of interest only if 60 per cent of its investments are in interest-bearing assets.

Para. 12

The tax charge on unauthorised unit trusts is set at the basic rate.

Para. 15

The trustees of non-resident discretionary trusts are denied relief on the proportion of their expenses corresponding to income which does not bear tax in the U.K.

Para. 16

The new ICTA 1988, ss.689A and 689B, provide new and amended rules for trust management expenses.

The new s.689A applies to trusts where a non-resident beneficiary has a right to the income. A proportion of the expenses equal to the proportion of the income which is untaxed is to be disregarded.

The new s.689B amends the existing rules on the order of set-off for trust management expenses (currently in the FA 1993, s.79(3)) to take account of the new system.

Para. 20

Savings income subject to deduction of lower rate tax will continue to be taxed under the anti-avoidance provisions of the ICTA 1988, s.739, at the transferor's marginal rate of tax.

Para. 26

The new FA 1989, s.88A, provides for part of the investment return received by a company carrying on life assurance business to be charged at a rate of corporation tax equivalent to the lower rate of income tax. The income concerned is limited to the company's basic life assurance and general annuity business (BLAGAB) profits [Standing Committee E, February 13, 1996, col. 273].

Section 79   SCHEDULE 7

TRANSFER OF CHARGE UNDER SCHEDULE C TO SCHEDULE D

Amendments of the Taxes Act 1988

1. The Taxes Act 1988 shall be amended in accordance with paragraphs 2 to 28 below.

2. In section 1(1) (the charge to income tax), for "Schedules A, C, D, E and F" there shall be substituted "Schedules A, D, E and F".

3. Section 17 (Schedule C) shall be omitted.

4.—(1) In section 18 (Schedule D), in subsection (1), in paragraph (b) of Schedule D, for "not charged under Schedule A, C or E" there shall be substituted "not charged under Schedule A or E".

(2) In subsection (3) of that section—

(a) in Case III, in paragraph (c) for the words from "except income charged under Schedule C" to the end of the paragraph there shall be substituted "from securities which is payable out of the public revenue of the United Kingdom or Northern Ireland";

(b) in Case IV, the words "except such income as is charged under Schedule C" shall be omitted; and

(c) in Case VI, for "Schedule A, C or E" there shall be substituted "Schedule A or E".

(3) Immediately before subsection (4) of section 18, there shall be inserted the following subsections—

"(3B) The references in Case IV of Schedule D to income arising from securities out of the United Kingdom, and in Case V of Schedule D to income arising from possessions out of the United Kingdom, shall be taken, in the case of relevant foreign holdings, to include references to the following—

(a) any proceeds of such a sale or other realisation of coupons for foreign dividends as is effected by a bank in the United Kingdom which pays the proceeds over or carries them into an account;

(b) any proceeds of a sale of such coupons to a dealer in coupons in the United Kingdom by a person who is not a bank or another dealer in coupons.

(3C) In this section 'relevant foreign holdings' means—

(a) any securities issued by or on behalf of a government or a public or local authority in a country outside the United Kingdom; or

(b) any shares or securities issued by or on behalf of a body of persons not resident in the United Kingdom;

and 'securities' here includes loan stock and similar securities.

(3D) In this section 'foreign dividends' means—

(a) in relation to relevant foreign holdings falling within subsection (3C)(a) above, interest or annual payments payable out of the revenue of the government or authority in question; and

(b) in relation to relevant foreign holdings falling within subsection (3C)(b) above, any dividends, interest or annual payments payable in respect of the holdings in question.

(3E) In this section—

(a) 'bank' has the meaning given by section 840A; and

(b) references to coupons include, in relation to any foreign dividends, warrants for and bills of exchange purporting to be drawn or made in payment of those dividends."

(4) In subsection (5) of that section, for "Part IV contains" there shall be substituted "Parts III and IV contain".

5. In section 19(1), in paragraph 2 of Schedule E, for the words "under Schedule C" there shall be substituted "under paragraph (c) of Case III of Schedule D".

6. For the heading to Part III there shall be substituted the following heading—

"GOVERNMENT SECURITIES"

7. Section 44 (mode of charge of tax under Schedule C) shall be omitted.

8. Section 45 (interpretation of Part III) shall be omitted.

9. Section 48 (securities of foreign states) shall be omitted.

10. In section 49 (stock and dividends in name of Treasury etc.), after subsection (2) there shall be inserted the following subsection—

"(3) In this section 'dividends' means any interest, public annuities, dividends or shares of annuities."

11. In sections 50(1) and 51A(1) (which provide for interest on certain securities to be paid without deduction of tax), the words "but shall be chargeable to tax under Case III of Schedule D" shall in each case be omitted.

12. Section 52 (taxation of interest on converted securities and interest which becomes subject to deduction) shall be omitted.

13. Section 123 (foreign dividends) shall be omitted.

14. In section 124—

(a) in subsection (6) (definitions in connection with quoted Eurobonds), the definitions of "recognised clearing system" and "relevant foreign securities", and the word "and" immediately preceding those definitions, and

(b) subsection (7),

shall be omitted.

15. In section 322(1) (consular officers and employees), the words "and he shall be treated as not resident in the United Kingdom for the purposes of sections 48 and 123(4)" shall be omitted.

16. In section 398 (transactions in deposits with and without certificates or in debts), in paragraph (b), the words "C or" shall be omitted.

17. In section 468M(4) (meaning of "eligible income" in connection with interest distributions of authorised unit trusts), for paragraphs (c) to (e) there shall be substituted the following paragraph—

"(cc) any foreign dividends (as defined by section 18(3D)) and any proceeds falling within section 18(3B)(a) or (b);".

18. In section 474 (treatment of tax-free income), subsections (1) and (3) shall be omitted.

19.—(1) In section 505 (exemptions for charities), in subsection (1), in paragraph (c), sub-paragraph (i) shall be omitted.

(2) For paragraph (d) of that subsection there shall be substituted the following paragraph—

"(d) exemption from tax under Schedule D in respect of public revenue dividends on securities which are in the name of trustees to the extent that the dividends are applicable and applied only for the repair of—

(i) any cathedral, college, church or chapel, or

(ii) any building used only for the purposes of divine worship;".

(3) After that subsection there shall be inserted the following subsection—

"(1A) In subsection (1)(d) above 'public revenue dividends' means—

(a) income from securities which is payable out of the public revenue of the United Kingdom or Northern Ireland;

(b) income from securities issued by or on behalf of a government or a public or local authority in a country outside the United Kingdom."

20.—(1) In section 512 (exemption from income tax for Atomic Energy Authority and National Radiological Protection Board)—

(a) in subsection (1)(a), for "Schedules A and C" there shall be substituted "Schedule A"; and

(b) in subsection (1)(b), after "annual payment" there shall be inserted "or in respect of public revenue dividends".

(2) After subsection (2) of that section there shall be inserted the following subsection—

"(3) In subsection (1) above 'public revenue dividends' means—

(a) income from securities which is payable out of the public revenue of the United Kingdom or Northern Ireland;

(b) income from securities issued by or on behalf of a government or a public or local authority in a country outside the United Kingdom."

21.—(1) In section 516 (government securities held by non-resident central banks), in subsection (1), for "dividends (within the meaning of Schedule C) paid out of the public revenue of the United Kingdom where they are" there shall be substituted "income from securities which is payable out of the public revenue of the United Kingdom and which is".

(2) In subsection (2) of that section, for "such dividends" there shall be substituted "such income".

22. In section 582A (designated international organisations), subsection (3) shall be omitted.

23. In section 730 (transfers of income arising from securities)—

(a) in subsections (2), (4)(b) and (6), for "under Schedule C or under section 123(3)", and

(b) in subsection (8), for "under Schedule C or section 123(3)",

there shall in each case be substituted "by virtue of section 18(3B)".

24. In section 828(2) (orders and regulations not required to be made by statutory instrument) for "section 124(6) or 841(1)(b) or paragraph 15(4) of Schedule 3" there shall be substituted "section 841(1)(b) or 841A".

25. In section 832(1) (interpretation of the Tax Acts), the definition of "recognised clearing system" shall be omitted.

26. After section 841 there shall be inserted the following section—

"Recognised clearing systems

841A.—(1) In the Tax Acts, 'recognised clearing system' means any system for clearing—

(a) quoted Eurobonds (as defined by section 124), or

(b) relevant foreign holdings (as defined by section 18(3C)),

which is for the time being designated for the purposes of this section as a recognised clearing system by an order made by the Board.

(2) An order under this section—

(a) may contain such transitional and other supplemental provision as appears to the Board to be necessary or expedient; and

(b) may be varied or revoked by a subsequent order."

27. Schedule 3 (machinery for payment of income tax under Schedule C and, in certain cases, Schedule D) shall be omitted.

28.—(1) In Schedule 23A (manufactured dividends and interest), in paragraph 1(1) (definitions)—

(a) in paragraph (b) of the definition of "overseas securities", and

(b) in the definition of "United Kingdom securities",
for "Eurobonds held in a recognised clearing system, within the meaning of section 124" there shall be substituted "Eurobonds (as defined by section 124) held in a recognised clearing system".

(2) In paragraph 4(8) of that Schedule, for paragraphs (a) to (d) there shall be substituted the following paragraphs—

"(b) a foreign dividend (as defined by section 18(3D)), or
(c) interest on a quoted Eurobond (as defined by section 124) held in a recognised clearing system,".

Other amendments

29. In the Table in section 98 of the Taxes Management Act 1970 (penalties in respect of certain information provisions)—
(a) in the first column, the entry relating to paragraph 13(1) of Schedule 3 to the Taxes Act 1988, and
(b) in the second column, the entry relating to paragraph 6C of that Schedule,
shall be omitted.

30. In section 178(2)(m) of the Finance Act 1989 (provisions to which power to set rates of interest applies), the words "and paragraph 6B of Schedule 3 to" shall be omitted.

31. In section 128 of the Finance Act 1995 (limit on income chargeable on non-residents: income tax), in subsection (3)(a), the words "Schedule C," shall be omitted.

Commencement, etc.

32. Subject to paragraphs 33 and 34 below, this Schedule has effect—
(a) for the purposes of income tax, for the year 1996–97 and subsequent years of assessment;
(b) for the purposes of corporation tax, for accounting periods ending after 31st March 1996.

Position of paying and collecting agents

33.—(1) Subject to the following provisions of this paragraph and paragraph 34 below—
(a) nothing in section 79 of this Act or this Schedule shall affect the obligations of any person under Schedule 3, in relation to times to which this paragraph applies, to set apart, retain or pay any amount of tax; and
(b) Schedule 3 shall have effect accordingly in relation to amounts set apart, retained or paid in pursuance of those obligations.

(2) The repeal of Schedule 3 shall not affect the operation of paragraph 6B of that Schedule in relation to any amount—
(a) which became due and payable in relation to a transaction occurring before the day on which this Act was passed; but
(b) which remains unpaid at any time on or after that day.

(3) The Board may by regulations make provision with respect to returns to be made for the quarter which includes both times before the day on which this Act was passed and times on and after that day.

(4) Regulations under sub-paragraph (3) above may, in particular, provide that section 98 of the Taxes Management Act 1970 shall have effect as if it included a reference in the second column of the Table to any specified provision of the regulations.

(5) In this paragraph "Schedule 3" means Schedule 3 to the Taxes Act 1988.

Position of taxpayers

34.—(1) Transitional payments of tax made on a person's behalf in relation to times to which this paragraph applies shall be treated as made only for the purpose of being applied in the discharge of that person's liability to tax charged under Schedule D.

(2) If a transitional payment of tax has been made on a person's behalf, but it appears to the Board that—
(a) that person was not liable to tax, or
(b) the sum paid exceeded his liability,
the Board shall make or allow such repayments, adjustments or set-offs against unpaid tax as they think appropriate.

(3) In this paragraph "transitional payment of tax" means a payment to which paragraph 33 above applies.

Times to which paragraphs 33 and 34 apply

35. Paragraphs 33 and 34 above apply in relation to times falling—
(a) within a year of assessment or an accounting period mentioned in paragraph 32 above, but

(b) before the day on which this Act was passed.

GENERAL NOTE
The Schedule makes amendments consequent on the abolition of the charge under Sched. C (the ICTA 1988, s.17) on interest on Government debt and its replacement by a charge under Sched. D, Cases III, IV or V.

Para. 4
Interest from U.K. Government securities is chargeable under Sched. D, Case III and interest from foreign governments is chargeable under Sched. D, Case IV or Case V.

Para. 26
The new ICTA 1988, s.841A, applies a new definition of "recognised clearing system", which currently relies on the repealed ICTA 1988, s.123.

Section 83   SCHEDULE 8

LOAN RELATIONSHIPS: CLAIMS RELATING TO DEFICITS

Claim to set off deficit against other profits for the deficit period

1.—(1) This paragraph applies where a claim is made under section 83(2)(a) of this Act for the whole or any part of the deficit to be set off against profits of any description for the deficit period.
(2) Subject to the following provisions of this paragraph—
(a) the amount to which the claim relates shall be set off against the profits of the company for the deficit period that are identified in the claim; and
(b) those profits shall be treated as reduced accordingly.
(3) Any reduction by virtue of sub-paragraph (2) above shall be made—
(a) after relief has been given for any loss incurred in a trade in an earlier accounting period; and
(b) before any relief is given against profits for that period either—
(i) under section 393A(1) of the Taxes Act 1988 (trading losses set against profits for the same or preceding accounting periods); or
(ii) by virtue of any claim made, in respect of a deficit for a subsequent period, under section 83(2)(c) of this Act.
(4) Relief shall not be given by virtue of a claim under section 83(2)(a) of this Act against any ring fence profits of the company within the meaning of Chapter V of Part XII of the Taxes Act 1988 (petroleum extraction activities).

Claim to treat deficit as eligible for group relief

2.—(1) This paragraph applies where the company makes a claim under section 83(2)(b) of this Act for the whole or any part of the deficit to be treated as eligible for group relief.
(2) The amount to which the claim relates shall be treated as if, for the purposes of subsection (1) of section 403 of the Taxes Act 1988 (group relief for trades)—
(a) it were a loss incurred in the deficit period by a company carrying on a trade; and
(b) the exclusions in subsection (2) of that section did not apply.

Claim to carry back deficit to previous accounting periods

3.—(1) This paragraph applies where a claim is made under section 83(2)(c) of this Act for the whole or any part of the deficit to be carried back to be set off against profits for earlier accounting periods.
(2) The claim shall have effect only if it relates to an amount that is equal to whichever is smaller of the following amounts, that is to say—
(a) so much of that deficit as is neither—
(i) an amount in relation to which a claim is made under subsection (2)(a) or (b) of section 83 of this Act, nor
(ii) an amount excluded by virtue of subsection (4) of that section from the amounts in relation to which claims may be made under subsection (2) of that section; and
(b) the total amount of the profits available for relief under this paragraph.
(3) Where the claim has effect, the amount to which the claim relates shall be set off against the profits available for relief under this paragraph—

(a) by treating those profits as reduced accordingly; and

(b) to the extent that those profits are profits for more than one accounting period, by applying the relief to profits for a later period before setting off any remainder of the amount to
which the claim relates against profits for an earlier period.

(4) Subject to sub-paragraph (5) below, the profits available for relief under this paragraph are
the amounts which, for accounting periods ending within the permitted period, would be
taken—

(a) apart from any relief under this paragraph, and

(b) after the giving of every relief which under sub-paragraph (6) below falls to be given in
priority to relief under this paragraph,

to be chargeable under Case III of Schedule D as profits and gains arising from the company's
loan relationships.

(5) Where any accounting period begins before the beginning of the permitted period but
ends in the course of it—

(a) any amount chargeable in respect of that accounting period under Case III of Schedule D
as profits and gains of the company's loan relationships shall be apportioned according to
the proportions of the accounting period falling before and after the beginning of the
permitted period; and

(b) the amount attributable, on that apportionment, to before the beginning of the permitted
period shall not be available for relief under this paragraph.

(6) The reliefs which fall to be given in priority to relief under this paragraph in respect of any
loss are—

(a) any relief in respect of a loss or deficit incurred or treated as incurred in an accounting
period before the deficit period;

(b) any relief under section 338 of the Taxes Act 1988 (charges on income) in respect of
payments made wholly and exclusively for the purposes of a trade;

(c) where the company is an investment company for the purposes of Part IV of that Act—

   (i) any allowance under section 28 of the Capital Allowances Act 1990 (machinery
   and plant of investment companies);

   (ii) any deduction in respect of management expenses under section 75 of the Taxes
   Act 1988; and

   (iii) any relief under section 338 of the Taxes Act 1988 in respect of payments made
   wholly and exclusively for the purposes of its business;

(d) any relief under section 393A of the Taxes Act 1988 (trading losses set against profits of
the same or any preceding accounting periods); and

(e) any relief in pursuance of a claim under section 83(2)(a) or (b) of this Act.

(7) In this paragraph "the permitted period" means the period of three years immediately
preceding the beginning of the deficit period so far as that three year period falls after 31st March
1996.

Claim to carry forward deficit to next accounting period

4.—(1) This paragraph applies where a claim is made under section 83(2)(d) of this Act for the
whole or any part of the deficit to be carried forward and set against non-trading profits for the
next accounting period.

(2) The amount to which the claim relates shall be set off against the non-trading profits of the
company for the accounting period immediately following the deficit period, and those profits
shall be treated as reduced accordingly.

(3) In this paragraph "non-trading profits", in relation to a company, means so much of any
profits of the company (of whatever description) as do not consist in trading income for the
purposes of section 393A of the Taxes Act 1988 (setting-off of trading losses against profits of the
same or an earlier period).

Construction of Schedule

5. In this Schedule "the deficit" and "the deficit period" shall be construed by reference to
section 83(1) of this Act.

GENERAL NOTE

The Schedule deals with the handling of claims regarding deficits on loan relationships under
s.83(2).

Para. 1

This deals with a claim to set a deficit against other corporation tax profits for the same period.
Relief is given after relief from trading losses from earlier periods or the current period or relief
carried back from subsequent periods. Relief cannot be given against ring-fenced North Sea
profits.

Para. 2

For group relief, the claim is treated as if it were for a trading loss, without the exclusions relating to non-commercial losses and losses in hobby farming.

Para. 3

For a carry-back claim, the profits are extinguished on a LIFO basis against Case III profits. An apportionment over three years takes place where accounting periods do not exactly match. Various other reliefs (listed in subpara. (6)) take precedence over this relief.

Para. 4

A carry-forward claim is set against non-trading profits for the following period.

Section 84   SCHEDULE 9

LOAN RELATIONSHIPS: SPECIAL COMPUTATIONAL PROVISIONS

Distributions

1. The credits and debits to be brought into account for the purposes of this Chapter shall not include any credits or debits relating to any amount falling, when paid, to be treated as a distribution.

Late interest

2.—(1) This paragraph applies for the purpose of bringing debits into account for the purposes of this Chapter in respect of a debtor relationship of a company where an authorised accruals basis of accounting is used as respects that relationship in pursuance of section 87 of this Act.

(2) If—

(a) interest payable under that relationship is not paid within the period of twelve months following the end of the accounting period in which it would (apart from this paragraph) be treated as accruing, and

(b) credits representing the full amount of the interest are not for any accounting period brought into account for the purposes of this Chapter in respect of the corresponding creditor relationship,

then debits relating to that interest shall be brought into account on the assumption that the interest does not accrue until it is paid.

Options etc.

3.—(1) This paragraph applies for determining the credits and debits to be brought into account for any accounting period in accordance with an authorised accruals basis of accounting, where—

(a) the answer to the question whether any amount will become due under a loan relationship after the end of that period,

(b) the amount which will become due under a loan relationship after the end of that period, or

(c) the time after the end of that period when an amount will become due under a loan relationship,

depends on the exercise of an option by a party to the relationship or an associate of his, or is otherwise under the control of such a party or an associate of his.

(2) It shall be assumed that the party or his associate will exercise his power to determine whether and on what date any amount will become due in the manner which (apart from taxation) appears, as at the end of the accounting period in question, to be the most advantageous to that party.

(3) In this paragraph "associate" has the meaning given for the purposes of Part XI of the Taxes Act 1988 by section 417(3) and (4) of that Act.

Foreign exchange gains and losses

4.—(1) The credits and debits to be brought into account for the purposes of this Chapter shall be computed disregarding so much of any authorised accounting method as, by requiring the translation or conversion of amounts from one currency into another, has the effect that credits and debits produced by that method include sums in which profits, gains or losses arising from fluctuations in the value of a currency are to any extent represented.

(2) This paragraph is without prejudice to the provisions of Chapter II of Part II of the Finance Act 1993 (exchange gains and losses).

Bad debt etc.

5.—(1) In determining the credits and debits to be brought into account in accordance with an accruals basis of accounting, a departure from the assumption in the case of the creditor relationships of a company that every amount payable under those relationships will be paid in full as it becomes due shall be allowed (subject to paragraph 6 below) to the extent only that—

(a) a debt is a bad debt;

(b) a doubtful debt is estimated to be bad; or

(c) a liability to pay any amount is released.

(2) Such a departure shall be made only where the accounting arrangements allowing the departure also require appropriate adjustments, in the form of credits, to be made if the whole or any part of an amount taken or estimated to represent an amount of bad debt is paid or otherwise ceases to be an amount in respect of which such a departure is allowed.

(3) Where—

(a) a liability to pay any amount under a debtor relationship of a company is released, and

(b) the release takes place in an accounting period for which an authorised accruals basis of accounting is used as respects that relationship,

no credit in respect of the release shall be required to be brought into account in the case of that company if the release is part of a relevant arrangement or compromise (within the meaning given by section 74(2) of the Taxes Act 1988) or the relationship is one as respects which section 87 of this Act requires the use of an authorised accruals basis of accounting.

Bad debt etc. where parties have a connection

6.—(1) This paragraph applies where for any accounting period section 87 of this Act requires an authorised accruals basis of accounting to be used as respects a creditor relationship of a company.

(2) The credits and debits which for that period are to be brought into account for the purposes of this Chapter in accordance with that accounting method shall be computed subject to sub-paragraphs (3) to (6) below.

(3) The assumption that every amount payable under the relationship will be paid in full shall be applied as if no departure from that assumption were authorised by virtue of paragraph 5 above except where it is allowed by sub-paragraph (4) below.

(4) A departure from that assumption shall be allowed in relation to a liability to pay any amount to the company ("the creditor company") under the creditor relationship where—

(a) in consideration of, or of any entitlement to, any shares forming part of the ordinary share capital of the company on whom the liability would otherwise have fallen, the creditor company treats the liability as discharged; and

(b) the condition specified in sub-paragraph (5) below is satisfied.

(5) That condition is that there would be no connection between the two companies for the accounting period in which that consideration is given if the question whether there is such a connection for that period fell to be determined, in accordance with section 87 of this Act, by reference only to times before the creditor company acquired possession of, or any entitlement to, the shares in question.

(6) Where the company ceases in the accounting period in question to be a party to the relationship—

(a) the debits brought into account for that period in respect of that relationship shall not (subject to sub-paragraph (7) below) be more than they would have been had the company not ceased to be a party to the relationship; and

(b) the credits brought into account for that period in respect of the relationship shall not (subject to that sub-paragraph) be less than they would have been in those circumstances.

(7) In determining for the purposes of sub-paragraph (6) above the debits and credits that would have been brought into account if a company had not ceased to be a party to a loan relationship, no account shall be taken of any amounts that would have accrued at times after it ceased to be a party to the relationship.

Writing-off of government investments

7.—(1) Where any government investment in a company is written off by the release of a liability to pay any amount under a debtor relationship of the company, no credit shall be required, in the case of that company, to be brought into account for the purposes of this Chapter in respect of that release.

(2) Subsections (7) and (8) of section 400 of the Taxes Act 1988 shall apply as they apply for the purposes of that section, for construing the reference in sub-paragraph (1) above to the writing-off of a government investment.

Restriction on writing off overseas sovereign debt etc.

8.—(1) This paragraph applies for the purposes of the use, as respects any loan relationship of a company and in conformity with paragraph 5 above, of an authorised accruals basis of accounting.

(2) Where the company is one to which a relevant overseas debt is owed, the debits and credits to be brought into account on that basis for the purposes of this Chapter shall be determined, for any accounting period of the company, on the assumption that it is not permissible for more than the relevant percentage of the debt to be estimated to be bad.

(3) For the purposes of this paragraph the relevant percentage of a debt for any accounting period of a company is (subject to sub-paragraph (4) below) such percentage (which may be zero) as may be determined, by reference to the position at the end of the relevant period of account, in accordance with regulations made by the Treasury.

(4) Where, apart from this sub-paragraph, the relevant percentage of a debt for any accounting period is more than the adjusted base percentage of that debt for that period, the relevant percentage of the debt for that period shall be taken to be equal to its adjusted base percentage for that period.

(5) For the purposes of this paragraph the adjusted base percentage of a debt for any accounting period shall be calculated by—

(a) taking the percentage which, in accordance with section 88B of the Taxes Act 1988 and any regulations made under that section, was or (assuming the debt to have been a debt of the company at the end of the base period) would have been the base percentage for that debt; and

(b) increasing that base percentage by five percentage points for every complete year (except the first) between—

(i) the time by reference to which the base percentage was, or would have been, determined, and

(ii) the end of the relevant period of account.

(6) In this paragraph "the relevant period of account", in relation to any accounting period of a company, means the period of account ending with that accounting period or, if a period of account does not end with that accounting period, the last period of account of the company to end before the end of that accounting period.

(7) In this paragraph "relevant overseas debt" means any debt which—

(a) satisfies one of the conditions specified in sub-paragraph (8) below; but

(b) is neither interest on a debt nor a debt which represents the consideration for the provision of goods or services.

(8) Those conditions are—

(a) that the debt is owed by an overseas State authority; or

(b) that payment of the debt is guaranteed by an overseas State authority; or

(c) that the debt is estimated to be bad for the purposes of this Chapter wholly or mainly because due payment is or may be prevented, restricted or subjected to conditions—

(i) by virtue of any law of a State or other territory outside the United Kingdom or any act of an overseas State authority; or

(ii) under any agreement entered into in consequence or anticipation of such a law or act.

(9) In this paragraph "overseas State authority" means—

(a) a State or other territory outside the United Kingdom;

(b) the government of such a State or territory;

(c) the central bank or other monetary authority of such a State or territory;

(d) a public or local authority in such a State or territory; or

(e) a body controlled by such a State, territory, government, bank or authority;

and for this purpose "controlled" shall be construed in accordance with section 840 of the Taxes Act 1988.

(10) The Treasury shall not make any regulations under this paragraph unless a draft of them has been laid before and approved by a resolution of the House of Commons.

Further restriction on bringing into account losses on overseas sovereign debt etc.

9.—(1) This paragraph applies where—

(a) for an accounting period in which a company ceases to be a party to a loan relationship ("the loss period") any amount falls for the purposes of this Chapter to be brought into account in respect of that relationship in accordance with an authorised accruals basis of accounting;

(b) by the bringing into account of that amount in that period a loss incurred in connection with a relevant overseas debt falling within sub-paragraph (2) below is treated for the purposes of this Chapter as arising in that period;

(c) the amount of the loss is greater than 5 per cent. of the debt; and

(d) the loss is not one incurred on a disposal of the debt to an overseas State authority in a case in which the State or territory by reference to which it is an overseas State authority is the same as that by reference to which the debt is a relevant overseas debt.

(2) A relevant overseas debt falls within this sub-paragraph if—

(a) a deduction has been made in respect of the debt in accordance with section 74(1)(j) of the Taxes Act 1988 for any period of account of the company ending before 1st April 1996;

(b) any debit relating to the debt has been brought into account for the purposes of this Chapter in accordance with so much of any authorised accruals basis of accounting as relates to the matters mentioned in paragraph 5(1)(a) to (c) above; or

(c) the debt is one acquired by the company on or after 20th March 1990 for a consideration greater than the price which it might reasonably have been expected to fetch on a sale in the open market at the time of acquisition.

(3) Where this paragraph applies, the amounts brought into account for the purposes of this Chapter in the loss period shall be such as to secure that only so much of the loss as does not exceed 5 per cent. of the debt is treated for the purposes of this Chapter as arising in the loss period; but sub-paragraph (4) below applies as respects further parts of that loss until the loss is exhausted.

(4) A part of the loss may, in accordance with sub-paragraph (5) below, be brought into account for the purposes of this Chapter in the form of a debit for any accounting period after the loss period ("a subsequent period").

(5) The amount of the debit brought into account under sub-paragraph (4) above for any subsequent period shall not exceed such amount as, together with any parts of the loss which for earlier periods have been represented by—

(a) the amount of the loss treated as arising in the loss period in accordance with sub-paragraph (3) above, or

(b) debits brought into account in accordance with this sub-paragraph,

is equal to 5 per cent. of the debt for each complete year that has elapsed between the beginning of the loss period and the end of the subsequent period.

(6) In this paragraph "overseas State authority" and "relevant overseas debt" have the same meanings as in paragraph 8 above.

(7) References in this paragraph to a loss do not include so much of any loss as falls to be disregarded for the purposes of this Chapter by virtue of paragraph 10 below or to any loss incurred before 1st April 1996.

Imported losses etc.

10.—(1) This paragraph applies in the case of a company ("the chargeable company") for an accounting period ("the loss period") where—

(a) an authorised accruals basis of accounting is used as respects a loan relationship of that company for the loss period;

(b) in accordance with that basis of accounting there is an amount which would fall (apart from this paragraph) to be brought into account for the purposes of this Chapter in respect of that relationship;

(c) by the bringing into account of that amount in that period a loss incurred in connection with that loan relationship would be treated for the purposes of this Chapter as arising in that period; and

(d) that loss is referable in whole or in part to a time when the relationship was not subject to United Kingdom taxation.

(2) The amounts brought into account for the purposes of this Chapter in the loss period shall be such as to secure that no part of the loss that is referable to a time when the relationship was not subject to United Kingdom taxation shall be treated for the purposes of this Chapter as arising in the loss period or any other accounting period of the chargeable company.

(3) For the purposes of this paragraph a loss is referable to a time when a relationship is not subject to United Kingdom taxation to the extent that, at the time to which the loss is referable, the chargeable company would not have been chargeable to tax in the United Kingdom on any profits or gains arising from the relationship.

(4) Sub-paragraph (3) above shall have effect where the chargeable company was not a party to the relationship at the time to which the loss is referable as if the reference to that company were a reference to the person who at that time was in the same position as respects the relationship as is subsequently held by the chargeable company.

Transactions not at arm's length

11.—(1) Subject to sub-paragraphs (2) and (3) below, where—
(a) debits or credits in respect of a loan relationship of a company fall to be brought into account for the purposes of this Chapter in accordance with an authorised accounting method,
(b) those debits or credits relate to amounts arising from, or incurred for the purposes of, a related transaction, and
(c) that transaction is not a transaction at arm's length,
the debits or credits given by that method shall be determined on the assumption that the transaction was entered into on the terms on which it would have been entered into between independent persons.

(2) Sub-paragraph (1) above shall not apply to debits arising from the acquisition of rights under a loan relationship where those rights are acquired for less than market value.

(3) Sub-paragraph (1) above does not apply—
(a) in the case of any related transaction between two companies that are members of the same group; or
(b) in relation to a member of a group of companies, in the case of any transaction which is part of a series of transactions having the same effect as a related transaction between two members of the same group.

(4) In this paragraph "related transaction" has the same meaning as in section 84 of this Act.

(5) Section 170 of the Taxation of Chargeable Gains Act 1992 (groups etc.) shall apply for the interpretation of this paragraph as it applies for the interpretation of sections 171 to 181 of that Act.

Continuity of treatment: groups etc.

12.—(1) Subject to paragraph 15 below, this paragraph applies where, as a result of—
(a) a related transaction between two members of the same group of companies,
(b) a series of transactions having the same effect as a related transaction between two companies each of which has been a member of the same group at any time in the course of that series of transactions,
(c) the transfer between two companies of the whole or part of the long term business of any insurance company in accordance with a scheme sanctioned by a court under Part I of Schedule 2C to the Insurance Companies Act 1982, or
(d) any transfer between two companies which is a qualifying overseas transfer within the meaning of paragraph 4A of Schedule 19AC to the Taxes Act 1988 (transfer of business of overseas life insurance company),
one of those companies ("the transferee company") directly or indirectly replaces the other ("the transferor company") as a party to a loan relationship.

(2) The credits and debits to be brought into account for the purposes of this Chapter in the case of the two companies shall be determined as follows—
(a) the transaction, or series of transactions, by virtue of which the replacement takes place shall be disregarded except for the purpose of identifying the company in whose case any debit or credit not relating to that transaction, or those transactions, is to be brought into account; and
(b) the transferor company and the transferee company shall be deemed (except for that purpose) to be the same company.

(3) This paragraph does not apply by virtue of sub-paragraph (1)(a) or (b) above in relation to any transfer of an asset, or of any rights under or interest in an asset, where the asset was within one of the categories set out in section 440(4)(a) to (e) of the Taxes Act 1988 (assets held for certain categories of long term business) either immediately before the transfer or immediately afterwards.

(4) This paragraph does not apply by virtue of sub-paragraph (1)(c) or (d) above in relation to any transfer of an asset, or of any rights under or interest in an asset, where—
(a) the asset was within one of the categories set out in section 440(4) of the Taxes Act 1988 immediately before the transfer; and
(b) is not within that category immediately afterwards.

(5) For the purposes of sub-paragraph (4) above, where one of the companies is an overseas life insurance company an asset shall be taken to be within the same category both immediately before the transfer and immediately afterwards if it—
(a) was within one category immediately before the transfer; and
(b) is within the corresponding category immediately afterwards.

(6) References in this paragraph to one company replacing another as a party to a loan relationship shall include references to a company becoming a party to any loan relationship

under which its rights are equivalent to those of the other company under a loan relationship of which that other company has previously ceased to be a party.

(7) For the purposes of sub-paragraph (6) above a person's rights under a loan relationship are equivalent to rights under another such relationship if they entitle the holder of an asset representing the relationship—

(a) to the same rights against the same persons as to capital, interest and dividends, and

(b) to the same remedies for the enforcement of those rights,

notwithstanding any difference in the total nominal amounts of the assets, in the form in which they are held or in the manner in which they can be transferred.

(8) Sub-paragraphs (4) and (5) of paragraph 11 above have effect for the purposes of this paragraph as they have effect for the purposes of that paragraph.

(9) In this paragraph "overseas life insurance company" has the same meaning as in Chapter I of Part XII of the Taxes Act 1988.

Loan relationships for unallowable purposes

13.—(1) Where in any accounting period a loan relationship of a company has an unallowable purpose, the debits which, for that period fall, in the case of that company, to be brought into account for the purposes of this Chapter shall not include so much of the debits given by the authorised accounting method used as respects that relationship as, on a just and reasonable apportionment, is attributable to the unallowable purpose.

(2) For the purposes of this paragraph a loan relationship of a company shall be taken to have an unallowable purpose in an accounting period where the purposes for which, at times during that period, the company—

(a) is a party to the relationship, or

(b) enters into transactions which are related transactions by reference to that relationship,

include a purpose ("the unallowable purpose") which is not amongst the business or other commercial purposes of the company.

(3) For the purposes of this paragraph the business and other commercial purposes of a company do not include the purposes of any part of its activities in respect of which it is not within the charge to corporation tax.

(4) For the purposes of this paragraph, where one of the purposes for which a company—

(a) is a party to a loan relationship at any time, or

(b) enters into a transaction which is a related transaction by reference to any loan relationship of the company,

is a tax avoidance purpose, that purpose shall be taken to be a business or other commercial purpose of the company only where it is not the main purpose, or one of the main purposes, for which the company is a party to the relationship at that time or, as the case may be, for which the company enters into that transaction.

(5) The reference in sub-paragraph (4) above to a tax avoidance purpose is a reference to any purpose that consists in securing a tax advantage (whether for the company or any other person).

(6) In this paragraph—

"related transaction" has the same meaning as in section 84 of this Act; and

"tax advantage" has the same meaning as in Chapter I of Part XVII of the Taxes Act 1988 (tax avoidance).

Debits and credits treated as relating to capital expenditure

14.—(1) This paragraph applies where any debit or credit given by an authorised accounting method for any accounting period in respect of a loan relationship of a company is allowed by normal accountancy practice to be treated, in the accounts of the company, as an amount brought into account in determining the value of a fixed capital asset or project.

(2) Notwithstanding the application to it of the treatment allowed by normal accountancy practice, the debit or credit shall be brought into account for the purposes of corporation tax, for the accounting period for which it is given, in the same way as a debit or credit which, in accordance with normal accountancy practice, is brought into account in determining the company's profit or loss for that period.

Repo transactions and stock-lending

15.—(1) In determining the debits and credits to be brought into account for the purposes of this Chapter in respect of any loan relationship, it shall be assumed that a disposal or acquisition to which this paragraph applies is not a related transaction for the purposes of section 84 of this Act.

(2) This paragraph applies to any such disposal or acquisition of rights or liabilities under the relationship as is made in pursuance of any repo or stock-lending arrangements.

(3) In this paragraph "repo or stock-lending arrangements" means any arrangements consisting in or involving an agreement or series of agreements under which provision is made—

(a) for the transfer from one person to another of any rights under that relationship; and

(b) for the transferor, or a person connected with him, subsequently to be or become entitled, or required—

(i) to have the same or equivalent rights transferred to him; or

(ii) to have rights in respect of benefits accruing in respect of that relationship on redemption.

(4) For the purposes of sub-paragraph (3) above rights under a loan relationship are equivalent to rights under another such relationship if they entitle the holder of an asset representing the relationship—

(a) to the same rights against the same persons as to capital, interest and dividends, and

(b) to the same remedies for the enforcement of those rights,

notwithstanding any difference in the total nominal amounts of the assets, in the form in which they are held or in the manner in which they can be transferred.

(5) Nothing in this paragraph shall prevent any redemption or discharge of rights or liabilities under a loan relationship to which any repo or stock-lending arrangements relate from being treated for the purposes of this Chapter as a related transaction (within the meaning of section 84 of this Act).

(6) This paragraph is without prejudice to section 730A(2) and (6) of the Taxes Act 1988 (deemed payments of loan interest in the case of the sale and repurchase of securities).

(7) Section 839 of the Taxes Act 1988 (connected persons) applies for the purposes of this paragraph.

Imputed interest

16.—(1) This paragraph applies where, in pursuance of sections 770 to 772 of the Taxes Act 1988 (transactions at an undervalue or overvalue), as those sections have effect by virtue of section 773(4) of that Act, any amount falls to be treated as interest payable under a loan relationship of a company.

(2) Those sections shall have effect, notwithstanding the provisions of any authorised accounting method, so as to require credits or debits relating to the deemed interest to be brought into account for the purposes of this Chapter to the same extent as they would be in the case of an actual amount of interest accruing or becoming due and payable under the loan relationship in question.

Discounted securities where companies have a connection

17.—(1) This paragraph applies as respects any accounting period ("the relevant period") where—

(a) a debtor relationship of a company ("the issuing company") is represented by a relevant discounted security issued by that company;

(b) the benefit of that security is available to another company at any time in that period;

(c) for that period there is a connection between the issuing company and the other company; and

(d) credits representing the full amount of the discount that is referable to that period are not for any accounting period brought into account for the purposes of this Chapter in respect of the corresponding creditor relationship.

(2) The debits falling in the case of the issuing company to be brought into account for the purposes of this Chapter in respect of the loan relationship shall be adjusted so that every debit relating to the amount of the discount that is referable to the relevant period is brought into account for the accounting period in which the security is redeemed, instead of for the relevant period.

(3) References in this paragraph to the amount of the discount that is referable to the relevant period are references to the amount relating to the difference between—

(a) the issue price of the security, and

(b) the amount payable on redemption,

which (apart from this paragraph) would for the relevant period be brought into account for the purposes of this Chapter in the case of the issuing company.

(4) In this paragraph "relevant discounted security" has the same meaning as in Schedule 13 to this Act, and the provisions of that Schedule shall apply for the purposes of this paragraph for

determining the difference between the issue price of a security and the amount payable on redemption as they apply for the purposes of paragraph 3(3) of that Schedule.

(5) For the purposes of this paragraph there is a connection between one company and another for the relevant period if (subject to the following provisions of this paragraph)—

(a) there is a time in that period, or in the period of two years before the beginning of that period, when one of the companies has had control of the other; or

(b) there is a time in that period, or in those two years, when both the companies have been under the control of the same person.

(6) Two companies which have at any time been under the control of the same person shall not, by virtue of that fact, be taken for the purposes of this paragraph to be companies between whom there is a connection if the person was the Crown, a Minister of the Crown, a government department, a Northern Ireland department, a foreign sovereign power or an international organisation.

(7) Section 88 of this Act shall apply for the purposes of this paragraph in the case of a debtor relationship of a company represented by a relevant discounted security as it would apply for the purposes of section 87 of this Act in the case of the corresponding creditor relationship of the company holding that security and, accordingly, as if—

(a) the reference to section 87 of this Act in section 88(4)(b) were a reference to this paragraph; and

(b) section 88(5) were omitted.

(8) For the purposes of this paragraph the benefit of a security is available to a company if—

(a) that security, or any entitlement to rights attached to it, is beneficially owned by that company; or

(b) that company is indirectly entitled, by reference to a series of loan transactions, to the benefit of any rights attached to the security.

(9) Subsections (2) to (6) of section 416 of the Taxes Act 1988 (meaning of "control") shall apply for the purposes of this paragraph as they apply for the purposes of Part XI of that Act.

Discounted securities of close companies

18.—(1) This paragraph applies for any accounting period where—

(a) a debtor relationship of a close company is represented by a relevant discounted security issued by the company; and

(b) at any time in or before that period that security has been beneficially owned by a person who at the time was—

(i) a participator in the company;

(ii) an associate of such a participator; or

(iii) a company of which such a participator has control.

(2) The debits falling in the case of the company to be brought into account for the purposes of this Chapter in respect of the loan relationship shall be adjusted so that no amount is brought into account in respect of the difference between—

(a) the issue price of the security, and

(b) the amount payable on redemption,

for any accounting period before that in which the security is redeemed.

(3) In this paragraph "relevant discounted security" has the same meaning as in Schedule 13 to this Act; and the provisions of that Schedule shall apply for the purposes of this paragraph for determining the difference between the issue price of a security and the amount payable on redemption as they apply for the purposes of paragraph 3(3) of that Schedule.

(4) In this paragraph—

"associate" has the meaning given in section 417(3) and (4) of the Taxes Act 1988;

"control" shall be construed in accordance with section 416(2) to (6) of that Act; and

"participator" means a person who, by virtue of section 417 of that Act, is a participator in the company for the purposes of Part XI of that Act, other than a person who is a participator for those purposes by virtue only of his holding a relevant discounted security issued by the company.

(5) In determining whether a person who carries on a business of banking is a participator in a company for the purposes of this paragraph, there shall be disregarded any securities of the company acquired by him in the ordinary course of his business.

GENERAL NOTE

This Schedule provides special computational rules for a variety of non-standard situations.

Para. 1

Dividends are excluded from account.

Para. 2
Debits under the accruals basis of accounting (see s.87) are not allowed if not actually paid within 12 months of accrual.

Para. 3
Where an option exists affecting a loan relationship, the party holding it is to be assumed to exercise the power in the way most favourable to it.

Para. 4
Exchange profits and losses dealt with under the FA 1993, ss.125–168 are excluded.

Para. 5
Bad debts are generally allowable. Where a debt is released as part of a "relevant arrangement or compromise" under the ICTA 1988, s.74(2), the debtor company does not have to bring a credit into account to recognise the release, unless the debt is released by a connected company.

Para. 6
Where the parties are connected (see s.87), the assumption that all amounts owed will be received in full prevails, except where the debt is discharged in consideration of an issue of shares.

Para. 7
The write-off of a Government investment under the ICTA 1988, s.400, does not require a credit to be brought into account.

Para. 8
Additional restrictions are imposed on the amount allowable as a bad debt provision in respect of certain overseas sovereign debt. The paragraph replaces the provisions in the ICTA 1988, ss.88A and 88B, which are repealed.

Para. 9
This paragraph, replacing the ICTA 1988, s.88C, imposes restrictions on losses arising from the disposal of overseas sovereign debt.

Para. 10
This paragraph prevents companies using an authorised accruals basis from obtaining relief on a loss on a loan relationship to the extent that the loss relates to a period when the loan relationship was outside the scope of U.K. tax.

Para. 11
For transactions not at arm's length, a rule applying the terms which would have been entered into between independent persons follows, except where this would be advantageous to the companies concerned.

Para. 12
Where a loan relationship is transferred from one company to another, the usual consequences of the transfer are to be ignored and the transferee is to be treated as standing in the shoes of the transferor. However, credits and debts relating to the loan which have nothing to do with the transfer itself continue to fall to the account of the actual holder of the loan relationship.

Para. 13
This is a general anti-avoidance provision disallowing debits incurred to obtain a tax advantage within the terms of the ICTA 1988, s.709.

Para. 14
Expenditure normally allowed to be capitalised may nevertheless be brought into account for the period in which it is incurred.

Para. 15

Transactions under which the economic ownership of a loan relationship remains with the original owner, such as sales and repurchase arrangements (repo) and stock lending, are not treated as disposals and acquisitions.

Para. 16

Imputed interest under the ICTA 1988, ss.770–773 is brought into account. See s.100 for imputed interest where there was no pre-existing loan relationship.

Para. 17

This paragraph provides for the taxation treatment of discounted securities where the companies which are parties to the loan relationship are connected (within the terms of subpara. (5)). Debits relating to the discount may not be brought into charge until the security is redeemed.

Para. 18

The same rule applies to discounted securities issued by a close company (see the ICTA 1988, s.414 *et seq.*) [Standing Committee E, February 29, 1996, col. 626].

Section 98   SCHEDULE 10

LOAN RELATIONSHIPS: COLLECTIVE INVESTMENT SCHEMES

Investment trusts

1.—(1) This paragraph applies for the purposes of the application of this Chapter in relation to investment trusts and venture capital trusts.

(2) If the Treasury by order approve the use of an accounting method for the creditor relationships of investment trusts or venture capital trusts—

(a) that method, instead of any method for which section 85 of this Act provides, shall be used as respects the creditor relationships of the trusts for which it is approved; and

(b) this Chapter shall have effect (subject to the provisions of the order) as if the accounting method were, for the purposes for which it is approved, an authorised accruals basis of accounting.

(3) Where an approval is given under this paragraph, it must be an approval of one of the following—

(a) the use of an accruals basis of accounting appearing to the Treasury to be recognised by normal accounting practice for use in the case of investment trusts;

(b) the use, with such modifications as may be provided for in the order, of an accruals basis of accounting appearing to them to be so recognised; or

(c) the use, with such modifications as may be so provided for, of an accounting method which, apart from the order, would be an authorised accruals basis of accounting.

(4) An order under this paragraph may provide for any approval of the use (with or without modifications) of a basis of accounting recognised by normal accounting practice to have effect in relation to accounting periods beginning before the time as from which the use of that method is recognised and before the making of the order.

Authorised unit trusts

2.—(1) The provisions of this Chapter so far as they relate to the creditor relationships of a company shall not apply for the purposes of corporation tax in computing the profits or losses of an authorised unit trust.

(2) For the purposes of corporation tax the profits and gains, and losses, that are to be taken to arise from the creditor relationships of an authorised unit trust shall be computed—

(a) in accordance with the provisions applicable, in the case of unauthorised unit trusts, for the purposes of income tax; and

(b) as if the provisions so applicable had effect in relation to an accounting period of an authorised unit trust as they have effect, in the case of unauthorised unit trusts, in relation to a year of assessment.

(3) In relation to the first accounting period of any authorised unit trust to end after 31st March 1996, the reference in sub-paragraph (2)(a) above to the provisions applicable for the purposes of income tax is a reference to the provisions so applicable for the year 1996–97.

(4) In this paragraph "unauthorised unit trust" means the trustees of any unit trust scheme which is not an authorised unit trust but is a unit trust scheme for the purposes of section 469 of the Taxes Act 1988.

Distributing offshore funds

3. For the purposes of paragraph 5(1) of Schedule 27 to the Taxes Act 1988 (computation of UK equivalent profit), the assumptions to be made in determining what, for any period, would be the total profits of an offshore fund are to include an assumption that paragraph 2 above applies in the case of that offshore fund as it applies in the case of any authorised unit trust.

Company holdings in unit trusts and offshore funds

4.—(1) This paragraph applies for the purposes of corporation tax in relation to any company where—

(a) at any time in an accounting period that company holds any of the following ("a relevant holding"), that is to say, any rights under a unit trust scheme or any relevant interests in an offshore fund; and

(b) there is a time in that period when that scheme or fund fails to satisfy the non-qualifying investments test.

   (2) The Corporation Tax Acts shall have effect for that accounting period in accordance with sub-paragraphs (3) and (4) below as if the relevant holding were rights under a creditor relationship of the company.

(3) An accruals basis of accounting shall not be used for the purposes of this Chapter as respects the company's relevant holdings.

(4) The authorised mark to market basis of accounting used for any accounting period as respects a relevant holding shall not be taken, for the purposes of this Chapter, to require the bringing into account of any credit relating to any distributions of an authorised unit trust which become due and payable in that period other than interest distributions within the meaning of section 468L(3) of the Taxes Act 1988.

Holding becoming or ceasing to be paragraph 4 holding

5.—(1) Section 116 of the 1992 Act (reorganisations etc. involving qualifying corporate bonds) shall have effect in accordance with the assumptions for which this paragraph provides if—

(a) a relevant holding is held by a company both at the end of one accounting period and at the beginning of the next; and

(b) paragraph 4 above applies to that holding for one of those periods but not for the other.

   (2) Where—

(a) the accounting period for which paragraph 4 above applies to the relevant holding is the second of the periods mentioned in sub-paragraph (1) above, and

(b) the first of those periods is not a period ending on 31st March 1996 or a period at the end of which there is deemed under section 212 of the 1992 Act to have been a disposal of the relevant holding,

the holding shall be assumed to have become a holding to which paragraph 4 above applies for the second of those periods in consequence of the occurrence, at the end of the first period, of a transaction such as is mentioned in section 116(1) of that Act.

(3) In relation to the transaction that is deemed to have occurred as mentioned in sub-paragraph (2) above—

(a) the relevant holding immediately before the beginning of the second accounting period shall be assumed to be the old asset for the purposes of section 116 of the 1992 Act; and

(b) the relevant holding immediately after the beginning of that period shall be assumed for those purposes to be the new asset.

(4) Where the accounting period for which paragraph 4 above applies to the relevant holding is the first of the periods mentioned in sub-paragraph (1) above, then, for the purposes of the 1992 Act—

(a) the holding shall be assumed to have become a holding to which paragraph 4 above does not apply for the second of those periods in consequence of the occurrence at the beginning of the second of those periods of a transaction such as is mentioned in section 116(1) of that Act;

(b) the relevant holding immediately before the beginning of that second period shall be assumed, in relation to that transaction, to be the old asset for the purposes of section 116 of the 1992 Act; and

(c) the relevant holding immediately after the beginning of that period shall be assumed, in relation to that transaction, to be the new asset for those purposes.

(5) In this paragraph "the 1992 Act" means the Taxation of Chargeable Gains Act 1992.

Opening valuation of paragraph 4 holding

6. Where—
(a) paragraph 5(2) above applies in the case of any relevant holding of a company, and
(b) for the purpose of bringing amounts into account for the purposes of this Chapter on the mark to market basis used for that period in pursuance of paragraph 4 above, an opening valuation of the holding falls to be made as at the beginning of that period,

the value of that asset at the beginning of that period shall be taken for the purpose of the opening valuation to be equal to whatever, in relation to a disposal immediately before the end of the previous accounting period, would have been taken to be the market value of the holding for the purposes of the Taxation of Chargeable Gains Act 1992.

Meaning of offshore funds

7.—(1) For the purposes of paragraph 4 above an interest is a relevant interest in an offshore fund if—
(a) it is a material interest in an offshore fund for the purposes of Chapter V of Part XVII of the Taxes Act 1988; or
(b) it would be such an interest if the assumption mentioned in sub-paragraph (2) below were made.

(2) That assumption is that the unit trust schemes and arrangements referred to in paragraphs (b) and (c) of subsection (1) of section 759 of the Taxes Act 1988 are not limited to those which are also collective investment schemes.

Non-qualifying investments test

8.—(1) For the purposes of paragraph 4 above a unit trust scheme or offshore fund fails to satisfy the non-qualifying investments test at any time when the market value of the qualifying investments exceeds 60 per cent. of the market value of all the investments of the scheme or fund.

(2) Subject to sub-paragraph (8) below, in this paragraph "qualifying investments", in relation to a unit trust scheme or offshore fund, means investments of the scheme or fund which are of any of the following descriptions—
(a) money placed at interest;
(b) securities;
(c) shares in a building society;
(d) qualifying holdings in a unit trust scheme or an offshore fund.

(3) For the purposes of sub-paragraph (2) above a holding in a unit trust scheme or offshore fund is a qualifying holding at any time if—
(a) at that time, or
(b) at any other time in the same accounting period,

that scheme or fund would itself fail (even on the relevant assumption) to satisfy the non-qualifying investments test.

(4) For the purposes of sub-paragraph (3) above the relevant assumption is that investments of the scheme or fund are qualifying investments in relation to that scheme or fund only if they fall within paragraphs (a) to (c) of sub-paragraph (2) above.

(5) References in this paragraph to investments of a unit trust scheme or offshore fund are references, as the case may be—
(a) to investments subject to the trusts of the scheme, or
(b) to assets of the fund,

but in neither case do they include references to cash awaiting investment.

(6) References in this paragraph to a holding—
(a) in relation to a unit trust scheme, are references to an entitlement to a share in the investments of the scheme; and
(b) in relation to an offshore fund, are references to shares in any company by which that fund is constituted or any entitlement to a share in the investments of the fund.

(7) In this paragraph "security" does not include shares in a company.

(8) The Treasury may by order amend this paragraph so as to extend or restrict the descriptions of investments of a unit trust scheme or offshore fund that are qualifying investments for the purposes of this paragraph.

Powers to make orders

9.—(1) An order made by the Treasury under any provision of this Schedule may—
(a) make different provision for different cases; and

(b) contain such incidental, supplemental, consequential and transitional provision as the Treasury may think fit.

(2) Without prejudice to the generality of sub-paragraph (1) above, an order under paragraph 8(8) above may make such incidental modifications of paragraph 8(4) above as the Treasury may think fit.

GENERAL NOTE

Para. 1
The Treasury may adopt by order a modified accounting method to be applied to creditor relationships of investment trusts, displacing the method provided for by s.85. The modified method must follow certain principles, for example a basis set out in an applicable Statement of Recommended Practice ("SORP").

Para. 2
Income from creditor relationships of authorised unit trusts is to be computed on the same basis as for unauthorised unit trusts.

Para. 3
Distributing offshore funds are to be treated in the same way as authorised unit trusts.

Para. 4
Holdings of corporate taxpayers in unit trusts and relevant offshore funds (see para. 7) are treated for tax purposes as if they were loan relationships and brought into account on a mark-to-market basis, where the holdings are invested as to 60 per cent or more in assets which are loan relationships or holdings in further funds themselves invested in loan relationships (see para. 8).

Para. 5
This paragraph deals with the consequences when unit trusts or offshore funds move in or out of the special rules for debt heavy funds.

Para. 6
The valuation of a holding within para. 4 follows that for capital gains purposes.

Para. 9
The Treasury is given power to make provision in its orders for special cases [Standing Committee E, March 5, 1996, col. 673].

Section 99   SCHEDULE 11

LOAN RELATIONSHIPS: SPECIAL PROVISIONS FOR INSURERS

PART I

INSURANCE COMPANIES

I minus E basis

1.—(1) Nothing in this Chapter shall be construed as preventing profits and gains arising from loan relationships of an insurance company from being included, where—
  (a) the relationship is referable to any life assurance business or capital redemption business carried on by the company, and
  (b) that business is business in respect of which the I minus E basis is applied,
in profits and gains on which the company is chargeable to tax in accordance with that basis.

(2) Where, for any accounting period, the I minus E basis is applied in respect of any life assurance business or capital redemption business carried on by an insurance company, the effect of applying that basis shall be—
  (a) that none of the credits or debits falling for the purposes of this Chapter to be brought into account in respect of loan relationships of the company that are referable to that business shall be brought into account as mentioned in section 82(2) of this Act; but
  (b) that (subject to the following provisions of this Schedule) all those credits and debits shall, instead, be brought into account, in applying that basis to that business, as non-trading credits or, as the case may be, non-trading debits;
and the reference in paragraph 2(1) below to non-trading credits and non-trading debits shall be construed accordingly.

Rules for different categories of business

2.—(1) Where an insurance company carries on basic life assurance and general annuity business or capital redemption business or both of them, a separate computation, using only the non-trading credits and non-trading debits referable to the business in question, shall be made for the purposes of this Chapter in relation to that business or, as the case may be, in relation to each of them.

(2) References in any enactment to the computation of any profits of an insurance company in accordance with the provisions of the Taxes Act 1988 applicable to Case I of Schedule D shall have effect as if those provisions included the provisions of this Chapter but, in accordance with sub-paragraph (3) below, only to the extent that they relate to the bringing into account in accordance with section 82(2) of this Act of credits and debits in respect of a company's debtor relationships.

(3) Where an insurance company carries on—

(a) life assurance business or any category of life assurance business, or

(b) capital redemption business,

the credits and debits referable to that business, or category of business, that are given by this Chapter in respect of creditor relationships of the company shall be disregarded for the purposes of any computations falling to be made, in relation to that business or category of business, in accordance with provisions applicable to Case I of Schedule D.

(4) Accordingly (and notwithstanding section 80(5) of this Act), the amounts which are to be brought into account in any computations such as are mentioned in sub-paragraph (3) above shall be determined under the provisions applicable apart from this Chapter.

(5) To the extent that any profits of an insurance company in respect of any business or category of business fall to be computed in accordance with provisions applicable to Case I of Schedule D the credits and debits referable to that business or category of business that fall to be disregarded under sub-paragraph (3) above shall also be disregarded in any computations falling to be made for the purposes of this Chapter otherwise than in accordance with sub-paragraph (1) above.

Apportionments

3. Where—

(a) any creditor relationship of an insurance company is represented by an asset which is an asset of a fund of the company or is linked to any category of insurance business, and

(b) any question arises for the purposes of the Corporation Tax Acts as to the extent to which credits or debits given for the purposes of this Chapter in respect of that relationship are referable to any category of the company's long term business,

section 432A of the Taxes Act 1988 (apportionment of insurance companies' income) shall have effect in relation to the credits and debits so given in respect of that relationship as it has effect in relation to the income arising from an asset.

Treatment of deficit

4.—Where, in the case of any insurance company, a non-trading deficit on its loan relationships is produced for any accounting period ("the deficit period") by any separate computation made under paragraph 2 above for—

(a) basic life assurance and general annuity business, or

(b) capital redemption business,

the following provisions of this paragraph shall apply in relation to that deficit, instead of section 83 of, and Schedule 8 to, this Act.

(2) On a claim made by the company in relation to the whole or any part of the deficit—

(a) the amount to which the claim relates shall be set off against any net income and gains of the deficit period referable to the relevant category of business and arising or accruing otherwise than in respect of loan relationships; and

(b) the amount of the net income and gains against which it is set off shall be treated as reduced accordingly;

and any such reductions shall be made before any deduction by virtue of section 76 of the Taxes Act 1988 of any expenses of management.

(3) Subject to the following provisions of this paragraph, on a claim made by the company in relation to the whole or any part of so much (if any) of the deficit as exceeds the amount of the net income and gains for the deficit period that are referred to in sub-paragraph (2)(a) above, the amount to which the claim relates shall be—

(a) carried back to the three immediately preceding accounting periods; and

(b) in accordance with sub-paragraph (5) below, set against the eligible profits of the company for those periods.

(4) If the whole or any amount of the deficit is not set off under sub-paragraph (2) or (3) above, so much of it as is not set off shall be—

(a) carried forward to the accounting period immediately following the deficit period; and

(b) treated for the purposes of the Corporation Tax Acts (including the following provisions of this paragraph) as an amount to be included in the company's expenses of management for the period following the deficit period.

(5) Subject to sub-paragraph (6) below, where, in pursuance of a claim under sub-paragraph (3) above, any amount falls to be carried back to be set off against the eligible profits of the company for the three accounting periods preceding the deficit period, that amount shall be set off against those profits as follows, that is to say—

(a) the amount shall be applied, up to the limit for the first set-off period in reducing the company's eligible profit for that period;

(b) any remainder of that amount after the limit for the first set-off period is reached shall be applied, up to the limit for the second set-off period in reducing the company's eligible profit for the second set-off period, and

(c) any remainder of that amount after the limit for the second set-off period has been reached shall be applied, up to the limit for the third set-off period, in reducing the company's eligible profit for the third set-off period.

(6) No reduction shall be made in pursuance of any such claim in a company's eligible profit for any accounting period ending before 1st April 1996.

(7) For the purposes of this paragraph the eligible profit of the company for an accounting period is the amount (if any) which, in pursuance of any separate computation made for that period for the relevant category of business, is chargeable to tax for that period under Case III of Schedule D as profits and gains arising from the company's loan relationships.

(8) For the purposes of this paragraph—

(a) the first set-off period is the accounting period immediately preceding the deficit period,

(b) the second set-off period is the accounting period immediately preceding the first set-off period,

(c) the third set-off period is the accounting period immediately preceding the second set-off period, and

(d) the limit for a set-off period is the amount equal to the adjusted amount of the company's eligible profit for that period.

(9) In sub-paragraph (8) above, the reference to the adjusted amount of a company's eligible profit for a set-off period is a reference to so much (if any) of the company's eligible profit for that period as remains after reducing it by an amount equal to the unused part of the relevant deductions for that period.

(10) For the purposes of sub-paragraph (9) above the unused part of the relevant deductions for any set-off period is the amount (if any) by which the aggregate of—

(a) so much of the amount of any deductions for the set-off period by virtue of section 76 of the Taxes Act 1988 as is referable to the relevant category of business, and

(b) so much of the aggregate of the deductions made in the case of the company in respect of charges on income for that period as is so referable,

exceeds the aggregate of the amounts referable to the relevant category of business that could for that period be applied in making deductions by virtue of that section, or in respect of charges on income, if the eligible profit of the company for that period were disregarded.

(11) In sub-paragraph (10) above, the references, in relation to a claim under sub-paragraph (3) above ("the relevant claim"), to deductions by virtue of section 76 of the Taxes Act 1988 for a set-off period are references to the deductions by way of management expenses that would have fallen to be made by virtue of that section for that period if—

(a) no account were taken of either—

    (i) the relevant claim; or

    (ii) any claim under sub-paragraph (3) above relating to a deficit for an accounting period after the deficit period;

but

(b) there were made all such adjustments required by virtue of any sum having been carried back to that set-off period—

    (i) under the Corporation Tax Acts, but

    (ii) otherwise than in pursuance of the relevant claim or of any other such claim as is mentioned in paragraph (a) above.

(12) Where—

(a) in pursuance of a claim under sub-paragraph (3) above any amount is set-off against the eligible profit of a company for any set-off period, and

(b) there is a section 76(5) amount for that period which is attributable to that claim,

that section 76(5) amount shall not be carried forward by virtue of section 75(3) of the Taxes Act 1988 but, if that set-off period is the first or second set-off period sub-paragraph (13) below shall apply to that amount instead.

(13) Where this sub-paragraph applies to a section 76(5) amount for any set-off period, the amount available in accordance with sub-paragraph (5) above to be carried back from that set-off period to be set off against eligible profits of previous set-off periods (or, as the case may be, against the eligible profit of the previous set-off period) shall be treated as increased by an amount equal to the amount to which this sub-paragraph applies.

(14) In relation to any claim under sub-paragraph (3) above, the amount which for any set-off period is, for the purposes of this paragraph, to be taken to be the section 76(5) amount attributable to that claim is the amount (if any) by which the amount specified in paragraph (a) below is exceeded by the amount specified in paragraph (b) below, that is to say—

(a) the amount that would have fallen to be carried forward by virtue of section 75(3) of the Taxes Act 1988 if the claim had not been made; and

(b) the amount which, after the making of the claim, would have fallen to be carried forward to a subsequent period by virtue of section 75(3) of that Act if sub-paragraphs (12) and (13) above, so far as they relate to that claim, were to be disregarded.

(15) A claim for the purposes of sub-paragraph (2) or (3) above must be made within the period of two years immediately following the end of the deficit period or within such further period as the Board may allow.

(16) In this paragraph—

"net income and gains" has the meaning given by subsection (1) of section 76 of the Taxes Act 1988; and

"the relevant category of business", in relation to a deficit, means the category of business in relation to which the deficit was produced.

Election for accruals basis for long term business assets

5.—(1) Subject to sub-paragraphs (3) to (6) below, sub-paragraph (2) below applies for any accounting period to so much of any creditor relationship of an insurance company as—

(a) for the whole or any part of that period is an asset within one of the categories set out in section 440(4)(d) and (e) of the Taxes Act 1988 (assets held for certain categories of long term business); and

(b) is an asset in relation to which an election under this paragraph is made by the company for that period.

(2) Where—

(a) this sub-paragraph applies for any accounting period to any asset, and

(b) apart from this paragraph, a mark to market basis of accounting would have had to be used for the purposes of this Chapter as respects that asset for the whole or any part of that period,

this Chapter shall have effect as if an authorised accruals basis of accounting had to be used for the purposes of this Chapter as respects that asset for that period or part.

(3) Sub-paragraph (2) above shall not apply to any holding to which paragraph 4(3) of Schedule 10 to this Act applies.

(4) An election under this paragraph shall not be made except by notice in writing given to an officer of the Board not more than three months after the end of the accounting period to which the election relates.

(5) An election under this paragraph shall be irrevocable, and shall not be varied, once it has been made.

(6) An election shall not be made under this paragraph for any accounting period ending after 31st March 1998.

(7) The Treasury may, if they think fit, by order—

(a) amend sub-paragraph (6) above to substitute a later date for the date for the time being specified in that sub-paragraph; or

(b) repeal that sub-paragraph.

Interpretation of Part I

6. In this Part of this Schedule—

"basic life assurance and general annuity business" and "long term business" have the same meanings as in Chapter I of Part XII of the Taxes Act 1988;

"capital redemption business" means any capital redemption business, within the meaning of section 458 of that Act, which is business to which that section applies;

"the I minus E basis" means the basis commonly so called (under which a company carrying on life assurance business or capital redemption business is charged to tax on that business otherwise than under Case I of Schedule D);

"life assurance business" includes any annuity business within the meaning of Chapter I of Part XII of that Act.

PART II

CORPORATE MEMBERS OF LLOYD'S

7.—(1) This Chapter does not apply as respects any loan relationship of a corporate member of Lloyd's in so far as rights or liabilities making up that relationship, or any securities representing them, are—

(a) assets forming part of that member's premiums trust fund; or

(b) liabilities attached to that fund.

(2) Section 230 of the Finance Act 1994 (interpretation of provisions applying to corporate members of Lloyd's) shall apply for the purposes of this paragraph as it applies for the purposes of Chapter V of Part IV of that Act.

GENERAL NOTE

The Schedule adapts the provisions regarding loan relationships to cater for the special circumstances of insurance companies.

Para. 1

This provides special rules where the profits of a company carrying on life assurance business are charged on the I minus E basis (see para. 6). Where this does apply, the relevant credits or debits are brought into account as non-trading credits or debits even though carrying on life assurance business is strictly the carrying on of a trade.

Para. 2

In any tax computation for BLAGAB or capital redemption business only those credits and debits specific to the business in question are to be taken into account for Case III. Also, where the profits of a life assurance business are computed under Case I and separate computations of profit from pension business, overseas life assurance business and life reinsurance business are made, the loan relationships provisions are disregarded and normal Case I rules apply, including the special rules in the FA 1989, s.83.

Para. 3

The normal apportionment rules in the ICTA 1988, s.432A, apply.

Para. 4

This sets out the method by which any deficits arising on BLAGAB or capital redemption business are to be relieved. A carry-back for three years is available.

Para. 5

A life assurance company may elect for the accruals basis rather than the mark-to-market basis to apply for its long-term business assets.

Para. 7

The loan relationship provisions do not apply to corporate members of Lloyd's in relation to assets which are part of the members' Premium Trust Fund or are liabilities attached to that fund [Standing Committee E, March 5, 1996, col. 679].

Section 101   SCHEDULE 12

MEANING OF DEBT CONTRACT OR OPTION

The section inserted after section 150 of the Finance Act 1994 by section 101(3) of this Act is as follows—

"Debt contracts and options

150A.—(1) A contract is a debt contract for the purposes of this Chapter if, not being an interest rate contract or option or a currency contract or option—

(a) it is a contract under which, whether unconditionally or subject to conditions being fulfilled, a qualifying company has any entitlement, or is subject to any duty, to become a party to a loan relationship; and

(b) the only transfers of money or money's worth for which the contract provides (apart from those that will be made under the loan relationship) are payments falling within subsection (5) below and payments falling within section 151 below.

(2) A contract is also a debt contract for the purposes of this Chapter if, not being a debt contract by virtue of subsection (1) above or an interest rate contract or option or a currency contract or option—

(a) it is a contract under which, whether unconditionally or subject to conditions being fulfilled, a qualifying company has any entitlement, or is subject to any duty, to become treated as a person with rights and liabilities corresponding to those of a party to a loan relationship; and

(b) the only transfers of money or money's worth for which the contract provides are payments falling within subsection (6) below and payments falling within section 151 below.

(3) In this section references to an entitlement to become a party to a loan relationship, or to a duty to become such a party, shall be taken to include references, in relation to a specified loan relationship, to either of the following, namely—

(a) an entitlement or, as the case may be, a duty to become a party to an equivalent relationship; and

(b) an entitlement or, as the case may be, a duty relating to the making of any one or more such payments as fall within subsection (5) below.

(4) Subsection (3) above shall apply in relation to references in this section to an entitlement or a duty to become treated as a person with rights and liabilities corresponding to those of a party to a loan relationship as it applies to references to an entitlement or, as the case may be, a duty to become such a party.

(5) The payments falling within this subsection are—

(a) a payment of an amount representing the price for becoming a party to the relationship;

(b) a payment of an amount determined by reference to the value at any time of the money debt by reference to which the relationship subsists;

(c) a settlement payment of an amount determined by reference to the difference at specified times between—

(i) the price for becoming a party to the relationship; and

(ii) the value of the money debt by reference to which the relationship subsists, or (if the relationship were in existence) would subsist.

(6) A payment falls within this subsection if it is a settlement payment of an amount determined by reference to the difference at specified times between—

(a) the price for becoming treated as a person with rights and liabilities corresponding to those of a party to a relationship; and

(b) the value of the money debt by reference to which the relationship subsists or (if the relationship existed) would subsist.

(7) Each of the following, namely—

(a) an option to enter into a contract which would be a debt contract, and

(b) an option to enter into such an option,

is a debt option for the purposes of this Chapter if the only transfers of money or money's worth for which the option provides are payments falling within section 151 below.

(8) For the purposes of this Chapter where any contract contains both—

(a) provisions under which, whether unconditionally or subject to conditions being fulfilled, a qualifying company has any entitlement, or is subject to any duty, to become a party to a loan relationship, and

(b) any provisions that have effect otherwise than for the purposes of or in relation to the provisions conferring that entitlement or imposing that duty,

the provisions mentioned in paragraph (a) above, together with the other contents of that contract so far as they are attributable on a just and reasonable basis to the provisions mentioned in that paragraph, shall be treated as a separate contract.

(9) For the purposes of this Chapter where—

(a) any attribution of the contents of a contract falls to be made between provisions falling within paragraph (a) of subsection (8) above and provisions falling within paragraph (b) of that subsection, and

(b) that contract provides for the making of any payment constituting a transfer of money or money's worth which cannot be attributed to the provisions falling within only one of those paragraphs,

that payment shall be treated as apportioned between the provisions falling within each of those paragraphs in such manner as may be just and reasonable.

(10) Expressions used in this section and in Chapter II of Part IV of the Finance Act 1996 have the same meanings in this section as in that Chapter; but references in this section to a loan relationship do not include—

(a) any loan relationship represented by an asset to which section 92 of that Act (convertible securities) applies; or

(b) any loan relationship to which section 93 of that Act (securities indexed to chargeable assets) applies.

(11) For the purposes of this section and, so far as it relates to a debt contract or option, of section 151 below the transfer of money's worth having a value of any amount shall be treated as the payment of that amount."

GENERAL NOTE

This Schedule inserts a new FA 1994, s.150A, which provides a definition of debt contracts and options for the purposes of the rules relating to financial instruments in the FA 1994, Part IV, Chapter II. Debt contracts are contracts under which a company has a right or duty to enter into a loan relationship or an equivalent relationship and debt options are options to enter into a debt contract.

The contract must not provide for any payment, apart from those made under the loan relationship, other than those covered in s.150A(5) and (6) and s.151.

Section 102   SCHEDULE 13

DISCOUNTED SECURITIES: INCOME TAX PROVISIONS

Charge to tax on realised profit comprised in discount

1.—(1) Where a person realises the profit from the discount on a relevant discounted security, he shall be charged to income tax on that profit under Case III of Schedule D or, where the profit arises from a security out of the United Kingdom, under Case IV of that Schedule.

(2) For the purposes of this Schedule a person realises the profit from the discount on a relevant discounted security where—

(a) he transfers such a security or becomes entitled, as the person holding the security, to any payment on its redemption; and

(b) the amount payable on the transfer or redemption exceeds the amount paid by that person in respect of his acquisition of the security.

(3) For the purposes of this Schedule the profit shall be taken—

(a) to be equal to the amount of the excess reduced by the amount of any relevant costs; and

(b) to arise, for the purposes of income tax, in the year of assessment in which the transfer or redemption takes place.

(4) In this paragraph "relevant costs", in relation to a security that is transferred or redeemed, are all the following costs—

(a) the costs incurred in connection with the acquisition of the security by the person making the transfer or, as the case may be, the person entitled to a payment on the redemption; and

(b) the costs incurred by that person in connection with the transfer or redemption of the security;

and for the purposes of this Schedule costs falling within paragraph (a) above shall not be regarded as amounts paid in respect of the acquisition of a security.

Realised losses on discounted securities

2.—(1) Subject to the following provisions of this Schedule, where—

(a) a person sustains a loss in any year of assessment from the discount on a relevant discounted security, and

(b) makes a claim for the purposes of this paragraph before the end of twelve months from the 31st January next following that year of assessment,

that person shall be entitled to relief from income tax on an amount of the claimant's income for that year equal to the amount of the loss.

(2) For the purposes of this Schedule a person sustains a loss from the discount on a relevant discounted security where—

(a) he transfers such a security or becomes entitled, as the person holding the security, to any payment on its redemption; and

(b) the amount paid by that person in respect of his acquisition of the security exceeds the amount payable on the transfer or redemption.

(3) For the purposes of this Schedule the loss shall be taken—

(a) to be equal to the amount of the excess increased by the amount of any relevant costs; and

(b) to be sustained for the purposes of this Schedule in the year of assessment in which the transfer or redemption takes place.

(4) Sub-paragraph (4) of paragraph 1 above applies for the purposes of this paragraph as it applies for the purposes of that paragraph.

Meaning of "relevant discounted security"

3.—(1) Subject to sub-paragraph (2) and paragraph 14(1) below, in this Schedule "relevant discounted security" means any security which (whenever issued) is such that—

(a) taking the security as at the time of its issue, and

(b) assuming redemption in accordance with its terms,

the amount payable on redemption is an amount involving a deep gain or might be an amount which would involve such a gain.

(2) The following are not relevant discounted securities for the purposes of this Schedule—

(a) shares in a company;

(b) gilt-edged securities that are not strips;

(c) excluded indexed securities;

(d) life assurance policies;

(e) capital redemption policies (within the meaning of Chapter II of Part XIII of the Taxes Act 1988); and

(f) subject to paragraph 10 below, securities issued (at whatever time) under the same prospectus as other securities which have been issued previously but (disregarding that paragraph) are not themselves relevant discounted securities.

(3) For the purposes of this Schedule the amount payable on redemption of a security involves a deep gain if—

(a) the issue price is less than the amount so payable; and

(b) the amount by which it is less represents more than the relevant percentage of the amount so payable.

(4) In this paragraph "the relevant percentage", in relation to the amount payable on redemption of a security, means—

(a) the percentage figure equal, in a case where the period between the date of issue and the date of redemption is less than thirty years, to one half of the number of years between those dates; and

(b) in any other case, 15 per cent.;

and for the purposes of this paragraph the fraction of a year to be used for the purposes of paragraph (a) above in a case where the period mentioned in that paragraph is not a number of complete years shall be calculated by treating each complete month, and any remaining part of a month, in that period as one twelfth of a year.

(5) References in this paragraph to redemption—

(a) do not include references to any redemption which may be made before maturity otherwise than at the option of the holder of the security; but

(b) in the case of a security that is capable of redemption at the option of the holder before maturity, shall have effect as references to the earliest occasion on which the holder of the security may require the security to be redeemed.

(6) For the purposes of this paragraph the amount payable on redemption shall not be taken to include any amount payable on that occasion by way of interest.

Meaning of "transfer"

4.—(1) Subject to sub-paragraph (2) below, in this Schedule references to a transfer, in relation to a security, are references to any transfer of the security by way of sale, exchange, gift or otherwise.

(2) Where an individual who is entitled to a relevant discounted security dies, then for the purposes of this Schedule—

(a) he shall be treated as making a transfer of the security immediately before his death;

(b) he shall be treated as obtaining in respect of the transfer an amount equal to the market value of the security at the time of the transfer; and

(c) his personal representatives shall be treated as acquiring the security for that amount on his death.

(3) For the purposes of this Schedule a transfer or acquisition of a security made in pursuance of an agreement shall be deemed to take place at the time when the agreement is made, if the person to whom the transfer is made, or who makes the acquisition, becomes entitled to the security at that time.

(4) If an agreement is conditional, whether on the exercise of an option or otherwise, it shall be taken for the purposes of this paragraph to be made when the condition is satisfied (whether by the exercise of the option or otherwise).

(5) This paragraph is without prejudice to paragraph 14(2) to (4) below.

Redemption to include conversion

5.—(1) This paragraph applies where a relevant discounted security is extinguished by being converted, in pursuance of rights conferred by the security, into shares in a company or into any other securities (including other relevant discounted securities).

(2) For the purposes of this Schedule the conversion shall be deemed—

(a) to constitute the redemption of the security which is extinguished; and

(b) to involve a payment on redemption of an amount equal to whatever, at the time of the conversion, is the market value of the shares or other securities into which the security in question is converted.

(3) This paragraph does not apply to an exchange to which paragraph 14 below applies.

Trustees and personal representatives

6.—(1) Where, on a transfer or redemption of a security by trustees, an amount is treated as income chargeable to tax by virtue of this Schedule—

(a) that amount shall be taken for the purposes of Chapters IA and IB of Part XV of the Taxes Act 1988 (settlements: liability of settlor etc.) to be income arising—
  (i) under the settlement of which the trustees are trustees; and
  (ii) from that security;

(b) that amount shall be taken for the purposes of Chapter IC of Part XV of that Act (settlements: liability of trustees) to be income arising to the trustees; and

(c) to the extent that tax on that amount is charged on the trustees, the rate at which it is chargeable shall be taken (where it would not otherwise be the case) to be the rate applicable to trusts for the year of assessment in which the transfer or redemption is made.

(2) Where the trustees are trustees of a scheme to which section 469 of the Taxes Act 1988 (unauthorised unit trusts) applies, sub-paragraph (1) above shall not apply if or to the extent that the amount is treated as income in the accounts of the scheme.

(3) Without prejudice to paragraph 12 below, paragraphs 1(1) and 2(1) above do not apply in the case of—

(a) any transfer of a security for the time being held under a settlement the trustees of which are not resident in the United Kingdom; or

(b) any redemption of a security which is so held immediately before its redemption.

(4) Relief shall not be given to trustees under paragraph 2 above except from income tax on income chargeable under paragraph 1 above.

(5) Sub-paragraph (6) below applies where, in the case of any trustees, the amount mentioned in paragraph (a) below exceeds in any year of assessment the amount mentioned in paragraph (b) below, that is to say—

(a) the aggregate amount of the losses in respect of which relief from income tax may be given to the trustees for that year under paragraph 2 above (including any amount treated as such a loss by virtue of that sub-paragraph); and

(b) the income of those trustees chargeable for that year to tax under paragraph 1 above.

(6) Subject to paragraph 7(2) below, the excess shall for the purposes of this Schedule be—

(a) carried forward to the immediately following year of assessment; and

(b) in relation to the year to which it is carried forward, treated as if it were a loss sustained in that year by the trustees from a discount on a relevant discounted security.

(7) Where a relevant discounted security is transferred by personal representatives to a legatee, they shall be treated for the purposes of this Schedule as obtaining in respect of the transfer an amount equal to the market value of the security at the time of the transfer.

(8) In this paragraph "legatee" includes any person taking (whether beneficially or as trustee) under a testamentary disposition or on an intestacy or partial intestacy, including any person taking by virtue of an appropriation by the personal representatives in or towards satisfaction of a legacy or other interest or share in the deceased's property.

Treatment of losses where income exempt

7.—(1) Where—
(a) on the transfer or redemption of any relevant discounted security, a loss is sustained from the discount on that security, and
(b) if the person sustaining that loss had realised a profit from that discount on that transfer or redemption, the profit would have been an exempt profit for the year of assessment in which the loss is sustained,
relief shall not be given to that person under paragraph 2 above in respect of that loss except from income tax on income chargeable for that year under paragraph 1 above.

(2) No part of any loss to which sub-paragraph (1) above applies shall be carried forward under paragraph 6(6) above.

(3) The reference in sub-paragraph (1) above to an exempt profit for a year of assessment is a reference to any income for that year which—
(a) is eligible for relief from tax by virtue of section 505(1) of the Taxes Act 1988, or would be so eligible but for section 505(3) of that Act (charities); or
(b) is eligible for relief from tax by virtue of section 592(2), 608(2)(a), 613(4), 614(2), (3), (4) or (5), 620(6) or 643(2) of that Act (pension scheme funds etc.).

(4) Where a loss to which sub-paragraph (1) above applies is sustained in a case in which the profit mentioned in paragraph (b) of that sub-paragraph would be eligible for relief under section 592(2) of the Taxes Act 1988—
(a) relief shall be given under paragraph 2 above in accordance with sub-paragraph (1) above before any computation is made under paragraph 7 of Schedule 22 to that Act, and
(b) that paragraph 7 shall have effect, accordingly, so that the amount of income to which the specified percentage is applied by virtue of sub-paragraph (3)(a) of that paragraph is reduced by the amount of the relief.

Transfers between connected persons

8.—(1) This paragraph applies where a relevant discounted security is transferred from one person to another and they are connected with each other.

(2) For the purposes of this Schedule—
(a) the person making the transfer shall be treated as obtaining in respect of it an amount equal to the market value of the security at the time of the transfer; and
(b) the person to whom the transfer is made shall be treated as paying in respect of his acquisition of the security an amount equal to that market value.

(3) Section 839 of the Taxes Act 1988 (connected persons) shall apply for the purposes of this paragraph.

Other transactions deemed to be at market value

9.—(1) This paragraph applies where a relevant discounted security is transferred from one person to another in a case in which—
(a) the transfer is made for a consideration which consists of or includes consideration not in money or money's worth; or
(b) the transfer is made otherwise than by way of a bargain made at arm's length.

(2) For the purposes of this Schedule—
(a) the person making the transfer shall be treated as obtaining in respect of it an amount equal to the market value of the security at the time of the transfer, and
(b) the person to whom the transfer is made shall be treated as paying in respect of his acquisition of the security an amount equal to that market value.

Issue of securities in separate tranches

10.—(1) In a case where—
(a) none of the securities issued on the occasion of the original issue of securities under a particular prospectus would be a relevant discounted security apart from this paragraph,
(b) some of the securities subsequently issued under the prospectus would be relevant discounted securities apart from paragraph 3(2)(f) above, and
(c) there is a time (whether before, at or after the beginning of the year 1996–97) when the aggregate nominal value as at that time of the securities falling within paragraph (b) above exceeds the aggregate nominal value as at that time of the securities which have been issued under the prospectus and do not fall within that paragraph,

sub-paragraph (2) below shall apply in relation to every security which has been or is issued under the prospectus at any time (whether before, at or after the time mentioned in paragraph (c) above).

(2) As regards any event occurring in relation to the security after the time mentioned in sub-paragraph (1)(c) above, this Schedule shall have effect as if the security—

(a) were a relevant discounted security; and

(b) had been acquired as such (whatever the time of its acquisition).

(3) For the purposes of sub-paragraph (2) above events, in relation to a security, include anything constituting a transfer, redemption or acquisition for the purposes of this Schedule.

Accrued income scheme

11. In a case where—

(a) paragraph 1 or 2 above applies on the transfer of any security, and

(b) apart from this paragraph, the transfer would be a transfer for the purposes of sections 710 to 728 of the Taxes Act 1988,

the transfer shall be treated as if it were not a transfer for those purposes.

Assets transferred abroad

12. For the purposes of sections 739 and 740 of the Taxes Act 1988 (prevention of avoidance of tax by transfer of assets abroad), where a person resident or domiciled outside the United Kingdom realises a profit from the discount on a relevant discounted security, that profit shall be taken to be income of that person.

Excluded indexed securities

13.—(1) For the purposes of this Schedule a security is an excluded indexed security if the amount payable on redemption is linked to the value of chargeable assets.

(2) For the purposes of this paragraph an amount is linked to the value of chargeable assets if, in pursuance of any provision having effect for the purposes of the security, it is equal to an amount determined by applying a relevant percentage change in the value of chargeable assets to the amount for which the security was issued.

(3) In sub-paragraph (2) above the reference to a relevant percentage change in the value of chargeable assets is a reference to the amount of the percentage change (if any) over the relevant period in the value of chargeable assets of any particular description or in any index of the value of any such assets.

(4) In sub-paragraph (3) above "the relevant period" means—

(a) the period between the time of the issue of the security and its redemption; or

(b) any other period in which almost all of that period is comprised and which differs from that period exclusively for purposes connected with giving effect to a valuation in relation to rights or liabilities under the security.

(5) If—

(a) there is a provision which, in the case of the amount payable on the redemption of any security,.falls within sub-paragraph (2) above,

(b) that provision is made subject to any other provision applying to the determination of that amount,

(c) that other provision is to the effect only that that amount must not be less than a specified percentage of the amount for which the security is issued, and

(d) the specified percentage is not more than 10 per cent.,

that other provision shall be disregarded in determining for the purposes of this paragraph whether the amount payable on redemption is linked to the value of chargeable assets.

(6) For the purposes of this paragraph an asset is a chargeable asset in relation to any security if any gain accruing to a person on a disposal of that asset would, on the assumptions specified in sub-paragraph (7) below, be a chargeable gain for the purposes of the Taxation of Chargeable Gains Act 1992.

(7) Those assumptions are—

(a) where it is not otherwise the case, that the asset is an asset of the person in question and that that person does not have the benefit of any exemption conferred by section 100 of that Act of 1992 (exemption for authorised unit trusts etc.);

(b) that the asset is not one the disposal of which by that person would fall to be treated for the purposes of income tax as a disposal in the course of a trade, profession or vocation carried on by that person; and

(c) that chargeable gains that might accrue under section 116(10) of that Act are to be disregarded.

(8) For the purposes of this paragraph neither—

  (a) the retail prices index, nor

  (b) any similar general index of prices published by the government of any territory or by the agent of any such government,

shall be taken to be an index of the value of chargeable assets.

Gilt strips

14.—(1) Every strip is a relevant discounted security for the purposes of this Schedule.

(2) For the purposes of this Schedule, where a person exchanges a gilt-edged security for strips of that security, the person who receives the strips in the exchange shall be deemed to have paid, in respect of his acquisition of each strip, the amount which bears the same proportion to the market value of the security as is borne by the market value of the strip to the aggregate of the market values of all the strips received in exchange for the security.

(3) For the purposes of this Schedule, where strips are consolidated into a single gilt-edged security by being exchanged by any person for that security, each of the strips shall be deemed to have been redeemed at the time of the exchange by the payment to that person of the amount equal to its market value.

(4) A person who holds a strip on the 5th April in any year of assessment, and who (apart from this sub-paragraph) does not transfer or redeem it on that day, shall be deemed for the purposes of this Schedule—

  (a) to have transferred that strip on that day;

  (b) to have received in respect of that transfer an amount equal to the strip's market value on that day; and

  (c) to have re-acquired the strip on the next day on payment of an amount equal to the amount for which it is deemed to have been disposed of on the previous day;

and the deemed transfer and re-acquisition shall be assumed for the purposes of paragraphs 1 and 2 above to be transactions in connection with which no relevant costs are incurred.

(5) Without prejudice to the generality of any power conferred by section 202 of this Act, the Treasury may by regulations provide that this Schedule is to have effect with such modifications as they may think fit in relation to any relevant discounted security which is a strip.

(6) Regulations made by the Treasury under this paragraph may—

  (a) make provision for the purposes of sub-paragraphs (2) to (4) above as to the manner of determining the market value at any time of any security;

  (b) make different provision for different cases; and

  (c) contain such incidental, supplemental, consequential and transitional provision as the Treasury may think fit.

(7) References in sub-paragraphs (2) and (3) above to the market value of a security given or received in exchange for another are references to its market value at the time of the exchange.

General interpretation

15.—(1) In this Schedule—

   "deep gain" shall be construed in accordance with paragraph 3(3) above;

   "excluded indexed security" has the meaning given by paragraph 13 above;

   "market value" (except in paragraph 14 above) has the same meaning as in the Taxation of Chargeable Gains Act 1992;

   "relevant discounted security" has the meaning given by paragraphs 3 and 14(1) above;

   "strip" means anything which, within the meaning of section 47 of the Finance Act 1942, is a strip of a gilt-edged security.

(2) Where a person, having acquired and transferred any security, subsequently re-acquires it, references in this Schedule to his acquisition of the security shall have effect, in relation to—

  (a) the transfer by him of that security, or

  (b) the redemption of the security in a case where he becomes entitled to any amount on its redemption,

as references to his most recent acquisition of the security before the transfer or redemption in question.

Application of Schedule for income tax purposes only

16.—(1) This Schedule does not apply for the purposes of corporation tax.

(2) Sub-paragraph (1) above is without prejudice to any enactment not contained in this Schedule by virtue of which the definition of a relevant discounted security, or any other provision of this Schedule, is applied for the purposes of corporation tax.

GENERAL NOTE

The Schedule makes provision for the taxation of securities issued at a discount and held by individuals.

Para. 1

Profits made on such securities are taxed under Case III or Case IV of Sched. D, as appropriate.

Para. 2

Losses can be set off against other income on a claim being made within 12 months.

Para. 3

The securities covered by this Schedule are defined. The definition, previously in the FA 1989, Sched. 11, comprises "deep gain" securities, subject to the exceptions listed. It applies when the discount is more than 0.5 per cent for each year of the bond's life or is more than 15 per cent of the amount payable on redemption.

Para. 4

The charge applies to transfers by way of sale, gift or exchange. The normal uplift to market value on death applies.

Para. 5

Conversion of a security is treated as redemption.

Para. 6

This deals with the position of trustees and personal representatives, applying relevant provisions of the ICTA 1988.

Para. 7

Where the income is exempt because it arises to a charity or a pension fund, losses may only be set off against profits of the same type in that year.

Para. 8

Transfers between connected persons are deemed to be made at market value.

Para. 9

The market value assumption also applies where the consideration is not all money or money's worth or the transfer is not an arm's length transaction.

Para. 10

Where further tranches are issued of a security which was not originally deep gain, they will all be treated as deep gain if they are predominantly so.

Paras. 11 and 12

The accrued income scheme does not apply but the anti-avoidance provisions of the ICTA 1988, ss.739 and 740 do.

Para. 13

Certain indexed securities are excluded from the Schedule. The securities concerned are those whose value on redemption is linked to the value of chargeable assets.

Para. 14

Strips of gilt-edged securities are brought within the Schedule. For gilt strips generally see s.202.

Section 104   SCHEDULE 14

LOAN RELATIONSHIPS: MINOR AND CONSEQUENTIAL AMENDMENTS

The Taxes Management Act 1970 (c. 9)

1.—(1) In subsection (4A) of section 87A of the Taxes Management Act 1970 (interest on overdue corporation tax)—

(a) in paragraph (a), for the words from "a relievable amount" to the end of the paragraph there shall be substituted "a non-trading deficit on the company's loan relationships,"; and

(b) in paragraph (b), for the words from "subsection (5)" to "subsection (10) of that section)" there shall be substituted "section 83(2)(c) of the Finance Act 1996 or paragraph 4(3) of Schedule 11 to that Act the whole or part of the deficit for the later period is set off against profits".

(2) In subsection (4B) of that section, for the words "section 131(5) or (6) of the Finance Act 1993", in each place where they occur, there shall be substituted "section 83(2)(c) of the Finance Act 1996 or paragraph 4(3) of Schedule 11 to that Act".

The Inheritance Tax Act 1984 (c. 51)

2.—(1) In section 174(1)(b) of the Inheritance Tax Act 1984 (unpaid tax relating to deep discount securities deemed to be transferred on death), for the words from "paragraph 4" onwards there shall be substituted "Schedule 13 to the Finance Act 1996 (discounted securities) on a transfer which is treated as taking place by virtue of paragraph 4(2) of that Schedule."

(2) This paragraph applies in relation to deaths on or after 6th April 1996.

The Airports Act 1986 (c. 31)

3. In section 77 of the Airports Act 1986 (taxation provisions), for subsection (3) there shall be substituted the following subsection—

"(3) For the purposes of Part VI of the Income and Corporation Taxes Act 1988 (company distributions) and Chapter II of Part IV of the Finance Act 1996 (loan relationships), any debentures of the company issued in pursuance of section 4 shall be treated as having been issued for new consideration equal to the principal sum payable under the debenture."

The Gas Act 1986 (c. 44)

4. In section 60 of the Gas Act 1986 (taxation provisions), for subsection (3) there shall be substituted the following subsection—

"(3) For the purposes of Part VI of the Income and Corporation Taxes Act 1988 (company distributions) and Chapter 11 of Part IV of the Finance Act 1996 (loan relationships), any debentures issued in pursuance of section 51 above shall be treated as having been issued for new consideration equal to the principal sum payable under the debenture."

The Taxes Act 1988

5. In section 18 of the Taxes Act 1988 (Schedule D), the following subsection shall be inserted after subsection (3)—

"(3A) For the purposes of corporation tax subsection (3) above shall have effect as if the following Case were substituted for Cases III and IV, that is to say—
'Case III:
tax in respect of—

    (a) profits and gains which, as profits and gains arising from loan relationships, are to be treated as chargeable under this Case by virtue of Chapter II of Part IV of the Finance Act 1996;

    (b) any annuity or other annual payment which—

        (i) is payable (whether inside or outside the United Kingdom and whether annually or at shorter or longer intervals) in respect of anything other than a loan relationship; and

        (ii) is not a payment chargeable under Schedule A;

    (c) any discount arising otherwise than in respect of a loan relationship;'

and as if Case V did not include tax in respect of any income falling within paragraph (a) of the substituted Case III."

6. In section 56 of that Act (transactions in deposits with or without certificates or in debts), after subsection (4) there shall be inserted the following subsections—

"(4A) This section and section 56A shall not apply for the purposes of corporation tax except in relation to rights in existence before 1st April 1996.

(4B) For the purposes of corporation tax, where any profits or gains arising from the disposal or exercise of a right in existence before 1st April 1996 are, or (if there were any) would be, chargeable under this section nothing in Chapter II of Part IV of the Finance Act 1996 (loan relationships) shall require any amount relating to that disposal, or to the exercise of that right, to be brought into account for the purposes of that Chapter."

7. In section 70(3) of that Act (extension of Cases IV and V of Schedule D to non-resident companies), for "Cases IV and V" there shall be substituted "Cases III and V".

8. In section 75 of that Act (expenses of management), after subsection (1) there shall be inserted the following subsection—

"(1A) The expenses of management of a company shall not include any expenses in relation to which a debit falls to be brought into account for the purposes of Chapter II of Part IV of the Finance Act 1996 (loan relationships) in computing the amount from which sums disbursed as expenses of management are deductible."

9. In section 77 of that Act (incidental costs of obtaining loan finance), after subsection (7) there shall be inserted the following subsection—

"(8) This section shall not apply for the purposes of corporation tax."

10.—(1) Section 78 of that Act (discounted bills of exchange) shall cease to have effect except in relation to bills of exchange drawn before 1st April 1996.

(2) Where any bill so drawn is paid on or after 1st April 1996—

(a) the amount which subsection (2) of that section provides to be treated as a deduction against total profits and as a charge on income shall (instead of being so treated) be brought into account for the purposes of this Chapter as a non-trading debit; and

(b) that amount shall be the only amount brought into account for the purposes of this Chapter in respect of the discount in question.

11.—(1) In section 209 of that Act (meaning of "distribution"), after subsection (3) there shall be inserted the following subsection—

"(3A) Where any security of a company is issued at a premium representing new consideration—

(a) the references in subsection (2)(d), (da) and (e) above to so much of any distribution as represents, or is an amount representing, the principal secured by a security shall be construed, in relation to a distribution in respect of the security issued at a premium, as references to the aggregate of—

(i) so much of the distribution as represents, or is an amount representing, that principal, and

(ii) so much of it as represents, or is an amount representing, the premium; and

(b) the reference in subsection (2)(d) above to so much of any distribution as represents a reasonable commercial return for the use of the principal secured by a security shall be construed, in relation to a distribution in respect of the security issued at a premium, as a reference to the aggregate of—

(i) so much of the distribution as represents a reasonable commercial return for the use of that principal, and

(ii) so much of it as (when regard is had to the extent to which distributions represent the premium) represents a reasonable commercial return for the use of the premium."

(2) Sub-paragraph (1) above does not apply to distributions made before 1st April 1996.

12.—(1) In subsection (2) of section 242 of that Act (set off of losses against surplus franked investment income), for paragraph (f) there shall be substituted—

"(f) the setting of amounts against profits in pursuance of a claim under section 83 of the Finance Act 1996 (non-trading deficits on loan relationships) or paragraph 4 of Schedule 11 to that Act (deficits of insurance companies)."

(2) In subsection (8) of that section, for paragraph (e) there shall be substituted the following paragraph—

"(e) if and so far as the purpose for which the claim is made is the setting of an amount against profits in pursuance of a claim under—

(i) section 83 of the Finance Act 1996 (non-trading deficits on loan relationships), or

(ii) paragraph 4 of Schedule 11 to that Act (deficits of insurance companies),

the time limit that by virtue of subsection (6) of that section or sub-paragraph (15) of that paragraph would be applicable to such a claim."

13.—(1) In subsection (4) of section 247 of that Act (payments between companies), for "for corporation tax charges on income of the payer company" there shall be substituted "deductible payments in relation to the payer company for the purposes of corporation tax".

(2) After that subsection there shall be inserted the following subsection—

"(4A) The reference in subsection (4) above to a payment which is a deductible payment in relation to a company for the purposes of corporation tax is a reference to any payment which is—

(a) a charge on income of that company for those purposes; or

(b) a payment of interest in relation to which a debit falls to be brought into account in the case of that company for the purposes of Chapter II of Part IV of the Finance Act 1996 (loan relationships)."

14.—(1) In subsection (2)(b) of section 337 of that Act (deduction of yearly interest etc. in computing income), for "yearly interest, annuity or other annual payment" there shall be substituted "annuity or other annual payment which is not interest".

(2) Subsection (3) of that section (deduction of yearly interest payable to a bank) shall cease to have effect.

15. After section 337 of that Act there shall be inserted the following section—

"Interest payable by companies

337A. No deduction shall be made in respect of interest in computing a company's income from any source except in accordance with Chapter II of Part IV of the Finance Act 1996 (loan relationships)."

16.—(1) Section 338 of that Act (charges on income) shall be amended as follows.

(2) In subsection (3)—

(a) in paragraph (a), for the words from "any yearly interest" to "annual payment" there shall be substituted "any annuity or annual payment payable otherwise than in respect of any of the company's loan relationships"; and

(b) the words from "and" at the end of paragraph (a) to the end of the subsection shall be omitted.

(3) In subsection (4), paragraphs (b) and (c) shall be omitted.

(4) In subsection (5)(a), the words ", not being interest," shall be omitted.

(5) Subsection (6) shall cease to have effect.

17. Sections 338A, 340 and 341 of that Act (charges on income to include certain loans to buy land, provisions relating to interest payable to non-residents and provisions relating to payments between related companies) shall cease to have effect.

18. In section 349(2) of that Act (deductions from interest payments), after "Schedule D" there shall be inserted "(as that Schedule has effect apart from the modification made for the purposes of corporation tax by section 18(3A))".

19. In section 400 of that Act (writing-off of government investment), after subsection (9) of that section there shall be inserted the following subsection—

"(9A) Nothing in section 80(5) of the Finance Act 1996 (matters to be brought into account in the case of loan relationships only under Chapter II of Part IV of that Act) shall be construed as preventing this section from applying where a government investment in a body corporate is written off by the extinguishment, in whole or in part, of any liability under a loan relationship."

20.—(1) In section 401 of that Act (relief for pre-trading expenditure), after subsection (1) there shall be inserted the following subsections—

"(1AA) Subsection (1) above shall not apply to any expenditure in relation to which any debit falls, or (but for subsection (1AB) below) would fall, to be brought into account for the purposes of Chapter II of Part IV of the Finance Act 1996 (loan relationships).

(1AB) Where, in the case of any company—

(a) a non-trading debit is given for any accounting period for the purposes of Chapter II of Part IV of the Finance Act 1996 (loan relationships), and

(b) an election for the purposes of this section is made by that company with respect to that debit within the period of 2 years beginning with the end of that accounting period,

that debit shall not be brought into account for the purposes of that Chapter as a non-trading debit for that period, but subsection (1AC) below shall apply instead.

(1AC) If a company—

(a) begins to carry on a trade within the period of seven years after the end of the accounting period for which a non-trading debit is given for the purposes of Chapter II of Part IV of the Finance Act 1996 (loan relationships),

(b) that debit is such that, if it had been given for the accounting period in which the company begins to carry on that trade, it would have been brought into account by reference to that trade in accordance with section 82(2) of that Act (trading debits and credits), and

(c) an election is or has been made with respect to that debit under subsection (1AB) above,

that debit shall be treated for the purposes of that Chapter as if it were a debit for the accounting period in which the company begins to carry on the trade and shall be brought into account for that period in accordance with section 82(2) of that Act."

(2) Subsection (1A) of that section shall cease to have effect.

21.—(1) In subsection (6) of section 404 of that Act (dual resident trading companies treated as investing companies)—

(a) in paragraph (a), after sub-paragraph (i) there shall be inserted the following sub-paragraph—
"(ia) making payments in relation to which, being payments under loan relationships, any debits fall to be brought into account for the purposes of Chapter II of Part IV of the Finance Act 1996;"
(b) in paragraph (c)(i), for "amount" there shall be substituted "aggregate of the debits relating to interest on the company's debtor relationships that fall to be brought into account for the purposes of Chapter II of Part IV of the Finance Act 1996 and the amounts";
(c) in paragraph (c)(ii), for "those charges include" there shall be substituted "that aggregate includes"; and
(d) in paragraph (c)(iii), for "the paying of those charges" there shall be substituted "the payment by the company of interest under its debtor relationships and of amounts treated as charges on income".
(2) After that subsection there shall be inserted the following subsection—
"(7) In this section 'debtor relationship' has the same meaning as in Chapter II of Part IV of the Finance Act 1996."
22.—(1) In subsection (1)(b) of section 407 of that Act (relationship between group relief and other relief), after "338(1)" there shall be inserted "of this Act or by virtue of section 83 of, or paragraph 4 of Schedule 11 to, the Finance Act 1996 (non-trading deficits)".
(2) In subsection (2) of that section, for paragraph (c) and the words after that paragraph there shall be substituted the following paragraph—
"(c) relief in pursuance of a claim under section 83(2) of, or paragraph 4 of Schedule 11 to, the Finance Act 1996 (non-trading deficits) in respect of any deficit for a deficit period after the accounting period the profits of which are being computed."
23.—(1) Where this Chapter has effect in relation to any accounting period in relation to which section 434A of that Act (computation of losses and limitation on relief) has effect without any of the amendments made by paragraph 2 of Schedule 31 to this Act, subsection (2) of that section of that Act shall have effect in relation to that period with the following amendments, that is to say—
(a) in paragraph (b), for "amount of interest and annuities treated as charges" there shall be substituted "aggregate amount treated as a charge", and at the end there shall be inserted "and"; and
(b) after that paragraph there shall be inserted the following paragraph—
"(c) any relevant non-trading deficit for that period on the company's debtor relationships."
(2) After that subsection there shall be inserted the following subsection—
"(2A) The reference in subsection (2)(c) above to a relevant non-trading deficit for any period on a company's debtor relationships is a reference to the non-trading deficit on the company's loan relationships which would be produced by any separate computation made under paragraph 2 of Schedule 11 to the Finance Act 1996 for the company's basic life assurance and general annuity business if credits and debits given in respect of the company's creditor relationships (within the meaning of Chapter II of Part IV of that Act) were disregarded."
(3) In subsection (3) of that section (losses not allowable against policy holders' share of relevant profits), for the words from "under" to the end of paragraph (b) there shall be substituted—
"(a) under Chapter II (loss relief) or Chapter IV (group relief) of Part X, or
(b) in respect of any amount representing a non-trading deficit on the company's loan relationships that has been computed otherwise than by reference to debits and credits referable to that business,".
24. Where this Chapter has effect in relation to any accounting period in relation to which section 434B of that Act (treatment of interest and annuities in the case of insurance companies) has effect without the amendments made by section 165 of this Act, that section of that Act shall have effect in relation to that period as if the words "interest or", in each place where they occur, were omitted.
25. In section 440 of that Act (transfer of assets between categories of business of insurance companies), after subsection (2) there shall be inserted the following subsection—
"(2A) Where under subsection (1) or (2) above there is a deemed disposal and re-acquisition of any asset representing a loan relationship of a company, any authorised accounting method used as respects that asset for the purposes of Chapter II of Part IV of the Finance Act 1996 shall be applied as respects that asset as if the asset that is deemed to be disposed of and the asset that is deemed to be re-acquired were different assets."
26. In section 468L(5) of that Act (interest distributions), for the words from the beginning to "complied with" there shall be substituted "Nothing in subsection (2) above or Chapter II of

Part IV of the Finance Act 1996 (loan relationships) shall require any amount relating to an interest distribution to be brought into account for the purposes of that Chapter otherwise than by virtue of paragraph 4(4) of Schedule 10 to that Act; but the interest distributions of an authorised unit trust for a distribution period".

27.—(1) In subsection (2) of section 475 of that Act (relief in relation to tax free Treasury securities in respect of borrowed money), for paragraph (b) there shall be substituted the following paragraph—

"(b) shall not be brought into account by way of any debit given for the purposes of Chapter II of Part IV of the Finance Act 1996 (loan relationships)."

(2) In subsection (4) of that section, for the words from "and is not" onwards there shall be substituted "or to be brought into account by way of a debit given for the purposes of Chapter II of Part IV of the Finance Act 1996 (loan relationships)."

28.—(1) In subsection (3) of section 477A of that Act (building societies: regulations for deducting tax), for paragraph (a) there shall be substituted the following paragraphs—

"(a) liability to pay the dividends or interest shall be treated for the purposes of Chapter II of Part IV of the Finance Act 1996 as a liability arising under a loan relationship of the building society;

(aa) if the dividends or interest are payable to a company, they shall be treated for those purposes as payable to that company in pursuance of a right arising under a loan relationship of that company;".

(2) Subsections (3A) to (3C) of that section shall cease to have effect.

29. Sections 484 and 485 of that Act (savings banks: exemption from tax) shall cease to have effect.

30. In section 486 of that Act (industrial and provident societies)—

(a) in subsection (1), for the words from "and, subject to subsection (7)" onwards there shall be substituted "but interest payable by such a society (whether as share interest or loan interest) shall be treated for the purposes of corporation tax as interest under a loan relationship of the society."; and

(b) in subsection (7), for the words from "not be deductible" onwards there shall be substituted "not be brought into account in that period for the purposes of Chapter II of Part IV of the Finance Act 1996 (loan relationships)."

31.—(1) In subsection (1) of section 487 of that Act (credit unions), for paragraph (b) there shall be substituted the following paragraph—

"(b) no credits shall be brought into account for the purposes of Chapter II of Part IV of the Finance Act 1996 in respect of any loan relationship of a credit union as respects which a member of the union stands in the position of a debtor as respects the debt in question."

(2) In subsection (3) of that section—

(a) for "No share interest, loan interest or annuity or other annual payment" there shall be substituted "An annuity or other annual payment (not being a payment of share interest or loan interest) which is"; and

(b) after "shall" there shall be inserted "not".

(3) After that subsection there shall be inserted the following subsection—

"(3A) No debits shall be brought into account for the purposes of Chapter II of Part IV of the Finance Act 1996 in respect of any loan relationship of a credit union as respects which a member of the union stands in the position of a creditor as respects the debt in question."

32.—(1) In subsection (1) of section 494 of that Act (charges on income and ring fence profits), after "Section 338" there shall be inserted "of this Act and Chapter II of Part IV of the Finance Act 1996 (loan relationships)".

(2) For the first sentence of subsection (2) of that section there shall be substituted the following—

"(2) Debits shall not be brought into account for the purposes of Chapter II of Part IV of the Finance Act 1996 in respect of any loan relationship of a company in any manner that results in a reduction of what would otherwise be the company's ring fence profits except—

(a) to the extent that the loan relationship is in respect of money borrowed by the company which has been—

(i) used to meet expenditure incurred by the company in carrying on oil extraction activities or in acquiring oil rights otherwise than from a connected person; or

(ii) appropriated to meeting expenditure to be so incurred by the company;

(b) in the case of debits falling to be brought into account by virtue of subsection (4) of section 84 of that Act in respect of a loan relationship that has not been entered into, to the extent that the relationship would have been one entered into for the purpose of borrowing money to be used or appropriated as mentioned in paragraph (a) above;

(c) in the case of debits in respect of a loan relationship deemed to exist for the purposes of section 100 of that Act, to the extent that the payment of interest under that relationship is expenditure incurred as mentioned in sub-paragraph (i) of paragraph (a) above; and

(d) in the case of debits in respect of a debtor relationship of the company which is a creditor relationship of a company associated with the company, to the extent that (subject always to paragraph (a) above) the debit does not exceed what, having regard to—

    (i) all the terms on which the money was borrowed, and

    (ii) the standing of the borrower,

would be the debit representing a reasonable commercial rate of return on the money borrowed.

In this subsection 'debtor relationship' and 'creditor relationship' have the same meanings as in Chapter II of Part IV of the Finance Act 1996, and references to a loan relationship, in relation to the borrowing of money, do not include references to any loan relationship deemed to exist for the purposes of section 100 of that Act."

(3) After subsection (2) of that section there shall be inserted the following subsection—

"(2A) Where any debit—

(a) falls to be brought into account for the purposes of Chapter II of Part IV of the Finance Act 1996 in respect of any loan relationship of a company, but

(b) in accordance with subsection (2) above cannot be brought into account in a manner that results in any reduction of what would otherwise be the company's ring fence profits,

then (notwithstanding anything in section 82(2) of that Act) that debit shall be brought into account for those purposes as a non-trading debit."

(4) For subsection (4) of that section (charges on income), there shall be substituted the following subsections—

"(4) Subsection (7) of section 403 shall have effect as if the reference in that subsection to the profits of the surrendering company for an accounting period did not include the relevant part of the company's ring fence profits for that period.

(5) For the purposes of subsection (4) above the relevant part of a company's ring fence profits for an accounting period are—

(a) if for that period—

    (i) there are no charges on income paid by the company that are allowable under section 338, or

    (ii) the only charges on income so allowable are charges to which subsection (3) above applies,

all the company's ring fence profits; and

(b) in any other case, so much of its ring fence profits as exceeds the amount of the charges on income paid by the company as are so allowable for that period and are not charges to which subsection (3) above applies."

33. In section 587A of that Act (extra return on new issues of securities), in subsection (1), after paragraph (e) there shall be inserted the following—

"but this section shall not apply for the purposes of corporation tax, except where the issue of the new securities was before 1st April 1996."

34. In section 614 of that Act (exemptions and reliefs in respect of income from certain pension funds etc.), after subsection (2) of that section there shall be inserted the following subsection—

"(2A) The reference in subsection (2) above to interest on sums forming part of a fund include references to any amount which is treated as income by virtue of paragraph 1 of Schedule 13 to the Finance Act 1996 (relevant discounted securities) and derives from any investment forming part of that fund."

35. In section 687(3) of that Act (payments under discretionary trusts), after paragraph (j) there shall be inserted the following paragraph—

"(k) the amount of any tax on an amount which is treated as income of the trustees by virtue of paragraph 1 of Schedule 13 to the Finance Act 1996 and is charged to tax at the rate applicable to trusts by virtue of paragraph 6 of that Schedule."

36. In section 710 of that Act (interpretation of sections 711 to 728), after subsection (1) there shall be inserted the following subsection—

"(1A) Sections 711 to 728 shall not apply for the purposes of corporation tax except as respects transfers of securities taking place before 1st April 1996."

37. In section 730A of that Act (treatment of price differential on repos) the following subsections shall be substituted for subsection (6)—

"(6) For the purposes of Chapter II of Part IV of the Finance Act 1996 (loan relationships)—
  (a) interest deemed by virtue of subsection (2) above to be paid or received by any company shall be deemed to be interest under a loan relationship; and
  (b) the debits and credits falling to be brought into account for the purposes of that Chapter so far as they relate to the deemed interest shall be those given by the use in relation to the deemed interest of an authorised accruals basis of accounting.
(6A) Any question whether debits or credits brought into account in accordance with subsection (6) above in relation to any company—
  (a) are to be brought into account under section 82(2) of the Finance Act 1996 (trading loan relationships), or
  (b) are to be treated as non-trading debits or credits,
shall be determined (subject to Schedule 11 to that Act (insurance companies)) according to the extent (if any) to which the company is a party to the repurchase in the course of activities forming an integral part of a trade carried on by the company."
38. In section 737(5A) of that Act (relief in respect of manufactured dividends) after "a manufactured dividend" there shall be inserted "that is not manufactured interest to which section 97 of the Finance Act 1996 applies".
39.—(1) For subsections (10) and (11) of section 768B of that Act (change in ownership of investment companies), there shall be substituted the following subsection—
"(10) Part IV of Schedule 28A shall have effect for the purpose of restricting, in a case where this section applies, the debits to be brought into account for the purposes of Chapter II of Part IV of the Finance Act 1996 (loan relationships) in respect of the company's loan relationships."
(2) In subsection (13) of that section (modified application of section 768(6)), after "company's total profits" there shall be inserted ", or the debits to be brought into account for the purposes of Chapter II of Part IV of the Finance Act 1996 in the case of a company in respect of its loan relationships,".
40. For subsections (9) and (10) of section 768C of that Act there shall be substituted the following subsection—
"(9) Part IV of Schedule 28A shall have effect for the purpose of restricting, in a case where this section applies, the debits to be brought into account for the purposes of Chapter II of Part IV of the Finance Act 1996 (loan relationships) in respect of the relevant company's loan relationships."
41. In section 795 of that Act (computation of income subject to foreign tax), after subsection (3) there shall be inserted the following subsection—
"(4) Subsections (2) and (3) above have effect for the purposes of corporation tax notwithstanding anything in section 80(5) of the Finance Act 1996 (matters to be brought into account in the case of loan relationships only under Chapter II of Part IV of that Act)."
42.—(1) In section 797 of that Act (limits on credit for foreign tax in the case of corporation tax), after subsection (3) there shall be inserted the following subsections—
"(3A) Where, in a case to which section 797A does not apply, a company has a non-trading deficit on its loan relationships for the relevant accounting period, then for the purposes of subsection (3) above that deficit shall be treated, to the extent that it is an amount to which a claim under—
  (a) subsection (2)(a) of section 83 of the Finance Act 1996 (deficit set against current year profits), or
  (b) paragraph 4(2) of Schedule 11 to that Act (set-off of deficits in the case of insurance companies),
relates, as an amount that can in that period be set against profits of any description but can be allocated in accordance with subsection (3) above only to the profits against which it is set off in pursuance of the claim.
(3B) For the purposes of subsection (3) above, where—
  (a) section 797A does not apply in the case of any company, and
  (b) any amount is carried forward to the relevant accounting period in pursuance of a claim under subsection (2)(d) of section 83 of the Finance Act 1996 or in accordance with subsection (3) of that section,
then that amount must be allocated to non-trading profits of the company for that period (so far as they are sufficient for the purpose) and cannot be allocated to any other profits."
(2) After subsection (5) of that section there shall be inserted the following subsection—
"(6) In this section 'non-trading profits' has the same meaning as in paragraph 4 of Schedule 8 to the Finance Act 1996."

43. After section 797 of that Act there shall be inserted the following section—

"Foreign tax on interest brought into account as a non-trading credit
797A.—(1) This section applies for the purposes of any arrangements where, in the case of any company—

(a) any non-trading credit relating to an amount of credit interest is brought into account for the purposes of Chapter II of Part IV of the Finance Act 1996 (loan relationships) for any accounting period ('the applicable accounting period'); and

(b) there is in respect of that amount an amount of foreign tax for which, under the arrangements, credit is allowable against United Kingdom tax computed by reference to that interest.

(2) It shall be assumed that tax chargeable under paragraph (a) of Case III of Schedule D on the profits and gains arising for the applicable accounting period from the company's loan relationships falls to be computed on the actual amount of its non-trading credits for that period, and without any deduction in respect of non-trading debits.

(3) Section 797(3) shall have effect (subject to subsection (7) below) as if—

(a) there were for the applicable accounting period an amount equal to the adjusted amount of the non-trading debits falling to be brought into account by being set against profits of the company for that period of any description; and

(b) different parts of that amount might be set against different profits.

(4) For the purposes of this section, the adjusted amount of a company's non-trading debits for any accounting period is the amount equal, in the case of that company, to the aggregate of the non-trading debits given for that period for the purposes of Chapter II of Part IV of the Finance Act 1996 (loan relationships) less the aggregate of the amounts specified in subsection (5) below.

(5) Those amounts are—

(a) so much of any non-trading deficit for the applicable accounting period as is an amount to which a claim under subsection (2)(b), (c) or (d) of section 83 of the Finance Act 1996 or paragraph 4(3) of Schedule 11 to that Act (group relief and transfer to previous or subsequent period of deficits) relates;

(b) so much of any non-trading deficit for that period as falls to be carried forward to a subsequent period in accordance with subsection (3) of that section or paragraph 4(4) of that Schedule; and

(c) any amount carried forward to the applicable accounting period in pursuance of a claim under section 83(2)(d) of that Act.

(6) Section 797(3) shall have effect as if any amount specified in subsection (5)(c) above were an amount capable of being allocated only to any non-trading profits of the company.

(7) Where—

(a) the company has a non-trading deficit for the applicable accounting period,

(b) the amount of that deficit exceeds the aggregate of the amounts specified in subsection (5) above, and

(c) in pursuance of a claim under—

(i) subsection (2)(a) of section 83 of the Finance Act 1996 (deficit set against current year profits), or

(ii) paragraph 4(2) of Schedule 11 to that Act (set-off of deficits in the case of insurance companies),

the excess falls to be set off against profits of any description,

section 797(3) shall have effect as if non-trading debits of the company which in aggregate are equal to the amount of the excess were required to be allocated to the profits against which they are set off in pursuance of the claim.

(8) In this section 'non-trading profits' has the same meaning as in paragraph 4 of Schedule 8 to the Finance Act 1996."

44.—(1) In section 798 of that Act (interest on certain overseas loans), after subsection (2) there shall be inserted the following subsection—

"(2A) For the purposes of corporation tax, this section shall apply only where the expenditure referred to in subsection (1)(b) above falls, in the case of the lender, to be brought into account for the purposes of Chapter II of Part IV of the Finance Act 1996 (loan relationships) in accordance with section 82(2) of that Act (trading debits and credits)."

(2) After subsection (3) of that section (deemed increase of interest) there shall be inserted the following subsection—

"(3A) Subsection (3) above has effect for the purposes of corporation tax notwithstanding anything in section 80(5) of the Finance Act 1996 (matters to be brought into account in the case of loan relationships only under Chapter II of Part IV of that Act)."

45. In section 807 of that Act (sale of securities with or without accrued interest), after subsection (5) there shall be inserted the following subsection—

"(6) This section does not apply for the purposes of corporation tax."
46. After section 807 of that Act there shall be inserted the following section—

"Disposals and acquisitions of company-loan relationships with or without interest
807A.—(1) This Part shall have effect for the purposes of corporation tax in relation to any company as if tax falling within subsection (2) below were to be disregarded.
(2) Tax falls within this subsection in relation to a company to the extent that it is—
(a) tax under the law of a territory outside the United Kingdom; and
(b) is attributable, on a just and reasonable apportionment, to interest accruing under a loan relationship at a time when the company is not a party to the relationship.
(3) Subject to subsections (1), (4) and (5) of this section, where—
(a) any non-trading credit relating to an amount of interest under a loan relationship is brought into account for the purposes of Chapter II of Part IV of the Finance Act 1996 (loan relationships) in the case of any company,
(b) that amount falls, as a result of any related transaction, to be paid to a person other than the company, and
(c) had the company been entitled, at the time of that transaction, to receive a payment of an amount of interest equal to the amount of interest to which the non-trading credit relates, the company would have been liable in respect of the amount of interest received to an amount of tax under the law of a territory outside the United Kingdom,
credit for that amount of tax shall be allowable under section 790(4) as if that amount of tax were an amount of tax paid under the law of that territory in respect of the amount of interest to which the non-trading credit relates.
(4) Subsection (3) above does not apply in the case of a credit brought into account in accordance with paragraph 1(2) of Schedule 11 to the Finance Act 1996 (the I minus E basis).
(5) The Treasury may by regulations provide for subsection (3) above to apply—
(a) in the case of trading credits, as well as in the case of non-trading credits;
(b) in the case of any credit ('an insurance credit') in the case of which, by virtue of subsection (4) above, it would not otherwise apply.
(6) Regulations under subsection (5) above may—
(a) provide for subsection (3) above to apply in the case of a trading credit or an insurance credit only if the circumstances are such as may be described in the regulations;
(b) provide for subsection (3) above to apply, in cases where it applies by virtue of any such regulations, subject to such exceptions, adaptations or other modifications as may be specified in the regulations;
(c) make different provision for different cases; and
(d) contain such incidental, supplemental, consequential and transitional provision as the Treasury think fit.
(7) In this section—
'related transaction' has the same meaning as in section 84 of the Finance Act 1996; and
'trading credit' means any credit falling to be brought into account for the purposes of Chapter II of Part IV of the Finance Act 1996 (loan relationships) in accordance with section 82(2) of that Act."
47. In section 811 of that Act (deduction of foreign tax where no credit available), after subsection (2) there shall be inserted the following subsection—
"(3) This section has effect for the purposes of corporation tax notwithstanding anything in section 80(5) of the Finance Act 1996 (matters to be brought into account in the case of loan relationships only under Chapter II of Part IV of that Act)."
48.—(1) In subsection (7C) of section 826 of that Act (interest on tax overpaid)—
(a) in paragraph (a), for the words from "a relievable amount" to the end of the paragraph there shall be substituted "a non-trading deficit on the company's loan relationships,";
(b) in paragraph (b), for the words from "subsection (5)" to "subsection (10) of that section)" there shall be substituted "section 83(2)(c) of the Finance Act 1996 or paragraph 4(3) of Schedule 11 to that Act the whole or part of the deficit for the later period is set off against profits"; and
(c) in the words after paragraph (c), for "subsection (5) or (6) (as the case may be) of that section" there shall be substituted "section 83(2)(c) of that Act or, as the case may be, paragraph 4(3) of Schedule 11 to that Act".
(2) In subsection (7CA) of that section, for the words "section 131 (5) or (6) of the Finance Act 1993", in each place where they occur, there shall be substituted "section 83(2)(c) of the Finance Act 1996 or paragraph 4(3) of Schedule 11 to that Act".

49. In subsection (1) of section 834 of that Act (definitions for the purposes of the Corporation Tax Acts), after the definition of "group relief" there shall be inserted the following definitions—

    " 'loan relationship' has the same meaning as it has for the purposes of Chapter II of Part IV of the Finance Act 1996;

    'non-trading deficit', in relation to a company's loan relationships shall be construed in accordance with section 82 of the Finance Act 1996."

50. Schedule 4 to that Act (deep discount securities) shall cease to have effect.

51. In paragraph 5B(2) of Schedule 19AC to that Act (overseas life companies), the following paragraph shall be inserted after paragraph (d)

    "(e) the setting of amounts against profits under, or in pursuance of a claim under, paragraph 4 of Schedule 11 to the Finance Act 1996 (loan relationships of insurance companies)."

52.—(1) Schedule 23A to that Act (manufactured payments) shall be amended as follows.

(2) In paragraph 3 (manufactured interest on UK securities), after sub-paragraph (4) there shall be inserted the following sub-paragraph—

    "(5) Without prejudice to section 97 of the Finance Act 1996 (manufactured interest), the references in this paragraph to all the purposes of the Tax Acts do not include the purposes of Chapter II of Part IV of that Act (loan relationships)."

(3) In paragraph 3A(3) (gilt-edged securities)—

    (a) for "Sub-paragraph (4)" there shall be substituted "Sub-paragraphs (4) and (5)"; and

    (b) for "it applies" there shall be substituted "they apply".

(4) In paragraph 4 (manufactured interest on overseas dividends), after sub-paragraph (8) there shall be inserted the following sub-paragraph—

    "(9) Without prejudice to section 97 of the Finance Act 1996 (manufactured interest), the references in this paragraph to all the purposes of the Tax Acts do not include the purposes of Chapter II of Part IV of that Act (loan relationships)."

(5) In paragraph 5 (dividends and interest passing through the market), in sub-paragraphs (2)(b) and (4)(b), at the end there shall be inserted, in each case, "and shall also be treated, in the case of interest the recipient of which is a company, as if for the purposes of Chapter II of Part IV of the Finance Act 1996 it were interest under a loan relationship to which the company is a party".

(6) In paragraph 6 (unapproved manufactured payments), sub-paragraphs (3), (4), (6) and (7) shall cease to have effect.

(7) In paragraph 7 (irregular manufactured payments), after sub-paragraph (1) there shall be inserted the following sub-paragraph—

    "(1A) Sub-paragraph (1) above does not apply in the case of the amount of any manufactured interest or manufactured overseas dividend which falls in accordance with section 97 of the Finance Act 1996 to be treated for the purposes of Chapter II of Part IV of that Act as interest under a loan relationship."

53. In Schedule 26 to that Act (controlled foreign companies), in paragraph 1(3), the word "and" shall be inserted at the end of paragraph (e), and after that paragraph there shall be inserted the following paragraph—

    "(f) any non-trading deficit on its loan relationships."

54.—(1) In paragraph 6 of Schedule 28A to that Act (amounts in issue for the purposes of section 768B of that Act), after sub-paragraph (d) there shall be inserted the following sub-paragraphs—

    "(da) the amount (if any) of the adjusted Case III profits and gains or non-trading deficit of the company for that accounting period;

    (db) the amount of any non-trading debit (other than one within sub-paragraph (dc) or (dd) below) that falls to be brought into account for that accounting period for the purposes of Chapter II of Part IV of the Finance Act 1996 (loan relationships) in respect of any debtor relationship of the company;

    (dc) the amount of any non-trading debit given for that accounting period by section 83(3) of the Finance Act 1996 (carried forward deficit not set off against profits);

    (dd) the amount of any non-trading debit given for that accounting period by paragraph 13 of Schedule 15 to the Finance Act 1996 (transitional adjustment for past interest) in respect of any debtor relationship of the company;".

(2) In Part II of that Schedule, after paragraph 6 there shall be inserted the following paragraph—

    "6A. For the purposes of paragraph 6(da) above, the amount for any accounting period of the adjusted Case III profits and gains or non-trading deficit of a company is the amount which, as the case may be, would be—

(a) the amount of the profits and gains chargeable under Case III of Schedule D as profits and gains arising from the company's loan relationships, or

(b) the amount of the company's non-trading deficit on those relationships for that period,

if, in computing that amount, amounts for that period falling within paragraph 6(db) to (dd) above were disregarded."

(3) In paragraph 7(1) of that Schedule (apportionment for the purposes of section 768B)—

(a) in paragraph (b), after "in paragraph 6(c) above," there shall be inserted "or in the case of the non-trading debit mentioned in paragraph 6(dc) above,";

(b) in paragraph (c), after "6(d)" there shall be inserted ", (da)"; and

(c) after paragraph (c) there shall be inserted the following paragraphs—

"(d) in the case of any such debit as—

(i) is mentioned in paragraph 6(db) above,

(ii) falls to be brought into account for the purposes of Chapter II of Part IV of the Finance Act 1996 in accordance with an authorised accruals basis of accounting, and

(iii) so falls to be brought into account otherwise than on the assumption, specified in paragraph 2(2) of Schedule 9 to that Act, that the interest to which it relates does not accrue until it is paid,

by reference to the time of accrual of the amount to which the debit relates;

(e) in the case of any such debit as—

(i) is mentioned in paragraph 6(db) above,

(ii) falls to be brought into account for the purposes of Chapter II of Part IV of the Finance Act 1996 in accordance with an authorised accruals basis of accounting, and

(iii) so falls to be brought into account on the assumption mentioned in paragraph (d)(iii) above,

by apportioning the whole amount of the debit to the first part of the accounting period being divided;

(f) in the case of any such debit as is mentioned in paragraph 6(dd) above, by apportioning the whole amount of the debit to the first part of the accounting period being divided."

(4) For Part IV of that Schedule (excess overdue interest) there shall be substituted the following Part—

"PART IV

DISALLOWED DEBITS

9.—(1) This paragraph has effect in a case to which section 768B applies for determining the debits to be brought into account for the purposes of Chapter II of Part IV of the Finance Act 1996 (loan relationships) for—

(a) the accounting period beginning immediately after the change in the ownership of the company; and

(b) any subsequent accounting period.

(2) The debits so brought into account shall not include the debits falling within paragraph 11 below to the extent (if at all) that the aggregate of—

(a) the amount of those debits, and

(b) the amount of any debits falling within that paragraph which have been brought into account for the purposes of that Chapter for any previous accounting period ending after the change in the ownership,

exceeds the profits for the accounting period ending with the change in the ownership.

(3) The reference in sub-paragraph (2) above to the profits is a reference to profits after making all deductions and giving all reliefs that for the purposes of corporation tax are made or given against the profits, including deductions and reliefs which under any provision are treated as reducing them for those purposes.

10.—(1) This paragraph has effect in a case to which section 768C applies for determining the debits to be brought into account for the purposes of Chapter II of Part IV of the Finance Act 1996 (loan relationships) for—

(a) the accounting period beginning immediately after the change in the ownership of the relevant company; and

(b) any subsequent accounting period.

(2) The debits so brought into account for any such accounting period shall not include the debits falling within paragraph 11 below to the extent (if at all) that the amount of those debits exceeds the modified total profits for the accounting period.

(3) The reference in sub-paragraph (2) above to the modified total profits for an accounting period is a reference to the total profits for that period—

(a) reduced, if that period is the period in which the relevant gain accrues, by an amount equal to the amount of the total profits for that period which represents the relevant gain; and

(b) after making all deductions and giving all reliefs that for the purposes of corporation tax are made or given against the profits, including deductions and reliefs which under any provision are treated as reducing them for those purposes, other than any reduction by virtue of paragraph 1(2) of Schedule 8 to the Finance Act 1996.

(4) Where by virtue of sub-paragraph (2) above a debit is to any extent not brought into account for an accounting period, that debit may (to that extent) be brought into account for the next accounting period, but this is subject to the application of sub-paragraphs (1) to (3) above to that next accounting period.

11.—(1) A debit falls within this paragraph if it is a non-trading debit which—

(a) falls to be brought into account for the purposes of Chapter II of Part IV of the Finance Act 1996 in accordance with an authorised accruals basis of accounting;

(b) so falls to be brought into account on the assumption, specified in sub-paragraph (2) of paragraph 2 of Schedule 9 to that Act, that the interest to which it relates does not accrue until it is paid; and

(c) apart from that sub-paragraph, would have fallen to be brought into account for those purposes for an accounting period ending before or with the change in the ownership of the company or, as the case may be, the relevant company.

(2) The debits that fall within this paragraph also include—

(a) any non-trading debit given by section 83(3) of the Finance Act 1996 (carried forward deficit from previous period not set off against non-trading profits of current period) for the post-change accounting period;

(b) any non-trading debit given by paragraph 13 of Schedule 15 to the Finance Act 1996 (transitional adjustment for past interest) in respect of any debtor relationship of the company or, as the case may be, the relevant company.

(3) The debits that fall within this paragraph also include any non-trading debit which—

(a) is not such a debit as is mentioned in sub-paragraph (1) or (2) above;

(b) is a debit in respect of a debtor relationship of the company or, as the case may be, the relevant company;

(c) falls to be brought into account for the purposes of Chapter II of Part IV of the Finance Act 1996 in accordance with an authorised accruals basis of accounting; and

(d) relates to an amount that accrued before the change in the ownership of that company.

(4) In this paragraph 'post-change accounting period' means the accounting period beginning immediately after the change in the ownership of the company or, as the case may be, the relevant company.

12. Expressions used both in this Part of this Schedule and in Chapter II of Part IV of the Finance Act 1996 have the same meanings in this Part of this Schedule as in that Chapter."

(5) In paragraph 13(1) of that Schedule (amounts in issue for the purposes of section 768C of that Act), after paragraph (e) there shall be inserted the following paragraphs—

"(ea) the amount (if any) of the adjusted Case III profits and gains or non-trading deficit of the company for that accounting period;

(eb) the amount of any non-trading debit (other than one within paragraph (ec) or (ed) below) that falls to be brought into account for that accounting period for the purposes of Chapter II of Part IV of the Finance Act 1996 (loan relationships) in respect of any debtor relationship of the company;

(ec) the amount of any non-trading debit given for that accounting period by section 83(3) of the Finance Act 1996 (carried forward deficit not set off against profits);

(ed) the amount of any non-trading debit given for that accounting period by paragraph 13 of Schedule 15 to the Finance Act 1996 (transitional adjustment for past interest) in respect of any debtor relationship of the company;".

(6) In Part V of that Schedule, after paragraph 13 there shall be inserted the following paragraph—

"13A. Paragraph 6A above shall apply for the purposes of paragraph 13(1)(ea) above as it applies for the purposes of paragraph 6(da) above."

(7) In paragraph 16(1) of that Schedule (apportionment for the purposes of section 768C)—

(a) in paragraph (b), after "in paragraph 13(1)(d) above," there shall be inserted "or in the case of the non-trading debit mentioned in paragraph 13(1)(ec) above,";

(b) in paragraph (c), after "13(1)(e)" there shall be inserted ", (ea)"; and

(c) after paragraph (c) there shall be inserted the following paragraphs—
"(d) in the case of any such debit as—
>(i) is mentioned in paragraph 13(1)(eb) above,
>(ii) falls to be brought into account for the purposes of Chapter II of Part IV of the Finance Act 1996 in accordance with an authorised accruals basis of accounting, and
>(iii) so falls to be brought into account otherwise than on the assumption, specified in paragraph 2(2) of Schedule 9 to that Act, that the interest to which it relates does not accrue until it is paid,

by reference to the time of accrual of the amount to which the debit relates;
(e) in the case of any such debit as—
>(i) is mentioned in paragraph 13(1)(eb) above,
>(ii) falls to be brought into account for the purposes of Chapter II of Part IV of the Finance Act 1996 in accordance with an authorised accruals basis of accounting, and
>(iii) so falls to be brought into account on the assumption mentioned in paragraph (d)(iii) above,

by apportioning the whole amount of the debit to the first part of the accounting period being divided;
(f) in the case of any such debit as is mentioned in paragraph 13(1)(ed) above, by apportioning the whole amount of the debit to the first part of the accounting period being divided."

The British Steel Act 1988 (c. 35)

55. In section 11 of the British Steel Act 1988 (taxation provisions), for subsection (7) there shall be substituted the following subsection—
"(7) For the purposes of Part VI of the Income and Corporation Taxes Act 1988 (company distributions) and Chapter II of Part IV of the Finance Act 1996 (loan relationships), any debentures issued in pursuance of section 3 above shall be treated as having been issued for new consideration equal to the principal sum payable under the debenture."

The Finance Act 1989 (c. 26)

56. In section 88(3) of the Finance Act 1989 (relevant profits of company), the following paragraph shall be inserted before paragraph (a)—
"(aa) amounts falling in respect of any non-trading deficits on the company's loan relationships to be brought into account in that period in accordance with paragraph 4 of Schedule 11 to the Finance Act 1996,".

57. Schedule 11 to that Act (deep gain securities) shall cease to have effect.

The Finance Act 1990 (c. 29)

58. Schedule 10 to the Finance Act 1990 (convertible securities) shall cease to have effect.

The Taxation of Chargeable Gains Act 1992 (c. 12)

59. In section 108(1) of the Taxation of Chargeable Gains Act 1992 (meaning of relevant securities), after paragraph (a) there shall be inserted the following paragraph—
"(aa) qualifying corporate bonds;".

60.—(1) Section 116 of that Act (reorganisations, conversions and reconstructions) shall be amended as follows.
(2) After subsection (4) there shall be inserted the following subsection—
"(4A) In determining for the purposes of subsections (1) to (4) above, as they apply for the purposes of corporation tax—
(a) whether sections 127 to 130 would apply in any case, and
(b) what, in a case where they would apply, would constitute the original shares and the new holding,
it shall be assumed that every asset representing a loan relationship of a company is a security within the meaning of section 132."
(3) After subsection (8) there shall be inserted the following subsection—
"(8A) Where subsection (6) above applies for the purposes of corporation tax in a case where the old asset consists of a qualifying corporate bond, Chapter II of Part IV of the

Finance Act 1996 (loan relationships) shall have effect so as to require such debits and credits to be brought into account for the purposes of that Chapter in relation to the relevant transaction as would have been brought into account if the transaction had been a disposal of the old asset at the market value mentioned in that subsection."

(4) After subsection (15) there shall be inserted the following subsection—

"(16) This section has effect for the purposes of corporation tax notwithstanding anything in section 80(5) of the Finance Act 1996 (matters to be brought into account in the case of loan relationships only under Chapter II of Part IV of that Act)."

61.—(1) In section 117 of that Act (meaning of "qualifying corporate bond"), before subsection (1) there shall be inserted the following subsection—

"(A1) For the purposes of corporation tax 'qualifying corporate bond' means (subject to sections 117A and 117B below) any asset representing a loan relationship of a company; and for purposes other than those of corporation tax references to a qualifying corporate bond shall be construed in accordance with the following provisions of this section."

(2) After subsection (2) of that section there shall be inserted the following subsection—

"(2AA) For the purposes of this section 'corporate bond' also includes any asset which is not included in the definition in subsection (1) above and which is a relevant discounted security for the purposes of Schedule 13 to the Finance Act 1996."

(3) After subsection (6A) of that section there shall be inserted the following subsections—

"(6B) An excluded indexed security issued on or after 6th April 1996 is not a corporate bond for the purposes of this section; and an excluded indexed security issued before that date shall be taken to be such a bond for the purposes of this section only if—

(a) it would be so taken apart from this subsection; and

(b) the question whether it should be so taken arises for the purposes of section 116(10).

(6C) In subsection (6B) above 'excluded indexed security' has the same meaning as in Schedule 13 to the Finance Act 1996 (relevant discounted securities)."

(4) After subsection (8) of that section there shall be inserted the following subsection—

"(8A) A corporate bond falling within subsection (2AA) above is a qualifying corporate bond whatever its date of issue."

62. After section 117 of that Act there shall be inserted the following sections—

"Assets that are not qualifying corporate bonds for corporation tax purposes

117A.—(1) An asset to which this section applies is not a qualifying corporate bond for the purposes of corporation tax in relation to any disposal of that asset.

(2) This section applies to any asset representing a loan relationship of a company where—

(a) subsection (3) or (4) below applies to the asset; and

(b) it is held in exempt circumstances.

(3) This subsection applies to an asset if—

(a) the settlement currency of the debt to which it relates is a currency other than sterling; and

(b) that debt is not a debt on a security.

(4) This subsection applies to an asset if the debt to which it relates is a debt on a security and is in a foreign currency.

(5) For the purposes of subsection (4) above a debt is a debt in a foreign currency if it is—

(a) a debt expressed in a currency other than sterling;

(b) a debt the amount of which in sterling falls at any time to be determined by reference to the value at that time of a currency other than sterling; or

(c) subject to subsection (6) below, a debt as respects which provision is made for its conversion into, or redemption in, a currency other than sterling.

(6) A debt is not a debt in a foreign currency for those purposes by reason only that provision is made for its redemption on payment of an amount in a currency other than sterling equal, at the rate prevailing at the date of redemption, to a specified amount in sterling.

(7) The provisions specified in subsection (8) below, so far as they require a disposal to be treated as a disposal on which neither a gain nor a loss accrues, shall not apply to any disposal of an asset to which this section applies.

(8) The provisions referred to in subsection (7) above are—

(a) sections 139, 140A, 171 and 172 of this Act; and

(b) section 486(8) of the Taxes Act.

(9) Paragraph 3 of Schedule 17 to the Finance Act 1993 shall have effect for construing the reference in subsection (2)(b) above to exempt circumstances as if references to a currency were references to the debt to which the relationship relates.

(10) In this section "security" includes a debenture that is deemed to be a security for the purposes of section 251 by virtue of subsection (6) of that section.

Holdings in unit trusts and offshore funds excluded from treatment as qualifying corporate bonds

117B.—(1) For the purposes of corporation tax an asset to which this section applies is not a qualifying corporate bond in relation to any disposal of that asset in an accounting period for which that asset falls, under paragraph 4 of Schedule 10 to the Finance Act 1996 (holdings in unit trusts and offshore funds), to be treated as a right under a creditor relationship of a company.

(2) This section applies to an asset which is comprised in a relevant holding (within the meaning of paragraph 4 of Schedule 10 to the Finance Act 1996) if—

(a) it is denominated in a currency other than sterling; and

(b) it is held in exempt circumstances.

(3) For the purposes of this section—

(a) a unit in a unit trust scheme, or

(b) a right (other than a share in a company) which constitutes a relevant interest in an offshore fund,

shall be taken to be denominated in a currency other than sterling if the price at which it may be acquired from, or disposed of to, persons concerned in the management of the trust or fund is fixed by those persons in a currency other than sterling.

(4) For the purposes of this section shares constituting a relevant interest in an offshore fund shall be taken to be denominated in a currency other than sterling if their nominal value is expressed in such a currency.

(5) The provisions specified in subsection (6) below, so far as they require a disposal to be treated as a disposal on which neither a gain nor a loss accrues, shall not apply to any disposal in relation to which this section applies.

(6) The provisions referred to in subsection (5) above are—

(a) sections 139, 140A, 171 and 172 of this Act; and

(b) section 486(8) of the Taxes Act.

(7) Paragraph 3 of Schedule 17 to the Finance Act 1993 shall have effect for construing the reference in subsection (2)(b) above to exempt circumstances as if references to a currency were references to the asset in question.

(8) Paragraph 7 Schedule 10 to the Finance Act 1996 shall apply for construing any reference in this section to a relevant interest in an offshore fund as it applies for the purposes of paragraph 4 of that Schedule."

63. In section 212 of that Act (annual deemed disposal of holdings of unit trusts), after subsection (2) there shall be inserted the following subsection—

"(2A) Subsection (1) above shall not apply to assets falling by virtue of paragraph 4 of Schedule 10 to the Finance Act 1996 (company holdings in unit trusts) to be treated for the accounting period in question as representing rights under a creditor relationship of the company."

64. In section 251 of that Act (exclusion for debts that are not debts on a security), after subsection (6) there shall be inserted the following subsections—

"(7) Where any instrument specified in subsection (8) below is not a security (as defined in section 132), that instrument shall be deemed to be such a security for the purposes of this section, other than the purposes of determining what is or is not an allowable loss in any case.

(8) The instruments mentioned in subsection (7) above are—

(a) any instrument that would fall to be treated for the purposes of this Act as an asset representing a loan relationship of a company if the provisions of sections 92(4) and 93(4) of the Finance Act 1996 (convertible securities and assets linked to the value of chargeable assets) were disregarded; or

(b) any instrument which (even apart from those provisions) is not a loan relationship of a company but which would be a relevant discounted security for the purposes of Schedule 13 to that Act if paragraph 3(2)(c) of that Schedule (excluded indexed securities) were omitted."

65. In section 253(3) of that Act (relief for loans to traders), in the words after paragraph (c), at the beginning there shall be inserted—

"then, to the extent that that amount is not an amount which, in the case of the claimant, falls to be brought into account as a debit given for the purposes of Chapter II of Part IV of the Finance Act 1996 (loan relationships),".

66.—(1) In section 254 of that Act (relief for debts on qualifying corporate bonds), in subsection (1)(c), after "bond" there shall be inserted "but is not a relevant discounted security for the purposes of Schedule 13 to the Finance Act 1996".

(2) After subsection (12) of that section there shall be inserted the following subsection—

"(13) This section does not apply for the purposes of corporation tax."

The Finance Act 1993 (c. 34)

67. In section 127 of the Finance Act 1993 (accrual of amounts where debts vary), after subsection (1) there shall be inserted the following subsections—

"(1A) For the purposes of this section if, in the case of any debt—

(a) an amount in respect of any discount or premium relating to that debt is treated, on an accruals basis of accounting, as accruing at any time for the purposes of Chapter II of Part IV of the Finance Act 1996 (loan relationships), or

(b) any such amount would be treated as so accruing if the authorised method of accounting used for those purposes as respects the loan relationship relating to that debt were an accruals basis of accounting, instead of a mark to market basis,

then, for the purposes of this section, there shall be deemed to be such a variation at that time of the nominal amount of the debt outstanding as is specified in subsection (1B) below.

(1B) That variation is—

(a) if the amount mentioned in paragraph (a) or (b) of subsection (1A) above relates to a discount, a variation that increases the nominal amount of the debt outstanding by the amount so mentioned; and

(b) if the amount so mentioned relates to a premium, a variation that decreases the nominal amount of the debt outstanding by the amount so mentioned."

68.—(1) In subsection (2) of section 129 of that Act (non-trading exchange gains), for the words after paragraph (b) there shall be substituted—

"and the rule in section 130(1) below shall apply."

(2) In subsection (4) of that section (non-trading exchange losses), for the words after paragraph (b) there shall be substituted—

"and the rule in section 130(2) below shall apply."

(3) Subsections (5) and (6) of that section (computation of net exchange gains or net exchange losses) shall cease to have effect.

(4) In subsection (7)(b) of that section (no gain or loss accruing on a right by virtue of a debt to receive income), for "(whether interest, dividend or otherwise)" there shall be substituted "that is not interest falling to be brought into account for the purposes of Chapter II of Part IV of the Finance Act 1996 (loan relationships) as interest accruing, or (according to the authorised method of accounting used) becoming due and payable, in an accounting period ending after 31st March 1996".

69. For sections 130 to 133 of that Act (charge to tax of non-trading gains and treatment of losses), there shall be substituted the following section—

"Non-trading gains and losses

130.—(1) Where a company is treated by virtue of section 129 above as receiving any amount in an accounting period, that amount shall be brought into account for that accounting period as if it were a non-trading credit falling for the purposes of Chapter II of Part IV of the Finance Act 1996 (loan relationships) to be brought into account in respect of a loan relationship of the company.

(2) Where a company is treated by virtue of section 129 above as incurring any loss in an accounting period, the amount of the loss shall be brought into account for that accounting period as if it were a non-trading debit falling for the purposes of Chapter II of Part IV of the Finance Act 1996 to be brought into account in respect of a loan relationship of the company."

70.—(1) For subsection (4) of section 153 of that Act (qualifying assets and liabilities) there shall be substituted the following subsection—

"(4) A right to settlement under a qualifying debt is not a qualifying asset where the company having the right holds an asset representing the debt and that asset is—

(a) an asset to which section 92 of the Finance Act 1996 applies (convertible securities); or

(b) an asset representing a loan relationship to which section 93 of that Act (relationships linked to the value of chargeable assets) applies."

(2) Subsection (6) of that section shall cease to have effect.

71. In section 154 of that Act (definitions connected with assets), after subsection (12) there shall be inserted the following subsection—

"(12A) So much of any asset as consists in a right to receive interest as respects which any sums fall to be brought into account for the purposes of Chapter II of Part IV of the Finance Act 1996 (loan relationships) shall be taken to be an asset to which the company became entitled at the following time (instead of the time for which subsection (12) above provides), that is to say—

    (a) where the sums fall to be brought into account for the purposes of that Chapter in accordance with an authorised accruals basis of accounting, the time when the interest is taken for those purposes to have accrued, and

    (b) where the sums fall to be brought into account for the purposes of that Chapter in accordance with an authorised mark to market basis of accounting, the time when the interest is taken for those purposes to have become due and payable."

72. In section 155 of that Act (definitions connected with liabilities), after subsection (11) there shall be inserted the following subsection—

    "(11A) So much of any liability consisting in a liability to pay interest as respects which debits fall to be brought into account for the purposes of Chapter II of Part IV of the Finance Act 1996 (loan relationships) shall be taken to be a liability to which the company became subject at the following time (instead of at the time for which subsection (11) above provides), that is to say—

    (a) where the debits fall to be brought into account for the purposes of that Chapter in accordance with an authorised accruals basis of accounting, the time when the interest is taken for those purposes to have accrued, and

    (b) where the debits fall to be brought into account for the purposes of that Chapter in accordance with an authorised mark to market basis of accounting, the time when the interest is taken for those purposes to have become due and payable."

73.—(1) For subsections (5) to (9) of section 159 of that Act (basic valuation where accrued income scheme applies) there shall be substituted the following subsection—

    "(5) Where—

    (a) a company becomes entitled, on any transfer by virtue of which it becomes a party to a loan relationship, to a right of settlement under a qualifying debt on a security, and

    (b) that transfer is a transfer with accrued interest,

the basic valuation of that right shall be found by taking the consideration for the company's becoming entitled to the right and then deducting the amount of the accrued interest the right to which is transferred."

(2) This paragraph does not apply in relation to transfers before 1st April 1996.

74. In section 167 of that Act (orders and regulations relating to exchange gains and losses), after subsection (5) there shall be inserted the following subsections—

    "(5A) Without prejudice to the generality of any power of the Treasury to amend regulations made under this Chapter, every such power shall include power to make such modifications of any regulations so made as the Treasury consider appropriate in consequence of the provisions of Chapter II of Part IV of the Finance Act 1996 (loan relationships).

    (5B) The power to make any such modifications as are mentioned in subsection (5A) above shall be exercisable so as to apply those modifications in relation to any accounting period of a company ending on or after 1st April 1996."

The Finance Act 1994 (c. 9)

75. In section 160 of the Finance Act 1994 (treatment of non-trading profits and losses on interest rate and currency contracts), for subsections (2) to (4) there shall be substituted the following subsections—

    "(2) Any amount which for the purposes of this section is treated as a non-trading profit of a company for any accounting period shall be brought into account for that accounting period as if it were a non-trading credit falling to be brought into account for the purposes of Chapter II of Part IV of the Finance Act 1996 in respect of a loan relationship of the company.

    (2A) Any amount which for the purposes of this section is treated as a non-trading loss of a company for any accounting period shall be brought into account for that accounting period as if it were a non-trading debit falling to be brought into account for the purposes of Chapter II of Part IV of the Finance Act 1996 in respect of a loan relationship of the company."

76.—(1) In subsection (9) of section 167 of that Act (factors to be taken into account when adjusting transactions not at arm's length), before the word "and" at the end of paragraph (b) there shall be inserted the following paragraph—

    "(ba) in a case where the qualifying contract is a debt contract or option, the amount of the debt by reference to which any loan relationship that would have been involved would have subsisted and any terms as to repayment, redemption or interest that, in the case of that debt or any asset representing it, would have been involved;".

(2) In paragraph (c) of that subsection, for "either" there shall be substituted "any such".

77. In section 173(5)(a) of that Act (references to the purposes of the Chapter), for the words from "subsections (5)" to "losses)" there shall be substituted "Chapter II of Part IV of the Finance Act 1996 (loan relationships), so far as that Chapter is applied by virtue of section 160(2) or (2A) above,".

78.—(1) In subsection (1) of section 177 of that Act (interpretation)—

(a) in the definition of "commencement day", after the words "'commencement day'" there shall be inserted "—

(a) for the purposes of this Chapter as it has effect in relation to any debt contract or option, means (subject to paragraph 25 of Schedule 15 to the Finance Act 1996) 1st April 1996; and

(b) for all other purposes";

and

(b) after the definitions of "currency contract" and "currency option" there shall be inserted—

" 'debt contract' and 'debt option' shall be construed in accordance with section 150A above;".

(2) In subsection (2)(a) of that section (time when company becomes entitled to a contract), for "or a currency contract or option," there shall be substituted "a currency contract or option or a debt contract or option".

79. For paragraphs 1 and 2 of Schedule 18 to that Act (special provision with respect to financial instruments for insurance companies) there shall be substituted the following paragraphs—

"Application of insurance companies provisions relating to loan relationships

1.—(1) Part I of Schedule 11 to the Finance Act 1996 (special provision with respect to loan relationships for insurance companies) shall have effect (subject to sub-paragraph (2) below) in relation to qualifying contracts as it has effect in relation to loan relationships which are creditor relationships within the meaning of Chapter II of Part IV of that Act.

(2) That Part of that Schedule shall have effect in its application in relation to qualifying contracts, as if—

(a) references to section 82(2) of the Finance Act 1996 were references to section 159 of this Act, and

(b) references to credits and debits given by Chapter II of Part IV of that Act in respect of a loan relationship were references, respectively, to the profits and losses deriving from the contract.

1A.—(1) Where the I minus E basis is applied for any accounting period in respect of the life assurance business or capital redemption business of any insurance company, this Chapter shall have effect for that period in relation to contracts and options held for the purposes of that business as if the words in subsection (10) of section 150A from 'but references' onwards were omitted.

(2) Expressions used in sub-paragraph (1) above and in Part I of Schedule 11 to the Finance Act 1996 have the same meanings in this paragraph as in that Part of that Schedule."

GENERAL NOTE

This Schedule, described by the minister as a "dustbin" or "rag bag" schedule, makes minor and consequential amendments to other legislation arising from the loan relationship provisions.

Para. 5

The new ICTA 1988, s.18(3A), provides that for corporation tax purposes foreign source loan relationships hitherto taxable under Cases IV or V of Sched. D are in future taxable under Case III.

Para. 11

The new ICTA 1985, s.209(3A), expands the definition of "distribution" to accommodate securities issued at a premium.

Para. 43

The new ICTA 1988, s.797A, together with the amendments made by paras. 41, 42 and 47, adapts the rules allowing companies double taxation relief where they suffer foreign tax on their interest income, so as to identify the U.K.-taxable income against which relief is allowed and match the accrual of foreign tax with the accrual of income for U.K. tax purposes.

Para. 46

The new ICTA 1988, s.807A, together with the amendment made by para. 45, adapts a provision which allows double taxation relief for foreign tax on interest income by reference to the amount of interest accrued rather than the amount actually received.

Para. 54

Together with the amendments made by paras. 39 and 40, this paragraph adapts anti-avoidance provisions involving the purchase of shell companies with surplus management expenses, a practice known as "expense buying".

Paras. 59–66

These amend the provisions of the Taxation of Chargeable Gains Act 1992 (c. 12) as they apply for corporation tax purposes to align their terminology with the loan relationship provisions and to disapply the TCGA in cases where previously chargeable gains and allowable losses are now charged or relieved on income account.

Paras. 67–74

These make consequential amendments to the provisions in the FA 1993 dealing with exchange gains and losses.

Section 105　　　　　　　　　　　　SCHEDULE 15

LOAN RELATIONSHIPS: SAVINGS AND TRANSITIONAL PROVISIONS

PART I

CORPORATION TAX

Application and interpretation of Part I

1.—(1) This Part of this Schedule has effect for the purposes of corporation tax.

(2) In this Part of this Schedule—

　　"the 1992 Act" means the Taxation of Chargeable Gains Act 1992;

　　"continuing loan relationship", in relation to any company, means any loan relationship to which the company was a party both immediately before and on 1st April 1996;

　　"first relevant accounting period", in relation to a company, means the first accounting period of the company to end after 31st March 1996; and

　　"transitional accounting period", in relation to a company, means any accounting period of the company beginning before and ending on or after 1st April 1996.

(3) Any question as to whether, or to what extent, credits or debits falling to be brought into account for the purposes of this Chapter by virtue of this Part of this Schedule are referable to any category of an insurance company's long term business shall be determined according to any apportionment in relation to the loan relationship in question which is made for the company's first relevant accounting period.

(4) In this Part of this Schedule references to this Chapter include references to any repeals having effect for the purposes of this Chapter.

Loan relationships terminated before 1st April 1996

2. Subject to paragraph 13(6) below, the amounts which are to be brought into account for the purposes of corporation tax in any transitional accounting period of a company by reference to any loan relationship to which it was a party only at a time before 1st April 1996—

　(a) shall not be computed in accordance with this Chapter; but

　(b) shall, instead, be computed as they would be for an accounting period ending on 31st March 1996.

Basic rules for transitional accounting periods

3.—(1) This paragraph applies as respects any continuing loan relationship of a company.

(2) In a transitional accounting period an amount accruing before 1st April 1996 in respect of a continuing loan relationship (whether it accrues as a right or liability) shall be brought into account for the purposes of this Chapter in accordance with an authorised accruals basis of accounting only if it is an amount accruing as interest.

(3) In a transitional accounting period an amount becoming due and payable before 1st April 1996 in respect of a continuing loan relationship shall be brought into account for the purposes of this Chapter in accordance with an authorised mark to market basis of accounting only if it is an amount becoming so due and payable as interest.

(4) Except where sub-paragraph (6) below applies and subject to the following provisions of this Part of this Schedule, any opening valuation that is to be made for the purpose of bringing amounts into account for the purposes of this Chapter in a transitional accounting period on a

mark to market basis of accounting shall be made as at 1st April 1996, instead of as at any earlier time.

(5) Where any opening valuation is made in accordance with sub-paragraph (4) above for any transitional accounting period—

(a) that valuation, and

(b) any closing valuation made as at the end of that period for the purposes mentioned in that sub-paragraph,

shall each be made disregarding any amount of interest that has accrued in respect of any part of that period.

(6) This sub-paragraph applies in the case of a continuing loan relationship if, apart from this Chapter—

(a) a mark to market basis of accounting would have been used, in the case of the relationship, for the purpose of bringing amounts into account in the transitional accounting period; and

(b) on that basis, an opening valuation as respects the relationship would have fallen to be made for that purpose as at a time before 1st April 1996.

(7) Notwithstanding anything in sub-paragraph (2) or (3) above, where—

(a) there is an amount that accrued or became due and payable before 1st April 1996 in respect of a continuing loan relationship of a company,

(b) that amount is not interest, and

(c) that amount would, apart from this Chapter, have been brought into account for the purposes of corporation tax in the accounting period in which it accrued or, as the case may be, became due and payable,

that amount shall be brought into account in that period for the purposes of corporation tax to the same extent as it would have been so brought into account apart from this Chapter and shall not otherwise be brought into account by virtue of the application in relation to times on or after 1st April 1996 of any authorised accounting method.

Application of accruals basis to pre-commencement relationships

4. Subject to the following provisions of this Schedule, any question for the purposes of this Chapter as to the amounts which are to be treated (in accordance with an authorised accruals basis of accounting) as accruing to a company on or after 1st April 1996 shall be determined by applying that basis of accounting for determining, first, what amounts had accrued before that date.

Adjustments in respect of pre-commencement trading relationships

5.—(1) This paragraph applies in the case of any continuing loan relationship of a company as respects which any amounts would have been brought into account for the purposes of corporation tax in computing the profits or losses of the company from any trade carried on by it if—

(a) the company had ceased to be a party to the relationship on 31st March 1996; and

(b) where it is not otherwise the case, an accounting period of the company had ended on that date.

(2) Where there is a difference between—

(a) the notional closing value of the relationship as at 31st March 1996, and

(b) the adjusted closing value of that relationship as at that date,

that difference shall be brought into account as provided for in paragraph 6 below.

(3) Except where sub-paragraph (4) or (6) below applies, the notional closing value as at 31st March 1996 of a loan relationship of a company shall be taken for the purposes of this paragraph to be the amount which, for the purposes of computing the profits or losses of the company from any trade carried on by it—

(a) was as at that date, or

(b) had an accounting period of the company ended on that date, would have been,

the amount falling to be brought into account as representing the value of the company's rights or liabilities under the relationship.

(4) Except where sub-paragraph (6) below applies, if no amount is given by sub-paragraph (3) above, the notional closing value as at 31st March 1996 of a loan relationship of a company shall be taken for the purposes of this paragraph to be the amount which, for the purposes of computing the profits or losses of the company from any trade carried on by it, would have been deductible as representing the cost of becoming a party to the relationship if the company had ceased to be a party to the relationship on 31st March 1996.

(5) Except where sub-paragraph (6) below applies, the adjusted closing value of that relationship as at that date shall be taken for the purposes of this paragraph to be the amount which for

the purposes of this Chapter is the opening value as at 1st April 1996 of the company's rights and liabilities under the relationship.

(6) For the purposes of this paragraph where the asset representing a loan relationship of a company is a relevant qualifying asset of the company, or the liabilities of the company under the relationship are relevant liabilities—

(a) the notional closing value of the relationship as at 31st March 1996 shall be taken for the purposes of this paragraph to be the value given by paragraph 12 below as the notional closing value as at 31st March 1996 of that asset or, as the case may be, of those liabilities; and

(b) the adjusted closing value of the relationship as at 31st March 1996 shall be taken for those purposes to be the amount which is as at 1st April 1996 the opening value of the asset or liabilities for the purposes of this Chapter.

(7) For the purposes of this paragraph, where an accruals basis of accounting is used as respects a loan relationship for the first relevant accounting period of the company, the opening value as at 1st April 1996 of the company's rights and liabilities under the relationship shall be taken to be the value which (disregarding interest) is treated in accordance with paragraph 4 above as having accrued to the company before that date.

(8) In this paragraph—

"attributed amount" means any attributed gain or loss falling to be calculated in accordance with any regulations made under Schedule 16 to the Finance Act 1993 (transitional provisions for exchange gains and losses) which contain any such provision as is mentioned in paragraph 3(1) of that Schedule;

"commencement day", in relation to a company, means its commencement day for the purposes of Chapter II of Part II of the Finance Act 1993;

"market value" has the same meaning as in the 1992 Act;

"relevant liability", in relation to a company, means any liability under a loan relationship the value of which has been determined as at the company's commencement day for the purpose of calculating any attributed amount;

"relevant qualifying asset", in relation to a company, means any qualifying asset for the purposes of Chapter II of Part II of the Finance Act 1993 the value of which has been determined as at the company's commencement day for the purpose of calculating any attributed amount.

Method of giving effect to paragraph 5 adjustments

6.—(1) Subject to sub-paragraph (4) below, the difference mentioned in paragraph 5(2) above shall be brought into account in accordance with sub-paragraph (2) or (3) below in the accounting period in which the company ceases to be a party to the relationship.

(2) If—

(a) the relationship is a creditor relationship and the difference consists in an excess of the amount mentioned in paragraph 5(2)(b) above over the amount mentioned in paragraph 5(2)(a) above, or

(b) the relationship is a debtor relationship and the difference consists in an excess of the amount mentioned in paragraph 5(2)(a) above over the amount mentioned in paragraph 5(2)(b) above,

the difference shall be brought into account as a credit given for the purposes of this Chapter for the period mentioned in sub-paragraph (1) above.

(3) In any other case, the difference shall be brought into account as a debit given for the purposes of this Chapter for the period so mentioned.

(4) Where the company, by notice in writing given on or before 30th September 1996 to an officer of the Board, makes an election for the purposes of this sub-paragraph—

(a) sub-paragraphs (1) to (3) above shall not apply; and

(b) instead, one sixth of every credit and debit which would have fallen, in accordance with those sub-paragraphs, to be brought into account on the relevant assumption shall be brought into account for each year in the period of six years beginning with the company's first relevant accounting period;

and for this purpose "the relevant assumption" is that the company had ceased on 1st April 1996 to be a party to every one of its continuing loan relationships to which paragraph 5 above applies.

(5) Where any amount representing a fraction of a credit or debit falls to be brought into account for any year under sub-paragraph (4) above, that amount shall be—

(a) apportioned between the accounting periods beginning or ending in that year; and

(b) brought into account in the periods to which it is allocated in accordance with that apportionment.

(6) An apportionment between accounting periods of an amount to be brought into account under sub-paragraph (4) above for any year shall be made according to how much of the year is

included in each period; and, if that year and the accounting period are the same, the apportionment shall be effected by the allocation of the whole amount to that accounting period.

(7) If the company ceases to be within the charge to corporation tax before the end of the six years mentioned in sub-paragraph (4)(b) above, the whole amount of the excess, so far as it has not fallen to be brought into account for an earlier accounting period, shall be brought into account as a debit or credit for the accounting period ending when the company ceases to be within that charge.

(8) Where any credit or debit falls to be brought into account under this paragraph for any accounting period for the whole or any part of which the company carries on the trade in question, the credit or debit shall be brought into account under section 82(2) of this Act in relation to that trade; and, in any other case, it shall be brought into account as a non-trading credit or non-trading debit.

General savings for the taxation of chargeable gains

7. The amendments of the 1992 Act contained in Schedule 14 to this Act and the related repeals made by this Act—
  (a) so far as they relate to section 253 of the 1992 Act, do not apply to any loan the outstanding amount of principal on which became irrecoverable before 1st April 1996;
  (b) so far as they relate to section 254 of the 1992 Act, do not apply to any security whose value became negligible before 1st April 1996;
  (c) so far as they relate to anything else, do not apply in relation to any disposal made, or deemed to be made, before 1st April 1996.

Transitional provision for chargeable assets held after commencement

8.—(1) This paragraph applies where—
  (a) on 31st March 1996 any company ("the relevant company") held any asset representing, in whole or in part, any loan relationship to which it was a party on that date;
  (b) the company did not dispose of that asset on that date and does not fall (apart from by virtue of this paragraph) to be treated for the purposes of the 1992 Act as having made a disposal of it on that date;
  (c) the asset is not one to which section 92 of this Act or paragraph 15 below applies;
  (d) that asset is not an asset representing a loan relationship to which section 93 of this Act applies;
  (e) that asset is not a relevant qualifying asset; and
  (f) a relevant event occurs.

(2) For the purposes of this paragraph a relevant event occurs on the first occasion after 31st March 1996 when the relevant company or any other company falls to be treated for the purposes of the 1992 Act as making a disposal, other than one to which section 139, 140A, 171(1) or 172 of that Act (disposals on which neither a gain nor a loss accrues) applies, of—
  (a) the asset in question, so far as it has not come to be represented by an asset falling within paragraph (b) below, or
  (b) any such asset as falls to be treated for the purposes of that Act as the same as that asset.

(3) The amount of any chargeable gain or allowable loss which would have been treated as accruing to the relevant company on the assumption—
  (a) that it had made a disposal of the asset on 31st March 1996, and
  (b) (so far as relevant for the purpose of computing the amount of that gain or loss) that the disposal had been for a consideration equal to the market value of the asset,

shall be brought into account (subject to the following provisions of this paragraph and to paragraph 9 below) as one accruing to the company ("the chargeable company") which makes the disposal constituting the relevant event, and shall be so brought into account in the accounting period in which that event occurs.

(4) The amount of the deemed chargeable gain or deemed allowable loss falling to be brought into account in accordance with sub-paragraph (3) above shall be treated as reduced by the extent (if any) to which it is, in relation to the company, an amount that already has been, or falls to be, taken into account for the purposes of corporation tax by virtue of the use of any accruals or mark to market basis of accounting—
  (a) for those purposes;
  (b) as respects times before 1st April 1996; and
  (c) in relation to the asset in question.

(5) To the extent that any deemed chargeable gain or deemed allowable loss falling to be brought into account under sub-paragraph (3) above includes any gain or loss deemed to accrue under section 116(10)(b) of the 1992 Act (qualifying corporate bonds acquired in a reorganis-

ation etc.), that gain or loss shall be deemed to have accrued for the purposes of that sub-paragraph and (without prejudice to its being brought into account in accordance with that sub-paragraph) shall not be taken to accrue again on the occurrence of the relevant event or any subsequent disposal of any asset.

(6) In any case where—

(a) the relevant company is one which at any time before 1st April 1996 was not resident in the United Kingdom,

(b) the asset was held by the relevant company at such a time, and

(c) if the asset had been disposed of at that time and a gain had accrued to the relevant company on that disposal, it would not have been included in the company's chargeable profits by virtue of section 10(3) of the 1992 Act (gain on a disposal by a branch or agency of a non-resident company),

the relevant company shall be deemed for the purposes of sub-paragraph (3) above to have acquired the asset, at market value, on the first day on which any relevant gain would have been included in the company's chargeable profits for the purposes of corporation tax (whether because it is a day on which the company became resident, or the asset became situated, in the United Kingdom or for any other reason).

(7) In sub-paragraph (6) above the reference, in relation to a company, to a relevant gain is a reference to any gain which would have accrued to the company on the following assumptions, that is to say—

(a) that the relevant company disposed of the asset on the day in question;

(b) that that disposal gave rise to a gain; and

(c) that any allowable losses which might have been available for deduction under section 8(1) of, or Schedule 7A to, the 1992 Act were to be disregarded.

(8) In any case where the company acquired the asset on a disposal on which, by virtue of any enactment specified in section 35(3)(d) of the 1992 Act, neither a gain nor a loss accrued to the person making the disposal, the reference in sub-paragraph (6) or (7) above to the relevant company includes—

(a) a reference to the company from which it acquired the asset; and

(b) if that company also acquired the asset on such a disposal, a reference to the company from which the asset was acquired by that company, and so on through any number of such disposals.

(9) In any case where section 176 of the 1992 Act (depreciatory transactions within a group) would have applied in relation to the disposal referred to in sub-paragraph (3) above if that disposal had actually taken place, that section shall apply for the calculation of any deemed allowable loss to be brought into account by virtue of that sub-paragraph.

(10) For the purposes of this paragraph a company that ceases to be within the charge to corporation tax shall be deemed to make a disposal of all its assets at their market value immediately before ceasing to be within that charge.

(11) In this section—

"market value" has the same meaning as in the 1992 Act; and

"relevant qualifying asset" has the same meaning as in paragraph 5 above.

Election for alternative treatment of amounts specified in paragraph 8

9.—(1) Subject to the following provisions of this paragraph, where (apart from this paragraph) any amount representing a deemed allowable loss would fall in the case of any company to be brought into account for any accounting period in accordance with sub-paragraph (3) of paragraph 8 above, the chargeable company may elect for that amount to be brought into account for that period for the purposes of this Chapter, instead of in accordance with that sub-paragraph.

(2) An amount brought into account for the purposes of this Chapter by virtue of an election under this paragraph shall be so brought into account as a debit given for that period for the purposes of this Chapter.

(3) The question whether or not any debit brought into account for any accounting period in accordance with sub-paragraph (2) above is to be brought into account for that period as a non-trading debit shall be determined according to how other credits or debits relating to the loan relationship in question are, or (if there were any) would be, brought into account for that period.

(4) No election shall be made under this paragraph in respect of any deemed allowable loss in any case where the asset in respect of which that loss is deemed to have accrued was one which, as at 1st April 1996, either—

(a) fell in accordance with section 127 or 214(9) of the 1992 Act (equation of new holding with previous holding) to be treated as the same as an asset which was not an asset representing a loan relationship; or

(b) would have so fallen but for section 116(5) of that Act.

(5) An election shall not be made under this paragraph at any time more than two years after the occurrence of the relevant event by virtue of which the amount to which the election relates would fall to be brought into account in accordance with paragraph 8(3) above.

Adjustments of opening value for mark to market accounting in the case of chargeable assets

10.—(1) Where—
  (a) a mark to market basis of accounting is used as respects any loan relationship of a company for the company's first relevant accounting period,
  (b) for the purpose of bringing amounts into account for the purposes of this Chapter on that basis, an opening valuation of an asset representing that relationship falls to be made as at 1st April 1996, and
  (c) that asset is a chargeable asset held by that company on 31st March 1996,
the value of that asset on 1st April 1996 shall be taken for the purpose of the opening valuation to be equal to whatever, in relation to a disposal on 31st March 1996, would have been taken to be its market value for the purposes of the 1992 Act.

(2) In this paragraph "chargeable asset", in relation to a company, means (subject to sub-paragraph (3) below) any asset in the case of which one of the following conditions is satisfied, that is to say—
  (a) a gain accruing to the company on a disposal of that asset on 31st March 1996 would have fallen to be treated in relation to the company as a chargeable gain; or
  (b) a chargeable gain or allowable loss would be deemed to have accrued to the company on any disposal of that asset on that date.

(3) An asset is not a chargeable asset for the purposes of this paragraph if (disregarding the provisions of this Chapter) it is an asset any disposal of which on 31st March 1996 would have fallen to be regarded for the purposes of the 1992 Act as a disposal of a qualifying corporate bond.

Other adjustments in the case of chargeable assets etc.

11.—(1) Where—
  (a) an authorised accruals basis of accounting is applied as respects any continuing loan relationship of a company for the company's first relevant accounting period,
  (b) an asset representing that relationship is a relevant asset or any liability under it is a relevant liability, and
  (c) the relationship is not one as respects which, if the company had ceased to be a party to the relationship on 31st March 1996, any amounts would have been brought into account in computing, for an accounting period ending on or after that date, the profits or losses of the company from any trade carried on by it,
that accounting method shall be taken for the purposes of this Chapter to require the asset or liability to be given a notional closing value as at 31st March 1996 in accordance with paragraph 12 below and the following provisions of this paragraph shall apply if there is any difference in the case of that relationship between the amounts mentioned in sub-paragraph (2) below.

(2) Those amounts are—
  (a) the amount which would have been brought into account as accruing in the first relevant accounting period of the company, if—
      (i) the company had become a party to the loan relationship on 1st April 1996;
      (ii) the opening value applicable as at that date for the purposes of an authorised accruals basis of accounting had been the notional closing value as at 31st March 1996; and
      (iii) the closing value applicable as at the end of that period for the purposes of such a basis of accounting were the same as the amount given as that closing value when applying such a basis for computing the amount mentioned in paragraph (b) below; and
  (b) the amount which is in fact treated as accruing in that period in accordance with paragraph 4 above.

(3) Where the amounts mentioned in paragraphs (a) and (b) of sub-paragraph (2) above are amounts falling to be brought into account as credits, the difference between them shall be brought into account—
  (a) where the amount mentioned in paragraph (a) exceeds the amount mentioned in paragraph (b), as a credit given for the purposes of this Chapter for the accounting period in which the company ceases to be a party to the relationship; and
  (b) in any other case, as a debit so given.

(4) Where the amounts mentioned in paragraphs (a) and (b) of sub-paragraph (2) above are amounts falling to be brought into account as debits, the difference between them shall be brought into account—

(a) where the amount mentioned in paragraph (a) exceeds the amount mentioned in paragraph (b), as a debit given for the purposes of this Chapter for the accounting period in which the company ceases to be a party to the relationship; and

(b) in any other case, as a credit so given.

(5) Where the company ceases to be within the charge to corporation tax, it shall be deemed for the purposes of this paragraph to have ceased to be a party to the relationship in question immediately before ceasing to be within that charge.

(6) A credit or debit brought into account under this paragraph shall be brought into account as a non-trading credit or non-trading debit.

(7) In this paragraph—

"chargeable asset", in relation to a company, means (subject to sub-paragraph (8) below) any asset held by the company on 31st March 1996 in the case of which one of the following conditions is satisfied, that is to say—

(a) a gain accruing to the company on a disposal of that asset on that date would have fallen to be treated in relation to the company as a chargeable gain; or

(b) a chargeable gain or allowable loss would be deemed to have accrued to the company on any disposal of that asset on that date;

and

"relevant asset" means a chargeable asset or a relevant qualifying asset.

(8) An asset is not a chargeable asset for the purposes of this paragraph if (disregarding the provisions of this Chapter) it is an asset any disposal of which on 31st March 1996 would have fallen to be regarded for the purposes of the 1992 Act as a disposal of a qualifying corporate bond.

(9) Expressions used in this paragraph and paragraph 5 above have the same meanings in this paragraph as in that paragraph.

Notional closing values of relevant assets

12.—(1) Subject to sub-paragraph (2) below, the notional closing value as at 31st March 1996 of any relevant asset representing a loan relationship of a company, or of any relevant liability, shall be taken for the purposes of paragraphs 5 and 11 above, to be an amount equal to the following amount, that is to say—

(a) in the case of a chargeable asset, its market value on that date;

(b) in the case of a relevant qualifying asset or relevant liability, the value given to it as at the company's commencement day for the purpose of computing any attributed amount.

(2) Sub-paragraph (3) below applies where a company, by notice in writing given on or before 30th September 1996 to an officer of the Board, makes an election for the purposes of that sub-paragraph in relation to all of its relevant qualifying assets which—

(a) apart from the election, would be given a notional closing value as at 31st March 1996 by sub-paragraph (1) above; and

(b) but for Chapter II of Part II of the Finance Act 1993 (exchange gains and losses), would be chargeable assets.

(3) Where such an election is made as respects those assets—

(a) sub-paragraph (1) above shall not apply as respects those assets; but

(b) the value of each of those assets as at 1st April 1996 shall be taken for the purposes of this Chapter to be its market value on that date.

(4) In this paragraph "chargeable asset" and "relevant asset" have the same meanings as in paragraph 11 above; and expressions used in this paragraph and paragraph 5 above have the same meanings in this paragraph as in that paragraph.

Further transitional rules for interest under loan relationships

13.—(1) Where—

(a) an amount of interest under a loan relationship of a company accrues or becomes due and payable in an accounting period ending on or after 1st April 1996, but

(b) the amount accruing or becoming due and payable has already, in the case of that company, been brought into account for the purposes of corporation tax for an old accounting period,

no credit or, as the case may be, debit relating to that amount shall be brought into account in the case of that company for the purposes of this Chapter.

(2) This Chapter shall have effect in accordance with sub-paragraphs (3) and (4) below in relation to any pre-commencement late interest, that is to say, interest which—

(a) has accrued or become due and payable in an old accounting period, but

(b) is paid in an accounting period ending on or after 1st April 1996.

(3) Where—

(a) an amount of pre-commencement late interest under a debtor relationship of a company is paid by that company,

(b) the amount paid is not interest which, in the case of that company, was brought into account for the purposes of corporation tax for any old accounting period,

(c) relief would have been allowable in respect of the amount paid if the provisions of this Chapter had not been enacted, and

(d) the amount paid is not interest in relation to which any debit falls (apart from under this sub-paragraph) to be brought into account for the purposes of this Chapter in the case of that company,

debits shall be brought into account for the purposes of this Chapter in the case of that company as if the amount paid were interest accruing, and becoming due and payable, at the time when it is paid.

(4) Where—

(a) an amount of pre-commencement late interest under a creditor relationship of a company is paid to that company,

(b) the amount paid is not interest which, in the case of that company, was brought into account for the purposes of corporation tax for any old accounting period,

(c) the amount paid is not interest in relation to which any credit falls (apart from under this sub-paragraph) to be brought into account for the purposes of this Chapter in the case of that company, and

(d) the amount paid is not an amount of interest which in relation to a transfer before 1st April 1996 was unrealised interest within the meaning of section 716 of the Taxes Act 1988,

credits shall be brought into account for the purposes of this Chapter in the case of that company as if the amount paid were interest accruing, and becoming due and payable, at the time when it is paid.

(5) Where—

(a) any interest under a debtor relationship of a company was paid by that company at a time on or after 20th December 1995 but during an old accounting period,

(b) the company was not required to make the payment at or before that time by virtue of any contractual obligation entered into by that company before 20th December 1995, and

(c) the interest paid is not interest which, if brought into account for the purposes of corporation tax in accordance with an authorised accruals basis of accounting, would fall to be so brought into account in an old accounting period,

the interest paid shall not, in the case of that company, be brought into account for the purposes of corporation tax in any old accounting period.

(6) Where on 1st April 1996 any interest under a loan relationship remains to be paid to or by a company that ceased to be a party to that relationship before that date, this Chapter (including the preceding provisions of this paragraph) shall have effect, so far as relating to interest under a loan relationship, as if the relationship were a continuing loan relationship.

(7) Sub-paragraphs (8) and (9) below apply where the accounting period for which any credits or debits relating to interest under a loan relationship are brought into account for the purposes of this Chapter is determined either—

(a) in accordance with an accruals basis of accounting, by reference to the time when by virtue of this paragraph that interest is deemed to accrue; or

(b) in accordance with a mark to market basis of accounting, by reference to the time when by virtue of this paragraph the interest is deemed to become due and payable.

(8) If—

(a) at the time when the interest in fact accrued or (as the case may be) when the interest in fact became due and payable, the company was a party to the relationship in question for the purposes of a trade carried on by it, and

(b) the credits or debits relating to that interest fall to be brought into account for an accounting period determined as mentioned in sub-paragraph (7) above which is a period for the whole or any part of which that company carries on that trade,

those credits or debits shall be so brought into account under section 82(2) of this Act.

(9) In a case not falling within sub-paragraph (8) above, credits or debits relating to any interest that fall to be brought into account for the purposes of this Chapter for an accounting period determined as mentioned in sub-paragraph (7) above shall be so brought into account as non-trading credits or, as the case may be, non-trading debits.

(10) References in this paragraph to interest under a loan relationship include references to any amounts brought into account for the purposes of corporation tax in accordance with the provisions of section 477A(3) of the Taxes Act 1988 (whether under those provisions as they had effect apart from the amendments made by this Act or under those provisions as amended by this Act).

(11) In this paragraph "old accounting period", in relation to a company, means any accounting period of that company ending before 1st April 1996.

Transitional in respect of incidental expenses already allowed

14. To the extent that any deduction in respect of any charges or expenses incurred as mentioned in section 84(3) of this Act has been made for the purposes of corporation tax in any accounting period ending before 1st April 1996, those charges or expenses shall not be included in the charges or expenses in relation to which debits may be brought into account for the purposes of this Chapter.

Holdings of unit trusts etc.

15.—(1) This paragraph applies to any asset which—
(a) is an asset of an insurance company's long term business fund (within the meaning of Chapter I of Part XII of the Taxes Act 1988) both on and immediately after 31st March 1996; and
(b) falls by virtue of paragraph 4 of Schedule 10 to this Act to be treated for a transitional accounting period of the company as representing rights under a creditor relationship of the company.

(2) Sections 212 and 213 of the 1992 Act (annual disposal of holdings of unit trusts etc.) shall have effect (without the amendment made by this Chapter) in relation to the assets to which this paragraph applies as if (where it would not otherwise be the case) 31st March 1996 were the last day of an accounting period of the company holding the asset.

(3) Nothing in this Chapter shall prejudice the effect of section 213 of the 1992 Act in relation to any disposal which (whether by virtue of sub-paragraph (2) above or otherwise) is deemed under section 212 of that Act to be made on or before 31st March 1996.

Bad debt relieved before commencement

16.—(1) This paragraph applies where—
(a) an amount becomes, or is to become, due and payable under a creditor relationship of a company in an accounting period ending on or after 1st April 1996, but
(b) by virtue of any of sub-paragraphs (i) to (iii) of section 74(1)(j) of the Taxes Act 1988 (or any enactment re-enacted in those sub-paragraphs), a deduction of an amount representing the whole or any part of the amount payable was authorised to be made, and was made, in computing for the purposes of corporation tax the profits of the company for any accounting period ending before that date.

(2) Subject to sub-paragraph (3) below, nothing in this Chapter shall require it to be assumed for the purposes of this Chapter that any part of the amount to which the deduction relates will be paid in full as it becomes due.

(3) Subject to sub-paragraph (4) below, where—
(a) the deduction relates to an amount payable under a creditor relationship of a company which has been proved or estimated to be a bad debt, but
(b) in an accounting period ending on or after 1st April 1996 the whole or any part of the liability under that relationship to pay that amount is discharged by payment,
this Chapter shall have effect, in the case of that company, as if there were a credit equal to the amount of the payment to be brought into account for the purposes of this Chapter for that period.

(4) Sub-paragraph (3) above does not apply to so much of any payment as is an amount in relation to which a credit falls to be brought into account for the purposes of this Chapter in accordance with paragraph 13(4) above.

Transitional for overseas sovereign debt etc.

17.—(1) Subject to any regulations under sub-paragraph (4) below and notwithstanding anything in the preceding provisions of this Schedule, the value which for the purposes of this Chapter is to be taken to be the value as at 1st April 1996 of a company's rights under any creditor relationship relating to a relevant overseas debt any part of which falls to be estimated as bad, is the following amount—

(a) where the company was not entitled to the debt before the end of its last period of account to end before 1st April 1996, the amount for which the company acquired those rights; and

(b) in any other case, the amount of so much of that debt as did not fall, in accordance with section 88B of the Taxes Act 1988, to be estimated as at the end of that period to be bad.

(2) Subject to any regulations under sub-paragraph (4) below, sub-paragraph (3) below shall apply where there is a loss incurred before 1st April 1996 to which section 88C of the Taxes Act 1988 has applied or applies by virtue of paragraph 2 above.

(3) Where, apart from this Chapter, any amount would have been allowed in respect of the loss as a deduction tor any accounting period ending after 31st March 1996, that amount shall not be so allowed but shall, instead, be brought into account for the purposes of this Chapter as if it were a debit given for that accounting period by paragraph 9 of Schedule 9 to this Act in respect of a loss incurred on or after 1st April 1996.

(4) The Treasury may by regulations—

(a) make such transitional provision as they consider appropriate for purposes connected with the coming into force of paragraphs 8 and 9 of Schedule 9 to this Act and the repeal of sections 88A to 88C of the Taxes Act 1988 (which contained corresponding provisions); and

(b) in connection with any such provision, make such modifications of this Schedule (including sub-paragraphs (1) to (3) above) as they consider appropriate;

and regulations made by virtue of this sub-paragraph may have retrospective effect in relation to any accounting periods ending on or after 1st April 1996.

(5) The Treasury shall not make any regulations under sub-paragraph (4) above unless a draft of them has been laid before and approved by a resolution of the House of Commons.

(6) In this paragraph "relevant overseas debt" has the same meaning as in paragraphs 8 and 9 of Schedule 9 to this Act.

Transitional for accrued income scheme

18.—(1) Subject to sub-paragraph (2) below, where, apart from this Chapter, any company would be treated under subsection (2) or (4) of section 714 of the Taxes Act 1988 (treatment of deemed sums and reliefs under accrued income scheme)—

(a) as receiving any amount at the end of a period beginning before and ending on or after 1st April 1996, or

(b) as entitled to any allowance of any amount in such a period,

that amount shall be brought into account as a non-trading credit or, as the case may be, non-trading debit given for the purposes of this Chapter for the company's first relevant accounting period, instead of in accordance with that subsection.

(2) A debit in respect of an allowance relating to a security shall not, in the case of any company, be brought into account for the purposes of this Chapter in accordance with sub-paragraph (1) above if—

(a) the security was transferred to that company with accrued interest in a transitional accounting period; and

(b) for the purposes of this Chapter an authorised accruals basis of accounting is used for that period as respects the creditor relationship of the company represented by that security.

(3) Where any excess would, apart from this Chapter, be available by virtue of section 103(4) of the Finance Act 1993 (transitional provision in connection with the repeal of section 724(7) of the Taxes Act 1988) to be applied in reducing the annual profits or gains of a company (if any) for its first relevant accounting period, that excess shall be brought into account for the purposes of this Chapter in the case of that company as a non-trading debit for that period.

(4) Subsection (6) of section 807 of the Taxes Act 1988 shall not prevent that section from having effect for an accounting period ending on or after 1st April 1996 in relation to amounts brought into account under this paragraph.

(5) The repeal by this Act of section 63 of the Finance Act 1993 (deemed transfers for the purposes of the accrued income scheme) and of enactments relating to that section shall not apply in relation to relevant days falling before 1st April 1996; but for the purposes of that section and this sub-paragraph 31st March 1996 shall be deemed (where it would not otherwise be so) to be the last day of an accounting period.

Deep discount securities

19.—(1) This Chapter shall not affect—

(a) the application of paragraph 3 of Schedule 4 to the Taxes Act 1988 (charge to tax after acquisition of deep discount securities) in relation to occasions before 1st April 1996;

(b) the application of paragraph 4 of that Schedule (charge to tax on disposal of such securities) in relation to any disposal before that date; or

(c) the application of paragraph 5 of that Schedule (relief in respect of the income element), in accordance (where applicable) with paragraphs 9 and 10 of that Schedule, in relation to income periods ending before that date.

(2) For the purposes of paragraph 5 of Schedule 4 to the Taxes Act 1988 and sub-paragraph (1)(c) above every income period current on 31st March 1996 shall be deemed to end on that date.

(3) The repeal by this Act of section 64 of the Finance Act 1993 (deemed transfers in the case of deep discount securities) and of enactments relating to that section shall not apply in relation to relevant times falling before 1st April 1996; but for the purposes of that section and this sub-paragraph 31st March 1996 shall be deemed (where it would not otherwise be so) to be the last day of an accounting period.

(4) Where—

(a) a company issued a deep discount security before 1st April 1996 which was not redeemed before that date, and

(b) there is a difference between the adjusted issue price of the security as at 31st March 1996 and the adjusted closing value of that security as at that date,

the amount of that difference shall, in the case of that company, be brought into account for the purposes of this Chapter in accordance with sub-paragraph (5) below.

(5) An amount falling to be brought into account for the purposes of this Chapter in accordance with this sub-paragraph shall be brought into account for those purposes for the accounting period in which the security is redeemed—

(a) if the adjusted issue price of the security as at 31st March 1996 is greater than the adjusted closing value of the security as at that date, as a non-trading credit; and

(b) if the adjusted closing value of the security as at that date is the greater, as a non-trading debit.

(6) Where—

(a) a company held a deep discount security on 31st March 1996,

(b) the company did not make any disposal of that security on that date,

(c) the security is not one in relation to which there is, or is deemed to be, a relevant time on that date for the purposes of section 64 of the Finance Act 1993, and

(d) there is an amount which, if the company had made a disposal of that security on that date, would have been treated under paragraph 4 of Schedule 4 to the Taxes Act 1988 as income chargeable to tax under Case III or IV of Schedule D,

that amount shall be brought into account as a non-trading credit given for the purposes of this Chapter for the accounting period mentioned in sub-paragraph (9) below.

(7) Where—

(a) a company held a deep discount security on 31st March 1996,

(b) the conditions specified in sub-paragraph (6)(b) and (c) above are satisfied in relation to that security,

(c) the security is not an asset falling to be treated as a relevant asset of the company for the purposes of paragraph 11 above, and

(d) there is a difference between the adjusted issue price of the security as at 31st March 1996 and the adjusted closing value of that security as at that date,

the amount of that difference (in addition to any amount given by sub-paragraph (6) above) shall, in the case of that company, be brought into account for the purposes of this Chapter in accordance with sub-paragraph (8) below.

(8) An amount falling to be brought into account for the purposes of this Chapter in accordance with this sub-paragraph shall be brought into account for those purposes for the accounting period mentioned in sub-paragraph (9) below—

(a) if the adjusted issue price of the security as at 31st March 1996 is greater than the adjusted closing value of the security as at that date, as a non-trading debit; and

(b) if the adjusted closing value of the security as at that date is the greater, as a non-trading credit.

(9) That period is the accounting period in which falls whichever is the earliest of the following, that is to say—

(a) the earliest day after 31st March 1996 on which, under the terms on which the security was issued, the company holding the security is entitled to require it to be redeemed;

(b) the day on which the security is redeemed; and

(c) the day on which the company makes a disposal of that security.

(10) The repeal by this Act of the reference in any enactment to, or to any provision of, paragraph 5 of Schedule 4 to the Taxes Act 1988 shall not have effect in relation to amounts treated as paid before 1st April 1996.

(11) For the purposes of this paragraph, in relation to any company—

(a) the adjusted issue price of a deep discount security as at 31st March 1996 is whatever for the purposes of Schedule 4 to the Taxes Act 1988 would have been the adjusted issue price of that security for an income period beginning with 1st April 1996; and

(b) the adjusted closing value of a security as at 31st March 1996 is the amount which for the purposes of this Chapter is the opening value as at 1st April 1996 of the company's rights and liabilities under the loan relationship of the company that is represented by that security;

and sub-paragraph (7) of paragraph 5 above shall apply for the purposes of this sub-paragraph as it applies for the purposes of that paragraph.

(12) In this paragraph "deep discount security", "disposal" and "income period" have the same meanings as in Schedule 4 to the Taxes Act 1988.

Deep gain securities

20.—(1) This Chapter shall not affect the application of paragraph 5 of Schedule 11 to the Finance Act 1989 (charge on deep gain securities) in relation to any transfer or redemption occurring before 1st April 1996.

(2) The repeal by this Act of section 65 of the Finance Act 1993 (deemed transfers in the case of deep gain securities) and of enactments relating to that section shall not apply in relation to relevant days falling before 1st April 1996; but for the purposes of that section and this sub-paragraph 31st March 1996 shall be deemed (where it would not otherwise be so) to be the last day of an accounting period.

(3) Where—

(a) a company held a deep gain security on 31st March 1996,

(b) the security was not transferred or redeemed by that company on that date,

(c) the security is not one in relation to which that date is, or is deemed to be, a relevant day for the purposes of section 65 of the Finance Act 1993, and

(d) there is an amount which, if the company had made a transfer of that security on that date by selling it for its adjusted closing value, would have been treated under paragraph 5 of Schedule 11 to the Finance Act 1989 as income chargeable to tax under Case III or IV of Schedule D,

that amount shall be brought into account as a non-trading credit given for the purposes of this Chapter for the accounting period mentioned in sub-paragraph (4) below.

(4) That period is the accounting period in which falls whichever is the earliest of the following, that is to say—

(a) the earliest day after 31st March 1996 on which, under the terms on which the security was issued, the company holding the security is entitled to require it to be redeemed;

(b) the day on which the security is redeemed; and

(c) the day on which the company makes a disposal of that security.

(5) For the purposes of this paragraph the adjusted closing value of a deep gain security held by a company on 31st March 1996 shall be the amount which for the purposes of this Chapter is the opening value as at 1st April 1996 of the company's rights and liabilities under the relationship represented by that security; and sub-paragraph (7) of paragraph 5 above shall apply for the purposes of this sub-paragraph as it applies for the purposes of that paragraph.

(6) In this paragraph "deep gain security" and "transfer" have the same meanings as in Schedule 11 to the Finance Act 1989.

Convertible securities

21.—(1) This Chapter shall not affect—

(a) the application of paragraph 12 of Schedule 10 to the Finance Act 1990 (charge in the case of convertible securities) in relation to any chargeable event occurring before 1st April 1996; or

(b) the application of paragraph 25 of that Schedule (relief in the case of convertible securities) in relation to any redemption occurring before that date.

(2) Where—

(a) a company held a qualifying convertible security on 31st March 1996,

(b) that date was not a date on which any chargeable event occurred in relation to that security, and

(c) there is an amount which, if there had been a chargeable event on that date, would have been treated under paragraph 12 of Schedule 10 to the Finance Act 1990 as income chargeable to tax under Case III or IV of Schedule D, that amount shall be brought into account, in the case of that company, as a non-trading credit given for the purposes of this Chapter for the accounting period mentioned in sub-paragraph (3) below.

(3) That period is the accounting period in which falls whichever is the earliest of the following, that is to say—

(a) the earliest day after 31st March 1996 on which, under the terms on which the security was issued, the company holding the security is entitled to require it to be redeemed;

(b) the day on which the security is redeemed; and

(c) the day on which the company makes a disposal of that security.

(4) Where—

(a) any qualifying convertible security is redeemed, and

(b) that security is one in the case of which any amount falls to be brought into account under sub-paragraph (2) above,

an amount equal to that amount shall be brought into account, in the case of the company that issued the security, as a non-trading debit given for the purposes of this Chapter for the accounting period in which the redemption occurs.

(5) In this paragraph "chargeable event" and "qualifying convertible security" have the same meanings as in Schedule 10 to the Finance Act 1990.

Transitional and savings for Chapter II of Part II of the Finance Act 1993

22.—(1) Chapter II of Part II of the Finance Act 1993 (exchange gains and losses) shall have effect in the case of any continuing loan relationship as follows.

(2) Subsection (1A) of section 127 of that Act (deemed variation of debt in respect of amounts accruing in respect of discounts and premiums) shall have effect in relation to the debt by reference to which the continuing loan relationship at any time subsists as if that debt is one to which the company became subject or entitled on 1st April 1996; and, accordingly, that subsection shall require the nominal amount of the debt outstanding to be treated as varied only where the time of the deemed variation is on or after 1st April 1996.

(3) Where section 127 of that Act has effect in relation to any debt by reference to which a continuing loan relationship at any time subsists, it shall so have effect, so far as the debt is one to which the company is deemed by virtue of sub-paragraph (2) above to have become subject or entitled on 1st April 1996, as if the nominal amount of the debt outstanding on that date were an amount equal to what it would have been if—

(a) sub-paragraph (2) above did not apply; and

(b) section 127(1A) of the Finance Act 1993 and the provisions to which it refers had always had effect.

(4) The amendment by this Act of section 153(4) of the Finance Act 1993 (assets excluded from being qualifying assets) shall not apply as respects times before 1st April 1996; and, where a company holds an asset immediately before and on 1st April 1996 and that asset is one which falls to be treated as a qualifying asset by virtue of that amendment—

(a) the company shall be treated as having become entitled to that asset on that date; and

(b) the basic valuation of the asset shall be taken to be its market value on 31st March 1996 (instead of any amount given by section 159 of that Act of 1993);

and in this sub-paragraph "market value" has the same meaning as in the 1992 Act.

(5) The repeal by this Act of section 153(6) of the Finance Act 1993 (liabilities excluded from being qualifying liabilities) shall not have effect as respects times before 1st April 1996; and, where a company is subject to a liability immediately before and on 1st April 1996 and that liability is one which falls to be treated as a qualifying liability by virtue of that repeal, the company shall be treated as having become subject to that liability on that date.

(6) The repeal by this Act of paragraphs 4 to 6 of Schedule 17 to the Finance Act 1993 (exchange gains and losses) shall not have effect in relation to any disposal before 1st April 1996.

Carrying back non-trading losses against exchange profits etc.

23.—(1) Subject to sub-paragraph (2) below, for the purpose of setting any amount against exchange profits for an accounting period beginning before 1st April 1996—

(a) a claim may be made under section 131(5) or (6) of the Finance Act 1993 (treatment of exchange gains and losses) in relation to any relievable amount for an accounting period ending on or after 1st April 1996; and

(b) the provisions of sections 129 to 133 of that Act shall be deemed to have effect for the purposes of that claim without the amendments made by Schedule 14 to this Act.

(2) If any claim is made by virtue of sub-paragraph (1) above in respect of the relievable amount for an accounting period beginning on or after 1st April 1996, then an amount equal to

the amount to which the claim relates shall be deemed, for the purposes of the computation falling to be made for that accounting period under section 82 of this Act, to be brought into account for that period as a non-trading credit.

(3) The references in this paragraph and paragraph 24 below to provisions of the Finance Act 1993 shall have effect as including references to those sections as applied by the provisions of Chapter II of Part IV of the Finance Act 1994.

(4) Sub-paragraph (3) above is without prejudice to the generality of section 20(2) of the Interpretation Act 1978 (references to other enactments).

Exchange losses etc. carried forward from before 1st April 1996

24. Where there is any amount which apart from this Chapter would fall under section 131(12) of the Finance Act 1993 (carrying forward of exchange gains and losses) to be carried forward to an accounting period ending on or after 1st April 1996, that amount shall be treated in relation to that period as an amount carried forward to that period in pursuance of section 83(3) of this Act.

Transitional for debt contracts and options to which Chapter II of Part IV of the Finance Act 1994 is applied

25.—(1) This paragraph applies in the case of any debt contract or option held by a company both immediately before and on 1st April 1996 if (apart from this Chapter)—

(a) the contract or option is an asset in the case of which the following condition is satisfied, that is to say, a gain accruing to the company on a disposal of that asset on 31st March 1996 would have fallen to be treated as a chargeable gain in relation to the company; or

(b) had there been a disposal of that asset on 31st March 1996, amounts with respect to it would have fallen to be brought into account for any accounting period beginning before 1st April 1996 in computing any profits or gains of the company from a trade carried on by it.

(2) Chapter II of Part IV of the Finance Act 1994 (provisions relating to certain financial instruments) shall have effect in relation to the debt contract or option as if references in that Chapter to 1st April 1996 were references to the beginning of the company's first relevant accounting period.

(3) For the accounting period mentioned in sub-paragraph (2) above, section 158(2) to (5) of that Act (adjustments for changes of basis of accounting) shall have effect in relation to the debt contract or option as if—

(a) any reference to the new basis were a reference to the basis of accounting on which, as regards the contract or option, the company's profit or loss for the accounting period so mentioned is calculated;

(b) any reference to being or not being included in amount A for a preceding accounting period were a reference to being or not being taken into account as receipts or increases in value in computing the company's profits or losses for such a period; and

(c) any reference to being or not being included in amount B for a preceding accounting period were a reference to being or not being taken into account as deductions or reductions in value in computing the company's profits or losses for such a period.

(4) Expressions used in this paragraph and in Chapter II of Part IV of the Finance Act 1994 have the same meanings in this paragraph as in that Chapter.

PART II

INCOME TAX AND CAPITAL GAINS TAX

Application and interpretation of Part II

26.—(1) This Part of this Schedule (except paragraph 29) has effect for the purposes of income tax and capital gains tax but not for the purposes of corporation tax.

(2) In this Part of this Schedule—

"the 1992 Act" means the Taxation of Chargeable Gains Act 1992;

"market value" has the same meaning as in the 1992 Act;

"qualifying indexed security" has the meaning given by paragraph 2 of Schedule 11 to the Finance Act 1989; and

"relevant discounted security" has the meaning given for the purposes of Schedule 13 to this Act.

(3) References in this Part of this Schedule to a disposal within marriage are references to any disposal to which section 58 of the 1992 Act applies.

Qualifying indexed securities

27.—(1) This paragraph applies where—
(a) on 5th April 1996 any person ("the relevant person") held a qualifying indexed security;
(b) that person did not dispose of that security on that date and does not fall (apart from by virtue of this paragraph) to be treated for the purposes of the 1992 Act as having made a disposal of it on that date; and
(c) a relevant event occurs.

(2) For the purposes of this paragraph a relevant event occurs on the first occasion after 5th April 1996 when the relevant person, or a person to whom that person has made a disposal of the security within marriage, falls to be treated for the purposes of the 1992 Act as making a disposal (otherwise than within marriage) which is—
(a) a disposal of the security in question; or
(b) a disposal of any such asset as falls to be treated for the purposes of that Act as the same as that security.

(3) The amount of any chargeable gain or allowable loss which would have been treated as accruing to the relevant person if—
(a) he had made a disposal of the asset on 5th April 1996, and
(b) that disposal had been for a consideration equal to the market value of the asset,
shall be brought into account as one accruing to the person who makes the disposal constituting the relevant event in the year of assessment in which that event occurs.

28. For the purposes of Schedule 13 to this Act where—
(a) a person held a qualifying indexed security both on and immediately after 5th April 1996, and
(b) that security is a relevant discounted security,
the amount which that person shall be taken to have paid in respect of his acquisition of that security on or before 5th April 1996 shall be an amount equal to its market value on that date.

29. For the purposes of paragraph 2 of Schedule 10 to this Act, paragraphs 27 and 28 above shall have effect in relation to an authorised unit trust for the first of its accounting periods to end after 31st March 1996 as if references in those paragraphs to 5th April 1996 were references to 31st March 1996.

Transitional in relation to qualifying corporate bonds

30.—(1) This paragraph applies where—
(a) any person holds any asset on and immediately after 5th April 1996;
(b) that asset is one which came to be held by that person as a result of a transaction to which section 127 of the 1992 Act applies; and
(c) that asset falls from 5th April 1996 to be treated as a relevant discounted security but is neither a qualifying indexed security nor such that it would have fallen to be treated as a qualifying corporate bond in relation to any disposal of it on that date.

(2) Section 116 of the 1992 Act (reorganisations etc. involving qualifying corporate bonds) shall have effect as if—
(a) there had been a transaction on 5th April 1996 by which the person holding the asset had disposed of it and immediately re-acquired it;
(b) the asset re-acquired had been a qualifying corporate bond; and
(c) the transaction had been a transaction to which section 127 of the 1992 Act would have applied but for section 116(5) of that Act.

GENERAL NOTE
The Schedule contains the transitional provisions for the new loan relationships rules.

Para. 2
Loan relationships ceasing before April 1, 1996 are not subject to the new provisions.

Para. 3
For loan relationships straddling April 1, 1996, any amounts due and accruing before that date are only brought into account if they are interest. For further transitional adjustments, see para. 13.

Para. 4
Where a company uses an accruals basis under the new provisions, that basis is assumed to have applied prior to April 1, 1996 in order to compute profits or losses arising from that date.

Para. 5

This deals with pre-April 1, 1996 trading loan relationships. The value under the new rules is compared with the value under the old rules and the balance is brought into account.

Para. 6

The balance identified under para. 5 is brought into account in the period in which the company ceases to be a party to the loan relationship, subject to a right to elect for a spread over six years.

Para. 7

The loan relationship provisions do not apply to loans treated as irrecoverable or securities whose value has become negligible under the TCGA 1992, ss.253 and 254, prior to April 1, 1996.

Para. 8

Chargeable assets held on March 31, 1996 which are not within the new provisions remain within the Taxation of Chargeable Gains Act 1992.

Para. 9

Where a loss arises under para. 8, the company may elect to have it treated as a non-trading debit, except where it arises under a reorganisation.

Para. 10

Previously chargeable assets brought into the mark-to-market basis are valued at market on March 31, 1996.

Para. 11

This provides for adjustments in respect of chargeable assets and assets which would have been chargeable but for the provisions in the FA 1993 dealing with the taxation of exchange differences. It ensures that overall profits and losses reflect pre-April 1, 1996 positions under the capital gains or foreign exchange codes.

Para. 12

Definitions are provided of the notional closing values for paras. 5 and 11 above. By election before September 30, 1996 an alternative method may be adopted by companies within para. 11.

Para. 13

This provides for adjustments in relation to interest accrued prior to April 1, 1996 but payable after that date.

Para. 14

Charges and expenses in connection with loans which have already been allowed cannot be allowed again.

Para. 15

This deals with the situation where an insurance company holds unit trusts or offshore funds. A deemed disposal under the TCGA 1992, s.212, will take place on March 31, 1996 but the seven-year deferral under s.213 will apply.

Para. 16

Bad debts already relieved will be brought into charge under the new provisions if they are repaid.

Para. 17

Special transitional rules are provided for overseas sovereign debt on which relief has been restricted by the ICTA 1988, ss.88A, 88B and 88C. Further modification may be made by Treasury order, subject to the affirmative resolution procedure.

Para. 18

This provides transitional rules following the repeal of the accrued income scheme legislation for companies. The FA 1993, s.63, applies as if March 31, 1996 was the last day of an accounting period.

Para. 19

Existing charges and reliefs for deep discount securities are preserved up to March 31, 1996, which is deemed to be a date on which an income period ceases. The accruing discount is charged as a non-trading credit on disposal or redemption. Where there is a disposal, any difference between the adjusted issue price and the adjusted closing value is brought into account as a non-trading debit or credit.

Para. 20
Similar transitional provisions (apart from the adjustment on disposal) apply for deep gain securities.

Para. 21
Similar transitional provisions apply for convertible securities.

Paras. 22–24
These provide consequential rules for the computation of exchange differences under the FA 1993.

Para. 25
This provides transitional rules for debt contracts and options in existence at April 1, 1996.

Para. 26
This introduces Part II of the Schedule, which applies only for income tax and corporation tax.

Para. 27
Any chargeable gain or allowable loss on a qualifying indexed security as at April 5, 1996, will be brought into account when it is disposed of.

Para. 28
The acquisition cost of a qualifying indexed security which is also a relevant discounted security within Sched. 13 will be treated as its market value.

Para. 29
Paragraphs 27 and 28 apply to authorised unit trusts for the purposes of Sched. 10, para. 2, with the substitution of March 31, 1996 for April 5, 1996.

Para. 30
Where there has been a share reorganisation resulting in a holding of relevant discounted securities which would not have been qualifying corporate bonds at that date, the capital gain or loss is preserved by a deemed disposal and reacquisition as a qualifying corporate bond [Standing Committee E, March 5, 1996, col. 690].

Section 114   SCHEDULE 16

SHARE OPTION SCHEMES APPROVED BEFORE PASSING OF THIS ACT

Preliminary

1.—(1) Subject to sub-paragraphs (2) and (3) below, this Schedule applies to any share option scheme approved by the Board before the day on which this Act is passed in consequence of their being satisfied that the scheme fulfils the requirements of Part IV of Schedule 9 to the Taxes Act 1988 (as well as such requirements of Parts I and II of that Schedule as apply in relation to the scheme).

(2) This Schedule shall not apply to a share option scheme if, before the end of 1996, the grantor gives notice to the Board that it is not to apply.

(3) Where a notice is given to the Board under sub-paragraph (2) above, the scheme shall, with effect from the day on which the notice is given, cease to be approved.

Limit on aggregate value of options

2.—(1) A scheme to which this Schedule applies shall have effect notwithstanding anything included in it to the contrary, as if it provided that no person shall, on or after the day on which this Act is passed, obtain rights under it which would, at the time they are obtained, cause the aggregate market value of the shares which that person may acquire in pursuance of rights obtained under the scheme or under any other share option scheme, not being a savings-related share option scheme, approved under Schedule 9 to the Taxes Act 1988 and established by the grantor or an associated company of the grantor (and not exercised) to exceed or further exceed £30,000.

(2) Sub-paragraph (3) of paragraph 28 of Schedule 9 to the Taxes Act 1988 (market value of shares to be calculated as at time when rights obtained etc) shall have effect for the purposes of sub-paragraph (1) above as it has effect for the purposes of sub-paragraph (1) of that paragraph.

Price at which scheme shares may be obtained

3. A scheme to which this Schedule applies shall have effect, notwithstanding anything included in it to the contrary, as if it provided that the price at which scheme shares may be acquired by the exercise of a right obtained, on or after the day on which this Act is passed, under the scheme must not be manifestly less than the market value of shares of the same class at that time or, if the Board and the grantor agree in writing, at such earlier time or times as may be provided in the agreement.

Approval of the Board to alterations

4. For the purposes of paragraph 4 of Schedule 9 to the Taxes Act 1988 (approval not to have effect from the date of any alteration in the scheme unless the Board have approved the alteration) the alterations made by paragraphs 2 and 3 above in any scheme to which this Schedule applies shall be taken to have been approved by the Board before the day on which this Act is passed.

Interpretation

5.—(1) Section 187 of the Taxes Act 1988 (interpretation of sections 185 and 186 and Schedules 9 and 10) applies for the purposes of this Schedule as it applies for the purposes of sections 185 and 186 of, and Schedules 9 and 10 to, that Act.

(2) In this Schedule "scheme shares" has the same meaning as in Part IV of Schedule 9 to the Taxes Act 1988.

GENERAL NOTE

This Schedule applies to existing share option schemes. A company can opt for the new provisions not to apply to the scheme. In such a case, it will cease to be approved. Where this is not done, the scheme will be deemed to include the new provisions limiting the value of options and precluding their issue at a discount.

Section 128   SCHEDULE 17

(Inserted as: Schedule 1B to the Taxes Management Act 1970)

CLAIMS FOR RELIEF INVOLVING TWO OR MORE YEARS

Preliminary

1.—(1) In this Schedule—
(a) any reference to a claim includes a reference to an election or notice; and
(b) any reference to the amount in which a person is chargeable to tax is a reference to the amount in which he is so chargeable after taking into account any relief or allowance for which a claim is made.

(2) For the purposes of this Schedule, two or more claims to which this Schedule applies which are made by the same person are associated with each other in so far as the same year of assessment is the earlier year in relation to each of those claims.

(3) In sub-paragraph (2) above, any reference to claims to which this Schedule applies includes a reference to amendments and revocations to which paragraph 4 below applies.

Loss relief

2.—(1) This paragraph applies where a person makes a claim requiring relief for a loss incurred or treated as incurred, or a payment made, in one year of assessment ("the later year") to be given in an earlier year of assessment ("the earlier year").

(2) Section 42(2) of this Act shall not apply in relation to the claim.

(3) The claim shall relate to the later year.

(4) Subject to sub-paragraph (5) below, the claim shall be for an amount equal to the difference between—
(a) the amount in which the person is chargeable to tax for the earlier year ("amount A"); and
(b) the amount in which he would be so chargeable on the assumption that effect could be, and were, given to the claim in relation to that year ("amount B").

(5) Where effect has been given to one or more associated claims, amounts A and B above shall each be determined on the assumption that effect could have been, and had been, given to the associated claim or claims in relation to the earlier year.

(6) Effect shall be given to the claim in relation to the later year, whether by repayment or set-off, or by an increase in the aggregate amount given by section 59B(1)(b) of this Act, or otherwise.

(7) For the purposes of this paragraph, any deduction made under section 62(2) of the 1992 Act (death: general provisions) in respect of an allowable loss shall be deemed to be made in pursuance of a claim requiring relief to be given in respect of that loss.

Relief for fluctuating profits of farming etc.

3.—(1) This paragraph applies where a person who is or has been carrying on a trade of farming or market gardening claims that subsection (2) or (3) of section 96 of the principal Act shall have effect in relation to his profits from that trade for two consecutive years of assessment ("the earlier year" and "the later year").

(2) The claim shall relate to the later year.

(3) Subject to sub-paragraph (4) below, in so far as the claim relates to the profits of the earlier year, the claim shall be for an amount equal to the difference between—
- (a) the amount in which the person is chargeable to tax for the earlier year ("amount A"); and
- (b) the amount in which he would be so chargeable on the assumption that effect could be, and were, given to the claim in relation to that year ("amount B").

(4) Where effect has been given to one or more associated claims, amounts A and B above shall each be determined on the assumption that effect could have been, and had been, given to the associated claim or claims in relation to the earlier year.

(5) In so far as the claim relates to the profits of the earlier year, effect shall be given to the claim in relation to the later year by an increase in the amount of tax payable or, as the case may require, in the aggregate amount given by section 59B(1)(b) of this Act.

(6) Where this paragraph applies twice in relation to the same year of assessment, the increase or reduction in the amount of tax payable for that year which is required by sub-paragraph (5) above on the earlier application shall be disregarded in determining amounts A and B above for the purposes of the later application.

Relief claimed by virtue of section 96(9)

4.—(1) This paragraph applies where—
- (a) a person who claims that subsection (2) or (3) of section 96 of the principal Act shall have effect for two consecutive years of assessment ("the earlier year" and "the later year") makes or amends a claim for relief under any other provision of the Income Tax Acts for either of those years; and
- (b) the making or amendment of the claim would be out of time but for subsection (9) of that section.

(2) The claim or amendment shall relate to the later year.

(3) Subject to sub-paragraph (4) below, in so far as the claim or amendment relates to income of the earlier year, the amount claimed, or (as the case may be) the increase or reduction in the amount claimed, shall be equal to the difference between—
- (a) the amount in which the person is chargeable to tax for the earlier year ("amount A"); and
- (b) the amount in which he would be so chargeable on the assumption that effect could be, and were, given to the claim or amendment in relation to that year ("amount B").

(4) Where effect has been given to one or more associated claims, amounts A and B above shall each be determined on the assumption that effect could have been, and had been, given to the associated claim or claims in relation to the earlier year.

(5) In so far as the claim or amendment relates to income of the earlier year, effect shall be given to the claim or amendment in relation to the later year by an increase in the amount of tax payable or, as the case may require, in the aggregate amount given by section 59B(1)(b) of this Act.

(6) In this paragraph "amend" includes revoke and "amendment" shall be construed accordingly.

Carry-back of post-cessation etc. receipts

5.—(1) This paragraph applies where a person who has received a sum to which section 108 of the principal Act applies (election for carry-back) makes an election under that section requiring tax to be charged as if the sum were received on the date on which the discontinuance took place or, as the case may be, on the last day of the period at the end of which the change of basis took place; and in this paragraph—

"the earlier year" means the year in which the sum is treated as received;
"the later year" means the year in which the sum is received.

(2) The claim shall relate to the later year.

(3) Subject to sub-paragraph (4) below, the claim shall be for an amount equal to the difference between—

(a) the amount in which the person is chargeable to tax for the earlier year ("amount A"); and

(b) the amount in which he would be so chargeable on the assumption that effect could be, and were, given to the claim in relation to that year ("amount B").

(4) Where effect has been given to one or more associated claims, amounts A and B above shall each be determined on the assumption that effect could have been, and had been, given to the associated claim or claims in relation to the earlier year.

(5) In computing amount B for the purposes of this paragraph, no further deduction or relief shall be made or given in respect of any loss or allowance deducted in pursuance of section 105 of the principal Act.

(6) Effect shall be given to the claim in relation to the later year by an increase in the amount of tax payable.

Backward spreading of certain payments

6.—(1) This paragraph applies where a person who has received a payment to which any of the following sections applies, namely—

(a) section 534 of the principal Act (relief for copyright payments etc.);

(b) section 537A of that Act (relief for payments in respect of designs); and

(c) section 538 of that Act (relief for painters, sculptors and other artists),

makes a claim under subsection (1) of that section requiring that effect be given to the following provisions of that section in connection with that payment.

(2) The claim shall relate to the year of assessment in which the payment in question is receivable ("the payment year"); and for the purposes of this sub-paragraph a payment shall be regarded as receivable in the year of assessment in computing the amount of the profits or gains of which it would, but for the relevant section, be included.

(3) Subject to sub-paragraph (4) below, in so far as the claim relates to the profits or gains of a year of assessment earlier than the payment year ("the earlier year"), the claim shall be for an amount equal to the difference between—

(a) the amount in which the person is chargeable to tax for the earlier year ("amount A"); and

(b) the amount in which he would be so chargeable on the assumption that effect could be, and were, given to the claim or amendment in relation to that year ("amount B").

(4) Where effect has been given to one or more associated claims, amounts A and B above shall each be determined on the assumption that effect could have been, and had been, given to the associated claim or claims in relation to the earlier year.

(5) In so far as the claim relates to the profits or gains of the earlier year, effect shall be given to the claim in relation to the payment year by an increase in the amount of tax payable.

GENERAL NOTE

The new TMA 1970, Sched. 1B, provides administrative rules regarding claims covering more than one tax year.

Para. 2

Claims for the loss of one year to be set against profits of an earlier year will be a claim for the later year.

Para. 3

Claims for the averaging of farm profits will be a claim for the later year.

Para. 4

Claims for other reliefs after a farmer's averaging claim will also be a claim for the later year.

Para. 5

Claims for carry-back of post-cessation receipts will be treated as a claim of the year in which the payment is received.

Para. 6

Claims for backward spreading under the ICTA 1988, ss.534, 537A and 538 will be treated as a claim of the later year.

SCHEDULE 18

OVERDUE TAX AND EXCESSIVE PAYMENTS BY THE BOARD

The Taxes Management Act 1970

1. In section 55 of the Taxes Management Act 1970 (recovery of tax not postponed) in subsection (1) (which specifies the appeals to which section 55 applies) for paragraph (b) (assessments under section 29) there shall be substituted—

"(b) an assessment to tax made otherwise than under section 9 of this Act,".

2.—(1) Section 59A of the Taxes Management Act 1970 (payments on account of income tax) shall be amended in accordance with the following provisions of this paragraph.

(2) In subsection (2) (requirement to make payments on account and determination, subject to subsections (4) and (4A), of the amount of such payments) for "(4) and (4A)" there shall be substituted "(4) to (4B)".

(3) In subsection (4A) (determination, subject to subsections (3) and (4), of amount of payments on account in the case of late or amended assessments), after "subsections (3) and (4) above" there shall be inserted "and subsection (4B) below".

(4) After subsection (4A) there shall be inserted—

"(4B) If as regards the year immediately preceding the year of assessment the taxpayer is assessed to income tax under section 29 of this Act in any amount, then, subject to subsections (3) and (4) above and to any subsequent application of this subsection, the amount of each payment on account shall be, and shall be deemed always to have been, the total of—

(a) the amount which, immediately before the making of the assessment under section 29, is the amount of that payment, and

(b) an amount equal to 50 per cent. of the amount in which he is assessed under that assessment;

and if that assessment is varied, the amount in which he is assessed under it shall be taken for the purposes of paragraph (b) above to be the amount of the assessment as varied."

(5) In subsection (5) (adjustments to be made where subsection (4A) applies) after "subsection (4A)" there shall be inserted "or (4B)".

3.—(1) Section 86 of the Taxes Management Act 1970 (interest on overdue income tax and capital gains tax) shall be amended in accordance with the following provisions of this paragraph.

(2) In subsection (4) (subsection (5) to apply with respect to interest in cases where taxpayer makes a claim under section 59A(3) or (4) but an amount becomes payable by him under certain provisions of section 59B) in paragraph (b), after "payable by him" there shall be inserted "(i)" and at the end of that paragraph there shall be added "or

(ii) in accordance with section 59B(6) of this Act in respect of income tax assessed under section 29 of this Act."

(3) In subsection (6) (determination of what amount is payable in accordance with section 59B(3), (4) or (5)) after "section 59B(3), (4) or (5) of this Act" there shall be inserted "or, in respect of income tax assessed under section 29 of this Act, in accordance with section 59B(6) of this Act".

4.—(1) Section 88 of the Taxes Management Act 1970 (which relates to interest on tax recovered to make good loss due to the taxpayer's fault and which is superseded by section 86 of that Act, as substituted by the Finance Act 1995) shall cease to have effect.

(2) In consequence of the repeal of section 88 of the Taxes Management Act 1970—

(a) section 88A of that Act (determinations under section 88) shall cease to have effect;

(b) in section 91 of that Act (effect of interest on reliefs) in subsection (1)—

(i) the words "or section 88" shall cease to have effect; and

(ii) for the words "those provisions", in each place where they occur, there shall be substituted "that section"; and

(c) in section 113 of that Act (form of returns and other documents) subsection (1C) shall cease to have effect.

The Taxes Act 1988

5. In section 307 of the Taxes Act 1988 (enterprise investment scheme and business expansion scheme: withdrawal of relief) in subsection (6) (application of section 86 of the Taxes Management Act 1970 to assessments made by virtue of section 307 as if the reckonable date were as specified in that subsection) for "the reckonable date" there shall be substituted "the relevant date".

6.—(1) Section 369 of the Taxes Act 1988 (MIRAS) shall be amended in accordance with the following provisions of this paragraph.

(2) In subsection (7)—

(a) for paragraph (a) (which applies section 29(3)(c) of the Taxes Management Act 1970) there shall be substituted—

"(a) section 29(1)(c) (excessive relief) as it has effect apart from section 29(2) to (10) of that Act;";

(b) in paragraph (b) (which applies section 30 of the Taxes Management Act 1970) after the words in parentheses there shall be inserted "apart from subsection (1B)";

(c) in paragraph (c) (which applies section 88 of the Taxes Management Act 1970) for "section 88" there shall be substituted "section 86"; and

(d) in the words following paragraph (d) after "as if it had been repaid" there shall be inserted "as respects a chargeable period".

(3) After subsection (7) there shall be inserted—

"(8) In the application of section 86 of the Management Act by virtue of subsection (7) above in relation to sums due and payable by virtue of an assessment made for the whole or part of a year of assessment ("the relevant year of assessment") under section 29(1)(c) or 30 of that Act, as applied by that subsection, the relevant date—

(a) is 1st January in the relevant year of assessment in a case where the person falling within subsection (6) above has made a relevant interim claim; and

(b) in any other case, is the later of the following dates, that is to say—

(i) 1st January in the relevant year of assessment; or

(ii) the date of the making of the payment by the Board which gives rise to the assessment.

(9) In this section—

"financial year", in relation to any person, means a financial year of that person for the purposes of the relevant regulations;

"interim claim" means an interim claim within the meaning of the relevant regulations;

"relevant interim claim" means, in relation to an assessment made for a period coterminous with, or falling wholly within, a person's financial year, an interim claim made for a period falling wholly or partly within that financial year; and

"the relevant regulations" means regulations made under section 378(3) for the purposes of subsection (6) above."

7. In section 374A of the Taxes Act 1988 (interest which never has been relevant loan interest etc) in subsection (4) (which provides for the application of the Taxes Management Act 1970 to an assessment under subsection (3) of that section as if it were an assessment to income tax and as if certain other things were the case) the words from "and as if" onwards shall be omitted.

8. In section 375 of the Taxes Act 1988 (interest ceasing to be relevant loan interest etc) in subsection (4) (which provides for the application of the Taxes Management Act 1970 to an assessment under subsection (3) of that section as it applies by virtue of section 374A(4) to an assessment under section 374A(3)) for "as it applies, by virtue of subsection (4) of section 374A, to an assessment under subsection (3) of that section" there shall be substituted "as if it were an assessment to income tax for the year of assessment in which the deduction was made".

9. In section 412(4) of the Taxes Act 1988 (group relief: power to assess under section 412(3) is without prejudice to the making of assessments under section 29(3)(c) of the Taxes Management Act 1970) for "section 29(3)(c)" there shall be substituted "section 29(1) (c)".

10. In section 588 of the Taxes Act 1988 (training courses: employee and employer may be assessed under section 29(3) of the Taxes Management Act 1970 if employee fails to comply with conditions for relief) for "section 29(3)" there shall be substituted "section 29(1)".

11.—(1) Schedule 14 to the Taxes Act 1988 (life assurance premium relief: provisions ancillary to section 266) shall be amended in accordance with the following provisions of this paragraph.

(2) In paragraph 6(2) (which provides for the application of the Taxes Management Act 1970 to an assessment under paragraph 6 of that Schedule as if it were an assessment to tax for the year of assessment in which the relief was given and as if certain other things were the case) the words from "and as if" onwards shall be omitted.

(3) In paragraph 7(3) (which applies specified provisions of the Taxes Management Act 1970 to the payment of a sum claimed under section 266(5)(b))—

(a) for paragraph (a) (which applies section 29(3)(c) of the Taxes Management Act 1970) there shall be substituted—

"(a) section 29(1)(c) (excessive relief) as it has effect apart from section 29(2) to (10) of that Act;";

(b) in paragraph (b) (which applies section 30 of the Taxes Management Act 1970) after the words in parentheses there shall be inserted "apart from subsection (1B)";

(c) in paragraph (c) (which applies section 88 of the Taxes Management Act 1970) for "section 88" there shall be substituted "section 86"; and

(d) for the words following paragraph (d) there shall be substituted—
"shall apply in relation to an amount which is paid to any person by the Board as an amount recoverable by virtue of section 266(5)(b) but to which that person is not entitled as if it were income tax which ought not to have been repaid and, where that amount was claimed by that person, as if it had been repaid as respects a chargeable period as a relief which was not due."

(4) After paragraph 7(3) there shall be added—
"(4) In the application of section 86 of the Management Act by virtue of sub-paragraph (3) above in relation to sums due and payable by virtue of an assessment made for the whole or part of a year of assessment ("the relevant year of assessment") under section 29(1)(c) or 30 of that Act, as applied by that sub-paragraph, the relevant date—
(a) is 1st January in the relevant year of assessment in a case where the person falling within section 266(5)(b) has made a relevant material claim; and
(b) in any other case, is the later of the following dates, that is to say—
(i) 1st January in the relevant year of assessment; or
(ii) the date of the making of the payment by the Board which gives rise to the assessment.
(5) In this paragraph—
"financial year", in relation to any person, means a financial year of that person for the purposes of the relevant regulations;
"interim claim" means an interim claim within the meaning of the relevant regulations;
"relevant interim claim" means, in relation to an assessment made for a period coterminous with, or falling wholly within, a person's financial year, an interim claim made for a period falling wholly or partly within that financial year;
"the relevant regulations" means regulations made under sub-paragraph (1) above."

12.—(1) Section 57 of the Finance Act 1989 (medical insurance: supplementary) shall be amended in accordance with the following provisions of this paragraph.

(2) In subsection (3) (which applies specified provisions of the Taxes Management Act 1970 to the payment of an amount claimed under section 54(6)(b))—
(a) for paragraph (a) (which applies section 29(3)(c) of the Taxes Management Act 1970) there shall be substituted—
"(a) section 29(1) (c) (excessive relief) as it has effect apart from section 29(2) to (10) of that Act;";
(b) in paragraph (b) (which applies section 30 of the Taxes Management Act 1970) after the words in parentheses there shall be inserted "apart from subsection (1B)";
(c) in paragraph (c) (which applies section 88 of the Taxes Management Act 1970) for "section 88" there shall be substituted "section 86"; and
(d) for the words following paragraph (d) there shall be substituted—
"shall apply in relation to an amount which is paid to any person by the Board as an amount recoverable by virtue of section 54(6)(b) above but to which that person is not entitled as if it were income tax which ought not to have been repaid and, where that amount was claimed by that person, as if it had been repaid as respects a chargeable period as a relief which was not due."

(3) After subsection (3) there shall be inserted—
"(3A) In the application of section 86 of the Taxes Management Act 1970 by virtue of subsection (3) above in relation to sums due and payable by virtue of an assessment made under section 29(1)(c) or 30 of that Act, as applied by that subsection, the relevant date—
(a) in a case where the person falling within section 54(6) above has made any interim claim, within the meaning of regulations made under subsection (1) and section 54(4) above, as respects some part of the year of assessment for which the assessment is made, is 1st January in that year of assessment; and
(b) in any other case, is the later of the following dates, that is to say—
(i) 1st January in the year of assessment for which the assessment is made; or
(ii) the date of the making of the payment by the Board which gives rise to the assessment."

13. In section 178 of the Finance Act 1989 (setting rates of interest) in subsection (2)(f) (which specifies the provisions of the Taxes Management Act 1970 to which the section applies) the words "88" shall be omitted.

The Finance Act 1991

14.—(1) Section 33 of the Finance Act 1991 (vocational training) shall be amended in accordance with the following provisions of this paragraph.

(2) In subsection (3) (which applies specified provisions of the Taxes Management Act 1970 to the payment of an amount claimed under section 32(5)(b))—

(a) for paragraph (a) (which applies section 29(3)(c) of the Taxes Management Act 1970) there shall be substituted—
"(a) section 29(1) (c) (excessive relief) as it has effect apart from section 29(2) to (10) of that Act;";
(b) in paragraph (b) (which applies section 30 of the Taxes Management Act 1970) after the words in parentheses there shall be inserted "apart from subsection (1B)";
(c) in paragraph (c) (which applies section 88 of the Taxes Management Act 1970) for "section 88" there shall be substituted "section 86"; and
(d) for the words following paragraph (d) there shall be substituted—
"shall apply in relation to an amount which is paid to any person by the Board as an amount recoverable by virtue of section 32(5)(b) above but to which that person is not entitled as if it were income tax which ought not to have been repaid and, where that amount was claimed by that person, as if it had been repaid as respects a chargeable period as a relief which was not due."
(3) After subsection (3) there shall be inserted—
"(3A) In the application of section 86 of the Taxes Management Act 1970 by virtue of subsection (3) above in relation to sums due and payable by virtue of an assessment made under section 29(1)(c) or 30 of that Act, as applied by that subsection, the relevant date—
(a) in a case where the person falling within section 32(5) above has made any interim claim, within the meaning of regulations made under subsection (1) above, as respects some part of the year of assessment for which the assessment is made, is 1st January in that year of assessment; and
(b) in any other case, is the later of the following dates, that is to say—
(i) 1st January in the year of assessment for which the assessment is made; or
(ii) the date of the making of the payment by the Board which gives rise to the assessment."

The Taxation of Chargeable Gains Act 1992

15.—(1) Section 281 of the Taxation of Chargeable Gains Act 1992 (payment by instalments of tax on gifts) shall be amended in accordance with the following provisions of this paragraph.
(2) In subsection (5), for paragraph (a) (tax payable by instalments to carry interest in accordance with Part IX of the Taxes Management Act 1970, except section 88) there shall be substituted—
"(a) tax payable by instalments by virtue of this section carries interest in accordance with Part IX of the Management Act as that Part applies where no election is made under subsection (2) above, and".
(3) In subsection (6) (power to pay at any time unpaid tax payable by instalments, with interest to the date of payment) after "with interest" there shall be inserted "(determined in accordance with subsection (5)(a) above)".
(4) In subsection (7) (cases where tax payable by instalments, with interest to the date of payment, becomes due and payable immediately) after "with interest" there shall be inserted "(determined in accordance with subsection (5)(a) above as if the tax were tax payable by instalments by virtue of this section)".

The Finance Act 1995

16. In section 73(4) of the Finance Act 1995 (power to apply certain provisions of the Taxes Management Act 1970 in relation to certain sums payable in connection with venture capital trusts)—
(a) for "section 29(3)(c)" there shall be substituted "section 29(1)(c)";
(b) for "section 88" there shall be substituted "section 86"; and
(c) after paragraph (d) there shall be added—
"and section 86 of that Act may be so applied with such modifications as respects the relevant date as may be specified in the regulations."

Commencement

17.—(1) Paragraphs 1 to 3, 6(2)(a) and (b), 8, 10, 11(3)(a) and (b), 12(2)(a) and (b), 14(2)(a) and (b) and 16(a) above have effect, subject to sub-paragraph (2) below—
(a) for the purposes of income tax and capital gains tax, as respects the year 1996–97 and subsequent years of assessment; and

(b) for the purposes of corporation tax, as respects accounting periods ending on or after the day appointed under section 199 of the Finance Act 1994 for the purposes of Chapter III of Part IV of that Act (self-assessment management provisions).

(2) Paragraphs 1, 3, 6(2)(a) and (b), 10, 11(3)(a) and (b), 12(2)(a) and (b) and 14(2)(a) and (b) above, so far as relating to partnerships whose trades, professions or businesses were set up and commenced before 6th April 1994, has effect as respects the year 1997–98 and subsequent years of assessment.

(3) Paragraphs 4, 5, 6(2)(c) and (3), 11(3)(c) and (4), 12(2)(c) and (3), 13, 14(2)(c) and (3), 15 and 16(b) and (c) above have effect, subject to sub-paragraph (4) below—
(a) as respects the year 1996–97 and subsequent years of assessment; and
(b) in relation to any income tax or capital gains tax which—
    (i) is charged by an assessment made on or after 6th April 1998; and
    (ii) is for the year 1995–96 or any earlier year of assessment;
and where sub-paragraph (4) of paragraph 11, sub-paragraph (3) of paragraph 12, or sub-paragraph (3) of paragraph 14 has effect by virtue of paragraph (b) of this sub-paragraph it shall have effect with the substitution, in the provision inserted by that sub-paragraph, for "section 29(1)(c)" of "section 29(3)(c)".

(4) Paragraphs 4, 6(2)(c) and (3), 11(3)(c) and (4), 12(2)(c) and (3), 13 and 14(2)(c) and (3) above, so far as relating to partnerships whose trades, professions or businesses were set up and commenced before 6th April 1994 have effect—
(a) as respects the year 1997–98 and subsequent years of assessment; and
(b) in relation to any income tax which—
    (i) is charged by an assessment made on or after 6th April 1998; and
    (ii) is for the year 1995–96 or any earlier year of assessment.

(5) Paragraphs 7 and 11(2) above have effect—
(a) as respects the year 1996–97 and subsequent years of assessment; and
(b) subject to sub-paragraphs (6) and (7) below, in relation to any income tax or capital gains tax which—
    (i) is charged by an assessment made on or after 6th April 1998; and
    (ii) is for the year 1995–96 or any earlier year of assessment.

(6) Sub-paragraph (5)(b) above does not apply to paragraph 7 above so far as paragraph 7 provides for the omission of—
(a) paragraph (a) of subsection (4) of section 374A of the Taxes Act 1988, and
(b) the words "and as if" so far as they relate to paragraph (a) of that subsection.

(7) Sub-paragraph (5)(b) above does not apply to paragraph 11(2) above so far as paragraph 11(2) provides for the omission of—
(a) the words "sections 55(1) (recovery of tax not postponed) and", and
(b) the words "and as if—
    (a) the assessment were among those specified in"
so far as those words relate to the words mentioned in paragraph (a) of this sub-paragraph.

(8) Paragraphs 6(2)(d), 11(3)(d), 12(2)(d) and 14(2)(d) above shall not apply in relation to any payment if the payment, or the claim on which it is made, was made before the day on which this Act is passed.

(9) Paragraph 9 above has effect as respects accounting periods ending on or after the day appointed under section 199 of the Finance Act 1994 for the purposes of Chapter III of Part IV of that Act (self-assessment management provisions).

(10) Any power to make regulations exercisable by virtue of an amendment made by any of the preceding provisions of this Schedule may be exercised so as to make provision having effect in relation to any year of assessment in relation to which that provision has effect in accordance with sub-paragraphs (1) to (9) above.

GENERAL NOTE

The Schedule makes various amendments to the provisions relating to interest where tax is paid late and enables excessive payments made by the Revenue to be recovered by assessment after the introduction of self-assessment.

Para. 17

The general position is that the starting dates for the Schedule are the years of assessment 1996/97 for income tax and capital gains tax, and accounting periods ending after the appointed day for corporation tax [Standing Committee E, February 20, 1996, col. 422].

SCHEDULE 19

SELF-ASSESSMENT: CLAIMS AND ENQUIRIES

Introductory

1. The Taxes Management Act 1970, as it has effect—
   (a) for the purposes of income tax and capital gains tax, as respects the year 1996–97 and subsequent years of assessment, and
   (b) for the purposes of corporation tax, as respects accounting periods ending on or after the day appointed under section 199 of the Finance Act 1994 for the purposes of Chapter III of Part IV of that Act (self-assessment management provisions),
shall be amended in accordance with the following provisions of this Schedule.

Matters subject to enquiry

2. In each of sections 9A(1), 11AB(1), 12AC(1), 19A(1), 28A(1) and 28B(1) (matters subject to enquiry), after paragraph (b) there shall be inserted "or
   (c) any claim or election included in the return (by amendment or otherwise)".

Power to call for documents

3.—(1) In section 19A (power to call for documents for the purposes of certain enquiries), after subsection (2) there shall be inserted the following subsection—
   "(2A) The officer of the Board may also (whether or not he imposes a requirement under subsection (2) above), by a notice in writing, require the taxpayer, within such time (which shall not be less than 30 days) as may be specified in the notice—
      (a) to produce to the officer such documents as are in the taxpayer's possession or power and as the officer may reasonably require for the purpose of making a determination for the purposes of section 28A(7A)(d) or 28B(6A)(d) of this Act, and
      (b) to furnish the officer with such accounts or particulars as he may reasonably require for that purpose."
   (2) In subsections (3), (5), (7), (9)(a) and (10) of that section, for the words "subsection (2)", in each place where they occur, there shall be substituted "subsection (2) or (2A)".
   (3) In subsection (4) of that section, for "subsection (2) or" there shall be substituted "subsection (2), (2A) or".
   (4) In section 97AA(1) (penalty for failure to comply with notice), for "section 19A(2) or (3)" there shall be substituted "section 19A(2), (2A) or (3)".

Further amendments of section 28A

4.—(1) In section 28A (amendment of self-assessment where enquiries made in the case of individuals, trustees and companies)—
   (a) in each of subsections (2)(a) and (4)(b), for "subsection (1)(b) above" there shall be substituted "subsection (1)(b) or (c) above";
   (b) in subsection (4)(a), for "the tax contained in the taxpayer's self-assessment" there shall be substituted "any amount set out in the return"; and
   (c) in subsection (5)(b), at the end there shall be inserted "and as to any claims or elections into which he has enquired."
   (2) After subsection (4) of that section there shall be inserted the following subsections—
   "(4A) If—
      (a) any claim or election is included in the return,
      (b) the officer is of opinion that the claim or election should be disallowed in whole or in part but that its disallowance to the extent he thinks appropriate would not require any amendment of the taxpayer's self-assessment, and
      (c) the claim or election, so far as the officer thinks it should be disallowed, is not, before the end of the period mentioned in subsection (3) above, amended to the officer's satisfaction or withdrawn,
   the officer shall, before the end of the period mentioned in subsection (4) above, give notice to the taxpayer of the extent to which he is disallowing the claim or election.
   (4B) Subsection (4A)(c) above is without prejudice to any provision by virtue of which any claim or election is irrevocable or unamendable."
   (3) Immediately before subsection (8) of that section there shall be inserted the following subsections—
   "(7A) Where, in the case of any return made in respect of any chargeable period—
      (a) alternative methods are allowed by the Tax Acts for bringing amounts into account in that return,

    (b) the return is made or amended using one of those methods,

    (c) a return could have been made in that case using an alternative method, and

    (d) an officer of the Board determines which of the alternative methods is to be used by the Board in relation to the taxpayer for that period,

any enquiry into that return or into an amendment of it shall be conducted, and this section shall have effect, as if the only method allowed for the purposes of the Tax Acts were the method determined by the officer.

(7B) For the purposes of subsection (7A) above the cases where the Tax Acts allow alternative methods for bringing amounts into account in a return are—

    (a) the case where those amounts may be brought into account either—

        (i) in making a computation for the purposes of Case I or II of Schedule D; or

        (ii) in making a computation for the purposes of any of Cases III to V of that Schedule;

    and

    (b) the case where the computation in which amounts are brought into account may be either—

        (i) a computation for the purposes of Case I of Schedule D; or

        (ii) a computation for the purpose of applying the basis (commonly called the I minus E basis) under which a company carrying on life assurance business or capital redemption business may be charged to tax on that business otherwise than under Case I of Schedule D.

(7C) In subsection (7B) above—

    'life assurance business' includes annuity business within the meaning of Chapter I of Part XII of the principal Act; and

    'capital redemption business' means any capital redemption business, within the meaning of section 458 of that Act, which is business to which that section applies."

Further amendments of section 28B

5.—(1) In section 28B (amendment of partnership statement following enquiry)—

(a) in subsection (3)(b), for "subsection (1)(b) above" there shall be substituted "subsection (1)(b) or (c) above"; and

(b) in subsection (5)(b), at the end there shall be inserted "and as to any claims or elections into which he has enquired."

(2) After subsection (6) of that section there shall be inserted the following subsections—

    "(6A) Where, in the case of any return made in relation to any period of account—

    (a) alternative methods are allowed by the Tax Acts for bringing amounts into account in that return,

    (b) the return is made or amended using one of those methods,

    (c) a return could have been made in that case using an alternative method, and

    (d) an officer of the Board determines which of the alternative methods is to be used by the Board in relation to the partnership for that period,

any enquiry into that return or into an amendment of it shall be conducted, and this section shall have effect, as if the only method allowed for the purposes of the Tax Acts were the method determined by the officer.

    (6B) In subsection (6A) above 'period of account' has the same meaning as in section 12AB of this Act; and subsection (7B) of section 28A of this Act applies for the purposes of subsection (6A) above as it applies for the purposes of subsection (7A) of that section."

Right of appeal against notice disallowing claim in return

6.—(1) In subsection (1) of section 31 (appeals)—

(a) after paragraph (a) there shall be inserted the following paragraph—

    "(aa) a decision contained in a notice under section 28A(4A) of this Act disallowing a claim or election in whole or in part, or";

    and

(b) in the words after paragraph (c), for "amendment or" there shall be substituted "amendment, the notice under section 28A(4A) of this Act or, as the case may be, the notice of".

(2) After that subsection there shall be inserted the following subsection—

    "(1AA) The matters that may be questioned on any appeal against—

    (a) an amendment under subsection (2) or (4) of section 28A of this Act,

    (b) a decision contained in a notice under subsection (4A) of that section disallowing a claim or election in whole or in part, or

(c) an amendment under section 28B(3) or 30B(1) of this Act,
do not include any determination made for the purposes of section 28A(7A)(d) or 28B(6A)(d) of this Act."

(3) In subsection (5) of that section, the words "against any assessment" shall be omitted.

7. In section 50 (procedure on appeals), after subsection (7) there shall be inserted the following subsection—

"(7A) If, on appeal, it appears to the Commissioners that a claim or election specified in a notice under section 28A(4A) of this Act should have been allowed or disallowed to an extent different from that specified in the notice, the claim or election shall be allowed or disallowed accordingly to the extent that appears to them appropriate, but otherwise the decision in the notice shall stand good."

Claims not included in returns

8.—(1) In Schedule 1A (claims not included in returns), in paragraph 4 (giving effect to claims and amendments), in sub-paragraph (1) for "(1A) and (3)" there shall be substituted "(1A), (3) and (4)".

(2) In sub-paragraph (2) of that paragraph, for "sub-paragraph (3)" there shall be substituted "sub-paragraphs (3) and (4)".

(3) After sub-paragraph (3) there shall be inserted the following sub-paragraph—

"(4) Nothing in this paragraph applies in relation to a claim or an amendment of a claim if the claim is not one for discharge or repayment of tax."

9.—(1) In paragraph 7 of Schedule 1A (amendment of claims where enquiries made), after sub-paragraph (3), there shall be inserted the following sub-paragraphs—

"(3A) If, in the case of a claim which is not a claim for discharge or repayment of tax—
(a) the officer is of opinion that the claim should be disallowed in whole or in part, and
(b) the claim, so far as the officer thinks it should be disallowed, is not, before the end of the period mentioned in sub-paragraph (2) above, amended to the officer's satisfaction or withdrawn,

the officer shall, before the end of the period mentioned in sub-paragraph (3) above, give notice to the taxpayer of the extent to which he is disallowing the claim.

(3B) Sub-paragraph (3A)(b) above is without prejudice to any provision by virtue of which any claim is irrevocable or unamendable."

(2) In sub-paragraph (4)(b) of that paragraph, for "the amount which" there shall be substituted "whether the claim should be allowed in whole or in part and as to what amount (if any)".

Right of appeal against notice disallowing claim not in return

10.—(1) In paragraph 9 of Schedule IA (appeals), for sub-paragraph (1) there shall be substituted the following sub-paragraph—

"(1) An appeal may be brought against—
(a) an amendment under paragraph 7(3) above, or
(b) a decision contained in a notice under paragraph 7(3A) above,

by giving notice to the officer within 30 days after the date on which the notice of amendment or, as the case may be, the notice under paragraph 7(3A) above was issued."

(2) In sub-paragraph (2) of that paragraph, for "making of the amendment under paragraph 7(3) above" there shall be substituted "date mentioned in sub-paragraph (1) above".

(3) In sub-paragraph (3) of that paragraph, for "under this paragraph" there shall be substituted "against an amendment under paragraph 7(3) above".

(4) After sub-paragraph (4) of that paragraph there shall be inserted the following sub-paragraph—

"(5) If, on appeal, it appears to the Commissioners that a claim specified in a notice under paragraph 7(3A) above should have been allowed or disallowed to an extent different from that specified in the notice, the claim shall be allowed or disallowed accordingly to the extent that appears to them appropriate, but otherwise the decision in the notice shall stand good."

GENERAL NOTE

The Schedule amends provisions relating to claims and enquiries.

Para. 3

Documents may be required for enquiries into the basis used for returning profits in cases where there is more than one possible basis.

Para. 4

The new TMA 1970, s.28A(7A), (7B) and (7C) allows the Revenue, in cases where it can determine which method is to be used for charging income to tax (the so-called "crown option"), to enquire into self-assessments made using a different method.

Para. 6

The exercise of the "crown option" cannot be questioned in any appeal.

Section 134   SCHEDULE 20

SELF-ASSESSMENT: DISCRETIONS EXERCISABLE BY THE BOARD ETC.

The Taxes Act 1988

1. In section 24(2) of the Taxes Act 1988 (presumption as to sums being paid by way of premium unless the contrary is shown) for "is" there shall be substituted "can be".

2. In section 38(4) of the Taxes Act 1988 (assumptions as to benefits and payments relating to leases) in the words after paragraph (b), for "is" there shall be substituted "can be".

3. In section 65(4) of the Taxes Act 1988 (assessments under Cases IV and V of Schedule D: subsections (1) to (3) not to apply to a person who satisfies the Board that he is not domiciled in the United Kingdom etc.) for "on a claim made to the Board, satisfies the Board" there shall be substituted "makes a claim to the Board stating".

4. In section 74(1)(j) of the Taxes Act 1988 (Case I or II of Schedule D: no deduction in respect of debts), in sub-paragraph (i) (deduction allowed for a bad debt proved to be such) the words "proved to be such" shall cease to have effect.

5.—(1) In section 109A of the Taxes Act 1988 (relief for post–cessation expenditure) in subsection (4) (relief for debt taken into account in computing profits or gains and later released or proved to be bad), in the first sentence, for the words following "entitled" there shall be substituted "is released in whole or in part as part of a relevant arrangement or compromise (within the meaning of section 74), he shall be treated as making a payment to which this section applies of—

(a) an amount equal to the amount released, or

(b) if he was entitled to only part of the benefit of the debt, an amount equal to an appropriate proportion of that amount."

(2) After that subsection there shall be inserted—

"(4A) Where a trade, profession or vocation carried on by a person has been permanently discontinued and subsequently an unpaid debt which was taken into account in computing the profits and gains of that trade, profession or vocation and to the benefit of which he is entitled, proves to be bad, then if—

(a) in making a claim for a year of assessment under subsection (1) above he gives notice that the debt was bad in any part of that year, and

(b) he has not given such a notice in respect of that debt in the making of any other such claim,

he shall be treated as making in that year a payment to which this section applies of an amount equal to the amount of the debt or, if he was entitled to only part of the benefit of the debt, to an appropriate proportion of that amount.

If any sum is subsequently received by him in payment of a debt for which relief has been given by virtue of this subsection, the sum shall be treated as one to which section 103 applies; and no deduction shall be made under section 105 in respect of any sum."

6. In section 132(1) of the Taxes Act 1988 (emoluments for period of absence treated as emoluments for duties performed in the UK except in so far as it is shown that but for that absence they would have been emoluments for duties performed outside the UK) for "it is shown that, but for that absence, they would" there shall be substituted "they would, but for that absence".

7. In section 145(7) of the Taxes Act 1988 (living accommodation provided for employee deemed to be provided by reason of his employment for the purposes of section 145(1) unless it can be shown that it is a case falling within paragraph (a) or (b)) in paragraphs (a) and (b) the words "it can be shown that" shall cease to have effect.

8. In section 159 of the Taxes Act 1988 (pooled cars)—

(a) in subsection (1) (which provides that the section is to apply to any car in the case of which the inspector is satisfied, whether on a claim under that section or otherwise, that it has been included in a car pool) for the words from "in the case" to "that it" there shall be substituted "which"; and

(b) subsections (4) to (6) (claims and appeals) shall cease to have effect.

9. In section 161 of the Taxes Act 1988 (exceptions from charge under section 160 on beneficial loans)—

   (a) in subsection (3) (exception for certain loans if it is shown that the interest rate is of a certain description) the words "it is shown that" shall cease to have effect; and

   (b) in subsection (4) (exception for loan to employee's relative from which employee shows that he derived no benefit) the words "shows that he" shall cease to have effect.

   10.—(1) In section 168 of the Taxes Act 1988 (interpretative provisions) in subsection (3) (exception from charge under Chapter II of Part V for any such payment or provision made by employer as can be shown to have been made in normal course of his domestic, family or personal relationships) for the words following "any such payment or provision" there shall be substituted "which is made by the employer, being an individual, in the normal course of his domestic, family or personal relationships".

   (2) In subsection (6) of that section—

   (a) in paragraph (b) (exception from charge for car made available by employer where it can be shown that the car was made available in normal course of his domestic, family or personal relationships) for "it can be shown that the car was" there shall be substituted "the car is"; and

   (b) in paragraph (d) (similar exception for vans) for "it can be shown that the van was" there shall be substituted "the van is".

   11. In section 186(10) of the Taxes Act 1988 (value of the proceeds of certain disposals)—

   (a) for paragraph (b) there shall be substituted the following paragraph—
     "(b) any other disposal falling within that subsection is not at arm's length,"; and

   (b) in paragraph (c) for "that sub-paragraph" there shall be substituted "that subsection".

   12. In section 231(3A) of the Taxes Act 1988 (restriction of tax credit where certain arrangements made by close investment-holding companies)—

   (a) in the words preceding paragraph (a), the words "it appears to the inspector that" shall cease to have effect; and

   (b) in the words following paragraph (b), for "appears to the inspector to be" there shall be substituted "is".

   13. In section 257 of the Taxes Act 1988 (personal allowance)—

   (a) in subsection (2) (claimant entitled to deduction if he proves that he is 65 or over), and

   (b) in subsection (3) (claimant entitled to deduction if he proves that he is 75 or over),
the words "proves that he" shall cease to have effect.

   14.—(1) Section 257A of the Taxes Act 1988 (married couple's allowance) shall be amended in accordance with the following provisions of this paragraph.

   (2) In subsection (1) (claimant entitled to reduction if he proves that he is a married man whose wife is living with him) for the words from the beginning to "he is" there shall be substituted "If the claimant is, for the whole or any part of the year of assessment,".

   (3) In—

   (a) subsection (2) (claimant entitled to reduction if he proves that he is a married man whose wife is living with him and that either of them is 65 or over), and

   (b) subsection (3) (similar provision on proof that claimant or wife is 75 or over),
for the words from the beginning to "and that" there shall be substituted "If the claimant is, for the whole or any part of the year of assessment, a married man whose wife is living with him, and".

   15. In section 257E(1) of the Taxes Act 1988 (claimant entitled to relief if his wife lives with him and he proves that for the year 1989–90 he was entitled as described in paragraph (a) or (b))—

   (a) the words "he proves" shall cease to have effect; and

   (b) the word "that", in the first and third places where it occurs in each of paragraphs (a) and (b), shall cease to have effect.

   16.—(1) Section 257F of the Taxes Act 1988 (transitional relief: effect of preceding sections where claimant who does not live with his wife proves that paragraphs (a) to (c) apply) shall be amended in accordance with the following provisions of this paragraph.

   (2) The words "the claimant proves" shall cease to have effect.

   (3) In paragraph (a)—

   (a) for "that he" there shall be substituted "the claimant"; and

   (b) the word "that" in the second place where it occurs shall cease to have effect.

   (4) In paragraph (b) the word "that" in the first place where it occurs shall cease to have effect.

   (5) In paragraph (c) the word "that" in the first and third places where it occurs shall cease to have effect.

   17.—(1) Section 259 of the Taxes Act 1988 (additional relief in respect of children) shall be amended in accordance with the following provisions of this paragraph.

   (2) In subsection (2) (claimant entitled to reduction if he proves that a qualifying child is resident with him) for the words from "if the claimant" to "he shall be entitled" there shall be substituted "if—

(a) the claimant is a person to whom this section applies, and

(b) a qualifying child is resident with him for the whole or a part of a year of assessment,

the claimant shall be entitled".

(3) In subsection (6) (circumstances in which the reference in subsection (5) to a child receiving full-time instruction includes a child undergoing training for a trade, profession or vocation) the second paragraph (inspector's power to require particulars of training) shall cease to have effect.

18. In section 261A(1) of the Taxes Act 1988 (person who proves that a qualifying child is resident with him in the year in which he and his wife separate is entitled to relief) for "who proves that a qualifying child is resident with him" there shall be substituted "with whom a qualifying child is resident".

19. In section 265(1) of the Taxes Act 1988 (claimant entitled to blind person's allowance if he proves that he is a registered blind person) the words "proves that he" shall cease to have effect.

20. In section 274(4) of the Taxes Act 1988 (effect of war insurance premiums on the limit on relief under section 266 or 273) in the second paragraph (definition of war insurance premiums: to include any part of any premium paid in respect of a life insurance policy which appears to the inspector to be attributable to risks arising from war or war service abroad) for "appears to the inspector to be" there shall be substituted "is".

21. In section 278(2) of the Taxes Act 1988 (bar on relief for non-residents not to apply to an individual who satisfies the Board that he or she is a Commonwealth citizen etc) the words "satisfies the Board that he or she" shall cease to have effect.

22. In section 306(2) of the Taxes Act 1988 (claim for relief in respect of eligible shares must be accompanied by a certificate issued by the company) for the words from the beginning to "accompanied by" there shall be substituted "No claim for relief in respect of eligible shares in a company may be made unless the person making the claim has received from the company".

23. In section 311(4) of the Taxes Act 1988 (application of section 306(2) to claims in respect of shares issued to the managers of an approved fund) for the words from "as if it required" to "accompanied by" there shall be substituted—

"(a) as if it required the certificate referred to in that section to be issued by the company to the managers; and

(b) as if it provided that no claim for relief may be made unless the person making the claim has received from the managers".

24. In section 381(4) of the Taxes Act 1988 (no relief unless it is shown that trade was on a commercial basis) the words "it is shown that" shall cease to have effect.

25.—(1) In section 384 of the Taxes Act 1988 (restrictions on right of set-off) in subsection (1) (no relief unless it is shown that trade was on a commercial basis and with a view to the realisation of profits) the words "it is shown that" shall cease to have effect.

(2) For subsection (9) of that section (conclusive evidence that a trade was carried on with a view to the realisation of profits) there shall be substituted—

"(9) Where at any time a trade is carried on so as to afford a reasonable expectation of profit, it shall be treated for the purposes of subsection (1) above as being carried on at that time with a view to the realisation of profits."

26. In section 393A of the Taxes Act 1988 (losses: set-off against profits of the same or an earlier accounting period)—

(a) in subsection (3)(b) (no relief unless trade was on commercial basis and with a view to the realisation of gain) for "it is shown that for" there shall be substituted "for"; and

(b) in subsection (4), for paragraph (a) (conclusive evidence that a trade was carried on with a view to the realisation of gain) there shall be substituted—

"(a) where at any time a trade is carried on so as to afford a reasonable expectation of gain, it shall be treated as being carried on at that time with a view to the realisation of gain; and".

27. In section 397(3) of the Taxes Act 1988 (farming and market gardening: relief not to be restricted in certain cases)—

(a) for ", if it is shown by the claimant" there shall be substituted "in any case"; and

(b) for the word "that", at the beginning of each of paragraphs (a) and (b), there shall be substituted "where".

28.—(1) Section 488 of the Taxes Act 1988 (co-operative housing associations) shall be amended in accordance with the following provisions of this paragraph.

(2) For subsection (9) (which provides for a claim to be made to the inspector within two years and excludes the operation of section 42 of the Taxes Management Act 1970) there shall be substituted—

"(9) A claim under this section may be made at any time not later than two years after the end of the year of assessment or accounting period to which, or to a part of which, it relates."

(3) In subsection (10) (no claim under the section to have effect unless it is proved that the conditions there specified are complied with) for the words from "no claim" to "it is proved that" there shall be substituted "no claim shall be made under this section unless".

(4) For subsection (11) (power of Board to direct that a claim shall have effect if they are satisfied that the conditions in subsection (10) are substantially complied with, and power to revoke the direction on subsequent information) there shall be substituted—

"(11) A housing association may make a claim under this section notwithstanding anything in subsection (10) above, if the association reasonably considers that the requirements of that subsection are substantially complied with.

(11A) If as a result of an enquiry—

(a) under section 11AB of the Management Act into a return, or an amendment of a return, in which a claim under this section by a housing association is included, or

(b) under paragraph 5 of Schedule 1A to that Act into a claim under this section by a housing association, or an amendment of such a claim,

an amendment is made to the association's self-assessment or, as the case may be, to the claim, the liability of all persons concerned to tax for all relevant years or accounting periods may also be adjusted by the making of assessments or otherwise."

(5) For subsection (12) (particulars required to be included in a claim may include an authority granted by the members for the use of information in their tax returns for determining the claim) there shall be substituted—

"(12) A housing association making a claim under this section may be required under or by virtue of section 11(1) of, or paragraph 2(5) of Schedule 1A to, the Management Act to deliver an authority, granted by all members of the association, for any relevant information contained in any return made by a member under the provisions of the Income Tax Acts to be used by an officer of the Board in such manner as he may think fit in connection with any enquiry under section 11AB of, or paragraph 5 of Schedule 1A to, the Management Act, so far as relating to the association's claim under this section."

29.—(1) Section 489 of the Taxes Act 1988 (self-build societies) shall be amended in accordance with the following provisions of this paragraph.

(2) For subsection (7) (which excludes the operation of section 42 of the Taxes Management Act 1970 but provides for a claim to be made to the inspector within two years) there shall be substituted—

"(7) A claim under this section may be made at any time not later than two years after the end of the year of assessment or accounting period to which, or to a part of which, it relates."

(3) In subsection (8) (no claim under the section to have effect unless it is proved that the conditions there specified are complied with) for the words from "no claim" to "it is proved that" there shall be substituted "no claim shall be made under this section unless".

(4) For subsection (9) (power of Board to direct that a claim shall have effect if they are satisfied that the conditions in subsection (8) are substantially complied with, and power to revoke the direction on subsequent information) there shall be substituted—

"(9) A self-build society may make a claim under this section notwithstanding anything in subsection (8) above, if the society reasonably considers that the requirements of that subsection are substantially complied with.

(9A) If as a result of an enquiry—

(a) under section 11AB of the Management Act into a return, or an amendment of a return, in which a claim under this section by a self-build society is included, or

(b) under paragraph 5 of Schedule 1A to that Act into a claim under this section by a self-build society or an amendment of such a claim,

an amendment is made to the society's self-assessment or, as the case may be, to the claim, the society's liability to tax for all relevant years or accounting periods may also be adjusted by the making of assessments or otherwise."

30. In section 503(6) of the Taxes Act 1988 (apportionments where a letting relates only in part to holiday accommodation) for "appear to the inspector, or on appeal the Commissioners, to be" there shall be substituted "are".

31. In section 570(2) of the Taxes Act 1988 (schemes for rationalizing industry: treatment of certain payments made under such schemes)—

(a) the words "on a claim it is shown in accordance with the provisions of Part II of Schedule 21 that" shall cease to have effect;

(b) after "the Tax Acts" there shall be inserted "and a claim is made to that effect,";

(c) for "that Schedule", where those words first occur, there shall be substituted "Schedule 21"; and

(d) at the end there shall be added—

"and paragraph 6 of that Schedule applies for the purposes of this subsection as it applies for the purposes of that Schedule."

32. In section 582(2)(b) of the Taxes Act 1988 (cases where retention of funding bonds is impracticable)—

    (a) the words "the Board are satisfied that" shall cease to have effect; and

    (b) in sub-paragraph (i), for the words from the beginning to "them" there shall be substituted—

        "(i) any such person shall be relieved from the obligation to retain bonds and account for income tax under that paragraph, on his furnishing to the Board".

33.—(1) Section 584 of the Taxes Act 1988 (relief for unremittable overseas income) shall be amended in accordance with the following provisions of this paragraph.

(2) For subsections (2) and (3) (the account to be taken of overseas income which the Board are satisfied is unremittable) there shall be substituted—

    "(2) Subject to subsection (2A) below, where a person so chargeable makes a claim under this subsection in relation to any overseas income—

    (a) which is unremittable; and

    (b) to which subsection (1)(a) above will continue to apply notwithstanding any reasonable endeavours on his part,

    then, in the first instance, account shall not be taken of that income, and tax shall be assessed, or, in the case of corporation tax, assessable, and shall be charged on all persons concerned and for all periods accordingly.

    (2A) If on any date paragraph (a) or (b) of subsection (2) above ceases to apply to any part of any overseas income in relation to which a claim has been made under that subsection—

    (a) that part of the income shall be treated as income arising on that date, and

    (b) account shall be taken of it, and of any tax payable in respect of it under the law of the territory where it arises, according to their value at that date."

(3) In subsection (4) (company chargeable to corporation tax in respect of source of income that it has ceased to possess) for "a company becomes chargeable to corporation tax in respect of income from any source by virtue of subsections (2) and (3)" there shall be substituted "a person becomes chargeable to income tax or corporation tax in respect of income from any source by virtue of subsection (2) or (2A)".

(4) In subsection (5) (where payment made by ECGD in respect of income, conditions in subsection (2) treated as not satisfied) for the words following "treated as income" there shall be substituted "to which paragraphs (a) and (b) of subsection (2) above do not apply (and accordingly cannot cease to apply)".

(5) For subsection (6) (delivery of notices under subsection (2) and making of assessments required by such notices) there shall be substituted—

    "(6) A claim under subsection (2) above—

    (a) for the purposes of income tax, shall be made on or before the first anniversary of the 31st January next following the year of assessment in which the income arises;

    (b) for the purposes of corporation tax, shall be made no later than two years after the end of the accounting period in which the income arises."

(6) In subsection (7) (charge to tax on executors and administrators) after "(2)" there shall be inserted "or (2A)".

(7) In subsection (8) (how to determine the amount of unremittable overseas income) for "(3)" there shall be substituted "(2A)".

34. In section 585(1) of the Taxes Act 1988 (relief for delayed remittances: claim may be made on showing that the conditions in paragraphs (a) to (c) are satisfied) for the words from "by making a claim" to "that is to say" there shall be substituted ", if the relevant conditions are satisfied, by making a claim require that the following provisions of this section shall apply; and for this purpose the relevant conditions are—".

35. In section 717(9) of the Taxes Act 1988 (which provides for section 713 to have effect for certain cases with the substitution of a new provision for subsections (3) to (6)) in the substituted subsection, for "an inspector decides is just and reasonable; and the jurisdiction of the General Commissioners or the Special Commissioners on any appeal shall include jurisdiction to review such a decision of the inspector" there shall be substituted "is just and reasonable".

36. In section 731(3) of the Taxes Act 1988 (cases of purchase and sale of securities where sections 732 to 734 do not apply)—

    (a) in paragraph (b) (it is shown to the satisfaction of the Board that certain conditions are satisfied in relation to the purchase and sale) for the words from "it is shown" to "and that" there shall be substituted "the purchase and sale were each effected at the current market price and"; and

    (b) the words following paragraph (b) (appeals) shall cease to have effect.

37. In section 769(2)(d) of the Taxes Act 1988 (acquisitions of shares on death and certain gifts of shares to be left out of account in applying the rules in subsection (1) for ascertaining change in ownership of company)—

(a) for "and, if it is shown that the gift" there shall be substituted ", and any gift of shares which"; and

(b) the words "any gift of shares" shall cease to have effect.

38.—(1) Section 812 of the Taxes Act 1988 (withdrawal of right to tax credit of certain non-resident companies connected with unitary states) shall be amended in accordance with the following provisions of this paragraph.

(2) In subsection (4), paragraph (a) (one of the conditions for the withdrawal of the right to tax credit treated as being satisfied unless, on making a claim under section 213(3), the claimant proves otherwise to the satisfaction of the Board) shall cease to have effect.

(3) In subsection (7) (power to substitute one of two sets of provisions for subsections (3) and (4)) for the words following "there shall be substituted" there shall be substituted "either the following subsection—

"(3) A company shall be treated as having a qualifying presence in a unitary state if it is liable in such a state to a tax charged on its income or profits by whatever name called for any period ending after the relevant date for which that state charges tax.";

or the following subsections—

"(3) A company shall be treated as having a qualifying presence in a unitary state if it has its principal place of business in such a state at any time after the relevant date.

(4) For the purposes of subsection (3) above the principal place of business of a company shall include both the place where central management and control of the company is exercised and the place where the immediate day-to-day management of the company as a whole is exercised."."

39. In section 815A of the Taxes Act 1988 (transfer of a non-UK trade) for subsections (2) to (4) there shall be substituted—

"(2) Where gains accruing to company A on the transfer would have been chargeable to tax under the law of the relevant member State but for the Mergers Directive, this Part, including any arrangements having effect by virtue of section 788, shall apply as if the amount of tax, calculated on the required basis, which would have been payable under that law in respect of the gains so accruing but for that Directive, were tax payable under that law."

40. In Schedule 6 to the Taxes Act 1988 (taxation of directors and others in respect of cars) in sub-paragraphs (1) and (2) of paragraph 2 (reduction for use of car for business travel) for "it is shown to the inspector's satisfaction that the employee was required by the nature of his employment to use, and did use" there shall be substituted "the employee is required by the nature of his employment to use and does use".

41. In Schedule 7 to the Taxes Act 1988 (taxation of benefit from loans obtained by reason of employment) in paragraph 1(5) (benefit of loan not obtained by reason of employment if made by an individual and shown to have been made in normal course of his domestic, family or personal relationships) the words "and shown to have been made" shall cease to have effect.

42. In Schedule 12 to the Taxes Act 1988 (foreign earnings) in paragraph 2(2) (emoluments in respect of which deduction under section 193(1) allowed not to exceed such proportion as is shown to be reasonable) the words "shown to be" shall cease to have effect.

43. In Schedule 21 to the Taxes Act 1988 (tax relief in connection with schemes for rationalizing industry and other redundancy schemes), paragraph 3 (no relief in respect of payments under schemes unless certain amounts are shown) shall cease to have effect.

The Capital Allowances Act 1990

44. In section 29(3) of the Capital Allowances Act 1990 (apportionments where a letting relates only in part to holiday accommodation) for "appear to the inspector, or on appeal the Commissioners, to be" there shall be substituted "are".

The Taxation of Chargeable Gains Act 1992

45. In the following provisions of this Schedule "the Gains Act" means the Taxation of Chargeable Gains Act 1992.

46. In section 30(4) of the Gains Act (section not to apply if it is shown that there was no tax avoidance purpose) for "if it is shown that" there shall be substituted "in a case where".

47. In each of—

(a) subsections (5) and (6) of section 30 of the Gains Act (consideration to be increased or reduced by such amount as appears to the inspector etc to be just and reasonable),

(b) section 32(4)(b) of the Gains Act (costs in cases of part disposal to be such proportion as appears to the inspector etc to be just and reasonable), and

(c) subsections (7) and (8) of section 33 of the Gains Act (amounts to be reduced to such amount as appears to the inspector etc to be just and reasonable),

for "appears to the inspector, or on appeal the Commissioners concerned, to be" there shall be substituted "is".

48. In section 48 of the Gains Act (consideration due after time of disposal and irrecoverable consideration) for the words following "if any part of the consideration so brought into account" there shall be substituted "subsequently proves to be irrecoverable, there shall be made, on a claim being made to that effect, such adjustment, whether by way of discharge or repayment of tax or otherwise, as is required in consequence."

49. In section 49 of the Gains Act (contingent liabilities) for subsection (2) (adjustment to be made if it is shown to the satisfaction of the inspector that a contingent liability has become enforceable) there shall be substituted—

"(2) If any such contingent liability subsequently becomes enforceable and is being or has been enforced, there shall be made, on a claim being made to that effect, such adjustment, whether by way of discharge or repayment of tax or otherwise, as is required in consequence."

50. In section 52(4) of the Gains Act (apportionments by such method as appears to the inspector etc to be just and reasonable) the words "such method as appears to the inspector or on appeal the Commissioners concerned to be" shall cease to have effect.

51. In section 116(13) of the Gains Act (subsection (12) not to apply where inspector, being satisfied sum is comparatively small, so directs) the words "the inspector is satisfied that" and "and so directs," shall cease to have effect.

52.—(1) In section 122 of the Gains Act (distribution which is not a new holding) in subsection (2) (treatment of distributions which the inspector is satisfied are comparatively small) the words "the inspector is satisfied that" and "and so directs" shall cease to have effect.

(2) Subsection (3) of that section (appeals from decisions of inspectors under subsection (2)) shall cease to have effect.

(3) In subsection (4)(a) of that section (subsections (2) and (3) not to apply in certain cases) for "subsections (2) and (3)" there shall be substituted "subsection (2)".

53.—(1) In section 133 of the Gains Act (premiums on conversion of securities) in subsection (2) (treatment of premiums which the inspector is satisfied are comparatively small) the words "the inspector is satisfied that" and "and so directs" shall cease to have effect.

(2) Subsection (3) of that section (appeals from decisions of inspectors under subsection (2)) shall cease to have effect.

(3) In subsection (4)(a) of that section (subsections (2) and (3) not to apply in certain cases) for "subsections (2) and (3)" there shall be substituted "subsection (2)".

54. In each of sections 150(10)(a) and 150A(9)(a) of the Gains Act (reductions in relief to be apportioned in such a way as appears to the inspector etc to be just and reasonable) for "such a way as appears to the inspector, or on appeal to the Commissioners concerned, to be" there shall be substituted "a way which is".

55. In section 164F(8)(a) of the Gains Act (section not to apply where it is shown that winding up etc is bona fide) the words "it is shown that" shall cease to have effect.

56. In section 164FG of the Gains Act (multiple claims for reductions under section 164A(2) or 164F(10A) of the Gains Act) in subsection (2) (reductions to be treated as claimed separately in such sequence as the claimant elects or an officer of the Board in default of an election determines) the words "or an officer of the Board in default of an election determines" shall cease to have effect.

57.—(1) In each of subsections (4) and (6) of section 176 of the Gains Act (losses or gains on disposals where there have been depreciatory transactions to be reduced to such extent as appears to the inspector etc to be just and reasonable) for "appears to the inspector, or, on appeal, the Commissioners concerned, to be" there shall be substituted "is".

(2) In subsection (5) of that section (footing on which decision under subsection (4) is to be made) for "The inspector or the Commissioners shall make the decision under subsection (4) above" there shall be substituted "A reduction under subsection (4) above shall be made".

58. In section 181(1)(b) of the Gains Act (sections 178 and 179 not to apply where it is shown that merger was bona fide) the words "it is shown that", and the word "that" in the second place where it occurs, shall cease to have effect.

59.—(1) Section 222 of the Gains Act (relief on disposal of residence and land up to the permitted area, which is 0.5 of a hectare) shall be amended in accordance with the following provisions of this paragraph.

(2) For subsection (3) (which provides for the permitted area in certain cases to be such area, larger than 0.5 of a hectare, as the Commissioners may determine) there shall be substituted—

"(3) Where the area required for the reasonable enjoyment of the dwelling-house (or of the part in question) as a residence, having regard to the size and character of the dwelling-house, is larger than 0.5 of a hectare, that larger area shall be the permitted area."

(3) In subsection (5) (determination of individual's main residence)—

(a) paragraph (b) (which, subject to conclusive notice by the individual under paragraph (a), provides for the question to be determined by an inspector), and

(b) the words following that paragraph (right of appeal against inspector's determination), shall cease to have effect.

(4) In subsection (6), paragraph (b) (further provision about the right of appeal against determinations under subsection (5)(b)) and the word "and" immediately preceding it shall cease to have effect.

60. In section 224(2) of the Gains Act (adjustment of relief given by section 223 for changes occurring during period of ownership) for "may be adjusted in such manner as the Commissioners concerned may consider to be just and reasonable" there shall be substituted "may be adjusted in a manner which is just and reasonable".

61. In section 226 of the Gains Act (relief in respect of private residence occupied by dependent relative before 6th April 1988) subsection (5) (power of inspector, before granting a claim for relief under that section, to require claimant to show that granting the claim will not preclude relief to claimant's wife or husband) shall cease to have effect.

62. In section 241(7) of the Gains Act (apportionments where a letting relates only in part to holiday accommodation) for "appear to the inspector, or on appeal the Commissioners, to be" there shall be substituted "are".

63.—(1) In section 271 of the Gains Act (miscellaneous exemptions) in subsections (1)(g) and (2), for "such extent as the Board are satisfied" there shall be substituted "the extent".

(2) In subsection (2) of that section, in the second paragraph, the words "the Board are satisfied that" shall cease to have effect.

64. In section 279(1) of the Gains Act (claimant for deduction in respect of gains accruing from the disposal of foreign assets must show that conditions in subsection (3) are satisfied) for paragraph (b) there shall be substituted—

"(b) the person charged or chargeable makes a claim, and

(c) the conditions set out in subsection (3) below are, so far as applicable, satisfied as respects those gains ("the qualifying gains");".

65. In section 280 of the Gains Act (payment of tax by instalments where consideration payable by instalments) for "if the person making the disposal satisfies the Board that he would otherwise suffer undue hardship, the tax on a chargeable gain accruing on the disposal may, at his option," there shall be substituted "at the option of the person making the disposal, the tax on a chargeable gain accruing on the disposal may".

66.—(1) Schedule 6 to the Gains Act (retirement relief) shall be amended in accordance with the following provisions of this paragraph.

(2) In paragraph 3, in sub-paragraphs (1), (3) and (4) (under each of which a person is treated as having retired on ill-health grounds if, on production of such evidence as the Board may reasonably require, the Board are satisfied as there mentioned)—

(a) the words "on production of such evidence as the Board may reasonably require, the Board are satisfied" shall cease to have effect, and

(b) for "that he" (in each place where those words occur) there shall be substituted "he".

(3) At the end of that paragraph there shall be added—

"(5) In any case where—

(a) an officer of the Board gives notice to any person under section 9A(1) of, or paragraph 5(1) of Schedule 1A to, the Management Act (notice of intention to enquire into a return or claim or an amendment of a return or claim), and

(b) the enquiry to any extent relates to the question whether or not a person falls to be treated as having retired on ill-health grounds by virtue of the foregoing provisions of this paragraph,

then, without prejudice to any other powers of such an officer in relation to such an enquiry, an officer of the Board may at the same or any subsequent time by notice in writing require that person, within such time (which shall not be less than 30 days) as may be specified in the notice, to produce such evidence relating to the question mentioned in paragraph (b) above as may reasonably be specified in the notice."

(4) In paragraph 10 (limitation of retirement relief in certain cases)—

(a) in sub-paragraph (1) for "appears to the Board to be" there shall be substituted "is"; and

(b) in sub-paragraph (2) for "the Board shall have regard" there shall be substituted "regard shall be had".

67. In Schedule 8 to the Gains Act (leases) in paragraph 10(2) (presumption as to sums being paid by way of premium unless the contrary is shown) for the words following "in so far as" there shall be substituted "other sufficient consideration for the payment can be shown to have been given".

The Finance Act 1993

68.—(1) In section 144 of the Finance Act 1993 (irrecoverable debts) in paragraph (b) of each of subsections (1) and (2) (cases where inspector is satisfied as to whole, or part, of a debt being irrecoverable) the words "the inspector is satisfied,", and the word "that" in the first place where it occurs, shall cease to have effect.

(2) In subsection (3)(b) of that section (debt to be treated as reduced by amount which was irrecoverable in the inspector's opinion) the words "in the opinion of the inspector" shall cease to have effect.

(3) Subsection (4) of that section (construction, for the purposes of appeals, of references in the section to the inspector) shall cease to have effect.

69.—(1) In section 145 of the Finance Act 1993, in subsections (1)(c) and (4)(b) (requirements that inspector is satisfied as to the recoverability of the outstanding amount) the words "the inspector is satisfied that" shall cease to have effect.

(2) In subsections (2)(b), (3)(b) and (5) of that section (opinion of inspector as to recoverability of the outstanding amount) the words "in the opinion of the inspector" shall cease to have effect.

(3) Subsection (6) of that section (construction, for the purposes of appeals, of references in the section to the inspector) shall cease to have effect.

70. In Schedule 15 to the Finance Act 1993 (exchange gains and losses: alternative calculations) in paragraph 3(4) (meaning of unremittable income), for paragraphs (a) to (c) there shall be substituted—

"(a) a claim under subsection (2) of section 584 of the Taxes Act 1988 (relief for unremittable income) has been made in relation to the income,

(b) paragraphs (a) and (b) of that subsection apply to it, and

(c) those paragraphs have not ceased to apply to it."

The Finance Act 1994

71.—(1) Section 163 of the Finance Act 1994 (interest rate and currency contracts: irrecoverable payments) shall be amended in accordance with the following provisions of this paragraph.

(2) In subsection (1) (application of subsections (2) and (3) where inspector is satisfied as to irrecoverability of qualifying payment) for the words from "where" to "made" there shall be substituted "where a qualifying company—

(a) is entitled to a right to receive a qualifying payment, and

(b) makes a claim".

(3) In subsections (2) and (3) (treatment of irrecoverable amounts) in paragraph (a) (amount is considered to have become irrecoverable in the period), for "is considered to have" there shall be substituted "may reasonably be regarded as having".

(4) In subsection (4) (treatment of amounts later recovered), in paragraph (b) (the whole or any part of so much of the qualifying payment as was considered irrecoverable is recovered in a later accounting period) for "was considered irrecoverable" there shall be substituted "fell within paragraphs (a) and (b) of that subsection".

GENERAL NOTE

Under self-assessment many provisions requiring a decision or other action to be taken by the Revenue before the making of an assessment are no longer appropriate and the Schedule removes them from the Taxes Act. The changes fall into four main categories:

(i) where a claimant is required to show or prove that a condition exists before a claim can be allowed, the claimant will in future need to be able to show that the condition exists only if asked by the Revenue;

(ii) the Revenue will no longer need to be satisfied that a condition exists before the taxpayer can complete his self-assessment;

(iii) where a judgment on whether a condition exists depends on how it appears to the Revenue (or on appeal to the Commissioners) it will in future depend on an objective appraisal of the facts of the case;

(iv) the Revenue, in the provisions operated on, will no longer need to "direct" that certain treatment should apply [Standing Committee E, February 20, 1996, col. 424].

SCHEDULE 21

SELF-ASSESSMENT: TIME LIMITS

The Taxes Act 1988

1. In section 62A(3) of the Taxes Act 1988 (time limit for giving notice of a change of basis period) for the words following "The second condition is" there shall be substituted—

"(a) in the case of a trade, profession or vocation carried on by an individual, that notice of the accounting change is given to an officer of the Board in a return under section 8 of the Management Act on or before the day on which that return is required to be made and delivered under that section;

(b) in the case of a trade, profession or vocation carried on by persons in partnership, that notice of the accounting change is given to an officer of the Board in a return under section 12AA of that Act on or before the day specified in relation to that return under subsection (2) or (3) of that section."

2.—(1) Section 84 of the Taxes Act 1988 (relief for gifts to educational establishments) shall be amended in accordance with the following provisions of this paragraph.

(2) In subsection (3), in the words following paragraph (b) (relief not available unless donor makes claim within two years of making the gift) for "two years of making the gift" there shall be substituted "the period specified in subsection (3A) below".

(3) After that subsection there shall be inserted—

"(3A) The period mentioned in subsection (3) above is—

(a) in the case of a claim with respect to income tax, the period ending with the first anniversary of the 31st January next following the year of assessment in whose basis period the gift is made;

(b) in the case of a claim with respect to corporation tax, the period of two years beginning at the end of the accounting period in which the gift is made.

(3B) In paragraph (a) of subsection (3A) above "basis period" means—

(a) in relation to a year of assessment for which a basis period is given by sections 60 to 63, that basis period,

(b) in relation to a year of assessment for which no basis period is given by those sections, the year of assessment."

3.—(1) Section 101 of the Taxes Act 1988 (valuation of work in progress at discontinuance of profession or vocation) shall be amended in accordance with the following provisions of this paragraph.

(2) In subsection (2) (election may be made within 12 months after discontinuance) for "12 months after the discontinuance" there shall be substituted "the period specified in subsection (2A) below".

(3) After that subsection there shall be inserted—

"(2A) The period mentioned in subsection (2) above is—

(a) in the case of an election for the purposes of income tax, the period ending with the first anniversary of the 31st January next following the year of assessment in which the profession or vocation is discontinued;

(b) in the case of an election for the purposes of corporation tax, the period of two years beginning at the end of the accounting period in which the profession or vocation is discontinued."

4. In section 257BB(5)(a) of the Taxes Act 1988 (notice to be given not later than six years after the end of the year of assessment to which it relates) for "not later than six years after" there shall be substituted "on or before the fifth anniversary of the 31st January next following".

5. In section 257D(9)(a) of the Taxes Act 1988 (notice to be given not later than six years after the end of the year of assessment to which it relates) for "not later than six years after" there shall be substituted "on or before the fifth anniversary of the 31st January next following".

6. In section 265(5)(a) of the Taxes Act 1988 (notice to be given not later than six years after the end of the year of assessment to which it relates) for "not later than six years after" there shall be substituted "on or before the fifth anniversary of the 31st January next following".

7. In section 306(1) of the Taxes Act 1988 (claim for relief in respect of eligible shares) as it has effect in relation to shares issued on or after 1st January 1994 (the enterprise investment scheme) for paragraph (b) (claim to be made not later than twelve months after the inspector authorises the issue of a certificate) there shall be substituted—

"(b) not later than the fifth anniversary of the 31st January next following that year of assessment".

8.—(1) Section 356B of the Taxes Act 1988 (residence basis: married couples) shall be amended in accordance with the following provisions of this paragraph.

(2) In subsection (2)(a) (election to be made before the end of the period of twelve months beginning with the end of the first year of assessment for which it is made or such longer period as the Board may in any particular case allow) for the words following "shall be made" there shall be substituted "on or before—
> (i) the first anniversary of the 31st January next following the first year of assessment for which it is made, or
> (ii) such later date as the Board may in any particular case allow,".

(3) In subsection (4)(b) (notice of withdrawal not to be given after the end of the period of twelve months beginning with the end of the first year of assessment for which it is given or such longer period as the Board may in any particular case allow) for the words following "shall not be given after" there shall be substituted—
> "(i) the first anniversary of the 31st January next following the year of assessment for which it is given, or
> (ii) such later date as the Board may in any particular case allow, and".

9. In section 356C(6) of the Taxes Act 1988, for paragraph (a) (election to have effect for the period in which it is made and subsequent periods) there shall be substituted—
> "(a) shall be made on or before the first anniversary of the 31st January next following the year of assessment in which falls the first period for which it is made and shall have effect for that period and subsequent periods,".

10. In section 381(1) of the Taxes Act 1988 (claim to be made by notice given within two years after year of assessment in which loss sustained) for "within two years after" there shall be substituted "on or before the first anniversary of the 31st January next following".

11. In section 392(5) of the Taxes Act 1988 (claim to be made within six years after the year of assessment in question)—
(a) for "within six years after" there shall be substituted "on or before the fifth anniversary of the 31st January next following"; and
(b) for "not later than six years after" there shall be substituted "on or before the fifth anniversary of the 31st January next following".

12. In section 471 of the Taxes Act 1988 (exchange of securities in connection with conversion operations, nationalisation etc.) for subsection (2) (tax treatment under subsection (1) not to apply to a person who gives notice to the inspector that he desires not to be treated as mentioned in that subsection) there shall be substituted—
> "(2) Subsection (1) above shall not apply to a person who elects, by notice given to an officer of the Board, not to be treated as mentioned in that subsection.
> (2A) A notice under subsection (2) above—
> (a) for the purposes of income tax, shall be given on or before the first anniversary of the 31st January next following the year of assessment in whose basis period the exchange takes place;
> (b) for the purposes of corporation tax, shall be given no later than two years after the end of the accounting period in which the exchange takes place.
> (2B) In paragraph (a) of subsection (2A) above "basis period" means—
> (a) in relation to a year of assessment for which a basis period is given by sections 60 to 63, that basis period;
> (b) in relation to a year of assessment for which no basis period is given by those sections, the year of assessment."

13.—(1) In section 472 of the Taxes Act 1988 (distribution of securities issued in connection with nationalisation etc.) in subsection (1) (dealer to be treated for tax purposes in the manner specified in subsections (2) and (3), unless he gives notice to the inspector that he desires not to be so treated) for "gives notice to the inspector not later than two years after the end of the chargeable period in which the distribution takes place that he desires" there shall be substituted "elects, by notice given to an officer of the Board,".

(2) After subsection (3) of that section there shall be inserted—
> "(3A) A notice under subsection (1) above—
> (a) for the purposes of income tax, shall be given on or before the first anniversary of the 31st January next following the year of assessment in whose basis period the distribution takes place;
> (b) for the purposes of corporation tax, shall be given no later than two years after the end of the accounting period in which the distribution takes place.
> (3B) In paragraph (a) of subsection (3A) above "basis period" means—
> (a) in relation to a year of assessment for which a basis period is given by sections 60 to 63, that basis period;
> (b) in relation to a year of assessment for which no basis period is given by those sections, the year of assessment."

14.—(1) Section 504 of the Taxes Act 1988 shall be amended in accordance with the following provisions of this paragraph.

(2) In subsection (6) (claim to be made within two years after the year of assessment or accounting period in which holiday accommodation is let) for "two years after that year or period" there shall be substituted "the time specified in subsection (6A) below".

(3) After subsection (6) there shall be inserted—

"(6A) The time mentioned in subsection (6) above is—

(a) in the case of a claim for the purposes of income tax, the period ending with the first anniversary of the 31st January next following the year of assessment in which the accommodation was let;

(b) in the case of a claim for the purposes of corporation tax, the period of two years beginning at the end of the accounting period in which the accommodation was let."

15.—(1) Section 524 of the Taxes Act 1988 (taxation of receipts from sale of patent rights) shall be amended in accordance with the following provisions of this paragraph.

(2) In subsection (2) (election to be made by notice served on the inspector not later than two years after end of chargeable period in which sum received)—

(a) for "the inspector not later than two years after the end of the chargeable period in which the sum was received" there shall be substituted "an officer of the Board within the period specified in subsection (2A) below"; and

(b) for "that chargeable period" there shall be substituted "the chargeable period in which it was received".

(3) After that subsection there shall be inserted—

"(2A) The period mentioned in subsection (2) above is—

(a) in the case of an election for the purposes of income tax, the period ending with the first anniversary of the 31st January next following the year of assessment in which the sum was received;

(b) in the case of an election for the purposes of corporation tax, the period of two years beginning at the end of the accounting period in which the sum was received."

(4) In subsection (4) (election to be made not later than two years after the end of the year of assessment in which the sum is paid) for "not later than two years after the end of" there shall be substituted "on or before the first anniversary of the 31st January next following".

16. In section 585(6) of the Taxes Act 1988 (no claim may be made more than six years after the end of the year of assessment in which the income to which it relates is received in the United Kingdom) for "more than six years after the end of" there shall be substituted "after the fifth anniversary of the 31st January next following".

17. In section 619(4) of the Taxes Act 1988 (election to be made before the end of the year of assessment in which qualifying premium paid) for "before the end of" there shall be substituted "on or before the 31st January next following".

18. In section 641(4) of the Taxes Act 1988 (election to be made not later than three months after the end of the year of assessment in which contributions are actually paid) for "not later than three months after the end of" there shall be substituted "on or before the 31st January next following".

19. In section 691(4) of the Taxes Act 1988 (election to be made within two years of the end of the year of assessment to which it relates) for "within two years of the end of" there shall be substituted "on or before the first anniversary of the 31st January next following".

20. In section 700(3) of the Taxes Act 1988 (time for making assessments, adjustments or claims shall not expire before the end of the third year following the year of assessment in which the administration of the estate was completed) for "third year" there shall be substituted "period of three years beginning with the 31st January next".

21.—(1) Section 781 of the Taxes Act 1988 (assets leased to traders and others) shall be amended in accordance with the following provisions of this paragraph.

(2) In subsection (8) (adjustment may be made at any time not more than six years from end of chargeable period in which payment made) for the words following "at any time" there shall be substituted "within the period specified in subsection (8A) below".

(3) After that subsection there shall be inserted—

"(8A) The period mentioned in subsection (8) above is—

(a) in the case of adjustments with respect to income tax, the period ending with the fifth anniversary of the 31st January next following the year of assessment in which the payment was made;

(b) in the case of adjustments with respect to corporation tax, the period of six years beginning at the end of the accounting period in which the payment was made."

22. In section 804(7) of the Taxes Act 1988 (claim for credit against tax for any year of assessment to be made within six years of the end of that year of assessment) for "within six years of the end of", in each place where those words occur, there shall be substituted "on or before the fifth anniversary of the 31st January next following".

23. In section 806(1) of the Taxes Act 1988 (claim to be made not later than six years from end of chargeable period for which income or gain falls to be charged to tax) for the words following "any income or chargeable gain" there shall be substituted—

"(a) shall, in the case of any income or chargeable gain which—
     (i) falls to be charged to income tax for a year of assessment, or
     (ii) would fall to be charged to income tax for a year of assessment if any income tax were chargeable in respect of the income or gain,
  be made on or before the fifth anniversary of the 31st January next following that year of assessment;
(b) shall, in the case of any income or chargeable gain which—
     (i) falls to be charged to corporation tax for an accounting period, or
     (ii) would fall to be charged to corporation tax for an accounting period if any corporation tax were chargeable in respect of the income or gain,
  be made not more than six years after the end of that accounting period."

24. In Schedule 11 to the Taxes Act 1988, in paragraph 12 (election to be made by notice given to the inspector within six years after the year of assessment in which payment made) for "the inspector within six years after" there shall be substituted "an officer of the Board on or before the fifth anniversary of the 31st January next following".

The Finance Act 1988 (c. 39)

25. In section 39(2)(b) of the Finance Act 1988 (election to be made not later than twelve months after the end of the first year of assessment for which it is to have effect) for "not later than twelve months after the end of" there shall be substituted "on or before the first anniversary of the 31st January next following".

The Capital Allowances Act 1990 (c. 1)

26.—(1) Section 25 of the Capital Allowances Act 1990 (qualifying expenditure) shall be amended in accordance with the following provisions of this paragraph.

(2) In subsection (3) (election to be made by notice given to the inspector not later than two years after the end of the chargeable period related to the incurring of expenditure) for "the inspector not later than two years after the end of that chargeable period" there shall be substituted "an officer of the Board within the period specified in subsection (3A) below".

(3) After subsection (3) there shall be inserted—

"(3A) The period mentioned in subsection (3) above is—
(a) for the purposes of income tax, the period ending with the first anniversary of the 31st January next following the year of assessment in which ends the chargeable period related to the incurring of the expenditure;
(b) for the purposes of corporation tax, the period of two years beginning at the end of the chargeable period related to the incurring of the expenditure."

27.—(1) Section 30 of the Capital Allowances Act 1990 (ships: first-year allowances) shall be amended in accordance with the following provisions of this paragraph.

(2) In subsection (1) (notices that may be given where first-year allowance falls to be made) for "the inspector not later than two years after the end of the period" there shall be substituted "an officer of the Board within the period specified in subsection (1A) below".

(3) After subsection (1) there shall be inserted—

"(1A) The period mentioned in subsection (1) above is—
(a) for the purposes of income tax, the period ending with the first anniversary of the 31st January next following the year of assessment in which ends the period of account for which the allowance mentioned in that subsection falls to be made;
(b) for the purposes of corporation tax, the period of two years beginning at the end of the accounting period for which the allowance mentioned in that subsection falls to be made."

28. For section 31(3) of the Capital Allowances Act 1990 (ships: notice to postpone writing-down allowance) there shall be substituted—

"(3) Where the shipowner has qualifying expenditure for a chargeable period in respect of his single ship trade, he may by notice given to an officer of the Board require the postponement of—
(a) the whole of the writing-down allowance to be made to him for that chargeable period, or

(b) so much of it as is specified in the notice.

(3A) A notice under subsection (3) above—

(a) for the purposes of income tax, shall be given on or before the first anniversary of the 31st January next following the year of assessment in which ends the chargeable period mentioned in that subsection;

(b) for the purposes of corporation tax, shall be given no later than two years after the end of the chargeable period mentioned in that subsection."

29.—(1) Section 33 of the Capital Allowances Act 1990 (ships: exclusion of section 31) shall be amended in accordance with the following provisions of this paragraph.

(2) For subsection (1) (notice to exclude section 31) there shall be substituted—

"(1) The shipowner may by notice given to an officer of the Board require that, with effect from the beginning of a chargeable period of a single ship trade, not being the chargeable period relating to the permanent discontinuance of that trade, section 31 shall not, or as the case may be, shall no longer apply."

(3) For subsection (4) (notice to have expenditure in respect of single ship trade attributed to actual trade) there shall be substituted—

"(4) The shipowner may by notice given to an officer of the Board require that an amount of expenditure specified in the notice, being less than the amount which, apart from this subsection, would be his qualifying expenditure in respect of a single ship trade for a chargeable period of that trade, shall be attributed to his actual trade."

(4) After subsection (5) there shall be substituted—

"(5A) A notice under subsection (1) or (4) above—

(a) for the purposes of income tax, shall be given on or before the first anniversary of the 31st January next following the year of assessment in which ends the chargeable period mentioned in that subsection;

(b) for the purposes of corporation tax, shall be given no later than two years after the end of the chargeable period mentioned in that subsection."

30.—(1) Section 37 of the Capital Allowances Act 1990 (election for certain machinery or plant to be treated as short life assets) shall be amended in accordance with the following provisions of this paragraph.

(2) In subsection (2) (elections)—

(a) in paragraph (c) (election may not be made more than two years after the end of the chargeable period in which the capital expenditure was incurred) for the words following "may not be made" there shall be substituted "after the end of the period specified in subsection (2A) below"; and

(b) the words following paragraph (d) shall cease to have effect.

(3) After that subsection there shall be inserted—

"(2A) The period mentioned in subsection (2) above is—

(a) for the purposes of income tax, the period ending with the first anniversary of the 31st January next following the year of assessment in which ends the chargeable period related to the incurring of the capital expenditure concerned;

(b) for the purposes of corporation tax, the period of two years beginning at the end of the chargeable period related to the incurring of the capital expenditure concerned; and if different parts of the capital expenditure are incurred at different times, only that part of the expenditure which is first incurred shall be taken into account for the purposes of this subsection."

31.—(1) Section 53 of the Capital Allowances Act 1990 (expenditure incurred by equipment lessor) shall be amended in accordance with the following provisions of this paragraph.

(2) In subsection (2) (election to be made by notice given to the inspector before the expiry of the period of two years beginning at the end of the chargeable period related to the incurring of the expenditure)—

(a) for "the inspector" there shall be substituted "an officer of the Board"; and

(b) for "of two years beginning at the end of the chargeable period related to the incurring of the expenditure referred to in subsection (1)(a) above" there shall be substituted "specified in subsection (2A) below".

(3) After that subsection there shall be inserted—

"(2A) The period mentioned in subsection (2) above is—

(a) for the purposes of income tax, the period ending with the first anniversary of the 31st January next following the year of assessment in which ends the chargeable period related to the incurring of the expenditure referred to in subsection (1)(a) above;

(b) for the purposes of corporation tax, the period of two years beginning at the end of the chargeable period related to the incurring of the expenditure referred to in subsection (1)(a) above."

32.—(1) Section 68 of the Capital Allowances Act 1990 (exclusion of certain expenditure relating to films, tapes and discs) shall be amended in accordance with the following provisions of this paragraph.

(2) In subsection (5) (claim to be made not later than two years after the end of the relevant period) for "not later than two years after the end of that period" there shall be substituted "within the period specified in subsection (5A) below".

(3) After that subsection there shall be inserted—

"(5A) The period mentioned in subsection (5) above is—

  (a) for the purposes of income tax, the period ending with the first anniversary of the 31st January next following the year of assessment in which ends the relevant period mentioned in that subsection;

  (b) for the purposes of corporation tax, the period of two years beginning at the end of the relevant period mentioned in that subsection."

(4) In subsection (9A)(b) (election to be made by giving notice to the inspector not later than two years after the end of the relevant period in which the film etc. is completed)—

  (a) for "the inspector" there shall be substituted "an officer of the Board"; and

  (b) for "not later than two years after the end of the relevant period in which the film, tape or disc is completed" there shall be substituted "within the period specified in subsection (9AA) below".

(5) After subsection (9A) there shall be inserted—

"(9AA) The period mentioned in subsection (9A)(b) above is—

  (a) in the case of an election for the purposes of income tax, the period ending with the first anniversary of the 31st January next following the year of assessment in which ends the relevant period in which the film, tape or disc is completed;

  (b) in the case of an election for the purposes of corporation tax, the period of two years beginning at the end of the relevant period in which the film, tape or disc is completed."

(6) In subsection (9B) for "(9A)(b)" there shall be substituted "(9AA)".

33. In section 129(2) of the Capital Allowances Act 1990 (election to be made by notice given to the inspector not more than two years after the end of the chargeable period related to the occurrence of the event) for the words following "by notice given to" there shall be substituted "an officer of the Board; and—

  (a) an election under this subsection for the purposes of income tax shall be made on or before the first anniversary of the 31st January next following the year of assessment in which ends the chargeable period related to the occurrence of the event; and

  (b) an election under this subsection for the purposes of corporation tax shall be made not more than two years after the end of the chargeable period related to the occurrence of the event."

34. In section 141(3) of the Capital Allowances Act 1990, in the second paragraph (election as respects an allowance for any year of assessment to be made by giving notice to the inspector not later than two years after the end of that year of assessment) for "the inspector not later than two years after the end of" there shall be substituted "an officer of the Board on or before the first anniversary of the 31st January next following".

The Taxation of Chargeable Gains Act 1992 (c. 12)

35. In section 35(6) of the Taxation of Chargeable Gains Act 1992 (elections under section 35(5) to be made by notice to the inspector within period ending 2 years after the end of the year of assessment or accounting period in which the disposal is made or at such later time as the Board may allow—

  (a) for "the inspector" there shall be substituted "an officer of the Board"; and

  (b) for paragraphs (a) and (b) there shall be substituted—

"(a) in the case of an election for the purposes of capital gains tax, with the first anniversary of the 31st January next following the year of assessment in which the disposal is made;

  (aa) in the case of an election for the purposes of corporation tax, 2 years after the end of the accounting period in which the disposal is made; or

  (b) in either case, at such later time as the Board may allow;".

36. In section 161 of the Taxation of Chargeable Gains Act 1992 (appropriations to and from stock) after subsection (3) there shall be inserted—

"(3A) An election under subsection (3) above shall be made—

  (a) for the purposes of capital gains tax, on or before the first anniversary of the 31st January next following the year of assessment in which ends the period of account in which the asset is appropriated for the purposes of the trade as trading stock;

  (b) for the purposes of corporation tax, within 2 years after the end of the accounting period in which the asset is appropriated for the purposes of the trade as trading stock;

and in paragraph (a) above "period of account" means a period for which the accounts of the trade are made up."

37. In section 242 of the Taxation of Chargeable Gains Act 1992 (small part disposals) after subsection (2) there shall be inserted—

"(2A) A claim under subsection (2) above shall be made—

(a) for the purposes of capital gains tax, on or before the first anniversary of the 31st January next following the year of assessment in which the transfer is made;

(b) for the purposes of corporation tax, within 2 years after the end of the accounting period in which the transfer is made."

38. In section 243 of the Taxation of Chargeable Gains Act 1992 (part disposal to authority with compulsory powers) after subsection (2) there shall be inserted—

"(2A) A claim under subsection (2) above shall be made—

(a) for the purposes of capital gains tax, on or before the first anniversary of the 31st January next following the year of assessment in which the transfer is made;

(b) for the purposes of corporation tax, within 2 years after the end of the accounting period in which the transfer is made."

39. In section 244 of the Taxation of Chargeable Gains Act 1992 (part disposal: consideration exceeding allowable expenditure) after subsection (2) there shall be inserted—

"(3) An election under subsection (2)(b) above shall be made—

(a) for the purposes of capital gains tax, on or before the first anniversary of the 31st January next following the year of assessment in which the part disposal is made;

(b) for the purposes of corporation tax, within 2 years after the end of the accounting period in which the part disposal is made."

40. In section 253 of the Taxation of Chargeable Gains Act 1992 (relief for loans to traders) after subsection (4) there shall be inserted—

"(4A) A claim under subsection (4) above shall be made—

(a) for the purposes of capital gains tax, on or before the fifth anniversary of the 31st January next following the year of assessment in which the payment was made;

(b) for the purposes of corporation tax, within 6 years after the end of the accounting period in which the payment was made."

41. In section 279 of the Taxation of Chargeable Gains Act 1992 (foreign assets: delayed remittances) for subsection (5) (no claim under section 279 to be made more than 6 years after end of year of assessment in which chargeable gain accrues) there shall be substituted—

"(5) No claim under this section in respect of a chargeable gain shall be made—

(a) in the case of a claim for the purposes of capital gains tax at any time after the fifth anniversary of the 31st January next following the year of assessment in which the gain accrues; or

(b) in the case of a claim for the purposes of corporation tax, more than 6 years after the end of the accounting period in which the gain accrues."

42.—(1) Schedule 2 to the Taxation of Chargeable Gains Act 1992 shall be amended in accordance with the following provisions of this paragraph.

(2) In paragraph 4 (election for pooling) in sub-paragraph (11) (election to be made by notice to the inspector not later than the expiration of 2 years from the end of the year of assessment or accounting period of a company in which the first relevant disposal is made, or such further time as the Board may allow) for the words following "notice to" there shall be substituted "an officer of the Board given—

(a) in the case of an election for the purposes of capital gains tax, on or before the first anniversary of the 31st January next following the year of assessment in which the first relevant disposal is made;

(b) in the case of an election for the purposes of corporation tax, not later than the expiration of 2 years from the end of the accounting period in which the first relevant disposal is made; or

(c) in either case, within such further time as the Board may allow."

(3) In paragraph 17 (election for valuation at 6th April) in sub-paragraph (3) (election to be made by notice to the inspector given within 2 years from the end of the year of assessment or accounting period of a company in which the disposal is made, or such further time as the Board may by notice allow) for the words following "by notice to" there shall be substituted "an officer of the Board given—

(a) in the case of an election for the purposes of capital gains tax, on or before the first anniversary of the 31st January next following the year of assessment in which the disposal is made;

(b) in the case of an election for the purposes of corporation tax, within 2 years from the end of the accounting period in which the disposal is made; or

(c) in either case, within such further time as the Board may by notice allow."

43. In Schedule 4 to the Taxation of Chargeable Gains Act 1992 (deferred charges on gains before 31st March 1982) in paragraph 9(1) (time for making claims)—
    (a) in paragraph (b)—
            (i) for "any other case" there shall be substituted "the case of a disposal made by, or a gain treated as accruing to, a person chargeable to corporation tax"; and
            (ii) the words "year of assessment or" shall be omitted;
    (b) after paragraph (b) there shall be inserted—
        "(c) in the case of a disposal made by, or a gain treated as accruing to, a person who is chargeable to capital gains tax, on or before the first anniversary of the 31st January next following the year of assessment in which the disposal in question is made or the gain in question is treated as accruing,"; and
    (c) in the words following paragraph (b), after "period" there shall be inserted "or (as the case may be) on or before such later date".

44.—(1) Schedule 6 to the Taxation of Chargeable Gains Act 1992 (retirement relief etc.) shall be amended in accordance with the following provisions of this paragraph.

(2) In paragraph 2(1) (election to be made by notice given to the Board not more than 2 years after the end of the year of assessment in which the disposal occurred) for "not more than 2 years after the end of" there shall be substituted "on or before the first anniversary of the 31st January next following".

(3) In paragraph 5(2) (claim for relief to be made not later than 2 years after the end of the year of assessment in which the disposal occurred) for "not later than 2 years after the end of" there shall be substituted "on or before the first anniversary of the 31st January next following".

(4) In paragraph 12(5)(b) (election to be made by giving notice to the inspector not later than 2 years after the end of the year of assessment in which capital distribution received)—
    (a) for "not later than 2 years after the end of" there shall be substituted "on or before the first anniversary of the 31st January next following"; and
    (b) for "the inspector" there shall be substituted "an officer of the Board".

(5) In paragraph 16 (aggregation of spouse's interest in the business: election to be made by giving notice to the inspector not later than 2 years after the end of the year of assessment in which material disposal occurred)—
    (a) in sub-paragraph (1)(e) for "not later than 2 years after the end of" there shall be substituted "on or before the first anniversary of the 31st January next following"; and
    (b) in sub-paragraph (2) for "the inspector" there shall be substituted "an officer of the Board".

The Finance (No. 2) Act 1992 (c. 48)

45. For section 41(6) of the Finance (No. 2) Act 1992 (claim to be made not later than two years after the end of the relevant period in which the expenditure to which it relates becomes payable) there shall be substituted—
    "(6) A claim under this section shall be made—
    (a) for the purposes of income tax, on or before the first anniversary of the 31st January next following the year of assessment in which ends the relevant period in which the expenditure to which it relates becomes payable;
    (b) for the purposes of corporation tax, not later than two years after the end of the relevant period in which the expenditure to which it relates becomes payable."

46. For section 42(6) of the Finance (No. 2) Act 1992 (claim to be made not later than two years after the end of the relevant period to which it relates) there shall be substituted—
    "(6) A claim under this section shall be made—
    (a) for the purposes of income tax, on or before the first anniversary of the 31st January next following the year of assessment in which ends the relevant period to which the claim relates,
    (b) for the purposes of corporation tax, not later than two years after the end of the relevant period to which the claim relates,
and shall be irrevocable."

47.—(1) Schedule 10 to the Finance (No. 2) Act 1992 (furnished accommodation) shall be amended in accordance with the following provisions of this paragraph.

(2) In paragraph 10(4) (election or notice to be made or given by notice in writing to the inspector before the end of the period of one year beginning with the end of the year of assessment concerned or such longer period as the Board may in any particular case allow)—
    (a) in paragraph (a) for the words following "must be made or given" there shall be substituted "on or before—
        (i) the first anniversary of the 31st January next following the year of assessment concerned, or

(ii) such later date as the Board may in any particular case allow, and"; and

(b) in paragraph (b) for "the inspector" there shall be substituted "an officer of the Board".

(3) In paragraph 10, in sub-paragraph (5) (assessment not to be out of time if made before the end of the period of one year beginning with the day when the election was made or the notice given) for "before the end of the period of one year beginning with the day when" there shall be substituted "on or before the first anniversary of the 31st January next following the year of assessment in which".

(4) In paragraph 12(2) (election must be made in writing to the inspector before the end of the period of one year beginning with the end of the year of assessment for which it is made or such longer period as the Board may in any particular case allow)—

(a) in paragraph (b) for the words following "must be made" there shall be substituted "on or before—

(i) the first anniversary of the 31st January next following the year of assessment for which it is made, or

(ii) such later date as the Board may in any particular case allow, and"; and

(b) in paragraph (c) for "the inspector" there shall be substituted "an officer of the Board".

(5) In paragraph 12(4) (notice of withdrawal to be given in writing to the inspector before the end of the period of one year beginning with the end of the year of assessment for which it is given or such longer period as the Board may in any particular case allow)—

(a) in paragraph (a) for the words following "must be given" there shall be substituted "on or before—

(i) the first anniversary of the 31st January next following the year of assessment for which it is given, or

(ii) such later date as the Board may in any particular case allow,"; and

(b) in paragraph (b) for "the inspector" there shall be substituted "an officer of the Board".

(6) In paragraph 12, in sub-paragraph (6)(b) (notice of withdrawal deemed to be given on the last day of the period of one year beginning with the end of the year of assessment concerned) for "last day of the period of one year beginning with the end of" there shall be substituted "first anniversary of the 31st January next following".

(7) In paragraph 12, in sub-paragraph (7) (assessment not to be out of time if made before the end of the period of one year beginning with the day when the election was made or the notice was given) for "before the end of the period of one year beginning with the day when" there shall be substituted "on or before the first anniversary of the 31st January next following the year of assessment in which".

The Finance Act 1994 (c. 9)

48.—(1) Section 118 of the Finance Act 1994 (expenditure on machinery or plant: notification) shall be amended in accordance with the following provisions of this paragraph.

(2) In subsection (3) (condition fulfilled with respect to a chargeable period if notice given to the inspector not later than two years after the end of the period) for "the inspector, in such form as the Board may require, not later than two years after the end of that period" there shall be substituted "an officer of the Board, in such form as the Board may require, within the period specified in subsection (3A) below".

(3) After subsection (3) there shall be inserted—

"(3A) A notice under subsection (3) above—

(a) for the purposes of income tax, shall be given on or before the first anniversary of the 31st January next following the year of assessment in which ends the chargeable period mentioned in that subsection;

(b) for the purposes of corporation tax, shall be given no later than two years after the end of the chargeable period mentioned in that subsection."

GENERAL NOTE

The amendments made by this Schedule align the time limits for making claims and elections, adjustments to assessments and the giving of notices with those within which a taxpayer has to file a return, or can amend a self-assessment or within which an assessment can ordinarily be made.

The time limit for filing an income tax and capital gains tax return is normally the January 31 next following the year of assessment, *i.e.* almost 10 months after the end of that year. The time limit for taxpayer amendment to a self-assessment is the first anniversary of the filing date, *i.e.* almost 22 months after the end of the year of assessment. The ordinary time limit for making assessments for income tax and capital gains tax is the fifth anniversary of the filing date, *i.e.* almost five years, 10 months after the end of the year of assessment.

The Schedule contains some amendments to sections affecting corporation tax as well as income tax and capital gains tax, but any references to two-year and six-year time limits for corporation tax are not being changed [Standing Committee E, February 20, 1996, col. 428].

Section 136   SCHEDULE 22

SELF-ASSESSMENT: APPEALS

The Taxes Management Act 1970

1. The Taxes Management Act 1970 shall be amended in accordance with paragraphs 2 to 10 below.

2. In section 19A (power to call for documents for purposes of certain enquiries), for subsection (11) there shall be substituted the following subsection—

"(11) The determination of the Commissioners of an appeal under subsection (6) above shall be final and conclusive (notwithstanding any provision having effect by virtue of section 56B of this Act)."

3. In section 28A (amendment of self-assessment where enquiries made), for subsections (6) and (7) there shall be substituted the following subsections—

"(6) At any time before a notice is given under subsection (5) above, the taxpayer may apply for a direction that the officer shall give such a notice within such period as may be specified in the direction.

(6A) Subject to subsection (7) below, an application under subsection (6) above shall be heard and determined in the same way as an appeal against an amendment of a self-assessment under subsection (2) or (4) above.

(7) The Commissioners hearing the application shall give the direction applied for unless they are satisfied that the officer has reasonable grounds for not giving the notice."

4. In section 31 (appeals in connection with assessments), for subsection (3) there shall be substituted the following subsection—

"(3) An appeal against an assessment made—

(a) by the Board, or

(b) under section 350 of the principal Act,

shall be to the Special Commissioners."

5. In section 33A (error or mistake in partnership statement), for subsection (8) there shall be substituted the following subsections—

"(8) Subject to subsection (8A) below, the determination of the Special Commissioners of an appeal under subsection (6) above shall be final and conclusive (notwithstanding any provision having effect by virtue of section 56B of this Act).

(8A) Subsection (8) above does not apply in relation to a point of law arising in connection with the computation of profits."

6. Section 42(12) and Schedule 2 (Commissioners to whom appeal lies where appeal is against amendment of claim not included in return) shall be omitted.

7. For section 47 there shall be substituted the following sections—

"Questions to be determined by Special Commissioners
46B.—(1) In so far as the question in dispute on an appeal to which this section applies is a question which under this section is to be determined by the Special Commissioners, the question shall be determined by them.

(2) This section applies to—

(a) an appeal against an amendment under section 28A(2) or (4) of this Act of a self-assessment;

(b) an appeal against a decision contained in a notice under section 28A(4A) of this Act disallowing a claim or election in whole or in part;

(c) an appeal against an amendment under section 28B(3) or 30B(1) of this Act of a partnership statement;

(d) an appeal against an assessment to tax which is not a self-assessment;

(e) an appeal against an amendment under paragraph 7(3) of Schedule 1A to this Act of a claim or election made otherwise than by being included in a return;

(f) an appeal against a decision contained in a notice under paragraph 7(3A) of Schedule 1A to this Act disallowing in whole or in part a claim or election made otherwise than by being included in a return.

(3) Any question—

(a) of the value of any shares or securities in a company resident in the United Kingdom, other than shares or securities quoted in The Stock Exchange Daily Official List, and

(b) arising in relation to the taxation of chargeable gains (whether under capital gains tax or corporation tax) or in relation to a claim under the 1992 Act,

is a question to be determined by the Special Commissioners.

(4) Any question as to the application of any of the following provisions of the principal Act is a question to be determined by the Special Commissioners—

(a) Chapter IA or IB of Part XV (settlements);

(b) Part XVI (administration of estates);

(c) sections 740 and 743(1) (liability in respect of transfer of assets abroad);

(d) section 747(4)(a) (liability in respect of controlled foreign company).

(5) Any question as to the application of—

(a) section 830 of the principal Act, or

(b) section 276 of the 1992 Act,

(liability in relation to territorial sea and designated areas) is a question to be determined by the Special Commissioners.

Jurisdiction of Special Commissioners over certain claims included in returns

46C.—(1) In so far as the question in dispute on an appeal to which this section applies concerns a claim made—

(a) to the Board, or

(b) under any of the provisions of the principal Act listed in subsection (3) below,

the question shall be determined by the Special Commissioners.

(2) This section applies to—

(a) an appeal against an amendment under section 28A(2) or (4) of this Act of a self-assessment;

(b) an appeal against an amendment under section 28B(3) or 30B(1) of this Act of a partnership statement.

(3) The provisions of the principal Act mentioned in subsection (1) above are—

(a) section 121(1) and (2) (management expenses of owner of mineral rights);

(b) sections 459 and 460 (exemption for certain friendly societies);

(c) section 467 (exemption for certain trade unions and employers' associations);

(d) sections 527, 534, 536 and 538 (reliefs in respect of royalties, copyright payments etc.);

(e) Chapter I of Part XVIII.

Questions to be determined by Lands Tribunal

46D.—(1) In so far as the question in dispute on an appeal to which this section applies—

(a) is a question of the value of any land or of a lease of land, and

(b) arises in relation to the taxation of chargeable gains (whether under capital gains tax or corporation tax) or in relation to a claim under the 1992 Act,

the question shall be determined by the relevant Lands Tribunal.

(2) This section applies to—

(a) an appeal against an amendment under section 28A(2) or (4) of this Act of a self-assessment;

(b) an appeal against a decision contained in a notice under section 28A(4A) of this Act disallowing a claim or election in whole or in part;

(c) an appeal against an amendment under section 28B(3) or 30B(1) of this Act of a partnership statement;

(d) an appeal against an assessment to tax which is not a self-assessment;

(e) an appeal against an amendment under paragraph 7(3) of Schedule 1A to this Act of a claim or election made otherwise than by being included in a return;

(f) an appeal against a decision contained in a notice under paragraph 7(3A) of Schedule 1A to this Act disallowing in whole or in part a claim or election made otherwise than by being included in a return.

(3) In this section 'the relevant Lands Tribunal' means—

(a) in relation to land in England and Wales, the Lands Tribunal;

(b) in relation to land in Scotland, the Lands Tribunal for Scotland;

(c) in relation to land in Northern Ireland, the Lands Tribunal for Northern Ireland."

8. In section 57(3)(c) (power to make regulations authorising conditional decisions where more than one tribunal is determining questions in the proceedings), for "section 47" there shall be substituted "section 46B, 46C or 46D".

9. In Schedule 1A (claims not included in returns), after paragraph 9 there shall be inserted the following paragraphs—

" 10. An appeal against an amendment under paragraph 7(3) above of a claim made—

(a) to the Board,

(b) under Part XVI of the principal Act (administration of estates), or

(c) under any of the provisions of the principal Act listed in section 46C(3) of this Act,

shall be to the Special Commissioners.

11.—(1) Subject to paragraph 10 above and the following provisions of this paragraph, an appeal under paragraph 9(1) above shall be to the General Commissioners.

(2) The appellant may elect (in accordance with section 46(1) of this Act) to bring the appeal before the Special Commissioners.

(3) Such an election shall be disregarded if—

(a) the appellant and the officer of the Board agree in writing, at any time before the determination of the appeal, that it is to be disregarded; or

(b) the General Commissioners have given a direction under sub-paragraph (5) below and have not revoked it.

(4) At any time before the determination of an appeal in respect of which an election has been made an officer of the Board after giving notice to the appellant may refer the election to the General Commissioners.

(5) On any such reference the Commissioners shall, unless they are satisfied that the appellant has arguments to present or evidence to adduce on the merits of the appeal, give a direction that the election be disregarded.

(6) If, at any time after the giving of such a direction (but before the determination of the appeal) the General Commissioners are satisfied that the appellant has arguments to present or evidence to adduce on the merits of the appeal, they shall revoke the direction.

(7) Any decision to give or revoke such a direction shall be final.

(8) If—

(a) a person bringing an appeal under paragraph 9(1) above has another appeal pending to either body of Commissioners concerning an assessment on him, and

(b) the appeals relate to the same source of income,

the appeal under paragraph 9(1) above shall be to the body of Commissioners before whom the appeal concerning the assessment is being brought.

(9) This paragraph is subject to provision made by or under Part V of this Act."

10. The following Schedule shall be substituted for Schedule 3—

"SCHEDULE 3

SMALL>RULES FOR ASSIGNING PROCEEDINGS TO GENERAL COMMISSIONERS</SMALL>

Introductory

1. In this Schedule—

'the relevant place' means the place referred to in section 44(1) of this Act, which is used to identify the General Commissioners before whom proceedings are to be brought; and

'the taxpayer', in relation to any proceedings, means the party to the proceedings who is neither the Board nor an officer of the Board.

General rule for income and capital gains tax proceedings

2.—(1) In the case of any proceedings relating to income tax or capital gains tax the relevant place is whichever of the places specified in sub-paragraph (2) below is identified—

(a) except where the proceedings are commenced by an officer of the Board, by an election made by the taxpayer; and

(b) where the proceedings are so commenced, by an election made by the officer.

(2) Those places are—

(a) the place (if any) in the United Kingdom which, at the time when the election is made, is the taxpayer's place of residence;

(b) the place (if any) which at that time is the taxpayer's place of business in the United Kingdom;

(c) the place (if any) in the United Kingdom which at that time is the taxpayer's place of employment;

and, in the case of a place of employment, it shall be immaterial for the purposes of this paragraph whether the proceedings in question relate to matters connected with the employment of the taxpayer.

(3) Where the taxpayer fails to make an election for the purposes of this paragraph before the time limit given by paragraph 5 below, an officer of the Board may elect which of the places specified in sub-paragraph (2) above is to be the relevant place.

(4) In sub-paragraph (2)(a) above 'place of residence' means—

(a) in relation to an election made by the taxpayer, his usual place of residence; and

(b) in relation to an election made by an officer of the Board, the taxpayer's usual place of residence or, if that is unknown, his last known place of residence.

(5) In sub-paragraph (2)(b) above 'place of business' means—

(a) the place where the trade, profession, vocation or business with which the proceedings are concerned is carried on, or

(b) if the trade, profession, vocation or business is carried on at more than one place, the head office or place where it is mainly carried on.

(6) This paragraph does not apply in the case of any proceedings to which paragraph 3, 4 or 7 below applies.

PAYE appeals

3.—(1) In the case of an appeal in exercise of a right of appeal conferred by regulations under section 203 of the principal Act, the relevant place is—

(a) except in a case falling in paragraph (b) below, the place determined by the regulations, and

(b) if the appellant elects for one of the places specified in paragraph 2(2) above to be the relevant place instead, the place identified by the election.

(2) This paragraph does not apply in the case of any proceedings to which paragraph 4 or 7 below applies.

Corporation tax etc.

4.—(1) In the case of the proceedings mentioned in sub-paragraph (2) below the relevant place is whichever of the places specified in sub-paragraph (3) below is identified—

(a) except where the proceedings are commenced by an officer of the Board, by an election made by the company or other body corporate which is a party to the proceedings ("the corporate taxpayer"); and

(b) where the proceedings are so commenced, by an election made by the officer.

(2) The proceedings are—

(a) proceedings relating to corporation tax;

(b) proceedings relating to income tax which are proceedings to which a company resident in the United Kingdom and within the charge to corporation tax is a party;

(c) proceedings relating to tax assessable under sections 419 and 420 of the principal Act (close company loans).

(3) The places are—

(a) the place where, at the time when the election is made, the corporate taxpayer carries on its trade or business;

(b) the place where, at that time, the head office or principal place of business of the corporate taxpayer is situated;

(c) the place where, at that time, the corporate taxpayer resides.

(4) Where the corporate taxpayer fails to make an election for the purposes of this paragraph before the time limit given by paragraph 5 below, an officer of the Board may elect which of the places specified in sub-paragraph (3) above is to be the relevant place.

(5) This paragraph does not apply in the case of any proceedings to which paragraph 7 below applies.

Procedure for making elections, etc.

5.—(1) An election by a taxpayer for the purposes of this Schedule shall be made by notice in writing to an officer of the Board.

(2) The time limit for the making of such an election in relation to proceedings is—

(a) the time when the taxpayer gives notice of appeal or, if the proceedings are not an appeal, otherwise commences the proceedings; or

(b) such later date as the Board allows.

(3) Such an election shall be irrevocable.

6. An election by an officer of the Board for the purposes of this Schedule shall be made by notice in writing served on the taxpayer.

Partnerships

7. In the case of proceedings relating to a partnership to which a partner of that partnership is a party, the relevant place is—

(a) the place where the trade, profession or business of the partnership is carried on, or

(b) if the trade, profession or business is carried on at more than one place, the place where it is mainly carried on.

Directions by the Board

8.—(1) The Board may give a direction in relation to any class of proceedings specified in the direction that, notwithstanding the preceding provisions of this Schedule, the relevant place shall be taken to be a place in a division specified in the direction.

(2) A direction given under this paragraph shall not have effect in relation to any proceedings unless an officer of the Board has served on the taxpayer a notice in writing stating the effect of the direction in relation to those proceedings.

(3) A direction given under this paragraph shall not have effect if the taxpayer gives a notice in accordance with sub-paragraph (4) below objecting to the direction.

(4) The taxpayer gives a notice in accordance with this sub-paragraph if he gives it in writing to the Board within the period of 30 days beginning with the day on which the notice under sub-paragraph (2) above was served on him.

9.—(1) The Board may give directions for determining the relevant place in cases where—

(a) the proceedings fall within paragraph 2, 4 or 7 above, but there is no place falling within paragraph 2(2), 4(3) or, as the case may be, paragraph 7; or

(b) the relevant place would, apart from the direction, be a place outside the United Kingdom.

(2) A direction given under this paragraph by the Board shall not have effect in relation to any proceedings unless an officer of the Board has served on the taxpayer a notice in writing stating the effect of the direction in relation to those proceedings.

(3) A direction under sub-paragraph (1) above may be given in relation to—

(a) proceedings falling within that sub-paragraph;

(b) any class of such proceedings specified in the direction; or

(c) proceedings specified in the direction.

Other provisions

10. The provisions of this Schedule have effect subject to sections 44(2), 46A and 57 of this Act, sections 102(1), 113(5), 343(10) and 783(9) of the principal Act and section 151 of the Capital Allowances Act 1990."

Section 102 of the Taxes Act 1988

11. In section 102(1)(a) of the Taxes Act 1988 (cases where jurisdiction exercised by General Commissioners) for "both the trades, professions or vocations" there shall be substituted "each of the persons whose trade, profession or vocation is one of those".

Commencement of Schedule

12. This Schedule has effect in relation to—

(a) any proceedings relating to the year 1996–97 or any subsequent year of assessment, and

(b) any proceedings relating to an accounting period ending on or after the day appointed under section 199 of the Finance Act 1994 for the purposes of Chapter III of Part IV of that Act (self-assessment).

GENERAL NOTE

The changes made by this Schedule do not affect the choice between having proceedings heard by the General or Special Commissioners that currently exists. However, where an appeal under self-assessment contains a question that, as an appeal against an assessment, would currently be heard by a specific tribunal, the new rules provide that the question, but not necessarily the entire appeal, will be heard by that tribunal.

Para. 2

This corrects an error in the TMA 1970, s.19A, and applies the same rules to direct appeals from the Special Commissioners as are applied to cases stated by the General Commissioners.

Para. 3

The amendments to the TMA 1970, s.28A, which deals with the way in which applications for a direction that an enquiry should be ended are to be heard, ensure that taxpayers have the same choice of commissioners as would be available if they appealed against amendment of self-assessment and that the procedure for considering the application is the same as that which would be used in those appeals.

Para. 4

This amendment excludes assessment which cannot be included as part of a self-assessment.

Para. 5

The amendment to the TMA 1970, s.33A, which allows partnerships to claim relief for errors or mistakes in their partnership statement, provides that the determination of the Special Commissioners on an appeal against the refusal of relief can only be appealed on a point of law connected with the way in which profits are computed. The same rule applies to individuals (see the TMA 1970, s.33(4)).

Para. 7

This codifies the rules enabling particular tribunals to determine specialist questions within an appeal against the amendment of a self-assessment.

The new s.46B ensures that the Special Commissioners retain exclusive jurisdiction to hear and determine questions relating to provisions formerly listed in ss.31 and 47.

The new s.46C ensures that the Special Commissioners have exclusive jurisdiction to hear and determine questions relating to claims currently listed in Sched. 2.

The new s.46D ensures that the Lands Tribunal continues to have exclusive jurisdiction to hear and determine questions currently listed in s.47.

Para. 9

This inserts additional provisions in Sched. 1A, which deals with the procedure for making claims under self-assessment that are not included in the return.

The new para. 10 provides that proceedings which would currently be heard by the Special Commissioners as appeals against the decision of an inspector will be heard and determined by them when the appeal is against amendment of a claim.

The new para. 11 ensures that in other circumstances the appeal against amendment of a claim is to be heard by the General Commissioners but with an option for the claimant to elect for the appeal to be heard by the Special Commissioners.

Para. 10

New Sched. 3 rationalises the rules for assigning proceedings to General Commissioners. The annotations below refer to paragraphs of the new Schedules:

Para. 2

For proceedings relating to income tax or capital gains tax, the taxpayer has the choice of the place where he lives, where he works or where he carries on business. Where the taxpayer does not choose, or where the Revenue begin proceedings themselves, the Revenue may make the choice.

Para. 3

For proceedings relating to PAYE, the place is determined by the PAYE regulations unless the taxpayer elects under para. 2.

Para. 4

Companies have a choice between the place where its business is carried on, where its head office is situated and where it resides. Where the company does not choose, or where the Revenue begin proceedings themselves, the Revenue may make the choice.

Paras. 5 and 6

Elections are made in writing at the inception of the appeal and are irrevocable. Elections by the Revenue are also made in writing.

Para. 7

For partnerships, the appropriate place is where the partnership's business is mainly carried on.

Paras. 8 and 9

The Revenue may give a direction in any case as to which division has jurisdiction, but this can be nullified by an objection from the taxpayer within 30 days. The Revenue may also give a direction in cases where the rules do not provide a place or give one which is outside the U.K. [Standing Committee E, February 20, 1996, col. 429].

           SCHEDULE 23

SELF-ASSESSMENT: SCHEDULES 13 AND 16 TO THE TAXES ACT 1988

PART I

SCHEDULE 13 TO THE TAXES ACT 1988

1. Schedule 13 to the Taxes Act 1988 (collection of advance corporation tax) shall be amended in accordance with the following provisions of this Part of this Schedule.

2. In paragraph 2 (contents of returns) in sub-paragraph (2) (specification of particular matters to be included in a return) after "The return shall specify" there shall be inserted "(a)" and at the end of that sub-paragraph there shall be inserted—

> "(b) whether any estimated amount of franked payments is included under that paragraph by virtue of paragraph 7(2) below and, if so, the amount so included;
>
> (c) whether any estimated amount of advance corporation tax is included under paragraph (c) of sub-paragraph (1) above by virtue of paragraph 7(2) below and, if so, the amount so included.

3. In paragraph 3(3) (power of the inspector to make an assessment in certain cases)—

(a) for "the inspector", where first occurring, there shall be substituted "an officer of the Board"; and

(b) for "or if the inspector is dissatisfied with any return, he may" there shall be substituted "or if an officer of the Board is of the opinion that a return is incorrect, any such officer may".

4.—(1) In sub-paragraph (1) of paragraph 3B (power of the inspector to make an assessment where he is not satisfied that there is a reasonable basis for the company treating itself as an international headquarters company)—

(a) for "the inspector is not satisfied that there was a reasonable basis" there shall be substituted "an officer of the Board is of the opinion that there was not a reasonable basis"; and

(b) for "he may" there shall be substituted "any such officer may".

(2) In sub-paragraph (3) of that paragraph for "the inspector" there shall be substituted "an officer of the Board".

5. In paragraph 5 (certain deemed claims for set-off in respect of franked investment income to be supported by such evidence as the inspector may reasonably require) for "the inspector" there shall be substituted "an officer of the Board".

6. In paragraph 6A(1) (certain deemed claims for set-off in respect of foreign income dividends to be supported by such evidence as the inspector may reasonably require) for "the inspector" there shall be substituted "an officer of the Board".

7.—(1) Paragraph 7 (special provision for qualifying distributions which are not payments and payments whose nature is not clear) shall be amended as follows.

(2) For sub-paragraph (2) (no amount to be shown under paragraph 2(1)(a) or (c) in respect of those qualifying distributions or payments) there shall be substituted—

> "(2) No amount is required to be shown under paragraph 2(1)(a) or (c) above in respect of the qualifying distribution or payment and, unless estimated amounts are shown by virtue of paragraph (a) below, paragraph 3(1) above shall not apply in relation to advance corporation tax in respect thereof; but—
>
> (a) the company making the return may include under paragraph 2(1)(a) and (c) above estimated amounts in respect of the qualifying distribution or payment; and
>
> (b) if it does so, paragraph 3(1) above shall apply in relation to advance corporation tax in respect thereof as it applies in relation to advance corporation tax in respect of franked payments which are required to be included in the return."

(3) In sub-paragraph (3) (particulars of the qualifying distribution or payment to be given separately in the return) at the beginning there shall be inserted "Whether or not estimated amounts are also included under paragraph 2(1)(a) or (c) above in respect of the qualifying distribution or payment,".

(4) For sub-paragraph (4) (assessment of advance corporation tax) there shall be substituted—

> "(3A) Sub-paragraph (4) below applies—
>
> (a) if an estimated amount is not included under paragraph 2(1)(a) or (c) above in respect of the qualifying distribution or payment; or
>
> (b) if an officer of the Board is of the opinion that an estimated amount which is included under paragraph 2(1)(a) or (c) above in respect of the qualifying distribution or payment is incorrect.

(4) Where this sub-paragraph applies, any advance corporation tax payable in respect of the qualifying distribution or payment shall be assessed on the company and shall be so assessed without regard to any franked investment income received by the company, but—

(a) relief shall be given in accordance with sub-paragraph (4A) or (4B) below;

(b) for the purposes of the application of paragraph 2(3) above to any subsequent return period, the amount of the franked payment comprising the qualifying distribution or payment shall be taken to be the amount calculated as mentioned in sub-paragraph (4A) or (4B) below, as the case may be; and

(c) any advance corporation tax due under an assessment made by virtue of this sub-paragraph shall be treated for the purposes of interest on unpaid tax as having been payable at the time when it would have been payable if correct amounts had been included under paragraph 2(1)(a) and (c) above in respect of the qualifying distribution or payment.

(4A) Where sub-paragraph (4) above applies by virtue of sub-paragraph (3A)(a) above, relief shall be given from the tax assessed (by discharge thereof) to the extent, if any, to which that tax exceeds the tax that would have been payable if the amount of the franked payment comprising the qualifying distribution or payment, calculated on the amount or value thereof shown in the assessment, had been included in the return under sub-paragraph (1)(a) of paragraph 2 above and the tax had been calculated in accordance with sub-paragraph (4) of that paragraph.

(4B) Where sub-paragraph (4) above applies by virtue of sub-paragraph (3A)(b) above, relief shall be given from the tax assessed (by discharge thereof) to the extent, if any, to which that tax exceeds the tax that would have been payable if the excess (if any) of—

(a) the amount of the franked payment comprising the qualifying distribution or payment, calculated on the amount or value thereof shown in the assessment, over

(b) the estimated amount specified under paragraph 2(2)(b) above in respect of that franked payment,

had been included in the return under sub-paragraph (1)(a) of paragraph 2 above and the tax had been calculated in accordance with sub-paragraph (4) of that paragraph."

8. After paragraph 7 there shall be inserted—

"Amended return where company becomes aware of an error

7A.—(1) If a company becomes aware—

(a) that anything which ought to have been included in a return made by it under this Schedule for any return period has not been so included,

(b) that anything which ought not to have been included in a return made by it under this Schedule for any return period has been so included,

(c) that an estimated amount included by virtue of paragraph 7(2)(a) above in a return under this Schedule for any period is incorrect, or

(d) that any other error has occurred in a return made by it under this Schedule for any return period,

it shall forthwith supply to the collector an amended return for that return period.

(2) The duty imposed by sub-paragraph (1) above is without prejudice to any duty that may also arise under paragraph 7A of Schedule 16.

(3) Where an amended return is supplied under this paragraph, all such assessments, adjustments, set-offs or payments or repayments of tax shall be made as may be required for securing that the resulting liabilities to tax (including interest on unpaid or overpaid tax) whether of the company or any other person are the same as they would have been if a correct return had been made."

9. In paragraph 8 (power of inspector to make assessments etc where items are included in returns under the Schedule in error) for "the inspector" there shall be substituted "an officer of the Board".

PART II

SCHEDULE 16 TO THE TAXES ACT 1988

10. Schedule 16 to the Taxes Act 1988 (collection of income tax on company payments which are not distributions) shall be amended in accordance with the following provisions of this Part of this Schedule.

11. In paragraph 4(2) (cases where the inspector may make an assessment)—

(a) for "the inspector", where first occurring, there shall be substituted "an officer of the Board"; and

(b) for "or if the inspector is dissatisfied with any return, he may" there shall be substituted "or if an officer of the Board is of the opinion that a return is incorrect, any such officer may".

12. After paragraph 7 there shall be inserted—

"Amended return where company becomes aware of an error

7A.—(1) If a company becomes aware—

(a) that anything which ought to have been included in a return made by it under this Schedule for any period has not been so included,

(b) that anything which ought not to have been included in a return made by it under this Schedule for any period has been so included, or

(c) that any other error has occurred in a return made by it under this Schedule for any period,

it shall forthwith supply to the collector an amended return for that period.

(2) The duty imposed by sub-paragraph (1) above is without prejudice to any duty that may also arise under paragraph 7A of Schedule 13.

(3) Where an amended return is supplied under this paragraph, all such assessments, adjustments, set-offs or payments or repayments of tax shall be made as may be required for securing that the resulting liabilities to tax (including interest on unpaid or overpaid tax) whether of the company or any other person are the same as they would have been if a correct return had been made."

13. In paragraph 8 (power of inspector to make assessments etc where items are included in returns under the Schedule in error) for "the inspector" there shall be substituted "an officer of the Board".

GENERAL NOTE

The Schedule makes prospective amendments to the ICTA 1988, Scheds. 13 and 16, which deal respectively with advance corporation tax (ACT) and returns of income tax deducted from payments made by a company.

Part I deals with the amendments to Sched. 13.

Para. 2

This allows a company to include in its return under Sched. 13, para. 2, an estimate of the amount of a franked payment whose nature is uncertain, or which is not a money payment.

Paras. 3–6 and 9

These amend certain powers in Sched. 13 which are currently given to an inspector, so that they are available to any Revenue official. They also amend the power to make an assessment so that it is only available where an official is of the opinion that a return is wrong rather than where he is dissatisfied with it.

Para. 7

Where a company opts not to include an estimate of franked payments in its return (see para. 2) or where an official is of the opinion that the estimate is wrong, he may raise an assessment.

Para. 8

The new Sched. 13, para. 7A, requires a company which becomes aware of an error to make an amended return.

Part II deals with the amendments to Sched. 16.

Paras. 11 and 13

These mirror the amendments made to Sched. 13 by paras. 3–6 and 9 above.

Para. 12

The new Sched. 16, para. 7A, requires a company which becomes aware of an error to make an amended return.

SCHEDULE 24

SELF-ASSESSMENT: ACCOUNTING PERIODS ETC.

PART I

AMENDMENTS OF THE TAXES MANAGEMENT ACT 1970

Introductory

1. The Taxes Management Act 1970 shall be amended in accordance with this Part of this Schedule.

2. In section 11 (return of profits), after subsection (9) there shall be inserted the following subsection—

"(10) In the following provisions of this Act 'section 11 notice' means a notice under this section."

Power to enquire into return for wrong period, etc.

3. In section 11AA (return of profits to include self-assessment), after subsection (4) there shall be inserted the following subsections—

"(5) This section, except subsection (4) above, applies in relation to a return for a period—
  (a) which ends in or at the end of the period specified in the section 11 notice;
  (b) which in the return is treated as an accounting period; but
  (c) which is not, or may not be, an accounting period.

(6) In relation to such a return, 'the filing date' means, in this section and section 11AB of this Act, the day which would be the day mentioned in section 11(4) of this Act if the period for which the return is made were an accounting period."

4.—(1) In section 11AB(1) (power to enquire into return of profits), after paragraph (c) (which is inserted by paragraph 2 of Schedule 19 to this Act), there shall be inserted "or
  (d) if it appears to the officer that a return delivered in response to a section 11 notice—
      (i) is or may be a return for the wrong period, or
      (ii) has become a return for the wrong period as a result of a direction under section 12(5A) of the principal Act,
    the period for which the return should have been made;".

(2) After subsection (3) of that section there shall be inserted the following subsections—

"(4) For the purposes of subsection (1)(d) above a return is a return for the wrong period in each of the cases set out below.

(5) The first case is where—
  (a) the return is made for a period which ends in or at the end of the period specified in the section 11 notice and which in the return is treated as an accounting period; but
  (b) the period for which the return is made is not an accounting period of the company.

(6) The second case is where—
  (a) the return is made for a part of the period specified in the section 11 notice which in the return is treated as not falling within an accounting period of the company; but
  (b) there is an accounting period ending in or at the end of the period specified in the section 11 notice."

5. In section 19A(1) (cases where officer has power to call for documents), after paragraph (c) (which is inserted by paragraph 2 of Schedule 19 to this Act) there shall be inserted "or
  (d) the period for which a return should have been made."

Amendment of return for wrong period

6. After section 28A there shall be inserted the following sections—

"Amendment of return of profits made for wrong period

28AA.—(1) Where an officer of the Board gives notice under section 11AB(1) of this Act to a company of his intention to enquire into the period for which a return should have been made, the officer's enquiries shall be treated as completed at such time as he by notice—
  (a) informs the company that he has completed his enquiries; and
  (b) states his conclusions on the subject of his enquiries.

(2) Subsections (3) and (4) below apply where the officer in the conclusions stated under subsection (1) above designates a period, in accordance with subsections (6) to (8) below, as the accounting period for which the return should have been made.

(3) At any time in the period of 30 days beginning with the day on which the officer's enquiries are completed, the company may amend the return for the purpose of making it a return appropriate to the designated period.

(4) At any time in the period of 30 days beginning immediately after the period mentioned in subsection (3) above, the officer may by notice to the company amend the return for the purpose of making it a return appropriate to the designated period.

(5) The power under subsections (3) and (4) above to amend a return includes the power to amend a self-assessment so as to make clear that it is a self-assessment for the designated period.

(6) If there is only one accounting period ending in or at the end of the period specified in the section 11 notice, the only period which the officer may designate is that period.

(7) If there is more than one accounting period ending in or at the end of the period specified in the section 11 notice, the only period which the officer may designate is the earliest of those accounting periods for which no return has been delivered.

(8) In designating a period, the officer must specify the dates on which the period begins and ends.

Provisions supplementary to section 28AA

28AB.—(1) On an application made by the company, the Commissioners shall direct the officer to give a notice under section 28AA(1) of this Act within a period specified in the direction, unless they are satisfied that the officer has reasonable grounds for not giving such a notice.

(2) Proceedings under subsection (1) above shall be heard and determined in the same way as an appeal.

(3) An appeal may be brought against an amendment made under section 28AA(4) of this Act within the period of 30 days beginning with the date on which the notice of the amendment was issued.

(4) The provisions of this Act relating to appeals shall have effect in relation to an appeal under subsection (3) above as they have effect in relation to an appeal against an assessment to tax.

(5) Subsection (6) below applies where—

(a) a return is delivered in response to a section 11 notice;

(b) following a statement of conclusions under section 28AA of this Act, a period is finally determined to be the accounting period for which the return should have been made;

(c) the effect of the determination is that there is a period ('a further period') which—

(i) before the determination was not an accounting period ending in or at the end of the period specified in the section 11 notice, and

(ii) as a result of the determination, becomes a period so ending;

and

(d) there is no return which can be amended under section 28AA of this Act so as to become a return for that further period.

(6) Where this subsection applies, the section 11 notice shall be taken to require a return for the further period before the postponed final day.

(7) The postponed final day is whichever is the later of—

(a) the final day determined under section 11(4) of this Act; and

(b) the last day of the period of 30 days beginning with the day on which the accounting period for the return mentioned in subsection (5)(a) above is finally determined.

(8) In relation to any return for the further period the provisions of this Act shall have effect as if any reference to the filing date in relation to that return were a reference to the postponed final day."

Failure to deliver return: determinations

7. After section 28C there shall be inserted the following sections—

"Determination of corporation tax where no return delivered

28D.—(1) Where—

(a) a section 11 notice has been served on a company, and

(b) no return is delivered to an officer of the Board in response to the notice before the relevant day,

the officer may make a determination of the amounts in which, to the best of his information and belief, the company is chargeable to corporation tax for the relevant period.

(2) In subsection (1) above 'the relevant period' means—

(a) if there is only one accounting period ending in or at the end of the period specified in the section 11 notice, that accounting period;

(b) if there is more than one accounting period ending in or at the end of the period so specified, each of those accounting periods;

(c) if the officer has insufficient information to identify the accounting periods of the company, such period or periods ending in or at the end of the period so specified as he may determine.

(3) Subject to subsections (4) and (5) below, a determination under subsection (1) above shall have effect for the purposes of Parts VA, VI, IX and XI of this Act as if—

(a) it were a self-assessment made under section 11AA of this Act; and

(b) (where subsection (2)(c) above applies) the period for which the determination is made were an accounting period of the company.

(4) If—

(a) the company delivers a return for a period ending in or at the end of the period specified in the section 11 notice,

(b) the period is, or is treated in the return as, an accounting period, and

(c) the return includes a self-assessment under section 11AA of this Act,

the self-assessment shall supersede the determination under subsection (1) above or, if there is more than one determination under that subsection, the determination for the period which is, or most closely approximates to, the period for which the return is made.

(5) If the company shows—

(a) that there is no period ending in or at the end of the period specified in the section 11 notice which is an accounting period of the company, or

(b) that it has delivered a return containing a self-assessment for the accounting period, or each accounting period, ending in or at the end of the period specified in the section 11 notice,

any determination under subsection (1) above shall be of no effect.

Determination of corporation tax where notice complied with in part

28E.—(1) Where—

(a) a company delivers a return for an accounting period ending in or at the end of the period specified in a section 11 notice served on the company, but

(b) there is another period so ending (an 'outstanding period') which it appears to an officer of the Board is or may be an accounting period but for which no return has been delivered before the relevant day,

the officer may make a determination of the amounts in which, to the best of his information and belief, the company is chargeable to corporation tax for the outstanding period.

(2) Subject to subsections (3) and (4) below, a determination under subsection (1) above shall have effect for the purposes of Parts VA, VI, IX and XI of this Act as if—

(a) it were a self-assessment made under section 11AA of this Act; and

(b) where the officer has insufficient information to determine whether the outstanding period is an accounting period, the period for which the determination is made were an accounting period of the company.

(3) If, after the determination is made—

(a) the company delivers a further return for a period ending in or at the end of the period specified in the section 11 notice,

(b) the period is, or is treated in the return as, an accounting period, and

(c) the return includes a self-assessment under section 11AA of this Act,

the self-assessment shall supersede the determination under subsection (1) above.

(4) If the company shows that it has delivered a return containing a self-assessment for the accounting period, or each accounting period, ending in or at the end of the period specified in the section 11 notice, the determination under subsection (1) above shall be of no effect.

Corporation tax determinations: supplementary

28F.—(1) Notice of any determination under section 28D or 28E of this Act shall be served on the person in respect of whom it is made and shall state the date on which it is issued.

(2) No determination may be made under section 28D or 28E of this Act after the end of the period of five years beginning with the relevant day.

(3) A self-assessment shall not supersede a determination under section 28D or 28E of this Act if it is made after whichever is the later of—

(a) the end of the period of five years beginning with the relevant day; and

(b) the end of the period of twelve months beginning with the date of the determination.

(4) Where—

(a) an officer of the Board has commenced any proceedings for the recovery of any tax charged by a determination under section 28D or 28E of this Act, and

(b) before those proceedings are concluded, the determination is superseded by a self-assessment,

those proceedings may be continued as if they were proceedings for the recovery of so much of the tax charged by the self-assessment as is due and payable and has not been paid.

(5) In sections 28D and 28E of this Act and this section 'the relevant day' means, in relation to a section 11 notice—

(a) if the final day for the delivery of any return required by the notice can be ascertained in accordance with section 11(4) of this Act, that day;

(b) in any other case, the day determined in accordance with subsection (6) below.

(6) The day is whichever is the later of—

(a) the last day of the period of 30 months from the end of the period specified in the section 11 notice; and

(b) the last day of the period of three months from the day on which the section 11 notice was served."

Commencement

8.—(1) Paragraphs 3 to 6 above have effect in relation to returns made for periods ending on or after the day appointed under section 199 of the Finance Act 1994 for the purposes of Chapter III of Part IV of that Act (self-assessment).

(2) Paragraph 7 above has effect in relation to notices under section 11 of the Taxes Management Act 1970 specifying a period ending on or after the day so appointed.

PART II

OTHER AMENDMENTS

General

9. In this Part of this Schedule "the appointed day" means the day appointed as mentioned in paragraph 8(1) above.

Repeal of section 8A of the Taxes Act 1988

10. Section 8A of the Taxes Act 1988 (resolutions to reduce corporation tax) shall cease to have effect.

Determination of accounting date

11.—(1) Section 12 of the Taxes Act 1988 (basis of, and periods for, assessment) shall be amended as follows.

(2) In subsection (5)—

(a) at the beginning there shall be inserted "Subject to subsection (5A) below"; and

(b) for the words "as the Board may determine" there shall be substituted "as the company may determine".

(3) After subsection (5) there shall be inserted the following subsection—

"(5A) If the Board is of the opinion, on reasonable grounds, that a date determined by a company for the purposes of subsection (5) above is inappropriate, they may by notice direct that the accounting date of such other of the trades referred to in that subsection as appears to them to be appropriate shall be used instead."

(4) This paragraph has effect where each of the different dates referred to in section 12(5) of the Taxes Act 1988 occurs on or after the appointed day.

Companies in liquidation

12.—(1) Section 342 of the Taxes Act 1988 (companies in liquidation) shall be amended as follows.

(2) In subsection (5) (assumption as to commencement date of final accounting period where company being wound up), for the words "the inspector may, with the concurrence of the liquidator" there shall be substituted "the liquidator may".

(3) In subsection (6) for the words from "as if" to the end there shall be substituted "as if the winding-up had commenced with the beginning of that new accounting period".

(4) This paragraph has effect in relation to the winding up of a company if the date on which the affairs of the company are completely wound up does not occur before the appointed day.

Construction of references to assessments

13. In section 197(1) of the Finance Act 1994 (construction of certain references), in paragraph (b) after "28C" there shall be inserted ", 28D or 28E".

GENERAL NOTE

The Schedule makes amendments, mainly to the Taxes Management Act 1970 (c. 9), in connection with returns by companies under the self-assessment system, to take effect from an appointed day.

Para. 3

This ensures that the provisions which require a company making a return to include a self-assessment applies in respect of every period that a company treats as an accounting period.

Paras. 4 and 5

These ensure that the power of the Revenue to enquire into a return of profits or to call for documents apply where the enquiry relates to the period for which the return has been made.

Para. 6

The new TMA 1970, ss.28AA and 28AB, set out the rules which apply where the Revenue gives notice of its intention to enquire into the period for which a return should have been made and provides for the same rules to apply to such an enquiry as apply to enquiries under the existing s.28A. Provision is also made for the case where, as the result of an enquiry, the period of a self-assessment is amended and as a result any further returns and self-assessments are due from the company.

Para. 7

The new TMA 1970, ss.28D and 28E, allow determinations to be made for any accounting period ending within the period for which a company has failed to make a return or returns, and also where, although the company has made a return for an accounting period, the Revenue believe that there are additional periods for which a return should have been made.

The new TMA 1970, s.28F, provides the time limits for making determinations and for self-assessments to supersede such determinations.

Para. 10

This repeals the ICTA 1988, s.8A, which deals with resolutions to reduce corporation tax retrospectively and ensures that assessments can be made in accordance with the resolution. Under self-assessment, the provisions of the Provisional Collection of Taxes Act 1968 (c. 2) will be sufficient to cater for this situation.

Para. 11

The amendment to the ICTA 1988, s.12, allows companies carrying on more than one trade which make up separate accounts for each to different dates, and do not make up general accounts, to choose which accounting date should determine their accounting period. This is subject to the Revenue determining a different date if it is of the opinion that the one chosen is inappropriate.

Para. 12

The amendment to the ICTA 1988, s.342, allows the liquidator of a company to make his own assumption as to the likely date of the end of the final accounting period of a company in liquidation without having to consult the inspector [Standing Committee E, February 20, 1996, col. 432].

Section 139   SCHEDULE 25

SELF-ASSESSMENT: SURRENDERS OF ADVANCE CORPORATION TAX

Amendments of section 240 of the Taxes Act 1988

1.—(1) Section 240 of the Taxes Act 1988 (set-off of company's advance corporation tax against subsidiary's liability to corporation tax) shall be amended as follows.

(2) For subsection (1) there shall be substituted the following subsections—

"(1) Where a company ('the surrendering company') has paid an amount of advance corporation tax in respect of a dividend or dividends paid by it in an accounting period, it may under this section surrender the benefit of so much of that amount as is available for surrender, or any part of that amount that is available for surrender, to any company which was a subsidiary of it throughout that accounting period.

(1A) The surrender shall take effect on the surrendering company making a claim in accordance with Schedule 13A.

(1B) A claim to surrender an amount exceeding the amount the benefit of which, at the time the claim is made, is available for surrender shall be of no effect."

(3) For subsections (6) and (7) there shall be substituted the following subsections—

"(5A) A claim under subsection (1A) above may be withdrawn by the surrendering company with the consent of the subsidiary to whom the surrender was made.

(5B) The withdrawal of a claim under subsection (1A) above to make a surrender for an accounting period of the surrendering company shall not prevent the making of a further claim under that subsection for that accounting period (whether to the same or a different subsidiary).

(5C) Where the surrendering company withdraws a claim by virtue of which an amount of advance corporation tax was treated under subsection (2) above as paid by its subsidiary in respect of a distribution made on a date determined under that subsection—

    (a) the subsidiary shall be treated as if it had not paid that amount in respect of a distribution made by it on the date so determined; and

    (b) subject to the effect of any further claim, the surrendering company shall be treated as having paid a corresponding amount of advance corporation tax in respect of a distribution made by it on the date so determined.

(5D) The amount of advance corporation tax the benefit of which is at any time available for surrender is the amount referred to in subsection (1) above less any amount which at that time falls within subsection (5E) below.

(5E) The amounts are—

    (a) any amount which has been repaid to the surrendering company;

    (b) any amount which has been dealt with under section 239(3);

    (c) any amount surrendered under a claim for that period which has not been withdrawn.

(5F) Subject to subsection (5C)(b) above, no amount of advance corporation tax the benefit of which has been surrendered under this section shall be treated for the purposes of section 239 as advance corporation tax paid by the surrendering company."

(4) After subsection (13) there shall be inserted the following subsection—

"(14) Schedule 13A (which makes supplementary provision with respect to surrenders of advance corporation tax) shall have effect."

The new Schedule 13A to the Taxes Act 1988

2. After Schedule 13 to the Taxes Act 1988 there shall be inserted the following Schedule—

"SCHEDULE 13A

SURRENDERS OF ADVANCE CORPORATION TAX

General

1.—(1) In this Schedule any reference to a claim is to a claim under section 240(1A).

(2) In this Schedule 'the relevant accounting period of the surrendering company' means, in relation to a claim by the surrendering company, the accounting period referred to in section 240(1).

Multiple claims

2.—(1) Surrenders to different subsidiaries or to the same subsidiary at different times shall be treated as made by separate claims (however the claims are presented).

(2) Where a surrendering company makes more than one claim at the same time, the claims shall be treated as made in such sequence as the surrendering company at that time elects or as, in default of such an election, an officer of the Board determines.

Content of claims etc.

3.—(1) A claim must specify—

    (a) the amount the benefit of which is surrendered; and

(b) the subsidiary to whom the surrender is made.

(2) The amount specified in compliance with sub-paragraph (1)(a) above must be an amount which is quantified at the time when the claim is made.

Time limit for claims

4. A claim by the surrendering company must be made within the period of six years from the end of the relevant accounting period of the surrendering company.

Claim to be included in return where possible

5.—(1) Where a claim could be made by being included in a return under section 11 of the Management Act, or an amendment of such a return, it must be so made.

(2) Section 42 of and Schedule 1A to the Management Act (procedure for making claims) shall not apply to the making of claims.

6.—(1) A claim not included in a return or an amendment of a return must be made to an officer of the Board and must be supported by such documents as the officer may require.

(2) The claim shall be made in such form as the Board may determine.

(3) The form of claim shall provide for a declaration to the effect that all the particulars given in the form are correctly stated to the best of the information and belief of the person making the claim.

Contents of notices of withdrawal, etc.

7.—(1) A claim shall not be withdrawn except by a notice given to an officer of the Board in such form as the Board may determine.

(2) A notice withdrawing a claim must specify—

(a) the surrendering company which made the claim;

(b) the amount the benefit of which was surrendered under the claim;

(c) the subsidiary to whom the surrender was made; and

(d) the relevant accounting period of the surrendering company in relation to the claim.

(3) A notice withdrawing a claim must be accompanied by a notice signifying the consent required by section 240(5A).

(4) Where a claim included in a return is withdrawn and the withdrawal could be made by an amendment of the return, it must be so made.

Simultaneous claims and withdrawals of claims

8. Where—

(a) a claim ('claim A') is withdrawn, and

(b) at the time when claim A is withdrawn, another claim ('claim B') is made,

claim A shall be treated as being withdrawn before claim B is treated as made.

Time limit for withdrawing claims

9.—(1) Subject to sub-paragraph (3) below, a claim shall not be withdrawn after the earlier of—

(a) the end of the period of six years from the end of the relevant accounting period of the surrendering company; and

(b) the date on which an assessment for any relevant accounting period of the subsidiary in whose favour the claim was made becomes final.

(2) In this paragraph 'relevant accounting period of the subsidiary' means, in relation to a claim, any period in which a distribution is treated under section 240(2) as made by virtue of the claim.

(3) In the circumstances given by sub-paragraph (4) below, a claim may be withdrawn at any time before the end of the period of six years from the end of the relevant accounting period of the surrendering company.

(4) The circumstances are that—

(a) the claim was made—

(i) after the date on which an assessment for a relevant accounting period of the subsidiary in whose favour the claim is made becomes final; and

(ii) after a further assessment has been made on the subsidiary for that period by an officer of the Board or the Board; and

(b) immediately before the claim is withdrawn, none of the advance corporation tax which, by virtue of the claim, is treated as paid by the subsidiary has been finally dealt with to the subsidiary's advantage.

(5) For the purposes of sub-paragraph (4) above, advance corporation tax is finally dealt with to the subsidiary's advantage if—

(a) it is set against any liability of the subsidiary under any assessment to corporation tax which has become final; or

(b) any of it is repaid to the subsidiary.

No amendment of claims

10. Nothing in the Management Act shall be read as allowing a claim to be amended.

Further self-assessments by the surrendering company

11.—(1) Where—

(a) a claim is made after an assessment to corporation tax for the relevant accounting period of the surrendering company has become final,

(b) under section 239(1), advance corporation tax has been set against the company's liability to corporation tax for that period, and

(c) the claim is a claim to surrender the benefit of an amount which is or includes the whole or a part of the amount set-off,

the claim must be accompanied by an assessment (a self-assessment) of the corporation tax due as a result of the claim.

(2) The tax shall be treated as due and payable, in accordance with section 59D of the Management Act, on the day following the expiry of nine months from the end of the relevant accounting period.

(3) The standard provisions about enquiries into self-assessments (given by paragraph 14 below) apply to self-assessments provided under this paragraph.

12.—(1) Where—

(a) by virtue of section 239(4), advance corporation tax paid in the relevant accounting period of the surrendering company has been set against the company's liability to corporation tax for a later accounting period,

(b) the claim is made after assessments to corporation tax for both periods have become final, and

(c) the claim is a claim to surrender the benefit of an amount which is or includes the whole or a part of the amount set-off,

the claim must be accompanied by an assessment (a self-assessment) of the corporation tax due as a result of the claim.

(2) The tax shall be treated as due and payable, in accordance with section 59D of the Management Act, on the day following the expiry of nine months from the end of the later accounting period.

(3) The standard provisions about enquiries into self-assessments (given by paragraph 14 below) apply to self-assessments provided under this paragraph.

(4) For the purposes of sub-paragraph (1)(a) above, advance corporation tax which was in fact paid in the relevant accounting period of the surrendering company shall be treated as set against the liability of the company to corporation tax for the later accounting period after any other advance corporation tax available to be so treated.

Further self-assessments by subsidiary

13.—(1) Sub-paragraph (3) below applies where—

(a) under section 239(1), advance corporation tax has been set against the subsidiary's liability to corporation tax for an accounting period ('the relevant accounting period'),

(b) the advance corporation tax is, includes or is part of advance corporation tax which is treated as paid by the subsidiary in respect of that period on the assumption that section 240(2) required that treatment, and

(c) after an assessment to corporation tax for that period has become final, the subsidiary becomes aware of facts ('the true facts') which, by virtue of section 240(1B), make that treatment incorrect.

(2) Sub-paragraph (3) below also applies where—

(a) by virtue of section 239(4), advance corporation tax has been set against the subsidiary's liability to corporation tax for an accounting period ('the relevant accounting period'),

(b) the advance corporation tax is, includes or is part of advance corporation tax which is treated as paid by the subsidiary in respect of a previous accounting period on the assumption that section 240(2) required that treatment, and

(c) after an assessment to corporation tax for that period has become final, the subsidiary becomes aware of facts ('the true facts') which, by virtue of section 240(1B), make that treatment incorrect.

(3) The subsidiary must, before the end of the period of three months beginning with the day on which it becomes aware of the true facts, provide an officer of the Board with an assessment (a self-assessment) of the amount of corporation tax which was due for the relevant accounting period on the basis of the true facts.

(4) The tax shall be treated as due and payable, in accordance with section 59D of the Management Act, on the day following the expiry of nine months from the end of the relevant accounting period of the subsidiary.

(5) The standard provisions about enquiries into self-assessments (given by paragraph 14 below) apply to self-assessments provided under this paragraph.

(6) For the purposes of this paragraph it shall be assumed that advance corporation tax actually paid (or correctly treated as paid) by the subsidiary has been set against the subsidiary's liability to corporation tax before any advance corporation tax incorrectly treated as paid by the subsidiary.

Standard provisions about enquiries into self-assessments

14.—(1) The standard provisions about enquiries into self-assessments (which correspond, in general terms, to certain provisions of section 28A of the Management Act) are as follows.

(2) An officer of the Board may, at any time before the end of the period of one year beginning with the day on which the self-assessment is received, give notice of his intention to enquire into the self-assessment.

(3) The officer's enquiries shall end on such day as he by notice—

(a) informs the company that he has completed his enquiries, and

(b) states his conclusions as to the amount of tax which should be contained in the company's self-assessment.

(4) At any time in the period of 30 days beginning with the day on which the enquiries end, the company may amend its self-assessment so as to make good any deficiency or eliminate any excess in the amount of tax contained in the self-assessment.

(5) At any time in the period of 30 days beginning immediately after the period mentioned in sub-paragraph (4) above, the officer may by notice to the company amend the company's self-assessment so as to make good any deficiency or eliminate any excess in the amount of tax contained in the self-assessment.

(6) The provisions of the Management Act apply to an amendment of a self-assessment under sub-paragraph (5) above as they apply to an amendment of a self-assessment under section 28A(4) of that Act.

(7) At any time before a notice is given under sub-paragraph (3) above, the company may apply for a direction that the officer shall give such a notice within such period as may be specified in the direction.

(8) Subject to sub-paragraph (9) below, an application under sub-paragraph (7) above shall be heard and determined in the same way as an appeal against an amendment of a self-assessment under section 28A(2) or (4) of the Management Act.

(9) The Commissioners hearing an application under sub-paragraph (7) above shall give the direction applied for unless they are satisfied that the officer has reasonable grounds for not giving the notice.

Repayments

15.—(1) Where—

(a) a claim is withdrawn after an assessment for the relevant accounting period of the surrendering company has become final, and

(b) an amount of corporation tax paid by the surrendering company in respect of that period would not have been payable if the claim had not been made,

the surrendering company shall be entitled by notice to claim repayment of that amount.

(2) Where—

(a) a claim is made after the date on which an assessment for any relevant accounting period of the subsidiary in whose favour the claim is made becomes final, and

(b) an amount of corporation tax paid by the subsidiary in respect of that period would not have been payable if the claim had not been made,

the subsidiary shall be entitled by notice to claim repayment of that amount.

(3) In this paragraph 'relevant accounting period of the subsidiary' has the same meaning as in paragraph 9."

3. Paragraphs 1 and 2 above have effect where the accounting period of the surrendering company ends on or after the day appointed under section 199 of the Finance Act 1994 for the purposes of Chapter III of Part IV of that Act (self-assessment).

Other amendments

4. Section 239(5) of the Taxes Act 1988 (manner in which claims under section 239(1) and (4) to be given effect) shall cease to have effect in relation to accounting periods ending on or after the day appointed as mentioned in paragraph 3 above.

5. In the Table in section 98 of the Taxes Management Act 1970 (penalties in respect of certain information provisions), after the entry in the second column relating to Schedule 13 to the Taxes Act 1988, there shall be inserted the following entry—

    "Schedule 13A, paragraphs 11, 12 and 13;".

GENERAL NOTE

The Schedule makes changes to facilitate surrenders of advance corporation tax (ACT) and taking the benefit of such surrenders in assessments. Companies may withdraw claims to surrender ACT and replace them with alternative claims where they so wish. A company must self-assess any additional liability produced as the result of the making or withdrawal of a claim.

Para. 1

This defines the amount of ACT which a company can surrender, provides for a claim to surrender to take effect as soon as it is made, allows withdrawals of a surrender where the subsidiary concerned consents and provides for claims to surrender to be subject to the new ICTA 1988, Sched. 13A.

Para. 2

The new ICTA 1988, Sched. 13A, sets out the rules governing claims to surrender.

The annotations below refer to paragraphs of the new Schedule.

Para. 2

Where a company surrenders ACT to more than one company at the same time each surrender is treated as a separate claim.

Para. 3

A claim must specify the subsidiary to which a surrender is being made, and quantify the amount.

Para. 4

The time limit for a claim remains at six years.

Paras. 5 and 6

A claim should be made, where possible, in a return, or an amendment to the return. Otherwise it will be made in a form prescribed by the Revenue.

Para. 7

The withdrawal of a claim must be made in such form as the Revenue may determine, and by amendment of return where possible. The consent of the subsidiary concerned is also required.

Para. 8

Where a claim is withdrawn, to be replaced by another claim made at the same time, the withdrawal takes effect before the new claim is regarded as made.

Para. 9

A general time limit of six years applies for the withdrawal of a claim. It cannot be withdrawn if the assessment of the subsidiary company concerned has become final.

Para. 10

Claims cannot be amended (but they can be withdrawn and replaced by a new claim).

Paras. 11 and 12

Where a surrendering company has already set the ACT which it is surrendering against its own corporation tax liability, the claim must be accompanied by a self assessment of the additional corporation tax due as a result of the claim.

Para. 13

Where a subsidiary becomes aware that surrendered ACT which it has utilised was not actually available for surrender, it must make a self-assessment within three months of the corporation tax which would have been due if the ACT had not been surrendered.

Para. 14

The provisions for enquiries into self-assessments under the TMA 1970, s.28A, apply to self-assessments under paras. 11–13 above.

Para. 15

Where as the result of the making or withdrawal of a claim the amount of ACT to be set against any corporation tax liabilities increases, repayment can be made to the company even where the assessment for the relevant accounting period has become final.

The annotations below refer to the main Schedule (Sched. 25).

Para. 3

The new system applies from the appointed day.

Para. 4

The amendment to the ICTA 1988, s.239, ensures that from the appointed day relief for ACT set against corporation tax is given automatically without claim.

Para. 5

The penalty provisions under the TMA 1970, s.98, apply for failure to provide the relevant information under the new Sched. 13A, paras. 11–13 [Standing Committee E, February 20, 1996, col. 433].

Section 150   SCHEDULE 26

DAMAGES AND COMPENSATION FOR PERSONAL INJURY

The sections inserted after section 329 of the Taxes Act 1988 by section 150 of this Act are as follows—

"Personal injury damages in the form of periodical payments

329AA.—(1) Where—

(a) an agreement is made settling a claim or action for damages for personal injury on terms whereby the damages are to consist wholly or partly of periodical payments; or

(b) a court awarding damages for personal injury makes an order incorporating such terms,

the payments shall not for the purposes of income tax be regarded as the income of any of the persons mentioned in subsection (2) below and accordingly shall be paid without any deduction under section 348(1)(b) or 349(1).

(2) The persons referred to in subsection (1) above are—

(a) the person ("A") entitled to the damages under the agreement or order;

(b) any person who, whether in pursuance of the agreement or order or otherwise, receives the payments or any of them on behalf of A;

(c) any trustee who, whether in pursuance of the agreement or order or otherwise, receives the payments or any of them on trust for the benefit of A under a trust under which A is during his lifetime the sole beneficiary.

(3) The periodical payments referred to in subsection (1) above, or any of them, may, if the agreement or order mentioned in that subsection or a subsequent agreement so provides, consist of payments under one or more annuities purchased or provided for, or for the benefit of, A by the person by whom the payments would otherwise fall to be made.

(4) Sums paid to, or for the benefit of, A by a trustee or trustees shall not be regarded as his income for the purposes of income tax if made out of payments which by virtue of this section are not to be regarded for those purposes as income of the trustee or trustees.

(5) In this section "personal injury" includes any disease and any impairment of a person's physical or mental condition.

(6) For the purposes of this section a claim or action for personal injury includes—

(a) such a claim or action brought by virtue of the Law Reform (Miscellaneous Provisions) Act 1934;

(b) such a claim or action brought by virtue of the Law Reform (Miscellaneous Provisions) Act (Northern Ireland) 1937;

(c) such a claim or action brought by virtue of the Damages (Scotland) Act 1976;

(d) a claim or action brought by virtue of the Fatal Accidents Act 1976;

(e) a claim or action brought by virtue of the Fatal Accidents (Northern Ireland) Order 1977.

(7) In relation to such an order as is mentioned in paragraph (b) of subsection (1) above "damages" includes an interim payment which the court, by virtue of rules of court in that behalf, orders the defendant to make to the plaintiff; and where, without such an order, the defendant agrees to make a payment on account of the damages that may be awarded against him in such an action as is mentioned in paragraph (a) of that subsection, that paragraph shall apply to the payment and the agreement as it applies to damages and to such an agreement as is there mentioned.

(8) In the application of subsection (7) above to Scotland for references to the plaintiff and the defendant there shall be substituted references to the pursuer and the defender.

Compensation for personal injury under statutory or other schemes

329AB.—(1) Section 329AA applies to annuity payments under an award of compensation made under the Criminal Injuries Compensation Scheme as it applies to payments of damages in that form under such an agreement or order as is mentioned in subsection (1) of that section.

(2) In subsection (1) above "the Criminal Injuries Compensation Scheme" means—
   (a) the scheme established by arrangements made under the Criminal Injuries Compensation Act 1995; or
   (b) arrangements made by the Secretary of State for compensation for criminal injuries and in operation before the commencement of that scheme.

(3) If it appears to the Treasury that any other scheme or arrangement, whether established by statute or otherwise, makes provision for the making of periodical payments by way of compensation for personal injury within the meaning of section 329AA, the Treasury may by order apply that section to those payments with such modifications as the Treasury consider necessary."

GENERAL NOTE
See the General Note to s.150.

Section 153   SCHEDULE 27

FOREIGN INCOME DIVIDENDS

Companies that pay FIDs

1.—(1) In section 246A(1) of the Taxes Act 1988 (foreign income dividends) after "a company" there shall be inserted "resident in the United Kingdom".

(2) This paragraph has effect in relation to dividends paid on or after 28th November 1995.

Recipients of FIDs

2. Section 246D(5) of that Act (exclusion of section 233(1) and (1A) in the case of foreign income dividends) shall have effect, and be deemed always to have had effect, as if at the end there were inserted "to which an individual is beneficially entitled, a foreign income dividend paid to personal representatives or a foreign income dividend paid to trustees in a case in which the dividend is income to which section 686 applies."

Calculation of the distributable foreign profit and the notional foreign source ACT

3.—(1) In section 246I(6) of that Act, for the words from "an amount equal" onwards there shall be substituted "the amount of corporation tax payable, before double taxation relief is afforded, in respect of the foreign source profit."

(2) In section 246P(2) of that Act (assumptions to apply for the purposes of calculating the notional foreign source ACT), the following paragraph shall be inserted before the "and" at the end of paragraph (e)—

"(ea) where any of the matched foreign source profits represent an amount ('a gross profit') reduced by one or more such deductions as are mentioned in section 246I(2), the amount of double taxation relief which is to be taken, in finding the amount of corporation tax falling finally to be borne, to have been available (after the reduction) to be allowed by reference to the amount representing the gross profit was equal to the amount that would have been available to be so allowed had no reduction been made;".

(3) In section 246P of that Act, after subsection (12) there shall be inserted the following subsection—

"(12A) In this section 'double taxation relief' has the same meaning as in section 246I."

(4) Subject to sub-paragraph (5) below, this paragraph has effect in relation to accounting periods ending after 28th November 1995.

(5) This paragraph, so far as applicable as respects authorised unit trusts, has effect in relation to any distribution period ending after 28th November 1995.

International headquarters company

4.—(1) Section 246S of that Act (conditions for treatment as international headquarters company) shall be amended as follows.

(2) In subsection (3) (wholly-owned subsidiary of foreign quoted parent company), in paragraph (a), for "wholly owned by" there shall be substituted "a 100 per cent. subsidiary of".

(3) Subsection (8) (extension of subsection (3)) shall cease to have effect.

(4) After subsection (10) there shall be inserted the following subsection—

"(10A) For the purposes of this section a company is a 100 per cent. subsidiary of another if and so long as it is a body corporate all of whose share capital would fall to be treated for the purposes of section 838 as owned directly or indirectly by the other and that other is a body corporate; but for this purpose references in that section to owning share capital shall be construed in accordance with subsection (12) below."

(5) Subject to sub-paragraph (6) below, this paragraph has effect in relation to any accounting period ending after 28th November 1995.

(6) Where—

(a) this paragraph has effect under sub-paragraph (5) above in relation to an accounting period in which a dividend is paid, and

(b) the immediately preceding period ended on or before 28th November 1995,

subsection (9) (requirement to be international headquarters company in the period before that in which a dividend is paid) shall have effect in the case of that dividend as if this paragraph also had effect in relation to that immediately preceding period.

Life assurance business charged under Case I of Schedule D

5.—(1) In section 440B of that Act (modifications for life assurance business charged under Case I of Schedule D), after subsection (1) there shall be inserted the following subsection—

"(1A) Nothing in section 208 shall prevent foreign income dividends from being taken into account in any computation of the profits of the company's life assurance business charged in accordance with Case I of Schedule D."

(2) This paragraph has effect in relation to accounting periods beginning on or after 1st January 1996.

Foreign income distributions to corporate unit holders

6.—(1) In section 468R of that Act (foreign income distributions to corporate unit holders), after subsection (3) there shall be inserted the following subsection—

"(4) No repayment shall be made of any tax which is deemed to have been deducted by virtue of the application of paragraph (b) of section 468Q(2) in relation to a foreign income distribution."

(2) This paragraph applies in relation to any distribution period ending on or after 28th November 1995.

GENERAL NOTE

The Schedule amends the foreign income dividend (FID) scheme which was introduced by the FA 1994, Sched. 16.

Para. 1

This makes it clear that a FID can only be paid by a U.K.-resident company.

Para. 2

This makes it clear that a non-resident company receiving a FID does not face a charge to lower rate income tax when such a charge would not apply in respect of other dividends.

Para. 3

This clarifies the basis set out in the ICTA 1988, s.246I(6), for the calculation of the distributable foreign profit where a company has a foreign source profit which has borne foreign tax at a lower rate than the rate of corporation tax in the U.K. It also amends s.246P(2) where foreign source profits have been reduced by charges on income, management expenses or other similar amounts. The changes will allow more relief for foreign tax.

Para. 4

An IHC (international headquarters company) may be owned by a foreign quoted company through any number of intermediate holding companies.

Para. 5

This corrects a mismatch between the treatment of FIDs received by life assurance companies charged under Sched. D Case I as compared with those charged on the "I minus E" basis by treating FIDs as part of the Case I profit. This is already done for the purposes of the "notional Case I test" between the profit calculated on the "I minus E" basis and the Case I basis. See also s.164.

Para. 6

When a foreign income distribution is made by an authorised unit trust to a corporate unit holder part of the distribution is deemed to have been paid under deduction of income tax at the lower rate. The new ICTA 1988, s.468R(4), makes it clear that no part of that notionally deducted tax is repayable.

Section 154　　　　　　　　SCHEDULE 28

FOTRA SECURITIES: CONSEQUENTIAL AMENDMENTS

The Taxes Act 1988

1. Section 47 of the Taxes Act 1988 (FOTRA securities) shall cease to have effect.

2. Section 474(2) of that Act (which prevents the deduction of expenses in respect of securities the income on which is exempt from tax) shall cease to have effect.

3.—(1) In section 475 of that Act (tax-free securities: exclusion of interest on borrowed money), for subsection (1) there shall be substituted the following subsection—

　"(1) This section has effect where a banking business, an insurance business or a business consisting wholly or partly in dealing in securities—
　(a) is carried on in the United Kingdom by a person not ordinarily resident there; and
　(b) in computing for any of the purposes of the Tax Acts the profits arising from, or loss sustained, in the business, any amount which would otherwise be brought into account is disregarded by virtue of a condition subject to which any 3½%, War Loan 1952 or after was issued;
　and for this purpose insurance business includes insurance business of any category."

(2) In subsections (3) and (8) of that section for the words "tax-free Treasury securities", in each place where they occur, there shall be substituted "3½% War Loan 1952 or after".

(3) Subsections (6) and (7) of that section shall cease to have effect.

4. In paragraph 5 of Schedule 19AA to that Act (designation of certain assets of overseas life assurance fund), for sub-paragraph (7) there shall be substituted the following sub-paragraph—

　"(7) For the purposes of sub-paragraph (5)(d) above, the reference to securities issued with a FOTRA condition is a reference to any FOTRA security within the meaning of section 154 of the Finance Act 1996."

5. In paragraph 5C of Schedule 19AC to that Act (modification for overseas life insurance companies in relation to tax-free securities), for sub-paragraph (2) there shall be substituted the following sub-paragraphs—

　"(2) Where, in computing the income to which this paragraph applies, any profits and gains arising from a FOTRA security, or from any loan relationship represented by it, are excluded by virtue of the tax exemption condition of that security, the amount which by virtue of section 76 is to be deductible by way of management expenses shall be reduced in accordance with sub-paragraph (3) below.

　(3) That amount shall be reduced so that it bears to the amount which would be deductible apart from this sub-paragraph the same proportion as the amount of the income to which this paragraph applies (after applying the provisions of section 154(2) to (7) of the Finance Act 1996) bears to what would be the amount of that income if the tax exemption condition were disregarded.

　(4) Subsection (8) of section 154 of the Finance Act 1996 (meaning of 'FOTRA security' and 'tax exemption condition') shall apply for the purposes of this paragraph as it applies for the purposes of that section."

6. In paragraph 1(3) of Schedule 24 to that Act and in paragraph 5(5) of Schedule 27 to that Act (amount taken into account in computing tax of company on the assumption that it is resident in the United Kingdom), for "by virtue of section 47 or 48" there shall be substituted, in each case, "and have been so received by virtue of section 154(2) of the Finance Act 1996".

The Inheritance Tax Act 1984 (c. 51)

7. In section 6(2) of the Inheritance Tax Act 1984 (FOTRA securities to be excluded property in specified circumstances), for the words from "neither" to "United Kingdom" there shall be substituted "of a description specified in the condition".

8. In each of paragraphs (a) and (b) of section 48(4) of that Act (excluded property in the case of settlements), for the words from "neither" to "United Kingdom" there shall be substituted "of a description specified in the condition in question".

GENERAL NOTE

The Schedule makes amendments consequential on the extension of relief from capital gains tax, as well as income tax, to holders of FOTRA ("free of tax to residents abroad") securities, also known as "exempt gilts", who are non-resident but not non-domiciled. The purpose is to facilitate the creation of a gilt strips market.

Paras. 1 and 2

These repeal the ICTA 1988, ss.47 and 474(2), which are replaced by s.154 above.

Para. 3

Consequential and simplifying amendments are made to the ICTA 1988, s.475, in particular making it clear that the section applies only to War Loan and making the restriction of relief concerned apply in the same way to all categories of insurance business.

Para. 5

The amendment to the ICTA 1988, Sched. 19AC, para. 5C is consequential, but also extends the application of that paragraph from interest on War Loan to the return on all FOTRA securities.

Section 156   SCHEDULE 29

PAYING AND COLLECTING AGENTS ETC.

PART I

THE NEW CHAPTER

1. In Part IV of the Taxes Act 1988 (provisions relating to the Schedule D charge) the following Chapter shall be inserted after Chapter VII—

"CHAPTER VIIA

PAYING AND COLLECTING AGENTS

Definitions

118A. In this Chapter—

(a) except in the terms "agent concerned", "collecting agent" and "paying agent", references to an "agent" include a person acting as nominee or sub-agent for an agent;

(b) "bank" has the meaning given by section 840A;

(c) the "chargeable date"—

(i) in the case of a relevant payment, has the meaning given by section 118B(5); and

(ii) in the case of a relevant receipt, has the meaning given by section 118C(4);

(d) "collecting agent" has the meaning given by section 118C(1), and in relation to any relevant receipt or chargeable receipt, a reference to the collecting agent is a reference to the collecting agent by virtue of whose performance of a relevant function that receipt was received or arose;

(e) in relation to any dividends, references to "coupons" include warrants for and bills of exchange purporting to be drawn or made in payment of those dividends;

(f) references to a depositary include references to a person acting as agent or nominee for a depositary;

(g) except in paragraph (h) below, references to "dividends" are references to foreign dividends, United Kingdom public revenue dividends or relevant dividends as the context requires;

(h) "foreign dividends" means any annual payments, interest or dividends payable out of or in respect of foreign holdings;

(i) "foreign holdings" means the stocks, funds, shares or securities of any body of persons not resident in the United Kingdom or of a government or public or local authority in a country outside the United Kingdom;

(j) "gilt-edged securities" means any securities which—

(i) are gilt-edged securities for the purposes of the 1992 Act; or

(ii) will be such securities on the making of any order under paragraph 1 of Schedule 9 to that Act the making of which is anticipated in the prospectus under which they were issued;

(k) "international organisation" has the meaning given by section 51A(8);

(l) references to a "nominee" include a person acting as agent or nominee for a nominee;

(m) "paying agent" has the meaning given by section 118B(1);

(n) "prescribed" means prescribed in regulations made by the Board under this Chapter or prescribed by the Board in accordance with such regulations;

(o) "quoted Eurobond" means a quoted Eurobond within the meaning of section 124 the interest on which is chargeable to tax under Case III of Schedule D, and "quoted Eurobond interest" means interest on such a quoted Eurobond;

(p) "relevant dividends" means foreign dividends and quoted Eurobond interest;

(q) "relevant holdings" means foreign holdings and quoted Eurobonds;

(r) "relevant payment" has the meaning given by section 118B(5);

(s) "relevant receipt" has the meaning given by section 118C(2);

(t) "securities" includes any loan stocks or similar securities, whether secured or unsecured; and

(u) "United Kingdom public revenue dividends" means income from securities which is payable out of the public revenue of the United Kingdom or Northern Ireland.

Paying agents

118B.—(1) A person specified in column 1 of Table A below shall be a paying agent for the purposes of this Chapter in relation to such dividends as are—

(a) of a description set out in column 2 of that Table opposite his specification; and

(b) entrusted to him for payment or distribution.

TABLE A

1	2
1. Any person in the United Kingdom.	United Kingdom public revenue dividends
2. The Bank of England	United Kingdom public revenue dividends paid on securities entered in the register of the Bank of Ireland in Dublin
3. Any person in the United Kingdom	Foreign dividends which are payable to persons in the United Kingdom and do not fall within subsection (4) below

(2) The Bank of England and the Bank of Ireland shall be treated as paying agents for the purposes of this Chapter in relation to United Kingdom public revenue dividends which are payable to them.

(3) The National Debt Commissioners shall be treated as paying agents for the purposes of this Chapter in relation to United Kingdom public revenue dividends payable by them.

(4) Foreign dividends fall within this subsection if they are payable out of, or in respect of, the stocks, funds, shares or securities of an organisation which is for the time being designated for the purposes of this subsection pursuant to section 582A(1).

(5) Any payment in relation to which a person is a paying agent shall be a relevant payment for the purposes of this Chapter; and the chargeable date is—

(a) in relation to such a payment as is mentioned in subsection (2) above, the date on which the payment is received; and

(b) in relation to any other relevant payment, the date on which the payment is made.

Collecting agents

118C.—(1) Subject to subsection (3) below, a person described in column 1 of Table B below shall be a collecting agent for the purposes of this Chapter in relation to such functions performed by him as are set out in that description, which shall be relevant functions for the purposes of this Chapter.

(2) Such dividends or proceeds of sale or other realisation as—

(a) are set out in column 2 of Table B below opposite the description of a collecting agent in column 1; and

(b) are received or arise by virtue of that collecting agent's performance of a relevant function comprised in that description

shall be relevant receipts for the purposes of this Chapter.

TABLE B

1	2
1. Any person in the United Kingdom who, in the course of a trade or profession, acts as custodian of any relevant holdings	any relevant dividends in respect of those relevant holdings which are received by him or are paid to another person at his direction or with his consent
2. Any person in the United Kingdom who, in the course of a trade or profession, by means of coupons collects or secures payment of or receives relevant dividends for another person	the relevant dividends which he so collects or receives or of which he so secures payment
3. any person in the United Kingdom who, in the course of a trade or profession, otherwise acts for another person in arranging to collect or secure payment of relevant dividends	the relevant dividends which he so collects or of which he so secures payment
4. Any bank in the United Kingdom which sells or otherwise realises coupons for relevant dividends and pays over the proceeds or carries them into an account	the proceeds of sale or other realisation of those coupons
5. Any dealer in coupons in the United Kingdom who purchases any coupons for relevant dividends otherwise than from a bank or another dealer in coupons	the proceeds of sale of those coupons

(3) Neither the clearing of a cheque, nor the arranging for the clearing of a cheque, shall of itself be a relevant function.

(4) The chargeable date. in relation to a relevant receipt, is—

(a) in the case of a relevant receipt falling within paragraph 4 or 5 of Table B above, the date on which the sale or realisation is effected, and

(b) in any other case, the date on which the dividends are paid.

(5) For the purposes of paragraph 1 of Table B above, a person acts as a custodian of relevant holdings if he holds them, or an entitlement to them, for another person.

(6) The Board may by regulations provide for the application of the provisions of this Chapter relating to collecting agents where—

(a) a person in the United Kingdom—

(i) holds, beneficially or otherwise, a right (the relevant right) which is a right to delivery of, or to amounts representing the whole or substantially the whole of the value of, a specified quantity of shares or securities comprised in a relevant holding which is held by a person outside the United Kingdom, and

(ii) is entitled to receive income (the relevant income) which is derived from, or which represents, foreign dividends or quoted Eurobond interest on that quantity of shares or securities; and

(b) apart from the provisions of the regulations, the relevant right is not a relevant holding, or the relevant income does not constitute foreign dividends or quoted Eurobond interest.

(7) Regulations under subsection (6) above may—

(a) treat the relevant right as a foreign holding or, as the case may be, a holding of quoted Eurobonds (the notional holding); and

(b) treat the relevant income as foreign dividends or, as the case may be, quoted Eurobond interest paid on the notional holding.

Chargeable payments and chargeable receipts

118D.—(1) For the purposes of this Chapter, every relevant payment shall be a chargeable payment unless—

(a) it is made in respect of a foreign dividend—

(i) which is payable on foreign holdings held in a recognised clearing system; and

(ii) in respect of which any conditions imposed by virtue of subsection (8) below are satisfied; or

(b) it is a payment of interest on an exempted certificate of deposit; or

(c) the making of the payment is excluded from being a chargeable payment by subsections (4), (5) or (6) below or by section 118G.

(2) For the purposes of this Chapter, every relevant receipt shall be a chargeable receipt, unless—

(a) it arises in respect of relevant holdings which are held in a recognised clearing system and—

(i) the collecting agent pays or accounts for the relevant receipt directly or indirectly to the recognised clearing system, and

(ii) any conditions imposed by virtue of subsection (8) below are satisfied; or

(b) it arises in respect of relevant holdings which are held in a recognised clearing system for which the collecting agent is acting as depositary; or

(c) it is excluded from being a chargeable receipt by subsection (7) below or by section 118G.

(3) In subsection (1)(b) above, "exempted certificate of deposit" means a certificate of deposit (within the meaning of section 56(5)) issued by a person in the United Kingdom relating to a deposit with a branch in the United Kingdom through which a company resident outside, and not resident in, the United Kingdom carries on a trade.

(4) The payment of United Kingdom public revenue dividends on securities the interest on which is, by virtue of directions given (or treated by section 51 as having been given) under section 50(1), payable without deduction of income tax shall not be a chargeable payment unless the interest is for the time being payable under deduction of income tax pursuant to an application made (or treated by section 51 as having been made) under section 50(2).

(5) The payment of United Kingdom public revenue dividends in respect of securities standing in the name of the official custodian for charities, or in respect of which there is given to the paying agent a certificate from the Board to the effect that the dividends are subject only to charitable trusts and are exempt from tax, shall not be a chargeable payment.

(6) In a case where—

(a) foreign dividends are entrusted by a company which at the time they are entrusted (the "relevant time") is not resident in the United Kingdom,

(b) they are entrusted for payment to a company which at the relevant time is resident in the United Kingdom, and

(c) at the relevant time the company mentioned in paragraph (b) above directly or indirectly controls not less than 10 per cent. of the voting power in the company mentioned in paragraph (a) above,

the payment of those dividends shall not be a chargeable payment.

(7) In a case where—

(a) foreign dividends are payable by a company which at the time of the payment (the "relevant time") is not resident in the United Kingdom,

(b) payment of those dividends is collected, received or secured, or coupons for those dividends are realised, on behalf of a company which at the relevant time is resident in the United Kingdom, and

(c) at the relevant time the company mentioned in paragraph (b) above directly or indirectly controls not less than 10 per cent. of the voting power in the company mentioned in paragraph (a) above,

those dividends or, as the case may be, the proceeds of realisation of those coupons shall not be a chargeable receipt.

(8) The Board may by regulations provide that subsection (1)(a) above does not apply in respect of a relevant payment, or that subsection (2)(a) above does not apply in respect of a relevant receipt, unless the paying agent or, as the case may be, the collecting agent has obtained a declaration from the recognised clearing system or its depositary in such form, and containing such information, as may be required by those regulations.

(9) The Board may by regulations make such provision as they may consider appropriate for requiring paying agents and collecting agents to deliver returns setting out particulars of—

(a) any relevant payments made by them which would have been chargeable payments but for the provisions of section 118D(1)(a);

(b) any relevant receipts which would have been chargeable receipts but for the provisions of section 118D(2)(a) or (b);

and for the keeping and production to, or to an officer of, the Board of any document in which any such declaration as is mentioned in subsection (8) above is contained.

Deduction of tax from chargeable payments and chargeable receipts

118E.—(1) Subject to subsection (2) below, where a paying agent makes a chargeable payment—

(a) he shall, on making the payment, deduct from it a sum representing the amount of income tax thereon;

(b) he shall become liable to account for that sum;

(c) the person to whom the chargeable payment is made shall allow the deduction on receipt of the residue of the payment, and the paying agent shall be acquitted and discharged of so much money as is represented by the deduction, as if that sum had actually been paid; and

(d) the deduction shall be treated as income tax paid by the person entitled to the chargeable payment.

(2) In relation to United Kingdom public revenue dividends payable to the Bank of Ireland out of the public revenue of the United Kingdom, or which are entrusted to the Bank of Ireland for payment and distribution and are not payable by that Bank out of its principal office in Belfast, subsection (1) above shall not apply, but—

(a) the money which, apart from this subsection, would be issuable to the Bank of Ireland under section 14 of the National Debt Act 1870, or otherwise payable to the Bank of Ireland for the purpose of dividends on securities of the United Kingdom government entered in the register of the Bank of Ireland in Dublin, shall be issued and paid to the Bank of England;

(b) the Bank of England shall deduct from the money so issued and paid to it a sum representing the amount of income tax on the dividends payable to the Bank of Ireland, and on the dividends on the securities of the United Kingdom government entered in the register of the Bank of Ireland in Dublin, and shall become liable to account for the same under section 118F(1);

(c) the Bank of England shall pay to the Bank of Ireland the residue of the money so issued and paid to it, to be applied by the Bank of Ireland in payment of the dividends; and

(d) the deduction shall be treated as income tax paid by the person entitled to the dividends, and the Bank of England and the Bank of Ireland shall be acquitted and discharged of so much money as is represented by the deduction, as if that sum had actually been paid.

(3) Where a collecting agent performs a relevant function—

(a) he shall on the chargeable date become liable to account for a sum representing the amount of income tax on any chargeable receipt in relation to which he is the collecting agent;

(b) he shall be entitled—

(i) to be indemnified by the person entitled to the chargeable receipt against the income tax for which he is liable to account in accordance with paragraph (a) above; and

(ii) to deduct out of the chargeable receipt or to retain from any other sums otherwise due from him to the person entitled to the chargeable receipt, or received by him on behalf of that person, amounts sufficient for meeting any liability to account for such income tax which he has discharged or to which he is subject;

(c) the person entitled to the chargeable receipt shall allow the deduction or retention on receipt of the residue of the chargeable receipt, and the collecting agent shall be acquitted and discharged of so much money as is represented by the deduction, as if that sum had actually been paid; and

(d) the amount for which the collecting agent is liable to account shall be treated as income tax paid by the person entitled to the chargeable receipt.

(4) A paying agent who makes a chargeable payment, or a collecting agent who is required to account for tax on a chargeable receipt, shall, if the person entitled to the chargeable payment or, as the case may be, the chargeable receipt so requests in writing, furnish him within thirty days after receiving that request with a certificate showing—

(a) the gross amount of the payment or receipt;

(b) the amount of income tax treated as paid by him;

(c) the actual amount actually paid or accounted for to him; and

(d) the chargeable date.

(5) The Board may by regulations—

(a) require a certificate furnished pursuant to subsection (4) above to contain information additional to that set out in paragraphs (a) to (d) of that subsection or a declaration made by or on behalf of the paying agent or collecting agent;

(b) make provision for the form of such a certificate or declaration.

(6) The duty imposed by subsection (4) above shall be enforceable at the suit or instance of the person requesting the certificate.

Accounting for tax on chargeable payments and chargeable receipts

118F.—(1) Income tax in respect of United Kingdom public revenue dividends for which the Bank of England, the Bank of Ireland, the National Debt Commissioners or any public office or department of the Crown are liable to account pursuant to section 118E(1) or (2) shall become due and payable on the seventh day after the chargeable date and shall be paid into the general account of the Board at the Bank of England or, in the case of the Bank of Ireland, at the Bank of Ireland.

(2) Any other income tax for which a paying agent is liable to account under section 118E(1), and any income tax for which a collecting agent is liable to account under section 118E(3), shall become due and payable on the fourteenth day from the end of the month in which the chargeable date falls.

(3) Any tax due under subsection (1) or (2) above shall carry interest, at the rate applicable under section 178 of the Finance Act 1989, from the date on which it becomes due until it is paid.

(4) The Board may by regulations make such provision as they may consider appropriate—

(a) for requiring paying agents and collecting agents to deliver returns setting out particulars of—

(i) chargeable payments made by them;

(ii) chargeable receipts in respect of which they are liable to account for tax;

(iii) any relevant payments made by them which would have been chargeable payments but for the provisions of section 118G;

(iv) any relevant receipts which would have been chargeable receipts but for the provisions of section 118G;

(v) the amount of any tax accounted for by them, or for which they are liable to account, in relation to chargeable payments or chargeable receipts;

(vi) in the case of relevant payments falling within sub-paragraph (iii) above, the paragraphs of subsection (3) or (4) of section 118G that applied to them;

(vii) in the case of relevant receipts falling within sub-paragraph (iv) above, the paragraphs of subsection (4) of section 118G that applied to them;

(viii) the names and addresses of the persons entitled to the relevant payments or relevant receipts;

(b) with respect to the furnishing of information by paying agents or collecting agents, including the inspection of books, documents and other records on behalf of the Board;

(c) for the assessment under the regulations of amounts due and for appeals against such assessments;

(d) for the repayment in specified circumstances of amounts paid (or purporting to be paid) under this Chapter.

Relevant securities of eligible persons

118G.—(1) Subject to subsection (2) below, and to the provisions of any regulations under section 118H—

(a) any relevant payment to which subsection (3) or (4) below applies shall not be a chargeable payment; and

(b) any relevant receipt to which subsection (4) below applies shall not be a chargeable receipt.

(2) Regulations made under paragraph (g), (h) or (i) of subsection (4) below may provide that only one of paragraphs (a) and (b) of subsection (1) above is to apply by virtue of those regulations in relation to relevant payments or relevant receipts of a particular kind or from a particular source.

(3) This subsection applies to payments of United Kingdom public revenue dividends so long as—

(a) they are exempt from tax by virtue of section 46, 49, 516 or 517;

(b) they are payable in respect of gilt-edged securities which for the time being are treated by section 51A as issued subject to the condition that interest on them is paid without deduction of income tax;

(c) they are payable in respect of securities which have been issued with such a condition as is authorised by section 22(1) of the Finance (No. 2) Act 1931 and which are for the time being beneficially owned by a person who is not ordinarily resident in the United Kingdom;

(d) they are eligible for relief from tax by virtue of section 505(1)(c) or (d), or would be so eligible but for section 505(3);

(e) they are eligible for relief from tax by virtue of section 592(2), 608(2)(a), 613(4), 614(2), (3) or (4) or 643(2); or

(f) they are payable in respect of securities held by or on behalf of a person of such a description as may be prescribed.

(4) This subsection applies to relevant payments (not being payments of United Kingdom public revenue dividends) and relevant receipts—

(a) to which a person who, at the chargeable date—
    (i) is not resident in the United Kingdom, and
    (ii) beneficially owns the relevant holdings from which they are derived,
  is beneficially entitled;

(b) which consist of, or of the proceeds of sale or other realisation of coupons for, interest (other than quoted Eurobond interest) to which a bank which, at the chargeable date—
    (i) is resident in the United Kingdom, and
    (ii) beneficially owns the foreign holdings from which they are derived,
  is beneficially entitled;

(c) which arise to the trustees of a qualifying discretionary or accumulation trust in their capacity as such in respect of relevant holdings held on the trusts thereof;

(d) which are eligible for relief from tax by virtue of section 505(1)(c) or (d), or would be so eligible but for section 505(3);

(e) which are eligible for relief from tax by virtue of section 592(2), 608(2)(a), 613(4), 614(2), (3) or (4), 620(6) or 643(2);

(f) which consist of, or of the proceeds of sale or other realisation of coupons for, dividends payable out of the public revenue of the Republic of Ireland or out of or in respect of shares or securities issued by or on behalf of any Republic of Ireland company, society, adventure or concern;

(g) to which a person of such a description as may be prescribed and who, at the chargeable date, beneficially owns the securities from which they are derived, is beneficially entitled;

(h) which are derived from relevant holdings held by or on behalf of a person of such a description as may be prescribed;

(i) which are of such a description as may be prescribed; or

(j) which fall to be treated as the income of, or of the government of, a sovereign power or of an international organisation.

(5) For the purposes of subsection (4)(c) above, a trust is a qualifying discretionary or accumulation trust if—

(a) it is such that some or all of any income arising to the trustees would fall (unless treated as income of the settlor or applied in defraying expenses of the trustees) to be comprised for the year of assessment in which it arises in income to which section 686 (liability to additional rate tax of certain income of discretionary trusts) applies;

(b) the trustees are not resident in the United Kingdom; and

(c) none of the beneficiaries of the trust is resident in the United Kingdom.

(6) The persons who are to be taken for the purposes of subsection (5) above to be the beneficiaries of a discretionary or accumulation trust shall be every person who, as a person falling wholly or partly within any description of actual or potential beneficiaries, is either—

(a) a person who is, or will or may become, entitled under the trust to receive the whole or any part of any income under the trust; or

(b) a person to or for the benefit of whom the whole or any part of such income may be paid or applied in exercise of any discretion conferred by the trust;

and for the purposes of this subsection references, in relation to a trust, to income under the trust shall include references to so much (if any) of any property falling to be treated as capital under the trust as represents amounts originally received by the trustees as income.

(7) The Board may by regulations provide that a paying agent who is entrusted with the payment or distribution of—

(a) United Kingdom public revenue dividends on securities which are held by a nominee approved for the purposes of this subsection, or

(b) foreign dividends on foreign holdings held by such a nominee,

shall treat those dividends as not being chargeable payments.

(8) For the purpose of giving relief from tax pursuant to arrangements which have effect by virtue of section 788, the Board may by regulations provide that a paying agent who is entrusted with the payment or distribution of United Kingdom public revenue dividends on gilt-edged securities held by a nominee approved for the purposes of this subsection shall—

(a) treat those dividends as not being chargeable payments, or

(b) deduct tax from them at such reduced rates (being lower than the rate that would otherwise be applicable by virtue of section 118E(1)) as may be prescribed.

(9) Where, pursuant to subsection (7) or (8) above, dividends are paid without deduction of tax, or subject to deduction of tax at a reduced rate, the provisions of this Chapter shall apply, subject to subsection (10) below and to the provisions of regulations under section 118H, as though the nominee was the paying agent in relation to those dividends and the chargeable date was the date on which he received them.

(10) Where tax has been deducted from dividends at a reduced rate pursuant to regulations under subsection (8) above, the tax for which the nominee is liable to account by virtue of subsection (9) above shall not exceed the difference between the amount of tax on those dividends at the rate that is applicable by virtue of section 118E(1) and the tax already deducted from them.

Relevant securities of eligible persons: administration

118H.—(1) The Board may by regulations provide that section 118G(1) shall not apply as regards relevant payments or relevant receipts—

(a) unless such conditions as may be prescribed are fulfilled;

(b) where the Board have reason to believe that section 118G(3) does not apply to, or to the whole of, any relevant payments; or

(c) where the Board have reason to believe that section 118G(4) does not apply to, or to the whole of, any relevant payments or relevant receipts.

(2) In subsection (3) below, references to the relevant exclusion are to exclusion from being a chargeable payment or chargeable receipt pursuant to section 118G(1) or regulations made under section 118G(7) or (8), or to the deduction of tax at a reduced rate pursuant to regulations under section 118G(8), as the case may be; and references to the agent concerned are to the paying agent or collecting agent or, as the case may be, to the nominee approved for the purpose of section 118G(7) or (8).

(3) Regulations under this section or section 118G(7) or (8) may—

(a) disapply the relevant exclusion in respect of any relevant payments or relevant receipts derived from any securities or relevant holdings unless the appropriate person has made a declaration in writing to the agent concerned, in such form as may be prescribed or authorised by the Board, confirming that the requirements for the exclusion are satisfied;

(b) require the person who makes such a declaration to undertake in the declaration to notify the agent concerned if the circumstances set out in the declaration change;

(c) require the agent concerned to consider the accuracy of any declaration made pursuant to a requirement imposed by virtue of paragraph (a) above;

(d) impose obligations—

(i) on persons having any rights in relation to relevant payments or relevant receipts in respect of which the relevant exclusion applies or is claimed to apply; and

(ii) on persons who are the agents concerned in relation to such relevant payments or relevant receipts as are mentioned in sub-paragraph (i) above

as to the provision of information, and the production of documents, to the Board or, on request, to an officer of the Board;

(e) provide for notices to be issued by the Board to persons who fail to comply with requirements for the provision of information or documents mentioned in paragraph (d) above, disapplying the relevant exclusion in relation to relevant payments or relevant receipts in relation to which they have any rights or in relation to which they are the agents concerned;

(f) impose requirements as to—

(i) the form and contents of any declaration to be made in accordance with the regulations under this section;

(ii) the appropriate person to make such a declaration;

(iii) the form and manner in which, and the time at which, any declaration is to be made or provided; and

(iv) the keeping and production to, or to an officer of, the Board of any document in which any such declaration is contained;

(g) provide for notices to be issued by the Board to such persons as may be described in the regulations where the Board are satisfied that the relevant exclusion applies, or where the Board are satisfied or have reason to believe that the relevant exclusion does not apply.

(4) Regulations under section 118G(7) or (8) may—

(a) prescribe conditions for the inclusion of securities or foreign holdings in arrangements established under that subsection;

(b) set out procedures for the approval of nominees for the purpose of that subsection and for the withdrawal of such approval.

Deduction of tax at reduced rate

118I. The Board may make regulations which provide for the amount of any income tax which a paying agent would otherwise be liable to deduct under section 118E(1)(a), or for which a collecting agent would otherwise be liable to account under section 118E(3)(a), to be reduced by reference to liabilities for such tax paid under the law of a territory outside the United Kingdom as may be prescribed.

Prevention of double accounting

118J.—(1) A relevant dividend the payment of which is a chargeable payment shall not be a chargeable receipt for the purpose of this Chapter.

(2) Subsection (1) above does not prevent the proceeds of sale or other realisation of a coupon from being a chargeable receipt.

(3) The Board may make regulations—

(a) for preventing more than one collecting agent from being liable to account for tax on the same dividend; or

(b) which provide that—

(i) where more than one person is a collecting agent in relation to a dividend, those persons may agree between themselves which one of their number shall be treated as the collecting agent in relation to that dividend; and

(ii) the person so identified shall for all the purposes of this Chapter be treated as the sole collecting agent in relation to that dividend.

Regulations

118K.—(1) Any power to make regulations under this Chapter—

(a) may be exercised as regards prescribed cases or descriptions of case; and

(b) may be exercised differently in relation to different cases or descriptions of case, or in relation to different persons or descriptions of person.

(2) Regulations under this Chapter may include such supplementary, incidental, consequential or transitional provisions as appear to the Board to be necessary or expedient.

(3) No specific provision of this Chapter about regulations shall prejudice the generality of subsections (1) and (2) above."

PART II

OTHER PROVISIONS

Penalties

2.—(1) In section 98 of the Taxes Management Act 1970 (penalties in respect of certain information provisions) the words "regulations under section 118D, 118F, 118G, 118H or 118I;" shall be inserted—

(a) in column 1 of the Table, after "regulations under section 42A"; and

(b) in column 2 of the Table, after "regulations under section 51B".

(2) In the same section—

(a) the words "regulations under section 124(3);" shall be inserted in column 1 of the Table after the words inserted by sub-paragraph (1)(a) above; and

(b) for the words "section 124(3)" in column 2 of the Table there shall be substituted "regulations under section 124(3)".

Amendments of the Taxes Act 1988

3. The Taxes Act 1988 shall be amended in accordance with paragraphs 4 to 7 below.

4. For section 124(2) to (5) there shall be substituted—

"(2) The conditions are—
(a) that a person who—
    (i) is not resident in the United Kingdom, and
    (ii) beneficially owns the quoted Eurobond
  is beneficially entitled to the interest;
(b) that the quoted Eurobond is held in a recognised clearing system.
(3) The Board may by regulations provide that subsection (1)(b) above shall be taken not to apply to a payment of interest unless—
(a) the person by or through whom the payment is made (the relevant payer) has received a declaration confirming that one of the conditions of subsection (2) above is satisfied, or
(b) they have issued a notice to the relevant payer stating that they consider that one (or both) of those conditions is satisfied.
(4) Regulations under subsection (3) above may—
(a) impose requirements as to—
    (i) the contents of any declaration to be made in accordance with regulations under subsection (3)(a) above,
    (ii) the form and manner in which any declaration is to be provided in accordance with any such regulations, and
    (iii) the keeping and production to, or to an officer of, the Board of any document in which any such declaration is contained;
(b) make provision for any such declaration to be made by the person entitled to the interest (or, as the case may be, the depositary for the recognised clearing system) or by such other person as may be prescribed by the regulations;
(c) require the relevant payer to consider the accuracy of any such declaration;
(d) make provision for notices to be issued by the Board to such persons as may be described in the regulations where the Board consider that
    (i) one (or both) of the conditions of subsection (2) above, or
    (ii) neither of those conditions
  is satisfied in relation to interest paid on any holding of quoted Eurobonds;
(e) make provision with respect to the furnishing of information by relevant payers, including the inspection of books and other records on behalf of the Board;
(f) require relevant payers to deliver returns setting out particulars of payments made by them to which subsection (1)(b) above applies and the names and addresses of the persons entitled to them;
(g) contain such supplementary, incidental, consequential or transitional provisions as appear to the Board to be necessary or expedient."
5.—(1) In section 348(3) and in section 349(1), at the end there shall be inserted "or to any payment which is a relevant payment for the purposes of Chapter VIIA of Part IV".
(2) In section 349(3), the following paragraph shall be inserted after paragraph (d)—
"(e) to any payment which is a relevant payment for the purposes of Chapter VIIA of Part IV; or"
6. In section 582A (designated international organisations: miscellaneous exemptions), in subsection (1) for "(2) to (6) below" there shall be substituted "(2) and (4) to (6) below and section 118B(4)".
7. In paragraph 4(8) of Schedule 23A (manufactured overseas dividends), for the words "subsection (2) or (3) of section 123 or under Part III, as the case may be, and for Parts III and IV of Schedule 3" there shall be substituted "Chapter VIIA of Part IV and for that Chapter".

Amendment of the Finance Act 1989

8. In section 178 of the Finance Act 1989 (setting rates of interest), in subsection (2)(m), before "160" there shall be inserted "118F,".

GENERAL NOTE
The Schedule provides a framework for the new arrangements under which paying and collecting agents have to deduct tax.

Para. 1
The framework is contained in the new ICTA 1988, Pt. IV, Chap. VIIA, ss.118A–K.

Section 118A
This provides definitions, in particular of "foreign dividends" and "United Kingdom public revenue dividends".

Section 118B
This determines who is a paying agent in relation to the dividends specified. The arrangements remain broadly as they are now.

Section 118C
Similarly, this determines who is a collecting agent in relation to certain activities, known as "relevant functions". The main circumstance in which collecting agents in future will have to deduct tax is where they act as custodian of shares or securities for a U.K. investor. Collecting agents who do no more than arrange to clear a cheque for foreign dividends or interest will no longer have to deduct tax.

Section 118D
This identifies the circumstances in which "relevant payments" and "relevant receipts" are not chargeable payments or receipts. These include payments and receipts on securities which are held in a recognised clearing system (subs. (1) and (2)), on exempted certificates of deposit (subs. (3)), on exempt gilts (subs. (4)), on U.K. Government securities held by charities (subs. (5)) and on dividends made to a U.K.-resident company by a foreign company in which it has at least a 10 per cent interest (subss. (6) and (7)).

Section 118E
This requires a paying agent when making a chargeable payment to deduct and account for tax on the payment. The tax is treated as paid by the person entitled to the chargeable payment.

Section 118F
This details when income tax deducted by paying and collecting agents becomes due and payable and imposes interest, at the rate due under the FA 1989, s.178, on late payments.

Section 118G
This provides for further exceptions where relevant payments and receipts are not chargeable payments and receipts. These include circumstances where tax is not due or there is an exemption from tax in other legislation or where the payments are to certain categories of person. The Revenue may make regulations determining that dividends shall not be chargeable payments in certain cases where the securities are held by approved nominees, *e.g.* within the terms of the Central Gilts Office schemes.

Section 118H
The Revenue are given power to make regulations specifying the conditions on which the exceptions in s.118G will apply.

Section 118I
The Revenue may make regulations providing for tax to be deducted at a reduced rate to take account of double taxation relief for overseas tax on the dividends.

Section 118J
This prevents a relevant dividend from being both a chargeable payment and a chargeable receipt and enables regulations to be made to prevent more than one collecting agent deducting tax on a dividend.

Section 118K
This specifies how the regulation-making powers may be exercised.

Para. 4
This sets out revised conditions under which interest on quoted Eurobonds paid by a person in the U.K. may be made without deduction of tax [Standing Committee E, February 22, 1996, col. 485].

Section 160   SCHEDULE 30

INVESTMENTS IN HOUSING

Reduced rate of corporation tax

1. After section 508 of the Taxes Act 1988 there shall be inserted the following sections—

"Investment trusts investing in housing
    508A.—(1) Where any company that is an investment trust has eligible rental income for any accounting period—

    (a) the rate of corporation tax chargeable for any financial year on the trust's housing investment profits for that period shall be deemed to be the small companies' rate for that year; and

    (b) its housing investment profits for that period shall be treated for the purposes of section 13 as excluded from its basic profits for that period.

  (2) For the purposes of this section—

    (a) a company's eligible rental income for any period is so much of its income for that period as consists in rents or other receipts deriving from lettings by the company of eligible properties; and

    (b) its housing investment profits for any period are so much of its profits for that period as represents the amount chargeable to tax under Schedule A in respect of its eligible rental income for that period.

  (3) In computing the amount mentioned in subsection (2)(b) above for any period, deductions shall be made which (except in so far as they exceed the amount from which they are deducted) are, in aggregate, not less than the sum of the following amounts—

    (a) every amount which is both—

        (i) deductible (otherwise than as a debit brought into account under Chapter II of Part IV of the Finance Act 1996) in the computation of any income of the company, or of its total profits, for that period, and

        (ii) referable to, or to activities connected with, the letting by the company on assured tenancies of dwelling-houses that are eligible properties when so let, and

    (b) any amount that is so referable that would represent a non-trading deficit on the company's loan relationships for that period.

  (4) For the purposes of subsection (3) above any question—

    (a) whether for any period there is an amount referable to any matter that would represent a non-trading deficit on a company's loan relationships, or

    (b) as to what that amount is for that period,

shall be determined by computing whether and to what extent there would for that period have been a non-trading deficit on the company's loan relationships if debits and credits fell to be brought into account under Chapter II of Part IV of the Finance Act 1996 to the extent only that they are referable to that matter.

Interpretation of section 508A

  508B.—(1) In section 508A 'eligible property' in relation to a company, means (subject to the following provisions of this section) any dwelling-house as respects which the following conditions are satisfied—

    (a) the company first acquired an interest in the dwelling-house on or after 1st April 1996;

    (b) that interest was not, at the time when it was acquired, subject to any letting or to any statutory tenancy;

    (c) at that time no arrangements had been made by the company or any person connected with it for the letting of the dwelling-house;

    (d) the interest of the company in the dwelling-house is a freehold interest or an interest under a long lease at a low rent;

    (e) the consideration given by the company for the acquisition of its interest in the dwelling-house did not exceed—

        (i) £125,000, in the case of a dwelling-house in Greater London, or

        (ii) £85,000, in any other case;

    (f) the dwelling-house is let by the company under an assured tenancy and is neither—

        (i) let by the company in consideration of a premium within the meaning of Schedule 8 to the 1992 Act, nor

        (ii) a dwelling-house in respect of which the person to whom it is let or any associate of his has been granted any option to purchase.

  (2) For the purposes of paragraph (b) of subsection (1) above, no account shall be taken of any shorthold tenancy or statutory shorthold tenancy to which the interest became subject before the time when it was acquired.

  (3) For the purposes of paragraph (c) of subsection (1) above, no account shall be taken of any arrangements made by a person connected with the company in question before the time when the interest was acquired by the company if—

    (a) that person had an interest in the dwelling-house when he made those arrangements;

    (b) that person did not dispose of his interest at any time after the arrangements were entered into and before the company acquired its interest; and

(c) the arrangements were such as to confer a relevant entitlement on a person who, at the time when the company acquired its interest, was a tenant under any shorthold tenancy of the dwelling-house (or any part of it).

(4) For the purposes of subsection (3)(c) above a relevant entitlement is an entitlement of a tenant under a shorthold tenancy of any premises, on the coming to an end of that tenancy, to such a further tenancy of the same or substantially the same premises as will itself be a shorthold tenancy.

(5) For the purposes of this section the consideration given by a company for the acquisition of an interest in a dwelling-house shall be taken (subject to subsection (6) below) to include—

(a) any amount expended by the company on the construction or renovation of the dwelling-house or on any conversion by virtue of which that dwelling-house came to be usable as such;

(b) any amount so expended by a person connected with the company; and

(c) any consideration given by a person connected with the company for the acquisition of any such interest in the dwelling-house as—

(i) is subsequently acquired by the company, or

(ii) is held by such a person at the same time as the company holds its interest in the premises.

(6) Where a company has acquired any interest in a dwelling-house from a person connected with that company—

(a) amounts expended by that person as mentioned in paragraph (a) of subsection (5) above, and

(b) the amount of any consideration given by that person for an interest in the dwelling-house,

shall be treated by virtue of that subsection as included in the consideration given by the company to the extent only that the aggregate of those amounts exceeds the consideration given by that company to that person for the interest acquired from that person by the company.

(7) In section 508A and this section—

'associate' has the meaning given by subsections (3) and (4) of section 417;

'assured tenancy' means—

(a) any letting which is an assured tenancy for the purposes of the Housing Act 1988 or the Housing (Scotland) Act 1988, or

(b) any tenancy in Northern Ireland which complies with such requirements or conditions as may be prescribed by regulations made by the Department of the Environment for Northern Ireland;

'letting' includes a letting by virtue of an agreement for a lease or under a licence, and 'let' shall be construed accordingly;

'long lease', in relation to the interest of a company in any dwelling-house, means a lease for a term of years certain of which at least 21 years remains unexpired at the time when that interest was acquired by the company;

'low rent' means a rent at an annual rate not exceeding—

(a) £1,000, in the case of a dwelling-house in Greater London; and

(b) £250, in any other case;

'rent' has the same meaning as it has for the purposes of Schedule A in its application to companies within the charge to corporation tax;

'shorthold tenancy' means any letting which is an assured shorthold tenancy for the purposes of the Housing Act 1988 or a short assured tenancy for the purposes of the Housing (Scotland) Act 1988;

'statutory shorthold tenancy' means—

(a) a statutory periodic tenancy within the meaning of the Housing Act 1988 which arose on the coming to an end of an assured shorthold tenancy which was a fixed term tenancy, or

(b) a statutory assured tenancy within the meaning of the Housing (Scotland) Act 1988 which arose on the coming to an end of a short assured tenancy;

'statutory tenancy'—

(a) in relation to England and Wales, has the same meaning as in the Rent Act 1977;

(b) in relation to Scotland, has the same meaning as in the Rent (Scotland) Act 1984; and

(c) in relation to Northern Ireland, has the same meaning as in the Rent (Northern Ireland) Order 1978.

(8) Section 839 shall apply for the purposes of this section.

(9) Section 508A shall have effect where—

(a) a company acquires an interest in any dwelling-house, and

(b) a person connected with the company has previously acquired an interest in the dwelling-house, being an interest subsequently acquired by the company or one held by that person at the same time as the company holds its interest,

as if references in this section (except in subsection (3) above) to the time when the company first acquired an interest in the premises included references to the time when the person connected with the company first acquired his interest.

(10) The Treasury may, if they think fit, by order vary the figures for the time being specified in paragraph (e) of subsection (1) above; and an order under this subsection may make different provision for different localities in Greater London or elsewhere.

(11) In the application of this section to Scotland—

(a) references to acquiring an interest shall be construed, if there is a contract to acquire the interest, as references to entering into that contract;

(b) references to the freehold interest shall be construed as references to the estate or interest of the proprietor of the *dominium utile* or, in the case of property other than feudal property, of the owner;

(c) in the definition of 'long lease' in subsection (7) above, the word 'certain' shall be omitted.

(12) Regulations made for the purposes of paragraph (b) of the definition of 'assured tenancy' in subsection (7) above shall be made by statutory rule for the purposes of the Statutory Rules (Northern Ireland) Order 1979, and shall be subject to negative resolution within the meaning of section 41(6) of the Interpretation Act (Northern Ireland) 1954."

Investments in housing by investment trusts

2.—(1) Section 842 of the Taxes Act 1988 (investment trusts) shall be amended as follows.

(2) In subsection (1) (conditions as to a company's income for approval as an investment trust)—

(a) in paragraph (a), for "derived wholly or mainly from shares or securities" there shall be substituted "consists wholly or mainly of eligible investment income"; and

(b) in paragraph (e), for "the income it derives from shares or securities" there shall be substituted "its eligible investment income".

(3) After that subsection there shall be inserted the following subsection—

"(1AA) Income is eligible investment income for the purposes of this section in so far as it is either—

(a) income deriving from shares or securities, or

(b) eligible rental income, within the meaning of section 508A."

Commencement

3. This Schedule has effect in relation to accounting periods beginning on or after the day on which this Act is passed.

GENERAL NOTE

The Schedule implements the extension of the investment powers of approved investment trusts to include rented residential property.

Para. 1

The new ICTA 1988, s.508A, applies the small companies' rate of corporation tax to the part of an investment trust's income which is referable to profits from investment in housing.

The new ICTA 1988, s.508B, defines the conditions governing housing investment. The conditions are:

(i) the property must be a residential property which the trust lets under an assured tenancy;

(ii) the property must not be let in consideration of a premium or to a person who has been granted an option to purchase it, or to any associate of such a person;

(iii) the trust, and any person connected with it, must not have acquired any interest in the property before April 1, 1996;

(iv) the interest held by the trust in the property must be a freehold or a long lease at low rent (£1,000 per annum in London, £250 elsewhere);

(v) the property must be unlet or let on a shorthold tenancy (or statutory shorthold tenancy) when it was acquired;

(vi) no prior arrangements must have been made by the trust or a connected person to let the property except in exceptional circumstances (see s.508B(3));

(vii) the total paid for the property must not exceed £125,000 in London or £85,000 elsewhere, including any amount spent in construction, renovation or conversion. The Treasury may vary these limits by statutory order.

Para. 2

At present, an investment trust must derive its income wholly or mainly from shares or securities and it must not retain more than 15 per cent of its income from such sources. Under the amendments to the ICTA 1988, s.482, its income may consist of any mix of investment and rental income. The 15 per cent rule is retained for investment income [Standing Committee E, February 22, 1996, col. 498].

Section 163   SCHEDULE 31

LIFE ASSURANCE BUSINESS LOSSES

Expenses of management

1. In section 76 of the Taxes Act 1988 (expenses of management: insurance companies) in subsection (1) (which applies section 75 of that Act with specified exceptions) before paragraph (a) there shall be inserted—

"(aa) where the whole or any part of a loss arising to the company in respect of its life assurance business in an accounting period is set off under section 393A or 403(1), there shall be deducted from the amount treated as the expenses of management for that period an amount equal to so much of the loss as, in the aggregate, is so set off, reduced by the amounts by which any losses for that period under section 436, 439B or 441 fall to be reduced under section 434A(2)(b); and

(ab) section 75(1) shall have effect with the substitution for "in computing profits apart from this section" of—

"(a) in computing income for the purposes of Schedule A, or

(b) by virtue of section 121(3) in computing income from the letting of rights to work minerals in the United Kingdom"; and".

Computation of losses and limitation on relief

2.—(1) In relation to accounting periods beginning on or after 1st January 1996 and ending after 31st March 1996, section 434A of the Taxes Act 1988 (life assurance business: computation of losses and limitation on relief) shall be amended as follows—

(a) for subsection (2) there shall be substituted the subsection (2) set out in sub-paragraph (2) below; and

(b) in subsection (2A) (which is inserted by paragraph 23(2) of Schedule 14 to this Act) for "(2)(c)" there shall be substituted "(2)(a)(ii)".

(2) The subsection (2) set out in this sub-paragraph is as follows—

"(2) Where for any accounting period the loss arising to an insurance company from its life assurance business falls to be computed in accordance with the provisions of this Act applicable to Case I of Schedule D—

(a) the loss resulting from the computation shall be reduced (but not below nil) by the aggregate of—

(i) the aggregate amount treated as a charge on income in computing for the period, otherwise than in accordance with those provisions, the profits or losses of the company's life assurance business; and

(ii) any relevant non-trading deficit for that period on the company's debtor relationships; and

(b) if the whole or any part of that loss as so reduced is set off—

(i) under section 393A, or

(ii) under section 403(1),

any losses for that period under section 436, 439B or 441 shall be reduced to nil, unless the aggregate of those losses exceeds the total of the amounts set off as mentioned in sub-paragraphs (i) and (ii) above, in which case each of those losses shall be reduced by an amount which bears to that total the proportion which the loss in question bears to that aggregate."

(3) In relation to accounting periods beginning on or after 1st January 1996 and ending on or before 31st March 1996, for subsection (2) of section 434A of the Taxes Act 1988 there shall be substituted the subsection (2) set out in sub-paragraph (2) above, but with the following amendments to paragraph (a), that is to say—

(a) in the words preceding sub-paragraph (i), the words "the aggregate of" shall be omitted;

(b) in sub-paragraph (i), for "aggregate amount treated as a charge on income" there shall be substituted "amount of interest and annuities treated as charges on income"; and

(c) sub-paragraph (ii) shall be omitted.

Spreading of relief for acquisition expenses

3.—(1) In section 86 of the Finance Act 1989 (spreading of relief for acquisition expenses) in subsection (1), for the words from "less any such repayments" to the end there shall be substituted—

"reduced by the items specified in subsection (1A) below."

(2) After that subsection there shall be inserted—

"(1A) Those items are—

(a) the appropriate portion of any deduction falling to be made under paragraph (aa) of subsection (1) of section 76 of the Taxes Act 1988 for the period in question;

(b) any such repayments or refunds falling within paragraph (c) of that subsection as are received in that period;

(c) any reinsurance commissions falling within paragraph (ca) of that subsection.

(1B) For the purposes of paragraph (a) of subsection (1A) above, "the appropriate portion" of the deduction there mentioned is the amount which bears to the whole of that deduction the proportion which the acquisition expenses, without making the reduction required by subsection (1) above, would bear to the whole of the expenses of management, without making the deductions required by paragraphs (aa), (a), (c) and (ca) of section 76(1) of the Taxes Act 1988."

Ascertainment of losses

4. In section 83 of the Finance Act 1989 (receipts to be brought into account) for subsection (3) (ascertainment of losses) there shall be substituted—

"(3) In ascertaining whether or to what extent a company has incurred a loss in respect of that business in a case where an amount is added to the company's long term business fund as part of or in connection with—

(a) a transfer of business to the company, or

(b) a demutualisation of the company not involving a transfer of business,

that amount shall (subject to subsection (4) below) be taken into account, for the period for which it is brought into account, as an increase in value of the assets of that fund within subsection (2)(b) above.

(4) Subsection (3) above does not apply where, or to the extent that, the amount concerned—

(a) would fall lo be taken into account as a receipt apart from this section,

(b) is taken into account under subsection (2) above otherwise than by virtue of subsection (3) above, or

(c) is specifically exempted from tax.

(5) Any amount which is to be taken into account pursuant to subsection (3) above for a period of account shall be so taken into account—

(a) after the making of any reduction under subsection (6) of section 83AA below in relation to that period, but

(b) before the making of any reduction under subsection (3) of that section in relation to an accounting period of the company ending in or with that period.

(6) In subsection (3) above "transfer of business" means—

(a) a transfer of the whole or part of the long term business of an insurance company in accordance with a scheme sanctioned by a court under Part I of Schedule 2C to the Insurance Companies Act 1982;

(b) a qualifying overseas transfer, within the meaning of paragraph 4A of Schedule 19AC to the Taxes Act 1988; or

(c) the making of a contract of reinsurance which, in whole or in part, constitutes or forms part of a total reinsurance by the reinsured, unless the reinsurer under the contract falls within section 439A of the Taxes Act 1988 (pure reinsurance).

(7) For the purposes of subsection (3)(a) above, a transfer of business falling within subsection (6)(c) above shall be treated as a transfer of business to the company which is the reinsurer under the contract of reinsurance.

(8) In this section—

"add", in relation to an amount and a company's long term business fund, includes transfer (whether from other assets of the company or otherwise);

"demutualisation" means the conversion, under the law of any territory, of a company which has been carrying on insurance business without having a share capital into a company with a share capital, without any change of legal personality;

"total reinsurance" means the reinsurance (whether effected by a single contract of reinsurance or by two or more such contracts, taken together, whether or not made with the same reinsurer) of the whole, or substantially the whole, of the reinsured's risk—

(a) under policies of a particular description issued in respect of insurances made in the course of carrying on life assurance business before the making of the contract of reinsurance (or, in a case where there are two or more contracts of reinsurance, the last of them); or

(b) under contracts of a particular description so made."

Application of surplus in reduction of certain losses

5. After section 83 of the Finance Act 1989 there shall be inserted—

"Amounts added to long-term business fund of a company in excess of that company's loss
83AA.—(1) If one or more relevant amounts are brought into account for a period of account of a company and either—

(a) the aggregate of those amounts exceeds the loss which, after the making of any reduction under subsection (6) below but before any application of section 83(3) above in relation to that period, would have arisen to the company in that period in respect of its life assurance business, or

(b) no such loss would have so arisen,

the surplus for that period shall be applied in accordance with the following provisions of this section and section 83AB below.

(2) In this section—

"relevant amount" means so much of any amount which is added to the long term business fund of a company as mentioned in subsection (3) of section 83 above as does not fall within any of the paragraphs of subsection (4) of that section;

"surplus", in relation to a period of account of a company, means (subject to section 83AB(2) below)—

(a) if the aggregate of the relevant amounts brought into account for that period exceeds the amount of any loss which, after the making of any reduction under subsection (6) below but before any application of section 83(3) above in relation to that period, would have arisen to the company in that period in respect of its life assurance business, the amount of the excess; or

(b) if no such loss would have so arisen, the aggregate of the relevant amounts brought into account for that period.

(3) Where, apart from section 83AB(2) below, there is a surplus for a period of account of a company for which there are brought into account one or more relevant amounts which were added to the company's long term business fund as part of, or in connection with, a particular transfer of business, the appropriate portion of the surplus for that period shall be treated as reducing (but not below nil) so much of any loss arising to the transferor company in the relevant accounting period as, on a just and reasonable apportionment of the loss, is referable to the business which is the subject of that particular transfer.

(4) For the purposes of subsection (3) above, the appropriate portion of the surplus for a period of account of a company is, in the case of any particular transfer of business, the amount which bears to that surplus (apart from any additions by virtue of section 83AB(2) below) the proportion which A bears to B, where—

A is the aggregate of such of the relevant amounts added to the company's long term business fund as part of, or in connection with, that particular transfer of business as are brought into account for that period, and

B is the aggregate of the relevant amounts brought into account for that period.

(5) Any reduction pursuant to subsection (3) above of the loss arising to the transferor company in the relevant accounting period shall be made after—

(a) the making of any reduction under subsection (6) below, and

(b) any application of section 83(3) above,

in relation to the period of account of that company in which falls the date of the particular transfer of business in question.

(6) Any loss arising to a company in respect of its life assurance business in a period of account subsequent to one for which there is a surplus shall be reduced (but not below nil) by so much of that surplus as cannot be applied—

(a) under subsection (3) above;

(b) under this subsection, in the reduction of a loss arising to the company in an earlier period of account; or

(c) under section 83AB below, in relation to a transfer of business from the company in that or any earlier period of account.

(7) Any reduction pursuant to subsection (6) above of a loss arising to a company in a period of account shall be made—

(a) before any application of section 83(3) above in relation to that period, and

(b) if the company is also the transferor company in relation to a particular transfer of business, before the making of any reduction under subsection (3) above in relation to that one of its accounting periods which is the relevant accounting period in relation to that transfer.

(8) A surplus in respect of an earlier period of account shall be applied under subsection (6) above before a surplus in respect of a later period of account.

(9) All such adjustments to the liability to tax of any person shall be made, whether by assessment or otherwise, as may be required to give effect to this section.

(10) In this section—

"add" has the same meaning as in section 83 above;

"the relevant accounting period" means the accounting period of the transferor company which—

(a) ends on the date of the transfer of business mentioned in subsection (3) above, or

(b) if that transfer of business falls with in section 83(6)(c) above and no accounting period of the transferor company ends on that date, ends next after that date;

"transfer of business" has the same meaning as in section 83(3) above;

"the transferor company" means the company from which the transfer of business mentioned in subsection (3) above is effected.

(11) A transfer of business falling within section 83(6)(c) above shall be treated for the purposes of this section as a transfer of business from the company which is the reinsured under the contract of reinsurance.

Treatment of surplus where there is a subsequent transfer of business from the company etc.

83AB.—(1) If an amount is added to the long term business fund of a company as part of or in connection with a transfer of business to the company, or a demutualisation of the company not involving a transfer of business, and—

(a) there is a surplus for the period of account of the company for which that amount is brought into account,

(b) at any time after the transfer of business or demutualisation, there is a transfer of business from the company (the "subsequent transfer"), and

(c) at the end of the relevant period of account there remains at least some of the surplus mentioned in paragraph (a) above which cannot be applied—

(i) under subsection (3) of section 83AA above,

(ii) under subsection (6) of that section, in the reduction of a loss arising to the company in an earlier period of account, or

(iii) under this section, in relation to an earlier subsequent transfer,

so much of the surplus falling within paragraph (c) above as, on a just and reasonable apportionment, is referable to business which is the subject of the subsequent transfer shall be applied under this section.

(2) An amount of surplus which is to be applied under this section shall be so applied by being treated as an amount of surplus (additional to any other amounts of surplus) for the period of account of the transferee company which last precedes the period of account of that company in which the subsequent transfer is effected, whether or not there is in fact any such preceding period of account.

(3) If, in a case where an amount is treated under subsection (2) above as an amount of surplus for a period of account of a company, the period is not one for which there is brought into account an amount added to the company's long term business fund in connection with the subsequent transfer, subsection (1) above shall have effect in relation to any transfer of business from the company subsequent to that transfer as if an amount had been so added and had been brought into account for that period.

(4) Any question as to what is a just and reasonable apportionment in any case for the purposes of subsection (1) above shall be determined by the Special Commissioners who shall determine the question in the same manner as they determine appeals; but any person

affected by the apportionment shall be entitled to appear and be heard or make representations in writing.

(5) A surplus in respect of an earlier period of account shall be applied under this section before a surplus in respect of a later period of account.

(6) All such adjustments to the liability to tax of any person shall be made, whether by assessment or otherwise, as may be required to give effect to this section.

(7) In this section—

"add" has the same meaning as in section 83 above;

"demutualisation" has the same meaning as in section 83 above;

"the relevant period of account" means the period of account of the company from which the subsequent transfer is effected which consists of or includes the accounting period of that company which—

(a) ends with the day on which the subsequent transfer is effected; or

(b) if the subsequent transfer is a transfer of business falling within section 83(6)(c) above and no accounting period of the company ends on that day, ends next after that day;

"surplus" has the same meaning as in section 83AA above;

"transfer of business" has the same meaning as in section 83(3) above;

"transferee company" means the company to which the subsequent transfer of business is effected.

(8) Where it is necessary for any purpose of this section to identify the time at which a demutualisation of a company takes place, that time shall be taken to be the time when the company first issues shares.

(9) A transfer of business falling within section 83(6)(c) above shall be treated for the purposes of this section as a transfer of business from the company which is the reinsured under the contract of reinsurance to the company which is the reinsurer under that contract."

Meaning of "brought into account" in sections 83AA and 83AB

6.—(1) In section 83A of the Finance Act 1989, in subsection (1) (meaning of "brought into account" in section 83)—

(a) for "In section 83" there shall be substituted "In sections 83 to 83AB"; and

(b) for "that section" there shall be substituted "those sections".

(2) In subsection (2) of that section (the accounts which are recognised for the purposes of that section) for "that section" there shall be substituted "those sections".

Enactments disapplying section 83(3) of the Finance Act 1989

7.—(1) The following provisions of the Taxes Act 1988 (each of which provides for section 83(3) of the Finance Act 1989 not to apply in certain cases) shall cease to have effect—

(a) section 436(3)(aa);

(b) section 439B(3)(b); and

(c) section 441(4)(aa).

(2) In consequence of sub-paragraph (1)(b) and (c) above, the word "and" shall be added at the end of section 439B(3)(a) and section 441 (4)(a) of the Taxes Act 1988.

Overseas life insurance companies

8.—(1) Schedule 8A to the Finance Act 1989 (modifications of sections 83 and 89 in relation to overseas life insurance companies) shall be amended in accordance with the following provisions of this paragraph.

(2) In the Heading "Modifications of sections 83 and 89 in relation to overseas life insurance companies" after "83" there shall be inserted "to 83A".

(3) In paragraph 1(1), for "sections 83 and 83A" there shall be substituted "sections 83 to 83A".

(4) In paragraph 1A, in sub-paragraph (4)—

(a) for the words from "being transferred" to "added to that fund" there shall be substituted "being added to the company's long term business fund"; and

(b) in the second sentence, for "a transfer" and "transferred" there shall be substituted respectively "an addition" and "added".

(5) After that sub-paragraph there shall be added—

"(5) Any reference in section 83AA(2), (3) or (4) or 83AB(1) or (3) to an amount being added to the relevant company's long term business fund shall be construed in accordance with sub-paragraph (4) above."

(6) In paragraph 1C(4), for "transfer" there shall be substituted "addition".

Transitional provisions

9.—(1) In the application of section 83AA or 83AB of the Finance Act 1989 in a case where one or more relevant amounts added to a company's long term business fund on or before 25th March 1996 are brought into account for a period of account beginning on or after 1st January 1996—

(a) the amount of any loss which, before any application of section 83(3) of that Act in relation to that period, would have arisen to the company in that period shall be treated as reduced (but not below nil) by the aggregate of those relevant amounts; and

(b) except as provided by paragraph (a) above, those relevant amounts shall be disregarded.

(2) In the application of sub-paragraph (1) above in relation to an overseas life insurance company, any reference to an amount added to a company's long term business fund shall be taken as a reference to any assets which became assets of the long term business fund of an overseas life insurance company used or held for the purposes of the company's United Kingdom branch or agency, having immediately previously been—

(a) held by the company otherwise than as assets of that fund, or

(b) used or held otherwise than for those purposes.

(3) If the relevant accounting period mentioned in subsection (3) of section 83AA of the Finance Act 1989 is a period beginning before 1st January 1996, only the appropriate portion of the eligible loss shall be reduced pursuant to that subsection; and for the purposes of this sub-paragraph—

(a) "the eligible loss" means so much of the loss arising to the transferor company in the relevant accounting period as, on a just and reasonable apportionment of the loss for the purposes of that subsection, is referable to the business which is the subject of the particular transfer of business in question; and

(b) "the appropriate portion" of the eligible loss is the amount which bears to the eligible loss the proportion which A bears to B where—

A is the number of days in the relevant accounting period which fall on or after 1st January 1996; and

B is the total number of days in the relevant accounting period.

(4) Paragraph 10(2) below shall not prevent—

(a) an amount of surplus for a period of account of a company beginning on or after 1st January 1996, or

(b) an amount of surplus for any period of account of a company which, by virtue of the operation of this sub-paragraph, derives from an amount of surplus falling within paragraph (a) above,

from being treated by virtue of section 83AB of the Finance Act 1989 as an amount of surplus for the period of account of another company last preceding its earliest period of account ending on or after 1st January 1996 (whenever beginning) or from being applied accordingly under section 83AA(6) or 83AB of that Act.

(5) In this paragraph—

"add" has the same meaning as in section 83 of the Finance Act 1989;

"brought into account" has the same meaning as it has in sections 83 to 83AB of that Act by virtue of section 83A of that Act;

"relevant amount" has the same meaning as in section 83AA of that Act;

"surplus" has the same meaning as in sections 83AA and 83AB of that Act.

Commencement

10.—(1) Subject to paragraph 2(1) and (3) above, paragraphs 1 to 3 above have effect in relation to accounting periods beginning on or after 1st January 1996.

(2) Subject to paragraph 9 above, paragraphs 4 to 8 above have effect in relation to periods of account beginning on or after 1st January 1996.

GENERAL NOTE

The Schedule modifies the provisions introduced in the FA 1995 regarding losses accruing to life assurance companies.

Para. 1

The rule that limits the amount of management expenses that a company can deduct from its income and gains is clarified. In particular, there are rules to determine how much of the management expenses that are reduced when a life assurance business loss is relieved consists of expenses incurred by the company in the acquisition of new business.

Para. 2
Losses on the whole of a company's life assurance business will, if set off against non-life profits or surrendered as group relief to other group companies, reduce the separately calculated losses arising on the company's pension business, overseas life assurance business or life reinsurance business.

Para. 3
Relief for acquisition expenses is spread forward over seven years.

Para. 4
The rule in the FA 1995 restricting losses incurred by life assurance companies is limited to cases where a transfer of funds arises in consequence of or as part of a transfer of business, including a transfer by way of reinsurance, or a demutualisation.

Para. 5
The new FA 1989, ss.83AA and 83AB, are designed to prevent "pre-funding", by providing that a cash injection may limit a loss for periods after that in which it is made, or of the accounting period of the transferor of business that ends with or after the transfer.

Paras. 6–10
These contain consequential amendments and transitional and commencement provisions [*Hansard*, H.C. Vol. 274, col. 1080].

Section 166   SCHEDULE 32

EQUALISATION RESERVES

1. In Chapter I of Part XII of the Taxes Act 1988 (insurance companies and capital redemption business), after section 444B there shall be inserted the following sections—

"*Equalisation reserves*

Equalisation reserves for general business
    444BA.—(1) Subject to the following provisions of this section and to sections 444BB to 444BD, the rules in subsection (2) below shall apply in making any computation, for the purposes of Case I or V of Schedule D, of the profits or losses for any accounting period of an insurance company whose business has at any time been or included business in respect of which it was required, by virtue of section 34A regulations, to maintain an equalisation reserve.
    (2) Those rules are—
    (a) that amounts which, in accordance with section 34A regulations, are transferred into the equalisation reserve in respect of the company's business for the accounting period in question are to be deductible;
    (b) that amounts which, in accordance with any such regulations, are transferred out of the reserve in respect of the company's business for that period are to be treated as receipts of that business; and
    (c) that it must be assumed that all such transfers as are required by section 34A regulations to be made into or out of the reserve in respect of the company's business for any period are made as required.
    (3) Where an insurance company having any business in respect of which it is required, by virtue of section 34A regulations, to maintain an equalisation reserve ceases to trade—
    (a) any balance which exists in the reserve at that time for the purposes of the Tax Acts shall be deemed to have been transferred out of the reserve immediately before the company ceases to trade; and
    (b) that transfer out shall be deemed to be a transfer in respect of the company's business for the accounting period in which the company so ceases and to have been required by section 34A regulations.
    (4) Where—
    (a) an amount is transferred into an equalisation reserve in respect of the business of an insurance company for any accounting period,
    (b) the rule in subsection (2)(a) above would apply to the transfer of that amount but for this subsection,
    (c) that company by notice in writing to an officer of the Board makes an election in relation to that amount for the purposes of this subsection, and

(d) the notice of the election is given not more than two years after the end of that period,

the rule mentioned in subsection (2)(a) above shall not apply to that transfer of that amount and, instead, the amount transferred (the 'unrelieved transfer') shall be carried forward for the purposes of subsection (5) below to the next accounting period and (subject to subsection (6) below) from accounting period to accounting period.

(5) Where—

(a) in accordance with section 34A regulations, a transfer is made out of an equalisation reserve in respect of an insurance company's business for any accounting period,

(b) the rule in subsection (2)(b) above would apply to the transfer but for this subsection, and

(c) the accounting period is one to which any amount representing one or more unrelieved transfers has been carried forward under subsection (4) above,

that rule mentioned in subsection (2)(b) above shall not apply to that transfer except to the extent (if any) that the amount of the transfer exceeds the aggregate of the amounts representing unrelieved transfers carried forward to that period.

(6) Where in the case of any company—

(a) any amount representing one or more unrelieved transfers is carried forward to an accounting period in accordance with subsection (4) above, and

(b) by virtue of subsection (5) above the rule in subsection (2)(b) above does not apply to an amount representing the whole or any part of any transfer out of an equalisation reserve in respect of the company's business for that period,

the amount mentioned in paragraph (a) above shall not be carried forward under subsection (4) above to the next accounting period except to the extent (if any) that it exceeds the amount mentioned in paragraph (b) above.

(7) To the extent that any actual or assumed transfer in accordance with section 34A regulations of any amount into an equalisation reserve is attributable to arrangements entered into wholly or mainly for tax purposes—

(a) the rule in subsection (2)(a) above shall not apply to that transfer; and

(b) the making of that transfer shall be disregarded in determining, for the purposes of the Tax Acts, whether and to what extent there is subsequently any requirement to make a transfer into or out of the reserve in accordance with section 34A regulations;

and this subsection applies irrespective of whether the insurance company in question is a party to the arrangements.

(8) For the purposes of this section the transfer of an amount into an equalisation reserve is attributable to arrangements entered into wholly or mainly for tax purposes to the extent that the arrangements to which it is attributable are arrangements—

(a) the sole or main purpose of which is, or

(b) the sole or main benefit accruing from which might (but for subsection (7) above) be expected to be,

the reduction by virtue of this section of any liability to tax.

(9) Where—

(a) any transfer made into or out of an equalisation reserve maintained by an insurance company is made in accordance with section 34A regulations in respect of business carried on by that company over a period ('the equalisation period'), and

(b) parts of the equalisation period are in different accounting periods,

the amount transferred shall be apportioned for the purposes of this section between the different accounting periods in the proportions that correspond to the number of days in the equalisation period that are included in each of those accounting periods.

(10) The Treasury may by regulations provide in relation to any accounting periods ending on or after 1st April 1996 for specified transitional provisions contained in section 34A regulations to be disregarded for the purposes of the Tax Acts in determining how much is required, on any occasion, to be transferred into or out of any equalisation reserve in accordance with the regulations.

(11) In this section and sections 444BB to 444BD 'section 34A regulations' means regulations made under section 34A of the Insurance Companies Act 1982 (equalisation reserves in respect of general business).

Modification of s. 444BA for mutual or overseas business and for non-resident companies

444BB.—(1) The Treasury may by regulations make provision modifying section 444BA so as, in cases mentioned in subsection (2) below—

(a) to require—

(i) sums by reference to which the amount of any transfer into or out of an equalisation reserve falls to be computed, or

(ii) the amount of any such transfer,

to be apportioned between different parts of the business carried on for any period by an insurance company; and

(b) to provide for the purposes of corporation tax for the amounts taken to be transferred into or out of an equalisation reserve to be computed disregarding any such sum or, as the case may be, any such part of a transfer as is attributed, in accordance with the regulations, to a part of the business described for the purpose in the regulations.

(2) Those cases are cases where an insurance company which, in accordance with section 34A regulations, is required to make transfers into or out of an equalisation reserve in respect of any business carried on by that company for any period is carrying on, for the whole or any part of that period—

(a) any business the income and gains of which fall to be disregarded in making a computation of the company's profits in accordance with the rules applicable to Case I of Schedule D, or

(b) any business by reference to which double taxation relief is afforded in respect of any income or gains.

(3) Section 444BA shall have effect (subject to any regulations under subsection (1) above) in the case of an equalisation reserve maintained by an insurance company which—

(a) is not resident in the United Kingdom, and

(b) carries on business in the United Kingdom through a branch or agency,

only if such conditions as may be prescribed by regulations made by the Treasury are satisfied in relation to that company and in relation to transfers into or out of that reserve.

(4) Regulations under this section prescribing conditions subject to which section 444BA is to apply in the case of any equalisation reserve maintained by an insurance company may—

(a) contain conditions imposing requirements on the company to furnish the Board with information with respect to any matters to which the regulations relate, or to produce to the Board documents or records relating to any such matters; and

(b) provide that, where any prescribed condition is not, or ceases to be, satisfied in relation to the company or in relation to transfers into or out of that reserve, there is to be deemed for the purposes of the Tax Acts to have been a transfer out of that reserve of an amount determined under the regulations.

(5) Regulations under this section may—

(a) provide for apportionments under the regulations to be made in such manner, and by reference to such factors, as may be specified or described in the regulations;

(b) make different provision for different cases;

(c) contain such supplementary, incidental, consequential and transitional provision as the Treasury may think fit;

(d) make provision having retrospective effect in relation to accounting periods beginning not more than one year before the time when the regulations are made;

and the powers conferred by this section in relation to transfers into or out of any reserve shall be exercisable in relation to both actual and assumed transfers.

(6) In this section 'double taxation relief' means—

(a) relief under double taxation arrangements which takes the form of a credit allowed against corporation tax, or

(b) unilateral relief under section 790(1) which takes that form;

and 'double taxation arrangements' here means arrangements having effect by virtue of section 788.

Modification of s. 444BA for non-annual accounting etc.

444BC.—(1) The Treasury may by regulations make provision modifying the operation of section 444BA in relation to cases where an insurance company has, for the purpose of preparing the documents it is required to prepare for the purposes of section 17 of the Insurance Companies Act 1982, applied for any period an accounting method described in paragraph 52 or 53 of Schedule 9A to the Companies Act 1985 (accounting on a non-annual basis).

(2) Subsection (5) of section 444BB applies for the purposes of this section as it applies for the purposes of that section.

Application of s. 444BA rules to other equalisation reserves

444BD.—(1) The Treasury may by regulations provide for section 444BA to have effect, in such cases and subject to such modifications as may be specified in the regulations, in relation to any equivalent reserves as it has effect in relation to equalisation reserves maintained by virtue of section 34A regulations.

(2) For the purposes of this section a reserve is an equivalent reserve if—
(a) it is maintained, otherwise than by virtue of section 34A regulations, either—
    (i) by an EC company carrying on business in the United Kingdom through a branch or agency, or
    (ii) in respect of any insurance business (within the meaning of the Insurance Companies Act 1982) which is carried on outside the United Kingdom by a company resident in the United Kingdom;
    and
(b) the purpose for which, or the manner in which, it is maintained is such as to make it equivalent to an equalisation reserve maintained by virtue of section 34A regulations.

(3) For the purposes of this section a reserve is also an equivalent reserve if it is maintained in respect of any credit insurance business in accordance with requirements imposed either—
(a) by or under any enactment, or
(b) under so much of the law of any territory as secures compliance with the requirements of Article 1 of the credit insurance directive (equalisation reserves for credit insurance).

(4) Without prejudice to the generality of subsection (1) above, the modifications made by virtue of that subsection may—
(a) provide for section 444BA to apply in the case of an equivalent reserve only where such conditions as may be specified in the regulations are satisfied in relation to the company maintaining the reserve or in relation to transfers made into or out of it; and
(b) contain any other provision corresponding to any provision which, in the case of a reserve maintained by virtue of section 34A regulations, may be made under sections 444BA to 444BC.

(5) Subsections (4) and (5) of section 444BB shall apply for the purposes of this section as they apply for the purposes of that section.

(6) Without prejudice to the generality of section 444BB(5), the transitional provision which by virtue of subsection (5) above may be contained in regulations under this section shall include—
(a) provision for treating the amount of any transfers made into or out of an equivalent reserve in respect of business carried on for any specified period as increased by the amount by which they would have been increased if no transfers into the reserve had been made in respect of business carried on for an earlier period; and
(b) provision for excluding from the rule in section 444BA(2)(b) so much of any amount transferred out of an equivalent reserve as represents, in pursuance of an apportionment made under the regulations, the transfer out of that reserve of amounts in respect of which there has been no entitlement to relief by virtue of section 444BA(2)(a).

(7) In this section—
    'credit insurance business' means any insurance business falling within general business class 14 of Schedule 2 to the Insurance Companies Act 1982 that is not reinsurance business;
    'the credit insurance directive' means Council Directive 87/343/EEC of 22nd June 1987 amending, as regards credit insurance and suretyship insurance, First Directive 73/239 on the coordination of laws, regulations and administrative provisions relating to the taking-up and pursuit of the business of direct insurance other than life assurance; and
    'EC company' has the same meaning as in the Insurance Companies Act 1982."

2. In the second column of the Table in section 98 of the Taxes Management Act 1970 (penalties in respect of certain information provisions), after the entry relating to regulations under section 431E(1) or 441A(3) of the Taxes Act 1988 there shall be inserted the following entries—
"regulations under section 444BB;
regulations under section 444BD;".

GENERAL NOTE

The Schedule makes tax provision for a new system of equalisation reserves which insurance companies will be required to maintain under DTI regulations, effective for accounting periods ending on or after December 23, 1996.

Para. 1

This introduces the new ICTA 1988, ss.444BA–BD.
The new s.444BA has the following main provisions:

(i) transfers into equalisation reserves will be treated as deductions from profits and transfers out will be taxed as receipts (subs. (2));

(ii) if an insurer which maintains an equalisation reserve ceases to trade, any balance on the reserve will be added to profits in the year of cessation (subs. (3));

(iii) companies may elect not to take full relief for amounts transferred to equalisation reserve. In such a case the unrelieved amount will not be charged to tax on a transfer out (subss. (4)–(6));

(iv) an anti-avoidance provision prevents relief where there are arrangements involving equalisation reserves entered into wholly or mainly for tax purposes.

The new s.444BB empowers the Treasury to make regulations covering special cases, such as companies operating through overseas branches, insurers operating part of their business on a mutual basis and non-resident companies operating through branches in the U.K.

The new s.444BC empowers the Treasury to make regulations to lay down detailed rules for insurers who use recognised forms of non-annual accounting.

The new s.444BD empowers the Treasury to make regulations allowing companies which are not subject to the new DTI supervisory rules to obtain relief on equalisation reserves if they voluntarily maintain these. These could include companies operating in the U.K. through a branch on the strength of an authorisation from another country in the EEA and companies resident in the U.K. for tax purposes but carrying on all their business abroad.

Regulations may also give tax relief for transfers into equalisation reserves maintained for credit insurance business, which is subject to EEC rules. Since the requirement to maintain equalisation reserves for credit insurance business pre-dates the tax relief scheme, the powers extend to making appropriate transitional arrangements.

Section 168   SCHEDULE 33

MANAGEMENT EXPENSES OF CAPITAL REDEMPTION BUSINESS

Amendment of section 76 of Taxes Act

1.—(1) In section 76 of the Taxes Act 1988 (management expenses of companies carrying on life assurance business), after subsection (5) there shall be inserted the following subsection—

"(5A) In the preceding provisions of this section references to life assurance business and references to basic life assurance and general annuity business shall be deemed, in each case, to include references to capital redemption business."

(2) In subsection (6) of that section, at the end there shall be inserted "or to any capital redemption business carried on by the company at or through that branch or agency."

(3) In subsection (8) of that section, before the definition of "investment business" there shall be inserted the following definition—

" 'capital redemption business' means any capital redemption business, within the meaning of section 458, which is business to which that section applies;".

Treatment of capital redemption business

2. In subsection (1) of section 458 of the Taxes Act 1988 (capital redemption business), at the end there shall be inserted "and where section 76 applies by virtue of subsection (5A) of that section, it shall apply separately to capital redemption business".

Overseas life insurance companies

3. In sub-paragraph (1) of paragraph 5 of Schedule 19AC to the Taxes Act 1988 (modification of section 76), at the end of paragraph (a) of the subsection (6A) which is treated as inserted by that sub-paragraph there shall be inserted "or capital redemption business".

Commencement

4. This Schedule has effect as respects accounting periods ending on or after the day appointed under section 199 of the Finance Act 1994 for the purposes of Chapter III of Part IV of that Act (self-assessment management provisions).

GENERAL NOTE

The Schedule makes amendments to the existing rules relating to management expenses of life assurance business so that they also apply to capital redemption business. It enacts concessions and will come into force when self-assessment for companies begins.

SCHEDULE 34

PROVISIONAL REPAYMENTS IN CONNECTION WITH PENSION BUSINESS

PART I

AMENDMENTS OF SCHEDULE 19AB TO THE TAXES ACT 1988

1.—(1) Paragraph 1 (entitlement to certain payments on account) shall be amended in accordance with the following provisions of this paragraph.

(2) In sub-paragraph (1) (entitlement to payment of an amount equal to the aggregate there mentioned) after "equal" there shall be inserted ", subject to paragraph 2 below,".

(3) For sub-paragraphs (3) and (4) (ascertainment of the "provisional fraction") there shall be substituted—

"(3) In the application of subsections (5) to (9) of section 432A for the purpose of determining the amounts to which a company is entitled by way of provisional repayments in the case of any accounting period of the company, the reference in subsection (5) to "the relevant fraction" shall be taken as a reference to the provisional fraction for that accounting period.

(4) For the purposes of this paragraph—
(a) the provisional fraction for an accounting period of a company is the fraction which would, on the basis of the company's latest section 11 return, be the relevant fraction for the purposes of section 432A(5) for the accounting period to which that return relates; but
(b) if there is no section 11 return on the basis of which that fraction can be ascertained, the provisional fraction shall be taken to be nil;
but this sub-paragraph is subject to paragraph 2 below."

(4) In sub-paragraph (5) (meaning of "the appropriate portion") in paragraph (b) (company carrying on more than one category of long term business) for sub-paragraph (ii) (income arising from assets not linked to pension business) there shall be substituted—

"(ii) if and to the extent that the payment or distribution in question is income which is not referable to a category of business by virtue of subsection (3) or (4) of section 432A, the provisional fraction; and

(iii) except as provided by sub-paragraph (i) or (ii) above, none."

(5) For sub-paragraph (6) (inspector not to give effect to claim unless he is satisfied he has been given sufficient information) there shall be substituted—

"(6) Section 42 of the Management Act (claims) shall not apply to a claim for a provisional repayment.

(6A) A claim for a provisional repayment shall be in such form as the Board may determine and the form of claim shall provide for a declaration to the effect that all the particulars given in the form are correctly stated to the best of the knowledge and belief of the person making the claim."

(6) For sub-paragraph (7) (provisional repayments to be treated as payments on account of certain payments or repayments which will eventually fall to be made in respect of income tax and tax credits) there shall be substituted—

"(7) A provisional repayment for a provisional repayment period shall be regarded as a payment on account of the amounts (if any) which the company would, apart from this Schedule, be entitled to be paid or repaid in respect of its pension business for the accounting period in which that provisional repayment period falls, in respect of—
(a) income tax borne by deduction on payments received by the company in that accounting period and referable to its pension business, and
(b) tax credits in respect of distributions received by the company in that accounting period and referable to its pension business,
on a claim such as is mentioned in section 7 of this Act or section 42(4) of the Management Act in respect of that accounting period."

(7) Sub-paragraph (8) (which relates to any case where an election is made under section 438(6) as respects franked investment income and which, having regard to amendments made by this Schedule, is unnecessary) shall cease to have effect.

(8) For sub-paragraph (10) (definitions) there shall be substituted—
"(10) In this paragraph—
"latest section 11 return", in the case of an accounting period of a company ("the current accounting period"), means, subject to sub-paragraph (11) below, the section 11 return for the latest preceding accounting period of the company for which such a return has been delivered before the making of the first claim for a provisional repayment for the current accounting period;

"section 11 return", in the case of any company, means a return delivered by the company pursuant to section 11 of the Management Act and includes a reference to any accounts, statements or reports delivered pursuant to that section together with the return;

"self-assessment" means an assessment included in a return under section 11 of the Management Act by virtue of section 11AA of that Act and includes a reference to such an assessment as amended under section 11AA(2) or 28A(3) or (4) of that Act.

(11) In any case where—

(a) there is a section 11 return which would, apart from this sub-paragraph, be the latest section 11 return in the case of an accounting period of a company,

(b) the self-assessment required to be included in that return pursuant to section 11AA of the Management Act has been amended under section 11AA(2) or 28A(3) or (4) of that Act, and

(c) that amendment was made before the making of the first claim for a provisional repayment for the accounting period mentioned in paragraph (a) above,

the return which is to be regarded as the latest section 11 return in the case of that accounting period shall be that return as it stands amended immediately after the making of that amendment of the self-assessment (or, if the self-assessment has been so amended more than once, that return as it stands amended immediately after the making of the last such amendment) but ignoring amendments which do not give rise to any change in the fraction which, on the basis of the return as it has effect from time to time, would be the relevant fraction for the purposes of section 432A(5) for the accounting period to which the return relates."

2.—(1) Paragraph 2 (changes in the provisional fraction) shall be amended in accordance with the following provisions of this paragraph.

(2) For sub-paragraphs (1) and (2) (cases where the paragraph applies, and consequences of its application) there shall be substituted—

"(1) This paragraph applies in any case where—

(a) a claim has been made for a provisional repayment for at least one provisional repayment period in an accounting period of a company;

(b) subsequently, a further such claim is made for a provisional repayment period falling within that accounting period; and

(c) had that further claim been the first claim made for a provisional repayment for that accounting period, the provisional fraction for the accounting period would have been a different fraction (whether in consequence of the delivery of a section 11 return for a later preceding accounting period or the application of paragraph 1(11) above);

and in this paragraph the "substituted provisional fraction" means the different fraction mentioned in paragraph (c) above.

(2) Where this paragraph applies—

(a) the amount of any provisional repayment to which the company is entitled for the provisional repayment period mentioned in sub-paragraph (1)(b) above shall be an amount determined in accordance with sub-paragraph (3) below or such lesser amount as may be specified in the claim; and

(b) in relation to any later provisional repayment period in the same accounting period, the substituted provisional fraction shall, subject to any further application of this paragraph, be treated as the provisional fraction for the accounting period."

(3) In sub-paragraph (3), in the definition of "total entitlement", for the words following paragraph (b) there shall be substituted—

"had the substituted provisional fraction been the provisional fraction for the accounting period as from the beginning of that period; and".

3.—(1) Paragraph 3 (repayment, with interest, of excessive provisional repayments) shall be amended in accordance with the following provisions of this paragraph.

(2) In sub-paragraph (1), for paragraphs (a) and (b) (which respectively refer to the company's assessment to corporation tax being finally determined and the amount referred to in paragraph 1(7)) there shall be substituted—

"(a) an insurance company's self-assessment for an accounting period becomes final, and

(b) the aggregate amount of the provisional repayments made to the company for that accounting period exceeds the appropriate amount,".

(3) After that sub-paragraph there shall be inserted—

"(1A) For the purposes of sub-paragraph (1)(b) above, the appropriate amount for an accounting period of a company is the amount (if any) which, on the assumptions in sub-paragraphs (1B) and (1C) below and disregarding any provisional repayments, the company would be entitled to be paid or repaid, when its self-assessment for the period becomes final, in respect of its pension business for that accounting period on a claim such as is mentioned in section 7 of this Act or section 42(4) of the Management Act in respect of—

(a) income tax borne by deduction on payments received by the company in that accounting period and referable to its pension business, and

(b) tax credits in respect of distributions received by the company in that accounting period and referable to its pension business.

(1B) The first assumption is that no payments or repayments have been made to the company in respect of—

(a) income tax such as is mentioned in paragraph (a) of sub-paragraph (1A) above, or

(b) tax credits such as are mentioned in paragraph (b) of that sub-paragraph,

before the company's self-assessment for the accounting period in question becomes final.

(1C) The second assumption is that in making any set off under—

(a) section 7(2),

(b) paragraph 5 of Schedule 16, or

(c) regulations made by virtue of section 51B,

income tax borne by deduction on income which is not referable to pension business is set off before income tax so borne on income which is referable to pension business.

(1D) In its application by sub-paragraph (1) above, section 30 of the Management Act shall have effect as if, instead of the provision made by subsection (5), it provided that an assessment under that section by virtue of sub-paragraph (1) above is not out of time under section 34 of that Act if it is made no later than the end of the accounting period following that in which the self-assessment mentioned in paragraph (a) of that sub-paragraph becomes final."

(4) In sub-paragraph (3) (application of section 87A of the Taxes Management Act 1970) in paragraph (b) (which provides for the specified words in subsection (1) of that section to be disregarded) for " "(in accordance with section 10 of the principal Act)" " there shall be substituted " "(in accordance with section 59D of this Act)" ".

(5) In sub-paragraph (4) (amount of principal outstanding to be determined in accordance with sub-paragraphs (5) to (7)) for "(7)" there shall be substituted "(8)".

(6) After sub-paragraph (7) there shall be added—

"(8) For the purposes of sub-paragraph (7) above, any repayment made by the company in respect of an amount paid or repaid to it in respect of—

(a) income tax such as is mentioned in paragraph (a) of sub-paragraph (1A) above, or

(b) tax credits such as are mentioned in paragraph (b) of that sub-paragraph,

shall be treated as a repayment in respect of the principal, taking an earlier such repayment by the company before a later.

(9) In this paragraph "self-assessment" means an assessment included in a return under section 11 of the Management Act by virtue of section 11AA of that Act and includes a reference to such an assessment as amended."

4.—(1) Paragraph 6 (interpretation) shall be amended in accordance with the following provisions of this paragraph.

(2) In sub-paragraph (1), for the definition of "provisional fraction" there shall be substituted—

" "provisional fraction" shall be construed in accordance with paragraphs 1(4) and 2 above;".

(3) Sub-paragraph (3) (which makes transitional provision for cases where an insurance company has not made a return under section 11 of the Taxes Management Act 1970 as amended by section 82 of the Finance (No. 2) Act 1987) shall cease to have effect.

(4) After that sub-paragraph there shall be added—

"(4) Sub-paragraph (5) below applies in any case where an insurance company—

(a) which has delivered a return under section 11 of the Management Act for an accounting period ending before the self-assessment appointed day, but

(b) which has not delivered its first return under that section for an accounting period ending on or after that day,

makes the first claim for a provisional repayment for a particular accounting period ending on or after that day.

(5) Where this sub-paragraph applies—

(a) the provisional fraction for the accounting period to which the claim mentioned in sub-paragraph (4) above relates shall be determined in accordance with paragraph

1(3), (4), and (6) and sub-paragraph (3) above, as they have effect in relation to accounting periods ending before that day; and

(b) paragraph 2 above, as originally enacted, shall have effect in relation to that accounting period as it has effect in relation to accounting periods ending before that day.

(6) In this paragraph "the self-assessment appointed day" means the day appointed under section 199 of the Finance Act 1994 for the purposes of Chapter III of Part IV of that Act (self-assessment management provisions)."

PART II

AMENDMENTS OF SCHEDULE 19AC TO THE TAXES ACT 1988

5.—(1) Paragraph 15 (modification of Schedule 19AB) shall be amended in accordance with the following provisions of this paragraph.

(2) Sub-paragraph (1) (which relates to paragraph 1(8) of Schedule 19AB) shall cease to have effect.

(3) At the end there shall be added—

"(3) In paragraph 3(1C) of Schedule 19AB, for paragraph (a) there shall be substituted—
"(a) section 11(3),"."

GENERAL NOTE

This amends various provisions of the ICTA 1988, Scheds. 19AB and 19AC, to comply with the self-assessment system for companies.

Part I deals with the amendments to Sched. 19AB.

Para. 1

The important changes made by this paragraph are:

(i) the fraction used to estimate how much of a company's income relates to its pension business will no longer be one with which the inspector needs to be satisfied, but the one shown in the company's most recent return and self-assessment;

(ii) the procedural rules on claims applying under self-assessment will not apply to claims under Sched. 19AB, because they are inappropriate, but a power is retained to prescribe the forms to be used. There is a clear statement that provisional repayments are on account of repayments ultimately due to the company when it makes its self-assessment return or as a result of subsequent amendments;

(iii) there are rules setting out what is meant by the latest return, particularly where the return and self-assessment has been amended.

Para. 2

The changes made reflect the change in the way the appropriate fraction is determined under para. 1.

Para. 3

The main change is that the new paragraph sets out more fully and clearly how excess repayments are calculated and what asssumptions are required to be made when calculating them. The changes also allow the time limit for recovering tax and interest on excess repayments to fit in with self-assessment procedures.

Para. 4

During the transition between Pay and File and self-assessment, claims may use a fraction calculated in accordance with the existing rules until there is a fraction that can be determined under self-assessment rules.

Part II deals with the amendments to Sched. 19AC. That Schedule contains the general modifications of the legislation relating to life assurance business which apply where the company concerned is a non-resident company trading in the U.K. through a branch.

Para. 5

This amends Sched. 19AC, para. 15, by deleting one subparagraph and inserting another. Both of these are consequential to the main changes.

SCHEDULE 35

ROLL-OVER RELIEF IN RESPECT OF SHIPS

Preliminary

1. The Capital Allowances Act 1990 shall be amended as follows.

Amendment of provisions relating to roll-over relief in respect of ships

2.—(1) In subsection (3) of section 33A (relief limited to expenditure on new shipping incurred or to be incurred by the shipowner), for paragraph (b) there shall be substituted the following paragraph—

"(b) the amount of any expenditure incurred or to be incurred by qualifying persons in the period of six years beginning with the day on which the event mentioned in subsection (1)(b) above occurs, so far as that expenditure is, or (when incurred) will be expenditure to which an addition made under this section in respect of that event may be attributed in accordance with subsection (5) below;".

(2) In subsection (4) of that section (relief not to apply where expenditure on new shipping not incurred by the shipowner within six years), for the words from the beginning of paragraph (b) onwards there shall be substituted the following—

"(b) circumstances arise in which the whole or any part of the addition ceases (otherwise than by being attributed) to be an amount that may be attributed, in accordance with subsection (5) below, to expenditure on new shipping incurred by qualifying persons in the period of six years mentioned in subsection (3)(b) above,

the shipowner shall be assumed not to have been entitled to so much of the addition as will not be so attributed."

(3) For subsection (5) of that section (attribution of relief to expenditure on new shipping) there shall be substituted the following subsections—

"(5) Subject to subsection (5A) below and to section 33D(6), where—

(a) an addition is made under this section to the shipowner's qualifying expenditure for the relevant period in respect of his actual trade, and

(b) expenditure on new shipping is incurred by a qualifying person in the period of six years mentioned in subsection (3)(b) above,

the shipowner may, by notice to an officer of the Board, attribute to that expenditure so much of the addition as is equal to so much of the expenditure as is not already the subject of an attribution under this subsection.

(5A) A notice under subsection (5) above shall not have effect in a case where the shipowner and the qualifying person to whose expenditure the notice relates are not the same person unless that person joins with the shipowner in the giving of that notice."

(4) After subsection (7) of that section there shall be inserted the following subsection—

"(8) In this section and the following provisions of this Chapter references to a qualifying person, in relation to any expenditure, are references to—

(a) the shipowner; and

(b) where the shipowner is a company, any company which, at the time when the expenditure is or is to be incurred, is or (as the case may be) would be a member of the same group of companies as the shipowner;

and for the purposes of this subsection two companies are members of the same group of companies at any time if, at that time, they are treated as members of the same group of companies for the purposes of Chapter IV of Part X of the principal Act (group relief)."

3.—(1) In subsection (1) of section 33C (re-imposition of deferred charge)—

(a) in paragraph (b), for "the shipowner" there shall be substituted "a qualifying person"; and

(b) for paragraph (c) there shall be substituted the following paragraph—

"(c) the expenditure is expenditure the whole or any part of which is expenditure to which the whole or any part of the addition is attributed in accordance with section 33A(5)."

(2) In subsection (2) of that section—

(a) the words "to be", in the first place where they occur, shall be omitted; and

(b) in paragraph (b), for "the shipowner" there shall be substituted "the qualifying person in question".

4.—(1) In section 33D (definition of expenditure on new shipping), in subsection (1)—

(a) in paragraph (a), for "the shipowner's actual trade" there shall be substituted "a trade carried on by the person who incurs that expenditure"; and

(b) in paragraph (b), for "the shipowner" there shall be substituted "that person".

(2) In subsection (2) of that section—

(a) in paragraph (a), for "the shipowner" there shall be substituted "the person who incurred the expenditure"; and

(b) in paragraph (c)(ii), for "the shipowner" there shall be substituted "the person who incurred the expenditure".

(3) After subsection (2) of that section there shall be inserted the following subsections—

"(2A) Subject to subsection (2B) below, expenditure incurred by a qualifying person other than the shipowner on the provision of a ship shall not be, and shall be deemed never to have been, expenditure on new shipping if—

(a) at any time after the time when the ship first belongs to that person in consequence of that expenditure, it ceases to belong to that person without having been brought into use for the purposes of a trade of that person;

(b) the ship is brought into use for the purposes of a trade of that person and an event falling within section 24(6)(c) occurs with respect to the ship before the end of the period of three years beginning with the time when it is first so brought into use; or

(c) there is a time falling—
(i) after the expenditure is incurred, and
(ii) where the ship is brought into use for the purposes of a trade of that person, before the end of the period of three years beginning with the time when it is first so brought into use,

when the shipowner and that person do not fall to be treated as members of the same group of companies for the purposes of Chapter IV of Part X of the principal Act (group relief).

(2B) Subsection (2A) above shall not apply by virtue of paragraph (a) or (b) of that subsection in any case if the event by virtue of which the case falls within that paragraph is, or is the result of—

(a) the total loss of the ship; or

(b) damage to the ship that puts it in a condition in which it is impossible, or not commercially worthwhile, for the repair required for restoring it to its previous use to be undertaken;

and that subsection shall have effect, where anything falling within paragraph (a) or (b) above occurs, as if times falling after the occurrence of the total loss or, as the case may be, after the occurrence of the damage were to be disregarded for the purposes of paragraph (c) of that subsection."

(4) In subsection (4) of that section—

(a) in paragraphs (a) and (b), for the words "the shipowner", in each place where they occur, there shall be substituted "the person who incurred the expenditure"; and

(b) in paragraph (c)(i), for "the shipowner's actual trade" there shall be substituted "a trade carried on by the person who incurred that expenditure".

(5) In subsection (6) of that section, for "by the shipowner" there shall be substituted "by a qualifying person".

(6) In subsection (7) of that section—

(a) for "any trade previously carried on by the shipowner" there shall be substituted "the shipowner's actual trade"; and

(b) in paragraph (a), for the words "by the persons for the time being carrying on that trade" there shall be substituted "for the purposes of that trade by the persons for the time being carrying it on".

(7) For subsection (8) of that section there shall be substituted the following subsection—

"(8) For the purposes of this section a person is connected with another person at any time if, at that time—

(a) he is, within the terms of section 839 of the principal Act, connected either with that other person or with a person who is connected with that other person by virtue of paragraph (b) below; or

(b) he is carrying on a trade previously carried on by that other person in a case in which the only changes in the persons engaged in carrying on that trade between—
(i) the time when it was previously carried on by that other person, and
(ii) the time in question,

are changes in respect of which the trade is to be treated by virtue of section 113(2) or 343(2) of the principal Act as not having been discontinued;

and the persons who shall be taken for the purposes of this section, in relation to expenditure incurred by a person who is not the shipowner, to be connected at any time with the person by whom the expenditure is or has been incurred shall include every person who at that time is connected (in accordance with the preceding provisions of this subsection) with the shipowner."

5.—(1) In section 33E (definition of a qualifying ship), after subsection (8) there shall be inserted the following subsection—

"(9) Subsections (5), (6) and (8) above shall have effect for the purposes of section 33D in relation to any ship on the provision of which expenditure is incurred on or after the passing of the Finance Act 1996 as if the references in those subsections to the shipowner included references to the person incurring that expenditure."

6.—(1) In section 33F (procedural provisions), in subsection (4)—

(a) for "An attribution made for the purposes of section 33A(5) or 33C" there shall be substituted "Subject to subsection (4A) below, an attribution in accordance with section 33A (5)"; and

(b) for "the person giving the notice" there shall be substituted "the shipowner".

(2) After that subsection there shall be inserted the following subsection—

"(4A) A notice by the shipowner under subsection (4) above shall not have effect in a case where the shipowner and the qualifying person to whose expenditure the notice relates are not the same person unless that person joins with the shipowner in the giving of that notice."

Commencement

7.—(1) Subject to sub-paragraph (2) below, this Schedule shall have effect in relation to any case in which the event mentioned in section 33A(1)(b) occurs on or after the day on which this Act is passed.

(2) Subject to sub-paragraph (3) below, this Schedule shall not apply for the purposes of claims, assessments and adjustments made on or after the day on which this Act is passed but before such day as the Treasury may by order appoint.

(3) Sub-paragraph (2) above shall not prevent the making on or after the day appointed under that sub-paragraph of any claims, assessments or adjustments in respect of the application of this Schedule, in accordance with sub-paragraph (1) above, in relation to times before that day; and nothing in any provision relating to the period within which any claim or assessment must be made shall prevent any such claim, assessment or adjustment from being made by reference to this Schedule if it is made no more than twelve months after the day so appointed.

GENERAL NOTE

The Schedule introduces amendments to the Capital Allowances Act 1990 (c. 1) so as to extend rollover relief for balancing charges arising on ships across groups of companies. The provision for deferment of balancing charges on ship disposals (commonly referred to as "rollover relief for balancing charges") was introduced by the FA 1995, ss.94–98.

Under the amendments, a company will be able to defer a balancing charge arising on the disposal of a qualifying ship and set it against the cost of new shipping bought by that company or other members of the group within the following six years. Ships bought by other members of the group will have to remain in the ownership of that other company and that company remain a member of the group for three years after the acquisition in order to qualify for the relief.

The new provisions will operate from a day to be appointed by the Treasury and will then apply to balancing charges arising on or after April 29, 1996, when the Finance Bill was passed [*Hansard*, H.C. Vol. 274, col. 1083].

Section 182   SCHEDULE 36

CONTROLLED FOREIGN COMPANIES

1.—(1) Section 747A of the Taxes Act 1988 (special rule for computing chargeable profits: currency) shall be amended as follows.

(2) Subsection (7) (first relevant accounting period of a trading company where subsection (6) does not apply) shall be omitted.

(3) In subsection (8) (first relevant accounting period of a company which is not a trading company)—

(a) the words "the company is not a trading company and" shall be omitted;

(b) for "its", where first occurring, there shall be substituted "the company's"; and

(c) after paragraph (b) (cases where direction under section 747 would have been given had the company not pursued an acceptable distribution policy) there shall be added—

"unless the company is a trading company, in which case paragraph (b) above shall be disregarded in the case of its accounting periods beginning before 28th November 1995."

2. In section 748(3) of the Taxes Act 1988 (direction under section 747(1) not to be given in cases where reduction in United Kingdom tax was not the main purpose etc) in paragraph (a), for "or any two or more of those transactions taken together" there shall be substituted "or any two or more transactions taken together, the results of at least one of which are so reflected,".

3.—(1) Schedule 24 to the Taxes Act 1988 (assumptions for calculating chargeable profits etc) shall be amended in accordance with the following provisions of this paragraph.

(2) In paragraph 1 (general) after sub-paragraph (3) there shall be inserted—

"(3A) In any case where—

(a) it is at any time necessary for any purpose of Chapter IV of Part XVII to determine the chargeable profits of the company for an accounting period, and

(b) at that time—

(i) no direction has been given under section 747(1) with respect to that or any earlier accounting period of the company, and

(ii) it has not been established that that or any earlier accounting period of the company is an ADP exempt period,

in determining the chargeable profits of the company for the accounting period mentioned in paragraph (a) above it shall be assumed, for the purpose of any of the following provisions of this Schedule which refer to the first accounting period in respect of which a direction is given under section 747(1) or which is an ADP exempt period, that that period (but not any earlier period) is an accounting period in respect of which such a direction is given or which is an ADP exempt period."

(3) After sub-paragraph (5) of that paragraph there shall be inserted—

"(6) Any reference in this Schedule to an "ADP exempt period", in the case of any company, is a reference to an accounting period of the company—

(a) which begins on or after 28th November 1995; and

(b) in respect of which the company pursued, within the meaning of Part I of Schedule 25, an acceptable distribution policy."

(4) In paragraph 2(1) (company assumed to have become resident in the United Kingdom at the beginning of the first accounting period in respect of which a direction is given under section 747(1) and to have continued so resident etc) for "in respect of which a direction is given under section 747(1) and" there shall be substituted—

"(a) in respect of which a direction is given under section 747(1), or

(b) which is an ADP exempt period,

and".

(5) In paragraph 4 (maximum reliefs assumed to have been claimed etc unless notice requesting other treatment is given by UK resident company or companies with a majority interest) after sub-paragraph (1) there shall be inserted—

"(1A) Sub-paragraph (2) below applies to any accounting period of the company—

(a) in respect of which a direction is given under section 747(1); or

(b) which is an ADP exempt period."

(6) In sub-paragraph (2) of that paragraph (notice to be given not later than the expiry of the time for making an appeal under s.753 or within such longer period as the Board may allow)—

(a) at the beginning there shall be inserted "Where this sub-paragraph applies to an accounting period of the company, then"; and

(b) for "the time for the making of an appeal under section 753" there shall be substituted "the appropriate period".

(7) After that sub-paragraph there shall be inserted—

"(2A) For the purposes of sub-paragraph (2) above, "the appropriate period"—

(a) in the case of an accounting period in respect of which a direction is given under section 747(1), means the time for the making of an appeal under section 753; and

(b) in the case of an accounting period which is an ADP exempt period, means the period of twenty months following the end of the accounting period."

(8) After sub-paragraph (3) of that paragraph (which defines the UK resident company or companies with a majority interest) there shall be inserted—

"(3A) Sub-paragraph (3) above shall apply in relation to an accounting period which is an ADP exempt period as it would apply if—

(a) that accounting period had instead been one in respect of which a direction had been duly given under section 747(1), and

(b) such apportionments and assessments as are mentioned in sub-paragraph (3) above had been made."

(9) In paragraph 9(1)(c) (losses incurred in accounting periods in which, among other things, the company was not resident in the United Kingdom) after "was not resident" there shall be inserted ", and is not to be assumed by virtue of paragraph 2(1)(b) above to have been resident,".

(10) In paragraph 10 (capital allowances for expenditure incurred on machinery or plant before the first accounting period in respect of which a direction is given under section 747(1)) for "in respect of which a direction is given under section 747(1), the" there shall be substituted—

"(a) in respect of which a direction is given under section 747(1), or
(b) which is an ADP exempt period,
the".

(11) In paragraph 11 (write-down of allowances for certain years preceding the first for which a direction is given under section 747(1)) in sub-paragraph (2) (which defines the starting period as the first accounting period for which a direction is given and makes provision in respect of claims under paragraph 9(3)) for "in respect of which a direction is given under section 747(1) and" there shall be substituted—

"(a) in respect of which a direction is given under section 747(1), or
(b) which is an ADP exempt period,
and".

4.—(1) Schedule 25 to the Taxes Act 1988 (cases excluded from direction-making powers) shall be amended as follows.

(2) In paragraph 2 (acceptable distribution policy)—
(a) in sub-paragraph (1)(d) (amount of the dividend etc paid to persons resident in the United Kingdom) for "50 per cent. of the company's available profits" there shall be substituted "90 per cent. of the company's net chargeable profits";
(b) in sub-paragraph (6) (computation of appropriate portion of profits in cases where there are two classes of issued shares) in the definition of "X", for "available profits" there shall be substituted "net chargeable profits".

(3) In paragraph 2A (further provisions to determine whether a controlled foreign company which is not a trading company pursues an acceptable distribution policy)—
(a) in sub-paragraph (1) (application) the words "which is not a trading company" shall be omitted;
(b) in sub-paragraph (5)(c) (which modifies the definition of "X" in paragraph 2(6) for certain purposes) for "available profits" there shall be substituted "net chargeable profits";
(c) sub-paragraphs (6) and (7) (which are superseded by amendments made to paragraph 2 by this Schedule) shall be omitted.

(4) In paragraph 3 ("available profits" and "net chargeable profits" for purposes of Part I of the Schedule)—
(a) sub-paragraphs (1) to (4) (ascertainment of "available profits") shall be omitted;
(b) in sub-paragraph (5) (certain dividends to be left out of account in determining available profits or, where the company is not a trading company, chargeable profits) the words "the available profits or, where the company is not a trading company," shall be omitted.

(5) In paragraph 6 (exempt activities) in sub-paragraph (2)(b) (less than 50 per cent. of gross trading receipts from wholesale, distributive or financial business to be derived from connected or associated persons) after "connected or associated persons" there shall be added "or persons who have an interest in the company at any time during that accounting period."

(6) In paragraph 16(2) (reductions in United Kingdom tax: extended meaning of "transaction" in paragraphs 17 and 18)—
(a) in paragraph (a), after "transaction" there shall be inserted "the results of which are"; and
(b) in paragraph (b), for "two or more such transactions taken together" there shall be substituted "two or more transactions taken together, the results of at least one of which are so reflected".

GENERAL NOTE

The Schedule amends the treatment of controlled foreign companies (CFCs) for tax purposes in relation to accounting periods beginning on or after November 28, 1995.

Para. 1

This abolishes the distinction between trading and non-trading companies in calculating chargeable profits.

Para. 2

In applying the "motive test", where two or more transactions are considered together, the results of only one of them need be reflected in the CFC's profits.

Para. 3

This amends the ICTA 1988, Sched. 24, which sets out rules for calculating the chargeable profits of a CFC. The following changes are made:

(i) the same consequences apply to an ADP (acceptable distribution policy) exempt period, *i.e.* an accounting period beginning on or after November 28, 1995, in which the company pursued an ADP, as they do to a period in which a direction is given, for the purposes of calculating chargeable profits;

(ii) other provisions regarding definition of accounting periods and the assumptions in respect of claims are extended to ADP exempt period;

(iii) losses arising after an ADP exempt period may not be set off against profits which are subject to a later direction;

(iv) capital allowances for pre-ADP exempt periods may be utilised as they are for pre-direction periods, subject to the power of the Revenue to restrict them.

Para. 4

This amends the ICTA 1988, Sched. 25, which sets out the conditions under which companies are excluded from the Revenue's direction-making powers. The distinction between trading and non-trading companies for the ADP test is abolished. Also, the definition for the purposes of the exempt activities test of gross trading receipts from connected or associated persons is extended to include persons with an interest in the CFC [Standing Committee E, February 27, 1996, col. 533].

Section 198   SCHEDULE 37

BANKS

PART I

"BANK" RE-DEFINED FOR CERTAIN PURPOSES

1.—(1) After section 840 of the Taxes Act 1988 there shall be inserted the following section—

"Banks

840A.—(1) In any provision in relation to which it is provided that 'bank' has the meaning given by this section 'bank' means—

(a) the Bank of England;

(b) an institution authorised under the Banking Act 1987;

(c) a relevant European institution; or

(d) a relevant international organisation which is designated as a bank for the purposes of that provision by an order made by the Treasury.

(2) For the purposes of subsection (1) above, an institution is a relevant European institution if—

(a) it is a European authorised institution within the meaning of the Banking Co-ordination (Second Council Directive) Regulations 1992; and

(b) the requirements of paragraph 1 of Schedule 2 to those regulations have been complied with in relation to its establishment of a branch.

(3) For the purposes of subsection (1) above, a relevant international organisation is an international organisation of which the United Kingdom is a member."

(2) In section 828 of the Taxes Act 1988 (regulations and orders), in subsection (4), for "or 791" there shall be substituted "791 or 840A(1)(d)".

PART II

AMENDMENTS OF THE TAXES ACT 1988

Provisions in which new meaning of "bank" applies

2.—(1) The following subsection—

"( ) In this section 'bank' has the meaning given by section 840A.",

shall be inserted in the Taxes Act 1988 in accordance with sub-paragraph (2) below.

(2) The subsection shall be inserted—

(a) in section 234A (information relating to distributions), after subsection (8), as subsection (8A);

(b) in section 349 (payment of interest under deduction of tax, etc.), after subsection (3), as subsection (3AA);

(c) in section 745 (obligation to furnish information not to apply to banks), after subsection (5), as subsection (5A);

(d) in section 816 (obligation to disclose certain particulars to apply to banks), after subsection (3), as subsection (3A).

(3) In Schedule 20 to the Taxes Act 1988 (charities: qualifying investments and loans), in paragraph 7 (certain deposits with banks to be qualifying investments), after sub-paragraph (2), there shall be inserted the following sub-paragraph—

"(3) In this paragraph 'bank' has the meaning given by section 840A."

(4) The provisions of paragraph 10 of that Schedule shall become sub-paragraph (1) of that paragraph and after that sub-paragraph there shall be inserted the following sub-paragraph—

"(2) In this paragraph 'bank' has the meaning given by section 840A."

Related amendments

3. In section 349(3) of the Taxes Act 1988—
(a) in paragraph (a), for the words from "in the United Kingdom" to the end there shall be substituted "on an advance from a bank, if at the time when the interest is paid the person beneficially entitled to the interest is within the charge to corporation tax as respects the interest";
(b) in paragraph (b), for "such a bank in the ordinary course of that" there shall be substituted "a bank in the ordinary course of its".

4. After subsection (3AA) of section 349 of the Taxes Act 1988 (inserted by paragraph 2 above) there shall be inserted the following subsection—

"(3AB) An order under section 840A(1)(d) designating an organisation as a bank for the purposes of paragraph (a) of subsection (3) above may provide that that paragraph shall apply to the organisation as if the words from "if" to the end were omitted."

5. In Schedule 20 to the Taxes Act 1988, in paragraphs 7(1) and 10, for "an institution authorised under the Banking Act 1987" there shall in each case be substituted "a bank".

Application

6. The amendments of the Taxes Act 1988 made by paragraphs 2 to 5 above apply as mentioned in paragraphs 7 to 10 below.

7. The amendment of section 234A applies in relation to payments made on or after the day on which this Act is passed.

8.—(1) The amendment of subsection (3)(a) of section 349, and inserted subsection (3AA) of that section so far as it relates to subsection (3)(a), apply in accordance with sub-paragraphs (2) to (6) below.

(2) The amendments do not apply in relation to interest payable before the day on which this Act is passed.

(3) In the case of an institution which—
(a) immediately before the day on which this Act is passed, is treated for the purposes of section 349(3)(a) as a bank carrying on a bona fide banking business in the United Kingdom, and
(b) on that day, falls within the definition of "bank" given by section 840A(1),
the amendments apply in relation to interest payable on an advance made before that day as well as in relation to interest payable on an advance made on or after that day.

(4) In the case of an institution which—
(a) immediately before the day on which this Act is passed, is not treated for the purposes of section 349(3)(a) as a bank carrying on a bona fide banking business in the United Kingdom, and
(b) on that day, falls within the definition of "bank" given by section 840A(1),
the amendments apply only in relation to interest payable on an advance made on or after that day.

(5) Sub-paragraph (6) below applies in the case of an institution which—
(a) immediately before the day on which this Act is passed, is treated for the purposes of section 349(3)(a) as a bank carrying on a bona fide banking business in the United Kingdom; and
(b) on that day does not fall within the definition of "bank" given by section 840A(1).

(6) The amendments apply in relation to—
(a) interest payable on an advance made on or after the day on which this Act is passed; and
(b) interest payable on an advance made before that day, if at the time when the interest is paid the person beneficially entitled to the interest is not within the charge to corporation tax as respects the interest.

(7) The amendment of subsection (3)(b) of section 349, and inserted subsection (3AA) of that section so far as it relates to subsection (3)(b), apply in relation to interest paid on or after the day on which this Act is passed on an advance made on or after that day.

(8) In relation to interest paid on an advance made before the day on which this Act is passed, section 349(3)(b) shall have effect as if for the words "such a bank" there were substituted "a bank carrying on a bona fide banking business in the United Kingdom" (and section 349(3AA) shall be disregarded).

9. The amendments of sections 745 and 816 apply in relation to requirements imposed on or after the day on which this Act is passed.

10. The amendments of paragraphs 7 and 10 of Schedule 20 apply in relation to deposits made or, as the case may be, money placed on or after the day on which this Act is passed.

PART III

OTHER AMENDMENTS

Amendments of the Management Act

11.—(1) The following subsection—

"( ) In this section 'bank' has the meaning given by section 840A of the principal Act.", shall be inserted in the Taxes Management Act 1970 in accordance with sub-paragraph (2) below.

(2) The subsection shall be inserted—

(a) in section 17 (returns from banks etc.), after subsection (1), as subsection (1A);

(b) in section 18 (obligation to supply certain information not to apply to banks), after subsection (3), as subsection (3AA);

(c) in section 24 (obligation to disclose certain particulars not to apply to banks), after subsection (3), as subsection (3A).

(3) In section 17(1) of that Act, for "person carrying on the trade or business of banking" there shall be substituted "such person who is a bank".

(4) In section 18(3) of that Act for the words from "carrying on" to the end there shall be substituted "in respect of any interest paid by the bank in the ordinary course of its business".

(5) This paragraph applies as follows—

(a) the amendments of section 17 apply in relation to interest paid on or after the day on which this Act is passed; and

(b) the amendments of sections 18 and 24 apply in relation to requirements imposed on or after the day on which this Act is passed.

Amendments of the Inheritance Tax Act 1984

12.—(1) In section 157 of the Inheritance Tax Act 1984 (non-residents' bank accounts), in subsection (5), for "the Bank of England, the Post Office or an authorised institution" there shall be substituted "a bank or the Post Office".

(2) After that subsection there shall be inserted the following subsection—

"(6) In this section 'bank' has the meaning given by section 840A of the Taxes Act 1988."

(3) This paragraph applies in relation to deaths occurring on or after the day on which this Act is passed.

GENERAL NOTE

Part I

Para. 1
The new ICTA 1988, s.840A, provides a statutory definition of "bank". This definition adopts the same criteria used by the Bank of England for regulatory purposes.

Part II

Para. 2
This provides for the new definition to apply for the purposes of a range of provisions in the ICTA 1988.

Para. 3
This amends the ICTA 1988, s.349(3), which allows yearly interest to be paid without deduction of tax in certain circumstances when paid by a bank or payable on an advance from a bank. For the latter, the changes make it clear that gross payment is dependent on the recipient being within the charge to corporation tax in respect of the interest. In many cases, where the U.K. has a double tax agreement with the country concerned, the payer in the U.K. will be able to seek the Revenue's agreement to continue to make the payment gross.

Para. 4

The new ICTA 1988, s.349(3AB), allows interest to be paid gross on advances from designated international institutions.

Paras. 5–10

These make further consequential amendments and commencement provisions.

Part III

Paras. 11 and 12

These make consequential amendments for the purposes of the Taxes Management Act 1970 (c. 9) and the Inheritance Tax Act 1984 (c. 51) [Standing Committee E, February 29, 1996, col. 571].

Section 199   SCHEDULE 38

QUOTATION OR LISTING OF SECURITIES

The Finance Act 1973

1.—(1) In section 38(2)(c) of the Finance Act 1973 (disposals of exploration or exploitation rights to include disposals of shares deriving their value from such rights), for "quoted" there shall be substituted "listed".

(2) This paragraph has effect in relation to disposals of shares on or after 1st April 1996.

The Inheritance Tax Act 1984

2.—(1) For the second and the last occurrences of the word "quoted" in each of—

(a) sections 105(1ZA) and 113A(3B) of the Inheritance Tax Act 1984 (meaning of "quoted" etc.), and

(b) the paragraph in section 272 of that Act (general interpretation) which defines "quoted" and "unquoted",

there shall be substituted "listed".

(2) This paragraph has effect—

(a) in relation to transfers of value on or after 1st April 1996; and

(b) for the purposes of any charge to tax by reason of an event occurring on or after 1st April 1996, in relation to transfers of value before that date.

3.—(1) In section 180(3) of that Act (whether two investments are of the same description), for "quoted" there shall be substituted "listed".

(2) This paragraph has effect in relation to any time falling on or after 1st April 1996.

4.—(1) In section 178(2) of that Act (shares or investments whose quotation is suspended at time of death)—

(a) for "quotation" there shall be substituted "listing"; and

(b) for "quoted" there shall be substituted "so listed or dealt in".

(2) In section 186B(1) of that Act (shares or investments whose quotation is suspended at the end of the relevant period), for "quotation" there shall be substituted "listing".

(3) This paragraph has effect in relation to investments sold, or treated as sold, on or after 1st April 1996.

5.—(1) In each of sections 227(1AA) and 228(5) of that Act (meaning of "unquoted"), for the word "quoted" there shall be substituted "listed".

(2) This paragraph has effect—

(a) in relation to transfers of value on or after 1st April 1996; and

(b) for the purposes of any charge to tax by reason of an event occurring on or after 1st April 1996, in relation to transfers of value before that date.

The Taxes Act 1988

6.—(1) In each of the provisions of the Taxes Act 1988 listed in sub-paragraph (2) below, for "quoted" (wherever occurring) there shall be substituted "listed".

(2) The provisions referred to in sub-paragraph (1) above are—

(a) paragraph (b) of the definition of "quoted Eurobond" in section 124(6);

(b) section 209(2)(e)(ii);

(c) section 246S(3)(c) and (e);

(d) section 254(11);

(e) section 349(3A)(b);

(f) section 415(1)(b);

(g) section 477A(1A);

(h) section 576(4);

(j) paragraph 11(a) and (c) of Schedule 9;

(k) paragraph (c) of paragraph 1(5C) of Schedule 18;

(l) paragraph 5 of Schedule 20; and

(m) paragraph 13(2)(c) of Schedule 25.

(3) So far as relating to the provision mentioned in sub-paragraph (2)(a) above, sub-paragraph (1) above has effect in relation to any interest paid on a quoted Eurobond on or after 1st April 1996.

(4) So far as relating to the provision mentioned in sub-paragraph (2)(b) above, sub-paragraph (1) above has effect in relation to any interest paid or other distribution made on or after 1st April 1996.

(5) So far as relating to the provisions mentioned in sub-paragraph (2)(c) and (m) above, sub-paragraph (1) above has effect in relation to accounting periods ending on or after 1st April 1996.

(6) So far as relating to the provision mentioned in sub-paragraph (2)(d) above, sub-paragraph (1) above has effect in relation to securities issued on or after 1st April 1996.

(7) So far as relating to the provisions mentioned in sub-paragraph (2)(e) and (g) above, sub-paragraph (1) above has effect in relation to dividends or interest which become payable on or after 1st April 1996.

(8) So far as relating to the provision mentioned in sub-paragraph (2)(f) above, sub-paragraph (1) above has effect in relation to periods of 12 months ending on or after 1st April 1996.

(9) So far as relating to the provision mentioned in sub-paragraph (2)(h) above, sub-paragraph (1) above has effect in relation to relevant periods ending on or after 1st April 1996.

(10) So far as relating to the provisions mentioned in sub-paragraph (2)(j) and (k) above, sub-paragraph (1) above has effect in relation to any time falling on or after 1st April 1996.

(11) So far as relating to the provision mentioned in sub-paragraph (2)(l) above, sub-paragraph (1) above has effect in relation to chargeable periods ending on or after 1st April 1996.

7.—(1) In each of the provisions of that Act listed in sub-paragraph (2) below, for "quoted on" there shall be substituted "listed in the Official List of".

(2) The provisions referred to in sub-paragraph (1) above are—

(a) paragraph (b) of the definition of "preference shares" in section 210(4);

(b) section 842(1)(c); and

(c) section 842AA(2)(e).

(3) Sub-paragraph (1) above, so far as relating to the provision mentioned in sub-paragraph (2)(a) above, has effect in relation to share capital repaid on or after 1st April 1996.

(4) Sub-paragraph (1) above, so far as relating to the provisions mentioned in sub-paragraph (2)(b) and (c) above, has effect in relation to accounting periods ending on or after 1st April 1996.

8.—(1) In section 251(5) of that Act (application of section 272(3) of the Taxation of Chargeable Gains Act 1992), for "listed" there shall be substituted "quoted".

(2) This paragraph has effect where the relevant date falls on or after 1st April 1996.

9.—(1) In section 735(3) of that Act (meaning of the "appropriate proportion")—

(a) after "the appropriate proportion" there shall be inserted ", in relation to securities listed in the Official List of the Stock Exchange,";

(b) in paragraph (a), for "first listed in The Stock Exchange Daily Official List at a price excluding the value of" there shall be substituted ", in accordance with announcements made by The Stock Exchange, first to be dealt in without carrying rights to"; and

(c) in paragraph (b), for "quoted in that List at a price excluding the value of" there shall be substituted ", in accordance with such announcements, first to be dealt in without carrying rights to".

(2) In section 735(4) of that Act (application of section 753(3) to securities purchased before their first interest payment), for "quoted" there shall be substituted "to be dealt in".

(3) In section 735(5) of that Act (application of section 735(3) to securities not listed in the Stock Exchange Daily Official List)—

(a) for "Stock Exchange Daily Official List" there shall be substituted "Official List of The Stock Exchange"; and

(b) after "shall have effect" there shall be inserted "as it has effect in relation to securities which are so listed but".

(4) This paragraph has effect in relation to cases where the first buyer purchases securities on or after 1st April 1996.

The Taxation of Chargeable Gains Act 1992

10.—(1) In each of the provisions of the Taxation of Chargeable Gains Act 1992 listed in sub-paragraph (2) below, for the word "quoted" (wherever occurring) there shall be substituted "listed".

(2) The provisions referred to in sub-paragraph (1) above are—

(a) section 144(8)(b);

(b) the definition of "unquoted company" in section 164N(1);

(c) section 165(2)(b)(i);

(d) section 276(2)(c) and (6);

(e) section 281(3)(c); and

(f) paragraph 2(2)(b)(i) of Schedule 7.

(3) So far as relating to the provisions mentioned in sub-paragraph (2)(a) and (c) to (f) above, sub-paragraph (1) above has effect in relation to disposals on or after 1st April 1996.

(4) So far as relating to the provision mentioned in sub-paragraph (2)(b) above, sub-paragraph (1) above has effect in relation to acquisitions of qualifying investments (within the meaning of section 164A of that Act) on or after 1st April 1996.

11.—(1) In section 146(4)(b) of that Act (definition of "quoted shares and securities"), for the words "have a quoted market value" there shall be substituted the words "are listed".

(2) This paragraph has effect in relation to disposals of options on or after 1st April 1996.

12.—(1) In section 272(3) of that Act (market value of certain listed shares or securities), for "listed" there shall be substituted "quoted".

(2) In Schedule 11 to that Act (transitional provisions and savings), in paragraph 7(1)(a) (modification of section 272(3) when ascertaining market values before 25th March 1973), for "listed" there shall be substituted "quoted".

(3) This paragraph has effect where the relevant date falls on or after 1st April 1996.

GENERAL NOTE

The Schedule makes necessary changes to the wording of a number of provisions in the FA 1973, the IHTA 1984, the ICTA 1988 and the TCGA 1992, resulting from changes in Stock Exchange practice.

Paras. 1–6, 8

These amendments substitute "listed" for "quoted" in the statutes mentioned.

Para. 7

This substitutes "listed on the Official List of" for "quoted on" in the provisions of the ICTA 1988 mentioned.

Para. 9

This ensures the continuity of the bond-washing anti-avoidance provisions after the forthcoming changes.

Paras. 10 and 12

This substitutes "listed" for "quoted" in a number of provisions in the TCGA 1992.

Para. 11

This replaces a reference to shares or securities "having a quoted market value" with a reference to their being listed.

Section 201   SCHEDULE 39

ENACTMENT OF CERTAIN INLAND REVENUE EXTRA-STATUTORY CONCESSIONS

PART I

INCOME TAX AND CORPORATION TAX

Capital Allowances

1.—(1) The Capital Allowances Act 1990 ("the 1990 Act") shall be amended as follows.

(2) The following section shall be inserted after section 15 of the 1990 Act:

"Balancing charge after cessation of trade

15A.—(1) This section applies where:

(a) a balancing charge falls to be made as provided in section 15 on any person in respect of a building or structure which is temporarily out of use but is deemed by virtue of subsection (1) of that section still to be an industrial building or structure; and

(b) when the building or structure was last in use, it was in use as an industrial building or structure for the purposes of a trade which was carried on by that person but which has since been permanently discontinued.

(2) Where this section applies, the amount of the balancing charge shall be treated for the purposes of section 105 of the principal Act (allowable deductions) as a sum received by that person which is chargeable to tax under section 103 or 104(1) of the principal Act (charges on receipts after discontinuance), and accordingly any loss, expense, debit or capital allowance such as is referred to in section 105(1) may be deducted from the amount of the balancing charge.

(3) Nothing in subsection (2) above shall prevent any amounts allowable under any other provisions of the Tax Acts from being deducted from the amount of the balancing charge.

(4) Section 15(3) shall apply for the purposes of this section."

(3) Section 35 of the 1990 Act (contributions to expenditure, and hiring of cars) shall be amended by the insertion of the following subsection after subsection (2):

"(2A) Where subsection (2) has operated to reduce any expenditure on the hiring of a motor car, and subsequently either any rebate (by whatever name called) of the rentals is made or any transaction occurs with regard to any rentals that falls within section 94 of the principal Act (debts deducted and subsequently released), then the amount otherwise taxable in respect of the rebate or transaction shall be reduced in the same proportion as the expenditure on hiring was reduced."

(4) The amendment made by subparagraph (2) above shall have effect where the balancing charge falls to be made on or after the day on which this Act is passed, and the amendment made by subparagraph (3) above shall have effect in relation to rebates made and transactions occurring on or after the day on which this Act is passed.

Contributions to overseas pension schemes

2.—(1) Section 76 of the Finance Act 1989 (non-approved retirement benefits schemes) shall be amended as follows.

(2) At the beginning of each of subsections (2), (3), (5) and (6), for "Expenses" there shall be substituted "Subject to subsection (6A) below, expenses".

(3) The following subsections shall be inserted after subsection (6):

"(6A) Expenses to which subsection (6B) or (6C) below applies shall be treated as not falling within any of subsections (2), (3), (5) or (6) above.

(6B) This subsection applies to expenses of paying any sum, or of providing benefits, pursuant to a superannuation fund which satisfies the requirements of section 615(6) of the Taxes Act 1988.

(6C) This subsection applies to expenses of paying any sum, or of providing benefits, pursuant to a retirement benefits scheme which is established outside the United Kingdom and which the Board are satisfied corresponds to such a scheme as is mentioned in paragraphs (a), (b) or (c) of section 596(1) of the Taxes Act 1988, where the expenses are incurred for the benefit of:

(a) employees whose emoluments are foreign emoluments within the meaning of section 192 of the Taxes Act 1988; or

(b) employees who are not resident in the United Kingdom and whose duties are performed wholly outside the United Kingdom (and for this purpose duties performed in the United Kingdom the performance of which is merely incidental to the performance of other duties outside the United Kingdom shall be treated as performed outside the United Kingdom)."

(4) The amendments made by this paragraph shall have effect in relation to expenses incurred on or after the day on which this Act is passed.

PART II

CHARGEABLE GAINS

Treatment of compensation and insurance money

3.—(1) Section 23 of the Taxation of Chargeable Gains Act 1992 (receipt of compensation and insurance money not treated as a disposal) shall be amended as follows.

(2) The following subsections shall be substituted for subsection (6):

"(6) If a building ("the old building") is destroyed or irreparably damaged, and all or part of a capital sum received by way of compensation for the destruction or damage, or under a policy of insurance of the risk of the destruction or damage, is applied by the recipient in constructing or otherwise acquiring a replacement building situated on other land ("the new building"), then for the purposes of subsections (4) and (5) above each of the old building and the new building shall be regarded as an asset separate from the land on which it is or was situated and the old building shall be treated as lost or destroyed.

(7) For the purposes of subsection (6) above:

(a) references to a building include references to any permanent or semi-permanent structure in the nature of a building; and

(b) the reference to a sum applied in acquiring the new building does not include a reference to a sum applied in acquiring the land on which the new building is situated; and

(c) all necessary apportionments shall be made of any expenditure, compensation or consideration, and the method of apportionment shall be such as is just and reasonable.

(8) This section shall apply in relation to a wasting asset with the following modifications:

(a) paragraphs (b) and (c) of subsection (1) above, and subsection (2) above, shall not apply; and

(b) in subsections (1) and (3) above, the amount of the expenditure from which the deduction is to be made shall be the amount which would have been allowable under Chapter III of this Part if the asset had been disposed of immediately after the application of the capital sum."

(3) The amendments made by this paragraph shall have effect in relation to capital sums received on or after 6th April 1996.

Assets of negligible value

4.—(1) Section 24 of the Taxation of Chargeable Gains Act 1992 (disposals where assets lost or destroyed, or become of negligible value) shall be amended by the substitution of the following subsection for subsection (2):

"(2) Where the owner of an asset which has become of negligible value makes a claim to that effect:

(a) this Act shall apply as if the claimant had sold, and immediately reacquired, the asset at the time of the claim or (subject to paragraphs (b) and (c) below) at any earlier time specified in the claim, for a consideration of an amount equal to the value specified in the claim.

(b) An earlier time may be specified in the claim if:

(i) the claimant owned the asset at the earlier time; and

(ii) the asset had become of negligible value at the earlier time; and either

(iii) for capital gains tax purposes the earlier time is not more than two years before the beginning of the year of assessment in which the claim is made; or

(iv) for corporation tax purposes the earlier time is on or after the first day of the earliest accounting period ending not more than two years before the time of the claim.

(c) Section 93 of and Schedule 12 to the Finance Act 1994 (indexation losses and transitional relief) shall have effect in relation to an asset to which this section applies as if the sale and reacquisition occurred at the time of the claim and not at any earlier time."

(2) The amendment made by this paragraph shall have effect in relation to claims made on or after 6th April 1996.

Settled Property

5.—(1) Section 72 of the Taxation of Chargeable Gains Act 1992 (termination of life interest on death of person entitled) shall be amended as follows.

(2) In subsections (1), (2) and (5), for the words "a life" wherever they occur, there shall be substituted "an" and, in subsection (5), the word "life", in the third place where it occurs, shall be omitted.

(3) For subsections (3) and (4) there shall be substituted the following subsections:

"(3) This section shall apply on the death of the person entitled to any annuity payable out of, or charged on, settled property or the income of settled property as it applies on the death of a person whose interest in possession in the whole or any part of settled property terminates on his death.

(4) Where, in the case of any entitlement to an annuity created by a settlement some of the settled property is appropriated by the trustees as a fund out of which the annuity is payable, and there is no right of recourse to, or to the income of, settled property not so appropriated, then without prejudice to subsection (5) below, the settled property so appropriated shall, while the annuity is payable, and on the occasion of the death of the person entitled to the annuity, be treated for the purposes of this section as being settled property under a separate settlement."

(4) The amendments made by this paragraph shall have effect in relation to deaths occurring on or after 6th April 1996.

6.—(1) Section 73 of the Taxation of Chargeable Gains Act 1992 (death of life tenant: exclusion of chargeable gain) shall be amended as follows.

(2) In subsection (1), for the words from "termination" to "that interest" there shall be substituted "death of a person entitled to an interest in possession in the settled property".

(3) In subsection (2), the word "life" shall be omitted.

(4) In subsection (3), for the words from "subsection (5)" to "subsection (2) above" there shall be substituted "subsections (3) to (5) of that section shall apply for the purposes of this section".

(5) The amendments made by this paragraph shall have effect in relation to deaths occurring on or after 6th April 1996.

Retirement Relief

7.—(1) Paragraph 14 of Schedule 6 to the Taxation of Chargeable Gains Act 1992 shall be amended as follows.

(2) In subparagraph (2), the word "original" shall be inserted before "qualifying period".

(3) The following subparagraphs shall be inserted at the end:

"(7) In relation to the expression "the original qualifying period", the questions whether a disposal is a qualifying disposal and whether the period relating to that disposal is a qualifying period shall be determined without regard to the requirement that the length of the period be at least one year.

(8) This paragraph shall not apply if the extended qualifying period resulting from the operation of subparagraphs (1) to (7) would be a period of less than one year."

(4) The amendments made by this paragraph shall have effect in relation to disposals made on or after 6th April 1996.

Relief for loans to traders

8.—(1) Section 253 of the Taxation of Chargeable Gains Act 1992 (relief for loans to traders) shall be amended as follows.

(2) In subsection (3):
(a) for the words from the beginning until "is satisfied that" there shall be substituted "Where a person who has made a qualifying loan makes a claim and at that time"; and
(b) for the words "when the claim was made" there shall be substituted "at the time of the claim or (subject to subsection (3A) below) any earlier time specified in the claim."

(3) The following subsection shall be inserted after subsection (3):

"(3A) For the purposes of subsection (3) above, an earlier time may be specified in the claim if:
(a) the amount to which that subsection applies was also irrecoverable at the earlier time; and either
(b) for capital gains tax purposes the earlier time falls not more than two years before the beginning of the year of assessment in which the claim is made; or
(c) for corporation tax purposes the earlier time falls on or after the first day of the earliest accounting period ending not more than two years before the time of the claim."

(4) In subsection (4) for the words from the beginning until "is satisfied that" there shall be substituted "Where a person who has guaranteed the repayment of a loan which is, or but for subsection (1)(c) above would be, a qualifying loan makes a claim and at that time".

(5) The amendments made by this paragraph shall have effect in relation to claims made on or after 6th April 1996.

Relief for debts on qualifying corporate bonds

9.—(1) Section 254 of the Taxation of Chargeable Gains Act 1992 (relief for debts on qualifying corporate bonds) shall be amended as follows.

(2) In subsection (2):
(a) for the words from the beginning until "is satisfied that" there shall be substituted "Where a person who has made a qualifying loan makes a claim and at that time"; and

(b) for the words "when the claim was made" there shall be substituted "at the time of the claim or (subject to subsection (8A) below) any earlier time specified in the claim".

(3) In subsections (6) and (7), the words "the inspector is satisfied that" shall be omitted.

(4) In subsection (8), the words "in the inspector's opinion" shall be omitted.

(5) The following subsection shall be inserted after subsection (8):

"(8A) For the purposes of subsection (2) above, an earlier time may be specified in the claim if:

(a) the condition which was fulfilled at the time of the claim was also fulfilled at the earlier time; and either

(b) for capital gains tax purposes the earlier time falls not more than two years before the beginning of the year of assessment in which the claim is made; or

(c) for corporation tax purposes the earlier time falls on or after the first day of the earliest accounting period ending not more than two years before the time of the claim."

(6) In subsection (11), the words "the inspector was satisfied that", "by the inspector" and "he was satisfied that" shall be omitted.

(7) The amendments made by this paragraph shall have effect in relation to claims made on or after 6th April 1996.

PART III

STAMP DUTY

Lost or spoiled instruments

10.—(1) The Stamp Duties Management Act 1891 ("the Management Act") shall be amended as follows.

(2) In section 9 of the Management Act (procedure for obtaining allowance), subsection (7), paragraph (e), the words "which is inadvertently and undesignedly spoiled, and in lieu whereof another instrument made between the same parties and for the same purpose is executed and duly stamped, or" shall be omitted.

(3) The following section shall be inserted after section 12 of the Management Act:

"Allowance for lost or spoiled instruments

Lost or spoiled instruments

12A.—(1) This section applies where the Commissioners are satisfied that:

(a) an instrument which was executed and duly stamped ("the original instrument") has been accidentally lost or spoiled; and

(b) in place of the original instrument, another instrument made between the same persons and for the same purpose ("the replacement instrument") has been executed; and

(c) an application for relief under this section is made to the Commissioners; and either

(d) where the original instrument has been lost, the applicant undertakes to deliver it up to the Commissioners to be cancelled if it is subsequently found; or

(e) where the original instrument has been spoiled:

(i) the application is made within two years after the date of the original instrument, or if it is not dated, within two years after the time when it was executed or within such further time as the Commissioners may allow; and

(ii) no legal proceeding has been commenced in which the original instrument has been or could or would have been given or offered in evidence; and

(iii) the original instrument is delivered up to the Commissioners to be cancelled.

(2) Where this section applies:

(a) the replacement instrument shall not be chargeable with any duty, but shall be stamped with the duty with which it would otherwise have been chargeable in accordance with the law in force at the time when it was executed, and shall be deemed for all purposes to be duly stamped; and

(b) if any duty, interest, fine or penalty was paid in respect of the replacement instrument before the application was made, the Commissioners shall pay to such person as they consider appropriate an amount equal to the duty, interest, fine or penalty so paid.

(3) For the purposes of this section the Commissioners may require the applicant to produce such evidence by statutory declaration or otherwise as they think fit."

(4) Subject to subparagraph (5) below, the amendments made by this paragraph shall have effect from the day on which this Act is passed.

(5) The amendments made by this paragraph shall not apply in relation to an instrument which has been accidentally spoiled if an application for allowance under section 9 of the Management Act was made before the day on which this Act is passed.

GENERAL NOTE

Extra-statutory concessions B19, B28, B39, D1, D19, D28, D36, D43, D48, G1 and G2 are given statutory effect. The capital gains tax concessions, prefixed D, take effect from April 6, 1996 and the remaining five from Royal Assent, April 29, 1996.

Para. 1

This gives statutory effect to the ESCs B19 and B28.

New Capital Allowances Act 1990 (c. 1), s.15A, applies where a person sells a building, which was last in use as an industrial building for the purposes of a trade carried on by that person, after the trade has ceased. It allows the person to set losses from the trade against any balancing charge which arises on the sale. It also allows any post-cessation expenses of the trade to be deducted from the balancing charge. The latter provision extends the ESC.

New CAA 1990, s.35(2A) gives statutory effect to ESC B28, which concerns rebates of hire charges on cars costing over £12,000. In computing the profits of a person hiring such a car, any allowable deduction for the rental payments is restricted by reference to the amount that the retail price of the car exceeds £12,000, using a formula laid down in s.35. Where a rebate is made of such rental payments, new s.35(2A) reduces the amount to be taxed using the same formula.

Para. 2

This gives effect to ESC B39 which provides that an employer may be entitled in certain circumstances to a deduction in computing his profits for tax purposes in respect of payments to a pension scheme not approved by the Revenue, even though the employee is not chargeable to income tax.

New FA 1989, s.76B, covers payments to a pension scheme to which the ICTA 1988, s.615(3), applies, *i.e.* a U.K. pension scheme solely for overseas employees.

New s.76C covers payments to a pension scheme established outside the U.K. which corresponds to a U.K.-approved scheme, if the payments are made for the benefit of employees who are in receipt of foreign emolument or who are not resident in the U.K. and whose duties are performed wholly outside the U.K.

Para. 3

This enacts ESCs D1 and D19. D1 provides that a capital sum received under an insurance policy and applied to restore a property held under a lease which has 50 years or less to run is not chargeable to capital gains tax. D19 provides that where a capital sum paid as compensation for loss or damage to a building is used to acquire a replacement building, the buildings are treated as separate assets from the land on which they stand, for the purposes of a claim under the TCGA 1992, s.23(4) or (5). The paragraph broadens the scope of D1 by applying it to wasting assets generally and to all capital sums, not just insurance policies. The enactment is effected by inserting new TCGA 1992, s.23(6)–(8).

Para. 4

This enacts ESC D28, which allows the owner of an asset which has become of negligible value to be treated, on the making of a claim, as if he had disposed of that asset at an earlier date, within stated limits, specified in the claim. New TCGA 1992, s.24(2), allows the previously concessionary carryback of two years, but ensures that indexation allowance for such a disposal cannot be used to create or increase a loss.

Paras. 5 and 6

These enact ESC D43. On the death of a person entitled to a life interest in possession in settled property, the trustees are deemed to have disposed of the property and re-acquired it at its market value, but, subject to certain conditions, there is no chargeable gain or allowable loss. D43 extends this treatment to the death of a person with any interest in possession, not just a life interest. The enactment of the concession is effected by amendments to the TCGA 1992, ss.72 and 73.

Para. 7

This enacts ESC D48, which deals with retirement relief. One of the factors taken into account in giving relief is the length of time throughout which the individual has carried on a qualifying business before the disposal of the assets. D48 allows a final qualifying business period of less than 12 months to be added to any earlier qualifying periods when calculating entitlement. It is enacted by amendments to TCGA 1992, Sched. 6, para. 14.

Paras. 8 and 9

These enact ESC D36, which enables a taxpayer to claim that a capital loss has accrued to him at an earlier date, within a two-year time limit, specified in the claim where he has made a loan, including one consisting of qualifying corporate bonds, which has become irrecoverable. The enactment is by way of amendments to the TCGA 1992, ss.253 and 254.

Para. 10

This enacts ESCs G1 and G2 which deal with the stamp duty position where stamped instruments are either lost or spoiled. The first concession is that the stamp duty on a lost instrument is allowed for, either by stamping a replica free, or by repayment of any duty paid on the replica. The second concession prevents any charge where the stamp duty liability on a replica is greater than that on the original instrument, *e.g.* because of an intervening increase in the rates of duty. This concession applies to both lost and spoiled instruments.

Allowance for the duty on instruments that are spoiled is already provided under the Stamp Duties Management Act 1891 (c. 38), s.9. The new SDMA 1891, s.12A, which enacts the concessions, restates that allowance with the minor change that a reduction in duty as between an original instrument and a replica is ignored in the case of spoiled instruments, as it is for lost instruments [Standing Committee E, February 29, 1996, col. 576].

Section 202   SCHEDULE 40

Gilt stripping: taxation provisions

The Stamp Act 1891 (c. 39)

1. In the definition of "stock" in section 122(1) of the Stamp Act 1891, after "Bank of Ireland," there shall be inserted "any strip (within the meaning of section 47 of the Finance Act 1942) of any such stocks or funds,".

2.—(1) At the end of paragraph (1) of the general exemptions at the end of Schedule 1 to the Stamp Act 1891 (exemption for Government stocks etc.) there shall be inserted "or strips (within the meaning of section 47 of the Finance Act 1942) of such stocks or funds".

(2) Where any day is appointed as the abolition day for the purposes of sections 107 to 110 of the Finance Act 1990, sub-paragraph (1) above shall cease to have effect in accordance with the provisions of that Act for the coming into force of the repeal of the paragraph mentioned in that sub-paragraph.

The Taxes Act 1988

3.—(1) At the end of subsection (5) of section 710 of the Taxes Act 1988 (meaning of "transfer"), there shall be inserted—

"(b) except as otherwise provided by subsections (1) and (3) of section 722A, does not include any transaction forming part of any such exchange as is mentioned in either of those subsections."

(2) After subsection (13) of that section there shall be inserted the following subsections—

"(13A) Where a security is deemed to have been transferred by virtue of section 722A(1), the interest period in which the exchange in question takes place shall be treated as ending on the day on which it would have ended had the exchange not taken place.

(13B) Where a security is deemed to have been transferred by virtue of section 722A(3), the interest period in which the exchange in question takes place shall be treated as having begun on such day as shall for that purpose be specified in the security."

4. In section 711 of the Taxes Act 1988 (interpretation of sections 710 and 712 to 728 of that Act), after subsection (6) there shall be inserted the following subsection—

"(6A) In any case where section 722A(1) or (3) applies, the deemed transfer shall be treated as made—

(a) without accrued interest in any such case where the exchange in question is made at any time after the balance has been struck for a dividend on the security but before the day on which that dividend is payable;

(b) with accrued interest in any other such case."

5. In section 712(4) of the Taxes Act 1988 (meaning of "settlement day"), after "722" there shall be inserted ", 722A".

6. In the Taxes Act 1988, the following section shall be inserted after section 722—

"Gilt strips: deemed transfer

722A.—(1) For the purposes of sections 710 to 728, where a gilt-edged security is exchanged by any person for strips of that security the security shall be deemed to have been transferred by that person.

(2) Nothing in subsection (1) above shall have effect to cause any person to be treated as the transferee of any securities for the purposes of section 713(2)(b).

(3) For the purposes of sections 710 to 728, where strips of gilt-edged securities are exchanged by any person for a single gilt-edged security consolidating those strips, that security shall be deemed to have been transferred to that person.

(4) Nothing in subsection (3) above shall have effect to cause any person to be treated as the transferor of any securities for the purposes of section 713(2)(a).

(5) In this section—
  'gilt-edged security' has the same meaning as in section 51A; and
  'strip' means anything which, within the meaning of section 47 of the Finance Act 1942, is a strip of a gilt-edged security."

7. In the Taxes Act 1988, the following section shall be inserted after section 730B—

"Exchanges of gilts: traders etc.

730C.—(1) This section has effect for the purposes of computing the profits and gains arising from any trade, profession or vocation carried on by any person in so far as the computation is such as to require amounts in respect of the acquisition or redemption of a gilt-edged security (including any strip) to be brought into account.

(2) Where a gilt-edged security is exchanged by any person for strips of that security—
  (a) the security shall be deemed to have been redeemed at the time of the exchange by the payment to that person of its market value; and
  (b) that person shall be deemed to have acquired each strip for the amount which bears the same proportion to that market value as is borne by the market value of the strip to the aggregate of the market values of all the strips received in exchange for the security.

(3) Where strips of a gilt-edged security are consolidated into a single security by being exchanged by any person for that security—
  (a) each of the strips shall be deemed to have been redeemed at the time of the exchange by the payment to that person of the amount equal to its market value; and
  (b) that person shall be deemed to have acquired the security for the amount equal to the aggregate of the market values of the strips given in exchange for the security.

(4) References in this section to the market value of a security given or received in exchange for another are references to its market value at the time of the exchange.

(5) Subsections (3) and (4) of section 473 shall not apply in the case of any exchange to which subsection (2) or (3) above applies.

(6) Without prejudice to the generality of any power conferred by section 202 of the Finance Act 1996, the Treasury may by regulations make provision for the purposes of this section as to the manner of determining the market value at any time of any gilt-edged security (including any strip).

(7) Regulations under subsection (6) above may—
  (a) make different provision for different cases; and
  (b) contain such incidental, supplemental, consequential and transitional provision as the Treasury may think fit.

(8) This section does not apply for the purposes of corporation tax.

(9) In this section—
  'gilt-edged security' has the same meaning as in section 51A; and
  'strip' means anything which, within the meaning of section 47 of the Finance Act 1942, is a strip of a gilt-edged security."

The Taxation of Chargeable Gains Act 1992 (c. 12)

8. In Schedule 9 to the Taxation of Chargeable Gains Act 1992 (gilt-edged securities), after paragraph 1 there shall be inserted the following paragraph—

"1A.—(1) Any security which is a strip of a security which is a gilt-edged security for the purposes of this Act is also itself a gilt-edged security for those purposes.

(2) In this paragraph 'strip' has the same meaning as in section 47 of the Finance Act 1942."

GENERAL NOTE

The Schedule deals with consequential changes to tax legislation following the introduction of gilt strips.

Paras. 1 and 2
These make consequential amendments to definitions in the Stamp Act 1891 (c. 39).

Paras. 3–7
These deal with the interaction of gilt stripping with the accrued income scheme and with the position of non-corporate traders, who are not covered by the scheme.

The new ICTA 1988, s.722A, ensures that when a person exchanges a gilt for strips, the accrued income scheme applies only to that person and not to the other person. Similarly, when a person reconstitutes a gilt the accrued income scheme applies only to that person.

The new ICTA 1988, s.730C, provides that where a non-corporate trader strips a gilt, it is treated as being redeemed for its market value and for the acquisition of the strips to take place at appropriate proportionate parts of that value. Where a gilt is reconstituted, the strips disposed of are treated as sold at their market values and the reconstituted gilt is deemed to be acquired for the aggregate of those values. The method of determining market value may be specified by regulation.

Para. 8
This makes a consequential amendment to a definition in the TCGA 1992.

Section 205   SCHEDULE 41

REPEALS

PART I

HYDROCARBON OIL DUTY: RELIEF FOR MARINE VOYAGES

Chapter	Short Title	Extent of repeal
1979 c. 2.	The Customs and Excise Management Act 1979.	In section 61(2), the words from "and in" to "waters)".
1979 c. 5.	The Hydrocarbon Oil Duties Act 1979.	Section 18 and in section 19(1), paragraph (a) and the words from "by the owner" to "be".
		In section 24(1), the words "section 18(1)".
		In Schedule 4, in paragraph 3, the word "18(1)".
1979 c. 8.	The Excise Duties (Surcharges or Rebates) Act 1979.	In section 1(7), paragraph (c) and in paragraph (d), the words "fishing boats".
1981 c. 35.	The Finance Act 1981.	In section 6(1) and (4), the word "18(1)".
1994 c. 9.	The Finance Act 1994.	In Schedule 4, paragraph 53.

The power in section 8(2) of this Act applies to these repeals as it applies to that section.

PART II

VEHICLE EXCISE AND REGISTRATION

(1) ELECTRICALLY PROPELLED VEHICLES

Chapter	Short Title	Extent of repeal
1994 c. 22.	The Vehicle Excise and Registration Act 1994.	In Schedule 1, paragraph 4F(2).

This repeal has effect in accordance with section 15(4) of this Act.

(2) VEHICLES CAPABLE OF CONVEYING LOADS

Chapter	Short Title	Extent of repeal
1994 c. 22.	The Vehicle Excise and Registration Act 1994.	In Schedule 1— (a) in paragraph 9(2), the word "and" immediately preceding paragraph (b); (b) in paragraph 11(2), the word "and" immediately preceding paragraph (b); (c) paragraph 15; and (d) in paragraph 16(1), paragraph (b) and the word "or" immediately preceding it.

These repeals have effect in accordance with section 17 of this Act.

(3) OLD VEHICLES

Chapter	Short Title	Extent of repeal
1994 c. 22.	The Vehicle Excise and Registration Act 1994.	In Schedule 1, paragraphs 1(3) to (5) and 2(2).
1995 c. 4.	The Finance Act 1995.	In Schedule 4, paragraph 6(2).

These repeals have effect in accordance with section 18(5) of this Act.

(4) EXEMPTIONS FOR VEHICLE TESTING

Chapter	Short Title	Extent of repeal
1994 c. 22.	The Vehicle Excise and Registration Act 1994.	In paragraph 22 of Schedule 2— (a) in each of paragraphs (b) and (d) of sub-paragraph (5), the word "goods"; (b) sub-paragraph (5)(c); (c) the word "and" at the end of sub-paragraph (7)(b); and (d) in sub-paragraph (10)(a), the words "(or, in Northern Ireland, a vehicle test certificate)".

These repeals have effect in accordance with section 20 of this Act.

(5) PROVISIONS RELATING TO NORTHERN IRELAND

Chapter	Short Title	Extent of repeal
1994 c. 22.	The Vehicle Excise and Registration Act 1994.	In paragraph 17 of Schedule 3, in sub-paragraph (1), "29(2)," and "34(6)," and sub-paragraph (2).

(6) LICENSING AND REGISTRATION

Chapter	Short Title	Extent of repeal
1994 c. 22.	The Vehicle Excise and Registration Act 1994.	In section 22— (a) in subsection (1), the word "and" immediately preceding paragraph (h); and (b) in subsection (1B), the word "above". In section 57(1), the words "(other than sections 7(2) and (3), 8, 26, 27, 52 and 54)".

PART III

EXCISE DUTIES: REPEAL OF DRAWBACKS ETC.

Chapter	Short Title	Extent of repeal
1977 c. 36.	The Finance Act 1977.	Section 3.
1979 c. 4.	The Alcoholic Liquor Duties Act 1979.	Section 22(6). Section 23. Section 92(6).
1979 c. 7.	The Tobacco Products Duty Act 1979.	Section 11(3).
1979 c. 58.	The Isle of Man Act 1979.	In section 9— (a) in subsection (1), the words "subsection (2) below and"; and (b) subsections (2) and (3).

PART IV

(1) FISCAL WAREHOUSING

Chapter	Short Title	Extent of repeal
1994 c. 23.	The Value Added Tax Act 1994.	In section 62(1)(a), the words "or" at the end of sub-paragraph (i) and "and" at the end of sub-paragraph (ii).

This repeal has effect in accordance with section 26(2) of this Act.

(2) WORK ON MATERIALS

Chapter	Short Title	Extent of repeal
1994 c. 23.	The Value Added Tax Act 1994.	Section 22. In section 55(5)(a), the word "or" at the end of the paragraph. Section 97(4)(b). In Schedule 4, paragraph 2.

(3) VALUE OF IMPORTED GOODS

Chapter	Short Title	Extent of repeal
1994 c. 23.	The Value Added Tax Act 1994.	In section 21(2)(a), the word "and" at the end of the paragraph.

This repeal has effect in accordance with section 27(4) of this Act.

(4) CONSTRUCTION AND CONVERSION OF BUILDINGS

Chapter	Short Title	Extent of repeal
1995 c. 4.	The Finance Act 1995.	Section 33(2).

This repeal has effect in accordance with section 30(4) of this Act.

(5) GROUPS

Chapter	Short Title	Extent of repeal
1994 c. 23.	The Value Added Tax Act 1994.	Section 43(1A).
1995 c. 4.	The Finance Act 1995.	In section 25(2), the words from the beginning to the word "and" immediately after the subsection (1A) inserted in section 43 of the Value Added Tax Act 1994.

These repeals have effect in accordance with section 31(5) of this Act.

PART V

INCOME TAX, CORPORATION TAX AND CAPITAL GAINS TAX

(1) APPLICATION OF LOWER RATE TO INCOME FROM SAVINGS

Chapter	Short Title	Extent of repeal
1988 c. 1.	The Income and Corporation Taxes Act 1988.	Section 207A. Sections 468E and 468EE. In section 469— (a) in subsection (1), paragraph (b) and the word "and" immediately preceding it; and (b) the second paragraph of subsection (3).
1990 c. 29.	The Finance Act 1990.	Section 51.
1992 c. 48.	The Finance (No. 2) Act 1992.	Section 19(4).
1993 c. 34.	The Finance Act 1993.	Section 77(1) and (2). Section 79(3). In Schedule 6, paragraph 14.
1994 c. 9.	The Finance Act 1994.	Section 111.

1. Subject to note 2 below, these repeals come into force in accordance with section 73 of, and Schedule 6 to, this Act.

2. The repeals in section 469 of the Taxes Act 1988 come into force for distribution periods ending on or after 6th April 1996.

(2) Transfer of Schedule C charge etc.

Chapter	Short Title	Extent of repeal
1970 c. 9.	The Taxes Management Act 1970.	In the Table in section 98— (a) in the first column, the entry relating to paragraph 13(1) of Schedule 3 to the Taxes Act 1988; and (b) in the second column, the entry relating to paragraph 6C of that Schedule.
1988 c. 1.	The Income and Corporation Taxes Act 1988.	Section 17. In section 18(3), in Case IV, the words "except such income as is charged under Schedule C". Sections 44 and 45. Section 48. In sections 50(1) and 51A(1), the words "but shall be chargeable to tax under Case III of Schedule D". Section 52. Section 123. In section 124— (a) in subsection (6), the definitions of "recognised clearing system" and "relevant foreign securities", and the word "and" immediately preceding those definitions; and (b) subsection (7). In section 322(1), the words "and he shall be treated as not resident in the United Kingdom for the purposes of sections 48 and 123(4)". In section 398(b), the words "C or". Section 474(1) and (3). Section 505(1)(c)(i). Section 582A(3). In section 832(1), the definition of "recognised clearing system". Schedule 3.
1988 c. 39.	The Finance Act 1988.	Section 76(1), (2), (3) and (5).
1989 c. 26.	The Finance Act 1989.	In section 178(2)(m), the words "and paragraph 6B of Schedule 3 to".
1992 c. 48.	The Finance (No. 2) Act 1992.	Section 30. In Schedule 11, paragraphs 1, 2, 4 and 5.
1993 c. 34.	The Finance Act 1993.	In Schedule 6, paragraphs 17 and 25(5).
1995 c. 4.	The Finance Act 1995.	In section 128(3)(a), the words "Schedule C".

These repeals have effect—
(a) in accordance with Schedule 7 to this Act; and
(b) without prejudice to paragraph 25 of Schedule 6 to this Act.

(3) Loan relationships

Chapter	Short Title	Extent of repeal
1970 c. 9.	The Taxes Management Act 1970.	In section 42 (as substituted by paragraph 13 of Schedule 19 to the Finance Act 1994), in subsection (7)(a), "484,".

Chapter	Short Title	Extent of repeal

1988 c. 1.	The Income and Corporation Taxes Act 1988.	Section 57.
		Section 78.
		Sections 88A to 88C.
		Sections 126 and 126A.
		In section 242, in each of subsections (2)(b) and (8)(b), the words "or paragraph 5 of Schedule 4".
		In section 337—
		  (a) in subsection (2), the words "to subsection (3) below and"; and
		  (b) subsection (3).
		In section 338—
		  (a) in subsection (3), the words from "and" at the end of paragraph (a) to the end of the subsection;
		  (b) in subsection (4), paragraphs (b) and (c);
		  (c) in subsection (5)(a), the words ", not being interest"; and
		  (d) subsection (6).
		Section 338A.
		Section 340.
		Section 341.
		Section 401(1A).
		In section 404(6)(c)(ii), the words "or paragraph 5(2) of Schedule 4".
		In section 477A, subsections (3A) to (3C).
		Sections 484 and 485.
		In section 494(3), the words "not consisting of a payment of interest".
		Section 714(6).
		Section 724.
		In section 804A(3), in paragraph (b) of the definition of "B", the words "and interest".
		Schedule 4.
		In Schedule 19AC, in paragraph 5B(2)(b), the words "or paragraph 5 of Schedule 4".
		In Schedule 23A, paragraphs 6(3), (4), (6) and (7).
		In Schedule 26, the word "and" at the end of paragraph 1(3)(d).

1989 c. 15.	The Water Act 1989.	Section 95(10).
1989 c. 26.	The Finance Act 1989.	Sections 93 to 95. Section 116. Schedules 10 and 11.
1990 c. 29.	The Finance Act 1990.	Section 56. Sections 58 and 59. Section 74. Schedule 10.
1991 c. 31.	The Finance Act 1991.	Section 52(2) and (3). In Schedule 12, paragraphs 3 and 4.
1992 c. 12.	The Taxation of Chargeable Gains Act 1992.	Section 108(1)(b). Section 117(2A), (3), (9) and (10). Section 118. In Schedule 10, paragraphs 14(6), (29) and (57), 19(6) and 22(4).
1992 c. 48.	The Finance (No. 2) Act 1992.	Section 33. In section 65(2)— (a) paragraphs (b) and (c); and

Chapter	Short Title	Extent of repeal
		(b) in paragraph (f), the words "to (c)".
		Schedule 7.
1993 c. 34.	The Finance Act 1993.	Sections 61 to 66.
		Section 103(4).
		Section 129(5) and (6).
		Section 152(2).
		Section 153(6) and (11A).
		Section 164(12).
		Section 176(3)(b) to (d).
		In Schedule 6—
		(a) paragraph 18;
		(b) in paragraph 20, the words "and in paragraph 11(1) of Schedule 11 to that Act"; and
		(c) paragraph 21.
		In Schedule 17, paragraphs 4 to 6.
		In Schedule 18, paragraphs 3 and 7.
1994 c. 9.	The Finance Act 1994.	Section 171.
		Section 251(12).
		In Schedule 18, in paragraph 4—
		(a) the definition of "the I minus E basis"; and
		(b) the words after the definition of "non-life mutual business".
		In Schedule 24, in paragraph 9—
		(a) the words "and 254" and the words "or 254", in each place where they occur; and
		(b) in sub-paragraph (9), the words "and subsection (10) of section 254 of that Act".
1995 c. 4.	The Finance Act 1995.	Section 42(6).
		Section 50.
		Section 87(6).
		Sections 88 and 89.
		Schedule 7.
		In Schedule 8, paragraphs 10 and 12(1)(c).
		In Schedule 24, paragraphs 4 to 6.

These repeals come into force in accordance with the provisions of Chapter II of Part IV of this Act.

(4) PROVISION OF LIVING ACCOMMODATION

Chapter	Short Title	Extent of repeal
1988 c. 1.	The Income and Corporation Taxes Act 1988.	In section 145(1), the words "and is not otherwise made the subject of any charge to him by way of income tax".

This repeal has effect in accordance with section 106 of this Act.

(5) SHARE OPTION SCHEMES ETC.

Chapter	Short Title	Extent of repeal
1988 c. 1.	The Income and Corporation Taxes Act 1988.	In section 187(8), paragraph (b) and the word "and" immediately preceding it. In Schedule 9, in paragraph 21(1), the word "and" immediately preceding paragraph (e), paragraph 28(2) and (4) and paragraph 29(8).
1989 c. 26.	The Finance Act 1989.	In Schedule 5, in paragraph 4(5)(a), the words "not less than one year and".
1992 c. 12.	The Taxation of Chargeable Gains Act 1992.	Section 149A(4). Section 238(4).

1. The repeal in section 187 of the Taxes Act 1988 has effect in accordance with section 117 of this Act.

2. The repeal in paragraph 21 of Schedule 9 to that Act has effect in accordance with section 113 of this Act.

3. The repeals in paragraphs 28 and 29 of that Schedule have effect in accordance with section 114 of this Act.

4. The repeal in the Finance Act 1989 has effect in accordance with section 119 of this Act.

5. The repeal of section 149A(4) of the Taxation of Chargeable Gains Act 1992 has effect in accordance with section 111(6) of this Act.

6. The repeal of section 238(4) of that Act has effect in accordance with section 112(2) and (3) of this Act.

(6) SELF-ASSESSMENT: RETURNS ETC.

Chapter	Short Title	Extent of repeal
1970 c. 9.	The Taxes Management Act 1970.	In section 8(1A), the words from "and the amounts referred to" to the end. In section 8A(1A), the words from "and the amounts referred to" to the end. In section 12AA(7)(a), the words "any part of". Section 12AC(6). In section 28C(3), the words "or 11AA". In section 42, subsections (3A) and (3B) and, in subsection (7)(a), the words "534, 535, 537A, 538".
1988 c. 1.	The Income and Corporation Taxes Act 1988.	In section 108, the words from "and, in any such case" to the end. In section 535, in subsection (4), the words "Subject to subsection (5) below", subsections (5) and (7) and, in subsection (6), the words from "unless the author" to the end. In section 547(5)(a), the words from "no assessment" to "but". In section 599A, in subsection (6), the words from "subject" to "and" and subsection (7).
1992 c. 12.	The Taxation of Chargeable Gains Act 1992.	In section 246, the words from "or, if earlier" to the end.
1994 c. 9.	The Finance Act 1994.	In Schedule 19, paragraph 23.

1. The repeals of subsections (3A) and (3B) of section 42 of the Taxes Management Act 1970 and the repeals in sections 108 and 535 of the Income and Corporation Taxes Act 1988 have effect in accordance with section 128(11) of this Act.

2. The repeal in subsection (7)(a) of section 42 of the Taxes Management Act 1970 has effect in accordance with section 128(12) of this Act.

3. The other repeals have effect in accordance with section 121(8) of this Act.

(7) SELF-ASSESSMENT: NOTICES

Chapter	Short Title	Extent of repeal
1970 c. 9.	The Taxes Management Act 1970.	In section 42, in subsection (7), in paragraph (a), "62A," and "401,", and in paragraph (c), "30,", "33,", "48, 49," and "124A," and in subsection (10) the words "and notices".

These repeals have effect in accordance with section 130 of this Act.

(8) OVERDUE TAX AND EXCESSIVE PAYMENTS BY THE BOARD

Chapter	Short Title	Extent of repeal
1970 c. 9.	The Taxes Management Act 1970.	Section 88. Section 88A. In section 91(1), the words "or section 88". Section 113(1C).
1971 c. 68.	The Finance Act 1971.	In Schedule 6, paragraph 87.
1975 c. 45.	The Finance (No. 2) Act 1975.	Section 46(4).
1980 c. 48.	The Finance Act 1980.	Section 61(4), so far as relating to section 88(5)(c) and (d) of the Taxes Management Act 1970.
1988 c. 1.	The Income and Corporation Taxes Act 1988.	In section 374A(4), the words from "and as if" onwards. In Schedule 14, in paragraph 6(2) the words from "and as if" onwards. In Schedule 29, in paragraph 32, the entries relating to section 88(2), section 88(5)(b) and section 88(5)(c) of the Taxes Management Act 1970.
1989 c. 26.	The Finance Act 1989.	Section 159. Section 160(1), (2) and (4). Section 161. In section 178(2)(f), the words "88". In section 179(1)(b)(i), the words "and 88(1)".

These repeals have effect in accordance with paragraph 17 of Schedule 18 to this Act.

(9) SELF-ASSESSMENT: CLAIMS AND ENQUIRIES

Chapter	Short Title	Extent of repeal
1970 c. 9.	The Taxes Management Act 1970.	In section 31(5), the words "against any assessment".

This repeal has effect in accordance with Schedule 19 to this Act.

(10) SELF-ASSESSMENT: DISCRETIONS ETC.

Chapter	Short Title	Extent of repeal
1988 c. 1.	The Income and Corporation Taxes Act 1988.	In section 74(1)(j)(i), the words "proved to be such".

Chapter	Short Title	Extent of repeal
		In section 145(7)(a) and (b), the words "it can be shown that".
		Section 159(4) to (6).
		In section 161, in subsection (3), the words "it is shown that" and, in subsection (4), the words "shows that he".
		In section 231(3A), the words "it appears to the inspector that".
		In section 257(2) and (3), the words "proves that he".
		In section 257E(1) the words "he proves" and, in each of paragraphs (a) and (b), the word "that" in the first and third places where it occurs.
		In section 257F, in the words preceding paragraph (a), the words "the claimant proves", and the word "that" in the second place where it occurs in paragraph (a), the first place where it occurs in paragraph (b) and the first and third places where it occurs in paragraph (c).
		In section 259(6), the second paragraph.
		In section 265(1), the words "proves that he".
		In section 278(2), the words "satisfies the Board that he or she".
		In section 381(4), the words "it is shown that".
		In section 384(1), the words "it is shown that".
		In section 570(2), the words "on a claim it is shown in accordance with the provisions of Part II of Schedule 21 that".
		In section 582(2)(b), the words "the Board are satisfied that".
		In section 731(3), the words following paragraph (b).
		In section 769(2)(d), the words "any gift of shares".
		In section 812(4), paragraph (a).
		In Schedule 7, in paragraph 1(5), the words "and shown to have been made".
		In Schedule 12, in paragraph 2(2), the words "shown to be".
		In Schedule 21, paragraph 3.
1992 c. 12.	The Taxation of Chargeable Gains Act 1992.	In section 52(4), the words "such method as appears to the inspector or on appeal the Commissioners concerned to be".
		In section 116(13), the words "the inspector is satisfied that" and "and so directs,".
		In section 122, in subsection (2), the words "the inspector is satisfied that" and "and so directs" and subsection (3).
		In section 133, in subsection (2), the words "the inspector is satisfied that" and "and so directs" and subsection (3).
		In section 164F(8)(a), the words "it is shown that".
		In section 164FG(2), the words "or an officer of the Board in default of an election determines".

Chapter	Short Title	Extent of repeal
1993 c. 34.	The Finance Act 1993.	In section 181(1)(b), the words "it is shown that" and the word "that" in the second place where it occurs. In section 222, in subsection (5), paragraph (b) and the words following it and, in subsection (6), paragraph (b) and the word "and" immediately preceding it. Section 226(5). In section 271(2), in the second paragraph, the words "the Board are satisfied that". In Schedule 6, in paragraph 3, in sub-paragraphs (1), (3) and (4), the words "on production of such evidence as the Board may reasonably require, the Board are satisfied". In section 144, in subsections (1)(b) and (2)(b), the words "the inspector is satisfied," and the word "that", in the first place where it occurs, and, in subsection (3)(b), the words "in the opinion of the inspector" and subsection (4). In section 145, in subsection (1)(c), the words "the inspector is satisfied that", in subsections (2)(b) and (3)(b), the words "in the opinion of the inspector", in subsection (4)(b), the words "the inspector is satisfied that" and in subsection (5), the words "in the opinion of the inspector" and subsection (6).

These repeals have effect in accordance with section 134 of, and Schedule 20 to, this Act.

(11) SELF-ASSESSMENT: TIME LIMITS

Chapter	Short Title	Extent of repeal
1990 c. 1.	The Capital Allowances Act 1990.	In section 37(2), the words following paragraph (d).
1992 c. 12.	The Taxation of Chargeable Gains Act 1992.	In Schedule 4, in paragraph 9(1)(b), the words "year of assessment or".
1994 c. 9.	The Finance Act 1994.	In Schedule 15, paragraph 21(a)(ii).

These repeals have effect in accordance with section 135 of, and Schedule 21 to, this Act.

(12) SELF-ASSESSMENT: APPEALS

Chapter	Short Title	Extent of repeal
1970 c. 9.	The Taxes Management Act 1970.	Section 42(12). In section 44— (a) subsections (1A) and (1B), and (b) in subsection (2), the words "and any direction under subsection (1A) above". Schedule 2.

Chapter	Short Title	Extent of repeal
1975 c. 7.	The Finance Act 1975.	Section 54.
1975 c. 45.	The Finance (No. 2) Act 1975.	Section 66.
1976 c. 40.	The Finance Act 1976.	In Schedule 9, paragraph 11.
1984 c. 43.	The Finance Act 1984.	In Schedule 22, paragraph 3(2).
1988 c. 1.	The Income and Corporation Taxes Act 1988.	In the Table in paragraph 32 of Schedule 29, the entries relating to Schedule 3 to the Taxes Management Act 1970.
1988 c. 39.	The Finance Act 1988.	Section 133(1).
1989 c. 26.	The Finance Act 1989.	Section 160(6). Section 168(8).
1990 c. 1.	The Capital Allowances Act 1990.	In Schedule 1, paragraph 1(4).
1994 c. 9.	The Finance Act 1994.	In Schedule 19, paragraph 36.
1995 c. 4.	The Finance Act 1995.	In Schedule 17, in paragraph 22, the words "(including that provision as proposed to be substituted by paragraph 7 of Schedule 19 to the Finance Act 1994)".

These repeals have effect in accordance with Schedule 22 to this Act.

(13) SELF-ASSESSMENT: ACCOUNTING PERIODS ETC.

Chapter	Short Title	Extent of repeal
1988 c. 1.	The Income and Corporation Taxes Act 1988.	Section 8A.
1993 c. 34.	The Finance Act 1993.	Section 206(2).

(14) SELF-ASSESSMENT: ADVANCE CORPORATION TAX

Chapter	Short Title	Extent of repeal
1988 c. 1.	The Income and Corporation Taxes Act 1988.	Section 239(5).

This repeal has effect in accordance with Schedule 25 to this Act.

(15) CLASS 4 CONTRIBUTIONS

Chapter	Short Title	Extent of repeal
1988 c. 1.	The Income and Corporation Taxes Act 1988.	Section 617(5).
1992 c. 4.	The Social Security Contributions and Benefits Act 1992.	In Schedule 2, in paragraph 3(2), the words "(e) section 617(5) (relief for Class 4 contributions)".
1992 c. 7.	The Social Security Contributions and Benefits (Northern Ireland) Act 1992.	In Schedule 2, in paragraph 3(2), the words "(e) section 617(5) (relief for Class 4 contributions)".

These repeals have effect in accordance with section 147 of this Act.

(16) PERSONAL INJURY DAMAGES AND COMPENSATION

Chapter	Short Title	Extent of repeal
1988 c. 1.	The Income and Corporation Taxes Act 1988.	Sections 329A to 329C.
1995 c. 4.	The Finance Act 1995.	Section 142.
1995 c. 53.	The Criminal Injuries Compensation Act 1995.	Section 8.

(17) FOREIGN INCOME DIVIDENDS

Chapter	Short Title	Extent of repeal
1988 c. 1.	The Income and Corporation Taxes Act 1988.	In section 246S— (a) in subsection (3), the words after paragraph (e); and (b) subsection (8).

These repeals have effect in accordance with Schedule 27 to this Act.

(18) FOTRA SECURITIES

Chapter	Short Title	Extent of repeal
1988 c. 1.	The Income and Corporation Taxes Act 1988.	Section 47. Section 474(2). In section 475— (a) in subsection (5), the words "Subject to subsection (6) below,"; (b) subsections (6) and (7); and (c) in subsection (8), the words from "and this subsection" onwards. In section 715— (a) in subsection (1), paragraphs (g) and (h); and (b) in subsection (8), the definition of "FOTRA securities".
1993 c. 34.	The Finance Act 1993.	In section 174— (a) subsection (6); and (b) in subsection (7), the definitions of "FOTRA securities" and "non-resident United Kingdom trader".
1994 c. 9.	The Finance Act 1994.	Section 222(6) and (7).

These repeals come into force in accordance with section 154(9) of this Act.

(19) PAYING AND COLLECTING AGENTS

Chapter	Short Title	Extent of repeal
1988 c. 39.	The Finance Act 1988.	Section 76(4) and (6).

(20) ACCRUED INCOME SCHEME

Chapter	Short Title	Extent of repeal
1988 c. 1.	The Income and Corporation Taxes Act 1988.	Section 721(1) and (4).

These repeals come into force in accordance with section 158 of this Act.

(21) MANUFACTURED PAYMENTS, REPOS, ETC.

Chapter	Short Title	Extent of repeal
1970 c. 9.	The Taxes Management Act 1970.	In the first column of the Table in section 98, the entry relating to section 729(11) of the Taxes Act 1988.
1988 c. 1.	The Income and Corporation Taxes Act 1988.	Section 729. Section 732(3). In section 737(5AA)(b), the words from "and the words" onwards. Section 737A(2)(b). Section 786(4). In Schedule 23A, paragraph 4(7A).
1994 c. 9.	The Finance Act 1994.	Section 124.
1995 c. 4.	The Finance Act 1995.	Section 80(2).

1. Subject to note 2 below, these repeals have effect in accordance with section 159(1) of this Act.

2. The repeals in section 737 of, and Schedule 23A to, the Taxes Act 1988, and the repeal of section 124 of the Finance Act 1994, come into force on the day on which this Act is passed.

(22) VENTURE CAPITAL TRUSTS

Chapter	Short Title	Extent of repeal
1988 c. 1.	The Income and Corporation Taxes Act 1988.	In Schedule 28B, in paragraph 9, in sub-paragraph (1) the words "subject to sub-paragraph (2) below" and sub-paragraph (2).

These repeals have effect in accordance with section 161 of this Act.

(23) LIFE ASSURANCE BUSINESS LOSSES

Chapter	Short Title	Extent of repeal
1988 c. 1.	The Income and Corporation Taxes Act 1988.	Section 436(3)(aa). Section 439B(3)(b). Section 441(4)(aa).
1995 c. 4.	The Finance Act 1995.	In Schedule 8, paragraph 16(4) and (5).

These repeals have effect in accordance with paragraph 10(2) of Schedule 31 to this Act.

(24) MANAGEMENT EXPENSES OF INSURANCE COMPANIES

Chapter	Short Title	Extent of repeal
1988 c. 1.	The Income and Corporation Taxes Act 1988.	In section 434(1)(b), the words from "of the tax" onwards. In section 434D(8), in paragraph (b) of the second sentence, the words from "of the tax" onwards. In section 442(3), the words "otherwise than for the purposes of section 76(2)". In section 473, subsection (5). In Schedule 19AC— (a) in paragraph 5(1), in the subsection (6B) deemed to be inserted in section 76, the words "and subsections (2) and (3)(b) above"; and (b) in paragraph 9, in the subsection (1A) deemed to be inserted in section 434, the words from "of the tax" onwards.
1992 c. 12.	The Taxation of Chargeable Gains Act 1992.	In Schedule 10, in paragraph 14(27)(a), the words "and (5)".

These repeals come into force in accordance with section 164(5) of this Act.

(25) ANNUAL PAYMENTS UNDER INSURANCE POLICIES

Chapter	Short Title	Extent of repeal
1988 c. 1.	The Income and Corporation Taxes Act 1988.	Section 434B(1).

This repeal has effect in accordance with section 165 of this Act.

(26) INDUSTRIAL ASSURANCE BUSINESS

Chapter	Short Title	Extent of repeal
1988 c. 1.	The Income and Corporation Taxes Act 1988.	In section 431(2)— (a) the definitions of "industrial assurance business" and of "ordinary long term business" and "ordinary life assurance business"; and (b) in the definition of "long term business fund", the words from "or, where" to "so maintained". Section 432(2). In section 458(3), the words "or industrial assurance business".
1989 c. 26.	The Finance Act 1989.	Section 83A(5).
1990 c. 29.	The Finance Act 1990.	In Schedule 6, paragraph 3.

These repeals come into force in relation to accounting periods beginning on or after 1st January 1996.

(27) Provisional repayments in connection with insurance companies' pension business

Chapter	Short Title	Extent of repeal
1988 c. 1.	The Income and Corporation Taxes Act 1988.	In Schedule 19AB, in paragraph 1(5)(b), the word "and" immediately preceding sub-paragraph (ii) and paragraphs 1(8) and 6(3). In Schedule 19AC, paragraph 15(1).

These repeals have effect in accordance with section 169 of, and Schedule 34 to, this Act.

(28) Friendly societies

Chapter	Short Title	Extent of repeal
1992 c. 48.	The Finance (No. 2) Act 1992.	In Schedule 9, paragraph 14(2).

This repeal has effect in accordance with section 171 of this Act.

(29) Loans to participators etc.

Chapter	Short Title	Extent of repeal
1988 c. 1.	The Income and Corporation Taxes Act 1988.	In section 419(6), the words "and to a company not resident in the United Kingdom".

This repeal has effect in accordance with section 173(6) of this Act.

(30) Chargeable gains: non-resident companies

Chapter	Short Title	Extent of repeal
1992 c. 12.	The Taxation of Chargeable Gains Act 1992.	Section 13(5)(a) and (6). In Schedule 5, paragraph 8(10).

These repeals come into force in relation to gains accruing on or after 28th November 1995.

(31) Cancellation of tax advantages: transactions in certain securities

Chapter	Short Title	Extent of repeal
1996 c. 8.	The Finance Act 1996.	In section 175, subsections (2) and (3) and, in subsection (4), the words "Except as provided by subsection (3) above,".

These repeals have effect in accordance with section 175(3) of this Act.

(32) Sub-contractors in the Construction Industry

Chapter	Short Title	Extent of repeal
1988 c. 1.	The Income and Corporation Taxes Act 1988.	In section 566(2), the words "and any such regulations may make different provision for different circumstances."

(33) Capital Allowances: Roll-over Relief in Respect of Ships

Chapter	Short Title	Extent of repeal
1990 c. 1.	The Capital Allowances Act 1990.	In section 33C(2), the words "to be", in the first place where they occur.

(34) Controlled Foreign Companies

Chapter	Short Title	Extent of repeal
1988 c. 1.	The Income and Corporation Taxes Act 1988.	In section 747A, subsection (7) and, in subsection (8), the words "the company is not a trading company and". In Schedule 25, in paragraph 2A, in sub-paragraph (1), the words "which is not a trading company" and sub-paragraphs (6) and (7) and, in paragraph 3, sub-paragraphs (1) to (4) and, in sub-paragraph (5), the words "the available profits or, where the company is not a trading company,".

These repeals have effect in accordance with section 182 of this Act.

Part VI

Inheritance Tax

Chapter	Short Title	Extent of repeal
1984 c. 51.	The Inheritance Tax Act 1984.	In section 105— (a) in subsection (1), "109A", the words "shares in or" in paragraph (b), and paragraph (c); (b) subsections (1A) and (1B); (c) in subsection (2), the words "(b) or"; and (d) subsection (2A). In section 107(4), the words "and section 109A below". Section 109A. Section 116(2A).
1987 c. 16.	The Finance Act 1987.	In Schedule 8, paragraphs 5 to 7.
1995 c. 4.	The Finance Act 1995.	Section 155(2).

1. Subject to note 2 below, these repeals have effect in accordance with section 184(6)(b) of this Act.

2. The repeal in section 116 of the Inheritance Tax Act 1984, and the related repeal in section 155 of the Finance Act 1995, have effect in accordance with section 185(3) and (6) of this Act.

PART VII

STAMP DUTY AND STAMP DUTY RESERVE TAX

Chapter	Short Title	Extent of repeal
1986 c. 41.	The Finance Act 1986.	In section 87, in subsection (2), the words "the expiry of the period of two months beginning with" and the words from "unless" to the end and subsections (4), (5) and (8). Section 88(2) and (3). Section 94(8). Section 96(12). Section 97(2).
1996 c. 8.	The Finance Act 1996.	Sections 186 to 196.

1. The repeals in sections 87 and 88 of the Finance Act 1986 have effect in accordance with sections 188 and 192 of this Act.

2. The repeals in sections 94 and 96 of the Finance Act 1986 have effect in accordance with section 194 of this Act.

3. The repeal in section 97 of the Finance Act 1986 has effect in accordance with section 196(4) of this Act.

4. The repeals in the Finance Act 1996 have effect—

(a) so far as relating to stamp duty, in accordance with section 108 of the Finance Act 1990; and

(b) so far as relating to stamp duty reserve tax, in accordance with section 110 of the Finance Act 1990.

PART VIII

MISCELLANEOUS

(1) RATES OF INTEREST

Chapter	Short Title	Extent of repeal
1994 c. 9.	The Finance Act 1994.	In Schedule 6, paragraph 11. In Schedule 7, paragraph 21(5).
1994 c. 23.	The Value Added Tax Act 1994.	Section 74(6).

Subsection (7) of section 197 of this Act applies in relation to these repeals as it applies in relation to subsection (6) of that section.

(2) BANKS

Chapter	Short Title	Extent of repeal
1984 c. 51.	The Inheritance Tax Act 1984.	In section 157(5), paragraph (b) and the word "and" immediately preceding it.
1987 c. 22.	The Banking Act 1987.	In Schedule 6, paragraph 17.

These repeals have effect in accordance with Schedule 37 to this Act.

(3) QUOTATION AND LISTING OF SECURITIES

Chapter	Short Title	Extent of repeal
1992 c. 12.	The Taxation of Chargeable Gains Act 1992.	Section 288(4).

This repeal has effect in relation to times falling on or after 1st April 1996.

(4) ENACTMENT OF EXTRA-STATUTORY CONCESSIONS

Chapter	Short Title	Extent of repeal
1891 c. 38.	The Stamp Duties Management Act 1891.	In section 9(7)(e), the words from "which is inadvertently" to "executed and duly stamped, or".
1992 c. 12.	The Taxation of Chargeable Gains Act 1992.	In section 72(5), the word "life" in the third place where it occurs. In section 73(2), the word "life". Section 75. In section 254— (a) in subsections (6) and (7), the words "the inspector is satisfied that"; (b) in subsection (8), the words "in the inspector's opinion"; and (c) in subsection (11), the words "the inspector was satisfied that", "by the inspector" and "he was satisfied that".

These repeals have effect in accordance with Schedule 39 to this Act.

INDEX

References are to sections and Schedules

EDUCATION (STUDENT LOANS) ACT 1996*

(1996 c. 9)

An Act to make provision for, and in consequence of, the payment of subsidy in respect of private sector student loans.   [29th April 1996]

PARLIAMENTARY DEBATES

Hansard, H.C. Vol. 267, col. 943; Vol. 269, col. 799; Vol. 275, col. 616. H.L. Vol. 568, col. 704; Vol. 569, col. 912; Vol. 570, cols. 739, 768, 816, 1472, 1504; Vol. 571, col. 72.

The Bill was considered in Standing Committee B between December 12, 1995 and January 9, 1996.

INTRODUCTION AND GENERAL NOTE

This Act makes changes to the system of publicly funded student support by allowing for public subsidy to private sector providers of loans to students. Prior to the passage of the Act public support for student maintenance took two forms. Under the Education Act 1962 (c. 12), s.1 (as amended by the Education Act 1980 (c. 20), s.19, Sched. 5) local education authorities are under a duty to pay an award to students ordinarily resident in their area, attending a course at a qualifying institution or taking a course designated as eligible. The Education (Student Loans) Act 1990 (c. 6) made provision for loans to students in addition to grants payable under these provisions. Government policy has since been to decrease the grant element of student maintenance and to replace it by loans. Present policy is to achieve parity between loans and grants in 1996–97 and maintain that parity thereafter (*Hansard*, H.C. Vol. 276, col. 948). By s.1(1) of the 1990 Act the Secretary of State was empowered to make arrangements for the payment of loans to eligible students. Under the arrangements loans are made through the Student Loans Company. This is a publicly owned company with two shareholders, the Secretary of State for Education and Employment and the Secretary of State for Scotland.

The present Act does not make any change to these powers granted under the 1990 Act and it is envisaged that present arrangements will continue, with the Student Loans Company continuing to make loans to students. What the Act does do is to permit the introduction of a parallel system of subsidised loan provision by the private financial sector. While the Student Loans Company would continue to make loans, the Government made it clear that students would have to choose between different forms of publicly subsidised loans. They would only be entitled to one such loan in any academic year, *either* a loan from the Student Loans Company *or* a subsidised loan from the public sector. The regulation making power under s.1(2)(b) of the 1990 Act would be used to ensure this (Mr E. Forth, Minister of State, *Hansard*, H.C. Vol. 275, col. 616). The Act authorises the Secretary of State to make arrangements for the provision of loans by private sector providers and to pay subsidies to those persons. While the nature of the arrangements is not specified in the Act it was envisaged by the Government that private financial institutions would engage in a competitive bidding exercise for a given level of subsidy and that up to four would then be chosen. Loans would be provided on the same terms as by the Student Loans Company. The details of the operation of the scheme were matters which would be determined by the contract between the Government and the financial institution concerned. In particular, while it was intended that the interest rate should not be higher than that charged by the Student Loan Company, there is no specific provision regarding this in the legislation nor as to other details of the scheme proposed. The 1990 Act made specific provision in Sched. 2 for the Secretary of State to make regulations relating to the maximum amount of loans, the time and manner of repayment, deferment and cancellation of repayment and for interest rates. The present Act confers no comparable regulation-making power in relation to subsidised loans provided by the private sector.

The Act is very short, but the scheme of the Act is complicated by the fact that it proceeds primarily by amending the Education (Student Loans) Act 1990. The principal provision is s.1 which confers power on the Secretary of State to make arrangements for subsidised private sector loans, by way of an amendment to the Education (Student Loans) Act 1990, and makes other amendments to that Act in order to take account of the new powers granted. The Act applies to England, Wales and Scotland but not (except in some minor respects) to Northern Ireland. It is proposed to establish similar arrangements in Northern Ireland (see *Hansard*, H.C. Vol. 276, col. 952). This will require an Order in Council under the Northern Ireland Act 1974 (c. 28) and s.2 provides for the procedure to be followed in relation to the making of such an Order.

---

* Annotations by William Hinds, Lecturer in Law, University of Leeds.

The other two sections contain financial provisions (s.3) and deal with the citation and extent of the Act (s.4).

COMMENCEMENT
   The Act entered into force on receipt of the Royal Assent on April 29, 1996. It was however envisaged that arrangements made under the Act would not be put into effect until October 1997 (Mr E. Forth, Minister of State, Standing Committee B, December 14, 1995).

ABBREVIATION
   "1990 Act": Education (Student Loans) Act 1990 (c. 6).

Subsidy in respect of private sector student loans

   1.—(1) In section 1 of the Education (Student Loans) Act 1990 (arrangements for loans for students out of money made available by Secretary of State), after subsection (1) insert—
      "(1A) The Secretary of State may, in pursuance of arrangements with persons by whom private sector student loans are made, pay subsidy to those persons in respect of such loans; and in this subsection "private sector student loans" means loans made to eligible students towards their maintenance otherwise than out of money made available by the Secretary of State."
   (2) The Schedule to this Act (which makes amendments in consequence of subsection (1) above) shall have effect.

DEFINITIONS
   "eligible students": s.1(2) of the Education (Student Loans) Act 1990.
   "private sector student loans": subs. (1).

GENERAL NOTE
   This section confers upon the Secretary of State power to subsidise private sector student loans provided in accordance with arrangements made between him and the provider of the loans (subs. (1)) and amends the Education (Student Loans) Act 1990 (subss. (1) and (2)).

Subs. (1)
   This inserts a new subs. (1A) in s.1 of the Education (Student Loans) Act 1990. The new subsection confers a power on the Secretary of State to make arrangements for the provision of student loans by the private sector and to pay subsidy in respect of such loans. The Act is an enabling Act and imposes no duty on the Secretary of State to make any such arrangements.

"*arrangements*": These are not defined by the Act, which is silent as to what form they should take. The Government proposed to invite private financial institutions to bid for the right to offer subsidised loans and it was envisaged that up to four institutions would be selected. Contracts to provide subsidised student loans would be awarded to institutions for a five year period in the first instance. The conditions on which loans were made would be regulated by the contract between the Government and the institution. It was intended that the contracts would include provisions to protect students, in particular rights to defer repayments and a maximum interest rate linked to the retail price index. It was intended that loans would be provided on comparable terms to those provided by the Student Loans Company (Mr E. Forth, Minister of State, *Hansard*, H.C. Vol. 267, cols. 951, 952). Loans from the Student Loans Company have their interest rates limited to the rise in the retail price index, so that, in real terms, students repay no more than they borrow. Repayments can be deferred if the borrower has an income of less than 85% of average earnings. Provision regarding interest rates and deferment of repayment in the case of Student Loan Company loans is contained in regulations made under Sched. 2 of the 1990 Act, currently the Education (Student Loans) Regulations 1994 (S.I. 1994 No. 3045). As noted above, the Government envisaged that the arrangements made under this subsection would regulate these matters in relation to subsidised private sector loans and the Act contains no regulation-making powers for such purposes.

"private sector student loans": These are defined for the purposes of this subsection as loans made to eligible students towards their maintenance otherwise than out of money made available by the Secretary of State. For the purposes of the remainder of the 1990 Act (as amended by the present Act) loans made under arrangements established in pursuance of this subsection are designated "subsidised private sector student loans". These are defined in s.1(1B) of the 1990 Act, as inserted by subs. (2) and para. 2(2) of the Schedule to the present Act.

"eligible students": An eligible student is one attending a course of higher education of at least one academic year's duration at an institution receiving support from public funds or courses at other institutions if so designated by or under regulations made by the Secretary of State (see s.1(2) of the 1990 Act). Subsection (2)(b) also empowers the Secretary of State to impose further conditions of eligibility. Such conditions are presently contained in the Education (Student Loans) Regulations 1994 (S.I. 1994 No. 3045), r. 4 and Schedule. Students must be attending a full-time course or a course for the initial training of teachers (whether full or part-time), be under the age of 50 at the date the course begins and satisfy residency and various procedural requirements. Courses of higher education are defined in Sched. 1 of the 1990 Act (which may be amended by order by the Secretary of State: s.1(4) and (6) of the 1990 Act). Institutions receiving support from public funds are defined by s.1(3) of the 1990 Act, as amended by s.93 and Sched. 8, para. 67 of the Further and Higher Education Act 1992 (c. 13), s.24 and Sched. 2, para. 9 of the Education Act 1994 (c. 30) and the Further and Higher Education (Scotland) Act 1992 (c. 37), s.62 and Sched. 9, para. 12(2).

Subs. (2)

This gives effect to the Schedule to the Act which makes amendments to the Education (Student Loans) Act 1990 in consequence of subs. (1) of the present Act. Some of these amendments are of more than technical significance and result in the creation in some respects of a different regime for "subsidised private sector student loans" as against "public sector student loans". Paragraph 2(2) of the Schedule inserts a new subs. (1B) into s.1 of the 1990 Act which defines these terms. "Subsidised private sector student loans" are loans made in accordance with arrangements made under the new subs. (1A) inserted in s.1 of the 1990 Act by s.1 of the present Act. "Public sector student loans" are loans made under arrangements made under s.1(1) of the 1990 Act.

Significant differences are, first, that under Sched. 2, para. 1 of the 1990 Act, the Secretary of State has a power to make regulations regarding the maximum amount of a loan, interest rates, repayment terms and deferment or cancellation of repayments. He is also required to make separate provision for the disabled. The present relevant regulations are the Education (Student Loans) Regulations 1994 (S.I. 1994 No. 3045). The effect of para. 3(2) and (3) of the Schedule to the present Act is to confine this regulation-making power to public sector student loans and to leave regulation of the same matters in relation to subsidised private sector loans to such arrangements, if any, as the Secretary of State may make with the providers of such loans.

Secondly, Sched. 2, para. 3(5) of the 1990 Act provides that any arrangements for the making of student loans must provide for an independent person to investigate and report on any dispute between borrowers or intending borrowers and the loan making body. The effect of para. 3(4)(c) of the Schedule to the present Act is that no such dispute procedure is provided in relation to subsidised private sector student loans.

Thirdly, there are also differences in relation to disclosure of information. Paragraph 4(1) of Sched. 2 of the 1990 Act (as amended by para. 3(6)(a) of the Schedule to the present Act) imposes an absolute prohibition on the disclosure of information held in relation to the making or recovering of public sector student loans if it is to be used for the purpose of soliciting custom for goods or services. Paragraph 3(6)(b) of the Schedule to the present Act inserts a new sub-para. (1A) in Sched. 2, para. 4 of the 1990 Act imposing a similar prohibition in relation to subsidised private sector student loans but with the exception that it is permissible for a member of a group (within the meaning of Pt. VII of the Companies Act 1985 (c. 6)) to make available information to another member of the group.

One other significant change applies to both public and subsidised private sector student loans. Under para. 2(1) of Sched. 2 of the 1990 Act (as amended by para. 3(3)(a) of the present Act) the Secretary of State has power to make regulations to require the governing bodies of institutions attended by eligible students to take certain steps, which include the provision of information, in relation to loan applications; this will now apply to both public sector student loans and subsidised private sector student loans. Paragraph 3(3)(b) of the Schedule inserts a new sub-para. (1A) in Sched. 2, para. 2 of the 1990 Act conferring a power to make regulations providing for payments to the governing bodies of institutions in respect of the administrative costs incurred in complying with such regulations.

Corresponding provision for Northern Ireland

2. An Order in Council under sub-paragraph (1)(b) of paragraph 1 of Schedule 1 to the Northern Ireland Act 1974 (legislation for Northern Ireland in the interim period) which contains a statement that it is made only for purposes corresponding to the purposes of section 1 above and the Schedule to this Act—

(a) shall not be subject to sub-paragraphs (4) and (5) of that paragraph (affirmative resolution of both Houses of Parliament), but

(b) shall be subject to annulment in pursuance of a resolution of either House of Parliament.

GENERAL NOTE

By virtue of s.4(3), the Act does not apply to Northern Ireland except for s.4(3) itself, para. 3(3) of the Schedule and s.2. Power exists to legislate for Northern Ireland by Order in Council under s.1(3) and Sched. 1, para. 1(1)(b) of the Northern Ireland Act 1974 (c. 28). Section 2 excludes the requirement in para. 1(4) and (5) of Sched. 1 of that Act that any such Order in Council shall be subject to the affirmative resolution procedure and substitutes by subs. (b) the negative resolution procedure, provided that the Order contains a statement that it is made only for purposes corresponding to s.1 and the Schedule to the present Act. The 1990 Act does not apply to Northern Ireland by virtue of s.4(4) of that Act (although there is a similar provision that any Order in Council under s.1(3) and Sched. 1, para. 1(1)(b) of the Northern Ireland Act 1974 shall be subject to the negative resolution procedure in s.2 and a power to make regulations under Sched. 2, para. 2 in respect of institutions in Northern Ireland, conferred by s.4(4)). The Education (Student Loans) (Northern Ireland) Order 1990 (S.I. 1990 No. 1506 (N.I. 11)), amended by the Education and Libraries (Northern Ireland) Order 1993 (S.I. 1993 No. 1506 (N.I. 12)) confers power upon the Department of Education for Northern Ireland to make arrangements for the payment of student loans in Northern Ireland. The provisions of the Order parallel those of the 1990 Act. It was the stated intention of the Government to introduce a scheme of subsidised private sector student loans in Northern Ireland: see *Hansard*, H.C. Vol. 276, col. 952.

Financial provisions

3. There shall be paid out of money provided by Parliament—

(a) any sums required by the Secretary of State for paying subsidy in respect of private sector student loans, and

(b) any increase attributable to this Act in the expenses of the Secretary of State under the Education (Student Loans) Act 1990.

GENERAL NOTE

This section contains the financial provisions authorising by s.3(a) the payment of subsidies by the Secretary of State to providers of subsidised private sector loans out of money provided by Parliament. Section 3(b) deals with increases in the expenditure of the Secretary of State under the 1990 Act resulting from this Act. As the principal substantive provisions of the present Act take the form of amendments to the 1990 Act, expenditure resulting from the introduction and administration of the subsidised private sector student loans scheme will constitute such expenditure. The subsection authorises the payment of such expenses out of money provided by Parliament.

Citation and extent

4.—(1) This Act may be cited as the Education (Student Loans) Act 1996.

(2) This Act and the Education Acts 1944 to 1994 may be cited together as the Education Acts 1944 to 1996.

(3) Apart from—

(a) section 2 above,

(b) (as respects institutions in Northern Ireland) paragraph 3(3) of the Schedule to this Act, and

(c) this section,

this Act does not extend to Northern Ireland.

GENERAL NOTE

This section provides for the citation of the Act and its extent. By virtue of subs. (2) the Act may be cited together with the Education Acts 1944 to 1994 as the Education Acts 1944 to 1996. The Act applies to England, Wales and Scotland but not, by virtue of subs. (3), to Northern Ireland with the exception of subs. (3) itself, s.2 and para. 3(3) of the Schedule. Power exists under s.1(3) and Sched. 1, para. 1(1)(b) of the Northern Ireland Act 1974 to legislate by Order in Council for Northern Ireland and s.2 of the present Act excludes the requirements of Sched. 1, para. 1(4) and (5) of that Act that any such Order should be subject to an affirmative resolution of both Houses of Parliament. Any such Order, if stating that it is made only for purposes corresponding to s.1 and the Schedule to the present Act, shall be subject to the negative resolution procedure only. Paragraph 3(3) of the Schedule amends Sched. 2, para. 2 of the 1990 Act (which applies to Northern Ireland by virtue of s.4(4) of the 1990 Act). This confers a power to make regulations requiring the governing bodies of institutions to which eligible students attend, to take prescribed steps in relation to eligible students. In its form as amended by para. 3(3)(a) of the Schedule to the present Act, this power can be exercised in relation to both public sector student loans and subsidised private sector student loans. In addition, para. 3(3)(b) of the Schedule confers a power to make regulations providing for the making of payments to governing bodies in relation to the taking of steps prescribed by any such regulations. These regulation-making powers will apply in relation to institutions in Northern Ireland.

SCHEDULE

CONSEQUENTIAL AMENDMENTS

1. The Education (Student Loans) Act 1990 is amended in accordance with this Schedule.

2.—(1) Section 1 (arrangements for loans for students out of money made available by Secretary of State) is amended as follows.

(2) After subsection (1A) (which is inserted by section 1 of this Act) insert—

"(1B) In this Act—
(a) references to public sector student loans are to loans under arrangements made under subsection (1) above; and
(b) references to subsidised private sector student loans are to loans in respect of which arrangements such as are mentioned in subsection (1A) above provide for the payment (at any time or in any circumstances) of subsidy under that subsection."

(3) In subsection (5), for "arrangements made under this section" substitute "public sector student loans and subsidised private sector student loans".

3.—(1) Schedule 2 (provisions about loans out of money made available by Secretary of State) is amended as follows.

(2) In paragraph 1—
(a) in sub-paragraph (1), before "loan" (in both places) and "loans" insert "public sector student", and
(b) in sub-paragraph (4), for "Loans" substitute "Public sector student loans",
and, accordingly, in the heading immediately preceding that paragraph, for "*Principal*," substitute "*Public sector student loans: principal,*".

(3) In paragraph 2—
(a) in sub-paragraph (1), for "loans under the arrangements made under section 1 of this Act," substitute "public sector student loans or subsidised private sector student loans,", and
(b) after that sub-paragraph insert—
"(1A) Regulations under sub-paragraph (1) above may include provision for the making of payments to governing bodies in respect of the taking by them of steps prescribed by the regulations."

(4) In paragraph 3—
(a) in sub-paragraph (1), for "The arrangements may provide for the" substitute "Arrangements made under section 1(1) of this Act may provide for public sector student" and for "to the loans" substitute "to such loans",
(b) in sub-paragraph (2), for "loans under the" substitute "such loans under those",
(c) in sub-paragraph (5), for "borrowers or intending borrowers under this Act" substitute "persons borrowing or intending to borrow by way of public sector student loans" and after "making" insert "such",
(d) in sub-paragraph (6), after "making" insert "public sector student", and

(e) in sub-paragraph (7), after "recovering" insert "public sector student" and for "under the arrangements" substitute "by virtue of this paragraph",

and, accordingly, for the heading immediately preceding that paragraph substitute "*Public sector student loans: administration*".

(5) For sub-paragraph (8) of paragraph 3 substitute—

"*Circulars to minors*

3A. No document sent—
 (a) in connection with public sector student loans by any such person or body as is mentioned in paragraph 3(1) above; or
 (b) in connection with subsidised private sector student loans by any person making or proposing to make such loans,

shall be regarded as sent with a view to financial gain within the meaning of section 50 of the Consumer Credit Act 1974 (circulars to minors)."

(6) In paragraph 4—
(a) in sub-paragraph (1), after "recovering" insert "public sector student",
(b) after that sub-paragraph insert—

 "(1A) No person making or proposing to make subsidised private sector student loans shall provide or make available to anyone else (whether for consideration or not) any information held in connection with such loans if the information is to be used for soliciting custom for goods or services; but this sub-paragraph does not prevent a member of a group (within the meaning of Part VII of the Companies Act 1985) providing or making available information to another member of the group.", and

(c) in sub-paragraph (2), for "sub-paragraph (1) above is" substitute "sub-paragraphs (1) and (1A) above are" and for "applies" substitute "apply".

(7) In paragraphs 5(3) and 6, for "loan under the arrangements" substitute "public sector student loan or subsidised private sector student loan".

DEFINITIONS
 "governing bodies": Sched. 2, para. 2(2) of the Education (Student Loans) Act 1990.
 "group": s.262(1) of the Companies Act 1985.
 "minors": s.189(1) of the Consumer Credit Act 1974.
 "public sector student loans": para. 2(2); s.1(1B)(a) of the Education (Student Loans) Act 1990.
 "subsidised private sector student loans": para. 2(2); s.1(1B)(b) of the Education (Student Loans) Act 1990.

GENERAL NOTE
 The Schedule amends the Education (Student Loans) Act 1990. As noted above in relation to s.1(2) the amendments are of some considerable importance.

Para. 1
 This provides that the 1990 Act shall be amended in accordance with the following paragraphs.

Para. 2
 Sub-paragraph (1) amends s.1 of the 1990 Act by inserting, by virtue of sub-para. (2), a new subs. (1B) in the 1990 Act after the new subs. (1A) as inserted by s.1 of this Act. The new subs. (1B) of the 1990 Act defines "public sector student loans" and "subsidised private sector student loans". The former are loans made under arrangements made under s.1(1) of the 1990 Act; the latter are loans made under arrangements made under s.1(1A) of the 1990 Act (inserted by s.1(1) of this Act). Sub-paragraph (3) amends s.1(5) of the 1990 Act to apply Sched. 2 of the 1990 Act to both public sector student loans and subsidised private sector student loans.

Para. 3

Sub-para. (1)
 This amends Sched. 2 to the 1990 Act as provided in the following sub-paragraphs.

Sub-para. (2)

Schedule 2, para. 1 of the 1990 Act confers upon the Secretary of State a power to make regulations in relation to student loans, regarding the maximum amount of loan in any one year, the time and manner of repayment and to provide for deferment or cancellation of liability (para. 1(1)). The maximum amount of loan that may be prescribed is limited by para. 1(2). Paragraph 1(3) imposes a duty to make such separate provision as the Secretary of State thinks appropriate for repayment of loans by disabled students. The prescribed interest on loans is regulated in sub-paras. (4) and (5). This provision for making regulations is retained, but Sched. 2, para. 1 of the 1990 Act is amended to confine it to public sector student loans. There is no comparable regulation-making power in relation to subsidised private sector student loans although s.1(2)(b) of the 1990 Act confers a power to make regulations regarding eligibility of students for loans. This power will apply to both public sector student loans and subsidised private sector loans. It was stated by the Government that this regulation-making power would be used to prevent a student obtaining more than one publicly subsidised loan in any one year (Mr E. Forth, Minister of State, *Hansard*, H.C. Vol. 275, col. 616).

Sub-para. (3)

Paragraph 2 of Sched. 2 to the 1990 Act confers a power to make regulations requiring governing bodies of institutions attended by students eligible for loans, to take prescribed steps, which may include the issue of certificates or provision of information. The effect of sub-para. (3)(a) is to extend that power to subsidised private sector student loans as well as public sector student loans. Sub-paragraph (3)(b) confers a power to make regulations providing for payments to governing bodies for taking the prescribed steps in relation to both types of loan.

Sub-para. (4)

This makes consequential amendments to para. 3 of Sched. 2 to the 1990 Act concerning administration of the existing student loans scheme to confine its operation to the administration of public sector student loans. One result is that the provision for investigation by an independent person of disputes between borrowers or intending borrowers and the loan making body only applies to such loans. No provision is made for any external complaints procedure in relation to subsidised private sector student loans. The view of the Government was that the Banking and Building Society ombudsmen could adequately deal with any complaints (*Hansard*, H.L. Vol. 570, col. 1518).

Sub-para. (5)

This repeals para. 3(8) of Sched. 2 to the 1990 Act and inserts a new para. 3A. The Consumer Credit Act 1974 (c. 39), s.50 makes it a criminal offence to send a document to a minor with a view to financial gain inviting him to, *inter alia*, borrow money or apply for information or advice on borrowing money. While only a small proportion of students are minors, some potential applicants will be and para. 3A provides that documents sent by providers of either public sector student loans or subsidised private sector loans shall not be regarded as sent with a view to financial gain for this purpose.

Sub-para. (6)

This amends para. 4 of Sched. 2 to the 1990 Act, regarding the disclosure of information by those concerned in the making or recovering of student loans. In the case of public sector student loans, para. 4(1)(a), as amended, prohibits information held for these purposes from being provided or made available for the purpose of soliciting custom for goods or services. In the case of subsidised private sector loans this prohibition is qualified. Paragraph 3(6)(b) of the Schedule inserts a new sub-para. (1A) in para. 4 of Sched. 2 to the 1990 Act which provides that such information may be provided or made available to one member of a group (within the meaning of Pt. VII of the Companies Act 1985) by another.

Consequential amendments are then made by sub-para. (6)(c) to para. 4(2) of Sched. 2 to the 1990 Act relating to the Data Protection Act 1984 (c. 35). Paragraph 4(2) now provides that para. 4(1) (as amended) and the new para. 4(1A) are without prejudice to the provisions of that Act, but that the Act applies irrespective of any consent given for the purpose of that Act by the person to whom the information relates.

Sub-para. (7)

This amends the provisions in paras. 5 and 6 of Sched. 2 to the 1990 Act relating to insolvency in England and Wales (para. 5) and Scotland (para. 6), to make it clear that they apply to both public sector student loans and subsidised private sector loans. The effect is that loans from either source are *not* to be treated as part of a bankrupt's estate and debts incurred in relation to such loans shall *not* be treated as bankruptcy debts.

INDEX

References are to sections and the Schedule

AUDIT (MISCELLANEOUS PROVISIONS) ACT 1996

(1996 c. 10)

An Act to extend the functions of the Audit Commission for Local Authorities and the National Health Service in England and Wales; to alter the financial year of that Commission and of the Accounts Commission for Scotland; to make provision about the manner of publication of certain information required to be published in pursuance of a direction of either Commission; and to repeal paragraph 5(4) of Schedule 3 to the Local Government Finance Act 1982. [29th April 1996]

PARLIAMENTARY DEBATES
Hansard, H.C. Vol. 268, col. 376. H.L. Vol. 569, col. 397; Vol. 570, col. 1117; Vol. 571, col. 900.

INTRODUCTION
This Act allows for the extension of the functions of the Audit Commission for Local Authorities and the National Health Service in England and Wales. Provision is made concerning information required to be published, and the alteration of the Commission's financial year.

Audit Commission: extension of functions, etc.

Collaborative studies of social services

1.—(1) After section 28 of the Local Government Finance Act 1982 insert—

"Collaborative studies of social services

28AA.—(1) At the request of the Secretary of State, the Commission may assist the Secretary of State in any study designed to improve economy, efficiency, effectiveness and quality of performance in the discharge of social services functions by local authorities.

(2) In this section "social services functions" means—

(a) any function under any enactment for the time being specified in Schedule 1 to the Local Authority Social Services Act 1970; and

(b) any function for the time being designated by an order made by the Secretary of State under section 2(2) of the 1970 Act as being appropriate for discharge through a local authority's social services committee.

(3) In the following provisions of this section "study" means a study of a description mentioned in subsection (1) above.

(4) If the Commission require—
(a) any local authority included in a study, or
(b) any officer or member of such an authority,
to supply the Commission or an authorised person with such information as is needed for the purposes of the study, the authority or officer or member shall supply the information.

(5) If the Commission require any local authority included in a study to make available for inspection by the Commission or an authorised person documents which relate to the authority and are needed for the purposes of the study, the authority shall make the documents available.

(6) Any information obtained under a requirement under subsection (4) or (5) above may be disclosed by the Commission to the Secretary of State for the purposes of any functions of his which are connected with the discharge of social services functions by local authorities.

(7) In subsections (4) and (5) above "authorised person" means a person authorised by the Commission for the purposes of this section.

(8) Any report of a study in which the Commission assists the Secretary of State shall be published by the Secretary of State in conjunction with the Commission.

(9) The Commission shall not provide assistance under subsection (1) above unless before it does so the Secretary of State has agreed to pay the Commission an amount equal to the full costs incurred by the Commission in providing the assistance."

(2) This section shall come into force at the end of the period of two months beginning with the day on which this Act is passed.

Consequential amendments

2.—(1) In section 30 of the Local Government Finance Act 1982 (restriction of disclosure of information) after subsection (1) insert—
"(1A) Subsection (1) above is subject to section 28AA(6)."

(2) In Schedule 3 to the 1982 Act (the Audit Commission) in paragraph 9(2) (income and expenditure with respect to functions in relation to health service bodies and in relation to other bodies to be managed separately) for the words from "the functions" to the end substitute "—
(a) the functions of the Commission under section 28AA of this Act in relation to the discharge of social services functions;
(b) its functions in relation to health service bodies; and
(c) its other functions."

Financial years of the Commissions

Financial year of Audit Commission

3.—(1) In section 36 of the Local Government Finance Act 1982 (interpretation of Part III of the Act) after subsection (1) insert—
"(1A) In this Part of this Act "financial year" means the period of 12 months ending with 31st October in any year."

(2) At the beginning of subsection (2) of that section (application of certain interpretation provisions of Local Government Act 1972) insert "Subject to subsection (1A) above".

(3) In Schedule 3 to the 1982 Act (the Audit Commission)—
(a) in paragraph 10(6) (date by which certain accounts must be sent to Comptroller and Auditor General) for "November" substitute "March"; and
(b) in paragraph 12(3) (date by which certain other accounts must be sent to Comptroller and Auditor General) for "30th November" substitute "31st March".

(4) Subsections (1) to (3) shall have effect in relation to the year ending with 31st October 1998 and subsequent years ending with 31st October.

(5) In relation to the period beginning on 1st April 1997 and ending with 31st October 1997—

(a) Part III of the 1982 Act (the Audit Commission) shall have effect as if "financial year" meant that period;

(b) paragraph 10(6) of Schedule 3 to that Act shall have effect so as to require the account there mentioned to be sent not later than 31st March 1998;

(c) paragraph 12(3) of Schedule 3 to that Act shall have effect so as to require the statement there mentioned to be transmitted on or before 31st March 1998.

Financial year of Accounts Commission for Scotland

4.—(1) In section 98 of the Local Government (Scotland) Act 1973 (expenses and accounts of Accounts Commission for Scotland)—

(a) in subsection (5), for the words "30th November" substitute "31st March"; and

(b) after subsection (6) add—

"(7) In this section, "financial year" means the period of twelve months ending with 31st October in any year.".

(2) In section 235(1) of the 1973 Act (interpretation), in the definition of "financial year", after the word "has" insert ", except in section 98,".

(3) Subsections (1) and (2)—

(a) shall first have effect in relation to—

(i) such year; or

(ii) such greater or lesser period than a year,

ending, in either case, with 31st October, as the Secretary of State may by order made by statutory instrument specify; and

(b) shall thereafter have effect in relation to years so ending,

and as respects any period specified under paragraph (a)(ii) the subsection added by subsection (1)(b) shall be construed as if referring to that period and not to a period of twelve months.

Miscellaneous and supplementary

Publication at direction of either Commission

5.—(1) In section 1 of the Local Government Act 1992 (direction of Audit Commission or Accounts Commission for Scotland requiring certain bodies to publish information about performance) in subsection (2)(b) (method of publication) for the words "in a newspaper circulating in the area of that body" substitute "and by one of the methods permitted by section 1A below".

(2) After section 1 of that Act insert—

"Permitted methods of publishing information

1A.—(1) The permitted methods of publication referred to in section 1(2)(b) above are as follows.

(2) The relevant body may publish the information in a newspaper printed for sale and circulating in their area.

(3) If the relevant body ensure that the distribution condition is satisfied with respect to the information, they may publish the information in a newspaper or periodical publication which is produced and distributed by another person (other than a local authority company) and which is free of charge to the recipient.

(4) For the purposes of subsection (3) above, a relevant body ensure that the distribution condition is satisfied with respect to information if—

   (a) they take all reasonable steps to secure that a copy of a publication containing the information is distributed to each dwelling in their area; and

   (b) in a case where they consider that the information is of concern to persons carrying on business in their area, they take such steps as they consider reasonable and practicable to secure that a copy of a publication containing the information is distributed to business premises in their area.

(5) For the purposes of subsection (3) above a local authority company is any company under the control of a local authority; and section 68(1) of the Local Government and Housing Act 1989 (company under control of local authority) shall have effect for the purposes of this subsection as it has effect for the purposes of Part V of that Act."

Remuneration etc. of members of Audit Commission

6.—(1) In paragraph 5 of Schedule 3 to the Local Government Finance Act 1982, sub-paragraph (4) (determination of remuneration etc. of members of Audit Commission requires Treasury consent) shall be omitted.

(2) This section shall apply to any determination made after the expiry of the period of two months beginning with the day on which this Act is passed.

Short title and extent

7.—(1) This Act may be cited as the Audit (Miscellaneous Provisions) Act 1996.

(2) This Act, apart from this section and sections 4 and 5, does not extend to Scotland.

(3) This Act does not extend to Northern Ireland.

INDEX

References are to sections

NORTHERN IRELAND
(ENTRY TO NEGOTIATIONS, ETC) ACT 1996

(1996 c. 11)

ARRANGEMENT OF SECTIONS

An Act to make provision for elections in Northern Ireland for the purpose of providing delegates from among whom participants in negotiations may be drawn; for a forum constituted by those delegates; for referendums in Northern Ireland; and for connected purposes. [29th April 1996]

PARLIAMENTARY DEBATES
Hansard, H.C. Vol. 275, cols. 716, 851; Vol. 276, cols. 88, 205. H.L. Vol. 571, cols. 1138, 1254.

INTRODUCTION

This Act introduces arrangements for elections to be held in Northern Ireland so that delegates can be chosen for participation in all-party negotiations. Provisions are also made for the constitution of a forum of such delegates until the end of May 1997 and for referendums to be held on any matter relating to Northern Ireland.

The elections

1.—(1) Elections shall be held in Northern Ireland for the purpose of providing delegates from among whom participants in negotiations may be drawn.

(2) Schedule 1 (which makes provision as to the holding of the elections and the provision of delegates) shall have effect.

The negotiations

2.—(1) The negotiations mentioned in section 1 are the negotiations referred to in Command Paper 3232 presented to Parliament on 16th April 1996.

(2) As soon as practicable after the elections, the Secretary of State shall invite the nominating representative of each party for which delegates have been returned in accordance with Schedule 1 to nominate, from among those delegates, a team to participate in the negotiations.

(3) The Secretary of State shall refrain from inviting nominations from the nominating representative of a party, and shall exclude delegates already nominated from entering into the negotiations, if and for as long as he considers that requirements set out in paragraphs 8 and 9 of Command Paper 3232 are not met in relation to the party.

(4) The nominating representative of a party may from time to time substitute for any member of the team nominated for that party another delegate returned for that party in accordance with Schedule 1.

The forum

3.—(1) The delegates returned in accordance with Schedule 1 shall constitute a forum for the discussion of issues relevant to promoting dialogue and understanding within Northern Ireland.

(2) The functions of the forum shall be deliberative only.

(3) Accordingly the forum shall not have any legislative, executive or administrative functions, or any power to determine the conduct, course or outcome of the negotiations mentioned in section 1.

(4) But if, in accordance with any rules of procedure adopted by them, the participants in the negotiations refer any matter to the forum, subsection (3) shall not be taken to prevent the forum from considering that matter.

(5) Schedule 2 shall have effect in relation to the forum.

Referendums

4.—(1) The Secretary of State may from time to time by order direct the holding of a referendum for the purpose of obtaining the views of the people of Northern Ireland on any matter relating to Northern Ireland.

(2) An order under subsection (1) shall be made by statutory instrument; but no order shall be made unless a draft has been laid before, and approved by resolution of, each House of Parliament.

(3) An order under subsection (1) may include such provision relating to the conduct of the referendum as appears to the Secretary of State expedient, including provision—

(a) setting out the wording of the question to be put;

(b) as to the persons entitled to vote;

(c) applying, with or without modifications, any enactment (and in particular any enactment relating to elections) or any provision made under an enactment.

(4) Nothing in this section shall be construed as authorising the Secretary of State to direct the holding of a poll otherwise than in accordance with Schedule 1 to the Northern Ireland Constitution Act 1973 in relation to the matters dealt with in section 1 of that Act (status of Northern Ireland as part of United Kingdom).

"Nominating representative" of a party

5.—(1) In this Act "nominating representative" in relation to a party means the person who at any time appears to the Secretary of State to be the leader of the party or otherwise the most appropriate person to act on behalf of the party for the purposes of this Act.

(2) The Secretary of State shall cause to be published in the Belfast Gazette—

(a) an initial list of the nominating representatives of the parties listed in Part II of Schedule 1;

(b) notice of any change in the nominating representative of any of those parties.

Allowances and Secretary of State's expenses

6.—(1) The Secretary of State may pay allowances to delegates returned in accordance with Schedule 1, whether by reference to days on which they attend the forum or participate in negotiations or otherwise.

(2) Any expenses incurred by the Secretary of State in connection with the elections or otherwise by virtue of this Act shall be paid out of money provided by Parliament.

Duration of sections 3 and 4

7.—(1) Section 3 shall cease to have effect at the end of May 1997.

(2) The Secretary of State may by order provide that section 3 shall—

(a) continue to have effect, or
(b) come into force again,
until a time, not later than the end of May 1998, specified in the order.

(3) The Secretary of State may by order provide that section 3 shall cease to have effect at a time specified in the order (being a time earlier than the time at which it would cease to have effect by virtue of subsection (1) or (2)).

(4) If it appears to the Secretary of State that the negotiations mentioned in section 1 are concluded or suspended, he shall by order under subsection (3) provide for section 3 to cease to have effect.

(5) Section 4 shall cease to have effect at the end of May 1999.

(6) An order under this section shall be made by statutory instrument; but no order shall be made unless a draft has been laid before, and approved by resolution of, each House of Parliament.

Short title

8. This Act may be cited as the Northern Ireland (Entry to Negotiations, etc) Act 1996.

SCHEDULES

Section 1(2)   SCHEDULE 1

THE ELECTIONS

PART I

GENERAL

Orders

1.—(1) The Secretary of State may by order make provision about the elections, and any other provision consequential on or supplementary to this Schedule.

(2) An order under this paragraph may apply, with or without modifications, any enactment (and in particular any enactment relating to elections) or any provision made under an enactment.

(3) An order under this paragraph shall be made by statutory instrument; but no order shall be made unless a draft has been laid before, and approved by resolution of, each House of Parliament.

Return of delegates

2.—(1) Five delegates shall be returned for each of the parliamentary constituencies in Northern Ireland and twenty for Northern Ireland as a whole.

(2) The constituencies referred to in sub-paragraph (1), and in the following provisions, are those provided for in the Parliamentary Constituencies (Northern Ireland) Order 1995.

Date of poll

3. The poll in the elections shall be held on a date provided for by an order under paragraph 1.

Franchise

4. The persons entitled to vote at the election in a constituency shall be those who both—
(a) would be entitled to vote as electors at a local election in a district electoral area wholly or partly comprised in the constituency, and
(b) are registered at an address within the constituency in a register of local electors.

Parties and party lists

5.—(1) The elections shall be conducted on the basis of lists submitted by the nominating representatives of parties.

(2) The parties for which lists may be submitted are those set out in Part II of this Schedule.

6.—(1) The nominating representative of each of those parties may (within such time as may be prescribed by an order under paragraph 1) submit to the Chief Electoral Officer for Northern Ireland separate lists of candidates for all or any of the constituencies ("constituency lists").

(2) If a nominating representative submits at least three constituency lists, he may also submit a list of candidates for Northern Ireland as a whole (a "regional list").

(3) The number of candidates on a constituency list must be at least two and not more than five.

(4) The number of candidates on a regional list must be at least two and not more than ten.

(5) A constituency list for a party may not include a candidate who is on another constituency list for the party.

(6) A party's regional list must include at least two candidates who are not on a constituency list for the party.

Method of election

7.—(1) Each elector shall have one vote, to be cast for a party named on the ballot paper for the constituency.

(2) The ballot paper shall show the names of each of the parties for which a constituency list has been submitted for the constituency.

Constituency delegates

8.—(1) For each constituency there shall be calculated—
(a) the total number of votes given;
(b) the quota for the constituency;
(c) the number of votes given for each party.

(2) The quota for a constituency is—

$$\frac{T}{6} + 1$$

where T is the total number of votes given.

9.—(1) If the number of votes given for a party in a constituency equals or exceeds the quota, one of the candidates on the party's constituency list shall be returned from the constituency as a delegate.

(2) But if the number of votes equals or exceeds a multiple of the quota, a correspondingly greater number of candidates shall be returned (up to the number appearing on the list).

10. If the application of paragraph 9 produces fewer than five delegates, then—
(a) there shall be calculated for each party (excluding any whose constituency list has been exhausted) the quotient representing—

$$\frac{V}{N + 1}$$

where V is the number of votes given for the party and N is the number of the party's candidates returned as delegates by the previous application of paragraph 9 (or paragraph 9 and this paragraph);
(b) a candidate on the list of the party with the highest quotient shall be returned as a delegate.

11. If the application of paragraph 10 produces fewer than five delegates, it shall be applied again until five delegates have been produced (or all the constituency lists have been exhausted).

12. The order in which the candidates on a party's list are returned for a constituency shall be the order in which they appear on the list.

13. An order under paragraph 1 shall make provision as to the return of delegates in the event of an equality of quotients.

Regional delegates

14.—(1) For each party having a regional list the aggregate number of votes given in all the constituencies shall be calculated.

(2) Two candidates from the regional list of each of the ten parties with the largest aggregates shall be returned as delegates.

15. The order in which the candidates on a party's regional list are returned shall be the order in which they appear on the list, except that a candidate returned at the election for a constituency shall be disregarded.

16. An order under paragraph 1 shall make provision as to the return of delegates in the event of an equality of votes.

Disqualification

17. A person is disqualified for being on a constituency or regional list if—

(a) he is a person to whom section 3 of the Representation of the People Act 1983 applies (disfranchisement of offenders in prison), or

(b) he is authorised to be detained on the ground (however formulated) that he is suffering from mental illness, or

(c) he is not of voting age within the meaning of section 1 of that Act.

Amendment of lists, and vacancies

18.—(1) A person's name shall be treated as removed from a party's constituency or regional list if he dies or is disqualified or if the Secretary of State receives a written request for removal from—

(a) that person, or

(b) the party's nominating representative.

(2) A person whose name is treated as removed from a list shall (if he is one) cease to be a delegate or a member of a team nominated under section 2(2) or (4).

19.—(1) This paragraph shall apply where a person ceases to be a delegate in accordance with paragraph 18.

(2) Where the delegate was appointed from a party's constituency list, there shall be returned as a delegate in his place—

(a) the next person on that list who is not a delegate, or

(b) if there is no such person, the next person on the party's regional list who is not a delegate.

(3) Where the delegate was appointed from a regional list, there shall be returned as a delegate in his place the next person on that list who is not a delegate.

(4) A vacancy which cannot be filled by the application of sub-paragraph (2) or (3) shall remain unfilled.

20. Where a party ceases to exist, any persons on its lists who are delegates or members of a team nominated under section 2(2) or (4) shall cease to be so.

PART II

THE PARTIES

Alliance Party
British Ulster Unionist Party
Communist Party of Ireland
Conservative Party
Democratic Left
Democratic Partnership
Democratic Unionist—DUP
Green Party
Independent Chambers
Independent Democratic Unionist Party
Independent Kerr
Independent McCaffrey
Independent McGrath
Independent McMullan
Independent Sinclair
Independent Templeton
Labour
Natural Law Party
No Going Back
Northern Ireland Party (NIP)
Northern Ireland Womens' Coalition
Progressive Unionist Party (PUP)
Sinn Fein
Social Democratic and Labour Party (SDLP)
UK Unionist Party—Robert McCartney
Ulster Christian Democrat Party
Ulster Democratic Party (UDP)
Ulster Independence
Ulster's Independent Voice
Ulster Unionist Party (UUP)
Workers' Party

SCHEDULE 2

THE FORUM

Chairman

1.—(1) There shall be a chairman of the forum.

(2) The chairman shall be elected by the members, but until the first election has taken place he shall be a member nominated by the Secretary of State.

Meetings

2.—(1) The first meeting of the forum shall be at a time decided by the Secretary of State.

(2) The time decided under sub-paragraph (1) shall be—

(a) after the commencement of negotiations within section 2, and

(b) within, or as soon as possible after expiry of, the period of four weeks beginning with the date of the poll in the elections.

(3) Subsequent meetings shall be at times determined by the members of the forum.

(4) But the forum shall not meet at any time notified by the Secretary of State to the chairman as being a time when, in the opinion of the Secretary of State, it would not be appropriate for the forum to meet because negotiations within section 2 are intended to take place; but the Secretary of State shall not prevent the holding of a meeting for more than four consecutive weeks.

Procedure

3.—(1) Subject to the provisions of this Schedule, the proceedings of the forum (and of any committee it may establish) shall be conducted in accordance with rules of procedure determined by the members of the forum and approved by the Secretary of State.

(2) The rules of procedure of the forum shall include provision for a quorum.

(3) Until rules of procedure have been determined and approved under sub-paragraph (1) proceedings shall be conducted in accordance with rules determined by the Secretary of State and notified by him to the chairman.

(4) In exercising his functions under sub-paragraphs (1) and (3) above, the Secretary of State shall make every effort to secure that the rules of procedure of the forum facilitate the promotion of dialogue, understanding and consensus across the communities of Northern Ireland.

4. A decision on the election or removal of a chairman or the adoption or alteration of rules of procedure shall not be regarded as taken by the members unless—

(a) no member present has objected to it, or

(b) it is approved on a vote by at least 75 per cent. of those voting.

Privilege

5. A written or oral statement made by a member of the forum in or for the purposes of the forum (or any committee it may establish) shall be privileged from action for defamation unless it is proved to have been made with malice.

Miscellaneous

6. The Secretary of State shall provide for the forum the services of such staff, the use of such premises and such other facilities as he thinks appropriate.

INDEX

References are to sections and Schedules

RATING (CARAVANS AND BOATS) ACT 1996

(1996 c. 12)

An Act to make provision about liability for non-domestic rates in England and Wales in relation to certain caravans and boats.   [29th April 1996]

PARLIAMENTARY DEBATES
Hansard, H.C. Vol. 267, col. 901; Vol. 269, col. 355; Vol. 276, col. 606. H.L. Vol. 568, col. 364; Vol. 570, col. 1137; Vol. 571, col. 900.

INTRODUCTION
This Act provides for certain caravans and boats to be liable for non-domestic rates where they are occupied as a sole or main residence.

Caravans and boats occupied as sole or main residence

1.—(1) Section 66 of the Local Government Finance Act 1988 (definition of "domestic property" for the purpose of exclusion from local rating lists) is amended as follows.

(2) For subsection (3) of that section (pitches for caravans) there is substituted—

"(3) Subsection (1) above does not apply in the case of a pitch occupied by a caravan, but if in such a case the caravan is the sole or main residence of an individual, the pitch and the caravan, together with any garden, yard, outhouse or other appurtenance belonging to or enjoyed with them, are domestic property".

(3) For subsection (4) of that section (moorings) there is substituted—

"(4) Subsection (1) above does not apply in the case of a mooring occupied by a boat, but if in such a case the boat is the sole or main residence of an individual, the mooring and the boat, together with any garden, yard, outhouse or other appurtenance belonging to or enjoyed with them, are domestic property.

(4A) Subsection (3) or (4) above does not have effect in the case of a pitch occupied by a caravan, or a mooring occupied by a boat, which is an appurtenance enjoyed with other property to which subsection (1)(a) above applies".

(4) Subsections (2) and (3) above are to be treated as having had effect on and after 1st April 1990 and any additional sums payable in respect of non-domestic rates by virtue of this subsection may accordingly be recovered.

(5) Subsection (4) does not apply in relation to a hereditament where—

(a) a proposal for the alteration of a local non-domestic rating list in respect of the hereditament has been made, and not withdrawn, before 30th January 1995 in accordance with regulations under section 55 of the Local Government Finance Act 1988,

(b) the ground for the proposal was that the list was inaccurate because the hereditament ought not to be shown in the list or, in the case of a composite hereditament, the rateable value shown in the list was too high, and

(c) the reason or one of the reasons given in the proposal, or on an appeal (in accordance with those regulations) to a tribunal against a refusal to make the proposed alteration, for the list being inaccurate was that any pitch occupied by a caravan or (as the case may be) mooring occupied by a boat was domestic property by virtue of section 66(1)(a) or (b) of that Act.

(6) Local non-domestic rating lists compiled on 1st April 1990, 1st April 1995 or 1st April 1996 must be altered so far as required in consequence of this section; and the alterations are to be treated as having had effect from 1st

April 1990 or, in the case of lists compiled on 1st April 1995 or 1st April 1996, from 1st April 1995 or from such other date as may be applicable in accordance with regulations under section 2.

Section 1: supplementary

2.—(1) The Secretary of State may make regulations for the purpose of giving effect to section 1 of this Act; and the regulations may have retrospective effect and may apply, with or without modifications, any of the provisions made by or under the Local Government Finance Act 1988 in relation to non-domestic rating.

(2) The power to make regulations under subsection (1) above is exercisable by statutory instrument, which shall be subject to annulment in pursuance of a resolution of either House of Parliament.

(3) Expressions used in section 1 of this Act and in sections 64 to 67 of the Local Government Finance Act 1988 have the same meaning in that section as in those sections.

(4) In consequence of section 1(2) of this Act, section 1(2) of the Caravans (Standard Community Charge and Rating) Act 1991 is repealed.

Short title, etc.

3.—(1) This Act may be cited as the Rating (Caravans and Boats) Act 1996.

(2) This Act extends to England and Wales only.

INDEX

References are to sections

BOATS,
  as main residence, 1(3)
  moorings, 1(3)

CARAVANS,
  as main residence, 1(2)–(3)
  pitches for, 1(2)

DOMESTIC PROPERTY,
  definition, 1(1)

EXTENT, 3(2)

INTERPRETATION, 2(3)

LOCAL RATING LISTS,
  alterations to, 1(6)
  exclusion from, 1(1)
  proposals for alteration of, 1(4)

REGULATIONS, 2(1)–(2)
REPEALS, 2(4)

SHORT TITLE, 3(1)

NON-DOMESTIC RATING (INFORMATION) ACT 1996

(1996 c.13)

An Act to make provision for and in connection with the disclosure by persons who are valuation officers or assessors to other such persons of information connected with non-domestic rating.   [22nd May 1996]

PARLIAMENTARY DEBATES
Hansard, H.C. Vol. 268, col. 1022; Vol. 271, col. 624. H.L. Vol. 569, col. 397; Vol. 571, cols. 749, 1476; Vol. 572, col. 394.

INTRODUCTION
  This Act provides for the disclosure by rating officials of information connected with non-domestic rating. An official shall not be prevented from disclosing information at the request of another official merely because it is held by him in connection with a statutory function.

Disclosure of information

1.—(1) Where a rating official requests another rating official to disclose any information to him in order to assist him in the performance of his statutory functions, the other official shall not be prevented from so disclosing the information merely because it is held by him in connection with his statutory functions.
  (2) In subsection (1)—
    "rating official" means a valuation officer or an assessor; and
    "statutory functions" means—
      (a) in relation to a valuation officer, functions under Part III of the Local Government Finance Act 1988; and
      (b) in relation to an assessor, functions under the Valuation Acts as defined in section 183(1) of the Local Government etc. (Scotland) Act 1994;
and in this subsection "valuation officer" means a person appointed under section 61(1)(a) or (b) of the Local Government Finance Act 1988 and "assessor" means a person appointed under section 27 of the Local Government etc. (Scotland) Act 1994.
  (3) In Schedule 11 to the Local Government Finance Act 1988 (valuation tribunals), in paragraph 8(3)(ea) (power to make regulations as to evidence)—
    (a) for "documents or" substitute "documents,"; and
    (b) insert after sub-paragraph (iv) (not as part of that sub-paragraph) "or of information disclosed by virtue of section 1(1) of the Non-Domestic Rating (Information) Act 1996;".

Short title and extent

2.—(1) This Act may be cited as the Non-Domestic Rating (Information) Act 1996.
  (2) This Act does not extend to Northern Ireland.

INDEX

References are to sections

RESERVE FORCES ACT 1996*

(1996 C. 14)

ARRANGEMENT OF SECTIONS

---

* Annotations by G.R. Rubin, Professor of Law at the University of Kent at Canterbury.

PART X

GENERAL OFFENCES

Offences against good order and discipline

Desertion and absence without leave from service, duty or training

General

PART XI

RESERVE ASSOCIATIONS

PART XII

MISCELLANEOUS AND GENERAL

Miscellaneous

General

An Act to make provision with respect to the reserve forces of the Crown and persons liable to be recalled for permanent service; to amend the provisions of the Reserve Forces Act 1980 relating to the lieutenancies; to amend the law relating to the postponement of the discharge or transfer to the reserve of regular servicemen; and for connected purposes.

[22nd May 1996]

PARLIAMENTARY DEBATES

Hansard, H.L. Vol. 567, col. 520; Vol. 568, cols. CWH1, CWH43, CWH99; Vol. 569, col. 1369; Vol. 570, col. 227. H.C. Vol. 274, col. 401; Vol. 278, col. 20.

The Bill was discussed in Standing Committee A between April 16–23, 1996.

INTRODUCTION AND GENERAL NOTE

The Reserve Forces Act 1996 brings the law with regard to the reserve forces up to date and will permit those reserves to be used more flexibly. The Act is a very complex measure and in parts contains highly technical provisions. Though parts of it are a re-enactment of provisions of the Reserve Forces Act 1980 (c. 9), experience has shown, for example, in the Gulf War, that the 1980 Act was insufficiently adaptable to the needs of the services. Consequently, the scope of the 1996 Act is wider than its predecessor and the new Act is consequently lengthy. It was enacted after an exhaustive consultation process with many interested parties, including representatives of employers' and employees' interests. For the most part, the Bill received the support of the Opposition parties in parliament, and many Opposition amendments were accepted by the government in the spirit of improving the objectives of the measure.

The underlying premise of the Act is that the reserve forces are conceived of as an integral component of the armed forces of the Crown (approximately 650 reservists have been called out to serve as part of the U.K.'s contribution to I-FOR, the NATO implementation force in former Yugoslavia). Thus, their central role in the defence of the realm is to be strengthened within the total defence effort. Moreover, they form, in the words of Lord Williams of Elvel, "a vital umbilical cord . . . between the regular forces and the civilian population (*Hansard*, H.L. Vol. 570, col. 231). In addition, and reflecting the geo-political changes in the nature of, and perceived combatants in, conflicts throughout the world since the end of the Cold War, reservists will now undertake new forms of service beyond those categories authorised by the 1980 Act. Built into the identification of these objectives is flexibility in the statutory provisions designed to attain them. That flexibility is a recognition both of the needs of civil society, including the needs of reservists themselves and their employers, and of the State (for example, the Secretary of State may lengthen reserve service by order in certain circumstances).

Part I   The Reserve Forces

This Part provides the legal (and constitutional) authority for the existence, maintenance and composition of the reserve forces of the Crown. There are two broad categories, the ex-regular reserve forces and the volunteer reserve forces. While parliament must authorise the maximum numbers, the government, discipline, organisation, pay and provisions of the reserve forces are governed by orders or regulations issued by Her Majesty or by the Defence Council under s.4.

Part II—Enlistment and Conditions of Service
This Part, together with Sched. 1 in regard to enlistment procedures, makes provision for enlistment, re-engagement, choice of reserve corps or unit, transfers, command, posting and discharge, including postponement of discharge in some circumstances, such as when a call-out order is in force.

Part III—Training and other Duties
While voluntary training and other voluntary activities can freely be assumed, Pt. III imposes, subject to qualifications, a training obligation on the reservist. It also introduces two new concepts, a full-time service commitment and an additional (or part-time) duties commitment. These will enable reservists to be employed more flexibly in the future, allowing them greater opportunities to increase their skills, and to undertake a wider range of tasks in peacetime, that is, in circumstances in which no call-out order has been made. The duties involved may well be operational, or could involve guard duty, maintenance, transporting or loading, signals work, or intelligence. Reservists will be subject to service discipline law for the duration. Previously, reservists undertaking such tasks were required, in the absence of call out or of statutory training days or annual camp, to leave the volunteer reserves, join the regular forces, obtain discharge from the latter and then rejoin the volunteer reserves whenever their full-time service commitment with the regulars had ceased. Such a wasteful and tortuous process will no longer be required under the new arrangements in Pt. III.

Part IV—Special Agreements for Call Out
This Part creates a new category of reservist, the high readiness reserve. The Act does not in fact use this phrase. Instead, it refers to a special agreement entered into by the reservist. It is implicit, rather than explicit, that the other party is the Secretary of State. The agreement imposes on the reservist an increased liability for call out, subject, however, to the agreement of his employer, if he is in "qualifying" employment. The high readiness reserve, the total number of which may be between 3000 and 5000, are persons with skills in short supply such as linguists, medical personnel, public relations specialists and electronics specialists. Provisions for entering into and terminating special agreements and for call out of members of the high readiness reserve for "permanent service" not exceeding nine months are included in Pt. IV.

Part V—Employee Agreements
This creates another new category of reservist, the sponsored reserve. Again, the Act does not employ this popular term. Instead, it refers to employee agreements entered into by an employee (implicitly with the Secretary of State), in pursuance of an "arrangement" between the employer and the Secretary of State. The employee then becomes a "special member" of a reserve force. The essence of the sponsored reserve is the deployment of persons (otherwise civilians) belonging to a Ministry of Defence contractor's workforce who accept a specific reserve liability to continue to provide a contracted service in an operational environment. Thus he might be involved in maintaining or repairing electrical or electronic equipment, tanks and other sophisticated vehicles or aircraft procured by the ministry from the sponsored reservist's employer. The special member will become subject to service discipline law while on service. He will probably replace regular service personnel on tasks when it is cost-effective to do so. Market testing of different tasks will be undertaken. In other words, the sponsored reserve extends contracting out to actual service. The provisions of Pt. V cover employee agreements, liabilities of special members for call out, call-out arrangements themselves and discharge and release from service. A maximum duration of liability may be specified in the employee agreement, though a six-month maximum (albeit renewable by the Secretary of State) applies when a call-out order under s.52 (with respect to national danger, great emergency or attack on the U.K.) or under s.54 (warlike operations) is also in force. See Pt. VI.

Part VI—Call Out for Permanent Service
This re-enacts the principal call-out powers in the 1980 Act in relation to national danger, great emergency and warlike operations. But it also expands the power of call out to include call out for peacekeeping, humanitarian and disaster relief operations. This reflects the changing nature of international conflict since the end of the Cold War and the changes in the tasks which service personnel now fulfil. As with the other categories of reservist, there is a maximum duration of call out. Provisions relating to general liability for call out, the different types of call out, acceptance into and release from service are covered in Pt. VI.

Part VII—Recall for Service of Officers and Former Servicemen

Certain commissioned officers and former regular service personnel who are no longer currently serving in the regular services are nonetheless liable for recall for service. Recall may apply only in the event of national danger, great emergency or apprehended or actual attack on the U.K. It therefore does not apply in relation to warlike operations or to peacekeeping, humanitarian or disaster relief operations. Part VII covers the authority for a recall order, the recall process, maximum duration of service, release and discharge and power to require information.

Part VIII—Schemes for Exemption and Financial Assistance

Two major safeguards are provided in the Act in relation to call out or recall. The first is provision for exemption or deferral, and the second is provision for financial assistance in consequence of call out or recall. The application in either case may be made by the person called out (or recalled), or by an affected employer. Note that in regard to the first safeguard, an application based on conscientious objection is not dealt with under these provisions. In regard to the second safeguard, pension rights are also protected. A compliance cost assessment was conducted to assess the financial implications for the government of making up an individual's service pay to the level of his civilian pay and of reimbursing employers for additional expenditure incurred as a result of call out or recall.

Part IX—Reserve Forces Appeal Tribunal

This Part creates a new appeal tribunal which will hear appeals from determinations by the Secretary of State in regard to applications for exemption, deferral, etc., and to claims for financial assistance. A legally qualified chairman and two ordinary members shall rehear a contested application or claim. There is no further provision for appeal.

Part X—General Offences

Under the Reserve Forces Act 1980, it was an offence for certain categories of reservist to fail to attend for call out or for training. In relation to other categories of reservists, the service discipline Acts were applicable to such offences. Part X of the 1996 Act now applies to all categories of reserve in cases of failure to attend for call out, duty or training. It also otherwise makes extensive provision in regard to desertion or absence without leave. It furthermore introduces new offences in relation to minor infringements, by reservists, of good order and discipline in circumstances when they would otherwise not be subject to service discipline law. It also provides that offences under Pt. X may be triable by court-martial or summarily in a civil court. In respect to deserters or illegal absentees, Sched. 2 contains detailed provisions regarding arrest, preliminary proceedings before a civil court, arrangements for custody, surrender to police, and certificates of arrest or surrender. In respect to court proceedings for offences under Pt. X, Sched. 3 contains general provisions as to evidence, particularly in regard to service documents.

Part XI—Reserve Associations

This Part updates the provisions of Pt. VI of the 1980 Act in regard to territorial, auxiliary and volunteer reserve associations (TAVRAs). These are the local bodies which have certain responsibilities in relation to the organisation of local reserve force units. Part XI makes provision for the creation, powers, duties and winding up of associations. Schedule 4 lays down a scheme for the constitution of local associations.

Part XII—Miscellaneous and General

This Part, as one would expect, contains a disparate group of provisions. It introduces Sched. 5 which makes provision in regard to the disposal or application of the charitable property of a disbanded reserve force unit. It removes any doubts as to the validity of the appointment and acts of lord-lieutenants and also introduces Sched. 6 which makes minor amendments in relation to the positions of deputy lord-lieutenant and vice lord-lieutenant (while most of the 1980 Act is to be repealed, ss.130–138 in relation to the lieutenancies remain in force). There are further minor provisions in Pt. XII in relation to such diverse matters as safeguard of employment, billeting, exemption from tolls, and voting in European, national and local elections. It also introduces the remaining Schedules which make consequential amendments to existing legislation. For example, Sched. 7 alters the service discipline Acts in relation to the postponement of transfer to the reserve or discharge from the regular services as a result of the introduction of the new categories of call out in the Act. Schedule 10 makes minor and consequential amendments to the service discipline Acts, that is, to the Army/Air Force Acts 1955 (c. 18, c. 19) and the Naval Discipline Act 1957 (c. 53), and to other legislation. Schedules 8 and 9 deal with transitory and transitional provisions. These cover, *inter alia*, those reservists who may remain subject to the limited call-out provisions of the 1980 Act, notwithstanding the wider call-out powers in the 1996

Act. It also makes provision for changes in reserve forces organisation and the termination of certain classes of reservist.

It should also be noted that provisions of the Armed Forces Act 1996 (c. 46) which received the Royal Assent on July 24, 1996 are applicable to members of the reserve forces. Thus the Armed Forces Act 1996, s.1, which continues in force the service discipline Acts, applies to the reserve forces insofar as the service discipline Acts do so. Similarly, a number of the provisions in regard to the trial and punishment of offences under service discipline law apply to reservists involved in disciplinary proceedings, whether dealt with summarily by a commanding officer or by court-martial. The provisions are s.5 and Sched. 1 in respect to procedure for dealing with offences under the service discipline Acts; s.6 regarding the abrogation of common law corroboration rules; s.7 concerning video recording evidence from children; s.8 and Sched. 2 relating to findings of unfitness to stand trial and insanity; and s.9 concerning the postponement of sentences of courts-martial.

Section 11 (fingerprinting of certain offenders); s.12 (taking of samples from certain offenders); s.13 and Sched. 4 (application of Rehabilitation of Offenders Act 1974 (c. 53)); s.14 (application of Rehabilitation of Offenders (Northern Ireland) Order 1978; ss.15–19 and Sched. 5 (review of court-martial findings and sentence, and appeal) are all applicable to reservists involved in service discipline procedures.

Section 20 (redress of complaints procedure) also applies to reservists who may invoke these procedures in respect to any matter relating to their reserve service. Sections 21–25 concerning complaints to industrial tribunals in regard to sex and racial discrimination and to equal treatment also apply to reservists. So do the provisions of ss.26 and 27. These amend s.192 of the Employment Rights Act 1996 (c. 18) (which re-enacts the Employment Protection (Consolidation) Act 1978 (c. 44), s.138A) and the Industrial Relations (Northern Ireland) Order 1993, para. 10. These provisions require the use of internal redress procedures by service personnel before they can make a complaint to an industrial tribunal on a matter not covered under ss.21–25. The matters relate to the terms and conditions of engagement, though the provisions in the Employment Rights Act 1996 and in the Industrial Relations (Northern Ireland) Order 1993 have not yet been brought into force. Section 28(2), which provides exemptions from gun certificate requirements under the Firearms (Amendment) Act 1988 (c. 45), applies to reservists to the extent that they are members of the armed forces. See the definition of "armed forces" in the 1988 Act, s.16A(3), as now amended, for the purpose of exercising supervision over persons who may be in possession of firearms without holding a certificate. Finally, s.32 of the Armed Forces Act 1996, concerning offences connected with the armed forces' drug testing programmes, will apply to reservists liable to participation in such programmes.

It may also be relevant to refer to the current armed forces' policy on homosexuality, which prohibits homosexuals from serving in the British armed forces and renders them subject to administrative discharge. The policy also applies to all members of the reserve forces. The policy, which was upheld by the Court of Appeal in *R. v. Ministry of Defence, ex p. Smith* [1996] 1 All E.R. 257, was reaffirmed in parliament during the debates on the Armed Forces Bill (*Hansard*, H.C. Vol. 277, col. 389). It also followed the publication of the report of the Ministry of Defence's Homosexuality Policy Assessment Team in March 1996 which recommended no change. The issue was discussed in the *Special Report from the Select Committee on the Armed Forces Bill*, 1995–96, H.C. Paper 143. Since those events, the Divisional Court has considered a further challenge to the legality of the administrative discharge of homosexuals. The application for judicial review by Terence Perkins, a leading medical assistant in the Royal Navy, discharged because of his sexual orientation, is based on the ruling of the European Court of Justice in *P. v. S. and Cornwall County Council* [1996] I.R.L.R. 347. The E.C.J. held in that case that the E.U. Equal Treatment Directive applied to transsexuals. The decision in *ex p. Perkins* is still awaited as at the date of this annotation. At the same time, the South London industrial tribunal has adjourned a claim by 18 ex-service personnel that they were unfairly dismissed from the services for being homosexual. The outcome of the industrial tribunal applications will be dependent on the Divisional Court's finding on the applicability of *P. v. S.* to the case of homosexual service personnel. The findings in these various legal proceedings involving regular and ex-regular service personnel will be applicable to reservists.

It is understood that it is the intention of the Ministry of Defence that the bulk of the provisions of the Armed Forces Act 1996 are due to be brought into force on April 1, 1997. Those provisions of the Act which came into effect following Royal Assent, are ss.1 and 34.

EXTENT

The Act extends to Northern Ireland (s.132(2)) and may be extended by Order in Council, with such exceptions and modifications, as appear to Her Majesty to be appropriate, to the Channel Islands and the Isle of Man (s.132(3)). Some of the provisions are made applicable by the Act to the Channel Islands and the Isle of Man (e.g. Pt. VII, s.77(1) and s.110(4)). It may be noted that service personnel including, where appropriate, personnel of the reserve forces, are subject to service discipline law ("service law" in s.127(1)), wherever they be serving throughout the world. Service discipline law extends to civil offences which are acts or omissions punishable by the law of England or which, if committed in England, would be punishable by that law. See, for example, Army Act 1955, s.70(2).

COMMENCEMENT
The Act comes into force on such day as the Secretary of State may, by order made by statutory instrument, appoint. Different days may be appointed for different purposes (s.132(4)). As at the date of this note, no commencement orders have been issued. Nor have any dates yet been intimated, though it is anticipated that it will come into force some time in the first half of 1997.

ABBREVIATIONS
"the 1980 Act": Reserve Forces Act 1980 (c. 9).
"the 1996 Act": Reserve Forces Act 1996 (c. 14).

PART I

THE RESERVE FORCES

Maintenance and composition

Power to maintain the reserve forces

1.—(1) Her Majesty may maintain each of the reserve forces in accordance with the provisions of this Act.

(2) In this Act "the reserve forces" means the following forces—

(a) the Royal Fleet Reserve, the Royal Naval Reserve and the Royal Marines Reserve ("the reserve naval and marine forces");

(b) the Army Reserve and the Territorial Army ("the reserve land forces"); and

(c) the Air Force Reserve and the Royal Auxiliary Air Force ("the reserve air forces").

DEFINITIONS
"reserve air forces": subs. 2(c).
"reserve forces": subs. (2).
"reserve land forces": subs. 2(a).
"reserve naval and marine forces": subs. 2(a).

GENERAL NOTE
This section provides for the Queen to maintain the reserve forces. Statute thereby preserves the prerogative power of maintaining an armed force. The division of legal authority, whether statutory or prerogative, is more or less a matter of convention. The Bill of Rights 1689 (1 Will. & Mary (c. 2)), art. 6, provides for parliamentary approval for a "standing army" in peacetime. A standing army means the regular forces as defined in the Army Act 1955, s.225(1). For the circumstances in which reference to the regular forces includes reference to the reserve forces, see, for example, Army Act 1955, s.211. The other service discipline Acts, the Air Force Act 1955 and the Naval Discipline Act 1957, contain comparable provision. The Minister of State recently declared, "As a matter of convention, parliamentary control over the armed forces has been limited to the numbers that may be maintained, matters of supply, the powers that are necessary to maintain the armed forces and, as we have recently done, review of the disciplinary powers that accompany the Armed Forces Bill . . . It has always been within the Crown's prerogative powers to decide which officers to appoint to particular positions, what their duties should be and the staff they should have" (*Hansard*, H.C. Vol. 278, col. 37). Military deployment and disposition are non-justiciable prerogative powers. See *China Navigation Co. v. Attorney-General* [1932] K.B. 197; *Chandler v. Director of Public Prosecutions* [1964] A.C. 736. But the courts were recently willing to review the administrative discharge procedure (a prerogative power,

albeit within a statutory framework) in relation to homosexuals in the armed forces. See *R. v. Ministry of Defence, ex p. Smith* [1995] 4 All E.R. 427 (Div. Ct); [1996] 1 All E.R. 257 (C.A.). In the Divisional Court, Simon Brown L.J. explained that, "No operational considerations are involved in this policy": [1995] 4 All E.R. 427, at p.446.

Subs. (1)
The armed forces are, of course, the armed forces of the Crown, though the Army is still the *British* Army, not the *Royal* Army. Cf., the Royal Navy, Royal Marines and Royal Air Force. The relation between parliamentary and prerogative authority in respect to the armed forces is explained in the General Note to s.1 (above).

Subs. (2)
The reserve forces comprise volunteers and ex-regular personnel. The terms of engagement of regular service personnel may require them to serve in the reserve forces after their period of regular service has expired.

Membership of the reserve forces

2.—(1) The reserve forces shall each consist of officers and men.

(2) The men of the Royal Fleet Reserve, the Army Reserve and the Air Force Reserve (referred to in this Act as "the ex-regular reserve forces") may only be—

    (a) men transferred to that force under the Army Act 1955, the Air Force Act 1955 or regulations under the Armed Forces Act 1966, as the case may be;

    (b) men enlisted or re-engaged in that force.

(3) The men of the Royal Naval Reserve, the Royal Marines Reserve, the Territorial Army and the Royal Auxiliary Air Force (referred to in this Act as "the volunteer reserve forces") may only be men enlisted or re-engaged in that force.

(4) In this Act, any reference (however expressed) to a man of any of the reserve forces is a reference to a person of either sex who is a member of that force and is of or below the rate or rank of warrant officer.

DEFINITIONS
    "ex-regular reserve forces": subs. (2).
    "man": subs. (4).
    "volunteer reserve forces": subs. (3).

GENERAL NOTE

Subss. (1) and (4)
This section makes provision for the two classes of reserve forces, the ex-regular reserve forces and the volunteer reserve forces. The former comprises the Royal Fleet Reserve, the Army Reserve and the Air Force Reserve (note that the last-named is not the *Royal* Air Force Reserve, even though, by notice dated March 7, 1918, and published in the *London Gazette*, March 15, 1918, King George V made known His Royal will and pleasure that the air force established pursuant to the Air Force (Constitution) Act 1917 (c. 51) should be styled the "Royal Air Force"). Section 6(1) of the 1917 Act makes provision for an Air Force Reserve. The volunteer reserve forces comprise the Royal Naval Reserve, the Royal Marine Reserve, the Territorial Army and the Royal Auxiliary Air Force.

Two amendments had been set down in the Lords. The first was to insert, after "officers", the phrase "who may be of either sex". The second was to insert after "men", the words "and women". However, as "officers" is gender-neutral and as subs. (4) states that any reference to a man of the reserve forces is a reference to a person of either sex, the first amendment was withdrawn and the second not moved (see *Hansard*, H.L. Vol. 568, col. CWH 43).

Subs. (2)
Regular service personnel have the right to be transferred in limited circumstances to the reserve. See, for example, Armed Forces Act 1966 (c. 45), s.2(1)(c). Terms of enlistment in the regular forces may also require the full term to be completed in the reserve forces. See, for example, Armed Forces Act 1966, s.2(1)(b). Enlistment and re-engagement are a species of contract between the Sovereign and the recruit. For enlistment or re-engagement in the ex-

regular reserve forces, see the 1996 Act, s.9(5), in respect to the reserve naval and marine forces, and s.12(2)(c) in respect to the Army Reserve and Air Force Reserve.

Subs. (3)

This describes the membership of the volunteer reserve forces, alluding to their historically "free-standing" organisational status vis-à-vis the regular forces, though a new role for the Territorial Army as a general reserve for the Regular Army was announced in July 1994. Prior to the coming into force of the 1996 Act, Territorial Army volunteers who wished to take part in peace-keeping or humanitarian aid operations or in training exercises in, say, the Falklands, were required to be embodied in the Regular Army by virtue of "S-type" engagements. This was a cumbersome procedure which s.56 of the 1996 Act will overcome, by permitting reservists to undertake those kinds of service.

Control of numbers in the reserve forces

3.—(1) Parliament shall authorise a maximum number of officers and a maximum number of men for each of the reserve forces; and, accordingly, the numbers of officers and men of a reserve force shall not exceed the numbers for the time being authorised for the force.

(2) The special members of a reserve force shall not be reckoned in the numbers of officers and men for the time being authorised for the force under this section.

DEFINITIONS

"men" ("man"): s.2(4).
"reserve forces": s.1(2).
"special member": s.127(1).

GENERAL NOTE

Parliament has asserted its authority over the executive to determine the size of all the armed forces. Section 3 also introduces the concept of the "special members", more commonly known as the sponsored reserve, for whom provision is made in Pt. V.

Subs. (1)

The original Bill reserved for the Secretary of State the power to determine appropriate numbers for the reserve naval and marine forces, while granting parliament the right to authorise maximum numbers for the reserve land and air forces. The underlying premise of the original provision was that the naval and marine forces are, by tradition, prerogative institutions. See, for example, the Naval Discipline Act 1957 (c. 53), s.138(1): "Nothing in this Act shall take away, abridge or prejudicially affect any right, power or prerogative of Her Majesty in right of Her Crown or in right of Her office of Admiralty". In respect to the other services, the Bill of Rights 1689, discussed previously, and the Air Force (Constitution) Act 1917 stress the primacy of parliament over prerogative. In respect to the 1996 Act, the government accepted that parliament should authorise the size of *all* the reserve forces, including the reserve naval and marine forces. See *Hansard*, H.L. Vol. 568, col. CWH 2. However, this still leaves some difficulties. First, for historical reasons, Bills dealing with the armed forces normally make reference to parliament, rather than to both or either Houses, in respect to approval for particular measures. Second, what does "parliament" mean in this context? See the Laying of Documents before Parliament (Interpretation) Act 1948 (c. 59) which refers to the laying of documents before each House. But control of maximum numbers of the reserve forces is intimately linked with the financing of the armed, including reserve, forces.

This is done through the Appropriation Act which, as a supply measure, is a Commons Bill and not debated in the Lords. Technically, the fixing of the numbers of the armed forces is achieved by a Commons motion under Standing Order 52 in respect to the Spring Supplementary Estimates (the Votes A Procedure), though the Lords, as well as the Commons, do debate a Motion on the Defence Estimates (deemed not to be a Supply Motion). For discussion, see *Hansard*, H.L. Vol. 568, col. CWH 46. As the Reserve Forces Bill was introduced in the Lords, it was necessary to add, in the Lords, a privilege amendment to the Bill, cl. 132(5), to avoid any inference that the Lords had infringed the Commons' privilege in dealing with a matter imposing a charge on public funds. The amendment, included in the Bill sent to the Commons (Bill 75, March 5, 1996), was removed in the Commons (*Hansard*, Standing Committee A, col. 85, April 23, 1996).

Subs. (2)

The special members of a reserve force refer to those members belonging to a contractor's work force. They will accept a liability to be called out and to continue to provide a contracted service in operational circumstances. The numbers in this "sponsored reserve", who might be welders, electricians, medical staff, electronics specialists, etc., will not be included in the maximum numbers of reserve forces personnel authorised by parliament in subs. (1). Indications in parliament have fixed the number as varying between 3000 and 5000.

Regulation and organisation

Orders and regulations concerning the reserve forces

4.—(1) Her Majesty may, by order signified under the hand of the Secretary of State, make orders with respect to—

(a) the government and discipline of any reserve force; and

(b) all other matters and things relating to that force,

and including any matter authorised to be prescribed by any provision of this Act or expressed to be subject to orders or regulations under this section.

(2) Subject to the provisions of any order under subsection (1), the Defence Council may make regulations with respect to any matters relating to any reserve force, being matters with respect to which Her Majesty may make orders under that subsection.

(3) Orders or regulations under this section may make different provision for different cases (including different forces), and may include such supplementary, consequential, incidental and transitional provisions as appear to Her Majesty or the Defence Council (as the case may be) to be necessary or expedient.

(4) Regulations under this section may be amended or revoked by an order or further regulations under this section; and an order under this section may be amended or revoked by another order under this section.

(5) Any order or regulations under this section shall be laid before each House of Parliament after being made.

DEFINITIONS
"prescribed": s.127(1).
"reserve forces": s.1(2).

GENERAL NOTE
The legal governance of the armed forces is wondrously complex. There are statutes, for example, the Army Act 1955; subordinate legislation in the form of statutory instruments issued by the Secretary of State under statutory authority, for example, the Rules of Procedure (Army) 1972 (S.I. 1972, No. 316) (and various amendments thereto); subordinate legislation in the form of regulations issued by the Defence Council under statutory authority, for example, the Army Summary Jurisdiction Regulations 1972, numbered as Defence Council (Army) Order 17 of 1972; Orders in Council issued under statutory authority, for example, any Order in Council issued under s.131(3) of the 1996 Act directing the extension of that Act to the Channel Islands and the Isle of Man; Orders in Council issued under the prerogative, for example, the Requisitioning of Ships Order relating to the Falklands conflict; the prerogative powers embodied in Queen's Regulations, which are regulations approved by the Sovereign and issued under the aegis of the Defence Council; the prerogative Royal Warrants for regulating pay and promotion, for example, the Pay Warrant; Defence Council Instructions; administrative instructions, for example, Army General Administrative Instructions (AGAIs); Letters of Policy Guidance on particular subjects, for example, in relation to sexual harassment or homosexuality, which may be issued by Heads of Staff such as the Adjutant-General of the Army; and, finally, "standing orders", which are permanent orders issued by a commander in respect to those under his command. Note that "pure" prerogative powers may be recognised by statute. For example, the Army Act 1955, s.144(3) states: "The foregoing provisions of this section shall not prevent the making by Royal Warrant or by any regulation, order or instruction of the Defence Council, of provision for the imposition of any forfeiture authorised by Act . . .".

Standing orders of a continuing nature are recognised by s.36(2) of the Army Act 1955 and by s.36 of the Air Force Act 1955 which make it an offence for those subject to them (including certain civilians working with a military command or formation abroad) to disobey such orders. Neither Queen's Regulations, nor AGAIs, nor letters of policy guidance fall within the definition of standing orders, and failure to comply with them is not on that account an offence under s.36. Technically, AGAIs are classified as "Restricted" and Letters of Policy Guidance are classified "In Confidence", though examples of the latter, in particular, are widely accessible to the general public.

Subs. (1)

The perennial issue of the relationship between parliament and prerogative in respect to control of the armed forces is reflected here. The Sovereign's prerogative power is recognised in respect to the government and discipline of any reserve force and to "all other matters and things relating to that force" (subs. 1(b)). This is a somewhat sweeping provision whose scope was justified by the minister, though perhaps not wholly convincingly (*Hansard*, H.L. Vol. 568, col. CWH 49), but the power is exercised through the Secretary of State. In other words, the constitutional convention of the Sovereign acting through and on the advice of Her ministers provides for the role of the Secretary of State who is, of course, answerable to the House of Commons. Thus subs. (1) ensures parliament has the final say. The subsection does not expressly refer to the Secretary of State for *Defence*. The Secretary of State is an indivisible office of all the Secretaries of State (see Interpretation Act 1978 and Sched. 1 thereto). Whether the other Secretaries of State could exercise the Defence Secretary's functions is difficult to envisage.

Subs. (2)

The Defence Council possesses similar powers to those available to the Sovereign, though the latter may restrict the scope of powers issued by the former. The Defence Council comprises the Secretary of State for Defence; the Minister of State (Armed Forces); the Minister of State (Defence Procurement); the Permanent Under-Secretary of State; the Chief Scientific Adviser; the Chief of the Procurement Executive; the Chief of Personnel and Logistics; the Chief of the Defence Staff; the Vice-Chief of the Defence Staff; the Chief of the Naval Staff; the Chief of the Air Staff and the Chief of the General Staff. See Defence (Transfer of Functions) Act 1964 (c. 15).

Subs. (5)

The words "each House of" were inserted before the word "Parliament" at the House of Lords Report Stage. The necessity for such a change is debatable. See *Hansard*, H.L. Vol. 569, col. 1369. The timetable for laying is not set down and words or phrases such as "forthwith" or "as soon as possible" are absent. Assurances were given for laying "at the earliest convenient moment". See *ibid.*, col. 1370. As the orders or regulations may concern the government and discipline of the armed forces, they could be significant from a "civil liberties" perspective rather than be dismissed merely as technical, "tidying up", provisions. There is an argument in favour of the negative resolution procedure, proposed, but subsequently withdrawn, by Opposition members of parliament (*ibid.*, Vol. 568, col. CWH 52), rather than notification through laying before both Houses. However, the H.L. Delegated Powers Scrutiny Committee report of December 1995 concluded that making orders or regulations under s.4 subject to parliamentary procedures would "burden Parliament with a mass of detailed provisions which it would be difficult to scrutinise effectively".

Organisation of the reserve forces

5.—(1) Any of the reserve forces may, by or in accordance with orders or regulations under section 4, be formed into such groupings as may be specified in the order or regulations concerned.

(2) Such orders or regulations may, in particular, include provision with respect to—

(a) the formation of the reserve naval or marine forces into divisions, classes or other naval or marine bodies;

(b) the formation of the reserve land forces into corps, regiments, battalions or other military bodies;

(c) the formation of the reserve air forces into wings, squadrons or other air-force bodies; and

(d) the formation of any such bodies as are mentioned in paragraphs (a) to (c) into higher formations, either alone or jointly with any other part of Her Majesty's armed forces.

DEFINITIONS
"reserve air forces": s.1(2)(c).
"reserve forces": s.1(2).

"reserve land forces": s.1(2)(b).
"reserve naval or marine forces": s.1(2)(a).

GENERAL NOTE
The reserve forces may be organised into specific groupings as a result of regulations or orders issued under s.4. The groupings are those currently employed in the organisation of the regular forces. Much discussion has taken place in parliament and elsewhere as to whether reserve personnel should be deployed as individual units (or even formations) or whether they should be deployed as component elements within regular forces units or formations ("cadreisation"). Currently, reserves are also deployed as individual personnel; for example, two reservist medical personnel were recently deployed in Rwanda, and individual reservists may make up shortfalls in regular units. A Territorial Army unit of one officer and 18 other ranks was recently serving with British Army regular forces in the NATO implementation force in Split. See *Hansard*, H.C. Vol. 274, col. 418. In a recent House of Commons Select Committee on Defence report on the Reserves, the term "cadreisation" in the Army referred to the difference between the Peace Establishment (PE) and the War Establishment (WE) of a unit. The WE increment is filled by members of the reserve forces (ex-regulars or volunteers) and/or by deployed regulars. Cadreisation may involve both individual posts and entire sub-units (see H.C. Paper 65, 1994–95, p.30).

Subs. (1)
To what does "in accordance with" refer? Under s.4, orders and regulations are made by, respectively, Her Majesty (signified under the hand of the Secretary of State) and the Defence Council. Presumably, it will enable administrative changes to be implemented by means of instructions without directly involving the Sovereign (or Secretary of State) or the Defence Council. *Cf.*, AGAIs. See the minister's amendment (*Hansard*, H.L. Vol. 568, col. CWH 3). Some matters, including pay and pensions (see ss.7 and 8), do not appear to permit of regulation "in accordance with", as distinct from "by", orders or regulations issued under s.4.

Subs. (2)
This states the specified groupings for each arm of the reserve forces which may be prescribed by or in accordance with orders or regulations issued under s.4. It is expected that the amalgamation of the Royal Air Force Volunteer Reserve and the Royal Auxiliary Air Force will occur on April 1, 1997, by virtue of subs. 2(c). The creation of joint formations with other reserve or regular forces ("any other part of Her Majesty's armed forces") is rendered possible by subs. 2(d). The phrase "armed forces" is defined, for different purposes, in various statutes. For "Her Majesty's forces" and "Her Majesty's military forces" see Army Act 1955, s.225(1).

Permanent staff of the reserve forces

6.—(1) Each reserve force may be served by a permanent staff consisting of persons who are members of that force or members of the regular services.

(2) Orders or regulations under section 4 may make provision with respect to the duties of, and any other matter relating to, the permanent staff of any reserve force.

DEFINITION
"reserve forces": s.1(2).

GENERAL NOTE
This section provides that the permanent staff of a reserve force may be members of that force or of the regular services. Different points of view exist as to whether the morale, profile and effectiveness of the reserve forces would be enhanced by appointing reservist generals (or other service equivalents) with access to Ministers and the chiefs of staff. Thus on Third Reading in the Commons, Julian Brazier M.P. moved a new clause on the "Appointment of Director-General Reserve Forces and Cadets", with the rank of not less than Major-General or naval or Royal Air Force equivalent. Apart from policy considerations, the Minister (Mr Soames) could not accept the amendment on technical grounds. One reason was that as the deployment of the armed forces and the appointment of officers are a prerogative power, parliament, as a matter of convention, should not legislate on such a proposal. See *Hansard*, H.C. Vol. 278, col. 20. Another concern is over the ratio between administrators and members of the reserve forces. One (disputed) estimate is of one administrator to every reservist (taking account of the limited time on reserve deployment by reservists). See *Hansard*, H.C. Vol. 274, cols. 405 and 425. See also Standing Committee A, col. 9, April 16, 1996. The Commons Select Committee on Defence (*op. cit*,

paras. 27–29) discussed the growth of Non-Regular [Forces] Permanent Staff as against a decline in the numbers of Regular [Forces] Permanent Staff and of the reserve forces themselves. There are also civilian staff employed full-time in non-military functions.

Subs. (1)
The word "may" is used, rather than the mandatory "shall". Apart from the flexibility this entails, it should be noted that reserve forces civilian staff are also employed full time in non-military functions, for example, as storemen, drivers, secretaries and caretakers. See *ibid.*, para. 27. Contractorisation (or "contracting-out") has also proceeded apace. Following government reassurances, an amendment calling for parliament to authorise a maximum number of reserve forces permanent staff was withdrawn. See *Hansard*, H.C. Vol. 278, col. 38. Of course, parliament annually authorises the maximum numbers of the regular forces by Order in Council, subject to affirmative resolution procedure; and by virtue of s.3 of the 1996 Act, it does the same in respect to the reserve forces.

Subs. (2)
The governance of the reserve forces by orders or regulations issued under s.4 is applied to the permanent staff of the reserve forces. Inasmuch as some permanent staff of the reserve forces may themselves be reservists, they may already be subject to the authority to issue orders or regulations under s.4. So subs. (2) may simply remove any doubts, especially if the career structure of administrators differs from that of the rest of the regular and reserve forces.

Pay and pensions

Pay, bounty and allowances of the reserve forces

7.—(1) Orders or regulations under section 4 may make provision with respect to pay, bounty and allowances for members of the reserve forces.
(2) Such orders or regulations may, in particular—
(a) make provision as to the manner in which payments of pay, bounty and allowances are made; and
(b) impose conditions or restrictions (including deductions) on the making of such payments.
(3) In relation to prescribed members of the reserve naval and marine forces, section 1(1) and (2) of the Naval Forces (Enforcement of Maintenance Liabilities) Act 1947 shall apply in relation to the restrictions which may be included in orders and regulations by virtue of this section as it applies in relation to the restrictions which may be included in an Order in Council regulating naval and marine pay.

DEFINITION
"reserve forces": s.1(2).

GENERAL NOTE
This section deals with matters of pay, bounty and allowances for reserve forces personnel. Service personnel are appointed under the prerogative and dismissed at will, even though provisions relating to enlistment are contained in statute. See the 1996 Act, Pt. II and Army Act 1955, Pt. I. The Armed Forces Act 1996 (see Introduction and General Note) contains provisions suggestive of a contractual relationship, for example, the entitlement of service personnel to "written particulars" of employment; the inclusion of an equality clause in their service conditions; a right to apply to an industrial tribunal to enforce the terms of their "contract" (as in civilian life, a provision not yet implemented by statutory instrument); the introduction of a geographically limited "local service engagement"; and statutory provisions in relation to service personnel who are under 18 years of age when they enlist. All these factors suggest that even if the common law principles of contract are not applicable to a service engagement, neither is the engagement governed purely by prerogative. A service engagement is now much closer to a contractual relationship than to one governed by the prerogative.
In the past, the courts have declined to enforce a soldier's pay claim (*Leaman v. R.* [1920] 3 K.B. 663). In *R. v. Secretary of State for War* [1891] 2 Q.B. 326, the Court of Appeal refused to enforce rights claimed by a retired lieutenant-colonel under the Royal Warrant regulating pay and retiring allowances. The Warrant, it was held, imposed no obligation on the Secretary of State beyond that owed to the Sovereign. In *Mitchell v. R.* [1896] 1 Q.B. 121, involving the same retired officer, Lord Esher M.R. stated at p.122, ". . . all engagements between those in the

military service of the Crown and the Crown are voluntary on the part of the Crown, and give no occasion for an action in respect of any alleged contract". See also *Re Tufnell* 3 Ch.D. 164. A complaint under the Army/Air Force Act 1955, s.180 or under the Naval Discipline Act 1957, s.130, each as amended by the Armed Forces Act 1996, s.20, would now be the 'redress of complaints' procedure to be followed. As Colonel Mitchell's claim derived from the Royal Warrant and not from regulations made under its authority, a different result might follow if a prerogative claim arises from a statutory or a common law duty owed to an individual (for further discussion, see Major-General A.P.V. Rogers, "Judicial Review and the Military" (1995) 2 Mil. L.J. 87, at p.88).

As the Armed Forces Act 1996, ss.24 and 25 now makes provision, as noted above, for equal pay and treatment claims by service personnel to be heard by an industrial tribunal, the prospects for regular and reserve personnel to take proceedings in respect to pay appear wholly different from those in the past.

Subs. (1)

The subject-matter of the orders and regulations authorised by s.4 may include the pay, bounty and allowances of members of the reserve forces. Whether court (apart from industrial tribunal) proceedings to enforce payments will be entertained will be keenly awaited. After the Gulf War, it has been alleged, some reservists who had been called out abandoned efforts to secure their financial entitlements in the face of Ministry of Defence bureaucracy.

Subs. (2)

Deductions are a routine feature of the pay of service personnel. Deductions may be made for messing, food and accommodation. They may also be made for barrack damage (see, for example, Army Act 1955, s.148), or for maintenance of dependants (Army Act 1955, ss.150–1). In the regular Army, service families have often complained of what they perceive as a humiliating official inspection of married quarters ("marching out") on departure or posting elsewhere, and the imposition of "charges raised" for particles of dust or minute stains. See Army Act 1955, s.147 and the Investigation (Lost or Damaged Property) (Army) Regulations 1956, Defence Council (Army) Order 113 of 1956. The latter appear to fall well short of the standards required in order to comply with the principles of natural justice.

So far as the reserve forces are concerned, it may be that deductions for barrack damage of a trivial nature will not be as vigorously pursued as in the regular services. Under the Army Act 1955, s.144, the power of deduction extends to the Territorial Army and to the Army Reserve when they are on permanent service, as a consequence of s.211 of the Army Act as amended by the Reserve Forces Act 1996, Sched. 10, para. 7. Note that the armed forces are exempt from the restrictions of the Wages Act 1986 (c. 48). See s.9(4) thereof, as amended by Sched. 10, para. 20 to the 1996 Act.

Subs. (3)

The Naval Forces (Enforcement of Maintenance Liabilities) Act 1947 (c. 24) declares that deductions may be made from the pay of naval and marine personnel in order to comply with a maintenance order. That provision may be extended to "prescribed members of the reserve naval and marine forces" by means of orders or regulations issued under s.4 of the 1996 Act. Presumably those "prescribed" are those who are subject to maintenance orders.

Pensions

8.—(1) Orders or regulations under section 4 may make provision for—

(a) the payment of pensions, allowances and gratuities by the Secretary of State to or in respect of any persons who are or have been members of the reserve forces;

(b) the making of payments towards the provision of pensions, allowances and gratuities to or in respect of any such persons.

(2) Orders or regulations under section 4 may also make provision for the payment of, or the making of payments towards the provision of, pensions, allowances and gratuities in respect of the death or disability of a person attributable to his service as a member of a reserve force.

(3) The provision made under this section may include provision for or towards the payment of lump sums instead of, or as well as, pensions.

DEFINITION
"reserve forces": s.1(2).

GENERAL NOTE
Some concern was expressed at the possibility of reservists prejudicing their entitlement to private occupational pensions in the event of extended call-out of, say, six to nine months. Entitlement is dependant normally upon continued membership of the scheme, including, of course, continuity of contributions. Doubts regarding pension entitlement, it was thought, might even deter enlistment in the reserve forces. In consequence, an amendment was proposed to insert at the end of s.8(1)(b) the following addition: "provided that the pensions of those in civilian life are fully safeguarded". The government successfully resisted on two grounds. First, the amendment was considered to be imprecise. Second, the minister gave assurances that as long as the employee paid his or her contribution, the government would pay the employer's contribution. See *Hansard*, H.L. Vol. 568, col. CWH 53; *ibid.*, Vol. 569, col. 1371.

Subs. (1)
The power to issue orders or regulations under s.4 expressly extends to the making of provision for the payment of pensions, allowances and gratuities to members of the reserve forces, and to the making of contributions towards the provision of pensions, allowances and gratuities (Allowance Regulations have in the past been issued by the Defence Council (and by its separate service predecessors), covering such items as casual charges for special transport, temporary extra issues of fuel, or in lieu of rations at either a higher or lower rate). See also s.83(2) regarding regulations in respect to payment to a third party towards pension provision. Presumably "allowances" has the same meaning in subs. (1) (and in subs. (2)) as in s.7(1). However, it is only in s.8(1)(a) that the Act specifically refers to payments by the Secretary of State. Whether this is sloppy drafting or whether it signifies a purely statutory, as distinct from a mixed statutory and prerogative, power (as in the case of pay) is obscure.

Subs. (2)
Orders or regulations may also be made for the payment of, or the making of contributions towards, pensions, allowances and gratuities in respect to reserve forces personnel who suffer death or disability attributed to reserve forces service. "Service" will include periods spent travelling from home to reserve force base, periods of training, and, of course, periods spent on operations. There may be other occasions when a reservist is on duty ("service") apart from those already mentioned. What of meal breaks, for example?

Subs. (3)
The opinion was expressed that lump sums were phased out after the Second World War. However, the government prefers to maintain flexibility by holding open the possibility of providing for a lump sum in addition to, or in lieu of, pension. See *Hansard*, H.C. Standing Committee A, col. 14, April 16, 1996.

PART II

ENLISTMENT AND CONDITIONS OF SERVICE

Enlistment and re-engagement

Enlistment of men in the reserve forces

9.—(1) An enlisting officer may enlist as men in any reserve force such persons as he considers suitable.

(2) In this Part "enlisting officer" means—

(a) a lord-lieutenant or deputy lieutenant holding office under Part VI of the Reserve Forces Act 1980;

(b) an officer of the regular services or of any reserve force;

(c) any consul-general, consul or vice consul or any other person duly exercising the functions of a British consul in any place outside the United Kingdom.

(3) A recruit may not be enlisted in any country or territory outside the United Kingdom which is specified for the purposes of this subsection by Her Majesty by Order in Council.

(4) Schedule 1 (enlistment of men in the reserve forces) shall have effect.

(5) In this Act any reference to men enlisted in a reserve force, so far as relating to any of the reserve naval and marine forces, is a reference to men entered for service in that force.

<small>DEFINITIONS</small>
"enlisting officer": subs. (2).
"men" ("man"): s.2(4).
"regular services": s.127(1).
"reserve forces": s.1(2).
"reserve naval and marine forces": s.1(2).

<small>GENERAL NOTE</small>
The intention of this section is, through simplified provisions, to bring the practice for enlisting reservists into line with the procedures in the Army Act 1955, s.1 and the Air Force Act 1955, s.1 (note that the relevant regulations relating to enlistment which are issued under the Army/Air Force Acts, s.22 are henceforth to be made by statutory instrument subject to the negative resolution procedure. See Armed Forces Act 1996, s.4). An enlisting officer exercises considerable powers when enlisting a recruit. The latter, after all, may be putting his or her life at risk. Those nominated as enlisting officers should therefore be precisely identified. The original Bill included as an enlisting officer "any other person authorised for the purpose of enlisting recruits by or in accordance with orders or regulations under section 4". This broad provision was removed at the Report stage in the Lords. See *Hansard*, H.L. Vol. 569, col. 1374.

Subs. (1)
The determination of who is "suitable" to be enlisted is to be read in the light of Sched. 1 to the 1996 Act ("Enlistment") where an "appropriate minimum age" is prescribed.

Subs. (2)
A lord-lieutenant or deputy lord-lieutenant is, under para. (a), the Sovereign's representative in the counties. Given the current constitutional arrangement that service personnel serve the Queen as commander-in-chief (and not parliament or the "constitution" as critics such as Tony Benn M.P. would prefer: see his Commonwealth of Britain Bill 1992, H.C. [1992–93] Bill 103, in which cl. 7 requires an oath of loyalty to the "Constitution of the Commonwealth of Britain", in place of the oath of allegiance to the Crown), a lord-lieutenant or his deputy as enlisting officer seems apposite. The Reserve Forces Act 1980, ss.130–138 regulates the appointment of lords-lieutenant and deputy lords-lieutenant (note that the bulk of the 1980 Act is repealed by the 1996 Act). Subsection 2(b) is somewhat broad. In the Army Act 1955, s.1, officers authorised by the Defence Council are the only officers who can enlist recruits (the former are referred to as recruiting officers rather than as enlisting officers). However, the wording of subs. 2(b) does not contain such qualification. Subsection 2(c) reflects the prudence of retaining the ability of the Crown to recruit overseas in the event that such a need were to arise.

Subs. (3)
While enlistment may occur overseas under subs. 2(b) and (c), subs. (3) makes provision for the prohibition on enlistment in countries specified by Order in Council.

Subs. (4)
This introduces Sched. 1 which lays down procedures for enlistment, including the signing of the attestation paper. For discussion of Sched. 1, see later.

Subs. (5)
A specific reference to the reserve naval and marine forces is an oblique reminder that the Royal Navy was not dependant for its existence on the procedures set out for the Regular Army in the Bill of Rights 1689.

Enlistment of foreign nationals and residents

10.—(1) Orders or regulations under section 4 may provide for the enlistment in any reserve force of persons who are not British citizens or who reside outside the United Kingdom.

(2) A person who is not a British citizen or who resides outside the United Kingdom may not be enlisted in a reserve force unless his enlistment is permitted by provision made for the purposes of subsection (1).

DEFINITION
"reserve forces": s.1(2).

GENERAL NOTE
Perhaps the most celebrated foreign nationals in the British armed forces today are the Gurkhas of the Brigade of Gurkhas. Their nationality is, of course, Nepalese. Apart from their case, the following rules *normally* apply to armed forces recruits: (a) at all times since birth, they have been either Commonwealth citizens or citizens of the Irish Republic; (b) they were born in the Irish Republic or in a country which is (or then was) in the Commonwealth; (c) each parent was born in such a country or in the Irish Republic and have always been or (if deceased) always were, Commonwealth citizens of the Irish Republic. The requirement at (c) is not an essential qualification for most non-commissioned specialisations in the Regular Army. A "Commonwealth citizen" includes a British citizen, a British Dependent Territories citizen, a British overseas citizen (*quaere*: does this include a British National (Overseas) citizen?), a British subject under the British Nationality Act 1981 (c. 61), and a citizen of an independent Commonwealth country. See *Hansard*, H.L. Vol. 559, col. 138 (WA), December 15, 1994. Earlier questions had raised the issue of U.K. compliance with the International Labour Organisation Discrimination (Employment and Occupation) Convention 1958. See *ibid.,* col. 98 (WA), December 7, 1994. A review of the rules relating to national extraction (as distinct from nationality or residence) and which govern eligibility for service in the armed forces was anticipated. The Army Act 1955, s.21, provides that the number of "aliens" serving at any one time in the Regular Army should not exceed one-fiftieth of the total, excluding those enlisted outside the U.K. and serving in prescribed units. The provisions do not apply to the reserve forces. Regulations to alter the percentage may be issued whenever a state of war exists or whenever the reserve forces are called out on permanent service. The restriction in the Act of Settlement 1700 (c. 2) on aliens holding certain offices or places of trust is inapplicable as long as the percentage authorised in s.21(1) and (3) of the Army Act 1955 is not exceeded. Regulations could dispense with the oath of allegiance in the case of aliens.

Subs. (1)
The versatile s.4 is once more at the disposal of the Sovereign, under the hand of the Secretary of State and of the Defence Council, to make orders or regulations regarding the enlistment in the reserve forces of foreign nationals or persons not resident in the U.K. A "British citizen", as the General Note to s.10 indicates, is defined in the British Nationality Act 1981. The "United Kingdom" is not defined in the 1996 Act. However, as s.132(2) extends the Act to Northern Ireland, and s.132(3) states that the Act may be extended by Order in Council to the Channel Islands and the Isle of Man, the meaning of "United Kingdom" in s.10 would appear to be limited to Great Britain and Northern Ireland. By contrast, the Army Act 1955, s.216(2) defines the U.K. normally as including the Channel Islands and the Isle of Man.

Subs. (2)
Persons who are not British citizens or who are resident outside the U.K. may be enlisted in the reserve forces only in accordance with orders or regulations issued under s.4.

Re-engagement for service

11.—(1) A man of a reserve force may be re-engaged for such period, beginning immediately after the end of his current term of service, as may be prescribed.

(2) A man wishing to re-engage—

(a) shall do so before being discharged, but not more than 12 months before the end of his current term of service; and

(b) on that re-engagement shall make such declaration as may be prescribed before an enlisting officer.

(3) A man who has re-engaged under this section may re-engage on a second or subsequent occasion.

DEFINITIONS
"man": s.2(4).
"prescribed": s.127(1).
"reserve forces": s.1(2).

GENERAL NOTE

This section makes provision for the re-engagement on one or more occasions of reservists for further periods of reserve service. Conditions for re-engagement are specified.

Subs. (1)

The word "may" is used, rather than "shall". Consequently, there is no automatic right to re-engagement. A proposed amendment to insert "provided that, in the opinion of the enlisting officer, his services continue to be required" after the word "prescribed", was not moved. See *Hansard*, H.L. Vol. 568, col. CWH 60. The Territorial Army Regulations (1978), para. 5.142, provides that applications for re-engagement are considered in the light of the applicant's efficiency, medical standard, age, and a recommendation from his commanding officer (Territorial Army Regulations are published separately by HMSO in a bulky volume). Moreover, s.19 of the 1996 Act enables orders or regulations to be issued in respect to, *inter alia*, re-engagement (see below). The length of re-engagement will be prescribed in orders or regulations issued under s.4.

Subs. (2)

Re-engagement must take place before discharge at the conclusion of his current term of service, but not earlier than 12 months before his current term of service expires. The nature of, and details specified in, the declaration to be made to the enlisting officer will be prescribed in orders or regulations issued under s.4. The matter is further regulated in Sched. 1, para. 3. "Discharge" is not defined in the 1996 Act, nor in the service discipline Acts.

Subs. (3)

Further re-engagements are possible, but, again, subject to meeting criteria set out in orders or regulations issued under s.4. Does "subsequent" mean "third" or does it permit of successive re-engagements?

Service in the reserve land and air forces on enlistment

12.—(1) Orders and regulations under section 4 may make provision as to the corps, units or bodies into which persons enlisting in a reserve land or air force may be enlisted.

(2) Subject to any restriction of choice imposed by or in accordance with orders or regulations under section 4—

(a) a man of the Territorial Army shall be enlisted for service in such corps and posted to such unit as he may select;

(b) a man of the Royal Auxiliary Air Force shall be enlisted for service in such unit as he may select; and

(c) a man enlisted in the Army Reserve or the Air Force Reserve shall be enlisted for service in such military body or air-force body (as the case may be) as he may select.

(3) A man of the Territorial Army may not (after his enlistment) be transferred to another corps, or posted or attached to any unit, without his consent.

(4) A man of the Royal Auxiliary Air Force may not (after his enlistment) be posted or attached to any unit without his consent.

(5) A man of the Army Reserve or Air Force Reserve may not (after his enlistment in or transfer to that force) be appointed, posted, transferred or attached to any military body or air-force body without his consent.

(6) Subsections (3), (4) and (5) do not apply to a man of a reserve force while he is in permanent service.

DEFINITIONS

"man": s.2(4).
"permanent service": s.127(1).
"reserve air force": s.1(2)(c).
"reserve land force": s.1(2)(b).

GENERAL NOTE

This section underlines the voluntary commitment of the members of the reserve forces. This applies both to volunteers of the Territorial Army and the Royal Auxiliary Air Force and also to the ex-regulars enlisting in the Army Reserve or Air Force Reserve. The issue is to what extent this voluntary commitment should be recognised by respecting the choice of corps, unit or body for which the reservist opts; or whether service exigencies dictate that personal choice be over-ridden. There is no equivalent provision for the reserve naval and marine forces, as they are not divided into corps, units and bodies such as exist within the reserve land and air forces. The view of the government, however, was that a recruit's identification with a unit was important to morale. Many units possess a strong local identity and recruiting base and enjoy a long and illustrious history. These factors, it is believed, encourage volunteer recruiting. The overriding requirement for the defence of the realm is reflected in subs. (6) and in s.20(2).

Subs. (1)

The orders or regulations made under s.4 may, for example, impose entry restrictions in respect to units which cater for particular specialisms, experience or age ranges. This is made clear by the opening words of subs. (2), below.

Subs. (2)

The essence of this subsection is to respect the choice of corps, unit or military or air force body which recruits, both volunteers and ex-regulars, select in respect to the reserve forces listed therein.

Subss. (3), (4) and (5)

These subsections prohibit the transfer, posting, attaching or appointing of reservists, without their consent, to units other than those which they have chosen. Note that regulations issued under the service discipline Acts may prescribe circumstances in which persons in one branch of the armed forces, whether naval, land or air, may be deemed to be attached to another. See, for example, Army Act 1955, s.179(2); Naval Discipline Act 1957, s.120(2). For the specific case of reservists, see, for example, Army Act 1955, s.211(8), as amended by the 1996 Act, Sched. 10, para. 7(6); Air Force Act 1955, s.210(8), as amended by the 1996 Act, Sched. 10, para. 11(6). The words "transfer", "posting" and "appointing", though obviously bearing different meanings, are not defined or explained in the service discipline Acts. See, for example, Armed Forces Act 1966, ss.2–4, 7 on provisions for transfer from the regular to the reserve service.

Subs. (6)

The right of reservists not to be transferred, posted, attached or appointed without their consent to another corps, unit or body will not apply while they are on actual service ("permanent service"). Service exigencies will therefore prevail over personal choice during this period, though s.20 makes clear (see below) that at the end of a period of permanent service (during which there may be a "hot" situation), the reservist is entitled to return to his original unit.

Transfer of men between reserve forces

13.—(1) A man serving in an ex-regular reserve force on transfer from the regular services may, with the consent of an authorised officer, enlist in another reserve force.

(2) A man enlisted in a reserve force (including a man enlisted by virtue of subsection (1)) may, with the consent of an authorised officer, enlist in another reserve force.

(3) On enlisting in a reserve force by virtue of this section the man concerned shall cease to be a member of the reserve force in which he was previously serving.

(4) A man originally serving in an ex-regular reserve force on transfer from the regular services who—

    (a) ceases to be a member of a reserve force in which he enlisted by virtue of this section without enlisting or re-enlisting in another reserve force; and

    (b) does so before the date on which his term of compulsory service in the ex-regular reserve force to which he was transferred would have

expired if he had not ceased to be a member of it on enlisting in
another reserve force,
shall, unless an authorised officer otherwise directs, again be a man of the
ex-regular reserve force to which he was transferred from the regular
services.

(5) A direction by an authorised officer under subsection (4) may be given
in respect of—

(a) one or more named individuals; or

(b) persons of any description specified in the direction.

(6) In this section "authorised officer" means an officer authorised by or in
accordance with directions of the Defence Council to exercise the powers
conferred by this section.

(7) In this Act "term of compulsory service" means the term for which a
person is required to serve in an ex-regular reserve force in pursuance of a
requirement imposed by or under the Army Act 1955, the Air Force Act 1955
or the Armed Forces Act 1966.

DEFINITIONS
"authorised officer": subs. (6).
"ex-regular reserve force": s.2(4).
"man": s.2(4).
"regular services": s.127(1).
"reserve forces": s.1(2).
"term of compulsory service": subs. (7).

GENERAL NOTE
This section deals with the transfer of reserve service personnel, whether volunteer or ex-
regular, between reserve forces. There are special provisions in respect to those liable to reserve
service consequent upon previous regular service.

Subs. (1)
An ex-regular reservist transferred from the regular services may enlist in another reserve
force. This seems wide enough to permit a Royal Fleet Reservist, for example, to transfer to, say,
the ex-regular Army Reserve or to the volunteer Territorial Army. The transfer may only be
with the consent of an authorised officer, that is, an officer authorised by or in accordance with
Defence Council directions (see subs. (6)).

Subs. (2)
A volunteer reservist may also join another volunteer or ex-regular reserve force with the
consent of an authorised officer. It is not wholly clear that the words in brackets are otiose, as the
phrase "man enlisted in a reserve force" covers both volunteer and ex-regular *personnel* and
volunteer and ex-regular *reserve forces*.

Subs. (3)
A transferee cannot simultaneously be a member of his previous and current reserve force.

Subs. (4)
Terms of enlistment in the regular services may require a recruit subsequently to serve a "term
of compulsory service" in an ex-regular reserve force. See, for example, Armed Forces Act 1966,
s.2 and Army Act 1955, s.12 and Army Terms of Service Regulations, 1992 (S.I. 1992, No. 1365).
However, let us suppose the ex-regular reservist has exercised his right to transfer between
reserve forces under s.13 of the 1996 Act, but he then ceases to be a member of the reserve force
to which he transferred (under s.13) from the ex-regular reserve force. If his total reserve service
does not add up to the "term of compulsory service" which he is required to complete on enlisting as a regular serviceman under the Army Act 1955 (or other service equivalent), then, unless
an authorised officer directs otherwise, he must revert to membership of the ex-regular reserve
force to which he was transferred from the regular services. In other words, under s.13, an ex-
regular reservist may, in exceptional circumstances, find himself serving in a reserve force in
which he may not be wholly comfortable.
Again, one should note the provisions of ss.12(2) and 20 of the 1996 Act, which assert service
priorities due to operational needs, including the exigencies of war.

Subs. (5)
The "direction" of the authorised officer in subs. (4) may be in respect to named individuals or to categories of persons described in the direction.

Subs. (6)
This is a definitional subsection. "In accordance with" Defence Council directions suggests implied authorisation may be permissible as well as the express authorisation connoted by the word "by". Directions may be in the form of Defence Council Instructions.

Subs. (7)
This explains "term of compulsory service" by reference to the service discipline Acts, though the phrase does not actually appear in that form in the Acts nor in the Terms of Service Regulations. See also the Army Act 1955 (Part 1) (Regular Army) (No. 2) Regulations 1986, issued by the Defence Council (Army) under powers contained in the Army Act 1955.

Discharge

General powers to discharge men of the reserve forces

14.—(1) The Defence Council may at any time discharge any man of any of the reserve forces.

(2) The power conferred by this section may also be exercised by any officer authorised by or in accordance with directions of the Defence Council to exercise that power.

(3) A man discharged by an authorised officer may appeal to the Defence Council, who may give such directions in his case (including a direction annulling the discharge) as they consider appropriate.

DEFINITIONS
"man": s.2(4).
"reserve forces": s.1(2).

GENERAL NOTE
Service personnel, including reservists, are appointed under the royal prerogative, albeit within a predominantly statutory framework. However, commissioned officers' terms of service in respect to their commissions (though not in respect to such matters as recall for service) are purely prerogative, albeit exercised by delegated authority. For the Regular Army, see Army Act 1955, ss.1–23; Army Terms of Service Regulations 1992 (S.I. 1992, No. 1365); Army Act 1955 (Part I) (Regular Army) (No. 2) Regulations 1986. Neither servicemen nor officers possess a contract of employment and consequently may be dismissed at will when their services are no longer required. However, the provisions of the Employment Rights Act 1996, s.192, as amended by the Armed Forces Act 1996, s.26, may alter this situation when the former section is implemented. Are discharge or dismissal decisions reviewable? Administrative discharge is the procedure which has recently attracted public attention in the wake of the discharge of homosexual service personnel. *Cf.*, discharges under regulations made under the authority of the Army Act 1955, s.11(3), and see annotations to subs. (1).

Subs. (1)
This governs the discharge of men, not officers, of the reserve forces, that is, those of warrant officer rank or below. The power of discharge, whether prerogative or statutory, or a combination of both, is exercised by the Defence Council, whose composition is regulated by the Defence (Transfer of Functions) Act 1964 (c. 15). While the exercise of the prerogative is now subject to judicial review after the GCHQ decision (*Council of Civil Service Unions v. Minister for the Civil Service* [1985] A.C. 374), and while the courts are prepared to review the exercise of service administrative decisions which do not involve "operational considerations" (see *R v. Ministry of Defence, ex p. Smith* [1995] 4 All E.R. 427 (Div. Ct.) *per* Simon Brown L.J., at p.446; [1996] 1 All E.R. 257 (C.A.)), the threshold for a successful challenge on the ground of irrationality is virtually insurmountable. But what if there are procedural inadequacies? Is there a right to be heard (*audi alteram partem*) where subs. (1) states that the Defence Council may *at any time* discharge a reservist? *Cf.*, *Bradley v. Attorney General* [1991] LRC [Law Reports of the Commonwealth, pub. Butterworths] (Const) 590 where a New Zealand naval officer (as distinct from a serviceman) was granted relief in the light of procedural defects. The exhaustion of internal remedies would presumably also be expected. See subs. (3) and s.15(2). See also the redress of grievance procedures in the service discipline Acts, for example, Army Act 1955, ss.180–1 as amended by the Armed Forces Act 1996, s.20.

Subs. (2)

An officer authorised by or in accordance with Defence Council directions may exercise that power of discharge. What if the discharge is exercised by an unauthorised officer? Or is exercised arbitrarily or capriciously? The older authorities such as *Mitchell v. R* [1896] 1 Q.B. 121 and *R v. Army Council, ex p. Ravenscroft* [1917] 2 K.B. 504 suggest that the courts will not intervene (cf., *Riordan v. War Office* [1959] 3 All E.R. 552). However, *GCHQ* and *ex p. Smith* (above), as well as decisions such as *Leech v. Deputy Governor of Parkhurst Prison* [1988] 2 W.L.R. 290 suggest a possibly more sensitive approach. For informed discussion of some of the cases accompanying the annotations to subss. (2) and (3), see A.P.V. Rogers, "Judicial Review and the Military" (1995) 2 Mil. L.J. 87.

Subs. (3)

Though the Defence Council itself appears to possess the right of instant discharge, a man discharged by an authorised officer may lodge an appeal with the Defence Council. Is the discharge suspended pending the appeal or is it immediately operative notwithstanding an appeal? As the Defence Council may, *inter alia*, annul the discharge, it seems that the latter is the correct interpretation. *Cf.*, courts-martial whose findings are subject to confirmation, which may occur considerably later. The confirmation stage is, however, to be abolished by the Armed Forces Act 1996, s.15. Elsewhere, within the court-martial system, there is no provision for a formal "appeal" to the Defence Council. Under the Army Act 1955, s.113, there is provision for petitioning the reviewing authorities, which includes the Defence Council. However, a formal appeal to the Courts-Martial Appeal Court must be preceded, by virtue of the Courts-Martial (Appeals) Act 1968 (c. 20), s.8(2), by a petition to the Defence Council. For a perceived 'Catch-22' element in the procedure, see John Mackenzie, "The Great Court-Martial Appeal Mystery", *New Law Journal*, February 16, 1996, pp.208, 219.

Discharge by commanding officer

15.—(1) A commanding officer may discharge any man of a reserve force under his command, in such manner and on such grounds as may be prescribed.

(2) A man discharged by his commanding officer may appeal to the Defence Council, who may give such directions in his case (including a direction annulling the discharge) as they consider appropriate.

DEFINITIONS
    "man": s.2(4).
    "prescribed": s.127(1).
    "reserve force": s.1(2).

GENERAL NOTE

The powers of a commanding officer in the regular forces to deal with disciplinary matters himself, without resort to courts-martial, were expanded in the Armed Forces Act 1976 (c. 52). However, his summary powers of punishment are limited and do not extend to discharge. Such a power of discharge is, however, granted to a commanding officer in the reserve forces. Under the 1980 Act, s.99(1), repealed by the 1996 Act, the commanding officer could discharge a Territorial Army or Royal Auxiliary Air Force reservist for, in broad terms, disobedience, neglect, misconduct or "other sufficient cause".

Subs. (1)

The manner in which, and grounds for, discharge may be prescribed in orders or regulations issued under s.4. Presumably, they will contain provisions similar to those in the now repealed s.99(1) of the 1980 Act. Presumably, also, no power of discharge can be lawfully exercised by a commanding officer in the absence of orders or regulations issued under s.4. For the prospects for judicial review of a commanding officer's discharge of a reservist, see annotations to s.14(1) and (2).

Subs. (2)

The right of appeal to the Defence Council by a man discharged by an authorised officer (s.14(3)) is mirrored by a similar right in the case of discharge by a commanding officer.

Entitlement to discharge

16.—(1) Any man of a reserve force shall (subject to the provisions of this Act) be entitled to be discharged on the expiry of his current term of service.

(2) Any enlisted man of a reserve force shall (subject to the provisions of this Act) be entitled to be discharged—

(a) before the end of his current term of service, on complying with the conditions mentioned in subsection (4); and

(b) in such other circumstances as may be prescribed.

(3) Subsection (2) shall also apply to any man of a reserve force who re-engages in the force; but in the case of a man who—

(a) is serving on transfer to the reserve from the regular services, and

(b) re-engages before the end of his term of compulsory service,

paragraph (a) of that subsection shall not apply until after the end of his term of compulsory service.

(4) The conditions for entitlement to discharge under subsection (2)(a) are that the man concerned—

(a) gives to his commanding officer 3 months' notice in writing, or such less notice as may be prescribed, of his desire to be discharged; and

(b) delivers up in good order, fair wear and tear excepted, all arms, clothing and other public property issued to him, or, in cases where for any good or sufficient cause the delivery of that property is impossible, paying its value,

but his commanding officer may, if it appears that the reasons for which the discharge is claimed are of sufficient urgency or weight, dispense either wholly or in part with either or both of the above conditions.

(5) A man of a reserve force who becomes entitled to be discharged shall be discharged in such manner as may be prescribed with all convenient speed (and shall continue as a man of that force until actually discharged).

DEFINITIONS

"man": s.2(4).

"prescribed": s.127(1).

"regular services": s.127(1).

"reserve force": s.1(2).

"term of compulsory service": s.13(7).

GENERAL NOTE

This section entitles a reservist to be discharged when his term of service expires or after submitting his notice in writing. This right does not apply if an ex-regular reservist has any unexpired reserve liability. As the right applies "subject to the provisions of this Act", it will not apply in circumstances such as those specified in s.17 or at times of national danger, great emergency or attack on the U.K.

There is also a conditional right of discharge prior to the expiry of a period of service. The flexibility reflects the voluntary spirit under which reserve service may be undertaken. It may also encourage recruitment where recruits are reassured that dislike of reserve service or changes in personal or employment circumstances may prompt them to leave the reserve forces.

Subs. (1)

This declares the right of discharge of both volunteers and ex-regulars on expiry of a current term of service. The last four words would appear to cover all the different categories of service commitment specified in the Act. These are: "term of compulsory service" (s.13(7)); "additional duties commitment" (s.25); "full-time service commitment (s.24); and "permanent service", which includes active service (s.127(1)). The phrase, "subject to the provisions of this Act" (used elsewhere in s.16), indicates that the right may be overridden by provisions elsewhere in the Act. See, for example, s.17 and Pt. VI ("Call out for Permanent Service"), and Pt. VII ("Recall for Service of Officers and Former Servicemen").

Subs. (2)

Paragraph (a) provides for premature discharge from reserve service, subject to the reservist meeting the conditions listed in subs. (4), below. In addition, para. (b) provides that orders or regulations issued under s.4 may prescribe the circumstances in which early discharge may be granted. Similar provisions already exist, for example, to permit a member of the Royal Naval Reserve to be discharged early in order to join the Merchant Navy. Other provisions of the Act may override this entitlement, for example, in the circumstances of war conditions.

Subs. (3)

Reservists who have re-engaged, that is, enlisted for a subsequent term of reserve service, will enjoy the same entitlement as in subs. (2). However, in the case of an ex-regular required to complete his term of compulsory service in the reserves, and who re-engaged for subsequent service *before* completing that compulsory reserve service, the entitlement to early discharge will apply only once that compulsory service has been completed.

Subs. (4)

This specifies the conditions to be met for early discharge under subs. (2)(a), above. A three-month period of written notice of the reservist's "desire" to be discharged (will "desire" be interpreted loosely or tightly?) is to be given to the reservist's commanding officer. This period is reducible in length (para. (a)) if so prescribed in orders or regulations issued under s.4. Three months is the maximum notice period. Will it act as a deterrent on seeking a discharge? The reservist's equipment, that is, "arms, clothing and other public property", must be delivered up in good order as a condition of early discharge (para. (b)). The paragraph does not specify to where the equipment should be returned. Could it be elsewhere than his former unit depot? The provision at the end of subs. (4) permits the commanding officer to dispense, in whole or in part, with the requirements for notice and/or the return of the equipment, if "it appears" (presumably a primarily objective test, and not dependant upon the commanding officer's whim) that the reservist's reasons for discharge are of "sufficient urgency or weight". Presumably, a reason which is urgent is also weighty, but not necessarily vice-versa. As to notice, it is not uncommon for the requirements as to notice to be waived. An unwilling reservist is not likely to be an asset to a unit premised on voluntary service. As to equipment, if illness prompts early discharge, then the kit would normally be collected by the reserve unit itself. Given an urgent or weighty reason for early discharge, the commanding officer could also overlook the failure to return equipment or the fact that the returned equipment is not in good order or has been damaged, whether accidentally, negligently or deliberately.

Subs. (5)

A person entitled to early discharge remains a reservist until actual discharge. Procedures for discharge "with all convenient speed" (convenient speed for the Ministry of Defence may be procrastination for others) may be prescribed in orders or regulations issued under s.4.

Postponement of discharge

17.—(1) Where, at the time he would (apart from this section) become entitled to be discharged under section 16, a man is in permanent service or full-time service under a full–time service commitment, he shall not be entitled to be discharged until he is released from that service.

(2) Where, at the time when a man not in permanent service or full-time service under a full-time service commitment would (apart from this section) become entitled to be discharged under section 16(1), an order under section 52 is in force authorising the call out of members of any reserve force, he may be required to prolong his service for such further term, not exceeding 12 months, as the Defence Council or an authorised officer may order.

(3) In subsection (2) "authorised officer" means an officer authorised by or in accordance with directions of the Defence Council to exercise the power conferred by that subsection.

(4) Where, at the time when a man not in permanent service or full-time service under a full-time service commitment would (apart from this section) become entitled to be discharged under section 16(2), an order under section 52 or 54 is in force authorising the call out of members of any reserve force, he shall not be entitled to be so discharged while that call-out order is in force.

DEFINITIONS

"authorised officer": subs. (3).
"call-out order": s.64.
"full-time service commitment": s.127(1).
"permanent service": s.127(1).
"reserve force": s.1(2).

    This section qualifies the entitlements to discharge and to early discharge provided in s.16, and enables the discharge of reservists to be delayed in time of crisis. Those reservists in permanent service, that is, those normally on active service, or those in full-time service, that is, those subject to a specific commitment made under s.24, are only entitled to discharge once they are released from that service. In the case of reservists in categories other than permanent or full-time service, discharge on expiry of a current term of service or early discharge can be postponed for up to 12 months when an order under s.52 is in force. Section 52 provides for call out of reservists in the event of national danger, great emergency or actual or apprehended attack on the U.K. Early discharge, but not discharge on expiry of a current term of service, can also be postponed for up to 12 months if an order under s.54 is in force. Section 54 provides for call out for "warlike operations", presumably considered a less serious crisis than those prescribed in s.52.

Subs. (1)
    Whereas s.16(2) grants a qualified entitlement to early discharge, this subsection removes that possibility in respect to reservists on active service or to those serving under a full-time service commitment, as detailed in s.24, below.

Subs. (2)
    This permits the postponement for up to 12 months of the discharge of a reservist on the expiry of his current term of service whenever a call-out order under s.52 is in force. The Defence Council or an authorised officer may determine the prolongation period.

Subs. (3)
    This defines an authorised officer for the purposes of subs. (2). It is identical to s.13(6) regarding the approval for transfer of men between reserve forces. *Cf.*, s.9(2)(b), where an enlisting officer need not be an "authorised officer".

Subs. (4)
    Early discharge is not available under s.16(2) whenever a call-out order under s.52 (in respect to national danger, etc.) or under s.54 (in respect to warlike operations) is in force.

Rights of men on being discharged

18.—(1) Where a man who is to be discharged from a reserve force is in permanent service and serving outside the United Kingdom—
    (a) if he requires to be released from that service and discharged in the United Kingdom, he shall be sent there free of charge with all convenient speed and shall be released from service and discharged on his arrival there; but
    (b) if at his request he is released from that service and discharged at the place where he is serving he shall have no claim to be sent to the United Kingdom or elsewhere.
    (2) If such a man is released from permanent service and discharged in the United Kingdom, he shall be entitled to be conveyed free of charge from the place where he is discharged to the place stated on his attestation paper to be the place where he was attested or to any place in the United Kingdom at which he intends to reside.

DEFINITIONS
    "man": s.2(4).
    "permanent service": s.127(1).
    "reserve forces": s.1(2).

    This section, broadly speaking, embodies an undertaking by the service authorities to return to the U.K. without charge, a reservist serving abroad who is to be discharged. He may, however, opt for discharge at the place where he has been serving. If discharged in the U.K., the released man has a further entitlement to free travel to his place of attestation or to his U.K. place of residence.

Subs. (1)

The entitlement in para. (a) to be returned free of charge and rapidly to the U.K. for discharge "on his arrival" (at his unit? at RAF Brize Norton?) applies to reservists on permanent service, that is, to those on active service (or "actual" service: s.127(1)). However, note that such entitlement will be subject to the restrictions on discharge imposed elsewhere in the Act. See, for example, s.16(4) and s.17(1), above. Section 18(1)(b) envisages the case of a reservist preferring to be discharged where he is serving abroad. In those circumstances, he has no entitlement to be sent to the U.K. or elsewhere.

Subs. (2)

The reservist conveyed to the U.K. after permanent service abroad and then discharged "on his arrival" has the right to free travel to his place of attestation or, to be precise, to the "place stated on his attestation paper", or to his intended U.K. place of residence.

Supplementary

Orders and regulations as to enlistment etc.

19.—(1) Orders or regulations under section 4 may make provision with respect to the enlistment and re-engagement of men in, and the discharge of men from, the reserve forces.

(2) Such orders or regulations may, in particular, include provision—

(a) specifying the duration of any term for which a person may enlist, whether by reference to a number of years or another criterion or a number of years and another criterion;

(b) enabling a man enlisted for a term of service of a description specified in the order or regulations concerned to be treated as if he had enlisted for a term of service of a different description;

(c) enabling a man to extend or reduce the term of his service; and

(d) enabling service in the reserve forces, or service otherwise than for the purposes of training, to be restricted to service in the United Kingdom or in any area of the United Kingdom.

(3) No order or regulations under section 4 may make provision such as is mentioned in subsection (1) which has the effect, in relation to any person who was a man of a reserve force immediately before the coming into force of the order or regulations concerned—

(a) of imposing a new or greater obligation on him without his consent, or

(b) of varying or revoking, without his consent, a right to which he is entitled, not being a right exercisable only with the consent of another person or an authority.

(4) The term for which, or any limited area within which, a man of a reserve force is liable to serve may not, without his consent, be affected or extended by or in accordance with orders or regulations under section 4.

DEFINITIONS

"men" ("man"): s.2(4).
"reserve forces": s.1(2).

GENERAL NOTE

Section 4 states that Her Majesty may make orders respecting the government and discipline of any reserve force and in respect to all other matters and things relative to that force. The Defence Council may also make regulations on the above matters subject to any exclusions contained in prerogative orders. Section 19 states that the orders or regulations may cover such matters as enlistment, re-engagement or discharge, that is, the subject-matter of Pt. II of the Act. The provision is analogous to s.2 of the Armed Forces Act 1966 (c. 45) which provides an equivalent power to make "terms of service" regulations for the regular forces. The details in orders or regulations may provide for the length, description and location of reserve service, for example, service confined to the U.K.

One legislative objective is to introduce flexibility into the terms of reserve engagement. The 1980 Act made provisions for fixed engagements of between one and five years for different reserve forces in different circumstances. This was thought to lead to inflexibility. Under the 1996 Act, orders or regulations may be issued to permit, for example, existing engagements to be lengthened, and to lay down a fixed period of notice to terminate the engagement (apart from the provision for early discharge in s.16(2)). This would replace the previous need for individuals to re-engage periodically, perhaps every year. The possibility is also created of entering into a reserve engagement to serve only in the U.K. or in a specific area of the U.K., a commitment which might be attractive to those willing to serve but unwilling or unable to serve abroad. Note the provision for local service engagements in the Armed Forces Act 1996 (c. 46), s.2. Personnel recruited to the regular services would only serve outside their local areas for a specified limited period for training or in exceptional circumstances. It is envisaged that the local service scheme in the regular forces will be applicable to certain guarding duties whose members would form a Military Provost Guarding Service (which some believe will be less expensive than either the Ministry of Defence Police or the existing regular forces).

The orders or regulations cannot operate retrospectively in such a manner as to impose a new or greater obligation on the reservist unless he consents. Nor may they remove unconditional entitlements from him without his consent.

Subs. (1)

The words "and generally for carrying out this Part into effect", which had appeared after the word "forces" when the Bill received its First Reading, were removed at the H.L. Report Stage (*Hansard*, H.L. Vol. 569, col. 1376). This followed concerns expressed that orders or regulations issued under s.4 in respect to enlistment, etc. could override the statutory provisions on enlistment etc in ss.9–18. See also the Committee Stage debate (Vol. 568, col. CWH 66). However, any such orders or regulations would surely be *ultra vires*.

Subs. (2)

The orders or regulations may specify in para. (a) the duration of service by reference to a number of years or to a criterion. The latter could be an event, such as the continuation of an armed conflict or state of war. Paragraph (b) permits the issue of orders or regulations to enable a man enlisted for one type of service to be treated as if enlisted for another kind of service. The phrase "term of service of a description specified" in orders or regulations is not defined in the Act. But throughout the statute, different kinds of service are stipulated, for example, s.22 (training obligations); s.24 (full-time service); s.25 (additional duties commitment): s.28 (special agreements for call out); s.13(7) (term of compulsory service); s.12(6) (reference to permanent service); and Sched. 1, para. 1(2) (reference to "general conditions of the engagement"). The relationship between the relevant order or regulation and the statutory provision as to the type of service involved would need to be examined in each case with respect to the *ultra vires* doctrine. Under para. (c), orders or regulations may permit a man to lengthen or shorten his term of service. As to the former, it will remove some bureaucratic procedures involved in discharge followed by re-enlistment. In respect to the latter, orders or regulations may amplify the conditions relating to the entitlement of a man to early discharge under s.16(2). Under para. (d), a local service commitment for reservists is provided. If the phrase "service in the reserve forces" includes training (which one presumes is the case), then the restricted undertaking will apply both to actual service and to training. The engagement may be confined to the U.K. or to "any area" of the U.K. Could "area" be, say, North Britain, or England, as distinct from, say, Salisbury Plain or Kent or Western Command district?

Subs. (3)

This prevents orders or regulations having the effect of making retrospective changes which increase a man's obligations to serve, unless he consents to such a new or greater obligation. Nor can they have the effect of varying or revoking an unconditional right to which he is entitled, unless he consents. Such an unconditional right is one whose exercise is not dependant on the consent or authority of another person or authority. It appears that the right to be discharged early under s.16(2), which is subject to conditions stipulated in s.16(4), may not be an unconditional right, even though the conditions in s.16(4) do not amount to a veto on early discharge by "another person or an authority".

Subs. (4)

The terms of service of a reservist in respect to time and space may not, without his consent, be affected or extended by or in accordance with orders or regulations under s.4. Does the subsection add anything to the prohibition in subs. (3)(a)? What does "affected" mean? Presumably it means "altered" (and therefore possibly resulting in a "new" obligation?) What does "extended" mean? Presumably it results in a "greater obligation".

Command, posting etc. of men in permanent service

20.—(1) Men of a reserve force who are in permanent service shall be placed under the command of such officers as the Defence Council or an authorised officer may direct and may be attached to any body or unit of Her Majesty's armed forces.

(2) Men of the reserve forces in permanent service may, without their consent—

(a) in the case of the reserve naval and marine forces, be drafted or posted, appointed or transferred to any naval or marine body or unit;

(b) in the case of the reserve land forces, be posted, appointed or transferred to any military body or unit (including, in the case of a man of the Territorial Army, transfer to any corps);

(c) in the case of the reserve air forces, be posted, appointed or transferred to any air-force unit or body,

by order of the Defence Council or an authorised officer.

(3) A man of a reserve force who has been the subject of an order under subsection (2) is entitled, if he continues as a member of that force on being released from permanent service, to be returned with all convenient speed to the corps, unit or body in which he was serving immediately before he was accepted into permanent service.

(4) In this section "authorised officer" means an officer authorised for the purposes of this section by or in accordance with directions of the Defence Council.

DEFINITIONS
"authorised officer": subs. (4).
"men" ("man"): s.2(4).
"permanent service": s.127(1).
"reserve air forces": s.1(2).
"reserve force": s.1(2).
"reserve land forces": s.1(2).
"reserve naval and marine forces": s.1(2).

GENERAL NOTE
This section enables reservists on actual service or call out to be placed under the command of any officers as the Defence Council or any authorised officer may so direct. Men of a reserve force may be attached to any body or unit of the armed forces, whether regular or reserve. Reservists have recently been serving in Bosnia on attachment to regular units. Reservists in each branch of the armed forces, that is, the naval, land and air forces, may be posted, appointed or transferred, without their consent, to any body or unit within their own branch of the armed forces. But once permanent service (of nine months, or the duration of emergency, national danger, or whatever) is ended, the reservist is entitled to rejoin his previous reserve body.

Subs. (1)
Reservists on actual service are placed under the command of officers appointed by the Defence Council or by an authorised officer. They may be attached to any regular or reserve unit or body. This appears to permit naval or marine reserves, for example, to be attached to regular or reserve air forces. "Attachment" in service discipline law usually applies to inter-service arrangements (and sometimes to enable disciplinary proceedings to be taken rapidly). See, for example, Naval Discipline Act 1957 (c. 53), ss.113, 120 and Sched. 2 thereto; Army Act 1955 (c. 18), ss.179, 208 and Sched. 6 thereto; Air Force Act 1955 (c. 19), ss.179, 208 and Sched. 6 thereto, and regulations issued thereunder. For the reserves, see Army Act 1955, s.211, Air Force Act 1955, s.210, and Naval Discipline Act 1957, s.111, all as amended by Sched. 10 to the 1996 Act. Though the word "attachment" is defined neither in the service discipline Acts nor in the 1996 Act, it connotes a temporary arrangement where separate armed forces organisational structures continue. In contrast, a posting or transfer has a more permanent and integrated organisational quality. Can a reservist be compelled to consent to attachment to a different branch of the armed forces? *Cf.*, subs. (2).

Subs. (2)
It might be inferred that a veto on attachment in subs. (1) does exist inasmuch as, by contrast, subs. (2) states expressly that the drafting, posting, appointment or transfer of reservists in

permanent service to any unit or body within their own branch (that is, naval, land or air) may, without the consent of the reservist, be ordered by the Defence Council or by an authorised officer.

Subs. (3)
Once his permanent service has ended, however, the draftee, etc. is entitled to be returned rapidly to his previous reserve corps, unit or body.

Subs. (4)
Authorisation may be implied as well as express. For the phrase "By or in accordance with ...", see annotations to s.13(6), above.

Service of marines in the Royal Fleet Reserve

21. Men of the Royal Fleet Reserve who were transferred to that force from the Royal Marines or are enlisted in that force as marines shall—
    (a) when in permanent service; or
    (b) when undergoing training or performing other duties,
be liable to serve as marine warrant officers, non-commissioned officers and men and not as warrant officers, petty officers and ratings of the Royal Navy.

DEFINITIONS
    "men" ("man"): s.2(4).
    "permanent service": s.127(1).

GENERAL NOTE
Far from being self-explanatory, the purpose of this short section is to affirm that former marines in the Royal Fleet Reserve, that is, in the naval ex-regular reserve force, are liable to serve as marines, with marine rank, and not as naval ratings with naval rank when in permanent service or undertaking duties or in training. The background to this provision is that whereas all men of the Royal Fleet Reserve are subject to the provisions of the Naval Discipline Act 1957 when called out or undergoing training or exercises, in the case of marines in the Royal Fleet Reserve, they are subject both to the Naval Discipline Act 1957, s.112 when aboard ship or part of a naval establishment, and also to the Army Act 1955, s.210, as is the case with regular Royal Marines. See also Sched. 10 to the 1996 Act. Moreover, subordinate or delegated legislation will have to reflect this dual service discipline liability. As the Royal Naval Reserve and the Royal Marine Reserve (the latter totalling just 1,400 men) are distinct legal entities, the problem in relation to the marines of the Royal Fleet Reserve does not arise in these volunteer reserve forces (there are too few ex-regular Royal Marines to justify a separate ex-regular marine reserve).

PART III

TRAINING AND OTHER DUTIES

Obligatory training

Training obligations of members of the reserve forces

22.—(1) A member of a reserve force may, in accordance with orders or regulations under section 4, be required by virtue of this section, in any year, to train in the United Kingdom or elsewhere for—
    (a) one or more periods not exceeding 16 days in aggregate; and
    (b) such other periods as may be prescribed, none of which shall exceed 36 hours without the consent of the person concerned;
and such a person may, while undergoing a period of training under this section, be attached to and trained with any body of Her Majesty's forces.
    (2) Such orders or regulations may, in particular, prescribe different periods under subsection (1)(b) for different forces or parts of a force.
    (3) This section has effect subject to section 23.

DEFINITIONS
    "prescribed": s.127(1).
    "reserve force": s.1(2).

This provides for obligatory training for all reservists, both ex-regular and volunteer, and prescribes the maximum commitment to be undertaken. Some ex-regular reservists undertake just one day's training a year as part of their annual reporting procedure. "Training" is not defined in the Act.

Subs. (1)
Orders or regulations issued under s.4 (assuming such to be issued) will provide for a training commitment of one or more periods not exceeding 16 days in aggregate (para. (a)), and such other periods, the number of which is not specified and therefore could be numerous, as may be prescribed in such orders or regulations (para. (b)). Each period of the latter category cannot exceed 36 hours without the consent of the reservist. The training may be undertaken in the U.K. or elsewhere, during which time the reservist may be attached to, and trained with, any body of regular or reserve forces.

Subs. (2)
The flexibility of the new reserve force regime is exemplified by orders or regulations issued under subs. (1)(b), which may prescribe different periods of training for different forces or parts thereof.

Subs. (3)
Section 23, below, contains provisions which may override the training obligation of a reservist.

Power to exempt persons from or relax training obligations

23.—(1) Orders or regulations under section 4 may provide for securing that persons of such descriptions as may be prescribed shall be exempted from liability to be required to undergo training under section 22.

(2) Such orders or regulations may also provide for relaxing, in such cases as may be prescribed, the liability to be required to undergo training under section 22.

(3) Officers authorised for the purposes of this subsection by or in accordance with directions of the Defence Council may, in accordance with such orders or regulations—

(a) exempt any unit or other group of members of a reserve force from liability to be required to undergo training under section 22; or

(b) relax that liability in the case of the unit or group.

(4) A commanding officer may, in accordance with orders or regulations under section 4—

(a) exempt any member of a reserve force who is under his command from liability to be required to undergo training under section 22; or

(b) relax that liability in the case of such a person.

DEFINITIONS
"prescribed": s.127(1).
"reserve force": s.1(2).

GENERAL NOTE
This section contains a number of provisions exempting certain persons from all or part of their training obligations. First, scope for general exemptions or for relaxations is provided by subss. (1) and (2). Then, wide discretion may be conferred by Defence Council regulations on authorised officers with respect to a unit or group, and on a commanding officer with respect to any individual member of a reserve force under his command, to waive or relax a training obligation (subss. (3) and (4)). The Commons Select Committee on the Reserves, H.C. Paper 65, 1994–95, para. 22, noted that, under Territorial Army regulations, training volunteers were required to take annual fitness and shooting tests. But, it added, "Surprisingly, they are not required to pass them". The government envisaged a general exemption power in s.23(1) for certain well-defined groups such as adult reservist leaders in the cadet forces. Provision for general relaxation (rather than exemption) in s.23(2) would apply to certain technical officers, perhaps linguists, who do not require the full training programme. The discretion exercised by authorised officers or commanding officers, and laid down in regulations, would possibly apply in cases where exemption or relaxation was appropriate for personal or for business reasons (in

the case of individuals), or where unusual circumstances prompted the cancellation of a unit's annual camp (in the case of a unit or group).

Subs. (1)
This is the general provision for exemption from training obligations by virtue of orders or regulations issued under s.4.

Subs. (2)
This is the general provision for relaxation of training obligations by virtue of orders or regulations issued under s.4.

Subs. (3)
This is the provision for exemption or relaxation of training obligations granted by officers who may be authorised by the Defence Council with respect to any specific unit or group of members of a reserve force. Orders or regulations issued under s.4 may authorise the exercise of authorised officers' discretion.

Subs. (4)
This is the provision for exemption or relaxation of training obligations which may be granted by a commanding officer with respect to any member of a reserve force under his command. Orders or regulations issued under s.4 may authorise the exercise of the commanding officer's discretion.

Commitments to perform additional duties

Commitments to a period of full-time service

24.—(1) A member of a reserve force may enter into a commitment in writing under this section (a "full-time service commitment") to undertake a period of full-time service of such duration as may be specified in the commitment.
(2) A person who has entered into such a commitment—
(a) shall be in full-time service from the time specified in the commitment as the beginning of the period of full-time service to be undertaken by him until the time at which he is released from that service;
(b) shall be subject to service law while in full-time service;
(c) shall perform such duties while he is in full-time service as he may, in accordance with the terms of the commitment and any orders or regulations under section 4, be required to perform.
(3) A full-time service commitment—
(a) shall specify the duties to be performed by the person concerned (in general or specific terms) and the period for which he has undertaken to be in full-time service;
(b) may, to the extent permitted by orders or regulations under section 4, limit the area within which he may be required to perform duties; and
(c) may contain such other terms relating to the duties to be performed by that person as are included in accordance with orders or regulations under section 4.
(4) A person who is in full-time service may be required—
(a) to serve with any of the regular services for the purposes of performing duties in accordance with the commitment concerned; and
(b) subject to any limitation in the commitment, to perform such duties anywhere in the world.
(5) A full-time service commitment—
(a) may, with the consent of the member concerned, be varied in accordance with orders or regulations under section 4;
(b) may be revoked before the beginning of the specified period of full-time service by an authorised officer (whether at the request of the

member concerned or otherwise) giving written notice to that effect to the member concerned; and

(c) shall terminate on the release of the member concerned from full-time service under the commitment.

(6) A person in full-time service shall, if not released from service sooner, be entitled to be released from service with all convenient speed in the prescribed manner at the end of the period of service specified in the commitment.

(7) Where a person in full-time service is accepted into permanent service under Part IV, V or VI—

(a) his full-time service shall cease while he is in permanent service; but

(b) if, on his release from permanent service, the period of full-time service undertaken by him has not expired, he shall resume his full-time service for the remainder of that period.

(8) A person in full-time service shall not be liable to be required to undergo training under section 22.

(9) The duties which a person in full-time service may be required to perform may include undertaking training.

(10) In this section—

"authorised officer" means an officer authorised by or in accordance with directions of the Defence Council for the purposes of this section;

"full-time service" means service under a full-time service commitment.

DEFINITIONS

"authorised officer": subs. (10).
"full-time service commitment": subs. (10).
"permanent service": s.127(1).
"prescribed": s.127(1).
"reserve force": s.1(2).
"service law": s.127(1).

GENERAL NOTE

This section embodies one of the major innovations of the 1996 Act (perhaps inevitably prompting some expressions of concern, vigorously dismissed by the government, regarding the maintenance of the regular forces "on the cheap"). It provides that a reservist may commit himself to undertaking a period of full-time service (which is distinct from permanent service), and lays down terms and conditions attached thereto. They include his subjection to service discipline law. The section permits a wider deployment than was authorised under the 1980 Act, and is also intended to avoid unnecessary bureaucracy. Under the 1980 Act, it was not possible for reservists to undertake periods of full-time service (or part-time service: see s.25 of the 1996 Act) in the absence of a call out "when warlike operations are in preparation or in progress", or for training functions. Reservists undertaking full-time service not involving warlike operations or training, for example, undertaking peacekeeping or humanitarian aid operations, were obliged to leave the volunteer reserve force and join the armed forces as regulars, and then leave the regular services and rejoin the volunteer reserves when their period of duty with the regulars was completed. Section 24 of the 1996 Act dispenses with the need for this complex process. Thus, if, hypothetically, a Royal Air Force station had to deploy a large number of aircraft elsewhere, leaving behind a limited number of personnel, and then a terrorist alert were to be sounded, the station could then be guarded by reservists called out on a s.24 full-time service commitment, leaving the remaining specialist personnel such as technicians to undertake their normal duties (see *Hansard*, H.C. Standing Committee A, col. 28, April 16, 1996). Full-time service with world-wide mobility will normally qualify for full regular rates of pay, with lower mobility justifying a lower "X" factor (which is the additional sum paid in recognition of the unique features of a service engagement). It is not expected that the reserve bounty would be available in such cases but this and other cognate matters are to be detailed in regulations.

Section 24 provides that the reservist, having undertaken in writing (subs. (1)) a full-time service commitment for a specified period (subs. (2)(a)), becomes subject to service discipline law for the duration. This means that even if the reservist is off-duty, he could be tried by court-martial for committing an offence under civil law involving another reservist (see, for example, Army/Air Force Act 1955, s.70; Naval Discipline Act 1957, s.42). His duties will be governed by the terms of his written commitment and by any orders or regulations issued under s.4 (subs.

(2)(c)). The full-time service commitment shall specify the length of the commitment and the duties, in general or in specific terms (subs. (3)(a)). The duties (a word not defined in the Act) may, of course, include participation in operations, as is the case with call out under Pts. IV–VI of the Act.

Additional duties commitments

25.—(1) A member of a reserve force may enter into a commitment in writing under this section (an "additional duties commitment") to perform such duties, for such period or periods, as may be specified in the commitment.

(2) A person who has entered into an additional duties commitment, in relation to each period of duty contemplated by the commitment—

(a) shall be subject to service law from any time specified in the commitment as the time at which he is to begin that period of duty until released from duty;

(b) while subject to service law, shall perform such duties as he may, in accordance with the terms of the commitment and any orders or regulations under section 4, be required to perform;

(c) shall, if not released from duty sooner, be entitled to be released from duty with all convenient speed in the prescribed manner at the end of that period.

(3) An additional duties commitment—

(a) shall specify—

(i) the duties to be performed by the person concerned (in general or specific terms);

(ii) the period or periods for which he is to perform duties;

(iii) the time and place at which he is to begin performing duties or, if there is to be more than one period of duty, the times and places at which he is to begin performing duties on each such occasion;

(b) may include terms requiring that person—

(i) to perform any duties outside the United Kingdom; or

(ii) to serve with any of the regular services for the purposes of performing any duties; and

(c) may contain such other terms relating to the duties to be performed by that person as are included in accordance with orders or regulations under section 4.

(4) An additional duties commitment—

(a) may, with the consent of the member concerned, be varied in accordance with orders or regulations under section 4;

(b) may be revoked at any time by an authorised officer (whether at the request of the member concerned or otherwise) giving written notice to that effect to the member concerned; and

(c) shall terminate (if not revoked sooner) on the release of the member concerned from the last period of duty contemplated by the commitment.

(5) A person's duties under an additional duties commitment are in addition to any other obligations of his as a member of a reserve force.

(6) The duties specified in an additional duties commitment may include undertaking training.

(7) In this section "authorised officer" means an officer authorised by or in accordance with directions of the Defence Council for the purposes of this section.

DEFINITIONS

"additional duties commitment": s.127(1).

"authorised officer": subs. (7).

"reserve force": s.1(2).

"service law": s.127(1).

This section enables a reservist to undertake additional (or part-time reserve) duties short of a full-time service commitment under s.24, in the absence of either a call out as specified in Pts. IV–VI or a training obligation. Its rationale, reflecting the flexibility of the statutory scheme, is to provide further opportunities for reservists to experience a wider range of tasks than was possible under the 1980 Act.

The additional duties commitment, according to the interpretation section, s.127(1), means a "commitment under section 25". The provisions of the section follow closely but not, of course, identically, those in s.24. While subs. (1) states that the written commitment may specify the period or periods of the commitment, thus allowing maximum flexibility regarding its duration, subs. (3)(a)(ii) states that the commitment *shall* specify the period or periods, etc.

Moreover, while a full-time service commitment may require service "anywhere in the world" (s.24(4)(b)), an additional duties commitment involves service "outside the United Kingdom" (s.25(3)(b)(i)). The additional duties commitment is in addition to any of the other obligations the reservist is required to meet (for example, training commitments or annual camp) as a reservist (subs. (5)).

In all other essentials, the statutory provisions with respect to a full-time service commitment under s.24 are applicable to an additional duties commitment under s.25.

Parliamentary control of commitments

26.—(1) Parliament may authorise for each of the reserve forces a maximum number of officers and a maximum number of men who may at any time be—

(a) in full-time service under full-time service commitments; or

(b) subject to additional duties commitments which are in force.

(2) Accordingly, the numbers of officers and men of a reserve force who are in full-time service, or subject to additional duties commitments which are in force, shall not exceed any numbers for the time being authorised by Parliament for that force.

(3) Any members of a reserve force who are in full-time service or who are subject to additional duties commitments shall not be reckoned in any numbers for the time being authorised by Parliament for any of the regular services.

DEFINITIONS
"additional duties commitment": s.127(1).
"full-time service": s.24(10).
"full-time service commitment": s.24(10).
"men" ("man"): s.2(4).
"regular services": s.127(1).
"reserve forces": s.1(2).

GENERAL NOTE

Subs. (1)
Parliament *may* authorise for each reserve force the maximum number of officers and men at any time in full-time service under full-time service commitments or subject to additional duties commitments. Note that under s.3, parliament *shall* authorise the maximum number of officers and men for each of the reserve forces.

Subs. (2)
If parliament authorises a maximum number under subs. (1), which, as we saw, uses the permissive "may", then the numbers entering into these commitments *shall* not exceed the authorised number.

Subs. (3)
Reservists who have entered into these commitments are not to be counted against the maximum numbers authorised by parliament for the regular services. For parliamentary control of the size of the armed forces, see note to s.3(1), above. Prior to its amendment, subs. (3) referred only to the regular Army and regular Air Force on the footing that the numbers of officers and men serving in the Royal Navy and Royal Marines had never been subject to parliamentary control through statute, though in practice parliament does so through its financial control.

Voluntary activities

Voluntary training and other duties

27.—(1) Nothing in this Part prevents a member of a reserve force—

(a) undertaking any voluntary training in the United Kingdom or elsewhere that is made available to him as a member of that force;

(b) undertaking any voluntary training or performing other voluntary duties in the United Kingdom or elsewhere, being training or duties undertaken or performed at his own request or following a request made to him by or on behalf of his commanding officer.

(2) Orders or regulations under section 4 may make provision as to the provision and use of training facilities for members of reserve forces and otherwise in connection with the undertaking of training or other duties as mentioned in subsection (1) of this section.

(3) A member of a reserve force shall be subject to service law while performing voluntary duties or training as mentioned in subsection (1).

DEFINITIONS
"reserve force": s.1(2).
"service law": s.127(1).

GENERAL NOTE
The requirements in Pt. III relating to training obligations, full-time service commitments and additional duties commitments do not prevent a reservist from undertaking voluntary training or duties in the U.K. or abroad. Opportunities may, for example, become available at short notice. In practice, reservists do undertake obligations beyond their minimum statutory requirements which, under the 1980 Act, could be as little as 19 or 27 days in a year. Section 27 formalises the situation, while replicating the provisions of s.43 of the 1980 Act. There is nothing stated in the section with regard to payment for the voluntary training or duties undertaken. Some concern was expressed in parliament that the line between training or duty which should attract payment and training or duty which is treated as voluntary, and consequently does not attract payment, may be extremely fine. See *Hansard*, H.C. Standing Committee A, col. 30, April 16, 1996; H.C. Vol. 278, col. 39, May 20, 1996.

Subs. (1)
The word "training" is not defined. Does para. (a) add anything to the subs. in the light of the wording of para. (b)? Paragraph (b) refers to voluntary training (or voluntary duties) undertaken by a reservist at his, or at his commanding officer's, request, while para. (a) refers to voluntary training "made available to him as a member of" a reserve force. Paragraph (b), with respect to voluntary duties, moves beyond the limits of s.43 of the 1980 Act which was restricted to voluntary training. The minister, in Standing Committee A, suggested that voluntary duties could extend from collecting a new truck from a storage depot, to a Territorial Army regiment spending a weekend moving ammunition from a depot to a port in anticipation of loading for an operation. He also suggested that duties would include parades and that preparation for a parade would be training. See *Hansard*, Standing Committee A, col. 30, April 16, 1996.

Subs. (2)
Orders or regulations may be required to ensure the availability of facilities for voluntary training or duties, given the complexity surrounding ownership of reserve forces property. Orders or regulations could also address the concern expressed that the dividing line between voluntary unpaid training or duties and obligatory paid training or duties requires clear definition.

Subs. (3)
Whether or not the dividing line between voluntary and obligatory training or duties is unclear, service discipline law applies in both cases. Would voluntary duty or training be a mitigating factor in sentencing an offender who has committed an offence against service discipline law?

PART IV

SPECIAL AGREEMENTS FOR CALL OUT

Special agreements

Special agreements

28.—(1) A member of a reserve force who has entered into a special agreement is liable, while the agreement is in force—

(a) to be called out for permanent service anywhere in the world; and

(b) to fulfil any training obligations specified in the agreement.

(2) A person in qualifying employment shall, before entering into a special agreement, obtain the consent of his employer in such form as may be prescribed.

(3) A special agreement—

(a) shall specify a period not exceeding 9 months as the maximum period for which the person concerned may be required to serve on being accepted into service under this Part; and

(b) may specify other terms relating to the obligations undertaken by the person entering into it.

(4) A person who has entered into a special agreement—

(a) shall fulfil any training obligations specified in the agreement;

(b) if accepted into service under this Part, shall serve,

in accordance with the terms of the agreement and (subject to those terms), on such other terms and conditions as may be prescribed and are applicable in his case.

(5) The obligations undertaken by a person who has entered into a special agreement are in addition to any other obligations he may have as a member of a reserve force.

DEFINITIONS

    "permanent service": s.127(1).

    "prescribed": s.127(1).

    "qualifying employment": s.37(1).

    "reserve force": s.1(2).

    "service under this Part": s.37(1).

    "special agreement": s.37(1).

GENERAL NOTE

Part IV creates a new category of reservist, one who enters into a "special agreement". The popular term is the "high readiness reserve", a phrase which does not appear in the Act. Such reservists are persons with a specialised skill in short supply in the regular or reserve forces. They are different from the existing administrative category, the "ready reserve list", who offer rapid availability but not necessarily specialist skills. High readiness reservists agree, with the consent of their employers, to undertake a higher liability for call out than ordinarily applies. The Ministry of Defence envisage around 3,000 members of this reserve category. They are likely to include linguists, air movements support staff, intelligence staff, public relations specialists, medical staff and specialist engineers and technicians. There is a maximum period of call out of nine months and an annual review to determine whether the high readiness reserve status is still appropriate in respect to individual members and their employers. Nonetheless, from the Ministry of Defence point of view, the existence of a pool of specialists whose skills are in short supply increases the certainty of services planning. Inevitably, however, some have argued that reservists should not be used as a stop-gap for skill shortages in the regular forces. Concern has been expressed about the possible reluctance (to put it no higher) by National Health Service trusts, given the internal market arrangements within the NHS, to permit medical staff to undertake high readiness reserve service for up to nine months, especially for humanitarian operations (notwithstanding the provisions in Pt. VIII for exemption from or deferral of call out). In some cases, it is alleged, NHS trusts might discriminate against reservists in appointing medical staff.

The government has claimed to find no evidence for this, however (though proof of discrimination in the appointment of staff is often elusive). In respect to high readiness reserve involvement in humanitarian operations, civilian aid agencies have voiced reservations if there is no long-term commitment.

Subs. (1)
The "special agreement" is a written agreement (presumably with the Ministry of Defence, though this is not stipulated). Under it, the reservist accepts the obligation to be called out for "permanent service" (which includes actual service) without limitation of area. He also accepts any training obligations specified in the agreement. In respect to training for high readiness reservists, the assumption is, however, that they already possess the requisite skills as linguists or medical staff, or whatever, and that the basic military skills are maintained. If he fails to comply with the terms of the agreement, then the high readiness reservist becomes subject to service discipline law remedies.

Subs. (2)
"Qualifying employment" is defined in s.37(1) as "employment under a contract of service which normally involves employment for 14 hours or more weekly". Thus it applies to employees and not to the self-employed; nor to business partners. Regarding the self-employed, the consent of an employer is obviously irrelevant; regarding business partners, it is assumed that the relationship of trust would conduce to the agreement of other partners to the reservist's entering into the special agreement. Orders or regulations under s.4 may prescribe the manner in which the employer's consent is obtained (see, also, ss.29–30). If there is no employer's consent, then there is no special agreement. There is no appeal against an employer's refusal of his consent.
As to the minimum 14 hours weekly period of employment normally undertaken, this contrasts with the norm of 16 hours for full-time employees in labour law (eight hours for part-time employees) for statutory entitlements. The figure of 14 hours was apparently reached after consultations involving the National Employers' Liaison Committee and trade unions, though s.37(5) permits the Secretary of State to reduce by order the specified minimum number of hours.
The consent of an employer for whom the reservist may, for example, work as a casual barman, is not required. There may be difficulties for some of those on short-term contracts meeting the requirements of the special agreement even if the definition of "qualifying employment" applies to their case. A person on a two-year contract, for example, who commits himself for up to nine months on high readiness reserve actual service is in a rather uncertain employment situation, notwithstanding his employer's agreement.

Subs. (3)
The special agreement must specify a period of high readiness reserve service up to a maximum of nine months (para. (a)) and may specify other terms relating to the reservist's obligations (para. (b)). The nine months period represents a compromise between call out for the duration of the operation (which could last longer than nine months) and the recognition that an employer is losing the services of a skilled specialist during the period. Paragraph (b) is very broadly worded. It may, for example, specify details regarding the training to be undertaken. But are the provisions wide enough to include matters relating to pay, pensions, or bounties?

Subs. (4)
This makes provision for the possibility of training obligations as a precursor to deployment in the high readiness reserve. Apart from the terms specified in the special agreement, orders or regulations under s.4 may also be applicable.

Subs. (5)
Given that under subs. (1), a member of the high readiness reserve is liable for call out for permanent service and for any training obligations specified in the special agreement, he is not discharged from any other obligations he may have as a reservist. Thus he may be obliged to fulfil his training obligations in accordance with s.22 or he may be called out for permanent service with his own unit under Pt. VI on operations where only his basic military skills and not his specialist skills may be required.

Employers' consent before entering agreements

29.—(1) Before entering into a special agreement, a person shall—
(a) submit a declaration to an authorised person in the prescribed form stating whether he is in employment and, if so, giving the name of his employer and such other particulars as may be prescribed;

(b) where the person concerned is in employment with an employer which is qualifying employment, produce to an authorised person a document recording the consent of that employer to his entering into the agreement.

(2) Where an authorised person is satisfied at the time a person enters into a special agreement that—

(a) he is not in qualifying employment; or

(b) he is in qualifying employment and the employer has consented to his entering into the agreement,

the validity of the agreement shall not be affected by any failure to comply with section 28(2); and a document purporting to be a certificate signed by the authorised person stating that he is satisfied of those matters shall be evidence of that fact.

(3) Where a person has more than one qualifying employment, subsections (1) and (2) apply separately in relation to each employer of his.

(4) In this section and section 30 "authorised person" means a person authorised by or in accordance with directions of the Defence Council for the purpose of exercising the functions concerned.

DEFINITIONS
"authorised person": subs. (4).
"prescribed": s.127(1).
"qualifying employment": s.37(1).
"special agreement": s.37(1).

GENERAL NOTE
As a reservist wishing to enter into a special agreement must obtain the prior consent of his employer, this section lays down the procedure to be followed to establish that such consent has been obtained. Note that there is no obligation on a reservist, apart from a special agreement situation, to inform his employer that he is, in fact, a reservist. In the event of call out, however, with the associated provisions for pensions protection (s.8) and the safeguards in Pt. VIII, reserve status could scarcely be concealed.

Subs. (1)
Prior to entering into a special agreement, the reservist must submit a declaration to a person authorised by the Defence Council for this purpose. It would seem that the person need not be an officer, though he normally would be. Could the Defence Council confer authority on a civilian? At least half the members of the Defence Council are themselves civilians. Orders or regulations under s.4 will prescribe the form which the declaration is to take. However, it must state whether the reservist is in employment; if so, the name of the employer and also any other particulars which might be prescribed by orders or regulations under s.4 (see para. (a)). Paragraph (a) therefore covers the situation both where the reservist is, and where he is not, in employment. Where the reservist is in qualifying employment, that is, normally working a minimum of 14 hours a week, he must submit to the "authorised person" a document which records his employer's consent to his entering into a special agreement.

Subs. (2)
This provides that as long as the authorised person is satisfied that the reservist is either not in qualifying employment, in which case the question of an employer's consent is irrelevant, or *is* in such employment and is satisfied that the employer has given his consent, the failure of the employee in fact to obtain the employer's consent in the prescribed manner will not invalidate the special agreement. It is, however, not clear why, if the reservist is not in qualifying employment, it is necessary to state that the failure of a reservist who *is* in qualifying employment to obtain an employer's consent in the prescribed form will not affect the validity of the special agreement of a reservist who is *not* in qualifying employment. Presumably, unemployed reservists who enter a special agreement will be deemed to be available for work for the purposes of employment benefit (or job seeker's allowance from October 1996), even though a maximum nine-month service with the high readiness reserve could materialise at any time.

Subs. (3)
The procedure to be followed regarding the obtaining of an employer's consent applies in respect to each employer if the reservist is in more than one qualifying employment.

Subs. (4)
The meaning of "authorised person" is given. Directions of the Defence Council may be in the form of Defence Council Instructions. For similar provisions in respect to authorised *officers*, see, for example, s.13(6) above.

New employer's consent to continuation of agreements

30.—(1) Where a person who has entered into a special agreement begins a new qualifying employment he shall, within 7 days of beginning that employment, submit a declaration to an authorised person in the prescribed form stating that he has begun a new qualifying employment and giving the name of his employer and such other particulars as may be prescribed.

(2) Subject to subsections (3) and (4), where a person has begun a new qualifying employment with an employer and submitted the declaration required by subsection (1), he is not liable to be called out under this Part or required to fulfil any training obligations specified in his special agreement unless and until—

   (a) the employer gives his written consent in the prescribed form to the continuation in force of the agreement; and

   (b) an authorised person certifies under subsection (5) that the employer has given that consent.

(3) Subsection (2) does not apply if the declaration is submitted by a person who is in service under this Part.

(4) If the declaration is submitted after the person concerned has been served with a call-out notice under section 32 but before the notice has ceased to have effect, the person concerned shall remain liable to be accepted into service until the notice ceases to have effect.

(5) Where, after a declaration under subsection (1) has been submitted, an authorised person is satisfied that the person concerned has begun a new qualifying employment and that his employer has given the requisite consent, he shall certify that fact in the prescribed form.

(6) For the purposes of subsection (2)(a), such a certificate shall be conclusive evidence that the employer has consented to the continuation in force of the special agreement in question.

(7) For the purposes of this section a person begins a new qualifying employment when, at any time after entering into a special agreement—

   (a) he begins a qualifying employment with a person who was not already his employer; or

   (b) where the hours for which he is employed, by a person who has not previously been required to give consent under this section or section 29, change so as to cause his employment by that person to become qualifying employment.

DEFINITIONS
   "authorised person": s.29(4).
   "call-out notice": s.37(1).
   "new qualifying employment": s.37(1).
   "service": s.37(1).
   "service under this Part": s.37(1).
   "special agreement": s.37(1).

GENERAL NOTE
The broad thrust of this section is to provide that where a reservist who has entered into a special agreement begins a new qualifying employment, he must secure the consent of his new employer.

Subs. (1)
On commencement of a new qualifying employment, normally involving a minimum of 14 hours per week, the reservist must submit his declaration with the necessary details to the authorised person within seven days.

Subs. (2)

Following submission of the declaration, the reservist is not liable to undertake high readiness reserve service or related training obligations unless both the new employer's written consent to the continuation to the agreement has been given in the prescribed form, and an authorised person has so certified.

Subs. (3)

If the reservist is currently on call out or other permanent service under the terms of the special agreement, then the procedures in subs. (2) are not required in the event of the reservist simultaneously beginning, presumably in terms of a contractual commencement date, a new qualifying employment.

Subs. (4)

This covers the situation where a call-out notice to serve with the high readiness reserve has been issued, and it is still in force, but the reservist has not actually begun his high readiness reserve service, other permanent service or training. In this case, even though he has commenced a new qualifying employment, he is liable for permanent service or training. Note, however, the employer's safeguard under s.31(2) regarding "Termination of agreement".

Subs. (5)

It is possible to envisage a reservist submitting a forged written consent (and drawing an extra bounty) to an authorised person. While that would constitute an offence under s.95(1)(d), the special agreement would appear to be valid by virtue of the authorised person's certification. For termination, see s.31.

Subs. (6)

As an evidentiary principle, a document can normally only be spoken to by its maker. This subsection anticipates the possibility that the authorised person will not be available to speak to the certificate issued by him.

Subs. (7)

This merely states when a new qualifying period begins. Under para. (b), there might not even be a change of employer.

Termination of agreements

31.—(1) A special agreement shall terminate when, before the person concerned has been accepted into service under this Part, any of the following events occurs—

    (a) the expiry of the period of 12 months beginning with the day on which the agreement was entered into;

    (b) the expiry of such period as may be prescribed after the giving in the prescribed manner of notice to terminate the agreement by the person concerned;

    (c) the giving by the Secretary of State of a direction that the agreement be terminated;

    (d) the acceptance of the person into permanent service under Part VI;

    (e) the coming into force of another special agreement; and

    (f) any other event specified in the agreement as an event which terminates the agreement.

(2) A direction under subsection (1)(c) may be given on the application of the person concerned or any employer of his or without any such application.

(3) A special agreement shall terminate on the release of the person concerned from a period of service under this Part.

(4) On the termination of a special agreement the obligations undertaken by the person concerned by entering the agreement shall cease and, accordingly, he may not be accepted into service under this Part.

(5) Any reference in this Part to a person who has entered into a special agreement does not include a reference to any person whose agreement has terminated.

DEFINITIONS
"permanent service": s.127(1).
"prescribed": s.127(1).
"service under this Part": s.37(1).
"special agreement": s.37(1).

GENERAL NOTE
This section identifies the events which result in the termination of special agreements.

Subss. (1), (2) and (3)
A special agreement will expire 12 months after it is entered into (subs. (1)(a)); or after the expiry of due notice given by the reservist ("the person concerned") in the manner prescribed by orders or regulations issued under s.4 (see subs. (1)(b)); or after a direction given by the Secretary of State (subs. (1)(c)), which may or may not be at the instance of the reservist or his employer (subs. (2)); or on the reservist being called out under Pt. VI, that is, in circumstances of national danger, great emergency, attack on the U.K., warlike operations, peacekeeping or humanitarian operations (subs. (1)(d)); or on the coming into effect of another special agreement (subs. (1)(e)); or on the occurrence of any other terminating event specified in the special agreement (subs. (1)(f)); or on the release of the reservist from high readiness reserve service (subs. (3)).

Subs. (4)
The reservist's liability for high readiness reserve service or for any related training obligations ceases on the termination of the special agreement. He will, of course, have to fulfil reserve obligations specified elsewhere in the Act, for example, in Pts. III and VI.

Subs. (5)
Since, as a matter of logic, a person whose special agreement has terminated is also one who has entered into a special agreement, the subsection declares that, for the purposes of Pt. IV, the latter does not include a reference to the former.

Call out for permanent service under Part IV

Call out of persons who have entered into special agreements

32.—(1) The Secretary of State may, if he considers it appropriate to do so, call out for service any person who has entered into a special agreement by serving a notice on him requiring him—
   (a) to present himself for service at a specified time and place; and
   (b) to remain at that place until he is either accepted into service or informed that he is not to be accepted into service in pursuance of the notice.

(2) A call-out notice shall also require the person concerned, if he fails to comply with the requirements mentioned in subsection (1)—
   (a) to present himself for service to any person specified in the notice or to any other authorised officer; and
   (b) having so presented himself, to remain until he is either accepted into service or informed that he is not to be accepted into service in pursuance of the notice.

(3) A call-out notice shall specify—
   (a) the person to whom the notice applies and the special agreement concerned; and
   (b) the time and place at which he is to present himself for service;
and it may also specify places and times at which and persons to whom the person may present himself for service if he fails to present himself at the time and place specified under paragraph (b) of this subsection.

(4) A call-out notice shall (without affecting any liability arising from a failure to comply with the notice) cease to have effect, if not revoked sooner, when—
   (a) the special agreement specified in the notice terminates under section 31(1); or

(b) the person concerned is either accepted into service or informed that he is not to be accepted into service in pursuance of the notice.

(5) A call-out notice served on a person may—

(a) be varied by the Secretary of State by serving a variation notice on him;

(b) be revoked by the Secretary of State by serving a revocation notice or a subsequent call-out notice on him.

(6) A notice under this section may be served on a person by delivering it to him or by leaving it at, or sending it by post to, his last known address; and any call-out or variation notice delivered to that address by registered post or recorded delivery shall be deemed to have been served on him.

(7) No steps may be taken against a person in respect of failure to comply with a call-out notice under this section unless the notice or, as the case may be, any variation notice was received by him or is deemed to have been served on him by virtue of subsection (6).

DEFINITIONS
"authorised officer": s.37(1).
"call-out notice": subs. (1).
"service": s.37(1).
"special agreement": s.37(1).

GENERAL NOTE
This section gives power to the Secretary of State to call out reservists who have signed special agreements, and it lays down the procedures to be followed in so doing. Actual deployment of the armed forces, including the reserve forces, is viewed as an exercise of the royal prerogative. But it is exercised by the Secretary of State within a statutory framework and therefore with the indulgence of parliament. Subsection (1) does not refer to the issue of a call-out order. This, however, seems to be implied in the light of the right to serve a call-out notice.

There are two initial steps for the reservist in receipt of a call-out notice for service in the high readiness reserve. First, he presents himself at the appointed time and place (subs. (1)(a)). Second, he remains there, pending selection for service; and if so selected, he awaits the processing of the papers and undergoes the carrying out of medical checks (subs. (1)(b)). There is no time limit specified for this stage to be completed. No doubt the service authorities would wish to complete the process as rapidly as possible, especially in the case of the high readiness reserve. The reservist himself, called out from his employment, or from his self-employed business or professional sole partnership would no doubt desire the same. The reservist's option of seeking, there and then, exemption or deferral under Pt. VIII if delay were unreasonable might additionally prompt a rapid processing of personnel (the processing of the reservists called out for service in Bosnia was completed in a single day).

If he fails to comply with the requirements in subs. (1), the high readiness reservist must present himself to, and remain with, any person specified in the notice or to any other officer authorised by the Defence Council, pending the decision on acceptance or otherwise into the high readiness reserve. Times and places where he may present himself in default of compliance with subs. (1) may be specified in the call-out notice (subs. (3)). Unless revoked sooner by the Secretary of State, the call-out notice expires when the special agreement itself terminates under s.31(1), for example, after the expiry of 12 months (subs. (4)(a)). It also expires on acceptance or rejection for high readiness reserve service in pursuance of the notice (subs. (4)(b)). The flexibility of the scheme is reflected in the power of the Secretary of State to vary (subs. (5)(a)), as well as to revoke (subs. (5)(b)) the call-out notice. Revocation of a call-out notice may also be achieved by the serving by the Secretary of State of a subsequent call-out notice on the reservist (subs. (5)(b)). Presumably this will re-start the nine month and 12 month countdowns in ss.28(3)(a) and 31(1)(a), respectively.

Reservists are required to provide the Posting Authority with information, including their address. It is not uncommon for ex-regulars to ignore their statutory obligations to reply to an annual letter from the Ministry of Defence. One assumes that high readiness reserves will comply with their reporting duties. But subs. (6) makes clear that, apart from personal delivery, the posting of a call-out notice or variation notice by registered post or by recorded delivery to the last-known address of the high readiness reservist is deemed to be a valid serving of a notice (subs. (6)). In that event, "steps may be taken against" a high readiness reservist's failure to comply with a call-out notice or variation notice (subs. (7)). The "steps" which can be taken for failure to comply with a notice are not specified in s.32 (nor, indeed, anywhere else in Pt. IV). However, s.96 makes it an offence triable by court-martial or summarily by a civil court, for a reservist to fail, without leave lawfully granted or without lawful excuse, to present himself for service at the time and place specified in the call-out notice.

Acceptance into service under Part IV

33.—(1) A person served with a call-out notice who—
  (a) presents himself for service to an authorised officer at the time and place specified in the notice under section 32(3)(b);
  (b) presents himself for service to an authorised officer at any other time or place; or
  (c) is brought before an authorised officer after the time so specified,
may be accepted into service by that officer.

(2) Where such a person is accepted into service, he shall be informed by the authorised officer in the prescribed manner that he has been accepted into service by virtue of subsection (1).

(3) If an authorised officer decides that such a person should not be accepted into service, he shall inform that person in the prescribed manner that he is not to be accepted into service in pursuance of the call-out notice concerned.

(4) Any liability of such a person arising from a failure to comply with a call-out notice is not affected by his acceptance into service or by a decision not to accept him into service.

(5) A person liable to be called out under this Part who—
  (a) is of a description for the time being specified in directions of the Secretary of State;
  (b) has not been served with a call-out notice; and
  (c) presents himself for service to an authorised officer,
may be accepted into service by that officer.

(6) Where a person is accepted into service by virtue of subsection (5)—
  (a) the authorised officer shall inform him in the prescribed manner that he has been accepted into service by virtue of that subsection; and
  (b) he shall be deemed to have been called out under this Part.

DEFINITIONS
  "authorised officer": s.37(1).
  "call-out notice": s.37(1).
  "prescribed": s.127(1).
  "service": s.37(1).

GENERAL NOTE
  This section makes provision, in respect to those reservists who have entered into a specific agreement, for the acceptance into permanent service of those in receipt of a call-out notice. Together with s.32, it is based on the premise that reservists may be unable to comply with the precise requirements of time and place in the call-out notice. Perhaps on hearing of the crisis through a government announcement, whether by newspapers or broadcast, the reservist will report to his usual drill hall or training centre, or a mobilisation centre other than that specified in the call-out notice. In other cases, he may not have been served with a call-out notice. In these cases, he should not be precluded from acceptance into service, though if there is no reasonable excuse for failure to comply, he may face disciplinary proceedings.

Subs. (1)
  As well as the situation where a reservist presents himself for service, para. (c) also provides for a reservist being brought before an authorised officer after the time so specified, following which he may be accepted into service by that officer. While Sched. 2 deals with arrest of deserters and absentees without leave, it does not appear to cover the case of para. (c). See also subs. (4). So the legal authority whereby a reservist is "brought" before an authorised officer is uncertain.

Subss. (2) and (3)

The authorised officer informs the reservist whether or not he is accepted into service. The manner of informing him will be laid down in orders or regulations issued under s.4. Some such phrase as "with all convenient speed" will be appropriate.

Subs. (4)

This makes clear that whether or not he is eventually accepted into permanent service with the high readiness reserve, disciplinary proceedings, for example, as provided in s.96, may be taken against a reservist who has failed to comply with a call-out notice. No doubt, if he is guilty, there will be powerful mitigating factors. Moreover, whether steps will be taken is, of course, a discretionary matter which may now involve the service prosecuting authorities created in the wake of the separation of the prosecuting function from the service command structure. See, on this, the Armed Forces Act 1996, Sched. 1, Pt. II.

Subss. (5) and (6)

These subsections cover the situation where a reservist of a specified description who has entered into a special agreement but who has not been served with a call-out notice may be accepted for service if he presents himself to an authorised officer.

Release from service under Part IV

34.—(1) A person who has been accepted into service under this Part shall remain in that service until released under subsection (2).

(2) A person who is in service under this Part shall be released from that service with all convenient speed in such manner as may be prescribed when he is no longer required by Her Majesty to be in that service or (if not released sooner) when he is entitled to be released under subsection (3).

(3) A person is entitled to be released from service under this Part—

(a) at the end of the period specified under section 28(3)(a); or

(b) when, on an application under section 78, it is determined that he is entitled to be released.

(4) Orders or regulations under section 4 may make provision enabling or requiring a person who has been accepted into service under this Part to be treated—

(a) if the circumstances of his call out or acceptance into service are of a prescribed description, and

(b) for the purpose of calculating when he is entitled to be released by virtue of subsection (3)(a),

as having been accepted into service on an earlier day than that on which he was actually accepted.

(5) Provision made for the purposes of subsection (4) shall secure—

(a) that any earlier day applicable for the purpose of calculating when a person is entitled to be released from service is to be notified to him as soon as is practicable after the day on which he was actually accepted into service; and

(b) that the period beginning with the earlier day is reckoned as part of his relevant service for the purposes of sections 53(13), 55(13), 57(11) and 69(8).

DEFINITIONS

"prescribed": s.127(1).

"service": s.37(1).

"service under this Part": s.37(1).

GENERAL NOTE

This makes provision for release from that service of individuals who have undertaken the obligations in a special agreement. This does not entail release from other reserve force obligations not involving permanent service in the high readiness reserve.

Subss. (1) and (2)

Orders or regulations issued under s.4 may prescribe the procedure for release which, in any case, must be conducted "with all convenient speed". Subsection (2) makes it clear that release relates to high readiness reserve service and not generally. Release may occur before or at the time when the reservist is entitled to release under subs. (3), but service cannot be extended beyond the maximum period of nine months service in any call-out period.

Subs. (3)
Section 28(3)(a) refers to the maximum period of nine months in permanent service (which is different from the maximum length of 12 months for a special agreement). Section 78 provides for individual exemption from call out.

Subs. (4)
This permits an individual in prescribed circumstances to be treated as if he had been accepted into service earlier than he actually was. Presumably it recognises that a delay in accepting him into service may be due to causes for which he cannot be held responsible. Therefore, he ought not to be prejudiced by being kept in high readiness reserve service for longer than he would have served without any delay in acceptance. The exact circumstances "enabling or requiring" an earlier acceptance date to be recorded are to be described in orders or regulations issued under s.4.

Subs. (5)
The earlier acceptance date is to be the commencement date when calculating the reservist's maximum liability for call out under Pt. VI (national danger, etc.) or the commissioned officer's or ex-serviceman's recall liability under Pt. VII.

Supplementary

Exercise of certain functions under section 32 or 33

35.—(1) The Secretary of State may authorise—
(a) the Defence Council;
(b) any particular officers; or
(c) any officers of a description specified in the authorisation,
to exercise any function of his under section 32 or 33, subject to such limitations and conditions as may be so specified.

(2) An authorisation under subsection (1) relating to the exercise of any function of the Secretary of State by the Defence Council shall (unless the authorisation provides otherwise) be deemed to permit the Defence Council to authorise—
(a) any particular officers; or
(b) any officers of a description determined by the Defence Council,
to exercise the function, subject to such limitations and conditions as may be so specified.

(3) Arrangements made under subsection (1) or (2) for the discharge of any function shall not prevent the exercise of the function by the Secretary of State or (in the case of arrangements under subsection (2)) the Defence Council.

GENERAL NOTE
This section enables the Secretary of State to authorise the Defence Council, or particular officers of a specified description, to fulfil his functions under ss.32 or 33. The authorisation may be subject to specified limitations and conditions. Unless the contrary is stated, the authorisation to the Defence Council is deemed to permit the latter to authorise, in turn, particular officers or officers of a description determined by the Defence Council. The granting of authorisation is not to be treated as preventing the exercise by the Secretary of State, or by the Defence Council (if sub-authorisation occurs) of the functions laid out in ss.32 and 33. Section 32 functions relate to serving, varying or revoking call-out notices. Under s.33(5)(a), the Secretary of State may give directions as to the description of persons liable to call out who, on presenting themselves to an authorised officer, may be accepted into high readiness reserve service, even if they have not been served with a call-out notice.

Parliamentary control of numbers and reports

36.—(1) The number of persons in a reserve force who are liable to be called out under this Part shall not exceed the number for that force for the time being authorised by Parliament.

(2) Any persons who are in service under this Part shall not be reckoned in any numbers for the time being authorised by Parliament for any of the regular services.

(3) The Secretary of State shall from time to time lay before each House of Parliament a report with respect to the exercise of his powers to call out persons under this Part.

(4) Any such report may be made either with respect to any use made, or with respect to any use proposed to be made, of those powers.

DEFINITIONS
    "regular services": s.127(1).
    "reserve force": s.1(2).
    "service under this Part": s.37(1).

GENERAL NOTE
    As with the total numbers in the reserve forces, parliament has asserted its authority to fix the maximum number in the high readiness reserve (subs. (1)). That figure shall not be taken into account in fixing the maximum numbers in the regular services, that is, the Royal Navy, Royal Marines, the regular Army, and the Royal Air Force (subs. (2)).

Subss. (3) and (4)
    The Secretary of State is required to lay a report before each House, detailing the exercise or proposed exercise of his powers to call out the high readiness reserve. Subsection (3) imposes this obligation "from time to time". Could a Secretary of State hide behind this phrase to conceal from parliament a proposed (or, indeed, a previous) call out of high readiness reserves in a sensitive operation? Or might it be diplomatically misguided to publicise to a foreign power a high readiness reserve call out? Under the 1980 Act, the successive call outs of individuals to man a small number of outposts took place. The information was lodged in the Commons Library but formal reporting to the House did not occur. A prolonged operation or the conclusion of the operation might, however, prompt a report to each House so that lessons might be drawn. On the other hand, if an annual reporting obligation had been imposed, it might only result in a blank report.

Interpretation of Part IV

37.—(1) In this Part—
    "authorised officer" means an officer authorised by or in accordance with directions of the Defence Council for the purposes of this Part;
    "call-out notice" means a notice under section 32(1);
    "service under this Part" and "service" mean permanent service on being called out under this Part;
    "qualifying employment" means employment under a contract of service which normally involves employment for 14 hours or more weekly (and "new qualifying employment" shall be construed in accordance with section 30(7)); and
    "special agreement" means a written agreement by which a person accepts the obligations mentioned in section 28(1).

(2) This Part shall have effect in relation to any member of a reserve force who is a Crown servant as if he were employed under a contract of service with such person as may be specified in directions of the Secretary of State as his employer for the purposes of this Part.

(3) The Secretary of State may by regulations make provision as to when a contract of service is to be treated for the purposes of this Part as normally involving or not involving employment for 14 hours or more weekly.

(4) Regulations under subsection (3) shall be made by statutory instrument which shall be subject to annulment in pursuance of a resolution of either House of Parliament.

(5) The Secretary of State may by order amend the definition of "qualifying employment" and subsection (3) so as to substitute, for the number of

hours for the time being specified, such number (not being more than 14) as is specified in the order.

(6) An order under subsection (5) shall be made by statutory instrument; but no such instrument shall be made unless a draft of it has been laid before, and approved by a resolution of, each House of Parliament.

DEFINITIONS
"authorised officer": subs. (1).
"call-out notice": subs. (1).
"new qualifying employment": subs. (1).
"qualifying employment": subs. (1).
"reserve force": s.1(2).
"service": subs. (1).
"service under this Part": subs. (1).
"special agreement": subs. (1).

GENERAL NOTE
This section defines certain terms used in Pt. IV in relation to the high readiness reserve. It clarifies that special agreements and employers' consent thereto apply in the case of Crown employment. It also enables the Secretary of State to alter the definition of qualifying employment and to determine related issues.

Subs. (1)
This interprets salient words or phrases used in Pt. IV.

Subs. (2)
Does a Crown servant have a contract of service? This has been considered by public and labour lawyers in recent years. Among the leading cases are *R. v. Secretary of State for the Home Department, ex p. Benwell* [1985] Q.B. 152; *R. v. Civil Service Appeal Board, ex p. Bruce* [1988] 3 All E.R. 686; and *R. v. Lord Chancellor's Department, ex p. Nangle* [1992] 1 All E.R. 897. Subsection (2) makes clear that at least for the purposes of the requirements of a special agreement, a Crown servant is to be treated as if employed under a contract of service.

Subss. (3) and (4)
The Secretary of State may issue regulations providing when a contract of employment is treated as normally involving or not involving employment for 14 hours or more weekly. While the number of hours of weekly employment may be fixed at any particular figure (whether 14 hours or less, or more than 14 hours), the actual hours worked may be different due to such factors as short-term working, sickness, overtime, public duties or even reserve service. Moreover, a contract of employment may not in fact specify the hours to be worked in terms of hours per week. There may be flexible hours or a number of hours per day or per month or per output.

Regulations issued by the Secretary of State and subject to negative resolution procedure in either House may take such factors into account in determining what is the "normal" length of the working week.

Subss. (5) and (6)
The qualifying employment of 14 hours may be reduced by order issued by the Secretary of State. Compared to the procedure set out in subs. (4), a more rigorous procedure involving a draft order and a positive resolution in each House is required.

PART V

EMPLOYEE AGREEMENTS

Preliminary

Purpose of Part V

38.—(1) This Part enables employees, in pursuance of arrangements between their employers and the Secretary of State, to enter into employee agreements and become special members of a reserve force.

(2) In this Part, references to an employee agreement are references to a written agreement by which a person agrees to accept the liability mentioned

in section 40(1) by becoming a special member of a reserve force specified in the agreement.

(3) Orders or regulations under section 4 may make provision—

(a) enabling a person to enlist in, or become an officer of, a reserve force for the purpose only of becoming a special member;

(b) as to any terms and conditions applicable to such a person, and for applying or disapplying any provisions of this Act, while such a person is a member of the force for that purpose;

(c) enabling the making of requests by a special member (whether before or after ceasing to be subject to the liability mentioned in section 40(1)) for permission to continue as a member of his force on ceasing to be a special member;

(d) as to any terms and conditions applicable to a special member who has ceased to be subject to the liability mentioned in section 40(1);

(e) as to the terms and conditions on which persons resume or begin service as ordinary members of a reserve force by virtue of section 42.

(4) Before orders or regulations under section 4 are made as to the terms and conditions of service of special members of a reserve force, the Secretary of State or, in the case of regulations, the Defence Council shall consult—

(a) one or more bodies appearing to that authority to represent the interests of employers concerned with the supply of goods or services to the armed forces;

(b) one or more bodies or persons appearing to that authority to represent the interests of employees of such employers; and

(c) one or more bodies or persons appearing to that authority to represent the interests of self-employed persons concerned with the supply of goods or services to the armed forces.

DEFINITIONS

"arrangements": s.48(2)(a).
"employee agreement": s.49.
"employer": s.48(2)(b).
"ordinary member": s.49.
"reserve force": s.1(2).
"special member": s.127(1).

GENERAL NOTE

This section introduces the new category of the sponsored reserve, which it describes as "special members of a reserve force". These are, in effect, civilians employed by a Ministry of Defence contractor. They agree by virtue of an "employee agreement" (as distinct from the "special agreement" in Pt. IV) to accept a reserve obligation to provide a contracted service such as maintaining equipment, but, crucially, in an operational context.

Subs. (1)

There are two stages to the process. First, an "arrangement" between the Crown contractor and the Ministry of Defence. Second, an "employee agreement" between an employee of the Crown contractor and the ministry. Whether or not an "arrangement" is an enforceable contract, it clearly cannot bind a third party who is the employee. Section 48(2)(a), however, states that "references to arrangements between an employer and the Secretary of State include references to arrangements between another person and the Secretary of State in pursuance of which the employer supplies, or is to supply, goods or services to or for the benefit of the armed forces".

But will the employee agreement be freely and voluntarily entered into without improper pressure from the employer? Will the employee be an unwilling (and therefore possibly a dangerous) sponsored reservist? Could the "employee agreement" be invalidated through duress? Will a Ministry of Defence contractor refuse to recruit new staff who decline to become sponsored reservists?

Subs. (2)

Is the employee agreement an enforceable contract? The Crown can, of course, enter into a contract but can the employee agreement be enforced by civil proceedings? Does the employee lose his civilian status and become subject to service discipline law when called out for permanent service? It does appear so. Indeed, is he subject to service discipline law even prior to undertaking permanent service? Section 40(1) refers only to liability for call out for permanent service as a sponsored reservist and for fulfilment of concomitant training obligations. It does not refer to the applicability of service discipline law. But s.38(3), while not explicit in this regard, appears designed for this purpose.

Subs. (3)

Orders or regulations issued under s.4 may make "tailor-made" provision for the specific case of the sponsored reserve. This might include the "disapplying" of any provisions of the Act in the case of the sponsored reserve. The maximum flexibility in terms and conditions can thereby be achieved. The possibility of becoming an officer in the sponsored reserve (para. (a)) may reflect the responsible and highly skilled tasks to be undertaken. A sponsored reservist may continue as a "member of his force" once his sponsored reserve liability has ceased (para. (c)). Is a "member of his force" the same as an "ordinary member", as defined in s.49? The last seven words of para. (c) seem to imply this, but the opposite might be inferred from the express reference to "ordinary members" in para. (e). A special member, no longer subject to the call out and training obligations provided for in s.40(1), may nonetheless be subject to other terms and conditions laid down in orders and regulations.

Subs. (4)

There must be formal consultation before the Secretary of State or the Defence Council makes orders or regulations on the terms and conditions applicable to the sponsored reserve. Consultation must be with those whom the Secretary of State or Defence Council consider are representatives of employers supplying goods and services to the armed forces; representatives of employees of those employers; and representatives of relevant self-employed persons. That is, a subjective test of who is appropriate to be consulted is laid down. But, of course, there is no such thing as an unfettered discretion: *Padfield v. M.A.F.F.* [1968] A.C. 997.

Employee agreements

39.—(1) An employee agreement may be entered into by any employee in pursuance of arrangements made between his employer and the Secretary of State.

(2) An employee of an employer who has made any such arrangements shall, before entering into an employee agreement, obtain the written consent of that employer in such form as may be prescribed.

(3) Where an authorised person is satisfied at the time a person enters into an employee agreement that his employer has consented to his entering into the agreement, the validity of the agreement shall not be affected by any failure to comply with subsection (2); and a document purporting to be a certificate signed by the authorised person stating that he is so satisfied shall be evidence of that fact.

(4) In subsection (3) "authorised person" means a person authorised by or in accordance with directions of the Defence Council for the purpose of exercising the functions mentioned in that subsection.

(5) An employee agreement shall, if the person concerned is not a member of the force when he enters into the agreement, specify the date by which he must enlist in, or become an officer of, the reserve force specified in the agreement.

(6) An employee agreement may specify—

(a) a maximum period for which the liability of the special member under section 40 is to subsist;

(b) events which will terminate his liability to be called out, and to fulfil training obligations, under the agreement; and

(c) other terms relating to the obligations undertaken by the person concerned or his service as a special member.

(7) On entering into an employee agreement a person who is already a member of the reserve force concerned shall become a special member of that force.

(8) Where a person entering into an employee agreement is not already a member of the reserve force concerned—

(a) he shall become a special member of the force concerned on enlisting in or becoming an officer of that force; but

(b) the agreement shall lapse if he has not enlisted in or become an officer of that force on or before the date specified in the agreement.

(9) An employee agreement entered into by any person shall terminate—

(a) on his entering into another employee agreement;

(b) on his ceasing to be a member of the reserve force concerned; or

(c) on his resuming service as, or becoming, an ordinary member of that force in accordance with section 42.

DEFINITIONS
"arrangements, etc.": s.48(2)(c).
"authorised person": subs. (4).
"employee agreement": s.49.
"employer, etc.": s.48(2)(b).
"ordinary member": s.49.
"prescribed": s.127(1).
"reserve force": s.1(2).
"special member": s.127(1).

GENERAL NOTE
The procedure for entering into the employee agreement is similar to that with respect to special agreements under Pt. IV. However, it presupposes a prior "arrangement" (see annotation to s.38(1)) between an employer and the Secretary of State. Thus the requirement for employer consent in subs. (2) and the certification of the authorised person (subs. (3) and (4)) are required. The certification procedure is justified in order to protect the armed forces from an unanticipated attempt by sponsored reservists to withdraw from their commitment at a crucial time on the pretext that the employer had not, in fact, consented. The details in the employee agreement include the date of joining a reserve force (subs. (5)); the maximum period of liability for call out and training (subs. (6)(a)); terminating events (subs. (6)(b)); and other terms relating to sponsored reserve obligations (subs. (6)(c)). Subsection (7) provides for an ordinary member of the "reserve force concerned" to become a special member of that force. Under subs. (8)(b), the employee agreement shall lapse if the prospective sponsored reservist has not joined the reserve force concerned by the date specified in the employee agreement. It is expected that the cap badge will, in many cases, be that of the Royal Electrical and Mechanical Engineers. Subsection (9) prescribes other events terminating an employee agreement.

Liabilities of special members

Liability of special members to be called out or to train

40.—(1) A special member of a reserve force is liable (until the liability ceases by virtue of section 41)—

(a) to be called out for permanent service under this Part; and

(b) to fulfil any training obligations which are specified in the agreement concerned or are prescribed for special members of the force and applicable in his case.

(2) A special member of a reserve force shall, subject to the terms of the agreement and the provisions of this Act, serve as a member of that force when he is not in permanent service, and when he is in permanent service, on any prescribed terms and conditions which are applicable in his case.

(3) Subject to any limitation in the agreement and any prescribed terms and conditions applicable in his case, a special member is liable to serve on being accepted into permanent service, and to be required to train, anywhere in the world.

(4) A period of service as a special member shall count towards any period for which a person may be required to serve on transfer to a reserve force from any of the regular services.

(5) Sections 16 and 22 and Parts IV and VI shall not apply to members of a reserve force while they are special members.

DEFINITIONS
"permanent service": s.127(1).
"prescribed": s.127(1).
"regular services": s.127(1).
"reserve force": s.1(2).
"special member": s.127(1).

GENERAL NOTE
This section lays down the liabilities of special members with respect to call out and training for the sponsored reserve.

Subs. (1)
The training obligation may be specified in the employee agreement or imported with reference to orders or regulations issued under s.4. It is obvious that training commitments may apply when the special member is not in permanent service.

Subs. (2)
Thus he must serve as a sponsored reservist in a reserve force even if not in permanent service, subject to the terms of his employee agreement and to any terms of the 1996 Act. While in permanent service, he is to serve subject to any terms and conditions, applicable to his case, issued under s.4.

Subs. (3)
This makes clear that unless his own employee agreement or orders or regulations issued under s.4 specify otherwise, he is liable to serve and to train anywhere in the world.

Subs. (4)
Ex-regulars with a reserve liability (see, for example, Army Act 1955, s.12 and Armed Forces Act 1966, s.2) may count their period of service in the sponsored reserve towards the period to be served in the reserves. That period of service as a special member is not, it appears, confined to permanent service. Periods of training, for example, therefore appear capable of being counted towards reserve liability of ex-regulars.

Subs. (5)
The obligations of high readiness reserves (Pt. IV) and of ordinary reserves (Pt. VI), together with the general entitlement to discharge (s.16) and the general training obligation (s.22) do not apply to the sponsored reserve.

Cessation of liabilities

41.—(1) The liability of a special member under section 40(1) to be called out, and to fulfil training obligations, shall cease when any of the following events occurs—

(a) the expiry of any period specified in his employee agreement as the maximum duration of that liability;

(b) the termination of his employment with the employer whose consent was required to his entry into the employee agreement;

(c) the expiry of a notice given by him—
    (i) to the Secretary of State; or
    (ii) to any other person specified by his agreement or prescribed for the purpose of receiving such notices;

(d) the expiry of a notice given by the Secretary of State to him; and

(e) any other event specified in his agreement or prescribed as an event leading to the cessation of that liability;

but that liability shall not cease by virtue of paragraph (c) while the operation of that paragraph in relation to him is suspended by an order made under subsection (6).

(2) A notice under paragraph (c) or (d) of subsection (1) shall expire at the end of such period not exceeding three months—

(a) as is specified in the employee agreement for the purpose of that paragraph, or

(b) if no such period is specified, as is prescribed for that purpose.

(3) Subsection (1) shall not apply to a special member who is in permanent service when an event mentioned in paragraph (a), (b), (d) or (e) of that subsection occurs until he is released from that service under section 45.

(4) A notice under subsection (1)(c) may not be given by a person who is in permanent service; and any such notice which a person has been given shall cease to have effect if he is accepted into permanent service before it has expired.

(5) The Secretary of State shall give a notice under subsection (1)(d) if it appears to him that his arrangements with the special member's employer have ceased to have effect.

(6) Where a call-out order under section 52 or 54 is in force, the Secretary of State may by order suspend the operation of paragraph (c) of subsection (1) of this section in relation to persons of a description specified in the order; and while an order under this subsection is in force—

- (a) no notices under that paragraph may be given by the persons so specified; and
- (b) any notice which was given by a person so specified before the order was made shall cease to have effect.

(7) An order under subsection (6) shall expire at the end of such period not exceeding six months as is specified in the order, without prejudice to the power of the Secretary of State to make more than one such order in relation to persons of the same description.

DEFINITIONS
"arrangements, etc.": s.48(2)(a).
"call-out order": s.64.
"employee agreement": s.49.
"employer, etc.": s.48(2)(b).
"permanent service": s.127(1).
"prescribed": s.127(1).
"special member": s.127(1).

GENERAL NOTE
This provides for the various circumstances which will bring about the cessation of the special member's liability to call out in the sponsored reserve and the cessation of his training commitment.

Subs. (1)
This lists the different events giving rise to the cessation of the reservist's liabilities as a special member of a reserve force. Conceivably, an employee could take the drastic step of terminating his employment in order to prevent being called out on permanent service as a sponsored reserve. The period of notice for paras. (c) and (d) is prescribed in subs. (2). An order under subs. (6) where a call-out notice under s.52 (in respect to national danger, etc.) or under s.54 (in respect to warlike operations) is in force, may suspend the operation of para. (c).

Subs. (2)
The period of notice, not exceeding three months, will either be specified in the employee agreement or in orders or regulations issued under s.4.

Subs. (3)
Permanent service will override the effectiveness of the terminating events mentioned in subs. (1)(a), (b), (d) and (e).

Subs. (4)
Engagement on permanent service will override a special member's right to give notice to terminate the employee agreement.

Subs. (5)
Whether the arrangements have ceased is subjectively determined by the Secretary of State who must, nonetheless, act reasonably in *Wednesbury* terms (*Associated Provincial Picture Houses Ltd v. Wednesbury Corporation* [1948] 1 K.B. 223), and must not act on the basis of no evidence: *Secretary of State for Education and Science v. Tameside M.B.C.* [1977] A.C. 1014 (H.L.).

Subs. (6)
As mentioned in subs. (1), the Secretary of State may issue an order to the effect that the call-out and training liability of a special member will not cease in spite of notice given, in the event of a call out under s.52 or s.54.

Subs. (7)
The Secretary of State's order will last for no longer than six months, though he may make more than one such order in relation to persons of the same description.

Discharge etc. of special members

42.—(1) This section applies when a man of a reserve force who is a special member ("the man") ceases by virtue of section 41 to be subject to the liability mentioned in section 40(1).

(2) The man shall be discharged with all convenient speed in such manner as may be prescribed unless he enters into a new employee agreement or continues as an ordinary member in accordance with subsection (3) or (4).

(3) If the man—

(a) was an ordinary member of the reserve force concerned immediately before becoming a special member; and

(b) was then serving for a term which has not expired,

he shall resume his service as an ordinary member (and so cease to be a special member) in accordance with orders or regulations under section 4.

(4) If the man has been given permission by an authorised officer to continue as a member on ceasing to be a special member he shall, unless he resumes service under subsection (3), become an ordinary member (and so cease to be a special member) in accordance with orders or regulations under section 4.

(5) Nothing in this section affects the exercise of any power apart from this section to discharge a man of a reserve force or the operation of section 13(4) in relation to a man who is discharged.

DEFINITIONS
"authorised officer": s.49.
"call-out order": s.64.
"employee agreement": s.49.
"man": s.2(4).
"ordinary member": s.49.
"prescribed": s.127(1).
"reserve force": s.1(2).
"special member": s.127(1).

GENERAL NOTE
This provides that when special members cease their liabilities for call out or training, they are then either discharged or, in some circumstances, will continue in reserve service other than the sponsored reserve.

Subss. (1), (2) and (3)
When the terminating events prescribed in s.41 have occurred, the sponsored reservist is to be discharged "with all convenient speed" in accordance with orders or regulations issued under s.4. Alternatively, he may enter into a new employee agreement (though nothing is stated in subs. (2) itself regarding the consent of the employer or the certification of the authorised person), or continue as an ordinary reservist, as defined in s.49, to complete his unexpired term of reserve service.

Subs. (4)
This makes provision for a man who has ceased to be a sponsored reservist to become (as distinct from resume as) an ordinary reservist. The permission of an authorised officer (who is defined in s.49) is required. What is involved in obtaining permission is not specified. As a

sponsored reservist, the man will already have gone through an enlistment or joining process, involving certification by an authorised person (see ss.38(2)(a) and 39(3)).

Subs. (5)
The right of the Defence Council, and of an authorised officer and of a commanding officer to discharge a reservist in accordance with ss.14 and 15 is preserved. The reference to s.13(4) means (somewhat tortuously) that an ex-regular sponsored reservist who had transferred out of the ex-regular reserve force will, on discharge from the sponsored reserve, again become a member of that ex-regular reserve force, unless an authorised officer directs otherwise.

Call out for permanent service under Part V

Call out of special members

43.—(1) The Secretary of State may call out for service any special member of a reserve force if he considers that it is appropriate, in the light of operational requirements and the arrangements he has made with the employer of that person, for that person to continue to undertake work of direct or indirect benefit to the armed forces.

(2) The Secretary of State may call out a special member by serving a notice on that person requiring him—
   (a) to present himself for service at a specified time and place; and
   (b) to remain at that place until he is either accepted into service or informed that he is not to be accepted into service in pursuance of the notice.

(3) A call-out notice shall also require the person concerned, if he fails to comply with the requirements mentioned in subsection (2)—
   (a) to present himself for service to any person specified in the notice or to any authorised officer; and
   (b) having so presented himself, to remain until either accepted into service or informed that he is not to be accepted into service in pursuance of the notice.

(4) A call-out notice shall specify—
   (a) the person to whom it applies and the agreement by virtue of which he is a special member; and
   (b) the time and place at which he is to present himself for service;
and it may also specify places and times at which and persons to whom the person may present himself for service if he fails to present himself at the time and place specified under paragraph (b) of this subsection.

(5) A call-out notice shall (without affecting any liability arising from a failure to comply with the notice) cease to have effect, if not revoked sooner, when the special member concerned—
   (a) ceases to be liable to be called out for service by virtue of section 41; or
   (b) is either accepted into service or informed that he is not to be accepted into service in pursuance of the notice.

(6) A call-out notice served on a special member may—
   (a) be varied by the Secretary of State by serving a variation notice on him;
   (b) be revoked by the Secretary of State by serving a revocation notice or a subsequent call-out notice on him.

(7) A notice under this section may be served on a person by delivering it to him or by leaving it at, or sending it by post to, his last known address; and any call-out or variation notice delivered to that address by registered post or recorded delivery shall be deemed to have been served on him.

(8) No steps may be taken against a person in respect of failure to comply with a call-out notice under this section unless the notice or, as the case may be, any variation notice was received by him or is deemed to have been served on him by virtue of subsection (7).

(9) In this section and section 44 "service" means permanent service.

GENERAL NOTE
This section lays down the conditions under which the Secretary of State may call out any sponsored reservist and makes provision for the procedure to be followed in calling him out.

Subs. (1)
The criteria to be met for call out are laid down. They are obviously couched in broad, somewhat loose, terms in accordance with the principle of maximum flexibility. They are, indeed, in accordance with the proposition that such questions are for the executive, not the courts. See the line of cases running from *The King's Prerogative in Saltpetre* (1606) 12 Co. Rep. 12; *The Case of Ship-money* (*R. v. Hampden*) (1637) 3 St. Tr. 825; *The Zamora* [1916] 2 A.C. 77; and *Council of Civil Service Unions v. Minister for the Civil Service* [1985] A.C. 374. These relate to operational questions. Policy questions in non-operational matters in respect to armed forces deployment may be justiciable: *R. v. M.o.D., ex p. Smith* [1995] 4 All E.R. 427 (Div.Ct.); [1996] 1 All E.R. 257 (C.A.). What is work of indirect, as distinct from direct, benefit to the armed forces? Clearly, work which involves maintaining sophisticated equipment or training other members of the armed forces in its use will be direct. But whether, for example, the preparation by a sponsored reservist of an instruction manual (whether or not in an operational environment) is deemed to be of direct or indirect benefit to the armed forces seems rather pedantic.

Subss. (2), (3), (4), (5), (6), (7) and (8)
Those provisions follow closely the arrangements for call out, call-out notices, and the serving of such notices, which are applicable in the case of the high readiness reserve who have entered into special agreements under Pt. IV. See annotations to s.32.

Acceptance into service of special members

44.—(1) A special member served with a call-out notice who—
(a) presents himself for service to an authorised officer at the time and place specified in the notice under section 43(4)(b);
(b) presents himself for service to an authorised officer at any other time or place; or
(c) is brought before an authorised officer after the time so specified,
may be accepted into service by that officer.

(2) Where such a person is accepted into service, he shall be informed by the authorised officer in the prescribed manner that he has been accepted into service by virtue of subsection (1).

(3) If an authorised officer decides that such a person should not be accepted into service, he shall inform that person in the prescribed manner that he is not to be accepted into service in pursuance of the call-out notice concerned.

(4) Any liability of such a person arising from a failure to comply with a call-out notice is not affected by his acceptance into service or by a decision not to accept him into service.

(5) A special member liable to be called out under this Part who—
(a) is of a description for the time being specified in directions of the Secretary of State;
(b) has not been served with a call-out notice; and
(c) presents himself for service to an authorised officer,
may be accepted into service by that officer.

(6) Where a person is accepted into service by virtue of subsection (5)—

(a) the authorised officer shall inform him in the prescribed manner that he has been accepted into service by virtue of that subsection; and

(b) he shall be deemed to have been called out under this Part.

DEFINITIONS

"authorised officer": s.49.

"call-out notice": s.49.

"prescribed": s.127(1).

"service": s.43(9).

"special member": s.127(1).

GENERAL NOTE

This section, which makes provision for the acceptance into permanent service of special members, also follows closely the comparable provisions in s.33 with respect to service in the high readiness reserve under Pt. IV. Thus presentation before an authorised officer (as defined in s.49); the decision as to acceptance or otherwise; the consequences of failure to comply with a call-out notice; and acceptance without a call-out notice reflect the similar provisions in s.33. See the annotations thereto.

Release from service of special members

45.—(1) A special member who has been accepted into permanent service shall remain in that service until released under subsection (2).

(2) A special member who is in permanent service shall be released from that service with all convenient speed in such manner as may be prescribed when he is no longer required by Her Majesty to be in that service or (if not released sooner) when he is entitled to be released under subsection (3).

(3) A special member is entitled to be released from permanent service—

(a) subject to paragraph (b), at the expiry of the period of 9 months beginning with the day on which he was accepted into service or of such shorter period as may be specified in the agreement concerned;

(b) if he extends (or further extends) his service under subsection (6), at the expiry of the period for which his service is extended;

(c) when, on an application under section 78, it is determined that he is entitled to be released.

(4) Orders or regulations under section 4 may make provision enabling or requiring a special member who has been accepted into permanent service to be treated—

(a) if the circumstances of his call out or acceptance into service are of a prescribed description, and

(b) for the purpose of calculating when he is entitled to be released by virtue of subsection (3)(a),

as having been accepted into service on an earlier day than that on which he was actually accepted.

(5) Provision made for the purposes of subsection (4) shall secure—

(a) that any earlier day applicable for the purpose of calculating when a person is entitled to be released from service is to be notified to him as soon as is practicable after the day on which he was actually accepted into service; and

(b) that the period beginning with the earlier day is reckoned as part of his relevant service for the purposes of sections 53(13), 55(13), 57(11) and 69(8).

(6) A special member who is in permanent service may, with the written consent of the employer whose consent was required for his entering into the agreement in such form as may be prescribed, extend his period of service beyond the day on which he would (apart from that extension) be entitled to be released.

    "permanent service": s.127(1).
    "prescribed": s.127(1).
    "special member": s.127(1).

GENERAL NOTE
    As with ss.43 and 44, the provisions relating to release from service as a sponsored reservist are similar to those regarding release from the high readiness reserve under Pt. IV. Thus the wording of subss. (1) to (5) inclusive is virtually identical to the wording of s.34(1) to (5), with "special member" in s.45 being substituted for "person" in s.34. Unless the period of service has been extended with the written approval of the employer, the special member will be released from permanent service in the sponsored reserve within nine months of acceptance, or after exemption has been granted under s.78.

Supplementary

Exercise of certain functions under section 43 or 44

46.—(1) The Secretary of State may authorise—
(a) the Defence Council;
(b) any particular officers; or
(c) any officers of a description specified in the authorisation,
to exercise any function of his under section 43 or 44, subject to such limitations and conditions as may be so specified.

(2) An authorisation under subsection (1) relating to the exercise of any function of the Secretary of State by the Defence Council shall (unless the authorisation provides otherwise) be deemed to permit the Defence Council to authorise—
(a) any particular officers; or
(b) any officers of a description determined by the Defence Council,
to exercise the function, subject to such limitations and conditions as may be so specified.

(3) Arrangements made under subsection (1) or (2) for the discharge of any function shall not prevent the exercise of the function by the Secretary of State or (in the case of arrangements under subsection (2)) the Defence Council.

GENERAL NOTE
    This section permits the Secretary of State to authorise the Defence Council or particular officers or officers of a specified description to exercise his functions under ss.43 and 44 to call out special members of a reserve force for permanent service. The authorisation may be subject to specified limitations or conditions. The wording in s.46 is identical to that in s.35 of Pt. IV relating to the high readiness reserve, except that the functions of the Secretary of State in respect to the sponsored reserve in Pt. V are exercised under ss.43 or 44 as compared with ss.32 or 33 for the high readiness reserve.

Parliamentary control of numbers and reports

47.—(1) The number of special members of a reserve force shall not exceed the number for that force for the time being authorised by Parliament.

(2) Any special members of a reserve force who are in permanent service shall not be reckoned in any numbers for the time being authorised by Parliament for any of the regular services.

(3) The Secretary of State shall from time to time lay before each House of Parliament a report with respect to the exercise of his powers to call out persons under this Part.

(4) Any such report may be made either with respect to any use made, or with respect to any use proposed to be made, of those powers.

DEFINITIONS
"permanent service": s.127(1).
"regular services": s.127(1).
"reserve force": s.1(2).
"special members": s.127(1).

GENERAL NOTE
It is for parliament to authorise the maximum number of sponsored reservists (subs. (1)). The number of sponsored reservists in permanent service, that is, those undertaking actual service, is not to be counted against the maximum numbers for the regular services authorised by parliament (for authorisation of the maximum numbers for the regular services, see annotations to s.3(1)). The wording of subss. (3) and (4) is identical to that in s.36(3) and (4) with respect to Pt. IV which authorises the high readiness reserve. The legal, constitutional and other (for example, service) issues raised are the same.

Application of Part V to Crown servants, employees of sub-contractors and self-employed persons

48.—(1) This Part shall have effect in relation to any Crown servant as if he were employed under a contract of service with such person as may be specified in directions made by the Secretary of State as his employer for the purposes of this Part.

(2) In this Part—

(a) references to arrangements between an employer and the Secretary of State include references to arrangements between another person and the Secretary of State in pursuance of which the employer supplies, or is to supply, goods or services to or for the benefit of the armed forces; and

(b) references to an employer who has made arrangements with the Secretary of State include references to an employer who supplies, or is to supply, goods or services to or for the benefit of the armed forces in pursuance of arrangements made by another person and the Secretary of State.

(3) This Part shall have effect in relation to any person who is self-employed as if—

(a) references to an employee were references to a self-employed person;

(b) references to arrangements between an employer and the Secretary of State were references to arrangements—

(i) between the self-employed person and the Secretary of State; or

(ii) between another person and the Secretary of State in pursuance of which the self-employed person concerned supplies, or is to supply, goods or services to or for the benefit of the armed forces;

(c) any requirement for the written consent of an employer were omitted;

(d) section 41(1)(b) were omitted.

DEFINITIONS
"arrangements, etc.": subs. (2)(a).
"employer, etc.": subs. (2)(b).

GENERAL NOTE
This section enables Crown servants, employees of sub-contractors and (notwithstanding the apparent contradiction) the self-employed to enter into employee agreements and join the sponsored reserve.

Subs. (1)
This follows closely the provision in s.37(2) with respect to the high readiness reserve. Thus, whether or not Crown servants legally are employees who work under a contract of employment, those Crown servants who work for a Crown body which has an "arrangement" with the Secretary of State to provide goods or services for the armed forces are eligible to enter into an "employee agreement" to join the sponsored reserve.

Subs. (2)
Where a Crown contractor ("an employer") makes an "arrangement" with the Secretary of State for the supply of goods and services, the contractor may, in some cases, be making a commitment to be fulfilled by a sub-contractor. Whether there are legally enforceable obligations would presumably depend on the existence and terms of relevant commercial contracts.

Subs. (3)
References to "employee" or to "employer" in Pt. V include references, where appropriate, to a "self-employed person". It follows that the need for an employer's consent in relation to an employee agreement and for termination of employment as an event resulting in the cessation of the special member's liabilities (s.41(1)(b)) is irrelevant.

Interpretation of Part V

49. In this Part—
    "authorised officer" means an officer authorised by or in accordance with directions of the Defence Council for the purposes of this Part;
    "call-out notice" means a notice under section 43;
    "employee agreement" has the meaning given in section 38;
    "ordinary member" means a member of a reserve force who—
        (i) is not a special member of that force; and
        (ii) is not a member of that force for the purpose only of becoming a special member.

DEFINITIONS
    "authorised officer": s.49.
    "call-out notice": s.43.
    "employee agreement": s.38.
    "ordinary member": s.49.
    "reserve force": s.1(2).
    "special member": s.127(1).

GENERAL NOTE
This interpretation section lays down definitions of phrases used in Pt. V.

PART VI

CALL OUT FOR PERMANENT SERVICE

General liability to be called out for permanent service

Liability of members of reserve forces under call-out orders

50.—(1) Members of a reserve force are liable to be called out under this Part for permanent service when any call-out order authorising the calling out of those members is in force.

(2) A call-out order authorises, subject to subsection (3), the calling out under this Part—
    (a) of any members of a reserve force; or
    (b) if the order is so limited, of any members of a reserve force of a description specified in the order;
and for the purposes of paragraph (b) a group of members of a force may be described by reference to the unit or body of the force to which they belong or any other criterion.

(3) A call-out order does not authorise the calling out under this Part of any person who is not liable to be called out under the order by virtue of regulations under section 62 or an exemption granted on an application under regulations under section 78.

(4) A person who is in service under a call-out order shall serve until released from that service under section 60.

(5) A person who is released from a period of service under a call-out order is, subject to the provisions of this Act, liable to be called out again on the authority of the same or any other call-out order.

(6) The number of persons who are in service under a call-out order shall not be reckoned in any numbers for the time being authorised by Parliament for any of the regular services.

GENERAL NOTE

Part VI re-enacts in a more simplified form the general call-out powers in the 1980 Act. It also introduces a new power to call out reserves for humanitarian disaster relief and peacekeeping duties, a power not authorised under the 1980 Act. Section 50 declares the general liability for call out for permanent service of members, whether one, some or all, of a reserve force while a call-out order is in force (subs. (1)). The word "members" is presumably to be distinguished from the special members (that is, the sponsored reservists and high readiness reservists) of a reserve force called out under Pts. V and IV respectively.

The call-out order may also be limited to members of a reserve force whose description is specified in the order (subs. (2)). Moreover, orders or regulations issued under s.4 may exempt any members (subs. (3) and s.62), while a successful application for exemption will also have this effect (subs. (3) and s.78). Liability to serve after a call-out order continues until release (subs. (4) and s.60), though provision is made for further call out under the same or any other order (subs. (5)). This may be significant if, following a call-out notice under s.58, a reservist is told he is not needed at that point. These provisions must, however, be read in the light of the provisions for maximum service on call out (see ss.53, 55 and 57).

Geographical extent of liability to service on call out

51.—(1) A person who is called out under this Part for service under a call-out order is liable to serve anywhere in the world unless the terms of service applicable in his case restrict his liability on being so called out to service within the United Kingdom or any area of the United Kingdom.

(2) A person whose liability for service is restricted as mentioned in subsection (1) may elect irrevocably in such manner as may be prescribed to be liable for worldwide service—

    (a) whenever he is called out for service under this Part;

    (b) whenever he is called out for service on the authority of a call-out order under any provision of this Part specified in the election; or

    (c) during any period of service (including a current period of service) under a call-out order specified in the election.

(3) The terms of service of a person who makes an election under subsection (2) are modified to the extent required by the election.

(4) In this section "the United Kingdom" includes the Channel Islands and the Isle of Man.

GENERAL NOTE

This section governs the geographical scope of the reservist's general liability to serve following call out.

Subs. (1)

There is a worldwide liability to service unless the reservist's terms of service confine his service to the U.K. or to any area of the U.K. Provision for local service will be in accordance with orders or regulations issued under s.4, the authority for which orders or regulations, in turn, is to be found in s.19(2)(d).

Subss. (2) and (3)
This enables a reservist on a local service obligation to elect to change his terms of service. Once made in the prescribed manner, the decision is irrevocable. It may be made even when he is called out for permanent service under any provision of Pt. VI; or called out in relation to any specific ground for call out in Pt. VI (for example, for humanitarian operations as distinct from warlike operations); or when he is in actual service.

Subs. (4)
Consequently, no Order in Council under s.132(3) is necessary to extend the Act to the Channel Islands or the Isle of Man.

Powers to authorise call out

Call out for national danger, great emergency or attack on the UK

52.—(1) Her Majesty may make an order authorising the call out under this Part of members of a reserve force—
  (a) if it appears to Her that national danger is imminent or that a great emergency has arisen; or
  (b) in the event of an actual or apprehended attack on the United Kingdom.

(2) A call-out order under this section shall have effect (subject to any order under subsection (3)) until it is revoked.

(3) Her Majesty may make an order providing that a call-out order under this section shall cease to authorise the call out of any person who is not in service under the order.

(4) An order under subsection (3) shall not affect the operation of any call-out notice which is served on any person before the day on which the order under that subsection is made.

(5) Her Majesty may make an order revoking a call-out order under this section (whether or not its effect has been restricted by an order under subsection (3)).

(6) Where an order under subsection (5) revoking a call-out order is made—
  (a) the call-out order shall cease to authorise the calling out of anyone who could otherwise be called out on the authority of that order (including anyone served with a call-out notice before the order under subsection (5) is made who has not been accepted into service); and
  (b) any person in service under the call-out order shall be entitled to be released.

(7) A call-out order under this section, and any order under subsection (3) or (5), shall be signified under the hand of the Secretary of State; and the making of such an order shall be reported forthwith to each House of Parliament.

(8) If, when a call-out order under this section is made, Parliament is separated by an adjournment or prorogation which will not expire within 5 days—
  (a) a proclamation shall be issued for the meeting of Parliament within 5 days; and
  (b) Parliament shall meet and sit upon the day appointed by the proclamation and shall continue to sit and act as if it had stood adjourned or prorogued to that day.

(9) In this section "the United Kingdom" includes the Channel Islands and the Isle of Man.

DEFINITIONS
  "call-out notice": s.64.
  "call-out order": s.64.

"members of a reserve force": s.127(1).
"service under a call-out order": s.64.

GENERAL NOTE

This section embodies the most obvious and traditional basis for the deployment of the reserve, that is, when the nation is in imminent danger or when an attack on the U.K. is in progress or is "apprehended". A further, less precise, ground for calling out the reserves is when there is a "great emergency".

It replaces both ss.10, 16, 18(1) and 22 of the 1980 Act and also the prerogative powers governing officers on the retired and emergency lists of the Royal Navy and Royal Marines, officers of the regular Army Reserve of officers, and retired officers of the Royal Air Force. In addition, some former air force officers, in particular, those in receipt of non-pensionable commissions, serve in the Air Force Reserve under statutory authority which is also superseded.

Subs. (1)

The gravity of the situation is symbolised by the call-out order being made by Her Majesty and not by the Secretary of State (contrast the cases under ss.32 and 43), although the order is actually signed by the Secretary of State (subs. (7)). Perhaps a case of concession by the efficient towards the dignified parts of the constitution. The subjective tone of "it appears to Her", in para. (a), adds to the argument that the exercise of the Crown's call-out power is unlikely to be justiciable. Admittedly, there is great scope for disagreement over what is a "national danger"; whether it is "imminent"; and what constitutes a "great emergency" (which does not appear to be confined to the U.K.). While para. (b) is couched in more objective terms (the phrase "if it appears to Her" is absent), an "actual . . . attack on the United Kingdom" could well be a pretty insignificant affair. Whether an attack is "apprehended" may also leave much room for argument. But the point is that, as discussed in the annotations to s.1 and s.4(3), it is, unless parliament were in the future to dictate otherwise, for the Crown, not the courts, to determine when the nation is in danger and what steps should be taken for the defence of the realm. It is submitted that this approach is as applicable to the objective determination of whether there is an actual or apprehended attack as it is to the subjective determination of the Crown that national danger is imminent or that a great emergency has arisen. So far as is known, there have been no legal challenges to the issue of Crown proclamations issued under the Emergency Powers Act 1920 (c. 55), s.1(1), as amended by the Emergency Powers Act 1964 (c. 38), s.1, where the subjective phrase, "it appears to Her Majesty", is employed (*cf.*, the Energy Act 1976 (c. 76), s.3(1)(b), employing an objective approach). Privy Council decisions in the past suggest that the courts will not intervene in such matters on the ground either that the exercise of such powers of proclamation are non-justiciable, or, if justiciable, the challenges will, in practical terms, and without access to government information, be unable to establish that the Crown has exercised its discretion unlawfully (see the cases cited in David Bonner, *Emergency Powers in Peacetime*, London: Sweet & Maxwell, 1985, p.64n.). Moreover, as the civil liberties of individuals are not restricted in the making of a call-out order (in the sense that no person becomes liable to executive detention or to an exclusion order, as has occurred with respect to Prevention of Terrorism legislation or to wartime Defence Regulations), a successful legal challenge is rendered even more unlikely.

Subss. (2), (3), (4) and (5)

Where a reservist is not in service under a call-out order, a subsequent order may remove his liability for call out unless he has already been served with a call-out notice prior to the making of the subsequent order. While the original order is not revoked in these circumstances, the Sovereign may revoke a call out under subs. (5). The effect of this is to withdraw the authority to call out those subject to that call-out order and to entitle those liable to service to be released therefrom.

Subss. (7) and (8)

As mentioned with respect to subs. (1), the Secretary of State will sign, in the Queen's name, the call-out order, any modification thereto, and the revocation order. Each House is to be notified "forthwith" (no doubt in the spirit of a national emergency) of the making of such order, and where parliament is prorogued or adjourned for at least five more days, it may be recalled within another five days by proclamation for this purpose. What would happen if parliament were dissolved and awaiting a general election is not clear, though the date of sitting of a new parliament is usually fixed on dissolution of the old. Moreover, there is usually (but not always) early warning of national danger, great emergency or attack on the U.K. In such circumstances, dissolution would be unlikely. If there is no early warning of, say, a nuclear attack on the U.K., then the constitutional niceties may be of only theoretical significance.

Maximum duration of service on call out under section 52

53.—(1) This section applies for the purpose of determining when members of a reserve force ("the force") who are in service under a call-out order made under section 52 ("the order") are, if not released sooner, entitled to be released from that service.

(2) A man is entitled to be released on the expiry of his current term as a member of the force.

(3) The Defence Council or any authorised officer may, before a man who is in service under the order becomes entitled to be released by virtue of this section, postpone his entitlement to be released by virtue of subsection (2).

(4) A man's entitlement to be released by virtue of subsection (2) may be postponed under subsection (3) more than once, but may not be postponed beyond the end of the period of 12 months beginning with the day on which (disregarding any postponement) that entitlement arises.

(5) A postponement of a man's entitlement to be released by virtue of subsection (2) shall not prevent him becoming entitled to be released by virtue of subsection (6) or, as the case may be, subsection (10).

(6) Any member of the force is entitled to be released when his current service under the order, or his current service under the order and any relevant service in aggregate, exceeds 3 years.

(7) A person may enter into a written agreement consenting to the extension of his period of service under the order beyond—

(a) the day on which he is entitled to be released by virtue of subsection (6), or

(b) the day on which, by virtue of a subsisting agreement under this subsection, he is entitled to be released by virtue of subsection (10),

until the end of such period beginning with that day, not exceeding 12 months, as may be specified in the agreement.

(8) An agreement under subsection (7) may not be entered into at any time—

(a) when the person concerned is not in service under the order;

(b) when he could not be served with a call-out notice on the authority of the order or any other call-out order under section 52; or

(c) more than 12 months before the day on which (disregarding the agreement) he is entitled to be released by virtue of subsection (6) or, as the case may be, subsection (10).

(9) An extension by an agreement under subsection (7) shall prevent the person concerned becoming entitled to be released on the day on which, apart from the agreement, he would be entitled to be released under subsection (6) or, as the case may be, subsection (10); but such an agreement shall not prevent a man becoming entitled to be released by virtue of subsection (2).

(10) A person who has entered into an agreement under subsection (7) is entitled to be released at the end of the period specified in the agreement as the period for which his permanent service is being extended.

(11) Her Majesty may by order signified under the hand of the Secretary of State provide that, in the case of such descriptions of person as may be specified in the order, subsection (6) shall apply as if for the words "3 years" there were substituted "5 years".

(12) The making of an order under subsection (11) shall be reported forthwith to each House of Parliament.

(13) In this section "relevant service", in relation to a person in service under the order, means any permanent service under this Part, or Part IV, V or VII, in the 6 years immediately preceding the first day of his current service under the order.

DEFINITIONS
"authorised officer": s.64.
"call-out notice": s.64.
"call-out order": s.64.
"man": s.2(4).
"members of a reserve force": s.127(1).
"permanent service": s.127(1).
"relevant service": subs. (13).
"service under a call-out order": s.64.

GENERAL NOTE
This lengthy and complicated section makes provision for the maximum duration of service on call-out under s.52, and for a reservist's entitlement to release from service.

Subss. (1) and (2)
If not released sooner (subs. (1)), a man is entitled to release on the expiry of his current term as a member of a reserve force (subs. (2)). Note that the phrase "current term" is not defined or fixed anywhere in the Act. It will, in each case, be found in the member's attestation paper (Sched. 1). Under s.19, orders or regulations issued under s.4 may make provision specifying the duration of service for which a person may enlist.

Subss. (3) and (4)
The Defence Council or an authorised officer, before entitlement to release arises, may postpone more than once the release of a person in permanent service. But the postponement cannot stretch beyond 12 months from the day on which entitlement to release arose.

Subss. (5), (6) and (7)
Notwithstanding a postponement, and unless he signs a written agreement to extend his service for no more than 12 months, a reservist is entitled to be released from service after three years. This period may be calculated under the order alone or aggregated with service as a high readiness reservist or a sponsored reservist or as a recalled officer or former serviceman under Pt. VII. The period of three years may be substituted by a period of five years in accordance with subs. (11).

Subss. (8) and (9)
The written extended agreement can only be made by those in service under the order or by those liable to be served a call-out notice, or by those entitled to release within 12 months before the completion of three years service. However, a proviso to subs. (9) states that notwithstanding the extension, a man is still entitled to be released on the expiry of his current term as a member of that force as *per* subs. (2). The logic of the proviso in the light of the provision for an extended written agreement is not wholly clear. In other words, can he sign an extended agreement and then ignore it and claim his release on the expiry of his current term? The answer appears to be that he can, although he can later re-enlist for the extended period of service.

Subs. (13)
With respect to the entitlement to release under subs. (6) of a reservist whose aggregate service exceeds three years, one is entitled to take account of any permanent service under Pts. IV–VII within the previous six years, prior to the start of his first day of current service.

Call out for warlike operations

54.—(1) The Secretary of State may make an order authorising calling out of members of a reserve force if it appears to him that warlike operations are in preparation or progress.
(2) A call-out order under this section—
(a) shall specify a date, not more than 12 months from the day on which the order is made, on which the order is (unless an order under subsection (3) is made) to cease to authorise the call out of any person who is not in service under the order; and
(b) shall have effect (subject to paragraph (a) or to any order under subsection (3)) until it is revoked.
(3) The Secretary of State may, before the date specified in the call-out order under subsection (2)(a), make an order providing that a call-out order

under this section shall cease to authorise the call out of any person who is not in service under the order.

(4) The restriction of the effect of a call-out order under this section—

(a) by an order under subsection (3), or

(b) by subsection (2)(a),

shall not affect the operation of any call-out notice served on any person before the day on which the order under subsection (3) is made or, as the case may be, the day specified in the call-out order.

(5) The Secretary of State may make an order revoking a call-out order under this section (whether or not its effect has been restricted as mentioned in subsection (4)).

(6) Where an order under subsection (5) revoking a call-out order is made—

(a) the call-out order shall cease to authorise the calling out of anyone who could otherwise be called out on the authority of that order (including anyone served with a call-out notice before the order under subsection (5) is made who has not been accepted into service); and

(b) any person in service under the call-out order shall be entitled to be released.

(7) The making of any call-out order under this section, or any order under subsection (3) or (5), shall be reported forthwith to each House of Parliament.

DEFINITIONS
  "call-out order": s.64.
  "members of a reserve force": s.127(1).
  "service": s.64.

GENERAL NOTE
  This section authorises another "mainstream" task of the reserves, to fulfil duties when called out as part of a war effort.

Subs. (1)
  It is the Secretary of State who makes the call-out order under s.54 (under s.52, it is Her Majesty). Again, the statute employs subjective phrasing ("if it appears to him . . ."). But for the reasons given in respect to s.52, the exercise of the Secretary of State's discretion is likely to be non-justiciable. Whether "warlike operations" are in preparation or in progress will not depend on a formal declaration of war. The U.K. government did not declare war on the Argentine Republic in 1982, nor on Iraq in 1990–91. The phrase is sufficiently flexible to be geographically unlimited. While the working assumption is that the "warlike operations" in question would be those by or directed against, the U.K., they may even relate to warlike operations by other states even if not immediately directed against the U.K. No doubt the Secretary of State will rely on military and diplomatic appreciations in guiding the exercise of his discretion.

Subs. (2)
  The call-out order shall be in force for no more than 12 months in respect to those liable to, but not yet in, service. The expiry date of the order is to be specified in the order.

Subs. (3)
  The specified expiry date in subs. (2) may be pre-empted by a later order specifying an earlier expiry date.

Subs. (4)
  Notwithstanding the expiry date provisions in subss. (2) and (3), a call-out notice already served before the expiry date will be effective.

Subs. (5)
  Notwithstanding the above provisions for expiry dates, the Secretary of State may revoke a call-out order.

Subs. (6)
The revocation would appear to have immediate effect even though this is not made explicit. On revocation, there is no longer authority to call out those not yet in service, or those in receipt of a call-out notice; nor to retain those in service.

Subs. (7)
The call-out order, the order substituting an earlier expiry date and/or the revocation order must be reported "forthwith" to each House.

Maximum duration of service on call out under section 54

55.—(1) This section applies for the purpose of determining when members of a reserve force ("the force") who are in service under a call-out order made under section 54 ("the order") are, if not released sooner, entitled to be released from that service.

(2) A man is entitled to be released on the expiry of his current term as a member of the force.

(3) The Defence Council or any authorised officer may, before a man who is in service under the order becomes entitled to be released by virtue of this section, postpone his entitlement to be released by virtue of subsection (2).

(4) A man's entitlement to be released by virtue of subsection (2) may be postponed under subsection (3) more than once, but may not be postponed beyond the end of the period of 12 months beginning with the day on which (disregarding any postponement) that entitlement arises.

(5) A postponement of a man's entitlement to be released by virtue of subsection (2) shall not prevent him becoming entitled to be released by virtue of subsection (6) or, as the case may be, subsection (10).

(6) Any member of the force is entitled to be released when his current service under the order, or his current service under the order and any relevant service in aggregate, exceeds 12 months.

(7) A person may enter into a written agreement consenting to the extension of his period of service under the order beyond—

    (a) the day on which he is entitled to be released by virtue of subsection (6), or

    (b) the day on which, by virtue of a subsisting agreement under this subsection, he is entitled to be released by virtue of subsection (10),

until the end of such period beginning with that day, not exceeding 6 months, as may be specified in the agreement.

(8) An agreement under subsection (7) may not be entered into at any time—

    (a) when the person concerned is not in permanent service under the order;

    (b) when he could not be served with a call-out notice on the authority of the order or any other call-out order under section 54; or

    (c) more than 6 months before the day on which (disregarding the agreement) he is entitled to be released by virtue of subsection (6) or, as the case may be, subsection (10).

(9) An extension by an agreement under subsection (7) shall prevent the person concerned becoming entitled to be released on the day on which, apart from the agreement, he would be entitled to be released under subsection (6) or, as the case may be, subsection (10); but such an agreement shall not prevent a man becoming entitled to be released by virtue of subsection (2).

(10) A person who has entered into an agreement under subsection (7) is entitled to be released at the end of the period specified in the agreement as the period for which his permanent service is being extended.

(11) Her Majesty may by order signified under the hand of the Secretary of State provide that, in the case of such descriptions of person as may be speci-

fied in the order, subsection (6) shall apply as if for the words "12 months" there were substituted "2 years".

(12) The making of an order under subsection (11) shall be reported forthwith to each House of Parliament.

(13) In this section "relevant service", in relation to a person in service under the order, means any permanent service under this Part, or Part IV, V or VII, in the 3 years immediately preceding the first day of his current service under the order.

DEFINITIONS
"authorised officer": s.64.
"call-out notice": s.64.
"call-out order": s.64.
"man": s.2(4).
"members of a reserve force": s.127(1).
"permanent service": s.127(1).
"relevant service": subs. (13).
"service": s.64.
"service under a call-out order": s.64.

GENERAL NOTE
This section provides for the ascertainment of when reservists called out for service in respect to warlike operations are entitled to be released from that service. The wording of all 13 subss. (in respect to warlike operations) is identical to that in all 13 subss. of s.53 (in respect to national danger, great emergency or attack on the U.K.) with the following exceptions:
(a) subsection (1) refers to "section 54", whereas s.53(1) refers to "section 52";
(b) subs. (6) refers to "12 months", whereas s.53(6) refers to "3 years";
(c) subs. (7) refers to "6 months", whereas s.53(7) refers to "12 months";
(d) subs. (8)(b) refers to "section 54", whereas s.53(8)(b) refers to "section 52";
(e) subs. (8)(c) refers to "6 months", whereas s.53(8)(c) refers to "12 months";
(f) subs. (11) refers to "12 months" and to "2 years", whereas s.53(11) refers to "3 years" and to "5 years";
(g) subs. (13) refers to "3 years", whereas s.53(13) refers to "6 years".
The rationale for the differences appears to be that those reservists called out under s.54 for warlike operations might experience more prolonged pressure than those called out under s.52 in respect to national danger, great emergency or attack on the U.K. The s.52 contingencies may be of shorter duration. Therefore, those called out under s.54 might be expected to sustain a shorter maximum period of actual service reserve duty and extended duty than those called out under s.52.

Call out for certain operations

56.—(1) The Secretary of State may make an order authorising the calling out of members of a reserve force if it appears to him that it is necessary or desirable to use armed forces—
  (a) on operations outside the United Kingdom for the protection of life or property; or
  (b) on operations anywhere in the world for the alleviation of distress or the preservation of life or property in time of disaster or apprehended disaster.

(2) A call-out order under this section—
  (a) shall specify a date, not more than 12 months from the day on which the order is made, on which the order is (unless an order under subsection (3) is made) to cease to authorise the call out of any person who is not in service under the order; and
  (b) shall have effect (subject to paragraph (a) or to any order under subsection (3)) until it is revoked.

(3) The Secretary of State may, before the date specified in the call-out order under subsection (2)(a), make an order providing that a call-out order under this section shall cease to authorise the call out of any person who is not in service under the order.

(4) The restriction of the effect of a call-out order under this section—
  (a) by an order under subsection (3), or

(b) by subsection (2)(a),

shall not affect the operation of any call-out notice served on any person before the day on which the order under subsection (3) is made or, as the case may be, the day specified in the call-out order.

(5) The Secretary of State may make an order revoking a call-out order under this section (whether or not its effect has been restricted as mentioned in subsection (4)).

(6) Where an order under subsection (5) revoking a call-out order is made—

(a) the call-out order shall cease to authorise the calling out of anyone who could otherwise be called out on the authority of that order (including anyone served with a call-out notice before the order under subsection (5) is made who has not been accepted into service); and

(b) any person in service under the call-out order shall be entitled to be released.

(7) The making of any call-out order under this section, or any order under subsection (3) or (5), shall be reported forthwith to each House of Parliament.

DEFINITIONS

"call-out notice": s.64.

"call-out order": s.64.

"members of a reserve force": s.127(1).

"service": s.64.

"service under a call-out order": s.64.

GENERAL NOTE

This section introduces for the first time legal authority to deploy reservists on peacekeeping operations and on disaster relief and humanitarian aid operations. The 1980 Act did not authorise such deployment, and to enable reservists to be deployed on such operations required them formally to leave the reserves, join the regular forces and then rejoin the reserves (if so desired) on completion of their service. Thus reservists serving in Bosnia had been called out (albeit as volunteers) under s.11 of the 1980 Act which related to "warlike operations".

Subs. (1)

It is on the footing that the circumstances of call out under s.56 are less grave than national danger, great emergency or attack on the U.K., as specified in s.52, that the Secretary of State and not the Sovereign may issue a call-out order. Again, subjective terminology ("if it appears to him") is employed, but this is conditioned by "necessary or desirable". The former obviously affords less discretionary authority than the latter. Paragraph (c), which refers to "operations outside the United Kingdom for the protection of life or property", would clearly cover peacekeeping in Bosnia. Would it also cover offensive action in Bosnia or participation in United Nations military operations against Iraq, as in the Gulf War, or would such a call out under s.56 be *ultra vires* on the footing that the authority for such a call out is to be found in s.54 in respect to warlike operations (one would have to make the questionable assumption that the matter is justiciable and that the burden of proof can be met by the applicant for review)?

As to disaster relief and humanitarian operations under para. (b), there is no geographical restriction (unlike the case with para. (a)). Therefore, flood relief activities, whether in Paisley in December 1994 or overseas, "for the alleviation of distress" are clearly covered. In respect to the "preservation of life or property in time of disaster or apprehended disaster", disaster might be natural (major earthquake) or man made (the Rwanda killings). Difficult issues might arise in respect to deployment to, say, Somalia, where reserve forces might be confronted by "warlords" and their armies or followers. Similarly, in the case of Operation Safe Haven (or Operation Provide Comfort in United States terminology) in 1991, designed to assist the Kurds in the wake of the Gulf War. While deployment in Somalia or in Operation Safe Haven would appear to fall within para. (a), that is, in relation to "operations outside the United Kingdom for the protection of life or property", it is not inconceivable that they would fall under the latter part of para (b); or even, particularly in respect to Somalia, under s.54(1), in respect to "warlike operations". The potential for overlap in respect to the different criteria for call out under s.56(1) does exist. Thus Bosnia operations might well fall under the "warlike operations" provisions in s.54 or the "peacekeeping operations" provision in s.56.

Whether it is appropriate for the armed forces to be involved in overseas humanitarian aid operations is a policy question on which differences of opinion have been voiced, not least by voluntary aid organisations which seek to stress the neutrality of non-governmental organisations. Reserve forces deployed as a governmental organisation may lack that aura. There are complex issues concerning cost-effectiveness, especially with the rundown of armed forces medical services which will require greater reliance on the reserve forces. There are also questions of expertise and of potential greater resistance to call out under s.56(1).

Subss. (2)–(7)
These subsections follow the exact wording in s.54(2)–(7). See annotations to s.54.

Maximum duration of service on call out under section 56

57.—(1) This section applies for the purpose of determining when members of a reserve force ("the force") who are in service under a call-out order made under section 56 ("the order") are, if not released sooner, entitled to be released from that service.

(2) A man is entitled to be released on the expiry of his current term as a member of the force.

(3) The Defence Council or any authorised officer may, before a man who is in service under the order becomes entitled to be released by virtue of this section, postpone his entitlement to be released by virtue of subsection (2).

(4) A man's entitlement to be released by virtue of subsection (2) may be postponed under subsection (3) more than once, but may not be postponed beyond the end of the period of 9 months beginning with the day on which (disregarding any postponement) that entitlement arises.

(5) A postponement of a man's entitlement to be released by virtue of subsection (2) shall not prevent him becoming entitled to be released by virtue of subsection (6) or, as the case may be, subsection (10).

(6) Any member of the force is entitled to be released when his current service under the order, or his current service under the order and any relevant service in aggregate, exceeds 9 months.

(7) A person may enter into a written agreement consenting to the extension of his period of service under the order beyond—

(a) the day on which he is entitled to be released by virtue of subsection (6), or

(b) the day on which, by virtue of a subsisting agreement under this subsection, he is entitled to be released by virtue of subsection (10),

until the end of such period not exceeding 6 months, as may be specified in the agreement.

(8) An agreement under subsection (7) may not be entered into at any time—

(a) when the person concerned is not in service under the order;

(b) when he could not be served with a call-out notice on the authority of the order or any other call-out order under section 56; or

(c) more than 3 months before the day on which (disregarding the agreement) he is entitled to be released by virtue of subsection (6) or, as the case may be, subsection (10).

(9) An extension by an agreement under subsection (7) shall prevent the person concerned becoming entitled to be released on the day on which, apart from the agreement, he would be entitled to be released under subsection (6) or, as the case may be, subsection (10); but such an agreement shall not prevent a man becoming entitled to be released by virtue of subsection (2).

(10) A person who has entered into an agreement under subsection (7) is entitled to be released at the end of the period specified in the agreement as the period for which his permanent service is being extended.

(11) In this section "relevant service", in relation to a person in service under the order, means any permanent service under this Part, or Part IV, V

or VII, in the 27 months immediately preceding the first day of his current service under the order.

DEFINITIONS
  "authorised officer": s.64.
  "call-out notice": s.64.
  "call-out order": s.64.
  "man": s.2(4).
  "members of a reserve force": s.127(2).
  "permanent service": s.127(1).
  "relevant service": subs. (11).
  "service": s.64.
  "service under a call-out order": s.64.

GENERAL NOTE
   This section provides for the determination of when a reservist called out for the operations specified in s.56 is entitled to be released from that service. Broadly speaking, and notwithstanding exceptions, he is liable to a maximum of nine months service in every 27 month period. Some members of parliament and employers felt that a six months maximum period was appropriate in respect to "non-military" operations, while the armed forces preferred a 12 month maximum period of service. It may be noted that regular army unaccompanied emergency tours generally do not exceed six months, though Royal Logistics Corps personnel usually serve for longer, while the Royal Navy normally employs a seven or nine month tour.
   With the exceptions noted below, the wording of subss. (1)–(10) in respect to call out for certain operations is identical to that in s.55(1)–(10) in respect to call out for warlike operations. The annotations to s.55 should also be consulted here. The minor differences in wording are: (a) subs. (1) refers to "section 56", whereas s.55(1) refers to "section 54"; (b) subs. (4) refers to "9 months", whereas s.55(4) refers to "12 months"; (c) subs. (6) refers to "9 months", whereas s.55(6) refers to "12 months"; (d) subs. (8) refers to "service", whereas s.55(8)(a) refers to "permanent service". This appears to be simply a drafting inconsistency; (e) subs. (8)(b) refers to "section 56", whereas s.55(8)(b) refers to "section 54"; (f) subs. (8)(c) refers to "3 months", whereas s.55(8)(c) refers to "6 months".
   In addition, the wording of subs. (11) is identical to that in s.55(13), except that subs. (11) refers to "27 months", whereas s.55(13) refers to "3 years".
   There is no equivalent in s.57 to s.53(11) or s.55(11), which permits Her Majesty to extend by order the aggregate length of service before entitlement to release arises. Consequently, provision for notification of an order to parliament similar to that in s.53(12) or s.55(12) does not arise.
   The rationale for the shorter duration of service compared to that in ss.53 and 55 is presumably that peacekeeping and humanitarian aid operations specified in s.56 are considered to be of lower priority to the national interest than the operations specified in ss.52 and 54. The willingness of employees to undertake s.56 operations and the willingness of employers to consent to their doing so may not be as great as in the case of ss.52 and 54 operations. Therefore, the period of service is shorter. Provision in Pt. VIII for exemption, etc. from call out will also, of course, be relevant.

Call out of members of a reserve force

Call out of members of a reserve force on authority of call-out order

   58.—(1) Where a call-out order is in force authorising the call out of members of a reserve force, the Secretary of State may call out any member who is liable to be called out under that order by serving a notice on him requiring him—
   (a) to present himself for service at a specified time and place; and
   (b) to remain at that place until he is either accepted into service or informed that he is not to be accepted into service in pursuance of the notice.
   (2) A call-out notice shall also require the person concerned, if he fails to comply with the requirements mentioned in subsection (1)—
   (a) to present himself for service to any person specified in the notice or to any other authorised officer; and

(b) having so presented himself, to remain until he is either accepted into service or informed that he is not to be accepted into service in pursuance of the notice.

(3) A call-out notice served on a person shall specify—

(a) the person to whom it applies;

(b) the call-out order authorising the calling out of that person and the provision of this Part under which the order is made; and

(c) the time and place at which the person is to present himself for service under that order;

and it may also specify places and times at which and persons to whom the person may present himself for service if he fails to present himself at the time and place specified under paragraph (c) of this subsection.

(4) A call-out notice served on a person may—

(a) be varied by the Secretary of State by serving a variation notice on him;

(b) be revoked by the Secretary of State by serving a revocation notice or a subsequent call-out notice on him.

(5) A call-out notice served on a person on the authority of a call-out order shall (without affecting any liability arising from a failure to comply with the notice) cease to have effect, if not revoked sooner—

(a) when an order revoking the call-out order is made after the day on which the notice was served but before the time mentioned in paragraph (b); or

(b) when the person concerned is either accepted into service or informed that he is not to be accepted into service in pursuance of the notice.

(6) The restriction of the effect of a call-out order—

(a) by an order under section 52(3), 54(3) or 56(3) (as the case may be); or

(b) in the case of a call-out order under section 54 or 56, by subsection (2)(a) of that section,

shall not affect the power of the Secretary of State under subsection (4) of this section to vary a call-out notice served before the effect of the call-out order is so restricted.

(7) A notice under this section may be served on a person by delivering it to him or by leaving it at, or sending it by post to, his last known address; and any call-out or variation notice delivered to that address by registered post or recorded delivery shall be deemed to have been served on him.

(8) No steps may be taken against a person in respect of failure to comply with a call-out notice under this section unless the notice or, as the case may be, any variation notice was received by him or is deemed to have been served on him by virtue of subsection (7).

DEFINITIONS

"authorised officer": s.64.
"call-out notice": s.64.
"call-out order": s.64.
"members of a reserve force": s.127(2).
"service": s.64.

GENERAL NOTE

This section makes provision for the call out of members of a reserve force under the authority of a call-out order issued by the Secretary of State. It does not deal with the call out of the high readiness reserve in Pt. IV or with the sponsored reserve in Pt. V or with the recall of ex-servicemen in Pt. VII, which categories have their own call out (or recall) provisions. Much of the wording in s.32 in respect to the call out of the high readiness reserve is repeated in s.58. Therefore, the annotations to s.32 may be consulted here (note that the wording in s.43 regarding the sponsored reserve is also similar). The following points should be noted: (a) in subs. (1), there is a specific reference to the existence of a call-out order, whereas such an order seems to be implied in s.32(1). Similarly, the discretion to serve a call-out notice is exercised without qualification in subs. (1), whereas in s.32(1), it is served when the Secretary of State considers it appropriate. In law, it is doubtful whether there is any difference. In every other respect, subs. (1) is identical to s.32(1); (b) subs. (2) is identical to s.32(2); (c) subs. (3) omits reference to a "special agreement" (which is mentioned in s.32(3)), but in its place refers, in para. (b), both to the call-out order authorising the serving of the notice and to the provision in Pt. V, whether that be s.52 or s.54 or s.56, under which the order is made. In every other respect, subs. (3) is identical to s.32(3); (d) subs. (4) is identical to s.32(5); (e) subs. (5) states, somewhat tortuously, that if a call-out notice served on a person has not already been revoked by virtue of a revocation notice under subs. (4)(b), then it will cease to have effect (generally, one presumes) when a revocation order is made subsequent to the serving of a call-out notice, but before a person is accepted into service; *or* it will cease to have effect when he is accepted into service or informed he is not being accepted into service. Any failure to comply with a call-out notice can still lead to "steps" being taken against a person, notwithstanding revocation of the notice; (f) subs. (6), which is even more tortuous than subs. (5), states that whereas the Secretary of State can both specify a 12-month expiry date for a call-out order in respect to any person not already in service under the order (see, for example, s.54(2)(a)), and can also make an order to terminate call-out authorisation before that expiry date (see for example, s.54(3)), the *variation* of a call-out notice can still be made by the Secretary of State under subs. (4)(a), as long as the notice has been served before the specification of an expiry date within 12 months, or before the pre-empting of that specified expiry date has been made. In short, the draftsman's *penchant* for lucidity unquestionably deserted him when he came to address s.58.

Acceptance into service under call-out order

59.—(1) A person served with a call-out notice who—

(a) presents himself for service to an authorised officer at the time and place specified in the notice under section 58(3)(c);

(b) presents himself for service to an authorised officer at any other time or place; or

(c) is brought before an authorised officer after the time so specified,

may be accepted into service by that officer.

(2) Where such a person is accepted into service, he shall be informed by the authorised officer in the prescribed manner that he has been accepted into service by virtue of subsection (1).

(3) If an authorised officer decides that such a person should not be accepted into service, he shall inform that person in the prescribed manner that he is not to be accepted into service in pursuance of the call-out notice concerned.

(4) Any liability of such a person arising from a failure to comply with a call-out notice is not affected by his acceptance into service or by a decision not to accept him into service.

(5) Where a call-out order is in force, any person who is liable to be called out under the order who—

(a) has not been served with a call-out notice; and

(b) presents himself for service to an authorised officer,

may be accepted into service under that call-out order by that officer.

(6) Where a person is accepted into service under a call-out order by virtue of subsection (5)—

(a) the authorised officer shall inform him in the prescribed manner that he has been accepted into service under that order by virtue of that subsection; and

(b) he shall be deemed to have been called out under this Part for service under that order.

<small>DEFINITIONS</small>
"authorised officer": s.64.
"call-out notice": s.64.
"call-out order": s.64.
"prescribed": s.127(1).
"service": s.64.

<small>GENERAL NOTE</small>
This section makes provision for the acceptance into permanent service of reservists who have been served with a call-out notice. The wording of all subsections with respect to ordinary

reservists is virtually identical to that in all subsections of s.33 with respect to the high readiness reserve. The exceptions are: (a) s.59(1) refers to a call-out notice under s.58(3)(c), whereas s.33(1) refers to a call-out notice under s.32(3)(b); (b) the words "where a call-out order is in force", at the commencement of s.59(5) do not appear in s.33(5); (c) the words "for service under that order" at the end of s.59(6) do not appear in s.33(6).

It is submitted that the slight variations in wording do not reflect any differences in the scheme of acceptance under the different call-out orders. Therefore, the annotations to s.33 may be consulted in ascertaining the meaning of s.59.

Release from service under call-out order

60.—(1) A person who has been accepted into service under a call-out order shall remain in that service until released under subsection (2).

(2) A person who is in service under a call-out order shall be released from that service with all convenient speed in such manner as may be prescribed when he is no longer required by Her Majesty to be in that service or (if not released sooner)—

(a) when he becomes entitled to be released by virtue of section 53, 55 or 57, as the case may be;

(b) when an order revoking that call-out order is made; or

(c) when, on an application under section 78, it is determined that he is entitled to be released.

(3) Orders or regulations under section 4 may make provision enabling or requiring a person who has been accepted into service under a call-out order to be treated—

(a) if the circumstances of his call out or acceptance into service are of a prescribed description, and

(b) for the purpose of calculating when he is entitled to be released by virtue of section 53, 55 or 57,

as having been accepted into service on an earlier day than that on which he was actually accepted.

(4) Provision made for the purposes of subsection (3) shall secure—

(a) that any earlier day applicable for the purpose of calculating when a person is entitled to be released from service is to be notified to him as soon as is practicable after the day on which he was actually accepted into service; and

(b) that the period beginning with the earlier day is reckoned as part of his relevant service for the purposes of section 53(13), 55(13), 57(11) and 69(8).

DEFINITIONS
"call-out order": s.64.
"prescribed": s.127(1).
"service": s.64.

GENERAL NOTE
This section provides for the release from service of ordinary reservists who have already been accepted into service. It also permits a reservist to be treated as if he had been accepted into service earlier than was actually the case. Again, the scheme of release from service under Pt. VI closely resembles that laid down for Pt. IV (high readiness reserve), and the annotations to s.34 should be applied accordingly to the provisions of s.60. Whereas s.60(2) is the equivalent to s.34(2) and (3), the provision in s.60(2)(b) regarding the revocation of a call-out order is inapplicable in the case of the high readiness reserve (though provision for revocation of a call-out *notice* served on a high readiness reservist is in s.32(5)(b)).

Alteration of authority for call out

61.—(1) The Secretary of State may direct that—

(a) a person who is in service under a call-out order ("the original order"), or

(b) a person who is in service under Part IV,

shall cease serving under that order or that Part and, in either case, shall continue in permanent service on the authority of a call-out order specified in the direction ("the new order").

(2) A call-out order may be specified in a direction under this section if it is in force on the day on which the direction is given and would, but for his being in permanent service already, authorise the calling out of the person concerned.

(3) A person in respect of whom a direction under this section is given—

(a) shall continue in permanent service after the direction is given as if he had been called out under the new order; and

(b) shall be deemed to have begun service under the new order at the time at which his service under the original order began (or is deemed under this subsection to have begun) or, as the case may be, his service under Part IV began.

(4) A direction under this section may be given in respect of two or more named persons or persons of a description specified in the direction.

(5) Any person in permanent service in respect of whom a direction under this section is given shall be informed of the effect of the direction as soon as is practicable after the direction is given.

DEFINITIONS
   "call-out order": s.64.
   "permanent service": s.127(1).
   "service": s.64.
   "service under a call-out order": s.64.

GENERAL NOTE
   In accordance with the aim of maximising the flexibility of the reserve forces scheme within a statutory framework, s.61 provides that the Secretary of State may direct that high readiness reserves on actual service under Pt. IV, or ordinary reservists in service under a call out under Pt. VI, will cease service under either of these orders, and continue in service under a new order. The Secretary of State's direction is in the form of an order ("the new order"). See subs. (1). The provision presumably refers to a new order under Pt. VI, notwithstanding that it might apply to those who were serving as high readiness reserves under Pt. IV. The reservist is deemed to have begun service under the new order at the time when his service under the original order under Pt. IV or Pt. VI had begun (subs. (3)(b)). The direction may relate to named persons or to those specified by description (subs. (4)). The reservists affected are to be informed "as soon as is practicable" of the effect of the direction (subs. (5)). That phrase is presumably weaker than "forthwith" used, for example, in s.54(7) in respect to the reporting of call-out orders to parliament. But perhaps the phrase is stronger in meaning than "with all convenient speed", in respect to release under s.60(2).

Supplementary

Power to exempt persons from or relax call-out liability

62.—(1) Orders or regulations under section 4 may provide for exempting any members of a reserve force, in such cases as may be prescribed, from liability to be called out under the authority of the provisions of this Part or, as the case may be, any of those provisions.

(2) Such orders or regulations may also provide for relaxing, in such cases as may be prescribed, the liability to be called out under the authority of the provisions of this Part or, as the case may be, any of those provisions.

DEFINITIONS
   " members of a reserve force": s.127(2).
   "prescribed": s.127(1).

GENERAL NOTE
   Orders or regulations issued by the Secretary of State or by the Defence Council under s.4 may exempt ordinary reservists from call-out liability in respect to some or all of the provisions

in Pt. VI. Orders or regulations may also relax the call-out liability. One could therefore envisage that reservists in certain civilian occupations may be exempt from call out with respect to, say, peacekeeping or humanitarian aid operations, but liable to call out in respect to national danger, great emergency or attack on the U.K. The regulations might also limit the duration of service in certain cases. For example, in respect to some medically qualified reservists, their services might be more urgent in the early days of disaster relief, after which the demand for their services might diminish, while at the same time, National Health Service needs in the U.K. remain high. For the different kinds of exemptions and relaxations suggested by the minister, see *Hansard*, H.C. Standing Committee A, April 23, 1996, col. 47.

Exercise of certain functions under section 58 or 61

63.—(1) The Secretary of State may authorise—
(a) the Defence Council;
(b) any particular officers; or
(c) any officers of a description specified in the authorisation,
to exercise any function of his under sections 58 and 61, subject to such limitations and conditions as may be so specified.

(2) An authorisation under subsection (1) above relating to the exercise of any function of the Secretary of State by the Defence Council shall (unless the authorisation provides otherwise) be deemed to permit the Defence Council to authorise—
(a) any particular officers; or
(b) any officers of a description determined by the Defence Council,
to exercise the function, subject to such limitations and conditions as may be so specified.

(3) Arrangements made under subsection (1) or (2) for the discharge of any function shall not prevent the exercise of the function by the Secretary of State or (in the case of arrangements under subsection (2)) the Defence Council.

GENERAL NOTE
This provides for the Secretary of State to authorise the Defence Council or particular officers or officers specified by description to exercise his functions, subject to specified limitations and conditions, in respect of call-out notices or orders issued by him. The words are identical to those in s.35 in respect to the high readiness reserve, apart from the reference to "sections 58 to 61" in s.63, in place of the reference to "section [sic] 32 or 33" in s.35.

Interpretation of Part VI

64. In this Part—
"authorised officer" means an officer authorised by or in accordance
    with directions of the Defence Council for the purposes of this Part;
"call-out notice" means a notice under section 58;
"call-out order" means an order under section 52, 54 or 56; and
"service under a call-out order", and "service" mean permanent service
    on being called out under this Part on the authority of a call-out
    order.

DEFINITIONS
"authorised officer": s.64.
"call-out notice": s.64.
"call-out order": s.64.
"service": s.64.
"scrvice under a call-out order": s.64.

GENERAL NOTE
This provides definitions of certain terms used in Pt. VI. Note that s.61 refers at different points to "service", meaning service under Pt. VI, and also to "service under Part IV".

PART VII

RECALL FOR SERVICE OF OFFICERS AND FORMER SERVICEMEN

Liability to be recalled for service

Liability of officers and former servicemen to be recalled

65.—(1) Persons to whom section 66 applies are liable, in accordance with this Part, to be recalled for service when any recall order which authorises their recall is in force.

(2) A person who is recalled for service as a man of any of the regular services shall, while in service under the recall order concerned, be deemed to be enlisted in the regular service concerned.

(3) A person who has been released or discharged from a period of service under a recall order may, subject to the provisions of this Act, be recalled again on the authority of the same or any other recall order.

(4) Any question whether a person may be recalled on the authority of a recall order shall be determined by reference to the circumstances at the time he is served with a recall notice or, if he is accepted into service under section 71(5), when he is accepted into service.

(5) The numbers of persons who are recalled for service under a recall order shall not be reckoned in any numbers for the time being authorised by Parliament for any of the regular services.

DEFINITIONS
   "man": s.77(1).
   "recall": s.77(1).
   "recall order": s.77(1).
   "regular services": s.127(1).
   "service": s.77(1).

GENERAL NOTE
   Part VII of the Act re-enacts without significant alteration, the provisions of the 1980 Act authorising the recall of officers and former servicemen. However, while the circumstances of recall have not been altered, the definition of those liable to recall has been changed. Only length of service since the termination of regular service is considered. There is no reference, as formerly, to whether a service pension is payable. The practical effect is that, in the case of the Army, at least, two categories of ex-regulars, the so-called "long-term Reserve" and service pensioners, are combined into a new single category subject to recall, independent of pensionability. The long-term Reserve and pensioner categories will, however, continue to exist as a transitional class for, it is anticipated, a maximum of another 28 and 43 years, respectively. Similarly, by virtue of Sched. 8, para. 9, the two other ex-regular Army categories, that is, the officers of the Regular Army Reserve of Officers, and the men of the Army Reserve are to be combined by the incorporation of the former into the latter.
   It should be noted that those recalled are not members of the reserve forces, but persons recalled to the regular services.

Subs. (1)
   This provision states the general liability for recall for permanent service of those specified in s.66 once a recall order is in force.

Subs. (2)
   Once recalled, the man who is at or below the rank of warrant officer is deemed to be an enlistee of the regular forces.

Subs. (3)
   A person subject to a recall order is liable to serve more than one period of service even if released or discharged from one period of service under a recall order.

Subs. (4)
   This subsection *appears* to state that a person's relevant status with respect to liability to recall is that which is in existence when he is served with a recall notice or when he is accepted into

service under s.71(5) (length of service since the end of regular service is, by its nature, changeable).

Subs. (5)
This repeats the constitutional point made previously that parliament must authorise the maximum numbers in the regular forces through the "Votes A" procedure (this is a legacy of the Bill of Rights prohibition on the maintenance of a standing army in peacetime without the consent of parliament). Though technically the naval and marine forces were not statutorily bound by the Bill of Rights restriction, the reference to the "regular services" in subs. (5) now brings the Royal Fleet Reserve, the Royal Naval Reserve and the Royal Marines Reserve within oversight of parliament. This in fact brings the legal position into line with the *practice* (but not with the obligation) of parliament voting the maximum numbers of the naval and marine forces.

Persons who may be recalled under Part VII

66.—(1) This section applies to any person not serving in the regular services or the reserve forces who—

(a) holds a commission as an officer; or

(b) has served as a man in the regular services and has not become an officer since being discharged or transferred to the reserve from the regular services,

unless he is excluded (whether permanently or temporarily) by any provision of this section.

(2) This section does not apply to any person falling within subsection (1)(b)—

(a) after he has attained the age of 55;

(b) in the case of a person who was discharged or transferred to the reserve from the regular army or the regular air force, after the end of the period of 18 years beginning with the day on which he was so discharged or transferred; or

(c) in the case of a person who was discharged or transferred to the reserve from the Royal Navy or the Royal Marines, after the end of the period of 6 years beginning with the day on which he was so discharged or transferred.

(3) The re-enlistment of a person falling within subsection (1)(b) in the regular services shall prevent or, as the case may be, shall terminate any application of this section to him by reference to an earlier discharge or transfer to the reserve.

(4) References to discharge or transfer to the reserve in subsections (1) and (2)—

(a) do not include discharge from a period of permanent service under a recall order; and

(b) in relation to a man who has been discharged or transferred to the reserve more than once, refer to his most recent discharge or transfer.

(5) This section does not apply to any person who is permanently exempted, or to any person while he is temporarily exempted, from all liability to be recalled under this Part—

(a) by regulations made by virtue of section 73; or

(b) by an exemption granted on an application made under regulations under section 79.

(6) Subject to any election made under subsection (7), this section does not apply to any person who—

(a) became an officer before the day on which this Part comes into force, or

(b) enlisted in the regular services before that day and has not re-enlisted, re-engaged or extended his service in the regular services, or become an officer, on or after that day.

(7) A person falling within paragraph (a) or (b) of subsection (6) may, with the consent of an authorised officer, irrevocably elect in such manner as may

be prescribed not to be excluded from the operation of this section by virtue of that subsection.

(8) An election under subsection (7) may be made by a person who is serving in the regular forces or the reserve forces as well as a person who is not so serving; and any election is without prejudice to the subsequent operation of subsections (1) to (5) in relation to the person concerned.

DEFINITIONS
"authorised officer": s.77(1).
"man": s.77(1).
"permanent service": s.127(1).
"prescribed": s.77(1).
"recall order": s.77(1).
"regular air force": s.127(1).
"regular army": s.127(1).
"regular services": s.127(1).
"reserve forces": s.1(2).

GENERAL NOTE

Subs. (1)
   This section identifies those who may be recalled under Pt. VII. Unless excluded by provisions elsewhere in s.66, they are, first, commissioned officers not serving in the regular services or reserve forces (subs. (1)(a)); second, ex-regular service personnel who have not become officers since discharge or transfer to the reserves (subs. (1)(b)). Commissions are, of course, an appointment by the Sovereign (and technically may be awarded to a man who has completed and been discharged from his regular service) and may be retained, whether with or without pension entitlement (in the absence of resignation thereof, accepted by the Sovereign), on the completion of one's service. See, for example, various Officers' Commission Orders. See also Sched. 10 to the 1996 Act for consequential amendments to the service discipline Acts.

Subs. (2)
   Liability to recall of ex-regulars in subs. (1)(b) does not apply to those who have reached the age of 55 (para. (a)); or to those who have served 18 years in the regular Army or regular Air Force before discharge or transfer to the reserve (para. (b)); or to those who have served six years in the (regular) Royal Navy or Royal Marines before discharge or transfer to the reserve.

Subs. (3)
   If an ex-regular has re-enlisted in the regular services, then he is not liable to recall in terms of subs. (1)(b).

Subs. (4)
   This makes clear that the discharge of an ex-regular, on completion of his service following a recall order, is not a reference to his discharge (or transfer to the reserve) in subss. (1) and (2) which refer to the termination of his *regular* service (para. (a)). Secondly, discharge or transfer to the reserve of an ex-regular who has re-enlisted in the regular services is a reference to his most recent discharge or transfer. Therefore, the 18 or six year time limits in subs. (2)(b) and (c), respectively, are calculated from the day of his most recent discharge or transfer to the reserve.

Subs. (5)
   The liability of officers and of ex-regulars under Pt. VII does not apply to those permanently or temporarily exempted by virtue of regulations made by the Defence Council under s.73, or by virtue of exemption following an application therefor under regulations made under s.79.

Subs. (6)
   This subsection has some puzzling aspects. The thrust of s.66 is that liability to recall applies to officers and ex-regulars who are not currently serving in the regular services or reserve forces. Subsection (6), which defines those *not* subject to recall liability, only makes sense if those not subject to recall liability are assumed to be currently serving in the regular services or reserve forces. Otherwise, the position is that in respect to officers: (a) officers not currently serving in the regular or reserve forces are liable to recall under s.66(1)(a); (b) according to subs. (6), s.66 does not apply to any person who became an officer before the day on which Pt. VII comes into force; but (c) an officer liable to be recalled under subs. (1)(a) must surely *include* one who

became an officer prior to Pt. VII coming into force. The position is even more complex in respect to enlisted men.

Subs. (7)

Notwithstanding the tortuous (and possibly unsuccessful) attempt in subs. (6) to exclude certain categories from liability to recall, such categories may, with the consent of an authorised officer, make an irrevocable election as prescribed in regulations issued by the Defence Council to be liable for recall.

Subs. (8)

Both serving and non-serving regulars and reservists may make the irrevocable election to be liable for recall, though the age and length of service restrictions in subs. (2), as well as any provisions in subss. (1)–(5) which are not in direct conflict with subs. (8) are not prejudiced. For example, whereas subs. (1) applies to any person "not serving in the regular services or the reserve forces", subs. (8) clearly applies both to those serving and those not serving in the regular or reserve forces. The use of the phrase "regular forces" instead of "regular services" in subs. (8) looks like a drafting oversight (as "regular services", but not "regular forces", is defined in s.127(1)).

Geographical extent of liability to service on recall

67.—(1) A person who is recalled shall, subject to the following provisions of this section, be liable to serve anywhere in the world.

(2) A person who, when he was last discharged or transferred to the reserve from the regular services, was liable only for service within the United Kingdom or any area of the United Kingdom, shall not be liable to serve outside the United Kingdom or, as the case may be, that area on being recalled.

(3) A person whose liability for service on recall is restricted as mentioned in subsection (2) may elect irrevocably in such manner as may be prescribed to be liable for worldwide service—

(a) whenever he is recalled for service;

(b) during any period of service (including a current period of service) under a recall order specified in the election.

(4) Subsection (2) shall not apply—

(a) to any person who makes an election under subsection (3)(a), or

(b) in relation to a period of service covered by the election, to a person who makes an election under subsection (3)(b).

(5) A person who is serving in the regular services or the reserve forces may make an election under subsection (3) before that service ceases.

DEFINITIONS

"prescribed": s.77(1).

"recall": s.77(1).

"recall order": s.77(1).

"regular services": s.127(1).

"reserve forces": s.1(2).

"service": s.77(1).

"the United Kingdom": s.77(1).

GENERAL NOTE

This section provides that a person, whether officer or otherwise, who is recalled, shall be liable to serve anywhere in the world (subs. (1)). However, if during his last service as a regular serviceman or officer, his terms of service restricted his service to within the U.K. (including the Channel Islands and Isle of Man) or any area of the U.K., then that restriction will apply in the event of recall (subs. (2)). He may, however, irrevocably elect in the manner prescribed in Defence Council regulations for world-wide service whenever he is recalled for service or during any period of service under the recall order specified in the election (subs. (3)). The election in subs. (3) overrides the geographical restriction on service in subs. (2) (see subs. (4)). If a person is currently serving in the regular services or in the reserve forces on geographically restricted terms of service, he may make that election during his current service (subs. (5)). The Armed Forces Act 1996, s.2 has recently made provision for a local service engagement in the regular services. It is anticipated that those enlisting or entering service on such terms will be engaged primarily on guarding duties.

Power to authorise recall

Recall for national danger, great emergency or attack on the UK

68.—(1) Her Majesty may make an order authorising the recall under this Part of persons to whom section 66 applies—

(a) if it appears to Her that national danger is imminent or that a great emergency has arisen; or

(b) in the event of an actual or apprehended attack on the United Kingdom.

(2) A recall order authorises, subject to subsection (3), the recall of any person to whom section 66 applies or, if the order is so limited, any such person who is of a description specified in the order.

(3) A recall order does not authorise the recall of any person to whom section 66 applies who is not liable to be recalled under the order by virtue of regulations made by virtue of section 73 or an exemption granted on an application under regulations under section 79.

(4) A recall order shall have effect (subject to any order under subsection (5)) until it is revoked.

(5) Her Majesty may make an order providing that any recall order shall cease to authorise the recall of any person who is not in service under the order.

(6) An order under subsection (5) shall not affect the operation of any recall notice which is served on any person on the authority of the recall order concerned before the day on which the order under that subsection is made.

(7) Her Majesty may make an order revoking any recall order (whether or not its effect has already been limited by an order under subsection (5)).

(8) Where an order under subsection (7) revoking a recall order is made—

(a) the recall order shall cease to authorise the recall of anyone who could otherwise be recalled on the authority of the recall order (including anyone served with a recall notice before the order under subsection (7) is made who has not been accepted into service); and

(b) anyone in service under the recall order shall be entitled to be released or discharged from that service.

(9) A recall order, or an order under subsection (5) or (7), shall be signified under the hand of the Secretary of State and the making of any such order shall be reported forthwith to each House of Parliament.

(10) If, when a recall order is made, Parliament is separated by an adjournment or prorogation which will not expire within 5 days—

(a) a proclamation shall be issued for the meeting of Parliament within 5 days; and

(b) Parliament shall meet and sit upon the day appointed by the proclamation and shall continue to sit and act as if it had stood adjourned or prorogued to that day.

DEFINITIONS
"recall": s.77(1).
"recall order": s.77(1).
"service": s.77(1).

GENERAL NOTE
This section provides for Her Majesty, conventionally acting on the advice of the Secretary of State (as subs. (9) emphasises), to issue an order authorising the recall of persons as defined in s.66 if it appears to her that national danger is imminent, a great emergency has arisen or an attack on the U.K. (which includes the Channel Islands and the Isle of Man) is apprehended or in

progress. Much of the section follows closely the provisions in s.52 regarding the call out of reserves in similar circumstances to those specified in s.68.

Subs. (1)
Notwithstanding the difference between recall in this section and call out in s.52(1), the wording of subs. (1) is virtually identical to that in s.52(1). Therefore, the annotations to the latter may be consulted with regard to national danger, great emergency and attack on the U.K.

Subs. (2)
The recall order may be limited in the coverage of those to whom it would otherwise apply under s.66.

Subs. (3)
There is provision for exclusions from recall under s.73 and for exemptions from recall under s.79. See also s.66(5).

Subs. (4)
The whole order may be revoked, and subs. (7) states who can make the revocation order.

Subs. (5)
The order may cease to authorise the recall of any person not already in actual service if a further order to that effect is made by Her Majesty. This would appear to cover any individual person, more than one person, or persons whose description may be specified in the further order.

Subs. (6)
A recall notice already served before the further "ceasing" order is made under subs. (5) will not affect the operation of that notice.

Subs. (7)
It is for Her Majesty to revoke by order any recall order, whether the latter is of unlimited scope or limited under subs. (5).

Subs. (8)
Taking account of the difference between recall and call out, the wording of subs. (8) is virtually identical to that in s.52(6). However, the words "or discharged from that service" in para. (b) do not appear in s.52(6)(b). This indicates that whereas release from call out to the reserves does not terminate membership of the reserves, discharge from the regular services after recall service has ceased, terminates, in the case of men (but not of officers), this "temporary" membership of the regular services.

Subss. (9) and (10)
Taking account of the difference between recall and call out, these subsections are identical in wording to s.52(7) and (8) respectively. The annotations thereto should therefore be consulted regarding reporting to, and meetings of, parliament.

Maximum duration of service on recall

69.—(1) This section applies for the purpose of determining when persons in service under a recall order ("the recall order") are entitled to be released from service (in the case of officers) or discharged (in the case of men).

(2) A person is (if not released or discharged sooner) entitled to be released from service or discharged when his current service under the recall order, or his current service and any relevant service in aggregate, exceeds 3 years.

(3) A person in service under the recall order may enter into a written agreement consenting to the extension of his period of service—

(a) beyond the day on which he is entitled to be released or discharged by virtue of subsection (2); or

(b) beyond the day on which, by virtue of a subsisting agreement under this subsection, he is entitled to be released or discharged by virtue of subsection (5),

until the end of such period, not exceeding 12 months, as may be specified in the agreement.

(4) An agreement under subsection (3) may not be entered into at any time—

    (a) when the person concerned could not be served with a recall notice on the authority of the order or any other recall order; or

    (b) more than 12 months before the day on which (apart from the agreement) he is entitled to be released or discharged by virtue of subsection (2) or subsection (5).

(5) A person who has entered into an agreement under subsection (3)—

    (a) shall no longer be entitled to be released or discharged on the day on which, apart from the agreement, he is so entitled by virtue of subsection (2) or, as the case may be, paragraph (b) of this subsection; and

    (b) is entitled to be released from service or discharged at the end of the period specified in the agreement as the period for which his service is being extended.

(6) Her Majesty may by order signified under the hand of the Secretary of State provide that, in the case of such descriptions of person as may be specified in the order, subsection (2) shall apply as if for the words "3 years" there were substituted "5 years".

(7) The making of an order under subsection (6) shall be reported forthwith to each House of Parliament.

(8) In this section "relevant service" means any service under this Part, or under Part IV, V or VI, within the 6 years immediately preceding the day on which a person's current service under the recall order began.

DEFINITIONS

    "man" ("men"): s.77(1).
    "recall order": s.77(1).
    "relevant service": subs. (8).
    "service": s.77(1).

GENERAL NOTE

    This section makes provision for determining when those in service under a recall order are entitled to release or discharge from that service. Its structure is similar in many respects to that in the provisions elsewhere in Pt. VI regarding maximum duration of service on call out to the reserves (see ss.53, 55 and 57).

Subs. (1)

    As officers normally retain their commissions after service, then release from service after recall duty is not release from "membership" of the regular services. In the case of men, however, as defined in s.77(1), release from service constitutes termination of "membership" of the regular services.

Subs. (2)

    The recall order authorised by s.68 does not itself specify its duration. It may, of course, be revoked (s.68(4), (7) and (8); and see also s.68(6)). But if such revocation does not occur, a person recalled to service is entitled to release or discharge, as the case might be, after three years of his current or aggregated service.

Subs. (3)

    Regarding the consent of a person already in service to the extension of his period of service, the wording is virtually identical (allowing for the difference between recall and call out) to that in s.53(7). The annotations to the latter may therefore be consulted in respect to subs. (3).

Subs. (4)

    This is a complicated provision, but it appears to state that only those liable to recall (as defined in s.66) can enter into an extended service agreement. The agreement cannot be entered into either more than 12 months before entitlement to release or discharge, which is to be no later than the three years specified in subs. (2), or not more than 12 months before entitlement to release or discharge, which is to be no later than the three years specified in subs. (2), or not more than 12 months before entitlement to release or discharge under the extended agreement (see subs. (5)).

Subs. (5)
Once having entered into an extended service agreement, a person is entitled to release or discharge at the end of the period specified therein, and is not entitled to release or discharge on the day he would have become entitled to release or discharge in the absence of the extended service agreement.

Subss. (6), (7) and (8)
Taking account of the difference between recall and call out, and of the different subsection numbers, the wording is virtually identical to that in s.53(11), (12) and (13). Thus the aggregate relevant service before entitlement to release or discharge arises may be extended by order (which order must be reported forthwith to both Houses of parliament) from three years in the six-year period immediately preceding the start of current service, to five years in the six-year period.

Recall for permanent service

Recall of persons on authority of recall order

70.—(1) Where a recall order is in force, the Secretary of State may recall any person who is liable to be recalled on the authority of that order by serving a notice on him requiring him—
(a) to present himself for service at a specified time and place; and
(b) to remain at that place until he is either accepted into service or informed that he is not to be accepted into service in pursuance of the notice.

(2) A recall notice shall also require the person concerned, if he fails to comply with the requirements mentioned in subsection (1)—
(a) to present himself for service to any person specified in the notice or to any other authorised officer; and
(b) having so presented himself, to remain until he is either accepted into service or informed that he is not to be accepted into service in pursuance of the notice.

(3) A recall notice served on a person shall specify—
(a) the person to whom it applies;
(b) the recall order which authorises his recall; and
(c) the time and place at which the person is to present himself for service under that order;
and it may also specify places and times at which and persons to whom that person may present himself for service if he fails to comply with the requirement to present himself at the time and place specified in paragraph (c) of this subsection.

(4) A recall notice served on a person may—
(a) be varied by the Secretary of State by serving a variation notice on him;
(b) be revoked by the Secretary of State by serving a revocation notice or a subsequent recall notice on him.

(5) A recall notice served on any person shall (without affecting any liability arising from a failure to comply with the notice) cease to have effect, if not revoked sooner, when—
(a) an order under section 68(7) is made; or
(b) the person concerned is either accepted into service or informed that he is not to be accepted into service in pursuance of the notice.

(6) The making of an order under section 68(5) shall not affect the power of the Secretary of State to vary a recall notice served before the order is made.

(7) A notice under this section may be served on a person by delivering it to him or by leaving it at, or sending it by post to, his last known address; and any

recall or variation notice delivered to that address by registered post or recorded delivery shall be deemed to have been served on him.

(8) No steps may be taken against a person in respect of failure to comply with a recall notice under this section unless the notice or, as the case may be, any variation notice, was received by him or is deemed to have been served on him by virtue of subsection (7).

DEFINITIONS

"authorised officer": s.77(1).
"recall notice": s.77(1).
"recall order": s.77(1).
"service": s.77(1).

GENERAL NOTE

This section makes provision for the procedures to be followed when a person has been served with a recall notice on the authority of a recall order. It follows closely the procedure applicable to those reservists called out under Pt. VI. Thus, those recalled must present themselves for service at a specified time and place, and remain there until accepted or not accepted for service. If they fail to present themselves thus, they must present themselves to any specified person and remain until acceptance or non-acceptance. Thus, the wording of subss. (1), (2), (3), (4), (7) and (8) is virtually identical to that in s.58(1), (2), (3), (4), (7), and (8), taking account of the differences between recall and call out. In addition, the wording of s.58(1)–(4), (7)–(8) is, in turn, virtually identical to that in s.32(1)–(7), though puzzlingly, s.32(5) corresponds to s.70(4) and s.32(4) corresponds to s.70(5). Therefore, the annotations to s.32 may sensibly be applied here.

Subs. (5)

The recall notice ceases to have effect when the recall order authorising the notice is revoked under s.68(7) or when the person on whom it is served is informed of his acceptance or non-acceptance into service. Any failure by the person to comply with the requirements of the notice may nonetheless expose him to the possibility of disciplinary measures even if the recall notice ceases to have effect for the reasons given above.

Subs. (6)

Whereas Her Majesty can make a further order providing that a recall order shall cease to authorise the recall of any person not yet in service under the order (s.68(5)), the Secretary of State may vary a recall notice served before the further "cessation" order is made.

Acceptance into service under recall order

71.—(1) A person served with a recall notice who—
  (a) presents himself for service to an authorised officer at the time and place specified in the notice under section 70(3)(c);
  (b) presents himself for service to an authorised officer at any other time or place; or
  (c) is brought before an authorised officer after the time so specified,
may be accepted into service by that officer.

(2) Where such a person is accepted into service, he shall be informed by the authorised officer in the prescribed manner that he has been accepted into service by virtue of subsection (1).

(3) If an authorised officer decides that such a person should not be accepted into service, he shall inform that person in the prescribed manner that he is not to be accepted into service in pursuance of the recall notice concerned.

(4) Any liability of such a person arising from a failure to comply with a recall notice is not affected by his acceptance into service or by a decision not to accept him into service.

(5) Where a recall order is in force, any person who is liable to be called out on the authority of the order who—
  (a) has not been served with a recall notice; and

(b) presents himself for service to an authorised officer,
may be accepted into service under that recall order by that officer.
(6) Where a person is accepted into service under a recall order by virtue of
subsection (5)—
(a) the authorised officer shall inform him in the prescribed manner that
he has been accepted into service under that order by virtue of that
subsection; and
(b) he shall be deemed to have been recalled for service under that order.

DEFINITIONS
"authorised officer": s.77(1).
"prescribed": s.77(1).
"recall": s.77(1).
"recall order": 7(1).
"service": s.77(1).

GENERAL NOTE
This section makes provision for the acceptance into permanent service of officers and ex-
servicemen served with a recall notice. Taking account of the difference between recall in Pt. VII
and call out in Pt. IV, the wording of subss. (1)–(6) is, with one exception, virtually identical to
that in s.33 (1)–(6). Therefore, the annotations to s.33 may usefully be consulted here. The minor
difference is that whereas subs. (5) refers to any person who is liable to recall "on the authority of
the order", s.35(5)(a) is more specific in identifying who is liable to call out under Pt. IV, by
referring to a person who "is of a description for the time being specified in directions of the
Secretary of State".

Release and discharge from service under recall order

72.—(1) A person who has been accepted into service under a recall order
shall remain in service until released from service or discharged.
(2) A person in service under a recall order shall be released or discharged
with all convenient speed in such manner as may be prescribed when he is no
longer required by Her Majesty to be in that service or (if not released or
discharged sooner) when he is entitled to be released or discharged—
(a) by virtue of section 68(8) or 69; or
(b) by virtue of a determination granted on an application made under
regulations under section 79.
(3) The Defence Council may by regulations make provision enabling or
requiring a person in service under a recall order—
(a) if the circumstances of his recall or acceptance into service are of a
prescribed description, and
(b) for the purpose of calculating when he is entitled to be released or
discharged by virtue of section 69,
to be treated as having been accepted into service on an earlier day than that
on which he was actually accepted.
(4) Provision made for the purposes of subsection (3) shall secure—
(a) that any earlier day applicable for the purpose of calculating when a
person is entitled to be released or discharged is to be notified to him
as soon as is practicable after the day on which he was actually
accepted into service; and
(b) that the period beginning with the earlier day is reckoned as part of his
relevant service for the purposes of sections 53(13), 55(13), 57(11) and
69(8).
(5) Notwithstanding anything in this Act, a person who is in service under a
recall order shall not be entitled to be released from service or discharged at a
time when he has become liable, as a person subject to service law, to be
proceeded against for an offence under service law.

(6) Subsection (5) shall not apply or, as the case may be, shall cease to apply to any person in relation to an offence if it has been determined that the offence will not be tried by court-martial.

DEFINITIONS
"prescribed": s.77(1).
"recall order": s.77(1).
"service": s.77(1).
"service law": s.127(1).

GENERAL NOTE
This section makes provision for the release or discharge from service of those officers or ex-servicemen liable to recall under s.66 who have been accepted into service with the regular services. Thus, entitlement arises under subs. (2) when Her Majesty has made an order revoking a recall order under s.68(7)–(8) or when the maximum duration of service has been reached under s.69, or when individual exemption from recall has been granted under s.79. It further enables provision to be made for those persons to be treated as if accepted into service on an earlier date than they actually were, thus entitling them to earlier release or discharge than otherwise would be the case. For example, if acceptance into service has been delayed through no fault of the person, then under subss. (3) and (4), the Defence Council may issue regulations to the effect that he may be treated as if he had reported for service earlier than he did. The calculation of his relevant service would be adjusted accordingly. It should be recalled that there is a maximum period of "relevant service" for recall set out in s.69(2), which is three years in any six-year period. This is capable of extension to five years in six under s.69(6). The definition of "relevant service" is in s.69(8).

Subss. (5) and (6)
Even if entitlement to release or discharge arises by virtue of the preceding subsections, it is overridden if the person is liable to be proceeded against by court-martial, but not if it is decided either not to take disciplinary proceedings against him or to subject him only to summary proceeding before his commanding officer. It may be noted that no similar provisions are contained in the Act in respect to reservists, even though service discipline law applies during their period of permanent service, and even though a number of provisions, for example, s.58(8), contemplate the possibility of "steps" being taken against any such person who fails to comply with a call-out notice.
Subsections (5) and (6) reflect similar provisions in service discipline law. These deem a person suspected of committing an offence triable by court-martial to be subject to service discipline law notwithstanding his ceasing at any time to be subject thereto, for example, by leaving the services. There are time limits for trial by court-martial in these cases. See, for example, Army Act 1955, ss.131–2.

Supplementary

Power to exempt persons from or relax recall liability

73. The Defence Council may by regulations make provision—
(a) securing that, in such cases as may be prescribed, persons otherwise liable to be recalled are exempt from that liability; and
(b) relaxing, in such cases as may be prescribed, the liability of any persons to be recalled.

DEFINITION
"prescribed": s.77(1).

GENERAL NOTE
In accordance with the principle of maximum flexibility, the Defence Council may issue regulations exempting persons from recall liability or relaxing their recall liability. The section reflects similar provisions in s.62 under Pt. VI, concerning the call out of reservists for permanent service. See the annotations to s.62.

Exercise of certain functions under section 70

74.—(1) The Secretary of State may authorise—
(a) the Defence Council;

(b) any particular officers; or

(c) any officers of a description specified in the authorisation,

to exercise any function of his under section 70, subject to such limitations and conditions as may be so specified.

(2) An authorisation under subsection (1) relating to the exercise of any function of the Secretary of State by the Defence Council shall (unless the authorisation provides otherwise) be deemed to permit the Defence Council to authorise—

(a) any particular officers; or

(b) any officers of a description determined by the Defence Council,

to exercise the function, subject to such limitations and conditions as may be so specified.

(3) Arrangements made under subsection (1) or (2) for the discharge of any function shall not prevent the exercise of the function by the Secretary of State or (in the case of arrangements under subsection (2)) the Defence Council.

GENERAL NOTE

This section makes provision for the Secretary of State to authorise, subject to such limitations and conditions as may be specified, the Defence Council or officers to exercise his functions under s.70. Section 74 is the counterpart to s.35 (in respect to Pt. IV) and to s.63 (in respect to Pt. VI), and the wording is virtually identical. The annotations to ss.35 and 63 may therefore be consulted accordingly in respect of s.74.

Power to require information

75.—(1) The Secretary of State may, for the purposes of carrying this Part into effect, make regulations requiring any person not serving in the regular services or the reserve forces who falls within paragraph (a) or (b) of section 66(1), to provide such information as may be specified in the regulations.

(2) The regulations shall secure that a person who falls within subsection (1)(b) of section 66 is under no obligation to provide information after he ceases to be a person to whom that section applies by virtue of subsection (2) of that section.

(3) Without prejudice to the generality of subsection (1), regulations under this section may include provision as to the manner in which, the times when and any person to whom specified information is to be provided.

(4) Any person who fails without reasonable excuse to comply with regulations under this section is guilty of an offence and liable on summary conviction to a fine not exceeding level 3 on the standard scale.

(5) Any person who, in providing information required by regulations under this section, knowingly or recklessly makes a statement false in any material particular is guilty of an offence and liable on summary conviction to imprisonment for a term not exceeding 3 months or a fine not exceeding level 4 on the standard scale (or both).

(6) Proceedings against any person for an offence under this section may be taken at any place at which he is for the time being.

(7) Regulations under this section shall be made by statutory instrument which shall be subject to annulment in pursuance of a resolution of either House of Parliament.

DEFINITIONS

"regular services": s.127(1).

"reserve forces": s.1(2).

GENERAL NOTE

Under this section, the Secretary of State may make regulations requiring those subject to recall to provide specified information. The section also makes it a punishable offence, subject to other requirements being met, to fail to provide, or to provide false, information. Proceedings would take place summarily in the civil courts.

Subs. (1)

The requirement by regulation to provide specified information applies to those holding a commission as an officer (even if not on actual service in the forces at the time), or to non-commissioned ex-servicemen. The information will relate to personal details of age, address, health, qualifications, training and occupation. But the statute itself does not impose restrictions on the nature of the information to be provided. Presumably, it must be information relevant to the needs of the ministry.

Subs. (2)

In the case of a non-commissioned ex-serviceman, the requirement under regulations to provide specified information ceases after he reaches the age of 55; or after the expiry of 18 years since his discharge or transfer to the reserve from the regular Army or regular Air Force; or after the expiry of six years in the case of discharge or transfer to the reserve from the Royal Navy or Royal Marines.

Subs. (3)

How, when and to whom the information is to be provided may be specified in the regulations.

Subs. (4)

What is a "reasonable excuse" for failure to comply with the regulations? There are some obvious answers, for example, wrongly addressed communication, hospitalisation, etc. Level 3 on the standard scale currently is a maximum fine of £1,000.

Subs. (5)

This lays down a more serious summary offence attracting a fine, not exceeding level 4, that is, £2,500, or imprisonment for a maximum of three months, or both. The elements for conviction are "knowingly and recklessly" making a "statement of fact in any material particular". As to the meaning of "knowingly", see, for example, Smith and Hogan, *Criminal Law*, 7th ed. (1992), p.105. It clearly imports *mens rea*. As to "recklessly", see *ibid*, pp.60–69.

Subs. (6)

The Act is applicable to the U.K. (see s.132(2)). Indeed, the wording appears to suggest that if the offence is committed within one jurisdiction, for example, in a place in England, proceedings may be taken against a person in a place in Scotland, if that is where he is for the time being. The offence is an offence against civil law, and triable before a civil court. The assumption appears to be that the person was not subject to service discipline law at the time of the alleged offence. If that assumption were mistaken in any particular case, then trial by court-martial for committing an offence under civil law would become a possibility inasmuch as the section does not *expressly* state that trial can only be before a civil court.

Subs. (7)

The negative resolution procedure will apply to the regulations (in the form of statutory instruments) made by the Secretary of State.

Recall not to affect service pensions

76. Where a person to or in respect of whom a service pension is payable has been accepted into service under a recall order—
  (a) any pay or other emoluments to which he is entitled in respect of his service on recall shall not be reduced by reason of the service pension;
  (b) the service pension shall not be withheld or reduced by reason of any such pay or emoluments.

DEFINITIONS

"recall order": s.77(1).
"service": s.77(1).

GENERAL NOTE

This provision was inserted by the government at the Report stage in the House of Lords. The normal Treasury rule is that when an individual in receipt of a public service pension is re-employed in a similar capacity, his pension ceases or is abated for the duration. Under the 1980 Act, s.31(5), that particular Treasury rule was waived for service pensioners recalled in an emergency. Section 76 of the 1996 Act now replicates that provision in respect to those former regulars liable to recall under Pt. VII. Does "emoluments" include allowances, gratuities and bounties? See s.7 in respect to the reserve forces. See also Army Act 1955, s.144(7). The notes to this section of the 1955 Act in the *Manual of Military Law* suggest that emoluments include pay, allowances and gratuities.

Interpretation of Part VII

77.—(1) In this Part—
　　"authorised officer" means an officer authorised by or in accordance with directions of the Defence Council for the purposes of this Part;
　　"man" means a person of either sex who is of or below the rank or rate of warrant officer;
　　"prescribed" means prescribed in regulations made by the Defence Council;
　　"recall order" means an order under section 68 and "recall" means recall for permanent service under such an order;
　　"service", in relation to service under a recall order, means permanent service; and
　　"the United Kingdom" includes the Channel Islands and the Isle of Man.
　　(2) Regulations made by the Defence Council under this Part may include incidental or supplementary provision and shall be laid before each House of Parliament after being made.

DEFINITIONS
　　"authorised officer": subs. (1).
　　"man": subs. (1).
　　"prescribed": subs. (1).
　　"recall order": subs. (1).
　　"service": subs. (1).
　　"United Kingdom": subs. (1).

GENERAL NOTE

Subs. (1)
This provides definitions of terms used in Pt. VII.

Subs. (2)
The regulations regarding the recall of commissioned officers and ex-regulars are laid before each House of parliament, but are not subject to any parliamentary proceedings. The regulations themselves will indicate whether they come into force immediately or at some specified date. The meaning of "incidental or supplementary provision" is vague and obscure. Judicial review of the legality of such regulations is, of course, not excluded.

PART VIII

SCHEMES FOR EXEMPTION AND FINANCIAL ASSISTANCE

Individual exemptions etc. from call out or recall

Individual exemptions etc. from call out

78.—(1) The Secretary of State may by regulations make provision enabling a person liable to be called out, or any employer of such a person, to apply for any deferral, revocation, entitlement to release or exemption which, under the regulations, may be granted to the person by or in respect of whom such an application is made.
　　(2) The regulations may provide for applications to be made by or in respect of a person—
　　(a) after the service on him of a call-out notice ("the original notice") but before he is accepted into service;

(b) after he has been accepted into service.

(3) The regulations may provide, in relation to an application made before a person is accepted into service, for the following to be available—

    (a) the deferral of his obligation to present himself for service in pursuance of the original notice;

    (b) the revocation of the original notice;

    (c) if the original notice was served under Part IV, an exemption from liability to be called out under that Part or Part VI;

    (d) if the original notice was served under Part V, an exemption from liability to be called out under that Part;

    (e) if the original notice was served under Part VI, an exemption from liability to be called out on the authority of—

        (i) the call-out order specified in that notice,

        (ii) any other call-out order made under the provision of Part VI so specified,

        (iii) any call-out order made under any provision of Part VI;

    (f) if the original notice was served under Part VI and the person concerned has entered into a special agreement, an exemption from liability to be called out under Part IV.

(4) The regulations may provide, in relation to an application made after a person has been accepted into service, for the following to be available—

    (a) a determination that he is entitled to be released from his current period of service;

    (b) if he is serving under Part IV, an exemption from liability to be called out under that Part or Part VI;

    (c) if he is serving under Part V, an exemption from liability to be called out under that Part;

    (d) if he is serving under Part VI, an exemption from any liability to be called out on the authority of—

        (i) the call-out order under which he is currently serving,

        (ii) any other call-out order made under the same provision of Part VI as the order under which he is currently serving,

        (iii) any call-out order made under any provision of Part VI; or

    (e) if a determination is given that he is entitled to be released from service under Part VI and provision such as is mentioned in section 80(2)(f) applies in his case, an exemption from liability to be called out under Part IV.

GENERAL NOTE

Section 78 authorises the Secretary of State to make regulations enabling a reservist liable to be called out, or his employer, to apply for deferral or exemption from liability (s.79 deals with exemptions, etc. from recall). The section goes on to lay down time limits for making applications, and the remedies available. It is implicit in the regulations issued by the Secretary of State after consultations, as required in s.81(5), that there may be many reasons why a deferral or exemption will be sought. Compassionate reasons relating to family sickness may be one. The reservist may be a self-employed businessman who cannot leave his business at that point without adverse consequences. Similarly, the employer may not be able to replace a highly skilled reservist at the crucial time. The reservist or former serviceman might, of course, have become a conscientious objector as a result of, or subsequent to, his former service duties. There is no express provision for exemption for conscientious objection in the Act. However, there are set procedures involving application to an advisory committee on conscientious objection whose recommendations the Secretary of State considers. See *Hansard*, H.L. Vol. 568, col. CWH 117. The balance between precision and discretion in the regulations will have to be struck in order, on the one hand, to avoid allegations of favouritism or unfairness in the manner in which exemptions are granted and, on the other, to ensure flexibility.

Subs. (1)

The application may be made by the person or by his employer. The options available under the regulations are the deferral of his call out, the revocation of his call-out notice, his release from call out or his exemption from call out. The call out of the reserve may, of course, occur under Pt. IV (in regard to the high readiness reserve); under Pt. V (in regard to the sponsored reserve); or under Pt. VI (in regard to general call out under the different circumstances in ss.52, 54 or 56).

Subs. (2)
This indicates that an application for deferral, etc. may be made before service but after receipt of a call-out notice, or after service has commenced. The phrase "call-out notice" is not defined in Pt. VIII. For its meaning for Pt. IV see s.32(1). For its meaning for Pt. V, see s.43. For its meaning for Pt. VI, see s.58.

Subs. (3)
This amplifies the options mentioned in subs. (1) in respect to a person not yet accepted into service. Under para. (c), exemption from call out under Pt. IV will also offer exemption from general call out under Pt. VI. Under para. (d), exemption from call out under Pt. V will only offer exemption from that type of call out. Under para. (e), exemption from an original general call-out notice under Pt. VI will offer exemption from any other call out under Pt. VI. Under para. (f), exemption from a general call out will also offer exemption from any call-out liability under Pt. IV in regard to the high readiness reserve.

Subs. (4)
Once accepted "into service" (which seems to be the same as being "in service"), the options which applicants might seek under regulations are:
   (a) release from a current period of service (para. (a));
   (b) exemption from call out for the high readiness reserve (notwithstanding already serving) and exemption from general call out;
   (c) exemption from call out to the sponsored reserve (notwithstanding already serving);
   (d) exemption from any call out liability under Pt. VI (notwithstanding already serving).
There is also a fifth possibility, in para. (e), which provides that when a high readiness reservist is accepted into permanent service under Pt. VI, his high readiness reserve liability ceases under s.31(1)(d). However, if he is released from general call-out liability following an application under s.78, he becomes exempt from any high readiness reserve liability.

Individual exemptions etc. from recall

79.—(1) The Secretary of State may by regulations make provision enabling any person liable to be recalled, or any employer of such a person, to apply for any deferral, revocation, entitlement to release or discharge or exemption which, under the regulations, may be granted to the person by or in respect of whom such an application is made.

(2) Regulations under this section may provide for applications to be made by or in respect of a person—
   (a) after the service on him of a recall notice ("the original notice") but before he is accepted into service; or
   (b) after he has been accepted into service.

(3) The regulations may provide, in relation to an application made before a person is accepted into service, for the following to be available—
   (a) the deferral of his obligation to present himself for service in pursuance of the original notice;
   (b) the revocation of the original notice;
   (c) an exemption from liability to be recalled on the authority of the recall order specified in the original notice or any other recall order.

(4) The regulations may provide, in relation to an application made after a person has been accepted into service, for the following to be available—
   (a) a determination that he is entitled to be released from service or discharged;
   (b) an exemption from liability to be recalled on the authority of the recall order under which he is currently serving or any other recall order.

(5) Regulations under this section may also make provision in relation to—
   (a) persons liable to be recalled under the Reserve Forces Act 1980, or
   (b) officers liable to be recalled otherwise than under this Act,

corresponding to the provision which may be made in relation to persons liable to be recalled under Part VII.

GENERAL NOTE

Whereas s.78 makes provision by regulation for exemption, deferral, etc. from call out in relation to reservists, s.79 makes similar provision in respect to recall to the regular services under Pt. VII in the case of commissioned officers and ex-servicemen. Thus the wording in subss. (1)–(3) is virtually identical to that in s.78(1)–(3), with two textual qualifications. First, "recall" and "recall notice" in s.79 are substituted for "call out" and "call out notice" in s.78. Note that neither "recall" nor "recall notice" ("the original notice") are defined in s.79. As used in Pt. VII, "recall" means "recall for permanent service under [a] recall order" (see s.77(1)), and the meaning of "recall order" therein is provided in s.68. Second, whereas s.78(3)(c)–(f) and s.78(4)(b)–(d) make reference to exemption in respect to Pts. IV–VI, the reference to exemption from recall liability in s.79(3) and (4) *implicitly* relates to Pt. VII.

Subs. (5)

Most of the 1980 Act is destined for repeal by the 1996 Act. However, the repeal of some provisions will only be brought into effect in due course, perhaps after a number of years when there are no more members of the "transitional class" of reservists whose call-out liabilities are still governed by the 1980 Act (see Scheds. 8 and 9). Similarly, there remains a class of officers whose recall liability is governed by the royal prerogative. Subs. (5) makes provision for regulations to be issued in regard to exemptions, deferrals, etc. in respect to these two residual categories.

Effect of exemptions etc.

80.—(1) The regulations may provide for an application for deferral or revocation which is not determined before the person concerned is accepted into service to be treated as an application for a determination that he is entitled to be released or discharged.

(2) The regulations may provide—

(a) for the terms on which deferrals, revocations, determinations of entitlement to release or discharge and exemptions may be granted (including any limitations or conditions subject to which they may be granted);

(b) for determinations of entitlement to release or discharge and exemptions to take effect immediately or at such other time as may be specified in the determination or exemption;

(c) for deferrals or exemptions to lapse at such time, at the end of such period or on the occurrence of such event as may be specified in the deferral or exemption;

(d) for determinations of entitlement to release or discharge which do not take effect immediately to lapse as mentioned in paragraph (c);

(e) for persons released from service under Part IV in pursuance of a determination of entitlement to release to be treated for the purposes of section 31(3) as if they had not been in that service and released;

(f) for persons released from service under Part VI in pursuance of a determination of entitlement to release to be treated for the purposes of section 31(1)(d) as if they had not been in that service;

(g) for waiver of deferrals, determinations of entitlement to release or discharge and exemptions.

(3) The regulations shall secure that deferrals or exemptions, or any determinations mentioned in subsection (2)(d), do not remain in force for more than 12 months from the day on which they take effect.

DEFINITION

"regulations": s.81(7).

GENERAL NOTE

Regulations made under s.78 or s.79 in respect to applications for deferral or revocation may cover cases where a person liable to be called out or recalled has already been accepted into service, in which case the application is treated as one for release or discharge.

Subs. (1)
    Guidance as to the scope of the regulations is given; for example, in relation to the terms, including any limitations or conditions, on which deferrals, etc. may be granted; or in relation to when a determination of entitlement will take effect or lapse (paras. (a)–(d)); or in relation to the high readiness reserve (paras. (e) and (f)); or for waivers of deferrals, etc. (para. (g)).

Subs. (2)
    Deferrals or exemptions last for no more than 12 months. Similarly, entitlements to release or discharge which do not take effect immediately will last for no more than 12 months.

Regulations under section 78 or 79: supplementary

    81.—(1) The regulations may, without prejudice to the generality of sections 78 to 80, make provision with respect to—
    (a) the persons by whom applications of any description may be made and the grounds on which applications may be made;
    (b) the persons who are to be regarded as employers for any purpose of the regulations;
    (c) the procedure for making applications (including the times when they may be made and any information to be provided by the applicant);
    (d) the determination of applications by any person or body identified by, or of a description specified in, the regulations;
    (e) any matters to be taken into account in determining applications;
    (f) the provision of information, in connection with any matter relevant to the lapse of a deferral, determination of entitlement to release or discharge or an exemption, by the person on whose application it was granted; and
    (g) any incidental or supplementary matters.
    (2) The persons who may be regarded under the regulations as the employer of a person in permanent service may include a former employer of that person who is, by virtue of the Reserve Forces (Safeguard of Employment) Act 1985, under an obligation to reinstate him at the end of his current period of permanent service.
    (3) The regulations may make different provision for different cases and may, in particular, make different provision for cases where the regulations enable an application to be made by or in respect of a person who is in permanent service on call-out or recall—
    (a) if he is serving under Part IV or a call-out order, after the making of an order under section 61 which extends the time at which he would (apart from the order) become entitled to be released from permanent service;
    (b) if he is serving under a call-out order—
        (i) after the making of an order under section 53(11) or 55(11) which extends the time at which he would (apart from the order) become entitled to be released from permanent service;
        (ii) after the postponement under section 53(3), 55(3) or 57(3) of his entitlement to be released;
    (c) if he is serving under a recall order, after the making of an order under section 69(6) which extends the time at which he would (apart from the order) become entitled to be released or discharged;
    (d) after he has agreed under any provision of this Act to extend (or further extend) his period of permanent service;
but the regulations need not enable applications to be made in every case where a person is served with a call-out or recall notice or is in permanent service.
    (4) Any person making an application under the regulations who is aggrieved by the determination of his application may appeal to a reserve forces appeal tribunal.

(5) Before making any regulations, the Secretary of State shall consult such bodies or persons as he considers appropriate, including—
(a) a body appearing to him to represent the interests of employers, a body appearing to him to represent the interests of employees and a body appearing to him to represent the interests of the self-employed; and
(b) the associations established under Part XI or a body appearing to him to represent those associations.
(6) The regulations shall be made by statutory instrument which shall be subject to annulment in pursuance of a resolution of either House of Parliament.
(7) In this section and section 80 "regulations" means any regulations made under section 78 or 79.

DEFINITIONS
"call-out order": s.64.
"permanent service": s.127(1).
"recall": s.77.
"regulations": subs. (7).

GENERAL NOTE
This section adds to the detail regarding the scope and coverage of the regulations in respect of deferral, revocation, entitlement to release or exemption in respect of call out or recall. It makes clear that a former employer may in some circumstances be treated as an employer entitled to apply for a determination. It makes provision for a reserve forces appeal tribunal; it requires the Secretary of State to consult interested parties before making regulations; and it stipulates that such regulations are statutory instruments subject to the negative resolution procedure.

Subs. (1)
This contains further details regarding the scope of the Secretary of State's regulations governing applications for determinations. They may prescribe who can apply, and the grounds therefor, the procedures to be followed, who can make the determination, and matters to be taken into account and information to be provided.

Subs. (2)
This clarifies that a former employer, subject to an obligation to reinstate a reservist after a current period of permanent service under the Reserve Forces (Safeguard of Employment) Act 1985 (c. 15), may be treated as the employer of that person for the purposes of these regulations. He would therefore appear to be entitled to apply for entitlement to release, as prescribed in s.78(4), and to any further exemption from liability.
The 1985 Act, which consolidates provisions which were previously contained in the National Service Act 1948 (c. 64), ss.35 *et seq.*, makes provision for the reinstatement in civil employment of members of the reserve forces who have been called into "whole-time service". It also provides "for the protection of the employment of those liable to be called into such service", that is, to prohibit discriminatory treatment in their employment.
Under s.1 of the 1985 Act, where a person has entered into "whole-time service", his "former employer" (which therefore implies that the contract of employment had ended on call out and was not merely "suspended") is obliged to reinstate him either in his previous occupation, or, if that is not reasonable and practicable, in the most favourable occupation and on the most favourable terms and conditions which are reasonable and practicable in his case. Reinstatement must be at the first opportunity which is reasonable and practicable to the former employer, and which is on or after the date notified to him of the reservist's availability for reinstatement. The applicant may, however, without prejudice, decline in writing the offer of reinstatement, giving reasons therefor. No obligation on the former employer continues after six months have elapsed from the end of the applicant's whole-time service. For a case where a reinstated reservist was shortly thereafter dismissed for redundancy, see *Slaven v. Thermo Engineers* [1992] I.C.R. 295, an appeal from a reinstatement committee under the 1985 Act.

Subs. (3)
It is not clear what "different provision" will be made in the regulations with respect to different cases, such as those where the Secretary of State has directed that a five-year maximum

duration of service on call out under s.52 is substituted for three years (see s.53(11)); or where the Defence Council or an authorised officer under s.53(3) has postponed a man's entitlement under s.53(2) to release on the expiry of his current term of permanent service. Perhaps the information to be provided (*cf*., subs. (1) (f)) may be specified in more detail, such as a minimum number of statements from third parties, as is the case with applications to the Advisory Committee on Conscientious Objectors.

Subs. (4)
This introduces the institution of the reserve forces appeal tribunal, the details of which are contained in Pt. IX. The ground for an appeal is that a person is "aggrieved" by the determination of his application. This is clearly a wide ground.

Subs. (5)
The Secretary of State is required to consult with persons or bodies "as he considers appropriate," including bodies representing employers, employees and the self-employed, and also territorial, auxiliary and volunteer reserve associations (TAVRAs) or representative bodies established under Pt. XI. *Cf*., s.38(4) in regard to consultations by the Secretary of State or by the Defence Council with representative bodies in relation to the issue of orders or regulations under s.4 governing the sponsored reserve.

Subs. (6)
The regulations in regard to exemptions, etc., are statutory instruments and therefore subject to parliamentary proceedings by way of the negative resolution procedure. The subsection does not state that they shall be laid before each House after being made (*cf*., s.86(5)).

Subs. (7)
"Regulations" in ss.80 and 81 mean those made under ss.78 and 79 in regard to exemptions, etc., and not those made under s.4.

Offences in connection with regulations under section 78 or 79

82.—(1) Any person who fails without reasonable excuse to provide information, in connection with the lapse of a deferral, entitlement to be released or discharged or an exemption, which he is required to provide under regulations under section 78 or 79 is guilty of an offence and liable, on summary conviction, to imprisonment for a term not exceeding 3 months or a fine not exceeding level 4 on the standard scale (or both).

(2) Any person who—

(a) in connection with an application under regulations under section 78 or 79, or

(b) in connection with the lapse of a deferral, determination of entitlement to release or discharge or an exemption granted under those regulations,

knowingly or recklessly provides information which is false or misleading in a material particular is guilty of an offence and liable, on summary conviction, to imprisonment for a term not exceeding 6 months or a fine not exceeding level 5 on the standard scale (or both).

GENERAL NOTE
This section makes it an offence to fail, without reasonable excuse, to provide information required by the regulations made under ss.78 and 79. If found guilty, the person concerned is liable on summary conviction to a maximum fine (currently) of £2,500 or three months imprisonment or both. What constitutes a reasonable excuse is likely to be determined on the facts of each case. The information in question may relate to changes in the circumstances entitling a person to deferral of his call out or recall, or to release or discharge or exemption. These criminal proceedings are, of course, under civil law, not service discipline law.

Subs. (2)
Knowingly or recklessly to provide false information in connection with an application for exemption or deferral will render a person liable on summary conviction to a maximum fine

(currently) of £5,000 or six months imprisonment or both. Again, the proceedings are civil, not service disciplinary. For "knowingly" and "recklessly", see annotations to s.75(5).

Financial assistance in respect of call out or recall

Payments to individuals in respect of call out or recall

83.—(1) The Secretary of State may by regulations provide for the making of payments by him to any persons in respect of any financial loss of a description prescribed by the regulations which is suffered by them and attributable to their being in permanent service under Part IV or Part V or under a call-out or recall order.

(2) The regulations may provide for payments to be made, in relation to any description of financial loss, towards the provision of pensions, allowances or gratuities to or in respect of a person making a claim.

(3) The regulations may, in relation to any payments to be made as mentioned in subsection (2)—

(a) provide for any such payments to be made to any person of a prescribed description;

(b) require such a person to accept such payments (notwithstanding anything which would otherwise prevent him from doing so) on such terms as may be determined by or under the regulations; and

(c) require persons of any such description to provide information in connection with claims for such payments or, where payments have been made to them, in connection with the use made of the money.

(4) A person making a claim under the regulations who is dissatisfied with the determination of his claim may appeal against the determination to a reserve forces appeal tribunal.

DEFINITIONS
    "call-out order": s.64.
    "permanent service": s.127(1).
    "prescribed": s.127(1).
    "recall order": s.77.

GENERAL NOTE
    A second safeguard in Pt. VIII (in addition to the right to seek exemption, deferral, etc.) is the availability of financial assistance to reservists and employers, to cover the additional costs, or to make up financial losses, incurred as a result of call out. The amounts recoverable are based on a compliance cost assessment produced in consultation with employers and reserve units. For employers, the intention is to reduce the average net cost of call out to zero. For reservists, it is to ensure they are not out of pocket (and to pay them for their time). In Standing Committee A, concern was expressed that protection of seniority and safeguards in respect to promotion prospects should be recognised as well as assistance for financial loss. See *Hansard*, H.C., Standing Committee A, col. 47, April 23, 1996.

Subs. (1)
    The financial assistance is payable under the regulations issued by the Secretary of State to high readiness reservists and sponsored reservists as a result of their permanent service, and to those in permanent service under general call out or recall. The nature of the regulations is described in s.85(4).

Subs. (2)
    As noted in relation to s.8(2), provision may be made for payments towards the provision of pensions, allowances or gratuities. This is in order to ensure that pensions policies do not lapse through non-payment when persons concerned are in permanent service.

Subs. (3)
    While para. (a) provides for payments to be made to any person, including an employer, pensions company or to the reservist himself, para. (b) appears to override any restrictions in pensions policies which might otherwise require the beneficiary, and no other, to contribute to the pension scheme. It also requires any person, including parties other than the reservist him-

self, such as relatives or a pensions company, to make available to the Secretary of State information regarding claims or payments. This is to check that payments made were, in fact, applied for their specified purpose. Presumably, no questions of qualified privilege, for example, in relation to solicitors acting on behalf of a beneficiary, would arise.

Subs. (4)
Presumably, the reference to "claim" is in respect to financial assistance and not to other matters in Pt. VIII, that is, to exemptions, deferrals, etc. The word "dissatisfied" is extremely broad. Could it therefore cover not only questions of quantum, but also the manner in which the claim was handled by the Secretary of State?

Payments to employers etc. in respect of call out or recall

84.—(1) The Secretary of State may by regulations provide for the making of payments by him to employers (including employers who are self-employed) in respect of any financial loss of a description prescribed by the regulations which is suffered by them and attributable to any of their employees being in permanent service under Part IV or Part V or under a call-out or recall order.

(2) Regulations under this section may also provide for the making of payments by the Secretary of State to the partners of a person carrying on business in partnership in respect of any financial loss of a description prescribed by the regulations which is suffered by them and attributable to that person being in permanent service under Part IV or Part V or under a call-out or recall order.

(3) A person making a claim under regulations under this section who is dissatisfied with the determination of his claim may appeal against the determination to a reserve forces appeal tribunal.

DEFINITIONS
"call-out order": s.64.
"permanent service": s.127(1).
"prescribed": s.127(1).
"recall order": s.77.

GENERAL NOTE
This is the counterpart provision to s.83 and makes provision for payment to employers, to the self-employed, and to a business partnership for any financial loss of a description prescribed in the Secretary of State's regulations. Perhaps even more so than in respect to financial assistance to reservists, etc., it is difficult to be certain that the payments to be made by virtue of regulations issued under s.84 will be an accurate reflection of particular firms' losses. The compliance cost assessment exercise was based on a limited survey of firms' anticipated costs. The basis for financial payments will, of course, be prescribed in the regulations. It is possible that payments to employers may be calculated as a percentage of the annual salary of the person called out. Dissatisfaction with the outcome of a claim will entitle the claimant to appeal to a reserve forces appeal tribunal (subs. (3)).

Regulations under section 83 or 84: supplementary

85.—(1) Regulations under section 83 or 84 ("the regulations") may, in particular, make provision with respect to—
  (a) the descriptions of persons who are entitled to claim payments and of the kinds of financial loss for which claims can be made;
  (b) the matters in respect of which, and any circumstances in which, persons are or are not entitled to any payment;
  (c) the sums, or the method of determining the sums, to be paid;
  (d) the procedure for making claims (including the time within which claims must be made and the information to be provided by persons making claims);
  (e) in the case of regulations under section 83, the provision of information by persons in connection with claims made by their employees or former employees;

(f) in the case of regulations under section 84, the provision of information by persons in respect of whom claims are made;

(g) the determination of claims by any person or body identified by, or of a description specified in, the regulations;

(h) any incidental or supplementary matters.

(2) The regulations may make different provision for different cases (but need not require payments to be made in all cases or for all losses).

(3) Before making any regulations under section 83 or 84 the Secretary of State shall consult such persons or bodies as he considers to be appropriate, including—

(a) a body appearing to him to represent the interests of employers, a body appearing to him to represent the interests of employees and a body appearing to him to represent the interests of the self-employed; and

(b) the associations established under Part XI or a body appearing to him to represent those associations.

(4) The regulations shall be made by statutory instrument which shall be subject to annulment in pursuance of a resolution of either House of Parliament.

(5) The regulations may also make provision for claims by or in respect of—

(a) persons recalled under the Reserve Forces Act 1980, or

(b) officers recalled otherwise than under this Act,

corresponding to the provision which may be made for claims by or in respect of persons recalled under Part VII.

GENERAL NOTE

In a similar fashion to s.81, which effectively makes provision for the obtaining of further and better particulars in regard to applications for exemption, deferral, etc., s.85 effectively makes provision for further and better particulars regarding claims for financial assistance in respect to call out or recall. Thus regulations may make provision for further details regarding claimants, the kinds of financial loss, the circumstances regarding payment or non-payment, the sums or methods of calculating them, procedures for claiming, provision of information, and determination of claims (subs. (1)). Different provision may be made for different cases (subs. (2); *cf.*, s.81(3)). The Secretary of State's duty to consult bodies before making regulations regarding financial assistance is laid down in subs. (3) (*cf.*, s.81(5)). The regulations will be in the form of statutory instruments subject to the negative resolution procedure (subs. (4); *cf.*, s.81(6)). Finally, regulations may make provision for claims for financial assistance by the residual categories of those liable to be recalled for service, that is, those not covered by Pt. VII of the 1996 Act. Those residual categories were discussed in the annotations to s.79(5).

Power to suspend payments due to national danger or great emergency

86.—(1) Where a call-out order under section 52 or a recall order under section 68 is in force, the Secretary of State may by order suspend the operation of any regulations under section 83 or 84.

(2) An order under subsection (1) may suspend the application of the regulations concerned in all cases or in such cases as may be specified in the order; and the effect of such an order is—

(a) to prevent any right to payments arising or (in relation to people who have already been called out or recalled) accruing further under the suspended regulations in respect of the period during which the order is in force; and

(b) to suspend for that period any obligation of the Secretary of State to make payments under the suspended regulations in respect of earlier periods.

(3) An order under subsection (1)—

(a) shall be made for such period not exceeding 12 months as may be specified in the order; and

(b) may (if it has not otherwise expired) be revoked by the Secretary of State by order.

(4) An order under subsection (1) shall be made by statutory instrument which shall be subject to annulment in pursuance of a resolution of either House of Parliament.

(5) An order revoking an order under subsection (1) shall be made by statutory instrument and shall be laid before each House of Parliament after being made.

DEFINITIONS
"call-out order": s.64.
"recall order": s.77.

GENERAL NOTE
This section confers a power on the Secretary of State to suspend payments in the case of call out or recall due to national danger, great emergency or apprehended or actual attack on the U.K. (subs. (1)). The order of the Secretary of State to suspend payments may apply in all or some cases, with the consequence that no right to payment arises during the currency of the order, or accrues further from the date of the order. Although the side-note suggests otherwise, the wording of subs. (2)(a): "to prevent any right to payments . . .", appears to preclude the *right* to payment as well as the *claim* to payment during the crisis, whereas any *claim* arising *prior* to the call-out order or recall order is merely suspended by subs. (2)(b). The order cannot exceed 12 months and may be revoked before then (subs. (3)). It is made by statutory instrument subject to the negative resolution procedure.

Offences in connection with claims for payments

87.—(1) Any person who, in connection with a claim by another person under regulations under section 83 or 84, fails without reasonable excuse to provide information which he is required to provide by the regulations is guilty of an offence and liable, on summary conviction, to imprisonment for a term not exceeding 3 months or a fine not exceeding level 4 on the standard scale (or both).

(2) Any person who, in connection with a claim under regulations under section 83 or 84, knowingly or recklessly provides information which is false or misleading in a material particular is guilty of an offence and liable, on summary conviction to imprisonment for a term not exceeding 6 months or a fine not exceeding level 5 on the standard scale (or both).

GENERAL NOTE
It is an offence to fail, without reasonable excuse, to provide information required by the regulations made under ss.83 or 84 in respect to the payment of financial assistance in the event of call out or recall. On summary conviction, the current maximum penalty is a fine of £2,500 (level 4 on the standard scale) or three months imprisonment or both. There is also a separate offence of knowingly or recklessly providing false information in connection with an application for financial assistance. On summary conviction, the current maximum penalty is a fine of £5,000 (level 5) or six months imprisonment or both. The section follows the format in s.82. For comments on the meaning of "knowingly" and "recklessly", see annotations to s.75(5).

PART IX

RESERVE FORCES APPEAL TRIBUNALS

The reserve forces appeal tribunals

88.—(1) Tribunals to be known as reserve forces appeal tribunals (referred to in this Part as "appeal tribunals") may be constituted for the purpose of exercising the jurisdiction mentioned in section 89.

(2) Such number of appeal tribunals shall be constituted, sitting at such times and such places, as the Secretary of State may from time to time determine.

(3) The Secretary of State may make available such officers and staff as he may consider necessary for carrying out the administrative work of appeal tribunals.

GENERAL NOTE
This section creates reserve forces appeal tribunals to hear appeals against determinations regarding both exemptions, deferrals, etc., and also claims to financial assistance. As seen above, the determinations of the applications, from which an appeal may be taken, will be made "by any person or body identified by, or of a description specified in" regulations made by the Secretary of State (see s.81(1)(d) and s.85(1)(g)). According to the minister (*Hansard*, H.L. Vol. 567, col. 522), the intention is to create an independent system of appeal tribunals to resolve disagreements and for such tribunals to operate informally and fairly. There was no equivalent institution in the 1980 Act. In respect to conscientious objectors, we have already noted the existence of the Advisory Committee (see annotations to s.78), while in respect to the Reserve Forces (Safeguard of Employment) Act 1985, mentioned in s.81(2), we have noted the existence of reinstatement committees with an appeal to the umpire (a High Court judge). In other countries such as Canada, the United States and Israel, there is a reserve forces ombudsman to whom issues for determination are sent. The number of appeal tribunals, and when and where they will sit, is within the discretion of the Secretary of State (subs. (2)), who will make provision for the administration, but not for the judicial staff, of the tribunal (subs. (3)).

Jurisdiction and powers of appeal tribunals

89.—(1) An appeal lies to an appeal tribunal by virtue of section 81(4) in respect of a determination of an application under regulations under section 78 or 79.

(2) An appeal lies to an appeal tribunal by virtue of sections 83(4) and 84(3) in respect of a determination of a claim under regulations under sections 83 and 84 respectively.

(3) An appeal to an appeal tribunal shall be by way of a rehearing of the application or claim.

(4) An appeal tribunal hearing an appeal may dismiss the appeal or may make any determination which the person or body hearing the original application or claim had the power to make.

(5) The person or body responsible for making determinations under the regulations under which the application or claim was made shall (so far as may be necessary) give effect under those regulations to the determination of the appeal tribunal.

GENERAL NOTE
This lays down the jurisdiction and powers of the appeal tribunal. It involves the rehearing of the application or claim (subs. (3)). This broad jurisdiction matches the broad basis for an appeal. The latter may arise where a person is "aggrieved" by the determination of his application (s.81(4)) or where he is "dissatisfied" with the determination of a claim for financial assistance (s.83(4)). The appeal tribunal may dismiss the appeal or make any determination which the person or body making the original determination has power to make (subs. (4)). The original jurisdiction is spelled out in regulations issued under ss.78–81 and ss.83–86. The person or body responsible for making the original determination must, so far as necessary, give effect to the appeal tribunal determination (subs. (5)). In effect, the person or body making the original determination must grant the claim, deferral, revocation, entitlement to release, discharge or exemption, as the case might be, when the appeal tribunal makes such a determination.

Appointment of panel of chairmen

90.—(1) There shall be a panel of chairmen of reserve forces appeal tribunals appointed by the Lord Chancellor and the Lord Advocate.

(2) No person may be appointed to the panel unless he is—

(a) a person who has a 10 year general qualification (within the meaning of section 71 of the Courts and Legal Services Act 1990);

(b) an advocate or solicitor in Scotland of at least 10 years' standing; or

(c) a member of the Bar of Northern Ireland or solicitor of the Supreme Court of Northern Ireland of at least 10 years' standing.

(3) The appointment of a person to the panel shall be for such term as may be determined by the Lord Chancellor and the Lord Advocate.

(4) A member of the panel shall vacate his office on the day on which he attains the age of 70 years; but this subsection is subject to section 26(4) to (6) of the Judicial Pensions and Retirement Act 1993 (power to authorise continuance in office up to the age of 75 years).

(5) There shall be paid to members of the panel such fees, allowances and expenses (if any) as the Secretary of State may determine.

GENERAL NOTE

The panel of chairmen of the appeal tribunals is appointed by the Lord Chancellor and by the Lord Advocate. Does this imply that the Lord Chancellor is wearing his executive rather than his judicial hat? If the latter, then it is arguable that the Lord President of the Court of Session, should appoint panel chairmen, and not the Lord Advocate, in order to reinforce the image of the independence of the appeal tribunal from government. *Cf.*, s.92(3) in regard to the appointment of members of an appeal tribunal, as distinct from the *panel* members.

The standard legal qualification for appointment as chairman is laid down. Similarly, standard terms of retirement are provided. Provision for fees, allowances, and expenses is also made. While lawyer-chairmen "adorn" the industrial tribunals and social security appeal tribunals, it is more open to debate whether reserve forces appeal tribunals will be required to interpret obscure and tortuous statutory provisions, rather than applying "common sense" as to whether exemptions or deferrals should be granted.

Appointment of panel of ordinary members

91.—(1) There shall be a panel of ordinary members of reserve forces appeal tribunals appointed by the Lord Chancellor and the Lord Advocate.

(2) Before appointing a member of the panel, the Lord Chancellor shall consult such persons or bodies as he considers to be appropriate, including—

(a) a body appearing to him to represent the interests of employers, a body appearing to him to represent the interests of employees and a body appearing to him to represent the interests of the self-employed; and

(b) the associations established under Part XI or a body appearing to him to represent those associations.

(3) The appointment of a person to the panel shall be for such term as may be determined by the Lord Chancellor and the Lord Advocate.

(4) A member of the panel shall vacate his office on the day on which he attains the age of 70 years; but this subsection is subject to section 26(4) to (6) of the Judicial Pensions and Retirement Act 1993 (power to authorise continuance in office up to the age of 75 years).

(5) There shall be paid to members of the panel such fees, allowances and expenses (if any) as the Secretary of State may determine.

GENERAL NOTE

This makes provision for the appointment of lay assessors ("ordinary members") to the reserve forces appeal tribunal. While they are to be appointed by the Lord Chancellor and by the Lord Advocate (*cf.*, s.92(3)), as in the case of the chairmen under s.90, an obligation to consult with appropriate bodies and associations before making the appointments is placed only on the Lord Chancellor (subs. (2)). The bodies and associations to be consulted are of the same description as those to be consulted by the Secretary of State under ss.81(5) and 85(3), in regard to the regulations to be made in respect to provision for exemption, deferral, etc., and for financial assistance. No specific bodies, such as the Trades Union Congress or the Confederation of British Industry, are mentioned and the appointees will not be representatives of the bodies consulted. The minister expressed the desire that a "good proportion" of women be appointed to the panels. The members would also receive appropriate training. The provision of subss. (3), (4) and (5) regarding duration of appointment, retirement, and fees, allowances and expenses, are identical to those in s.90(3), (4) and (5).

Membership of tribunals etc.

92.—(1) An appeal tribunal shall consist of a chairman and two other members selected by the Lord Chancellor from the appropriate panel appointed under section 90 or 91.

(2) Where a tribunal is hearing an appeal in respect of a determination of an application under regulations under section 78 or 79, the Lord Chancellor shall, if requested to do so by the tribunal, appoint a serving or retired officer of any regular service or reserve force to advise the tribunal on any relevant service matters.

(3) In the case of an appeal tribunal which is to sit in Scotland or Northern Ireland, the members shall be selected and any officer appointed by the Lord President of the Court of Session or the Lord Chief Justice of Northern Ireland, as the case may be.

DEFINITIONS
"reserve force": s.1(2).
"regular service": s.127(1).

GENERAL NOTE
This states that the appeal tribunal is composed of a chairman and two lay assessors selected by the Lord Chancellor from the panels appointed under ss.90 and 91 (see subs. (1)). Under subs. (2), if the appeal tribunal is considering any determinations made in respect to the matters in ss.78 or 79, that is, to exemptions, deferrals, revocations, releases or discharges, then the appeal tribunal can request the Lord Chancellor to appoint a serving or retired regular or reserve officer to advise on any relevant service matters. Presumably the Lord Chancellor would take advice from the Secretary of State, but must, of course, exercise the power of appointment himself and must not effectively delegate his statutory function to the Secretary of State.

In respect of the wording of subs. (2), the appeal tribunal may lodge a "request", but if the Lord Chancellor is so "requested", he "shall" appoint such an officer. While the latter may advise, it is unlikely that his advice *must* be followed. Under subs. (3), the Lord President of the Court of Session and the Lord Chief Justice of Northern Ireland will appoint panel members and any officer (the latter presumably after consultations with the Secretary of State) if an appeal tribunal sits in Scotland or in Northern Ireland respectively.

General power to make rules

93.—(1) The Secretary of State may make rules with respect to the practice and procedure to be followed on appeals to appeal tribunals.

(2) Rules under this section may, in particular, include provision—
(a) limiting the time within which appeals may be brought;
(b) specifying the parties to any proceedings;
(c) allowing the chairman of an appeal tribunal to determine preliminary and incidental matters;
(d) requiring persons to produce documents, to attend to give evidence, and to give evidence on oath;
(e) as to the payment of expenses and allowances to persons producing documents or attending to give evidence;
(f) enabling or requiring proceedings to be held in private;
(g) as to the person who may represent the parties; and
(h) as to the award and recovery of costs.

(3) No person shall be required by any rules under this section to give any evidence or produce any document or other material at a hearing held by an appeal tribunal which he could not be compelled to give or produce in civil proceedings in any court in that part of the United Kingdom in which the hearing takes place.

(4) Rules under this section shall be made by statutory instrument which shall be subject to annulment in pursuance of a resolution of either House of Parliament.

GENERAL NOTE
This confers on the Secretary of State (and not on the Lord Chancellor) a power to make rules regarding the practice and procedure to be followed by the appeal tribunal (subs. (1)). Under the Tribunals and Inquiries Act 1992 (c. 53), s.8, the Secretary of State is bound to consult the Council on Tribunals before making his rules. The subject-matter of the rules is laid down (subs. (2)). They will cover such matters as time limits; the parties; the chairman's rulings on preliminary and incidental matters; requirements regarding the production of documents; attendance to give evidence; evidence on oath; paying expenses and allowances; hearings in private; representation of the parties (for example, by persons other than lawyers, such as an applicant's commanding officer if the intention is to widen rather than to narrow the choice of representative); and awards and costs. Until the rules are actually published, it is not possible to comment on how they compare with the rules governing, say, industrial tribunals. However, the possibility exists of the Secretary of State's rules not complying with the Salmon Commission recommendation that the parties should be represented, that there should be cross-examination, and that a party's lawyer should be entitled to cross-examine if so desired by the party. The rules of evidence and of discovery of documents in civil proceedings elsewhere in the U.K. are applicable to the appeal tribunal (subs. (3)). The rules are to be made by statutory instrument, subject to the negative resolution procedure (subs. (4)) which parliament might wish to invoke if the Secretary of State's rules are considered to be unsatisfactory in regard to such matters as restricting hearings in public (where no classified or commercially sensitive material may be involved).

Offences in connection with appeals

94.—(1) Any person who, in connection with an appeal to an appeal tribunal, knowingly or recklessly provides information which is false or misleading in a material particular is guilty of an offence.

(2) Any person who without reasonable excuse—

(a) fails to provide information in connection with an appeal to an appeal tribunal which he is required to provide by rules under section 93; or

(b) fails to attend an appeal tribunal when required to do so by rules under that section,

is guilty of an offence.

(3) Any person guilty of an offence under this section is liable on summary conviction to imprisonment for a term not exceeding 6 months or a fine not exceeding level 5 on the standard scale (or both).

GENERAL NOTE
This parallels the provisions elsewhere in Pt. IX regarding the provision of information which is false or misleading in a material particular in regard to applications for exemptions, etc., and to claims for financial assistance. If such false information is knowingly or recklessly provided in connection with an appeal, the person responsible is guilty of an offence. The current maximum penalty is a fine of £5,000 (level 5) or six months imprisonment or both. Similarly, a failure without reasonable excuse to provide information to an appeal tribunal which he is required to do by rules under s.93, or a failure without reasonable excuse to attend the appeal tribunal when so required by rules under s.93 is an offence punishable by a (current) maximum penalty of £5,000 (level 5) or six months imprisonment or both. *Cf.*, the annotations to ss.75(5), 82 and 87.

PART X

GENERAL OFFENCES

Offences against good order and discipline

Offences against orders and regulations under section 4

95.—(1) A member of a reserve force who—

(a) when required by or in pursuance of orders or regulations under section 4 to attend at any place, fails without reasonable excuse to attend in accordance with the requirement;

(b) uses threatening or insulting language or behaves in an insubordinate manner to any officer, warrant officer, non-commissioned officer or petty officer who in pursuance of orders or regulations under section 4 is acting in the execution of his office, and who would be the superior officer of the offender if he were subject to service law;

   (c) by any fraudulent means obtains or is an accessory to the obtaining of any pay or other sum contrary to orders or regulations under section 4;
   (d) knowingly or recklessly makes a statement false in any material particular in giving any information required by orders of regulations under section 4; or
   (e) fails without reasonable excuse to comply with orders or regulations under section 4,

is guilty of an offence triable by court-martial or summarily by a civil court.

(2) A person guilty of an offence under this section is liable—
   (a) on conviction by court-martial to suffer imprisonment, or such less punishment provided for by service law;
   (b) on summary conviction by a civil court—
      (i) in the case of an offence under subsection (1)(a), (b), or (e), to a fine not exceeding level 3 on the standard scale; and
      (ii) in the case of an offence under subsection (1)(c) or (d), to imprisonment for a term not exceeding 6 months or a fine not exceeding level 5 on the standard scale (or both).

(3) A person convicted of an offence under this section is liable, if sentenced to a term of imprisonment or if such a term is imposed in default of payment of any fine, to be taken into military custody, air-force custody or naval custody (as the case may be).

DEFINITIONS
"civil court": s.109.
"reserve force": s.1(2).
"service law": s.127(1).

GENERAL NOTE
Section 95 extends to all the reserve forces the offences of failure to comply with regulations, insubordination, etc., which, under s.76 of the 1980 Act, applied only to members of the Army Reserve and Air Force Reserve. The section provides a limited framework for discipline, ranging from the requirement to notify changes of address, to behaviour at reserve unit social functions at times when, because they are not on duty, the majority of reserve personnel are not subject to service discipline law.

Subs. (1)
This creates a number of offences triable either by court-martial or summarily in the civil courts. The offences are listed in subs. (1)(a)–(e). One would presume that the offence in para. (b), that is, using threatening or insulting language or behaving in an insubordinate manner to any officer, warrant officer, non-commissioned officer or petty officer in the execution of their office would be tried by court-martial rather than by a civil court, in view of the distinctive service discipline terminology of behaving in an insubordinate manner (*cf.*, Army/Air Force Acts 1955, s.33; Naval Discipline Act 1957, s.11, which employ slightly different wording).

It should be noted that the offences specified may be committed in circumstances when a reservist may not at the time be subject to service discipline law under the Army/Air Force Acts 1955 and the Naval Discipline Act 1957. In that respect, s.95 now renders 60,000 reservists subject to limited service jurisdiction at all times, whereas reservists are subject to the service discipline Acts generally only when they are in permanent service; on full-time reserve service under s.24; under an additional duties commitment under s.25; on the permanent staff; or when undertaking training and duty (officers in the Territorial Army, the Royal Auxiliary Air Force and the Royal Air Force Volunteer Reserve are subject to service discipline law at all times. However, if they are in the sponsored reserve, there is some uncertainty as to whether service discipline law applies to them when they are not in permanent service, or in training, or on duty, or undertaking the commitments in ss.24 and 25).

In para. (b), threatening language (a term familiar as a civil offence) is language from which a person may reasonably infer that violence may be used. Insulting language may be difficult to define. However, it is intended to, and does, display disrespect to a superior officer. It may also be a form of insubordinate behaviour. But the latter may, of course, involve conduct as distinct from language (*cf.*, the much beloved charge of "dumb insolence"). The language itself need not be discourteous in order to amount to behaving in an insubordinate manner.

But as indicated above, a difficulty is to apply those offences to circumstances which are neither actual service offences nor purely "civilian" offences.

Consider the scenario suggested by the minister (*Hansard*, H.C. Vol. 278, col. 48, May 20, 1996). A Territorial Army unit is dismissed at the end of the muster parade and they retire to socialise at the bar. The members are now off-duty and not subject to service discipline law. However, an argument breaks out at bar closing time and insulting and threatening words are spoken, and a member behaves in an insubordinate manner to the senior officer present who is responsible for closing the bar. The member may be charged under s.95(b)(1), whereas prior to the 1996 Act, no offence involving insubordination could be committed and any threatening or insulting language would provide the basis for a purely "civilian" offence.

Subs. (2)

Though military and air force discipline law permit a district court-martial to award a maximum of two years imprisonment (spent in a civilian prison) and a general court-martial to award life imprisonment, a court-martial, in sentencing a person guilty of an offence under s.95, may be guided by the maximum penalty imposed by a civil court for such offences, where applicable. That maximum penalty is currently £5,000 (level 5) or six months imprisonment or both in relation to the offences in paras. (c) and (d); and £1,000 (level 3) in the case of offences in paras. (a), (b) and (e). Nonetheless, courts-martial tend to impose heavier sentences for offences than would be imposed for the same or equivalent offence by a civil court.

Lesser punishments imposed by courts-martial include custodial orders for young offenders, combined with dismissal; dismissal with or without disgrace; detention (but not in the case of officers) at the Military Corrective Training Centre, Colchester, which may be combined with dismissal; forfeiture of seniority in the case of officers; reduction in rank (not in respect to officers); fine up to 28 days (not exceeding civil fine); reprimand or severe reprimand (but not in relation to privates or aircraftmen); stoppages of pay (entailing payment of compensation if loss proved); and minor punishments such as restriction of privileges (non-commissioned officers and privates/aircraftmen only). It may be noted that a general court-martial still has power to award the death penalty for five separate military offences in wartime (including armed rebellion and armed rioting), involving mutiny or assisting the enemy. The death sentence is mandatory in the case of treason, though treason is a civil offence and is only triable by court-martial abroad.

Subs. (3)

Service "custody" is not defined in the 1996 Act; nor in the service discipline Acts. It could mean being kept in the guardroom, but here it would appear to mean detention at the Military Corrective Training Centre. Within the services, a person may be in custody under close arrest or open arrest.

Desertion and absence without leave from service, duty or training

Failure to attend for service on call out or recall

96.—(1) A member of a reserve force served with a call-out notice under any provision of this Act who, without leave lawfully granted or reasonable excuse—

    (a) fails to present himself for service at the time and place specified in the call-out notice under section 32(3)(b), 43(4)(b) or 58(3)(c) (as the case may be);

    (b) having so presented himself, fails to remain there until accepted into service or informed that he is not to be accepted into service in pursuance of that notice; or

    (c) where he has for any reason failed to present himself at the time and place so specified or to remain there, fails—

        (i) to present himself to a person specified in the call-out notice or to any other authorised officer; or

        (ii) having so presented himself, to remain until accepted into service or informed that he is not to be accepted into service in pursuance of that notice,

is guilty, according to the circumstances, of desertion or absence without leave.

    (2) Subsection (1) applies to a person liable to recall as it applies to a member of a reserve force—

(a) with the substitution for references to a call-out notice of references to a recall notice; and

(b) as if paragraph (a) of that subsection referred to the time and place specified in the recall notice under section 70(3)(c).

(3) An offence under this section is triable by court-martial or summarily by a civil court.

DEFINITIONS
"authorised officer": s.64.
"call-out notice": s 58.
"civil court": s.109.
"reserve force": s.1(2).
"service": s.64.

GENERAL NOTE
Section 96 makes special provision for both reservists who fail to report as required on call out and persons liable to recall who fail to report as required. Prior to the 1996 Act, the law was inconsistent. Some categories of reservists, in particular, naval and marine reservists, were assumed or deemed or declared to be subject to service discipline law from the time they were obliged to report for service. If they failed, they could, according to circumstances, be prosecuted for desertion under the service discipline Acts. In contrast, the 1980 Act created distinct offences for other groups of reservists (see, for example, s.73 and Sched. 5 to the 1980 Act in regard to the Army Reserve and Air Force Reserve; and s.106 and Sched. 5 in relation to the Territorial Army and the Royal Auxiliary Air Force; and s.143 in relation to the Ulster Defence Regiment). The 1996 Act now creates distinct offences applicable to all categories of reservists as well as to those subject to recall. Thus the section creates the offences of desertion and absence without leave for service on call out or recall. Consequently, when, having received his call-out notice or recall notice, a person fails to present himself for service at the time or place specified; or fails to remain there pending acceptance or non-acceptance into service; or, failing which, fails to present himself to a specified person or authorised officer; or, having presented himself there, he fails to remain there till acceptance or non-acceptance; then he is guilty of either desertion or absence without leave. Trial is either by court-martial or summarily by civil court. The basic difference between desertion and absence without leave is in the intention, in the case of the former, of permanently being absent from duty. It may involve fraudulent enlistment without resigning a commission or without previously securing a discharge. It may also involve being absent without leave with intent to avoid serving at any place overseas or to avoid service when before the enemy (see Army/Air Force Act 1955, s.37; Naval Discipline Act 1957, s.15).

Failure to attend for duty or training

97.—(1) A member of a reserve force who has entered into a full-time service commitment or an additional duties commitment and, without leave lawfully granted or reasonable excuse, fails to appear at the time and place at which he is required to attend—

(a) in the case of a full-time service commitment, to begin the period of full-time service contemplated by the commitment;

(b) in the case of an additional duties commitment, to begin a period of service under the commitment,

is guilty, according to the circumstances, of desertion or absence without leave.

(2) A member of a reserve force who—

(a) is required to undergo a period of training in accordance with section 22, a special agreement or an employee agreement (or any other requirement applicable to special members), and

(b) fails, without leave lawfully granted or reasonable excuse, to appear at any time and place at which he is required to attend,

is guilty of absence without leave.

(3) An offence under this section is triable by court-martial or summarily by a civil court.

DEFINITIONS
"additional duties commitment": s.25.
"civil court": s.109.
"employee agreement": s.38(2).
"full-time service commitment": s.24.
"reserve force": s.1(2).
"special agreement": s.28(1).
"special member": s.127(1).

GENERAL NOTE
It is desertion or absence without leave, according to the circumstances of the case (as explained in the annotations to s.96), to fail to attend, without leave lawfully granted or without reasonable excuse, when required to do so by the terms of the following: a full-time service commitment, as provided in s.24; an additional duties commitment, as provided by s.25; a commitment under a special agreement, as provided by s.28(1); a commitment under an employee agreement, as provided in ss.38(2) and 40(1); or a training obligation under s.22.

Punishment etc. of offences of desertion or absence without leave

98.—(1) An offence under section 37 or 38 of the Army Act 1955 or the Air Force Act 1955 or section 16 or 17 of the Naval Discipline Act 1957 (offences under service law of desertion or absence without leave) committed by a member of a reserve force is triable summarily by a civil court as well as by court-martial.

(2) A member of a reserve force convicted by court-martial of an offence under section 96(1) or 97(1) is punishable as for an offence under service law of desertion or absence without leave (as the case may be).

(3) A member of a reserve force convicted by a civil court of—
(a) an offence under section 96(1) or 97(1), or
(b) an offence under service law of desertion or absence without leave,
is liable to imprisonment for a term not exceeding 6 months or a fine not exceeding level 5 on the standard scale (or both).

(4) A person convicted of an offence under section 97(2) is liable—
(a) if convicted by court-martial, to the same punishment as for an offence under service law of absence without leave;
(b) if convicted by a civil court, to imprisonment for a term not exceeding 6 months or a fine not exceeding level 5 on the standard scale (or both).

(5) A person convicted by a civil court of an offence mentioned in this section, if sentenced to a term of imprisonment or if such a term is imposed in default of payment of any fine, is liable to be taken into military, air-force or naval custody (as the case may require).

(6) Where a member of a reserve force or a person liable to recall is convicted of an offence of desertion, the time which elapsed between the time of his desertion and the time of his apprehension or voluntary surrender shall not be taken into account in reckoning his service for the purpose of release from permanent service or discharge.

DEFINITIONS
"civil court": s.109.
"permanent service": s.127(1).
"recall": s.127(1).
"reserve force": s.1(2).
"service law": s.127(1).

GENERAL NOTE
A civil court, as well as a court-martial, can try a reservist charged with the commission of service discipline Act offences in relation to desertion or absence without leave (subs. (1); *cf.* similar provisions in s.73 of the 1980 Act, albeit it was limited to members of the Army Reserve and Air Force Reserve). One presumes that the desertion or absence without leave had occurred once the reservist had *commenced* actual service or his full-time service commitment or additional duties commitment, or his training obligations. Subsection (2) seems more appropriate in those cases of failure to attend prior to commencing his training obligation. However,

the wording of the provisions does not require this division. Under subss. (3) and (4), the same current maximum penalty of a £5,000 fine or six months imprisonment or both applies, whether the trial is by court-martial or by a civil court. A convicted offender, sentenced to imprisonment by a civil court, may be taken into service custody. The wording of subs. (5) is similar to that in s.95(3). See the annotations thereto. Subsection (6) reflects the standard practice of not counting as reckonable service the period spent on desertion. The same rule, however, does not apply to the case of absence without leave.

False pretence of illegal absence

99. Any person who falsely represents himself to be a deserter or absentee without leave from any reserve force is guilty of an offence and liable on summary conviction to imprisonment for a term not exceeding 3 months or a fine not exceeding level 4 on the standard scale (or both).

DEFINITION
"reserve force": s.1(2).

GENERAL NOTE
It is an offence for a person falsely to represent himself to be a deserter or absentee without leave from any reserve force. Whoever would wish to represent himself in that way, for what reason, and under what circumstances, is not clear. Might a regular serviceman, when apprehended, wish to do so? Would a civilian wish to do so? Summary proceedings would take place in a civil court, with a current maximum penalty of £2,500 or three months imprisonment or both. The provision bears similarities to the Army/Air Force Act 1955, s.191 in respect of the regular forces, though it is confined to pretending to be a deserter.

Treatment of deserters etc.

100.—(1) Schedule 2 (arrest and subsequent treatment of suspected deserters or absentees without leave from the reserve forces) shall have effect.

(2) Schedule 2 shall apply to a person liable to recall who is a suspected deserter or absentee without leave by virtue of this Part and is not otherwise subject to service law as it applies to a member of a reserve force.

(3) The delivery under that Schedule of a member of a reserve force or a person liable to recall into military, air-force or naval custody, or the committal of any such person for the purpose of being so delivered, shall not prevent his subsequently being tried summarily in accordance with this Part.

DEFINITIONS
"recall": s.127(1).
"reserve forces": s.1(2).
"service law": s.127(1).

GENERAL NOTE
The procedures governing the arrest and subsequent treatment of suspected deserters or absentees without leave from the reserve forces are in Sched. 2. Schedule 2 also applies to former servicemen not otherwise subject to service discipline law (commissioned officers, whether or not pensioners, do not remain subject to service discipline law after they have left the regular forces).

Following the arrest of a suspected deserter or absentee without leave, he is brought before a magistrates' court (or equivalent in Scotland or Northern Ireland). The court may then cause the suspect to be delivered into service custody or commit him to a prison, police station or other place until delivered into service custody (see Sched. 2, paras. 4(2) and 5(3)). Subsection (3) makes it clear that delivery into service custody does not preclude his subsequently being tried summarily in a civil court.

Inducing a person to desert or absent himself

101.—(1) A person who, in the United Kingdom or elsewhere, by any means—

(a) procures or persuades, or attempts to procure or persuade, a member of a reserve force to commit an offence of desertion or absence without leave;

(b) knowing that a member of a reserve force is about to commit such an offence, aids or assists him in so doing; or

(c) knowing a member of a reserve force to be a deserter or an absentee without leave, procures or persuades or assists him to remain a deserter or absentee, or assists in his rescue from custody,

is guilty of an offence.

(2) A person who—

(a) procures or persuades, or attempts to procure or persuade, a person liable to recall to commit an offence of desertion or absence without leave;

(b) knowing that such a person is about to commit such an offence, aids or assists him in so doing; or

(c) knowing a person liable to recall to be a deserter or absentee without leave, procures or persuades or assists him to remain a deserter or absentee, or assists in his rescue from custody,

is guilty of an offence.

(3) A person guilty of an offence under subsection (1) or (2) is liable on summary conviction—

(a) in the case of an offence involving an offence of desertion or a deserter, to imprisonment for a term not exceeding 6 months or a fine not exceeding level 5 on the standard scale (or both); and

(b) in the case of an offence of absence without leave or an absentee without leave, to a fine not exceeding level 5 on the standard scale.

DEFINITION

"reserve force": s.1(2).

GENERAL NOTE

This creates offences, committed in the U.K. or abroad, of inducing, aiding or abetting a member of a reserve force, or a person liable to recall, to desert or remain a deserter or absentee without leave (subss. (1) and (2)). The section employs a number of different terms, that is, "procures or persuades" in subs. (1)(a), and "aids or assists" in subs. (1)(b). It is substantially but not wholly based on the wording in the Army/Air Force Acts 1955, s.192; Naval Discipline Act, 1957, s.97. It is also an offence to attempt to procure or persuade a reservist to desert or to go absent without leave. The prosecution must prove that the person charged with aiding or assisting knew the reservist or person liable to recall was about to commit such an offence. Therefore, the civilian friend who drives the reservist or person liable to recall to a holiday destination, for example, may be innocent if unaware of the passenger's real motive. *Cf.*, the provisions in the Accessories and Abettors Act 1861 (c. 94), s.8, as amended by the Criminal Law Act 1977 (c. 45), s.1, that is, aiding, abetting, counselling and procuring, as discussed in, for example, Smith and Hogan, *Criminal Law* (7th ed.), Butterworth, 1992, Chap. 7. See also the Incitement to Disaffection Act 1934 (c. 56), whereby an endeavour by a person to "seduce a member of the armed forces from his duty or allegiance to the Crown" is a criminal offence under s.1, and also aiding, abetting, counseling or procuring the commission of the offence under s.1 is itself an offence under s.2.

In respect of the offences involving desertion, the current maximum penalty is a £5,000 fine (level 5) or six months imprisonment or both. With respect to offences in relation to going absent without leave, the current maximum penalty is £5,000 (subs. (3)). There is no court-martial jurisdiction under s.101, presumably because it is assumed that the person committing the offence will be a civilian. If a person subject to service discipline law, including a reservist on duty, were to commit the offence, there would presumably be concurrent jurisdiction, with trial either before a civil court or by court-martial.

Record of illegal absence

102.—(1) Where a member of a reserve land, air or marine force is subject to service law and is unlawfully absent from his duty—

(a) a board of inquiry under section 135 of the Army Act 1955 or the Air Force Act 1955, as the case may be, may be assembled after the expiry of 21 days from the date of his absence, notwithstanding that the period during which he was subject to service law is less than 21 days, or has expired before the expiry of 21 days; and

(b) the record mentioned in section 136 of the Army Act 1955 or the Air Force Act 1955, as the case may be, may be entered in the manner there provided, or in such regimental or service books and by such officer as may be prescribed.

(2) Where a member of a reserve land, air or marine force—

(a) having been served with a call-out notice under any provision of this Act, fails, without leave lawfully granted, to do anything mentioned in section 96(1)(a), (b) or (c);

(b) having entered into a full-time service commitment fails, without leave lawfully granted, to appear at any time or place at which he is required to attend to begin the period of full-time service contemplated by the commitment;

(c) having entered into an additional duties commitment fails, without leave lawfully granted, to appear at any time or place at which he is required to begin a period of duty under the commitment;

(d) having been required to undergo a period of training as mentioned in section 97(2) fails, without leave lawfully granted, to appear at any time or place at which he is required to appear,

and his absence continues for not less than 14 days, an entry of his absence shall be made by such officer as may be prescribed in such manner, and in such regimental or service books, as may be prescribed.

DEFINITIONS

"additional duties commitment": s.25.
"call-out notice": s.58.
"full-time service commitment": s.24.
"prescribed": s.127(1).
"reserve air force": s.1(2).
"reserve land force": s.1(2).
"reserve marine force": s.127(1).
"service law": s.127(1).

GENERAL NOTE

Subs. (1)

This provision lays down procedures which may be followed when an Army, Air Force or Marine reservist, subject to service law, is unlawfully absent from his duty. It presupposes he has already commenced his duty. In the absence of "duty", he would not, of course, be subject to *service* law, though perhaps he would be subject to s.95 of the 1996 Act. The provision does not appear to extend to naval reservists inasmuch as it refers to a member of a "reserve land, air or marine force", as distinct from the "reserve naval, marine, land and air forces". The procedures permit (the word "may" in subs. (1)(a) and (b) is employed) the assembling of a board of enquiry and the keeping of appropriate records in accordance with the provisions of the Army/Air Force Acts 1955, ss.135 and 136. These make provision for the assembling, jurisdiction, composition, rules of evidence and procedure, and representation in respect to a board of enquiry. Note that s.135(5) of the 1955 Acts states that evidence given before a board of enquiry shall not be admissible against any person in proceedings before a court-martial, or before a commanding officer or appropriate superior authority except in respect to perjury which can be chargeable as a civil offence under the Army/Air Force Acts 1955, s.70. However, s.136 states that the entering in the regimental or service books of the record of the board's report, to the effect that the person has been absent without leave for not less than 21 days, has the like effect as a conviction by court-martial for desertion. Whether such a provision would pass muster under Art. 6 (right to a fair trial) of the European Convention on Human Rights, is to be doubted. The provision in s.136 does not apply if the absentee subsequently surrenders or is arrested or the report is annulled by the Army/Air Force Board or by a subsequent board of enquiry.

Subs. (2)

This covers the situation where the reservist is required to present himself for a category of duty before that duty has actually commenced. The categories are those described in paras. (a), (b), (c) and (d). A record of his absences, if lasting not less than 14 days, is then to be made in the service or regimental books in accordance with orders or regulations issued under s.4. This provision should be read in the light of s.96(1) regarding failure to attend for service on call out and in the light of s.97 regarding failure to attend for duty or training. Such failures, as we have noted above, are offences triable by court-martial or summarily by a civil court.

General

Trial of offences as offences under service law

103.—(1) Any offence which is by virtue of this Part triable by court-martial shall for all purposes of and incidental to the arrest, trial and punishment of the offender (including the summary disposal of the case by an officer having power to deal with the case) be deemed to be an offence under the Army Act 1955, the Air Force Act 1955 or the Naval Discipline Act 1957, as the case may require.

(2) References in those Acts to forfeitures and stoppages shall be construed in relation to any such offence as references to such forfeitures and stoppages as may be prescribed.

DEFINITION
"prescribed": s.127(1).

GENERAL NOTE

Subs. (1)
This provides that an offence under Pt. X, which is triable by court-martial, is for purposes incidental to arrest, trial and punishment, deemed to be an offence under service discipline law, even though the 1996 Act is not service law as otherwise defined in s.127(1). This means that subordinate legislation such as the Army Summary Jurisdiction Regulations 1972; the Rules of Procedure (Army) 1972; and the Police and Criminal Evidence Act 1984 (c. 60) codes of practice made applicable to service discipline law, are applicable in respect to proceedings against reservists or those liable to recall.

Subs. (2)
For forfeitures and stoppages, see annotations to s.95(2).

Jurisdiction of civil courts

104.—(1) A civil court in the United Kingdom with jurisdiction in the place where a person is for the time being shall have jurisdiction to try him for any offence under this Part which is triable by such a court.

(2) Subsection (1) applies notwithstanding that the alleged offence was committed outside the jurisdiction of the court, except that where it was committed in any part of the United Kingdom it shall be triable only by a court in that part of the United Kingdom.

(3) Every fine imposed under this Part by a court-martial shall be paid to such authority as may be prescribed.

DEFINITIONS
"civil court": s.109.
"prescribed": s.127(1).

GENERAL NOTE

Subs. (1)
This makes provision for a civil court in the U.K. to try an alleged offender for an offence under Pt. X even if the offence was committed outside the jurisdiction of the court. The person tried must, for the time being, be within the jurisdiction of the court. It appears that if the offence is committed abroad, for example, an offence under s.95(1) while on an operation or in training abroad (though a court-martial would be the most appropriate forum), the civil court will still have jurisdiction.

Subs. (2)

However, if the offence were committed in England and the alleged offender was in Scotland for the time being, a Scottish civil court would have no jurisdiction (and vice-versa, of course).

Subs. (3)

The recipient of the fine, whether that be central funds or the local Territorial Army unit, or whatever, will be prescribed in regulations or orders issued under s.4. Note that, generally speaking, Army and Royal Air Force courts-martial, both general and district, may award fines of up to 28 days, the amount not to exceed that imposed under civil law for the equivalent offence.

Trial of offences by civil court

105.—(1) Any offence to which this section applies which is triable by a court-martial is also triable summarily by a civil court and punishable with imprisonment for a term not exceeding 3 months or a fine not exceeding level 4 on the standard scale (or both).

(2) Nothing in this section affects the liability of a person charged with an offence to which this section applies to be taken into military, air-force or naval custody.

(3) This section applies to an offence under service law (other than an offence of desertion or absence without leave) committed by a member of a reserve force when not in permanent service under Part IV or Part V or under a call-out order.

DEFINITIONS
"civil court": s.109.
"reserve force": s.1(2).
"service law": s.127(1).

GENERAL NOTE

Replicating the effect of s.110 of the 1980 Act which applied only to the Territorial Army and to the Royal Auxiliary Air Force, this section provides that a civil court, as well as a court-martial, will have jurisdiction to try summarily a reservist who is alleged to have committed an offence, other than desertion or absence without leave, under service law. Jurisdiction arises when the reservist is on duty in the following cases: when serving under a full-time service commitment, under an additional duties commitment, when on training, or when serving as permanent staff.

The current maximum punishment is a fine of £2,500 (level 4) or three months imprisonment or both. If the reservist is in actual service (permanent service) with the high readiness reserve, with the sponsored reserve or on call out under Pt. VI, then the civil court will have no jurisdiction in such cases. A civil court may, however, choose to commit the reservist to service custody for disposal under service discipline law.

Offences triable by court-martial or civil court

106.—(1) A person charged with an offence which under this Part is triable both by a court-martial and by a civil court may be tried either by a court-martial (or by an officer having power to deal summarily with the case) or by a civil court but not by both of them.

(2) It is immaterial, for the purposes of any provision of this Part making an offence triable by court-martial, whether the person concerned is otherwise subject to service law.

DEFINITIONS
"civil court": s.109.
"service law": s.127(1).

Subs. (1)

This makes clear that dual jurisdictions are alternatives, trial either by court-martial or summarily by civil court, but not by both.

Subs. (2)
Courts-martial will have jurisdiction under provisions of Pt. X notwithstanding that the person may otherwise not be subject at that time to service discipline law. See the example given in the annotation to s.95(1).

Time for institution of proceedings

107.—(1) Proceedings against a person before either—
(a) a court-martial or an officer having power to deal with the case summarily; or
(b) a civil court,
in respect of an offence under this Act or under service law and alleged to have been committed by him during his period of service in a reserve force may be instituted whether or not he has ceased to be a member of that reserve force.

(2) Such proceedings may, notwithstanding anything in any other enactment, be instituted at any time within 2 months after—
(a) the time at which the offence becomes known to his commanding officer; or
(b) the time at which he is apprehended, whichever is later.

DEFINITIONS
"civil court": s.109.
"reserve force": s.1(2).
"service law": s.127(1).

GENERAL NOTE
This provision reflects the filling of the "*Boydell* gap" (*R. v. Governor of Wormwood Scrubs, ex p. Boydell* [1948] 2 K.B. 193) in which an officer's conviction by court-martial for a civil offence was quashed on the ground that he was no longer subject to military law when he was tried. Now the Army/Air Force Acts 1955, s.132 and Naval Discipline Act 1957, s.52 provide a six-month time limit by which a person must be tried by court-martial after he has ceased to be subject to service discipline law (the period is three months if summary disposal by the commanding officer). Reservists therefore would ordinarily remain liable to court-martial proceedings within six months (or three months in regard to summary disposal) of completion of call out, training or other duties, including permanent staff duties. Pre-trial procedures of arrest, custody, investigation of charges, etc., are therefore also available to the service authorities even if the person is no longer subject to service discipline law (Army/Air Force Acts 1955, s.131; Naval Discipline Act 1957, s.51). Now under s.107 of the 1996 Act, civil or court-martial proceedings for an offence under service law or under the 1996 Act, and committed by a reservist during reserve service, must commence within two months of the time when the offence became known to the reservist's commanding officer or of the time of the alleged offender's apprehension, whichever is the later. This time limit applies whether or not the reservist has ceased to be a member of that reserve force. It therefore appears to override the above provision in respect to reservists who had ceased to be subject to service discipline law, for example, after their day's training, but who were still liable to court-martial proceedings for a further six months thereafter. Subsection (2) does, however, employ the phrase "notwithstanding anything in any other enactment". How that relates to the interplay between s.205(1)(g) and (h) of the Army/Air Force Acts 1955, as amended by the 1996 Act, Sched. 10, para. 1, which extends service discipline law to reservists, and s.132 of the Army/Air Force Acts 1955, which set a time limit for the trial of offences under service discipline law is not wholly clear.

Evidence

108.—(1) Schedule 3 (evidence) shall have effect in relation to proceedings under this Part and any other proceedings for an offence under any other Part of this Act.

(2) Paragraphs 2 to 8 of that Schedule apply to a member of a reserve force who is tried by a civil court, whether or not he is at the time of the trial subject to service law.

(3) Where by virtue of any provision of this Act a document is admissible in evidence or is evidence of any matter stated in it in proceedings before a civil court in England and Wales, it shall be sufficient evidence of the matter so stated in such proceedings in Scotland.

DEFINITIONS
"civil court": s.109.
"reserve force": s.1(2).
"service law": s.127(1).

GENERAL NOTE
This section introduces Sched. 3 which contains general provisions with respect to evidence in proceedings under Pt. X, and in relation to any other proceedings for an offence under any other part of the Act (for example, the offence in s.94 of providing false information in connection with an appeal to the reserve forces appeal tribunal). Virtually every section of Pt. IX is concerned with "offences" (though see s.102 in regard to record keeping). So why omit "offences" in relation to "proceedings under this Part" (*i.e.* Pt. X)? Schedule 3 provides broadly that letters or documents purporting to be issued on behalf of the Defence Council are evidence of the service details of any person in the armed forces. They include his rank, post and decorations. Defence Council letters and documents are also evidence of relevant records or regulations.

Subs. (3)
Documents admissible as evidence in English civil courts will be admissible in Scottish civil courts. Whether the reverse is the case is not stated. Service discipline law enables service personnel to be charged with any offence punishable by the law of England wherever the offence is committed, and allows any defences thereto which English law permits. See Army/Air Force Acts 1955, s.70(1) and (2); Naval Discipline Act 1957, s.42(1) and (2). Some Scots lawyers and members of parliament consider this unacceptable. *Cf.*, *Hansard*, H.C. Vol. 240, col. 658.

Meaning of "civil court"

109. In this Part a reference to a civil court shall be construed as a reference—
(a) in England and Wales, to a magistrates' court;
(b) in Scotland, to the sheriff sitting as a court of summary jurisdiction; and
(c) in Northern Ireland, to a court of summary jurisdiction.

GENERAL NOTE
This defines "civil court" within England and Wales, Scotland and Northern Ireland.

PART XI

RESERVE ASSOCIATIONS

Establishment of associations for areas in the UK

110.—(1) A territorial, auxiliary and volunteer reserve association (in this Part referred to as an "association") may be established for any area in the United Kingdom determined by the Defence Council.

(2) If the Defence Council alters the areas into which the United Kingdom has for the time being been divided for the purposes of subsection (1), the Defence Council may by order alter the area for which an existing association is established.

(3) An order under subsection (2)—
(a) may make supplemental, incidental and transitional provision (including provision as respects the transfer of property, rights and liabilities and financial adjustments); and
(b) shall be made by statutory instrument which shall be subject to annulment in pursuance of a resolution of either House of Parliament.

(4) In this section "the United Kingdom" includes the Channel Islands and the Isle of Man.

DEFINITION
   "association": subs. (1).

GENERAL NOTE
   Subsection (1) declares that territorial, auxiliary and volunteer reserve associations (TAVRAs) may be established for any area of the U.K., including the Channel Islands and Isle of Man (see subs. (4)), determined by the Defence Council. The subsection does not actually state in so many words that the Defence Council is given power to make orders creating such TAVRAs, but this might be inferred, especially in the light of s.111(1). Moreover, if the Defence Council makes alterations in the areas for this purpose, then subs. (2) states explicitly that the area covered by an existing association may be adjusted by Defence Council order. The order is a statutory instrument subject to the negative resolution procedure by either House (subs. (3)(b)). The additional scope of the order embracing property and financial or other aspects of TAVRAs is adverted to in subs. (3)(a). The section does not explain what is a TAVRA. For brief discussion, see Introduction and General Note, s.113 and Sched. 4.

Constitution of associations

111.—(1) An association shall be constituted, and its members shall be appointed and hold office, in accordance with a scheme made by the Defence Council.
   (2) Schedule 4 (schemes made under subsection (1)) shall have effect.
   (3) The Secretary of State may by order make such modifications (whether by way of addition, substitution or otherwise) to Schedule 4 as he considers appropriate.
   (4) An order under subsection (3)—
   (a) may contain such supplemental, incidental and transitional provision as the Secretary of State considers appropriate; and
   (b) shall be made by statutory instrument which shall be subject to annulment in pursuance of a resolution of either House of Parliament.

DEFINITION
   "association": s.110(1).

GENERAL NOTE
   The constitution, membership and office holding of TAVRAs is to be in accordance with a scheme made by the Secretary of State. The scheme is outlined in Sched. 4 ("Provisions of Schemes for the Constitution of Associations") to which the Secretary of State may make, by order, appropriate modifications, including supplemental, incidental and transitional provisions.

General duties of associations

112.—(1) It shall be the duty of an association to make itself acquainted with, and conform to, the plan of the Defence Council for the organisation within the area for which the association is established of—
   (a) Her Majesty's land and air forces; and
   (b) the reserve naval and marine forces in so far as the plan relates to matters with respect to which functions are conferred on the association under section 113(1).
   (2) It shall also be the duty of an association to give advice and assistance in relation to the military and air-force resources and capabilities of the area for which the association is established to the Defence Council and to such officers as the Defence Council may direct.
   (3) The advice and assistance which an association may be required to give under subsection (2) includes advice or assistance relating to any matter in connection with—
   (a) local support for, or for the activities of, Her Majesty's land and air forces, the reserve naval and marine forces and the cadet forces mentioned in section 113(1)(c); and

    (b) the availability of financial and material assistance (including land and buildings) for any activity or requirement of those forces or for any other defence purpose,

which the association is requested to provide by the Defence Council or any officer mentioned in subsection (2).

    "association": s.110(1).
    "reserve naval and marine forces": s.1(2).

GENERAL NOTE
    A TAVRA is required to fulfil the different functions of recruitment and welfare (with regard to the Territorial Army and the Royal Auxiliary Air Force), and the provision and maintenance of accommodation (with regard to the Royal Naval Reserve, the Royal Marine Reserve, the Territorial Army, the Royal Auxiliary Air Force and the Cadet Forces). It must liaise with the civilian community, including employers. It must also acquaint itself with, and conform to, the Defence Council's plan for the organisation of both military and air forces in its area and also (to an extent limited by the provisions of s.113(1)) of the reserve naval and marine forces. The words "acquainted with" are imprecise; and "conform to" is perhaps not as strong an injunction as "comply with".
    Note that while para. (a) refers to the land and air forces, para. (b) specifically refers to the naval and marine forces. This is because the associations provide no real support for the (regular) Royal Navy or Royal Marines, though some support is provided for the reserve naval and marine forces.

Subs. (2)
    In relation to local military and air force resources and capabilities, TAVRAs have a duty to offer advice and assistance thereon to the Defence Council or to appointed officers.

Subs. (3)
    The nature of the advice and assistance, primarily logistical and financial, is laid down.

Powers and duties assignable to associations

    113.—(1) An association shall have such powers and duties connected with the organisation and administration of—
    (a) Her Majesty's land and air forces;
    (b) the reserve naval and marine forces; or
    (c) the Army Cadet Force, the Air Training Corps, the Combined Cadet Force and the Sea Cadet Corps,
as may for the time being be transferred or assigned to it by order of Her Majesty signified under the hand of the Secretary of State or, subject to such an order, by regulations under this Part.
    (2) The powers and duties which may be so transferred or assigned include any powers conferred on or vested in Her Majesty, and any powers or duties conferred or imposed on the Defence Council or the Secretary of State, by statute or otherwise, and in particular respecting the following matters—
    (a) the organisation of the units of the Territorial Army and the Royal Auxiliary Air Force and their administration (including maintenance) at all times other than when training or on duty or when in permanent service;
    (b) the recruiting of members for the volunteer reserve forces;
    (c) the provision and maintenance of buildings, rifle ranges, magazines, sites of camps, aerodromes, landing grounds and hangars;
    (d) facilitating the provision of areas to be used for manoeuvres;
    (e) arranging with employers as to leave of absence for training, and ascertaining, after consultation with the representatives of the main employers in the area for which the association is established, the times of training which having regard to their businesses are best suited to the circumstances of civil life;
    (f) establishing or assisting cadet units and also rifle and aviation clubs;

(g) the provision of transport for the peace-time requirements of the reserve forces;

(h) providing accommodation for the safe custody of arms or equipment;

(i) the supply of the requirements, when called out, of the units of the reserve forces within the area for which the association is established in so far as those requirements are directed by the Defence Council to be met locally;

(j) the welfare of members and former members of Her Majesty's land and air forces and of members and former members of the reserve naval and marine forces.

(3) For the purposes of subsection (2)(i) the Defence Council shall make and issue to associations regulations specifying, so far as practicable, the requirements mentioned in that paragraph which are to be met locally.

(4) An association shall not have any powers of command or training over any part of Her Majesty's forces.

(5) The members of an association shall not be under any pecuniary liability for any act done by them in their capacity as members in carrying out the provisions of this Part.

DEFINITIONS
"association": s.110(1).
"permanent service": s.127(1).
"reserve forces": s.1(2).
"reserve naval and marine forces": s.127(1).
"volunteer reserve forces": s.2(3).

GENERAL NOTE
This section substantially re-enacts s.124 of the 1980 Act. It provides details of the powers and duties in connection with the various forces, including the principal cadet forces, which may be transferred or assigned to a TAVRA by Her Majesty or by regulations issued by the Defence Council (on the latter, see s.117). The powers and duties embody a division of responsibility as between TAVRAs on the one hand and Her Majesty, the Defence Council or the Secretary of State on the other. See, for example, subs. (2)(a) where the organisation and administration of certain reserve units are in the hands of a TAVRA except when the unit is engaged in training, is on duty, or is in permanent service. In such cases its organisation and administration are in the hands of the Crown (however represented).

Some tasks, such as those specified in subs. (2)(e) and (f), seem highly appropriate for local organisation and administration, though, depending on what is meant by "consultation", the needs of business may appear to some to supersede those of the reserve forces. Other tasks such as that in subs. (2)(h) might, to some, be more appropriately the responsibility of the Secretary of State. Subsection (4) makes it clear, however, that a TAVRA has no power of command or of training over any part of Her Majesty's forces. A clear division is laid down here. Arguably, this is consistent with the thrust of the Act, which is, as Lord Judd suggested, "to strengthen the central role of the reserve forces in the total defence effort" in new circumstances. These are where, "There will be less flexibility within the regular permanent services and a more immediate demand for a critical role by the reserve forces" (*Hansard*, H.L. Vol. 568, cols. CWH 122, 125).

Some of the provisions are couched in general or vague terms, for example, subs. (2)(j) which imposes a duty in respect to the welfare of members and former members of the reserve forces. Given the terminology of "Her Majesty's land and air forces" (subs. (2)(j)), the welfare duty may extend to certain regulars as to well as to ex-regulars of those services (though not to members of the Royal Navy or Royal Marines). Members and full-time staff of reserve forces may themselves be ex-regulars.

Finally, subs. (5) states that members of TAVRAs will not incur any financial liability for any acts done in their capacity as members in carrying out the provisions of Pt. XI. For the provisions in regard to lawful expenditure and the recovery of expenses incurred by associations, see s.114. If there is unauthorised expenditure, presumably there may be personal liability.

Expenses of associations

114. —(1) The Defence Council shall pay to an association, out of money provided by Parliament, such sums as in the opinion of the Defence Council are required to meet the necessary expenditure incurred by the association.

(2) An association—

(a) shall annually at such time as may be specified in regulations under this Part; and

(b) may at any other time for any special purpose,

submit in such form and manner as may be so specified a statement of its necessary requirements to the Defence Council; and all payments under this section to an association shall be made upon the basis of such a statement, so far as approved by the Defence Council.

(3) Subject to regulations under this Part, any money paid to an association by the Defence Council shall be applicable to any of the purposes specified in the approved statements in accordance with which money has been granted and, except with the written consent of the Defence Council or an officer authorised by or in accordance with directions of the Defence Council for the purpose of giving consents, shall not be applicable otherwise.

(4) Nothing in this section shall be construed as enabling the Defence Council or an authorised officer to give consent to the application of money to any purpose to which, apart from this section, it could not lawfully be applied, or to give consent without the authority of the Treasury in any case in which, apart from this section, the authority of the Treasury would be required.

(5) All money received by an association otherwise than from the Defence Council (except such money, if any, as may be received by the association for specified purposes) shall be available for the purposes of any of the powers and duties of the association.

(6) The income from investments representing money originally received for the purposes of any of the reserve forces, or the cadet forces mentioned in section 113(1)(c), shall be applied only to that purpose, unless the Defence Council otherwise direct.

DEFINITIONS

"association": s.110(1).

"reserve forces; the": s.1(2).

GENERAL NOTE

This section makes provision for an association to submit a budget relating to necessary expenditure. It is submitted annually to the Defence Council or at any other time for any special purpose (subs. (2)). The Defence Council shall then make such payments as, in its opinion, are required to meet that necessary expenditure (subs. (1)). The money must then be applied to those purposes, unless written permission in relation to another purpose is granted (subs. (4)). The Defence Council or an authorised officer can only authorise lawful expenditure which includes Treasury approved expenditure (subs. (4)). Funds generated from any other sources may be used for any association purposes unless specified otherwise, perhaps by the donor (subs. (5)). Income from investments received for the purposes of any of the reserve forces or the cadet forces (see s.113(1)(c)) can only be used for those purposes unless the Defence Council directs otherwise (subs. (6)).

Accounts of associations

115.—(1) An association shall cause its accounts to be made up and audited annually in such manner as may be specified in regulations under this Part.

(2) An association shall send copies of its accounts, together with any report of the auditors on them, to—

(a) the Defence Council; or

(b) such authority or person as may be directed by regulations under this Part.

DEFINITION

"association": s.110(1).

GENERAL NOTE

This reproduces s.126 of the 1980 Act and makes provision for the annual making up and auditing of association accounts. The manner of their compilation is to be specified in regulations, and the accounts have to be sent to the Defence Council or as directed by regulations. The normal practice is for the audited association accounts to be sent for his scrutiny to the Command Secretary, HQ Land, who has responsibility for the day-to-day management of TAVRA funding. The TAVRA regulations require public and private funds to be separately identified in association accounts. Private funds for this purpose appear to include income generated from that element of the TAVRA grant which represents the general administration of the Territorial Army or the Royal Auxiliary Air Force, the Royal Naval Reserve or the Royal Marine Reserve, as the case might be. It does not include income generated from the grant allocated for TAVRA administration or for the TAVRA estates. TAVRAs may invest an element of their grant representing the general administration of the Territorial Army or of the Royal Auxiliary Air Force, as the case might be, and use the income generated thereby, without prior Ministry of Defence approval. It is treated as private income inasmuch as it does not come directly from the ministry but from the institution in which the money has been invested. This allows scope for flexibility in respect to local decision making, and reflects the ministry's views in regard to delegation of responsibility.

Joint committees of associations

116.—(1) Two or more associations may from time to time join in appointing from among their respective members a joint committee for any purpose in respect of which they are jointly interested.

(2) An association joining in appointing a joint committee under this section may delegate to it any power which such an association may exercise for the purpose for which the committee is appointed.

(3) Subject to the terms of delegation, a joint committee appointed under this section shall in respect of any matter delegated to it have the same power in all respects as the associations appointing it.

(4) The costs of such a joint committee shall be defrayed by the associations by whom it has been appointed in such proportion as may be agreed between them.

(5) The accounts of such joint committees and their officers shall for the purposes of this Part be deemed to be accounts of the associations appointing them and of their officers.

DEFINITION

"association": s.110(1).

GENERAL NOTE

The broad thrust of this provision is to enable two or more local associations to form a joint committee for any purpose in which they may have a joint interest (subs. (1)). The mode of appointment will be provided in the constitution of the association, the scheme for which is contained in Sched. 4, para. 1(e). Powers of delegation to the joint committee may be granted, though the powers conferred may not exceed those possessed by the associations appointing it (subss. (2) and (3)). Provisions relating to costs and to maintaining accounts of a joint committee are laid down (subss. (4) and (5)). The phrase "any purpose in respect of which they are jointly interested" must, of course, be read in the light of the powers possessed by each association. The powers and duties specified in s.113(2) will set the parameters of what a joint committee may organise.

Regulations as to associations

117.—(1) Regulations for carrying into effect the provisions of this Part as respects associations may be made by the Defence Council and such regulations may, in particular, provide for the following matters

(a) for regulating the manner in which powers are to be exercised and duties performed by associations, and for specifying the services to which money paid by the Defence Council is to be applicable;

(b) for authorising and regulating the acquisition by or on behalf of associations of land for the purposes of this Part and the disposal of any land so acquired;

(c) for authorising and regulating the borrowing of money by associations;

(d) for authorising the acceptance of any money or other property, and the taking over of any liability, by associations, and for regulating the administration of any money or property so acquired and the discharge of any liability so taken over;

(e) for facilitating the co-operation of an association with any other association or with any local authority or other body (whether by the constitution of joint committees or otherwise) and for the provision of assistance by one association to another;

(f) for affiliating cadet units, rifle and aviation clubs and other bodies to any of the reserve forces or any part of any such force;

(g) for or in respect of anything directed or authorised by any provision of this Part to be done or provided for by or in regulations or to be done in such manner as may be specified.

(2) Regulations under this section made for the purposes of section 114 or 115 shall be subject to the Treasury's consent.

(3) Regulations under this section shall be laid before each House of Parliament after being made.

DEFINITIONS
"association": s.110(1).
"reserve forces": s.1(2).

GENERAL NOTE
We have noted previously the delicate balance between the local autonomy of associations and central control of the defence effort. See, especially, s.113(2), (3) and (4). Section 117 elaborates on this balance by conferring on the Defence Council the power to issue regulations for the carrying into effect of the provisions in Pt. XI regarding the powers and duties of associations. The regulations issued by the Defence Council, and which are to be laid before each House after being made (subs. (3)), will set the framework or agenda for, and mode of carrying out, the activities of local associations. The areas covered are listed in subs. (1)(a)–(g), but this is not an exhaustive list. As many of the activities involve expenditure of public funds, the need for Treasury approval is laid down (subs. (2)). On provisions regarding associations' expenditure and the accounts thereof, see ss.114 and 115.

Compensation of displaced employees

118.—(1) The Secretary of State may make regulations providing for the payment by the Secretary of State of compensation to, or in respect of, any person who in the Secretary of State's opinion falls within subsection (2) or (3).

(2) A person falls within this subsection if he has ceased to be employed by an association established for the purposes of this Part, or has suffered a diminution in the emoluments of his employment by such an association, in consequence of—

(a) the winding-up of the association;
(b) any change in its activities or in the area for which it is established; or
(c) any proposal for such a winding-up or change.

(3) A person falls within this subsection if he—

(a) has ceased to be employed by the body known as the Council of Territorial, Auxiliary and Volunteer Reserve Associations; or
(b) has suffered a diminution in the emoluments of his employment by that body,

in consequence of the winding-up of associations established for the purposes of this Part or of changes in their activities or the areas for which they are established.

(4) Regulations under this section shall be made by statutory instrument which shall be subject to annulment in pursuance of a resolution of either House of Parliament.

DEFINITION
"association": s.110(1).

GENERAL NOTE
This is a "redundancy payments" provision, substantially reproducing s.129 of the 1980 Act. It provides that the Secretary of State may make regulations in respect to compensation for loss of employment or for diminution in emoluments in respect to persons employed by an association or by the Council of TAVRAs. The section provides that where, in the Secretary of State's opinion (subs. (1)), a person's cessation of employment or a diminution in his emoluments (in effect, a reduction in pay) occurs in consequence of the events specified in subss. (2)(a)–(c) and (3), then, under the regulations, compensation will be payable to or in respect of that person.

On the footing that he is a civilian, and in the event of a winding up of an association or a reduction in its area or activities, then existing labour law provisions in respect to redundancy payments, and to the Transfer of Undertakings (Protection of Employment) Regulations 1981 (as amended), will be applicable. The Secretary of State's proposed regulations, to be made by statutory instrument, and subject to the negative resolution procedure, cannot override them. Regulations under the 1980 Act provided for compensation payments higher than the statutory minimum under redundancy payments legislation. Section 118 does not itself make provision for the settlement of any disputes as to entitlement or quantum in respect to compensation. Subsection (1) does in fact lay down a subjective test of entitlement ("in the Secretary of State's opinion") rather than an objective test. Perhaps greater financial control from the centre can be secured, thus minimising judicial scrutiny of ministerial actions or decisions which concern armed forces organisation. But unless a dispute resolution forum is created in the regulations (and, legally, it is doubtful whether this would be *intra vires*), then an aggrieved party may only have the option of an industrial tribunal application under labour law provisions, or resort to judicial review.

Winding-up of associations

119.—(1) The Defence Council may make an order providing for the winding-up of an association.

(2) An order under subsection (1)—

(a) may make supplemental, incidental and transitional provision (including provision as respects the transfer of property, rights and liabilities and financial adjustments); and

(b) shall be made by statutory instrument which shall be subject to annulment in pursuance of a resolution of either House of Parliament.

DEFINITION
"association": s.110(1).

GENERAL NOTE
Whereas the Defence Council may create (by order? See s.110(1) which is silent on this point) an association, so also may it, by an order subject to the negative resolution procedure, wind up an association (subss. (1) and (2)(b)). The scope of the order may cover the arrangements to be made regarding the transfer of property, the settlement of rights and liabilities and the settling of financial matters.

PART XII

MISCELLANEOUS AND GENERAL

Miscellaneous

Disbanding of units: charitable property

120. Schedule 5 (treatment of charitable property held for purposes of any body of a reserve force which has been, or is to be, disbanded or amalgamated with another body) shall have effect.

DEFINITION
"reserve force": s.1(2).

GENERAL NOTE
This section introduces Sched. 5 which will apply in relation to charitable property held for the purposes of any reserve force unit which has been or is to be disbanded or amalgamated with another body. What constitutes "charitable property" is defined (unhelpfully) in Sched. 5 as "any property belonging to a charity" (paras. 3(2) and 15(2) in respect to England and Wales and to Northern Ireland, respectively), or "any property belonging to a recognised body" (para. 9(2) in respect to Scotland). No doubt in such cases, it would be such property as a Territorial Army unit's drill hall or a Royal Naval Reserve unit's training vessel. For further details, see annotations to Sched. 5.

The lieutenancies

121.—(1) Schedule 6 (minor amendments and pre-consolidation amendments relating to the lieutenancies) shall have effect.

(2) It is hereby declared that the validity of the appointment of a lord-lieutenant after 20th April 1980 is not affected by the fact that the instrument appointing him refers to the power of appointment previously contained in the Local Government Act 1972 or the Local Government (Scotland) Act 1973 and not the corresponding power under the Reserve Forces Act 1980.

This subsection shall come into force on the passing of this Act.

GENERAL NOTE
As previously indicated, the provisions of the 1980 Act, ss.130–138 dealing with the appointment and duties of lord-lieutenants are not repealed. However, this section introduces Sched. 6 which makes minor amendments to those provisions of the 1980 Act.

Subs. (2)
This provision was introduced by the government at the Third Reading stage in the Lords. The background is that the statutory powers governing the appointment by Her Majesty of lord-lieutenants for each county of England and Wales are contained in s.130 of the 1980 Act. That provision was a consolidation measure which repeated verbatim provisions previously contained in the local government legislation of 1972 (England and Wales) and 1973 (Scotland). It transpired, however, that a number of instruments appointing lord-lieutenants omitted reference to the 1980 Act and referred instead to the 1972 and 1973 Acts. Whatever the validity of the appointments of lord-lieutenants after 1980, subs. (2) removes any doubt in that regard or in respect to any acts done by a lord-lieutenant whose instrument of appointment did not refer to the 1980 Act. The subs. came into effect immediately on the passing of the 1996 Act.

Safeguard of employment for members of reserve forces

122.—(1) The Reserve Forces (Safeguard of Employment) Act 1985 shall be amended as follows.

(2) For subsection (1) of section 1 (obligation to reinstate) there shall be substituted the following subsections—

"(1) This section applies to any person who is in permanent service under—

(a) Part IV (special agreements for call out) or Part V (special members) of the Reserve Forces Act 1996;

(b) a call-out order under Part VI of that Act (orders authorising general call out of members of reserve forces); or

(c) a recall order under section 68 (recall of officers and former servicemen) of that Act.

(1A) In this Act "whole-time service" means permanent service to which this section applies."

(3) For subsection (1) of section 17 (prohibition of dismissal for liability to whole-time service) there shall be substituted the following subsection—

"(1) If the employer of a person who may be required to enter upon a period of whole-time service—

(a) terminates that person's employment without his consent at any time when he is not in that service, and

(b) does so solely or mainly by reason of any duties or liabilities which that person may be liable to perform or discharge—
(i) if required to report at any time or place with a view to entering into whole-time service; or
(ii) if he enters upon a period of whole-time service,
the employer is guilty of an offence and liable on summary conviction to a fine not exceeding level 3 on the standard scale."

(4) In section 20(1) (interpretation), for the definition of "whole-time service" there shall be substituted the following definition—
" 'whole-time service' has the meaning given by section 1(1A)."

(5) For subsections (3) and (4) of section 20 (interpretation) there shall be substituted the following subsection—

"(3) A period of whole time service shall not be regarded as having ceased by reason of any absence on leave (including sick leave or maternity leave) before release from service or discharge."

(6) The amendments made by this section do not affect the operation of the Reserve Forces (Safeguard of Employment) Act 1985 in its application to persons liable to be called out or recalled for permanent service under the Reserve Forces Act 1980 or officers liable to be called out or recalled otherwise than under this Act.

DEFINITIONS
"call-out order": s.127(1).
"permanent service": s.127(1).
"recall": s.77.
"recall order": s.77.
"reserve forces": s.1(2).
"special agreement": s.28(1).
"special member": s.127(1).
"whole-time service": subs. (2); Reserve Forces (Safeguard of Employment) Act 1985, s.1A.

GENERAL NOTE
This makes amendments to the Reserve Forces (Safeguard of Employment) Act 1985 (c. 17), which was discussed in the annotation to s.81(2). The effect is to ensure that those called out or recalled for permanent service under Pts. IV to VII of the 1996 Act (that is, the high readiness reserve, sponsored reserve, "general" reservists, and commissioned officers and ex-servicemen subject to recall) receive the same protection in regard to safeguarding their civilian employment as those liable to be called out under the 1980 Act whose protection is continued (subs. (2), substituting a new s.1(1) and 1(A) of the 1985 Act). It further provides that those who report at any time or place in accordance with a call-out notice remain within the protection of the 1985 Act even if they are not accepted into service (subs. (3), substituting a new s.17(1) of the 1985 Act).

It should be noted that the scope of the 1985 Act is limited to the cases of reinstatement and dismissal of employees already in employment (it is, indeed, a criminal offence for an employer to dismiss an employee on the ground that the latter has a call out liability). As noted earlier, the 1985 Act does not make it unlawful for an employer to discriminate against a reservist or intended reservist in deciding whom to appoint to a job vacancy. Nor is it unlawful under the Act to dismiss, or to discriminate against, or to subject to any other detriment, an employee on the ground that he is or may become a reservist, in relation to terms of employment, access to opportunities for promotion, transfer or training, or any other benefits, facilities or services relating to that employment (applications in respect to unfair dismissal, unfair selection for redundancy, sex or racial discrimination may, of course, be made to an industrial tribunal under labour legislation). As noted previously, complaints have been levelled that National Health Service trusts have declined to appoint as medical staff, job applicants who are or may wish to become reservists. It has also been alleged that some trusts are issuing contracts which forbid medical staff from joining the reserves. The 1996 Act does, of course, contain provisions in Pt. VIII whereby employers may seek exemption or deferral in relation to their staff, or seek financial assistance to cover additional costs in securing replacements for reservists. On those grounds, the government believed that it could not accept various amendments to s.122 with a view to prohibiting discrimination (as outlined above) in relation to the employment of reservists or potential reservists. However, one would have thought that an employer, offered the choice of two job applicants with equivalent qualifications and experience, and concerned to secure uninterrupted service (and apart from any training commitments and other duties short of permanent service), is more likely to appoint the non-reservist rather than appoint the reservist and then seek to invoke the provisions of Pt. VIII in the event of call out for, say, humanitarian aid operations in another Continent.

Subs. (5)
The reference to maternity leave relates to the position under the 1985 Act of a female reservist granted maternity leave from her employment while she is on call out. Any doubt as to her entitlement to reinstatement under the 1985 Act (reinstatement being subject to a time limit of six months after release from service or discharge) in view of her absence from employment being extended by maternity leave, is removed by the amendment in subs. (5), which substitutes a new s.20(3) of the 1985 Act.

Subs. (6)
Any residual categories of those still liable to call out or recall, whether under the 1980 Act or under any other provision not covered by the 1996 Act (for example, under the royal prerogative) continue to receive the employment safeguards in the 1985 Act.

Billeting

123.—(1) All provisions for the time being in force in relation to the billeting of the Royal Marines shall be applicable to the men of the reserve naval and marine forces during such time as they attend training or are in permanent service or full-time service under a full-time service commitment.

(2) All powers and authorities in relation to the billeting of the Royal Marines which may be exercised by any colonel, commandant, or commanding officer of any division of Royal Marines, may, for the purpose of billeting the men of the reserve naval and marine forces, be exercised by any officer in the Royal Navy holding the rank of commander, or any higher rank, authorised for the purpose by orders or regulations under section 4.

DEFINITIONS
"full-time service commitment": s.127(1).
"men" ("man"): s.2(4).
"permanent service": s.127(1).
"reserve naval and marine forces": s.127(1).

GENERAL NOTE
This provision appears to deal with a lacuna respecting the men of the reserve naval and marine forces whose existence in peacetime is not subject to the restrictions on a standing army in the Bill of Rights 1689. Billeting provisions in respect to the land forces are to be found in the Army Act 1955, Pt. IV. For the application of the Army Act to the Royal Marines, see s.210 of the 1955 Act. For the application of the Army Act to the reserve forces, see s.211 of the 1955 Act, as amended by Sched. 10 to the 1996 Act.

Exemption from tolls etc.

124.—(1) This section applies to a member of any reserve land, air or marine force when going to or returning from any place at which he is required to attend, and for non-attendance at which he is liable to be punished.

(2) For the purposes of section 184 of the Army Act 1955, section 184 of the Air Force Act 1955 and all other enactments relating to the duties, tolls and ferries which are mentioned in those sections, a person to whom this section applies shall be deemed to be a member of the regular army on duty or (as the case may be) the regular air force on duty.

DEFINITIONS
"member": s.127(2).
"regular air force": s.127(1).

"regular army": s.127(1).
"reserve air force": s.1(2).
"reserve land force": s.1(2).
"reserve marine force": s.127(1).

GENERAL NOTE
This quaint provision enables members of the reserve land, air and marine forces, when travelling to or from a place as part of their duty, to secure exemption, on the same footing as the regular non-naval forces, from the duties and tolls mentioned in s.184 Army/Air Force Acts 1955. Note that under s.184(3), a member of the regular (and, now, reserve) forces, when on duty, is entitled to be carried on a ferry in Scotland at half the normal rate. No comparable provision in regard to ferries elsewhere in the U.K. is mentioned in the section! The provision does not extend to members of the Royal Fleet Reserve.

Absence for voting

125. No member of a reserve force shall be liable, when not in permanent service, to any penalty or punishment on account of his absence from duty in the United Kingdom for voting at—
   (a) any election of a Member of Parliament or a Member of the European Parliament, or
   (b) any local election,
or going to or returning from such voting.

DEFINITIONS
"member of a reserve force": s.127(2).
"permanent service": s.127(1).
"reserve force": s 1(2).

GENERAL NOTE
Liability to punishment will clearly only arise if their absence from duty in order to vote occurs when they are in permanent service. As noted on more than one occasion above, permanent service is service under Pts. IV–VII. Training and other duties under Pt. III, the latter meaning a full-time service commitment or an additional duties commitment do not constitute permanent service (though they do constitute "duty" in relation to service discipline law and for other purposes). Inasmuch as obligations under Pt. III may well be undertaken on the other side of the world, the non-liability to punishment for absence for the purpose of voting in the U.K. during an election will scarcely matter.

Postponement of transfer to the reserve or discharge of servicemen

126. Schedule 7 (amendments of the enactments concerning the postpone-ment of transfer to the reserve or discharge from the regular services of sol-diers, marines, airmen and ratings) shall have effect.

DEFINITION
"regular services": s.127(1).

GENERAL NOTE
Given the new categories of, and conditions for, call out in the 1996 Act, s.126 introduces Sched. 7 which amends the provisions in the Army/Air Force Acts 1955 and the Armed Forces Act 1966 relating to the postponement of transfer to the reserve or discharge from the regular services. It does not affect the situation of commissioned officers. For Sched. 7, see later.

General

Interpretation

127.—(1) In this Act—
      "additional duties commitment" means a commitment under section 25;
      "call-out order" has the meaning given by section 64;
      "the ex-regular reserve forces" has the meaning given by section 2(2);
      "full-time service commitment" means a commitment under section 24;

"man" (except in Part VII) has the meaning given by section 2(4);
"permanent service" includes actual service;
"prescribed" means (except in Part VII) prescribed by orders or regulations under section 4;
"recall" and "recall order" have the meanings given by section 77;
"regular air force" has the same meaning as in the Air Force Act 1955;
"regular army" means the regular forces within the meaning of the Army Act 1955 (but does not include the Royal Marines);
"regular services" means the Royal Navy, the Royal Marines, the regular army or the regular air force;
"the reserve forces", "the reserve naval and marine forces", "the reserve land forces" and "the reserve air forces" have the meaning given by section 1(2);
"reserve marine force" means the Royal Marines Reserve;
"service law" means military law, air-force law or the Naval Discipline Act 1957 (as the case may require);
"special member" means a member of a reserve force who is, by virtue of Part V, a special member of that force;
"term of compulsory service" has the meaning given by section 13(7);
"the volunteer reserve forces" has the meaning given by section 2(3).

(2) Any reference in this Act to a member of a reserve force or a member of the reserve forces is to an officer in, or a man of, that force or any of those forces, as the case may be.

DEFINITIONS
See list in subs. (1).

GENERAL NOTE

Subs. (1)
This is the principal interpretation section which provides definitions of terms used throughout the Act. Note the definition of "regular army". The Army Act 1955, s.225(1) refers to the "regular forces" which are the regular Army and the Royal Marines.

Subs. (2)
A "member" of a reserve force is either an officer or a man (or woman) of a reserve force.

Transitory provisions

128. Schedule 8 (transitory and transitional provisions relating to the organisation of the reserve forces as maintained under the Reserve Forces Act 1980) shall have effect.

DEFINITIONS
"reserve forces": s.1(2).

GENERAL NOTE
This applies Sched. 8 which deals with transitional provisions concerning the organisation of the reserve forces. See annotations to Sched. 8.

Application of Act to persons currently serving in the reserve forces or regular services

129.—(1) Schedule 9 shall have effect with respect to the application of this Act in relation to members of the reserve forces who are members of the transitional class.

(2) Nothing in the Reserve Forces Act 1980 shall apply to a member of a reserve force who is not a member of the transitional class or, in the case of a person who is to be transferred to the reserve from the regular services, is not capable of becoming a member of the transitional class.

(3) In this Act "the transitional class", in relation to members of the reserve forces, shall be construed in accordance with Part I of Schedule 9.

DEFINITIONS
"members of the reserve forces": s.127(2).
"regular services": s.127(1).
"transitional class; the": subs. (3).

GENERAL NOTE
Section 129 introduces Sched. 9 which applies to members of a "transitional class" of reservists (in which one may find "transitional members", "transitional officers" and "transitional men"!). A detailed explanation of the transitional class and its members is provided in Pt. I of the Sched. Subsection (1) indicates that Sched. 9 specifies those sections of the 1996 Act (in addition to the transitional provisions of the 1980 Act) which apply to members of the transitional class. In other words, this transitional class covers both those individuals with "reserved" rights to be called out under the not-yet-repealed provisions of the 1980 Act, and also those officers whose liability for call out is effectively governed by the royal prerogative rather than by statute. Such categories will be able to elect to become fully subject to the 1996 Act prior to the repeal of the residual provisions of the 1980 Act. In this event, the residual provisions of the 1980 Act, though as yet unrepealed, will no longer apply to their cases. The obverse is that certain sections of the 1980 Act continue to be in force while there are individuals subject to them. The transitional period could even last for a further 43 years from the commencement of the 1996 Act. Presumably this would apply only in respect to a "transitional officer" liable for service up to the age of 65. It would be a shorter maximum period in the case of those who had more recently joined the regular services without electing to become subject to the call out liability of the 1996 Act.

Power to make transitional, consequential etc. provisions

130.—(1) The Secretary of State may by regulations make such transitional and consequential provisions and such savings as he considers necessary or expedient in preparation for, in connection with, or in consequence of—
  (a) the coming into force of any provision of this Act; or
  (b) the operation of any enactment repealed or amended by a provision of this Act during any period when the repeal or amendment is not wholly in force.
  (2) Regulations under this section—
  (a) may make modifications of any enactment contained in this or in any other Act;
  (b) shall be made by statutory instrument which shall be subject to annulment in pursuance of a resolution of either House of Parliament.

GENERAL NOTE

Subs. (1)
The kind of regulation authorised under subs. (1)(a) might be one relating to s.93(1), authorising the Secretary of State to make rules with respect to the practice and procedure in regard to appeal tribunals. With respect to subs. (1)(b), it might be one which laid down when the repeal of provisions under the 1980 Act, as envisaged in s.129, comes into effect.

Subs. (2)
Paragraph (a) confers enormous and, perhaps, disturbing power on the Secretary of State, particularly in relation to the words "in any other Act". The constitutional propriety of such power may be open to question. *Cf.*, the enormous power of the Secretary of State, under the Deregulation and Contracting Out Act 1994 (c. 40), s.1, to repeal by regulation provisions in previous statutes inconsistent with the objectives of the 1994 Act.

Consequential amendments and repeals

131.—(1) Schedule 10 (consequential amendments) shall have effect.
  (2) The enactments specified in Schedule 11 (which include some that are spent) are repealed to the extent specified.

GENERAL NOTE
Schedules 10 and 11 are given effect. See below.

Short title, extent and commencement

132.—(1) This Act may be cited as the Reserve Forces Act 1996.

(2) This Act extends to Northern Ireland.

(3) Her Majesty may by Order in Council direct that any of the provisions of this Act shall extend, with such exceptions and modifications as appear to Her Majesty to be appropriate, to the Channel Islands and the Isle of Man.

(4) This Act shall come into force on such day as the Secretary of State may by order made by statutory instrument appoint; and different days may be appointed for different purposes.

GENERAL NOTE
See the "Extent" and "Commencement" comments after the Introduction and General Note, above.

SCHEDULES

Section 9   SCHEDULE 1

ENLISTMENT

Conditions for enlistment

1.—(1) An enlisting officer shall not enlist any person as a man in a reserve force unless he is satisfied that the person concerned has been given a notice under sub-paragraph (2), understands it and wishes to be enlisted.

(2) A person offering to enlist shall be given a notice in such form as may be prescribed setting out the questions to be answered on attestation and stating the general conditions of the engagement to be entered into by him and such other matters as may be prescribed.

(3) The attestation paper to be used for the purpose of attesting recruits to a reserve force shall be in such form as may be prescribed.

2.—(1) An enlisting officer shall not enlist a person under the appropriate minimum age unless consent to the enlistment has been given in writing by a person with—

(a) parental responsibility (within the meaning of the Children Act 1989 or the Children (Northern Ireland) Order 1995) for the person offering to enlist; or

(b) parental responsibilities (within the meaning of section 1(3) of the Children (Scotland) Act 1995) in relation to that person.

(2) Where the enlisting officer is satisfied, by the production of a certified copy of an entry in the register of births or by any other evidence appearing to him to be sufficient, that a person offering to enlist has or has not attained the appropriate minimum age, that person shall be deemed for the purposes of this Act to have attained, or as the case may be, not to have attained, that age.

(3) A document purporting to be a certificate signed by the enlisting officer, stating that he is satisfied as mentioned in sub-paragraph (2), shall be sufficient evidence, until the contrary is proved, that he was so satisfied.

Procedure on attestation

3.—(1) The procedure for enlisting a person (in this paragraph referred to as "the recruit") in a reserve force is as follows.

(2) The enlisting officer shall warn the recruit that if he makes any false answers to the questions to be read out to him he will be liable to be punished as provided by this Act.

(3) He shall then read, or cause to be read, to the recruit the questions set out in the attestation paper and satisfy himself that he understands each of those questions and that his answers have been duly recorded in the attestation paper.

(4) He shall then ask the recruit to make and sign the declaration set out in the attestation paper as to the truth of the answers and shall administer to him the oath of allegiance as set out in the attestation paper.

(5) Upon signing the declaration and taking the oath the recruit shall become a man of the reserve force in question.

(6) The enlisting officer shall by signature attest, in the manner required by the attestation paper, that the requirements of this Act as to the attestation of the recruit have been carried out and deliver the attestation paper duly dated to such person as may be prescribed.

(7) When, in accordance with orders or regulations under section 4, the recruit is finally approved for service, the officer by whom he is approved shall at his request furnish him with a certified copy of the attestation paper.

Validity of attestation and enlistment

4.—(1) This paragraph applies where a person has signed the declaration required by paragraph 3.

(2) The validity of the person's enlistment shall not be called in question on the ground of any error or omission in his attestation paper.

(3) If within 3 months from the date on which the person signed the declaration he claims that his enlistment is invalid—

(a) by reason of any non-compliance with the requirements of this Act as to enlistment or attestation; or

(b) on any other ground whatsoever (not being an error or omission in his attestation paper) on which apart from this sub-paragraph the validity of his enlistment could have been called in question,

the claim shall be submitted as soon as may be to the Defence Council, and, if the claim is well founded, the Defence Council shall cause him to be discharged with all convenient speed.

(4) If when the person signed the declaration he had not attained the appropriate minimum age, and within 3 months from the date on which he signed the declaration he, or any person whose consent to the enlistment was required under paragraph 2(1) but who did not duly consent, claims that his enlistment is invalid—

(a) by reason of any non-compliance with the requirements of this Act as to enlistment or attestation; or

(b) on any other ground whatsoever (not being an error or omission in his attestation paper) on which apart from this sub-paragraph the validity of his enlistment could have been called in question,

the claim shall be submitted as soon as may be to the Defence Council, and, if the claim is well founded, the Defence Council shall cause him to be discharged with all convenient speed.

(5) If no claim under sub-paragraph (3) or (4) is made within 3 months from the date on which he signed the declaration, the person shall be deemed to have been validly enlisted notwithstanding any such non-compliance or other grounds as aforesaid.

(6) Notwithstanding any such non-compliance or other grounds as aforesaid, or the making of a claim under sub-paragraph (3) or (4), the person shall be deemed to be a man of the reserve force in question until his discharge.

(7) Nothing in this paragraph shall be construed as prejudicing the determination of any question as to the term for which a person was enlisted or as preventing the discharge of a person who has not claimed his discharge.

False answers in attestation papers

5.—(1) Any person appearing before an enlisting officer for the purpose of being attested who knowingly or recklessly makes a false answer to any question contained in the attestation paper and put to him by or by the direction of the enlisting officer is guilty of an offence.

(2) A person guilty of an offence under sub-paragraph (1) is liable on summary conviction to imprisonment for a term not exceeding 3 months or a fine not exceeding level 4 on the standard scale (or both); and he may be proceeded against summarily notwithstanding that he has since become subject to service law.

(3) A person guilty of an offence under sub-paragraph (1) who has since become and remains subject to service law is liable on conviction by court-martial to imprisonment for a term not exceeding 3 months or to any less punishment provided by service law.

Evidence as to attestation papers

6.—(1) With respect to evidence in proceedings under Part X, whether before a court-martial, a civil court or otherwise—

(a) a document purporting—

(i) to be a copy of the attestation paper signed by any person; and

(ii) to be certified to be a true copy by a person stated in the certificate to have the custody of the attestation paper,

shall be evidence of the enlistment of the person attested; and

(b) the attestation paper purporting to be signed by a person on his enlistment shall be evidence of his having given the answers to questions which he is recorded in that paper as having given.

(2) In this paragraph "civil court" has the same meaning as in Part X.

Meaning of "appropriate minimum age"

7. In this Schedule "appropriate minimum age" means the age of 17 years and 6 months, except that in such classes of case as may be prescribed it means the age of 17 years.

DEFINITIONS
"appropriate minimum age": para. 7.
"civil court": s.109.
"enlisting officer": s.9(2).
"man": s.127(1).
"parental responsibilities": Children (Scotland) Act 1995 (c. 36), s.1(3).
"parental responsibility": Children Act 1989 (c. 41), s.3; Children (Northern Ireland) Order 1995 (S.I 1995, No. 755 (N.I. 2)).
"prescribed": s.127(1).
"recruit; the": para. 3(1).
"reserve force": s.1(2).
"service law": s.127(1).

GENERAL NOTE

Paras. 1 and 2
These paragraphs lay down the detailed procedures for enlistment in the reserves, supplemented by orders or regulations issued under s.4 in respect of particular matters. The latter will cover, for example, the form of the notice to be given to the potential recruit, which sets out the attestation questions, general conditions of engagements and any other matters prescribed in the order or regulation (see para. 2(2)). The enlistment procedure is not applicable to officers. The latter may be granted commissions from the Sovereign. With respect to the conditions for enlistment, the duties on the enlisting officer (as he is defined in s.9(2)) to satisfy himself as to certain matters are laid down. He must be satisfied, for example, that the notice is understood by the potential recruit and that the latter has attained the appropriate minimum age. Alternatively, the enlisting officer must be satisfied that there is written parental consent. See paras. 1(2) and 2(1).

Para. 3
The formal attestation procedure itself is laid down in para. 3. Whereas sub-para. (5) states that the recruit becomes a member of a reserve force on signing a declaration and on taking the oath of allegiance, sub-para. (7) refers to the recruit being "finally approved for service" by an officer. Does sub-para. (7) therefore qualify in some way sub-para. (5)?

Para. 4
Under para. 4 regarding the validity of attestation and enlistment, the recruit has three months in which to claim his enlistment was invalid (not being based on any error or omission in his attestation paper). On submission of a claim, the Defence Council will cause the matter to be investigated to discover whether the claim is well-founded. In the Lords, it was unsuccessfully proposed to substitute "proved" for "well-founded". The latter is in fact the terminology which applies in respect to enlistment in the regular forces. See Army/Air Force Acts 1955, s.18 and Armed Forces Act 1966, s.10. It does not seem to be the case that final approval for service in para. 3(7) only occurs after the three-month period has expired. Note also in regard to non-acceptance, para. 4(5) in respect to valid enlistment and membership of a reserve force.

Para. 5
Note the need for intent in sub-para. (1). As to "recklessly", is it objective or subjective recklessness? See, for example, *R. v. Caldwell* [1982] A.C. 341 for the objective approach (although not extended to the circumstances envisaged in para. 5(1)), and *R. v. Cunningham* [1957] 2 Q.B. 396 for the subjective approach. Under sub-para. (2), the level 4 maximum is currently set at £2,500 under the Criminal Justice Act 1982 (c. 48), s.37. Alternative jurisdictions, either service or civil, are available (but not, of course, both). Under service law, imprisonment (sub-para. (3)) is served in a civil prison. The service authorities only maintain a tri-service detention centre, the Military Corrective Training Centre, Colchester.

Section 100   SCHEDULE 2

DESERTERS AND ABSENTEES WITHOUT LEAVE

Preliminary

1.—(1) This Schedule applies in relation to anyone who is, or is suspected of being, a deserter or absentee without leave from a reserve force.

(2) In the application of this Schedule to Scotland and Northern Ireland, for references to a magistrates' court there shall be substituted–
  (a) in Scotland, references to the sheriff sitting as a court of summary jurisdiction; and
  (b) in Northern Ireland, references to a court of summary jurisdiction.

Arrest

2.—(1) Where a constable has reasonable grounds for suspecting that a person is a member of a reserve force who has deserted or is absent without leave, he may arrest that person without a warrant.

(2) Where no constable is available, any person may arrest a person he has reasonable grounds for suspecting is a member of a reserve force who has deserted or is absent without leave.

(3) Any person having authority to issue a warrant for the arrest of a person charged with a criminal offence, if satisfied by evidence on oath that there is, or is reasonably suspected of being, within his jurisdiction a member of a reserve force who—
  (a) has deserted or is absent without leave; or
  (b) is reasonably suspected of having deserted or being absent without leave,
may issue a warrant authorising his arrest.

(4) Any person arrested as a deserter or absentee without leave from a reserve force shall as soon as practicable be brought before a magistrates' court.

Proceedings before a civil court where persons suspected of illegal absence

3.—(1) Paragraphs 4 and 5 apply in the case of a person ("the accused") who is brought before a magistrates' court and alleged to be a member of a reserve force who has deserted or is absent without leave.

(2) The provisions of the Magistrates' Courts Act 1980—
  (a) relating to the constitution and procedure of magistrates' courts acting as examining Justices and conferring powers of adjournment and remand on such courts so acting; and
  (b) as to evidence and the issue and enforcement of summonses or warrants to secure the attendance of witnesses,
shall apply to proceedings to which paragraph 4 or 5 applies.

(3) In the application of this Schedule to Scotland and Northern Ireland, the reference in sub-paragraph (2) to provisions of the Magistrates' Courts Act 1980 shall be construed as a reference to any corresponding enactment in force as respects courts of summary jurisdiction.

4.—(1) This paragraph applies where the accused admits that he is illegally absent from a reserve force and the court is satisfied of the truth of the admission.

(2) If the accused is not in custody for some cause other than illegal absence from his reserve force, the court shall—
  (a) cause him to be delivered into military, air-force or naval custody (as the case may require) in such manner as the court may think fit; or
  (b) commit him to a prison, police station or other place provided for the confinement of persons in custody, to be kept there for such reasonable period as the court may specify or until sooner delivered into military, air-force or naval custody (as the case may require).

(3) If the accused is in custody for some other cause, the court may act as mentioned in sub-paragraph (2).

(4) Any period specified as mentioned in sub-paragraph (2)(b)—
  (a) shall not exceed such time as appears to the court reasonably necessary to enable the accused to be delivered into military, air-force or naval custody; and
  (b) may be extended by the court from time to time if it appears to the court reasonably necessary to do so for that purpose.

5.—(1) This paragraph applies where—
  (a) the accused does not admit that he is illegally absent from a reserve force; or
  (b) the court is not satisfied of the truth of any such admission.

(2) The court shall consider the evidence with a view to determining whether there is sufficient evidence to justify his being tried under this Act for an offence of desertion or absence without leave.

(3) Where the court considers that there is sufficient evidence to justify his being tried under this Act for an offence of desertion or absence without leave, the court shall (unless he is in custody for some other cause) cause him to be delivered into military, air-force or naval custody (as the case may require) or commit him as mentioned in paragraph 4(2)(b).

If the accused is in custody for some other cause, the court may act as mentioned in this paragraph.

(4) If the court does not consider that there is sufficient evidence to justify the trial of the accused for an offence of desertion or absence without leave, he shall be discharged.

Surrender to police

6.—(1) Where a person surrenders himself to a constable as being illegally absent from a reserve force—
- (a) the constable shall, unless the person concerned surrenders himself at a police station, bring him to a police station; and
- (b) the police officer in charge of the police station to which that person is brought, or at which he surrendered himself, shall forthwith inquire into his case.

(2) If it appears to that police officer that the person concerned is illegally absent from a reserve force, he may—
- (a) cause him to be delivered into military, air-force or naval custody (as the case may require) without bringing him before a magistrates' court; or
- (b) bring him before a magistrates' court.

Certificates of arrest or surrender

7.—(1) Where a person is delivered into military, air-force or naval custody under this Schedule, there shall be handed over with him a certificate in such form as may be prescribed signed by a justice of the peace.

(2) The certificate shall contain such particulars as may be prescribed as to the arrest or surrender of the person concerned and the proceedings before the court.

(3) For any such certificate there shall be payable to the clerk of the court, by such person as the Defence Council may direct, such fee (if any) as may be prescribed.

(4) In this paragraph and paragraph 8, "prescribed" means prescribed by regulations made by the Secretary of State by statutory instrument under section 189 of the Army Act 1955 (for a person delivered into military custody), section 189 of the Air Force Act 1955 (for a person delivered into air-force custody) or section 110 of the Naval Discipline Act 1957 (for a person delivered into naval custody).

8.—(1) Where a person is delivered into military, air-force or naval custody under this Schedule without being brought before a court, there shall be handed over with him a certificate in such form as may be prescribed signed by the police officer who caused him to be delivered into custody.

(2) The certificate shall contain such particulars as may be prescribed relating to the surrender of the person concerned.

9.—(1) In proceedings for an offence under section 96 a document purporting to be a duly signed certificate under paragraph 7 or 8 shall be evidence of the matters stated in the document.

(2) In proceedings for such an offence against a person who was taken into military, air-force or naval custody on arrest or surrender, a certificate—
- (a) purporting to be signed by a provost officer or by any other officer in charge of the guard-room or other place where that person was confined on being taken into custody; and
- (b) stating the fact, date, time and place of arrest or surrender,

shall be evidence of the matters stated in the certificate.

Duties of governors of prisons and others to receive deserters and absentees

10.—(1) It shall be the duty of the governor of a civil prison—
- (a) to receive any person duly committed to that prison by a magistrates' court as being illegally absent from a reserve force; and
- (b) to detain him until (in accordance with the directions of the court) he is delivered into military, air-force or naval custody.

(2) Sub-paragraph (1) shall apply to the person having charge of any police station or other place (not being a prison) provided for the confinement of persons in custody as it applies to the governor of a prison.

DEFINITIONS
"accused": para. 3.
"civil court": s.109.
"prescribed": para. 7(4).

GENERAL NOTE
This Schedule deals with the arrest and subsequent treatment of deserters and absentees without leave from a reserve force. Arrest powers without a warrant are granted to a constable or to

any person if a constable is not available. Reasonable grounds for suspicion must exist, although it is not necessary for the arrester to establish that the arrestee would otherwise have escaped (para. 2(1) and (2)). Following arrest and his appearance before a magistrates' court (or equivalent in Scotland or Northern Ireland), further disposal is dependant on whether he admits or disputes illegal absence (a secular term which clearly covers both absence without leave and desertion). Note that under para. 4(2), the court "shall" dispose of him in accordance with sub-sub-paras. (a) and (b). However, under para. 4(3), if the accused is already in civilian custody for a separate matter, the court has the option ("may") to hand him over to service custody. Thus the civilian authorities could retain custody of him with a view to criminal proceedings in the civil courts in respect of matters other than illegal absence from the reserve forces. If the accused disputes the charge of illegal absence, but the magistrates conclude there is sufficient *prima facie* evidence thereof, then para. 5(3) states that he must be disposed of in the same manner as in para. 4(2)(a) and (b). If, however, there are also charges other than illegal absence, then according to the last sentence in para. 5(3), the civil court has the same option ("may") as is indicated in para. 4(3).

With respect to surrender to the police in para. 6, note that a constable has discretion either to have the person concerned delivered into service custody or to bring him before a magistrates' court (para. 6(2)). This contrasts with the situation in para. 2(4) where, on arrest, a person is to be brought as soon as practicable before a magistrates' court. The surrender to the police of an illegal absentee from the reserve forces would appear to be a "clear-cut" case otherwise justifying an immediate transfer of the person to service custody. However, the fact that the draftsman saw fit to make provision in para. 6(2)(b) for procedure before a magistrates' court (which would no doubt seek to satisfy itself that the person was indeed an illegal absentee who surrendered to the police) raises the question why individual responsibility, and possibly subjective judgment, is granted to a constable in the form of the option in para. 6(2)(a). *Cf.*, similar provisions in the Army/Air Force Acts 1955, s.188. Paragraphs 7, 8 and 9 deal with certificates of arrest or of surrender, and para. 10 states the duties of prison governors and others to receive and detain illegal absentees or alleged illegal absentees.

Section 108   SCHEDULE 3

EVIDENCE

General provisions as to evidence

1. This Schedule has effect with respect to evidence in proceedings under Part X and proceedings for an offence under any other Part of this Act, whether before a court-martial, a civil court or otherwise.

2. A letter, return or other document stating that any person—
   (a) was or was not serving at any specified time or during any specified period in any part of Her Majesty's forces or was discharged from any part of those forces at or before any specified time;
   (b) held or did not hold at any specified time any specified rank or appointment in any of those forces, or had at or before any specified time been attached, posted or transferred to any part of those forces;
   (c) at any specified time or during any specified period was or was not serving or held or did not hold any rank or appointment in any particular country or place; or
   (d) was or was not at any specified time authorised to use or wear any decoration, badge, wound stripe or emblem,
shall, if it purports to be issued by or on behalf of the Defence Council or by a person authorised by them, be evidence of the matters stated in the document.

3.—(1) A record made in any service book or other document prescribed by Queen's Regulations for the purposes of this paragraph, being a record—
   (a) made in pursuance of any Act or of Queen's Regulations, or otherwise in pursuance of military, air-force or naval duty, as the case may be; and
   (b) purporting to be signed by the commanding officer or by any person whose duty it was to make the record,
shall be evidence of the facts stated therein.

(2) A copy of a record (including the signature thereto) in any book or other document to which sub-paragraph (1) applies, if it purports to be certified to be a true copy by a person stated in the certificate to have the custody of the book or other document, shall be evidence of the record.

4. A document purporting to be issued by order of the Defence Council and to contain instructions or regulations given or made by the Defence Council shall be evidence of the giving of the instructions or making of the regulations and of their contents.

5. A certificate purporting to be issued by or on behalf of the Defence Council or by a person authorised by them, and stating—
  (a) that a decoration of a description specified in or annexed to the certificate is or is not a military, naval or air-force decoration; or
  (b) that a badge, wound stripe or emblem of a description specified in or annexed to the certificate is or is not one supplied or authorised by the Defence Council,
shall be evidence of the matters stated in the certificate.

6. A certificate purporting to be signed by a person's commanding officer or any officer authorised by him to give the certificate, and stating the contents of, or of any part of, standing orders or other routine orders of a continuing nature made for—
  (a) any formation, unit or body of—
    (i) the regular army or any reserve land force;
    (ii) the Royal Marines or the Royal Marines Reserve; or
    (iii) the regular air force or any reserve air force;
  (b) any division, class or other body of the Royal Navy, the Royal Fleet Reserve or the Royal Naval Reserve;
  (c) any command or other area, garrison or place; or
  (d) any ship, submarine, train or aircraft,
shall in proceedings against the person concerned be evidence of the matters stated in the certificate.

7. Where, in relation to one reserve force, any document would be evidence in any proceedings under Part X by virtue of this Schedule, or paragraph 6 of Schedule 1, that document shall in like manner, subject to the same conditions and for the like purpose be evidence in the like proceedings in relation to any other reserve force.

Proceedings for offences under section 95

8. Where a man of any reserve force is required by or in pursuance of orders or regulations under section 4 to attend at any place, a certificate—
  (a) purporting to be signed by any officer or person who is mentioned in it as being appointed to be present at that place for the purpose of inspecting men of the force in question or for any other purpose connected with that force; and
  (b) stating that the man failed to attend in accordance with that requirement,
shall without proof of the signature or appointment of the officer or person be evidence of the failure in any proceedings relating to such a failure under section 95.

Proof of outcome of civil trial

9.—(1) Where a person subject to service law has been tried before a civil court (whether at the time of the trial he was or was not subject to service law), a certificate signed by the clerk of the court and stating all or any of the following matters—
  (a) that the person concerned was tried before the court for an offence specified in the certificate;
  (b) the result of the trial;
  (c) what judgment or order was given or made by the court; and
  (d) that other offences specified in the certificate were taken into consideration at the trial,
shall be evidence of the matters stated in the certificate.

(2) The clerk of the court shall, if required by the commanding officer of the person in question or any other officer, furnish a certificate under this paragraph and shall be paid such fee as may be prescribed by regulations made by the Secretary of State under section 199 of the Army Act 1955, section 199 of the Air Force Act 1955 or section 129B of the Naval Discipline Act 1957, as the case may be.

(3) A document purporting to be a certificate under this paragraph and to be signed by the clerk of the court shall, unless the contrary is shown, be deemed to be such a certificate.

(4) References in this paragraph to the clerk of the court include references to his deputy and to any other person having the custody of the records of the court.

DEFINITIONS
  "civil court": s.109.
  "regular air force": s.127(1).
  "regular army": s.127(1).
  "reserve air force": s.1(2).
  "reserve force": s.1(2).
  "reserve land force": s.1(2).
  "service law": s.127(1).

GENERAL NOTE

This Schedule contains provisions concerning evidence in proceedings under the Act. Broadly, it provides that letters or documents purporting to be issued by or on behalf of the Defence Council are to be evidence of various matters relating to the service of any person in the armed forces, whether regular or reserve. These matters may include details as to his rank, post (para. 2) and decorations (paras. 2 and 5). The letters or documents may also be evidence of records to be kept in accordance with Queen's Regulations (para. 3) or of instructions or regulations given or made by the Defence Council (para. 4), or of standing or routine orders (para. 6).

The Schedule is introduced by s.108 to which reference back should be made. Note that the general provisions as to evidence relate to proceedings under Pt. X, which is the part dealing with offences against good order and discipline. This includes the wide-ranging s.95, which expands the reach of both civilian and service law in relation to reservists (see para. 8), and also offences relating to illegal absences (ss.96–102). Note, also, that the provisions as to evidence are applicable in both courts-martial and in civil courts (para. 1); see also para. 9 in respect to a certificate from the clerk of a civil court.

Section 111   SCHEDULE 4

PROVISIONS OF SCHEMES FOR THE CONSTITUTION OF ASSOCIATIONS

1.—(1) A scheme for the constitution of an association ("a scheme") shall provide—

(a) for the date of the establishment of the association;

(b) for the incorporation of the association by an appropriate name;

(c) for appointment as members of the association of naval members, marine members, military members and air force members;

(d) for the appointment as members of the association by the Defence Council, after consultation with, and on the recommendation of, the bodies to be represented, of representatives of such of the local authorities wholly or partly within the area for which the association is established as the Defence Council may from time to time determine;

(e) for the mode of appointment, dismissal, term of office and rotation of members of the association and the filling of casual vacancies;

(f) for the election of a chairman and a vice-chairman or vice-chairmen by the association and for defining their powers and duties;

(g) for the appointment by the association, subject to the approval of the Defence Council, of a secretary and other officers and members of the staff of the association;

(h) for the procedure to be adopted, including the appointment of committees and the delegation to committees of any of the powers or duties of the association;

(i) for enabling flag, general or air officers of any part of Her Majesty's forces, or officers deputed by them, to attend the meetings of the association, and to speak but not to vote.

(2) A scheme shall secure that the aggregate number of naval members, marine members, military members and air force members are not less than half of the whole number of members of the association.

(3) A secretary or other officer or member of the staff who is in the employment of the association by virtue of the provisions of an order made by the Defence Council in exercise of the powers conferred upon the Defence Council by section 119 shall be deemed for the purposes of sub-paragraph (1)(g) above (and the corresponding purposes of the scheme concerned) to have been appointed by the association.

2. A scheme for an association in England and Wales or Northern Ireland (but not for an association established for an area that includes Greater London) shall provide—

(a) for constituting as president of the association the lord-lieutenant of one of the counties or parts of counties for which the association is established, as the Defence Council may from time to time think fit, or, failing any of those lord-lieutenants, such other person as the Defence Council may think fit; and

(b) for constituting as vice-presidents of the association the lord-lieutenants of any of those counties or parts of counties (if they are willing to act) and such other persons (if any) as the Defence Council may think fit.

3. A scheme for an association in Scotland shall provide—

(a) in the case where an association area coincides with a local government area or where a local government area contains two or more association areas, for the selection by the Defence Council of the president and vice-presidents of the association from the lord-lieutenants residing in the local government area or from such other persons as the Defence Council may think fit; or

(b) in the case where an association area falls within two or more local government areas, for the selection by the Defence Council of the president and vice-presidents of the association from the lord-lieutenants residing in those local government areas or from such other persons as the Defence Council may think fit.

4. A scheme for an association established for an area including Greater London shall provide for constituting the lord-lieutenant of Greater London or failing him, such other person as the Defence Council may think fit, president of the association.

5. A scheme may provide—

(a) for the appointment as members of the association by the Defence Council, of representatives of universities whose activities are carried on wholly or partly within the area for which the association is established;

(b) for the appointment as members of the association by the Defence Council, of persons representing the Army Cadet Force, the Air Training Corps, the Combined Cadet Force and the Sea Cadet Corps;

(c) for the appointment as members of the association by the Defence Council, of persons representing employers, and persons employed, in the area for which the association is established;

(d) for the appointment of co-opted members;

(e) for dividing the area for which the association is established into two or more parts and for establishing sub-associations for any of the parts; and

(f) for delegating to a sub-association such of the powers and duties of the association as may be approved by the Defence Council and regulating the relations of a sub-association to the association and, where any association has established more than one sub-association, regulating the relations of one sub-association to another.

6. A scheme shall provide that of the chairman and the vice-chairman or vice-chairmen at least one shall be a naval or marine member of the association and at least one shall be a military member of the association and at least one an air force member of the association.

7. A scheme may contain any consequential, supplemental or transitory provisions which may appear to be necessary or expedient for the purposes of the scheme, and also as respects any matter for which provision may be made by regulations under Part XI and for which it appears desirable to make special provision affecting the association established by the scheme.

8.—(1) A scheme for an association established for an area including or including any part of the counties of Kent, East Sussex and West Sussex may provide that the Lord Warden of the Cinque Ports shall ex-officio be a member of the association.

(2) A scheme for an association established for an area including or including any part of the counties of Devon and Cornwall may provide that the Warden of the Stannaries shall ex-officio be a member of the association.

9.—(1) The Governor of the Isle of Wight shall ex-officio be a member of an association established for an area including the Isle of Wight.

(2) The Lieutenant-Governor of the Isle of Man shall ex-officio be a member of an association established for an area including the Isle of Man.

(3) The Lord Mayor of the City of London shall ex-officio be president of a sub-association established for the City of London.

10. In this Schedule—

"air force member" means one who is a member or former member of Her Majesty's air forces or who is specially qualified by his interest in and knowledge of matters relating to aviation;

"county" means, in relation to Wales, a preserved county (as defined by section 64 of the Local Government (Wales) Act 1994);

"marine member" means one who is a member or former member of the Royal Marines or the Royal Marines Reserve or who is specially qualified by his interest in and knowledge of matters affecting marine forces;

"military member" means one who is a member or former member of Her Majesty's military forces or who is specially qualified by his interest in and knowledge of military matters;

"naval member" means one who is a member or former member of the Royal Navy or the Royal Naval Reserve or who is specially qualified by his interest in and knowledge of naval matters.

DEFINITIONS

"air force member": para. 10.

"association": s.110(1).

"county": para. 10.

"marine member": para. 10.

"military member": para. 10.

"naval member": para. 10.

"scheme": para. 1(1).

GENERAL NOTE
Section 110 confers power on the Defence Council to make orders creating local TAVRAs for any area of the U.K. Section 111 states that such local associations shall be constituted and its members appointed and hold office in accordance with a scheme for the constitution of such associations. That scheme is drawn up in Sched. 4. The membership comprises service and civilian members, the former being not less than half the total membership (paras. 1(1)(c) and (d) and 2). No maximum numbers are laid down. Provision is made for electing a chairman and vice-chairman (paras. 1(1)(f) and 6) and for appointing committees to whom powers may be delegated (para. 1(1)(h)). Ex-officio members are identified by their office (paras. 8 and 9). Civilian members may also be co-opted or appointed from universities, from the cadet forces and from representatives of employers and employees (para. 5(a)).

Section 120   SCHEDULE 5

CHARITABLE PROPERTY ON DISBANDING OF UNITS

PART I

PRELIMINARY

Designation of successor to disbanded unit

1.—(1) A warrant of Her Majesty may designate, for the purposes of this Schedule, any unit of a reserve force as the successor to any unit or other body of the same or any other reserve force which has been or is to be disbanded.

(2) The Secretary of State shall send a copy of any such warrant to—

(a) the Charity Commissioners;

(b) the Lord Advocate;

(c) the Department of Health and Social Services for Northern Ireland; and

(d) a trustee of each charity in England and Wales or Northern Ireland, or a person concerned in the management or control of each recognised body, affected by the warrant by virtue of the following provisions of this Schedule.

(3) A copy of a warrant required to be sent under this paragraph may be sent by post; and any such copy shall be sent so as to arrive on or before the day on which the warrant comes into force and, in any event, not more than 14 days from the day on which the warrant is made.

General interpretation

2. In this Schedule—

"disbanded unit" means a unit for which a successor is designated under paragraph 1;

"charity" has the same meaning (in relation to England and Wales) as in the Charities Act 1993 and (in relation to Northern Ireland) as in the Charities Act (Northern Ireland) 1964;

"recognised body" has the same meaning as in Part I of the Law Reform (Miscellaneous Provisions) (Scotland) Act 1990;

"warrant" means a warrant making such a designation,

and references to disbandment of a body of a reserve force (however expressed) include references to its amalgamation with another unit or body.

PART II

SUCCESSION TO CHARITABLE PROPERTY: ENGLAND AND WALES

Effect of designation of successor to disbanded unit

3.—(1) On and after the day on which a warrant comes into force, any charitable property which is held for the purposes of the disbanded unit in question shall (subject to the provisions of this Part of this Schedule) be held for the corresponding purposes, or most nearly corresponding purposes, of the successor unit designated by the warrant.

(2) In this Part of this Schedule "charitable property" means any property belonging to a charity.

(3) The same jurisdiction and powers shall be exercisable in relation to any charity owning property to which sub-paragraph (1) applies as would be exercisable if that sub-paragraph were not a provision of an Act of Parliament regulating that charity.

Exclusion of charitable property from paragraph 3

4.—(1) If the Charity Commissioners consider that paragraph 3(1) should not apply to all or any of the charitable property held for the purposes of a disbanded unit, they may make an order providing that paragraph 3(1) shall not apply or shall cease to apply to that property or part.

(2) An order under this paragraph may be made at any time within the period of 6 months beginning with the day on which the warrant is made.

5.—(1) If a charity affected by a warrant or any trustee of, or person interested in, such a charity considers that paragraph 3(1) should not apply to all or any of the property held by the charity for the purposes of the disbanded unit in question, then the charity, trustee or person interested, as the case may be, may apply to the court for an order providing that paragraph 3(1) shall cease to apply to that property or part.

(2) An application under this paragraph—
(a) may be made at any time within the period of 6 months beginning with the day on which the warrant comes into force; and
(b) is subject to subsections (2) to (5) of section 33 of the Charities Act 1993 (proceedings not to be begun without the consent of the Charity Commissioners or leave of a judge of the High Court),

and for the purposes of subsection (5) of that section an application for an order of the Commissioners authorising proceedings under this paragraph shall be deemed to be refused if it is not granted during the period of one month beginning with the day on which the application is received by the Commissioners.

(3) In this paragraph "the court" has the same meaning as in the Charities Act 1993.

Application of property otherwise than under paragraph 3

6. In any case where—
(a) the Secretary of State requests the Charity Commissioners to make provision with respect to any charitable property which is held for the purposes of a unit of a reserve force that has been or is to be disbanded; or
(b) an order is made under paragraph 4 or 5 excluding any charitable property so held from the operation of paragraph 3(1),

the Commissioners may, notwithstanding anything in subsection (4) of section 16 of the Charities Act 1993 (limit on jurisdiction to make schemes etc. for the protection of charities), exercise their jurisdiction under that section with respect to the property to which the request or order relates.

Validity of certain acts by trustees

7. Neither a warrant nor any order under paragraph 4 or 5 shall affect the validity of anything done or omitted with respect to any property affected by the warrant or order before a copy of the warrant or order is received by a trustee of the charity in question.

Saving for interests in property contingent on disbandment of unit

8. Nothing in this Part of this Schedule applies to any property held by a charity for the purposes of a unit that has been or is to be disbanded if, under the terms on which the property is so held—
(a) any interest of the charity in the property is determined on the disbanding of that unit; and
(b) any other person or charity has an interest in the property contingent upon the determination of the interest of the charity.

PART III

SUCCESSION TO CHARITABLE PROPERTY: SCOTLAND

Effect of designation of successor to disbanded unit

9.—(1) On and after the day on which a warrant comes into force, any charitable property which is held for the purposes of the disbanded unit in question shall (subject to the provisions of this Part of this Schedule) be held for the corresponding purposes, or most nearly corresponding purposes, of the successor unit designated by the warrant.

(2) In this Part of this Schedule "charitable property" means any property belonging to a recognised body.

Exclusion of charitable property from paragraph 9

10.—(1) If the Lord Advocate considers that paragraph 9 should not apply to all or any of the charitable property held for the purposes of a disbanded unit, he may give a direction providing that paragraph 9 shall not apply or shall cease to apply to that property or part.

(2) A direction under this paragraph may be given at any time during the period of 6 months beginning with the day on which the warrant is made.

11.—(1) If a recognised body affected by a warrant or any person concerned in the management or control of, or interested in, such a body considers that paragraph 9 should not apply to all or any of the charitable property held by the recognised body for the purposes of the disbanded unit in question, then the recognised body, person concerned in its management or control or person interested, as the case may be, may apply by petition to the Court of Session for the court to make an order—

(a) providing that paragraph 9 shall cease to apply to that property or part; and

(b) exercising, with respect to that property or part, any of the court's powers relating to a charitable or other permanent endowment.

(2) On an application under sub-paragraph (1), the court may exercise any such power as is mentioned in sub-paragraph (1)(b) to make such order as it considers to be appropriate, whether or not that power would normally be exercisable at the instance of such a petitioner.

(3) An application under this paragraph may be made at any time within the period of 6 months beginning with the day on which the warrant comes into force.

Power of Lord Advocate to apply to Court of Session

12.—(1) Where a body of a reserve force has been or is to be disbanded, the Lord Advocate—

(a) if he has not given a direction under paragraph 9, may; and

(b) if he has given such a direction, shall,

apply by petition to the Court of Session for the court to make an order exercising, with respect to any charitable property which is held for the purposes of the disbanded unit, any of the court's powers relating to a charitable or other permanent endowment.

(2) On an application under sub-paragraph (1), the court may, subject to any such direction, exercise any such power to make such order as it considers to be appropriate, whether or not that power would normally be exercisable at the instance of the Lord Advocate.

Validity of certain acts

13. None of the following, that is to say, a warrant, a direction under paragraph 10 or an order under paragraph 11 or 12 shall affect the validity of anything done or omitted with respect to any property affected by the warrant, direction or order before a copy of the warrant, direction or order is received by a person concerned in the management or control of the recognised body in question.

Saving for interests in property contingent on disbandment of unit

14. Nothing in this Part of this Schedule applies to any property held by a recognised body for the purposes of a unit that has been or is to be disbanded if, under the terms on which the property is so held—

(a) any interest of the recognised body in the property is determined on the disbanding of that unit; and

(b) any other person or recognised body has an interest in the property contingent upon the determination of the interest of the recognised body.

Part IV

Succession to charitable property: Northern Ireland

Effect of designation of successor to disbanded unit

15.—(1) On and after the day on which a warrant comes into force, any charitable property which is held for the purposes of the disbanded unit in question and administered for those purposes according to the law of Northern Ireland shall (subject to the provisions of this Part of this Schedule) be held for the corresponding purposes, or most nearly corresponding purposes, of the successor unit designated by the warrant.

(2) In this Part of this Schedule "charitable property" means any property belonging to a charity.

(3) The same jurisdiction and powers shall be exercisable in relation to any charity owning property to which sub-paragraph (1) applies as would be exercisable if that sub-paragraph were not a provision of an Act of Parliament regulating the charity.

Exclusion of charitable property from paragraph 15

16.—(1) If the Department of Health and Social Services for Northern Ireland considers that paragraph 15(1) should not apply to all or any of the charitable property held for the purposes of a disbanded unit, that Department may make an order providing that paragraph 15(1) shall not apply or shall cease to apply to that property.

(2) An order under this paragraph may be made at any time during the period of 6 months beginning with the day on which the warrant is made.

17.—(1) If a charity affected by a warrant or any trustee of, or person interested in, such a charity considers that paragraph 15(1) should not apply to all or any of the property held by the charity for the purposes of the disbanded unit in question, then the charity, trustee or person interested, as the case may be, may apply to the court for an order providing that paragraph 15(1) shall cease to apply to that property or part.

(2) An application under this paragraph—

(a) may be made at any time within the period of 6 months beginning with the day on which the warrant comes into force; and

(b) is subject to section 29(3) of the Charities Act (Northern Ireland) 1964 (under which an application for an order of the court in connection with the administration of a charity may not be made without the consent of the Attorney General for Northern Ireland).

(3) In this paragraph "the court" has the same meaning as in the Charities Act (Northern Ireland) 1964.

Application of property otherwise than under paragraph 15

18. In any case where—

(a) the Secretary of State requests the Department of Health and Social Services for Northern Ireland to make provision with respect to any charitable property held for the purposes of a unit of a reserve force which has been or is to be disbanded; or

(b) an order is made under paragraph 16 or 17 excluding any charitable property so held from the operation of paragraph 15(1),

the Department may, notwithstanding anything in subsection (1) of section 13 of the Charities Act (Northern Ireland) 1964 and irrespective of the value of the property in question, exercise its jurisdiction under that section with respect to the property to which the request or order relates.

Validity of certain acts by trustees

19. Neither a warrant nor any order under paragraph 16 or 17 shall affect the validity of anything done or omitted with respect to any property affected by the warrant or order before a copy of the warrant or order is received by a trustee of the charity in question.

Saving for interests in property contingent on disbandment of unit

20. Nothing in this Part of this Schedule applies to any property held by a charity for the purposes of a unit which has been or is to be disbanded if, under the terms on which the property is so held—

(a) any interest of the charity in the property is determined on the disbanding of that unit; and

(b) any other person or charity has an interest in the property contingent upon the determination of the interest of the charity.

DEFINITIONS
"charitable property": para. 3(2).
"charitable property" [Northern Ireland]: para. 15(2).
"charitable property" [Scotland]: para. 9(2).
"charity": para. 2.
"court; the": Charities Act 1993, s.97(1).
"court; the" [Northern Ireland]: Charities Act (Northern Ireland) 1964.
"disbanded unit": para. 2.
"recognised body": para. 2.
"reserve force": s.1(2).
"warrant": para. 2.

GENERAL NOTE

Schedule 5, introduced by s.120, makes provision for the treatment of charitable property held for the purpose of any unit of a reserve force which has been, or is to be, disbanded or amalgamated with another body. According to the minister, Mr Soames, on the drafting of this provision, "We have gone into mind-numbing detail on the arcane technicalities of charity law as a whole and Schedule 5 in particular. It is a hellish subject" (*Hansard*, H.C. Standing Committee A, col. 73, April 23, 1996). Hellish or not, the thrust of the Schedule is that where a reserve force unit is disbanded, Her Majesty may designate by warrant a unit as the successor to the disbanded one (para. 1). The effect of this is that the charitable property of the disbanded unit will now be held for the corresponding purposes of the successor unit (para. 3(1)). The Charity Commissioners may, however, make an order excluding certain property of a disbanded unit from the above arrangement (para. 4(1)). An interested trustee or an affected charity may also apply within six months to a court to the same effect (para. 5(1) and (2)). The Secretary of State may also intervene (para. 6).

The minister offered an illustration in Standing Committee A. Envisage a charitable trust for unit A, both to help its recruiting and also to make welfare payments to its former soldiers' widows. On amalgamation of units A and B to form unit C, the trustees would formerly have had to obtain a scheme from the Charity Commissioners if they wished to assist unit C in any way. However, with a warrant under Sched. 5, payments could be made, if the trustees so wished, to unit C for recruiting, without the need for a new, approved scheme. The trustees could also continue to make welfare payments to the widows of former members of unit A, but not, in due course, to widows of former members of unit C (the minister did not, of course, even mention unit B), as this is a charitable purpose unaffected by the warrant (see *Hansard*, H.C. Standing Committee A, col. 74, April 23, 1996).

Section 121(1) SCHEDULE 6

AMENDMENTS TO THE RESERVE FORCES ACT 1980 RELATING TO THE LIEUTENANCIES

1. Part VI of the Reserve Forces Act 1980 (the lieutenancies) shall be amended as follows.
2. In section 133 (deputy lieutenants)—
(a) in subsection (2), the words "to the satisfaction of the Secretary of State" and "in the Secretary of State's opinion" shall cease to have effect;
(b) at the end of subsection (4) there shall be added the words "; but the commission may be revoked by the lord-lieutenant of the county or area.";
(c) in subsection (5)—
(i) the words from "(at" to "rate)" shall cease to have effect;
(ii) after the words "London Gazette" there shall be inserted the words "or the Edinburgh Gazette"; and
(iii) the words from "in like manner" to the end shall cease to have effect.
3. In section 135 (vice lord-lieutenants), after subsection (1) there shall be inserted the following subsections—
"(1A) The commission of a vice lord-lieutenant may, with Her Majesty's approbation, be revoked by the lord-lieutenant of the county or area.
(1B) Where the person who appointed a vice lord-lieutenant dies or otherwise ceases to be lord-lieutenant, the commission of the vice lord-lieutenant shall not be vacated until a new lord-lieutenant is appointed."
4. In section 136 (removal of vice lord-lieutenant and deputy lieutenants), paragraph (b) (and the word "and" immediately preceding it) shall cease to have effect.
5. In section 137 (statutory functions)—
(a) in subsection (1)—
(i) after the word "lord-lieutenant" (in both places) there shall be inserted the word ", lieutenants";
(ii) for the words from "jurisdiction" to "are" there shall be substituted the words "functions and privileges (whether provided for under any enactment or otherwise) as are for the time being exercisable by or"; and
(iii) the words from "area" (in the second place it appears) shall cease to have effect;
(b) in subsection (2), the words from "and appoint" to the end shall cease to have effect.

GENERAL NOTE

This makes minor amendments to the provisions of the 1980 Act in relation to the appointment of deputy lieutenants and vice lord-lieutenants of counties. See the annotations to s.121(2) regarding the removal of doubts as to the validity of appointments of lord-lieutenants and as to the validity of their acts.

Section 126   SCHEDULE 7

POSTPONEMENT OF TRANSFER TO THE RESERVE OR DISCHARGE FROM THE REGULAR SERVICES

The Army

1.—(1) Sections 9 (postponement of transfer to the reserve or discharge) and 10 (continuation of army service in imminent national danger) of the Army Act 1955 shall be amended as follows.

(2) For subsections (1) to (4) of section 9 there shall be substituted the following subsections—

"(1) This section applies to a soldier of the regular forces if, on the relevant date, a call-out order under section 52, 54 or 56 of the Reserve Forces Act 1996 is in force authorising the call out for permanent service of members of the reserve.

For the purposes of this section, "the relevant date", in relation to a soldier, means the date on which he would, apart from this section, fall to be transferred to the reserve or he would be entitled to be discharged, as the case may be.

(1A) A soldier to whom this section applies may be retained in army service after the relevant date in accordance with this section for such period as the competent military authority may order, and his service may be prolonged accordingly.

(1B) The period for which a soldier may be retained in service after the relevant date by virtue of this section shall be limited as follows, that is to say—

(a) a soldier who would otherwise have fallen to be transferred to the reserve may not be retained for longer than the period for which, if the assumptions mentioned in sub-section (1C) below are made in relation to him, he could have been required to serve on being called out under Part VI of the Reserve Forces Act 1996; or

(b) a soldier who would otherwise have been discharged may not be retained for longer than twelve months;

and a soldier who is retained in service is (if not transferred or discharged sooner) entitled to be transferred to the reserve or discharged, as the case may require, at the end of whichever of the above periods applies to him.

(1C) The assumptions to be made in relation to a soldier for the purposes of subsection (1B)(a) above are that—

(a) he was transferred to the reserve in time to be called out for permanent service starting on the relevant date; and

(b) he was so called out on the authority of the call-out order which justified his retention in service."

(3) After subsection (6) of section 9 there shall be inserted the following subsection—

"(6A) Where a soldier is retained in service by virtue of this section but would otherwise have fallen to be transferred to the reserve—

(a) any period for which he is liable to serve in the reserve after the completion of his army service shall be reduced by the period for which he is so retained; and

(b) the period for which he is so retained shall be treated as a period of relevant service for the purposes of any provision of Part IV, V, VI or VII of the Reserve Forces Act 1996."

(4) In subsection (1) of section 10, for the words from "men" to the end there shall be substituted the words "a call-out order under section 52 of the Reserve Forces Act 1996 authorising the call out of members of the reserve is in force".

2. The Army Act 1955 shall continue to apply without the amendments made by paragraph 1 in relation to any soldier who is in service immediately before the date on which that paragraph comes into force unless—

(a) he re-enters, re-engages or extends his army service after that day; or

(b) he elects irrevocably in such manner as may be prescribed to be a person to whom that Act shall apply with those amendments.

The Royal Marines

3.—(1) Paragraphs 4A (postponement of transfer to Royal Fleet Reserve or discharge) and 4B (continuation of service in Royal Marines in imminent national danger) of Schedule 7 to the Army Act 1955 (provisions as to Royal Marines) shall be amended as follows.

(2) For sub-paragraphs (1) to (4) of paragraph 4A there shall be substituted the following sub-paragraphs—

"(1) This paragraph applies to a marine serving in the Royal Marines if, on the relevant date, a call-out order under section 52, 54 or 56 of the Reserve Forces Act 1996 is in force authorising the call out for permanent service of members of the Royal Fleet Reserve.

For the purposes of this paragraph, "the relevant date", in relation to a marine, means the date on which he would, apart from this paragraph, fall to be transferred to the Royal Fleet Reserve or he would be entitled to be discharged, as the case may be.

(1A) A marine to whom this paragraph applies may be retained in service in the Royal Marines after the relevant date in accordance with this paragraph for such period as the competent authority may order, and his service may be prolonged accordingly.

(1B) The period for which a marine may be retained in service after the relevant date by virtue of this paragraph shall be limited as follows, that is to say—

    (a) a marine who would otherwise have fallen to be transferred to the Royal Fleet Reserve may not be retained for longer than the period for which, if the assumptions mentioned in sub-paragraph (1C) below are made in relation to him, he could have been required to serve on being called out under Part VI of the Reserve Forces Act 1996; or

    (b) a marine who would otherwise have been discharged may not be retained for longer than twelve months;

and a marine who is retained in service is (if not transferred or discharged sooner) entitled to be transferred to the Royal Fleet Reserve or discharged as the case may require, at the end of whichever of the above periods applies to him.

(1C) The assumptions to be made in relation to a marine for the purposes of sub-paragraph (1B)(a) above are that—

    (a) he was transferred to the Royal Fleet Reserve in time to be called out for permanent service starting on the relevant date; and

    (b) he was so called out on the authority of the call-out order which justified his retention in service."

(3) After sub-paragraph (6) of paragraph 4A there shall be inserted the following sub-paragraph—

"(6A) Where a marine is retained in service by virtue of this paragraph but would otherwise have fallen to be transferred to the Royal Fleet Reserve—

    (a) any period for which he is liable to serve in the Royal Fleet Reserve after the completion of his service in the Royal Marines shall be reduced by the period for which he is so retained; and

    (b) the period for which he is so retained shall be treated as a period of relevant service for the purposes of any provision of Part IV, V, VI or VII of the Reserve Forces Act 1996."

(4) Sub-paragraph (8) of paragraph 4A shall cease to have effect.

(5) In sub-paragraph (1) of paragraph 4B, for the words from "men" to the end there shall be substituted the words "a call-out order under section 52 of the Reserve Forces Act 1996 authorising the call out of members of the Royal Fleet Reserve is in force".

4. The Army Act 1955 shall continue to apply without the amendments made by paragraph 3 in relation to any marine who is in service immediately before the date on which that paragraph comes into force unless—

    (a) he re-enters, re-engages or extends his service in the Royal Marines after that day; or

    (b) he elects irrevocably in such manner as may be prescribed to be a person to whom that Act shall apply with those amendments.

The Royal Air Force

5.—(1) Sections 9 (postponement of transfer to the reserve or discharge) and 10 (continuation of air-force service in imminent national danger) of the Air Force Act 1955 shall be amended as follows.

(2) For subsections (1) to (4) of section 9 there shall be substituted the following subsections—

"(1) This section applies to an airman of the regular air force if, on the relevant date, a call-out order under section 52, 54 or 56 of the Reserve Forces Act 1996 is in force authorising the call out for permanent service of members of the reserve.

For the purposes of this section, "the relevant date", in relation to an airman, means the date on which he would, apart from this section, fall to be transferred to the reserve or he would be entitled to be discharged, as the case may be.

(1A) An airman to whom this section applies may be retained in air-force service after the relevant date in accordance with this section for such period as the competent air-force authority may order, and his service may be prolonged accordingly.

(1B) The period for which an airman may be retained in service after the relevant date by virtue of this section shall be limited as follows, that is to say—

    (a) an airman who would otherwise have fallen to be transferred to the reserve may not be retained for longer than the period for which, if the assumptions mentioned in

subsection (1C) below are made in relation to him, he could have been required to serve on being called out under Part VI of the Reserve Forces Act 1996; or
  (b) an airman who would otherwise have been discharged may not be retained for longer than twelve months;
and an airman who is retained in service is (if not transferred or discharged sooner) entitled to be transferred to the reserve or discharged, as the case may require, at the end of whichever of the above periods applies to him.

(1C) The assumptions to be made in relation to an airman for the purposes of subsection (1B)(a) above are that—
  (a) he was transferred to the reserve in time to be called out for permanent service starting on the relevant date; and
  (b) he was so called out on the authority of the call-out order which justified his retention in service."

(3) After subsection (6) of section 9 there shall be inserted the following subsection—
  "(6A) Where an airman is retained in service by virtue of this section but would otherwise have fallen to be transferred to the reserve—
  (a) any period for which he is liable to serve in the reserve after the completion of his air-force service shall be reduced by the period for which he is so retained; and
  (b) the period for which he is so retained shall be treated as a period of relevant service for the purposes of any provision of Part IV, V, VI or VII of the Reserve Forces Act 1996."

(4) In subsection (1) of section 10, for the words from "men" to the end there shall be substituted the words "a call-out order under section 52 of the Reserve Forces Act 1996 authorising the call out of members of the reserve is in force".

6. The Air Force Act 1955 shall continue to apply without the amendments made by paragraph 5 in relation to any airman who is in service immediately before the date on which that paragraph comes into force unless—
  (a) he re-enters, re-engages or extends his air-force service after that day; or
  (b) he elects irrevocably in such manner as may be prescribed to be a person to whom that Act shall apply with those amendments.

The Royal Navy

7.—(1) Sections 4 (postponement of transfer to Royal Fleet Reserve or discharge) and 5 (continuation of service in Royal Navy in imminent national danger) of the Armed Forces Act 1966 shall be amended as follows.

(2) For subsections (1) to (4) of section 4 there shall be substituted the following subsections—
  "(1) This section applies to a rating if, on the relevant date, a call-out order under section 52, 54 or 56 of the Reserve Forces Act 1996 is in force authorising the call out for permanent service of members of the Royal Fleet Reserve.
  For the purposes of this section, "the relevant date", in relation to a rating, means the date on which he would, apart from this section, fall to be transferred to the Royal Fleet Reserve or he would be entitled to be discharged, as the case may be.

(1A) A rating to whom this section applies may be retained in service in the Royal Navy after the relevant date in accordance with this section for such period as the competent authority may order, and his service may be prolonged accordingly.

(1B) The period for which a rating may be retained in service after the relevant date by virtue of this section shall be limited as follows, that is to say—
  (a) a rating who would otherwise have fallen to be transferred to the Royal Fleet Reserve may not be retained for longer than the period for which, if the assumptions mentioned in subsection (1C) below are made in relation to him, he could have been required to serve on being called out under Part VI of the Reserve Forces Act 1996; or
  (b) a rating who would otherwise have been discharged may not be retained for longer than twelve months;
and a rating who is retained in service is (if not transferred or discharged sooner) entitled to be transferred to the Royal Fleet Reserve or discharged, as the case may require, at the end of whichever of the above periods applies to him.

(1C) The assumptions to be made in relation to a rating for the purposes of subsection (1B)(a) above are that—
  (a) he was transferred to the Royal Fleet Reserve in time to be called out for permanent service starting on the relevant date; and
  (b) he was so called out on the authority of the call-out order which justified his retention in service."

(3) After subsection (6) of section 4 there shall be inserted the following subsection—

"(6A) Where a rating is retained in service by virtue of this section but would otherwise have fallen to be transferred to the Royal Fleet Reserve—

(a) any period for which he is liable to serve in the Royal Fleet Reserve after the completion of his service in the Royal Navy shall be reduced by the period for which he is so retained; and

(b) the period for which he is so retained shall be treated as a period of relevant service for the purposes of any provision of Part IV, V, VI or VII of the Reserve Forces Act 1996."

(4) Subsection (9) of section 4 shall cease to have effect.

(5) In subsection (1) of section 5, for the words from "men" to the end there shall be substituted the words "a call-out order under section 52 of the Reserve Forces Act 1996 authorising the call out of members of the Royal Fleet Reserve is in force".

8. The Armed Forces Act 1966 shall continue to apply without the amendments made by paragraph 7 in relation to any rating who is in service immediately before the date on which that paragraph comes into force unless—

(a) he re-enters, re-engages or extends his service in the Royal Navy after that day; or

(b) he elects irrevocably in such manner as may be prescribed to be a person to whom that Act shall apply with those amendments.

DEFINITIONS

"call-out order": s.64.
"member of the reserve": s.127(2).
"permanent service": s.127(1).
"prescribed": s.127(1).
"relevant date; the" [Army]: para. 2 and Army Act 1955, s.9(1), as amended.
"relevant date; the" [Royal Air Force]: para. 5(2) and Air Force Act 1955, s.9(1), as amended.
"relevant date; the" [Royal Marines]: para. 3(2) and Army Act 1955, Sched. 7, para. 4A, as amended.
"relevant date; the" [Royal Navy]: para. 7(2) and Armed Forces Act 1966, s.4(1), as amended.

GENERAL NOTE

Section 126 introduces Schedule 7. This provides for the amendment of the provisions in the Army/Air Force Acts 1955 and the Armed Forces Act 1966, which permit the postponement, in the first instance for no more than 12 months, of the discharge or transfer to the reserve of a regular serviceman in specified circumstances. There are two categories of circumstances. The first is that a state of war exists between Her Majesty and a foreign power, that men have been called out on permanent service and that the regular serviceman is serving abroad. The second, which postpones the regular serviceman's transfer to the reserve, is that there is imminent national danger or great emergency.

Schedule 7 amends the relevant service laws to take account of the revised powers of call out in the 1996 Act. For example, under the Army Act 1955, s.9(1)–(4), as amended by the 1996 Act, a regular soldier who falls to be transferred to the reserve or who is entitled to be discharged on a date when a call-out order under ss.52, 54 and 56 of the 1996 Act (in respect of national danger, etc.; warlike operations; and peacekeeping and humanitarian operations, respectively) is in force, may be retained in Army service for a maximum extended period before transfer or discharge. In relation to soldiers in service immediately before the date on which para. 1 comes into force and which thereby amends the Army Act 1955, ss.9 and 10, para. 2 makes clear that such additional liability is not retrospective. The position is otherwise if such a soldier re-enters, re-engages or extends his army service *after* the day on which these amendments to the Army Act come into force; or if he elects irrevocably in a prescribed manner to be bound by the relevant provisions of the 1955 Act as amended by the 1996 Act. There are similar provisions amending service law in relation to regular service personnel in the Royal Marines, Royal Navy and Royal Air Force.

Section 128 SCHEDULE 8

TRANSITORY AND TRANSITIONAL PROVISIONS

Existing members of the reserve forces

1.—(1) Nothing in section 2 shall prevent a person who, immediately before the day on which that section comes into force, is a man of a reserve force from continuing as a man of that force.

(2) If men of the Air Force Reserve are transferred to the Royal Auxiliary Air Force under paragraph 7(2) after the day on which section 2 comes into force, nothing in that section shall prevent them continuing as men of the Royal Auxiliary Air Force.

Royal Fleet Reserve

2.—(1) The Royal Fleet Reserve shall cease to be maintained as a division of the Royal Naval Reserve and shall, accordingly, be a separate reserve force.

(2) Sub-paragraph (1) does not affect the continuity of membership of the Royal Fleet Reserve.

3. Any reference in any enactment or other instrument to the Royal Naval Reserve which, immediately before the commencement of paragraph 2(1), included a reference to the Royal Fleet Reserve shall continue to have effect as if it included a reference to the Royal Fleet Reserve.

The special class of the Royal Fleet Reserve

4.—(1) The special class of the Royal Fleet Reserve existing by virtue of sections 2 and 57 of the Reserve Forces Act 1980 may continue in existence subject to sub-paragraphs (2) and (3) of this paragraph.

(2) No man, after the commencement of this paragraph—
  (a) may on entering or re-engaging in the Royal Fleet Reserve or during a term of service in that force, be entered in or transferred to the special class or undertake the liability for service in that class; or
  (b) may be transferred to that class otherwise than as mentioned in section 57(2) and section 58 of the Reserve Forces Act 1980.

(3) Persons in the special class immediately before the commencement of this paragraph shall continue in that class (subject to the provisions of the Reserve Forces Act 1980) until the end of their terms of service as mentioned in section 57(3) of that Act.

(4) A member of the special class who elects to be subject to Part VI of this Act shall cease to be a member of that class and shall become subject to the provisions of that Part.

(5) A person liable under the Reserve Forces Act 1980 to serve in the special class on transfer to the reserve who elects to be subject to Part VI of this Act shall cease to be liable to serve in that class.

5. If it appears to the Secretary of State that—
  (a) the special class of the Royal Fleet Reserve has no members; and
  (b) no person remains liable to serve in that class on transfer to the reserve,
the Secretary of State may by order made by statutory instrument repeal section 2(3) and (4), section 57 and section 58 of the Reserve Forces Act 1980.

Home Service Force

6. Section 6 of the Reserve Forces Act 1980 shall cease to have effect.

Royal Air Force Volunteer Reserve

7.—(1) Her Majesty may continue to maintain a force known as the Royal Air Force Volunteer Reserve as a division of the Air Force Reserve.

(2) On a day appointed by the Secretary of State by order, any officers or men of the Royal Air Force Volunteer Reserve who, immediately before that day, fall within any description of member specified in the order shall cease to be members of the Air Force Reserve and become members of the Royal Auxiliary Air Force.

(3) An order under sub-paragraph (2) may describe the members who are to be transferred by reference to the unit or part of the Royal Air Force Volunteer Reserve to which they belong or by reference to any other criterion.

Reserves of Officers

8.—(1) On a day appointed by the Secretary of State by order officers of the retired list of the Royal Navy and officers of the emergency list of the Royal Navy shall become members of the Royal Fleet Reserve.

(2) On a day appointed by the Secretary of State by order officers of the retired list of the Royal Marines and officers of the emergency list of the Royal Marines shall become members of the Royal Fleet Reserve.

9. On a day appointed by the Secretary of State by order, the members of the Regular Army Reserve of Officers shall become members of the Army Reserve.

Training of existing members of the Royal Auxiliary Air Force

10. Section 41(1) of the Reserve Forces Act 1980 shall apply, in relation to any person who may be required to undergo training under that section, with the omission of the words "within the United Kingdom".

Effect of transfers under this Schedule

11.—(1) Any officers transferred to a reserve force under paragraph 7(2), 8 or 9 shall continue to serve in that force on the same conditions as they served immediately before their transfer.

(2) Any men transferred to the Royal Auxiliary Air Force under paragraph 7(2) shall serve for the same term and on the same conditions as they served in the Air Force Reserve.

(3) Anything done by or to any such officer or man before his transfer shall be treated so far as is necessary on and after that day as if it had been done by or to a member of the reserve force to which he was transferred.

(4) If any such officer or man is transferred to a reserve force on or after the day appointed for the purposes of Part I of Schedule 9—

    (a) he shall be regarded for the purposes of paragraph 2 of that Schedule as if he had been a member of that force since immediately before the appointed day;

    (b) the references in that paragraph to "that time" shall be taken to refer to the time at which he was transferred to the reserve force.

Parliamentary control

12. A determination by Parliament of the permitted numbers of officers or men for any reserve force under any provision of Part I of the Reserve Forces Act 1980 shall have effect as a determination under section 3 of this Act.

DEFINITIONS
    "man": s.2(4).
    "member": s.127(2).
    "reserve forces": s.1(2).
    "special class of the Royal Fleet Reserve": Reserve Forces Act 1980, s.57(1).

GENERAL NOTE
    Section 128 introduces Sched. 8 which deals with transitional provisions in connection with the organisation of different branches of the reserve forces. The Schedule brings about, and enables the Secretary of State by order to bring about, a number of organisational changes. One is to create as a separate body rather than as a division of the Royal Naval Reserve, the Royal Fleet Reserve to which ex-regular naval personnel may be transferred (paras. 2 and 3). Another change is the abolition of the special class of the Royal Fleet Reserve when it has no members and when there is no longer any person who is liable to serve in that class. For the composition of this special class, see the 1980 Act, s.57(1). It includes, *inter alia*, men who had been entered for non-continuous service in the naval service before December 16, 1949 or who had enlisted in the marines and who, on later transfer to the Royal Fleet Reserve, had accepted liability for service in the special class. Once the passage of time has taken its toll, the Secretary of State may repeal by order the sections of the 1980 Act relating to the special class (para. 5).

    Other provisions in the Schedule include powers granted to the Secretary of State to issue orders transferring the officers of the retired and emergency lists of the Royal Navy and Royal Marines into the Royal Fleet Reserve (para. 8(4)); orders transferring the officers of the Regular Army Reserve of Officers into the Army Reserve (para. 9); and orders transferring specified members of the Royal Air Force Volunteer Reserve into the Royal Auxiliary Air Force. A proposal specifically to identify the Royal Air Force Volunteer Reserve (Training) in the Schedule, in order to ensure that all branches of the Volunteer Reserve can be called out by agreement in an emergency was withdrawn. The Volunteer Reserve (Training) makes provision for air-experience flights, volunteer gliding schools and air cadet squadrons. However, their training and equipping activities are not in fact assigned for the immediate reinforcing of the Royal Air Force (if such were required). Nonetheless, the Volunteer Reserve (Training) is legally part of the Air Force Reserve and its members theoretically are qualified to be considered for inclusion in the call out provisions of the Act, though individual call outs of Volunteer Reserve (Training) members, who do not require to meet full reserve medical and training standards, would be most unlikely. See *Hansard*, H.C. Standing Committee A, col. 79, April 23, 1996.

SCHEDULE 9

APPLICATION OF ACT TO TRANSITIONAL MEMBERS

PART I

THE TRANSITIONAL CLASS OF MEMBERS OF THE RESERVE FORCES

1.—(1) The transitional class consists of persons who—
(a) are members of a reserve force;
(b) for the time being fall within paragraph 2 or 3; and
(c) have not made an election under paragraph 4.

(2) In this Schedule "transitional member" means a member of a reserve force who for the time being is a member of the transitional class; and "transitional officer" and "transitional man" shall be construed accordingly.

(3) In this Part of this Schedule "the appointed day" means such day as the Secretary of State may by order made by statutory instrument appoint for the purposes of this Part of this Schedule.

2. A person who, immediately before the appointed day, was an officer or man of a reserve force falls within this paragraph if—
(a) he has remained a member of that force without interruption since that time; and
(b) he has not extended his service in, or become an officer of, that force since that time.

3. An officer or man who becomes a member of a reserve force on or after the appointed day, on transfer to the reserve from the regular services, falls within this paragraph if—
(a) he joined the regular services before the appointed day and did not re-enlist, re-engage or extend his service, or become an officer, in the regular services on or after that day;
(b) he has remained a member of the reserve force concerned without interruption since being transferred from the regular services; and
(c) he has not extended his service in, or become an officer of, that force since being so transferred.

4.—(1) A person who is a transitional member of a reserve force by virtue of paragraph 2 or 3 may elect to cease being a transitional member.

(2) An officer or man serving in the regular services who—
(a) joined those services before the appointed day; and
(b) has not re-enlisted, re-engaged or extended his service, or become an officer, on or after that day,
may elect not to be a transitional member on his transfer to the reserve.

(3) An election under this paragraph is irrevocable and must be made in the prescribed manner.

(4) A person who has made an election under this paragraph shall cease to be or, as the case may be, shall not become a transitional member of the reserve force concerned.

5.—(1) In this Part of this Schedule "man", in relation to the regular services, means a person of or below the rank or rate of warrant officer.

(2) A person in permanent service on recall (whether under the Reserve Forces Act 1980 or, in the case of an officer, otherwise than under this Act) shall not be regarded for the purposes of this Part of this Schedule as serving in the regular services.

PART II

APPLICATION OF ACT TO MEMBERS OF THE TRANSITIONAL CLASS

6. The provisions of this Act (other than section 129 and this Schedule) apply in relation to members of the transitional class in accordance with this Part of this Schedule.

7.—(1) Any reference in this Act to a reserve force, to two or more of the reserve forces or to all the reserve forces shall, unless the context otherwise requires, be construed as a reference to the whole of the force, or of each force, concerned, including any transitional members.

(2) Any reference in this Act to members, officers or men of a reserve force includes, unless the context otherwise requires, a reference to members, officers or men who are transitional members.

(3) This paragraph has effect subject to the exceptions and modifications in the following provisions of this Part of this Schedule.

8.—(1) In the application of section 17(1) to a transitional man, the reference to permanent service includes a reference to permanent service under the Reserve Forces Act 1980.

(2) Section 17(2), (3) and (4) do not apply to transitional men.

9.—(1) In the application of sections 18, 20 and 21 to a transitional man, the reference to permanent service includes a reference to permanent service under the Reserve Forces Act 1980.

(2) In the application of section 21 to a transitional man of the Royal Fleet Reserve, the reference to training and other duties includes a reference to training or other duties in pursuance of any provision of the Reserve Forces Act 1980.

10. Section 22 does not apply to transitional members of a reserve land, air or marine force.

11. In the application of section 24 to a transitional member who has entered into a full-time service commitment—

(a) for the reference in subsection (7) to permanent service under Part VI there shall be substituted a reference to permanent service on call out under the Reserve Forces Act 1980 or, as the case may be, under any other call-out obligations of an officer; and

(b) for the reference in subsection (8) to training under section 22 there shall (except in the case of a member of a reserve naval force) be substituted a reference to training required under the Reserve Forces Act 1980 or, as the case may be, under any other training obligations of an officer.

12.—(1) Transitional members may (subject to the provisions of this Act) enter into a special agreement or an employee agreement; and Parts IV and V apply accordingly.

(2) Transitional members of a reserve force do not lose their status as transitional members by virtue of either becoming special members of the force or (where they continue as ordinary members under section 42) ceasing to be special members of the force.

13. In the application of section 31(1) to a special agreement entered into by a transitional member, for the reference in paragraph (d) to permanent service under Part VI there shall be substituted a reference to permanent service under the Reserve Forces Act 1980 or, as the case may be, under any other call-out obligations of an officer.

14. In the application of section 34(5) to transitional members, the reference in paragraph (b) to section 57(11) shall be omitted.

15. In the application of section 40(5) to a transitional special member—

(a) for the reference to section 22 there shall (except in the case of a member of a reserve naval force) be substituted a reference to the corresponding provision of the Reserve Forces Act 1980 or, as the case may be, of any other training obligations of an officer;

(b) for the reference to Part VI there shall be substituted a reference to the corresponding provisions of the Reserve Forces Act 1980 or, as the case may be, of any other call-out obligations of an officer.

16. An order may be made under section 41(6) suspending the operation of section 41(1)(c) in relation to transitional special members, notwithstanding that Part VI does not apply to transitional members.

17. In the application of section 45(5) to transitional members, the reference in paragraph (b) to section 57(11) shall be omitted.

18. Part VI does not apply to transitional members.

19. Regulations under section 78, 83 or 84 may make provision, in relation to transitional members liable to be called out under—

(a) the Reserve Forces Act 1980, or

(b) any other call-out obligations of officers,

corresponding to the provision which may be made in regulations under that section in relation to members of the reserve forces liable to be called out under Part VI of this Act.

20. In the application of section 96(1) to a transitional member—

(a) the reference to any provision of this Act includes a reference to any provision of the Reserve Forces Act 1980 or, as the case may be, of any other call-out obligations of an officer; and

(b) for the reference in paragraph (a) to section 58(3)(c) there shall be substituted a reference to the corresponding provision of that Act or those obligations.

21. In the application of section 97(2) to a transitional member, for the reference to section 22 there shall (except in the case of a member of a reserve naval force) be substituted a reference to the corresponding provision of the Reserve Forces Act 1980 or, as the case may be, of any other training obligations of an officer.

22. In the application of section 102(2) to transitional members—

(a) the reference in paragraph (a) to any provision of this Act includes a reference to the corresponding provision of the Reserve Forces Act 1980 or, as the case may be, of any other call-out obligations of an officer;

(b) the reference in paragraph (d) to training includes (except in the case of members of a reserve naval force) a reference to the corresponding training required under the Reserve Forces Act 1980 or, as the case may be, under any other training obligations of an officer.

23. In the application of section 123(1) to a transitional man, the reference to permanent service includes a reference to permanent service under the Reserve Forces Act 1980.

24. In the application of section 125 to a transitional member, the reference to permanent service includes a reference to permanent service under the Reserve Forces Act 1980 or, as the case may be, under any other call-out obligations of an officer.

DEFINITIONS
"appointed day": para. 1(3).
"employee agreement": s.38(2).
"full-time reserve commitment": s.24.
"man": para. 5(1).
"member of a reserve force": s.127(2).
"permanent service": s.127(1).
"prescribed": s.127(1).
"recall": s.127(1).
"regular services": s.127(1).
"reserve . . . air force": s.1(2).
"reserve force": s.1(2).
"reserve land . . . force": s.1(2).
"reserve . . . marine force": s.127(1).
"special agreement": s.28.
"special member": s.127(1).
"transitional class": para. 1(1).
"transitional man": para. 1(2).
"transitional member": para. 1(2).
"transitional officer": para. 1(2).

GENERAL NOTE
By virtue of s.129, Pt. II of Sched. 9 sets out the provisions of the 1996 Act which apply, with modifications, to members of a transitional class of reservists, or which do not apply to that class. Part I of Sched. 9 defines the members of this class to whom call-out provisions of the 1980 Act still apply (unless the members elect irrevocably to be bound by the call-out liabilities of the 1996 Act) until the Secretary of State, by order, brings the repeal of those provisions of the 1980 Act, as provided by the 1996 Act, into effect. Repeals will be brought into effect when, for example, there are no more members of, or no more persons liable to be members of, the transitional class. See, for example, the case of the special class of the Royal Fleet Reserve, discussed in the general note to Schedule 8. It should be noted that (with minor exceptions in relation to, for example, pension protection for members of the Ulster Defence Regiment) the 1980 Act in regard to the reserve forces no longer applies to anyone who is not a member of the transitional class or capable of becoming one.

Part I of this Schedule defines a transitional member, first, as a member of a reserve force who has remained a member of that force without interruption since immediately before an "appointed day" (as fixed by the Secretary of State) and who has not extended his service in, or become an officer of, that reserve force since that day (para. 2). Second, a transitional member may be an officer or man who joined a reserve force on or after the appointed day on transfer from the regular services. The conditions are that he joined the regulars before the appointed day and did not re-enlist, re-engage, etc., in the regular services on or after that day; that he has remained a member of that reserve force without interruption since his transfer from the regulars; and that he has not extended his service in or become an officer of that force since his transfer (para. 3). The transitional member reservist or ex-regular reservist may, however, elect irrevocably to cease or not be (as the case might be) a transitional member (para. 4), in which case his liabilities are governed exclusively by the 1996 Act. Among the provisions of the 1996 Act which do not apply to the transitional class, as defined in Pt. I of Sched. 9, are s.17 (in respect to postponement of discharge in certain circumstances); s.22 (in respect to training obligations, except in relation to naval reservists); and Pt. VI (in regard to general liability to be called out for permanent service).

Section 131(1)   SCHEDULE 10

MINOR AND CONSEQUENTIAL AMENDMENTS

Army Act 1955 (c. 18)

1.—(1) Section 205(1) (persons subject to military law) of the Army Act 1955 shall be amended as follows.

(2) For paragraph (e) there shall be substituted the following paragraphs—

"(e) every officer of the Territorial Army who is not a special member;

(ea) every officer of the Territorial Army who is a special member when in permanent service, in full-time service or undertaking any training or duty (whether in pursuance of an obligation or not);

(eb) every officer of the army reserve when in permanent service, in full-time service or undertaking any training or duty (whether in pursuance of an obligation or not) or when serving on the permanent staff of the army reserve;".

(3) In paragraph (g) for the words from "called" to the end there shall be substituted the words "in permanent service, in full-time service or undertaking any training or duty (whether in pursuance of an obligation or not) or when serving on the permanent staff of the army reserve;".

(4) In paragraph (h) for the words from "embodied" to "parades" there shall be substituted the words "in permanent service, in full-time service, called out for home defence service or undertaking any training or duty".

2. At the end of section 205 of that Act there shall be inserted the following subsection—

"(4) In this section—

"full-time service" means service under a commitment entered into under section 24 of the Reserve Forces Act 1996;

"permanent service" means permanent service on call out under any provision of the Reserve Forces Act 1980, the Reserve Forces Act 1996 or any other call-out obligations of an officer; and

"special member" has the same meaning as in the Reserve Forces Act 1996."

3.—(1) Section 210(2) (application of section 205 to Royal Marines) of that Act shall be amended as follows.

(2) After paragraph (a) there shall be inserted the following paragraph—

"(aa) any reference to an officer of the army reserve shall be construed as including a reference to an officer of the Royal Marines Reserve or a marine officer of the Royal Fleet Reserve;".

(3) For paragraph (b) there shall be substituted the following paragraphs—

"(b) any reference to a warrant officer, non-commissioned officer or man of the army reserve shall be construed as including a reference to a warrant officer, non-commissioned officer or a marine of the Royal Marines Reserve and to a marine warrant officer or non-commissioned officer or a marine of the Royal Fleet Reserve; and

(ba) any reference to the permanent staff of the army reserve shall be construed as including a reference to the permanent staff of the Royal Marines Reserve or the Royal Fleet Reserve."

4. In section 210(3) of that Act, for the words "the Royal Marines Reserve or" there shall be substituted the words "or the Royal Marines Reserve and a marine officer, marine warrant officer or non-commissioned officer or a marine of".

5. In section 210(4) of that Act, for the word "or" there shall be substituted the words "and to marine officers, marine warrant officers or non-commissioned officers and marines of".

6. After subsection (5) of section 210 of that Act there shall be inserted the following subsection—

"(6) For the purposes of this section references to marine warrant officers or non-commissioned officers and marines of the Royal Fleet Reserve shall be construed as references to persons who were transferred to that force from the Royal Marines or who enlisted in that force as marines."

7.—(1) Section 211 (application of Act to reserve forces) of that Act shall be amended as follows.

(2) In subsection (1)—

(a) in paragraph (a), for the words "any reserve of officers" there shall be substituted the words "the army reserve"; and

(b) for paragraph (b) there shall be substituted the following paragraph—

"(b) officers of the Territorial Army when in permanent service, in full-time service, called out for home defence service or undertaking any training or duty (whether in pursuance of an obligation or not) or when serving on the permanent staff of the Territorial Army,".

(3) For subsection (2) there shall be substituted the following subsection—

"(2) Subsections (5) and (6) of section 17 shall apply to warrant officers, non-commissioned officers and men of the army reserve and the Territorial Army as if the references to forfeited service were references to a period of permanent service or, as the case may be, of service as a member of the force concerned, which is to be disregarded under section 98(6) of the Reserve Forces Act 1996."

(4) For subsections (4) and (5) there shall be substituted the following subsections—

"(4) The provisions of this Act mentioned in subsection (4A) below shall apply to officers, warrant officers, non-commissioned officers and men of the army reserve and the Territorial Army only when they are in permanent service, in full-time service, called out for home defence service or serving on the permanent staff of the army reserve or the Territorial Army.

(4A) The provisions referred to in subsection (4) above are—

(a) sections 150 to 153 of this Act;

(b) except insofar as they may be applied by regulations made under section 103(2) of the Reserve Forces Act 1996, the provisions of Part II of this Act relating to the award of stoppages and sections 144 to 149 of this Act."

(5) For subsection (6) there shall be substituted the following subsection—

"(6) Section 182 of this Act shall not apply at any time to officers, warrant officers, non-commissioned officers or men of the Territorial Army."

(6) For subsection (8) there shall be substituted the following subsection—

"(8) An officer of the army reserve or the Territorial Army may be attached temporarily to any of Her Majesty's naval or air forces whether or not he is in permanent service but, if not in permanent service, shall not be so attached except with his consent."

(7) After subsection (8) there shall be inserted the following subsection—

"(9) In this section—

"full-time service" means service under a commitment entered into under section 24 of the Reserve Forces Act 1996; and

"permanent service" means permanent service on call-out under any provision of the Reserve Forces Act 1980, the Reserve Forces Act 1996 or any other call-out obligations of an officer."

8. In paragraph 22 of Schedule 7 (provisions as to Royal Marines: application of section 211) to that Act—

(a) after the words "Royal Marines Reserve" there shall be inserted the words "or marine officers, marine warrant officers or non-commissioned officers or marines of"; and

(b) for the words "any reserve of officers" there shall be substituted the words "the army reserve".

Air Force Act 1955 (c. 19)

9.—(1) Section 205(1) (persons subject to air-force law) of the Air Force Act 1955 shall be amended as follows.

(2) Paragraph (c) shall cease to have effect.

(3) For paragraph (f) there shall be substituted the following paragraphs—

"(f) every officer of the air force reserve or Royal Auxiliary Air Force who is not a special member;

(ff) every officer of the air force reserve or Royal Auxiliary Air Force who is a special member, when in permanent service, in full-time service or undertaking any training or duty (whether in pursuance of an obligation or not);".

(4) In paragraph (h), for the words from "called" to the end there shall be substituted the words "in permanent service, in full-time service or undertaking any training or duty (whether in pursuance of an obligation or not) or when serving on the permanent staff of the air force reserve;".

(5) In paragraph (i), for the words from "embodied" to "parades" there shall be substituted the words "in permanent service, in full-time service, called out for home defence service or undertaking any training or duty".

10. For subsection (3) of section 205 of that Act there shall be substituted the following subsection—

"(3) In this section—

"air forces commission" means a commission in the Royal Air Force, the air force reserve or the Royal Auxiliary Air Force;

"full-time service" means service under a commitment entered into under section 24 of the Reserve Forces Act 1996;

"permanent service" means permanent service on call out under any provision of the Reserve Forces Act 1980, the Reserve Forces Act 1996 or any other call-out obligations of an officer;

"special member" has the same meaning as in the Reserve Forces Act 1996."

11.—(1) Section 210 (application of Act to reserve forces) of that Act shall be amended as follows.

(2) In subsection (1)—

(a) for paragraph (a) there shall be substituted the following paragraph—
"(a) officers of the air force reserve when in permanent service, in full-time service or undertaking any training or duty (whether in pursuance of an obligation or not) or when serving on the permanent staff of the air force reserve,"; and
(b) for paragraph (c) there shall be substituted the following paragraph—
"(c) officers of the Royal Auxiliary Air Force when in permanent service, in full-time service, called out for home defence service or undertaking any training or duty (whether in pursuance of an obligation or not) or when serving on the permanent staff of the Royal Auxiliary Air Force,".
(3) For subsection (2) there shall be substituted the following subsection—
"(2) Subsection (4) of section 17 shall apply to warrant officers, non-commissioned officers and men of the air force reserve and the Royal Auxiliary Air Force as if the references to forfeited service were references to a period of permanent service or, as the case may be, of service as a member of the force concerned, which is to be disregarded under section 98(6) of the Reserve Forces Act 1996."
(4) For subsections (4) and (5) there shall be substituted the following subsections—
"(4) The provisions of this Act mentioned in subsection (4A) below shall apply to officers, warrant officers, non-commissioned officers and men of the air force reserve and the Royal Auxiliary Air Force only when they are in permanent service, in full-time service, called out for home defence service or serving on the permanent staff of the air force reserve or the Royal Auxiliary Air Force.
(4A) The provisions referred to in subsection (4) above are—
(a) sections 150 to 153 of this Act;
(b) except insofar as they may be applied by regulations made under section 103(2) of the Reserve Forces Act 1996, the provisions of Part II of this Act relating to the award of stoppages and sections 144 to 149 of this Act."
(5) For subsection (6) there shall be substituted the following subsection—
"(6) Section 182 of this Act shall not apply at any time to officers, warrant officers, non-commissioned officers or men of the Royal Auxiliary Air Force."
(6) For subsection (8) there shall be substituted the following subsection—
"(8) An officer of the air force reserve or the Royal Auxiliary Air Force may be attached temporarily to any of Her Majesty's naval or military forces whether or not he is in permanent service but, if not in permanent service, shall not be so attached except with his consent."
(7) After subsection (8) there shall be inserted the following subsection—
"(9) In this section—
"full-time service" means service under a commitment entered into under section 24 of the Reserve Forces Act 1996;
"permanent service" means permanent service on call out under any provision of the Reserve Forces Act 1980, the Reserve Forces Act 1996 or any other call-out obligations of an officer."

Naval Discipline Act 1957 (c. 53)

12.—(1) Section 111 (application of Act to naval forces etc.) of the Naval Discipline Act 1957 shall be amended as follows.
(2) For subsection (3) there shall be substituted the following subsection—
"(3) Any officer or rating of any of the naval reserve forces is subject to this Act while—
(a) in permanent service on call out under any provision of the Reserve Forces Act 1980, the Reserve Forces Act 1996 or any other call-out obligations of an officer;
(b) in full-time service under a commitment entered into under section 24 of the Reserve Forces Act 1996;
(c) undertaking any training or duty (whether in pursuance of an obligation or not); or
(d) serving on the permanent staff of the Royal Fleet Reserve or the Royal Naval Reserve."
(3) In subsection (4), for the words from "naval" to the end there shall be substituted the words "person recalled to the Royal Navy under section 30 of the Reserve Forces Act 1980 or Part VII of the Reserve Forces Act 1996 is subject to this Act from the time he is accepted into service until duly released or discharged".
13. In section 132 (definitions of Her Majesty's forces, etc.) of that Act—
(a) in subsection (7), for the words from "warrant" to the end there shall be substituted the words "marine officers and persons who were transferred to that force from the Royal Marines or who enlisted as marines.";
(b) for subsection (8) there shall be substituted the following subsection—

"(8) In this Act "naval reserve forces" means the Royal Fleet Reserve (except so far as it consists of marine officers and persons who were transferred from the Royal Marines or who enlisted as marines) and the Royal Naval Reserve."

Reserve Forces Act 1966 (c. 30): old references to RMFVR

14. Any reference to the Royal Marine Forces Volunteer Reserve in any Act or instrument shall continue to be construed as may be necessary in consequence of the change of name made by section 1 of the Reserve Forces Act 1966 as a reference to the Royal Marines Reserve.

House of Commons Disqualification Act 1975 (c. 24)

15. In section 3 (certain reserve officers and persons liable to recall not to be regarded as members of regular services) of the House of Commons Disqualification Act 1975, in subsection (1)(b), after the word "pensioner" there shall be inserted the words ", or former soldier,".

Northern Ireland Assembly Disqualification Act 1975 (c. 25)

16. In section 2 (certain reserve officers and persons liable to recall not to be regarded as members of regular services) of the Northern Ireland Assembly Disqualification Act 1975, in subsection (1)(b), after the word "pensioner" there shall be inserted the words ", or former soldier,".

Employment Protection (Consolidation) Act 1978 (c. 44)

17. In section 138(3) (application of Act to service in the armed forces) of the Employment Protection (Consolidation) Act 1978, for the words "Part VI of the Reserve Forces Act 1980" there shall be substituted the words "Part XI of the Reserve Forces Act 1996".

Magistrates' Courts Act 1980 (c. 43)

18. In section 125 (warrants) of the Magistrates' Courts Act 1980, in subsection (4)(b), for the words "Schedule 5 to the Reserve Forces Act 1980" there shall be substituted the words "Schedule 2 to the Reserve Forces Act 1996".

Reserve Forces Act 1982 (c. 14): old references to TAVR

19. Any reference to the Territorial and Army Volunteer Reserve in any Act or instrument shall continue to be construed as may be necessary in consequence of the change of name made by section 1 of the Reserve Forces Act 1982 as a reference to the Territorial Army.

Wages Act 1986 (c. 48)

20. In section 9(4) (exclusion of service as a member of the armed forces) of the Wages Act 1986, for the words "Part VI of the Reserve Forces Act 1980" there shall be substituted the words "Part XI of the Reserve Forces Act 1996".

Wages (Northern Ireland) Order 1988 (S.I. 1988/796 (N.I. 7))

21. In Article 11(3) (exclusion of service as a member of the armed forces) of the Wages (Northern Ireland) Order 1988 for the words "Part VI of the Reserve Forces Act 1980" there shall be substituted the words "Part XI of the Reserve Forces Act 1996".

Official Secrets Act 1989 (c. 6)

22. In section 12(1) (meaning of "Crown servant") of the Official Secrets Act 1989, in paragraph (d), for the words "the Reserve Forces Act 1980" there shall be substituted the words "Part XI of the Reserve Forces Act 1996".

Army Act 1992 (c. 39)

23. In section 2(3) of the Army Act 1992 (application of Reserve Forces (Safeguard of Employment) Act 1985) for the words "in the circumstances mentioned in section 1(1)(a)" there shall be substituted the words "within the meaning".

Trade Union and Labour Relations (Consolidation) Act 1992 (c. 52)

24. In section 274 (armed forces) of the Trade Union and Labour Relations (Consolidation) Act 1992, in subsection (2), for the words "Part VI of the Reserve Forces Act 1980" there shall be substituted the words "Part XI of the Reserve Forces Act 1996".

Tribunals and Inquiries Act 1992 (c. 53)

25. In Schedule 1 to the Tribunals and Inquiries Act 1992 (tribunals under the supervision of the Council on Tribunals), in paragraph 38 (the Reserve Forces) at the end there shall be inserted—

"(c) the appeal tribunals constituted under Part IX of the Reserve Forces Act 1996."

Judicial Pensions and Retirement Act 1993 (c. 8)

26. In Schedule 5 to the Judicial Pensions and Retirement Act 1993 (offices to which retirement provisions apply), at the end there shall be added the following entry—

"Chairman or other member of a reserve forces appeal tribunal constituted under Part IX of the Reserve Forces Act 1996".

Industrial Relations (Northern Ireland) Order 1993 (S.I. 1993/2668 (N.I. 11))

27. In Article 9 (application of industrial relations legislation to the Crown) of the Industrial Relations (Northern Ireland) Order 1993, for the words "Part VI of the Reserve Forces Act 1980" there shall be substituted the words "Part XI of the Reserve Forces Act 1996".

DEFINITIONS

"air forces commission": para. 10 and Air Force Act 1955, s.205(3).
"full-time service": s.24.
"permanent service": s.127(1).
"special member": s.127(1).

GENERAL NOTE

The principal effect of Sched. 10 is to make consequential amendments to the service discipline Acts, the Army/Air Force Acts 1955 and the Naval Discipline Act 1957. The application of the service discipline Acts to the reserves is governed by ss.205, 210 and 211 of the Army Act 1955 (in respect to the land forces); Sched. 7 to the Army Act (in respect of the marine forces); ss.205 and 210 of the Air Force Act 1955 (in respect of the air forces); and ss.111 and 132 of the Naval Discipline Act 1957 (in respect of the naval forces). The changes to these statutes implemented by paras. 1–13 of Sched. 10 to the 1996 Act take account of the new forms of service introduced by the 1996 Act. The opportunity has also been taken to remove some obsolete terminology, such as the reference to the Women's Royal Naval Service in s.132(5) of the Naval Discipline Act 1957; or to the Royal Marine Forces Volunteer Reserve as changed by the Reserve Forces Act 1966, s.1, or to the Territorial and Army Volunteer Reserve as changed by the Reserve Forces Act 1982, s.1. The following effects may be particularly noted. Special members under Pt. V who have signed employee agreements become subject to service discipline law only when they are on duty. In contrast, persons undertaking a full-time service commitment under s.24 and also permanent staff members of a reserve force will be subject to service discipline law at all times.

        SCHEDULE 11

REPEALS

Chapter	Short Title	Extent of repeal
1951 c. 8.	Home Guard Act 1951.	The whole Act.
1955 c. 18.	Army Act 1955.	Section 205(1)(k). Section 212. In section 225(1), in the definition of "regular forces" the words "or the Home Guard".
1955 c. 19.	Air Force Act 1955.	Section 205(1)(c).
1966 c. 45.	Armed Forces Act 1966.	In section 3, the words from "the provisions so" to the end. Section 4(9) and (10).
1980 c. 9.	Reserve Forces Act 1980.	The whole Act, except sections 48, 55, 130 to 138, 140, 151, 156, 157 and 158.
1982 c. 14.	Reserve Forces Act 1982.	The whole Act.
1984 c. 60.	Police and Criminal Evidence Act 1984.	In Schedule 2, the entry relating to the Reserve Forces Act 1980.
1985 c. 17.	Reserve Forces (Safeguard of Employment) Act 1985.	In section 20(1), the definitions of "regular forces", "reserve or auxiliary force" and "service in the armed forces of the Crown" and, in the definition of "permanent service", the words from "and" to the end. In Schedule 4, paragraph 7.
1991 c. 62.	Armed Forces Act 1991.	In Schedule 2, paragraph 11(4).
1992 c. 39.	Army Act 1992.	Section 3(1).
1993 c. 86.	Charities Act 1993.	In Schedule 6, paragraph 16.
1994 c. 19.	Local Government (Wales) Act 1994.	Section 61(4) and (6).
1994 c. 39.	Local Government etc. (Scotland) Act 1994.	In Schedule 13, paragraph 116(3) and (5).

GENERAL NOTE

The Home Guard is now history by virtue of the repeal of the Home Guard Act 1951 (c. 8). See Sheena N. McMurtrie, "Farewell to Dad's Army", *New Law Journal*, April 26, 1996, p.610. There remains, however, in s.66, provision for the recall of certain members of the Long-term Reserve and pensioners under the age of 55 (as well as the recall of the Regular Army Reserve of Officers who are to be combined with the Army Reserve by virtue of Sched. 8, para. 9) who would no doubt take unkindly to an "ageist" description. Note that while most of the 1980 Act is to be repealed, the repeal of the provisions affecting the transitional class will only take effect in the fullness of time on the issuance of an order by the Secretary of State. Among the provisions of the 1980 Act left unrepealed (apart from ss.130–138 in relation to the lieutenancies) are ss.140 and 151. These give authority for the payment of war pensions to former members of the Ulster Defence Regiment and the Home Guard. These provisions were initially destined for repeal. However, they were preserved in order not to give the impression either that the government intended to cease paying pensions to the individuals concerned or to exclude new applicants who might develop a disability attributable to their service.

INDEX

NATIONAL HEALTH SERVICE
(RESIDUAL LIABILITIES) ACT 1996

(1996 c. 15)

An Act to make provision with respect to the transfer of liabilities of certain National Health Service bodies in the event of their ceasing to exist.

[22nd May 1996]

PARLIAMENTARY DEBATES
Hansard, H.C. Vol. 272, col. 913; Vol. 273, col. 808; Vol. 276, cols. 544, 1168. H.L. Vol. 571, col. 1752; Vol. 572, col. 765.

INTRODUCTION
Before the introduction of this Act the Secretary of State had a power to transfer property, rights and liabilities of a National Health Service trust, a Health Authority or a Special Health Authority if any such body ceases to exist. He is now obliged to do so in order to secure that all liabilities are dealt with.

Transfer of residual liabilities: England and Wales

1.—(1) If a National Health Service trust, a Health Authority or a Special Health Authority ceases to exist, the Secretary of State must exercise his statutory powers to transfer property, rights and liabilities of the body so as to secure that all of its liabilities are dealt with.

(2) For the purposes of subsection (1), a liability is dealt with by being transferred to—

(a) the Secretary of State;
(b) a National Health Service trust;
(c) a Health Authority; or
(d) a Special Health Authority.

Transfer of residual liabilities: Scotland

2.—(1) If a National Health Service trust, a Health Board or a Special Health Board ceases to exist, the Secretary of State must exercise his statutory powers to transfer property, rights and liabilities of the body so as to secure that all of its liabilities are dealt with.

(2) For the purposes of subsection (1), a liability is dealt with by being transferred to—

(a) the Secretary of State;
(b) a National Health Service trust;
(c) a Health Board;
(d) a Special Health Board; or
(e) the Common Services Agency for the Scottish Health Service.

Provision for Northern Ireland

3. An Order in Council under paragraph 1(1)(b) of Schedule 1 to the Northern Ireland Act 1974 (legislation for Northern Ireland in the interim period) which contains a statement that it is made only for purposes corresponding to those of section 1—

(a) shall not be subject to paragraph 1(4) and (5) of that Schedule (affirmative resolution of both Houses of Parliament); but

(b) shall be subject to annulment in pursuance of a resolution of either House of Parliament.

Short title and extent

4.—(1) This Act may be cited as the National Health Service (Residual Liabilities) Act 1996.

(2) Section 1 extends only to England and Wales, section 2 extends only to Scotland and section 3 extends only to Northern Ireland.

INDEX

References are to sections

POLICE ACT 1996*

(1996 c. 16)

---

* Annotations by Steve Uglow, Senior Lecturer at Law, University of Kent.

Part III

Police Representative Institutions

Part IV

Complaints, disciplinary proceedings etc.

Chapter I

Complaints

Interpretation

The Police Complaints Authority

Handling of Complaints etc.

CHAPTER II

DISCIPLINARY AND OTHER PROCEEDINGS

PART V

MISCELLANEOUS AND GENERAL

Offences

Miscellaneous financial provisions

Miscellaneous

Supplemental

An Act to consolidate the Police Act 1964, Part IX of the Police and Criminal Evidence Act 1984, Chapter I of Part I of the Police and Magistrates' Courts Act 1994 and certain other enactments relating to the police.

[22nd May 1996]

PARLIAMENTARY DEBATES

Hansard, H.L. Vol. 567, col. 1406; Vol. 568, col. 467; Vol. 570, cols. 8, 418, 1836. H.C. Vol. 278, col. 199.

INTRODUCTION AND GENERAL NOTE

This statute is consolidating legislation, drawing together the provisions of the Police Act 1964 (c. 48), Police and Criminal Evidence Act 1984 (c. 60) and the Police and Magistrates' Courts Act 1994 (c. 29) and putting most police legislation into a single enactment.

Parts I and II lay down the different functions and responsibilities of the new free-standing police authorities, the chief constables (or commissioners in the London forces) and the Secretary of State. Despite the objective of consolidation, it retains the anachronistic distinctions between the governance of the metropolitan forces and that of the provincial forces. The legislation also continues the complex arrangements for police financing.

In Part III, the Act continues the legislation on the various police representative institutions such as the Police Federation, the Police Negotiating Board and the Police Advisory Board.

Part IV of the Act lays down the statutory procedures for dealing with complaints from the public and, to a lesser extent, for disciplinary proceedings against police officers.

PART I

ORGANISATION OF POLICE FORCES

Police areas

Police areas

1.—(1) England and Wales shall be divided into police areas.

(2) The police areas referred to in subsection (1) shall be—

(a) those listed in Schedule 1 (subject to any amendment made to that Schedule by an order under section 32 below, section 58 of the Local Government Act 1972, or section 17 of the Local Government Act 1992),

(b) the metropolitan police district, and

(c) the City of London police area.

(3) References in Schedule 1 to any local government area are to that area as it is for the time being, but excluding any part of it within the metropolitan police district.

GENERAL NOTE

This section is derived from s.1(1) of the Police Act 1964 (c. 48) and s.1 of the Police and Magistrates' Courts Act 1994 (c. 29).

The requirement for police forces in all areas dates from the Municipal Corporations Act 1835 for boroughs and the County and Borough Police Act 1856 for counties. The responsibility rested upon the justices of the peace to establish forces for each county and upon watch committees for the boroughs. There were a large number of police areas until the Police Act 1964 since when the absorption of borough forces into county forces and amalgamations of county forces has reduced the number to 43, two in London (Metropolitan and City of London) and 41 provincial forces. These are specified in Sched. 1 to the Act—there are three categories: metropolitan districts, counties and groups of counties. Non-metropolitan districts (unitary authorities) created under s.14 of the Local Government Act 1992 (c. 14) are included in county forces.

The Home Secretary has the power to alter the size of police areas under ss.32–34 of the Act, taking into account recommendations made by the Welsh Local Government Commission under s.58 of the Local Government Act 1972 (c. 70) or by the Local Government Commission under s.17 of the Local Government Act 1992 (c. 14).

The area of the Metropolitan Police Force is defined under s.76(1)(a)–(d) of the Local Government Act 1972, s.62 and Sched. 8 to the Police Act 1964 (c. 48) and s.101 of this Act. Although the Secretary of State can amend the size of the Metropolitan Police Force area (s.34(2)(a)), he cannot make alterations that result in the abolition of the metropolitan police district (s.32(2)).

The area of the City of London Police was initially laid down in the City of London Police Act 1839 and is defined by s.32 and Sched. 8 to the Police Act 1964 (c. 48) and s.101 of this Act. The area of the City force cannot be altered by the Secretary of State (s.32(1)).

Forces outside London

Maintenance of police forces

2. A police force shall be maintained for every police area for the time being listed in Schedule 1.

GENERAL NOTE

This section is derived from ss.1(1) and 4 of the Police Act 1964 (c. 48) and s.2 of the Police and Magistrates' Courts Act 1994 (c. 29).

A police force shall be maintained for every police area outside London—a police force means "a force maintained by a police authority" under s.101.

Establishment of police authorities

3.—(1) There shall be a police authority for every police area for the time being listed in Schedule 1.

(2) A police authority established under this section for any area shall be a body corporate to be known by the name of the area with the addition of the words "Police Authority".

GENERAL NOTE

This section is derived from s.2 of the Police and Magistrates' Courts Act 1994 (c. 29).

Prior to 1964, the bodies responsible for policing were watch committees in the boroughs and joint standing committees in the counties (under the Local Government Act 1888 (c. 41)). These bodies were abolished by the Police Act 1964 (c. 48) and replaced by police authorities. Prior to 1994, the customary name was "local police authority". Under subs. (2) of this Act the authority is to be known by the name of the area (*e.g.* Cumbria, Thames Valley) with the addition of the words "Police Authority".

Under s.101 of this Act, a police authority is an authority established under this section in relation to a police area listed in Sched. 1. Its membership is laid down under s.4. The authority for the Metropolitan Police Force is the Secretary of State and for the City of London, the Common Council (s.101).

Under s.2(1) of the Police Act 1964 (c. 48) the local police authority was a committee of the main council of the local authority. Under the Police and Magistrates' Courts Act 1994 (c. 29) and subs. (2) of this section, it has become a body corporate with its members presumably individually and collectively liable. It is also less constrained—the Police and Magistrates' Courts Act 1994 (c. 29) repeals s.9 of the Police Act 1964 (c. 48) which gave the authority the necessary powers to acquire and hold land which are no longer necessary.

The authority's accountability to the local authority is under s.20 whereby each relevant council makes arrangements for questions to be put on the discharge of the police authority's functions and for these questions to be answered by a person nominated by the authority. There are no such arrangements for the Metropolitan Police Force or the City of London Police Force.

Membership of police authorities etc.

4.—(1) Subject to subsection (2), each police authority established under section 3 shall consist of seventeen members.

(2) The Secretary of State may by order provide in relation to a police authority specified in the order that the number of its members shall be a specified odd number greater than seventeen.

(3) A statutory instrument containing an order under subsection (2) shall be laid before Parliament after being made.

(4) Schedules 2 and 3 shall have effect in relation to police authorities established under section 3 and the appointment of their members.

GENERAL NOTE

This section is derived from ss.3A and 3B of the Police Act 1964 (c. 48) and s.3 of the Police and Magistrates' Courts Act 1994 (c. 29).

The membership of local police authorities under the Police Act 1964 (c. 48) consisted of two thirds being drawn from the elected members of the council of the relevant local authority and one third being drawn from justices of the peace for the area. The original provisions of the Police and Magistrates' Courts Act 1994 (c. 29) were somewhat controversial (*Current Law Statutes 1994 Vol. 3 at 29–13*) as the size of the authority was to be 16, with eight to be nominated from the local authority, three to be drawn from local justices of the peace and five (including the chairman) to be nominees of the Secretary of State. Parliamentary debate suggested that this threatened the traditional tripartite division of responsibility for the police, between the Home Secretary, chief constable and police authority. The outcome was that membership was to be a minimum of 17, although the Secretary of State may increase that number to any odd number greater than 17 (s.4(2)). The authority is responsible for appointing its own chairman under Sched. 2, para. 9.

The balance and appointment of the authority is laid down in Sched. 2, para. 1(1). Nine members are to be drawn from relevant councils (these are the councils specified in Sched. 1); five are to be independent members and three are to be justices of the peace. Where the size is greater than 17, the council members shall still be in the majority (para. 1(2)).

Council members are appointed by the relevant council to reflect the balance of political parties on the council (para. 4). When more than one council is involved, a joint committee of the councils is set up, again reflecting the overall political balance on the councils as a whole. Where that balance changes, the council or joint committee can remove a member of the authority with a view to restoring that balance (para. 20).

There are similar provisions for magistrates so that where there is a selection panel (constituted under s.21(1A) of the Justices of the Peace Act 1979 (c. 55)) for the police area, that panel shall make the appointments. Where the area covers more than one panel, the appointments shall be made by a joint committee (para. 8).

The independent members are appointed by the existing members of the authority (para. 5) from a shortlist prepared by the Secretary of State according to the provisions of Sched. 3. This provides for a selection panel consisting of three members, one nominated by the authority and one by the Secretary of State. These two, once nominated, then decide on the third member. This panel then submits a list of candidates to the Secretary of State who, if there are fewer candidates than twice the number of vacancies, may nominate additional candidates to bring the overall number up to that figure (Sched. 3, para. 13). These names are then sent to the police authority concerned.

Members of the authority are normally appointed for four years (Sched. 2, para. 16) and should live or work within the area of the authority (para. 13). They should be aged between 21 and 70 (paras. 10 and 13). Under para. 11, a person is disqualified if they have any financial interests in the work of the authority, are a bankrupt, are disqualified to act as a company director or have been sentenced to a sentence of imprisonment (including suspended sentences) of three months or more within the past five years.

Reductions in size of police authorities

5.—(1) This section applies to any order under section 4(2) which varies or revokes an earlier order so as to reduce the number of a police authority's members.

(2) Before making an order to which this section applies, the Secretary of State shall consult—

(a) the authority,

(b) the councils which are relevant councils in relation to the authority for the purposes of Schedule 2, and

(c) any selection panel, constituted under regulations made in accordance with section 21(1A) of the Justices of the Peace Act 1979, which is responsible, or is represented on a joint committee which is responsible, for the appointment of members of the authority.

(3) An order to which this section applies may include provision as to the termination of the appointment of the existing members of the authority and the making of new appointments or re-appointments.

GENERAL NOTE

This section is derived from s.3B of the Police Act 1964 (c. 48) and s.3 of the Police and Magistrates' Courts Act 1994 (c. 29).

Under s.4(2) of the Act, the Secretary of State is empowered to increase the size of the police authority. Where this has happened, s.5 permits the Secretary of State to reduce the number again, provided that he has consulted the police authority itself as well as the relevant councils and selection panels. For the duty to "consult", see *R. v. Secretary of State for Social Services, ex p. Association of Metropolitan Authorities* [1986] 1 All E.R. 164. The Secretary of State must exercise his powers in a manner to promote the efficiency and effectiveness of the police under s.36 of the Act.

General functions of police authorities

6.—(1) Every police authority established under section 3 shall secure the maintenance of an efficient and effective police force for its area.

(2) In discharging its functions, every police authority established under section 3 shall have regard to—

(a) any objectives determined by the Secretary of State under section 37,

(b) any objectives determined by the authority under section 7,

(c) any performance targets established by the authority, whether in compliance with a direction under section 38 or otherwise, and

(d) any local policing plan issued by the authority under section 8.

(3) In discharging any function to which a code of practice issued under section 39 relates, a police authority established under section 3 shall have regard to the code.

(4) A police authority shall comply with any direction given to it by the Secretary of State under section 38 or 40.

GENERAL NOTE

This section is derived from s.4 of the Police Act 1964 (c. 48) and s.4 of the Police and Magistrates' Courts Act 1994 (in part) (c. 29).

Under s.6(1) the primary duty of the police authority is to "maintain" a police force, namely to deploy in a proper fashion, a trained, disciplined and sufficient body of constables.

Under the Police Act 1964 (c. 48), s.4, this primary responsibility was expressed as the maintenance of an "adequate and efficient" force. This was changed by the Police and Magistrates' Courts Act 1994 (c. 29), s.4 to an "efficient and effective" force. Whether this adds anything is to be doubted—can an ineffective force ever be said to be efficient? However the wording stresses the authority's part in ensuring that the force met its objectives, whether those were related to crime control, maintenance of public order or crime prevention. The change of wording is to be found throughout the Act—see ss.11(2), 23(1), 32(3)(b), 36(1), 40(2)(a), 54(2), 57(1) and 58.

This Act changes the wording again so that it is no longer the "duty" of the authority to secure the maintenance of such a force but simply that the authority "shall secure". This wording does not change the statutory duty placed on the authority who would be liable for breach of that duty. *Inter alia* a breach of statutory duty can be an indictable offence at common law or a tort: *Halsbury's Laws (4th ed) Vol. 41 at 543.*

The general exhortation of the 1964 legislation has given way to more specific methods of evaluating police performance—the 1994 legislation provided that authorities should set local policing objectives and issue local policing plans (s.4 of the Police and Magistrates' Courts Act 1994 (c. 29) and ss.7 and 8 of this Act); it also empowered the Home Secretary to set national policing objectives and performance targets for the police (s.15 of the Police and Magistrates' Courts Act 1994 (c. 29) and s.37 of this Act). Initially the key national objectives were to:

- maintain and if possible increase the number of detections for violent crimes
- increase the number of detections for burglaries
- target and prevent crimes which are particular local problems in partnership with the public and other local agencies
- provide high visibility policing to reassure the public
- respond promptly to emergency calls.

Allied to these, the Secretary of State may specify performance indicators to assess forces' attainment of these objectives (s.38 of this Act). An authority must comply with such performance indicators (s.6(4)).

In discharging their functions generally, a police authority "shall have regard" to all such objectives, performance indicators and plans. They must not unreasonably and inconsistently ignore any of them.

The Secretary of State in the past has had no residual functions with regard to police authorities. However by s.15 of the Police and Magistrates' Courts Act 1994 (c. 29) (s.40 of this Act) he was empowered to instruct the inspectors of constabulary to carry out an inspection of any force at any time and, if the force were not efficient or not effective, the Secretary of State could direct the police authority to take such measures as are necessary. By s.6(4) an authority must comply with such directions.

Local policing objectives

7.—(1) Every police authority established under section 3 shall, before the beginning of each financial year, determine objectives for the policing of the authority's area during that year.

(2) Objectives determined under this section may relate to matters to which objectives determined under section 37 also relate, or to other matters, but in any event shall be so framed as to be consistent with the objectives determined under that section.

(3) Before determining objectives under this section, a police authority shall—

(a) consult the chief constable for the area, and
(b) consider any views obtained by the authority in accordance with arrangements made under section 96.

GENERAL NOTE

This section is derived from s.4A of the Police Act 1964 and s.4 of the Police and Magistrates' Courts Act 1994 (in part).

This reflects the move towards more concrete functions for the police authority introduced in 1994. It is mandatory for the authority to determine local policing objectives which may simply reflect national objectives established under s.37 or, more usually, will include particular issues important within a force area. However, local objectives must not be inconsistent with national objectives. Under s.40 the Secretary of State may direct the authority to embrace a particular objective.

By setting objectives, it is inevitable that police authorities will be more involved in operational issues, although by subs. (3) the authority must consult with the chief constable before determining the objectives. The authority must also consult with the local community. This latter function is achieved through local consultative committees which were originally organised under s.106 of the Police and Criminal Evidence Act 1984 (c. 60) as a general mechanism for obtaining the views of the local community. Section 106 is repealed by this Act and replaced by s.96. The only situation when a local community must be consulted on a specific policing issue is under s.7(3)(b).

Local policing plans

8.—(1) Every police authority established under section 3 shall, before the beginning of each financial year, issue a plan setting out the proposed arrangements for the policing of the authority's area during the year ("the local policing plan").

(2) The local policing plan shall include a statement of the authority's priorities for the year, of the financial resources expected to be available and of the proposed allocation of those resources, and shall give particulars of—

(a) any objectives determined by the Secretary of State under section 37,
(b) any objectives determined by the authority under section 7, and
(c) any performance targets established by the authority, whether in compliance with a direction under section 38 or otherwise.

(3) A draft of the local policing plan shall be prepared by the chief constable for the area and submitted by him to the police authority for it to consider.

(4) Before issuing a local policing plan which differs from the draft submitted by the chief constable under subsection (3), a police authority shall consult the chief constable.

(5) A police authority shall arrange for every local policing plan issued by it under this section to be published in such manner as appears to it to be appropriate, and shall send a copy of the plan to the Secretary of State.

GENERAL NOTE

This section is derived from s.4B of the Police Act 1964 (c. 48) and s.4 of the Police and Magistrates' Courts Act 1994 (c. 29) (in part) and provides for the issuing and publication of an annual local policing plan for the force area. The plan must contain (subs. (2)) a financial plan, national and local policing objectives, national and local performance indicators and a statement of the authority's priorities for the year.

Although the plan is the responsibility of the authority, a draft is prepared (subs. (3)) by the chief constable and the authority must consult with him (subs. (4)) if they intend to differ from that draft.

Annual reports by police authorities

9.—(1) As soon as possible after the end of each financial year every police authority established under section 3 shall issue a report relating to the policing of the authority's area for the year.

(2) A report issued by a police authority under this section for any year shall include an assessment of the extent to which the local policing plan for that year issued under section 8 has been carried out.

(3) A police authority shall arrange for every report issued by it under this section to be published in such manner as appears to it to be appropriate, and shall send a copy of the report to the Secretary of State.

GENERAL NOTE

This section is derived from s.4C of the Police Act 1964 (c. 48) and s.4 of the Police and Magistrates' Courts Act 1994 (c. 29) and provides for the issuing and publication of an annual report on the policing of the area, including an assessment (under subs. (2)) of the extent to which the previous year's policing plan has been implemented.

General functions of chief constables

10.—(1) A police force maintained under section 2 shall be under the direction and control of the chief constable appointed under section 11.

(2) In discharging his functions, every chief constable shall have regard to the local policing plan issued by the police authority for his area under section 8.

GENERAL NOTE

This section is derived from s.5 of the Police Act 1964 (c. 48) and s.5 of the Police and Magistrates' Courts Act 1994 (in part) (c. 29).

Under this section, the chief constable has "direction and control" of the force, although at common law there are limits on what a police constable can be ordered to do. Constitutionally each police officer, having been sworn in before a justice of the peace, is the holder of an unpaid and independent Crown office, recognised by the common law as the office of constable (Lustgarten L, *The Governance of Police* (1986) Chap. 2). Constables were historically subordinate to justices of the peace and these origins can still be seen in the fact that commissioners are themselves sworn in as justices. Officers exercise their authority and their powers independently by virtue of the common law, as amended by statute (especially Police and Criminal Evidence Act 1984 (c. 60)). But the modern reality is that there is little independence and the "contemporary police officer is less a descendant of the nineteenth century constable than a distant cousin several times removed." Above street level, there is a tight and hierarchical chain of command (see s.13), culminating in the chief constable.

The chief constable is the director of policing services in his or her area. However, his or her position is quite different from that of the other directors of public services such as health, welfare or education. Such directors would normally be answerable, in terms of planning and performance, initially to local authorities themselves, then to regional and national levels of management and through Secretaries of State to Parliament. Contrary to this, the chief constable's operational control is to a large extent autonomous and does not accord to the normal principles of local democratic scrutiny or parliamentary accountability.

That power is constrained as the chief constable is seen as part of a tripartite system of control with the Home Secretary (Pt. II of this Act) and the police authority being the other parts. But the chief constable is not subject to direct control by either of these. He can only be dismissed by the authority in the "interests of efficiency" (s.11(2)) and only then with Home Office approval. He has the power of appointment, conditions of employment, discipline and dismissal of all the constables and civilian personnel within the force. He is responsible for the operational deployment of the force and its financial management. That "direction and control" also extends to those officers seconded to his or her force under the mutual aid provisions (s.24(3) and also s.1(3) of the Police Act 1969). However, under subs. (2) he must have regard to the local policing plan issued under s.8, a power which will give the authority a limited input into operational matters.

Appointment and removal of chief constables

11.—(1) The chief constable of a police force maintained under section 2 shall be appointed by the police authority responsible for maintaining the force, but subject to the approval of the Secretary of State and to regulations under section 50.

(2) Without prejudice to any regulations under section 50 or under the Police Pensions Act 1976, the police authority, acting with the approval of the Secretary of State, may call upon the chief constable to retire in the interests of efficiency or effectiveness.

(3) Before seeking the approval of the Secretary of State under subsection (2), the police authority shall give the chief constable an opportunity to make representations and shall consider any representations that he makes.

(4) A chief constable who is called upon to retire under subsection (2) shall retire on such date as the police authority may specify or on such earlier date as may be agreed upon between him and the authority.

GENERAL NOTE

This section is derived from ss.4(2) and 5A of the Police Act 1964 (c. 48) and s.5 of the Police and Magistrates' Courts Act 1994 (c. 29) (part).

Under the pre-existing and current legislation, the chief constable was appointed by the police authority. This requires the approval of the Secretary of State and the practice is that the authority chooses their preferred candidate from a short list from the Home Office. Under the 1964 legislation it was possible to be the chief constable of more than one force. This is no longer the case.

Under the Police Act 1964 (c. 48), s.5(4) the chief constable could be called upon to retire in the interests of efficiency. The Police and Magistrates' Courts Act 1994 (c. 29) and this Act expand that so that retirement can be in "the interests of efficiency or effectiveness" (s.11(2)). Before determining the issue, the police authority must give the chief constable the opportunity to make representations and only then should the authority seek the approval of the Secretary of State.

These provisions apply equally to assistant chief constables under s.12(3) as these officers may be called on to deputise for the chief constable (s.12(4)).

The Secretary of State has power under s.42 to require an authority to call on the chief constable (or an assistant chief constable) to resign. On analogy with s.11(2), before determining the issue, the Secretary of State must give the chief constable the opportunity to make representations and may, if necessary, hold an inquiry (s.42(3)).

Assistant chief constables

12.—(1) The ranks that may be held in a police force maintained under section 2 shall include that of assistant chief constable; and in every such police force there shall be at least one person holding that rank.

(2) Appointments and promotions to the rank of assistant chief constable shall be made, in accordance with regulations under section 50, by the police authority after consultation with the chief constable and subject to the approval of the Secretary of State.

(3) Subsections (2), (3) and (4) of section 11 shall apply to an assistant chief constable as they apply to a chief constable.

(4) A chief constable shall, after consulting his police authority, designate a person holding the rank of assistant chief constable to exercise all the powers and duties of the chief constable—

    (a) during any absence, incapacity or suspension from duty of the chief constable, or

    (b) during any vacancy in the office of chief constable.

(5) No more than one person shall be authorised to act by virtue of a designation under subsection (4) at any one time; and a person so authorised shall not have power to act by virtue of that subsection for a continuous period exceeding three months except with the consent of the Secretary of State.

(6) The provisions of subsection (4) shall be in addition to, and not in substitution for, any other enactment which makes provision for the exercise by any other person of powers conferred on a chief constable.

GENERAL NOTE

This section is derived from s.6(1) of the Police Act 1964 (c. 48) and s.6 of the Police and Magistrates' Courts Act 1994 (c. 29).

The rank of assistant chief constable is immediately subordinate to that of chief constable. Each force must have at least one assistant chief constable.

Under the Police Act 1964 (c. 48), s.6, there was an additional rank of deputy chief constable and under s.108(3) of the Police and Criminal Evidence Act 1984 it was possible to have more than one deputy chief constable. These provisions were repealed by the Police and Magistrates' Courts Act 1994 (c. 29) which specifically excluded the rank of deputy chief constable. This was the result of the Sheehy Report (*Inquiry into Police Responsibilities and Rewards* (Cm. 2280) (1993)) which sought to streamline the management hierarchy of the police by removing certain ranks.

However, the need for a substitute for the chief constable in certain circumstances still exists and under subs. (4) an assistant chief constable may be designated (with the approval of the policy authority) to act as chief constable in the absence, incapacity or suspension of the chief constable. This can only last for a maximum of three months unless there is the further approval of the Secretary of State under subs. (5).

Other members of police forces

13.—(1) The ranks that may be held in a police force maintained under section 2 shall be such as may be prescribed by regulations under section 50 and the ranks so prescribed shall include, in addition to chief constable and assistant chief constable, the ranks of superintendent, chief inspector, inspector, sergeant and constable.

(2) The ranks prescribed by regulations under section 50 for the purposes of subsection (1) above shall not include that of deputy chief constable.

(3) Appointments and promotions to any rank below that of assistant chief constable in any police force maintained under section 2 shall be made, in accordance with regulations under section 50, by the chief constable.

GENERAL NOTE

This section is derived from s.7 of the Police Act 1964 (c. 48) and s.7 of the Police and Magistrates' Courts Act 1994 (c. 29).

The ranks of police officers are prescribed by Home Office regulations made under s.50(2)(a) but any ranks so prescribed must include the ranks detailed in s.13.

The precursor of this section, s.7 of the Police Act 1964 (c. 48), was amended as a result of the Sheehy Report (*supra*). This Report recommended the abolition of the ranks of chief inspector, chief superintendent and deputy chief constable. However the rank of chief inspector, previously included only in the regulations under s.50, was retained and is now included as a statutory rank.

Police fund

14.—(1) Each police authority established under section 3 shall keep a fund to be known as the police fund.

(2) Subject to any regulations under the Police Pensions Act 1976, all receipts of the police authority shall be paid into the police fund and all expenditure of the authority shall be paid out of that fund.

(3) Accounts shall be kept by each police authority of payments made into or out of the police fund.

GENERAL NOTE

This section is derived from s.8 of the Police Act 1964 (c. 48) and s.8 of the Police and Magistrates' Courts Act 1994 (c. 29).

Under s.8 of the Police Act 1964, the police authority's accounts were treated as accounts of the local authority under the Local Government Finance Act 1982 (c. 32) and designated as the "police fund". Under s.8(4), approval was needed from the local authority in certain circumstances. Since 1994, as a "body corporate" (s.3 of this Act) the authority has greater flexibility. Whether such an express provision is still necessary is debateable.

The receipts for police expenditure can come from central government, either through the police grant (s.46) or other grants (ss.47 and 48) from the Home Office, through revenue support or non-domestic rates from the Department of the Environment or from the council tax from local government. The authority can also accept gifts and loans under s.93.

Civilian employees

15.—(1) A police authority established under section 3 may employ persons to assist the police force maintained by it or otherwise to enable the authority to discharge its functions.

(2) A police authority shall exercise its powers under section 101 (and section 107) of the Local Government Act 1972 so as to secure that, subject to subsection (3) below, any person employed by the authority under this section is under the direction and control of the chief constable of the police force maintained by the authority.

(3) Subsection (2) shall not apply to such of the persons employed by the authority as may be agreed between the chief constable and the authority or, in the absence of agreement, as may be determined by the Secretary of State.

(4) The powers of direction and control referred to in subsection (2) include the powers of engagement and dismissal.

GENERAL NOTE

This section is derived from s.10 of the Police Act 1964 (c. 48) and s.10 of the Police and Magistrates' Courts Act 1994 (c. 29).

Under s.6(1), the primary duty of the police authority is to "maintain" a police force, namely to employ a trained and disciplined body of constables. This section enables the authority to employ civilians to assist the police or the authority in the performance of their functions. As the authority is a "body corporate" (s.3), whether such an express power is necessary is debateable.

Such a power existed under the Police Act 1964 (c. 48) but the 1994 legislation (repeated in subs. (2)) ensures that where such non-constables are employed (for example, scenes of crime officers), the authority shall ensure (through the conditions of the contract of employment) that they work under the direction and control of the chief constable. However, not all civilian employees work directly under the chief constable and where he or she is working directly for the authority (for example, as treasurer), subs. (3) provides that, with consent, the chief constable shall not direct that employment.

Appointment of clerk

16. A police authority established under section 3 shall appoint a person to be the clerk to the authority.

GENERAL NOTE

This section is derived from s.10A of the Police Act 1964 (c. 48) and s.11 of the Police and Magistrates' Courts Act 1994 (c. 29) (in part) and was introduced in 1994, to act as chief officer and administrative head of the authority's work.

Appointment of persons not employed by police authorities

17. Where a police authority established under section 3 is required or authorised by any Act—

(a) to appoint a person to a specified office under the authority, or

(b) to designate a person as having specified duties or responsibilities,

then, notwithstanding any provision of that Act to the contrary, the authority may appoint or designate either a person employed by the authority under section 15, or a person not holding any office or employment under the authority.

GENERAL NOTE

This section is derived from s.10B of the Police Act 1964 (c. 48) and s.11 of the Police and Magistrates' Courts Act 1994 (c. 29).

Where the authority is required to appoint or designate a person to a task, then the authority can appoint either a civilian employee or someone not employed by the authority. For example, the authority is required to appoint a clerk under s.16 of this Act. Many authorities have appointed an officer from the local authority who remains an employee of the local authority.

Supply of goods and services

18. Subsections (1) to (3) of section 1 of the Local Authorities (Goods and Services) Act 1970 (supply of goods and services by local authorities) shall apply to a police authority established under section 3 as they apply to a local authority, except that in their application to a police authority the references in those subsections to a public body shall be read as references to any person.

GENERAL NOTE

This section is derived from s.8A of the Police Act 1964 (c. 48) and s.9 of the Police and Magistrates' Courts Act 1994 (c. 29).

Section 1 of the Local Authorities (Goods and Services) Act 1970 (c. 39) permits local authorities to enter into a range of contracts. This section enables the police authority to enter such contracts on its own behalf with no involvement of local government. However, as the authority is a "body corporate" (s.3), whether such an express power is necessary is debateable. The authority must comply with compulsory competitive tendering regulations.

Approval of decisions about precepts

19.—(1) A police authority established under section 3 shall not—
  (a) issue a precept under section 40 of the Local Government Finance Act 1992, or
  (b) make the calculations required by section 43 of that Act,
except by a decision of the authority which complies with subsection (2) below.

  (2) A decision complies with this subsection only if the members approving it—
  (a) constitute at least half of the total membership at the time of the decision, and
  (b) include more than half of the members (at that time) appointed under paragraph 2 of Schedule 2.

GENERAL NOTE

This section is derived from s.28 of the Police and Magistrates' Courts Act 1994 (c. 29).

Part of the authority's income is from the council tax collected by the relevant councils. The new autonomy of the police authority requires that for this purpose it becomes a precepting authority. That is, the authority has a statutory responsibility to set a budget for the year, the total amount of which is determined by the Secretary of State. Having set its budget, the authority issues a precept to the relevant councils under s.40 of the Local Government Finance Act 1992 as a result of which the authority will receive a proportion of the council tax collected by that council.

Section 27 of the Police and Magistrates' Courts Act 1994 (c. 29) (still in force) established the police authority as a precepting authority with a limited budget under s.39 of the Local Government Finance Act 1992 (c. 14). However, this section imposes certain conditions before a precept is issued, namely that at least half of the total membership and at least half of the "council appointed" members approve of the precept.

Questions on police matters at council meetings

20.—(1) Every relevant council shall make arrangements (whether by standing orders or otherwise) for enabling questions on the discharge of the functions of a police authority to be put by members of the council at a meeting of the council for answer by a person nominated by the authority for that purpose.

  (2) On being given reasonable notice by a relevant council of a meeting of that council at which questions on the discharge of the police authority's functions are to be put, the police authority shall nominate one or more of its members to attend the meeting to answer those questions.

(3) In this section "relevant council" has the same meaning as in Schedule 2.

GENERAL NOTE

This section is derived from s.11 of the Police Act 1964 (c. 48) and s.12 of the Police and Magistrates' Courts Act 1994 (c. 29).

This provides for some residual democratic accountability through the local authority. Each relevant council should make arrangements for questions to be put on the discharge of the police authority's functions and for these questions to be answered by a person nominated by the authority, who need not be a council member. There are no such arrangements for the Metropolitan Police Force or the City of London Police Force.

Application of certain provisions to police authorities

21.—(1) Any relevant legislative provision which, immediately before 21st July 1994, applied to police authorities constituted in accordance with section 2 of the Police Act 1964 shall, except where the context otherwise requires, apply in the same way to police authorities established under section 3 above.

(2) Subsection (1) is subject to any provision to the contrary made—

(a) by this Act, or

(b) by any other Act passed, or subordinate legislation made, on or after 21st July 1994.

(3) For the purposes of subsection (1), a provision is a "relevant legislative provision" if it is a provision (other than a provision which applies only to specified police authorities) of an instrument which—

(a) was made before 21st July 1994 under a public general Act, and

(b) is of a legislative character.

GENERAL NOTE

This section is derived from s.45 of the Police and Magistrates' Courts Act 1994 (c. 29).

This is a facilitative, fall-back, section so that where there is pre-existing legislation which applied to the old police authorities constituted under the Police Act 1964, such legislation shall continue to apply to the new authorities constituted under this Act.

General provisions

Reports by chief constables to police authorities

22.—(1) Every chief constable shall, as soon as possible after the end of each financial year, submit to the police authority a general report on the policing during that year of the area for which his force is maintained.

(2) A chief constable shall arrange for a report submitted by him under subsection (1) to be published in such manner as appears to him to be appropriate.

(3) The chief constable of a police force shall, whenever so required by the police authority, submit to that authority a report on such matters as may be specified in the requirement, being matters connected with the policing of the area for which the force is maintained.

(4) A report submitted under subsection (3) shall be in such form as the police authority may specify.

(5) If it appears to the chief constable that a report in compliance with subsection (3) would contain information which in the public interest ought not to be disclosed, or is not needed for the discharge of the functions of the police authority, he may request that authority to refer the requirement to submit the report to the Secretary of State; and in any such case the requirement shall be of no effect unless it is confirmed by the Secretary of State.

(6) The police authority may arrange, or require the chief constable to arrange, for a report submitted under subsection (3) to be published in such manner as appears to the authority to be appropriate.

(7) This section shall apply in relation to the City of London police force as if for references to a chief constable there were substituted references to the Commissioner.

GENERAL NOTE

This section is derived from s.12 of the Police Act 1964 (c. 48) and Police and Magistrates' Courts Act 1994 (c. 29), Sched. 5, para. 1.

This section provides for chief constables to furnish their police authority with two types of report—firstly, under subs. (1) an annual report on the general policing of the force area and secondly, when required by the authority under subs. (3), a report on some specific matter connected with the policing of the area. The publication of an annual report remains a mandatory duty, although the words "in writing" are now omitted (Police and Magistrates' Courts Act 1994, Sched. 5, para. 1). This power of authorities to require reports caused some friction between police authorities (especially in metropolitan areas) and their chief constables in the 1970s. The chief constable can initially refuse to comply with such a requirement if he or she believes that disclosure would not be in the public interest or that the matters are outside of the functions of the police authority's functions. In such a case, the requirement to furnish a report is reviewed by the Secretary of State under subs. (5) who must consent before a report need be produced.

The Secretary of State can also require reports from both authorities and chief constables— ss.43 and 44.

Collaboration agreements

23.—(1) If it appears to the chief officers of police of two or more police forces that any police functions can more efficiently or effectively be discharged by members of those forces acting jointly, they may, with the approval of the police authorities which maintain those forces, make an agreement for that purpose.

(2) If it appears to any two or more police authorities that any premises, equipment or other material or facilities can with advantage be provided jointly for the police forces maintained by those authorities, they may make an agreement for that purpose.

(3) Any expenditure incurred under an agreement made under this section shall be borne by the police authorities in such proportions as they may agree or as may, in the absence of agreement, be determined by the Secretary of State.

(4) An agreement under subsection (1) or (2) may be varied or determined by a subsequent agreement.

(5) If it appears to the Secretary of State that an agreement should be made under subsection (1), (2) or (4), he may, after considering any representations made by the parties concerned, direct those parties to enter into such an agreement under those provisions as may be specified in the direction.

(6) The reference in subsection (1) to members of a police force includes a reference to special constables appointed for the area for which that force is maintained.

(7) The provisions of this section shall not prejudice the power of a police authority to act jointly, or co-operate in any other way, with any person where to do so is calculated to facilitate, or is conducive or incidental to, the discharge of any of the authority's functions.

GENERAL NOTE

This section is derived from s.13 of the Police Act 1964 (c. 48) and Police and Magistrates' Courts Act 1994 (c. 29), Sched. 5, para. 5.

This section provides for formal collaboration between forces where the sharing of premises, equipment or facilities seems appropriate. For example, police forces are to a limited extent regionalised and within the region might have shared training facilities or specialist investigative squads such as the regional crime squads. The oldest of these, dating from 1965, are the five regional crime squads (RCS). RCS responsibilities are to identify and arrest those responsible for serious offences which transcend force boundaries, to cooperate with regional criminal intelligence officers in generating intelligence and to assist in the investigation of serious crime, usually for a limited period. The current terms of reference are set out in *Home Office Circular No. 28/1987*. For a discussion of RCS work, see *Maguire M. and Norris C. (1992): The Conduct and*

Supervision of Criminal Investigations (Royal Commission on Criminal Justice Research Study No. 5) (HMSO). The squads are staffed by detectives from adjacent forces. Further, the National Crime Intelligence Service (NCIS) was set up in 1992, to develop along the lines of the FBI. Such co-ordination can be seen in the area of drugs, where every force has a dedicated Drugs Squad and these also exist at RCS and NCIS level. This also occurs in areas such as immigration, terrorism or political surveillance through the work of Special Branch. However such formal schemes do not prejudice more informal methods (subs. (7)).

Such collaboration can be initiated by the chief constable or the authority, although the authority must consent to any such scheme. Where forces or authorities are refusing to co-operate, there is a residual power under subs. (5) for the Secretary of State to direct the parties to enter into an agreement.

Aid of one police force by another

24.—(1) The chief officer of police of any police force may, on the application of the chief officer of police of any other police force, provide constables or other assistance for the purpose of enabling the other force to meet any special demand on its resources.

(2) If it appears to the Secretary of State to be expedient in the interests of public safety or order that any police force should be reinforced or should receive other assistance for the purpose of enabling it to meet any special demand on its resources, and that satisfactory arrangements under subsection (1) cannot be made, or cannot be made in time, he may direct the chief officer of police of any police force to provide such constables or other assistance for that purpose as may be specified in the direction.

(3) While a constable is provided under this section for the assistance of another police force he shall, notwithstanding section 10(1), be under the direction and control of the chief officer of police of that other force.

(4) The police authority maintaining a police force for which assistance is provided under this section shall pay to the police authority maintaining the force from which that assistance is provided such contribution as may be agreed upon between those authorities or, in the absence of any such agreement, as may be provided by any agreement subsisting at the time between all police authorities generally, or, in the absence of such general agreement, as may be determined by the Secretary of State.

GENERAL NOTE

This section is derived from s.14 of the Police Act 1964 (c. 48) and provides another technique for co-ordination between individual forces. Mutual assistance between forces was first given statutory recognition in s.25 of the Police Act 1890. The chief constable (or commissioner as this section applies to all forces including the Metropolitan force) is empowered to provide assistance, normally police officers, to other forces. Such constables are under the direction and control of the chief constable of the receiving force (subs. (3)). Although such mutual aid has the appearance of voluntary collaboration under subs. (1), the Home Secretary has powers to require that such assistance be given under subs. (2). For a discussion of the legal basis of mutual aid, see Lustgarten, *Governance of the Police* (1986), Chap. 8.

Such mutual aid can be temporary, providing extra officers for public order duties, or permanent when personnel are seconded to regional or national specialist squads.

Collaboration is also seen in the changing role of the Association of Chief Police Officers (ACPO), who have been described as a "focal part of the policy-making scene" and the "vertebrae of more centrally co-ordinated policing" and who are an influential lobby group on all matters of criminal justice policy. Operationally they have developed their own operational manuals on topics such as public order tactics and also set up in 1972 the National Reporting Centre, based in New Scotland Yard, to organise the provision of mutual aid, co-ordinating the movement of constables between forces in times of emergency. It has been activated on occasions such as the prison officers' dispute of 1980–81, the inner city disturbances in 1981, the papal visit in 1982 and, most controversially, the miners' strike in 1984–85. The demands on policing of this last event placed financial demands on both provider and receiver authorities and demonstrated the difficulties of arriving at mutually acceptable financial settlements envisaged in subs. (4). The Secretary of State's powers for covering such expenditure is quite limited, s.48 only envisages such grants in cases involving national security.

Provision of special services

25.—(1) The chief officer of police of a police force may provide, at the request of any person, special police services at any premises or in any locality in the police area for which the force is maintained, subject to the payment to the police authority of charges on such scales as may be determined by that authority.

(2) In the application of this section to the metropolitan police force, for the reference in subsection (1) to the police authority there shall be substituted a reference to the Receiver for the Metropolitan Police District.

GENERAL NOTE

This provision derives from s.15 of the Police Act 1964 (c. 48) and is unaltered. Chief officers are permitted to provide special services to individuals or organisations and to charge for such services. A modern example is policing at sporting events—*Harris v. Sheffield United Football Club* [1987] 2 All E.R. 838 where the court held that the police presence inside the ground was beyond that which the club was entitled to expect from the chief constable's duty to enforce the law and was therefore special police services within the terms in this section. See also *Glasbrook Bros v. Glamorgan County Council* [1924] All E.R. 579 where, during a strike, the colliery manager insisted that the police officers were billeted on the premises. The House of Lords upheld the practice that in such circumstances the colliery would be expected to pay the additional cost.

Provision of advice and assistance to international organisations etc.

26.—(1) Subject to the provisions of this section, a police authority may provide advice and assistance—

(a) to an international organisation or institution, or

(b) to any other person or body which is engaged outside the United Kingdom in the carrying on of activities similar to any carried on by the authority or the chief officer of police for its area.

(2) The power conferred on a police authority by subsection (1) includes a power to make arrangements under which a member of the police force maintained by the authority is engaged for a period of temporary service with a person or body within paragraph (a) or (b) of that subsection.

(3) The power conferred by subsection (1) shall not be exercised except with the consent of the Secretary of State or in accordance with a general authorisation given by him.

(4) A consent or authorisation under subsection (3) may be given subject to such conditions as appear to the Secretary of State to be appropriate.

(5) Nothing in this section authorises a police authority to provide any financial assistance by—

(a) making a grant or loan,

(b) giving a guarantee or indemnity, or

(c) investing by acquiring share or loan capital.

(6) A police authority may make charges for advice or assistance provided by it under this section.

(7) In its application in relation to the metropolitan police force this section shall apply—

(a) as if the power conferred by subsection (1) were conferred on the Commissioner of Police of the Metropolis (and accordingly as if the references in subsections (1)(b) and (2) to a police authority were omitted), and

(b) as if in subsection (6) the reference to a police authority were a reference to the Receiver for the Metropolitan Police District.

(8) The provisions of this section are without prejudice to the Police (Overseas Service) Act 1945 and section 10 of the Overseas Development and Co-operation Act 1980.

GENERAL NOTE

This section is derived from s.15A of the Police Act 1964 (c. 48) as inserted by s.13 of the Police and Magistrates' Courts Act 1994 (c. 29).

This permits the police authority to provide, with the consent of the Secretary of State, advice and assistance, including the secondment of officers, to international organisations. Previously under the Police (Overseas Service) Act 1945 (c. 17), police officers could be seconded to act on behalf of foreign governments and under the Overseas Development and Co-operation Act 1980 (c. 63), s.10, authorities could provide officers to assist with public services. This is a broader and more flexible provision, permitting the authority to assist the U.N., Europol or any individuals or bodies engaged in policing functions.

Special constables

27.—(1) The chief officer of police of the police force maintained for a police area may, in accordance with regulations under section 51, appoint special constables for that area.

(2) Subject to regulations under section 51, all special constables appointed for a police area shall be under the direction and control of, and subject to dismissal by, the chief officer of police.

GENERAL NOTE

This section is derived from s.16 of the Police Act 1964 (c. 48).

The "special" is the descendant of the citizen in uniform. The special constable possesses the powers and privileges of constable within the area for which he or she is appointed—see s.30(2) (3) and (4). There was a Special Constables Act 1831 empowering justices to appoint specials on the occasion of a riot or the threat of a riot. This section, replacing s.16 of the Police Act 1964, maintains the power for chief constables to appoint special constables in accordance with the regulations promulgated by the Secretary of State under s.51.

Police cadets

28.—(1) The chief officer of police of a police force may, in accordance with regulations under section 52, appoint persons as police cadets to undergo training with a view to becoming members of that police force.

(2) Subject to regulations under section 52, all police cadets shall be under the control of, and subject to dismissal by, the chief officer of police.

(3) Without prejudice to subsection (2), for the purposes of any enactment relating to the functions of employers and of any rule of law with respect to the vicarious liability of employers, the police authority that maintains a police force shall be treated as the employer of any police cadets undergoing training with the force.

(4) In the application of this section to the metropolitan police force, for the reference in subsection (3) to the police authority there shall be substituted a reference to the Receiver for the Metropolitan Police District.

GENERAL NOTE

This section is derived from s.17 of the Police Act 1964 (c. 48).

Police cadets were first given statutory recognition in the Police Act 1964 (c. 48), although the employment of youths undergoing training with a view to them becoming police officers had existed for some decades before that time. In the 1960s and 1970s, ex-cadets formed a significant part of recruit intake. That has now substantially declined. This section, replacing s.17 of the Police Act 1964 (c. 48), maintains the power for chief constables to appoint cadets in accordance with the regulations promulgated by the Secretary of State under s.52. The cadets are under the control of the chief constable, although not the "direction and control" which is the phrase used in ss.10 and 27.

Under subs. (3), although the police authority is to be treated as the employer of the cadet, this does not give an industrial tribunal jurisdiction to hear a complaint for unfair dismissal—*Wiltshire Police Authority v. Wynn* [1980] 3 W.L.R. 445.

Attestation of constables

29. Every member of a police force maintained for a police area and every special constable appointed for a police area shall, on appointment, be attested as a constable by making a declaration in the form set out in Schedule 4—

    (a) in the case of a member of the metropolitan police force or a special constable appointed for the metropolitan police district, before the Commissioner or an Assistant Commissioner of Police of the Metropolis, and

    (b) in any other case, before a justice of the peace having jurisdiction within the police area.

GENERAL NOTE

This section is derived from s.18 of the Police Act 1964 (c. 48).

The attestation is to be found in Sched. 4. The office of constable is an office under the Crown and as such the police officer exercises his or her authority and powers independently by virtue of the common law, as amended by statute. But all officers are members of a police force and subject to the chief constable's power to "direct and control" his or her force under s.10. Thus the modern reality is that there is little independence and the "*contemporary police officer is less a descendant of the nineteenth century constable than a distant cousin several times removed.*"

There is a contradiction since an officer at street level operates independently of direct control, exercises a discretion on whether to stop, search and question. This is of low visibility and almost impossible to supervise. But above street level, there is a tight and hierarchical chain of command, culminating in the chief constable. The officer's autonomy disappears and there is a military quality to policing which is seen at its extreme in the control of public disorder, when the officer works as part of a squad, directly responding to an officer's commands and where individual discretion is non-existent.

Constables are sworn in before a justice of the peace. The members of the Metropolitan Force are sworn in before the commissioner or assistant commissioner, who are justices of the peace in their own right by virtue of the Metropolitan Police Acts of 1829 and 1856.

Jurisdiction of constables

30.—(1) A member of a police force shall have all the powers and privileges of a constable throughout England and Wales and the adjacent United Kingdom waters.

(2) A special constable shall have all the powers and privileges of a constable in the police area for which he is appointed and, where the boundary of that area includes the coast, in the adjacent United Kingdom waters.

(3) Without prejudice to subsection (2), a special constable appointed for a police area shall have all the powers and privileges of a constable—

    (a) in the case of a special constable appointed for a police area other than the City of London police area, in any other police area which is contiguous to his own police area; and

    (b) in the case of a special constable appointed for the City of London police area, in the metropolitan police district and in any police area which is contiguous to that district.

(4) A special constable who is for the time being required by virtue of section 23 or 24 to serve with another police force shall have all the powers and privileges of a constable in any area in which special constables appointed for the area for which that force is maintained have those powers and privileges under this section.

(5) In this section—

    "powers" includes powers under any enactment, whenever passed or made;

    "United Kingdom waters" means the sea and other waters within the seaward limits of the territorial sea;

and this section, so far as it relates to powers under any enactment, makes them exercisable throughout the United Kingdom waters whether or not the enactment applies to those waters apart from this provision.

(6) This section is without prejudice to—

(a) sections 98 and 99 below, and
(b) any other enactment conferring powers on constables for particular purposes.

GENERAL NOTE

This section is derived from s.19 of the Police Act 1964 (c. 48) as amended by s.160 of the Criminal Justice and Public Order Act 1994 (c. 33), Police and Magistrates' Courts Act 1994 (c. 29), Sched. 5, para. 4 and Local Government Act 1972, s.196(1) and (5).

The most basic powers exercised by a police officer are ones that can be exercised by any citizen but there are now many others which have been given to a police officer by statute, notably the Police and Criminal Evidence Act 1984 (c. 60). An example of a power that a citizen does not possess would be the constable's power to stop and search under s.1 of the Police and Criminal Evidence Act 1984.

Before 1964, a constable could only exercise such powers within the area for which the officer had been appointed. Since 1964, the police officer's jurisdiction is not limited to the area of the force to which he or she belongs but extends throughout England and Wales. If seconded to the Royal Ulster Constabulary or a Scottish force under s.98, the constable has the powers and privileges of any member of that force.

Under subss. (2) (3) and (4), the jurisdiction of special constables is more limited. It is generally restricted to the force area and any police area which is contiguous—this latter term is probably narrowly defined as "touching"—*James A. Jobling & Co v. Sunderland County Borough Assessment Committee* [1944] 1 All E.R. 207.

Rewards for diligence

31. A police authority may, on the recommendation of the chief officer of police, grant out of the police fund to members of the police force maintained by that authority rewards for exceptional diligence or other specially meritorious conduct.

GENERAL NOTE

This section is derived from s.20 of the Police Act 1964 (c. 48) and allows a police authority to reward police officers for meritorious conduct. Presumably this is exhortatory since such bonuses are unlikely to be *ultra vires.*

Alteration of police areas

GENERAL NOTE

Sections 32–34

These sections derive from s.21 of the Police Act 1964 (c. 48) as amended by s.14 of the Police and Magistrates' Courts Act 1994 (c. 29).

The power to alter the size of police areas is carefully scrutinised as this is a mechanism by which central government can reduce the number of forces, limit the local connection with a force and be seen as moving towards a "national" police force. The Secretary of State has the power to alter the size of any force, except that of the City of London (s.32(1)) and can thereby abolish any force except that of the Metropolitan force (s.32(2) and by implication that of the City of London). This power can be exercised on his or her own initiative (s.32(3)(b)) although this may be subject to judicial review were such changes in the interest of neither efficiency nor effectiveness. Although the Secretary of State must, under s.33, give notice of any changes to the local authorities and the police authorities concerned, and must consider any objections, there is no requirement for a local inquiry of any kind, although any order under s.32 must be laid before each House of Parliament (s.34(3)).

Demographic changes and alterations in local government boundaries obviously require a flexible mechanism to allow police force areas to reflect such changes. But such flexibility brings in its wake the possibility that a small number of regional forces will replace the current 43 local forces.

Power to alter police areas by order

32.—(1) The Secretary of State may by order make alterations in police areas in England and Wales other than the City of London police area.

(2) The alterations that may be made by an order under this section include alterations that result in a reduction or an increase in the number of police

areas, but not alterations that result in the abolition of the metropolitan police district.

(3) The Secretary of State shall not exercise his power under this section to make alterations unless either—

    (a) he has received a request to make the alterations from the police authority for each of the areas (other than the metropolitan police district) affected by them, or

    (b) it appears to him to be expedient to make the alterations in the interests of efficiency or effectiveness.

(4) The Secretary of State shall exercise his power to make orders under this section in such a way as to ensure that none of the following areas—

    (a) a county in which there are no district councils,

    (b) a district in any other county,

    (c) a county borough in Wales, and

    (d) a London borough,

is divided between two or more police areas.

(5) Subsection (4) shall not have effect so as to prevent the maintenance of any part of the boundary of the metropolitan police district as it existed immediately before 1st April 1995.

Objections to alterations proposed by Secretary of State

33.—(1) Before making an order under section 32 by virtue of subsection (3)(b) of that section, the Secretary of State shall give notice of his proposal to—

    (a) the police authority for every area (other than the metropolitan police district) that he proposes to alter,

    (b) the council of every county, district, county borough or London borough wholly or partly within any area (other than the metropolitan police district) that he proposes to alter,

    (c) the council of every London borough, county or district all or part of which would under the proposal be brought into or left out of the metropolitan police district, and

    (d) such other persons as he considers appropriate.

(2) A notice under subsection (1) shall—

    (a) specify the proposed alterations and describe the general nature of any related provisions proposed to be included in the order,

    (b) set out the Secretary of State's reasons for proposing the alterations, and

    (c) specify a date before which any objections to the proposals are to be delivered to the Secretary of State.

(3) The date specified under subsection (2)(c) shall fall after the end of the period of four months beginning with the date of the notice.

(4) Where objections have been duly delivered to the Secretary of State by a person notified under subsection (1), the Secretary of State shall before making the order under section 32—

    (a) consider the objections, and

    (b) give to that person a further notice stating whether he accepts the objections and, if he does not, giving his reasons.

(5) Where the Secretary of State has given a notice under subsection (1) specifying proposed alterations, the provisions of an order making the alterations may be inconsistent with the notice so far as it describes the general nature of the provisions, and may contain provisions not referred to in the notice.

Orders altering police areas: supplementary provisions

34.—(1) The power to make orders under section 32 includes power to make such supplementary and transitional provision as the Secretary of State thinks necessary or expedient, including—
(a) provision as to the membership of a police authority;
(b) provision for the transfer of property, rights and liabilities;
(c) provision for the transfer of members of police forces and other persons;
(d) provision as to pending legal proceedings.
(2) Without prejudice to subsection (1), the power to make orders under section 32 includes power—
(a) to amend Schedule 1 to this Act and section 76 of the London Government Act 1963 (extent of metropolitan police district), and
(b) to amend any other enactment, and any instrument made under any enactment, where the amendment is consequential on any provision of the order.
(3) No order shall be made under section 32 by virtue of subsection (3)(b) of that section unless a draft of the order has been laid before and approved by resolution of each House of Parliament.
(4) An order to which subsection (3) applies, and which would apart from this subsection be treated for the purposes of the standing orders of either House of Parliament as a hybrid instrument, shall proceed in that House as if it were not such an instrument.
(5) A statutory instrument containing an order made under section 32 by virtue of subsection (3)(a) of that section shall be subject to annulment in pursuance of a resolution of either House of Parliament.

Supplemental

The Scilly Isles

35. For the purposes of the application of this Part to the Isles of Scilly—
(a) the Isles shall be treated as if they were a county, and
(b) references to the council of a county shall be construed as references to the Council of the Isles.

GENERAL NOTE
This section is derived from s.26 of the Police Act 1964 (c. 48).

PART II

CENTRAL SUPERVISION, DIRECTION AND FACILITIES

Functions of Secretary of State

General duty of Secretary of State

36.—(1) The Secretary of State shall exercise his powers under the provisions of this Act referred to in subsection (2) in such manner and to such extent as appears to him to be best calculated to promote the efficiency and effectiveness of the police.
(2) The provisions of this Act mentioned in subsection (1) are—
(a) Part I;
(b) this Part;
(c) Part III (other than sections 61 and 62);
(d) in Chapter II of Part IV, section 85 and Schedule 6; and
(e) in Part V, section 95.

GENERAL NOTE
This section is derived from s.28 of the Police Act 1964 (c. 48) and Police and Magistrates' Courts Act 1994 (c. 29), Sched. 5, para. 6.

There is still no residual power for the Secretary of State to take over the running of a police force which is failing in its duties. However this establishes a general duty for the Secretary of State to exercise his powers in a manner calculated to promote the efficiency and effectiveness of the police service. The wording was amended in 1994 to include "effectiveness" alongside "efficiency". It is a section that may facilitate parliamentary questions about the powers of the Secretary of State under the Act and might also form a basis for judicial review of any decisions which the Secretary of State takes under subs. (2).

Setting of objectives for police authorities

37.—(1) The Secretary of State may by order determine objectives for the policing of the areas of all police authorities established under section 3.

(2) Before making an order under this section the Secretary of State shall consult—

(a) persons whom he considers to represent the interests of police authorities established under section 3, and

(b) persons whom he considers to represent the interests of chief constables of forces maintained by those authorities.

(3) A statutory instrument containing an order under this section shall be laid before Parliament after being made.

GENERAL NOTE

This section is derived from s.28A of the Police Act 1964 (c. 48) as inserted by s.15 of the Police and Magistrates' Courts Act 1994 (c. 29).

The legislation of 1994 and 1996 has put in place specific methods of evaluating police performance. The 1994 legislation provided that authorities should set local policing objectives and issue local policing plans (s.4 of the Police and Magistrates' Courts Act 1994 (c. 29) and ss.7 and 8 of this Act). Such local plans must be consistent with the Home Secretary's power to set national policing objectives and performance targets for the police. These have been laid down by statutory instrument: Police (Secretary of State's Objectives) Order 1994 (S.I. 1994 No. 2678). The key national objectives are to:

- maintain and if possible increase the number of detections for violent crimes
- increase the number of detections for burglaries
- target and prevent crimes which are particular local problems in partnership with the public and other local agencies
- provide high visibility policing to reassure the public
- respond promptly to emergency calls.

Setting of performance targets

38.—(1) Where an objective has been determined under section 37, the Secretary of State may direct police authorities to establish levels of performance ("performance targets") to be aimed at in seeking to achieve the objective.

(2) A direction under this section may be given to all police authorities established under section 3 or to one or more particular authorities.

(3) A direction given under this section may impose conditions with which the performance targets must conform, and different conditions may be imposed for different authorities.

(4) The Secretary of State shall arrange for any direction given under this section to be published in such manner as appears to him to be appropriate.

GENERAL NOTE

This section is derived from s.28B of the Police Act 1964 (c. 48) as inserted by s.15 of the Police and Magistrates' Courts Act 1994 (c. 29).

Allied to the power to determine objectives under s.37, the Secretary of State may specify performance indicators to assess forces' attainment of these objectives (s.38). An authority must comply with such performance indicators under s.38(2).

Codes of practice

39.—(1) The Secretary of State may issue codes of practice relating to the discharge by police authorities established under section 3 of any of their functions.

(2) The Secretary of State may from time to time revise the whole or part of any code of practice issued under this section.

(3) The Secretary of State shall lay before Parliament a copy of any code of practice, and of any revision of a code of practice, issued by him under this section.

GENERAL NOTE

This section is derived from s.28C of the Police Act 1964 (c. 48) as inserted by s.15 of the Police and Magistrates' Courts Act 1994 (c. 29).

Codes of Practice have become a familiar technique for regulating criminal justice agencies, especially those promulgated under Police and Criminal Evidence Act 1984 (c. 60). Section 39 provides for such Codes for the work of police authorities. The first of these was *Financial Management (1993/94 HCP 673)*.

Power to give directions to police authorities after adverse reports

40.—(1) The Secretary of State may at any time require the inspectors of constabulary to carry out, for the purposes of this section, an inspection under section 54 of any police force maintained under section 2.

(2) Where a report made to the Secretary of State under section 54 on an inspection carried out for the purposes of this section states—

(a) that, in the opinion of the person making the report, the force inspected is not efficient or not effective, or

(b) that in his opinion, unless remedial measures are taken, the force will cease to be efficient or will cease to be effective,

the Secretary of State may direct the police authority responsible for maintaining the force to take such measures as may be specified in the direction.

GENERAL NOTE

This section is derived from s.28D of the Police Act 1964 (c. 48), as inserted by s.15 of the Police and Magistrates' Courts Act 1994 (c. 29).

The power of the Secretary of State to influence local policing has been significantly increased by this section. Where there is an adverse report on the policing of an area by an inspector of constabulary acting under s.54, the Secretary of State can direct the police authority to take such measures as he or she specifies, although such measures must be those that will improve the efficiency or effectiveness of the force.

Directions as to minimum budget

41.—(1) The power of the Secretary of State to give directions under section 40 to a police authority established under section 3 shall include power to direct the authority that the amount of its budget requirement for any financial year (under section 43 of the Local Government Finance Act 1992) shall not be less than an amount specified in the direction.

(2) The power exercisable by virtue of subsection (1), and any direction given under that power, are subject to any limitation imposed under Chapter V of Part I of the Local Government Finance Act 1992.

(3) A direction shall not be given by virtue of subsection (1) in relation to a financial year at any time after the end of the preceding December.

(4) Where the Secretary of State gives a direction to a police authority by virtue of subsection (1), any precept issued or calculation made by the authority under Part I of the Local Government Finance Act 1992 which is inconsistent with the direction shall be void.

GENERAL NOTE

This section is derived from s.29 of the Police and Magistrates' Courts Act 1994 (c. 29).

This is a further new power for the Secretary of State. It is again contingent upon an adverse report on a force by an inspector of constabulary acting under s.54. Where there is such a report, the Secretary of State can direct the police authority that expenditure must reach at least a specified amount. Thus the Secretary of State can prevent the local authority members of a police authority from, for example, cutting back on the police budget rather than expenditure on education or social services. However, it has to be demonstrated that such expenditure cuts would affect the efficiency or effectiveness of the force.

Removal of chief constables, etc.

42.—(1) The Secretary of State may require a police authority to exercise its power under section 11 to call upon the chief constable to retire in the interests of efficiency or effectiveness.

(2) Before requiring the exercise of that power or approving the exercise of that or the similar power exercisable with respect to an assistant chief constable, the Secretary of State shall give the chief constable or assistant chief constable an opportunity to make representations to him and shall consider any representations so made.

(3) Where representations are made under this section the Secretary of State may, and in a case where he proposes to require the exercise of the power mentioned in subsection (1) shall, appoint one or more persons (one at least of whom shall be a person who is not an officer of police or of a Government department) to hold an inquiry and report to him and shall consider any report made under this subsection.

(4) The costs incurred by a chief constable or assistant chief constable in respect of an inquiry under this section, taxed in such manner as the Secretary of State may direct, shall be defrayed out of the police fund.

GENERAL NOTE

This section is derived from s.29 of the Police Act 1964 (c. 48) and Police and Magistrates' Courts Act 1994 (c. 29), Sched. 5, para. 7.

Under s.11, the chief constable can be called upon by the police authority to retire in "the interests of efficiency or effectiveness" (s.11(2)). Before determining the issue, the police authority must give the chief constable the opportunity to make representations and only then should the authority seek the approval of the Secretary of State.

These provisions apply equally to assistant chief constables under s.12(3) as these officers may be called on to deputise for the chief constable (s.12(4)).

Similarly the Secretary of State has power under s.42 to require an authority to call on the chief constable (or an assistant chief constable) to resign. On analogy with s.11(2), before determining the issue, the Secretary of State must give the chief constable the opportunity to make representations and may, if necessary, hold an inquiry (s.42(3)). Any inquiry would be subject to the Tribunals and Inquiries Act 1992 (c. 53) by virtue of s.16(1) of that Act.

Reports from police authorities

43.—(1) A police authority shall, whenever so required by the Secretary of State, submit to the Secretary of State a report on such matters connected with the discharge of the authority's functions, or otherwise with the policing of its area, as may be specified in the requirement.

(2) A requirement under subsection (1) may specify the form in which a report is to be given.

(3) The Secretary of State may arrange, or require the police authority to arrange, for a report under this section to be published in such manner as appears to him to be appropriate.

GENERAL NOTE

This section is derived from s.29A of the Police Act 1964 (c. 48) as inserted by s.16 of the Police and Magistrates' Courts Act 1994 (c. 29).

Whereas the Secretary of State has had the power to require reports from chief constables for many years under s.30 of the Police Act 1964 (c. 48) and now under s.44 of this Act, he or she has not had the power to require reports from police authorities. This section empowers the Secretary of State to require a report from a police authority on any matter connected with the discharge of the authority's functions, the reason given being that it was incongruous to be able to require a report from the chief constable but not from the authority.

While such provisions can be seen to undermine the local autonomy of the police authority, the section might again have the incidental effect of facilitating the asking of parliamentary questions. The Secretary of State is only responsible to Parliament for the Metropolitan force (and even then will not answer questions on operational issues). The Secretary of State refuses to answer questions on the subject of provincial forces. However since the Secretary of State's general duty under s.36 is supported by specific powers under this Act, he or she should be less able to argue that he or she bears no responsibility at all for the policing of provincial forces and thus need not answer parliamentary questions relating to the work of such forces.

Reports from chief constables

44.—(1) The Secretary of State may require a chief constable to submit to him a report on such matters as may be specified in the requirement, being matters connected with the policing of the chief constable's police area.

(2) A requirement under subsection (1) may specify the form in which a report is to be given.

(3) The Secretary of State may arrange, or require the chief constable to arrange, for a report under this section to be published in such manner as appears to the Secretary of State to be appropriate.

(4) Every chief constable shall, as soon as possible after the end of each financial year, submit to the Secretary of State the like report as is required by section 22(1) to be submitted to the police authority.

(5) This section shall apply in relation to the City of London police force as if for references to a chief constable there were substituted references to the Commissioner.

GENERAL NOTE

This section derives from s.30 of the Police Act 1964 (c. 48) and the Police and Magistrates' Courts Act 1994 (c. 29), Sched. 5, para. 8.

The chief constable of a force must submit two different sorts of report to the Secretary of State. The first of these is the routine annual report submitted to the police authority, a copy of which must also be sent to the Secretary of State under subs. (4). The second situation concerns the power of the Secretary of State to require reports from a chief constable on a matter concerned with the policing of an area. The chief constable must comply with such a request. This might be compared with the position with regard to requests by police authorities under s.22(5). Such a report can be in whatever form (written or otherwise) that the Secretary of State may direct (subs. (2)). Whether the report is published depends on whether the Secretary of State deems it appropriate (subs. (3)).

Criminal statistics

45.—(1) The chief officer of police of every police force shall, at such times and in such form as the Secretary of State may direct, transmit to the Secretary of State such particulars with respect to offences, offenders, criminal proceedings and the state of crime in the chief officer's police area as the Secretary of State may require.

(2) The Secretary of State shall cause a consolidated and classified abstract of the information transmitted to him under this section to be prepared and laid before Parliament.

GENERAL NOTE

This section derives from s.54 of the Police Act 1964 (c. 48).

The annual volume of criminal statistics produced by the Home Office is more detailed and accurate than those of other western countries and provides an invaluable source of information for policy makers, criminal justice practitioners and criminologists. This section is responsible for that since it empowers the Secretary of State to require the chief constables to collect and transmit such data and then requires him to lay a digest of the data before Parliament.

Police grant

46.—(1) Subject to the following provisions of this section, the Secretary of State shall for each financial year make grants for police purposes to—

(a) police authorities for areas other than the metropolitan police district, and

(b) the Receiver for the Metropolitan Police District;

and in those provisions references to police authorities shall be taken as including references to the Receiver.

(2) For each financial year the Secretary of State shall with the approval of the Treasury determine—

(a) the aggregate amount of grants to be made under this section, and

(b) the amount of the grant to be made to each authority;

and any determination may be varied by further determinations under this subsection.

(3) The Secretary of State shall prepare a report setting out any determination under subsection (2), and stating the considerations which he took into account in making the determination.

(4) In determining the allocation among police authorities of the whole or any part of the aggregate amount of grants, the Secretary of State may exercise his discretion by applying such formulae or other rules as he considers appropriate.

(5) The considerations which the Secretary of State takes into account in making a determination under subsection (2), and the formulae and other rules referred to in subsection (4), may be different for different authorities or different classes of authority.

(6) A copy of every report prepared under subsection (3) shall be laid before the House of Commons, and no payment of grant shall be made unless the report setting out the determination of its amount has been approved by resolution of that House.

(7) A grant to a police authority under this section shall be paid at such time, or in instalments of such amounts and at such times, as the Secretary of State may with the approval of the Treasury determine; and any such time may fall within or after the financial year concerned.

(8) Where in consequence of a further determination under subsection (2) the amount of an authority's grant is less than the amount already paid to it for the year concerned, a sum equal to the difference shall be paid by the authority to the Secretary of State on such day as he may specify; but no sum shall be payable by an authority under this subsection unless the report setting out the further determination has been approved by resolution of the House of Commons.

GENERAL NOTE

This section derives from s.31 of the Police Act 1964 (c. 48) and s.17 of the Police and Magistrates' Courts Act 1994 (part) (c. 29).

In the debate on the (now) Police and Magistrates' Courts Act 1994, the Lord Chancellor explained that the new provisions replaced the old system by which 51 per cent of police expenditure was refunded through the police grant "... *In future, each police authority will receive a cash limited amount of police grant. The Secretary of State is required to report in another place on how he proposes to allocate police grant and he must secure the approval of that House to his proposal. The new police authorities will also receive funding through revenue support grant, non-domestic rates and the council tax. Section 27 establishes the new police authorities as major precepting bodies for local government finance purposes...*" (*Hansard*, H.L. Vol. 551, col. 459). One significant impact for the new free-standing authorities is that they are able to determine the size of their own establishment, whereas previously the size of a force was decided centrally.

The section lays down a specific procedure in determining the overall amount of grant and the amount to go to each authority. This must be decided in consultation with the Treasury but there is no similar statutory provision for consultation with police authorities or with chief constables. Under subs. (4) the Secretary of State is entitled to apply rules or formulae at his or her discretion. These rules may be different for different authorities or different classes of authority (subs. (5)), thereby allowing the Secretary of State to adopt different considerations for metropolitan forces as opposed to shire forces. The amounts themselves and the considerations taken into account must be published in a report to be laid before the House of Commons.

Grants for capital expenditure

47.—(1) The Secretary of State may make grants in respect of capital expenditure incurred (or to be incurred) for police purposes by—
    (a) police authorities for areas other than the metropolitan police district, and
    (b) the Receiver for the Metropolitan Police District.

(2) Grants under this section may be made either unconditionally or subject to conditions.

(3) The Secretary of State shall exercise his powers under this section only with the approval of the Treasury.

GENERAL NOTE

This section is derived from s.31A of the Police Act 1964 (c. 48) as inserted by s.17 of the Police and Magistrates' Courts Act 1994 (c. 29).

The police grant is presumably not intended to cover major capital expenditure. This section provides that, with the consent of the Treasury, the Secretary of State can make grants to police authorities for such expenditure.

Grants for expenditure on safeguarding national security

48.—(1) The Secretary of State may make grants in respect of expenditure incurred (or to be incurred) for police purposes by—
    (a) police authorities for areas other than the metropolitan police district, and
    (b) the Receiver for the Metropolitan Police District,
in connection with safeguarding national security.

(2) Grants under this section may be made either unconditionally or subject to conditions.

(3) The Secretary of State shall exercise his powers under this section only with the approval of the Treasury.

GENERAL NOTE

This section is derived from s.31B of the Police Act 1964 (c. 48) as inserted by s.17 of the Police and Magistrates' Courts Act 1994 (in part) (c. 29).

Police authorities incur large and unforeseen expenditures. For example, the policing of the miners' strike in 1984/85 involved a large amount of mutual assistance provided by one force for the benefit of another, normally for the policing of picket lines. Many authorities found the cost of this difficult to meet and yet had little control over the expenditure. Under this section, and with the consent of the Treasury, the Secretary of State can make grants to police authorities for expenditure incurred in connection with safeguarding national security. However, this criterion is quite limited and while it might encompass the extra costs of policing a nuclear missile base, it would be difficult to argue that the cost of extra officers required to police a blockade of a port by animal rights demonstrators or picketing in the course of an industrial action could also be met from central funds.

Local inquiries

49.—(1) The Secretary of State may cause a local inquiry to be held by a person appointed by him into any matter connected with the policing of any area.

(2) An inquiry under this section shall be held in public or in private as the Secretary of State may direct.

(3) Subsections (2) and (3) of section 250 of the Local Government Act 1972 (power to summon and examine witnesses) shall apply to an inquiry held under this section as they apply to an inquiry held under that section.

(4) Where the report of the person holding an inquiry under this section is not published, a summary of his findings and conclusions shall be made

known by the Secretary of State so far as appears to him consistent with the public interest.

(5) The Secretary of State may direct that the whole or part of the costs incurred by any person for the purposes of an inquiry held under this section shall be defrayed—

(a) out of the police fund, or

(b) if the inquiry relates to more than one police area, out of the police funds concerned in such proportions as may be specified in the direction,

and any costs payable under this section shall be subject to taxation in such manner as the Secretary of State may direct.

GENERAL NOTE

This section derives from s.32 of the Police Act 1964 (c. 48).

The Home Secretary is able to institute an inquiry into policing matters. Examples are the Scarman Report into the Brixton disturbances (*The Brixton Disturbances* Cmnd. 8427 (1982)) or the investigation into the brick-planting techniques of Detective Sergeant Challenor in London in the 1960s (*Report of Inquiry by A.E. James Q.C.* Cmnd. 2735 (1965)).

The Secretary of State may appoint the person holding the inquiry, may direct whether the proceedings are to be held in public or not and may decide the form of any publication of the report. As with s.22 (reports by chief constables to police authorities), publication of any report may be limited by considerations of public interest (subs. (4)). A public interest is to be distinguished from the private interest of individuals and judges have treated it as akin to the notion of the greatest good of the greatest number. It is a question of fact, probably subject to judicial review: *Re Amalgamated Anthracite Collieries Ltd's Application* (1927) 43 T.L.R. 672.

Witnesses can be compelled to attend and presumably produce documents (defined by s.13 of the Civil Evidence Act 1995 (c. 38)).

Regulations for police forces

50.—(1) Subject to the provisions of this section, the Secretary of State may make regulations as to the government, administration and conditions of service of police forces.

(2) Without prejudice to the generality of subsection (1), regulations under this section may make provision with respect to—

(a) the ranks to be held by members of police forces;

(b) the qualifications for appointment and promotion of members of police forces;

(c) periods of service on probation;

(d) voluntary retirement of members of police forces;

(e) the conduct, efficiency and effectiveness of members of police forces and the maintenance of discipline;

(f) the suspension of members of a police force from membership of that force and from their office as constable;

(g) the maintenance of personal records of members of police forces;

(h) the duties which are or are not to be performed by members of police forces;

(i) the treatment as occasions of police duty of attendance at meetings of the Police Federations and of any body recognised by the Secretary of State for the purposes of section 64;

(j) the hours of duty, leave, pay and allowances of members of police forces; and

(k) the issue, use and return of police clothing, personal equipment and accoutrements.

(3) Without prejudice to the powers conferred by this section, regulations under this section shall—

(a) establish, or make provision for the establishment of, procedures for cases in which a member of a police force may be dealt with by dismissal, requirement to resign, reduction in rank, reduction in rate of pay, fine, reprimand or caution, and

   (b) make provision for securing that any case in which a senior officer may be dismissed or dealt with in any of the other ways mentioned in paragraph (a) is decided—
      (i) where he is a member of the metropolitan police force, by the Commissioner of Police of the Metropolis, and
      (ii) where he is a member of any other force, by the police authority which maintains the force or by a committee of that authority.
For the purposes of this subsection "senior officer" means a member of a police force holding a rank above that of superintendent.

   (4) In relation to any matter as to which provision may be made by regulations under this section, the regulations may, subject to subsection (3)(b),—

   (a) authorise or require provision to be made by, or confer discretionary powers on, the Secretary of State, police authorities, chief officers of police or other persons, or
   (b) authorise or require the delegation by any person of functions conferred on that person by or under the regulations.

   (5) Regulations under this section for regulating pay and allowances may be made with retrospective effect to any date specified in the regulations, but nothing in this subsection shall be construed as authorising pay or allowances payable to any person to be reduced retrospectively.

   (6) Regulations under this section as to conditions of service shall secure that appointments for fixed terms are not made except where the person appointed holds the rank of superintendent or a higher rank.

   (7) Regulations under this section may make different provision for different cases and circumstances.

   (8) Any statutory instrument containing regulations under this section shall be subject to annulment in pursuance of a resolution of either House of Parliament.

GENERAL NOTE

   This section derives from s.33 of the Police Act 1964 (c. 48) and s.18 of the Police and Magistrates' Courts Act 1994 (c. 29).

   The Secretary of State has wide ranging powers to make regulations, not least concerning pay and conditions of service and discipline. The Police Regulations 1995 (S.I. 1995 No. 215) and the Police (Discipline) Regulations 1985 (S.I. 1985 No. 518 as amended) which incorporates the police code of discipline are major examples.

   The Secretary of State must take into consideration any recommendations of the Police Negotiating Board (established under Police Negotiating Board Act 1980 (c. 10) and continued under s.61 of this Act) over questions relating to hours of duty, leave, pay and allowances, pensions or the issue, use and return of police equipment and clothing (under s.62(1)). The Secretary of State must take into consideration any representations of the Police Advisory Board (established under s.46 of the Police Act 1964 (c. 48) and continued under s.63 of this Act) over questions relating to matters other than those mentioned above (under s.63(3)).

Regulations for special constables

   51.—(1) The Secretary of State may make regulations as to the government, administration and conditions of service of special constables.

   (2) Without prejudice to the generality of subsection (1), regulations under this section may make provision with respect to—

   (a) the qualifications for appointment of special constables;
   (b) the retirement of special constables;
   (c) the suspension of special constables from their office as constable;
   (d) the allowances payable to special constables; and
   (e) the application to special constables, subject to such modifications as may be prescribed by the regulations, of any provisions made by or under any enactment relating to the pensions payable to or in respect of members of police forces.

(3) If regulations under this section provide for the calculation of any pension payable to or in respect of special constables by reference to a scale of notional remuneration specified in the regulations, regulations under this section increasing any such notional remuneration may be made with retrospective effect to any date specified in the regulations.

(4) Subsections (7) and (8) of section 50 shall apply to regulations under this section.

GENERAL NOTE

This section derives from s.34 of the Police Act 1964 (c. 48).

The Secretary of State has analogous powers to make regulations relating to the administration and conditions of service of special constables. The Police (Special Constables) Regulations 1965 (S.I. 1965 No. 536 as amended) are the relevant rules.

Unlike constables and police cadets, there is no role in relation to these regulations for the Police Negotiating Board or the Police Advisory Board.

Regulations for police cadets

52.—(1) The Secretary of State may make regulations as to the government, administration and conditions of service of police cadets.

(2) Subsections (5), (7) and (8) of section 50 shall apply to regulations under this section.

GENERAL NOTE

This section derives from s.35 of the Police Act 1964 (c. 48).

The Secretary of State has powers to make regulations regarding the administration and conditions of service of police cadets. The relevant regulations are the Police (Cadets) Regulations 1979 (S.I. 1979 No. 1727 as amended).

As under s.50, the Secretary of State must take into consideration any recommendations of the Police Negotiating Board over questions relating to hours of duty, leave, pay and allowances, pensions or the issue, use and return of police equipment and clothing (under s.62). He or she must take into consideration any representations of the Police Advisory Board over questions relating to matters other than those mentioned above (under s.63).

Regulations as to standard of equipment

53. The Secretary of State may make regulations requiring equipment provided or used for police purposes to satisfy such requirements as to design and performance as may be prescribed in the regulations.

GENERAL NOTE

This section derives from s.36 of the Police Act 1964 (c.48) and allows the Secretary of State to ensure that equipment used by the police meets certain specifications. No regulations have been made prior to 1996.

Inspectors of constabulary

Appointment and functions of inspectors of constabulary

54.—(1) Her Majesty may appoint such number of inspectors (to be known as "Her Majesty's Inspectors of Constabulary") as the Secretary of State may with the consent of the Treasury determine, and of the persons so appointed one may be appointed as chief inspector of constabulary.

(2) The inspectors of constabulary shall inspect, and report to the Secretary of State on the efficiency and effectiveness of, every police force maintained for a police area.

(3) The inspectors of constabulary shall carry out such other duties for the purpose of furthering police efficiency and effectiveness as the Secretary of State may from time to time direct.

(4) The chief inspector of constabulary shall in each year submit to the Secretary of State a report in such form as the Secretary of State may direct, and the Secretary of State shall lay a copy of that report before Parliament.

(5) The inspectors of constabulary shall be paid such salary and allowances as the Secretary of State may with the consent of the Treasury determine.

GENERAL NOTE
This section derives from s.38 of the Police Act 1964 (c. 48) and s.20 of the Police and Magistrates' Courts Act 1994 (c. 29).

The inspectorate of constabulary was first established by the County and Borough Police Act 1856, s.15. That provision was only repealed in 1964. The Queen, acting on the recommendation of the Secretary of State appoints inspectors who, under subs. (2), have a statutory duty to inspect and report to the Secretary of State on the "efficiency and effectiveness" of police forces—this wording was introduced by s.20 of the Police and Magistrates' Courts Act 1994 (c. 29).

"Her Majesty's Inspectors of Constabulary" (HMI) now inspect all the police forces—previously the Metropolitan force was excluded from these provisions. The form and content of the inspections has never been defined although the HMI provides guidance in the shape of 400 policy statements and 300 questions in relation to seven key areas: personnel and organisation; technology; operational performance; quality of service; community relations; complaints and discipline; counter-terrorism and war planning. Each of the five inspectors (all ex-chief officers) has his own administrative staff (including assistant inspectors appointed under s.56) and is attached to a particular region, not only inspecting the forces but also acting as convenor and chairman of regional conferences and promoting co-operation. Local forces are inevitably influenced by the HMI, a crucial conduit between them and central government, by which the policy concerns of the Home Office are communicated as well as being the means by which the Home Office gains information on how those policy priorities are being implemented in the field.

There is an annual report from the chief inspector of constabulary on the work of the HMI laid before Parliament each year (subs. (4)).

Publication of reports

55.—(1) Subject to subsection (2), the Secretary of State shall arrange for any report received by him under section 54(2) to be published in such manner as appears to him to be appropriate.

(2) The Secretary of State may exclude from publication under subsection (1) any part of a report if, in his opinion, the publication of that part—
  (a) would be against the interests of national security, or
  (b) might jeopardise the safety of any person.

(3) The Secretary of State shall send a copy of the published report—
  (a) (except where he is himself the police authority) to the police authority maintaining the police force to which the report relates, and
  (b) to the chief officer of police of that police force.

(4) The police authority shall invite the chief officer of police to submit comments on the published report to the authority before such date as it may specify.

(5) The police authority shall prepare comments on the published report and shall arrange for—
  (a) its comments,
  (b) any comments submitted by the chief officer of police in accordance with subsection (4), and
  (c) any response which the authority has to the comments submitted by the chief officer of police,
to be published in such manner as appears to the authority to be appropriate.

(6) The police authority (except where it is the Secretary of State) shall send a copy of any document published under subsection (5) to the Secretary of State.

GENERAL NOTE
This section derives from s.38A of the Police Act 1964 (c. 48) as inserted by s.21 of the Police and Magistrates' Courts Act 1994 (c. 29).

Reports on individual forces have been published informally since 1990. This was made statutory in 1994 and the Secretary of State shall arrange for publication of all reports. Under subs. (2)

any such report or any part of it may be excluded from publication if the Secretary of State feels that it would be against the interests of national security or might jeopardise the safety of an individual. This appears to be a narrower criterion than the normal "public interest" formula.

Assistant inspectors and staff officers

56.—(1) The Secretary of State may appoint assistant inspectors of constabulary.

(2) Members of a police force may be appointed by the Secretary of State to be assistant inspectors of constabulary or to be staff officers to the inspectors of constabulary.

(3) Persons appointed under this section shall be paid such salary and allowances as the Secretary of State may with the consent of the Treasury determine.

GENERAL NOTE

This section derives from s.39 of the Police Act 1964 (c. 48) as amended by s.22 of the Police and Magistrates' Courts Act 1994 (c. 29).

The expansion in the work of the inspectorate is reflected in the provisions (new in 1994) allowing for the appointing of assistant inspectors of constabulary. Previously officers from forces had been seconded to the HMI as staff officers to inspectors. Such officers may now either be staff officers or assistant inspectors in their own right and presumably with more authority than a mere staff officer.

Central services

Common services

57.—(1) The Secretary of State may provide and maintain, or may contribute to the provision or maintenance of, such organisations, facilities and services as he considers necessary or expedient for promoting the efficiency or effectiveness of the police.

(2) Charges may be made for the use of facilities and services provided by the Secretary of State (or by organisations provided or maintained by him) under subsection (1).

(3) The Secretary of State may by regulations make provision for requiring all police forces in England and Wales to use specified facilities or services, or facilities or services of a specified description, (whether or not provided under subsection (1)) if he considers that it would be in the interests of the efficiency or effectiveness of the police for them to do so.

(4) Before making regulations under this section, the Secretary of State shall consult—

(a) persons whom he considers to represent the interests of police authorities, and

(b) persons whom he considers to represent the interests of chief officers of police.

GENERAL NOTE

This section is derived from s.41 of the Police Act 1964 (c. 48) as amended by s.23 of the Police and Magistrates' Courts Act 1994 (c. 29).

The Secretary of State was given the power to provide common services in the Police Act 1964 which specifically mentioned matters such as the police college, district training, forensic science, wireless departments and other services. Section 23 of the Police and Magistrates' Courts Act 1994 (c. 29) makes this provision more general, permitting the Secretary of State to provide such services as are thought necessary to promote the efficiency and effectiveness of the police service.

Under subss. (2) and (3) the police forces can be required to use such services and be charged for their use—however no such regulations have yet been issued.

In *R. v. Secretary of State for the Home Department ex p. Northumbria Police Authority* [1988] 1 All E.R. 556, s.41 of the Police Act 1964 was held to authorise the Secretary of State to supply equipment (in this case CS gas and plastic baton rounds) from a central store if he considered it necessary or expedient for promoting the efficiency of the police and his right to do so was not restricted to an emergency nor did he need the consent of the police authority.

Research

58. The Secretary of State may set up such bodies and take such other steps as appear to him to be necessary or expedient for the purpose of undertaking research into matters affecting the efficiency or effectiveness of the police.

GENERAL NOTE
This section derives from s.42 of the Police Act 1964 (c. 48) and the Police and Magistrates' Courts Act 1994 (c. 29), Sched. 5, para. 9.
The Police Research and Planning Branch was set up in the Home Office in 1963 and put on a statutory footing a year later. Although the branch no longer exists, research on matters relevant to the police is still carried on in the Home Office by the Research and Statistics Directorate as well as the Police Research Group.

PART III

POLICE REPRESENTATIVE INSTITUTIONS

Police Federations

59.—(1) There shall continue to be a Police Federation for England and Wales and a Police Federation for Scotland for the purpose of representing members of the police forces in those countries respectively in all matters affecting their welfare and efficiency, except for—
 (a) questions of promotion affecting individuals, and
 (b) (subject to subsection (2)) questions of discipline affecting individuals.
 (2) A Police Federation may represent a member of a police force at any proceedings brought under regulations made in accordance with section 50(3) above or section 26(2A) of the Police (Scotland) Act 1967 or on an appeal from any such proceedings.
 (3) Except on an appeal to a police appeals tribunal or as provided by section 84, a member of a police force may only be represented under subsection (2) by another member of a police force.
 (4) The Police Federations shall act through local and central representative bodies.
 (5) The Police Federations and every branch of a Federation shall be entirely independent of, and subject to subsection (6) unassociated with, any body or person outside the police service, but may employ persons outside the police service in an administrative or advisory capacity.
 (6) The Secretary of State—
 (a) may authorise a Police Federation or a branch of a Federation to be associated with a person or body outside the police service in such cases and manner, and subject to such conditions and restrictions, as he may specify, and
 (b) may vary or withdraw an authorisation previously given;
and anything for the time being so authorised shall not be precluded by subsection (5).
 (7) This section applies to police cadets as it applies to members of police forces, and references to the police service shall be construed accordingly.

GENERAL NOTE
This section derives from s.44 of the Police Act 1964 (c. 48) as amended by s.109 of the Police and Criminal Evidence Act 1984 (c. 60).
The existence of the Police Federation as the representative organ of police officers must be understood in the light of police history. In 1918, there were widespread strikes by the police organised by the National Union of Police and Prison Officers. In the wake of these events and given the discontent of police officers about their pay and conditions, there was an inquiry and report by the Desborough Committee (Cmd. 874 and Cmd. 574), shortly followed by the Police Act 1919. This legislation banned police officers from belonging to trade unions, a ban continued in s.47 of the Police Act 1964 and by s.64 of this Act. Instead a representative organisation, the Police Federation, was set up in 1919 in each force with branches representing constables,

sergeants and inspectors. This division between the ranks operates at local and national level so that there are, for example, three central committees representing each level. There is also a national joint committee. Chief officers (through the Association of Chief Police Officers) and superintendents (through the Superintendents' Association) have their separate non-statutory organisations.

The purpose of the Federation was to "enable members of the police forces to consider and bring to the notice of the police authorities and the Secretary of State, all matters affecting their welfare and efficiency other than questions of discipline and promotion affecting individuals". That statement of purpose in the Police Act 1919 (c. 46) is reflected in s.59(1) of this Act. However the Federation does play a role in disciplinary matters and under subss. (2) and (3) can represent members at disciplinary hearings or in front of appeals tribunals. It is one of their most effective roles.

In many ways the Federation is a quasi-trade union, limited only in its isolation from organised labour (emphasised in subs. (5) whereby the Federation must not be associated with any person or body outside the police service (for example, the TUC)) and by its inability to call out its members on strike (see s.91 of this Act). It has sought repeal of these restrictions from time to time and campaigns hard on issues affecting the pay and conditions of its members. It is also influential as a lobby group seeking change in criminal justice policy.

Regulations for Police Federations

60.—(1) The Secretary of State may by regulations—

(a) prescribe the constitution and proceedings of the Police Federations, or

(b) authorise the Federations to make rules concerning such matters relating to their constitution and proceedings as may be specified in the regulations.

(2) Without prejudice to the generality of subsection (1), regulations under this section may make provision—

(a) with respect to the membership of the Federations;

(b) with respect to the raising of funds by the Federations by voluntary subscription and the use and management of funds derived from such subscriptions;

(c) with respect to the manner in which representations may be made by committees or bodies of the Federations to police authorities, chief officers of police and the Secretary of State;

(d) for the payment by the Secretary of State of expenses incurred in connection with the Federations and for the use by the Federations of premises provided by police authorities for police purposes; and

(e) for modifying any regulations under the Police Pensions Act 1976, section 50 above or section 26 of the Police (Scotland) Act 1967 in relation to any member of a police force who is the secretary or an officer of a Police Federation and for requiring the appropriate Federation to make contributions in respect of the pay, pension or allowances payable to or in respect of any such person.

(3) Regulations under this section may contain such supplementary and transitional provisions as appear to the Secretary of State to be appropriate, including provisions adapting references in any enactment (including this Act) to committees or other bodies of the Federations.

(4) Before making any regulations under this section the Secretary of State shall consult the three Central Committees of the Police Federation to which the regulations will relate, sitting together as a Joint Committee.

(5) A statutory instrument containing regulations under this section shall be subject to annulment in pursuance of a resolution of either House of Parliament.

(6) This section applies to police cadets as it applies to members of police forces.

GENERAL NOTE

This section derives from s.44(3) of the Police Act 1964 (c. 48) as amended by s.109 of the Police and Criminal Evidence Act 1984 (c. 60).

The power to make regulations underlines the Secretary of State's power over the Federation, not least by the power to control the raising of funds. The Federation's income is relatively small. The Police (Police Federation) Regulations 1969 (S.I. 1969 No. 1787 as amended) are the relevant rules.

The Police Negotiating Board for the United Kingdom

GENERAL NOTE

Sections 61, 62, 63
These sections are derived from ss.45 and 46 of the Police Act 1964 (c. 48) and Police Negotiating Board Act 1980 (c. 10).
Another result of the report of the Desborough Committee in 1919 was the creation of the Police Council "for the consideration of general questions affecting the police" which sat for the first time in 1920. It was an advisory committee working on police regulations and a code of discipline. The Council was reconstituted under s.45 of the Police Act 1964 (c. 48) and its functions split into two by the creation of the Police Advisory Board by s.46 of the Police Act 1964 (c. 48). This division of function was continued by the Police Negotiating Board Act 1980 (c. 10) which abolished the Police Council replacing it with a new body—the Police Negotiating Board which is continued by s.61 of this Act. The Police Advisory Board is also continued by s.63. The difference between the bodies is that the Negotiating Board brings together police officers with representatives of the police authorities, chief officers and the Secretary of State to discuss and make recommendations regarding the pay and conditions of service of constables. The Advisory Board's role is to advise the Secretary of State on general policy issues affecting the police service. The Secretary of State is under a statutory obligation to consult both bodies before drafting regulations under ss.50 or 52 (see s.62 and s.63(3)).

61.—(1) There shall continue to be a Police Negotiating Board for the United Kingdom for the consideration by persons representing the interests of—
  (a) the authorities who between them maintain the police forces in Great Britain and the Royal Ulster Constabulary,
  (b) the persons who are members of those police forces or of that Constabulary or are police cadets,
  (c) the Commissioner of Police of the Metropolis, and
  (d) the Secretary of State,
of questions relating to hours of duty, leave, pay and allowances, pensions or the issue, use and return of police clothing, personal equipment and accoutrements.

(2) The Chairman and any deputy chairman or chairmen of the Board shall be appointed by the Prime Minister.

(3) Subject to subsection (2), the Board shall continue to be constituted in accordance with such arrangements, made after consultations between the Secretary of State and organisations representing the interests of the persons referred to in paragraphs (a), (b) and (c) of subsection (1), as appear to the Secretary of State to be satisfactory.

(4) The Secretary of State may—
  (a) pay to the Chairman and to any deputy chairman or chairmen of the Board such fees as the Secretary of State may, with the approval of the Treasury, determine, and
  (b) defray any expenses incurred by the Board.

Functions of the Board with respect to regulations

62.—(1) Before making—
  (a) regulations under section 50 or 52;
  (b) regulations under section 26 or 27 of the Police (Scotland) Act 1967 (other than regulations relating to special constables); or
  (c) regulations under section 10(4) or 25 of the Police Act (Northern Ireland) 1970,
with respect to any of the matters mentioned in section 61(1) (other than pensions), the Secretary of State shall take into consideration any rec-

ommendation made by the Police Negotiating Board for the United Kingdom and shall supply the Board with a draft of the regulations.

(2) The arrangements referred to in section 61(3) shall regulate the procedure for reaching agreement on a recommendation to be made by the Board for the purposes of subsection (1) above and shall include provision for arriving at such a recommendation by arbitration in such circumstances as may be determined by or under the arrangements.

(3) No regulations relating to pensions shall be made under section 52 above, section 27 of the Police (Scotland) Act 1967 or section 10(4) or 25 of the Police Act (Northern Ireland) 1970 except after consultation with the Board.

Police Advisory Boards for England and Wales and for Scotland

63.—(1) There shall continue to be a Police Advisory Board for England and Wales and a Police Advisory Board for Scotland for the purpose of advising the Secretary of State on general questions affecting the police in those countries respectively.

(2) The constitution and proceedings of each of the Police Advisory Boards shall be such as the Secretary of State may determine after consulting organisations representing the interests of police authorities and of members of police forces and police cadets.

(3) Before making—
(a) regulations under section 50 or 52, other than regulations with respect to any of the matters mentioned in section 61(1), or
(b) regulations under Chapter I of Part IV,
the Secretary of State shall supply the Police Advisory Board for England and Wales with a draft of the regulations, and take into consideration any representations made by that Board.

Membership of trade unions

64.—(1) Subject to the following provisions of this section, a member of a police force shall not be a member of any trade union, or of any association having for its objects, or one of its objects, to control or influence the pay, pensions or conditions of service of any police force.

(2) Where a person was a member of a trade union before becoming a member of a police force, he may, with the consent of the chief officer of police, continue to be a member of that union during the time of his service in the police force.

(3) If any question arises whether any body is a trade union or an association to which this section applies, the question shall be determined by the chief registrar of friendly societies.

(4) This section applies to police cadets as it applies to members of a police force, and references to a police force or to service in a police force shall be construed accordingly.

(5) Nothing in this section applies to membership of the Police Federations, or of any body recognised by the Secretary of State for the purposes of this section as representing members of police forces who are not members of those Federations.

GENERAL NOTE

This section derives from s.47 of the Police Act 1964 (c. 48) and prevents police officers from belonging to a trade union and from any formal association with organised labour outside of the police service. Questions relating to officers' welfare and conditions of employment are dealt with by the Police Federation (see s.59). The definition of a trade union is to be found in s.1 of the Trade Union and Labour Relations Act 1992 and if there is any dispute, the matter falls to be determined by the chief registrar of friendly societies under subs. (3). The chief registrar is appointed under the Friendly Societies Act 1974, s.1.

PART IV

COMPLAINTS, DISCIPLINARY PROCEEDINGS ETC.

CHAPTER I

COMPLAINTS

GENERAL NOTE

This chapter of Pt. IV of the Act deals with complaints. A complaint is a complaint about the conduct of an individual officer or officers and not about the direction and control of the force by the chief constable (s.67(4)). There is no formal machinery for dealing with complaints about operational policy except through the police authority or through the community liaison provisions under s.96.

The basic machinery for investigation of complaints against the police for many years was under s.49 of the Police Act 1964 (c. 48) which left the investigation and adjudication of the complaint to other police officers, often from the same force. Originally the only independent element was the D.P.P. who had to decide whether or not an allegation of crime against an officer should be prosecuted. Reform of this system was initially through the Police Act 1976 which introduced the Police Complaints Board, an independent body which looked at all reports of investigations into complaints except those involving possible criminal charges which still went to the D.P.P. The Board had neither the power nor the staff to carry out its own inquiries but they could request further information and advise that disciplinary action be taken.

The system did not inspire great public confidence. There was demand for an increased independent element and criticism of the requirement that all complaints had to be recorded and an investigating officer appointed. This led to a host of trivial matters being dealt with formally. In 1984 there was further reform under the Police and Criminal Evidence Act 1984. It is this system which in the main is retained in this Act. The regulations governing complaints can be found in the Police (Complaints) (General) Regulations 1985 (S.I. 1985 No. 520). A summary of the process of handling complaints may be useful:

- initially all complaints are recorded unless the conduct is the subject of criminal or disciplinary proceedings (s.67(5)).
- there are then separate processes for senior officers through s.68 (for those above the rank of superintendent) and a standard procedure through s.69 for other officers.
- in both cases, an investigating officer is not appointed if it is possible to resolve the matter informally by way of explanation or apology (s.68(2) and s.69(4)).
- in both cases, if it is pursued formally, then an investigating officer will be appointed, normally from the same force but from other forces if the complaint is serious (s.68(2) and s.69(5)).
- in both cases, certain complaints must be referred to the Police Complaints Authority (PCA) and other complaints or other matters may be so referred (ss.70 and 71).
- in both cases, certain investigations must be supervised by the PCA (s.72(1)(a) and (b)) and other complaints which have been referred may be so supervised (s.72(1)(c)) may be. The powers of the PCA include approval of the investigating officer and the appointment of a supervisor from within the PCA itself.
- in both cases, at the end of an investigation, the investigating officer submits a report whether the investigation has been supervised by the PCA (s.73) or not (ss.68(6) or 69(9)). Where the PCA has been involved, the report goes both to the PCA and the police authority (or commissioner for the Metropolitan force). Where the investigation has not been supervised the report goes to the police authority or the chief constable.
- in the case of senior officers, on receiving the report, the police authority either refer the matter to the D.P.P. under s.74 or, if they are satisfied that no criminal offence has been committed, may take action under the Police (Discipline) (Senior Officers) Regulations 1985 (S.I. 1985 No. 519).
- in the case of junior officers, if the report indicates a criminal offence may have been committed, the chief constable must send a copy to the D.P.P. (s.75(4)). If no criminal offence is indicated by the report, the chief constable may bring disciplinary proceedings under the Police (Discipline) Regulations 1985 (S.I. 1985 No. 518) or take no further formal action.
- in the case of junior officers, the chief constable must send a memorandum to the PCA indicating the action which has been taken and, if no action was taken, what reason there was for not bringing disciplinary proceedings (s.75(4) (5) and (6)). If the PCA is unhappy with the decision not to take disciplinary proceedings, they have the power to require the chief constable to take such proceedings under s.76.

One recent issue has been the application of public interest immunity to documents which related to inquiries into police misconduct. This exemption was originally based on the long-recognised refusal to disclose the names of informants to crime—*Marks v. Beyfus* (1890) 25 QBD 494; *D v. National Society for the Prevention of Cruelty to Children* [1977] 1 All E.R. 589. Immunity from disclosure had become automatic, without consideration of the original pur-pose—*Neilson v. Laugharne* [1981] 1 All E.R. 829; *Hehir v. Commissioner of Police for the Metropolis* [1982] 2 All E.R. 335; but also see *Peach v. Metropolitan Police Commissioner* [1986] 2 All E.R. 129; *ex p. Coventry Newspapers* [1993] 1 All E.R. 86. This view was reconsidered by the House of Lords in *R. v. Chief Constable of the West Midlands Police, ex p. Wiley* [1994] 3 All E.R. 420 which no longer accepts blanket claims to immunity for such documents, allowing the trial court to inspect the documents to determine whether a claim to public interest immunity should be upheld.

Interpretation

Interpretation of Chapter I

65. In this Chapter—
"the appropriate authority" means—
　　　　(a) in relation to a member of the metropolitan police force, the Commissioner of Police of the Metropolis, and
　　　　(b) in relation to a member of any other police force—
　　　　　　(i) if he is a senior officer, the police authority for the force's area, and
　　　　　　(ii) if he is not a senior officer, the chief officer of police of the force;
"the Authority" means the Police Complaints Authority;
"complaint" means a complaint about the conduct of a member of a police force which is submitted—
　　　　(a) by a member of the public, or
　　　　(b) on behalf of a member of the public and with his written consent;
"disciplinary proceedings" means proceedings identified as such by regulations under section 50;
"investigating officer" means a member of a police force appointed under section 68(3) or, as the case may be, section 69(5) or (6) to investigate a complaint;
"senior officer" means a member of a police force holding a rank above that of superintendent;
"serious injury" means a fracture, damage to an internal organ, impair-ment of bodily function, a deep cut or a deep laceration.

GENERAL NOTE
　　This section is derived from ss.83, 84 and 87 of the Police and Criminal Evidence Act 1984 (c. 60) (in part).
　　This section defines certain regularly used expressions—the "appropriate authority" is the body or person responsible for the proper handling of a complaint by a member of the public; "senior officer" means chief constables and assistant chief constable. One change of wording from the Police and Criminal Evidence Act 1984 (c. 60) is that the current Act does not talk of "criminal or disciplinary charges" but of "criminal or disciplinary proceedings".

The Police Complaints Authority

The Police Complaints Authority

66.—(1) The authority known as "the Police Complaints Authority" shall continue in existence as a body corporate.
　　(2) Schedule 5 shall have effect in relation to the Authority.

GENERAL NOTE
　　This section is derived from s.83 of the Police and Criminal Evidence Act 1984 (c. 60).
　　The Police Complaints Authority was established by the Police and Criminal Evidence Act

1984 (c. 60) and continues in existence in this Act. It is a body corporate, as are the police authorities—see *Halsbury's Laws (4th ed.) Vol. 9 paras. 1201 ff esp. para. 1245*. The constitution, membership, financing *etc.* are dealt with in Sched. 5 of this Act. The PCA consists of not less than eight members, appointed by the Secretary of State (although the chairman is appointed by the Queen). The members are not and have not been police officers. The Authority is financed through the Home Office but is an independent body. The Authority must report to the Secretary of State, both annually on the discharge of their functions, and on any other matter that should be drawn to the Secretary of State's attention (s.79 of this Act).

Handling of Complaints etc.

Preliminary

67.—(1) Where a complaint is submitted to the chief officer of police for a police area, he shall take any steps that appear to him to be desirable for the purpose of obtaining or preserving evidence relating to the conduct complained of.

(2) After complying with subsection (1), the chief officer shall determine whether he is the appropriate authority in relation to the member of a police force whose conduct is the subject of the complaint.

(3) If the chief officer determines that he is not the appropriate authority, he shall—

(a) send the complaint or, if it was submitted orally, particulars of it, to the appropriate authority, and

(b) give notice that he has done so to the person by whom or on whose behalf the complaint was submitted.

(4) Nothing in this Chapter shall have effect in relation to a complaint in so far as it relates to the direction or control of a police force by the chief officer of police or the person performing the functions of the chief officer of police.

(5) If any conduct to which a complaint wholly or partly relates is or has been the subject of criminal or disciplinary proceedings, none of the provisions of this Chapter which relate to the recording and investigation of complaints shall have effect in relation to the complaint in so far as it relates to that conduct.

GENERAL NOTE

This section derives from s.84 of the Police and Criminal Evidence Act 1984 (c. 60).

On receiving a complaint, the chief officer (although responsibility is normally delegated to an assistant chief constable) must determine that it is a complaint about the conduct of an officer and not about operational issues (subs. (4)). The chief officer must then determine who is the "appropriate authority" as defined in s.65—if the complaint concerns a senior officer, that appropriate authority is the police authority; if it concerns the lower ranks, the appropriate authority is the chief constable. It should be noted that in some cases the complaint must also be referred to the PCA under s.70—for example, if the complaint concerns death or serious injury.

Investigation of complaints: senior officers

68.—(1) Where a complaint about the conduct of a senior officer—

(a) is submitted to the appropriate authority, or

(b) is sent to the appropriate authority under section 67(3),

the appropriate authority shall record and, subject to subsection (2), investigate it.

(2) If satisfied that the conduct complained of, even if proved, would not justify criminal or disciplinary proceedings, the appropriate authority may deal with the complaint according to the appropriate authority's discretion.

(3) In any other case, the appropriate authority shall appoint a member of the appropriate authority's force or of some other force to investigate the complaint.

(4) If the appropriate authority requests the chief officer of police of a police force to provide a member of his force for appointment under subsection (3), the chief officer shall comply with the request.

(5) No member of a police force of a rank lower than that of the member whose conduct is the subject of the complaint may be appointed under subsection (3).

(6) Unless an investigation under this section is supervised by the Authority under section 72, the investigating officer shall submit his report on it to the appropriate authority.

GENERAL NOTE

This section derives from s.86 of the Police and Criminal Evidence Act 1984 (c. 60) and the Police and Magistrates' Courts Act 1994 (c. 29), Sched. 5, para. 26.

This section deals with complaints against senior officers, that is, chief constables and assistant chief constables (or their equivalents in the Metropolitan and City forces). On receiving the complaint, the police authority must make a preliminary decision (subs. (2)) whether, if the facts complained of were true, they would justify criminal or disciplinary proceedings. If not, the authority are entitled to use their discretion—that is, seek to resolve the matter informally by explanation or apology.

If there is a prima facie case which might justify disciplinary or criminal proceedings, the authority must appoint an investigating officer. The legislation does not seek to specify when that officer should come from another force but where the complaint is at all serious, this would be customary. The chief constable of another force cannot refuse to provide such an investigating officer (subs. (4)).

The investigating officer will work either independently or under the supervision of the PCA. The PCA is involved where there has been a reference under s.70. The investigating officer will report either to the police authority (s.68(6)) if the PCA is not supervising the inquiry or to both the chief officer and the PCA (s.73(1)) if they are.

Investigation of complaints: standard procedure

69.—(1) If a chief officer of police determines that he is the appropriate authority in relation to a member of a police force—

(a) whose conduct is the subject of a complaint, and

(b) who is not a senior officer,

he shall record the complaint.

(2) After recording a complaint under subsection (1), the chief officer of police shall consider whether the complaint is suitable for informal resolution and may appoint a member of his force to assist him.

(3) A complaint is not suitable for informal resolution unless—

(a) the member of the public concerned gives his consent, and

(b) the chief officer of police is satisfied that the conduct complained of, even if proved, would not justify criminal or disciplinary proceedings.

(4) If it appears to the chief officer of police that the complaint is suitable for informal resolution, he shall seek to resolve it informally and may appoint a member of his force to do so on his behalf.

(5) If it appears to the chief officer of police that the complaint is not suitable for informal resolution, he shall appoint a member of his own or some other force to investigate it formally.

(6) If, after attempts have been made to resolve a complaint informally, it appears to the chief officer of police—

(a) that informal resolution of the complaint is impossible, or

(b) that the complaint is for any other reason not suitable for informal resolution,

he shall appoint a member of his own or some other force to investigate it formally.

(7) A member of a police force may not be appointed to investigate a complaint formally if he has previously been appointed to act in relation to it under subsection (4).

(8) If a chief officer of police requests the chief officer of police of some other force to provide a member of that other force for appointment under subsection (5) or (6), that chief officer shall comply with the request.

(9) Unless the investigation is supervised by the Authority under section 72, the investigating officer shall submit his report on it to the chief officer of police who appointed him.

GENERAL NOTE

This section is derived from s.85 of the Police and Criminal Evidence Act 1984 (c. 60) and the Police and Magistrates' Courts Act 1994 (c. 29), Sched. 5, para. 25(b).

This section deals with complaints against junior officers, that is, those holding the rank of superintendent or below. If the chief officer has received the complaint, he or she must record it and deal with it unless he or she is dispensed from that duty under the regulations which allow anonymous or repetitious complaints to be ignored (Police (Anonymous, Repetitious etc. Complaints) Regulations 1985 (S.I. 1985 No. 672)). The chief officer must determine that he or she is the appropriate authority under s.67. After that, he or she must consider whether the matter is suitable for informal resolution (subss. (2) (3) and (4)). A complaint is suitable to be dealt with informally where the matter is such that, even if the facts were proved, they would not justify criminal or disciplinary proceedings against the officer. In addition, the complainant must consent to such a resolution. See the Police (Complaints) (Informal Resolution) Regulations 1985 (S.I. 1985 No. 671).

If the matter is not suitable for informal resolution (or where it has been tried and failed (subs. (6)), the chief officer must appoint an investigating officer. The legislation does not seek to specify when that officer should come from another force but where the complaint is at all serious, this would be customary. The chief constable of another force cannot refuse to provide such an investigating officer (subs. (8)).

The investigating officer will work either independently or under the supervision of the PCA. The PCA is involved where there has been a reference under s.70. The investigating officer will report either to the chief officer (s.69(9)) if the PCA is not supervising the inquiry or to both the chief officer and the PCA (s.73(1)) if they are.

References of complaints to Authority

70.—(1) The appropriate authority—
(a) shall refer to the Authority—
     (i) any complaint alleging that the conduct complained of resulted in the death of, or serious injury to, some other person, and
     (ii) any complaint of a description specified for the purposes of this section in regulations made by the Secretary of State, and
(b) may refer to the Authority any complaint which is not required to be referred to them.

(2) The Authority may require the submission to them for consideration of any complaint not referred to them by the appropriate authority; and the appropriate authority shall comply with any such requirement not later than the end of the period specified for the purposes of this subsection in regulations made by the Secretary of State.

(3) Where a complaint falls to be referred to the Authority under subsection (1)(a), the appropriate authority shall refer it to them not later than the end of the period specified for the purposes of sub-paragraph (i) or, as the case may be, (ii) of that subsection in regulations made by the Secretary of State.

GENERAL NOTE

This section derives from s.87 of the Police and Criminal Evidence Act 1984 (c. 60).

This section deals with the involvement of the PCA in the investigation of complaints. Complaints may be referred to the Authority in two ways—there are mandatory referrals and voluntary referrals. Under subs. (1)(a)(i), all complaints involving death or serious injury (as defined in s.65) must be referred to the Authority. Under regulations made under subs. (1)(a)(ii) the Secretary of State has also required that complaints involving actual bodily harm, corruption and serious arrestable offences (as defined in s.116 of the Police and Criminal Evidence Act 1984) be referred to the PCA. In addition to these two types of mandatory referral, the police authority or the chief constable may refer other complaints even though they are not compelled to do so (subs. (1)(b)). Finally where a complaint comes to the attention of the PCA, they may themselves require under subs. (2) that a complaint be referred to them.

References of other matters to Authority

71.—(1) The appropriate authority may refer to the Authority any matter to which this section applies, if it appears to the appropriate authority that the matter ought to be referred by reason—

(a) of its gravity, or

(b) of exceptional circumstances.

(2) This section applies to any matter which—

(a) appears to the appropriate authority to indicate that a member of a police force may have committed a criminal offence or behaved in a manner which would justify disciplinary proceedings, and

(b) is not the subject of a complaint.

GENERAL NOTE

This section derives from s.88 of the Police and Criminal Evidence Act 1984 (c. 60) and s.34 of the Police and Magistrates' Courts Act 1994 (c. 29).

This deals with those situations where no complaint has been made but an officer has behaved in a manner which may justify criminal or disciplinary proceedings. Where this comes to the attention of the appropriate authority, if at the same time, the appropriate authority consider that it is a grave matter or there are exceptional circumstances, they may at their discretion refer it to the PCA.

However, the PCA cannot in these circumstances act on their own initiative. If a complaint has been made, they can require it to be referred to them under s.70(2) but if no complaint is forthcoming, even where the Authority are aware of the circumstances, the Authority is subject to the discretion of the "appropriate authority".

Supervision of investigations by Authority

72.—(1) The Authority shall supervise the investigation of—

(a) any complaint alleging that the conduct of a member of a police force resulted in the death of, or serious injury to, some other person,

(b) any other description of complaint specified for the purposes of this section in regulations made by the Secretary of State, and

(c) any complaint which is not within paragraph (a) or (b), and any matter referred to the Authority under section 71, if the Authority determine that it is desirable in the public interest that they should do so.

(2) Where the Authority have made a determination under subsection (1)(c), they shall notify it to the appropriate authority.

(3) Where an investigation is to be supervised by the Authority, they may require—

(a) that no appointment is made under section 68(3) or 69(5) unless they have given notice to the appropriate authority that they approve the person whom that authority propose to appoint, or

(b) if such an appointment has already been made and the Authority are not satisfied with the person appointed, that—

(i) the appropriate authority, as soon as is reasonably practicable, select another member of a police force and notify the Authority that it proposes to appoint him, and

(ii) the appointment is not made unless the Authority give notice to the appropriate authority that they approve that person.

(4) The Secretary of State shall by regulations authorise the Authority, subject to any restrictions or conditions specified in the regulations, to impose requirements as to a particular investigation additional to any requirements imposed by virtue of subsection (3).

(5) A member of a police force shall comply with any requirement imposed on him by virtue of regulations under subsection (4).

GENERAL NOTE

This section derives from s.89 of the Police and Criminal Evidence Act 1984 (c. 60) (in part) and governs the supervision of investigations by the PCA. They must supervise investigations where there is a mandatory referral under s.70(a)(i) or (ii). If there is a voluntary referral under s.70(b) or under s.71, the PCA must determine that it is in the public interest for them to supervise any investigation (subs. (1)(c)). A public interest is to be distinguished from the private interest of individuals and judges have treated it as akin to the notion of the greatest good of the greatest number. It is a question of fact, probably subject to judicial review: *Re Amalgamated Anthracite Collieries Ltd's Application* (1927) 43 TLR 672.

Where the PCA supervises an investigation, they have the power to approve the appointment of the investigating officer and this includes, where an investigating officer has already been appointed, the replacement of that officer with another of whom the PCA does approve (subs. (3)).

Reports on investigations etc.

73.—(1) At the end of an investigation which the Authority have supervised, the investigating officer shall—

(a) submit a report on the investigation to the Authority, and

(b) send a copy of the report to the appropriate authority.

(2) After considering a report submitted to them under subsection (1), the Authority shall submit an appropriate statement to the appropriate authority.

(3) If it is practicable to do so, the Authority, when submitting the appropriate statement under subsection (2), shall send a copy of it to the member of a police force whose conduct has been investigated.

(4) If—

(a) the investigation related to a complaint, and

(b) it is practicable to do so,

the Authority shall also send a copy of the appropriate statement to the person by or on behalf of whom the complaint was submitted.

(5) The power to issue an appropriate statement includes power to issue separate statements in respect of the disciplinary and criminal aspects of an investigation.

(6) No disciplinary proceedings shall be brought before the appropriate statement is submitted to the appropriate authority.

(7) Subject to subsection (8), neither the appropriate authority nor the Director of Public Prosecutions shall bring criminal proceedings before the appropriate statement is submitted to the appropriate authority.

(8) The restriction imposed by subsection (7) does not apply if it appears to the Director that there are exceptional circumstances which make it undesirable to wait for the submission of the appropriate statement.

(9) In this section "appropriate statement" means a statement—

(a) as to whether the investigation was or was not conducted to the Authority's satisfaction,

(b) specifying any respect in which it was not so conducted, and

(c) dealing with any such other matters as the Secretary of State may by regulations provide.

GENERAL NOTE

This section is derived from s.89 of the Police and Criminal Evidence Act 1984 (c. 60) (in part) and the Police and Magistrates' Courts Act 1994 (c. 29), Sched. 5, para. 27.

At the end of an investigation, the investigating officer submits a report whether the investigation has been supervised by the PCA (s.73) or not (ss.68(6) or 69(9)). Under this section, where the PCA has been involved, the report goes both to the PCA and the police authority (or commissioner for the Metropolitan force). The PCA is under a duty to comment on the report (subs. (2)) by issuing an "appropriate statement"—by subs. (9) such a statement shall cover whether the investigation was satisfactorily conducted and detailing any aspect of the investigation which was not satisfactory. Copies of the statement should also go to the police officer whose conduct was in question and to the complainant. This is dealt with by the Police (Complaints) (General) Regulations 1985 (S.I. 1985 No. 520).

Steps to be taken after investigation: senior officers

74. On receiving—

    (a) a report concerning the conduct of a senior officer which is submitted to it under section 68(6), or

    (b) a copy of a report concerning the conduct of a senior officer which is sent to it under section 73(1),

the appropriate authority shall send a copy of the report to the Director of Public Prosecutions unless the report satisfies the appropriate authority that no criminal offence has been committed.

GENERAL NOTE

    This section is derived from s.90(1) of the Police and Criminal Evidence Act 1984 (c. 60).

    In the case of senior officers, after the conclusion of the investigation and submission of the report the police authority or commissioner must refer the matter to the D.P.P. unless they are satisfied that no criminal offence has been committed. After the D.P.P. has dealt with the question of criminal proceedings or if the appropriate authority are satisfied that no criminal offence has been committed, action may be taken under the Police (Discipline) (Senior Officers) Regulations 1985 (S.I. 1985 No. 519). Under these regulations the senior officer may be brought in front of a disciplinary tribunal and be required to resign, reduced in rank, fined or reprimanded. Appeal against such punishment is possible under s.85 of this Act.

Steps to be taken after investigation: standard procedure

75.—(1) Nothing in this section or section 76 has effect in relation to senior officers.

    (2) On receiving—

    (a) a report concerning the conduct of a member of a police force who is not a senior officer which is submitted to him under section 69(9), or

    (b) a copy of a report concerning the conduct of such a member which is sent to him under section 73(1),

a chief officer of police shall determine whether the report indicates that a criminal offence may have been committed by a member of the police force for his area.

    (3) If the chief officer determines that the report indicates that a criminal offence may have been committed by a member of the police force for his area, he shall send a copy of the report to the Director of Public Prosecutions.

    (4) After the Director has dealt with the question of criminal proceedings, the chief officer shall, in such cases as may be prescribed by regulations made by the Secretary of State, send the Authority a memorandum which—

    (a) is signed by the chief officer,

    (b) states whether he has brought (or proposes to bring) disciplinary proceedings in respect of the conduct which was the subject of the investigation, and

    (c) if he has not brought (or does not propose to bring) such proceedings, gives his reasons.

    (5) If the chief officer considers that the report does not indicate that a criminal offence may have been committed by a member of the police force for his area, he shall, in such cases as may be prescribed by regulations made by the Secretary of State, send the Authority a memorandum to that effect which—

    (a) is signed by the chief officer,

    (b) states whether he has brought (or proposes to bring) disciplinary proceedings in respect of the conduct which was the subject of the investigation, and

    (c) if he has not brought (or does not propose to bring) such proceedings, gives his reasons.

    (6) Where the investigation—

    (a) related to conduct which was the subject of a complaint, and

    (b) was not supervised by the Authority,

the chief officer shall, if he is required by virtue of regulations under subsection (4) or (5) to send the Authority a memorandum, at the same time send them a copy of the complaint, or of the record of the complaint, and a copy of the report of the investigation.

(7) Where a chief officer has sent the Authority a memorandum under subsection (4) or (5), he shall—

    (a) if the memorandum states that he proposes to bring disciplinary proceedings, bring and proceed with them, and

    (b) if the memorandum states that he has brought such proceedings, proceed with them.

GENERAL NOTE

This section is derived from s.90(2)–(10) of the Police and Criminal Evidence Act 1984 (c. 60) and s.35 of the Police and Magistrates' Courts Act 1994 (c. 29).

In the case of junior officers, after the conclusion of the investigation and submission of the report by the investigating officer and if the report indicates a criminal offence may have been committed, the chief constable must send a copy to the D.P.P. (s.75(4)). Previously, under s.90(3) of the Police and Criminal Evidence Act 1984 (c. 60) the chief officer retained some discretion since he or she had to consider whether the officer "ought" to be charged. This discretion no longer exists.

After the D.P.P. has dealt with the question of criminal proceedings, or if no criminal offence is indicated by the report, the chief constable may bring disciplinary proceedings under the Police (Discipline) Regulations 1985 (S.I. 1985 No. 518) or take no further formal action. In either case the chief constable must send a memorandum to the PCA indicating the action which has been taken and, if no action was taken, why no disciplinary proceedings were brought (s.75(4) (5) and (6)). If no further action is to be taken by the chief constable, the PCA do have the power to require it under s.76. If the chief constable indicates to the PCA that disciplinary proceedings are to be brought, he or she must proceed with them.

Powers of Authority as to disciplinary proceedings

76.—(1) Where a memorandum under section 75 states that a chief officer of police has not brought disciplinary proceedings or does not propose to bring such proceedings, the Authority may recommend him to bring such proceedings.

(2) Where a chief officer has brought disciplinary proceedings in accordance with a recommendation under subsection (1), he shall proceed with them.

(3) If after the Authority have made a recommendation under this section and consulted the chief officer he is still unwilling to bring disciplinary proceedings, they may direct him to do so.

(4) Where the Authority give a chief officer a direction under this section, they shall supply him with a written statement of their reasons for doing so.

(5) Subject to subsection (6), it shall be the duty of a chief officer to comply with such a direction.

(6) The Authority may withdraw a direction given under this section.

(7) A chief officer shall—

    (a) advise the Authority of what action he has taken in response to a recommendation or direction under this section, and

    (b) supply the Authority with such other information as they may reasonably require for the purposes of discharging their functions under this section.

GENERAL NOTE

This section derives from s.93 of the Police and Criminal Evidence Act 1984 (c. 60) and s.36 of the Police and Magistrates' Courts Act 1994 (c. 29).

Where the chief officer has received a report on a complaint from an investigating officer and has chosen not to institute disciplinary proceedings, that will emerge from the memorandum sent to the PCA by the chief officer under s.75. If dissatisfied with such an outcome, the PCA is empowered firstly to recommend that he or she take such steps (subs. (1)) and, if the chief officer is still unwilling, to require him or her to do so (subs. (4)). The chief officer is under a duty to comply with this direction (subs. (5)). See *R. v. Police Complaints Board, ex p. Madden* [1983] 2 All E.R. 353 which interprets similar provisions in the Police Act 1976.

Information as to the manner of dealing with complaints etc.

77. Every police authority in carrying out its duty with respect to the maintenance of an efficient and effective police force, and inspectors of constabulary in carrying out their duties with respect to the efficiency and effectiveness of any police force, shall keep themselves informed as to the working of sections 67 to 76 in relation to the force.

GENERAL NOTE

This section is derived from s.95 of the Police and Criminal Evidence Act 1984 (c. 60) and the Police and Magistrates' Courts Act 1994 (c. 29), Sched. 5, para. 29.

This places a duty upon both the police authority and the inspectorate of constabulary to ensure that they are properly informed about the functioning of the complaints machinery. The former, perhaps, should address the issue in their annual report while it should be a matter of attention for the latter during any periodic inspection.

Constabularies maintained by authorities other than police authorities

78.—(1) An agreement for the establishment in relation to any body of constables maintained by an authority, other than a police authority, of procedures corresponding or similar to any of those established by or by virtue of this Chapter may, with the approval of the Secretary of State, be made between the Authority and the authority maintaining the body of constables.

(2) Where no such procedures are in force in relation to a body of constables, the Secretary of State may by order establish such procedures.

(3) An agreement under this section may at any time be varied or terminated with the approval of the Secretary of State.

(4) Before making an order under this section the Secretary of State shall consult—

(a) the Authority, and

(b) the authority maintaining the body of constables to whom the order would relate.

(5) A statutory instrument containing an order under this section shall be subject to annulment in pursuance of a resolution of either House of Parliament.

(6) Nothing in any other enactment passed or made before 31st October 1984 shall prevent an authority who maintain a body of constables from carrying into effect procedures established by virtue of this section.

(7) No such procedures shall have effect in relation to anything done by a constable outside England and Wales.

GENERAL NOTE

This section is derived from s.96 of the Police and Criminal Evidence Act 1984 (c. 60) and the Police and Magistrates' Courts Act 1994 (c. 29), Sched. 5, para. 30.

This provides for the complaints machinery put in place by this Part of the Act to be used for police forces, other than those maintained by a police authority. There are voluntary agreements under subs. (1) which cover, for example, the British Transport Police, the U.K. Atomic Energy Authority Police, the Ministry of Defence Police and the Royal Parks Police. The Secretary of State is empowered to establish such procedures in the absence of agreement (subs. (2)) but no such orders have been made before 1996.

Reports

79.—(1) The Authority shall, at the request of the Secretary of State, report to him on such matters relating generally to their functions as the Secretary of State may specify, and the Authority may for that purpose carry out research into any such matters.

(2) The Authority may make a report to the Secretary of State on any matters coming to their notice under this Chapter to which they consider that

his attention should be drawn by reason of their gravity or of other exceptional circumstances.

(3) The Authority shall send a copy of any report under subsection (2)—

(a) to the police authority and the chief officer of police of any police force which appears to the Authority to be concerned, or

(b) if the report concerns a body of constables such as is mentioned in section 78, to the authority maintaining it and the officer having the direction and the control of it.

(4) As soon as practicable after the end of each calendar year the Authority shall make to the Secretary of State a report on the discharge of their functions during that year.

(5) The Secretary of State shall lay before Parliament a copy of every report received by him under this section and shall cause every such report to be published.

(6) The Authority shall send to each police authority—

(a) a copy of every report made under subsection (4), and

(b) any statistical or other general information—

(i) which relates to the year dealt with by the report and to the area of that police authority, and

(ii) which the Authority consider should be brought to the police authority's attention in connection with its functions under section 77.

GENERAL NOTE

This section is derived from s.97 of the Police and Criminal Evidence Act 1984 (c. 60).

The PCA firstly must report, at the request of the Secretary of State, on any matter relating to their functions (subs. (1)); secondly they may make a report to the Secretary of State if there is a grave or exceptional matter that should be brought to his or her attention (subs. (2)); thirdly they are under a duty to issue an annual report (subs. (4)). The annual reports and other research still questions the effectiveness of the PCA—see *Maguire M. and Corbett C.: A Study of the Police Complaints System (HMSO) 1991*. Very few complaints succeed and the level of withdrawal is still high. The PCA only supervises in the most serious of cases and is in the position of evaluating the police's work on the basis of the police's own paperwork. The Authority still only publishes annual reports and not detailed reports on individual incidents. The Home Affairs Committee of the House of Commons has been receiving evidence on the operation of the complaints machinery—*House of Commons Papers 1995/96 112*.

Restriction on disclosure of information

80.—(1) No information received by the Authority in connection with any of their functions under sections 67 to 79 or regulations made by virtue of section 81 shall be disclosed by any person who is or has been a member, officer or servant of the Authority except—

(a) to the Secretary of State or to a member, officer or servant of the Authority or, so far as may be necessary for the proper discharge of the functions of the Authority, to other persons,

(b) for the purposes of any criminal, civil or disciplinary proceedings, or

(c) in the form of a summary or other general statement made by the Authority which does not identify the person from whom the information was received or any person to whom it relates.

(2) Any person who discloses information in contravention of this section shall be guilty of an offence and liable on summary conviction to a fine of an amount not exceeding level 5 on the standard scale.

GENERAL NOTE

This section derives from s.98 of the Police and Criminal Evidence Act 1984 (c. 60).

This creates a criminal offence which prevents members or employees of the PCA from revealing information gathered in connection with PCA functions. The exceptions are: firstly under subs. (1)(a) where information can be disclosed for the purpose of the functions of the PCA to the Secretary of State, members and servants of the PCA and to of "other persons", for example, the complainant and his or her lawyer; secondly under subs. (1)(b) where information must also be revealed for the purpose of court or disciplinary proceedings—public interest immunity can no longer be automatically claimed in such circumstances (see *R. v. Chief Constable of the West Midlands Police, ex p. Wiley* [1994] 3 All E.R. 420 and the general note to this Part of the Act); thirdly under subs. (1)(c) where the Authority itself can issue general statements as long as they do not reveal the identity of any informant.

Regulations

81.—(1) The Secretary of State may make regulations as to the procedure to be followed under this Chapter.

(2) The Secretary of State shall by regulations provide—

(a) that, subject to such exceptions, and in accordance with such procedures, as may be specified in the regulations, the chief officer of police of a police force shall supply a copy of, or of the record of, any complaint concerning the conduct of a member of his force—
  (i) to that member, and
  (ii) to the person by or on behalf of whom the complaint was submitted;

(b) procedures for the informal resolution of complaints of such descriptions as may be specified in the regulations, and for giving the person by or on behalf of whom the complaint was submitted a record of the outcome of any such procedure if he applies for one within such period as the regulations may provide;

(c) procedures for giving a member of a police force, whose conduct is the subject of a complaint which falls to be resolved informally, an opportunity to comment orally or in writing on the complaint;

(d) for cases in which any provision of this Chapter is not to apply where—
  (i) a complaint, other than a complaint which falls to be resolved informally, is withdrawn, or
  (ii) the complainant indicates that he does not wish any further steps to be taken;

(e) for enabling the Authority to dispense with any requirement of this Chapter;

(f) for enabling the Authority to relinquish the supervision of the investigation of any complaint or other matter;

(g) procedures for the reference or submission of complaints or other matters to the Authority;

(h) for the time within which the Authority are to give a notification under section 72(2);

(i) that the Authority shall be supplied with such information or documents of such description as may be specified in the regulations at such time or in such circumstances as may be so specified;

(j) that any action or decision of the Authority which they take in consequence of their receipt of a memorandum under section 75 shall, if it is an action or decision of a description specified in the regulations, be notified to the person concerned and that, in connection with such a notification, the Authority shall have power to supply that person with any relevant information;

(k) that chief officers of police shall have power to delegate any functions conferred on them by or by virtue of this Chapter.

(3) In this section "document" means anything in which information of any description is recorded.

GENERAL NOTE

These sections 81 and 82 are derived from ss.99 and 100 of the Police and Criminal Evidence Act 1984 (c. 60).

These sections 81 and 82 provide for the Secretary of State to make regulations governing the procedure to be followed in relation to complaints. Significant rules include the Police (Complaints) (General) Regulations 1985 (S.I. 1985 No. 520 as amended); Police (Discipline) (Senior Officers) Regulations 1985 (S.I. 1985 No. 519 as amended); Police (Discipline) Regulations 1985

(S.I. 1985 No. 518 as amended); Police (Complaints) (Informal Resolution) Regulations 1985 (S.I. 1985 No. 671 as amended).

The definition of "document" is to be found in s.13 of the Civil Evidence Act 1995 (c. 38).

Regulations—supplementary

82.—(1) Regulations under this Chapter may make different provision for different circumstances and may authorise the Secretary of State to make provision for any purposes specified in the regulations.

(2) Subject to subsection (3), a statutory instrument containing regulations under this Chapter shall be subject to annulment in pursuance of a resolution of either House of Parliament.

(3) Regulations to which this subsection applies shall not be made unless a draft of them has been laid before and approved by resolution of each House of Parliament.

(4) Subsection (3) applies to regulations made by virtue of section 70(1)(a)(ii), 72(1)(b) or (4), 75(4) or (5) or 81(2)(b), (e) or (f).

Guidance concerning complaints etc.

83.—(1) The Secretary of State may issue guidance to police authorities, chief officers of police and other members of police forces concerning the discharge of their functions under this Chapter and they shall have regard to any such guidance in the discharge of their functions.

(2) Guidance may not be issued under subsection (1) in relation to the handling of a particular case.

(3) A failure on the part of a person to whom guidance is issued under subsection (1) to have regard to such guidance shall be admissible in evidence on any appeal from a decision taken in proceedings under regulations made in accordance with section 50(3).

(4) In discharging their functions under section 76 the Authority shall have regard to any guidance given to them by the Secretary of State with respect to such matters as are for the time being the subject of guidance under subsection (1), and they shall have regard in particular, but without prejudice to the generality of this subsection, to any such guidance as to the principles to be applied in cases that involve any question of criminal proceedings.

(5) The report of the Authority under section 79(4) shall contain a statement of any guidance given to the Authority under subsection (4) above during the year to which the report relates.

GENERAL NOTE

This section is derived from s.105 of the Police and Criminal Evidence Act 1984 (c. 60) and the Police and Magistrates' Courts Act 1994 (c. 29), Sched. 5, para. 34.

The Secretary of State's guidance is just guidance and those with a function in dealing with complaints (especially chief constables and police authorities) must still address their minds to relevant issues. Where such guidance is provided by the Secretary of State, authorities should not consider themselves bound by it. See *R. v. Police Complaints Board, ex p. Madden* [1983] 2 All E.R. 353.

CHAPTER II

DISCIPLINARY AND OTHER PROCEEDINGS

GENERAL NOTE

Discipline in the police forces comes under the Police (Discipline) (Senior Officers) Regulations 1985 (S.I. 1985 No. 519 as amended) and the Police (Discipline) Regulations 1985 (S.I. 1985 No. 518 as amended). The latter regulations contain the Police Discipline Code in Sched. 1.

A breach of the Code of Discipline by a senior officer may lead to disciplinary proceedings. In this case there will be a disciplinary tribunal, consisting of an independent lawyer from a panel kept by the Secretary of State.

Disciplinary proceedings against a junior officer will be heard by a chief officer, probably an assistant chief constable, under para. 13 of the 1985 Regulations. There is no longer the possibility of involvement by members of the PCA as existed with the previous procedures under s.94 of the Police and Criminal Evidence Act 1984 (c. 60).

Punishments include reprimands, fines, reductions in rank, requirement to resign or dismissal. There was the possibility of an appeal to the Secretary of State under s.37 of the Police Act 1964 but this cumbersome process was abolished by s.19(1) of the Police and Magistrates' Courts Act 1994 (c. 29) and has been replaced by the police appeals tribunals, now constituted under s.85 and Sched. 6 of this Act.

Representation at disciplinary and other proceedings

84.—(1) A member of a police force of the rank of superintendent or below may not be dismissed, required to resign or reduced in rank by a decision taken in proceedings under regulations made in accordance with section 50(3)(a) unless he has been given an opportunity to elect to be legally represented at any hearing held in the course of those proceedings.

(2) Where a member of a police force makes an election to which subsection (1) refers, he may be represented at the hearing, at his option, either by counsel or by a solicitor.

(3) Except in a case where a member of a police force of the rank of superintendent or below has been given an opportunity to elect to be legally represented and has so elected, he may be represented at the hearing only by another member of a police force.

(4) Regulations under section 50 shall specify—

(a) a procedure for notifying a member of a police force of the effect of subsections (1) to (3) above,

(b) when he is to be notified of the effect of those subsections, and

(c) when he is to give notice whether he wishes to be legally represented at the hearing.

(5) If a member of a police force—

(a) fails without reasonable cause to give notice in accordance with the regulations that he wishes to be legally represented, or

(b) gives notice in accordance with the regulations that he does not wish to be legally represented,

he may be dismissed, required to resign or reduced in rank without his being legally represented.

(6) If a member of a police force has given notice in accordance with the regulations that he wishes to be legally represented, the case against him may be presented by counsel or a solicitor whether or not he is actually so represented.

GENERAL NOTE

This section is derived from s.102 of the Police and Criminal Evidence Act 1984 (c. 60) and the Police and Magistrates' Courts Act 1994 (c. 29), Sched. 5, para. 33.

This section provides for legal representation for police officers at disciplinary proceedings. It only applies in serious cases where there is a possibility of reduction in rank, requirement to resign or dismissal. In less serious cases, officers are entitled to be represented by the Police Federation (s.59(2) of this Act) and can only be represented by another police officer (s.59(3)).

However, officers subject to disciplinary proceedings in serious cases where there is a possibility of reduction in rank, requirement to resign or dismissal must be asked whether they are electing to be legally represented. A failure to ask the officer limits the possible sanctions available to the tribunal. A failure to elect on the part of the police officer can lead to sanctions being imposed without recourse to legal representation (subs. (4)). Where the officer has elected to be legally represented, the police force itself can also be represented by counsel or solicitor, even where the officer is ultimately not represented by solicitor or counsel.

Appeals against dismissal etc.

85.—(1) A member of a police force who is dismissed, required to resign or reduced in rank by a decision taken in proceedings under regulations made in accordance with section 50(3) may appeal to a police appeals tribunal against the decision except where he has a right of appeal to some other person; and in that case he may appeal to a police appeals tribunal from any decision of that other person as a result of which he is dismissed, required to resign or reduced in rank.

(2) Where a police appeals tribunal allows an appeal it may, if it considers that it is appropriate to do so, make an order dealing with the appellant in a way—

(a) which appears to the tribunal to be less severe than the way in which he was dealt with by the decision appealed against, and

(b) in which he could have been dealt with by the person who made that decision.

(3) The Secretary of State may make rules as to the procedure on appeals to police appeals tribunals under this section.

(4) Rules made under this section may make provision for enabling a police appeals tribunal to require any person to attend a hearing to give evidence or to produce documents, and may, in particular, apply subsections (2) and (3) of section 250 of the Local Government Act 1972 with such modifications as may be set out in the rules.

(5) A statutory instrument containing rules made under this section shall be laid before Parliament after being made.

(6) Schedule 6 shall have effect in relation to appeals under this section.

GENERAL NOTE

This section is derived from s.37 of the Police Act 1964 (c. 48) as amended by s.19(1) of the Police and Magistrates' Courts Act 1994 (c. 29).

Under s.37 of the Police Act 1964 (c. 48), appeals against the findings of any disciplinary proceedings involved an appeal to the Secretary of State. But this cumbersome process was abolished by s.19(1) of the Police and Magistrates' Courts Act 1994 (c. 29) and has been replaced by police appeals tribunals. There is only a right of appeal where the officer concerned has been reduced in rank, required to resign or dismissed (subs. (1)). In the draft Police and Magistrates' Courts Bill, mere reduction in rank was not included. The government changed its mind on that issue but did not introduce any general right of appeal against a decision to fine or reprimand a police officer.

The constitution of the appeals tribunal can be found in Sched. 6.

For appeals by senior officers, the panel is appointed by the Secretary of State and includes: (a) a lawyer of seven years' experience, chosen from a list maintained by the Lord Chancellor; (b) a member of a police authority (other than the authority involved); and (c) either a present or past Inspector of Constabulary or an ex-Commissioner of the Metropolitan Police.

For appeals by junior officers, the panel is appointed by the police authority and consists of four persons including: (a) a lawyer of seven years' experience, chosen from a list maintained by the Lord Chancellor; (b) a member of the police authority; (c) a chief officer chosen from a list maintained by the Secretary of State; and (d) a retired officer of appropriate rank.

The tribunal will be chaired in both cases by the lawyer member. The tribunal has the power to compel witnesses to attend and produce documents in accordance with s.250(2) and (3) of the Local Government Act 1972 (c. 70) (subs. (4)). "Document" has a wide meaning incorporating any medium on which information is stored—see s.13 of the Civil Evidence Act 1995 (c. 38).

Admissibility of statements in subsequent proceedings

86.—(1) Subject to subsection (2), no statement made by a person for the purpose of the informal resolution of a complaint shall be admissible in any subsequent criminal, civil or disciplinary proceedings.

(2) A statement is not rendered inadmissible by subsection (1) if it consists of or includes an admission relating to a matter which does not fall to be resolved informally.

(3) In this section "complaint" and "disciplinary proceedings" have the meanings given in section 65.

GENERAL NOTE

This section is derived from ss.84(4), 104(3) and (4) of the Police and Criminal Evidence Act 1984 (c. 60) and the Police and Magistrates' Courts Act 1994 (c. 29), Sched. 5, para. 24.

The policy of the Act is to encourage informal resolution of disputes wherever possible. Obviously such resolution may well involve inculpatory statements by the police officer involved. He or she would be unwise to make such statements if they were then admissible in evidence in subsequent proceedings, be they disciplinary or in court. Under subs. (1) any such statement is not admissible evidence in subsequent proceedings. The officer is thereby able to take part in the informal procedures without prejudicing himself or herself. The only exception is that, if the officer admits to some other matter not the subject of the complaint or the informal resolution, that admission will still be admissible evidence.

Note that the previous incarnation of this section, s.104(1) of the Police and Criminal Evidence Act 1984 (c. 60), incorporated a version of the double jeopardy rule that where an officer had been convicted or acquitted in criminal proceedings, he or she should not be liable in any further disciplinary proceedings. This was questioned in *R. v. Police Complaints Board, ex p. Madden* [1983] 2 All E.R. 353. Consequently this subsection has now been omitted.

Guidance concerning disciplinary proceedings etc.

87.—(1) The Secretary of State may issue guidance to police authorities, chief officers of police and other members of police forces concerning the discharge of their functions under regulations made under section 50 in relation to the matters mentioned in subsection 2(e) of that section, and they shall have regard to any such guidance in the discharge of their functions.

(2) Subsections (2) to (5) of section 83 shall apply in relation to guidance issued under subsection (1) above as they apply in relation to guidance issued under subsection (1) of that section.

GENERAL NOTE

This section is derived from s.105(1) of the Police and Criminal Evidence Act 1984 (c. 60) and the Police and Magistrates' Courts Act 1994 (c. 29), Sched. 5, para. 34.

Where such guidance is provided, authorities should not consider themselves bound by it. See *R. v. Police Complaints Board, ex p. Madden* [1983] 2 All E.R. 353.

Liability for wrongful acts of constables

88.—(1) The chief officer of police for a police area shall be liable in respect of torts committed by constables under his direction and control in the performance or purported performance of their functions in like manner as a master is liable in respect of torts committed by his servants in the course of their employment, and accordingly shall in respect of any such tort be treated for all purposes as a joint tortfeasor.

(2) There shall be paid out of the police fund—

(a) any damages or costs awarded against the chief officer of police in any proceedings brought against him by virtue of this section and any costs incurred by him in any such proceedings so far as not recovered by him in the proceedings; and

(b) any sum required in connection with the settlement of any claim made against the chief officer of police by virtue of this section, if the settlement is approved by the police authority.

(3) Any proceedings in respect of a claim made by virtue of this section shall be brought against the chief officer of police for the time being or, in the case of a vacancy in that office, against the person for the time being performing the functions of the chief officer of police; and references in subsections (1) and (2) to the chief officer of police shall be construed accordingly.

(4) A police authority may, in such cases and to such extent as appear to it to be appropriate, pay out of the police fund—

(a) any damages or costs awarded against a person to whom this subsection applies in proceedings for a tort committed by that person,

(b) any costs incurred and not recovered by such a person in such proceedings, and

(c) any sum required in connection with the settlement of a claim that has or might have given rise to such proceedings.

(5) Subsection (4) applies to a person who is—

(a) a member of the police force maintained by the police authority,

(b) a constable for the time being required to serve with that force by virtue of section 24 or 98, or

(c) a special constable appointed for the authority's police area.

GENERAL NOTE

This section is derived from s.48 of the Police Act 1964 (c. 48) and the Criminal Justice and Public Order Act 1994 (c. 33), Sched. 10, para. 13.

This section ensures that the general principles of vicarious liability (*i.e.* that an employer is responsible for damage caused by the torts of his employees acting in the course of employment) apply to the police. Such liability is a form of strict liability because it arises from the employer-employee (or master-servant) relationship, without reference to any fault of the employer. In all cases of vicarious liability the employer is liable in addition to the employee, who remains legally responsible for his tort. The essential requirements for vicarious liability are the existence of a tort, committed by a police officer who was acting in the course of his or her employment.

This is straightforward where the plaintiff has suffered an injury or damage as a direct result of the acts or omissions of a police officer—*Knightley v. Johns* [1982] 1 All E.R. 851; *Rigby v. Chief Constable of Northamptonshire* [1985] 2 All E.R. 985. However, where damage has been caused by a third party, civil actions against the police force have failed on the grounds that a legal duty cannot arise in the absence of a special relationship between the police and the injured party. It must be noted, however, that even if a special relationship be established in an extremely exceptional case, the appellate courts may refuse to impose a legal duty on grounds of public policy considerations, if to do so would be unjust and unreasonable—*Hill v. Chief Constable of West Yorkshire* [1988] 2 All E.R. 238; *Clough v. Bussan* [1990] 1 All E.R. 431; *Alexandrou v. Oxford* [1993] 4 All E.R. 328; *Osman v. Ferguson* [1993] 4 All E.R. 344; *Hughes v. National Union of Mineworkers* [1991] 4 All E.R. 278. Such a special relationship probably exists where it is assumed by the police: *Swinney v. Chief Constable of Northumbria* (1996) N.L.J. 878.

PART V

MISCELLANEOUS AND GENERAL

Offences

Assaults on constables

89.—(1) Any person who assaults a constable in the execution of his duty, or a person assisting a constable in the execution of his duty, shall be guilty of an offence and liable on summary conviction to imprisonment for a term not exceeding six months or to a fine not exceeding level 5 on the standard scale, or to both.

(2) Any person who resists or wilfully obstructs a constable in the execution of his duty, or a person assisting a constable in the execution of his duty, shall be guilty of an offence and liable on summary conviction to imprisonment for a term not exceeding one month or to a fine not exceeding level 3 on the standard scale, or to both.

(3) This section also applies to a constable who is a member of a police force maintained in Scotland or Northern Ireland when he is executing a warrant, or otherwise acting in England or Wales, by virtue of any enactment conferring powers on him in England and Wales.

GENERAL NOTE

This section is derived from s.51 of the Police Act 1964 (c. 48), ss.15, 30 and 31 of the Criminal Law Act 1977, the Criminal Justice Act 1982 (c. 48), ss.37, 46, Sched. 1, para. 18, Sched. 6, and the Criminal Justice and Public Order Act 1994 (c. 33), Sched. 10, para. 4.

This section consolidates the two offences previously contained in s.51 of the Police Act 1964 (c. 48).

Under subs. (1) is the offence of assault on a police constable in the execution of his or her duty. The *actus reus* requires at least a common law assault (*R. v. Fagan* [1968] 3 All E.R. 442; *Donnelly v. Jackman* [1970] 1 All E.R. 987; *Collins v. Wilcock* [1984] 3 All E.R. 374).

The police officer must be in the execution of his or her duty—*R. v. Riley* (1989) 91 Cr.App.R. 14; *Collins v. Wilcock (supra)*; *R. v. Brazil* [1983] 3 All E.R. 537; *Kenlin v. Gardiner* [1966] 3 All E.R. 931.

There is no requirement to prove that the defendant was aware that the victim was a police officer—*R. v. Forbes and Webb* (1865) 10 Cox CC 362. However if the defendant honestly believes that he is acting lawfully, he does not have the *mens rea* for the assault—*R. v. Williams* [1987] 3 All E.R. 411; *R. v. Ball* [1989] Crim.L.R. 579.

Under subs. (2) is the offence of obstruction of a police constable in the execution of his or her duty. This does not require violence and the offence is committed if the defendant makes it more difficult for the aforementioned police constable to carry out his or her duty—*Hinchcliffe v. Sheldon* [1955] 3 All E.R. 406. Not helping a police officer or refusing to answer questions does not constitute obstruction—*Rice v. Connelly* [1966] 2 Q.B. 414. The obstruction must be wilful which means intentional—*R. v. Senior* (1899) 1 Q.B. 283; *R. v. Wershof* [1978] 3 All E.R. 540; *R. v. Sheppard* [1980] 3 All E.R. 899.

Impersonation, etc.

90.—(1) Any person who with intent to deceive impersonates a member of a police force or special constable, or makes any statement or does any act calculated falsely to suggest that he is such a member or constable, shall be guilty of an offence and liable on summary conviction to imprisonment for a term not exceeding six months or to a fine not exceeding level 5 on the standard scale, or to both.

(2) Any person who, not being a constable, wears any article of police uniform in circumstances where it gives him an appearance so nearly resembling that of a member of a police force as to be calculated to deceive shall be guilty of an offence and liable on summary conviction to a fine not exceeding level 3 on the standard scale.

(3) Any person who, not being a member of a police force or special constable, has in his possession any article of police uniform shall, unless he proves that he obtained possession of that article lawfully and has possession of it for a lawful purpose, be guilty of an offence and liable on summary conviction to a fine not exceeding level 1 on the standard scale.

(4) In this section—
   (a) "article of police uniform" means any article of uniform or any distinctive badge or mark or document of identification usually issued to members of police forces or special constables, or anything having the appearance of such an article, badge, mark or document, and
   (b) "special constable" means a special constable appointed for a police area.

General Note

This section is derived from s.52 of the Police Act 1964 (c. 48) as amended by ss.37, 38, 39 and 46 of the Criminal Justice Act 1982 (c. 48).

This section contains three separate offences relating to impersonating a police officer. The most serious, punishable with a maximum of six months' imprisonment, under subs. (1) is where the defendant impersonates a police officer with intent to deceive. To deceive someone is to induce a person to believe a thing to be true which is in fact false—*Re London and Globe Finance* [1903] 1 Ch. 728, namely that the accused is a police officer. This will require a specific intent, recklessness is not enough although it may constitute some evidence of intent under *R. v. Nedrick* [1986] 3 All E.R. 1. It does not have to be an intent to deceive a specific individual—*R. v. Greenberg* [1942] 2 All E.R. 344. There is no need to show that the defendant obtained any benefit as a result of the deception.

Where proof of intent to deceive is difficult, there is a lesser offence under subs. (2) of wearing police uniform, in circumstances where it is "calculated" to deceive. In *Turner v. Shearer* [1973] 1 All E.R. 397 "calculated" was interpreted as "likely to deceive" and did not require subjective intent or foresight on the part of the accused.

Under subs. (3) possession of police uniform is an offence unless the defendant proves that he or she came by the uniform lawfully. The burden of proof is on the defendant and this will be satisfied by proof on the balance of probabilities—*R. v. Carr-Briant* [1943] 2 All E.R. 156.

Causing disaffection

91.—(1) Any person who causes, or attempts to cause, or does any act calculated to cause, disaffection amongst the members of any police force, or induces or attempts to induce, or does any act calculated to induce, any member of a police force to withhold his services, shall be guilty of an offence and liable—

    (a) on summary conviction, to imprisonment for a term not exceeding six months or to a fine not exceeding the statutory maximum, or to both;

    (b) on conviction on indictment, to imprisonment for a term not exceeding two years or to a fine, or to both.

(2) This section applies to special constables appointed for a police area as it applies to members of a police force.

GENERAL NOTE

This section is derived from s.53 of the Police Act 1964 (c. 48); the Interpretation Act 1978 (c. 30), Sched. 1; the Magistrates' Court Act 1980 (c. 43), s.32(2); Criminal Justice Act 1988 (c. 33), Sched. 15, para. 58(b).

This offence covers, *inter alia*, any encouragement of police officers to strike. It is not necessary to show that the defendant was seeking to induce any particular officer to go on strike or commit a breach of discipline. The attempt can be directed at the members of the force generally—*R. v. Bowman* (1912) 76 JP 271. The prosecution would need to be shown that the defendant knew that the persons concerned were police officers.

Miscellaneous financial provisions

Grants by local authorities

92.—(1) The council of a county, district, county borough or London borough may make grants to any police authority established under section 3 whose police area falls wholly or partly within the county, district, county borough or borough.

(2) The council of a London borough, county, or district which falls wholly or partly within the metropolitan police district may make grants for police purposes to the Receiver for the Metropolitan Police District.

(3) Grants under this section may be made unconditionally or, with the agreement of the chief officer of police for the police area concerned, subject to conditions.

(4) This section applies to the Council of the Isles of Scilly as it applies to a county council.

GENERAL NOTE

This section is derived from s.53B of the Police Act 1964 (c. 48), as inserted by s.24 of the Police and Magistrates' Courts Act 1994 (c. 29).

This provides for local authorities to make grants to police forces other than the contribution from police funds from precepts raised against council tax. Such grants can be earmarked for use on particular projects under subs. (3) so that a district council may advance money to the police on the condition that it is spent, for example, on the provision of closed circuit TV cameras in a specific location.

Acceptance of gifts and loans

93.—(1) A police authority may, in connection with the discharge of any of its functions, accept gifts of money, and gifts or loans of other property, on such terms as appear to the authority to be appropriate.

(2) The terms on which gifts or loans are accepted under subsection (1) may include terms providing for the commercial sponsorship of any activity of the police authority or of the police force maintained by it.

(3) In the application of this section in relation to the metropolitan police force, for the references to the police authority there shall be substituted references to the Receiver for the Metropolitan Police District.

GENERAL NOTE

This section is derived from s.53B of the Police Act 1964 (c. 48), as inserted by the Police and Magistrates' Courts Act 1994 (c. 29).

This was a more controversial measure when it was introduced in the Police and Magistrates' Courts Act 1994 (c. 29). This empowers police authorities to accept what is the equivalent of commercial sponsorship of police work. However it is not intended to reward the police for success in particular operations and there will be a Code of Practice for the guidance of police authorities in such matters. The section means that the police can accept grants to cover the capital cost of setting up a crime prevention or community relations scheme. One example was the sponsorship of a regional conference on neighbourhood watch schemes which was undertaken by General Accident.

Financing of new police authorities

94.—(1) The Secretary of State may make grants to any police authority established under section 3 in respect of expenditure incurred (or to be incurred) by it at any time before the beginning of its first precepting year.

(2) Without prejudice to any other powers to borrow, a police authority established under section 3 may borrow by way of temporary loan or overdraft from a bank or otherwise any sums which it may require for the purpose of meeting its expenditure before the beginning of its first precepting year.

(3) The sums borrowed by an authority under this section shall not exceed such amount as the Secretary of State may determine, and shall be repaid before the end of its first precepting year.

(4) For the purposes of this section the "first precepting year" of a police authority is the financial year in which revenue is first received by it as a result of a precept issued by it under Part I of the Local Government Finance Act 1992.

GENERAL NOTE

This section is derived from s.32 of the Police and Magistrates' Courts Act 1994 (c. 29).

This provides for the initial funding of new police authorities in the transitional period before they are able to issue precepts.

Metropolitan and City of London police funds

95. There shall be paid out of the metropolitan police fund and the City of London police fund respectively (subject, in the case of the metropolitan police fund, to the approval of the Secretary of State) any expenditure incurred under this Act in respect of—

  (a) any special constables appointed for the metropolitan police district or the City of London police area; and

  (b) any police cadets appointed in relation to the metropolitan police force or the City of London police force.

GENERAL NOTE

This section derives from s.56 of the Police Act 1964 (c. 48) and the Police and Magistrates' Courts Act 1994 (c. 29), Sched. 5, para. 13.

Miscellaneous

Arrangements for obtaining the views of the community on policing

96.—(1) Arrangements shall be made for each police area for obtaining—

  (a) the views of people in that area about matters concerning the policing of the area, and

  (b) their co-operation with the police in preventing crime in that area.

(2) Except as provided by subsections (3) to (6), arrangements for each police area shall be made by the police authority after consulting the chief constable as to the arrangements that would be appropriate.

(3) The Secretary of State shall issue guidance to the Commissioner of Police of the Metropolis concerning arrangements for the metropolitan police district; and the Commissioner shall make arrangements under this section after taking account of that guidance.

(4) The Commissioner shall make separate arrangements—
(a) for each London borough;
(b) for each district which falls wholly within the metropolitan police district; and
(c) in the case of districts which fall partly within the metropolitan police district, for each part of such a district which falls within that police district.

(5) The Commissioner shall—
(a) consult the council of each London borough as to the arrangements that would be appropriate for the borough,
(b) consult the council of each district mentioned in subsection (4)(b) as to the arrangements that would be appropriate for the district, and
(c) consult the council of each district mentioned in subsection (4)(c) as to the arrangements that would be appropriate for the part of the district which falls within the metropolitan police district.

(6) The Common Council of the City of London shall issue guidance to the Commissioner of Police for the City of London concerning arrangements for the City of London police area; and the Commissioner shall make arrangements under this section after taking account of that guidance.

(7) A body or person whose duty it is to make arrangements under this section shall review the arrangements so made from time to time.

(8) If it appears to the Secretary of State that arrangements for a police area are not adequate for the purposes set out in subsection (1), he may require the body or person whose duty it is to make arrangements for that area to submit a report to him concerning the arrangements.

(9) After considering a report submitted under subsection (8), the Secretary of State may require the body or person who submitted it to review the arrangements and submit a further report to him concerning them.

(10) A body or person whose duty it is to make arrangements shall be under the same duties to consult when reviewing arrangements as when making them.

GENERAL NOTE

This section derives from s.106 of the Police and Criminal Evidence Act 1984 (c. 60).

Prior to 1984, there were no statutory arrangements for the police to consult with the local community. As a result of the Scarman Report into the Brixton disturbances (*The Brixton Disturbances Cmnd. 8427 (1982)*), s.106 of the Police and Criminal Evidence Act 1984 (which are replicated in this section) made the local police authority, in consultation with the chief constable, responsible for making arrangements to obtain the views of local people living in the area about matters concerning local policing and for obtaining their co-operation with the police in preventing crime. If the arrangements are inadequate, then the Home Secretary retains the power to require a report from the authority (subss. (8) and (9)). While consultative arrangements may provide a forum for local people to express their genuine feelings on crime and policing, these arrangements pose the same fundamental problem for democratic theory as the police authorities themselves. In the authorities there are the independent members elected under Sched. 3 of this Act and under this section, there is a non-elected body between the police and, for example, local elected representatives. The development of consultative committees in the 10 years since 1984 has been criticised as they often operate as little more than talking shops dominated by a police agenda. However, as changes in police organisation now stresses the local area with devolution of management and financial functions, such consultative bodies will provide a natural link with such areas and a forum for the articulation of views on policing objectives and police performance in a locality which will be required by the police authority itself in producing local policing objectives and local policing plans under ss.7 and 8 of this Act.

The arrangements for London are slightly different. There is no local input into the management of the police whatsoever, whether elected or not. The Secretary of State acts as the authority for the Metropolitan force (and the Common Council of the City of London for the City force). The justification for this is partly historical, partly functional, as the Metropolitan force does perform some national duties. However, the vast preponderance of its work is for the people of London. There are consultative arrangements but as the Secretary of State is the police authority, the duty for making arrangements with the localities for consultation falls on the Commissioner under subss. (3) (4) and (5).

Police officers engaged on service outside their force

97.—(1) For the purposes of this section "relevant service" means—

(a) temporary service on which a person is engaged in accordance with arrangements made under section 26;

(b) temporary service under section 56 on which a person is engaged with the consent of the appropriate authority;

(c) temporary service under the Crown in connection with the provision by the Secretary of State of—

(i) such organisations and services as are described in section 57, or

(ii) research or other services connected with the police,

on which a person is engaged with the consent of the appropriate authority;

(d) temporary service as an adviser to the Secretary of State on which a person is engaged with the consent of the appropriate authority;

(e) service the expenses of which are payable under section 1(1) of the Police (Overseas Service) Act 1945, on which a person is engaged with the consent of the appropriate authority;

(f) service in the Royal Ulster Constabulary, on which a person is engaged with the consent of the Secretary of State and the appropriate authority; or

(g) service pursuant to an appointment under section 10 of the Overseas Development and Co-operation Act 1980, on which a person is engaged with the consent of the appropriate authority.

(2) In subsection (1) "appropriate authority", in relation to a member of a police force, means the chief officer of police acting with the consent of the police authority, except that in relation to the chief officer of police it means the police authority.

(3) Subject to subsections (4) to (8), a member of a police force engaged on relevant service shall be treated as if he were not a member of that force during that service; but, except where a pension, allowance or gratuity becomes payable to him out of money provided by Parliament by virtue of regulations made under the Police Pensions Act 1976—

(a) he shall be entitled at the end of the period of relevant service to revert to his police force in the rank in which he was serving immediately before the period began, and

(b) he shall be treated as if he had been serving in that force during the period of relevant service for the purposes of any scale prescribed by or under regulations made under section 50 above fixing his rate of pay by reference to his length of service.

(4) In the case of relevant service to which subsection (1)(e) refers, the reference in subsection (3) to regulations made under the Police Pensions Act 1976 shall be read as including a reference to regulations made under section 1 of the Police (Overseas Service) Act 1945.

(5) A person may, when engaged on relevant service, be promoted in his police force as if he were serving in that force; and in any such case—

(a) the reference in paragraph (a) of subsection (3) to the rank in which he was serving immediately before the period of relevant service began shall be construed as a reference to the rank to which he is promoted, and

(b) for the purposes mentioned in paragraph (b) of that subsection he shall be treated as having served in that rank from the time of his promotion.

(6) A member of a police force who—

(a) has completed a period of relevant service within paragraph (a), (b), (c), (d) or (g) of subsection (1), or

(b) while engaged on relevant service within paragraph (e) of that subsection, is dismissed from that service by the disciplinary authority established by regulations made under section 1 of the Police (Overseas Service) Act 1945 or is required to resign as an alternative to dismissal, or

(c) while engaged on relevant service within paragraph (f) of that subsection, is dismissed from that service or is required to resign as an alternative to dismissal,

may be dealt with under regulations made in accordance with section 50(3) for anything done or omitted while he was engaged on that service as if that service had been service in his police force; and section 85 shall apply accordingly.

(7) For the purposes of subsection (6) a certificate certifying that a person has been dismissed, or required to resign as an alternative to dismissal, shall be evidence of the fact so certified, if—

(a) in a case within paragraph (b) of that subsection, it is given by the disciplinary authority referred to in that paragraph, or

(b) in a case within paragraph (c) of that subsection, it is given by or on behalf of the chief constable of the Royal Ulster Constabulary, or such other person or authority as may be designated for the purposes of this subsection by order of the Secretary of State.

(8) A member of a police force engaged on relevant service within paragraph (b), (c) or (d) of subsection (1)—

(a) shall continue to be a constable, and

(b) shall be treated for the purposes of sections 30, 59, 60, 64 and 90 as if he were a member of his police force.

(9) The Secretary of State shall be liable in respect of torts committed by a member of a police force engaged on relevant service within paragraph (b), (c) or (d) of subsection (1) in the performance or purported performance of his functions in like manner as a master is liable in respect of torts committed by his servants in the course of their employment, and shall in respect of any such tort be treated for all purposes as a joint tortfeasor.

GENERAL NOTE

   This section derives from ss.43 and 53 of the Police Act 1964 (c. 48) as amended by s.26 of the Police and Magistrates' Courts Act 1994 (c. 29).

   This is designed to provide for continuity of service and entitlements for officers who are engaged in service outside of their own forces, for example, under ss.26 or 98 of this Act. Subsection (1) defines the relevant periods of service. Under subs. (3), although the police officer is not a member of his or her own force during this period, he or she is entitled to revert to his or her original force and is to be treated as if he or she had been serving in that force for purposes, for example, of calculating length of service.

Cross-border aid of one police force by another

98.—(1) The chief officer of police of a police force in England or Wales may, on the application of the chief officer of a police force in Scotland or the chief constable of the Royal Ulster Constabulary, provide constables or other assistance for the purpose of enabling the Scottish force or the Royal Ulster Constabulary to meet any special demand on its resources.

(2) The chief officer of a police force in Scotland may, on the application of the chief officer of police of a police force in England or Wales or the chief constable of the Royal Ulster Constabulary, provide constables or other assistance for the purpose of enabling the English or Welsh force or the Royal Ulster Constabulary to meet any special demand on its resources.

(3) The chief constable of the Royal Ulster Constabulary may, on the application of the chief officer of police of a police force in England or Wales or the chief officer of a police force in Scotland, provide constables or other

assistance for the purpose of enabling the English or Welsh force or the Scottish force to meet any special demand on its resources.

(4) If it appears to the Secretary of State—

(a) to be expedient in the interests of public safety or order that a police force should be reinforced or should receive other assistance for the purpose of enabling it to meet any special demand on its resources, and

(b) that satisfactory arrangements under subsection (1), (2) or (3) cannot be made, or cannot be made in time,

he may direct the chief officer of police of any police force in England or Wales, the chief officer of any police force in Scotland or the chief constable of the Royal Ulster Constabulary, as the case may be, to provide such constables or other assistance for that purpose as may be specified in the direction.

(5) While a constable is provided under this section for the assistance of another police force he shall, notwithstanding any enactment,—

(a) be under the direction and control of the chief officer of police of that other force (or, where that other force is a police force in Scotland or the Royal Ulster Constabulary, of its chief officer or the chief constable of the Royal Ulster Constabulary respectively); and

(b) have in any place the like powers and privileges as a member of that other force has in that place as a constable.

(6) The police authority maintaining a police force for which assistance is provided under this section shall pay to the police authority maintaining the force from which that assistance is provided such contribution as may be agreed upon between those authorities or, in the absence of any such agreement, as may be provided by any agreement subsisting at the time between all police authorities generally, or, in the absence of such general agreement, as may be determined by the Secretary of State.

(7) In the application of this section to Scotland, any expression used in this section and in the Police (Scotland) Act 1967 shall have the same meaning in this section as in that Act.

(8) In the application of this section to Northern Ireland, any expression used in this section and in the Police Act (Northern Ireland) 1970 shall have the same meaning in this section as in that Act.

(9) For the purposes of this section "constable", in relation to Northern Ireland, means a member of the Royal Ulster Constabulary or the Royal Ulster Constabulary Reserve.

GENERAL NOTE

This section is derived from s.141 of the Criminal Justice and the Public Order Act 1994 (c. 33).

This section is analogous to s.24 of this Act which provides for mutual assistance between police forces in England and Wales. Similar provisions are required across jurisdictional borders within the U.K., for example, assistance from Scottish forces or from the Royal Ulster Constabulary to English or Welsh forces (and vice versa). This section empowers chief officers to give such mutual aid. However the Secretary of State retains the residual power to direct that such mutual assistance be given where it is expedient in the interests of public safety or order (subs. (4)).

Where police officers are provided under this section, they are under the direction and control of the chief officer of the force which has requested assistance (subs. (5)(a)) and have the powers and privileges of a constable of that jurisdiction while engaged on such duties (subs. (5)(b)).

Jurisdiction of metropolitan police officers

99.—(1) A member of the metropolitan police force who is assigned to the protection of any person or property in Scotland shall, in the discharge of that duty, have the powers and privileges of a constable of a police force maintained under the Police (Scotland) Act 1967.

(2) A member of the metropolitan police force who is assigned to the protection of any person or property in Northern Ireland shall, in the discharge

of that duty, have the powers and privileges of a constable of the Royal Ulster Constabulary.

GENERAL NOTE
This section is derived from s.112 of the Police and Criminal Evidence Act 1984 (c. 60).

The Metropolitan force have specialist duties wholly different in nature from other forces. For example, metropolitan officers will be responsible for the protection of members of the government or of the royal family. These duties can take the officers to other jurisdictions (Scotland and Northern Ireland) within the U.K. This section ensures that they have the powers and privileges of a constable of that jurisdiction while engaged on such duties.

Chief constables affected by police area alterations or local government reorganisations

100.—(1) If the chief constable of a police force which ceases to exist in consequence of an order under section 32 above, section 58 of the Local Government Act 1972 or section 17 of the Local Government Act 1992 is not appointed chief constable or other member of the successor force as from the date of transfer, he shall on that date become a member of that force (or, if there is more than one successor force, of such of them as may be provided by or under the order) by virtue of this section.

(2) While a person is a member of a police force by virtue only of this section he shall hold the rank of assistant chief constable but shall be treated for the purposes of his pay, pension and other conditions of service as if he had continued to be chief constable of the force which ceased to exist, subject however to section 10(1).

(3) A chief constable who becomes a member of a police force by virtue of this section shall, subject to regulations under section 50, cease to be a member of that force at the end of three months unless he has then accepted and taken up an appointment in that force.

(4) If a chief constable was appointed for a term which expires within three months of his becoming a member of a police force by virtue of this section, subsection (3) shall have effect as if the reference to three months were a reference to that term.

(5) Where—
  (a) the chief constable of a police force is engaged for a period of relevant service within paragraph (b), (c), (d) or (e) of section 97(1), and
  (b) before the end of that period that force ceases to exist as mentioned in subsection (1) above,
subsection (1) shall apply to the chief constable as if he were still the chief constable of that force, but with the substitution for references to the date of transfer of references to the end of the same period.

(6) In this section—
  (a) "successor force", in relation to a police force which ceases to exist in consequence of an order, means a force to which members of that police force are transferred by virtue of the order; and
  (b) "date of transfer" means the date as from which those members are so transferred.

GENERAL NOTE
This section is derived from s.58 of the Police Act 1964 (c. 48) and the Police and Magistrates' Courts Act 1994 (c. 29), Sched. 5, para. 14.

Amalgamations of forces under s.32 of this Act prejudices the position of existing chief constables whose job ceases to exist and who may not be appointed to a new position. This provision protects the position of chief constables so affected ensuring that, for a transition period of three months, the chief constable will be treated as an assistant chief constable for the new force and that pay, pension rights and other conditions of service are unaffected and as if he or she had continued to serve for this period.

Supplemental

Interpretation

101.—(1) Except where the context otherwise requires, in this Act—
"chief officer of police" means—
　　　　(a) in relation to a police force maintained under section 2, the chief constable,
　　　　(b) in relation to the metropolitan police force, the Commissioner of Police of the Metropolis, and
　　　　(c) in relation to the City of London police force, the Commissioner of Police for the City of London;
"City of London police area" means the City of London as defined for the purposes of the Acts relating to the City of London police force;
"metropolitan police district" means that district as defined in section 76 of the London Government Act 1963;
"police area" means a police area provided for by section 1;
"police authority" means—
　　　　(a) in relation to a police area listed in Schedule 1, the authority established under section 3,
　　　　(b) in relation to the metropolitan police district, the Secretary of State, and
　　　　(c) in relation to the City of London police area, the Common Council;
"police force" means a force maintained by a police authority;
"police fund" means—
　　　　(a) in relation to a force maintained under section 2, the fund kept by that force's police authority under section 14,
　　　　(b) in relation to the metropolitan police force, the metropolitan police fund, and
　　　　(c) in relation to the City of London police force, the fund out of which the expenses of that force are paid.
(2) In this Act "police purposes", in relation to a police area, includes the purposes of—
　(a)　special constables appointed for that area,
　(b)　police cadets undergoing training with a view to becoming members of the police force maintained for that area, and
　(c)　civilians employed for the purposes of that force or of any such special constables or cadets.

Orders, rules and regulations

102. Any power of the Secretary of State to make orders, rules or regulations under this Act shall be exercisable by statutory instrument.

Consequential amendments, transitional provisions, repeals, etc.

103.—(1) The enactments mentioned in Schedule 7 shall be amended as provided in that Schedule.
(2) Schedule 8 (which contains transitional and transitory provisions, savings etc.) shall have effect.
(3) The enactments mentioned in Parts I and II of Schedule 9 are repealed, and the instruments mentioned in Part III of that Schedule are revoked, to the extent specified in the third column of the Schedule.

Commencement

104.—(1) Except as provided by subsection (2), this Act shall come into force at the end of the period of three months beginning with the day on which it is passed.

(2) The following provisions of this Act—
section 50(3),
Part IV (including Schedules 5 and 6) other than section 88,
paragraphs 43, 45 and 46 of Schedule 7,
paragraph 12 of Schedule 8, and
Part II of Schedule 9,
shall come into force on such day as the Secretary of State may by order appoint.

(3) An order under this section may appoint different days for different purposes or different areas.

(4) The power to make orders under this section includes power to make such transitional provisions and savings as appear to the Secretary of State to be necessary or expedient.

(5) Where an order under this section contains provisions made by virtue of subsection (4), the statutory instrument containing that order shall be subject to annulment in pursuance of a resolution of either House of Parliament.

Extent

105.—(1) Except as provided by subsections (2) to (5), this Act extends to England and Wales only.

(2) The following provisions of this Act extend to Scotland (and in the case of section 99(1) to Scotland only)—
section 21;
Part III;
paragraph 8 of Schedule 5 (and section 66 so far as it relates to that paragraph);
sections 98, 99(1), 101(2), 102 and 104 to 106 and paragraphs 1 to 5, 7 and 11(1), (2) and (4) of Schedule 8 (and section 103 so far as it relates to those paragraphs).

(3) The following provisions of this Act extend to Northern Ireland (and in the case of section 99(2) to Northern Ireland only)—
sections 61 and 62;
sections 98, 99(2), 102 and 104 to 106 and paragraphs 1 to 4 of Schedule 8 (and section 103 so far as it relates to those paragraphs).

(4) Subject to subsection (5), the amendments in Schedule 7 and the repeals and revocations in Schedule 9 have the same extent as the enactments to which they refer and section 103 extends accordingly.

(5) Paragraphs 2 to 6 of Schedule 7 extend to England, Wales and Scotland only.

Short title

106. This Act may be cited as the Police Act 1996.

SCHEDULES

Section 1 SCHEDULE 1

POLICE AREAS

England (except London)

Name of police area	Extent
Avon and Somerset	The county of Somerset and the non-metropolitan districts of Bath and North East Somerset, Bristol, North West Somerset and South Gloucestershire
Bedfordshire	The county of Bedfordshire and the non-metropolitan district of Luton

Name of police area	*Extent*
Cambridgeshire	The county of Cambridgeshire
Cheshire	The county of Cheshire
Cleveland	The non-metropolitan districts of Hartlepool, Middlesbrough, Redcar and Cleveland and Stockton-on-Tees
Cumbria	The county of Cumbria
Derbyshire	The county of Derbyshire and the non-metropolitan district of Derby
Devon and Cornwall	The counties of Devon and Cornwall and the Isles of Scilly
Dorset	The county of Dorset and the non-metropolitan districts of Bournemouth and Poole
Durham	The county of Durham and the non-metropolitan district of Darlington
Essex	The county of Essex
Gloucestershire	The county of Gloucestershire
Greater Manchester	The metropolitan districts of Bolton, Bury, Manchester, Oldham, Rochdale, Salford, Stockport, Tameside, Trafford and Wigan
Hampshire	The counties of Hampshire and Isle of Wight and the non-metropolitan districts of Portsmouth and Southampton
Hertfordshire	The county of Hertfordshire
Humberside	The non-metropolitan districts of the East Riding of Yorkshire, Kingston upon Hull, North East Lincolnshire and North Lincolnshire
Kent	The county of Kent
Lancashire	The county of Lancashire
Leicestershire	The county of Leicestershire and the non-metropolitan districts of Leicester and Rutland
Lincolnshire	The county of Lincolnshire
Merseyside	The metropolitan districts of Knowsley, Liverpool, St. Helens, Sefton and Wirral
Norfolk	The county of Norfolk
Northamptonshire	The county of Northamptonshire
Northumbria	The county of Northumberland and the metropolitan districts of Gateshead, Newcastle upon Tyne, North Tyneside, South Tyneside and Sunderland
North Yorkshire	The county of North Yorkshire and the non-metropolitan district of York
Nottinghamshire	The county of Nottinghamshire
South Yorkshire	The metropolitan districts of Barnsley, Doncaster, Rotherham and Sheffield
Staffordshire	The county of Staffordshire and the non-metropolitan district of Stoke-on-Trent
Suffolk	The county of Suffolk
Surrey	The county of Surrey
Sussex	The counties of East Sussex and West Sussex and the non-metropolitan district of Brighton and Hove
Thames Valley	The counties of Berkshire, Buckinghamshire and Oxfordshire and the non-metropolitan district of Milton Keynes
Warwickshire	The county of Warwickshire
West Mercia	The counties of Hereford and Worcester and Shropshire
West Midlands	The metropolitan districts of Birmingham, Coventry, Dudley, Sandwell, Solihull, Walsall and Wolverhampton
West Yorkshire	The metropolitan districts of Bradford, Calderdale, Kirklees, Leeds and Wakefield

Name of police area	*Extent*
Wiltshire	The county of Wiltshire and the non-metropolitan district of Thamesdown

Wales

Name of police area	*Extent*
Dyfed Powys	The counties of Cardiganshire, Carmarthenshire, Pembrokeshire and Powys
Gwent	The county of Monmouthshire and the county boroughs of Blaenau Gwent, Caerphilly, Newport and Torfaen
North Wales	The counties of Anglesey, Caernarfonshire and Merionethshire, Denbighshire and Flintshire and the county boroughs of Aberconwy and Colwyn and Wrexham
South Wales	The counties of Cardiff and Swansea and the county boroughs of Bridgend, Merthyr Tydfil, Neath and Port Talbot, Rhondda, Cynon, Taff and the Vale of Glamorgan

Section 4 SCHEDULE 2

POLICE AUTHORITIES ESTABLISHED UNDER SECTION 3

Membership of police authorities

1.—(1) Where, by virtue of section 4, a police authority is to consist of seventeen members—
(a) nine of those members shall be members of a relevant council appointed under paragraph 2,
(b) five shall be persons appointed under paragraph 5, and
(c) three shall be magistrates appointed under paragraph 8.

(2) Where, by virtue of an order under subsection (2) of that section, a police authority is to consist of more than seventeen members—
(a) a number which is greater by one than the number of members provided for in paragraphs (b) and (c) below shall be members of a relevant council appointed under paragraph 2,
(b) such number as may be prescribed by the order, not exceeding one third of the total membership, shall be persons appointed under paragraph 5, and
(c) the remainder shall be magistrates appointed under paragraph 8.

Appointment of members by relevant councils

2.—(1) In the case of a police authority in relation to which there is only one relevant council, the members of the police authority referred to in paragraph 1(1)(a) or (2)(a) shall be appointed by that council.

(2) In any other case, those members shall be appointed by a joint committee consisting of persons appointed by the relevant councils from among their own members.

3. The number of members of the joint committee, and the number of those members to be appointed by each relevant council, shall be such as the councils may agree or, in the absence of agreement, as may be determined by the Secretary of State.

4.—(1) A council or joint committee shall exercise its power to appoint members of a police authority under paragraph 2 so as to ensure that, so far as practicable, the members for whose appointment it is responsible reflect—
(a) in the case of appointments by a council, the balance of parties for the time being prevailing among the members of the council, and
(b) in the case of appointments by a joint committee, the balance of parties for the time being prevailing among the members of the relevant councils taken as a whole.

(2) The members referred to in sub-paragraph (1)(a) and (b) do not include any member of a relevant council who is disqualified for being appointed as or being a member of the police authority under paragraph 12.

Appointment of independent members

5. The members of a police authority referred to in paragraph 1(1)(b) or (2)(b) shall be appointed—

(a) by the members of the police authority appointed under paragraph 2 or 8,

(b) from among persons on a short-list prepared by the Secretary of State in accordance with Schedule 3.

6.—(1) Every police authority shall arrange for a notice stating—

(a) the name of each of its members appointed under paragraph 5, and

(b) such other information relating to him as the authority considers appropriate,

to be published in such manner as appears to it to be appropriate.

(2) A police authority shall send to the Secretary of State a copy of any notice which it has arranged to be published under sub-paragraph (1).

Appointment of magistrates

7. The members of a police authority referred to in paragraph 1(1)(c) or (2)(c)—

(a) must be magistrates for an area all or part of which constitutes or forms part of the authority's area, and

(b) shall be appointed in accordance with paragraph 8;

and in that paragraph references to a panel are references to a selection panel constituted under regulations made in accordance with section 21(1A) of the Justices of the Peace Act 1979.

8.—(1) Where there is a panel for an area which constitutes or includes the police authority's area, that panel shall make the appointment.

(2) Where the area of more than one panel falls wholly or partly within the police authority's area, the appointment shall be made by a joint committee consisting of representatives from the panels concerned.

(3) The number of members of a joint committee, and the number of those members to be appointed by each panel, shall be such as the panels may agree or, in the absence of agreement, as may be determined by the Lord Chancellor.

Chairman

9.—(1) A police authority shall at each annual meeting appoint a chairman from among its members.

(2) The appointment under sub-paragraph (1) shall be the first business transacted at the meeting.

(3) On a casual vacancy occurring in the office of chairman, an appointment to fill the vacancy shall be made—

(a) at the next meeting of the authority (other than an extraordinary meeting), or

(b) if that meeting is held within fourteen days after the date on which the vacancy occurs and is not an annual meeting, not later than the next following meeting.

Disqualification

10. A person shall be disqualified for being appointed as a member of a police authority if he has attained the age of seventy years.

11.—(1) Subject to sub-paragraphs (3) and (4), a person shall be disqualified for being appointed as or being a member of a police authority if—

(a) he holds any paid office or employment appointments to which are or may be made or confirmed by the police authority or any committee or sub-committee of the authority, or by a joint committee on which the authority is represented, or by any person holding any such office or employment;

(b) a bankruptcy order has been made against him or his estate has been sequestrated or he has made a composition or arrangement with, or granted a trust deed for, his creditors;

(c) he is subject to a disqualification order under the Company Directors Disqualification Act 1986, or to an order made under section 429(2)(b) of the Insolvency Act 1986 (failure to pay under county court administration order); or

(d) he has within five years before the date of his appointment or since his appointment been convicted in the United Kingdom, the Channel Islands or the Isle of Man of an offence, and has had passed on him a sentence of imprisonment (whether suspended or not) for a period of not less than three months.

(2) A paid employee of a police authority who is employed under the direction of a joint board, joint authority or joint committee on which the authority is represented and any member of which is appointed on the nomination of some other police authority shall be disqualified for being appointed as or being a member of that other police authority.

(3) Where a person is disqualified under sub-paragraph (1)(b) by reason that a bankruptcy order has been made against him or his estate has been sequestrated, the disqualification shall cease—

(a) unless the bankruptcy order is previously annulled or the sequestration of his estate is recalled or reduced, on his obtaining a discharge; and

(b) if the bankruptcy order is annulled or the sequestration of his estate is recalled or reduced, on the date of that event.

(4) Where a person is disqualified under sub-paragraph (1)(b) by reason of his having made a composition or arrangement with, or granted a trust deed for, his creditors and he pays his debts in full, the disqualification shall cease on the date on which the payment is completed, and in any other case it shall cease at the end of the period of five years beginning with the date on which the terms of the deed of composition or arrangement or trust deed are fulfilled.

(5) For the purposes of sub-paragraph (1)(d), the date of a conviction shall be taken to be the ordinary date on which the period allowed for making an appeal or application expires or, if an appeal or application is made, the date on which the appeal or application is finally disposed of or abandoned or fails by reason of its non-prosecution.

12. Without prejudice to paragraphs 10 and 11, a member of a relevant council shall be disqualified for being appointed as or being a member of a police authority under paragraph 2 if he was elected for an electoral division or ward wholly within the metropolitan police district.

13.—(1) Without prejudice to paragraphs 10 and 11, a person shall be disqualified for being appointed as a member of a police authority under paragraph 5 if—

(a) he has not yet attained the age of twenty-one years, or

(b) neither his principal or only place of work, nor his principal or only place of residence, has been in the area of the authority during the whole of the period of twelve months ending with the day of appointment.

(2) Without prejudice to paragraphs 10 and 11, a person shall be disqualified for being a member so appointed if, at any time, neither his principal or only place of work, nor his principal or only place of residence, is within that area.

14.—(1) Without prejudice to paragraphs 10 and 11, a person shall be disqualified for being appointed as a member of a police authority under paragraph 5, and for being a member so appointed, if he is—

(a) a member of the council for a county, district, county borough or London borough which is wholly or partly within the area of the police authority;

(b) a magistrate eligible for appointment to the police authority under paragraph 8;

(c) a member of the selection panel for the police authority's area established under Schedule 3;

(d) a member of a police force;

(e) an officer or employee of a police authority; or

(f) an officer or employee of a relevant council.

(2) A person shall not be regarded for the purposes of sub-paragraph (1)(f) as an employee of a relevant council by reason of his holding—

(a) the post of head teacher or principal of a school, college or other educational institution or establishment which is maintained or assisted by a local education authority; or

(b) any other post as a teacher or lecturer in any such school, college, institution or establishment.

Tenure of office

15. Subject to the following paragraphs (and to the provisions of any order under section 4(2)) a person shall hold and vacate office as a member of a police authority in accordance with the terms of his appointment.

16.—(1) A person shall be appointed to hold office as a member for—

(a) a term of four years or a term expiring on his attaining the age of seventy years, whichever is the shorter, or

(b) such shorter term as the body appointing him may determine in any particular case.

(2) A person shall not, by virtue of sub-paragraph (1)(b), be appointed under paragraph 5 for a term shorter than four years without the approval of the Secretary of State.

17.—(1) A person may at any time resign his office as a member, or as chairman, by notice in writing to the police authority.

(2) Where a member appointed under paragraph 5 resigns his office as a member under sub-paragraph (1) of this paragraph, he shall send a copy of the notice to the Secretary of State.

18.—(1) A member of a relevant council appointed to be a member of a police authority under paragraph 2 shall cease to be a member of the authority if he ceases to be a member of the council (and does not on the same day again become a member of the council).

(2) A magistrate appointed to be a member of a police authority under paragraph 8 shall cease to be a member of the authority if he ceases to be a magistrate for an area all or part of which constitutes or forms part of the authority's area.

19.—(1) A police authority may remove a member from office by notice in writing if—

(a) he has been absent from meetings of the police authority for a period longer than three consecutive months without the consent of the authority,

(b) he has been convicted of a criminal offence (but is not disqualified for being a member under paragraph 11),

(c) the police authority is satisfied that the member is incapacitated by physical or mental illness, or

(d) the police authority is satisfied that the member is otherwise unable or unfit to discharge his functions as a member.

(2) Where a police authority removes a member under sub-paragraph (1), it shall give notice of that fact—

(a) in the case of a member appointed under paragraph 2 or 8, to the body which appointed him, and

(b) in the case of a member appointed under paragraph 5, to the Secretary of State.

20. A council or joint committee may remove from office a member of a police authority appointed by it under paragraph 2 with a view to appointing another in his place if it considers that to do so would further the object provided for by paragraph 4.

21. If a chairman of a police authority ceases to be a member, he shall also cease to be chairman.

Eligibility for re-appointment

22. A person who ceases to be a member, otherwise than by virtue of paragraph 19, or ceases to be chairman, may (if otherwise eligible) be re-appointed.

Validity of acts

23. The acts and proceedings of any person appointed to be a member or chairman of a police authority and acting in that office shall, notwithstanding his disqualification or want of qualification, be as valid and effectual as if he had been qualified.

24. The proceedings of a police authority shall not be invalidated by a vacancy in the membership of the authority or in the office of chairman or by any defect in the appointment of a person as a member or as chairman.

Allowances

25.—(1) A police authority may make to its chairman and other members such payments by way of reimbursement of expenses and allowances as the Secretary of State may, with the approval of the Treasury, determine.

(2) Payments made under sub-paragraph (1) may differ according to whether the recipient is a chairman or other member or was appointed under paragraph 2, 5 or 8.

Interpretation

26.—(1) For the purposes of this Schedule, a council is a "relevant council" in relation to a police authority if—

(a) it is the council for a county, district, county borough or London borough which constitutes, or is wholly within, the authority's police area, and

(b) in the case of a district council, the district is not in a county having a county council within paragraph (a).

(2) In determining for the purposes of sub-paragraph (1) whether a county or district is wholly within a police area, any part of the county or district which is within the metropolitan police district shall be disregarded.

27. In this Schedule "magistrate" has the same meaning as in the Justices of the Peace Act 1979.

Section 4 SCHEDULE 3

POLICE AUTHORITIES: SELECTION OF INDEPENDENT MEMBERS

Selection panels

1.—(1) There shall be a selection panel for each police area for the time being listed in Schedule 1.

(2) Each selection panel shall consist of three members, one of whom shall be appointed by each of the following—

(a) the designated members of the police authority for the area;

(b) the Secretary of State;

(c) the two members of the panel appointed by virtue of paragraphs (a) and (b).

(3) A designated member may be appointed as a member of a selection panel by virtue of paragraph (a) (but not paragraph (b) or (c)) of sub-paragraph (2).

(4) In this Schedule "designated member" means a member appointed under paragraph 2 or 8 of Schedule 2.

2. A person shall be disqualified for being appointed as or being a member of a selection panel if, by virtue of paragraph 10, 11, 13 or 14(1)(d) to (f) of Schedule 2, he is disqualified—

(a) for being appointed under paragraph 5 of that Schedule as a member of the police authority for the panel's area, or

(b) for being a member so appointed.

3.—(1) A person shall be appointed to hold office as a member of a selection panel for a term of two years, or for a term expiring on his attaining seventy years of age, whichever is the shorter.

(2) A person may at any time resign his office as a member by notice in writing to the persons who under paragraph 1 would be required to appoint his successor.

(3) A person shall not cease to be a member by reason only that any of the persons appointing him cease to hold the positions by virtue of which they appointed him.

4. A member of a selection panel may be removed from office by notice in writing by the persons who, under paragraph 1, would be required to appoint his successor ("the appointer") if—

(a) the member has been absent from two consecutive meetings of the selection panel without the consent of the panel,

(b) the member has been convicted of a criminal offence (but is not disqualified for being a member under paragraph 2),

(c) the appointer is satisfied that the member is incapacitated by physical or mental illness, or

(d) the appointer is satisfied that the member is otherwise unable or unfit to discharge his functions as a member.

5. A person who ceases to be a member of a selection panel, otherwise than by virtue of paragraph 4, may (if otherwise eligible) be re-appointed.

6.—(1) The acts and proceedings of any person appointed to be a member of a selection panel and acting in that office shall, notwithstanding his disqualification or want of qualification, be as valid and effectual as if he had been qualified.

(2) Subject to the provisions of any regulations made under paragraph 11, the proceedings of a selection panel shall not be invalidated by—

(a) a vacancy in the membership of the panel, or

(b) a defect in the appointment of a person as a member.

7.—(1) A police authority shall make to members of the selection panel for the authority's area such payments by way of reimbursement of expenses and allowances as it may determine.

(2) A police authority shall—

(a) provide the selection panel for the authority's area with such accommodation, and such secretarial and other assistance, as they may reasonably require, and

(b) meet any expenses incurred by the panel in the exercise of their functions.

Functions of selection panel

8.—(1) Where appointments to a police authority are to be made under paragraph 5 of Schedule 2, the selection panel for the authority's area shall nominate persons willing to be candidates for appointment.

(2) Unless the selection panel are able to identify only a smaller number, the number of persons to be nominated by a selection panel under this paragraph on any occasion shall be a number four times greater than the number of appointments to be made under paragraph 5 of Schedule 2.

(3) A selection panel shall notify the Secretary of State of—

(a) the name of each person nominated by it under this paragraph, and

(b) such other information regarding those persons as it considers appropriate.

9. A person shall not be nominated under paragraph 8 in relation to an authority if, by virtue of paragraph 10, 11, 13 or 14 of Schedule 2, he is disqualified for being appointed as a member of the authority under paragraph 5 of that Schedule.

10. In exercising their functions a selection panel shall have regard to the desirability of ensuring that, so far as reasonably practicable, the persons nominated by them under paragraph 8—

(a) represent the interests of a wide range of people within the community in the police area, and

(b) include persons with skills, knowledge or experience in such fields as may be specified for the purposes of this paragraph in regulations made under paragraph 11.

11.—(1) The Secretary of State may make regulations as to—

(a) the procedures to be followed in relation to the selection of persons for nomination under paragraph 8, and

(b) the conduct of the proceedings of selection panels.

(2) Without prejudice to the generality of sub-paragraph (1), regulations under this paragraph may—

(a) make provision (including provision imposing time limits) as to the procedures to be adopted when inviting applications or suggestions for nomination under paragraph 8, and for dealing with applications and suggestions received;

(b) make provision specifying the fields referred to in paragraph 10;

(c) prescribe matters, in addition to those mentioned in paragraph 10, to which a selection panel is to have regard in carrying out any of its functions;

(d) provide for decisions of a selection panel to be taken by a majority of the members.

(3) Regulations under this paragraph may make different provision for different cases and circumstances.

(4) A statutory instrument containing regulations under this paragraph shall be subject to annulment in pursuance of a resolution of either House of Parliament.

Secretary of State's short-list

12.—(1) Where the Secretary of State receives a notice under paragraph 8(3), he shall as soon as practicable prepare a short-list of candidates and send it to the police authority concerned.

(2) Subject to paragraph 13, the candidates on the short-list prepared by the Secretary of State shall be persons nominated by the selection panel, and their number shall be one half of the number of those persons.

(3) Where the number of persons nominated by the panel is an odd number, the number to be short-listed by the Secretary of State shall be one half of the number nominated reduced by one.

13.—(1) This paragraph has effect where the number of persons nominated by the selection panel is less than twice the number of vacancies to be filled by appointments under paragraph 5 of Schedule 2.

(2) The Secretary of State may himself nominate such number of candidates as, when added to the number nominated by the selection panel, equals twice the number of vacancies; and if he does so, paragraph 12 shall have effect as if the selection panel had nominated the Secretary of State's nominees as well as their own.

14. The Secretary of State shall give to the designated members any information regarding the persons on his short-list which they request and which he has received under paragraph 8.

Section 29   SCHEDULE 4

FORM OF DECLARATION

I,......... of......... do solemnly and sincerely declare and affirm that I will well and truly serve Our Sovereign Lady the Queen in the office of constable, without favour or affection, malice or ill will; and that I will to the best of my power cause the peace to be kept and preserved, and prevent all offences against the persons and properties of Her Majesty's subjects; and that while I continue to hold the said office I will to the best of my skill and knowledge discharge all the duties thereof faithfully according to law.

Section 66   SCHEDULE 5

THE POLICE COMPLAINTS AUTHORITY

Constitution of Authority

1.—(1) The Police Complaints Authority shall consist of a chairman and not less than eight other members.

(2) The chairman shall be appointed by Her Majesty.

(3) The other members shall be appointed by the Secretary of State.

(4) The members of the Authority shall not include any person who is or has been a constable in any part of the United Kingdom.

(5) Persons may be appointed as whole-time or part-time members of the Authority.

(6) The Secretary of State may appoint not more than two of the members of the Authority to be deputy chairmen.

Status of Authority

2. The Authority shall not be regarded as the servant or agent of the Crown or as enjoying any status, privilege or immunity of the Crown; and the Authority's property shall not be regarded as property of or property held on behalf of the Crown.

Members

3.—(1) Subject to the following provisions of this Schedule, a person shall hold an office to which he is appointed under paragraph 1(2), (3) or (6) in accordance with the terms of his appointment.

(2) A person shall not be appointed to such an office for more than three years at a time.

(3) A person may at any time resign such an office.

(4) The Secretary of State may at any time remove a person from such an office if satisfied that—

(a) he has without reasonable excuse failed to carry out his duties for a continuous period of three months beginning not earlier than six months before that time;

(b) he has been convicted of a criminal offence;

(c) he has become bankrupt or made an arrangement with his creditors;

(d) he is incapacitated by physical or mental illness;

(e) he has acted improperly in relation to his duties; or

(f) he is otherwise unable or unfit to perform his duties.

4. The Secretary of State may pay, or make such payments towards the provision of, such remuneration, pensions, allowances or gratuities to or in respect of persons appointed to office under paragraph 1(2), (3) or (6) or any of them as he may, with the consent of the Treasury, determine.

5. Where a person ceases to hold such an office otherwise than on the expiry of his term of office, and it appears to the Secretary of State that there are special circumstances which make it right for that person to receive compensation, the Secretary of State may, with the consent of the Treasury, direct the Authority to make to the person a payment of such amount as the Secretary of State may, with the consent of the Treasury, determine.

Staff

6. The Authority may, after consultation with the Secretary of State, appoint such officers and servants as appear to the Authority to be appropriate, subject to the approval of the Treasury as to numbers and as to remuneration and other terms and conditions of service.

7. Where a person who is employed by the Authority and is by reference to that employment a participant in a scheme under section 1 of the Superannuation Act 1972 is appointed to an office under paragraph 1(2), (3) or (6), the Treasury may determine that his service in that office shall be treated for the purposes of the scheme as service as an employee of the Authority; and his rights under the scheme shall not be affected by paragraph 4.

8. The Employers' Liability (Compulsory Insurance) Act 1969 shall not require insurance to be effected by the Authority.

Power of Authority to set up regional offices

9.—(1) If it appears to the Authority that it is necessary to do so in order to discharge their duties efficiently, the Authority may, with the consent of the Secretary of State and the Treasury, set up a regional office in any place in England and Wales.

(2) The Authority may delegate any of their functions to a regional office.

Proceedings

10.—(1) Subject to the provisions of Chapter I of Part IV and section 87, the arrangements for the proceedings of the Authority (including the quorum for meetings) shall be such as the Authority may determine.

(2) The arrangements may, with the approval of the Secretary of State, provide for the discharge, under the general direction of the Authority, of any of the Authority's functions by a committee or by one or more of the members, officers or servants of the Authority.

11. The validity of any proceedings of the Authority shall not be affected by—

(a) any defect in the appointment of the chairman or any other member, or

(b) any vacancy in the office of chairman or among the other members.

Finance

12. The Secretary of State—
(a) shall pay to the Authority expenses incurred or to be incurred by the Authority under paragraphs 5 and 6, and
(b) shall, with the consent of the Treasury, pay to the Authority such sums as appear to the Secretary of State to be appropriate for enabling the Authority to meet other expenses.

13.—(1) The Authority shall—
(a) keep proper accounts and proper records in relation to the accounts,
(b) prepare in respect of each financial year of the Authority a statement of accounts in such form as the Secretary of State may, with the approval of the Treasury, direct, and
(c) send copies of the statement to the Secretary of State and the Comptroller and Auditor General before the end of the month of August next following the financial year to which the statement relates.

(2) The Comptroller and Auditor General shall examine, certify and report on each statement received by him in pursuance of this paragraph and shall lay copies of each statement and of his report before Parliament.

(3) The financial year of the Authority shall be the twelve months ending on 31st March.

Section 85   SCHEDULE 6

APPEALS TO POLICE APPEALS TRIBUNALS

Police appeals tribunals

1.—(1) In the case of an appeal by a senior officer, the police appeals tribunal shall consist of three members appointed by the Secretary of State, of whom—
(a) one shall be a person chosen from a list of persons who have a seven year general qualification within the meaning of section 71 of the Courts and Legal Services Act 1990 and have been nominated by the Lord Chancellor for the purposes of this Schedule,
(b) one shall be a member of a police authority, other than the relevant police authority, and
(c) one shall be a person who—
(i) is (or has within the previous five years been) an Inspector of Constabulary, or
(ii) has within the previous five years been (and is no longer) the Commissioner of Police of the Metropolis.

(2) The member of the police appeals tribunal to whom sub-paragraph (1)(a) applies shall be the chairman.

2.—(1) In the case of an appeal by a member of a police force who is not a senior officer, the police appeals tribunal shall consist of four members appointed by the relevant police authority, of whom—
(a) one shall be a person chosen from the list referred to in paragraph 1(1)(a),
(b) one shall be a member of the authority or, where the authority is the Secretary of State, a person nominated by him,
(c) one shall be a person chosen from a list maintained by the Secretary of State of persons who are (or have within the last five years been) chief officers of police, other than a person who is (or has at any time been) the chief officer of police of the force maintained by the relevant police authority, and
(d) one shall be a retired officer of appropriate rank.

(2) The member of the police appeals tribunal to whom sub-paragraph (1)(a) applies shall be the chairman.

Notice of appeal

3. An appeal shall be instituted by giving notice of appeal within the time prescribed by rules made under section 85.

Respondent

4. On any appeal the respondent shall be such person as may be prescribed by rules made under section 85.

Casting vote

5. Where there is an equality of voting among the members of a police appeals tribunal, the chairman shall have a second or casting vote.

Hearing

6.—(1) A police appeals tribunal may determine a case without a hearing but shall not decide to do so unless both the appellant and the respondent have been afforded an opportunity to make written or, if either so requests, oral representations and any such representations have been considered.

(2) Where a hearing is held, the appellant shall have the right to appear by a serving member of a police force or by counsel or a solicitor; and the respondent shall have the right to appear by an officer of the police force or by the clerk or other officer of the police authority or by counsel or a solicitor.

Effect of orders

7.—(1) Where an appeal is allowed, the order shall take effect by way of substitution for the decision appealed against, and as from the date of that decision or, where that decision was itself a decision on appeal, the date of the original decision appealed against.

(2) Where the effect of the order made by the police appeals tribunal is to reinstate the appellant in the force or in his rank, he shall, for the purpose of reckoning service for pension and, to such extent (if any) as may be determined by the order, for the purpose of pay, be deemed to have served in the force or in his rank continuously from the date of the original decision to the date of his reinstatement.

(3) Where the effect of the order made by the police appeals tribunal is to reinstate the appellant in the force and he was suspended for a period immediately preceding the date of the original decision or any subsequent decision, the order shall deal with the suspension.

Remuneration and expenses

8. Members of a police appeals tribunal shall be—
(a) paid such remuneration, and
(b) reimbursed for such expenses,
as the Secretary of State may determine.

Costs

9.—(1) An appellant shall pay the whole of his own costs unless the police appeals tribunal directs that the whole or any part of his costs are to be defrayed out of the police fund of the relevant police authority.

(2) Subject to sub-paragraph (1), all the costs and expenses of an appeal under section 85, including the costs of the respondent and any remuneration or expenses paid by virtue of paragraph 8, shall be defrayed out of the police fund of the relevant police authority.

Interpretation

10. In this Schedule—
(a) "senior officer" means a member of a police force holding a rank above that of superintendent,
(b) "relevant police authority" means the police authority which maintains the police force of which the appellant is a member, and
(c) "retired officer of appropriate rank" means—
    (i) where the appellant was, immediately before the proceedings, of the rank of superintendent, a retired member of a police force who at the time of his retirement was of that rank, and
    (ii) in any other case a retired member of a police force who at the time of his retirement was of the rank of chief inspector or below.

Section 103 SCHEDULE 7

CONSEQUENTIAL AMENDMENTS

PART I

REFERENCES TO POLICE AUTHORITIES ESTABLISHED UNDER SECTION 3 OF POLICE ACT 1964

1.—(1) In the provisions referred to in sub-paragraph (2), for "section 3 of the Police Act 1964", in each place where it occurs, there shall be substituted "section 3 of the Police Act 1996".

(2) The provisions referred to in sub-paragraph (1) are—
(a) section 11(4)(a) of, and paragraph 9(d) of Part II of Schedule 1 to, the Trustee Investments Act 1961;

(b) sections 2(6) and 8(1) of the Local Government (Records) Act 1962;

(c) section 11(2) of the Local Government Act 1966;

(d) section 28(5)(a) of the Leasehold Reform Act 1967;

(e) section 1(3) of the Local Government Grants (Social Need) Act 1969;

(f) section 7(1AA) of the Post Office Act 1969;

(g) the definition of "public body" in section 1(4) of the Local Authorities (Goods and Services) Act 1970;

(h) sections 98(1A), 99, 100J(1)(e) and (4)(a), 146A(1) and (1A), 223(2), 228(7A), 229(8), 231(4), 232(1A), 233(11) and 234(4) of, and paragraphs 6A(1), 6B(b) and 46 of Schedule 12 to, the Local Government Act 1972;

(i) section 13(7)(f) of the Employment Agencies Act 1973;

(j) section 25(1)(ca) of the Local Government Act 1974;

(k) paragraph (a) of the definition of "local authority" in section 44(1) of the Local Government (Miscellaneous Provisions) Act 1976;

(l) section 71 of the Race Relations Act 1976;

(m) section 5(3)(baa) of the Rent (Agriculture) Act 1976;

(n) section 14(caa) of the Rent Act 1977;

(o) section 64(6) of the Justices of the Peace Act 1979;

(p) paragraphs (a)(i) and (aa) of the definition of "local authority" in section 20(1) of the Local Government, Planning and Land Act 1980 and section 99(4)(dc) of, and paragraph 5C of Schedule 16 to, that Act;

(q) paragraphs (a) and (b) of the definition of "local authority" in section 17(4) of the Acquisition of Land Act 1981;

(r) section 33(9)(a) of, and paragraph (ca) of the definition of "local authority" in section 41(13) of, the Local Government (Miscellaneous Provisions) Act 1982;

(s) sections 12(2)(g), 19(7), 20(10) and 28B(1) and (2)(a) of the Local Government Finance Act 1982;

(t) paragraph 7(1)(ba) of Schedule 1 to the Stock Transfer Act 1982;

(u) the definition of "local authority" in section 60(3) of the County Courts Act 1984;

(v) section 4(e) of the Housing Act 1985;

(w) the definition of "local authority" in section 106(1) of the Housing Associations Act 1985;

(x) the definition of "local authority" in section 38 of the Landlord and Tenant Act 1985;

(y) sections 6(2)(a) and 9(1)(a) of the Local Government Act 1986;

(z) section 58(1)(a) of the Landlord and Tenant Act 1987;

(za) section 1(1)(e) of, and Schedule 2 to, the Local Government Act 1988;

(zb) sections 111(2)(e) and 112(2)(a) of the Local Government Finance Act 1988;

(zc) paragraph 12(2)(g) of Schedule 1 to the Housing Act 1988;

(zd) sections 5(1), 21(1)(g), 39(1)(j), 67(3)(i), 101(3)(ea), 155(4)(ea) and 157(6)(g) of the Local Government and Housing Act 1989;

(ze) the definition of "local authority" in section 252(12) of the Town and Country Planning Act 1990;

(zf) sections 19(3)(c), 39(1)(b) and 54(3)(f) and (3A)(b) of the Local Government Finance Act 1992.

PART II

OTHER CONSEQUENTIAL AMENDMENTS

Pedlars Act 1871 (c. 96)

2. In section 5 of the Pedlars Act 1871, in paragraph 1 for "of the police district" there shall be substituted "for the police area".

3. In section 8 of that Act—

(a) for "police district" there shall be substituted "police area", and

(b) for "such district" there shall be substituted "the area".

4. In section 9 of that Act for "police district", in both places where it occurs, there shall be substituted "police area".

5. In section 21 of that Act for "district" there shall be substituted "police area".

6. In Schedule 2 to that Act for "police district" in each place where it occurs in Form A and Form B there shall be substituted "police area".

Parks Regulation Act 1872 (c. 15)

7. In section 7 of the Parks Regulation Act 1872 for "police district" there shall be substituted "police area".

8. In section 8 of that Act for "of the district" there shall be substituted "for the police area".

Riot (Damages) Act 1886 (c. 38)

9. In section 2(1) of the Riot (Damages) Act 1886—
(a) for "any police district" there shall be substituted "a police area", and
(b) for "such district" there shall be substituted "the area".
10. In section 3 of that Act—
(a) in subsection (1) for "district" there shall be substituted "police area", and
(b) in subsection (3) for "police district" there shall be substituted "police area".
11. In section 9 of that Act—
(a) for "police district" there shall be substituted "police area",
(b) for "the Police Act 1964" there shall be substituted "the Police Act 1996", and
(c) for "any other district" there shall be substituted "any other police area".

Local Government Act 1958 (c. 55)

12. In section 60(2) of the Local Government Act 1958 after "Part I of the Police Act 1964" there shall be inserted "or section 32 of the Police Act 1996".

Superannuation (Miscellaneous Provisions) Act 1967 (c. 28)

13.—(1) Section 13 of the Superannuation (Miscellaneous Provisions) Act 1967 shall be amended as follows.
(2) In subsection (1)—
(a) for "section 35 of the Police Act 1964" there shall be substituted "section 52 of the Police Act 1996", and
(b) in paragraph (a) for "section 17 of that Act" there shall be substituted "section 28 of that Act".
(3) In subsection (3) for "sections 35 and 17 of the Police Act 1964" there shall be substituted "sections 52 and 28 of the Police Act 1996".

Police (Scotland) Act 1967 (c. 77)

14.—(1) Section 26 of the Police (Scotland) Act 1967 shall be amended as follows.
(2) In subsection (2)(i) for "section 47 of the Police Act 1964" there shall be substituted "section 64 of the Police Act 1996".
(3) In subsection (9) for the words from "other than" to "1980" there shall be substituted "other than regulations with respect to any of the matters mentioned in section 61(1) of the Police Act 1996".
15. In section 39(4) of that Act, for "or section 141 of the Criminal Justice and Public Order Act 1994" there shall be substituted "or section 98 of the Police Act 1996".

Firearms Act 1968 (c. 27)

16. In Schedule 1 to the Firearms Act 1968, in paragraph 5 for "section 51(1) of the Police Act 1964" there shall be substituted "section 89(1) of the Police Act 1996".

Police Act (Northern Ireland) 1970 (c. 9 (N.I.))

17. In section 14(5) of the Police Act (Northern Ireland) 1970 for "section 141 of the Criminal Justice and Public Order Act 1994" there shall be substituted "section 98 of the Police Act 1996".

Pensions (Increase) Act 1971 (c. 56)

18.—(1) Schedule 2 to the Pensions (Increase) Act 1971 shall be amended as follows.
(2) In paragraph 15—
(a) in sub-paragraph (b) for "section 53C of the Police Act 1964" there shall be substituted "section 97 of the Police Act 1996",
(b) in sub-paragraph (ba) for "section 15A(2) of the Police Act 1964" there shall be substituted "section 26(2) of the Police Act 1996",
(c) in sub-paragraph (c) for "the Police Act 1964" there shall be substituted "the Police Act 1996", and
(d) for sub-paragraph (d) there shall be substituted—
"(d) was engaged—
(i) on relevant service within paragraph (b), (c) or (d) of section 97(1) of the Police Act 1996, or

(ii) on central service pursuant to section 38 of the Police (Scotland) Act 1967."

(3) In paragraph 43, for sub-paragraph (b) there shall be substituted—
"(b) section 51 or 52 of the Police Act 1996;".

(4) In paragraph 51(a) for "section 10 of the Police Act 1964" there shall be substituted "section 15 of the Police Act 1996".

Superannuation Act 1972 (c. 11)

19. In section 15(5)(b) of the Superannuation Act 1972 for "section 34 or 35 of the Police Act 1964" there shall be substituted "section 51 or 52 of the Police Act 1996".

20. Schedule 1 to that Act shall continue to have effect with the following entry (originally inserted by paragraph 7(1) of Schedule 4 to the Police and Criminal Evidence Act 1984) in the list of "Other Bodies"—
"Police Complaints Authority".

Local Government Act 1972 (c. 70)

21. In section 94(5)(b) of the Local Government Act 1972 for "or paragraph 26 of Schedule 1B to the Police Act 1964" there shall be substituted "or paragraph 25 of Schedule 2 to the Police Act 1996".

Overseas Pensions Act 1973 (c. 21)

22. In section 2(2)(d)(i) of the Overseas Pensions Act 1973 for the words from "section 53C(1)(a), (c) or (e)" to "1980)" there shall be substituted "section 97(1)(a), (e) or (g) of the Police Act 1996 (service under section 26 of the Police Act 1996, under section 1(1) of the Police (Overseas Service) Act 1945 or pursuant to an appointment under section 10 of the Overseas Development and Co-operation Act 1980)".

Juries Act 1974 (c. 23)

23. In Schedule 1 to the Juries Act 1974, in Part I, in Group B—
(a) for the words from "(including" to "1964)" there shall be substituted "(including a person on relevant service within paragraph (b), (c) or (d) of section 97(1) of the Police Act 1996)",
(b) for "the Police Act 1964", in the second place where it occurs, there shall be substituted "the Police Act 1996", and
(c) for "section 10 of the Police Act 1964" there shall be substituted "section 15 of the Police Act 1996".

House of Commons Disqualification Act 1975 (c. 24)

24. In section 1(3) of the House of Commons Disqualification Act 1975, in the definition of "police authority", for "the Police Act 1964" there shall be substituted "the Police Act 1996".

Northern Ireland Assembly Disqualification Act 1975 (c. 25)

25. In section 1(2) of the Northern Ireland Assembly Disqualification Act 1975, in the definition of "police authority", for "the Police Act 1964" there shall be substituted "the Police Act 1996".

Salmon and Freshwater Fisheries Act 1975 (c. 51)

26. In Schedule 3 to the Salmon and Freshwater Fisheries Act 1975, in Part III, in paragraph 39(1)(c) for "section 15 of the Police Act 1964" there shall be substituted "section 25 of the Police Act 1996".

Sex Discrimination Act 1975 (c. 65)

27.—(1) Section 17 of the Sex Discrimination Act 1975 shall be amended as follows.

(2) In subsection (2) for "section 33, 34 or 35 of the Police Act 1964" there shall be substituted "section 50, 51 or 52 of the Police Act 1996".

(3) In subsection (7) for "the Police Act 1964", in each place where it occurs, there shall be substituted "the Police Act 1996".

(4) In subsection (8)—
(a) for "the Police Act 1964" there shall be substituted "the Police Act 1996", and
(b) for "sections 33, 34 and 35" there shall be substituted "sections 50, 51 and 52".

Police Pensions Act 1976 (c. 35)

28. Section 1(1) of the Police Pensions Act 1976 shall continue to have effect with a reference to the Police Negotiating Board for the United Kingdom substituted for the reference to the Police Council for the United Kingdom (the substitution originally made by section 2(3) of the Police Negotiating Board Act 1980).

29.—(1) Section 7(2) of that Act shall be amended as follows.

(2) In paragraph (ba) for "section 15A(2) of the Police Act 1964" there shall be substituted "section 26(2) of the Police Act 1996".

(3) In paragraph (bb) for "section 53C of the Police Act 1964" there shall be substituted "section 97 of the Police Act 1996".

30.—(1) Section 11 of that Act (interpretation) shall be amended as follows.

(2) In subsection (1)—

(a) in paragraph (aa) for "section 15A(2) of the Police Act 1964" there shall be substituted "section 26(2) of the Police Act 1996",

(b) in paragraph (ab) for "section 53C of the Police Act 1964" there shall be substituted "section 97 of the Police Act 1996", and

(c) for paragraph (c) there shall be substituted—

"(c) central service in respect of which the provisions of section 97 of the Police Act 1996 or (as the case may be) section 38A of the Police (Scotland) Act 1967 have effect.".

(3) In subsection (2) for "the Police Act 1964" there shall be substituted "the Police Act 1996".

(4) In subsection (3) for "the Police Act 1964" there shall be substituted "the Police Act 1996".

(5) In subsection (5) for the definition of "central service" there shall be substituted—

" "central service"—

(a) means relevant service within paragraph (b), (c) or (d) of section 97(1) of the Police Act 1996, or

(b) has the meaning given in section 38(5) of the Police (Scotland) Act 1967,

(as the case may require)."

Race Relations Act 1976 (c. 80)

31. In section 16(5) of the Race Relations Act 1976, in the definition of "the Police Act", for "the Police Act 1964" there shall be substituted "the Police Act 1996".

Interpretation Act 1978 (c. 30)

32. In Schedule 1 to the Interpretation Act 1978 (words and expressions defined), in the definition of "police area" etc., for "section 62 of the Police Act 1964" there shall be substituted "section 101(1) of the Police Act 1996".

Finance Act 1981 (c. 35)

33. In section 107(3)(k) of the Finance Act 1981 for "section 62 of the Police Act 1964" there shall be substituted "section 101(1) of the Police Act 1996".

Police and Criminal Evidence Act 1984 (c. 60)

34. In section 5(1) of the Police and Criminal Evidence Act 1984 for paragraph (a) there shall be substituted—

"(a) under section 22 of the Police Act 1996; or".

35. In section 50(2) of that Act for paragraph (a) there shall be substituted—

"(a) under section 22 of the Police Act 1996; or".

36. In section 55(14) of that Act for paragraph (a) there shall be substituted—

"(a) under section 22 of the Police Act 1996; or".

37. In section 64(6B) of that Act—

(a) the definition of "chief officer of police" shall be omitted, and

(b) in the definition of "the responsible chief officer of police" after "whose" there shall be inserted "police".

38. In section 77(3) of that Act, in the definition of "police purposes", for "section 64 of the Police Act 1964" there shall be substituted "section 101(2) of the Police Act 1996".

Prosecution of Offences Act 1985 (c. 23)

39. In section 3(3) of the Prosecution of Offences Act 1985, in the definition of "police force", for "the Police Act 1964" there shall be substituted "the Police Act 1996".

Housing Act 1985 (c. 68)

40. In Schedule 1 to the Housing Act 1985, in paragraph 2(2), for "section 33 of the Police Act 1964" there shall be substituted "section 50 of the Police Act 1996".

Ministry of Defence Police Act 1987 (c. 4)

41. In section 1(2)(a) of the Ministry of Defence Police Act 1987 for "the Police Act 1964" there shall be substituted "the Police Act 1996".

Football Spectators Act 1989 (c. 37)

42. In section 14(7) of the Football Spectators Act 1989 for "section 41 of the Police Act 1964" there shall be substituted "section 57 of the Police Act 1996".

Aviation and Maritime Security Act 1990 (c. 31)

43. In section 22(4)(b)(i) of the Aviation and Maritime Security Act 1990 for "section 96(1) of the Police and Criminal Evidence Act 1984" there shall be substituted "section 78(1) of the Police Act 1996".

Local Government Act 1992 (c. 19)

44. In section 17(6) of the Local Government Act 1992 for "at the commencement of section 1 of the Police and Magistrates' Courts Act 1994" there shall be substituted "on 1st April 1995".

Tribunals and Inquiries Act 1992 (c. 53)

45. In section 7 of the Tribunals and Inquiries Act 1992, in subsection (2), after "36(a)," there shall be inserted "36A,".

46. In Schedule 1 to that Act, in Part I, after paragraph 36 there shall be inserted—

> "Police
> 36A. An appeals tribunal constitu-
> ted in accordance with Schedule
> 6 to the Police Act 1996 (c.00)."

Criminal Appeal Act 1995 (c. 35)

47. In section 22(2)(c) of the Criminal Appeal Act 1995 for "section 2 of the Police Act 1964" there shall be substituted "section 2 of the Police Act 1996".

Section 103   SCHEDULE 8

TRANSITIONAL PROVISIONS, SAVINGS ETC.

PART I

GENERAL PROVISIONS

Continuity of the law

1.—(1) The repeal (or revocation) and re-enactment of provisions in this Act does not affect the continuity of the law.

(2) Any subordinate legislation made or other thing done, or having effect as if done, under or for the purposes of any provision repealed and re-enacted by this Act shall, if in force or effective immediately before the commencement of the corresponding provision of this Act, have effect thereafter as if made or done under or for the purposes of that corresponding provision.

(3) Any reference (express or implied) in this Act or any other enactment or in any instrument or document—

(a) to any provision of this Act, or

(b) to things done or falling to be done under or for the purposes of any provision of this Act,

shall (so far as the context permits) be construed as including, in relation to times, circumstances or purposes in relation to which the corresponding provision repealed by this Act had effect, a reference—

(i) to that corresponding provision, or

(ii) to things done or falling to be done under or for the purposes of that corresponding provision, as the case may be.

(4) Any reference (express or implied) in any enactment or in any instrument or document—

(a) to any provision repealed and re-enacted by this Act, or

(b) to things done or falling to be done under or for the purposes of any such provision,

shall (so far as the context permits) be construed as including, in relation to times, circumstances or purposes in relation to which the corresponding provision of this Act has effect, a reference—

(i) to that corresponding provision, or

(ii) to things done or falling to be done under or for the purposes of that corresponding provision,

as the case may be.

(5) Without prejudice to the generality of sub-paragraph (4), where a power conferred by an Act is expressed to be exercisable in relation to enactments contained in Acts passed before or in the same Session as the Act conferring the power, the power is also exercisable in relation to provisions of this Act which reproduce such enactments.

(6) Sub-paragraphs (1) to (5) have effect instead of section 17(2) of the Interpretation Act 1978 (but are without prejudice to any other provision of that Act).

(7) This paragraph is to be read subject to the provisions of any order made under section 104 or under paragraph 11 below.

General saving for old transitional provisions and savings

2. The repeal by this Act of any provision of Part II of Schedule 4 to the Police and Criminal Evidence Act 1984, or any other transitional provision or saving relating to the coming into force of a provision reproduced in this Act, does not affect the operation of the transitional provision or saving in so far as it is not specifically reproduced in this Act but remains capable of having effect in relation to the corresponding provision of this Act or otherwise.

3. The repeal by this Act of an enactment previously repealed subject to savings does not affect the continued operation of those savings.

Use of existing forms, etc.

4. Any reference to an enactment repealed by this Act which is contained in a document made, served or issued on or after the commencement of that repeal shall be construed, except so far as a contrary intention appears, as a reference or, as the context may require, as including a reference to the corresponding provision of this Act.

PART II

PROVISIONS RELATING TO PARTICULAR ENACTMENTS

Pedlars Act 1871

5. Any reference to a police district contained in—

(a) an application for a pedlar's certificate under the Pedlars Act 1871 made before the commencement of paragraphs 2 to 6 of Schedule 7 to this Act, or

(b) a pedlar's certificate granted under that Act before that commencement,

shall on and after that commencement be read as if it were a reference to the equivalent police area.

Savings relating to the Police Act 1964

6. Notwithstanding the repeal by this Act of subsection (4) of section 58 of the Police Act 1964 (provision made by regulations for chief constables affected by amalgamations or reorganisations not to be less favourable than that under the Police Pensions Act 1976), that subsection shall continue to have effect in relation to any person who was the chief constable of a police force on 1st July 1964 and became a member of another police force by virtue of that section.

7. Notwithstanding the repeal by this Act of subsection (4) of section 64 of that Act (power to make consequential amendments to local Acts by order), any local enactment which immediately before the coming into force of that repeal had effect with modifications by virtue of an order made under that subsection shall continue to have effect with those modifications.

Saving for transitional provisions under the Police and Magistrates' Courts Act 1994

8. Without prejudice to the generality of paragraph 1(4) above, any transitional provision which—

(a) is contained in an order made under section 94(1) of the Police and Magistrates' Courts Act 1994, and

(b) relates to the coming into force of a provision of that Act reproduced in this Act,

shall, in so far as it remains capable of having effect, continue to operate in relation to the corresponding provision of this Act.

Police areas

9. For the period beginning with the commencement of Schedule 1 to this Act and ending on 31st March 1997, that Schedule shall have effect as if—

(a) for the entry in the second column opposite the name of the Bedfordshire police area there were substituted—

"The county of Bedfordshire".

(b) for the entry in that column opposite the name of the Derbyshire police area there were substituted—

"The county of Derbyshire",

(c) for the entry in that column opposite the name of the Dorset police area there were substituted—

"The county of Dorset",

(d) for the entry in that column opposite the name of the Durham police area there were substituted—

"The county of Durham",

(e) for the entry in that column opposite the name of the Hampshire police area there were substituted—

"The counties of Hampshire and Isle of Wight",

(f) for the entry in that column opposite the name of the Leicestershire police area there were substituted—

"The county of Leicestershire",

(g) for the entry in that column opposite the name of the Staffordshire police area there were substituted—

"The county of Staffordshire",

(h) for the entry in that column opposite the name of the Sussex police area there were substituted—

"The counties of East Sussex and West Sussex",

(i) for the entry in that column opposite the name of the Thames Valley police area there were substituted—

"The counties of Berkshire, Buckinghamshire and Oxfordshire",

(j) for the entry in that column opposite the name of the Wiltshire police area there were substituted—

"The county of Wiltshire".

10. Notwithstanding the repeal by this Act of sections 21A and 21C of the Police Act 1964 (power to amend Welsh police areas in relation to the Welsh local government reorganisation), any order made under section 21A of that Act shall continue to have effect.

Part III

Provisions relating to complaints and discipline

Modification of enactments pending commencement of new discipline procedures

11.—(1) Until such day as the Secretary of State may by order appoint, the provisions of this Act mentioned in sub-paragraphs (2) and (3) shall have effect subject to the modifications set out in those sub-paragraphs.

(2) Section 59 shall have effect as if—

(a) in subsection (2) for "proceedings brought under regulations made in accordance with section 50(3) above or section 26(2A) of the Police (Scotland) Act 1967" there were substituted "disciplinary proceedings", and

(b) in subsection (3) for "a police appeals tribunal" there were substituted "the Secretary of State".

(3) Section 91(1) shall have effect as if after "services" there were inserted "or to commit breaches of discipline".

(4) Subsections (3) to (5) of section 104 shall have effect in relation to an order under this paragraph as they have effect in relation to an order under that section.

Modification of section 81

12. Until such day as the Lord Chancellor may appoint under section 16(2) of the Civil Evidence Act 1995 (commencement orders) for the commencement of paragraph 9(3) of Schedule 1 to that Act, section 81 of this Act shall have effect as if for subsection (3) there were substituted—

"(3) In this section "document" has the same meaning as in Part I of the Civil Evidence Act 1968."

Saving for complaints procedures established for other bodies of constables

13. The coming into force of any provision of Part IV of this Act which re-enacts a provision of Part IX of the Police and Criminal Evidence Act 1984 (police complaints), as amended by the Police and Magistrates' Courts Act 1994, shall not affect any procedures established by virtue of section 96 of the 1984 Act (constabularies maintained by authorities other than police authorities) before that provision comes into force.

Section 103   SCHEDULE 9

REPEALS AND REVOCATIONS

PART I

REPEALS: GENERAL

Chapter	Short title	Extent of repeal
23 Geo. 5 c. 12.	Children and Young Persons Act 1933.	In section 107(1), in the definition of "Chief officer of police" the words "as regards England has the same meaning as in the Police Act 1964,".
1964 c. 48.	The Police Act 1964.	The whole Act (except sections 37 and 60 to 65, Schedule 5 and the provisions of Schedule 9 other than the entry relating to the Children and Young Persons Act 1933).
1967 c. 77.	The Police (Scotland) Act 1967.	In Schedule 4, the paragraphs under the heading "The Police Act 1964".
1971 c. 56.	Pensions (Increase) Act 1971.	In Schedule 2, in paragraph 51 the words "other than a local authority".
1972 c. 39.	The Police Act 1972.	The whole Act.
1972 c. 70.	The Local Government Act 1972.	Section 196.
1976 c. 35.	The Police Pensions Act 1976.	In Schedule 2, paragraph 5.
1977 c. 45.	The Criminal Law Act 1977.	In Schedule 1, paragraph 18. In Schedule 6, the entry headed "Police Act 1964".
1980 c. 10.	The Police Negotiating Board Act 1980.	The whole Act.
1982 c. 48.	The Criminal Justice Act 1982.	In Schedule 3, the entry headed "the Police Act 1964".
1984 c. 60.	The Police and Criminal Evidence Act 1984.	In section 64(6B), the definition of "chief officer of police" and the word "and" immediately after it. Sections 106, 109 and 112.
1988 c. 41.	The Local Government Finance Act 1988.	Sections 64(7)(e) and (f) and 144(4).
1989 c. 11.	The Police Officers (Central Service) Act 1989.	Sections 1 and 3. The Schedule.
1994 c. 29.	The Police and Magistrates' Courts Act 1994.	Sections 1 to 26, 28, 29, 32, 34 to 38, 45 and 95. Schedules 1 to 3.

Chapter	Short title	Extent of repeal
		In Schedule 4, paragraph 6.
		In Schedule 5, paragraphs 1 to 16, 21, 22, 24(b), 25 to 28, 31 to 34, 39(a) and 40(2).
		In Schedule 9, in Part I, the entries relating to sections 53(1), 60(1) and 60(2) of the Police Act 1964.
		In Schedule 9, in Part I, the entries relating to the Police and Criminal Evidence Act 1984 (except for the entries relating to section 108 of, and Schedules 4 and 6 to, that Act).
		In Schedule 9, in Part I, the entry relating to the Courts and Legal Services Act 1990.
1994 c. 33.	The Criminal Justice and Public Order Act 1994.	Section 141.
		Section 160(1).
		In Schedule 10, paragraphs 13, 14, 17 and 27.

PART II

REPEALS CONSEQUENTIAL ON NEW DISCIPLINE AND COMPLAINTS PROCEDURES

Chapter	Short title	Extent of repeal
1964 c. 48.	The Police Act 1964.	Section 37.
		Sections 60 to 62.
		Section 64 (except subsection (2)).
		Section 65(2) to (4).
		Schedule 5.
1984 c. 60.	The Police and Criminal Evidence Act 1984.	Section 67(8).
		Sections 83 to 105.
		Schedule 4.
1990 c. 41.	The Courts and Legal Services Act 1990.	In Schedule 10, paragraph 22.
1994 c. 29.	The Police and Magistrates' Courts Act 1994.	In Schedule 5, in paragraph 24 the opening words and sub-paragraph (a).
		In Schedule 5, paragraphs 29, 30 and 36.

PART III

REVOCATIONS

Number	Title	Extent of revocation
S.I. 1995/493	The Avon (Structural Change) Order 1995.	Article 13.
S.I. 1995/600	The Humberside (Structural Change) Order 1995.	Article 11.
S.I. 1995/610	The North Yorkshire (District of York) (Structural and Boundary Changes) Order 1995.	Article 12.
S.I. 1995/1747	The Cleveland (Further Provision) Order 1995.	Article 4.
S.I. 1995/1769	The Buckinghamshire (Borough of Milton Keynes) (Structural Change) Order 1995.	Article 5.

Number	Title	Extent of revocation
S.I. 1995/1770	The East Sussex (Boroughs of Brighton and Hove) (Structural Change) Order 1995.	Article 7.
S.I. 1995/1771	The Dorset (Boroughs of Poole and Bournemouth) (Structural Change) Order 1995.	Article 5.
S.I. 1995/1772	The Durham (Borough of Darlington) (Structural Change) Order 1995.	Article 5.
S.I. 1995/1773	The Derbyshire (City of Derby) (Structural Change) Order 1995.	Article 5.
S.I. 1995/1774	The Wiltshire (Borough of Thamesdown) (Structural Change) Order 1995.	Article 5.
S.I. 1995/1775	The Hampshire (Cities of Portsmouth and Southampton) (Structural Change) Order 1995.	Article 5.
S.I. 1995/1776	The Bedfordshire (Borough of Luton) (Structural Change) Order 1995.	Article 5.
S.I. 1995/1779	The Staffordshire (City of Stoke-on-Trent) (Structural and Boundary Changes) Order 1995.	Article 7.
S.I. 1996/507	The Leicestershire (City of Leicester and District of Rutland) (Structural Change) Order 1996.	Article 5.

TABLE OF DERIVATIONS

Notes:

1. This Table shows the derivation of the provisions of the Act.
2. The following abbreviations are used in the Table:

1964	= Police Act 1964 (c. 48)
1972	= Police Act 1972 (c. 39)
1980	= Police Negotiating Board Act 1980 (c. 10)
1984	= Police and Criminal Evidence Act 1984 (c. 60)
1989	= Police Officers (Central Service) Act 1989 (c. 11)
1994	= Police and Magistrates' Courts Act 1994 (c. 29)
1994 (c. 33)	= Criminal Justice and Public Order Act 1994 (c. 33)

Provision	Derivation
1(1)	1964 s.1(1); 1994 s.1(1) (part).
(2)	1964 s.1(2) (part); 1994 s.1(1) (part).
(3)	1964 s.1(3); 1994 s.1(1) (part).
2	1964 s.2; 1994 s.2 (part).
3	1964 s.3; 1994 s.2 (part).
4	1964 s.3A; 1994 s.3(1) (part).
5(1)	1964 s.3B(1); 1994 s.3(1) (part).
(2)	1964 s.3B(2) (part); 1994 s.3(1) (part).
(3)	1964 s.3B(3); 1994 s.3(1) (part).
6	1964 s.4; 1994 s.4 (part).
7	1964 s.4A; 1994 s.4 (part).
8	1964 s.4B; 1994 s.4 (part).

Provision	Derivation
9	1964 s.4C; 1994 s.4 (part).
10	1964 s.5; 1994 s.5 (part).
11	1964 s.5A; 1994 s.5 (part).
12(1)	1964 s.6(1) (part); 1994 s.6 (part).
(2) to (6)	1964 s.6(2) to (6); 1994 s.6 (part).
13(1)	1964 s.7(1); 1994 s.7.
(2)	1964 s.6(1) (part); 1994 s.6 (part).
(3)	1964 s.7(2).
14	1964 s.8; 1994 s.8.
15	1964 s.10; 1994 s.10.
16	1964 s.10A; 1994 s.11 (part).
17	1964 s.10B; 1994 s.11 (part).
18	1964 s.8A; 1994 s.9.
19	1994 s.28.
20	1964 s.11; 1994 s.12.
21	1994 s.45; drafting.
22(1)	1964 s.12(1); 1994 Sch. 5 para. 1(1), (2).
(2)	1964 s.12(1A); 1994 Sch. 5 para. 1(1), (3).
(3)	1964 s.12(2).
(4)	1964 s.12(2A); 1994 Sch. 5 para. 1(1), (5).
(5)	1964 s.12(3).
(6)	1964 s.12(3A); 1994 Sch. 5 para. 1(1), (6).
(7)	1964 s.12(4).
23(1)	1964 s.13(1); 1994 Sch. 5 para. 2(1), (2).
(2) to (6)	1964 s.13(2) to (6).
(7)	1964 s.13(7); 1994 Sch. 5 para. 2(1), (3).
24	1964 s.14.
25	1964 s.15.
26	1964 s.15A; 1994 s.13.
27(1)	1964 s.16(1).
(2)	1964 s.16(2) (part).
28(1)	1964 s.17(1).
(2)	1964 s.17(2) (part).
(3), (4)	1964 s.17(3), (4).
29	1964 s.18.
30(1)	1964 s.19(1); 1994 (c. 33) s.160(1) (part).
(2)	1964 s.19(2); 1994 (c. 33) s.160(1) (part).
(3)	1964 s.19(3); Local Government Act 1972 (c. 70) s.196(1), (5); 1994 Sch. 5 para. 4.
(4)	1964 s.19(4).
(5)	1964 s.19(5A); 1994 (c. 33) s.160(1) (part).
(6)	1964 s.19(6) (part); drafting.
31	1964 s.20.
32	1964 s.21; 1994 s.14 (part).
33	1964 s.21B; 1994 s.14 (part).
34(1)	1964 s.21C(1) (part); 1994 s.14 (part).
(2)	1964 s.21C(2) (part); 1994 s.14 (part).
(3), (4)	1964 s.21C(3), (4); 1994 s.14 (part).
(5)	1964 s.21C(5) (part); 1994 s.14 (part).
35	1964 s.26(1).
36	1964 s.28; 1994 Sch. 5 para. 6.
37	1964 s.28A; 1994 s.15 (part).
38	1964 s.28B; 1994 s.15 (part).
39	1964 s.28C; 1994 s.15 (part).
40	1964 s.28D; 1994 s.15 (part).
41	1994 s.29.
42(1)	1964 s.29(1); 1994 Sch. 5 para. 7(1), (2).
(2)	1964 s.29(2); 1994 Sch. 5 para. 7(1), (3).
(3)	1964 s.29(3).

Provision	Derivation
42(4)	1964 s.29(4).
43	1964 s.29A; 1994 s.16.
44(1)	1964 s.30(1).
(2), (3)	1964 s.30(1A), (1B); 1994 Sch. 5 para. 8(1), (2).
(4)	1964 s.30(2); 1994 Sch. 5 para. 8(1), (3).
(5)	1964 s.30(3).
45	1964 s.54.
46	1964 s.31; 1994 s.17 (part).
47	1964 s.31A; 1994 s.17 (part).
48	1964 s.31B; 1994 s.17 (part).
49(1), (2)	1964 s.32(1), (2).
(3)	1964 s.32(3); Interpretation Act 1978 (c. 30) s.17(2)(a) (converts reference to Local Government Act 1933 s.290(2), (3)).
(4), (5)	1964 s.32(4), (5).
50(1)	1964 s.33(1).
(2)	1964 s.33(2); 1994 s.18(1), (2).
(3)	1964 s.33(3); 1994 s.18(1), (3) (part).
(4)	1964 s.33(3A); 1994 s.18(1), (3) (part).
(5)	1964 s.33(4).
(6)	1964 s.33(4A); 1994 s.18(1), (4).
(7)	1964 s.33(5).
(8)	1964 s.33(6).
51	1964 s.34.
52	1964 s.35.
53	1964 s.36.
54(1)	1964 s.38(1).
(2)	1964 s.38(2); 1994 s.20(1), (2).
(3)	1964 s.38(3);1994 s.20(1), (3).
(4), (5)	1964 s.38(4), (5).
55	1964 s.38A; 1994 s.21.
56(1)	1964 s.39(1); 1994 s.22 (part).
(2)	1964 s.39(1A); 1994 s.22 (part).
(3)	1964 s.39(2).
57	1964 s.41; 1994 s.23.
58	1964 s.42; 1994 Sch. 5 para. 9.
59(1)	1964 s.44(1); 1984 s.109(a).
(2)	1964 s.44(1A); 1984 s.109(b) (part); 1994 Sch. 5 para. 11(1), (2).
(3)	1964 s.44(1B); 1984 s.109(b) (part); 1994 Sch. 5 para. 11(1), (3).
(4)	1964 s.44(2) (part).
(5)	1964 s.44(2) (part); 1972 s.1(1), (2).
(6)	1964 s.44(2A); 1972 s.1(1), (3) (part).
(7)	1964 s.44(6) (part).
60(1)	1964 s.44(3) (part); 1984 s.109(c).
(2)	1964 s.44(3) (part); Police (Scotland) Act 1967 (c. 77) Sch. 4 (part); Interpretation Act 1978 (c. 30) s.17(2)(a) (converts reference to Police Pensions Act 1948).
(3)	1964 s.44(4).
(4), (5)	1964 s.44(5).
(6)	1964 s.44(6) (part).
61(1)	1980 s.1(1); 1994 Sch. 5 para. 21(1), (2).
(2)	1980 s.1(2).
(3)	1980 s.1(3); 1994 Sch. 5 para. 21(1), (3).
(4)	1980 s.1(4) (part); Transfer of Functions (Minister for the Civil Service and Treasury) Order 1981 (S.I. 1981/1670).
62(1), (2)	1980 s.2(1), (2).
(3)	1980 s.2(3) (part).
63(1), (2)	1964 s.46(1), (2).
(3)	1964 s.46(3); 1980 s.2(4); 1984 s.100(2).
64(1), (2)	1964 s.47(1).

Provision	Derivation
64(3) to (5)	1964 s.47(2) to (4).
65	"the appropriate authority": 1984 s.84(4) ("the appropriate authority").
	"the Authority": 1984 s.83(1) (part).
	"complaint": 1984 s.84(4) ("complaint").
	"disciplinary proceedings": 1984 s.84(4) ("disciplinary proceedings"); 1994 Sch. 5 para. 24 (part).
	"investigating officer": drafting.
	"senior officer": 1984 s.84(4) ("senior officer"); 1994 Sch. 5 para. 24 (part).
	"serious injury": 1984 s.87(4) ("serious injury").
66(1)	1984 s.83(1) (part), Sch. 4 para. 2(1).
(2)	1984 s.83(2).
67(1) to (3)	1984 s.84(1) to (3).
(4), (5)	1984 s.84(5), (6).
68(1)	1984 s.86(1).
(2)	1984 s.86(2); 1994 Sch. 5 para. 26.
(3) to (6)	1984 s.86(3) to (6).
69(1), (2)	1984 s.85(1), (2).
(3)	1984 s.85(10); 1994 Sch. 5 para. 25(b).
(4)	1984 s.85(4).
(5)	1984 s.85(3).
(6) to (8)	1984 s.85(5) to (7).
(9)	1984 s.85(9).
70(1) to (3)	1984 s.87(1) to (3).
71(1)	1984 s.88 (part).
(2)	1984 s.88 (part); 1994 s.34.
72(1)	1984 s.89(1), (2).
(2), (3)	1984 s.89(3), (4).
(4), (5)	1984 s.89(5).
73(1) to (4)	1984 s.89(6) to (9).
(5)	1984 s.89(11).
(6)	1984 s.89(12); 1994 Sch. 5 para. 27.
(7), (8)	1984 s.89(13), (14).
(9)	1984 s.89(10).
74	1984 s.90(1).
75(1) to (3)	1984 s.90(2) to (4).
(4)	1984 s.90(5); 1994 s.35(1), (4).
(5)	1984 s.90(7); 1994 s.35(1), (6).
(6)	1984 s.90(9); 1994 s.35(1), (8).
(7)	1984 s.90(10) (part); 1994 s.35(1), (9).
76(1)	1984 s.93(1); 1994 s.36(1), (2).
(2)	1984 s.93(2) (part); 1994 s.36(1), (3).
(3)	1984 s.93(3); 1994 s.36(1), (4).
(4)	1984 s.93(4).
(5)	1984 s.93(5); 1994 s.36(1), (5).
(6)	1984 s.93(6); 1994 s.36(1), (6).
(7)	1984 s.93(7); 1994 s.36(1), (7).
77	1984 s.95; 1994 Sch. 5 para. 29.
78(1)	1984 s.96(1); 1994 Sch. 5 para. 30.
(2) to (4)	1984 s.96(2) to (4).
(5)	1984 s.96(5) (part).
(6), (7)	1984 s.96(6), (7).
79(1)	1984 s.97(1).
(2), (3)	1984 s.97(2).
(4)	1984 s.97(3).
(5), (6)	1984 s.97(5), (6).
80	1984 s.98.
81(1)	1984 s.99(1).
(2)	1984 s.99(2); 1994 Sch. 5 para. 31.
(3)	1984 s.118(1) ("document"); Civil Evidence Act 1995 (c. 38) Sch. 1 para. 9(3).

Provision	Derivation
82(1)	1984 s.100(1).
(2), (3)	1984 s.100(4), (5).
(4)	1984 s.100(6); 1994 Sch. 5 para. 32.
83(1)	1984 s.105(1) (part); 1994 Sch. 5 para. 34(1), (2).
(2)	1984 s.105(2) (part).
(3)	1984 s.105(3) (part); 1994 Sch. 5 para. 34(1), (3).
(4), (5)	1984 s.105(4) (part), (5) (part).
84	1984 s.102; 1994 Sch. 5 para. 33.
85	1964 s.37; 1994 s.19(1).
86(1), (2)	1984 s.104(3), (4).
(3)	1984 s.84(4); 1994 Sch. 5 para. 24.
87(1)	1984 s.105(1) (part); 1994 Sch. 5 para. 34(1), (2).
(2)	1984 s.105(2) to (5) (part); 1994 Sch. 5 para. 34(1), (3).
88(1) to (3)	1964 s.48(1) to (3).
(4)	1964 s.48(4) (part).
(5)	1964 s.48(4) (part); 1994 (c. 33) Sch. 10 para. 13.
89(1)	1964 s.51(1); Criminal Law Act 1977 (c. 45) ss.15(1), 30(1), (2), Sch. 1 para. 18; Criminal Justice Act 1982 (c. 48) ss.37(1), (2), 46(1).
(2)	1964 s.51(3); Criminal Law Act 1977 (c. 45) s.31, Sch. 6; Criminal Justice Act 1982 (c. 48) ss.37(1), (2), 46(1).
(3)	1964 s.51(4); 1994 (c. 33) Sch. 10 para. 14.
90(1)	1964 s.52(1); Criminal Justice Act 1982 (c. 48) ss.37(1), (2), 39(2), 46(1), Sch. 3.
(2)	1964 s.52(2); Criminal Justice Act 1982 (c. 48) ss.37(1), (2), 38(1), (6), (8), 46(1).
(3)	1964 s.52(3); Criminal Justice Act 1982 (c. 48) ss.37(1), (2), 38(1), (6), (8), 46(1).
(4)	1964 s.52(4).
91(1)	1964 s.53(1); Interpretation Act 1978 (c. 30) Sch. 1 ("statutory maximum"); Magistrates' Courts Act 1980 (c. 43) s.32(2); Criminal Justice Act 1988 (c. 33) Sch. 15 para. 58(b).
(2)	1964 s.53(2).
92	1964 s.53A; 1994 s.24.
93	1964 s.53B; 1994 s.25.
94	1994 s.32.
95	1964 s.56; 1994 Sch. 5 para. 13.
96(1) to (4)	1984 s.106(1) to (4).
(5)	1984 s.106(5) to (7).
(6) to (10)	1984 s.106(8) to (12).
97(1)(a)	1964 s.53C(1)(a); 1994 s.26 (part).
(b)	1964 ss.43(5) (part), 53C(1)(b) (part); 1994 s.26 (part), Sch. 5 para. 10(1), (3).
(c)	1964 ss.43(5) (part), 53C(1)(b) (part); 1994 s.26 (part).
(d)	1964 s.43(3C); 1989 s.1(1) (part).
(e)	1964 s.53C(1)(c) (part); 1994 s.26 (part).
(f)	1964 s.53C(1)(d) (part); 1994 s.26 (part).
(g)	1964 s.53C(1)(e) (part); 1994 s.26 (part).
(2)	1964 ss.43(5) (part), 53C(2); 1994 s.26 (part).
(3)	1964 ss.43(3A) (part), 53C(3); 1989 s.1(1) (part); 1994 s.26 (part), Sch. 5 para. 10(1), (2).
(4) to (7)	1964 s.53C(4) to (7); 1994 s.26 (part).
(8)	1964 s.43(3A) (part); 1989 s.1(1) (part).
(9)	1964 s.43(3B) (part); 1989 s.1(1) (part).
98(1) to (6)	1994 (c. 33) s.141(1) to (6).
(7), (8)	1994 (c. 33) s.141(7) (part).
(9)	1994 (c. 33) s.141(8).
99	1984 s.112.
100(1)	1964 s.58(1); 1994 Sch. 5 para. 14(1), (2).

Provision	Derivation
100(2)	1964 s.58(2); 1994 Sch. 5 para. 14(1), (3).
(3)	1964 s.58(3).
(4)	1964 s.58(3A); 1994 Sch. 5 para. 14(1), (4).
(5)	1964 s.58(5) (part).
(6)	1964 s.58(7).
101(1)	1964 s.62; 1994 Sch. 5 para. 15.
(2)	1964 s.64(1).
102	1964 s.60(1); 1984 ss.96(5) (part), 100(3); 1994 s.94(8) (part).
103	Drafting.
104(1), (2)	Drafting.
(3), (4)	1994 s.94(4), (5).
(5)	1994 s.94(8).
105	Drafting.
106	Drafting.
Sch. 1	1964 Sch. 1A; 1994 s.1(2), Sch. 1; Avon (Structural Change) Order 1995 (S.I. 1995/493) Art. 13; Humberside (Structural Change) Order 1995 (S.I. 1995/600) Art. 11; North Yorkshire (District of York) (Structural and Boundary Changes) Order 1995 (S.I. 1995/610) Art. 12; Cleveland (Further Provision) Order 1995 (S.I. 1995/1747) Art. 4; Buckinghamshire (Borough of Milton Keynes) (Structural Change) Order 1995 (S.I. 1995/1769) Art. 5; East Sussex (Boroughs of Brighton and Hove) (Structural Change) Order 1995 (S.I. 1995/1770) Art. 7; Dorset (Boroughs of Poole and Bournemouth) (Structural Change) Order 1995 (S.I. 1995/1771) Art. 5; Durham (Borough of Darlington) (Structural Change) Order 1995 (S.I. 1995/1772) Art. 5; Derbyshire (City of Derby) (Structural Change) Order 1995 (S.I. 1995/1773) Art. 5; Wiltshire (Borough of Thamesdown) (Structural Change) Order 1995 (S.I. 1995/1774) Art. 5; Hampshire (Cities of Portsmouth and Southampton) (Structural Change) Order 1995 (S.I. 1995/1775) Art. 5; Bedfordshire (Borough of Luton) (Structural Change) Order 1995 (S.I. 1995/1776) Art. 5; Staffordshire (City of Stoke-on-Trent) (Structural and Boundary Changes) Order 1995 (S.I. 1995/1779) Art. 7; Police Areas (Wales) Order 1995 (S.I. 1995/2864) Art. 2; Leicestershire (City of Leicester and District of Rutland) (Structural Change) Order 1996 (S.I. 1996/507) Art. 5.
Sch. 2	
paras. 1 to 26	1964 Sch. 1B paras. 1 to 6, 7 (part), 8 and 10 to 27; 1994 s.3(2), Sch. 2 (part).
para. 27	1964 s.27 ("magistrate"); Interpretation Act 1978 s.17(2)(a) (converts reference to Justices of the Peace Act 1949).
Sch. 3	1964 Sch. 1C; 1994 s.3(2), Sch. 2.
Sch. 4	1964 Sch. 2.
Sch. 5	
Para. 1	1984 Sch. 4 para. 1; 1994 Sch. 5 para. 36(1), (2).
Para. 2	1984 Sch. 4 para. 2(2).
Para. 3	1984 Sch. 4 para. 3; 1994 Sch. 5 para. 36(1), (3).
Paras. 4 to 6	1984 Sch. 4 paras. 4 to 6.
Para. 7	1984 Sch. 4 para. 7(2).
Paras. 8 to 13.	1984 Sch. 4 paras. 8 to 13.
Sch. 6	1964 Sch. 5; 1994 s.19(2), Sch. 3.
Sch. 7	
Paras. 1 to 13	Drafting.
Para. 14	Drafting; 1980 s.2(4).
Para. 15	Drafting; 1994 (c. 33) Sch. 10 para. 17.
Para. 16	Drafting.
Para. 17	Drafting; 1994 (c. 33) Sch. 10 para. 27.
Paras. 18, 19	Drafting.
Para. 20	1984 Sch. 4 para. 7(1).
Paras. 21 to 27	Drafting.
Para. 28	1980 s.2(3) (part).
Paras. 29 to 44	Drafting.

Provision	Derivation
Paras. 45, 46	1994 Sch. 5 paras. 39(a), 40(2).
Para. 47	Drafting.
Sch. 8	
Paras. 1 to 8	Drafting.
Para. 9	1964 Sch. 1A; 1994 s.1(2), Sch. 1; Buckinghamshire (Borough of Milton Keynes) (Structural Change) Order 1995 (S.I. 1995/1769) Arts. 1 and 5; East Sussex (Boroughs of Brighton and Hove) (Structural Change) Order 1995 (S.I. 1995/1770) Arts. 1 and 7; Dorset (Boroughs of Poole and Bournemouth) (Structural Change) Order 1995 (S.I. 1995/1771) Arts. 1 and 5; Durham (Borough of Darlington) (Structural Change) Order 1995 (S.I. 1995/1772) Arts. 1 and 5; Derbyshire (City of Derby) (Structural Change) Order 1995 (S.I. 1995/1773) Arts. 1 and 5; Wiltshire (Borough of Thamesdown) (Structural Change) Order 1995 (S.I. 1995/ 1774) Arts. 1 and 5; Hampshire (Cities of Portsmouth and Southampton) (Structural Change) Order 1995 (S.I. 1995/1775) Arts. 1 and 5; Bedfordshire (Borough of Luton) (Structural Change) Order 1995 (S.I. 1995/1776) Arts. 1 and 5; Staffordshire (City of Stoke-on-Trent) (Structural and Boundary Changes) Order 1995 (S.I. 1995/1779) Arts. 1 and 7; Leicestershire (City of Leicester and District of Rutland) (Structural Change) Order 1996 (S.I. 1996/507) Arts. 1 and 5.
Paras. 10 to 12	Drafting.
Para. 13	1994 s.38.
Sch. 9	Drafting; 1994 s.37.

TABLE OF DESTINATIONS

POLICE ACT 1964
(c. 48)

POLICE (SCOTLAND) ACT 1967
(c. 77)

TABLE OF DESTINATIONS

POLICE ACT 1972
(C. 39)

1972	1996
s.1(1), (2)	s.59(5)
(1), (3)	
(part)	59(6)

LOCAL GOVERNMENT ACT 1972
(C. 70)

1972	1996
s.196(1), (5) . . .	s.30(3)

CRIMINAL LAW ACT 1977
(C. 45)

1977	1996
s.15(1)	s.89(1)
30(1), (2)	89(1)
31	89(2)
Sched.1,	
para.18	89(1)
Sched.6	89(2)

INTERPRETATION ACT 1978
(C. 30)

1978	1996
s.17(2)(a)	
(converts	
reference to	
Local	
Government	
Act 1933	
s.290(2), (3))	s.49(3)
17(2)(a)	
(converts	
reference to	
Police	
Pensions Act	
1948)	60(2)
17(2)(a)	
(converts	
reference to	
Justices of	
the Peace	
Act 1949) . .	Sched.2,
	para.27
Sched.1	
("statutory	
maximum")	s.91(1)

POLICE NEGOTIATING BOARD ACT 1980
(C. 10)

1980	1996
s.1(1)	s.61(1)
(2)	61(2)
(3)	61(3)
(4) (part) . . .	61(4)
2(1), (2)	62(1), (2)
(3) (part) . . .	62(3),
	Sched.7,
	para.28
(4)	63(3),
	Sched.7,
	para.14

TABLE OF DESTINATIONS

MAGISTRATES' COURTS ACT 1980
(c. 43)

1980	1996
s.32(2)........	s.91(1)

CRIMINAL JUSTICE ACT 1982
(c. 48)

1982	1996
s.37(1), (2)....	ss.89(1), (2), 90(1), (2), (3)
38(1)........	s.90(2), (3)
(6)........	90(2), (3)
(8)........	90(2), (3)
39(2)........	90(1)
46(1)........	ss.89(1), (2), 90(1), (2), (3)
Sched.3.......	s.90(1)

POLICE AND CRIMINAL EVIDENCE ACT 1984
(c. 60)

1984	1996
s.83(1) (part)	ss.65, 66(1)
(2)........	s.66(2)
84(1)–(3)....	67(1)–(3)
(4)........	86(3)
(4) ("the appropriate authority")	65
(4) ("complaint")	65
(4) ("disciplinary proceedings")	65
(4) ("senior officer")....	65
(4) ("serious injury")	65
(5), (6)....	67(4), (5)
85(1), (2)....	69(1), (2)
(3)........	69(5)
(4)........	69(4)
(5)–(7)....	69(6)–(8)
(9)........	69(9)
(10)	69(3)
86(1)........	68(1)
(2)........	68(2)
(3)–(6)....	68(3)–(6)
87(1)–(3)....	70(1)–(3)
88 (part)	71(1), (2)
89(1), (2)....	72(1)
(3), (4)....	72(2), (3)
(5)........	72(4), (5)
(6)–(9)....	73(1)–(4)
(10)	73(9)
(11)	73(5)
(12)	73(6)
(13), (14)..	73(7), (8)

1984	1996
s.90(1)........	s.74
(2)–(4)....	75(1)–(3)
(5)........	75(4)
(7)........	75(5)
(9)........	75(6)
(10) (part)	75(7)
93(1)........	76(1)
(2) (part) .	76(2)
(3)........	76(3)
(4)........	76(4)
(5)........	76(5)
(6)........	76(6)
(7)........	76(7)
95	77
96(1)........	78(1)
(2)–(4)....	78(2)–(4)
(5) (part) .	ss.78(5), 102
(6), (7)....	s.78(6), (7)
97(1)........	79(1)
(2)........	79(2), (3)
(3)........	79(4)
(5), (6)....	79(5), (6)
98	80
99(1)........	81(1)
(2)........	81(2)
100(1)........	82(1)
(2)	63(3)
(3)	102
(4), (5)...	82(2), (3)
(6)	82(4)
102	84
104(3), (4)...	86(1), (2)
105(1) (part)	83(1), 87(1)
(2)–(5)	
(part)	87(2)

1984	1996
s.105(2) (part)	s.83(2)
(3) (part)	83(3)
(4) (part)	83(4)
(5) (part)	83(4)
106(1)–(4)...	96(1)–(4)
(5)–(7)...	96(5)
(8)–(12)..	96(6)–(10)
109(a)	59(1)
(b) (part)	59(2), (3)
(c)......	60(1)
112	99
118(1)	
("document")	81(3)
Sched.4, para.1	Sched.5, para.1
Sched.4, para.2(1) ...	s.66(1)
Sched.4, para.2(2) ...	Sched.5, para.2
Sched.4, para.3	Sched.5, para.3
Sched.4, paras.4–6...	Sched.5, paras.4–6
Sched.4, para.7(1) ...	Sched.7, para.20
Sched.4, para.7(2) ...	Sched.5, para.7
Sched.4, paras.8–13..	Sched.5, paras.8–13

16–93

TABLE OF DESTINATIONS

CRIMINAL JUSTICE ACT 1988
(c. 33)

POLICE OFFICERS (CENTRAL SERVICE) ACT 1989
(c. 11)

POLICE AND MAGISTRATES' COURTS ACT 1994
(c. 29)

TABLE OF DESTINATIONS

CRIMINAL JUSTICE AND PUBLIC ORDER ACT 1994
(c. 33)

1994	1996
s.141(1)–(6)...	s.98(1)–(6)
(7) (part)	98(7), (8)
(8)	98(8)
160(1) (part)	30(1), (2), (5)
Sched.10,	
para.13.....	88(5)
para.14.....	89(3)
para.17.....	Sched.7,
	para.15
para.27.....	Sched.7,
	para.17

CRIMINAL EVIDENCE ACT 1995
(c. 38)

1995	1996
Sched.1,	
para.9(3) ...	s.81(3)

TRANSFER OF FUNCTIONS (MINISTER FOR THE CIVIL SERVICE AND TREASURY) ORDER 1981 (S.I. 1981 No. 1670)

S.I. 1981 No.	
1670	1996
....	s.61(4)

AVON (STRUCTURAL CHANGE) ORDER 1995 (S.I. 1995 No. 493)

S.I. 1995 No.	
493	1996
art.13	Sched.1

HUMBERSIDE (STRUCTURAL CHANGE) ORDER 1995 (S.I. 1995 No. 600)

S.I. 1995 No.	
600	1996
art.11	Sched.1

NORTH YORKSHIRE (DISTRICT OF YORK) (STRUCTURAL AND BOUNDARY CHANGES) ORDER 1995 (S.I. 1995 No. 610)

S.I. 1995 No.	
610	1996
art.12	Sched.1

CLEVELAND (FURTHER PROVISION) ORDER 1995 (S.I. 1995 No. 1747)

S.I. 1995 No.	
1747	1996
art.4.........	Sched.1

TABLE OF DESTINATIONS

BUCKINGHAMSHIRE (BOROUGH OF MILTON KEYNES) (STRUCTURAL CHANGE) ORDER 1995 (S.I. 1995 No. 1769)

S.I. 1995 No. 1769	1996
art.1.........	Sched.8, para.9
art.5.........	Sched.1, Sched.8, para.9

EAST SUSSEX (BOROUGHS OF BRIGHTON AND HOVE) (STRUCTURAL CHANGE) ORDER 1995 (S.I. 1995 No. 1770)

S.I. 1995 No. 1770	1996
art.1.........	Sched.8, para.9
art.7.........	Sched.1, Sched.8, para.9

DORSET (BOROUGHS OF POOLE AND BOURNEMOUTH) (STRUCTURAL CHANGE) ORDER 1995 (S.I. 1995 No. 1771)

S.I. 1995 No. 1771	1996
art.1.........	Sched.8, para.9
art.5.........	Sched.1, Sched.8, para.9

DURHAM (BOROUGH OF DARLINGTON) (STRUCTURAL CHANGE) ORDER 1995 (S.I. 1995 No. 1772)

S.I. 1995 No. 1772	1996
art.1.........	Sched.8, para.9
art.5.........	Sched.1, Sched.8, para.9

DERBYSHIRE (CITY OF DERBY) (STRUCTURAL CHANGE) ORDER 1995 (S.I. 1995 No. 1773)

S.I. 1995 No. 1773	1996
art.1.........	Sched.8, para.9
art.5.........	Sched.1, Sched.8, para.9

WILTSHIRE (BOROUGH OF THAMESDOWN) (STRUCTURAL CHANGE) ORDER 1995 (S.I. 1995 No. 1774)

S.I. 1995 No. 1774	1996
art.1.........	Sched.8, para.9
art.5.........	Sched.1, Sched.8, para.9

TABLE OF DESTINATIONS

HAMPSHIRE (CITIES OF PORTSMOUTH AND SOUTHAMPTON) (STRUCTURAL CHANGE) ORDER 1995 (S.I. 1995 No. 1775)

S.I. 1995 No.
1775	**1996**
art.1..........	Sched.8,
	para.9
art.5..........	Sched.1,
	Sched.8,
	para.9

BEDFORDSHIRE (BOROUGH OF LUTON) (STRUCTURAL CHANGE) ORDER 1995 (S.I. 1995 No. 1776)

S.I. 1995 No.
1776	**1996**
art.1..........	Sched.8,
	para.9
art.5..........	Sched.1,
	Sched.8,
	para.9

STAFFORDSHIRE (CITY OF STOKE-ON-TRENT) (STRUCTURAL AND BOUNDARY CHANGES) ORDER 1995 (S.I. 1995 No. 1779)

S.I. 1995 No.
1779	**1996**
art.1..........	Sched.8,
	para.9
art.7..........	Sched.1,
	Sched.8,
	para.9

POLICE AREAS (WALES) ORDER 1995 (S.I. 1995 No. 2864)

S.I. 1995 No.
2864	**1996**
art.2..........	Sched.1

LEICESTERSHIRE (CITY OF LEICESTER AND DISTRICT OF RUTLAND) (STRUCTURAL CHANGE) ORDER 1996 (S.I. 1996 No. 507)

S.I. 1996 No.
507	**1996**
art.1..........	Sched.8,
	para.9
art.5..........	Sched.1,
	Sched.8,
	para.9

INDEX

INDUSTRIAL TRIBUNALS ACT 1996

(1996 c. 17)

[A table showing the derivation of the provisions of this consolidation Act will be found at the end of the Act. The Table has no official status.]

ARRANGEMENT OF SECTIONS

PART I

INDUSTRIAL TRIBUNALS

Introductory

PART II

THE EMPLOYMENT APPEAL TRIBUNAL

Introductory

An Act to consolidate enactments relating to industrial tribunals and the Employment Appeal Tribunal. [22nd May 1996]

PARLIAMENTARY DEBATES
   Hansard, H.L. Vol. 568, cols. 11, 468; Vol. 570, col. 9; Vol. 572, col. 557. H.C. Vol. 278, col. 200.

INTRODUCTION
   This Act revises the law relating to industrial tribunals and to the Employment Appeal Tribunal. Certain enactments are consolidated in the Act, while those listed in Schedule 3 are repealed or revoked. Amendments also cover the areas of jurisdiction, membership and procedure. The Act came into force on August 22, 1996 by virtue of s.46.

PART I

INDUSTRIAL TRIBUNALS

Introductory

Industrial tribunals

   1.—(1) The Secretary of State may by regulations make provision for the establishment of tribunals to be known as industrial tribunals.

(2) Regulations made wholly or partly under section 128(1) of the Employment Protection (Consolidation) Act 1978 and in force immediately before this Act comes into force shall, so far as made under that provision, continue to have effect (until revoked) as if made under subsection (1); and the tribunals established in pursuance of such regulations shall continue to be known as industrial tribunals.

Jurisdiction

Enactments conferring jurisdiction on industrial tribunals

2. Industrial tribunals shall exercise the jurisdiction conferred on them by or by virtue of this Act or any other Act, whether passed before or after this Act.

Power to confer further jurisdiction on industrial tribunals

3.—(1) The appropriate Minister may by order provide that proceedings in respect of—
  (a) any claim to which this section applies, or
  (b) any claim to which this section applies and which is of a description specified in the order,
may, subject to such exceptions (if any) as may be so specified, be brought before an industrial tribunal.

(2) Subject to subsection (3), this section applies to—
  (a) a claim for damages for breach of a contract of employment or other contract connected with employment,
  (b) a claim for a sum due under such a contract, and
  (c) a claim for the recovery of a sum in pursuance of any enactment relating to the terms or performance of such a contract,
if the claim is such that a court in England and Wales or Scotland would under the law for the time being in force have jurisdiction to hear and determine an action in respect of the claim.

(3) This section does not apply to a claim for damages, or for a sum due, in respect of personal injuries.

(4) Any jurisdiction conferred on an industrial tribunal by virtue of this section in respect of any claim is exercisable concurrently with any court in England and Wales or in Scotland which has jurisdiction to hear and determine an action in respect of the claim.

(5) In this section—
  "appropriate Minister", as respects a claim in respect of which an action could be heard and determined by a court in England and Wales, means the Lord Chancellor and, as respects a claim in respect of which an action could be heard and determined by a court in Scotland, means the Lord Advocate, and
  "personal injuries" includes any disease and any impairment of a person's physical or mental condition.

(6) In this section a reference to breach of a contract includes a reference to breach of—
  (a) a term implied in a contract by or under any enactment or otherwise,
  (b) a term of a contract as modified by or under any enactment or otherwise, and
  (c) a term which, although not contained in a contract, is incorporated in the contract by another term of the contract.

Membership etc.

Composition of a tribunal

4.—(1) Subject to the following provisions of this section, proceedings before an industrial tribunal shall be heard by—

    (a) the person who, in accordance with regulations made under section 1(1), is the chairman, and

    (b) two other members, or (with the consent of the parties) one other member, selected as the other members (or member) in accordance with regulations so made.

  (2) Subject to subsection (5), the proceedings specified in subsection (3) shall be heard by the person mentioned in subsection (1)(a) alone.

  (3) The proceedings referred to in subsection (2) are—

    (a) proceedings on an application under section 161, 165 or 166 of the Trade Union and Labour Relations (Consolidation) Act 1992,

    (b) proceedings on a complaint under section 126 of the Pension Schemes Act 1993,

    (c) proceedings on a complaint under section 23 or 188 of the Employment Rights Act 1996 or on an application under section 128, 131 or 132 of that Act,

    (d) proceedings in respect of which an industrial tribunal has jurisdiction by virtue of section 3 of this Act,

    (e) proceedings in which the parties have given their written consent to the proceedings being heard in accordance with subsection (2) (whether or not they have subsequently withdrawn it),

    (f) proceedings in which the person bringing the proceedings has given written notice withdrawing the case, and

    (g) proceedings in which the person (or, where more than one, each of the persons) against whom the proceedings are brought does not, or has ceased to, contest the case.

  (4) The Secretary of State may by order amend the provisions of subsection (3).

  (5) Proceedings specified in subsection (3) shall be heard in accordance with subsection (1) if a person who, in accordance with regulations made under section 1(1), may be the chairman of an industrial tribunal, having regard to—

    (a) whether there is a likelihood of a dispute arising on the facts which makes it desirable for the proceedings to be heard in accordance with subsection (1),

    (b) whether there is a likelihood of an issue of law arising which would make it desirable for the proceedings to be heard in accordance with subsection (2),

    (c) any views of any of the parties as to whether or not the proceedings ought to be heard in accordance with either of those subsections, and

    (d) whether there are other proceedings which might be heard concurrently but which are not proceedings specified in subsection (3).

decides at any stage of the proceedings that the proceedings are to be heard in accordance with subsection (1).

  (6) Where (in accordance with the following provisions of this Part) the Secretary of State makes industrial tribunal procedure regulations, the regulations may provide that, in such circumstances as the regulations may specify, any act required or authorised by the regulations to be done by an industrial tribunal may be done by the person mentioned in subsection (1)(a) alone.

  (7) Where a Minister of the Crown so directs in relation to any proceedings on grounds of national security—

    (a) the proceedings shall be heard and determined, and

    (b) any act required or authorised by industrial tribunal procedure regulations to be done by an industrial tribunal in relation to the proceedings shall be done,

by the President of the Industrial Tribunals (England and Wales) appointed in accordance with regulations made under section 1(1), or by the President of the Industrial Tribunals (Scotland) so appointed, alone.

Remuneration, fees and allowances

5.—(1) The Secretary of State may pay to—

(a) the President of the Industrial Tribunals (England and Wales),

(b) the President of the Industrial Tribunals (Scotland), and

(c) any person who is a member on a full-time basis of a panel of chairmen of tribunals which is appointed in accordance with regulations made under section 1(1).

such remuneration as he may with the consent of the Treasury determine.

(2) The Secretary of State may pay to—

(a) members of industrial tribunals,

(b) any assessors appointed for the purposes of proceedings before industrial tribunals, and

(c) any persons required for the purposes of section 2A(1)(b) of the Equal Pay Act 1970 to prepare reports,

such fees and allowances as he may with the consent of the Treasury determine.

(3) The Secretary of State may pay to any other persons such allowances as he may with the consent of the Treasury determine for the purposes of, or in connection with, their attendance at industrial tribunals.

Procedure

Conduct of hearings

6.—(1) A person may appear before an industrial tribunal in person or be represented by—

(a) counsel or a solicitor,

(b) a representative of a trade union or an employers' association, or

(c) any other person whom he desires to represent him.

(2) The Arbitration Act 1950 does not apply to any proceedings before an industrial tribunal.

Industrial tribunal procedure regulations

7.—(1) The Secretary of State may by regulations ("industrial tribunal procedure regulations") make such provision as appears to him to be necessary or expedient with respect to proceedings before industrial tribunals.

(2) Proceedings before industrial tribunals shall be instituted in accordance with industrial tribunal procedure regulations.

(3) Industrial tribunal procedure regulations may, in particular, include provision—

(a) for determining by which tribunal any proceedings are to be determined,

(b) for enabling an industrial tribunal to hear and determine proceedings brought by virtue of section 3 concurrently with proceedings brought before the tribunal otherwise than by virtue of that section,

(c) for treating the Secretary of State (either generally or in such circumstances as may be prescribed by the regulations) as a party to any proceedings before an industrial tribunal (where he would not otherwise be a party to them) and entitling him to appear and to be heard accordingly,

(d) for requiring persons to attend to give evidence and produce documents and for authorising the administration of oaths to witnesses,

(e) for enabling an industrial tribunal, on the application of any party to the proceedings before it or of its own motion, to order—

(i) in England and Wales, such discovery or inspection of documents, or the furnishing of such further particulars, as might be ordered by a county court on application by a party to proceedings before it, or

(ii) in Scotland, such recovery or inspection of documents as might be ordered by a sheriff,

(f) for prescribing the procedure to be followed in any proceedings before an industrial tribunal, including provision—

(i) as to the persons entitled to appear and to be heard on behalf of parties to such proceedings, and

(ii) for enabling an industrial tribunal to review its decisions, and revoke or vary its orders and awards, in such circumstances as may be determined in accordance with the regulations,

(g) for the appointment of one or more assessors for the purposes of any proceedings before an industrial tribunal, where the proceedings are brought under an enactment which provides for one or more assessors to be appointed,

(h) for authorising an industrial tribunal to require persons to furnish information and produce documents to a person required for the purposes of section 2A(1)(b) of the Equal Pay Act 1970 to prepare a report, and

(j) for the registration and proof of decisions, orders and awards of industrial tribunals.

(4) A person who without reasonable excuse fails to comply with—

(a) any requirement imposed by virtue of subsection (3)(d) or (h), or

(b) any requirement with respect to the discovery, recovery or inspection of documents imposed by virtue of subsection (3)(e),

is guilty of an offence and liable on summary conviction to a fine not exceeding level 3 on the standard scale.

(5) Subject to any regulations under section 11(1)(a), industrial tribunal procedure regulations may include provision authorising or requiring an industrial tribunal, in circumstances specified in the regulations, to send notice or a copy of—

(a) any document specified in the regulations which relates to any proceedings before the tribunal, or

(b) any decision, order or award of the tribunal,

to any government department or other person or body so specified.

(6) Where in accordance with industrial tribunal procedure regulations an industrial tribunal determines in the same proceedings—

(a) a complaint presented under section 111 of the Employment Rights Act 1996, and

(b) a question referred under section 163 of that Act,

subsection (2) of that section has no effect for the purposes of the proceedings in so far as they relate to the complaint under section 111.

Procedure in contract cases

8.—(1) Where in proceedings brought by virtue of section 3 an industrial tribunal finds that the whole or part of a sum claimed in the proceedings is due, the tribunal shall order the respondent to the proceedings to pay the amount which it finds due.

(2) An order under section 3 may provide that an industrial tribunal shall not in proceedings in respect of a claim, or a number of claims relating to the same contract, order the payment of an amount exceeding such sum as may be specified in the order as the maximum amount which an industrial tribunal may order to be paid in relation to a claim or in relation to a contract.

(3) An order under section 3 may include provisions—

(a) as to the manner in which and time within which proceedings are to be brought by virtue of that section, and

(b) modifying any other enactment.

(4) An order under that section may make different provision in relation to proceedings in respect of different descriptions of claims.

Pre-hearing reviews and preliminary matters

9.—(1) Industrial tribunal procedure regulations may include provision—

(a) for authorising the carrying-out by an industrial tribunal of a preliminary consideration of any proceedings before it (a "pre-hearing review"), and

(b) for enabling such powers to be exercised in connection with a pre-hearing review as may be prescribed by the regulations.

(2) Such regulations may in particular include provision—

(a) for authorising any tribunal carrying out a pre-hearing review under the regulations to make, in circumstances specified in the regulations, an order requiring a party to the proceedings in question, if he wishes to continue to participate in those proceedings, to pay a deposit of an amount not exceeding £150, and

(b) for prescribing—

(i) the manner in which the amount of any such deposit is to be determined in any particular case,

(ii) the consequences of non-payment of any such deposit, and

(iii) the circumstances in which any such deposit, or any part of it, may be refunded to the party who paid it or be paid over to another party to the proceedings.

(3) The Secretary of State may from time to time by order substitute for the sum specified in subsection (2)(a) such other sum as is specified in the order.

(4) Industrial tribunal procedure regulations may also include provision for authorising an industrial tribunal to hear and determine any issue relating to the entitlement of any party to proceedings to bring or contest the proceedings in advance of the hearing and determination of the proceedings by that or any other industrial tribunal.

National security etc.

10.—(1) A Minister of the Crown may on grounds of national security direct an industrial tribunal to sit in private when hearing or determining any proceedings specified in the direction.

(2) Industrial tribunal procedure regulations may enable an industrial tribunal to sit in private for the purpose of—

(a) hearing evidence which in the opinion of the tribunal relates to matters of such a nature that it would be against the interests of national security to allow the evidence to be given in public, or

(b) hearing evidence from any person which in the opinion of the tribunal is likely to consist of—

(i) information which he could not disclose without contravening a prohibition imposed by or by virtue of any enactment,

(ii) information which has been communicated to him in confidence or which he has otherwise obtained in consequence of the confidence reposed in him by another person, or

(iii) information the disclosure of which would, for reasons other than its effect on negotiations with respect to any of the matters mentioned in section 178(2) of the Trade Union and Labour Relations (Consolidation) Act 1992, cause substantial injury to any undertaking of his or in which he works.

(3) The reference in subsection (2)(b)(iii) to any undertaking of a person or in which he works shall be construed—

(a) in relation to a person in Crown employment, as a reference to the national interest,

(b) in relation to a person who is a relevant member of the House of Lords staff, as a reference to the national interest or (if the case so requires) the interests of the House of Lords, and

    (c) in relation to a person who is a relevant member of the House of Commons staff, as a reference to the national interest or (if the case so requires) the interests of the House of Commons.

    (4) If on a complaint under—

    (a) section 146 of the Trade Union and Labour Relations (Consolidation) Act 1992, or

    (b) section 111 of the Employment Rights Act 1996,

it is shown that the action complained of was taken for the purpose of safeguarding national security, the industrial tribunal shall dismiss the complaint.

    (5) Except where the complaint is that a dismissal is unfair by virtue of—

    (a) section 99(1) to (3), 100 or 103 of the Employment Rights Act 1996, or

    (b) subsection (1) of section 105 of that Act by reason of the application of subsection (2), (3) or (6) of that section,

a certificate purporting to be signed by or on behalf of a Minister of the Crown and certifying that the action specified in the certificate was taken for the purpose of safeguarding national security is for the purposes of subsection (4) of this section conclusive evidence of that fact.

    (6) The reference in subsection (5) to "dismissal" shall be construed—

    (a) in relation to a person in Crown employment, as a reference to the termination of Crown employment, and

    (b) in relation to a person who is a relevant member of the House of Commons staff, as a reference to the termination of his employment as such.

Restriction of publicity in cases involving sexual misconduct

    11.—(1) Industrial tribunal procedure regulations may include provision—

    (a) for cases involving allegations of the commission of sexual offences, for securing that the registration or other making available of documents or decisions shall be so effected as to prevent the identification of any person affected by or making the allegation, and

    (b) for cases involving allegations of sexual misconduct, enabling an industrial tribunal, on the application of any party to proceedings before it or of its own motion, to make a restricted reporting order having effect (if not revoked earlier) until the promulgation of the decision of the tribunal.

    (2) If any identifying matter is published or included in a relevant programme in contravention of a restricted reporting order—

    (a) in the case of publication in a newspaper or periodical, any proprietor, any editor and any publisher of the newspaper or periodical,

    (b) in the case of publication in any other form, the person publishing the matter, and

    (c) in the case of matter included in a relevant programme—

        (i) any body corporate engaged in providing the service in which the programme is included, and

        (ii) any person having functions in relation to the programme corresponding to those of an editor of a newspaper,

shall be guilty of an offence and liable on summary conviction to a fine not exceeding level 5 on the standard scale.

    (3) Where a person is charged with an offence under subsection (2) it is a defence to prove that at the time of the alleged offence he was not aware, and neither suspected nor had reason to suspect, that the publication or programme in question was of, or included, the matter in question.

    (4) Where an offence under subsection (2) committed by a body corporate is proved to have been committed with the consent or connivance of, or to be attributable to any neglect on the part of—

(a) a director, manager, secretary or other similar officer of the body corporate, or

(b) a person purporting to act in any such capacity,

he as well as the body corporate is guilty of the offence and liable to be proceeded against and punished accordingly.

(5) In relation to a body corporate whose affairs are managed by its members "director", in subsection (4), means a member of the body corporate.

(6) In this section—

"identifying matter", in relation to a person, means any matter likely to lead members of the public to identify him as a person affected by, or as the person making, the allegation,

"relevant programme" has the same meaning as in the Sexual Offences (Amendment) Act 1992,

"restricted reporting order" means an order—

(a) made in exercise of a power conferred by regulations made by virtue of this section, and

(b) prohibiting the publication in Great Britain of identifying matter in a written publication available to the public or its inclusion in a relevant programme for reception in Great Britain,

"sexual misconduct" means the commission of a sexual offence, sexual harassment or other adverse conduct (of whatever nature) related to sex, and conduct is related to sex whether the relationship with sex lies in the character of the conduct or in its having reference to the sex or sexual orientation of the person at whom the conduct is directed,

"sexual offence" means any offence to which section 4 of the Sexual Offences (Amendment) Act 1976, the Sexual Offences (Amendment) Act 1992 or section 274(2) of the Criminal Procedure (Scotland) Act 1995 applies (offences under the Sexual Offences Act 1956, Part I of the Criminal Law (Consolidation) (Scotland) Act 1995 and certain other enactments), and

"written publication" has the same meaning as in the Sexual Offences (Amendment) Act 1992.

Restriction of publicity in disability cases

12.—(1) This section applies to proceedings on a complaint under section 8 of the Disability Discrimination Act 1995 in which evidence of a personal nature is likely to be heard by the industrial tribunal hearing the complaint.

(2) Industrial tribunal procedure regulations may include provision in relation to proceedings to which this section applies for—

(a) enabling an industrial tribunal, on the application of the complainant or of its own motion, to make a restricted reporting order having effect (if not revoked earlier) until the promulgation of the decision of the tribunal, and

(b) where a restricted reporting order is made in relation to a complaint which is being dealt with by the tribunal together with any other proceedings, enabling the tribunal to direct that the order is to apply also in relation to those other proceedings or such part of them as the tribunal may direct.

(3) If any identifying matter is published or included in a relevant programme in contravention of a restricted reporting order—

(a) in the case of publication in a newspaper or periodical, any proprietor, any editor and any publisher of the newspaper or periodical,

(b) in the case of publication in any other form, the person publishing the matter, and

(c) in the case of matter included in a relevant programme—

(i) any body corporate engaged in providing the service in which the programme is included, and

(ii) any person having functions in relation to the programme corresponding to those of an editor of a newspaper,

shall be guilty of an offence and liable on summary conviction to a fine not exceeding level 5 on the standard scale.

(4) Where a person is charged with an offence under subsection (3), it is a defence to prove that at the time of the alleged offence he was not aware, and neither suspected nor had reason to suspect, that the publication or programme in question was of, or included, the matter in question.

(5) Where an offence under subsection (3) committed by a body corporate is proved to have been committed with the consent or connivance of, or to be attributable to any neglect on the part of—

(a) a director, manager, secretary of other similar officer of the body corporate, or

(b) a person purporting to act in any such capacity,

he as well as the body corporate is guilty of the offence and liable to be proceeded against and punished accordingly.

(6) In relation to a body corporate whose affairs are managed by its members "director", in subsection (5), means a member of the body corporate.

(7) In this section—

"evidence of a personal nature" means any evidence of a medical, or other intimate, nature which might reasonably be assumed to be likely to cause significant embarrassment to the complainant if reported,

"identifying matter" means any matter likely to lead members of the public to identify the complainant or such other persons (if any) as may be named in the order,

"promulgation" has such meaning as may be prescribed by regulations made by virtue of this section,

"relevant programme" means a programme included in a programme service, within the meaning of the Broadcasting Act 1990,

"restricted reporting order" means an order—

(a) made in exercise of a power conferred by regulations made by virtue of this section, and

(b) prohibiting the publication in Great Britain of identifying matter in a written publication available to the public or its inclusion in a relevant programme for reception in Great Britain, and

"written publication" includes a film, a sound track and any other record in permanent form but does not include an indictment or other document prepared for use in particular legal proceedings.

Costs and expenses

13.—(1) Industrial tribunal procedure regulations may include provision—

(a) for the award of costs or expenses, including any allowances payable under section 5(2)(c) or (3), and

(b) for taxing or otherwise settling any such costs or expenses (and, in particular in England and Wales, for enabling such costs to be taxed in a county court).

(2) In relation to proceedings under section 111 of the Employment Rights Act 1996—

(a) where the employee has expressed a wish to be reinstated or re-engaged which has been communicated to the employer at least seven days before the hearing of the complaint, or

(b) where the proceedings arise out of the employer's failure to permit the employee to return to work after an absence due to pregnancy or childbirth,

industrial tribunal procedure regulations shall include provision for requiring the employer to pay the costs or expenses of any postponement or adjournment of the hearing caused by his failure, without a special reason, to adduce reasonable evidence as to the availability of the job from which the complainant was dismissed, or which she held before her absence, or of comparable or suitable employment.

Interest

14.—(1) The Secretary of State may by order made with the approval of the Treasury provide that sums payable in pursuance of decisions of industrial tribunals shall carry interest at such rate and between such times as may be prescribed by the order.

(2) Any interest due by virtue of such an order shall be recoverable as a sum payable in pursuance of the decision.

(3) The power conferred by subsection (1) includes power—

(a) to specify cases or circumstances in which interest is not payable,

(b) to provide that interest is payable only on sums exceeding a specified amount or falling between specified amounts,

(c) to make provision for the manner in which and the periods by reference to which interest is to be calculated and paid,

(d) to provide that any enactment—

(i) does or does not apply in relation to interest payable by virtue of subsection (1), or

(ii) applies to it with such modifications as may be specified in the order,

(e) to make provision for cases where sums are payable in pursuance of decisions or awards made on appeal from industrial tribunals,

(f) to make such incidental or supplemental provision as the Secretary of State considers necessary.

(4) In particular, an order under subsection (1) may provide that the rate of interest shall be the rate specified in section 17 of the Judgments Act 1838 as that enactment has effect from time to time.

Enforcement

15.—(1) Any sum payable in pursuance of a decision of an industrial tribunal in England and Wales which has been registered in accordance with industrial tribunal procedure regulations shall, if a county court so orders, be recoverable by execution issued from the county court or otherwise as if it were payable under an order of that court.

(2) Any order for the payment of any sum made by an industrial tribunal in Scotland (or any copy of such an order certified by the Secretary of the Tribunals) may be enforced as if it were an extract registered decree arbitral bearing a warrant for execution issued by the sheriff court of any sheriffdom in Scotland.

(3) In this section a reference to a decision or order of an industrial tribunal—

(a) does not include a decision or order which on being reviewed, has been revoked by the tribunal, and

(b) in relation to a decision or order which on being reviewed, has been varied by the tribunal, shall be construed as a reference to the decision or order as so varied.

Recoupment of social security benefits

Power to provide for recoupment of benefits

16.—(1) This section applies to payments which are the subject of proceedings before industrial tribunals and which are—

(a) payments of wages or compensation for loss of wages,

(b) payments by employers to employees under sections 146 to 151, sections 168 to 173 or section 192 of the Trade Union and Labour Relations (Consolidation) Act 1992,

(c) payments by employers to employees under—
    (i) Part III, V, VI or VII,
    (ii) section 93, or
    (iii) Part X,
of the Employment Rights Act 1996, or

(d) payments by employers to employees of a nature similar to, or for a purpose corresponding to the purpose of, payments within paragraph (b) or (c),

and to payments of remuneration under a protective award under section 189 of the Trade Union and Labour Relations (Consolidation) Act 1992.

(2) The Secretary of State may by regulations make with respect to payments to which this section applies provision for any or all of the purposes specified in subsection (3).

(3) The purposes referred to in subsection (2) are—

(a) enabling the Secretary of State to recover from an employer, by way of total or partial recoupment of jobseeker's allowance or income support—
    (i) a sum not exceeding the amount of the prescribed element of the monetary award, or
    (ii) in the case of a protective award, the amount of the remuneration,

(b) requiring or authorising an industrial tribunal to order the payment of such a sum, by way of total or partial recoupment of either benefit, to the Secretary of State instead of to an employee, and

(c) requiring an industrial tribunal to order the payment to an employee of only the excess of the prescribed element of the monetary award over the amount of any jobseeker's allowance or income support shown to the tribunal to have been paid to the employee and enabling the Secretary of State to recover from the employer, by way of total or partial recoupment of the benefit, a sum not exceeding that amount.

(4) Regulations under this section may be framed—

(a) so as to apply to all payments to which this section applies or to one or more classes of those payments, and

(b) so as to apply to both jobseeker's allowance and income support, or to only jobseeker's allowance or income support.

(5) Regulations under this section may—

(a) confer powers and impose duties on industrial tribunals or adjudication officers or other persons,

(b) impose on an employer to whom a monetary award or protective award relates a duty—
    (i) to furnish particulars connected with the award, and
    (ii) to suspend payments in pursuance of the award during any period prescribed by the regulations,

(c) provide for an employer who pays a sum to the Secretary of State in pursuance of this section to be relieved from any liability to pay the sum to another person,

(d) confer on an employee a right of appeal to a social security appeal tribunal against any decision of an adjudication officer as to the total or partial recoupment of an income-based jobseeker's allowance or of income support in pursuance of the regulations, and

(e) provide for the proof in proceedings before industrial tribunals (whether by certificate or in any other manner) of any amount of jobseeker's allowance or income support paid to an employee.

(6) Regulations under this section may make different provision for different cases.

Recoupment: further provisions

17.—(1) Where in pursuance of any regulations under section 16 a sum has been recovered by or paid to the Secretary of State by way of total or partial recoupment of jobseeker's allowance or income support—

(a) no sum shall be recoverable under Part III or V of the Social Security Administration Act 1992, and

(b) no abatement, payment or reduction shall be made by reference to the jobseeker's allowance or income support recouped.

(2) Any amount found to have been duly recovered by or paid to the Secretary of State in pursuance of regulations under section 16 by way of total or partial recoupment of jobseeker's allowance shall be paid into the National Insurance Fund.

(3) In section 16—

"monetary award" means the amount which is awarded, or ordered to be paid, to the employee by the tribunal or would be so awarded or ordered apart from any provision of regulations under that section, and

"the prescribed element", in relation to any monetary award, means so much of that award as is attributable to such matters as may be prescribed by regulations under that section.

(4) In section 16 "income-based jobseeker's allowance" has the same meaning as in the Jobseekers Act 1995.

Conciliation

Conciliation

18.—(1) This section applies in the case of industrial tribunal proceedings and claims which could be the subject of industrial tribunal proceedings—

(a) under—

(i) section 2(1) of the Equal Pay Act 1970,

(ii) section 63 of the Sex Discrimination Act 1975, or

(iii) section 54 of the Race Relations Act 1976,

(b) arising out of a contravention, or alleged contravention, of section 64, 68, 137, 138, 146, 168, 169, 170, 174, 188 or 190 of the Trade Union and Labour Relations (Consolidation) Act 1992,

(c) under section 8 of the Disability Discrimination Act 1995,

(d) arising out of a contravention, or alleged contravention, of section 8, 13, 15, 18(1), 21(1), 28 or 92, or of Part V, VI, VII or X, of the Employment Rights Act 1996,

(e) which are proceedings in respect of which an industrial tribunal has jurisdiction by virtue of section 3 of this Act, or

(f) arising out of a contravention, or alleged contravention, of a provision specified by an order under subsection (8)(b) as a provision to which this paragraph applies.

(2) Where an application has been presented to an industrial tribunal, and a copy of it has been sent to a conciliation officer, it is the duty of the conciliation officer—

(a) if he is requested to do so by the person by whom and the person against whom the proceedings are brought, or

(b) if, in the absence of any such request, the conciliation officer considers that he could act under this subsection with a reasonable prospect of success,

to endeavour to promote a settlement of the proceedings without their being determined by an industrial tribunal.

(3) Where at any time—

(a) a person claims that action has been taken in respect of which proceedings could be brought by him before an industrial tribunal, but

(b) before any application relating to that action has been presented by him a request is made to a conciliation officer (whether by that person or by the person against whom the proceedings could be instituted) to make his services available to them,

the conciliation officer shall act in accordance with subsection (2) as if an application had been presented to an industrial tribunal.

(4) Where a person who has presented a complaint to an industrial tribunal under section 111 of the Employment Rights Act 1996 has ceased to be employed by the employer against whom the complaint was made, the conciliation officer shall (for the purpose of promoting a settlement of the complaint in accordance with subsection (2)) in particular—

(a) seek to promote the reinstatement or re-engagement of the complainant by the employer, or by a successor of the employer or by an associated employer, on terms appearing to the conciliation officer to be equitable, or

(b) where the complainant does not wish to be reinstated or re-engaged, or where reinstatement or re-engagement is not practicable, and the parties desire the conciliation officer to act, seek to promote agreement between them as to a sum by way of compensation to be paid by the employer to the complainant.

(5) Where at any time—

(a) a person claims that action has been taken in respect of which a complaint could be presented by him to an industrial tribunal under section 111 of the Employment Rights Act 1996, but

(b) before any complaint relating to that action has been presented by him a request is made to a conciliation officer (whether by that person or by the employer) to make his services available to them,

the conciliation officer shall act in accordance with subsection (4) as if a complaint had been presented to an industrial tribunal under section 111.

(6) In proceeding under this section a conciliation officer shall, where appropriate, have regard to the desirability of encouraging the use of other procedures available for the settlement of grievances.

(7) Anything communicated to a conciliation officer in connection with the performance of his functions under this section shall not be admissible in evidence in any proceedings before an industrial tribunal, except with the consent of the person who communicated it to that officer.

(8) The Secretary of State may by order—

(a) direct that further provisions of the Employment Rights Act 1996 be added to the list in subsection (1)(d), or

(b) specify a provision of any other Act as a provision to which subsection (1)(f) applies.

Conciliation procedure

19. Industrial tribunal procedure regulations shall include in relation to industrial tribunal proceedings in the case of which any enactment makes provision for conciliation—

(a) provisions requiring a copy of the application by which the proceedings are instituted, and a copy of any notice relating to it which is lodged by or on behalf of the person against whom the proceedings are brought, to be sent to a conciliation officer,

(b) provisions securing that the applicant and the person against whom the proceedings are brought are notified that the services of a conciliation officer are available to them, and

(c) provisions postponing the hearing of any such proceedings for such period as may be determined in accordance with the regulations for the purpose of giving an opportunity for the proceedings to be settled by way of conciliation and withdrawn.

PART II

THE EMPLOYMENT APPEAL TRIBUNAL

Introductory

The Appeal Tribunal

20.—(1) The Employment Appeal Tribunal ("the Appeal Tribunal") shall continue in existence.

(2) The Appeal Tribunal shall have a central office in London but may sit at any time and in any place in Great Britain.

(3) The Appeal Tribunal shall be a superior court of record and shall have an official seal which shall be judicially noticed.

Jurisdiction

Jurisdiction of Appeal Tribunal

21.—(1) An appeal lies to the Appeal Tribunal on any question of law arising from any decision of, or arising in any proceedings before, an industrial tribunal under or by virtue of—

(a) the Equal Pay Act 1970,

(b) the Sex Discrimination Act 1975,

(c) the Race Relations Act 1976,

(d) the Trade Union and Labour Relations (Consolidation) Act 1992,

(e) the Disability Discrimination Act 1995, or

(f) the Employment Rights Act 1996.

(2) No appeal shall lie except to the Appeal Tribunal from any decision of an industrial tribunal under or by virtue of the Acts listed in subsection (1).

(3) Subsection (1) does not affect any provision contained in, or made under, any Act which provides for an appeal to lie to the Appeal Tribunal (whether from an industrial tribunal, the Certification Officer or to any other person or body) otherwise than on a question to which that subsection applies.

Membership etc.

Membership of Appeal Tribunal

22.—(1) The Appeal Tribunal shall consist of—

(a) such number of judges as may be nominated from time to time by the

Lord Chancellor from the judges (other than the Lord Chancellor) of the High Court and the Court of Appeal,

(b) at least one judge of the Court of Session nominated from time to time by the Lord President of the Court of Session, and

(c) such number of other members as may be appointed from time to time by Her Majesty on the joint recommendation of the Lord Chancellor and the Secretary of State ("appointed members").

(2) The appointed members shall be persons who appear to the Lord Chancellor and the Secretary of State to have special knowledge or experience of industrial relations either—

(a) as representatives of employers, or

(b) as representatives of workers (within the meaning of the Trade Union and Labour Relations (Consolidation) Act 1992).

(3) The Lord Chancellor shall, after consultation with the Lord President of the Court of Session, appoint one of the judges nominated under subsection (1) to be the President of the Appeal Tribunal.

(4) No judge shall be nominated a member of the Appeal Tribunal except with his consent.

Temporary membership

23.—(1) At any time when—

(a) the office of President of the Appeal Tribunal is vacant, or

(b) the person holding that office is temporarily absent or otherwise unable to act as the President of the Appeal Tribunal,

the Lord Chancellor may nominate another judge nominated under section 22(1)(a) to act temporarily in his place.

(2) At any time when a judge of the Appeal Tribunal nominated under paragraph (a) or (b) of subsection (1) of section 22 is temporarily absent or otherwise unable to act as a member of the Appeal Tribunal—

(a) in the case of a judge nominated under paragraph (a) of that subsection, the Lord Chancellor may nominate another judge who is qualified to be nominated under that paragraph to act temporarily in his place, and

(b) in the case of a judge nominated under paragraph (b) of that subsection, the Lord President of the Court of Session may nominate another judge who is qualified to be nominated under that paragraph to act temporarily in his place.

(3) At any time when an appointed member of the Appeal Tribunal is temporarily absent or otherwise unable to act as a member of the Appeal Tribunal, the Lord Chancellor and the Secretary of State may jointly appoint a person appearing to them to have the qualifications for appointment as an appointed member to act temporarily in his place.

(4) A person nominated or appointed to act temporarily in place of the President or any other member of the Appeal Tribunal, when so acting, has all the functions of the person in whose place he acts.

(5) No judge shall be nominated to act temporarily as a member of the Appeal Tribunal except with his consent.

Temporary additional judicial membership

24.—(1) at any time when it appears to the Lord Chancellor that it is expedient to do so in order to facilitate in England and Wales the disposal of business in the Appeal Tribunal, he may appoint a qualified person to be a temporary additional judge of the Appeal Tribunal during such period or on such occasions as the Lord Chancellor thinks fit.

(2) In subsection (1) "qualified person" means a person who—

(a) is qualified for appointment as a judge of the High Court under section 10 of the Supreme Court Act 1981, or

(b) has held office as a judge of the High Court or the Court of Appeal.

(3) A person appointed to be temporary additional judge of the Appeal Tribunal has all the functions of a judge nominated under section 22(1)(a).

Tenure of appointed members

25.—(1) Subject to subsections (2) to (4), an appointed member shall hold and vacate office in accordance with the terms of his appointment.

(2) An appointed member—

(a) may at any time resign his membership by notice in writing addressed to the Lord Chancellor and the Secretary of State, and

(b) shall vacate his office on the day on which he attains the age of seventy.

(3) Subsection (2)(b) is subject to section 26(4) to (6) of the Judicial Pensions and Retirement Act 1993 (Lord Chancellor's power to authorise continuance of office up to the age of seventy-five).

(4) If the Lord Chancellor, after consultation with the Secretary of State, is satisfied that an appointed member—

(a) has been absent from sittings of the Appeal Tribunal for a period longer than six consecutive months without the permission of the President of the Appeal Tribunal,

(b) has become bankrupt or made an arrangement with his creditors, or has had his estate sequestrated or made a trust deed for behoof of his creditors or a composition contract,

(c) is incapacitated by physical or mental illness, or

(d) is otherwise unable or unfit to discharge the functions of a member,

the Lord Chancellor may declare his office as a member to be vacant and shall notify the declaration in such manner as the Lord Chancellor thinks fit; and when the Lord Chancellor does so, the office becomes vacant.

Staff

26. The Secretary of State may appoint such officers and servants of the Appeal Tribunal as he may determine, subject to the approval of the Minister for the Civil Service as to numbers and terms and conditions of service.

Remuneration, pensions and allowances

27.—(1) The Secretary of State shall pay—

(a) the appointed members,

(b) any person appointed to act temporarily in the place of an appointed member, and

(c) the officers and servants of the Appeal Tribunal,

such remuneration and such travelling and other allowances as he may, with the relevant approval, determine; and for this purpose the relevant approval is that of the Treasury in the case of persons within paragraph (a) or (b) and the Minister for the Civil Service in the case of persons within paragraph (c).

(2) A person appointed to be a temporary additional judge of the Appeal Tribunal shall be paid such remuneration and allowances as the Lord Chancellor may, with the approval of the Treasury, determine.

(3) If the Secretary of State determines, with the approval of the Treasury, that this subsection applies in the case of an appointed member, the Secretary of State shall—

(a) pay such pension, allowance or gratuity to or in respect of that person on his retirement or death, or

(b) make to the member such payments towards the provision of a pension, allowance or gratuity for his retirement or death,

as the Secretary of State may, with the approval of the Treasury, determine.

(4) Where—

(a) a person ceases to be an appointed member otherwise than on his retirement or death, and

(b) it appears to the Secretary of State that there are special circumstances which make it right for him to receive compensation,
the Secretary of State may make to him a payment of such amount as the Secretary of State may, with the approval of the Treasury, determine.

Composition of Appeal Tribunal

28.—(1) The Appeal Tribunal may sit, in accordance with directions given by the President of the Appeal Tribunal, either as a single tribunal or in two or more divisions concurrently.

(2) Subject to subsections (3) to (5), proceedings before the Appeal Tribunal shall be heard by a judge and either two or four appointed members, so that in either case there is an equal number—
  (a) of persons whose knowledge or experience of industrial relations is as representatives of employers, and
  (b) of persons whose knowledge or experience of industrial relations is as representatives of workers.

(3) With the consent of the parties, proceedings before the Appeal Tribunal may be heard by a judge and one appointed member or by a judge and three appointed members.

(4) Proceedings on an appeal on a question arising from any decision of, or arising in any proceedings before, an industrial tribunal consisting of the person mentioned in section 4(1)(a) alone shall be heard by a judge alone unless a judge directs that the proceedings shall be heard in accordance with subsections (2) and (3).

(5) Where a Minister of the Crown so directs in relation to any proceedings on grounds of national security, the proceedings shall be heard by the President of the Appeal Tribunal alone.

Procedure

Conduct of hearings

29.—(1) A person may appear before the Appeal Tribunal in person or be represented by—
  (a) counsel or a solicitor,
  (b) a representative of a trade union or an employers' association, or
  (c) any other person whom he desires to represent him.

(2) The Appeal Tribunal has in relation to—
  (a) the attendance and examination of witnesses,
  (b) the production and inspection of documents, and
  (c) all other matters incidental to its jurisdiction,
the same powers, rights, privileges and authority (in England and Wales) as the High Court and (in Scotland) as the Court of Session.

Appeal Tribunal procedure rules

30.—(1) The Lord Chancellor, after consultation with the Lord President of the Court of Session, shall make rules ("Appeal Tribunal procedure rules") with respect to proceedings before the Appeal Tribunal.

(2) Appeal Tribunal procedure rules may, in particular, include provision—
  (a) with respect to the manner in which, and the time within which, an appeal may be brought,

   (b) with respect to the manner in which any application to the Appeal Tribunal may be made,

   (c) for requiring persons to attend to give evidence and produce documents and for authorising the administration of oaths to witnesses,

   (d) for requiring or enabling the Appeal Tribunal to sit in private in circumstances in which an industrial tribunal is required or empowered to sit in private by virtue of section 10 of this Act,

   (e) for the registration and proof of any award made on an application to the Appeal Tribunal under section 67 or 176 of the Trade Union and Labour Relations (Consolidation) Act 1992 and

   (f) for interlocutory matters arising on any appeal or application to the Appeal Tribunal to be dealt with otherwise than in accordance with section 28(2) to (5) of this Act.

(3) Subject to Appeal Tribunal procedure rules, the Appeal Tribunal has power to regulate its own procedure.

Restriction of publicity in cases involving sexual misconduct

31.—(1) Appeal Tribunal procedure rules may, as respects proceedings to which this section applies, include provisions—

   (a) for cases involving allegations of the commission of sexual offences, for securing that the registration or other making available of documents or decisions shall be so effected as to prevent the identification of any person affected by or making the allegation, and

   (b) for cases involving allegations of sexual misconduct, enabling the Appeal Tribunal, on the application of any party to the proceedings before it or of its own motion, to make a restricted reporting order having effect (if not revoked earlier) until the promulgation of the decision of the Appeal Tribunal.

(2) This section applies to—

   (a) proceedings on an appeal against a decision of an industrial tribunal to make, or not to make, a restricted reporting order, and

   (b) proceedings on an appeal against any interlocutory decision of an industrial tribunal in proceedings in which the industrial tribunal has made a restricted reporting order which it has not revoked.

(3) If any identifying matter is published or included in a relevant programme in contravention of a restricted reporting order—

   (a) in the case of publication in a newspaper or periodical, any proprietor, any editor and any publisher of the newspaper or periodical,

   (b) in the case of publication in any other form, the person publishing the matter, and

   (c) in the case of matter included in a relevant programme—

        (i) any body corporate engaged in providing the service in which the programme is included, and

        (ii) any person having functions in relation to the programme corresponding to those of an editor of a newspaper,

shall be guilty of an offence and liable on summary conviction to a fine not exceeding level 5 on the standard scale.

(4) Where a person is charged with an offence under subsection (3) it is a defence to prove that at the time of the alleged offence he was not aware, and neither suspected nor had reason to suspect, that the publication or programme in question was of, or included, the matter in question.

(5) Where an offence under subsection (3) committed by a body corporate is proved to have been committed with the consent or connivance of, or to be attributable to any neglect on the part of—

   (a) a director, manager, secretary or other similar officer of the body corporate, or

   (b) a person purporting to act in any such capacity,

he as well as the body corporate is guilty of the offence and liable to be proceeded against and punished accordingly.

(6) In relation to a body corporate whose affairs are managed by its members "director", in subsection (5), means a member of the body corporate.

(7) "Restricted reporting order" means—

(a) in subsections (1) and (3), an order—

> (i) made in exercise of a power conferred by rules made by virtue of this section, and
>
> (ii) prohibiting the publication in Great Britain of identifying matter in a written publication available to the public or its inclusion in a relevant programme for reception in Great Britain, and

(b) in subsection (2), an order which is a restricted reporting order for the purposes of section 11.

(8) In this section—

"identifying matter", in relation to a person, means any matter likely to lead members of the public to identify him as a person affected by, or as the person making, the allegation,

"relevant programme" has the same meaning as in the Sexual Offences (Amendment) Act 1992,

"sexual misconduct" means the commission of a sexual offence, sexual harassment or other adverse conduct (of whatever nature) related to sex, and conduct is related to sex whether the relationship with sex lies in the character of the conduct or in its having reference to the sex or sexual orientation of the person at whom the conduct is directed,

"sexual offence" means any offence to which section 4 of the Sexual Offences (Amendment) Act 1976, the Sexual Offences (Amendment) Act 1992 or section 274(2) of the Criminal Procedure (Scotland) Act 1995 applies (offences under the Sexual Offences Act 1956, Part I of the Criminal Law (Consolidation) (Scotland) Act 1995 and certain other enactments) and

"written publication" has the same meaning as in the Sexual Offences (Amendment) Act 1992.

Restriction of publicity in disability cases

32.—(1) This section applies to proceedings—

(a) on an appeal against a decision of an industrial tribunal to make, or not to make, a restricted reporting order, or

(b) on an appeal against any interlocutory decision of an industrial tribunal in proceedings in which the industrial tribunal has made a restricted reporting order which it has not revoked.

(2) Appeal Tribunal procedure rules may, as respects proceedings to which this section applies, include provision for—

(a) enabling the Appeal Tribunal, on the application of the complainant or of its own motion, to make a restricted reporting order having effect (if not revoked earlier) until the promulgation of the decision of the Appeal Tribunal, and

(b) where a restricted reporting order is made in relation to an appeal which is being dealt with by the Appeal Tribunal together with any other proceedings, enabling the Appeal Tribunal to direct that the order is to apply also in relation to those other proceedings or such part of them as the Appeal Tribunal may direct.

(3) If any identifying matter is published or included in a relevant programme in contravention of a restricted reporting order—

(a) in the case of publication in a newspaper or periodical, any proprietor, any editor and any publisher of the newspaper or periodical,

(b) in the case of publication in any other form, the person publishing the matter, and

(c) in the case of matter included in a relevant programme—

　　(i) any body corporate engaged in providing the service in which the programme is included, and

　　(ii) any person having functions in relation to the programme corresponding to those of an editor of a newspaper,

shall be guilty of an offence and liable on summary conviction to a fine not exceeding level 5 on the standard scale.

(4) Where a person is charged with an offence under subsection (3), it is a defence to prove that at the time of the alleged offence he was not aware, and neither suspected nor had reason to suspect, that the publication or programme in question was of, or included, the matter in question.

(5) Where an offence under subsection (3) committed by a body corporate is proved to have been committed with the consent or connivance of, or to be attributable to any neglect on the part of—

(a) a director, manager, secretary or other similar officer of the body corporate, or

(b) a person purporting to act in any such capacity,

he as well as the body corporate is guilty of the offence and liable to be proceeded against and punished accordingly.

(6) In relation to a body corporate whose affairs are managed by its members "director", in subsection (5), means a member of the body corporate.

(7) "Restricted reporting order" means—

(a) in subsection (1), an order which is a restricted reporting order for the purposes of section 12, and

(b) in subsections (2) and (3), and order—

　　(i) made in exercise of a power conferred by rules made by virtue of this section, and

　　(ii) prohibiting the publication in Great Britain of identifying matter in a written publication available to the public or its inclusion in a relevant programme for reception in Great Britain.

(8) In this section—

"complainant" means the person who made the complaint to which the proceedings before the Appeal Tribunal relate,

"identifying matter" means any matter likely to lead members of the public to identify the complainant or such other persons (if any) as may be named in the order,

"promulgation" has such meaning as may be prescribed by rules made by virtue of this section,

"relevant programme" means a programme included in a programme service, within the meaning of the Broadcasting Act 1990, and

"written publication" includes a film, a sound track and any other record in permanent form but does not include an indictment or other document prepared for use in particular legal proceedings.

Restriction of vexatious proceedings

33.—(1) If, on an application made by the Attorney General or the Lord Advocate under this section, the Appeal Tribunal is satisfied that a person has habitually and persistently and without any reasonable ground—

(a) instituted vexatious proceedings, whether in an industrial tribunal or before the Appeal Tribunal, and whether against the same person or against different persons, or

(b) made vexatious applications in any proceedings, whether in an industrial tribunal or before the Appeal Tribunal, the Appeal Tribunal may, after hearing the person or giving him an opportunity of being heard, make a restriction of proceedings order.

(2) A "restriction of proceedings order" is an order that—

(a) no proceedings shall without the leave of the Appeal Tribunal be instituted in any industrial tribunal or before the Appeal Tribunal by the person against whom the order is made,

(b) any proceedings instituted by him in any industrial tribunal or before the Appeal Tribunal before the making of the order shall not be continued by him without the leave of the Appeal Tribunal, and

(c) no application (other than one for leave under this section) is to be made by him in any proceedings in any industrial tribunal or before the Appeal Tribunal without the leave of the Appeal Tribunal.

(3) A restriction of proceedings order may provide that it is to cease to have effect at the end of a specified period, but otherwise it remains in force indefinitely.

(4) Leave for the institution or continuance of, or for the making of an application in, any proceedings in an industrial tribunal or before the Appeal Tribunal by a person who is the subject of a restriction of proceedings order shall not be given unless the Appeal Tribunal is satisfied—

(a) that the proceedings or application are not an abuse of the process of the tribunal in question, and

(b) that there are reasonable grounds for the proceedings or application.

(5) A copy of a restriction of proceedings order shall be published in the London Gazette and the Edinburgh Gazette.

Costs and expenses

34.—(1) Appeal Tribunal procedure rules may include provision empowering the Appeal Tribunal to order a party to any proceedings before the Appeal Tribunal to pay to any other party to the proceedings the whole or part of the costs or expenses incurred by the other party in connection with the proceedings where in the opinion of the Appeal Tribunal—

(a) the proceedings were unnecessary, improper or vexatious, or

(b) there has been unreasonable delay or other unreasonable conduct in bringing or conducting the proceedings.

(2) Except as provided by subsection (1), Appeal Tribunal procedure rules shall not enable the Appeal Tribunal to order the payment of costs or expenses by any party to proceedings before the Appeal Tribunal.

Decisions and further appeals

Powers of Appeal Tribunal

35.—(1) For the purpose of disposing of an appeal, the Appeal Tribunal may—

(a) exercise any of the powers of the body or officer from whom the appeal was brought, or

(b) remit the case to that body or officer.

(2) Any decision or award of the Appeal Tribunal on an appeal has the same effect, and may be enforced in the same manner, as a decision or award of the body or officer from whom the appeal was brought.

Enforcement of decisions etc.

36.—(1) Any sum payable in England and Wales in pursuance of an award of the Appeal Tribunal—

(a) made under section 67 or 176 of the Trade Union and Labour Relations (Consolidation) Act 1992, and

(b) registered in accordance with Appeal Tribunal procedure rules,

is, if a county court so orders, recoverable by execution issued from the county court or otherwise as if it were payable under an order of that court.

(2) Any order by the Appeal Tribunal for the payment in Scotland of any sum in pursuance of such an award (or any copy of such an order certified by the Secretary of the Tribunals) may be enforced as if it were an extract registered decree arbitral bearing a warrant for execution issued by the sheriff court of any sheriffdom in Scotland.

(3) Any sum payable in pursuance of an award of the Appeal Tribunal under section 67 or 176 of the Trade Union and Labour Relations (Consolidation) Act 1992 shall be treated as if it were a sum payable in pursuance of a decision of an industrial tribunal for the purposes of section 14 of this Act.

(4) No person shall be punished for contempt of the Appeal Tribunal except by, or with the consent of, a judge.

(5) A magistrates' court shall not remit the whole or part of a fine imposed by the Appeal Tribunal unless it has the consent of a judge who is a member of the Appeal Tribunal.

Appeals from Appeals Tribunal

37.—(1) Subject to subsection (3), an appeal on any question of law lies from any decision or order of the Appeal Tribunal to the relevant appeal court with the leave of the Appeal Tribunal or of the relevant appeal court.

(2) In subsection (1) the "relevant appeal court" means—

(a) in the case of proceedings in England and Wales, the Court of Appeal, and

(b) in the case of proceedings in Scotland, the Court of Session.

(3) No appeal lies from a decision of the Appeal Tribunal refusing leave for the institution or continuance of, or for the making of an application in, proceedings by a person who is the subject of a restriction of proceedings order made under section 33.

(4) This section is without prejudice to section 13 of the Administration of Justice Act 1960 (appeal in case of contempt of court).

PART III

SUPPLEMENTARY

Crown employment and Parliamentary staff

Crown employment

38.—(1) This Act has effect in relation to Crown employment and persons in Crown employment as it has effect in relation to other employment and other employees.

(2) In this Act "Crown employment" means employment under or for the purposes of a government department or any officer or body exercising on behalf of the Crown functions conferred by a statutory provision.

(3) For the purposes of the application of this Act in relation to Crown employment in accordance with subsection (1)—

(a) references to an employee shall be construed as references to a person in Crown employment, and

(b) references to a contract of employment shall be construed as references to the terms of employment of a person in Crown employment.

(4) Subsection (1) applies to—

(a) service as a member of the naval, military or air forces of the Crown, and

(b) employment by an association established for the purposes of Part XI of the Reserve Forces Act 1996;

but Her Majesty may by Order in Council make any provision of this Act apply to service as a member of the naval, military or air forces of the Crown subject to such exceptions and modifications as may be specified in the Order in Council.

Parliamentary staff

39.—(1) This Act has effect in relation to employment as a relevant member of the House of Lords staff or a relevant member of the House of Commons staff as it has effect in relation to other employment.

(2) Nothing in any rule of law or the law or practice of Parliament prevents a relevant member of the House of Lords staff or a relevant member of the House of Commons staff from bringing before an industrial tribunal proceedings of any description which could be brought before such a tribunal by a person who is not a relevant member of the House of Lords staff or a relevant member of the House of Commons staff.

(3) For the purposes of the application of this Act in relation to a relevant member of the House of Commons staff—

(a) references to an employee shall be construed as references to a relevant member of the House of Commons staff, and

(b) references to a contract of employment shall be construed as including references to the terms of employment of a relevant member of the House of Commons staff.

(4) In this Act "relevant member of the House of Lords staff" means any person who is employed under a contract of employment with the Corporate Officer of the House of Lords.

(5) In this Act "relevant member of the House of Commons staff" has the same meaning as in section 195 of the Employment Rights Act 1996; and (subject to an Order in Council under subsection (12) of that section)—

(a) subsections (6) and (7) of that section have effect for determining who is the employer of a relevant member of the House of Commons staff for the purposes of this Act, and

(b) subsection (8) of that section applies in relation to proceedings brought by virtue of this section.

General

Power to amend Act

40.—(1) The Secretary of State may by order—

(a) provide that any provision of this Act to which this section applies and which is specified in the order shall not apply to persons, or to employments, of such classes as may be prescribed in the order, or

(b) provide that any provision of this Act to which this section applies shall apply to persons or employments of such classes as may be prescribed in the order subject to such exceptions and modifications as may be so prescribed.

(2) This section applies to sections 3, 8, 16 and 17 and to section 18 so far as deriving from section 133 of the Employment Protection (Consolidation) Act 1978.

Orders, regulations and rules

41.—(1) Any power conferred by this Act on a Minister of the Crown to make an order, and any power conferred by this Act to make regulations or rules, is exercisable by statutory instrument.

(2) No recommendation shall be made to Her Majesty to make an Order in Council under section 38(4), and no order shall be made under section 3, 4(4)

or 40, unless a draft of the Order in Council or order has been laid before Parliament and approved by a resolution of each House of Parliament.

(3) A statutory instrument containing—

(a) an order made by a Minister of the Crown under any other provision of this Act except Part II of Schedule 2, or

(b) regulations or rules made under this Act.

is subject to annulment in pursuance of a resolution of either House of Parliament.

(4) Any power conferred by this Act which is exercisable by statutory instrument includes power to make such incidental, supplementary or transitional provision as appears to the Minister exercising the power to be necessary or expedient.

Interpretation

42.—(1) In this Act—

"the Appeal Tribunal" means the Employment Appeal Tribunal,

"Appeal Tribunal procedure rules" shall be construed in accordance with section 30(1),

"appointed member" shall be construed in accordance with section 22(1)(c),

"conciliation officer" means an officer designated by the Advisory, Conciliation and Arbitration Service under section 211 of the Trade Union and Labour Relations (Consolidation) Act 1992,

"contract of employment" means a contract of service or apprenticeship, whether express or implied, and (if it is express) whether oral or in writing,

"employee" means an individual who has entered into or works under (or, where the employment has ceased, worked under) a contract of employment,

"employer", in relation to an employee, means the person by whom the employee is (or, where the employment has ceased, was) employed,

"employers' association" has the same meaning as in the Trade Union and Labour Relations (Consolidation) Act 1992,

"employment" means employment under a contract of employment and "employed" shall be construed accordingly,

"industrial tribunal procedure regulations" shall be construed in accordance with section 7(1),

"statutory provision" means a provision, whether of a general or a special nature, contained in, or in any document made or issued under, any Act, whether of a general or special nature,

"successor", in relation to the employer of an employee, means (subject to subsection (2)) a person who in consequence of a change occurring (whether by virtue of a sale or other disposition or by operation of law) in the ownership of the undertaking, or of the part of the undertaking, for the purposes of which the employee was employed, has become the owner of the undertaking or part, and

"trade union" has the meaning given by section 1 of the Trade Union and Labour Relations (Consolidation) Act 1992.

(2) The definition of "successor" in subsection (1) has effect (subject to the necessary modifications) in relation to a case where—

(a) the person by whom an undertaking or part of an undertaking is owned immediately before a change is one of the persons by whom (whether as partners, trustees or otherwise) it is owned immediately after the change, or

(b) the persons by whom an undertaking or part of an undertaking is owned immediately before a change (whether as partners, trustees or

otherwise) include the persons by whom, or include one or more of the persons by whom, it is owned immediately after the change,
as it has effect where the previous owner and the new owner are wholly different persons.

(3) For the purposes of this Act any two employers shall be treated as associated if—

(a) one is a company of which the other (directly or indirectly) has control, or

(b) both are companies of which a third person (directly or indirectly) has control;

and "associated employer" shall be construed accordingly.

Final provisions

Consequential amendments

43. Schedule 1 (consequential amendments) shall have effect.

Transitionals, savings and transitory provisions

44. Schedule 2 (transitional provisions, savings and transitory provisions) shall have effect.

Repeals and revocations

45. The enactments specified in Part I of Schedule 3 are repealed, and the instruments specified in Part II of that Schedule are revoked, to the extent specified in the third column of that Schedule.

Commencement

46. This Act shall come into force at the end of the period of three months beginning with the day on which it is passed.

Extent

47. This Act does not extend to Northern Ireland.

Short title

48. This Act may be cited as the Industrial Tribunals Act 1996.

SCHEDULES

Section 43   SCHEDULE 1

CONSEQUENTIAL AMENDMENTS

The Transport Act 1968 (c. 73)

1. Section 135(4)(b) of the Transport Act 1968 shall continue to have effect with the substitution (originally made by paragraph 6 of Schedule 16 to the Employment Protection (Consolidation) Act 1978) of "an industrial tribunal" for the words from "a tribunal" to the end.

The Transport Holding Company Act 1972 (c. 14)

2. Section 2 of the Transport Holding Company Act 1972 shall continue to have effect with the substitution (originally made by paragraph 13 of Schedule 16 to the Employment Protection (Consolidation) Act 1978) of "an industrial tribunal" for —

(a) in subsection (3)(c), the words from "a tribunal" to the end, and

(b) in subsection (7), "a tribunal established under section 12 of the Industrial Training Act 1964".

The Sex Discrimination Act 1975 (c. 65)

3. In section 75(5)(c) of the Sex Discrimination Act 1975, for "regulations made under paragraph 1 of Schedule 9 to the Employment Protection (Consolidation) Act 1978" substitute "industrial tribunal procedure regulations under Part I of the Industrial Tribunals Act 1996".

The Race Relations Act 1976 (c. 74)

4.—(1) The Race Relations Act 1976 is amended as follows.

(2) In section 56(6), for "paragraph 6A of Schedule 9 to the Employment Protection (Consolidation) Act 1978" substitute "section 14 of the Industrial Tribunals Act 1996".

(3) In section 66(7)(c), for "regulations made under paragraph 1 of Schedule 9 to the Employment Protection (Consolidation) Act 1978" substitute "industrial tribunal procedure regulations under Part I of the Industrial Tribunals Act 1996".

The Aircraft and Shipbuilding Industries Act 1977 (c. 3)

5. In the Aircraft and Shipbuilding Industries Act 1977—
(a) section 49(10), and
(b) section 50(3)(b),
shall continue to have effect with the substitution (originally made by paragraph 28 of Schedule 16 to the Employment Protection (Consolidation) Act 1978) of "an industrial tribunal or, as the case may require, a tribunal established under" for "a tribunal established under section 12 of the Industrial Training Act 1964 or, as the case may require".

The Judicial Pensions Act 1981 (c. 20)

6. In section 12(1) of the Judicial Pensions Act 1981, for "section 128 of the Employment Protection (Consolidation) Act 1978" substitute "section 1(1) of the Industrial Tribunals Act 1996".

The Social Security Administration Act 1992 (c. 5)

7. In section 58(4) of the Social Security Administration Act 1992, for "section 132 of the Employment Protection (Consolidation) Act 1978" substitute "section 16 of the Industrial Tribunals Act 1996".

The Trade Union and Labour Relations (Consolidation) Act 1992 (c. 52)

8. In section 288 of the Trade Union and Labour Relations (Consolidation) Act 1992—
(a) in subsection (2), for paragraphs (a) and (b) substitute "section 18 of the Industrial Tribunals Act 1996 (conciliation)", and
(b) in subsection (2A), for "section 290" substitute "subsection (1)(b) of that section".

The Tribunals and Inquiries Act 1992 (c. 53)

9.—(1) The Tribunals and Inquiries Act 1992 is amended as follows.

(2) In section 11(2), for "section 136(1) of the Employment Protection (Consolidation) Act 1978" substitute "section 21(1) of the Industrial Tribunals Act 1996".

(3) In Schedule 1—
(a) in Part I, in paragraph 16, and
(b) in Part II, in paragraph 51,
for "section 128 of the Employment Protection (Consolidation) Act 1978 (c. 44)" substitute "section 1(1) of the Industrial Tribunals Act 1996 (c. 17)".

The Judicial Pensions and Retirement Act 1993 (c. 8)

10.—(1) The Judicial Pensions and Retirement Act 1993 is amended as follows.

(2) In Schedule 1, in Part II, in the entry relating to the office of chairman of industrial tribunals, for "section 128 of the Employment Protection (Consolidation) Act 1978" substitute "section 1(1) of the Industrial Tribunals Act 1996".

(3) In Schedule 5—
(a) in the entry relating to the office of chairman of industrial tribunals, for "section 128 of the Employment Protection (Consolidation) Act 1978" substitute "section 1(1) of the Industrial Tribunals Act 1996", and
(b) in the entry relating to the office of member of the Employment Appeal Tribunal, for "section 135(2)(c) of the Employment Protection (Consolidation) Act 1978" substitute "section 22(1)(c) of the Industrial Tribunals Act 1996".

(4) In paragraph 5 of Schedule 7—
(a) in sub-paragraphs (2)(g) and (5)(vii), for "section 128 of the Employment Protection (Consolidation) Act 1978" substitute "section 1(1) of the Industrial Tribunals Act 1996", and
(b) in sub-paragraph (7), for "section 135(2)(c) of the Employment Protection (Consolidation) Act 1978" substitute "section 22(1)(c) of the Industrial Tribunals Act 1996".

The Pension Schemes Act 1993 (c. 48)

11. In section 181(1) of the Pension Schemes Act 1993, in the definition of "industrial tribunal" for "section 128 of the Employment Protection (Consolidation) Act 1978" substitute "section 1(1) of the Industrial Tribunals Act 1996".

The Disability Discrimination Act 1995 (c. 50)

12.—(1) The Disability Discrimination Act 1995 is amended as follows.

(2) In section 8(7), for "paragraph 6A of Schedule 9 to the Employment Protection (Consolidation) Act 1978" substitute "section 14 of the Industrial Tribunals Act 1996".

(3) In section 9(2)(a) for "paragraph 1 of Schedule 3" substitute "section 18 of the Industrial Tribunals Act 1996".

Section 44   SCHEDULE 2

TRANSITIONAL PROVISIONS, SAVINGS AND TRANSITORY PROVISIONS

PART I

TRANSITIONAL PROVISIONS AND SAVINGS

1. The substitution of this Act for the provisions repealed or revoked by this Act does not affect the continuity of the law.

2. Anything done, or having effect as done, (including the making of subordinate legislation) under or for the purposes of any provision repealed or revoked by this Act has effect as if done under or for the purposes of any corresponding provision of this Act.

3. Any reference (express or implied) in this Act or any other enactment, or in any instrument or document, to a provision of this Act is (so far as the context permits) to be read as (according to the context) being or including in relation to times, circumstances, and purposes before the commencement of this Act a reference to the corresponding provision repealed or revoked by this Act.

4.—(1) Any reference (express or implied) in any enactment, or in any instrument or document, to a provision repealed or revoked by this Act is (so far as the context permits) to be read as (according to the context) being or including in relation to times, circumstances and purposes after the commencement of this Act a reference to the corresponding provision of this Act.

(2) In particular, where a power conferred by an Act is expressed to be exercisable in relation to enactments contained in Acts passed before or in the same Session as the Act conferring the power, the power is also exercisable in relation to provisions of this Act which reproduce such enactments.

5. Paragraphs 1 to 4 have effect in place of section 17(2) of the Interpretation Act 1978 (but are without prejudice to any other provision of that Act).

6. The repeal by this Act of section 130 of, and Schedule 10 to, the Employment Protection (Consolidation) Act 1978 (jurisdiction of referees under specified provisions to be exercised by industrial tribunals) does not affect—

(a) the operation of those provisions in relation to any question which may arise after the commencement of this Act, or

(b) the continued operation of those provisions after the commencement of this Act in relation to any question which has arisen before that commencement.

PART II

TRANSITORY PROVISIONS

Disability discrimination

7.—(1) If section 62 of the Disability Discrimination Act 1995 has not come into force before the commencement of this Act, this Act shall have effect with the omission of section 12 until the relevant commencement date.

(2) The reference in sub-paragraph (1) to the relevant commencement date is a reference—

(a) if an order has been made before the commencement of this act appointing a day after that commencement as the day on which section 62 of the Disability Discrimination Act 1995 is to come into force, to the day so appointed, and

(b) otherwise, to such day as the Secretary of State may by order appoint.

(3) If paragraph 1 of Schedule 3 to the Disability Discrimination Act 1995 has not come into force before the commencement of this Act, this Act shall have effect with the omission of section 18(1)(c) until the relevant commencement date.

(4) The reference in sub-paragraph (3) to the relevant commencement date is a reference—

(a) if an order has been made before the commencement of this Act appointing a day after the commencement as the day on which paragraph 1 of Schedule 3 to the Disability Discrimination Act 1995 is to come into force, to the day so appointed, and

(b) otherwise, to such day as the Secretary of State may by order appoint.

(5) If paragraph 2 of Schedule 6 to the Disability Discrimination Act 1995 has not come into force before the commencement of this Act, this Act shall have effect with the omission of section 21(1)(e) until the relevant commencement date.

(6) The reference in sub-paragraph (5) to the relevant commencement date is a reference—

(a) if an order has been made before the commencement of this Act appointing a day after that commencement as the day on which paragraph 2 of Schedule 6 to the Disability Discrimination Act 1995 is to come into force, to the day so appointed, and

(b) otherwise, to such day as the Secretary of State may by order appoint.

(7) If section 63 of the Disability Discrimination Act 1995 has not come into force before the commencement of this Act, this Act shall have effect with the omission of section 32 until the relevant commencement date.

(8) The reference in sub-paragraph (7) to the relevant commencement date is a reference—

(a) if an order has been made before the commencement of this Act appointing a day after that commencement as the day on which section 63 of the Disability Discrimination Act 1995 is to come into force, to the day so appointed, and

(b) otherwise, to such day as the Secretary of State may by order appoint.

Jobseeker's allowance

8.—(1) If paragraph 2 of Schedule 2 to the Jobseekers Act 1995 has not come into force before the commencement of this Act, this Act shall have effect until the relevant commencement date as if a reference to unemployment benefit were substituted for—

(a) each of the references to jobseeker's allowance in subsections (3) and (4) of section 16,

(b) the second reference to jobseeker's allowance in subsection (5) of that section,

(c) the first reference to jobseeker's allowance in subsection (1) of section 17, and

(d) the reference to jobseeker's allowance in subsection (2) of that section.

(2) The reference in sub-paragraph (1) to the relevant commencement date is a reference—

(a) if an order has been made before the commencement of this Act appointing a day after that commencement as the day on which paragraph 2 of Schedule 2 to the Jobseekers Act 1995 is to come into force, to the day so appointed, and

(b) otherwise, to such day as the Secretary of State may by order appoint.

Armed forces

9.—(1) If section 31 of the Trade Union Reform and Employment Rights Act 1993 has not come into force before the commencement of this Act, section 38 shall have effect until the relevant commencement date as if for subsection (4) there were substituted—

"(4) Subsection (1)—

(a) does not apply to service as a member of the naval, military or air forces of the Crown, but

(b) does apply to employment by an association established for the purposes of Part XI of the Reserve Forces Act 1996."

(2) The reference in sub-paragraph (1) to the relevant commencement date is a reference—

(a) if an order has been made before the commencement of this Act appointing a day after that commencement as the day on which section 31 of the Trade Union Reform and Employment Rights Act 1993 is to come into force, to the day so appointed, and

(b) otherwise, to such day as the Secretary of State may by order appoint.

10.—(1) If Part XI of the Reserve Forces Act 1996 has not come into force before the commencement of this Act, section 38 of this Act shall have effect until the relevant commencement date as if for "Part XI of the Reserve Forces Act 1996" there were substituted "Part VI of the Reserve Forces Act 1980".

(2) The reference in sub-paragraph (1) to the relevant commencement date is a reference—

(a) if an order has been made before the commencement of this Act appointing a day after that commencement as the day on which Part XI of the Reserve Forces Act 1996 is to come into force, to the day so appointed, and

(b) otherwise, to such day as the Secretary of State may by order appoint.

SCHEDULE 3

REPEALS AND REVOCATIONS

PART I

REPEALS

Chapter	Short Title	Extent of repeal
1963 c. 2.	The Betting, Gaming and Lotteries Act 1963.	In Schedule 5A, paragraph 21.
1975 c. 65.	The Sex Discrimination Act 1975.	Section 64.
1976 c. 74.	The Race Relations Act 1976.	Section 55.
1978 c. 44.	The Employment Protection (Consolidation) Act 1978.	Section 128. Sections 130 to 136A. Section 138(7)(e). Section 139(1)(d). Section 139A(3)(a). Schedules 9 to 11. In Schedule 15, paragraph 18. In Schedule 16, paragraphs 3, 6, 13, 16, 20(2), 25(3) and 28.
1980 c. 30.	The Social Security Act 1980.	In Schedule 4, paragraph 13.
1980 c. 42.	The Employment Act 1980.	In Schedule 1, paragraphs 16 to 18 and 26 to 29.
1981 c. 49.	The Contempt of Court Act 1981.	Section 16(6).
1981 c. 54.	The Supreme Court Act 1981.	In Schedule 5, the entry relating to the Employment Protection (Consolidation) Act 1978.
1982 c. 46.	The Employment Act 1982.	In Schedule 3, in Part I, paragraphs 7 to 9.
1986 c. 48.	The Wages Act 1986.	In Schedule 4, paragraphs 9 and 10.
1986 c. 50.	The Social Security Act 1986.	In Schedule 10, in Part II, paragraph 50.
1989 c. 38.	The Employment Act 1989.	Section 20. In Schedule 6, paragraph 26.
1992 c. 6.	The Social Security (Consequential Provisions) Act 1992.	In Schedule 2, paragraph 50.
1992 c. 52.	The Trade Union and Labour Relations (Consolidation) Act 1992.	Section 290. Section 291(2) and (3). In Schedule 2, paragraphs 19, 20, 24(1) and (2) and 25.
1993 c. 8.	The Judicial Pensions and Retirement Act 1993.	In Schedule 6, paragraph 30.
1993 c. 19.	The Trade Union Reform and Employment Rights Act 1993.	Sections 36 to 38. Sections 40 to 42. In Schedule 7, paragraphs 6 and 7. In Schedule 8, paragraphs 19, 20, 28 to 30, 86 and 87.
1993 c. 48.	The Pension Schemes Act 1993.	In Schedule 8, paragraph 11(2).
1994 c. 20.	The Sunday Trading Act 1994.	In Schedule 4, paragraph 21.
1995 c. 18.	The Jobseekers Act 1995.	In Schedule 2, paragraph 2.
1995 c. 26.	The Pensions Act 1995.	In Schedule 3, paragraphs 8 and 9.

Chapter	Short Title	Extent of repeal
1995 c. 50.	The Disability Discrimination Act 1995.	Section 62. Section 63. In Schedule 3, paragraph 1. In Schedule 6, paragraph 2.

PART II

REVOCATIONS

Number	Title	Extent of revocation
S.I. 1983/1794.	The Equal Pay (Amendment) Regulations 1983.	Regulation 3(3) and (4).
S.I. 1995/2587.	The Collective Redundancies and Transfer of Undertakings (Protection of Employment) (Amendment) Regulations 1995.	Regulation 12(3). Regulation 13(3). In Regulation 14(4), the words ", and paragraph 2(2) of Schedule 9 to,".

TABLE OF DERIVATIONS

Notes:

1. This Table shows the derivation of the provisions of the consolidation.
2. The following abbreviations are used in the Table:

EP(C)A	= Employment Protection (Consolidation) Act 1978 (c. 44)
TULR(C)A	= Trade Union and Labour Relations (Consolidation) Act 1992 (c. 52)
TURERA	= Trade Union Reform and Employment Rights Act 1993 (c. 19)

Provision	Derivation
1(1)	EP(C)A s.128(1).
(2)	—
2	EP(C)A s.128(1).
3(1)	EP(C)A s.131(1); TURERA s.38(a).
(2)	EP(C)A s.131(2).
(3)	EP(C)A s.131(3); TURERA s.38(b).
(4)	EP(C)A s.131(6).
(5)	EP(C)A s.131(7); TURERA s.38(e).
(6)	EP(C)A s.131(7).
4(1), (2)	EP(C)A s.128(2A), (2B); TURERA s.36(2).
(3)	EP(C)A s.128(2C); TURERA s.36(2); Pension Schemes Act 1993 (c. 48) Sch.8 para.11(2).
(4)	EP(C)A s.128(2D); TURERA s.36(2).
(5)	EP(C)A s.128(2F); TURERA s.36(2).
(6), (7)	EP(C)A s.128(5), (6); TURERA s.36(3).
5(1)	EP(C)A Sch.9 para.9; Transfer of Functions (Minister for the Civil Service and Treasury) Order 1981 (S.I. 1981/1670).
(2)	EP(C)A Sch.9 para.10; Transfer of Functions (Minister for the Civil Service and Treasury) Order 1981 (S.I.1981/1670); Equal Pay (Amendment) Regulations 1983 (S.I.1983/1794) Reg.3(4).

Provision	Derivation
(3)	EP(C)A Sch.9 para.10; Transfer of Functions (Minister for the Civil Service and Treasury) Order 1981 (S.I.1981/1670).
6(1)	EP(C)A Sch.9 para.6.
(2)	EP(C)A Sch.9 para.4.
7(1)	EP(C)A Sch.9 para.1(1).
(2)	EP(C)A s.128(4); Employment Act 1980 (c. 42) Sch.1 para.16.
(3)	EP(C)A Sch.9 para.1(2)(a) to (ga), (j); Employment Act 1980 (c. 42) Sch.1 para.26; Equal Pay (Amendment) Regulations 1983 (S.I. 1983/1794) Reg.3(3); Employment Act 1989 (c. 38) Sch.6 para.26.
(4)	EP(C)A Sch.9 para.1(7); Criminal Justice Act 1982 (c. 48) ss.38, 46; Equal Pay (Amendment) Regulations 1983 (S.I.1983/1794) Reg.3(3); Criminal Procedure (Consequential Provisions) (Scotland) Act 1995 (c. 40) Sch.1.
(5)	EP(C)A Sch.9 para.1(6); TURERA s.40(3).
(6)	EP(C)A Sch.9 para.5.
8(1)	EP(C)A s.131(4).
(2)	EP(C)A s.131(4A); TURERA s.38(c).
(3)	EP(C)A s.131(5).
(4)	EP(C)A s.131(5A); TURERA s.38(d).
9(1)	EP(C)A Sch.9 para.1A(1); Employment Act 1989 (c. 38) s.20; TURERA Sch.8 para.28(b).
(2), (3)	EP(C)A Sch.9 para.1A(2), (3); Employment Act 1989 (c. 38) s.20.
(4)	EP(C)A Sch.9 para.1B; TURERA Sch.8 para.28(c).
10(1)	EP(C)A Sch.9 para.1(4A); TURERA Sch.7 para.6(a).
(2)	EP(C)A Sch.9 para.1(5); TULR(C)A Sch.3 para.1(4).
(3)	EP(C)A ss.138(7)(e), 139(1)(d), 139A(3)(a); TURERA Sch.7 para.11.
(4)	EP(C)A Sch.9 para.2(1); TULR(C)A Sch.2 para.24(1), (2).
(5)	EP(C)A Sch.9 para.2(2); TURERA Sch.7 para.6(b); Collective Redundancies and Transfer of Undertakings (Protection of Employment) (Amendment) Regulations (S.I.1995/2587) Reg.14(4).
(6)	EP(C)A ss.138(7)(c), 139(1)(c).
11(1)	EP(C)A Sch.9 para.1(5A); TURERA s.40(2).
(2) to (5)	EP(C)A Sch.9 para.1(8) to (11); TURERA s.40(4).
(6)	EP(C)A Sch.9 para.1(5A), (8); TURERA s.40(2), (4); Criminal Procedure (Consequential Provisions) (Scotland) Act 1995 (c. 40) s.2(4).
12	Disability Discrimination Act 1995 (c. 50) s.62.
13(1)	EP(C)A Sch.9 para.1(2)(h), (i).
(2)	EP(C)A Sch.9 para.1(4); TURERA Sch.8 para.28(a).
14	EP(C)A Sch.9 para.6A; Employment Act 1982 (c. 46) Sch.3 Pt.I para.7.
15(1)	EP(C)A Sch.9 para.7(1).
(2)	EP(C)A Sch.9 para.7(2); Employment Act 1980 (c. 42) Sch.1 para.27.
(3)	EP(C)A Sch.9 para.7(3).
16(1)	Betting, Gaming and Lotteries Act 1963 (c. 2) Sch.5A para.16; EP(C)A s.132(1); TULR(C)A Sch.2 para.19; TURERA Sch.8 para.19; Sunday Trading Act 1994 (c. 20) Sch.4 para.16; Deregulation and Contracting Out Act 1994 (c. 40) Sch.8.
(2)	EP(C)A s.132(2).
(3)	EP(C)A s.132(2); Social Security Act 1986 (c. 50) Sch.10 Pt.II para.50(a); Jobseekers Act 1995 (c. 18) Sch.2 para.2(2).
(4)	EP(C)A s.132(3)(a); Social Security Act 1986 (c. 50) Sch.10 Pt.II para.50(b)(i); Jobseekers Act 1995 (c. 18) Sch.2 para.2(2).
(5)	EP(C)A s.132(3)(b) to (f); Social Security Act 1980 (c. 30) Sch.4 para.13; Health and Social Services and Social Security Adjudications Act 1983 (c. 41) Sch.8 Pt.I para.1; Social Security Act 1986 (c. 50) Sch.10 Pt.II para.50(b); Jobseekers Act 1995 (c. 18) Sch.2 para.2(2), (3).
(6)	EP(C)A s.132(3)(g).
17(1)	EP(C)A s.132(4); Social Security Act 1986 (c. 50) Sch.10 Pt.II para.50(c); Social Security (Consequential Provisions) Act 1992 (c. 6) Sch.2 para. 50(1); Jobseekers Act 1995 (c. 18) Sch.2 para.2(2), (4).
(2)	EP(C)A s.132(5); Jobseekers Act 1995 (c. 18) Sch.2 para.2(2).
(3)	EP(C)A s.132(6).
(4)	EP(C)A s.132(6); Jobseekers Act 1995 (c. 18) Sch.2 para.2(5).

Provision	Derivation
18(1)	Betting, Gaming and Lotteries Act 1963 (c. 2) Sch.5A para.21; Sex Discrimination Act 1975 (c. 65) s.64(1); Race Relations Act 1976 (c. 74) s.55(1); EP(C)A ss.133(1), 134(1); Employment Act 1980 (c. 42) Sch.1 para.17; Wages Act 1986 (c. 48) Sch.4 para.9; TULR(C)A s.290; TURERA Sch.8 paras.20, 86; Sunday Trading Act 1994 (c. 20) Sch.4 para.21; Deregulation and Contracting Out Act 1994 (c. 40) Sch.8; Pensions Act 1995 (c. 26) Sch.3 para.8; Disability Discrimination Act 1995 (c. 50) Sch.3 para.1; Collective Redundancies and Transfer of Undertakings (Protection of Employment) (Amendment) Regulations (S.I. 1995/2587) Regs. 12(3), 13(3).
(2)	Sex Discrimination Act 1975 (c. 65) s.64(1); Race Relations Act 1976 (c. 74) s.55(1); EP(C)A ss.133(2), (4), 134(1); Disability Discrimination Act 1995 (c. 50) Sch.3 para.1(1).
(3)	Sex Discrimination Act 1975 (c. 65) s.64(2); Race Relations Act 1976 (c. 74) s.55(2); EP(C)A ss.133(3), (4), 134(3); Employment Act 1980 (c. 42) Sch.1 para.18; Disability Discrimination Act 1995 (c. 50) Sch.3 para.1(2).
(4)	EP(C)A s.134(2).
(5)	EP(C)A s.134(3); Employment Act 1980 (c. 42) Sch.1 para.18.
(6)	Sex Discrimination Act 1975 (c. 65) s.64(3); Race Relations Act 1976 (c. 74) s.55(3); EP(C)A ss.133(5), 134(4); Disability Discrimination Act 1995 (c. 50) Sch.3 para.1(3).
(7)	Sex Discrimination Act 1975 (c. 65) s.64(4); Race Relations Act 1976 (c. 74) s.55(4); EP(C)A ss.133(6), 134(5); Disability Discrimination Act 1995 (c. 50) Sch.3 para.1(4).
(8)	EP(C)A s.133(7).
19	EP(C)A Sch.9 para.1(3).
20(1)	EP(C)A s.135(1).
(2)	EP(C)A Sch.11 paras.13, 14.
(3)	EP(C)A Sch.11 para.12.
21(1)	Betting, Gaming and Lotteries Act 1963 (c. 2) Sch.5A para.16; EP(C)A s.136(1); Wages Act 1986 (c. 48) Sch.4 para.10; TULR(C)A s.291(2); Sunday Trading Act 1994 (c. 20) Sch.4 para.16; Deregulation and Contracting Out Act 1994 (c. 40) Sch.8; Pensions Act 1995 (c. 26) Sch.3 para.9; Disability Discrimination Act 1995 (c. 50) Sch.6 para.2.
(2)	EP(C)A s.136(5); TULR(C)A s.291(3).
(3)	—
22(1)	EP(C)A s.135(2).
(2)	EP(C)A s.135(3); TULR(C)A Sch.2 para.20.
(3), (4)	EP(C)A s.135(4), (5).
23(1)	EP(C)A Sch.11 para.4.
(2)	EP(C)A Sch.11 paras.5, 6.
(3)	EP(C)A Sch.11 para.7.
(4)	EP(C)A Sch.11 para.9.
(5)	EP(C)A Sch.11 para.11.
24(1)	EP(C)A Sch.11 para.8(1).
(2)	EP(C)A Sch.11 para.8(2); Supreme Court Act 1981 (c. 54) Sch.5, entry relating to EP(C)A.
(3)	EP(C)A Sch.11 para.10.
25(1)	EP(C)A Sch.11 para.1.
(2), (3)	EP(C)A Sch.11 para.2; Judicial Pensions and Retirement Act 1993 (c. 8) Sch.6 para.30.
(4)	EP(C)A Sch.11 para.3.
26	EP(C)A Sch.11 para.24; Transfer of Functions (Treasury and Minister for the Civil Service) Order 1995 (S.I.1995/269).
27(1)	EP(C)A Sch.11 para.25; Transfer of Functions (Minister for the Civil Service and Treasury) Order 1981 (S.I.1981/1670); Transfer of Functions (Treasury and Minister for the Civil Service) Order 1995 (S.I.1995/269).
(2) to (4)	EP(C)A Sch.11 paras.26 to 28; Transfer of Functions (Minister for the Civil Service and Treasury) Order 1981 (S.I.1981/670).
28(1)	EP(C)A Sch.11 para.15.
(2) to (5)	EP(C)A Sch.11 para.16; TURERA s.37.

Provision	Derivation
29(1)	EP(C)A Sch.11 para.20.
(2)	EP(C)A Sch.11 para.22(1).
30(1)	EP(C)A Sch.11 para.17(1).
(2)	EP(C)A Sch.11 para.18; Employment Act 1980 (c. 42) Sch.1 para.28; Employment Act 1982 (c. 46) Sch.3 Pt.I para.8(1); TULR(C)A Sch.2 para.25(a); TURERA Sch.7 para.7, Sch.8 paras.29, 30.
(3)	EP(C)A Sch.11 para.17(2).
31(1) to (6)	EP(C)A Sch.11 para.18A(1) to (6); TURERA s.41.
(7)	EP(C)A Sch.11 para.18A(7); TURERA s.41.
(8)	EP(C)A Sch.11 para.18A(7); TURERA s.41; Criminal Procedure (Consequential Provisions) (Scotland) Act 1995 (c. 40) s.2(4).
32(1), (2)	Disability Discrimination Act 1995 (c. 50) s.63(1), (2).
(3) to (6)	Disability Discrimination Act 1995 (c. 50) ss.62(3) to (6), 63(3)
(7)	Disability Discrimination Act 1995 (c. 50) s.63(4), (5).
(8)	Disability Discrimination Act 1995 (c. 50) ss.62(7), 63(6).
33(1) to (4)	EP(C)A s.136A(1) to (4); TURERA s.42.
(5)	EP(C)A s.136A(6); TURERA s.42.
34	EP(C)A Sch.11 para.19.
35	EP(C)A Sch.11 para.21.
36(1)	EP(C)A Sch.11 para.21A(1); Employment Act 1980 (c. 42) Sch.1 para.29; TULR(C)A Sch.2 para.25(b).
(2)	EP(C)A Sch.11 para.21A(2); Employment Act 1980 (c. 42) Sch.1 para.29.
(3)	EP(C)A Sch.11 para.21A(3); Employment Act 1982 (c. 46) Sch.3 Pt.I para.9; TULR(C)A Sch.2 para.25(b).
(4)	EP(C)A Sch.11 para.22(2).
(5)	EP(C)A Sch.11 para.23(2).
37(1), (2)	EP(C)A s.136(4).
(3)	EP(C)A s.136A(5); TURERA s.42.
(4)	EP(C)A s.136(4).
38(1), (2)	EP(C)A s.138(1), (2).
(3)	EP(C)A s.138(7)(a), (b).
(4)	EP(C)A s.138(3), 138A(2)(b); TURERA s.31; Reserve Forces Act 1996 (c. 14) Sch.10 para.17.
39(1)	EP(C)A ss.139(1), 139A(1); TURERA Sch.7 para.11.
(2)	EP(C)A ss.139(2), 139A(2); TURERA Sch.7 para.11.
(3)	EP(C)A s.139(1)(a), (b).
(4)	EP(C)A s.139A(5); TURERA Sch.7 para.11.
(5)	EP(C)A s.139(3) to (9).
40(1)	EP(C)A s.149(1).
(2)	EP(C)A s.149(2).
41(1)	EP(C)A s.154(1).
(2)	EP(C)A ss.128(2E), 131(8), 138A(6), 149(4); TURERA ss.31(2), 36(2).
(3), (4)	EP(C)A s.154(2), (3).
42(1)	
"Appeal Tribunal"	—
"Appeal Tribunal procedure rules"	—
"appointed member"	—
"conciliation officer"	—
"contract of employment", "employee", "employer"	EP(C)A s.153(1).
"employers' association"	EP(C)A s.153(1); TULR(C)A Sch.2 para.21(2)(a).

Provision	Derivation
"employment", "employed", "statutory provision"	EP(C)A s.153(1).
"industrial tribunal procedure rules"	—
"successor"	EP(C)A s.153(1); TULR(C)A Sch.2 para.21(2)(d).
"trade union"	EP(C)A s.153(1); TULR(C)A Sch.2 para.21(2)(f).
(2)	EP(C)A s.153(4A); TULR(C)A Sch.2 para.21(3).
(3)	EP(C)A s.153(4).
43	—
44	—
45	—
46	—
47	—
48	—
Sch.1	—
Sch.2	—
Sch.3	—

TABLE OF DESTINATIONS

Betting, Gaming and Lotteries Act 1963
(c. 2)

1963	1996
Sched. 5A,	
para. 16	ss.16(1), 21(1)
para. 21	s.18(1)

Sex Discrimination Act 1975
(c. 65)

1975	1996
s.64(1).......	s.18(1), (2)
(2).......	18(3)
(3).......	18(6)
(4).......	18(7)

Race Relations Act 1976
(c. 74)

1976	1996
s.55(1).......	s.18(1), (2)
(2).......	18(3)
(3).......	18(6)
(4).......	18(7)

Employment Protection (Consolidation) Act 1978
(c. 44)

1978	1996	1978	1996	1978	1996
s.128(1)	ss.1(1), (2)	s.134(1)	s.18(1), (2)	s.149(1)	s.40(1)
(4)	s.7(2)	(2)	18(4)	(2)	40(2)
(5),(6)...	4(6), (7)	(3)	18(3), (5)	(4)	41(2)
(2A).....	4(1), (2)	(4)	18(6)	153(1)	42(1),
(2B).....	4(1), (2)	(5)	18(7)		"contract of
(2C).....	4(3)	135(1)	20(1)		employment"
(2D).....	4(4)	(2)	22(1)		"employers'
(2E).....	41(2)	(3)	22(2)		association"
(2F)	4(5)	(4), (5)...	22(3), (4)		"employment"
131(1)	3(1)	136(1)	21(1)		"successor"
(2)	3(2)	(4)	37(1), (2), (4)		"trade union"
(3)	3(3)	(5)	21(2)	(4)	42(3)
(4)	9(1)	136A(1)–(4).	33(1)–(4)	(4A).....	42(2)
(4A)	8(2)	136A(5).....	37(3)	154(1)	41(1)
(5)	8(3)	(6).....	33(5)	(2)	41(3), (4)
(5A).....	8(4)	138(1), (2)...	38(1), (2)	(3)	41(3), (4)
(6)	3(4)	(3)	38(4)	Sched. 9,	
(7)	3(5), (6)	(7)(a)....	38(3)	para. 1(1)...	7(1)
(8)	41(2)	(b)....	38(3)	para. 1(2)	
132(1)	16(1)	(c)....	10(6)	(a)–(ga)...	7(3)
(2)	16(2), (3)	(e)....	10(3)	para. 1(2)(j)	7(3)
(3)(a)....	16(4)	A(2)(b)..	38(4)	para. 1(2)(h)	13(1)
(b)–(f)	16(5)	(6).....	41(2)	para. 1(2)(i)	13(1)
(g)....	16(6)	139(1)	39(1)	para. 1(3)...	19
(4)	17(1)	(a)....	39(3)	para. 1(4)...	13(2)
(5)	17(2)	(b)....	39(3)	para. 1(4A).	10(1)
(6)	17(3), (4)	(c)....	10(6)	para. 1(5)...	10(2)
133(1)	18(1)	(d)....	10(3)	para. 1(5A).	11(1), (6)
(2)	18(2)	(2)	39(2)	para. 1(6)...	7(5)
(3)	18(3)	(3)–(9)...	39(5)	para. 1(7)...	7(4)
(4)	18(2), (3)	139A(1).....	39(1)	para. 1(8)...	11(2)–(5), (6)
(5)	18(6)	(2).....	39(2)	para. 1(9),	
(6)	18(7)	(3)(a)..	10(3)	(10), (11)..	11(2)–(5)
(7)	18(8)	(5).....	39(4)	para. 1A(1).	9(1)
				para. 1A	
				(2), (3)	9(2), (3)

SOCIAL SECURITY ACT 1980
(c. 30)

EMPLOYMENT ACT 1980
(c. 42)

SUPREME COURT ACT 1981
(c. 54)

EMPLOYMENT ACT 1982
(c. 46)

TABLE OF DESTINATIONS

CRIMINAL JUSTICE ACT 1982
(c. 48)

1982	1996
s.38	s.7(4)
46	7(4)

HEALTH AND SOCIAL SERVICES AND SOCIAL SECURITY ADJUDICATIONS ACT 1983
(c. 41)

1983	1996
Sched. 8,	
Pt. I,	
para. 1	s.16(5)

WAGES ACT 1986
(c. 48)

1986	1996
Sched. 4,	
para. 9	s.18(1)
para. 10	21(1)

SOCIAL SECURITY ACT 1986
(c. 50)

1986	1996
Sched. 10,	
Pt. II,	
para. 50(a)	s.16(3)
para. 50(b)	16(5)
para. 50(b)	
(i)	16(4)
para. 50(c) .	17(1)

EMPLOYMENT ACT 1989
(c. 38)

1986	1996
s.20	s.9(1), (2), (3)
Sched. 6,	
para. 26	7(3)

SOCIAL SECURITY (CONSEQUENTIAL PROVISIONS) ACT 1992
(c. 6)

1992	1996
Sched. 2,	
para. 50(1) .	s.17(1)

TABLE OF DESTINATIONS

TRADE UNION AND LABOUR RELATIONS (CONSOLIDATION) ACT 1992
(c. 52)

1992	1996	1992	1996	1992	1996
s.290 .... s.18(1)		Sched. 2—*cont.*		Sched. 2—*cont.*	
291(2) ...... 21(1)		para. 21(2)		para. 24(2) . s.10(4)	
(3) ...... 21(2)		(d) .... s.42(1),		para. 25(a) . 30(2)	
Sched. 2,		"successor"		para. 25(b) . 36(1), (3)	
para. 19 .... 16(1)		para. 21(2)		Sched. 3,	
para. 20 .... 22(2)		(f)......... 42(1),		para.1(4)... 10(2)	
para. 21(2)		"trade union"			
(a) .... 42(1),		para. 21(3) . 42(2)			
"employers'		para. 24(1) . 10(4)			
association"					

JUDICIAL PENSIONS AND RETIREMENT ACT 1993
(c. 8)

1993	1996
Sched. 6,	
para. 30 .... s.25(2), (3)	

TRADE UNION REFORM AND EMPLOYMENT RIGHTS ACT 1993
(c. 19)

1993	1996	1993	1996	1993	1996
s.31 .... s.38(4)		s.40(2)........ s.11(1), (6)		Sched. 8,	
(2).......... 41(2)		(3)........ 7(5)		para. 19 .... s.16(1)	
36(2)........ ss.4(1), (2), (3),		(4)........ 11(2)–(5), (6)		para. 20 .... 18(a)	
(4), (5), 41(2)		41 .... 31(1)–(6), (7),		para. 28(a) . 13(2)	
(3)........ s.41(6), (7)		(8)		para. 28(b) . 9(1)	
37 .... 28(2)–(5)		42 .... ss.33(1)–(4),		para. 28(c).. 9(4)	
38(a)........ 3(1)		(5), 37(3)		para. 29 .... 30(2)	
(b) ...... 3(3)		Sched. 7,		para. 30 .... 30(2)	
(c)........ 8(2)		para. 6(a)... 10(1)		para. 86 .... 18(1)	
(d) ...... 8(4)		para. 6(b) .. 10(5)			
(3)........ 3(5)		para. 7 ..... 30(2)			
		para. 11 .... ss.10(3), 39(1),			
		(2), (4)			

PENSIONS SCHEMES ACT 1993
(c. 48)

1993	1996
Sched. 8,	
para. 11(2) . s.4(3)	

SUNDAY TRADING ACT 1994
(c. 20)

1994	1996
Sched. 4,	
para. 16 .... ss.16(1), 21(1)	
para. 21 .... s. 18(1)	

TABLE OF DESTINATIONS

DEREGULATION AND CONTRACTING OUT ACT 1994
(C. 40)

1994	1996
Sched. 8	ss.16(1), 18(1), 21(1)

JOBSEEKERS ACT 1995
(C. 18)

1995	1996
Sched. 2,	
para. 2(2). . .	ss.16(3), (4), (5), 17(1), (2)
para. 2(3). . .	s.16(5)
para. 2(4). . .	17(1)
para. 2(5). . .	17(4)

PENSIONS ACT 1995
(C. 54)

1995	1996
Sched. 3,	
para. 8	s.18(1)
para. 9	21(1)

CRIMINAL PROCEDURE (CONSEQUENTIAL PROVISIONS) (SCOTLAND) ACT 1995
(C. 40)

1995	1996
s.2(4).	ss.11(6), 31(8)
Sched. 1	s.7(4)

DISABILITY DISCRIMINATION ACT 1995
(C. 50)

1995	1996	1995	1996	1995	1996
s.62	s.12	s.63(4), (5). . . .	s.32(7)	Sched. 3—*cont.*	
(3)–(6). . . .	32(3)–(6)	(6).	32(8)	para. 1(2). . .	s.18(3)
(7).	32(8)	Sched. 3,		para. 1(3). . .	18(6)
63(1), (2). . . .	32(1), (2)	para. 1	18(1)	para. 1(4). . .	18(7)
(3).	32(3)–(6)	para. 1(1). . .	18(2)	Sched. 6,	
				para. 2	21(1)

RESERVE FORCES ACT 1996
(C. 14)

1996	1996
Sched. 10,	
para. 17	s.38(4)

17–40

TABLE OF DESTINATIONS

TRANSFER OF FUNCTIONS (MINISTER FOR THE CIVIL SERVICE AND TREASURY) ORDER 1981
(S.I. 1981 No. 1670)

S.I. 1981 No.
1670   **1996**
S.I. 1981 No.
1670. . . . . ss.5(1), (2), (3),
27(1), (2)–(4)

EQUAL PAY (AMENDMENT) REGULATIONS 1983
(S.I. 1983 No. 1794)

S.I. 1983 No.
1794   **1996**
reg. 3(3) . . . . . . s.7(3), (4)
reg. 3(4) . . . . . . 5(2)

TRANSFER OF FUNCTIONS (TREASURY AND MINISTER FOR THE CIVIL SERVICE) ORDER 1995
(S.I. 1995 No. 269)

S.I. 1995 No.
269   **1996**
S.I. 1995 No.
269. . . . . ss.26, 27(1)

COLLECTIVE REDUNDANCIES AND TRANSFER OF UNDERTAKINGS
(PROTECTION OF EMPLOYMENT) (AMENDMENT) REGULATIONS 1995
(S.I. 1995 No. 2587)

S.I. 1995 No.
2587   **1996**
reg. 12(3) . . . . . s.18(1)
reg. 13(3) . . . . . 18(1)
reg. 14(4) . . . . . 10(5)

INDEX

References are to sections and Schedules

EMPLOYMENT RIGHTS ACT 1996*

(1996 c. 18)

[A Table showing the derivation of the provisions of this consolidation Act will be found at the end of the Act. The Table has no official status.]

ARRANGEMENT OF SECTIONS

PART I

EMPLOYMENT PARTICULARS

PART II

PROTECTION OF WAGES

---

* Annotations by Gareth Thomas, LL.B., B.C.L., Senior Lecturer in Law, University of East Anglia, and Robert Upex, M.A., LL.M., of the Middle Temple, Barrister, Professor of Law, Kingston University.

CHAPTER II

A WEEK'S PAY

Introductory

Employments with normal working hours

Employments with no normal working hours

The calculation date

Maximum amount of week's pay

Miscellaneous

CHAPTER III

OTHER INTERPRETATION PROVISIONS

PART XV

GENERAL AND SUPPLEMENTARY

General

Reciprocal arrangements

Final provisions

An Act to consolidate enactments relating to employment rights.
[22nd May 1996]

PARLIAMENTARY DEBATES
   Hansard, H.L. Vol. 568, cols. 11, 467; Vol. 570, col. 9; Vol. 572, col. 556. H.C. Vol. 278, col. 200.

INTRODUCTION AND GENERAL NOTE

The Employment Rights Act 1996 (c. 18) consolidates most of the existing law relating to individual employment rights. The Employment Rights Bill was first introduced in the summer of 1995, but failed to receive Royal Assent during that parliamentary session. The Bill was subsequently re-introduced in the next session, received Royal Assent on May 22, 1996, and came into force on August 22, 1996. The Act has been widely welcomed as a necessary (and long overdue) rationalisation of the previous morass of legislative provisions on employment rights. The consolidation itself is a model of clarity and logic. Sadly, however, the extent to which the notorious complexity of modern employment law can be alleviated by a mere consolidation of the existing provisions is strictly limited, no matter how clever the drafting, and the inherent difficulty of much of the law in this area remains largely unaffected.

The Act contains most of the provisions formerly contained in the Employment Protection (Consolidation) Act 1978 (c. 44) (other than those concerning industrial tribunals and the Employment Appeal Tribunal, which are consolidated in the Industrial Tribunals Act 1996 (c. 17)), and the Wages Act 1986 (c. 48). Also included are the employment rights provisions from the Sunday Trading Act 1994 (c. 20) and the Pensions Act 1995 (c. 26). There are however some important omissions. In particular, the Act does not include any of the provisions on discrimination in employment, which are still to be found in the Equal Pay Act 1970 (c. 41), Sex Discrimination Act 1975 (c. 65), Race Relations Act 1976 (c. 74) and Disability Discrimination Act 1995 (c. 50); nor does it include the rights enjoyed by employees in relation to trade union membership and activities (which remain in Pt. III of the Trade Union and Labour Relations (Consolidation) Act 1992 (c. 52)) or the Transfer of Undertakings (Protection of Employment) Regulations 1981 (S.I. 1981 No. 1794) (TUPE).

The Act organises the relevant material into 15 Parts. The first 12 Parts contain the substantive material concerning, respectively, Employment Particulars (written statements and itemised pay statements), Protection of Wages, Guarantee Payments, Sunday Working, Protection against Detriment, Time Off Work, Suspension from Work, Maternity Rights, Termination (notice and reasons), Unfair Dismissal, Redundancy Payments and Insolvency. The remaining three Parts deal with a range of subsidiary matters, including the excluded classes of employment, the restrictions on contracting out, the computation of periods of continuous employment and other matters of interpretation. The material is organised in a clear and systematic way, although in a number of areas it is still necessary to consult several different Parts of the Act in order to gain a complete picture of the relevant law. So for example, Pt. VIII (Maternity Rights) only covers the general right to maternity leave and the right to return to work; to obtain a full picture of the Act's provisions concerning maternity rights, it is also necessary to consult, *inter alia*, Pt. VI (time off work for ante-natal care), Pt. VII (suspension from work on maternity grounds) and Pt. X (dismissal for a reason connected with pregnancy or childbirth). A similar point could be made in relation to the organisation of the material concerning Sunday working, occupational pension scheme trustees, employee representatives and health and safety cases. Such minor quibbles will no doubt diminish in importance as those using the Act become more familiar with the reorganised material.

As is often the case, the consolidation process has served to highlight some curious inconsistencies in the legislative provisions (although in this context some variation is only to be expected, given the turbulent history of the subject, and the fact that provisions which are superficially very similar may derive from legislation originally introduced by governments of very different political persuasions). This is nowhere better exemplified than in Pt. VI (Time Off Work), where the consolidation process has helped to expose the subtle but nonetheless significant variations in the drafting of the various provisions.

PART I

EMPLOYMENT PARTICULARS

Right to statements of employment particulars

Statement of initial employment particulars

1.—(1) Where an employee begins employment with an employer, the employer shall give to the employee a written statement of particulars of employment.

(2) The statement may (subject to section 2(4)) be given in instalments and (whether or not given in instalments) shall be given not later than two months after the beginning of the employment.

(3) The statement shall contain particulars of—

(a) the names of the employer and employee,

(b) the date when the employment began, and

(c) the date on which the employee's period of continuous employment began (taking into account any employment with a previous employer which counts towards that period).

(4) The statement shall also contain particulars, as at a specified date not more than seven days before the statement (or the instalment containing them) is given, of—

(a) the scale or rate of remuneration or the method of calculating remuneration,

(b) the intervals at which remuneration is paid (that is, weekly, monthly or other specified intervals),

(c) any terms and conditions relating to hours of work (including any terms and conditions relating to normal working hours),

(d) any terms and conditions relating to any of the following—

(i) entitlement to holidays, including public holidays, and holiday pay (the particulars given being sufficient to enable the employee's entitlement, including any entitlement to accrued holiday pay on the termination of employment, to be precisely calculated),

(ii) incapacity for work due to sickness or injury, including any provision for sick pay, and

(iii) pensions and pension schemes,

(e) the length of notice which the employee is obliged to give and entitled to receive to terminate his contract of employment,

(f) the title of the job which the employee is employed to do or a brief description of the work for which he is employed,

(g) where the employment is not intended to be permanent, the period for which it is expected to continue or, if it is for a fixed term, the date when it is to end,

(h) either the place of work or, where the employee is required or permitted to work at various places, an indication of that and of the address of the employer,

(j) any collective agreements which directly affect the terms and conditions of the employment including, where the employer is not a party, the persons by whom they were made, and

(k) where the employee is required to work outside the United Kingdom for a period of more than one month—

(i) the period for which he is to work outside the United Kingdom,

(ii) the currency in which remuneration is to be paid while he is working outside the United Kingdom,

(iii) any additional remuneration payable to him, and any benefits to be provided to or in respect of him, by reason of his being required to work outside the United Kingdom, and

(iv) any terms and conditions relating to his return to the United Kingdom.

(5) Subsection (4)(d)(iii) does not apply to an employee of a body or authority if—

(a) the employee's pension rights depend on the terms of a pension scheme established under any provision contained in or having effect under any Act, and

(b) any such provision requires the body or authority to give to a new employee information concerning the employee's pension rights or the determination of questions affecting those rights.

DEFINITIONS
"collective agreement": s.235(1).
"employee": s.230(1).
"employer": s.230(4).
"employment": s.230(5).
"job": s.235.
"normal working hours": s.234.

GENERAL NOTE
The right of an employee to be provided with a written statement of the main particulars of his or her employment was introduced by the Contracts of Employment Act 1963 (c. 49), and subsequently re-enacted in the Contracts of Employment Act 1972 (c. 53). The provisions were amended by the Trade Union Reform and Employment Rights Act 1993 (c. 19), implementing EEC Directive No. 91/533 (adopted on October 14, 1991) on information concerning employment conditions, which requires employers to notify their employees of "the essential aspects of the contract or employment relationship". For the most part, the pre-TURERA provisions already satisfied the requirements of the directive (indeed, in certain respects they exceeded them), and the emphasis in the directive on providing information to employees on terms and conditions on an individual basis was clearly in tune with the government's preference for individual contracting. The main changes made by the 1993 Act were as follows:

(i) the time within which a written statement must be provided was reduced from 13 weeks of the start of employment to only two months;

(ii) the working hours threshold was reduced from 16 to eight hours a week (the exclusion of part-timers was subsequently removed altogether following the House of Lords' decision in *R. v. Secretary of State for Employment ex p. Equal Opportunities Commission* [1994] IRLR 176);

(iii) the information to be included in a written statement was extended to cover a range of additional matters, for example, the length of time for which a non-permanent job is expected to continue, the employee's place of work, the existence of any relevant collective agreements, and any special arrangements where the employee is required to work outside the U.K. for more than one month;

(iv) the ability of an employer to provide a written statement which refers to some other document (*e.g.* a company handbook or a collective agreement) for all or any of the relevant particulars was significantly restricted;

(v) the rules concerning the notification of changes in terms and conditions were tightened up, with employees being given the right to receive individual written notification of any changes.

With two important exceptions, the new requirements do not apply to "pre-TURERA employees", *i.e.* those whose employment with their employer began before November 30, 1993 (the day on which the amending provisions came into force). The provisions of ss.1–6 of the EP(C)A 1978 (as they had effect *before* the 1993 amendments) continue in force for such employees: see Sched. 2, para. 7(2). However, pre-TURERA employees are entitled to request a new-style statement, either before or within three months of the end of employment (*ibid.* para. 7(3)), although such a request may only be made once (*ibid.* para. 7(4)); and the new requirements concerning notification of changes in the particulars apply to pre-TURERA employees, even if those employees have not previously requested a new-style statement (*ibid.* para. 7(5)).

Subs. (1)

Employee. The right to receive a written statement of employment particulars arises where an "employee" begins employment with an employer. Self-employed workers are therefore excluded: see the note to s.230. Also excluded are employees working wholly or mainly outside Great Britain (s.196), employees who are employed for less than one month (s.198), and mariners (s.199). The exclusion of those in Crown employment and of Parliamentary staff from the right to a written statement was removed by the 1993 Act. There was also formerly an exclusion for part-time workers whose contracts involved employment for less than 16 hours weekly. This exclusion was modified by the 1993 Act to meet the requirements of the directive, so that an employee only needed to be employed under a contract normally involving employment for at least eight hours a week to qualify for a written statement; and was subsequently removed altogether (with effect from February 6, 1995) by the Employment Protection (Part-time Employees) Regulations 1995 (S.I. 1995 No. 31) following the House of Lords' decision in *R. v. Secretary of State for Employment ex p. Equal Opportunities Commission* [1994] IRLR 176, that the hours of work thresholds for certain employment protection rights were contrary to E.C. law.

Where an employee ceases to fall within one of the excluded categories, his or her employment is deemed to begin at that time: see the note to s.5.

Written statement of particulars of employment. A written statement is not a contract of employment *per se*, nor does it become one simply because the employee signs a receipt for it without objecting to the terms set out therein, unless the evidence is that the employee in fact signed the written statement as a contract: see *Gascol Conversions v. Mercer* [1974] I.C.R. 420. In normal circumstances the written statement simply provides evidence of what the main terms of employment are: see *Turriff Construction v. Bryant* (1967) 2 I.T.R. 292, and *Parkes Classic Confectionery v. Ashcroft* (1973) 8 I.T.R. 43. In *System Floors (U.K.) v. Daniel* [1982] I.C.R. 54 (a case where the employer was arguing that the written statement was not accurate), Browne-Wilkinson J. put it thus:

"It seems to us, therefore, that in general the status of the statutory statement is this. It provides very strong prima facie evidence of what were the terms of the contract between the parties, but does not constitute a written contract between the parties. Nor are the statements of the terms finally conclusive: at most, they place a heavy burden on the employer to show that the actual terms of the contract are different from those which he has set out in the statutory statement."

Browne-Wilkinson J. added that as against an *employee* the written statement will be "no more than persuasive, though not conclusive" evidence, which might be rebutted, *e.g.*, by evidence of statements made at a job interview or in letters of appointment. These dicta were subsequently approved by the Court of Appeal in *Robertson v. British Gas Corp.* [1983] I.C.R. 351.

Before the 1993 amendments, the EP(C)A 1978, s.5 specifically provided that the right to a written statement did not apply where the employee had a written contract of employment which covered all the matters required to be included in the written statement, provided the employee had been given a copy of that contract or a copy was made reasonably accessible to him. The substituted provisions contain no such exemption, inviting the argument that an employee must be provided with a written statement even where he or she has been given a full written contract. Such an interpretation would be unfortunate, particularly in view of the limited circumstances in which a written statement may refer the employee to some other document (see the note to s.2). It is therefore likely that a tribunal would hold it to be implicit in the new provisions that a written contract which covers all the prescribed matters constitutes a "written statement" within the meaning of the section, an interpretation which would have the distinct advantage of avoiding what might be considered needless duplication.

Subs. (2)

As seen in the General Note, the time within which a written statement must be given was reduced by the 1993 Act to two months after the beginning of employment, rather than 13 weeks as was previously the case. The particulars may be given in instalments, provided they are all supplied within the two-month deadline, but the main particulars must be included in a single document: see the note to s.2(4). The right to receive a written statement is not lost if the employment ends before the two-month deadline expires (see s.2(6)), although as seen above, s.198 provides that the employment must have continued for at least one month in order for the right to arise in the first place.

Subs. (3)

Period of continuous employment. This is to be calculated in accordance with the provisions of ss.210–219. Employment with a previous employer must be taken into account if it counts towards the employee's period of continuous employment, although whether in fact continuity is preserved through a change of employer for the purposes of the employee's statutory rights must be determined in accordance with the statutory provisions. A promise by an employer that an employee's previous period of continuous employment will count towards his or her continuity of employment with the new employer may only take effect, if at all, as a separate contract: see *Secretary of State for Employment v. Globe Elastic Thread Co.* [1979] I.C.R. 706, overruling *Evenden v. Guildford City Association Football Club* [1975] I.C.R. 367.

It should be noted that while "the date on which the employee's period of continuous employment began" will normally be the employee's first day at work with that employer, in certain circumstances the start of the employee's period of continuous employment will be deemed to be postponed; see the notes to ss.210–219, below.

Subs. (4)

This subsection lists the terms and conditions of employment of which particulars must be given in the written statement. The particulars in paras. (g)–(k) were added by the 1993 Act, as was the provision in para. (f) concerning the employee's job description. The list of required particulars may be added to by the Secretary of State under s.7. For the position where there are no terms and conditions relating to any of the specified heads, see the note to s.2(1).

Normal working hours. For the calculation of normal working hours, see the note to s.234.

Pensions and pension schemes. Note that by virtue of subs. (5), the duty to give particulars of any terms and conditions relating to pensions and pension schemes does not apply where the scheme in question places a statutory duty on the employer to give information to new employees concerning their pension rights.

Length of notice. For the statutory minimum periods of notice, see the note to s.234.

Place of work. This is not defined. *Cf.* the definition in TULR(C)A 1992, s.228, where an employee's "place of work" is defined (for the purposes of the law on separate workplace ballots) as "the premises occupied by his employer at or from which that person works or, where he does not work at or from any such premises or works at or from more than one set of premises, the premises occupied by his employer with which his employment has the closest connection".

Work outside the United Kingdom. Certain additional information relating to employment overseas must be included in the written statement where relevant. The position of those working outside the U.K. is further strengthened by the requirement in s.2(5) that where within two months of starting employment the employee is to begin work outside the U.K. for a period of more than one month, the written statement must be given before the employee departs.

Statement of initial particulars: supplementary

2.—(1) If, in the case of a statement under section 1, there are no particulars to be entered under any of the heads of paragraph (d) or (k) of subsection (4) of that section, or under any of the other paragraphs of subsection (3) or (4) of that section, that fact shall be stated.

(2) A statement under section 1 may refer the employee for particulars of any of the matters specified in subsection (4)(d)(ii) and (iii) of that section to the provisions of some other document which is reasonably accessible to the employee.

(3) A statement under section 1 may refer the employee for particulars of either of the matters specified in subsection (4)(e) of that section to the law or to the provisions of any collective agreement directly affecting the terms and conditions of the employment which is reasonably accessible to the employee.

(4) The particulars required by section 1(3) and (4)(a) to (c), (d)(i), (f) and (h) shall be included in a single document.

(5) Where before the end of the period of two months after the beginning of an employee's employment the employee is to begin to work outside the United Kingdom for a period of more than one month, the statement under section 1 shall be given to him not later than the time when he leaves the United Kingdom in order to begin so to work.

(6) A statement shall be given to a person under section 1 even if his employment ends before the end of the period within which the statement is required to be given.

DEFINITIONS
"collective agreement": s.235(1).
"employee": s.230(1).
"employment": s.230(5).

GENERAL NOTE

Subs. (1)
Where there are no terms and conditions relating to any of the specified heads, that fact must be stated in the written statement. On the face of it, this seems to suggest that no particulars need be given under *any* of the headings where none have been agreed, but in *Eagland v. British Telecommunications* [1990] IRLR 328, E.A.T., Wood P. distinguished between "mandatory terms", *i.e.* essential terms which the written statement must contain, and "non-mandatory terms", where no particulars need be given if there is no evidence that the parties have reached an agreement on that matter. The particulars now contained in s.1(3)(a) to (c) (the parties, commencement of employment, and continuity of employment), and s.1(4)(a),(b),(e) and (f) (rate of pay, the interval of payment, notice requirements and job title) were said to be mandatory terms, while the particulars in s.1(4)(c) and (d) (hours of work, holidays, sickness and pensions) were non-mandatory, since the wording of the section ("any terms and conditions relating to . . .") clearly envisaged that there might not be any agreed terms on those matters. This distinction was subsequently approved on appeal by the Court of Appeal: [1992] IRLR 323. In the case of non-mandatory terms such as pensions, holidays and sick pay, Parker L.J. (giving the leading judgment of the court) stated that the tribunal has no power to impose any such terms on the employer if the parties had agreed that there should be no such terms, or if no agreement at all had been reached on those matters (there being no entitlement to such terms as a necessary legal incident of the employment relationship). The employer's obligation is simply to give details of any such terms that exist, not to have a particular term in the first place. In *Morley v. Heritage* [1993] IRLR 400, a case concerning entitlement to pay in lieu of untaken holiday entitlement, the Court of Appeal confirmed that, in the case of non-mandatory terms, the mere fact that a particular type of term is mentioned in s.1(4) (*e.g.* entitlement to accrued holiday pay) does not mean that there *has* to be such a term; the section simply requires writing if there *is* such a term.
In the case of mandatory terms, however, Parker L.J. considered that it was difficult to imagine how a case could arise where there were no terms on the relevant matters; one possibility might be where there is no evidence of any agreement on the length of notice, but in such a case the tribunal would be able to imply a term that there must be reasonable notice (that being the term which would normally be implied in the absence of an express agreement, as one of the ordinary incidents of the employment relationship). He disapproved of the suggestion in *Mears v. Safecar Security* [1982] IRLR 183, that the tribunal has a duty under s.11(1) to "invent" a term in circumstances where no express term has been agreed and where there is no evidence upon which a term can be implied, simply to fill the gap in the written statement: "I do not consider that even in mandatory cases the Tribunal have power to impose on parties terms which have not been agreed.". Taking this to its logical conclusion, Leggatt L.J. suggested that a failure to reach agreement on one of the mandatory terms might well lead to a finding that the contract fails for uncertainty: "If an essential term, such as a written statement must contain, has not been agreed, there will be no agreement."
Of the new particulars added by the 1993 Act, those in s.1(4)(g) and (h) (non-permanent employment and place of work) would appear to be mandatory, while those in s.1(4)(j) (any collective agreements) are presumably non-mandatory; the particulars in s.1(4)(k) relating to employment abroad appear to be a mixture of the two.

Subss. (2), (3), (4)
Before the 1993 amendments, the employer enjoyed a wide power to refer the employee to some other document (*e.g.* a company handbook or collective agreement) for all or any of the particulars which had to be included in the written statement, provided that document was reasonably accessible to the employee; however, that power of reference was significantly restricted by the 1993 Act, and the current position is that the employer may only refer the employee to another document for particulars relating to sickness and sickpay, pensions and, under s.3(1), any relevant disciplinary rules and procedures; subs. (3) allows the employer to refer the employee to the provisions of the general law or to a reasonably accessible collective agreement, but only for details of notice periods. In the past, employers made widespread use of this power of incorporation by reference, particularly through the provision of company handbooks, and the restriction of this practice has been criticised as adding significantly to the administrative costs of employers. In a modest concession, s.1(2) allows the employer to give the

written statement in instalments (provided all the particulars are given within the two-month deadline), but the particulars set out in subs. (4) must be included within a single document.
Reasonably accessible. See the note to s.6.

Subs. (6)
While an employee cannot insist on being given a written statement within two months of the start of his or her employment (see s.1(2)), the right to receive a written statement is not lost if the employment ends before that period expires, provided the employment has continued for at least one month (see s.198).

Note about disciplinary procedures and pensions

3.—(1) A statement under section 1 shall include a note—
  (a) specifying any disciplinary rules applicable to the employee or referring the employee to the provisions of a document specifying such rules which is reasonably accessible to the employee,
  (b) specifying (by description or otherwise)—
            (i) a person to whom the employee can apply if dissatisfied with any disciplinary decision relating to him, and
            (ii) a person to whom the employee can apply for the purpose of seeking redress of any grievance relating to his employment,
      and the manner in which any such application should be made, and
  (c) where there are further steps consequent on any such application, explaining those steps or referring to the provisions of a document explaining them which is reasonably accessible to the employee.
  (2) Subsection (1) does not apply to rules, disciplinary decisions, grievances or procedures relating to health or safety at work.
  (3) The note need not comply with the following provisions of subsection (1)—
  (a) paragraph (a),
  (b) in paragraph (b), sub-paragraph (i) and the words following sub-paragraph (ii) so far as relating to sub-paragraph (i), and
  (c) paragraph (c),
if on the date when the employee's employment began the relevant number of employees was less than twenty.
  (4) In subsection (3) "the relevant number of employees", in relation to an employee, means the number of employees employed by his employer added to the number of employees employed by any associated employer.
  (5) The note shall also state whether there is in force a contracting-out certificate (issued in accordance with Chapter I of Part III of the Pension Schemes Act 1993) stating that the employment is contracted-out employment (for the purposes of that Part of that Act).

DEFINITIONS
    "associated employer": s.231.
    "employee": s.230(1).
    "employer": s.230(4).
    "employment": s.230(5).

GENERAL NOTE
    This section sets out the information relating to disciplinary rules and procedures and pensions which must be included in the written statement. In brief, the statement must contain a note specifying any disciplinary rules applicable to the employee (or referring the employee to a reasonably accessible document which specifies those rules); it must specify a person to whom the employee may apply if dissatisfied with a disciplinary decision relating to him or her, or if seeking redress of a grievance relating to his or her employment, and the manner in which such an application should be made; it must explain any further steps in the employer's disciplinary or grievance procedures consequent on such an application, or refer the employee to a reasonably accessible document which explains those steps; and it must state whether a contracting-out certificate issued by the Occupational Pensions Board under Pt. III of the Pension Schemes Act 1993 is in force for the employment in question. Subsection (2) provides that the above require-

ments do not apply to rules, procedures, etc., relating to health and safety at work, while subs. (3) exempts small firms from most of the requirements concerning disciplinary rules and procedures (see below).

Reasonably accessible. See the note to s.6.

Subss. (3), (4)

Small firms (*i.e.* those employing less than 20 employees on the date when the employee's employment began) are exempt from all the requirements concerning notification of disciplinary procedures, other than the requirement in subs. (1)(b) to specify how and to whom the employee may apply if seeking redress of a grievance relating to his employment. The small firm exemption was first floated in the White Paper, *Building Businesses ... Not Barriers* (Cmnd. 9794, 1986), and was subsequently enacted in the Employment Act 1989 (c. 38).

Relevant number of employees. In determining the "relevant number of employees" for the purposes of the small firm exemption, the tribunal must take account of all the employees of the employer, irrespective of their employment status, and must also include in the head-count those employed by any associated employer (see below). The exemption applies where the number employed by the employer is less than 20 on the date when the employee's employment began; the fact that the number of employees subsequently rises above the threshold does not entitle an employee originally covered by the exemption to be supplied with the additional particulars. It follows that in order to determine each employee's entitlement an employer would need to keep an accurate record not only of the number of employees from time to time, but also when they were taken on and in what order. In situations where there is a significant turnover in the workforce this is likely to be both difficult and burdensome. A situation where there are within the same workforce some employees who are entitled to full statement while others are only entitled to an abbreviated version is both anomalous and administratively inconvenient, particularly where the terms and conditions of those concerned are largely the same, and many small employers, particularly those with fluctuating workforces, have continued to issue all their employees with the full statement in order to avoid these potential problems.

Associated employer. See the note to s.231.

Statement of changes

4.—(1) If, after the material date, there is a change in any of the matters particulars of which are required by sections 1 to 3 to be included or referred to in a statement under section 1, the employer shall give to the employee a written statement containing particulars of the change.

(2) For the purposes of subsection (1)—

(a) in relation to a matter particulars of which are included or referred to in a statement given under section 1 otherwise than in instalments, the material date is the date to which the statement relates,

(b) in relation to a matter particulars of which—

(i) are included or referred to in an instalment of a statement given under section 1, or

(ii) are required by section 2(4) to be included in a single document but are not included in an instalment of a statement given under section 1 which does include other particulars to which that provision applies,

the material date is the date to which the instalment relates, and

(c) in relation to any other matter, the material date is the date by which a statement under section 1 is required to be given.

(3) A statement under subsection (1) shall be given at the earliest opportunity and, in any event, not later than—

(a) one month after the change in question, or

(b) where that change results from the employee being required to work outside the United Kingdom for a period of more than one month, the time when he leaves the United Kingdom in order to begin so to work, if that is earlier.

(4) A statement under subsection (1) may refer the employee to the provisions of some other document which is reasonably accessible to the employee for a change in any of the matters specified in sections 1(4)(d)(ii) and (iii) and 3(1)(a) and (c).

(5) A statement under subsection (1) may refer the employee for a change in either of the matters specified in section 1(4)(e) to the law or to the provisions of any collective agreement directly affecting the terms and conditions of the employment which is reasonably accessible to the employee.

(6) Where, after an employer has given to an employee a statement under section 1, either—

(a) the name of the employer (whether an individual or a body corporate or partnership) is changed without any change in the identity of the employer, or

(b) the identity of the employer is changed in circumstances in which the continuity of the employee's period of employment is not broken,

and subsection (7) applies in relation to the change, the person who is the employer immediately after the change is not required to give to the employee a statement under section 1; but the change shall be treated as a change falling within subsection (1) of this section.

(7) This subsection applies in relation to a change if it does not involve any change in any of the matters (other than the names of the parties) particulars of which are required by sections 1 to 3 to be included or referred to in the statement under section 1.

(8) A statement under subsection (1) which informs an employee of a change such as is referred to in subsection (6)(b) shall specify the date on which the employee's period of continuous employment began.

DEFINITIONS
"associated employer": s.231.
"collective agreement": s.235(1).
"employee": s.230(1).
"employer": s.230(4).
"employment": s.230(5).

GENERAL NOTE
This section sets out the procedures which employers must follow in notifying employees of changes in any of the matters covered by the written statement. The rules on notifying changes were tightened up considerably by the 1993 Act. Previously the employer was not required to give employees individual notice of any changes, but was allowed to notify employees of those changes by means of a written statement which they had a reasonable opportunity of reading at work or which was reasonably accessible to them in some other way; alternatively, the employer could simply refer the employees to some other document, once again provided they had a reasonable opportunity of reading that document at work or it was otherwise reasonably accessible to them. Furthermore, the employer was entitled to indicate in the original written statement that any future changes in the particulars would be recorded in that document, and if the changes were duly noted up within one month of the change this relieved the employer of the need to take other steps to inform employees of the change. As a result of the changes made in 1993, the employer is now normally required to give each individual employee a written statement containing particulars of the changes; this must be provided at the earliest opportunity, and at the latest within one month of the change (or, where the change results from the employee being sent to work outside the U.K. for more than one month, the time when the employee leaves the U.K. in order to begin work, if earlier).

The statement must normally set out the details of the changes in full, and may not be given in instalments (even if the original statement was so provided), but there are two relatively minor concessions: first, the statement of changes may refer the employee to some other reasonably accessible document, to the general law or to a relevant collective agreement for the details of those changes where a cross-reference on those matters would have been permissible in the original written statement (subss. (4),(5)); and secondly, where the name or the identity of the employer changes, the employee does not have to be issued with a new s.1 statement unless the employee's continuity of employment is broken by the change of identity or there are changes in any of the matters (other than the names of the parties) required to be included in the written statement (sub. (6)).

It is important to recognise that observance of the statutory duty to notify employees of changes in their terms and conditions of employment does not of itself entitle the employer to vary the terms of the contract of employment unilaterally. Any such variation is subject to the ordinary common law rules concerning the variation of contracts, and it has long been established that the mere fact that an employee does not object to a unilateral alteration of his or her written particulars does not imply assent to a variation of the contract, particularly where the change in question has no immediate practical effect (see *Jones v. Associated Tunnelling Co.* [1981] IRLR 477; *Robertson v. British Gas Corp.* [1983] IRLR 302). Conversely, a failure by the employer to comply with the statutory requirements will not nullify a variation which is in fact contractually valid (*e.g.* where there has been an agreed oral variation of the contract).

Reasonably accessible. See the note to s.6.

Period of continuous employment. See the notes to ss.210–219.

Exclusion from rights to statements

5.—(1) Sections 1 to 4 apply to an employee who at any time comes or ceases to come within the exceptions from those sections provided by sections 196 and 199, and under section 209, as if his employment with his employer terminated or began at that time.

(2) The fact that section 1 is directed by subsection (1) to apply to an employee as if his employment began on his ceasing to come within the exceptions referred to in that subsection does not affect the obligation under section 1(3)(b) to specify the date on which his employment actually began.

DEFINITIONS
"employee": s.230(1).
"employment": s.230(5).

GENERAL NOTE
Certain classes of employees are excluded from the right to a written statement: see the note to s.1(1). Subsection (1) provides that where an employee ceases to fall within one of the excluded categories, that employee is to be treated as if his employment began at that time, save that by virtue of subs. (2), the written statement must specify the date on which his employment actually began. Under the pre-1993 provisions the employer was required to provide a written statement within one month of the employee ceasing to fall within an excluded category (as opposed to the usual time-limit of 13 weeks), but under the present law no special provision is made for such cases, and it therefore appears that the normal two-month time-limit applies.

Reasonably accessible document or collective agreement

6. In sections 2 to 4 references to a document or collective agreement which is reasonably accessible to an employee are references to a document or collective agreement which—

(a) the employee has reasonable opportunities of reading in the course of his employment, or

(b) is made reasonably accessible to the employee in some other way.

DEFINITIONS
"collective agreement": s.235(1).
"employee": s.230(1).
"employment": s.230(5).

GENERAL NOTE
This section defines a "reasonably accessible" document or collective agreement as one which the employee has reasonable opportunities of reading in the course of his or her employment, or one which is made reasonably accessible to him or her in some other way.

Power to require particulars of further matters

7. The Secretary of State may by order provide that section 1 shall have effect as if particulars of such further matters as may be specified in the order were included in the particulars required by that section; and, for that purpose, the order may include such provisions amending that section as appear to the Secretary of State to be expedient.

GENERAL NOTE
This section empowers the Secretary of State to add to the list of matters about which particulars must be included in the written statement. At the time of writing no order had been made under this section, or under any of its predecessors.

Right to itemised pay statement

Itemised pay statement

8.—(1) An employee has the right to be given by his employer, at or before the time at which any payment of wages or salary is made to him, a written itemised pay statement.

(2) The statement shall contain particulars of—

(a) the gross amount of the wages or salary,

(b) the amounts of any variable, and (subject to section 9) any fixed, deductions from that gross amount and the purposes for which they are made,

(c) the net amount of wages or salary payable, and

(d) where different parts of the net amount are paid in different ways, the amount and method of payment of each part-payment.

DEFINITIONS
"employee": s.230(1).
"employer": s.230(4).

GENERAL NOTE
This section gives an employee the right to be given a written, itemised pay statement by the employer on each payment of wages or salary. The statement must give a breakdown of the employee's gross pay, the amount of any variable and fixed deductions made therefrom, and the purposes for which they are made, the net amount of pay, and where different parts of the net pay are paid in different ways, the amount and method of payment of each part-payment. The right to receive an itemised pay statement is not conditional upon the employee having requested such a statement: see *Coales v. Wood (John) & Co.* [1986] IRLR 129, E.A.T.

The right only applies to "employees"; self-employed workers are therefore excluded (see the note to s.230). Certain classes of employee are also excluded from the right, namely, employees ordinarily working outside Great Britain (s.196(3)), share fishermen (s.199(2)), merchant seamen (s.199(4)) and police officers (s.200). The right does however extend to those in Crown employment and to Parliamentary staff. There was formerly an exclusion for part-time workers whose contracts involved employment for less than 16 hours weekly. This exclusion was modified by s.27 of the Trade Union Reform and Employment Rights Act 1993, which extended the right to receive an itemised pay statement to employees working under a contract normally involving employment for between eight and 16 hours a week (albeit with an exception for small employers), to meet the requirements of EEC Directive No. 91/533; the exclusion was however subsequently removed altogether, with effect from February 6, 1995, by the Employment Protection (Part-time Employees) Regulations 1995 (S.I. 1995 No. 31): see the note to s.1(1), above.

Wages or salary. The statement only has to include sums payable to the employee from the employer, not sums payable from other sources, *e.g.* tips (*Cofone v. Spaghetti House* [1980] I.C.R. 155, E.A.T.).

Deductions. The statement must contain details of the amount of each variable deduction and the purpose for which it was made; merely describing a deduction as a "miscellaneous deduction" will not be sufficient (*Milsom v. Leicestershire County Council* [1978] IRLR 433). Where the deductions are of a fixed amount they need not be itemised in each pay statement as long as the aggregate amount of those deductions is given, and the employee has been provided with a standing statement of fixed deductions: see the note to s.9. For the special rules concerning unauthorised deductions from wages, see Pt. II, below.

Standing statement of fixed deductions

9.—(1) A pay statement given in accordance with section 8 need not contain separate particulars of a fixed deduction if—

(a) it contains instead an aggregate amount of fixed deductions, including that deduction, and

(b) the employer has given to the employee, at or before the time at which the pay statement is given, a standing statement of fixed deductions which satisfies subsection (2).

(2) A standing statement of fixed deductions satisfies this subsection if—

(a) it is in writing,

(b) it contains, in relation to each deduction comprised in the aggregate amount of deductions, particulars of—

(i) the amount of the deduction,

(ii) the intervals at which the deduction is to be made, and

(iii) the purpose for which it is made, and

(c) it is (in accordance with subsection (5)) effective at the date on which the pay statement is given.

(3) A standing statement of fixed deductions may be amended, whether by—

(a) addition of a new deduction,

(b) a change in the particulars, or

(c) cancellation of an existing deduction,

by notice in writing, containing particulars of the amendment, given by the employer to the employee.

(4) An employer who has given to an employee a standing statement of fixed deductions shall—

(a) within the period of twelve months beginning with the date on which the first standing statement was given, and

(b) at intervals of not more than twelve months afterwards,

re-issue it in a consolidated form incorporating any amendments notified in accordance with subsection (3).

(5) For the purposes of subsection (2)(c) a standing statement of fixed deductions—

(a) becomes effective on the date on which it is given to the employee, and

(b) ceases to be effective at the end of the period of twelve months beginning with that date or, where it is re-issued in accordance with subsection (4), with the end of the period of twelve months beginning with the date of the last re-issue.

DEFINITIONS

"employee": s.230(1).

"employer": s.230(4).

GENERAL NOTE

Where the deductions are of a fixed amount, the employer need not include separate details of each deduction in each pay statement, but may instead give the employee a standing statement of fixed deductions, in which case the employer need only include the aggregate amount of the fixed deductions in each pay statement. The standing statement must be in writing, and must contain the amount of each fixed deduction, the intervals at which the deduction is to be made, and the purpose for which it is made (subs. (2)). The employer may amend the standing statement at any time by notice in writing (subs. (3)). The standing statement is valid for 12 months from the date on which it is given to the employee (subs. (5)), and must be reissued in consolidated form (taking account of any amendments) within 12 months of issue, and at intervals of not more than 12 months thereafter (subs. (4)).

Power to amend provisions about pay and standing statements

10. The Secretary of State may by order—

(a) vary the provisions of sections 8 and 9 as to the particulars which must be included in a pay statement or a standing statement of fixed deductions by adding items to, or removing items from, the particulars listed in those sections or by amending any such particulars, and

(b) vary the provisions of subsections (4) and (5) of section 9 so as to shorten or extend the periods of twelve months referred to in those subsections, or those periods as varied from time to time under this section.

This section empowers the Secretary of State to amend the provisions concerning itemised pay statements and standing statements of fixed deductions. At the time of writing no order had been made under this section, or under any of its predecessors.

Enforcement

References to industrial tribunals

11.—(1) Where an employer does not give an employee a statement as required by section 1, 4 or 8 (either because he gives him no statement or because the statement he gives does not comply with what is required), the employee may require a reference to be made to an industrial tribunal to determine what particulars ought to have been included or referred to in a statement so as to comply with the requirements of the section concerned.

(2) Where—

(a) a statement purporting to be a statement under section 1 or 4, or a pay statement or a standing statement of fixed deductions purporting to comply with section 8 or 9, has been given to an employee, and

(b) a question arises as to the particulars which ought to have been included or referred to in the statement so as to comply with the requirements of this Part,

either the employer or the employee may require the question to be referred to and determined by an industrial tribunal.

(3) For the purposes of this section—

(a) a question as to the particulars which ought to have been included in the note required by section 3 to be included in the statement under section 1 does not include any question whether the employment is, has been or will be contracted-out employment (for the purposes of Part III of the Pension Schemes Act 1993), and

(b) a question as to the particulars which ought to have been included in a pay statement or standing statement of fixed deductions does not include a question solely as to the accuracy of an amount stated in any such particulars.

(4) An industrial tribunal shall not consider a reference under this section in a case where the employment to which the reference relates has ceased unless an application requiring the reference to be made was made—

(a) before the end of the period of three months beginning with the date on which the employment ceased, or

(b) within such further period as the tribunal considers reasonable in a case where it is satisfied that it was not reasonably practicable for the application to be made before the end of that period of three months.

DEFINITIONS
"employee": s.230(1).
"employer": s.230(4).
"employment": s.230(5).

Enforcement of the provisions on written statements and itemised pay statements is by way of reference to an industrial tribunal under this section, subject to a time limit of three months from the date on which the employment ceased, or a further reasonable period where the tribunal is satisfied that it was not reasonably practicable for the application to be made within that time (subs. (4)). Where the employer has failed to provide a statement, or has provided an incomplete statement, or has failed to give proper notice of a change in the particulars, the employee may refer the matter to an industrial tribunal, which must determine what matters "ought to have been included or referred to in a statement" so as to comply with the statutory requirements (subs. (1)). Where a statement has been given but a question arises as to whether the particulars are correct, either the employer or the employee may refer the matter to a tribunal (subs. (2)), which may either confirm the particulars given or amend or replace them as the tribunal considers appropriate (see the note to s.12). It should be noted that the tribunal has no jurisdiction under this section to hear complaints that relate solely to the accuracy of an amount stated in a pay statement or standing statement (subs. (3)).

Unfortunately the construction of these provisions has been far from straightforward. The following points can be made with a reasonable degree of confidence:

(i) after some initial doubts (see in particular *Construction Industry Training Board v. Leighton* [1978] IRLR 60, E.A.T., per Kilner Brown J., and *Brown v. Stuart Scott & Co.* [1981] I.C.R. 166, E.A.T.), it is now clearly established that an industrial tribunal has jurisdiction under s.11 to amend particulars which are incorrect, in the sense that they do not accurately reflect what the parties in fact agreed upon. In *Mears v. Safecar Security* [1982] 2 All E.R. 865, the Court of Appeal held that a tribunal has jurisdiction under subs. (2) to hear complaints of inaccurate particulars, and also has the power to correct those particulars if necessary (under the provisions now contained in s.12(2));

(ii) the function of the tribunal is merely to find and declare what has been agreed between the parties, and where necessary to amend the written statement where it does not accurately reflect that agreement; the tribunal has no jurisdiction under s.11 to interpret the terms and conditions of the contract, still less to rectify the contract, that being the function of the ordinary courts: *Cuthbertson v. AML Distributors* [1975] IRLR 228, I.T. (tribunal refused to quantify what length of notice would have been "reasonable" at common law as this would have been to interpret the contract); *Construction Industry Training Board v. Leighton* [1978] IRLR 60, E.A.T. (tribunal had no jurisdiction to determine entitlement to a salary increment mentioned in the written statement); but *cf. Owens v. Multilux* [1974] IRLR 113, N.I.R.C.

(iii) where the employer has failed to provide a statement, or has provided an incomplete statement, the tribunal is empowered under subs. (1) "to determine what particulars *ought to have been included or referred to*" in the statement so as to comply with the statutory requirements. In *Mears v. Safecar Security* (above), the Court of Appeal held that in determining what particulars to include, the tribunal should first consider whether the parties had reached agreement on the matter; if not, the tribunal should consider whether, in the light of all the facts and circumstances (including the conduct of the parties subsequent to the formation of the contract), a term should be implied; controversially, Stevenson L.J. then went on to suggest, *obiter*, that in the absence of any evidence of an express or implied agreement on a particular matter, the tribunal might as a last resort have to "invent" a term on the basis of what it considers to be just and equitable in all the circumstances, in order to fulfil its statutory duty to determine what particulars ought to have been included in the statement: "... if the tribunal have not enough materials in the facts and circumstances to determine what *would* have been agreed, they must determine what *should* have been agreed ..." This unconventional approach conflicted with the normal common law rules on the implication of terms into contracts, and was subsequently disapproved in *Eagland v. British Telecommunications* [1992] IRLR 323, where the Court of Appeal held that the tribunal has no power under subs. (1) to invent a term, but may only determine what in fact has been expressly or impliedly agreed between the parties. The Court of Appeal adopted the distinction drawn by Wood P. ([1990] IRLR 328, E.A.T.) between "mandatory" and "non-mandatory" terms (see the note to s.2(1)), and Parker L.J. said that even in the case of mandatory terms, a tribunal does not have the power to impose terms on the parties which have not been agreed, except to the limited extent of implying a term which would normally be implied (in the absence of an express agreement) as one of the ordinary incidents of the employment relationship (*e.g.* a term that there must be reasonable notice).

Not reasonably practicable. For the interpretation of this phrase in unfair dismissal law, see the note to s.111.

Determination of references

12.—(1) Where, on a reference under section 11(1), an industrial tribunal determines particulars as being those which ought to have been included or referred to in a statement given under section 1 or 4, the employer shall be deemed to have given to the employee a statement in which those particulars were included, or referred to, as specified in the decision of the tribunal.

(2) On determining a reference under section 11(2) relating to a statement purporting to be a statement under section 1 or 4, an industrial tribunal may—

　(a) confirm the particulars as included or referred to in the statement given by the employer,

　(b) amend those particulars, or

　(c) substitute other particulars for them,

as the tribunal may determine to be appropriate; and the statement shall be deemed to have been given by the employer to the employee in accordance with the decision of the tribunal.

(3) Where on a reference under section 11 an industrial tribunal finds—

(a) that an employer has failed to give an employee any pay statement in accordance with section 8, or

(b) that a pay statement or standing statement of fixed deductions does not, in relation to a deduction, contain the particulars required to be included in that statement by that section or section 9,

the tribunal shall make a declaration to that effect.

(4) Where on a reference in the case of which subsection (3) applies the tribunal further finds that any unnotified deductions have been made from the pay of the employee during the period of thirteen weeks immediately preceding the date of the application for the reference (whether or not the deductions were made in breach of the contract of employment), the tribunal may order the employer to pay the employee a sum not exceeding the aggregate of the unnotified deductions so made.

(5) For the purposes of subsection (4) a deduction is an unnotified deduction if it is made without the employer giving the employee, in any pay statement or standing statement of fixed deductions, the particulars of the deduction required by section 8 or 9.

DEFINITIONS

"contract of employment": s.230(2).
"employee": s.230(1).
"employer": s.230(4).
"week": s.235(1).

GENERAL NOTE

This section sets out the powers of a tribunal on a reference under s.11. Subsection (1) applies where no written statement has been given, or the statement which has been given is incomplete; subs. (2) applies where the statement is inaccurate. In both cases, the employer will be deemed to have given the employee a statement which complies with the decision of the tribunal. See the note to s.11 above.

Where the failure relates to an itemised pay statement or standing statement of fixed deductions, the tribunal will make a declaration to that effect (subs. (3)), and in the case of an unnotified deduction (*i.e.* a deduction made otherwise than in accordance with ss.8 or 9), the tribunal may order the employer to pay the employee a sum not exceeding the total amount of any such deductions made during the 13 weeks immediately preceding the date of the application to the tribunal, whether or not those deductions were made in accordance with the employee's contract of employment (subs. (4)). This power is penal in nature, and within the overall limit the tribunal has a broad discretion as to the amount which the employer may be ordered to pay: see *Milsom v. Leicestershire County Council* [1978] IRLR 433; *Scott v. Creager* [1979] IRLR 162. These provisions are separate from the provisions in Pt. II of the Act concerning unauthorised deductions from wages, save that the aggregate of any amounts ordered by a tribunal to be paid under subs. (4) and under s.24 of the Act (complaints of unauthorised deductions) in respect of a particular deduction must not exceed the amount of that deduction: see s.26.

PART II

PROTECTION OF WAGES

Deductions by employer

Right not to suffer unauthorised deductions

13.—(1) An employer shall not make a deduction from wages of a worker employed by him unless—

(a) the deduction is required or authorised to be made by virtue of a statutory provision or a relevant provision of the worker's contract, or

(b) the worker has previously signified in writing his agreement or consent to the making of the deduction.

(2) In this section "relevant provision", in relation to a worker's contract, means a provision of the contract comprised—

(a) in one or more written terms of the contract of which the employer has given the worker a copy on an occasion prior to the employer making the deduction in question, or

(b) in one or more terms of the contract (whether express or implied and, if express, whether oral or in writing) the existence and effect, or combined effect, of which in relation to the worker the employer has notified to the worker in writing on such an occasion.

(3) Where the total amount of wages paid on any occasion by an employer to a worker employed by him is less than the total amount of the wages properly payable by him to the worker on that occasion (after deductions), the amount of the deficiency shall be treated for the purposes of this Part as a deduction made by the employer from the worker's wages on that occasion.

(4) Subsection (3) does not apply in so far as the deficiency is attributable to an error of any description on the part of the employer affecting the computation by him of the gross amount of the wages properly payable by him to the worker on that occasion.

(5) For the purposes of this section a relevant provision of a worker's contract having effect by virtue of a variation of the contract does not operate to authorise the making of a deduction on account of any conduct of the worker, or any other event occurring, before the variation took effect.

(6) For the purposes of this section an agreement or consent signified by a worker does not operate to authorise the making of a deduction on account of any conduct of the worker, or any other event occurring, before the agreement or consent was signified.

(7) This section does not affect any other statutory provision by virtue of which a sum payable to a worker by his employer but not constituting "wages" within the meaning of this Part is not to be subject to a deduction at the instance of the employer.

DEFINITIONS
  "employed": s.230(5).
  "employer": s.230(4).
  "relevant provision": subs. (2).
  "statutory provision": s.235(1).
  "wages": s.27(1).
  "worker": s.230(3).

GENERAL NOTE
  This Part of the Act contains the restrictions on deductions from wages which were originally introduced by Pt. I of the Wages Act 1986 (c. 48). The Wages Act repealed the restrictions on deductions from wages previously imposed by the Truck Acts 1831–1940, which had proved to be unsatisfactory in several respects, not least in the fact that they only applied to manual workers. The main impetus for the repeal of the Truck Acts was the desire to facilitate the extension of cashless pay to manual workers, previously hindered by the right of a manual worker under the Truck Act 1831 (c. 37) to be paid entirely in current coin of the Realm. However, simply repealing the Truck Acts without putting anything in their place would have removed all protection against deductions from wages, and it was widely felt that some protection was still necessary, particularly for workers in retail employment where deductions for cash or stock shortages were still commonplace, and often draconian (see for example *Bristow v. City Petroleum* [1987] 2 All E.R. 45n, H.L.; *Sealand Petroleum v. Barratt* [1986] 2 All E.R. 360). Consequently, Pt. I of the Wages Act 1986 replaced the Truck Acts provisions with a new set of restrictions on deductions from wages, applicable to all workers (as defined in s.230(3)), with additional protection for those in retail employment. One major difference between the two sets of provisions is that the current restrictions are mainly procedural, turning on whether the worker has authorised the deduction in question, whereas the restrictions in the Truck Acts were (at least in part) substantive, as the court was able to examine whether a particular deduction was fair and reasonable in all the circumstances. The protection does not apply to Parliamentary staff (ss.194(2) and 195(2)), members of the armed forces (s.192(2)), employees ordinarily working outside Great Britain (s.196(3)) or mariners (s.199(1)), but it does extend to those in Crown employment and

to police officers (s.200). For the parallel provisions which apply where an employer demands a payment from a worker instead of deducting it at source, see s.15, below.

Subs. (1)

An employer may not make a deduction from the wages of a worker employed by him unless that deduction is required or authorised to be made by statute (*e.g.* deductions of income tax or National Insurance contributions, or an attachment of earnings order), or by a "relevant provision" of the worker's contract (as defined in subs. (2)), or the worker has previously signified in writing his agreement or consent to the making of the deduction. In *Fairfield v. Skinner* [1993] IRLR 4, the E.A.T. held that even where the employer is authorised by the contract to make a particular type of deduction, the tribunal must still consider whether the employer is entitled to deduct the amount in question. In that case, the employer deducted sums from the complainant's wages under a contractual provision which authorised the making of deductions of that type, but the tribunal was not satisfied on the evidence that the sums deducted were in fact due from the complainant, and held that the contract did not authorise the employer to make the deductions in question. The E.A.T. upheld the tribunal's decision, holding that where there is a dispute as to the amount deducted, the tribunal must consider whether that particular deduction was justified on the facts of the case. This ruling is a significant limitation on the scope of an employer's authorisation to make deductions.

A deduction. The early case law on the Wages Act revealed a lamentable degree of confusion over the proper interpretation of its provisions, and in particular over the meaning of a "deduction". Diametrically opposed views were expressed by different divisions of the E.A.T. before the Court of Appeal finally settled the matter in *Delaney v. Staples (R.J.) (t/a De Montford Recruitment)* [1991] 1 All E.R. 609, [1991] IRLR 112 (upheld on other grounds: [1992] 1 All E.R. 944, [1992] IRLR 191, H.L.: see the note to s.27). The narrow interpretation, advanced by the E.A.T. in *Barlow v. A.J. Whittle (t/a Micro Management)* [1990] IRLR 79 and *Alsop v. Star Vehicle Contracts* [1990] IRLR 83, was that the statutory restrictions on deductions from wages only apply where an amount £X is due to the worker as wages, and the employer claims to be entitled to recover an amount £Y by deducting it from the amount £X. On this view, the provisions have no application in a complaint of non-payment where the employer argues that the sum claimed is not due to the worker under the contract, as such a complaint is essentially one of breach of contract and therefore within the jurisdiction of the County Court rather than the industrial tribunal. In *Barlow*, the E.A.T. held that the withholding of bonus payments to which the worker claimed to be entitled was a failure to pay, not a deduction within the meaning of the Act: "Basically, it is for the Industrial Tribunals to deal with deductions and for County Courts to deal with failures to pay" (at p.82). On a broad interpretation, however, a failure to pay does constitute a "deduction" within the meaning of the Act, even where the employer denies liability to make the payment in question. This view, preferred by the E.A.T. in *Greg May (C.F. & C.) v. Dring* [1990] IRLR 9, and in *Kournavous v. J.R. Masterson & Sons* [1990] IRLR 119, is supported by subs. (3), which provides that there is a deduction for these purposes "where the total amount of wages paid on any occasion ... is less than the total amount of the wages properly payable ... on that occasion", unless the deficiency is attributable to an error of computation (on which, see the note to subs. (4)). On this view, if there is any doubt as to what is properly payable to a worker, the Industrial Tribunal in exercising its statutory jurisdiction must resolve that doubt by determining whether the sum was in fact owed by the employer under the contract of employment. In *Delaney v. Staples,* the Court of Appeal preferred the broad approach of the E.A.T. in *Greg May* and *Kournavous,* and rejected the distinction between deductions and non-payments drawn by the E.A.T. in *Barlow* and *Alsop.* The worker therefore succeeded in claiming that the employer's failure to pay her unpaid commission and holiday pay was an unauthorised deduction from her wages, as she had not given her prior consent to any such deduction. The Court of Appeal's decision was upheld by the House of Lords, but on other grounds, there being no appeal on this point. The Court of Appeal's ruling has subsequently been applied by the E.A.T. in a wide range of situations where a disputed non-payment has been held to be a deduction: see *e.g. McCree v. Tower Hamlets London Borough Council* [1992] IRLR 56 (phasing-out of a bonus); *Bruce v. Wiggins Teape (Stationery)* [1994] IRLR 536 (withdrawal of a night shift premium); *Morgan v. West Glamorgan County Council* [1995] IRLR 68 (salary cut); and *Saavedra v. Aceground* [1995] IRLR 198 (retention of part of service charge).

There will be a deduction from wages within the meaning of the section where the amount of the deduction is such that the employer pays the worker nothing, *i.e.* a case of total non-payment. In *Kournavous v. J.R. Masterson & Sons*, above, Mayfield L.J. considered that a total non-payment was no different from a deduction of 100 per cent, and was therefore covered by the provisions; see also *Alsop v. Star Vehicle Contracts*, above. In *New Centurion Trust v. Welch* [1990] IRLR 123, it was argued on behalf of the employers that since they had claims against the worker which they were entitled to set-off against the worker's wages, and since those claims exceeded any wages which might otherwise have been due to the worker, there were in fact no wages payable to the worker from which any deduction could be made. The E.A.T. refused to accept this submission without a detailed examination of the facts, but it is submitted that the argument is fundamentally flawed, as the only reason why no wages were payable in that case was because a deduction had already been made by way of equitable set-off.

From wages. See the note to s.27.

Previously signified . . . his agreement or consent to the making of the deduction. To be valid, the worker's agreement or consent must predate the event giving rise to the deduction, not just the making of the deduction itself: *Discount Tobacco & Confectionery v. Williamson* [1993] I.C.R. 371, E.A.T. (and see the note to subs. (6)). In *Potter v. Hunt Contracts* [1992] IRLR 108, the E.A.T. refused to infer an agreement to a deduction from wages from a written undertaking by the worker to repay the outstanding balance of a loan to the employer upon leaving the company, emphasising that, to fulfil the requirement in subs. (1)(b), there must be a document signed by the worker which clearly states that the deduction is to be made from the worker's wages, and it must be clear that the worker agrees to a deduction being made from that source.

In writing. The worker must signify his or her agreement or consent to the making of the deduction in writing. In *Pename v. Paterson* [1989] IRLR 195, E.A.T., the worker was informed at his interview that if he left without giving notice he would forfeit a week's wages, and this was subsequently reiterated in the letter confirming his appointment. The E.A.T. held that as the worker had not signified his agreement *in writing* to such a deduction, the employer could not lawfully deduct the sum in question (*aliter* if the deduction was authorised by a relevant provision of the worker's contract?).

Subs. (3)

Less than the total amount of wages properly payable. In determining the amount of wages that are "properly payable" by the employer, the tribunal has jurisdiction to determine whether the worker is in fact entitled to receive the amount in question. It follows that cases of non-payment where the employer disputes the amount payable fall within the scope of the provisions: *Delaney v. Staples (R.J.) (t/a De Montford Recruitment)* [1991] 1 All E.R. 609, [1991] IRLR 112, C.A. (see the note to subs. (1)).

On any occasion. See *Murray v. Strathclyde Regional Council* [1992] IRLR 396, E.A.T.

Subs. (4)

A conscious decision not to pay, even if based on a mistaken belief as to contractual entitlement, is not an error of computation: see *Yemm v. British Steel* [1994] IRLR 117, E.A.T.; *Morgan v. West Glamorgan County Council* [1995] IRLR 68, E.A.T.

Subs. (5)

Where a contract of employment has been varied so as to authorise the making of a deduction, that variation must predate the conduct or other event on account of which the deduction was made, and must have been notified to the worker in writing before the deduction was made: see *York City and District Travel v. Smith* [1990] IRLR 213, E.A.T.

Subs. (6)

The worker's agreement to the deduction must predate the conduct or other event on account of which the deduction was made, not just the making of the deduction itself: see *Discount Tobacco v. Williamson* [1993] I.C.R. 371 (and see the note to subs. (1)).

Excepted deductions

14.—(1) Section 13 does not apply to a deduction from a worker's wages made by his employer where the purpose of the deduction is the reimbursement of the employer in respect of—

    (a) an overpayment of wages, or

    (b) an overpayment in respect of expenses incurred by the worker in carrying out his employment,

made (for any reason) by the employer to the worker.

(2) Section 13 does not apply to a deduction from a worker's wages made by his employer in consequence of any disciplinary proceedings if those proceedings were held by virtue of a statutory provision.

(3) Section 13 does not apply to a deduction from a worker's wages made by his employer in pursuance of a requirement imposed on the employer by a

statutory provision to deduct and pay over to a public authority amounts determined by that authority as being due to it from the worker if the deduction is made in accordance with the relevant determination of that authority.

(4) Section 13 does not apply to a deduction from a worker's wages made by his employer in pursuance of any arrangements which have been established—

(a) in accordance with a relevant provision of his contract to the inclusion of which in the contract the worker has signified his agreement or consent in writing, or

(b) otherwise with the prior agreement or consent of the worker signified in writing,

and under which the employer is to deduct and pay over to a third person amounts notified to the employer by that person as being due to him from the worker, if the deduction is made in accordance with the relevant notification by that person.

(5) Section 13 does not apply to a deduction from a worker's wages made by his employer where the worker has taken part in a strike or other industrial action and the deduction is made by the employer on account of the worker's having taken part in that strike or other action.

(6) Section 13 does not apply to a deduction from a worker's wages made by his employer with his prior agreement or consent signified in writing where the purpose of the deduction is the satisfaction (whether wholly or in part) of an order of a court or tribunal requiring the payment of an amount by the worker to the employer.

DEFINITIONS
"employer": s.230(4).
"statutory provision": s.235(1).
"wages": s.27(1).
"worker": s.230(3).

GENERAL NOTE
A wide range of deductions are excluded from the Act's provisions, thus enabling an employer to make such a deduction without satisfying the requirements imposed by s.13. The extent of the exclusion is however unclear. On a narrow interpretation, the exclusion only applies where the employer is lawfully entitled to make the deduction in question (the point being that the statutory provisions do not affect the legality of a deduction at common law, so that even if the statutory requirements are satisfied, a worker may still be able to argue that the employer had no right to make the deduction in the first place). In *Home Office v. Ayres* [1992] IRLR 59, E.A.T., a case involving a deduction to reimburse an overpayment of wages, the E.A.T. held that subs. (1) only allows an employer to make such a deduction where the reimbursement is of monies to which the employer is lawfully entitled, in the sense that the employer could successfully recover them in a court of law. On this interpretation, if a common law claim for reimbursement by the employer would be defeated, *e.g.* by a defence of estoppel or change of position (on which see *Lipkin Gorman v. Karpnale* [1991] A.C. 548, H.L.), the worker can argue that the deduction was unlawful at common law and therefore not covered by the statutory exclusion, so that the employer must comply with the s.13 requirements. In *Ayres*, the worker successfully argued before the tribunal that the employer had no right to recover the overpayment because the worker had innocently spent the money on normal living expenses. The exclusion did not therefore apply, and in the absence of prior written consent, the worker could recover the deduction under the statutory provisions.

On a broad interpretation, however, the exclusion applies whenever a deduction is made for one of the stated purposes, irrespective of whether that deduction was one which the employer was entitled to make at common law. In *Sunderland Polytechnic v. Evans* [1993] IRLR 196, E.A.T., a case involving a deduction for taking part in industrial action, the E.A.T. held, exercising its power to look at *Hansard* (following *Pepper v. Hart* [1993] A.C. 593) that Parliament's intention in enacting the exceptions in s.14 was that they were to be applied literally, and that any issue as to the lawfulness of a deduction at common law was a matter for the ordinary courts to determine. This ruling was subsequently applied in a case under subs. (1) by the E.A.T. in *S.I.P. Industrial Products v. Swinn* [1994] IRLR 323, placing the correctness of the earlier decision in *Ayres* in doubt.

Subs. (1)

See *Home Office v. Ayres* [1992] IRLR 59, E.A.T., and *S.I.P. Industrial Products v. Swinn* [1994] IRLR 323, discussed above.

Subs. (2)

In *Chiltern House v. Chambers* [1990] IRLR 88, E.A.T., it was suggested by Wood P., *obiter*, that this exception probably refers to certain disciplined services such as the police and fire service, not to private employment.

Subs. (3)

This exception covers, *e.g.* deductions of unpaid tax, and payments in response to an attachment of earnings order.

Subs. (4)

This exception covers, *e.g.* the deduction of pension contributions and the check-off of union subscriptions (although *cf.* the Trade Union and Labour Relations (Consolidation) Act 1992 (c. 52), s.68, as amended by TURERA 1993, which requires the authorisation of check-off arrangements to be renewed periodically).

Subs. (5)

Strike or other industrial action. There is no statutory definition of "strike" or "industrial action" here; for the interpretation of "strike" for the purposes of continuity of employment, see the note to s.235. For the interpretation of these terms in the context of unfair dismissal law, see the case law under the Trade Union and Labour Relations (Consolidation) Act 1992 (c. 52), ss.237 and 238. In *Sunderland Polytechnic v. Evans* [1993] IRLR 196, the E.A.T. held that this provision excludes any deduction made on account of the worker's participation in a strike or other industrial action, whether or not the deduction is lawful at common law (see the General Note, above). On the legality at common law of a deduction for taking part in a strike or other industrial action, see *Sweet and Maxwell's Encyclopedia of Employment Law*, para. 1·8403.

Payments to employer

Right not to have to make payments to employer

15.—(1) An employer shall not receive a payment from a worker employed by him unless—

(a) the payment is required or authorised to be made by virtue of a statutory provision or a relevant provision of the worker's contract, or

(b) the worker has previously signified in writing his agreement or consent to the making of the payment.

(2) In this section "relevant provision", in relation to a worker's contract, means a provision of the contract comprised—

(a) in one or more written terms of the contract of which the employer has given the worker a copy on an occasion prior to the employer receiving the payment in question, or

(b) in one or more terms of the contract (whether express or implied and, if express, whether oral or in writing) the existence and effect, or combined effect, of which in relation to the worker the employer has notified to the worker in writing on such an occasion.

(3) For the purposes of this section a relevant provision of a worker's contract having effect by virtue of a variation of the contract does not operate to authorise the receipt of a payment on account of any conduct of the worker, or any other event occurring, before the variation took effect.

(4) For the purposes of this section an agreement or consent signified by a worker does not operate to authorise the receipt of a payment on account of any conduct of the worker, or any other event occurring, before the agreement or consent was signified.

(5) Any reference in this Part to an employer receiving a payment from a worker employed by him is a reference to his receiving such a payment in his capacity as the worker's employer.

DEFINITIONS
　"employed": s.230(5).
　"employer": s.230(4).
　"relevant provision": subs. (2).
　"statutory provision": s.235(1).
　"wages": s.27(1).
　"worker": s.230(3).

GENERAL NOTE
　This section gives a worker the right not to have to make a payment to his or her employer. The provisions mirror those which apply in the case of deductions: see the note to s.13, above.

Excepted payments

16.—(1) Section 15 does not apply to a payment received from a worker by his employer where the purpose of the payment is the reimbursement of the employer in respect of—

(a)　an overpayment of wages, or

(b)　an overpayment in respect of expenses incurred by the worker in carrying out his employment,

made (for any reason) by the employer to the worker.

(2) Section 15 does not apply to a payment received from a worker by his employer in consequence of any disciplinary proceedings if those proceedings were held by virtue of a statutory provision.

(3) Section 15 does not apply to a payment received from a worker by his employer where the worker has taken part in a strike or other industrial action and the payment has been required by the employer on account of the worker's having taken part in that strike or other action.

(4) Section 15 does not apply to a payment received from a worker by his employer where the purpose of the payment is the satisfaction (whether wholly or in part) of an order of a court or tribunal requiring the payment of an amount by the worker to the employer.

DEFINITIONS
　"employer": s.230(4).
　"statutory provision": s.235(1).
　"wages": s.27(1).
　"worker": s.230(3).

GENERAL NOTE
　This section contains a number of exceptions to the right not to have to make a payment to the employer. The exceptions mirror those which apply in the case of deductions: see the note to s.14, above.

Cash shortages and stock deficiencies in retail employment

Introductory

17.—(1) In the following provisions of this Part—

"cash shortage" means a deficit arising in relation to amounts received in connection with retail transactions, and

"stock deficiency" means a stock deficiency arising in the course of retail transactions.

(2) In the following provisions of this Part "retail employment", in relation to a worker, means employment involving (whether or not on a regular basis)—

(a)　the carrying out by the worker of retail transactions directly with members of the public or with fellow workers or other individuals in their personal capacities, or

(b)　the collection by the worker of amounts payable in connection with retail transactions carried out by other persons directly with members of the public or with fellow workers or other individuals in their personal capacities.

(3) References in this section to a "retail transaction" are to the sale or supply of goods or the supply of services (including financial services).

(4) References in the following provisions of this Part to a deduction made from wages of a worker in retail employment, or to a payment received from such a worker by his employer, on account of a cash shortage or stock deficiency include references to a deduction or payment so made or received on account of—

(a) any dishonesty or other conduct on the part of the worker which resulted in any such shortage or deficiency, or

(b) any other event in respect of which he (whether or not together with any other workers) has any contractual liability and which so resulted,

in each case whether or not the amount of the deduction or payment is designed to reflect the exact amount of the shortage or deficiency.

(5) References in the following provisions of this Part to the recovery from a worker of an amount in respect of a cash shortage or stock deficiency accordingly include references to the recovery from him of an amount in respect of any such conduct or event as is mentioned in subsection (4)(a) or (b).

(6) In the following provisions of this Part "pay day", in relation to a worker, means a day on which wages are payable to the worker.

DEFINITIONS
  "cash shortage": subs. (1).
  "employer": s.230(4).
  "employment": s.230(5).
  "pay day": subs. (6).
  "retail employment": subs. (2).
  "retail transaction": subs. (3).
  "stock deficiency": subs. (1).
  "wages": s.27(1).
  "worker": s.230(3).

GENERAL NOTE

Sections 17–22 give special protection to workers in retail employment where an employer makes a deduction or receives a payment in respect of a cash shortage or stock deficiency. These provisions are additional to the requirements of ss.13 and 15, which must also be complied with. The gist of the additional provisions is that where an employer makes a deduction from the wages of a worker in retail employment on account of cash shortages or stock deficiencies, the amount deducted must not exceed one-tenth of the gross amount of wages payable on a pay day (s.18(1)). Deductions may however be made in instalments over successive pay days, as long as no more than 10 per cent is deducted on each pay day, and the first deduction is made within 12 months of the discovery of the shortage or deficiency, or within 12 months of the date when it ought to have been discovered (s.18(2)); and any amount still outstanding on a worker's final pay day may be deducted at that time (s.22(2)). Demands for payment are subject to similar limitations (s.20(3); s.21), but with the additional requirements that the demand must be made in writing on one of the worker's pay days (s.20(2)), and the employer must notify the worker in writing of his or her total liability in respect of the shortage or deficiency (s.20(1)).

This additional protection was included in the Wages Act 1986 (c. 48) because of widespread concern that the procedural requirements applicable to deductions generally would provide insufficient protection against unreasonable deductions for those in retail employment, where terms entitling the employer to make deductions for stock shortages or cash deficiencies occurring during a worker's shift, whether or not caused by the neglect or default of that worker, were (and still are) commonplace. The protection is however of limited effect. It only applies to retail workers, and to deductions and payments on account of cash shortages and stock deficiencies. Deductions and payments for other reasons, *e.g.* misconduct, dishonesty, poor workmanship or absenteeism, are not covered (subject to subs. (4)), and may therefore be made without limit. Moreover, the protection only affords a temporary stay of execution, as the employer may recover the full amount claimed in instalments, or from the worker's final instalment of wages, and there is no requirement that the total amount deducted be fair and reasonable in all the circumstances. In this respect, at least, the present protection compares unfavourably with that previously afforded by the Truck Act 1896 (c. 44), s.1: see *Sealand Petroleum Co. v. Barratt* [1986] 2 All E.R. 360; *Bristow v. City Petroleum* [1987] 2 All E.R. 45n, H.L.

Subs. (4)

The special protection applies whether or not the amount of the deduction or payment reflects the exact amount of the shortage or deficiency in question. A fine which does not reflect the actual amount of the shortage or deficiency is therefore covered by these provisions.

Subs. (6)

Pay day. The relevant day is the day on which wages are payable, not the day on which they are in fact paid.

Limits on amount and time of deductions

18.—(1) Where (in accordance with section 13) the employer of a worker in retail employment makes, on account of one or more cash shortages or stock deficiencies, a deduction or deductions from wages payable to the worker on a pay day, the amount or aggregate amount of the deduction or deductions shall not exceed one-tenth of the gross amount of the wages payable to the worker on that day.

(2) Where the employer of a worker in retail employment makes a deduction from the worker's wages on account of a cash shortage or stock deficiency, the employer shall not be treated as making the deduction in accordance with section 13 unless (in addition to the requirements of that section being satisfied with respect to the deduction)—

   (a) the deduction is made, or
   (b) in the case of a deduction which is one of a series of deductions relating to the shortage or deficiency, the first deduction in the series was made,

not later than the end of the relevant period.

(3) In subsection (2) "the relevant period" means the period of twelve months beginning with the date when the employer established the existence of the shortage or deficiency or (if earlier) the date when he ought reasonably to have done so.

DEFINITIONS

   "cash shortage": s.17(1).
   "employer": s.230(4).
   "gross amount": s.27(4).
   "pay day": s.17(6).
   "the relevant period": subs. (3).
   "retail employment": s.17(2).
   "stock deficiency": s.17(1).
   "wages": s.27(1).
   "worker": s.230(3).

GENERAL NOTE

This section provides that where an employer makes a deduction from the wages of a worker in retail employment on account of cash shortages or stock deficiencies, the amount deducted must not exceed one-tenth of the gross amount of wages payable on any one pay day (subs. (1)), and the employer must make the deduction (or the first deduction, as the case may be) within 12 months of discovering the shortage or deficiency (s.18(2), (3)). See also the note to s.22 (final instalment of wages). These requirements are additional to the provisions of s.13, which must also be complied with.

For the background to the provisions concerning deductions on account of cash shortages and stock deficiencies, see the note to s.17.

Gross amount of the wages payable. This means the total amount of wages payable, before any deductions of whatever nature: see the note to s.27(4).

Subs. (3)

The limitation period of 12 months was chosen in order to prevent employers from dredging up old events in respect of which memories may have become blurred, while still allowing a sufficient time for cash shortages or stock deficiencies to be discovered in an annual stock-taking.

Wages determined by reference to shortages etc.

19.—(1) This section applies where—

(a) by virtue of an agreement between a worker in retail employment and his employer, the amount of the worker's wages or any part of them is or may be determined by reference to the incidence of cash shortages or stock deficiencies, and

(b) the gross amount of the wages payable to the worker on any pay day is, on account of any such shortages or deficiencies, less than the gross amount of the wages that would have been payable to him on that day if there had been no such shortages or deficiencies.

(2) The amount representing the difference between the two amounts referred to in subsection (1)(b) shall be treated for the purposes of this Part as a deduction from the wages payable to the worker on that day made by the employer on account of the cash shortages or stock deficiencies in question.

(3) The second of the amounts referred to in subsection (1)(b) shall be treated for the purposes of this Part (except subsection (1)) as the gross amount of the wages payable to him on that day.

(4) Accordingly—

(a) section 13, and

(b) if the requirements of section 13 and subsection (2) of section 18 are satisfied, subsection (1) of section 18,

have effect in relation to the amount referred to in subsection (2) of this section.

DEFINITIONS

"cash shortage": s.17(1).
"employer": s.230(4).
"gross amount": s.27(4).
"pay day": s.17(6).
"retail employment": s.17(2).
"stock deficiency": s.17(1).
"wages": s.27(1).
"worker": s.230(3).

GENERAL NOTE

This section prevents the 10 per cent limit on deductions from being circumvented in circumstances where a cash shortage or stock deficiency is taken into account in calculating a worker's pay in the first place, rather than being deducted from an already-fixed amount. So, for example, if an employer pays retail workers a basic rate which takes account of likely cash shortages or stock deficiencies, but with an additional bonus payment if there are no such shortages or deficiencies, the worker's gross wages will be deemed to be the amount which he or she would have received, had there been no shortages or deficiencies. The difference between the amount actually received and the amount which would have been received had there been no shortages or deficiencies will be treated as a deduction, and therefore subject to the requirements of s.13, and will also be subject to the 10 per cent limit imposed by s.18.

Limits on method and timing of payments

20.—(1) Where the employer of a worker in retail employment receives from the worker a payment on account of a cash shortage or stock deficiency, the employer shall not be treated as receiving the payment in accordance with section 15 unless (in addition to the requirements of that section being satisfied with respect to the payment) he has previously—

(a) notified the worker in writing of the worker's total liability to him in respect of that shortage or deficiency, and

(b) required the worker to make the payment by means of a demand for payment made in accordance with the following provisions of this section.

(2) A demand for payment made by the employer of a worker in retail employment in respect of a cash shortage or stock deficiency—

(a) shall be made in writing, and

(b) shall be made on one of the worker's pay days.

(3) A demand for payment in respect of a particular cash shortage or stock deficiency, or (in the case of a series of such demands) the first such demand, shall not be made—

(a) earlier than the first pay day of the worker following the date when he is notified of his total liability in respect of the shortage or deficiency in pursuance of subsection (1)(a) or, where he is so notified on a pay day, earlier than that day, or

(b) later than the end of the period of twelve months beginning with the date when the employer established the existence of the shortage or deficiency or (if earlier) the date when he ought reasonably to have done so.

(4) For the purposes of this Part a demand for payment shall be treated as made by the employer on one of a worker's pay days if it is given to the worker or posted to, or left at, his last known address—

(a) on that pay day, or

(b) in the case of a pay day which is not a working day of the employer's business, on the first such working day following that pay day.

(5) Legal proceedings by the employer of a worker in retail employment for the recovery from the worker of an amount in respect of a cash shortage or stock deficiency shall not be instituted by the employer after the end of the period referred to in subsection (3)(b) unless the employer has within that period made a demand for payment in respect of that amount in accordance with this section.

DEFINITIONS

"cash shortage": s.17(1).
"employer": s.230(4).
"gross amount": s.27(4).
"pay day": s.17(6).
"retail employment": s.17(2).
"stock deficiency": s.17(1).
"wages": s.27(1).
"worker": s.230(3).

GENERAL NOTE

This section gives special protection to retail workers where an employer makes a demand for payment on account of cash shortages or stock deficiencies, rather than deducting it at source. As with deductions, the demand for payment must be made within 12 months of the discovery of the shortage or deficiency, or within 12 months of the date when it ought to have been discovered (subs. (3)(b)), and the total amount of the payment must not exceed one-tenth of the gross amount of wages payable on a pay day (see the note to s.21). There is a 12 month limitation period on the institution of proceedings to recover such sums, unless the employer has made a demand for payment within that period (subs. (5)). In addition, the demand must be made in writing on one of the worker's pay days (subs. (2)), and the employer must have notified the worker in writing of his or her total liability in respect of the shortage or deficiency (s.20(1)), before any demand for payment is made (subs. (3)(a)). These requirements are additional to the provisions of s.15, which must also be complied with.

For the background to the provisions concerning demands for payment on account of cash shortages and stock deficiencies, see the note to s.17.

Limit on amount of payments

21.—(1) Where the employer of a worker in retail employment makes on any pay day one or more demands for payment in accordance with section 20, the amount or aggregate amount required to be paid by the worker in pursuance of the demand or demands shall not exceed—

(a) one-tenth of the gross amount of the wages payable to the worker on that day, or

(b) where one or more deductions falling within section 18(1) are made by the employer from those wages, such amount as represents the balance of that one-tenth after subtracting the amount or aggregate amount of the deduction or deductions.

(2) Once an amount has been required to be paid by means of a demand for payment made in accordance with section 20 on any pay day, that amount shall not be taken into account under subsection (1) as it applies to any subsequent pay day, even though the employer is obliged to make further requests for it to be paid.

(3) Where in any legal proceedings the court finds that the employer of a worker in retail employment is (in accordance with section 15 as it applies apart from section 20(1)) entitled to recover an amount from the worker in respect of a cash shortage or stock deficiency, the court shall, in ordering the payment by the worker to the employer of that amount, make such provision as appears to the court to be necessary to ensure that it is paid by the worker at a rate not exceeding that at which it could be recovered from him by the employer in accordance with this section.

DEFINITIONS
     "cash shortage": s.17(1).
     "employer": s.230(4).
     "gross amount": s.27(4).
     "pay day": s.17(6).
     "retail employment": s.17(2).
     "stock deficiency": s.17(1).
     "wages": s.27(1).
     "worker": s.230(3).

GENERAL NOTE
     The total amount of a demand for payment on account of cash shortages or stock deficiencies must not exceed one-tenth of the gross amount of wages payable on any pay day (subs. (1)(a)). Where the employer makes a deduction for cash shortages or stock deficiencies on the same pay day as a demand for payment, the total amount of those deductions and payments must not exceed the 10 per cent limit (subs. (1)(b)). If however the employer has made a demand for payment which has not been met, that demand will not count against the 10 per cent limit for any subsequent pay day, even if the employer makes a further request for payment (subs. (2)). See also the note to s.22 (final instalment of wages).

Final instalments of wages

22.—(1) In this section "final instalment of wages", in relation to a worker, means—

(a) the amount of wages payable to the worker which consists of or includes an amount payable by way of contractual remuneration in respect of the last of the periods for which he is employed under his contract prior to its termination for any reason (but excluding any wages referable to any earlier such period), or

(b) where an amount in lieu of notice is paid to the worker later than the amount referred to in paragraph (a), the amount so paid,

in each case whether the amount in question is paid before or after the termination of the worker's contract.

(2) Section 18(1) does not operate to restrict the amount of any deductions which may (in accordance with section 13(1)) be made by the employer of a worker in retail employment from the worker's final instalment of wages.

(3) Nothing in section 20 or 21 applies to a payment falling within section 20(1) which is made on or after the day on which any such worker's final instalment of wages is paid; but (even if the requirements of section 15 would otherwise be satisfied with respect to it) his employer shall not be treated as receiving any such payment in accordance with that section if the payment

was first required to be made after the end of the period referred to in section 20(3)(b).

(4) Section 21(3) does not apply to an amount which is to be paid by a worker on or after the day on which his final instalment of wages is paid.

"employer": s.230(4).
"final instalment of wages": subs. (1).
"retail employment": s.17(2).
"wages": s.27(1).
"worker": s.230(3).

GENERAL NOTE
This section provides that the 10 per cent limit on deductions and demands for payment in respect of cash shortages and stock deficiencies does not apply to the final instalment of wages due to a worker on the termination of employment. Note however that the usual 12 month time-limit on the making of deductions or demands for payment in respect of cash shortages or stock deficiencies continues to apply, so that an employer may not make a deduction or demand a payment on a worker's final instalment of wages in respect of a shortage or deficiency which was discovered or ought to have been discovered more than 12 months before the final instalment is paid. Any deduction or demand for payment on a worker's final instalment of wages remains subject to the general requirements of ss.13 and 15.

For the background to the provisions concerning deductions and demands for payment on account of cash shortages and stock deficiencies, see the note to s.17.

Enforcement

Complaints to industrial tribunals

23.—(1) A worker may present a complaint to an industrial tribunal—
(a) that his employer has made a deduction from his wages in contravention of section 13 (including a deduction made in contravention of that section as it applies by virtue of section 18(2)),
(b) that his employer has received from him a payment in contravention of section 15 (including a payment received in contravention of that section as it applies by virtue of section 20(1)),
(c) that his employer has recovered from his wages by means of one or more deductions falling within section 18(1) an amount or aggregate amount exceeding the limit applying to the deduction or deductions under that provision, or
(d) that his employer has received from him in pursuance of one or more demands for payment made (in accordance with section 20) on a particular pay day, a payment or payments of an amount or aggregate amount exceeding the limit applying to the demand or demands under section 21(1).

(2) Subject to subsection (4), an industrial tribunal shall not consider a complaint under this section unless it is presented before the end of the period of three months beginning with—
(a) in the case of a complaint relating to a deduction by the employer, the date of payment of the wages from which the deduction was made, or
(b) in the case of a complaint relating to a payment received by the employer, the date when the payment was received.

(3) Where a complaint is brought under this section in respect of—
(a) a series of deductions or payments, or
(b) a number of payments falling within subsection (1)(d) and made in pursuance of demands for payment subject to the same limit under section 21(1) but received by the employer on different dates,
the references in subsection (2) to the deduction or payment are to the last deduction or payment in the series or to the last of the payments so received.

(4) Where the industrial tribunal is satisfied that it was not reasonably practicable for a complaint under this section to be presented before the end

of the relevant period of three months, the tribunal may consider the complaint if it is presented within such further period as the tribunal considers reasonable.

<small>DEFINITIONS</small>
    "employer": s.230(4).
    "pay day": s.17(6).
    "wages": s.27(1).
    "worker": s.230(3).

<small>GENERAL NOTE</small>
The remedy for an infringement of the provisions on deductions or demands for payment is by way of complaint to an industrial tribunal (subs. (1)), subject to a time limit of three months beginning with the date of the deduction or payment complained of (subs. (2)), or, in the case of a series of deductions or payments, the date of the last deduction or payment (subs. (3)). The time limit may be extended by a further reasonable period if the tribunal is satisfied that it was not reasonably practicable for the complaint to be presented within that time (subs. (4)). The time-limit only relates to the presentation of complaints; it does not place a temporal limit on the tribunal's power to order the repayment of deductions or payments which contravene the statutory provisions: see *Reid v. Camphill Engravers* [1990] IRLR 268, E.A.T.

The remedy for any contravention of the statutory provisions on deductions or demands for payment is by way of complaint under this section: see s.205(2). This does not however affect the common law right of a worker to bring proceedings in the ordinary courts for wages due under the contract of employment where a deduction is made in breach of contract: see *Rickard v. P.B. Glass Supplies* [1990] I.C.R. 150, C.A.

Has received ... a payment. The right to complain of a demand for payment which does not comply with the statutory requirements only arises where the employer has received a payment from the worker in contravention of those requirements; there is no right to complain where the employer has made a demand for payment but where no payment has in fact been made.

Not reasonably practicable. For the interpretation of this phrase in unfair dismissal law, see the note to s.111.

Determination of complaints

24. Where a tribunal finds a complaint under section 23 well-founded, it shall make a declaration to that effect and shall order the employer—
    (a) in the case of a complaint under section 23(1)(a), to pay to the worker the amount of any deduction made in contravention of section 13,
    (b) in the case of a complaint under section 23(1)(b), to repay to the worker the amount of any payment received in contravention of section 15,
    (c) in the case of a complaint under section 23(1)(c), to pay to the worker any amount recovered from him in excess of the limit mentioned in that provision, and
    (d) in the case of a complaint under section 23(1)(d), to repay to the worker any amount received from him in excess of the limit mentioned in that provision.

<small>DEFINITIONS</small>
    "employer": s.230(4).
    "worker": s.230(3).

<small>GENERAL NOTE</small>
If the tribunal finds a complaint under s.23 to be well-founded, it must make declaration to that effect, and must order the employer to repay any deduction or payment received in breach of the statutory provisions. Where the complaint is of a deduction or payment in excess of the 10 per cent limit which applies in the case of retail workers, the tribunal may only order repayment of the amount received in excess of that 10 per cent limit. There is no provision for compensation for consequential loss.

These remedies compare unfavourably with those available under the Truck Acts, which could give rise to criminal liability (although prosecutions were rare), and were enforceable by the Wages Inspectorate. There is however a sting in the tail, in that once an employer has been ordered under this section to repay an amount which has been improperly received, the right to recover that amount is lost altogether by virtue of s.25(4) and (5), irrespective of any right which the employer might have to it under the contract, so that the employer will be unable to recover it by an ordinary common law action: see *Potter v. Hunt Contracts* [1992] IRLR 108, E.A.T.

Determinations: supplementary

25.—(1) Where, in the case of any complaint under section 23(1)(a), a tribunal finds that, although neither of the conditions set out in section 13(1)(a) and (b) was satisfied with respect to the whole amount of the deduction, one of those conditions was satisfied with respect to any lesser amount, the amount of the deduction shall for the purposes of section 24(a) be treated as reduced by the amount with respect to which that condition was satisfied.

(2) Where, in the case of any complaint under section 23(1)(b), a tribunal finds that, although neither of the conditions set out in section 15(1)(a) and (b) was satisfied with respect to the whole amount of the payment, one of those conditions was satisfied with respect to any lesser amount, the amount of the payment shall for the purposes of section 24(b) be treated as reduced by the amount with respect to which that condition was satisfied.

(3) An employer shall not under section 24 be ordered by a tribunal to pay or repay to a worker any amount in respect of a deduction or payment, or in respect of any combination of deductions or payments, in so far as it appears to the tribunal that he has already paid or repaid any such amount to the worker.

(4) Where a tribunal has under section 24 ordered an employer to pay or repay to a worker any amount in respect of a particular deduction or payment falling within section 23(1)(a) to (d), the amount which the employer is entitled to recover (by whatever means) in respect of the matter in relation to which the deduction or payment was originally made or received shall be treated as reduced by that amount.

(5) Where a tribunal has under section 24 ordered an employer to pay or repay to a worker any amount in respect of any combination of deductions or payments falling within section 23(1)(c) or (d), the aggregate amount which the employer is entitled to recover (by whatever means) in respect of the cash shortages or stock deficiencies in relation to which the deductions or payments were originally made or required to be made shall be treated as reduced by that amount.

DEFINITIONS
"employer": s.230(4).
"worker": s.230(3).

GENERAL NOTE

Subss. (4), (5)
See the note to s.24.

Complaints and other remedies

26. Section 23 does not affect the jurisdiction of an industrial tribunal to consider a reference under section 11 in relation to any deduction from the wages of a worker; but the aggregate of any amounts ordered by an industrial tribunal to be paid under section 12(4) and under section 24 (whether on the same or different occasions) in respect of a particular deduction shall not exceed the amount of the deduction.

DEFINITIONS
"wages": s.27(1).
"worker": s.230(3).

GENERAL NOTE
Under s.12(4) of the Act, where a tribunal finds that an employer has made any unnotified deductions from an employee's pay (*i.e.* deductions which have not been specified in a pay state-

ment or a standing statement of fixed deductions, in accordance with ss.8 or 9), the tribunal may order the employer to repay the total amount of any such deductions made during the preceding 13 weeks, whether or not those deductions were made in accordance with the employee's contract of employment. This section prevents double recovery, by providing that where an order has been made under s.12(4), the aggregate of any amounts ordered to be paid under that section and under s.24 in respect of a particular deduction must not exceed the amount of that deduction.

Supplementary

Meaning of "wages" etc.

27.—(1) In this Part "wages", in relation to a worker, means any sums payable to the worker in connection with his employment, including—

(a) any fee, bonus, commission, holiday pay or other emolument referable to his employment, whether payable under his contract or otherwise,

(b) statutory sick pay under Part XI of the Social Security Contributions and Benefits Act 1992,

(c) statutory maternity pay under Part XII of that Act,

(d) a guarantee payment (under section 28 of this Act),

(e) any payment for time off under Part VI of this Act or section 169 of the Trade Union and Labour Relations (Consolidation) Act 1992 (payment for time off for carrying out trade union duties etc.),

(f) remuneration on suspension on medical grounds under section 64 of this Act and remuneration on suspension on maternity grounds under section 68 of this Act,

(g) any sum payable in pursuance of an order for reinstatement or re-engagement under section 113 of this Act,

(h) any sum payable in pursuance of an order for the continuation of a contract of employment under section 130 of this Act or section 164 of the Trade Union and Labour Relations (Consolidation) Act 1992, and

(j) remuneration under a protective award under section 189 of that Act,

but excluding any payments within subsection (2).

(2) Those payments are—

(a) any payment by way of an advance under an agreement for a loan or by way of an advance of wages (but without prejudice to the application of section 13 to any deduction made from the worker's wages in respect of any such advance),

(b) any payment in respect of expenses incurred by the worker in carrying out his employment,

(c) any payment by way of a pension, allowance or gratuity in connection with the worker's retirement or as compensation for loss of office,

(d) any payment referable to the worker's redundancy, and

(e) any payment to the worker otherwise than in his capacity as a worker.

(3) Where any payment in the nature of a non-contractual bonus is (for any reason) made to a worker by his employer, the amount of the payment shall for the purposes of this Part—

(a) be treated as wages of the worker, and

(b) be treated as payable to him as such on the day on which the payment is made.

(4) In this Part "gross amount", in relation to any wages payable to a worker, means the total amount of those wages before deductions of whatever nature.

(5) For the purposes of this Part any monetary value attaching to any payment or benefit in kind furnished to a worker by his employer shall not be treated as wages of the worker except in the case of any voucher, stamp or similar document which is—

(a) of a fixed value expressed in monetary terms, and

(b) capable of being exchanged (whether on its own or together with other vouchers, stamps or documents, and whether immediately or only after a time) for money, goods or services (or for any combination of two or more of those things).

DEFINITIONS

"employer": s.230(4).
"employment": s.230(5).
"gross amount": subs. (4).
"wages": subs. (1).
"worker": s.230(3).

GENERAL NOTE

Any sums payable to the worker in connection with his employment. "Wages" are widely defined for present purposes as "any sums payable to the worker in connection with his employment". The payments listed in subs. (1) are specifically identified as being included within the definition, while those in subs. (2) are specifically excluded. Also excluded are payments or benefits in kind, unless falling within subs. (5).

One type of sum which is not specifically mentioned is a payment of wages in lieu of notice. In *Delaney v. Staples (R.J.) (t/a De Montford Recruitment)* [1992] 1 All E.R. 944, [1992] IRLR 191, the House of Lords held that a payment of wages in lieu of notice (*i.e.* where the employer terminates the contract without notice and makes a payment to the worker as damages for breach of contract), is not "wages" within the meaning of the section, as it is a sum payable not in connection with employment but in connection with the termination of employment. In adopting this narrow interpretation, the House of Lords in effect approved the earlier decisions of the E.A.T. in *Delaney* (see [1990] IRLR 86) and in *Jackson v. Foster Wheeler (London)* [1990] IRLR 412, and disapproved the decisions in *Kournavous v. J.R. Masterson & Sons* [1990] IRLR 119, and in *Janstorp International (U.K.) v. Allen* [1990] IRLR 417, where the E.A.T. had held that, notwithstanding the fact that at common law a payment in lieu of notice is characterised as damages for wrongful dismissal rather than wages, on a literal interpretation of subs. (1), pay in lieu of notice is a sum payable to a worker "in connection with his employment", and therefore falls within the statutory definition of wages. The result of the decision in *Delaney* is that an employer can withhold some or all of a payment in lieu of notice without the need to comply with the requirements of this Part of the Act.

In the House of Lords in *Delaney*, Browne-Wilkinson L.J. considered that the definition of wages was in principle wide enough to include a payment in lieu of notice made in connection with the termination of employment, but he considered that the provisions would be unworkable if all such payments were included within the meaning of wages. Lord Browne-Wilkinson was however careful to distinguish between payments in lieu relating to the termination of employment, which were held to fall outside the statutory definition of wages because such a payment is not a payment of wages in the ordinary sense (*i.e.* a payment for services rendered under a contract of employment), and payments in respect of "garden leave", which he characterised as advance payments of wages falling due under a subsisting contract of employment, and which therefore fall within the statutory definition of wages.

Whether payable under his contract or otherwise. This has been held to include non-payment of an *ex gratia* payment of commission where the payment was within the reasonable contemplation of the parties as being payable: see *Kent Management Services v. Butterfield* [1992] IRLR 394, E.A.T.

PART III

GUARANTEE PAYMENTS

Right to guarantee payment

28.—(1) Where throughout a day during any part of which an employee would normally be required to work in accordance with his contract of employment the employee is not provided with work by his employer by reason of—

(a) a diminution in the requirements of the employer's business for work of the kind which the employee is employed to do, or

(b) any other occurrence affecting the normal working of the employer's business in relation to work of the kind which the employee is employed to do,

the employee is entitled to be paid by his employer an amount in respect of that day.

(2) In this Act a payment to which an employee is entitled under subsection (1) is referred to as a guarantee payment.

(3) In this Part—

(a) a day falling within subsection (1) is referred to as a "workless day", and

(b) "workless period" has a corresponding meaning.

(4) In this Part "day" means the period of twenty-four hours from midnight to midnight.

(5) Where a period of employment begun on any day extends, or would normally extend, over midnight into the following day—

(a) if the employment before midnight is, or would normally be, of longer duration than that after midnight, the period of employment shall be treated as falling wholly on the first day, and

(b) in any other case, the period of employment shall be treated as falling wholly on the second day.

DEFINITIONS

"contract of employment": s.230(2).
"day": subs. (4).
"employee": s.230(1).
"employer": s.230(4).
"employment": s.230(5).
"guarantee payment": subs. (2).
"workless day": subs. (3).
"workless period": subs. (3).

GENERAL NOTE

Part III of the Act contains a set of provisions which are intended to give a limited degree of financial protection to an employee who is laid off by his or her employer without pay or on reduced pay, by providing that for a specified period and in specified circumstances the employee is entitled to receive a statutory guarantee payment from the employer for each workless day. These provisions were introduced by the Employment Protection Act 1975 (c. 71) as part of a statutory "floor of rights". The entitlements are modest: statutory guarantee payments may be claimed for a maximum of five workless days in any three month period, and the amount payable is subject to a limit of only £14.50 per day. Many employees are covered by collectively-negotiated guaranteed week agreements, which guarantee a minimum weekly level of income during lay-off or short-time working. Such arrangements are particularly important for hourly-paid workers and those paid according to output, who are more likely to be adversely affected by temporary unavailability of work than salaried and weekly-paid employees. Any payments made under the employee's contract of employment operate to reduce the employer's obligation to make guarantee payments under the statute, and vice versa. In recognition of the prevalence of guaranteed week agreements, many of which pre-dated the 1975 Act, the statutory guarantee payments provisions are a rare exception to the normal rule which prohibits contracting out of statutory employment rights, as the Secretary of State may make an exemption order exempting from these provisions employers who are parties to a collective agreement which gives employees a right to guaranteed remuneration during lay-off, or where there is a wages order in force to like effect. Finally, it should be noted that an employee who is entitled to receive a statutory guarantee payment, or a payment under a collective agreement or wages order in respect of which an exemption order is in force, will be disqualified from claiming a jobseeker's allowance for the workless day in question (S.I. 1983 No. 1598, as amended by S.I. 1990 No. 1487).

In order for an employee to be eligible for a guarantee payment in respect of a "workless day", the following requirements must be satisfied:

(i) the whole day must be workless, *i.e.* the employee must not be provided with work by the employer throughout the day. If the employee does some work for the employer on the day in question, no matter how small, he or she will not be entitled to a guarantee payment. "Day" is defined in subs. (4) as the period of 24 hours from midnight to midnight. Night shift workers whose shift extends over two days may only claim one workless day per shift lost, as subs. (5) deems the whole of a night shift to fall either on the first or the second day, depending on whether the shift mostly falls before or after midnight;

(ii) the workless day must be a day during which the employee would normally be required to work in accordance with his or her contract of employment;

(iii) the failure to provide work must have been caused by (a) a diminution in the requirements of the employer's business for work of the kind which the employee is employed to do; or (b) any other occurrence affecting the normal working of the employer's business in relation to that work;

(iv) the employee must not fall within one of the exclusions from the right: see the note to s.29.

Normally required to work in accordance with his contract of employment. As the purpose of the guarantee payment provisions is to compensate the employee for what he or she would have earned if work had been available, an employee cannot claim a guarantee payment for a day on which he or she would not normally have been required to work, *e.g.* holidays, or days of sickness absence: *York and Reynolds v. Colledge Hosiery Co.* [1978] IRLR 53, I.T. It might reasonably be assumed that the provisions were intended to apply in a situation where the employee's contractual working days are reduced from, say, five days a week to four, but the requirement that the employee must normally be required to work on the day in question has been restrictively interpreted as meaning that an employee whose working days are reduced in such a way will not be able to claim a guarantee payment for the fifth day because he or she is no longer contractually required to work on that day: see *Clemens v. Richards (Peter) (t/a John Bryan)* [1977] IRLR 332, I.T.; *Daley v. Strathclyde Regional Council* [1977] IRLR 414, I.T. In both cases, the tribunals refused to interpret subs. (1) as referring to the original contracts of employment of the applicants, although such an interpretation would not have unduly strained the wording of the section, and would surely have been more in line with parliamentary intentions. It is interesting to note that for the purposes of calculating the amount and duration of a guarantee payment, the Act specifically provides that where the employee's contract has been varied, or a new contract has been entered into, in connection with a period of short-time working, it is the original contract which is relevant, not the amended version: see s.30(5) and s.31(6). No such provision is however made in relation to the initial conditions of entitlement.

Any other occurrence. According to the Industrial Tribunal in *North v. Pavleigh* [1977] IRLR 461, this would cover an involuntary closure caused by an event such as a natural disaster or a power cut, but not a voluntary closure by the employer to observe a religious holiday.

Exclusions from right to guarantee payment

29.—(1) An employee is not entitled to a guarantee payment unless he has been continuously employed for a period of not less than one month ending with the day before that in respect of which the guarantee payment is claimed.

(2) An employee who is employed—

(a) under a contract for a fixed term of three months or less, or

(b) under a contract made in contemplation of the performance of a specific task which is not expected to last for more than three months,

is not entitled to a guarantee payment unless he has been continuously employed for a period of more than three months ending with the day before that in respect of which the guarantee payment is claimed.

(3) An employee is not entitled to a guarantee payment in respect of a workless day if the failure to provide him with work for that day occurs in consequence of a strike, lock-out or other industrial action involving any employee of his employer or of an associated employer.

(4) An employee is not entitled to a guarantee payment in respect of a workless day if—

(a) his employer has offered to provide alternative work for that day which is suitable in all the circumstances (whether or not it is work which the employee is under his contract employed to perform), and

(b) the employee has unreasonably refused that offer.

(5) An employee is not entitled to a guarantee payment if he does not comply with reasonable requirements imposed by his employer with a view to ensuring that his services are available.

DEFINITIONS
"associated employer": s.231.
"day": s.28(4).
"employee": s.230(1).
"employer": s.230(4).
"guarantee payment": s.28(2).
"workless day": s.28(3).

GENERAL NOTE
The following categories are excluded from the right to a guarantee payment:
  (i) employees who have not been continuously employed by their employer for at least one
     month ending with the day before that in respect of which a guarantee payment is claimed
     (subs. (1));
 (ii) casual employees employed under a fixed term contract of three months or less, and those
     employed to perform a specific task which is not expected to last for more than three
     months, unless in either case the employee has already been continuously employed for a
     period of more than three months ending with the day before that in respect of which a
     guarantee payment is claimed (subs. (2)).
(iii) the right to a guarantee payment is lost where the failure to provide work occurs in conse-
     quence of a strike, lock-out or other industrial action involving the employer or an associ-
     ated employer (subs. (3)). In their original form, the provisions excluded a claim for a
     guarantee payment where the failure was in consequence of a "trade dispute"; the present
     wording was substituted by the Employment Act 1982 (c. 46) on account of the narrowing
     of the trade dispute definition in that Act. On the pre-1982 wording, see *Thomson v. Priest*
     (Lindley) [1978] IRLR 99, I.T.; *Garvey v. Maybank (J. & J.) (Oldham)* [1979] IRLR 408,
     I.T. This exclusion is wider than the trade dispute qualification in the case of social secur-
     ity benefits, as it applies irrespective of whether the employee was directly interested in
     the dispute. The definitions of "strike" and "lock-out" in s.235(4) and (5) do not apply to
     this section;
(iv) the right to a guarantee payment is lost where the employee has unreasonably refused an
     offer of suitable alternative work for the workless day in question (subs. (4)); the alterna-
     tive work can be work outside the employee's contract of employment, provided it is
     suitable in all the circumstances: *Purdy v. Willowbrook International* [1977] IRLR 388,
     I.T.;
 (v) the right to a guarantee payment is lost where the employee fails to comply with any
     reasonable requirements imposed by the employer with a view to ensuring that the
     employee is available for work (subs. (5)); see, *e.g. Meadows (C.) v. Faithfull Overalls*
     [1977] IRLR 330, I.T. (employees who went home because their factory ran out of heating
     oil were not entitled to guarantee payments because they failed to comply with the
     employer's reasonable requirement to stay on the premises until a delivery of oil arrived).
In addition to the above exclusions, the following categories of employee are also excluded
from the right to a guarantee payment: employees who ordinarily work outside Great Britain
(s.196); share fishermen (s.199(2)); police officers (s.200); and employees covered by an exemption order issued by the Secretary of State under s.35 (see the note to that section). The right
does however extend to those in Crown employment and to Parliamentary staff. The restriction
of the right to "employees" (as defined in s.230) means that a self-employed casual worker does
not enjoy any right to a guarantee payment on a workless day: see, *e.g. Mailway (Southern) v.*
Willsher [1978] IRLR 322, E.A.T.

Calculation of guarantee payment

   30.—(1) Subject to section 31, the amount of a guarantee payment payable
to an employee in respect of any day is the sum produced by multiplying the
number of normal working hours on the day by the guaranteed hourly rate;
and, accordingly, no guarantee payment is payable to an employee in whose
case there are no normal working hours on the day in question.
   (2) The guaranteed hourly rate, in relation to an employee, is the amount
of one week's pay divided by the number of normal working hours in a week
for that employee when employed under the contract of employment in force
on the day in respect of which the guarantee payment is payable.
   (3) But where the number of normal working hours differs from week to
week or over a longer period, the amount of one week's pay shall be divided
instead by—

(a) the average number of normal working hours calculated by dividing by twelve the total number of the employee's normal working hours during the period of twelve weeks ending with the last complete week before the day in respect of which the guarantee payment is payable, or

(b) where the employee has not been employed for a sufficient period to enable the calculation to be made under paragraph (a), a number which fairly represents the number of normal working hours in a week having regard to such of the considerations specified in subsection (4) as are appropriate in the circumstances.

(4) The considerations referred to in subsection (3)(b) are—

(a) the average number of normal working hours in a week which the employee could expect in accordance with the terms of his contract, and

(b) the average number of normal working hours of other employees engaged in relevant comparable employment with the same employer.

(5) If in any case an employee's contract has been varied, or a new contract has been entered into, in connection with a period of short-time working, subsections (2) and (3) have effect as if for the references to the day in respect of which the guarantee payment is payable there were substituted references to the last day on which the original contract was in force.

DEFINITIONS
"contract of employment": s.230(2).
"day": s.28(4).
"employee": s.230(1).
"employer": s.230(4).
"employment": s.230(5).
"guarantee payment": s.28(2).
"normal working hours": s.234.
"week": s.235(1).
"week's pay": s.220.

GENERAL NOTE
The complexity of the formula for the calculation of a guarantee payment is out of all proportion to the sums involved. Where the employee has regular working hours, the amount of a guarantee payment for a workless day is calculated by multiplying the number of normal working hours for that day by the "guaranteed hourly rate", *i.e.* a week's pay divided by the number of normal working hours in a week for that employee (subs. (2)). Where the employee's working hours vary from week to week, the guaranteed hourly rate is calculated by dividing a week's pay by the average number of working hours for that employee over the preceding 12 weeks (subs. (3)(a)); if the employee has not been employed for 12 weeks, a number which fairly represents the employee's normal working hours will be taken (subs. (3)(b)), based on what the employee could expect under his or her contract, and the average working hours of comparable employees of the same employer (subs. (4)). This is of course all subject to s.31, which limits the amount payable to £14.50 per day, for a maximum of five workless days in any three month period.

Subs. (1)
Normal working hours. For the calculation of normal working hours, see the note to s.234; see also subs. (2) below. An employee who has no normal working hours on the day in question will not be entitled to a guarantee payment in respect of that day.

Subs. (2)
In calculating the guaranteed hourly rate, the employee's normal working hours will usually be those under the contract of employment in force on the workless day; where however the employee's contractual hours have been varied in connection with the short-time working, the guaranteed weekly rate is to be calculated by reference to the employee's normal working hours under his or her original contract: see subs. (5).
Week's pay. For the calculation of a week's pay, see the note to s.220.

Limits on amount of and entitlement to guarantee payment

31.—(1) The amount of a guarantee payment payable to an employee in respect of any day shall not exceed £14.50.

(2) An employee is not entitled to guarantee payments in respect of more than the specified number of days in any period of three months.

(3) The specified number of days for the purposes of subsection (2) is the number of days, not exceeding five, on which the employee normally works in a week under the contract of employment in force on the day in respect of which the guarantee payment is claimed.

(4) But where that number of days varies from week to week or over a longer period, the specified number of days is instead—

(a) the average number of such days, not exceeding five, calculated by dividing by twelve the total number of such days during the period of twelve weeks ending with the last complete week before the day in respect of which the guarantee payment is claimed, and rounding up the resulting figure to the next whole number, or

(b) where the employee has not been employed for a sufficient period to enable the calculation to be made under paragraph (a), a number which fairly represents the number of the employee's normal working days in a week, not exceeding five, having regard to such of the considerations specified in subsection (5) as are appropriate in the circumstances.

(5) The considerations referred to in subsection (4)(b) are—

(a) the average number of normal working days in a week which the employee could expect in accordance with the terms of his contract, and

(b) the average number of such days of other employees engaged in relevant comparable employment with the same employer.

(6) If in any case an employee's contract has been varied, or a new contract has been entered into, in connection with a period of short-time working, subsections (3) and (4) have effect as if for the references to the day in respect of which the guarantee payment is claimed there were substituted references to the last day on which the original contract was in force.

(7) The Secretary of State may by order made in accordance with section 208 vary any of the limits specified in this section, and (in particular) vary the length of the period specified in subsection (2), after a review under that section.

DEFINITIONS
  "contract of employment": s.230(2).
  "day": s.28(4).
  "employee": s.230(1).
  "employer": s.230(4).
  "employment": s.230(5).
  "guarantee payment": s.28(2).
  "week": s.235(1).

GENERAL NOTE
  The amounts available by way of statutory guarantee payment are far from generous. The upper limit is currently set at £14.50 for any one workless day, and an employee may not claim for more than five workless days in any period of three months. Any contractual payments received by an employee in respect of a workless day must be set off against the statutory entitlement, and any such days will count against the statutory maximum of five days: see the note to s.32. If under the contract of employment the employee normally works for *less* than five days a week, entitlement to a guarantee payment is limited to that lesser number of days in any three-month period (subs. (3)). Where the employee's number of working days varies from week to week, then, as with the calculation of normal working hours under s.30, the average number of working days over the preceding 12 weeks will be taken (subs. (4)(a)), and if the employee has been employed for less than 12 weeks, the number will be that which is fairly representative of the employee's normal working days in a week (subs. (4)(b)), based on what the employee could expect under

his or her contract, and the average number of working days of comparable employees of the same employer (subs. (5)).

Subs. (3)

  The number of days ... on which the employee normally works. As this must be determined in accordance with s.28(5), a shift worker who worked four 10-hour night-shifts spanning Monday to Friday was only entitled to guarantee payments for four days: *Trevethan v. Sterling Metals* [1977] IRLR 416, I.T. Note that where the employee's contract has been varied in connection with a period of short-time working, the number of normal working days should be determined by reference to the original contract (subs. (6)).

Subs. (7)

  The limits on both the amount of and duration of a statutory guarantee payment must be reviewed by the Secretary of State annually, taking into consideration the general level of earnings in Great Britain at the time, the national economic situation and any other matters he thinks relevant: see the note to s.208. The present figure of £14.50 has effect as regards any day in respect of which an employee becomes entitled to a guarantee payment on or after September 27, 1995: see S.I. 1995 No. 1953. The previous figure (for the period from April 1, 1992 to September 26, 1995) was £14.10.

Contractual remuneration

32.—(1) A right to a guarantee payment does not affect any right of an employee in relation to remuneration under his contract of employment ("contractual remuneration").

(2) Any contractual remuneration paid to an employee in respect of a workless day goes towards discharging any liability of the employer to pay a guarantee payment in respect of that day; and, conversely, any guarantee payment paid in respect of a day goes towards discharging any liability of the employer to pay contractual remuneration in respect of that day.

(3) For the purposes of subsection (2), contractual remuneration shall be treated as paid in respect of a workless day—

  (a) where it is expressed to be calculated or payable by reference to that day or any part of that day, to the extent that it is so expressed, and

  (b) in any other case, to the extent that it represents guaranteed remuneration, rather than remuneration for work actually done, and is referable to that day when apportioned rateably between that day and any other workless period falling within the period in respect of which the remuneration is paid.

DEFINITIONS

  "contract of employment": s.230(2).
  "contractual remuneration": subs. (1).
  "day": s.28(4).
  "employee": s.230(1).
  "employer": s.230(4).
  "guarantee payment": s.28(2).
  "workless day": s.28(3).
  "workless period": s.28(3).

GENERAL NOTE

  Any contractual remuneration paid by the employer in respect of a workless day will go towards discharging the employer's liability to pay statutory guarantee payments, and similarly any payments made for a workless day under the statutory provisions will be set off against the contractual entitlement (subs. (2)). Any workless day for which the employee receives contractual remuneration will also count against the statutory maximum entitlement, so that an employee who has already been paid for five workless days under his contract will not be entitled to claim a further five days of statutory guarantee payments within the same three-month period: *Cartwright v. Clancey (G.)* [1983] IRLR 355, E.A.T. If the contractual payment does not relate to a particular day (*e.g.* as in the case of a guaranteed week agreement which provides for a weekly guarantee of earnings rather than a daily guarantee), the employer may apportion the weekly payment rateably between the workless days: see subs. (3)(b).

In practice, an employee's contractual entitlement to a guaranteed level of income during lay-off or short-time working often derives from a collectively-negotiated guaranteed week agreement. For the power of the Secretary of State to make an exemption order excluding employees from the statutory guarantee payments provisions in such circumstances, see the note to s.35.

Power to modify provisions about guarantee payments

33. The Secretary of State may by order provide that in relation to any description of employees the provisions of—
  (a) sections 28(4) and (5), 30, 31(3) to (5) (as originally enacted or as varied under section 31(7)) and 32, and
  (b) so far as they apply for the purposes of those provisions, Chapter II of Part XIV and section 234,
shall have effect subject to such modifications and adaptations as may be prescribed by the order.

DEFINITIONS
  "employee": s.230(1).

GENERAL NOTE
  This section empowers the Secretary of State to amend the provisions concerning guarantee payments. At the time of writing no order had been made under this section, or under any of its predecessors.

Complaints to industrial tribunals

34.—(1) An employee may present a complaint to an industrial tribunal that his employer has failed to pay the whole or any part of a guarantee payment to which the employee is entitled.

(2) An industrial tribunal shall not consider a complaint relating to a guarantee payment in respect of any day unless the complaint is presented to the tribunal—
  (a) before the end of the period of three months beginning with that day, or
  (b) within such further period as the tribunal considers reasonable in a case where it is satisfied that it was not reasonably practicable for the complaint to be presented before the end of that period of three months.

(3) Where an industrial tribunal finds a complaint under this section well-founded, the tribunal shall order the employer to pay to the employee the amount of guarantee payment which it finds is due to him.

DEFINITIONS
  "day": s.28(4).
  "employee": s.230(1).
  "employer": s.230(4).
  "guarantee payment": s.28(2).

GENERAL NOTE
  A complaint that an employer has failed to pay the whole or any part of a statutory guarantee payment lies to an industrial tribunal within three months of the day for which it is claimed to be payable, or within a further reasonable period where the tribunal is satisfied that it was not reasonably practicable for the complaint to be made within that period. If the tribunal finds the complaint well-founded it will order the employer to pay the amount due.
  Not reasonably practicable. For the interpretation of this phrase in unfair dismissal law, see the note to s.111.

Exemption orders

35.—(1) Where—
  (a) at any time there is in force a collective agreement, or an agricultural

wages order, under which employees to whom the agreement or order relates have a right to guaranteed remuneration, and

(b) on the application of all the parties to the agreement, or of the Board making the order, the appropriate Minister (having regard to the provisions of the agreement or order) is satisfied that section 28 should not apply to those employees,

he may make an order under this section excluding those employees from the operation of that section.

(2) In subsection (1) "agricultural wages order" means an order made under—

(a) section 3 of the Agricultural Wages Act 1948, or

(b) section 3 of the Agricultural Wages (Scotland) Act 1949.

(3) In subsection (1) "the appropriate Minister" means—

(a) in relation to a collective agreement or to an order such as is referred to in subsection (2)(b), the Secretary of State, and

(b) in relation to an order such as is referred to in subsection (2)(a), the Minister of Agriculture, Fisheries and Food.

(4) The Secretary of State shall not make an order under this section in respect of an agreement unless—

(a) the agreement provides for procedures to be followed (whether by arbitration or otherwise) in cases where an employee claims that his employer has failed to pay the whole or any part of any guaranteed remuneration to which the employee is entitled under the agreement and those procedures include a right to arbitration or adjudication by an independent referee or body in cases where (by reason of an equality of votes or otherwise) a decision cannot otherwise be reached, or

(b) the agreement indicates that an employee to whom the agreement relates may present a complaint to an industrial tribunal that his employer has failed to pay the whole or any part of any guaranteed remuneration to which the employee is entitled under the agreement.

(5) Where an order under this section is in force in respect of an agreement indicating as described in paragraph (b) of subsection (4) an industrial tribunal shall have jurisdiction over a complaint such as is mentioned in that paragraph as if it were a complaint falling within section 34.

(6) An order varying or revoking an earlier order under this section may be made in pursuance of an application by all or any of the parties to the agreement in question, or the Board which made the order in question, or in the absence of such an application.

DEFINITIONS
  "agricultural wages order": subs. (2).
  "appropriate Minister": subs. (3).
  "collective agreement": s.235(1).
  "employee": s.230(1).
  "employer": s.230(4).

GENERAL NOTE
  This section contains a rare exception to the normal rule against contracting out of statutory employment rights. It empowers the Secretary of State to make an exemption order excluding employees from the statutory guarantee payments provisions where there is in force a collective agreement or agricultural wages order which gives the employees a right to guaranteed remuneration. Such an order may only be made on the application of all the parties to the agreement, or of the Board making the order, and the Secretary of State must be satisfied that the agreement provides for a complaints procedure to deal with disputed claims, including the right to independent arbitration or adjudication, or allows the employee to go to an industrial tribunal.
  The collective contracting out procedure has been widely used, and there are currently 26 orders in force which have effect under this section; they are: S.I. 1977 Nos. 145, 157, 902, 1096, 1158, 1322, 1349, 1522, 1523, 1538, 1601 and 2032; S.I. 1978 Nos. 153, 429, 737 and 826; S.I. 1979

No. 1403; S.I. 1980 No. 1715; S.I. 1981 No. 6; S.I. 1987 No. 1757; S.I. 1989 Nos. 1326, 1575 and 2163; S.I. 1990 Nos. 927 and 2330; S.I. 1994 No. 1409.

On the restrictions on contracting-out, and the exception for collective agreements excluding rights to guarantee payments, see s.203(2)(a).

PART IV

SUNDAY WORKING FOR SHOP AND BETTING WORKERS

Protected shop workers and betting workers

Protected shop workers and betting workers

36.—(1) Subject to subsection (5), a shop worker or betting worker is to be regarded as "protected" for the purposes of any provision of this Act if (and only if) subsection (2) or (3) applies to him.

(2) This subsection applies to a shop worker or betting worker if—

(a) on the day before the relevant commencement date he was employed as a shop worker or a betting worker but not to work only on Sunday,

(b) he has been continuously employed during the period beginning with that day and ending with the day which, in relation to the provision concerned, is the appropriate date, and

(c) throughout that period, or throughout every part of it during which his relations with his employer were governed by a contract of employment, he was a shop worker or a betting worker.

(3) This subsection applies to any shop worker or betting worker whose contract of employment is such that under it he—

(a) is not, and may not be, required to work on Sunday, and

(b) could not be so required even if the provisions of this Part were disregarded.

(4) Where on the day before the relevant commencement date an employee's relations with his employer had ceased to be governed by a contract of employment, he shall be regarded as satisfying subsection (2)(a) if—

(a) that day fell in a week which counts as a period of employment with that employer under section 212(2) or (3) or under regulations under section 219, and

(b) on the last day before the relevant commencement date on which his relations with his employer were governed by a contract of employment, the employee was employed as a shop worker or a betting worker but not to work only on Sunday.

(5) A shop worker is not a protected shop worker, and a betting worker is not a protected betting worker, if—

(a) he has given his employer an opting-in notice on or after the relevant commencement date, and

(b) after giving the notice, he has expressly agreed with his employer to do shop work, or betting work, on Sunday or on a particular Sunday.

(6) In this Act "opting-in notice", in relation to a shop worker or a betting worker, means written notice, signed and dated by the shop worker or betting worker, in which the shop worker or betting worker expressly states that he wishes to work on Sunday or that he does not object to Sunday working.

(7) In this Act "the relevant commencement date" means—

(a) in relation to a shop worker, 26th August 1994, and

(b) in relation to a betting worker, 3rd January 1995.

DEFINITIONS
   "betting work": s.233(2).
   "betting worker": s.233(1).
   "contract of employment": s.230(2).
   "employee": s.230(1).
   "employer": s.230(4).

"opting-in notice": subs. (6).
"protected betting worker": s.36(1).
"protected shop worker": s.36(1).
"relevant commencement date": subs. (7).
"shop": s.232(4).
"shop work": s.232(2).
"shop worker": s.232(1).

GENERAL NOTE

When the Sunday Trading Act 1994 (c. 20) removed the restrictions on Sunday trading by shops, part of the deal worked out by the government to ensure parliamentary approval of the deregulatory measures was the inclusion in the Act of a scheme of protection for employees not wishing to work on Sundays. The protection was extended to betting workers by the Deregulation and Contracting Out Act 1994 (c. 40), when that Act legalised betting on Sundays.

To benefit from the protection against Sunday working, an employee must either be a "protected" shop worker or betting worker, as defined in this section, or an "opted-out" shop worker or betting worker, as defined in s.41. There are two categories of protected worker; the first category consists of those who were already working as shop workers or betting workers, but not solely to work on Sunday, when the restrictions on Sunday trading were removed (subs. (2)); the second category consists of those who are not contractually required to work on Sunday (subs. (3)). A protected worker will lose this protected status if he or she gives the employer an "opting-in notice" expressly stating that he or she wishes to work on Sunday or does not object to Sunday working (subs. (6)), and subsequently expressly agrees with the employer to do shop work or betting work on Sunday or on a particular Sunday (subs. (5)).

A worker will be an "opted-out" shop worker or betting worker if he or she has given the employer notice of objection to Sunday working, and has continued to be employed in that job up to the appropriate date: see the note to s.41. The opting-out procedure is significant because it enables a worker who was not in employment when the restrictions on Sunday trading were removed, and who may be required to work on Sunday under his or her contract of employment, to gain protection against Sunday working. The only limit on the right to opt-out of Sunday working is that the worker concerned must not have been employed to work only on Sunday: see the note to s.40(3).

The scope of the protection for protected and opted-out shop workers and betting workers against Sunday working is as follows:

  (i) dismissal of a protected or opted-out shop worker or betting worker for refusing to do shop work or betting work on Sunday, or for giving an opting-out notice to the employer objecting to Sunday working, is automatically unfair, irrespective of length of service: see the note to s.101;
 (ii) it is automatically unfair to select an employee for redundancy on the above grounds: see the note to s.105(4);
(iii) a protected or opted-out shop worker or betting worker has the right not to be subjected to any detriment (short of dismissal) by his employer for refusing to do shop work or betting work on Sunday, or for giving an opting-out notice to the employer objecting to Sunday working: see the note to s.45;
 (iv) the contracts of employment of protected or opted-out shop workers or betting workers are unenforceable to the extent that they require the employee to work (or the employer to provide work) on Sundays: see the notes to ss.37 and 43;
  (v) an employee who is employed to do shop work or betting work on Sunday must be given an explanatory statement by the employer in a prescribed form setting out his or her statutory rights in relation to Sunday working, unless he or she is employed to work only on Sunday: see the note to s.42.

Subs. (1)

Shop worker. This is defined in s.232(1) as "an employee who, under his contract of employment, is or may be required to do shop work"; "shop work" is defined in s.232(2) as "work in or about a shop in England or Wales on a day on which the shop is open for the serving of customers"; "shop" includes any premises where any retail trade or business is carried out (s.232(4)), including hairdressing, the hiring of goods for private use and retail auction sales (s.232(6)), but does not include catering or the sale of programmes, etc., at theatres and places of amusement (s.232(7)). See the note to s.232.

Betting worker. This is defined in s.233(1) as "an employee who, under his contract of employment, is or may be required to do betting work"; "betting work" is defined in s.232(2) as (a) "work at a track in England or Wales for a bookmaker on a day on which the bookmaker acts as such at the track, being work which consists of or includes dealing with betting transactions", and

(b) "work in a licensed betting office in England or Wales on a day on which the office is open for use for the effecting of betting transactions"; "betting transactions" includes the collection or payment of winnings on a bet and any transaction in which one or more of the parties is acting as a bookmaker (s.233(3)), and "bookmaker" is defined as a person who carries on the business of receiving or negotiating bets or conducting pool betting operations, whether or not on his own account, or who holds himself out, or permits himself to be held out, as such a person (s.233(4)). See the note to s.233.

Subs. (2)

The first category of protected worker covers those who were employed as shop workers or betting workers on the day before the "relevant commencement date" (see below), but not to work only on Sunday, and who have been continuously employed as shop workers or betting workers up to the "appropriate date" for the provision concerned (see below). Special provision is made in subs. (4) for an employee whose contract of employment ended before the relevant commencement date, but whose continuity of employment is preserved by virtue of s.212(2) or (3), or under s.219 (*e.g.* an employee absent from work because of sickness or injury, or pregnancy or childbirth).

Relevant commencement date. This refers to the date on which the provisions removing the restrictions on Sunday trading came into force, *i.e.* August 26, 1994, for shop workers; January 3, 1995, for betting workers: see subs. (7).

Continuously employed. An employee's period of continuous employment is to be calculated in accordance with the provisions of ss.210–219.

Appropriate date. To fall within the first category of protected worker, a worker must have been continuously employed up to the "appropriate date" for the provision concerned. The "appropriate date" will differ depending on the nature of the complaint; for example, in an unfair dismissal complaint, it will be the effective date of termination (see s.101(4)); where the complaint is that the employee has been subjected to a detriment, it will be the date of the act or failure to act (see s.45(9)); for the provisions in s.37 concerning the enforceability of contracts of employment, the "appropriate date" will be the day on which the agreement is entered into, or, where the employee is returning to work after pregnancy or childbirth, the day on which she returns to work (see s.37(5)); see also s.38(5) (contracts with guaranteed hours) and s.39(5) (reduction of pay, etc.).

Subs. (3)

The second category of protected worker covers shop workers and betting workers who were employed after the provisions removing the restrictions on Sunday trading came into force, and who are not, and may not be, contractually required to work on Sunday, even if the provisions of this Part of the Act were to be disregarded. This category was added to the Sunday Trading Act 1994 at the instance of the Union of Shop Distributive and Allied Workers, and is designed to protect shop workers and betting workers who come under pressure from their employers to agree to Sunday working.

Subs. (5)

The statutory protection ceases where a protected shop worker or betting worker gives the employer a written, signed and dated "opting-in notice" in which the worker expressly states that he or she wishes to work on Sunday or has no objection to doing so (see subs. (6)), and, after giving the notice, expressly agrees with the employer to do shop work or betting work on Sunday or on a particular Sunday. In such a case, the worker's contract of employment will be taken to be varied to the extent necessary to give effect to the terms of the agreement: see s.37(3).

Contractual requirements relating to Sunday work

37.—(1) Any contract of employment under which a shop worker or betting worker who satisfies section 36(2)(a) was employed on the day before the relevant commencement date is unenforceable to the extent that it—

    (a) requires the shop worker to do shop work, or the betting worker to do betting work, on Sunday on or after that date, or

    (b) requires the employer to provide the shop worker with shop work, or the betting worker with betting work, on Sunday on or after that date.

(2) Subject to subsection (3), any agreement entered into after the relevant commencement date between a protected shop worker, or a protected betting worker, and his employer is unenforceable to the extent that it—

(a) requires the shop worker to do shop work, or the betting worker to do betting work, on Sunday, or

(b) requires the employer to provide the shop worker with shop work, or the betting worker with betting work, on Sunday.

(3) Where, after giving an opting-in notice, a protected shop worker or a protected betting worker expressly agrees with his employer to do shop work or betting work on Sunday or on a particular Sunday (and so ceases to be protected), his contract of employment shall be taken to be varied to the extent necessary to give effect to the terms of the agreement.

(4) The reference in subsection (2) to a protected shop worker, or a protected betting worker, includes a reference to an employee who although not a protected shop worker, or protected betting worker, at the time when the agreement is entered into is a protected shop worker, or protected betting worker, on the day on which she returns to work in accordance with section 79, or in pursuance of an offer made in the circumstances described in section 96(3), after a period of absence from work occasioned wholly or partly by pregnancy or childbirth.

(5) For the purposes of section 36(2)(b), the appropriate date—

(a) in relation to subsections (2) and (3) of this section, is the day on which the agreement is entered into, and

(b) in relation to subsection (4) of this section, is the day on which the employee returns to work.

DEFINITIONS
"betting work": s.233(2).
"betting worker": s.233(1).
"contract of employment": s.230(2).
"employee": s.230(1).
"employer": s.230(4).
"opting-in notice": s.36(6).
"protected betting worker": s.36(1).
"protected shop worker": s.36(1).
"relevant commencement date": s.36(7).
"shop": s.232(4).
"shop work": s.232(2).
"shop worker": s.232(1).

GENERAL NOTE
This section amends the contracts of employment of protected shop workers and betting workers by rendering unenforceable any contractual requirement relating to Sunday work, whether on the worker to do such work or on the employer to provide it, irrespective of whether the contract in question was entered into before or after the relevant commencement date. Special provision is made in subs. (4) for those returning to work after pregnancy or childbirth. Provision is also made for the automatic variation of a protected worker's contract of employment where he or she has given the employer an opting-in notice and has expressly agreed to work on Sunday, in accordance with s.36(5); in such a case, the worker's contract of employment will be taken to be varied to the extent necessary to give effect to the terms of the agreement (subs. (3)).

Relevant commencement date. See the note to s.36(2).

Appropriate date. See the note to s.36(2).

Contracts with guaranteed hours

38.—(1) This section applies where—

(a) under the contract of employment under which a shop worker or betting worker who satisfies section 36(2)(a) was employed on the day before the relevant commencement date, the employer is, or may be, required to provide him with shop work, or betting work, for a specified number of hours each week,

(b) under the contract the shop worker or betting worker was, or might have been, required to work on Sunday before that date, and

(c) the shop worker has done shop work, or the betting worker betting work, on Sunday in that employment (whether or not before that day) but has, on or after that date, ceased to do so.

(2) So long as the shop worker remains a protected shop worker, or the betting worker remains a protected betting worker, the contract shall not be regarded as requiring the employer to provide him with shop work, or betting work, on weekdays in excess of the hours normally worked by the shop worker or betting worker on weekdays before he ceased to do shop work, or betting work, on Sunday.

(3) For the purposes of section 36(2)(b), the appropriate date in relation to this section is any time in relation to which the contract is to be enforced.

DEFINITIONS
"betting work": s.233(2).
"betting worker": s.233(1).
"contract of employment": s.230(2).
"employee": s.230(1).
"employer": s.230(4).
"protected betting worker": s.36(1).
"protected shop worker": s.36(1).
"relevant commencement date": s.36(7).
"shop": s.232(4).
"shop work": s.232(2).
"shop worker": s.232(1).
"week": s.235(1).

GENERAL NOTE
This section provides that where before the relevant commencement date a protected shop worker's or betting worker's contract of employment guaranteed a certain specified number of hours of work each week, and that worker previously worked on a Sunday but no longer does so, the employer is not obliged to make up any shortfall in hours caused by the fact that the worker no longer works on Sunday by providing him or her with work on weekdays in excess of the hours normally worked on weekdays before the worker ceased to work on Sunday.
Relevant commencement date. See the note to s.36(2).

Reduction of pay etc.

39.—(1) This section applies where—
(a) under the contract of employment under which a shop worker or betting worker who satisfies section 36(2)(a) was employed on the day before the relevant commencement date, the shop worker or betting worker was, or might have been, required to work on Sunday before the relevant commencement date,
(b) the shop worker has done shop work, or the betting worker has done betting work, on Sunday in that employment (whether or not before that date) but has, on or after that date, ceased to do so, and
(c) it is not apparent from the contract what part of the remuneration payable, or of any other benefit accruing, to the shop worker or betting worker was intended to be attributable to shop work, or betting work, on Sunday.

(2) So long as the shop worker remains a protected shop worker, or the betting worker remains a protected betting worker, the contract shall be regarded as enabling the employer to reduce the amount of remuneration paid, or the extent of the other benefit provided, to the shop worker or betting worker in respect of any period by the relevant proportion.

(3) In subsection (2) "the relevant proportion" means the proportion which the hours of shop work, or betting work, which (apart from this Part) the shop worker, or betting worker, could have been required to do on Sunday in the period ("the contractual Sunday hours") bears to the aggregate of those hours and the hours of work actually done by the shop worker, or betting worker, in the period.

(4) Where, under the contract of employment; the hours of work actually done on weekdays in any period would be taken into account in determining the contractual Sunday hours, they shall be taken into account in determining the contractual Sunday hours for the purposes of subsection (3).

(5) For the purposes of section 36(2)(b), the appropriate date in relation to this section is the end of the period in respect of which the remuneration is paid or the benefit accrues.

DEFINITIONS
"betting work": s.233(2).
"betting worker": s.233(1).
"contract of employment": s.230(2).
"employee": s.230(1).
"employer": s.230(4).
"protected betting worker": s.36(1).
"protected shop worker": s.36(1).
"relevant commencement date": s.36(7).
"shop": s.232(4).
"shop work": s.232(2).
"shop worker": s.232(1).

GENERAL NOTE
This section entitles an employer to make a proportionate reduction in the pay of a protected shop worker or betting worker who worked on a Sunday before the relevant commencement date, but who no longer does so, in circumstances where it is not apparent from the worker's contract what part of his or her remuneration was attributable to Sunday working (*e.g.* a weekly or monthly paid worker). It varies the contract so as to enable the employer to reduce amount of the remuneration paid (or any other benefit provided) in respect of any period by the proportion which that worker's "contractual Sunday hours" (*i.e.* the hours which he or she could have been required to do on Sunday in that period) bears to the aggregate of those hours and the hours of work actually done in that period.
Relevant commencement date. See the note to s.36(2).

Opting-out of Sunday work

Notice of objection to Sunday working

40.—(1) A shop worker or betting worker to whom this section applies may at any time give his employer written notice, signed and dated by the shop worker or betting worker, to the effect that he objects to Sunday working.

(2) In this Act "opting-out notice" means a notice given under subsection (1) by a shop worker or betting worker to whom this section applies.

(3) This section applies to any shop worker or betting worker who under his contract of employment—

(a) is or may be required to work on Sunday (whether or not as a result of previously giving an opting-in notice), but

(b) is not employed to work only on Sunday.

DEFINITIONS
"betting worker": s.233(1).
"employer": s.230(4).
"opting-in notice": s.36(6).
"opting-out notice": subs. (2).
"shop worker": s.232(1).

GENERAL NOTE
This section enables a shop worker or betting worker who may be contractually required to work on Sunday (whether or not as a result of having previously given an opting-in notice) to opt out of Sunday working by giving the employer a written, signed and dated "opting-out notice" stating that he or she objects to Sunday working. An opting-out notice will usually take effect after three months beginning with the day on which it was given (see s.41(3)), although the

waiting period will be reduced to one month if the employer fails to comply with the duty under s.42 to give that shop worker or betting worker an explanatory statement setting out his or her statutory rights in relation to Sunday working: see s.42(2). In addition to conferring the same protection against dismissal or other detriment as is enjoyed by protected workers (see the note to s.36), an opting-out notice renders unenforceable any existing contractual requirement relating to Sunday work, whether on the worker to do such work or on the employer to provide it, and also makes any subsequent agreement between an opted-out worker and his or her employer unenforceable to the extent that it requires the employee to work, or the employer to provide work, on Sundays: see the note to s.43.

The significance of the opting-out procedure is that it enables shop workers and betting workers who have entered employment since the restrictions on Sunday trading were removed, and who may have a contractual requirement to work on Sunday, to gain protection against Sunday working. The only limit on the right to opt-out of Sunday working is that the worker concerned must not have been employed to work *only* on Sunday (see subs. (3)(b)).

Opted-out shop workers and betting workers

41.—(1) Subject to subsection (2), a shop worker or betting worker is to be regarded as "opted-out" for the purposes of any provision of this Act if (and only if)—

(a) he has given his employer an opting-out notice,

(b) he has been continuously employed during the period beginning with the day on which the notice was given and ending with the day which, in relation to the provision concerned, is the appropriate date, and

(c) throughout that period, or throughout every part of it during which his relations with his employer were governed by a contract of employment, he was a shop worker or a betting worker.

(2) A shop worker is not an opted-out shop worker, and a betting worker is not an opted-out betting worker, if—

(a) after giving the opting-out notice concerned, he has given his employer an opting-in notice, and

(b) after giving the opting-in notice, he has expressly agreed with his employer to do shop work, or betting work, on Sunday or on a particular Sunday.

(3) In this Act "notice period", in relation to an opted-out shop worker or an opted-out betting worker, means, subject to section 42(2), the period of three months beginning with the day on which the opting-out notice concerned was given.

DEFINITIONS
"betting work": s.233(2).
"betting worker": s.233(1).
"contract of employment": s.230(2).
"employer": s.230(4).
"notice period": subs. (3).
"opting-in notice": s.36(6).
"opted-out betting worker": s.41(1).
"opted-out shop worker": s.41(1).
"opting-out notice": s.40(2).
"shop work": s.232(2).
"shop worker": s.232(1).

GENERAL NOTE
A shop worker or betting worker will only be regarded as "opted-out" if the conditions set out in subs. (1) are satisfied, *i.e.* (i) he or she must have given the employer an opting-out notice (see the note to s.40); (ii) he or she must have been continuously employed from the day on which the notice was given up to the "appropriate date" for the provision in question; and (iii) throughout that period, he or she must have been a shop worker or betting worker.

A worker will cease to be opted-out if, having given an opting-out notice, he or she gives the employer an "opting-in notice" (see the note to s.36(5)), and after giving that notice, expressly agrees with the employer to do shop work or betting work on Sunday or on a particular Sunday (subs. (2)). In such a case, the worker's contract of employment will be taken to be varied to the extent necessary to give effect to the terms of the agreement: see s.43(3).

Appropriate date. See the note to s.36(2).

Continuously employed. An employee's period of continuous employment is to be calculated in accordance with the provisions of ss.210–219.

Explanatory statement

42.—(1) Where a person becomes a shop worker or betting worker to whom section 40 applies, his employer shall, before the end of the period of two months beginning with the day on which that person becomes such a worker, give him a written statement in the prescribed form.

(2) If—

(a) an employer fails to comply with subsection (1) in relation to any shop worker or betting worker, and

(b) the shop worker or betting worker, on giving the employer an opting-out notice, becomes an opted-out shop worker or an opted-out betting worker,

section 41(3) has effect in relation to the shop worker or betting worker with the substitution for "three months" of "one month".

(3) An employer shall not be regarded as failing to comply with subsection (1) in any case where, before the end of the period referred to in that subsection, the shop worker or betting worker has given him an opting-out notice.

(4) Subject to subsection (6), the prescribed form in the case of a shop worker is as follows—

"STATUTORY RIGHTS IN RELATION TO SUNDAY SHOP WORK

You have become employed as a shop worker and are or can be required under your contract of employment to do the Sunday work your contract provides for.

However, if you wish, you can give a notice, as described in the next paragraph, to your employer and you will then have the right not to work in or about a shop on any Sunday on which the shop is open once three months have passed from the date on which you gave the notice.

Your notice must—

be in writing;

be signed and dated by you;

say that you object to Sunday working.

For three months after you give the notice, your employer can still require you to do all the Sunday work your contract provides for. After the three month period has ended, you have the right to complain to an industrial tribunal if, because of your refusal to work on Sundays on which the shop is open, your employer—

dismisses you, or

does something else detrimental to you, for example, failing to promote you.

Once you have the rights described, you can surrender them only by giving your employer a further notice, signed and dated by you, saying that you wish to work on Sunday or that you do not object to Sunday working and then agreeing with your employer to work on Sundays or on a particular Sunday."

(5) Subject to subsection (6), the prescribed form in the case of a betting worker is as follows—

"STATUTORY RIGHTS IN RELATION TO SUNDAY BETTING WORK

You have become employed under a contract of employment under which you are or can be required to do Sunday betting work, that is to say, work—

at a track on a Sunday on which your employer is taking bets at the track, or in a licensed betting office on a Sunday on which it is open for business.

However, if you wish, you can give a notice, as described in the next paragraph, to your employer and you will then have the right not to do Sunday betting work once three months have passed from the date on which you gave the notice.

Your notice must—

be in writing;

be signed and dated by you;

say that you object to doing Sunday betting work.

For three months after you give the notice, your employer can still require you to do all the Sunday betting work your contract provides for. After the three month period has ended, you have the right to complain to an industrial tribunal if, because of your refusal to do Sunday betting work, your employer—

dismisses you, or

does something else detrimental to you, for example, failing to promote you.

Once you have the rights described, you can surrender them only by giving your employer a further notice, signed and dated by you, saying that you wish to do Sunday betting work or that you do not object to doing Sunday betting work and then agreeing with your employer to work on Sundays or on a particular Sunday."

(6) The Secretary of State may by order amend the prescribed forms set out in subsections (4) and (5).

DEFINITIONS
"betting work": s.233(2).
"betting worker": s.233(1).
"contract of employment": s.230(2).
"employer": s.230(4).
"opting-in notice": s.36(6).
"opted-out betting worker": s.41(1).
"opted-out shop worker": s.41(1).
"opting-out notice": s.40(2).
"shop": s.232(4).
"shop work": s.232(2).
"shop worker": s.232(1).

GENERAL NOTE
This section imposes a duty on an employer to give an explanatory statement of statutory rights in relation to Sunday working to any shop worker or betting worker who is or may be required under his or her contract of employment to work on Sunday. The statement must be given in the prescribed form, and must normally be given within two months of the start of employment (subs. (1)). There are however two circumstances where no statement need be given: (i) where the employee is employed to work only on Sunday (by virtue of s.40(3)(b)); and secondly, where before the end of the two-month time-limit referred to above, the employee has given the employer an opting-out notice (subs. (3)).

If an employer fails to comply with the requirement to give an explanatory statement in the prescribed form and within the prescribed time-limit, the result is that the statutory notice period after which the opting-out notice takes effect (usually three months beginning with the day on which the notice is given) is reduced to only one month (subs. (2)).

Contractual requirements relating to Sunday work

43.—(1) Where a shop worker or betting worker gives his employer an opting-out notice, the contract of employment under which he was employed immediately before he gave that notice becomes unenforceable to the extent that it—

(a) requires the shop worker to do shop work, or the betting worker to do betting work, on Sunday after the end of the notice period, or

(b) requires the employer to provide the shop worker with shop work, or the betting worker with betting work, on Sunday after the end of that period.

(2) Subject to subsection (3), any agreement entered into between an opted-out shop worker, or an opted-out betting worker, and his employer is unenforceable to the extent that it—

(a) requires the shop worker to do shop work, or the betting worker to do betting work, on Sunday after the end of the notice period, or

(b) requires the employer to provide the shop worker with shop work, or the betting worker with betting work, on Sunday after the end of that period.

(3) Where, after giving an opting-in notice, an opted-out shop worker or an opted-out betting worker expressly agrees with his employer to do shop work or betting work on Sunday or on a particular Sunday (and so ceases to be opted-out), his contract of employment shall be taken to be varied to the extent necessary to give effect to the terms of the agreement.

(4) The reference in subsection (2) to an opted-out shop worker, or an opted-out betting worker, includes a reference to an employee who although not an opted-out shop worker, or an opted-out betting worker, at the time when the agreement is entered into—

(a) had given her employer an opting-out notice before that time, and

(b) is an opted-out shop worker, or an opted-out betting worker, on the day on which she returns to work in accordance with section 79, or in pursuance of an offer made in the circumstances described in section 96(3), after a period of absence from work occasioned wholly or partly by pregnancy or childbirth.

(5) For the purposes of section 41(1)(b), the appropriate date—

(a) in relation to subsections (2) and (3) of this section, is the day on which the agreement is entered into, and

(b) in relation to subsection (4) of this section, is the day on which the employee returns to work.

DEFINITIONS
"betting work": s.233(2).
"betting worker": s.233(1).
"contract of employment": s.230(2).
"employer": s.230(4).
"notice period": s.41(3).
"opted-out betting worker": s.41(1).
"opted-out shop worker": s.41(1).
"opting-in notice": s.36(6).
"opting-out notice": s.40(2).
"shop": s.232(4).
"shop work": s.232(2).
"shop worker": s.232(1).

GENERAL NOTE
This section makes similar provision in relation to the contracts of employment of opted-out workers as is made for protected workers by s.37. Where a shop worker or betting worker has given an opting-out notice, any contractual requirement relating to Sunday work, whether on the worker to do such work or on the employer to provide it, is unenforceable once the notice period has elapsed (subs. (1)); any subsequent agreement between an opted-out shop worker or betting worker and his or her employer is also unenforceable to the extent that it requires the employee to work, or the employer to provide work, on Sundays (subs. (2)). Special provision is made for those returning to work after pregnancy or childbirth (subs. (4)), and also for the automatic variation of an opted-out worker's contract of employment where he or she has given the employer an opting-in notice and has expressly agreed to work on Sunday; in such a case, the worker's contract of employment will be taken to be varied to the extent necessary to give effect to the terms of the agreement (subs. (3)).

Appropriate date. See the note to s.36(2).

PART V

PROTECTION FROM SUFFERING DETRIMENT IN EMPLOYMENT

Rights not to suffer detriment

Health and safety cases

44.—(1) An employee has the right not to be subjected to any detriment by any act, or any deliberate failure to act, by his employer done on the ground that—

(a) having been designated by the employer to carry out activities in connection with preventing or reducing risks to health and safety at work, the employee carried out (or proposed to carry out) any such activities,

(b) being a representative of workers on matters of health and safety at work or member of a safety committee—

(i) in accordance with arrangements established under or by virtue of any enactment, or

(ii) by reason of being acknowledged as such by the employer, the employee performed (or proposed to perform) any functions as such a representative or a member of such a committee,

(c) being an employee at a place where—

(i) there was no such representative or safety committee, or

(ii) there was such a representative or safety committee but it was not reasonably practicable for the employee to raise the matter by those means,

he brought to his employer's attention, by reasonable means, circumstances connected with his work which he reasonably believed were harmful or potentially harmful to health or safety,

(d) in circumstances of danger which the employee reasonably believed to be serious and imminent and which he could not reasonably have been expected to avert, he left (or proposed to leave) or (while the danger persisted) refused to return to his place of work or any dangerous part of his place of work, or

(e) in circumstances of danger which the employee reasonably believed to be serious and imminent, he took (or proposed to take) appropriate steps to protect himself or other persons from the danger.

(2) For the purposes of subsection (1)(e) whether steps which an employee took (or proposed to take) were appropriate is to be judged by reference to all the circumstances including, in particular, his knowledge and the facilities and advice available to him at the time.

(3) An employee is not to be regarded as having been subjected to any detriment on the ground specified in subsection (1)(e) if the employer shows that it was (or would have been) so negligent for the employee to take the steps which he took (or proposed to take) that a reasonable employer might have treated him as the employer did.

(4) Except where an employee is dismissed in circumstances in which, by virtue of section 197, Part X does not apply to the dismissal, this section does not apply where the detriment in question amounts to dismissal (within the meaning of that Part).

DEFINITIONS
"act": s.235.
"employee": s.230(1).
"employer": s.230(4).

GENERAL NOTE
This section is one of a number of measures originally introduced in the Trade Union Reform and Employment Rights Act 1993 to implement EEC Directive No. 89/391 on the introduction

of measures to encourage improvements in the health and safety of workers at work (the "Framework Directive"). Most of the directive's requirements were implemented by the Management of Health and Safety at Work Regulations 1992 (S.I. 1992 No. 2051), but primary legislation was necessary in order to implement the requirement to protect workers with designated health and safety responsibilities, and workers who leave their workstations in circumstances of serious, imminent and unavoidable danger, against being placed at a disadvantage by their employers because of their actions.

This section gives an employee the right not to be subjected to any detriment by his or her employer (whether by an act or a deliberate failure to act) on any of the health and safety grounds specified in subs. (1); in addition, s.100 makes it automatically unfair to dismiss an employee for one of the specified health and safety reasons, and s.105(3) makes it automatically unfair to select an employee for redundancy on those grounds. Similar protection is conferred by ss.45 to 47 on shop and betting workers, occupational pension scheme trustees and employee representatives. In many respects the protection against suffering detriment on health and safety grounds mirrors the long-standing protection against victimisation on trade union grounds conferred by ss.146 to 167 of the Trade Union and Labour Relations (Consolidation) Act 1992 (c. 52), but there are some important differences.

Subs. (1)

The protection applies where the employee is subjected to any detriment on one of the five grounds set out in subs. (1): the first two grounds concern employees with some specific health and safety responsibility at the workplace, *viz.*, (a) where an employer-designated health and safety officer suffers detriment for carrying out or proposing to carry out health and safety activities at work; and (b) where an employee who is a health and safety representative or member of a safety committee (whether in accordance with arrangements made under statute or by reason of being acknowledged as such by the employer) suffers detriment for performing or proposing to perform any of his or her functions as such. The other three grounds concern employees with no specific health and safety responsibility, but who take action (which might include "whistleblowing" or walking off the job) in response to a perceived health and safety risk, *i.e.*, (c) where an employee (in circumstances where there is no safety representative or safety committee, or it was not reasonably practicable to raise the matter with them) suffers a detriment for bringing to the employer's attention, by reasonable means, circumstances which he or she reasonably believes to be harmful or potentially harmful to health or safety; (d) where an employee suffers a detriment for leaving or proposing to leave his or her place of work, or for refusing to return to it, in circumstances of danger which the employee reasonably believed to be serious and imminent and which he or she could not reasonably be expected to avert; and finally (e) where an employee suffers a detriment in such circumstances for taking or proposing to take "appropriate steps" (see the note to subs. (2)) to protect himself/herself or others from the danger.

Employee. The right not to suffer detriment on health and safety grounds only extends to employees; self-employed workers are therefore excluded (see the note to s.230). Note however that under s.209(7), the Secretary of State has the power to extend the right conferred by this section to cover persons other than employees. It is unclear whether the confinement of the rights to employees is in conformity with EEC Directive No. 89/391, which requires measures protecting the health and safety of "workers". The right is not subject to any qualifying period of continuous employment, and applies irrespective of the number of hours worked or the employee's age. The right does not apply to members of the armed forces (s.192(2)), employees working wholly or mainly outside Great Britain (s.196), share fishermen (s.199(2)) or police officers (s.200), but it does extend to those in Crown employment and to Parliamentary staff.

Subjected to any detriment. "Detriment" is not defined for these purposes. That concept is also used in the Sex Discrimination Act 1975 (c. 65), where it forms part of the definition of indirect discrimination in s.1(1)(b); it is also used in s.6(2)(b) of that Act to define the scope of unlawful discrimination in the employment field (see also the Race Relations Act 1976 (c. 74), s.1(1)(b) and s.4(2)(c)). In that context it has been held that "detriment" is to be given its ordinary, common-sense meaning of being put under a disadvantage (*Ministry of Defence v. Jeremiah* [1979] IRLR 436). There is similar protection against victimisation for trade union reasons in the Trade Union and Labour Relations (Consolidation) Act 1992, s.146, but in that context the terminology is different in that s.146 gives an employee the right not to have "action short of dismissal" taken against him: see below. One form of detriment is normally excluded from the protection of this section, *i.e.* where the detriment in question amounts to a dismissal: see the note to subs. (4).

By any act, or any deliberate failure to act. The employer must not subject the employee to any detriment by any act, or by any deliberate failure to act. This is wide enough to cover the imposition of a variety of forms of discipline, *e.g.* suspension, demotion, transfer to less desirable work, withholding of bonuses or overtime, or the imposition of some other financial penalty. Initially, it was thought that the protection afforded by this section was narrower than the protection against action short of dismissal for trade union reasons under s.146 of the 1992 Act, because s.298 of that Act defines "action" as including an omission. It therefore seemed that the s.146 protection could apply where there was a simple omission to act (see, for example, *Ridgway v. National Coal Board* [1987] IRLR 80, C.A., where the employer's refusal to extend a wage increase agreed with one union to members of another union was held to constitute action short of dismissal), whereas under this section the protection only applies where there is a *deliberate* failure to act. However, in *Associated Newspapers v. Wilson; Associated British Ports v. Palmer* [1995] IRLR 259, the House of Lords overruled *Ridgway*, and held that the withholding of pay increases to those who refused to sign individual contracts did not constitute "action" within the meaning of s.146, because the extended definition of action in s.298 does not apply to s.146 for reasons of legislative history (the argument being that as the original provisions on action short of dismissal for trade union reasons in the Employment Protection Act 1975 (c. 71) did not contain the extended definition of "action", it must be assumed that the subsequent consolidation in the Employment Protection (Consolidation) Act 1978 (c. 44) was not intended to change the substantive law). As a result of the narrow interpretation of s.146 in *Associated Newspapers v. Wilson*, it seems that the protection under this section is wider than the protection against action short of dismissal for trade union reasons, as it does at least cover a deliberate failure to act, whereas s.146 is restricted to positive acts.

It is unclear whether an employee is "subjected to any detriment" for present purposes where the employer *threatens* to subject the employee to some disadvantage. Under s.146, it has been held that "action short of dismissal" includes a threat to report employees to a disciplinary tribunal for holding a union meeting on the employer's premises without permission (*Carter v. Wiltshire County Council* [1979] IRLR 331), but there are dicta to the contrary in *Brassington v. Cauldon Wholesale* [1977] IRLR 479.

Representative of workers on matters of health and safety at work; member of a safety committee. The protection against suffering detriment applies to health and safety representatives and members of safety committees appointed in accordance with the Safety Representatives and Safety Committees Regulations 1977 (S.I. 1977 No. 500) (issued under s.2(4)–(7) of the Health and Safety at Work etc. Act 1974 (c. 37)), and also to *de facto* safety representatives and committee members, provided they are acknowledged as such by the employer.

Any functions as such a representative. The functions of safety representatives are set out in s.2(4) of the Health and Safety at Work etc. Act 1974 and reg. 4 of the Safety Representatives and Safety Committees Regulations 1977.

Subs. (2)

Appropriate steps. Whether the steps taken by the employee were "appropriate" must be judged by reference to all the circumstances, including the employee's state of knowledge and the facilities and advice available to the employee at the time. The employer has a defence under subs. (3) if the employer can show that it was (or would have been) so negligent for the employee to take those steps that a reasonable employer might have treated the employee as the employer did.

Subs. (4)

While the dismissal of an employee will undoubtedly be to subject that employee to a detriment, any complaint of a dismissal on health and safety grounds must normally be brought under s.100, not under this section. However, an employee who is employed under a fixed-term contract of one year or more and who has contracted out of his right to complain of unfair dismissal under s.197 will be entitled to bring a complaint under this section if his or her fixed-term contract is not renewed on any of the health and safety grounds set out in subs. (1).

Sunday working for shop and betting workers

45.—(1) An employee who is—

  (a) a protected shop worker or an opted-out shop worker, or

  (b) a protected betting worker or an opted-out betting worker,

has the right not to be subjected to any detriment by any act, or any deliberate failure to act, by his employer done on the ground that the employee refused (or proposed to refuse) to do shop work, or betting work, on Sunday or on a particular Sunday.

  (2) Subsection (1) does not apply to anything done in relation to an opted-out shop worker or an opted-out betting worker on the ground that he refused (or proposed to refuse) to do shop work, or betting work, on any Sunday or Sundays falling before the end of the notice period.

(3) An employee who is a shop worker or a betting worker has the right not to be subjected to any detriment by any act, or any deliberate failure to act, by his employer done on the ground that the employee gave (or proposed to give) an opting-out notice to his employer.

(4) Subsections (1) and (3) do not apply where the detriment in question amounts to dismissal (within the meaning of Part X).

(5) For the purposes of this section a shop worker or betting worker who does not work on Sunday or on a particular Sunday is not to be regarded as having been subjected to any detriment by—

(a) a failure to pay remuneration in respect of shop work, or betting work, on a Sunday which he has not done,

(b) a failure to provide him with any other benefit, where that failure results from the application (in relation to a Sunday on which the employee has not done shop work, or betting work) of a contractual term under which the extent of that benefit varies according to the number of hours worked by the employee or the remuneration of the employee, or

(c) a failure to provide him with any work, remuneration or other benefit which by virtue of section 38 or 39 the employer is not obliged to provide.

(6) Where an employer offers to pay a sum specified in the offer to any one or more employees—

(a) who are protected shop workers or opted-out shop workers or protected betting workers or opted-out betting workers, or

(b) who under their contracts of employment are not obliged to do shop work, or betting work, on Sunday,

if they agree to do shop work, or betting work, on Sunday or on a particular Sunday subsections (7) and (8) apply.

(7) An employee to whom the offer is not made is not to be regarded for the purposes of this section as having been subjected to any detriment by any failure to make the offer to him or to pay him the sum specified in the offer.

(8) An employee who does not accept the offer is not to be regarded for the purposes of this section as having been subjected to any detriment by any failure to pay him the sum specified in the offer.

(9) For the purposes of section 36(2)(b) or 41(1)(b), the appropriate date in relation to this section is the date of the act or failure to act.

(10) For the purposes of subsection (9)—

(a) where an act extends over a period, the "date of the act" means the first day of that period, and

(b) a deliberate failure to act shall be treated as done when it was decided on;

and, in the absence of evidence establishing the contrary, an employer shall be taken to decide on a failure to act when he does an act inconsistent with doing the failed act or, if he has done no such inconsistent act, when the period expires within which he might reasonably have been expected to do the failed act if it was to be done.

DEFINITIONS

"act": s.235.
"betting work": s.233(2).
"betting worker": s.233(1).
"contract of employment": s.230(2).
"employee": s.230(1).
"employer": s.230(4).
"notice period": s.232(8); s.233(6).
"opted-out betting worker": s.41(1).
"opted-out shop worker": s.41(1).
"opting-out notice": s.40(2).
"protected betting worker": s.36(1).

"protected shop worker": s.36(1).
"shop": s.232(4).
"shop work": s.232(2).
"shop worker": s.232(1).

GENERAL NOTE

This section gives "protected" and "opted-out" shop workers and betting workers the right not to be subjected to any detriment (short of dismissal) by their employers, whether by an act or a deliberate failure to act, for refusing to do shop work or betting work on Sunday, or on a particular Sunday, or for giving an opting-out notice to the employer objecting to Sunday working, or for proposing to do either of the above; s.101 makes it automatically unfair to dismiss a protected or opted-out shop worker or betting worker for refusing to do shop work or betting work on Sunday, and s.105(4) makes it automatically unfair to select an employee for redundancy on those grounds. The provisions are similar to those in ss.44, 46 and 47 concerning health and safety cases, occupational pension scheme trustees and employee representatives. As with those provisions, the protection does not apply where the detriment in question amounts to a dismissal; any such complaint must be brought under s.101 instead. Note however that as the provisions which allow an employee employed for a fixed term to contract-out of the right to complain of unfair dismissal do not apply to a dismissal for refusing to do Sunday work (see s.197(2)), the usual exception which allows a dismissed employee to claim protection against suffering detriment where s.197 applies is not applicable here: see subs. (4), and compare the note to s.44(4), above.

The statutory protection for employees not wishing to work on Sundays was introduced for shop workers by the Sunday Trading Act 1994, as part of the deal worked out by the government to obtain parliamentary approval of the repeal of the prohibition on Sunday trading in shops. Similar protection was extended to betting workers by the Deregulation and Contracting Out Act 1994, when that Act legalised betting on Sundays. The right not to suffer detriment conferred by this section only applies to employees, not to self-employed workers (see the note to s.230), and is not subject to any qualifying period of continuous employment. The right does not apply to those in Crown employment (s.191(1)), members of the armed forces (s.192(2)), Parliamentary staff (ss.194(2) and 195(2)), employees working wholly or mainly outside Great Britain (s.196), share fishermen (s.199(2)), or police officers (s.200).

To benefit from the protection against Sunday working, an employee must be either a "protected" or an "opted-out" shop worker or betting worker, within the meaning of the Act: see the notes to ss.36 and 41. Essentially, a worker will be "protected" for these purposes if he or she was employed in the job in question before the deregulatory provisions came into force (unless employed to work only on Sunday), and has continued to be employed in that job up to the date of the act or the deliberate failure to act complained of (s.36(2)), or alternatively if under his or her contract of employment the worker may not be required to work on Sunday (s.36(3)); a worker will be regarded as "opted-out" if, being a worker who may be contractually required to work on Sunday (but who is not employed only to work on Sunday), he or she has given the employer notice of objection to Sunday working, and has continued to be employed in that job up to the date of the act or the deliberate failure to act complained of (s.41(1)).

There are limits to the protection. In particular, a shop worker or betting worker who does not work on Sunday will not be regarded as having been subjected to any detriment where the employer fails to pay that worker remuneration in respect of Sunday work which he or she has not done, or to provide that worker with any other benefit, contractual entitlement to which depends upon remuneration or the number of hours worked, or to provide that worker with work, remuneration or any other benefit which, by virtue of ss.38 or 39 above, the employer is not obliged to provide (subs. (5)). Similarly, where an employer offers to pay a specified amount to protected or opted-out shop workers or betting workers if they agree to do shop work or betting work on Sunday or on a particular Sunday, an employee to whom the offer is not made, or who does not accept the offer, will not be regarded as having been subjected to any detriment by any failure to make the offer to him or to pay him the sum specified in the offer (subss. (6)–(8)).

Protected shop worker; protected betting worker. See the note to s.36(1).
Opted-out shop worker; opted-out betting worker. See the note to s.41(1).
Subjected to any detriment by any act, or any deliberate failure to act. See the note to s.44(1).

Trustees of occupational pension schemes

46.—(1) An employee has the right not to be subjected to any detriment by any act, or any deliberate failure to act, by his employer done on the ground that, being a trustee of a relevant occupational pension scheme which relates to his employment, the employee performed (or proposed to perform) any functions as such a trustee.

(2) Except where an employee is dismissed in circumstances in which, by virtue of section 197, Part X does not apply to the dismissal, this section does not apply where the detriment in question amounts to dismissal (within the meaning of that Part).

(3) In this section "relevant occupational pension scheme" means an occupational pension scheme (as defined in section 1 of the Pension Schemes Act 1993) established under a trust.

DEFINITIONS
"act": s.235.
"employee": s.230(1).
"employer": s.230(4).
"employment": s.230(5).
"relevant occupational pension scheme": subs. (3).

COMMENCEMENT
This section comes into force on a date to be fixed by regulations: see Sched. 2, para 15. At the time of writing no such order had been made.

GENERAL NOTE
This section gives an employee who is a trustee of a "relevant occupational pension scheme" (see below) which relates to his or her employment the right not to be subjected to any detriment (short of dismissal) by his or her employer, whether by an act or a deliberate failure to act, for performing (or proposing to perform) any functions as such a trustee. This protection was introduced by the Pensions Act 1995 (c. 26) as part of a package of employment rights for the trustees of occupational pension schemes, all of which are now contained in this Act. Section 102 makes it automatically unfair to dismiss an employee for performing (or proposing to perform) his or her functions as a trustee of an occupational pension scheme, s.105(5) makes it automatically unfair to select an employee for redundancy on those grounds, and s.58 gives an occupational pension fund trustee the right to a reasonable amount of paid time off during working hours to perform his or her duties as such a trustee, or to undergo training relevant to the performance of those duties. The provisions are similar to those in ss.44, 45 and 47 concerning health and safety cases, shop and betting workers and employee representatives. As with ss.44 and 47, the protection does not apply where the detriment in question amounts to a dismissal, unless the employee has contracted out of his or her right to bring an unfair dismissal complaint under s.197, in which case the employee will be entitled to bring a complaint under this section if his or her fixed-term contract is not renewed because he or she performed or proposed to perform the functions of a trustee (subs. (2)).

The right not to suffer detriment conferred by this section only applies to employees, not to self-employed workers (see the note to s.230), and is not subject to any qualifying period of continuous employment. The right does not apply to members of the armed forces (s.192(2)), Parliamentary staff (ss.194(2) and 195(2)), or employees working wholly or mainly outside Great Britain (s.196), but it does apply to those in Crown employment (s.191(1)) and (somewhat unusually) to share fishermen (s.199(2)), and police officers (s.200).

Subjected to any detriment by any act, or any deliberate failure to act. See the note to s.44(1).

Relevant occupational pension scheme. This refers to an occupational pension scheme established under a trust (subs. (3)). "Occupational pension scheme" is defined for these purposes in s.1 of the Pension Schemes Act 1993 (c. 48), as "any scheme or arrangement which is comprised in one or more instruments or agreements and which has, or is capable of having, effect in relation to one or more descriptions or categories of employments so as to provide benefits, in the form of pensions or otherwise, payable on termination of service, or on death or retirement, to or in respect of earners with qualifying service in an employment of any such description or category".

Employee representatives

47.—(1) An employee has the right not to be subjected to any detriment by any act, or any deliberate failure to act, by his employer done on the ground that, being—

(a) an employee representative for the purposes of Chapter II of Part IV of the Trade Union and Labour Relations (Consolidation) Act 1992 (redundancies) or Regulations 10 and 11 of the Transfer of Undertakings (Protection of Employment) Regulations 1981, or

(b) a candidate in an election in which any person elected will, on being elected, be such an employee representative,

he performed (or proposed to perform) any functions or activities as such an employee representative or candidate.

(2) Except where an employee is dismissed in circumstances in which, by virtue of section 197, Part X does not apply to the dismissal, this section does not apply where the detriment in question amounts to a dismissal (within the meaning of that Part).

DEFINITIONS
"act": s.235.
"employee": s.230(1).
"employer": s.230(4).
"employment": s.230(5).

GENERAL NOTE

This section gives an employee who is an employee representative for the purposes of the statutory requirements concerning consultation over collective redundancies or transfers of undertakings (under Pt. IV of the Trade Union and Labour Relations (Consolidation) Act 1992 and the Transfer of Undertakings (Protection of Employment) Regulations 1981 (S.I. 1981 No. 1794) respectively), or who is a candidate for election as such a representative, the right not to be subjected to any detriment (short of dismissal) by his or her employer, whether by an act or a deliberate failure to act, for performing (or proposing to perform) any functions or activities as such a representative or candidate. This protection was originally introduced by the Collective Redundancies and Transfer of Undertakings (Protection of Employment) (Amendment) Regulations 1995 (S.I. 1995 No. 2587), which made provision for the election of employee representatives with whom an employer may consult over collective redundancies and transfers of undertakings where there are no recognised trade unions. Section 103 makes it automatically unfair to dismiss an employee for performing (or proposing to perform) his or her functions or activities as an employee representative or candidate, s.105(6) makes it automatically unfair to select an employee for redundancy on those grounds, and s.61 gives an employee representative the right to a reasonable amount of paid time off during working hours to perform his or her functions as such a representative or candidate.

Once again, the provisions are similar to those in ss.44 to 46 concerning health and safety cases, shop and betting workers and occupational pension fund trustees. As with ss.44 and 46, the protection does not apply where the detriment in question amounts to a dismissal, unless the employee has contracted out of his or her right to bring an unfair dismissal complaint under s.197, in which case the employee will be entitled to bring a complaint under this section if his or her fixed-term contract is not renewed because he or she performed or proposed to perform any functions or activities as an employee representative or candidate (subs. (2)).

The right not to suffer detriment conferred by this section only applies to employees, not to self-employed workers (see the note to s.230), and is not subject to any qualifying period of continuous employment. The right does not apply to members of the armed forces (s.192(2)), employees working wholly or mainly outside Great Britain (s.196), share fishermen (s.199(2)), or police officers (s.200), but it does apply to those in Crown employment (s.191(1)), and to Parliamentary staff (ss.194(2) and 195(2)).

Subjected to any detriment by any act, or any deliberate failure to act. See the note to s.44(1).

Employee representative. Section 196(1) of the Trade Union and Labour Relations (Consolidation) Act 1992 (as substituted by S.I. 1995 No. 2587) provides that for the purposes of Chap. II of Pt. IV of the 1992 Act (Procedure for handling redundancies), "persons are employee representatives if—

(a) they have been elected by employees for the specific purpose of being consulted by their employer about dismissals proposed by him, or

(b) having been elected by employees (whether before or after dismissals have been proposed by their employer) otherwise than for that specific purpose, it is appropriate (having regard to the purposes for which they were elected) for the employer to consult them about dismissals proposed by him,

and (in either case) they are employed by the employer at the time when they are elected."

There is a similar definition in reg. 11A of the Transfer of Undertakings (Protection of Employment) Regulations 1981 (as added by S.I. 1995 No. 2587), for the purposes of regs. 10 and 11 (Duty to inform and consult representatives).

Enforcement

Complaints to industrial tribunals

48.—(1) An employee may present a complaint to an industrial tribunal that he has been subjected to a detriment in contravention of section 44, 45, 46 or 47.

(2) On such a complaint it is for the employer to show the ground on which any act, or deliberate failure to act, was done.

(3) An industrial tribunal shall not consider a complaint under this section unless it is presented—

(a) before the end of the period of three months beginning with the date of the act or failure to act to which the complaint relates or where that act or failure is part of a series of similar acts or failures, the last of them, or

(b) within such further period as the tribunal considers reasonable in a case where it is satisfied that it was not reasonably practicable for the complaint to be presented before the end of that period of three months.

(4) For the purposes of subsection (3)—

(a) where an act extends over a period, the "date of the act" means the last day of that period, and

(b) a deliberate failure to act shall be treated as done when it was decided on;

and, in the absence of evidence establishing the contrary, an employer shall be taken to decide on a failure to act when he does an act inconsistent with doing the failed act or, if he has done no such inconsistent act, when the period expires within which he might reasonably have been expected to do the failed act if it was to be done.

DEFINITIONS
"date of the act": subs. (4).
"employee": s.230(1).
"employer": s.230(4).

GENERAL NOTE
Enforcement of the right not to be subjected to a detriment within employment lies through a complaint to an industrial tribunal (subs. (1)), subject to a time limit of three months from the date of the act or failure to act complained of, or within a further reasonable period where the tribunal is satisfied that it was not reasonably practicable for the complaint to be made within that period (subs. (3)). Where an act extends over a period, the time limit runs from the last day of that period (subs. (4)(a)). A deliberate failure to act will be treated as done when it was decided upon; in the absence of evidence to the contrary, this will be taken to be when the employer does an act inconsistent with doing the act in question, or if he has not done any such inconsistent act, at the end of the period within which he might reasonably have been expected to do the act if it was to be done (subs. (4)(b)). It will be for the employee to show at the outset that the employer has subjected him or her to a detriment, but the burden of proof is placed squarely on the employer to show the ground on which the act (or deliberate failure to act) was done (subs. (2)). This echoes the position under s.146 of the 1992 Act, where the employer has to show the purpose for which action was taken against the complainant.

If the tribunal upholds the complaint it will make a declaration to that effect, and may in addition award such compensation as it considers just and equitable in all the circumstances: see the note to s.49.

Not reasonably practicable. For the interpretation of this phrase in unfair dismissal law, see the note to s.111.

Where an act extends over a period. Where an act extends over a period, the time limit will not begin to run until the last day of that period, *i.e.* until the act complained of ceases. This phrase also appears in s.76(6)(c) of the Sex Discrimination Act 1975 and s.68(7)(c) of the Race

Relations Act 1976. In that context, it has been held to apply only to a *continuing* act of discrimination, and not to a *single* act or event which has continuing *consequences*, where the time limit runs from the act itself. So, for example, in *Amies v. Inner London Education Authority* [1977] I.C.R. 308, the E.A.T. held that the employer's failure to appoint the complainant to a particular post was not a continuing act of sex discrimination; in contrast, in *Calder v. James Findlay Corp.* [1989] IRLR 55, the employer's refusal to allow the complainant access to a mortgage subsidy scheme was held by the E.A.T. to amount to a continuing discrimination against her, so that she was entitled to bring her complaint more than three months after the refusal. The distinction was approved by the House of Lords in the leading case of *Barclays Bank v. Kapur* [1991] IRLR 136, where the employer's refusal to recognise the complainant's previous service for pensions purposes was held to be a continuing act of race discrimination. That decision was followed in *Littlewoods Organisation v. Traynor* [1993] IRLR 154, where the employer's failure to take promised remedial action in relation to a complaint of discrimination was also held to constitute a continuing act of discrimination, but was distinguished in *Sougrin v. Haringey Health Authority* [1991] IRLR 447, where the employer's decision on grading was held by the Court of Appeal to be a single act of discrimination with continuing consequences, not a continuing act of discrimination. However, in *Owusu v. London Fire & Civil Defence Authority* [1995] IRLR 574, the E.A.T. held that a succession of specific instances of discrimination (*e.g.* a failure to re-grade over a number of years) may indicate the existence of a discriminatory policy, rule or practice, which can constitute a continuing act extending over a period.

Deliberate failure to act. A deliberate failure to act will be treated as done when it was decided on. In *Swithland Motors v. Clarke* [1994] I.C.R. 231, a case under the parallel provisions in the Sex Discrimination Act 1975 involving an alleged deliberate omission to offer employment, the E.A.T. held that "decided" means "decided at a time and in circumstances when [the person] was in a position to implement that decision".

Remedies

49.—(1) Where an industrial tribunal finds a complaint under section 48 well-founded, the tribunal—

    (a) shall make a declaration to that effect, and

    (b) may make an award of compensation to be paid by the employer to the complainant in respect of the act or failure to act to which the complaint relates.

(2) The amount of the compensation awarded shall be such as the tribunal considers just and equitable in all the circumstances having regard to—

    (a) the infringement to which the complaint relates, and

    (b) any loss which is attributable to the act, or failure to act, which infringed the complainant's right.

(3) The loss shall be taken to include—

    (a) any expenses reasonably incurred by the complainant in consequence of the act, or failure to act, to which the complaint relates, and

    (b) loss of any benefit which he might reasonably be expected to have had but for that act or failure to act.

(4) In ascertaining the loss the tribunal shall apply the same rule concerning the duty of a person to mitigate his loss as applies to damages recoverable under the common law of England and Wales or (as the case may be) Scotland.

(5) Where the tribunal finds that the act, or failure to act, to which the complaint relates was to any extent caused or contributed to by action of the complainant, it shall reduce the amount of the compensation by such proportion as it considers just and equitable having regard to that finding.

Definitions
    "employee": s.230(1).
    "employer": s.230(4).

General Note
    The remedies for a breach of the right not to be subjected to any detriment within employment mirror those available in cases of action short of dismissal for trade union reasons under s.149 of the Trade Union and Labour Relations (Consolidation) Act 1992. Where the tribunal finds a complaint well-founded, it must make a declaration to that effect, and may order the

employer to pay compensation to the complainant in respect of the act or failure to act to which the complaint relates (subs. (1)). The amount of compensation will be assessed on a just and equitable measure, having regard to the infringement to which the complaint relates and to any loss attributable to the act or failure to act complained of (subs. (2)). This can include any expenses reasonably incurred by the employee in consequence of the employer's act or failure to act, and the loss of any benefit which the employee might reasonably have expected but for that act or failure to act (subs. (3)). Compensation is not expressly restricted to pecuniary loss, and may therefore cover other matters such as injury to feelings. Awards of compensation are subject to the usual rules on mitigation of loss (subs. (4)) and contributory fault (subs. (5)), but there is no statutory upper limit on the amount of compensation which may be awarded for an infringement of the provisions.

PART VI

TIME OFF WORK

Public duties

Right to time off for public duties

50.—(1) An employer shall permit an employee of his who is a justice of the peace to take time off during the employee's working hours for the purpose of performing any of the duties of his office.

(2) An employer shall permit an employee of his who is a member of—

(a) a local authority,

(b) a statutory tribunal,

(c) a police authority,

(d) a board of prison visitors or a prison visiting committee,

(e) a relevant health body,

(f) a relevant education body, or

(g) the Environment Agency or the Scottish Environment Protection Agency,

to take time off during the employee's working hours for the purposes specified in subsection (3).

(3) The purposes referred to in subsection (2) are—

(a) attendance at a meeting of the body or any of its committees or sub-committees, and

(b) the doing of any other thing approved by the body, or anything of a class so approved, for the purpose of the discharge of the functions of the body or of any of its committees or sub-committees.

(4) The amount of time off which an employee is to be permitted to take under this section, and the occasions on which and any conditions subject to which time off may be so taken, are those that are reasonable in all the circumstances having regard, in particular, to—

(a) how much time off is required for the performance of the duties of the office or as a member of the body in question, and how much time off is required for the performance of the particular duty,

(b) how much time off the employee has already been permitted under this section or sections 168 and 170 of the Trade Union and Labour Relations (Consolidation) Act 1992 (time off for trade union duties and activities), and

(c) the circumstances of the employer's business and the effect of the employee's absence on the running of that business.

(5) In subsection (2)(a) "a local authority" means—

(a) a local authority within the meaning of the Local Government Act 1972,

(b) a council constituted under section 2 of the Local Government etc. (Scotland) Act 1994,

(c) the Common Council of the City of London,

(d) a National Park authority, or

(e) the Broads Authority.

(6) The reference in subsection (2) to a member of a police authority is to a person appointed as such a member under Schedule 2 to the Police Act 1996.

(7) In subsection (2)(d)—

(a) "a board of prison visitors" means a board of visitors appointed under section 6(2) of the Prison Act 1952, and

(b) "a prison visiting committee" means a visiting committee appointed under section 19(3) of the Prisons (Scotland) Act 1989 or constituted by virtue of rules made under section 39 (as read with section 8(1)) of that Act.

(8) In subsection (2)(e) "a relevant health body" means—

(a) a National Health Service trust established under Part I of the National Health Service and Community Care Act 1990 or the National Health Service (Scotland) Act 1978,

(b) a Health Authority established under section 8 of the National Health Service Act 1977 or a Special Health Authority established under section 11 of that Act, or

(c) a Health Board constituted under section 2 of the National Health Service (Scotland) Act 1978.

(9) In subsection (2)(f) "a relevant education body" means—

(a) a managing or governing body of an educational establishment maintained by a local education authority,

(b) a governing body of a grant-maintained school, further education corporation or higher education corporation,

(c) a school council appointed under section 125(1) of the Local Government (Scotland) Act 1973,

(d) a school board within the meaning of section 1(1) of the School Boards (Scotland) Act 1988,

(e) a board of management of a self-governing school within the meaning of section 135(1) of the Education (Scotland) Act 1980,

(f) a board of management of a college of further education within the meaning of section 36(1) of the Further and Higher Education (Scotland) Act 1992,

(g) a governing body of a central institution within the meaning of section 135(1) of the Education (Scotland) Act 1980, or

(h) a governing body of a designated institution within the meaning of Part II of the Further and Higher Education (Scotland) Act 1992.

(10) The Secretary of State may by order—

(a) modify the provisions of subsections (1) and (2) and (5) to (9) by adding any office or body, removing any office or body or altering the description of any office or body, or

(b) modify the provisions of subsection (3).

(11) For the purposes of this section the working hours of an employee shall be taken to be any time when, in accordance with his contract of employment, the employee is required to be at work.

DEFINITIONS

"board of prison visitors": subs. (7).
"local authority": subs. (5).
"prison visiting committee": subs. (7).
"relevant education body": subs. (9).
"relevant health body": subs. (8).
"employee": s.230(1).
"employer": s.230(4).
"working hours": subs. (11).

GENERAL NOTE

An employee is entitled to a reasonable amount of unpaid time off during his or her working hours to perform certain specified public duties. The public duties for which time off may be claimed are those specified in subss. (1) to (3), although the list of bodies and purposes may be modified by order of the Secretary of State under sub. (10). Justices of the peace are entitled under subs. (1) to time off to perform any of the duties of their office, but members of the bodies listed in subs. (2) are only entitled to time off to attend meetings of the body concerned (including committees and sub-committees) and to do other activities approved by that body for the purpose of discharging its functions (sub. (3)). The statutory right to time off for public duties does not carry any entitlement to pay during the time off, although there may be a contractual right to that effect.

There is no minimum qualifying period of continuous employment for this right, but following categories of employee are excluded: employees who ordinarily work outside Great Britain (s.196); share fishermen (s.199(2)); merchant seamen (s.199(4)); and police officers (s.200). The right extends to those in Crown employment and to Parliamentary staff, save that where the terms of employment of a person in Crown employment restrict that person's right to take part in certain political activities or activities which may conflict with his or her official functions, that person may not claim time off under this section for public duties which are connected with any such activities (see s.191(5)).

During the employee's working hours. The employee is entitled to time off during "working hours", defined in subs. (11) as any time when, in accordance with his or her contract of employment, the employee is required to be at work. Merely allowing the employee to rearrange his or her contractual duties so that the time spent on public duties can be made up at some other time will not be sufficient: *Ratcliffe v. Dorset County Council* [1978] IRLR 191, I.T.

Reasonable in all the circumstances. The amount of time off which it would be reasonable for an employer to allow an employee to take must be determined in the light of matters such as the overall amount of time off required for the performance of the duties in question, how much time off the employee has already been permitted (whether for public duties or for trade union duties or activities), and the needs of the employer's business (subs. (4)). While an employer may not entirely avoid the obligation to permit time off for public duties by requiring the employee to rearrange his or her contractual duties around those public duties (see *Ratcliffe v. Dorset County Council*, above), where an employee has extensive public duties it may be reasonable to expect the employee to give up some of his or her own time to those duties rather than expecting all the time to come out of working hours (*Emmerson v. I.R.C.* [1977] IRLR 458, I.T.), and where possible to plan the absences from work so as to produce a reasonable pattern of time off. In *Borders Regional Council v. Maule* [1993] IRLR 199, E.A.T., the employee had been allowed time off to sit as a member of the Social Security Appeals Tribunal, but was refused a day off to attend an annual SSAT training session. The industrial tribunal upheld the employee's complaint on the basis that, having allowed the employee time off to sit on the SSAT, the employer should have accepted the need to allow additional time off for training. The E.A.T. upheld the employer's appeal, explaining the correct approach in the following terms:

"An employee who is undertaking a variety of public and other duties may have some responsibility to plan the absences from work, and to scale the level of commitment which such public duties involve so as to produce a pattern which can be regarded as reasonable in all the circumstances."

Subs. (10)
The Time Off for Public Duties Orders 1990 and 1995 (S.I. 1990 No. 1870 and S.I. 1995 No. 694) were made under the predecessor to this subsection.

Complaints to industrial tribunals

51.—(1) An employee may present a complaint to an industrial tribunal that his employer has failed to permit him to take time off as required by section 50.

(2) An industrial tribunal shall not consider a complaint under this section that an employer has failed to permit an employee to take time off unless it is presented—

(a) before the end of the period of three months beginning with the date on which the failure occurred, or

(b) within such further period as the tribunal considers reasonable in a case where it is satisfied that it was not reasonably practicable for the complaint to be presented before the end of that period of three months.

(3) Where an industrial tribunal finds a complaint under this section well-founded, the tribunal—

(a) shall make a declaration to that effect, and
(b) may make an award of compensation to be paid by the employer to the employee.

(4) The amount of the compensation shall be such as the tribunal considers just and equitable in all the circumstances having regard to—

(a) the employer's default in failing to permit time off to be taken by the employee, and
(b) any loss sustained by the employee which is attributable to the matters to which the complaint relates.

DEFINITIONS
"employee": s.230(1).
"employer": s.230(4).

GENERAL NOTE
A complaint that an employer has failed to allow an employee to take reasonable time off under s.50 lies to an industrial tribunal (subs. (1)), subject to a time limit of three months from the date of the failure, or within a further reasonable period where the tribunal is satisfied that it was not reasonably practicable for the complaint to be made within that period (subs. (2)). If the tribunal upholds the complaint it will make a declaration to that effect, and may in addition award such compensation as it considers just and equitable in all the circumstances, having regard to the employer's default and any loss sustained by the employee which is attributable to that failure (subss. (3) & (4)). The tribunal's function under this section is to determine whether the employer acted reasonably in all the circumstances, not to attempt to determine what amount of time off would have been reasonable (*Emmerson v. I.R.C.*; *Ratcliffe v. Dorset County Council*, above), and the tribunal has no jurisdiction to impose conditions on the parties (*Corner v. Buckinghamshire County Council* [1978] IRLR 320, E.A.T., where the tribunal had found that 21 days off per annum for public duties was reasonable, but sought to impose a condition that 10 of those days should be unpaid).

Not reasonably practicable. For the interpretation of this phrase in unfair dismissal law, see the note to s.111.

Looking for work and making arrangements for training

Right to time off to look for work or arrange training

52.—(1) An employee who is given notice of dismissal by reason of redundancy is entitled to be permitted by his employer to take reasonable time off during the employee's working hours before the end of his notice in order to—

(a) look for new employment, or
(b) make arrangements for training for future employment.

(2) An employee is not entitled to take time off under this section unless, on whichever is the later of—

(a) the date on which the notice is due to expire, and
(b) the date on which it would expire were it the notice required to be given by section 86(1),

he will have been (or would have been) continuously employed for a period of two years or more.

(3) For the purposes of this section the working hours of an employee shall be taken to be any time when, in accordance with his contract of employment, the employee is required to be at work.

DEFINITIONS
"dismissal by reason of redundancy": s.235(3).
"employee": s.230(1).
"employer": s.230(4).
"employment": s.230(5).
"working hours": subs. (3).

GENERAL NOTE
An employee who is under notice of dismissal for redundancy is entitled to a reasonable amount of time off during working hours to look for new work or to make arrangements for

training for future employment. There is also a right to be paid for that time off, but the right to payment is strictly limited: see the note to s.53.

Unlike the other rights to time off in this Part, the right to time off to look for work or arrange training is subject to a qualifying period of continuous employment of at least two years ending with the date on which the notice of dismissal is due to expire, or, where less than the statutory minimum period of notice has been given, the date on which that minimum notice period would have expired (subs. (2)). The following categories of employee are also excluded: employees who ordinarily work outside Great Britain (s.196); share fishermen (s.199(2)); merchant seamen (s.199(4)); and police officers (s.200). The right extends to those in Crown employment and to Parliamentary staff.

Given notice of dismissal. The employee must have been given actual notice of dismissal in order to qualify for this right; a mere warning of impending redundancies is not sufficient: on this distinction, see *Morton Sundour Fabrics v. Shaw* (1966) 2 I.T.R. 84; *Pritchard-Rhodes v. Boon and Milton* [1979] IRLR 19, E.A.T.; *Doble v. Firestone Tyre and Rubber Co.* [1981] IRLR 300, E.A.T.

By reason of redundancy. This is to be construed in accordance with s.139: see s.235(3). Note that the right to time off is not dependent on the employee having a valid claim for a redundancy payment, and so it may be claimed even where, for example, the employee has refused a reasonable offer of alternative employment: *Dutton v. Hawker Siddeley Aviation* [1978] I.C.R. 1057, E.A.T.

Reasonable time off. The amount of *paid* time off which an employee is entitled to claim under these provisions is subject to a maximum of 40 per cent of a week's pay for any one period of notice (see the note to s.53), but this does not mean that the right to time off is itself similarly limited, merely that time off in excess of that limit will (in the absence of a more generous contractual entitlement) be unpaid. The employee need not provide documentary proof of appointments or interviews in order to claim time off, but his or her failure to do so may be relevant in determining whether a refusal of time off was unreasonable within the meaning of s.54: see *Dutton v. Hawker Siddeley Aviation*, above.

During the employee's working hours. The employee is entitled to time off during "working hours", defined in subs. (3) as any time when, in accordance with his or her contract of employment, the employee is required to be at work.

Continuously employed. An employee's period of continuous employment is to be calculated in accordance with the provisions of ss.210–219.

Right to remuneration for time off under section 52

53.—(1) An employee who is permitted to take time off under section 52 is entitled to be paid remuneration by his employer for the period of absence at the appropriate hourly rate.

(2) The appropriate hourly rate, in relation to an employee, is the amount of one week's pay divided by the number of normal working hours in a week for that employee when employed under the contract of employment in force on the day when the notice of dismissal was given.

(3) But where the number of normal working hours differs from week to week or over a longer period, the amount of one week's pay shall be divided instead by the average number of normal working hours calculated by dividing by twelve the total number of the employee's normal working hours during the period of twelve weeks ending with the last complete week before the day on which the notice was given.

(4) If an employer unreasonably refuses to permit an employee to take time off from work as required by section 52, the employee is entitled to be paid an amount equal to the remuneration to which he would have been entitled under subsection (1) if he had been permitted to take the time off.

(5) The amount of an employer's liability to pay remuneration under subsection (1) shall not exceed, in respect of the notice period of any employee, forty per cent. of a week's pay of that employee.

(6) A right to any amount under subsection (1) or (4) does not affect any right of an employee in relation to remuneration under his contract of employment ("contractual remuneration").

(7) Any contractual remuneration paid to an employee in respect of a period of time off under section 52 goes towards discharging any liability of the employer to pay remuneration under subsection (1) in respect of that

period; and, conversely, any payment of remuneration under subsection (1) in respect of a period goes towards discharging any liability of the employer to pay contractual remuneration in respect of that period.

DEFINITIONS
"contract of employment": s.230(2).
"employee": s.230(1).
"employer": s.230(4).
"employment": s.230(5).
"normal working hours": s.234.
"week": s.235(1).
"week's pay": s.220.

GENERAL NOTE
This section contains the convoluted formula for determining the amount of pay to which an employee is entitled during a period of time off under s.52. The gist of the provisions is that an employee who is permitted to take time off to look for work or arrange training is entitled under subs. (1) to be paid during such time off at his or her normal hourly rate (the "appropriate hourly rate", as defined in subs. (2)), but subject to a maximum amount of 40 per cent of a week's pay for any one period of notice (subs. (5)). Where the employee also has a contractual right to be paid while looking for work or arranging training, any contractual remuneration which he or she receives in respect of a period of time off will go towards discharging the employer's liability under subs. (1), and similarly any payments under subs. (1) will be set off against the employer's liability under the contract (subs. (7)). If the employer unreasonably refuses to allow time off, the employee is entitled to be paid an amount equivalent to the amount which would have been received under the statute, had he or she in fact been allowed to take the time off (subs. (4)). Such a claim will still be subject to the limit of 40 per cent of a week's pay, but need not be set off against any contractual payments for the period in question, as the set off provisions in subs. (7) only apply to payments of remuneration under subs. (1) (*i.e.* where time off has been allowed), not to payments of compensation under subs. (4) (*i.e.* where time off has been unreasonably refused). If this were not the case, there would be no sanction against an employer who refused to allow time off under these provisions.

The appropriate hourly rate. This is calculated by dividing one "week's pay" by the employee's "normal working hours" (see below). Where the employee has regular working hours, the appropriate hourly rate is calculated by dividing his or her week's pay by the number of normal working hours in a week for that employee under the contract of employment in force at the date on which the notice of dismissal was given (subs. (2)). Where the employee's working hours vary from week to week, the appropriate hourly rate is calculated by dividing a week's pay by the average number of working hours for that employee over the preceding 12 weeks, ending with the last complete week before the day on which notice was given (subs. (3)).

Week's pay. For the calculation of a week's pay, see the note to s.220.

Normal working hours. For the calculation of normal working hours, see the note to s.234.

Complaints to industrial tribunals

54.—(1) An employee may present a complaint to an industrial tribunal that his employer—
  (a) has unreasonably refused to permit him to take time off as required by section 52, or
  (b) has failed to pay the whole or any part of any amount to which the employee is entitled under section 53(1) or (4).

(2) An industrial tribunal shall not consider a complaint under this section unless it is presented—
  (a) before the end of the period of three months beginning with the date on which it is alleged that the time off should have been permitted, or
  (b) within such further period as the tribunal considers reasonable in a case where it is satisfied that it was not reasonably practicable for the complaint to be presented before the end of that period of three months.

(3) Where an industrial tribunal finds a complaint under this section well-founded, the tribunal shall—

(a) make a declaration to that effect, and

(b) order the employer to pay to the employee the amount which it finds due to him.

(4) The amount which may be ordered by a tribunal to be paid by an employer under subsection (3) (or, where the employer is liable to pay remuneration under section 53, the aggregate of that amount and the amount of that liability) shall not exceed, in respect of the notice period of any employee, forty per cent. of a week's pay of that employee.

DEFINITIONS
"employee": s.230(1).
"employer": s.230(4).

GENERAL NOTE

A complaint that an employer has unreasonably refused to allow an employee to take time off under s.52 or has failed to pay the employee what is due under s.53 lies to an industrial tribunal (subs. (1)), subject to a time limit of three months from the date on which it is alleged that the time off should have been permitted, or within a further reasonable period where the tribunal is satisfied that it was not reasonably practicable for the complaint to be made within that period (subs. (2)). If the tribunal upholds the complaint it will make a declaration to that effect, and order the employer to pay the amount due (subs. (3)), subject to a maximum of 40 per cent of a week's pay for any one period of notice (subs. (4): see the note to s.53). As seen in the note to s.52, the fact that the amount of paid time off which an employee is entitled to claim is subject to a maximum of 40 per cent of a week's pay does not mean that the right to time off is itself similarly limited, merely that time off in excess of that limit will be unpaid (unless of course the contract of employment provides otherwise). The effect of the limit on compensation in subs. (4) is that where an employer has already permitted an employee to take paid time off up to the statutory maximum of 40 per cent of a week's pay, a tribunal which finds that the employer acted unreasonably by refusing to allow the employee a further period of unpaid time off would be restricted to making a declaration to that effect.

Not reasonably practicable. For the interpretation of this phrase in unfair dismissal law, see the note to s.111.

Ante-natal care

Right to time off for ante-natal care

55.—(1) An employee who—

(a) is pregnant, and

(b) has, on the advice of a registered medical practitioner, registered midwife or registered health visitor, made an appointment to attend at any place for the purpose of receiving ante-natal care,

is entitled to be permitted by her employer to take time off during the employee's working hours in order to enable her to keep the appointment.

(2) An employee is not entitled to take time off under this section to keep an appointment unless, if her employer requests her to do so, she produces for his inspection—

(a) a certificate from a registered medical practitioner, registered midwife or registered health visitor stating that the employee is pregnant, and

(b) an appointment card or some other document showing that the appointment has been made.

(3) Subsection (2) does not apply where the employee's appointment is the first appointment during her pregnancy for which she seeks permission to take time off in accordance with subsection (1).

(4) For the purposes of this section the working hours of an employee shall be taken to be any time when, in accordance with her contract of employment, the employee is required to be at work.

DEFINITIONS
"contract of employment": s.230(2).
"employee": s.230(1).

"employer": s.230(4).
"working hours": subs. (4).

GENERAL NOTE

A pregnant employee has the right not to be unreasonably refused time off with pay during working hours in order to receive ante-natal care. To qualify for the right, an employee must be pregnant, and she must have made an appointment for ante-natal care, on the advice of a registered medical practitioner, registered midwife or registered health visitor (subs. (1)). The employer is entitled to ask the employee to produce a medical certificate stating that she is pregnant, and an appointment card or other document showing that an appointment has been made (subs. (2)), but not for the first appointment (subs. (3)).

The section does not place any limit on the amount of time off which an employee may claim, merely stating that the time off must be "to enable her to keep the appointment" (contrast ss.50 and 52, where the right is to take "reasonable" time off), but an employee denied time off for ante-natal care may only complain to an industrial tribunal where the employer has "unreasonably refused" to permit her to take time off: see the note to s.57.

There is no minimum qualifying period of continuous employment for this right, but following categories of employee are excluded: employees who ordinarily work outside Great Britain (s.196); share fisherwomen (s.199(2)); and police officers (s.200). The right extends to those in Crown employment and to Parliamentary staff.

An employee who ... is pregnant. To qualify for the right to time off under this section, the employee must be pregnant, which suggests that the right is not intended to be used for an initial appointment to confirm a pregnancy. On the other hand, an employee who is *in fact* pregnant, but whose pregnancy has not yet been confirmed, could argue that, as she satisfies the requirements of the section, she is entitled to paid time off for an appointment to confirm the pregnancy. Some support for this interpretation can be found in the fact that the employer may not ask the employee for a medical certificate stating that she is pregnant until her *second* appointment, which could be taken to imply that the first appointment may be used for the purpose of confirming the pregnancy. Ultimately, the point may turn on whether an appointment for that purpose could properly be described as an appointment "for the purpose of receiving ante-natal care".

During the employee's working hours. The employee is entitled to time off during "working hours", defined in subs. (4) as any time when, in accordance with her contract of employment, the employee is required to be at work.

Right to remuneration for time off under section 55

56.—(1) An employee who is permitted to take time off under section 55 is entitled to be paid remuneration by her employer for the period of absence at the appropriate hourly rate.

(2) The appropriate hourly rate, in relation to an employee, is the amount of one week's pay divided by the number of normal working hours in a week for that employee when employed under the contract of employment in force on the day when the time off is taken.

(3) But where the number of normal working hours differs from week to week or over a longer period, the amount of one week's pay shall be divided instead by—

(a) the average number of normal working hours calculated by dividing by twelve the total number of the employee's normal working hours during the period of twelve weeks ending with the last complete week before the day on which the time off is taken, or

(b) where the employee has not been employed for a sufficient period to enable the calculation to be made under paragraph (a), a number which fairly represents the number of normal working hours in a week having regard to such of the considerations specified in subsection (4) as are appropriate in the circumstances.

(4) The considerations referred to in subsection (3)(b) are—

(a) the average number of normal working hours in a week which the employee could expect in accordance with the terms of her contract, and

(b) the average number of normal working hours of other employees engaged in relevant comparable employment with the same employer.

(5) A right to any amount under subsection (1) does not affect any right of an employee in relation to remuneration under her contract of employment ("contractual remuneration").

(6) Any contractual remuneration paid to an employee in respect of a period of time off under section 55 goes towards discharging any liability of the employer to pay remuneration under subsection (1) in respect of that period; and, conversely, any payment of remuneration under subsection (1) in respect of a period goes towards discharging any liability of the employer to pay contractual remuneration in respect of that period.

DEFINITIONS

"contract of employment": s.230(2).
"employee": s.230(1).
"employer": s.230(4).
"employment": s.230(5).
"normal working hours": s.234.
"week": s.235(1).
"week's pay": s.220.

GENERAL NOTE

An employee who is permitted to take time off for ante-natal care under s.55 is entitled to be paid during that time off at the "appropriate hourly rate", as defined in subs. (2). Where the employee also has a contractual right to be paid during the time off, any contractual remuneration which she receives in respect of a period of time off will go towards discharging the employer's liability under subs. (1), and similarly any payments under subs. (1) will be set off against the employer's liability under the contract (subs. (6)).

If the employer allows the employee to take time off for ante-natal care but fails to pay for it, the tribunal will order the employer to pay the amount due; if, on the other hand, the employer unreasonably refuses to allow time off, the employee is entitled to be paid an amount equivalent to the amount which she would have received under the statute, had she in fact been allowed to take the time off (see the note to s.57).

Entitled to be paid. If the employer allows time off for ante-natal care, that time off must be paid. The right to payment follows automatically from a finding that the time off is reasonable, and it is not open to an employer to separate off the question of whether it would be reasonable to allow time off from the question of whether that time off should be paid, by claiming, for example, that it would be reasonable to allow time off only if it is unpaid: see *Gregory v. Tudsbury* [1982] IRLR 267, I.T.; (but *cf. Thomas Scott & Sons (Bakers) v. Allen* [1983] IRLR 329, C.A., a case on time off for trade union duties under what is now s.168 of the Trade Union and Labour Relations (Consolidation) Act 1992, where May L.J. attempted to make just such a distinction).

The appropriate hourly rate. This is calculated by dividing one "week's pay" by the employee's "normal working hours" (see below). Where the employee has regular working hours, the appropriate hourly rate is calculated by dividing her week's pay by the number of normal working hours in a week for that employee under the contract of employment in force on the day when the time off is taken (subs. (2)). Where the employee's working hours vary from week to week, the appropriate hourly rate is calculated by dividing a week's pay by the average number of working hours for that employee over the preceding 12 weeks, ending with the last complete week before the day on which time off is taken (subs. (3)(a)); if the employee has not been employed for 12 weeks, a number which fairly represents her normal working hours will be taken (subs. (3)(b)), based on what she could expect under the terms of her contract, and the average working hours of comparable employees of the same employer (subs. (4)).

Week's pay. For the calculation of a week's pay, see the note to s.220.

Normal working hours. For the calculation of normal working hours, see the note to s.234.

Complaints to industrial tribunals

57.—(1) An employee may present a complaint to an industrial tribunal that her employer—
(a) has unreasonably refused to permit her to take time off as required by section 55, or

(b) has failed to pay the whole or any part of any amount to which the employee is entitled under section 56.

(2) An industrial tribunal shall not consider a complaint under this section unless it is presented—

(a) before the end of the period of three months beginning with the date of the appointment concerned, or

(b) within such further period as the tribunal considers reasonable in a case where it is satisfied that it was not reasonably practicable for the complaint to be presented before the end of that period of three months.

(3) Where an industrial tribunal finds a complaint under this section well-founded, the tribunal shall make a declaration to that effect.

(4) If the complaint is that the employer has unreasonably refused to permit the employee to take time off, the tribunal shall also order the employer to pay to the employee an amount equal to the remuneration to which she would have been entitled under section 56 if the employer had not refused.

(5) If the complaint is that the employer has failed to pay the employee the whole or part of any amount to which she is entitled under section 56, the tribunal shall also order the employer to pay to the employee the amount which it finds due to her.

DEFINITIONS
  "employee": s.230(1).
  "employer": s.230(4).

GENERAL NOTE
  A complaint that an employer has unreasonably refused to allow an employee to take time off under s.55 or has failed to pay her what is due under s.56 lies to an industrial tribunal (subs. (1)), subject to a time limit of three months from the date of the appointment concerned, or within a further reasonable period where the tribunal is satisfied that it was not reasonably practicable for the complaint to be made within that period (subs. (2)). If the tribunal upholds the complaint it will make a declaration to that effect (subs. (3)). If the employer has unreasonably refused to allow time off for ante-natal care, the tribunal will order the employer to pay the employee an amount equivalent to the amount which she would have received under the statute, had she in fact been allowed to take the time off (subs. (4)). If the employer has allowed the employee to take time off, but has failed to pay for it, the tribunal will order the employer to pay the amount due (subs. (5)).
  Not reasonably practicable. For the interpretation of this phrase in unfair dismissal law, see the note to s.111.

Occupational pension scheme trustees

Right to time off for pension scheme trustees

58.—(1) The employer in relation to a relevant occupational pension scheme shall permit an employee of his who is a trustee of the scheme to take time off during the employee's working hours for the purpose of—

(a) performing any of his duties as such a trustee, or

(b) undergoing training relevant to the performance of those duties.

(2) The amount of time off which an employee is to be permitted to take under this section and the purposes for which, the occasions on which and any conditions subject to which time off may be so taken are those that are reasonable in all the circumstances having regard, in particular, to—

(a) how much time off is required for the performance of the duties of a trustee of the scheme and the undergoing of relevant training, and how much time off is required for performing the particular duty or for undergoing the particular training, and

(b) the circumstances of the employer's business and the effect of the employee's absence on the running of that business.

(3) In this section—

(a) "relevant occupational pension scheme" means an occupational pension scheme (as defined in section 1 of the Pension Schemes Act 1993) established under a trust, and

(b) references to the employer, in relation to such a scheme, are to an employer of persons in the description or category of employment to which the scheme relates.

(4) For the purposes of this section the working hours of an employee shall be taken to be any time when, in accordance with his contract of employment, the employee is required to be at work.

DEFINITIONS

"contract of employment": s.230(2).
"employee": s.230(1).
"employer": s.230(4).
"employment": s.230(5).
"relevant occupational pension scheme": subs. (3).
"working hours": subs. (4).

COMMENCEMENT

This section comes into force on a date to be fixed by regulations: see Sched. 2, para 15. At the time of writing no such order had been made.

GENERAL NOTE

This section gives an employee who is a trustee of a "relevant occupational pension scheme" (as defined in subs. (3)) the right to a reasonable amount of time off with pay during working hours to perform his or her duties as such a trustee, or to undergo training relevant to the performance of those duties (subs. (1)). This right derives from the Pensions Act 1995, which extended a number of important employment rights to the trustees of occupational pension schemes, all of which are now contained in this Act. In addition to the right to time off, s.46 gives pension fund trustees a right not to be subjected to any detriment for performing or proposing to perform their functions as a trustee, s.102 makes it automatically unfair to dismiss an employee for performing or proposing to perform his or her functions as a trustee and s.105(5) makes it automatically unfair to select an employee for redundancy on those grounds.

The employee is entitled to take such time off as is reasonable in all the circumstances, in terms of the amount that is taken, the purposes for which it is taken, the occasions on which it is taken, and any conditions which are attached to it. In determining what is reasonable, regard must be had to matters such as the overall amount of time off required for the performance of the duties of a trustee and the undergoing of relevant training, the circumstances of the employer's business, and the effect of the employee's absence on the running of the business (subs. (2)). An employee who is permitted to take time off under these provisions is entitled to be paid for the time taken off, in accordance with s.59: see below. If the employer fails to permit an employee to take time off in accordance with the statutory provisions, or fails to pay the employee the amount due in respect of the time off, the employee may complain to an industrial tribunal under s.60.

There is no minimum qualifying period of continuous employment for this right, and the usual exclusions for employees who ordinarily work outside Great Britain, share fishermen, merchant seamen and police officers do not apply. Parliamentary staff are however excluded (see ss.194(2)(d) and 195(2)(d)), although the right extends to those in Crown employment.

During the employee's working hours. The employee is entitled to time off during "working hours", defined in subs. (4) as any time when, in accordance with his or her contract of employment, the employee is required to be at work.

Subs. (2)

Reasonable in all the circumstances. This is very similar to the formula used in s.50(4) (time off for public duties), although in that context the tribunal is expressly directed to have regard to the amount of time off the employee has already been permitted for public duties or for trade union duties or activities.

Subs. (3)
Relevant occupational pension scheme. See the note to s.46(3).

Right to payment for time off under section 58

59.—(1) An employer who permits an employee to take time off under section 58 shall pay him for the time taken off pursuant to the permission.

(2) Where the employee's remuneration for the work he would ordinarily have been doing during that time does not vary with the amount of work done, he must be paid as if he had worked at that work for the whole of that time.

(3) Where the employee's remuneration for the work he would ordinarily have been doing during that time varies with the amount of work done, he must be paid an amount calculated by reference to the average hourly earnings for that work.

(4) The average hourly earnings mentioned in subsection (3) are—

(a) those of the employee concerned, or

(b) if no fair estimate can be made of those earnings, the average hourly earnings for work of that description of persons in comparable employment with the same employer or, if there are no such persons, a figure of average hourly earnings which is reasonable in the circumstances.

(5) A right to be paid an amount under subsection (1) does not affect any right of an employee in relation to remuneration under his contract of employment ("contractual remuneration").

(6) Any contractual remuneration paid to an employee in respect of a period of time off under section 58 goes towards discharging any liability of the employer under subsection (1) in respect of that period; and, conversely, any payment under subsection (1) in respect of a period goes towards discharging any liability of the employer to pay contractual remuneration in respect of that period.

DEFINITIONS
"contract of employment": s.230(2).
"employee": s.230(1).
"employer": s.230(4).
"employment": s.230(5).

COMMENCEMENT
This section comes into force on a date to be fixed by regulations: see Sched. 2, para 15. At the time of writing no such order had been made.

GENERAL NOTE
An employee who is permitted to take time off to perform his or her duties as a trustee or to undergo training under s.58 is entitled to be paid during that time off. In contrast with the other provisions in this Act concerning the right to payment for time off, which use a highly technical formula based on the "appropriate hourly rate" to calculate the amount due (see the notes to ss.53, 56 and 62), this section uses the much less technical formula used in s.169 of the Trade Union and Labour Relations (Consolidation) Act 1992 (payment for time off for trade union duties). It provides that where the employee's remuneration does not vary according to the amount of work done, the employee must be paid the amount which he or she would have earned during the period of time off, as if he or she had worked for the whole of that time (subs. (2)). Where the employee's remuneration varies according to the amount of work done, the employee is entitled to be paid an amount calculated by reference to his or her average hourly earnings for that work (subs. (3)), or, where no fair estimate can be made of those earnings, the average hourly earnings of those in comparable employment with the same employer; if there are none, a figure of average hourly earnings which is reasonable in all the circumstances must be applied. Where the employee also has a contractual right to be paid during the time off, any contractual remuneration which he or she receives in respect of a period of time off will go towards discharging the employer's liability under subs. (1), and similarly any payments under subs. (1) will be set off against the employer's liability under the contract (subs. (6)).

If the employer fails to pay the employee the amount due in respect of the time off, the employee may complain to an industrial tribunal, which will order the employer to pay the employee the amount which it finds to be due: see the note to s.60.

Complaints to industrial tribunals

60.—(1) An employee may present a complaint to an industrial tribunal that his employer—

(a) has failed to permit him to take time off as required by section 58, or

(b) has failed to pay him in accordance with section 59.

(2) An industrial tribunal shall not consider a complaint under this section unless it is presented—

(a) before the end of the period of three months beginning with the date when the failure occurred, or

(b) within such further period as the tribunal considers reasonable in a case where it is satisfied that it was not reasonably practicable for the complaint to be presented before the end of that period of three months.

(3) Where an industrial tribunal finds a complaint under subsection (1)(a) well-founded, the tribunal—

(a) shall make a declaration to that effect, and

(b) may make an award of compensation to be paid by the employer to the employee.

(4) The amount of the compensation shall be such as the tribunal considers just and equitable in all the circumstances having regard to—

(a) the employer's default in failing to permit time off to be taken by the employee, and

(b) any loss sustained by the employee which is attributable to the matters complained of.

(5) Where on a complaint under subsection (1)(b) an industrial tribunal finds that an employer has failed to pay an employee in accordance with section 59, it shall order the employer to pay the amount which it finds to be due.

DEFINITIONS
"employee": s.230(1).
"employer": s.230(4).

COMMENCEMENT
This section comes into force on a date to be fixed by regulations: see Sched. 2, para 15. At the time of writing no such order had been made.

GENERAL NOTE
A complaint that an employer has failed to allow an employee to take time off under s.58 or has failed to pay the employee what is due under s.59 lies to an industrial tribunal (subs. (1)), subject to a time limit of three months from the date of the failure, or within a further reasonable period where the tribunal is satisfied that it was not reasonably practicable for the complaint to be made within that period (subs. (2)). If the tribunal upholds the complaint it will make a declaration to that effect (subs. (3)), and may in addition award such compensation as it considers just and equitable in all the circumstances, having regard to the employer's default and any loss sustained by the employee which is attributable to that failure (subs. (3) & (4)). For the similar provisions in relation to time off for public duties, see the note to s.51. Where the complaint is that the employer has failed to pay the employee the amount due in respect of the time off, the tribunal will order the employer to pay the employee the amount which it finds to be due (subs. (4)).

Not reasonably practicable. For the interpretation of this phrase in unfair dismissal law, see the note to s.111.

Employee representatives

Right to time off for employee representatives

61.—(1) An employee who is—

(a) an employee representative for the purposes of Chapter II of Part IV of the Trade Union and Labour Relations (Consolidation) Act 1992 (redundancies) or Regulations 10 and 11 of the Transfer of Undertakings (Protection of Employment) Regulations 1981, or

(b) a candidate in an election in which any person elected will, on being elected, be such an employee representative,

is entitled to be permitted by his employer to take reasonable time off during the employee's working hours in order to perform his functions as such an employee representative or candidate.

(2) For the purposes of this section the working hours of an employee shall be taken to be any time when, in accordance with his contract of employment, the employee is required to be at work.

DEFINITIONS
  "contract of employment": s.230(2).
  "employee": s.230(1).
  "employer": s.230(4).
  "employment": s.230(5).
  "working hours": subs. (2).

GENERAL NOTE
  This section gives an employee who is an employee representative for the purposes of the statutory requirements concerning consultation over collective redundancies or transfers of undertakings (under Pt. IV of the Trade Union and Labour Relations (Consolidation) Act 1992) and the Transfer of Undertakings (Protection of Employment) Regulations 1981 respectively), or who is a candidate for election as such a representative, the right to a reasonable amount of time off with pay during working hours to perform his or her functions as such a representative or candidate.
  This right was introduced by the Collective Redundancies and Transfer of Undertakings (Protection of Employment) (Amendment) Regulations 1995 (S.I. 1995 No. 2587) which made provision for the election of employee representatives with whom an employer may consult over collective redundancies and transfers of undertakings, *e.g.* where there are no recognised trade unions. In addition to the right to time off, s.47 gives employee representatives (and candidates for election as representatives) the right not to be subjected to any detriment for performing or proposing to perform their functions or activities as an employee representative or candidate, s.103 makes it automatically unfair to dismiss an employee representative or candidate for performing or proposing to perform his or her functions, and s.105(6) makes it automatically unfair to select an employee for redundancy on those grounds.
  An employee who is permitted to take time off under these provisions is entitled to be paid for that time off in accordance with s.62, and if the employer unreasonably refuses to permit an employee to take time off, or fails to pay the whole or any part of the amount due to the employee in respect of the time off, the employee may complain to an industrial tribunal under s.63: see below.
  There is no minimum qualifying period of continuous employment for this right, but following categories of employee are excluded: employees who ordinarily work outside Great Britain (s.196); share fishermen (s.199(2)); and police officers (s.200). The right extends to those in Crown employment and to Parliamentary staff.
  Employee representative. See the note to s.47(1).
  During the employee's working hours. The employee is entitled to time off during "working hours", defined in subs. (2) as any time when, in accordance with his or her contract of employment, the employee is required to be at work.

Right to remuneration for time off under section 61

62.—(1) An employee who is permitted to take time off under section 61 is entitled to be paid remuneration by his employer for the time taken off at the appropriate hourly rate.

(2) The appropriate hourly rate, in relation to an employee, is the amount of one week's pay divided by the number of normal working hours in a week for that employee when employed under the contract of employment in force on the day when the time off is taken.

(3) But where the number of normal working hours differs from week to week or over a longer period, the amount of one week's pay shall be divided instead by—

(a) the average number of normal working hours calculated by dividing by twelve the total number of the employee's normal working hours during the period of twelve weeks ending with the last complete week before the day on which the time off is taken, or

(b) where the employee has not been employed for a sufficient period to enable the calculation to be made under paragraph (a), a number which fairly represents the number of normal working hours in a week having regard to such of the considerations specified in subsection (4) as are appropriate in the circumstances.

(4) The considerations referred to in subsection (3)(b) are—

(a) the average number of normal working hours in a week which the employee could expect in accordance with the terms of his contract, and

(b) the average number of normal working hours of other employees engaged in relevant comparable employment with the same employer.

(5) A right to any amount under subsection (1) does not affect any right of an employee in relation to remuneration under his contract of employment ("contractual remuneration").

(6) Any contractual remuneration paid to an employee in respect of a period of time off under section 61 goes towards discharging any liability of the employer to pay remuneration under subsection (1) in respect of that period; and, conversely, any payment of remuneration under subsection (1) in respect of a period goes towards discharging any liability of the employer to pay contractual remuneration in respect of that period.

DEFINITIONS
"contract of employment": s.230(2).
"employee": s.230(1).
"employer": s.230(4).
"employment": s.230(5).
"normal working hours": s.234.
"week": s.235(1).
"week's pay": s.220.

GENERAL NOTE
An employee who is permitted to take time off to perform his or her functions as an employee representative or candidate under s.61 is entitled to be paid during that time off at the "appropriate hourly rate", as defined in subs. (2). Where the employee also has a contractual right to be paid during the time off, any contractual remuneration which he or she receives in respect of a period of time off will go towards discharging the employer's liability under subs. (1), and similarly any payments under subs. (1) will be set off against the employer's liability under the contract (subs. (6)).

If the employer fails to pay the employee the amount due in respect of the time off, the employee may complain to an industrial tribunal, which will order the employer to pay the employee the amount which it finds to be due: see the note to s.63.

The appropriate hourly rate. See the note to s.56.

Week's pay. For the calculation of a week's pay, see the note to s.220.

Normal working hours. For the calculation of normal working hours, see the note to s.234.

Complaints to industrial tribunals

63.—(1) An employee may present a complaint to an industrial tribunal that his employer—

(a) has unreasonably refused to permit him to take time off as required by section 61, or

(b) has failed to pay the whole or any part of any amount to which the employee is entitled under section 62.

(2) An industrial tribunal shall not consider a complaint under this section unless it is presented—

(a) before the end of the period of three months beginning with the day on which the time off was taken or on which it is alleged the time off should have been permitted, or

(b) within such further period as the tribunal considers reasonable in a case where it is satisfied that it was not reasonably practicable for the complaint to be presented before the end of that period of three months.

(3) Where an industrial tribunal finds a complaint under this section well-founded, the tribunal shall make a declaration to that effect.

(4) If the complaint is that the employer has unreasonably refused to permit the employee to take time off, the tribunal shall also order the employer to pay to the employee an amount equal to the remuneration to which he would have been entitled under section 62 if the employer had not refused.

(5) If the complaint is that the employer has failed to pay the employee the whole or part of any amount to which he is entitled under section 62, the tribunal shall also order the employer to pay to the employee the amount which it finds due to him.

DEFINITIONS
"employee": s.230(1).
"employer": s.230(4).

GENERAL NOTE
A complaint that an employer has unreasonably refused to allow an employee to take time off under s.61 or has failed to pay the employee what is due under s.62 lies to an industrial tribunal (subs. (1)), subject to a time limit of three months from the date on which the time off was taken or on which it is alleged that the time off should have been permitted, or within a further reasonable period where the tribunal is satisfied that it was not reasonably practicable for the complaint to be made within that period (subs. (2)). If the tribunal upholds the complaint it will make a declaration to that effect (subs. (3)). If the employer has unreasonably refused to allow the employee time off to perform his or her functions as an employee representative or candidate, the tribunal will order the employer to pay the employee an amount equivalent to the amount which he or she would have received under the statute, had the employee in fact been allowed to take the time off (subs. (4)). If the employer has allowed the employee to take time off, but has failed to pay for it, the tribunal will order the employer to pay the amount due (subs. (5)). These provisions mirror those in s.57 governing complaints in relation to time off for ante-natal care.

Not reasonably practicable. For the interpretation of this phrase in unfair dismissal law, see the note to s.111.

PART VII

SUSPENSION FROM WORK

Suspension on medical grounds

Right to remuneration on suspension on medical grounds

64.—(1) An employee who is suspended from work by his employer on medical grounds is entitled to be paid by his employer remuneration while he is so suspended for a period not exceeding twenty-six weeks.

(2) For the purposes of this Part an employee is suspended from work on medical grounds if he is suspended from work in consequence of—

(a) a requirement imposed by or under a provision of an enactment or of an instrument made under an enactment, or

(b) a recommendation in a provision of a code of practice issued or approved under section 16 of the Health and Safety at Work etc. Act 1974,

and the provision is for the time being specified in subsection (3).

(3) The provisions referred to in subsection (2) are—

Regulation 16 of the Control of Lead at Work Regulations 1980,

Regulation 16 of the Ionising Radiations Regulations 1985, and

Regulation 11 of the Control of Substances Hazardous to Health Regulations 1988.

(4) The Secretary of State may by order add provisions to or remove provisions from the list of provisions specified in subsection (3).

(5) For the purposes of this Part an employee shall be regarded as suspended from work on medical grounds only if and for so long as he—

(a) continues to be employed by his employer, but

(b) is not provided with work or does not perform the work he normally performed before the suspension.

DEFINITIONS
"employee": s.230(1).
"employer": s.230(4).
"week": s.235(1).

GENERAL NOTE

This section gives an employee who is suspended from work on certain specified medical grounds a right to be paid his or her normal remuneration (calculated in accordance with s.69) during medical suspension, for a period of up to 26 weeks. These provisions apply where the employee is capable of work (see s.65(3)), but where the employer is unable to provide the employee with work because of the effect of health and safety legislation on the employer's undertaking. An employee may only claim medical suspension pay if he or she is suspended from work in consequence of a requirement or recommendation contained in one of the provisions specified in subs. (3). Those provisions mainly concern medical checks on workers engaged in work involving exposure to lead, ionising radiations or certain other chemical substances or processes hazardous to health. The employee may complain to an industrial tribunal under s.70 if the employer fails to pay the amount due under this section.

An employee who is dismissed, rather than suspended, as a result of a requirement or recommendation specified in subs. (3) may bring an unfair dismissal complaint after only one month's continuous employment, instead of the usual two years (see s.108(2)); such a dismissal will not however be automatically unfair. Where an employee is taken on as a replacement for another employee who is suspended from work on medical grounds, the dismissal of the replacement will be deemed to be for a substantial reason for the purposes of s.98(1)(b) where it was in order to make it possible to allow the other employee to resume work, provided the replacement was informed in writing at the time of his or her engagement that the employment would terminate when the employee's suspension ended: see the note to s.106(3).

Suspended from work. As defined in subs. (5), this refers to the situation where the employee continues to be employed by the employer, but is not provided with work or does not perform the work he normally performed before the suspension.

Subs. (4)

The Secretary of State may by order add to or remove from the list of provisions in subs. (3). The Employment Protection (Medical Suspension) Order 1980 (S.I. 1980 No. 1581) (as amended by S.I. 1985 No. 1787 and S.I. 1988 No. 1746) had effect under the predecessor of this section.

Exclusions from right to remuneration

65.—(1) An employee is not entitled to remuneration under section 64 unless he has been continuously employed for a period of not less than one month ending with the day before that on which the suspension begins.

(2) An employee who is employed—

(a) under a contract for a fixed term of three months or less, or

(b) under a contract made in contemplation of the performance of a specific task which is not expected to last for more than three months,

is not entitled to remuneration under section 64 unless he has been continuously employed for a period of more than three months ending with the day before that on which the suspension begins.

(3) An employee is not entitled to remuneration under section 64 in respect of any period during which he is incapable of work by reason of disease or bodily or mental disablement.

(4) An employee is not entitled to remuneration under section 64 in respect of any period if—

   (a) his employer has offered to provide him with suitable alternative work during the period (whether or not it is work which the employee is under his contract, or was under the contract in force before the suspension, employed to perform) and the employee has unreasonably refused to perform that work, or

   (b) he does not comply with reasonable requirements imposed by his employer with a view to ensuring that his services are available.

DEFINITIONS
"employee": s.230(1).
"employer": s.230(4).

GENERAL NOTE
The following categories are excluded from the right to medical suspension pay:

   (i) employees who have not been continuously employed by their employer for at least one month ending with the day before that on which the suspension begins (subs. (1));

   (ii) casual employees employed under fixed term contracts of three months or less, and those employed to perform a specific task which is not expected to last for more than three months, unless in either case the employee has already been continuously employed for a period of more than three months ending with the day before that on which the suspension begins (subs. (2)).

   (iii) an employee is excluded from the right to medical suspension pay in respect of any period during which he or she is incapable of work by reason of disease or bodily or mental disablement (subs. (3));

   (iv) the right to medical suspension pay in respect of any period is lost if the employee unreasonably refuses an offer of "suitable alternative work" for that period (see below), whether or not the alternative work is work which the employee is employed to perform under the contract of employment (subs. (4)(a));

   (v) the right to medical suspension pay in respect of any period is lost if the employee fails to comply with any reasonable requirements imposed by the employer with a view to ensuring that the employee is available for work (subs. (4)(b)).

With the exception of category (iii), the above exclusions also apply to the right to a statutory guarantee payment under s.29. In addition, the following categories are also excluded from the right to medical suspension pay: employees who ordinarily work outside Great Britain (s.196); share fishermen (s.199(2)); and police officers (s.200). The right does however extend to those in Crown employment and to Parliamentary staff.

Continuously employed. Continuous employment is to be calculated in accordance with the provisions of ss.210–219.

Suitable alternative work. This is not defined for present purposes. Section 67(2) defines "suitable alternative work" for the purposes of the provisions on suspension on maternity grounds as work which is suitable in relation to the employee, appropriate for her to do in the circumstances, and on terms and conditions which are not substantially less favourable than those under which she normally works.

Suspension on maternity grounds

Meaning of suspension on maternity grounds

66.—(1) For the purposes of this Part an employee is suspended from work on maternity grounds if, in consequence of any relevant requirement or relevant recommendation, she is suspended from work by her employer on the ground that she is pregnant, has recently given birth or is breastfeeding a child.

(2) In subsection (1)—

   "relevant requirement" means a requirement imposed by or under a specified provision of an enactment or of an instrument made under an enactment, and

   "relevant recommendation" means a recommendation in a specified provision of a code of practice issued or approved under section 16 of the Health and Safety at Work etc. Act 1974;

and in this subsection "specified provision" means a provision for the time being specified in an order made by the Secretary of State under this subsection.

(3) For the purposes of this Part an employee shall be regarded as suspended from work on maternity grounds only if and for so long as she—

(a) continues to be employed by her employer, but

(b) is not provided with work or (disregarding alternative work for the purposes of section 67) does not perform the work she normally performed before the suspension.

DEFINITIONS
"employee": s.230(1).
"employer": s.230(4).

GENERAL NOTE

The Trade Union Reform and Employment Rights Act 1993 introduced new rights for women suspended from work on maternity grounds, implementing EEC Directive No. 92/85 on the introduction of measures to encourage improvements in the safety and health at work of pregnant workers and workers who have recently given birth or are breastfeeding. Although similar in some respects to the rights enjoyed by those suspended from work on medical grounds (see ss.64 and 65, above), these rights are more advantageous, in that they give an employee suspended from work on maternity grounds a right to be offered suitable alternative employment by her employer where there is an available vacancy (see the note to s.67), and a right to be paid her normal remuneration by her employer during the period of suspension, unless she has unreasonably refused an offer of suitable alternative work for the period in question (see the note to s.68). There is a right of complaint to an industrial tribunal under s.70 if the employer fails to make an offer of alternative employment or fails to pay her the amount due.

Before the 1993 reforms, a dismissal on grounds of pregnancy was not unfair where the employee could not continue working without contravening a statutory provision. The 1993 Act removed that exception, and made it automatically unfair to dismiss an employee on grounds of pregnancy or childbirth, irrespective of length of service, even where the dismissal was because of a statutory requirement that she be suspended from work on maternity grounds: see the note to s.99(1). Under the new regime an employer is therefore expected to comply with a statutory prohibition on continued working by suspending the employee rather than by dismissing her.

This section defines the circumstances in which an employee will be regarded as suspended from work on maternity grounds for the purposes of the above provisions. It provides that an employee is "suspended from work on maternity grounds" where she is suspended from work by her employer on the ground that she is pregnant, has recently given birth or is breastfeeding; the suspension must be in consequence of a "relevant requirement" or a "relevant recommendation" in a "specified provision", *i.e.* a provision specified by the Secretary of State for these purposes.

Suspended from work. This is defined in subs. (3) as referring to the situation where an employee continues to be employed by her employer, but is not provided with work or does not perform the work she normally performed before the suspension.

Specified provision. The Suspension from Work (on Maternity Grounds) Order 1994 (S.I. 1994 No. 2930) which had effect under the predecessor of this section, specifies the following provisions of the Management of Health and Safety at Work Regulations (S.I. 1992 No. 2051) (as amended by S.I. 1994 No. 2865), as relevant provisions for these purposes:

(i) Regulation 13A(3), which requires the suspension of an employee where the employee is a woman of child-bearing age, doing work of a kind which could involve risk, by reason of her condition, to the health and safety of a new or expectant mother, or to that of her baby, from any processes, working conditions or physical, biological or chemical agents (including those specified in Annexes I and II of EEC Directive No. 92/85), and where it is not reasonable to alter her working conditions or hours of work to avoid such a risk, or where to do so would not avoid such a risk; in such a case the woman must be suspended from work for so long as is necessary to avoid that risk. The employer need not take any action under this provision unless notified by the employee in writing that she is pregnant, has given birth within the previous six months, or is breastfeeding (reg. 13C(1)); and the duty to suspend the employee will lapse in the following three circumstances: (a) if the employee fails, within a reasonable time of being requested to do so in writing by her employer, to produce a medical certificate from a registered medical practitioner or a registered midwife showing that she is pregnant; (b) once the employer knows that the employee is no longer a new or expectant mother; or (c) if the employer cannot establish whether she remains a new or expectant mother (reg. 13C(2)).

(ii) Regulation 13B, which requires the suspension of an employee where the employee is a new or expectant mother who works at night, and who has a medical certificate from a registered medical practitioner or a registered midwife which shows that it is necessary for her health and safety that she should not be at work for any period of night work identified in the certificate; in such a case the woman must be suspended from work for so long as is necessary for her health and safety. As before, the duty to suspend the employee will lapse once the employer knows that the employee is no longer a new or expectant mother, or if the employer cannot establish whether she remains a new or expectant mother (reg. 13C(2)).

Right to offer of alternative work

67.—(1) Where an employer has available suitable alternative work for an employee, the employee has a right to be offered to be provided with the alternative work before being suspended from work on maternity grounds.

(2) For alternative work to be suitable for an employee for the purposes of this section—

(a) the work must be of a kind which is both suitable in relation to her and appropriate for her to do in the circumstances, and

(b) the terms and conditions applicable to her for performing the work, if they differ from the corresponding terms and conditions applicable to her for performing the work she normally performs under her contract of employment, must not be substantially less favourable to her than those corresponding terms and conditions.

DEFINITIONS
"contract of employment": s.230(2).
"employee": s.230(1).
"employer": s.230(4).

GENERAL NOTE
An employee who is suspended from work on maternity grounds has the right to be offered suitable alternative work by her employer where there is an available vacancy (subs. (1)). The work must be suitable in relation to the employee, appropriate for her to do in the circumstances, and on terms and conditions which are not substantially less favourable than those under which she normally works (subs. (2)). If the employer fails to make such an offer, the employee may complain to a tribunal under s.70(4), and if the tribunal upholds the complaint it may award such compensation as it considers just and equitable in all the circumstances. If the employee unreasonably refuses an offer of suitable alternative work she will lose her right to be paid while she is suspended from work: see the note to s.68.

The following categories of employee are excluded from this right: employees who ordinarily work outside Great Britain (s.196); share fisherwomen (s.199(2)); and police officers (s.200). The right extends to those in Crown employment and to Parliamentary staff.

Dismissal of an employee engaged as a replacement for another employee suspended from work on maternity grounds will be deemed to be for a substantial reason for the purposes of s.98(1)(b) where the dismissal was in order to make it possible to allow the other employee to resume work, provided the replacement was informed in writing at the time of his or her engagement that the employment would terminate when the employee's suspension ended: see the note to s.106(3).

Suitable alternative work. The definition of "suitable alternative work" in subs. (2) echoes the familiar concept of "suitable available vacancy" which applies in the case of redundancy during the maternity leave period: see the note to s.77.

Right to remuneration

68.—(1) An employee who is suspended from work on maternity grounds is entitled to be paid remuneration by her employer while she is so suspended.

(2) An employee is not entitled to remuneration under this section in respect of any period if—

(a) her employer has offered to provide her during the period with work which is suitable alternative work for her for the purposes of section 67, and

(b) the employee has unreasonably refused to perform that work.

GENERAL NOTE

An employee who is suspended from work on maternity grounds has the right to be paid by her employer while she is suspended from work (subs. (1)). As with the right to medical suspension pay under s.64, the amount payable under this section will be calculated in accordance with s.69, but the right to remuneration under this section is not subject to a 26-week limit. The right to remuneration will be lost if the employer has offered her suitable alternative work for the period in question, and she has unreasonably refused that offer (subs. (2)). The employee may complain to an industrial tribunal under s.70(1) if the employer fails to pay her the amount due, and if the tribunal upholds her complaint it will order the employer to pay her the amount which it finds is due to her.

The following categories of employee are excluded from this right: employees who ordinarily work outside Great Britain (s.196); share fishermen (s.199(2)); and police officers (s.200). The right extends to those in Crown employment and to Parliamentary staff.

Suitable alternative work. The definition of suitable alternative work in s.67(2) applies to this section.

General

Calculation of remuneration

69.—(1) The amount of remuneration payable by an employer to an employee under section 64 or 68 is a week's pay in respect of each week of the period of suspension; and if in any week remuneration is payable in respect of only part of that week the amount of a week's pay shall be reduced proportionately.

(2) A right to remuneration under section 64 or 68 does not affect any right of an employee in relation to remuneration under the employee's contract of employment ("contractual remuneration").

(3) Any contractual remuneration paid by an employer to an employee in respect of any period goes towards discharging the employer's liability under section 64 or 68 in respect of that period; and, conversely, any payment of remuneration in discharge of an employer's liability under section 64 or 68 in respect of any period goes towards discharging any obligation of the employer to pay contractual remuneration in respect of that period.

GENERAL NOTE

The amount of remuneration payable to an employee while suspended from work on medical grounds under s.64 or on maternity grounds under s.68 is a week's pay for each full week of suspension, with a proportionate reduction for any week in which remuneration is only payable for part of that week (subs. (1)). The statutory rights do not affect any contractual rights to payment which the employee might have (subs. (2)), but any payment by the employer under the contract of employment in respect of any period goes towards discharging the employer's liability under the statute in respect of that period, and vice versa (subs. (3)). The right to medical suspension pay is limited to a maximum period of 26 weeks, but no such limit applies to the right to be paid while suspended on maternity grounds.

Week's pay. This is to be calculated in accordance s.220 *et seq.* The maximum amount of a week's pay set by s.227 for the purposes of unfair dismissal compensation and redundancy payments does not apply in this context.

Complaints to industrial tribunals

70.—(1) An employee may present a complaint to an industrial tribunal that his or her employer has failed to pay the whole or any part of remuneration to which the employee is entitled under section 64 or 68.

(2) An industrial tribunal shall not consider a complaint under subsection (1) relating to remuneration in respect of any day unless it is presented—

(a) before the end of the period of three months beginning with that day, or

(b) within such further period as the tribunal considers reasonable in a case where it is satisfied that it was not reasonably practicable for the complaint to be presented within that period of three months.

(3) Where an industrial tribunal finds a complaint under subsection (1) well-founded, the tribunal shall order the employer to pay the employee the amount of remuneration which it finds is due to him or her.

(4) An employee may present a complaint to an industrial tribunal that in contravention of section 67 her employer has failed to offer to provide her with work.

(5) An industrial tribunal shall not consider a complaint under subsection (4) unless it is presented—

(a) before the end of the period of three months beginning with the first day of the suspension, or

(b) within such further period as the tribunal considers reasonable in a case where it is satisfied that it was not reasonably practicable for the complaint to be presented within that period of three months.

(6) Where an industrial tribunal finds a complaint under subsection (4) well-founded, the tribunal may make an award of compensation to be paid by the employer to the employee.

(7) The amount of the compensation shall be such as the tribunal considers just and equitable in all the circumstances having regard to—

(a) the infringement of the employee's right under section 67 by the failure on the part of the employer to which the complaint relates, and

(b) any loss sustained by the employee which is attributable to that failure.

DEFINITIONS
"day": subs. (4).
"employee": s.230(1).
"employer": s.230(4).

GENERAL NOTE
A complaint that the employer has failed to pay the whole or any part of the remuneration payable to an employee suspended from work under s.64 or s.68 lies to an industrial tribunal (subs. (1)). The complaint must be brought within three months beginning with the day for which payment is claimed, or within a further reasonable period where the tribunal is satisfied that it was not reasonably practicable for the complaint to be made within that period (subs. (2)). If the tribunal finds the complaint well-founded it will order the employer to pay the remuneration which it finds due (subs. (3)).

Similarly, a complaint that the employer has failed to make an offer of alternative work under s.67 also lies to an industrial tribunal (subs. (4)), although in this case the complaint must be brought within three months of the first day of suspension, unless not reasonably practicable to do so (subs. (5)). If the tribunal upholds the complaint, it may award such compensation as it considers just and equitable in all the circumstances, having regard to the infringement of the employee's right to be offered alternative work, and any loss sustained by the employee which is attributable to that failure (subss. (6) & (7)).

Not reasonably practicable. For the interpretation of this phrase in unfair dismissal law, see the note to s.111.

PART VIII

MATERNITY RIGHTS

General right to maternity leave

General right to maternity leave

71.—(1) An employee who is absent from work at any time during her maternity leave period is (subject to sections 74 and 75) entitled to the benefit of the terms and conditions of employment which would have been applicable to her if she had not been absent (and had not been pregnant or given birth to a child).

(2) Subsection (1) does not confer any entitlement to remuneration.

DEFINITIONS
　"employee": s.230(1).
　"employer": s.230(4).
　"employment": s.230(5).
　"maternity leave period": s.235(1).

GENERAL NOTE
　This section enacts a general right to 14 weeks' maternity leave for all employees, irrespective of length of service, hours of work or size of firm, during which an employee is entitled to the benefit of all her normal contractual rights except for remuneration, which is specifically excluded: see the note to subs. (2). The right to maternity leave was introduced by the Trade Union Reform and Employment Rights Act 1993, implementing the requirements of EEC Directive No. 92/85 on the introduction of measures to encourage improvements in the safety and health at work of pregnant workers and workers who have recently given birth or are breast-feeding. It is additional to the right of employees with at least two years' continuous employment to return to work after up to 29 weeks' maternity absence (see ss.79–85), and like the right to return it is subject to detailed notice requirements. An employee with a separate contractual right to maternity leave is entitled to exercise a "composite" right by taking advantage of whichever right is, in any particular respect, the more favourable.

Subs. (1)
　An employee absent from work during the maternity leave period will be "entitled to the benefit of the terms and conditions of employment which would have been applicable to her if she had not been absent"; this stops short of stating expressly that the employee's contract of employment continues to subsist during the maternity leave period, but it probably amounts to the same thing. In the absence of any specific provision concerning the remedies available to a woman denied the benefits of her contract of employment during the maternity leave period, it seems that the remedy will be an action for breach of contract in the ordinary courts. On the vexed question of the status of the contract of employment during the extended period of maternity absence, see the note to s.85.

Subs. (2)
　The right to the continuation of the terms and conditions of employment during the maternity leave period does not confer any right to remuneration during that period. Instead, entitlement to be paid during the maternity leave period is governed by the provisions on Statutory Maternity Pay (SMP) in Pt. XII of the Social Security Contributions and Benefits Act 1992 (c. 4), which gives all those who satisfy the qualifying conditions a right to receive SMP for a maximum of 18 weeks, the first six weeks at the higher rate of nine-tenths of normal weekly earnings, and thereafter at a lower rate fixed by regulations (£54.44 per week, at the time of writing). Payments of SMP must be set off against any contractual payments (*e.g.* under a contractual maternity scheme) for the weeks in question, and vice versa. Employers are entitled to recover 92 per cent of the cost of SMP from the state by deducting it from N.I. contributions; small employers (*i.e.* those whose gross N.I. contributions do not exceed £20,000 for the qualifying tax year) may recover the full amount paid out, and are also entitled to deduct an additional amount equal to 5.5 per cent of the SMP paid, to compensate for the additional N.I. contributions.
　Remuneration. As originally drafted in the Trade Union Reform and Employment Rights Bill, this provision excluded any entitlement to "pay", which would have included the totality of the consideration which an employee receives from her employer, whether in the form of wages or salary, or non-wage benefits such as private medical insurance, company car, accommodation allowance, etc. The Bill was however amended in Committee, and the reference to "pay" was replaced by "remuneration", the intention being to exclude the employee's entitlement to wages and salary, but not to any other non-wage benefits. The term "remuneration" is used in several other places in the Act, in particular in the calculation of a "week's pay" under s.220 *et seq*, where it is similarly undefined; in that context, it has been held to include, in addition to wages or salary, any regular bonuses, commission or supplements to which the employee is entitled (*Weevsmay v. Kings* [1977] I.C.R. 244; *Marcusfield (A & B) v. Melhuish* [1977] IRLR 484), but not payments in kind, payments from a third party (*e.g.* tips: *Palmanor v. Cedron* [1978] I.C.R. 1008), unless distributed by the employer *(Keywest Club (t/a Veeraswamys Restaurant) v. Choudhury* [1988] IRLR 51), or expenses, unless there is an element of profit or surplus (*S & U Stores v. Wilkes*

[1974] IRLR 283). It seems likely that the same interpretation will be applied in this context. If so, an employee will be entitled to the benefit of the non-wage elements of her remuneration package throughout her statutory maternity leave period. Whether she continues to be entitled to those benefits after the end of the maternity leave period will be a matter of her contract of employment.

Commencement of maternity leave period

72.—(1) Subject to subsection (2), an employee's maternity leave period commences with the earlier of—

(a) the date which, in accordance with section 74(1) to (3), she notifies to her employer as the date on which she intends her period of absence from work in exercise of the right conferred by section 71 to commence, and

(b) the first day after the beginning of the sixth week before the expected week of childbirth on which she is absent from work wholly or partly because of pregnancy.

(2) Where the employee's maternity leave period has not commenced by virtue of subsection (1) when childbirth occurs, her maternity leave period commences with the day on which childbirth occurs.

(3) The Secretary of State may by order vary subsections (1) and (2).

DEFINITIONS
"childbirth": s.235(1).
"employee": s.230(1).
"employer": s.230(4).
"employment": s.230(5).
"expected week of childbirth": s.235(1).
"maternity leave period": s.235(1).

GENERAL NOTE
Within certain limits, an employee can choose when she wishes her maternity leave to begin. The maternity leave period will normally commence on the date notified by her to the employer as the date on which she intends her maternity leave period to begin (subs. (1)(a)), although she may not choose a date which falls before the beginning of the eleventh week before the expected week of childbirth (EWC): see s.74(2). There are however two specific instances in which the start of the maternity leave period will be triggered automatically: the first is where the employee is absent from work wholly or partly because of pregnancy after the start of the sixth week before the expected week of childbirth, in which case her maternity leave period will begin to run from the first day of absence (subs. (1)(b)); the second is where childbirth occurs early, before the maternity leave period would otherwise have commenced, in which case her maternity leave period begins to run from the date of the birth (subs. (2)).

The first of the automatic triggering provisions is intended to remove the possibility of a woman who is suffering from ante-natal illness delaying the start of her maternity leave period by taking sick leave instead. Under the original proposals in the Trade Union Reform and Employment Rights Bill, the maternity leave period would have commenced automatically with the first day of pregnancy absence after the beginning of the *eleventh* week before the EWC, but this was amended in Committee following objections that it removed a woman's right to choose when to start her maternity leave. Under the provisions as enacted, a woman suffering from ante-natal illness who does not qualify for the right to return to work after maternity absence under s.79 will still have the possibility of up to eight weeks' leave post-childbirth. However, in such cases the temptation will always be to delay the start of the maternity leave period for as long as possible so as to guarantee the maximum period of leave after childbirth, and there is an obvious danger that a woman might try to continue working through ante-natal illness in an attempt to avoid the automatic triggering provisions. Such a consequence would be particularly unfortunate given the fact that the EEC Directive from which the maternity leave provisions derive was intended to improve the health and safety protection of pregnant women at work.

On which she is absent from work wholly or partly because of pregnancy. It is only absence "wholly or partly because of pregnancy" which automatically sets the clock running, and given the widespread propensity to assume that *any* illness during pregnancy is pregnancy-related, some difficult conflicts of evidence are likely to arise where the reason for the absence is disputed. One assumes that a woman who is permitted by her employer to take time off work for ante-natal care under s.55 will not be "absent from work wholly or partly because of pregnancy or childbirth" within these provisions, although this is not made explicit. It would be most unfortunate if this were not the case.

Expected week of childbirth. This is defined in s.235(1) as "the week, beginning with midnight between Saturday and Sunday, in which it is expected that childbirth will occur". There are two definitions of "week" in s.235(1), and although it appears from that section that the more complex definition should apply in this context, the E.A.T. held under the previous provisions that it is the simple definition ("week means a week ending with Saturday") that is to be applied in maternity rights cases, as it is more appropriate to the definition of "expected week of childbirth": *Secretary of State for Employment v. Ford (A.) & Son (Sacks)* [1986] I.C.R. 882. "Childbirth" is defined in s.235(1) as "the birth of a living child or the birth of a child whether living or dead after 24 weeks of pregnancy". Before the 1993 reforms, the maternity provisions used the concept of the "expected week of *confinement*", which referred to the birth of a child after *28* weeks of pregnancy.

Duration of maternity leave period

73.—(1) Subject to subsections (2) and (3), an employee's maternity leave period continues for the period of fourteen weeks from its commencement or until the birth of the child, if later.

(2) Subject to subsection (3), where any requirement imposed by or under any relevant statutory provision prohibits the employee from working for any period after the end of the period mentioned in subsection (1) by reason of her having recently given birth, her maternity leave period continues until the end of that later period.

(3) Where the employee is dismissed after the commencement of her maternity leave period but before the time when (apart from this subsection) that period would end, the period ends at the time of the dismissal.

(4) In subsection (2) "relevant statutory provision" means a provision of—

(a) an enactment, or

(b) an instrument made under an enactment,

other than a provision for the time being specified in an order made under section 66(2).

(5) The Secretary of State may by order vary subsections (1) to (4).

DEFINITIONS

"employee": s.230(1).
"maternity leave period": s.235(1).
"relevant statutory provision": subs. (4).

GENERAL NOTE

The maternity leave period normally lasts for a maximum of 14 weeks, but it may continue beyond the end of that period in two situations. First, subs. (1) provides that if childbirth is late, the maternity leave period will continue until the birth of the child, even if this extends it beyond the normal 14-week limit; and secondly, subs. (2) provides that where the employee is prohibited by law from working within a certain period after childbirth, her maternity leave period will continue until the expiry of that period. The Maternity (Compulsory Leave) Regulations 1994 (S.I. 1994 No. 2479) provide for two weeks' compulsory leave beginning with the day of childbirth, in compliance with Art. 8(2) of EEC Directive No. 92/85, and the maternity leave period will therefore be deemed to continue until the expiry of that period. The requirement of two weeks' leave after childbirth is compulsory on both the employer and the employee, and an employer who infringes the prohibition is liable on summary conviction to a fine not exceeding level 2 on the standard scale; there does not appear to be any sanction on the employee in such a case.

Where an employee is dismissed during maternity leave, the maternity leave period will end at the time of the dismissal (subs. (3)). Such a dismissal will however be automatically unfair if the reason for the dismissal is that the employee has given birth to a child or any other reason connected with her having given birth to a child: see the note to s.99. Special rules apply where the employee is redundant during the maternity leave period, in that she is entitled to be offered alternative employment with her employer where there is a suitable available vacancy: see the note to s.77. Failure to make such an offer will render the dismissal automatically unfair, but an employee who unreasonably refuses an offer of suitable alternative employment will lose her right to a redundancy payment, and her dismissal is likely to be held fair.

Relevant statutory provision. See the Maternity (Compulsory Leave) Regulations 1994 (S.I. 1994 No. 2479) made under s.2(2) of the European Communities Act 1972.

Requirement to notify commencement of leave

74.—(1) Subject to subsections (4) and (5), an employee does not have the right conferred by section 71 unless she notifies her employer of the date on which she intends her period of absence from work in exercise of the right to commence.

(2) No date occurring before the beginning of the eleventh week before the expected week of childbirth may be notified under subsection (1).

(3) Notification under subsection (1) shall be given by an employee—

(a) not less than twenty-one days before the date on which she intends her period of absence from work in exercise of the right conferred by section 71 to commence, or

(b) if that is not reasonably practicable, as soon as is reasonably practicable.

(4) Where an employee's maternity leave period commences with the first day after the beginning of the sixth week before the expected week of childbirth on which she is absent from work wholly or partly because of pregnancy—

(a) subsection (1) does not require her to notify her employer of the date specified in that subsection, but

(b) (whether or not she has notified him of that date) she does not have the right conferred by section 71 unless she notifies him as soon as is reasonably practicable that she is absent from work wholly or partly because of pregnancy.

(5) Where an employee's maternity leave period commences with the day on which childbirth occurs—

(a) subsection (1) does not require her to notify her employer of the date specified in that subsection, but

(b) (whether or not she has notified him of that date) she does not have the right conferred by section 71 unless she notifies him as soon as is reasonably practicable after the birth that she has given birth.

(6) Any notification required by this section shall, if the employer so requests, be given in writing.

DEFINITIONS

"childbirth": s.235(1).
"employee": s.230(1).
"employer": s.230(4).
"expected week of childbirth": s.235(1).
"maternity leave period": s.235(1).

GENERAL NOTE

The right to maternity leave is subject to detailed notice requirements set out in ss.74 and 75; these notice requirements also apply to the right to return to work after maternity absence under s.79, but an employee who wishes to exercise her right to return to work under that section must include with the information required by s.75 the information that she intends to exercise her right to return to work: see the note to s.79.

This section requires the employee to notify her employer of the date on which she intends her maternity leave period to commence, at least 21 days before that date, or, if that is not reasonably practicable, as soon as is reasonably practicable (subs. (3)); the notice must be given in writing, if the employer so requests (subs. (6)). For obvious reasons, this requirement does not apply where the maternity leave period is automatically triggered by a day of absence wholly or partly because of pregnancy after the sixth week before the EWC, but in such a case the employee must notify her employer as soon as is reasonably practicable (in writing, if he so requests) that she is absent from work for that reason (subs. (4)); similarly, where the maternity leave period begins with the day of childbirth, she must notify her employer as soon as is reasonably practicable (again, in writing if he so requests) that she has given birth (subs. (5)).

Not reasonably practicable. In *Nu-Swift International v. Mallinson* [1978] IRLR 537 (decided under the pre-1993 provisions on the right to return to work), the E.A.T. held that in determining whether it was "not reasonably practicable" for an employee to give the required 21 days' notice of her intention to return to work, the tribunal should adopt the interpretation given to those words in unfair dismissal law: see the note to s.111. In *Nu-Swift*, the employee failed to give 21 days' notice of her intention to return to work because she was unable to make up her mind whether or not to return; the E.A.T. held that this did not make it "not reasonably practicable" for her to give the employer the required notice, and she therefore lost her right to return.

Expected week of childbirth. See the note to s.72.

Requirement to notify pregnancy etc.

75.—(1) An employee does not have the right conferred by section 71 unless at least twenty-one days before her maternity leave period commences or, if that is not reasonably practicable, as soon as is reasonably practicable, she informs her employer in writing of—

(a) her pregnancy, and

(b) the expected week of childbirth,

or, if childbirth has occurred, of the date on which it occurred.

(2) An employee does not have the right conferred by section 71 unless, if requested to do so by her employer, she produces for his inspection a certificate from—

(a) a registered medical practitioner, or

(b) a registered midwife,

stating the expected week of childbirth.

DEFINITIONS

"childbirth": s.235(1).
"employee": s.230(1).
"employer": s.230(4).
"expected week of childbirth": s.235(1).
"maternity leave period": s.235(1).

GENERAL NOTE

In addition to giving notice in accordance with s.74, the employee must notify her employer in writing at least 21 days before her maternity leave period commences (or as soon as is reasonably practicable thereafter) that she is pregnant, and of the expected week of childbirth (or, if childbirth has already occurred, the date of the birth) (subs. (1)). The employer may also request her to produce a medical certificate from a registered medical practitioner or registered midwife confirming the expected week of confinement (subs. (2)). If the employee wishes to exercise her right to return to work under s.79, she must include with the information required by subs. (1) the information that she intends to exercise her right to return to work: see the note to s.79.

Not reasonably practicable. See the note to s.74.

Expected week of childbirth. See the note to s.72.

Requirement to notify return during maternity leave period

76.—(1) An employee who intends to return to work earlier than the end of her maternity leave period shall give to her employer not less than seven days' notice of the date on which she intends to return.

(2) If an employee attempts to return to work earlier than the end of her maternity leave period without complying with subsection (1), her employer shall be entitled to postpone her return to a date such as will secure, subject to subsection (3), that he has seven days' notice of her return.

(3) An employer is not entitled under subsection (2) to postpone an employee's return to work to a date after the end of her maternity leave period.

(4) If an employee whose return to work has been postponed under subsection (2) has been notified that she is not to return to work before the date to which her return was postponed, the employer is under no contractual obligation to pay her remuneration until the date to which her return was postponed if she returns to work before that date.

DEFINITIONS
   "employee": s.230(1).
   "employer": s.230(4).
   "maternity leave period": s.235(1).

GENERAL NOTE
   A woman who is absent from work on maternity leave does not have to notify her employer of her intention to return to work at the end of the 14 week maternity leave period, either before, during or towards the end of that period. This contrasts with the right to return to work after extended maternity absence, where notice of the intention to return must be given at the beginning and at the end of the period of absence, and where the employer is entitled to ask for written confirmation of that intention during the period of maternity leave (see the note to s.80). However, this section provides that a woman who wishes to return to work *before* the end of her maternity leave period must give her employer at least seven days' notice (not necessarily in writing) of the date of her intended return (subs. (1)); if she attempts to return to work early without doing so, the employer may postpone her return to the extent necessary to give the required seven days' notice (subs. (2)), although not beyond the end of the maternity leave period (subs. (3)), and is under no obligation to pay her if she insists on returning to work before that notice period expires (subs. (4)).

Redundancy during maternity leave period

   77.—(1) This section applies where during an employee's maternity leave period it is not practicable by reason of redundancy for the employer to continue to employ her under her existing contract of employment.

   (2) Where there is a suitable available vacancy, the employee is entitled to be offered (before the ending of her employment under her existing contract) alternative employment with her employer or his successor, or an associated employer, under a new contract of employment which complies with subsection (3) (and takes effect immediately on the ending of her employment under the previous contract).

   (3) The new contract of employment must be such that—

   (a) the work to be done under it is of a kind which is both suitable in relation to the employee and appropriate for her to do in the circumstances, and

   (b) its provisions as to the capacity and place in which she is to be employed, and as to the other terms and conditions of her employment, are not substantially less favourable to her than if she had continued to be employed under the previous contract.

DEFINITIONS
   "associated employer": s.231.
   "by reason of redundancy": s.235(3).
   "contract of employment": s.230(2).
   "employee": s.230(1).
   "employer": s.230(4).
   "maternity leave period": s.235(1).
   "successor": s.235(1).

GENERAL NOTE
   A woman who becomes redundant during her maternity leave period is entitled to be offered alternative employment with her employer or his successor, or an associated employer, where there is a suitable available vacancy, defined in subs. (3) as work which is suitable in relation to the employee, appropriate for her to do in the circumstances, and on terms and conditions which are not substantially less favourable to her than those which she enjoyed under her previous contract. The offer of alternative employment must be made before her original contract ends, and must take effect immediately on the ending of that contract (subs. (2)). Failure to make such an offer will render the dismissal automatically unfair under s.99(1)(e), but an employee who unreasonably refuses an offer of suitable alternative employment will lose her right to a redundancy payment (see the note to s.141(2)), and her dismissal is likely to be held to be fair. The right conferred by this section mirrors the long-standing right of a woman who is made redundant during extended maternity absence to be offered suitable alternative employment, and the cases decided under those provisions are likely to be held in point here. See the note to s.81.

By reason of redundancy. This is to be construed in accordance with s.139: see s.235(3).

Suitable available vacancy. The alternative work must be "suitable" in relation to the employee and "appropriate" for her to do in the circumstances. Neither requirement is defined. In the context of entitlement to redundancy payments it has been held that the suitability of an offer of alternative employment is a question of fact and degree for the tribunal (see *Taylor v. Kent County Council* [1969] 2 Q.B. 560). The issue of suitability is likely to turn on matters such as the nature and status of the job, pay, hours of work, place of work and working conditions in general. The alternative employment must also be "appropriate for her to do in the circumstances"; the tribunal must therefore take into account the particular personal circumstances of the employee, including the fact that she has a new baby, in considering the suitability of the offer of alternative employment. Factors likely to be relevant include the location of the work, hours of work, domestic considerations, etc. The requirement of appropriateness does not appear in the redundancy payments provisions, although in that context the tribunal must consider whether the employee's refusal of an offer of alternative employment was unreasonable, a test which probably performs a similar function. The terms and conditions of the new contract of employment must not be "substantially less favourable" to her than if she had continued in her original job. In other words, the terms and conditions of the new contract *may* be less favourable, provided they are not *substantially* so. This contrasts with the right to return to work under s.79, where the employee is entitled to return to work on terms and conditions which are not less favourable than those which would have been applicable to her had she not been absent from work: see the note to s.39(2).

Associated employer. See the note to s.231.

Contractual rights to maternity leave

78.—(1) An employee who has both the right to maternity leave under section 71 and another right to maternity leave (under a contract of employment or otherwise) may not exercise the two rights separately but may, in taking maternity leave, take advantage of whichever right is, in any particular respect, the more favourable.

(2) The provisions of sections 72 to 77 apply, subject to any modifications necessary to give effect to any more favourable contractual terms, to the exercise of the composite right described in subsection (1) as they apply to the exercise of the right under section 71.

DEFINITIONS
"contract of employment": s.230(2).
"employee": s.230(1).

GENERAL NOTE
This section allows a woman who has both a contractual and a statutory right to maternity leave to create a composite right by taking advantage of whichever is, in any particular respect, the more favourable (subs. (1)). In exercising this composite right, the normal statutory requirements still apply, suitably modified to give effect to any more favourable terms in the contract (subs. (2)). This mirrors the long-standing provisions on the composite right to return to work after maternity absence, and the cases decided under those provisions are likely to be held in point here: see the note to s.85. In that context, the Court of Appeal has held that the statutory requirements will continue to apply unless there is evidence that the parties have expressly or impliedly agreed to some modification of them: see *Lavery v. Plessey Telecommunications* [1983] IRLR 202.

In any particular respect. See *Bovey v. Board of Governors of the Hospital for Sick Children* [1978] IRLR 241, a case under the equivalent provisions relating to the right to return to work after maternity absence: see the note to s.85.

Right to return to work

Right to return to work

79.—(1) An employee who—
(a) has the right conferred by section 71, and
(b) has, at the beginning of the eleventh week before the expected week of childbirth, been continuously employed for a period of not less than two years,

also has the right to return to work at any time during the period beginning at the end of her maternity leave period and ending twenty-nine weeks after the beginning of the week in which childbirth occurs.

(2) An employee's right to return to work under this section is the right to return to work with the person who was her employer before the end of her maternity leave period, or (where appropriate) his successor, in the job in which she was then employed—

(a) on terms and conditions as to remuneration not less favourable than those which would have been applicable to her had she not been absent from work at any time since the commencement of her maternity leave period,

(b) with her seniority, pension rights and similar rights as they would have been if the period or periods of her employment prior to the end of her maternity leave period were continuous with her employment following her return to work (but subject to the requirements of paragraph 5 of Schedule 5 to the Social Security Act 1989 (credit for the period of absence in certain cases)), and

(c) otherwise on terms and conditions not less favourable than those which would have been applicable to her had she not been absent from work after the end of her maternity leave period.

(3) The Secretary of State may by order vary the period of two years specified in subsection (1) or that period as varied by an order under this subsection.

DEFINITIONS
"childbirth": s.235(1).
"contract of employment": s.230(2).
"employee": s.230(1).
"employer": s.230(4).
"expected week of childbirth": s.235(1).
"job": s.235(1).
"maternity leave period": s.235(1).
"week": s.235(1).

GENERAL NOTE
This section defines the scope of the right to return to work after extended maternity absence. It gives an employee who has been continuously employed for at least two years at the beginning of the eleventh week before the EWC the right to return to work up to 29 weeks after the week of childbirth. The right to extended maternity absence co-exists with the right to 14 weeks' maternity leave (see the note to s.71), and an employee must have qualified for the right to maternity leave in order to be eligible for the right to return. She must also satisfy the additional notice requirements for the right to return to work (see s.80, below).

The right to return to work is not dependent upon the continuance of the contract of employment through the period of absence. Before the 1993 reforms, s.33(3) of the EP(C)A provided that an employee who satisfied the statutory requirements was entitled to return to work after maternity absence "whether or not a contract of employment subsists during the period of her absence". This is no longer stated expressly, but it is implicit in the other provisions. Whether the contract of employment subsists through the period of absence is a matter of contract to be determined on the facts of each individual case. See the note to s.85.

The position of an employee who is dismissed during maternity absence is especially complicated. If she is dismissed before the beginning of the eleventh week before the EWC, she will not qualify for the right to maternity leave or the right to return to work, but if the reason for the dismissal was connected with her pregnancy, the dismissal will be automatically unfair under s.99. Where the dismissal takes place after the beginning of the eleventh week before the EWC, her right to return to work will be unaffected, provided she satisfies the statutory requirements. She may also be able to bring an unfair dismissal claim, but this will depend upon when the dismissal takes place. If she is dismissed during the 14-week maternity leave period, the dismissal will bring her maternity leave period to an end (see s.73(3)), and the dismissal will be automatically unfair under s.99 if it is for a reason connected with her pregnancy. If however the dismissal takes place during the extended maternity absence (*i.e.* after the end of the 14-week maternity leave period), otherwise than in the course of attempting to return to work, this will only give rise to an unfair dismissal claim if her contract of employment subsisted during that period. As stated above, claiming unfair dismissal (or a redundancy payment) will not prevent the employee from exercising her right to return to work, although the employer may make the exercise of her right to return to work conditional on her repaying any unfair dismissal compensation or redundancy payment paid in respect of that dismissal: see the note to s.84. Finally, if she is dismissed in the course of attempting to exercise her statutory right to return to work, she will be deemed to have been dismissed from the notified day of return (see the note to s.96), whether or not her contract of employment subsisted during her maternity absence. The position is the same if she is dismissed while attempting to exercise a "composite" (*i.e.* a combined statutory and contractual) right to return: see the note to s.85(2).

If the conditions set out in subs. (1) are satisfied, an employee has the right to return to work at any time up to 29 weeks after the beginning of the actual week of childbirth. The right is a right to return to work with her original employer (or, where appropriate, a successor of that employer), in the job in which she was employed before the end of her maternity leave period, and on terms and conditions which are "not less favourable than those which would have been applicable to her had she not been absent from work" (see the note to subs. (2)). This means that she will be entitled to benefit from any improvement in the terms and conditions applicable to her job, but will also have to accept any deterioration in those terms which would have applied to her had she not been absent. In general, she is entitled to return on terms and conditions not less favourable than those which would have been applicable to her had she not been absent from work after the end of her maternity leave period (subs. (2)(c)), but in the case of terms and conditions as to remuneration, the entitlement is to terms and conditions not less favourable than those which would have been applicable to her had she not been absent from work at any time since the commencement of her maternity leave period (subs. (2)(a)); this reflects the fact that there is no statutory entitlement to remuneration during the maternity leave period. It is expressly provided in subs. (2)(b) that as regards the employee's seniority, pension rights and other similar rights, her period of employment before the end of the maternity leave period is to be treated as continuous with her employment following her return to work, so that she will be entitled to return at the same level of seniority, etc., as she enjoyed when she left, but this does not mean that the time during which she is absent from work actually counts in the entitlement to such rights, unless her contract provides otherwise. There are however two major qualifications to this: first, Sched. 5, para. 5 of the Social Security Act 1989 (implementing EEC Directive No. 86/378 on equal treatment for men and women in occupational social security schemes), provides that a provision in an employment-related benefit scheme (*e.g.* a pension or sickness scheme) will be an "unfair maternity provision" unless, in determining rights and entitlements under the scheme, an employee who is on paid maternity absence (whether statutory or contractual maternity pay) is given credit for her period of absence as if she were working normally and receiving the pay likely to be paid for doing so during that period; and secondly, for the purposes of statutory rights dependent upon continuity of employment, an employee's period of maternity absence does count towards entitlement: see the note to s.212.

Subs. (1)
At the beginning of the eleventh week before the expected week of childbirth. The definition of "week" to be applied here is the simple definition ("a week ending with Saturday") used for the purpose of calculating periods of continuous employment: *Secretary of State for Employment v. Ford (A.) & Son (Sacks)* [1986] I.C.R. 882. See the note to s.72.
The week in which childbirth occurs. This refers to the actual week of childbirth, not the expected week of childbirth: see *F.W. Woolworth & Co. v. Smith* [1990] I.C.R. 45, E.A.T.

Subs. (2)
In the job in which she was then employed. "Job", as defined in s.235(1), means "the nature of the work which [she] is employed to do in accordance with [her] contract, and the capacity and place in which [she] is so employed". It follows that if the employee's job description in her contract of employment defines her "job" more widely than the work which she in fact did, the employer may be able to offer her a different job on her return to work. See for example *Edgell v. Lloyd's Register of Shipping* [1977] IRLR 463 (employee was given less responsibility on her return to work, but as the nature of her job remained the same, the employer had fulfilled his statutory obligations). An employee is however given additional protection by the requirement that the terms and conditions be "not less favourable than those which would have been applicable to her had she not been absent from work" (see below).
Not less favourable. See *McFadden (N.) v. Greater Glasgow Passenger Transport Executive* [1977] IRLR 327 (the employee was re-employed on the same grade as before, but her terms and conditions were held to be less favourable than before, because she no longer had her own desk, had suffered a drop in status, and was more vulnerable to redundancy).

Requirement to notify return

80.—(1) An employee does not have the right conferred by section 79 unless she includes with the information required by section 75(1) the information that she intends to exercise the right.

(2) Where, not earlier than twenty-one days before the end of her maternity leave period, an employee is requested in accordance with subsection (3) by her employer, or a successor of his, to give him written confirmation that she intends to exercise the right conferred by section 79, the employee is not entitled to that right unless she gives the requested confirmation—

(a) within fourteen days of receiving the request, or

(b) if that is not reasonably practicable, as soon as is reasonably practicable.

(3) A request under subsection (2) shall be—

(a) made in writing, and

(b) accompanied by a written statement of the effect of that subsection.

DEFINITIONS
"employee": s.230(1).
"employer": s.230(4).
"maternity leave period": s.235(1).

GENERAL NOTE
To qualify for the right to return to work after maternity absence, the employee must have satisfied the requirements set out in s.79(1), and she must also have notified her employer at the time that she gave the information required under s.75 that she intends to exercise her right to return to work (subs. (1)). The right to return arises once the employee has complied with these initial notice requirements (*i.e.* before she gives notice of her intended day of return under s.82): see *Philip Hodges & Co. v. Kell* [1994] I.C.R. 656, E.A.T., discussed in the note to s.81.

In addition, while she is on leave her employer may request that she confirm in writing her intention to return to work, and she must comply with that request within 14 days or, if not reasonably practicable, within a further reasonable period (subs. (2)). The request for confirmation must be in writing, accompanied by a written statement explaining the consequences of a failure to give confirmation (subs. (3)), and may be made no earlier than 21 days before the end of the 14-week maternity leave period. As that period may have started anything up to 11 weeks before the EWC, this may leave the employee with very little time after giving birth to decide whether or not she still wishes to return to work. Indeed, where childbirth is delayed by more than two weeks (which is by no means uncommon) she could even be required to give confirmation of her intention to return to work before she has given birth! This is a significant (and, arguably, highly undesirable) departure from the pre-1993 provisions, which stated that a request for confirmation could not be made earlier than 49 days after the beginning of the EWC. The period immediately around the time of childbirth is hardly the most appropriate time for a woman to be expected to make important decisions about her future employment. The latitude with which the tribunals are prepared to interpret the test of reasonable practicability in subs. (2)(b) will be crucial here. It should also be remembered that there is nothing in the Act's provisions which prevents a woman who has confirmed her intention to return to work from subsequently changing her mind (although *quaere* whether in such a case she might be disqualified from receiving the jobseeker's allowance on the grounds that she has "without good cause, neglected to avail [herself] of a reasonable opportunity of employment" within the Jobseekers Act 1995 (c. 18), s.19(6)(d)).

Redundancy before return

81.—(1) This section applies where an employee has the right conferred by section 79 but it is not practicable by reason of redundancy for the employer to permit her to return in accordance with that right.

(2) Where there is a suitable available vacancy, the employee is entitled to be offered alternative employment with her employer or his successor, or an associated employer, under a new contract of employment which complies with subsection (3).

(3) The new contract of employment must be such that—

(a) the work to be done under it is of a kind which is both suitable in relation to the employee and appropriate for her to do in the circumstances, and

(b) its provisions as to the capacity and place in which she is to be employed, and as to the other terms and conditions of her employment, are not substantially less favourable to her than if she had returned to work pursuant to the right conferred by section 79.

DEFINITIONS

"associated employer": s.231.
"by reason of redundancy": s.235(3).
"contract of employment": s.230(2).
"employee": s.230(1).
"employer": s.230(4).
"successor": s.235(1).

GENERAL NOTE

If a genuine redundancy situation arises during the employee's maternity absence which makes it impracticable for the employer to permit her to return to work, she is entitled to be offered alternative employment with her employer, or his successor, or an associated company, if there is a suitable available vacancy (subss. (1), (2)). The alternative work must be suitable in relation to the employee, appropriate for her to do in the circumstances, and on terms and conditions which are not substantially less favourable than if she had returned to work in accordance with her statutory right (subs. (3)). Failure to make such an offer will be treated as an automatically unfair dismissal under s.99(4), irrespective of the reasonableness of the employer's actions. So, for example, in *Community Task Force v. Rimmer* [1986] I.C.R. 491, the employers had a vacancy which would have been suitable and appropriate for the employee, but the job was not offered to her because that would have led to the withdrawal of funding from the Manpower Services Commission. The E.A.T. held that the failure to offer the job to the employee rendered her dismissal automatically unfair: "The test of availability ... is not expressed to be qualified by considerations of what is economic or reasonable. The tribunal must simply ask themselves whether a suitable vacancy is available".

An employee who unreasonably refuses an offer of suitable alternative employment will lose her right to a redundancy payment (see the note to s.141(2)), and her dismissal is likely to be held to be fair. If there is no suitable available vacancy, the employee will be able to claim unfair dismissal if she was unfairly selected for redundancy. She will also be entitled to a redundancy payment, but if the employer can show that she would in any event have been dismissed for redundancy before the notified day of return, she will be treated as having been dismissed from that earlier date: see s.137(2).

The E.A.T. has held that an employee acquires the right to return to work once she has complied with the initial notice requirements contained in ss.75(1) and 80(1) (*i.e.* before she gives notice of her intended day of return under s.82), which means that in a redundancy situation she has the right to be offered any suitable alternative employment which becomes available during her maternity absence, even if at the time when she gives notice of her intended day of return, no such alternative employment is available: see *Philip Hodges &Co. v. Kell* [1994] I.C.R. 656.

By reason of redundancy. This is to be construed in accordance with s.139: see s.235(3).

Suitable available vacancy. See the note to s.81.

Associated employer. See the note to s.231.

Exercise of right to return

82.—(1) An employee shall exercise the right conferred by section 79 giving written notice to the employer (who may be her employer before the end of her maternity leave period or a successor of his) at least twenty-one days before the day on which she proposes to return of her proposal to return on that day (the "notified day of return").

(2) An employer may postpone an employee's return to work until a date not more than four weeks after the notified day of return if he notifies her before that day that for specified reasons he is postponing her return until that date; and, accordingly, she will be entitled to return to work with him on that date.

(3) An employee to whom subsection (4) applies may—

(a) postpone her return to work until a date not more than four weeks after the notified day of return (even if that date falls after the end of the period of twenty-nine weeks beginning with the week in which childbirth occurred), and

(b) where no day of return has been notified to the employer, extend the time during which she may exercise her right to return in accordance with subsection (1), so that she returns to work not more than four weeks after the end of that period of twenty-nine weeks.

(4) This subsection applies to an employee if she gives to her employer, before the notified day of return (or the end of the period of twenty-nine weeks), a certificate from a registered medical practitioner stating that by reason of disease or bodily or mental disablement she will be incapable of work on the notified day of return (or at the end of that period).

(5) Where an employee has once exercised a right of postponement or extension under subsection (3), she is not entitled again to exercise a right of postponement or extension under that subsection in connection with the same return to work.

(6) If an employee has notified a day of return but there is an interruption of work (whether due to industrial action or some other reason) which renders it unreasonable to expect the employee to return to work on the notified day of return, she may instead return to work when work resumes after the interruption or as soon as reasonably practicable afterwards.

(7) Where in the case of an employee who has not already notified a day of return—

(a) there is an interruption of work (whether due to industrial action or some other reason) which renders it unreasonable to expect the employee to return to work before the end of the period of twenty-nine weeks beginning with the week in which childbirth occurred, or which appears likely to have that effect, and

(b) in consequence, the employee does not notify a day of return,

the employee may exercise her right to return in accordance with subsection (1) so that she returns to work at any time before the end of the period of twenty-eight days after the end of the interruption even though that means that she returns to work outside the period of twenty-nine weeks.

(8) Where an employee has exercised the right under subsection (3)(b) to extend the period during which she may exercise her right to return, subsection (7) applies as if for the reference to the end of the period of twenty-nine weeks there were substituted a reference to the end of the further period of four weeks after the end of that period.

(9) Where in the case of an interruption of work an employee has refrained from notifying the day of return in the circumstances described in subsection (7), subsection (3)(b) applies as if for the reference to the end of the period of twenty-nine weeks there were substituted a reference to the end of the period of twenty-eight days after the end of the interruption of work.

DEFINITIONS
"childbirth": s.235(1).
"employee": s.230(1).
"employer": s.230(4).
"notified day of return": subs. (1).
"successor": s.235(1).
"week": s.235(1).

GENERAL NOTE
In order to exercise her right to return to work under the Act, an employee must give her employer (or his successor) at least 21 days' notice in writing of her intention to return to work on a specified date (the "notified day of return") (subs. (1)), and that date must be not later than 29 weeks after the beginning of the week of childbirth (see the note to s.79(1)). This is a mandatory requirement, not qualified by any test of reasonable practicability, and failure to comply with

it to the letter will result in loss of the right to return: see *Lavery v. Plessey Telecommunications* [1982] IRLR 180, C.A., where the employee lost her right to return by giving only five day's notice of her intention to return, instead of the seven days required at that time, even though at the time she gave the incorrect notice she could have satisfied the statutory requirements and still have stayed within the 29-week limit (so that her failure was a purely technical one). An employee who has failed to satisfy the statutory requirements may however be able to claim a separate contractual right to return to work: see the note to s.85.

An employee who has the right to return to work under s.79, and has exercised it in accordance with this section, will be deemed to have been dismissed with effect from the notified date of return if she is not permitted by her employer to return to work: see the note to s.96(1).

In certain limited circumstances either party may postpone the return to work beyond the 29-week limit. The employer may postpone the employee's return to work for to up to four weeks after her notified day of return; the postponement may be for any reason, but the employer must tell her (not necessarily in writing) before the notified day of return that he is postponing her return until a certain date, and he must specify the reason for the postponement (subs. (2)).

The employee may postpone her return to work in two situations. First, she may be able to postpone her return to work for medical reasons (subss. (3), (4)). If she has already notified the employer of her intended day of return, she may delay her return for up to four weeks beyond that date if she is able to produce a medical certificate stating that she will be incapable of work because of disease or bodily or mental disablement on the notified date of return; if she has not yet notified the employer of her intended day of return, she may delay her return for up to four weeks beyond the end of the 29-week period, provided her medical certificate states that she will be incapable of work on the expiry of that period. She may only delay her return to work in this way on one occasion (subs. (5)). If at the end of the extended period she is still unfit to return to work, she will lose her right to return, and it appears that she will be unable to claim unfair dismissal either. In *Kelly v. Liverpool Maritime Terminals* [1988] IRLR 310, the employee's pregnancy aggravated a back injury, which made her unable to return to work at the end of the four-week period. She wrote to the employer explaining that she would be unable to return to work for some time, and continued to send in medical certificates. The Court of Appeal was unwilling to interpret the letter and medical certificates as an attempt to return to work coupled with a request for sick leave, and held that her employment had terminated (without any dismissal or resignation) when she failed to return to work at the end of the four-week period. On this analysis, it seems that the only way in which the employee could have preserved her right to return to work would have been to drag herself back to work in order to claim sick leave. The decision in *Kelly* is highly unsatisfactory, and, it is submitted, out of step with the current emphasis in European law, and in particular EEC Directive No. 92/85, on the need to improve the health and safety at work of pregnant workers and workers who have recently given birth.

The employee may also postpone her return to work if there is an interruption of work (whether due to industrial action or some other reason) which makes it unreasonable to expect her to return. Again, the extent to which she can delay her return will depend upon whether she has already notified her employer of her intended day of return. If she has, she may delay her return until work resumes after the interruption, or as soon as reasonably practicable thereafter (subs. (6)); if she has not, she may wait until the stoppage is over and then give written notice to her employer in the usual way (*i.e.* at least 21 days before her intended day of return) that she intends to return to work, provided she returns within 28 days of the end of the interruption (subs. (7)). In practice this means that she must give the employer notice of her intention to return no later than a week after the end of the stoppage.

Shall exercise the right ... by giving written notice. Although nowhere stated in the Act, it seems that in addition to notifying the employer of her intended date of return, the employee must physically present herself at work on the appropriate date in order to exercise her right to return effectively: see *Kelly v. Liverpool Maritime Terminals* [1988] IRLR 310, C.A., above.

Notified day of return

83.—(1) Subject to subsection (2), in this Act "notified day of return" shall be construed in accordance with section 82(1).

(2) Where—

(a) an employee's return is postponed under subsection (2) or (3)(a) of section 82, or

(b) the employee returns to work on a day later than the notified day of return in the circumstances described in subsection (6) of that section,

then, subject to subsection (5) of that section, references in subsections (2), (3)(a) and (6) of that section and the following provisions of this Act to the notified day of return shall be construed as references to the day to which the return is postponed or that later day.

DEFINITIONS
   "employee": s.230(1).

Employee dismissed at or after end of maternity leave period

84.—(1) This section applies where an employee has the right to return to work conferred by section 79 and either—

  (a) her maternity leave period ends by reason of dismissal, or

  (b) she is dismissed after the end of her maternity leave period, otherwise than in the course of attempting to return to work in accordance with her contract in circumstances in which section 85 applies.

(2) Where this section applies, the right conferred by section 79 is exercisable only on the employee repaying any compensation for unfair dismissal, or redundancy payment, paid in respect of the dismissal if the employer requests repayment.

DEFINITIONS
   "employee": s.230(1).
   "employer": s.230(4).
   "maternity leave period": s.235(1).

GENERAL NOTE

The effect of a dismissal during maternity leave or maternity absence has long been regarded as one of the most difficult and troublesome areas of employment law. Unfortunately, since much of the confusion results from the inherent complexity of the provisions rather than any lack of clarity in their drafting, the extent to which matters can be improved by a simple consolidation of the earlier provisions is strictly limited, no matter how ingenious the draftsmanship. It is however arguable that in redrafting the provisions in this section on dismissal during maternity absence, formerly contained in Sched. 2, para. 6 of the 1978 Act, one notorious source of confusion has (perhaps unwittingly) been removed.

The confusion arises because different provision is made, depending on whether the dismissal occurs during maternity leave, during extended maternity absence or in the course of attempting to return to work after maternity absence (see the note to s.79). A dismissal during maternity leave or maternity absence will not affect an employee's right to return to work, provided she satisfies the statutory requirements; it may also give rise to an ordinary unfair dismissal claim under s.95 if her contract of employment subsisted during her maternity absence. This section provides that if the employee has received compensation for unfair dismissal or a redundancy payment in respect of such a dismissal, the employer may make the exercise of her right to return to work conditional on her repaying any such payment.

On the face of it this section seems perfectly innocuous, but it has a deeper significance, because its predecessor (Sched. 2, para. 6 of the EP(C)A) was controversially interpreted by the Court of Appeal in *Lavery v. Plessey Telecommunications* [1982] IRLR 180 as preventing an employee who has not exercised her right to return to work effectively from claiming that she has been dismissed under the ordinary definition of dismissal in what is now s.95. In that case, the employee had no statutory right to return to work because she had given insufficient notice of her intended date of return. This meant that she could not rely on s.56 of the EP(C)A (now s.96) to establish a deemed dismissal. She argued instead that as her contract of employment had continued to exist through her maternity absence, she had a contractual right to return to work, and the employer's refusal to allow her to return therefore constituted an ordinary dismissal under s.55 of the EP(C)A (now s.95). The Court of Appeal held that since the dismissal occurred in the course of her attempting to exercise a composite right to return to work, she could not claim that she had been dismissed under s.55, so that she had no remedy for the employer's refusal to permit her to return. The Court of Appeal considered that it was driven to this conclusion by para. 6(2) of Sched. 2, which at that time stated that: "*For the purposes of sub-paragraph (1)*, an employee shall not be taken to be dismissed during the period of her absence if the dismissal occurs in the course of the employee's attempting to return to work in accordance with her contract in circumstances in which section 48 [now s.85] applies." (emphasis supplied).

It has long been argued that in interpreting para. 6(2) as a substantive provision, the Court of Appeal misinterpreted the statutory provisions. Paragraph 6(2) did not expressly state that an employee dismissed while attempting to exercise a composite right to return could not bring an ordinary unfair dismissal claim; it merely provided that such a dismissal was not to be regarded as a dismissal during the period of maternity absence *for the purposes of para. 6(1)*, which itself was concerned only to define the scope of para. 6. The only substantive provisions in para. 6 were those in para. 6(3), which disapplied certain sections of the Act from any dismissal within the scope of para. 6, and para. 6(4), which stated that a dismissal during maternity absence did not affect the right to return to work, and regulated the relationship between such a dismissal and the right to return by providing for the repayment of compensation, etc. In *Crouch v. Kidsons Impey* [1996] IRLR 79, the E.A.T., *obiter*, agreed with the interpretation of para. 6(2) as a non-substantive provision, and by implication disagreed with *Lavery*.

The provision formerly contained in para. 6(2) is now contained in subs. (1)(a) of this section, and it is submitted that, in its new form, it is utterly incapable of bearing the interpretation given to para. 6(2) by the Court of Appeal in *Lavery*. It follows that there is no longer any reason why an employee whose contract of employment subsists through maternity absence, but who has not exercised her composite right to return to work effectively, should not be able to claim an ordinary dismissal under s.95 if she is not permitted to return to work.

Contractual rights to return

85.—(1) An employee who has both the right to return to work conferred by section 79 and another right to return to work after absence because of pregnancy or childbirth (under a contract of employment or otherwise) may not exercise the two rights separately but may, in returning to work, take advantage of whichever right is, in any particular respect, the more favourable.

(2) Sections 79 and 81 to 84, and the provisions of the following Parts of this Act relating to the right conferred by section 79 (other than section 137(2)), apply, subject to any modifications necessary to give effect to any more favourable contractual terms, to the exercise of the composite right described in subsection (1) as they apply to the exercise of the right conferred by section 79.

DEFINITIONS
"childbirth": s.235(1).
"contract of employment": s.230(2).
"employee": s.230(1).

GENERAL NOTE
This section allows a woman who has a contractual and a statutory right to return to work after maternity absence to create a composite right by taking advantage of whichever is, in any particular respect, the more favourable (subs. (1)). The statutory right can therefore be seen as a basic minimum entitlement which may be improved upon by the employee's contract of employment. In exercising this composite right, the normal statutory requirements will apply, modified to give effect to any more favourable contractual terms (subs. (2)), and it appears that the statutory requirements will continue to apply unless there is evidence that the parties have expressly or impliedly agreed to some modification of them: *Kolfor Plant v. Wright* [1982] IRLR 311, E.A.T.; *Lavery v. Plessey Telecommunications* [1983] IRLR 202, C.A. If the employee fails to comply with the requirements of her composite right, she is likely to lose both her statutory *and* her contractual right to return, even if her contract of employment continues during her maternity absence.

An employee who is prevented by her employer from exercising a composite right to return will be deemed to have been dismissed from the notified day of return (see the note to s.96). The corollary of this, however, is that there can be no deemed dismissal under s.96 if she has failed to comply with the requirements of her composite right. In *Lavery v. Plessey Telecommunications*, above, the Court of Appeal held that there can be no ordinary dismissal under s.55 (now s.95) in such a situation either, even if the employee's contract of employment continued during her maternity absence. It is submitted that this argument is no longer valid in the light of the rewording of the EP(C)A provisions (see the note to s.84), but the courts have in any event succeeded in circumventing the ruling in *Lavery* where an employee who has failed to establish a statutory or a composite right to return is able to establish a wholly independent contractual right to return. In such a case, it has been held that the employer's refusal to permit her to return to work entitles her to bring an ordinary unfair dismissal action. In *Lucas v. Norton of London* [1984] IRLR 86, the employee made no attempt to comply with the statutory scheme, but had reached a "nebulous agreement" with her employer that she should be able to return to work a reasonable time after childbirth. She was subsequently not permitted to return to work, and the E.A.T. held that as her contract of employment had continued throughout her absence, the employer's refusal to permit her to return to work entitled her to bring an ordinary unfair dismissal complaint. *Lavery* was distinguished on the basis that in *Lucas*, the employee had never sought to establish a statutory right to return and was relying solely on the agreement which she had reached with her employer, whereas in *Lavery* the employee had initially taken the necessary steps to enjoy her statutory right to return, but by giving insufficient notice of her intention to return had failed to exercise her composite right effectively.

It is unclear whether the reasoning in *Lucas* only applies where there is evidence of a positive agreement for the woman to return to work, rather than the mere continuance of the contract of employment, but it is clear that for *Lucas* to apply, the contract of employment must continue to subsist throughout the maternity absence. Unfortunately, the Act is silent on that point. In *Hilton International Hotels (UK) v. Kaissi* [1994] IRLR 270, the E.A.T. held that the applicant was entitled to claim unfair dismissal on ordinary principles when she was not allowed to return to work, even though she had no contractual right to return and had made no attempt to comply with the statutory procedures for the right to return, because her contract continued to exist until it was brought to an end by her employers. According to the E.A.T., the continuance or discontinuance of the contract of employment through maternity absence is a matter of contract, not statute (so that a failure to satisfy the statutory requirements for the right to return does not automatically terminate the contract), and whether or not the contract comes to an end depends on the agreement and actions of the parties. However, in *Crouch v. Kidsons Impey* [1996] IRLR 79, a different division of the E.A.T. distinguished *Kaissi* on its facts and emphasised that there is no presumption that the contract continues during maternity absence, holding that where an employee simply leaves work because she is pregnant and does not fulfil the requirements for the right to return to work, the appropriate inference (in the absence of any relevant contractual terms) is that the contract is to be regarded as terminating by consent at the time when she leaves (unless she continues to receive maternity pay after that date, in which case the contract is likely to terminate by consent at the end of the maternity pay period). The ruling in *Crouch* makes it less likely that a contract will be found to continue during maternity absence, unless there is an express or implied agreement to that effect, but the matter is in need of clarification by a higher court.

In any particular respect, the more favourable. In *Bovey v. Board of Governors of the Hospital for Sick Children* [1978] IRLR 241, the E.A.T. held that there is a limit on the extent to which an employee may seek to sub-divide her statutory and contractual rights in order to take advantage of more favourable contractual provision. In that case, the employee had been employed before maternity absence as a full-time physiotherapist. She wished to return to work part-time, but her employers were only prepared to allow her to do so on a lower grade. She claimed a composite right to return to work part-time on her original grade, but the E.A.T. held that the respective rights were "essentially indivisible". She had a statutory right to return to work full-time on her original grade, and a contractual right to return to work part-time on a lower grade, and she had to choose between them: "There must be a limit to the extent to which the right in question, to return to work, can be sub-divided, so as to identify the particular respects in which it is more favourable". It could however be argued that what the applicant was attempting to do was wholly consistent with the wording of the section, which states that an employee may take advantage "of whichever right is, *in any particular respect*, the more favourable". (emphasis supplied). The explanation for the E.A.T.'s reluctance to accept her argument probably lies in their concern that the "most unfortunate and inconvenient consequences" would result if such a precedent were to be applied generally in industry.

PART IX

TERMINATION OF EMPLOYMENT

Minimum period of notice

Rights of employer and employee to minimum notice

86.—(1) The notice required to be given by an employer to terminate the contract of employment of a person who has been continuously employed for one month or more—

    (a) is not less than one week's notice if his period of continuous employment is less than two years,

    (b) is not less than one week's notice for each year of continuous employment if his period of continuous employment is two years or more but less than twelve years, and

(c) is not less than twelve weeks' notice if his period of continuous employment is twelve years or more.

(2) The notice required to be given by an employee who has been continuously employed for one month or more to terminate his contract of employment is not less than one week.

(3) Any provision for shorter notice in any contract of employment with a person who has been continuously employed for one month or more has effect subject to subsections (1) and (2); but this section does not prevent either party from waiving his right to notice on any occasion or from accepting a payment in lieu of notice.

(4) Any contract of employment of a person who has been continuously employed for three months or more which is a contract for a term certain of one month or less shall have effect as if it were for an indefinite period; and, accordingly, subsections (1) and (2) apply to the contract.

(5) Subsections (1) and (2) do not apply to a contract made in contemplation of the performance of a specific task which is not expected to last for more than three months unless the employee has been continuously employed for a period of more than three months.

(6) This section does not affect any right of either party to a contract of employment to treat the contract as terminable without notice by reason of the conduct of the other party.

DEFINITIONS
  "continuously employed": ss.210–219.
  "contract of employment": s.230(2).
  "employee": s.230(1).
  "employer": s.230(4).

GENERAL NOTE
  This section gives a statutory right to a minimum period of notice, but it does not extend to the following categories of persons: (1) Crown employees: s.191(1) and (2); (2) House of Commons staff: s.195(1) and (2); (3) House of Lords staff: s.194(1) and (2); (4) employees who work outside Great Britain: s.196(1); (5) employees who are engaged under a contract made in contemplation of the performance of a specific task which is not expected to last for more than three months (unless continuously employed for more than three months): s.86(5); and (6) merchant seamen: s.199(1).

  Subsection (1) entitles employees continuously employed for one month or more but for less than two years to at least one week's notice. After two years' employment, they are entitled to one week's notice for each year of continuous employment, but, if they have been employed for more than 12 years, their statutory entitlement will not exceed 12 weeks. Subsection (2) obliges an employee continuously employed for one month or more to give at least one week's notice. The notice must be definite and explicit and must specify the date of termination or give sufficient facts from which the date of termination can be ascertained: *Morton Sundour Fabrics v. Shaw* (1967) 2 I.T.R. 84 and *Walker v. Cotswold Chine Home School* (1977) 12 I.T.R. 342. Once a notice has been given, it cannot be withdrawn unilaterally, but only with the agreement of the other party: *Riordan v. War Office* [1959] 3 All E.R. 552 and *Harris & Russell v. Slingsby* [1973] I.C.R. 454.

  Although an attempt to provide for a shorter period will be ineffective, subs. (3) provides that either side may waive his or her right to notice or accept a payment in lieu of notice. In *Staffordshire County Council v. Secretary of State for Employment* [1989] I.C.R. 664 the Court of Appeal held that this provision is only relevant to an employee's rights in contract, not to the statutory rights on termination of employment. Although the Court of Appeal's remarks in this case are directed to subs. (3) in the context of the employee's statutory right to a redundancy payment, there is no reason why they should not also extend to the right not to be unfairly dismissed.

  Subsection (6) makes it clear that the right of either party to treat the contract as terminable without notice because of a serious breach by the other party is not affected by the statutory provisions.

  The statutory periods may also be used for other purposes under the legislation. For example, a failure to give the notice required by s.86 may cause the "effective date of termination" (in cases of unfair dismissal) or "relevant date" (in redundancy payments cases) to be postponed: see ss.97(2)–(4) and 145(5). The statutory notice period is also used as a basis for computing the obligatory period for the purposes of a counter-notice given by an employee dismissed for redundancy, and for the purpose of s.140: see ss.142 and 136(3).

Note the provisions of s.91(5).

Rights of employee in period of notice

87.—(1) If an employer gives notice to terminate the contract of employment of a person who has been continuously employed for one month or more, the provisions of sections 88 to 91 have effect as respects the liability of the employer for the period of notice required by section 86(1).

(2) If an employee who has been continuously employed for one month or more gives notice to terminate his contract of employment, the provisions of sections 88 to 91 have effect as respects the liability of the employer for the period of notice required by section 86(2).

(3) In sections 88 to 91 "period of notice" means—

(a) where notice is given by an employer, the period of notice required by section 86(1), and

(b) where notice is given by an employee, the period of notice required by section 86(2).

(4) This section does not apply in relation to a notice given by the employer or the employee if the notice to be given by the employer to terminate the contract must be at least one week more than the notice required by section 86(1).

DEFINITIONS

"continuously employed": ss.210–219.
"contract of employment": s.230(2).
"employee": s.230(1).
"employer": s.230(4).

GENERAL NOTE

This section sets out the general entitlement of employees during their notice period and applies whether it is they or their employer who gave notice. Section 88 applies to employees with normal working hours; s.89 to employees without normal working hours. Section 90 makes provision for the deduction of sick pay in certain circumstances. Note the provisions of s.91(1) and (5).

It is clear that employees claiming damages for breach of contract are under a duty to mitigate their loss and that the assessment of the employer's liability should be calculated in the same way, and subject to the same deductions, as damages for breach of contract: see *Westwood v. Secretary of State for Employment* [1985] I.C.R. 209 and *Secretary of State for Employment v. Cooper* [1987] I.C.R. 766.

Employments with normal working hours

88.—(1) If an employee has normal working hours under the contract of employment in force during the period of notice and during any part of those normal working hours—

(a) the employee is ready and willing to work but no work is provided for him by his employer,

(b) the employee is incapable of work because of sickness or injury,

(c) the employee is absent from work wholly or partly because of pregnancy or childbirth, or

(d) the employee is absent from work in accordance with the terms of his employment relating to holidays,

the employer is liable to pay the employee for the part of normal working hours covered by any of paragraphs (a), (b), (c) and (d) a sum not less than the amount of remuneration for that part of normal working hours calculated at the average hourly rate of remuneration produced by dividing a week's pay by the number of normal working hours.

(2) Any payments made to the employee by his employer in respect of the relevant part of the period of notice (whether by way of sick pay, statutory

sick pay, maternity pay, statutory maternity pay, holiday pay or otherwise) go towards meeting the employer's liability under this section.

(3) Where notice was given by the employee, the employer's liability under this section does not arise unless and until the employee leaves the service of the employer in pursuance of the notice.

DEFINITIONS
"childbirth": s.235(1).
"contract of employment": s.230(2).
"employee": s.230(1).
"employer": s.230(4).

Employments without normal working hours

89.—(1) If an employee does not have normal working hours under the contract of employment in force in the period of notice, the employer is liable to pay the employee for each week of the period of notice a sum not less than a week's pay.

(2) The employer's liability under this section is conditional on the employee being ready and willing to do work of a reasonable nature and amount to earn a week's pay.

(3) Subsection (2) does not apply—
(a) in respect of any period during which the employee is incapable of work because of sickness or injury,
(b) in respect of any period during which the employee is absent from work wholly or partly because of pregnancy or childbirth, or
(c) in respect of any period during which the employee is absent from work in accordance with the terms of his employment relating to holidays.

(4) Any payment made to an employee by his employer in respect of a period within subsection (3) (whether by way of sick pay, statutory sick pay, maternity pay, statutory maternity pay, holiday pay or otherwise) shall be taken into account for the purposes of this section as if it were remuneration paid by the employer in respect of that period.

(5) Where notice was given by the employee, the employer's liability under this section does not arise unless and until the employee leaves the service of the employer in pursuance of the notice.

DEFINITIONS
"childbirth": s.235(1).
"contract of employment": s.230(2).
"employee": s.230(1).
"employer": s.230(4).

Short-term incapacity benefit and industrial injury benefit

90.—(1) This section has effect where the arrangements in force relating to the employment are such that—
(a) payments by way of sick pay are made by the employer to employees to whom the arrangements apply, in cases where any such employees are incapable of work because of sickness or injury, and
(b) in calculating any payment so made to any such employee an amount representing, or treated as representing, short-term incapacity benefit or industrial injury benefit is taken into account, whether by way of deduction or by way of calculating the payment as a supplement to that amount.

(2) If—
(a) during any part of the period of notice the employee is incapable of work because of sickness or injury,
(b) one or more payments by way of sick pay are made to him by the employer in respect of that part of the period of notice, and

(c) in calculating any such payment such an amount as is referred to in paragraph (b) of subsection (1) is taken into account as mentioned in that paragraph,

for the purposes of section 88 or 89 the amount so taken into account shall be treated as having been paid by the employer to the employee by way of sick pay in respect of that part of that period, and shall go towards meeting the liability of the employer under that section accordingly.

DEFINITIONS
  "employee": s.230(1).
  "employer": s.230(4).

Supplementary

91.—(1) An employer is not liable under section 88 or 89 to make any payment in respect of a period during which an employee is absent from work with the leave of the employer granted at the request of the employee, including any period of time off taken in accordance with—
  (a) Part VI of this Act, or
  (b) section 168 or 170 of the Trade Union and Labour Relations (Consolidation) Act 1992 (trade union duties and activities).

(2) No payment is due under section 88 or 89 in consequence of a notice to terminate a contract given by an employee if, after the notice is given and on or before the termination of the contract, the employee takes part in a strike of employees of the employer.

(3) If, during the period of notice, the employer breaks the contract of employment, payments received under section 88 or 89 in respect of the part of the period after the breach go towards mitigating the damages recoverable by the employee for loss of earnings in that part of the period of notice.

(4) If, during the period of notice, the employee breaks the contract and the employer rightfully treats the breach as terminating the contract, no payment is due to the employee under section 88 or 89 in respect of the part of the period falling after the termination of the contract.

(5) If an employer fails to give the notice required by section 86, the rights conferred by sections 87 to 90 and this section shall be taken into account in assessing his liability for breach of the contract.

(6) Sections 86 to 90 and this section apply in relation to a contract all or any of the terms of which are terms which take effect by virtue of any provision contained in or having effect under an Act (whether public or local) as in relation to any other contract; and the reference in this subsection to an Act includes, subject to any express provision to the contrary, an Act passed after this Act.

DEFINITIONS
  "contract of employment": s.230(2).
  "employee": s.230(1).
  "employer": s.230(4).

GENERAL NOTE
  Subsections (1) and (2) remove liability from the employer where (a) the employee takes time off with the employer's permission and (b) the employee takes part in a strike. It should be noted that the definition of "strike" in s.235(5) does not apply here.
  Subsection (5) provides that an employer who fails to comply with the notice requirements of s.86 will be liable to pay damages for breach of contract and the rights given by ss.87–90 and this section will be taken into account in assessing liability for breach of contract. It is clear that employees claiming damages for breach of contract under these provisions are under a duty to mitigate their loss and that the assessment of the employer's liability should be calculated in the same way, and subject to the same deductions, as damages for breach of contract: see *Westwood v. Secretary of State for Employment* [1985] I.C.R. 209 and *Secretary of State for Employment v. Cooper* [1987] I.C.R. 766.

Written statement of reasons for dismissal

Right to written statement of reasons for dismissal

92.—(1) An employee is entitled to be provided by his employer with a written statement giving particulars of the reasons for the employee's dismissal—

(a) if the employee is given by the employer notice of termination of his contract of employment,

(b) if the employee's contract of employment is terminated by the employer without notice, or

(c) if the employee is employed under a contract for a fixed term and that term expires without being renewed under the same contract.

(2) Subject to subsection (4), an employee is entitled to a written statement under this section only if he makes a request for one; and a statement shall be provided within fourteen days of such a request.

(3) Subject to subsection (4), an employee is not entitled to a written statement under this section unless on the effective date of termination he has been, or will have been, continuously employed for a period of not less than two years ending with that date.

(4) An employee is entitled to a written statement under this section without having to request it and irrespective of whether she has been continuously employed for any period if she is dismissed—

(a) at any time while she is pregnant, or

(b) after childbirth in circumstances in which her maternity leave period ends by reason of the dismissal.

(5) A written statement under this section is admissible in evidence in any proceedings.

(6) Subject to subsection (7), in this section "the effective date of termination"—

(a) in relation to an employee whose contract of employment is terminated by notice, means the date on which the notice expires,

(b) in relation to an employee whose contract of employment is terminated without notice, means the date on which the termination takes effect, and

(c) in relation to an employee who is employed under a contract for a fixed term which expires without being renewed under the same contract, means the date on which the term expires.

(7) Where—

(a) the contract of employment is terminated by the employer, and

(b) the notice required by section 86 to be given by an employer would, if duly given on the material date, expire on a date later than the effective date of termination (as defined by subsection (6)),

the later date is the effective date of termination.

(8) In subsection (7)(b) "the material date" means—

(a) the date when notice of termination was given by the employer, or

(b) where no notice was given, the date when the contract of employment was terminated by the employer.

DEFINITIONS

"contract of employment": s.230(2).

"effective date of termination": subss. (6)–(8).

"employee": s.230(1).

"employer": s.230(4).

GENERAL NOTE

This section gives to a dismissed employee the right to be given a written statement giving particulars of the reasons for the dismissal by his or her employer. By virtue of subs. (1) employees who are entitled are those dismissed with or without notice or whose fixed-term contract has expired.

The following categories of employees are excluded from the right: (1) employees who ordinarily work outside Great Britain: see s.196(2) and (3); (2) employees continuously employed for less than two years: s.92(3); (3) share fishermen: s.199(2); and (4) those employed in police service: s.200. It should be noted that Crown employees are included within the statutory entitlement, as are members of the armed forces, House of Commons staff, and House of Lords staff: see ss.191, 192, 194 and 195.

The employee's entitlement is to be provided with a written statement giving particulars of the reasons for the dismissal. But the employee must first ask for the written statement, which should be given by the employer within 14 days of the employee's request. In addition, an employee who is dismissed, either while she is pregnant, or after childbirth in circumstances in which her maternity leave period ends by reason of her dismissal, will be entitled under subs. (4) to be provided with a written statement. The entitlement is irrespective of length of employment and does not depend upon the employee first making a request.

Written statements are admissible in evidence in any proceedings: see subs. (5). If the employer gives another reason in subsequent litigation, the tribunal would either ignore that other reason and hold the employer to the original statement or treat the change of reason as going to the employer's credibility.

Complaints to industrial tribunal

93.—(1) A complaint may be presented to an industrial tribunal by an employee on the ground that—

   (a) the employer unreasonably failed to provide a written statement under section 92, or

   (b) the particulars of reasons given in purported compliance with that section are inadequate or untrue.

(2) Where an industrial tribunal finds a complaint under this section well-founded, the tribunal—

   (a) may make a declaration as to what it finds the employer's reasons were for dismissing the employee, and

   (b) shall make an award that the employer pay to the employee a sum equal to the amount of two weeks' pay.

(3) An industrial tribunal shall not consider a complaint under this section relating to the reasons for a dismissal unless it is presented to the tribunal at such a time that the tribunal would, in accordance with section 111, consider a complaint of unfair dismissal in respect of that dismissal presented at the same time.

DEFINITIONS
   "employee": s.230(1).
   "employer": s.230(4).

GENERAL NOTE
This section gives the right to an employee to complain to an industrial tribunal on the grounds that the employer has unreasonably *failed* to provide a written statement as required by s.92 or has provided one containing inadequate or untrue particulars. In that case the employee must present a complaint to the industrial tribunal within three months of the date of termination: see subs. (3).

It should be noted that the highlighted word "fails" was introduced by the Trade Union Reform and Employment Rights Act 1993 (c. 19). The previous word was "refuses". This change clearly extends the possible circumstances in which an employer may be held liable and overrules a previous decision of the E.A.T. in *Ladbroke Entertainments v. Clark* [1987] I.C.R. 585 that a failure to provide written reasons cannot be equated with a refusal. The case law relating to the previous version of this section (s.53 of the 1978 Act, as amended by the 1993 Act) is set out below, but should be considered in the light of the amendment to the section already mentioned.

If the tribunal finds the complaint well-founded, it may make a declaration as to what it finds to have been the employer's reasons for dismissing the employee; it *must* also award the employee two weeks' pay: see subs. (2).

This section is a penal section. The E.A.T. has therefore held that it should be rigidly construed and that there should be clear evidence that there has been an unreasonable refusal: *Charles Lang & Sons v. Aubrey* [1978] I.C.R. 168. See also *Lowson v. Percy Main & District Social Club & Institute* [1979] I.C.R. 568 and *Newland v. Simons and Willer (Hairdressers)* [1981]

IRLR 359, where the E.A.T. held not to be unreasonable a failure to reply for seven weeks. A refusal (and, it may be, failure) cannot be said to be unreasonable where it is based upon a conscientious belief that there has been no dismissal: *Brown v. Stuart Scott & Co.* [1981] I.C.R. 166. See also *Broomsgrove v. Eagle Alexander* [1981] IRLR 127. *Cf. Daynecourt Insurance Brokers v. Iles* [1978] IRLR 335.

A statement of reasons is not untrue if the employer genuinely believes that the reason given is the reason for the dismissal. It is not necessary for the industrial tribunal to embark upon a consideration of whether the reason was good or bad: *Harvard Securities v. Younghusband* [1990] IRLR 17. It is not sufficient compliance with s.92 merely to rely upon the answer put into the employee's original application; the statute clearly contemplates an independent and separate document: *Rowan v. Machinery Installations (South Wales)* [1981] IRLR 122.

The document must be of such a kind that the employee, or anyone to whom he or she may wish to show it, can know from reading the document itself why the employee has been dismissed, and it may refer to other documents provided that the document the employee receives contains a simple statement of the essential reasons for the dismissal: *Horsley Smith & Sherry v. Dutton* [1977] I.C.R. 594, at p.597. See also *Marchant v. Earley Town Council* [1979] I.C.R. 891. In *Gilham v. Kent County Council (No. 1)* [1985] I.C.R. 227, the Court of Appeal said that s.92 is sufficiently complied with if the employer's response to a request refers to other documents containing reasons. It also said that where the employee appoints a legal adviser, the employer need only communicate with the adviser; it is not necessary to communicate with the employee personally.

The industrial tribunal may only hear complaints relating to statements issued in response to an employee's request: see *Catherine Haigh Harlequin Hair Design v. Seed* [1990] IRLR 175. If the employer voluntarily gives a written statement, the employee will not be able to complain about it unless the employer refers to it and effectively adopts it in response to the employee's request, as happened in *Marchant v. Earley Town Council*, above.

PART X

UNFAIR DISMISSAL

CHAPTER I

RIGHT NOT TO BE UNFAIRLY DISMISSED

The right

The right

94.—(1) An employee has the right not to be unfairly dismissed by his employer.

(2) Subsection (1) has effect subject to the following provisions of this Part (in particular sections 108 to 110) and to the provisions of the Trade Union and Labour Relations (Consolidation) Act 1992 (in particular sections 237 to 239).

DEFINITIONS
"employee": s.230(1).
"employer": s.230(4).

GENERAL NOTE
On the face of it, s.94(1) gives *all* employees a general right not to be unfairly dismissed, though this is not without qualification. Broadly speaking, unfair dismissals fall into two categories: (1) those in which the dismissal is for a "potentially fair" reason: capability or qualifications, conduct, redundancy, statutory requirements, or "some other substantial reason"; or (2) those in which the dismissal is for a reason to which special rules apply, for example, a dismissal for trade union or health and safety reasons. This means that at the outset it is necessary to identify the reason for the dismissal. In unfair dismissal cases falling within the first category, an employee must have been continuously employed for two years (s.108(1)) and must not be excluded. One of the more common exclusions is of employees over the "normal retiring age": s.209.

In unfair dismissal cases falling within the second category, the two-year qualification period and age exclusion do not apply: ss.108(3) and 109(2). These cases are as follows: (1) dismissals for pregnancy and childbirth: s.99; (2) dismissals in health and safety cases: s.100; (3) dismissals of shop workers and betting workers who refuse Sunday work: s.101; (4) dismissals of employees who are trustees of occupational pension schemes: s.102; (5) dismissals of employee representatives: s.102; and (6) dismissals for assertion of a statutory right: s.104. The special rules apply not only to *dismissals* for any of these reasons, but to *selection for redundancy*: s.105.

Sections 191–195 deal with particular types of employment, *e.g.* Crown employment. Sections 196–201 contain the provisions excluding certain classes of employment.

Dismissal

Circumstances in which an employee is dismissed

95.—(1) For the purposes of this Part an employee is dismissed by his employer if (and, subject to subsection (2) and section 96, only if)—
 (a) the contract under which he is employed is terminated by the employer (whether with or without notice),
 (b) he is employed under a contract for a fixed term and that term expires without being renewed under the same contract, or
 (c) the employee terminates the contract under which he is employed (with or without notice) in circumstances in which he is entitled to terminate it without notice by reason of the employer's conduct.

(2) An employee shall be taken to be dismissed by his employer for the purposes of this Part if—
 (a) the employer gives notice to the employee to terminate his contract of employment, and
 (b) at a time within the period of that notice the employee gives notice to the employer to terminate the contract of employment on a date earlier than the date on which the employer's notice is due to expire;
and the reason for the dismissal is to be taken to be the reason for which the employer's notice is given.

DEFINITIONS
 "employee": s.230(1).
 "employer": s.230(4).

GENERAL NOTE
It is fundamental to a complaint of unfair dismissal that the employee should have been dismissed. Unless the industrial tribunal is satisfied that there has been a dismissal, the case will fail. Section 95 contains the definition of dismissal. It should be noted that the statutory provision is exhaustive: it uses the phrase "if, but only if". The combined effect of the statutory provisions and judicial interpretations of them is that some situations clearly fall within them, *e.g.* an actual dismissal; some situations are deemed to be a dismissal, *e.g.* a resignation prompted by a repudiatory breach on the employer's part or the expiry of a fixed term contract. Some situations, *e.g.* a frustrating event or a voluntary resignation unprompted by action on the employer's part, are outside the definition.

It is important when determining whether an action falls within the definition of dismissal, to start with the statutory language and then to examine the relevant judicial decisions. This is different from the common law position involving wrongful dismissal, to which the statutory definition does not apply. It is also important to bear in mind that an event which is treated as a dismissal by the statute may not be a dismissal at common law. For example, the expiry of a fixed-term contract is expressly treated as a dismissal by s.95(2)(b). At common law, however, it will not amount to a dismissal.

If there is any dispute in tribunal proceedings as to whether the employee was dismissed or not, the burden is upon the employee to satisfy the tribunal that he or she was dismissed.

Subs. (1)(a)

Termination with or without notice. As a general rule, termination occurs when either party informs the other clearly and unequivocally that the contract is to end or the circumstances are such that it is clear that termination was intended or that it can be inferred that termination was intended. The words used to terminate the contract must be capable of being construed as words of termination. The principles are the same whether the termination consists of a dismissal by the employer or a resignation by the employee.

A notice of termination must be definite and explicit and must state the date of termination (or enable it to be inferred); a mere warning of impending dismissal or resignation would not be enough: see *Morton Sundour Fabrics v. Shaw* (1967) 2 I.T.R. 84. Once a notice of termination has been given, it cannot be withdrawn by the party giving it without the agreement of the other party: see *Riordan v. War Office* [1961] 1 W.L.R. 210 and *Harris and Russell v. Slingsby* [1973] I.C.R. 454.

In the case of a dismissal by the employer, phrases such as "I hereby give you notice of dismissal" are clear. Problems, however, arise where there is a row between the employer and the employee and words are used in the heat of the moment. If the words used by the employer are not ambiguous or could only be interpreted as amounting to words of dismissal, then the conclusion is clear. If, on the other hand, the words used are ambiguous and it is not clear whether they do amount to words of dismissal (*e.g.* "You're finished with me"), it is necessary to look at all the circumstances of the case, particularly the intention with which the words were spoken, and consider how a reasonable employee would, in all the circumstances have understood them: see *Gale (B.G.) v. Gilbert* [1978] I.C.R. 1149, *Tanner v. Kean* [1978] IRLR 110, *Sothern v. Franks Charlesly & Co.* [1981] IRLR 278, *Stern (J. & J.) v. Simpson* [1983] IRLR 52 and *Martin v. Yeoman Aggregates* [1983] I.C.R. 314.

An employee may be treated as dismissed where the employer unilaterally imposes radically different terms of employment so that, on an objective construction of the employer's conduct, there is a removal or withdrawal of the old contract: see *Hogg v. Dover College* [1990] I.C.R. 39 and *Alcan Extrusions v. Yates* [1996] IRLR 327 (which involved the unilateral imposition of a new shift system on a group of employees).

A dismissal with notice may be converted into a summary dismissal if the employer dismisses the employee on the spot during his or her notice period. Such an action would amount to a wrongful dismissal, but also would have the effect of bringing forward the date of termination for the purposes of the statutory rights: see *Stapp v. The Shaftesbury Society* [1982] IRLR 326.

The statutory provisions governing notice are set out in s.86.

Employee repudiation. In the case of an employee whose actions amount to a repudiation of his or her contract of employment, the employer's acceptance of that repudiation will be treated as a dismissal for the purposes of the statutory definition of dismissal: see *London Transport Executive v. Clarke* [1981] I.C.R. 355. This analysis is sometimes applied to sentences of imprisonment passed on employees. If it is, the employee's conduct is treated as repudiatory and the employer's action in accepting the repudiation, by dismissing him or her or treating the contract as frustrated, as amounting to a dismissal within the statutory definition: see *Norris v. Southampton City Council* [1982] I.C.R. 177, *Shepherd (F.C.) & Co. v. Jerrom* [1986] I.C.R. 802 and *Chakki v. United Yeast Co.* [1982] I.C.R. 140.

Frustration. Frustration occurs when circumstances beyond the control of either party to a contract make it incapable of being performed in the form which was undertaken by the contracting parties. In that case, the contract will terminate automatically and the frustrating event will not be treated as a dismissal for the purposes of the employee's statutory rights. For an exposition of the basic principles of frustration, see Lord Radcliffe's observations in *Davis Contractors v. Fareham U.D.C.* [1956] A.C. 696, at pp. 728–729. In the context of a contract of employment, the most common examples are illness and imprisonment. The death of either party is also best treated as a frustrating event. The effect of frustration is to terminate the contract automatically without either party having to take steps to bring it to an end. Since the employee will not be treated as having been dismissed, a complaint of unfair dismissal or a claim for a redundancy payment will fail: see *Marshall v. Harland & Wolff* [1972] I.C.R. 101.

Frustration through illness has come to be reconsidered in the last few years because of its operation in the context of the statutory rights. *Marshall v. Harland & Wolff* [1972] I.C.R. 101 sets out the basic principles. For an application of these principles in relation to short-term periodic contracts, see *Egg Stores (Stamford Hill) v. Leibovici* [1977] I.C.R. 260 and *Hart (R.N.) v. Marshall (A.R.) & Sons (Bulwell)* [1977] I.C.R. 539. The doctrine of frustration can in appropriate circumstances be applied to a periodic contract terminable by the employer by short notice: see *Notcutt v. Universal Equipment Co. (London)* [1986] I.C.R. 414 and also *Williams v. Watsons Luxury Coaches* [1991] I.C.R. 536. In this last case, the E.A.T. made it clear that tribunals should be reluctant to decide that a contract of employment has been frustrated by an employee's illness and that the party alleging frustration should not be allowed to rely upon the frustrating event if that event was caused by the fault of that party.

It is likely that the imposition of a custodial sentence upon an employee frustrates the contract or terminates it by making it impossible for the employee to perform his or her part of the contract: see *Shepherd (F.C.) & Co. v. Jerrom* [1986] I.C.R. 802.

Termination by mutual agreement. At common law, the parties are free to enter into an agreement that the contract should terminate and may insert a term into the contract stipulating for the employee to accept an agreed sum in satisfaction of any claims he or she may have in the event of certain specified events occurring. In the context of the statutory rights, however, the courts have shown reluctance to find that there is a genuine bilateral termination as opposed to an apparent agreement engineered by the employer. The E.A.T. has held that a resignation on agreed terms will not amount to a dismissal, even if preceded by difficulties between the parties: see *Sheffield v. Oxford Controls Co.* [1979] I.C.R. 396, *Staffordshire County Council v. Donovan* [1981] IRLR 108, *Birch v. University of Liverpool* [1985] I.C.R. 470 and *Logan Salton v. Durham County Council* [1989] IRLR 99.

The effect of s.203(1) (formerly s.140 of the 1978 Act) should be noted. This makes void any agreement which purports to exclude or limit any provision in the Act.

What amounts to a resignation? The requirements in the case of a resignation by an employee are very similar to those for a dismissal. It is important for employers to know whether an employee has resigned, since if they treat the employee as having resigned when that is not in fact the case, they may be held to have dismissed the employee. If the employee's resignation is prompted by a repudiatory act or breach of contract by the employer, that may be treated as a constructive dismissal by the employer: see below. As with dismissal, similar questions have arisen as to what amounts to a resignation, particularly where there has been a row between the employer and the employee and it is not clear from the language used whether the employee was in fact intending to resign. If the employee's words are not ambiguous (*e.g.* "I am resigning") or, when construed, have a clear meaning, he or she will be treated as having resigned, irrespective of whether they were intended to bear that meaning, unless the words of resignation were uttered in the heat of the moment or as a result of pressure exerted by the employer: see *Sovereign House Security Services v. Savage* [1989] IRLR 115, *Sothern v. Franks Charlesly & Co.* [1981] IRLR 278 and *Kwik-Fit (G.B.) v. Lineham* [1992] I.C.R. 183. See also the cases mentioned earlier in this note.

A resignation will be treated as a dismissal if the employee is invited to resign and it is made clear that, unless he or she does so, he or she will be dismissed: see *East Sussex County Council v. Walker* (1972) 7 I.T.R. 280 and *Martin v. Glynwed Distribution (t/a MBS Fastenings)* [1983] I.C.R. 511. The tribunal will take the same view if an employee is inveigled into resigning: see *Caledonian Mining Co. v. Bassett* [1987] I.C.R. 425.

A resignation may also be turned into a dismissal if the employee is forced to leave earlier than the date of expiry of his or her notice of resignation: see *British Midland Airways v. Lewis* [1978] I.C.R. 782. There will be no dismissal, however, where the employee resigns and the employer invokes a contractual provision entitling him or her to terminate the contract early by making a payment in lieu of notice so that the contract ends before the expiry of the employee's notice: see *Marshall (Cambridge) v. Hamblin* [1994] I.C.R. 362.

Subs. (1)(b)

Expiry of fixed-term contract. Fixed-term contracts may take a number of forms. The contract may specify that it is to continue for a stated period (*e.g.* five years from January 1, 1996). In that case, it cannot be terminated before the expiry of that period, unless its terms empower the parties to terminate it earlier or they agree to bring it to an end: see, for example, *Nelson v. James Nelson & Sons* [1914] 2 K.B. 770. A second type of fixed-term contract is one which provides for a definite period of employment but specifies that it may be brought to a premature end by either party giving the other a stated period of notice of termination, for example six months or a year. In *Dixon v. British Broadcasting Corp.* [1979] I.C.R. 281 the Court of Appeal held that, in the context of employment protection legislation, such a contract is a contract for a fixed term even though it is terminable by notice on either side before the expiry of the term. Lord Denning M.R. emphasised that a fixed-term contract must be for a specified period.

In recent years, it has become important to decide whether or not a particular contract is a fixed-term contract for the purposes of the employment protection legislation. Decisions on the relevant provision have drawn a distinction between contracts to perform a particular task or carry out a particular purpose (which are held not to be fixed-term contracts) and contracts for a particular period (which are): see, for example, *Wiltshire County Council v. National Association of Teachers in Further and Higher Education and Guy* [1981] I.C.R. 455. See also *Pfaffinger v. City of Liverpool Community College* [1986] IRLR 508.

The expiry and non-renewal of a fixed-term contract can constitute "some other substantial reason" for dismissal within s.98(1)(b): see *Fay v. North Yorkshire County Council* [1986] I.C.R. 133.

Note s.197, which excludes certain types of fixed-term contracts from the statutory provisions.

Subs. (1)(c)

Constructive dismissal. Constructive dismissal is the term applied to a resignation by the employee in circumstances such that he or she is entitled to terminate the contract without notice because of the employer's conduct. In *Western Excavating (E.C.C.) v. Sharp* [1978] I.C.R. 221, the Court of Appeal affirmed that the question whether an employee is entitled to terminate without notice should be answered according to the rules of the law of contract; see, for example, *per* Lord Denning M.R. at p.226. The evaluation of whether the employer's conduct is repudiatory depends upon whether the conduct, viewed objectively, showed an intention no longer to be bound by the contract. It does not depend upon whether the employer intended the conduct to be repudiatory or could reasonably have believed that it would be accepted as such; nor is the fact that the employer acted on a genuine, though mistaken, belief of fact enough to prevent his or her conduct amounting to a repudiation: see *Lewis v. Motorworld Garages* [1986] I.C.R. 157, *Post Office v. Roberts* [1980] IRLR 347, *Millbrook Furnishing Industries v. McIntosh* [1981] IRLR 309, *British Broadcasting Corp. v. Beckett* [1983] IRLR 43 and *Brown v. J.B.D. Engineering* [1993] IRLR 568. In *Bridgen v. Lancashire County Council* [1987] IRLR 58, Sir John Donaldson M.R. said that the mere fact that a party to a contract takes a view of its construction which is ultimately shown to be wrong does not of itself constitute repudiatory conduct. "It has to be shown that he did not intend to be bound by the contract as properly construed".

It is not necessary that the person of whose conduct the employee complains should have authority to dismiss, provided that the person concerned acted in the course of employment: see *Hilton International Hotels (U.K.) v. Protopapa* [1990] IRLR 316. Similarly, an employee who resigns as a result of an *ultra vires* action on the part of the employer may claim constructive dismissal: see *Warnes v. Trustees of Cheriton Oddfellows Social Club* [1993] IRLR 58.

In cases of constructive dismissal, the industrial tribunal must first consider whether the employer's action is in breach of his or her contractual obligations or is a repudiation of them. That will involve ascertaining the express terms of the contract and considering whether any terms should be implied. But it should be borne in mind that, once the breach or repudiation has been established it must be serious enough to entitle the employee to leave without notice. This is a mixed question of fact and law. See *Gillies v. Daniels (Richard) & Co.* [1979] IRLR 457, *White v. London Transport Executive* [1981] IRLR 261, *Pedersen v. Camden London Borough Council* [1981] I.C.R. 674, *Milbrook Furnishing Industries v. McIntosh* [1981] IRLR 309 and *Woods v. W.M. Car Services (Peterborough)* [1982] I.C.R. 693.

Examples of a breach of an express term are a failure to pay wages, a refusal of holiday entitlement, the withdrawal of an employee's company car and unilateral alterations in the employee's pay, status or place of work: see *Lytlarch v. Reid* [1991] I.C.R. 216, *Tritan Oliver (Special Products) v. Bromage* (E.A.T. 709/91; I.D.S. Brief 511), *Millbrook Furnishing Industries v. McIntosh* [1981] IRLR 309, *Wadham Stringer Commercials (London) and Wadham Stringer Vehicles v. Brown* [1983] IRLR 46 and *McNeil v. Charles Crimin (Electrical Contractors)* [1984] IRLR 179. In this last type of case, the tribunal will need to consider whether the employee was subject to an express or implied mobility obligation: see *Courtaulds Northern Spinning v. Sibson* [1988] I.C.R. 451 and *Aparau v. Iceland Frozen Foods* [1996] IRLR 119. A proposed unilateral variation in the employee's terms of employment will amount to an anticipatory breach entitling the employee to resign and claim constructive dismissal: see *Greenaway Harrison v. Wiles* [1994] IRLR 380.

Examples of terms *implied* into employees' contracts are terms obliging the employer to maintain the relationship of trust between employer and employee, or not to treat the employees arbitrarily, capriciously or inequitably, or not to behave intolerably and not in accordance with good industrial practice: see *Woods v. W.M. Car Services (Peterborough)* [1981] I.C.R. 666 and [1982] I.C.R. 693 (C.A.), *Courtaulds Northern Textiles v. Andrew* [1979] IRLR 84, *Wigan Borough Council v. Davies* [1981] I.C.R. 411 and *White v. London Transport Executive* [1981] IRLR 261. See also *Bliss v. South East Thames Regional Health Authority* [1987] I.C.R. 700, where the Court of Appeal held that the employer was in breach of the implied term of trust and confidence by requiring the employee to submit to a medical examination and suspending him when he refused. A failure to deal with a female employee's complaint of alleged sexual harassment will be treated as a breach of this type of implied term, as will a failure to provide employees with a procedure for dealing with their grievances: see *Bracebridge Engineering v. Darby* [1990] IRLR 3 and *W.A. Goold (Pearmak) v. McConnell* [1995] IRLR 516. The courts are reluctant, however, to imply into an employee's contract terms such as an entitlement to be provided with regular pay increases: see *Murco Petroleum v. Forge* [1987] I.C.R. 282. In cases where there is an implied right for the employer to transfer an employee from one place of employment to another, the right must be subject to an implied qualification that reasonable notice must be given: see *Prestwick Circuits v. McAndrew* [1990] IRLR 191.

The E.A.T. has applied the implied term that an employer should not behave in a manner calculated or likely to destroy or seriously damage the relationship of trust and confidence between employer and employer to the employer's conduct in the exercise of powers conferred by an *express* term: see *United Bank v. Akhtar* [1989] IRLR 507.

A series of actions on the part of the employer may cumulatively amount to a breach of the implied contractual obligation of mutual trust and confidence, although each individual action may not. The course of conduct relied upon may include a breach of an express term of the contract committed by the employer but waived by the employee at the time: see *Lewis v. Motorworld Garages* [1986] I.C.R. 157.

Once the industrial tribunal has decided that there has been a breach or repudiation and that it was sufficiently serious to entitle the employee to end the contract immediately, it must then be satisfied that the employee's departure was caused by the breach: see *British Leyland (U.K.) v. McQuilken* [1978] IRLR 245 and *Walker v. Wedgwood (Josiah) & Sons* [1978] I.C.R. 744. It must be satisfied also that he or she has not waived the right to terminate by staying on too long after the conduct in question. Otherwise he or she may be taken to have elected to affirm the contract: see *Western Excavating (E.C.C.) v. Sharp* [1978] I.C.R. 221 at p.226, *per* Lord Denning M.R., and *Cox Toner (W.E.) v. Crook* [1981] I.C.R. 823. In the event of a subsequent resignation, it will not be possible to claim constructive dismissal. The employee must also accept a repudiation unequivocally: *Harrison v. Norwest Holst Group Administration* [1985] I.C.R. 668.

Finally, it may be noted that a constructive dismissal is not automatically unfair and that in certain circumstances it may be fair: see *Savoia v. Chiltern Herb Farms* [1982] IRLR 166 and *Cawley v. South Wales Electricity Board* [1985] IRLR 89.

Subs. (2)

Employee leaving early. The effect of this provision is that if an employee, upon being given notice by the employer, walks out without giving any notice at all, he or she will be treated as not having been dismissed: see *Walker v. Cotswold Chine Home School* (1977) 12 I.T.R. 342. Provided, however, that he or she gives some notice (not necessarily that which is required to be given under the contract or under s.86(2)), the statutory requirement will have been satisfied: see *Ready Case v. Jackson* [1981] IRLR 312 and *T.B.A. Industrial Products v. Morland* [1982] I.C.R. 686. On that view, notice amounts to no more than notification. In cases of this kind, the effective date of termination of the employee's contract will be the date on which he or she ceases working in accordance with the counter-notice and not the date when the employer's notice would have expired: *Thompson v. G.E.C. Avionics* [1991] IRLR 488. This means that the three-month limitation period for presenting a complaint of unfair dismissal will start to run from the date when the counter-notice takes effect.

Failure to permit return after childbirth treated as dismissal

96.—(1) Where an employee who—

(a) has the right conferred by section 79, and

(b) has exercised it in accordance with section 82,

is not permitted to return to work, she shall (subject to the following provisions of this section) be taken for the purposes of this Part to be dismissed for the reason for which she was not permitted to return with effect from the notified day of return (being deemed to have been continuously employed until that day).

(2) Subsection (1) does not apply in relation to an employee if—

(a) immediately before the end of her maternity leave period (or, if it ends by reason of dismissal, immediately before the dismissal) the number of employees employed by her employer, added to the number employed by any associated employer of his, did not exceed five, and

(b) it is not reasonably practicable for the employer (who may be the same employer or a successor of his) to permit her to return to work under section 79 or for him or an associated employer to offer her employment under a contract of employment satisfying the conditions specified in subsection (4).

(3) Subsection (1) does not apply in relation to an employee if—

    (a) it is not reasonably practicable for a reason other than redundancy for the employer (who may be the same employer or a successor of his) to permit her to return to work under section 79,

    (b) he or an associated employer offers her employment under a contract of employment satisfying the conditions specified in subsection (4), and

    (c) she accepts or unreasonably refuses that offer.

(4) The conditions referred to in subsections (2) and (3) are—

    (a) that the work to be done under the contract is of a kind which is both suitable in relation to the employee and appropriate for her to do in the circumstances, and

    (b) that the provisions of the contract as to the capacity and place in which she is to be employed, and as to the other terms and conditions of her employment, are not substantially less favourable to her than if she had returned to work under section 79.

(5) Where on a complaint of unfair dismissal any question arises as to whether the operation of subsection (1) is excluded by the provisions of subsection (2) or (3), it is for the employer to show that the provisions in question were satisfied in relation to the complainant.

(6) Where subsection (1) applies to an employee who was employed as a shop worker, or a betting worker, under her contract of employment on the last day of her maternity leave period, she shall be treated for the purposes of this Act as if she had been employed as a shop worker, or a betting worker, on the day with effect from which she is treated as dismissed.

DEFINITIONS
    "associated employer": s.231.
    "betting worker": s.233.
    "employee": s.230(1).
    "employer": s.230(4).
    "maternity leave period": ss.72 and 73.
    "notified day of return": s.83.
    "shop worker": s.232.
    "successor": s.235(1) and (2).

GENERAL NOTE
The general rule is set out in subs. (1): an employee will be treated as dismissed if she is not permitted to return to work and the reason for dismissal will be taken to be the reason for which she is not allowed to return. This, however, is subject to the proviso that she has the right to return within s.79 and that she has complied with s.82 in exercising it.

This general rule will not apply in the following cases: (1) the employer is a small employer with five or less employees (including employees of an associated employer) and it is not reasonably practicable to allow the employee to return or to offer her suitable alternative employment (including employment with an associated employer): or (2) it is not reasonably practicable to allow the employee to return to work, but the employer or an associated employer offers suitable alternative employment which she accepts or unreasonably refuses.

Note subs. (5), which places upon the employer the burden of showing that either of these exceptions is satisfied.

Effective date of termination

97.—(1) Subject to the following provisions of this section, in this Part "the effective date of termination"—

    (a) in relation to an employee whose contract of employment is terminated by notice, whether given by his employer or by the employee, means the date on which the notice expires,

    (b) in relation to an employee whose contract of employment is terminated without notice, means the date on which the termination takes effect, and

(c) in relation to an employee who is employed under a contract for a fixed term which expires without being renewed under the same contract, means the date on which the term expires.

(2) Where—

(a) the contract of employment is terminated by the employer, and

(b) the notice required by section 86 to be given by an employer would, if duly given on the material date, expire on a date later than the effective date of termination (as defined by subsection (1)),

for the purposes of sections 108(1), 119(1) and 227(3) the later date is the effective date of termination.

(3) In subsection (2)(b) "the material date" means—

(a) the date when notice of termination was given by the employer, or

(b) where no notice was given, the date when the contract of employment was terminated by the employer.

(4) Where—

(a) the contract of employment is terminated by the employee,

(b) the material date does not fall during a period of notice given by the employer to terminate that contract, and

(c) had the contract been terminated not by the employee but by notice given on the material date by the employer, that notice would have been required by section 86 to expire on a date later than the effective date of termination (as defined by subsection (1)),

for the purposes of sections 108(1), 119(1) and 227(3) the later date is the effective date of termination.

(5) In subsection (4) "the material date" means—

(a) the date when notice of termination was given by the employee, or

(b) where no notice was given, the date when the contract of employment was terminated by the employee.

(6) Where an employee is taken to be dismissed for the purposes of this Part by virtue of section 96, references in this Part to the effective date of termination are to the notified date of return.

DEFINITIONS
"contract of employment": s.230(2).
"employee": s.230(1).
"employer": s.230(4).

GENERAL NOTE
It is important to decide what the effective date of termination is since the limitation period for presenting a complaint of unfair dismissal starts to run from that date. Section 97 contains two sets of rules, one applying to actual dismissal cases, the other to postponement of the date of termination. The position in constructive dismissal cases, for which there are no specific statutory provisions is also discussed below.

Actual dismissals
The date of termination is one of the following: (1) if the dismissal is with notice, the date on which the notice expires; or (2) if the dismissal is without notice, the date on which the notice takes effect; or (3) if the dismissal is constituted by the expiry of a fixed-term contract, the date on which the term expires. This date of termination is called the "effective date of termination" in the unfair dismissal provisions.

It can often be difficult to decide the difference between a dismissal with notice when the employee is not required to work out the notice and a summary dismissal, particularly if in both cases the employee receives a payment of wages. The speech of Lord Browne-Wilkinson in *Delaney v. Staples (R.J.) (t/a De Montfort Recruitment)* [1992] I.C.R. 483, at pp.488–9 contains a discussion of what is meant by payments in lieu of notice, which is certainly helpful in the present context, although it should be borne in mind that the case in question arose in the context of the Wages Act 1986 (c. 48) (now Pt. II of this Act).

For an employee dismissed with notice who is told that there is no need to work out the notice and given a payment attributable to the notice period in a lump sum (*i.e.* effectively on paid or "garden" leave), the date of termination will be the date when the notice expires: *Dixon v. Stenor* [1973] I.C.R. 157, *Adams v. G.K.N. Sankey* [1980] IRLR 416 and *Chapman v. Letheby & Chris-*

topher [1981] IRLR 440. If, on the other hand, he or she is dismissed without notice and with a payment in lieu of notice, the date of termination is either the date when the summary dismissal is communicated, or, if he or she is given notice of an impending dismissal with wages in lieu of notice, the date when the dismissal takes effect: *Dedman v. British Building and Engineering Appliances* [1974] I.C.R. 53, *Cort (Robert) & Son v. Charman* [1981] I.C.R. 816, and *Belling & Lee v. Burford* [1982] I.C.R. 454. See also *West v. Kneels* [1987] I.C.R. 146. A summary dismissal effected by letter will not take effect until the employee reads the letter or has a reasonable opportunity of reading it: see *Brown v. Southall & Knight* [1980] I.C.R. 617 at pp.628–629.

In cases involving payments in lieu of notice, the tribunal must hear evidence of what actually was said when the employee was dismissed to enable it to decide whether the dismissal was summary or was with notice but without a requirement to work during the notice period: *Leech v. Preston Borough Council* [1985] I.C.R. 192. The P45 form, which an employer should give to the employee when the employment is terminated, has nothing to do with the date on which the employment terminates: *London Borough of Newham v. Ward* [1985] IRLR 509. There is nothing in s.97(1) to prevent the parties retrospectively agreeing a date of termination, even though the employee's contract subsists after that date: *Crank v. Her Majesty's Stationery Office* [1985] I.C.R. 1.

In cases where the employee gives a counter-notice to terminate the contract on a date earlier than the date when the employer's notice would expire, the effective date of termination of the employee's contract will be the date on which he or she ceases working in accordance with the counter-notice and not the date when the employer's notice would have expired: *Thompson v. G.E.C. Avionics* [1991] IRLR 488. The three-month limitation period for presenting a complaint of unfair dismissal will start to run from the date when the counter-notice takes effect.

A dismissal with notice may be converted into a summary dismissal if the employer dismisses the employee on the spot during his or her notice period. That will bring forward the date of termination to the date of the summary dismissal: *Stapp v. The Shaftesbury Society* [1982] IRLR 326.

In cases where the employee invokes a domestic appeals procedure much will depend upon what the contract actually provides. For example, it may provide that the contract is to continue until the appeal is determined. In that case, there will be no difficulty. See *Sainsbury (J.) v. Savage* [1981] I.C.R. 1, *Crown Agents for Overseas Governments and Administration v. Lawal* [1979] I.C.R. 103, *Batchelor v. British Railways Board* [1987] IRLR 136, *Board of Governors National Heart and Chest Hospitals v. Nambiar* [1981] I.C.R. 441 and *High v. British Railways Board* [1978] IRLR 52.

Constructive dismissals

There is no express provision dealing with the date of termination in constructive dismissal cases. This means that a tribunal will need to apply by analogy the provisions of s.97(1). In many constructive dismissal cases, the employer commits a repudiatory act and the employee continues to work until such time as he or she decides to resign. In such a case, the earliest date for the ending of the employment would be the date of the resignation, but, if it is a resignation with notice, the effective date of termination should be the date when the notice expires. That should be the general rule. In exceptional cases, the repudiatory act may be treated as putting an immediate end to the relationship, in which case the effective date of termination will be the date when the employment relationship is to be treated as having ended. See *B.M.K. v. Logue* [1993] I.C.R. 601, which involved an employee removed as a director by resolutions of his fellow-directors.

Postponement of the date of termination

The statutory date of termination may be postponed in the following circumstances: (1) where the notice given by the employer is shorter than the notice which the employee is entitled to under s.86; and (2) where the employee terminates the contract with or without notice but the notice required by s.86 to be given to the employee would have expired later, had the employer given such notice.

Where the notice given by the employer would expire earlier than the notice required to be given by s.86, the later date is treated by s.97(2) and (3) as the date of termination. For example, if the employee is entitled under s.86 to eight weeks' notice and only receives four, he or she will be treated as having received eight weeks' notice and the date of termination will be when the eight weeks' notice would have expired. This postponement of the date of termination is only for certain purposes, however. The main purposes are: (1) qualifying for a written statement of reasons for dismissal under s.92; (2) calculating whether an employee has sufficient continuity of employment under s.108(1); and (3) calculating the years of employment for the purposes of a basic award of compensation. It should be noted that the date of termination is only extended by the statutory minimum notice entitlement, not by any minimum contractual notice entitlement:

Fox Maintenance v. Jackson [1978] I.C.R. 110. It should also be noted that the purposes for which the extensions may take place are limited to those specified in this Act and to no others: see *Staffordshire County Council v. Secretary of State for Employment* [1989] I.C.R. 664, at p.672G.

It is important to have the statutory provisions in mind in the case of employees who are dismissed with less notice than they are entitled to under s.86. An employee dismissed summarily shortly before the expiry of a complete year of continuous employment may be treated as dismissed on a date falling after the expiry of the complete year of continuous employment with the result that he or she is treated as having an extra year of continuous employment; that, in turn, will affect the size of the basic award or redundancy payment.

The second type of postponement of the date of termination (see above) only operates in relation to unfair dismissal claims where the *employee* terminates the contract either with or without notice and for the same purposes as those set out above. In that case the date on which the employer's notice under s.86 (had it been given) would have been required to expire is treated as the effective date of termination.

Fairness

General

98.—(1) In determining for the purposes of this Part whether the dismissal of an employee is fair or unfair, it is for the employer to show—
  (a) the reason (or, if more than one, the principal reason) for the dismissal, and
  (b) that it is either a reason falling within subsection (2) or some other substantial reason of a kind such as to justify the dismissal of an employee holding the position which the employee held.
(2) A reason falls within this subsection if it—
  (a) relates to the capability or qualifications of the employee for performing work of the kind which he was employed by the employer to do,
  (b) relates to the conduct of the employee,
  (c) is that the employee was redundant, or
  (d) is that the employee could not continue to work in the position which he held without contravention (either on his part or on that of his employer) of a duty or restriction imposed by or under an enactment.
(3) In subsection (2)(a)—
  (a) "capability", in relation to an employee, means his capability assessed by reference to skill, aptitude, health or any other physical or mental quality, and
  (b) "qualifications", in relation to an employee, means any degree, diploma or other academic, technical or professional qualification relevant to the position which he held.
(4) Where the employer has fulfilled the requirements of subsection (1), the determination of the question whether the dismissal is fair or unfair (having regard to the reason shown by the employer)—
  (a) depends on whether in the circumstances (including the size and administrative resources of the employer's undertaking) the employer acted reasonably or unreasonably in treating it as a sufficient reason for dismissing the employee, and
  (b) shall be determined in accordance with equity and the substantial merits of the case.
(5) Where the employee is taken to be dismissed for the purposes of this Part by virtue of section 96, subsection (4)(a) applies as if for the words "acted reasonably" onwards there were substituted the words "would have been acting reasonably or unreasonably in treating it as a sufficient reason for dismissing the employee if she had not been absent from work, and".
  (6) Subsections (4) and (5) are subject to—
  (a) sections 99 to 107 of this Act, and

(b) sections 152, 153 and 238 of the Trade Union and Labour Relations (Consolidation) Act 1992 (dismissal on ground of trade union membership or activities or in connection with industrial action).

DEFINITIONS
"employee": s.230(1).
"employer": s.230(4).
"position": s.235(1).

GENERAL NOTE
Once it has been established that the employee has been dismissed, an unfair dismissal claim will fall to be decided in two stages. The first stage consists of establishing what was the reason for the dismissal. Reasons may be divided into two categories (1) what may be called "potentially fair" reasons, and (2) reasons which, subject to certain exceptions, make a dismissal automatically unfair (*e.g.* dismissals for health and safety reasons or on grounds of pregnancy). This second category is discussed in the notes to ss.100–104. The provisions of ss.152, 153 and 238 of the Trade Union and Labour Relations (Consolidation) Act 1992 (c. 52) should be noted. These deal with dismissals on the grounds of trade union membership or activities and dismissals in connection with industrial action.

At the second stage, the tribunal must be satisfied that the employer acted reasonably in dismissing for the given reason, unless the reason is one of those which makes the dismissal automatically unfair. The "potentially fair" reasons are so called because they can potentially justify dismissal, but they do not necessarily justify dismissal, since s.98(4) obliges the tribunal to decide whether the employer acted reasonably or unreasonably in treating the reasons as sufficient for dismissing the employee.

In a complaint of unfair dismissal involving the potentially fair reasons, s.98(1)(a) places the burden on the employer to show the reason (or, if there was more than one, the principal reason) for the dismissal. He or she must then show that the reason falls within one of the four specific categories set out in s.98(2), namely: (1) capability or qualifications; (2) the employee's conduct; (3) redundancy; or (4) statutory requirements. In addition, there is what may be called a residual category, which, in the phraseology of the statute, is "some other substantial reason of a kind such as to justify the dismissal of an employee holding the position which that employee held".

Subs. (1)
In unfair dismissal cases where the reason is redundancy (which is one of the potentially fair reasons set out above), s.7(6) of the Industrial Tribunals Act 1996 (formerly Sched. 9, para. 5 of the 1978 Act) suspends the operation of the presumption of redundancy where in the same proceedings the industrial tribunal determines a claim for a redundancy payment and a complaint of unfair dismissal. Thus, as in other unfair dismissal cases, the burden is on the employer to show the reason for the dismissal.

The burden of establishing the reason, or principal reason, for the dismissal lies upon the employer. If he or she fails to do so, the dismissal will be deemed unfair: see, for example, *Adams v. Derby City Council* [1986] IRLR 163. See also *Maund v. Penwith District Council* [1984] I.C.R. 143. An incorrect label will not be fatal to the employer's case: see *Abernethy v. Mott Hay and Anderson* [1974] I.C.R. 323, especially *per* Cairns L.J., at p. 330. See also *Trust Houses Forte Leisure v. Aquilar* [1976] IRLR 251, *Yusuf v. Aberplace* [1984] I.C.R. 850, *Clarke v. Trimoco Motor Group* [1993] I.C.R. 237 and *Ely v. Y.K.K. Fasteners (U.K.)* [1994] I.C.R. 164.

If the employer relies upon one particular reason and the reason is not established, it is not possible to try to rely upon an entirely different reason either at the tribunal hearing or upon appeal, though it may, of course, be possible to apply for leave to amend the notice of appearance: see *Nelson v. British Broadcasting Corp.* [1977] I.C.R. 649 and *Burkett v. Pendletons (Sweets)* [1992] I.C.R. 407. The employer may not adduce evidence of what happened after the dismissal or of events which occurred before the dismissal but which did not come to his or her knowledge until afterwards: see *Devis (W.) & Sons v. Atkins* [1977] I.C.R. 662, applied by the E.A.T. in *Vauxhall Motors v. Ghafoor* [1993] I.C.R. 376. It should also be noted that s.107 debars the tribunal from taking into account any industrial pressure exerted on the employer to obtain the dismissal, when determining the reason for the dismissal.

Subs. (2)

Capability and qualifications. "Capability" means "capability assessed by reference to skill, aptitude, health or any other physical or mental quality", and "qualifications" means "any degree, diploma or other academic, technical or professional qualification relevant to the position which the employee held": s.98(3). See *Shook v. Ealing London Borough Council* [1986] I.C.R. 314, in which the E.A.T. stressed that under s.98(2)(a) the reason for dismissal must relate to the employee's capacity and to the performance of his or her duties under the contract of employment. It is not necessary to show that the employee's incapacity (in this case disabilities caused by back trouble) would have affected the performance of all that he or she might be required to do under the contract. A failure to pass aptitude tests may relate to both capability and qualifications: see *Blackman v. Post Office* [1974] I.C.R. 151. The most common case to arise under this heading is ill-health, which can include mental health: *O'Brien v. Prudential Assurance Co.* [1979] IRLR 140 and *Shook v. London Borough of Ealing* [1986] I.C.R. 314.

The other case which commonly arises is lack of capability. This should be viewed relatively narrowly as applying mainly to cases where the employee is incapable of satisfactory work. Cases where a person has not come up to standard through his or her own carelessness, negligence or idleness, are better dealt with as cases of conduct rather than capability. The difference is between "sheer incapability due to an inherent incapacity to function" and "a failure to exercise to the full such talent as is possessed": *Sutton & Gates (Luton) v. Boxall* [1978] I.C.R. 67 at p.71. See also *James v. Waltham Holy Cross U.D.C.* [1973] I.C.R. 398 and *Cook v. Linnell (Thomas) & Sons* [1977] I.C.R. 770.

Conduct. There is no statutory definition of "conduct". Apart from the overlap between conduct and capability, conduct itself has been held to embrace a wide range of actions. Its scope includes gross misconduct, such as theft, violence, negligence and working in competition with the employer, and lesser matters, such as clocking offences or swearing. What may be called "off-duty" conduct will fall within this head if it in some way bears upon the relationship between the employer and the employee, particularly where criminal offences are involved: see *Singh v. London County Bus Services* [1976] IRLR 176, *Nottinghamshire County Council v. Bowly* [1978] IRLR 252, *Norfolk County Council v. Bernard* [1978] IRLR 220, *Moore v. C. & A. Modes* [1981] IRLR 71 and *P. v. Nottinghamshire County Council* [1992] I.C.R. 706. The category may also embrace the situation where the employee conceals previous convictions in order to obtain a job: *Torr v. British Railways Board* [1977] I.C.R. 785. It should be noted that, as in the case of capability and qualifications, the reason must *relate* to the conduct in question.

Redundancy. See the notes to s.139.

Statutory requirements. An example of this type of reason would be the loss of a driving licence in the case of a person employed as a driver, or a teacher declared unsuitable by the Department of Education and Science: see *Sandhu v. Department of Education and Science and Hillingdon London Borough* [1978] IRLR 208 and *Sutcliffe & Eaton v. Pinney* [1977] IRLR 349. The fact that the employers genuinely but erroneously believe that they will contravene a statutory requirement cannot be a reason falling within s.98(2)(d), though it might be "some other substantial reason": *Bouchaala v. Trust House Forte Hotels* [1980] I.C.R. 721. The fact that the continued employment of the employee contravenes a statutory requirement does not exonerate the employer from acting reasonably: *Sandhu v. Department of Education and Science and Hillingdon London Borough*, above.

Some other substantial reason. The fifth category of reason is what was earlier called a residual category. It is stated in s.98(1)(b) as being "some other substantial reason of a kind such as to justify the dismissal of an employee holding the position which the employee held". These words are not to be construed *ejusdem generis* with the other four potentially fair reasons. That means that this is a fairly wide category of reasons: *R.S. Components v. Irwin* [1973] I.C.R. 535. The most common examples, thrown up by the cases, relate to the business needs of the employer and have tended to involve a refusal by the employee to agree to a change in contractual terms (as in *R.S. Components*, above) or a refusal to agree to a reorganisation falling short of redundancy: see *St. John of God (Care Services) v. Brooks* [1992] I.C.R. 715 and *Hollister v. National Farmers' Union* [1979] I.C.R. 542. It is open to an industrial tribunal to find that an employee's dismissal following a reorganisation was for some other substantial reason, despite the fact that the dismissal was by reason of redundancy and the alternative ground was not pleaded nor canvassed in argument at the tribunal hearing: *Hannan v. TNT-IPEC* [1986] IRLR 165.

A number of cases involving this category of reason have reached the Court of Appeal in recent years. In those cases "some other substantial reason" has been held to include dismissals instigated by a third party, the expiry and non-renewal of a fixed-term contract, the imposition of a sentence of imprisonment and a mistake as to the employee's intentions (brought about by his late notification to the employers that he had changed his mind about resigning): see *Dobie v. Burns International Security Services (U.K.)* [1984] I.C.R. 812, *Grootcon (U.K.) v. Keld* [1984] IRLR 302, *Kingston v. British Railways Board* [1984] I.C.R. 781, *Fay v. North Yorkshire County*

Council [1986] I.C.R. 133 and *Ely v. Y.K.K. Fasteners (U.K.)* [1993] IRLR 500. In *Kent County Council v. Gilham (No. 2)* [1985] I.C.R. 233 the Court of Appeal said that the burden on the employer of showing a substantial reason is designed to deter employers from dismissing employees for some trivial or unworthy reason. If, on the face of it, the reason could justify the dismissal, then it passes as a substantial reason. This test must not be confused with the s.98(4) test.

Note the provisions of s.106, which deals with replacements. Note also reg. 8(2) of the 1981 Regulations which provide that where, either before or after a relevant transfer, the employee is dismissed because of economic, technical or organisational reasons entailing changes in the workforce of either the transferor or transferee, the dismissal will be treated as being for some other substantial reason; the tribunal will then have to consider s.98(4).

Subs. (4)

Generally

Once a potentially fair reason has been established, it is then necessary to consider whether the employer acted fairly in dismissing for that reason. It is important to remember that the effect of s.98(4) is that there is no burden of proof on either the employer or the employee. It is therefore wrong for an industrial tribunal to place the burden on the employer of satisfying them that he or she acted reasonably: see *Post Office Counters v. Heavey* [1990] I.C.R. 1 and *Boys and Girls Welfare Society v. McDonald* [1996] IRLR 129. The Court of Appeal has stressed that appeals to the E.A.T. and beyond only lie on points of law and has discouraged attempts to dress up questions of fact as questions of law: see *Bailey v. B.P. Oil (Kent Refinery)* [1980] I.C.R. 642, *Thomas & Betts Manufacturing Co. v. Harding* [1980] IRLR 255, *Wass (W. & J.) v. Binns* [1982] I.C.R. 486, *Woods v. W.M. Car Services (Peterborough)* [1982] IRLR 413, *O'Kelly v. Trusthouse Forte* [1983] I.C.R. 728, *Martin v. Glynwed Distribution (t/a MBS Fastenings)* [1983] I.C.R. 511, *Dobie v. Burns International Security Services (U.K.)* [1984] I.C.R. 812 and *Gilham v. Kent County Council (No. 2)* [1985] I.C.R. 233. The most recent reiteration of this view is to be found in *Piggott Brothers v. Jackson* [1992] I.C.R. 85. See also *East Berkshire Health Authority v. Matadeen* [1992] I.C.R. 723. It is clear, however, that the question of fairness cannot be considered solely as one of fact, and therefore unappealable. It is best described as a mixed question of fact and law. The tenor of the Court of Appeal decisions is to restrict considerably the circumstances in which appeals may be made to the E.A.T. from industrial tribunals' decisions and to discourage the E.A.T. from reversing the tribunals' decisions because it would have reached a different conclusion.

For a discussion of the approach to be taken see the remarks of May L.J. in *Neale v. Hereford and Worcester County Council* [1986] I.C.R. 471, at p.483, and the critique of them by Lord Donaldson of Lymington M.R. in *Piggott Brothers v. Jackson* [1992] I.C.R. 85, at p.92. This approach may be characterised as the "reasonable decision" approach. It was summarised by Browne-Wilkinson J. (as he then was) in *Iceland Frozen Foods v. Jones* [1983] I.C.R. 17, at pp.24–25, in words quoted with approval by the Court of Appeal in *Neale's* case, above:

"The correct approach ... is as follows: (1) the starting point should always be the words of section 57(3) themselves; (2) in applying the section an industrial tribunal must consider the reasonableness of the employer's conduct, not simply whether they (the members of the industrial tribunal) consider the dismissal to be fair; (3) in judging the reasonableness of the employer's conduct an industrial tribunal must not substitute its decision as to what was the right course to adopt for that of the employer; (4) in many, though not all, cases there is a band of reasonable responses to the employee's conduct within which one employer might take one view, another quite reasonably take another; (5) the function of the industrial tribunal, as an industrial jury, is to determine whether in the particular circumstances of each case the decision to dismiss the employee fell within the band of reasonable responses which a reasonable employer might have adopted. If the dismissal falls within the band the dismissal is fair: if the dismissal falls outside the band, it is unfair".

In taking this approach, the Court of Appeal has laid emphasis on the autonomy of the industrial tribunals, and attempts by the E.A.T. to provide guidance to the tribunals have been regarded as misconceived: see *Bailey v. B.P. Oil (Kent Refinery)*, above, at p.648 (Lawton L.J.), *cf.* the E.A.T.'s attitude in *Iceland Frozen Foods v. Jones* [1983] I.C.R. 17.

Another aspect of the tribunal's role concerns the question it should ask, since, if it asks the wrong question, its decision will be liable to be upset on appeal. The appellate courts have stressed that the relevant question is whether it was reasonable of the employer to dismiss the employee and that in many cases there may be a range of courses of action open to the employer, all of which fall within the band of reasonableness; for an industrial tribunal to prefer one course of action to another will cause it to apply the test of what it would have done itself and not the test of what a reasonable employer would have done: see *British Leyland (U.K.) v. Swift* [1981]

IRLR 91 (C.A.), *Watling (N.C.) & Co. v. Richardson* [1978] 13 I.C.R. 1049, *Iceland Frozen Food v. Jones* [1983] I.C.R. 17 and *Neale v. Hereford and Worcester County Council* [1986] I.C.R. 471. See also *Whitbread & Co. v. Mills* [1988] I.C.R. 776.

In deciding upon the fairness or otherwise of the dismissal, the tribunal must take into account any relevant provision of the Code of Practice on Disciplinary Practice and Procedures in Employment. Section 207(1) of the Trade Union and Labour Relations (Consolidation) Act 1992 stresses that a failure by the employer does not "of itself" make him or her liable to any legal proceedings; it goes on to say that the Code is admissible in evidence in proceedings in industrial tribunals and that "any provision of the Code which appears to the tribunal ... to be relevant to any question in the proceedings shall be taken into account in determining that question". In *Devis (W.) & Sons v. Atkins* [1977] I.C.R. 662, at p.679 Viscount Dilhorne said that non-compliance with the Code does not necessarily make a dismissal unfair, but that a failure to follow a procedure prescribed in the Code may lead to the conclusion that a dismissal was unfair, which, if that procedure had been followed, would have been held to have been fair. The effect of the existence of s.98(4) (and its predecessors) and the Code of Practice is that considerable importance has been attached to the notion of procedural fairness, *i.e.* the possibility that a dismissal may be made unfair by the use of an unfair procedure (*e.g.* lack of warnings or opportunity for the employee to state his or her side of the case) even where the reason is a perfectly good one. This has been highlighted by the decision of the House of Lords in *Polkey v. Dayton (A.E.) Services* [1988] I.C.R. 142.

Capability and qualifications

Two aspects of this potentially fair reason have given rise to a considerable amount of litigation: unsatisfactory work performance and ill-health.

In cases involving unsatisfactory work performance, the employer must satisfy the industrial tribunal that he or she honestly believed on reasonable grounds that the employee was incapable. A full and careful investigation of the facts should be undertaken; if, however, that is done, the employer does not have to satisfy the tribunal that he or she drew the correct conclusion, only that he or she had sufficient evidence upon which he or she could reach that conclusion. It is necessary for the employer to follow a reasonable procedure and, in particular, to give the employee a warning and an opportunity to improve. A failure to do so will not automatically make the dismissal unfair, particularly if it can be shown that the employee is incapable of improving or already knows clearly what is expected, or that the giving of a warning would have made no difference to the result. See *Alidair v. Taylor* [1978] I.C.R. 445, *Cook v. Thomas Linnell & Sons* [1977] I.C.R. 770, *Hollister v. National Farmers' Union* [1979] I.C.R. 542, *James v. Waltham Holy Cross Urban District Council* [1973] I.C.R. 398 and *Dunning (A.J.) & Sons (Shopfitters) v. Jacomb* [1973] I.C.R. 448.

The employer must deal with ill employees carefully, particularly if the employee is suffering from mental illness as in *O'Brien v. Prudential Assurance Co.* [1979] IRLR 140. In cases of prolonged absence, the question is whether the employer can be expected to wait any longer and, if so, how much longer: *Spencer v. Paragon Wallpapers* [1977] I.C.R. 301 at p.307. Except in exceptional circumstances, the employee should be consulted and the employer should take reasonable steps to find out the true medical position, preferably by means of a sufficiently detailed medical report to enable an informed decision to be made: *East Lindsey District Council v. Daubney* [1977] I.C.R. 566, *Williamson v. Alcan* [1978] I.C.R. 104, *A. Links & Co. v. Rose* [1991] IRLR 353, *Eclipse Blinds v. Wright* [1992] IRLR 133 and *Seymour v. British Airways Board* [1983] I.C.R. 148 (which concerned the dismissal of a disabled employee). There is no equivalent duty on an employee to indicate to the employer his or her prospects of recovery: *Mitchell v. Arkwood Plastics (Engineering)* [1993] I.C.R. 471. The E.A.T. has stressed that the decision to dismiss is managerial, not medical, but the employer should consider the possibility of offering alternative work within the employee's capabilities, if it is available: *Merseyside and North Wales Electricity Board v. Taylor* [1975] I.C.R. 185, *cf. Taylorplan Catering (Scotland) v. McInally* [1980] IRLR 53. In cases of persistent, intermittent absence for minor illness, the employer should conduct a fair review of the employee's attendance record and the reasons for it, and give the employee appropriate warnings and an opportunity to make representations. This type of situation was considered by the E.A.T. in *Lynock v. Cereal Packaging* [1988] I.C.R. 670.

Conduct

The employer must show that his or her view of the facts stemmed from an honest belief based upon reasonable grounds; it is also important to undertake a careful investigation which provides sufficient evidence for the conclusion reached. In *British Home Stores v. Burchell* [1980] I.C.R. 303, the E.A.T. set out the following guidelines for tribunals to apply when dealing with cases of alleged misconduct:

"First ... there must be established by the employer the fact of that belief; that the employer did believe it. Secondly, that the employer had in his mind reasonable grounds upon which to sustain that belief. And thirdly ... that the employer at the stage at which he formed that belief on those grounds, had carried out as much investigation into the matter as was reasonable in all the circumstances of the case".

The case in question arose from alleged dishonesty, but the *Burchell* test is generally applied to those cases where the reason for the employee's dismissal is the employer's belief that there has been misconduct of some kind. In *Boys and Girls Welfare Society v. McDonald* [1996] IRLR 129, the E.A.T. stressed that industrial tribunals should not fall into the error of placing the burden on employers of satisfying them as to the reasonableness of the dismissal. *Burchell's* case was decided before the enactment of what is now s.98(4) in its present form, which expressly establishes a neutral burden of proof. The E.A.T. also pointed out that once the tribunal has considered the three-part test of *Burchell* it must still go on to consider whether the dismissal fell within the range of reasonable responses of a reasonable employer.

In this note, dismissals for conduct will be considered under the following headings: (i) conduct of investigations; (ii) decision to dismiss; (iii) procedural fairness; and (iv) criminal offences.

(i) Conduct of investigations. In considering an employer's conduct of an investigation, an industrial tribunal will generally follow the three-stage approach set out in *Burchell's* case above and widely followed. It should not be followed slavishly, however, particularly where the facts of a particular case do not easily fit within its scope. It is useful in cases where a single employee's misconduct is involved, but may not assist in more complicated cases. Thus, for example, in cases where employers conduct an investigation but cannot identify the persons responsible for the acts or omissions in question, they are entitled to dismiss a group of employees, even where it is possible that not all in the group were guilty of the act. But the industrial tribunal must be satisfied that the employer conducted a proper investigation; it need not be a quasi-judicial investigation with cross-examination of witnesses: see *Whitbread & Co. v. Thomas* [1988] I.C.R. 135, *Parr v. Whitbread, t/a Threshers Wine Merchants* [1990] I.C.R. 427 and *Ulsterbus v. Henderson* [1989] IRLR 251. See also *Chamberlain Vinyl Products v. Patel* [1996] I.C.R. 113 and *Scottish Daily Record & Sunday Mail (1986) v. Laird* [1986] IRLR 665.

It is important, however, that employers are careful in their handling of the evidence used in the investigation of alleged misconduct. See *Linfood Cash and Carry v. Thomson* [1989] I.C.R. 518 (approved by the Court of Appeal in *Morgan v. Electrolux* [1991] I.C.R. 369), which involved an investigation based on allegations made by an anonymous informant, *Vauxhall Motors v. Ghafoor* [1993] I.C.R. 376, which concerned notes taken at a disciplinary meeting and *Louies v. Coventry Hood & Seating Co.* [1990] I.C.R. 54, which involved written statements whose contents were kept from the employee under investigation.

(ii) Decision to dismiss. An employer who treats employees differently (for example, by dismissing one and not another) will not be held to have dismissed unfairly provided that the decision was one which a reasonable employer could reach. See *Securicor v. Smith* [1989] IRLR 356, *Cain v. Leeds Western Health Authority* [1990] IRLR 168, *Frames Snooker Centre v. Boyce* [1992] IRLR 472 and *London Borough of Harrow v. Cunningham* [1996] IRLR 256. In *Paul v. East Surrey District Health Authority* [1995] IRLR 305 the Court of Appeal stressed that in cases of this kind ultimately the question for the employer is whether in the particular case dismissal is a reasonable response to the misconduct and warned that tribunals should scrutinise arguments based upon disparity of treatment with particular care. Similar considerations arise where the employee in question is dismissed for an offence (*e.g.* assaulting another employee) but there is evidence that in the past other employees have not been dismissed for a similar offence: see *Procter v. British Gypsum* [1991] IRLR 7.

A similar problem arises in situations where there is a theft, but the employer cannot determine which employee is responsible and dismisses a group of employees (so-called "blanket dismissal" cases): see *Parr v. Whitbread & Co.* [1990] I.C.R. 427, in which the E.A.T. suggested an approach for dealing with this type of case. See also *Whitbread & Co. v. Thomas* [1988] I.C.R. 135.

The *Burchell* test does not apply where misconduct in fact takes place; in that case the question is not whether the employer had a reasonable belief, but whether the act of dismissal was a reasonable response.

(iii) Procedural fairness. There are two House of Lords decisions which have a particularly important bearing on this area. The first, *Polkey v. A.E. Dayton* [1998] I.C.R. 142, involves the question whether a dismissal which would be unfair because of a failure to follow a fair pro-

cedure can be held to be fair if the employer is able to establish that following a fair procedure would have made no difference to the outcome. The House of Lords said that the correct question is whether the employer was reasonable or unreasonable in deciding that the reason for dismissing the employee was a sufficient reason, not whether the employee would nevertheless have been dismissed even if there had been prior consultation or warning. Whether the employer could reasonably have concluded that consultation or warning would be useless so that the failure to consult or warn would not necessarily render the dismissal unfair was a matter for the industrial tribunal to consider in the light of the circumstances known to the employer at the time of the decision to dismiss. Lord Mackay of Clashfern L.C., who delivered the main speech, adopted the analysis of Browne-Wilkinson J. in *Sillifant v. Powell Duffryn Timber* [1983] IRLR 91, at p.97. Although *Polkey's* case was decided in the context of a dismissal for redundancy, it is applicable to other reasons for dismissal, particularly conduct dismissals. The second House of Lords decision which is important in the present context is *West Midlands Co-operative Society v. Tipton* [1986] I.C.R. 192, which concerns appeals.

Another question which arises from the role of internal appeals procedures in the dismissal process is whether a fair appeal can rectify an unfair disciplinary hearing and thus render fair a dismissal which might otherwise be unfair. In *Whitbread & Co. v. Mills* [1988] I.C.R. 776 the E.A.T. answered the question in the affirmative. The Court of Appeal reached a similar conclusion in *Sartor v. P. & O. European Ferries (Felixstowe)* [1992] IRLR 271, although the above case was not referred to in its judgment. The court did stress, however, that for a procedural defect to be cured by an appeal the appeal must be by way of rehearing. Procedural fairness is particularly important in cases of conduct, though the requirements are not absolute. Generally, the employer should go through a procedure appropriate to the nature and size of the organisation and a failure to do so, except in the exceptional cases considered below, will cause the dismissal to be unfair. In *Clarke v. Trimoco Motor Group* [1993] I.C.R. 237, at p.248, the E.A.T. said:

"... [A]n employee before being dismissed must, in order to satisfy the requirements of natural justice, be given an opportunity of giving an explanation, save in those rare cases where there is no possibility of the employee giving an explanation of the conduct alleged or where it is plainly admitted so that there may be no cause to ask for an explanation ... The present case is quite plainly not in one of those exceptional categories ... ".

A failure to apply a procedure, however, will not cause the dismissal to be unfair if, for example, the employee shows himself to be "determined to go his own way" or has taken up a position which is unlikely to be altered by being given a hearing: see *Retarded Children's Aid Society v. Day* [1978] I.C.R. 437, at p. 442 and *James v. Waltham Holy Cross Urban District Council* [1973] I.C.R. 398. But it is important to bear in mind that the decision in *Polkey's* case means that in most cases such questions are not generally relevant. Lord Bridge of Harwich did, however, say, at p. 163:

"It is quite a different matter if the tribunal is able to conclude that the employer himself, at the time of the dismissal, acted reasonably in taking the view that, in the exceptional circumstances of the particular case, the procedural steps normally appropriate would have been futile, could not have altered the decision to dismiss and therefore could be dispensed with".

The procedure will probably involve the application of the employer's disciplinary rules, which should make clear what amounts to an offence and what the result of a breach of the rule will be, and they should have been brought sufficiently to the employee's notice. If there are no rules, or the rules make no provision of the particular offence, the provisions of the Code of Practice will be relevant. In most cases (with the exception of a dismissal for a single act of gross misconduct), the employer should employ a warnings system, *e.g.* an oral warning followed by a written warning and then by a final written warning specifying that a further recurrence will lead to dismissal: see *Bevan Ashford v. Malin* [1995] I.C.R. 453, which involved a dismissal relying upon a spent warning.

The employee should also be interviewed and given the opportunity to state his or her case (including the right to be accompanied at the interview); he or she should also be told of any right to appeal. In cases where the employee has a contractual right to have an appeal against dismissal heard and decided by an appeals panel constituted in a particular way, a defect in the composition of such a body will not inevitably make the dismissal of an employee after a flawed hearing unfair: see *Westminster City Council v. Cabaj* [1996] I.C.R. 960. This decision is significant in that it suggests a partial retreat from the views of the House of Lords in *Polkey's* case. It also suggests that further attention should be given to the question of whether an employer who breaks a contractual obligation can be said to be acting reasonably. See also *Blundell v. Christie Hospital NHS Trust* [1996] I.C.R. 347.

A failure to follow a fair procedure will not automatically make the dismissal unfair. It is important, however, that the procedures are checked from time to time and kept up to date: see, for example, *Denco Ltd. v. Joinson* [1991] I.C.R. 172.

(iv) Criminal offences. One aspect of misconduct which has caused difficulty is the commission by the employee of a criminal offence. The employer must have a genuine belief based upon reasonable grounds, and this requirement has been applied to employees under suspicion of having committed an offence within the employment: see *British Home Stores v. Burchell* [1980] I.C.R. 303, approved by the Court of Appeal in *W. Weddel & Co. v. Tepper* [1980] I.C.R. 286, though another division of the Court of Appeal, in *Monie v. Coral Racing* [1981] I.C.R. 109, emphasised that each case must depend upon its facts. See also *Royal Society for the Protection of Birds v. Croucher* [1984] I.C.R. 604 and *Whitbread & Co. v. Thomas* [1988] I.C.R. 135. In *McLaren v. National Coal Board* [1988] I.C.R. 370 the Court of Appeal made it clear that the standards of fairness which require an employer to give an employee the opportunity of explaining his or her conduct before dismissal are immutable. See also *Dillett v. National Coal Board* [1988] I.C.R. 218, *Clarke v. Trimoco Motor Group* [1993] I.C.R. 237 and *Securicor Guarding v. R.* [1994] IRLR 633.

The employer does not have to prove the employee's guilt and, provided his or her belief is genuine and reasonable, the dismissal of the employee will not be made unfair by the latter's subsequent acquittal: see *Da Costa v. Optolis* [1976] IRLR 178. This is likely also to be the case where an employee accused of a crime pleads guilty and the employer refuses to accept his or her explanation that he or she was not guilty but had bowed to pressure to plead guilty to avoid a prison sentence. In such a case, the question is whether on the facts which were known or ought to have been known to the employers, they genuinely believed on reasonable grounds that the employee was guilty. If the procedure by which the employers reached their conclusion was faulty, they will have failed to act reasonably. But, in the absence of any lapse of procedure, it is an error of law for the industrial tribunal to seek to reopen the factual issues on the basis of which the employers reached their conclusion: see *British Gas v. McCarrick* [1991] IRLR 305. In *P. v. Nottinghamshire County Council* [1992] I.C.R. 706, which involved a school groundsman dismissed after he had admitted an offence of gross indecency with his daughter, the Court of Appeal said that where an employee has become unsuitable for his or her current work the possibility of alternative employment, depending on the size and administrative resources of the employers' undertaking, may be a relevant factor for them to take into account. Section 98(4) does not, however, require the employers to undertake that investigation before giving the employee notice of dismissal, provided that they do so before the notice takes effect.

Redundancy

If the tribunal is satisfied that the reason was redundancy, it is likely that the dismissal will be held to be fair, unless the employer acts with blatant unfairness. In recent years the E.A.T. has shown greater preparedness to hold a dismissal for redundancy unfair, by emphasising standards of good industrial relations practice: see *Williams v. Compair Maxam* [1982] I.C.R. 156, *Freud v. Bentalls* [1983] I.C.R. 77, *Grundy (Teddington) v. Plummer and Salt* [1983] IRLR 98 and *Stacey v. Babcock Power (Construction Division)* [1986] IRLR 3, *cf. Grundy (Teddington) v. Willis* [1976] I.C.R. 323, *N.C. Watling & Co. v. Shaw* [1978] I.C.R. 1049 and *Holden v. Bradville* [1985] IRLR 483. It has, however, expressed the view that, provided the selection process is fair, an industrial tribunal should scrutinise critically a complaint that the dismissal was unfair on some other grounds: *British United Shoe Machinery Co. v. Clarke* [1978] I.C.R. 70 and *Hinckley & Bosworth Borough Council v. Ainscough* [1979] I.C.R. 590. See also *Robinson v. British Island Airways* [1978] I.C.R. 304, *Carry All Motors v. Pennington* [1980] I.C.R. 806 and *Cowen v. Haden Carrier* [1982] IRLR 225 (reversed by the Court of Appeal on the meaning of redundancy: see [1983] I.C.R. 1) for examples of the E.A.T.'s reluctance to hold a dismissal for redundancy unfair; *cf. N.C. Watling & Co. v. Richardson* [1978] I.C.R. 1049, where the selection process was unfair. Further, if the employee would still have been made redundant had the employer taken reasonable steps to consult with the employee or find him other employment, the tribunal may either find that the dismissal was fair or order that (if it was unfair) no compensation, other than the basic award, should be paid: *British United Show Machinery Co. v. Clarke* [1978] I.C.R. 70, and *Pink v. White and White & Co. (Earls Barton)* [1985] IRLR 489, *cf. Howarth Timber (Leeds) v. Biscomb* [1986] IRLR 52. In such a case, in view of the House of Lords decision in *Polkey v. A.E. Dayton Services* [1988] I.C.R. 142 the tribunal would normally find the dismissal unfair and award no compensation, though it is open to them to find that the employer could reasonably have concluded that consultation or warning would be useless so that the failure to consult or warn in the light of the circumstances known to the employer at the time the decision to dismiss was taken was not unreasonable: see, for example, *Duffy v. Yeomans & Partners* [1994] IRLR 642. A tribunal may also conclude that, on the facts as found by it, the dismissal was unfair, but that, had a fair procedure been followed, the employee could have been fairly dismissed within a given period of time. In that case, it may confine the period of loss, for the purposes of assessing compensation, to that period of time. A further alternative is that the tribunal may conclude that the dismissal was unfair, but that, had the employer gone through a fair procedure, the employee would have stood a chance of being fairly dismissed at the end of the procedure. If the tribunal reaches such a decision, it may go on to reduce the compensation by the relevant percentage. It is important, however, that the tribunal should consider what would have been the result if the proper procedure had been followed: *Red Bank Manufacturing Co. v. Meadows* [1992] IRLR 209.

The two main obligations laying upon an employer proposing to dismiss an employee for redundancy are to make reasonable efforts, where practicable, to find him or her suitable alternative employment in the undertaking, or, where appropriate, with an associated employer and to consult with him or her and give reasonable warning of impending redundancy: see *Vokes v. Bear* [1974] I.C.R. 1, *Holliday Concreting (Testing) v. Woods* [1979] IRLR 301, *Thomas & Betts Manufacturing v. Harding* [1980] IRLR 255, *Barratt Construction v. Dalrymple* [1984] IRLR 385 and *Wood v. Coverage Care* [1996] IRLR 266 (in which the E.A.T. said that the tribunal had not erred in taking into account the employee's spent convictions when considering her for alternative posts in a residential home which included elderly persons); *Kelly v. Upholstery and Cabinet Works (Amesbury)* [1977] IRLR 91 and *Williams v. Compair Maxam* [1982] I.C.R. 156 (which contains a particularly useful discussion of this area). See also *Freud v. Bentalls* [1983] I.C.R. 77, *Grundy (Teddington) v. Plummer and Salt* [1983] IRLR 98, *Gray v. Shetland Norse Preserving Co.* [1985] IRLR 53, *Rolls-Royce Motors v. Dewhurst* [1985] IRLR 184 and *Holden v. Bradville* [1985] IRLR 483 and *King v. Eaton* [1996] IRLR 199.

The important decision of the House of Lords in *Polkey v. A.E. Dayton Services* [1988] I.C.R. 142 is the general starting-point for a consideration of the employer's obligations when dismissing for redundancy. Lord Mackay of Clashfern L.C. said, at p.152:

"If the employer could reasonably have concluded in the light of the circumstances known to him at the time of dismissal that consultation or warning would be utterly useless he might well act reasonably even if he did not observe the provisions of the code. Failure to observe the requirement of the code relating to consultation or warning will not necessarily render a dismissal unfair. Whether in any particular case it did so is a matter for the industrial tribunal to consider in the light of the circumstances known to the employer at the time he dismissed the employee".

See also Lord Bridge of Harwich at pp.162–163; *Hooper v. British Railways Board* [1988] IRLR 517 and *Duffy v. Yeomans & Partners* [1994] IRLR 642.

The E.A.T. has thus continued to emphasise the need, even in a recession, for prior consultation and warning, and has been reluctant to find exceptional circumstances which would obviate this requirement. It has said that these requirements are not avoided by the fact that the employers are a small company or that immediate decisions needed to be made: see *Heron v. Citylink-Nottingham* [1993] IRLR 372, *Ferguson v. Prestwick Circuits* [1992] IRLR 266, *De Grasse v. Stockwell Tools* [1992] IRLR 269, and *Rolls-Royce Motor Cars v. Price* [1993] IRLR 203. A dismissal for redundancy may be made unfair by events which happen during the period of notice given to the employee, for example by the employer's failure to offer new employment to an employee under notice of dismissal for redundancy when it became available during the notice period: *Stacey v. Babcock Power* [1986] I.C.R. 221.

The provisions of s.105 should be noted: they make automatically unfair a selection for redundancy for any of the reasons set out in ss.99–104. See the notes to those sections.

Statutory requirements

The fact that the employer shows that it is not possible to continue to employ the employee in the particular job he or she does, without contravening a statutory requirement, does not mean that there is not the need to go through a fair procedure before dismissing the employee: *Sutcliffe and Eaton v. Pinney* [1977] IRLR 349 and *Sandhu v. Department of Education and Science and London Borough of Hillingdon* [1978] IRLR 208.

Some other substantial reason

The two main areas which have evolved through the cases are re-organisations which fall short of redundancy and changes in the employee's terms of employment. They show the difficulty of drawing the line between fairness and unfairness where there is a clear conflict between the employer's legitimate business interests and the employee's contractual rights, since the employee's contract is static and, *prima facie*, he or she can insist upon continued performance of it as it stands. The effect of the Court of Appeal's decision in *Hollister v. National Farmers' Union* [1979] I.C.R. 542 is, in effect, to whittle down the need to comply with s.98(4). There, the court said that, provided the industrial tribunal has found that there was a substantial reason justifying dismissal, it is not necessary for the employers to consult the employee about the re-organisation of the business. All that needs to be shown is a sound commercial reason for making the re-organisation. See also *Bowater Containers v. McCormack* [1980] IRLR 50, *Genower v. Ealing, Hammersmith and Hounslow Area Health Authority* [1980] IRLR 297, *Lad-*

broke Courage Holidays v. Asten [1981] IRLR 59, *Richmond Precision Engineering v. Pearce* [1985] IRLR 179 and *Labour Party v. Oakley* [1988] I.C.R. 403.

Often, but not always, allied with re-organisations are unilateral changes in the terms of the employee's contract, which raise difficult issues of law and practice. One of the first cases to be decided on some other substantial reason, *R.S. Components v. Irwin* [1973] I.C.R. 535, concerned the introduction into the employee's contract of a restraint of trade clause. His refusal to accept it made his consequent dismissal fair. See also *St. John of God (Care Services) v. Brooks* [1992] I.C.R. 715, *Catamaran Cruisers v. Williams* [1994] IRLR 386 and *Leicester University Students' Union v. Mahomed* [1995] IRLR 292.

Pregnancy and childbirth

99.—(1) An employee who is dismissed shall be regarded for the purposes of this Part as unfairly dismissed if—
  (a) the reason (or, if more than one, the principal reason) for the dismissal is that she is pregnant or any other reason connected with her pregnancy,
  (b) her maternity leave period is ended by the dismissal and the reason (or, if more than one, the principal reason) for the dismissal is that she has given birth to a child or any other reason connected with her having given birth to a child,
  (c) her contract of employment is terminated after the end of her maternity leave period and the reason (or, if more than one, the principal reason) for the dismissal is that she took, or availed herself of the benefits of, maternity leave,
  (d) the reason (or, if more than one, the principal reason) for the dismissal is a relevant requirement, or a relevant recommendation, as defined by section 66(2), or
  (e) her maternity leave period is ended by the dismissal, the reason (or, if more than one, the principal reason) for the dismissal is that she is redundant and section 77 has not been complied with.
(2) For the purposes of subsection (1)(c)—
  (a) a woman takes maternity leave if she is absent from work during her maternity leave period, and
  (b) a woman avails herself of the benefits of maternity leave if, during her maternity leave period, she avails herself of the benefit of any of the terms and conditions of her employment preserved by section 71 during that period.
(3) An employee who is dismissed shall also be regarded for the purposes of this Part as unfairly dismissed if—
  (a) before the end of her maternity leave period she gave to her employer a certificate from a registered medical practitioner stating that by reason of disease or bodily or mental disablement she would be incapable of work after the end of that period,
  (b) her contract of employment was terminated within the period of four weeks beginning immediately after the end of her maternity leave period in circumstances in which she continued to be incapable of work and the certificate remained current, and
  (c) the reason (or, if more than one, the principal reason) for the dismissal is that she has given birth to a child or any other reason connected with her having given birth to a child.
(4) Where—
  (a) an employee has the right conferred by section 79,
  (b) it is not practicable by reason of redundancy for the employer to permit her to return in accordance with that right, and
  (c) no offer is made of such alternative employment as is referred to in section 81,
the dismissal of the employee which is treated as taking place by virtue of section 96 is to be regarded for the purposes of this Part as unfair.

DEFINITIONS
   "childbirth": s.235(1).
   "employee": s.230(1).
   "employer": s.230(4).

GENERAL NOTE
   This section provides that the dismissal of a woman will be treated as automatically unfair if the dismissal is for any of the reasons set out in subss. (1), (3) or (4). It should also be noted that selection for redundancy for most of these reasons (excluding a dismissal for a reason falling within subs. (1)(e) or a deemed dismissal falling within s.99(4)) will also be automatically unfair: see s.105(1) and (2). There is no minimum qualifying period of continuous employment for employees dismissed contrary to this section; nor are they excluded if they are over the normal retirement age: see ss.108(3) and 109(2).
   The provisions of s.10(4) and (5) of the Industrial Tribunals Act 1996 should be noted. Section 10(4) says that an industrial tribunal is to dismiss a complaint of unfair dismissal if it is shown that the action complained of was taken for the purpose of safeguarding national security. Section 10(5) goes on to state that a certificate purporting to be signed by or on behalf of a Minister of the Crown and certifying that the action was taken for that purpose is to be conclusive evidence of that fact. But there is an exception for complaints under this section. Presumably that means that, in cases arising under s.99 and involving national security, a tribunal is not bound to regard a Ministerial certificate as conclusive and is not bound to dismiss the complaint. Although it is not clear what the relationship between the general unfair dismissal provisions and s.99 is, it seems logical to suggest that the tribunal should consider s.99 first. If it decides that the employer has satisfied that section, it should then go on to consider the reasonableness of the employer's behaviour under s.98(4). In *Brown v. Stockton-on-Tees*, above, the House of Lords did not need to consider the effect of s.98 in view of the decision it reached on what is now s.99 (formerly s.60), but Lord Griffiths, who gave the main speech, pointed out that s.98(4) is made expressly subject to s.99. Although this decision was based on a previous version of these provisions, the position has not been changed by subsequent amendments.

Subs. (1)
   This subsection sets out five reasons which will cause a dismissal to be automatically unfair.
   The first reason is that the employee was pregnant or any other reason connected with her pregnancy. This follows the wording of the predecessor to this provision, s.60 of the 1978 Act before it was amended by the Trade Union Reform and Employment Rights Act 1993, and there is no reason to suppose that cases which considered the words in that provision (which are in the present version) do not remain good law. Thus, under the old s.60(1), reasons connected with pregnancy were held to include miscarriages and hypertension: see *George v. Beecham Group* [1977] IRLR 43 and *Elegbede v. The Wellcome Foundation* [1977] IRLR 383. The House of Lords considered the phrase "any other reason connected with her pregnancy" in *Brown v. Stockton-on-Tees Borough Council* [1988] I.C.R. 410 and held that the phrase ought to be read widely. So a pregnant employee who was selected for redundancy because she would require maternity leave was held to have been dismissed for a reason connected with her pregnancy; her dismissal was therefore unfair.
   The second reason is that the employee's maternity leave period is ended by the dismissal and the reason (or principal reason) is that she has given birth to a child or is any other reason connected with her having given birth to a child. For provisions relating to the maternity leave period, see ss.72 and 73.
   The third reason applies where her contract of employment was terminated after the end of her maternity leave period and the reason for the dismissal is that she took, or availed herself of the benefits of, maternity leave. A woman will be treated as taking maternity leave if she is absent from work during her maternity leave period; she will be treated as availing herself of the benefits of maternity leave if, during her maternity leave period, she avails herself of the benefit of any of the terms and conditions of her employment preserved by section 71 during that period: see subs. (2). Section 71 gives her entitlement to the benefit of the terms and conditions of employment which would have been applicable to her if she had not been absent and had not been pregnant or given birth to a child, but it does not give any entitlement to remuneration. It is subject to the conditions set out in ss.74 and 75.
   The fourth reason applies where she was dismissed because of a requirement imposed by or under any relevant provision of an enactment or instrument made under an enactment or a recommendation in any relevant provision of a code of practice issued or approved under s.16 of the Health and Safety at Work etc. Act 1974 (c. 37). See also s.66.
   The fifth reason arises where her maternity leave period is ended by the dismissal and the reason is that she is redundant and s.77 has not been complied with. Section 77 comes into play

where during an employee's maternity leave period it is not practicable by reason of redundancy for the employer to continue to employ her under her existing contract. In that case, she is entitled to be offered alternative employment, where there is a suitable available vacancy. The offer must be made before her employment ends and the alternative employment must be with her employer or the employer's successor or an associated employer. The employment must take effect immediately on the ending of her employment under the previous contract. The alternative employment must comply with s.77(3). It must be suitable in relation to her and appropriate for her to do in the circumstances; the terms of the new contract must not be substantially less favourable than if she had continued to be employed under her old contract. In *Community Task Force v. Rimmer* [1986] I.C.R. 491, the E.A.T. held that a suitable "available" vacancy is not qualified by consideration of what is economic or reasonable. It should be noted that a selection for redundancy for this fifth reason is not protected by the provisions of s.105(2).

Subs. (3)

A dismissal falling within this subsection will be automatically unfair. It applies where, before the end of her maternity leave period, she gave to the employer a certificate from a registered medical practitioner stating that by reason of disease or bodily or mental disablement she would be incapable of work after the end of that period, and her contract of employment was terminated within the four-week period following the end of her maternity leave period in circumstances where she continued to be incapable of work and the certificate relating to her incapacity remained current. If these conditions are complied with and the reason for the dismissal is that she has given birth to a child "or any other reason connected with her having given birth to a child", the dismissal will be unfair.

Subs. (4)

This subsection applies where the employee has the right to return given by s.79 but it is not practicable for the employer to allow her to return because of redundancy. If she is not offered alternative employment complying with s.81, she will be treated as having been dismissed and the dismissal will be unfair.

Health and safety cases

100.—(1) An employee who is dismissed shall be regarded for the purposes of this Part as unfairly dismissed if the reason (or, if more than one, the principal reason) for the dismissal is that—

(a) having been designated by the employer to carry out activities in connection with preventing or reducing risks to health and safety at work, the employee carried out (or proposed to carry out) any such activities,

(b) being a representative of workers on matters of health and safety at work or member of a safety committee—
(i) in accordance with arrangements established under or by virtue of any enactment, or
(ii) by reason of being acknowledged as such by the employer, the employee performed (or proposed to perform) any functions as such a representative or a member of such a committee,

(c) being an employee at a place where—
(i) there was no such representative or safety committee, or
(ii) there was such a representative or safety committee but it was not reasonably practicable for the employee to raise the matter by those means,
he brought to his employer's attention, by reasonable means, circumstances connected with his work which he reasonably believed were harmful or potentially harmful to health or safety,

(d) in circumstances of danger which the employee reasonably believed to be serious and imminent and which he could not reasonably have been expected to avert, he left (or proposed to leave) or (while the danger persisted) refused to return to his place of work or any dangerous part of his place of work, or

(e) in circumstances of danger which the employee reasonably believed to be serious and imminent, he took (or proposed to take) appropriate steps to protect himself or other persons from the danger.

(2) For the purposes of subsection (1)(e) whether steps which an employee took (or proposed to take) were appropriate is to be judged by reference to all the circumstances including, in particular, his knowledge and the facilities and advice available to him at the time.

(3) Where the reason (or, if more than one, the principal reason) for the dismissal of an employee is that specified in subsection (1)(e), he shall not be regarded as unfairly dismissed if the employer shows that it was (or would have been) so negligent for the employee to take the steps which he took (or proposed to take) that a reasonable employer might have dismissed him for taking (or proposing to take) them.

DEFINITIONS
  "employee": s.230(1).
  "employer": s.230(4).

GENERAL NOTE
  The Trade Union Reform and Employment Rights Act 1993 introduced the right to claim unfair dismissal in health and safety cases. A new s.57A was inserted into the 1978 Act; this is now s.100. For employees covered by this provision there is no minimum qualifying period of continuous employment; nor are they excluded if they are over the normal retirement age: see ss.108(3) and 109(2). It should also be noted that selection for redundancy for any of the reasons set out in this section will also be automatically unfair: see s.105(1) and (2).

  An employee dismissed for one of the reasons set out below may apply to the industrial tribunal for interim relief under s.128. He or she may also be entitled to a special award of compensation and interim relief: see s.125. The provisions of s.10(4) and (5) of the Industrial Tribunals Act 1996 should be noted. Section 10(4) says that an industrial tribunal is to dismiss a complaint of unfair dismissal if it is shown that the action complained of was taken for the purpose of safeguarding national security. Section 10(5) goes on to state that a certificate purporting to be signed by or on behalf of a Minister of the Crown and certifying that the action was taken for that purpose is to be conclusive evidence of that fact. But there is an exception for complaints under this section. Presumably that means that, in cases arising under s.100 and involving national security, a tribunal is not bound to regard a Ministerial certificate as conclusive and is not bound to dismiss the complaint.

Subs. (1)
  This subsection provides that the dismissal of an employee will be automatically unfair if the reason (or principal reason) for it is one of the five reasons specified there. The five reasons are as follows.

  (1) The employee carried out, or proposed to carry out activities in connection with preventing or reducing risks to health and safety at work, after being designated by the employer to do so.

  (2) The employee, as a workers' representative on health and safety matters or member of a safety committee, performed, or proposed to perform, any functions as such a representative or committee member, in accordance with arrangements established under or by virtue of any enactment or by reason of being acknowledged as representative or committee member by the employer.

  (3) In the case of employees at a place where there was no workers' representative or safety committee or, where there was a representative or a committee, but it was not reasonably practicable for the employees to raise the matter by those means, they brought to the employer's attention by reasonable means circumstances connected with their work which they reasonably believed were harmful or potentially harmful to health and safety.

  (4) There were circumstances of danger which the employee reasonably believed to be serious and imminent, and which he or she could not reasonably be expected to avert, and he or she left, proposed to leave, or (while the danger persisted) refused to return to, the place of work or any dangerous part of it.

  (5) There were circumstances of danger which the employee reasonably believed to be serious and imminent and he or she took, or proposed to take, appropriate steps to protect himself or herself or other persons from the danger. Whether the steps were appropriate is to be judged by reference to all the circumstances including, in particular, his or her knowledge and the facilities and advice available to him or her at the time: s.100(2). In the case of a dismissal for this fifth reason, the dismissal will not be automatically unfair if the employer shows that it was (or would have been) so negligent for the employee to take the steps which he or she took, or proposed to

take, that a reasonable employer might have dismissed him or her for taking, or proposing to take, them: s.100(3).

The first two cases set out above relate only to the defined activities of safety representatives, employees with designated health and safety functions and members of safety committees. The third case covers any employee, but it should be noted that an employee wishing to raise health and safety issues must go through any safety committee or representative where possible, unless it is not reasonably practicable to do so. Thus, an employee with a grievance must first raise it through the relevant representative; he or she will only be able to rely upon the third reason above if it is possible to satisfy the tribunal that it was not reasonably practicable to use that avenue. Employees who take the issue into their own hands run the risk, therefore, of falling outside s.100(1)(c). In a case covered by this provision, the employee must show that he or she *reasonably believed* that the circumstances were harmful or potentially harmful to health or safety. In *Kerr v. Nathan's Wastesavers* (EAT 91/95) which involved an employee who was dismissed for refusing to drive a vehicle which, in his opinion, might become overloaded by the end of the working day, the E.A.T. said that the duty placed on the employee to show reasonable belief should not be too heavy, since the purpose of the legislation is to protect employees who raise matters of health and safety. They upheld the tribunal's decision that the case should be dismissed on the grounds that although the employee's belief was genuine it was not based on reasonable grounds. Clearly, in cases of this kind, tribunals will need to be careful when deciding upon the reasonableness of the employee's belief.

Employees who are tempted to report a health and safety matter to an outside body such as the Health and Safety Executive again run the risk of putting themselves outside s.100. In such a case, the question would be whether the case was covered by s.100(1)(e) and whether the steps taken by the employee were "appropriate steps to protect himself or other persons from the danger". Again, the question would arise as to whether the employee should have raised other matters internally with a safety official or the employer before taking more serious action.

Although s.100 talks in terms of dismissal, there is no reason why the provision should not also apply to constructive dismissals. By analogy with *W.A. Goold (Pearmak) v. McConnell* [1995] IRLR 516, which involved a (successful) claim by an employee that a failure to provide a proper grievance procedure amounted to a breach of an implied term in the contract, it may be argued that an employer's continued or persistent failure to deal with an employee's complaints about health and safety amounts to a breach of a similar sort of implied term.

Shop workers and betting workers who refuse Sunday work

101.—(1) Where an employee who is—

(a) a protected shop worker or an opted-out shop worker, or

(b) a protected betting worker or an opted-out betting worker,

is dismissed, he shall be regarded for the purposes of this Part as unfairly dismissed if the reason (or, if more than one, the principal reason) for the dismissal is that he refused (or proposed to refuse) to do shop work, or betting work, on Sunday or on a particular Sunday.

(2) Subsection (1) does not apply in relation to an opted-out shop worker or an opted-out betting worker where the reason (or principal reason) for the dismissal is that he refused (or proposed to refuse) to do shop work, or betting work, on any Sunday or Sundays falling before the end of the notice period.

(3) A shop worker or betting worker who is dismissed shall be regarded for the purposes of this Part as unfairly dismissed if the reason (or, if more than one, the principal reason) for the dismissal is that the shop worker or betting worker gave (or proposed to give) an opting-out notice to the employer.

(4) For the purposes of section 36(2)(b) or 41(1)(b), the appropriate date in relation to this section is the effective date of termination.

DEFINITIONS
    "betting work": s.233(2).
    "betting worker": s.233(1).
    "notice period": s.41(3).
    "opted-out betting worker": s.233(6) and 41(1) and (2).
    "opted-out shop worker": ss.232(8) and 41(1) and (2).
    "opting-out notice": s.40(2).
    "protected betting worker": s.233(6) and 36(1) to (5).
    "protected shop worker": s.232(8) and 36(1) to (5).

"shop work": s.232(2).
"shop worker": s.232(1).

GENERAL NOTE

The Sunday Trading Act 1994 (c. 20) introduced a scheme of protection for shop workers, including protection against dismissal. This was extended to betting workers by amendments introduced into the Betting, Gaming and Lotteries Act 1963 (c. 2) by the Deregulation and Contracting Out Act 1994 (c. 40). These provisions have all now been consolidated into the present section. Section 101 embraces "protected shop workers", "opted-out shop workers", "protected betting workers" and "opted-out betting workers". A shop worker or betting worker is protected if he or she satisfies the conditions set out in s.36(2) or (3). The conditions in s.36(2) are: (a) he or she must be employed as a shop worker on the day before August 26, 1994 or as a betting worker on the day before January 3, 1995; (b) on that day, he or she was not employed to work only on Sunday; (c) he or she has been continuously employed from the day before the commencement date to the "appropriate date"; and (d) throughout that period, he or she was a shop worker or betting worker. The "appropriate date" is defined by s.101(4) as the effective date of termination.

The conditions in s.36(3) apply to any shop worker or betting worker whose contract of employment is such that under it he or she is not, and may not be, required to work on Sunday, and could not be required to do so, even if the provisions of Pt. IV of the Employment Rights Act 1996 (which deal with Sunday working) were disregarded. Note the provisions of s.36(4), which deal with employees who have ceased to be employed on the day before the commencement date for reasons falling within s.212(2) or (3) of this Act or because the Employment Protection (Continuity of Employment) Regulations 1993 (S.I. 1993 No. 2165) apply.

A shop worker or betting worker will be regarded as "opted-out" if the following conditions, set out in s.41, are satisfied: (a) he or she has given an opting-out notice (as defined by s.40(1) and (2)); (b) he or she has been continuously employed from the date on which the notice was given to the "appropriate date"; and (c) throughout that period he or she was a shop worker or betting worker. The "appropriate date" is defined by s.101(4) as the effective date of termination. A shop worker or betting worker will cease to be protected or opted-out if he or she gives the employer an opting-in notice and, after giving the notice, has expressly agreed with the employer to work on Sunday or on a particular Sunday: ss.41(2) and 36(6).

Under subs. (1) a protected shop worker or betting worker will automatically be treated as having been unfairly dismissed if the reason (or principal reason) was that he or she refused, or proposed to refuse, to do shop work on Sunday or on a particular Sunday. This provision will not apply, however, to an opted-out shop worker or betting worker where the reason for the dismissal was that he or she refused or proposed to refuse to do shop work or betting work on any Sunday or Sundays falling before the end of the "notice period". The notice period is defined by s.41(3) as "the period of three months beginning with the day on which the opting-out notice was given". In other words, the statutory protection given by s.101(1) does not come into effect until three months after the opting-out notice was given.

Under subs. (3) a shop worker or betting worker will be treated as unfairly dismissed if the reason for the dismissal is that he or she gave, or proposed to give, an opting-out notice to the employer. It should be noted that selection for redundancy for a reason set out in subs. (1) or (3) is also automatically unfair: s.105(1) and (4).

An employee covered by these provisions may complain of unfair dismissal irrespective of age, length of service or the number of weekly hours worked: ss.108(3) and 109(2).

Trustees of occupational pension schemes

102.—(1) An employee who is dismissed shall be regarded for the purposes of this Part as unfairly dismissed if the reason (or, if more than one, the principal reason) for the dismissal is that, being a trustee of a relevant occupational pension scheme which relates to his employment, the employee performed (or proposed to perform) any functions as such a trustee.

(2) In this section "relevant occupational pension scheme" means an occupational pension scheme (as defined in section 1 of the Pension Schemes Act 1993) established under a trust.

DEFINITIONS
"employee": s.230(1).
"employment": s.230(5).
"relevant occupational pension scheme": s.102(2).

Section 102 of this Act gives the right not to be unfairly dismissed to employees who are trustees of a relevant occupational pension scheme relating to their employment. If the reason for the dismissal is that the employee performed, or proposed to perform, any functions as such a trustee, the dismissal will be automatically unfair. Selection for redundancy on these grounds is also automatically unfair: s.105(1) and (5). It is not necessary for employees covered by this provision to serve a minimum qualifying period of employment; nor are employees over the normal retiring age excluded: ss.108(3) and 109(2).

Employee representatives

103. An employee who is dismissed shall be regarded for the purposes of this Part as unfairly dismissed if the reason (or, if more than one, the principal reason) for the dismissal is that the employee, being—

(a) an employee representative for the purposes of Chapter II of Part IV of the Trade Union and Labour Relations (Consolidation) Act 1992 (redundancies) or Regulations 10 and 11 of the Transfer of Undertakings (Protection of Employment) Regulations 1981, or

(b) a candidate in an election in which any person elected will, on being elected, be such an employee representative,

performed (or proposed to perform) any functions or activities as such an employee representative or candidate.

DEFINITIONS
"employee": s.230(1).
"employee representative": s.196 of the Trade Union and Labour Relations (Consolidation) Act 1992 (inserted by the Collective Redundancies and Transfer of Undertakings (Protection of Employment) (Amendment) Regulations 1995 (S.I. 1995 No. 2587), reg. 6).

GENERAL NOTE
This section gives the right not to be unfairly dismissed to employee representatives. If the reason for the dismissal is that the employee, as an employee representative, performed, or proposed to perform, any functions or activities as an employee representative, the dismissal will be automatically unfair. This also applies to employees who are candidates for election as an employee representative. Selection for redundancy on these grounds is also automatically unfair: s.105(1) and (6). It is not necessary for employees covered by this provision to serve a minimum qualifying period of employment; nor are employees over the normal retiring age excluded: ss.108(3) and 109(2).

The provisions of s.10(4) and (5) of the Industrial Tribunals Act 1996 should be noted. Section 10(4) says that an industrial tribunal is to dismiss a complaint of unfair dismissal if it is shown that the action complained of was taken for the purpose of safeguarding national security. Section 10(5) goes on to state that a certificate purporting to be signed by or on behalf of a Minister of the Crown and certifying that the action was taken for that purpose is to be conclusive evidence of that fact. But there is an exception for complaints under this section. Presumably that means that, in cases arising under s.103 and involving national security, a tribunal is not bound to regard a Ministerial certificate as conclusive and is not bound to dismiss the complaint.

Assertion of statutory right

104.—(1) An employee who is dismissed shall be regarded for the purposes of this Part as unfairly dismissed if the reason (or, if more than one, the principal reason) for the dismissal is that the employee—

(a) brought proceedings against the employer to enforce a right of his which is a relevant statutory right, or

(b) alleged that the employer had infringed a right of his which is a relevant statutory right.

(2) It is immaterial for the purposes of subsection (1)—

(a) whether or not the employee has the right, or

(b) whether or not the right has been infringed;

but, for that subsection to apply, the claim to the right and that it has been infringed must be made in good faith.

(3) It is sufficient for subsection (1) to apply that the employee, without specifying the right, made it reasonably clear to the employer what the right claimed to have been infringed was.

(4) The following are relevant statutory rights for the purposes of this section—

    (a) any right conferred by this Act for which the remedy for its infringement is by way of a complaint or reference to an industrial tribunal,

    (b) the right conferred by section 86 of this Act, and

    (c) the rights conferred by sections 68, 86, 146, 168, 169 and 170 of the Trade Union and Labour Relations (Consolidation) Act 1992 (deductions from pay, union activities and time off).

DEFINITIONS

    "employee": s.230(1).
    "employer": s.230(4).

GENERAL NOTE

The Trade Union Reform and Employment Rights Act 1993 introduced a right to claim unfair dismissal on the grounds of assertion of a statutory right. This is now to be found in s.104. It is not necessary for employees covered by this provision to serve a minimum qualifying period of employment; nor are employees over the normal retiring age excluded: ss.108(3) and 109(2). Selection for redundancy on these grounds is also automatically unfair: s.105(1) and (7).

The dismissal of an employee will be automatically unfair if the reason (or principal reason) for it was that the employee brought proceedings against the employer to enforce a "relevant statutory right" or alleged that the employer had infringed a "relevant statutory right". In both cases the right must be a right of the dismissed employee, but it is immaterial whether the employee has the right or not and whether it was infringed or not, provided that the claim to the right and its infringement are made in good faith: subs. (2). It is sufficient for this section to apply that the employee made it reasonably clear to the employer what the right claimed to have been infringed was; it is not necessary to specify the right: subs. (3).

Subsection (4) sets out the statutory rights which are relevant. These are: (1) any right conferred by the 1996 Act, for which the remedy for its infringement is by way of a complaint or reference to the industrial tribunal; (2) the right conferred by s.86 to a minimum period of notice; and (3) the right conferred by ss.68, 86, 146, 168, 169 and 170 of the Trade Union and Labour Relations (Consolidation) Act 1992, which deal with deductions of union dues, action short of dismissal on grounds related to trade union membership and activities, and time off for trade union duties and activities. The only decision reported at the time of going to press is *Mennell v. Newell & Wright (Transport Contractors)* [1996] I.C.R. 607.

Redundancy

105.—(1) An employee who is dismissed shall be regarded for the purposes of this Part as unfairly dismissed if—

    (a) the reason (or, if more than one, the principal reason) for the dismissal is that the employee was redundant,

    (b) it is shown that the circumstances constituting the redundancy applied equally to one or more other employees in the same undertaking who held positions similar to that held by the employee and who have not been dismissed by the employer, and

    (c) it is shown that any of subsections (2) to (7) applies.

(2) This subsection applies if the reason (or, if more than one, the principal reason) for which the employee was selected for dismissal was that specified in any of paragraphs (a) to (d) of subsection (1) of section 99 (read with subsection (2) of that section) or subsection (3) of that section (and any requirements of the paragraph, or subsection, not relating to the reason are satisfied).

(3) This subsection applies if the reason (or, if more than one, the principal reason) for which the employee was selected for dismissal was one of those specified in subsection (1) of section 100 (read with subsections (2) and (3) of that section).

(4) This subsection applies if either—

(a) the employee was a protected shop worker or an opted-out shop worker, or a protected betting worker or an opted-out betting worker, and the reason (or, if more than one, the principal reason) for which the employee was selected for dismissal was that specified in subsection (1) of section 101 (read with subsection (2) of that section), or

(b) the employee was a shop worker or a betting worker and the reason (or, if more than one, the principal reason) for which the employee was selected for dismissal was that specified in subsection (3) of that section.

(5) This subsection applies if the reason (or, if more than one, the principal reason) for which the employee was selected for dismissal was that specified in section 102(1).

(6) This subsection applies if the reason (or, if more than one, the principal reason) for which the employee was selected for dismissal was that specified in section 103.

(7) This subsection applies if the reason (or, if more than one, the principal reason) for which the employee was selected for dismissal was one of those specified in subsection (1) of section 104 (read with subsections (2) and (3) of that section).

(8) For the purposes of section 36(2)(b) or 41(1)(b), the appropriate date in relation to this section is the effective date of termination.

(9) In this Part "redundancy case" means a case where paragraphs (a) and (b) of subsection (1) of this section are satisfied.

DEFINITIONS
"employee": s.230(1).
"redundant": s.139.

GENERAL NOTE
This section serves as an adjunct to the special rules governing certain types of dismissal set out in ss.99–104. Those provisions state that employees dismissed for any of the reasons set out there will be treated automatically as unfairly dismissed. This section applies where there is a selective dismissal for redundancy and the employee dismissed is complaining that the reason for the selection was one of the reasons set out in those sections. It should go without saying, however, that these provisions only apply where the reason for the dismissal is redundancy; if the tribunal is satisfied that redundancy was not the reason, then the provisions do not apply.

A dismissal for redundancy will be in contravention of s.105 and automatically unfair if the following conditions are satisfied: (1) the circumstances constituting the redundancy applied equally to one or more employees in the same undertaking who held positions similar to that held by the dismissed employee; (2) those employees have not been dismissed; and (3) the employee in question was selected for a reason falling within any of the provisions of ss.99–104.

It should be noted that the two-year qualifying period does not apply to employees selected for dismissal for redundancy in these circumstances; nor are employees over the normal retiring age excluded: ss.108(3)(h) and 109(2)(h). Subsections (2)–(7) set out the reasons covered by s.105. If the dismissal does not infringe s.105, the industrial tribunal should then go on to consider whether the employer fulfilled the requirements of s.98(4): *Thomas & Betts Manufacturing v. Harding* [1980] IRLR 255 and *McDowell v. Eastern British Road Services* [1981] IRLR 482.

The provisions of s.10(4) and (5) of the Industrial Tribunals Act 1996 should be noted. Section 10(4) says that an industrial tribunal is to dismiss a complaint of unfair dismissal if it is shown that the action complained of was taken for the purpose of safeguarding national security. Section 10(5) goes on to state that a certificate purporting to be signed by or on behalf of a Minister of the Crown and certifying that the action was taken for that purpose is to be conclusive evidence of that fact. But there is an exception for complaints under this section where the reason for selection for redundancy is alleged to be one of those provided for in ss.99, 100 or 103. Presumably that means that, in cases arising under s.105 and involving national security, a tribunal is not bound to regard a Ministerial certificate as conclusive and is not bound to dismiss the complaint.

Although s.7(6) of the Industrial Tribunals Act 1996 places upon the employer the burden of showing that the reason for the dismissal in an unfair dismissal case is redundancy, the burden of showing that s.105 applies lies upon the employee. He or she must show that the dismissal satisfied the three conditions set out above.

Replacements

106.—(1) Where this section applies to an employee he shall be regarded for the purposes of section 98(1)(b) as having been dismissed for a substantial reason of a kind such as to justify the dismissal of an employee holding the position which the employee held.

(2) This section applies to an employee where—

(a) on engaging him the employer informs him in writing that his employment will be terminated on the resumption of work by another employee who is, or will be, absent wholly or partly because of pregnancy or childbirth, and

(b) the employer dismisses him in order to make it possible to give work to the other employee.

(3) This section also applies to an employee where—

(a) on engaging him the employer informs him in writing that his employment will be terminated on the end of a suspension of another employee from work on medical grounds or maternity grounds (within the meaning of Part VII), and

(b) the employer dismisses him in order to make it possible to allow the resumption of work by the other employee.

(4) Subsection (1) does not affect the operation of section 98(4) in a case to which this section applies.

DEFINITIONS
"childbirth": s.235(1).
"employee": s.230(1).
"employer": s.230(4).
"employment": s.230(5).

GENERAL NOTE
In view of the fact that the qualifying period for the right not to be unfairly dismissed is two years, the provisions of this section are not likely to be needed very often. An employee absent for pregnancy or childbirth who fails to return within two years of going off on maternity leave is likely to have lost her right to return by the time the replacement's qualifying period has elapsed. Subsections (2) and (3) apply to employees engaged to replace employees absent on maternity leave or as a consequence of a medical suspension or suspension on maternity grounds under s.66. The replacement must be told in writing that the employment will be ended when the absent employee returns. When he or she is dismissed, the dismissal will be treated by subs. (1) as being for some other substantial reason, but the employer will still need to satisfy the requirements of s.98(4), which should not be difficult: see subs. (4).

Pressure on employer to dismiss unfairly

107.—(1) This section applies where there falls to be determined for the purposes of this Part a question—

(a) as to the reason, or principal reason, for which an employee was dismissed,

(b) whether the reason or principal reason for which an employee was dismissed was a reason fulfilling the requirement of section 98(1)(b), or

(c) whether an employer acted reasonably in treating the reason or principal reason for which an employee was dismissed as a sufficient reason for dismissing him.

(2) In determining the question no account shall be taken of any pressure which by calling, organising, procuring or financing a strike or other industrial action, or threatening to do so, was exercised on the employer to dismiss the employee; and the question shall be determined as if no such pressure had been exercised.

DEFINITIONS
"employee": s.230(1).
"employer": s.230(4).

GENERAL NOTE

This section requires the tribunal to ignore certain kinds of pressure from third parties and to decide upon the reason for the dismissal and its fairness as if there had been no pressure. "Pressure" is defined in subs. (2) as "any pressure which, by calling, organising, procuring or financing a strike or other industrial action, or threatening to do so, was exercised on the employer to dismiss the employee". See *Trend v. Chiltern Hunt* [1977] I.C.R. 612, *Hazells Offset v. Luckett* [1977] IRLR 430, *Ford Motor Co. v. Hudson* [1978] I.C.R. 482 and *Colwyn Borough Council v. Dutton* [1980] IRLR 420.

If the pressure was exercised because the employee was not a trade union member, the employer or the employee may ask the industrial tribunal, under s.160 of the 1992 Act, to join as a party to the proceedings the person claimed to have exerted the pressure. That person may have to make a total or partial contribution to any compensation awarded against the employer: the 1992 Act, s.160(3).

It should be noted that the definition of strike in s.235(5) does not apply to this section.

Exclusion of right

Qualifying period of employment

108.—(1) Section 94 does not apply to the dismissal of an employee unless he has been continuously employed for a period of not less than two years ending with the effective date of termination.

(2) If an employee is dismissed by reason of any such requirement or recommendation as is referred to in section 64(2), subsection (1) has effect in relation to that dismissal as if for the words "two years" there were substituted the words "one month".

(3) Subsection (1) does not apply if—

(a) section 84 or 96(1) applies,

(b) subsection (1) of section 99 (read with subsection (2) of that section) or subsection (3) of that section applies,

(c) subsection (1) of section 100 (read with subsections (2) and (3) of that section) applies,

(d) subsection (1) of section 101 (read with subsection (2) of that section) or subsection (3) of that section applies,

(e) section 102 applies,

(f) section 103 applies,

(g) subsection (1) of section 104 (read with subsections (2) and (3) of that section) applies, or

(h) section 105 applies.

DEFINITIONS

"continuously employed": ss.210–219.
"effective date of termination": s.97.
"employee": s.230(1).

GENERAL NOTE

The general rule as set out in subs. (1) is that an employee must have been continuously employed for two years. It should be noted, however, that the Order raising the qualifying period to two years has been the subject of litigation, on the grounds that it is incompatible with the Equal Treatment Directive (76/207/EEC). In *R. v. Secretary of State for Employment, ex p. Seymour-Smith and Perez* [1995] I.C.R. 889 the Court of Appeal held that, on the evidence, it had been demonstrated that for the period leading up to the dismissal of the employees the qualifying period had a disparate impact upon women and that the Secretary of State for Employment had failed to prove that the increase in the threshold had increased employment opportunities, so that the discriminatory impact of the Order had not been justified. The Court of Appeal granted a declaration that the Order was discriminatory but refused to make an order quashing it. They granted leave to appeal to the House of Lords. The case has now been heard by the House of Lords, but at the time of going to press, judgment had not been given.

Subsection (2) reduces the qualifying period of employment to one month in cases covered by s.64(2), where an employee is suspended from work on medical grounds.

Subsection (3) sets out the situations in which s.108(1) does not apply, for which there is, therefore, no qualifying period of employment. These are: (1) dismissal of an employee at or after the end of her maternity leave period; (2) failure to permit an employee to return after childbirth; (3) dismissal in connection with pregnancy or childbirth; (4) dismissal for reasons connected with health and safety; (5) dismissal of a shop or betting worker; (6) dismissal of a pension fund trustee; (7) dismissal of an employee representative; (8) dismissal for assertion of a statutory right; and (9) selection for redundancy in situations (3)–(8). In cases where subs. (3) is alleged to apply, the burden will be on the employee to satisfy the tribunal that the reason for the dismissal is one of those which avoids the operation of the two-year rule.

Upper age limit

109.—(1) Section 94 does not apply to the dismissal of an employee if on or before the effective date of termination he has attained—
    (a) in a case where—
        (i) in the undertaking in which the employee was employed there was a normal retiring age for an employee holding the position held by the employee, and
        (ii) the age was the same whether the employee holding that position was a man or a woman,
    that normal retiring age, and
    (b) in any other case, the age of sixty-five.
  (2) Subsection (1) does not apply if—
    (a) section 84 or 96(1) applies,
    (b) subsection (1) of section 99 (read with subsection (2) of that section) or subsection (3) of that section applies,
    (c) subsection (1) of section 100 (read with subsections (2) and (3) of that section) applies,
    (d) subsection (1) of section 101 (read with subsection (2) of that section) or subsection (3) of that section applies,
    (e) section 102 applies,
    (f) section 103 applies,
    (g) subsection (1) of section 104 (read with subsections (2) and (3) of that section) applies, or
    (h) section 105 applies.

DEFINITIONS
"effective date of termination": s.97.
"employee": s.230(1).
"position": s.235(1).

GENERAL NOTE
Subsection (1) contains the general exclusion of employees over the normal retiring age or, where there is no such age, sixty-five. But this exclusion does not apply to employees protected by the provisions of subs. (2): see the note below.

Subs. (1)
In *Nothman v. Barnet London Borough Council* [1979] I.C.R. 111 the House of Lords held, by a majority, that this subsection (formerly s.64(1)(b) of the 1978 Act) "sets up only one barrier to be overcome by the class of employee whose conditions of employment specify a normal retiring age, and another and entirely different barrier to be overcome by the class of employee whose conditions of employment specify no retiring age": *per* Lord Salmon at p.116. So it is necessary to determine first whether there is a normal retiring age; if there is, the second barrier will not apply; if, on the other hand, there is no normal retiring age, the second barrier will then operate. It should be noted that although the statutory provisions have been amended since the decision in *Nothman's* case, the decision is not affected by the changes.
    The House of Lords, however, did not specifically discuss what is meant by the phrase "normal retiring age", though Lord Salmon indicated that it will be necessary to look at the conditions of employment to see if they specify a normal retiring age: see p.116. After differences of opinion in the Court of Appeal about the meaning of the phrase, the House of Lords decided, in *Waite v. Government Communications H.Q.* [1983] I.C.R. 653, that it means the retiring age laid down in the terms and conditions upon which the employee was employed ("the contractual retiring age"). The presumption that the contractual retiring age is the normal retiring age may be displaced by evidence that there is in practice some higher age at which employees holding the

position are regularly retired, and which they have reasonably come to regard as their normal retiring age. Lord Fraser of Tullybelton said, at pp.662–663:

"The proper test is … not merely statistical. It is to ascertain what would be the reasonable expectation or understanding of the employees holding that position at the relevant time. The contractual retiring age will prima facie be displaced by evidence that it is regularly departed from in practice. The evidence may show that the contractual retirement age has been superseded by some definite higher age, and, if so, that will have become the normal retiring age. Or the evidence may show merely that the contractual retirement age has been abandoned and that employees retire at a variety of higher ages. In that case there will be no normal retiring age and the statutory alternatives of 65 for a man and 60 for a woman will apply".

This test was applied in *Hughes and Coy v. D.H.S.S.* [1985] I.C.R. 419, in the context of changes in retirement policy in the civil service, *Brooks v. British Telecommunications* [1992] I.C.R. 414, in the context of British Telecom's retirement policy and *Barclays Bank v. O'Brien* [1994] I.C.R. 865.

A further question which arises is whether the normal retiring age may be below the contractual retiring age. In *Bratko v. Beloit Walmsley* [1996] I.C.R. 76 the E.A.T. said that the employer cannot reduce the normal retiring age below the contractual age of retirement, without going through the normal steps necessary to change a contractual term. They said that the decision of the House of Lords in *Waite's* case contemplates only the possibility of a normal retiring age higher than the contractual retiring age, and not lower. An employee who agrees to a change in the terms of the pension scheme applicable to him or her, involving a reduction of the pension age, is not automatically taken to have agreed to a change in his normal retiring age. The industrial tribunal must ascertain whether the contractual position between the parties has altered, and see whether the employee has understood the change and generally agreed to it: *Stepney Cast Stone Co. v. MacArthur* [1979] IRLR 181 and *B.P. Chemicals v. Joseph* [1980] IRLR 55. The phrase "normal retiring age" is not synonymous with "pensionable age": see *Ord v. Maidstone and District Hospital Management Committee* [1979] I.C.R. 369 and *Stepney Cast Stone Co. v. MacArthur* [1979] IRLR 181.

An employee who is taken on after the age of 65 may be held to have a normal retiring age which is later than 65, but it remains necessary to look at the terms of the contract. The fact that an employee is taken on when over 65 does not mean that there must be implied a later retiring age: see *Dixon v. London Production Tools and Phildon Instrumentation (London)* [1980] IRLR 385.

A further point to note is the meaning of the word "position"; it is defined in s.235(1). The statute refers to a normal retiring age for an employee holding the position the employee in question held. In *Brooks v. British Telecommunications* [1992] I.C.R. 414 the E.A.T. held that the statutory definition of "position" included consideration of the nature of an employee's work, which of necessity related to the work actually done and not merely to the employee's grade. They upheld the industrial tribunal's conclusion that it was necessary to look and see whether as a matter of common sense and practicality the work done by two people was sufficiently similar for it to be sensible to treat them as holding the same position. In *Barber v. Thames Television* [1992] I.C.R. 661 the Court of Appeal said that in applying the definition of "position" the matters to be taken into account include terms, whether contractual or by virtue of the expectation of the person concerned, which fall within the phrase "terms and conditions of the employee's employment" as used in the definition of "position" in s.235(1). It is thus possible to have employees who have the same job title, but who occupy different positions.

Finally, there is the question of how industrial tribunals should deal with issues relating to the normal retiring age. The question whether there is a normal retiring age is a question of fact: see *Barclays Bank v. O'Brien* [1994] I.C.R. 865 and *Secretary of State for Education v. Birchall* [1994] IRLR 630. The tribunal will therefore need to consider all the circumstances to enable it to determine the question and will have to make relevant findings of fact. The President of the E.A.T. has suggested that in cases such as this it is not appropriate to proceed by way of preliminary hearing and on the basis of assumed facts, separately from the rest of the case. In such cases it is often better to hear all the facts first and then resolve the issues: see *Secretary of State for Education v. Birchall* [1994] IRLR 630.

Subs. (2)

Subsection (2) sets out the situations in which s.109(1) does not apply, for which there is, therefore, age exclusion. These are: (1) dismissal of an employee at or after the end of her maternity leave period; (2) failure to permit an employee to return after childbirth; (3) dismissal in connection with pregnancy or childbirth; (4) dismissal for reasons connected with health and safety; (5) dismissal of a shop or betting worker; (6) dismissal of a pension fund trustee; (7) dismissal of an employee representative; (8) dismissal for assertion of a statutory right; and (9) selection for redundancy in situations (3)–(8). In cases where subs. (2) is alleged to apply, the burden will be on the employee to satisfy the tribunal that the reason for the dismissal is one of those which avoids the operation of the two-year rule.

Dismissal procedures agreements

110.—(1) Where a dismissal procedures agreement is designated by an order under subsection (3) which is for the time being in force—

  (a) the provisions of that agreement relating to dismissal shall have effect in substitution for any rights under section 94, and

  (b) accordingly, section 94 does not apply to the dismissal of an employee from any employment if it is employment to which, and he is an employee to whom, those provisions of the agreement apply.

(2) Subsection (1) does not apply if—

  (a) section 84 or 96(1) applies,

  (b) subsection (1) of section 99 (read with subsection (2) of that section) or subsection (3) of that section applies,

  (c) subsection (1) of section 101 (read with subsection (2) of that section) or subsection (3) of that section applies,

  (d) subsection (1) of section 104 (read with subsections (2) and (3) of that section) applies, or

  (e) section 105(1) and (4) applies.

(3) An order designating a dismissal procedures agreement may be made by the Secretary of State, on an application being made to him jointly by all the parties to the agreement, if he is satisfied that—

  (a) every trade union which is a party to the agreement is an independent trade union,

  (b) the agreement provides for procedures to be followed in cases where an employee claims that he has been, or is in the course of being, unfairly dismissed,

  (c) those procedures are available without discrimination to all employees falling within any description to which the agreement applies,

  (d) the remedies provided by the agreement in respect of unfair dismissal are on the whole as beneficial as (but not necessarily identical with) those provided in respect of unfair dismissal by this Part,

  (e) the procedures provided by the agreement include a right to arbitration or adjudication by an independent referee, or by a tribunal or other independent body, in cases where (by reason of an equality of votes or for any other reason) a decision cannot otherwise be reached, and

  (f) the provisions of the agreement are such that it can be determined with reasonable certainty whether or not a particular employee is one to whom the agreement applies.

(4) If at any time when an order under subsection (3) is in force in relation to a dismissal procedures agreement the Secretary of State is satisfied, whether on an application made to him by any of the parties to the agreement or otherwise, either—

  (a) that it is the desire of all the parties to the agreement that the order should be revoked, or

  (b) that the agreement no longer satisfies all the conditions specified in subsection (3),

the Secretary of State shall revoke the order by an order under this subsection.

(5) The transitional provisions which may be made in an order under subsection (4) include, in particular, provisions directing—

  (a) that an employee—

      (i) shall not be excluded from his right under section 94 where the effective date of termination falls within a transitional period which

ends with the date on which the order takes effect and which is
specified in the order, and
   (ii) shall have an extended time for presenting a complaint under
   section 111 in respect of a dismissal where the effective date of termination falls within that period, and
(b) that, where the effective date of termination falls within such a transitional period, an industrial tribunal shall, in determining any complaint of unfair dismissal presented by an employee to whom the
   dismissal procedures agreement applies, have regard to such considerations as are specified in the order (in addition to those specified in this
   Part and section 10(4) and (5) of the Industrial Tribunals Act 1996).

DEFINITIONS
   "dismissal procedures agreement": s.235(1).
   "employee": s.230(1).
   "employment": s.230(5).

GENERAL NOTE
   Employees covered by a dismissal procedures agreement are excluded from the statutory
provisions and the agreement takes effect in substitution: subs. (1). Subsection (2) sets out the
situations in which subs. (1) does not apply. These are: (1) dismissal of an employee at or after
the end of her maternity leave period; (2) failure to permit an employee to return after childbirth; (3) dismissal in connection with pregnancy or childbirth; (4) dismissal of a shop or betting
worker; (5) dismissal for assertion of a statutory right; and (6) selection for redundancy in situations (3)–(5).
   Subsection (3) sets out the requirements to be met for an agreement to be approved by the
Secretary of State. Such an agreement takes the form of an order. Subsection (4) specifies the
conditions to be met before an order may be revoked; subsection (5) provides for the Secretary
of State to make appropriate transitional provisions when revoking an order.
   The only agreement so far approved is the Dismissal Procedure Agreement between the Electrical Contractors' Association and the Electrical Electronic Telecommunications and Plumbing Union (EETPU), made on September 14, 1979.

CHAPTER II

REMEDIES FOR UNFAIR DISMISSAL

Introductory

Complaints to industrial tribunal

   111.—(1) A complaint may be presented to an industrial tribunal against
an employer by any person that he was unfairly dismissed by the employer.
   (2) Subject to subsection (3), an industrial tribunal shall not consider a
complaint under this section unless it is presented to the tribunal—
   (a) before the end of the period of three months beginning with the effec-
      tive date of termination, or
   (b) within such further period as the tribunal considers reasonable in a
      case where it is satisfied that it was not reasonably practicable for the
      complaint to be presented before the end of that period of three
      months.
   (3) Where a dismissal is with notice, an industrial tribunal shall consider a
complaint under this section if it is presented after the notice is given but
before the effective date of termination.
   (4) In relation to a complaint which is presented as mentioned in subsection (3), the provisions of this Act, so far as they relate to unfair dismissal,
have effect as if—
   (a) references to a complaint by a person that he was unfairly dismissed by
      his employer included references to a complaint by a person that his
      employer has given him notice in such circumstances that he will be
      unfairly dismissed when the notice expires,

(b) references to reinstatement included references to the withdrawal of the notice by the employer,

(c) references to the effective date of termination included references to the date which would be the effective date of termination on the expiry of the notice, and

(d) references to an employee ceasing to be employed included references to an employee having been given notice of dismissal.

DEFINITIONS
"effective date of termination": s.97.
"employer": s.230(4)

GENERAL NOTE
This section provides for the method of taking action against an employer to enforce the rights conferred by s.94. Subsection (2) is the main provision and sets a basic limitation period of three months from the effective date of termination. This period may be extended where the tribunal considers that it was not "reasonably practicable" to present the complaint within that period, but, as will be seen from the note on subs. (2), the requirement is strict. Subsection (3) provides for complaints to be presented before the effective date of termination, but it is a provision which is rarely encountered.

Subs. (2)
Subsection (2) provides that an industrial tribunal may not consider a complaint of unfair dismissal unless it is presented to the tribunal within three months of the "effective date of termination" or such further period as the tribunal considers reasonable in a case where it is satisfied that it was not reasonably practicable for the complaint to be presented within three months. This period will be extended to six months in cases involving dismissals in connection with a strike or lock-out under s.238 of the Trade Union and Labour Relations (Consolidation) Act 1992 where the tribunal is given jurisdiction: the 1992 Act, s.239(2).

This provision goes to the tribunal's jurisdiction. So if the complaint is presented out of time, the tribunal must consider as a preliminary issue whether to allow the complaint to proceed; the employer cannot agree to raise no objection to the claim being presented out of time. The burden is on the applicant to satisfy the tribunal that it was not reasonably practicable to present the complaint in time: *Porter v. Bandridge* [1978] I.C.R. 943. When dealing with a question involving the time limit, the industrial tribunal has essentially four questions to consider: (1) when was the complaint presented? (2) when did the limitation period expire? (3) was it reasonably practicable for the complaint to be presented within three months of the effective date of termination? (4) within what period was it reasonably practicable for the complaint to have been presented?

The industrial tribunal must first decide when the effective date of termination was: see the note to s.97.

Date of presentation of complaint. Once the effective date of termination has been established, the first question is when the date of presentation was. A complaint is "presented" when it arrives at the Central Office of Industrial Tribunals or an Office of the Tribunals: *P.O. v. Moore* [1981] I.C.R. 623. See also *Hammond v. Haigh Castle & Co.* [1973] I.C.R. 261, *Bengey v. North Devon District Council* [1977] I.C.R. 15, *House v. Emerson Electric Industrial Controls* [1980] I.C.R. 795, and *Hetton Victory Club v. Swainston* [1983] I.C.R. 341. It can be pushed through the letter-box (if the relevant office has one), but it should be marked with the date and time at which that happens. If the tribunal office does not have a letter-box, for example because it is in multiple occupation, the time limit may be extended to the next working day: *Hetton Victory Club v. Swainston* [1983] I.C.R. 341. If the office of the tribunal does not have a letter-box and the date of presentation is a Sunday or bank holiday, the day will be treated as a "*dies non*" and the time for presentation will be extended to the next day: see *Ford v. Stakis Hotels & Inns* [1987] I.C.R. 943. Special arrangements exist between the C.O.I.T. and the Post Office (that post which arrives on a Saturday will be held until the following Monday) and an application may be treated as arriving earlier: see, for example, *Lang v. Devon General* [1987] I.C.R. 4.

Date of expiry of three-month period. The complaint must be presented within three months of that date. That means, for example, that an employee whose effective date of termination is September 16 must present the complaint by midnight on December 15. The question which arises, however, concerns the position when the effective date of termination is the last day of a month and there is no corresponding date in the month three months later. An example of this would be an employee whose effective date of termination was November 30. The corresponding date three months later is the end of February. The question is whether the limitation period expires on February 28. (It should be noted that that date will also be the expiry date for a dismissal who effective date of termination was December 1.) A further complication arises where the effective date of termination is the end of a short month, for example February, but the relevant month three months later is longer. So, for example, an employee is dismissed and the effective date of termination is February 28. Does the limitation period expire on June 27 or June 30? In this last case, the argument is that, since the effective date of termination is the end of a month, so the expiry of the limitation period should be the end of the month three months later.

These issues were considered by the E.A.T. in *University of Cambridge v. Murray* [1993] I.C.R. 460. The E.A.T. said that the three-month limitation period must be computed by reference to the day before the corresponding date in the third month after the date of termination; if there is no such day, for example because the dismissal takes place on 30 November and the following year is not a leap year, the date of expiry is 28 February. In *Pruden v. Cunard Ellerman* [1993] IRLR 317 another division of the E.A.T., presided over by the President, reached the same conclusion but by a simpler route. They said that the tribunal should determine the effective date of termination, take the day before and then go forward three months. When February is involved, because the effective date of termination is November 30 or December 1, the limitation period expires on the last day of February.

Practicability of presentation within limitation period. Once it has been determined that the complaint was presented out of time, the next question is whether it was reasonably practicable for the complaint to have been presented within the limitation period. The approach of the Court of Appeal in *Dedman v. British Building & Engineering Appliances* [1974] I.C.R. 53 is still followed, although that case was decided under provisions whose relevant wording was "practicable," and in the context of a 28-day limitation period. This approach has been affirmed in subsequent Court of Appeal decisions, and it has been stressed that industrial tribunals should be fairly strict in enforcing the time limits and that questions of reasonable practicability are questions of fact: see *Wall's Meat Co. v. Khan* [1979] I.C.R. 52. In *Palmer v. Southend-on-Sea Borough Council* [1984] I.C.R. 372, May L.J. said (at p.384) that "reasonably practicable" means more than what is reasonably capable physically of being done and that to construe the words as "reasonable" would be to take a view too favourable to the employee. He also emphasised that, since the issue is pre-eminently one of fact, the E.A.T. and the Court of Appeal should be slow to interfere with the industrial tribunal's decision. The decided cases can be grouped into various categories, which are considered separately below. It should be noted, however, that a theme which is common to all of them is that there is a noticeable, and regrettable, tendency to erect the dicta of the Court of Appeal into principles to be followed in the various categories and to move away from the words of the statute, which are fairly simple and straightforward. The words of Stephenson L.J. in *Riley v. Tesco Stores* [1980] I.C.R. 323, at p.334, should be borne in mind:

"When judges elaborate, or qualify, the plain words of a statute by gloss upon gloss, the meaning of the words may be changed, the intention of Parliament not carried out but defeated, and injustice done instead of justice".

Ignorance. This category embraces ignorance both of the right to claim and of the time limit. The approach of the Court of Appeal to ignorance of the law is fairly strict: if the employee ought to have known, but did not know, of the right then it was reasonably practicable to present the complaint in time: *Porter v. Bandridge* [1978] I.C.R. 943 and *Wall's Meat Co. v. Khan* [1979] I.C.R. 52. Although such ignorance might be excusable in the circumstances of the case, the publicity given to the right not to be unfairly dismissed must make it unlikely that ignorance will be excused. Ignorance will not be excused if it arises from the fault of the complainant in not making such inquiries as he or she should reasonably in all the circumstances have made: *Wall's Meat Co. v. Khan* [1979] I.C.R. 52. See also *Riley v. Tesco Stores* [1980] I.C.R. 323, *Avon County Council v. Haywood-Hicks* [1978] I.C.R. 646, *Churchill v. A. Yeates & Sons* [1983] I.C.R. 380 and *Trevelyans (Birmingham) v. Norton* [1991] I.C.R. 488. In *Machine Tool Industry Research Association v. Simpson* [1988] I.C.R. 558 the Court of Appeal said that it is not reasonably practicable for an employee to bring a complaint of unfair dismissal until he or she has knowledge of a fundamental fact that rendered the dismissal unfair. The court accepted the argument that, in cases of this kind, the subjective state of mind of the employee must be approached in three stages. First, it must have been reasonable for the employee not to be aware of the factual basis on which he or she could bring an application during the limitation period. Second, the applicant must establish that the knowledge which he or she gains has, in the circumstances, been reasonably gained and that the knowledge is crucial to his or her change of belief from one in which he or she does not believe that there are grounds for making an application to a belief which he or she reasonably or genuinely holds that there is a ground for making an application. Third, the acquisition of this knowledge must be crucial to the decision to bring the claim in any event. See also *Marley (U.K.) v. Anderson* [1996] I.C.R. 728, in which the Court of Appeal reviewed the case law in this area.

Considerations similar to those set out above arise in relation to ignorance of the time limit, though there have been suggestions that such ignorance may make it harder to prove that it was not reasonably practicable to present the complaint within the time limit: see, for example, *Riley v. Tesco Stores* [1980] I.C.R. 323, at p.328 (Stephenson L.J.). A reasonable mistake is capable of affording just cause, as in *Wall's Meat Co. v. Khan* [1979] I.C.R. 52.

Reliance upon advisers and others. The second category of cases concerns employees who rely upon advisers. It is immaterial whether or not they are skilled or whether or not they are engaged. In *Riley v. Tesco Stores*, above, at p.330, which concerned wrong advice given by a Citizens' Advice Bureau, Stephenson L.J. said:

"What matters is that the employee cannot of necessity prove reasonable impracticability by saying 'I took advice': and a third party, skilled or unskilled, only comes to be considered a possible excuse for the employee's delay if he gives advice or is authorised to act in time and fails to act or advise acting in time".

It should be noted that the Lord Justice is not saying that the effect of taking advice from a third party is that the employee is necessarily prevented from establishing reasonable practicability. This has been extended to delay in presenting a claim because of reliance on the advice of the Free Representation Unit: see *Croydon Health Authority v. Jaufurally* [1986] I.C.R. 4, *cf. Papparis v. Charles Fulton & Co.* [1981] IRLR 104. See also *Harrington v. Kent County Council* [1980] IRLR 353.

A failure by an adviser to give correct advice will generally prevent the employee from claiming that it was not reasonably practicable to apply in time. In *Rybak v. Jean Sorelle Ltd.* [1991] I.C.R. 127, the E.A.T. upheld the tribunal's decision that it was not reasonably practicable for the employee to have presented her complaint in time as a result of being misled by a member of the industrial tribunal staff. In *London International College Ltd. v. Sen* [1993] IRLR 333 the Court of Appeal considered anew the cases involving the taking of advice. The case concerned an employee who took legal advice from a solicitor but then sought further advice by contacting the industrial tribunal office, from which he received erroneous advice. As a result, his complaint was presented out of time. The tribunal found that the effective cause of his failure was the advice of the industrial tribunal and concluded that it was not reasonably practicable for him to present his complaint in time. In the course of giving the judgment of the Court of Appeal upholding the decision of the tribunal, the Master of the Rolls, Sir Thomas Bingham, accepted that the authorities suggest that an employee who consults an adviser can no longer say that it was not reasonably practicable to comply with the time limit even if the advice was wrong. But he went on to question the rationale of the principle and also to question whether the previous cases were purporting to lay down a rule of law "to govern what is essentially a question of fact". He concluded his judgment with an expression of unease that "the overlay of authority does seem . . . to have distracted attention from what started out . . . as a simple and readily comprehensible statutory test": see pp.335 and 336.

Criminal proceedings. This category embraces employees who are prosecuted for alleged crimes. A failure by the employee to present a claim of unfair dismissal because of outstanding criminal charges is not an acceptable reason for saying that it was not reasonably practicable to present the complaint in time: *Wall's Meat Co. v. Khan* [1979] I.C.R. 52 and *Porter v. Bandridge* [1978] I.C.R. 943. See also *Norgett v. Luton Industrial Co-operative Society* [1976] I.C.R. 442 and *Trevelyans (Birmingham) v. Norton* [1991] I.C.R. 488.

Delay for good reason. The fourth category concerns employees who delay presenting a complaint of unfair dismissal for what appear to them at the time good reasons. An example is delay because of the operation of domestic appeals procedures. Here, the question is whether the fact of a pending appeal makes it not reasonably practicable to present a complaint: see *Palmer v. Southend-on-Sea Borough Council* [1984] I.C.R. 372. The Court of Appeal said that "reasonably practicable" should not be construed so widely as to mean simply "reasonable" nor so narrowly as to mean "reasonably capable physically of being done" and that its meaning lay between those two limits. See also *James W. Cook & Co. (Wivenhoe) (in liquidation) v. Tipper* [1990] IRLR 386 and *Birmingham Optical Group v. Johnson* [1995] I.C.R. 459.

Postal delays. The postal system has added its own problems to this area of the law, by such matters as delay and loss of applications: see *Beanstalk Shelving v. Horn* [1981] I.C.R. 273, *Burton v. Field Sons & Co.* [1977] I.C.R. 106 and *House v. Emerson Electric Industrial Controls* [1980] I.C.R. 795. A common feature of cases in this area is that the application is posted by first class post the day before the expiry of the limitation period, but, instead of arriving the next day, arrives the day after. It is, of course, risky to leave the posting of an application so late and the E.A.T. has regularly warned against it: see, for example, *Beanstalk Shelving v. Horn* [1980] I.C.R. 273, at p.277, and *Midshires Building Society v. Horton* [1991] I.C.R. 648, at p.651. In cases of this kind, the tribunal should go into the circumstances in which the application was posted and, if solicitors were involved, whether they could reasonably have expected the application to be delivered the next day. "It is not a question of what can be guaranteed of the postal services; it is a question of what a reasonable solicitor would have expected, or might reasonably have expected, at the time, date and place in question": *Burton v. Field Sons & Co.* [1977] I.C.R. 106, at p.111, quoted in *St. Basil's Centre v. McCrossan* [1992] I.C.R. 140, at p.142. In *Birmingham Midshires Building Society v. Horton* [1991] I.C.R. 648, the E.A.T. refused to interfere with the tribunal's decision to accept the evidence of the applicant's solicitor that he believed that 99 per cent of first class post arrived the day after it was posted, and to allow the complaint to proceed out of time. In such cases it is open to the industrial tribunal to examine the procedures in a solicitor's office to see whether it considers they are reasonable in the circumstances: *Birmingham Midshires Building Society v. Horton* [1991] I.C.R. 648, at p.652. In *St. Basils' Centre v. McCrossan* [1992] I.C.R. 140 the E.A.T. said that to encourage uniformity it would be reasonable for tribunals to look to the guidance given in the Rules of the Supreme Court and work on the basis that first class mail is delivered on the second working day after posting. That general approach should be subject, however, to evidence to the contrary in a particular situation.

If the application is delayed and arrives outside the time limit, it has not been "presented" within the time limit. In such a case, however, the tribunal should consider all the relevant evidence and decide whether in the circumstances it was reasonably practicable for the complaint to have been presented in time. Thus, if the application is completed and signed but there is then a delay in posting it, the tribunal is likely to take the view that, since the application was ready to be sent on the day it was signed, it was reasonably practicable to have presented it within the limitation period.

The problem is much the same with applications which are lost in the post. A lost application cannot be said to be presented, but it is arguable that the assumption that the application had arrived would make it not reasonably practicable to present a second application in time. The E.A.T.'s decision in *Capital Foods Retail v. Corrigan* [1993] IRLR 430, however, suggests that caution should be exercised here. See also *Camden & Islington Community Services NHS Trust v. Kennedy* [1996] IRLR 381.

Presentation outside limitation period. It is important to bear in mind that the decision that it was not reasonably practicable for a complaint to be presented within the time limit is not the end of the matter. The tribunal must go on to decide upon the period within which it was reasonably practicable to present the complaint: see *James W. Cook & Co. (Wivenhoe) v. Tipper* [1990] I.C.R. 716, for example. This case suggests that a tribunal should be careful about extending the time for presenting a complaint much beyond a month, except in exceptional circumstances. Clearly, too, the longer the period that elapses after the expiry of the limitation period, the less likely becomes an extension of time. In cases of this kind, however, the industrial tribunal should give proper consideration to all the relevant circumstances in which the delay occurred, rather than concentrate upon the length of the delay itself. There are no laid down time limits as to what should and should not be regarded as a reasonable period: see *Marley (U.K.) v. Anderson* [1996] I.C.R. 728.

Subs. (4)
Subsection (4) enables a complaint to be presented during the currency of the notice of termination or of an employee's notice of termination in a constructive dismissal case: see *Presley v. Llanelli Borough Council* [1979] I.C.R. 419. It does not apply where the dismissal consists of the expiry of a fixed term of contract without its renewal: see *Throsby v. Imperial College of Science and Technology* [1978] I.C.R. 357, at p.367.

Subsection (4) applies to an employee who is dismissed with notice and, during the notice period, presents a complaint but is subsequently summarily dismissed: see *Patel v. Nagesan* [1995] I.C.R. 988.

The remedies: orders and compensation

112.—(1) This section applies where, on a complaint under section 111, an industrial tribunal finds that the grounds of the complaint are well-founded.

(2) The tribunal shall—

(a) explain to the complainant what orders may be made under section 113 and in what circumstances they may be made, and

(b) ask him whether he wishes the tribunal to make such an order.

(3) If the complainant expresses such a wish, the tribunal may make an order under section 113.

(4) If no order is made under section 113, the tribunal shall make an award of compensation for unfair dismissal (calculated in accordance with sections 118 to 127) to be paid by the employer to the employee.

DEFINITIONS
   "employee": s.230(1).
   "employer": s.230(4).

GENERAL NOTE
   This section provides for the steps to be taken by the industrial tribunal once it has decided to uphold a complaint of unfair dismissal. The main remedies for unfair dismissal were intended to be reinstatement and re-engagement orders, and the whole tenor of ss.112–116 is to suggest that the industrial tribunal should apply those remedies first. The statistics show, however, that few re-employment orders are made. The first step the tribunal should take, in the case of successful complaints of unfair dismissal, is to explain to the employees what re-employment orders may be made and the circumstances in which they may be made, and to ask them whether they wish the tribunal to make an order; if they do so, the tribunal may then make an order, but is not obliged to do so: s.112(3). If the tribunal decides to consider making a re-employment order, it must first consider whether to make a reinstatement order: s.116(1). If it decides not to do so, it must then consider whether to make a re-engagement order: s.116(2). If it decides not to make any order, it must make an award of compensation: s.112(4).
   A failure by the industrial tribunal to comply with s.112(2) by explaining to the successful complainant what orders for re-employment may be made and to ask whether he or she wishes the tribunal to make an order will not make their decision on relief a nullity; it is voidable if it results in injustice or unfairness to the complainant: *Cowley v. Manson Timber* [1995] I.C.R. 367.

Orders for reinstatement or re-engagement

The orders

   113. An order under this section may be—
   (a) an order for reinstatement (in accordance with section 114), or
   (b) an order for re-engagement (in accordance with section 115),
as the tribunal may decide.

Order for reinstatement

   114.—(1) An order for reinstatement is an order that the employer shall treat the complainant in all respects as if he had not been dismissed.
   (2) On making an order for reinstatement the tribunal shall specify—
   (a) any amount payable by the employer in respect of any benefit which the complainant might reasonably be expected to have had but for the dismissal (including arrears of pay) for the period between the date of termination of employment and the date of reinstatement,
   (b) any rights and privileges (including seniority and pension rights) which must be restored to the employee, and
   (c) the date by which the order must be complied with.
   (3) If the complainant would have benefited from an improvement in his terms and conditions of employment had he not been dismissed, an order for reinstatement shall require him to be treated as if he had benefited from that improvement from the date on which he would have done so but for being dismissed.
   (4) In calculating for the purposes of subsection (2)(a) any amount payable by the employer, the tribunal shall take into account, so as to reduce the employer's liability, any sums received by the complainant in respect of the period between the date of termination of employment and the date of reinstatement by way of—
   (a) wages in lieu of notice or ex gratia payments paid by the employer, or
   (b) remuneration paid in respect of employment with another employer,
and such other benefits as the tribunal thinks appropriate in the circumstances.
   (5) Where a dismissal is treated as taking place by virtue of section 96, references in this section to the date of termination of employment are to the notified date of return.

DEFINITIONS
    "employer": s.230(4).

GENERAL NOTE
    A reinstatement order is an order to the employer to treat the applicant as if he or she had not been dismissed. In deciding whether to make an order, the tribunal must comply with the requirements of s.116(1), and take into account the factors set out there. The effect of an order of reinstatement is to give the employee his or her old job back.

Subs. (2)
    On making the order, the tribunal must make ancillary orders in relation to the following matters: (1) any amount payable by the employer in respect of any benefit which the employee might reasonably be expected to have had but for the dismissal, including arrears of pay, for the period between the date of termination and the date of reinstatement; (2) any rights and privileges, including seniority and pension rights, which must be restored to the employee; and (3) the date by which the order must be complied with. There is no statutory maximum to the amount which may be ordered to be paid under s.114(2)(a). This is the effect of the amendments introduced by s.30 of the Trade Union Reform and Employment Rights Act 1993, which reversed the effect of the decision of the Court of Appeal in *O'Laoire v. Jackel International* [1990] I.C.R. 197.
    A question which arises in the light of these amendments is whether an award of arrears of pay under s.114(2)(a) is subject to the rules of mitigation. In *City & Hackney Health Authority v. Crisp* [1990] I.C.R. 95 the E.A.T. said that the award should not be reduced because of the employee's failure to take steps to mitigate her loss, since an order for reinstatement requires an employer to treat the employee in all respects as if he or she had not been dismissed. If, however, the employee did take steps to mitigate the loss, the earnings by way of mitigation between the date of termination and the date of the reinstatement order are required by s.114(4) to be brought into account. The continuity of employment of an employee who is reinstated will be preserved: see s.219 and the Employment Protection (Continuity of Employment) Regulations 1993 (S.I. 1993 No. 2165).

Subs. (4)
    In calculating the amount of arrears of pay, the tribunal should deduct any sums by way of wages in lieu of notice or *ex gratia* payment or remuneration paid in respect of employment with another employer received by the employee. It may also deduct "such other benefits" as it thinks appropriate in the circumstances: s.114(4). This only affects receipts or benefits between the date of termination of employment and the date of reinstatement.

Order for re-engagement

115.—(1) An order for re-engagement is an order, on such terms as the tribunal may decide, that the complainant be engaged by the employer, or by a successor of the employer or by an associated employer, in employment comparable to that from which he was dismissed or other suitable employment.
    (2) On making an order for re-engagement the tribunal shall specify the terms on which re-engagement is to take place, including—
    (a) the identity of the employer,
    (b) the nature of the employment,
    (c) the remuneration for the employment,
    (d) any amount payable by the employer in respect of any benefit which the complainant might reasonably be expected to have had but for the dismissal (including arrears of pay) for the period between the date of termination of employment and the date of re-engagement,
    (e) any rights and privileges (including seniority and pension rights) which must be restored to the employee, and
    (f) the date by which the order must be complied with.
    (3) In calculating for the purposes of subsection (2)(d) any amount payable by the employer, the tribunal shall take into account, so as to reduce the employer's liability, any sums received by the complainant in respect of the period between the date of termination of employment and the date of re-engagement by way of—

(a) wages in lieu of notice or ex gratia payments paid by the employer, or

(b) remuneration paid in respect of employment with another employer,

and such other benefits as the tribunal thinks appropriate in the circumstances.

(4) Where a dismissal is treated as taking place by virtue of section 96, references in this section to the date of termination of employment are to the notified date of return.

DEFINITIONS

"associated employer": s.231.

"employer": s.230(4).

"employment": s.230(5).

"successor": s.235(1) and (2).

GENERAL NOTE

A re-engagement order is an order that the employee should be engaged by the employer, or by a successor of the employer or an associated employer, in employment comparable to that from which he or she was dismissed. In deciding whether to make the order, the tribunal must have regard to the requirements of s.116(3). The three factors it must take into account under that subsection are similar to those mentioned above in relation to reinstatement orders. Although subs. (1) says that the terms of the order may be "such terms as the tribunal may decide", s.116(4) makes it clear that, except in cases of contributory conduct, the terms of the re-engagement must be as favourable as an order of re-instatement, so far as reasonably practicable: see s.116(4) and the note to that subsection.

There is an obvious difference between a re-engagement order and an order to make an offer of re-engagement. The difference is that a re-engagement order writes a new contract for the parties, whereas an order to offer re-engagement merely orders the employer to offer terms. In the latter case, the employee may return to the industrial tribunal for its decision as to whether he or she should accept the terms. This matter was considered in *Lilley Construction v. Dunn* [1984] IRLR 483 by the E.A.T. It suggested that it is unwise for tribunals to make orders to offer re-engagement, because of the possible sources of confusion. There is also the point that it is doubtful whether tribunals have jurisdiction to make such orders.

Subs. (2)

This subsection requires the tribunal when making the order to specify the terms of re-engagement. These include remuneration, "any amount payable by the employer in respect of any benefit which the complainant might reasonably be expected to have had but for the dismissal, including arrears of pay, for the period between the date of termination of employment and the date of re-engagement", and "any rights and privileges, including seniority and pension rights, which must be restored to the employee". See *Electronic Data Processing v. Wright* [1986] I.C.R. 76, in which the tribunal ordered the employee to be re-engaged at a salary less than her previous salary, and ordered the employers to pay compensation under s.115(2)(d) on the basis of her pre-dismissal salary. The E.A.T. upheld the award.

As with reinstatement orders, this provision cannot be frustrated by an employer's refusal to comply with the re-engagement order. This is the result of the amendments introduced by s.30 of the Trade Union Reform and Employment Rights Act 1993.

A question which arises is whether an award of arrears of pay under s.69(4)(d) is subject to the rules of mitigation. In *City & Hackney Health Authority v. Crisp* [1990] I.C.R. 95 the E.A.T. rejected the employers' argument that the amount in respect of arrears of pay between the date of termination and the date of re-engagement should be reduced because of the industrial tribunal's finding that had the employee pursued her claim more vigorously she would probably have been re-engaged earlier. In effect, the employers were arguing that the employee should be subject to a duty to mitigate his or her loss of earnings. If, however, the employee did take steps to mitigate the loss, the earnings by way of mitigation between the date of termination and the date of the re-engagement order are required by subs. (3) to be brought into account.

Subs. (3)

In calculating the amount of arrears of pay, the tribunal should deduct any sums by way of wages in lieu of notice or *ex gratia* payment or remuneration paid in respect of employment with another employer received by the employee. It may also deduct "such other benefits" as it thinks appropriate in the circumstances. This only affects receipts or benefits between the date of termination of employment and the date of reinstatement.

Choice of order and its terms

116.—(1) In exercising its discretion under section 113 the tribunal shall first consider whether to make an order for reinstatement and in so doing shall take into account—

(a) whether the complainant wishes to be reinstated,

(b) whether it is practicable for the employer to comply with an order for reinstatement, and

(c) where the complainant caused or contributed to some extent to the dismissal, whether it would be just to order his reinstatement.

(2) If the tribunal decides not to make an order for reinstatement it shall then consider whether to make an order for re-engagement and, if so, on what terms.

(3) In so doing the tribunal shall take into account—

(a) any wish expressed by the complainant as to the nature of the order to be made,

(b) whether it is practicable for the employer (or a successor or an associated employer) to comply with an order for re-engagement, and

(c) where the complainant caused or contributed to some extent to the dismissal, whether it would be just to order his re-engagement and (if so) on what terms.

(4) Except in a case where the tribunal takes into account contributory fault under subsection (3)(c) it shall, if it orders re-engagement, do so on terms which are, so far as is reasonably practicable, as favourable as an order for reinstatement.

(5) Where in any case an employer has engaged a permanent replacement for a dismissed employee, the tribunal shall not take that fact into account in determining, for the purposes of subsection (1)(b) or (3)(b), whether it is practicable to comply with an order for reinstatement or re-engagement.

(6) Subsection (5) does not apply where the employer shows—

(a) that it was not practicable for him to arrange for the dismissed employee's work to be done without engaging a permanent replacement, or

(b) that—

(i) he engaged the replacement after the lapse of a reasonable period, without having heard from the dismissed employee that he wished to be reinstated or re-engaged, and

(ii) when the employer engaged the replacement it was no longer reasonable for him to arrange for the dismissed employee's work to be done except by a permanent replacement.

DEFINITIONS

"associated employer": s.231.
"employer": s.230(4).
"employment": s.230(5).
"successor": s.235(1) and (2).

GENERAL NOTE

The first step the tribunal should take, in the case of successful complaints of unfair dismissal, is to explain to the employees what re-employment orders may be made and the circumstances in which they may be made, and to ask them whether they wish the tribunal to make an order; if they do so, the tribunal may then make an order, but is not obliged to do so: s.112(3). If the tribunal decides to consider making a re-employment order, it must first consider whether to make a reinstatement order: s.116(1). If it decides not to do so, it must then consider whether to make a re-engagement order: s.116(2). If it decides not to make any order, it must make an award of compensation: s.112(4). A failure by the industrial tribunal to comply with s.112(2) by explaining to the successful complainant what orders for re-employment may be made and to ask whether he or she wishes the tribunal to make an order will not make their decision on relief a nullity; it is voidable if it results in injustice or unfairness to the complainant: *Cowley v. Manson Timber* [1995] I.C.R. 367.

Subs. (1)

In deciding whether to make an order, the tribunal must comply with the requirements of s.116(1), and take into account the following factors: (1) the complainant's wishes; (2) the practicability for the employer of compliance with the order; and (3) where the complainant caused or contributed to some extent to the dismissal, whether it would be just to order reinstatement. The tribunal must consider all these factors: *cf. Qualcast (Wolverhampton) v. Ross* [1979] I.C.R. 386, where the tribunal apparently failed to do so. Although it may be thought that the first factor is paramount, the second and third factors have given rise to such case law as there is.

Practicability. The tribunal may have to consider the practicability of complying with the order at two separate stages: first, when considering whether to make the order; and second, if the employer fails to comply with the order, whether it was practicable for the employer to comply with the order. This approach has received the approval of the Court of Appeal in *Port of London Authority v. Payne* [1994] I.C.R. 555. At the first stage, the tribunal has to look forward and "take into account" whether it is practicable to make the order; at the second stage, the tribunal is looking back: see *Cold Drawn Tubes v. Middleton* [1992] I.C.R. 318, at 320. In *Freemans v. Flynn* [1984] I.C.R. 874 the E.A.T. said that at the first stage, the tribunal is not required to make a finding that it would be practicable for the employer to comply. This proposition is at variance with the later decision of the E.A.T. in *Port of London Authority v. Payne* [1993] I.C.R. 30 which in fact concerned a re-engagement order. There, they said that before making an order the tribunal must determine whether it is practicable for the employers to comply with the order and should make a decision on the issue of practicability at this first stage. They refused to follow an earlier decision of the E.A.T., in *Timex Corporation v. Thomson* [1981] IRLR 522 in which Browne-Wilkinson J. (as he then was) said that the tribunal need only "have regard" to the practicability of making the order. When the Court of Appeal came to consider this question, they took the view that the E.A.T's decision on this point did less than justice to the careful assessment which the tribunal made. They said that the determination at the first stage was only provisional, a conclusion in accord with common sense and the authorities: [1994] I.C.R. 555, at p.569. At the first stage, therefore, the tribunal should not be required to make a decision on the practicability of making the reinstatement order; in making their provisional determination, they should be obliged merely to take it into account in the sense of having regard to it. Clearly, however, they will fall into error if they completely fail to take into account the practicability of making the order.

One consideration is whether the employee is likely to be a satisfactory employee if reinstated, but the industrial tribunal should take a broad common sense view of what is practicable: see *Nothman v. London Borough of Barnet* [1980] IRLR 65 at p.66, para. 4, (Ormrod L.J.) and *Meridian v. Gomersall* [1977] I.C.R. 597 at pp.601–602; *cf. Enessy Co. S.A. t/a The Tulchan Estate v. Minoprio* [1978] IRLR 489 at p.490, para. 2. See also *Coleman v. Magnet Joinery* [1975] I.C.R. 46. They should use their experience and common sense, looking at what has occurred in the past and what can reasonably be expected for the future and maintaining a fair balance between the parties: *Rao v. Civil Aviation Authority* [1992] I.C.R. 503. "Practicable" does not, however, mean expedient: *Qualcast (Wolverhampton) v. Ross* [1979] I.C.R. 386. The second stage of practicability, in cases of non-compliance with a reinstatement order, is considered in the note to s.117(4).

Contributory fault. In *Boots Co. v. Lees-Collier* [1986] I.C.R. 728 an employee who was dismissed on the grounds of suspected theft of company property was found by the tribunal to have acted absent-mindedly but not dishonestly. The tribunal made an order for reinstatement, but made no express finding as to the practicability of the employer's compliance with such an order or as to whether the employee's conduct had caused or contributed to his dismissal. The tribunal accepted evidence that the employee's superior had lost confidence in his honesty and competence to carry out his duties but did not consider that factor to be a bar to reinstatement. The employers appealed to the E.A.T. on the grounds that in accepting that evidence the tribunal made a finding inconsistent with a conclusion that reinstatement was practicable and that it had failed to make any finding under s.116(1)(c). The E.A.T. dismissed the appeal. They said that the tribunal was justified in not considering the question of contributory fault for the express purposes of s.116(1)(c), having concluded that the explanation for the employee's conduct was not dishonesty. Since they had concluded that the employee's conduct had not caused or contributed to the dismissal for the purposes of compensation, there was no room for a finding that he had caused or contributed to his dismissal for the purposes of s.116(1)(c). The tribunal was also not obliged to make a definite finding under s.116(1)(b) that the reinstatement order was practicable, since it was sufficient for them to have examined the relevant evidence relating to practicability.

Note the provisions of subss. (5) and (6) in relation to the engagement of replacements.

Subs. (3)

In deciding whether to make a re-engagement order under this subsection, the tribunal must consider the requirements of subs. (3). The three factors it must take into account are similar to those mentioned above in relation to reinstatement orders. In relation to the second factor (practicability), however, the tribunal must consider the practicability of re-engagement with a successor of the employer or an associated employer. The engagement of a permanent replacement by the employer does not automatically mean that reinstatement or re-engagement are impracticable: see subss. (5) and (6), below. The effect of a re-engagement order will be to give the employee a job similar to the one from which he or she was dismissed: subs. (4).

The fact that the tribunal considers it practicable for the employer to comply does not mean that the issue of practicability is settled once and for all. Practicability falls to be considered at two stages, as with reinstatement orders: at the first stage, it is a consideration which the tribunal must have in mind when considering whether to order re-engagement; at the second stage, the employer may escape the consequences of non-compliance with an order by discharging the burden of showing that it was not practicable to comply with the order, under s.117(4). The same considerations arise in relation to "practicability" as with reinstatement orders. The relevant case law has been fully considered in that context: see the note to subs. (2), above.

Subs. (4)

Except in cases of contributory conduct, the terms of the re-engagement must be as favourable as an order of re-instatement, so far as reasonably practicable. In *Freemans v. Flynn* [1984] I.C.R. 874 for example, the industrial tribunal found that the employee had contributed to his own dismissal to the extent of 20 per cent. Accordingly, the re-engagement order was that he should be re-engaged at a salary comparable to 80 per cent of his salary at the effective date of termination of his contract. See also *Morganite Crucible Carbon v. Donne* [1988] I.C.R. 18, where the tribunal found that there was a degree of contributory conduct on the employee's part and made a re-engagement order with the requirement that he should forfeit four weeks' pay; and *Nairne v. Highlands & Islands Fire Brigade* [1989] IRLR 366, where the Court of Session upheld the E.A.T.'s decision that in a case where the employee's degree of contributory fault was assessed at 75 per cent a re-engagement order was not appropriate.

Subss. (5) and (6)

It should be noted that the engagement of a permanent replacement by the employer does not automatically mean that reinstatement is not practicable. When considering the practicability of making an order, the tribunal is not allowed to take that fact into account, unless the employer shows one of the following: either that it was not practicable to arrange for the dismissed employee's work to be done without engaging a permanent replacement or that the replacement was engaged after a reasonable period had passed without the employer having heard from the dismissed employee that he or she wished to be reinstated and that when the replacement was engaged it was no longer reasonable for the employer to arrange for the dismissed employee's work to be done except by a permanent replacement.

Enforcement of order and compensation

117.—(1) An industrial tribunal shall make an award of compensation, to be paid by the employer to the employee, if—

    (a) an order under section 113 is made and the complainant is reinstated or re-engaged, but

    (b) the terms of the order are not fully complied with.

(2) Subject to section 124, the amount of the compensation shall be such as the tribunal thinks fit having regard to the loss sustained by the complainant in consequence of the failure to comply fully with the terms of the order.

(3) Subject to subsections (1) and (2), if an order under section 113 is made but the complainant is not reinstated or re-engaged in accordance with the order, the tribunal shall make—

    (a) an award of compensation for unfair dismissal (calculated in accordance with sections 118 to 127), and

    (b) except where this paragraph does not apply, an additional award of compensation of the appropriate amount,

to be paid by the employer to the employee.

(4) Subsection (3)(b) does not apply where—

    (a) the employer satisfies the tribunal that it was not practicable to comply with the order, or

(b) the reason (or, if more than one, the principal reason)—
        (i) in a redundancy case, for selecting the employee for dismissal, or
        (ii) otherwise, for the dismissal,
is one of those specified in section 100(1)(a) and (b), 102(1) or 103.

(5) In subsection (3)(b) "the appropriate amount" means—
(a) where the dismissal is of a description referred to in subsection (6), not less than twenty-six nor more than fifty-two weeks' pay, and
(b) in any other case, not less than thirteen nor more than twenty-six weeks' pay.

(6) The descriptions of dismissal in respect of which an employer may incur a higher additional award in accordance with subsection (5)(a) are—
(a) a dismissal which is an act of discrimination within the meaning of the Sex Discrimination Act 1975 which is unlawful by virtue of that Act, and
(b) a dismissal which is an act of discrimination within the meaning of the Race Relations Act 1976 which is unlawful by virtue of that Act.

(7) Where in any case an employer has engaged a permanent replacement for a dismissed employee, the tribunal shall not take that fact into account in determining for the purposes of subsection (4)(a) whether it was practicable to comply with the order for reinstatement or re-engagement unless the employer shows that it was not practicable for him to arrange for the dismissed employee's work to be done without engaging a permanent replacement.

(8) Where in any case an industrial tribunal finds that the complainant has unreasonably prevented an order under section 113 from being complied with, in making an award of compensation for unfair dismissal (in accordance with sections 118 to 127) it shall take that conduct into account as a failure on the part of the complainant to mitigate his loss.

DEFINITIONS
    "employee": s.230(1).
    "employer": s.230(4).
    "redundancy case": s.105(9).

GENERAL NOTE
    This section comes into play where the tribunal makes a re-employment order under ss.114 or 155 and the order is not complied with. Subsections (1) and (2) make provision for partial non-compliance; subss. (3)–(7) deal with total non-compliance. Subsection (8) deals with the situation where the employee has unreasonably prevented an order from being complied with. If the employer does not comply fully with the terms of a reinstatement or re-engagement order, the tribunal must award such an amount of compensation as it thinks fit having regard to the loss sustained by the employee, subject to the maximum permissible under s.124. If the employer totally fails to comply, then the tribunal must go on to award compensation in the usual way and it must also make an additional award of compensation under subs. (3) or a special award, in accordance with s.125 or the 1992 Act, s.157.
    The E.A.T. considered the difference between partial and total non-compliance in *Artisan Press v. Srawley and Parker* [1986] I.C.R. 328. In that case the industrial tribunal made a reinstatement order in respect of employees employed as security staff with minor general duties. The employers re-employed them as cleaners with a few security duties. The employees complained, and the tribunal found, that the employers had failed to comply with the order. The employers appealed on the grounds that, since the terms of the reinstatement order had not been fully complied with, the tribunal should have applied s.117(1) and (2). The E.A.T. dismissed their appeal. They said that an employer failed to reinstate the employee if the employee was re-employed on a less favourable basis than previously, since the requirement of s.114(1) is that the employee should be treated as if he or she had not been dismissed. Since the employers had re-employed the employees as cleaners with minor security duties, they had failed to comply with the reinstatement order. The E.A.T. pointed out that the reason for an award of compensation under s.117(2) is to compensate an employee where the employer fails to comply fully with the orders made by the tribunal under s.114(2)(a), (b) and (c) relating to ancillary matters.

Subss. (3) and (4)

In cases of total non-compliance, the employer may escape the consequences of non-compliance by showing that it was not "practicable" to comply with the re-employment order. In deciding whether it was practicable to re-employ the employee, the tribunal should not take into account the fact that the employer has engaged a permanent replacement, unless the employer shows that it was not practicable for the dismissed employee's work to be done without taking such a step: subs. (7) and the 1992 Act, s.158(6). The issue of practicability at this stage is different from the question of practicability as one of the considerations the tribunal must have in mind when deciding whether to order re-employment: see *Freemans v. Flynn* [1984] I.C.R. 874. The burden is on the employer to show that re-employment was not practicable, but the E.A.T. has stressed that the industrial tribunal must not impose too high a duty on the employer to find the employee a job. It is enough for the employer to try to find a suitable job for the employee; if there is none, the duty has been discharged. As the E.A.T. pointed out in *Cold Drawn Tubes v. Middleton* [1992] I.C.R. 318, at p.320, there is a difference between the two stages at which practicability falls to be considered. At the first stage, when considering whether to make the re-employment order, the tribunal has to look forward and "take into account" whether it is practicable to make the order; at the second stage, the tribunal is looking back. In doing so, it should take a broad common sense view.

In *Port of London Authority v. Payne* [1994] I.C.R. 555 which was commented upon in the note to s.116, the Court of Appeal said that the standard must not be set too high: the test is practicability not possibility. They said that a tribunal should pay due regard to the commercial judgement of the employer unless the employer was to be disbelieved, but that an employer could not be expected "to explore every possible avenue which ingenuity might suggest": see p.574.

The tribunal must go on to award compensation in the usual way: subs. (3)(a). In addition, the employee will be entitled to be paid any amount of arrears of pay ordered by the tribunal, under ss.114(2)(a) or 115(2)(d), when making the reinstatement or re-engagement order. The tribunal must also make an additional award of between 13 and 26 weeks' pay, unless the dismissal was an unlawful act of discrimination on grounds of sex or race; in that case, the tribunal should make a higher additional award of between 26 and 52 weeks' pay: subs. (3)(b), (5) and (6). Additional awards will be made where the following conditions are fulfilled: (1) the employer totally fails to comply with a re-employment order; (2) the employer fails to satisfy the tribunal that it was not practicable to comply with the order; and (3) the case is one where a special award is not payable.

If the failure is partial, the tribunal may award whatever amount it considers fit with regard to the employee's loss caused by the non-compliance, under subs. (1) above. This is subject to the statutory limit of £11,300 (at the time of going to press), but the statutory limit does not apply to ancillary orders for arrears of pay in cases where the tribunal has made a reinstatement or re-engagement order: see s.124(3). For an analysis of the difference between total and partial non-compliance, see *Artisan Press v. Srawley* [1986] I.C.R. 328, and the note to subs. (1) above.

In the case of a total failure to comply, the additional award will be between 13 and 26 weeks' pay. The maximum at the time of going to press was £5,460 (*i.e.* 26 × £210). If the dismissal was an unlawful act of sex or race discrimination, the tribunal will order the employer to pay a higher additional award of between 26 and 52 weeks' pay. The maximum is at present £10,920 (*i.e.* 52 × £210). The employer will be liable to pay the award unless the tribunal is satisfied that it was not practicable to comply with the re-employment order.

In *Mabirizi v. National Hospital for Nervous Diseases* [1990] I.C.R. 281 the E.A.T. said that the additional award is not intended to be a precisely calculated substitute for financial loss but a general solatium to be arrived at by fixing the appropriate point on the scale specified. The tribunal must exercise its discretion in deciding where in the range of 13 to 26 weeks the award should fall. In deciding where to pitch the award, it must address its mind to the fact that it is exercising a discretionary power and must consider what factors ought properly to affect the exercise of that discretion. Some sort of proper assessment and balancing must take place: *Morganite Electrical Carbon v. Donne* [1988] I.C.R. 18, at pp.28–29. In considering the amount of the award, the tribunal is entitled to have regard to the employer's conduct and to make an award which registers disapproval of that conduct: see *Motherwell Railway Club v. McQueen* [1989] I.C.R. 418.

The following points should also be noted: (1) In addition to awarding an additional or higher additional award of compensation, the tribunal will also award compensation in the usual way. It should be noted, however, that in cases where the employee has unreasonably prevented a re-employment order from being complied with by the employer, the tribunal must take that conduct into account when making a compensatory award of compensation and treat it as a failure to mitigate: see subs. (8). (2) Additional and higher additional awards are not subject to deductions for contributory conduct or, indeed, to any other form of deduction. (3) There is no reason why an employer should not make an *ex gratia* payment to an employee which is expressed to be in satisfaction of, or as a contribution towards, any additional or higher additional award which may be made by a tribunal in due course: see *Darr v. L.R.C. Products* [1993] IRLR 257. (4) An employee entitled to receive a special award may not also receive an additional or higher additional award. Instead he or she will be entitled to an increased special award of one week's pay multiplied by 156, or £20,600, whichever is the greater: see s.125(2). See also the 1992 Act, s.158(2).

In cases in which there is a total failure to comply and the dismissal is unfair because it is contrary to s.100(1)(a) and (b) (in cases involving dismissals in health and safety cases), s.102(1) (in cases involving the dismissal of a employee trustee of an occupational pension scheme), s.103 (in cases involving the dismissal of an employee representative) or ss.152 or 153 of the 1992 Act (which makes dismissals and selections for redundancy for trade union reasons unfair), the employee will be eligible for a special award calculated in accordance with s.125 or s.158 of the 1992 Act (in trade union cases).

Compensation

General

118.—(1) Where a tribunal makes an award of compensation for unfair dismissal under section 112(4) or 117(3)(a) the award shall consist of—
  (a) a basic award (calculated in accordance with sections 119 to 122 and 126), and
  (b) a compensatory award (calculated in accordance with sections 123, 124, 126 and 127).

(2) Where this subsection applies, the award shall also include a special award calculated in accordance with section 125 unless—
  (a) the complainant does not request the tribunal to make an order under section 113, or
  (b) the case falls within section 121.

(3) Subsection (2) applies where the reason (or, if more than one, the principal reason)—
  (a) in a redundancy case, for selecting the employee for dismissal, or
  (b) otherwise, for the dismissal,
is one of those specified in section 100(1)(a) and (b), 102(1) or 103.

DEFINITIONS
  "redundancy case": s.105(9).

GENERAL NOTE
  An industrial tribunal will award compensation if it makes no order for re-employment, or if it makes such an order but the employer totally fails to comply with it. Compensation may consist of the following elements: (1) a basic award; (2) a compensatory award; and (3) an additional or higher additional award or a special award. The Employment Act 1982 (c. 46), Sched. 3, para. 7, empowered the Secretary of State to order sums payable by virtue of industrial tribunals' decisions to carry interest. This provision was implemented by the Industrial Tribunals (Interest) Order 1990 (S.I. 1990 No. 479), which came into operation on April 1, 1990. Its effect is that a monetary award carries interest if it is unpaid for more than six weeks after the date of the award. The rate of interest from April 1, 1993 is 8 per cent per annum in relation to decisions made on or after April 1, 1993: see the Judgement Debts (Rate of Interest) Order 1993 (S.I. 1993 No. 564). See *Secretary of State for Employment v. Reeves* [1993] I.C.R. 508, which involved claims for redundancy payments against the employer, followed by a claim from the National Insurance Fund. The tribunal upheld their claims and also awarded interest calculated by reference to the dates of the original decisions against the employers. The E.A.T upheld the Secretary of State's appeal, on the grounds that time only started to run from the date of the decision made against the Secretary of State, not against the employers. Note the definitions of "calculation date" and "relevant decision" in art. 2(1) of the 1990 Order.

Subs. (1)
  If the industrial tribunal makes a finding of unfair dismissal, it must first consider whether to make an order for the re-employment of the applicant. If he or she does not wish such an order to

be made or if the tribunal decides against making an order, it will proceed to award compensation. If it does make an order, but the employer totally fails to comply with it, the tribunal will make an award of compensation in the usual way and will also award an additional or higher additional award of compensation or a special award. In most cases, compensation usually consists of a basic award and a compensatory award.

Subss. (2) and (3)

A special award is only available to employees in two types of unfair dismissal case: (1) where the dismissal is automatically unfair because they were dismissed, or selected for redundancy, for a reason falling within s.100(1)(a) or (b) (dismissals in health and safety cases), s.102(1) (dismissals of trustees of occupational pension schemes) or s.103 (dismissals of employee representatives); and (2) where their dismissal is automatically unfair by virtue of the provisions of ss.152 or 153 of the Trade Union and Labour Relations (Consolidation) Act 1992: see subs. (3) and the 1992 Act, s.157(1).

The employee will only qualify for the award if he or she has asked for an order of reinstatement or re-engagement and the tribunal has either not made one and has proceeded to assess compensation or has made an order with which the employer has totally failed to comply. In cases where the dismissal is not made automatically unfair by virtue of the provisions of ss.100(1)(a) or (b), 102(1) or 103 of the 1996 Act or s.152 or 153 of the 1992 Act, the employee will receive an additional award or a higher additional award of compensation, rather than a special award. The remedy is not available where s.121 applies: s.118(2)(b). This is in cases where an employee is entitled to a minimum basic award of two weeks' pay, where the dismissal was by reason of redundancy but he or she is disentitled because of the provisions of s.141, or where an employee is treated as not having been dismissed because of the operation of s.138.

Basic award

119.—(1) Subject to the provisions of this section, sections 120 to 122 and section 126, the amount of the basic award shall be calculated by—
  (a) determining the period, ending with the effective date of termination, during which the employee has been continuously employed,
  (b) reckoning backwards from the end of that period the number of years of employment falling within that period, and
  (c) allowing the appropriate amount for each of those years of employment.
(2) In subsection (1)(c) "the appropriate amount" means—
  (a) one and a half weeks' pay for a year of employment in which the employee was not below the age of forty-one,
  (b) one week's pay for a year of employment (not within paragraph (a)) in which he was not below the age of twenty-two, and
  (c) half a week's pay for a year of employment not within paragraph (a) or (b).
(3) Where twenty years of employment have been reckoned under subsection (1), no account shall be taken under that subsection of any year of employment earlier than those twenty years.
(4) Where the effective date of termination is after the sixty-fourth anniversary of the day of the employee's birth, the amount arrived at under subsections (1) to (3) shall be reduced by the appropriate fraction.
(5) In subsection (4) "the appropriate fraction" means the fraction of which—
  (a) the numerator is the number of whole months reckoned from the sixty-fourth anniversary of the day of the employee's birth in the period beginning with that anniversary and ending with the effective date of termination, and
  (b) the denominator is twelve.
(6) Subsections (4) and (5) do not apply to a case within section 96(1).

DEFINITIONS
  "effective date of termination": s.97.
  "employee": s.230(1).
  "employment": s.230(5).

GENERAL NOTE

The basic award is calculated in the same way as a redundancy payment. It is necessary to take the complainant's age, length of continuous employment (calculated in accordance with ss.210–219) on the effective date of termination and the amount of gross weekly pay (calculated in accordance with ss.220–229). Starting with the effective date of termination and working backwards, the number of years of continuous employment should be reckoned. For each year of employment between 41 and 64, one and a half weeks' pay should be allowed; for each year between 22 and 41, one week's pay; and for each year between the time the employee started work and 22, half a weeks' pay: subs. (2). Employment before the age of 18 may count, which is not the case with redundancy payments. The week's pay used in the calculation should not include overtime, bonuses and tips: see *Brownson v. Hire Service Shops* [1978] I.C.R. 517 and *Palmanor v. Cedron* [1978] I.C.R. 1008. Subsection (3) provides that no more than 20 years of employment may be counted and subss. (4) and (5) contain tapering provisions which will reduce the amount of the basic award of an employee over 64. The tapering provisions do not apply to employees who are treated as dismissed because of a failure by the employer to allow them to return after pregnancy or childbirth: subs. (6).

In this context, it is important to bear in mind the provisions of s.97(2), since their operation may affect the effective date of termination of the employment and, in consequence, the length of continuous employment for the purposes of calculating the basic award. So, for example, an employee with nearly eight years' employment, who is given one week's notice, may in fact be treated as having been continuously employed for eight years instead of seven by s.97(2) operating to extend the effective date of termination into the ninth year of continuous employment.

Basic award: minimum in certain cases

120.—(1) The amount of the basic award (before any reduction under section 122) shall not be less than £2,770 where the reason (or, if more than one, the principal reason)—

(a) in a redundancy case, for selecting the employee for dismissal, or

(b) otherwise, for the dismissal,

is one of those specified in section 100(1)(a) and (b), 102(1) or 103.

(2) The Secretary of State may by order increase the sum specified in subsection (1).

DEFINITIONS

"redundancy case": s.105(9).

GENERAL NOTE

The employee is entitled to a minimum basic award of £2,770 in cases where the dismissal, or, in redundancy cases, the selection of the employee for dismissal, was for a reason falling within s.100(1)(a) or (b) (dismissals in health and safety cases), s.102(1) (dismissals of trustees of occupational pension schemes) or s.103 (dismissals of employee representatives).

It is unclear how this provision is intended to operate. If, for example, the employee would be entitled to a basic award of £750, is that award increased to £2,770 or £3,520? If he or she would be entitled to £3000 anyway, should anything more be awarded? There is no clear answer to these questions, but a close reading of this provision would tend to suggest that if the basic award would be less than £2,770, it is raised to that amount and, if the basic award would exceed £2,770, that higher amount should be awarded. Reductions from the figure of £2770 may be made, however, under s.122.

Basic award of two weeks' pay in certain cases

121. The amount of the basic award shall be two weeks' pay where the tribunal finds that the reason (or, where there is more than one, the principal reason) for the dismissal of the employee is that he was redundant and the employee—

(a) by virtue of section 138 is not regarded as dismissed for the purposes of Part XI, or

(b) by virtue of section 141 is not, or (if he were otherwise entitled) would not be, entitled to a redundancy payment.

GENERAL NOTE
  The employee is entitled to a minimum basic award of two weeks' pay, where the dismissal was by reason of redundancy but he or she is disentitled because of the provisions of s.141, or where he or she is not treated as dismissed because of the operation of s.138.

Basic award: reductions

122.—(1) Where the tribunal finds that the complainant has unreasonably refused an offer by the employer which (if accepted) would have the effect of reinstating the complainant in his employment in all respects as if he had not been dismissed, the tribunal shall reduce or further reduce the amount of the basic award to such extent as it considers just and equitable having regard to that finding.

(2) Where the tribunal considers that any conduct of the complainant before the dismissal (or, where the dismissal was with notice, before the notice was given) was such that it would be just and equitable to reduce or further reduce the amount of the basic award to any extent, the tribunal shall reduce or further reduce that amount accordingly.

(3) Subsection (2) does not apply in a redundancy case unless the reason for selecting the employee for dismissal was one of those specified in section 100(1)(a) and (b), 102(1) or 103; and in such a case subsection (2) applies only to so much of the basic award as is payable because of section 120.

(4) The amount of the basic award shall be reduced or further reduced by the amount of—
  (a) any redundancy payment awarded by the tribunal under Part XI in respect of the same dismissal, or
  (b) any payment made by the employer to the employee on the ground that the dismissal was by reason of redundancy (whether in pursuance of Part XI or otherwise).

GENERAL NOTE
  The following reductions in the basic award may be made under this section: (1) where the employee unreasonably refuses an offer of reinstatement: subs. (1); (2) where the employee's conduct before the dismissal makes it just and equitable to reduce the compensation: subs. (2) and (3); and (3) where the employee has already received a redundancy payment. Although it is not mentioned in the statutory provisions, the amount of any *ex gratia* payment made by the employer will also be deducted.

Subss. (2) and (3)
  The tribunal has the power to reduce the basic award to any extent, where it considers that any conduct of the employee before dismissal (or before notice was given, if that is the case) makes it just and equitable to do so. If the tribunal finds that the employee has contributed to some degree to the dismissal, it must reflect that finding in the award of compensation: see *Morganite Electrical Carbon v. Donne* [1988] I.C.R. 18. The effect of this rule is that any conduct before the dismissal is relevant, not merely conduct which caused or contributed to it. So evidence of misconduct before the dismissal, which came to light after the dismissal, would justify a reduction in the basic award. This is what would happen now if a case like *W. Devis & Sons v. Atkins* [1977] I.C.R. 662 were to recur. The legislation under which that case was decided has been considerably changed since then, however. Further, except in redundancy cases, it is perfectly feasible for the employee to receive no basic award at all. The equivalent provision in relation to compensa-

tory awards, s.123(6), is somewhat narrower, since it only enables reduction to be made where the conduct *caused or contributed* to the dismissal. There is no reason, therefore, why different percentages of reduction should not be made from the basic award and the compensatory award, though the E.A.T. has suggested that this should only be done in exceptional circumstances: see *Royal Society for the Prevention of Cruelty to Animals v. Cruden* [1986] I.C.R. 205. See also *Les Ambassadeurs Club v. Bainda* [1982] IRLR 5 and *Thompson v. Woodland Designs* [1980] IRLR 423, where the basic award was reduced by 85 per cent, and the compensatory award by 100 per cent, for contributory conduct. In *Charles Robertson (Developments) v. White* [1995] I.C.R. 349 the E.A.T. considered this issue and concluded that a discrepancy in reductions made to the basic and compensatory awards is not wrong in principle but flows from the fact that the discretions in the respective provisions are worded differently and require different factors to be taken into account. In many cases, however, the reductions are likely to be the same.

In *Courtaulds Northern Spinning v. Moosa* [1984] I.C.R. 218 the E.A.T. suggested that the taking of industrial action should not be characterised as contributory fault meriting a reduction in the amount of compensation. The E.A.T. subsequently decided that this decision should not be followed and that, when considering any reduction of compensation under this subsection, the tribunal was entitled to examine the facts and circumstances surrounding the dismissal, including the circumstances surrounding the industrial action: see *T.N.T. Express (U.K.) v. Downes* [1994] I.C.R. 1. In *Tracey v. Crosville Wales* [1996] I.C.R. 237, however, the Court of Appeal approved the E.A.T.'s decision in *Courtaulds Northern Spinning v. Moosa* and said that the tribunal should ignore the conduct represented by the industrial action in which the applicant had participated but that other blameworthy conduct of the applicant causing or contributing to the dismissal should be taken into account when deciding upon a reduction in compensation.

Reductions under this subsection are not permissible, however, if the dismissal was for redundancy, unless it was made unfair because the employee was selected for a reason falling within s.100(1)(a) or (b) (dismissals in health and safety cases), s.102(1) (dismissals of trustees of occupational pension schemes) or s.103 (dismissals of employee representatives); in such cases, only the basic award payable by virtue of s.120(1) is susceptible of reduction.

Subs. (4)

The basic award will be reduced (or further reduced if there have been reductions under the previous headings) by the amount of any redundancy payment awarded by the tribunal, or paid by the employer to the employee whether in pursuance of the statutory obligations or otherwise. If the amount of the redundancy payment exceeds the amount of the basic award which would be payable but for subs. (4), the amount of the excess will be deducted from the compensatory award: s.123(7). Subsection (4) only applies, however, to payments made where the dismissal is in fact due to redundancy. So if a payment is expressed to be made to satisfy an employee's entitlement to a redundancy payment but the circumstances are such that there is in fact no redundancy situation, the payment will not fall to be deducted under s.122(4): see *Boorman v. Allmakes* [1995] I.C.R. 842.

Minimum basic awards where the dismissal or selection for redundancy is for a reason falling within s.100(1)(a) or (b) (dismissals in health and safety cases), s.102(1) (dismissals of trustees of occupational pension schemes) or s.103 (dismissals of employee representatives) are susceptible to reduction under this provision: see s.120(1).

Deduction of ex gratia *payments.* If the employer makes a lump sum payment to a dismissed employee before a complaint is presented to the industrial tribunal and does not specifically state that it is referable to any possible future liability to pay a basic award, it is a question of construction whether the payment is to be taken to include any liability the employer may have because of the statutory provisions. Although there is a risk that the employer will remain liable to pay a basic award (and also a compensatory award), it seems probable, particularly if the payment is fairly substantial, that it will be held to be compensation for any rights the employee may have under the legislation: see *Chelsea Football Club and Athletic Co. v. Heath* [1981] I.C.R. 323, at pp.327–328. In that case, the *ex gratia* payment will be deducted first from the basic award; if there is a surplus, that will then be deducted from the compensatory award: see *Rushton v. Harcos Timber & Building Supplies* [1993] I.C.R. 230 and *Darr v. L.R.C. Products* [1993] IRLR 257.

Order of deductions. A question (which has also arisen in relation to the calculation of compensatory awards) is whether any *ex gratia* payment should be deducted before any contribution in respect of the employee's misconduct or after. There is no direct authority on the question in relation to basic awards, but, in relation to compensatory awards the E.A.T. has held that a payment in lieu of notice (and presumably an *ex gratia* payment) should be deducted after the contribution for contributory conduct: see *Derwent Coachworks v. Kirby* [1995] I.C.R. 48. The

E.A.T. did not follow its earlier decision in *Parker & Farr v. Shelvey* [1979] I.C.R. 896. It would be sensible to apply the same approach to basic awards.

Adopting that approach, the order (except if the dismissal was for redundancy) should be: (1) calculate basic award; (2) deduct from net amount in (1): (a) contribution for refusal of employer's reinstatement offer and (b) contribution for conduct; (3) deduct *ex gratia* payment.

If the dismissal was for redundancy, step (2) will consist of deducting (a) and (b) and then any redundancy payment paid to the employee. If the redundancy dismissal was automatically unfair by virtue of s.100(1)(a) or (b) (in health and safety cases), s.102(1) (dismissals of trustees of occupational pension schemes) or s.103 (dismissals of employee representatives), the order will be: (1) calculate basic award; (2) add £2,770; (3) deduct: (a) contribution for refusal of employer's reinstatement offer; (b) contribution for conduct (but only from the £2,700, or so much of it as represents the basic award); (c) redundancy payment; (4) deduct *ex gratia* payment.

A special award will also be payable: see s.125.

Compensatory award

123.—(1) Subject to the provisions of this section and sections 124 and 126, the amount of the compensatory award shall be such amount as the tribunal considers just and equitable in all the circumstances having regard to the loss sustained by the complainant in consequence of the dismissal in so far as that loss is attributable to action taken by the employer.

(2) The loss referred to in subsection (1) shall be taken to include—

(a) any expenses reasonably incurred by the complainant in consequence of the dismissal, and

(b) subject to subsection (3), loss of any benefit which he might reasonably be expected to have had but for the dismissal.

(3) The loss referred to in subsection (1) shall be taken to include in respect of any loss of—

(a) any entitlement or potential entitlement to a payment on account of dismissal by reason of redundancy (whether in pursuance of Part XI or otherwise), or

(b) any expectation of such a payment,

only the loss referable to the amount (if any) by which the amount of that payment would have exceeded the amount of a basic award (apart from any reduction under section 122) in respect of the same dismissal.

(4) In ascertaining the loss referred to in subsection (1) the tribunal shall apply the same rule concerning the duty of a person to mitigate his loss as applies to damages recoverable under the common law of England and Wales or (as the case may be) Scotland.

(5) In determining, for the purposes of subsection (1), how far any loss sustained by the complainant was attributable to action taken by the employer, no account shall be taken of any pressure which by—

(a) calling, organising, procuring or financing a strike or other industrial action, or

(b) threatening to do so,

was exercised on the employer to dismiss the employee; and that question shall be determined as if no such pressure had been exercised.

(6) Where the tribunal finds that the dismissal was to any extent caused or contributed to by any action of the complainant, it shall reduce the amount of the compensatory award by such proportion as it considers just and equitable having regard to that finding.

(7) If the amount of any payment made by the employer to the employee on the ground that the dismissal was by reason of redundancy (whether in pursuance of Part XI or otherwise) exceeds the amount of the basic award which would be payable but for section 122(4), that excess goes to reduce the amount of the compensatory award.

DEFINITIONS
    "employee": s.230(1).

"employer": s.230(4).
"redundancy": s.139.

GENERAL NOTE

The heads of loss which the compensatory award may cover were set out in *Norton Tool Co. v. Tewson* [1972] I.C.R. 501 and are: (1) immediate loss of wages; (2) manner of dismissal; (3) future loss of wages; and (4) loss of protection in respect of unfair dismissal or dismissal by reason of redundancy. To this, there has been added subsequently a fifth head—loss of pension rights. The tribunal must make sure that the various heads of compensation are considered; it is up to the complainant to prove the loss: see *Tidman v. Aveling Marshall* [1977] I.C.R. 506, at p.508. But "it is not ... to be expected that precise and detailed proof of every item of loss will be presented": *Norton Tool Co. v. Tewson* [1972] I.C.R. 501, at pp.504–505. The common law rules on assessment of damages are irrelevant: *Norton Tool*, at p.504.

In general, the purpose of the compensatory award is only to compensate the employee for financial loss sustained as a result of the dismissal, not for injury to pride or feelings and the like: *Norton Tool*, at pp.504 and 505. This can have the effect that, if the tribunal finds as a fact that the employee has suffered no loss as a result of the employer's action, there should be no compensatory award: *W. Devis & Sons v. Atkins* [1977] I.C.R. 662; *cf. Devonshire v. Trico-Folberth* [1989] I.C.R. 747. An example would be where the employee immediately found another job at the same, or a better, rate of pay; in such a case, however, he or she would still be entitled to receive a basic award, but the tribunal should not make a compensatory award: *Isleworth Studios v. Rickard* [1988] I.C.R. 432. Another example would be where evidence of misconduct which came to light after the dismissal shows that the employee suffered no injustice: *W. Devis & Sons v. Atkins*, above. In *Tele-Trading v. Jenkins* [1990] IRLR 430 the Court of Appeal said that in such a case s.123(1) applies rather than s.123(6), since conduct which came to light after the dismissal cannot be said to have caused or contributed to it. Conduct which occurs after the dismissal is not relevant, however, in calculating the compensatory award: *Soros v. Davison* [1994] I.C.R. 590.

It may also be appropriate for a tribunal to make no award of compensation under s.123(1) in cases where there was a procedural omission by the employer which made the dismissal unfair, but it is clear that, had the employer not acted unfairly, the result would still have been the same (particularly in redundancy cases): *Earl v. Slater & Wheeler (Airlyne)* [1972] I.C.R. 508, *Clarkson International Tools v. Short* [1973] I.C.R. 70 and *Robertson v. Magnet* [1993] IRLR 512. See also *Tele-Trading v. Jenkins* [1990] IRLR 430. The extent to which the compensatory award should be reduced in such circumstances is an issue whose ramifications are still being worked out in the light of the House of Lords decision in *Polkey v. A. E. Dayton Services* [1988] I.C.R. 142. In that case, Lord Bridge of Harwich said, at p.163:

"If it is held that taking the appropriate steps which the employer failed to take before dismissing the employee would not have affected the outcome, this will often lead to the result that the employee, though unfairly dismissed, will recover no compensation or, in the case of redundancy, no compensation in excess of his redundancy payment".

He went on to quote with approval the dictum of Browne-Wilkinson J. (as he then was) in *Sillifant v. Powell Duffryn Timber* [1993] IRLR 91, at p.96:

"If the tribunal thinks there is a doubt whether or not the employee would have been dismissed, this element can be reflected by reducing the normal amount of compensation by a percentage representing the chance that the employee would still have lost his employment".

See also *Mining Supplies (Longwall) v. Baker* [1988] IRLR 417. In *Red Bank Manufacturing Co. v. Meadows* [1992] I.C.R. 204 the E.A.T. said that when calculating compensation in circumstances where a dismissal is unfair because of a failure to go through a fair procedure, the tribunal must ask a two-stage question when calculating the compensation to be awarded: (1) if the proper procedure had been followed, would it have resulted in an offer of employment? and (2) if so, what would that employment have been and what wage would have been paid in respect of it? See also *Campbell v. Dunoon & Cowal Housing Association* [1993] IRLR 496, where the reduction was 75 per cent. Similarly, if the tribunal takes the view that there is a degree of uncertainty as whether the employee would have been fairly dismissed if the proper procedure had been followed, then a calculation has to be made of the chances of the employee continuing to receive his or her wages or receiving nothing. If the tribunal takes the view that there is a X per cent chance of receiving the wages, then there should be a reduction to X per cent of those wages: *Rao v. Civil Aviation Authority* [1994] I.C.R. 495 and *Campbell v. Dunoon & Cowal Housing Association* [1993] IRLR 496. See also *Wolesley Centers v. Simmons* [1994] I.C.R. 503.

More recently, the E.A.T. in Scotland has taken the view that the reduction of compensation suggested by Lord Bridge in *Polkey's* case should be confined to cases in which the unfairness of the dismissal arises from a failure to take steps which can properly be categorised as "procedural"; his observations do not apply where the grounds for holding a dismissal unfair arise from the substance of the decision: see *Steel Stockholders (Birmingham) v. Kirkwood* [1993] IRLR 515. This decision should be treated with considerable caution, however, in view of the criticisms to which it was subjected by the Court of Appeal in *O'Dea v. ISC Chemicals, t/a Rhône-Poulenc Chemicals* [1995] IRLR 599, particularly the observations of Peter Gibson, L.J. at p.604, paras. 24 and 25. See also *Boulton & Paul v. Arnold* [1994] IRLR 532. In cases such as those which have been discussed above, the burden is in effect on the employer: *Charles Letts & Co. v. Howard* [1976] IRLR 248. Theoretically, once an unfair dismissal has been established, the burden of proof in relation to loss lies on the employee. But, particularly where the tribunal is satisfied that the dismissal suffers from procedural unfairness, the employee will have a prima facie loss and very little is then required to cause the evidential burden to shift to the employer to show that the dismissal could, or would be likely to, have occurred in any event. If the employer fails to discharge that burden, there should be no reduction in compensation: *Britool v. Roberts* [1993] IRLR 481.

The degree of unfairness of the employer in dismissing an employee is not a relevant consideration in the assessment of what award is just and equitable in all the circumstances. So it is not permissible for the industrial tribunal to take into account a finding of fact that the employers, when dismissing an employee, intended to behave fairly towards their employees: *Morris v. Acco Co.* [1985] I.C.R. 306. The tribunal should not take into account the employee's conduct after the dismissal when assessing compensation: *Soros v. Davison* [1994] I.C.R. 590.

Ex gratia payments

The effect of *ex gratia* payments paid by the employer should also be noted. If such a payment is made, it should first be set off against the basic award and any surplus should then be carried forward and set off against the compensatory award: *Chelsea Football Club and Athletic Co. v. Heath* [1981] I.C.R. 323 and *Rushton v. Harcos Timber & Building Supplies* [1993] I.C.R. 230, *cf. Roadchef v. Hastings* [1988] IRLR 142, where the tribunal did not offset an *ex gratia* payment since they considered that an employer acting reasonably would have made the same payment after a period of prior warning. The E.A.T. held that the tribunal was entitled to make that finding: there was nothing to indicate that the employers would not have paid the same monies after a period of warning. If there is any surplus after the set off against the compensatory award, and an additional award falls to be made, the surplus should be set off against the additional award: *Darr v. L.R.C. Products* [1993] IRLR 257. The *ex gratia* payment or any other amount of money paid by the employer must be expressly or impliedly referable to the award of compensation: *Chelsea Football Club & Athletic Co. v. Heath* [1981] I.C.R. 323, at p.327. If the dismissal is for redundancy and the employer pays a redundancy payment and an *ex gratia* payment, the redundancy payment will be set off against the basic award and the *ex gratia* payment against the compensatory and, if appropriate, additional award: *Rushton v. Harcos Timber & Building Supplies* [1993] I.C.R. 230.

The order of calculation

Section 124(5) provides that the statutory maximum for a compensatory award (£11,300 at the time of going to press) should be ignored until the very end of the calculation. Any *ex gratia* payment should be deducted before the statutory maximum is applied and after any contribution for contributory fault: *McCarthy v. B.I.C.C.* [1985] IRLR 94 and *Derwent Coachworks v. Kirby* [1995] I.C.R. 48 (not following the previous decision in *Parker & Farr v. Shelvey* [1979] I.C.R. 896).

A further question here concerns the correct order of calculation when a "*Polkey*" reduction falls to be made in circumstances where a severance payment has been paid to an employee, the severance payment being in effect an enhanced redundancy payment. In *Cox v. Camden London Borough Council* [1996] I.C.R. 815, one division of the E.A.T. held that the deduction of the severance payment should be made first, followed by the "*Polkey*" reduction. In *Digital Equipment Co. v. Clements* [1996] I.C.R. 829, on the other hand, another division of the E.A.T., presided over by the then President, Mummery J., said that the correct order was to make a "*Polkey*" reduction *first*, followed by deduction of the severance payment. The second of the two cases, which was the later, did not consider the decision in the first. Pending clarification of the issue by the Court of Appeal, this area must remain in a state of confusion.

The order is as follows.

(1) Take the loss of earnings to the date of hearing (after allowing for failure to mitigate); then

(2) deduct any earnings received to the date of the hearing (but excluding wages earned from alternative employment during the period covered by any wages in lieu);

(3) deduct any amount for contributory fault;

(4) (a) deduct the amount of the *ex gratia* payment not deducted from the basic award; (b) deduct the amount of any wages paid in lieu of notice;

(5) the total thus far is the "prescribed element";

(6) add up the other heads of compensation as follows: (a) estimated future loss of wages; (b) loss of other benefits (before and after hearing); (c) loss of statutory industrial rights; (d) loss of

redundancy rights in excess of statutory entitlement; (e) loss of pension rights; (f) expenses incurred; then

(7) from sub-total arrived at after step 6, deduct amount for contributory fault;

(8) if appropriate, make a *"Polkey"* reduction, but only from compensatory award;

(9) deduct: (a) any excess of *ex gratia* payment not already deducted; (b) the amount of any wages paid in lieu of notice; (c) any excess of redundancy payment over basic award if paid by employer;

(10) if total exceeds £11,300, reduce to £11,300.

It is important when reducing the total to £11,300 to reduce all the elements in the compensatory award *pro rata*.: see reg. 5(2) of the Recoupment Regulations 1977–88 [full title given below], *Mason v. Wimpey Waste Management and Secretary of State for Employment* [1982] IRLR 454 and *Tipton v. West Midlands Co-operative Society (No. 2)* (E.A.T. 859/86). Otherwise, the prescribed element would bear the wrong proportion to the rest of the compensatory award, and there would be either too little or too much recoupment.

Subs. (1)

The calculation of the compensatory award is considered under the following headings: (1) loss of earnings to date of hearing; (2) future loss of earnings; (3) manner of dismissal; (4) loss of future protection; (5) loss of pension rights; and (6) other losses.

Expenses are considered in the note to subs. (2). The issues of mitigation, contributory fault, and other deductions are considered in the notes to subss. (3), (4), (6) and (7). Note the provisions of subs. (4), which requires the tribunal to ignore industrial pressure when calculating the compensatory award. See also s.107.

Loss of earnings to date of hearing. This head of loss is called the "prescribed element", since it is affected by the Recoupment Regulations 1977–88. The prescribed element should relate to the period for which the loss of earnings is awarded: see *Honan v. A1 Bacon Co.* [1996] I.C.R. 721. The general rule is that loss of earnings should be assessed to the date of the tribunal hearing and the employee is required to bring into account earnings from any new employment: *Ging v. Ellward Lancs.* (1978) 13 I.T.R. 265; see also the note on mitigation under subs. (4), below. If there is a dispute about the level of pay the employee was receiving at the time of dismissal, the tribunal must resolve the dispute: *Kinzley v. Minories Finance* [1988] I.C.R. 113. There may be exceptions to the general rule, for example where a long period elapses between the date of dismissal and the date of assessment and the employee obtains new employment. In that case, the loss should be assessed up to the start of the new employment and any loss caused by events after the start of the new employment becomes irrelevant: *Courtaulds Spinning v. Moosa* [1984] I.C.R. 218. See also *Gilham v. Kent County Council (No. 3)* [1986] I.C.R. 52. In dealing with cases of this kind, it is important that tribunals should not allow themselves to be bound by the formulae established by case law, but should remember the overriding words of s.74(1) and award the amount they consider just and equitable. See *Fentiman v. Fluid Engineering Products* [1991] I.C.R. 570, where the E.A.T. refused to apply the general rule in a case where a dismissed employee obtained new employment at a significantly higher rate of pay between the date of the dismissal and the date of the industrial tribunal hearing and where there was a considerable gap between the date of dismissal and the promulgation of the tribunal's decision.

A further problem arises in cases where the employee is dismissed, obtains a job at a lower rate of pay, and is then dismissed from that second job, as to whether the compensation against the first employer should be awarded in respect of a time after the dismissal by the second employer. According to the Court of Appeal in *Mabey Plant Hire v. Richens* (Court of Appeal, May 6, 1993) I.D.S. Brief 495, the tribunal should award compensation in respect of the difference between the wages paid in the first job and the second job, had the employee continued in it. They should not award compensation in respect of the loss of wages from the first job only, since the dismissal from the second job breaks the chain of causation. If there was a reduction for contributory fault in respect of the first dismissal, that should continue to affect the compensation awarded, but there should be no reduction for contributory fault in respect of the second: see the note to subs. (6), for a discussion of contributory fault.

Loss under this head is based on the employee's net take-home pay (after deduction of tax and social security contributions) but it may include regular overtime (net) and bonus earnings and tips: *Norton Tool Co. v. Tewson* [1972] I.C.R. 501 at p.506, *Brownson v. Hire Service Shops* [1978] I.C.R. 517 and *Palmanor v. Cedron* [1978] I.C.R. 1008. If the employee was dismissed without wages or wages in lieu of notice, the net wages for the notice period to which he or she was entitled will be included here.

The figure thus arrived at is subject to deductions. Wages paid in lieu of notice are deductible, but not wages earned by the employee during the period covered by the wages in lieu of notice: *Addison v. Babcock FATA* [1987] I.C.R. 805 and *T.B.A. Industrial Products v. Locke* [1984]

I.C.R. 228. If, as is usual, the wages in lieu of notice are paid gross, the gross amount should be deducted: *ibid.*, at p.235. No deduction will be made in respect of any unemployment or income support received, since this will be subject to recoupment by the Department of Employment: under the Employment Protection (Recoupment of Unemployment Benefit and Supplementary Benefit) Regulations 1977–1988 (S.I. 1977 No. 674, as amended by S.I. 1980 No. 1608 and S.I. 1988 No.419). There is no need for the industrial tribunal to make a reduction for an educational grant received by the employee in connection with a course embarked upon following the dismissal: see *Justfern v. D'Ingerthorpe* [1994] I.C.R. 286, at p.294. On the other hand, statutory sick pay and invalidity benefit should be deducted: see *Puglia v. C. James & Sons* [1996] I.C.R. 301. The E.A.T. did not follow the earlier decision of another division in *Hilton International Hotels (U.K.) v. Faraji* [1994] I.C.R. 259. *Cf. Rubenstein and Roskin t/a McGuffies Dispensing Chemist v. McGloughlin* [1996] IRLR 557, in which it was decided that it was just and equitable to deduct *half* of the invalidity benefit received by the employee. A deduction should only be made in respect of sickness benefit received by the employee if, had the employment continued, the benefit would have been deducted from his or her wages or he or she would have been disentitled from receiving any sickness benefit: *Sun & Sand v. Fitzjohn* [1979] I.C.R. 268.

If the employee receives a tax rebate of any size, that may be deductible, as may any damages for wrongful dismissal already awarded. No deductions are made in respect of unemployment benefit or supplementary benefit received by the employee, but part of the compensatory award is subject to the Employment Protection (Recoupment of Unemployment Benefit and Supplementary Benefit) Regulations 1977–1988.

The loss of benefits in kind (*e.g.* low interest mortgage, use of company car, medical insurance) should not be dealt with under this head, since the Recoupment Regulations only affect loss of earnings. Such losses should be dealt with under the heading of other losses: see below. It may be proper to include an amount in respect of loss of holiday leave and loss of a tax rebate; the tribunal should generally disregard the incidence of tax in respect of the tax on loss of earnings: *Tradewinds Airways v. Fletcher* [1981] IRLR 272, *Lucas v. Lawrence Scott Electromotors* [1983] I.C.R. 309 and *M.B.S. v. Calo* [1983] I.C.R. 459.

Future loss of earnings. This should be calculated on the basis of the difference between the employee's net take-home pay in the former job and that in the new job, if he or she has obtained one: *Norton Tool Co. v. Tewson* [1972] I.C.R. 501. Although the calculation of future loss is speculative, particularly where the employee has not obtained another job at the time of the tribunal hearing, the tribunal must have some evidence of the probable future loss and its scale before making an award: *Adda International v. Curcio* [1976] I.C.R. 407. Awards for future loss in respect of a period of six or nine months are not unlikely. In *Morganite Electric Carbon v. Donne* [1988] I.C.R. 18, the E.A.T. said that the award for future loss is not restricted to 26 to 52 weeks' pay and that the range must be determined by the evidence in any particular case. This is subject to the statutory maximum. Where, however, the unfair dismissal arises from the closure of the employer's business, the future loss element cannot extend beyond the date of complete closure of the business: *James W. Cook (Wivenhoe) v. Tipper* [1990] I.C.R. 716.

Where the employee has obtained another job, a comparison between the two jobs must obviously be made. If the new job is at the same or a higher salary the amount of compensation under this head is likely to be nominal. If, on the other hand, there is a shortfall, the tribunal will first need to compare the employee's salary prospects for the future in each job and see as best they can how long it will be before he or she reaches with the new employers the equivalent salary to that which he or she would have reached but for the dismissal: *Tradewinds Airways v. Fletcher* [1981] IRLR 272 at p.274, para. 8. See also *Mabey Plant Hire v. Richens* (Court of Appeal, May 6, 1993) I.D.S. Brief 495. They should then select an appropriate multiplier. The multiplier should reflect the tribunal's estimate of the future loss but should also take into account various discounting factors, such as the possibility that the employee might have resigned in the future. The fact that the receipt of earnings will be accelerated by the payment to the employee of a lump sum of compensation will also be a discount factor. See also *Cartiers Superfoods v. Laws* [1978] IRLR 315.

If the employee has not obtained another job, the exercise becomes more speculative. The tribunal will again have to find an appropriate multiplier, based on its local knowledge and experience of the labour market, but it should make clear its reasons for the period chosen: *Qualcast (Wolverhampton) v. Ross* [1979] I.C.R. 386. In arriving at a multiplier, the tribunal must also consider the circumstances of the employee's age and state of health or injuries suffered by him or her, which may make finding another job more difficult: *Fougère v. Phoenix Motor Co.* [1976] I.C.R. 495 and *Brittains (Arborfield) v. Van Uden* [1977] I.C.R. 211. See also *Devine v. Designer Flowers Wholesale Florist Sundries* [1993] IRLR 517, which considered *Fougère's* case. The tribunal must decide upon an appropriate cut-off point for the award for future loss. In *Holroyd v. Gravure Cylinders* [1984] IRLR 259, the dismissed employee embarked on a

12-month postgraduate university course. He tried to argue that the tribunal should have allowed for loss of earnings during the period of study and for some unspecified time after that. The E.A.T. rejected that argument, on the grounds that the employee effectively took himself out of the labour market by deciding to embark on the course. Any future loss at the end of the course was so remote as to be incapable of calculation. See also *Forth Estuary Engineering v. Litster* [1986] IRLR 59 and *Gilham v. Kent County Council (No. 3)* [1986] I.C.R. 52.

Compensation may be awarded for a time beyond the normal retiring age, if the tribunal finds that the employee would probably have stayed on beyond that time: *Barrel Plating & Phosphating Co. v. Danks* [1976] I.C.R. 503. If the employee in fact succeeds in finding another job fairly soon after the tribunal hearing, the employer may be able to apply to the tribunal for a review to consider reducing the amount of compensation: see the Industrial Tribunal (Constitution and Rules of Procedure) Regulations 1993 (S.I. 1993 No. 2687), reg. 11; see also *Yorkshire Engineering & Welding Co. v. Burnham* [1974] I.C.R. 77 and *Help The Aged Housing Association (Scotland) v. Vidler* [1977] IRLR 104.

Manner of dismissal. This will not generally be a head of compensation, unless there is cogent evidence that the manner of the dismissal caused financial loss, for example by making it more difficult to find future employment: *Vaughan v. Weighpack* [1974] I.C.R. 261, at pp.265–266.

Loss of future protection. An employee who succeeds in finding another job will not acquire the right not to be unfairly dismissed and the right to receive a redundancy payment for two years. This head of loss is effectively compensated for by the basic award, and so a nominal amount is usually awarded: see *S. H. Muffett v. Head* [1987] I.C.R. 1, where the E.A.T. said that £100 was the correct sum under this head. That case was decided some years ago, however, and the figure of £100 should presumably be revised, *cf.*, however, *Daley v. A. E. Dorsett (Almar Dolls)* [1982] I.C.R. 1, where an amount to reflect loss of notice entitlement was awarded.

Loss of an advantageous position in relation to redundancy (*e.g.* where the employee's contract gives an entitlement to a larger redundancy payment, if he or she is made redundant, than he or she would receive under the statutory entitlement) is a matter to be taken into account: *Lee v. I.P.C. Business Press* [1984] I.C.R. 306.

Loss of pension rights. This head has provided considerable difficulty and it is potentially capable of substantially increasing the amount of compensation. A committee of chairmen of industrial tribunals has considered this question and, in consultation with the Government Actuary's Department, produced guidelines, *Industrial Tribunals: Compensation for Loss of Pension Rights* (H.M.S.O. 1991). In *Bingham v. Hobourn Engineering* [1992] IRLR 298 the E.A.T. said that there is no duty on an industrial tribunal to follow the guidelines and, therefore, no error of law in not giving precise effect to the scheme they recommend. In each case, it is a question of evaluating the factors on either side to see what adjustment should be made or whether the guidelines are a safe guide at all. Even so, it is likely that the methods set out will be the most commonly used, since they are fairly simple to use and utilise information which the tribunal is likely to have before it by the end of the hearing.

The one figure which is likely to trouble tribunals is the percentage of reduction for the likelihood of withdrawal (*i.e.* that the employee would have left before retirement for reasons other than death or disability). This is a matter for the tribunal to assess after hearing all the evidence. In *T.B.A. Industrial Products v. Locke* [1984] I.C.R. 228 the tribunal applied a withdrawal factor of 70 per cent because of their view that there was "a very high degree of probability that the employee would have left the employment in any event due either to a continuation of his unsatisfactory work performance or to overall redundancy". They also applied a 70 per cent reduction in the total compensation awarded for contributory conduct. The employee appealed on the grounds that he had been penalised twice. The E.A.T. upheld the tribunal's approach, saying that the employee's unsatisfactory work performance had to be taken into account for two quite separate purposes.

Under the guidelines, loss of pension rights falls to be assessed under three heads: (1) loss of pension rights from the date of dismissal to the date of hearing; (2) loss of future pension rights; and (3) loss of enhancement of accrued pension rights. Appendix 2 of the guidelines contains a set of tables, in the form of flow charts, for calculating each head of loss. The first head is calculated by taking the employee's gross weekly pensionable pay and the employer's normal contribution as a percentage of the payroll. If the tribunal does not know it or cannot find it out from the employers, it should assume 10 per cent for contributory schemes and 15 per cent for noncontributory schemes. The weekly continuing pension loss thus ascertained should then be multiplied by the number of weeks between the effective date of termination and the date of the hearing: see Appendix 2, table 1. This figure is not part of the prescribed element. The second head is calculated by ascertaining the employee's weekly continuing pension loss in the same way as under the first head. From the figure there should be deducted the new employer's weekly contribution in the new pension scheme (if the employee has found a new job); if there is no scheme, 3 per cent of the weekly wages should be deducted. The figure thus arrived at should be multiplied by the number of weeks allowed for future loss of earnings whether total or partial. See Appendix 2, table 2. The third head, loss of enhancement of accrued pension rights, is arrived at by taking the deferred pension the employee will receive based on salary at leaving and his or her anticipated age of retirement. The appropriate multiplier should then be applied as set out in the table in Appendix 4. This amount should then be reduced by a percentage reflecting the tribunal's view of the likelihood of withdrawal. See Appendix 2, table 3. There are various situations in which an employee will receive no award under this head. They are also catered for in the flow chart in Appendix 2, table 3. Examples are employees in public sector schemes, employees in private sector who are near retirement age, and employees in whose case the tribunal has found that their employment would have terminated in any event within a period of up to a year.

Other losses. As was mentioned earlier, compensation will only be awarded in respect of financial loss, so that, for example, injury to pride or feelings, or loss of job satisfaction, will not be compensated. The E.A.T. has also said that the calculation of the compensatory award should exclude loss of allowances, since allowances are either a component of the employee's remuneration and chargeable to tax accordingly, or are paid to reimburse expenses actually incurred. In the latter case, the employee will suffer no loss if the new job has fewer allowances than the old job: *Tradewinds Airways v. Fletcher* [1981] IRLR 272. Loss caused to the employee by the employer's delay in giving a promised written reference, or failure to do so, should not be included in the calculation of the award: *Gallear v. J. F. Watson & Son* [1979] IRLR 306. Compensation in respect of the loss of fringe benefits will also be dealt with under this head, rather than under the head of loss of earnings to date of hearing. This is because the Recoupment Regulations only affect actual earnings. A common head of loss, which would fall to be dealt with here, is the loss of a company car. There is little guidance on how to calculate this loss, and the calculation will depend upon whether the employee has the use of the car as well as for the purposes of the job. One way to assess the loss is to take the scale charge for the car and for the petrol provided by the employer for private mileage by reference to which the employee is assessed to tax. For the purposes of taxation, this scale charge is increased if there is a low element of business mileage and decreased if there is a high element of business mileage. An alternative method of calculating the loss would be to use the schedule of running costs published by the Automobile Association. This tends to give a higher figure, particularly where the car involved is an expensive model with a large engine capacity.

There is no direct authority which offers any guidance on which of these two methods of calculating the loss is to be preferred. In *Shove v. Downs Surgical* [1984] I.C.R. 532, at pp.541–542, (a wrongful dismissal case), Sheen J. took the view that the scale charges used to calculate an employee's liability to tax do not afford a useful guide to calculating this head of loss as part of the damages to be awarded; he seems to have preferred the A.A. guidelines. Other fringe benefits which may be included under this head are loss of medical insurance, loss of preferential treatment (for example, low interest or interest-free loans) and loss of rights under a share option scheme.

Subs. (2)

This subsection enables any expense reasonably incurred to be included. This may include the cost of setting up one's own business but not the cost of presenting a complaint of unfair dismissal: *Gardiner-Hill v. Roland Berger Technics* [1982] IRLR 498 and *Nohar v. Granitstone* (1974) 9 I.T.R. 155. The costs of travel to interviews and of subscribing to appropriate trade journals or papers with job advertisements would be properly included under this head. It is arguable that the tribunal should take into account interest on an overdraft incurred as a result of the dismissal. Assuming that the employee can satisfy the tribunal that the overdraft interest was incurred as a result of the dismissal, s.74(2)(a) is wide enough to cover such an expense.

Subs. (3)

The loss to be included here is to include only the amount by which the amount of the redundancy payment would have exceeded the amount of the basic award, apart from any reductions under s.122. This is likely to arise where the employee is contractually entitled to a payment on redundancy which is in excess of his or her statutory entitlement. So if, for example, the contractual entitlement is to a payment of double the statutory amount, so that the employee is entitled to £1,500 by way of statutory payment and £3,000 by way of contractual entitlement, the £3,000 will be brought in at this stage. If it has already been paid, then it will be deducted by virtue of subs. (7): see the note to that subsection.

Subs. (4)

This subsection requires the industrial tribunal to apply the common law rules relating to mitigation of damages. It does not prevent a tribunal taking into account, as a failure on the part of an employee to mitigate, his or her conduct in unreasonably preventing a re-employment order from being complied with by the employer: see s.117(8).

The tribunal must address its mind to the question of mitigation; a failure to do so will be good grounds for an appeal: *Morganite Electrical Carbon v. Donne* [1988] I.C.R. 18. It should be noted, however, that the burden of proving mitigation lies on the employer: *Sturdy Finance v. Bardsley* [1979] IRLR 65 and *Fyfe v. Scientific Furnishings* [1989] I.C.R. 648. The employee's conduct before the dismissal should not be taken into account in determining the question of mitigation: *Prestwick Circuits v. McAndrew* [1990] IRLR 191. The rules require a dismissed employee to take reasonable steps to minimise his or her loss by looking for another job. If he or she fails to accept a reasonable offer, or to take any reasonable steps, an appropriate amount representing what he or she could have earned, will be deducted from the award of compensation. The general rule is that if the employee has obtained another job, the earnings from that job will go towards reducing the amount of compensation; this general rule is subject, however, to exceptions: see note to subs. (1) above. Earnings from part-time employment should be deducted: see *Justfern v. D'Ingerthorpe* [1994] I.C.R. 286. The rule to be applied in making deductions for mitigation is that, if the employee is dismissed without notice, net wages will be awarded for the notice period without making a deduction for earnings or potential earnings during the notice period: *Norton Tool Co. v. Tewson* [1972] I.C.R. 501, *Everwear Candlewick v. Isaac* [1974] I.C.R. 525 and *T.B.A. Industrial Products v. Locke* [1984] I.C.R. 229; *cf. Tradewinds Airways v. Fletcher* [1981] IRLR 272. But credit must be given for payment of salary or wages in lieu of notice received from the employers: *T.B.A. Industrial Products v. Locke*, above. This position was confirmed by the Court of Appeal in *Addison v. Babcock FATA* [1987] I.C.R. 805.

It is clear that the employee may be awarded no compensation in respect of loss of earnings, if he or she unreasonably refuses the employer's offer to consider him or her for vacancies which arise after the dismissal or unreasonably refuses an offer of reinstatement (in which case the tribunal may make no compensation award at all): *Gallear v. J. F. Watson & Son* [1979] IRLR 306 and *Sweetlove v. Redbridge & Waltham Forest Area Health Authority* [1979] IRLR 195. If, however, the employee's refusal of alternative employment precedes the dismissal, the industrial tribunal should treat that as contributory conduct rather than a failure to mitigate: *Trimble v. Supertravel* [1982] IRLR 451; see also *Martin v. Yeoman Aggregates* [1983] I.C.R. 314. In an appropriate case, for example where the employee is in his or her fifties, has occupied a senior position, and tries to utilise the experience gained in the employment by setting up his or her own business, it may be reasonable to try to do that rather than seek alternative employment, and it will not be right to treat that failure as a failure to mitigate: *Gardiner-Hill v. Roland Berger Technics* [1982] IRLR 498. In such cases, it is important to make sure that adequate evidence is put before the tribunal. If the evidence shows that the employee's earnings as a self-employed person will be lower than his or her previous earnings, that fall must be reflected in the amount of compensation awarded: *Lee v. I.P.C. Business Press* [1984] I.C.R. 306.

A failure by a dismissed employee to utilise an employer's internal appeal procedure cannot as a matter of law amount to a failure to mitigate his or her loss: see *Lock v. Connell Estate Agents* [1994] I.C.R. 983. In that case, the E.A.T. did not follow its previous decision in *Hoover v. Forde* [1980] I.C.R. 239, but instead followed the later decision of the Scottish division of the E.A.T. in *William Muir (Bond 9) v. Lamb* [1985] IRLR 95. When the industrial tribunal decides that there should be a reduction in the compensatory award for failure to mitigate, it should find the date by which the employee should have found work (or accepted an offer of reinstatement or re-employment) and assess the loss of wages, taking into account the failure to mitigate, up to that time; in other words, only that part of the compensatory award relating to loss of wages should be subject to the deduction. The tribunal should not calculate the compensatory award and reduce the whole award by a percentage: *Peara v. Enderlin* [1979] I.C.R. 804; see also *Gardiner-Hill v. Roland Berger Technics* [1982] IRLR 498.

Subs. (5)

Sections 107 and 123(5) of the Act oblige an industrial tribunal to ignore industrial pressure when determining the reason for the employee's dismissal and to determine the amount of the compensatory award, ignoring the effect of any actual or threatened industrial pressure. However, the employee's conduct in provoking the pressure (*e.g.* by ceasing to pay union subscriptions) may be relevant in reducing the amount of compensation: see *Morris v. Gestetner* [1973] I.C.R. 587 and *Sulemanji v. Toughened Glass* [1979] I.C.R. 799.

In cases of this kind, where the pressure was exercised because the employee was not a member of any trade union or a particular trade union (or one of a number of particular trade unions), s.160 of the Trade Union and Labour Relations (Consolidation) Act 1992 enables the employer or employee to ask the tribunal to join as a party to the proceedings anyone claimed to have exercised the pressure. The tribunal must grant the request if it is made before the hearing, but has a discretion as to whether to do so once the hearing has begun; once compensation has been awarded or a re-employment order made, no request for joinder may be made. If the tribunal considers the claim made by the employer or employee against the third party well-founded, s.160(3) enables it to order the party to make a total or partial contribution to the compensation, as it considers just and equitable in the circumstances.

Subs. (6)

The wording of this provision is narrower than the equivalent provision relating to the basic award, s.122(2). If the tribunal finds that the employee has contributed to some extent to the dismissal, it must reflect that finding in the award of compensation: *Morganite Electrical Carbon v. Donne* [1988] I.C.R. 18. A finding of contributory fault may also affect the tribunal's decision as to whether to make a re-employment order: see s.116. To make a reduction, the tribunal must make three findings: (1) that there was conduct on the part of the employee which was culpable or blameworthy, in the sense that it was "perverse or foolish, or ... bloody-minded ... or unreasonable in all the circumstances"; (2) that the dismissal was caused or contributed to to some extent by that conduct; and (3) that it was just and equitable, having regard to the first and second findings, to reduce the assessment of the employee's loss to a specified extent: *Nelson v. B.B.C. (No. 2)* [1979] I.C.R. 110 at pp.121–122 (Brandon L.J.).

Of the second, the E.A.T. has said: "... [W]hen one looks at what the Act requires, which is a finding that the dismissal was to any extent caused or contributed by any action of the complainant it is ... clear that no such direct and exclusive causal connection as a sole or principal or operative cause, is to be discerned in the statutory requirements. It is much looser than that ...": see *Polentarutti v. Autokraft* [1991] I.C.R. 757 at p.769. It appears also to be possible to make a reduction in cases of dismissal for lack of capacity: see *Finnie v. Top Hat Frozen Foods* [1985] I.C.R. 433. It will not amount to unreasonable conduct if the employee's action is lawful and proper, such as a refusal to obey an unlawful order: *Morrish v. Henlys (Folkestone)* [1973] I.C.R. 482.

The assessment of contributory fault is a separate stage in the procedure of fixing compensation, which should be clearly indicated by the tribunal: *Nudds v. W. & J. B. Eastwood* [1978] I.C.R. 171. There is no reason why a person held to have been constructively dismissed should not have their compensation reduced on the grounds of contributory fault: *Morrison v. Amalgamated Transport & General Workers' Union* [1989] IRLR 361 and *Polentarutti v. Autokraft* [1991] I.C.R. 757. The tribunal should approach the question of contributory fault in a broad common sense manner and the E.A.T. is not entitled to interfere with its conclusion unless the tribunal is wrong in law or its conclusion is one which no reasonable tribunal could have reached on the evidence; the apportionment of responsibility for the dismissal is a matter of impression, opinion and discretion: *Maris v. Rotherham C.B.C.* [1974] I.C.R. 435, *Hollier v. Plysu* [1983] IRLR 260 and *Warrilow v. Robert Walker* [1984] IRLR 304. There must be a causal connection between the actions of the employee and the dismissal, but the connection need not be direct and exclusive: see *Hutchinson v. Enfield Rolling Mills* [1981] IRLR 318. In assessing contributory fault the statutory provisions require the tribunal to confine its inquiry to the conduct of the employee and decide whether that conduct requires the amount of compensation to be reduced: *Parker Foundry v. Slack* [1992] I.C.R. 302; see also *Allders International v. Parkins* [1981] IRLR 68. In assessing contributory fault, acts of the employee's agent (*e.g.* advice given by solicitors) may be taken into account: *Allen v. Hammett* [1982] I.C.R. 227.

A further question concerns the effect of contributory fault on a "*Polkey*" reduction. This question was considered by the E.A.T. in *Rao v. Civil Aviation Authority* [1991] I.C.R. 503 and [1994] I.C.R. 495. The question arises in cases where the tribunal takes the view that there is a degree of uncertainty as to whether the employee would have been fairly dismissed if the proper procedure had been followed. In that case, the tribunal should calculate the loss of earnings and make appropriate deductions for mitigation. It should then make a reduction for contributory conduct. If it takes the view that there is a X per cent chance of receiving the amount so calculated, then there should be a reduction to X per cent of that amount. It is important to note that a *Polkey* reduction is separate from a reduction for contributory fault under this subsection: *Campbell v. Dunoon & Cowal Housing Association* [1993] IRLR 496.

Finally, the effect of the taking of industrial action needs to be considered in relation to contributory fault. In *Courtaulds Northern Spinning v. Moosa* [1984] I.C.R. 218 the E.A.T. said that the taking of industrial action should not be characterised as contributory fault. In *T.N.T. Express (U.K.) v. Downes* [1994] I.C.R. 1, however, it decided that the previous decision should not be followed, and industrial tribunals are entitled to examine the facts and circumstances surrounding the dismissal, including the circumstances surrounding the industrial action. In *Tracey v. Crosville Wales* [1996] I.C.R. 237, however, the Court of Appeal approved the E.A.T.'s decision in *Courtaulds Northern Spinning v. Moosa* and said that the tribunal should ignore the conduct represented by the industrial action in which the applicant had participated but that other blameworthy conduct of the applicant causing or contributing to the dismissal should be taken into account when deciding upon a reduction in compensation. The actual amount of the reduction for contributory fault is a question of fact for the tribunal, but it may be up to 100 per cent: see, for example, *Smith v. Lodge Bros. (Funerals)* (E.A.T. 92/88) and *Chaplin v. H. J. Rawlinson* [1991] I.C.R. 553. Although subs. (5) does not allow compensation to reflect the loss suffered by the employee as a consequence of industrial pressure, his or her conduct in provoking that pressure may be relevant in assessing contributory fault: *Sulemanji v. Toughened Glass* [1979] I.C.R. 799 (the employee stopped paying his union subscriptions); see also *Colwyn B.C. v. Dutton* [1980] IRLR 420.

In certain cases, the industrial tribunal may have to consider carefully whether to categorise the employee's conduct as amounting to a failure to mitigate or as contributory conduct: see, for example, *Trimble v. Supertravel* [1981] IRLR 68. The amount of the contribution should be deducted from the total amount of the compensatory award, ignoring the statutory maximum (£11,300 at the time of going to press). The maximum only operates if the reduced figure exceeds £11,300: see s.124(5) and *Walter Braund (London) v. Murray* [1991] I.C.R. 327.

The general note to this section sets out the order in which the compensatory award should be calculated, including cases where contributory fault is involved.

Subs. (7)

This subsection provides that, if the amount by which any redundancy payment paid by the employer to the employee (whether paid in pursuance of the employer's statutory obligation or otherwise) exceeds the basic award which would be payable but for s.122(4), that amount will be deducted from the compensatory award. This provision is the obverse of s.123(3), which provides for the tribunal to take into account an employee's entitlement to a redundancy payment in excess of the statutory amount. The entitlement is to be taken into account in calculating the compensatory award, but must be deducted if actually paid. The sort of payments likely to be affected here are payments to which employees are contractually entitled on redundancy under schemes set up by their employers. Such payments are likely to be calculated by reference to the employee's statutory entitlement but to exceed it. Thus an employee entitled to a statutory payment of £1,500 may also be entitled to receive £3,000 from an employer's scheme, if, for example, the scheme provides for payments to be made of double the statutory amount.

The decision of the E.A.T. in *Boorman v. Allmakes* [1995] I.C.R. 842 should be noted. Although it is a decision on the equivalent provision relating to basic awards, s.122(4), it is arguable that its reasoning applies in this context also. If that is correct, subs. (7) will only apply to payments made where the dismissal is in fact due to redundancy. See also the note to s.122(4), above.

Limit of compensatory award etc.

124.—(1) The amount of—

(a) any compensation awarded to a person under section 117(1) and (2), or

(b) a compensatory award to a person calculated in accordance with section 123,

shall not exceed £11,300.

(2) The Secretary of State may by order increase the sum specified in subsection (1).

(3) In the case of compensation awarded to a person under section 117(1) and (2), the limit imposed by this section may be exceeded to the extent necessary to enable the award fully to reflect the amount specified as payable under section 114(2)(a) or section 115(2)(d).

(4) Where—

(a) a compensatory award is an award under paragraph (a) of subsection (3) of section 117, and

(b) an additional award falls to be made under paragraph (b) of that subsection,

the limit imposed by this section on the compensatory award may be exceeded to the extent necessary to enable the aggregate of the compensatory and additional awards fully to reflect the amount specified as payable under section 114(2)(a) or section 115(2)(d).

(5) The limit imposed by this section applies to the amount which the industrial tribunal would, apart from this section, award in respect of the subject matter of the complaint after taking into account—
  (a) any payment made by the respondent to the complainant in respect of that matter, and
  (b) any reduction in the amount of the award required by any enactment or rule of law.

GENERAL NOTE

This section provides for a limit to the compensatory award, which may be raised by the Secretary of State by order under subs. (2). It is not necessary before deciding whether to increase the limit to have regard to the matters set out in s.208(2), which only applies when considering the limit on a week's pay. It should be noted that subss. (3) and (4) exclude from the ambit of subs. (1) awards of arrears of pay made in the context of a reinstatement or re-engagement order which has not been complied with. There is thus no statutory maximum to the amount which may be ordered to be paid under ss.114(2)(a) or 115(2)(d). This is the effect of the amendments introduced by s.30 of the Trade Union Reform and Employment Rights Act 1993, which reversed the effect of the decision in *O'Laoire v. Jackel International* [1990] I.C.R. 197.

Subsection (5) provides that the statutory maximum for a compensatory award (£11,300 at the time of going to press) should be ignored until the very end of the calculation. Any *ex gratia* payment should be deducted before the statutory maximum is applied and after any contribution for contributory fault: *McCarthy v. B.I.C.C.* [1985] IRLR 94 and *Derwent Coachworks v. Kirby* [1995] I.C.R. 48 (not following the previous decision in *Parker & Farr v. Shelvey* [1979] I.C.R. 896). The amount of any contribution should be deducted from the total amount of the compensatory award, ignoring the statutory maximum (£11,300 at the time of going to press). The maximum only operates if the reduced figure exceeds £11,300: see s.124(5) and *Walter Braund (London) v. Murray* [1991] I.C.R. 327. If the compensatory award falls to be reduced to £11,300 because it exceeds that limit, all the elements in the compensatory award should be reduced *pro rata*: see reg. 5(2) of the Recoupment Regulations, *Mason v. Wimpey Waste Management and Secretary of State for Employment* [1982] IRLR 454 and *Tipton v. West Midlands Co-operative Society (No. 2)* (E.A.T. 859/86). Otherwise, the prescribed element will bear the wrong proportion to the rest of the compensatory award, and there will be either too little or too much recoupment.

Special award

125.—(1) Subject to the following provisions, the amount of the special award shall be—
  (a) one week's pay multiplied by 104, or
  (b) £13,775,
whichever is the greater, but shall not exceed £27,500.

(2) Where the award of compensation is made under section 117(3)(a) then, unless the employer satisfies the tribunal that it was not practicable to comply with the order under section 113, the amount of the special award shall be increased to—
  (a) one week's pay multiplied by 156, or
  (b) £20,600,
whichever is the greater (but subject to the following provisions).

(3) In a case where the amount of the basic award is reduced under section 119(4), the amount of the special award shall be reduced by the same fraction.

(4) Where the tribunal considers that any conduct of the complainant before the dismissal (or, where the dismissal was with notice, before the notice was given) was such that it would be just and equitable to reduce or further reduce the amount of the special award to any extent, the tribunal shall reduce or further reduce that amount accordingly.

(5) Where the tribunal finds that the complainant has unreasonably—
  (a) prevented an order under section 113 from being complied with, or

(b) refused an offer by the employer (made otherwise than in compliance with such an order) which, if accepted, would have the effect of reinstating the complainant in his employment in all respects as if he had not been dismissed,

the tribunal shall reduce or further reduce the amount of the special award to such extent as it considers just and equitable having regard to that finding.

(6) Where the employer has engaged a permanent replacement for the complainant, the tribunal shall not take that fact into account in determining for the purposes of subsection (2) whether it was practicable to comply with an order under section 113 unless the employer shows that it was not practicable for him to arrange for the complainant's work to be done without engaging a permanent replacement.

(7) The Secretary of State may by order increase any of the sums specified in subsections (1) and (2).

DEFINITIONS
"employer": s.230(4).
"week's pay": ss.220–229.

GENERAL NOTE
A special award is only available under this section to employees where the dismissal is automatically unfair because they were dismissed, or selected for redundancy, for reasons connected with health and safety (contrary to s.100(1)(a) or (b)), performance of the functions of the trustee of an occupational pension scheme (contrary to s.102(1)) or performance of the functions or activities of an employee representative (contrary to s.103). A special award is also available under s.157(1) of the Trade Union and Labour Relations (Consolidation) Act 1992 where the dismissal is automatically unfair by virtue of the provisions of ss.152 or 153 of that Act (which deal with dismissal for trade union membership and activities). The employee will only qualify for the award if he or she has asked for an order of reinstatement or re-engagement and the tribunal has either not made one and has proceeded to assess compensation or has made an order with which the employer has totally failed to comply: see s.118(2). In cases where the dismissal is not made automatically unfair by virtue of the provisions set out above, the employee will receive an additional award or a higher additional award of compensation, rather than a special award. The remedy is not available where s.121 applies: see s.118(2)(b). This is in cases where an employee is entitled to a minimum basic award of two weeks' pay, where the dismissal was by reason of redundancy but he or she is disentitled because of the provisions of s.141, or where an employee is treated as not having been dismissed because of the operation of s.138.

Where the tribunal decides not to make an order for re-employment and goes on to award compensation, the amount of the award will be either one week's pay multiplied by 104 or £13,775, whichever is the greater; it may not exceed £27,500: see subs. (1). If, however, the tribunal is making an award of compensation because of the employer's total failure to comply with a re-employment order, the amount will be one week's pay multiplied by 156 or £20,600, whichever is greater, unless the employer can show that it was not practicable to comply with the order: see subs. (2). (Note also the provisions of subs. (6) in cases where the employer has engaged a permanent replacement). It should be noted that the amount of a week's pay in this context is not subject to a statutory ceiling imposed by s.227(1): see *Port of London Authority v. Payne* [1994] IRLR 9, at p.17.

There are few reported examples of a special award. In *Artisan Press v. Srawley* [1986] I.C.R. 328 the E.A.T. held that there had been a total failure to comply with a re-employment order, in a case where employees were held to have been unfairly dismissed because of their membership of a trade union. The E.A.T. upheld the tribunal's award of £18,367 and £20,080 to the two employees concerned. See also *Port of London Authority v. Payne* [1994] IRLR 9.

The Secretary of State is empowered by subs. (7) to raise the amounts of £13,775, £20,600 and £27,500. The award will be reduced in the case of employees over 64: see subs. (3) and s.119(4). It is liable to reduction under subs. (4) in cases where the employee's conduct before the dismissal makes it just and equitable to reduce the award, and under subs. (5) in cases where the employee has unreasonably prevented a re-employment order from being complied with or unreasonably refused an offer of reinstatement made by the employer. In the case where the employee has unreasonably prevented a re-employment order from being complied with by the employer, the tribunal must take that conduct into account when making a compensatory award of compensation and treat it as a failure to mitigate: see s.117(8).

Acts which are both unfair dismissal and discrimination

126.—(1) This section applies where compensation falls to be awarded in respect of any act both under—

(a) the provisions of this Act relating to unfair dismissal, and

(b) either or both of the Sex Discrimination Act 1975 and the Race Relations Act 1976.

(2) An industrial tribunal shall not award compensation under any one of those two or three Acts in respect of any loss or other matter which is or has been taken into account under the other, or any of the others, by the tribunal (or another industrial tribunal) in awarding compensation on the same or another complaint in respect of that act.

GENERAL NOTE

This section is aimed at preventing double recovery in cases where compensation falls to be awarded for an unlawful act of sex or racial discrimination and an unfair dismissal. Thus, for example, compensation in respect of loss of wages from the date of dismissal to the date of the hearing should only be awarded once, even if the dismissal is also an unlawful act of discrimination.

Dismissal of woman at or after end of maternity leave period

127. Where section 84 applies in relation to an employee, compensation in any unfair dismissal proceedings shall be assessed without regard to the right conferred on the employee by section 79.

DEFINITIONS

"employee": s.230(1).

GENERAL NOTE

A dismissal after the end of the maternity leave period will not affect the employee's right to return to work under s.79. This section provides that compensation in any unfair dismissal proceedings arising out of the dismissal will be assessed without regard to her right to return. But the employer may make it a condition of her exercising her right that she repays any redundancy payment or compensation for unfair dismissal paid in respect of that dismissal: see s.84(2).

Interim relief

Interim relief pending determination of complaint

128.—(1) An employee who presents a complaint to an industrial tribunal—

(a) that he has been unfairly dismissed by his employer, and

(b) that the reason (or, if more than one, the principal reason) for the dismissal is one of those specified in section 100(1)(a) and (b), 102(1) or 103,

may apply to the tribunal for interim relief.

(2) The tribunal shall not entertain an application for interim relief unless it is presented to the tribunal before the end of the period of seven days immediately following the effective date of termination (whether before, on or after that date).

(3) The tribunal shall determine the application for interim relief as soon as practicable after receiving the application.

(4) The tribunal shall give to the employer not later than seven days before the date of the hearing a copy of the application together with notice of the date, time and place of the hearing.

(5) The tribunal shall not exercise any power it has of postponing the hearing of an application for interim relief except where it is satisfied that special circumstances exist which justify it in doing so.

DEFINITIONS

"effective date of termination": s.97.

"employee": s.230(1).
"employer": s.230(4).

GENERAL NOTE
    The remedy of interim relief is available under this section to employees who allege that they
were dismissed for a reason connected with health and safety (contrary to s.100(1)(a) and (b)),
or performance of the functions of the trustee of an occupational pension scheme (contrary to
s.102(1)) or performance of the functions or activities of an employee representative (contrary
to s.103). It may be noted that interim relief is also available under s.161(1) of the Trade Union
and Labour Relations (Consolidation) Act 1992 where they allege that they were dismissed for
trade union reasons contrary to s.152 of that Act. See *Barley v. Amey Roadstone Corporation*
[1977] I.C.R. 546.
    The employee is required by subs. (2) to apply within seven days of the effective date of
termination. The subsection uses the term "present" in relation to the application. See the note
to s.111(2), where this term is considered. Subsections (3) and (4) require the tribunal to determine the application as soon as practicable after receiving the application, and to give the
employer a copy of both and a notice of the date, time and place of the hearing at least seven days
before the hearing. It may only postpone the hearing in special circumstances: see subs. (5).

Procedure on hearing of application and making of order

    129.—(1) This section applies where, on hearing an employee's appli-
cation for interim relief, it appears to the tribunal that it is likely that on
determining the complaint to which the application relates the tribunal will
find that the reason (or, if more than one, the principal reason) for his dismissal is one of those specified in section 100(1)(a) and (b), 102(1) or 103.
    (2) The tribunal shall announce its findings and explain to both parties (if
present)—
    (a) what powers the tribunal may exercise on the application, and
    (b) in what circumstances it will exercise them.
    (3) The tribunal shall ask the employer (if present) whether he is willing,
pending the determination or settlement of the complaint—
    (a) to reinstate the employee (that is, to treat him in all respects as if he
        had not been dismissed), or
    (b) if not, to re-engage him in another job on terms and conditions not less
        favourable than those which would have been applicable to him if he
        had not been dismissed.
    (4) For the purposes of subsection (3)(b) "terms and conditions not less
favourable than those which would have been applicable to him if he had not
been dismissed" means, as regards seniority, pension rights and other similar
rights, that the period prior to the dismissal should be regarded as continuous
with his employment following the dismissal.
    (5) If the employer states that he is willing to reinstate the employee, the
tribunal shall make an order to that effect.
    (6) If the employer—
    (a) states that he is willing to re-engage the employee in another job,
        and
    (b) specifies the terms and conditions on which he is willing to do so,
the tribunal shall ask the employee whether he is willing to accept the job on
those terms and conditions.
    (7) If the employee is willing to accept the job on those terms and con-
ditions, the tribunal shall make an order to that effect.
    (8) If the employee is not willing to accept the job on those terms and
conditions—
    (a) where the tribunal is of the opinion that the refusal is reasonable, the
        tribunal shall make an order for the continuation of his contract of
        employment, and
    (b) otherwise, the tribunal shall make no order.
    (9) If on the hearing of an application for interim relief the employer—
    (a) fails to attend before the tribunal, or

(b) states that he is unwilling either to reinstate or re-engage the employee as mentioned in subsection (3),

the tribunal shall make an order for the continuation of the employee's contract of employment.

DEFINITIONS
"contract of employment": s.230(2).
"employee": s.230(1).
"employer": s.230(4).

GENERAL NOTE

At the interim relief hearing, if the tribunal considers it "likely" that on hearing the substantive complaint the tribunal will find that the dismissal was unfair by virtue of ss.100(1)(a) or (b), 102(1) or 103, it must announce its findings and explain the powers it has: subss. (1) and (2). It must also ask the employer if he or she is prepared to re-employ the employee: subs. (3). If he or she is prepared to do so, the tribunal will make an appropriate order under subss. (5) or (7). In the case of a re-engagement order, the tribunal must also ask the employee whether he or she is willing to accept the proposed terms and conditions. If the employer does not appear, or refuses to re-employ the employee, the tribunal must make an order for the continuation of the employee's contract under s.130. The word "likely" was interpreted by Slynn J. as meaning that the employee must have a "pretty good" chance of success: see *Taplin v. C. Shippam* [1978] I.C.R. 1068.

Order for continuation of contract of employment

130.—(1) An order under section 129 for the continuation of a contract of employment is an order that the contract of employment continue in force—

(a) for the purposes of pay or any other benefit derived from the employment, seniority, pension rights and other similar matters, and

(b) for the purposes of determining for any purpose the period for which the employee has been continuously employed,

from the date of its termination (whether before or after the making of the order) until the determination or settlement of the complaint.

(2) Where the tribunal makes such an order it shall specify in the order the amount which is to be paid by the employer to the employee by way of pay in respect of each normal pay period, or part of any such period, falling between the date of dismissal and the determination or settlement of the complaint.

(3) Subject to the following provisions, the amount so specified shall be that which the employee could reasonably have been expected to earn during that period, or part, and shall be paid—

(a) in the case of a payment for any such period falling wholly or partly after the making of the order, on the normal pay day for that period, and

(b) in the case of a payment for any past period, within such time as may be specified in the order.

(4) If an amount is payable in respect only of part of a normal pay period, the amount shall be calculated by reference to the whole period and reduced proportionately.

(5) Any payment made to an employee by an employer under his contract of employment, or by way of damages for breach of that contract, in respect of a normal pay period, or part of any such period, goes towards discharging the employer's liability in respect of that period under subsection (2); and, conversely, any payment under that subsection in respect of a period goes towards discharging any liability of the employer under, or in respect of breach of, the contract of employment in respect of that period.

(6) If an employee, on or after being dismissed by his employer, receives a lump sum which, or part of which, is in lieu of wages but is not referable

to any normal pay period, the tribunal shall take the payment into account in determining the amount of pay to be payable in pursuance of any such order.

(7) For the purposes of this section, the amount which an employee could reasonably have been expected to earn, his normal pay period and the normal pay day for each such period shall be determined as if he had not been dismissed.

DEFINITIONS
"contract of employment": s.230(2).
"employee": s.230(1).
"employer": s.230(4).

GENERAL NOTE
This section sets out what is meant by an order for the continuation of the employee's contract of employment. Such an order is an order that the employee's contract is to continue in force until the complainant is determined (or settled), for the purposes of pay, seniority, pension rights and "any other benefit derived from the employment" and for calculating continuity of employment. Subsections (2) to (4) require the tribunal to make ancillary orders dealing specifically with pay; subss. (5) and (6) require it to take into account payments made by the employer to the employee.

Application for variation or revocation of order

131.—(1) At any time between—
(a) the making of an order under section 129, and
(b) the determination or settlement of the complaint,
the employer or the employee may apply to an industrial tribunal for the revocation or variation of the order on the ground of a relevant change of circumstances since the making of the order.

(2) Sections 128 and 129 apply in relation to such an application as in relation to an original application for interim relief except that, in the case of an application by the employer, section 128(4) has effect with the substitution of a reference to the employee for the reference to the employer.

DEFINITIONS
"employee": s.230(1).
"employer": s.230(4).

GENERAL NOTE
This section enables either the employer or the employee to apply to the tribunal for the revocation or variation of the tribunal's order on the ground of a relevant change of circumstances since the making of the order. The application may be made between the making of the order and the determination or settlement of the complaint of unfair dismissal: see subs. (1). The tribunal which hears the application need not be the tribunal which made the original order: *British Coal Corporation v. McGinty* [1987] I.C.R. 912.

Consequence of failure to comply with order

132.—(1) If, on the application of an employee, an industrial tribunal is satisfied that the employer has not complied with the terms of an order for the reinstatement or re-engagement of the employee under section 129(5) or (7), the tribunal shall—
(a) make an order for the continuation of the employee's contract of employment, and
(b) order the employer to pay compensation to the employee.

(2) Compensation under subsection (1)(b) shall be of such amount as the tribunal considers just and equitable in all the circumstances having regard—
(a) to the infringement of the employee's right to be reinstated or re-engaged in pursuance of the order, and
(b) to any loss suffered by the employee in consequence of the non-compliance.

(3) Section 130 applies to an order under subsection (1)(a) as in relation to an order under section 129.

(4) If on the application of an employee an industrial tribunal is satisfied that the employer has not complied with the terms of an order for the continuation of a contract of employment subsection (5) or (6) applies.

(5) Where the non-compliance consists of a failure to pay an amount by way of pay specified in the order—

(a) the tribunal shall determine the amount owed by the employer on the date of the determination, and

(b) if on that date the tribunal also determines the employee's complaint that he has been unfairly dismissed, it shall specify that amount separately from any other sum awarded to the employee.

(6) In any other case, the tribunal shall order the employer to pay the employee such compensation as the tribunal considers just and equitable in all the circumstances having regard to any loss suffered by the employee in consequence of the non-compliance.

DEFINITIONS
"employee": s.230(1).
"employer": s.230(4).

GENERAL NOTE
This section contains provisions which apply in cases where the employer fails to comply with an interim relief order. If the tribunal made a reinstatement or re-engagement order and the employer fails to comply, the employee may apply to the tribunal. It will make an order for the continuation of the employee's contract and order the employer to pay the employee whatever amount of compensation it considers just and equitable. Section 130 will then apply: see subs. (3).

If the employer fails to comply with an order for the continuation of the employee's contract and the non-compliance consists of a failure to pay an amount of pay specified in the order, the tribunal must determine the amount owed by the employer on the date of its determination: see subss. (4) and (5). In any other case, the tribunal will order the employer to pay whatever amount of compensation it considers just and equitable in all the circumstances having regard to any loss suffered by the employee in consequence of the non-compliance: see subs. (6).

CHAPTER III

SUPPLEMENTARY

Death of employer or employee

133.—(1) Where—

(a) an employer has given notice to an employee to terminate his contract of employment, and

(b) before that termination the employee or the employer dies,

this Part applies as if the contract had been duly terminated by the employer by notice expiring on the date of the death.

(2) Where—

(a) an employee's contract of employment has been terminated,

(b) by virtue of subsection (2) or (4) of section 97 a date later than the effective date of termination as defined in subsection (1) of that section is to be treated for certain purposes as the effective date of termination, and

(c) the employer or the employee dies before that date,

subsection (2) or (4) of section 97 applies as if the notice referred to in that subsection as required by section 86 expired on the date of the death.

(3) Where an employee has died, sections 113 to 116 do not apply; and, accordingly, if the industrial tribunal finds that the grounds of the complaint

are well-founded, the case shall be treated as falling within section 112(4) as a case in which no order is made under section 113.

(4) Subsection (3) does not prejudice an order for reinstatement or re-engagement made before the employee's death.

(5) Where an order for reinstatement or re-engagement has been made and the employee dies before the order is complied with—

(a) if the employer has before the death refused to reinstate or re-engage the employee in accordance with the order, subsections (3) to (6) of section 117 apply, and an award shall be made under subsection (3)(b) of that section, unless the employer satisfies the tribunal that it was not practicable at the time of the refusal to comply with the order, and

(b) if there has been no such refusal, subsections (1) and (2) of that section apply if the employer fails to comply with any ancillary terms of the order which remain capable of fulfilment after the employee's death as they would apply to such a failure to comply fully with the terms of an order where the employee had been reinstated or re-engaged.

DEFINITIONS
    "contract of employment": s.230(2).
    "effective date of termination": s.97.
    "employee": s.230(1).
    "employer": s.230(4).

GENERAL NOTE
    This section contains ancillary provisions dealing with the situation where the employer or employee dies. If either of them dies before the notice of dismissal, the Act applies as if the employee's contract had been terminated with notice expiring on the date of the death: subs. (1). Subsection (2) applies where the provisions of s.97(2) or (4) operate to postpone the effective date of termination. The provisions relating to re-employment orders do not apply, unless an order was made before the employee's death: see subss. (3) and (4). Subsection (5) applies where the employee dies after the making of an order but before it is complied with.

Teachers in aided schools

134.—(1) Where a teacher in an aided school is dismissed by the governors of the school in pursuance of a requirement of the local education authority under paragraph (a) of the proviso to section 24(2) of the Education Act 1944, this Part has effect in relation to the dismissal as if—

(a) the local education authority had at all material times been the teacher's employer,

(b) the local education authority had dismissed him, and

(c) the reason or principal reason for which they did so had been the reason or principal reason for which they required his dismissal.

(2) For the purposes of a complaint under section 111 as it has effect by virtue of subsection (1)—

(a) section 117(4)(a) applies as if for the words "not practicable to comply" there were substituted the words "not practicable for the local education authority to permit compliance", and

(b) section 123(5) applies as if the references in it to the employer were to the local education authority.

Part XI

Redundancy payments etc.

Chapter I

Right to redundancy payment

The right

135.—(1) An employer shall pay a redundancy payment to any employee of his if the employee—

(a) is dismissed by the employer by reason of redundancy, or

(b) is eligible for a redundancy payment by reason of being laid off or kept on short-time.

(2) Subsection (1) has effect subject to the following provisions of this Part (including, in particular, sections 140 to 144, 149 to 152, 155 to 161 and 164).

Definitions

"employee": s.230(1).
"employer": s.230(4).
"redundancy": s.235(3).
"redundancy payment": s.162.

General Note

Employees dismissed for redundancy have two main statutory rights: (i) the right to complain of unfair dismissal under the provisions of Pt. X of the Act (ss.94–134); and (ii) the right to claim a redundancy payment under the provisions of Pt. XI of the Act (ss.135–181). In addition, they have the right to time off during their notice period to look for new employment or make arrangements for training for further employment. Both main rights require a two-year qualifying period; in the case of the right not to be unfairly dismissed, that requirement is sometimes lifted: see the notes to s.108. As with unfair dismissal claims, the employee must have been dismissed. The definition of "dismiss" is considered in the notes to ss.136–138. It should be noted that, in the case of redundancy payments claims, the definition is extended in cases where the employee is offered alternative employment. The definition of "redundancy" is common to both the Pt. X and the Pt. XI rights. Apart from the definition of redundancy, however, the two Parts are completely self-contained. This means that the provisions of Pt. XI are not applicable to unfair dismissal claims, nor are those of Pt. X applicable to redundancy payments claims. It will be an error of law if a tribunal applies the wrong provisions to the wrong type of claim: *Hempell v. W. H. Smith & Sons* [1986] I.C.R. 365.

In general, an employee dismissed for redundancy will be advised to complain of unfair dismissal or make a dual claim. This is because a complaint under the unfair dismissal provisions enables the industrial tribunal to decide whether the employer's decision to dismiss was reasonable in all the circumstances, whereas the redundancy payments provisions merely enable the tribunal to decide whether the statutory presumption of redundancy has or has not been rebutted. Further, the unfair dismissal provisions give an employee the possibility of receiving greater compensation, in the form of the basic award, which is calculated in the same way as a redundancy payment, and a compensatory award, which is not available under the redundancy payments provisions. In the case of a dual claim, the successful employee will either receive a basic award or a redundancy payment, but not both, since s.122 contains set-off provisions.

Although s.135 provides for redundancy payments to be paid where employees are dismissed for redundancy or where they are laid off or kept on short-time, the large majority of cases concern the first type of payment.

Chapter II

Right on dismissal by reason of redundancy

Dismissal by reason of redundancy

Circumstances in which an employee is dismissed

136.—(1) Subject to the provisions of this section and sections 137 and 138, for the purposes of this Part an employee is dismissed by his employer if (and only if)—

(a) the contract under which he is employed by the employer is terminated by the employer (whether with or without notice),

(b) he is employed under a contract for a fixed term and that term expires without being renewed under the same contract, or

(c) the employee terminates the contract under which he is employed (with or without notice) in circumstances in which he is entitled to terminate it without notice by reason of the employer's conduct.

(2) Subsection (1)(c) does not apply if the employee terminates the contract without notice in circumstances in which he is entitled to do so by reason of a lock-out by the employer.

(3) An employee shall be taken to be dismissed by his employer for the purposes of this Part if—

(a) the employer gives notice to the employee to terminate his contract of employment, and

(b) at a time within the obligatory period of notice the employee gives notice in writing to the employer to terminate the contract of employment on a date earlier than the date on which the employer's notice is due to expire.

(4) In this Part the "obligatory period of notice", in relation to notice given by an employer to terminate an employee's contract of employment, means—

(a) the actual period of the notice in a case where the period beginning at the time when the notice is given and ending at the time when it expires is equal to the minimum period which (by virtue of any enactment or otherwise) is required to be given by the employer to terminate the contract of employment, and

(b) the period which—

(i) is equal to the minimum period referred to in paragraph (a), and

(ii) ends at the time when the notice expires,

in any other case.

(5) Where in accordance with any enactment or rule of law—

(a) an act on the part of an employer, or

(b) an event affecting an employer (including, in the case of an individual, his death),

operates to terminate a contract under which an employee is employed by him, the act or event shall be taken for the purposes of this Part to be a termination of the contract by the employer.

DEFINITIONS
"employee": s.230(1).
"employer": s.230(4).

GENERAL NOTE

The provisions of subs. (1) are identical to those of s.95(1) in Pt. X, and reference should therefore be made to the notes to that subsection. In addition, however, the provisions of subs. (2) should be noted; these are not to be found in s.95 and disapply the constructive dismissal provisions where an employee is entitled to terminate the contract by reason of a lock-out by the employer.

Subsection (3) obliges an employee who is given notice of dismissal for redundancy (but not unfair dismissal) and who wishes to leave before the expiry of that notice to give a counter-notice *in writing* during the "obligatory period of notice"; the counter-notice must terminate the contract earlier than the date of expiry of the employer's notice. An employee who fails to comply with subs. (3) will be treated as not dismissed. The definition of obligatory period is given in subs. (4) and has the effect that, for an employee who is entitled to four weeks' notice and receives four weeks' notice, the obligatory period is the whole of the notice period; if he or she is entitled to four weeks' notice but receives eight weeks' notice, the obligatory period is the last four weeks of that eight-week period. These provisions are unnecessarily complex and provide a trap for the unwary or ignorant, though the E.A.T. has managed to mitigate their rigour in some cases by finding a mutually agreed variation of the date of expiry of the employer's notice, and thus to protect employees who might otherwise have fallen outside the statutory provisions: see, for example, *Pritchard-Rhodes v. Boon* [1979] IRLR 19, *Tunnel Holdings v. Woolf* [1976] I.C.R. 387 and *C.P.S. Recruitment, t/a Blackwood Associates v. Bowen and Secretary of State for Employment* [1982] IRLR 54; cf. *T.B.A. Industrial Products v. Morland* [1982] I.C.R. 686. Note the provisions of s.145(3), which state that the relevant date in this context is the date on which the employee's counter-notice expires.

The provisions of subs. (5) should be noted. They only protect an employee's right to a redundancy payment where the frustrating event relates to the employer, not the employee, though if the event affects both, it will be enough that some of the effect is upon the employer: see *Fenerty v. British Airports Authority* [1976] I.C.R. 361. Note also the provisions of s.139(4).

Failure to permit return after childbirth treated as dismissal

137.—(1) Subject to subsection (2) and section 138, where an employee who—

(a) has the right conferred by section 79, and

(b) has exercised it in accordance with section 82,

is not permitted to return to work, she shall be taken for the purposes of this Part to be dismissed for the reason for which she was not permitted to return with effect from the notified day of return (being deemed to have been continuously employed until that day).

(2) Where in proceedings arising out of a failure to permit an employee to return to work pursuant to the right conferred by section 79 the employer shows—

(a) that the reason for the failure is that the employee is redundant, and

(b) that the employee was, or (had she continued to be employed by him) would have been, dismissed by reason of redundancy on a day falling after the commencement of her maternity leave period and before the notified day of return,

for the purposes of this Part the employee shall not be taken to be dismissed with effect from the notified day of return but shall be taken to be dismissed by reason of redundancy with effect from that earlier day (being deemed to have been continuously employed until that earlier day).

DEFINITIONS

"employee": s.230(1).

"employer": s.230(4).

"maternity leave period": ss. 72 and 73.

"notified day of return": s.83.

GENERAL NOTE

The general rule is set out in subs. (1): an employee will be treated as dismissed if she is not permitted to return to work and the reason for dismissal will be taken to be the reason for which she is not allowed to return. This, however, is subject to the proviso that she has the right to return within s.79 and that she has complied with s.82 in exercising it.

Subsection (2) provides that this general rule will not apply where the employer shows that the reason for the failure to permit the employee to return is that she is redundant and that she would in any case have been dismissed before the notified day of return. In that case the date of dismissal will be the earlier date of dismissal, not the notified day of return. This also applies where the employee is in fact dismissed after the start of the maternity leave period but before the notified day of return. Note the provisions of s.145(7), which define the "relevant date" as the notified day of return, and s.146(3).

No dismissal in cases of renewal of contract or re-engagement

138.—(1) Where—

(a) an employee's contract of employment is renewed, or he is re engaged under a new contract of employment in pursuance of an offer (whether in writing or not) made before the end of his employment under the previous contract, and

(b) the renewal or re-engagement takes effect either immediately on, or after an interval of not more than four weeks after, the end of that employment,

the employee shall not be regarded for the purposes of this Part as dismissed by his employer by reason of the ending of his employment under the previous contract.

(2) Subsection (1) does not apply if—

(a) the provisions of the contract as renewed, or of the new contract, as to
 (i) the capacity and place in which the employee is employed, and
 (ii) the other terms and conditions of his employment, differ (wholly or in part) from the corresponding provisions of the previous contract, and

(b) during the period specified in subsection (3)—
 (i) the employee (for whatever reason) terminates the renewed or new contract, or gives notice to terminate it and it is in consequence terminated, or
 (ii) the employer, for a reason connected with or arising out of any difference between the renewed or new contract and the previous contract, terminates the renewed or new contract, or gives notice to terminate it and it is in consequence terminated.

(3) The period referred to in subsection (2)(b) is the period—

(a) beginning at the end of the employee's employment under the previous contract, and

(b) ending with—
 (i) the period of four weeks beginning with the date on which the employee starts work under the renewed or new contract, or
 (ii) such longer period as may be agreed in accordance with subsection (6) for the purpose of retraining the employee for employment under that contract;

and is in this Part referred to as the "trial period".

(4) Where subsection (2) applies, for the purposes of this Part—

(a) the employee shall be regarded as dismissed on the date on which his employment under the previous contract (or, if there has been more than one trial period, the original contract) ended, and

(b) the reason for the dismissal shall be taken to be the reason for which the employee was then dismissed, or would have been dismissed had the offer (or original offer) of renewed or new employment not been made, or the reason which resulted in that offer being made.

(5) Subsection (2) does not apply if the employee's contract of employment is again renewed, or he is again re-engaged under a new contract of employment, in circumstances such that subsection (1) again applies.

(6) For the purposes of subsection (3)(b)(ii) a period of retraining is agreed in accordance with this subsection only if the agreement—

(a) is made between the employer and the employee or his representative before the employee starts work under the contract as renewed, or the new contract,

(b) is in writing,

(c) specifies the date on which the period of retraining ends, and

(d) specifies the terms and conditions of employment which will apply in the employee's case after the end of that period.

DEFINITIONS
 "contract of employment": s.230(2).
 "employee": s.230(1).
 "employer": s.230(4).
 "renewal": s.235(1).

GENERAL NOTE

The provisions governing offers of re-engagement and alternative employment are amongst the most complex to be found in Pt. XI of the Act. They operate in two separate ways: either they affect the question whether or not employees are to be treated as having been dismissed, considered here; or they operate to disentitle them from receiving a redundancy payment which would otherwise be payable; this aspect is considered in the note to s.141. There is the additional complicating factor of the trial period: this comes into operation in both cases where the offer of new employment differs at all from the terms of the previous employment. The trial period provisions are considered separately in the note to subs. (3), below.

Section 138 deals with the situation where an employee who is under notice of redundancy (or who has been constructively dismissed) is offered alternative employment. The point of its provisions, which follow on from the basic definition of dismissal in s.136, is to determine in what circumstances the employee is to be treated as having been dismissed. As will be seen from the discussion below, there are circumstances in which an employee will be treated as not having been dismissed. In such circumstances, there will be no entitlement to a redundancy payment, simply because entitlement to a payment depends upon having been dismissed for redundancy and, therefore, if there is no dismissal, there can be no entitlement. Once, however, the employee is found to have been dismissed, he or she may be disentitled from receiving the payment which would otherwise be payable if there is held to have been an unreasonable refusal of a suitable offer: see the notes to s.141 below.

The trial period provisions in s.138 build on the basic structure of s.136 by setting out the circumstances in which a trial period will come into operation. If an employee unreasonably terminates the employment during the trial period, that act will disentitle him or her from the right to receive a payment. Note the provisions of s.146(1), which make clear that references to re-engagement are to re-engagement by the employer or an associated employer, and references to offers are to offers made by the employer or an associated employer.

Subss. (1) and (2)

These subsections cater for two alternative possibilities: either that the terms and conditions of the new employment are the same as those of the old, or that they are different. In both cases, there must be an offer of a renewal of the contract or of re-engagement under a new contract; an offer of re-engagement must be made before the ending of the employment under the previous contract. The renewal or re-engagement must take effect immediately on the ending of the previous employment or within four weeks: for what constitutes a valid offer, see *The Singer Co. (U.K.) v. Ferrier* [1980] IRLR 300. If any of the conditions are not complied with, there will be a dismissal. Where the new contract is the same as the old, and all the conditions of s.138(1) are complied with, there will be no dismissal and s.213(1) will preserve continuity of employment during the gap (if any) between the two contracts. In *S.I. (Systems and Instruments) v. Grist and Riley* [1983] I.C.R. 788 the E.A.T. said that, on a proper construction of what is now s.138(1) (formerly s.84(1)), a distinction is to be drawn between cases of renewal and re-engagement. In cases of renewal, the offer need not be made before the termination of the contract of employment, but in cases of re-engagement under a new contract, the offer must be made before termination. This view was also taken by another division of the E.A.T. in *EBAC v. Wymer* [1995] I.C.R. 466, although the decuision in the *S.I. Systems* case, above, was not cited.

Where the provisions of the new contract differ at all from the provisions of the employee's previous contract, subs. (2) brings a trial period into operation. If the employee leaves or is dismissed during the trial period, he or she will be treated as having been dismissed under the previous contract. An employee whose termination of the contract during the trial period is held to be unreasonable will be disentitled from receiving a redundancy payment: see note to s.141. An employee who leaves during the trial period or who is dismissed by the employer (for a reason connected with or arising out of the change in the contract) will be treated as having been dismissed on the date on which the previous contract ended and for the reason for which that contract was ended: see subs. (4). Note the extended meaning of "relevant date" in s.145(4) for situations covered by this provision.

"Renewal" includes "extension": see s.235(1). Note also the provisions of s.146(2) in relation to contracts which end on a Friday, Saturday or Sunday.

Subs. (3)

The coming into operation of the trial period occurs in all cases whether the old contract is renewed or the employee is re-engaged under a new contract and where there is a difference between the terms and conditions of the new contract and the corresponding provisions of the previous contract, unless it is one to which the *de minimis* rule applies: *Rose v. Henry Trickett & Sons* (1971) 6 I.T.R. 211 at p.215. The trial period generally starts with the ending of the previous contract and ends four weeks from the date on which the employee starts work under the new contract, by virtue of subs. (3). In *Benton v. Sanderson Kayser* [1989] I.C.R. 136 the question arose as to the meaning "period of four weeks" used by what is now subs. (3)(b)(i) (formerly s.84(4)). The Court of Appeal held that this phrase means a period of four consecutive weeks calculated according to the calendar rather than the period of time actually worked. The trial period may only be extended, by agreement between the parties, for the purpose of retraining the employee and the agreement must comply with the requirements of subs. (6). An extension for any other reason will have no effect. This means that an employee who decides to leave during the period of the extension will be held to have resigned: *Meek v. J. Allen Rubber Co. and Secretary of State for Employment* [1980] IRLR 21. Similar considerations apply where there is more than one renewal of the original contract or the employee is again re-engaged under a new contract. Section 138 applies also to offers of re-engagement with associated employers: see s.146(1). It may be noted that a refusal to offer an employee a trial period may cause the dismissal to be unfair: *Elliot v. Richard Stump* [1987] I.C.R. 579.

In cases of constructive dismissal, the rules set out above will apply, but with the added complication that a so-called common law trial period will come into existence. This means that if, in breach of the contract, the employee is transferred to another department and takes the job there on trial, he or she has a reasonable period in which to decide whether to take the new job or leave (the "common law" trial period). If he or she decides to take it, the statutory trial period then comes into operation: *Air Canada v. Lee* [1978] I.C.R. 1202 and *Turvey v. C.W. Cheyney & Son* [1979] I.C.R. 341. The difficulty with this is that since the employee is granted a reasonable time under the common law trial period to make up his or her mind, it is not easy to know when the statutory trial period has started and whether, when the employee left the employment, the statutory period had ended or not. If it had, there will have been no dismissal and the employee will be held to have resigned.

If the employee leaves during the trial period, entitlement to a redundancy payment will be lost if the new employment was suitable, and the termination of the employment during the trial period was unreasonable: see s.141(4) and the note to that subsection.

Redundancy

139.—(1) For the purposes of this Act an employee who is dismissed shall be taken to be dismissed by reason of redundancy if the dismissal is wholly or mainly attributable to—
  (a) the fact that his employer has ceased or intends to cease—
      (i) to carry on the business for the purposes of which the employee was employed by him, or
      (ii) to carry on that business in the place where the employee was so employed, or
  (b) the fact that the requirements of that business—
      (i) for employees to carry out work of a particular kind, or
      (ii) for employees to carry out work of a particular kind in the place where the employee was employed by the employer,
  have ceased or diminished or are expected to cease or diminish.

(2) For the purposes of subsection (1) the business of the employer together with the business or businesses of his associated employers shall be treated as one (unless either of the conditions specified in paragraphs (a) and (b) of that subsection would be satisfied without so treating them).

(3) For the purposes of subsection (1) the activities carried on by a local education authority with respect to the schools maintained by it, and the activities carried on by the governors of those schools, shall be treated as one business (unless either of the conditions specified in paragraphs (a) and (b) of that subsection would be satisfied without so treating them).

(4) Where—
  (a) the contract under which a person is employed is treated by section 136(5) as terminated by his employer by reason of an act or event, and
  (b) the employee's contract is not renewed and he is not re-engaged under a new contract of employment,
he shall be taken for the purposes of this Act to be dismissed by reason of redundancy if the circumstances in which his contract is not renewed, and he

is not re-engaged, are wholly or mainly attributable to either of the facts stated in paragraphs (a) and (b) of subsection (1).

(5) In its application to a case within subsection (4), paragraph (a)(i) of subsection (1) has effect as if the reference in that subsection to the employer included a reference to any person to whom, in consequence of the act or event, power to dispose of the business has passed.

(6) In subsection (1) "cease" and "diminish" mean cease and diminish either permanently or temporarily and for whatever reason.

DEFINITIONS
    "associated employer": s.231.
    "business": s.235(1).
    "employee": s.230(1).
    "employer": s.230(4).

GENERAL NOTE
    The definition of redundancy serves a dual purpose: redundancy is one of the potentially fair reasons in unfair dismissal cases, and an employee who is dismissed by reason of redundancy is also entitled to a redundancy payment, by virtue of s.135. In cases involving only a claim for a redundancy payment, s.163(2) enacts a presumption of redundancy. This means that the burden is on the employer who wishes to dispute liability to make the payment to prove that the employee was not redundant. In cases involving a complaint of unfair dismissal and a claim for a redundancy payment, however, the presumption will not operate in relation to the unfair dismissal complaint: see s.7(6) of the Industrial Tribunals Act 1996. In unfair dismissal cases, the burden is on the employer to show what the reason (or principal reason) for the dismissal was. If an employer fails to discharge that burden the dismissal will be automatically held to be unfair. It is therefore possible for an employer to fail to rebut the presumption of redundancy in the redundancy payment claim and thus become liable for a redundancy payment, and to fail to establish the reason for the dismissal in the unfair dismissal claim and thus be held to have dismissed the employee unfairly: see *Midland Foot Comfort Centre v. Moppett* [1973] I.C.R. 219.

    A preliminary question which arises is whether the dismissal is *by reason* of the particular circumstances which constitute a redundancy. In *Hindle v. Percival Boats* [1969] 1 W.L.R. 174, the Court of Appeal held that, provided the employer honestly believes that the dismissal of the employee is due to some reason other than redundancy (however mistaken the belief may be), the dismissal will not be by reason of redundancy. But it emphasised that industrial tribunals must be wary of dishonest employers or employers who misdirect themselves into thinking that they were influenced by the employee's deficiencies, when the main factor was that the requirements of the business had declined. See also *Baxter v. Limb Group of Companies* [1994] IRLR 572.

Subs. (1)
    The definition of redundancy uses the phrase "in the place where the employee was ... employed". In such cases, the question is whether the employer has contractual authority, express or implied, to order the employee to move; or, in other words, what degree of mobility the employee is subject to. The industrial tribunal must consider, therefore, whether there is an express or implied mobility term in the employee's contract. If the employee is required to move to another factory within the radius of the mobility obligation because of the closure of the factory where he or she works, it is not possible to claim a redundancy payment, since there has not been a cessation of the business in the place where he or she is employed: see, for example, *Stevenson v. Teesside Bridge and Engineering* [1971] 1 All E.R. 296. If, on the other hand, he or she is employed in a factory in East Anglia and, because of its closure, is required to move to the Midlands, to which the mobility obligation does not extend, the refusal to move will be justified and any dismissal will be by reason of redundancy: *O'Brien v. Associated Fire Alarms* [1968] 1 W.L.R. 1916. An employee who can be required to work anywhere in the United Kingdom will not be justified in refusing to move: *United Kingdom Atomic Energy Authority v. Claydon* [1974] I.C.R. 128.

    The one qualification to the above rules is that, if the employee is redundant, he or she may lose the entitlement to a redundancy payment if he or she is held to have unreasonably refused a suitable offer of alternative employment: see s.141. The E.A.T. has made it clear that an employer cannot rely on a mobility clause to argue that there is no redundancy unless he or she invokes it: see *Curling v. Securicor* [1992] IRLR 549. "... [A]n employer who does not invoke a mobility clause can[not] be heard to say that its mere existence entitles him to claim, after he has closed down the workplace where his employees were employed, that he might have required them to work elsewhere, although he did not do so, and therefore they were redundant": see p.553, para. 17.

Care needs to be taken over the construction of mobility clauses. In *Rank Xerox v. Churchill* [1988] IRLR 280, for example, six employees were employed at the company's London headquarters. Their contracts specified that as their place of work, but added: "The company may require you to transfer to another location". The company decided to move its headquarters to Marlow, but the six employees declined to go and left their employment. They claimed redundancy payments. The E.A.T. said that the words in the employees' contracts were simple and clear and there was no room for any implication of a requirement of reasonableness. The transfers involved a move to a place where the employees could be required to work. The employers had not therefore ceased to carry out their business in the place where the employees were employed and there was no redundancy. See also *Sutcliffe v. Hawker Siddeley Aviation* [1973] IRLR 304. In *Securicor v. Reid* (E.A.T. 540/92, I.D.S. Brief 495) the employee's contract said that he was "based at Edinburgh branch" and the relevant mobility clause stated: "Should the interests of the Company demand it, you may be required to serve at the Company's Head Office in London or at one of the Company's branches… " The E.A.T. construed the clause as entitling the employers to move employees not only from branch to branch but from site to site.

The case of *Rank Xerox v. Churchill* above should be contrasted with *Bass Leisure v. Thomas* [1994] IRLR 104, in which the E.A.T. (Judge Hicks, Q.C. and colleagues) said that "the place" where an employee is employed does not extend to any place where the employee may be contractually required to work; the question is primarily a factual one and the only relevant contractual terms are those which define the place of employment and its extent. This is a surprising decision; leave was given to appeal to the Court of Appeal.

Note subs. (2) which says that the employer's business and that of any associated employer are to be treated as one and subs. (3) which states that the activities carried on by a local education authority with respect to schools maintained by it and the activities carried on by the governors of those schools are to be treated as one business for the purposes of subs. (1).

Subsection (6) makes clear that "cease" and "diminish" mean cease and diminish either permanently or temporarily and for whatever reason.

Subs. (1)(a)

Of the two definitions of redundancy given in subs. (1), that relating to cessation of a business in subs. (1)(a) has caused little difficulty. It is not necessary to show that the employer is the legal owner of the business in question, only that that person is in control of the business: *Thomas v. Jones* [1978] I.C.R. 274.

Subs. (1)(b)

The second definition, in subs. (1)(b), that there is a cessation or diminution in the requirements of a business for work of a particular kind, is by no means straightforward and has caused considerable difficulties. In a series of cases, the Court of Appeal has held that, provided the amount of work remains the same or increases, the employer is entitled to re-organise the business: *Chapman v. Goonvean and Rostowrack China Clay Co.* [1973] I.C.R. 310, and *Lesney Products & Co. v. Nolan* [1977] I.C.R. 235. See also *Murphy v. Epsom College* [1985] I.C.R. 80 and *MacFisheries v. Findlay* [1985] I.C.R. 160; *cf. Halfords v. Roche* (E.A.T. 803/87). In *Johnson v. Nottinghamshire Police Authority* [1974] I.C.R. 170, at p.176 Lord Denning M.R. said:

"[A]n employer is entitled to reorganise his business so as to improve its efficiency and, in doing so, to propose to his staff a change in the terms and conditions of their employment: and to dispense with their services if they do not agree. Such a change does not automatically give the staff a right to a redundancy payment. It only does so if the change in the terms and conditions is due to a redundancy situation".

Cf. the approach of the E.A.T. in *Robinson v. British Midland Airways* [1978] I.C.R. 304. See also *North Riding Garages v. Butterwick* [1967] 2 Q.B. 56.

The Court of Appeal has made it clear that, in considering whether there has been a diminution in the requirements of the business for employees to carry out work of a particular kind, the tribunal must look at the terms of the employee's contract. An example of this is *Cowen v. Haden* [1983] I.C.R. 1, where an employee was employed as a divisional contracts surveyor and was "required to undertake, at the direction of the company, any and all duties which reasonably fall within the scope of his capabilities". The Court of Appeal held that the requirement that the employee should perform the duties within the scope of his capabilities was restricted to the duties of a divisional contracts surveyor; the employers therefore had no right to require him to transfer from that work to assume the job of a quantity surveyor. See also *Pink v. White and White & Co. (Earls Barton)* [1985] IRLR 489 and *Perkins Engine Group v. Overend* (E.A.T. 479/88).

It should be borne in mind that a reorganisation which does not fall within the statutory definition of redundancy may amount to "some other substantial reason," the fifth potentially fair reason: see s.98(1)(b).

Another problem has been caused by economic policy considerations. In *O'Hare v. Rotaprint* [1980] I.C.R. 94 the E.A.T. suggested that if the work-force is expanded to meet a scale of production which fails to materialise, there may not be a cessation or diminution of work because the requirement never materialised. This is arguably inconsistent with the later Court of Appeal decision in *Nottinghamshire County Council v. Lee* [1980] I.C.R. 635 in which the court held that if there is a diminution in the requirement at the time of the dismissal, it makes no difference that when the employee was engaged he or she knew of the diminishing work requirements. In such cases, however, the tribunal may hold the dismissal to be for some other substantial reason, an approach followed more recently by the Court of Appeal in *North Yorkshire County Council v. Fay* [1986] I.C.R. 133. In *Association of University Teachers v. University of Newcastle-upon-Tyne* [1987] I.C.R. 317 the E.A.T. stressed that the task of the industrial tribunal in such cases is to consider whether, on the facts, the dismissal is due to redundancy; it should not consider the reason for the redundancy situation. In that case, an employee was dismissed at the end of his three-year fixed-term contract because funding for the course on which he taught had run out. The industrial tribunal's decision was that this did not amount to a redundancy situation, but it was reversed by the E.A.T., which said that because of the lack of funds the course could no longer be continued and there ceased to be a requirement for the employee's services.

Exclusions

Summary dismissal

140.—(1) Subject to subsections (2) and (3), an employee is not entitled to a redundancy payment by reason of dismissal where his employer, being entitled to terminate his contract of employment without notice by reason of the employee's conduct, terminates it either—

(a) without notice,

(b) by giving shorter notice than that which, in the absence of conduct entitling the employer to terminate the contract without notice, the employer would be required to give to terminate the contract, or

(c) by giving notice which includes, or is accompanied by, a statement in writing that the employer would, by reason of the employee's conduct, be entitled to terminate the contract without notice.

(2) Where an employee who—

(a) has been given notice by his employer to terminate his contract of employment, or

(b) has given notice to his employer under section 148(1) indicating his intention to claim a redundancy payment in respect of lay-off or short-time,

takes part in a strike at any relevant time in circumstances which entitle the employer to treat the contract of employment as terminable without notice, subsection (1) does not apply if the employer terminates the contract by reason of his taking part in the strike.

(3) Where the contract of employment of an employee who—

(a) has been given notice by his employer to terminate his contract of employment, or

(b) has given notice to his employer under section 148(1) indicating his intention to claim a redundancy payment in respect of lay-off or short-time,

is terminated as mentioned in subsection (1) at any relevant time otherwise than by reason of his taking part in a strike, an industrial tribunal may determine that the employer is liable to make an appropriate payment to the employee if on a reference to the tribunal it appears to the tribunal, in the circumstances of the case, to be just and equitable that the employee should receive it.

(4) In subsection (3) "appropriate payment" means—

(a) the whole of the redundancy payment to which the employee would have been entitled apart from subsection (1), or

(b) such part of that redundancy payment as the tribunal thinks fit.

(5) In this section "relevant time"—

(a) in the case of an employee who has been given notice by his employer to terminate his contract of employment, means any time within the obligatory period of notice, and

(b) in the case of an employee who has given notice to his employer under section 148(1), means any time after the service of the notice.

DEFINITIONS

"contract of employment": s.230(2).
"employee": s.230(1).
"employer": s.230(4).
"strike": s.235(5).

GENERAL NOTE

This section deals with misconduct and also contains special provisions which apply in the case of strikes. The provisions contained in this section suffer from considerable complexity.

Subss. (1) and (3)

If an employee is dismissed for misconduct, albeit in a redundancy situation, the presumption of redundancy will be rebutted and the dismissal will not have been by reason of redundancy. In such a case, the tribunal should scrutinise the employer's reason carefully, to ensure that it is not a reason trumped up to defeat a legitimate claim. If, on the other hand, the employer dismisses the employee for redundancy, but discovers misconduct on his or her part, s.140(1) must be complied with. This provision operates so as to disentitle an employee where the employer, "being entitled to terminate his contract of employment by reason of the employee's conduct," terminates it in one of three ways: (1) without notice, or (2) by giving shorter notice than the employee is entitled to, or (3) by giving the correct notice but also stating in writing that the employer would be entitled to terminate the contract summarily because of the employee's conduct.

The E.A.T. has expressed the view that subs. (1) applies where there is a single dismissal (*i.e.* a dismissal for redundancy and not explicitly for misconduct) as well as a double dismissal (*i.e.* a dismissal for redundancy followed by a dismissal for misconduct): see *Simmons v. Hoover* [1977] I.C.R. 61, at p.80. So if, for example, the employer gives the employee less notice than he or she is entitled to and subsequently misconduct on the part of the employee comes to light, subs. (1) will relieve the employer of liability; if, on the other hand, the employer gives the correct notice, liability to pay a redundancy payment will not be extinguished unless the employee is dismissed a second time.

Subsection (1) uses the phrase "where the employer, *being entitled* to terminate his contract …" The effect of the italicised words was considered by the E.A.T. in *Bonner v. H. Gilbert* [1989] IRLR 475. It held that where the employer raises a defence to a redundancy payments claim based on subs. (1), the question of whether or not he or she is entitled to terminate the employee's contract must be determined according to the contractual approach propounded in *Western Excavating (E.C.C.) v. Sharp* [1978] I.C.R. 221. In other words, the employer must show that the employee was guilty of conduct which was a significant breach of contract or which showed that he or she no longer intended to be bound by one or more of the essential terms of the contract. A reasonable belief that the employee has committed a breach of contract will not be enough.

Subsection (3) gives the industrial tribunal power to award all or part of the redundancy payment, where the employer terminates the contract in accordance with subs. (1) and the second dismissal takes place at any "relevant time", which is defined as "any time within the obligatory period of notice". That phrase is defined in s.136(4); see the note above. In *Simmons v. Hoover* [1977] I.C.R. 61 the E.A.T. expressed the view that subs. (3) applies only where there are two dismissals. If their analysis of subss. (1) and (3) is correct, the result is that some serious anomalies exist, which tend to favour employers who act wrongfully.

Subs. (2)

This subsection contains provisions dealing with the situation where an employee takes part in a strike, to which special considerations apply. The employee's action in taking part in a strike has been held to be "employee's conduct" within subs. (1): see *Simmons v. Hoover*, above. If the dismissal provokes a strike, subs. (2) operates to negate the effect of subs. (1), so that the employee does not lose the entitlement to a redundancy payment. Subsection (2) will not operate, however, if the strike came first. In that case, subs. (1) will operate. It is a moot point whether subs. (3) will operate, but it is submitted that it will not, since its terms exclude termination by reason of taking part in a strike.

Relationship of subss. (1), (2) and (3)

The report of *Simmons v. Hoover* contains an appendix setting out the various possibilities. In it, the E.A.T. takes an example of a redundant employee (X) who is entitled to three months' notice and postulates seven hypothetical situations.

Situation 1. X is dismissed on January 1 with two months' notice. The employer knew on January 1 that he or she had been stealing. In that case, according to the E.A.T., subs. (1) applies and subs. (3) does not, since there has not been a double dismissal.

Situation 2. X is dismissed on January 1 with two months' notice and the employers subsequently discover that he or she had been stealing before the dismissal. The result is the same as in situation 1.

Situation 3. X is dismissed on January 1 with three months' notice. On February 1 the employers discover that he or she has been stealing and terminate the contract immediately. The employee is within subss. (1) and (3) and is entitled to a discretionary payment.

Situation 4. Z is dismissed on January 1 with six months' notice. The employers terminate the contract immediately or on short notice in the following circumstances: (a) X had been found stealing on February 1 and was dismissed on that day. (b) The employers discovered that X had been stealing before January 1 and dismissed him on February 1. (c) X was found stealing on May 1 and was dismissed on that day. In cases (a) and (b), X is covered by subs. (1) but not by subss. (2)–(5) (formerly s.92) and therefore receives no payment. In case (c), X is covered by subss. (1) and (3) and receives a discretionary payment.

Situation 5. X is dismissed on January 1 with three months' notice and goes on strike immediately afterwards. The employers terminate the contract immediately on February 1 by reason of the strike. X is covered by subss. (1) and (2) and receives a redundancy payment.

Situation 6. X is dismissed on January 1 with six months' notice and goes on strike immediately afterwards. The employers terminate the contract on February 1. X is covered by subs. (1) but not subss. (2)–(5) and does not receive a redundancy payment.

Situation 7. X is dismissed with six months' notice on January 1. On February 1 he or she is caught stealing. The employers give X one month's notice and the contract terminates on March 1. X is covered by subs. (1) but not subss. (2)–(5), and receives no payment.

As can be seen from the above examples, much depends on the coincidence of timing, for example, whether the second dismissal takes place during the obligatory period. The complexity of this area is unfortunate.

Renewal of contract or re-engagement

141.—(1) This section applies where an offer (whether in writing or not) is made to an employee before the end of his employment—
(a) to renew his contract of employment, or
(b) to re-engage him under a new contract of employment,
with renewal or re-engagement to take effect either immediately on, or after an interval of not more than four weeks after, the end of his employment.

(2) Where subsection (3) is satisfied, the employee is not entitled to a redundancy payment if he unreasonably refuses the offer.

(3) This subsection is satisfied where—
(a) the provisions of the contract as renewed, or of the new contract, as to—
(i) the capacity and place in which the employee would be employed, and
(ii) the other terms and conditions of his employment,
would not differ from the corresponding provisions of the previous contract, or

(b) those provisions of the contract as renewed, or of the new contract, would differ from the corresponding provisions of the previous contract but the offer constitutes an offer of suitable employment in relation to the employee.

(4) The employee is not entitled to a redundancy payment if—

(a) his contract of employment is renewed, or he is re-engaged under a new contract of employment, in pursuance of the offer,

(b) the provisions of the contract as renewed or new contract as to the capacity or place in which he is employed or the other terms and conditions of his employment differ (wholly or in part) from the corresponding provisions of the previous contract,

(c) the employment is suitable in relation to him, and

(d) during the trial period he unreasonably terminates the contract, or unreasonably gives notice to terminate it and it is in consequence terminated.

DEFINITIONS
"contract of employment": s.230(2).
"employee": s.230(1).
"employer": s.230(4).
"renewal": s.235(1).

GENERAL NOTE
The provisions governing offers of re-engagement and alternative employment operate in two separate ways: either they affect the question whether or not the employee is to be treated as having been dismissed; or they operate to disentitle him or her from receiving a redundancy payment which would otherwise be payable. The first set of provisions is considered in the note to s.138. There is the additional complicating factor of the trial period: this comes into operation in both cases where the offer of new employment differs at all from the terms of the previous employment. The trial period provisions are considered in the note to s.138(3).

Section 138 deals with the situation where an employee who is under notice of redundancy (or who has been constructively dismissed) is offered alternative employment. Its provisions have been considered above; they follow on from the basic definition of dismissal in s.136. Once the employee is found to have been dismissed, he or she may be disentitled from receiving the payment which would otherwise be payable if there is held to have been an unreasonable refusal of a suitable offer. The effect of the trial period provisions is that, if an employee unreasonably terminates the employment during the trial period, that act will disentitle him or her from the right to receive a payment: see s.141(4).

The provisions of this section affect an employee treated as dismissed for redundancy by virtue of the provisions of s.138. An employee will be disentitled from receiving a redundancy payment where he or she unreasonably refuses an offer of suitable new employment. Subsection (1) applies to an offer made before the ending of the previous employment to renew the contract or re-engage him or her under a new one, the renewal or re-engagement taking effect no more than four weeks after the ending of the previous contract. If the provisions of the new contract are the same as those of the old, the employee will be disentitled, if he or she unreasonably refuses the offer: see subss. (2) and (3). Where the provisions of the new contract differ, the first question is whether the offer is suitable, since subs. (3)(b) will only disentitle the employee in the case of an unreasonable refusal of a suitable offer. If he or she actually gives the new contract a try, the statutory trial period will come into operation; if then he or she leaves during it, entitlement will be lost if the new employment was suitable, and the termination of the employment during the trial period was unreasonable: subs. (4). Whether there has been an offer is essentially an issue of fact for the tribunal to decide. A multiplicity of insufficiently specific offers may not be an adequate substitute for an offer of a single suitable alternative employment: see *Curling v. Securicor* [1992] IRLR 549.

The two significant questions here concern what is meant by "suitable" and "unreasonable". They must be kept separate and dealt with separately by the tribunal: *Carron Co. v. Robertson* (1967) 2 I.T.R. 484 at p.486, and *Hindes v. Supersine* [1979] I.C.R. 517. See also *Taylor v. Kent County Council* [1969] Q.B. 560. The suitability of the offer is to be looked at objectively by the industrial tribunal and is regarded by the appellate courts as being a matter of fact and degree for it to decide: *Carron Co. v. Robertson*, above, at p.486 and *Taylor v. Kent County Council*, above, at pp.565–566. In *Taylor v. Kent County Council* [1969] Q.B. 560, Lord Parker C.J. said that suitability "means employment which is substantially equivalent to the employment which has ceased," but there are suggestions in later cases that an objectively unsuitable offer may be made suitable (or vice versa) by the employee's attitude towards it: see, for example, *Hindes v. Supersine*, above, at p.523 and *Executors of J.F. Everest v. Cox* [1980] I.C.R. 415. See also *Standard Telephones and Cables v. Yates* [1981] IRLR 21.

In the case of an offer found not to be suitable, it will not be necessary to go on to consider the reasonableness of the employee's refusal. If, however, the offer is found to be suitable, the tribunal must then consider the reasonableness of the refusal by looking at the personal reasons that relate to the employee: *Carron Co. v. Robertson*, above, and *Hindes v. Supersine*, above. This is a subjective matter to be considered from the employee's point of view: *Cambridge & District Co-operative Society v. Ruse* [1993] IRLR 156. This must be judged as at the time the offer is made and not with hindsight, taking account of the personal circumstances of the individual employee, and also his or her reaction in those circumstances; all the relevant factors should be considered as a whole: see *Lambert v. Warren Bros. (Plymstock)* (E.A.T. 85/88), *Thomas Wragg & Sons v. Wood* [1976] I.C.R. 313, *Paton Calvert & Co. v. Westerside* [1979] IRLR 108, and *Executors of J.F. Everest v. Cox*, above. In looking at the two separate factors of suitability and reasonableness, the industrial tribunal is entitled to look at factors which may be common to both questions: *Spencer v. Gloucestershire County Council* [1985] IRLR 393.

Note the provisions of s.146(1) and (2), in relation to re-engagement and offers made by the employer and to contracts under which the employment ends on a Friday, Saturday or Sunday.

Employee anticipating expiry of employer's notice

142.—(1) Subject to subsection (3), an employee is not entitled to a redundancy payment where—
  (a) he is taken to be dismissed by virtue of section 136(3) by reason of giving to his employer notice terminating his contract of employment on a date earlier than the date on which notice by the employer terminating the contract is due to expire,
  (b) before the employee's notice is due to expire, the employer gives him a notice such as is specified in subsection (2), and
  (c) the employee does not comply with the requirements of that notice.
(2) The employer's notice referred to in subsection (1)(b) is a notice in writing—
  (a) requiring the employee to withdraw his notice terminating the contract of employment and to continue in employment until the date on which the employer's notice terminating the contract expires, and
  (b) stating that, unless he does so, the employer will contest any liability to pay to him a redundancy payment in respect of the termination of his contract of employment.
(3) An industrial tribunal may determine that the employer is liable to make an appropriate payment to the employee if on a reference to the tribunal it appears to the tribunal, having regard to—
  (a) the reasons for which the employee seeks to leave the employment, and
  (b) the reasons for which the employer requires him to continue in it,
to be just and equitable that the employee should receive the payment.
(4) In subsection (3) "appropriate payment" means—
  (a) the whole of the redundancy payment to which the employee would have been entitled apart from subsection (1), or
  (b) such part of that redundancy payment as the tribunal thinks fit.

DEFINITIONS
  "employee": s.230(1).
  "employer": s.230(4).
  "redundancy": s.235(3).
  "redundancy payment": s.162.

GENERAL NOTE
  These provisions follow on from the provisions of s.136(3) and (4), which deal with the situation where the employee gives a counter-notice during the period of the employer's notice. They only apply, however, where the employee is taken to have been dismissed, that is where the

employee has given a counter-notice during the "obligatory period of notice", as defined by s.136(4). If the employee's counter-notice is not within that period, he or she will not be taken to have been dismissed anyway.

Where s.136(3) applies, and the employer gives a notice during the period of the employee's notice, the tribunal has a discretion as to how much of the redundancy payment the employee should be awarded. The employer's notice must comply with the requirements of subs. (2). In practice, these provisions are seldom, if ever, encountered.

Strike during currency of employer's notice

143.—(1) This section applies where—
(a) an employer has given notice to an employee to terminate his contract of employment ("notice of termination"),
(b) after the notice is given the employee begins to take part in a strike of employees of the employer, and
(c) the employer serves on the employee a notice of extension.
(2) A notice of extension is a notice in writing which—
(a) requests the employee to agree to extend the contract of employment beyond the time of expiry by a period comprising as many available days as the number of working days lost by striking ("the proposed period of extension"),
(b) indicates the reasons for which the employer makes that request, and
(c) states that the employer will contest any liability to pay the employee a redundancy payment in respect of the dismissal effected by the notice of termination unless either—
    (i) the employee complies with the request, or
    (ii) the employer is satisfied that, in consequence of sickness or injury or otherwise, the employee is unable to comply with it or that (even though he is able to comply with it) it is reasonable in the circumstances for him not to do so.
(3) Subject to subsections (4) and (5), if the employee does not comply with the request contained in the notice of extension, he is not entitled to a redundancy payment by reason of the dismissal effected by the notice of termination.
(4) Subsection (3) does not apply if the employer agrees to pay a redundancy payment to the employee in respect of the dismissal effected by the notice of termination even though he has not complied with the request contained in the notice of extension.
(5) An industrial tribunal may determine that the employer is liable to make an appropriate payment to the employee if on a reference to the tribunal it appears to the tribunal that—
(a) the employee has not complied with the request contained in the notice of extension and the employer has not agreed to pay a redundancy payment in respect of the dismissal effected by the notice of termination, but
(b) either the employee was unable to comply with the request or it was reasonable in the circumstances for him not to comply with it.
(6) In subsection (5) "appropriate payment" means—
(a) the whole of the redundancy payment to which the employee would have been entitled apart from subsection (3), or
(b) such part of that redundancy payment as the tribunal thinks fit.
(7) If the employee—
(a) complies with the request contained in the notice of extension, or
(b) does not comply with it but attends at his proper or usual place of work and is ready and willing to work on one or more (but not all) of the available days within the proposed period of extension,
the notice of termination has effect, and shall be deemed at all material times to have had effect, as if the period specified in it had been appropriately

extended; and sections 87 to 91 accordingly apply as if the period of notice required by section 86 were extended to a corresponding extent.

(8) In subsection (7) "appropriately extended" means—

(a) in a case within paragraph (a) of that subsection, extended beyond the time of expiry by an additional period equal to the proposed period of extension, and

(b) in a case within paragraph (b) of that subsection, extended beyond the time of expiry up to the end of the day (or last of the days) on which he attends at his proper or usual place of work and is ready and willing to work.

DEFINITIONS
"contract of employment": s.230(2).
"employee": s.230(1).
"employer": s.230(4).
"strike": s.235(5).

GENERAL NOTE

These provisions apply where the employer gives notice of termination to the employee and during the currency of the notice the employee takes part in a strike. If the employer serves a notice of extension complying with subs. (2) and the employee fails to comply with it, the tribunal has a discretion as to how much of the redundancy payment the employee should be awarded. This does not apply if the employer agrees to make a payment to the employee despite the failure to comply with the employer's notice.

Subsection (7) applies where the employee complies with the notice of extension or attends at the usual place of work and is ready and willing to work on some of the available days within the proposed period of extension. Its effect is to extend the notice of termination by the amount of time specified by subs. (8). Note the provisions of s.144(3).

Provisions supplementary to section 143

144.—(1) For the purposes of section 143 an employee complies with the request contained in a notice of extension if, but only if, on each available day within the proposed period of extension, he—

(a) attends at his proper or usual place of work, and

(b) is ready and willing to work,

whether or not he has signified his agreement to the request in any other way.

(2) The reference in section 143(2) to the number of working days lost by striking is a reference to the number of working days in the period—

(a) beginning with the date of service of the notice of termination, and

(b) ending with the time of expiry,

which are days on which the employee in question takes part in a strike of employees of his employer.

(3) In section 143 and this section—

"available day", in relation to an employee, means a working day beginning at or after the time of expiry which is a day on which he is not taking part in a strike of employees of the employer,

"available day within the proposed period of extension" means an available day which begins before the end of the proposed period of extension,

"time of expiry", in relation to a notice of termination, means the time at which the notice would expire apart from section 143, and

"working day", in relation to an employee, means a day on which, in accordance with his contract of employment, he is normally required to work.

(4) Neither the service of a notice of extension nor any extension by virtue of section 143(7) of the period specified in a notice of termination affects—

(a) any right either of the employer or of the employee to terminate the contract of employment (whether before, at or after the time of expiry) by a further notice or without notice, or

(b) the operation of this Part in relation to any such termination of the contract of employment.

DEFINITIONS
  "employee": s.230(1).
  "employer": s.230(4).
  "strike": s.235(5).

GENERAL NOTE
  The provisions contained in this section are supplemental to the provisions of s.143. Subsection (1) sets out what amounts to compliance with a notice of extension; and subs. (2) amplifies the reference in s.143(2) to the number of working days lost by striking. Subsection (3) defines terms used in ss.143 and 144.

Supplementary

The relevant date

145.—(1) For the purposes of the provisions of this Act relating to redundancy payments "the relevant date" in relation to the dismissal of an employee has the meaning given by this section.

(2) Subject to the following provisions of this section, "the relevant date"—

(a) in relation to an employee whose contract of employment is terminated by notice, whether given by his employer or by the employee, means the date on which the notice expires,

(b) in relation to an employee whose contract of employment is terminated without notice, means the date on which the termination takes effect, and

(c) in relation to an employee who is employed under a contract for a fixed term which expires without being renewed under the same contract, means the date on which the term expires.

(3) Where the employee is taken to be dismissed by virtue of section 136(3) the "relevant date" means the date on which the employee's notice to terminate his contract of employment expires.

(4) Where the employee is regarded by virtue of section 138(4) as having been dismissed on the date on which his employment under an earlier contract ended, "the relevant date" means—

(a) for the purposes of section 164(1), the date which is the relevant date as defined by subsection (2) in relation to the renewed or new contract or, where there has been more than one trial period, the last such contract, and

(b) for the purposes of any other provision, the date which is the relevant date as defined by subsection (2) in relation to the previous contract or, where there has been more than one such trial period, the original contract.

(5) Where—

(a) the contract of employment is terminated by the employer, and

(b) the notice required by section 86 to be given by an employer would, if duly given on the material date, expire on a date later than the relevant date (as defined by the previous provisions of this section),

for the purposes of sections 155, 162(1) and 227(3) the later date is the relevant date.

(6) In subsection (5)(b) "the material date" means—

(a) the date when notice of termination was given by the employer, or

(b) where no notice was given, the date when the contract of employment was terminated by the employer.

(7) Where an employee is taken to be dismissed for the purposes of this Part by virtue of section 137(1), references in this Part to the relevant date are (unless the context otherwise requires) to the notified date of return.

GENERAL NOTE
With the exception of subss. (3) and (4) which contain definitions of "relevant date" specific to the situations catered for by ss.136(3) and 138(4) respectively, subss. (2) and (5)–(6) are identical to s.97(1)–(3), which define "effective date of termination" for the purpose of the unfair dismissal provisions. Reference should therefore be made to the notes to those provisions. Note s.153, which defines the "relevant date" in relation to claims for redundancy payments by virtue of the provisions governing lay-off or short-time working.

Provisions supplementing sections 138 and 141

146.—(1) In sections 138 and 141—
(a) references to re-engagement are to re-engagement by the employer or an associated employer, and
(b) references to an offer are to an offer made by the employer or an associated employer.
(2) For the purposes of the application of section 138(1) or 141(1) to a contract under which the employment ends on a Friday, Saturday or Sunday—
(a) the renewal or re-engagement shall be treated as taking effect immediately on the ending of the employment under the previous contract if it takes effect on or before the next Monday after that Friday, Saturday or Sunday, and
(b) the interval of four weeks to which those provisions refer shall be calculated as if the employment had ended on that next Monday.
(3) Where section 138 or 141 applies in a case within section 137(1)—
(a) references to a renewal or re-engagement taking effect immediately on, or after an interval of not more than four weeks after, the end of the employment are to a renewal or re-engagement taking effect on, or after an interval of not more than four weeks after, the notified day of return, and
(b) references to provisions of the previous contract are to the provisions of the contract under which the employee worked immediately before the beginning of her maternity leave period.

GENERAL NOTE
These provisions are supplemental to the provisions of ss.138 and 141, and have been commented upon in the notes to those sections.

CHAPTER III

RIGHT BY REASON OF LAY-OFF OR SHORT-TIME

Lay-off and short-time

Meaning of "lay-off" and "short-time"

147.—(1) For the purposes of this Part an employee shall be taken to be laid off for a week if—
(a) he is employed under a contract on terms and conditions such that his remuneration under the contract depends on his being provided by the employer with work of the kind which he is employed to do, but
(b) he is not entitled to any remuneration under the contract in respect of the week because the employer does not provide such work for him.

(2) For the purposes of this Part an employee shall be taken to be kept on short-time for a week if by reason of a diminution in the work provided for the employee by his employer (being work of a kind which under his contract the employee is employed to do) the employee's remuneration for the week is less than half a week's pay.

DEFINITIONS
"employee": s.230(1).
"employer": s.230(4).

GENERAL NOTE
For an employee to be able to claim a redundancy payment by reason of being laid off, he or she must be employed under a contract on such terms and conditions that the remuneration depends upon being provided by the employer with work of the kind which he or she is employed to do; he or she will be taken to be laid off in any week in respect of which he or she is not entitled to any remuneration under the contract because such work is not provided: see subs. (1) and *Puttick v. John Wright & Sons (Blackwall)* [1972] I.C.R. 457, *A. Dakri Co. v. Tiffen* [1981] I.C.R. 256 and *Kenneth Macrae & Co. v. Dawson* [1984] IRLR 4. If the employee's contract provides for a guaranteed minimum wage in the event of a lay-off, there will be no statutory lay-off for the purposes of these provisions: see *Powell v. Duffryn Wagon Co.* [1974] I.C.R. 123.
Subsection (2) provides that an employee will be taken to be on short-time where there is a diminution in the work provided by the employer which causes his or her remuneration for any week to be less than half a week's pay.

Eligibility by reason of lay-off or short-time

148.—(1) Subject to the following provisions of this Part, for the purposes of this Part an employee is eligible for a redundancy payment by reason of being laid off or kept on short-time if—
   (a) he gives notice in writing to his employer indicating (in whatever terms) his intention to claim a redundancy payment in respect of lay-off or short-time (referred to in this Part as "notice of intention to claim"), and
   (b) before the service of the notice he has been laid off or kept on short-time in circumstances in which subsection (2) applies.
   (2) This subsection applies if the employee has been laid off or kept on short-time—
   (a) for four or more consecutive weeks of which the last before the service of the notice ended on, or not more than four weeks before, the date of service of the notice, or
   (b) for a series of six or more weeks (of which not more than three were consecutive) within a period of thirteen weeks, where the last week of the series before the service of the notice ended on, or not more than four weeks before, the date of service of the notice.

DEFINITIONS
"employee": s.230(1).
"employer": s.230(4).

GENERAL NOTE
This section sets out the conditions which must be satisfied for the employee to be able to claim a redundancy payment: (1) he or she must have been laid off or kept on short-time working for four or more consecutive weeks ending with the date of service of the notice of intention to claim a redundancy payment or within four weeks of the date of service *or* he or she must have been laid off or kept on short-time working for a series of six or more weeks (of which not more than three were consecutive) within a period of 13 weeks, and the last week of the series must have ended on the date of the service of the notice or within four weeks of that date; and (2) he or she must have given written notice of the intention to claim a redundancy payment no earlier than the last day of the last week of the period of lay-off or short-time working. In addition, the

employee must also resign: see s.150(1). See *Allinson v. Drew Simmonds Engineering* [1985] I.C.R. 488. Note also the provisions of s.154.

Exclusions

Counter-notices

149. Where an employee gives to his employer notice of intention to claim but—
  (a) the employer gives to the employee, within seven days after the service of that notice, notice in writing (referred to in this Part as a "counter-notice") that he will contest any liability to pay to the employee a redundancy payment in pursuance of the employee's notice, and
  (b) the employer does not withdraw the counter-notice by a subsequent notice in writing,
the employee is not entitled to a redundancy payment in pursuance of his notice of intention to claim except in accordance with a decision of an industrial tribunal.

Definitions
  "employee": s.230(1).
  "employer": s.230(4).

General Note
  Sections 149–152 contain a series of exclusions. This section provides that if the employer gives a counter-notice within seven days of the service of the employee's notice of intention to claim and does not withdraw it, the employee will only be entitled to a redundancy payment in accordance with the decision of an industrial tribunal.

Resignation

150.—(1) An employee is not entitled to a redundancy payment by reason of being laid off or kept on short-time unless he terminates his contract of employment by giving such period of notice as is required for the purposes of this section before the end of the relevant period.
  (2) The period of notice required for the purposes of this section—
  (a) where the employee is required by his contract of employment to give more than one week's notice to terminate the contract, is the minimum period which he is required to give, and
  (b) otherwise, is one week.
  (3) In subsection (1) "the relevant period"—
  (a) if the employer does not give a counter-notice within seven days after the service of the notice of intention to claim, is three weeks after the end of those seven days,
  (b) if the employer gives a counter-notice within that period of seven days but withdraws it by a subsequent notice in writing, is three weeks after the service of the notice of withdrawal, and
  (c) if—
         (i) the employer gives a counter-notice within that period of seven days, and does not so withdraw it, and
         (ii) a question as to the right of the employee to a redundancy payment in pursuance of the notice of intention to claim is referred to an industrial tribunal,
      is three weeks after the tribunal has notified to the employee its decision on that reference.
  (4) For the purposes of subsection (3)(c) no account shall be taken of—

(a) any appeal against the decision of the tribunal, or
(b) any proceedings or decision in consequence of any such appeal.

DEFINITIONS
"contract of employment": s.230(2).
"employee": s.230(1).
"employer": s.230(4).

GENERAL NOTE
In addition to satisfying the conditions set out in s.148, an employee must also terminate the contract by giving the notice required to be given by subs. (2) before the end of the "relevant period" as set out in subs. (3). The notice required is *either* the minimum specified by the employee's contract (if more than one week) *or* one week. The "relevant period" is as follows: (a) if the employer does not give a counter-notice within seven days after the service of the notice of intention to claim, three weeks after the end of the seven days; (b) if the employer gives a counter-notice within the seven days, but withdraws it by a subsequent notice in writing, three weeks after the notice of withdrawal; (c) if the employer gives a counter-notice within seven days and does not withdraw it, and a question as to the employee's right to a redundancy payment is referred to an industrial tribunal, three weeks after the tribunal has notified the employee of its decision on the reference. In this last case, no account should be taken of any appeal against the decision of the tribunal or any proceedings or decision in consequence of any such appeal: see subs. (4).

Dismissal

151.—(1) An employee is not entitled to a redundancy payment by reason of being laid off or kept on short-time if he is dismissed by his employer.

(2) Subsection (1) does not prejudice any right of the employee to a redundancy payment in respect of the dismissal.

DEFINITIONS
"contract of employment": s.230(2).
"employee": s.230(1).
"employer": s.230(4).

GENERAL NOTE
An employee will not be entitled to a redundancy payment in pursuance of the notice of intention to claim if he or she is dismissed by the employer, but this will not prejudice any right to claim a redundancy payment by reason of the dismissal.

Likelihood of full employment

152.—(1) An employee is not entitled to a redundancy payment in pursuance of a notice of intention to claim if—
(a) on the date of service of the notice it was reasonably to be expected that the employee (if he continued to be employed by the same employer) would, not later than four weeks after that date, enter on a period of employment of not less than thirteen weeks during which he would not be laid off or kept on short-time for any week, and
(b) the employer gives a counter-notice to the employee within seven days after the service of the notice of intention to claim.
(2) Subsection (1) does not apply where the employee—
(a) continues or has continued, during the next four weeks after the date of service of the notice of intention to claim, to be employed by the same employer, and
(b) is or has been laid off or kept on short-time for each of those weeks.

DEFINITIONS
"employee": s.230(1).
"employer": s.230(4).

GENERAL NOTE
An employee will not be entitled if, on the date of the service of the notice of intention to claim, it was reasonably to be expected that he or she (if the employment continued) would enter

a period of employment of not less than 13 weeks within four weeks of that date, during which there would not be a lay-off or short-time working for any week. In that case, the employer must give the employee a counter-notice in writing stating that liability to pay the redundancy payment will be contested. The counter-notice must be given within seven days after the service of the employee's notice of intention to claim. The provisions of subs. (1) do not apply where the employee continues or has continued to be employed by the same employer during the four weeks after the date of the service of the notice of intention to claim and is or has been laid off or kept on short-time work for each of those weeks: subs. (2). Note also s.154.

Supplementary

The relevant date

153. For the purposes of the provisions of this Act relating to redundancy payments "the relevant date" in relation to a notice of intention to claim or a right to a redundancy payment in pursuance of such a notice—
  (a) in a case falling within paragraph (a) of subsection (2) of section 148, means the date on which the last of the four or more consecutive weeks before the service of the notice came to an end, and
  (b) in a case falling within paragraph (b) of that subsection, means the date on which the last of the series of six or more weeks before the service of the notice came to an end.

Provisions supplementing sections 148 and 152

154. For the purposes of sections 148(2) and 152(2)—
  (a) it is immaterial whether a series of weeks consists wholly of weeks for which the employee is laid off or wholly of weeks for which he is kept on short-time or partly of the one and partly of the other, and
  (b) no account shall be taken of any week for which an employee is laid off or kept on short-time where the lay-off or short-time is wholly or mainly attributable to a strike or a lock-out (whether or not in the trade or industry in which the employee is employed and whether in Great Britain or elsewhere).

CHAPTER IV

GENERAL EXCLUSIONS FROM RIGHT

Qualifying period of employment

155. An employee does not have any right to a redundancy payment unless he has been continuously employed for a period of not less than two years ending with the relevant date.

DEFINITIONS
  "continuously employed": ss.210–219.
  "employee": s.230(1).
  "relevant date": s.145.

Upper age limit

156.—(1) An employee does not have any right to a redundancy payment if before the relevant date he has attained—
  (a) in a case where—
      (i) in the business for the purposes of which the employee was employed there was a normal retiring age of less than sixty-five for an employee holding the position held by the employee, and
      (ii) the age was the same whether the employee holding that position was a man or woman,
    that normal retiring age, and
  (b) in any other case, the age of sixty-five.

(2) Subsection (1) does not apply to a case within section 137(1).

DEFINITIONS
"employee": s.230(1).
"position": s.235(1).
"relevant date": s.145.

GENERAL NOTE
Subsection (1) contains the general exclusion of employees over the normal retiring age or, where there is no such age, 65. But this exclusion does not apply to employees who fall within s.137. These provisions are identical to those contained in s.109(1) and the notes to that subsection should therefore be referred to.

Exemption orders

157.—(1) Where an order under this section is in force in respect of an agreement covered by this section, an employee who, immediately before the relevant date, is an employee to whom the agreement applies does not have any right to a redundancy payment.
(2) An agreement is covered by this section if it is an agreement between—
(a) one or more employers or organisations of employers, and
(b) one or more trade unions representing employees,
under which employees to whom the agreement applies have a right in certain circumstances to payments on the termination of their contracts of employment.
(3) Where, on the application of all the parties to an agreement covered by this section, the Secretary of State is satisfied, having regard to the provisions of the agreement, that the employees to whom the agreement applies should not have any right to a redundancy payment, he may make an order under this section in respect of the agreement.
(4) The Secretary of State shall not make an order under this section in respect of an agreement unless the agreement indicates (in whatever terms) the willingness of the parties to it to submit to an industrial tribunal any question arising under the agreement as to—
(a) the right of an employee to a payment on the termination of his employment, or
(b) the amount of such a payment.
(5) An order revoking an earlier order under this section may be made in pursuance of an application by all or any of the parties to the agreement in question or in the absence of such an application.
(6) Subsection (1) does not apply to a case within section 137(1).

DEFINITIONS
"contract of employment": s.230(2).
"employee": s.230(1).
"employer": s.230(4).
"relevant date": s.145.
"trade union": s.235 (1).

GENERAL NOTE
The provisions of this section apply where a collective agreement is in force which gives employees to whom it relates a right in certain circumstances to receive payments on the termination of their contracts of employment. The parties to the agreement must apply to the Secretary of State for the agreement to be exempted. If an order is made, the employees to whom the agreement applies will be excluded from the statutory right to receive a redundancy payment and will have to rely on their rights under the agreement. The Secretary of State must be satisfied that the agreement indicates that the parties are willing to submit to an industrial tribunal questions arising under the agreement concerning the right of an employee to the payment or to the amount of a payment. An exemption order may be revoked by a later order, whether or not the parties to the agreement have applied for it to be revoked: see subs. (5). Note subs. (6).

Pension rights

158.—(1) The Secretary of State shall by regulations make provision for excluding the right to a redundancy payment, or reducing the amount of any redundancy payment, in such cases to which subsection (2) applies as are prescribed by the regulations.

(2) This subsection applies to cases in which an employee has (whether by virtue of any statutory provision or otherwise) a right or claim (whether or not legally enforceable) to a periodical payment or lump sum by way of pension, gratuity or superannuation allowance which—

(a) is to be paid by reference to his employment by a particular employer, and

(b) is to be paid, or to begin to be paid, at the time when he leaves the employment or within such period after he leaves the employment as may be prescribed by the regulations.

(3) The regulations shall secure that the right to a redundancy payment shall not be excluded, and that the amount of a redundancy payment shall not be reduced, by reason of any right or claim to a periodical payment or lump sum, in so far as the payment or lump sum—

(a) represents compensation for loss of employment or for loss or diminution of emoluments or of pension rights, and

(b) is payable under a statutory provision (whether passed or made before or after the passing of this Act).

(4) In relation to any case where (in accordance with any provision of this Part) an industrial tribunal determines that an employer is liable to pay part (but not the whole) of a redundancy payment the references in this section to a redundancy payment, or to the amount of a redundancy payment, are to the part of the redundancy payment, or to the amount of the part.

DEFINITIONS
"employee": s.230(1).
"employer": s.230(4).
"employment": s.230(5).

GENERAL NOTE
Employees with pension rights are subject to regulations made by the Secretary of State under this section which may exclude their right to a redundancy payment or reduce the amount of any redundancy payment. The relevant regulations are the Redundancy Payments Pensions Regulations 1965 (S.I. 1965 No. 1932) particularly reg. 3. See *Stowe-Woodward B.T.R. v. Beynon* [1978] I.C.R. 609, *British Telecommunications v. Burwell* [1986] I.C.R. 35 and *Royal Ordnance v. Pilkington* [1989] I.C.R. 737.

Public offices etc.

159. A person does not have any right to a redundancy payment in respect of any employment which—

(a) is employment in a public office within the meaning of section 39 of the Superannuation Act 1965, or

(b) is for the purposes of pensions and other superannuation benefits treated (whether by virtue of that Act or otherwise) as service in the civil service of the State.

DEFINITIONS
"employment": s.230(5).

GENERAL NOTE
Holders of certain public offices are excluded from the right to receive a redundancy payment since special schemes exist for them which are more beneficial than the statutory scheme. An example of such a scheme is the Whitley Council Agreement, which provides for redundancy payments. Such schemes may include a provision for referring disputes to an industrial tribunal, as does the Whitley Council Agreement. In that case, they are governed by s.177, which does not

provide a limitation period for the bringing of claims. References under s.177 are, therefore, governed by the ordinary limitation rules and must be brought within six years: see *Greenwich Health Authority v. Skinner* [1989] I.C.R. 220 and *Stevens v. Bexley Health Authority* [1989] I.C.R. 224.

Overseas government employment

160.—(1) A person does not have any right to a redundancy payment in respect of employment in any capacity under the Government of an overseas territory.

(2) The reference in subsection (1) to the Government of an overseas territory includes a reference to—
(a) a Government constituted for two or more overseas territories, and
(b) any authority established for the purpose of providing or administering services which are common to, or relate to matters of common interest to, two or more overseas territories.

(3) In this section references to an overseas territory are to any territory or country outside the United Kingdom.

Domestic servants

161.—(1) A person does not have any right to a redundancy payment in respect of employment as a domestic servant in a private household where the employer is the parent (or step-parent), grandparent, child (or step-child), grandchild or brother or sister (or half-brother or half-sister) of the employee.

(2) Subject to that, the provisions of this Part apply to an employee who is employed as a domestic servant in a private household as if—
(a) the household were a business, and
(b) the maintenance of the household were the carrying on of that business by the employer.

DEFINITIONS
"employment": s.230(5).

GENERAL NOTE
The redundancy payments provisions do not apply where the employer is one of the following in relation to the employee: parent, step-parent, grandparent, child, step-child, grandchild, brother, sister, half-brother or half-sister. Subject to this exclusion, subs. (2) provides for the household to be treated as if it were a business.

CHAPTER V

OTHER PROVISIONS ABOUT REDUNDANCY PAYMENTS

Amount of a redundancy payment

162.—(1) The amount of a redundancy payment shall be calculated by—
(a) determining the period, ending with the relevant date, during which the employee has been continuously employed,
(b) reckoning backwards from the end of that period the number of years of employment falling within that period, and
(c) allowing the appropriate amount for each of those years of employment.

(2) In subsection (1)(c) "the appropriate amount" means—
(a) one and a half weeks' pay for a year of employment in which the employee was not below the age of forty-one,
(b) one week's pay for a year of employment (not within paragraph (a)) in which he was not below the age of twenty-two, and
(c) half a week's pay for each year of employment not within paragraph (a) or (b).

(3) Where twenty years of employment have been reckoned under subsection (1), no account shall be taken under that subsection of any year of employment earlier than those twenty years.

(4) Where the relevant date is after the sixty-fourth anniversary of the day of the employee's birth, the amount arrived at under subsections (1) to (3) shall be reduced by the appropriate fraction.

(5) In subsection (4) "the appropriate fraction" means the fraction of which—

(a) the numerator is the number of whole months reckoned from the sixty-fourth anniversary of the day of the employee's birth in the period beginning with that anniversary and ending with the relevant date, and

(b) the denominator is twelve.

(6) Subsections (1) to (5) apply for the purposes of any provision of this Part by virtue of which an industrial tribunal may determine that an employer is liable to pay to an employee—

(a) the whole of the redundancy payment to which the employee would have had a right apart from some other provision, or

(b) such part of the redundancy payment to which the employee would have had a right apart from some other provision as the tribunal thinks fit,

as if any reference to the amount of a redundancy payment were to the amount of the redundancy payment to which the employee would have been entitled apart from that other provision.

(7) Subsections (4) and (5) do not apply to a case within section 137(1).

(8) This section has effect subject to any regulations under section 158 by virtue of which the amount of a redundancy payment, or part of a redundancy payment, may be reduced.

DEFINITIONS

"continuously employed": ss.210–219.
"employee": s.230(1).
"employment": s.230(5).
"relevant date": s.145.

GENERAL NOTE

To calculate a redundancy payment, it is necessary to find out the following information: (1) the employee's age at the relevant date; (2) the number of years of continuous employment; and (3) the amount of gross weekly pay, calculated in accordance with ss.220–229. See *Secretary of State for Employment v. John Woodrow & Sons (Builders)* [1983] IRLR 11 and *Donelan v. Kerrby Construction and Secretary of State for Employment* [1983] I.C.R. 237. The calculation is subject to the following limits: (a) the number of years used in the calculation may not exceed 20: subs. (2); and (b) the amount of a week's pay may not exceed a figure set by the Secretary of State for Employment and usually raised annually, the amount being £210 at the time of going to press: s.227(1).

Redundancy payments are calculated in accordance with the provisions of subss. (2)–(8). The total amount arrived at may be subject to a deduction in certain cases, mainly in the case of misconduct or where employees are near retirement age. Social security benefits paid to the employee are not deductible. It should be noted that statutory redundancy payments are exempt from income tax, but they must be aggregated with other termination payments received: Income and Corporation Taxes Act 1988, ss.579(1) and 580(3). The effect of this is to bring them within s.148. Similar considerations apply to *ex gratia* payments paid to compensate employees for loss of their statutory or contractual redundancy rights: see *Mairs v. Haughey* [1993] IRLR 551.

When the employer pays the redundancy payment, the employee must be given a written statement setting out the calculation of the payment. This does not apply to payments made as a result of a tribunal decision: see s.165.

Subs. (2)

This subsection sets out the method of calculation. This is to take each year of continuous employment, working backwards from the relevant date. For each year of continuous employment the amount of the redundancy payment is assessed on the basis of the employee's age at the beginning of the year. For each year in which the employee was 41 or more (but not more than 64), one and a half weeks' pay is payable; for each year in which he or she was between 22 and 41, one week's pay; for each year over the age of 18 between the time he or she started work and 22, half a week's pay. Thus, an employee employed for 20 years and made redundant at 62 will receive a redundancy payment reckoned on the basis of the years of continuous employment from 62 going back to 42. The maximum redundancy payment that can be awarded at present is thus £6,300. Employment before the age of 18 may not be counted: s.211(2). The effect of this last provision is that the employee's period of continuous employment will be treated as starting on his or her eighteenth birthday if that date is later than the starting date. Note also s.211(1).

Subss. (3) and (4)

Employees dismissed after their 64th birthday will have their redundancy payments reduced by one-twelfth for each complete month between the 64th birthday and the relevant date. In cases where subs. (4) applies, the amount of the redundancy payment to which the employee would ordinarily be entitled is reduced by one-twelfth for each complete month which has passed between the 64th birthday and the relevant date. In such cases, it will be particularly important to ascertain the relevant date; according to the E.A.T., the provisions in what is now s.145(5) for extending the relevant date do not apply to these cases: see *Slater v. John Swain & Son* [1981] I.C.R. 554.

References to industrial tribunals

163.—(1) Any question arising under this Part as to—
(a) the right of an employee to a redundancy payment, or
(b) the amount of a redundancy payment,
shall be referred to and determined by an industrial tribunal.

(2) For the purposes of any such reference, an employee who has been dismissed by his employer shall, unless the contrary is proved, be presumed to have been so dismissed by reason of redundancy.

(3) Any question whether an employee will become entitled to a redundancy payment if he is not dismissed by his employer and he terminates his contract of employment as mentioned in section 150(1) shall for the purposes of this Part be taken to be a question as to the right of the employee to a redundancy payment.

(4) Where an order under section 157 is in force in respect of an agreement, this section has effect in relation to any question arising under the agreement as to the right of an employee to a payment on the termination of his employment, or as to the amount of such a payment, as if the payment were a redundancy payment and the question arose under this Part.

DEFINITIONS
　"contract of employment": s.230(2).
　"employee": s.230(1).
　"employer": s.230(4).

GENERAL NOTE
　This section provides for claims for redundancy payments—both as to entitlement and to amount—to be heard and determined by an industrial tribunal. Note the provisions of subs. (2), which enact the presumption of redundancy. This does not apply, however, to the unfair dismissal part of a claim where an employee makes a dual claim for unfair dismissal and a redundancy payment: see s.6(7) of the Industrial Tribunals Act 1996.

Claims for redundancy payment

164.—(1) An employee does not have any right to a redundancy payment unless, before the end of the period of six months beginning with the relevant date—
(a) the payment has been agreed and paid,
(b) the employee has made a claim for the payment by notice in writing given to the employer,

(c) a question as to the employee's right to, or the amount of, the payment has been referred to an industrial tribunal, or

(d) a complaint relating to his dismissal has been presented by the employee under section 111.

(2) An employee is not deprived of his right to a redundancy payment by subsection (1) if, during the period of six months immediately following the period mentioned in that subsection, the employee—

(a) makes a claim for the payment by notice in writing given to the employer,

(b) refers to an industrial tribunal a question as to his right to, or the amount of, the payment, or

(c) presents a complaint relating to his dismissal under section 111,

and it appears to the tribunal to be just and equitable that the employee should receive a redundancy payment.

(3) In determining under subsection (2) whether it is just and equitable that an employee should receive a redundancy payment an industrial tribunal shall have regard to—

(a) the reason shown by the employee for his failure to take any such step as is referred to in subsection (2) within the period mentioned in subsection (1), and

(b) all the other relevant circumstances.

DEFINITIONS
    "employee": s.230(1).
    "employer": s.230(4).
    "relevant date": s.145.

GENERAL NOTE
    In contrast to the problems encountered with the limitation provision in unfair dismissal claims, s.111(2), the limitation period for claims for redundancy payments appears to have caused relatively little litigation. It is a jurisdictional provision: *Secretary of State for Employment v. Atkins Auto Laundries* [1972] I.C.R. 76. By virtue of subs. (1) an employee will be deprived of the right to a redundancy payment, unless before the end of a six-month period beginning with the relevant date one of the following events occurs: (a) the payment has been agreed and paid; or (b) the employee has made a claim for the payment by notice in writing given to the employer; or (c) a question as to the right to a payment, or the amount of the payment, has been referred to an industrial tribunal; or (d) he or she has presented a complaint of unfair dismissal to the tribunal. In *Price v. Smithfield & Zwanenberg Group* [1978] I.C.R. 93, the E.A.T. said that the test of whether there was sufficient written notice of a claim within subs. (1)(b) was whether the notice or writing relied upon was of such a character that the recipient would reasonably understand in all the circumstances of the case that it was the employee's intention to seek a redundancy payment. In *Nash v. Ryan International* [1977] I.C.R. 560, the E.A.T. held that it will be sufficient if the employee's application is posted, even though it is not received. This case was distinguished in *Secretary of State for Employment v. Bank* [1983] I.C.R. 48, in which the E.A.T. held that an application was referred when it was received by the tribunal office, not on the date it was sent by the employee. In *Duffin v. Secretary of State for Employment* [1983] I.C.R. 766, the E.A.T. held that a complaint of unfair dismissal presented within six months entitles the employee to a redundancy payment even though the complaint would have been out of time for the purposes of the tribunal's unfair dismissal jurisdiction.
    If the six-month limit is not observed, the tribunal has power, by virtue of subs. (2), to award a payment if it considers it just and equitable to do so, having regard to the reason shown by the employee for failing to take the relevant steps and all the other relevant circumstances. But he or she must make the claim, in one of the three ways described in (b) to (d) above, during the six-month period immediately following the initial six-month period. A claim which is made outside 12 months after the relevant date will be time-barred. The employee will be protected if he or she makes a claim within (b) above. There is no requirement that the application to the industrial tribunal should follow within any particular time: *Price v. Smithfield & Zwanenberg Group* [1978] I.C.R. 93. See also *Bentley Engineering Co. v. Miller* [1976] I.C.R. 225.
    It should be noted that the employee's claim will be invalid if it is made before his employment comes to an end: see *Watts v. Rubery Owen Conveyancer* [1977] I.C.R. 429 and *cf.* s.111(3), which allows complaints of unfair dismissal to be presented during the notice period.

Written particulars of redundancy payment

165.—(1) On making any redundancy payment, otherwise than in pursuance of a decision of a tribunal which specifies the amount of the payment to be made, the employer shall give to the employee a written statement indicating how the amount of the payment has been calculated.

(2) An employer who without reasonable excuse fails to comply with subsection (1) is guilty of an offence and liable on summary conviction to a fine not exceeding level 1 on the standard scale.

(3) If an employer fails to comply with the requirements of subsection (1), the employee may by notice in writing to the employer require him to give to the employee a written statement complying with those requirements within such period (not being less than one week beginning with the day on which the notice is given) as may be specified in the notice.

(4) An employer who without reasonable excuse fails to comply with a notice under subsection (3) is guilty of an offence and liable on summary conviction to a fine not exceeding level 3 on the standard scale.

DEFINITIONS
  "employee": s.230(1).
  "employer": s.230(4).

GENERAL NOTE
  When the employer pays the redundancy payment, the employee must be given a written statement setting out the calculation of the payment. This does not apply to payments made as a result of a tribunal decision. An employer who fails to comply without reasonable excuse is guilty of an offence and liable on summary conviction to a fine.
  A failure by an employer to give a written statement, as required by this provision, does not of itself prevent a payment from being a redundancy payment: see *Barnsley M.B.C. v. Frest* [1996] I.C.R. 85.

CHAPTER VI

PAYMENTS BY SECRETARY OF STATE

Applications for payments

166.—(1) Where an employee claims that his employer is liable to pay to him an employer's payment and either—
  (a) that the employee has taken all reasonable steps, other than legal proceedings, to recover the payment from the employer and the employer has refused or failed to pay it, or has paid part of it and has refused or failed to pay the balance, or
  (b) that the employer is insolvent and the whole or part of the payment remains unpaid,
the employee may apply to the Secretary of State for a payment under this section.

(2) In this Part "employer's payment", in relation to an employee, means—
  (a) a redundancy payment which his employer is liable to pay to him under this Part, or
  (b) a payment which his employer is, under an agreement in respect of which an order is in force under section 157, liable to make to him on the termination of his contract of employment.

(3) In relation to any case where (in accordance with any provision of this Part) an industrial tribunal determines that an employer is liable to pay part (but not the whole) of a redundancy payment the reference in subsection (2)(a) to a redundancy payment is to the part of the redundancy payment.

(4) In subsection (1)(a) "legal proceedings"—
(a) does not include any proceedings before an industrial tribunal, but
(b) includes any proceedings to enforce a decision or award of an industrial tribunal.

(5) An employer is insolvent for the purposes of subsection (1)(b)—
(a) where the employer is an individual, if (but only if) subsection (6) is satisfied, and
(b) where the employer is a company, if (but only if) subsection (7) is satisfied.

(6) This subsection is satisfied in the case of an employer who is an individual—
(a) in England and Wales if—
(i) he has been adjudged bankrupt or has made a composition or arrangement with his creditors, or
(ii) he has died and his estate falls to be administered in accordance with an order under section 421 of the Insolvency Act 1986, and
(b) in Scotland if—
(i) sequestration of his estate has been awarded or he has executed a trust deed for his creditors or has entered into a composition contract, or
(ii) he has died and a judicial factor appointed under section 11A of the Judicial Factors (Scotland) Act 1889 is required by that section to divide his insolvent estate among his creditors.

(7) This subsection is satisfied in the case of an employer which is a company—
(a) if a winding up order or an administration order has been made or a resolution for voluntary winding up has been passed, with respect to the company,
(b) if a receiver or (in England and Wales only) a manager of the company's undertaking has been duly appointed, or (in England and Wales only) possession has been taken, by or on behalf of the holders of any debentures secured by a floating charge, of any property of the company comprised in or subject to the charge, or
(c) if a voluntary arrangement proposed in the case of the company for the purposes of Part I of the Insolvency Act 1986 has been approved under that Part of that Act.

Definitions
  "employee": s.230(1).
  "employer": s.230(4).

General Note
  An employee may apply under this section to the Secretary of State for a payment direct from the National Insurance Fund. This course of action is available where the employer refuses or fails to pay all or part of a redundancy payment to which the employee claims to be entitled and the employee has taken reasonable steps (other than legal proceedings) to recover the payment; it is also available where the employer is insolvent, as defined in subss. (6) and (7), and the whole or part of the payment remains unpaid. If the Secretary of State makes a payment, he will be subrogated to the employee's rights and remedies: see s.167(3). Disputes are dealt with by the industrial tribunal: see s.170. The Employment Act 1990, s.13, provided for the merger of the Redundancy Fund with the National Insurance Fund.

Making of payments

167.—(1) Where, on an application under section 166 by an employee in relation to an employer's payment, the Secretary of State is satisfied that the requirements specified in subsection (2) are met, he shall pay to the employee out of the National Insurance Fund a sum calculated in accordance with section 168 but reduced by so much (if any) of the employer's payment as has already been paid.

(2) The requirements referred to in subsection (1) are—

(a) that the employee is entitled to the employer's payment, and

(b) that one of the conditions specified in paragraphs (a) and (b) of subsection (1) of section 166 is fulfilled,

and, in a case where the employer's payment is a payment such as is mentioned in subsection (2)(b) of that section, that the employee's right to the payment arises by virtue of a period of continuous employment (computed in accordance with the provisions of the agreement in question) which is not less than two years.

(3) Where under this section the Secretary of State pays a sum to an employee in respect of an employer's payment—

(a) all rights and remedies of the employee with respect to the employer's payment, or (if the Secretary of State has paid only part of it) all the rights and remedies of the employee with respect to that part of the employer's payment, are transferred to and vest in the Secretary of State, and

(b) any decision of an industrial tribunal requiring the employer's payment to be paid to the employee has effect as if it required that payment, or that part of it which the Secretary of State has paid, to be paid to the Secretary of State.

(4) Any money recovered by the Secretary of State by virtue of subsection (3) shall be paid into the National Insurance Fund.

DEFINITIONS
"employee": s.230(1).
"employer's payment": s.166(2).

GENERAL NOTE
See General Note to preceding section.

Amount of payments

168.—(1) The sum payable to an employee by the Secretary of State under section 167—

(a) where the employer's Payment to which the employee's application under section 166 relates is a redundancy payment or a part of a redundancy payment, is a sum equal to the amount of the redundancy payment or part, and

(b) where the employer's payment to which the employee's application under section 166 relates is a payment which the employer is liable to make under an agreement in respect of which an order is in force under section 157, is a sum equal to the amount of the employer's payment or of the relevant redundancy payment, whichever is less.

(2) The reference in subsection (1)(b) to the amount of the relevant redundancy payment is to the amount of the redundancy payment which the employer would have been liable to pay to the employee on the assumptions specified in subsection (3).

(3) The assumptions referred to in subsection (2) are that—

(a) the order in force in respect of the agreement had not been made,

(b) the circumstances in which the employer's payment is payable had been such that the employer was liable to pay a redundancy payment to the employee in those circumstances,

(c) the relevant date, in relation to any such redundancy payment, had been the date on which the termination of the employee's contract of employment is treated as having taken effect for the purposes of the agreement, and

(d) in so far as the provisions of the agreement relating to the circumstances in which the continuity of an employee's period of employment is to be treated as broken, and the weeks which are to count in computing a period of employment, are inconsistent with the provisions of Chapter I of Part XIV, the provisions of the agreement were substituted for those provisions.

DEFINITIONS
"employee": s.230(1).
"employer's payment": s.166(2).

Information relating to applications for payments

169.—(1) Where an employee makes an application to the Secretary of State under section 166, the Secretary of State may, by notice in writing given to the employer, require the employer—
(a) to provide the Secretary of State with such information, and
(b) to produce for examination on behalf of the Secretary of State documents in his custody or under his control of such description,
as the Secretary of State may reasonably require for the purpose of determining whether the application is well-founded.

(2) Where a person on whom a notice is served under subsection (1) fails without reasonable excuse to comply with a requirement imposed by the notice, he is guilty of an offence and liable on summary conviction to a fine not exceeding level 3 on the standard scale.

(3) A person is guilty of an offence if—
(a) in providing any information required by a notice under subsection (1), he makes a statement which he knows to be false in a material particular or recklessly makes a statement which is false in a material particular, or
(b) he produces for examination in accordance with a notice under subsection (1) a document which to his knowledge has been wilfully falsified.

(4) A person guilty of an offence under subsection (3) is liable—
(a) on summary conviction, to a fine not exceeding the statutory maximum or to imprisonment for a term not exceeding three months, or to both, or
(b) on conviction on indictment, to a fine or to imprisonment for a term not exceeding two years, or to both.

DEFINITIONS
"employer": s.230(4).

References to industrial tribunals

170.—(1) Where on an application made to the Secretary of State for a payment under section 166 it is claimed that an employer is liable to pay an employer's payment, there shall be referred to an industrial tribunal—
(a) any question as to the liability of the employer to pay the employer's payment, and
(b) any question as to the amount of the sum payable in accordance with section 168.

(2) For the purposes of any reference under this section an employee who has been dismissed by his employer shall, unless the contrary is proved, be presumed to have been so dismissed by reason of redundancy.

DEFINITIONS
"employee": s.230(1).
"employer": s.230(4).
"employer's payment": s.166(2).

CHAPTER VII

SUPPLEMENTARY

Application of Part to particular cases

Employment not under contract of employment

171.—(1) The Secretary of State may by regulations provide that, subject to such exceptions and modifications as may be prescribed by the regulations, this Part and the provisions of this Act supplementary to this Part have effect in relation to any employment of a description to which this section applies as may be so prescribed as if—

(a) it were employment under a contract of employment,

(b) any person engaged in employment of that description were an employee, and

(c) such person as may be determined by or under the regulations were his employer.

(2) This section applies to employment of any description which—

(a) is employment in the case of which secondary Class 1 contributions are payable under Part I of the Social Security Contributions and Benefits Act 1992 in respect of persons engaged in it, but

(b) is not employment under a contract of service or of apprenticeship or employment of any description falling within subsection (3).

(3) The following descriptions of employment fall within this subsection—

(a) any employment such as is mentioned in section 159 (whether as originally enacted or as modified by an order under section 209(1)),

(b) any employment remunerated out of the revenue of the Duchy of Lancaster or the Duchy of Cornwall,

(c) any employment remunerated out of the Queen's Civil List, and

(d) any employment remunerated out of Her Majesty's Privy Purse.

DEFINITIONS
"contract of employment": s.230(2).
"employee": s.230(1).
"employer": s.230(4).
"employment": s.230(5).

GENERAL NOTE
This section gives the Secretary of State power to make regulations providing for specified office-holders to be embraced by the coverage of the redundancy provisions. These are the Redundancy Payments Office Holders Regulations 1965 (S.I. 1965 No. 2007) and the Redundancy Payments Office Holders (Scotland) Regulations 1966 (S.I. 1966 No. 1436).

Termination of employment by statute

172.—(1) The Secretary of State may by regulations provide that, subject to such exceptions and modifications as may be prescribed by the regulations, this Part has effect in relation to any person who by virtue of any statutory provisions—

(a) is transferred to, and becomes a member of, a body specified in those provisions, but

(b) at a time so specified ceases to be a member of that body unless before that time certain conditions so specified have been fulfilled,

as if the cessation of his membership of that body by virtue of those provisions were dismissal by his employer by reason of redundancy.

(2) The power conferred by subsection (1) is exercisable whether or not membership of the body in question constitutes employment within the meaning of section 230(5); and, where that membership does not constitute such employment, that power may be exercised in addition to any power exercisable under section 171.

DEFINITIONS
  "employer": s.230(4).
  "employment": s.230(5).

GENERAL NOTE
  This section gives the Secretary of State power to make regulations treating the termination of certain employments by statute as equivalent to dismissal. Regulations made under this section have extended the redundancy provisions to chief constables and chief officers of fire brigades: see the Redundancy Payments Termination of Employment Regulations 1965 (S.I. 1965 No. 2022).

Employees paid by person other than employer

173.—(1) For the purposes of the operation of the provisions of this Part (and Chapter I of Part XIV) in relation to any employee whose remuneration is, by virtue of any statutory provision, payable to him by a person other than his employer, each of the references to the employer specified in subsection (2) shall be construed as a reference to the person by whom the remuneration is payable.

(2) The references referred to in subsection (1) are the first reference in section 135(1), the third reference in section 140(3), the first reference in section 142(3) and the first reference in section 143(2)(c) and the references in sections 142(2)(b), 143(4) and (5), 149(a) and (b), 150(3), 152(1)(b), 158(4), 162(6), 164 to 169, 170(1) and 214(5).

DEFINITIONS
  "employee": s.230(1).
  "employer": s.230(4).

Death of employer or employee

Death of employer: dismissal

174.—(1) Where the contract of employment of an employee is taken for the purposes of this Part to be terminated by his employer by reason of the employer's death, this Part has effect in accordance with the following provisions of this section.

(2) Section 138 applies as if—

(a) in subsection (1)(a), for the words "in pursuance" onwards there were substituted "by a personal representative of the deceased employer",

(b) in subsection (1)(b), for the words "either immediately" onwards there were substituted "not later than eight weeks after the death of the deceased employer", and

(c) in subsections (2)(b) and (6)(a), for the word "employer" there were substituted "personal representative of the deceased employer".

(3) Section 141(1) applies as if—

(a) for the words "before the end of his employment" there were substituted "by a personal representative of the deceased employer", and

(b) for the words "either immediately" onwards there were substituted "not later than eight weeks after the death of the deceased employer."

(4) For the purposes of section 141—

(a) provisions of the contract as renewed, or of the new contract, do not differ from the corresponding provisions of the contract in force immediately before the death of the deceased employer by reason only that the personal representative would be substituted for the deceased employer as the employer, and

(b) no account shall be taken of that substitution in determining whether refusal of the offer was unreasonable or whether the employee acted reasonably in terminating or giving notice to terminate the new or renewed employment.

(5) Section 146 has effect as if—

  (a) subsection (1) were omitted, and

  (b) in subsection (2), paragraph (a) were omitted and, in paragraph (b), for the word "four" there were substituted "eight".

(6) For the purposes of the application of this Part (in accordance with section 161(2)) in relation to an employee who was employed as a domestic servant in a private household, references in this section and sections 175 and 218(4) and (5) to a personal representative include a person to whom the management of the household has passed, otherwise than in pursuance of a sale or other disposition for valuable consideration, in consequence of the death of the employer.

<small>DEFINITIONS</small>
  "contract of employment": s.230(2).
  "employee": s.230(1).
  "employer": s.230(4).
  "employment": s.230(5).

<small>GENERAL NOTE</small>
  This section makes appropriate adjustments to the redundancy payments provisions in cases where the employer dies.

Death of employer: lay-off and short-time

175.—(1) Where an employee is laid off or kept on short-time and his employer dies, this Part has effect in accordance with the following provisions of this section.

(2) Where the employee—

  (a) has been laid off or kept on short-time for one or more weeks before the death of the employer,

  (b) has not given the deceased employer notice of intention to claim before the employer's death,

  (c) after the employer's death has his contract of employment renewed, or is re-engaged under a new contract, by a personal representative of the deceased employer, and

  (d) after renewal or re-engagement is laid off or kept on short-time for one or more weeks by the personal representative,

the week in which the employer died and the first week of the employee's employment by the personal representative shall be treated for the purposes of Chapter III as consecutive weeks (and references to four weeks or thirteen weeks shall be construed accordingly).

(3) The following provisions of this section apply where—

  (a) the employee has given the deceased employer notice of intention to claim before the employer's death,

  (b) the employer's death occurred before the end of the period of four weeks after the service of the notice, and

  (c) the employee has not terminated his contract of employment by notice expiring before the employer's death.

(4) If the contract of employment is not renewed, and the employee is not re-engaged under a new contract, by a personal representative of the deceased employer before the end of the period of four weeks after the service of the notice of intention to claim—

  (a) sections 149 and 152 do not apply, but

  (b) (subject to that) Chapter III applies as if the employer had not died and the employee had terminated the contract of employment by a week's notice, or by the minimum notice which he is required to give to terminate the contract (if longer than a week), expiring at the end of that period.

(5) If—

  (a) the contract of employment is renewed, or the employee is re-engaged under a new contract, by a personal representative of the deceased employer before the end of the period of four weeks after the service of the notice of intention to claim, and

(b) the employee was laid off or kept on short-time by the deceased employer for one or more of those weeks and is laid off or kept on short-time by the personal representative for the week, or for the next two or more weeks, following the renewal or re-engagement,

subsection (6) has effect.

(6) Where this subsection has effect Chapter III applies as if—

(a) all the weeks mentioned in subsection (5) were consecutive weeks during which the employee was employed (but laid off or kept on short-time) by the same employer, and

(b) the periods specified by section 150(3)(a) and (b) as the relevant period were extended by any week or weeks any part of which was after the death of the employer and before the date on which the renewal or re-engagement took effect.

DEFINITIONS
"contract of employment": s.230(2).
"employee": s.230(1).
"employer": s.230(4).

GENERAL NOTE
This section makes appropriate adjustments to the provisions relating to lay-off and short-time in cases where the employer dies.

Death of employee

176.—(1) Where an employee whose employer has given him notice to terminate his contract of employment dies before the notice expires, this Part applies as if the contract had been duly terminated by the employer by notice expiring on the date of the employee's death.

(2) Where—

(a) an employee's contract of employment has been terminated by the employer,

(b) (by virtue of subsection (5) of section 145) a date later than the relevant date as defined by the previous provisions of that section is the relevant date for the purposes of certain provisions of this Act, and

(c) the employee dies before that date,

that subsection applies as if the notice to which it refers would have expired on the employee's death.

(3) Where—

(a) an employer has given notice to an employee to terminate his contract of employment and has offered to renew his contract of employment or to re-engage him under a new contract, and

(b) the employee dies without having accepted or refused the offer and without the offer having been withdrawn,

section 141(2) applies as if for the words "he unreasonably refuses" there were substituted "it would have been unreasonable on his part to refuse".

(4) Where an employee's contract of employment has been renewed or he has been re-engaged under a new contract—

(a) if he dies during the trial period without having terminated, or given notice to terminate, the contract, section 141(4) applies as if for paragraph (d) there were substituted—

"(d) it would have been unreasonable for the employee during the trial period to terminate or give notice to terminate the contract.", and

(b) if during that trial period he gives notice to terminate the contract but dies before the notice expires, sections 138(2) and 141(4) apply as if the notice had expired (and the contract had been terminated by its expiry) on the date of the employee's death.

(5) Where in the circumstances specified in paragraphs (a) and (b) of subsection (3) of section 136 the employee dies before the notice given by him under paragraph (b) of that subsection expires—

    (a) if he dies before his employer has given him a notice such as is specified in subsection (2) of section 142, subsections (3) and (4) of that section apply as if the employer had given him such a notice and he had not complied with it, and

    (b) if he dies after his employer has given him such a notice, that section applies as if the employee had not died but did not comply with the notice.

(6) Where an employee has given notice of intention to claim—

    (a) if he dies before he has given notice to terminate his contract of employment and before the relevant period (as defined in subsection (3) of section 150) has expired, that section does not apply, and

    (b) if he dies within the period of seven days after the service of the notice of intention to claim, and before the employer has given a counter-notice, Chapter III applies as if the employer had given a counter-notice within that period of seven days.

(7) Where a claim for a redundancy payment is made by a personal representative of a deceased employee—

    (a) if the employee died before the end of the period of six months beginning with the relevant date, subsection (1) of section 164, and

    (b) if the employee died after the end of the period of six months beginning with the relevant date but before the end of the following period of six months, subsection (2) of that section,

applies as if for the words "six months" there were substituted "one year".

DEFINITIONS
    "contract of employment": s.230(2).
    "employee": s.230(1).
    "employer": s.230(4).

GENERAL NOTE
    This section deals with a number of situations where an employee dies after being given notice of dismissal.

Equivalent payments

References to industrial tribunals

177.—(1) Where the terms and conditions (whether or not they constitute a contract of employment) on which a person is employed in employment of any description mentioned in section 171(3) include provision—

    (a) for the making of a payment to which this section applies, and

    (b) for referring to an industrial tribunal any question as to the right of any person to such a payment in respect of that employment or as to the amount of such a payment,

the question shall be referred to and determined by an industrial tribunal.

(2) This section applies to any payment by way of compensation for loss of employment of any description mentioned in section 171(3) which is payable in accordance with arrangements falling within subsection (3).

(3) The arrangements which fall within this subsection are arrangements made with the approval of the Treasury (or, in the case of persons whose service is for the purposes of pensions and other superannuation benefits treated as service in the civil service of the State, of the Minister for the Civil Service) for securing that a payment will be made—

    (a) in circumstances which in the opinion of the Treasury (or Minister) correspond (subject to the appropriate modifications) to those in which a right to a redundancy payment would have accrued if the provisions of this Part (apart from section 159 and this section) applied, and

(b) on a scale which in the opinion of the Treasury (or Minister), taking into account any sums payable in accordance with—

(i) a scheme made under section 1 of the Superannuation Act 1972, or

(ii) the Superannuation Act 1965 as it continues to have effect by virtue of section 23(1) of the Superannuation Act 1972,

to or in respect of the person losing the employment in question, corresponds (subject to the appropriate modifications) to that on which a redundancy payment would have been payable if those provisions applied.

DEFINITIONS
"employment": s.230(5).

GENERAL NOTE
Holders of certain public offices are excluded from the right to receive a redundancy payment by s.159, since special schemes exist for them which are more beneficial than the statutory scheme. An example of such a scheme is the Whitley Council Agreement, which provides for redundancy payments. Such schemes may include a provision for referring disputes to an industrial tribunal, as does the Whitley Council Agreement. In that case, they are governed by this section, which does not provide a limitation period for the bringing of claims. References under this section are, therefore, governed by the ordinary limitation rules and must be brought within six years: see *Greenwich Health Authority v. Skinner* [1989] I.C.R. 220 and *Stevens v. Bexley Health Authority* [1989] I.C.R. 224.

Other supplementary provisions

Old statutory compensation schemes

178.—(1) The Secretary of State may make provision by regulations for securing that where—

(a) (apart from this section) a person is entitled to compensation under a statutory provision to which this section applies, and

(b) the circumstances are such that he is also entitled to a redundancy payment,

the amount of the redundancy payment shall be set off against the compensation to which he would be entitled apart from this section; and any statutory provision to which any such regulations apply shall have effect subject to the regulations.

(2) This section applies to any statutory provision—

(a) which was in force immediately before 6th December 1965, and

(b) under which the holders of such situations, places or employments as are specified in that provision are, or may become, entitled to compensation for loss of employment, or for loss or diminution of emoluments or of pension rights, in consequence of the operation of any other statutory provision referred to in that provision.

Notices

179.—(1) Any notice which under this Part is required or authorised to be given by an employer to an employee may be given by being delivered to the employee, or left for him at his usual or last-known place of residence, or sent by post addressed to him at that place.

(2) Any notice which under this Part is required or authorised to be given by an employee to an employer may be given either by the employee himself

or by a person authorised by him to act on his behalf, and (whether given by or on behalf of the employee)—

  (a) may be given by being delivered to the employer, or sent by post addressed to him at the place where the employee is or was employed by him, or

  (b) if arrangements have been made by the employer, may be given by being delivered to a person designated by the employer in pursuance of the arrangements, left for such a person at a place so designated or sent by post to such a person at an address so designated.

(3) In this section any reference to the delivery of a notice includes, in relation to a notice which is not required by this Part to be in writing, a reference to the oral communication of the notice.

(4) Any notice which, in accordance with any provision of this section, is left for a person at a place referred to in that provision shall, unless the contrary is proved, be presumed to have been received by him on the day on which it was left there.

(5) Nothing in subsection (1) or (2) affects the capacity of an employer to act by a servant or agent for the purposes of any provision of this Part (including either of those subsections).

(6) In relation to an employee to whom section 173 applies, this section has effect as if—

  (a) any reference in subsection (1) or (2) to a notice required or authorised to be given by or to an employer included a reference to a notice which, by virtue of that section, is required or authorised to be given by or to the person by whom the remuneration is payable,

  (b) in relation to a notice required or authorised to be given to that person, any reference to the employer in paragraph (a) or (b) of subsection (2) were a reference to that person, and

  (c) the reference to an employer in subsection (5) included a reference to that person.

DEFINITIONS
  "employee": s.230(1).
  "employer": s.230(4).

Offences

180.—(1) Where an offence under this Part committed by a body corporate is proved—

  (a) to have been committed with the consent or connivance of, or

  (b) to be attributable to any neglect on the part of,

any director, manager, secretary or other similar officer of the body corporate, or any person who was purporting to act in any such capacity, he (as well as the body corporate) is guilty of the offence and liable to be proceeded against and punished accordingly.

(2) In this section "director", in relation to a body corporate established by or under any enactment for the purpose of carrying on under national ownership any industry or part of an industry or undertaking, being a body corporate whose affairs are managed by its members, means a member of that body corporate.

Interpretation

181.—(1) In this Part—

  "counter-notice" shall be construed in accordance with section 149(a),
  "dismissal" and "dismissed" shall be construed in accordance with sections 136 to 138,
  "employer's payment" has the meaning given by section 166,
  "notice of intention to claim" shall be construed in accordance with section 148(1),

"obligatory period of notice" has the meaning given by section 136(4), and

"trial period" shall be construed in accordance with section 138(3).

(2) In this Part—

(a) references to an employee being laid off or being eligible for a redundancy payment by reason of being laid off, and

(b) references to an employee being kept on short-time or being eligible for a redundancy payment by reason of being kept on short-time,

shall be construed in accordance with sections 147 and 148.

PART XII

INSOLVENCY OF EMPLOYERS

Employee's rights on insolvency of employer

182. If, on an application made to him in writing by an employee, the Secretary of State is satisfied that—

(a) the employee's employer has become insolvent,

(b) the employee's employment has been terminated, and

(c) on the appropriate date the employee was entitled to be paid the whole or part of any debt to which this Part applies,

the Secretary of State shall, subject to section 186, pay the employee out of the National Insurance Fund the amount to which, in the opinion of the Secretary of State, the employee is entitled in respect of the debt.

DEFINITIONS
"appropriate date": s.185.
"employee": s.230(1).
"employer": s.230(4).
"insolvent": s.183.

GENERAL NOTE
Employees are given a limited amount of statutory protection when their employer becomes insolvent. First, under the insolvency laws, employees are treated as preferential creditors in respect of unpaid wages for the four months prior to the insolvency, up to a limit of £800 (Insolvency Act 1986 (c. 45), s.386 and Sched. 6); secondly, under Pt. XI of this Act, an employee may recover an unpaid redundancy payment (or other employer's payment payable to the employee on termination of employment) from the National Insurance Fund where the employer is insolvent (see the notes to ss.166–170); thirdly, under this Part of the Act, certain debts owed by an insolvent employer to employees are treated as guaranteed debts which can be recovered by employees from the National Insurance Fund; and finally, the administrator of an occupational pension scheme may claim unpaid employer's contributions to the scheme from the State where the employer is insolvent (Pension Schemes Act 1993, ss.123–127).

Under the provisions in this Part of the Act, an employee is entitled to apply for payment of certain guaranteed debts (as set out in s.184) from the Secretary of State. The application must be made in writing, and before making any payment the Secretary of State must be satisfied: (i) that the applicant's employer has become insolvent; (ii) that the applicant's employment has terminated; and (iii) that on the "appropriate date" (see s.185) the applicant was entitled to be paid in whole or in part any debt to which these provisions apply (subs. (1)). The following categories of employee are excluded from the right to claim payment of guaranteed debts: employees who ordinarily work outside the territory of the Member States of the European Communities and of Norway and Iceland (s.196(7)); share fishermen (s.199(2)); merchant seamen (s.199(4)), and, for obvious reasons, Crown employees (s.191(2)) and Parliamentary Staff (ss.194(2) and 195(2)).

These provisions are underpinned by EEC Directive No. 80/987 (the Insolvency Protection Directive), and must wherever possible be construed so as to comply with the requirements of the Directive: see *Secretary of State for Employment v. Mann* [1996] IRLR 4, where the E.A.T. held that the Secretary of State, when making a payment of a protective award under the equivalent EP(C)A provisions, was not entitled to set off against the protective award sums paid in lieu of notice, or wages paid for the protected period. The E.A.T. so held because in *Commission v. United Kingdom* [1994] IRLR 412, the E.C.J. held that the power formerly contained in s.190(3) (now repealed) of the Trade Union and Labour Relations (Consolidation) Act 1992, which allowed an employer to set off such payments against a protective award was not compatible with EEC Directive No. 75/129 (the Collective Redundancies Directive), and it would not be compatible with the Insolvency Directive for the Secretary of State to set off such payments where the employer could not do so. The E.A.T. also ruled that the eight-week limit on the arrears of pay recoverable from the Secretary of State imposed by s.184(1), and the ceiling on the total amount payable by the Secretary of State in respect of any week imposed by s.186(1), are not incompatible with Community law. See the notes to those sections.

Insolvent. This is defined for these purposes in s.183: see the note to that section.

The appropriate date. See the note to s.185.

Any debt to which this Part applies. See the note to s.184.

Insolvency

Insolvency

183.—(1) An employer has become insolvent for the purposes of this Part—

(a) where the employer is an individual, if (but only if) subsection (2) is satisfied, and

(b) where the employer is a company, if (but only if) subsection (3) is satisfied.

(2) This subsection is satisfied in the case of an employer who is an individual—

(a) in England and Wales if—

(i) he has been adjudged bankrupt or has made a composition or arrangement with his creditors, or

(ii) he has died and his estate falls to be administered in accordance with an order under section 421 of the Insolvency Act 1986, and

(b) in Scotland if—

(i) sequestration of his estate has been awarded or he has executed a trust deed for his creditors or has entered into a composition contract, or

(ii) he has died and a judicial factor appointed under section 11A of the Judicial Factors (Scotland) Act 1889 is required by that section to divide his insolvent estate among his creditors.

(3) This subsection is satisfied in the case of an employer which is a company—

(a) if a winding up order or an administration order has been made, or a resolution for voluntary winding up has been passed, with respect to the company,

(b) if a receiver or (in England and Wales only) a manager of the company's undertaking has been duly appointed, or (in England and Wales only) possession has been taken, by or on behalf of the holders of any debentures secured by a floating charge, of any property of the company comprised in or subject to the charge, or

(c) if a voluntary arrangement proposed in the case of the company for the purposes of Part I of the Insolvency Act 1986 has been approved under that Part of that Act.

DEFINITIONS

"employee": s.230(1).

"employer": s.230(4).

GENERAL NOTE

This section defines insolvency for the purposes of this Part of the Act. The same definition is used in s.166(5) for the purposes of the payment of redundancy payments, etc., by the Secretary of State.

Adjudged bankrupt. See the Insolvency Act 1986, Pt. IX *et seq.*

Composition or arrangement with his creditors. See the Pt. VIII of the Insolvency Act 1986 (c. 45).

Winding up order. See Pt. IV, Chap. VI *et seq.* of the Insolvency Act 1986.

Administration order. See Pt. II of the Insolvency Act 1986.

Resolution for voluntary winding up. See Pt. IV, Chap. II of the Insolvency Act 1986.

Receiver or ... manager has been appointed. See Pt. III of the Insolvency Act 1986. To fall within this head, the receiver must have been appointed for the purposes stated in subs. (3)(b): *Secretary of State for Employment v. Stone* [1994] IRLR 761, E.A.T.

Debts to which Part applies

184.—(1) This Part applies to the following debts—

(a) any arrears of pay in respect of one or more (but not more than eight) weeks,

(b) any amount which the employer is liable to pay the employee for the period of notice required by section 86(1) or (2) or for any failure of the employer to give the period of notice required by section 86(1),

(c) any holiday pay—

(i) in respect of a period or periods of holiday not exceeding six weeks in all, and

(ii) to which the employee became entitled during the twelve months ending with the appropriate date,

(d) any basic award of compensation for unfair dismissal, and

(e) any reasonable sum by way of reimbursement of the whole or part of any fee or premium paid by an apprentice or articled clerk.

(2) For the purposes of subsection (1)(a) the following amounts shall be treated as arrears of pay—

(a) a guarantee payment,

(b) any payment for time off under Part VI of this Act or section 169 of the Trade Union and Labour Relations (Consolidation) Act 1992 (payment for time off for carrying out trade union duties etc.),

(c) remuneration on suspension on medical grounds under section 64 of this Act and remuneration on suspension on maternity grounds under section 68 of this Act, and

(d) remuneration under a protective award under section 189 of the Trade Union and Labour Relations (Consolidation) Act 1992.

(3) In subsection (1)(c) "holiday pay", in relation to an employee, means—

(a) pay in respect of a holiday actually taken by the employee, or

(b) any accrued holiday pay which, under the employee's contract of employment, would in the ordinary course have become payable to him in respect of the period of a holiday if his employment with the employer had continued until he became entitled to a holiday.

(4) A sum shall be taken to be reasonable for the purposes of subsection (1)(e) in a case where a trustee in bankruptcy, or (in Scotland) a permanent or interim trustee (within the meaning of the Bankruptcy (Scotland) Act 1985), or liquidator has been or is required to be appointed—

(a) as respects England and Wales, if it is admitted to be reasonable by the trustee in bankruptcy or liquidator under section 348 of the Insolvency Act 1986 (effect of bankruptcy on apprenticeships etc.), whether as originally enacted or as applied to the winding up of a company by rules under section 411 of that Act, and

(b) as respects Scotland, if it is accepted by the permanent or interim trustee or liquidator for the purposes of the sequestration or winding up.

DEFINITIONS

"employee": s.230(1).

"employer": s.230(4).

"holiday pay": subs. (3).

GENERAL NOTE

This section sets out the debts which are guaranteed debts for the purposes of this Part. Note that the total amount payable is subject to the limit of £210 per week set by s.186(1).

Any arrears of pay. "Pay" for these purposes includes any of the statutory payments set out in subs. (2).

In respect of one or more (but not more than eight) weeks. In *Secretary of State for Employment v. Mann* [1996] IRLR 4, the E.A.T. ruled that the eight-week limit on the arrears of pay recoverable from the Secretary of State under these provisions is not incompatible with Community law, as the setting of that limit is expressly permitted under Arts. 3(2) and 4(2) of the Insolvency Directive. It was argued in that case that by allowing such a limit, the provisions of the Directive are themselves in breach of the fundamental principle of equality in Community law, but that argument was rejected by the E.A.T., which refused to make a reference to the E.C.J. on the matter.

Any amount which the employer is liable to pay the employee for the period of notice. Section 86 makes provision for certain minimum periods of notice to be given to terminate a contract of employment. During that period of notice, the employee is entitled to be paid in accordance with ss.88–91, and if the employee serves out that period of notice, that amount can be claimed from the employer as a liquidated sum, or from the National Insurance Fund as a guaranteed debt in the event of the employer's insolvency. However, the right to notice conferred by the Act is essentially a contractual right, so that if the employee is dismissed without notice, the employee's claim against the employer will be a claim for damages for breach of contract, and therefore subject to the usual contractual rules on mitigation of loss, and if the employer is insolvent the amount which may be claimed from the National Insurance Fund will be subject to the same rules. See *Westwood v. Secretary of State for Employment* [1984] IRLR 209, H.L., where it was held that the Secretary of State was entitled to deduct the amount of unemployment benefit received by the employee during the statutory notice period from the amount payable to the employee from the National Insurance Fund. See also *Secretary of State for Employment v. Cooper* [1987] I.C.R. 766, where the E.A.T. held, following *Westwood*, that it was also appropriate to deduct, by way of mitigation, any wages received during the notice period from another source, and any income tax otherwise payable on the amount due.

The appropriate date

185. In this Part "the appropriate date"—
- (a) in relation to arrears of pay (not being remuneration under a protective award made under section 189 of the Trade Union and Labour Relations (Consolidation) Act 1992) and to holiday pay, means the date on which the employer became insolvent,
- (b) in relation to a basic award of compensation for unfair dismissal and to remuneration under a protective award so made, means whichever is the latest of—
  - (i) the date on which the employer became insolvent,
  - (ii) the date of the termination of the employee's employment, and
  - (iii) the date on which the award was made, and
- (c) in relation to any other debt to which this Part applies, means whichever is the later of—
  - (i) the date on which the employer became insolvent, and
  - (ii) the date of the termination of the employee's employment.

DEFINITIONS

"employee": s.230(1).
"employer": s.230(4).
"holiday pay": s.184(3).

Limit on amount payable under section 182

186.—(1) The total amount payable to an employee in respect of any debt to which this Part applies, where the amount of the debt is referable to a period of time, shall not exceed—
- (a) £210 in respect of any one week, or
- (b) in respect of a shorter period, an amount bearing the same proportion to £210 as that shorter period bears to a week.

(2) The Secretary of State may vary the limit specified in subsection (1), after a review under section 208, by order made in accordance with that section.

DEFINITIONS
  "employee": s.230(1).

GENERAL NOTE
  The statutory limit on the amount payable under s.182 in respect of any week relates to the employee's gross wages, so that the correct approach is for the maximum to be applied before any reduction is made for the amount which would have been deducted for tax and National Insurance contributions: see *Morris v. Secretary of State for Employment* [1985] I.C.R. 492, E.A.T.
  In *Secretary of State for Employment v. Mann* [1996] IRLR 4, the E.A.T. rejected the argument that the statutory ceiling (then set at £205 per week, but raised to £210 from September 27, 1995) is not compatible with Community law. The E.A.T. pointed out that Art. 4(3) of the Insolvency Directive (Directive No. 80/987) expressly permits Member States to set a ceiling to the liability for employees' outstanding claims "in order to avoid the payment of sums going beyond the social objectives of the Directive". According to the E.A.T., the ceiling must be consistent with the social objective of the Directive, but that objective is the protection of employees, not the absolute guarantee of payments; the limit set by U.K. law represented a legitimate choice within the terms of the Directive, which could be justified as avoiding the payment of sums going beyond the protection aimed at by the Directive; it could not be said that the limit set was a derisory one.

Role of relevant officer

187.—(1) Where a relevant officer has been, or is required to be, appointed in connection with an employer's insolvency, the Secretary of State shall not make a payment under section 182 in respect of a debt until he has received a statement from the relevant officer of the amount of that debt which appears to have been owed to the employee on the appropriate date and to remain unpaid.
  (2) If the Secretary of State is satisfied that he does not require a statement under subsection (1) in order to determine the amount of a debt which was owed to the employee on the appropriate date and remains unpaid, he may make a payment under section 182 in respect of the debt without having received such a statement.
  (3) A relevant officer shall, on request by the Secretary of State, provide him with a statement for the purposes of subsection (1) as soon as is reasonably practicable.
  (4) The following are relevant officers for the purposes of this section—
  (a) a trustee in bankruptcy or a permanent or interim trustee (within the meaning of the Bankruptcy (Scotland) Act 1985),
  (b) a liquidator,
  (c) an administrator,
  (d) a receiver or manager,
  (e) a trustee under a composition or arrangement between the employer and his creditors, and
  (f) a trustee under a trust deed for his creditors executed by the employer.
  (5) In subsection (4)(e) "trustee" includes the supervisor of a voluntary arrangement proposed for the purposes of, and approved under, Part I or VIII of the Insolvency Act 1986.

DEFINITIONS
  "employee": s.230(1).
  "employer": s.230(4).
  "relevant officer": subs. (4).
  "trustee": subs. (5).

GENERAL NOTE
If a trustee in bankruptcy, liquidator or any of the other officers listed in subs. (4) has been appointed or is required to be appointed in connection with the employer's insolvency, this section provides that a payment may not be made out of the National Insurance Fund under s.182 until the official in question provides the Secretary of State with a statement of what is due to the employee (subs. (1)), unless the Secretary of State is satisfied that no such statement is needed in order to determine the amount due (subs. (2)). The Secretary of State may require a statement to be provided as soon as reasonably practicable (subs. (3)).

Complaints to industrial tribunals

188.—(1) A person who has applied for a payment under section 182 may present a complaint to an industrial tribunal—

(a) that the Secretary of State has failed to make any such payment, or

(b) that any such payment made by him is less than the amount which should have been paid.

(2) An industrial tribunal shall not consider a complaint under subsection (1) unless it is presented—

(a) before the end of the period of three months beginning with the date on which the decision of the Secretary of State on the application was communicated to the applicant, or

(b) within such further period as the tribunal considers reasonable in a case where it is not reasonably practicable for the complaint to be presented before the end of that period of three months.

(3) Where an industrial tribunal finds that the Secretary of State ought to make a payment under section 182, the tribunal shall—

(a) make a declaration to that effect, and

(b) declare the amount of any such payment which it finds the Secretary of State ought to make.

GENERAL NOTE
A complaint of non-payment or underpayment of a guaranteed debt must be presented within three months "beginning with the date on which the decision of the Secretary of State on the application was communicated to the applicant", unless it is not reasonably practicable for the complaint to be presented within that period, in which case the tribunal may allow a further reasonable period (subs. (2)). It seems that there is no right under this section to complain of a delay on the part of the Secretary of State in reaching a decision, as a claim of non-payment cannot be made until the Secretary of State's decision on the application has been communicated to the applicant.

Not reasonably practicable. For the interpretation of this phrase in unfair dismissal law, see the note to s.111.

Transfer to Secretary of State of rights and remedies

189.—(1) Where, in pursuance of section 182, the Secretary of State makes a payment to an employee in respect of a debt to which this Part applies—

(a) on the making of the payment any rights and remedies of the employee in respect of the debt (or, if the Secretary of State has paid only part of it, in respect of that part) become rights and remedies of the Secretary of State, and

(b) any decision of an industrial tribunal requiring an employer to pay that debt to the employee has the effect that the debt (or the part of it which the Secretary of State has paid) is to be paid to the Secretary of State.

(2) Where a debt (or any part of a debt) in respect of which the Secretary of State has made a payment in pursuance of section 182 constitutes—

(a) a preferential debt within the meaning of the Insolvency Act 1986 for the purposes of any provision of that Act (including any such provision as applied by any order made under that Act) or any provision of the Companies Act 1985, or

(b) a preferred debt within the meaning of the Bankruptcy (Scotland) Act 1985 for the purposes of any provision of that Act (including any such provision as applied by section 11A of the Judicial Factors (Scotland) Act 1889),

the rights which become rights of the Secretary of State in accordance with subsection (1) include any right arising under any such provision by reason of the status of the debt (or that part of it) as a preferential or preferred debt.

(3) In computing for the purposes of any provision mentioned in subsection (2)(a) or (b) the aggregate amount payable in priority to other creditors of the employer in respect of—

(a) any claim of the Secretary of State to be paid in priority to other creditors of the employer by virtue of subsection (2), and

(b) any claim by the employee to be so paid made in his own right,

any claim of the Secretary of State to be so paid by virtue of subsection (2) shall be treated as if it were a claim of the employee.

(4) But the Secretary of State shall be entitled, as against the employee, to be so paid in respect of any such claim of his (up to the full amount of the claim) before any payment is made to the employee in respect of any claim by the employee to be so paid made in his own right.

(5) Any sum recovered by the Secretary of State in exercising any right, or pursuing any remedy, which is his by virtue of this section shall be paid into the National Insurance Fund.

DEFINITIONS
"employee": s.230(1).
"employer": s.230(4).

GENERAL NOTE
Where the Secretary of State makes a payment of a guaranteed debt to an employee under s.182, the employee's rights in respect of that debt (including any rights as a preferential creditor under the Insolvency Act 1986 (c. 45)) are transferred to the Secretary of State.

Power to obtain information

190.—(1) Where an application is made to the Secretary of State under section 182 in respect of a debt owed by an employer, the Secretary of State may require—

(a) the employer to provide him with such information as he may reasonably require for the purpose of determining whether the application is well-founded, and

(b) any person having the custody or control of any relevant records or other documents to produce for examination on behalf of the Secretary of State any such document in that person's custody or under his control which is of such a description as the Secretary of State may require.

(2) Any such requirement—

(a) shall be made by notice in writing given to the person on whom the requirement is imposed, and

(b) may be varied or revoked by a subsequent notice so given.

(3) If a person refuses or wilfully neglects to furnish any information or produce any document which he has been required to furnish or produce by a notice under this section he is guilty of an offence and liable on summary conviction to a fine not exceeding level 3 on the standard scale.

(4) If a person, in purporting to comply with a requirement of a notice under this section, knowingly or recklessly makes any false statement he is guilty of an offence and liable on summary conviction to a fine not exceeding level 5 on the standard scale.

(5) Where an offence under this section committed by a body corporate is proved—

(a) to have been committed with the consent or connivance of, or

(b) to be attributable to any neglect on the part of,
any director, manager, secretary or other similar officer of the body corporate, or any person who was purporting to act in any such capacity, he (as well as the body corporate) is guilty of the offence and liable to be proceeded against and punished accordingly.

(6) Where the affairs of a body corporate are managed by its members, subsection (5) applies in relation to the acts and defaults of a member in connection with his functions of management as if he were a director of the body corporate.

DEFINITIONS
    "employer": s.230(4).

GENERAL NOTE
    This section gives the Secretary of State the power to obtain information from the employer, and from any other person who has relevant records or other documents, in order to establish the employee's claim (subs. (1)). Refusal or wilful neglect to comply with such a request will be an offence (subs. (3)).

PART XIII

MISCELLANEOUS

CHAPTER I

PARTICULAR TYPES OF EMPLOYMENT

Crown employment etc.

Crown employment

191.—(1) Subject to sections 192 and 193, the provisions of this Act to which this section applies have effect in relation to Crown employment and persons in Crown employment as they have effect in relation to other employment and other employees or workers.

(2) This section applies to—
    (a) Parts I to III,
    (b) Part V, apart from section 45,
    (c) Parts VI to VIII,
    (d) in Part IX, sections 92 and 93,
    (e) Part X, apart from section 101, and
    (f) this Part and Parts XIV and XV.

(3) In this Act "Crown employment" means employment under or for the purposes of a government department or any officer or body exercising on behalf of the Crown functions conferred by a statutory provision.

(4) For the purposes of the application of provisions of this Act in relation to Crown employment in accordance with subsection (1)—
    (a) references to an employee or a worker shall be construed as references to a person in Crown employment,
    (b) references to a contract of employment, or a worker's contract, shall be construed as references to the terms of employment of a person in Crown employment,
    (c) references to dismissal, or to the termination of a worker's contract, shall be construed as references to the termination of Crown employment,
    (d) references to redundancy shall be construed as references to the existence of such circumstances as are treated, in accordance with any arrangements falling within section 177(3) for the time being in force, as equivalent to redundancy in relation to Crown employment, and
    (e) references to an undertaking shall be construed—

(i) in relation to a Minister of the Crown, as references to his functions or (as the context may require) to the department of which he is in charge, and

(ii) in relation to a government department, officer or body, as references to the functions of the department, officer or body or (as the context may require) to the department, officer or body.

(5) Where the terms of employment of a person in Crown employment restrict his right to take part in—

(a) certain political activities, or

(b) activities which may conflict with his official functions,

nothing in section 50 requires him to be allowed time off work for public duties connected with any such activities.

(6) Sections 159 and 160 are without prejudice to any exemption or immunity of the Crown.

DEFINITIONS

"contract of employment": s.230(2).

"Crown employment": subs. (3).

"employee": s.230(1).

"employer": s.230(4).

GENERAL NOTE

This section extends most of the Act's provisions to those in Crown employment, the principal exceptions being the right to a minimum period of notice under Pt. IX, and the provisions on redundancy payments in Pt. XI.

The employment status of civil servants has long been a source of controversy, and there is still doubt as to whether Crown servants have a contract with the Crown, and if so, whether that contract is a contract of employment. In *I.R.C. v. Hambrook* [1956] 2 Q.B. 641, Goddard C.J. said, *obiter*: "an established civil servant is appointed to an office and is a public officer, remunerated by moneys provided by Parliament, so that his employment depends not on a contract with the Crown but on appointment by the Crown ...". There is however strong support for the view that the relationship must be contractual, although not necessarily involving a contract of employment (see, *e.g. Kodeeswaran (Chelliah) v. Att.-Gen. of Ceylon* [1970] A.C. 1111, P.C.; *Cresswell v. Board of Inland Revenue* [1984] I.C.R. 508; *R. v. Lord Chancellor's Department, ex p. Nangle* [1991] IRLR 343, C.A.), but the point has yet to be finally settled. For a useful account of the status of Crown employees, see *Sweet and Maxwell's Encyclopedia of Employment Law*, para. 1·2202, and S. Fredman and G.S. Morris, *The State as Employer: Labour Law in the Public Services*, Mansell, London, 1989, pp. 61–71.

Note that under s.245 of the Trade Union and Labour Relations (Consolidation) Act 1992, a person who holds any office or employment under the Crown is deemed to be an employee for the purposes of liability for the economic torts. That provision is designed to ensure that any doubt about the contractual status of civil servants does not affect the liability in tort of the civil service unions for organising industrial action.

Armed forces

192.—(1) Section 191—

(a) applies to service as a member of the naval, military or air forces of the Crown but subject to the following provisions of this section, and

(b) applies to employment by an association established for the purposes of Part XI of the Reserve Forces Act 1996.

(2) The provisions of this Act which have effect by virtue of section 191 in relation to service as a member of the naval, military or air forces of the Crown are—

(a) Part I,

(b) in Part VI, sections 55 to 57,

(c) Parts VII and VIII,

(d) in Part IX, sections 92 and 93,

(e) Part X, apart from sections 100 to 103 and 134, and

(f) this Part and Parts XIV and XV.

(3) Her Majesty may by Order in Council—

(a) amend subsection (2) by making additions to, or omissions from, the provisions for the time being specified in that subsection, and

(b) make any provision for the time being so specified apply to service as a member of the naval, military or air forces of the Crown subject to such exceptions and modifications as may be specified in the Order in Council,

but no provision contained in Part II may be added to the provisions for the time being specified in subsection (2).

(4) Modifications made by an Order in Council under subsection (3) may include provision precluding the making of a complaint or reference to any industrial tribunal unless the person aggrieved has availed himself of the service redress procedures applicable to him.

(5) Where modifications made by an Order in Council under subsection (3) include provision such as is mentioned in subsection (4), the Order in Council shall also include provision designed to secure that the service redress procedures result in a determination, or what is to be treated under the Order in Council as a determination, in sufficient time to enable a complaint or reference to be made to an industrial tribunal.

(6) In subsections (4) and (5) "the service redress procedures" means the procedures, excluding those which relate to the making of a report on a complaint to Her Majesty, referred to in—

(a) sections 180 and 181 of the Army Act 1955,

(b) sections 180 and 181 of the Air Force Act 1955, and

(c) section 130 of the Naval Discipline Act 1957.

(7) No provision shall be made by virtue of subsection (4) which has the effect of substituting a period longer than six months for any period specified as the normal period for a complaint or reference.

(8) In subsection (7) "the normal period for a complaint or reference", in relation to any matter within the jurisdiction of an industrial tribunal, means the period specified in the relevant enactment as the period within which the complaint or reference must be made (disregarding any provision permitting an extension of that period at the discretion of the tribunal).

DEFINITIONS
"normal period for a complaint or reference": subs. (8).
"service redress procedures": subs. (6).

COMMENCEMENT
This section comes into force on a date to be fixed by regulations: see Sched. 2, para. 16. At the time of writing, no such order had been made. Until this section comes into force, the provisions in Sched. 2, para. 16 continue to have effect.

GENERAL NOTE
This section extends most of the provisions of the Act to members of the armed forces. The provisions which apply are listed in subs. (2), and include the right to a statement of employment particulars and to itemised pay statements, the right to time off for ante-natal care, the right to suspension from work on medical or maternity grounds, maternity rights, the right to a written statement of reasons for dismissal, and (with certain exceptions) the right not to be unfairly dismissed. The following rights are *not* on the list: protection of wages; the right to guarantee payments; protection from suffering detriment in employment; the right to time off work (other than for ante-natal care); the right to a minimum period of notice; redundancy payments; and rights on the employer's insolvency.

The application of the above provisions to the armed forces is subject to subs. (3), which permits the normal provisions to be modified by an Order in Council. Subs. (4) provides that such an Order may preclude the making of a complaint or reference to an industrial tribunal unless the complainant "has availed himself of the service redress procedures applicable to him", where those procedures result in a determination in sufficient time to enable a complaint or reference to be made to a tribunal (subs. (5)); subs. (7) provides that the normal limitation period for a complaint or reference to a tribunal may not be replaced under these powers by a period of longer than six months.

National security

193.—(1) The provisions of this Act to which this section applies do not have effect in relation to any Crown employment in respect of which there is in force a certificate issued by or on behalf of a Minister of the Crown certifying that employment of a description specified in the certificate, or the employment of a particular person so specified, is (or, at a time specified in the certificate, was) required to be excepted from those provisions for the purpose of safeguarding national security.

(2) This section applies to—

(a) Part I, so far as it relates to itemised pay statements,

(b) Part III,

(c) in Part VI, sections 50 to 54,

(d) in Part VII, sections 64 and 65, and sections 69 and 70 so far as relating to those sections,

(e) in Part IX, sections 92 and 93, except where they apply by virtue of section 92(4),

(f) Part X, except so far as relating to a dismissal which is treated as unfair—

(i) by section 99(1) to (3), 100 or 103, or

(ii) by subsection (1) of section 105 by reason of the application of subsection (2), (3) or (6) of that section, and

(g) this Part and Parts XIV and XV (so far as relating to any of the provisions specified in paragraphs (a) to (f)).

(3) Any document purporting to be a certificate issued as mentioned in subsection (1)—

(a) shall be received in evidence, and

(b) unless the contrary is proved, shall be deemed to be such a certificate.

DEFINITIONS
"Crown employment": s.191(3).
"employment": s.230(5).

Parliamentary staff

House of Lords staff

194.—(1) The provisions of this Act to which this section applies have effect in relation to employment as a relevant member of the House of Lords staff as they have effect in relation to other employment.

(2) This section applies to—

(a) Part I,

(b) Part III,

(c) in Part V, sections 44 and 47, and sections 48 and 49 so far as relating to those sections,

(d) Part VI, apart from sections 58 to 60,

(e) Parts VII and VIII,

(f) in Part IX, sections 92 and 93,

(g) Part X, apart from sections 101 and 102, and

(h) this Part and Parts XIV and XV.

(3) For the purposes of the application of the provisions of this Act to which this section applies in relation to a relevant member of the House of Lords staff references to an undertaking shall be construed as references to the House of Lords.

(4) Nothing in any rule of law or the law or practice of Parliament prevents a relevant member of the House of Lords staff from bringing before the High Court or a county court—

(a) a claim arising out of or relating to a contract of employment or any other contract connected with employment, or

(b) a claim in tort arising in connection with employment.

(5) Where the terms of the contract of employment of a relevant member of the House of Lords staff restrict his right to take part in—

(a) certain political activities, or

(b) activities which may conflict with his official functions,

nothing in section 50 requires him to be allowed time off work for public duties connected with any such activities.

(6) In this section "relevant member of the House of Lords staff" means any person who is employed under a contract of employment with the Corporate Officer of the House of Lords.

(7) For the purposes of the application of—

(a) the provisions of this Act to which this section applies, or

(b) a claim within subsection (4),

in relation to a person continuously employed in or for the purposes of the House of Lords up to the time when he became so employed under a contract of employment with the Corporate Officer of the House of Lords, his employment shall not be treated as having been terminated by reason only of a change in his employer before or at that time.

DEFINITIONS

"contract of employment": s.230(2).

"employer": s.230(4).

"employment": s.230(5).

"relevant member of the House of Lords staff": subs. (6).

GENERAL NOTE

This section extends most of the Act's provisions to House of Lords staff. The reference to employment "under a contract of employment" in, for example, subs. (6) could be taken to imply that House of Lords staff are employed under contracts of service, although their status has never been firmly established. Note that in relation to House of Commons staff, it is specifically provided in s.195(3) that references to a "contract of employment" are to be construed as including references to the terms of employment of such staff, thus avoiding any inference being drawn from the use of that term; there is no similar provision in this section.

For an account of the status of Parliamentary staff, see *Sweet and Maxwell's Encyclopedia of Employment Law*, para. 1·2203.

House of Commons staff

195.—(1) The provisions of this Act to which this section applies have effect in relation to employment as a relevant member of the House of Commons staff as they have effect in relation to other employment.

(2) This section applies to—

(a) Part I,

(b) Part III,

(c) in Part V, sections 44 and 47, and sections 48 and 49 so far as relating to those sections,

(d) Part VI, apart from sections 58 to 60,

(e) Parts VII and VIII,

(f) in Part IX, sections 92 and 93,

(g) Part X, apart from sections 101 and 102, and

(h) this Part and Parts XIV and XV.

(3) For the purposes of the application of the provisions of this Act to which this section applies in relation to a relevant member of the House of Commons staff—

(a) references to an employee shall be construed as references to a relevant member of the House of Commons staff,

(b) references to a contract of employment shall be construed as including references to the terms of employment of a relevant member of the House of Commons staff,

(c) references to dismissal shall be construed as including references to the termination of the employment of a relevant member of the House of Commons staff, and

(d) references to an undertaking shall be construed as references to the House of Commons.

(4) Nothing in any rule of law or the law or practice of Parliament prevents a relevant member of the House of Commons staff from bringing before the High Court or a county court—

(a) a claim arising out of or relating to a contract of employment or any other contract connected with employment, or

(b) a claim in tort arising in connection with employment.

(5) In this section "relevant member of the House of Commons staff" means any person—

(a) who was appointed by the House of Commons Commission or is employed in the refreshment department, or

(b) who is a member of the Speaker's personal staff.

(6) Subject to subsection (7), for the purposes of—

(a) the provisions of this Act to which this section applies,

(b) Part XI (where applicable to relevant members of the House of Commons staff), and

(c) a claim within subsection (4),

the House of Commons Commission is the employer of staff appointed by the Commission and the Speaker is the employer of his personal staff and of any person employed in the refreshment department and not appointed by the Commission.

(7) Where the House of Commons Commission or the Speaker designates a person to be treated for all or any of the purposes mentioned in subsection (6) as the employer of any description of staff (other than the Speaker's personal staff), the person so designated shall be treated for those purposes as their employer.

(8) Where any proceedings are brought by virtue of this section against—

(a) the House of Commons Commission,

(b) the Speaker, or

(c) any person designated under subsection (7),

the person against whom the proceedings are brought may apply to the court or industrial tribunal concerned to have some other person against whom the proceedings could at the time of the application be properly brought substituted for him as a party to the proceedings.

(9) For the purposes mentioned in subsection (6)—

(a) a person's employment in or for the purposes of the House of Commons shall not (provided he continues to be employed in such employment) be treated as terminated by reason only of a change in his employer, and

(b) (provided he so continues) his first appointment to such employment shall be deemed after the change to have been made by his employer for the time being.

(10) In accordance with subsection (9)—

(a) an employee shall be treated for the purposes mentioned in subsection (6) as being continuously employed by his employer for the time being from the commencement of his employment until its termination, and

(b) anything done by or in relation to his employer for the time being in respect of his employment before the change shall be so treated as having been done by or in relation to the person who is his employer for the time being after the change.

(11) In subsections (9) and (10) "employer for the time being", in relation to a person who has ceased to be employed in or for the purposes of the House of Commons, means the person who was his employer immediately before he ceased to be so employed, except that where some other person

would have been his employer for the time being if he had not ceased to be so employed it means that other person.

(12) If the House of Commons resolves at any time that any provision of subsections (5) to (8) should be amended in its application to any member of the staff of that House, Her Majesty may by Order in Council amend that provision accordingly.

DEFINITIONS
"contract of employment": s.230(2).
"employee": s.230(1).
"employer": s.230(4).
"employer for the time being": subs. (11).
"employment": s.230(5).
"relevant member of the House of Commons staff": subs. (5).

GENERAL NOTE
This section extends most of the Act's provisions to House of Commons staff. For an account of the status of Parliamentary staff, see *Sweet and Maxwell's Encyclopedia of Employment Law*, para. 1·2203.

Excluded classes of employment

Employment outside Great Britain

196.—(1) Sections 1 to 7 and sections 86 to 91 do not apply in relation to employment during any period when the employee is engaged in work wholly or mainly outside Great Britain unless—
   (a) the employee ordinarily works in Great Britain and the work outside Great Britain is for the same employer, or
   (b) the law which governs his contract of employment is the law of England and Wales or the law of Scotland.

(2) The provisions to which this subsection applies do not apply to employment where under the employee's contract of employment he ordinarily works outside Great Britain.

(3) Subsection (2) applies to—
   (a) in Part I, sections 8 to 10,
   (b) Parts II, III and V,
   (c) Part VI, apart from sections 58 to 60,
   (d) Parts VII and VIII,
   (e) in Part IX, sections 92 and 93, and
   (f) (subject to subsection (4)) Part X.

(4) Part X applies to employment where under her contract of employment the employee ordinarily works outside Great Britain if—
   (a) section 84 applies to her dismissal, or
   (b) she is treated as dismissed by section 96.

(5) For the purposes of subsections (2) and (4), a person employed to work on board a ship registered in the United Kingdom shall be regarded as a person who under his contract ordinarily works in Great Britain unless—
   (a) the ship is registered at a port outside Great Britain,
   (b) the employment is wholly outside Great Britain, or
   (c) the person is not ordinarily resident in Great Britain.

(6) An employee—
   (a) is not entitled to a redundancy payment if he is outside Great Britain on the relevant date unless under his contract of employment he ordinarily worked in Great Britain, and
   (b) is not entitled to a redundancy payment if under his contract of employment he ordinarily works outside Great Britain unless on the relevant date he is in Great Britain in accordance with instructions given to him by his employer.

(7) Part XII does not apply to employment where, under the employee's contract of employment, he ordinarily works outside the territory of the member States of the European Communities and of Norway and Iceland.

DEFINITIONS
"contract of employment": s.230(2).
"employee": s.230(1).
"employer": s.230(4).
"employment": s.230(5).
"redundancy payment": s.235(1).
"relevant date": s.235(1).

GENERAL NOTE
Ordinarily works outside Great Britain. This phrase has proved to be especially problematic, particularly when applied to peripatetic employees (*e.g.* airline pilots) and those employed by multinational employers. After some initial uncertainty, it is now well established that a person cannot at the same time be said to be working both inside and outside Great Britain. In *Wilson v. Maynard Shipbuilding Consultants A.B.* [1977] IRLR 491, the Court of Appeal (overruling the decision of the E.A.T. in *Portec (U.K.) v. Mogensen* [1976] IRLR 209), held that the question should be determined not by looking at the proportions of time spent inside or outside Great Britain, but by considering the terms of the contract, and if the contract is not determinative of the issue, by looking to see where the employee is based. The factors which may help to indicate the employee's base include the location of his headquarters, where the travels involved in his employment begin and end, where his place of residence is, where he is to be paid and in what currency, and whether he is to pay national insurance contributions. This approach was affirmed by the Court of Appeal in *Todd v. British Midland Airways* [1978] IRLR 370, although in that case Eveleigh L.J. stressed that the employee's base is not conclusive, and that in determining whether an employee ordinarily works outside Great Britain, the tribunal should consider the whole of the employee's employment, past and future, not just the terms of the contract. A similar view was expressed by Donaldson L.J. in *Janata Bank v. Ahmed* [1981] IRLR 457. The need to consider the realities of the situation ensures that an employer cannot evade his statutory responsibilities merely by including a mobility clause in an employee's contract empowering the employer to require the employee to work outside Great Britain: see *Sonali Bank v. Rahman* [1989] I.C.R. 314, E.A.T. Note that in considering the terms of the employee's contract, it is the contract subsisting at the relevant date which must be taken into account, not any earlier contract (*Western v. Vega Space Systems Engineering* [1989] IRLR 429).
Wholly outside Great Britain. Employment will be wholly outside Great Britain where no part of the employee's work is done within Great Britain, even if the employee regularly returns to the U.K. on leave and is paid in sterling with U.K. tax and national insurance deducted: see *Wood v. Cunard Line* [1990] IRLR 281.
On the position of those in off-shore employment, see the note to s.201.

Fixed-term contracts

197.—(1) Part X does not apply to dismissal from employment under a contract for a fixed term of one year or more if—
   (a) the dismissal consists only of the expiry of that term without its being renewed, and
   (b) before the term expires the employee has agreed in writing to exclude any claim in respect of rights under that Part in relation to the contract.
(2) Subsection (1) does not prevent Part X from applying if the dismissal is regarded as unfair by virtue of section 101.
(3) An employee employed under a contract of employment for a fixed term of two years or more is not entitled to a redundancy payment in respect of the expiry of that term without its being renewed (whether by the employer or by an associated employer of his) if, before the term expires, the employee has agreed in writing to exclude any right to a redundancy payment in that event.
(4) An agreement such as is mentioned in subsection (1) or (3) may be contained—
   (a) in the contract itself, or

(b) in a separate agreement.

(5) Where—

(a) an agreement such as is mentioned in subsection (3) is made during the currency of a fixed term, and

(b) the term is renewed,

the agreement shall not be construed as applying to the term as renewed; but this subsection is without prejudice to the making of a further agreement in relation to the renewed term.

DEFINITIONS

"associated employer": s.231.

"contract of employment": s.230(2).

"dismissal": s.95.

"employee": s.230(1).

"employer": s.230(4).

"employment": s.230(5).

"redundancy payment": s.235(1).

GENERAL NOTE

This section is an exception to the normal restrictions on contracting-out of the Act's provisions (see s.203). While a contract for a fixed term will be held at common law to terminate by expiry at the end of the period fixed in the contract, non-renewal of a fixed-term contract will be deemed to be a dismissal for the purposes of unfair dismissal law and redundancy payments (see ss.95 and 136(1)). An employee with a fixed-term contract of one year or more may however contract-out of his or her rights to claim unfair dismissal, where the dismissal consists of the expiry of that term without renewal (subs. (1)), unless the dismissal is for refusing to do shop work or betting work on a Sunday (subs. (2)); similarly, an employee with a fixed-term contract of two years or more may contract-out of his or her right to a redundancy payment, but again only where the dismissal consists of the expiry of that term without renewal (subs. (3)). Any such agreement may be in the contract or in a separate agreement (subs. (4)), but it must be in writing, and it must be made before the term expires.

Contract for a fixed term. To qualify as a fixed-term contract, a contract must be certain in its duration, at least to the extent that the date of termination is ascertainable, *e.g.* from the terms of the contract. A contract of indefinite or uncertain duration (*e.g.* a contract to perform a specific task), is not a fixed-term contract: *Wiltshire County Council v. National Association of Teachers in Further and Higher Education* [1980] IRLR 198, C.A. However, a contract may be for a fixed term even if it can be terminated by notice before the expiry date: *Dixon v. British Broadcasting Corp.* [1979] 2 All E.R. 112, C.A., disapproving *British Broadcasting Corp. v. Ioannou* [1975] 2 All E.R. 999, C.A., on this point.

Difficulties can arise where an employee works under a series of fixed-term contracts, or where the length of a fixed-term contract is extended. In *B.B.C. v. Ioannou*, above, Denning L.J. suggested that in such a case the tribunal should look at the final contract to see whether it is of sufficient length for the contracting-out provisions to operate. He rejected the distinction drawn by Stevenson and Geoffrey Lane L.JJ. in that case between an extension or renewal of an existing fixed-term contract, where the court could treat the periods as falling under one contract, and a re-engagement under a new contract, describing it as "too fine a distinction for ordinary mortals to comprehend". Denning L.J.'s approach was applied by the E.A.T. in *Open University, The v. Triesman* [1978] IRLR 114. In that case, the employee was originally employed under a fixed-term contract for 18 months, but her employment was subsequently extended by a further seven months. The E.A.T. interpreted this as a new fixed-term contract for a seven month period, rather than an extension of the original contract, so that the employee could not contract out of her rights. However, in *Mulrine v. University of Ulster* [1993] IRLR 545, a case involving the extension of a two-year fixed-term contract for a further four months, the Northern Ireland Court of Appeal declined to follow Denning L.J.'s approach, preferring the distinction drawn by Stevenson and Geoffrey Lane L.JJ. in *Ioannou*. On the facts, the court held that there was not a separate contract for four months, but that the original contract had been extended, so that the clause in that contract whereby the employee contracted-out of her right to pursue an unfair dismissal claim was still operative.

Where a fixed-term contract is renewed for a further term, subs. (5) expressly provides that an agreement to contract-out of the right to a redundancy payment on the expiry of the original contract will not apply to the renewed contract, although the parties may make a further agreement in relation to the new contract. There is no equivalent provision in relation to the right to claim unfair dismissal, which could be taken as indicating that an agreement to contract-out is to apply to the new contract unless specifically excluded. Against that, it could be argued that, as a matter of policy, the right to claim unfair dismissal on the expiry of a fixed-term contract should only be excluded under these provisions where there is an agreement to that effect in relation to that particular contract.

Short-term employment

198. Sections 1 to 7 do not apply to an employee if his employment continues for less than one month.

DEFINITIONS
"employee": s.230(1).
"employment": s.230(5).

GENERAL NOTE
See the note to s.1.

Mariners

199.—(1) Sections 1 to 7, Part II and sections 86 to 91 do not apply to a person employed as a seaman in a ship registered in the United Kingdom under a crew agreement the provisions and form of which are of a kind approved by the Secretary of State.

(2) Sections 8 to 10, Part III, sections 44, 45, 47, 50 to 57 and 61 to 63, Parts VII and VIII, sections 92 and 93 and (subject to subsection (3)) Parts X to XII do not apply to employment as master, or as a member of the crew, of a fishing vessel where the employee is remunerated only by a share in the profits or gross earnings of the vessel.

(3) Part X applies to employment such as is mentioned in subsection (2) if—

(a) section 84 applies to the employee's dismissal, or
(b) she is treated as dismissed by section 96,

and Part XI applies to employment such as is so mentioned if the employee is treated as dismissed by section 137.

(4) Sections 8 to 10 and 50 to 54 and Part XII do not apply to employment as a merchant seaman.

(5) In subsection (4) "employment as a merchant seaman"—

(a) does not include employment in the fishing industry or employment on board a ship otherwise than by the owner, manager or charterer of that ship except employment as a radio officer, but
(b) subject to that, includes—

(i) employment as a master or a member of the crew of any ship,
(ii) employment as a trainee undergoing training for the sea service, and
(iii) employment in or about a ship in port by the owner, manager or charterer of the ship to do work of the kind ordinarily done by a merchant seaman on a ship while it is in port.

(6) Section 196(6) does not apply to an employee, and section 197(3) does not apply to a contract of employment, if the employee is—

(a) employed as a master or seaman in a British ship, and
(b) ordinarily resident in Great Britain.

DEFINITIONS
"contract of employment": s.230(2).
"employee": s.230(1).
"employer": s.230(4).
"employment": s.230(5).
"employment as a merchant seaman": subs. (5).

GENERAL NOTE
Crew agreement. See s.1 of the Merchant Shipping Act 1970 (c. 36).
Remunerated only by a share in the profits ... of the vessel. See *Goodeve v. Gilsons* [1985]

I.C.R. 401, C.A., where the exclusion was held not to apply to a fisherman remunerated by a share in the profits of the employer's fleet, rather than of the vessel upon which the employee was employed.

Police officers

200.—(1) Sections 8 to 10, Part III, sections 44, 45, 47, 50 to 57 and 61 to 63, Parts VII and VIII, sections 92 and 93, Part X and section 137 do not apply to employment under a contract of employment in police service or to persons engaged in such employment.

(2) In subsection (1) "police service" means—

(a) service as a member of a constabulary maintained by virtue of an enactment, or

(b) subject to section 126 of the Criminal Justice and Public Order Act 1994 (prison staff not to be regarded as in police service), service in any other capacity by virtue of which a person has the powers or privileges of a constable.

DEFINITIONS
"contract of employment": s.230(2).
"employee": s.230(1).
"employer": s.230(4).
"employment": s.230(5).
"police service": subs. (2).

GENERAL NOTE
For an account of the employment status of those employed in the police service, see *Sweet and Maxwell's Encyclopedia of Employment Law*, para. 1·2207.

The powers or privileges of a constable. In *Home Office v. Robinson* [1982] I.C.R. 31, the E.A.T. held that this exclusion included prison officers, who are accorded the powers and privileges of a constable by virtue of the Prison Act 1952 (c. 52), but this was changed by s.126 of the Criminal Justice and Public Order Act 1994 (c. 33), which states that a prison officer is not to be regarded as in police service for the purposes of this Act or the Trade Union and Labour Relations (Consolidation) Act 1992 (c. 52).

Offshore employment

Power to extend employment legislation to offshore employment

201.—(1) In this section "offshore employment" means employment for the purposes of activities—

(a) in the territorial waters of the United Kingdom,

(b) connected with the exploration of the sea-bed or subsoil, or the exploitation of their natural resources, in the United Kingdom sector of the continental shelf, or

(c) connected with the exploration or exploitation, in a foreign sector of the continental shelf, of a cross-boundary petroleum field.

(2) Her Majesty may by Order in Council provide that—

(a) the provisions of this Act, and

(b) any Northern Ireland legislation making provision for purposes corresponding to any of the purposes of this Act,

apply, to such extent and for such purposes as may be specified in the Order (with or without modification), to or in relation to a person in offshore employment.

(3) An Order in Council under this section—

(a) may make different provision for different cases,

(b) may provide that all or any of the provisions referred to in subsection (2), as applied by such an Order in Council, apply—

(i) to individuals whether or not they are British subjects, and

(ii) to bodies corporate whether or not they are incorporated under the law of a part of the United Kingdom, and apply even where the application may affect their activities outside the United Kingdom,

(c) may make provision for conferring jurisdiction on any court or class of court specified in the Order in Council, or on industrial tribunals, in respect of offences, causes of action or other matters arising in connection with offshore employment,

(d) may (without prejudice to subsection (2) and paragraph (a)) provide that the provisions referred to in subsection (2), as applied by the Order in Council, apply in relation to any person in employment in a part of the areas referred to in subsection (1)(a) and (b),

(e) may exclude from the operation of section 3 of the Territorial Waters Jurisdiction Act 1878 (consents required for prosecutions) proceedings for offences under the provisions referred to in subsection (2) in connection with offshore employment,

(f) may provide that such proceedings shall not be brought without such consent as may be required by the Order in Council,

(g) may (without prejudice to subsection (2)) modify or exclude the operation of any or all of sections 196, 199 and 215(2) to (6) or of any corresponding Northern Ireland legislation.

(4) Any jurisdiction conferred on a court or tribunal under this section is without prejudice to jurisdiction exercisable apart from this section by that or any other court or tribunal.

(5) In this section—

"cross-boundary petroleum field" means a petroleum field that extends across the boundary between the United Kingdom sector of the continental shelf and a foreign sector of the continental shelf,

"foreign sector of the continental shelf" means an area outside the territorial waters of any state, within which rights with respect to the sea-bed and subsoil and their natural resources are exercisable by a state other than the United Kingdom,

"petroleum field" means a geological structure identified as an oil or gas field by the Order in Council concerned, and

"United Kingdom sector of the continental shelf" means the area designated under section 1(7) of the Continental Shelf Act 1964.

DEFINITIONS

"cross-boundary petroleum field": subs. (5).
"employment": s.230(5).
"foreign sector of the continental shelf": subs. (5).
"offshore employment": subs. (1).
"petroleum field": subs. (5).
"United Kingdom sector of the continental shelf": subs. (5).

GENERAL NOTE

The Employment Protection (Offshore Employment) Order 1976 (S.I. 1976 No. 766) has effect under this section, as amended by S.I. 1977 No. 588, S.I. 1981 No. 208 and S.I. 1984 No. 1149.

CHAPTER II

OTHER MISCELLANEOUS MATTERS

Restrictions on disclosure of information

National security

202.—(1) Where in the opinion of any Minister of the Crown the disclosure of any information would be contrary to the interests of national security—

(a) nothing in any of the provisions to which this section applies requires any person to disclose the information, and

(b) no person shall disclose the information in any proceedings in any court or tribunal relating to any of those provisions.

(2) This section applies to—

(a) Part I, so far as it relates to employment particulars,

(b) in Part V, sections 44 and 47, and sections 48 and 49 so far as relating to those sections,

(c) in Part VI, sections 55 to 57 and 61 to 63,

(d) in Part VII, sections 66 to 68, and sections 69 and 70 so far as relating to those sections,

(e) Part VIII,

(f) in Part IX, sections 92 and 93 where they apply by virtue of section 92(4),

(g) Part X so far as relating to a dismissal which is treated as unfair—
    (i) by section 99(1) to (3), 100 or 103, or
    (ii) by subsection (1) of section 105 by reason of the application of subsection (2), (3) or (6) of that section, and

(h) this Part and Parts XIV and XV (so far as relating to any of the provisions in paragraphs (a) to (g)).

Contracting out etc. and remedies

Restrictions on contracting out

203.—(1) Any provision in an agreement (whether a contract of employment or not) is void in so far as it purports—

(a) to exclude or limit the operation of any provision of this Act, or

(b) to preclude a person from bringing any proceedings under this Act before an industrial tribunal.

(2) Subsection (1)—

(a) does not apply to any provision in a collective agreement excluding rights under section 28 if an order under section 35 is for the time being in force in respect of it,

(b) does not apply to any provision in a dismissal procedures agreement excluding the right under section 94 if that provision is not to have effect unless an order under section 110 is for the time being in force in respect of it,

(c) does not apply to any provision in an agreement if an order under section 157 is for the time being in force in respect of it,

(d) does not apply to any provision of an agreement relating to dismissal from employment such as is mentioned in section 197(1) or (3),

(e) does not apply to any agreement to refrain from instituting or continuing proceedings where a conciliation officer has taken action under section 18 of the Industrial Tribunals Act 1996, and

(f) does not apply to any agreement to refrain from instituting or continuing before an industrial tribunal any proceedings within section 18(1)(d) (proceedings under this Act where conciliation available) of the Industrial Tribunals Act 1996 if the conditions regulating compromise agreements under this Act are satisfied in relation to the agreement.

(3) For the purposes of subsection (2)(f) the conditions regulating compromise agreements under this Act are that—

(a) the agreement must be in writing,

(b) the agreement must relate to the particular complaint,

(c) the employee or worker must have received independent legal advice from a qualified lawyer as to the terms and effect of the proposed agreement and, in particular, its effect on his ability to pursue his rights before an industrial tribunal,

(d) there must be in force, when the adviser gives the advice, a policy of insurance covering the risk of a claim by the employee or worker in respect of loss arising in consequence of the advice,

(e) the agreement must identify the adviser, and

(f) the agreement must state that the conditions regulating compromise agreements under this Act are satisfied.

(4) In subsection (3)—

"independent", in relation to legal advice received by an employee or worker, means that the advice is given by a lawyer who is not acting in the matter for the employer or an associated employer, and

"qualified lawyer" means—

(a) as respects England and Wales, a barrister (whether in practice as such or employed to give legal advice), or a solicitor who holds a practising certificate, and

(b) as respects Scotland, an advocate (whether in practice as such or employed to give legal advice), or a solicitor who holds a practising certificate.

DEFINITIONS

"collective agreement": s.235(1).
"conciliation officer": s.235(1).
"contract of employment": s.230(2).
"dismissal": s.95.
"dismissal procedures agreement": s.235(1).
"employee": s.230(1).
"employer": s.230(4).
"employment": s.230(5).

GENERAL NOTE

This section contains a general restriction on contracting out of the Act's provisions, subject to the exceptions in subs. (2).

Compromise agreements. The provisions on compromise agreements were introduced by the Trade Union Reform and Employment Rights Act 1993, s.39. Before the 1993 Act, an agreement to refrain from instituting or continuing industrial tribunal proceedings was only valid where an ACAS conciliation officer had "taken action" in relation to the agreement (see now subs. (2)(e)). During the 1980s there was a sharp rise in the number of cases referred to ACAS where no formal complaint had been made to an industrial tribunal (non-IT1 cases), and where ACAS was in effect being asked to rubber-stamp an agreement which had already been reached. It was open to doubt whether in such cases a conciliation officer could be said to have "taken action", and following legal advice ACAS adopted a new policy in July 1990 of refusing to rubber-stamp agreements reached independently unless the terms of the agreement were capable of being changed as a result of the intervention of the conciliation officer (ACAS Annual Report 1991, p.45). As a result, the number of non-IT1 cases received by ACAS fell from 17,724 (or 36 per cent of the total caseload) in 1989, to only 2,431 (3 per cent of the total) in 1992. One important consequence of the adoption of this more restrictive policy was that there was no longer any mechanism whereby a settlement freely reached between the parties but without the assistance of an ACAS conciliator could be given legal force, and this led to the risk of IT1 applications being made simply in order to ensure that such a settlement might become binding, and the tribunal system becoming even more overloaded with unnecessary applications. Hence the introduction of compromise agreements, whereby the parties can reach a binding agreement without ACAS involvement.

Subs. (3)

A compromise agreement will only be binding if it satisfies all the requirements set out in subs. (3):

(i) the agreement must be in writing (unlike agreements reached with the involvement of an ACAS conciliation officer, which do not have to be in writing);

(ii) the agreement must relate to the particular complaint; in other words, a blanket agreement which purports to cover any statutory complaint which the individual might bring will not be valid. If an agreement is intended to cover more than one type of complaint, it must spell out each complaint to which it is intended to apply;

(iii) the individual must have received independent legal advice from a "qualified lawyer" (defined in subs. (4)) as to the terms and effect of the proposed agreement and its effect on the individual's ability to pursue his or her rights before an industrial tribunal; advice will be "independent" for these purposes if it is given by a lawyer "who is not acting *in the matter* for the employer or an associated employer" (subs. (4), italics supplied), which seems to imply that the lawyer may be acting or have acted for the employer in some *other* capacity; curiously, the parallel provisions in the Sex Discrimination Act 1975, Race Relations Act 1976, Trade Union and Labour Relations (Consolidation) Act 1992 and the Disability Discrimination Act 1995 (c. 50) require that the lawyer "is not acting for the other party or for a person who is connected with that other party", which on the face of it seems to rule out the possibility of the lawyer acting for the employer in *any* capacity; *quaere* whether the different wording is intended to imply that a greater degree of independence is required in such cases;

(iv) there must be a policy of insurance in force at the time when the advice is given covering the risk of a claim (*e.g.* of professional negligence) by the individual in respect of loss arising in consequence of the advice;

(v) the agreement must identify the adviser;

(vi) the agreement must state that the conditions regulating compromise agreements under the Act are satisfied; where a single compromise agreement is intended to cover claims under more than one of the Acts referred to in (iii) above, it seems that the agreement must expressly state that the requirements of *each* of those Acts are satisfied, because the relevant provisions all require a compromise agreement to state that "the conditions regulating compromise agreements *under this Act* are satisfied" (italics supplied). This is presumably designed to avoid the type of confusion which arose in *Livingstone v. Hepworth Refractories* [1992] IRLR 63, where the E.A.T. held that a conciliated settlement "in full and final settlement of all claims" reached under the Employment Protection (Consolidation) Act 1978 was not binding in respect of a subsequent claim of unlawful sex discrimination.

Where these requirements are satisfied, a compromise agreement may preclude an individual from instituting or continuing proceedings in relation to any of the matters set out in s.18(1)(d) of the Industrial Tribunals Act 1996 (c. 17), *i.e.* itemised pay statements, protection of wages, guarantee payments, protection from suffering detriment in employment, time off work, suspension from work on medical or maternity grounds, written statement of reasons for dismissal, and unfair dismissal.

Law governing employment

204.—(1) For the purposes of this Act it is immaterial whether the law which (apart from this Act) governs any person's employment is the law of the United Kingdom, or of a part of the United Kingdom, or not.

(2) Subsection (1) is subject to section 196(1)(b).

DEFINITIONS
"employment": s.230(5).

Remedy for infringement of certain rights

205.—(1) The remedy of an employee for infringement of any of the rights conferred by section 8, Part III, Parts V to VIII, section 92, Part X and Part XII is, where provision is made for a complaint or the reference of a question to an industrial tribunal, by way of such a complaint or reference and not otherwise.

(2) The remedy of a worker in respect of any contravention of section 13, 15, 18(1) or 21(1) is by way of a complaint under section 23 and not otherwise.

DEFINITIONS
"employee": s.230(1).
"worker": s.230(3).

General provisions about death of employer or employee

Institution or continuance of tribunal proceedings

206.—(1) Where an employer has died, any tribunal proceedings arising under any of the provisions of this Act to which this section applies may be defended by a personal representative of the deceased employer.

(2) This section and section 207 apply to—

(a) Part I, so far as it relates to itemised pay statements,
(b) Part III,
(c) Part V,
(d) Part VI, apart from sections 58 to 60,
(e) Parts VII and VIII,
(f) in Part IX, sections 92 and 93, and
(g) Parts X to XII.

(3) Where an employee has died, any tribunal proceedings arising under any of the provisions of this Act to which this section applies may be instituted or continued by a personal representative of the deceased employee.

(4) If there is no personal representative of a deceased employee, any tribunal proceedings arising under any of the provisions of this Act to which this section applies may be instituted or continued on behalf of the estate of the deceased employee by any appropriate person appointed by the industrial tribunal.

(5) In subsection (4) "appropriate person" means a person who is—
(a) authorised by the employee before his death to act in connection with the proceedings, or
(b) the widow or widower, child, parent or brother or sister of the deceased employee;
and in Part XI and the following provisions of this section and section 207 references to a personal representative include a person appointed under subsection (4).

(6) In a case where proceedings are instituted or continued by virtue of subsection (4), any award made by the industrial tribunal shall be—
(a) made in such terms, and
(b) enforceable in such manner,
as the Secretary of State may by regulations provide.

(7) Any reference in the provisions of this Act to which this section applies to the doing of anything by or in relation to an employer or employee includes a reference to the doing of the thing by or in relation to a personal representative of the deceased employer or employee.

(8) Any reference in the provisions of this Act to which this section applies to a thing required or authorised to be done by or in relation to an employer or employee includes a reference to a thing required or authorised to be done by or in relation to a personal representative of the deceased employer or employee.

(9) Subsections (7) and (8) do not prevent a reference to a successor of an employer including a personal representative of a deceased employer.

DEFINITIONS
"appropriate person": subs. (5).
"employee": s.230(1).
"employer": s.230(4).

GENERAL NOTE
This section provides that, where an employee has died, tribunal proceedings arising under any of the provisions referred to in subs. (2) may be instituted or continued by a personal representative of the deceased employee (subs. (3)), or, if the deceased employee has no personal representative, by an "appropriate person" appointed by the industrial tribunal (subs. (4)); similarly, where an employer has died, any such tribunal proceedings may be defended by a personal representative of the deceased employer (subs. (1)).

For the position regarding rights and liabilities accruing after death, see s.207; and for the provisions concerning the death of an employer or employee in relation to claims of unfair dismissal and the right to a redundancy payment, see the notes to ss.133 and 174–176 respectively.

Subs. (6)
The Industrial Tribunals Awards (Enforcement in case of death) Regulations 1976 (S.I. 1976 No. 663) have effect under this subsection.

Rights and liabilities accruing after death

207.—(1) Any right arising under any of the provisions of this Act to which this section applies which accrues after the death of an employee devolves as if it had accrued before his death.

(2) Where an industrial tribunal determines under any provision of Part XI that an employer is liable to pay to a personal representative of a deceased employee—

(a) the whole of a redundancy payment to which he would have been entitled but for some provision of Part XI or section 206, or

(b) such part of such a redundancy payment as the tribunal thinks fit,

the reference in subsection (1) to a right includes any right to receive it.

(3) Where—

(a) by virtue of any of the provisions to which this section applies a personal representative is liable to pay any amount, and

(b) the liability has not accrued before the death of the employer,

it shall be treated as a liability of the deceased employer which had accrued immediately before his death.

DEFINITIONS
  "employee": s.230(1).
  "employer": s.230(4).

Modifications of Act

Review of limits

208.—(1) The Secretary of State shall in each calendar year review—

(a) the limits specified in section 31,

(b) the limit specified in section 186(1), and

(c) the limits imposed by subsection (1) of section 227 for the purposes specified in paragraphs (a) to (c) of that subsection,

and shall determine whether any of those limits should be varied.

(2) In making a review under subsection (1) the Secretary of State shall consider—

(a) the general level of earnings obtaining in Great Britain at the time of the review,

(b) the national economic situation as a whole, and

(c) such other matters as he thinks relevant.

(3) If on a review under subsection (1) the Secretary of State determines that, having regard to the considerations mentioned in subsection (2), any of the limits specified in subsection (1) should be varied, he shall prepare and lay before each House of Parliament the draft of an order giving effect to his decision.

(4) Where a draft of an order under this section is approved by resolution of each House of Parliament the Secretary of State shall make an order in the form of the draft.

(5) If, following the completion of a review under subsection (1), the Secretary of State determines that any of the limits referred to in that subsection should not be varied, he shall lay before each House of Parliament a report containing a statement of his reasons for that determination.

(6) The Secretary of State may at any time, in addition to the annual review provided by in subsection (1), conduct a further review of the limits specified in subsection (1) so as to determine whether any of them should be varied.

(7) Subsections (2) to (4) shall apply to a review under subsection (6) as if it were a review under subsection (1).

Powers to amend Act

209.—(1) The Secretary of State may by order—

(a) provide that any provision of this Act, other than any to which this paragraph does not apply, which is specified in the order shall not apply to persons, or to employments, of such classes as may be prescribed in the order,

(b) provide that any provision of this Act, other than any to which this paragraph does not apply, shall apply to persons or employments of such classes as may be prescribed in the order subject to such exceptions and modifications as may be so prescribed, or

(c) vary, or exclude the operation of, any of the provisions to which this paragraph applies.

(2) Subsection (1)(a) does not apply to—

(a) Parts II and IV,

(b) in Part V, sections 45 and 46, and sections 48 and 49 so far as relating to those sections,

(c) in Part VI, sections 58 to 60,

(d) in Part IX, sections 87(3), 88 to 90, 91(1) to (4) and (6) and 92(6) to (8),

(e) in Part X, sections 95, 97(1) to (5), 98(1) to (4) and (6), 100, 101, 102, 103, 105, 107, 110, 111, 120(2), 124(1), (2) and (5), 125(7) and 134,

(f) in Part XI, sections 143, 144, 160(2) and (3), 166 to 173 and 177 to 180,

(g) in Part XIII, sections 196(1) and 197(1),

(h) Chapter I of Part XIV, or

(j) in Part XV, section 236(3) so far as relating to sections 120(2), 124(2) and 125(7).

(3) Subsection (1)(b) does not apply to—

(a) any of the provisions to which subsection (1)(a) does not apply,

(b) sections 1 to 7, or

(c) the provisions of sections 86 to 91 not specified in subsection (2).

(4) The provision which may be made by virtue of paragraph (b) of subsection (1) in relation to section 94 does not include provision for application subject to exceptions or modifications; but this subsection does not prejudice paragraph (a) of that subsection.

(5) Subsection (1)(c) applies to sections 29(2), 65(2), 86(5), 92(3), 108(1), 109(1), 159, 160(1), 196(2), (3) and (5) and 199(1), (2), (4) and (5).

(6) The Secretary of State may by order amend any of—

(a) sections 84, 85, 97(6), 98(5) and 99(4),

(b) sections 108(3), 109(2) and 110(2) so far as relating to section 84, and

(c) sections 114(5), 115(4), 119(6), 127, 137(2), 145(7), 146(3), 156(2), 157(6), 162(7), 196(4), 199(3), 226(3)(a) and (5)(a) and 227(4)(a),

or modify the application of any of those provisions to any description of case.

(7) The Secretary of State may by order provide that, subject to any such modifications and exceptions as may be prescribed in the order, section 44, and any other provisions of this Act so far as relating to that section, shall apply to such descriptions of persons other than employees as may be so prescribed as to employees (but as if references to their employer were to such person as may be so prescribed).

(8) The provisions of this section are without prejudice to any other power of the Secretary of State to amend, vary or repeal any provision of this Act or to extend or restrict its operation in relation to any person or employment.

PART XIV

INTERPRETATION

CHAPTER I

CONTINUOUS EMPLOYMENT

Introductory

210.—(1) References in any provision of this Act to a period of continuous employment are (unless provision is expressly made to the contrary) to a period computed in accordance with this Chapter.

(2) In any provision of this Act which refers to a period of continuous employment expressed in months or years—

(a) a month means a calendar month, and

(b) a year means a year of twelve calendar months.

(3) In computing an employee's period of continuous employment for the purposes of any provision of this Act, any question—

(a) whether the employee's employment is of a kind counting towards a period of continuous employment, or

(b) whether periods (consecutive or otherwise) are to be treated as forming a single period of continuous employment,

shall be determined week by week; but where it is necessary to compute the length of an employee's period of employment it shall be computed in months and years of twelve months in accordance with section 211.

(4) Subject to sections 215 to 217, a week which does not count in computing the length of a period of continuous employment breaks continuity of employment.

(5) A person's employment during any period shall, unless the contrary is shown, be presumed to have been continuous.

DEFINITIONS
   "employment": s.230(5).
   "week": s.235(1).

GENERAL NOTE
   Most of the statutory employment rights conferred by this Act depend upon the employee having served the appropriate qualifying period of continuous employment. For example, the right to complain of unfair dismissal is subject to a qualifying period of two years' continuous service (albeit with several important exceptions), as is the right to return to work after pregnancy or childbirth. The concept of continuous employment is also used to calculate the amount of a number of statutory awards and payments, *e.g.*, the amount of a redundancy payment, and of a basic award for unfair dismissal. The rules for determining continuity, formerly contained in Schedule 13 of the 1978 Act, are set out in this Chapter of the Act.
   The concept of "continuous employment" is purely a creature of statute. Questions of continuity are governed by the statutory provisions alone, so that an agreement between an employer and an employee (*e.g.* that continuity is to be preserved through a change of employer) will not be effective for statutory purposes, although such an agreement may well be enforceable by the employee as a separate contract: see *Secretary of State for Employment v. Globe Elastic Thread Co.* [1979] IRLR 327, H.L.
   Continuity of employment involves two main elements: first, the existence of a continuous (*i.e.* unbroken) relationship between employer and employee; and secondly, an unbroken relationship which lasts the requisite length of time. In essence, the rules provide that an employee who works for one employer will be deemed to have been employed continuously by that employer irrespective of any changes in the terms of the employee's contract during that period of service. It follows that a single period of continuous employment can span a range of different jobs with the same employer, provided the requirements of this Chapter are satisfied. In certain circumstances, continuity will also be preserved where there has been a change of employer: see the note to s.218.
   The overall length of an employee's period of continuous employment is computed in calendar months and years of 12 calendar months (subs. (2)), but whether a particular period of

employment counts towards the total period of continuous employment, or whether continuity has been broken, is to be determined on a week by week basis (subs. (3)). The general rule is that any week which does not count under the provisions of this Chapter will break the employee's continuity of employment (subs. (4)). The effect of a break in continuity is that the entire period of continuous employment before that week will be wiped out, and the employee will have to start building up a period of continuous employment all over again. The provisions determining which weeks count for the purposes of computing continuous employment are to be found in s.212. A person's employment will be presumed to have been continuous unless the contrary is shown (subs. (5)).

There are a number of exceptional circumstances in which a week which does not count towards the period of continuous employment will not break the continuity of that period, for example, a week during which the employee is absent from work due to a strike or lock-out: see the notes to ss.215–217. In such a case, the beginning of the period of continuous employment will be treated as postponed by the length of the period which does not count; thus a month's strike will mean that the start of continuous employment will be taken to have been a month later: see s.211(3).

The provisions on continuous employment were the subject of major change in 1995 following the landmark decision of the House of Lords in *R. v. Secretary of State for Employment ex p. Equal Opportunities Commission* [1994] IRLR 176. An employee's continuity of employment used to depend on how many hours a week he or she worked, or was employed under the contract of employment to work. In the *EOC* case, the House of Lords held that these hours of work thresholds were contrary to E.C. law, as they indirectly discriminated against women (who represent the majority of part-time workers), and it had not been shown that they were objectively justified. The rules were subsequently amended by the Employment Protection (Part-time Employees) Regulations 1995 (S.I. 1995 No. 31) so that, as from February 6, 1995, any week during which the employee has a contract of employment with the employer counts towards his or her period of continuous employment, regardless of the employee's hours of work. See the note to s.212.

Subs. (5)

Where there is a dispute about continuity, the burden is on the employer to rebut the presumption of continuity by showing that it was broken at some stage. It should be noted, however, that the presumption only applies to employment by one employer; it cannot be applied to employment with different employers, unless the case falls within one of the exceptional situations where continuity is preserved through a change of employer. This is clear from the wording of s.218(1). In *Secretary of State for Employment v. Cohen* [1987] IRLR 169, the E.A.T. held that an industrial tribunal had erred in applying the presumption of continuity to an employee's employment with three successive employers. They said that the presumption only applies to employment with one employer, unless the case can be brought within the provisions now contained in s.218. This means that in a case where there are successive employers, the industrial tribunal must make findings as to whether there have been transfers falling within the appropriate provisions.

Period of continuous employment

211.—(1) An employee's period of continuous employment for the purposes of any provision of this Act—

(a) (subject to subsections (2) and (3)) begins with the day on which the employee starts work, and

(b) ends with the day by reference to which the length of the employee's period of continuous employment is to be ascertained for the purposes of the provision.

(2) For the purposes of sections 155 and 162(1), an employee's period of continuous employment shall be treated as beginning on the employee's eighteenth birthday if that is later than the day on which the employee starts work.

(3) If an employee's period of continuous employment includes one or more periods which (by virtue of section 215, 216 or 217) while not counting in computing the length of the period do not break continuity of employment, the beginning of the period shall be treated as postponed by the number of days falling within that intervening period, or the aggregate number of days falling within those periods, calculated in accordance with the section in question.

DEFINITIONS
"employee": s.230(1).

GENERAL NOTE

An employee's period of continuous employment is computed by identifying the starting date and the finishing date, and calculating the length of the period which falls within those dates (subs. (1)), with an appropriate deduction for any non-counting periods which do not break the employee's continuity (subs. (3)). This differs from the pre-1982 regime, under which the period of continuous employment was calculated by adding up the number of weeks that counted. The present rules were introduced by the Employment Act 1982 (c. 46).

Begins with the day on which the employee starts work. The starting-date for the calculation of the period of continuous employment is the day on which the employee "starts work". This has been interpreted as meaning the day on which the employment under the contract begins, not the day on which the employee actually starts to perform his or her duties. In *General of the Salvation Army v. Dewsbury* [1984] I.C.R. 498, the employee's contract started on May 1, 1982, a Saturday, but as the following Monday was a bank holiday, she actually started teaching on May 4. The E.A.T. held that her period of employment was to be calculated from May 1, 1982.

An employee's period of continuous employment ends with the day by reference to which the length of his or her continuous employment falls to be ascertained for the purposes of the employment right in question: subs. (1)(b). So for example, in the case of unfair dismissal, the end day of the period of continuous employment would be the effective date of termination of employment (see the note to s.97), whereas for the provisions on statutory minimum notice periods, the end day is the date on which notice is given (see the note to s.86).

Weeks counting in computing period

212.—(1) Any week during the whole or part of which an employee's relations with his employer are governed by a contract of employment counts in computing the employee's period of employment.

(2) Any week (not within subsection (1)) during an employee's period of absence from work occasioned wholly or partly by pregnancy or childbirth after which the employee returns to work in accordance with section 79, or in pursuance of an offer described in section 96(3), counts in computing the employee's period of employment.

(3) Subject to subsection (4), any week (not within subsection (1)) during the whole or part of which an employee is—

    (a) incapable of work in consequence of sickness or injury,

    (b) absent from work on account of a temporary cessation of work,

    (c) absent from work in circumstances such that, by arrangement or custom, he is regarded as continuing in the employment of his employer for any purpose, or

    (d) absent from work wholly or partly because of pregnancy or childbirth,

counts in computing the employee's period of employment.

(4) Not more than twenty-six weeks count under subsection (3)(a) or (subject to subsection (2)) subsection (3)(d) between any periods falling under subsection (1).

DEFINITIONS
"childbirth": s.235(1).
"contract of employment": s.230(2).
"employee": s.230(1).
"employer": s.230(4).
"week": s.235(1).

GENERAL NOTE

Subs. (1)

This provides that a week will count towards an employee's period of continuous employment if during the whole or part of the week the employee has a contract of employment with the employer. Continuity will only be preserved through a week where there is no subsisting contract of employment if that week falls within subss. (2) or (3): see below. An employee's continuity of employment used to depend on how many hours a week he or she worked, or was employed under the contract of employment to work. The basic rule was that a week would only count if the employee was actually employed for 16 hours or more during that week, or if during the whole or part of that week the employee's relations with the employer were governed by a contract normally involving employment for 16 hours or more weekly. An employee whose contract of employment normally involved employment for between eight and 16 hours a week and who had been continuously employed for five years or more, was however treated as if the contract normally involved employment for 16 hours or more a week. The effect of these rules was that many part-time workers did not qualify for the statutory employment rights.

However, in 1994 the hours of work thresholds were held by the House of Lords to be contrary to E.C. law, as they indirectly discriminated against women, who represent the majority of part-time workers: *R. v. Secretary of State for Employment ex p. Equal Opportunities Commission* [1994] I.R.L.R. 176. The rules were subsequently amended by the Employment Protection (Part-time Employees) Regulations 1995 (S.I. 1995 No. 31), with effect from February 6, 1995, and subs. (1) now provides that any week during the whole or part of which the employee has a contract of employment with the employer counts towards his or her period of continuous employment, regardless of the employee's hours of work.

Week. This is defined in s.235(1) as "a week ending with Saturday".

During the whole or part of which. The whole week counts, even if the employee only works for the employer for a part of the week. This provision was particularly important under the pre-1982 law, when continuity was computed by adding up the number of weeks which counted (see *e.g. Coulson v. City of London Polytechnic* [1976] I.C.R. 433; *IPC Business Press v. Gray* [1977] I.C.R. 858; *Wynne v. Hair Control* [1978] I.C.R. 870; *Cookson & Zinn v. Morgan* [1979] I.C.R. 425; *Jennings v. Salford Community Service Agency* [1981] I.C.R. 399); it is of less practical significance now that an employee's period of continuous employment is computed by calculating the number of months and years which fall within the start and the finish of employment: see the note to s.211.

Subs. (2)

This preserves continuity throughout a period of maternity absence where the employee returns to work after pregnancy or childbirth in accordance with s.79 ("Right to return to work") or in pursuance of an offer of alternative employment under s.95(3) ("Failure to permit return after childbirth ..."), but not, it seems, her contractual right or any composite right she may have under s.85. Note that under this provision, the employee is entitled to count every week of such absence, whereas under subs. (3)(d), below, a maximum of only 26 weeks may be counted.

Subs. (3)

Generally, continuity of employment is broken by a week during which there is no contract of employment (*i.e.* a week which falls outside subs. (1)), even if the employee is subsequently re-employed by the same employer after the break. However, this important provision, formerly contained in Sched. 13, para. 9 of the 1978 Act, safeguards continuity of employment through periods during which there is no contract of employment, by providing for four exceptional situations where a week will still count even where there is no subsisting contract of employment: *Ford v. Warwickshire County Council* [1983] I.R.L.R. 126, H.L.

Any week (not within subs. (1)). Under the previous provisions, there was no express requirement that para. 9 only applied where there was no subsisting contract of employment; the only reference to there being no contract was in the marginal heading to para. 9, which referred to "Periods in which there is no contract of employment". In *Ford v. Warwickshire County Council,* above, the House of Lords held that para. 9 only applied during periods when there was no contract of employment in existence, but prior to that decision, para. 9 had been applied by the courts in cases where there *was* a contract of employment during the period in question (see *e.g. Lloyds Bank v. Secretary of State for Employment* [1979] I.R.L.R. 41, E.A.T.). The new wording makes it clear that subss. (1) and (3) are mutually exclusive, consistent with the ruling in *Ford.*

Incapable of work in consequence of sickness or injury. Continuity will be preserved under this heading for up to 26 weeks of absence (see subs. (4)), provided the employee returns to work at the end of that period. "Incapable of work" means incapable of carrying out the duties which the employee was employed to perform before the period in question; the employee need not be incapable of any kind of work in order to fall within this exception: *Donnelly v. Kelvin International Services* [1992] I.R.L.R. 496, E.A.T. There must however be some causal connection between the employee's absence and sickness or injury: *Scarlett v. Abbott (Godfrey) Group* [1978] I.C.R. 1106, E.A.T.; *Green v. Wavertree Heating and Plumbing Co.* [1978] I.C.R. 928; *Pearson v. Kent County Council* [1993] I.R.L.R. 165, C.A. Where the employee's absence from work due to sickness or injury does not terminate the contract, as will normally be the case, the weeks of absence will count under subs. (1), although there may come a stage when illness causes the contract to be frustrated.

Temporary cessation of work. Continuity will be preserved during a week where the employee is absent from work on account of a temporary cessation of work, due *e.g.* to disruption of supplies, mechanical breakdown, fire, flood, seasonal lay-off due to fluctuating demand, etc. If the employee's contract of employment subsists during such a period, continuity will usually be preserved under subs. (1). For continuity to be preserved where the contract does not subsist, the following three requirements must be satisfied:

(i) there must be a *cessation of work*; *i.e.*, there must be a diminution in the quantum of work required by the employer, with the consequence that work is no longer available for the employee to do. In *Fitzgerald v. Hall, Russell & Co.* [1970] A.C. 984, the House of Lords held that it is not necessary that the employer should have ceased operations in the factory or part of it in which the employee works; the relevant issue is whether there was no longer any work available for him personally. The exception will not apply where work is available for the employee to do, but the employer decides not to offer him that work, *e.g.*, where the employee is a member of a pool of workers amongst whom the employer distributes work, and where the work is allocated to another member of the pool: see *Byrne v. Birmingham District Council* [1987] I.C.R. 519, C.A., followed in *Letheby & Christopher v. Bond* [1988] I.C.R. 480, E.A.T. (the employee was a casual worker who ran a bar at race meetings. On one particular week, work was available but was not offered to her; her absence during that week was held not to be an absence on account of a temporary cessation of work).

(ii) the cessation of work must be *temporary*; the question of whether a cessation of work is "temporary" must be determined with hindsight, looking back over the history of the whole period of employment and taking account of all the circumstances: *Ford v. Warwickshire County Council* [1983] I.R.L.R. 126, H.L.; *Fitzgerald v. Hall, Russell & Co.* [1970] A.C. 984, H.L. Evidence of the intentions of the parties is relevant, but absence of such evidence is not conclusive. The test is an objective one, and the question of whether a cessation of work is temporary is one of fact and degree in each case. There is no limit on the length of the absence, but if it is lengthy the question will arise whether it is to be regarded as temporary or permanent: see *e.g. Stephens (G W) & Son v. Fish* [1989] I.C.R. 324, E.A.T. (the employee was employed as a coach driver whose main duty was to drive coal miners to and from work. He stopped driving the miners during the miners' strike, but the cessation of work was held to be temporary).

Attempts to decide whether any particular absence is or is not "temporary" have given rise to some difficult case law. The cases reveal two different approaches to the question of whether a cessation of work can properly be described as "temporary". In *Ford v. Warwickshire County Council* [1983] I.C.R. 273, H.L., Lord Diplock appeared to favour a mathematical approach, whereby the tribunal should compare the length of the periods during which the employee was in work with the length of the intervening gaps, to see if the gaps could properly be described as temporary. In that case, the House of Lords held that the exception applied to a teacher employed under a series of fixed-term contracts for each academic year, but with a gap during each summer vacation; the fact that the breaks in employment were regular, predictable and agreed in advance between the parties did not defeat the operation of the exception, provided the interruption could properly be regarded as transient, in the sense that it lasted only for a relatively short time in relation to the periods of normal working:

"... [T]he whole scheme of the Act appears to me to show that it is in the sense of 'transient', *i.e.* lasting only for a relatively short time, that the word 'temporary' is used [in s.212(3)(b)] ..." (per Diplock L.J., at p.284).

Ford was followed in *University of Aston, Birmingham v. Malik* [1984] I.C.R. 492, E.A.T., in which a lecturer employed under a series of consecutive yearly contracts was held to have been continuously employed during a period when there was no paid work for her to do because the employer was temporarily short of money, and in *Sillars v. Charringtons Fuels* [1989] I.C.R. 475, which involved a regular seasonal pattern of approximately six months in work, followed by approximately six months out of work. The Court of Appeal upheld the industrial tribunal's use of the mathematical approach, which had led to a finding that as the period out of work relative to the period in work was not short, and therefore not "temporary", the employee had not been in continuous employment. See also *Berwick Salmon Fisheries Co. v. Rutherford* [1991] I.R.L.R. 203, E.A.T., which involved seasonal workers with a salmon netting company, which appears to confirm that under the mathematical approach, a cessation of work will not be regarded as temporary where the periods in work are shorter than the periods out of work.

The mathematical approach was however rejected as inappropriate by the Court of Appeal in *Flack v. Kodak* [1986] I.C.R. 775. In that case, the employee was employed according to seasonal needs on an intermittent basis, and her employment revealed an irregular pattern. Within the final two years of her employment she had bursts of employment and non-employment, following which she worked for 542 days until her dismissal. The Court of Appeal said that in such a case the tribunal should adopt a broad rather than a mathematical approach, having regard to all the circumstances over the whole period of employment (including the intentions of the parties) to ascertain whether the breaks in employment were temporary, and should not confine themselves to looking only at each such break in relation to the adjoining periods of employment. Such an approach enables the tribunal to look at all the factors, and it therefore gives far greater flexibility.

These decisions show that in all cases the process of judging whether a cessation is temporary involves the use of hindsight and consideration of all relevant factors, but it is equally clear that the approach to be taken depends upon whether the pattern of employment and unemployment is regular or irregular. The mathematical approach is appropriate where there is a regular pattern of employment and non-employment, but where the pattern of work is irregular, the broad approach is preferable.

(iii) the absence from work must be *on account of* the temporary cessation of work, *i.e.* there must be a causal link between the cessation of work and the employee's absence: see *Bentley Engineering Co. v. Crown* [1976] I.C.R. 225, E.A.T. An employee who resigns or who is dismissed by his employer for misconduct only to be re-engaged later will not be able to benefit from subs. (3)(b), because the employee's absence was not caused by the temporary unavailability of work. So, for example, in *Roach v. CSB (Moulds)* [1991] I.C.R. 349, the E.A.T. held that continuity of employment was broken in the case of an employee who was dismissed by his employers, went to work for another employer for about 12 days, and then returned to his previous employers at a lower grade for some seven months before being finally dismissed by them. See also *Ryan v. Shipboard Maintenance* [1980] I.C.R. 88, and *Hellyer Brothers v. McLeod* [1986] I.C.R. 122. Where however there is a temporary cessation of work, an employee who takes other employment during that period will still be regarded as absent from work on account of that temporary cessation, provided the new job is clearly intended only to be a stop-gap until the employee is able to resume work with his original employer: *Thompson v. Bristol Channel Ship Repairers and Engineers* (1970) 5 ITR 85, C.A.

Absent ... in circumstances such that, by arrangement or custom, he is regarded as continuing in ... employment. Continuity will be preserved where the employee is absent from work but is regarded "by arrangement or custom" as continuing in employment for all or any purposes. This exception covers the type of situation where an employee is granted unpaid leave of absence, or is laid off, or is seconded by the employer to a third party, in circumstances where the contract of employment does not subsist throughout the period of absence but where there is an arrangement or understanding or custom whereby the employee is regarded as continuing in the employment of the employer for all or any purposes. See *Wishart v. National Coal Board* [1974] I.C.R. 460; *Lane v. Wolverhampton Die Casting Co.* (1967) 2 ITR 120; *Rhodes v. Pontins* (1971) 6 ITR 88; *Murray v. Kelvin Electronics Co.* (1967) 2 ITR 622; *Southern Electricity Board v. Collins* [1970] 1 Q.B. 83. The arrangement or custom must predate the absence from work (*Murphy v. Birrell & Sons* [1978] I.R.L.R. 458, E.A.T.), although in one case a reinstatement agreement made after dismissal was held to be effective to preserve continuity under this head (*Ingram v. Foxon* [1984] I.C.R. 685, E.A.T.). In *Lloyds Bank v. Secretary of State for Employment* [1979] I.R.L.R. 41, E.A.T., this provision was applied in a case where the employee's contract provided for work on a "week on, week off" basis, but the correctness of that decision (and of the decision in *Corton House v. Skipper* [1981] I.C.R. 307, where a similar approach was adopted) has been placed in doubt by the ruling of the House of Lords in *Ford v. Warwickshire County Council* (above), that the exceptions in subs. (3) only apply where there is no subsisting contract during the employee's absence from work. See also *Harber v. North London Polytechnic* [1990] I.R.L.R. 195, C.A. If the interpretation of subs. (3) in *Ford* is correct, it should not be used to protect employees whose hours fluctuate, nor should it be used as a safety net provision to catch hours of work, or periods of employment, which cannot be accommodated within the other provisions of this Chapter.

In *Letheby & Christopher v. Bond* [1988] I.C.R. 480, the E.A.T. refused to apply the provisions of subs. (3)(c) to a casual worker who was absent from work for a week while she was on holiday, holding that the tribunal should have asked whether, when the absence took place, the parties regarded the employment as continuing. Since she was employed under a series of single, separate contracts, it was not possible to say that her employment was regarded as continuing during her absence.

Absent ... because of pregnancy or childbirth. Continuity will be preserved for up to 26 weeks where the employee is absent from work wholly or partly because of pregnancy or childbirth. Note however that by virtue of subs. (2), above, if the employee returns to work after pregnancy or childbirth in accordance with s.79 ("Right to return to work") or in pursuance of an offer of alternative employment under s.95(3) ("Failure to permit return after childbirth ..."), she is entitled to count every week of such absence, whereas under this exception a maximum of only 26 weeks may be counted. Absence from work caused by the employee's resignation will be within this exception, provided the absence is wholly or partly because of pregnancy or child-birth: see *Mitchell v. Royal British Legion Club* [1981] I.C.R. 18, E.A.T.

Intervals in employment

213.—(1) Where in the case of an employee a date later than the date which would be the effective date of termination by virtue of subsection (1) of section 97 is treated for certain purposes as the effective date of termination by virtue of subsection (2) or (4) of that section, the period of the interval between the two dates counts as a period of employment in ascertaining for the purposes of section 108(1) or 119(1) the period for which the employee has been continuously employed.

(2) Where an employee is by virtue of section 138(1) regarded for the purposes of Part XI as not having been dismissed by reason of a renewal or re-engagement taking effect after an interval, the period of the interval counts as a period of employment in ascertaining for the purposes of section 155 or 162(1) the period for which the employee has been continuously employed (except so far as it is to be disregarded under section 214 or 215).

(3) Where in the case of an employee a date later than the date which would be the relevant date by virtue of subsections (2) to (4) of section 145 is treated for certain purposes as the relevant date by virtue of subsection (5) of that section, the period of the interval between the two dates counts as a period of employment in ascertaining for the purposes of section 155 or 162(1) the period for which the employee has been continuously employed (except so far as it is to be disregarded under section 214 or 215).

DEFINITIONS
"employee": s.230(1).
"effective date of termination": s.97.
"employment": s.230(5).

Special provisions for redundancy payments

214.—(1) This section applies where a period of continuous employment has to be determined in relation to an employee for the purposes of the application of section 155 or 162(1).

(2) The continuity of a period of employment is broken where—
(a) a redundancy payment has previously been paid to the employee (whether in respect of dismissal or in respect of lay-off or short-time), and
(b) the contract of employment under which the employee was employed was renewed (whether by the same or another employer) or the employee was re-engaged under a new contract of employment (whether by the same or another employer).

(3) The continuity of a period of employment is also broken where—
(a) a payment has been made to the employee (whether in respect of the termination of his employment or lay-off or short-time) in accordance with a scheme under section 1 of the Superannuation Act 1972 or arrangements falling within section 177(3), and
(b) he commenced new, or renewed, employment.

(4) The date on which the person's continuity of employment is broken by virtue of this section—
(a) if the employment was under a contract of employment, is the date which was the relevant date in relation to the payment mentioned in subsection (2)(a) or (3)(a), and
(b) if the employment was otherwise than under a contract of employment, is the date which would have been the relevant date in relation

to the payment mentioned in subsection (2)(a) or (3)(a) had the employment been under a contract of employment.

(5) For the purposes of this section a redundancy payment shall be treated as having been paid if—

(a) the whole of the payment has been paid to the employee by the employer,

(b) a tribunal has determined liability and found that the employer must pay part (but not all) of the redundancy payment and the employer has paid that part, or

(c) the Secretary of State has paid a sum to the employee in respect of the redundancy payment under section 167.

DEFINITIONS
"contract of employment": s.230(2).
"employee": s.230(1).
"employer": s.230(4).
"employment": s.230(5).

GENERAL NOTE
Continuity of employment will be broken by the payment of a redundancy payment, but only for the purposes of claiming a redundancy payment (subs. (1)). In order for this provision to apply, there must be payment in full in accordance with the statutory redundancy payments scheme: *Rowan v. Machinery Installations (South Wales)* [1981] I.R.L.R. 122, E.A.T. Note however that if the employee is subsequently re-employed on terms which require the repayment of the redundancy payment, this section does not apply: see the Employment Protection (Continuity of Employment) Regulations 1993 (S.I. 1993 No. 2165).

Employment abroad etc.

215.—(1) This Chapter applies to a period of employment—

(a) subject to the following provisions of this section) even where during the period the employee was engaged in work wholly or mainly outside Great Britain, and

(b) even where the employee was excluded by or under this Act from any right conferred by this Act.

(2) For the purposes of sections 155 and 162(1) a week of employment does not count in computing a period of employment if the employee—

(a) was employed outside Great Britain during the whole or part of the week, and

(b) was not during that week an employed earner for the purposes of the Social Security Contributions and Benefits Act 1992 in respect of whom a secondary Class 1 contribution was payable under that Act (whether or not the contribution was in fact paid).

(3) Where by virtue of subsection (2) a week of employment does not count in computing a period of employment, the continuity of the period is not broken by reason only that the week does not count in computing the period; and the number of days which, for the purposes of section 211(3), fall within the intervening period is seven for each week within this subsection.

(4) Any question arising under subsection (2) whether—

(a) a person was an employed earner for the purposes of the Social Security Contributions and Benefits Act 1992, or

(b) if so, whether a secondary Class 1 contribution was payable in respect of him under that Act,

shall be determined by the Secretary of State.

(5) Any legislation (including regulations) as to the determination of questions which under the Social Security Administration Act 1992 the Secretary of State is empowered to determine (including provisions as to the reference of questions for decision, or as to appeals, to the High Court or the Court of Session) apply to the determination of any question by the Secretary of State under subsection (4).

(6) Subsection (2) does not apply in relation to a person who is—
(a) employed as a master or seaman in a British ship, and
(b) ordinarily resident in Great Britain.

DEFINITIONS
"contract of employment": s.230(2).
"employee": s.230(1).
"employment": s.230(5).

GENERAL NOTE
Periods of employment during which an employee is engaged in work wholly or mainly outside Great Britain generally count towards the employee's period of continuous employment (subs. (1)). However, for the purposes of the redundancy payments provisions, a week will not count towards an employee's continuous employment if during any part of that week the employee was employed outside Great Britain, and the employee was not during that week an employed earner in respect of whom an employer's contribution was payable (subs. (2)); it is however expressly stated that the employee's continuity of employment will not be broken by such a week (subs. (3)).
Wholly or mainly outside Great Britain. See the note to s.196.

Industrial disputes

216.—(1) A week does not count under section 212 if during the week, or any part of the week, the employee takes part in a strike.
(2) The continuity of an employee's period of employment is not broken by a week which does not count under this Chapter (whether or not by virtue only of subsection (1)) if during the week, or any part of the week, the employee takes part in a strike; and the number of days which, for the purposes of section 211(3), fall within the intervening period is the number of days between the last working day before the strike and the day on which work was resumed.
(3) The continuity of an employee's period of employment is not broken by a week if during the week, or any part of the week, the employee is absent from work because of a lock-out by the employer; and the number of days which, for the purposes of section 211(3), fall within the intervening period is the number of days between the last working day before the lock-out and the day on which work was resumed.

DEFINITIONS
"employee": s.230(1).
"employer": s.230(4).
"lock-out": s.235(4).
"strike": s.235(5).
"week": s.235(1).

GENERAL NOTE
Special rules operate for weeks during all or part of which an employee takes part in a strike or is absent from work because of a lock-out by the employer. The basic position is that a week will not count towards an employee's period of continuous employment if during any part of that week the employee took part in a "strike", no matter how short (subs. (1)). Continuity of employment will not however be broken by such a week (subs. (2)), even if the employee is dismissed during the strike and re-engaged once it is over: *Hanson v. Fashion Industries (Hartlepool)* [1980] I.R.L.R. 393, E.A.T. In such a case, the beginning of the employee's period of continuous employment will be postponed by the number of days the strike lasts (by virtue of s.211(3)), so that a dispute lasting nine days will cause the starting date of the employee's period of continuous employment to be treated as nine days later than it actually was.
These rules operate whether or not the strike is unlawful (*e.g.* without due strike notice) or unofficial: see *Bloomfield v. Springfield Hosiery Finishing Co.* [1972] I.C.R. 91; *Clarke Chapman-John Thompson v. Walters* [1972] I.C.R. 83. A period of time after the end of the strike but before the employee returns to work is likely to be treated as a temporary cessation of work, and therefore covered by s.212(3)(b): *Clarke Chapman-John Thompson v. Walters*, above. Employees who are laid off because of a strike or lock-out at another plant will probably also be covered by s.212(3)(b). Any attempt to contract out of these rules, for example by asking

the employee, when taken on again after the strike, to sign a new contract excluding the previous period of employment with the employer, will be void: see the note to s.203.

Similarly, continuity will not be broken by a week during which the employee is absent from work because of a "lock-out" by the employer (subs. (3)); the Act does not specifically state that such a week does not count (contrast subs. (1), above), and it would therefore seem that the week during which the lock-out occurs will still count under s.212(1), provided the employee's contract of employment continues in existence during that week.

Strike. This is defined for present purposes in s.235(5).

Lock-out. This is defined for present purposes in s.235(4).

Reinstatement after military service

217.—(1) If a person who is entitled to apply to his former employer under the Reserve Forces (Safeguard of Employment) Act 1985 enters the employment of the employer not later than the end of the six month period mentioned in section 1(4)(b) of that Act, his period of service in the armed forces of the Crown in the circumstances specified in section 1(1) of that Act does not break his continuity of employment.

(2) In the case of such a person the number of days which, for the purposes of section 211(3), fall within the intervening period is the number of days between the last day of his previous period of employment with the employer (or, if there was more than one such period, the last of them) and the first day of the period of employment beginning in the six month period.

DEFINITIONS
"employer": s.230(4).
"employment": s.230(5).

GENERAL NOTE
Where an employee is re-engaged by his former employer after military service, in accordance with the Reserve Forces (Safeguard of Employment) Act 1985 (c. 17), his continuity of employment with his employer is not broken by the period of service in the armed forces (subs. (1)), although that period will not count towards his period of continuous employment (subs. (2)).

Change of employer

218.—(1) Subject to the provisions of this section, this Chapter relates only to employment by the one employer.

(2) If a trade or business, or an undertaking (whether or not established by or under an Act), is transferred from one person to another—

    (a) the period of employment of an employee in the trade or business or undertaking at the time of the transfer counts as a period of employment with the transferee, and

    (b) the transfer does not break the continuity of the period of employment.

(3) If by or under an Act (whether public or local and whether passed before or after this Act) a contract of employment between any body corporate and an employee is modified and some other body corporate is substituted as the employer—

    (a) the employee's period of employment at the time when the modification takes effect counts as a period of employment with the second body corporate, and

    (b) the change of employer does not break the continuity of the period of employment.

(4) If on the death of an employer the employee is taken into the employment of the personal representatives or trustees of the deceased—

    (a) the employee's period of employment at the time of the death counts as a period of employment with the employer's personal representatives or trustees, and

  (b) the death does not break the continuity of the period of employment.

  (5) If there is a change in the partners, personal representatives or trustees who employ any person—

    (a) the employee's period of employment at the time of the change counts as a period of employment with the partners, personal representatives or trustees after the change, and

    (b) the change does not break the continuity of the period of employment.

  (6) If an employee of an employer is taken into the employment of another employer who, at the time when the employee enters the second employer's employment, is an associated employer of the first employer—

    (a) the employee's period of employment at that time counts as a period of employment with the second employer, and

    (b) the change of employer does not break the continuity of the period of employment.

  (7) If an employee of the governors of a school maintained by a local education authority is taken into the employment of the authority or an employee of a local education authority is taken into the employment of the governors of a school maintained by the authority—

    (a) his period of employment at the time of the change of employer counts as a period of employment with the second employer, and

    (b) the change does not break the continuity of the period of employment.

  (8) If a person employed in relevant employment by a health service employer is taken into relevant employment by another such employer, his period of employment at the time of the change of employer counts as a period of employment with the second employer and the change does not break the continuity of the period of employment.

  (9) For the purposes of subsection (8) employment is relevant employment if it is employment of a description—

    (a) in which persons are engaged while undergoing professional training which involves their being employed successively by a number of different health service employers, and

    (b) which is specified in an order made by the Secretary of State.

  (10) The following are health service employers for the purposes of subsections (8) and (9)—

    (a) Health Authorities established under section 8 of the National Health Service Act 1977,

    (b) Special Health Authorities established under section 11 of that Act,

    (c) National Health Service trusts established under Part I of the National Health Service and Community Care Act 1990,

    (d) the Dental Practice Board, and

    (e) the Public Health Laboratory Service Board.

DEFINITIONS

  "associated employer": s.231.
  "business": s.235(1).
  "employee": s.230(1).
  "employer": s.230(4).
  "employment": s.230(5).

GENERAL NOTE

  The statutory provisions on continuity of employment normally relate only to employment by the one employer (subs. (1)), so that a change of employer usually breaks continuity. However, this section provides for a number of situations where continuity of employment is preserved despite a change of employer. These provisions are supplemented by the Transfer of Undertakings (Protection of Employment) Regulations 1981 (S.I. 1981 No. 1794), which automatically transfer the contracts of employment of those employed in the transferred undertaking to the transferee employer in certain circumstances.

Subs. (1)

Employment by the one employer. Provided that the employee is employed by the same employer, continuity of employment is not affected by the fact that the employee may have a number of consecutive contracts of employment with that employer involving different types of work or different terms: *Re Mack Trucks (Britain)* [1967] 1 W.L.R. 780.

Subs. (2)

Where there is a transfer of a "trade or business or an undertaking" from one person to another, continuity of employment will be preserved through the change of employer in the case of an employee employed in the trade or business or undertaking "at the time of the transfer". Note that the presumption of continuity in s.210(5) does not apply to a transfer of business case under subs. (2): *Secretary of State for Employment v. Cohen* [1987] IRLR 169, E.A.T.

Trade or business, or an undertaking. This provision only applies to the transfer of a trade, business or undertaking, or a part thereof; it does not apply to a transfer of physical assets. See generally, *Melon v. Powe (Hector)* [1981] IRLR 477, H.L.; *Ault (G.D.) (Isle of Wight) v. Gregory* (1967) 2 I.T.R. 301; *Kenmir v. Frizzell* [1968] 1 All E.R. 414; *Lloyd v. Brassey* [1969] 2 Q.B. 98, C. A.; *Woodhouse v. Brotherhood (Peter)* [1972] 2 Q.B. 520, C.A.; *Green v. Wavertree Heating and Plumbing Co.* [1978] I.C.R. 928, E.A.T.; *Teesside Times v. Drury* [1980] IRLR 72, C.A.; *Ward v. Haines Watts* [1983] IRLR 285, E.A.T.

Business. As defined in s.235(1), this includes a trade or profession and includes any activity carried on by a body of persons, whether corporate or unincorporated.

At the time of the transfer. This provision only preserves the continuity of employment of an employee in the trade or business or undertaking at the time of the transfer. It is unclear whether this means that, in order for continuity to be preserved, the employee must be in employment at the actual moment of the transfer (echoing the restrictive interpretation of the phrase "immediately before the transfer" in reg. 5(3) of the Transfer of Undertakings (Protection of Employment) Regulations 1981 in *Secretary of State for Employment v. Spence* [1986] IRLR 248), or whether a broader view should be taken. The point was considered, but not resolved, by the Court of Appeal in *Teesside Times v. Drury* (above), but in *Macer v. Abafast* [1990] IRLR 137, the E.A.T. held that the provision should be interpreted in such a way as to preserve continuity, and that a short gap between the two employments did not destroy continuity, even where it included one or more weeks which would not otherwise count. This broad interpretation avoids the possibility of an employer circumventing the provisions by dismissing the employees before the transfer, but unfortunately it leaves open the crucial question as to how long a gap can be before the provision will cease to apply. The decision in *Macer* was applied by the E.A.T. in *Tuck (A & G) v. Bartlett* [1994] IRLR 162 and in *Justfern v. Skaife D'Ingerthorpe* [1994] IRLR 164.

Subs. (3)

This provision only applies where one body corporate is substituted for another as employer by an Act of Parliament: see *Gale v. Northern General Hospital NHS Trust* [1994] IRLR 292, C.A.

Subs. (5)

This provision safeguards continuity where, for example, one partner retires and is replaced by another. In *Fielding (Harold) v. Mansi* [1974] IRLR 79, it was held not to apply where a partnership was dissolved and the employee was subsequently employed by one of the former partners; similarly, in *Wynne v. Hair Control* [1978] I.C.R. 870, where employment by an individual was followed by employment by a partnership which included that person. This narrow interpretation of subs. (5) was doubted by the E.A.T. in *Allen & Son v. Coventry* [1980] I.C.R. 9, and in *Jeetle v. Elster* [1985] I.C.R. 389, but in both cases the E.A.T. was able to find that continuity was preserved under subs. (2) as a transfer of business.

Subss. (6)–(8)

Associated employer. This is defined in s.231: see the note to that section. The requirement for associated employers to be limited companies in order for this provision to apply could, potentially, adversely affect public sector employees who move from one public body to another. This result is partially avoided by the Redundancy Payments (Local Government) (Modification) Order 1983 (S.I. 1983 No. 1160), which deems the employment of local government employees who move from one local government body to another to be continuous, but only for redundancy payments purposes. Special provision is also made for teachers who move between employment by a local education authority and employment by the governors of a LEA-maintained school (see subs. (7)), and for trainee health service employees who move from employment by one health service employer to another such employer (see subs. (8)). See also the Employment Protection (Continuity of Employment of National Health Service Employees) (Modification) Order 1996 (S.I. 1996 No. 1023).

Reinstatement or re-engagement of dismissed employee

219.—(1) Regulations made by the Secretary of State may make provision—

   (a) for preserving the continuity of a person's period of employment for the purposes of this Chapter or for the purposes of this Chapter as applied by or under any other enactment specified in the regulations, or

   (b) for modifying or excluding the operation of section 214 subject to the recovery of any such payment as is mentioned in that section,

in cases where, in consequence of action to which subsection (2) applies, a dismissed employee is reinstated or re-engaged by his employer or by a successor or associated employer of that employer.

(2) This subsection applies to any action taken in relation to the dismissal of an employee which consists of—

   (a) his making a claim in accordance with a dismissal procedures agreement designated by an order under section 110,

   (b) the presentation by him of a relevant complaint of dismissal,

   (c) any action taken by a conciliation officer under section 18 of the Industrial Tribunals Act 1996, or

   (d) the making of a relevant compromise contract.

(3) In subsection (2)(b) "relevant complaint of dismissal" means—

   (a) a complaint under section 111 of this Act,

   (b) a complaint under section 63 of the Sex Discrimination Act 1975 arising out of a dismissal,

   (c) a complaint under section 54 of the Race Relations Act 1976 arising out of a dismissal, or

   (d) a complaint under section 8 of the Disability Discrimination Act 1995 arising out of a dismissal.

(4) In subsection (2)(d) "relevant compromise contract" means—

   (a) an agreement or contract authorised by—

      (i) section 203(2)(f) of this Act,

      (ii) section 77(4)(aa) of the Sex Discrimination Act 1975,

      (iii) section 72(4)(aa) of the Race Relations Act 1976, or

      (iv) section 9(2)(b) of the Disability Discrimination Act 1995, or

   (b) an agreement to refrain from instituting or continuing any proceedings before an industrial tribunal where the tribunal has jurisdiction in respect of the proceedings by virtue of an order under section 3 of the Industrial Tribunals Act 1996.

DEFINITIONS
"associated employer": s.231.
"employee": s.230(1).
"employer": s.230(4).

GENERAL NOTE
Regulations made by the Secretary of State. The Employment Protection (Continuity of Employment) Regulations 1993 (S.I. 1993 No. 2165) have effect under this section.

CHAPTER II

A WEEK'S PAY

Introductory

Introductory

220. The amount of a week's pay of an employee shall be calculated for the purposes of this Act in accordance with this Chapter.

DEFINITIONS
  "employee": s.230(1).

GENERAL NOTE
  This Chapter lays down the rules for determining the calculation of a week's pay for the purposes of the Act. The calculation of a week's pay is important for a number of statutory employment rights, including the calculation of the basic and additional awards for unfair dismissal, redundancy payments, guarantee payments and payments under the insolvency provisions. The amount of a week's pay for statutory purposes is subject to a statutory maximum (see s.227) which can be varied by order.
  The calculation of a week's pay depends on whether the employee has "normal working hours" (as defined in s.234), and whether the employee's remuneration varies with the amount of work done. Employments where there are normal working hours are governed by ss.221 to 223; where there are no normal working hours, the method of calculation is laid down in s.224. Sections 225 and 226 set out the relevant calculation dates, which vary according to the particular statutory rights involved; s.227 determines the maximum amount of a week's pay; and s.228 deals with the situation where the employee has not been employed for a sufficient period to enable the calculation to be made in the usual way.
  A week's pay. For the purposes of the calculation of a week's pay, the amount of gross weekly pay should be taken, not the net amount: see *Secretary of State for Employment v. Woodrow (John) & Sons (Builders)* [1983] IRLR 11, E.A.T.

Employments with normal working hours

General

221.—(1) This section and sections 222 and 223 apply where there are normal working hours for the employee when employed under the contract of employment in force on the calculation date.
  (2) Subject to section 222, if the employee's remuneration for employment in normal working hours (whether by the hour or week or other period) does not vary with the amount of work done in the period, the amount of a week's pay is the amount which is payable by the employer under the contract of employment in force on the calculation date if the employee works throughout his normal working hours in a week.
  (3) Subject to section 222, if the employee's remuneration for employment in normal working hours (whether by the hour or week or other period) does vary with the amount of work done in the period, the amount of a week's pay is the amount of remuneration for the number of normal working hours in a week calculated at the average hourly rate of remuneration payable by the employer to the employee in respect of the period of twelve weeks ending—
  (a) where the calculation date is the last day of a week, with that week, and
  (b) otherwise, with the last complete week before the calculation date.
  (4) In this section references to remuneration varying with the amount of work done includes remuneration which may include any commission or similar payment which varies in amount.
  (5) This section is subject to sections 227 and 228.

DEFINITIONS
  "contract of employment": s.230(2).
  "employee": s.230(1).

"employer": s.230(4).
"employment": s.230(5).
"normal working hours": s.234.
"week": s.235(1).

GENERAL NOTE

Where the employee has normal working hours and the employee's remuneration does not vary with the amount of work done, subs. (2) provides that the employee's "week's pay" is the amount which is payable under the contract of employment which is in force on the relevant calculation date (see ss.225 and 226) if the employee works throughout the normal working hours of the week. This could include any regular bonuses paid to the employee: see *e.g. Marcusfield (A. & B.) v. Melhuish* [1977] IRLR 484; *Donelan v. Kerby Constructions* [1983] I.C.R. 237. The relevant amount has been held to exclude a back-dated pay increase agreed after the calculation date: *Leyland Vehicles v. Reston* [1981] I.C.R. 403, E.A.T. On the meaning of "remuneration" in this context, see below.

If the employee has normal working hours, but his or her remuneration varies with the amount of work done (*e.g.* piece workers, or those eligible for bonuses or commission which varies in amount: see subs. (4)), the employee's "week's pay" is the amount of remuneration for the number of normal working hours in the week, calculated at the average hourly rate payable in respect of the 12-week period preceding the calculation date (if that day is the last day of the week), or otherwise ending with the last complete week before the calculation date (subs. (3)). This provision has been held to apply to waiters remunerated according to a system by which a fixed charge of 15 per cent was placed in a fund and distributed to all waiters (and some kitchen staff) in proportions calculated by reference to the relative importance of the various employees in the service hierarchy: see *Keywest Club (t/a Veeraswamy's Restaurant) v. Choudhury* [1988] IRLR 51, E.A.T. Different rules apply where the employee's remuneration varies according to the time of work (*e.g.* shift and rota workers): see the note to s.222.

Average hourly rate. In calculating the average hourly rate of remuneration, only those hours when the employee was working, and the remuneration payable for, or apportionable to, those hours of work may be taken into account: see s.223(1). Note also that any premium in respect of overtime working must be ignored: see s.223(3), applied in *British Coal Corp. v. Cheesbrough* [1990] I.C.R. 317, H.L.

Remuneration. This key concept is not defined in the Act. It has been held to include, in addition to wages or salary, any regular bonuses, commission or supplements to which the employee is entitled (*Weevsmay v. Kings* [1977] I.C.R. 244; *Ogden v. Ardphalt Asphalt* [1977] I.C.R. 604; *Marcusfield (A. & B.) v. Melhuish*, above), but not payments in kind, payments from a third party (*e.g.* tips: *Palmanor v. Cedron* [1978] I.C.R. 1008), unless distributed by the employer (*Keywest Club (t/a Veeraswamy's Restaurant) v. Choudhury*, above; *Nerva v. RL & G (A Firm)* [1995] IRLR 200), or expenses, unless there is an element of profit or surplus in the employee's hands (*S. & U. Stores v. Wilkes* [1974] IRLR 283). Commission or bonuses which are payable on a periodic basis (*e.g.* yearly) may be apportioned pro rata where they are payable at a time outside the calculation period: s.229(2) (see *e.g. Bickley (J. & S.) v. Washer* [1977] I.C.R. 425).

Remuneration varying according to time of work

222.—(1) This section applies if the employee is required under the contract of employment in force on the calculation date to work during normal working hours on days of the week, or at times of the day, which differ from week to week or over a longer period so that the remuneration payable for, or apportionable to, any week varies according to the incidence of those days or times.

(2) The amount of a week's pay is the amount of remuneration for the average number of weekly normal working hours at the average hourly rate of remuneration.

(3) For the purposes of subsection (2)—

(a) the average number of weekly hours is calculated by dividing by twelve the total number of the employee's normal working hours during the relevant period of twelve weeks, and

(b) the average hourly rate of remuneration is the average hourly rate of remuneration payable by the employer to the employee in respect of the relevant period of twelve weeks.

(4) In subsection (3) "the relevant period of twelve weeks" means the period of twelve weeks ending—
(a) where the calculation date is the last day of a week, with that week, and
(b) otherwise, with the last complete week before the calculation date.
(5) This section is subject to sections 227 and 228.

DEFINITIONS
"contract of employment": s.230(2).
"employee": s.230(1).
"employer": s.230(4).
"employment": s.230(5).
"normal working hours": s.234.
"week": s.235(1).

GENERAL NOTE
This section applies where the employee has normal working hours, but where his or her time of work varies from week to week or over a longer period, and the amount of remuneration payable varies accordingly, *e.g.* shift and rota workers. Here, it is necessary to average *both* the rate of remuneration *and* the weekly number of working hours, so that the amount of a week's pay is the average weekly number of normal working hours payable at the average hourly rate (subs. (2)). As in s.221(3), the averages are calculated over the 12-week period preceding the calculation date (subs. (3)). Special rules apply where the employee has not been employed long enough for a calculation to be made under the above rules: see s.228(1). In such a case, the tribunal must determine an amount "which fairly represents a week's pay."

Supplementary

223.—(1) For the purposes of sections 221 and 222, in arriving at the average hourly rate of remuneration, only—
(a) the hours when the employee was working, and
(b) the remuneration payable for, or apportionable to, those hours,
shall be brought in.
(2) If for any of the twelve weeks mentioned in sections 221 and 222 no remuneration within subsection (1)(b) was payable by the employer to the employee, account shall be taken of remuneration in earlier weeks so as to bring up to twelve the number of weeks of which account is taken.
(3) Where—
(a) in arriving at the average hourly rate of remuneration, account has to be taken of remuneration payable for, or apportionable to, work done in hours other than normal working hours, and
(b) the amount of that remuneration was greater than it would have been if the work had been done in normal working hours (or, in a case within section 234(3), in normal working hours falling within the number of hours without overtime),
account shall be taken of that remuneration as if the work had been done in such hours and the amount of that remuneration had been reduced accordingly.

DEFINITIONS
"employee": s.230(1).
"employer": s.230(4).
"normal working hours": s.234.
"week": s.235(1).

Employments with no normal working hours

Employments with no normal working hours

224.—(1) This section applies where there are no normal working hours for the employee when employed under the contract of employment in force on the calculation date.

(2) The amount of a week's pay is the amount of the employee's average weekly remuneration in the period of twelve weeks ending—

    (a) where the calculation date is the last day of a week, with that week, and

    (b) otherwise, with the last complete week before the calculation date.

(3) In arriving at the average weekly remuneration no account shall be taken of a week in which no remuneration was payable by the employer to the employee and remuneration in earlier weeks shall be brought in so as to bring up to twelve the number of weeks of which account is taken.

(4) This section is subject to sections 227 and 228.

DEFINITIONS

    "contract of employment": s.230(2).
    "employee": s.230(1).
    "employer": s.230(4).
    "employment": s.230(5).
    "normal working hours": s.234.
    "week": s.235(1).

GENERAL NOTE

    This section applies where the employee has no normal working hours. In such a case the week's pay is determined by calculating the amount of the employee's average weekly remuneration in the 12-week period preceding the calculation date (if that day is the last day of the week), or otherwise ending with the last complete week before the calculation date (subs. (2)). Subsection (3) provides that no account is to be taken of a week in which no remuneration was payable by the employer to the employee; see *Secretary of State for Employment v. Crane* [1988] IRLR 238, E.A.T.

The calculation date

Rights during employment

    225.—(1) Where the calculation is for the purposes of section 30, the calculation date is—

    (a) where the employee's contract has been varied, or a new contract entered into, in connection with a period of short-time working, the last day on which the original contract was in force, and

    (b) otherwise, the day in respect of which the guarantee payment is payable.

    (2) Where the calculation is for the purposes of section 53 or 54, the calculation date is the day on which the employer's notice was given.

    (3) Where the calculation is for the purposes of section 56, the calculation date is the day of the appointment.

    (4) Where the calculation is for the purposes of section 62, the calculation date is the day on which the time off was taken or on which it is alleged the time off should have been permitted.

    (5) Where the calculation is for the purposes of section 69—

    (a) in the case of an employee suspended on medical grounds, the calculation date is the day before that on which the suspension begins, and

    (b) in the case of an employee suspended on maternity grounds, the calculation date is—

        (i) where the day before that on which the suspension begins falls within either the employee's maternity leave period or the further period up to the day on which the employee exercises the right conferred on her by section 79, the day before the beginning of the maternity leave period, and

        (ii) otherwise, the day before that on which the suspension begins.

DEFINITIONS

    "employee": s.230(1).

"employer": s.230(4).
"maternity leave period": s.235(1).

Rights on termination

226.—(1) Where the calculation is for the purposes of section 88 or 89, the calculation date is the day immediately preceding the first day of the period of notice required by section 86(1) or (2).

(2) Where the calculation is for the purposes of section 93, 117 or 125, the calculation date is—

(a) if the dismissal was with notice, the date on which the employer's notice was given, and

(b) otherwise, the effective date of termination.

(3) Where the calculation is for the purposes of section 119 or 121, the calculation date is—

(a) if the employee is taken to be dismissed by virtue of section 96(1), the last day on which the employee worked under her contract of employment immediately before the beginning of her maternity leave period,

(b) if by virtue of subsection (2) or (4) of section 97 a date later than the effective date of termination as defined in subsection (1) of that section is to be treated for certain purposes as the effective date of termination, the effective date of termination as so defined, and

(c) otherwise, the date specified in subsection (6).

(4) Where the calculation is for the purposes of section 147(2), the calculation date is the day immediately preceding the first of the four, or six, weeks referred to in section 148(2).

(5) Where the calculation is for the purposes of section 162, the calculation date is—

(a) if the employee is taken to be dismissed by virtue of section 137(1), the last day on which the employee worked under her contract of employment immediately before the beginning of her maternity leave period,

(b) if by virtue of subsection (5) of section 145 a date is to be treated for certain purposes as the relevant date which is later than the relevant date as defined by the previous provisions of that section, the relevant date as so defined, and

(c) otherwise, the date specified in subsection (6).

(6) The date referred to in subsections (3)(c) and (5)(c) is the date on which notice would have been given had—

(a) the contract been terminable by notice and been terminated by the employer giving such notice as is required by section 86 to terminate the contract, and

(b) the notice expired on the effective date of termination, or the relevant date,

(whether or not those conditions were in fact fulfilled).

DEFINITIONS
"effective date of termination": s.97.
"employee": s.230(1).
"employer": s.230(4).
"maternity leave period": s.235(1).

Maximum amount of week's pay

Maximum amount

227.—(1) For the purpose of calculating—

(a) a basic award of compensation for unfair dismissal,

(b) an additional award of compensation for unfair dismissal, or

(c) a redundancy payment,

the amount of a week's pay shall not exceed £210.

(2) The Secretary of State may vary the limits imposed by subsection (1), after a review under section 208, by order made in accordance with that section.

(3) Such an order may provide that it applies in the case of a dismissal—

(a) in relation to which the date which is the effective date of termination for the purposes of this subsection by virtue of section 97(2) or (4) falls after the order comes into force, or

(b) in relation to which the date which is the relevant date for the purposes of this subsection by virtue of section 145(5) falls after the order comes into force,

even if the date which is the effective date of termination, or the relevant date, for other purposes of this Act falls before the order comes into force.

(4) Subsection (3)—

(a) does not apply to a case within section 96(1) or 137(1), but

(b) is without prejudice to section 236(5).

DEFINITIONS
"effective date of termination": s.97.

GENERAL NOTE
The figure in subs. (1) was introduced by the Employment Protection (Increase of Limits) Order 1995 (S.I. 1995 No. 1953) with effect from September 27, 1995.

Miscellaneous

New employments and other special cases

228.—(1) In any case in which the employee has not been employed for a sufficient period to enable a calculation to be made under the preceding provisions of this Chapter, the amount of a week's pay is the amount which fairly represents a week's pay.

(2) In determining that amount the industrial tribunal—

(a) shall apply as nearly as may be such of the preceding provisions of this Chapter as it considers appropriate, and

(b) may have regard to such of the considerations specified in subsection (3) as it thinks fit.

(3) The considerations referred to in subsection (2)(b) are—

(a) any remuneration received by the employee in respect of the employment in question,

(b) the amount offered to the employee as remuneration in respect of the employment in question,

(c) the remuneration received by other persons engaged in relevant comparable employment with the same employer, and

(d) the remuneration received by other persons engaged in relevant comparable employment with other employers.

(4) The Secretary of State may by regulations provide that in cases prescribed by the regulations the amount of a week's pay shall be calculated in such manner as may be so prescribed.

DEFINITIONS
"employee": s.230(1).
"employer": s.230(4).
"employment": s.230(5).

Supplementary

229.—(1) In arriving at—

(a) an average hourly rate of remuneration, or

(b) average weekly remuneration,

under this Chapter, account shall be taken of work for a former employer within the period for which the average is to be taken if, by virtue of Chapter I of this Part, a period of employment with the former employer counts as part of the employee's continuous period of employment.

(2) Where under this Chapter account is to be taken of remuneration or other payments for a period which does not coincide with the periods for which the remuneration or other payments are calculated, the remuneration or other payments shall be apportioned in such manner as may be just.

DEFINITIONS
"employee": s.230(1).
"employer": s.230(4).
"employment": s.230(5).

CHAPTER III

OTHER INTERPRETATION PROVISIONS

Employees, workers etc.

230.—(1) In this Act "employee" means an individual who has entered into or works under (or, where the employment has ceased, worked under) a contract of employment.

(2) In this Act "contract of employment" means a contract of service or apprenticeship, whether express or implied, and (if it is express) whether oral or in writing.

(3) In this Act "worker" (except in the phrases "shop worker" and "betting worker") means an individual who has entered into or works under (or, where the employment has ceased, worked under)—

(a) a contract of employment, or
(b) any other contract, whether express or implied and (if it is express) whether oral or in writing, whereby the individual undertakes to do or perform personally any work or services for another party to the contract whose status is not by virtue of the contract that of a client or customer of any profession or business undertaking carried on by the individual;

and any reference to a worker's contract shall be construed accordingly.

(4) In this Act "employer", in relation to an employee or a worker, means the person by whom the employee or worker is (or, where the employment has ceased, was) employed.

(5) In this Act "employment"—

(a) in relation to an employee, means (except for the purposes of section 171) employment under a contract of employment, and
(b) in relation to a worker, means employment under his contract;

and "employed" shall be construed accordingly.

GENERAL NOTE
Employee; contract of employment. The benefits of most of the Act's provisions are restricted to employees, as defined in subs. (1); that definition turns upon the existence of a contract of employment, which in turn is defined in subs. (2) in terms of a contract of service or apprenticeship. Those terms are not further defined. The key distinction for present purposes is therefore between an employee who works under a contract of employment or service, and an independent contractor who works under a contract for services, although certain people may not fit into either category, *e.g.* police cadets (see *Wiltshire Police Authority v. Wynn* [1981] Q.B. 95, C.A.). The distinction between an employee and an independent contractor is of crucial importance in a number of other areas of law, including the distinction between taxation under Schedule D and Schedule E, payment of national insurance contributions, entitlement to social security benefits, the vicarious liability of an employer in tort, and industrial health and safety legislation.

Whether or not a person is an employee for the purposes of this Act has been clearly established to be a question of fact for the industrial tribunal, and the tribunal's decision on the matter is unlikely to be overturned on appeal unless the tribunal has misdirected itself on the law, or has reached a perverse decision (*i.e.* a decision which no reasonable tribunal would have made): *O'Kelly v. Trusthouse Forte* [1983] IRLR 369, C.A.; *Nethermere (St. Neots) v. Taverna* [1984] IRLR 240, C.A.; *McLeod v. Hellyer Brothers* [1987] IRLR 232, C.A.; *Clifford v. Union of Democratic Mineworkers* [1991] IRLR 518, C.A.; see also *Lee Ting Sang v. Chung Chi-Keung* [1990] IRLR 236, P.C. In *Davies v. Presbyterian Church of Wales* [1986] IRLR 194, H.L., it was suggested by Lord Templeman in the House of Lords that the employment status of a presbyterian minister was a question of law, but that case was subsequently distinguished in *Hellyer* on the grounds that it turned on the construction of a written document. In *Lee Ting Sang*, Griffiths L.J. (at p. 239) explained that the characterisation of employee status as a question of fact was due to the "difficulty of devising a conclusive test to resolve the question and the threat of the appellate courts being crushed by the weight of appeals if the many borderline cases were considered to be questions of law". The inevitable result of such a fact-based approach is an undesirable degree of uncertainty over the scope of the definition of employee, and consequently over the applicability of the employment rights conferred by the Act.

A variety of tests (*e.g.* the "control" test, the "integration" test, the "economic reality" test and the "mutuality of obligation" test) have been used by the courts and tribunals over the years to determine whether or not a person is an employee. These tests are all still relevant, but the current approach (usually referred to as the "mixed" or "multiple" test) is to consider the arrangement as a whole, taking into account all the relevant factors. The different tests are as follows:

The "control" test. In some of the earlier cases, the courts tended to focus on the degree of control exercisable by the employer, not just over what a person did but over the way in which he or she did it: see *e.g. Yewens v. Noakes* (1880) 6 Q.B. 530, C.A.; *Simmons v. Health Laundry Co.* [1910] 1 K.B. 543, C.A. However, this test is not a reliable indicator of the employment relationship, not least because it is difficult to apply to highly skilled or professional workers, of whom it would be unrealistic to say that the employer is able to control the way in which work is done (see *e.g. Cassidy v. Ministry of Health* [1951] 2 K.B. 343, C.A.). Control, in the wider sense of "the power of deciding the thing to be done, the means to be employed in doing it, the time when and the place where it shall be done" (per MacKenna J., *Ready Mixed Concrete (South East) v. Minister of Pensions and National Insurance* [1968] 2 Q.B. 497) is still highly relevant (see *Clifford v. Union of Democratic Mineworkers* [1991] IRLR 518, C.A.), but it is no longer regarded as a sufficient indicator.

The "integration" test. This test focuses on the extent to which an individual is integrated into a business, in the sense that his or her work is done "as an integral part of the business" (*Stevenson Jordan & Harrison v. McDonald & Evans* [1952] 1 T.L.R. 101, C.A., per Denning L.J.). It has proved useful in overcoming the difficulties in applying the control test to professional employees (see *e.g. Beloff v. Pressdram* [1973] 1 All E.R. 241), but like the control test, it should be regarded as only one of a number of relevant factors.

The "economic reality" test. This test involves the tribunal in asking whether the worker is in business on his or her own account: see *Market Investigations v. Minister of Social Security* [1969] 2 Q.B. 173, applied in *Young & Woods v. West* [1980] IRLR 201, C.A.; *Lee Ting Sang v. Chung Chi-Keung* [1990] IRLR 236, P.C. Under this test, attention is likely to focus on matters such as which of the parties bears the risk of loss and the chance of profit. For a variant of the economic reality test, see *Withers v. Flackwell Heath Football Supporters' Club* [1981] IRLR 307, E.A.T. (how would a person answer the question, "are you your own boss?"). A person may be in business on his or her own account even where that person does not carry on an identifiable business, provided he or she is not economically dependent on a particular employer: see *Hall (Inspector of Taxes) v. Lorimer* [1994] IRLR 171, C.A.; *Wickens v. Champion Employment* [1984] I.C.R. 365, E.A.T.

The "mutuality of obligation" test. In cases of casual or sporadic employment, it may be held that there is insufficient mutuality of obligation between the parties (*i.e.* mutual obligations on the employer to provide work and on the worker to accept it) to justify a finding that there is a contract of employment between them: see *e.g. Airfix Footwear v. Cope* [1978] IRLR 396, E.A.T.; *O'Kelly v. Trusthouse Forte* [1983] IRLR 369, C.A.; *Nethermere (St. Neots) v. Taverna* [1984] IRLR 240, C.A.; *McLeod v. Hellyer Brothers* [1987] IRLR 232, C.A.

The "mixed" or "multiple" test. The modern approach to the question whether a person is or is not an employee is to consider the arrangement as a whole, taking into account all the relevant factors: *Ready Mixed Concrete (South East) v. Minister of Pensions and National Insurance* [1968] 2 Q.B. 497; *Construction Industry Training Board v. Labour Force* [1970] 3 All E.R. 220, D.C.; *Global Plant v. Secretary of State for Social Services* [1972] 1 Q.B. 139. In *Ready Mixed Concrete*, MacKenna J. stated that for a contract of employment to exist, the following conditions must be satisfied: (i) the worker must undertake to provide his own work and skill; (ii) the worker must be "subject to the other's control in a sufficient degree"; (iii) the other provisions of the contract must be "consistent with its being a contract of service". This approach gives the tribunal considerable discretion in determining whether or not a contract of employment exists, and makes it extremely difficult to predict the outcome of individual cases.

The label which the parties use to describe their relationship is a relevant consideration, especially where the other factors are evenly balanced, but it is not conclusive, and the parties cannot alter the reality of their relationship by putting a different label on it: *Young & Woods v. West* [1980] IRLR 201, C.A.; *Ferguson v. Dawson (John) and Partners (Contractors)* [1976] IRLR 346, C.A.; *Massey v. Crown Life Insurance Co.* [1978] IRLR 31, C.A.; *McMeecham v. Secretary of State for Employment* [1995] I.C.R. 444, E.A.T. The fact that a person has obtained tax advantages by adopting the label of self-employed may make a court reluctant to allow him to change that label in order subsequently to claim unfair dismissal (see *e.g. Massey v. Crown Life Insurance Co.*, above), but the court may disregard the label altogether if there is evidence that the worker was forced to accept it (see *Young & Woods v. West*, above).

Worker. The definition of "worker" is wider than the definition of "employee", as in addition to those who work under contracts of service or apprenticeship, it also includes certain self-employed persons who undertake to perform work personally. This wider definition, which applies for the purposes of the provisions in Pt. II on deductions from pay, derives from s.8 of the Wages Act 1986 (c. 48). There is a similar definition of "worker" in s.296(1) of the Trade Union and Labour Relations (Consolidation) Act 1992 (c. 52); *cf.* the extended definitions of "employed" and "employment" in s.1(6) of the Equal Pay Act 1970 (c. 41), s.82 of the Sex Discrimination Act 1975 (c. 65), s.78 of the Race Relations Act 1976 (c. 74), and s.68 of the Disability Discrimination Act 1995 (c. 50), which also include (albeit in slightly different terms) those employed under contracts personally to do any work.

Associated employers

231. For the purposes of this Act any two employers shall be treated as associated if—

(a) one is a company of which the other (directly or indirectly) has control, or

(b) both are companies of which a third person (directly or indirectly) has control;

and "associated employer" shall be construed accordingly.

DEFINITIONS
"employer": s.230(4).

GENERAL NOTE
The definition of "associated employer" contained in this section has been held to be exhaustive: *Gardiner v. Merton London Borough Council* [1981] I.C.R. 186. The definition is considerably restricted by the requirement that, under the first limb of the definition, at least one of the employers must be a limited company, and under the second limb, both employers must be limited companies. "Company" in this context means a limited company, but it does not include other statutory corporate bodies: *Hasley v. Fair Employment Agency* [1989] IRLR 106, N.I.C.A. This means that bodies such as unincorporated associations, partnerships, public utilities, local authorities and universities can only be treated as associated employers under the first limb of the definition. In *Pinkney v. Sandpiper Drilling* [1989] IRLR 425, the E.A.T. avoided this conclusion in the case of a partnership of companies by treating employment by the partnership as employment by each of the companies in the partnership; and the definition was extended to foreign companies in *Hancill v. Marcon Engineering* [1990] IRLR 51, E.A.T. The employment of local government employees who move from one local government body to another is deemed to be continuous by the Redundancy Payments (Local Government) (Modification) Order 1983 (S.I. 1983 No. 1160), but only for redundancy payments purposes. See also s.218(7), which preserves the continuity of employment of teachers who move between employment by a local education authority and employment by the governors of an LEA-maintained school, and s.218(8), which makes similar provision for health workers undergoing professional training who move between health service employers.

Control. "Control" here means voting control (*i.e.* control of a majority of the votes carried by the shares) rather than *de facto* control: *Secretary of State for Employment v. Newbold and Joint Liquidators of David Armstrong (Catering Services)* [1981] IRLR 305, E.A.T.; *Umar v. Pliastar* [1981] I.C.R. 727, E.A.T.; *Washington Arts Association v. Forster* [1983] I.C.R. 346, E.A.T.; *South West Launderettes v. Laidler* [1986] IRLR 305, C.A. There must be voting control of 51 per cent or more of the shares (*Hair Colour Consultants v. Mena* [1984] IRLR 386, E.A.T.), although in *Payne v. Secretary of State for Employment* [1989] IRLR 352, C.A., this requirement was held to be satisfied where one shareholder held her 50 per cent shareholding as nominee for the holder of the other 50 per cent shareholding. There is conflicting authority on whether control by "a third person" can include control by two or more persons acting in concert. Such an argument was accepted by the E.A.T. in *Zarb and Samuels v. British & Brazilian Produce Co. (Sales)* [1978] IRLR 78, followed in *Harford v. Swiftrim* [1987] IRLR 360, E.A.T., but was doubted by the Court of Appeal in *South West Launderettes v. Laidler*, above, and by the E.A.T. in *Strudwick v. Iszatt Bros.* [1988] IRLR 457, and *Russell v. Elmdon Freight Terminal* [1989] I.C.R. 629. It is however clearly established that the same group of people must be in control of both companies: *Poparm v. Weekes* [1984] IRLR 388, E.A.T.; *Strudwick v. Iszatt Bros.*, above.

Shop workers

232.—(1) In this Act "shop worker" means an employee who, under his contract of employment, is or may be required to do shop work.

(2) In this Act "shop work" means work in or about a shop in England or Wales on a day on which the shop is open for the serving of customers.

(3) Subject to subsection (4), in this Act "shop" includes any premises where any retail trade or business is carried on.

(4) Where premises are used mainly for purposes other than those of retail trade or business and would not (apart from subsection (3)) be regarded as a shop, only such part of the premises as—

(a) is used wholly or mainly for the purposes of retail trade or business, or

(b) is used both for the purposes of retail trade or business and for the purposes of wholesale trade and is used wholly or mainly for those two purposes considered together,

is to be regarded as a shop for the purposes of this Act.

(5) In subsection (4)(b) "wholesale trade" means the sale of goods for use or resale in the course of a business or the hire of goods for use in the course of a business.

(6) In this section "retail trade or business" includes—

(a) the business of a barber or hairdresser,

(b) the business of hiring goods otherwise than for use in the course of a trade or business, and

(c) retail sales by auction,

but does not include catering business or the sale at theatres and places of amusement of programmes, catalogues and similar items.

(7) In subsection (6) "catering business" means—

(a) the sale of meals, refreshments or intoxicating liquor for consumption on the premises on which they are sold, or

(b) the sale of meals or refreshments prepared to order for immediate consumption off the premises;

and in paragraph (a) "intoxicating liquor" has the same meaning as in the Licensing Act 1964.

(8) In this Act—

"notice period", in relation to an opted-out shop worker, has the meaning given by section 41(3),

"opted-out", in relation to a shop worker, shall be construed in accordance with section 41(1) and (2),

"opting-in notice", in relation to a shop worker, has the meaning given by section 36(6),

"opting-out notice", in relation to a shop worker, has the meaning given by section 40(2), and

"protected", in relation to a shop worker, shall be construed in accordance with section 36(1) to (5).

Betting workers

233.—(1) In this Act "betting worker" means an employee who, under his contract of employment, is or may be required to do betting work.

(2) In this Act "betting work" means—

(a) work at a track in England or Wales for a bookmaker on a day on which the bookmaker acts as such at the track, being work which consists of or includes dealing with betting transactions, and

(b) work in a licensed betting office in England or Wales on a day on which the office is open for use for the effecting of betting transactions.

(3) In subsection (2) "betting transactions" includes the collection or payment of winnings on a bet and any transaction in which one or more of the parties is acting as a bookmaker.

(4) In this section "bookmaker" means any person who—

(a) whether on his own account or as servant or agent to any other person, carries on (whether occasionally or regularly) the business of receiving or negotiating bets or conducting pool betting operations, or

(b) by way of business in any manner holds himself out, or permits himself to be held out, as a person who receives or negotiates bets or conducts such operations.

(5) Expressions used in this section and in the Betting, Gaming and Lotteries Act 1963 have the same meaning in this section as in that Act.

(6) In this Act—

"notice period", in relation to an opted-out betting worker, has the meaning given by section 41(3),

"opted-out", in relation to a betting worker, shall be construed in accordance with section 41(1) and (2),

"opting-in notice", in relation to a betting worker, has the meaning given by section 36(6),

"opting-out notice", in relation to a betting worker, has the meaning given by section 40(2), and

"protected", in relation to a betting worker, shall be construed in accordance with section 36(1) to (5).

Normal working hours

234.—(1) Where an employee is entitled to overtime pay when employed for more than a fixed number of hours in a week or other period, there are for the purposes of this Act normal working hours in his case.

(2) Subject to subsection (3), the normal working hours in such a case are the fixed number of hours.

(3) Where in such a case—

(a) the contract of employment fixes the number, or minimum number, of hours of employment in a week or other period (whether or not it also provides for the reduction of that number or minimum in certain circumstances), and

(b) that number or minimum number of hours exceeds the number of hours without overtime,

the normal working hours are that number or minimum number of hours (and not the number of hours without overtime).

DEFINITIONS

"contract of employment": s.230(2).
"employee": s.230(1).
"employed": s.230(5).
"employment": s.230(5).
"week": s.235(1).

GENERAL NOTE

If the employee's contract of employment specifies the number of hours which the employee is obliged to work, that will usually be conclusive, even if in practice the employee often works longer hours than those specified in the contract (*ITT Components (Europe) v. Kolah (Y.)* [1977] I.C.R. 740, E.A.T.), unless the employee can prove that the contract of employment has been varied to reflect the increased hours (see *e.g. Armstrong Whitworth Rolls v. Mustard* [1971]

1 All E.R. 598). The employee's working hours may be specified in the written statement issued under s.1 of the Act. If there is no express term, the tribunal may have to infer a term from all the facts: *Dean v. Eastbourne Fishermen's and Boatmen's Protection Society and Club* [1977] I.C.R. 556, E.A.T.; *Larkin v. Cambos Enterprises (Stretford)* [1978] I.C.R. 1247, E.A.T.

This section makes clear that, in general, "normal working hours" will not include overtime. If the contract states that overtime is payable after a certain number of hours per week have been worked, the hours of overtime will not count for present purposes (see *e.g. Fox v. Wright (C.) (Farmers)* [1978] I.C.R. 98), even if the employee regularly works overtime. The only exception is where the overtime is clearly obligatory on *both* sides, in the sense that the employer is obliged to provide it, and the employee is obliged to work it: *Tarmac Roadstone Holdings v. Peacock* [1973] I.C.R. 273, C.A., followed in *Lotus Cars v. Sutcliffe and Stratton* [1982] I.R.L.R. 381, C.A.

Other definitions

235.—(1) In this Act, except in so far as the context otherwise requires—
"act" and "action" each includes omission and references to doing an act or taking action shall be construed accordingly,
"basic award of compensation for unfair dismissal" shall be construed in accordance with section 118,
"business" includes a trade or profession and includes any activity carried on by a body of persons (whether corporate or unincorporated),
"childbirth" means the birth of a living child or the birth of a child whether living or dead after twenty-four weeks of pregnancy,
"collective agreement" has the meaning given by section 178(1) and (2) of the Trade Union and Labour Relations (Consolidation) Act 1992,
"conciliation officer" means an officer designated by the Advisory, Conciliation and Arbitration Service under section 211 of that Act,
"dismissal procedures agreement" means an agreement in writing with respect to procedures relating to dismissal made by or on behalf of one or more independent trade unions and one or more employers or employers' associations,
"employers' association" has the same meaning as in the Trade Union and Labour Relations (Consolidation) Act 1992,
"expected week of childbirth" means the week, beginning with midnight between Saturday and Sunday, in which it is expected that childbirth will occur,
"guarantee payment" has the meaning given by section 28,
"independent trade union" means a trade union which—
(a) is not under the domination or control of an employer or a group of employers or of one or more employers' associations, and
(b) is not liable to interference by an employer or any such group or association (arising out of the provision of financial or material support or by any other means whatever) tending towards such control,
"job", in relation to an employee, means the nature of the work which he is employed to do in accordance with his contract and the capacity and place in which he is so employed,
"maternity leave period" shall be construed in accordance with sections 72 and 73,
"notified day of return" shall be construed in accordance with section 83,
"position", in relation to an employee, means the following matters taken as a whole—
(a) his status as an employee,
(b) the nature of his work, and

(c) his terms and conditions of employment,

"redundancy payment" has the meaning given by Part XI,

"relevant date" has the meaning given by sections 145 and 153,

"renewal" includes extension, and any reference to renewing a contract or a fixed term shall be construed accordingly,

"statutory provision" means a provision, whether of a general or a special nature, contained in, or in any document made or issued under, any Act, whether of a general or special nature,

"successor", in relation to the employer of an employee, means (subject to subsection (2)) a person who in consequence of a change occurring (whether by virtue of a sale or other disposition or by operation of law) in the ownership of the undertaking, or of the part of the undertaking, for the purposes of which the employee was employed, has become the owner of the undertaking or part,

"trade union" has the meaning given by section 1 of the Trade Union and Labour Relations (Consolidation) Act 1992,

"week"—

   (a) in Chapter I of this Part means a week ending with Saturday, and

   (b) otherwise, except in section 86, means, in relation to an employee whose remuneration is calculated weekly by a week ending with a day other than Saturday, a week ending with that other day and, in relation to any other employee, a week ending with Saturday.

(2) The definition of "successor" in subsection (1) has effect (subject to the necessary modifications) in relation to a case where—

(a) the person by whom an undertaking or part of an undertaking is owned immediately before a change is one of the persons by whom (whether as partners, trustees or otherwise) it is owned immediately after the change, or

(b) the persons by whom an undertaking or part of an undertaking is owned immediately before a change (whether as partners, trustees or otherwise) include the persons by whom, or include one or more of the persons by whom, it is owned immediately after the change,

as it has effect where the previous owner and the new owner are wholly different persons.

(3) References in this Act to redundancy, dismissal by reason of redundancy and similar expressions shall be construed in accordance with section 139.

(4) In sections 136(2), 154 and 216(3) and paragraph 14 of Schedule 2 "lock-out" means—

(a) the closing of a place of employment,

(b) the suspension of work, or

(c) the refusal by an employer to continue to employ any number of persons employed by him in consequence of a dispute,

done with a view to compelling persons employed by the employer, or to aid another employer in compelling persons employed by him, to accept terms or conditions of or affecting employment.

(5) In sections 91(2), 140(2) and (3), 143(1), 144(2) and (3), 154 and 216(1) and (2) and paragraph 14 of Schedule 2 "strike" means—

(a) the cessation of work by a body of employed persons acting in combination, or

(b) a concerted refusal, or a refusal under a common understanding, of any number of employed persons to continue to work for an employer in consequence of a dispute,

done as a means of compelling their employer or any employed person or body of employed persons, or to aid other employees in compelling their employer or any employed person or body of employed persons, to accept or not to accept terms or conditions of or affecting employment.

PART XV

GENERAL AND SUPPLEMENTARY

General

Orders and regulations

236.—(1) Any power conferred by any provision of this Act to make any order (other than an Order in Council) or regulations is exercisable by statutory instrument.

(2) A statutory instrument made under any power conferred by this Act to make an Order in Council or other order or regulations, except—

 (a) an Order in Council or other order to which subsection (3) applies,

 (b) an order under section 35 or Part II of Schedule 2, or

 (c) an order made in accordance with section 208,

is subject to annulment in pursuance of a resolution of either House of Parliament.

(3) No recommendation shall be made to Her Majesty to make an Order in Council under section 192(3), and no order shall be made under section 72(3), 73(5), 79(3), 120(2), 124(2) or 125(7) or (subject to subsection (4)) section 209, unless a draft of the Order in Council or order has been laid before Parliament and approved by a resolution of each House of Parliament.

(4) Subsection (3) does not apply to an order under section 209(1)(b) which specifies only provisions contained in Part XI.

(5) Any power conferred by this Act which is exercisable by statutory instrument includes power to make such incidental, supplementary or transitional provisions as appear to the authority exercising the power to be necessary or expedient.

Financial provisions

237. There shall be paid out of the National Insurance Fund into the Consolidated Fund sums equal to the amount of—

 (a) any expenses incurred by the Secretary of State in consequence of Part XI, and

 (b) any expenses incurred by the Secretary of State (or by persons acting on his behalf) in exercising his functions under Part XII.

Reciprocal arrangements

Reciprocal arrangements with Northern Ireland

238.—(1) If provision is made by Northern Ireland legislation for purposes corresponding to any of the purposes of this Act, other than an excepted provision, the Secretary of State may, with the consent of the Treasury, make reciprocal arrangements with the appropriate Northern Ireland authority for co-ordinating the relevant provisions of this Act with the corresponding provisions of the Northern Ireland legislation so as to secure that they operate, to such extent as may be provided by the arrangements, as a single system.

(2) The following provisions of this Act are excepted provisions for the purposes of subsection (1)—

 (a) in Part I, sections 1 to 7,

 (b) Parts II and IV,

 (c) in Part V, sections 45 and 46,

 (d) in Part VI, sections 58 to 60,

(e) in Part IX, sections 86 to 91, and

(f) in Part X, sections 101 and 102.

(3) The Secretary of State may make regulations for giving effect to any arrangements made under subsection (1).

(4) Regulations under subsection (3) may make different provision for different cases.

(5) Such regulations may provide that the relevant provisions of this Act have effect in relation to persons affected by the arrangements subject to such modifications and adaptations as may be specified in the regulations, including provision—

(a) for securing that acts, omissions and events having any effect for the purposes of the Northern Ireland legislation have a corresponding effect for the purposes of this Act (but not so as to confer a right to double payment in respect of the same act, omission or event), and

(b) for determining, in cases where rights accrue both under this Act and under the Northern Ireland legislation, which of those rights is available to the person concerned.

(6) In this section "the appropriate Northern Ireland authority" means such authority as may be specified in the Northern Ireland legislation.

Reciprocal arrangements with Isle of Man

239.—(1) If an Act of Tynwald is passed for purposes similar to the purposes of Part XI, the Secretary of State may, with the consent of the Treasury, make reciprocal arrangements with the appropriate Isle of Man authority for co-ordinating the provisions of Part XI with the corresponding provisions of the Act of Tynwald so as to secure that they operate, to such extent as may be provided by the arrangements, as a single system.

(2) For the purposes of giving effect to any arrangements made under subsection (1) the Secretary of State may, in conjunction with the appropriate Isle of Man authority, make any necessary financial adjustments between the National Insurance Fund and any fund established under the Act of Tynwald.

(3) The Secretary of State may make regulations for giving effect to any arrangements made under subsection (1).

(4) Regulations under subsection (3) may provide that Part XI has effect in relation to persons affected by the arrangements subject to such modifications and adaptations as may be specified in the regulations, including provision—

(a) for securing that acts, omissions and events having any effect for the purposes of the Act of Tynwald have a corresponding effect for the purposes of Part XI (but not so as to confer a right to double payment in respect of the same act, omission or event), and

(b) for determining, in cases where rights accrue both under this Act and under the Act of Tynwald, which of those rights is available to the person concerned.

(5) In this section "the appropriate Isle of Man authority" means such authority as may be specified in an Act of Tynwald.

Final provisions

Consequential amendments

240. Schedule 1 (consequential amendments) shall have effect.

Transitionals, savings and transitory provisions

241. Schedule 2 (transitional provisions, savings and transitory provisions) shall have effect.

Repeals and revocations

242. The enactments specified in Part I of Schedule 3 are repealed, and the instruments specified in Part II of that Schedule are revoked, to the extent specified in the third column of that Schedule.

Commencement

243. This Act shall come into force at the end of the period of three months beginning with the day on which it is passed.

Extent

244.—(1) Subject to the following provisions, this Act extends to England and Wales and Scotland but not to Northern Ireland.

(2) The provisions of this Act which refer to shop workers and betting workers extend to England and Wales only.

(3) Sections 201 and 238 (and sections 236 and 243, this section and section 245) extend to Northern Ireland (as well as to England and Wales and Scotland).

(4) Sections 240 and 242 and Schedules 1 and 3 have the same extent as the provisions amended or repealed by this Act.

Short title

245. This Act may be cited as the Employment Rights Act 1996.

SCHEDULES

Section 240

SCHEDULE 1

CONSEQUENTIAL AMENDMENTS

The Equal Pay Act 1970 (c. 41)

1.—(1) Section 1 of the Equal Pay Act 1970 is amended as follows.

(2) In subsection (10A)—

(a) for "section 139 of the Employment Protection (Consolidation) Act 1978" substitute "section 195 of the Employment Rights Act 1996", and

(b) for "subsections (4) to (9)" substitute "subsections (6) to (12)".

(3) In subsection (10B)—

(a) for "section 139A of the Employment Protection (Consolidation) Act 1978" substitute "section 194 of the Employment Rights Act 1996", and

(b) for "subsection (6)" substitute "subsection (7)".

The Atomic Energy Authority Act 1971 (c. 11)

2.—(1) Section 10 of the Atomic Energy Authority Act 1971 is amended as follows.

(2) In subsection (2)—

(a) in paragraph (a), for "the said sections 1 to 4" substitute "sections 1 to 7 of the Employment Rights Act 1996", and

(b) in paragraph (b)—

(i) for "section 5 of the said Act of 1978" substitute "the Employment Rights Act 1996", and

(ii) for "subsection (1) of that section" substitute "section 1 of that Act".

(3) In subsection (3)—

(a) for "the Employment Protection (Consolidation) Act 1978" substitute "the Employment Rights Act 1996", and

(b) for "sections 1 to 4" substitute "section 1".

(4) In subsection (4)—

(a) for "Schedule 13 to the said Act of 1978" substitute "Chapter I of Part XIV of the Employment Rights Act 1996", and

(b) for the words from "sub-paragraph (2)" to "that sub-paragraph" substitute "subsection (2) of section 218 of that Act, be taken to be such a transfer of an undertaking as is mentioned in that subsection".

The Attachment of Earnings Act 1971 (c. 32)

3. Paragraph 3 of Part I of Schedule 3 to the Attachment of Earnings Act 1971 shall continue to have effect with the substitution (originally made by paragraph 4 of Schedule 4 to the Wages Act 1986) of the following paragraph for paragraph (c)—

"(c) amounts deductible under any enactment, or in pursuance of a request in writing by the debtor, for the purposes of a superannuation scheme, namely any enactment, rules, deed or other instrument providing for the payment of annuities or lump sums—

(i) to the persons with respect to whom the instrument has effect on their retirement at a specified age or on becoming incapacitated at some earlier age, or

(ii) to the personal representatives or the widows, relatives or dependants of such persons on their death or otherwise,

whether with or without any further or other benefits."

The British Library Act 1972 (c. 54)

4. In paragraph 13(3)(a) of the Schedule to the British Library Act 1972, for "the Employment Protection (Consolidation) Act 1978" substitute "the Employment Rights Act 1996".

The Health and Safety at Work etc. Act 1974 (c. 37)

5. In section 80(2A) of the Health and Safety at Work etc. Act 1974, for "the Employment Protection (Consolidation) Act 1978 which re-enact" substitute "the Employment Rights Act 1996 or the Trade Union and Labour Relations (Consolidation) Act 1992 which derive from provisions of the Employment Protection (Consolidation) Act 1978 which re-enacted".

The Sex Discrimination Act 1975 (c. 65)

6.—(1) The Sex Discrimination Act 1975 is amended as follows.

(2) In section 85A(2)—

(a) for "section 139 of the Employment Protection (Consolidation) Act 1978" substitute "section 195 of the Employment Rights Act 1996", and

(b) for "subsections (4) to (9)" substitute "subsections (6) to (12)".

(3) In section 85B(2)—

(a) for "section 139A of the Employment Protection (Consolidation) Act 1978" substitute "section 194 of the Employment Rights Act 1996", and

(b) for "subsection (6)" substitute "subsection (7)".

The Scottish Development Agency Act 1975 (c. 69)

7. In paragraph 6 of Schedule 3 to the Scottish Development Agency Act 1975, for "the Employment Protection (Consolidation) Act 1978" substitute "the Employment Rights Act 1996".

The Welsh Development Agency Act 1975 (c. 70)

8. In paragraph 7 of Schedule 2 to the Welsh Development Agency Act 1975, for "the Employment Protection (Consolidation) Act 1978" substitute "the Employment Rights Act 1996".

The Lotteries and Amusements Act 1976 (c. 32)

9. In section 23(1) of the Lotteries and Amusements Act 1976, for "meanings given by section 153(1) of the Employment Protection (Consolidation) Act 1978" substitute "same meanings as in the Employment Rights Act 1996".

The Race Relations Act 1976 (c. 74)

10.—(1) The Race Relations Act 1976 is amended as follows.

(2) In section 75A(2)—

(a) for "section 139 of the Employment Protection (Consolidation) Act 1978" substitute "section 195 of the Employment Rights Act 1996", and

(b) for "subsections (4) to (9)" substitute "subsections (6) to (12)".

(3) In section 75B(2)—

(a) for "section 139A of the Employment Protection (Consolidation) Act 1978" substitute "section 194 of the Employment Rights Act 1996", and

(b) for "subsection (6)" substitute "subsection (7)".

(4) In paragraph 11(4) of Schedule 2, for paragraphs (a) and (c) substitute—

"(a) the Employment Rights Act 1996 except Part XI;
 (b) the Trade Union and Labour Relations (Consolidation) Act 1992; and".

The Development of Rural Wales Act 1976 (c. 75)

11. In—
(a) paragraph 6 of Schedule 2, and
(b) paragraph 6 of Schedule 6,
to the Development of Rural Wales Act 1976, for "the Employment Protection (Consolidation) Act 1978" substitute "the Employment Rights Act 1996".

The New Towns (Scotland) Act 1977 (c. 16)

12. In section 3(6) of the New Towns (Scotland) Act 1977, for "Parts I, IV, V and VI of the Employment Protection (Consolidation) Act 1978" substitute "Parts I and IX to XI of the Employment Rights Act 1996".

The National Health Service (Scotland) Act 1978 (c. 29)

13. In section 12C(3) of the National Health Service (Scotland) Act 1978—
(a) for "Part VI of the Employment Protection (Consolidation) Act 1978" substitute "Part XI of the Employment Rights Act 1996", and
(b) for "Part VI of that Act" substitute "that Part of that Act".

The House of Commons (Administration) Act 1978 (c. 36)

14. In paragraph 1 of Schedule 2 to the House of Commons (Administration) Act 1978, for "section 139 of the Employment Protection (Consolidation) Act 1978" substitute "section 195 of the Employment Rights Act 1996".

The New Towns Act 1981 (c. 64)

15. In section 54(5) of the New Towns Act 1981, for "Schedule 13 to the Employment Protection (Consolidation) Act 1978" substitute "Chapter I of Part XIV of the Employment Rights Act 1996".

The Wildlife and Countryside Act 1981 (c. 69)

16. In paragraph 8(4) of Schedule 13 to the Wildlife and Countryside Act 1981, for the words from "Schedule" to "continuous)" substitute "Chapter I of Part XIV of the Employment Rights Act 1996".

The Hops Marketing Act 1982 (c. 5)

17. In section 2(7) of the Hops Marketing Act 1982, for "the Employment Protection (Consolidation) Act 1978" substitute "the Employment Rights Act 1996".

The Oil and Gas (Enterprise) Act 1982 (c. 23)

18.—(1) In Schedule 3 to the Oil and Gas (Enterprise) Act 1982, after paragraph 45 add—

"The Employment Rights Act 1996

46.—(1) For subsection (1) of section 201 of the Employment Rights Act 1996 (offshore employment) there shall be substituted the following subsection—
 (1) In this section "offshore employment" means employment for the purposes of—
  (a) any activities in the territorial waters of the United Kingdom, or
  (b) any such activities as are mentioned in section 23(2) of the Oil and Gas (Enterprise) Act 1982 in waters within subsection (6)(b) or (c) of that section."
(2) Subsection (5) of that section shall be omitted."
(2) The paragraph inserted by sub-paragraph (1) is subject to section 38(2) of the Oil and Gas (Enterprise) Act 1982 (power to bring provisions into force by order).

The Local Government Finance Act 1982 (c. 32)

19. In paragraph 8(3) of Schedule 3 to the Local Government Finance Act 1982, for "the Employment Protection (Consolidation) Act 1978" substitute "the Employment Rights Act 1996".

The Administration of Justice Act 1982 (c. 53)

20. In section 10(d) of the Administration of Justice Act 1982—
(a) for "the Employment Protection (Consolidation) Act 1978" substitute "the Employment Rights Act 1996", and
(b) for "section 81" substitute "section 135".

The Health and Social Services and Social Security Adjudications Act 1983 (c. 14)

21. In paragraph 23 of Part II of Schedule 3 to the Health and Social Services and Social Security Adjudications Act 1983, for "the Employment Protection (Consolidation) Act 1978" substitute "the Employment Rights Act 1996".

The National Audit Act 1983 (c. 44)

22. In paragraph 2(3) of Schedule 2 to the National Audit Act 1983, for "the Employment Protection (Consolidation) Act 1978" substitute "the Employment Rights Act 1996".

The National Heritage Act 1983 (c. 47)

23. In—
(a) paragraph 5(5) of Part I of Schedule 1,
(b) paragraph 15(5) of Part II of Schedule 1,
(c) paragraph 25(5) of Part III of Schedule 1,
(d) paragraph 35(5) of Part IV of Schedule 1,
(e) paragraph 2(5) of Schedule 2, and
(f) paragraph 5(5) of Schedule 3,
to the National Heritage Act 1983, for "the Employment Protection (Consolidation) Act 1978" substitute "the Employment Rights Act 1996".

The National Heritage (Scotland) Act 1985 (c. 16)

24. In—
(a) paragraph 5(5) of Part I, and
(b) paragraph 16(5) of Part II,
of Schedule 1 to the National Heritage (Scotland) Act 1985, for "the Employment Protection (Consolidation) Act 1978" substitute "the Employment Rights Act 1996".

The Prosecution of Offences Act 1985 (c. 23)

25.—(1) The Prosecution of Offences Act 1985 is amended as follows.
(2) In section 11(5), for "Schedule 13 to the Employment Protection (Consolidation) Act 1978" substitute "Chapter I of Part XIV of the Employment Rights Act 1996".
(3) In section 15(6), for the words from "be treated as" to "shall not be so treated" substitute "not be treated as transferred functions".

The Local Government Act 1985 (c. 51)

26.—(1) The Local Government Act 1985 is amended as follows.
(2) In section 54(2), for "Schedule 13 to the said Act of 1978" substitute "Chapter I of Part XIV of the Employment Rights Act 1996".
(3) In section 105(1), for "the Employment Protection (Consolidation) Act 1978" substitute "the Employment Rights Act 1996".

The Trustee Savings Banks Act 1985 (c. 58)

27. In section 3(7) of the Trustee Savings Banks Act 1985, for "paragraph 17(3) of Schedule 13 to the Employment Protection (Consolidation) Act 1978" substitute "section 218(3) of the Employment Rights Act 1996".

The Housing (Consequential Provisions) Act 1985 (c. 71)

28. In paragraph 7(2)(b) of Schedule 4 to the Housing (Consequential Provisions) Act 1985, for "Schedule 13 to that Act" substitute "Chapter I of Part XIV of the Employment Rights Act 1996".

The Insolvency Act 1986 (c. 45)

29. In paragraph 13 of Schedule 6 to the Insolvency Act 1986, for sub-paragraph (2) substitute—

"(2) An amount falls within this sub-paragraph if it is—

(a) a guarantee payment under Part III of the Employment Rights Act 1996 (employee without work to do);

(b) any payment for time off under section 53 (time off to look for work or arrange training) or section 56 (time off for ante-natal care) of that Act or under section 169 of the Trade Union and Labour Relations (Consolidation) Act 1992 (time off for carrying out trade union duties etc.);

(c) remuneration on suspension on medical grounds, or on maternity grounds, under Part VII of the Employment Rights Act 1996; or

(d) remuneration under a protective award under section 189 of the Trade Union and Labour Relations (Consolidation) Act 1992 (redundancy dismissal with compensation)."

The Legal Aid (Scotland) Act 1986 (c. 47)

30. In paragraph 10(1) of Schedule 1 to the Legal Aid (Scotland) Act 1986, for "the Employment Protection (Consolidation) Act 1978" substitute "the Employment Rights Act 1996".

The Debtors (Scotland) Act 1987 (c. 18)

31. In section 73(3)(g) of the Debtors (Scotland) Act 1987, for "section 81(1) of the Employment Protection (Consolidation) Act 1978" substitute "the Employment Rights Act 1996".

The Pilotage Act 1987 (c. 21)

32. In section 25(6) of the Pilotage Act 1987, for "Schedule 13 to the Employment Protection (Consolidation) Act 1978" substitute "Chapter I of Part XIV of the Employment Rights Act 1996".

The Housing (Scotland) Act 1987 (c. 26)

33. In paragraph 10(2)(b) of Schedule 22 to the Housing (Scotland) Act 1987, for "Schedule 13 to that Act" substitute "Chapter I of Part XIV of the Employment Rights Act 1996".

The Consumer Protection Act 1987 (c. 43)

34. In section 22(5) of the Consumer Protection Act 1987, for "the Employment Protection (Consolidation) Act 1978" substitute "the Employment Rights Act 1996".

The Income and Corporation Taxes Act 1988 (c. 1)

35.—(1) The Income and Corporation Taxes Act 1988 is amended as follows.

(2) In section 579—

(a) in subsections (3)(a) and (5)(a) and in subsection (4)(a) as it has effect for the purposes of corporation tax, for the words from "by which" to "rebate" substitute "of the redundancy payment or the corresponding amount of the other employer's payment", and

(b) in subsection (6), for "section 106 of the Employment Protection (Consolidation) Act 1978" substitute "section 166 of the Employment Rights Act 1996".

(3) In section 580(1)—

(a) in paragraph (a), for ", "employer's payment" and "rebate" have the same meaning as in the Employment Protection (Consolidation) Act 1978 ("the 1978 Act")" substitute "and "employer's payment" have the same meaning as in Part XI of the Employment Rights Act 1996",

(b) in paragraph (b), for the words "of the relevant redundancy payment" onwards substitute "which would have been payable as a redundancy payment had one been payable;", and

(c) in paragraph (c), for "the 1978 Act" substitute "the Employment Rights Act 1996".

(4) In—

(a) paragraph 19(a) of Part III of Schedule 9, and

(b) paragraph 2 of Schedule 10,

for "the Employment Protection (Consolidation) Act 1978" substitute "the Employment Rights Act 1996".

The Legal Aid Act 1988 (c. 34)

36. In paragraph 7(1) of Schedule 7 to the Legal Aid Act 1988, for "the Employment Protection (Consolidation) Act 1978" substitute "the Employment Rights Act 1996".

The Education Reform Act 1988 (c. 40)

37.—(1) The Education Reform Act 1988 is amended as follows.

(2) In section 174(2), for "Schedule 13 to that Act" substitute "Chapter I of Part XIV of the Employment Rights Act 1996".

(3) In section 203(7), for "section 55 of the Employment Protection (Consolidation) Act 1978" substitute "Part X of the Employment Rights Act 1996".

(4) In section 221(2)(b), for "section 81 of the Employment Protection (Consolidation) Act 1978" substitute "section 135 of the Employment Rights Act 1996".

(5) In section 235—

(a) in subsection (1), for "the Employment Protection (Consolidation) Act 1978" substitute "the Employment Rights Act 1996", and

(b) in subsection (2)(f), for "section 81 of the Employment Protection (Consolidation) Act 1978" substitute "section 139 of the Employment Rights Act 1996".

The Local Government Finance Act 1988 (c. 41)

38. In paragraph 6(4) of Schedule 11 to the Local Government Finance Act 1988, for "the Employment Protection (Consolidation) Act 1978" substitute "the Employment Rights Act 1996".

The Housing (Scotland) Act 1988 (c. 43)

39. In paragraph 12(1) of Schedule 1 to the Housing (Scotland) Act 1988, for "the Employment Protection (Consolidation) Act 1978" substitute "the Employment Rights Act 1996".

The Health and Medicines Act 1988 (c. 49)

40. In section 18 of the Health and Medicines Act 1988, for "the Employment Protection (Consolidation) Act 1978" substitute "the Employment Rights Act 1996".

The Housing Act 1988 (c. 50)

41. In paragraph 10(1) of Schedule 5 to the Housing Act 1988, for "the Employment Protection (Consolidation) Act 1978" substitute "the Employment Rights Act 1996".

The Dock Work Act 1989 (c. 13)

42. In section 6(3) of the Dock Work Act 1989—

(a) for "the 1978 Act" substitute "the Employment Rights Act 1996",

(b) for "section 151 of, and Schedule 13 to," substitute "Chapter I of Part XIV of",

(c) for "paragraph 15 of Schedule 13" substitute "section 216 of that Act", and

(d) for "paragraph 4 of that Schedule" substitute "section 212(1) of that Act".

The Electricity Act 1989 (c. 29)

43.—(1) The Electricity Act 1989 is amended as follows.

(2) In section 56(3), for "Schedule 13 to the said Act of 1978" substitute "Chapter I of Part XIV of the Employment Rights Act 1996".

(3) In—

(a) paragraph 4(1) of Schedule 14, and

(b) paragraph 4(1) of Schedule 15,

for the words from the beginning to "continuous" substitute "Chapter I of Part XIV of the Employment Rights Act 1996".

The Local Government and Housing Act 1989 (c. 42)

44. In section 10 of the Local Government and Housing Act 1989—

(a) in subsection (1), for "subsection (4) of section 29 of the Employment Protection (Consolidation) Act 1978" substitute "section 50(4) of the Employment Rights Act 1996", and

(b) in subsection (2)—

(i) for "the Employment Protection (Consolidation) Act 1978" substitute "the Employment Rights Act 1996", and

(ii) for "subsection (1) of section 29" substitute "subsection (2) of section 50".

The National Health Service and Community Care Act 1990 (c. 19)

45.—(1) The National Health Service and Community Care Act 1990 is amended as follows.

(2) In section 7(3)—

    (a) for "Part VI of the Employment Protection (Consolidation) Act 1978" substitute "Part XI of the Employment Rights Act 1996", and

    (b) for "the said Part VI" substitute "that Part of that Act".

    (3) In—

    (a) section 20(6), and

    (b) section 49(3)(b),

for "the Employment Protection (Consolidation) Act 1978" substitute "the Employment Rights Act 1996".

    (4) In section 60(3)—

    (a) for "Part VI of the Employment Protection (Consolidation) Act 1978" substitute "Part XI of the Employment Rights Act 1996", and

    (b) for "the said Part VI" substitute "that Part of that Act".

The Enterprise and New Towns (Scotland) Act 1990 (c. 35)

46. In paragraph 17(1) of Schedule 1 to the Enterprise and New Towns (Scotland) Act 1990, for "the Employment Protection (Consolidation) Act 1978" substitute "the Employment Rights Act 1996".

The Environmental Protection Act 1990 (c. 43)

47. In paragraph 15 of Schedule 10 to the Environmental Protection Act 1990, for "the Employment Protection (Consolidation) Act 1978" substitute "the Employment Rights Act 1996".

The Natural Heritage (Scotland) Act 1991 (c. 28)

48. In paragraph 4 of Schedule 4 to the Natural Heritage (Scotland) Act 1991, for "the Employment Protection (Consolidation) Act 1978" substitute "the Employment Rights Act 1996".

The Coal Mining Subsidence Act 1991 (c. 45)

49. In section 30(7) of the Coal Mining Subsidence Act 1991—

    (a) for "section 153(4) of the Employment Protection (Consolidation) Act 1978" substitute "section 231 of the Employment Rights Act 1996", and

    (b) for "meaning given by section 153(1) of the Employment Protection (Consolidation) Act 1978" substitute "same meaning as in the Employment Rights Act 1996".

The Ports Act 1991 (c. 52)

50. In section 24(8) of the Ports Act 1991, for the words from the beginning to "continuous" substitute "Chapter I of Part XIV of the Employment Rights Act 1996".

The Social Security Contributions and Benefits Act 1992 (c. 4)

51.—(1) The Social Security Contributions and Benefits Act 1992 is amended as follows.

    (2) In section 6(5), for "section 81" onwards substitute "Part XI of the Employment Rights Act 1996 (redundancy payments) does not apply by virtue of section 199(2) or 209 of that Act."

    (3) In—

    (a) section 27(2)(b), and

    (b) section 28(4),

for "section 81(2) of the Employment Protection (Consolidation) Act 1978" substitute "section 139(1) of the Employment Rights Act 1996".

    (4) In section 112(3)—

    (a) in paragraph (a), for "the Employment Protection (Consolidation) Act 1978" substitute "the Employment Rights Act 1996",

    (b) in paragraph (b), after "that Act" insert "or the Trade Union and Labour Relations (Consolidation) Act 1992", and

    (c) in paragraph (c), for "the Employment Protection Act 1975" substitute "the Trade Union and Labour Relations (Consolidation) Act 1992".

    (5) In section 171(1), for "section 55(2) to (7) of the Employment Protection (Consolidation) Act 1978" substitute "Part X of the Employment Rights Act 1996".

The Further and Higher Education Act 1992 (c. 13)

52.—(1) The Further and Higher Education Act 1992 is amended as follows.

    (2) In section 35—

(a) in subsection (1)(c)—
  (i) for "section 84 of the Employment Protection (Consolidation) Act 1978" substitute "section 138 of the Employment Rights Act 1996", and
  (ii) for "Part VI" substitute "Part XI", and
(b) in subsection (2), for "Schedule 13 to" substitute "Chapter I of Part XIV of".
(3) In section 49(2)(b), for "section 81 of the Employment Protection (Consolidation) Act 1978" substitute "Part XI of the Employment Rights Act 1996".
(4) In section 90(1), for "the Employment Protection (Consolidation) Act 1978" substitute "the Employment Rights Act 1996".

The Timeshare Act 1992 (c. 35)

53. In section 1 of the Timeshare Act 1992—
(a) in subsection (3)(b), for "as defined in section 153 of the Employment Protection (Consolidation) Act 1978" substitute "within the meaning of the Employment Rights Act 1996", and
(b) in subsection (8)(b), for "section 153 of the Employment Protection (Consolidation) Act 1978" substitute "the Employment Rights Act 1996".

The Further and Higher Education (Scotland) Act 1992 (c. 37)

54. In section 33(3)(b) of the Further and Higher Education (Scotland) Act 1992, for "section 81 of the Employment Protection (Consolidation) Act 1978" substitute "section 135 of the Employment Rights Act 1996".

The Museums and Galleries Act 1992 (c. 44)

55. In section 1(7) of the Museums and Galleries Act 1992, for "paragraph 17(3) of Schedule 13 to the Employment Protection (Consolidation) Act 1978" substitute "section 218(3) of the Employment Rights Act 1996".

The Trade Union and Labour Relations (Consolidation) Act 1992 (c. 52)

56.—(1) The Trade Union and Labour Relations (Consolidation) Act 1992 is amended as follows.
(2) In section 67(8)—
(a) in paragraph (a), for "paragraph 8(1)(b) of Schedule 14 to the Employment Protection (Consolidation) Act 1978" substitute "section 227(1)(a) of the Employment Rights Act 1996", and
(b) in paragraph (b), for "section 75" substitute "section 124(1)".
(3) In section 68(11), for "Part I of the Wages Act 1986" substitute "the Employment Rights Act 1996".
(4) In section 68A(4)—
(a) in paragraph (a), for "the Employment Protection (Consolidation) Act 1978" substitute "the Employment Rights Act 1996", and
(b) in paragraph (b), for "section 1(1) of the Wages Act 1986" substitute "section 13 of that Act".
(5) In section 88—
(a) in subsection (2), for "section 1 of the Wages Act 1986" substitute "section 13 of the Employment Rights Act 1996",
(b) in subsection (3), for "section 5 of the Wages Act 1986" substitute "section 23 of the Employment Rights Act 1996", and
(c) in subsection (4), for "section 5(2) of the Wages Act 1986" substitute "section 23(2) of the Employment Rights Act 1996".
(6) In section 140(4), for "section 75 of the Employment Protection (Consolidation) Act 1978" substitute "section 124(1) of the Employment Rights Act 1996".
(7) In—
(a) section 152(1), and
(b) section 153,
for "Part V of the Employment Protection (Consolidation) Act 1978" substitute "Part X of the Employment Rights Act 1996".
(8) In section 154, for "Section 64 of the Employment Protection (Consolidation) Act 1978 (qualifying period and upper age limit for unfair dismissal protection) does" substitute "Sections 108 and 109 of the Employment Rights Act 1996 (qualifying period and upper age limit for unfair dismissal protection) do".
(9) In section 156—

(a) in subsection (1), for "subsection (7A), (7B) or (9) of section 73 of the Employment Protection (Consolidation) Act 1978" substitute "section 122 of the Employment Rights Act 1996", and

(b) in subsection (2), for "subsection (7B)" substitute "subsection (2)".

(10) In section 157—

(a) in subsection (1), for "section 73(2) of the Employment Protection (Consolidation) Act 1978" substitute "section 121 of the Employment Rights Act 1996", and

(b) in subsection (2), for "section 71(2)(b) of the Employment Protection (Consolidation) Act 1978" substitute "section 117(3)(b) of the Employment Rights Act 1996".

(11) In section 158—

(a) in subsection (2), for "section 71(2)(a) of the Employment Protection (Consolidation) Act 1978" substitute "section 117(3)(a) of the Employment Rights Act 1996",

(b) in subsection (3), for "section 73(5) of the Employment Protection (Consolidation) Act 1978" substitute "section 119(4) of the Employment Rights Act 1996", and

(c) in subsection (7), for the words from the beginning to "Part" substitute—

"(7) Chapter II of Part XIV of the Employment Rights Act 1996 (calculation of a week's pay) applies for the purposes of this section with the substitution for section 226 of the following—

For the purposes of this Chapter".

(12) In section 167—

(a) in subsection (1), for "Part V of the Employment Protection (Consolidation) Act 1978" substitute "Part X of the Employment Rights Act 1996", and

(b) in subsection (2)—

(i) for "section 67 of the Employment Protection (Consolidation) Act 1978" substitute "section 111 of the Employment Rights Act 1996",

(ii) for "section 68(2) or 71(2)(a)" substitute "section 112(4) or 117(3)(a)", and

(iii) for "section 69" substitute "section 113".

(13) In section 176(6)—

(a) in paragraph (a), for "paragraph 8(1)(b) of Schedule 14 to the Employment Protection (Consolidation) Act 1978" substitute "section 227(1)(a) of the Employment Rights Act 1996", and

(b) in paragraph (b), for "section 75" substitute "section 124(1)".

(14) In section 190—

(a) in subsection (4)—

(i) for "Schedule 3 to the Employment Protection (Consolidation) Act 1978" substitute "sections 87 to 91 of the Employment Rights Act 1996", and

(ii) for "section 49(1)" substitute "section 86(1)", and

(b) in subsection (5)—

(i) for "Schedule 14 to the Employment Protection (Consolidation) Act 1978" substitute "Chapter II of Part XIV of the Employment Rights Act 1996",

(ii) for "Part II of that Schedule" substitute "that Chapter", and

(iii) for "paragraph 7(1)(k) or (l) of that Schedule" substitute "section 226(5)".

(15) In sections 237(1A) and 238(2A)—

(a) for "section 57A, 57AA or 60 of the Employment Protection (Consolidation) Act 1978 (dismissal in health and safety cases, employee representative and maternity cases)" substitute "section 99(1) to (3), 100 or 103 of the Employment Rights Act 1996 (dismissal in maternity, health and safety and employee representative cases)", and

(b) for "section 59" substitute "section 105(9)".

(16) In section 239—

(a) in subsection (1), for "Part V of the Employment Protection (Consolidation) Act 1978" substitute "Part X of the Employment Rights Act 1996",

(b) in subsection (2), for "section 67(2)" substitute "section 111(2)", and

(c) in subsection (3), for "sections 57 to 61 of the Employment Protection (Consolidation) Act 1978" substitute "sections 98 to 106 of the Employment Rights Act 1996".

(17) In section 278(6), for "Subsections (4) to (9) of section 139 of the Employment Protection (Consolidation) Act 1978" substitute "Subsections (6) to (12) of section 195 of the Employment Rights Act 1996".

(18) In section 282, for subsection (2) substitute—

"(2) Chapter I of Part XIV of the Employment Rights Act 1996 (computation of period of continuous employment), and any provision modifying or supplementing that Chapter for the purposes of that Act, apply for the purposes of this section."

(19) In section 298, for "section 55 of the Employment Protection (Consolidation) Act 1978" substitute "Part X of the Employment Rights Act 1996".

The Tribunals and Inquiries Act 1992 (c. 53)

57. In section 11(2) of the Tribunals and Inquiries Act 1992, for "Subsection (1)" substitute "This section".

The Social Security Act 1993 (c. 3)

58. In section 2(4)(b) of the Social Security Act 1993, for "sections 106(2) and 122(1) of the Employment Protection (Consolidation) Act 1978" substitute "sections 167(1) and 182 of the Employment Rights Act 1996".

The Education Act 1993 (c. 35)

59. In section 305(1) of the Education Act 1993, for "the Employment Protection (Consolidation) Act 1978" substitute "the Employment Rights Act 1996".

The Railways Act 1993 (c. 43)

60.—(1) The Railways Act 1993 is amended as follows.
(2) In section 93(5), (6) and (12), for "the Employment Protection (Consolidation) Act 1978" substitute "the Employment Rights Act 1996".
(3) In paragraph 6 of Schedule 11, for sub-paragraphs (10) to (12) substitute—
   "(10) Chapter I of Part XIV of the Employment Rights Act 1996, except section 218(6), shall apply for the purposes of this paragraph as it applies for the purposes of that Act."

The Pension Schemes Act 1993 (c. 48)

61.—(1) The Pension Schemes Act 1993 is amended as follows.
(2) In section 123(3), for "the Employment Protection (Consolidation) Act 1978" substitute "the Employment Rights Act 1996".
(3) In section 124(4), for ", maternity pay under Part III" onwards substitute "and any payment such as is referred to in section 184(2) of the Employment Rights Act 1996".
(4) In section 165—
(a) in subsection (7), for "section 137 of the Employment Protection (Consolidation) Act 1978" substitute "section 201 of the Employment Rights Act 1996", and
(b) in subsection (8), for "section 144(5) of the Employment Protection (Consolidation) Act 1978" substitute "section 199(5) of the Employment Rights Act 1996".

The Finance Act 1994 (c. 9)

62. In paragraph 27 of Schedule 24 to the Finance Act 1994—
(a) for sub-paragraphs (9) to (11) substitute—
   "(9) Chapter I of Part XIV of the Employment Rights Act 1996, except section 218(6), shall apply for the purposes of this paragraph as it applies for the purposes of that Act.", and
(b) in sub-paragraph (13), for "sub-paragraphs (11) and" substitute "sub-paragraph".

The Local Government (Wales) Act 1994 (c. 19)

63.—(1) The Local Government (Wales) Act 1994 is amended as follows.
(2) In section 41—
(a) in subsection (1)—
      (i) for "section 84 of the Employment Protection (Consolidation) Act 1978" substitute "section 138 of the Employment Rights Act 1996", and
      (ii) for "Part VI" substitute "Part XI", and
(b) in subsection (2), for "Schedule 13 to the Act of 1978" substitute "Chapter I of Part XIV of the Employment Rights Act 1996".
(3) In section 43—
(a) in subsection (6), for "section 82(5) or (6) or 84(3) of the Employment Protection (Consolidation) Act 1978" substitute "section 138 or 141 of the Employment Rights Act 1996", and
(b) in subsection (7), for "Part VI of the Act of 1978" substitute "Part XI of the Employment Rights Act 1996".
(4) In section 44—
(a) in subsection (1), for "Part IV, V or VI of the Employment Protection (Consolidation) Act 1978" substitute "Part IX, X or XI of the Employment Rights Act 1996",
(b) in subsection (3), for "sections 101, 102, 108 and 119 of the Act of 1978" substitute "sections 164, 165, 170 and 179 of the Employment Rights Act 1996", and

(c) in subsection (4), for "sections 81(4), 82(1) and 101 of the Act of 1978, and in Schedule 4 to that Act," substitute "sections 155, 156, 162 and 164 of the Employment Rights Act 1996".
(5) In section 45(5), for "the Employment Protection (Consolidation) Act 1978" substitute "the Employment Rights Act 1996".

The Coal Industry Act 1994 (c. 21)

64. In paragraph 4(11) of Schedule 5 to the Coal Industry Act 1994, for the words from the beginning to "that Schedule" substitute "Chapter I of Part XIV of the Employment Rights Act 1996, except section 218(6),".

The Criminal Justice and Public Order Act 1994 (c. 33)

65. In section 126(2) of the Criminal Justice and Public Order Act 1994, for paragraph (a) substitute—
"(a) the Trade Union and Labour Relations (Consolidation) Act 1992 and the Employment Rights Act 1996;".

The Local Government etc. (Scotland) Act 1994 (c. 39)

66.—(1) The Local Government etc. (Scotland) Act 1994 is amended as follows.
(2) In section 10—
(a) in subsection (1)—
(i) for "section 84 of the Employment Protection (Consolidation) Act 1978" substitute "section 138 of the Employment Rights Act 1996", and
(ii) for "Part VI" substitute "Part XI", and
(b) in subsection (2), for "Schedule 13 to the said Act of 1978" substitute "Chapter I of Part XIV of the Employment Rights Act 1996".
(3) In section 13—
(a) in subsection (5), for the words from "subsections" to "1978" substitute "section 138 or 141 of the Employment Rights Act 1996 (renewal of contract or re-engagement)", and
(b) in subsection (6), for "Part VI of the said Act of 1978" substitute "Part XI of the Employment Rights Act 1996".
(4) In section 14(1), for "Part VI of the Employment Protection (Consolidation) Act 1978" substitute "Part XI of the Employment Rights Act 1996".

The Jobseekers Act 1995 (c. 18)

67.—(1) The Jobseekers Act 1995 is amended as follows.
(2) In—
(a) section 14(3)(b), and
(b) section 19(7),
for "section 81(2) of the Employment Protection (Consolidation) Act 1978" substitute "section 139(1) of the Employment Rights Act 1996".
(3) In paragraph 6(2)(a)(i) of Schedule 1, for "the Employment Protection (Consolidation) Act 1978" substitute "the Employment Rights Act 1996".

The Environment Act 1995 (c. 25)

68. In paragraph 3 of Schedule 2 to the Environment Act 1995—
(a) in sub-paragraph (6), for "section 84 of the Employment Protection (Consolidation) Act 1978" substitute "section 138 of the Employment Rights Act 1996", and
(b) in sub-paragraph (7), for "Schedule 13 to the Employment Protection (Consolidation) Act 1978" substitute "Chapter I of Part XIV of the Employment Rights Act 1996".

The Disability Discrimination Act 1995 (c. 50)

69.—(1) The Disability Discrimination Act 1995 is amended as follows.
(2) In section 50(9)(a), for "the Employment Protection (Consolidation) Act 1978" substitute "the Employment Rights Act 1996".
(3) In section 65(2), for "section 139 of the Employment Protection (Consolidation) Act 1978" substitute "section 195 of the Employment Rights Act 1996".

SCHEDULE 2

TRANSITIONAL PROVISIONS, SAVINGS AND TRANSITORY PROVISIONS

PART I

TRANSITIONAL PROVISIONS AND SAVINGS

General transitionals and savings

1. The substitution of this Act for the provisions repealed or revoked by this Act does not affect the continuity of the law.

2.—(1) Anything done, or having effect as done, (including the making of subordinate legislation) under or for the purposes of any provision repealed or revoked by this Act has effect as if done under or for the purposes of any corresponding provision of this Act.

(2) Sub-paragraph (1) does not apply to the making of any subordinate legislation to the extent that it is reproduced in this Act.

3. Any reference (express or implied) in this Act or any other enactment, or in any instrument or document, to a provision of this Act is (so far as the context permits) to be read as (according to the context) being or including in relation to times, circumstances and purposes before the commencement of this Act a reference to the corresponding provision repealed or revoked by this Act.

4.—(1) Any reference (express or implied) in any enactment, or in any instrument or document, to a provision repealed or revoked by this Act is (so far as the context permits) to be read as (according to the context) being or including in relation to times, circumstances and purposes after the commencement of this Act a reference to the corresponding provision of this Act.

(2) In particular, where a power conferred by an Act is expressed to be exercisable in relation to enactments contained in Acts passed before or in the same Session as the Act conferring the power, the power is also exercisable in relation to provisions of this Act which reproduce such enactments.

5. Paragraphs 1 to 4 have effect in place of section 17(2) of the Interpretation Act 1978 (but are without prejudice to any other provision of that Act).

Preservation of old transitionals and savings

6.—(1) The repeal by this Act of an enactment previously repealed subject to savings (whether or not in the repealing enactment) does not affect the continued operation of those savings.

(2) The repeal by this Act of a saving made on the previous repeal of an enactment does not affect the operation of the saving in so far as it remains capable of having effect.

(3) Where the purpose of an enactment repealed by this Act was to secure that the substitution of the provisions of the Act containing that enactment for provisions repealed by that Act did not affect the continuity of the law, the enactment repealed by this Act continues to have effect in so far as it is capable of doing so.

Employment particulars

7.—(1) In this paragraph "pre-TURERA employee" means an employee whose employment with his employer began before 30th November 1993 (the day on which section 26 of the Trade Union Reform and Employment Rights Act 1993 came into force), whether or not the provisions of sections 1 to 6 of the Employment Protection (Consolidation) Act 1978, as they had effect before the substitution made by that section, applied to him before that date.

(2) Subject to the following provisions of this paragraph, sections 1 to 7 of this Act do not apply to a pre-TURERA employee (but the provisions of sections 1 to 6 of the Employment Protection (Consolidation) Act 1978, as they had effect before the substitution made by section 26 of the Trade Union Reform and Employment Rights Act 1993, continue in force in his case).

(3) Where a pre-TURERA employee, at any time—

(a) on or after the day on which this Act comes into force, and

(b) either before the end of his employment or within the period of three months beginning with the day on which his employment ends,

requests from his employer a statement under section 1 of this Act, the employer shall (subject to section 5 and any other provision disapplying or having the effect of disapplying sections 1 to 4) be treated as being required by section 1 to give him a written statement under that section not later than two months after the request is made; and section 4 of this Act shall (subject to that) apply in relation to the employee after he makes the request.

(4) An employer is not required to give an employee a statement under section 1 pursuant to sub-paragraph (3)—

(a) on more than one occasion, or

(b) if he has already given him a statement pursuant to paragraph 3(3) of Schedule 9 to the Trade Union Reform and Employment Rights Act 1993.

(5) Where—

(a) on or after the day on which this Act comes into force there is in the case of a pre-TURERA employee a change in any of the matters particulars of which would, had he been given a statement of particulars on 30th November 1993 under section 1 of the Employment Protection (Consolidation) Act 1978 (as substituted by section 26 of the Trade Union Reform and Employment Rights Act 1993), have been included or referred to in the statement, and

(b) he has not previously requested a statement under sub-paragraph (3) or paragraph 3(3) of Schedule 9 to the Trade Union Reform and Employment Rights Act 1993,

subsections (1) and (6) of section 4 of this Act shall be treated (subject to section 5 and any other provision disapplying or having the effect of disapplying section 4) as requiring his employer to give him a written statement containing particulars of the change at the time specified in subsection (3) of section 4; and the other provisions of section 4 apply accordingly.

Monetary limits in old cases

8. In relation to any case in which (but for this Act) a limit lower than that set by Article 3 of the Employment Protection (Increase of Limits) Order 1995 would have applied in accordance with Article 4 of that Order, this Act has effect as if it reproduced that lower limit.

Shop workers and betting workers to whom old maternity provisions applied

9.—(1) This paragraph applies where an employee exercised a right to return to work under Part III of the Employment Protection (Consolidation) Act 1978 at a time when the amendments of that Part made by the Trade Union Reform and Employment Rights Act 1993 did not have effect in her case (so that her right was a right to return to work in the job in which she was employed under the original contract of employment).

(2) Section 36(4) shall have effect as if for paragraph (b) there were substituted—

"(b) under her original contract of employment, she was a shop worker, or a betting worker, but was not employed to work only on Sunday."

(3) If the employee was employed as a shop worker under her original contract of employment, she shall not be regarded as failing to satisfy the condition in section 36(2)(a) or (c) or 41(1)(c) merely because during her pregnancy she was employed under a different contract of employment by virtue of section 60(2) of the Employment Protection (Consolidation) Act 1978 (as it had effect before the commencement of section 24 of the Trade Union Reform and Employment Rights Act 1993) or otherwise by reason of her pregnancy.

(4) In this paragraph, and in section 36(4)(b) as substituted by sub-paragraph (2), "original contract of employment" has the meaning given by section 153(1) of the Employment Protection (Consolidation) Act 1978 as originally enacted.

Validity of provisions deriving from certain regulations

10. Any question as to the validity of any of sections 47, 61, 62, 63 and 103, which derive from the Collective Redundancies and Transfer of Undertakings (Protection of Employment) (Amendment) Regulations 1995 made under subsection (2) of section 2 of the European Communities Act 1972, shall be determined as if those provisions were contained in regulations made under that subsection.

Unfair dismissal

11. Part X does not apply to a dismissal from employment under a contract for a fixed term of two years or more (not being a contract of apprenticeship) if—

(a) the contract was made before 28th February 1972, and

(b) the dismissal consists only of the expiry of that term without its being renewed.

Redundancy payments

12.—(1) Section 135 does not apply to an employee who immediately before the relevant date is employed under a contract for a fixed term of two years or more (not being a contract of apprenticeship) if the contract was made before 6th December 1965.

(2) Section 197(3) does not apply if the contract was made before 6th December 1965.

Periods of employment

13.—(1) The reference in section 215(2)(b) to a person being an employed earner for the purposes of the Social Security Contributions and Benefits Act 1992 in respect of whom a secondary Class 1 contribution was payable under that Act (whether or not it was in fact paid) shall be construed—

(a) as respects a week of employment after 1st June 1976 and before 1st July 1992, as a reference to a person being an employed earner for the purposes of the Social Security Act 1975 in respect of whom a secondary Class 1 contribution was payable under that Act (whether or not it was in fact paid),

(b) as respects a week of employment after 6th April 1975 and before 1st June 1976, as a reference to a person being an employed earner for the purposes of the Social Security Act 1975, and

(c) as respects a week of employment before 6th April 1975, as a reference to a person being an employee in respect of whom an employer's contribution was payable in respect of the corresponding contribution week (whether or not it was in fact paid).

(2) For the purposes of the application of sub-paragraph (1) to a week of employment where the corresponding contribution week began before 5th July 1948, an employer's contribution shall be treated as payable as mentioned in that sub-paragraph if such a contribution would have been so payable had the statutory provisions relating to national insurance in force on 5th July 1948 been in force in that contribution week.

(3) The references in subsection (4) of section 215 to the Social Security Contributions and Benefits Act 1992 include the Social Security Act 1975; and that subsection applies to any question arising whether an employer's contribution was or would have been payable as mentioned in sub-paragraph (1) or (2).

(4) In this paragraph—

"employer's contribution" has the same meaning as in the National Insurance Act 1965, and

"corresponding contribution week", in relation to a week of employment, means a contribution week (within the meaning of that Act) of which so much as falls within the period beginning with midnight between Sunday and Monday and ending with Saturday also falls within that week of employment.

14.—(1) Subject to paragraph 13 and sub-paragraphs (2) and (3) of this paragraph, Chapter I of Part XIV applies to periods before this Act comes into force as it applies to later periods.

(2) If, during the whole or any part of a week beginning before 6th July 1964, an employee was absent from work—

(a) because he was taking part in a strike, or

(b) because of a lock-out by his employer,

the week counts as a period of employment.

(3) Any week which counted as a period of employment in the computation of a period of employment for the purposes of the Employment Protection (Consolidation) Act 1978 counts as a period of employment for the purposes of this Act; and any week which did not break the continuity of a person's employment for the purposes of that Act shall not break the continuity of a period of employment for the purposes of this Act.

PART II

TRANSITORY PROVISIONS

Occupational pension scheme trustees

15.—(1) If sections 42 to 46 of the Pensions Act 1995 have not come into force before the commencement of this Act, this Act shall have effect with the omission of sections 46, 58 to 60 and 102 until the relevant commencement date.

(2) The reference in sub-paragraph (1) to the relevant commencement date is a reference—

(a) if an order has been made before the commencement of this Act appointing a day after that commencement as the day on which sections 42 to 46 of the Pensions Act 1995 are to come into force, to the day so appointed, and

(b) otherwise, to such day as the Secretary of State may by order appoint.

Armed forces

16.—(1) If section 31 of the Trade Union Reform and Employment Rights Act 1993 has not come into force before the commencement of this Act, this Act shall have effect until the relevant commencement date as if for section 192 there were substituted—

"**Armed forces**

192. Section 191—

(a) does not apply to service as a member of the naval, military or air forces of the Crown, but

(b) does apply to employment by an association established for the purposes of Part XI of the Reserve Forces Act 1996."

(2) The reference in sub-paragraph (1) to the relevant commencement date is a reference—

(a) if an order has been made before the commencement of this Act appointing a day after that commencement as the day on which section 31 of the Trade Union Reform and Employment Rights Act 1993 is to come into force, to the day so appointed, and

(b) otherwise, to such day as the Secretary of State may by order appoint.

17.—(1) If Part XI of the Reserve Forces Act 1996 has not come into force before the commencement of this Act, section 192 of this Act shall have effect until the relevant commencement date as if for "Part XI of the Reserve Forces Act 1996" there were substituted "Part VI of the Reserve Forces Act 1980".

(2) The reference in sub-paragraph (1) to the relevant commencement date is a reference—

(a) if an order has been made before the commencement of this Act appointing a day after that commencement as the day on which Part XI of the Reserve Forces Act 1996 is to come into force, to the day so appointed, and

(b) otherwise, to such day as the Secretary of State may by order appoint.

Disability discrimination

18.—(1) If paragraph 3 of Schedule 6 to the Disability Discrimination Act 1995 has not come into force before the commencement of this Act, this Act shall have effect with the omission of subsections (3)(d) and (4)(a)(iv) of section 219 until the relevant commencement date.

(2) The reference in sub-paragraph (1) to the relevant commencement date is a reference—

(a) if an order has been made before the commencement of this Act appointing a day after that commencement as the day on which paragraph 3 of Schedule 6 to the Disability Discrimination Act 1995 is to come into force, to the day so appointed, and

(b) otherwise, to such day as the Secretary of State may by order appoint.

Section 242   SCHEDULE 3

REPEALS AND REVOCATIONS

PART I

REPEALS

Chapter	Short Title	Extent of repeal
1963 c. 2.	The Betting, Gaming and Lotteries Act 1963.	Section 31A. In Schedule 5A, paragraphs 1 to 20 and 22.
1969 c. 48.	The Post Office Act 1969.	In Schedule 9, paragraph 33.
1971 c. 11.	The Atomic Energy Authority Act 1971.	Section 10(1).
1976 c. 74.	The Race Relations Act 1976.	In Schedule 2, in paragraph 11, in sub-paragraph (1), the words "and the following" and sub-paragraphs (2), (3) and (5) and paragraphs 12 and 13.
1978 c. 44.	The Employment Protection (Consolidation) Act 1978.	Section 1 to 6. Sections 8 to 22C. Sections 29 to 47. Sections 49 to 57A. Sections 59 to 61. Sections 63 to 93. Section 96. Sections 98 to 102. Sections 106 to 108. Sections 110 to 112. Sections 114 to 120.

Chapter	Short Title	Extent of repeal
		Section 122.
		Sections 124 to 127.
		Section 129.
		Section 137.
		Section 138(1) to (6), (7)(a) to (d) and (f) and (8).
		Section 139(1)(a) to (c) and (e) and (2) to (9).
		Section 139A(1), (2), (3)(b) and (4) to (6).
		Sections 140 to 142.
		Section 144.
		Section 146.
		Section 146A.
		Sections 148 to 160.
		Schedules 1 to 4.
		Schedule 7.
		Schedule 8.
		Schedules 12 to 17.
1980 c. 20.	The Education Act 1980.	In Schedule 1, paragraph 30.
1980 c. 42.	The Employment Act 1980.	Section 6.
		Section 8(2).
		Section 9.
		Sections 12 to 14.
		Section 20.
		Section 21.
		In Schedule 1, paragraphs 1, 8, 11, 13, 20, 22, 23, 25, 31 and 33.
		Schedule 2.
1980 c. 43.	The Magistrates' Courts Act 1980.	In Schedule 7, paragraph 175.
1980 c. 48.	The Finance Act 1980.	In Schedule 19, paragraph 5(4).
1981 c. 64.	The New Towns Act 1981.	Section 54(6).
1982 c. 16.	The Civil Aviation Act 1982.	In Schedule 3, paragraphs 6 and 8(1).
1982 c. 23.	The Oil and Gas (Enterprise) Act 1982.	In Schedule 3, paragraph 40.
1982 c. 24.	The Social Security and Housing Benefits Act 1982.	In Schedule 2, paragraph 13.
1982 c. 46.	The Employment Act 1982.	Section 20.
		Section 21(1) and (3).
		In Schedule 2, paragraphs 1 to 5, 6(2), (4) and (5), 7(1) and (2) and 9.
		In Schedule 3, in Part I, paragraphs 1, 2, 4 and 6 and, in Part II, paragraphs 15, 21 to 23, 25, 26, 27(1) and 28 to 30.
		Schedule 4.
1983 c. 23.	The Water Act 1983.	In Schedule 2, in Part I, paragraph 8(1)(b).
1983 c. 41.	The Health and Social Services and Social Security Adjudications Act 1983.	In Schedule 9, in Part I, paragraph 25.
1984 c. 36.	The Mental Health (Scotland) Act 1984.	Section 126(2)(c).

Chapter	Short Title	Extent of repeal
1985 c. 17.	The Reserve Forces (Safeguard of Employment) Act 1985.	In Schedule 4, paragraph 6.
1985 c. 51.	The Local Government Act 1985.	In section 53, subsection (5) and, in subsection (6), the words "Except as provided in subsection (5) above" and "a redundancy payment under Part VI of the said Act of 1978 or to". Section 55(3) to (5). Section 59(1) to (3).
1985 c. 65.	The Insolvency Act 1985.	Section 218. In Schedule 8, paragraph 31(1), (2) and (5).
1985 c. 66.	The Bankruptcy (Scotland) Act 1985.	In Schedule 7, in Part I, paragraph 14(1), (2) and (4).
1985 c. 71.	The Housing (Consequential Provisions) Act 1985.	In Schedule 4, paragraph 7(2)(a).
1986 c. 45.	The Insolvency Act 1986.	In Schedule 14, the entries relating to the Employment Protection (Consolidation) Act 1978.
1986 c. 47.	The Legal Aid (Scotland) Act 1986.	In Schedule 1, in paragraph 10(2)(a), the words "Part VI of the Employment Protection (Consolidation) Act 1978 shall not apply to him and".
1986 c. 48.	The Wages Act 1986.	Sections 1 to 11. Sections 28 to 33. Schedule 1. In Schedule 4, paragraph 4. Schedule 5. In Schedule 6, paragraph 10.
1986 c. 50.	The Social Security Act 1986.	In Schedule 10, in Part IV, paragraphs 76 and 81.
1986 c. 59.	The Sex Discrimination Act 1986.	Section 3.
1987 c. 26.	The Housing (Scotland) Act 1987.	In Schedule 22, in Part II, paragraph 10(2)(a).
1988 c. 1.	The Income and Corporation Taxes Act 1988.	Section 150(b). In section 579, subsection (2)(a), in subsections (2)(b) and (3)(b) and in subsection (4)(b) as it has effect otherwise than for the purposes of corporation tax, the word "net" and, in subsection (5)(b), the words ", and the full amount of the rebate". Section 580(2).
1988 c. 4.	The Norfolk and Suffolk Broads Act 1988.	In Schedule 6, paragraph 19.
1988 c. 20.	The Dartford-Thurrock Crossing Act 1988.	In Schedule 5, in Part I, paragraph 2(2).
1988 c. 34.	The Legal Aid Act 1988.	In Schedule 7, in paragraph 7(3), the words "Part VI of the Employment Protection (Consolidation) Act 1978 shall not apply to him and".

Chapter	Short Title	Extent of repeal
1988 c. 40.	The Education Reform Act 1988.	In section 173, subsection (6) and, in subsection (7), the words "Except as provided in subsection (6) above" and "a redundancy payment under Part VI of the Act of 1978 mentioned above or to". Section 175(3) to (5). Section 178(1) and (2). In Schedule 12, in Part I, paragraph 23 and, in Part III, paragraph 80.
1988 c. 43.	The Housing (Scotland) Act 1988.	In Schedule 1, in paragraph 12(2), the words "Part VI of the Employment Protection (Consolidation) Act 1978 shall not apply to him and".
1988 c. 50.	The Housing Act 1988.	In Schedule 5, in paragraph 10(2), the words "Part VI of the Employment Protection (Consolidation) Act 1978 shall not apply to him and".
1989 c. 13.	The Dock Work Act 1989.	Section 6(2). Section 7(4). In Schedule 2, paragraphs 6 and 7.
1989 c. 15.	The Water Act 1989.	In section 194(7)(d), the words "and the Employment Protection (Consolidation) Act 1978". In Schedule 25, paragraph 56.
1989 c. 29.	The Electricity Act 1989.	Section 56(2).
1989 c. 38.	The Employment Act 1989.	Sections 15 to 18. Section 19(1). In section 27(1), the words "and 16 to 19". In section 29(1), the definition of "the 1978 Act". Section 30(3)(f). In Schedule 6, paragraphs 21 to 25. In Schedule 9, paragraphs 3 to 5.
1989 c. 39.	The Self-Governing Schools etc. (Scotland) Act 1989.	In Schedule 10, paragraph 7.
1990 c. 19.	The National Health Service and Community Care Act 1990.	In Schedule 9, paragraph 20.
1990 c. 35.	The Enterprise and New Towns (Scotland) Act 1990.	In Schedule 1, in paragraph 17(2), the words "Part VI of the said Act of 1978 shall not apply to him and".
1990 c. 38.	The Employment Act 1990.	Section 13(1), (2) and (4). Section 16. In section 17, subsection (1) and, in subsection (2), the words "Apart from this section,". In Schedule 2, paragraph 1(1) and (3) to (6). Schedule 3.
1990 c. 43.	The Environmental Protection Act 1990.	In Schedule 10, in paragraph 16, the words "Part VI of the Employment Protection (Consolidation) Act 1978 shall not apply to him and".

Chapter	Short Title	Extent of repeal
1991 c. 28.	The Natural Heritage (Scotland) Act 1991.	In Schedule 4, in paragraph 5, the words "Part VI of the Employment Protection (Consolidation) Act 1978 shall not apply to him and".
1992 c. 6.	The Social Security (Consequential Provisions) Act 1992.	In Schedule 2, paragraphs 51 and 74.
1992 c. 13.	The Further and Higher Education Act 1992.	In Schedule 8, in Part II, paragraph 89.
1992 c. 37.	The Further and Higher Education (Scotland) Act 1992.	In Schedule 9, paragraph 6.
1992 c. 52.	The Trade Union and Labour Relations (Consolidation) Act 1992.	In Schedule 2, paragraphs 11 to 14, 16 to 18, 21 to 23, 29(2), 30, 33 and 34(1) and (2).
1993 c. 19.	The Trade Union Reform and Employment Rights Act 1993.	Sections 23 to 26. Sections 28 to 31. In section 39, subsection (1) and, in subsection (2), the words ", the Wages Act 1986". Section 54(2)(a) to (e). Schedules 2 to 5. In Schedule 6, paragraph 3. In Schedule 7, paragraphs 2 to 5, 11, 13, 14 and 16. In Schedule 8, paragraphs 10 to 18, 21 to 27, 31, 32, 35 to 37 and 67. In Schedule 9, paragraph 3.
1993 c. 48.	The Pension Schemes Act 1993.	Section 164(6). In Schedule 8, paragraphs 11(1) and 45(a).
1994 c. 10.	The Race Relations (Remedies) Act 1994.	Section 1(2).
1994 c. 18.	The Social Security (Incapacity for Work) Act 1994.	In Schedule 1, in Part II, paragraph 54.
1994 c. 20.	The Sunday Trading Act 1994.	In Schedule 4, paragraphs 1 to 20 and 22.
1994 c. 40.	The Deregulation and Contracting Out Act 1994.	Section 20(3) and (5). Section 36(1). Schedule 8.
1995 c. 17.	The Health Authorities Act 1995.	In Schedule 1, paragraph 103.
1995 c. 25.	The Environment Act 1995.	In Schedule 7, in paragraph 11(3), the words from the beginning to "but".
1995 c. 26.	The Pensions Act 1995.	Sections 42 to 46. In Schedule 3, paragraphs 1 to 7 and 10.
1995 c. 50.	The Disability Discrimination Act 1995.	In Schedule 6, paragraph 3.
1996 c. 14.	The Reserve Forces Act 1996.	In Schedule 10, paragraph 17.

PART II

REVOCATIONS

Number	Title	Extent of revocation
S.I. 1983/624.	The Insolvency of Employer (Excluded Classes) Regulations 1983.	The whole instrument.
S.I. 1993/2798.	The Sex Discrimination and Equal Pay (Remedies) Regulations 1993.	In the Schedule, in paragraph 1, the entry relating to the Employment Protection (Consolidation) Act 1978 and paragraph 2.
S.I. 1995/31.	The Employment Protection (Part-time Employees) Regulations 1995.	The whole instrument.
S.I. 1995/278.	The Insolvency of Employer (Excluded Classes) Regulations 1995.	The whole instrument.
S.I. 1995/2587.	The Collective Redundancies and Transfer of Undertakings (Protection of Employment) (Amendment) Regulations 1995.	Regulation 12(1), (2) and (4). Regulation 13(1), (2) and (4) to (6). Regulation 14.
S.I. 1996/593.	The Environment Act 1995 (Consequential Amendments) Regulations 1996.	In Schedule 1, paragraph 19.
S.I. 1996/973.	The Environment Act 1995 (Consequential and Transitional Provisions) (Scotland) Regulations 1996.	In the Schedule, paragraph 4.

TABLE OF DERIVATIONS

Notes:

1. This Table shows the derivation of the provisions of the consolidation.
2. The following abbreviations are used in the Table:

BGLA	=	Betting, Gaming and Lotteries Act 1963 (c.2)
EP(C)A	=	Employment Protection (Consolidation) Act 1978 (c.44)
EA 1980	=	Employment Act 1980 (c.42)
EA 1982	=	Employment Act 1982 (c.46)
WA	=	Wages Act 1986 (c.48)
EA 1989	=	Employment Act 1989 (c.38)
TULR(C)A	=	Trade Union and Labour Relations (Consolidation) Act 1992 (c.52)
TURERA	=	Trade Union Reform and Employment Rights Act 1993 (c.19)
STA	=	Sunday Trading Act 1994 (c.20)
D & COA	=	Deregulation and Contracting Out Act 1994 (c.40)
PA	=	Pensions Act 1995 (c.26)
CRTUPER	=	Collective Redundancies and Transfer of Undertakings (Protection of Employment) (Amendment) Regulations (S.I.1995/2587)

Provision	Derivation
1(1), (2)	EP(C)A s.1(1); TURERA Sch.4.

Provision	Derivation
(3) to (5)	EP(C)A s.1(2) to (4); TURERA Sch.4.
2(1)	EP(C)A s.2(1); TURERA Sch.4.
(2)	EP(C)A s.2(2)(a); TURERA Sch.4.
(3)	EP(C)A s.2(2)(b), (3); TURERA Sch.4.
(4) to (6)	EP(C)A s.2(4) to (6); TURERA Sch.4.
3(1)	EP(C)A s.3(1)(a) to (c); TURERA Sch.4.
(2) to (4)	EP(C)A s.3(2) to (4); TURERA Sch.4.
(5)	EP(C)A s.3(1)(d); TURERA Sch.4.
4(1)	EP(C)A s.4(1); TURERA Sch.4.
(2)	EP(C)A s.4(1), (2); TURERA Sch.4.
(3)	EP(C)A s.4(1); TURERA Sch.4.
(4)	EP(C)A s.4(3)(a); TURERA Sch.4.
(5)	EP(C)A s.4(3 (b), (4); TURERA Sch.4.
(6), (7)	EP(C)A s.4(5); TURERA Sch.4.
(8)	EP(C)A s.4(6); TURERA Sch.4.
5	EP(C)A s.5(2), (3); TURERA Sch.4.
6	EP(C)A ss.2(2)(a), (3), 3(1)(a), (c), 4(3)(a), (4); TURERA Sch.4.
7	EP(C)A s.6; TURERA Sch.4.
8	EP(C)A s.8.
9(1), (2)	EP(C)A s.9(1).
(3) to (5)	EP(C)A s.9(2) to (4).
10	EP(C)A s.10.
11(1)	EP(C)A s.11(1); TURERA Sch.8 para. 10(a).
(2)	EP(C)A s.11(2).
(3)	EP(C)A s.11(4); TURERA Sch.8 para.10(b); Pension Schemes Act 1993 (c.48) Sch. 8 para.11(1).
(4)	EP(C)A s.11(9); TURERA Sch.8 para 10(c).
12(1), (2)	EP(C)A s.11(5), (6).
(3) to (5)	EP(C)A s.11(8).
13(1)	WA s.1(1).
(2)	WA s.1(3).
(3)	WA s.8(3).
(4)	WA s.8(3), (4).
(5)	WA s.1(4)(a).
(6)	WA s.1(4)(b).
(7)	WA s.1(6).
14(1)	WA s.1(5)(a).
(2)	WA s.1(5)(b).
(3)	WA s.1(5)(c).
(4)	WA s.1(5)(d).
(5)	WA s.1(5)(e).
(6)	WA s.1(5)(f).
15(1)	WA s.1(1), (2).
(2)	WA s.1(3).
(3)	WA s.1(4)(a).
(4)	WA s.1(4)(b).
(5)	WA s.8(5).
16(1)	WA s.1(5)(a).
(2)	WA s.1(5)(b).
(3)	WA s.1(5)(e).
(4)	WA s.1(5)(f).
17(1)	WA s.2(2) ("cash shortage", "stock deficiency").
(2)	WA s.2(2) ("retail employment").
(3)	WA s.2(2) ("retail transaction").
(4), (5)	WA s.4(6).
(6)	WA s.2(2) ("pay day").

Provision	Derivation
18(1)	WA s.2(1).
(2), (3)	WA s.2(3).
19(1)	WA s.2(4).
(2) to (4)	WA s.2(5).
20(1) to (3)	WA s.3(1) to (3).
(4)	WA s.3(6).
(5)	WA s.4(4).
21(1), (2)	WA s.3(4), (5).
(3)	WA s.4(5), first sentence.
22(1) to (3)	WA s.4(1) to (3).
(4)	WA s.4(5), second sentence.
23(1) to (3)	WA s.5(1) to (3).
(4)	WA s.5(2).
24	WA s.5(4).
25(1), (2)	WA s.5(5).
(3) to (5)	WA s.5(6) to (8).
26	WA s.6(2).
27(1)	EP(C)A s.122(4); WA s.7(1); Social Security Act 1986 (c.50) Sch.10 Pt.IV para.81; Social Security (Consequential Provisions) Act 1992 (c.6) Sch.2 para.74; TULR(C)A Sch.2 paras.18(3), 34(1), (2); TURERA Sch.8 para.18.
(2), (3)	WA s.7(2), (3).
(4)	WA s.8(1) ("gross amount").
(5)	WA s.7(4).
28(1) to (3)	EP(C)A s.12(1).
(4), (5)	EP(C)A s.12(2).
29(1), (2)	EP(C)A s.13(1), (2); EA 1982 Sch.2 para. 1.
(3)	EP(C)A s.13(3); EA 1982 Sch.2 para.1, Sch.3 Pt.II para.15.
(4), (5)	EP(C)A s.13(4); EA 1982 Sch.2 para.1.
30(1)	EP(C)A s.14(1).
(2) to (4)	EP(C)A s.14(2).
(5)	EP(C)A s.14(3).
31(1)	EP(C)A s.15(1); Employment Protection (Increase of Limits) Order 1995 (S.I. 1995 (S.I.1995/1953) Art.3, Sch.
(2)	EP(C)A s.15(2); EA 1980 s.14.
(3) to (5)	EP(C)A s.15(3).
(6)	EP(C)A s.15(4).
(7)	EP(C)A s.15(5); EA 1980 Sch.1 para.8.
32	EP(C)A s.16(1) to (3).
33	EP(C)A s.16(4).
34	EP(C)A s.17.
35(1) to (3)	EP(C)A s.18(1) to (3).
(4), (5)	EP(C)A s.18(4).
(6)	EP(C)A s.18(5).
36(1)	BGLA Sch.5A para.2(1); STA Sch.4 para.2(1); D & COA Sch.8.
(2)	BGLA Sch.5A para.2(2); STA Sch.4 para.2(2); D & COA Sch.8.
(3)	BGLA Sch.5A para.2(3); STA Sch.4 para.2(3); D & COA Sch.8.
(4)	BGLA Sch.5A para.2(7); STA Sch.4 para.2(7); D & COA Sch.8.
(5)	BGLA Sch.5A para.3(1); STA Sch.4 para.3(1); D & COA Sch.8.
(6)	BGLA Sch.5A para.3(2); STA Sch.4 para.3(2); D & COA Sch.8.
(7)	BGLA Sch.5A para.1(1); ("the commencement date"); STA Sch.4 para.1(1) ("the commencement date"); D & COA Sch.8.
37(1)	BGLA Sch.5A para.12(1); STA Sch.4 para.12(1); D & COA Sch.8.
(2)	BGLA Sch.5A para.12(2); STA Sch.4 para.12(2); D & COA Sch.8.
(3)	BGLA Sch.5A paras.3(1)(b), 12(3); STA Sch.4 paras.3(1)(b), 12(3); D & COA Sch.8.

Provision	Derivation
(4)	BGLA Sch.5A para.12(4); EP(C)A Sch.13 para.10; EA 1980 Sch.1 para.31; TURERA Sch.8 para.31(b); STA Sch.4 para.12(4); D & COA Sch.8.
(5)	BGLA Sch.5A para.2(4)(c), (d); STA Sch.4 para.2(4)(c), (d); D & COA Sch.8.
38(1), (2)	BGLA Sch.5A para.14; STA Sch.4 para.14; D & COA Sch.8.
(3)	BGLA Sch.5A para.2(4)(e); STA Sch.4 para.2(4)(e); D & COA Sch.8.
39(1) to (3)	BGLA Sch.5A para.15(1); STA Sch.4 para.15(1); D & COA Sch.8.
(4)	BGLA Sch.5A para.15(2); STA Sch.4 para.15(2); D & COA Sch.8.
(5)	BGLA Sch.5A para.2(4)(f); STA Sch.4 para.2(4)(f); D & COA Sch.8.
40(1)	BGLA Sch.5A para.4(2); STA Sch.4 para.4(2); D & COA Sch.8.
(2)	BGLA Sch.5A para.4(3); STA Sch.4 para.4(3); D & COA Sch.8.
(3)	BGLA Sch.5A para.4(1); STA Sch.4 para.4(1); D & COA Sch.8.
41(1)	BGLA Sch.5A para.5(1); STA Sch.4 para.5(1); D & COA Sch.8.
(2)	BGLA Sch.5A para.5(5); STA Sch.4 para.5(5); D & COA Sch.8.
(3)	BGLA Sch.5A para.6; STA Sch.4 para.6; D & COA Sch.8.
42(1) to (3)	BGLA Sch.5A para.11(1) to (3); STA Sch.4 para.11(1) to (3); D & COA Sch.8.
(4)	STA Sch.4 para.11(4).
(5)	BGLA Sch.5A para.11(4); D & COA Sch.8.
(6)	BGLA Sch.5A para.11(5); STA Sch.4 para.11(5); D & COA Sch.8.
43(1), (2)	BGLA Sch.5A para.13(1), (2); STA Sch.4 para.13(1), (2); D & COA Sch.8.
(3)	BGLA Sch.5A paras.5(5)(b), 13(3); STA Sch.4 paras.5(5)(b); 13(3); D & COA Sch.8.
(4)	BGLA Sch.5A para.13(4); EP(C)A Sch.13 para.10; EA 1980 Sch.1 para.31; TURERA Sch.8 para. 31(b); STA Sch.4 para.13(4); D & COA Sch.8.
(5)	BGLA Sch.5A para.5(2)(c), (d); STA Sch.4 para.5(2)(c), (d); D & COA Sch.8.
44	EP(C)A s.22A; TURERA Sch.5 para.1.
45(1) to (3)	BGLA Sch.5A para.10(1) to (3); STA Sch.4 para.10(1) to (3); D & COA Sch.8.
(4)	BGLA Sch.5A paras.1(1) ("dismissal"), 10(4); STA Sch.4 paras.1(1) ("dismissal"), 10(4); D & COA Sch.8.
(5)	BGLA Sch.5A para.10(5); STA Sch.4 para.10(5); D & COA Sch.8.
(6) to (8)	BGLA Sch.5A para.10(6); STA Sch.4 para.10(6); D & COA Sch.8.
(9)	BGLA Sch.5A paras.2(4)(b), 5(2)(b); STA Sch.4 paras.2(4)(b); 5(2)(b); D & COA Sch.8.
(10)	BGLA Sch.5A paras.2(6), 5(4); STA Sch.4 paras.2(6), 5(4); D & COA Sch.8.
46(1)	PA s.46(1).
(2)	PA s.46(2), (10).
(3)	PA ss.124(1) ("trust scheme"), 176 ("occupational pension scheme").
47	EP(C)A s.22AA; CRTUPER Reg.12(1).
48(1)	BGLA Sch.5A para.16; EP(C)A s.22B(1); TURERA Sch.5 para.1; STA Sch.4 para.16; D & COA Sch.8; PA s.46(3); CRTUPER Reg.12(2).
(2) to (4)	EP(C)A s.22B(2) to (4); TURERA Sch.5 para.1.
49	EP(C)A s.22C; TURERA Sch.5 para.1
50(1)	EP(C)A s.29(1).
(2)	EP(C)A s.29(1); Time Off for Public Duties Order 1990 (S.I.1990/1870) Art.2; Time Off for Public Duties Order 1995 (S.I.1995/694) Art.2; Environment Act 1995 (Consequential Amendment) Regulations 1996 (S.I.1996/593) Sch.1 para.19; Environment Act 1995 (Consequential and Transitional Provisions) (Scotland) Regulations 1996 (S.I.1996/973) Sch. para.4.
(3)	EP(C)A s.29(3).
(4)	EP(C)A s.29(4); TULR(C)A Sch.2 para.11.
(5)	EP(C)A s.29(1), (2)(a); Norfolk and Suffolk Broads Act 1988 (c.4) Sch.6

Provision	Derivation
	para.19; Local Government etc. (Scotland) Act 1994 (c.39) s.183(2)(a); Environment Act 1995 (c.25) Sch.7 para.11(3).
(6)	EP(C)A s.29(1)(bc); Police Act 1996 (c.16) Sch.8 para.1(4); Time Off for Public Duties Order 1995 (S.I.1995/694) Art.2.
(7)	EP(C)A s.29(1)(cc); Time Off for Public Duties Order 1990 (S.I.1990/1870) Art.2.
(8)	EP(C)A s.29(1)(d), (2)(b); National Health Service (Scotland) Act 1978 (c.29) Sch.15 para.2; National Health Service and Community Care Act 1990 (c.19) Sch.9 para.20; Health Authorities Act 1995 (c.17) Sch.1 para.103(2).
(9)	EP(C)A s.29(1)(e) to (eg), (2)(c); Education Reform Act 1988 (c.40) Sch.12 Pt.I para.23, Pt.III para.80; Self-governing Schools etc. (Scotland) Act 1989 (c.39) Sch.10 para.7; Further and Higher Education Act 1992 (c.13) Sch.8 Pt.II para.89; Further and Higher Education (Scotland) Act 1992 (c.37) Sch.9 para.6.
(10)	EP(C)A s.29(5).
(11)	EP(C)A s.32, TULR(C)A Sch.2 para.13.
51(1)	EP(C)A s.29(6).
(2)	EP(C)A s.30(1); TULR(C)A Sch.2 para.12(a).
(3)	EP(C)A s.30(2); TULR(C)A Sch.2 para.12(b).
(4)	EP(C)A s.30(2).
52(1), (2)	EP(C)A s.31(1), (2).
(3)	EP(C)A s.32; TULR(C)A Sch.2 para.13.
53(1)	EP(C)A s.31(3)
(2), (3)	EP(C)A s.31(4).
(4)	EP(C)A s.31(5).
(5)	EP(C)A s.31(9).
(6), (7)	EP(C)A s.31(10), (11).
54	EP(C)A s.31(6) to (9).
55(1) to (3)	EP(C)A s.31A(1) to (3); EA 1980 s.13.
(4)	EP(C)A s.32; TULR(C)A Sch.2 para.13.
56(1)	EP(C)A s.31A(4); EA 1980 s.13.
(2) to (4)	EP(C)A s.31A(5); EA 1980 s.13.
(5), (6)	EP(C)A s.31A(9), (10); EA 1980 s.13.
57(1), (2)	EP(C)A s.31A(6), (7); EA 1980 s.13.
(3) to (5)	EP(C)A s.31A(8); EA 1980 s.13.
58(1), (2)	PA s.42(1), (2).
(3)	PA ss.124(1) ("employer", trust scheme"), 176 ("occupational pension scheme").
(4)	PA s.42(4).
59(1) to (4)	PA s.43(1) to (4).
(5), (6)	PA s.43(5).
60(1)	PA ss.42(3), 43(6).
(2)	PA s 44.
(3) to (5)	PA s ·5(1) to (3).
61(1)	EP(C)A s.31AA(1); CRTUPER Reg.13(1).
(2)	EP(C)A s.32; TULR(C)A Sch.2 para.13; CRTUPER Reg.13(2).
62(1)	EP(C)A ss.31A(4), 31AA(2), (3)(a); EA 1980 s.13; CRTUPER Reg.13(1).
(2) to (4)	EP(C)A ss.31A(5), 31AA(2); EA 1980 s.13; CRTUPER Reg.13(1).
(5), (6)	EP(C)A ss.31A(9), (10), 31AA(2); EA 1980 s.13; CRTUPER Reg.13(1).
63(1)	EP(C)A ss.31A(6), 31AA(2); EA 1980 s.13; CRTUPER Reg.13(1).
(2)	EP(C)A ss.31A(7), 31AA(2), (3)(b); EA 1980 s.13; CRTUPER Reg. 13(1).
(3) to (5)	EP(C)A ss.31A(8), 31AA(2); EA 1980 s.13; CRTUPER Reg.13(1).
64(1), (2)	EP(C)A s.19(1).
(3)	EP(C)A Sch.1; Employment Protection (Medical Suspension) Order 1980 (S.I.1980/1581); Employment Protection (Medical Suspension) Order

Provision	Derivation
	1985 (S.I.1985/1787); Employment Protection (Medical Suspension) Order 1988 (S.I. 1988/1746).
(4)	EP(C)A s.19(3).
(5)	EP(C)A s.19(2).
65	EP(C)A s.20; EA 1982 Sch.2 para.2.
66(1)	EP(C)A s.45(1); TURERA Sch.3.
(2)	EP(C)A s.45(1), (3); TURERA Sch.3.
(3)	EP(C)A s.45(2); TURERA Sch.3.
67	EP(C)A s.46(1), (2); TURERA Sch.3.
68	EP(C)A s.47(1), (2); TURERA Sch.3.
69(1)	EP(C)A ss.21(1), 47(3); TURERA Sch.3.
(2)	EP(C)A ss.21(2), 47(4); TURERA Sch.3.
(3)	EP(C)A ss.21(3), 47(5); TURERA Sch.3.
70(1)	EP(C)A ss.22(1), 47(6); TURERA Sch.3.
(2)	EP(C)A ss.22(2), 47(7); TURERA Sch.3.
(3)	EP(C)A ss.22(3), 47(8); TURERA Sch.3.
(4) to (7)	EP(C)A s.46(3) to (6); TURERA Sch.3.
71	EP(C)A s.33; TURERA s.23(2).
72	EP(C)A s.34(1) to (3); TURERA s.23(2).
73(1) to (3)	EP(C)A s.35(1) to (3); TURERA s.23(2).
(4)	EP(C)A s.35(2); TURERA s.23(2).
(5)	EP(C)A s.35(4).
74(1)	EP(C)A s.36(1)(a), (3); TURERA s.23(2).
(2)	EP(C)A s.36(2); TURERA s.23(2).
(3)	EP(C)A s.36(1)(a); TURERA s.23(2).
(4)	EP(C)A s.36(1)(b), (3); TURERA s.23(2).
(5)	EP(C)A s.36(1)(c), (3); TURERA s.23(2).
(6)	EP(C)A s.36(1); TURERA s.23(2)
75	EP(C)A s.37; TURERA s.23(2).
76	EP(C)A s.37A; TURERA s.23(2)
77(1), (2)	EP(C)A s.38(1); TURERA s.23(2).
(3)	EP(C)A s.38(2); TURERA s.23(2)
78	EP(C)A s.38A; TURERA s.23(2).
79	EP(C)A s.39(1) to (3); TURERA Sch.2.
80	EP(C)A s.40; TURERA Sch.2.
81	EP(C)A s.41; TURERA Sch.2.
82(1), (2)	EP(C)A s.42(1), (2); TURERA Sch.2.
(3), (4)	EP(C)A s.42(3); TURERA Sch.2.
(5) to (7)	EP(C)A s.42(4) to (6); TURERA Sch.2.
(8), (9)	EP(C)A s.42(7), (4); TURERA Sch.2.
83	EP(C)A s.43(3), (4); TURERA Sch.2.
84	EP(C)A Sch.2 Pt.III para.6(1), (2), (4)(b); TURERA Sch.8 para.26(d)
85	EP(C)A s.44; TURERA Sch.2.
86(1) to (3)	EP(C)A s.49(1) to (3); EA 1982 Sch.2 para.3(1).
(4)	EP(C)A s.49(4); EA 1982 Sch.2 para.3(2).
(5)	EP(C)A s.49(4A); EA 1982 Sch.2 para.3(3).
(6)	EP(C)A s.49(5).
87(1), (2)	EP(C)A s.50(1), (2); EA 1982 Sch.2 para.3(1).
(3)	EP(C)A Sch.3 para.1.
(4)	EP(C)A s.50(3).
88(1)	EP(C)A Sch.3 para.2(1); TURERA Sch.8 para.27(a)(i), (ii).
(2)	EP(C)A Sch.3 para.2(2); Social Security and Housing Benefits Act 1982 (c.24) Sch.2 para.13; TURERA Sch.8 para.27(a)(iii).
(3)	EP(C)A Sch.3 para.2(3).
89(1), (2)	EP(C)A Sch.3 para.3(1), (2).
(3)	EP(C)A Sch.3 para.3(3); TURERA Sch.8 para.27(b)(i).

Provision	Derivation
(4)	EP(C)A Sch.3 para.3(3; Social Security and Housing Benefits Act 1982 (c.24) Sch.2 para.13; TURERA Sch.8 para.27(b)(ii).
(5)	EP(C)A Sch.3 para.3(4).
90(1)	EP(C)A Sch.3 para.4(1); Social Security (Incapacity for Work) Act 1994 (c.18) Sch.1 Pt.II para.54.
(2)	EP(C)A Sch.3 para.4(2).
91(1)	EP(C)A Sch.3 para.5; TURLR(C)A Sch.2 para.23.
(2)	EP(C)A Sch.3 para.6.
(3)	EP(C)A Sch.3 para.7(1).
(4)	EP(C)A Sch.3 para.7(2).
(5)	EP(C)A s.51.
(6)	EP(C)A s.52.
92(1), (2)	EP(C)A s.53(1).
(3)	EP(C)A s.53(2); EA 1982 Sch.2 para.4; EA 1989 s.15(1).
(4)	EP(C)A s.53(2A); TURERA s.24(4).
(5)	EP(C)A s.53(3).
(6)	EP(C)A s.55(4); 153(1) ("effective date of termination").
(7)	EP(C)A ss.55(5), 153(1) ("effective date of termination"); EA 1982 Sch.3 Pt.I para.1.
(8)	EP(C)A s.55(7)(a); EA 1982 Sch.3 Pt.I para.1.
93(1)	EP(C)A s.53(4); TURERA Sch.8 para.11.
(2)	EP(C)A s.53(4).
(3)	EP(C)A s.53(5).
94(1)	EP(C)A s.54(1).
(2)	EP(C)A s.54(2).
95	EP(C)A s.55(1) to (3).
96(1)	EP(C)A s.56; EA 1980 Sch.1 para.11; TURERA Sch.8 para.12.
(2) to (4)	EP(C)A s.56A(1) to (3); EA 1980 s.12; TURERA Sch.8 para.13.
(5)	EP(C)A s.56A(4); EA 1980 s.12.
(6)	BGLA Sch.5A para.1(4); STA Sch.4 para.1(6); D & COA Sch.8.
97(1)	EP(C)A s.55(4).
(2)	EP(C)A s.55(5); EA 1982 Sch.3 Pt.I para.1.
(3)	EP(C)A s.55(7)(a); EA 1982 Sch.3 Pt.I para.1.
(4)	EP(C)A s.55(6); EA 1982 Sch.3 Pt.I para.1.
(5)	EP(C)A s.55(7)(b); EA 1982 Sch.3 Pt.I para.1.
(6)	EP(C)A Sch.2 Pt.I paras.1, 2(3)(a), (4).
98(1), (2)	EP(C)A s.57(1), (2).
(3)	EP(C)A s.57(4).
(4)	EP(C)A s.57(3); EA 1980 s.6.
(5)	EP(C)A Sch.2 Pt.I paras.1, 2(1); EA 1980 Sch.1 para.23.
(6)	EP(C)A s.57(3); Sch.2 Pt.I para.2(1); TULR(C)A Sch.2 paras.14, 22; TURERA Sch.5 para.2, Sch.8 para.26(a)(i).
99(1) to (3)	EP(C)A s.60; TURERA s.24(1).
(4)	EP(C)A Sch.2 Pt.I paras.1, 2(2); TURERA Sch.8 para.26(a)(ii).
100	EP(C)A s.57A; TURERA Sch.5 para.3.
101(1) to (3)	BGLA Sch.5A para.7(1) to (3); STA Sch.4 para.7(1) to (3); D & COA Sch.8.
(4)	BGLA Sch.5A paras.2(4)(a), 5(2)(a); STA Sch.4 paras.2(4)(a), 5(2)(a); D & COA Sch.8.
102(1)	PA s.46(5).
(2)	PA ss.124(1) ("trust scheme"), 176 ("occupational pension scheme").
103	EP(C)A s.57AA; CRTUPER Reg.14(1).
104(1) to (3)	EP(C)A s.60A(1) to (3); TURERA s.29(1).
(4)	BGLA Sch.5A para.19; EP(C)A s.60A(4); TURERA s.29(1); STA Sch.4 para.19; D & COA Sch.8; PA Sch.3 para.2.
105(1)	BGLA Sch.5A para.8; EP(C)A s.59(1); TURERA s.24(2), Sch.8 para.14(a); STA Sch.4 para.8; D&COA Sch.8; PA s.46(6).

Provision	Derivation
(2)	EP(C)A s.59(2); TURERA s.24(2).
(3)	EP(C)A s.59(2); TURERA s.24(2), Sch.5 para.4.
(4)	BGLA Sch.5A para.8; STA Sch.4 para.8; D & COA Sch.8.
(5)	PA s.46(6).
(6)	EP(C)A s.59(2); CRTUPER Reg.14(2).
(7)	EP(C)A s.59(2); TURERA ss.24(2), 29(2).
(8)	BGLA Sch.5A paras.2(4)(a), 5(2)(a); STA Sch.4 paras.2(4)(a), 5(2)(a); D & COA Sch.8.
(9)	EP(C)A s.59(3); TURERA Sch.8 para.14(c).
106(1)	EP(C)A s.61.
(2)	EP(C)A ss.19(2), 45(2), 61(1); TURERA Sch.3, Sch.8 para.15(a).
(3)	EP(C)A s.61(2); TURERA Sch.8 para.15(b).
(4)	EP(C)A s.61.
107	EP(C)A s.63.
108(1)	EP(C)A s.64(1)(a); Unfair Dismissal (Variation of Qualifying Period) Order 1985 (S.I.1985/782) Art.3(1).
(2)	EP(C)A s.64(2); EA 1982 Sch.2 para.5(1)(b); Unfair Dismissal (Variation of Qualifying Period) Order 1985 (S.I.1985/782) Art.4.
(3)	BGLA Sch.5A para.9; EP(C)A s.64(3) to (5), Sch.2 Pt.I paras.1, 2(4), Pt.III para.6(3); TURERA ss.24(3), 29(3), Sch.5 para.5; STA Sch.4 para.9; D & COA Sch.8; PA s.46(7); CRTUPER Reg.14(2).
109(1)	EP(C)A s.64(1)(b); Sex Discrimination Act 1986 (c.59) s.3(1).
(2)	BGLA Sch.5A para.9; EP(C)A s.64(3) to (5), Sch.2 Pt.I paras.1, 2(4), Pt.III para.6(3); TURERA ss.24(3), 29(3), Sch.5 para.5; STA Sch.4 para.9; D & COA Sch.8; PA s.46(7); CRTUPER Reg.14(2).
110(1)	EP(C)A s.65(3).
(2)	BGLA Sch.5A para.20; EP(C)A s.65(4), Sch.2 Pt.I paras.1, 2(4), Pt.III para.6(3); TURERA Sch.8 para.16; STA Sch.4 para.20; D & COA Sch.8.
(3)	EP(C)A s.65(1), (2).
(4)	EP(C)A s.66(2); EA 1980 Sch.1 para.13(b).
(5)	EP(C)A s.66(3).
111(1), (2)	EP(C)A s.67(1), (2).
(3), (4)	EP(C)A s.67(4).
112(1)	EP(C)A s.68(1), (2).
(2), (3)	EP(C)A s.68(1).
(4)	EP(C)A s.68(2); EA 1982 Sch.3 Pt.II para.21.
113	EP(C)A s.69(1).
114(1), (2)	EP(C)A s.69(2).
(3)	EP(C)A s.69(3).
(4)	EP(C)A s.70(2).
(5)	EP(C)A Sch.2 Pt.I paras.1, 2(3)(b).
115(1)	EP(C)A s.69(1), (4).
(2)	EP(C)A s.69 (4).
(3)	EP(C)A s.70(2).
(4)	EP(C)A Sch.2 Pt.I paras.1, 2(3)(b).
116(1)	EP(C)A s.69(5).
(2) to (4)	EP(C)A s.69(6).
(5), (6)	EP(C)A s.70(1).
117(1)	EP(C)A s.71(1).
(2)	EP(C)A s.71(1); TURERA s.30(2)(a).
(3)	EP(C)A s.71(2); EA 1982 Sch.3 Pt.II para.22; TURERA Sch.5 para.6(a).
(4)	EP(C)A s.71(2) to (2B); TURERA Sch.5 para.6(b); PA Sch.3 para.3; CRTUPER Reg.14(3).
(5)	EP(C)A s.71(2).
(6), (7)	EP(C)A s.71(3), (4)
(8)	EP(C)A s.71(5); EA 1982 Sch.3 Pt.II para.22.

Provision	Derivation
118(1)	EP(C)A s.72(1); TULR(C)A Sch.2 para.16; TURERA Sch.5 para.7.
(2)	EP(C)A s.72(2); TURERA Sch.5 para.7.
(3)	EP(C)A s.72(2), (3); TURERA Sch.5 para.7; PA Sch.3 para.4; CRTUPER Reg.14(3).
119(1)	EP(C)A s.73(1), (3); EA 1980 s.9(2); TURERA Sch.5 para.8(a).
(2)	EP(C)A s.73(3); EA 1980 s.9(3).
(3)	EP(C)A s.73(4),
(4)	EP(C)A s.73(5), (6); Sex Discrimination Act 1986 (c.59) s.3(2).
(5)	EP(C)A s.73(6).
(6)	EP(C)A Sch.2 Pt.I paras.1, 2(4).
120(1)	EP(C)A s.73(6A), (6B); TURERA Sch.5 para.8(b); PA Sch.3 para.5; Employment Protection (Increase of Limits) Order 1995 (S.I.1995/1953) Art.3, Sch.; CRTUPER Reg.14(3).
(2)	EP(C)A s.73(6C); TURERA Sch.5 para.8(b).
121	EP(C)A s.73(2).
122(1), (2)	EP(C)A s.73(7A), 7B; EA 1980 s.9(4).
(3)	EP(C)A s.73(6B), (7C); TULR(C)A Sch.2 para.17; TURERA Sch.5 para.8(b), (c); PA Sch.3 para.5; CRTUPER Reg.14(3).
(4)	EP(C)A s.73(9).
123(1)	EP(C)A s.74(1); TURERA s.30(3)(a).
(2)	EP(C)A s.74(2).
(3)	EP(C)A s.74(3); EA 1982 Sch.3 Pt.II para.23.
(4) to (7)	EP(C)A s.74(4) to (7).
124(1)	EP(C)A s.75(1); Employment Protection (Increase of Limits) Order 1995 (S.I.1995/1953) Art.3, Sch.
(2)	EP(C)A s.75(2).
(3)	EP(C)A s.71(1A); TURERA s.30(2)(b).
(4)	EP(C)A s.74(8); TURERA s.30(3)(b).
(5)	EP(C)A s.75(3).
125(1), (2)	EP(C)A s.75A(1), (2); TURERA Sch.5 para.9; Employment Protection (Increase of Limits) Order 1995 (S.I.1995/1953) Art.3, Sch.
(3) to (7)	EP(C)A s.75A(3) to (7); TURERA Sch.5 para.9.
126	EP(C)A s.76(1).
127	EP(C)A Sch.2 Pt.III para.6(1), (4)(a).
128(1)	EP(C)A s.77(1); TURERA Sch.5 para.10; PA Sch.3 para.6; CRTUPER Reg.14(3).
(2) to (5)	EP(C)A s.77(2) to (5); TURERA Sch.5 para.10.
129(1)	EP(C)A s.77A(1); TURERA Sch.5 para.10; PA Sch.3 para.7; CRTUPER Reg.14(3).
(2), (3)	EP(C)A s.77A(2); TURERA Sch.5 para.10.
(4), (5)	EP(C)A s.77A(3), (4); TURERA Sch.5 para.10.
(6) to (8)	EP(C)A s.77A(5); TURERA Sch.5 para.10.
(9)	EP(C)A s.77A(6); TURERA Sch.5 para.10.
130	EP(C)A s.78; TURERA Sch.5 para.10.
131	EP(C)A s.78A; TURERA Sch.5 para.10.
132	EP(C)A s.79; TURERA Sch.5 para.10.
133(1)	EP(C)A Sch.12 Pt.II paras.7, 8.
(2)	EP(C)A Sch.12 Pt.II para.9; EA 1982 Sch.3 Pt.II para.28.
(3), (4)	EP(C)A Sch.12 Pt.II para.10.
(5)	EP(C)A Sch.12 Pt.II para.11.
134	EP(C)A s.80.
135	EP(C)A s.81(1).
136(1)	EP(C)A s.83(1), (2).
(2)	EP(C)A ss.83(2), 92(4).
(3)	EP(C)A s.85(1), (2).
(4)	EP(C)A s.85(5).
(5)	EP(C)A s.93(1).

Provision	Derivation
137(1)	EP(C)A s.86, Sch.2 Pt.II paras.3, 4(2); TURERA Sch.8 para.17.
(2)	EP(C)A Sch.2 Pt.II paras.3, 5; TURERA Sch.8 para.26(c).
138(1)	EP(C)A s.84(1).
(2)	EP(C)A s.84(3), (6).
(3)	EP(C)A s.84(4).
(4), (5)	EP(C)A s.84(6).
(6)	EP(C)A s.84(5).
139(1), (2)	EP(C)A s.81(2).
(3)	EP(C)A s.81(2A), EA 1982 Sch.3 Pt.I para.2(1).
(4), (5)	EP(C)A s.93(2), (3).
(6)	EP(C)A s.81(3).
140(1)	EP(C)A s.82(2).
(2)	EP(C)A s.92(1).
(3), (4)	EP(C)A s.92(3).
(5)	EP(C)A s.92(2).
141(1)	EP(C)A s.82(3).
(2), (3)	EP(C)A s.82(5).
(4)	EP(C)A s.82(6).
142(1), (2)	EP(C)A s.85(3).
(3), (4)	EP(C)A s.85(4).
143(1)	EP(C)A s.110(1).
(2)	EP(C)A s.110(1), (2).
(3), (4)	EP(C)A s.110(5).
(5), (6)	EP(C)A s.110(6).
(7), (8)	EP(C)A s.110(4).
144(1)	EP(C)A s.110(3).
(2)	EP(C)A s.110(8).
(3)	EP(C)A s.110(9).
(4)	EP(C)A s.110(7).
145(1) to (4)	EP(C)A s.90(1).
(5), (6)	EP(C)A s.90(3).
(7)	EP(C)A Sch.2 Pt.II paras.3, 4(1)(a).
146(1)	EP(C)A ss.82(3), (5), (6), (7), 84(1), (3), (6), (7).
(2)	EP(C)A ss.82(4), 84(2).
(3)	EP(C)A Sch.2 Pt.II paras.3, 4(1)(b) (c); TURERA Sch.8 para.26(b)(i).
147	EP(C)A s.87.
148	EP(C)A s.88(1).
149	EP(C)A ss.88(4), 89(1), (4).
150(1), (2)	EP(C)A s.88(2).
(3), (4)	EP(C)A s.89(5), (6).
151	EP(C)A s.88(2)(b).
152(1)	EP(C)A s.88(3), (4).
(2)	EP(C)A s.89(1).
153	EP(C)A s.90(2).
154	EP(C)A s.89(2), (3).
155	EP(C)A s.81(1), (4).
156(1)	EP(C)A s.82(1); EA 1989 s.16(1)
(2)	EP(C)A Sch.2 Pt.II paras.3, 4(3).
157(1)	EP(C)A s.96(3)(a).
(2), (3)	EP(C)A s.96(1).
(4)	EP(C)A s.96(2).
(5)	EP(C)A s.96(4).
(6)	EP(C)A Sch.2 Pt.II paras.3, 4(3).
158	EP(C)A s.98.
159	EP(C)A s.99(1).
160(1)	EP(C)A s.99(2).

Provision	Derivation
(2), (3)	EP(C)A s.114.
161	EP(C)A s.100.
162(1)	EP(C)A s.81(1), Sch.4 paras.1, 2.
(2), (3)	EP(C)A Sch.4 paras.2, 3.
(4), (5)	EP(C)A Sch.4 para.4; EA 1989 s.16(2).
(6)	EP(C)A Sch.4 para.5.
(7)	EP(C)A Sch.2 Pt.II paras.3, 4(3)
(8)	EP(C)A Sch.4 para.6.
163(1) to (3)	EP(C)A s.91.
(4)	EP(C)A s.96(3)(b).
164	EP(C)A s.101.
165(1)	EP(C)A s.102(1).
(2)	EP(C)A s.102(2); Criminal Justice Act 1982 (c.48) ss.38, 46; Criminal Procedure (Consequential Provisions) (Scotland) Act 1995 (c.40) Sch.1.
(3)	EP(C)A s.102(3).
(4)	EP(C)A s.102(3); Criminal Justice Act 1982 (c.48) ss.35, 38, 46; Criminal Procedure (Consequential Provisions) (Scotland) Act 1995,(c.40) Sch.1.
166(1)	EP(C)A s.106(1).
(2), (3)	EP(C)A s.106(1A), (1B); EA 1989 Sch.6 para.21(2).
(4)	EP(C)A s.106(7).
(5)	EP(C)A s.106(5), (6).
(6)	EP(C)A s.106(5)(a), (b), (6)(a), (b); Insolvency Act 1985 (c.65) Sch.8 para.31(2); Bankruptcy (Scotland) Act 1985 (c.66) Sch.7 Pt.I para.14(1); Insolvency Act 1986 (c.45) Sch.14.
(7)	EP(C)A s.106(5)(c), (6)(c); Insolvency Act 1985 (c.65) Sch.8 para.31(2); Insolvency Act 1986 (c.45) Sch.14.
167(1)	EP(C)A s.106(2); Employment Act 1990 (c.38) Sch.2 para.1(3).
(2)	EP(C)A s.106(2); EA 1982 Sch.2 para.6(4); EA 1989 Sch.6 para.21(3).
(3)	EP(C)A s.106(3).
(4)	EP(C)A s.106(3); Employment Act 1990 (c.38) Sch.2 para.1(3).
168	EP(C)A Sch.7; EA 1989 Sch.6 para.25.
169(1)	EP(C)A s.107(1).
(2)	EP(C)A s.107(2); Criminal Justice Act 1982 (c.48) ss.38, 46; Criminal Procedure (Consequential Provisions) (Scotland) Act 1995 (c.40) Sch.1.
(3)	EP(C)A s.107(3).
(4)	EP(C)A s.107(4), (5); Magistrates' Courts Act 1980 (c.43) Sch.7 para.175.
170	EP(C)A s.108; EA 1989 Sch.6 para.22.
171(1)	EP(C)A s.115(2).
(2)	EP(C)A s.115(1); Social Security (Consequential Provisions) Act 1992 (c.6) s.2(4).
(3)	EP(C)A s.111(1), 115(1).
172	EP(C)A s.116.
173(1)	EP(C)A s.117(1), (2), (4).
(2)	EP(C)A Sch.8.
174(1) to (3)	EP(C)A Sch.12 Pt.III paras.12, 14, 15.
(4)	EP(C)A Sch.12 Pt.III paras.12, 16.
(5)	EP(C)A Sch.12 Pt.III paras.12, 14, 15.
(6)	EP(C)A Sch.12 Pt.III paras.12, 21.
175(1)	EP(C)A Sch.12 Pt.III paras.12, 17 to 20.
(2) to (4)	EP(C)A Sch.12 Pt.III paras.12, 17 to 19.
(5), (6)	EP(C)A Sch.12 Pt.III paras.12, 20.
176(1), (2)	EP(C)A Sch.12 Pt.IV para.22.
(3)	EP(C)A Sch.12 Pt.IV para.23(1).
(4)	EP(C)A Sch.12 Pt.IV paras.23(2), 24.
(5) to (7)	EP(C)A Sch.12 Pt.IV paras.25 to 27.
177(1)	EP(C)A s.112(2).
(2)	EP(C)A s.112(1).

Provision	Derivation
(3)	EP(C)A s.111(3); Transfer of Functions (Minister for the Civil Service and Treasury) Order 1981 (S.I.1981/1670); Transfer of Functions (Treasury and Minister for the Civil Service) Order 1995 (S.I.1995/269).
178	EP(C)A s.118.
179(1) to (5)	EP(C)A s.119.
(6)	EP(C)A s.117(3).
180	EP(C)A s.120.
181	—
182	EP(C)A s.122(1); Insolvency Act 1985 (c.65) s.218(2); Employment Act 1990 (c.38) Sch.2 para.1(4).
183(1)	EP(C)A s.127(1), (2).
(2)	EP(C)A s.127(1)(a), (b), (2)(a), (b); Insolvency Act 1985 (c.65) Sch.8 para.31(5); Bankruptcy (Scotland) Act 1985 (c.66) Sch.7 Pt.I para.14(4); Insolvency Act 1986 (c.45) Sch.14; EA 1989 Sch.6 para.23.
(3)	EP(C)A s.127(1)(c), (2)(c); Insolvency Act 1985 (c.65) Sch.8 para.31(5); Insolvency Act 1986 (c.45) Sch.14.
184(1)	EP(C)A s.122(3); EA 1982 Sch.3 Pt.I para.4.
(2)	EP(C)A s.122(4); Insolvency Act 1985 (c.65) s.218(4); TULR(C)A Sch.2 para.18(3); TURERA Sch.8 para.18.
(3)	EP(C)A s.127(3).
(4)	EP(C)A s.122(7), (8); Insolvency Act 1985 (c.65) s.218(5); Bankruptcy (Scotland) Act 1985 (c.66) s.75(11), Sch.7 Pt.I para.14(2); Insolvency Act 1986 (c.45) Sch.14.
185	EP(C)A s.122(2); Insolvency Act 1985 (c.65) s.218(3); TULR(C)A Sch.2 para.18(2).
186(1)	EP(C)A s.122(5); Employment Protection (Increase of Limits) Order 1995 (S.I.1995/1953) Art.3, Sch.
(2)	EP(C)A s.122(6).
187(1)	EP(C)A s.122(9), (10).
(2)	EP(C)A s.122(11); EA 1989 s.18(2).
(3)	EP(C)A s.122(10).
(4)	EP(C)A s.122(9); Insolvency Act 1985 (c.65) s.218(6)(a); Bankruptcy (Scotland) Act 1985 (c.66) s.75(11).
(5)	EP(C)A s.122(9); Insolvency Act 1985 (c.65) s.218(6)(b); Insolvency Act 1986 (c.45) Sch.14.
188(1), (2)	EP(C)A s.124(1).
(3)	EP(C)A s.124(3).
189(1)	EP(C)A s.125(1).
(2)	EP(C)A s.125(2); EA 1989 s.19(1).
(3), (4)	EP(C)A s.125(2A); EA 1989 s.19(1).
(5)	EP(C)A s.125(4); Employment Act 1990 (c.38) Sch.2 para.1(4).
190(1), (2)	EP(C)A s.126(1), (2).
(3), (4)	EP(C)A s.126(3), (4); Criminal Justice Act 1982 (c.48) ss.38, 46; Criminal Procedure (Consequential Provisions) (Scotland) Act 1995 (c.40) Sch.1.
(5), (6)	EP(C)A s.155(1), (2).
191(1), (2)	EP(C)A s.138(1), Sch.13 para.19(1); WA s.9(1); PA Sch.3 para.10.
(3)	EP(C)A s.138(2), Sch.13 para.19(2); WA s.9(2).
(4)	EP(C)A s.138(7), Sch.13 para.19(5); WA s.9(5).
(5)	EP(C)A s.138(8).
(6)	EP(C)A s.99.
192(1)	EP(C)A s.138(3), Sch.13 para.19(3); WA s.9(4); TURERA s.31(1); Reserve Forces Act 1996 (c.14) Sch.10 para.17.
(2)	EP(C)A s.138A(1); TURERA s.31(2); CRTUPER Reg.14(5).
(3) to (5)	EP(C)A s.138A(2) to (4); TURERA s.31(2).
(6)	EP(C)A s.138A(7) TURERA s.31(2).
(7)	EP(C)A s.138A(5); TURERA s.31(2)
(8)	EP(C)A s.138A(7); TURERA s.31(2).

Provision	Derivation
193(1)	EP(C)A s.138(4); TURERA Sch.7 para.3(b).
(2)	EP(C)A s.138(4); TURERA Sch.7 para.3(b); CRTUPER Regs.13(4), 14(4).
(3)	EP(C)A s.138(4).
194(1), (2)	EP(C)A s.139A(1); TURERA Sch.7 para.11.
(3)	EP(C)A s.139A(3)(b); TURERA Sch.7 para.11.
(4)	EP(C)A s.139A(2), (5); TURERA Sch.7 para.11.
(5) to (7)	EP(C)A s.139A(4) to (6); TURERA Sch.7 para.11.
195(1) to (3)	EP(C)A s.139(1).
(4)	EP(C)A s.139(2), (3).
(5) to (8)	EP(C)A s.139(3) to (6).
(9), (10)	EP(C)A s.139(7).
(11), (12)	EP(C)A s.139(8), (9).
196(1)	EP(C)A s.141(1); TURERA Sch.8 para.22.
(2)	EP(C)A s.141(2).
(3)	BGLA Sch.5A para.22; EP(C)A s.141(2); Insolvency of Employer (Excluded Classes) Regulations 1983 (S.I.1983/624) Reg.3(1); WA s.30(1); STA Sch.4 para.22; D & COA Sch.8; PA s.46(4)(b).
(4)	EP(C)A Sch.2 Pt.I paras.1, 2(4), PT.III para.6(1) to (3).
(5)	EP(C)A s.141(5); WA s.30(2).
(6)	EP(C)A s.141(3), (4).
(7)	EP(C)A s.141(2A); Insolvency of Employer (Excluded Classes) Regulations 1983 (S.I.1983/624) Reg.3(2); Insolvency of Employer (Excluded Classes) Regulations 1995 (S.I.1995/278) Reg.3.
197(1)	EP(C)A s.142(1); EA 1980 s.8(2).
(2)	BGLA Sch.5A para.7(4); STA Sch.4 para.7(4); D & COA Sch.8.
(3) to (5)	EP(C)A s.142(2) to (4).
198	EP(C)A s.5(1)(a); TURERA Sch.4.
199(1)	EP(C)A s.144(1); WA s.30(3); TURERA Sch.8 para.23.
(2)	EP(C)A s.144(2).
(3)	EP(C)A Sch.2 Pt.I paras.1, 2(4), PT.II paras.3, 4(3), PT.III para.6(1) to (3); Dock Work Act 1989 (c.13) s.7(4).
(4), (5)	EP(C)A s.144(4), (5).
(6)	EP(C)A s.144(3).
200(1)	EP(C)A s.146(2); Insolvency of Employer (Excluded Classes) Regulations 1983 (S.I.1983/624) Reg.3(3).
(2)	EP(C)A s.146(3); Criminal Justice and Public Order Act 1994 (c.33) s.126.
201(1)	EP(C)A s.137(2); WA s.10(1).
(2)	EP(C)A s.137(1); WA s.10(1).
(3), (4)	EP(C)A s.137(3), (4); WA s.10.
(5)	EP(C)A s.137(2). (5); WA s.10(1).
202(1)	EP(C)A s.146A(1); TURERA Sch.7 para.5.
(2)	EP(C)A s.146A(2); TURERA Sch.7 para.5. CRTUPER Regs.13(5), 14(4).
203(1)	BGLA Sch.5A para.17(1); EP(C)A s.140(1); WA s.6(3); STA Sch.4 para.17(1); D & COA Sch.8; PA s.46(8).
(2)	BGLA Sch.5A para.17(2); EP(C)A s.140(2); WA s.6(3); TURERA s.39(1)(a), Sch.6 para.3(a); STA Sch.4 para.17(2); D & COA Sch.8; PA s.46(9).
(3), (4)	EP(C)A s.140(3), (4); WA s.6(4), (5); TURERA s.39(1)(b), Sch.6 para.3(b).
204(1)	EP(C)A s.153(5).
(2)	EP(C)A s.153(5); TURERA Sch.8 para.25(b).
205(1)	BGLA Sch.5A para.22; EP(C)A s.129; STA Sch.4 para.22; D&COA Sch.8; PA ss.45(4), 46(4)(a).
(2)	WA s.6(1).
206(1)	EP(C)A Sch.12 Pt.I para.2

Provision	Derivation
(2)	BGLA Sch.5A para.22; EP(C)A Sch.12 Pt.I para.1; STA Sch.4 para.22; D & COA Sch.8; PA s.46(4)(c).
(3)	EP(C)A Sch.12 PT.I para.2.
(4), (5)	EP(C)A Sch.12 Pt.I para.3(1).
(6)	EP(C)A Sch.12 Pt.I para.3(2).
(7), (8)	EP(C)A Sch.12 Pt.I para.4(1).
(9)	EP(C)A Sch.12 Pt.I para.4(2).
207(1)	EP(C)A Sch.12 Pt.I para.5.
(2)	EP(C)A Sch.12 Pt.IV para.28.
(3)	EP(C)A Sch.12 Pt.I para.6.
208(1) to (5)	EP(C)A s.148(1) to (5).
(6), (7)	EP(C)A s.148(6).
209(1)	EP(C)A s.149(1).
(2)	EP(C)A s.149(2); EA 1982 Sch.2 para.9(1)(b), Sch.3 Pt.II para.25; TURERA Sch.8 para.24; CRTUPER Reg.14(6).
(3)	EP(C)A s.149(2).
(4)	EP(C)A s.149(1)(b).
(5)	EP(C)A s.149(1)(c); EA 1982 Sch.2 para.9(1)(a); EA 1989 s.15(2).
(6)	EP(C)A Sch.2 Pt.III para.7(1); TURERA Sch.8 para.26(e).
(7)	EP(C)A s.149(2A); TURERA Sch.7 para.13; CRTUPER Reg.12(4).
(8)	EP(C)A s.149(3).
210(1), (2)	BGLA Sch.5A para.1(2); EP(C)A s.151(1); EA 1982 Sch.2 para.7(1); STA Sch.4 para.1(4); D & COA Sch.8.
(3)	BGLA Sch.5A para.1(2), (3); EP(C)A s.151(2); EA 1982 Sch.2 para.7(1); STA Sch.4 para.1(4), (5); D & COA Sch.8.
(4)	EP(C)A Sch.13 para.1(1); EA 1982 Sch.2 para.7(2); Employment Protection (Part-time Employees) Regulation 1995 (S.I.1995/31) Reg.4(2).
(5)	EP(C)A Sch.13 para.1(3); EA 1982 Sch.2 para.7(1).
211	EP(C)A s.151(3) to (5); EA 1982 Sch.2 para.7(1).
212(1)	EP(C)A Sch.13 para.4.
(2)	EP(C)A Sch.13 para.10; EA 1980 Sch.1 para.31; TURERA Sch.8 para.31(b).
(3)	EP(C)A Sch.13 opara.9(1); TURERA Sch.8 para.31(a).
(4)	EP(C)A Sch.13 para.9(2).
213(1)	EP(C)A Sch.13 para.11(1); EA 1982 Sch.3 Pt.II para.29.
(2), (3)	EP(C)A Sch.13 para.11(2), (3).
214(1) to (3)	EP(C)A Sch.13 para.12(1), (2).
(4)	EP(C)A Sch.13 para.12(1).
(5)	EP(C)A Sch.13 para.12(3).
215(1)	EP(C)A Sch.13 para.1(2); EA 1982 Sch.2 para.7(2).
(2)	EP(C)A Sch.13 para.14(1); Social Security (Consequential Provisions) Act 1992 (c.6) Sch.2 para.51(1).
(3)	EP(C)A s.15(6)(a), Sch.13 para.14(3); EA 1982 Sch.2 para.7(1).
(4)	EP(C)A Sch.13 para.14(4); Social Security (Consequential Provisions) Act 1992 (c.6) Sch.2 para.51(2).
(5)	EP(C)A Sch.13 para.14(4).
(6)	EP(C)A Sch.13 para.14(6).
216(1)	EP(C)A Sch.13 para.15(1).
(2)	EP(C)A s.151(6)(b), Sch.13 para.15(2), (3); EA 1982 Sch.2 para.7(1).
(3)	EP(C)A s.151(6)(b), Sch.13 para.15(4); EA 1982 Sch.2 para.7(1).
217(1)	EP(C)A Sch.13 para.16(1); Reserve Forces (Safeguard of Employment) Act 1985 (c.17) Sch.4 para.6.
(2)	Interpretation Act 1978 (c.30) s.17(2)(a); EP(C)A s.151(6)(c); EA 1982 Sch.2 para.7(1).
218(1)	EP(C)A Sch.13 para.17(1); EA 1982 Sch.3 Pt.I para.2(2); Health Authorities Act 1995 (c.17) Sch.1 para.103(3).
(2) to (5)	EP(C)A Sch.13 para.17(2) to (5).

Provision	Derivation
(6)	EP(C)A Sch.13 para.18.
(7)	EP(C)A Sch.13 para.18A; EA 1982 Sch.3 Pt.I para.2(3).
(8) to (10)	EP(C)A Sch.13 para.18B; Health Authorities Act 1995 (c.17) Sch.1 para.103(3).
219(1)	EP(C)A Sch.13 para.20(1).
(2)	EP(C)A Sch.13 para.20(2), (3) ("relevant conciliation powers"); TURERA Sch.7 para.14; Disability Discrimination Act 1995 (c.50) Sch.6 para.3(b).
(3)	EP(C)A Sch.13 para.20(3) ("relevant complaint of dismissal"); TURERA Sch.7 para.14(d); Disability Discrimination Act 1995 (c.50) Sch.6 para.3(a).
(4)	EP(C)A Sch.13 para.20(3) ("relevant compromise contract"); TURERA Sch.7 para.14(d); Disability Discrimination Act 1995 (c.50) Sch.6 para.3(c).
220	—
221	EP(C)A Sch.14 Pt.II para.3.
222	EP(C)A Sch.14 Pt.II para.4.
223	EP(C)A Sch.14 Pt.II para.5.
224	EP(C)A Sch.14 Pt.II para.6.
225(1), (2)	EP(C)A Sch.14 Pt.II para.7.
(3)	EP(C)A Sch.14 Pt.II para.7; EA 1980 Sch.1 para.33.
(4)	EP(C)A Sch.14 Pt.II para.7; CRTUPER Reg.13(6).
(5)	EP(C)A Sch.14 Pt.II para.7; TURERA Sch.8 para.32(a).
226(1)	EP(C)A Sch.14 Pt.II para.7.
(2)	EP(C)A Sch.14 Pt.II para.7; TURERA Sch.8 para.32(b).
(3)	EP(C)A Sch.2 Pt.I paras.1, 2(4), (5), Sch.14 Pt.II para.7; EA 1982 Sch.3 Pt.II para.30(2); TURERA Sch.8 para.26(a)(iii).
(4)	EP(C)A Sch.14 Pt.II para.7.
(5)	EP(C)A Sch.2 Pt.I paras.3, 4(3), (4), Sch.14 Pt.II para.7; EA 1982 Sch.3 Pt.II para.30(2); TURERA Sch.8 para.26(b)(ii).
(6)	EP(C)A Sch.14 Pt.II para.7.
227(1)	EP(C)A Sch.14 Pt.II para.8(1); Employment Protection (Increase of Limits) Order 1995 (S.I.1995/1953) Art.3, Sch.
(2)	EP(C)A Sch.14 Pt.II para.8(2).
(3)	EP(C)A Sch.14 Pt.II para.8(3), (4); EA 1982 Sch.3 Pt.II para.30(3).
(4)	EP(C)A Sch.2 Pt.I paras.1, 2(4), Pt.II paras.3, 4(3), Sch.14 Pt.II para.8(3), (4).
228(1) to (3)	EP(C)A Sch.14 Pt.II para.9.
(4)	EP(C)A Sch.14 Pt.II para.12.
229(1)	EP(C)A Sch.14 Pt.II para.10.
(2)	EP(C)A Sch.14 Pt.II para.11.
230(1)	BGLA Sch.5A para.1(2); EP(C)A s.153(1) ("employee"); STA Sch.4 para.1(4); D & COA Sch.8; PA s.46(11).
(2)	BGLA Sch.5A para.1(2); EP(C)A s.153(1) ("contract of employment"); STA Sch.4 para.1(4); D & COA Sch.8; PA s.46(11).
(3)	WA s.8(1) ("worker"), (2).
(4)	BGLA Sch.5A para.1(2); EP(C)A s.153(1) ("employer"); WA s.8(1) ("employer"); STA Sch.4 para.1(4); D & COA Sch.8; PA s.46(11).
(5)	BGLA Sch.5A para.1(2); EP(C)A s.153(1) ("employment"); WA s.8(1) ("employment", "employed"); STA Sch.4 para.1(4); D & COA Sch.8; PA s.46(11).
231	EP(C)A s.153(4); WA s.6(6); TURERA Sch.6 para.3(b).
232(1)	STA Sch.4 para.1(1) ("shop worker").
(2)	STA Sch.4 para.1(1) ("shop work").
(3)	STA Sch.4 para.1(1) ("shop").
(4), (5)	STA Sch.4 para.1(2), (3).
(6)	STA Sch.4 para.1(1) ("retail trade or business").

Provision	Derivation
(7)	STA Sch.4 para.1(1) ("catering business", "intoxicating liquor").
(8)	STA Sch.4 para.1(1) ("notice period", "opted-out", "opting-in notice", "opting-out notice", "protected").
233(1)	BGLA Sch.5A para.1(1) ("betting worker"); D & COA Sch.8.
(2)	BGLA Sch.5A para.1(1) ("betting work"); D & COA Sch.8.
(3)	BGLA Sch.5A para.1(1) ("betting transaction"); D & COA Sch.8.
(4)	BGLA Sch.5A para.1(1) ("bookmaker"); D & COA Sch.8.
(5)	—
(6)	BGLA Sch.5A para.1(1) ("notice period", "opted-out", "opting-in notice", "opting-out notice", "protected"); D & COA Sch.8.
234(1), (2)	EP(C)A Sch.14 Pt.I para.1.
(3)	EP(C)A Sch.14 Pt.I para.2.
235(1)	
"act", "action"	BGLA Sch.5A para.1(2); EP(C)A s.153(1); STA Sch.4 para.1(4); D & COA Sch.8; PA s.46(11).
"basic award of compensation for unfair dismissal"	—
"business"	EP(C)A s.153(1).
"childbirth"	EP(C)A s.153(1); TURERA Sch.8 para.25(a)(i).
"collective agreement"	EP(C)A s.153(1); TULR(C)A Sch.2 para.21(2)(a).
"conciliation officer"	—
"dismissal procedures agreement"	EP(C)A s.153(1).
"employers' association"	EP(C)A s.153(1); TULR(C)A Sch.2 para.21(b).
"expected week of childbirth"	EP(C)A s.153(1); TURERA Sch.8 para.25(a)(ii).
"guarantee payment", "independent trade union", "job"	EP(C)A s.153(1).
"maternity leave period"	EP(C)A s.153(1); TURERA Sch.8 para.25(a)(iii).
"notified day of return"	EP(C)A s.153(1); TURERA Sch.8 para.25(a)(iv).
"position", "redundancy payment", "renewal"	EP(C)A s.153(1).
"statutory provision"	EP(C)A s.153(1); WA s.8(1).
"successor"	EP(C)A s.153(1); TULR(C)A Sch.2 para.21(2)(d).
"trade union"	EP(C)A s.153(1); TULR(C)A Sch.2 para.21(2)(f).
"week"	EP(C)A ss.49(6), 153(1), Sch.13 para.24(1).
(2)	EP(C)A s.153(4A); TULR(C)A Sch.2 para.21(3).
(3)	EP(C)A s.153(2).
(4)	EP(C)A ss.89(3), 92(5), Sch.13 para.24(1).
(5)	EP(C)A ss.89(3), 92(5), 110(9), Sch.3 para.6, Sch.13 para.24(1).
236(1)	BGLA Sch.5A para.11(6); EP(C)A s.154(1); STA Sch.4 para.11(6); D & COA Sch.8.
(2)	BGLA Sch.5A para.11(6); EP(C)A s.154(2); STA Sch.4 para.11(6); D & COA Sch.8.

Provision	Derivation
(3)	EP(C)A ss.34(4), 35(5), 39(4), 73(6D), 75(2), 75A(8), 138A(6), 149(4), Sch.2 Pt.III para.7(2); TURERA ss.23(2), 31(2), Sch.2, Sch.5 paras.8(b), 9, Sch.7 para.16(a).
(4)	EP(C)A s.149(5); TURERA Sch.7 para.16(b).
(5)	EP(C)A s.154(3).
237	EP(C)A s.156(2).
238(1)	EP(C)A s.157(1).
(2)	EP(C)A s.157(1); EA 1982 Sch.2 para.9(2).
(3) to (5)	EP(C)A s.157(3).
(6)	EP(C)A s.157(4).
239(1)	EP(C)A s.158(1).
(2)	EP(C)A s.158(2); Employment Act 1990 (c.38) Sch.2 para.1(6).
(3), (4)	EP(C)A s.158(3).
(5)	EP(C)A s.158(4).
240	—
241	—
242	—
243	—
244	—
245	—
Sch. 1	—
Sch. 2	—
Sch.3	—

TABLE OF DESTINATIONS

Betting, Gaming and Lotteries Act 1963
(c. 2)

1963	1996
Sched.5A	
para.1(1) ("betting transaction")	s.233(3)
para.1(1) ("betting work")	233(2)
para.1(1) ("betting worker")	233(1)
para.1(1) ("bookmaker")	233(4)
para.1(1) ("dismissal")	45(4)
para.1(1) ("notice period", "opted-out", "opting-in notice", "opting-out notice", "protected")	233(6)
para.1(1) ("the commencement date")	36(6)
para.1(2)	ss.210(1)–(3), 230(1), (2), (4), (5) s.235(1) "act", "action"

1963	1996
Sched.5A—cont.	
para.1(3)	s.210(3)
(4)	96(6)
para.2(1)	36(1)
(2)	36(2)
(3)	36(3)
(4)(a)	ss.101(4), 105(8)
(b)	s.45(9)
(e)	38(3)
(f)	39(5)
(6)	45(10)
(7)	36(4)
para.3(1)	36(5)
(b)	37(3)
(2)	36(6)
para.4(1)	40(3)
(2)	40(1)
(3)	40(2)
para.5(1)	41(1)
(2)(a)	ss.101(4), 105(8)
(b)	s.45(9)
(c)	43(5)
(d)	43(5)
(4)	45(10)
(5)	41(2)
(b)	43(3)
para.6	41(3)
para.7(1)–(3)	101(1)–(3)
(4)	197(2)
para.8	105(1), (4)

1963	1996
Sched.5A—cont.	
para.9	ss.108(3), 109(2)
para.10(1)–(3)	s.45(1)–(3)
(4)	45(4)
(5)	45(5)
(6)	45(6)–(8)
para.11(1)–(3)	42(1)–(3)
(4)	42(5)
(5)	42(6)
(6)	236(1), (2)
para.12(1)	37(1)
(2)	37(2)
(3)	37(3)
(4)	37(4)
(c)	37(5)
(d)	37(5)
para.13(1), (2)	43(1), (2)
(3)	43(3)
(4)	43(4)
para.14	38(1), (2)
para.15(1)	39(1)–(3)
(2)	39(4)
para.16	48(1)
para.17(1)	203(1)
(2)	203(2)
para.19	104(4)
para.20	110(2)
para.22	ss.196(3), 205(1), 206(2)

National Health Service (Scotland) Act 1978
(c. 29)

1978	1996
Sched.15, para.2	s.50(8)

Interpretation Act 1978
(c. 30)

1978	1996
s.17(2)(a)	s.217(2)

Employment Protection (Consolidation) Act 1978
(c. 44)

1978	1996
s.1(1)	s.1(1), (2)
(2)–(4)	1(3)–(5)
2(1)	2(1)
(2)(a)	ss.2(2), 6
(b)	s.2(3)
(3)	2(3)

1978	1996
(4)–(6)	2(4)–(6)
3(1)(a)	ss.3(1), 6
s.3(1)(b)	s.3(1)
(c)	ss.3(1), 6
(d)	s.3(5)
(2)–(4)	3(2)–(4)

1978	1996
s.4(1)	s.4(1), (2), (3)
(2)	4(2)
(3)(a)	ss.4(4), 6
(b)	s.4(5)
(4)	4(5), 6
(5)	4(6), (7)
(6)	4(8)

1978	1996
s.71(3), (4)....	s.117(6), (7)
(5)........	117(8)
72(1)........	118(1)
(2)........	118(2), (3)
(3)........	118(3)
73(1)........	119(1)
(2)........	121
(3)........	119(1), (2)
(4)........	119(3)
(5)........	119(4)
(6)........	119(4), (5)
(6A)......	120(1)
(6B)......	ss.120(1), 122(3)
(6C)......	s.120(2)
(6D)......	236(3)
73(7A), (7B)	122(1), (2)
(7C)......	122(3)
(9)......	122(4)
74(1)........	123(1)
(2)........	123(2)
(3)........	123(3)
(4)–(7)....	123(4)–(7)
(8)........	124(4)
75(1)........	124(1)
(2)........	ss.124(2), 236(3)
(3)........	s.124(5)
75A(1), (2)..	125(1), (2)
(3)–(7)..	125(3)–(7)
(8)......	236(3)
76(1)........	126
77(1)........	128(1)
(2)–(5)....	128(2)–(5)
77A(1)......	129(1)
(2)......	129(2), (3)
(3), (4)..	129(4), (5)
(5)......	129(6)–(8)
(6)......	129(9)
78	130
78A	131
79	132
80	134
81(1)........	ss.135, 155, 162(1)
(2)........	s.139(1), (2)
(2A)......	139(3)
(3)........	139(6)
(4)........	155
82(1)........	156(1)
(2)........	140(1)
(3)........	ss.141(1), 146(1)
(4)........	s.146(2)
(5)........	ss.141(2), (3), 146(1)
(6)........	141(4), 146(1)
(7)........	146(1)
83(1)........	136(1)
(2)........	136(1), (2)
84(1)........	ss.138(1), 146(1)
(2)........	s.146(2)
(3)........	ss.138(2), 146(1)
(4)........	s.138(3)
(5)........	138(6)
(6)........	ss.138(2), (4), (5), 146(1)

1978	1996
s.84(7)........	s.146(1)
85(1), (2)....	136(3)
(3)........	142(1), (2)
(4)........	142(3), (4)
(5)........	136(4)
86	137(1)
87	147
88(1)........	148
(2)........	150(1), (2)
(b)....	151
(3)........	152(1)
(4)........	ss.149, 152(1)
89(1)........	s.149
(2)........	154
(3)........	ss.154, 235(4), (5)
(4)........	s.149
89(5), (6)....	150(3), (4)
90(1)........	145(1)–(4)
(2)........	153
(3)........	145(5)
91	163(1)–(3)
92(1)........	140(2)
(2)........	140(5)
(3)........	140(3), (4)
(4)........	136(2)
(5)........	235(4), (5)
93(1)........	136(5)
(2), (3)........	139(4), (5)
96(1)........	157(2), (3)
(2)........	157(4)
(3)(a)....	157(1)
(b)....	163(4)
(4)........	157(5)
98	158
99	191(6)
(1)........	159
(2)........	160(1)
100	161
101	164
102(1)......	165(1)
(2)......	165(2)
(3)......	165(3), (4)
106(1)......	166(1)
106(1A), (B)	166(2), (3)
(2)......	167(1), (2)
(3)......	167(3), (4)
(5)......	166(5)
(a), (b)	166(6)
(c)....	166(7)
(6)	166(5)
(a), (b)	166(6)
(c)....	166(7)
(7)	166(4)
107(1)......	169(1)
(2)......	169(2)
(3)......	169(3)
(4), (5)...	169(4)
108	170
110(1)......	143(1), (2)
(2)......	143(2)
(3)......	144(1)
(4)......	143(7), (8)
(5)......	143(3), (4)
(6)......	143(5), (6)
(7)......	144(4)
(8)......	144(2)
(9)......	ss.144(3), 235(5)
s.111(1), (3)...	s.171(3)

1978	1996
s.112(1)	s.177(2)
(2)	177(1)
114	160(2), (3)
115(1)	171(2), (3)
(2)	171(1)
116	171
117(1), (2)...	173(1)
(3)	179(6)
(4)	173(1)
118	178
119	179(1)–(5)
120	180
122(1)	182
(2)	185
(3)	184(1)
(4)	ss.27(1), 184(1)
(5)	s.186(1)
(6)	186(2)
(9)	187(1), (4), (5)
(10)	187(1), (3)
(11)	187(2)
124(1)	188(1), (2)
(3)	188(3)
125(1)	189(1)
(2)	189(2)
(2A).....	189(3), (4)
(4)	189(5)
126(1), (2)...	190(1), (2)
126(3), (4)...	190(3), (4)
127(1)	183(1)
(a), (b)	183(2)
(c)....	183(3)
(2)	183(1)
(a), (b)	183(2)
(c)....	183(3)
(3)	s.184(3)
(7), (8)...	184(4)
129	205(1)
137(1)	201(2)
(2)	201(1), (5)
(3), (4)...	201(3), (4)
(5)	201(5)
138(1)	191(1), (2)
(2)	191(3)
(3)	192(1)
(4)	193(1), (2), (3)
(7)	191(4)
(8)	191(5)
138A(1).....	192(2)
(2)–(4).	192(3)–(5)
(5).....	192(7)
(6).....	236(3)
(7).....	192(6), (8)
139(1)	195(1)–(3)
(2)	195(4)
(3)	195(4), (5)–(8)
(4)–(6)...	195(5)–(8)
(7)	195(9), (10)
(8), (9)...	195(11), (12)
139A(1).....	194(1), (2)
(2).....	194(4)
(3)(b)..	194(3)
(5).....	s.194(4)
(4)–(6).	194(5)–(7)
140(1)	203(1)
(2)	203(2)
(3), (4)...	203(3), (4)

EMPLOYMENT ACT 1980
(C. 42)

MAGISTRATES' COURTS ACT 1980
(C. 43)

SOCIAL SECURITY AND HOUSING BENEFITS ACT 1982
(C. 24)

EMPLOYMENT ACT 1982
(c. 42)

1982	1996
Sched.2,	
para.1	s.29(1), (2), (3), (4)
para.2	65
para.3(1) . . .	ss.86(1)–(3), 87(1), (2)
(2) . . .	s.86(4)
(3) . . .	86(5)
para.4	92(3)
para.5(1)(b)	108(2)
para.6(4) . . .	167(2)
para.7(1) . . .	ss.210(1), (2), (3), (5), 211, 215(3), 216(2), (3), 217(2)

1982	1996
Sched.2—cont.	
para.7(2) . . .	s.210(4), 215(1)
para.9(1)(a)	209(5)
(b)	209(2)
(2) . . .	238(2)
Sched.3,	
Pt.I,	
para.1	ss.92(7), 92(8), 97(2), (3), (4), (5)
para.2(1) . . .	139(3)
(2) . . .	218(1)

1982	1996
Sched.3,	
Pt.I—cont.	
para.2(3) . . .	s.218(7)
para.4	184(1)
Pt.II,	
para.15	29(3)
para.21	112(4)
para.22	117(3), (8)
para.23	123(3)
para.25	209(2)
para.28	133(2)
para.29	213(1)
para.30(2) . .	226(3), (5)
(3) . .	227(3)

CRIMINAL JUSTICE ACT 1982
(c. 48)

1982	1996
s.35	s.165(4)
38	ss.165(2), (4), 169(2), 190(3), (4)
46	165(2), (4), 169(2), 190(3), (4)

RESERVE FORCES (SAFEGUARD OF EMPLOYMENT) ACT 1985
(c. 17)

1985	1996
Sched.4,	
para.6	s.217(1)

INSOLVENCY ACT 1985
(c. 65)

1985	1996
s.218(2)	s.182
218(4)	184(2)
218(3)	185
218(5)	184(4)
218(6)(a)	187(4)
(b)	187(5)
Sched.8,	
para.31(2) . .	166(6), (7)
(5) . .	183(2), (3)

BANKRUPTCY (SCOTLAND) ACT 1985
(c. 66)

1985	1996
s.75(11)	ss.184(4), 187(4)
Sched.7,	
Pt.I,	
para.14(1) . .	s.166(6)
(2) . .	184(4)
(4) . .	183(2)

TABLE OF DESTINATIONS

DOCK WORK ACT 1989
(C. 13)

EMPLOYMENT ACT 1989
(C. 38)

SELF-GOVERNING SCHOOLS ETC. (SCOTLAND) ACT 1989
(C. 39)

NATIONAL HEALTH SERVICE AND COMMUNITY CARE ACT 1990
(C. 19)

EMPLOYMENT ACT 1990
(C. 38)

SOCIAL SECURITY (CONSEQUENTIAL PROVISIONS) ACT 1992
(C. 6)

FURTHER AND HIGHER EDUCATION ACT 1992
(C. 13)

FURTHER AND HIGHER EDUCATION (SCOTLAND) ACT 1992
(C. 37)

TRADE UNION AND LABOUR RELATIONS (CONSOLIDATION) ACT 1992
(C. 52)

TRADE UNION REFORM AND EMPLOYMENT RIGHTS ACT 1993
(C. 19)

TABLE OF DESTINATIONS

PENSION SCHEMES ACT 1993
(C. 48)

1993	1996
Sched.8,	
para.11(1) . . .	s.11(3)

SOCIAL SECURITY (INCAPACITY FOR WORK) ACT 1994
(C. 18)

1994	1996
Sched.1,	
Pt.II,	
para.54	s.90(1)

SUNDAY TRADING ACT 1994
(C. 20)

1994	1996	1994	1996	1993	1996
Sched.4,		Sched.4—cont.		Sched.4—cont.	
para.1(1),		para.1(5)	s.210(3)	para.7(4)	s.197(2)
"the		(6)	96(6)	para.8	105(1), (4)
commence-		para.2(1)	36(1)	para.9	ss.108(3),
ment date" .	s.36(7)	(2)	36(2)		109(2)
"dismissal" .	45(4)	(3)	36(3)	para.10(1)–(3)	s.45(1)–(3)
"catering		(4)(a) .	ss.101(4),	(4) . . .	45(4)
business" . . .	232(7)		105(8)	(5) . . .	45(5)
"intoxicating		(b) .	s.45(9)	(6) . . .	45(6)–(8)
liquor"	232(7)	(c)..	37(5)	para.11(1)–(3)	42(1)–(3)
"notice		(d) .	37(5)	(4) . . .	42(4)
period"	232(8)	(e) .	38(3)	(5) . . .	42(6)
"opted-out"	232(8)	(f)..	39(5)	(6) . . .	236(1), (2)
"opting-in		(6)	45(10)	para.12(1) . . .	37(1)
notice"	232(8)	(7)	36(4)	(2) . . .	37(2)
"opting-out		para.3(1)	36(5)	(3) . . .	37(3)
notice"	232(8)	(1)(b) .	37(3)	(4) . . .	37(4)
"protected".	232(8)	(2)	36(6)	para.13(1) . . .	43(1), (2)
"retail trade		para.4(1)	40(3)	(2) . . .	43(1), (2)
or business"	232(6)	(2)	40(1)	(3) . . .	43(3)
"shop"	232(3)	(3)	40(2)	(4) . . .	43(4)
"shop work"	232(2)	para.5(1)	41(1)	para.14	38(1), (2)
"shop		(2)(a) .	ss.101(4),	para.15(1) . . .	39(1)–(3)
worker"	232(1)		105(8)	(2) . . .	39(4)
(2)	232(4), (5)	(b) .	s.45(9)	para.16	48(1)
(3)	232(4), (5)	(c)..	43(5)	para.17(1) . . .	203(1)
(4)	ss.210(1), (2),	(d) .	43(5)	(2) . . .	203(2)
	(3), 230(1),	(4)	45(10)	para.19	104(4)
	(2), (4), (5)	(5)	41(2)	para.20	110(2)
	s.235(1),	(b) .	43(3)	para.22	ss.196(3),
	"act"	para.6	41(3)		205(1), 206(2)
	"action"	para.7(1)–(3)	101(1)–(3)		

CRIMINAL JUSTICE AND PUBLIC ORDER ACT 1994
(C. 33)

1994	1996
s.126	s.200(2)

TABLE OF DESTINATIONS

LOCAL GOVERNMENT ETC. (SCOTLAND) ACT 1994
(C. 39)

1994	1996
s.183(2)(a)....	s.50(5)

DEREGULATION AND CONTRACTING OUT ACT 1994
(C. 40)

1994	1996
Sched.8.......	ss.36(1), (2),
	(3), (4), (5),
	(6), (7), 37(1),
	(2), (3), (4),
	(5), 38(1), (2),
	(3), 39(1)–(3),
	(4), (5), 40(1),
	(2), (3), 41(1),
	(2), (3),
	42(1)–(3), (5),
	(6), 43(1), (2),
	(3), (4), (5),
	45(1)–(3), (4),
	(5), (6)–(8),
	(9), (10),
	48(1), 96(6),
	101(1)–(3),
	(4) 104(4),
	105(1), (4),
	(8), 108(3),
	109(2),
	110(2),
	196(3),
	197(2),
	203(1), (2),
	205(1),
	206(2),
	210(1), (2),
	(3), 230(1),
	(2), (4), (5),
	233(1), (2),
	(3), (4), (6),
	235(1),
	"act"
	"action"
	236(1), (2)

HEALTH AUTHORITIES ACT 1995
(C. 17)

1995	1996
Sched.1,	
para.103(3) ..	ss.50(8), 218(1),
	(8)–(10)

ENVIRONMENT ACT 1995
(C. 25)

1995	1996
Sched.7,	
para.11(3) ...	s.50(5)

18–316

PENSIONS ACT 1995
(c. 26)

1995	1996	1995	1996	1995	1996
s.42(1), (2)....	s.58(1), (2)	s.46(6)........	s.105(1), (5)	s.176,	
(3)........	60(1)	(7)........	108(3), 109(2)	"occupational	
(4)........	58(4)	(8)........	203(1)	pension	
(6)........	60(1)	(9)........	203(2)	scheme".....	ss.46(3), 58(3),
43(1)–(4)....	59(1)–(4)	(10)	46(2)		102(2)
(5)........	59(5), (6)	(11)	230(1), (2),	Sched.3,	
44	60(2)		(4), (5)	para.2.......	s.104(4)
45(1)–(3)....	60(3)–(5)		235(1),	para.3.......	117(4)
(4)........	205(1)		"act"	para.4.......	118(3)
46(1)........	46(1)		"action"	para.5.......	ss.120(1),
(2)........	46(2)	124(1),			122(3)
(3)........	48(1)	"employer"..	58(3)	para.6.......	s.128(1)
(4)(a)....	205(1)	"trust		para.7.......	129(1)
(c)....	206(1)	scheme".....	ss.46(3), 58(3),		
(5)........	102(1)		102(2)		

CRIMINAL PROCEDURE (CONSEQUENTIAL PROVISIONS) (SCOTLAND) ACT 1995
(c. 40)

1995	1996
Sched.1.......	ss.165(2), (4),
	169(2),
	190(3), (4)

DISABILITY DISCRIMINATION ACT 1995
(c. 50)

1995	1996
Sched.6,	
para.3(a)	s.219(3)
(b)	219(2)
(c)	219(4)

RESERVE FORCES ACT 1996
(c. 14)

1996 (c.14)	1996
Sched.10,	
para.17......	s.192(1)

POLICE ACT 1996
(c. 16)

1996 (c. 16)	1996
Sched.8,	
para.1(4)	s.50(6)

EMPLOYMENT PROTECTION (MEDICAL SUSPENSION) ORDER 1980
(S.I. 1980 No. 1581)

1980	1996
	s.64(3)

TRANSFER OF FUNCTIONS (MINISTER FOR THE CIVIL SERVICE AND TREASURY) ORDER 1981
(S.I. 1981 No. 1670)

1981	1996
	s.177(3)

TABLE OF DESTINATIONS

TABLE OF DESTINATIONS

EMPLOYMENT PROTECTION (INCREASE OF LIMITS) ORDER 1995
(S.I. 1995 No. 1953)

COLLECTIVE REDUNDANCIES AND TRANSFER OF UNDERTAKINGS (PROTECTION OF EMPLOYMENT) (AMENDMENT) REGULATIONS 1995
(S.I. 1995 No. 2587)

ENVIRONMENT ACT 1995 (CONSEQUENTIAL AMENDMENTS) REGULATIONS 1996
(S.I. 1996 No. 593)

ENVIRONMENT ACT 1995 (CONSEQUENTIAL AND TRANSITIONAL PROVISIONS) (SCOTLAND) REGULATIONS 1996
(S.I. 1996 No. 973)

INDEX

References are to sections and Schedules

LAW REFORM (YEAR AND A DAY RULE) ACT 1996*

(1996 c. 19)

An Act to abolish the "year and a day rule" and, in consequence of its abolition, to impose a restriction on the institution in certain circumstances of proceedings for a fatal offence. [17th June 1996]

PARLIAMENTARY DEBATES
Hansard, H.C. Vol. 268, col. 1022; Vol. 271, col. 624. H.L. Vol. 569, col. 397; Vol. 571, col. 1227; Vol. 572, cols. 560, 980.

INTRODUCTION AND GENERAL NOTE
This short Act extending to England and Wales and Northern Ireland abolishes the long established common law rule whereby a person can only be charged with an offence of homicide if the victim dies within a year and a day of the defendant's act or omission. The Act provides procedural safeguards in respect of prosecution, in particular, to prevent any risk of double jeopardy. The Act is prospective in effect and abolishes the rule without replacement.

Although the rule has existed since the thirteenth century, the state of medical science has changed so significantly that not only can there now be a more accurate linking of injury with death, but also, victims can be kept artificially alive for long periods, thus rendering impossible prosecutions for their ultimate death. The Home Affairs Select Committee of the House of Commons examined the rule and recommended its abolition (Second Report, House of Commons, Home Affairs Committee, H.C. 428 Session 1994–95). The Law Commission issued a consultation paper in 1994 ("*The Year and a Day Rule in Homicide*", Law Commission Consultation Paper No. 136) and in its final report recommended abolition ("*Legislating the Criminal Code: The Year and a Day Rule in Homicide*", Law Com. No. 230, 1995). Much work in highlighting the effect of the rule had been carried out by Mr Alan Milburn M.P. as a result of a case involving one of his constituents.

The Bill introduced on December 13, 1995 was not amended in its progress through Parliament. The text of the Act is based largely on the draft Bill set out in Appendix A of the Law Commission Final Report.

COMMENCEMENT
Section 1 of the Act came into force on the date of Royal Assent (June 17, 1996). Section 2 comes into force at the end of the period of two months beginning with the day on which the Act was passed. In relation to the applicability of these provisions;
  (a) the year and a day rule will continue to apply to a case where the act or omission causing death occurred before June 17, 1996 (s.3(2)), and
  (b) the provisions of s.2 (when in force) will apply not only to the institution of proceedings in relation to a death which occurs after that date, but also in relation to a death which occurred after June 17, 1996 but before the commencement of s.2 (s.3(3)).

EXTENT
By virtue of s.3(4) the Act extends to England and Wales and Northern Ireland.

Abolition of "year and a day rule"

1. The rule known as the "year and a day rule" (that is, the rule that, for the purposes of offences involving death and of suicide, an act or omission is conclusively presumed not to have caused a person's death if more than a year and a day elapsed before he died) is abolished for all purposes.

GENERAL NOTE
The purpose of this section is to abolish the year and a day rule for all purposes.

"The rule"
Coke's definition of murder required that "the party wounded, or hurt, *etc.* die of the wound, or hurt, *etc.* within a year and a day after the same" (3 Coke's Institutes 47). That this require-

---

* Annotations by Ruth Harrison, LL.M.

ment still applied to homicide offences in the twentieth century was confirmed in *R v. Dyson* [1908] 2 K.B. 454 and in *R v. Inner West London Coroner ex p. De Luca* [1989] Q.B. 249. That the victim should die within a year and a day was not so much a "rule", therefore, as an element of the definition of the offence. The drafting of the Act may appear a little strange in this respect but it seems clear that it is intended to delete this aspect of Coke's definition.

"Offences involving death"
Apart from murder, the rule has also been held to apply to manslaughter (*R v. Dyson* [1908] 2 K.B. 454), infanticide by virtue of s.1(1) of the Infanticide Act 1938 (c. 36) (*R v. Inner West London Coroner ex p. De Luca* [1989] Q.B. 249), killings pursuant to a suicide pact under s.4(1) of the Homicide Act 1957 (c. 11) (*ex p. De Luca*), aiding and abetting suicide under s.2(1) of the Suicide Act 1961 (c. 60) (*ex p. De Luca*), verdicts of suicide returned by coroner's juries (*ex p. De Luca*) and probably, but there is no judicial authority, motoring offences under the Road Traffic Acts—causing death by dangerous driving (s.1 of the Road Traffic Act 1988 (c. 52)), causing death by careless driving when under the influence of drink or drugs (s.3A Road Traffic Act 1988 (c. 52)), and aggravated vehicle taking causing death (s.12(A) of the Theft Act 1968 (c. 60)).

Restriction on institution of proceedings for a fatal offence

2.—(1) Proceedings to which this section applies may only be instituted by or with the consent of the Attorney General.
    (2) This section applies to proceedings against a person for a fatal offence if—
   (a) the injury alleged to have caused the death was sustained more than three years before the death occurred, or
   (b) the person has previously been convicted of an offence committed in circumstances alleged to be connected with the death.
    (3) In subsection (2) "fatal offence" means—
   (a) murder, manslaughter, infanticide or any other offence of which one of the elements is causing a person's death, or
   (b) the offence of aiding, abetting, counselling or procuring a person's suicide.
    (4) No provision that proceedings may be instituted only by or with the consent of the Director of Public Prosecutions shall apply to proceedings to which this section applies.
    (5) In the application of this section to Northern Ireland—
   (a) the reference in subsection (1) to the Attorney General is to the Attorney General for Northern Ireland, and
   (b) the reference in subsection (4) to the Director of Public Prosecutions is to the Director of Public Prosecutions for Northern Ireland.

GENERAL NOTE
This section provides safeguards in relation to prosecutions, by requiring the consent of the Attorney General in two situations. The first is where the death of the victim occurs over three years after the injury is sustained (s.2(2)(a)). Section 2(2)(a) uses the word "injury" although s.1 refers to the "act of omission" causing death. Time will run from when the "injury" is sustained. Unlike the rule which has been abolished, delay between injury and death will not trigger the conclusive presumption, but it will activate the requirement for the Attorney General's consent to prosecute. The second situation is where the accused has previously been convicted of an offence in connection with the death (s.2(2)(b)). The plea of *autrefois convict* (or *autrefois acquit*) does not prevent a prosecution for a homicide offence (*R v. Thomas* [1950] 1 K.B. 26). It is to be noted there is no further elaboration of the type of offence nor any reference to the type or length of sentence imposed, save that the offence be "committed in circumstances alleged to be connected with the death".

"Fatal Offence"
See note to s.1 above. Whatever the doubts may have been over the applicability of the common law rule, the Act now clearly sets out the offences covered for the purposes of s.2(2).

Short title, commencement and extent

3.—(1) This Act may be cited as the Law Reform (Year and a Day Rule) Act 1996.

(2) Section 1 does not affect the continued application of the rule referred to in that section to a case where the act or omission (or the last of the acts or omissions) which caused the death occurred before the day on which this Act is passed.

(3) Section 2 does not come into force until the end of the period of two months beginning with the day on which this Act is passed; but that section applies to the institution of proceedings after the end of that period in any case where the death occurred during that period (as well as in any case where the death occurred after the end of that period).

(4) This Act extends to England and Wales and Northern Ireland.

GENERAL NOTE

The year and a day rule was not part of the law of Scotland.

INDEX

References are to sections

DOGS (FOULING OF LAND) ACT 1996

(1996 c. 20)

ARRANGEMENT OF SECTIONS

An Act to make provision with respect to the fouling of land by dogs.

[17th June 1996]

PARLIAMENTARY DEBATES
    Hansard, H.C. Vol. 268, col. 1022; Vol. 269, col. 1063; Vol. 274, col. 611. H.L. Vol. 570, col. 1640; Vol. 572, cols. 182, 1024, 1367.

INTRODUCTION
    This Act assists local authorities in the control of dog fouling in public areas and is applicable to all land in the open air to which the public have access. A list of exceptions to which the Act does not apply is provided in s.1(2) and (3).

Land to which Act applies

1.—(1) Subject to subsections (2) to (4) below, this Act applies to any land which is open to the air and to which the public are entitled or permitted to have access (with or without payment).

(2) This Act does not apply to land comprised in or running alongside a highway which comprises a carriageway unless the driving of motor vehicles on the carriageway is subject, otherwise than temporarily, to a speed limit of 40 miles per hour or less.

(3) This Act does not apply to land of any of the following descriptions, namely—

(a) land used for agriculture or for woodlands;

(b) land which is predominantly marshland, moor or heath; and

(c) common land to which the public are entitled or permitted to have access otherwise than by virtue of section 193(1) of the Law of Property Act 1925 (right of access to urban common land).

(4) Where a private Act confers powers for the regulation of any land, the person entitled to exercise those powers may, by notice in writing given to the local authority in whose area the land is situated, exclude the application of this Act to that land.

(5) For the purposes of this section, any land which is covered shall be treated as land which is "open to the air" if it is open to the air on at least one side.

(6) In this section—

"agriculture" includes horticulture, fruit growing, seed growing, dairy farming and livestock breeding and keeping, and the use of land as grazing land, meadow land, osier land, market gardens and nursery grounds;

"carriageway" has the same meaning as in the Highways Act 1980;

"common land" has the same meaning as in the Commons Registration Act 1965;

"speed limit" means a speed limit imposed or having effect as if imposed under the Road Traffic Regulation Act 1984.

Designation of such land

2.—(1) A local authority may by order designate for the purposes of this Act any land in their area which is land to which this Act applies; and in this Act "designated land" means land to which this Act applies which is for the time being so designated.

(2) The power conferred by subsection (1) above includes power to designate land either specifically or by description, and to revoke or amend orders previously made.

(3) The Secretary of State shall by regulations prescribe the form of orders under subsection (1) above, and the procedure to be followed in the making of such orders.

(4) Such regulations shall in particular include provision requiring local authorities to publicise the making and effect of such orders.

Offence

3.—(1) If a dog defecates at any time on designated land and a person who is in charge of the dog at that time fails to remove the faeces from the land forthwith, that person shall be guilty of an offence unless—

(a) he has a reasonable excuse for failing to do so; or

(b) the owner, occupier or other person or authority having control of the land has consented (generally or specifically) to his failing to do so.

(2) A person who is guilty of an offence under this section shall be liable on summary conviction to a fine not exceeding level 3 on the standard scale.

(3) Nothing in this section applies to a person registered as a blind person in a register compiled under section 29 of the National Assistance Act 1948.

(4) For the purposes of this section—

(a) a person who habitually has a dog in his possession shall be taken to be in charge of the dog at any time unless at that time some other person is in charge of the dog;

(b) placing the faeces in a receptacle on the land which is provided for the purpose, or for the disposal of waste, shall be a sufficient removal from the land; and

(c) being unaware of the defecation (whether by reason of not being in the vicinity or otherwise), or not having a device for or other suitable means of removing the faeces, shall not be a reasonable excuse for failing to remove the faeces.

Fixed penalty notices

4.—(1) Where on any occasion an authorised officer of a local authority finds a person who he has reason to believe has on that occasion committed an offence under section 3 above in the area of that authority, he may give that person a notice offering him the opportunity of discharging any liability to conviction for that offence by payment of a fixed penalty.

(2) Subsections (2) to (8) of section 88 of the Environmental Protection Act 1990 shall apply for the purposes of this section as they apply for the purposes of that section but as if references to a litter authority were references to a local authority.

(3) In subsection (8) of that section as it applies for the purposes of this section "chief finance officer", in relation to a local authority, means the person having responsibility for the financial affairs of the authority.

(4) In this section "authorised officer", in relation to a local authority, means any employee of the authority who is authorised in writing by the authority for the purpose of issuing notices under this section.

(5) In subsection (4) above, the reference to any employee of the authority includes references to—

(a) any person by whom, in pursuance of arrangements made with the authority, any functions relating to the enforcement of this Act fall to be discharged; and

(b) any employee of any such person.

Orders and regulations by Secretary of State

5.—(1) Any power of the Secretary of State to make an order or regulations under this Act shall be exercisable by statutory instrument.

(2) A statutory instrument containing an order or regulations under this Act shall be subject to annulment in pursuance of a resolution of either House of Parliament.

Effect of Act on byelaws

6.—(1) Subsections (2) and (3) below apply to any byelaw made by a local authority which has the effect of making any person in charge of a dog guilty of an offence if—

(a) he permits the dog to defecate on any land; or

(b) in a case where the dog defecates on any land, he fails to remove the faeces from the land.

(2) In so far as any byelaw to which this subsection applies would, apart from this subsection, have effect in relation to any designated land, the byelaw—

(a) shall cease to have effect in relation to the land; or

(b) where it is made after the order under section 2(1) above, shall not have effect in relation to the land.

(3) In so far as any byelaw to which this subsection applies still has effect at the end of the period of 10 years beginning with the day on which this Act comes into force, it shall cease to have effect at the end of that period in relation to any land to which this Act applies.

(4) Where any omission would, apart from this subsection, constitute an offence both under section 3 above and under any byelaw other than one to which subsections (2) and (3) above apply, the omission shall not constitute an offence under the byelaw.

Interpretation

7.—(1) In this Act "local authority"—

(a) in relation to England, means any unitary authority or any district council so far as they are not a unitary authority; and

(b) in relation to Wales, means the council of any county or county borough.

(2) The following are unitary authorities for the purposes of subsection (1)(a) above, namely—

(a) any county council so far as they are the council for an area for which there are no district councils;

(b) the council of any district comprised in an area for which there is no county council;

(c) any London borough council;

(d) the Common Council of the City of London; and

(e) the Council of the Isles of Scilly.

Short title, commencement and extent

8.—(1) This Act may be cited as the Dogs (Fouling of Land) Act 1996.

(2) This Act shall come into force at the end of the period of two months beginning with the day on which it is passed.

(3) This Act extends to England and Wales only.

INDEX

References are to sections

LONDON REGIONAL TRANSPORT ACT 1996

(1996 c. 21)

ARRANGEMENT OF SECTIONS

An Act to extend, and facilitate the exercise of, the powers of London Regional Transport to enter into and carry out agreements; and for connected purposes.   [17th June 1996]

PARLIAMENTARY DEBATES
Hansard, H.C. Vol. 272, col. 913, Vol. 273, col. 988, Vol. 275, col. 424. H.L. Vol. 571, col. 432, Vol. 572, cols. 77, 735, 1491.

INTRODUCTION
This Act extends the general and operating powers of London Regional Transport to enter into and carry out agreements.

Extension of general powers

1. After subsection (2) of section 3 of the London Regional Transport Act 1984 (general powers) there shall be inserted the following subsections—
"(2A) London Regional Transport shall also have power, with the consent of the Secretary of State, to enter into and carry out an agreement with any person for the carrying on by that person ('the contractor') of any activities which London Regional Transport does not have power to carry on if the agreement includes provision for one or more of the following, namely—
(a) the carrying on by the contractor of such activities as are mentioned in subsection (2) above;
(b) the provision by the contractor to London Regional Transport of services ancillary to the provision of public passenger transport services; and
(c) the use by the contractor of land or other property owned by London Regional Transport, or transferred to the contractor by London Regional Transport for the purposes of the agreement.
(2B) Where an agreement has been entered into under subsection (2) or (2A) above, the powers conferred on London Regional Transport by that subsection include power to enter into and carry out other agreements with other persons for the purpose of—
(a) fulfilling any condition which must be fulfilled before the agreement can have effect; or
(b) satisfying any requirement imposed by or under the agreement."

Extension of operating powers

2.—(1) After sub-paragraph (1) of paragraph 14 of Schedule 2 to the London Regional Transport Act 1984 (operating powers) there shall be inserted the following sub-paragraph—
"(1A) London Regional Transport may acquire land by agreement for the purposes of any agreement entered into by them under section 3(2) or (2A) of this Act."
(2) After paragraph 23 of that Schedule there shall be inserted the following paragraph—

"23A. Where any activities for which provision is made by an agreement under section 3(2) or (2A) of this Act cease to be carried on by the other party (whether by reason of the expiry or termination of the agreement or otherwise), London Regional Transport may, with the consent of the Secretary of State—

(a) acquire by agreement any land or other property used for the purpose of carrying on those activities; and

(b) in the case of an agreement under section 3(2A) of this Act, themselves carry on those activities notwithstanding that they would not otherwise have power to do so."

(3) At the end of paragraph 24 of that Schedule there shall be inserted the words ", or to secure the performance of any agreement entered into by them under section 3(2) or (2A) of this Act".

Supplementary transfers of functions

3. After section 31A of the London Regional Transport Act 1984 there shall be inserted the following section—

"Power of Secretary of State to transfer functions

31B.—(1) For the purpose of enabling any person to carry on any activities for which provision is made by an agreement under section 3(2) or (2A) of this Act, the Secretary of State may by order provide for any functions of London Regional Transport under any statutory provisions to be exercisable by that person (whether to the exclusion of or concurrently with London Regional Transport).

(2) An order under this section may—

(a) provide for the functions to cease to be so exercisable when the activities cease to be carried on by that person (whether by reason of the expiry or termination of the agreement or otherwise); and

(b) make such supplementary, incidental and consequential provision as the Secretary of State considers necessary or expedient.

(3) This section does not apply to any function of London Regional Transport under this Act or any other statutory provision specifically amended by any provision of this Act.

(4) Any reference in this section to London Regional Transport includes a reference to any subsidiary of theirs.

(5) A statutory instrument containing an order under this section shall be subject to annulment in pursuance of a resolution of either House of Parliament."

Minor and consequential amendments

4.—(1) In section 3 of the London Regional Transport Act 1984 (general powers)—

(a) in subsections (3) and (4), for the words "subsection (2)" there shall be substituted the words "subsection (2) or (2A)(a)";

(b) in subsections (5) and (6), for the words "subsection (2)" there shall be substituted the words "subsection (2) or (2A)"; and

(c) in subsection (8), for the words "subsection (2) or (7)" there shall be substituted the words "subsection (2), (2A) or (7)".

(2) In the following provisions, namely—

(a) section 11(3)(bb) of the Competition Act 1980;

(b) sections 8(a), 30(1)(a), 34(3)(c), 40(4)(b), 50(8)(a) and 51(3)(e) of, and paragraph 5(2)(a) of Schedule 2 to, the London Regional Transport Act 1984;

(c) subsections (1)(b), (2)(b), (4)(b), (5) and (7) of section 36 of the Transport Act 1985; and

(d) section 3(1)(b) of the London Regional Transport (Penalty Fares) Act 1992,

for the words "section 3(2)" there shall be substituted the words "section 3(2) or (2A)(a)".

(3) In sections 12(2)(b), 17(4) and 52(8)(b) of the London Regional Transport Act 1984, for the words "section 3(2)" there shall be substituted the words "section 3(2) or (2A)".

(4) In Schedule 2 to that Act (operating powers)—

(a) in paragraph 14(3), for the words "sub-paragraph (2)" there shall be substituted the words "sub-paragraph (1A) or (2)"; and

(b) in paragraphs 15(4) and 16, for the words "paragraph 8(4) or 14(2)" there shall be substituted the words "paragraph 8(4) or 14(1A) or (2)".

Financial provision

5. There shall be paid out of money provided by Parliament any increase attributable to this Act in the sums so payable under any other Act.

Short title, commencement and extent

6.—(1) This Act may be cited as the London Regional Transport Act 1996.

(2) This Act shall come into force at the end of the period of two months beginning with the day on which it is passed.

(3) This Act does not extend to Scotland or Northern Ireland.

INDEX

References are to sections

NORTHERN IRELAND (EMERGENCY PROVISIONS) ACT 1996*

(1996 c. 22)

ARRANGEMENT OF SECTIONS

PART I

SCHEDULED OFFENCES

The scheduled offences

* Annotations by Gary Scanlan and Sarah Gale of City University.

An Act to re-enact, with omissions and amendments, the Northern Ireland (Emergency Provisions) Act 1991; and for connected purposes.

[17th June 1996]

PARLIAMENTARY DEBATES
Hansard, H.C. Vol. 269, col. 31, Vol. 272, col. 41, Vol. 279, col. 448. H.L. Vol. 569, col. 1118, Vol. 570, col. 1386, Vol. 571, cols. 848, 1807, Vol. 572, col. 625.

INTRODUCTION AND GENERAL NOTE
This Act is principally a re-enactment of the Northern Ireland (Emergency Provisions) Act 1991 (c. 24). For the legislative history of the 1991 Act see the annotations to that Act in Current Law Statutes Annotated. The present Act differs however, in one major respect to the 1991 Act, namely that Part VII of the 1991 Act relating to confiscation of proceeds of terrorist related activities has not been re-enacted in the 1996 Act. These provisions will be the subject of a proposed Bill which it is intended will form the subject of a separate Act.

ABBREVIATIONS
"1991 Act": Northern Ireland (Emergency Provisions) Act 1991.

PART I

SCHEDULED OFFENCES

The scheduled offences

The scheduled offences

1.—(1) In this Act "scheduled offence" means an offence specified in Part I or III of Schedule 1 to this Act but subject to any relevant note in Part I of that Schedule.

(2) Part II of that Schedule shall have effect with respect to offences related to those specified in Part I of that Schedule.

(3) The Secretary of State may by order amend Parts I and II of that Schedule whether by adding an offence to, or removing an offence from, either of those Parts or otherwise; and an order under this subsection may contain such transitional provisions as appear to the Secretary of State to be necessary or expedient.

GENERAL NOTE
This section substantially re-enacts s.1 of the 1991 Act. The section preserves the scheduled offence which derives from the Diplock report of 1972.

Scheduled offences, though in most respects crimes with no political overtones, are nevertheless offences which are frequently committed by terrorist organisations in pursuit of their terrorist aims. In such circumstances these offences are to be tried by a single judge without jury.

Scheduled offences within Pt. I of the Schedule fall into the following principal categories. By note 1 to Pt. I of the Schedule the offences set out in Pt. I (which are made subject to note 1) may in a particular instance be certified by the Attorney General for Northern Ireland not to be a scheduled offence and therefore to be subject to trial by jury. A prime example being a "domestic murder".

By notes 2, 3 and 4 to Pt. I of the Schedule, certain specified offences within Pt. I are only to be scheduled offences when the conditions set out in the notes are satisfied. Thus the offence of robbery where explosives or firearms are used will be a scheduled offence. Offences not subject to note 1 remain scheduled offences.

Part II of the Schedule provides that inchoate forms of the offences listed in Pt. I are to be regarded as scheduled offences. Part III of the Schedule provides that extra-territorial offences as defined in s.1(3) of the Criminal Jurisdiction Act 1975 (c. 59) are scheduled offences.

Preliminary inquiries, bail and young persons in custody

Preliminary inquiry into scheduled offences

2.—(1) Where in any proceedings before a magistrates' court for a scheduled offence (not being an extra-territorial offence as defined in section 1(3) of the Criminal Jurisdiction Act 1975) the prosecution requests the court to conduct a preliminary inquiry into the offence under the Magistrates' Courts (Northern Ireland) Order 1981, the court shall, notwithstanding anything in Article 31 of that Order, conduct a preliminary inquiry into the offence unless the court is of opinion that in the interests of justice a preliminary investigation should be conducted into the offence under that Order.

(2) Where in any proceedings a person charged with a scheduled offence is also charged with another offence which is not a scheduled offence, that other offence shall be treated as a scheduled offence for the purposes of this section.

DEFINITIONS
    "extra-territorial offence": General Note to s.1 above; Criminal Jurisdiction Act 1975, s.1(3).
    "scheduled offence": s.1, Sched. 1.

GENERAL NOTE
    A preliminary inquiry in Northern Ireland is akin to a "section 1 committal" in England and Wales though the resident magistrate is required to consider the evidence and to commit or dismiss accordingly. A preliminary investigation in Northern Ireland is akin to full oral committal proceedings in England and Wales.
    The above section which reproduces s.2 of the 1991 Act, provides that in most circumstances, without objection by the accused, an accused charged with a scheduled offence (not being a territorial offence) will be committed for trial by way of preliminary inquiry and on the written evidence alone.
    The defence, in accepting such a form of committal, must have regard to the fact that the subsequent trial will be by judge alone, and that the judge may see evidence admitted at the preliminary inquiry which is highly prejudicial yet of little probative value.

Subs. (2)
    Where a scheduled and non-scheduled offence are the subject of a prosecution the mode of trial should be determined by the offence which is the most serious.

Limitation of power to grant bail in case of scheduled offences

3.—(1) This section applies to any person who has attained the age of fourteen and is charged with a scheduled offence which is neither being tried summarily nor certified by the Director of Public Prosecutions for Northern Ireland as in his opinion suitable to be so tried.

(2) Subject to subsection (7), a person to whom this section applies shall not be admitted to bail except—
    (a) by a judge of the High Court or the Court of Appeal; or
    (b) by the judge of the court of trial on adjourning the trial of a person charged with a scheduled offence.

(3) A judge may, in his discretion, admit to bail in pursuance of subsection (2) a person to whom this section applies except where he is satisfied that there are substantial grounds for believing that that person, if released on bail (whether subject to conditions or not), would—

(a) fail to surrender to custody, or

(b) commit an offence while on bail, or

(c) interfere with any witness, or

(d) otherwise obstruct or attempt to obstruct the course of justice, whether in relation to himself or in relation to any other person,

or, if released subject to conditions, would fail to comply with all or any of those conditions.

(4) In exercising his discretion in accordance with subsection (3) in relation to a person, a judge shall have regard to such of the following considerations as appear to him to be relevant, namely—

(a) the nature and seriousness of the offence with which the person is charged,

(b) the character, antecedents, associations and community ties of the person,

(c) the time which the person has already spent in custody and the time which he is likely to spend in custody if he is not admitted to bail, and

(d) the strength of the evidence of his having committed the offence,

as well as to any others which appear to be relevant.

(5) Without prejudice to any other power to impose conditions on admission to bail, a judge may impose such conditions on admitting a person to bail under this section as appear to him to be likely to result in that person's appearance at the time and place required, or to be necessary in the interests of justice or for the prevention of crime.

(6) Where a person to whom this section applies is a serving member of—

(a) any of Her Majesty's forces; or

(b) the Royal Ulster Constabulary or the Royal Ulster Constabulary Reserve,

he may be admitted to bail on condition that he is held in military or (as the case may be) police custody if the judge is satisfied that suitable arrangements have been made for holding him in such custody; and where a person is admitted to bail on such a condition it shall be lawful for him to be held in such custody in accordance with the conditions of his bail.

(7) The power to admit a person to bail in accordance with subsection (6) shall, notwithstanding subsection (2), be exercisable by a resident magistrate as well as by a judge.

GENERAL NOTE

This section re-enacts s.3 of the 1991 Act. The section limits the power to grant bail to persons charged with scheduled offences to a judge of the High Court or Court of Appeal, or the judge of the court of trial, and places the onus of proof in bail applications on the prosecution. Subsection (6) makes it lawful for a serving member of Her Majesty's forces or of the Royal Ulster Constabulary Reserve to be held on bail in military or police custody.

Subs. (1)

Note that bail may be granted by a resident magistrate where the scheduled offence is to be tried or has been certified as suitable for being tried summarily.

Subss. (3), (4) and (5)

These subsections give the judge wide discretion when considering whether to admit a person charged with a scheduled offence to bail. Subsection (3) makes it clear that the burden is on the prosecution to satisfy the judge that the accused will breach the conditions laid down in the subsection, which would militate against admitting to bail.

Subs. (6)

Members of the security forces admitted to bail within the terms of the subsection are kept in secure accommodation within police or military establishments.

Legal aid to applicants for bail in case of scheduled offences

4.—(1) Where it appears to a judge of the High Court or the Court of Appeal—
(a) that a person charged with a scheduled offence intends to apply to be admitted to bail; and
(b) that it is desirable in the interests of justice that that person should have legal aid but that he has not sufficient means to enable him to obtain that aid,
the judge may assign to him a solicitor and counsel, or counsel only, in the application for bail.

(2) If, on a question of granting a person free legal aid under this section, there is a doubt whether his means are sufficient to enable him to obtain legal aid or whether it is desirable in the interests of justice that he should have free legal aid, the doubt shall be resolved in favour of granting him free legal aid.

(3) Articles 32, 36 and 40 of the Legal Aid, Advice and Assistance (Northern Ireland) Order 1981 (statements, payments, rules and stamp duty) shall apply in relation to legal aid under this section as they apply in relation to legal aid under Part III of that Order as if any legal aid under this section were given in pursuance of a criminal aid certificate under Article 29 of that Order.

GENERAL NOTE

This section re-enacts s.4 of the 1991 Act. It makes provision for legal aid to applicants for bail where persons are charged with scheduled offences. It enables a judge to assign a solicitor and counsel, or counsel only, to a person who intends to apply to be admitted to bail, where it is desirable in the interests of justice to allow him legal aid. Though the discretion to refuse to grant legal aid is limited, the section would permit refusal where a renewed bail application was made without any further evidence to support the application.

Subs. (2)

This subsection provides that a judge in exercising the jurisdiction to grant legal aid in cases of doubt as to the accused's means, must resolve to grant legal aid to an applicant for bail.

Maximum period of remand in custody in case of scheduled offences

5. Notwithstanding Article 47(2) and (3) of the Magistrates' Courts (Northern Ireland) Order 1981, the period for which a person charged with a scheduled offence (or with a scheduled offence and another offence which is not a scheduled offence) may be remanded in custody by a magistrates' court shall be a period of not more than twenty-eight days beginning with the day following that on which he is so remanded.

GENERAL NOTE

This provision re-enacts s.5 of the 1991 Act. The section enables a magistrate to remand in custody for up to 28 days a person charged with a scheduled offence. The section clarifies the remand period in respect of individuals charged with offences which are a mixture of scheduled and non-scheduled offences.

Holding in custody of young persons charged with scheduled offences

6.—(1) Where a young person charged with a scheduled offence has been remanded or committed for trial as respects that offence and is not released on bail, he may—
(a) notwithstanding the provisions of any enactment, and
(b) whether or not he was remanded or committed for trial at a time when this section was not in force,
be held in custody in such prison or other place as may be specified in a direction given by the Secretary of State under this section.

(2) The Secretary of State may give a direction in respect of a person to

whom this section applies if he considers that it is necessary, in order to prevent his escape or to ensure his safety or the safety of others, to make special arrangements as to the place at which that person is to be held in custody while on remand or while committed for trial.

(3) A direction may be given by the Secretary of State at any time after the young person to whom it relates has been charged with a scheduled offence, and may be varied or revoked by a further direction.

(4) In this section "young person" means a person who has attained the age of fourteen and is under the age of seventeen.

DEFINITIONS
"young person": subs. (4).

GENERAL NOTE
The section re-enacts s.6 of the 1991 Act. The Secretary of State is empowered to issue directions in respect of young persons charged with a scheduled offence and who are not on bail, permitting the holding of such persons in prison or other secure institutions pending trial. A court has the limited power to order a young person to be detained under the same circumstances only when he is certified as unruly.

Directions under section 6

7.—(1) A direction under section 6 shall, if it has not previously ceased to have effect, cease to have effect at the expiry of such period as may be specified in the direction (being a period not exceeding two months beginning with the date of the direction) unless continued in force by a further direction.

(2) Where, by virtue of a direction, a young person is held in custody in a prison or other place and the direction ceases to have effect (whether or not by reason of the expiry or cesser of section 6) it shall be lawful for him to continue to be held in custody in that prison or place until arrangements can be made for him to be held in custody in accordance with the law then applicable to his case.

(3) Nothing in subsection (2) above shall be taken to make lawful the holding in custody of any person who would, disregarding that subsection, be entitled to be released from custody.

GENERAL NOTE
This section re-enacts s.7 of the 1991 Act and relates to the duration and renewal of directions made under s.6 noted above. The section provides for the lapsing and renewal of directions made under s.6 by the Secretary of State. Though a direction may be renewed by further directions, without renewal, it will lapse after a two-month period.

Time limits on preliminary proceedings

Power of Secretary of State to set time limits in relation to preliminary proceedings for scheduled offences

8.—(1) The Secretary of State may by regulations make provision, with respect to any specified preliminary stage of proceedings for a scheduled offence, as to the maximum period—
  (a) to be allowed to the prosecution to complete that stage;
  (b) during which the accused may, while awaiting completion of that stage, be—
        (i) in the custody of a magistrates' court; or
        (ii) in the custody of the Crown Court,
    in relation to that offence.

(2) The regulations may, in particular—
(a) provide for—
(i) the Magistrates' Courts (Northern Ireland) Order 1981,
(ii) section 3 above, or
(iii) any other enactment, or any rule of law, relating to bail,
to apply in relation to cases to which custody or overall time limits apply subject to such modifications as may be specified (being modifications which the Secretary of State considers necessary in consequence of any provision made by the regulations);
(b) provide for time limits imposed by the regulations to cease to have effect in cases where, after the institution of proceedings for a scheduled offence, the Attorney General for Northern Ireland has certified that the offence in question is not to be treated as a scheduled offence;
(c) make such provision with respect to the procedure to be followed in criminal proceedings as the Secretary of State considers appropriate in consequence of any other provision of the regulations; and
(d) make such transitional provision in relation to proceedings instituted before the commencement of any provision of the regulations as the Secretary of State considers appropriate.

(3) Where separate counts of an indictment allege a scheduled offence and an offence which is not a scheduled offence, then (subject to, and in accordance with, the provisions of the regulations) the regulations shall have effect in relation to the latter offence as if it were a scheduled offence.

(4) The Crown Court may, in circumstances prescribed by the regulations, extend or further extend a time limit at any time before it expires.

(5) Where, in relation to any proceedings for a relevant offence, an overall time limit has expired before the completion of the stage of the proceedings to which the limit applies, the accused shall be treated, for all purposes, as having been acquitted of that offence.

GENERAL NOTE
See note to s.9 below.

Section 8: supplementary provisions

9.—(1) Where—
(a) a person escapes from the custody of a magistrates' court or of the Crown Court before the expiry of a custody time limit which applies in his case; or
(b) a person who has been released on bail in consequence of the expiry of a custody time limit—
(i) fails to surrender himself into the custody of the court at the appointed time; or
(ii) is arrested by a constable in connection with any breach, or apprehended breach, of any condition of his bail,
the regulations under section 8 shall, so far as they provide for any custody time limit in relation to the preliminary stage in question, be disregarded.

(2) Where—
(a) a person escapes from the custody of a magistrates' court or of the Crown Court; or
(b) a person who has been released on bail fails to surrender himself into the custody of the court at the appointed time,
the overall time limit which applies in his case in relation to the stage which the proceedings have reached at the time of the escape or, as the case may be, at the appointed time shall, so far as the relevant offence in question is concerned, cease to have effect.

(3) Where a person is convicted of a relevant offence in any proceedings, the exercise, in relation to any preliminary stage of those proceedings, of the

power conferred by section 8(4) shall not be called into question on any appeal against that conviction.

(4) In the application of section 8 in relation to proceedings on indictment, "preliminary stage" does not include any stage—

(a) after the time when the case for the prosecution is opened; or

(b) if the court accepts a plea of guilty before the case for the prosecution is opened, after that plea is accepted.

(5) In the application of section 8 in relation to summary proceedings, "preliminary stage" does not include any stage—

(a) after the court begins to hear evidence for the prosecution at the trial;

(b) if the court accepts a plea of guilty before it has begun to hear evidence for the prosecution, after that plea is accepted; or

(c) after the court begins to consider whether to exercise its power under Article 44(4) of the Mental Health (Northern Ireland) Order 1986 (power to make hospital order without convicting the accused).

(6) In this section and section 8—

"custody of the Crown Court" includes custody to which a person is committed in pursuance of—

(a) Article 37 or 40(4) of the Magistrates' Courts (Northern Ireland) Order 1981 (magistrates' court committing accused for trial); or

(b) section 51(8) of the Judicature (Northern Ireland) Act 1978 (magistrates' court dealing with a person brought before it following his arrest in pursuance of a warrant issued by the Crown Court);

"custody of a magistrates' court" means custody to which a person is committed in pursuance of Article 47 or 49 of the Magistrates' Courts (Northern Ireland) Order 1981 (remand);

"custody time limit" means a time limit imposed by the regulations in pursuance of section 8(1)(b) or, where any such limit has been extended by the Crown Court under section 8(4), the limit as so extended;

"overall time limit" means a time limit imposed by the regulations in pursuance of section 8(1)(a) or, where any such limit has been extended by the Crown Court under section 8(4), the limit as so extended;

"relevant offence" means—

(a) a scheduled offence, or

(b) an offence in relation to which the regulations have effect in accordance with section 8(3); and

"specified" means specified in the regulations.

(7) For the purposes of the application of any custody time limit in relation to a person who is in the custody of a magistrates' court or of the Crown Court—

(a) all periods during which he is in the custody of a magistrates' court in respect of the same offence shall be aggregated and treated as a single continuous period; and

(b) all periods during which he is in the custody of the Crown Court in respect of the same offence shall be aggregated and treated similarly.

DEFINITIONS

"custody of a magistrates' court": subs. (6).
"custody of the Crown Court": subs. (6).
"custody time limit": subs. (6).
"overall time limit": subs. (6).
"preliminary stage": subs. (6).
"relevant offence": subs. (6).
"specified": subs. (6).

GENERAL NOTE

This section and s.8 above re-enact with amendments, s.8 of the 1991 Act. Both sections collectively empower the Secretary of State by regulation to apply time limits to any specified preliminary stage of proceedings for a scheduled offence up to the beginning of taking evidence for the prosecution in a magistrate's court or arraignment of the accused in the Crown Court. The powers in this section have never been invoked. Section 8 also provides that time limits may be set for the stage of proceeedings leading up to trial in scheduled offences.

When regulations under the sections come into force, breach of any time limits will result in an accused being bailed, see s.8(2). By s.8(4) the time limits before expiration may be extended in a given case by application to the Crown Court. Where an "overall time limit" has been breached the accused shall be treated for all purposes as having been acquitted of that offence: s.8(5).

Court and mode of trial

Court for trial of scheduled offences

10.—(1) A trial on indictment of a scheduled offence shall be held only at the Crown Court sitting in Belfast, unless—

(a) the Lord Chancellor after consultation with the Lord Chief Justice of Northern Ireland directs that the trial, or a class of trials within which it falls, shall be held at the Crown Court sitting elsewhere; or

(b) the Lord Chief Justice of Northern Ireland directs that the trial, or part of it, shall be held at the Crown Court sitting elsewhere.

(2) A person committed for trial for a scheduled offence, or for two or more offences at least one of which is a scheduled offence, shall be committed—

(a) to the Crown Court sitting in Belfast, or

(b) where a direction has been given under subsection (1) which concerns the trial, to the Crown Court sitting at the place specified in the direction;

and section 48 of the Judicature (Northern Ireland) Act 1978 (committal for trial on indictment) shall have effect accordingly.

(3) Where—

(a) in accordance with subsection (2) any person is committed for trial to the Crown Court sitting in Belfast, and

(b) a direction is subsequently given under subsection (1), before the commencement of the trial, altering the place of trial,

that person shall be treated as having been committed for trial to the Crown Court sitting at the place specified in the direction.

GENERAL NOTE

This section re-enacts, with amendments, s.9 of the 1991 Act. It enables the trial of scheduled offences to be held other than at the Crown Court in Belfast. The Lord Chancellor may by this provision after consultation with the Chief Justice, direct the trial on indictment or committal of any scheduled offence at another Crown Court venue within the province other than at Belfast Crown Court.

Mode of trial on indictment of scheduled offences

11.—(1) A trial on indictment of a scheduled offence shall be conducted by the court without a jury.

(2) The court trying a scheduled offence on indictment under this section shall have all the powers, authorities and jurisdiction which the court would have had if it had been sitting with a jury, including power to determine any question and to make any finding which would, apart from this section, be required to be determined or made by a jury, and references in any enactment to a jury or the verdict or finding of a jury shall be construed accordingly in relation to a trial under this section.

(3) Where separate counts of an indictment allege a scheduled offence and an offence which is not a scheduled offence, the trial on indictment shall, without prejudice to section 5 of the Indictments Act (Northern Ireland)

1945 (orders for amendment of indictment, separate trial and postponement of trial), be conducted as if all the offences alleged in the indictment were scheduled offences.

(4) Without prejudice to subsection (2), where the court trying a scheduled offence on indictment—

(a) is not satisfied that the accused is guilty of that offence, but

(b) is satisfied that he is guilty of some other offence which is not a scheduled offence, but of which a jury could have found him guilty on a trial for the scheduled offence,

the court may convict him of that other offence.

(5) Where the court trying a scheduled offence convicts the accused of that or some other offence, then, without prejudice to its power apart from this subsection to give a judgment, it shall, at the time of conviction or as soon as practicable thereafter, give a judgment stating the reasons for the conviction.

(6) A person convicted of any offence on a trial under this section without a jury may, notwithstanding anything in sections 1 and 10(1) of the Criminal Appeal (Northern Ireland) Act 1980, appeal to the Court of Appeal under Part I of that Act—

(a) against his conviction, on any ground, without the leave of the Court of Appeal or a certificate of the judge of the court of trial; and

(b) against sentence passed on conviction, without that leave, unless the sentence is one fixed by law.

(7) Where a person is so convicted, the time for giving notice of appeal under subsection (1) of section 16 of that Act of 1980 shall run from the date of judgment if later than the date from which it would run under that subsection.

GENERAL NOTE

This section re-enacts s.10 of the 1991 Act. The section provides the statutory authority for the trial of scheduled offences by a single judge without a jury, first introduced in the Northern Ireland (Emergency Provisions) Act 1973 (c. 53). This mode of trial for such offences was recommended by the Diplock Commission in 1972.

Safeguards for the accused are provided in subs. (5), which requires a trial judge to give reasons for the conviction of an accused, and in subs. (6), which gives an unfettered right of appeal from the verdict of the trial judge.

Subs. (3)

The rules governing amendment of the indictment and application for separate trials are the same as in England and Wales.

Subs. (4)

This subsection allows for alternative verdicts in trials in "Diplock Courts", *i.e.* courts which try scheduled offences by a single judge, as is provided for in jury trials both in Northern Ireland and in England and Wales; see the Criminal Law Act (Northern Ireland) 1967, s.6 and the Criminal Law Act 1967 (c. 58), s.6.

Subs. (5)

When introduced in 1973 this provision was as novel as the trial of indictable offences tried by judge alone. It is a necessary provision enabling the appeal procedure to work effectively: see subs. (6). The judgment is, for appeal purposes, the equivalent of a judge's direction in a jury trial. It is a requirement of the provision that the judgment should contain every reason or detail relied upon by the judge in coming to a guilty verdict. The judgment should explain where the judge has come to a decision apparently at variance with the evidence and no obvious or apparent reason for the judge's finding appears in the transcript. Though there is no statutory obligation, the practice has grown up for the trial judge to give his reasons on an acquittal.

Subss. (6) and (7)

A person convicted on indictment before a "Diplock Court" for a scheduled offence has an unfettered right of appeal against conviction or sentence without leave of the Court of Criminal Appeal or the certificate of the trial judge. These provisions are a valuable counterbalance to the removal of the right to trial by jury for scheduled offences.

Evidence and onus of proof

Admissions by persons charged with scheduled offences

12.—(1) In any criminal proceedings for a scheduled offence, or for two or more offences at least one of which is a scheduled offence, a statement made by the accused may be given in evidence by the prosecution in so far as—
  (a) it is relevant to any matter in issue in the proceedings, and
  (b) it is not excluded by the court in pursuance of subsection (2) or in the exercise of its discretion referred to in subsection (3) (and has not been rendered inadmissible by virtue of such a direction as is mentioned in subsection (2)(iii)).
(2) Where in any such proceedings—
  (a) the prosecution proposes to give, or (as the case may be) has given, in evidence a statement made by the accused, and
  (b) prima facie evidence is adduced that the accused was subjected to torture, to inhuman or degrading treatment, or to any violence or threat of violence (whether or not amounting to torture), in order to induce him to make the statement,
then, unless the prosecution satisfies the court that the statement was not obtained by so subjecting the accused in the manner indicated by that evidence, the court shall do one of the following things, namely—
  (i) in the case of a statement proposed to be given in evidence, exclude the statement;
  (ii) in the case of a statement already received in evidence, continue the trial disregarding the statement; or
  (iii) in either case, direct that the trial shall be restarted before a differently constituted court (before which the statement in question shall be inadmissible).
(3) It is hereby declared that, in the case of any statement made by the accused and not obtained by so subjecting him as mentioned in subsection (2)(b), the court in any such proceedings as are mentioned in subsection (1) has a discretion to do one of the things mentioned in subsection (2)(i) to (iii) if it appears to the court that it is appropriate to do so in order to avoid unfairness to the accused or otherwise in the interests of justice.
(4) This section does not apply to a summary trial.

GENERAL NOTE
  The origins of this section lie in the Northern Ireland (Emergency Provisions) Act 1973 (c. 53). Most trials of scheduled offences involve reliance on admissions or confessions made by the accused. The section provides for two principal safeguards against the admission of such evidence. The exclusion of admissions and confessions is provided for where the grounds set out in subs. (2) are satisfied. It is for the prosecution to negate these grounds in any given case.
  Subsection (3) spells out a clear statutory judicial discretion to exclude statement evidence. It would appear that any common law discretion to exclude evidence is preserved (see *R. v. Dillon* [1985] N.I. 292).

Onus of proof in relation to offences of possession

13.—(1) Where a person is charged with possessing a proscribed article in such circumstances as to constitute an offence to which this section applies and it is proved that at the time of the alleged offence—
  (a) he and that article were both present in any premises; or
  (b) the article was in premises of which he was the occupier or which he habitually used otherwise than as a member of the public,
the court may accept the fact proved as sufficient evidence of his possessing (and, if relevant, knowingly possessing) that article at that time unless it is further proved that he did not at that time know of its presence in the premises in question, or, if he did know, that he had no control over it.

(2) This section applies to vessels, aircraft and vehicles as it applies to premises.

(3) In this section "proscribed article" means an explosive, firearm, ammunition, substance or other thing (being a thing possession of which is an offence under one of the enactments mentioned in subsection (4)).

(4) This section applies to scheduled offences under the following enactments, that is to say—

The Explosive Substances Act 1883

Section 3, so far as relating to subsection (1)(b) thereof (possessing explosive with intent to endanger life or cause serious damage to property).

Section 4 (possessing explosive in suspicious circumstances).

The Protection of the Person and Property Act (Northern Ireland) 1969

Section 2 (possessing petrol bomb, etc, in suspicious circumstances).

The Firearms (Northern Ireland) Order 1981

Article 6(1) (manufacturing, dealing in or possessing certain weapons, etc.).

Article 17 (possessing firearm or ammunition with intent to endanger life or cause serious damage to property).

Article 18(2) (possessing firearm or imitation firearm at time of committing, or being arrested for, a specified offence).

Article 22(1), (2) or (4) (possession of a firearm or ammunition by a person who has been sentenced to imprisonment, etc.).

Article 23 (possessing firearm or ammunition in suspicious circumstances).

(5) This section does not apply to a summary trial.

DEFINITIONS
"premises": subs. (2).
"proscribed article": subs. (3).
"vehicle": s.58.

GENERAL NOTE
This section re-enacts s.12 of the 1991 Act. This section enables a court to infer knowledge or control on the part of an accused charged with offences listed in the section of possession, once arms or explosives are shown to have been on the premises (including vehicles), where the accused was, or which he occupied or habitually used.

The section derives from a recommendation of the Diplock Commission. It reverses the position at common law (see *R. v. Whelan* [1972] N.I. 153). This provision does not apply to summary trials, see subs. (5).

Subs. (1)
If the facts of either subs. (1)(a) or (b) are established by the prosecution, the court, in its discretion, may invoke the section and establish the ingredients of possession prescribed for a conviction of an offence charged. Possession requires (a) knowledge of the existence of the article; (b) physical contact; and (c) assent to having control of the article.

The section has a long legislative history. Its effect remains unclear. It has been suggested (see *R. v. Laverty* (1976) 6 N.I.J.B.) that the section comes into operation as soon as the circumstances of the case point with reasonable clarity to guilty possession though strict proof is lacking as to the fact of possession. On this interpretation the section will require an accused in the above circumstances to provide some explanation of the relevant circumstances.

In the case of *R. v. Killen* [1974] N.I. 220, it was held that the effect of the section is to establish a *prima facie* case of possession or knowingly possessing an article or explosive within the terms of the offence. At the end of the defence case the section may be invoked again as a matter of discretion in determining whether the accused's guilt has been established beyond reasonable doubt. Despite the above, it must be accepted that there are conceptual difficulties in the interpretation of the evidential effects of this section.

Treatment of offenders

Treatment of young persons convicted of scheduled offences

14.—(1) Section 73(2) of the Children and Young Persons Act (Northern Ireland) 1968 (under which a court may sentence a child or young person convicted on indictment of an offence punishable in the case of an adult with imprisonment for fourteen years or more to detention for a period specified in the sentence) shall have effect in relation to a young person convicted of a scheduled offence committed while this subsection is in force with the substitution of the word "five" for the word "fourteen".

(2) Subsection (3) of section 74 of that Act (under which the maximum length of the term or the aggregate of the terms for which a person may be committed in custody to a remand home under section 74(1)(e) is one month) shall have effect in relation to a young person found guilty of a scheduled offence committed while this subsection is in force with the substitution of the words "six months" for the words "one month".

DEFINITIONS

"young person": Children and Young Persons Act (Northern Ireland) 1968, s.180.

GENERAL NOTE

This section which re-enacts s.13 of the 1991 Act, deals with the treatment of young persons convicted of scheduled offences. It enables a court to order the detention of a young person following a conviction for a wide range of scheduled offences and extends the limit of one month to six months for the maximum period of committal to a remand home.

The section amends s.73 of the Children and Young Persons Act (Northern Ireland) 1968, by determining that in the case of scheduled offences where the maximum sentence which can be imposed is not less than five years, the court can authorise the detention of a young person convicted of such an offence. In respect of other serious offences not being scheduled offences the maximum sentence that can be imposed must not be less than 14 years before a young person so convicted can be detained under s.73. The period of detention provided by the sentence for a young person, though in the court's discretion, is subject to the young person being discharged on licence by the Secretary of State. This sentencing option, since it involves a young person being deprived of liberty, can only be imposed when the court is of the opinion that no other options are suitable. By virtue of subs. (2) the courts may commit a young person convicted of a scheduled offence to a remand home for up to six months. The subsection applies to young persons whether convicted on indictment or after summary proceedings before a magistrates' or juvenile court. Committal to a remand home requires the young person to be convicted of a scheduled offence punishable in the case of an adult with imprisonment. Furthermore, the court must consider that no other method of dealing with the young person is suitable.

A young person may not be committed to a remand home for a period which exceeds that for which an adult convicted of the same offence could be imprisoned, and in no event for longer than six months (see s.74(3) of the 1968 Act).

Restricted remission for persons sentenced for scheduled offences

15.—(1) The remission granted under prison rules in respect of a sentence of imprisonment passed in Northern Ireland for a scheduled offence shall not, where it is for a term of five years or more, exceed one-third of that term.

(2) Where a person is sentenced on the same occasion for two or more such offences to terms which are consecutive subsection (1) shall apply as if those terms were a single term.

(3) Where a person is serving two or more terms which are consecutive but not all subject to subsection (1), the maximum remission granted under prison rules in respect of those terms taken together shall be arrived at by calculating the maximum remission for each term separately and aggregating the result.

(4) In this section "prison rules" means rules made under section 13 of the Prison Act (Northern Ireland) 1953.

(5) The Secretary of State may by order substitute a different length of sentence and a different maximum period of remission for those mentioned in subsection (1).

(6) This section applies where—

(a) the scheduled offence is committed while this section is in force;

(b) the offence (being a scheduled offence within the meaning of the Northern Ireland (Emergency Provisions) Act 1991) was committed while section 14 of that Act was in force; or

(c) the offence (being a scheduled offence within the meaning of the Northern Ireland (Emergency Provisions) Act 1978) was committed while section 22 of the Prevention of Terrorism (Temporary Provisions) Act 1989 was in force.

GENERAL NOTE

This section which re-enacts s.14 of the 1991 Act, provides for the maximum rate of remission for persons convicted of scheduled offences under the Northern Ireland (Emergency Provisions) Acts 1978 and 1991.

Subsections (2) and (3) provide for the differing methods of calculation of remission in respect of consecutive sentences, which are subject to s.15(1), and situations where not all the consecutive sentences that have been imposed are subject to s.15(1).

Subs. (5)

This subsection empowers the Secretary of State to vary the threshold and/or rate of remission set out in s.15(1) by statutory instrument, subject to a negative resolution.

Conviction of scheduled offence during period of remission

16.—(1) This section applies where a person who has been sentenced to imprisonment or a term of detention in a young offenders centre for a period exceeding one year—

(a) is discharged from prison or the centre in pursuance of prison rules; and

(b) before that sentence or term of detention would (but for that discharge) have expired he commits, and is convicted on indictment of, a scheduled offence.

(2) If the court before which he is convicted of the scheduled offence sentences him to imprisonment or a term of detention it shall in addition order him to be returned to prison or, where appropriate, to a young offenders centre for the period between the date of the order and the date on which the sentence of imprisonment or term of detention mentioned in subsection (1) would have expired but for his discharge.

(3) No order shall be made under subsection (2) if the sentence imposed by the court is a suspended sentence or a sentence of life imprisonment or of detention during the Secretary of State's pleasure under section 73(1) of the Children and Young Persons Act (Northern Ireland) 1968; and any order made by a court under that subsection shall cease to have effect if an appeal results in the acquittal of the person concerned or in the substitution of a sentence other than one in respect of which the duty imposed by that subsection applies.

(4) The period for which a person is ordered under this section to be returned to prison or a young offenders centre—

(a) shall be taken to be a sentence of imprisonment or term of detention for the purposes of the Prison Act (Northern Ireland) 1953 and for the purposes of the Treatment of Offenders Act (Northern Ireland) 1968 other than section 26(2) (reduction for time spent in custody);

(b) shall not be subject to any provision of prison rules for discharge before expiry; and

(c) shall be served before, and be followed by, the sentence or term imposed for the scheduled offence and be disregarded in determining the appropriate length of that sentence or term.

(5) For the purposes of this section a certificate purporting to be signed by the governor or deputy governor of a prison or young offenders centre which specifies—

(a) the date on which a person was discharged from prison or a young offenders centre;

(b) the sentence or term which the person was serving at the time of his discharge, the offence in respect of which the sentence or term was imposed and the date on which he was convicted of that offence;

(c) the date on which the person would, but for his discharge in pursuance of prison rules, have been discharged from prison or a young offenders centre,

shall be evidence of the matters so specified.

(6) In this section—

"prison rules" means rules made under section 13 of the Prison Act (Northern Ireland) 1953;

"sentence of imprisonment" does not include a committal in default of payment of any sum of money or for want of sufficient distress to satisfy any sum of money or for failure to do or abstain from doing anything required to be done or left undone;

"young offenders centre" has the meaning assigned to it by section 2(a) of the Treatment of Offenders Act (Northern Ireland) 1968.

(7) For the purposes of subsection (1) consecutive terms of imprisonment or of detention in a young offenders centre shall be treated as a single term and a sentence of imprisonment or detention in a young offenders centre includes—

(a) a sentence or term passed by a court in the United Kingdom, the Channel Islands or the Isle of Man;

(b) in the case of imprisonment, a sentence passed by a court-martial on a person found guilty of a civil offence within the meaning of the Army Act 1955, the Air Force Act 1955 and the Naval Discipline Act 1957.

(8) The Secretary of State may by order substitute a different period for the period of one year mentioned in subsection (1).

(9) This section applies irrespective of when the discharge from prison or a young offenders centre took place but only if—

(a) the scheduled offence is committed while this section is in force;

(b) the offence (being a scheduled offence within the meaning of the Northern Ireland (Emergency Provisions) Act 1991) was committed while section 15 of that Act was in force; or

(c) the offence (being a scheduled offence within the meaning of the Northern Ireland (Emergency Provisions) Act 1978) was committed while section 23 of the Prevention of Terrorism (Temporary Provisions) Act 1989 was in force.

GENERAL NOTE

This section which re-enacts s.15 of the 1991 Act, provides that a person who is serving a sentence of over 12 months and who is subsequently discharged early from a prison or young offenders' centre situated in Northern Ireland will, if he commits and is convicted of a scheduled offence as provided for under the Northern Ireland (Emergency Provisions) Acts 1978 and 1991, before the earlier sentence would have expired, be returned to custody to complete the first sentence in full before serving any further term for the latter offence.

Subs. (3)

Subsection (3) sets out, *inter alia*, the forms of sentence which, although imposed upon a person following conviction for a scheduled offence, will not result in the convicted person having to serve the unexpired portion of an earlier sentence for which he has been discharged from custody early.

Subs. (9)

This is a transitional provision authorising the reactivation of a sentence, whether the offence which brings about the reactivation was committed during the operation of the present section or a precursor.

PART II

POWERS OF ARREST, SEARCH AND SEIZURE, ETC.

Entry and search of premises for purpose of arresting terrorists

17. For the purpose of arresting a person under section 14(1)(b) of the Prevention of Terrorism (Temporary Provisions) Act 1989 (arrest of persons suspected of being concerned in acts of terrorism) a constable may enter and search any premises or other place where that person is or where the constable has reasonable grounds for suspecting him to be.

GENERAL NOTE

The general powers of arrest which are available to the forces of law and order in connection with violence in Northern Ireland are currently contained in s.14 of the Prevention of Terrorism (Temporary Provisions) Act 1989 (c. 4). This provision applies throughout the U.K. One ground justifying the arrest of a suspect, set out in s.14(1)(b), is where a constable has reasonable grounds for suspecting that the person arrested is or has been concerned in the commission, preparation or instigation of acts of terrorism, as defined in s.14(2) of the 1989 Act. There would appear to be no requirement that there be a specified or particular offence committed or suspected to have been committed to justify the exercise of this power of arrest. This power of arrest is considerably wider than the power of arrest under s.24 of the Police and Criminal Evidence Act 1984 (c. 60). The section enables a constable to enter and search premises for the purpose of making an arrest of a suspected terrorist. This supplementary power is only applicable in Northern Ireland.

Constables' general power of arrest and seizure

18.—(1) Any constable may arrest without warrant any person who he has reasonable grounds to suspect is committing, has committed or is about to commit a scheduled offence or an offence under this Act which is not a scheduled offence.

(2) For the purpose of arresting a person under this section a constable may enter and search any premises or other place where that person is or where the constable has reasonable grounds for suspecting him to be.

(3) A constable may seize anything which he has reasonable grounds to suspect is being, has been or is intended to be used in the commission of a scheduled offence or an offence under this Act which is not a scheduled offence.

GENERAL NOTE

This section re-enacts s.17 of the 1991 Act. The section gives the police a general power of arrest without warrant for all offences under the Act, whether or not they are scheduled offences. Although it mirrors many of the aspects of arts. 19 and 26 of the Police and Criminal Evidence (Northern Ireland) Order 1989, the section is not a duplication of those latter provisions. Section 18 is concerned with arrest powers in relation to scheduled offences and offences set out in the Act. The powers of arrest under the Police and Criminal Evidence (Northern Ireland) Order 1989 are concerned with arrestable offences, *i.e.* offences which may attract a penalty of 5 years or more. Offences under the Act may not attract such a high tariff. The section requires all powers, be they of arrest or search and seizure, to be exercised only where there is reasonable cause.

Subss. (1) and (2)

It would appear that the police, in exercising the powers under subss. (1) and (2), are authorised to use force by virtue of the Criminal Law Act (Northern Ireland) 1967, s.2(b), s.3 and s.20(3). A constable must also inform a person arrested under this section of the grounds of arrest and of the fact that the powers under the section have been invoked.

Subs. (3)

The powers of seizure under this subsection are governed by the necessity for the constable to have reasonable grounds to suspect any object seized is being or has been used or may be used for the purposes proscribed. Nevertheless, the powers, since they authorise seizure of objects which may be used for unlawful purposes, are clearly wider than the common law powers of seizure. The right of seizure, furthermore, is dependent upon the power of arrest under the section and, where appropriate, consequential powers to enter premises.

Powers of arrest and seizure by members of Her Majesty's forces

19.—(1) Any member of Her Majesty's forces on duty may arrest without warrant, and detain for not more than four hours, a person who he has reasonable grounds to suspect is committing, has committed or is about to commit any offence.

(2) A person effecting an arrest under this section complies with any rule of law requiring him to state the ground of arrest if he states that he is effecting the arrest as a member of Her Majesty's forces.

(3) For the purpose of arresting a person under this section a member of Her Majesty's forces may enter and search any premises or other place—

(a) where that person is, or

(b) if there are reasonable grounds for suspecting that that person is a terrorist or has committed an offence involving the use or possession of an explosive substance or firearm, where there are reasonable grounds for suspecting him to be.

(4) Any member of Her Majesty's forces may seize, and detain for not more than four hours, anything which he has reasonable grounds to suspect is being, has been or is intended to be used in the commission of an offence under section 26 or 27.

GENERAL NOTE

This section re-enacts s.18 of the 1991 Act. In view of the general lack of training of the armed forces in police duties, who are in any event generally only on short tours of duty in the province, the provision eases the normal common law requirements for a member of the armed forces when making an arrest. As a balance to this extended power of arrest the person arrested in respect of any alleged offence can only be detained for a maximum of four hours. Such an individual, if he is to be detained beyond the the four-hour period, must be re-arrested under s.18.

Subs. (2)

This subsection determines that in respect of an arrest under the section the common law requirements of stating the grounds of arrest are satisfied where a member of Her Majesty's forces states that he is effecting the arrest in his capacity as a member of those forces.

Subs. (3)

This subsection authorises a member of Her Majesty's forces to enter and search premises or any other place to effect an arrest. As in all the provisions of this section, the use of reasonable force in exercising the power is justified. In contrast to the general power of arrest set out in subs. (1), the entry of premises or other places for the purpose of effecting an arrest requires reasonable grounds for suspicion that a person to be arrested is a terrorist or has committed or is suspected of committing offences specified in s.19(3)(b).

Subs. (4)

This provision creates a power of seizure in respect of objects connected with offences under the Act which concern interfering with rights of property, highways and road closures.

Power to search for munitions, radio transmitters, and scanning receivers

20.—(1) Any member of Her Majesty's forces on duty or any constable may enter any premises or other place other than a dwelling-house for the purpose of ascertaining—

(a) whether there are any munitions unlawfully at that place; or

(b) whether there is a transmitter at that place;
and may search the place for any munitions or transmitter with a view to exercising the powers conferred by subsection (7).

(2) Any member of Her Majesty's forces on duty authorised by a commissioned officer of those forces or any constable authorised by an officer of the Royal Ulster Constabulary not below the rank of inspector may enter any dwelling-house in which there are reasonable grounds for suspecting that there are unlawfully any munitions or that there is a transmitter and may search it for any munitions or transmitter with a view to exercising the said powers.

(3) If it is necessary for the purpose of effectively carrying out a search—

(a) a member of Her Majesty's forces or constable exercising the powers conferred by subsection (1) may be accompanied by other persons; and

(b) any authority given under subsection (2) may authorise other persons to accompany the member of Her Majesty's forces or constable to whom the authority is given.

(4) If the member of Her Majesty's forces or constable carrying out a search under subsection (1) or (2) reasonably believes that it is necessary to do so for the purpose of effectively carrying out the search or of preventing the frustration of its object he may—

(a) require any person who when the search begins is on, or during the search enters, the premises or other place where the search is carried out ("the place of search") to remain in, or in a specified part of, that place, to refrain from entering a specified part of it or to go from one specified part of it to another specified part;

(b) require any person who is not resident in the place of search to refrain from entering it; and

(c) use reasonable force to secure compliance with any such requirement.

(5) No requirement imposed under subsection (4) shall have effect after the conclusion of the search in relation to which it was imposed; and no such requirement shall be imposed or have effect after the end of the period of four hours beginning with the time when that or any other requirement was first imposed under that subsection in relation to the search in question but an officer of the Royal Ulster Constabulary not below the rank of superintendent may extend that period by a further period of four hours if he reasonably believes that it is necessary to do so for the purpose mentioned in that subsection.

(6) Any member of Her Majesty's forces on duty or any constable may—

(a) stop any person in any public place and, with a view to exercising the powers conferred by subsection (7), search him for the purpose of ascertaining whether he has any munitions unlawfully with him or any transmitter with him; and

(b) with a view to exercising the said powers—

(i) search any person not in a public place who he has reasonable grounds to suspect has any munitions unlawfully with him or any transmitter with him; and

(ii) search any person entering or found in a dwelling-house entered under subsection (2).

(7) Where a member of Her Majesty's forces or a constable is empowered by virtue of any provision of this Act to search any premises or other place or any person—

(a) he may seize any munitions found in the course of the search (unless it appears to him that the munitions are being, have been and will be used only lawfully) and may retain and, if necessary, destroy them; and

(b) he may seize any transmitter found in the course of the search (unless it appears to him that the transmitter has been, is being and is likely to be used only lawfully) and may retain it.

(8) The preceding provisions of this section shall have effect in relation to scanning receivers as they have effect in relation to transmitters.

(9) In this section—

"munitions" means—

(a) explosives, explosive substances, firearms and ammunition; and

(b) anything used or capable of being used in the manufacture of any explosive, explosive substance, firearm or ammunition;

"scanning receiver" means—

(a) any apparatus for wireless telegraphy designed or adapted for the purpose of automatically monitoring selected frequencies, or automatically scanning a selected range of frequencies, so as to enable transmissions on any of those frequencies to be detected or intercepted; or

(b) part of any such apparatus;

"transmitter" means any apparatus for wireless telegraphy designed or adapted for emission, as opposed to reception, or part of any such apparatus;

"wireless telegraphy" has the same meaning as in section 19(1) of the Wireless Telegraphy Act 1949.

DEFINITIONS

"munitions": s.20(9).
"scanning receiver": s.20(9).
"transmitter": s.20(9).
"wireless telegraphy": s.20(9).

GENERAL NOTE

Sections 20 and 21 re-enact, with amendments, s.19 of the 1991 Act. Subsection (1) authorises the security forces to search premises or other places other than dwelling houses, for munitions or transmitters, including 35 scanning receivers (see subs. (8)). The purpose of the provision, *inter alia*, is to prevent the use by terrorists of communication equipment intended to be used to broadcast, monitor, or interfere with the communications of the security forces.

To search a dwelling house for munitions or transmitters, a member of Her Majesty's forces or a constable must be authorised to do so by either a commissioned officer or an officer of the Royal Ulster Constabulary, not below the rank of Inspector, respectively. Furthermore, there must be reasonable grounds for suspicion that there are munitions and/or transmitters within the dwelling house. Under neither s.21(1) nor s.21(2) is there a requirement for a search warrant to be obtained.

Subs. (3)

This provision creates the statutory authority for the various civilian or technical specialists to accompany the security forces on house searches. The subsection requires those persons to be individually authorised by a commissioned officer or a senior police officer in the same way as policemen and soldiers.

Depending on the circumstances and the nature of the search, such specialists may include forensic scientists and crime officers, who will examine any weapons, explosives and transmitters found during the search. It also includes police photographers for the purpose of records and Army technical officers who are trained to destroy munitions.

Safeguards in the operation of this provision are as follows. Anyone accompanying a search must be individually authorised to do so. The search damage report form, a copy of which is handed to the householder on completion of the search, must contain information about those conducting the search, including their names and professional rank and those of the officer who authorised the search.

Subs. (4)

The imposition of "specific requirements"upon a person within the terms of s.21(4) requires a reasonable belief on the part of the person carrying out the search that the imposition of such a requirement is necessary. This obviously requires the person imposing the requirement to show, on an objective standard, that the imposition of the requirement was necessary to conduct the search. Reasonable force may be used to impose the specific requirement upon a person. The provision determines the legal position regarding the powers of the security forces to restrict people's movements during a house search, where it is necessary to do so for the purpose of carrying out an effective search of premises.

Subs. (5)

Although a "specific requirement" imposed by virtue of s.21(4) upon a person may not extend in the first instance for longer than four hours, an officer of the Royal Ulster Constabulary not below the rank of superintendent may extend that period to a maximum of eight hours in total if he reasonably believes it is necessary to carry out a search.

Subs. (6)

The powers of search under this subsection which permit the stopping and searching of persons in a public place are designed to meet the situation where the security forces have no suspicion about a particular individual or car, but wish to search every person or vehicle entering an area. The powers of search are to be exercised with a view to exercising the powers conferred by subs. (7) (see below).

Subs. (7)

This subsection permits as a result of any search authorised under the Act of either premises or other places or any person: (a) the seizure, retention and destruction of unlawfully held munitions; and (b) the seizure and retention, but not the destruction of a transmitter.

An example of a lawful purpose for the purposes of this section would be the possession of a transmitter used as a hobby by a radio "ham".

By virtue of s.21 it is an offence wilfully to fail to comply with a "specific requirement" or wilfully to obstruct a search carried out under the authority of subss. (1) (2) and (4). The term wilful does not necessarily connote an intention on the part of an accused to bring about the external elements of the offences created by that section. It may be interpreted as no more than acting voluntarily and consciously in such a way as to give rise to the commission of an offence under s.20. These offences are triable either way (see also subs. (6)).

Section 20: supplementary provisions

21.—(1) Where a member of Her Majesty's forces or a constable carries out a search under section 20(1) or (2) he shall, unless it is not practicable to do so, make a written record of the search which shall specify—

    (a) the address of the premises, or a description of the place, which is searched;

    (b) the date and time of the search;

    (c) any damage caused in the course of the search; and

    (d) anything seized in the course of the search.

(2) Such a record shall also include the name (if known) of any person appearing to the person making the record to be the occupier of the premises or other place searched; but—

    (a) a person may not be detained to find out his name; and

    (b) if the person making the record does not know the name of a person appearing to him to be the occupier of the premises or other place searched, he shall include in the record a note otherwise describing him.

(3) Such a record shall identify the person by whom the search is carried out—

    (a) in the case of a constable, by reference to his police number; and

    (b) in the case of a member of Her Majesty's forces, by reference to his service number, rank and regiment.

(4) Where a record of a search is made under this section a copy of the record shall be supplied at once or, where that is not practicable, as soon as is practicable to any person appearing to the person making the record to be the occupier of the premises or other place searched.

(5) A person who wilfully fails to comply with a requirement imposed under section 20(4) or wilfully obstructs, or seeks to frustrate the object of, a search in relation to which such a requirement has been or could be imposed is guilty of an offence and liable—

    (a) on conviction on indictment, to imprisonment for a term not exceeding two years or a fine or both;

    (b) on summary conviction, to imprisonment for a term not exceeding six months or a fine not exceeding the statutory maximum or both.

(6) A person who fails to stop when required to do so under subsection (6) of section 20 is guilty of an offence and liable on summary conviction to a fine not exceeding level 5 on the standard scale.

GENERAL NOTE
    See note to s.20 above.

Powers of explosives inspectors

22.—(1) An inspector appointed under section 53 of the Explosives Act 1875 may, for the purpose of ascertaining whether there is unlawfully in any premises or other place other than a dwelling-house any explosive or explosive substance, enter that place and search it with a view to exercising the powers conferred by subsection (3).

(2) Any such inspector may, with a view to exercising those powers, stop any person in a public place and search him for the purpose of ascertaining whether he has any explosive or explosive substance unlawfully with him.

(3) Any such inspector may seize any explosive or explosive substance found in the course of a search under this section unless it appears to him that it is being, has been and will be used only for a lawful purpose and may retain and, if necessary, destroy it.

DEFINITIONS
    "premises": s.28(1).

GENERAL NOTE
    Section 22 re-enacts s.20 of the 1991 Act, and empowers an inspector of explosives to search any premises other than a dwelling house, and any person in a public place for explosives or explosive substances; and where necessary, to seize and destroy any explosives or explosive substances found in a course of a search.

    The powers of an explosive inspector to search premises and seize explosives is provided for in ss.73 and 74 of the Explosives Act 1875 (c. 17). Such powers are exercisable only where there is reasonable suspicion. This section supplements these powers. Entry of premises under this section does not require prior suspicion.

Subs. (2)
    This subsection also empowers the stopping of a vehicle for the purposes of conducting a search (see s.28(1)(a)).

Entry to search for persons unlawfully detained

23.—(1) Where any person is believed to be unlawfully detained in such circumstances that his life is in danger, any member of Her Majesty's forces on duty or any constable may, subject to subsection (2), enter any premises or other place for the purpose of ascertaining whether that person is so detained there.

(2) A dwelling-house may be entered in pursuance of subsection (1)—

    (a) by a member of Her Majesty's forces, only when authorised to do so by a commissioned officer of those forces; and

    (b) by a constable, only when authorised to do so by an officer of the Royal Ulster Constabulary not below the rank of inspector.

GENERAL NOTE
    This section re-enacts s.21 of the 1991 Act with amendments, and empowers the police and members of the armed forces to enter any premises or other place, including (where authorisation is given by an appropriate senior officer) a dwelling house, to search for persons when they are believed to be unlawfully detained in such circumstances that their life is in danger.

The section thus creates a special power to enter and search for persons believed to be kidnapped or in danger of death. No search warrant is required to conduct a search under this provision, though as with all the search powers under the Act, there is a distinction between search procedures when the search is conducted in respect of a dwelling house (subs. (2)) as opposed to searching a public or other place. The section now permits authorisation for entry by a police officer of the rank of inspector.

Examination of documents

24.—(1) Where a member of Her Majesty's forces or a constable is empowered by virtue of any provision of this Act to search any premises or other place or any person he may examine any document or record found in the course of the search so far as reasonably required for ascertaining whether it contains any such information as is mentioned in section 33(1)(a) or (b).

(2) A document or record which cannot be conveniently or thoroughly examined at the place where it is found may be removed for examination to another place and retained there until the examination has been completed.

(3) This section shall not be taken to authorise the examination, removal or retention of a document or record by a person at a time when he has reasonable cause for believing it to be an item subject to legal privilege (within the meaning of the Police and Criminal Evidence (Northern Ireland) Order 1989).

(4) Where a document or record is examined under this section it shall not be photographed or copied.

(5) Where a document or record is examined under this section the person who examines it shall make a written record of the examination at once or, where it is not practicable to make one at once, as soon as is practicable.

(6) A record of an examination of a document or record which is made under this section shall specify—

(a) a description of the document or record;

(b) the object of the examination;

(c) the address of the premises, or a description of the place, where the document or record was found;

(d) where the document or record was found in the course of a search of a person, the name of that person;

(e) where the document or record was found in the course of a search of any premises or other place, the name of any person appearing to the person making the record to be the occupier of the premises or other place or to have had custody or control of the document or record when it was found;

(f) where the document or record was removed for examination from the place where it was found, the date and time when it was removed from that place; and

(g) where the document or record was examined at the place where it was found, the date and time when it was examined.

(7) Such a record shall identify the person by whom the examination was carried out—

(a) in the case of a constable, by reference to his police number; and

(b) in the case of a member of Her Majesty's forces, by reference to his service number, rank and regiment.

(8) Where a record of an examination of a document or record is made under this section a copy of the record shall be supplied at once or, if that is not practicable, as soon as is practicable—

(a) in a case where the document or record was found in the course of a search of a person, to that person; and

(b) in a case where the document or record was found in the course of a search of any premises or other place, to any person appearing to the person making the record to be the occupier of the premises or other place or to have had custody or control of the document or record when it was found.

(9) Subject to subsection (10), a document or record may not be retained by virtue of subsection (2) for more than forty-eight hours.

(10) An officer of the Royal Ulster Constabulary not below the rank of chief inspector may authorise the retention of a document or record by a constable for a further period or periods; but no such authorisation shall permit the retention of a document or record beyond the end of the period of ninety-six hours from the time when it was removed for examination from the place where it was found.

(11) Any person who wilfully obstructs a member of Her Majesty's forces or a constable in the exercise of the powers conferred by this section is guilty of an offence and liable—

(a) on conviction on indictment, to imprisonment for a term not exceeding two years or a fine or both;

(b) on summary conviction, to imprisonment for a term not exceeding six months or a fine not exceeding the statutory maximum or both.

GENERAL NOTE

This section re-enacts s.22 of the 1991 Act. It enables the police and armed forces following a search carried out under any provision of the Act, to examine any document or record so found, in so far as is reasonably required for ascertaining whether such documents or records contain any information of a kind likely to be of use to terrorists in carrying out or planning acts of terrorism (see s.33(1)(a) and (b)). The section further provides (see subs. (2)) that such a document or record so found which cannot be conveniently or thoroughly examined at the place in which it was found, may be moved to another place for the purpose of examination. Although s.33 prescribes offences relating to the collection by persons, of information about certain categories of individual and other information that could be useful to terrorists in planning or carrying out acts of violence, there would, in the absence of s.24, be no clear statutory power for the security forces to detect such offences. The section therefore only allows the examination of documents or records to the extent reasonably required for ascertaining whether they contain such information. The nature of the power is such that it cannot be exercised subject to any statutory test of reasonable suspicion. The section was intended to enable the security forces to examine documents or records found during a search authorised by the Act, before the requisite suspicion about such items (as prescribed by the section) have been formed. The security forces in exercising the power must, however, have acted reasonably. This latter requirement falls to be determined by the courts. If there is already a reasonable suspicion concerning any documents or records, the police have powers of seizure under the PACE order (the Police and Criminal Evidence (Northern Ireland) Order 1989 (see subs. (3)). The section not only forbids indiscriminate searches, it also constrains the security forces in their exercise of the power (see subss. (4)–(8)).

Subss. (9) and (10)

These subsections restrict the time for which documents or records seized and carried away by the security forces under the section may be retained. Provision is also made for the police to retain such items for an extended time, which cannot in any event exceed 96 hours.

Subs. (11)

The offence under this section requires the accused to act wilfully. This term needs to be authoritatively determined by the courts, but may mean no more than that the accused has acted voluntarily. The accused may not need to appreciate that his conduct amounts to an obstruction.

Power to stop and question

25.—(1) Any member of Her Majesty's forces on duty or any constable may stop any person for so long as is necessary in order to question him for the purpose of ascertaining—

(a) that person's identity and movements;

(b) what he knows concerning any recent explosion or any other recent incident endangering life or concerning any person killed or injured in any such explosion or incident; or

(c) any one or more of the matters referred to in paragraphs (a) and (b).

(2) Any person who—
(a) fails to stop when required to do so under this section, or
(b) refuses to answer, or fails to answer to the best of his knowledge and ability, any question addressed to him under this section,
is guilty of an offence and liable on summary conviction to a fine not exceeding level 5 on the standard scale.

GENERAL NOTE

This section re-enacts s.23 of the 1991 Act. It permits the security forces, within the constraints of the section, to stop and question persons as to their identity, movement or knowledge of recent explosions or other incidents which endanger life.

The section, contrary to the principles of common law, makes it an offence for a person either to fail to stop when requested to do so or answer any questions put to him and authorised under the section. Any question must be fully and accurately answered to the best of the person's knowledge. A person may be arrested without warrant for an offence under this section (see ss.18 and 19). A prosecution under this section in respect of an offence in Northern Ireland requires the consent of the D.P.P. for Northern Ireland (s.57), as do all prosecutions for offences within the Act.

General powers of entry and interference with rights of property and with highways

26.—(1) Any member of Her Majesty's forces on duty or any constable may enter any premises or other place—
(a) if he considers it necessary to do so in the course of operations for the preservation of the peace or the maintenance of order; or
(b) if authorised to do so by or on behalf of the Secretary of State.

(2) Any member of Her Majesty's forces on duty, any constable or any person specifically authorised to do so by or on behalf of the Secretary of State may, if authorised to do so by or on behalf of the Secretary of State—
(a) take possession of any land or other property;
(b) take steps to place buildings or other structures in a state of defence;
(c) detain any property or cause it to be destroyed or moved;
(d) do any other act interfering with any public right or with any private rights of property, including carrying out any works on any land of which possession has been taken under this subsection.

(3) Any member of Her Majesty's forces on duty, any constable or any person specifically authorised to do so by or on behalf of the Secretary of State may, so far as he considers it immediately necessary for the preservation of the peace or the maintenance of order—
(a) wholly or partly close a highway or divert or otherwise interfere with a highway or the use of a highway; or
(b) prohibit or restrict the exercise of any right of way or the use of any waterway.

(4) Any person who, without lawful authority or reasonable excuse (the proof of which lies on him), interferes with works executed, or any apparatus, equipment or any other thing used, in or in connection with the exercise of powers conferred by this section is guilty of an offence and liable on summary conviction to imprisonment for a term not exceeding six months or a fine not exceeding level 5 on the standard scale or both.

(5) Any authorisation to exercise any powers under any provision of this section may authorise the exercise of all those powers, or powers of any class or a particular power specified, either by all persons by whom they are capable of being exercised or by persons of any class or a particular person specified.

GENERAL NOTE

This section re-enacts s.24 of the 1991 Act. By virtue of this section any member of the security forces is authorised to enter on property, including private property, to take possession of it, or even to destroy it or otherwise interfere with private or public proprietary rights. With the exception of the powers to enter premises or any other place, authorised by s.26(1)(a) and (3) which concern highways and waterways (see below), the exercise of any powers under this section requires the authorisation of the Secretary of State. The section also empowers interference by the security forces with highways.

As in all cases under the Act where there is interference with property rights, there is provision for compensation (see s.55).

Subs. (1)

This subsection gives to members of the security forces, either with or without the authority of the Secretary of State, a general power of entry upon property under s.26(1)(a), this would be authorised by this section where a member of the security forces sought refuge from a terrorist attack.

Subs. (2)

All the powers set out in the subsection can only be exercised on the authority of the Secretary of State, though such power to authorise may be delegated by him. Such powers may be used, *inter alia*, to allow for the construction of army posts upon private (though usually derelict) property or on roadways and public pavements.

Subs. (3)

This provision allows the security forces to interfere with the use of the highways or waterways where it is immediately necessary to do so for the preservation of the peace or maintenence of order. One of the principal uses of this power is to block off roadways in order to deal with parked motor vehicles which are or are suspected to be car bombs. The security forces do not require the prior authorisation of the Secretary of State to exercise these powers.

Subs. (4)

An offence under this section is a non-scheduled offence. A power of arrest without warrant of a person suspected of committing an offence under the section is authorised under ss.18 and 19 of the Act.

Subs. (5)

This subsection provides for types of authorisation by the Secretary of State to the security forces or other persons for the purposes of the section.

Power of Secretary of State to direct the closure, etc. of roads

27.—(1) If the Secretary of State considers it necessary to do so for the preservation of the peace or the maintenance of order he may by order direct—
  (a) that any highway specified in the order shall either be wholly closed or be closed to such extent, or diverted in such manner, as may be so specified;
  (b) that any highway specified in the order, being a highway which has already been wholly or partly closed or diverted—
      (i) under this section; or
      (ii) in the exercise or purported exercise of any power conferred by or under a relevant enactment,
    shall continue to be so closed or diverted by virtue of the order.
  (2) A person is guilty of an offence if, without lawful authority or reasonable excuse (the proof of which lies on him), he interferes with—
  (a) works executed in connection with the closure or diversion of any highway specified in an order under this section (whether executed in pursuance of any such order or in pursuance of the exercise or purported exercise of any such power as is mentioned in subsection (1)(b)(ii)); or
  (b) apparatus, equipment or any other thing used in pursuance of any such order in connection with the closure or diversion of any such highway.
  (3) A person is guilty of an offence if—

(a) within 200 metres of any road closure works—
    (i) he executes any bypass works; or
    (ii) without lawful authority or reasonable excuse (the proof of which lies on him) he has in his possession or under his control any materials or equipment suitable for executing bypass works; or
(b) he knowingly permits on land occupied by him the doing or occurrence of anything which is an offence under paragraph (a).

(4) A person guilty of an offence under this section is liable on summary conviction to imprisonment for a term not exceeding six months or a fine not exceeding level 5 on the standard scale or both.

(5) In this section—
"bypass works" means works that would facilitate the bypassing by vehicles of the road closure works in question;
"relevant enactment" means section 26(2) or (3) above, section 17(2) or (3) of the Northern Ireland (Emergency Provisions) Act 1973, section 19(2) or (3) of the Northern Ireland (Emergency Provisions) Act 1978, section 24(2) or (3) of the Northern Ireland (Emergency Provisions) Act 1991 or the Civil Authorities (Special Powers) Act (Northern Ireland) 1922;
"road closure works" means works which have been executed in connection with the closure of a highway specified in an order under this section or with the closure of a highway in pursuance of the exercise or purported exercise of any power conferred by or under a relevant enactment.

(6) Nothing in this section prejudices the operation of section 26(2) or (3).

DEFINITIONS
"bypass works": subs. (5).
"relevant enactment": subs. (5).
"road closure works": subs. (5).

GENERAL NOTE
By virtue of this section, which re-enacts s.25 of the 1991 Act, the authority for road closures is vested in the Secretary of State. The Secretary of State is thus empowered to direct the closure of highways. The section is required because of the vast numbers of road crossings between the province and the Republic of Ireland. In general the exercise of this power is exceptional and will be exercised only where security demands it.

Subss. (2)–(4)
The offences under this section are not scheduled offences. There is by virtue of ss.18 and 19 a power of arrest, without warrant, of a person suspected of committing any offence under the section.

Supplementary provisions

28.—(1) Any power conferred by this Part of this Act—
(a) to enter any premises or other place includes power to enter any vessel, aircraft or vehicle;
(b) to search any premises or other place includes power to stop and search any vehicle or vessel or any aircraft which is not airborne and search any container;
and in this Part of this Act references to any premises or place shall be construed accordingly.

(2) Where a document or record examined under section 24 was found in the course of a search of a vehicle, vessel or aircraft—
(a) the reference in subsection (6) of that section to the address of the premises, or a description of the place, where the document or record was found shall be construed as a reference to the location of the vehicle, vessel or aircraft where it was found together (in the case of a vehicle) with its registration number; and

(b) the references in that section to the occupier of the premises or place where it was found shall be construed as references to the person in charge of the vehicle, vessel or aircraft.

(3) In this Part of this Act references to a dwelling-house include references to a vessel or vehicle which is habitually stationary and used as a dwelling.

(4) Any power conferred by this Part of this Act to enter any place, vessel, aircraft or vehicle shall be exercisable, if need be, by force.

(5) Any power conferred by virtue of this section to search a vehicle or vessel shall, in the case of a vehicle or vessel which cannot be conveniently or thoroughly searched at the place where it is, include power to take it or cause it to be taken to any place for the purpose of carrying out the search.

(6) Where by virtue of this section a search under section 20(1) or (2) is carried out in relation to a vessel, aircraft or vehicle, the person carrying out the search may, if he reasonably believes that it is necessary to do so for the purpose mentioned in subsection (4) of that section—

(a) require any person in or on the vessel, aircraft or vehicle to remain with it or, in the case of a vessel or vehicle which by virtue of subsection (5) above is removed for the purpose of the search, to go to and remain at the place to which it is removed; and

(b) use reasonable force to secure compliance with any such requirement; and sections 20(5) and 21(5) shall apply to a requirement imposed under this subsection as they apply to a requirement imposed under section 20(4).

(7) The requirement to make a record of a search under subsection (1) or (2) of section 20 shall apply in the case of a vehicle, vessel or aircraft (other than one which is habitually stationary) searched by virtue of this section only where the search takes place after the vehicle, vessel or aircraft is removed for the purpose of the search by virtue of subsection (5) above; and in the case of such a search—

(a) the reference in section 21(1) to the address of the premises, or a description of the place, which is searched shall be construed as a reference to the location where the vehicle, vessel or aircraft is searched together (in the case of a vehicle) with its registration number; and

(b) the references in section 21 to the occupier of the premises or place searched shall be construed as references to the person in charge of the vehicle, vessel or aircraft.

(8) Any power conferred by virtue of this section to search any vessel, aircraft, vehicle or container includes power to examine it.

(9) Any power conferred by this Part of this Act to stop any person includes power to stop a vessel or vehicle or an aircraft which is not airborne.

(10) Any person who, when required by virtue of this section to stop a vessel or vehicle or any aircraft which is not airborne, fails to do so is guilty of an offence and liable on summary conviction to imprisonment for a term not exceeding six months or a fine not exceeding level 5 on the standard scale or both.

(11) A member of Her Majesty's forces exercising any power conferred by this Part of this Act when he is not in uniform shall, if so requested by any person at or about the time of exercising that power, produce to that person documentary evidence that he is such a member.

(12) The Documentary Evidence Act 1868 shall apply to any authorisation given in writing under this Part of this Act by or on behalf of the Secretary of State as it applies to any order made by him.

GENERAL NOTE
   This section re-enacts s.26 of the 1991 Act. The supplementary provisions in this section relate to the powers of entry and search in this Part of the Act and concern the application of these powers to vehicles, vessels and aircraft.

Subs. (1)

The powers of entry and search authorised under this Part of this Act are contained in ss.17, 20–24 and 26. By virtue of this section every power to search vehicles and other entities listed in the subsection which are *sui generis*, includes a power to stop such vehicles and other entities in order to carry out a search. The power of search includes the power to search containers on a vehicle and to examine the same (see subs. (8)).

Subs. (2)

This provision supplements s.24 and determines the position where the making of a record under s.24(6) of an examination of a document concerns documents which have been found in the course of the search of a vehicle, vessel or aircraft. It accordingly determines for the purposes of such a record where such documents, *etc.* are to be regarded as located and, where appropriate, who shall be deemed to be the occupier, where there is ambiguity in either case.

Subs. (4)

All powers of entry may, if necessary, be exercised by force. This presumably means reasonable force in all the circumstances of the case (see also subs. (6)(b)).

Subs. (6)

Where, in the course of a search under s.20(1) or (2) of a vessel, vehicle or aircraft, there is a need to impose specific requirements, there is a requirement for a reasonable belief on the part of the person carrying out the search that the imposition of such a requirement is necessary. This obviously requires the person imposing the requirement to show, on an objective standard, that the imposition of the requirement was necessary to conduct the search. Reasonable force may be used to impose the specific requirement upon a person.

Subss. (9) and (10)

The powers conferred by this Part of the Act to stop any person are contained in ss.20, 21, 22 and 24. It is an offence to fail to stop a vehicle when requested to do so. The offence is non-scheduled, though there is a power to arrest for the offence without warrant, by virtue of ss.18 and 19.

Subs. (11)

This subsection provides a safeguard for the citizen where security considerations may require a member of Her Majesty's forces to operate in plain clothes.

Part III

Offences against Public Security and Public Order

Directing terrorist organisation

29. Any person who directs, at any level, the activities of an organisation which is concerned in the commission of acts of terrorism is guilty of an offence and liable on conviction on indictment to imprisonment for life.

Definitions

"terrorism": s.58.

General Note

This section re-enacts s.27 of the 1991 Act. A prosecution for an offence (which is a scheduled offence) under this section which takes place in Northern Ireland requires the consent of the D.P.P. for Northern Ireland (see s.57). It can be said to be an offence designed to bring to justice those who manipulate others, frequently young persons, to engage in terrorist activity. The requirement that an accused "directs" "at any level" the activities of an organisation could include within the ambit of the offence not only the commanders of such organisations, *i.e.* the "directors", but also intermediate commanders, or any individual who supervises or directs activity proscribed by the section in respect of individuals who are in a subordinate position to such directors within the organisation. The provision is widely drafted to include any organisation involved with terrorism including organisations involved *e.g.* in "animal liberation" by violent means.

Proscribed organisations

30.—(1) Subject to subsection (6), any person who—

(a) belongs or professes to belong to a proscribed organisation; or

(b) solicits or invites support for a proscribed organisation other than support with money or other property; or

(c) solicits or invites any person to become a member of a proscribed organisation or to carry out on behalf of a proscribed organisation orders or directions given, or requests made, by a member of that organisation; or

(d) arranges or assists in the arrangement or management of, or addresses, any meeting of three or more persons (whether or not it is a meeting to which the public are admitted) knowing that the meeting—

    (i) is to support a proscribed organisation;

    (ii) is to further the activities of such an organisation; or

    (iii) is to be addressed by a person belonging or professing to belong to such an organisation,

is guilty of an offence and liable on conviction on indictment to imprisonment for a term not exceeding ten years or a fine or both and on summary conviction to imprisonment for a term not exceeding six months or a fine not exceeding the statutory maximum or both.

(2) The organisations specified in Schedule 2 to this Act are proscribed organisations for the purposes of this Act; and any organisation which passes under a name mentioned in that Schedule shall be treated as proscribed, whatever relationship (if any) it has to any other organisation of the same name.

(3) The Secretary of State may by order add to Schedule 2 to this Act any organisation that appears to him to be concerned in terrorism or in promoting or encouraging it.

(4) The Secretary of State may also by order remove an organisation from Schedule 2 to this Act.

(5) The possession by a person of a document—

(a) addressed to him as a member of a proscribed organisation; or

(b) relating or purporting to relate to the affairs of a proscribed organisation; or

(c) emanating or purporting to emanate from a proscribed organisation or officer of a proscribed organisation,

shall be evidence of that person belonging to the organisation at the time when he had the document in his possession.

(6) A person belonging to a proscribed organisation shall—

(a) if the organisation is a proscribed organisation by virtue of an order under subsection (3); or

(b) if this section has ceased to be in force but has been subsequently brought into force by an order under section 62(3),

not be guilty of an offence under this section by reason of belonging to the organisation if he has not after the coming into force of the order under subsection (3) or the coming into force again of this section, as the case may be, taken part in any activities of the organisation.

(7) Subsection (6) shall apply in relation to a person belonging to the Red Hand Commando, the Ulster Freedom Fighters, the Ulster Volunteer Force, the Irish National Liberation Army, the Irish People's Liberation Organisation or the Ulster Defence Association as if the organisation were proscribed by virtue of an order under subsection (3) with the substitution in

subsection (6) for the reference to the coming into force of such an order of a reference—
  (a) as respects a person belonging to the Red Hand Commando or the Ulster Freedom Fighters, to 12th November 1973;
  (b) as respects a person belonging to the Ulster Volunteer Force, to 4th October 1975;
  (c) as respects a person belonging to the Irish National Liberation Army, to 3rd July 1979;
  (d) as respects a person belonging to the Irish People's Liberation Organisation, to 29th March 1990;
  (e) as respects a person belonging to the Ulster Defence Association, to 11th August 1992.

GENERAL NOTE
  This section re-enacts s.28 of the 1991 Act. It gives effect to Sched. 2 to the Act which lists the proscribed organisations and enables the Secretary of State, by order, to add to, or remove organisations from the list. It is an offence under the section to be a member of, or to support such organisations.

Subs. (1)
  This provision makes it an offence to belong to or otherwise support the activities of a proscribed organisation (as set out in Sched. 2) by engaging in any forms of conduct set out in the subsection. It is an offence under the subsection to profess membership of a proscribed organisation.

Subs. (5)
  This subsection provides that certain documents in the possession of an accused as prescribed within the section shall be evidence that the possessor belonged to a proscribed organisation at the time of possession. The evidential effect of the subsection may be interpreted as satisfying the legal burden normally borne by the prosecution in establishing the principal element of an offence under s.30(1)(a).

Subs. (6)
  Where an individual is a member of a proscribed organisation which is proscribed by subsequent operation of either subs. (3) or s.62(3) of the Act and which concerns the duration, expiry or revival of temporary provisions in the Act (including the present section), that individual will not commit an offence within the section if, following the proscription of that organisation in either of the circumstances above, he has not taken part in any of the activities of the organisation.

Subs. (7)
  This provides that for the purposes of applying subs. (6) to the members of organisations listed in the present subsection, an order made under subs. (3) will be deemed to have come into force in relation to each of the organisations on the respective dates set out in the subsection.

Display of support in public for a proscribed organisation

  31. Any person who in a public place—
  (a) wears any item of dress; or
  (b) wears, carries or displays any article,
in such a way or in such circumstances as to arouse reasonable apprehension that he is a member or supporter of a proscribed organisation is guilty of an offence and liable—
  (i) on conviction on indictment, to imprisonment for a term not exceeding one year or a fine or both;
  (ii) on summary conviction, to imprisonment for a term not exceeding six months or a fine not exceeding the statutory maximum or both.

DEFINITIONS
   "public place": s.58.

GENERAL NOTE
   This section re-enacts s.29 of the 1991 Act. It constitutes a scheduled offence and a prosecution in Northern Ireland requires the consent of the D.P.P. for Northern Ireland (see s.57).

Subs. (1)
   The wearing of berets, dark glasses and dark clothing while escorting the coffin of a supporter of the I.R.A. has been held to constitute the wearing of a uniform and an item of dress for the purposes of the section (see *Morgan v. D.P.P., The Times,* December 12, 1974 in the context of a precursor to the present section).

Possession of items intended for terrorist purposes

   32.—(1) A person is guilty of an offence if he has any article in his possession in circumstances giving rise to a reasonable suspicion that the item is in his possession for a purpose connected with the commission, preparation or instigation of acts of terrorism connected with the affairs of Northern Ireland.
   (2) It is a defence for a person charged with an offence under this section to prove that at the time of the alleged offence the article in question was not in his possession for such a purpose as is mentioned in subsection (1).
   (3) A person guilty of an offence under this section is liable—
   (a) on conviction on indictment, to imprisonment for a term not exceeding ten years or a fine or both;
   (b) on summary conviction, to imprisonment for a term not exceeding six months or a fine not exceeding the statutory maximum or both.
   (4) Subsections (1), (2) and (5) of section 13 shall apply where a person is charged with possessing an article in such circumstances as to constitute an offence under this section as they apply where a person is charged with possessing a proscribed article in such circumstances as are there mentioned.

GENERAL NOTE
   This section re-enacts s.30 of the 1991 Act. The offence requires a person to have an article in their possession in circumstances which give rise to a reasonable suspicion that the item has a connection with terrorism. Articles such as agricultural fertiliser and diesel oil may be used as explosive, and gas cylinders can be converted to mortar tubes. Even rubber gloves can protect individuals making explosives.
   It is a defence for a person charged with an offence under the section to prove on a balance of probabilities that such articles as may satisfy the terms of the section, were not in his possession for such a purpose as set out in the section. The offence is a scheduled offence (see also s.57 of the Act).

Subs. (4)
   The section attracts and applies the provisions of s.13 of the Act, *i.e.* "onus of proof in relation to offences of possession" as set out in the subsection, to any offence charged under the present section.

Unlawful collection, etc. of information

   33.—(1) No person shall, without lawful authority or reasonable excuse (the proof of which lies on him)—
   (a) collect, record, publish, communicate or attempt to elicit any information with respect to any person to whom this paragraph applies which is of such a nature as is likely to be useful to terrorists;
   (b) collect or record any information which is of such a nature as is likely to be useful to terrorists in planning or carrying out any act of violence; or

(c) have in his possession any record or document containing any such information as is mentioned in paragraph (a) or (b).

(2) Subsection (1)(a) applies to any of the following persons, that is to say—

(a) any constable or member of Her Majesty's forces;

(b) any person holding judicial office;

(c) any officer of any court;

(d) any person employed for the whole of his time in the prison service in Northern Ireland; and

(e) any person who has at any time been a person falling within any of the preceding paragraphs.

(3) In subsection (1) any reference to recording information includes a reference to recording it by means of photography or by any other means.

(4) Any person who contravenes this section is guilty of an offence and liable—

(a) on conviction on indictment, to imprisonment for a term not exceeding ten years or a fine or both;

(b) on summary conviction, to imprisonment for a term not exceeding six months or a fine not exceeding the statutory maximum or both.

(5) The court by or before which a person is convicted of an offence under this section may order the forfeiture of any record or document mentioned in subsection (1) which is found in his possession.

(6) Subsections (1), (2) and (5) of section 13 shall apply where a person is charged with an offence under subsection (1)(c) above as they apply where a person is charged with possessing a proscribed article in such circumstances as are mentioned in section 13.

(7) Without prejudice to section 18 of the Interpretation Act 1978 (offences under two or more laws), nothing in this section shall derogate from the operation of the Official Secrets Acts 1911 to 1989.

DEFINITIONS
"recording of information": subs. (3).
"terrorist": s.58.

GENERAL NOTE
This section re-enacts s.31 of the 1991 Act with an amendment, namely the application of s.13(1) (2) and (5) where a person is charged with an offence under s.33(1)(c) (see note to s.13). It is an offence under the section for an accused without lawful authority or reasonable excuse (the proof of which the accused must establish) to collect information about specified categories of individuals which would prove likely to be useful to terrorists, or to collect any information which by its nature would be likely to be useful to terrorists in planning or carrying out any act of violence. The section is aimed, *inter alia*, at interfering with the intelligence-gathering activities of terrorist organisations. The section would, however, include the activities of persons such as newspaper editors who have information at their disposal which if used ill-advisedly could be useful to terrorists. The offences within the section are scheduled offences. See also the notes to s.24 of the 1991 Act.

Subs. (1)
The accused has a defence to a charge under the section of lawful authority in which the onus of proof to establish lawful authority lies on him. The most common type of case which will arise under s.33(1)(d) is likely to be the recording of movements of the security forces and includes the communicating or conveying of information by lookouts to the principal participators in acts of violence.

Training in making or use of firearms, explosives or explosive substances

34.—(1) Subject to subsection (2), any person who instructs or trains another or receives instruction or training in the making or use of firearms, explosives or explosive substances is guilty of an offence and liable—

(a) on conviction on indictment, to imprisonment for a term not exceeding ten years or a fine or both;

(b) on summary conviction, to imprisonment for a term not exceeding six months or a fine not exceeding the statutory maximum or both.

(2) In any prosecution for an offence under this section it shall be a defence for the person charged to prove that the instruction or training was given or received with lawful authority or for industrial, agricultural or sporting purposes only or otherwise with good reason.

(3) The court by or before which a person is convicted of an offence under this section may order the forfeiture of any thing which appears to the court to have been in his possession for purposes connected with the offence.

(4) Without prejudice to section 18 of the Interpretation Act 1978 (offences under two or more laws), nothing in this section shall derogate from the operation of the Unlawful Drilling Act 1819.

GENERAL NOTE

This section re-enacts s.32 of the 1991 Act. The offence proscribed under this section is a scheduled offence. It is an offence to instruct or to train another or to receive instructions or training in the making or use of firearms, explosives or explosive substances.

Subs. (2)

Although training in firearms, *etc.* carried on in good faith is a defence to a charge under the section, the onus of the defence is borne by the accused.

Wearing of hoods, etc. in public places

35. Any person who, without lawful authority or reasonable excuse (the proof of which lies on him), wears in a public place or in the curtilage of a dwelling-house (other than one in which he is residing) any hood, mask or other article whatsoever made, adapted or used for concealing the identity or features is guilty of an offence and liable—

(a) on conviction on indictment, to imprisonment for a term not exceeding one year or a fine or both;

(b) on summary conviction, to imprisonment for a term not exceeding six months or a fine not exceeding the statutory maximum or both.

DEFINITIONS

"dwelling house": s.58.

GENERAL NOTE

This section re-enacts s.33 of the 1991 Act. The offence can be tried on indictment and it is also a scheduled offence. A prosecution requires the consent of the D.P.P. for Northern Ireland (see s.57).

PART IV

DETENTION ORDERS

Detention orders

36. Schedule 3 to this Act shall have effect with respect to the detention of terrorists and persons suspected of being terrorists.

GENERAL NOTE

Schedule 3 contains the powers and procedures for the holding of persons suspected of being terrorists under interim custody orders and for the detention of terrorists under detention orders.

Sched. (3)

It is the intention of the Government, as it has been in the past, to suspend the power of detention when the Act comes into force (see s.62(5) of the Act). No one has been detained under these provisions from the time they were first introduced by the Northern Ireland (Emergency Provisions) (Amendment) Act 1975. The present procedure of detention involves an extra-judicial system whereby decisions relating to detention are made by the Secretary of State after advice from an Adviser. The appointment of Advisers and their prescribed qualifications are set out in paras. 1 and 2 of Sched. 3.

Persons suspected of involvement in terrorism can be made the subject of an interim custody order (see para. 4 of Sched. 3). If the order is to exceed 14 days in duration then the relevant case must be referred to an Adviser (see para. 6 of Sched. 3); under para. 7 of Sched. 3 the Adviser in considering any relevant information (see para. 7.2. *ibid*) must determine if the person detained has been concerned in terrorist activities and whether detention is necessary for the protection of the public (para. 7.1. *ibid*).

The Secretary of State, following receipt of an Adviser's report, may, if he is satisfied that the person detained is concerned in acts of terrorism and furthermore that the detention of the person concerned is necessary, make a Detention Order under para. 8 of Sched. 3.

Paragraphs 9–15 contain supplemental provisions. These include the power of the Secretary of State to refer a detention order case to an Adviser (para. 9), to direct the discharge or release of a person who is detained under an interim custody order or in respect of a detention order direct an unconditional discharge or conditional release and/or a release for a specified period (para. 10).

Paragraph 11 provides, *inter alia*, for the institutions that may hold persons who are the subject of interim custody orders or detention orders.

Paragraph 12 deals with the status of persons the subject of interim custody orders, who are at large.

Paragraph 13 provides for offences that may be committed by persons subject to interim custody orders or persons who assist in such activities.

Paragraph 14 deals, *inter alia*, with the evidential status of any orders, notices, or directions made or given by the Secretary of State in exercising his powers under Sched. 3.

Paragraph 15 deals with the power to award compensation to a person released, or about to be released from detention.

Part V

Regulation of the Provision of Private Security Services

GENERAL NOTE
Part V of the Act contains provisions dealing with private security services and re-enacts ss.35–42 of the 1991 Act. These provisions are designed to prevent paramilitary organisations in Northern Ireland from setting up security firms to raise funds through extortion. The scheme requires that anyone who offers security guard services in Northern Ireland must hold a valid certificate for such purposes and that such a certificate is renewable annually by the Secretary of State.

Section 37 makes it an offence for a person to provide or offer security services for a reward unless he is, or is acting on behalf of, the holder of a certificate issued by the Secretary of State under Pt. V of the Act. It is also an offence for a person who does not hold a certificate to advertise the provision of such services. The offences under this section are scheduled offences.

Section 38 deals with the procedures to be followed on the application for a certificate under Pt. V of the Act and the information such an application should contain.

Section 39 provides that the Secretary of State may refuse to issue a certificate or revoke a certificate if satisfied that a proscribed organisation or an organisation closely associated with a proscribed organisation would benefit from the issue of a certificate. The section further provides that the Secretary of State may issue or revoke a certificate if the applicant has persistently failed to comply with the provisions of Pt. V of the Act.

Section 40 determines that there is a duty to notify the Secretary of State of changes in personnel in a security business following the granting of a certificate to that business.

Section 41 empowers the police to enter any premises where a business involving the provision of security services is carried out. It further creates a power for the police to inspect any records kept there of persons employed as security guards. It thus enables the police to check that the information provided to the Secretary of State in support of an application for a certificate is both current and accurate.

The section proscribes offences of failing to produce records for inspection and of knowingly keeping false or misleading records.

Section 42 makes it an offence to pay money for the provision of security services to a person who does not hold a certificate or is not acting on behalf of the holder of a certificate. Section 43 deals with the liability of directors and other officers for offences committed by a body corporate under Pt. V of the Act. Section 44 makes provision concerning notifications which must be given under Pt. V of the Act.

Prohibition on provision of security services without a certificate

37.—(1) A person shall not provide, or offer to provide, security services for reward, unless he is, or is acting on behalf of, the holder of a certificate in force under this Part of this Act.

(2) A person shall not publish, or cause to be published, any advertisement for the provision of such services by a person who is not the holder of such a certificate.

(3) Any person who contravenes subsection (1) or (2) is guilty of an offence and liable—

(a) on conviction on indictment, to imprisonment for a term not exceeding five years or a fine or both;

(b) on summary conviction, to imprisonment for a term not exceeding six months or a fine not exceeding the statutory maximum or both.

(4) Where a person is charged with an offence under this section in respect of an advertisement it shall be a defence for him to prove—

(a) that he is a person whose business it is to publish or arrange for the publication of advertisements; and

(b) that he received the advertisement for publication in the ordinary course of business; and

(c) that he had reasonable grounds for believing that the person advertised as the provider of the security services in question was the holder of a certificate in force under this Part of this Act.

(5) In this Part of this Act "security services" means the services of one or more individuals as security guards (whether with or without any other services relating to the protection of property or persons).

Applications for certificates

38.—(1) An application for a certificate under this Part of this Act—

(a) shall be made to the Secretary of State in such manner and form as he may specify, and

(b) shall be accompanied by such information as he may specify concerning—

    (i) the applicant;

    (ii) any business carried on or proposed to be carried on by the applicant and involving the provision of security services for reward;

    (iii) any persons whom the applicant employs, or proposes to employ, as security guards;

    (iv) any partners or proposed partners of the applicant or (if the applicant is a partnership) the members, and any proposed members, of the partnership; and

    (v) if the applicant is a body corporate, the officers, and any proposed officers, of that body.

(2) Any person who, in connection with any such application, knowingly or recklessly furnishes the Secretary of State with information which is false or misleading in a material respect is guilty of an offence and liable—

(a) on conviction on indictment, to imprisonment for a term not exceeding two years or a fine or both;

(b) on summary conviction, to imprisonment for a term not exceeding six months or a fine not exceeding the statutory maximum or both.

(3) In this section—

(a) "officer" includes a director, manager or secretary; and

(b) any reference to the employment or proposed employment of any person or persons by an applicant for a certificate under this Part of this Act shall, in relation to an applicant who is, or is a member of, a partnership, be construed as a reference to the employment or proposed employment of any person or persons by the partnership or any of the partners.

(4) For the purposes of this section a person in accordance with whose directions or instructions the directors of a body corporate are accustomed to act shall be treated as an officer of that body, except that a person shall not be so treated by reason only that the directors act on advice given by him in a professional capacity.

Issue, duration and revocation of certificates

39.—(1) Where an application for a certificate under this Part of this Act has been made to the Secretary of State in accordance with section 38, the Secretary of State may only refuse to issue such a certificate to the applicant in a case where he is satisfied that an organisation falling within subsection (8) below would be likely to benefit from the issue of the certificate or that the applicant has persistently failed to comply with the requirements of this Part of this Act or of Part V of the Northern Ireland (Emergency Provisions) Act 1991; and if the Secretary of State refuses to issue a certificate he shall notify the applicant of the refusal.

(2) A certificate under this Part of this Act shall come into force at the beginning of the day on which it is issued and, subject to subsection (3), shall expire at the end of the period of twelve months beginning with that day.

(3) Where the certificate is issued to a person who already holds a certificate in force under this Part of this Act, the new certificate shall expire at the end of the period of twelve months beginning with the day following that on which that person's current certificate expires.

(4) The Secretary of State may from time to time by order substitute for the period specified in each of subsections (2) and (3) such period exceeding twelve months as is specified in the order.

(5) Subject to subsection (6), the Secretary of State may revoke a certificate in force under this Part of this Act if he is satisfied that an organisation falling within subsection (8) would be likely to benefit from the certificate remaining in force or that the holder of the certificate has persistently failed to comply with the requirements of this Part of this Act or of Part V of the Northern Ireland (Emergency Provisions) Act 1991.

(6) The Secretary of State shall not revoke a certificate under subsection (5) unless the holder of the certificate—

(a) has been notified of the Secretary of State's intention to revoke it, and

(b) has been given a reasonable opportunity of making representations to the Secretary of State.

(7) If the Secretary of State revokes a certificate under subsection (5), he shall forthwith notify the holder of the certificate of its revocation.

(8) An organisation falls within this subsection if—

(a) it is for the time being a proscribed organisation; or

(b) it appears to the Secretary of State to be closely associated with an organisation which is for the time being a proscribed organisation.

(9) In this section "benefit" means benefit whether directly or indirectly and whether financially or in any other way.

Duty to notify Secretary of State of changes of personnel

40.—(1) Where—

(a) an application has been made by any person under section 38, and

(b) that person proposes to employ a person as a security guard as from a relevant time, and

(c) information concerning the proposed employee was not furnished to the Secretary of State in pursuance of section 38(1)(b)(iii) at the time when the application was made, the person who made the application shall, not later than fourteen days before that relevant time, notify to the Secretary of State such information concerning the proposed employee as the Secretary of State may specify.

(2) Where an application has been made by any person under section 38, that person shall notify to the Secretary of State such information concerning any change to which this subsection applies as the Secretary of State may specify, and shall so notify any such information—

(a) not later than fourteen days before the change occurs; or

(b) if that is not reasonably practicable, as soon as is reasonably practicable.

(3) Subsection (2) applies—

(a) in relation to an application made by a partnership or by a member of a partnership, to any change occurring at a relevant time in the members of the partnership, and

(b) in relation to an application made by a body corporate, to any change occurring at a relevant time in the officers of that body,

unless the change involves a person becoming a partner or officer and information relating to that change was furnished to the Secretary of State in pursuance of section 38(1)(b)(iv) or (v) at the time when the application was made.

(4) Any person who contravenes subsection (1) or (2) is guilty of an offence and liable on summary conviction to imprisonment for a term not exceeding six months or a fine not exceeding level 5 on the standard scale or both.

(5) In this section "relevant time", in relation to an application made under section 38, means a time when—

(a) the application has been neither granted nor refused by the Secretary of State; or

(b) a certificate issued in pursuance of the application is in force under this Part of this Act;

and subsections (3) and (4) of that section apply also for the purposes of this section.

Records of employees

41.—(1) A constable may enter any premises where a business involving the provision of security services is carried on and require to be produced for his inspection any records kept there of persons employed as security guards.

(2) A constable exercising the powers conferred by subsection (1) shall identify himself to the person appearing to be in charge of the premises in question and, if not in uniform, shall produce to that person documentary evidence that he is a constable.

(3) Any person who without reasonable excuse fails to produce for inspection any records required to be produced under subsection (1) is guilty of an offence and liable on summary conviction to imprisonment for a term not exceeding six months or a fine not exceeding level 5 on the standard scale or both.

(4) Any person providing security services for reward who makes or keeps records of persons employed by him as security guards which he knows to be false or misleading in a material respect is guilty of an offence and liable—

(a) on conviction on indictment, to imprisonment for a term not exceeding two years or a fine or both;

(b) on summary conviction, to imprisonment for a term not exceeding six months or a fine not exceeding the statutory maximum or both.

Payments in respect of the provision of security services

42.—(1) Any person who, in respect of the provision of security services, pays any sum of money to a person who is neither—

(a) the holder of a certificate in force under this Part of this Act, nor

(b) a person acting on behalf of the holder of such a certificate,

is guilty of an offence.

(2) A person guilty of an offence under subsection (1) is liable on summary conviction to imprisonment for a term not exceeding six months or a fine not exceeding level 5 on the standard scale or both.

(3) It shall be a defence for a person charged with an offence under subsection (1) to prove that, at the time when he paid the money in question, he had reasonable grounds for believing that the person to whom he paid it was, or was acting on behalf of, the holder of a certificate in force under this Part of this Act.

Liability of directors, etc.

43.—(1) Where an offence under this Part of this Act which has been committed by a body corporate is proved to have been committed with the consent or connivance of, or to be attributable to any neglect on the part of, any director, manager, secretary or other similar officer of the body corporate, or any person purporting to act in any such capacity, he as well as the body corporate shall be guilty of that offence and be liable to be proceeded against and punished accordingly.

(2) Where the affairs of a body corporate are managed by its members, subsection (1) shall apply in relation to the acts and defaults of a member in connection with his functions of management as if he were a director of the body corporate.

Notifications

44.—(1) Any notification given under this Part of this Act shall be in writing.

(2) Any notification required by this Part of this Act to be given by any person to the Secretary of State may be sent to him by post.

(3) Any notification required by this Part of this Act to be given by the Secretary of State to any person may—

(a) if that person is an individual, be sent to him by post addressed to him at his usual or last-known place of residence or business;

(b) if that person is a partnership, be sent to a partner, or to a person having the control or management of the partnership business, at the principal office of the partnership; or

(c) if that person is a body corporate, be sent to the secretary or clerk of that body at its registered or principal office.

(4) This section is without prejudice to any other lawful method of giving a notification.

Part VI

Persons in Police Custody under Terrorism Provisions

The terrorism provisions and police custody

45.—(1) In this Part of this Act "the terrorism provisions" means section 14 of the Prevention of Terrorism (Temporary Provisions) Act 1989 and any provision of Schedule 2 or 5 to that Act conferring a power of arrest or detention.

(2) A person is held in police custody for the purposes of this Part of this Act if he is detained at a police station or is detained elsewhere in the charge of a constable except that a person who is at a court after being charged with an offence is not held in police custody for the purposes of section 46 below.

GENERAL NOTE

This section, which re-enacts s.43 of the 1991 Act, deals with the interpretation of terms used in this part of the Act. The effect of this section, *inter alia*, is to apply s.14 of the Prevention of Terrorism Act 1989, which concerns the arrest, detention and control of entry of persons suspected of terrorism under that Act, together with those parts of Sched. 2 "Exclusion Orders" and Sched. 5 "Post and Border Control" to the 1989 Act which concern arrest and detention to any persons detained under any of the provisions of the present Act.

Right to have someone informed of detention under terrorism provisions

46.—(1) A person who is detained under the terrorism provisions and is being held in police custody shall be entitled, if he so requests, to have one friend or relative or other person who is known to him or is likely to take an interest in his welfare told that he is being detained under those provisions and where he is being held in police custody.

(2) A person shall be informed of the right conferred on him by subsection (1) as soon as practicable after he has become a person to whom that subsection applies.

(3) A request made by a person under subsection (1), and the time at which it is made, shall be recorded in writing.

(4) If a person makes such a request, it must be complied with as soon as is practicable except to the extent that any delay is permitted by this section.

(5) Any delay in complying with such a request is only permitted if—

(a) it is authorised by an officer of at least the rank of superintendent; and

(b) it does not extend beyond the end of the period referred to in subsection (6).

(6) That period is—

(a) except where paragraph (b) applies, the period of forty-eight hours beginning with the time when the detained person was first detained under the terrorism provisions;

(b) where the detained person was, prior to the time when he was first so detained, being examined in accordance with paragraph 2 of Schedule 5 to the Prevention of Terrorism (Temporary Provisions) Act 1989, the period of forty-eight hours beginning with the time when he was first so examined.

(7) An officer may give an authorisation under subsection (5) orally or in writing but, if he gives it orally, he shall confirm it in writing as soon as is practicable.

(8) An officer may only authorise a delay in complying with a request under subsection (1) where he has reasonable grounds for believing that telling the person named in the request of the detention of the detained person—

(a) will lead to interference with or harm to evidence connected with a scheduled offence or interference with or physical injury to any person; or

(b) will lead to the alerting of any person suspected of having committed such an offence but not yet arrested for it; or

(c) will hinder the recovery of any property obtained as a result of such an offence; or

(d) will lead to interference with the gathering of information about the commission, preparation or instigation of acts of terrorism; or

(e) by alerting any person, will make it more difficult—

    (i) to prevent an act of terrorism; or

    (ii) to secure the apprehension, prosecution or conviction of any person in connection with the commission, preparation or instigation of an act of terrorism.

(9) If any delay is authorised, then, as soon as is practicable—

(a) the detained person shall be told the reason for authorising it; and

(b) the reason shall be recorded in writing.

(10) Any authorisation under subsection (5) shall cease to have effect once the reason for giving it ceases to subsist.

(11) The right conferred by subsection (1) may be exercised by a person to whom that subsection applies on each occasion when he is transferred from one place to another; and this section applies to each subsequent occasion on which that right is so exercised as it applies to the first such occasion.

(12) Subsection (11) shall not be construed as prejudicing the operation of a request by a person to whom subsection (1) applies which was made, but not complied with, before he was transferred.

DEFINITIONS
"delay": subss. (5) and (6).

GENERAL NOTE
This provision re-enacts s.44 of the 1991 Act.

Under this provision a person arrested for suspected involvement in terrorist offences has the right to have someone informed of his detention and of his whereabouts "as soon as practicable", unless a delay is justified on the basis of one of the grounds set out in subs. (8). The maximum period of delay is 48 hours; this period is calculated, in the cases where a person was, prior to being detained, being examined on arrival or departure from the U.K. under para. 2 of Sched. 5 to the 1989 Act, from the moment the examination under para. 2 began.

A person detained must be informed of his right to communicate with a friend, relative or other person (subs. (2)), and to be informed of any delay and the ground(s) for the delay (subs. (9)).

The section follows s.56 of the Police and Criminal Evidence Act 1984. By s.61 of that Act, the Secretary of State is empowered to make codes of practice in connection with the detention, treatment, questioning, and identification of persons detained under "terrorism provisions".

Detention beyond 48 hours is permitted under s.14(5) of the 1989 Act on the authorisation of the Secretary of State, but in no case is detention under the terrorism provisions to exceed five days.

Right of access to legal advice

47.—(1) A person who is detained under the terrorism provisions and is being held in police custody shall be entitled, if he so requests, to consult a solicitor privately.

(2) A person shall be informed of the right conferred on him by subsection (1) as soon as practicable after he has become a person to whom that subsection applies.

(3) A request made by a person under subsection (1), and the time at which it is made, shall be recorded in writing unless it is made by him while at a court after being charged with an offence.

(4) If a person makes such a request, he must be permitted to consult a solicitor as soon as is practicable except to the extent that any delay is permitted by this section.

(5) Any delay in complying with a request under subsection (1) is only permitted if—

    (a) it is authorised by an officer of at least the rank of superintendent; and

    (b) it does not extend beyond the relevant time.

(6) In subsection (5) "the relevant time" means—

    (a) where the request is the first request made by the detained person under subsection (1), the end of the period referred to in section 46(6); or

    (b) where the request follows an earlier request made by the detained person under that subsection in pursuance of which he has consulted a solicitor, the end of the period of forty-eight hours beginning with the time when that consultation began.

(7) An officer may give an authorisation under subsection (5) orally or in writing but, if he gives it orally, he shall confirm it in writing as soon as is practicable.

(8) An officer may only authorise a delay in complying with a request under subsection (1) where he has reasonable grounds for believing that the exercise of the right conferred by that subsection at the time when the detained person desires to exercise it—
(a) will lead to interference with or harm to evidence connected with a scheduled offence or interference with or physical injury to any person; or
(b) will lead to the alerting of any person suspected of having committed such an offence but not yet arrested for it; or
(c) will hinder the recovery of any property obtained as a result of such an offence; or
(d) will lead to interference with the gathering of information about the commission, preparation or instigation of acts of terrorism; or
(e) by alerting any person, will make it more difficult—
(i) to prevent an act of terrorism; or
(ii) to secure the apprehension, prosecution or conviction of any person in connection with the commission, preparation or instigation of an act of terrorism.
(9) If any delay is authorised, then, as soon as is practicable—
(a) the detained person shall be told the reason for authorising it; and
(b) the reason shall be recorded in writing.
(10) If an officer of at least the rank of Assistant Chief Constable has reasonable grounds for believing that, unless he gives a direction under subsection (11), the exercise by a person of the right conferred by subsection (1) will have any of the consequences specified in subsection (8), he may give a direction under subsection (11).
(11) A direction under this subsection is a direction that a person desiring to exercise the right conferred by subsection (1) may only consult a solicitor in the sight and hearing of a qualified officer of the uniformed branch of the Royal Ulster Constabulary.
(12) An officer is qualified for the purposes of subsection (11) if—
(a) he is of at least the rank of inspector; and
(b) in the opinion of the officer giving the direction, he has no connection with the case.
(13) Any authorisation under subsection (5) or direction under subection (11) shall cease to have effect once the reason for giving it ceases to subsist.

DEFINITIONS
"relevant time": subs. (6).

GENERAL NOTE
This section re-enacts s.45 of the 1991 Act. It provides a statutory right for a person detained under this part of the Act to have access to a solicitor. The person detained must also be informed of this right (subs. (2)). The right to access is exercisable "as soon as is practicable", subject to a permitted delay of 48 hours (see subs. (5) and (6)). The grounds for delay are set out in subs. (8). Any delay in granting access must be communicated to the detained person, together with the reason for the delay.
By subs. (1) an officer of at least the rank of Assistant Chief Constable may, if he has reasonable grounds for suspecting that one of the consequences set out in subs. (8) will occur if a consultation takes place between a detained person and their solicitor in private, direct that such a consultation shall take place in the sight and hearing of a qualified officer of the uniformed branch of the Royal Ulster Constabulary.
This section follows closely s.58 of the Police and Criminal Evidence Act 1984.
Both ss.46 and 47 fail to set out the consequences that flow from a failure of the police to observe the provisions of both sections. Guidance may be given on this point once the Codes of Practice authorised under s.52 (see notes to s.44 above) are promulgated.

Fingerprinting

48. Article 61(1) to (8) of the Police and Criminal Evidence (Northern Ireland) Order 1989 (fingerprinting) shall apply to the taking of a person's fingerprints by a constable under section 15(9) of the Prevention of Terrorism (Temporary Provisions) Act 1989 as if for Article 61(4) there were substituted—

"(4) An officer may only give an authorisation if he is satisfied that it is necessary to do so in order to assist in determining—

(a) whether that person is or has been concerned in the commission, preparation or instigation of acts of terrorism to which section 14 of the Prevention of Terrorism (Temporary Provisions) Act 1989 applies; or

(b) whether he is subject to an exclusion order under that Act;

or if the officer has reasonable grounds for suspecting that person's involvement in an offence under any of the provisions mentioned in subsection (1)(a) of that section and for believing that his fingerprints will tend to confirm or disprove his involvement.".

GENERAL NOTE

Section 15(9) of the 1989 Act provides statutory authority for a police officer to take the fingerprints of a person detained under s.14 of the Act. Article 61(1)–(8) of the Police and Criminal Evidence (Northern Ireland) Order 1989, which concerns fingerprinting and which reproduces the equivalent provisions governing the taking of fingerprints under s.61 of the Police and Criminal Evidence Act 1984, are by virtue of the present section to be applied (as amended by s.48) to the taking of fingerprints of persons detained under Pt. VI of the Act.

The amendment made by the present section to the provisions of the Police and Criminal Evidence (Northern Ireland) Order, when applied to the taking of fingerprints of persons detained under Pt. VI of the Act, mirrors the equivalent amendments made by s.15(10) of the 1989 Act to s.61 of the Police and Criminal Evidence Act 1984, which now governs the taking of fingerprints of persons detained under the "Terrorism Provisions" in England and Wales. Accordingly, in Northern Ireland, fingerprints may not be taken within the terms of the "terrorism provisions" without consent, unless an officer of at least the rank of superintendent authorises them to be taken.

It would appear that a person's fingerprints taken under the above-mentioned provisions will not necessarily be destroyed if no charge is brought. The fingerprints may be kept for as long as the terrorist emergency continues. The practice is different where fingerprints are taken under the Police and Criminal Evidence (Northern Ireland) Order without reference to the "terrorism provisions".

PART VII

MISCELLANEOUS

Supplementary regulations for preserving the peace, etc.

49.—(1) The Secretary of State may by regulations make provision additional to the foregoing provisions of this Act for promoting the preservation of the peace and the maintenance of order.

(2) Regulations under this section may authorise the Secretary of State to make orders for such purposes as may be specified in the regulations.

(3) Any person contravening or failing to comply with the provisions of any regulations under this section or any instrument or directions under any such regulations is guilty of an offence and liable on summary conviction to imprisonment for a term not exceeding six months or a fine not exceeding level 5 on the standard scale or both.

GENERAL NOTE

This section re-enacts s.58 of the 1991 Act with consequential amendments. The section gives the Secretary of State power to make orders under the Act promoting the preservation of the peace and the maintenance of order. Under subs. (2) are the purposes for which the regulations made under s.49 may be specified in those regulations. This potentially wide power is limited in the sense that a breach of any provision of such regulations is a summary offence only. Furthermore, judicial review would be available to question the legality of any regulations made under the section.

Explosives factories, magazines and stores

50.—(1) The grounds on which the Secretary of State may reject an application for a licence under section 6 of the Explosives Act 1875 (new explosives factories and magazines) shall include the ground that the establishment of the factory or magazine in question is undesirable in the interests of safeguarding national security or protecting public safety; and a licence granted under that section may be withdrawn by him on that ground at any time before it comes into force.

(2) The Secretary of State may also refuse a licence under section 15 or registration under section 21 of that Act (explosives stores and other premises for keeping explosives) on the ground that the establishment of the store or, as the case may be, the keeping of explosives on the premises in question is undesirable in the interests of safeguarding national security or protecting public safety.

GENERAL NOTE
    This section re-enacts s.59 of the 1991 Act. Prior to the original passing of this section as s.24 of the 1989 Act there were, because of the security situation in Northern Ireland, strict controls on the manufacture and storage of commercial explosives in the Province. The controls are exercised by the Secretary of State as the licensing authority for the manufacture and storage of explosives under the provisions of the Explosives Act 1875. Once a licence has been granted, the Chief Constable's consent is required, *inter alia*, for the sale, acquisition, movement or manufacture of explosives under the Explosives Act (Northern Ireland) 1970.
    Prior to the passing of what is now s.50, the controls under the above legislation were seriously weakened, since the licensing powers of the Secretary of State were laid down solely in the context of safety requirements. In the circumstances of Northern Ireland it was regarded by the Government as essential that the Secretary of State had the power to prevent the extension of the manufacture and storage of explosives in Northern Ireland on the basis of the security of the Province. The section when originally enacted removed any doubt that such a power to refuse a licence on this ground exists. The section as reproduced still applies only to Northern Ireland. The Government gave assurances that in refusing a licence the Secretary of State would only take into account security considerations and would have no regard to the commercial advantages of firms already in the explosives market. Subsection (1) thus provides this additional power of refusal to grant a licence and also enables the Secretary of State to refuse to confirm a licence granted but not yet in force. Such a power was already available under the relevant legislation in such a case but was limited only to safety considerations. Subsection (2) applies the same criteria to licences in respect of explosives stores or the registration of premises for the keeping of explosives.
    Anyone wishing to establish a new explosives factory or magazine in Northern Ireland must comply with the licensing procedures in ss.6 and 7 of the Explosives Act 1875. Section 6 requires the applicant to submit a draft of the proposed licence to the Secretary of State. Under s.7 the Secretary of State may not grant a licence until he has held an inquiry, at which objections may be heard.

Independent Assessor of Military Complaints Procedures in Northern Ireland

51.—(1) The Secretary of State may appoint a person to be known as the Independent Assessor of Military Complaints Procedures in Northern Ireland (in this Act referred to as "the Independent Assessor").

(2) A person shall not be eligible for appointment as the Independent Assessor if he is, or at any time during the period of twenty years ending with the date of the appointment has been, a serving member of Her Majesty's forces.

(3) Schedule 4 to this Act shall have effect with respect to the Independent Assessor.

(4) The Independent Assessor—
   (a) shall keep under review the procedures adopted by the General Offi-
       cer Commanding Northern Ireland ("the GOC") for receiving, inves-
       tigating and responding to relevant complaints;
   (b) shall receive and investigate any representations concerning those
       procedures;
   (c) may investigate the operation of those procedures in relation to any
       particular complaint or group of complaints;
   (d) may require the GOC to review any particular case or group of cases in
       which the Independent Assessor considers any of those procedures to
       have operated inadequately; and
   (e) may make to the GOC recommendations concerning any inadequa-
       cies in those procedures, including inadequacies in the way in which
       they operate in relation to any particular complaint, group of com-
       plaints or description of complaints.
(5) In this section "relevant complaint" means a complaint relating to the
behaviour of any member of Her Majesty's forces under the command of the
GOC, other than—
   (a) any complaint which has been referred by the GOC to the Royal
       Ulster Constabulary and not remitted by the Royal Ulster Constabu-
       lary to the GOC to be dealt with by him; and
   (b) any complaint relating to a matter in respect of which a claim for com-
       pensation has been made under section 55 below or which is the sub-
       ject of proceedings involving a claim for compensation which have
       been instituted in any court.
(6) The GOC shall—
   (a) furnish such information;
   (b) disclose such documents; and
   (c) provide such assistance,
as the Independent Assessor may reasonably require for the purpose of the
performance of his functions.

DEFINITIONS
"relevant complaint": subs. (5).

GENERAL NOTE
   Although there have been informal procedures for dealing with complaints concerning the
armed forces, Lord Colville, during his review of the emergency legislation prior to the enactment of the 1991 Act, suggested that an "ombudsman type" official could be responsible for
investigations of complaints against the Army. The present section is a result of that suggestion.
The police are already subject to a formal statutory complaints procedure (see the Independent
Commission for Police Complaints, established by the Police (Northern Ireland) Order 1987).
   The official created under the section to review complaints against the army is the Independent Assessor of Military Complaints Procedures in Northern Ireland. The Independent
Assessor is appointed by the Secretary of State. His qualifications for appointment are set out in
subs. (2).

Subs. (4)
   This subsection sets out the principal functions of the Independent Assessor. Subsection (3)
gives effect to Sched. 6 which deals, *inter alia*, with the tenure of the Independent Assessor and
prescribes some of his responsibilities. One of the principal functions of the Independent
Assessor is to keep under review the procedures adopted by the General Officer Commanding
Northern Ireland (the GOC) for receiving, investigating, and responding to non-criminal complaints relating to the behaviour of members of the armed forces under his command. It is thus
with complaints that the functions of the Independent Assessor are concerned. Criminal complaints of misconduct by the armed forces remain subject to the independent investigation by the
Royal Ulster Constabulary.
   The Independent Assessor is also to act as adviser to the GOC, although his duties are confined to the five matters set out in subs. (4), *i.e.* keeping the complaints procedure under review,
investigating the operation of the procedure, receiving and investigating representations and
making recommendations relating to the procedure to the GOC. There is, however, no indepen-

dent element which looks into the actual consideration of a particular complaint. Although the Independent Assessor may make recommendations to the GOC, there is no specific duty on the GOC to pay regard to such recommendations.

All the duties of the Independent Assessor under subs. (4) relate to "relevant complaints", a term defined in subs. (5). The GOC is under a duty (see subs. (6)) to supply the Independent Assessor with such information, documents or assistance as are reasonably required by him.

Schedule 6 may be regarded as dealing with what were described, when the section was first introduced, as housekeeping matters. These include the Independent Assessor's term of office (see para. 1), his remuneration (see para. 2) and the appointment of staff (see para. 3). The Independent Assessor under para. 4 will be required to submit an annual report to the Secretary of State, meaning the Secretary of State for Northern Ireland or the Secretary of State for Defence.

Paragraph 5 sets out the offices from which the Independent Assessor is disqualified.

Codes of practice: police powers

52.—(1) The Secretary of State shall make codes of practice in connection with the detention, treatment, questioning and identification of persons detained under the Prevention of Terrorism (Temporary Provisions) Act 1989.

(2) The Secretary of State may make codes of practice in connection with—

(a) the exercise by police officers of any power conferred by Part II of this Act or by that Act; and

(b) the seizure and retention of property found by police officers when exercising powers of search conferred by any provision of this Act or that Act.

(3) The Secretary of State may make codes of practice in connection with the exercise by members of Her Majesty's forces of any of their powers under Part II of this Act.

(4) In this section "police officer" means a member of the Royal Ulster Constabulary or the Royal Ulster Constabulary Reserve.

<small>DEFINITIONS</small>
"police officer": subs. (4).

<small>GENERAL NOTE</small>
This section places a mandatory obligation on the Secretary of State to make a code of practice in connection with the exercise by the forces of law and order of the powers of detention under the Prevention of Terrorism (Temporary Provisions) Act 1989 (see subs. (1)). There is also an enabling power for the Secretary of State to make codes of practice in connection with the exercise by the police and armed forces of the emergency powers conferred by Pt. II of the Act, or in relation to the seizure and retention of property found by police officers when exercising powers of search conferred by any provision of this Act or the 1989 Act (see subs. (1)(a) and (b)).

Video recording

53.—(1) The Secretary of State shall—

(a) make a code of practice in connection with the silent video recording of interviews to which this section applies; and

(b) make an order requiring the silent video recording of interviews to which this section applies in accordance with the code as it has effect for the time being.

(2) This section applies to interviews held by police officers of persons detained under section 14(1)(a) or (b) of the Prevention of Terrorism (Temporary Provisions) Act 1989 (arrest and detention of suspected persons).

(3) In this section "police officer" means a member of the Royal Ulster Constabulary or the Royal Ulster Constabulary Reserve.

GENERAL NOTE

This is a new provision. It provides for the silent video recording of interviews of persons detained under s.14(1)(a) or (b) of the 1989 Act. It imposes a requirement upon the Secretary of State to make a code of practice.

The provision was regarded as an acceptable compromise between ensuring that persons being questioned under the anti-terrorism legislation at holding centres should be protected from threats or the use of violence, while preserving the anonymity of such individuals, who could otherwise be recognised by terrorists or those sympathetic to terrorists by their voices.

Codes of practice: supplementary

54.—(1) This section applies to a code of practice under section 52 or 53.

(2) When the Secretary of State proposes to issue a code of practice he shall prepare and publish a draft of the code, shall consider any representations made to him about the draft and may modify the draft accordingly.

(3) The Secretary of State shall lay before both Houses of Parliament a draft of any code of practice prepared by him; and when he has laid the draft of the code before both Houses he may by order bring the code into operation.

(4) An order bringing a code of practice into operation may contain such transitional provisions or savings as appear to the Secretary of State to be necessary or expedient.

(5) The Secretary of State may from time to time revise the whole or any part of a code of practice issued by him and issue the code as revised; and subsections (2) to (4) shall apply (with appropriate modifications) to such a revised code as they apply to the first issue of a code.

(6) A failure on the part of a police officer to comply with any provision of a code shall not of itself render him liable to any criminal or civil proceedings.

(7) A failure on the part of a member of Her Majesty's forces to comply with any provision of a code shall not of itself render him liable to any criminal or civil proceedings other than—

(a) proceedings under any provision of the Army Act 1955 or the Air Force Act 1955 other than section 70 (civil offences); and

(b) proceedings under any provision of the Naval Discipline Act 1957 other than section 42 (civil offences).

(8) In all criminal and civil proceedings any code shall be admissible in evidence; and if any provision of a code appears to the court or tribunal conducting the proceedings to be relevant to any question arising in the proceedings it shall be taken into account in determining that question.

(9) In this section—

"criminal proceedings" includes proceedings in Northern Ireland before a court-martial constituted under the Army Act 1955, the Air Force Act 1955 or the Naval Discipline Act 1957 or a disciplinary court constituted under section 50 of the 1957 Act and proceedings in Northern Ireland before the Courts-Martial Appeal Court;

"police officer" means a member of the Royal Ulster Constabulary or the Royal Ulster Constabulary Reserve.

GENERAL NOTE

This section sets out the procedures for promulgating any codes of practice made under ss.52 and 53 or for revising any such codes. Subsection (4) permits the codes of practice to contain transitional provisions.

Although a police officer will be liable to disciplinary proceedings for failure to comply with any provision of any code under the section, the breach of any such provision will not *per se* render an officer liable to criminal or civil proceedings (see s.54(7)).

Subs. (8)

This makes any code made under the section admissible where it, or any of its provisions, are relevant in any criminal or civil proceedings. Subsection (9) defines the terms relevant to the section.

Right to compensation

55.—(1) Where under this Act any real or personal property is taken, occupied, destroyed or damaged, or any other act is done interfering with private rights of property, compensation shall, subject to the provisions of this section, be payable by the Secretary of State to any person who—
    (a) has an estate or interest in that property or (as the case may be) is entitled to those rights of property, and
    (b) suffers loss or damage as a result of the act.
    (2) No compensation shall be payable under this section in respect of any act falling within subsection (1) unless an application for such compensation is made to the Secretary of State, in such manner as he may specify, within—
    (a) the period of four months beginning with the date when the act was done, or
    (b) such longer period beginning with that date and not exceeding twelve months as—
        (i) the Secretary of State on a request being made to him in writing, or
        (ii) the county court on an appeal under subsection (3), may in a particular case allow.
    (3) Where the Secretary of State refuses any request made to him for the purposes of subsection (2)(b), he shall serve a notice of his refusal on the person who made the request, and that person may, within the period of six weeks beginning with the date of service of the notice, appeal to the county court against that refusal.
    (4) Where the Secretary of State has determined any application for compensation made in accordance with subsection (2), he shall serve on the applicant either—
    (a) a notice stating that he has decided to award the applicant compensation in pursuance of his application and specifying the amount of the award, or
    (b) a notice stating that he has decided to refuse the application;
and the applicant may within the period of six weeks beginning with the date of service of the notice appeal to the county court against the decision of the Secretary of State to pay the amount of compensation specified in the notice or (as the case may be) to refuse the application and unless he so appeals within that period that decision shall become in all respects final and binding.
    (5) Any notice served under subsection (3) or (4) shall contain particulars of the right of appeal under that subsection and, in the case of a notice served under subsection (4), of the consequences of a failure to exercise that right.
    (6) Where—
    (a) a person having a right to compensation under this section has made an application in accordance with subsection (2), and
    (b) by virtue of any assignment or operation of law that right has passed to any other person,
that other person (or, if he is subject to any legal disability, the person appearing to the Secretary of State to be entitled to act on his behalf) may be treated by the Secretary of State as the applicant for the purposes of any provision of this section.
    (7) Where—
    (a) a person has a right to compensation in respect of any act falling within subsection (1), and
    (b) the act was done in connection with, or revealed evidence of the commission of—
        (i) a scheduled offence, or
        (ii) an offence under this Act other than a scheduled offence, and
    (c) proceedings for that offence are brought against that person,

his right to such compensation shall not be enforceable at any time when any such proceedings have not been concluded or if he is convicted of the offence.

GENERAL NOTE

In carrying out certain duties and powers under the Act, the security forces may in some way adversely affect or interfere with the proprietary rights of third parties. This section provides for compensation for the class of persons who come within the terms of s.55 where they have suffered loss through the exercise by the security forces of such duties or powers—subject however to s.55 (see below). Compensation will only be payable for direct damage, interference, etc. Indirect damage, for example, loss of trade due to the erection of security barriers, would not be the subject of compensation under the section (see *R. v. C.; McCreesh v. County Court Judge of Armagh* unreported).

Subs. (2)

This subsection sets out the procedures to be followed by an applicant seeking compensation under the section. The manner of the application is to be specified by the Secretary of State, to whom the application for compensation should be made. There are strict time limits for the making of an application for compensation, which must be made in any event within 12 months from the date of the damage, either because the Secretary of State had agreed to entertain the application outside the usual four-month time limit or because he has refused to extend the time limit and the applicant has appealed against the decision to the county court under subs. (3).

Subs. (4)

This provides that where the Secretary of State has determined any application for compensation under the section he shall serve notice upon the applicant of his decision. The applicant may appeal against the decision to the county court. Failure to appeal within the time limit specified in the subsection makes the Secretary of State's determination binding.

Subs. (5)

This specifies that a notice served under subs. (4) must contain full information on the right of appeal and the consequences of failing to appeal.

Subss. (6) and (7)

This permits successors in title to property rights to recover compensation which a predecessor in title applied for in respect of relevant property, dependent upon the terms of the section being satisfied. A person may not recover compensation while he is the subject of proceedings or has been convicted of an offence under the Act and where the claim for compensation arises from conduct connected with an offence (whether scheduled or not) which is the subject of those proceedings or such a conviction.

Compensation notices

56. Any notice required by section 55 to be served on any person by the Secretary of State may—
   (a) if that person is an individual, be served on him—
         (i) by delivering it to him, or
         (ii) by sending it by post addressed to him at his usual or last-known place of residence or business, or
         (iii) by leaving it for him there;
   (b) if that person is a partnership, be served on the partnership—
         (i) by sending it by post to a partner, or to a person having the control or management of the partnership business, at the principal office of the partnership, or
         (ii) by addressing it to a partner or any such person and leaving it at that office;
   (c) if that person is a body corporate, be served on the body—
         (i) by sending it by post to the secretary or clerk of the body at its registered or principal office, or

(ii) by addressing it to the secretary or clerk of the body and leaving it at that office; or

(d) in any case, be served on that person's solicitor by delivering it to the solicitor, or by sending it by post to him at his office, or by leaving it for him there.

GENERAL NOTE

This section, which re-enacts s.64 of the 1991 Act, determines how a notice issued by the Secretary of State under s.55 may be served upon parties who have applied for compensation under that section, be they individuals, partnerships or corporations.

PART VIII

SUPPLEMENTARY

Restriction of prosecutions

57. A prosecution in respect of an offence under this Act shall not be instituted except by or with the consent of the Director of Public Prosecutions for Northern Ireland.

General interpretation

58. In this Act, except so far as the context otherwise requires—

"dwelling-house" means any building or part of a building used as a dwelling;

"explosive" means any article or substance manufactured for the purpose of producing a practical effect by explosion;

"explosive substance" means any substance for the time being specified in regulations made under section 3 of the Explosives Act (Northern Ireland) 1970;

"firearm" includes an air gun or air pistol;

"proscribed organisation" means an organisation for the time being specified in Schedule 2 to this Act, including an organisation which is to be treated as a proscribed organisation by virtue of section 30(2);

"public place" means a place to which for the time being members of the public have or are permitted to have access, whether on payment or otherwise;

"scheduled offence" has the meaning given by section 1;

"terrorism" means the use of violence for political ends and includes any use of violence for the purpose of putting the public or any section of the public in fear;

"terrorist" means a person who is or has been concerned in the commission or attempted commission of any act of terrorism or in directing, organising or training persons for the purpose of terrorism;

"vehicle" includes a hovercraft.

Repeal of Northern Ireland (Emergency Provisions) Act 1991

59. The Northern Ireland (Emergency Provisions) Act 1991 shall cease to have effect.

Orders and regulations

60.—(1) Subject to subsection (4), any power to make orders or regulations conferred by this Act shall be exercisable by statutory instrument.

(2) No order under section 1, 30 or 62(3) and no regulations under section 49 shall be made unless—

(a) a draft of the order or regulations has been approved by resolution of each House of Parliament; or

(b) it is declared in the order or regulations that it appears to the Secretary of State that by reason of urgency it is necessary to make the order or regulations without a draft having been so approved.

(3) Orders and regulations under the provisions mentioned in subsection (2) shall, if not so approved in draft, be laid before Parliament after being made and, if at the end of the period of forty days (computed in accordance with section 7(1) of the Statutory Instruments Act 1946) after the day on which the Secretary of State made such an order or regulations a resolution has not been passed by each House approving the order or regulations in question, the order or regulations shall then cease to have effect (but without prejudice to anything previously done or to the making of a new order or new regulations).

(4) Subsection (1) does not apply to any order under section 27 or Schedule 3 or any order under regulations made by virtue of section 49.

(5) Any regulations under section 8 and any order under section 15(5), 16(8), 53 or 54 shall be subject to annulment in pursuance of a resolution of either House of Parliament.

(6) Any order under section 39(4) shall be laid before Parliament after being made.

GENERAL NOTE

This section determines that the power to make orders and regulations under the various sections of the Act shall in general be exercisable by statutory instrument (but see subs. (4) below) and requires such orders to be laid before Parliament for approval. The section lays down the various differing procedures for the making of orders and regulations under the many sections in the Act which authorise such delegated legislation.

Subs. (4)

This provides that orders made by the Secretary of State under s.27, which relates to road closures, or under Sched. 3, covering detention of terrorists, or under s.49 regarding supplementary regulations for preserving the peace, *etc.* will not be in the form of statutory instruments and so will not be subject to the procedures set out in s.60.

Expenses

61. Any expenses of the Secretary of State under this Act shall be defrayed out of money provided by Parliament.

Commencement, duration, expiry and revival of provisions of this Act

62.—(1) This Act shall come into force on 25th August 1996.

(2) The temporary provisions of this Act, that is to say, Parts I to VII except—

(a) section 7, Part III of Schedule 1 and, so far as they relate to offences which are scheduled offences by virtue of that Part, sections 3, 10 and 11; and

(b) sections 55 and 56,

shall (subject and without prejudice to subsection (3)) expire with 15th June 1997.

(3) The Secretary of State may by order provide—

(a) that all or any of the temporary provisions of this Act which are for the time being in force (including any in force by virtue of an order under this section) shall continue in force for a period not exceeding twelve months from the coming into operation of the order;

(b) that all or any of those provisions which are for the time being in force shall cease to be in force; or

(c) that all or any of those provisions which are not for the time being in force shall come into force again and remain in force for a period not exceeding twelve months from the coming into operation of the order.

(4) An order under subsection (3) which relates to section 20, 23, 24, 25 or 26 may provide for the continuance, cessation or revival of that section—

(a) generally,

(b) only in so far as it concerns powers of members of Her Majesty's Forces, or

(c) except in so far as it concerns powers of members of Her Majesty's Forces.

(5) The Secretary of State shall be deemed to have made an order under subsection (3)(b) above in respect of the provisions of section 36 and Schedule 3 with effect immediately after the coming into force of those provisions on 25th August 1996.

(6) The coming into force of any provision of sections 10 to 13 by virtue of an order made under subsection (3)(c) above shall not affect any trial on indictment where the indictment has been presented before the coming into force of that provision, and any such trial shall be conducted as if the provision had not come into force.

(7) Where before the coming into force of subsection (1) of section 10 by virtue of such an order a person has been committed for trial for a scheduled offence and the indictment has not been presented, then, on the coming into force of that subsection, he shall, if he was committed to the Crown Court sitting elsewhere than in Belfast, be treated as having been committed—

(a) to the Crown Court sitting in Belfast; or

(b) where a direction has been given under that subsection which concerns the trial, to the Crown Court sitting at the place specified in the direction.

(8) The expiry or cesser of any provision mentioned in subsection (6) shall not affect the application of that provision to any trial on indictment where the indictment has been presented before the expiry or cesser; and the expiry or cesser of section 15 or 16 shall not affect the operation of that section in relation to an offence committed while it, or a corresponding earlier enactment, was in force.

(9) It is hereby declared that the expiry or cesser of any provision of section 10 shall not affect—

(a) any committal of a person for trial in accordance with that provision to the Crown Court sitting either in Belfast or elsewhere, or

(b) any committal of a person for trial which, in accordance with that provision, has taken effect as a committal for trial to the Crown Court sitting elsewhere than in Belfast,

in a case where the indictment has not been presented.

(10) This Act shall, by virtue of this subsection, be repealed as from the end of 24th August 1998.

GENERAL NOTE

The Act will come into force on August 25, 1996. This section sets out the timetable for implementation of the various parts of the Act.

Subs. (2)

This deals with the automatic expiry of the temporary provisions of the Act unless such provisions are continued in force under the procedures laid down in subs. (3). The provisions of the Act excluded from the ambit of subs. (2) are set out in the subsection.

Subs. (3)
Subs. (3)
    This provides the machinery for the continuance, renewal or cessation of the temporary provisions of the Act.

Subs. (5)
    By this subsection, the powers of detention (see s.36) are not to be brought into force. It is the Government's intention that the power of detention authorised by the Act should be retained on the statute book as a reserve power.

Subs. (10)
    By this subsection, the Act is given a lifespan of two years.

Savings, amendments and repeals

    63.—(1) Neither any rule of law nor any enactment other than this Act shall be construed as limiting or otherwise affecting the operation of any provision of this Act for the time being in force, but—
        (a) subject to the foregoing, any power conferred by this Act shall not derogate from Her Majesty's prerogative or any powers exercisable apart from this Act by virtue of any rule of law or enactment; and
        (b) subject to the foregoing and to section 62(8) above, a provision of this Act shall not affect the operation of any rule of law or enactment at a time when the provision is not in force.
    (2) Schedule 5 (which makes transitional provisions in relation to scheduled offences) shall have effect.
    (3) Where this Act repeals and re-enacts provisions of the Northern Ireland (Emergency Provisions) Act 1991, the repeal and re-enactment shall not, unless the contrary intention appears, affect the continuity of the law.
    (4) Any document made, served or issued after the commencement of this Act which contains a reference to an enactment repealed by this Act shall, so far as the context permits, be construed as referring to or (as the context may require) including a reference to the corresponding provision of this Act.
    (5) Any document made, served or issued after the commencement of this Act which contains a reference to a provision of this Act shall, so far as the context permits, be construed as referring to or (as the context may require) including a reference to the corresponding provision of the Northern Ireland (Emergency Provisions) Act 1991.
    (6) The enactments mentioned in Schedule 6 to this Act shall be amended in accordance with that Schedule.
    (7) The enactments mentioned in Part I of Schedule 7 to this Act are hereby repealed, and the instruments mentioned in Part II of that Schedule are hereby revoked, to the extent there specified.

GENERAL NOTE
Subs. (1)
    This preserves, *inter alia*, the prerogative of the Executive to keep in reserve powers beyond those conceded in the Act. That is to say, the Act should not be regarded as exclusive; thus, powers conferred by other Acts or the operation of Her Majesty's prerogative are not limited by the provisions of the Act.

Short title and extent

    64.—(1) This Act may be cited as the Northern Ireland (Emergency Provisions) Act 1996.
    (2) This Act extends to Northern Ireland only, except that the amendments and repeals in Schedules 6 and 7 have the same extent as the enactments to which they relate.

SCHEDULES

SCHEDULE 1

THE SCHEDULED OFFENCES

PART I

SUBSTANTIVE OFFENCES

Common law offences

1. Murder subject to note 1 below.
2. Manslaughter subject to note 1 below.
3. Riot.
4. Kidnapping subject to note 1 below.
5. False imprisonment subject to note 1 below.

Malicious Damage Act 1861 (c. 97)

6. Offences under section 35 of the Malicious Damage Act 1861 (interference with railway) subject to note 1 below.

Offences against the Person Act 1861 (c. 100)

7. Offences under the following provisions of the Offences against the Person Act 1861—
  (a) section 4 (offences relating to murder) subject to note 1 below;
  (b) section 16 (threats to kill) subject to note 1 below;
  (c) section 18 (wounding with intent to cause grievous bodily harm) subject to note 1 below;
  (d) section 20 (causing grievous bodily harm) subject to note 1 below;
  (e) section 29 (causing explosion or sending explosive substance or throwing corrosive liquid with intent to cause grievous bodily harm);
  (f) section 47 (assault occasioning actual bodily harm) subject to note 1 below.

Explosive Substances Act 1883 (c. 3)

8. Offences under the following provisions of the Explosive Substances Act 1883—
  (a) section 2 (causing explosion likely to endanger life or damage property);
  (b) section 3 (intending or conspiring to cause any such explosion, and making or possessing explosive with intent to endanger life or cause serious damage to property);
  (c) section 4 (making or possessing explosives in suspicious circumstances).

Prison Act (Northern Ireland) 1953 (c. 18 (N.I.))

9. Offences under the following provisions of the Prison Act (Northern Ireland) 1953 subject to note 1 below—
  (a) section 25 (being unlawfully at large while under sentence);
  (b) section 26 (escaping from lawful custody and failing to surrender to bail);
  (c) section 27 (attempting to break prison);
  (d) section 28 (breaking prison by force or violence);
  (e) section 29 (rescuing or assisting or permitting to escape from lawful custody persons under sentence of death or life imprisonment);
  (f) section 30 (rescuing or assisting or permitting to escape from lawful custody persons other than persons under sentence of death or life imprisonment);
  (g) section 32 (causing discharge of prisoner under pretended authority);
  (h) section 33 (assisting prisoners to escape by conveying things into prisons).

Theft Act (Northern Ireland) 1969 (c. 16 (N.I.))

10. Offences under the following provisions of the Theft Act (Northern Ireland) 1969—
  (a) section 1 (theft) subject to note 2 below;
  (b) section 8 (robbery) subject to notes 1 and 3 below;
  (c) section 9 (burglary) subject to note 2 below;
  (d) section 10 (aggravated burglary) subject to notes 1 and 3 below;
  (e) section 15 (obtaining property by deception) subject to note 2 below;
  (f) section 20 (blackmail) subject to notes 1 and 2 below.

Protection of the Person and Property Act (Northern Ireland) 1969 (c. 29 (N.I.))

11. Offences under the following provisions of the Protection of the Person and Property Act (Northern Ireland) 1969—
    (a) section 1 (intimidation) subject to note 1 below;
    (b) section 2 (making or possessing petrol bomb, etc. in suspicious circumstances);
    (c) section 3 (throwing or using petrol bomb, etc).

Hijacking

12. Offences under section 1 of the Aviation Security Act 1982 (aircraft).

13. Offences in Northern Ireland under section 2 of the Criminal Jurisdiction Act 1975 (vehicles or ships).

Criminal Damage (Northern Ireland) Order 1977 (S.I. 1977/426 (N.I. 4))

14. Offences under the following provisions of the Criminal Damage (Northern Ireland) Order 1977 subject to note 1 below—
    (a) Article 3(1) and (3) or Article 3(2) and (3) (arson);
    (b) Article 3(2) (destroying or damaging property with intent to endanger life);
    (c) Article 4 (threats to destroy or damage property);
    (d) Article 5 (possessing anything with intent to destroy or damage property).

Criminal Law (Amendment) (Northern Ireland) Order 1977 (S.I. 1977/1249 (N.I. 16))

15. Offences under Article 3 of the Criminal Law (Amendment) (Northern Ireland) Order 1977 (bomb hoaxes) subject to note 1 below.

Firearms (Northern Ireland) Order 1981 (S.I. 1981/155 (N.I. 2))

16. Offences under the following provisions of the Firearms (Northern Ireland) Order 1981—
    (a) Article 4(1), (2), (3) or (4) (manufacturing, dealing in, repairing, etc, firearm or ammunition without being registered) subject to note 1 below;
    (b) Article 5 (shortening barrel of shot gun or converting imitation firearm into firearm) subject to note 1 below;
    (c) Article 6(1) (manufacturing, dealing in or possessing certain weapons, etc.) subject to note 1 below;
    (d) Article 17 (possessing firearm or ammunition with intent to endanger life or cause serious damage to property);
    (e) Article 18 (use or attempted use of firearm or imitation firearm to prevent arrest of self or another etc.);
    (f) Article 19 (carrying firearm or imitation firearm with intent to commit indictable offence or prevent arrest of self or another);
    (g) Article 20 (carrying firearm, etc, in public place) subject to notes 1 and 4 below;
    (h) Article 22 (possession of firearm or ammunition by person who has been sentenced to imprisonment, etc, and sale of firearm or ammunition to such a person) subject to note 1 below;
    (i) Article 23 (possessing firearm or ammunition in suspicious circumstances).

Taking of Hostages Act 1982 (c. 28)

17. Offences under the Taking of Hostages Act 1982.

Nuclear Material (Offences) Act 1983 (c. 18)

18. Offences under section 2 of the Nuclear Material (Offences) Act 1983 (offences involving nuclear material: preparatory acts and threats).

Prevention of Terrorism (Temporary Provisions) Act 1989 (c. 4)

19. Offences under the following provisions of the Prevention of Terrorism (Temporary Provisions) Act 1989—
    (a) section 8 (breach of exclusion order);
    (b) sections 9, 10 and 11 (financial assistance for terrorism);
    (c) section 17 and Schedule 7 (terrorist investigations);
    (d) section 18 (information about acts of terrorism);
    (e) section 18A (failure to disclose knowledge or suspicion of financial assistance for terrorism);
    (f) paragraph 25B of Schedule 4 (contravention of restraint orders).

Aviation and Maritime Security Act 1990 (c. 31)

20. Offences under the following provisions of the Aviation and Maritime Security Act 1990—
(a) section 1 (endangering safety at aerodromes);
(b) section 9 (hijacking of ships);
(c) section 10 (seizing or exercising control of fixed platforms).

Channel Tunnel (Security) Order 1994 (S.I. 1994/570)

21. Offences under the following provisions of the Channel Tunnel (Security) Order 1994—
(a) Article 4 (hijacking of Channel Tunnel trains);
(b) Article 5 (seizing or exercising control of the tunnel system).

This Act

22. Offences under the following provisions of this Act—
(a) section 21(5);
(b) section 29;
(c) section 30;
(d) section 31;
(e) section 32;
(f) section 33;
(g) section 34;
(h) section 35;
(i) section 37;
(j) paragraph 13 of Schedule 3.

Notes

1. Any offence specified in this Part of this Schedule which is stated to be subject to this note is not a scheduled offence in any particular case in which the Attorney General for Northern Ireland certifies that it is not to be treated as a scheduled offence.

2. An offence specified in paragraph 10(a), (c) or (e) is a scheduled offence only where it is charged that the offence was committed in relation to or by means of nuclear material within the meaning of the Nuclear Material (Offences) Act 1983; and the Attorney General for Northern Ireland shall not certify that the offence specified in paragraph 10(f) is not to be treated as a scheduled offence in a case where it is charged that the offence was so committed.

3. An offence specified in paragraph 10(b) or (d) is a scheduled offence only where it is charged—
(a) that an explosive, firearm, imitation firearm or weapon of offence was used to commit the offence; or
(b) that the offence was committed in relation to or by means of nuclear material within the meaning of the Nuclear Material (Offences) Act 1983;
and expressions defined in section 10 of the Theft Act (Northern Ireland) 1969 have the same meaning when used in this note.

4. The offence specified in paragraph 16(g) is a scheduled offence only where it is charged that the offence relates to a weapon other than an air weapon.

PART II

INCHOATE AND RELATED OFFENCES

Each of the following offences, that is to say—
(a) aiding, abetting, counselling, procuring or inciting the commission of an offence specified in Part I of this Schedule (hereafter in this paragraph referred to as a "substantive offence");
(b) attempting or conspiring to commit a substantive offence;
(c) an offence under section 4 of the Criminal Law Act (Northern Ireland) 1967 of doing any act with intent to impede the arrest or prosecution of a person who has committed a substantive offence;
(d) an offence under section 5(1) of the Criminal Law Act (Northern Ireland) 1967 of failing to give information to a constable which is likely to secure, or to be of material assistance in securing, the apprehension, prosecution or conviction of a person for a substantive offence,
shall be treated for the purposes of this Act as if it were the substantive offence.

Part III

Extra-Territorial Offences

Any extra-territorial offence as defined in section 1(3) of the Criminal Jurisdiction Act 1975.

Section 30(2) SCHEDULE 2

Proscribed Organisations

The Irish Republican Army.
Cumann na mBan.
Fianna na hEireann.
The Red Hand Commando.
Saor Eire.
The Ulster Freedom Fighters.
The Ulster Volunteer Force.
The Irish National Liberation Army.
The Irish People's Liberation Organisation.
The Ulster Defence Association.

Section 36 SCHEDULE 3

Detention of Terrorists

Advisers

1. The Secretary of State shall for the purposes of this Schedule appoint such number of Advisers as he may determine to advise him on matters concerning the detention and release of terrorists.

2. An Adviser shall be a person who holds or has held judicial office in any part of the United Kingdom or who is—
    (a) a person who has a ten year general qualification within the meaning of section 71 of the Courts and Legal Services Act 1990; or
    (b) an advocate or solicitor in Scotland of at least ten years' standing; or
    (c) a member of the Bar of Northern Ireland or solicitor of the Supreme Court of Northern Ireland of at least ten years' standing.

3.—(1) An Adviser shall hold and vacate his office in accordance with the terms of his appointment and shall, on ceasing to hold office, be eligible for reappointment.

(2) An Adviser may at any time by notice in writing to the Secretary of State resign his office.

(3) The Secretary of State may pay to the Advisers such remuneration and allowances as he may determine.

Interim custody orders

4.—(1) Where it appears to the Secretary of State that there are grounds for suspecting that a person has been concerned—
    (a) in the commission or attempted commission of any act of terrorism, or
    (b) in directing, organising or training persons for the purpose of terrorism,
the Secretary of State may make an interim custody order for the temporary detention of that person.

(2) An interim custody order shall be signed by the Secretary of State or a Minister of State or Under Secretary of State.

5.—(1) The Secretary of State may, at any time before the expiry of the period of fourteen days following the date of an interim custody order, refer the case to an Adviser and, unless the case is so referred, the order shall cease to have effect at the expiry of that period.

(2) A reference to an Adviser under this paragraph shall be by notice in writing signed on behalf of the Secretary of State and a copy of the notice shall be sent to the person detained.

Reference to an Adviser

6.—(1) As soon as possible after a case is referred to an Adviser under paragraph 5, the person detained shall be served with a statement in writing as to the nature of the terrorist activities of which he is suspected.

(2) A person detained may, within seven days following the date on which he receives any such statement as is mentioned in sub-paragraph (1), send to the Secretary of State—

    (a) written representations concerning his case; and

    (b) a written request that he be seen personally by an Adviser;

and the Secretary of State shall send a copy of such representations or request to the Adviser concerned.

(3) The Secretary of State may pay any reasonable costs or expenses incurred by a person detained in obtaining legal advice or legal assistance in connection with the preparation of any representations he may make concerning his case.

7.—(1) Where the case of a person detained under an interim custody order is referred to an Adviser, he shall consider it and report to the Secretary of State whether or not in his opinion—

    (a) the person detained has been concerned in terrorist activities; and

    (b) the detention of that person is necessary for the protection of the public.

(2) In considering any case referred to him an Adviser shall have regard to any information (whether oral or in writing) which is made available to, or obtained by, him and to any representations (whether oral or in writing) made by the person detained.

(3) No person shall be present during the consideration by an Adviser of the case of any person referred to him, except—

    (a) any person who for the time being is being seen by the Adviser;

    (b) any assistant to the Adviser; and

    (c) any person who is present in the interests of security.

(4) The Secretary of State may, at the request of an Adviser, pay any reasonable expenses incurred by any person in connection with a reference to the Adviser.

Detention orders

8.—(1) After receiving a report made by an Adviser under paragraph 7(1), the Secretary of State shall consider the case of the person to whom it relates and, if he is satisfied—

    (a) that the person has been concerned in the commission or attempted commission of any act of terrorism, or in directing, organising or training persons for the purpose of terrorism, and

    (b) that the detention of that person is necessary for the protection of the public,

the Secretary of State may make a detention order for the detention of that person.

(2) If, on considering any case under sub-paragraph (1), the Secretary of State is not satisfied as mentioned in that sub-paragraph, he shall direct the release of the person concerned.

(3) Subject to sub-paragraphs (4) and (5), where—

    (a) a person is detained under an interim custody order; and

    (b) a detention order is not made in respect of that person within the period of seven weeks following the date of the interim custody order,

the interim custody order shall cease to have effect.

(4) The Secretary of State may, where a person is required to be detained under an interim custody order, give a direction in writing extending the period of seven weeks mentioned in sub-paragraph (3) (or that period as extended under this sub-paragraph) for a further period of one week if it is stated in the direction that the report of the Adviser in relation to that person's case has not been received before the sixth day immediately preceding the day on which the interim custody order would, but for the direction, cease to have effect.

(5) Not more than three directions under sub-paragraph (4) shall be given in respect of any one interim custody order.

(6) A detention order shall be signed by the Secretary of State, and a direction under sub-paragraph (4) shall be signed by the Secretary of State or a Minister of State or Under Secretary of State.

Supplemental

9.—(1) The Secretary of State may at any time refer the case of a person detained under a detention order to an Adviser and, if so requested in writing in accordance with sub-paragraph (2) by a person so detained, shall do so within fourteen days beginning with the receipt of the request.

(2) A person detained under a detention order shall not be entitled to make a request for the purposes of sub-paragraph (1)—

    (a) before the expiry of the period of one year beginning with the date of the detention order; or

(b) within a period of six months from the date of the last notification under sub-paragraph (5) below.

(3) On any reference under this paragraph, an Adviser shall consider the case and report to the Secretary of State whether or not the person's continued detention is necessary for the protection of the public.

(4) Paragraphs 6(3) and 7(2) to (4) shall apply for the purposes of a reference under this paragraph as they apply for the purposes of a reference under paragraph 5.

(5) Where a case is referred to an Adviser in consequence of a request made in accordance with this paragraph, the Secretary of State shall, after receiving the report of the Adviser, reconsider the case of the person to whom it relates and, if he decides not to release that person, shall notify him of his decision.

(6) A notification under sub-paragraph (5) shall be by notice in writing and signed by the Secretary of State.

10.—(1) The Secretary of State may, as respects a person detained under an interim custody order—

(a) direct his discharge unconditionally; or

(b) direct his release (whether or not subject to conditions) for a specified period.

(2) The Secretary of State may, as respects a person detained under a detention order—

(a) direct his discharge unconditionally; or

(b) direct his release subject to conditions or for a specified period, or both.

(3) The Secretary of State may recall to detention a person released under sub-paragraph (1)(b) or (2)(b) and a person so recalled may be detained under the original interim custody or detention order, as the case may be.

(4) Where a person is released under sub-paragraph (1)(b), any period during which he is not in detention shall be left out of account for the purposes of paragraphs 5(1), 6(2) and 8(3).

11.—(1) A person required to be detained under an interim custody order or a detention order may be detained in a prison or in some other place approved for the purposes of this paragraph by the Secretary of State.

(2) A person for the time being having custody of a person required to be detained as aforesaid shall have all the powers, authorities, protection and privileges of a constable.

(3) Subject to any directions of the Secretary of State, a person required to be detained as aforesaid shall be treated as nearly as may be as if he were a prisoner detained in a prison on remand and any power of temporary removal for judicial, medical or other purposes shall apply accordingly.

(4) A person required to be detained as aforesaid who is unlawfully at large may be arrested without warrant by any constable or any member of Her Majesty's forces on duty.

12. Where a person required to be detained under an interim custody order is unlawfully at large, the interim custody order shall not cease to have effect under paragraph 5 or 8 while he remains at large; and, upon his being taken again into custody, those paragraphs shall have effect as if the date of the interim custody order were that of his being taken again into custody.

13. Any person who—

(a) being detained under an interim custody order or detention order, escapes;

(b) rescues any person detained as aforesaid, or assists a person so detained in escaping or attempting to escape;

(c) fails to return to detention at the expiry of a period for which he was released under paragraph 10(1)(b) or (2)(b); or

(d) knowingly harbours any person required to be detained under an interim custody order or detention order, or gives him any assistance with intent to prevent, hinder or interfere with his being taken into custody,

is guilty of an offence and liable on conviction on indictment to imprisonment for a term not exceeding five years or a fine or both.

14.—(1) Any document purporting to be an order, notice or direction made or given by the Secretary of State for the purposes of this Schedule and to be signed in accordance with this Schedule shall be received in evidence and shall, until the contrary is proved, be deemed to be duly made or given and signed.

(2) Prima facie evidence of any such order, notice or direction may, in any legal proceedings, be given by the production of a document bearing a certificate purporting to be signed by or on behalf of the Secretary of State stating that the document is a true copy of the order, notice or direction, and the certificate shall be received in evidence, and shall, until the contrary is proved, be deemed to be duly made and signed.

15. The Secretary of State may make such payments to persons released or about to be released from detention under this Schedule as he may, with the consent of the Treasury, determine.

Section 51   SCHEDULE 4

Independent Assessor of Military Complaints Procedures in Northern Ireland

Tenure of office

1.—(1) Subject to the following provisions of this paragraph, the Independent Assessor shall hold and vacate office in accordance with the terms of his appointment.

(2) The Independent Assessor shall be appointed for a term not exceeding three years.

(3) The Independent Assessor may at any time resign his office by notice in writing addressed to the Secretary of State.

(4) The Secretary of State may remove the Independent Assessor from office—

(a) if he has without reasonable excuse failed to carry out his duties for a continuous period of six months or more;

(b) if he has been convicted of a criminal offence;

(c) if a bankruptcy order has been made against him, his estate has been sequestrated or he has made a composition or arrangement with, or granted a trust deed for, his creditors; or

(d) if the Secretary of State is satisfied that he is otherwise unable or unfit to perform his functions.

(5) At the end of a term of appointment the Independent Assessor shall be eligible for re-appointment.

Remuneration etc.

2.—(1) There shall be paid to the Independent Assessor such remuneration and such travelling and other allowances as the Secretary of State may determine.

(2) In the case of any such holder of the office of Independent Assessor as may be determined by the Secretary of State, there shall be paid such pension, allowances or gratuities to or in respect of him, or such payments towards the provision of a pension to or in respect of him, as may be so determined.

Staff

3.—(1) The Independent Assessor may appoint such number of employees as he may determine.

(2) The remuneration and other terms and conditions of service of persons employed by the Independent Assessor shall be such as he may determine.

(3) The approval of the Secretary of State shall be required for the making of a determination under this paragraph.

Reports

4.—(1) The Independent Assessor shall prepare an annual report on the performance of his functions which he shall submit to the Secretary of State who shall cause it to be published and lay copies of it before each House of Parliament.

(2) The Independent Assessor may make a report to the Secretary of State about any matter which comes to his attention in the course of the performance of his functions.

Disqualification

5. In Part III of Schedule 1 to the Northern Ireland Assembly Disqualification Act 1975 (other disqualifying offices), the following entry shall be inserted at the appropriate place—
"Independent Assessor of Military Complaints Procedures in Northern Ireland."

Section 63(2)   SCHEDULE 5

Scheduled Offences: Transitional Provisions

1. In this Schedule "commencement" means the time when this Act comes into force.

2.—(1) This Schedule applies to offences which—

(a) were immediately before commencement specified in Part I of Schedule 1 to the Northern Ireland (Emergency Provisions) Act 1991, but

(b) are not immediately after commencement specified in Part I of Schedule 1 to this Act.

(2) In relation to offences committed (or alleged to have been committed) before commencement, this Act shall apply as if offences to which this Schedule applies were specified in Part I of Schedule 1.

(3) Sub-paragraph (2) is subject to the following provisions.

3. Paragraph 2(2) shall not apply in relation to section 2 (preliminary inquiry) unless a request that a preliminary inquiry be held has been granted under section 2 of the 1991 Act.

4. Paragraph 2(2) shall not apply in relation to section 3 (limitation of power to grant bail).

5. Paragraph 2(2) shall not apply in relation to section 4 (legal aid to applicants for bail) except for the purposes of assignments made before commencement.

6. Paragraph 2(2) shall not apply in relation to section 5 (maximum period of remand in custody) except for the purposes of orders for remand made before commencement.

7. Paragraph 2(2) shall not apply in relation to section 6 (custody of young persons).

8. Paragraph 2(2) shall not apply in relation to section 8 (time limits for preliminary proceedings).

9. Paragraph 2(2) shall not apply in relation to sections 10 to 13 (court, mode of trial, evidence and onus of proof) except in cases where the case for the prosecution was opened, or a plea of guilty was accepted, before commencement.

10. Paragraph 2(2) shall not apply in relation to sections 14 to 16 (treatment of offenders) except where the conviction of the offence in question occurred before commencement.

11. Paragraph 2(2) shall not apply in relation to section 18 (constable's general power of arrest and seizure) except where the arrest, entry, search or seizure occurred before commencement.

12. Paragraph 2(2) shall not apply in relation to section 46(8)(a) to (c) (right to have someone informed of detention: delay related to scheduled offence) except for the purposes of authorisations given before commencement.

13. Paragraph 2(2) shall not apply in relation to section 47(8)(a) to (c) (right of access to legal advice: delay related to scheduled offence) except for the purposes of authorisations given before commencement.

14. Paragraph 2(2) shall not apply in relation to section 53(7) (compensation: restriction) except where the act in question was done before commencement.

15. Note 1 of Part I of Schedule 1 shall apply to any offence to which the corresponding note in the Northern Ireland (Emergency Provisions) Act 1991 applied.

Section 63(6)   SCHEDULE 6

CONSEQUENTIAL AMENDMENTS

The Elected Authorities (Northern Ireland) Act 1989 (c. 3)

1. The Elected Authorities (Northern Ireland) Act 1989 shall be amended as follows.

2. In section 6(5) (breach of terms of declaration), in the definition of "proscribed organisation" for the words "section 28 of the Northern Ireland (Emergency Provisions) Act 1991" there shall be substituted the words "section 30 of the Northern Ireland (Emergency Provisions) Act 1996".

3. In Schedule 2 (declaration against terrorism), for the words "Schedule 2 to the Northern Ireland (Emergency Provisions) Act 1991" there shall be substituted the words "Schedule 2 to the Northern Ireland (Emergency Provisions) Act 1996".

The Prevention of Terrorism (Temporary Provisions) Act 1989 (c. 4)

4. The Prevention of Terrorism (Temporary Provisions) Act 1989 shall be amended as follows.

5. In section 10(3) (contributions to resources of proscribed organisations), for the words "section 28 of the Northern Ireland (Emergency Provisions) Act 1991" there shall be substituted the words "section 30 of the Northern Ireland (Emergency Provisions) Act 1996".

6.—(1) Section 17 (investigation of terrorist activities) shall be amended as follows.

(2) In subsection (1)(a)(ii) for the words "section 27, 28, 53, 54 or 54A of the Northern Ireland (Emergency Provisions) Act 1991" there shall be substituted the words "section 29 or 30 of the Northern Ireland (Emergency Provisions) Act 1996".

(3) In subsection (1)(a)(iii) for the words "section 28 of the said Act of 1991" there shall be substituted the words "section 30 of the said Act of 1996".

(4) In subsection (1)(b) for the words "section 28(3) of that Act" there shall be substituted the words "section 30(3) of the Act of 1996".

(5) In subsection (2A) the words "or section 53, 54 or 54A of the Northern Ireland (Emergency Provisions) Act 1991" shall be omitted.

(6) In subsection (2B) the words "or section 53(4A), 54(5D) or 54A(5) of the Act of 1991" shall be omitted.

(7) In subsection (6) the words "or section 54A of the Act of 1991" shall be omitted.

7.—(1) Section 27 (commencement and duration) shall be amended as follows.

(2) In subsection (10) for the words "section 28 of the Northern Ireland (Emergency Provisions) Act 1991" there shall be substituted the words "section 30 of the Northern Ireland (Emergency Provisions) Act 1996".

(3) For subsection (11) there shall be substituted—

"(11) The provisions excluded by subsection (10) above from subsection (5) shall remain in force until 15th June 1997 and then expire but shall be—

(a) included in the provisions to which subsection (3) of section 62 of the said Act of 1996 applies (provisions that can be continued in force, repealed or revived by order); and

(b) treated as part of that Act for the purposes of subsection (10) of that section (repeal at end of two years).".

8. In paragraph 7(4) of Schedule 3 (supervision of detention and examination powers), for the words "sections 44 and 45 of the Northern Ireland (Emergency Provisions) Act 1991" there shall be substituted the words "sections 46 and 47 of the Northern Ireland (Emergency Provisions) Act 1996".

9.—(1) Schedule 4 (forfeiture orders) shall be amended as follows.

(2) In paragraph 8(1), in the definition of "a Northern Ireland order" for paragraph (b) there shall be substituted—

"(b) an order made under paragraph 23 or 25A below ("a Northern Ireland restraint order"); or".

(3) In paragraph 18(1), in the definition of "a Northern Ireland order" for paragraph (b) there shall be substituted—

"(b) an order made under paragraph 23 or 25A below ("a Northern Ireland restraint order"); or".

(4) After paragraph 25 there shall be inserted—

"25A.—(1) The power to make a restraint order under the provisions of paragraphs 23 and 24 above shall be exercisable by the Secretary of State in any case in which it appears to him that the information which it would be necessary to provide in support of an application to the High Court or a judge under those provisions would, if disclosed, be likely to place any person in danger or prejudice the capability of members of the Royal Ulster Constabulary to investigate an offence under Part III of this Act.

(2) In their application by virtue of sub-paragraph (1) above paragraphs 23 to 25 above shall have effect with the necessary modifications and as if references to the High Court were references to the Secretary of State.

(3) An order made by the Secretary of State by virtue of this paragraph may be varied or discharged by the High Court under paragraph 23(5) or 24(2) above.

25B.—(1) A person who, without lawful authority or reasonable excuse (the proof of which lies on him), contravenes a restraint order is guilty of an offence and liable—

(a) on conviction on indictment, to imprisonment for a term not exceeding fourteen years or a fine or both;

(b) on summary conviction, to imprisonment for a term not exceeding six months or a fine not exceeding the statutory maximum or both.

(2) Nothing in sub-paragraph (1) above shall be taken to prejudice any power of the High Court to deal with the contravention of a restraint order as a contempt of court."

10. In paragraph 8(1) of Schedule 7 (terrorist investigations), for the words "or an offence under section 27 of the Northern Ireland (Emergency Provisions) Act 1991" there shall be substituted the words "or an offence under section 29 of the Northern Ireland (Emergency Provisions) Act 1996".

The Police and Criminal Evidence (Northern Ireland) Order 1989 (S.I. 1989/1341 (N.I. 12))

11.—(1) The Police and Criminal Evidence (Northern Ireland) Order 1989 shall be amended as follows.

12. In Article 4(3) (provisions relating to powers to stop and search), for sub-paragraph (b) there shall be substituted—

"(b) sections 20, 22 and 28 of the Northern Ireland (Emergency Provisions) Act 1996, and".

13. In Article 30(3) (information to be given on arrest), for the words "section 18(2) of the Northern Ireland (Emergency Provisions) Act 1991" there shall be substituted the words "section 19(2) of the Northern Ireland (Emergency Provisions) Act 1996".

14. In Article 54(2) (abolition of certain powers of constables to search persons), the words "section 19(6)(b) of the Northern Ireland (Emergency Provisions) Act 1991 or" shall cease to have effect.

15. At the beginning of Article 61(9)(b) (fingerprinting), there shall be inserted the words "except as provided by section 48 of the Northern Ireland (Emergency Provisions) Act 1996,".

16. In Article 74(9) (confessions), for the words "section 11 of the Northern Ireland (Emergency Provisions) Act 1991" there shall be substituted the words "section 12 of the Northern Ireland (Emergency Provisions) Act 1996".

17. In Article 76(2)(b) (exclusion of unfair evidence), for the words "subsection (1) of section 11 of the Northern Ireland (Emergency Provisions) Act 1991" there shall be substituted the words "subsection (1) of section 12 of the Northern Ireland (Emergency Provisions) Act 1996".

The Northern Ireland (Remission of Sentences) Act 1995 (c. 47)

18.—(1) Section 1 of the Northern Ireland (Remission of Sentences) Act 1995 (release on licence of persons subject to restricted remission) shall be amended as follows.

(2) In subsection (1) for the words "section 14 of the Northern Ireland (Emergency Provisions) Act 1991" there shall be substituted the words "section 15 of the Northern Ireland (Emergency Provisions) Act 1996".

(3) In subsection (2) for the words "section 14" there shall be substituted the words "section 15 of that Act".

(4) In subsection (6) for the words "Section 15 of the Northern Ireland (Emergency Provisions) Act 1991" there shall be substituted the words "Section 16 of the Northern Ireland (Emergency Provisions) Act 1996".

Section 63(7) SCHEDULE 7

REPEALS AND REVOCATIONS

PART I

ENACTMENTS

Chapter	Short Title	Extent of repeal
1980 c. 47.	The Criminal Appeal (Northern Ireland) Act 1980.	Section 30(2).
1989 c. 4.	The Prevention of Terrorism (Temporary Provisions) Act 1989.	In section 17(2A), the words "or section 53, 54 or 54A of the Northern Ireland (Emergency Provisions) Act 1991". In section 17(2B), the words "or section 53(4A), 54(5D) or 54A(5) of the Act of 1991". In section 17(6), the words "or section 54A of the Act of 1991".
1991 c. 24.	The Northern Ireland (Emergency Provisions) Act 1991.	The whole Act.
1993 c. 36.	The Criminal Justice Act 1993.	Sections 36 to 48. Section 50(2)(b). Section 78(8) and (12). Section 79(6). Paragraph 6 of Schedule 4. Paragraphs 3 and 17 of Schedule 5.
1994 c. 33.	The Criminal Justice and Public Order Act 1994.	Section 83(1)(c), (3) and (5). Paragraph 51 of Schedule 9. Paragraph 63(2) of Schedule 10.
1995 c. 35.	The Criminal Appeal Act 1995.	Section 22(5)(b), and the word "and" immediately before it.
1995 c. 40.	The Criminal Procedure (Consequential Provisions) (Scotland) Act 1995.	Paragraph 79 of Schedule 4.

PART II

ORDERS AND REGULATIONS

Number	Title	Extent of revocation
S.I. 1989/1341 (N.I. 12).	The Police and Criminal Evidence (Northern Ireland) Order 1989.	In Article 54(2), the words "section 19(6)(b) of the Northern Ireland (Emergency Provisions) Act 1991 or".
S.I. 1992/1958.	The Northern Ireland (Emergency Provisions) Act 1991 (Amendment) Order 1992.	The whole Order.
S.I. 1994/570.	The Channel Tunnel (Security) Order 1994.	Paragraph 1 of Schedule 3.
S.I. 1994/764.	The Northern Ireland (Emergency Provisions) Act 1991 (Guernsey) Order 1994.	The whole Order.
S.I. 1994/1696.	The Insurance Companies (Third Insurance Directives) Regulations 1994.	Paragraph 21 of Schedule 8.
S.I. 1995/2993 (N.I. 17).	The Police (Amendment) (Northern Ireland) Order 1995.	Article 9(4).

INDEX

References are to sections and schedules